The Pitman Dictionary
of English and Shorthand

The Pitman Dictionary

of English and Shorthand

New Era Edition

Pitman

PITMAN PUBLISHING LIMITED
39 Parker Street, London WC2B 5PB

Associated Companies
Copp Clark Ltd, Toronto
Fearon-Pitman Publishers Inc, Belmont, California
Pitman Publishing New Zealand Ltd, Wellington
Pitman Publishing Pty Ltd, Melbourne

Text set in 6/7 pt Monotype Times New Roman, printed by letterpress
and bound in Great Britain at The Pitman Press, Bath

ISBN 0 273 36137 6

G8-(173:24)

Preface

THE PITMAN DICTIONARY OF ENGLISH AND SHORTHAND, based on the original work of Sir Isaac Pitman, was first compiled more than half a century ago by Arthur Reynolds, M.A. The work that he did in providing definitions for each shorthand outline has stood the test of time well and from its first publication the dictionary has proved extremely popular and has served shorthand writers and office workers everywhere throughout these years.

Nearly ten years ago, an Appendix was added containing some 6,000 words with shorthand outlines only. This updated the dictionary by including a large number of words that had arrived in the language since 1920.

The present dictionary is a completely reset and rewritten new edition, using a larger page to provide extra space. The words from the Appendix have been entered in their alphabetical position and have been provided with definitions. A large number of the original definitions have been rewritten to take account of modern idiom and structural changes in the language that the passage of years always brings.

By the courtesy of the Oxford University Press, a further 5,000 words, drawn from the Fifth Edition of *The Concise Oxford Dictionary*, have also been added with rewritten definitions. In addition, there are some 6,500 words accumulated by Pitman editors over the years. All these additions bring the total number of shorthand outlines now presented to nearly 100,000.

Because of limitations of space, it has not been possible to illustrate the uses of words by inserting appropriate passages from literature or to enter the vast field of origin and etymology. The guiding principle throughout has been to issue the dictionary in as modern an idiom as possible, always having in mind the needs of users in the classrooms and offices of the world today as the paramount consideration. Arthur Reynolds's words in the preface to his edition remain true today: "The modest role assumed confines the ambition of this dictionary within the limit of a desire to explain simply and usefully the words of the vocabulary."

The Introduction to this dictionary, originally contributed by the great shorthand authority, H. W. B. Wilson, has been retained in a slightly revised form. It contains more than 1,500 shorthand outlines as examples of the applications of rules and has for years been regarded by many teachers and would-be teachers of Pitman's Shorthand as an indispensable part of the study of the system

A greatly extended Appendix of Proper Names appears at the end of the main part of the dictionary. Considerations of space have, however, prevented the repetition in this Appendix of any names which appear in the main dictionary in the same word form, e.g. the name "Perry" is omitted from the Appendix because the word "perry" is given and defined in the body of the work.

For the first time in the long history of Pitman's Shorthand, the dictionary now shows position writing. No one who consults the work will have any doubt about how the shorthand outline should be written in relation to the line. There are many words in English (such as *received, below, sedate, define*) which begin with a consonant and vowel, usually "*e*," and which have two or more syllables the first of which is unstressed. The vowel sound actually uttered by English speakers is often indeterminate, varying between an "e" as in "bet," an "i" as in "bit" and an "e" as in "beat." Not only does the pronunciation differ

v

regionally in the English-speaking world, but it also differs even for the same speaker at different times according to the speed of utterance and the context in which the word occurs. In these instances it has seemed best to regard this indeterminate vowel as being a second position one, and to allow those which were included in the first edition to remain unaltered.

On the other hand, there are some such words the pronunciation of which has positively changed during the last few decades to a clearly sounded vowel, as in "retail." Such words are, of course, written phonetically in the usual way.

There are many words however (such as *after, bath, path, dance, master*) which begin with the vowel "a" or with a consonant followed by the vowel "a," and which in the first edition of this dictionary were given the pronunciation with the short "a" as in "patch." In the present day this group of words has a different pronunciation in large areas of the English-speaking world, where the long "a" as in "ah" is used. To reflect these two definite pronunciations, alternative shorthand outlines have been given.

Pronunciation and usage change slowly and subtly without our being aware of it, but a dictionary that has been current for more than half a century will surely show signs of becoming out of date in these respects. The necessary changes have, therefore, been made; but it is important to emphasize that no changes in the Pitman Shorthand system have been introduced in this edition.

The question of hyphenation has been a particular difficulty, as it must always be to modern lexicographers. In the main, the principle has been to use as few hyphens as possible consistent with good sense and easy comprehension. Hyphens have been abandoned whenever it has been possible to find reputable modern precedents for doing so.

The shorthand outlines given in this work are not always necessarily the only theoretically correct ones. They have been carefully selected—(i) for ease of writing; (ii) for ease of distinguishing from other similar outlines; and (iii) for ease of continuing with the next outline and the prevention of interference with the lines above or below wherever possible.

The fully vocalized outlines will obviously be of great help to all shorthand writers with the problem of pronunciation, but they cannot indicate which syllable is stressed. A stress mark has therefore been placed immediately *after* the syllable that is stressed. Three examples, not likely to be mispronounced, will make this clear:

> ter'minus—the stress is on the "-ter-"
> deduc'tion—the stress is on the "-duc-"
> lemonade'—the stress is on the "-ade"

Words of one syllable do not need a stress mark. In words of more than one syllable where no stress mark is given, the syllables are regarded as being of equal stress.

The publishers are confident that this edition of the work will uphold the tradition of the original and justly celebrated *Pitman English and Shorthand Dictionary* and they wish to express their appreciation to those who have contributed to its production.

Contents

Introduction

In this dictionary standard forms are furnished for the words of the English language, written in accordance with the rules of Pitman Shorthand. Every writer of the system is aware that there is often a choice between two or more possible shorthand forms, and the dictionary provides those outlines which experience has shown can be recommended for general adoption. Hence the importance and usefulness of the work as a book of reference for teachers, students and practitioners.

Every effort has been made to render the dictionary reliable and consistent in regard to pronunciation and the selection of the shorthand forms. There will, no doubt, be differences of opinion about the outlines for certain words, since a form which is the most convenient to one writer is not invariably so to another writer. It is strongly recommended, however, that the closest possible adherence to dictionary outlines be observed, since they have been decided upon as the result of experience and careful thought. No dictionary outline, therefore, should be rejected in favour of another until an attempt has been made to ascertain whether there is not some special reason for its adoption. It is obvious that uniformity of outlines is especially helpful in the case of writers who have to read or transcribe one another's notes.

Representation of Vowels, etc.

The following observations with regard to the vowel sounds, etc., in certain classes of words may be found helpful:

(*a*) The sound of the vowel "*a*" in such words as *bar*, *harm*, *embark*, is *ah*.

There are, on the other hand, many words in which the vowel "*a*" before *r* has a short or indistinct sound; *e.g.*, ... *tariff*; .... *globular*, ... *pillar*. Compare .... *tarry* (adjective) with .... *tarry* (verb).

(*b*) *aw* and not *ah* is used in such words as *taunt*, *launch*, *saunter*.

(*c*) "*o*" when occurring medially and sounded indistinctly is represented by *ŭ*, as in *custom*, *mason*, *London*, *monopoly*, *gallop*.

A long vowel tends to become short when it is unaccented, and in some words, such as *proclaim*, *biograph*, the vowels *ō* and *ŭ* are practically indistinguishable as ordinarily pronounced. In others, however, *e.g.*, *flotation*, *hotel*, *rotate*, *nobility*, the vowel is unmistakably *ō* although unaccented.

(*d*) The unaccented "*a*" in such words as *accurate*, *breakage*, *palace*, including most adjectives ending in *-ate*, is represented by *ĕ*.

Here, again, the long vowel tends to become short when it is unaccented.

Compare .... *lace* with .... *palace*. In some cases, however, including all *verbs* ending in *-ate*, the vowel "*a*" is long, although it may be unaccented.

Compare .... *moderate* (adjective) with .... *moderate* (verb).

(e) *ĭ* is used in .... *marriage,* .... *carriage,* etc.

(f) The diphthong *ī* is used in words ending in *-ization,* e.g., ... *realization,* .... *capitalization.*

(g) The vowel sound after *j* or *r* in such words as *Jew, juice, peruse,* is *ōō* and not *ū.* After *l,* also, *ū* is generally represented as *ōō* unless it begins a syllable; e.g., ... *include,* .... *flute,* .... *solution,* but .... *soluble,* .... *valuer.*

(h) Triphones are used to represent a diphthong and any following vowel (either short or long) as, ... *hyena.*

(i) In French words such as *patois, boudoir, soirée,* etc., *oi* is pronounced *wah,* approximately.

(j) *French eu.* When the usual sign representing the vowel sound of *eu* in French words cannot be conveniently employed, it may be treated as *ŭ;* thus, ... *raconteur,* .... *restaurateur.*

(k) In such words as *ranch, French, inch, punch,* with regard to which authorities differ, *ch,* which represents the more usual pronunciation, is employed.

Notes as to the Placing of Vowel-signs, etc.

1. DIPHTHONG *ū* BETWEEN TWO STROKES. The diphthong *ū* when occurring between two strokes is treated in the same way as a third-place vowel; *i.e.,* it is always written before the second of the two strokes; thus, ... *Hercules,* .... *culinary,* .... *valueless.*

2. DIPHTHONGS *ī* AND *ow.* The diphthong *ī* is written out of its ordinary position for the purpose of joining finally to .... *n,* as in .... *deny;* and also in a few instances when following a third-place vowel; *e.g.,* .... *radii,* .... *nuclei,* .... *genii.* The diphthong *ow* is written out of its ordinary position for the purpose of joining initially to .... *l,* as in .... *owl.*

3. DIPHTHONG *oi.* It is permissible to write the first tick of the diphthong *oi* upward (i.e. as in the diphone *awī*), instead of horizontally, when it is more convenient to do so. This is the case especially when it is joined initially to .... *l,* thus .... *oil.*

4. The small circle used to represent a vowel occurring between the two consonants expressed by a stroke hooked for *r* or *l* is written *after* the stroke unless the presence of a hook or a stroke or of another vowel-sign renders the other side more convenient; thus, ... *garnish,* but .... *regard;* ....

side car, but ⎯⎯ *motor-car;* ⎯⎯ *shilling,* but ⎯⎯ *virulent;* ⎯⎯
parlour, but ⎯⎯ *parallel.*

5. THIRD-PLACE VOWEL OCCURRING ON SAME SIDE OF STROKE AS *shun* HOOK.
Any vowel- (or diphthongal-) sign other than a *dot* vowel is placed *outside*
final shun hook; thus ⎯⎯ *delusion,* ⎯⎯ *fusion,* ⎯⎯ *alleviation* (but
⎯⎯ *vision*). All third-place signs are written inside medial *shun* hook; thus,
⎯⎯ *educational.*

6. VOCALIZATION IN DERIVATIVE WORDS. A vowel in a derivative word,
whether occurring in a (grammatical) prefix or suffix, such as *re-, pre-, -able,
-ance,* or in the portion representing the root word, follows the ordinary rules as
regards the stroke to which it is to be placed, and if it is immediately followed
by another vowel, a diphone is used; thus, ⎯⎯ *re-examine,* ⎯⎯ *prefigure,*
⎯⎯ *measurable,* ⎯⎯ *severance,* ⎯⎯ *singer,* ⎯⎯ *unopened,* ⎯⎯
unaccented.

This does not apply to Compound Words, in which case the vowel-signs
are generally placed as in the original words unless there is some special reason
to the contrary; thus, ⎯⎯ *headache,* ⎯⎯ *steam-engine,* ⎯⎯ *crab-
apple;* but ⎯⎯ *seaman,* ⎯⎯ *black-eyed,* to avoid placing a vowel-sign
in an angle.

Supplementary Rules for the Choice of Outlines

The following rules and explanations are given in order to show the practice
which has been followed in the selection of the outlines for various classes of
words:

Diphthong ū and Consonant ⎯⎯ Y

Stroke ⎯⎯ is used whenever convenient in words beginning with the sound
of *ū;* thus, ⎯⎯ *Europe,* ⎯⎯ *utilize,* ⎯⎯ *eulogy,* ⎯⎯ *unique.* Note,
however, ⎯⎯ *usury* and ⎯⎯ *Euphrates.*

Abbreviated W Used Medially

The abbreviated form of the consonant *w* is not joined medially to a preceding
stroke except in a few COMPOUNDS of "woman," in which it joins easily, such as
⎯⎯ *needlewoman,* ⎯⎯ *charwoman,* and in ⎯⎯ *sidewalk;* hence ⎯⎯
woodwork, ⎯⎯ *saleswoman,* ⎯⎯ *workwoman,* ⎯⎯ *silkworm.*

W (Semicircle and Stroke)

The right motion semicircle is used to express initial *w* only before *k, g, m,* and
r (upward or downward); thus: ⎯⎯ *week,* ⎯⎯ *wagon,* ⎯⎯ *woman,*
⎯⎯ *wiry,* ⎯⎯ *were.* In all other cases, the stroke *w* is used for initial *w.*

Initial *w* followed by a DIPHONE or a TRIPHONE is represented by the stroke ......; thus, ... *weigher,* ...... *wooer,* ...... *Wyoming.*

S (Direction of Circle) in N-S-M words

In writing *n s m* the circle *s* is placed *inside* the *m* in the following cases:

(*a*) In DERIVATIVES and COMPOUNDS from words in which the circle is written inside the *m; e.g.,* ...... *unseemly,* ...... *unsummoned,* ...... *tinsmith,* (compare ...... *newsmonger*).

(*b*) In words containing the syllable *-some, e.g.,* ...... *noisome,* ...... *handsome.*

NOTE. It will be found that, with only two or three exceptions, *e.g.,* ...... *mincemeat,* ...... *Norseman,* and ...... *nursemaid,* the form ...... is used for *n s m* and the form ...... for *n z m,* most of the examples of the latter being words ending in *-ism, e.g.,* ...... *communism,* ...... *galvanism.*

S, Z (Circle and Stroke)

1. Words ending in *-nese* and *-nize,* most of which are DERIVATIVES, are written with stroke *n* and circle *s* (*z*) whenever convenient; thus, ... *Japanese,* ...... *Americanize,* ...... *humanize,* ...... *modernize.* Note, however, ... *revolutionize.*

2. Words ending in *-nism* are written with ...... unless a better outline is obtained by writing hook *n* and ...... The latter is found to be the more convenient form after ...... (but not ...... or ......) ...... or ...... Examples: ...... *Puritanism,* ...... *religionism,* ...... *anachronism;* but ...... *mechanism,* ...... *paganism,* ...... *modernism,* ...... *Wesleyanism.*

3. Words ending in *-ess.* All words (feminines) ending in *-ess* cannot conveniently be treated uniformly, but the following shows the practice which has been followed:

(*a*) In words ending with the *syllable -ess,* stroke *s* is used if necessary for the purpose of distinguishing the feminine singular from the masculine plural when no other means of distinction is available; thus, ... *poetess,* (...... *poets*), ... *heiress,* (...... *heirs*), ... *Jewess,* (...... *Jews*).

(*b*) With regard to those words ending in *-eress, -oress, -dess, -n(t)ess* or *-fess* in which alternative methods of distinction are available, stroke *s* is used

after .... or ......: thus, ... *archeress*, ... *manageress*, ... *tutoress*, ... *murderess*, ... *vicaress*, ... *deaconess*, ... *countess*: but in other cases the circle is written, *e.g.*, ... *viscountess*, ... *giantess*, ... *lioness*, ... *baroness*, ... *mayoress*, ... *authoress*.

(*c*) In words ending in *-ress* immediately preceded by a consonant, the final *s* sound is always represented by the circle; thus, ... *actress*, ... *waitress*, ... *tigress*.

4. Words ending in *-zoon* are written with stroke *z;* thus, ... *epizoon*, ... *polyzoon* (plural ...... *polyzoa*); but adjectives ending in *-zoic* have the circle; thus, ... *paleozoic*, ... *protozoic*.

5. Derivatives from words with outlines containing stroke *s* formed by adding a suffix beginning with a vowel to a *primitive* word ending with *s* or *z* and a vowel, retain stroke *s* or *z;* thus, ... *cosier*, ... *lazier*, ... *pursuance*, ... *Sadducean*, ... *Puseyism*, ... *laziest*, ... *busiest* (see also 3(*a*) below).

Compare—(*a*) Secondary derivatives, such as ...... *spiciest*, ... *sauciest*, ... *glossier*, the primitives of which are written with circle *s;* and (*b*) Derivatives in which the suffix does not commence with a vowel; *e.g.*, ... *drowsiness*, ... *merciless*, ... *busily*.

S (Stroke and Circle); ST (...... and Loop)

1. Initial *s* or *st* followed by a diphone is written as follows:

(*a*) With stroke *s* or ...... in derivatives such as ...... *sower*, ... *seer*, ... *stayer*.

(*b*) With the circle or loop in other words, such as ...... *sahib*, ... *séance*, ... *sienna*, ... *stoic*, ... *Styrian*.

Initial *s* or *st* followed by a triphone is written with stroke *s* or ......; thus, ... *Siam*, ... *suet*, ... *Stuart*, ... *steward*, ... *Stowell*.

2. Contrary to the general rule for words beginning with *s* vowel *s*, several words beginning with *sĭst* or (*con*)*sĭst* are more easily written with circle *s* first; *e.g.*, ... *system*, ... *cistern*, ... *consist*, ... *consistent*, ... *sisterly*.

3(*a*). While words ending in *-ous* preceded by a diphthong are written with stroke *s*, their derivatives ending in *-ĭously*, *-uously*, *-uousness* and *-uosity* are

generally written with the circle; thus, ... *piously*, ... *continuously*, ... *strenuousness*, ... *impetuosity*.

The following, however, are cases in which the stroke is retained for the purpose of distinction: .... *joyously*, ... *joyousness*, ... *ingenuously*, ... *ingenuousness*, ... *tenuously*, ... *tenuousness*, ... *sinuosity*.

(*b*) In other words containing *s*, *z* or *st* preceded by a TRIPHONE or by a DIPHONE, the circle or loop is used; *e.g.*, ... *bias*, ... *biased*, ... *quiesce*, ... *acquiesce*, ... *Genoese*, ... *essayist*, ... *truest*, ... *deist*, ... *Judaism*, ... *statuesque*. The following are exceptions to this: .... *prowess*, (........ *principles*), ... *dais*, ... *chaos*, ... *newest*, (........ *next*), ... *highest*.

4. Words ending in *-astic* or *-istic* are written as follows:

(*a*) With *st* loop after *t, d, j* or *l*; thus, ... *artistic*, ... *deistic*, ... *logistic*, ... *elastic*, ... *statistics*.

(*b*) With .... in other cases; thus, ... *plastic*, ... *theistic*, ... *sophistic*.

5. .... is retained in DERIVATIVES from words with outlines containing .... , except the monosyllabic past tenses .... *stayed*, ... *stewed*, etc.; thus, ... *stowage*, ... *dustiness*, ... *majestic*, ... *lustier*, but the loop is used freely in words like; .... *steady*, ... *steadied*, ... *study*, ... *studio*.

ST (Loop and .... ST)

Words ending in *-nest, -nist; -fest, -vest, -vist; -test, -tist, -dest*, etc., are written with the *st* loop unless a distinctly better outline is obtained by means of the stroke; thus, ... *keenest*, ... *greenest*, ... *organist*, ... *briefest*, ... *bravest*, ... *faintest*, ... *fondest*, ... *artist*, but .... *plainest*, ... *earnest*, ... *toughest*, ... *positivist*, ... *kindest*, ... *hardest*.

SST (........ , ... and ....)

Words ending in *-cest, -cist* and *-sest* are generally written with .... ; thus, ... *fiercest*, ... *publicist*, ... *closest;* but .... is more convenient after .... *n* or .... *r*, as in .... *nicest*, ... *empiricist;* .... *densest*. .... is used in verbs ending in *-sist, e.g.,* .... *subsist*, ... *desist*.

SZD (...?... and ...?....)

COMPOUND WORDS ending in -*sized* are written with ...?.... except when ...?.... gives a better joining (as after *f, v* or *n*); thus, ...⸝... *fair-sized,* ...⸝... *full-sized,* ...⸝.... *large-sized;* but ...⸝. *oversized,* ...⸝. *undersized.*

SS, SZ (Large Circle, ...?..?... and ...?....)

1. Words ending in -*sis* and -*sus* are written with the large circle; thus, ...⸝.... *basis,* (plural ...⸝.... *bases*), ...⸝.... *narcissus.* Note also ...⸝... *Francis.*

2. Words ending with the sound of *sĕs* or *zĕs*, or with *s* plus *s/z* separated by a diphthong or a diphone (including words ending in -*cess*, -*cize* and -*size*), are generally written with ...?.... or ...?....; thus, ...?.... *access,* ...?.... *possess,* ...?.... *capsize,* ...?.... *gaseous;* but after *th, n* or upward *r,* ...?.... affords a better joining, e.g., ...?.... *Gothicize,* ...?.... *princess,* ...?.... *Frances,* ...?.... *recess,* ...?.... *exorcize.* The form ...?.... is used also in ...?... *diocese* and ...?... *decease* for distinction; and the common words ...?... *success,* ...?... *exercise* and ...?... *emphasize,* are written with the large circle for convenience.

3. Words ending in -*cism* are generally written with the large circle; thus, ...?... *fanaticism,* ...?... *Gallicism;* but after ...?... *th,* ...?... *n* or ...?... *r,* the form ...?.... gives more convenient and distinctive outlines; thus, ...?.... *Gothicism,* ...?.... *cynicism,* ...?.... *laconicism,* ...?.... *exorcism,* ...?.... *Doricism.*

Hooked Stroke and Stroke R or L

1. Words ending in -*metry* and -*metric* are written with stroke *r* whenever practicable; thus ...?... *geometry,* ...?... *barometric,* but ...?... *planimetry.*

2. Words ending in -*able* or -*ible* are generally written with the hooked stroke ...?...; thus, ...?.... *obtainable,* ...?.... *illegible.* The separate strokes ...?..., however, are used when a better outline is thus obtained; e.g.:

(*a*) After ...?., ...?., ...?., ...?... or after a circle following a "right" curve (but not after ...?. or ...?.); thus, ...?... *excusable,* ...?.... *accessible,* ...?.... *invincible,* ...?.... *reversible,* ...?.... *forcible* (but ...?.... *feasible,* ...?.... *serviceable*).

(*b*) After ...?.... or ...?....; thus, ...?... *contestable,* ...?... *digestible.*

(c) After ...., ... or a downstroke hooked for *v;* thus, ...*explainable,* ....*discernible,* ....*provable.*

(d) After a half-length stroke hooked for *n;* thus, ... *accountable,* .... *lamentable.* (But note .... *insurmountable.*)

(e) After a *shun* hook; thus, ... *actionable,* but in .... *mentionable* .... disjoined is more convenient.

3. Words ending in *-tal* or *-dal* preceded by .... *r* are written with stroke *l;* thus, ... *parietal,* .... *spheroidal.* Compare the words .... *rattle,* .... *riddle.* A number of words ending in *-tal* preceded by *n* are also written with stroke *l; e.g.,* .... *mental,* .... *horizontal.* Compare the word .... *mantle.*

4. Words ending in *-ful* and *-fully* are written with stroke *l* in cases where a distinction between the adjective and the adverb can easily be shown by means of the downward and the upward *l* respectively; *e.g.,* after ...., ..., ..., ..., or a straight upstroke; thus, ... *wakeful,* .... *wakefully,* .... *manful,* .... *wrongful,* .... *sorrowful.* In other words, including verbs, *fl* and *vl* occurring after the strokes mentioned above are represented by the hooked forms ....; thus, ... *scuffle,* .... *interval,* .... *upheaval,* .... *cavalry,* .... *gravel,* .... *rifle,* .... *hovel.*

5. Words ending in *-shly* are generally written with ...., thus, ... *foolishly,* .... *freshly.* But note .... *harshly,* in which the stroke *l* is more convenient. The stroke *shl* is always written upwards, as; .... *official,* .... *palatial.*

6. On the other hand words beginning with *enr-, unr-, unl-, enl-,* formed by a prefix from words beginning with *r* or *l* generally retain the separate *r* or *l;* thus, ... *enrage,* .... *unreasoning,* .... *unleavened,* .... *enlist.* But note .... *enlighten* and .... *enliven.*

7. Words ending in *-ary, -ery, -ory,* etc., are treated as follows:

(a) The hooked strokes are used when they give a more easily written outline than the separate *r;* thus, ... *drapery,* .... *rookery,* .... *treasury,* .... *luminary.*

(b) The hooked strokes are retained in adjectives derived from words written with a final hooked stroke, such as .... *tottery,* .... *silvery,* .... *savoury.*

(*c*) In other cases the separate *r* or *l* is written; thus, ... *statutory,* ....
notary, ... *factory,* .... *fishery.*

8. DERIVATIVES ending in *-ally* and *-alize* from words written with a final
hooked stroke retain the hooked form; thus, ... *brutally,* .... *brutalize,*
.... *locally,* .... *localize.* But note .... *totally* which is considered a
useful distinguishing outline from .... *total.*

9. Words ending in *-erate* or *-orate* are often written with separate .... *rt*
if the latter gives an easily written outline and one which enables that of the past
tense to be easily formed from it; thus, ... *exaggerate,* .... *exaggerated;*
.... *adulterate,* .... *adulterated;* .... *enumerate,* .... *enumerated.*
Compare .... *deliberate,* .... *deliberated,* .... *decorate,* .... *decorated.*
The outline .... *elaborate* is necessary for distinction (........*laboured*).

10. DERIVATIVES from words written with hooked forms of the *pr, pl* series
are generally also written with the hooked forms if practicable, even if the *r* or
l is no longer in the same syllable as the preceding consonant; thus, ...
tippler, ... *trampling,* .... *saddling,* .... *tackling,* .... *doubly.* Compare such words as .... *seedling,* .... *duckling,* which are not so derived.

11. The hooked form *shr* is always written downward (*cp. para.* 5); ....
Devonshire, ... *pressure.*

12. In COMPOUND WORDS, when the second part of the compound begins
with *r* or *l*, that *r* or *l* is, as a rule, not combined with the last letter of the first
part; hence, ... *typewritten,* .... *bricklayer,* .... *necklace.*
But note .... *typewriter* and .... *typewriting,* these outlines being preferred
for their speed, the words being of frequent occurrence.

13. In the case of *verbs* the hooked forms are generally preferred so as to
enable past tenses to be written on the same principle; thus, ... *bridle,*
.... *bridled* (compare .... *bridal*), ... *model,* .... *modelled.*

14. The hooked forms for *ng-gr, ng-kr* are used in all cases except when they
occur initially or follow a circle or an upstroke. Then the doubled form is
used, as; .... *anchor,* .... *hanker,* .... *sinker,* but .... *conger,*
.... *banker.* The outline .... *shrinker* uses the doubled form.

Duplicate (Alternative) Forms for FR, VR, etc.

1. In DERIVATIVES and COMPOUNDS from words written with ...., etc.,
the form of *fr* or *vr* used in the primitive should, when convenient, also be used

in the derivative or compound, without regard to the practice adopted in other words; thus, ⏜ *freeness* (compare ⏜ *furnace*), ⏜ *offerer* (compare ⏜ *friar*).

Subject to the above:

2. The "left" curves ⏜⏜ are used if more convenient for joining than the "right" curves. This is the case:

(*a*) When *fr* or *vr* occurs either before or after *t, d, ch, j, f, v, th, s* or *z*, as in ⏜ *tougher*, ⏜ *leverage*, ⏜ *effervesce*, ⏜ *survivor*, ⏜ *froth*, ⏜ *zephyr*.

(*b*) Generally before a character beginning with the same motion, viz. the "left" motion, as in ⏜ *friable*, ⏜ *freckle*, ⏜ *frank*, ⏜ *France*.

3. In other cases the "right" curves ⏜⏜ are generally used, as ⏜ *verbose*, ⏜ *Africa*, ⏜ *fresh*, ⏜ *frame*.

4. As regards *thr* and *THr*, ⏜⏜ are used initially when preceded by a vowel (*i.e.*, as when standing alone); thus, ⏜ *Atherton*, ⏜ *Atherley*, ⏜ *otherwise;* and

5. In other cases the "right" curves ⏜⏜ are used, as ⏜ *thread*, ⏜ *thrive*, ⏜ *thrash*, ⏜ *throttle*, ⏜ *tether*, ⏜ *zither*, ⏜ *Arthur*.

6. There are no right-motion forms for *thl;* ⏜ *Ethel,* but ⏜ *lethal*.

7. When circles to initial hooks follow another stroke, both circle and hook are shown; thus, ⏜ *prosper*, ⏜ *destroy*, ⏜ *display*.

Double Consonants (Vocalized) and Separate R or L

1. Medial *r* or *l* preceded by a strongly-sounded vowel is generally represented by separate *r* or *l* unless a hooked form is necessary in order to avoid an awkward or a too lengthy outline; thus ⏜ *ulterior*, ⏜ *internal*, ⏜ *fraternal*, ⏜ *repel*, but ⏜ *repulsive*.

2. Words ending in *-torial* are generally written with separate *r*, but the hooked form is used in a few cases to avoid an awkward or a very lengthy outline; thus, ⏜ *tutorial*, ⏜ *equatorial*, ⏜ *piscatorial*, but ⏜ *reportorial*, ⏜ *spectatorial*, ⏜ *dictatorial*.

3. Words ending in *-tarium, -torium*, etc., are generally written with the hooked *tr;* thus, ⏜ *planetarium*, ⏜ *moratorium*.

4. Words ending in *-chord* are written with half-length *kr;* thus, ⎍ *tetrachord*, ⌇ *monochord*.

5. Words ending in *-form* are written with the hooked form, ⌒ or ⌒, after | | / ( ) ⌒ ⌒ or ⌒; thus, ⌒ *stalactiform*, ⌒ *spongiform*, ⌒ *aciform*, ⌒ *curviform*, ⌒ *vermiform*. In other cases separate *r* is used; thus, ⌒ *napiform*, ⌒ *cuneiform*, ⌒ *metalliform*, ⌒ *variform*.

6. Words ending in *-culate, -gulate, -cular, -gular,* and *-culum* are generally written with the hooked strokes *kl* or *gl;* thus, ⌒ *calculate*, ⌒ *speculate*, ⌒ *gesticulate*, ⌒ *reticulate*, ⌒ *articulate*, ⌒ *circulate*, ⌒ *matriculate*, ⌒ *coagulate*, ⌒ *regulate*, ⌒ *binocular*, ⌒ *angular*, ⌒ *singular*, ⌒ *curriculum*.

7. The prefix *for-* is represented by ⌒ or, when this is inconvenient, by ⌒; thus, ⌒ *forsake*, ⌒ *forbear*, but ⌒ *forget*. This does not apply to the prefix *fore-*, which should be written with separate *r* (downward in preference) when convenient; thus, ⌒ *forecast*, ⌒ *forenoon*, ⌒ *foresight* (compare ⌒ *ferocity*); otherwise the hooked form is used; thus, ⌒ *foretell*, ⌒ *foreshorten*, ⌒ *forewarn*.

8. Compound words ending in *-bird* and *-board* are written with the halflength *br* whenever convenient; thus, ⌒ *jailbird*, ⌒ *mocking-bird*, ⌒ *blackboard*, ⌒ *switchboard*. But note ⌒ *pasteboard;* also ⌒ *keyboard*, for distinction (⌒ *cupboard*).

Final N (Stroke and Hook)

1. Words ending in *-nian* are generally written with the hook for the final *n*, even in the case of DERIVATIVES from words with outlines ending with hook *n;* thus, ⌒ *Etonian*, ⌒ *Hamiltonian*, but note ⌒ *Gladstonian*, ⌒ *Augustinian*, ⌒ *Athenian*.

2. Words ending in *-n nt* are generally written with hook *n* finally; thus, ⌒ *anent*, ⌒ *assonant*, ⌒ *dissonant*. Final *-n nt* preceded by *p*, stroke *t* or *v* or *m* is, however, written with stroke *nt* finally; thus, ⌒ *pennant*, ⌒ *tenant*, ⌒ *convenient*, ⌒ *dominant*, as are also the words ⌒ *consonant* and ⌒ *sonant*.

3. Words ending in *-t n* or *-d n* are generally written with the hook for the final *n;* thus, ⟍⌐ *fatten,* ⟍⟋ *wheaten,* ⟋⟍ *abandon.*

4. The final *n* is, however, represented by the stroke in the following cases:

(*a*) Words ending in *-rt n* or *-j st n,* such as ⟍⟍ *Spartan,* ⟍⟍ *martin,* ⟍⟋ *congestion.* Compare ⟍⟋ *puritan,* ⟍⟋ *baritone,* ⟍⟋ *Samaritan,* in which a vowel occurs between the *r* and the *t.*

(*b*) Most words ending in *-ntine,* e.g. ⟍⟍ *turpentine.*

(*c*) The words ⟍⟍ *fountain,* ⟍⟍ *mountain,* ⟍⟍ *plantain,* ⟍⟍ *pontoon,* ⟍⟍ *bounden* and ⟍⟍ *garden.*

N Preceded by Two Vowel Sounds

Stroke *n* is used: (*a*) After a TRIPHONE consisting of *ū* and a vowel; thus, ⟍⟍ *genuine,* ⟍⟍ *constituent,* ⟍⟍ *pursuant.* Compare ⟍⟍ *lion,* ⟍⟍ *client,* ⟍⟍ *compliance,* ⟍⟍ *buoyancy,* in which the *n* is preceded by other triphones.

(*b*) After two separate vowel-signs; thus, ⟍⟍ *triune.*

(*c*) In the words ⟍⟍ *pioneer,* ⟍⟍ *giant,* ⟍⟍ *buoyant,* ⟍⟍ *heroine,* ⟍⟍ *ruin,* and several words ending in *-fluent,* e.g., ⟍⟍ *fluent,* ⟍⟍ *mellifluent.* Compare other words in which *n* occurs after a diphone, e.g., ⟍⟍ *crayon,* ⟍⟍ *cayenne,* ⟍⟍ *hygiene.*

Note also words like ⟍⟍ *recurrence,* ⟍⟍ *concurrent,* in which stroke *n* is used although the two vowel sounds do not occur together.

Medial N

1. In the absence of any special reason to the contrary, stroke *n* is used between *p, b, t, d, ch* or *j* and *full-length t* or *d;* thus, ⟍⟍ *pantaloon,* ⟍⟍ *bountiful,* ⟍⟍ *tantalize,* ⟍⟍ *dental,* ⟍⟍ *legendary.*

2. But the hook is used between the same strokes and *half-length t* or *d,* unless the *n* is followed by a vowel; thus, ⟍⟍ *painted,* ⟍⟍ *potentate,* ⟍⟍ *daunted,* ⟍⟍ *enchanted,* ⟍⟍ *jointed,* but ⟍⟍ *penitent,* ⟍⟍ *originated.*

Note, however, ⟍⟍ *abandon* and ⟍⟍ *urbanity,* in which the other circular movement in the outlines renders the hook more convenient.

Stroke *n* is used after only one downstroke having an initial attachment on the opposite side; thus, ⟍⟍ *stranded,* ⟍⟍ *reprinted,* ⟍⟍ *branded.* Compare ⟍⟍ *disappointed,* ⟍⟍ *suspended.*

3. Hook *n* is used between ⟋ *r* and ⟍ *n* in such words as ⟍⟋ barrenness, ⟍⟋ modernness, but stroke *n* is preferred between ⟋ *sr* or ⟋ *w* and ⟍ *n;* thus, ⟋ sereneness, ⟋ oneness. Similarly ⟋ roundness, but ⟋ windiness.

4. Stroke *n* is generally retained in DERIVATIVES from words written with the stroke, other than a few ending in -*ic* or -*cy;* thus, ⟍ funnier, ⟍ puniness; but ⟋ euphonic, ⟋ subserviency.

Medial NS

1. Stroke *n* is used medially before *s* or *z*, unless the hook is clearly more convenient; thus, ⟋ Wednesday, ⟋ wainscot, ⟋ caravansary, but ⟋ ransom, ⟋ lonesome, ⟍ ironside.

2. Two hooks together are generally avoided; hence ⟍ plunger, ⟍ ranger. They are, however, allowed in ⟍ kindred, ⟍ hundred, ⟍ manger, ⟍ philanthropist, and one or two uncommon words, as well as certain compound words (see next paragraph).

3. In COMPOUND WORDS hook *n* is often retained medially, even where it would be avoided in other words; e.g., ⟍ open-mouthed, ⟍ penman, ⟍ mainmast, ⟍ rainproof, ⟍ earthenware.

F, V (Hook and Stroke)

1. Words ending in -*tive* (other than those which are contracted) are generally written with ⟍; thus, ⟍ receptive, ⟍ inventive. Exceptions to the above are ⟍ captive, ⟍ plaintive, ⟍ comparative, and such words as ⟍ attentive, ⟍ retentive, ⟍ digestive, ⟍ suggestive.

2. The stroke is used for *f* or *v* occurring between *p* or *b* (without an initial attachment) and *t* or *d;* thus, ⟍ pivot, ⟍ buffet. After ⟍ or ⟍, however, the hook is more convenient; thus, ⟍ private, ⟍ brevity.

3. Hook *f* or *v* is used between *t*, *d* or *ch* and *t* or *d* in DERIVATIVES as well as other words; thus ⟍ sanctified, ⟍ Cheviot. Note, however, ⟍ defied, ⟍ edified and ⟍ deified, for distinction.

Direction of "Shun" Hook

Words like ⟍ probation, ⟍ correction, etc., are written in accordance with the principle that when the *shun* hook is added to a straight stroke which

has an initial attachment, the hook is written on the side *opposite* to the initial attachment; and ⌐‾‾, *decoction,* ⌐‾‾ *adoption,* ⌐‾‾ *inaction,* etc., are written to follow the general rule that the hook is added on the side *opposite* the last-sounded vowel when there is no initial attachment. It must be remembered, however, that the hook is always added to the right side of simple *t, d* or *j;* thus ⌐‾‾ *rotation,* ⌐‾‾ *gradation,* ⌐‾‾ *logician.*

The Aspirate

1. Initial *h* followed by a TRIPHONE is represented by the upward or the downward stroke, and not by the tick; thus, ⌐‾‾ *Higham,* ⌐‾‾ *Howard,* ⌐‾‾ *hierarchy,* ⌐‾‾ *hyaline,* ⌐‾‾ *Howell.*

2. Downward *h* is used in a few cases to create a clear distinction of outline as ⌐‾‾ *heritor, cp.* ⌐‾‾ *inheritor;* ⌐‾‾ *heritable, cp.* ⌐‾‾ *inheritable,* or to provide a more easily written form, as ⌐‾‾ *heritage.*

3. Words beginning with *hetero-* are written with ⌐‾‾ except before ⌐‾‾ or ⌐‾‾ when ⌐‾‾ is more convenient; thus, ⌐‾‾ *heterogeneous,* ⌐‾‾ *heterodox;* but ⌐‾‾ *heterogamous,* ⌐‾‾ *heteromorphous,* ⌐‾‾ *heterology.*

4. COMPOUND WORDS ending in *-house* are written as under:

(*a*) With ⌐‾‾ if convenient for joining, *i.e.* after *p, b, t, d, f* or a straight upstroke; thus, ⌐‾‾ *chop-house,* ⌐‾‾ *club-house,* ⌐‾‾ *gate-house,* ⌐‾‾ *coffee-house,* ⌐‾‾ *warehouse,* ⌐‾‾ *hothouse.*

(*b*) With ⌐‾‾ after *k, g, m* or *l;* thus ⌐‾‾ *workhouse,* ⌐‾‾ *log-house,* ⌐‾‾ *summer-house,* ⌐‾‾ *ale-house.*

(*c*) When stroke *s* gives a better joining than either ⌐‾‾ or ⌐‾‾, *i.e.* after *ch, s, sh, n, ng,* a circle or a hook; thus, ⌐‾‾ *coach-house,* ⌐‾‾ *ice-house,* ⌐‾‾ *washhouse,* ⌐‾‾ *pigeon-house,* ⌐‾‾ *alms-house,* ⌐‾‾ *greenhouse.*

5. Downward *h* is retained in DERIVATIVES and COMPOUNDS of words in which *h* is the only consonant, if a *syllable* is added to the primitive word; thus, ⌐‾‾ *highness,* ⌐‾‾ *highest,* ⌐‾‾ *hoer,* ⌐‾‾ *high-bred,* ⌐‾‾ *hay-loft.* Compare ⌐‾‾ *hoed,* ⌐‾‾ *hewn,* etc., in which there is no added syllable.

6. Medial *h.* With regard to words ending in *-hold, -holed,* etc.:

(*a*) The form ⌐‾‾ is used after *p, b, f, v,* TH, or *h;* thus ⌐‾‾ *uphold,* ⌐‾‾

copyhold, ⟍⟋ behold, ⟍⟋ foothold, ⟍⟋ overhauled, ⟋⟋ withhold, ⟋ high-heeled.

(b) In other cases dot h and either ⟋ or, if more convenient, ⟋ are written; thus, ⟍ pigeonholed, ⟋ stronghold, ⟍ strangle-hold, ⟋ leasehold. ⟋

7. The use of initial Tick h is confined to the aspirate before m, l and r downward. The Tick h may be used when appropriate in a phrase, as; ⟍ for whom.

Upward and Downward R and L

1. Words beginning with st (*vowel*) r followed by stroke n have upward r; thus, ⟋ consternation, ⟋ sternutation, ⟋ Stornoway.

2. Final r is written upward (among other cases) after kr, gr or lk; thus, ⟋ crier, ⟋ grower, ⟋ luckier; but downward after sk or fk; thus, ⟍ obscure, ⟍ fakir.

3. Final r in COMPOUNDS, as in other words, is written upward after two downstrokes; thus ⟍⟋ tax-gatherer, ⟍⟋ shooting-star.

4. In words ending in -rest, -rist, -lest or -list the r or l is written upward or downward as when followed by a final vowel; thus, ⟍ barest, ⟍ fairest, ⟋ imperialist, ⟍ fullest, ⟍ annalist.

5. Medial r is nearly always written downward before m; thus, ⟍ barium, ⟍ emporium, ⟍ forum. After th, however, it is written upward; thus, ⟋ theorem.

6. Medial r is also written downward in most DERIVATIVES from words written with downward r; thus, ⟍ declarable, ⟍ powerful, ⟍ barely, ⟍ furrier, ⟍ maturely; but in words ending in -rial, -ral or -rhal upward r is used; thus, ⟋ armorial, ⟋ mayoral, ⟋ catarrhal.

7. Final l after ⟍ ⟍ or ⟋ is written as after ⟍; thus, ⟍ egotistical, ⟍ methodistical, ⟍ logistical, ⟍ fantastically.

8. L occurring finally, or with only a circle or loop following, is written downward after a half-length or double-length stroke if a more convenient outline is so obtained; thus, ⟍ completely, ⟍ shiftless, ⟍ vividly, ⟍ pectoral, ⟍ structural. Note ⟍ actual and ⟍ actually for distinction.

9. Final *l* is written upward after downward *l* in ⎰ genteelly, ⎰ foully, etc., but downward after ⌐ *ld* or ⌐ *lr* in ⎰ mildly, ⎰ scholarly, etc.

10. Final *l* is written downward in COMPOUNDS of words written with upward *l* if the upward form would be quite inconvenient for joining, as in ⎰ sand-eel, ⎰ train-oil, but the upward form is retained if at all practicable, as in ⎰ port-hole, ⎰ stock-list.

11. Medial *l* is written upward in ⎰ biliousness and ⎰ supercilious-ness, but downward in words ending in *-lescence* or *-lescent;* e.g., ⎰ opalescence, ⎰ coalescent. It is also written upward before ⎰ whenever practicable; thus, ⎰ realism, ⎰ imperialism, but ⎰ sensational-ism, ⎰ naturalism.

Upward and Downward SH

1. Final *sh* is written downward after *t* (or *st*); but upward after *d;* thus, ⎰ latish, ⎰ coquettish, ⎰ Crustacea, ⎰ moustache, but ⎰ radish, ⎰ Swedish. Exception: ⎰ brutish.

2. Final *-shŭs* is written upward after *t, d* or *sd,* but downward after *st;* thus, ⎰ fictitious, ⎰ seditious, but ⎰ superstitious.

3. The words ⎰ mopish and ⎰ mobbish are written with upward *sh* on the same principle as ⎰ brush, that after a straight downstroke which has an initial attachment, *sh* is written on the side opposite to the initial attachment.

4. Final *sh* or *sh s* after upward *l* is written downward; thus, ⎰ lash, ⎰ slash, ⎰ polish, ⎰ malicious; but in the past tenses ⎰ lashed, ⎰ polished, etc., upward *sh* is more convenient.

Compound Consonants

1. *Wl* and *wh l.* The compound consonants ⎰ and ⎰ are used in all words beginning with *w l d* and *wh l d* respectively; thus, ⎰ wailed, ⎰ weld, ⎰ wild, ⎰ wilder, ⎰ wheeled.

2. *Rr* and *ler.* The use of ⎰ and ⎰ is strictly confined to derivatives from words written with final downward *r* or final downward *l;* hence, ⎰ sorcerer, ⎰ fruiterer, ⎰ boiler, but note ⎰ cellarer.

3. The word ..../. *queer* is so written in order to keep it quite distinct from
.... *clear.*

4. *Kw* and *mp, mb* in COMPOUND WORDS. A consonant at the end of the first
part of a compound word is not combined with a consonant beginning the
second part; hence .... *silkworm,* .... *dumb-bell,* .... *tomboy.*
An exception to this is the word .... *lukewarm.*

5. When *mpr* or *mbr* follow *k, g* or an upstroke, they are represented by the
hooked form, as; .... *camber,* .... *Humber,* .... *lumber,* but in other
instances, the doubled form is used, as: .... *chamber,* .... *bumper.*

Halving Principle

1. A stroke is not halved when a better outline is obtained by means of the
full *t* or *d;* thus, ... *hotel,* .... *flotsam,* .... *graduation,* .... *indulge,*
.... *integer,* .... *interior,* .... *tautology,* .... *litigious,* .... *lemonade.*

2. Words ending in *-tatory, -datory, -ditary,* etc., are treated as follows:

(*a*) In the case of the termination *-tatory* the last *t* is generally written in full;
thus, ... *rotatory,* .... *excitatory,* .... *saltatory;* but

(*b*) When the termination is *-datory, -ditary,* the halving principle is generally
applied; thus, ... *consolidatory,* .... *hereditary.*

3. Words ending in *-tively* following stroke *t* or *tr* are written with full *t;*
thus, ... *authoritatively,* .... *illustratively.*

4. Words ending in *-ctary, -ctory, -catory, -gatory, -ctarian,* etc., are generally
written with full *t;* thus, ... *directory,* .... *purgatory,* .... *Tractarian.*
A better outline, however, is obtained by halving in such words as .... *secretary.*
.... *migratory.*

5. Words ending in *-taceous* and *-dacious* are written with full *t* or *d;* thus,
.... *cretaceous,* .... *mendacious.*

6. Although the halving principle is generally applied for the addition of
either *t* or *d* in words of more than one syllable, in primitive words a light
stroke (other than .... or ......) which can be thickened as well as
halved) is not halved standing alone to add *d,* or a heavy stroke standing alone to
add *t,* unless there is a final hook or a joined diphthong; thus, ... *acrid,*
.... *applaud,* .... *adroit,* .... *sedate,* .... *seclude.* Exceptions to this are: ....
convert, ... *concord* and .... *conclude.*

In past tenses of more than one syllable, however, a light stroke may generally be halved; thus, ...𝒫.... *seated,* ...:𝒫.... *stated,* ...𝒜.... *uttered,* ⌒ℂ .... *offered,* ....𝒮ᵛ .... *supplied,* ...𝒮... *construed,* ...𝒾:.... *committed,* ...ₒ𝒾:.... *commuted;* but note .....⌐⌐.. *echoed* and ..)⁚. *essayed.*

7. The more common words ending in *-pid* are written with half-length *p;* thus, ...𝒾⁚.... *tepid,* ⸝⸜₰ *insipid;* but

8. Words ending in *-pade, -ped, -pede* or *-pod* are generally written with full *d;* thus, ..)⌐⌐⌐. *escapade,* ∕⌒⌐⌐ *uniped,* ....⌐⌐. *centipede,* ...ᐸ⌐⌐ *tripod.* But note ⌐⌐⌐⌐⌐⌐ₗ.... *quadruped,* to avoid a lengthy outline.

9. Words ending in *k (vowel) d* are generally written with full *d;* thus ....⌐⌐⌐.ₗ... *arcade,* ......⌐⌐⌐.. *naked,* ...𝒾ₗ.... *decoyed;* but half-length *k* is used in a few words of more than two syllables, *e.g.,* ⌣⌣⁚... *barricade,* ....⌐⌐⌐⁚. *cavalcade,* and in the word ...∕⌐⌐.. *rescued.*

10. Words ending in *g (vowel) t,* however, are generally written with half-length *g;* thus, ..⸜⌐⌐... *frigate,* ....⌐⌐.. *target,* ..⸜⌐⌐... *nugget.*

11. As a rule the halving principle is not applied if the resulting outline would not be capable of full vocalization. It is, however, applied in the case of a number of words ending in *-tism* or *-dism* in which a more facile outline is obtained by disregarding the "*i,*" viz., ..𝒾⁚⌐⌐.... *despotism,* ...⌐⌐⸜ᵧ.. *Jacobitism,* ......⸝ₖ.... *patriotism,* ⸜⌐ₒ⌐ *blackguardism,* ⸜⌐⸝⌐ *favouritism,* ⌐ₒ⌐⌐ *scepticism,* and several words ending in *-matism* such as, ⸜⌐⸝ₗ.... *rheumatism.* Compare such words as ⸜ᵧ⌐ₜ *absolutism,* .⸝⌐ₓ.. *conservatism,* etc., in which the full outline is quite convenient.

12. The halving principle is, as a rule, applied when *t* or *d* is preceded by a DIPHONE; thus, ..⸝⌐ₜ.. *create,* ..)ₗ.. *druid,* ..∕⌐ᵛ.... *radiate;* but the *t* is written in full in ..⸜⌐... *poet,* ..⸝⌐ₗ..... *silhouette,* and a few uncommon words and proper names.

13. Stroke *t* or *d* is retained when convenient in the following classes of DERIVATIVES, viz.:

(*a*) Words derived, either directly or indirectly, from *primitive* words with outlines containing stroke *t* or *d* and not more than one other stroke consonant; *e.g.,* ....⸝⌐.... *pitiful,* ⌐⌐⌐⁚. *cottony,* ⌐⌐⸝ₒ *gluttonous,* ...⸜........ *bedeck,* ......⸝ₗ.... *undivided,* ⌐⌐⸜ *becloud,* ⌣⌐⸝ *overrate,* ..⸝ₗ........ *outspread,* ⸜⌐⸝ *overcrowd.*

The following are exceptions: .... *beautify,* .... *beautiful,* .... *written,* .... *writing,* .... *undefined,* .... *indebted,* .... *subdivide.*

(*b*) Certain secondary derivatives from *primary derivatives* written with stroke *t* or *d*, in which the stroke is retained for the purpose of distinction; *e.g.,* .... *weightiness,* .... *greediness,* .... *heartily,* .... *flightiness.*

(*c*) In words ending in -*tieth*, in order to prevent the possibility of confusion between .... *seventieth* and .... *seventh;* .... *fiftieth* and .... *fifth,* etc.

14. In COMPOUNDS of words with outlines ending in stroke *t* or *d*, that *t* or *d* is generally expressed by halving; thus, ... *copyright,* .... *backbite,* .... *ice-boat,* .... *cow-hide,* .... *go-ahead,* .... *brushwood.* Stroke *t* or *d* is, however, retained after one half-length stroke, as in .... *tit-bit,* .... *catboat,* and also in a few cases in which the full *t* or *d* gives a more distinct outline, *e.g.,* .... *rosewood,* .... *jolly-boat,* .... *row-boat.*

15. In COMPOUNDS of words commencing with *t* or *d*, that *t* or *d* is not expressed by halving; thus, ... *timetable,* .... *gravedigger,* .... *quarterdeck.* Exceptions: .... *sometimes* and .... *beforetime.*

16. *Rt* is written upward:

(*a*) finally, as in .... *port,* .... *fort* and .... *alert.*

(*b*) When circled initially, as .... *sort,* .... *concert,* and .... *consort;* and

(*c*) Initially and medially before stroke *n*, as in .... *certain,* .... *ascertain* and .... *fortune, cp.* .... *fourteen.*

It is written downward:

(*d*) In such words as .... *art* and .... *artful,* following the rule for initial *r* with a preceding vowel;

(*e*) When more convenient for joining and vocalization, as in .... *shirt* and .... *snort;* and

(*f*) When used medially, as in .... *assortment,* for the convenience of joining *ment.*

17. *Lt* is generally written upward as in .... *fault,* .... *quilt,* .... *exult;* but it is written downward:

(a) When preceded by an initial vowel and followed by *m*, as in .....⌐..... *ultimate*, and

(b) After *n*, *ng*, *vs* or *ns* as in ....⌐.... *knelt*, ...⌐.... *ringlet*, ...⌐.... *vacillate*, ...⌐... *insult;* also in the word ....⌐.... *dwelt*.

18. *Rd*. With regard to final *rd*, the forms .....⌐...... *veered*, ...⌐...... *persevered*, etc., are adopted, but in such words as *geared*, ...⌐.... is a better form than ......⌐...., which would become indistinct in fast writing.

19. In addition to cases in which ....⌐.... would be actually inconvenient, ...⌐.... is used for final *rd* in such past tenses as ....⌐.... *rendered*, ...⌐.... *surrendered*, ...⌐.... *wintered*. (Compare ....⌐.... *windward*.)

20. *Ld*. When ....⌐.... would be inconvenient *ld* is represented by the full form ....⌐....; thus, ...⌐.... *quarrelled*, ...⌐.... *belittled*, ...⌐.... *scheduled*, ...⌐.... *leasehold*. Note: ....⌐.... is sufficiently convenient in ....⌐.... *retailed*, ...⌐.... *mild*, ...⌐.... *lulled*, etc.

Doubling Principle

1. The doubling principle is not applied in words ending in *-lateral* and *-literal*, double-length *l* being used only in words in which it occurs *finally* and in words derived from these; hence, ...⌐.... *lateral*, *cp*. ....⌐.... *latterly*, ...⌐.... *pluriliteral*, ...⌐.... *poulterer*, *cp*. ....⌐.... *slaughterer*, ...⌐.... *liturgy*, *cp*. ....⌐.... *lighterage*.

2. The doubling principle, which is applied in the case of most common words ending in *-ture*, is not applied in the following instances: ....⌐.... *literature*, ...⌐.... *capture* (the outline ....⌐.... being required for *captor*), ...⌐.... *furniture*, and words like ....⌐.... *departure* and ....⌐.... *candidature*.

3. When the vowel in the termination *-tor* is sounded distinctly, as in the legal terms ....⌐.... *grantor*, ...⌐.... *vendor*, ...⌐.... *guarantor*, the doubling principle is not applied.

4. The doubling principle is applied in a few cases although there is an accented vowel between *t* and *r;* e.g., ...⌐.... *interpret*, ...⌐.... *enteric*, ...⌐.... *dysenteric*, ...⌐.... *tartaric*, ...⌐.... *material*.

5. The doubling principle is also applied in the following cases, notwithstanding that there is no vowel between the *t* or *d* and the *r:*

(*a*) Several words containing *central, centri-* or *-centric*, e.g., ... central, ... concentric, ... eccentric, ... centrifugal.

(*b*) .... theatrical, ... cylindric.

6. Words ending in *-erate* or *-orate*, which are derived from words written with a double-length stroke, are written by means of the halving principle (*i.e.*, in the same way as past tenses such as .... centred); thus, ... directorate, ... stadtholderate.

7. The doubling principle is not applied when *tr* is preceded by a triphone representing a diphthong and a long vowel; thus, ... extenuator, ... punctuator. Compare .... proprietor, ... radiator.

8. Joining of Strokes of Unequal Length. The rule that unless the difference in thickness, or an angle at the point of junction, shows the inequality of length, strokes of unequal length may not be joined, applies to double-length as well as half-length strokes. Double-length *n*, however, is sufficiently distinct after *t* or downward *l*; thus, ... detonator, ... alienator.

9. Double-length *l* is written upward, except after *n, ng, ns* or *sk*; thus, ... filter, ... beholder, ... gilder, but .... penholder, ... ringleader, ... insulter, ... scolder, ... helter-skelter.

10. Double-length strokes may be used in such COMPOUND WORDS as the following: .... backbiter, ... chaffcutter, ... muzzle-loader.

Prefixes

1. (*a*) The prefix *com-* or *con-* initially is represented by means of a light dot written at the beginning of the outline; *e.g.*, ... confess, ... commence.

(*b*) *Medially* (in words or phrases) it is indicated by proximity, as in .... subcommittee and .... *I am content*.

(*c*) Where the dot would be of no advantage, or for the sake of legibility, the *com-* or *con-* is written in full; thus .... comedian, ... commotion.

2. (*a*) The prefix *cum-* or *cog-* used *medially* is also indicated by proximity, in the same way as medial *com-* or *con-*, as in .... circumference, ... recognize.

(*b*) As *cum-* or *cog-* do not frequently occur initially, they are always represented by the consonants in full and never by the dot, as in .... cumbent, ... cog-wheel.

3. *Accommo-* (or *accom-*) is represented by a joined or disjoined *k;* thus .... *accommodation,* but .... *accommodate,* .... *accomplish,* but .... *accompany.*

4. The prefix *intro-* is represented by double-length *n,* as in .... *introduce.*

5. The prefix for *magna-, magne-, magni-,* is represented by a disjoined *m;* thus .... *magnanimous,* .... *magnetized,* .... *magnificent.*

6. (*a*) *Trans-* is contracted by the omission of the *n,* when it is followed by *p, m,* upward *l* or the hooked letters *pl, kr, gr, fr* and *fl,* thus, ... *transparent,* .... *transmit,* .... *translation,* .... *transplant,* .... *transcribe,* .... *transgress,* .... *transfer,* .... *transfluent.*

(*b*) The full form is sometimes written in order to give distinguishing outlines or more facile forms; thus, ... *transverse, cp.* .... *transfers.*

7. (*a*) The prefix *self-* is represented by means of a small disjoined circle, written in the second vowel-place, as in .... *self-made.*

(*b*) *Self-con-* is represented by a disjoined circle written in the place of the *con-* dot, e.g. .... *self-control.*

8. (*a*) The prefix *in-* is represented by a small initial hook written with the right motion before the treble consonants *str, skr* and upward *h;* thus .... *instruct,* .... *inscriber,* .... *inhabit.*

(*b*) This small hook is not used in negative words, i.e. where *in-* means *not;* e.g. .... *hospitable,* but .... *inhospitable.*

9. Words which have the prefix *il-, im-, in-, ir-, un-,* are represented thus:

(*a*) .... *reparable,* but .... *irreparable;* .... *limitable,* but .... *illimitable,* i.e. by writing the downward *r* or *l* when the rules for writing initial *r* or *l* allow this to be done.

(*b*) The strokes *l, m, n,* or *r* are repeated in cases where a distinction cannot otherwise be obtained, thus, ... *illegible,* .... *immaterial,* .... *unnamed,* .... *irradiate,* .... *innumerable.*

10. Logograms are sometimes used as prefixes in such words as, ... *gentlemanlike,* .... *undertake,* being joined to the following outline if convenient.

Suffixes

1. With reference to -ing the stroke is used after ⌒, although it does not give a very convenient joining, as the dot might be mistaken for a vowel-sign; thus, ⟋⌣ utilizing, ⌒ releasing.

2. When adding -ing, the outline of the original word is almost invariably left unaltered; thus, ⟍ fancying, ⟋ freezing, ⌒ shelling, ⌢. cleansing, ⟋ hoeing, ⟋ allowing, ⟍ failing, ⟍ piercing, ⟍ pushing, ⟋ rating. Exceptions to this are ⟋ losing, ⟋ lacing, etc., ⟋ ailing, ⟋ coalescing, ⟋ convalescing and ⟋ writing.

3. When the outline of the present tense ends with a joined diphthong, the latter is not retained if stroke ⟋ can be joined; thus, ⟋ renewing, ⟋ pursuing, ⟋ bowing.

4. Outlines containing stroke ng, when used in the representation of the suffix -ing are vocalized in the ordinary way, whether the vowel is a third-place vowel or otherwise; thus, ⟋ laying, ⟋ gnawing.

5. -ality, -ility, -arity, etc., are expressed by means of a disjoined stroke in the great majority of cases, including practically all of the large number of words ending in -bility. The words which are written in full include:

(a) Words ending in -alty, -iality, erty, or -iority, if the full outline is quite convenient; thus, ⟍ penalty, ⟋ cordiality, ⟋ partiality, ⟋ veniality, ⟋ inferiority.

(b) Words in which the full outline is particularly facile, especially after a half-length stroke; e.g., ⟋ fertility, ⟋ austerity, ⟋ maturity, ⟋ verticality, ⟋ personality.

(c) Words in which the -ality, etc., is preceded by only one stroke or by s or shun; thus, ⟋ hilarity, ⟋ facility, ⟋ nationality.

(d) In a few cases for the purpose of distinction; e.g., ⟋ juniority, cp. ⟋ geniality; ⟋ locality, cp. ⟋ legality; ⟋ disparity, cp. ⟋ disability.

(e) ⟋ compatibility, ⟋ accessibility, ⟋ asperity, and a few other miscellaneous words.

A vowel preceding the disjoined consonant indicating the suffix -ality, etc., may, if necessary, be disregarded; thus, ⟋ visibility.

6. *-ment* is represented by .... after .... or ......, or a hook to which the full form ...... cannot conveniently be joined; thus, ... *consignment,* .... *preferment,* .... *effacement,* .... *commencement,* .... *enchantment,* .... *pavement;* also in ...... *enlistment.* When ...... can be made convenient, it is often written in preference to the contracted form; thus, ... *discernment,* .... *amendment,* .... *assortment.*

7. The suffix .... may be joined when occurring after full-length .... *r,* .... *n* or .... *ng;* also, when convenient, after a hook (the preceding part of the outline remaining unaltered); thus, ... *censorship,* .... *companionship,* .... *kingship,* .... *friendship,* .... *relationship.* *-ship* is written in full after .... *l,* as in .... *fellowship;* also in .... *airship.*

8. Disjoined .... may be used in compound and other words in which *-ship* is not grammatically a suffix; thus, ... *battleship,* .... *midshipman,* .... *lightship.*

9. *-fulness* is represented by the disjoined suffix ...... except in .... *delightfulness,* .... *doubtfulness* and .... *beautifulness.*

10. *-lessness* and *-lousness* are represented by the disjoined suffix ....; thus, ... *sleeplessness,* .... *carelessness,* .... *ridiculousness,* .... *credulousness.*

11. Unvocalized short forms, joined or disjoined, may be used as suffixes, as in ...... *rebuild,* ...... *safeguard,* ...... *indifference,* ...... *become.*

12. Compound words, joined or disjoined, with their primary outlines; thus, ... *brother-in-law,* .... *watertight.*

13. Compound words beginning with *here, there, where,* etc., are written as follows; .... *hereby,* .... *therefrom,* .... *whereupon.*

14. Compounds of *further-, -much* and *-soever,* are written thus; .... *furthermore,* .... *inasmuch,* .... *whatsoever.*

Short Forms

DERIVATIVES and COMPOUNDS from single-stroke short forms are written by retaining the unvocalized shorthand in the outline whenever a convenient and legible form is so obtained; thus, ... *golden,* .... *thankless,* .... *deliverer,* .... *would-be,* .... *twofold.*

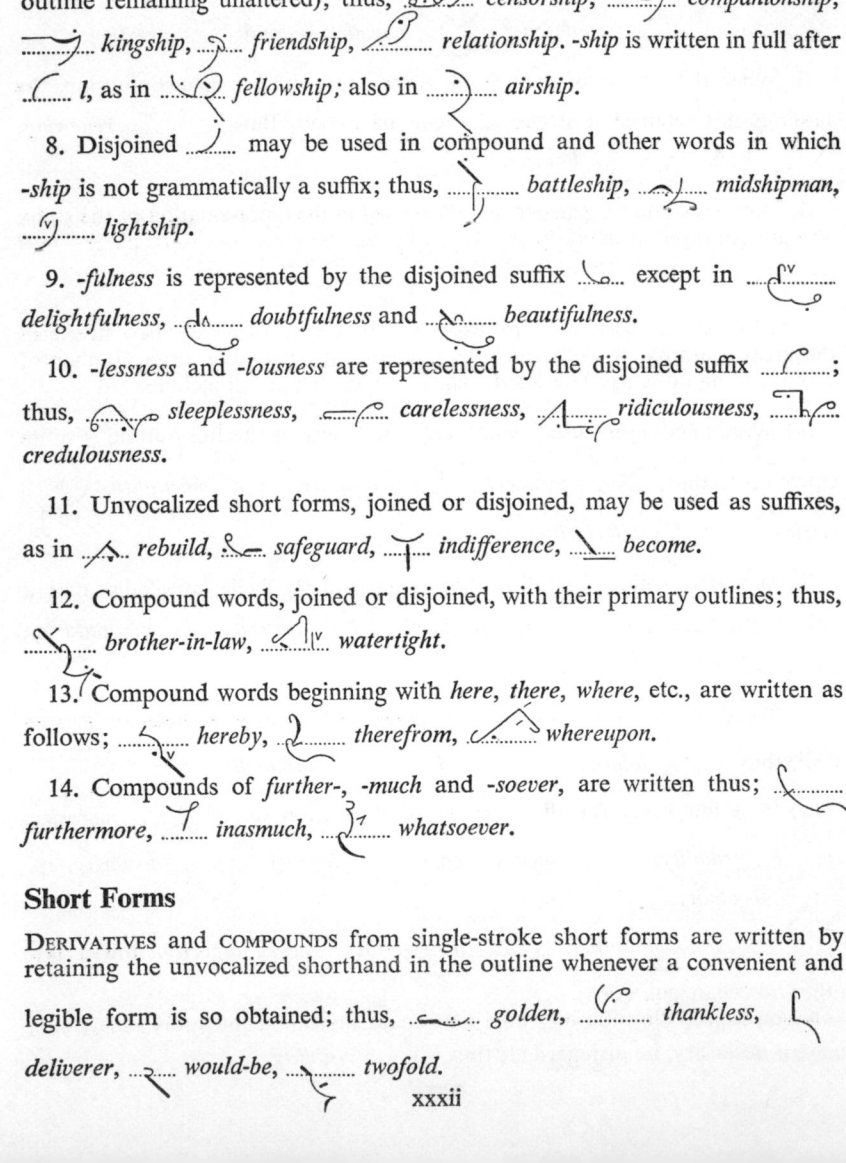

Contracted Forms

1. Although medial *t* after *s* may often be omitted, this is not permissible when a vowel occurs immediately after the *t* except in the following instances; viz. ⟍ *postal*, ⟍ *postage*, ⟍ *post-office*, ⟍ *testament*, ⟍ *testimony*, ⟍ *procrastinate*, ⟍ *investigate*, ⟍ *mistake*, ⟍ *domestic*, ⟍ *pessimistic*, ⟍ *optimistic*, ⟍ *euphemistic*, ⟍ *mediumistic*, ⟍ *bombastic*, ⟍ *futuristic*, ⟍ *substitute*, ⟍ *sub-stitution*, ⟍ *destitute*, ⟍ *destitution*, ⟍ *institute*, ⟍ *institution*, ⟍ *celestial* and derivatives from these words (⟍ *mistook* excepted). Compare ⟍ *pistol*, ⟍ *vestige*, ⟍ *sophisticate*, ⟍ *mystic*, ⟍ *plastic*, ⟍ *rustic*, etc., in which the *t* is expressed.

2. In addition to the contracted forms appearing in the lists in the textbooks, contracted forms are also given in the dictionary, as alternatives to the full outlines, for some other words, which are not considered to be of such frequent occurrence in general matter as to warrant their inclusion in the lists; thus, ⟍ or ⟍ *generation*, ⟍ or ⟍ *constitutional-ly*.

Derivative Words

The derivation of words must be regarded as one of a number of considerations affecting the choice of outlines, but while in the outlines of many derivatives the outline of the primitive word, or some particular feature of it, is retained, there are, on the other hand, many cases in which derivatives are written in accordance with the ordinary rules and principles of the system, without regard to derivation; *e.g.*, ⟍ *remove*, ⟍ *remover*; ⟍ *bitter*, ⟍ *embitter*; ⟍ *hawk*, ⟍ *hawker*; ⟍ *ail*, ⟍ *ailment*; ⟍ *royal*, ⟍ *royalist*.

Words described as "derivatives" are taken to include any words that are *apparently* derived from other English words.

Derivatives Anticipated

In certain cases, including some verbs previously mentioned, words are written in a particular way so that their outlines may agree with those of derivatives formed from them, *e.g.*, ⟍ *meddle*, ⟍ *meddled*; ⟍ *wanton*, ⟍ *wantonly*; ⟍ *clandestine*, ⟍ *clandestinely*; ⟍ *captive*, ⟍ *captivate*; ⟍ *inadvertent*, ⟍ *inadvertently*; ⟍ *exist*, ⟍ *existence*; ⟍ *sister*, ⟍ *sisterly*; ⟍ *scientific*, ⟍ *scientifically*; ⟍ *shelter*, ⟍ *sheltered*.

Compound Words

A number of classes of compound words have already been dealt with in connection with the various principles involved. With regard to cases in which the outlines of the primary words will not join conveniently, they are written disjoined if a better outline is not obtainable by altering one or both of them so as to admit of joining. (See also the paragraph that follows.)

Disjoining

1. Disjoining is not resorted to if a better outline can otherwise be obtained; thus, _____ *tactics,* _____ *locate,* _____ *densely,* _____ *rearrange,* but _____ *misfeasance,* _____ *steadfast,* _____ *mentionable,* _____ *deaf-mute,* _____ *spendthrift.*

2. Three straight strokes that would not make an angle are not joined together; hence _____ *picture-gallery,* _____ *turkey-cock.*

3. Outlines in which one at least of three strokes is a curve are generally allowable although there is no angle; thus, _____ *papacy,* _____ *clockwork;* but the combination _____ is avoided; hence, _____ *luckier.*

4. Sometimes an angle is shown in order to make a joining allowable; thus, _____ *escheat,* _____ *Hebraized.*

5. More than two successive downstrokes including *p b, d t,* etc., are generally avoided by disjoining in such words as _____ *top-boots,* _____ *red-tapism,* _____ *quarterdeck.* Compare _____ *copybook,* _____ *seed-time,* _____ *tea-dealer,* in which there are only two downstrokes.

Outlines and Vowels

Outlines, as a rule, are not varied in order to permit of a vowel-sign being placed exactly in its proper place; thus, _____ *legislation,* _____ *ceaseless,* _____ *ingeniously,* _____ *appropriately,* _____ *meanwhile.* In a few cases, however, in which an outline that can be more accurately vocalized is a better one from a practical point of view, it is adopted, *e.g.,* _____ *doubtless,* _____ *unsoiled.*

In certain cases, in which it would be difficult to insert an intersected vowel-sign, it is disregarded; *e.g.,* _____ *figurative,* _____ *calculated,* _____ *partiality.*

Special Outlines

It will be recognized that there are many pairs or groups of words which, from their meaning, are liable to clash, and every precaution is necessary in such

cases to avoid the risk of confusion. In a great majority of cases the application of the ordinary rules of the system affords adequate means of distinction, but in a comparatively few of these pairs of words, such as .... *favoured,* .... *favourite;* .... *Australian,* .... *Australasian;* .... *birth,* .... *burial;* which otherwise would be written with the same or a very similar form, a special outline is adopted for one of them in order to provide a clear distinction. Again, in a few instances, such as .... *solicitor,* .... *affidavit,* .... *oxyhydrogen,* .... *tartaric,* .... *sincerely,* .... *necessarily,* it has been found advisable, in order to secure the most convenient outline, to adopt a form which is not capable of being fully vocalized, or which is not written in accordance with the usual practice. A list of these special outlines, in addition to those already mentioned in this Introduction, is given below. It should be borne in mind that such outlines, except in the case of some derivatives from the words in question, must not necessarily be regarded as models for the formation of other outlines.

The following outlines are written out of their proper position for the purpose of distinction: .... *human,* .... *woman,* (cp. .... *humane,* .... *women).*

The Index to the Introduction will be found most useful where it is desired to refer to any word or class of word.

List of Special Outlines

afresh	capital	editor
agent	caused	editorial
alcohol	*child*less	erudite
alkali	conciliatory	eventually
alliance	considerate	explode
allowance	constitute	*eye*sight
antithesis	*dear*est	*eye*sore
assuredly	delightful	fallen
avert	descriptions	farmer
avoidance	desert	farther
bachelor	destiny	fiscal
bankrupt	diffract	flannelette
beerhouse	discern	foundation
bold	downright	further
candlestick	edification	futile

xxxv

futurism	needless	revere
garnet	notable	reverie
Gentile	officiated	secretariat
girth	omniscient	secretary
gradually	orator	separate
guidance	ordinal	shortened
hardiest	ornament	shrinker
heartily	ornamental	sightseer
hearty	outburst	solitary
hospital	oval	standardize
hyoid	partake	start
ignominy	*particular*ly	statute
illness	pattern	subvert
imperceptible	pennon	swerved
indigent	persecute	synod
indolent	poorest	temperate
inert	preciseness	transept
inevitable	pre-eminent	trivial
intromission	proprietary	undoubted
junior	Protestant	unlikely
marital	protestation	unluckily
merchandise	pure	upright
moodily	qualify	ursiform
moral	quality	verbal
mortal	queerly	veritable
Mrs.	railroad	vesture
narrate	rebate	virile
needful	rebut	vitiated
	regret	vitiation

Proper Names

Proper names have frequently more than one accepted pronunciation. In some instances, such as *Grantham, Evesham*, etc., there is a local and also an "outside" pronunciation, and in the case of foreign names some have an anglicized pronunciation while others are given a native pronunciation only. From the shorthand point of view some proper names require special consideration, and the following observations will serve to indicate the practice which has been adopted in various groups of words:

1. When the *nses* circle is used, the vowel is understood to be *ĕ:* it is therefore necessary to write stroke *n* and the *ses* circle when another vowel occurs, as in ⟨⟩ *Albigenses*, ⟨⟩ *Waldenses*.

2. Proper names ending in *-ley* preceded by the sound of *k* are generally written with the hooked form; thus, ⟨⟩ *Brockley*, ⟨⟩ *Hinckley*.

3. Words ending in *-shire* are generally written with the hooked form *shr;* thus, ⟨⟩ *Ayrshire*, ⟨⟩ *Aberdeenshire*.

4. Words ending in *-ford* are generally written with the half-length hooked form (⟨⟩ or ⟨⟩); thus, ⟨⟩ *Woodford*, ⟨⟩ *Catford*, ⟨⟩ *Oxford*. The separate ⟨⟩, however, is used after ⟨⟩, etc., as in ⟨⟩ *Swinford*, ⟨⟩ *Cinderford*, ⟨⟩ *Chingford*.

5. The hooked form ⟨⟩ is used for the terminations *-borough, -burgh, -bury,* when it is more convenient than the separate *b-r*, including cases in which it occurs after *t, d, m, ms, l, ls;* thus, ⟨⟩ *Attleborough*, ⟨⟩ *Flamborough*, ⟨⟩ *Aldeburgh*, ⟨⟩ *Bloomsbury*, ⟨⟩ *Tilbury*, ⟨⟩ *Halsbury*.

6. Proper names ending in *-ton* or *-don* are treated in the same way as other words having those terminations (see page xx); thus, ⟨⟩ *Merton*, ⟨⟩ *Pemberton*, ⟨⟩ *Cheriton*, ⟨⟩ *Clifton*, ⟨⟩ *Bandon*.

7. Words ending in *-field* are generally written with ⟨⟩ but after ⟨⟩ or ⟨⟩ hook *f* is used; thus, ⟨⟩ *Duffield*, but ⟨⟩ *Lichfield*, ⟨⟩ *Sedgfield*.

8. In the majority of words ending in *-ham* the *h* is silent, *e.g.,* ⟨⟩ *Clapham*, ⟨⟩ *Seaham*, ⟨⟩ *Ashburnham*, ⟨⟩ *Tottenham*, ⟨⟩ *Rotherham*, but in a few names of more than two syllables ending in *-ingham*, such as *Birmingham, Nottingham*, the aspirate is pronounced by some persons. There are also a number of names ending in *-sham* or *-tham* in which custom has sanctioned the sound of *sh* and *th* respectively, *e.g.,* ⟨⟩ *Horsham*, ⟨⟩ *Waltham*, ⟨⟩ *Bentham*, though in others the *s* or *t* sound is retained, *e.g.,* ⟨⟩ *Topsham*, ⟨⟩ *Cheetham*, ⟨⟩ *Greatham*.

9. The *h* in the termination *-hurst* is generally represented by the **dot**; thus, Lyndhurst, Billingshurst. In a few instances, however, it is disregarded in order to obtain a more convenient outline, *e.g.*, Pankhurst, Parkhurst.

10. After *k* (among other cases) the terminations *-wall*, *-well*, are most conveniently written with ; thus, Kirkwall, Bakewell. After upward *l*, however, is sufficiently convenient; as Holywell.

11. When the vowel in the termination *-ville* is sounded distinctly, the separate *l* is written if convenient; thus, Sackville, Granville, but Nashville.

12. The termination *-gate* is written with full *t;* thus, Bishopsgate, Deansgate, Cripplegate.

13. *-wood*, however, is generally written with half-length *w;* thus, Attwood, Kingswood. Exception, Heywood, to distinguish from Hayward.

14. Words having the termination *-worth* are written with ; thus, Saddleworth, Nailsworth; or when necessary to avoid an awkward or too lengthy outline, with vocalized with *wŭ;* thus, Wandsworth, Wordsworth.

15. In words ending in *-ing*, the dot is used after or or after following another stroke; thus, Epping, Wapping, Hastings, Twining, Spalding. In other cases stroke is written; thus, Tooting, Kettering, Hutchings, Harding, Jennings.

16. In proper names *p* is not omitted when it occurs between *m* and *t* or *m* and *sh; e.g.,* Hampstead (Hamstead), Ampthill, Compton, Assumption, Hampshire. In Campden the *p* is silent.

17. In proper names having their origin in short forms the shorthand outlines are retained, but may be vocalized; thus, Child, Gold, Short. Proper names having their origin in contracted outlines are written in full; thus, Lord, Liberty, Wordsworth, Yardley, Goodyear, Young.

18. In several place names such as .... Kingston-on-Thames, ... Stratford-on-Avon, ...: Burton-on-Trent, ... Clacton-on-Sea, ... Southend-on-Sea the preposition *on* may be omitted.

19. The following are so written in order to obtain an easy or distinct outline:

.... Surat, ... Shetland, ... Thetford, ... Dudley, ... Jedburgh, ... Ushant, ... London, ... Carruthers, ... Sutherland, ... Weymouth.

Distinguishing Outlines

The following distinguishing outlines should be noted: .... Frances, ... Francis; .... Persia, ... Prussia; .... Tenby, ... Denbigh; .... Dunbar, ... Edinburgh; .... Didsbury, ... Dewsbury; .... Bute, ... Bude; .... Symonds, ... Simmons; .... Wyndham, ... Wenham; .... Cobbett, ... Cobb; .... Hindley, ... Huntley; .... Wales, ... Wells; .... Mather, ... Modder; .... Barmen, ... Bremen.

Index to Introduction

Abbreviations Used in the Dictionary

abbrev.,	abbreviation, abbreviated	impers.,	impersonal
adj.,	adjective, adjectival	Ind.,	India, Indian
adv.,	adverb, adverbial	indef.,	indefinite
aero.,	aeronautics, aeronautical	interj.,	interjection
Amer.,	America, American	interrog.,	interrogative
anat.,	anatomy, anatomical	i.q.,	same as
Anglo-Ind.,	Anglo-Indian	Ir.,	Ireland, Irish
Arab.,	Arabic	It.,	Italy, Italian
arch.,	archaic	ital.,	italic
archit.,	architecture, architectural		
art.,	article, artistic	Jap.,	Japan, Japanese
astron.,	astronomy, astronomical	journ.,	journalism, journalistic
Aust.,	Austria, Austrian		
Austral.,	Australia, Australian	Lat.,	Latin
		leg.,	legal
bel.,	belonging	lit.,	literary
biol.,	biology, biological	liter.,	literal, literally
bot.,	botany, botanical		
		math.,	mathematics, mathematical
chem.,	chemistry, chemical	mech.,	mechanics, mechanical
colloq.,	colloquial	med.,	medicine, medical
comp.,	comparative	meteorol.,	meteorology, meteorological
conj.,	conjunction		
cp.,	compare	mil.,	military
		mus.,	music, musical
def.,	definite	myth.,	mythology, mythological
dem. pron.,	demonstrative pronoun		
derog.,	derogatory	n.,	noun
dial.,	dialect	naut.,	nautical
		n. pl.,	noun plural
elec.,	electric, electrical		
eng.,	engineering	obs.,	obsolete
erron.,	erroneous	opp.,	opposite
esp.,	especially	orig.,	original, originally
eth.,	ethics, ethically		
exclam.,	exclamation	path.,	pathology, pathological
		pedant.,	pedantry, pedantic
fem.,	female, feminine	pers.,	personal
fig.,	figuratively	pers. pron.,	personal pronoun
Fr.,	France, French	pert.,	pertaining
		philos.,	philosophy, philosophical
geol.,	geology, geological	phonet.,	phonetic(s), phonetically
Ger.,	Germany, German	phr.,	phrase
Gr.,	Greek, Grecian	phys.,	physics, physical
gram.,	grammar, grammatical	physiol.,	physiology, physiological
		pl.,	plural
Heb.,	Hebrew	poet.,	poetry, poetical
her.,	heraldry, heraldic	Pol.,	Poland, Polish
Hind.,	Hindustani	Port.,	Portugal, Portuguese
hist.,	history, historical	poss. adj.,	possessive adjective
i.e.,	that is	p.p.,	past participle
illit.,	illiterate	pred.,	predicate

prep.,	preposition	Span.,	Spain, Spanish
pres.,	present	super.,	superlative
pret.,	preterite	surg.,	surgery, surgical
pron.,	pronoun		
prov.,	provincial	theol.	theology, theological
pr.p.,	present participle	Turk.,	Turkey, Turkish
psych.,	psychology, psychological		
q.v.,	which see	U.S.A.,	United States of America
		usu.,	usual, usually
refl. pron.,	reflexive pronoun		
rel.,	relating to, relative		
rel. pron.,	relative pronoun	v.i.,	verb intransitive
rep.,	representing	v. refl.,	verb reflexive
Russ.,	Russia, Russian	v.t.,	verb transitive
		vulg.,	vulgar
Scot.,	Scotland, Scottish		
sing.,	singular	zool.,	zoology, zoological

NOTES

(a) All short forms, other than those which are fully vocalized (such as .... *cramped*), are printed in italic; also any portions of derivative or compound words for which short form outlines are retained.

(b) Position of outlines in relation to the line is indicated throughout.

(c) Capitals are employed initially only where such is the ordinary usage, as in the case of proper names and terms. In botanical, zoological and similar scientific terms, the names of genera are capitalized; with species bearing the same name a capital would not, of course, be used. For example, *Ranunculus*, the genus; but *ranunculus*, a plant of this genus.

A

a, *indef. art.* or *adj.*, (*an* before vowel or mute *h*), one, any.

Aaron'ic, *adj.*, pert. or rel. to Aaron.

Ab, (Av), *n.*, the eleventh month of the Jewish civil year.

a'baca, *n.*, a fibrous plantain providing manilla hemp.

ab'acist, *n.*, a mathematician.

aback', *adv.*, behind, at the back.

ab'acus, *n.*, the top portion of a pillar; a device for arithmetical calculations consisting of a frame of parallel wires on which coloured balls run.

Abad'don, *n.*, the Destroying Angel; the bottomless pit.

abaft', *prep.* and *adv.*, astern, or towards the stern of a ship.

abalo'ne, *n.*, an edible mollusc found in California.

aban'don, *v.t.*, to give up, forsake, leave.

aban'doned, *p.p.*, abandon; *adj.*, shameless, profligate.

abandonee', *n.*, one to whom something is relinquished.

aban'doner, *n.*, one who abandons.

aban'doning, *pr.p.*, abandon.

aban'donment, *n.*, the act of abandoning; shamelessness.

abarticula'tion, *n.*, a dislocation.

abase', *v.t.*, to lower, degrade, humiliate.

abased', *p.p.*, abase.

abase'ment, *n.*, the act of lowering or humiliating; the state of humiliation.

abash', *v.t.*, to put to confusion or shame.

abashed', *p.p.*, abash.

abash'ing, *pr.p.*, abash.

abash'ment, *n.*, the state of being abashed.

abas'ing, *pr.p.*, abase.

abask', *adv.*, in warm light.

---

abat'able, *n.*, reduceable.

abate', *v.i.* and *t.*, to diminish, decrease.

aba'ted, *p.p.*, abate.

abate'ment, *n.*, the act of abating; the state of being abated; the reduction of an amount or quantity.

abat'ing, *pr.p.*, abate.

ab'atis, ab'attis, *n.*, a military obstruction of felled trees.

ab'atised, *adj.*, having an abatis.

abattoir', *n.*, a slaughterhouse (*Fr.*).

abax'ial, *adj.*, away from the axis.

abb, *n.*, a weaving term = yarn of warp.

Ab'ba, *n.*, a Semitic word = father.

ab'bacy, *n.*, the office of an abbot; an abbot's jurisdiction.

abba'tial, *adj.*, pert. or rel. to an abbot or abbey.

abbat'ical, *adj.*, i.q. abbatial.

ab'bé, *n.*, the French word for abbot; unbeneficed priests often have the title given to them as a dignified appellation.

ab'bess, *n.*, the lady head of an abbey.

ab'bey, *n.*, a religious house under the rule of an abbot.

ab'bot, *n.*, the superior of an abbey.

ab'botship, *n.*, an abbot's office or dignity.

abbre'viate, *v.t.*, to shorten.

abbre'viated, *p.p.*, abbreviate.

abbre'viating, *pr.p.*, abbreviate.

abbrevia'tion, *n.*, the act of shortening; the abbreviated state; a shortened formula, as B.A. for Bachelor of Arts.

abbre'viator, *n.*, one who abbreviates; the drafter of ecclesiastical briefs at the Vatican.

---

abbre'viatory, *adj.*, shortening.

abbre'viature, *n.*, the sign marking a contraction; also an abridgment.

Ab'derite, *n.*, an inhabitant of Abdera, a place noted for stupidity; a stupid person.

ab'dicant, *adj.*, abdicating; also *n.*, one who abdicates.

ab'dicate, *v.t.*, to resign, to renounce.

ab'dicated, *p.p.*, abdicate.

ab'dicating, *pr.p.*, abdicate.

abdica'tion, *n.*, the act of abdicating.

ab'dicative, *adj.*, disposed to abdicate.

ab'dicator, *n.*, one who abdicates.

ab'ditory, *n.*, a place to hide things in.

abdo'men, *n.*, the belly, the container for the viscera.

abdom'inal, *adj.*, bel. to the abdomen.

abdominos'copy, *n.*, a surgical examination of the abdomen.

abdom'inous, *adj.*, rel. to the abdomen; gross.

abduce', *v.t.*, to draw away or aside.

abduced', *p.p.*, abduce.

abdu'cent, *adj.*, drawing away or aside.

abdu'cing, *pr.p.*, abduce.

abduct', *v.t.*, to carry off forcibly or by stealth.

abduct'ed, *p.p.*, abduct.

abduct'ing, *pr.p.*, abduct.

abduc'tion, *n.*, the act of abducting.

abduct'or, *n.*, one who abducts.

abeam', *adv.*, at right angles to the keel.

abear', *v.t.*, to put up with.

abed', *adv.*, in bed.

abele', *n.*, the white poplar.

Abel'ian, *adj.*, pert. or rel. to Abel, the Norwegian mathematician; *n.*, a member of

the sect of Abelites or Abelians.

A′belite, *n.*, a member of the ancient African sect of followers of Abel.

a′belmosk, *n.*, a North-African evergreen shrub.

aberdevine′, *n.*, a song-bird related to the goldfinch.

a′berglaube, *n.*, excessive belief, superstition.

aber′rancy, *n.*, a straying from the truth.

aber′rant, *adj.*, straying from the truth.

aberra′tion, *n.*, the act of straying from the truth; mental confusion; a deviation from type (*biol.*); an optical defect in a lens or mirror; the seeming displacement of a heavenly body (*astron.*).

abet′, *v.t.*, to aid, to encourage, to help in some action, frequently in a misdeed. (The phrase in such a context is "to aid and abet".)

abet′ment, *n.*, assistance, aid.

abet′ted, *p.p.*, abet.

abet′ter, abet′tor, *n.*, one who abets.

abet′ting, *pr.p.*, abet.

ab extra, *adv.*, from outside.

abey′ance, *n.*, suspension; the state of suspension or of being held over.

abey′ant, *adj.*, holding over.

abhor′, *v.t.*, to hate, to abominate, to shudder at.

abhorred′, *p.p.*, abhor.

abhor′rence, *n.*, hatred with loathing.

abhor′rent, *adj.*, repulsive, hateful.

abhor′rently, *adv.*, in an abhorrent way.

abhor′rer, *n.*, one who abhors.

abhor′ring, *pr.p.*, abhor.

abi′dance, *n.*, an abiding.

abide′, *v.i.*, to stay, to remain, to dwell.

abi′der, *n.*, one who abides.

abid′ing, *pr.p.*, abide.

abid′ingly, *adv.*, permanently, continually.

ab′ies, *n.*, the fir-tree, a member of the pine-family.

Ab′igail, *n.*, the Bible name of a woman attendant; hence, by transference, denoting any lady's maid.

abil′ity, *n.*, the state of being able; the capacity.

abintest′ate, *adj.* and *n.*, inheriting from (or the inheritor of) an intestate person.

abiogen′esis, *n.*, a spontaneous generation.

abitur′ient, *n.*, a school-leaver entering university.

ab′ject, *adj.*, sunk to a low state, grovelling, mean; also *n.*, (but rare), a mean fellow.

abject′, *v.t.*, to degrade.

abjec′tion, *n.*, the state of one who is abject, or cast down.

ab′jectly, *adv.*, meanly; in a grovelling manner.

ab′jectness, *n.*, meanness, a grovelling attitude.

abjudica′tion, *n.*, judicial rejection.

abjura′tion, *n.*, a solemn denial or repudiation of some doctrine or opinion.

abju′ratory, *adj.*, of the nature of an abjuration.

abjure′, *v.t.*, to make a solemn denial or repudiation of some doctrine or opinion.

abjured′, *p.p.*, abjure.

abjur′er, *n.*, one who abjures.

abjur′ing, *pr.p.*, abjure.

ablacta′tion, *n.*, the act of weaning.

abla′tion, *n.*, the act of carrying off or removing.

ab′lative, *adj.*, tending to remove or separate. As a *n.* the ablative is the grammatical name for the case denoting separation.

ab′laut, *n.*, vowel changes to show different meanings, *e.g.* sing, sang.

ablaze′, *adv.*, on fire.

a′ble, *adj.*, having power, means or capacity.

a′ble-bodied, *adj.*, in a physically fit condition.

ableg′ate, *n.*, a papal envoy; a bearer to new cardinals of their insignia.

ab′len, *n.*, a small fresh-water fish.

ab′let, *n.*, *i.q.* ablen.

ab′lings, *adv.*, perhaps (*Scot.*).

abloom′, *adv.*, in or into bloom.

ab′luent, *adj.*, cleansing, purifying; *n.*, that which cleanses.

ablush′, *adv.*, blushingly.

ablu′tion, *n.*, the act of cleansing.

ablu′tionary, *adj.*, pert. or rel. to ablution.

a′bly, *adv.*, in an able manner; with ability.

ab′negate, *v.t.*, to give up, to renounce.

ab′negated, *p.p.*, abnegate.

ab′negating, *pr.p.*, abnegate.

abnega′tion, *n.*, the act of abnegating.

abnor′mal, *adj.*, contrary to rule, unusual.

abnormal′ity, *n.*, the state of being abnormal.

abnor′mity, *n.*, the state or quality of the abnormal; an irregularity.

aboard′, *adv.*, on board, on a vessel.

abode′, *n.*, a place of abiding or dwelling; the act of abiding; *p.p.*, abide.

aboil′, *adv.*, boiling.

abol′ish, *v.t.*, to destroy, to put an end to.

abol′ishable, *adj.*, that which can be abolished.

abol′ished, *p.p.*, abolish.

abol′isher, *n.*, one who abolishes.

abol′ishing, *pr.p.*, abolish.

abol′ishment, *n.*, the act or state of abolishing.

aboli′tion, *n.*, *i.q.* abolishment.

aboli′tionism, *n.*, the anti-slavery doctrine or principle.

aboli′tionist, *n.*, one who opposes slavery.

ab′oma, *n.*, a large tree-boa found in tropical South America.

aboma'sus, *n.*, the name of the "fourth stomach" of ruminating animals.

A'-bomb, *n.*, an atomic bomb.

abom'inable, *adj.*, detestable, hateful.

abom'inably, *adv.*, in an abominable way.

abom'inate, *v.t.*, to detest, to abhor.

abom'inated, *p.p.*, abominate.

abomina'tion, *n.*, loathing; something detestable.

a bon marché, *adj.*, cheap; *n.*, a good bargain (*Fr.*).

aboral', *adj.*, belonging to parts of an animal away from the mouth.

aborig'inal, *adj.*, indigenous; *n.*, a primitive native.

aborig'ines, *n.*, the original natives.

abort', *v.i.*, to miscarry; deliberately to end.

abort'ed, *adj.*, undeveloped; brought to a premature end.

abort'ient, *adj.*, barren, sterile.

abort'ifacient, *n.*, a drug or other agent causing abortion.

abor'tion, *n.*, a birthmiscarriage; the procuring of a miscarriage.

abor'tionist, *n.*, one who causes abortion.

abor'tive, *adj.*, premature, ineffectual.

abor'tively, *adv.*, ineffectually.

abor'tiveness, *n.*, the state of being abortive.

abou'lia, *n.*, a mental disorder causing the loss of will-power. Also *abulia*.

abound', *v.i.*, to be in a state of plenty; to be in great quantity or numbers.

abound'ed, *p.p.*, abound.

abound'ing, *pr.p.*, abound.

about', *adv.*, around; nearly; *prep.*, around, concerning.

about'-sledge, *n.*, the largest of the blacksmith's hammers.

above', *adv.*, over, higher up; *prep.*, over, beyond, in excess of.

above'-board, *adj.* and *adv.*, without concealment, open.

abracadab'ra, *n.*, a cabalistic word used as a charm.

abrade', *v.t.*, to wear or scrape off.

abrad'ed, *p.p.*, abrade.

abrad'ing, *pr.p.*, abrade.

Abraham'ic, *adj.*, rel. to Abraham the patriarch.

A'brahamite, *n.*, a follower of the Gnostic preacher, Abraham.

abranc'hial, *adj.*, having no gills.

abra'sion, *n.*, the act or operation of abrading, wearing or rubbing off.

abra'sive, *adj.*, tending to abrasion; useful for abrading purposes; *n.*, a material used for rubbing purposes.

ab'razite, *n.*, a hydrous silicate of aluminium and calcium.

abreac'tion, *n.*, the getting rid of an emotion by re-enacting its first occurrence.

abreast', *adv.*, on a level with, in line with.

abridge', *v.t.*, to shorten, to epitomize.

abridged', *p.p.*, abridge.

abridg'ing, *pr.p.*, abridge.

abridg'ment, *n.*, the act or state of abridging; an epitome.

abroach', *adv.*, on tap, broached.

abroad', *adv.*, outside one's home or fatherland; in foreign parts.

ab'rogate, *v.t.*, to cancel, to annul, to repeal.

ab'rogated, *p.p.*, abrogate.

ab'rogating, *pr.p.*, abrogate.

abroga'tion, *n.*, the act of abrogating; the repeal of a law.

ab'rogative, *adj.*, cancelled, repealed.

ab'rogator, *n.*, one who abrogates.

abrupt', *adj.*, broken off short, precipitous, sudden, rude.

abrup'tion, *n.*, a sudden breaking off or separation.

abrupt'ly, *adv.*, steeply, suddenly, rudely.

abrupt'ness, *n.*, steepness, rudeness.

ab'scess, *n.*, a sore, a tumour.

abscind', *v.t.*, to sever, to cut off.

abscis'sion, *n.*, the act of severance.

abscond', *v.i.*, to make off, to flee into retirement.

abscond'ed, *p.p.*, abscond.

abscond'er, *n.*, one who absconds.

abscond'ing, *pr.p.*, abscond.

ab'sence, *n.*, the state of being away or absent; a lack.

ab'sent, *adj.*, away; not present; inattentive.

absent', *v.t.*, to withdraw (oneself).

absent'ed, *p.p.*, absent.

absentee', *n.*, one who absents himself or is away; a non-resident.

absentee'ism, *n.*, the practice of not being present, usually of workers absent from their duties.

absent'ing, *pr.p.*, absent.

ab'sently, *adv.*, in an absent manner.

ab'sent-mind'ed, *adj.*, preoccupied, inattentive to one's surroundings.

ab'sent-mindedly, *adv.*, in an inattentive way.

ab'sent-mindedness, *n.*, inattention.

ab'sinth(e), *n.*, a liqueur made from wormwood and brandy.

absin'thian, *adj.*, rel. to absinth.

absin'thiate, *v.t.*, to make bitter with wormwood.

absin'thiated, *p.p.*, absinthiate.

absin'thin, *n.*, the bitter quality in absinth.

ab'sinthism, *n.*, the state induced by indulgence in absinth.

ab'solute, *adj.*, free, independent; unlimited; perfect; despotic.

ab'solutely, *adv.*, perfectly, quite; despotically.

ab'soluteness, *n.*, the quality of being absolute.

absolu'tion, *n.*, the act of loosing or absolving from sin.

ab'solutism, *n.*, the state or condition of the absolute; despotic rule.

ab'solutist, *n.*, one who advocates despotic rule.

absol′utory, *adj.*, able to absolve; loosing from sin.

absol′vatory, *adj.*, capable of absolving.

absolve′, *v.t.*, to release from sin, to pardon.

absolved′, *p.p.*, absolve.

absolv′er, *n.*, one who absolves.

absolv′ing, *pr.p.*, absolve.

ab′sonant, *adj.*, discordant; unreasonable.

absorb′, *v.t.*, to draw in; to swallow; to engross; to incorporate by mechanical or chemical action.

absorbabil′ity, *n.*, the condition of being absorbable.

absorb′able, *adj.*, capable of absorption.

absorbed′, *p.p.*, absorb.

absorb′ent, *adj.*, absorbing; *n.*, a substance capable of absorbing.

absorb′ing, *pr.p.*, absorb; *adj.*, engrossing.

absorb′ivity, *n.*, the power of absorption.

absorp′tion, *n.*, the act of absorbing; mental preoccupation.

absorp′tive, *adj.*, capable of absorbing.

absquat′ulate, *v.*, to run away, to make off.

abstain′, *v.i.*, to keep aloof from, to refrain.

abstained′, *p.p.*, abstain.

abstain′er, *n.*, one who abstains, particularly from alcohol.

abstain′ing, *pr.p.*, abstain.

abste′mious, *adj.*, moderate in the use of food and drink.

abste′miously, *adv.*, with moderation in regard to food and drink.

abste′miousness, *n.*, the habit of moderation in regard to eating and drinking.

absten′tion, *n.*, the act of abstaining.

absterge′, *v.t.*, to cleanse by wiping.

absterged′, *p.p.*, absterge.

abster′gent, *adj.*, cleansing; *n.*, that which cleanses.

abster′ging, *pr.p.*, absterge.

absterse′, *adj.*, wiped clean.

abster′sion, *n.*, the act of wiping clean.

abster′sive, *adj.*, of cleansing property.

ab′stinence, *n.*, the act or state of abstaining.

ab′stinency, *n.*, a refraining from pleasures, especially food and drink.

ab′stinent, *adj.*, not self-indulgent.

ab′stinently, *adv.*, in a manner not self-indulgent.

abstract′, *v.t.*, to draw away, to remove, to epitomize.

ab′stract, *adj.*, apart from matter (which is concrete); also *n.*, an epitome or summary.

abstract′ed, *p.p.*, abstract; also *adj.*, absent-minded.

abstract′edly, *adv.*, in an absent-minded way.

abstract′edness, *n.*, a mentally absent state.

abstract′er, *n.*, one who abstracts.

abstract′ing, *pr.p.*, abstract.

abstrac′tion, *n.*, the act of abstracting; the state of being abstracted; mental concentration.

abstrac′tive, *adj.*, capable of abstracting.

ab′stractly, *adv.*, in an abstract manner.

ab′stractness, *n.*, the quality of being abstract.

abstruse′, *adj.*, hidden, profound, hard to comprehend.

abstruse′ly, *adv.*, in an abstruse way.

abstruse′ness, *n.*, the quality of the abstruse.

absurd′, *adj.*, irrational, ridiculous.

absurd′ity, *n.*, the absurd state, an absurd thing.

absurd′ly, *adv.*, in an absurd way.

absurd′ness, *n.*, *i.q.* absurdity.

abu′lia, *n.*, *i.q.* aboulia.

abun′dance, *n.*, plenty.

abun′dant, *adj.*, plentiful.

abun′dantly, *adv.*, plentifully, richly.

abus′able, *adj.*, capable of being abused.

abuse′, *n.*, ill-treatment, an insult, a misuse; *v.t.*, to ill-treat, to violate, to insult, to misuse.

abused′, *p.p.*, abuse.

abus′er, *n.*, one who abuses.

abus′ing, *pr.p.*, abuse.

abu′sive, *adj.*, of the nature of abuse; insulting.

abu′sively, *adv.*, in an insulting way.

abu′siveness, *n.*, the abusive tendency.

abut′, *v.i.*, to adjoin; *v.t.*, to make to touch at the side or end.

abut′ment, *n.*, the act of abutting; that which is abutted upon or abuts.

abut′tal, *n.*, the relation of abutting; an abutment.

abut′ted, *p.p.*, abut.

abut′ter, *n.*, the owner of the adjoining property (*leg.*).

abut′ting, *pr.p.*, abut.

abysm′, *n.*, an abyss, a gulf, vast depth.

abys′mal, *adj.*, profound, of vast depth.

abyss′, *n.*, *i.q.* abysm.

abyss′al, *adj.*, over 300 fathoms below the sea.

Abyssin′ian, *n.*, a native of Abyssinia; *adj.*, pert. or rel. to A.

aca′cia, *n.*, a shrub so named (one kind yields gum arabic).

academ′ic, *adj.*, concerned with intellectual study unrelated to vocational needs; theoretical; scholarly; bel. to the Platonic School.

academ′ical, *adj.*, *i.q.* academic.

academ′ically, *adv.*, in an academic way.

academic′ian, *n.*, a member of an Academy.

Acad′emist, *n.*, an academic philosopher.

acad′emy, *n.*, a place of learning; originally the School of Plato.

Aca′dian, *adj.*, pert. or rel. to Nova Scotia.

ac′ajou, *n.*, gum obtained from the cashew tree; also a wood resembling mahogany.

Acale′phae, *n. pl.*, marine stinging zoophytes.

acan′tha, *n.*, a plant's prickle; a fish's fin; a spinous growth.

acantha′ceous, *adj.*, prickly.

acan′thine, *adj.*, rel. to the acanthus; *n.*, the

acanthus-leaf orna-
ment (*archit.*).

acan'thous, *adj.*, prickly,
spinous.

acan'thus, *n.*, a prickly-
leaved plant.

acar'diac, *adj.*, not having a heart.

acar'icide, *n.*, a mite
killer.

acarpell'ous, *adj.*, without carpels.

acarp'ous, *adj.*, without
fruit.

ac'arus, *n.*, a mite.

acatalec'tic, *adj.*, not
catalectic, *i.e.*, not
lacking in metre.

acat'alepsy, *n.*, epilepsy.

acatalep'tic, *adj.*, in a
state of acatalepsy.

acaules'cent, *adj.*, apparently stemless.

acau'lous, *adj.*, without
a stem.

Acca'dian, *n.*, the language of ancient
Babylon.

accede', *v.i.*, to agree to.

acced'ed, *p.p.*, accede.

acced'ing, *pr.p.*, accede.

accel'erate, *v.i.* and *t.*, to
quicken, to hasten.

accel'erated, *p.p.*, accelerate.

accel'erating, *pr.p.*, accelerate.

accelera'tion, *n.*, the
quickening of speed.

accel'erative, *adj.*, causing acceleration.

accel'erator, *n.*, a quickening agent; any de-
vice to increase speed;
the throttle control of
motor vehicles.

accel'eratory, *adj.*, causing acceleration.

accelerom'eter, *n.*, an
instrument for mea-
suring the accelera-
tion of aircraft, etc.

accend'ible, *adj.*, inflammable.

accen'sion, *n.*, the act of
lighting altar candles.

accen'sor, *n.*, a person in
the R.C. Church who
lights and trims the
candles.

ac'cent, *n.*, the stress of
voice; a printed or
written sign on a
syllable or letter or
musical note; a pecu-
liar distinction of
speech or pronuncia-
tion.

accent', *v.t.*, to lay stress
in speech or music.

accent'ed, *p.p.*, accent.

accent'ing, *pr.p.*, accent.

Accent'or, *n.*, the sparrow genus.

accent'ual, *adj.*, rel. to
accent.

accent'uate, *v.t.*, to mark
with an accent; to
give prominence to.

accent'uated, *p.p.*,
accentuate.

accent'uating, *pr.p.*,
accentuate.

accentua'tion, *n.*, the act
of accentuating.

accept', *v.t.*, to take or
receive; to approve;
to agree to pay.

acceptabil'ity, *n.*, the
quality or state of
being acceptable.

accept'able, *adj.*, able to
be accepted; agree-
able; welcome.

accept'ableness, *n.*, *i.q.*
acceptability.

accept'ably, *adv.*, in an
acceptable way.

accept'ance, *n.*, the act of
accepting; a state of
acceptability; a bill of
exchange; an agree-
ment to meet a bill.

accepta'tion, *n.*, the state
of being accepted;
the meaning, sense.

accept'ed, *p.p.*, accept.

accept'er, *n.*, one who
accepts.

accept'ing, *pr.p.*, accept.

accep'tion, *n.*, favouritism.

accept'or, *n.*, one who
accepts; one who has
given his acceptance
on a draft.

ac'cess, *n.*, an approach
or the means of ap-
proach; an increase;
an attack (of disease).

ac'cessary, *adj.*, aiding,
contributing to; *n.*,
an accomplice.

accessibil'ity, *n.*, the
state or quality of
being approachable.

acces'sible, *adj.*, easily
approached.

acces'sibly, *adv.*, in an
accessible way.

acces'sion, *n.*, an approach; the act of
acceding; an increase;
a coming to the
throne.

acces'sional, *adj.*, rel.
to an accession.

acces'sive, *adj.*, tending
to accession.

accesso'rial, *adj.*, rel. to
an accessory.

ac'cessory, *adj.*, *i.q.* ac-
cessary; *n.*, some-
thing additional.

acciaccatu'ra, *n.*, a grace
note struck with an-
other note but in-
stantly released, while
the other continues to
sound (*It.*, *mus.*).

ac'cidence, *n.*, the rudimentary part of gram-
mar.

ac'cident, *n.*, a chance
occurrence; a mishap.

acciden'tal, *adj.*, happening by chance;
fortuitous; *n.*, a musi-
cal sharp or flat not
belonging to the key.

acciden'tally, *adv.*, by
accident.

ac'cidie, *n.*, a loss of interest; ennui; world
weariness. Also *acedia*.

accip'ient, *n.*, a receiver.

accip'iter, *n.*, the hawk;
also name for birds of
prey.

accip'itral, *adj.*, hawk-
like; keensighted.

accip'itrine, *adj.*, like the
hawk.

acclaim', *n.*, loud approval; *v.t.*, to wel-
come or approve with
shouting.

acclama'tion, *n.*, loud
applause.

acclam'atory, *adj.*, expressing loud ap-
plause.

acclimatiza'tion, *n.*, the
act of adapting to
climate.

accli'matize, *v.t.*, to
adapt to climate.

accli'matized, *p.p.*, ac-
climatize.

accli'matizing, *pr.p.*, ac-
climatize.

accli'mature, *n.*, the act
of habituating to cli-
mate.

accliv'itous, *adj.*, rising,
sloping upwards.

accliv'ity, *n.*, an upward
slope; a hill.

accli'vous, *adj.*, *i.q.* ac-
clivitous.

accolade', *n.*, the stroke
with the sword in
conferring knight-
hood; the brace that
couples musical staves
together.

accom'modate, *v.t.*, to
do a service or con-
venience; to fit, adapt;
to find lodging for.

accom'modated, *p.p.*,
accommodate.

accom'modating, *pr.p.*,
accommodate; *adj.*,
obliging.

accommoda'tion, *n.*, a
favour, a con-
venience; hospitality,
room; living space.

accom'modative, *adj.*, willing to accommodate.

accom'modator, *n.*, one who accommodates.

accom'panied, *p.p.*, accompany.

accom'panier, *n.*, one who accompanies.

accom'paniment, *n.*, something that accompanies. In music, an instrumental support to the voice or to other instruments.

accom'panist, *n.*, one who plays the musical accompaniment.

accom'pany, *v.t.*, to go with. Musically, to play the accompaniment.

accom'panying, *pr.p.*, accompany.

accom'plice, *n.*, a partner in crime.

accom'plish, *v.t.*, to perform, to finish.

accom'plishable, *adj.*, able to be performed.

accom'plished, *p.p.*, accomplish; *adj.*, skilful, proficient.

accom'plisher, *n.*, one who accomplishes.

accom'plishing, *pr.p.*, accomplish.

accom'plishment, *n.*, the act or state of accomplishing; an elegant acquirement.

accord', *n.*, an agreement, consent, harmony; *v.i.*, to agree; *v.t.*, to grant.

accord'ance, *n.*, *i.q.* accord.

accord'ancy, *n.*, *i.q.* accord.

accord'ant, *adj.*, in a state of agreement.

accord'antly, *adv.*, agreeably.

accord'ed, *p.p.*, accord.

accord'er, *n.*, one who accords.

accord'ing, *pr.p.*, accord. (Helps to form the prepositional phrase, "according to".)

accord'ingly, *adv.*, in agreement. In special sense = therefore.

accord'ion, *n.*, a portable reed instrument with bellows and a keyboard.

accord'ionist, *n.*, a player on the accordion.

accost', *n.*, a greeting (usually unwelcome); *v.t.*, to greet, to address in words.

accost'able, *adj.*, able to be accosted.

accost'ed, *p.p.*, accost.

accost'ing, *pr.p.*, accost.

accouche'ment, *n.*, bringing to bed; confinement (*Fr.*).

accoucheur', *n.*, a male "midwife" (*Fr.*).

accoucheuse', *n.*, a midwife (*Fr.*).

account', *n.*, a sum, a bill; a description; a statement of a financial situation; *v.i.* and *t.*, to esteem, to reckon.

accountabil'ity, *n.*, the state of being accountable; a liability to be called to account.

account'able, *adj.*, able to account; responsible.

account'ableness, *n.*, the state of being accountable.

account'ancy, *n.*, the work of an accountant.

account'ant, *n.*, one who proves or keeps accounts.

account'antship, *n.*, the art or function of an accountant.

account'-book, *n.*, a book in which accounts are entered.

account'ed, *p.p.*, account.

account'ing, *pr.p.*, account.

accou'ple, *v.t.*, to join one thing to another.

accou'pled, *p.p.*, accouple.

accou'pling, *pr.p.*, accouple.

accou'tre, *v.t.*, to clothe, to equip (*Fr.*).

accou'tred, *p.p.*, accoutre.

accou'trements, *n.*, military equipment (*Fr.*).

accou'tring, *pr.p.*, accoutre.

accred'it, *v.t.*, to recommend, to authorize.

accred'ited, *p.p.*, accredit.

accred'iting, *pr.p.*, accredit.

accres'cence, *n.*, a growth, an addition.

accres'cent, *adj.*, growing, being added.

accrete', *v.i.*, to grow together; *v.t.*, to unite.

accre'tion, *n.*, a growth, an addition.

accre'tive, *adj.*, tending to growth.

accroach'ment, *n.*, usurpation.

accrue', *v.i.*, to increase, to be added.

accrued', *p.p.*, accrue.

accru'ing, *pr.p.*, accrue.

accuba'tion, *n.*, the act of reclining.

accum'bent, *adj.*, reclining at table.

accu'mulate, *v.i.* and *t.*, to pile up, to amass, to grow.

accu'mulated, *p.p.*, accumulate.

accu'mulating, *pr.p.*, accumulate.

accumula'tion, *n.*, the act of accumulating; a piled-up mass.

accu'mulative, *adj.*, tending to accumulate.

accu'mulatively, *adv.*, increasingly; in piles.

accu'mulator, *n.*, one who accumulates; an apparatus for storing electric power.

ac'curacy, *n.*, the state or faculty of being accurate.

ac'curate, *adj.*, correct; exact.

ac'curately, *adv.*, carefully, precisely.

ac'curateness, *n.*, *i.q.* accuracy.

accurse', *v.t.*, to invoke curses against.

accursed', *p.p.*, accurse.

accurs'ed, *adj.*, ill-fated.

accurs'ing, *pr.p.*, accurse.

accu'sable, *adj.*, able to be accused.

accu'sant, *adj.*, accusing; *n.*, an accuser.

accusa'tion, *n.*, a charge, an indictment.

accu'sative, *adj.*, bringing a charge; *n.*, the objective case in grammar.

accu'satively, *adv.*, in the manner of an accusation.

accu'satory, *adj.*, incriminating, accusing.

accuse', *v.t.*, to charge, to indict.

accused', *p.p.*, accuse.

accus'er, *n.*, one who brings a charge.

accus'ing, *pr.p.*, accuse.

accus'tom, *v.t.*, to habituate.

accus'tomarily, *adv.*, habitually, in wonted manner.

accus'tomary, *adj.*, habitual, wonted.

accus'tomed, *p.p.*, accustom.

accus'tomedness, *n.*, the fact of being accustomed.

accus'toming, *pr.p.*, accustom.

ace, *n.*, a single pip on a playing-card; a unit; an expert.

ace'dia, *n.*, *i.q.* accidie.

Acel'dama, *n.*, the field of blood.

acen'tric, *adj.*, without a centre.

Aceph'ala, *n. pl.*, bivalves; headless molluscs.

aceph'alous, *adj.*, headless.

a'cer, *n.*, the maple-tree.

ac'erate, *adj.*, needle-pointed.

acerb', *adj.*, sour, bitter.

a'cerbate, *v.t.*, to embitter, to exasperate.

acerb'ic, *adj.*, *i.q.* acerb.

acerb'ity, *n.*, a bitter quality, bitterness.

ac'erose, *adj.*, needle-shaped.

a'cervate, *adj.*, massed or heaped together.

aces'cence, *n.*, a souring.

aces'cency, *n.*, the quality or state of turning sour.

aces'cent, *adj.*, turning sour.

acetab'ulum, *n.*, a cup to hold vinegar; the thigh-bone socket.

aceta'rious, *adj.*, used in salad.

acet'ary, *n.*, the sour pulp in a pear, etc.

ac'etate, *n.*, the salt of acetic acid.

ac'etated, *adj.*, combined with acetic acid.

ace'tic, *adj.*, of the nature of vinegar.

acet'ified, *p.p.*, acetify.

acet'ify, *v.i.*, to become sour; *v.t.*, to turn into vinegar.

acet'ifying, *pr.p.*, acetify.

acetom'eter, *n.*, an instrument for ascertaining the strength of acetic acid.

ac'etone, *n.*, an inflammable liquid; a solvent of organic materials.

ac'etose, *adj.*, producing or rel. to vinegar.

acetos'ity, *n.*, acidity.

ac'etous, *adj.*, *i.q.* acetose.

ace'tum, *n.*, vinegar (*Lat.*).

a'cetyl, *n.*, the radical of acetic acid.

acet'ylene, *n.* and *adj.*, a colourless inflammable gas, so named.

Achai'an, *adj.*, bel. to the Achaioi; *i.q.* Achean.

acharne'ment, *n.*, ferocity, gusto (*Fr.*).

acha'tes, *n.*, any faithful friend.

ache, *n.* and *v.i.*, pain; to be painful.

Ache'an, *adj.*, bel. to Achaia (a tribal district of ancient Greece).

ached, *p.p.*, ache.

A'cheron, *n.*, a fabled river in Hades.

achiev'able, *adj.*, able to be achieved.

achieve', *v.t.*, to accomplish by courage, skill or perseverance; to finish successfully.

achieved', *p.p.*, achieve.

achieve'ment, *n.*, something achieved; a full escutcheon in heraldry.

achiev'er, *n.*, one who achieves.

achiev'ing, *pr.p.*, achieve.

achil'ous, *adj.*, without lips.

ach'ing, *pr.p.*, ache.

a'chor, *n.*, a variety of eczema.

achromat'ic, *adj.*, colourless; forming images without their prismatic colouring.

achro'matism, *n.*, the achromatic state or quality.

achro'matize, *v.t.*, to make achromatic.

acic'ular, *adj.*, sharp-pointed.

acic'ulate, *adj.*, bearing prickles or bristles.

acic'uliform, *adj.*, needle-shaped.

ac'id, *adj.*, sour, tart; *n.*, a chemical compound.

acidif'erous, *adj.*, acid-yielding.

acidifica'tion, *n.*, the act of converting to acid.

acid'ified, *p.p.*, acidify.

acid'ifier, *n.*, one who, that which, acidifies.

acid'ify, *v.i.* and *t.*, to make or become acid.

acid'ifying, *pr.p.*, acidify.

acidim'eter, *n.*, an apparatus for testing the strength of an acid.

acid'ity, *n.*, the acid quality, sourness.

acidos'is, *n.*, an acid condition of the blood, as in diabetes.

acid'ulae, *n. pl.*, cold acid mineral water-springs.

acid'ulate, *v.t.*, to make acid.

acid'ulated, *adj.*, bitter-tempered; *p.p.*, acidulate.

acid'ulating, *pr.p.*, acidulate.

acidula'tion, *n.*, the act of acidulating.

acid'ulous, *adj.*, slightly acid.

a'ciform, *adj.*, *i.q.* acciculiform.

a'cinus, *n.*, the seed of a grape or berry.

ack'-ack', *adj.* and *n.*, pert. and rel. to anti-aircraft (*colloq.*).

ack'-emm'a, *adv.* and *n.*, morning, ante meridiem (*slang*).

acknowl'edge, *v.t.*, to own, to admit.

acknowl'edged, *p.p.*, acknowledge.

acknowl'edger, *n.*, one who acknowledges.

acknowl'edging, *pr.p.*, acknowledge.

acknowl'edgment, *n.*, the act of acknowledging; the return of a favour.

aclin'ic, *adj.*, not dipping (of a magnet, and therefore at the magnetic equator).

ac'me, *n.*, the highest point; the point of perfection (*Gr.*).

ac'ne, *n.*, a skin disorder; a pimple.

acock', *adv.*, in a cocked position.

acol'ogy, *n.*, therapeutics, the science of remedies.

ac'olyte, *n.*, the attendant on a priest.

ac'onite, *n.*, the plant monk's-hood, or wolf's-bane.

acon'itine, *adj.*, of the quality of aconite.

a'corn, *n.*, the fruit of the oak.

a'corned, *adj.*, acorn-bearing.

acos'mism, *n.*, the disbelief in an eternal world.

acotyle'don, *n.*, a plant not having seed-lobes.

acotyle'donous, *adj.*, destitute of cotyledons (or seed-lobes).

acou'chy, *n.*, the Surinam rat.

acous'tic, *adj.*, rel. to hearing.

acoust'ical, *adj.*, *i.q.* acoustic.

acous'tics, *n. pl.*, the science of sound characteristics of particular environments.

acquaint', *v.t.*, to make known, to make oneself familiar with.

acquaint'ance, *n.*, the state of being acquainted; a person known, but not intimately.

acquaint'anceship, *n.*, *i.q.* acquaintance.

acquaint'ed, *p.p.*, acquaint; *adj.*, informed about.

acquaint'ing, *pr.p.*, acquaint.

acquest', *n.*, property acquired otherwise than by inheritance.

acquiesce', *v.i.*, to take passively, to submit to.

acquiesced', *p.p.*, acquiesce.

acquies'cence, *n.*, the state or act of acquiescing.

acquies'cent, *adj.*, ready to acquiesce or submit.

acquies'cing, *pr.p.*, acquiesce.

acquirabil'ity, *n.*, the state of being acquirable.

acquir'able, *adj.*, able to be acquired.

acquire', *v.t.*, to obtain, to attain, to gain possession of.

acquired', *p.p.*, acquire.

acquire'ment, *n.*, the act or state of acquiring; a thing acquired.

acquir'er, *n.*, one who acquires.

acquir'ing, *pr.p.*, acquire.

acquisi'tion, *n.*, the act of acquiring; a valuable gain.

acquis'itive, *adj.*, of an acquiring tendency.

acquis'itively, *adv.*, in an acquisitive manner.

acquis'itiveness, *n.*, the acquiring tendency.

acquit', *v.t.*, to free or clear, to exculpate; reflexively, to bear oneself.

acquit'ment, *n.*, the act of acquitting.

acquit'tal, *n.*, the act or state of acquitting.

acquit'tance, *n.*, a discharge, a release.

acquit'ted, *p.p.*, acquit.

acquit'ting, *pr.p.*, acquit.

a'cre, *n.*, a measure of surface, a field.

a'creage, *n.*, the extent in acres.

a'cred, *adj.*, possessing or containing acres.

ac'rid, *adj.*, sharp, pungent, corrosive.

acrid'ity, *n.*, the acrid state or quality.

ac'ridness, *n.*, *i.q.* acridity.

acrimo'nious, *adj.*, full of bitterness, spiteful.

acrimo'niously, *adv.*, in an acrimonious way.

acrimo'niousness, *n.*, the acrimonious quality.

ac'rimony, *n.*, bitterness, spitefulness.

Ac'rita, *n. pl.*, animals with no distinct nervous system (*zool.*).

acrit'ical, *adj.*, without a crisis.

acroamat'ic, *adj.*, communicated orally; esoteric.

acroat'ic, *adj.*, rel. to esoteric teaching.

ac'robat, *n.*, a gymnast, rope dancer, tumbler and the like.

acrobat'ic, *adj.*, pertaining to acrobatics.

acrobat'ics, *n. pl.*, performances by an acrobat.

Acrocerau'nian, *adj.*, bel. to Acroceraunia, a Grecian promontory.

ac'rogen, *n.*, an organism that grows at the apex only.

acrog'enous, *adj.*, growing at the apex.

acrog'raphy, *n.*, the process of making a relief printing-block.

ac'rolith, *n.*, a figure with a head made of stone.

acron'yc(h)al, *adj.*, occurring at nightfall.

ac'ronym, *n.*, a word from the initials of others, *e.g.* Anzac.

acrop'etal, *adj.*, developing from below upwards.

acrophob'ia, *n.*, a morbid dread of heights.

acroph'ony, *n.*, the phonetic use of hieroglyphs.

Acrop'olis, *n.*, a city stronghold (*Gr.*).

ac'rospire, *n.*, the first sprout; *v.t.*, to germinate.

ac'rospired, *p.p.*, acrospire.

across', *adv.* and *prep.*, athwart, to the opposite side, over.

acros'tic, *adj.* and *n.*, a composition, in which certain letters, usually the first in a line, make words.

acros'tically, *adv.*, acrostic-wise.

acrote'ria, *n. pl.*, ornaments above a building or pediment.

acryl'ic, *adj.*, resinous; derived from polymethyl acrilate.

act, *n.*, a thing done or performed; the doing of a thing; a Parliamentary measure made law; a main division of a drama; *v.i.* and *t.*, to perform, to do, to play.

act'ed, *p.p.*, act.

Ac'tian, *adj.*, pert. or rel. to Actium (a promontory of ancient Greece).

act'ing, *n.*, an actor's business; *pr.p.*, act.

actin'ia, *n.*, a sea anemone.

actin'ic, *adj.*, rel. to rays and their penetrative power.

actin'iform, *adj.*, radiated.

ac'tinism, *n.*, radiation; the property of radiant energy.

actin'ium, *n.*, a radioactive metal found in pitchblende.

actin'ograph, *n.*, a ray-recording instrument.

actinol'ogy, *n.*, the science or study of rays.

actinom'eter, *n.*, an instrument for measuring rays.

ac'tion, *n.*, the state of doing or acting; the thing done; a lawsuit; the mechanism of a piano.

ac'tionable, *adj.*, liable to an action or lawsuit.

ac'tionary, *n.*, a stockholder.

ac'tionist, *n.*, *i.q.* actionary.

ac'tionless, *adj.*, without action.

ac'tivate, *v.t.*, to render active.

activa'tion, *n.*, the process of rendering active.

ac'tivator, *n.*, that which renders active.

ac′tive, *adj.*, full of action, lively.

ac′tively, *adv.*, in an active way.

activ′ity, *n.*, the active state.

ac′ton, *n.*, a padded jacket worn under mail.

act′or, *n.*, one who acts; a player.

act′ress, *n.*, a woman who acts.

act′ual, *adj.*, real, existing.

actual′ity, *n.*, the state of being actual.

act′ualize, *v.t.*, to make real.

act′ually, *adv.*, really, in fact.

actua′rial, *adj.*, pert. or rel. to an actuary.

actua′rially, *adv.*, by actuarial methods.

act′uary, *n.*, a registrar; one skilled in insurance business, rates of mortality, etc.

act′uate, *v.t.*, to move, to influence.

act′uated, *p.p.*, actuate.

act′uating, *pr.p.*, actuate.

actua′tion, *n.*, the state of being actuated.

acu′ity, *n.*, sharpness, acuteness.

acu′leate, *adj.*, armed with a sting.

acu′leated, *adj.*, *i.q.* aculeate.

acul′eus, *n.*, a sting, a prickle.

acu′men, *n.*, sharpness, wit, sagacity.

acu′minate, *adj.*, tapering.

acu′minated, *adj.*, *i.q.* acuminate.

acumina′tion, *n.*, the ending in a point.

acu′minous, *adj.*, pointed.

acupress′ure, *n.*, stopping bleeding by means of a suture.

acupunctura′tion, *n.*, the act of pricking with a needle.

acupunct′ure, *n.*, the pricking with a needle as a medical cure.

acu′shla, *n.*, beloved.

acute′, *adj.*, pointed, sharp; shrill.

acute′ly, *adv.*, sharply, cleverly.

acute′ness, *n.*, the state or quality of being acute.

adac′tyl, *adj.*, having neither fingers nor toes.

ad′age, *n.*, a common or old saying.

ada′gio, *adj.* and *adv.*, in slow time (*mus.*); *n.*, a slow movement, so named.

Ad′am, *adj.*, a decorative style in houses; *n.*, the first man.

ad′amant, *n.*, a hard stone; the diamond.

adamante′an, *adj.*, like adamant; hardhearted.

adaman′tine, *adj.*, of adamant; hardhearted.

Adam′ic, *adj.*, rel. to Adam.

Ad′amite, *n.*, a human, sprung from Adam.

Adamit′ic, *adj.*, *i.q.* Adamic.

Ad′am's-ap′ple, *n.*, the projecting thyroid cartilage of the throat.

adapt′, *v.t.*, to fit, to make suitable, to alter.

adaptabil′ity, *n.*, the power to be adapted.

adapt′able, *adj.*, able to be adapted.

adapt′ableness, *n.*, the adaptable capacity.

adapta′tion, *n.*, the act of adapting; a thing adapted.

adapt′ed, *p.p.*, adapt.

adapt′er, *n.*, one who adapts.

adapt′ing, *pr.p.*, adapt.

adapt′ive, *adj.*, capable of adapting.

Adar′, *n.*, the sixth month of the Jewish civil year.

adax′ial, *adj.*, attached to the axis.

add, *v.t.*, to put one thing to another; to say something more.

add′ax, *n.*, a large antelope with twisted horns.

ad′ded, *p.p.*, add.

adden′da, *n. pl.*, things to be added.

adden′dum, *n.*, a thing to be added.

ad′der, *n.*, a poisonous reptile; one who adds.

addibil′ity, *n.*, the fitness to be added.

ad′dible, *adj.*, capable of addition.

addict′, *v.t.*, to give over to.

addic′ted, *p.p.*, addict, generally in sense of prone to, given up to; strongly attached to.

addict′edness, *n.*, the state of addiction.

addict′ing, *pr.p.*, addict.

addic′tion, *n.*, the act of addicting oneself; a powerful attachment to.

addic′tive, *adj.*, inclined to addict.

ad′ding, *pr.p.*, add.

addit′ament, *n.*, an addition.

addi′tion, *n.*, the act of adding; a thing added.

addi′tional, *adj.*, added.

addi′tionally, *adv.*, as well as; also.

add′itive, *adj.* and *n.*, to be added.

ad′dle, *v.i.*, to become muddled; *v.t.*, to muddle.

ad′dle-brained, *adj.*, muddled.

ad′dled, *p.p.*, addle; rotten, confused.

ad′dle-head′ed, *adj.*, with a confused brain.

ad′dle-pa′ted, *adj.*, *i.q.* addle-headed.

ad′dling, *adj.*, confusing; *pr.p.*, addle.

address′, *n.*, a congratulatory speech or letter; a public lecture or discourse; skilfulness; manners; direction; *v.t.*, to speak to; to direct something to; to prepare to strike (a golf ball).

addressed′, *p.p.*, address.

addressee′, *n.*, one to whom a thing is addressed.

address′er, *n.*, one who addresses.

address′ing, *pr.p.*, address.

adduce′, *v.t.*, to bring forward or cite.

adduced′, *p.p.*, adduce.

addu′cent, *adj.*, drawing together.

addu′cer, *n.*, one who adduces.

addu′cible, *adj.*, able to be adduced.

addu′cing, *pr.p.*, adduce.

adduct′, *v.t.*, to draw towards the axis of a limb or body.

adduc′tion, *n.*, the act of adducting, as of muscles.

adduc′tive, *adj.*, with power to adduct.

adduc′tor, *n.*, an adducting muscle.

ad′eling, *n.*, one of princely descent.

adel′opode, *adj.*, having concealed feet.

adel′phia, *n.*, a brotherhood; a group of stamens.

ademp′tion, *n.*, the act of depriving.

adenog′raphy, *n.*, a descriptive anatomy of the glands.

ad′enoid, *adj.*, glandiform; glandular.

ad′enoidal, *adj.*, pert. or rel. to the adenoids.

ad′enoids, *n. pl.*, spongy glands in the upper throat.

adenolog′ical, *adj.*, pert. or rel. to the study of the glands.

adenol′ogy, *n.*, the study of the glands.

adeno′ma, *n.*, a glandular kind of tumour.

ad′enose, *adj.*, glandular.

adenot′omy, *n.*, the cutting of a gland.

ad′enous, *adj.*, glandular.

ad′eps, *n.*, fat (*Lat.*).

adept′, *adj.*, skilled, expert; *n.*, an expert person.

ad′equacy, *n.*, the state of being adequate.

ad′equate, *adj.*, equal to, competent, sufficient.

ad′equately, *adv.*, in an adequate manner or degree.

ad′equateness, *n.*, the state of being adequate.

ades′pota, *n. pl.*, literary works without an owner.

à deux, *adv.* and *adj.*, for two (*Fr.*).

adhere′, *v.i.*, to stick to, to cling to, to support.

adhered′, *p.p.*, adhere.

adhe′rence, *n.*, the act of adhering.

adhe′rency, *n.*, the tendency to adhere.

adhe′rent, *adj.*, sticking to; *n.*, a supporter; a sticking substance.

adhe′rently, *adv.*, in a clinging or closely joined way.

adhe′rer, *n.*, one who supports or clings.

adhe′ring, *pr.p.*, adhere.

adhe′sion, *n.*, the act or quality of adhering; a thing that adheres.

adhe′sive, *adj.*, sticky, clinging.

adhe′sively, *adv.*, with adhesion.

adhe′siveness, *n.*, the tendency to adhere.

adhib′it, *v.t.*, to let in; to attach; to use.

adhib′ited, *p.p.*, adhibit.

adhib′iting, *pr.p.*, adhibit.

adhibi′tion, *n.*, the act of adhibiting.

ad hoc, *adj.*, arranged for this purpose (*Lat.*).

adiabat′ic, *adj.*, impervious to heat.

adian′tum, *n.*, a maidenhair fern.

adiaph′orism, *n.*, theological indifference.

adiaph′orist, *n.*, one who holds dogma or rites as indifferent.

adiaph′oron, *n.*, a thing indifferent in the eyes of the Church.

adiaph′orous, *adj.*, indifferent, neutral.

adieu′, orig. a *Fr.* phrase, à Dieu = to God, now used as "farewell", *interj.* and *n.*

ad infinitum, to infinity; and so on (*Lat.*).

adipes′cent, *adj.*, becoming fatty.

adipoc′erate, *v.t.*, to convert into adipocere.

ad′ipocere, *n.*, a light, a fatty substance.

ad′ipose, *adj.* and *n.*, fat.

adipo′sity, *n.*, a tendency to fat.

ad′ipsy, *n.*, the absence of thirst.

ad′it, *n.*, an approach, an entrance, esp. in a mine.

adja′cence, *n.*, the state of being near.

adja′cency, *n.*, the neighbourhood.

adja′cent, *adj.*, situated near.

adja′cently, *adv.*, close by.

adject′, *v.t.*, to join.

adject′ed, *p.p.*, adject.

adject′ing, *pr.p.*, adject.

adjec′tion, *n.*, the act of adjecting.

adjecti′val, *adj.*, of the nature of an adjective.

adjecti′vally, *adv.*, in the manner of adjectives.

ad′jective, *n.*, the grammatical term for a word denoting a

quality or describing a noun.

adjoin′, *v.t.*, to lie near, to be joined to.

adjoined′, *p.p.*, adjoin.

adjoin′ing, *adj.*, next to, contiguous, *pr.p.*, adjoin.

adjourn′, *v.t.* and *i.*, to put off to another time; to postpone; to leave off.

adjourned′, *p.p.*, adjourn.

adjourn′ing, *pr.p.*, adjourn.

adjourn′ment, *n.*, the act of adjourning.

adjudge′, *v.t.*, to decide judicially.

adjudged′, *p.p.*, adjudge.

adjudg′ing, *pr.p.*, adjudge.

adjudg′ment, *n.*, the act of judging; the verdict.

adju′dicate, *v.t.*, to sit or decide as a judge.

adju′dicated, *p.p.*, adjudicate.

adju′dicating, *pr.p.*, adjudicate.

adjudica′tion, *n.*, the act of adjudicating.

adju′dicator, *n.*, one who adjudicates.

adjud′icature, *n.*, *i.q.* adjudication.

ad′junct, *n.*, something added.

adjunc′tion, *n.*, the act of joining; a thing joined.

adjunc′tive, *adj.*, tending to join.

adjunc′tively, *adv.*, in an adjunctive way.

adjunct′ly, *adv.*, as something added.

adjura′tion, *n.*, a solemn appeal; a solemn oath; the act of adjuring.

adju′ratory, *adj.*, of the nature of an adjuration.

adjure′, *v.t.*, to make a solemn charge or appeal.

adjured′, *p.p.*, adjure.

adjur′er, *n.*, one who adjures.

adjur′ing, *pr.p.*, adjure.

adjust′, *v.t.*, to fit, to make exact, to settle.

adjust′able, *adj.*, able to be adjusted.

adjust′ed, *p.p.*, adjust.

adjust′er, *n.*, one who adjusts.

adjust′ing, *pr.p.*, adjust

adjust'ive, *adj.,* capable of adjusting.

adjust'ment, *n.,* the act or state of adjusting; a regulating means, as in a watch; a settlement.

adj'utage, *n.,* the mouthpiece of a fountain.

ad'jutancy, *n.,* the office or rank of adjutant.

ad'jutant, *n.,* an assistant to a commanding officer.

ad'jutant-gen'eral, *n.,* the principal assistant to a general.

ad'juvant, *adj.,* assisting.

ad'mass, *n.,* people easily influenced by mass methods of publicity.

admeas'ure, *v.t.,* to apportion.

admeas'ured, *p.p.,* admeasure.

admeas'urement, *n.,* the act or state of admeasuring.

admeas'uring, *pr.p.,* admeasure.

admin'icle, *n.,* aid; additional evidence.

admin'ister, *v.t.,* to perform, to execute; to control; to dispense.

admin'istered, *p.p.,* administer.

administe'rial, *adj.,* rel. to administration.

admin'istering, *pr.p.,* administer.

admin'istrable, *adj.,* able to be administered.

admin'istrant, *n., i.q.* administrator.

admin'istrate, *v.t.,* to manage, to govern.

admin'istrated, *p.p.,* administrate.

admin'istrating, *pr.p.,* administrate.

administra'tion, *n.,* the act of governing; the government.

admin'istrative, *adj.,* capable of administering; executive.

admin'istratively, *adv.,* in an administrative way.

admin'istrator, *n.,* one who administers.

admin'istratorship, *n.,* the function of administering.

admin'istratrix, *n.,* the fem. of administrator.

admirabil'ity, *n.,* the fitness to be admired.

ad'mirable, *adj.,* worthy of admiration.

ad'miral, *n.,* the commander of a fleet.

ad'miralship, *n.,* skill in commanding a fleet.

Ad'miralty, *n.,* the governing body of a navy.

admira'tion, *n.,* wonder, regard.

admire', *v.t.,* to wonder at, to esteem.

admired', *p.p.,* admire.

admir'er, *n.,* one who admires.

admir'ing, *pr.p.,* admire.

admir'ingly, *adv.,* like one who admires.

admissibil'ity, *n.,* the being admissible.

admis'sible, *adj.,* able to be admitted or permitted or conceived.

admis'sion, *n.,* the act of letting in or admitting; a concession.

admis'sive, *adj.,* tending to admit.

admis'sory, *adj.,* giving admission.

admit', *v.t.,* to let in; to acknowledge, to concede.

admit'table, *adj.,* able to be admitted.

admit'tance, *n.,* permission to enter.

admit'ted, *p.p.,* admit.

admit'tedly, *adv.,* acknowledge a thing to be.

admit'ter, *n.,* one who admits.

admit'ting, *pr.p.,* admit.

admix', *v.t.,* to mix together.

admixed', *p.p.,* admix.

admix'ing, *pr.p.,* admix.

admix'tion, *n.,* the act or state of admixing.

admix'ture, *n.,* the act of admixing; an assembly of mixed things.

admon'ish, *v.t.,* to warn, to reprove.

admon'ished, *p.p.,* admonish.

admon'isher, *n.,* one who admonishes.

admon'ishing, *pr.p.,* admonish.

admonish'ment, *n.,* a rebuke.

admoni'tion, *n.,* the act of admonishing; a warning.

admon'itor, *n.,* one who admonishes.

admon'itory, *adj.,* rel. to admonition; warning.

adnas'cence, *n.,* an adhesion, a growing on to.

ad'nate, *adj.,* grown together.

ad nau'seam, *Lat. phr.,* to a disgusting extent.

adnom'inal, *adj.,* adjectival.

ado', *n.,* a stir, trouble, fuss.

ado'be, *adj.,* made of sun-dried brick; *n.,* sun-dried brick (*Span.*).

adoles'cence, *n.,* the state of growing up.

adoles'cency, *n.,* the period of growing up.

adoles'cent, *adj.,* in the growing-up stage; *n.,* one between childhood and adulthood.

adon'is, *n.,* a beauty, a dandy.

ad'onize, *v.t.,* to adorn, to beautify oneself.

adopt', *v.t.,* to take to oneself, to choose; to take as one's own child.

adopt'ed, *p.p.,* adopt.

adopt'er, *n.,* one who adopts.

adopt'ing, *pr.p.,* adopt.

adop'tion, *n.,* the act of adopting.

adop'tive, *adj.,* rel. to adoption.

ador'able, *adj.,* fit to be adored.

ador'ableness, *n.,* the adorable state; the fitness to be adored.

ador'ably, *adv.,* in an adorable way.

adora'tion, *n.,* the act of adoring.

adore', *v.t.,* to worship; to love exceedingly.

adored', *p.p.,* adore.

ador'er, *n.,* one who adores.

ador'ing, *pr.p.,* adore.

ador'ingly, *adv.,* in an adoring way.

adorn', *v.t.,* to beautify, to decorate.

adorned', *p.p.,* adorn.

adorn'er, *n.,* one who adorns.

adorn'ing, *pr.p.,* adorn.

adorn'ment, *n.,* the act of adorning; an embellishment.

adoscula'tion, *n.,* the impregnation of flowers or ova.

adown', *adv.* and *prep.,* down; down along.

adren'al, *adj.,* in the region of the kidneys.

adren'alin, *n.,* a glandular secretion affecting circulation and muscular action.

adrift', *adj.* and *adv.,* not under control; lacking rational purpose.

adrip', *adv.*, in a dripping state.

adroga'tion, *n.*, adoption.

adroit', *adj.*, skilful, nimble.

à droite, to the right (*Fr.*).

adroit'ly, *adv.*, in an adroit manner.

adroit'ness, *n.*, the adroit state or faculty.

adry', *adj.*, thirsty.

adsciti'tious, *adj.*, additional, unessential.

adsciti'tiously, *adv.*, in an adscititious way.

ad'script, *adj.*, written later; *n.*, a serf attached to the soil.

adsorb', *v.t.*, to attract to its surface.

adsorbed', *p.p.*, adsorb.

adsorb'ing, *pr.p.*, adsorb.

adsorp'tion, *n.*, the attraction to its surface.

ad'ulate, *v.t.*, to bestow fulsome flattery on.

adula'tion, *n.*, fulsome flattery.

ad'ulator, *n.*, one who adulates.

ad'ulatory, *adj.*, fulsomely flattering.

adult', *n.*, one grown up; *adj.*, grown up, of full age.

adul'terant, *adj.*, adulterating; *n.*, a person or thing that adulterates.

adul'terate, *v.t.*, to corrupt, to make impure.

adul'terated, *p.p.*, adulterate.

adul'terating, *pr.p.*, adulterate.

adultera'tion, *n.*, the act or effect of adulterating.

adul'terator, *n.*, one who adulterates.

adul'terer, *n.*, one who commits adultery.

adul'teress, *n.*, the fem. of adulterer.

adul'terine, *adj.*, adulterated, illegal.

adul'terous, *adj.*, rel. to adultery.

adul'terously, *adv.*, in the manner of an adulterer.

adul'tery, *n.*, sexual intercourse of a married person with one not that person's spouse.

adult'hood, *n.*, maturity, the state of being grown up; adultness.

adult'ness, *n.*, *i.q.* adulthood.

adum'bra, *n.*, the penumbra of an eclipse of the moon.

adum'bral, *adj.*, overshadowing, shady.

adum'brant, *adj.*, in outline, foreshadowing.

ad'umbrate, *v.t.*, to sketch in outline, to typify.

ad'umbrated, *p.p.*, adumbrate.

ad'umbrating, *pr.p.*, adumbrate.

adumbra'tion, *n.*, the act of adumbrating.

adunc', *adj.*, hooked.

adunc'ate, *adj.*, *i.q.* adunc.

adun'city, *n.*, hookedness.

adunc'ous, *adj.*, hooked.

adust', *adj.*, burnt, dried up; *adv.*, in the dust.

ad valor'em, *Lat. phr.*, according to value.

advance', *n.*, the act of advancing, progress; payment in advance; *v.i.* and *t.*, to put forward, to move forward, to give beforehand, to increase.

advanced', *p.p.*, advance.

advance'ment, *n.*, the act or state of advancing; promotion.

advan'cer, *n.*, one who advances.

advan'cing, *pr.p.*, advance.

advan'tage, *n.*, a gain, profit, superiority; *v.t.*, to be of service to, to benefit.

advan'taged, *p.p.*, advantage.

advanta'geous, *adj.*, profitable, useful.

advanta'geously, *adv.*, with advantage.

advanta'geousness, *n.*, the state of being advantageous.

advant'aging, *pr.p.*, advantage.

advene', *v.i.*, to come to, to arrive; to be added.

adve'nient, *adj.*, additional.

ad'vent, *n.*, the coming, the arrival; the four weeks before Christmas.

Ad'ventist, *n.*, a believer in Christ's second coming.

adventi'tious, *adj.*, additional, casual; by chance.

adventi'tiously, *adv.*, additionally, casually.

adventi'tiousness, *n.*, the quality of being casual.

advent'ual, *adj.*, rel. to Advent.

adven'ture, *n.*, a hazardous enterprise, a risk; *v.i.* and *t.*, to embark on an enterprise.

adven'tured, *p.p.*, adventure.

adven'turer, *n.*, one who adventures; a trickster.

adven'turesome, *adj.*, prone to adventure.

adven'turess, *n.*, the fem. of adventurer.

adven'turing, *pr.p.*, adventure.

adven'turous, *adj.*, bold, ready to take risks.

adven'turously, *adv.*, daringly.

adven'turousness, *n.*, boldness, daring.

ad'verb, *n.*, a word that qualifies verbs, adjectives or adverbs.

adverb'ial, *adj.*, rel. to an adverb.

adverb'ially, *adv.*, in the manner of an adverb.

adversa'ria, *n. pl.*, miscellaneous notes (*Lat.*).

ad'versary, *n.*, the opponent, an enemy.

adver'sative, *adj.*, contrary, antithetical.

ad'verse, *adj.*, opposed, contrary to.

ad'versely, *adv.*, in a contrary or hostile way.

ad'verseness, *n.*, the adverse state.

adver'sity, *n.*, bad fortune, misfortune, misery.

advert', *v.i.* and *t.*, to turn, to direct; to refer to.

advert'ed, *p.p.*, advert.

advert'ence, *n.*, attention; reference to.

advert'ency, *n.*, the attentive state.

advert'ent, *adj.*, attentive.

advert'ently, *adv.*, attentively.

advert'ing, *pr.p.*, advert.

ad'vertise, *v.t.*, to proclaim publicly, to make known.

ad'vertised, *p.p.*, advertise.

adver'tisement, *n.*, a publication, a notice.

ad'vertiser, *n.*, one who advertises.

ad'vertising, *n.*, the art of publicizing goods and services; *pr.p.*, advertise.

advice', *n.*, counsel, warning.

advisabil'ity, *n.*, the state of being advisable.

advis'able, *adj.*, able to be recommended; wise, prudent.

advis'ableness, *n.*, *i.q.* advisability.

advis'ably, *adv.*, wisely, in a way to be approved.

advise', *v.t.*, to give notice; to warn; to inform.

advised', *p.p.*, advise.

advis'edly, *adv.*, upon consideration, with all care.

advis'er, *n.*, one who advises.

advis'ing, *pr.p.*, advise.

advis'ory, *adj.*, with power to advise.

ad'vocaat, *n.*, a liqueur containing eggs.

ad'vocacy, *n.*, the act of advocating.

ad'vocate, *n.*, the pleader of a cause; *v.t.*, to plead, to urge, to support.

ad'vocated, *p.p.*, advocate.

ad'vocateship, *n.*, the office of advocate.

ad'vocating, *pr.p.*, advocate.

advoca'tion, *n.*, the act of transferring a lawcase to another court (*Scot.*); an appeal.

advow'ee, *n.*, a patron holding an advowson.

advow'son, *n.*, the right of presentation to a benefice.

adynam'ia, *n.*, the loss of physical strength.

adynam'ic, *adj.*, pert. or rel. to adynamia; unaffected by force.

ad'ytum, *n.*, an inner shrine; a recess (*Lat.*).

adze, *n.*, an axe-like tool.

ae'dile, *n.*, a Roman magistrate.

Aege'an, *adj.*, pert. or rel. to a Greek sea and archipelago.

ae'ger, *n.*, a note certifying a student's illness (in Eng. university).

ae'gis, *n.*, the protecting shield of Zeus; any protective government.

aegro'tat, *n.*, a certificate of sickness.

Aene'id, *n.*, Virgil's poem on Aeneas.

Aeneolith'ic, *adj.*, rel. to the end of the neolithic period.

Aeo'lian, *adj.*, bel. to Aeolia, an ancient Greek province.

ae'on, *n.*, an age, a great length of time.

aer'ate, *v.t.*, to impregnate with air.

aer'ated, *p.p.*, aerate.

aer'ating, *pr.p.*, aerate.

aera'tion, *n.*, the process of aerating.

aer'ator, *n.*, an apparatus for supplying air.

ae'rial, *adj.*, of the air; *n.*, a radio antenna.

ae'rie, *n.*, a bird of prey's nest.

aerifica'tion, *n.*, the process or state of aerifying.

aer'ified, *p.p.*, aerify.

aer'iform, *adj.*, having the form of air, unreal.

aer'ify, *v.t.*, to fill with air.

aerify'ing, *pr.p.*, aerify.

aerobat'ics, *n. pl.*, aerial acrobatics.

aer'obe, *n.*, a microbe that can live only on oxygen.

aerobi'oscope, *n.*, an instrument for surveying germs in the air.

aer'obomb, *n.*, a bomb dropped from an aircraft.

aer'obus, *n.*, an aerial omnibus.

aer'o-cam'era, *n.*, a camera for use on an aircraft.

aer'odart, *n.*, an arrow-headed missile.

aer'odrome, *n.*, an airfield, airport (*becoming obs.*).

aerodynam'ics, *n.*, the science of the laws of motion of gases.

aer'ofoil, *n.*, the lifting surface of an aircraft.

aer'ogram(me), *n.*, a message by radio or telephone; an airletter.

aerog'raphy, *n.*, a description of the atmosphere.

aer'olite, *n.*, a meteoric stone.

aer'olith, *n.*, *i.q.* aerolite.

aerolit'ic, *adj.*, pert. or rel. to aerolites.

aerolog'ical, *adj.*, pert. or rel. to aerology.

aerol'ogist, *n.*, a student of aerology.

aerol'ogy, *n.*, the science of the atmosphere.

aer'omancy, *n.*, divination by means of the sky.

aerom'eter, *n.*, an apparatus for discovering the tension of air.

aeromet'ric, *adj.*, pert. or rel. to aerometry.

aerom'etry, *n.*, the science of measuring air and gases.

aer'omotor, *n.*, an aircraft engine.

aer'onaut, *n.*, a professional flyer.

aeronau'tic, *adj.*, pert. or rel. to air navigation.

aeronaut'ical, *adj.*, *i.q.* aeronautic.

aeronau'tics, *n.*, the art and science of flying aircraft.

aer'ophyte, *n.*, a plant that grows in the air.

aer'oplane, *n.*, an aircraft; a flying machine heavier than air (*becoming obs.*).

aeros'copy, *n.*, the observation of atmospheric phenomena.

aer'osol, *n.*, a container of liquid used for fine spraying.

aer'ostat, *n.*, an air balloon.

aerostat'ics, *n.*, the science of stable gases; air navigation.

aeru'ginous, *adj.*, like verdigris, copper-rust.

aer'y, *adj.*, high in the air; spiritual.

Aescula'pian, *adj.*, rel. to Aesculapius. Also *Esculapian*.

Aescula'pius, *n.*, the Roman god of healing.

aesthet'ic, *adj.*, pert. or rel. to good taste or fine perception. Also *esthetic*.

aesthet'ical, *adj.*, *i.q.* aesthetic.

aesthet'icism, *n.*, the quality of being aesthetic.

aesthet'ics, *n. pl.*, the principles of good taste.

aestho-physiol'ogy, *n.*, the scientific study of the sensory organs.

aesti'val, *adj.,* relating to summer.

aes'tivate, *v.i.,* to spend the summer.

aestiva'tion, *n.,* dormancy in summer; the internal arrangement of a flower-bud.

aetiol'ogy, *n.,* the science of causes.

afar', *adv.,* at a distance, far off.

afeard', *adj.,* afraid, frightened.

affabil'ity, *n.,* the quality of being affable.

af'fable, *adj.,* ready to be spoken to, gracious; genially well disposed.

af'fableness, *n.,* the quality of being affable.

af'fably, *adv.,* graciously, agreeably.

affair', *n.,* a thing, a matter, a business, a military engagement; an association.

affect', *v.t.,* to influence, to modify, to act upon; to assume, to adopt, to pretend.

affecta'tion, *n.,* an assumed pose, a pretence.

affect'ed, *adj.,* showing affectation; *p.p.,* affect.

affect'edly, *adv.,* in an affected way.

affect'edness, *n.,* *i.q.* affectation.

affectibil'ity, *n.,* an affectible condition.

affect'ible, *adj.,* capable of being affected.

affect'ing, *pr.p.,* affect.

affect'ingly, *adv.,* touchingly.

affec'tion, *n.,* love, tender feeling, a fondness for; an ailment.

affec'tional, *adj.,* rel. to affections.

affec'tionate, *adj.,* loving, fond.

affec'tionately, *adv.,* lovingly, fondly.

affec'tionateness, *n.,* the quality of being affectionate.

affec'tioned, *adj.,* disposed.

affec'tive, *adj.,* emotional; with power to affect.

affec'tively, *adv.,* in an affective way.

aff'erent, *adj.,* conducting inwards towards a centre (mainly nerves).

affettuo'so, *adv.,* with emotion (*It., mus.*).

affi'ance, *n.,* a promise, a pledge, a trust; *v.t.,* to plight faith, to betroth.

affi'anced, *p.p.,* affiance; *adj.,* betrothed.

affi'ancer, *n.,* one who affiances.

affi'ancing, *pr.p.,* affiance.

affiche, *n.,* a notice (*Fr.*).

affida'vit, *n.,* a sworn written statement.

affied', *adj.,* affianced.

affil'iate, *v.t.,* to adopt a child; to fix a child's parentage; to associate.

affil'iated, *p.p.,* affiliate.

affil'iating, *pr.p.,* affiliate.

affilia'tion, *n.,* the act of affiliating.

af'finage, *n.,* refining.

affined', *adj.,* related, connected.

affin'ity, *n.,* a near relationship; a resemblance of nature; attraction (*chem.*).

affirm', *v.i.* and *t.,* to state confidently; to state as the truth.

affirm'able, *adj.,* able to be affirmed.

affirm'ably, *adv.,* in an affirmable manner.

affirm'ance, *n.,* a ratification.

affirm'ant, *n.,* one who affirms.

affirma'tion, *n.,* the act of affirming; a positive statement.

affirm'ative, *adj.,* asserting; saying yes.

affirm'atively, *adv.,* in an affirmative way.

affirmed', *p.p.,* affirm.

affirm'er, *n.,* one who affirms.

affirm'ing, *pr.p.,* affirm.

affix', *v.t.,* to fix, to join.

af'fix, *n.,* an addition; a syllable or syllables added at the end of a word.

affixed', *p.p.,* affix.

affix'ing, *pr.p.,* affix.

affix'ture, *n.,* the act of affixing; that which is affixed.

affla'ted, *adj.,* inspired.

affla'tion, *n.,* inspiration.

affla'tus, *n.,* a breath of wind; an inspiration.

afflict', *v.t.,* to cause pain or grief to.

afflict'ed, *p.p.,* afflict.

afflict'er, *n.,* one who afflicts.

afflict'ing, *pr.p.,* afflict.

afflic'tion, *n.,* distress, grief, oppression.

afflic'tive, *adj.,* causing affliction.

af'fluence, *n.,* abundance, wealth.

af'fluency, *n.,* an affluent state.

af'fluent, *adj.,* abundantly wealthy.

af'fluently, *adv.,* in an affluent manner.

af'flux, *n.,* a flowing towards; a concourse.

afford', *v.t.,* to bestow, to yield; to be able to spend.

afford'ed, *p.p.,* afford.

afford'ing, *pr.p.,* afford.

affor'est, *v.t.,* to turn into a forest by planting.

afforesta'tion, *n.,* the act of afforesting.

affran'chise, *v.t.,* to liberate.

affran'chisement, *n.,* the act of liberating.

affray', *n.,* an alarming or noisy fight; *v.t.,* to alarm.

affreight', *v.t.,* to charter a trading vessel.

affreight'ment, *n.,* the chartering of a cargo vessel.

aff'ricate, *n.,* the combination of an explosive consonant with a spirant (*phonet.*).

affright', *n.,* terror, dread; *v.t.,* to cause terror.

affright'ed, *p.p.,* affright.

affright'er, *n.,* one who affrights.

affright'ing, *pr.p.,* affright.

affront', *n.,* an insult; *v.t.,* to insult.

affront'ed, *p.p.,* affront.

affront'ing, *pr.p.,* affront.

affront'ive, *adj.,* ready to insult.

affuse', *v.t.,* to pour (water) on.

affused', *p.p.,* affuse.

affus'ing, *pr.p.,* affuse.

affu'sion, *n.,* the pouring on (of water).

Af'ghan, n., a native of Afghanistan.

afield', adv., to a distance, far.

afire', adv., on fire.

aflame', adv., in flames; in a glow.

afloat', adv., floating, sailing.

aflow', adj., inundated; overrun; filled.

afoot', adv., on foot.

afore', adv., formerly, before.

afore'going, adj., previous, preceding.

afore'hand, adv., previously, in anticipation.

afore'mentioned, adj., previously spoken of.

afore'named, adj., previously named.

afore'said, adj., previously said or mentioned.

afore'thought, adv. and adj., with premeditation.

afore'time, adv., in former times.

a fortio'ri, for a stronger reason (Lat.).

afoul', adv., running foul.

afraid', adj., frightened.

af'reet, n., an evil spirit, a demon.

afresh', adv., over again.

Af'ric, adj., rel. to Africa.

Af'rican, adj., i.q. Afric.; n., a native of Africa.

Afrikaans', n., the South African Dutch language; adj., South African Dutch.

Afrikan'der, n., a South African breed of cattle; also formerly i.q. Afrikaner.

Afrika'ner, n., a person born of white parents in South Africa.

af'rit, n., i.q. afreet.

afront', adv. and prep., in front (of).

aft', adj. and adv., behind, in the stern of a ship.

aft'er, adv., conj. and prep., behind; later; later than; according to.

aft'er-birth, n., the placenta.

aft'er-care, n., the care of a person following illness or wrongdoing.

aft'erglow, n., the luminosity in the sky after sunset.

aft'erguard, n., the sailors stationed abaft the mainmast.

aft'erlight, n., hindsight.

aft'ermath, n., a second crop; anything that succeeds a main event.

afternoon', n., the period between midday and night.

aft'ers, n. pl., a course following the main course (colloq.).

aft'erthought, n., a later reflection.

aft'erward, adv., later in time.

aft'erwards, adv., i.q. afterward.

aft'er-wit, n., belated wisdom; wisdom after the event.

a'ga, n., a Turkish gentleman or magistrate.

again', adv., once more.

against', prep., opposite, in opposition to.

agal'ma, n., an impression on a seal.

ag'ama, n., an African or Indian lizard.

ag'ami, n., the trumpeter bird of South America.

agam'ic, adj., the absence of sexual organs in lower animals and plants (zool.).

ag'amist, n., one opposed to marriage.

ag'amous, adj., unfit to marry; produced without sexual union.

ag'apae, n., pl. of agape.

ag'ape, n., a love feast.

agape', adv., gaping, in astonishment.

Agapem'one, n., the abode of Love.

ag'aric, n., a fungus or mushroom.

agasp', adv., gasping; adj., eager for.

ag'ate, n., a precious stone so named.

à gauche, to the left (Fr.).

aga've, n., an American plant (bot.).

agaze', adv., in a gazing attitude.

agazed', adj., astounded.

age, n., a time-period; the length of a life; v.i., to grow old.

a'ged, adj., old.

aged, p.p., age.

a'gedly, adv., like an old person.

a'gedness, n., the characteristics of being aged.

a'geing, pr.p., age.

age'less, adj., never growing old; endless; timeless.

a'gency, n., the function of an agent.

agen'da, n., things to be done or considered.

a'gene, n., nitrogen trichloride, used for whitening flour.

a'gent, n., one who acts; an intermediary.

aggera'tion, n., a heaping up.

agglom'erate, v.t. and i., to gather into a mass, to collect; n., a heap.

agglom'erated, p.p., agglomerate.

agglom'erating, pr.p., agglomerate.

agglomera'tion, n., the act of agglomerating; a mass.

agglu'tinant, adj., tending to agglutinate.

agglu'tinate, v.t. and i., to join (as if with glue).

agglu'tinated, p.p., agglutinate.

agglu'tinating, pr.p., agglutinate.

agglutina'tion, n., the process of agglutinating.

agglu'tinative, adj., tending to agglutination.

ag'grandize, v.t., to increase power or property; to exalt.

ag'grandized, p.p., aggrandize.

aggrand'izement, n., an increase, an exaltation.

ag'grandizer, n., one who aggrandizes.

ag'grandizing, pr.p., aggrandize.

ag'gravate, *v.t.*, to make heavier or more serious; to exasperate (*colloq.*).

ag'gravated, *p.p.*, aggravate.

ag'gravating, *pr.p.*, aggravate; *adj.*, exasperating (*colloq.*).

aggrava'tion, *n.*, the making worse or more serious.

ag'gregate, *adj.*, taken together; *n.*, a total.

ag'gregate, *v.t.*, to collect.

ag'gregated, *p.p.*, aggregate.

ag'gregately, *adv.*, collectively.

ag'gregating, *pr.p.*, aggregate.

aggrega'tion, *n.*, the act of aggregating.

ag'gregative, *adj.*, tending to aggregate.

aggress', *v.t.*, to assault; to open a quarrel; to invade another man's rights.

aggressed', *p.p.*, aggress.

aggress'ing, *pr.p.*, aggress.

aggres'sion, *n.*, an unprovoked assault; an encroachment.

aggress'ive, *adj.*, assaulting, encroaching, belligerent.

aggress'iveness, *n.*, a tendency to be aggressive.

aggress'or, *n.*, one who begins a quarrel, or who invades another man's rights.

aggriev'ance, *n.*, an offence.

aggrieve', *v.t.*, to offend, to give cause for complaint.

aggrieved', *p.p.*, aggrieve; *adj.*, offended.

aggriev'ing, *pr.p.*, aggrieve.

aghast', *adj.* and *adv.*, struck with amazement and horror.

ag'ile, *adj.*, nimble, active.

ag'ileness, *n.*, *i.q.* agility.

agil'ity, *n.*, nimbleness, activity.

ag'ing, *pr.p.*, *i.q.* ageing.

ag'io, *n.*, the exchange premium; the allowance on a worn coin.

ag'iotage, *n.*, brokerage.

agist', *v.t.*, to look after cattle for hire; to assess for the public.

agist'ment, *n.*, the contract with an agistor;

the agistor's profit; an assessment.

agist'or, *n.*, one who takes care of cattle for hire.

ag'itable, *adj.*, able to be agitated.

ag'itate, *v.t.*, to set in motion; to perturb; to excite.

ag'itated, *p.p.*, agitate; *adj.*, disturbed.

ag'itating, *pr.p.*, agitate.

agita'tion, *n.*, an agitated state; a disturbance; public movement.

ag'itative, *adj.*, causing agitation.

agita'to, *adv.*, agitatedly (*mus.*).

ag'itator, *n.*, one who excites the public; a shaking or mixing device.

Aglai'a, *n.*, one of the Graces (*Gr.*).

a'glet, *n.*, the metal sheath at the end of a lace; a bullion ornament on a uniform; a particular kind of stay-lace (round and white).

agley', *adv.*, askew, awry.

aglow', *adv.*, glowing.

agmatol'ogy, *n.*, the study of fractures.

ag'nail, *n.*, a whitlow, a corn, a misshapen finger-end.

ag'nate, *adj.*, related on the paternal side; akin; collaterally related.

agnat'ic, *adj.*, rel. to the male descent.

agna'tion, *n.*, the relationship through male descent.

agni'tion, *n.*, an acknowledgment.

agno'men, *n.*, an additional name.

agnos'tic, *adj.*, refusing to believe in the existence of a God; *n.*, one who refuses to believe in the existence of a God.

agnos'ticism, *n.*, the belief of the agnostic.

ago', *adv.*, in time past.

agog', *adv.*, in an excited, eager state.

ago'ing, *adv.*, in movement.

agone', *adv.*, past.

agon'ic, *adj.*, without an angle.

ag'onist, *n.*, one who agonizes or contends.

agonis'tes, *n.*, one who strives.

agonis'tic, *adj.*, striving, agonizing.

agonis'tical, *adj.*, *i.q.* agonistic.

ag'onize, *v.i.* and *t.*, to endure anguish; to distress.

ag'onized, *p.p.*, agonize.

ag'onizing, *pr.p.*, agonize.

ag'onizingly, *adv.*, in a distressing manner.

ag'ony, *n.*, extreme pain or anguish.

ag'ora, *n.*, a market-place, a market (*Gr.*).

agoraphob'ia, *n.*, a morbid fear of open spaces.

agou'ti, *n.*, a rodent with three hind toes.

ag'rapha, *n. pl.*, sayings of Christ not in the Gospels.

agraph'ia, *n.*, the loss of the power to write.

agra'rian, *adj.*, rel. to the land; *n.*, a supporter of agrarianism.

agra'rianism, *n.*, the doctrine of equal distribution of land.

agra'rianize, *v.t.*, to divide the land equally.

agree', *v.i.*, to consent, to be of one mind with.

agreeabil'ity, *n.*, being agreeable.

agree'able, *adj.*, pleasant, consenting.

agree'ableness, *n.*, pleasantness.

agree'ably, *adv.*, pleasantly; in accordance with.

agreed', *p.p.*, agree.

agree'ing, *pr.p.*, agree.

agree'ment, *n.*, consent, a formal document of consent.

agres'tic, *adj.*, rel. to the country.

ag'ricultor, *n.*, *i.q.* agriculturist.

agricul'tural, *adj.*, rel. to agriculture.

agricul'turalist, *n.*, *i.q.* agriculturist.

ag'riculture, *n.*, land cultivation.

agricul'turist, *n.*, one engaged in agriculture.

ag'rimony, *n.*, the plant *agrimonia*.

ag'rimotor, *n.*, a motor or tractor for farm work.

agriol'ogy, n., the study of uncivilized peoples.

agron'omy, n., husbandry; economy in the management of the land.

agrostog'raphy, n., the description of grasses.

agrostol'ogy, n., the study of grasses.

aground', adv., resting on a sea or river bed.

a'gue, n., a feverish, shivering complaint.

a'gued, adj., suffering from ague.

a'guish, adj., inclined to ague, shivering.

agu'ti, n., i.q. agouti.

ah, interj., expressing pain or surprise.

aha', interj., expressing glee or surprise.

ahead', adv., in advance, beyond.

aheap', adv., piled up.

ahem', interj., expressing hesitation or incredulity.

ahim'sa, n., non-violence —the highest form of duty acclaimed in Hindu Scriptures.

ahoy', interj., a sailor's challenge of another ship.

ahull', adv., lying almost broadside to wind and sea.

aid', n., help, assistance; v.t., to help, to assist.

aid'ance, n., i.q. aid.

aid'ed, p.p., aid.

aide'-de-camp, n., a general officer's assistant.

aide-mém'oire, n., an aid to memory.

aid'er, n., one who aids.

aid'ful, adj., helping.

aid'ing, pr.p., aid.

aid'less, adj., without help or aid.

ai'glet, i.q. aglet.

ai'gret, n., a heron or egret.

ai'grette, n., an ornament of feathers or jewels worn on the headdress.

ai'guille, n., a sharp mountain peak; a drill.

ail, v.i., to be ill.

ailed, p.p., ail.

ail'eron, n., the movable flap on the wing-tip of an aeroplane.

ail'ing, pr.p., ail; adj., in a sick state.

ail'ment, n., an illness.

aim, n., a striving to hit a mark; a thing aimed at; direction; intention; v.i., to strive to hit a mark; v.t., to point; to direct.

aimed, p.p., aim.

aim'ing, pr.p., aim.

aim'less, adj., without aim or intention.

aim'lessly, adv., in an aimless way.

aim'lessness, n., the absence of aim or intention.

ain't, am I not? is he, she, it not?; are we, you, they not? (colloq.).

air, n., the atmosphere; a person's bearing; a melody; v.t., to expose to the air, to dry, to display boastfully.

air'base, n., a place where aircraft are housed and maintained.

air'bed, n., an inflated bed.

air'borne, adj., carried by air.

air'brake, n., a brake actuated by air.

air'-cells, n. pl., cells containing air.

air'craft, n., flying machine(s).

air'craftman, n., the lowest rank in the Royal Air Force.

air'craftsman, n., one associated with aircraft; an aeronaut.

air'craftwoman, n., the lowest rank in the Women's Royal Air Force.

aired, p.p., air.

Aire'dale, n., a large, rough-haired terrier.

air'field, n., an open area used by aircraft for taking off and landing.

air' force, n., a country's strength in military aircraft.

air'-gas, n., the gas made by mixing air with petroleum vapour.

air'graph, n., a micro-film for facsimile transmission by air.

air'gun, n., a gun in which the force is air.

air'-hole, n., an opening to admit air.

air'ily, adv., lightly, gaily.

air'iness, n., sprightliness, breeziness.

air'ing, pr.p., air; n., a walk or drive in the air.

air'jacket, n., an inflatable jacket.

air'less, adj., without air.

air'-lift, n., an air-transport operation.

air'line, n., a direct air route; an air traffic system.

air'lin'er, n., a passenger-carrying aircraft.

air'lock, n., a small pneumatic chamber; an air bubble in a pipe.

air'mail, n., post conveyed by air.

air'man, n., an aviator.

air'manship, n., the art of handling aircraft.

Air' Marsh'al, n., an Air Force officer ranking with vice-admiral or lieutenant-general.

air'-mechan'ic, n., one who services aircraft.

air'minded, adj., having special thought for the development of air transport.

air'plane, n., i.q. aeroplane, aircraft.

air'-pock'et, n., a region of rarefied atmosphere.

air'port, n., a passenger aircraft station.

air'-pump, n., a pump for forcing out air.

air'-raid, n., an attack by aircraft.

air'-screw, n., an aircraft propeller.

air'-shaft, n., a ventilating shaft.

air'ship, n., a dirigible balloon.

air'strip, n., a runway for aircraft.

air'tight, adj., excluding the air.

Air'-Vice-Marsh'al, n., a Royal Air Force officer ranking with a British Army Major-General.

air'way, n., an air route.

air'worthi'ness, n., fitness for flying.

air'worthy, adj., safe for flying.

air'y, adj., having plenty of air; light, sprightly.

aisle, n., a division in a building flanking

the central division; a passage or gangway between things arranged in rows.

ait, *n.*, a little island in a river.

aitch'bone, *n.*, the cut of beef over the rump bone.

ajar', *adv.*, slightly opened.

aj'utage, *n.*, a tub for discharging liquid.

akim'bo, *adv.*, with hands on hips and the elbows pointed outwards.

akin', *adj.*, rel. by blood; of like nature.

al'abaster, *n.*, a semitransparent stone so named; *adj.*, made of alabaster.

à la carte', *adv.*, by the bill of fare (*Fr.*).

alack', *interj.*, expressing grief.

alack'-a-day, interjectional phrase, expressing grief.

alac'rity, *n.*, speed, alertness, smartness.

à la mode', *adv.*, in the fashion; *n.*, a thin silk material (*Fr.*).

a'lar, *adj.*, winged.

alarm', *n.*, sudden fear; a sense of coming danger; an alarum; *v.t.*, to cause sudden fright; to call to arms.

alarmed', *p.p.*, alarm.

alarm'ing, *pr.p.*, alarm; *adj.*, startling, disquieting.

alarm'ingly, *adv.*, startlingly.

alarm'ist, *n.*, one who, without reason, causes alarm.

alar'um, *n.*, a clockwork contrivance for waking people up.

a'lary, *adj.*, rel. to wings; wing-like.

alas', *interj.*, expressing sorrow.

a'late, *adj.*, *i.q.* alar.

alb, *n.*, a long, close-fitting white robe so named.

al'bacore, *n.*, a large species of tunny fish.

Alba'nian, *adj.*, bel. to Albania; *n.*, a native of Albania (an old name for Scotland).

alba'ta, *n.*, a white alloy of nickel, zinc and copper.

al'batross, *n.*, a great sea bird; the emblem of the R.A.F.

albe'it, *conj.*, although, even granting that.

al'bert, *n.*, a particular kind of watch-chain.

albes'cent, *adj.*, growing white.

Al'bin, *n.*, an old name for Scotland.

albi'ness, *n.*, the fem. of albino.

al'binism, *n.*, the physical character of the albino.

albi'no, *n.*, a man or beast having white hair and skin and pink eyes; a plant deficient in colouring matter.

albi'noism, *n.*, *i.q.* albinism.

albugin'eous, *adj.*, rel. to the white of the eye.

albu'go, *n.*, an eye disease affecting the cornea.

al'bum, *n.*, a book of blank pages.

albu'men, *n.*, the white of an egg; the nutritive matter found in a seed.

albu'min, *n.*, any substance composed like or resembling albumen; a proteid.

albu'minize, *v.t.*, to apply to paper an albuminous solution.

albu'minized, *p.p.*, albuminize.

albu'minizing, *pr.p.*, albuminize.

albu'minoid, *adj.*, resembling albumen.

albu'minous, *adj.*, with the quality of albumin.

albuminu'ria, *n.*, the presence of albumen in the urine.

albumin'ric, *adj.*, rel. to albuminuria.

albur'num, *n.*, a tree's sap-wood.

alcade', *n.*, a Spanish, Portuguese or Moorish Governor.

Alca'ic, *adj.*, in the metre of Alcaeus (a Greek poet).

al'cazar, *n.*, a Spanish or Moorish palace.

alchem'ic, *adj.*, rel. to alchemy.

alchem'ical, *adj.*, *i.q.* alchemic.

al'chemist, *n.*, one who practises alchemy.

alchemis'tic, *adj.*, rel. to an alchemist.

al'chemize, *v.t.*, to change as by alchemy.

al'chemy, *n.*, the spurious art of turning

base metals into gold; the forerunner of chemistry.

al'cohol, *n.*, a pure spirit so named; the active constituent in intoxicating drinks.

al'coholate, *n.*, a compound having alcohol as its acid radical.

alcohol'ic, *adj.*, rel. to alcohol.

al'coholism, *n.*, alcoholic poisoning.

al'coholist, *n.*, one who favours or is addicted to alcohol.

alcoholiza'tion, *n.*, the act of alcoholizing.

al'coholize, *v.t.*, to produce an alcoholic effect.

al'coholized, *p.p.*, alcoholize.

alcoholom'eter, *n.*, an instrument for testing the alcoholic strength of liquors.

Al'coran, *n.*, the sacred book of the Mohammedan religion.

Alcoran'ic, *adj.*, rel. to the Alcoran.

Alcoran'ist, *n.*, one who studies the Alcoran.

al'cove, *n.*, a recess.

Aldeb'aran, *n.*, one of the Hyades group of stars.

al'dehyde, *n.*, a volatile liquid derived from alcohol.

al'der, *n.*, a tree so named.

al'derman, *n.*, a municipal dignitary so named.

alderman'ic, *adj.*, resembling, or bel. to, an alderman.

Al'derney, *n.*, a small dairy cow bred in the Channel Islands.

al'derwoman, *n.*, the fem. of alderman.

Al'dine, *adj.*, bel. to Aldus Manutius, the Venetian 16th cent. printer.

ale, *n.*, an intoxicating malt liquor, brewed with hops; beer.

aleak', *adv.*, having sprung a leak.

a'leatory, *adj.*, rel. to dicing and gambling.

ale'-conner, *n.*, an inspector of ale and alemeasures.

alec'tryomancy, *n.*, divination by means of cocks.

alee', *adv.*, on or towards the lee side.

a'legar, *n.*, malt vinegar.

ale'hoof, n., ground-ivy.

ale'house, n., a place where ale is sold.

alem'bic, n., a distilling vessel.

alem'broth, n., a mixture used in alchemy.

alert', adj., on the watch, spry.

alert'ness, n., the quality of being alert.

alette', n., a small wing in a building; a side of a pier.

aleu'romancy, n., divination by means of flour.

aleurom'eter, n., an instrument for testing the properties of flour.

Aleu'tian, adj., rel. to the Aleuts, who live in the Aleutian islands off Alaska.

aleu'tic, adj., i.q. Aleutian.

ale'wife, n., a woman-seller of ale; an American herring-like fish.

Alexan'drian, adj., rel. to Alexander or Alexandria.

Alexan'drine, adj., rel. to Alexandria; n., a twelve-syllabled iambic verse.

alex'ia, n., the inability to see words; word-blindness.

alex'in, n., a substance found in blood serum able to destroy bacteria.

alexiphar'mic, adj., antidotal.

alfal'fa, n., a plant used as fodder.

alfres'co, an Italian phrase = in the fresh air.

al'gae, n. pl., seaweeds and water-weeds.

al'gal, adj., pert. to algae.

al'gebra, n., the method of calculating by means of letters, signs and figures.

algebra'ic, adj., rel. to algebra.

algebra'ical, adj., i.q. algebraic.

al'gebraist, n., one skilled in algebra.

Algerine', adj., rel. to Algiers.

al'gid, adj., cold, with particular reference to the cold stage of the ague.

algid'ity, n., the cold stage of the ague.

al'gist, n., a specialist in seaweeds.

Al'gol, n., the variable star *Beta in Perseus*; a computer language.

al'gor, n., chilliness.

al'gorism, n., Arabic numeration; arithmetic.

al'gorithm, n., a logical device of ordered and progressive questions leading to desired conclusions.

al'gum, n., a Biblical tree, sandal-wood.

Alham'bra, n., the famous Moorish palace at Granada.

a'lias, adv., at another time; n., a false name.

al'ibi, adv., in another place; n., the being in another place (leg.).

al'idad, n., the degree marker on a quadrant or similar instrument. Also *alidade*.

a'lien, adj., foreign, strange; n., a foreigner, a stranger.

alienabil'ity, n., the capacity to be alienated.

a'lienable, adj., able to be alienated.

a'lienage, n., the state of being an alien.

a'lienate, v.t., to make over to another; to appropriate; to estrange.

a'lienated, p.p., alienate.

a'lienating, pr.p., alienate.

aliena'tion, n., the act or state of alienating.

a'lienator, n., one who alienates.

alienee', n., one to whom a property is transferred (leg.).

a'lienism, n., the state of being an alien; the treatment of mental derangement.

a'lienor, n., one who transfers property (leg.).

alif'erous, adj., winged.

al'iform, adj., wing-shaped.

alight', v.i., to descend, to light down, to dismount; adv., on fire.

alight'ed, p.p., alight.

alight'ing, pr.p., alight.

align', v.t., to arrange in line.

align'ed, p.p., align.

align'ing, pr.p., align.

align'ment, n., the act or state of aligning.

alike', adj., resembling, like; adv., in a similar way, equally.

al'iment, n., nourishment, support.

aliment'al, adj., rel. to aliment.

aliment'ary, adj., rel. to aliment, giving nourishment.

alimenta'tion, n., the giving of aliment.

aliment'iveness, n., a liking for food and drink.

alimo'nious, adj., nutritious.

al'imony, n., support; a living allowance to a wife legally separated from her husband.

aline', v.t., i.q. align.

al'iped, adj., wing-footed.

aliphat'ic, adj., of fat.

al'iquant, adj., forming a fractional part of a number.

al'iquot, adj., contained so many times in a whole; n., an aliquot part.

a'lish, adj., resembling ale.

alive', adj., living, alert.

aliz'arine, n., a coal product, used for red-dyeing.

al'kahest, n., the universal solvent in alchemy.

alkales'cency, n., a tendency to become alkaline.

alkales'cent, adj., becoming alkaline.

al'kali, n., a chemical substance of a neutralizing nature.

al'kalifiable, adj., able to be alkalified.

al'kalified, p.p., alkalify.

al'kalify, v.t., to change into an alkali.

al'kalifying, pr.p., alkalify.

alkalig'enous, adj., producing alkali.

alkalim'eter, n., an apparatus for ascertaining the percentage of alkali in a solution.

alkalimet'ric, adj., rel. to alkalimetry.

alkalimet'rical, adj., i.q. alkalimetric.

alkalim'etry, n., the process of discovering the percentage of alkali in a solution.

al'kaline, adj., rel. to alkali.

alkalin′ity, *n.*, the state of being alkaline.

alkaliza′tion, *n.*, the act or state of alkalizing.

al′kalize, *v.t.*, to turn into alkali.

al′kalized, *p.p.*, alkalize.

al′kalizing, *pr.p.*, alkalize.

al′kaloid, *n.*, a chemical substance with properties like alkali.

al′kanet, *n.*, the name of a plant producing red dye.

Al′koran, *i.q.* Alcoran.,

all, *adj.*, the entire number; the whole.

al′la breve, *adv.*, in quick common time (*mus.*).

Al′lah, *n.*, the Mohammedan (Arabic) name for God.

al′lanite, *n.*, a mineral so named.

allanto′ic, *adj.*, rel. to the allantois.

allan′toid, *adj.*, like an allantois.

allan′tois, *n.*, a membranous appendage like a sac.

allay′, *v.t.*, to lighten, to make quiet, to alleviate.

allayed′, *p.p.*, allay.

allay′ing, *pr.p.*, allay.

all′-clear, *n.*, a signal that danger is passed.

allega′tion, *n.*, the act of making a charge.

allege′, alledge′, *v.t.*, to assert, to make a statement.

allege′able, alledge′able, *adj.*, able to be alleged.

alleged′, alledged′, *p.p.*, allege.

alleg′er, alledg′er, *n.*, one who alleges.

alle′giance, *n.*, plighted loyalty.

alleg′ing,   alledg′ing, *pr.p.*, allege.

allegor′ic, *adj.*, in the manner of allegory.

allegor′ical, *adj.*, *i.q.* allegoric.

allegor′ically, *adv.*, in an allegorical manner or sense.

al′legorist, *n.*, a writer of allegory.

al′legorize, *v.t.*, to make into allegory.

al′legorized, *p.p.*, allegorize.

al′legorizer, *n.*, one who allegorizes.

al′legorizing, *pr.p.*, allegorize.

al′legory, *n.*, a figurative story.

allegret′to, *adj.*, in fairly quick time (slower than allegro); *n.*, a movement in fairly quick time (*mus.*).

allegris′simo, *adj.*, in very fast time; *n.*, a movement in very fast time (*mus.*).

alle′gro, *adj.*, in fast time; *n.*, a fast movement (*mus.*).

allelu′ia, *interj.*, praise the Lord (*Heb.*).

alle′mande, *n.*, a dance movement in moderate tempo (*Fr.*).

all′ergen, *n.*, any substance causing allergic reaction.

aller′gic, *adj.*, highly susceptible to; having an aversion from.

all′ergy, *n.*, extreme sensitiveness to certain substances.

alle′viate, *v.t.*, to lighten, to assuage.

alle′viated, *p.p.*, alleviate.

alle′viating, *pr.p.*, alleviate.

allevia′tion, *n.*, the act of alleviating.

alle′viative, *adj.*, tending to alleviate.

alle′viator, *n.*, one who alleviates.

al′ley, *n.*, a narrow passage.

al′leyway, *n.*, *i.q.* alley.

All Fools′ Day, *n.*, 1 April.

all-fours′, *adv.*, on all four legs, or on hands and knees.

all-hail′, *interj.*, expressing greeting.

All-Hal′lows, *n.*, the feast of All Hallows or Saints, 1 Nov.

allia′ceous, *adj.*, pert. or rel. to garlic.

alli′ance, *n.*, a union by treaty.

al′lied, *p.p.*, ally.

al′lies, *n. pl.*, those who are closely or solemnly united.

all′igate, *v.t.*, to perform an alligation.

alliga′tion, *n.*, the act of binding.

al′ligator, *n.*, the crocodile of America.

all′-important, *adj.*, of the greatest importance.

all′-in, *adj.*, unrestricted; exhausted (*colloq.*).

allit′erate, *v.t.*, to make alliterative; *adj.*, alliterating in character.

allit′erated, *p.p.*, alliterate.

allit′erating, *pr.p.*, alliterate.

allitera′tion, *n.*, the repetition of a sound, usually initial, in a succession of words.

allit′erative, *adj.*, with a tendency to alliteration.

allit′eratively, *adv.*, in an alliterative way.

al′lium, *n.*, garlic; the name of a large class of *liliaceae.*

al′locate, *v.t.*, to assign a place or portion to.

al′located, *p.p.*, allocate.

al′locating, *pr.p.*, allocate.

alloca′tion, *n.*, the act of allocating.

alloca′tur, *n.*, a judge's allowance of an order of costs.

al′lochroite, *n.*, a species of garnet, so named from its changing colour under heat.

allocu′tion, *n.*, a spoken address, esp. one delivered by the Pope.

allo′dial, *adj.*, rel. to absolute ownership.

allo′dium, *n.*, an estate held in fee simple.

allog′amy, *n.*, cross-fertilization (*bot.*).

al′lograph, *n.*, a deed drawn by someone who is not a party to it.

allonge′, *v.i.*, to lunge; *n.*, a lunge; a paper slip attached to a bill of exchange, enabling further endorsement.

allopath′ic, *adj.*, rel. to allopathy.

allopath′ically, *adv.*, on allopathic principles or methods.

allop′athist, *n.*, one who practises allopathy.

allop′athy, *n.*, the medical system which employs counter remedies as distinguished from homoeopathy.

allot′, *v.t.*, to give as a portion or lot, to apportion.

all′otheism, *n.*, the worship of strange gods.

allot′ment, *n.*, an allotted portion; a small piece of land used for growing fruit, flowers and vegetables.

allot′ropism, *n.*, the principle or process of allotropy.

allot'ropy, n., a variation in physical properties.

allot'ted, p.p., allot.

allottee', n., one to whom an allotment is made.

allot'ting, pr.p., allot.

allow', v.t., to permit; to concede or admit.

allow'able, adj., able to be allowed.

allow'ableness, n., the state of being allowable.

allow'ably, adv., in a way that can be allowed.

allow'ance, n., permission, a privilege; a grant; v.t., to give a grant to.

allow'anced, p.p., allowance.

allow'ancing, pr.p., allowance.

allowed', p.p., allow.

allow'ing, pr.p., allow.

alloy', n., a mixture of metals; v.t., to spoil by a mixture of the base with the good.

alloy'age, n., the act of alloying.

alloyed', p.p., alloy.

alloy'ing, pr.p., alloy.

all'-round', adj., complete; competent in all ways.

all'-rounder, n., one competent in all things.

All Saints' Day, see All Hallows.

all'seed, n., the name of various plants giving much seed.

all'-seeing, adj., seeing all things.

All Souls' Day, n., 2 Nov., a Christian day of prayer for the dead.

all'spice, n., the pepperplant berry of Jamaica.

allude', v.i., to refer to.

allud'ed, p.p., allude.

allud'ing, pr.p., allude.

allure', v.t., to entice, to draw on.

allured', p.p., allure.

allure'ment, n., the act of alluring.

allur'er, n., one who allures.

allur'ing, pr.p., allure.

allur'ingly, adv., in an alluring way.

allu'sion, n., a reference to, a hinting at.

allu'sive, adj., making reference.

allu'sively, adv., in an allusive way.

allu'siveness, n., the quality of being allusive.

allu'sory, adj., i.q. allusive.

allu'via, n., pl. of alluvium.

allu'vial, adj., rel. to alluvium.

allu'vion, n., the act of depositing soil.

allu'vium, n., soil deposited by the sea or a river.

all-wise', adj., omniscient.

al'ly, n., a person or state joined to another by compact; a close friend; v.t., to attach, to bind.

ally'ing, pr.p., ally.

al'ma(h), n., an Egyptian dancing-girl.

Al'magest, n., the treatise of Pliny on astronomy; any learned treatise.

al'ma ma'ter, n., one's university or college.

al'manac, n., a year's calendar.

al'mandine, adj., rel. to the almandite.

al'mandite, n., a species of garnet.

almight'iness, n., the state of being almighty.

almight'y, adj., omnipotent; n., the Almighty, i.e., God.

a'lmond, n., the nut of the almond-tree.

al'moner, n., a distributor of alms; a hospital social worker.

al'monry, n., the place where alms are distributed.

al'most, adv., nearly, all but.

alms, n., a charitable gift.

alms'-house, n., a house where poor persons are lodged without charge.

al'muce, n., i.q. amess.

al'mug, n., i.q. algum.

al'oe, n., a bitter tropical plant.

aloet'ic, adj., rel. to the aloe.

aloet'ical, adj., i.q. aloetic.

aloft', adv., up above, on high.

alog'ical, adj., not logical, not rational.

alogot'rophy, n., irregular nutrition.

alone', adj. and adv., solitary, solitarily, by oneself.

along', adv., in line, in company with; prep., from end to end or through a part of; forward.

along'side, adv. and prep., side by side with.

aloof', adv., at a distance, apart, aside.

aloof'ness, n., a distant, stand-offish manner.

alope'cia, n., a form of baldness.

aloud', adv., so as to be heard.

alp, n., a mountain (literally, a snow-top).

alpac'a, n., a Peruvian goat; the material made from its hair.

alp'enstock, n., a mountaineer's staff.

al'pha, n., the Greek A.

al'phabet, n., all the letters of a language arranged in order.

alphabeta'rian, n., the learner or maker of an alphabet.

alphabet'ic, adj., in the order of the alphabet.

alphabet'ical, adj., rel. to the alphabet.

alphabet'ically, adv., i.q. alphabetic.

al'phus, n., a form of leprosy.

Alp'ine, adj., rel. to the Alps.

Alpi'ni, n., the Italian mountain soldiery.

al'pinist, n., an Alpine climber.

alread'y, adv., by this time.

Alsa'tia, n., Alsace; also the name given to the Whitefriars in London, a famous sanctuary.

Alsa'tian, adj., rel. to Alsatia; n., a native of A.; a German wolfhound.

al'sike, n., a sort of clover.

al'so, adv., in addition, as well.

Alta'ic, adj., rel. to the Altaic mountains.

al'tar, n., the stone or table of sacrifice.

al'tarage, *n.,* the endowments of an altar.

al'tar-cloth, *n.,* the cloth with which an altar is vested.

al'tar-piece, *n.,* a picture behind an altar.

al'tar-plate, *n.,* the communion plate.

al'tar-rails, *n. pl.,* the rails separating the altar from the rest of the chancel.

altaz'imuth, *n.,* an instrument for determining altitude and azimuth.

al'ter, *v.t.,* to change, to make different; *v.i.,* to become different.

alterabil'ity, *n.,* the alterable state.

al'terable, *adj.,* able to be altered.

al'terableness, *n.,* a tendency to change.

al'terably, *adv.,* with change.

al'terant, *adj.,* change-producing; *n.,* a substance that modifies a colour.

altera'tion, *n.,* a change, a variation.

al'terative, *n.,* a medicine which alters the bodily functions.

al'tercate, *v.i.,* to dispute.

al'tercating, *pr.p.,* altercate.

alterca'tion, *n.,* a dispute, a wrangle.

al'tered, *p.p.,* alter.

al'tering, *pr.p.,* alter.

al'tern, *adj.,* with opposite parts alternating.

al'ternate, *v.t. and i.,* to make alternate; to be alternate; to occur in turn (of two items).

altern'ate, *adj.,* occurring one after the other in turn.

al'ternated, *p.p.,* alternate.

altern'ately, *adv.,* in succession (of two items].

al'ternating, *pr.p.,* alternate.

alterna'tion, *n.,* the act of alternating.

alter'native, *adj. and n.,* a choice between one and another.

altern'atively, *adv.,* one way or another.

al'ternator, *n.,* a dynamo for generating alternating electric current.

althae'a, *n.,* the marsh-mallow and other plants.

although', *conj.,* admitted, granted that; notwithstanding that.

alti'meter, *n.,* an instrument for measuring vertical angular elevation.

alti'metry, *n.,* the science of measuring vertical angular elevation.

al'tisonant, *adj.,* high-sounding.

al'titude, *n.,* height.

al'to, *adj.,* high-pitched (of a male voice); *n.,* the alto part, an alto singer or instrument, as the viola.

altogeth'er, *adv.,* entirely, wholly.

alto-relie'vo, *adj.,* in high relief; *n.,* a carving in high relief.

alto-rilie'vo, *i.q.* alto-relievo (*It.*).

al'truism, *n.,* the guiding philosophy of acting on behalf of others.

al'truist, *n.,* one who professes altruism.

altruis'tic, *adj.,* rel. to altruism.

alu'del, *n.,* a pear-shaped glass vessel used in condensing.

al'ula, *n.,* a bird's winglet.

al'um, *n.,* a chemical compound so named.

alu'mina, *n.,* aluminium oxide.

alu'minate, *v.t.,* to blend with a salt of aluminium.

aluminif'erous, *adj.,* producing alum, aluminium or alumin.

alu'minite, *n.,* a white hydrous aluminium sulphate.

alumin'ium, *n.,* a whitish metallic element so named. Also *aluminum.*

alu'minous, *adj.,* rel. to aluminium, alumina or alum.

alu'minum, *n., i.q.* aluminium.

al'umish, *adj.,* somewhat resembling alum.

alum'na, *n.,* the fem. of alumnus (*Lat.*).

alum'ni, *n. pl., i.q.* alumnus.

alum'nus, *n.,* one who has been brought up in a college or a place of learning.

al'veary, *n.,* a beehive.

al'veolar, *adj.,* rel. to alveoli.

al'veolary, *adj., i.q.* alveolar.

al'veolate, *adj.,* full of cavities.

al'veoli, *n. pl.,* small cavities.

al'veolus, *n.,* a small cavity.

al'vine, *adj.,* rel. to the belly.

al'way, *adv.,* at all times.

al'ways, *adv.,* at all times.

al'yssum, *n.,* a rock plant.

am, *v.i., pr.p.,* 1st pers. of to be.

amadavat', *n.,* a small Indian song-bird; (place name).

am'adou, *n.,* a kind of tinder produced from fungi.

a'mah, *n.,* a child's nurse (*Ind.*).

amain', *adv.,* with full strength.

amal'gam, *n.,* an alloy of a metal with mercury; an intimate mixture.

amal'gamate, *v.t.,* to mix together.

amal'gamated, *p.p.,* amalgamate.

amal'gamating, *pr.p.,* amalgamate.

amalgama'tion, *n.,* the act of amalgamating; a compound.

amal'gama'tor, *n.,* one who amalgamates.

amanuen'sis, *n.,* a secretary; one who writes from dictation or copy.

am'aranth, *n.,* the plant love-lies-bleeding; a flower said in poetry never to fade.

amaranth'ine, *adj.,* rel. to amaranth.

amaranth'us, *n.,* also amarantus, which gives its name to the Amarantaceae (*bot.*).

Amaryl'lis, *n.,* a Greek rustic nymph's name; a hothouse flowering plant of South Africa.

amass', *v.t.,* to pile together.

amassed', *p.p.,* amass.

amass'ing, *pr.p.,* amass.

amass'ment, *n.,* the act or state of amassing.

am'ateur, *n.,* one who merely for love, not for a livelihood, pursues a study or art.

amateur'ish, adj., unskilled, unprofessional.

amateur'ishly, adv., in an unskilled way.

amateur'ishness, n., unprofessionalism.

amateur'ism, . n., i.q. amateurishness.

am'ative, adj., sexually loving.

am'atively, adv., in a sexually loving way.

am'ativeness, n., the amative state.

am'atol, n., a high explosive made from TNT and ammonium nitrate.

am'atory, adj., of a loving tendency.

amauro'sis, n., blindness.

amauro'tic, adj., rel. to amaurosis.

amaze', v.t., to astonish; to stagger with surprise.

amazed', p.p., amaze.

amaze'ment, n., a state of astonishment.

amaz'ing, pr.p., amaze; adj., astonishing.

amaz'ingly, adv., in an astonishing way.

Am'azon, n., one of the race of women-warriors; the river of that name.

amazo'nian, adj., rel. to the Amazons; bold, mannish.

am'bages, n. pl., circumlocutions.

am'ban, n., a resident Chinese representative in Tibet.

ambas'sador, n., a representative, usually of a sovereign or state.

ambassador'ial, adj., rel. to ambassador.

ambas'sadress, n., the fem. of ambassador.

am'ber, n., a yellow, resinous substance, fossilized.

am'bergris, n., a fragrant substance obtained from the sperm whale.

ambidex'ter, adj. and n., (one) using both hands equally well.

ambidexter'ity, n., the power to use both hands equally well.

ambidex'trous, adj., i.q. ambidexter.

ambidex'trously, adv., in an ambidextrous way.

am'bient, adj., going about, surrounding.

ambigu'ity, n., a double meaning, uncertainty.

ambig'uous, adj., of double meaning, uncertain.

ambig'uously, adv., equivocally.

ambig'uousness, n., a tendency to be ambiguous.

am'bit, n., bounds, scope.

ambi'tion, n., aiming at high things.

ambi'tionless, adj., without ambition.

ambi'tious, adj., inclined to ambition.

ambi'tiously, adv., in an ambitious way.

ambiv'alence, n., a conflict of emotions.

ambiv'alent, adj., emotionally drawn in two directions.

am'bivert, n., a person who is neither introvert nor extrovert.

am'ble, n., the walk of certain quadrupeds; v.i., to go at a slow pace.

am'bled, p.p., amble.

am'bler, n., one who ambles.

am'bling, pr.p., amble.

amblyo'pia, n., dimness of vision.

am'bo, adj., both together (Lat.); n., a pulpit for the reading of the epistle or the gospel.

amboy'na (wood), n., finely marked wood of an Asian tree.

ambro'sia, n., a divine drink or fragrance; a weed so named.

ambro'sial, adj., rel. to ambrosia.

Ambro'sian, adj., rel. to St. Ambrose.

am'brotype, n., a photographic negative which, being thin, gave the effect of a positive.

am'bry, n., a cupboard, a locker. Also aumbry.

ambs-ace, n., the lowest throw at dice; bad luck. Also ames-ace.

am'bulance, n., a vehicle for conveying the sick or wounded.

am'bulant, adj., walking, moving.

ambula'tion, n., the act of walking.

am'bulator, n., a walker; a wheel for road-measuring.

am'bulatory, adj., rel. to walking; n., a processional path round the altar of a church or in a cloister.

am'bury, n., a tumour affecting cattle and horses; a disease in turnips and some other plants.

ambuscade', n., the act of hiding; a place of hiding, for the purpose of a secret attack; the men in hiding; v.t., to attack from an ambush.

ambusca'ded, p.p., ambuscade.

ambusca'ding, pr.p., ambuscade.

am'bush, n. and v.t., i.q. ambuscade.

am'bushed, p.p., ambush.

am'busher, n., one who lies in ambush.

am'bushing, pr.p., ambush.

am'bushment, n., i.q. ambuscade.

ameer', amir', n., a Mohammedan ruler; the ruler of Afghanistan.

ame'liorate, v.t. and i., to make better, to improve.

ame'liorated, p.p., ameliorate.

ame'liorating, pr.p., ameliorate.

ameliora'tion, n., the act or state of ameliorating.

ame'liorative, adj., tending to ameliorate.

ame'liorator, n., one who ameliorates.

amen', interj., so be it; the ending of an oath or a prayer.

amenabil'ity, n., the amenable quality.

ame'nable, adj., adaptable; ready to fall in with the ideas and wishes of others.

ame'nably, adv., in an amenable way.

amend', v.t. and i., to improve.

amend'able, adj., capable of amending.

amend'ed, p.p., amend.

amend'er, n., one who amends.

amend'ing, pr.p., amend.

amend'ment, n., the act of amending; an alternative proposal.

amends', n. pl., satisfactory compensation for a wrong done.

amen'ity, *n.*, pleasantness; a service provided for better comfort or satisfaction.

am'ent, *n.*, a catkin.

amenta'ceous, *adj.*, resembling the catkin.

amen'tia, *n.*, the state of being out of one's mind.

ament'um, *n.*, *i.q.* ament.

amerce', *v.t.*, to punish with a fine.

amerce'able, *adj.*, able or fit to be amerced.

amerced', *p.p.*, amerce.

amerce'ment, *n.*, the act of amercing.

amerc'er, *n.*, one who amerces.

amerc'ing, *pr.p.*, amerce.

Amer'ican, *adj.*, rel. to America; *n.*, a native of A.

Amer'icanism, *n.*, something peculiar to Americans.

Amer'icanist, *n.*, a student of subjects pertaining to America.

Amer'icanize, *v.t.* and *i.*, to change to American.

ameri'cium, *n.*, an atomic element from America.

Am'erind, *adj.* and *n.*, an American Indian.

ames-ace, *n.*, *i.q.* ambsace.

amess', *n.*, a hood with long ends in front.

am'ethyst, *n.*, a gem of a violet-blue colour; a kind of quartz.

amethyst'ine, *adj.*, of, or like, an amethyst.

Amhar'ic, *n.*, the court language of Abyssinia.

amiabil'ity, *n.*, lovableness, goodheartedness.

a'miable, *adj.*, lovable, goodhearted.

a'miableness, *n.*, the lovable quality.

a'miably, *adv.*, in a lovable way.

amian'thus, *n.*, a species of asbestos.

amicabil'ity, *n.*, an amicable tendency.

am'icable, *adj.*, of a friendly character.

am'icableness, *n.*, friendliness.

am'icably, *adv.*, in a friendly way.

am'ice, *n.*, any kind of clothing or hooded mantle; the linen collar, with ornamental border, worn by the priest and ministers at the Mass.

amid', *prep.*, in the midst of, surrounded by.

am'idine, *n.*, a chemical compound so named; a solution of starch in hot water.

amid'most, *adv.* and *prep.*, in the very centre.

amid'ships, *adv.*, in the middle of a ship.

amidst', *prep.*, *i.q.* amid.

amiss', *adv.*, wrongly, in error, lacking.

amito'sis, *n.*, the division of a nucleus directly.

am'ity, *n.*, friendship.

am'meter, *n.*, an instrument for measuring electric current.

am'monal, *n.*, a high-explosive compound.

ammo'nia, *n.*, a strong-smelling gas, much used in the arts and in medicine.

ammo'niac, *adj.*, rel. to ammonia.

ammoni'acal, *adj.*, *i.q.* ammonia.

ammo'niated, *adj.*, impregnated with ammonia.

am'monite, *n.*, a fossil shell-fish so named.

ammuni'tion, *n.*, the means of defence, war material.

amne'sia, *n.*, the loss of memory.

amne'sic, *adj.*, losing the memory.

am'nesty, *n.*, the act of overlooking an offence; a pardon.

am'nion, *n.*, a membranous sac found in embryos.

amniot'ic, *adj.*, rel. to an amnion.

amoe'ba, *n.*, a class of Protozoans so named.

amoe'bic, *adj.*, rel. to an amoeba.

amok', *adv.*, *i.q.* amuck.

Amo'mum, *n.*, an aromatic herb of the ginger family.

among', *prep.*, in the midst of, together with.

amongst', *prep.*, *i.q.* among.

Amontilla'do, *n.*, a variety of sherry.

amo'ral, *adj.*, without a moral code, non-moral.

amoral'ity, *n.*, the state of being amoral.

amorce', *n.*, a percussion cap for a toy pistol.

am'oret, *n.*, *i.q.* amourette.

am'orist, *n.*, one with a propensity for amours.

amoro'so, *adj.* and *adv.*, in a tender way (*mus.*).

am'orous, *adj.*, very loving.

am'orously, *adv.*, in an amorous way.

am'orousness, *n.*, an amorous tendency.

amor'phism, *n.*, the state of being amorphous.

amor'phous, *adj.*, shapeless, without form.

amortiza'tion, *n.*, the act of conveying property to a corporation with perpetual succession; the reduction of a debt by means of a sinking fund.

amor'tize, *v.t.*, to effect an amortization of.

amor'tizement, *n.*, *i.q.* amortization; the finishing off on the top of an architectural member.

amount', *n.*, the sum, a total; *v.i.*, to equal in total.

amount'ed, *p.p.*, amount.

amount'ing, *pr.p.*, amount.

amour', *n.*, a love adventure.

amourette', *n.*, a petty love-affair.

amour-propre, *n.*, self-esteem (*Fr.*).

amp', *n.*, the abbrev. of ampère.

ampelop'sis, *n.*, a climbing plant allied to the vine.

amper'age, *n.*, the strength of current in ampères.

ampère', *n.*, the unit of electric current.

am'persand, *n.*, the sign &.

am'phi, a prefix = around, about.

Amphib'ia, *n. pl.*, creatures that can live both on land and in water.

amphib'ian, *adj.*, of the nature of amphibia.

amphib'ious, *adj.*, *i.q.* amphibian.

amphib'iously, *adv.*, in the manner of amphibia.

amphib'iousness, *n.*, the quality of being amphibious.

amphibol'ogy, n., the ambiguity of expression.

amphib'olous, adj., equivocal; spreading on both sides.

am'phibrach, n., a metrical foot containing three syllables, of which the middle one is long and the others are short.

amphigour'i, ·n., meaningless nonsense.

amphisbae'na, n., a fabled snake with a head at either end.

amphithe'atre, amphithe'ater, n., a theatre with seats all round.

amphitheat'ric, adj., in the form of an amphitheatre.

amphitheat'rical, adj., i.q. amphitheatric.

Amphit'ryon, n., a host, an entertainer.

am'phora, n., a two-handled jar of earthenware.

am'phoral, adj., rel. to an amphora.

ampho'ric, adj., sound obtained by blowing into a large vessel with a small mouth.

am'ple, adj., full, abundant, large, spacious.

am'pleness, n., the condition of ample.

am'pliative, adj., extending a simple conception (logic).

amplifica'tion, n., an enlarging.

am'plified, p.p., amplify.

am'plifier, n., one who amplifies; electronic apparatus for increasing audio signal strength.

am'plify, v.t., to enlarge; to add to a previous statement.

am'plifying, pr.p., amplify.

am'plitude, n., extent, largeness.

am'ply, adv., abundantly, largely.

am'poule, n., a sealed container holding a single dose.

ampul'la, n., a flask (Lat.).

am'putate, v.t., to cut off (a limb).

am'putated, p.p., amputate.

am'putating, pr.p., amputate.

amputa'tion, n., the operation of cutting off.

am'putator, n., one who performs amputations.

am'track, n., an amphibious land-craft.

amuck', adv., in a frenzied way, used in the phrase "to run amuck," or "amok."

am'ulet, n., a charm consisting of a jewel or ornament.

amus'able, adj., able to be amused.

amuse', v.t., to entertain, to delight.

amused', p.p., amuse.

amus'edly, adv., with amusement.

amuse'ment, n., a diversion, a pleasure.

amus'er, n., one who amuses.

amus'ing, pr.p., amuse; adj., diverting.

amus'ingly, adv., in an amusing way.

amus'ive, adj., tending to amusement.

amyg'dalate, n., a salt of amygdalic acid; an emulsion of almonds; adj., rel. to almonds.

amyg'dal'ic, adj., of almonds.

amyg'dalin, n., a glucoside found in stone fruit.

amyg'daline, adj., rel. to almonds.

amyg'daloid, adj., almond-shaped.

am'yl, n., starch, fine flour.

amyla'ceous, adj., starchy.

am'ylin, n., starch-cellulose.

am'yloid, adj., starchy.

amylop'sin, n., the pancreatic juice ferment that converts starch into sugar.

am'yss, n., i.q. amess.

an, indef. art.; a before a consonant.

an'a, n., collected sayings; usually suffix, as Eliana.

Anabap'tism, n., rebaptizing.

Anabap'tist, n., one who re-baptizes a person already baptized. An A. is now called a Baptist.

Anabaptist'ic, adj., rel. to Anabaptist teaching.

an'abas, n., an Indian tree-climbing fish.

anab'asis, n., an up-country march.

anabat'ic, adj., rel. to an air current flowing upwards (meteor.).·

anab'olism, n., a biological term describing the constructive processes. in the making of a cell.

an'abranch, n., a stream that leaves and then re-enters a river.

anacamp'tic, adj., reflecting.

anacathars'is, n., vomiting.

anacathar'tic, adj., purging upwards.

anachron'ic, adj., out of date.

anach'ronism, n., an error in point of time.

anachronis'tic, adj., involving an error of time.

anaclas'tic, adj., rel. to refraction.

anacolu'thon, n., a mixture of syntactical constructions in a sentence.

anacon'da, n., a large S. American water-snake.

Anacreon'tic, adj., rel. to, or like, the poet Anacreon.

anacrus'is, n., an unstressed syllable at the beginning of verse.

an'adem, n., a band, a fillet, a garland.

anad'romous, adj., ascending rivers to spawn (of fish).

anae'mia, n., a bloodless condition. Also anemia.

anaem'ic, adj., suffering from anaemia.

anaerobe, n., a minute organism able to live without free oxygen.

anaesthe'sia, n., a state of insensibility to pain.

anaesthet'ic, adj. and n., producing insensibility.

an'aglyph, n., an ornament in relief.

anaglyph'ic, adj., rel. to anaglyph.

anaglyp'tic, adj., i.q. anaglyphic.

anagno'risis, n., recognition.

an'agogy, n., a mystical interpretation.

an'agram, n., the letters of a word rearranged to make a new word.

anagrammat'ic, adj., of the nature of an anagram.

anagrammat'ical, adj., i.q. anagrammatic.

anagram'matize, v.t., to make an anagram out of a word.

an'agraph, n., a recipe.

a'nal, adj., rel. to the anus.

analec'ta, n., i.q. analects.

analec'tic, adj., composed of selections.

an'alects, n. pl., selections, gleanings.

analem'ma, n., a scale for ·finding the sun's declination on a given day; a surgical support.

an'alepsy, n., a form of epilepsy.

analep'tic, adj. and n., a medicine; restorative.

analges'ia, n., insensibility to pain.

analges'ic, adj., unable to feel pain; n., a pain-relieving drug.

analog'ical, adj., of the nature of an analogy.

anal'ogist, n., one who draws analogies.

anal'ogize, v.i., to draw analogies.

anal'ogized, p.p., analogize.

anal'ogizing, pr.p., analogize.

anal'ogous, adj., bearing a likeness or analogy to.

anal'ogously, adv., in an analogous way.

an'alogue, n., something that corresponds with another.

anal'ogy, n., a correspondence or likeness of one thing to another.

analphabet'ic, adj., illiterate; n., someone ignorant of the alphabet.

an'alysable, adj., capable of analysis.

analysa'tion, n., the act of analysing.

an'alyse, v.t., to separate into parts or elements; to trace a thing to the source.

an'alysed, p.p., analyse.

an'alyser, n., one who analyses.

an'alysing, pr.p., analyse.

anal'ysis, n., the process of analysing.

an'alyst, n., one who analyses.

analyt'ic, adj., bel. to analysis.

analyt'ical, adj., i.q. analytic.

anamnes'is, n., recollection (esp. of a previous existence).

anamor'phosis, n., a distortion.

ana'nas, n., the pineapple.

anan'drous, adj., without stamens; a description of female plants.

an'apaest, an'apest, n., a metrical foot of two short syllables before a long one.

anapaes'tic, anapes'tic, adj., rel. to an anapest.

anaph'ora, n., the portion of the liturgy of the Eastern Church which corresponds to the canon of the Western Church.

anarch'ic, adj., tending to, or in a state of, anarchy.

anarch'ical, adj., i.q. anarchic.

an'archism, n., the state of, or tending to, anarchy.

an'archist, n., one who teaches the overthrow of all government.

an'archy, n., a state of lawlessness.

anar'throus, adj., without the use of the article attached to a noun; without joints.

anasar'ca, n., a dropsical condition of the cellular tissue; a somewhat similar affection of plants in wet weather.

anasar'cous, adj., subject to anasarca.

anas'tasis, n., resurrection, recovery.

anastat'ic, adj., in relief.

anastig'mat, n., an anastigmatic lens.

anastigmat'ic, adj., free from astigmatism.

anastig'matism, n., freedom from astigmatism.

anas'tomose, v.t., to join by running together.

anastomos'is, n., the cross-connection of arteries, branches, rivers, etc.

anas'trophe, n., an inversion.

anath'ema, n., a solemn curse; the person or thing cursed.

anathemat'ical, adj., rel. to anathema.

anath'ematism, n., the pronouncing of anathemas.

anathematiza'tion, n., the act of anathematizing.

anath'ematize, v.t., to pronounce an anathema on.

anath'ematized, p.p., anathematize.

anath'ematizer, n., one who anathematizes.

anath'ematizing, pr.p., anathematize.

anatif'erous, adj., geese-producing.

anatom'ic, adj., rel. to anatomy.

anatom'ical, adj., i.q. anatomic.

anat'omist, n., one who studies or practises anatomy.

anatomiza'tion, n., dissection.

anat'omize, v.t., to practise anatomy; to cut into parts.

anat'omized, p.p., anatomize.

anat'omizing, pr.p., anatomize.

anat'omy, n., the study or art of cutting a body to examine its structure; the structural arrangement of a body.

anatrep'tic, adj., upsetting, refuting.

an(n)at'ta, n., an orange-red dye used in cheese-making.

an(n)at'to, n., i.q. an(n)atta.

an'bury, n., i.q. ambury.

an'cestor, n., one of an earlier generation, a forefather.

ancesto'rial, adj., rel. to ancestors.

ances'tral, adj., rel. to ancestors.

an'cestress, n., the fem. of ancestor.

an'cestry, n., the line of one's ancestors.

anchithere, n., a fossil animal; the size of a small pony.

anch'or, n., a mechanical device preventing a ship from drifting by gripping the sea bottom; v.i. and t., to come, or to bring a ship, to rest.

anch'orable, adj., able to be anchored.

anch'orage, n., a place where a vessel may be anchored or lie at anchor.

anch'ored, p.p., anchor.

anch'oress, n., the fem. of anchoret or anchorite.

anch'oret, *n.,* one who retires from the world; a hermit.

anchoret'ic, *adj.,* rel. to an anchoret.

anchoret'ical, *adj., i.q.* anchoretic.

anch'oring, *pr.p.,* anchor.

anch'orite, *n., i.q.* anchoret.

ancho'vy, *n.,* a small fish, found in the Mediterranean.

anchu'sa, *n.,* kinds of a hairy-stemmed plant.

an'chylose, *v.t.* and *i.,* to stiffen.

anchylo'sis, *n.,* the stiffening of a joint.

an'cient, *adj.,* rel. to long-past time; of great age; *n.,* a very old man; in old English, an ensign.

an'ciently, *adv.,* in ancient times.

an'cientry, *n.,* the people of old time.

ancill'ary, *adj.,* serving (like a handmaid), and so helping.

ancip'ital, *adj.,* double headed, two edged.

ancip'itous, *adj., i.q.* ancipital.

an'con, *n.,* a bracket, a quoin.

and, *conj.,* expressing addition.

Andalu'sian, *adj.* and *n.,* a native of, or bel. to, Andalusia, a province of Spain.

andan'te, *adv.,* in moderately slow (musical) time; *n.,* a movement in moderately slow time.

andanti'no, *adv.,* not quite so slow as andante.

Ande'an, *adj.,* rel. to the Andes.

And'ine, *adj., i.q.* Andean.

and'iron, *n.,* a fire-dog or iron bar supporting a log on a hearth.

andranat'omy, *n.,* dissection of the (male) body.

androe'cium, *n.,* the stamens taken collectively (*bot.*).

an'drogen, *n.,* any substance capable of developing sexual characteristics.

androg'ynal, *adj.,* hermaphrodite.

androg'ynism, *n.,* the change in plants from dioecious to monoecious.

androg'ynous, *adj., i.q.* androgynal.

an'droid, *adj.,* like a human; *n.,* an automaton.

android'al, *adj.* and *n., i.q.* android.

an'dron, *n.,* the men's quarters in a Greek house.

an'ecdotage, *n.,* anecdotes collectively; garrulous old age.

an'ecdotal, *adj.,* rel. to anecdote.

an'ecdote, *n.,* a short tale or story.

anecdot'ic, *adj.,* with a tendency to anecdote.

anecdot'ical, *adj., i.q.* anecdotic.

an'ecdotist, *n.,* one who tells anecdotes.

anele', *v.t.,* to anoint with oil.

ane'mia, *n., i.q.* anaemia.

ane'mic, *adj., i.q.* anaemic.

anem'ograph, *n.,* an instrument for recording wind phenomena.

anemog'raphy, *n.,* the recording of the wind's velocity.

anemol'ogy, *n.,* the study or science of the winds.

anemom'eter, *n.,* a wind gauge.

anemom'etry, *n.,* the art or science of gauging the winds.

anem'one, *n.,* the wind-flower.

anemoph'ilous, *adj.,* wind-fertilized.

anem'oscope, *n.;* an apparatus indicating the force and direction of the wind.

anent', *prep.,* towards, concerning.

an'eroid, *adj.,* without liquid (descriptive of a barometer, the barometric pressure being measured without the use of a fluid).

anesthe'sia, *n., i.q.* anaesthesia.

anesthet'ic, *adj.* and *n., i.q.* anaesthetic.

an'eurin, *n.,* the vitamin B.

an'eurism, *n.,* a condition caused by the swelling of an artery.

anew', *adv.,* afresh, over again.

anfract'uous, *adj.,* winding.

ang'ary, *n.,* a belligerent's right to seize or destroy neutral property in war.

an'gel, *n.,* a heavenly messenger; an old coin so named.

angel'ic, *adj.,* like, or rel. to, the angels.

angel'ica, *n.,* an aromatic plant, used in medicine and sweets.

angel'ical, *adj., i.q.* angelic.

angelol'ogy, *n.,* the study of angel ministry.

an'gelot, *n.,* the name of a coin and a musical instrument.

an'gelus, *n.,* a religious devotion; the bell rung for it.

an'ger, *n.,* wrath, fury; *v.t.,* to provoke to wrath.

an'gered, *p.p.,* anger.

an'gering, *pr.p.,* anger.

An'gevin, *adj.* and *n.,* of Anjou; a Plantagenet.

an'gina, *n.,* an intense pain in the throat or chest.

angin'a pec'toris, *n.,* a disease of the heart.

angiocarp'ous, *adj.,* with fruit covered by an envelope.

angiog'raphy, *n.,* a description of the vascular system.

angiol'ogy, *n.,* the study of the vascular system and lymphatics.

angio'ma, *n.,* a blood-filled tumour.

angiot'omy, *n.,* the dissection of the vascular system.

an'gle, *n.,* a figure resulting from the inclination of one straight line to another; the inclination of two lines to one another; also a fishing hook, rod and line; *v.i.,* to fish with a rod and line.

an'gled, *p.p.,* angle.

an'gle iron, *n.,* a strengthening piece used in structural work.

an'gler, *n.,* one who angles.

An'glican, *adj.,* of the English type.

An'glicanism, *n.,* the method and spirit of the English Church.

An'glice, *adv.,* in the English way or language (*Lat.*).

An'glicism, *n.,* a peculiarity of English speech and idioms.

an'glicize, *v.t.,* to convert into English.

an'glicized, *p.p.*, anglicize.

an'glicizing, *pr.p.*, anglicize.

an'gling, *pr.p.*, angle; *n.*, the fisherman's pursuit.

Ang'lo-, *prefix*, English (used conjointly, as in Anglo-American).

Ang'lo-Cath'olic, *adj.* and *n.*, of Catholic as opposed to Protestant tendencies.

Ang'lophil, Ang'lophile, *adj.* and *n.*, a friend and admirer of the English.

Ang'lophobe, *adj.* and *n.*, one who fears or dislikes the English.

Ang'lo-Sax'on, *adj.* and *n.*, rel. to the fused races of Angles and Saxons.

ango'la, *n.*, the wool of the angora goat.

an'gor, *n.*, extreme distress.

ango'ra, *n.*, a fine kind of wool; a breed of cats.

an'grily, *adv.*, in an angry way.

an'griness, *n.*, *i.q.* anger.

an'gry, *adj.*, showing or feeling wrath or passion.

Ang'ström un'it, *n.*, a hundred-millionth of a centimetre, used for measuring short wavelengths.

ang'uiform, *adj.*, snake-shaped.

Anguil'la, *n.*, the common-eel genus.

anguil'liform, *adj.*, like an eel in form.

ang'uine, *adj.*, snake-like.

anguin'eal, *adj.*, rel. to snakes.

anguin'eous, *adj.*, *i.q.* anguin'eal.

an'guish, *n.*, acute pain or distress, physical or mental.

an'guished, *adj.*, feeling anguish.

an'guishing, *adj.*, causing anguish.

an'gular, *adj.*, pointed, corner-wise.

angular'ity, *n.*, an angular quality or character.

an'gularly, *adv.*, corner-wise, pointedly.

an'gulated, *adj.*, having angles.

anhela'tion, *n.*, a panting.

anhy'drous, *adj.*, waterless.

anicon'ic, *adj.*, not shaped as humans or animals.

an'icut, *n.*, a river-dam in S. India built for irrigation purposes.

anigh', *adv.* and *prep.*, near.

an'il, *n.*, an indigo plant found in the W. Indies.

an'ile, *adj.*, old-woman-ish.

an'iline, *n.*, a coal-tar product, from which certain dyes are made.

anil'ity, *n.*, old age in woman.

an'ima, *n.*, a breath, a spirit.

animadver'sion, *n.*, consideration, reflexion; adverse comment.

animadvert', *v.i.*, to make comment on.

animadvert'ed, *p.p.*, animadvert.

animadvert'er, *n.*, one who animadverts.

animadvert'ing, *pr.p.*, animadvert.

an'imal, *adj.*, having life and will to move; brutal; rel. to animals; *n.*, a living creature; a brute; a carnal person.

animal'cula, *n.*, pl. of animalculum.

animal'cular, *adj.*, pert. or rel to, an animalculum.

animal'cule, *n.*, *i.q.* animalcula.

animal'culine, *adj.*, of the nature of animalcules.

animal'culist, *n.*, a student of animalcules.

animal'culum, *n.*, a diminutive animal.

an'imalism, *n.*, the condition of animal being; sensuality.

animal'ity, *n.*, the quality of animals.

animaliza'tion, *n.*, the act of animalizing.

an'imalize, *v.t.*, to turn into animals; to brutalize; to add an animal quality to anything.

an'imalized, *p.p.*, animalize.

an'imalizing, *pr.p.*, animalize.

an'imate, *adj.*, having life; *v.t.*, to quicken, to give life or spirit to.

an'imated, *p.p.*, animate; *adj.*, lively, brisk.

an'imatedly, *adv.*, full of spirit.

an'imating, *pr.p.*, animate; *adj.*, inspiriting.

an'imatingly, *adv.*, in an inspiriting way.

anima'tion, *n.*, life, vigour, briskness.

an'imative, *adj.*, causing animation.

an'imé, *n.*, a West Indian resin used in making varnish (*Fr.*).

an'imism, *n.*, the belief in the existence of a spiritual world apart from matter; the tendency to endow the material world and material objects with a soul.

an'imist, *n.*, a believer in animism.

animos'ity, *n.*, resentment, anger.

an'imus, *n.*, adverse feeling.

an'ise, *n.*, an aromatic plant.

an'iseed, *n.*, the seed of anise.

an'isette, *n.*, a cordial made from aniseed.

an'ker, *n.*, a Dutch wine measure.

ankh, *n.*, a key-like cross as a symbol of enduring life (*Egyptian*).

an'kle, *n.*, the part between the foot and the leg.

an'kle-bone, *n.*, the joint of the ankle.

an'kled, *adj.*, having ankles.

an'klet, *n.*, an ornamental ring for the ankle.

ankylos'is, *n.*, *i.q.* anchylosis.

an'na, *n.*, a small Indian coin, 1-16th of a rupee.

an'nalist, *n.*, one who writes or compiles annals.

an'nalize, *v.t.*, to compile annals.

an'nals, *n.*, the record of yearly events.

ann'ates, *n. pl.*, *i.q.* annats.

an'nats, *n.*, the first-fruits of a benefice, formerly payable to the Pope, later to Queen Anne's Bounty (*Lat.* annates).

anneal', *v.t.*, to temper with furnace-heat.

annealed', *p.p.*, anneal.

anneal'ing, *pr.p.*, anneal.

annec'tent, *adj.*, connecting, linking.

annel'idan, *adj.*, rel. to Annelida (*i.e.*, earthworms and similar water-worms).

annex', *n.*, something joined on (usu. a building); *v.t.*, to join or to add.

annex'able, *adj.*, able to be annexed.

annexa'tion, *n.*, the act of annexing; appropriation.

annexa'tionist, *n.*, one who advocates annexation.

annexe', *n.*, *i.q.* annex.

annexed', *p.p.*, annex.

annex'ing, *pr.p.*, annex.

anni'hilable, *adj.*, able to be annihilated.

anni'hilate, *v.t.*, to reduce to nothing, to destroy entirely.

anni'hilated, *p.p.*, annihilate.

anni'hilating, *pr.p.*, annihilate.

annihila'tion, *n.*, the complete destruction.

anni'hilator, *n.*, one who annihilates.

anniver'sary, *n.*, a yearly commemoration.

an'no Dom'ini, a Lat. phrase = in the year of Our Lord.

an'no mun'di, a Lat. phrase = in the year of the world.

an'notate, *v.t.*, to make notes or comments on.

an'notated, *p.p.*, annotate.

an'notating, *pr.p.*, annotate.

annota'tion, *n.*, the act of making notes on; a note made.

an'notator, *n.*, one who annotates.

an'notatory, *adj.*, having annotation.

annot'to, *n.*, a yellowish-red dye.

announce', *v.t.*, to make publicly known.

announced', *p.p.*, announce.

announce'ment, *n.*, a thing announced; the act of announcing.

announc'er, *n.*, one who announces.

announc'ing, *pr.p.*, announce.

annoy', *v.t.*, to vex, to irritate.

annoy'ance, *n.*, that which annoys; the act of annoying.

annoyed', *p.p.*, annoy.

annoy'er, *n.*, one who annoys.

annoy'ing, *pr.p.*, annoy.

an'nual, *adj.*, yearly, happening year by year; *n.*, a plant that lives only for one year.

an'nually, *adv.*, year by year.

annu'itant, *n.*, one who receives an annuity.

annu'ity, *n.*, a yearly payment of money.

annul', *v.t.*, to cancel, to make null and void.

an'nular, *adj.*, ring-like.

an'nulate, *adj.*, having rings, ringed.

an'nulated, *adj.*, *i.q.* annulate.

annula'tion, *n.*, the act or state of being ringed; ring formation.

an'nulet, *n.*, a little ring. In heraldry it denotes a fifth son.

annulled', *p.p.*, annul.

annul'ling, *pr.p.*, annul.

annul'ment, *n.*, the act of annulling.

ann'uloid, *adj.*, ring-like.

Annulo'sa, *n.*, a class of animals under which arthropods and the higher worms are grouped.

an'nulose, *adj.*, ringed; rel. to the Annulosa.

an'nulus, *n.*, a ring.

annu'merate, *v.t.*, to add in.

annu'merated, *p.p.*, annumerate.

annu'merating, *pr.p.*, annumerate.

annumera'tion, *n.*, the process of annumerating.

annun'ciate, *v.t.*, to proclaim or publish tidings.

annun'ciated, *p.p.*, annunciate.

annun'ciating, *pr.p.*, annunciate.

annuncia'tion, *n.*, the act of announcing.

annun'ciator, *n.*, an announcer; an indicator (*e.g.* in hotels) to show where attendance is needed.

annun'ciatory, *adj.*, bringing an announcement.

an'ode, *n.*, the point where the electric current enters.

ano'dontia, *n.*, the absence of teeth.

ano'dontis, *n.*, *i.q.* anodontia.

an'odyne, *adj.*, soothing; *n.*, something that eases pain.

anoet'ic, *adj.*, being conscious with sensation but without thought.

anoint', *v.t.*, to smear with oil or ointment.

anoint'ed, *p.p.*, anoint.

anoint'er, *n.*, one who anoints.

anoint'ing, *pr.p.*, anoint.

anoint'ment, *n.*, the act of anointing.

anom'alism, *n.*, an irregular tendency.

anom'alist, *n.*, one who commits irregularities.

anomalist'ic, *adj.*, tending to irregularity.

anomalist'ical, *adj.*, *i.q.* anomalistic.

anom'alous, *adj.*, irregular, exceptional.

anom'alously, *adv.*, irregularly.

anom'alure, *n.*, an African scale-tailed squirrel.

anom'aly, *n.*, an irregularity; an exceptional proceeding.

anon', *adv.*, immediately.

anona'ceous, *adj.*, pert. or rel. to the pineapple.

an'onym, *n.*, a nameless person; a pseudonym.

anonym'ity, *n.*, going without a name.

anon'ymous, *adj.*, not ascribed; nameless.

anon'ymously, *adv.*, without a name.

anon'ymousness, *n.*, the act or state of anonymity.

anoph'eles, *n.*, a malarial mosquito.

an'orak, *n.*, a jacket with a hood attached.

anorex'ia, *n.*, the want of appetite.

anos'mia, *n.*, inodorousness.

anoth'er, *adj.*, some person or thing else; one added.

anot'ta, *n.*, *i.q.* annotto.

anour'ous, *adj.*, tailless.

anox'ia, *n.*, a lack of oxygen.

an'serated, *adj.*, (of an heraldic cross) with terminations cleft and ornamented with birds' or reptiles' heads, etc.

an'serine, *adj.*, rel. to a goose; silly.

an'swer, *v.i.*, to make reply; to suit; to be sufficient for a purpose.

an'swerable, *adj.*, held to account.

an'swered, *p.p.*, answer.

an'swerer, *n.*, one who answers.

an'swering, *pr.p.*, answer.

an'swerless, *adj.*, without answer.

ant, *n.*, a tiny insect, an emmet.

an'ta, *n.*, a pilaster corresponding to one opposite.

antac'id, *adj.*, corrective of acidity.

antag'onism, *n.*, the act or state of opposing.

antag'onist, *n.*, one who strives against or opposes.

antagonist'ic, *adj.*, opposing.

antag'onize, *v.t.*, to resist, to struggle against, to neutralize; to arouse hostility in.

antag'onized, *p.p.*, antagonize.

antag'onizing, *pr.p.*, antagonize.

antal'gic, *adj.*, pain-relieving.

antal'kali, *n.*, a substance that counteracts alkali.

Antarc'tic, *adj.*, opposite to the Arctic; rel. to the South Pole.

antarthrit'ic, *adj.*, curing or relieving arthritis.

antasthmat'ic, *adj.*, relieving asthma.

ant'eater, *n.*, a four-footed animal that devours ants.

an'te-bellum, before the war (*Lat.*).

antecede', *v.t.*, to go before.

antece'ded, *p.p.*, antecede.

antece'dence, *n.*, the act of going before.

antece'dent, *adj.*, going before; *n.*, something that has gone before; in pl. = past conduct.

antece'dently, *adv.*, previously.

antece'ding, *pr.p.*, antecede.

anteces'sor, *n.*, one who has anteceded.

an'techamber, *n.*, a room leading into another.

an'tedate, *v.t.*, to anticipate the proper date.

an'tedated, *p.p.*, antedate.

an'tedating, *pr.p.*, antedate.

antedilu'vial, *adj.*, before the flood.

antedilu'vian, *adj.*, i.q. antediluvial; *n.*, one who lived before the flood.

an'telope, *n.*, a kind of deer.

antemerid'ian, *adj.*, before midday.

an'te merid'iem, before noon (*Lat.*).

antemun'dane, *adj.*, before the world's making.

antemu'ral, *adj.*, before the wall or walls.

antenat'al, *adj.*, before birth.

anteni'cene, *adj.*, before the Council of Nicaea, A.D. 325.

anten'na, *n.*, a feeler or horn of a crustacean or an insect; a radio aerial.

anten'nae, *n.*, pl. of antenna.

antenup'tial, *adj.*, before marriage.

antepas'chal, *adj.*, before Easter.

antepenult', *n.*, the last syllable but two.

antepenult'imate, *adj.*, preceding the last but one.

antepilep'tic, *adj.*, rel. to the treatment of epilepsy.

ante-post', *adj.*, made before the runners' numbers are put on board (of racing bets).

antepran'dial, *adj.*, before dinner.

ante'rior, *adj.*, preceding, earlier in date.

anterior'ity, *n.*, a precedence in the date.

ante'riorly, *adv.*, earlier.

an'te-room, *n.*, an outer room leading into another.

anthel'ion, *n.*, a luminous ring on a cloud or fog bank opposite the sun.

anthelmin'tic, *adj.* and *n.*, of use against intestinal worms (*med.*).

an'them, *n.*, a solemn piece of vocal music for solo or chorus.

an'ther, *n.*, the part of a flower's stamen containing the pollen.

an'theroid, *adv.*, like an anther.

anthe'sis, *n.*, the opening of a flower-bud; full bloom.

ant'-hill, *n.*, the mound raised by ants.

anthol'ogist, *n.*, the compiler of an anthology.

anthol'ogize, *v.t.*, to make an anthology.

anthol'ogy, *n.*, a selection of choice literary passages.

an'thracene, *n.*, a product of coal-tar distillation.

an'thracite, *n.*, a smokeless kind of coal.

anthracit'ic, *adj.*, rel. to anthracite.

an'thrax, *n.*, a carbuncle; an infectious disease among sheep and cattle, and communicable to man.

anthropog'eny, *n.*, the study of man's origin.

anthropog'ony, *n.*, i.q. anthropogeny.

anthropog'raphy, *n.*, the description of the human race.

an'thropoid, *adj.*, resembling the human.

anthropol'ogist, *n.*, a student of anthropology.

anthropol'ogy, *n.*, the study of humanity as a branch of natural science.

anthropomor'phism, *n.*, the likening of divine things to human.

anthropomor'phist, *n.*, one who likens the divine to the human.

anthropomor'phize, *v.i.*, to liken the divine to the human.

anthropomor'phized, *p.p.*, anthropomorphize.

anthropomor'phizing, *pr.p.*, anthropomorphize.

anthropomor'phous, *adj.*, in human shape.

anthropop'athy, *n.*, the attribution of human passions to the Deity.

anthropoph'agi, *n. pl.*, cannibals.

anthropoph'agous, *adj.*, cannibalistic.

anthropoph'agy, *n.*, cannibalism.

an'ti-, a Greek prefix = against, opposite to, instead of.

antiadi'tis, *n.*, tonsillitis.

anti-air'craft, *adj.*, employed against hostile aircraft.

an'tiar, *n.*, the upas tree of Java; poison obtained from it.

antibil'ious, *adj.*, corrective of bile.

antibiot'ic, *adj.*, inimical to growth; *n.*, any substance inimical to growth, particularly of disease-bearing bacteria.

an'tibody, *n.*, a substance in the blood that will counteract poisons.

an'tic, *adj.*, odd, quaint; *n.*, a buffoon; a merry caper.

An'tichrist, *n.*, the rival to Christ.

antichrist'ian, *adj.*, hostile to Christianity; rel. to Antichrist.

antic'ipant, *n.*, one who anticipates.

antic'ipate, *v.t.*, to act in advance; to forestall; to foresee.

antic'ipated, *p.p.*, anticipate.

antic'ipating, *pr.p.*, anticipate.

anticipa'tion, *n.*, the act of anticipating.

antic'ipative, *adj.*, anticipating.

antic'ipatively, *adv.*, with the purpose of forestalling.

antic'ipator, *n.*, one who anticipates.

antic'ipatory, *adj.*, forestalling, in advance.

anticlimac'tic, *adj.*, of the nature of an anticlimax.

anticli'max, *n.*, a drop from a previous ascent; bathos.

anticli'nal, *adj.*, bent with the convex side upward.

an'ti-clock'wise, *adj.*, in a circular left to right direction.

anticy'clone, *n.*, the opposite of a cyclone; an atmospheric system of high pressure at the centre.

an'tidotal, *adj.*, of the nature of an antidote.

an'tidote, *n.*, a remedy for poison or other trouble.

antidot'ical, *adj.*, rel. to antidotes.

antifeb'rile, *adj.*, fever-arresting.

antifed'eral, *adj.*, opposed to federalism.

antifed'eralism, *n.*, a

movement opposed to federalism.

an'tigen, *n.*, substance put into the blood to stimulate the production of antibodies.

antigrop'elos, *n. pl.*, waterproof leggings.

antihist'amine, *n.*, a drug used to combat histamines in conditions of allergy.

anti-Jac'obin, *adj.* and *n.*, (one) opposed to the Jacobins.

antijuda'ic, *adj.* and *n.*, contrary to what is Jewish.

antilog'arithm, *n.*, a number that corresponds to a given logarithm.

antil'ogy, *n.*, a contradiction, inconsistency.

antimacas'sar, *n.*, a protection against soiling chairs, etc.

antimalar'ial, *adj.*, used against malaria.

antimonarch'ical, *adj.*, opposed to monarchy.

antimo'nial, *adj.*, rel. to antimony.

antimo'niate, *adj.*, having antimony in it.

antimo'nious, *adj.*, *i.q.* antimonial.

an'timony, *n.*, a metallic element used in medicine, the arts and alloys.

Antino'mian, *adj.*, opposed to law. The word is applied to those sectaries who hold that, in virtue of their belief, they are subject to no moral law.

Antino'mianism, *n.*, the theory or principles of Antinomians.

antin'omy, *n.*, a violation of law.

antipa'pal, *adj.*, opposed to the papacy.

antipathet'ic, *adj.*, repugnant, disliking.

antipath'ic, *adj.*, in a state of antipathy.

antip'athy, *n.*, a feeling of repugnance or dislike.

anti-personnel', *adj.*, designed to kill or injure human beings, *e.g.* bombs.

antiphlogis'tic, *adj.*, preventive of inflammation.

an'tiphon, *n.*, a passage sung or recited during a church service.

antiph'onal, *adj.*, singing or reciting in alternate verses or

passages; *n.*, a collection of antiphons.

antiph'onary, *n.*, a book of antiphons.

antiph'ony, *n.*, alternate or responsory singing.

antiph'rasis, *n.*, the use of a word in a sense contrary to its proper meaning.

antip'odal, *adj.*, rel. to the antipodes.

an'tipode, *adj.*, opposite.

antipode'an, *adj.*, in or of the antipodes.

antip'odes, *n. pl.*, countries exactly on the opposite side of the globe; any extreme contrast.

an'tipole, *n.*, the direct opposite.

an'tipope, *n.*, a usurper to the papacy.

antipyret'ic, *adj.*, relieving fever.

antipy'rin, *n.*, a preparation derived from coal tar, used in relief of fever.

antiqua'rian, *adj.*, rel. to antiquity; often incorrectly used as a noun.

antiqua'rianism, *n.*, a fondness for antiquarian research.

an'tiquary, *n.*, one who studies ancient things.

an'tiquate, *v.t.*, to make out-of-date; to abolish.

an'tiquated, *p.p.*, antiquate; *adj.*, old-fashioned, out-of-date.

an'tiquating, *pr.p.*, antiquate.

antiqua'tion, *n.*, the act of antiquating.

antique', *adj.*, old, old-fashioned; *n.*, a specimen of old work, a curiosity.

antique'ly, *adv.*, in an old-fashioned way.

antique'ness, *n.*, age, old-world style.

antiq'uities, *n. pl.*, relics of ancient times.

antiq'uity, *n.*, the olden days.

antirheumat'ic, *adj.*, relieving rheumatism.

Antirrhin'um, *n.*, a genus of plants, the snapdragon.

antisabbatar'ian, *adj.* and *n.*, (person) opposed to observance of the Sabbath.

antiscorbu'tic, *adj.*, remedial in cases of scurvy.

antiscript'ural, adj., contrary to holy scripture.

anti-sem'ite, adj. and n., (person) hostile to Jews.

anti-semit'ic, adj., opposed to Jews.

antisep'tic, adj., resisting or arresting putrefaction; n., a substance with antiseptic properties.

antislav'ery, n., opposition to slavery.

antiso'cial, adj., opposed to the interests of society.

antispasmod'ic, adj., spasm-relieving.

antis'tasis, n., a rhetorical argument that an act is justified on the ground that its omission would have led to something worse.

antis'trophe, n., the lyrical passages that alternate with the strophe of a Greek chorus.

antistroph'ic, adj., rel. to antistrophe.

an'ti-tank, adj., for use against tanks.

antitet'anin, n., a toxin used to prevent tetanus.

antithe'ist, n., one opposed to the belief in God.

antith'eses, n., pl. of antithesis.

antith'esis, n., opposition, contrast.

antithet'ic, adj., opposed to, in contrast with.

antithet'ical, adj., i.q. antithetic.

antithet'ics, n., the science of opposition in industry.

antitox'in, n., a substance that counteracts poison.

an'ti-trade, adj. and n., a wind that blows in the opposite direction to a trade wind.

antitrinita'rian, adj., opposed to belief in the Holy Trinity.

an'titype, n., that which is represented by a type, e.g., the Cross is the antitype to the Brazen Serpent in the Wilderness.

antityp'ical, adj., not corresponding to the type.

anti-vac'cinationist, n., one opposed to vaccination.

antivenene', n., an antitoxin, esp. a snake-poison antidote.

anti-vivisec'tion, n., opposition to vivisection.

ant'ler, n., a stag's horn.

ant'lered, adj., having antlers.

ant'like, adj., resembling an ant.

antonoma'sia, n., the substitution of names.

ant'onym, n., a word of opposite meaning.

an'trum, n., a body cavity—esp. in the upper jaw-bone.

Ant'werp, n., a city in Belgium; a kind of homing or carrier pigeon.

Anu'bis, n., the Egyptian dog-headed deity.

a'nus, n., the terminal opening of the alimentary canal in animals.

an'vil, n., a blacksmith's hammering-block.

anxi'ety, n., care, uneasiness, strong concern.

anx'ious, adj., careworn, uneasy, desirous.

anx'iously, adv., in an anxious way.

anx'iousness, n., a state of anxiety.

an'y, adj., some (one or more).

an'ybody, pron., some individual.

an'yhow, adv., in any way.

an'yone, pron., anybody.

an'ything, pron., something not particularized.

an'ytime, adv., at any time.

an'yway, adv., in any manner; conj., in any case.

an'ywhere, adv., in any place.

an'ywise, adv., in any way.

Anz'ac, adj. and n., an acronym for the Australian and New Zealand Army Corps.

Ao'nian, adj., rel. to Aonia. Mt. Helicon in Aonia was sacred to the Muses.

a'orist, adj. and n., indefinite; e.g., the aorist tense relates to no particular time.

aoris'tic, adj., rel. to the aorist.

aor'ta, n., the main artery, leading from the left side of the heart.

aorti'tis, n., inflammation of the aorta.

apace', adv., quickly, at a faster rate.

apa'che, n., a hooligan; a N. American Indian tribe (Fr.).

ap'agoge, n., proof by showing the absurdity of the opposite.

ap'anage, n., a perquisite; orig., the provision for maintenance of the younger members of a family. Also appanage.

apart', adv., separately, at a distance from each other.

apart'heid, n., race segregation (Afrikaans).

apart'ment, n., a room or self-contained suite of rooms in a house or building.

apathet'ic, adj., listless, indifferent.

apathet'ical, adj., i.q. apathetic.

apathet'ically, adv., listlessly, indifferently.

ap'athist, n., one of an apathetic tendency.

ap'athy, n., indifference, listlessness.

ap'atite, n., a substance once used as a gem.

ape, n., one of the monkey tribe; v.t., to imitate, to copy.

apeak', adv., on the peak or summit of a flagstaff.

aped, p.p., ape.

apel'lous, adj., not skinned over, uncicatrized.

ape'-man', n., a hypothetical being intermediate between an ape and a man.

apep'sia, n., the inability to digest.

apep'sy, n., i.q. apepsia.

aperçu, n., a brief summary (Fr.).

ape'rient, adj., opening, laxative; n., a laxative medicine.

ape'ritif, n., an appetizer.

aper'itive, adj., having aperient properties.

ap'erture, n., an opening.

ap'ery, n., apish conduct; a colony of apes.

apet'alous, adj., without petals.

a'pex, *n.,* the top, the summit.

aphae'resis, *n.,* the elision of an unaccented syllable. Also *apheresis.*

apha'sia, *n.,* loss of speech.

aphe'lion, *n.,* the point most distant from the sun. Its opposite is the perihelion.

aphe'resis, *n., i.q.* aphaeresis.

aph'esis, *n.,* a special form of apheresis (*e.g.* squire for esquire).

aphet'ic, *adj.,* rel. to aphesis.

aph'icide, *n.,* an aphis killer.

aph'id, *n.,* the anglicized form of aphis.

aph'ides, *n.,* pl. of aphis.

a'phis, *n.,* the green-fly.

aphlogis'tic, *adj.,* non-inflammatory.

apho'nia, *n.,* soundlessness.

aph'ony, *n.,* loss of voice.

aph'orism, *n.,* a short, pithy saying; a maxim.

aph'orist, *n.,* an utterer of aphorisms.

aphorist'ic, *adj.,* in the manner of an aphorism.

aphorist'ical, *adj., i.q.* aphoristic.

aph'orize, *v.i.,* to utter aphorisms.

aph'rite, *n.,* the foam-spar.

aphrodis'iac, *adj.,* sexually exciting; *n.,* a drug that excites sexually.

aphrodis'ian, *adj.,* belonging to Venus; rel. to sensual love.

aph'thae, *n. pl.,* small ulcerous vesicles, seen in the complaint called milk-thrush.

aph'thong, *n.,* a non-sounded letter or syllable of a word.

aphyll'ous, *adj.,* naturally leafless.

ap'ian, *adj.,* rel. to bees.

apia'rian, *adj., i.q.* apian.

a'piarist, *n.,* a bee-keeper.

a'piary, *n.,* a bee-house.

ap'ical, *adj.,* placed at the tip.

ap'ices, *n.,* pl. of apex.

apic'ulated, *adj.,* pointed, peaked.

apicul'tural, *adj.,* rel. to apiculture.

a'piculture, *n.,* bee-keeping.

apicul'turist, *n.,* one who practises apiculture.

apiece', *adv.,* in shares.

a'ping, *pr.p.,* ape.

a'pis, *n.,* a bee (*Lat.*).

a'pish, *adj.,* ape-like, imitative.

a'pishly, *adv.,* in an ape-like manner.

a'pishness, *n.,* an apish habit.

aplas'tic, *adj.,* not easily moulded.

aplomb', *adj. and adv.,* perpendicular; *n.,* cool self-possession.

apnoe'a, *n.,* the suspension or stopping of breathing.

apoc'alypse, *n.,* a revelation.

apocalyp'tic, *adj.,* rel. to or resembling apocalypse.

apocalyp'tical, *adj., i.q.* apocalyptic.

apocar'pous, *adj.,* with separate carpels.

ap'ocentre, *n.,* the most distant point in an orbit.

apoc'opate, *v.t.,* to perform apocope; to cut off or shorten.

apoc'ope, *n.,* a cutting off or elision of a final syllable or letter.

apocrus'tic, *adj.,* astringent.

apoc'rypha, *n.,* the name given to the Christian gospels omitted from the New Testament.

apoc'ryphal, *adj.,* rel. to the apocrypha; of uncertain authority.

ap'od, *adj. and n.,* without feet or ventral fins. Also *apode.*

a'podal, *adj.,* not having ventral fins.

a'pode, *adj.,* without feet.

apod'osis, *n.,* the clause answering to an *if-*clause in syntax.

apog'amy, *n.,* asexual reproduction.

ap'ogee, *n.,* the point in the moon's orbit most distant from the earth.

ap'ograph, *n.,* an exact transcript.

apolaus'tic, *adj.,* self-indulgent.

Apollinar'ian, *adj.,* rel. to Apollo, and to Apollinaris.

Apollinar'is, *n.,* the heretical Bishop of Laodicea; a mineral water from Apollinarisbu.

Apol'lo, *n.,* a Greek and Roman deity, the patron of music; worshipped as the sun-god Phoebus Apollo.

Apoll'yon, *n.,* the great Power of Darkness; the Devil.

apologet'ic, *adj.,* conveying an apology, making a defence.

apologet'ical, *adj., i.q.* apologetic.

apologet'ically, *adv.,* in an apologetic way.

apolo'gia, *n.,* a written defence.

apol'ogist, *n.,* one who makes an apology or defence.

apol'ogize, *v.i.,* to make an apology.

apol'ogized, *p.p.,* apologize.

apol'ogizer, *n.,* one who makes an apology.

apol'ogizing, *pr.p.,* apologize.

ap'ologue, *n.,* a fable with a moral.

apol'ogy, *n.,* a defence; an expression of regret; a makeshift.

ap'ophthegm, *n.,* a brief saying; a maxim.

apoph'yge, *n.,* a hollow curve at the base or top of a column.

apoplec'tic, *adj.,* rel. to apoplexy; *n.,* a sufferer from apoplexy.

apoplec'tical, *adj., i.q.* apoplectic.

ap'oplexy, *n.,* a stroke caused by brain affection.

aposi'tia, *n.,* a distaste for food.

apos'tasy, *n.,* a falling away from, a revolt against one's religion.

apos'tate, *n.,* one who apostatizes.

apostat'ical, *adj.,* tending to apostasy.

apos'tatize, *v.i.,* to revolt against one's former faith.

apos'tatized, *p.p.,* apostatize.

apos'tatizing, *pr.p.,* apostatize.

a posterio'ri, a Lat. phrase = arguing from effect to cause.

apos'til, *v.t.,* to annotate marginally; *n.,* a marginal note.

apos'tle, *n.,* one who is commissioned, esp. one of the Twelve

Apostles; a leader in a movement or cause.

apos'tleship, *n.,* an apostle's office.

apos'tolate, *n.,* the order of apostles; an apostle's function.

apostol'ic, *adj.,* rel. to apostles.

apostol'ical, *adj., i.q.* apostolic.

apostolic'ity, *n.,* the apostolic character.

apos'trophe, *n.,* an aside address to some person or thing; a typographical mark of possession.

apostroph'ic, *adj.,* rel. to apostrophe.

apos'trophize, *v.t.,* to address with an apostrophe.

apos'trophized, *p.p.,* apostrophize.

apos'trophizing, *pr.p.,* apostrophize.

apoth'ecary, *n.,* a storer of medicinal drugs; formerly an irregular practitioner in medicine.

ap'othegm, *n., i.q.* apophthegm.

apothegmat'ic, *adj.,* of the nature of apothegm.

apotheo'sis, *n.,* deification, making into a god.

apothe'osize, *v.t.,* to deify.

apot'omy, apot'ome, *n.,* a major semitone.

appal', *v.t.,* to terrify, to dismay.

Appalach'ian, *adj.,* rel. to the Appalachian mountains.

appalled', *p.p.,* appal.

appall'ing, *pr.p.,* appal; *adj.,* frightful.

appall'ingly, *adv.,* in an appalling way.

ap'panage, *n., i.q.* apanage.

appara'tus, *n.,* appliances for doing work.

appar'el, *n.,* clothing; embroidered work on alb and amice; *v.t.,* to clothe.

appar'elled, *or* **-eled,** *p.p.,* apparel; *adj.,* ornamented with apparels.

appar'elling, *pr.p.,* apparel.

appa'rent, *adj.,* visible, manifest, seeming.

appa'rently, *adv.,* clearly, seemingly.

appari'tion, *n.,* the act of appearing; something that appears, a ghost.

appar'itor, *n.,* an officer in a law court; a church beadle.

appeal', *n.,* reference to a superior court, a call for aid; *v.i.,* to call upon; to carry a case to a superior court.

appeal'able, *adj.,* able to be pleaded before a higher court.

appealed', *p.p.,* appeal.

appeal'er, *n.,* one who appeals.

appeal'ing, *pr.p.,* appeal; *adj.,* compelling interest.

appeal'ingly, *adv.,* in an appealing way.

appear', *v.i.,* to become visible; to seem.

appear'ance, *n.,* a showing, becoming visible; a seeming; an outward aspect.

appeared', *p.p.,* appear.

appear'er, *n.,* one who appears.

appear'ing, *pr.p.,* appear.

appeas'able, *adj.,* able to be appeased.

appeas'ableness, *n.,* an appeasable state or temper.

appease', *v.t.,* to calm, to allay.

appeased', *p.p.,* appease.

appease'ment, *n.,* the act of appeasing.

appeas'er, *n.,* one who appeases.

appeas'ing, *pr.p.,* appease.

appel'lant, *n.,* one who appeals.

appel'late, *adj.,* having appeal jurisdiction.

appella'tion, *n.,* a name.

appel'lative, *adj.,* rel. to appeal; *n.,* a nickname, a title.

appel'latively, *adv.,* by way of an appeal.

appel'latory, *adj.,* conveying an appeal.

appellee', *n.,* the person against whom an appeal is lodged.

appel'lor, *n., i.q.* appellant.

append', *v.t.,* to hang to, to fix to, to add.

append'age, *n.,* something appended.

append'ant, *n., i.q.* appendage; *adj.,* joined to, added.

appen'dectomy, *n., i.q.* appendicectomy.

append'ed, *p.p.,* append.

appendicec'tomy, *n.,* the surgical removal of the appendix.

appen'dices, *n.,* pl. of appendix (*med.*).

appendici'tis, *n.,* the disease of the vermiform appendix to the great intestine.

append'ing, *pr.p.,* append.

appen'dix, *n.,* additional matter at the end of a book; a part of the great intestine.

appen'dixes, *n.,* pl. of appendix.

apperceive', *v.t.,* to assimilate and understand a mass of ideas already possessed.

apperceived', *p.p.,* apperceive.

apperceiv'ing, *pr.p.,* apperceive.

appercep'tion, *n.,* self-consciousness; the ability to be conscious of perceiving.

appertain', *v.i.,* to belong to, to be related to.

appertained', *p.p.,* appertain.

appertain'ing, *pr.p.,* appertain.

appertain'ment, *n.,* the state of appertaining.

ap'petence, *n.,* a strong desire, an appetite, a tendency.

ap'petency, *n., i.q.* appetence.

ap'petent, *adj.,* craving, impulsive.

ap'petite, *n.,* a desire (chiefly for food).

ap'petitive, *adj.,* producing appetite.

ap'petize, *v.t.,* to excite appetite.

ap'petizer, *n.,* something that promotes appetite.

ap'petizing, *adj.,* stimulating the appetite, tempting.

Ap'pian, *adj.,* named from Appius, as the Appian Way.

applaud', *v.t.,* to clap the hands at, to approve.

applaud'ed, *p.p.,* applaud.

applaud'er, *n.,* one who applauds.

applaud'ing, *pr.p.,* applaud.

applause', *n.,* the act of applauding; open praise.

applau'sive, *adj.,* expressing applause.

ap'ple, *n.,* the fruit so named; the pupil of an eye.

ap'ple-tree, n., a tree bearing apples.

appli'ance, n., something applied.

appli'ancy, n., the habit of applying, adaptability.

applicabil'ity, n., the ability to be applied, fitness.

ap'plicable, adj., able to be applied, fit.

ap'plicableness, n., suitability, fitness to be applied.

ap'plicancy, n., the state of applying.

ap'plicant, n., one who applies for some gift or position.

applica'tion, n., the act of applying; steady industry; the moral of a story or discourse.

ap'plicative, adj., rel. to application; able to be applied.

ap'plicatory, adj., fit for application.

applied', p.p., apply.

appli'er, n., one who applies.

appli'qué, n., something laid on (Fr.).

apply', v.t. and i., to put one thing to another, to exert; to request; to concern, to be related to.

apply'ing, pr.p., apply.

appoggiatu'ra, n., an ornamental note in music, taking its time out of a principal note (It.).

appoint', v.t., to fix; to confer office; to settle.

appoint'ed, p.p., appoint; adj., equipped.

appointee', n., a person appointed.

appoint'er, n., one who appoints.

appoint'ing, pr.p., appoint.

appoint'ment, n., the act of appointing; an office or post; an engagement; equipment.

appoint'ments, n., pl. of appointment.

appor'tion, v.t., to assign portions or parts.

appor'tioned, p.p., apportion.

appor'tioner, n., one who apportions.

appor'tioning, pr.p., apportion.

appor'tionment, n., the act of apportioning.

appose', v.t., to put one thing to another.

appos'er, n., one who apposes.

ap'posite, adj., fitting, to the point.

ap'positely, adv., fittingly, to the point.

ap'positeness, n., applicability, the state of being to the point.

apposi'tion, n., the act of placing side by side. In grammar, apposition is the juxta-position of two nouns or equivalents in the same case, the latter explaining the former, as Elizabeth Regina.

appos'itive, adj., rel. to apposition.

apprais'al, n., the act of appraising.

appraise', v.t., to take the value of, to price.

appraised', p.p., appraise.

appraise'ment, n., the act of appraising.

apprais'er, n., a valuer, one who appraises.

apprais'ing, pr.p., appraise.

appre'ciable, adj., able to be appreciated.

appre'ciably, adv., sensibly, in a way to be felt.

appre'ciate, v.t. and i., to set a value on; to esteem highly; to increase in value.

appre'ciated, p.p., appreciate.

appre'ciating, pr.p., appreciate.

apprecia'tion, n., the act of valuing, the recognition of value; a rise in price, a critique.

appre'ciative, adj., showing appreciation.

appre'ciatively, adv., in an appreciative way.

appre'ciatory, adj., i.q. appreciative.

apprehend', v.t., to seize, to arrest; to understand; to anticipate with fear.

apprehend'ed, p.p., apprehend.

apprehend'er, n., one who apprehends.

apprehend'ing, pr.p., apprehend.

apprehen'sible, adj., able to be apprehended.

apprehen'sion, n., nervous fear.

apprehen'sive, adj., nervously fearful.

apprehen'sively, adv., in an apprehensive way.

apprehen'siveness, n., an apprehensive state.

appren'tice, n., a young person learning a trade or profession; v.t., to bind a youth to an employer.

appren'ticed, p.p., apprentice.

appren'ticeship, n., the state of an apprentice; the period of being an apprentice.

appren'ticing, pr.p., apprentice.

apprise', v.t., to give notice of, to inform.

apprised', p.p., apprise.

appris'er, n., one who apprises.

appris'ing, pr.p., apprise.

apprize', v.t., to value.

ap'pro, n., the abbrev. for approval.

approach', n., a coming near, a path to; v.t. and i., to come near to, to make advances.

approach'able, adj., able to be approached, affable.

approached', p.p., approach.

approach'er, n., one who approaches.

approach'ing, pr.p., approach.

approach'ment, n., the act of approaching.

ap'probate, v.t., to approve, to sanction.

ap'probated, p.p., approbate.

ap'probating, pr.p., approbate.

approba'tion, n., approval, sanction.

ap'probative, adj., approving, sanctioning.

ap'probatively, adv., in an approving way.

ap'probativeness, n., a state of approving.

ap'probatory, adj., i.q. approbative.

appro'priable, adj., able to be appropriated.

appro'priate, v.t., to make one's own; to set aside; adj., fitting, suitable.

appro'priated, p.p., appropriate.

appro'priately, adv., in an appropriate way.

appro'priateness, n., fitness, suitability.

appro'priating, pr.p., appropriate.

appropria'tion, n., the act of appropriating.

appro'priative, adj., given to appropriating.

appro'priator, *n.*, one who appropriates.

approv'able, *adj.*, worthy to be approved.

approv'al, *n.*, approbation, sanction.

approve', *v.t.*, to think well of, to sanction.

approved', *p.p.*, approve.

approve'ment, *n.*, the act of approving.

approv'er, *n.*, one who approves.

approv'ing, *pr.p.*, approve.

approv'ingly, *adv.*, in an approving way.

approx'imate, *adj.*, coming very near to, almost correct.

approx'imate, *v.i.*, to approach, to come near to.

approx'imated, *p.p.*, approximate.

approx'imately, *adv.*, nearly, closely.

approx'imating, *pr.p.*, approximate.

approxima'tion, *n.*, the act of approximating; a calculation or statement almost exact.

approx'imative, *adj.*, coming close to, approaching.

appui', *n.*, support (*Fr.*).

appul'sion, *n.*, the act of striking against.

appur'tenance, *n.*, that which pertains or belongs.

appur'tenant, *adj.*, bel. or pert. to.

a'pricot, *n.*, a fruit of the plum kind.

A'pril, *n.*, the fourth month of the year.

A'pril-fool, *n.*, one who is made a fool of on All Fools' Day, 1 April.

a prio'ri, from something antecedent, *i.e.*, reasoning from cause to effect (*Lat.*).

a'pron, *n.*, an outside garment protecting other clothes; an advanced strip of stage in the theatre.

a'proned, *adj.*, wearing an apron.

apropos', a French phrase = to the purpose; in that connection.

apse, *n.*, the round or multilateral end of a chancel, aisle, chapel or recess.

ap'sidal, *adj.*, rel. to an apse; in shape like an apse.

ap'sides, *n.*, pl. of apsis.

ap'sis, *n.*, a point in an eccentric orbit furthest from or nearest to the centre of attraction; an apse.

apt, *adj.*, fit, apposite, liable to, well qualified.

ap'tera, *n.*, wingless creatures.

ap'teral, *adj.*, rel. to aptera.

ap'terous, *adj.*, wingless.

ap'teryx, *n.*, a bird with rudimentary wings.

apt'itude, *n.*, fitness, quickness, capacity for.

apt'ly, *adv.*, fitly, appropriately.

apt'ness, *n.*, a capacity for doing things, appropriateness.

ap'tote, *adj.*, not having case-endings.

aptot'ic, *adj.*, uninflected.

a'qua, *n.*, water (*Lat.*).

aquafor'tis, *n.*, nitric acid.

a'qualung, *n.*, a portable diving apparatus.

aquamarine', *adj.*, bluish-green; *n.*, bluish-green beryl.

a'quaplane, *n.* and *v.i.*, (to ride on) a plank towed behind a speedboat.

a'qua-planing, *n.*, the buoyancy caused by a film of water on an aircraft runway or road surface.

aquarelle', *n.*, a water-colour.

aqua'rial, *adj.*, rel. to water.

aqua'rian, *adj.*, living in water.

aqua'rium, *n.*, a receptacle for water animals or plants.

Aqua'rius, *n.*, the water carrier—one of the signs of the Zodiac.

aquat'ic, *adj.*, rel. to, living in, water.

aq'uatint, *n.*, a special kind of engraving; an engraving printed from an aquatint plate.

a'quavi'tae, *n.*, strong water, especially brandy (*eau de vie*).

a'queduct, *n.*, a channel for conveying water.

a'queous, *adj.*, watery, of water.

a'queousness, *n.*, a watery state.

A'quila, *n.*, a type of eagle; the name of a constellation in the N. hemisphere.

aquile'gia, *n.*, a buttercup type of plant.

a'quiline, *adj.*, eagle-like; hooked like an eagle's beak.

a'quilon, *n.*, the N.E. wind.

aquos'ity, *n.*, wateriness.

Ar'ab, *n.*, a native of Arabia.

arabesque', *n.*, an ornamentation or carving in the Moorish style.

arabesqued', *adj.*, in the arabesque style.

Ara'bian, *adj.*, rel. to Arabia.

Ar'abic, *adj.*, *i.q.* Arabian; *n.*, the language of the Arab world.

A'rabist, *n.*, a student of Arabic.

ar'able, *adj.*, fit for the plough and tilling.

Arach'nida, *n.*, insects of the spider tribe (*zool.*).

arach'noid, *adj.*, spider-like.

arachnol'ogy, *n.*, the study of spider-nature.

ar'agonite, *n.*, a calcium carbonate. Also *arragonite*.

Arama'ic, *adj.* and *n.*, the name of an ancient language of Syria.

Arama'ism, *n.*, an Aramaic idiom.

Arame'an, *adj.*, rel. to Aram (Mesopotamia) or Aramaea.

aran'eology, *n.*, the study of spiders.

arapai'ma, *n.*, a gigantic river-fish of S. America.

ara'tion, *n.*, ploughing, tilling.

Araucar'ia, *n.*, a tree genus including the monkey-puzzle.

ar'balist, *n.*, a military engine so named; a crossbow. Also *arcubalist*.

ar'balister, *n.*, a crossbowman.

ar'biter, *n.*, a judge or umpire.

ar'bitrable, *adj.*, able to go to arbitration.

arb'itrage, *n.*, a profitable type of dealing on the Stock Exchange.

arbit'rageur, *n.*, a dealer in arbitrage.

arb'itral, *adj.*, pertaining to arbitration.

arbit′rament, *n.*, a decision, an umpire's verdict.

ar′bitrarily, *adv.*, of one's own will, despotically.

ar′bitrariness, *n.*, an arbitrary temper.

ar′bitrary, *adj.*, acting on one's own will or decision.

ar′bitrate, *v.i.*, to decide between disputants.

ar′bitrated, *p.p.*, arbitrate.

ar′bitrating, *pr.p.*, arbitrate.

arbitra′tion, *n.*, the act of arbitrating.

arbitra′tional, *adj.*, rel. to arbitration.

arbitra′tionist, *n.*, one who favours arbitration.

ar′bitrator, *n.*, one who arbitrates.

ar′bitratrix, *n.*, the fem. of arbitrator.

arb′or, *n.*, a shaft, a spindle; a tree.

arbora′ceous, *adj.*, treelike; wooded.

Arb′or Day, *n.*, a day set apart annually for public tree-planting.

arbor′eal, *adj.*, *i.q.* arboreous.

arbo′reous, *adj.*, rel. to trees.

arbores′cence, *n.*, the growth of trees.

arbores′cent, *adj.*, growing like a tree.

arbore′tum, *n.*, a collection of trees for scientific study.

ar′boriculture, *n.*, scientific tree-culture.

arboricult′urist, *n.*, one engaged in arboriculture.

ar′boriform, *adj.*, treelike.

ar′borist, *n.*, one who cultivates trees.

arboriza′tion, *n.*, an appearance like a tree.

ar′borous, *adj.*, rel. to trees.

arb′or vit′ae, *n.*, popular name of several evergreens.

ar′bour, **ar′bor**, *n.*, a tree-shaded bower.

ar′boured, *adj.*, recessed with arbours.

ar′buscle, *n.*, a tuft.

arbu′tean, *adj.*, rel. to the arbutus.

ar′butus, *n.*, the wild strawberry.

arc, *n.*, a curve, a part

---

of the periphery of a circle or other curve.

arcade′, *n.*, an arched structure; the range of arches in a church or other building; an arched passage with shops on either side.

arca′ded, *adj.*, in the form of an arcade.

Arca′dian, *adj.*, native to Arcadia; rustic, simple, pastoral.

arca′na, *n. pl.*, secrets, mysteries.

arca′num, *n.*, a secret; something hidden.

arch, *adj.*, sly, roguish; *n.*, a structural curve over an opening, or on the face of a wall; *v.t.*, to form into an arch.

arch-, **ar′chi-**, a prefix denoting eminence, as archbishop.

Archae′an, *adj.*, rel. to the earliest geological period.

archaeolog′ic, *adj.*, *i.q.* archaeological.

archaeolog′ical, *adj.*, rel. to archaeology.

archaeol′ogist, *n.*, one who studies archaeology.

archaeol′ogy, *n.*, the study of architectural antiquities.

archaeop′teryx, *n.*, the earliest known bird; the link between birds and reptiles.

archa′ic, *adj.*, rel. to the remote past, obsolete.

ar′chaism, *n.*, an antiquated usage or expression.

archais′tic, *adj.*, affectedly or imitatively archaic.

archan′gel, *n.*, an angel of the highest rank.

archangel′ic, *adj.*, rel. to an archangel.

archbish′op, *n.*, a bishop who rules a province.

archbish′opric, *n.*, the office or rule of an archbishop.

archdea′con, *n.*, a chief deacon; the bishop's diocesan deputy.

archdea′conry, *n.*, an archdeacon's dignity or office.

archdea′conship, *n.*, an archdeacon's service.

archdru′id, *n.*, the chief of the Order of Druids.

archdu′cal, *adj.*, rel. to an archduke.

---

archduch′ess, *n.*, the fem. of archduke.

archduch′y, *n.*, an archduke's territory.

archduke′, *n.*, a duke of the highest rank.

archduke′dom, *n.*, an archduke's office or territorial jurisdiction.

arched, *adj.*, covered with or forming an arch; *p.p.*, arch.

arch′-en′emy, *n.*, the chief enemy; the devil.

arch′er, *n.*, one who shoots with a bow.

arch′eress, *n.*, the fem. of archer.

arch′ery, *n.*, the sport of shooting with a bow.

ar′chetypal, *adj.*, rel. to an archetype.

ar′chetype, *n.*, the original on which a type is modelled.

archfiend′, *n.*, the chief among the fiends, Satan.

arch-foe′, *n.*, the chief foe.

arch′ical, *adj.*, governmental; original.

archidiac′onal, *adj.*, pert. to an archdeacon.

archiepis′copacy, *n.*, an archbishop's incumbency.

archiepis′copal, *adj.*, pert. to an archbishop.

archiepis′copate, *n.*, *i.q.* archiepiscopacy.

ar′chil, *n.*, a lichen so named.

Archilo′chian, *adj.*, rel. to Archilochus, an ancient Greek satirical poet, inventor of the iambus.

archiman′drite, *n.*, the title of a Greek priest of the higher rank, ruler of a large monastery or of several smaller ones.

Archime′dean, *adj.*, rel. to Archimedes, the famous mathematician of antiquity.

arch′ing, *adj.*, curving; *pr.p.*, arch.

archipel′ago, *n.*, a group of sea islands.

ar′chitect, *n.*, a master-builder, one who designs buildings.

ar′chitected, *adj.*, designed by an architect.

ar′chitective, *adj.*, rel. to architecture; constructive.

architecton′ic, *adj.*, *i.q.* architective.

architecton'ics, *n.*, the architectural science.

architect'ural, *adj.*, rel. to architecture.

ar'chitecture, *n.*, the art or work of an architect.

ar'chitrave, *n.*, a principal beam, being the part of the entablature which rests on the capitals of the columns.

archi'val, *adj.*, rel. to archives.

ar'chives, *n. pl.*, ancient public records.

ar'chivist, *n.*, a student of archives.

ar'chivolt, *n.*, the under surface of an arch.

arch'let, *n.*, a small arch.

arch'ly, *adv.*, slyly, roguishly.

arch'ness, *n.*, slyness, roguishness.

ar'chon, *n.*, a magistrate, a ruler (*Gr.*).

archpres'byter, *n.*, a presbyter of the higher rank.

archpres'bytery, *n.*, the office of an arch-presbyter.

archpriest', *n.*, the title anciently given to the leading priest in a diocese.

archtrait'or, *n.*, the greatest of traitors.

arch'vill'ain, *n.*, one supremely villainous.

arch'way, *n.*, a passage through an arch.

arch'wise, *adv.*, in the form of an arch.

arc'-lamp, *n.*, a lamp illuminated by an electric arc.

ar'cograph, *n.*, a device for drawing circles without striking from a centre.

arcta'tion, *n.*, constriction, constipation.

Arc'tic, *adj.*, rel. to the Arctic or North Pole.

Arctu'rus, *n.*, the Great Bear constellation.

ar'cuate, *adj.*, arched in structure.

arcua'tion, *n.*, the arch formation.

ar'cubalist, *n.*, *i.q.* arbalist.

ar'dency, *n.*, fervent emotion, ardour.

ar'dent, *adj.*, heated, impetuous, zealous.

ar'dently, *adv.*, in an ardent way.

ar'dour, ar'dor, *n.*, heat, passion, zeal.

ar'duous, *adj.*, steep, difficult.

ar'duously, *adv.*, laboriously, with difficulty.

ar'duousness, *n.*, difficulty.

are, the pl. of the present tense of the copulative verb *to be*.

are, *n.*, a unit of superficial measurement about 119.6 sq. yd. (*Fr.*).

a'rea, *n.*, a surface measurement; a space enclosed; the sunk space round a building; the extent, the range.

ar'eca, *n.*, a kind of tropical palm.

arefac'tion, *n.*, withering.

ar'efy, *v.t.*, to wither up, to dry up.

are'na, *n.*, the open space of a Roman amphitheatre; a place or scene of contest.

arena'ceous, *adj.*, sandy.

arena'tion, *n.*, the use of hot sand.

arenose', *adj.*, *i.q.* arenaceous.

are'ola, *n.*, a small space in the marking on insects' wings, veins of leaves, etc.

are'olate, *adj.*, marked with *areolae*.

areola'tion, *n.*, the act or state of being marked with *areolae*.

areom'eter, *n.*, a surface measuring instrument.

areomet'ric, *adj.*, rel. to surface measurement.

areomet'rical, *adj.*, *i.q.* areometric.

areom'etry, *n.*, the science of surface-measurement.

Areop'agist, *n.*, *i.q.* Areopagite.

Areop'agite, *n.*, a member of the Areopagus.

Areop'agus, *n.*, the Hill of Ares in Athens, on which the most ancient of the Courts was held. Called Mars' Hill in the Acts of the Apostles.

areop'agy, *n.*, a secret tribunal.

ar'gal, *conj.*, a corruption of *ergo* = therefore. Used in Shakespeare.

ar'gala, *n.*, a large Indian stork.

ar'gali, *n.*, Asian wild sheep.

ar'gand, *adj.* and *n.*, rel. to Argand's method of lighting; a lamp with a tubular wick.

ar'gent, *adj.* and *n.*, silver, silvery.

argent'al, *adj.*, silvery.

argent'ic, *adj.*, rel. to silver.

argentif'erous, *adj.*, silver-producing.

Ar'gentine, *adj.*, rel. to Argentina; *n.*, a native of A.

ar'gentine, *adj.*, silvery; *n.*, a white metal so named.

ar'gil, *n.*, white clay.

argilla'ceous, *adj.*, of white clay.

argillif'erous, *adj.*, producing white clay.

argil'lous, *adj.*, containing, or consisting of, white clay.

Ar'give, *adj.*, a native of Argos.

ar'gle-bar'gle, *n.* and *v.i.*, *i.q.* argy-bargy.

ar'gol, *n.*, the grape-juice deposit in fermentation.

ar'gon, *n.*, an inert gas in the atmosphere.

Ar'gonaut, *n.*, a sailor on the mythical ship *Argo*.

Argonaut'ic, *adj.*, rel. to the Argonauts.

ar'gosy, *n.*, a richly-laden merchant vessel.

ar'got, *n.*, the French name for slang.

ar'guable, *adj.*, capable of being argued.

ar'gue, *v.t.* and *i.*, to discuss, to try to prove; to show.

ar'gued, *p.p.*, argue.

ar'guer, *n.*, one who argues.

ar'gufier, *n.*, one who is given to arguing.

ar'gufy, *v.i.* (*illit.*), to dispute, to wrangle.

ar'guing, *pr.p.*, argue.

ar'gument, *n.*, a debate, a discussion, an attempt to prove; a summarized purport of a book or speech.

argumenta'tion, *n.*, a dispute.

argumen'tative, *adj.*, rel. to argument; fond of disputing.

argumen'tatively, *adv.*, in an argumentative way.

argumen'tativeness, *n.*, a fondness for disputing.

Ar'gus, *n.*, a Greek mythological being,

having a hundred eyes.

ar'gus, *n.*, an E. Indian pheasant.

argute', *adj.*, sharp, shrewd; (of sounds) shrill.

ar'gy-bar'gy, **ar'gie-bar'gie**, *n.* and *v.i.*, tedious argument, wrangling.

a'ria, *n.*, a melody, a song, an air.

A'rian, *adj.*, rel. to Arius, the heretical leader opposed by St. Athanasius.

A'rianism, *n.*, the profession of Arian teaching.

ar'id, *adj.*, dry, parched, waste.

arid'ity, *n.*, a state of dryness.

ar'idness, *n.*, *i.q.* aridity.

ar'iel, *n.*, a species of gazelle in Western Asia and Africa.

A'ries, *n.*, the Ram, one of the signs of the Zodiac.

ariet'ta, *n.*, a short aria or melody.

aright', *adv.*, rightly, correctly.

ar'il, *n.*, a secondary covering of a seed.

Ar'imasp, *n.*, one of the Arimaspi; a mythical one-eyed race of N. Europe.

Arimas'pian, *adj.*, rel. to the Arimaspi.

ario'so, *adj.* and *adv.*, aria-like; melodiously.

arise', *v.i.*, to spring forth, to ascend, to leave one's bed.

aris'en, *p.p.*, arise.

aris'ing, *pr.p.*, arise.

aris'ta, *n.*, awn; bristle-like points or beard of grain and grasses.

ar'istarch, *n.*, a critic like Aristarchus.

aristarch'ian, *adj.*, rel. to Aristarchus.

aris'tate, *adj.*, awned, bearded.

aristoc'racy, *n.*, government by the best citizens; the aristocrats as a class or body.

ar'istocrat, *n.*, a member of the aristocracy; a person with pride of birth.

aristocrat'ic, *adj.*, like an aristocrat.

aristocrat'ical, *adj.*, *i.q.* aristocratic.

aristol'ogy, *n.*, the art or science of dining.

Aristote'lian, *adj.*, belonging to Aristotle, the Greek philosopher.

Aristote'lic, *adj.*, *i.q.* Aristotelian.

ar'ithmancy, *n.*, divining by means of numbers.

arith'metic, *n.*, the science of numbers.

arithmet'ical, *adj.*, rel. to arithmetic.

arithmeti'cian, *n.*, one who practises arithmetic.

ark, *n.*, a chest, a box (Noah's Ark was a large floating vessel); a place of refuge.

arles, *n. pl.*, earnest-money (*dial.*).

arm, *n.*, a limb of the body; an inlet of the sea; a weapon; *v.t.* and *i.*, to furnish with weapons, to equip for war.

arma'da, *n.*, a fleet of armed ships.

armadil'lo, *n.*, a four-footed creature, small, having a horny shell.

Armagedd'on, *n.*, the final battle at the Day of Judgment; any great final conflict.

ar'mament, *n.*, an armed force; the collected munitions of war; defence.

ar'mature, *n.*, defensive armour; part of an electrical machine.

arm'chair, *n.*, a chair with supporting arms.

armed, *p.p.*, arm; *adj.*, having arms.

Arme'nian, *adj.*, bel. to Armenia; *n.*, a native of A.

arm'ful, *n.*, a gathering of things to fill the arms.

arm'hole, *n.*, a hole to let the arm through.

ar'miger, *n.*, the Lat. name for our Esquire; a person entitled to bear arms.

armig'erous, *adj.*, entitled to bear arms (*her.*).

armil'la, *n.*, a bracelet, a ring.

armil'lary, *adj.*, rel. to an armilla.

arm'ing, *pr.p.*, arm.

Armin'ian, *adj.*, rel. to Arminius, a 16th cent. Dutch anti-Calvinist teacher.

Armin'ianism, *n.*, the teaching of the school of Arminius.

armip'otence, *n.*, armed superiority.

armip'otent, *adj.*, superior in arms.

arm'istice, *n.*, a temporary suspension of hostilities.

arm'less, *adj.*, without arms.

arm'let, *n.*, a badge or ornament worn round the arm.

armor'ial, *adj.* and *n.*, (book) pertaining to heraldic arms.

Armor'ic, *adj.*, rel. to Armorica, the western part of France between the Loire and the Seine.

Armor'ican, *n.*, *i.q.* Armoric.

arm'ory, *n.*, heraldry.

ar'mour, **ar'mor**, *n.*, defensive arms worn on the body, or used in the plating of a man-of-war.

armoured, *p.p.*, armour.

ar'mourer, **ar'morer**, *n.*, one who makes armour.

ar'mourist, *n.*, an heraldic expert.

ar'mour-pla'ted, *adj.*, covered with defensive plates (*naut.*).

ar'moury, **ar'mory**, *n.*, a place for the making or the keeping of arms.

arm'pit, *n.*, the hollow under the arms.

arm's'-length, a phrase, "at arm's-length" = at a distance as long as one's arm.

ar'my, *n.*, an armed body of men; a large number.

ar'nica, *n.*, a medicinal herb so named, useful for bruises.

arnot'to, *n.*, an American tree resembling the Indian plum.

aroint', *v.i.* (generally found in the imperative), to remove, to get out of the way.

aro'ma, *n.*, a fragrant smell or taste; metaphorically, an intangible quality.

aromat'ic, *adj.*, possessing aroma.

aromat'ical, *adj.*, *i.q.* aromatic.

aro'matize, *v.t.*, to season, to perfume.

aro'matizer, *n.*, something that gives aroma.

aro'matous, *adj.*, *i.q.* aromatic.

arose', *p.p.*, arise.

around', *adv.* and *prep.*, all about, round.

arouse', *v.t.*, to stir up, to awaken.

aroused', *p.p.*, arouse.

arous'ing, *pr.p.*, arouse.

arpeg'gio, *n.*, the harp-like striking of the notes of a chord separately (*It.*, *mus.*).

ar'pent, *n.*, a former French land measure = an acre.

arquebusade', *n.*, a volley from arquebuses.

ar'quebuse, ar'quebus, *n.*, an old fire-arm, supported on a rest.

arquebusier', *n.*, one who fires an arquebus.

ar'rack, *n.*, a heady liquor distilled from rice and other plants.

ar'ragonite, *n.*, *i.q.* aragonite.

arraign', *v.t.*, to indict before a judge.

arraigned', *p.p.*, arraign.

arraign'er, *n.*, one who arraigns.

arraign'ing, *pr.p.*, arraign.

arraign'ment, *n.*, a legal indictment.

arrange', *v.t.*, to place in order, to settle.

arrange'able, *adj.*, able to be arranged.

arranged', *p.p.*, arrange.

arrange'ment, *n.*, the act of arranging; an agreed plan; a musical setting.

arrang'er, *n.*, one who arranges.

arrang'ing, *pr.p.*, arrange.

ar'rant, *adj.*, thorough, downright.

ar'rantly, *adv.*, in a downright way.

ar'ras, *n.*, a tapestry (derived from Arras in France).

array', *n.*, order (as battle array), dress; *v.t.*, to vest, to dress.

arrayed', *p.p.*, array.

array'er, *n.*, one who arrays.

array'ing, *pr.p.*, array.

arrear', *n.*, a position in the rear.

arrear'age, *n.*, the amount in arrears.

arrears', *n.*, an unpaid debt.

arrect', *adj.*, raised, pricked up, attentive.

arrest', *v.t.*, to seize, to attract (the mind or attention); *n.*, a seizure by legal warrant, a stopping.

arrest'ed, *p.p.*, arrest.

arrest'er, arrest'or, *n.*, one who arrests.

arrest'ing, *pr.p.*, arrest.

arrest'ment, *n.*, the act of arresting.

arride', *v.t.*, to please, to gratify.

ar'ris, *n.*, a ridge, as that between the channels of a Doric pillar.

arri'val, *n.*, a coming, the act of arriving.

arrive', *v.i.*, to come, to reach a place.

arrived', *p.p.*, arrive.

arriv'ing, *pr.p.*, arrive.

ar'rogance, *n.*, overbearing pride.

ar'rogancy, *n.*, *i.q.* arrogance.

ar'rogant, *adj.*, overbearingly proud, exacting.

ar'rogantly, *adv.*, in an arrogant way.

ar'rogate, *v.t.*, to claim unduly or in excess.

ar'rogated, *p.p.*, arrogate.

ar'rogating, *pr.p.*, arrogate.

arroga'tion, *n.*, the act of arrogating.

arrondisse'ment, *n.*, a French territorial division so named (*Fr.*).

arro'sion, *n.*, destruction by biting.

ar'row, *n.*, a sharp-pointed missile, shot from a bow.

ar'row-head, *n.*, an arrow's pointed end.

ar'rowroot, *n.*, a starchy plant (*Maranta arundinacea*), very nutritious.

ar'row-shaped, *adj.*, shaped like an arrow.

ar'rowy, *adj.*, like an arrow.

arroy'o, *n.*, a creek; a dried-up watercourse.

ar'senal, *n.*, a factory or store of war munitions.

ar'senate, *n.*, *i.q.* arseniate.

arse'niate, *n.*, an arsenic acid salt.

ar'senic, *n.*, a metal, a strong poison.

arsen'ical, *adj.*, containing or rel. to arsenic.

arsen'icate, *v.t.*, to charge with arsenic.

arsen'icated, *p.p.*, arsenicate.

arse'nious, *adj.*, pert. to arsenic.

ar'senite, *n.*, an arsenious acid salt.

ar'sis, *n.*, the stress of the voice where the accent comes; the conductor's beat at the beginning of a bar.

ar'son, *n.*, the act of wilfully setting on fire.

art, *n.*, a skill, knowledge, cunning; any human activity (as painting, sculpture) in which creative imagination is allied to sensory skill.

art'efact, *n.*, an artificially made product. Also *artifact*.

artel', *n.*, the collective enterprise of Soviet Union workers (*Russ.*).

arte'rial, *adj.*, bel. to the arteries.

arterializa'tion, *n.*, the changing of venous into arterial blood.

arte'rialize, *v.t.*, to change venous into arterial blood.

arte'rialized, *p.p.*, arterialize.

arte'rializing, *pr.p.*, arterialize.

arteriol'ogy, *n.*, the study of the arteries.

arterioscleros'is, *n.*, the hardening of the arteries esp. due to old age.

arteriot'omy, *n.*, the act of cutting arteries.

ar'tery, *n.*, a blood-vessel leading direct from the heart.

arte'sian, *adj.*, very deeply bored. (Artesian wells were first made in Artois.)

art'ful, *adj.*, cunning, designing.

art'fully, *adv.*, cunningly.

art'fulness, *n.*, cunning.

arthral'gia, *n.*, neuralgic pains in a joint.

arthrit'ic, *adj.*, rel. to arthritis.

arthri'tis, *n.*, inflammation of a joint.

ar'thropod, *n.*, a creature with jointed body and limbs.

Arthu'rian, *adj.*, rel. to King Arthur.

ar'tichoke, *n.*, an edible vegetable so named.

ar'ticle, *n.*, a separate part, a member, a thing or commodity; a doctrine, a treaty-clause; a piece of literary work; *v.t.*, to bind by indenture.

ar'ticled, *p.p.*, article.

ar'ticling, *pr.p.*, article.

artic'ular, *adj.*, rel. to a joint or articulation.

artic'ularly, *adv.*, in an articulate way; in detail.

articula'ta, *n. pl.*, creatures with segmented bodies.

artic'ulate, *adj.*, jointed; clear, distinct.

artic'ulate, *v.i.*, to speak distinctly.

artic'ulated, *p.p.*, articulate.

artic'ulately, *adv.*, with distinct utterance.

artic'ulating, *pr.p.*, articulate.

articula'tion, *n.*, a joint (*anat.*); clear utterance.

art'ifact, *n.*, *i.q.* artefact.

art'ifice, *n.*, a contrivance, a cunning device.

artif'icer, *n.*, one who practises an art, a workman.

artifi'cial, *adj.*, made by art, unreal.

artificial'ity, *n.*, an artificial or unnatural character.

artifi'cially, *adv.*, in an artificial way.

artifi'cialness, *n.*, *i.q.* artificiality.

artil'lerist, *n.*, an expert in artillery.

artil'lery, *n.*, military guns; also the men who use them.

artil'leryman, *n.*, a man in the artillery force.

ar'tisan, *n.*, one who practises a trade.

ar'tisanship, *n.*, the work of or state of being an artisan.

art'ist, *n.*, one who practises a fine art.

artiste', *n.*, a stage performer (*Fr.*).

artist'ic, *adj.*, rel. to art and artists.

artist'ical, *adj.*, *i.q.* artistic.

artist'ically, *adv.*, in an artistic way.

ar'tistry, *n.*, artistic skill, artistic expression.

art'less, *adj.*, simple, natural.

art'lessly, *adv.*, simply, naturally.

art'lessness, *n.*, a simple state or character.

art'y, *adj.*, pretentiously artistic (*colloq.*).

ar'um, *n.*, kinds of plant including the wake-robin; a lily.

Arunde'lian, *adj.*, rel. to Arundel.

arundif'erous, *adj.*, reed-producing.

arus'pex, *n.*, *i.q.* haruspex.

arus'pice, *n.*, a soothsayer, a diviner.

arus'picy, *n.*, divining by means of the entrails of sacrificed beasts.

Ar'yan, *adj.* and *n.*, stemming from the original Indo-Europeans; such a one.

as, *n.*, a Roman coin and weight.

as, *adv.* and *conj.*, denoting similarity of cause.

asafoet'ida, *n.*, an extract from the *Ferula* and other strong-smelling bitter plants.

asbes'tic, *adj.*, *i.q.* asbestine.

asbes'tine, *adj.*, made of or rel. to asbestos.

asbes'tos, *n.*, a fireproof substance.

as'caris, *n.*, a round worm.

ascend', *v.t.* and *i.*, to go up, to mount.

ascend'able, *adj.*, able to be ascended.

ascen'dancy, *n.*, supremacy, superiority.

ascend'ant, *n.*, a state of upward advance; predominance.

ascend'ed, *p.p.*, ascend.

ascend'ency, *n.*, *i.q.* ascendancy.

ascend'ent, *adj.*, mounting upward.

ascend'er, *n.*, one who ascends.

ascend'ing, *pr.p.*, ascend.

ascen'sion, *n.*, the act of ascending.

ascen'sional, *adj.*, rel. to ascension.

Ascen'sion Day, *n.*, the day of Christ's ascent to heaven.

Ascen'siontide, *n.*, Ascension Day to Whitsunday.

ascen'sive, *adj.*, rising, progressive.

ascent', *n.*, a rising, climbing, a degree of acclivity.

ascertain', *v.t.*, to find out for certain.

ascertain'able, *adj.*, capable of being ascertained.

ascertained', *p.p.*, ascertain.

ascertain'er, *n.*, one who ascertains.

ascertain'ing, *pr.p.*, ascertain.

ascertain'ment, *n.*, the act of ascertaining.

asce'sis, *n.*, the practice of self-discipline.

ascet'ic, *adj.*, practising severe self-denial; *n.*, one who lives the ascetic life.

ascet'icism, *n.*, the practice or life of an ascetic.

ascid'ium, *n.*, a mollusc with a leathery covering.

ascititious, *adj.*, additional, supplemental. Also adscititious.

ascor'bic, *adj.*, antiscorbutic.

As'cot, *n.*, a famous English racecourse in Berkshire.

ascrib'able, *adj.*, able to be ascribed.

ascribe', *v.t.*, to impute or attribute.

ascribed', *p.p.*, ascribe.

ascrib'ing, *pr.p.*, ascribe.

ascrip'tion, *n.*, the act of ascribing.

as'dic, *n.*, apparatus for detecting submarines (acronym of Allied Submarine Detection Investigation Committee).

ase'ity, *n.*, underived existence.

asep'sis, *n.*, the absence of putrefaction.

asep'tic, *adj.*, not decaying or putrefying.

asex'ual, *adj.*, sexless.

ash, *n.*, the tree so named; burnt remains.

ashamed', *adj.*, filled with shame.

ashamed'ness, *n.*, the state of feeling shame.

ash'en, *adj.*, bel. to or resembling the ash or ashes; pale.

ash'ery, *n.*, an ashbin.

Ash'es, (The), *n.*, a mock term applied in cricket

to the defeat of England by the Australians in 1882; the mythical trophy in any cricket series of games between Australia and England.

ash'es, *n. pl.*, the remains of a human body after cremation.

ash'et, *n.*, a big oval plate.

ash'-hole, *n.*, a hole where ashes are thrown.

ash'lar, *n.*, a hewn or squared stone.

ash'laring, *n.*, the wooden plaster-studs between the floor and the rafters of a garret; ashlar stonework.

ashore', *adv.*, on shore.

ash'-pan, *n.*, a pan for ashes.

ash'pit, *n.*, a pit where ashes are thrown.

Ash Wed'nesday, *n.*, the first day of Lent, when ashes are sprinkled on penitents' heads.

ash'y, *adj.*, pale, ash-like in colour.

A'sian, *adj.*, bel. to Asia; *n.*, a native of Asia.

Asian'ic, *adj.*, *i.q.* Asian.

Asiat'ic, *adj.*, *i.q.* Asian.

Asiat'icism, *n.*, an Asiatic peculiarity.

aside', *adv.*, on one side, apart; *n.*, a remark spoken aside.

as'inine, *adj.*, rel. to or resembling an ass.

asinin'ity, *n.*, stupid obstinacy.

asit'ia, *n.*, loss of appetite; lack of food.

ask, *v.t.*, to question, to beg.

askance', *adv.*, sideways; with a suspicious look.

askant', *adv.*, *i.q.* askance.

Askar'i(s), *n. pl.*, European-trained native soldiers of E. Africa.

asked, *p.p.*, ask.

askel'etal, *adj.*, having no skeleton.

askew', *adv.*, obliquely.

ask'ing, *pr.p.*, ask.

aslant', *adv.*, sloping, slanting.

asleep', *adv.*, in a state of sleep.

aslope', *adv.*, sloping.

Asmone'an, *adj.*, pert. to a great Jewish family.

aso'cial, *adj.*, not sociable.

aso'matous, *adj.*, without body.

asp, *n.*, a venomous snake.

aspar'agine, *adj.*, rel. to asparagus.

aspar'agus, *n.*, a vegetable esteemed as a delicacy.

as'pect, *n.*, sight, look, position, prospect.

as'pen, *adj.*, shivering; *n.*, a kind of poplar that shivers.

as'perate, *v.t.*, to make harsh or uneven.

as'perated, *p.p.*, asperate.

as'perating, *pr.p.*, asperate.

aspera'tion, *n.*, the act or state of harshness; making uneven.

asper'ges, *n.*, the sprinkling with holy water.

as'pergil, *n.*, *i.q.* aspergillum.

aspergil'lum, *n.*, the holy water sprinkler.

aspergil'lus, *n.*, a fungus.

asper'ity, *n.*, roughness, harshness.

asperm'ous, *adj.*, not seeding.

asperse', *v.t.*, to accuse injuriously, to slander.

aspersed', *p.p.*, asperse.

aspers'er, *n.*, one who asperses.

aspers'ing, *pr.p.*, asperse.

asper'sion, *n.*, a slander.

aspers'ive, *adj.*, slanderous.

aspers'ively, *adv.*, in a slanderous way.

asperso'rium, *n.*, a holy water vessel.

aspers'ory, *n.*, *i.q.* aspersorium.

as'phalt, *n.*, a species of pitch.

asphal'tic, *adj.*, rel. to asphalt.

asphal'tum, *n.*, the name of asphalt (*Lat.*).

as'phodel, *n.*, a plant; the "fabulous asphodel" of Hades in Greek poetry.

asphyx'ia, *n.*, suffocation, a temporary stoppage of breathing.

asphyx'iant, *adj.* and *n.*, causing asphyxia.

asphyx'iate, *v.t.*, to produce asphyxia.

asphyx'iated, *p.p.*, asphyxiate.

asphyx'iating, *pr.p.*, asphyxiate; *adj.*, causing asphyxia.

asphyxia'tion, *n.*, the act or state of suffocation.

asphyx'y, *n.*, *i.q.* asphyxia.

as'pic, *n.*, a savoury jelly.

aspidis'tra, *n.*, a plant of the asparagus group, usually grown indoors.

aspi'rant, *n.*, one who aspires.

as'pirate, *n.*, the sounded letter *h*.

as'pirate, *v.t.*, to pronounce with a heavy breath.

as'pirated, *p.p.*, aspirate.

as'pirating, *pr.p.*, aspirate.

aspira'tion, *n.*, the act of aspiring; a strong desire.

as'pirator, *n.*, an instrument for drawing in gas or air; also for drawing off fluid from abscesses, etc.

aspi'ratory, *adj.*, rel. to aspiration.

aspire', *v.i.*, to desire strongly, to strive after.

aspired', *p.p.*, aspire.

aspir'er, *n.*, one who aspires.

aspir'in, *n.*, a depressant drug.

as'piring, *pr.p.*, aspire; *adj.*, ambitious.

aspir'ingly, *adv.*, ambitiously.

asquint', *adv.*, with a squint.

ass, *n.*, an animal (sometimes domesticated as a beast of burden); a donkey.

as'sagai, *n.*, a Kaffir spear.

assa'i, *adv.*, a musical term = very (*It.*).

assail', *v.t.*, to attack.

assail'able, *adj.*, open to attack.

assail'ant, *n.*, one who attacks.

assailed', *p.p.*, assail.

assail'er, *n.*, *i.q.* assailant.

assail'ing, *pr.p.*, assail.

assas'sin, *n.*, a treacherous murderer.

assas'sinate, *v.t.,* to murder treacherously.

assas'sinated, *p.p.,* assassinate.

assas'sinating, *pr.p.,* assassinate.

assassina'tion, *n.,* the act of assassinating.

assas'sinator, *n., i.q.* assassin.

assault', *v.t.,* to attack with violence; *n.,* a hostile attack.

assault'ed, *p.p.,* assault.

assault'ing, *pr.p.,* assault.

assay', *v.t.,* to try, to test; *n.,* a trial, a test.

assay'able, *adj.,* able to be assayed.

assayed', *p.p.,* assay.

assay'er, *n.,* one who assays.

assay'ing, *pr.p.,* assay.

assem'blage, *n.,* a gathering together.

assem'ble, *v.t.* and *i.,* to call or gather together; to meet together.

assem'bled, *p.p.,* assemble.

assem'bler, *n.,* one who assembles.

assem'bling, *pr.p.,* assemble.

assem'bly, *n.,* a meeting together.

assent', *v.i.,* to agree to, to approve; *n.,* an agreement, an approval.

assenta'tion, *n.,* obsequious concurrence.

assent'ed, *p.p.,* assent.

assen'ter, *n.,* one who assents.

assen'tient, *adj.,* giving approval.

assent'ing, *pr.p.,* assent.

assert', *v.t.,* to affirm, to state positively.

assert'ed, *p.p.,* assert.

assert'ing, *pr.p.,* assert.

asser'tion, *n.,* a positive affirmation.

assert'ive, *adj.,* making strong affirmation.

assert'ively, *adv.,* in an assertive way.

assert'or, *n.,* one who asserts.

assert'ory, *adj.,* rel. to assertion; affirmative.

assess', *v.t.,* to fix a value.

assess'able, *adj.,* liable to assessment.

assessed', *p.p.,* assess.

assess'ing, *pr.p.,* assess.

assess'ment, *n.,* valuation for rating or taxing purposes.

assess'or, *n.,* one who assesses.

as'sets, *n. pl.,* property owned; items to be set against liabilities.

assev'erate, *v.i.,* to assert strongly.

assev'erated, *p.p.,* asseverate.

assev'erating, *pr.p.,* asseverate.

asservera'tion, *n.,* a strong assertion.

assib'ilate, *v.t.,* to hiss.

assibila'tion, *n.,* a hissing sound.

as'sident, *adj.,* usually present with; in constant attendance on.

assidu'ity, *n.,* steady diligence.

assid'uous, *adj.,* steadily diligent.

assid'uously, *adv.,* with untiring diligence.

assid'uousness, *n., i.q.* assiduity.

assign', *v.t.,* to allot, to make over to.

assign'able, *adj.,* able to be assigned.

as'signat, *n.,* Government promissory note issued during the French Revolution.

assigna'tion, *n.,* an agreed (usually clandestine) meeting.

assigned', *p.p.,* assign.

assignee', *n.,* one to whom something is assigned.

assign'er, *n.,* one who assigns. Also *assignor.*

assign'ing, *pr.p.,* assign.

assign'ment, *n.,* a deed of transfer, the act of assigning.

assignor', *n., i.q.,* assigner.

assigns', *n. pl.,* persons to whom property is transferred.

assim'ilable, *adj.,* able to be assimilated.

assim'ilate, *v.t.,* to make like; to absorb.

assim'ilated, *p.p.,* assimilate.

assim'ilating, *pr.p.,* assimilate.

assimila'tion, *n.,* the act of assimilating.

assim'ilative, *adj.,* capable of assimilating.

assim'ilatory, *adj.,* tending to assimilation.

assist', *v.t.* and *i.,* to help; to be present at a ceremony.

assist'ance, *n.,* help, aid; presence at a ceremony.

assist'ant, *n.,* one who assists, a helper.

assist'ed, *p.p.,* assist.

assist'ing, *pr.p.,* assist.

assize', *n.,* a court of justice, with judge and jury; *v.t.,* to fix price, weight and measure by authority.

assized', *p.p.,* assize.

assize'ment, *n.,* the act of assizing.

assiz'er, *n.,* one who assizes; one of a grand jury. Also *assizor.*

assiz'es, *n.,* pl. of assize.

assiz'ing, *pr.p.,* assize.

assiz'or, *n., i.q.* assizer.

associabil'ity, *n.,* the character of being associable.

asso'ciable, *adj.,* capable of being associated.

asso'ciate, *adj.,* connected; *n.,* one who is associated; *v.t.* and *i.,* to join to oneself, or to be in company with.

asso'ciated, *p.p.,* associate.

asso'ciateship, *n.,* the state of being an associate.

asso'ciating, *pr.p.,* associate.

associa'tion, *n.,* the act of joining; a body of associated members.

associa'tional, *adj.,* rel. to an association.

asso'ciative, *adj.,* tending to an association.

assoii', *v.t.,* to pardon (*arch.*).

assoil'zie, *v.t., i.q.* assoil (*Scot.*).

as'sonance, *n.,* the correspondence in sounds —consonants or vowels; any sort of correspondence.

as'sonant, *adj.,* making assonance.

assort', *v.t.,* to arrange in kinds, to classify; *v.i.,* to agree, to fall in with.

assort'ed, *p.p.,* assort.

assort'er, *n.,* one who assorts.

assort'ing, *pr.p.,* assort.

assort'ment, *n.,* a variety; a mixture.

assuage', *v.t.* and *i.*, to abate; to subside; to satisfy.

assuaged', *p.p.*, assuage.

assuage'ment, *n.*, the act of allaying.

assuag'er, *n.*, one who assuages.

assuag'ing, *pr.p.*, assuage.

assua'sive, *adj.*, tending to assuage.

assume', *v.t.*, to take upon oneself; to accept without proof.

assumed', *p.p.*, assume.

assum'er, *n.*, one who assumes.

assum'ing, *pr.p.*, assume.

assum'ingly, *adv.*, in an assuming way.

assump'sit, *n.*, an unsealed agreement; an action at law rel. to such an agreement.

assump'tion, *n.*, the act of assuming; the taking for granted.

assump'tive, *adj.*, inclined to assume.

assump'tively, *adv.*, in an assumptive way.

assur'ance, *n.*, confidence; excessive confidence; a confident statement; a life-security.

assure', *v.t.*, to make secure; to affirm with certainty; to take out a policy on.

assured', *p.p.*, assure.

assur'edly, *adv.*, certainly, without doubt.

assur'edness, *n.*, a confident state of mind.

assur'er, *n.*, one who assures.

assur'gent, *adj.*, rising obliquely; aggressive.

assur'ing, *pr.p.*, assure; *adj.*, confidence-inspiring.

assur'ingly, *adv.*, in an assuring way.

Assyr'ian, *adj.*, rel. to Assyria; *n.*, a native of A.

Assyriol'ogy, *n.*, a study of the language and history of Assyria.

Astar'te, *n.*, the Syro-Phoenician moon-goddess, also known as Ashtoreth.

astat'ic, *adj.*, in equilibrium; not tending to move in either direction.

as'ter, *n.*, a plant with star-shaped flora.

aste'ria, *n.*, a sapphire cut star-wise.

aste'riated, *adj.*, radiating like a star.

as'terid, *n.*, a starfish.

as'terisk, *n.*, a star-shaped mark of reference.

as'terism, *n.*, a cluster of stars; three asterisks marking a passage in a book.

astern', *adv.*, on the stern, i.e., to the rear of a vessel.

as'teroid, *adj.*, star-like; like an aster.

asteroid'al, *adj.*, *i.q.* asteroid.

asthen'ia, *n.*, the loss of power.

asthen'ic, *adj.*, suffering from the loss of power.

asthenol'ogy, *n.*, the study of asthenia.

asth'ma, *n.*, a disease in which the patient breathes with difficulty.

asthmat'ic, *adj.*, suffering from asthma; rel. to asthma.

asthmat'ical, *adj.*, *i.q.* asthmatic.

astigmat'ic, *adj.*, rel. to astigmatism.

astig'matism, *n.*, a focal disorder of the sight.

Astil'be, *n.*, a genus of herbaceous perennial plant having feathery plumes of flowers.

astir', *adv.*, on the move.

aston'ied, *adj.*, dismayed, astounded (*obs.*).

aston'ish, *v.t.*, to fill with amazement, to cause excessive surprise.

aston'ished, *p.p.*, astonish.

aston'ishing, *pr.p.*, astonish.

aston'ishingly, *adv.*, surprisingly, amazingly.

aston'ishment, *n.*, surprise, amazement.

astound', *v.t.*, to amaze.

astound'ed, *p.p.*, astound.

astound'ing, *pr.p.*, astound.

astrad'dle, *adv.*, in straddling fashion.

as'tragal, *n.*, a convex moulding (*archit.*).

astrakhan', *n.*, the skin of Astrakhan lamb, with woolly fur.

as'tral, *adj.*, rel. to the stars; starry.

astray', *adv.*, off the right path.

astrict', *v.t.*, to bind; to limit.

astrict'ed, *p.p.*, astrict.

astrict'ing, *pr.p.*, astrict.

astric'tion, *n.*, the act or state of astricting.

astric'tive, *adj.*, with power to astrict.

astric'tively, *adv.*, in a limited way.

astride', *adv.* and *prep.*, with one foot only on either side of something.

astringe', *v.t.*, to bind together; to compress.

astrin'gency, *n.*, the quality of binding.

astrin'gent, *adj.*, binding, contracting; *n.*, a binding medicine.

as'trodome, *n.*, a dome window in an aircraft.

astrograph'ic, *adj.*, rel. to astrography.

astrog'raphy, *n.*, star-mapping.

as'troid, *n.*, a star exceeding 5 points magnitude.

as'troite, *n.*, an ancient name for the sapphire.

as'trolabe, *n.*, an apparatus for finding the altitude of stars.

astrol'oger, *n.*, one who professes astrology.

astrolog'ic, *adj.*, rel. to astrology.

astrolog'ical, *adj.*, *i.q.* astrologic.

astrol'ogize, *v.i.*, to profess astrology.

astrol'ogy, *n.*, the pretended art of foretelling the future by the stars.

as'tronaut, *n.*, one engaged in space travel; a spaceman.

astronaut'ical, *adj.*, rel. to space travel.

astronaut'ics, *n.*, the science of interplanetary travel.

astron'omer, *n.*, one who practises astronomy.

astronom'ic, *adj.*, rel. to astronomy.

astronom'ical, *adj.*, *i.q.* astronomic.

astron'omy, *n.*, the science of the heavenly bodies.

astrophotog'raphy, *n.*, the use of photography in astronomy.

astrophys'ics, *n.*, the science of the properties of the sun, moon, planets, etc.

as'troscope, *n.*, a celestial globe; a celestial telescope.

astrut', *adv.*, in strutting fashion.

astute', *adj.*, shrewd, cunning.

astute'ly, *adv.*, shrewdly, cunningly.

astute'ness, *n.*, shrewdness, cunning.

asun'der, *adv.*, apart, in separate pieces.

a-swirl', *adv.*, in a swirl.

asy'lum, *n.*, any place of refuge; a shelter for poor or afflicted persons; a mental home.

asymmet'ric, *adj.*, lacking symmetry.

asymmet'rical, *adj.*, *i.q.* asymmetric.

asym'metry, *n.*, want of symmetry or proportion.

as'ymptote, *n.*, a straight line which an ever-approaching curve never reaches.

asynch'ronism, *n.*, a lack of coincidence in time.

asyntac'tic, *adj.*, ungrammatical.

at, *prep.*, denoting station or position.

at'abal, *n.*, a Moorish name for a kettledrum.

at'avism, *n.*, a reversion to ancestral type.

atax'ia, *n.*, disorder, loss of muscular control.

atax'ic, *adj.*, characterized by ataxia.

A'tē, *n.*, the Greek goddess of mischief; retribution (*Gr.*).

ate, *p.p.*, eat.

ateleio'sis, atelio'sis, *n.*, arrested development.

atelier', *n.*, a work-shop studio (*Fr.*).

athal'amous, *adj.*, without thalami.

Athana'sian, *adj.*, bel. to Athanasius.

a'theism, *n.*, the denial of God's existence.

a'theist, *n.*, a professor of atheism.

atheist'ic, *adj.*, rel. to atheists and atheism.

atheist'ical, *adj.*, *i.q.* atheistic.

ath'eling, *adj.*, of princely family (*obs.*).

athenae'um, *n.*, orig. the temple of Athene; now any institution for the promotion of culture.

Athen'e, *n.*, the Greek goddess of wisdom.

Athe'nian, *adj.*, bel. to Athens; *n.*, a native of A.

atherm'ic, *adj.*, impervious to heat.

atheto'sis, *n.*, involuntary movement of the limbs.

athirst', *adj.*, in a thirsty state.

ath'lete, *n.*, one trained and skilled in physical accomplishment.

athlet'ic, *adj.*, strong, exercised; rel. to athletes.

athlet'ics, *n. pl.*, games and exercises for athletes.

at home, *adv.*, phrase = in one's own house; familiar with; *n.*, a reception; a party.

athwart', *adv.* and *prep.*, across.

ati'choo, *n.*, a representation of the sound of a sneeze.

atilt', *adv.*, in tilting fashion.

Atlante'an, *adj.*, rel. to Atlas.

atlan'tes, *n. pl.*, figures of men supporting, like caryatids, a super-structure (*archit.*).

Atlan'tic, *adj.* and *n.*, the name of the ocean between Europe, Africa and America.

Atlan'tis, *n.*, the traditional lost island of the Atlantic.

atlan'tosaur'us, *n.*, kinds of gigantic fossil reptile.

At'las, at'las, *n.*, a mountain in Africa; the mythological giant who bore the world on his shoulders; a book of maps.

atmol'ogy, *n.*, the study of vapour.

atmom'eter, *n.*, a vapour-measuring instrument.

at'mosphere, *n.*, the earth's air-envelope.

atmospher'ic, *adj.*, rel. to the atmosphere.

atmospher'ical, *adj.*, *i.q.* atmospheric.

atmosphe'rics, *n. pl.*, electrical disturbances on transmission and reception of sound waves.

ato'cia, *n.*, sterility in a female.

atoll', *n.*, a ring-shaped coral island, with a lagoon inside it.

at'om, *n.*, a particle of matter; any very small thing.

atom'ic, *adj.*, rel. to atoms.

atom'ical, *adj.*, *i.q.* atomic.

at'omism, *n.*, the atomic theory; a belief in that theory.

at'omist, *n.*, one who holds with atomism.

atomiza'tion, *n.*, conversion into fine spray.

at'omize, *v.t.*, to reduce to atoms; to convert into spray.

at'omizer, *n.*, an instrument for converting liquids into fine spray.

atomol'ogy, *n.*, the study of atoms.

at'omy, *n.*, a skeleton; an emaciated body; an atom; a tiny being.

aton'able, *adj.*, able to be atoned for.

aton'al, *adj.*, not in any key (*mus.*).

atone', *v.i.*, to make amends; to reconcile.

atoned', *p.p.*, atone.

atone'ment, *n.*, satisfaction, reconciliation.

aton'er, *n.*, one who atones.

aton'ic, *adj.*, wanting tone; unaccented.

aton'ing, *pr.p.*, atone.

at'ony, *n.*, want of tone.

atop', *adv.*, on the top.

atrabila'rian, *adj.*, *i.q.* atrabilious.

atrabil'ious, *adj.*, suffering from black bile, depressed, melancholy.

atramenta'ceous, *adj.*, inky.

atrament'al, *adj.*, rel. to ink.

atramenta'rious, *adj.*, *i.q.*, atramentaceous.

atrament'ous, *adj.*, *i.q.* atramentaceous.

atrip', *adv.*, trippingly.

a'trium, *n.*, the central hall of a house (*Lat.*).

atro'cious, *adj.*, savage, brutal, heinous.

atro'ciously, *adv.*, savagely, brutally.

atro'ciousness, *n.*, savage character.

atroc'ity, *n.*, a brutal act; brutality.

at'rophied, *adj.*, wasting through lack of nourishment.

at'rophy, *n.*, a wasting away; *v.t.*, to cause

wasting; *v.i.*, to waste away.

at'ropine, *n.*, an alkaloid contained in deadly nightshade.

ATS, *n.*, women of the Auxiliary Territorial Service (now Women's Royal Army Corps).

att'aboy, an exclamation of encouragement or admiration (*interj.*).

attach', *v.t.*, to bind, to fasten; to seize under warrant.

attach'able, *adj.*, able to be attached.

atta'ché, *n.*, one attached to a legation (*Fr.*).

atta'ché-case, *n.*, a carrying case for papers, etc.

attached', *p.p.*, attach.

attach'ing, *pr.p.*, attach.

attach'ment, *n.*, a fastening; a close tie of affection; legal seizure.

attack', *v.t.*, to assault; *n.*, an assault.

attack'able, *adj.*, liable to attack.

attacked', *p.p.*, attack.

attack'er, *n.*, one who attacks.

attack'ing, *pr.p.*, attack.

attain', *v.t.* and *i.*, to reach, to arrive at.

attainabil'ity, *n.*, the being able to be attained.

attain'able, *adj.*, able to be attained.

attain'ableness, *n.*, *i.q.* attainability.

attaind'er, *n.*, the forfeiture of civil rights.

attained', *p.p.*, attain.

attain'ing, *pr.p.*, attain.

attain'ment, *n.*, the act of attaining, something attained; an intellectual gift.

attaint', *n.*, the act of attainting; *v.t.*, to impose attainder upon.

attaint'ed, *p.p.*, attaint.

attaint'ing, *pr.p.*, attaint.

attaint'ment, *n.*, the act of attainting.

attaint'ure, *n.*, a dishonouring imputation; attainder.

at'tar, *n.*, the Oriental word for perfume made from flowers.

attem'per, *v.t.*, to modify, to adapt.

attem'pered, *p.p.*, attemper.

attem'pering, *pr.p.*, attemper.

attempt', *n.*, an endeavour; *v.t.* and *i.*, to try, to endeavour.

attempt'able, *adj.*, able to be attempted.

attempt'ed, *p.p.*, attempt.

attempt'er, *n.*, one who attempts.

attempt'ing, *pr.p.*, attempt.

attend', *v.i.* and *t.*, to wait on, to wait for; to be present; to pay attention to.

attend'ance, *n.*, the act of attending; persons present.

attend'ant, *n.*, one who is present to look after persons or things.

attend'ed, *p.p.*, attend.

attend'ing, *pr.p.*, attend.

attent', *n.*, attention.

atten'tion, *n.*, the giving of heed.

atten'tive, *adj.*, giving heed.

atten'tively, *adv.*, with attention.

atten'tiveness, *n.*, the character of being attentive.

atten'uant, *adj.*, making thin.

atten'uate, *v.t.*, to make thin.

atten'uated, *p.p.*, attenuate.

atten'uating, *pr.p.*, attenuate.

attenua'tion, *n.*, the act of making thin; thinness.

attest', *v.t.*, to bear witness to.

attesta'tion, *n.*, the act of attesting.

attest'ed, *p.p.*, attest.

attest'er, attest'or, *n.*, one who attests.

attest'ing, *pr.p.*, attest.

At'tic, *adj.*, bel. to Attica in Greece.

at'tic, *n.*, a room in the roof of a house; a low storey above the entablature.

At'ticism, *n.*, the usage of Attica or the Athenians.

At'ticize, *v.t.* and *i.*, to make Attic, to become Attic.

At'ticized, *p.p.*, atticize.

At'ticizing, *pr.p.*, atticize.

attire', *n.*, dress, clothes; *v.t.*, to dress, to array.

attired', *p.p.*, attire.

attir'er, *n.*, one who attires.

attir'ing, *pr.p.*, attire.

at'titude, *n.*, posture; a state of mind.

attitu'dinal, *adj.*, rel. to attitude.

attitu'dinize, *v.i.*, to posture, to assume false airs.

attitu'dinized, *p.p.*, attitudinize.

attitu'dinizing, *pr.p.*, attitudinize.

attol'lent, *adj.*, elevating.

attorn', *v.t.* and *i.*, to transfer; to make a legal acknowledgement of a new landlord (*leg.*).

attor'ney, *n.*, the legal agent for another.

Attor'ney-Gen'eral, *n.*, the highest legal adviser of the Crown.

attor'neyship, *n.*, the office or function of an attorney.

attract', *v.t.*, to draw, to allure, to charm.

attractabil'ity, *n.*, the state of being subject to attraction.

attract'able, *adj.*, subject to attraction.

attract'ed, *p.p.*, attract.

attract'ing, *pr.p.*, attract.

attract'ingly, *adv.*, in an attracting way.

attrac'tion, *n.*, the act of attracting; charm; the unseen force in nature drawing particles to each other.

attract'ive, *adj.*, able to attract; charming.

attract'ively, *adv.*, charmingly.

attract'iveness, *n.*, a power to charm.

at'trahent, *adj.*, drawing to.

attrib'utable, *adj.*, able to be attributed.

at'tribute, *n.*, something attributed; a quality or property.

attrib'ute, *v.t.*, to impute, to ascribe.

attrib'uted, *p.p.*, attribute.

attrib'uting, *pr.p.*, attribute.

attribu'tion, *n.*, the act of attributing.

attrib′utive, *adj.*, rel. to an attribute; expressing an attribute; assigned to; *n.*, an adjective.

attrib′utively, *adv.*, as an attribute.

attrite′, *adj.*, worn down.

attri′tion, *n.*, wearing down by rubbing.

attui′tion, *n.*, animal consciousness (*psych.*).

attune′, *v.t.*, to make in tune.

attuned′, *p.p.*, attune.

attun′ing, *pr.p.*, attune.

atyp′ical, *adj.*, acquired by specialization; not according to type.

aubade, *n.*, opposite to serenade; a sunrise song.

auberge′, *n.*, an inn (*Fr.*).

aub′ergine, *n.*, the egg plant and its fruit.

aubin′, *n.*, a kind of canter (*Fr.*).

aubrie′tia, *n.*, a purple-flowered rock plant.

au′burn, *adj.*, reddish brown in colour.

au courant, *pred. adj.*, well-informed (*Fr.*).

auc′tion, *n.*, a public sale, where the prices are raised by the bidders; a variety of the card game, bridge.

auc′tioneer′, *n.*, one who sells by auction.

auctioneer′ing, *adj.*, rel. to auctioneers; *n.*, an auctioneer's profession.

auctor′ial, *adj.*, rel. to an author or his works.

auda′cious, *adj.*, bold, daring, impudent.

auda′ciously, *adv.*, daringly, impudently.

auda′ciousness, *n.*, impudence.

audac′ity, *n.*, daring, impudence.

audibil′ity, *n.*, ability to be heard.

au′dible, *adj.*, able to be heard.

au′dibleness, *n.*, *i.q.* audibility.

au′dibly, *adv.*, in a way that can be heard.

au′dience, *n.*, a hearing; collected hearers.

au′dile, *adj.*, rel. to hearing; *n.*, one who remembers mainly through sound.

au′dio-, *adj.*, using transmitted sound; *prefix*, rel. to sound.

aud′io-fre′quency, *n.*, frequency comparable to that of sound.

audiom′eter, *n.*, an apparatus for testing the power of hearing.

au′diophil(e), *n.*, an enthusiast for true sound reproduction.

aud′io-typist, *n.*, one who types from sound.

aud′io-vis′ual, *adj.*, having simultaneous appearance and sound.

au′diphone, *n.*, an instrument for conveying sound through the teeth.

au′dit, *n.*, an inspection of accounts; *v.t.*, to hold an examination of accounts.

au′dited, *p.p.*, audit.

au′diting, *pr.p.*, audit.

audi′tion, *n.*, the sense of hearing; the judging of a performance for suitability.

aud′itive, *adj.*, concerned with hearing.

au′ditize, *v.t.*, to represent in sounds.

au′ditor, *n.*, a hearer; one who conducts an audit.

auditor′ial, *adj.*, connected with an audit.

audito′rium, *n.*, the part of a building occupied by the audience.

au′ditory, *n.*, a body of hearers; an auditorium.

au fait, adjectival phrase = versed in; instructed (*Fr.*).

au fond, *adv.*, at the bottom (*Fr.*).

Auge′an, *adj.*, rel. to Augeas, a mythical king whose stables Hercules cleansed.

au′ger, *n.*, a boring instrument.

au′get, *n.*, a priming-tube so named.

aught, *n.*, anything.

au′gite, *n.*, another name for pyroxene.

aug′ment, *n.*, the addition to, or lengthening of, an initial syllable.

augment′, *v.t.*, to increase, to make larger.

augment′able, *adj.*, able to be augmented.

augmenta′tion, *n.*, the act of augmenting; an increase.

augment′ative, *adj.*, tending to increase.

augment′ed, *p.p.*, augment.

augment′er, *n.*, one who augments.

augment′ing, *pr.p.*, augment.

au′gur, *n.*, a Roman soothsayer who divined by the flight of birds; *v.t.* and *i.*, to practise augury; to foretell.

au′gural, *adj.*, rel. to augury.

au′gured, *p.p.*, augur.

au′guring, *pr.p.*, augur.

au′gurship, *n.*, the office of an augur.

au′gury, *n.*, the art of an augur; an omen.

Au′gust, *n.*, the 8th month of the year, named from the Emperor Augustus.

august′, *adj.*, grand, venerable.

Augus′tan, *adj.*, rel. to the period of Augustus.

Augus′tine, *n.*, the saintly bishop of Hippo; also his later namesake, the Apostle of the English.

Augustin′ian, *adj.* and *n.*, (of) one who follows the rule of the Order named after St. Augustine.

august′ly, *adv.*, in an august manner.

august′ness, *n.*, stateliness, majesty.

auk, *n.*, an aquatic bird.

aula′rian, *adj.*, rel. to a hall.

au′lic, *adj.*, rel. to a court, as the Aulic Council.

aum′bry, *n.*, *i.q.* ambry.

au naturel, *adv.* or *pred. adj.*, (cooked) in the simplest way (*Fr.*).

aunt, *n.*, a female relative (a mother's or father's sister).

aunt′ie, *n.*, the childish name for aunt.

au pair, *adj.*, paid for by mutual services; *n.*, a person acting in this capacity (*Fr.*).

au′ra, *n.*, a breeze, an air, a subtle emanation.

au′ral, *adj.*, rel. to the ear.

au′rally, *adv.*, through the ear.

au′rated, *adj.*, eared.

au′reate, *adj.*, golden, gilded.

aure′lia, *n.*, a chrysalis.

aure'lian, *adj.,* in the chrysalis state.

aure'ola, *n.,* a halo; the sun's corona.

au'reole, *n.,* a halo or circlet of light.

au revoir, *adv.,* (goodbye) till we meet again (*Fr.*).

au'ric, *adj.,* containing gold.

au'ricle, *n.,* the projecting body of an ear; one of the heart's cavities.

au'ricled, *adj.,* having auricles.

auric'ula, *adj.,* earshaped; like an auricle; *n.,* the Alpine primrose; a little appendage.

auric'ular, *adj.,* rel. to the ear or hearing.

auric'ularly, *adv.,* privately.

auric'ulate, *adj.,* having auricles.

auric'ulated, *adj.,* *i.q.* auriculate.

aurif'erous, *adj.,* gold-producing.

au'riform, *adj.,* ear-shaped.

au'rify, *v.t.* and *i.,* to turn into gold.

Auri'ga, *n.,* a Northern constellation, the Waggoner.

aurig'raphy, *n.,* gold-engraving.

aur'ilave, *n.,* an instrument for cleaning ears.

au'rist, *n.,* one who treats ear complaints.

au'rochs, *n.,* the bison or wild ox of Europe.

auro'ra, *n.,* the dawn.

auro'ra borea'lis, *n.,* the northern lights.

auro'ral, *adj.,* rel. to the dawn.

aur'ous, *adj.,* containing gold.

au'rum, *n.,* gold (*Lat.*).

ausculta'tion, *n.,* hearing through a stethoscope.

auscult'ative, *adj.,* *i.q.* auscultatory.

aus'cultator, *n.,* one who examines a patient with a stethoscope.

auscul'tatory, *adj.,* rel. to auscultation.

au'spicate, *v.t.,* to invoke good luck on.

au'spicated, *p.p.,* auspicate.

au'spicating, *pr.p.,* auspicate.

au'spice, *n.,* an omen.

au'spices, *n. pl.,* influence, protection.

auspi'cious, *adj.,* lucky, of good omen.

auspi'ciously, *adv.,* luckily, with good omen.

auspi'ciousness, *n.,* a state of good omen.

Auss'ie, *n.,* an. Australian (*slang*).

austere', *adj.,* severe, stern, harsh.

austere'ly, *adv.,* severely, sternly, harshly.

auster'ity, *n.,* severity, sternness, harshness.

aus'tral, *adj.,* southern.

Australa'sian, *adj.,* rel. to Australasia.

Austra'lian, *adj.,* rel. to Australia; *n.,* a native of A.

Austra'lianism, *n.,* a phrase, etc., characteristic of Australia.

Aus'trian, *adj.,* pert. to Austria and the Austrians; *n.,* a native of A.

aus'tromancy, *n.,* divination by means of the wind.

aut'archy, *n.,* absolute sovereignty.

aut'arky, *n.,* self-sufficiency.

authen'tic, *adj.,* true, real, actual.

authen'tical, *adj.,* *i.q.* authentic.

authen'ticate, *v.t.,* to verify, to prove real.

authen'ticated, *p.p.,* authenticate.

authen'ticating, *pr.p.,* authenticate.

authentica'tion, *n.,* the act of authenticating.

authentic'ity, *n.,* truth, reality.

authigen'ic, *adj.,* originating where found.

au'thor, *n.,* a beginner, a creator, a writer.

au'thoress, *n.,* the fem. of author.

authoritar'ian, *adj.* and *n.,* favouring obedience to authority.

authoritar'ianism, *n.,* authoritarian principles.

author'itative, *adj.,* having authority.

author'itatively, *adv.,* as having authority.

author'itativeness, *n.,* having authority.

author'ity, *n.,* power, right; a recognized expert; *n. pl.,* the powers that be.

au'thorizable, *adj.,* able to be authorized.

authoriza'tion, *n.,* the granting of authority.

au'thorize, *v.t.,* to give authority to.

au'thorized, *p.p.,* authorize.

au'thorizing, *pr.p.,* authorize.

au'thorship, *n.,* the writing of anything.

aut'ism, *n.,* morbid šelf-admiration (*psych.*).

aut'o, *n.,* abbrev. of automobile; *pref.,* of one's self or of itself.

aut'obahn, *n.,* a German motorway.

autobiog'rapher, *n.,* one who writes his own biography.

autobiograph'ic, *adj.,* rel. to autobiography.

autobiograph'ical, *adj.,* *i.q.* autobiographic.

autobiog'raphist, *n.,* *i.q.* autobiographer.

autobiog'raphy, *n.,* a biography of oneself by oneself.

aut'obus, *n.,* a motorbus.

aut'ocar, *n.,* an automobile vehicle.

autoceph'alous, *adj.,* having its own head; independent.

autoch'thon, *n.,* a native of the soil.

autoch'thonous, *adj.,* native, indigenous.

autocop'yist, *n.,* an apparatus for producing facsimiles.

autoc'racy, *n.,* government by an absolute monarch.

au'tocrat, *n.,* one who rules absolutely.

autocrat'ic, *adj.,* ruling absolutely.

autocrat'ical, *adj.,* *i.q.* autocratic.

autocrit'ical, *adj.,* self-critical.

aut'ocycle, *n.,* a motor-propelled cycle.

au'to-da-fé, *n.,* phrase = an act of faith (*Span.*).

autodiagno'sis, *n.,* the diagnosis of one's own disease.

autodidac'tic, *adj.,* self-teaching.

autoerot'ic, *adj.,* sexually self-gratifying.

autogen'esis, *n.,* self-generation.

autog'enous, *adj.,* self-producing.

autog'eny, *n.,* spontaneous generation.

autogir'o, *n.,* a flying machine with overhead rotating blades. Also *Autogyro.*

au'tograph, *n.,* writing in one's own hand.

autograph'ic, *adj.*, written in one's own hand.

autograph'ical, *adj.*, *i.q.* autographic.

autog'raphy, *n.*, writing in one's own hand.

autogravure', *n.*, a process of photocopying.

autogyr'o, *n.*, *i.q.* autogiro.

aut'oharp, *n.*, a type of mechanical zither.

auto'latry, *n.*, self-worship.

autol'ogy, *n.*, the scientific study of self.

autol'ysis, *n.*, the self-destruction of the body's cells.

aut'omat, *n.*, a café or restaurant where meals are provided in slot-machines.

autom'ata, *n.*, pl. of automaton.

aut'omate, *v.t.*, to apply automation.

automa'ted, *p.p.*, automate.

au'tomath, *n.*, a self-taught person.

automat'ic, *adj.*, self-moving, self-acting.

automat'ical, *adj.*, *i.q.* automatic.

automat'ically, *adv.*, mechanically.

automati'city, *n.*, the working of itself.

automa'ting, *pr.p.*, automate.

automa'tion, *n.*, automatic mechanical handling.

autom'atism, *n.*, the principle of self-action.

automat'ograph, *n.*, a scientific form of planchette.

autom'aton, *n.*, a self-moving, self-acting instrument.

automobile', *adj.*, self-moving; *n.*, a wheeled vehicle having its own motive power.

automot'ive, *adj.*, self-propelled.

au'tomotor, *n.*, a self-moving engine.

autonom'ic, *adj.*, *i.q.* autonomous.

auton'omism, *n.*, *i.q.* autonomy.

autonomist'ic, *adj.*, *i.q.* autonomous.

auton'omize, *v.t.*, to make autonomous.

auton'omous, *adj.*, obeying one's own laws, self-governing.

auton'omy, *n.*, self-government, independence.

aut'onym, *n.*, a real name, not a pseudonym.

autopian'o, *n.*, a piano with automatic playing apparatus.

auto-port'rait, *n.*, a self-portrait.

autop'sia, *n.*, *i.q.* autopsy.

autop'sy, *n.*, a personal examination (usu. of a dead body); a post-mortem examination.

autostrada, *n.*, an Italian arterial road.

auto-sugges'tion, *n.*, a subconscious suggestion.

autotox'in, *n.*, a poisonous substance produced by changes within the organism.

au'totype, *n.*, a facsimile; a photographic print in monochrome in a carbon pigment.

aut'ovac, *n.*, an apparatus supplying petrol to a carburettor.

aut'o-wheel, *n.*, a small motor attachable to the back wheel of a bicycle.

au'tumn, *n.*, the third of the seasons.

autum'nal, *adj.*, of the autumn.

auxanom'eter, *n.*, an instrument for measuring plant-growth.

auxil'iaries, *n. pl.*, assistant troops, not forming part of the regular forces.

auxil'iary, *adj.*, helping; *n.*, a helper.

aux'in, *n.*, a growth hormone.

auxom'eter, *n.*, an instrument for measuring magnification.

avail', *v.i.*, to profit, to be of use, to serve a purpose.

availabil'ity, *n.*, the ability to be used.

avail'able, *adj.*, able to be used.

avail'ableness, *n.*, *i.q.* availability.

availed, *p.p.*, avail.

avail'ing, *pr.p.*, avail.

av'alanche, *n.*, a sudden slide of snow and ice in mountainous regions, often with catastrophic consequences.

avant-courier, *n.*, one who goes before; an advance-guard (*Fr.*).

avant-garde, *n.*, the pioneers in any art in a particular period (*Fr.*).

av'arice, *n.*, greed for gain.

avari'cious, *adj.*, greedy for gain.

avari'ciously, *adv.*, greedily.

avari'ciousness, *n.*, insatiable greediness.

avast', *interj.*, = stop! (*naut.*).

avatar', *n.*, a descent; an incarnation.

avaunt', *interj.* = stand! keep off!

a've, an exclamation = Hail! *n.*, the act of devotion so named.

A've Mari'a, phrase = Hail Mary! the salutation to the Virgin Mary.

avenge', *v.t.*, to exact satisfaction for a wrong.

avenged', *p.p.*, avenge.

aveng'er, *n.*, one who avenges.

aveng'ing, *pr.p.*, avenge.

av'ens, *n.*, a plant of the genus *Rosaceae*.

av'entail, *n.*, an air hole, a ventail.

aven'turine, *n.*, a brownish glass with copper crystals.

av'enue, *n.*, an approach or passage, esp. through trees.

aver', *v.t.*, to state firmly.

av'erage, *adj.*, conforming to a general estimate; *n.*, a mean or middle; a general estimate; *v.t.* and *i.*, to get or conform to a general estimate.

av'eraged, *p.p.*, average.

av'eraging, *pr.p.*, average.

aver'ment, *n.*, a positive statement.

averred', *p.p.*, aver.

averr'ing, *pr.p.*, aver.

averruncat'or, *n.*, an instrument for cutting off very high branches of trees.

averse', *adj.*, turned away from; disinclined, unfavourable to.

averse'ly, *adv.*, disapprovingly.

aver'sion, *n.*, a strong dislike.

avert', *v.t.*, to turn aside; to ward off.

avert'ed, *p.p.*, avert.

avert'er, *n.*, one who averts.

avert'ible, *adj.*, able to be averted.

avert'ing, *pr.p.*, avert.

av'ian, *adj.*, pertaining to birds.

av'iarist, *n.*, one who keeps an aviary.

a'viary, *n.*, a collection of birds; a large cage.

av'iate, *v.i.*, to fly in an aircraft.

avia'tion, *n.*, the art and science of aerial flight.

a'viator, *n.*, one who practises aviation.

a'viculture, *n.*, bird-rearing; bird-fancying.

av'id, *adj.*, greedy, very desirous.

avid'ious, *adj.*, *i.q.* avid.

avid'ity, *n.*, greediness, eagerness.

av'idly, *adv.*, greedily, with avidity.

aviette', *n.*, an engineless aircraft; a glider.

av'ifauna, *n.*, birds of a district or country collectively.

a'vion, *n.*, the earliest type of heavier-than-air machine (*Fr.*).

avionics, *n. pl.*, the science of electronic and technical apparatus for use in aircraft.

avi'so, *n.*, a boat for carrying dispatches.

avoca'do, *n.*, a pear-shaped tropical fruit.

avoca'tion, *n.*, a calling, a vocation, chosen employment.

avoc'ative, *adj.*, calling one aside.

av'ocet, *n.*, a wader-bird so named; also a humming-bird.

avoid', *v.t.*, to get away from, to escape.

avoid'able, *adj.*, that can be avoided.

avoid'ably, *adv.*, in an avoidable way.

avoid'ance, *n.*, the act of avoiding.

avoid'ed, *p.p.*, avoid.

avoid'er, *n.*, one who avoids.

avoid'ing, *pr.p.*, avoid.

avoirdupois', *adj.*, and *n.* a standard of weight, reckoning 16 oz. to the pound.

av'oset, *n.*, *i.q.* avocet.

avoset'ta, *n.*, *i.q.* avocet.

avouch', *v.i.*, to affirm strongly.

avouched', *p.p.*, avouch.

avouch'er, *n.*, one who avouches.

avouch'ing, *pr.p.*, avouch.

avouch'ment, *n.*, a strong affirmation.

avow', *v.t.*, to state openly, to confess.

avow'able, *adj.*, able to be avowed.

avow'al, *n.*, the act of avowing, an admission.

avowed', *p.p.*, avow.

avow'edly, *adv.*, admittedly, openly.

avowee', *n.*, a patron possessing an advowson.

avow'er, *n.*, one who avows.

avow'ing, *pr.p.*, avow.

avow'ry, *n.*, a law term for the acknowledgment of having taken the goods.

avulse', *v.t.*, to tear off.

avul'sion, *n.*, the act of rending.

avun'cular, *adj.*, rel. to an uncle.

await', *v.t.*, to wait for, to expect.

await'ed, *p.p.*, await.

await'ing, *pr.p.*, await.

awake', *v.t.* and *i.*, to rouse from sleep, to rise from sleep; *adj.*, not asleep, alert.

awaked', *p.p.*, awake.

awa'ken, *v.t.*, to rouse from sleep.

awa'kened, *p.p.*, awaken.

awa'kening, *pr.p.*, awaken; *n.*, the act or effect of becoming aware.

awa'king, *pr.p.*, awake.

award', *n.*, a final judgment; *v.t.*, to make over, to adjudge.

award'ed, *p.p.*, award.

award'er, *n.*, one who awards.

award'ing, *pr.p.*, award.

aware', *adj.*, knowing, on the look out.

aware'ness, *n.*, the condition of being aware.

awash', *adj.* and *adv.*, just covered by water.

away', *adv.*, at, or to, a distance off.

awe, *n.*, reverential fear; *v.t.*, to strike awe into.

awear'y, *adj.*, tired.

aweath'er, *adv.*, towards the windy side.

awed, *p.p.*, awe.

aweigh', *adv.*, in a position when the anchor just clears the bottom.

awe'less, *adj.*, without awe.

awe'some, *adj.*, *i.q.* awful.

awe'-struck, *adj.*, struck with awe.

aw'ful, *adj.*, producing awe, terrible.

aw'fully, *adv.*, terribly.

aw'fulness, *n.*, terrifying character.

awheel', *adv.*, on wheels.

awhile', *adv.*, for a time.

awhirl', *adv.*, in a whirling state.

aw'ing, *pr.p.*, awe.

awk'ward, *adj.*, clumsy, embarrassing.

awk'wardly, *adv.*, clumsily.

awk'wardness, *n.*, clumsiness, difficulty.

awl, *n.*, a cobbler's tool for piercing.

awn, *n.*, the beard of wheat.

awn'ing, *n.*, a cover for shelter.

awoke', *p.p.*, awake.

awry', *adv.*, twisted aside.

axe, *n.*, a tool for cutting timber.

axe'-head, *n.*, the iron head of an axe.

ax'ial, *adj.*, rel. to an axis.

axif'erous, *adj.*, bearing an axis.

ax'iform, *adj.*, like an axis.

ax'il, *n.*, the angle at the junction of the upper side of a lateral member with the stem.

ax'ile, *adj.*, rel. to an axis.

axil'la, *n.*, the armpit.

ax'illar, *adj.*, *i.q.* axillary; *n.*, one of the under feathers of a bird where the wing joins the body.

ax'illary, *adj.*, rel. to an axil or axilla.

ax'inite, *n.*, a mineral so named.

ax'iom, *n.*, a universally agreed principle or proposition.

axiomat'ic, *adj.*, universally agreed upon, unarguable.

axiomat'ical, *adj.*, *i.q.* axiomatic.

ax'is, *n.*, a straight line on which a body revolves; the stem of a plant.

ax'le, *n.*, the pin round which a wheel turns.

ax'le-box, *n.*, the metal lining of a hub.

ax'led, *adj.*, having an axle.

ax'le-tree, *n.*, *i.q.* axle.

Ax'minster, *adj.* and *n.*, a carpet of that name.

ax'olotl, *n.*, a newt-like amphibian found in Mexican lakes.

ax'on, *n.*, a nerve cell appendage which carries a signal from the cell.

ay, *interj.*, = yes.

ayah, *n.*, a Hindu female nurse.

aye, *adv.*, always, for ever.

aye-aye, *n.*, a squirrel-like animal found only in Madagascar.

Ayles'bury, *adj.* and *n.*, a breed of table ducks.

aza'lea, *n.*, a flowering shrub so named.

azan', *n.*, the Mohammedan call to prayer.

Azil'ian, *adj.* and *n.*, of the period between palaeolithic and neolithic.

az'imuth, *n.*, an arc of the horizon intercepted between the meridian and another vertical circle.

az'imuthal, *adj.*, rel. to an azimuth.

azo'ic, *adj.*, without organic life.

az'ote, *n.*, an older name for nitrogen.

azote'a, *n.* the flat roof of a house (*Span.*).

az'oth, *n.*, the alchemist's name for mercury.

azot'ic, *adj.*, nitrogenous.

Az'tec, *adj.* and *n.*, a person of the ancient Cental American civilization so named; descriptive of this culture.

az'ure, *adj.*, sky-blue; *n.*, the blue sky.

az'urine, *n.*, an aniline colour, deep blue.

az'ygous, *adj.*, unpaired.

az'ymite, *n.*, a user of unleavened bread.

az'ymous, *adj.*, rel. to unleavened bread.

B

baa, *interj.* and *n.*, the cry of a sheep.

Ba'al, *n.*, a Canaanitish deity, supposed to represent the sun.

bab'ble, *v.t.* and *i.*, to talk indistinctly or idly, to murmur; *n.*, idle talk.

bab'bled, *p.p.*, babble.

bab'blement, *n.*, *i.q.* babble.

bab'bler, *n.*, one who babbles, a teller of secrets.

bab'bling, *pr.p.*, babble.

babe, *n.*, *i.q.* baby.

Ba'bel, *n.*, the city where the confusion of tongues took place; a confused mixture of sounds; disorder.

ba'bery, *n.*, tawdry finery.

babirous'sa, *n.*, an Asian wild hog found in Ceylon.

ba'boo, ba'bu, *n.*, a Hindu word = master.

baboon', *n.*, a large species of ape.

babouche', *n.*, an oriental loose slipper.

ba'by, *n.*, an infant, a young child of either sex.

bab'y-farm, *n.*, a nursery for babies.

ba'byhood, *n.*, the state of being a baby: infancy.

ba'byish, *adj.*, childish.

Babylo'nian, *adj.*, rel. to Babylon or Babel.

Babylo'nish, *adj.*, *i.q.* Babylonian.

bab'y-ribb'on, *n.*, very narrow ribbon.

bab'y-sitt'er, *n.*, a babyminder.

baccalau'reate, *n.*, an academic degree (*Fr.*).

baccara', *n.*, a game of cards (*Fr.*).

baccarat', *n.*, *i.q.* baccara.

bac'cate, *adj.*, bearing berries; like a berry.

bac'chanal, *adj.*, *i.q.* bacchanalian; *n.*, a votary of Bacchus, a drunken reveller.

bacchana'lian, *adj.*, riotous, characterized by intemperate drinking.

bac'chant, *n.*, a priest of Bacchus.

bacchan'te, *n.*, a priestess of Bacchus, a female bacchanal.

bac'chic, *adj.*, rel. to Bacchus, drunken.

Bac'chus, *n.*, the classical god of wine.

baccif'erous, *adj.*, producing berries.

bacciv'orous, *adj.*, feeding on berries.

bach'elor, *n.*, an unmarried man; a university man who has taken his first degree.

bach'elor-girl', *n.*, a single woman living alone.

bach'elorhood, *n.*, the state or period of being a bachelor.

bacill'ary, *adj.*, connected with bacilli.

bacil'li, *n.*, pl. of bacillus.

bacill'icide, *n.*, a bacilli killer.

bacill'iform, *adj.*, rod-shaped.

bacil'lus, *n.*, a microscopic organism; the source of disease, a bacterium.

back, *adj.*, lying in the rear; *adv.*, toward a former place, state, or condition; *n.*, the hinder part; a shallow vat used by brewers, dyers, etc.; a ferryboat; *v.t.*, to support; to endorse; to. move backward; *v.i.*, to move or go back.

back'bar, *n.*, a bar to support the back.

back'ben'cher, *n.*, an occupant of a back bench (e.g. in the House of Commons).

back'bite, *v.t.*, to slander an absent person.

back'biter, *n.*, one who backbites.

back'biting, *pr.p.*, backbite; *n.*, a secret calumny.

back'board, *n.*, a board used to give erectness to the spine.

back'bone, *n.*, the spine; *fig.*, firmness of character.

back'chat, *n.*, impertinent answering back.

back'cloth, *n.*, the painted cloth at the rear of a stage.

back'-door', *n.*, a door at the back of a building.

back'-down, *n.*, and *v.i.* surrender.

back'drop, *n.*, *i.q.* backcloth.

backed, *p.p.*, back; *adj.*, having a back; supported (*colloq.*).

back'er, *n.*, one who backs; one who supports a particular party in a contest.

back'fire, *n.*, the act of backfiring; *v.i.*, to explode prematurely.

back'fired, *p.p.*, backfire.

back'firing, *pr.p.*, backfire.

back'fisch, *n.*, a young girl; a flapper (*Ger.*).

back'-front, *n.*, the rear elevation of a building.

backgam'mon, *n.*, a game for two played on a prepared board with pieces or men and dice.

back'ground, *n.*, the part of a picture represented as farthest from the spectator; the facts and information needed to understand a topic.

back'handed, *adj.*, with the hand turned backward; oblique; sloping back; unfair.

back'hander, *n.*, an indirect blow.

back'house, *n.*, an outbuilding behind a house.

back'ing, *pr.p.*, back; *n.*, support.

back'lash, *n.*, the motion that has been missed between working parts of a machine; any reactive situation.

back'log, *n.*, an accumulation of business not yet dealt with.

back'marker, *n.*, an old issue; anything out of date (*fig.*); a person last to begin an activity.

back'num'ber, *n.*, an old issue; anything out of date (*fig.*).

back′ped′al, *v.i.,* to hold back; to withdraw from a formerly held position.

back′scratch′er, *n.,* an appliance for scratching the back; a flatterer (*colloq.*).

back′scratch′ing, *n.,* flattery, toadyism.

back′side, *n.,* the back part of anything; the buttocks.

back′sight, *n.,* the rear sight of a gun or rifle.

back′slang, *n.,* a kind of slang in which words are pronounced backwards.

back′slide, *v.i.,* to fall away from religion or morality.

back′slider, *n.,* one who backslides.

back′sliding, *n.,* falling away from faith or practice.

backspa′cer, *n.,* a typewriter key which, on pressure, reverses the carriage movement.

back′stairs, *adj.,* secret and unfair, underhand; *n.,* stairs in the back of a house.

back′stay, *n.,* a long rope from the top of a mast backwards to the side of a ship helping to support the mast.

back′sword, *n.,* a single sharp-edged sword.

back′ward, *adj.,* and *adv.,* toward the back; in a contrary manner or direction.

backwarda′tion, *n.,* consideration by a seller of stock for power to delay delivery.

back′wardly, *adv.,* unwillingly.

back′wardness, *n.,* the state of being backward.

backwards, *adv.,* *i.q.* backward.

back′wash, *n.,* the movement of a retiring wave; an unfavourable reaction (*colloq.*).

back′water, *n.,* water turned back in its course by an obstruction; a reach of water not part of the main stream; *v.i.,* to reverse the rowing.

back′woods, *n. pl.,* (U.S.A. and Canada), forest districts remote from the more thickly settled parts.

back′woodsman, *n.,* an inhabitant of the backwoods.

back′yard, *n.,* an enclosure in the rear of a house.

ba′con, *n.,* pig meat pickled and dried.

Baco′nian, *adj.,* pert. to Bacon, his philosophy and theories; *n.,* esp. one who believes that Bacon was the author of the works of Shakespeare.

bacte′ria, *n.,* pl. of bacterium.

bacte′rial, *adj.,* rel. to bacteria.

bacte′rian, *adj.,* *i.q.* bacterial.

bacte′ricide, *n.,* a substance that destroys bacteria.

bacte′riform, *adj.,* resembling bacteria.

bacteriol′ogist, *n.,* one who studies disease germs.

bacteriol′ogy, *n.,* the science rel. to bacteria.

bacteriol′ysis, *n.,* the destruction of bacteria by a serum.

bacteriolyt′ic, *adj.,* capable of destroying bacteria.

bacter′iophage, *n.,* a minute organism which destroys bacteria.

bacte′rium, *n.,* a minute organism found in organic matter, diseased animal tissues, etc.

bac′terize, *v.t.,* to infect with bacteria.

bac′uline, *adj.,* of the stick or flogging.

bad, *adj.,* the opposite of good; lacking good qualities, physical or moral.

bad′dish, *adj.,* rather bad.

bade, *p.p.,* bid.

badge, *n.,* a mark or token worn to show a connection between the wearer and some other person, occupation or condition.

badg′er, *n.,* a small mammal of nocturnal habits, carnivorous, and living in a burrow, *v.t.,* to worry or annoy.

badg′ered, *p.p.,* badger.

badg′ering, *pr.p.,* badger.

badi′geon, *n.,* a mixture of plaster and other substances used to fill up small holes in joiners' work.

bad′inage, *n.,* playful talk; chaff.

bad′ly, *adv.,* in a bad manner, unskilfully.

badmash, *n.,* a rascal, a bad character.

bad′minton, *n.,* a game like lawn-tennis, but played with shuttlecocks; a kind of claret-cup.

bad′ness, *n.,* the state of being bad.

ba′el, *n.,* an orange-like fruit of the Indian tree used specifically for diarrhoea, etc.

baf′fle, *n.,* a board or plate to reflect or dissipate sound; *v.t.,* to elude; to perplex, to defeat.

baf′fled, *p.p.,* baffle.

baf′fler, *n.,* one who baffles.

baf′fling, *pr.p.,* baffle; *adj.,* baulking.

baff′y, *n.,* a short wooden golf club for lofting.

bag, *n.,* a sack; *v.t.,* to put into a bag; *v.i.,* to swell or hang like a bag.

bagasse′, *n.,* the waste after extracting juice from sugar-cane and sugar-beet (*Fr.*).

bagatelle′, *n.,* a trifle; a game played with a cue and balls on a board having nine holes at one end.

bag′gage, *n.,* luggage; the necessaries of an army; a wanton woman (*colloq.*).

bagged, *p.p.,* bag.

bag′ging, *pr.p.,* bag; *n.,* the cloth or other materials for bags.

bag′gy, *adj.,* puffy; looking like a bag.

bag′man, *n.,* a commercial traveller (slang).

bagn′io, *n.,* a bath; a brothel (*It.*).

bag′pipe, *n.,* a musical instrument of great antiquity, consisting of a leather wind bag and pipes, now regarded as the Scottish national instrument.

bag′piper, *n.,* one who plays on a bagpipe.

baguette′, *n.,* a long rectangular gem; a small moulding in architecture (*Fr.*).

bail, bale, *n.,* a little stick placed on the

stumps at cricket; legal security; *v.t.*, to free from water with a bucket or the like; to liberate from imprisonment on security.

bail'able, *adj.*, admitting of bail.

bailed, *p.p.*, bail.

bailee', *n.*, a person to whom goods are entrusted.

bail'er, *n.*, one who, or that which, bails.

bail'ey, *n.*, the outer wall of a castle.

Bail'ey bridge, *n.*, a prefabricated bridge of lattice steel.

bai'lie, *n.*, a Scottish alderman.

bai'liff, *n.*, a subordinate civil officer; an understeward on an estate.

bail'ing, *pr.p.*, bail.

bai'liwick, *n.*, the precincts within which a bailiff has authority.

bail'ment, *n.*, the act of bailing an accused person.

bailor', *n.*, one who delivers goods or money to another in trust.

bails'man, *n.*, one who gives bail for another.

bairn, *n.*, a child (*Scot.*).

bait, *v.t.*, to feed horses when travelling; to lure fish or other animals; to harass by dogs; to provoke or annoy; *n.*, a lure to catch fish or animals; a temptation.

bait'ed, *p.p.*, bait.

bait'ing, *pr.p.*, bait.

baize, *n.*, a coarse woollen stuff with a long nap.

bake, *v.t.*, to dry and harden by heat; to prepare in an oven.

baked, *p.p.*, bake.

bake'house, *n.*, a building for baking.

bak'elite, *n.*, a widely used plastic substance.

bake'meat, *n.*, meat cooked in an oven; a meat-pie.

bak'er, *n.*, one who bakes.

bak'ery, *n.*, *i.q.* bakehouse.

bak'ing, *pr.p.*, bake.

bak'sheesh, bakh'shish, *n.*, a gratuity of money (an Eastern term); a tip.

bal'aam, *n.*, matter used to pad a newspaper column (*journ.*).

balaclav'a, *n.*, a woollen helmet covering the ears and back of the head, named from a Crimean village.

balalaik'a, *n.*, a Russian musical instrument of the guitar type.

bal'ance, *n.*, an instrument for ascertaining the weight of a body; surplus—the difference of two sums; the part of a clock that regulates the beats; *v.t.*, to weigh; to examine a merchant's books by summation; to be equal on both sides of an account.

bal'anced, *p.p.*, balance.

bal'ancer, *n.*, one who, or that which, balances.

bal'ance-sheet, *n.*, a statement of assets and liabilities.

bal'ancing, *pr.p.*, balance.

bal'as-ru'by, *n.*, a species of ruby.

bal'ata, *n.*, a gum resembling rubber, and used for insulating purposes and as a substitute for shoe-leather.

balbo'a, *n.*, the monetary unit of Panama.

Balbrig'gan, *n.*, knitted cotton fabric used in hose, underwear, etc. (*Ir.*).

bal'conied, *adj.*, having balconies.

bal'cony, *n.*, a projecting gallery in a theatre; a projecting platform, with a balustrade, on the outside of a building.

bald, *adj.*, without, or with little, hair; unadorned.

bal'dachin, *n.*, a canopy; also *baldachino* and *baudequin* (orig. the canopy was of cloth from Bajdacca, *i.e.* Bagdad).

bald'coot, *n.*, the waterfowl with a bare white forehead; a bald person.

bal'derdash, *n.*, nonsense.

bald'-faced, *adj.*, having white on the face.

bald'head, *n.*, a man bald on the head.

bald'headed, *adj.*, bald; *adj.* and *adv.* without restraint.

bald'icoot, *n.*, *i.q.* baldcoot.

bald'ish, *adj.*, somewhat bald.

bald'ly, *adv.*, meanly, inelegantly.

baldmoney, *n.*, a yellow-flowered umbelliferous plant.

bald'ness, *n.*, the state of being bald.

bal'dric, *n.*, a broad belt worn diagonally across the body.

bale, *n.*, a bundle of goods; a calamity; *v.t.*, *i.q.* bail.

Balear'ic, *adj.*, pert. to a Spanish group of islands in the Mediterranean.

baled, *p.p.*, bale.

baleen', *adj.*, and *n.*, whalebone.

bale'-fire, *n.*, an alarm fire.

bale'ful, *adj.*, pernicious, calamitous, harmful, sorrowful.

bale'fully, *adv.*, in a baleful manner.

bale'fulness, *n.*, the state of being baleful.

bal'ing, *pr.p.*, bale.

balize', *n.*, a landmark or sea-beacon.

balk, *n.*, a thick beam; a disappointment; *v.t.*, to bar the way of. (Also *baulk*.)

Bal'kan, *adj.*, of the peninsula bounded by the Adriatic, Aegean and Black Seas.

balked, *p.p.*, balk.

balk'ing, *pr.p.*, balk.

ball, *n.*, a round body, a bullet; *v.t.* and *i.*, to form into a ball.

bal'lad, *n.*, a short narrative poem adapted for song.

bal'lad-mon'ger, *n.*, a dealer in ballads, an inferior poet.

bal'last, *n.*, heavy matter carried in a ship which has no cargo; material between the rails of a railway; *v.t.*, to steady.

bal'lasted, *p.p.*, ballast.

bal'lasting, *n.*, materials for ballast; *pr.p.*, ballast.

ball'-cock, *n.*, an automatic stopcock consisting of a hollow

sphere floating on the surface of a liquid and attached to a lever operating a valve.

balled, *p.p.*, ball.

ballerin'a, *n.*, a leading female ballet-dancer (*It.*).

bal'let, *n.*, an elaborate dance in which several persons take part, the action conveying a story (*Fr.*).

bal'let, *n.*, a little ball (*her.*).

balletomane', *n.*, a ballet enthusiast.

balletoma'nia, *n.*, enthusiasm for ballet.

ball'ing, *pr.p.*, ball.

ballis'ta, *n.*, an ancient military engine for throwing heavy missiles; a sort of catapult.

ballis'ter, *n.*, a crossbow.

ballis'tic, *adj.*, pert. to the ballista.

ballis'tics, *n.*, the science rel. to projectiles.

ballis'tite, *n.*, a very high explosive.

ballonet, *n.*, *i.q.*, balloonet.

balloon', *n.*, a large hollow sphere, esp. a large bag filled with a light gas, capable of rising in the air.

balloonet', *n.*, a small balloon.

balloon'ing, *n.*, the art of managing balloons.

balloon'ist, *n.*, one who ascends in a balloon.

bal'lot, *n.*, a ball or paper by which one votes secretly; the system of voting in this way; a lottery; *v.i.*, to vote secretly.

bal'lot-box, *n.*, a box for receiving ballots.

bal'loted, *p.p.*, ballot.

bal'loting, *pr.p.*, ballot.

ball'ot-pap'er, *n.*, a voting-paper.

ball'-room, *n.*, a large room for dancing.

ball'y, *adj.*, circumlocution for *bloody* (*slang*).

ballyhoo', *n.*, blarney, eyewash.

ball'yrag, *v.t.* and *i.*, to indulge in horseplay.

balm, *n.*, a fragrant ointment; anything that soothes pain.

balm'ily, *adv.*, in a balmy manner.

balm'iness, *n.*, the quality of being balmy.

Balmo'ral, *n.*, the site of a royal residence in Scotland; a kind of laced boot, petticoat and Scotch cap.

balm'y, *adj.*, fragrant; soothing; refreshing; gently restful.

bal'neal, *adj.*, pert. to a bath.

balneol'ogy, *n.*, a scientific study of bathing and medicinal springs.

bal'sa, *n.*, a raft; corkwood.

bal'sam, *n.*, an aromatic, resinous substance flowing from certain plants, and used in medicine.

balsam'ic, *adj.*, having the qualities of balsam.

balsam'ical, *adj.*, *i.q.* balsamic.

balsamif'erous, *adj.*, producing balsam.

Bal'tic, *adj.*, pert. to the Baltic Sea.

bal'timore, *n.*, a north-American orange-and-black starling.

bal'uster, *n.*, a small column used for balustrades.

bal'ustered, *adj.*, having balusters.

balustrade', *n.*, a row of balusters joined by a rail.

bam, *n.*, and *v.t.* hoax.

bambi'no, *n.*, a baby, a figure of Christ as a baby (*It.*).

bamboo', *n.*, a tropical grass with large, jointed stems.

bamboo'zle, *v.t.*, to impose upon, to deceive.

bamboo'zled, *p.p.*, bamboozle.

bamboo'zling, *pr.p.*, bamboozle.

ban, *n.*, a prohibition; a curse *v.t.*, to put under a curse; to proscribe.

ban'al, *adj.*, commonplace, vulgar.

banal'ity, *n.*, that which is banal.

bana'na, *n.*, a herbaceous plant akin to the plantain, bearing soft, luscious fruit.

Ban'bury cake, *n.*, a spiced cake originally from Banbury, Oxfordshire.

ban'co, *n.*, a standard of money in which some banks keep their accounts; a seat or bench of justice.

band, *n.*, a connection; a narrow strip; a company of men, esp. soldiers; a body of instrumental musicians; *v.t.* and *i.*, to associate for some common purpose.

band'age, *n.*, a roller used in binding up wounds; the binding material itself; *v.t.*, to put a bandage on.

band'aged, *p.p.*, bandage.

band'aging, *pr.p.*, bandage.

bandan'na, *n.*, an Indian silk handkerchief.

band'box, *n.*, a light box of pasteboard for containing bonnets, etc.

band'eau, *n.*, a ribbon for the forehead.

band'ed, *p.p.*, band.

band'elet, *n.*, a small band or fillet.

ban'der, *n.*, one banded with others.

ban'derole, *n.*, a little flag; a military weapon; a trumpet.

ban'dicoot, *n.*, a large edible Indian rat.

band'ied, *p.p.*, bandy.

band'ing, *pr.p.*, band.

ban'dit, *n.*, a robber, an outlaw.

band'itry, *n.*, the state of being bandits.

bandit'ti, *n.*, pl. of bandit.

band'master, *n.*, the conductor of a band.

ban'dog, *n.*, a large, fierce dog, a mastiff, usually kept chained.

bandoleer', **bandolier'**, *n.*, a shoulder-belt for cartridges.

bandoler'o, *n.*, a highwayman (*Span.*).

ban'doline, *n.*, a sticky preparation for fixing the hair or moustache.

bandore', *n.*, a stringed musical instrument, a sort of lyre (*Span.*).

band'roll, *n.*, *i.q.* banderole.

band'saw, *n.*, an endless steel saw.

bands'man, *n.*, a player in a band.

bandstand, *n.*, an open-air platform for a band of musicians.

band'wag'on, *n.*, the wagon for the band in a circus procession; hence, an important position.

band'-wheel, n., a wheel on which a strap runs.

ban'dy, adj., bent; n., a sort of hockey-stick; the game played with these sticks and a ball; v.t., to toss to and fro.

ban'dying, pr.p., bandy.

ban'dy-leg, n., a bent or crooked leg.

ban'dy-legged, adj., having bent legs.

bane, n., any cause of destruction; deadly poison.

bane'ful, adj., destructive, poisonous.

bane'fully, adv., in a baneful way.

bane'fulness, n., the quality of being baneful.

bang, n., a loud noise, a heavy blow; v.t., to beat; to make a loud noise.

banged, p.p., bang.

bang'ing, pr.p., bang.

ban'gle, n., an ornamental ring for wrist or ankle.

bangue, i.q., bhang.

ban'ian, n., i.q., banyan.

ban'ish, v.i., to drive away, to exile.

ban'ished, p.p., banish.

ban'isher, n., one who banishes.

ban'ishing, pr.p., banish.

ban'ishment, n., exile; the act of banishing.

ban'ister, n., a baluster, an upright in a stair-rail.

ban'jo, n., a musical instrument with six strings, a body like a tambourine, and a neck like a guitar.

ban'jolin, n., a sort of combined banjo and mandolin.

banjule'le, n., a sort of combined banjo and ukulele.

bank, n., a mound; any acclivity; an establishment that trades in money; v.i., to enclose with a bank, to put money in a bank; to turn quickly (an aircraft term).

bank'able, adj., receivable at a bank (securities), etc.

bank'-bill, n., a bill of exchange payable to order and negotiable.

bank'book, n., a book in which debits and credits are entered by the officials of a bank.

banked, p.p., bank.

bank'er, n., one who keeps a bank; an Eastern labourer; a hunting horse that does not clear large banks; a mason's wooden or stone bench used for trimming.

bank'ing, n., the business of a banker; making a turn with an aeroplane, inner side downwards; pr.p., bank.

bank'note, n., a promissory note payable on demand, issued by a bank.

bank'rupt, n., a person declared by legal authority to be unable to pay his debts.

bank'ruptcy, n., the state of being a bankrupt.

bank'rupted, adj., declared bankrupt.

bank'sia, n., an Australian flowering shrub now grown in Europe.

banks'man, n., an overseer at a pit-mouth.

bank'-stock, n., a share or shares in the capital of a bank.

banned, p.p., ban.

ban'ner, n., a large square flag bearing heraldic devices.

ban'nered, adj., having a banner.

ban'neret, n., a knight intermediate in rank between a baron and a knight bachelor, raised to this rank for bravery in the field.

ban'nerol, n., a little flag, a banderole.

ban'ning, pr.p., ban.

ban'nock, n., an unleavened cake made of meal and baked on an iron plate over a fire (Scot.).

banns, n. pl., a proclamation in church of an intended marriage.

ban'quet, n., a feast; v.t. and i., to feast.

ban'queted, p.p., banquet.

ban'queter, n., one who banquets.

ban'queting, pr.p., banquet.

banquette, n., a little raised bank inside the parapet of a fortification; the raised footway of a bridge.

ban'shee, n., a female fairy whose appearance foretells a death (Ir.).

ban'stickle, n., a stickleback.

bant, v.i., to treat obesity by abstinence from sugar, starch and fat.

ban'tam, n., a small domestic fowl of great courage.

ban'ter, n., humorous raillery, chaff; v.t., to make fun of, to attack with jests.

ban'tered, p.p., banter.

ban'terer, n., one who banters.

ban'tering, pr.p., banter.

ban'thine, n., a drug used for peptic ulcers.

ban'ting, n., the treatment of obesity by abstinence from sugar, starch and fat.

bant'ling, n., an infant (contemptuous).

Bantu', n., a group of negroid races in Central and Southern Africa.

ban'yan, n., a Hindu trader; a loose jacket; a kind of Indian fig tree whose branches send down shoots which take root and become trunks.

banzai', n., a Japanese greeting to their Emperor, used in battle, etc. (interj.).

ba'obab, n., a large African tree bearing a pulpy-fruit called monkey-bread.

bap, n., a small loaf or roll of bread (Scot.).

bap'tism, n., immersion; the ceremony of admittance to a religion.

baptis'mal, adj., pert. to baptism.

Bap'tist, n., one who baptizes, esp. St. John, the forerunner of Christ; a member of the Baptist sect.

bap'tistery, n., a building or portion of a building where baptism is administered.

baptis'tic, adj., rel. to baptism.

bap'tistry, n., i.q. baptistery.

bapti'zable, adj., capable of being baptized.

baptize', v.t., to administer the sacrament of baptism to; to christen.

baptized', p.p., baptize.

bapti'zer, n., one who baptizes.

baptizing, pr.p., baptize.

bar, n., a pole; an obstruction; a bank of sand, etc., at the mouth of a river; the place in court where prisoners are placed; the profession of barrister; the enclosed place in a tavern where liquor is served; in music, a vertical line on the staff; a large European seafish; a unit of atmospheric pressure; v.t., to fasten with a bar; to hinder; to exclude.

barathe'a, n., a fine cloth of silk (or cotton) and wool.

ba'rathrum, n., a pit at Athens where criminals were thrown; an abyss.

barb, n., the sharp point projecting backwards of an arrow, fish hook, etc.; a Barbary horse; a kind of pigeon; v.t., to furnish with barbs, as an arrow.

bar'bacan, n., a watchtower; a small outwork before the gate of a walled town or castle.

Barba'dian, adj., bel. to Barbados; n., an inhabitant of Barbados.

barba'rian, n., an uncivilized person; a brutal man.

barbar'ic, adj., savage, wild; ornate, but not in good taste.

bar'barism, n., an outrage; any offence against good taste; any form of speech contrary to correct idiom.

barbar'ity, n., savageness, ferocity.

bar'barize, v.i., to become barbarous; v.t. to make barbarous.

bar'barized, p.p., barbarize.

bar'barizing, pr.p., barbarize.

bar'barous, adj., uncivilized, ignorant; cruel; brutal.

bar'barously, adv., in a barbarous manner.

bar'barousness, n., i.q. barbarity.

Barb'ary ape, n., a large tailless monkey of N. Africa and Gibraltar.

bar'bate, adj., bearded.

bar'becue, n., a large animal roasted whole; an open-air party where this is done; v.t., to cook whole by roasting.

bar'becued, p.p., barbecue.

bar'becuing, pr.p., barbecue.

barbed, adj., furnished with barbs; p.p., barb.

bar'bel, n., a freshwater fish with four beard-like appendages on its upper jaw.

bar'bellate, adj., having short, stiff hairs, often barbed.

bar'ber, n., a men's hairdresser.

bar'berry, n., a shrub bearing small acid berries, common in hedges.

bar'bet, n., a dog with curly hair, a poodle.

barbette', n., a platform in a fortification or on a ship of war, from which a cannon may be fired over the parapet instead of through an embrasure.

bar'bican, n., a barbacan.

barb'itone, n., a hypnotic drug; a veronal.

barbiturate', n., a salt of barbituric acid.

barbitur'ic, adj., applied to an acid used as a sedative.

barbol'a, n., an embellishment by attaching plastic flowers, fruit, etc.

bar'bule, n., a small barb; a little beard.

bar'carole, n., a Venetian boat-song.

Barcelon'a, adj. and n., a Spanish city; a hazel-nut imported from Spain.

bard, n., a poet, esp. a Celtic poet or singer; the armour for breast and flanks of a war-horse.

bard'ic, adj., pert. to bards.

bard'ism, n., bardic lore.

bardol'atry, n., the worship of Shakespeare.

bare, adj., naked, empty, much worn; v.t., to strip naked.

bare'bone, adj., very lean.

bared, p.p., bare.

bare'faced, adj., impudent.

bare'facedness, n., effrontery, impudence.

bare'foot, adj., with bare feet.

bare'footed, adj., i.q. barefoot.

barège', n., a thin, gauze-like fabric (Fr.).

bare'headed, adj., having the head uncovered.

bare'ly, adv., nakedly, without decoration; scarcely.

bare'ness, n., the state of being bare.

bar'er, adj., comp. of bare.

bare'sark, adv. and n., a wild Norse warrior; shirtless; without armour.

bar'est, adj., super. of bare; v., 2nd pers.; pr.t. of bare.

bar'gain, n., an agreement; the thing stipulated for; something bought or sold cheap; v.i., to make an agreement.

bar'gained, p.p., bargain.

bargainee', n., the party who receives the property bargained for.

bar'gainer, n., one who bargains.

bar'gaining, pr.p., bargain.

barge, n., a boat used ceremonially; a flat-bottomed boat for carrying goods.

bargee', n., one who works on a barge.

barge'man, n., a man who manages a barge.

barg'ing, n., transport by barge; pr.p. barge.

bar'ic, adj., of or containing barium.

baril'la, n., an impure soda got by burning certain plants, esp. sea-weeds.

bar'ing, pr.p., bare.

bar'-iron, n., iron smelted from the ore in long rods.

bar'itone, adj., between tenor and bass; n., a baritone voice or singer.

ba'rium, n., a metal (chem.).

bark, n., the outer rind of a tree, shrub, etc.; a barque; the cry of a dog; v.t., to peel; v.i., to cry like a dog.

barked, *p.p.*, bark.

bar'keeper, *n.*, a server at a tavern bar.

bark'entine, *n.*, *i.q.* barque.

bark'er, *n.*, one who, or that which, barks; a pistol (*slang*); a person who attracts custom at a show.

bark'ery, *n.*, a tanhouse.

bark'ing, *pr.p.*, bark.

bark'y, *adj.*, having the qualities of bark.

bar'ley, *n.*, a kind of grain.

bar'ley-broth, *n.*, broth containing barley.

bar'leycorn, *n.*, a grain of barley; a measure equal to a third of an inch; a rifle foresight.

bar'ley-meal, *n.*, a meal made by crushing barley.

barl'ow, *n.*, a large, single-bladed pocket-knife.

barm, *n.*, yeast.

bar'maid, *n.*, a woman who serves in a tavern.

barm'ecidal, *adj.*, *i.q.* barmecide.

bar'mecide, *adj.*, unreal, illusory.

barm'y, *adj.*, containing barm; frothy; soft; silly (*slang*).

barn, *n.*, a covered building for storing farm produce.

bar'nacle, *n.*, a stalked sea shell-fish, often found attached to ships' bottoms; a species of goose.

barocyclonom'eter, *n.*, an aneroid barometer for detecting distant storms.

bar'ograph, *n.*, a recording barometer.

bar'olite, *n.*, a kind of barytes.

barom'eter, *n.*, an instrument for measuring the weight or pressure of the atmosphere.

baromet'ric, *adj.*, pert. to the barometer.

baromet'rical, *adj.*, *i.q.* barometric.

barom'etry, *n.*, the science underlying the use of the barometer.

bar'on, *n.*, a peer holding the lowest rank in the hereditary peerage.

bar'onage, *n.*, the whole body of barons; the dignity of baron.

bar'oness, *n.*, the wife of a baron.

bar'onet, *n.*, one holding hereditary rank below a baron, not a peer, but an hereditary knight.

bar'onetage, *n.*, the whole body of baronets.

bar'onetcy, *n.*, the title and dignity of a baronet.

bar'onetize, *v.t.*, to make a baronet.

baro'nial, *adj.*, pert. or bel. to a baron.

bar'ony, *n.*, the title or honour of a baron; in Ireland, a territorial division corresponding to the hundred.

baroque', *adj.*, in baroque style; *n.*, grotesque or whimsical architecture and art, prevalent in the 18th century.

bar'oscope, *n.*, an instrument for forecasting weather.

baroscop'ic, *adj.*, pert. to a baroscope.

baroscop'ical, *adj.*, *i.q.* baroscopic.

barouche', *n.*, a four-wheeled carriage with a falling top.

barque, *n.*, a three-masted sailing vessel, the two forward masts square-rigged, the mizzen mast rigged fore-and-aft.

bar'quentine, *n.*, *i.q.* barque. (Also *barkentine*.)

bar'racan, *n.*, a kind of camlet.

bar'rack, *n.*, a house for soldiers.

barracoon', *n.*, a negro barrack, a slave depot.

barracoot'a, *n.*, *i.q.* barracuda.

barracud'a, *n.*, a large, West Indian sea-fish.

bar'rage, *n.*, the formation of an artificial bar on a river or water course, to increase the depth of water; a bar thus formed, esp. on the Nile; a defensive screen of gunfire.

bar'ras, *n.*, a kind of resin; a galipot.

bar'rator, *n.*, an encourager of litigation; the master or any of the crew of a ship who commits barratry.

bar'ratrous, *adj.*, tainted with barratry.

bar'ratry, *n.*, fraud by the master of a ship; the encouragement of lawsuits and quarrels.

barred, *adj.*, marked with thick lines; *p.p.*, bar.

bar'rel, *n.*, a cask; a hollow cylinder or tube.

bar'relage, *n.*, the accommodation for barrels.

bar'relled, *adj.*, having a barrel or barrels.

bar'rel-organ, *n.*, a musical instrument in which a barrel furnished with pegs opens valves as it turns and admits air to a set of pipes.

bar'ren, *adj.*, not fertile; unproductive.

bar'renness, *n.*, the state of being barren.

ba'rret, *n.*, a flat cap.

barrette', *n.*, the hilt of a rapier.

barricade', *n.*, a temporary fortification made of trees, earth, etc.; *v.t.*, to stop up by a barricade.

barrica'ded, *p.p.*, barricade.

barrica'ding, *pr.p.*, barricade.

bar'rier, *n.*, an obstruction, an obstacle.

bar'ring, *pr.p.*, bar; *prep.*, excepting.

bar'rister, *n.*, a lawyer who acts as an advocate.

bar'row, *n.*, a prehistoric sepulchral mound; a wheelbarrow.

ba'rrow-boy, *n.*, a fruit vendor with a barrow.

Bar'sac, *n.*, a sweet, white wine from Barsac in France.

bar'-shot, *n.*, a double shot consisting of two round-shot united by a bar.

bar'ter, *n.*, the act of exchanging; *v.t.*, to exchange one commodity for another and not for money.

bar'tered, *p.p.*, barter.

bar'terer, *n.*, one who barters.

bar'tering, *pr.p.*, barter.

bartizan', *n.*, a turret for archers.

bar'ton, *n.*, a demesne; a farmyard.

Barts, *n.*, St. Bartholomew's Hospital in London (*abbrev.*).

bar'ysphere, n., that part of the earth within the lithosphere.

bary'ta, n., oxide of barium.

bary'tes, n., baryta, or its sulphate (heavy-spar).

baryt'ic, adj., containing baryta.

bar'ytone, adj., i.q. baritone.

bary'tum, n., barium.

ba'sal, adj., pert. to a base.

basalt', n., a black igneous rock.

basalt'ic, adj., pert. to basalt.

basalt'iform, adj., in the form of basalt; columnar.

basalt'ine, adj., i.q. basaltic.

bas'an, baz'an, n., sheepskin tanned in oak or larch bark.

bas'anite, n., touchstone.

bas bleu, n., a bluestocking (Fr.).

bascol'ogy, n., the study of the Basques.

bas'cule, n., an apparatus on the see-saw principle.

base, adj., worthless, low, mean; n., the bottom of anything; a military depôt; v.t., to lay the foundation of.

base'ball, n., a ballgame like rounders.

base'born, adj., of illegitimate birth.

based, p.p., base.

base'less, adj., without foundations.

base'ly, adv., in a base manner.

base'ment, n., the lowest story of a building.

base'ness, n., meanness, vileness.

ba'ses, n. pl., of basis.

bash, n., a heavy blow; v.t., to strike heavily.

bashaw', n., a pasha.

bashed, p.p., bash.

bash'ful, adj., modest to excess; shy.

bash'fully, adv., in a bashful manner.

bash'fulness, n., excessive modesty; shyness.

bash'i-bazouk', n., an irregular Turkish soldier.

bash'ing, pr.p., bash; n., the act of striking.

ba'sic, adj., rel. to a base.

bas'ically, adv., fundamentally.

basi'city, n., an acid's relative power of combining with bases.

bas'ified, p.p., basify.

bas'ifier, n., that which basifies.

bas'ify, v.t., to convert into a chemical base.

bas'ifying, pr.p., basify.

bas'il, n., the slope at the edge of a cutting tool, a bezel; an aromatic pot-herb.

bas'ilar, adj., i.q. basal.

bas'ilary, adj., i.q. basal.

basil'ic, adj., royal; kingly.

basil'ica, n., a Roman public hall; a church with a similar plan.

basil'ical, adj., pert. to a basilica.

basil'icon, n., an ointment made of wax, pitch and resin.

bas'ilisk, n., a fabulous creature, a serpent or cockatrice.

ba'sin, n., a round shallow vessel; a tract of country, drained by a river.

bas'inet, n., a light steel headpiece.

ba'sing, pr.p., base.

ba'sis, n., a base, a foundation.

bask, v.t., to lie in warmth or at ease.

basked, p.p., bask.

bask'er, n., one who basks.

bas'ket, n., a container made of plaited twigs, rushes, osiers, etc.

bas'ketball, n., a ballgame played with suspended nets as goals.

bask'ing, pr.p., bask.

bas'net, n., i.q. basinet.

bas'on, n., a bench for felting hat material; v.t., to felt.

Basque, adj., pert. to this language or people; n., the language of the Biscayans, French and Spanish.

basque, n., a short continuation of a bodice below the waist (Fr.).

bas-relief', n., a sculpture in low relief.

bass, n., a weaving material of lime bark; a sea-fish like a perch; a kind of bitter ale.

bass, adj., pert. to the lowest part or male voice; n., this part or voice (mus.).

bas'set, n., a game at cards; a miner's term for an outcrop; v.i., to crop out.

bas'seted, p.p., basset.

bass'et-horn, n., a tenor clarinet.

bas'seting, pr.p., basset.

bassinet', -ette', n., a cradle or perambulator (Fr.).

bass'o, n., bass (It., mus.).

bassoon', n., a bass wind instrument.

bassoon'ist, n., a bassoon player.

bass'o-profun'do, n., a deep bass.

bass'-viol', n., a violoncello.

bass'wood, n., the American lime-tree.

bast, n., a fibrous inner bark of the lime and other trees.

bas'tard, adj., spurious, not genuine; n., an illegitimate child.

bas'tardize, v.t., to prove to be a bastard.

bas'tardized, p.p., bastardize.

bas'tardizing, pr.p., bastardize.

bas'tardy, n., the state of being a bastard.

baste, v.t., to cudgel; to drip fat upon roasting meat; to sew slightly with long stitches.

bast'ed, p.p., baste.

bastile', bastille', n., a fortress, esp. the state prison in Paris destroyed in 1789.

bastina'do, n., punishment in Mohammedan countries by beating the soles of the feet; v.t., to inflict this punishment.

bastina'doed, p.p., bastinado.

bast'ing, pr.p., baste; n., the long, loose stitches which fasten pieces of a garment together during the making.

bast'ion, n., a mound at the angle of a fortification.

bast'ioned, *adj.,* having bastions.

Basu'to, *n.,* a member of one of the Bantu tribes.

bas'yle, *n.,* a non-acid constituent of a compound.

bat, *n.,* a club used in cricket and similar games; a winged mammal; *v.i.,* to play with a bat at cricket.

batat'a, *n.,* a West Indian plant; a sweet or Spanish potato.

batch, *n.,* a quantity of bread baked at one time; a number of individuals or articles similar to each other.

bate, *v.i.* and *t.,* to lessen.

bateau', *n.,* a light, broad flat-bottomed Canadian boat; the pontoon of a floating bridge (*Fr.*).

ba'ted, *p.p.,* bate.

bath, *n.,* a vessel in which the body is washed; a Hebrew liquid measure; *Knights of the Bath,* a British order of knighthood; *v.t.,* to immerse the body in water for washing.

bath'-chair, *n.,* a wheeled chair for invalids.

bathe, *v.t.,* to immerse in liquid, the sun, etc.; *v.i.,* to take a bath.

bathed, *p.p.,* bath.

bathed, *p.p.,* bathe.

bath'er, *n.,* one who bathes.

bathet'ic, *adj.,* characterized by bathos.

bathing, *pr.p.,* bath.

bath'ing, *pr.p.,* bathe.

bathom'eter, *n.,* a spring balance for sounding water.

bath'os, *n.,* a ludicrous descent from the elevated to the mean in literary composition; an anti-climax.

bath'room, *n.,* a room for bathing in.

bathyb'ius, *n.,* an inorganic slimy substance dredged from ocean depths.

bathygraph'ical, *adj.,* indicating depths of water.

bathym'eter, *n.,* a sounding instrument.

bathy'metry, *n.,* the science of sounding seas and lakes.

bath'yscaphe, *n.,* a bathyscope.

bath'yscope, *n.,* a modern type of bathysphere.

bath'ysphere, *n.,* a submersible observation chamber.

bat'ik, *n.,* a method of printing coloured designs on textiles.

bat'ing, *pr.p.,* bate; *prep.,* excepting.

batiste', *n.,* a kind of cambric.

bat'let, *n.,* a small bat for beating linen in the wash.

bat'man, *n.,* a man who provides personal services for officers in the army; a marshaller of aircraft on landing or take off.

bat'on, *n.,* a truncheon; a conductor's stick; in heraldry, a diminutive of the band sinister, couped (*Fr.*).

Batra'chia, *n. pl.,* a group of amphibious animals, including frogs and toads.

batra'chian, *adj.,* pert. to the Batrachia; *n.,* one of them.

bat'rachite, *n.,* a fossilized frog.

bat'rachoid, *adj.,* resembling a frog.

bats'man, *n.,* a cricketer using the bat.

bat'ta, *n.,* an extra allowance made to British officers in India.

battal'ia, *n. pl.,* an old plural of battalion.

battal'ion, *n.,* a body of infantry of about 1,000 men, forming part of a regiment.

battal'ioned, *adj.,* formed into battalions.

bat'ted, *p.p.,* bat.

bat'teler, bat'tler, *n.,* an undergraduate who gets his batteis free.

bat'tels, *n.,* food ordered from the buttery at an Oxford college.

bat'ten, *n.,* a long slip of wood; *v.t.,* to fatten; to fasten with battens; *v.i.,* to grow fat, to gorge.

bat'tened, *p.p.,* batten.

bat'tening, *pr.p.,* batten.

bat'ter, *n.,* a mixture of flour, eggs, etc., beat-

en with some liquid into a paste; *v.t.,* to beat with successive blows.

bat'tered, *p.p.,* batter.

bat'terer, *n.,* one who batters.

bat'tering, *pr.p.,* batter.

bat'tering-ram, *n.,* an engine of war used to beat down walls.

bat'tery, *n.,* a number of guns placed near one another; a parapet, etc., to cover guns and gunners; a storage device for electricity; personal assault.

bat'ting, *pr.p.,* bat.

bat'tish, *adj.,* like a bat.

bat'tle, *n.,* a great combat; *v.i.,* to fight.

bat'tle-array, *n.,* the arrangement of an army ready to give battle.

bat'tle-axe, *n.,* an axe used as a weapon.

bat'tle-cruiser, *n.,* an armoured cruiser.

bat'tled, *adj.,* furnished with battlements; *p.p.,* battle.

bat'tledore, *n.,* a racket used to strike a ball or shuttlecock.

bat'tlefield, *n.,* the scene of a battle.

bat'tlement, *n.,* an indented parapet.

bat'tlemented, *adj.,* having battlements.

bat'tler, *n.,* one who battles.

bat'tleship, *n.,* a large ship of war.

bat'tleworthy, *adj.,* fit for battle.

bat'tling, *pr.p.,* battle.

battol'ogy, *n.,* babbling; a needless repetition of words.

battue', *n.,* the shooting of driven game (*Fr.*).

batt'y, *adj.,* crazy (*slang*); batlike.

baubee', *n.,* a halfpenny (*Scot.*).

bau'ble, *n.,* a short stick bearing a fool's-head; a showy trifle.

baulk, *i.q.* balk.

baux'ite, *n.,* a clay, the main source of aluminium.

Bava'rian, *adj.,* pert. to Bavaria; *n.,* an inhabitant of Bavaria.

ba'vin, *n.,* a faggot of brushwood.

bawbee′, *n.*, *i.q.* baubee.

bawd, *n.*, a brothel-keeper; a pander.

bawd′ily, *adv.*, in a bawdy manner.

bawd′y, *adj.*, lewd; obscene; unchaste.

bawl, *n.*, a vehement cry; *v.t.* and *i.*, to shout.

bawled, *p.p.*, bawl.

bawl′er, *n.*, one who bawls.

bawl′ey, *n.*, a fishing boat peculiar to the Essex and Kentish coasts (*dial.*).

bawl′ing, *n.*, loud shouting; *pr.p.*, bawl.

bawn, *n.*, an enclosure with mud walls (for cattle).

bay, *adj.*, of a reddish chestnut colour; *n.*, an expanse of water between two headlands; the laurel-tree; the bark of a dog; a recess; a space between columns or buttresses, or projecting beyond the wall line, as a window; *v.t.*, and *i.*, to bark.

bayadère′, *n.*, a Hindu dancing-girl (*Fr.*).

bay′ard, *n.*, a bay horse.

bay′berry, *n.*, the wax-myrtle and its fruit.

bayed, *adj.*, having a bay or bays; *p.p.*, bay.

bay′ing, *pr.p.*, bay.

bay′onet, *n.*, a short sword to fix on the muzzle of a rifle; *v.t.*, to stab with a bayonet.

bay′oneted, *p.p.*, bayonet.

bay′oneting, *pr.p.*, bayonet.

bay′ou, *n.*, a channel proceeding from a lake (*Amer.*).

bay′-rum, *n.*, an aromatic used as a hair-dressing.

bay′-salt, *n.*, salt obtained by evaporating sea-water.

bay′-tree, *n.*, a kind of laurel.

bay′-window, *n.*, a window forming a recess in a room, often polygonal in plan.

bazaar′, **bazar′**, *n.*, an Oriental street-market; a charity sale of miscellaneous articles.

bazoo′ka, *n.*, a slide wind instrument; an anti-tank weapon.

bdell′ium, *n.*, an Arabian aromatic gum-resin.

be, *v.i.*, to exist; to become; to remain. (It forms a connection between the subject and predicate of a sentence; it also helps to form the compound tenses of other verbs.)

beach, *n.*, the strand; the part of the shore washed by the tide; *v.t.*, to run (a vessel) on to the beach.

beach′comber, *n.*, a long, rolling wave; a long-shore vagrant.

beached, *p.p.*, beach.

beach′ing, *pr.p.*, beach.

beach′-res′cue, *n.*, a beach lifeguard.

beach′wards, *adv.*, towards the beach.

beach′y, *adj.*, having a beach.

bea′con, *n.*, an object, light or signal used as a warning; *v.i.*, to serve as a beacon.

bea′conage, *n.*, money paid to maintain a beacon.

bea′coned, *adj.*, having a beacon; *p.p.*, beacon.

bea′coning, *pr.p.*, beacon.

bead, *n.*, a little perforated ball of gold, glass, etc., strung with others on a thread; any small globular body; *v.t.*, to adorn with beads; *v.i.*, to form into beads.

bead′ed, *adj.*, beadlike; *p.p.*, bead.

bead′ing, *n.*, a small round moulding in architecture or joinery; *pr.p.*, bead.

bead′le, *n.*, a subordinate officer of a court, church or parish.

bea′dledom, *n.*, stupid officiousness.

bead′-roll, *n.*, a list of persons for whose souls prayers are requested; a catalogue.

beads′man, *n.*, one whose employment is to pray for another; a recipient of alms.

bead′y, *adj.*, (of eyes) small and bright; covered with beads or small drops.

bea′gle, *n.*, a small hound kept to hunt hares.

beak, *n.*, the bill of a bird.

beaked, *adj.*, having a beak; beak-shaped.

beak′er, *n.*, a large drinking cup or glass; any receptacle for liquid.

beam, *n.*, a long straight piece of wood; a collection of parallel rays of light; *v.i.*, to emit rays of light; to show affection, satisfaction, etc.

beamed, *p.p.*, beam.

beam′ing, *pr.p.*, beam.

beam′less, *adj.*, emitting no rays of light.

beam′y, *adj.*, heavy, massive; radiant.

bean, *n.*, the seed of a leguminous plant; the plant itself; a term of greeting, usually with the prefix "old" (*slang*).

beanfeast, *n.*, merry-making.

bean′o, *n.*, a jollification (*slang*).

bear, *v.t.*, to support; to covey; to bring forth; *n.*, a large carnivorous, flat-footed animal; a rude or uncouth man; a Stock Exchange operator who sells in the hope of re-purchase at a lower price.

bear′able, *adj.*, able to be borne.

bear′-baiting, *n.*, the sport of baiting bears with dogs.

beard, *n.*, the hair on the face; *v.t.*, to defy.

beard′ed, *adj.*, having a beard; *p.p.*, beard.

beard′ing, *pr.p.*, beard.

beard′less, *adj.*, without a beard.

beard′lessness, *n.*, the state of being without a beard.

bear′er, *n.*, one who bears.

bear′garden, *n.*, a place where bears were kept for sport; any place of disorder.

bear′ing, *n.*, demeanour, mien; in a machine it is the support in which a revolving part rotates; *pr.p.*, bear.

bear′ish, *adj.*, resembling a bear; rude; surly.

bear′like, *adj.*, like a bear.

bear′s′-foot, *n.*, a kind of hellebore.

bear′s′-grease, *n.*, a pomade for the hair.

bear′skin, *n.*, the dressed fur of a bear.

beast, *n.,* any four-footed animal; a brutal or disgusting person.

beast'liness, *n.,* brutality; filthiness.

beast'ly, *adj.,* like a beast.

beat, *n.,* a stroke or blow; the round of a policeman; *v.t.,* to strike; to overcome.

beaten, *adj.,* made smooth by beating or treading; *p.p.,* beat.

beat'er, *n.,* one who beats.

beatifi'ic, *adj.,* imparting bliss.

beatif'ical, *adj.,* *i.q.* beatific.

beatifica'tion, *n.,* blessedness; an act of the Pope by which he declares a person beatified but not canonized.

beat'ified, *p.p.,* beatify.

beat'ify, *v.t.,* to make blessed.

beat'ifying, *pr.p.,* beatify.

beat'ing, *n.,* a defeat; *pr.p.,* beat.

beat'itude, *n.,* consummate bliss; one of the eight blessings invoked by Christ.

beau, *n.,* a fop; a sweetheart (*Fr.,* pl. *beaux*).

Beauf'ort scale, *n.,* a large scale of wind velocity.

beau geste, *n.,* a display of magnanimity (*Fr.*).

beau-ide'al, *n.,* the highest type of excellence (*Fr.*).

Beaujolais, *n.,* a claret from the district of Beaujolais (*Fr.*).

beau-monde', *n.,* the fashionable world (*Fr.*).

beaumon'tage, *n.,* a composition for hiding cracks in wood or iron.

Beaune, *n.,* a red burgundy from Beaune.

beau'teous, *adj.,* beautiful.

beau'teously, *adv.,* in a beautiful manner.

beau'teousness, *n.,* beauty.

beauti'cian, *n.,* a specialist in cosmetics; one engaged in beauty culture.

beautifica'tion, *n.,* the act of beautifying.

beau'tified, *p.p.,* beautify.

beau'tifier, *n.,* one who beautifies.

beau'tiful, *adj.,* highly pleasing to the eye, the ear or the mind.

beau'tifulness, *n.,* *i.q.* beauty.

beau'tify, *v.t.,* to render beautiful.

beau'tifying, *pr.p.,* beautify.

beau'ty, *n.,* a combination of qualities and characteristics of a person or object held to be delightful to the senses and intellect; a beautiful woman or thing.

beau'ty-spot, *n.,* something that heightens beauty by contrast; a patch on the face to do this; an outstandingly attractive place.

beaux'ite, *i.q.* bauxite.

bea'ver, *n.,* a small quadruped haunting rivers and lakes, valuable for its fur; the fur itself; the vizor of a helmet.

bea'vered, *adj.,* having a beaver or vizor.

beav'erteen, *n.,* a course, twilled cotton with pile of loops.

bebee'rine, *n.,* the active principle of the bark of the *bebeeru,* a kind of laurel found in Guyana.

be'bop, *n.,* a variety of jazz.

becalm', *v.t.,* to render calm; to reduce (a ship) to motionlessness.

becalmed', *p.p.,* becalm.

becalm'ing, *pr.p.,* becalm.

became', *p.p.,* become.

because', *conj.,* by reason that.

beccafi'co, *n.,* a bird like the nightingale; the garden warbler.

be'chamel, *n.,* a kind of white sauce (inventor's name).

bechance', *v.t.* and *i.,* to happen to; to happen.

bechanced', *p.p.,* bechance.

bechan'cing, *pr.p.,* bechance.

becharm', *v.t.,* to charm.

bêche'-de-mer, *n.,* the trepang, a sea-slug.

beck, *n.,* a brook; a nod intended as a signal; *v.t.,* to call by a nod.

becked, *p.p.,* beck.

beck'et, *n.,* in ships a contrivance for fastening loose ropes.

beck'ing, *pr.p.,* beck.

beck'on, *v..,* to make a sign with the hand or finger.

beck'oned, *p.p.,* beckon.

beck'oning, *pr.p.,* beckon.

becloud', *v.t.,* to cover with clouds; to render obscure.

becloud'ed, *p.p.,* becloud.

becloud'ing, *pr.p.,* becloud.

become', *v.i.,* to pass from one state to another; *v.t.,* to suit.

becom'ing, *pr.p.,* become; *adj.,* suitable.

becom'ingly, *adv.,* in a becoming manner.

becom'ingness, *n.,* suitability.

Becquerel rays, *n. pl.,* the rays emitted by radio-active matter.

bed, *n.,* that on which one sleeps; a plot of ground in a garden; that on which anything rests; a layer; *v.t.,* to place in a bed; to plant.

bedab'ble, *v.t.,* to wet; to sprinkle.

bedab'bled, *p.p.,* bedabble.

bedab'bling, *pr.p.,* bedabble.

bedark'en, *v.t.,* to make dark.

bedash', *v.t.,* to bespatter.

bedaub', *v.t.,* to smear with anything thick or slimy.

bedaubed', *p.p.,* bedaub.

bedaub'ing, *pr.p.,* bedaub.

bedaze', *i.q.,* bedazzle.

bedaz'zle, *v.t.,* to blind by excess of light.

bed'-chair, *n.,* a chair with a movable back which can be lowered so as to form a bed.

bed'chamber, *n.,* a bedroom.

bed'clothes, *n. pl.,* blankets, coverlets, etc.

bed'cover, *n.,* an upper bed covering.

bed'ded, *p.p.,* bed.

bedd'er, *n.,* a plant for bedding out; an upholsterer.

bed'ding, *n.,* a bed and its furniture; *pr.p.,* bed.

bedeck′, *v.t.*, to adorn.

bedecked′, *p.p.*, bedeck.

bedeck′ing, *pr.p.*, bedeck.

bed′eguar, *n.*, a spongy excrescence found on roses, produced by insects.

be′del(l), *n.*, a beadle in a university or lawcourt.

bedev′il, *v.t.*, to torment, as by evil spirits.

bedev′il(l)ed, *p.p.*, bedevil.

bedev′il(l)ing, *pr.p.*, bedevil.

bedev′ilment, *n.*, possession by the devil; disorder; besetting.

bedew′, *v.t.*, to moisten as with dew.

bedewed′, *p.p.*, bedew.

bedew′ing, *pr.p.*, bedew.

bed′fast, *adj.*, confined to bed.

bed′fellow, *n.*, one who occupies the same bed with another.

bed′-hangings, *n. pl.*, curtains hung about a bed.

bedight′, *v.t.*, to dress gaily, *p.p.*, bedight.

bedim′, *v.t.*, to make dim; to obscure.

bedi′zen, *v.t.*, to deck in a tawdry manner.

bed′-key, *n.*, a wrench for tightening a bedstead.

bed′lam, *n.*, a madhouse (orig. a Bethlehem Hospital).

bed′lamite, *n.*, a madman.

Bed′lington, *n.*, a shorthaired sporting terrier.

bed′maker, *n.*, a womanservant who has the care of college rooms.

bed′mate, *n.*, a bedfellow.

Bed′ouin, *n.*, a nomadic Arab.

bed′pan, *n.*, a utensil for use in a sick-bed.

bed′plate, *n.*, the foundation plate of an engine.

bed′post, *n.*, one of the corner pillars of a bed.

bed′quilt, *n.*, a coverlet or counterpane.

bedrab′bled, *adj.*, dirty with rain and mud.

bedrag′gle, *v.t.*, to soil by dragging through mud.

bed′rid, *adj.*, *i.q.* bedridden.

bed′ridden, *adj.*, long confined to bed.

bed′rock, *n.*, underlying rock formations; basic principles.

bed′room, *n.*, a sleeping room.

bed′side, *adj.*, beside a bed; *n.*, the space adjoining a bed.

bed′sitt′er, *n.*, abbrev. for bed-sitting-room.

bed′sitt′ing-room, *n.*, a bedroom and sitting-room combined.

bed′spread, *n.*, a top coverlet for a bed.

bed′stead, *n.*, the framework of a bed.

bed′straw, *n.*, a plant growing wild in Britain, bearing yellow or white flowers.

bed′tick, *n.*, stout linen or cotton forming a bag to hold the packing of a bed.

bed′time, *n.*, the hour for bed.

bee, *n.*, an insect, one species of which is kept in hives for its wax and honey.

bee′bee, *n.*, a lady (*Hindustani*).

bee′bread, *n.*, the pollen of flowers collected by bees as food for their young.

beech, *n.*, a large, smooth-barked tree yielding a hard timber.

beech′en, *adj.*, bel. to the beech.

beech′nut, *n.*, a nut or fruit of the beech.

beech′y, *adj.*, abounding in beeches.

beef, *n.*, the flesh of cattle.

beef′eater, *n.*, a yeoman of the guard.

beef′steak, *n.*, a slice of beef for broiling.

beeftea′, *n.*, beef juice, for invalids.

beef′y, *adj.*, fleshy.

bee′hive, *n.*, a box used as a habitation for bees.

bee′house, *n.*, a house to contain bee-hives; an apiary.

beele, *n.*, an Indian tree akin to the quince.

bee′line, *n.*, the direct path between two places.

Be′elzebub, *n.*, a Philistine god (O.T.); the prince of devils (N.T.).

bee′-master, *n.*, one who keeps bees.

been, *p.p.*, be.

beer, *n.*, a fermented alcoholic drink made from malted barley.

beer′-barrel, *n.*, a barrel to contain beer.

beer′house, *n.*, a house where malt liquors are sold.

beer′-pump, *n.*, a pump to draw beer from cask to bar.

beer′shop, *n.*, a shop where beer is sold.

beer′y, *adj.*, of or like beer; betraying the influence of beer.

beest′ings, *n.*, the first milk given by a cow after calving.

bees′wax, *n.*, the wax secreted by bees.

bees′wing, *n.*, a film which forms in old port wine.

beet, *n.*, a plant with a thick, fleshy root, the red beet used as a vegetable, the white to produce sugar.

beet′le, *n.*, an insect with four wings, the front pair horny; a wooden mallet; *v.i.*, to overhang.

beet′le-brow, *n.*, a prominent brow.

beet′led, *p.p.*, beetle.

beet′ling, *adj.*, overhanging (said of cliffs, etc.); *pr.p.*, beetle.

beet′root, *n.*, the root of a beet; the plant itself.

beeves, *n. pl.*, oxen.

beez′er, *n.*, nose (*slang*).

befall′, *v.t.*, to happen to; *v.i.*, to come to pass.

befal′len, *p.p.*, befall.

befal′ling, *pr.p.*, befall.

befell′, *p.p.*, befall.

befit, *v.t.*, to be suitable to.

befit′ted, *p.p.*, befit.

befit′ting, *pr.p.*, befit.

befog′, *v.t.*, to involve in fog; to confuse.

befogged′, *p.p.*, befog.

befogg′ing, *pr.p.*, befog.

befool′, *v.t.*, to delude.

befooled′, *p.p.*, befool.

befool′ing, *pr.p.*, befool.

before′, *prep.*, in front of; *adv.*, previously; *conj.*, rather than; sooner than.

before'hand, *adv.,* in advance.

before'-mentioned, *adj.,* previously mentioned.

before'time, *adv.,* formerly.

befoul', *v.t.,* to soil.

befriend', *v.t.,* to act as a friend to.

befriend'ed, *p.p.,* befriend.

befriend'ing, *pr.p.,* befriend.

befringe', *v.t.,* to supply with a fringe.

beg, *v.t.* and *i.,* to ask for earnestly; to solicit alms; to assume.

begad', *interj.,* by God.

began, *p.p.,* begin.

beget', *v.t.,* to procreate; to produce.

beget'ter, *n.,* one who begets; a father.

beget'ting, *pr.p.,* beget.

beg'gar, *n.,* one who begs; *v.t.,* to reduce to beggary.

beg'gared, *p.p.,* beggar.

beg'garing, *pr.p.,* beggar.

beg'garliness, *n.,* meanness.

beg'garly, *adj.,* like a beggar.

beg'gary, *n.,* the state of a beggar.

begged, *p.p.,* beg.

beg'ging, *pr.p.,* beg.

begin', *v.t.* and *i.,* to originate.

begin'ner, *n.,* one who begins; a tiro.

begin'ning, *n.,* the origin; the commencement; *pr.p.,* begin.

begird', *v.t.,* to surround with a girdle.

begird'ing, *pr.p.,* begird.

begirt', *p.p.,* begird.

begone', *interj.,* go away!

bego'nia, *n.,* a flowering tropical plant.

begor'ra, *exclam.,* Irish expletive for *By God.*

begot', *p.p.,* beget.

begot'ten, *p.p.,* beget.

begrime', *v.t.,* to make grimy.

begrimed', *p.p.,* begrime.

begrim'ing, *pr.p.,* begrime.

begrudge', *v.t.,* to envy someone the possession of.

begrudged', *p.p.,* begrudge.

begrudg'ing, *pr.p.,* begrudge.

beguile', *v.t.,* to deceive; to while away (time).

beguiled', *p.p.,* beguile.

beguile'ment, *n.,* the act or effect of beguiling.

beguil'er, *n.,* one who beguiles.

beguil'ing, *pr.p.,* beguile.

beguine, *n.,* a dance in bolero rhythm.

begun', *p.p.,* begin.

behalf', *n.,* interest; support; defence.

behave', *v.i.* and *refl.,* to conduct oneself.

behaved', *p.p.,* behave.

beha'ving, *pr.p.,* behave.

behav'io(u)r, *n.,* a manner of behaving.

behav'iourism, *n.,* the study and analysis of behaviour (*psych.*).

behav'iourist, *n.,* one who practises behaviourism.

behead', *v.t.,* to decapitate.

behead'ed, *p.p.,* behead.

behead'ing, *pr.p.,* behead.

beheld', *p.p.,* behold.

be'hemoth, *n.,* a Biblical monster; perhaps the hippopotamus.

behest', *n.,* a command.

behind', *prep.* and *adv.,* at the back of; later.

behind'hand, *adj.,* tardy; *adv.,* insufficiently advanced.

behold', *interj.,* fix your attention on; *v.t.* and *i.,* to look at with attention.

behold'en, *adj.,* bound in gratitude.

behold'er, *n.,* a spectator.

behold'ing, *pr.p.,* behold.

behoof', *n.,* an advantage; a benefit.

behoove', *v.t. impers., i.q.* behove.

behooved', *p.p.,* behoove.

behove', *v.t. impers.,* to be fit, meet, or necessary for.

behoved', *p.p.,* behove.

beige, *adj.,* greyish; *n.,* unbleached woollen fabric.

bei'gnet, *n.* a fritter (*Fr.*).

be'ing, *pr.p.,* be; *n.,* existence, a living creature, usually human.

bel, *n.,* a unit of measurement for sound, etc.

bela'bour, *v.t.,* to beat soundly.

bela'boured, *p.p.,* belabour.

bela'bouring, *pr.p.,* belabour.

belat'ed, *adj.,* having lingered till late; benighted.

belat'edness, *n.,* delay.

belaud', *v.t.,* to load with praise.

belay', *v.t.,* to make fast by winding round something.

belayed', *p.p.,* belay.

belay'ing, *pr.p.,* belay.

belay'ing-pin, *n.,* a stout post for belaying ropes about.

bel can'to, *n.,* a special form of operatic singing (*It.*).

belch, *n.,* the act of belching; *v.i.,* to eject wind from the stomach.

belched, *p.p.,* belch.

bel'cher, *n.,* a partly-coloured neckerchief.

belch'ing, *n.,* the act of ejecting wind from the stomach orally; *pr.p.,* belch.

bel'dam, bel'dame, *n.,* an ugly old woman.

belea'guer, *v.t.,* to blockade with an army.

belea'guered, *p.p.,* beleaguer.

belea'guering, *pr.p.,* beleaguer.

belem'nite, *n.,* a dart-shaped fossil shell found in chalk.

bel'fry, *n.,* a bell-tower; a campanile.

bel'ga, *n.,* the Belgian unit of currency = 5 paper francs.

Bel'gian, *adj.,* pert. to Belgium; *n.,* an inhabitant of B.

Bel'gic, *adj.,* Belgian; pert. to the Belgae.

Belgrav'ia, *n.,* a once fashionable residential part of London containing Belgrave Square.

Be'lial, *n.,* wickedness; a wicked person; Satan.

be'lie, *v.t.,* to show to be false; to calumniate.

belied', *p.p.,* belie.

belief', *n.,* an assent of the mind to the truth of a declared fact without personal knowledge of it; a creed.

believ'able, *adj.*, credible.

believe', *v.t.* and *i.*, to be firmly persuaded of the truth of anything.

believed', *p.p.*, believe.

believ'er, *n.*, one who believes.

believ'ing, *pr.p.*, believe.

believ'ingly, *adv.*, in a believing manner.

belike', *adv.*, probably, perhaps.

Belish'a beacon, *n.*, a post with a yellow globe on top marking a pedestrian street-crossing.

belit'tle, *v.t.*, to disparage.

belit'tled, *p.p.*, belittle.

belit'tler, *n.*, one who belittles.

belit'tling, *pr.p.*, belittle.

bell, *n.*, a metallic vessel which gives a clear, musical sound on being struck; any bell-shaped thing; *v.t.*, to put a bell on.

belladon'na, *n.*, a poisonous, medicinal plant.

bell'-animal'cule, *n.*, a family of plants of the Vorticella genus.

bell'-bird, *n.*, a South American bird; also an Australian bird of a different species.

bell'-boy, *n.*, a hotel attendant.

bell'-buoy, *n.*, a buoy fitted with a bell.

belle, *n.*, a lady of distinguished beauty.

belles-let'tres, *n. pl.*, elegant literature (*Fr.*).

bellet'rist, *n.*, a student of belles-lettres.

belletris'tic, *adj.*, pert. to belles-lettres.

bell'-founder, *n.*, a maker of bells.

bell'-foundry, *n.*, a bell-caster's works.

bel'licose, *adj.*, warlike; pugnacious.

bel'lied, *p.p.*, belly; *adj.*, protuberant.

bellig'erency, *n.*, warfare; aggressive and hostile conduct.

bellig'erent, *n.*, one engaged in fighting; *adj.*, carrying on war; aggressively hostile.

bel'lite, *n.*, a kind of explosive.

bell'man, *n.*, a public crier with a bell.

bell'-metal, *n.*, an alloy of copper and tin used in making bells.

Bellon'a, *n.*, a woman of commanding presence; the goddess of war.

bel'low, *n.*, a loud outcry; *v.i.*, to roar; to make a loud, hollow noise like a bull.

bel'lowed, *p.p.*, bellow.

bel'lower, *n.*, one who bellows.

bel'lowing, *n.*, the act or the sound itself; *pr.p.*, bellow.

bel'lows, *n.*, sing., or pl., an instrument for making a strong current of air.

bell'pull, *n.*, a bellrope or wire and its attachment.

bell'-punch, *n.*, a ticket punch with a signal bell.

bell'push, *n.*, a button which, if pressed, rings a bell.

bell'ringer, *n.*, one who rings bells.

bell'-wether, *n.*, a sheep that leads the flock, having a bell on his neck.

bel'ly, *n.*, that part of the body below the thorax or chest; a protuberance, generally hollow; *v.i.*, to swell out.

bel'ly-band, *n.*, a band round the belly of a horse.

bel'lyful, *n.*, as much as satisfies the appetite.

bel'lying, *pr.p.*, belly.

belong', *v.i.*, to be the property of; to pertain to.

belonged', *p.p.*, belong.

belong'ing, *pr.p.*, belong.

belong'ings, *n. pl.*, possessions.

belov'ed, *adj.* and *n.*, (one) greatly loved.

below', *adv.* and *prep.*, under.

belt, *n.*, a girdle; a band, esp. one round two wheels transferring motion from one to the other; *v.t.*, to fasten or surround with a belt.

Bel'tane, *n.*, an ancient Celtic festival in which bonfires on hills were lighted.

bel'ted, *adj.*, wearing a belt; *p.p.*, belt.

belt'ing, *n.*, the materials of which belts for machinery are made; *pr.p.*, belt.

bel'vedere, *n.*, a summer-

house on a knoll; a look-out turret.

bely'ing, *pr.p.*, belie.

bem'a, *n.*, a platform in ancient Athenian public assembly (*Gr.*).

bemire', *v.t.*, to soil with mud or mire.

bemired', *p.p.*, bemire.

bemir'ing, *pr.p.*, bemire.

bemoan', *v.t.*, to lament.

bemoaned', *p.p.*, bemoan.

bemoan'er, *n.*, one who bemoans.

bemoan'ing, *n.*, lamentation; *pr.p.*, bemoan.

bemuse', *v.t.*, to muddle or stupefy.

bemused', *p.p.*, bemuse.

bemus'edly, *adv.*, in a bewildered manner.

bemuse'ment, *n.*, a bemused condition.

bemus'ing, *pr.p.*, bemuse.

ben, *n.*, a mountain peak (*Scot.*).

benatu'ra, *n.*, a vessel for holy water.

bench, *n.*, a long seat; a table on which carpenters, etc., do their work; a judge's seat, the judges, their court.

bench'er, *n.*, a senior barrister in an inn of court who is a governor of the society.

bend, *n.*, a curve; one of the ordinaries in heraldry; *v.t.*, to curve or make crooked; *v.i.*, to deviate from the straight.

bend'able, *adj.*, capable of being bent.

bend'ed, *p.p.*, bend.

bend'er, *n.*, one who bends.

bend'ing, *n.*, the act; *pr.p.*, bend.

bend'let, *n.*, a diminutive of a bend in heraldry.

bend'y, *adj.*, divided into an even number of bends of a shield in heraldry.

beneaped', *adj.*, left aground by a neap-tide.

beneath', *adv.* and *prep.*, below; under.

benedi'cite, *interj. n.*, bless you; a blessing; *or* a grace at table, the Church canticle beginning with the word.

ben'edick, *n.*, *i.q.* benedict.

ben'edict, n., a married man, esp. a formerly confirmed bachelor.

Benedic'tine, adj., rel. to St. Benedict's rule; n., a monk of the Order of St. Benedict; a kind of liqueur.

Benedic'tiness, n., a Benedictine nun.

benedic'tion, n., a blessing; a solemn invocation of happiness.

benedic'tive, adj., i.q. benedictory.

benedic'tory, adj., giving a blessing.

ben'efact, v.t., to confer a benefit on.

benefac'tion, n., a charitable donation.

benefac'tor, n., one who confers a benefit.

benefac'tress, n., fem. of benefactor.

ben'efice, n., an ecclesiastical endowment providing for the maintenance of divine service.

ben'eficed, adj., possessed of a benefice.

benef'icence, n., active charity.

benef'icent, adj., performing acts of charity; well-disposed.

benef'icently, adv., in a beneficent manner.

bénéficiaire', n., a player who takes a benefit (Fr.).

benefi'cial, adj., advantageous.

benefi'cially, adv., in a beneficial manner.

benefi'ciary, n., one who is in the receipt of benefits or profits.

ben'efit, n., an advantage or profit; v.t., to do good to; v.i., to gain advantage.

ben'efited, p.p., benefit.

ben'efiting, pr.p., benefit.

Ben'elux, n., a name for Belgium, the Netherlands and Luxemburg.

benev'olence, n., charitableness; a euphemism for a tax illegally exacted.

benev'olent, adj., charitable; kindly.

benev'olently, adv., in a benevolent manner.

Bengal', n., a province in India; a signal firework; a striped gingham.

Bengalese', adj., pert. to Bengal.

Bengal'i, n., the language of Bengal; a native of B.

benight', v.t., to overtake with night.

benight'ed, adj., morally dark, ignorant; p.p., benight.

benight'ing, pr.p., benight.

benign', adj., kind; gracious; not severe.

benig'nancy, n., i.q. benignity.

benig'nant, adj., gracious, kind.

benig'nantly, adv., in a benignant manner.

benig'nity, n., graciousness; kindness of superiors.

benign'ly, adv., in a benign manner.

ben'ison, n., a benediction.

beni'tier, n., a receptacle for holy water.

benj'amin, n., a North American shrub with aromatic bark; the youngest child.

ben'net, n., a yellow herb.

bent, n., a natural tendency; a wiry grass; p.p., bend.

benth'al, adj., pert. to depth.

ben'thos, n., the flora and fauna found at the bottom of the ocean (biol.).

ben'thoscope, n., a bathysphere.

bent'wood, adj., made of this material; n., wood artificially bent.

benumb', v.t., to deprive of sensation.

benumbed', p.p., benumb.

benumb'ing, pr.p., benumb.

ben'zedrine, n., a drug used to relieve respiratory trouble by inhalation.

ben'zene, n., a solvent for grease prepared from coal tar.

ben'zine, n., i.q. benzene.

benzo'ic, adj., obtained from benzoin.

benzo'in, n., gum benjamin, obtained from the fragrant resin of a tree of Sumatra, used in incense, cosmetics, etc.

ben'zol, n., i.q. benzene.

ben'zoline, n., i.q. benzene.

benzyp'rine, n., a cancer-inducing hydrocarbon.

bequeath', v.t., to leave by will.

bequeathed', p.p., bequeath.

bequeath'er, n., one who bequeaths.

bequeath'ing, pr.p., bequeath.

bequest', n., a legacy; the act of bequeathing.

berate', v.t., to scold.

berat'ed, p.p., berate.

berat'ing, pr.p., berate.

Berb'er, adj., rel. to Barbary or N. Africa; n., a native of Barbary or N. Africa.

ber'berine, n., a yellow dye obtained from the root of the barberry tree.

ber'beris, n., a shrub bearing red or yellow berries.

berceuse, n., a cradle-song; a lullaby (Fr.).

bere, n., barley.

Berœ'an, adj., rel. to Berœa.

bereave', v.t., to deprive of something prized.

bereaved', p.p., bereave.

bereave'ment, n., deprivation, esp. loss by death.

bereav'ing, pr.p., bereave.

bereft', p.p., bereave.

ber'et, n., a flat, round, cloth cap (Fr.).

berg, n., a mountain or hill.

ber'gamot, n., a kind of pear; a fragrant oil or perfume prepared from lime fruit; a coarse tapestry.

ber'gander, n., a wild duck.

berg'mote, n., a Derbyshire miners' court for settling disputes.

beri'beri, n., a tropical disease.

berlin', n., an old-fashioned four-wheeled carriage.

berm, n., a ledge in fortification.

Bermud'ian, adj., pert. to Bermuda; n., an inhabitant of the Bermudas.

Ber'nardine, n., a Cistercian monk.

Bernese', adj., pert. to Berne; n. a citizen of Berne.

ber'ried, adj., having berries.

ber′ry, *n.*, a small pulpy fruit.

ber′ryless, *adj.*, devoid of berries.

ber′serk, *adj.*, frenzied.

ber′serker, *n.*, a Scandinavian warrior; a person of extreme violence.

berth, *n.*, a station in which a ship can lie; a sleeping space in a ship; an appointment or situation; *v.t.*, to assign a ship's anchorage.

Berth′a, *n.*, a German long-range gun named after Bertha Krupp.

berthed′, *p.p.*, berth.

berth′ing, *pr.p.*, berth.

Ber′thon-boat, *n.*, a collapsible boat.

bertillonage′, *n.*, the identification of criminals by their physical characteristics (*Fr.*).

Bertill′on sys′tem, *n.*, a method of criminal identification by measurements.

ber′yl, *n.*, a kind of inferior emerald.

ber′ylline, *adj.*, like a beryl; bluish-green.

beryll′ium, *n.*, a metal resembling magnesium.

beseech′, *v.t.*, to entreat.

beseech′ed, *p.p.*, beseech.

beseech′er, *n.*, one who beseeches.

beseech′ing, *adj.*, entreating; *pr.p.*, beseech.

beseech′ingly, *adv.*, in a beseeching manner, entreatingly.

beseem′, *v.t.*, to be worthy of.

beseemed′, *p.p.*, beseem.

beseem′ing, *adj.*, becoming; fit; worthy of; *pr.p.*, beseem.

beseem′ingly, *adv.*, in a beseeming manner.

beset′, *v.t.*, to hem in; to press hard upon.

beset′ment, *n.*, a state of being closed in.

beset′ting, *adj.*, habitually assailing.

beshrew′, *v.t.*, to wish a curse upon; to execrate mildly.

besiclom′eter, *n.*, an optical instrument for measuring the breadth of the forehead.

beside′, *prep.*, at the side of; in comparison with.

besides′, *adv.*, moreover; *prep.*, in addition to.

besiege′, *v.t.*, to surround with armed forces with the intention of compelling surrender; to harass.

besieged′, *p.p.*, besiege.

besieg′er, *n.*, one who besieges.

besieg′ing, *pr.p.*, besiege.

beslav′er, *v.t.*, to overflatter.

beslobb′er, *v.t.*, to kiss effusively.

beslubb′er, *v.t.*, to besmear.

besmear′, *v.t.*, to smear all over.

besmeared′, *p.p.*, besmear.

besmear′ing, *pr.p.*, besmear.

besmirch′, *v.t.*, to soil.

besmirched′, *p.p.*, besmirch.

besmirch′ing, *pr.p.*, besmirch.

be′som, *n.*, a broom; a brush of twigs.

besot′, *v.t.*, to stupefy with drink.

besot′ted, *p.p.*, besot.

besot′ting, *pr.p.*, besot.

besought′, *p.p.*, beseech.

bespang′le, *v.t.*, to adorn with spangles.

bespang′led, *adj.*, adorned with spangles; *p.p.*, bespangle.

bespang′ling, *pr.p.*, bespangle.

bespat′ter, *v.t.*, to soil by spattering.

bespat′tered, *p.p.*, bespatter.

bespat′tering, *pr.p.*, bespatter.

bespeak′, *n.*, (among actors), a benefit performance; *v.t.*, to order beforehand; to betoken.

bespeak′er, *n.*, one who bespeaks.

bespeak′ing, *pr.p.*, bespeak.

bespoke′, *p.p.*, bespeak.

bespok′en, *p.p.*, bespeak.

bespread′, *v.t.*, to form a coating over.

besprent′, *adj.*, sprinkled with; scattered about.

besprin′kle, *v.t.*, to sprinkle over.

besprin′kled, *p.p.*, besprinkle.

besprin′kling, *pr.p.*, besprinkle.

Bes′semer, *adj.*, descriptive of steel made by Sir Henry Bessemer's process.

best, *adj.*, good in the highest degree; *v.t.*, to surpass, to overcome.

bestead′, *v.t.* and *i.*, to help.

best′ed, *adj.*, overpowered (*colloq.*).

bes′tial, *adj.*, brutal; brutish.

bestial′ity, *n.*, beastliness; the quality of a beast.

best′ialize, *v.t.*, to reduce to the condition of a beast.

bes′tiary, *n.*, a moralizing book on animals.

bestir′, *v.t.* and *refl.*, to put into brisk action.

bestirred′, *p.p.*, bestir.

bestir′ring, *pr.p.*, bestir.

bestow′, *v.t.*, to confer; to impart; to stow away.

bestow′al, *n.*, the act of bestowing.

bestowed′, *p.p.*, bestow.

bestow′er, *n.*, one who bestows.

bestow′ing, *pr.p.*, bestow.

bestrad′dle, *v.t.*, to bestride.

bestrew′, *v.t.*, to strew.

bestrewed′, *p.p.*, bestrew.

bestrew′ing, *pr.p.*, bestrew.

bestrid′, *p.p.*, bestride.

bestrid′den, *p.p.*, bestride.

bestride′, *v.t.*, to stand or sit with the legs on each side of.

bestrid′ing, *pr.p.*, bestride.

bet, *v.t.*, to wager.

bet′a, *n.*, the second letter of the Greek alphabet.

betake′, *v.t. refl.*, to repair; to resort.

betak′en, *p.p.*, betake.

bet′atron, *n.*, an apparatus for increasing the speed of electrons.

be′tel, *n.*, a kind of pepper, chewed in Malaysia.

bête-noire, *n.*, a pet aversion (*Fr.*).

Beth′din, *n.*, a Jewish tribunal.

beth′el, *n.*, a place of worship.

bethes'da, *n.*, a Nonconformist chapel.

bethink', *v.t. refl.*, to call or recall to mind.

bethink'ing, *pr.p.*, bethink.

bethought', *p.p.*, bethink.

betide', *v.t.*, to happen to; *v.i.*, to happen.

beti'ded, *p.p.*, betide.

beti'ding, *pr.p.*, betide.

betimes', *adv.*, seasonably; at an early hour.

bêtise, *n.*, a foolish remark or action (*Fr.*).

beto'ken, *v.t.*, to serve as a token of; to foreshadow.

beto'kened, *p.p.*, betoken.

beto'kening, *pr.p.*, betoken.

bet'on, *n.*, a kind of concrete.

bet'ony, *n.*, a British plant once used in medicine and dyeing.

betook', *p.p.*, of betake.

betray', *v.t.*, to be unfaithful to.

betray'al, *n.*, the act of betraying.

betrayed', *p.p.*, betray.

betray'er, *n.*, one who betrays.

betray'ing, *pr.p.*, betray.

betray'ment, *n.*, *i.q.* betrayal.

betroth', *v.t.*, to contract with a view to marriage.

betroth'al, *n.*, the act of betrothing.

betrothed', *p.p.*, betroth.

betroth'ing, *pr.p.*, betroth.

bet'ted, *p.p.*, bet.

bet'ter, *adj.*, good in a higher degree; *adv.*, in a more excellent manner; *n.*, a superior; *v.t.*, to improve.

bet'tered, *p.p.*, better.

bet'tering, *pr.p.*, better.

bet'terment, *n.*, an improvement.

bet'ters, *n. pl.*, superiors.

bet'ting, *n.*, the act of wagering; *pr.p.*, bet.

bet'ty, *n.*, a short jemmy; a Florence flask.

between', *adv.* and *prep.*, in the space or interval separating two things or groups.

between'ness, *n.*, the circumstance of being between.

between'time, *adv.*, at intervals.

between'whiles, *adv.*, *i.q.* betweentime.

betwixt', *prep.*, between.

beu'lah, *n.*, a Nonconformist chapel.

bev'atron, *n.*, an atomic accelerator of high capacity.

bev'el, *n.*, the inclination of two surfaces of a solid body to one another; *v.t.*, to cut to a bevel.

bev'el(l)ed, *adj.*, having a bevel; *p.p.*, bevel.

bev'el(l)er, *n.*, an operative who bevels plate glass, etc.

bev'el(l)ing, *pr.p.*, bevel.

bev'el-wheels, *n.*, the machinery in which the shafts of two wheels that work on each other form an angle.

bev'erage, *n.*, a drink.

bev'y, *n.*, a flock of birds; a company of ladies.

bewail', *v.t.*, to lament.

bewail'able, *adj.*, worthy of being bewailed.

bewailed', *p.p.*, bewail.

bewail'er, *n.*, one who bewails.

bewail'ing, *n.*, lamentation; *pr.p.*, bewail.

beware', *v.i.*, to guard against; to be suspicious of.

bewil'der, *v.t.*, to puzzle, to confuse.

bewil'dered, *p.p.*, bewilder.

bewil'dering, *pr.p.*, bewilder.

bewil'derment, *n.*, a state of being bewildered.

bewitch', *v.t.*, to subject to the influence of witchcraft; to charm.

bewitched', *p.p.*, bewitch.

bewitch'er, *n.*, one who bewitches.

bewitch'ery, *n.*, fascination; charm.

bewitch'ing, *adj.*, having power to bewitch; *pr.p.*, bewitch.

bewitch'ment, *n.*, *i.q.* bewitchery.

bewray', *v.t.*, to betray.

bey, *n.*, a Turkish governor.

beyond', *adv.* and *prep.*, on the farther side of.

bez'ant, *n.*, a gold coin current in Europe about the 9th century; an heraldic charge.

bez'el, *n.*, that part of a finger ring which holds the stone; the groove in which the glass of a watch is set.

bezique', *n.*, a card game.

be'zoar, *n.*, the intestinal concretions of certain animals, formerly believed to be antidotes to poison.

bezoar'dic, *adj.*, compounded with bezoar.

bezon'ian, *n.*, a rascally fellow.

bhang, *n.*, a narcotic prepared from Indian hemp.

bhis'ti, bhees'ty, *n.*, an Indian water-carrier.

bian'gular, *adj.*, having two angles.

bian'nual, *adj.*, happening twice yearly; *n.*, a plant that flowers twice a year.

bi'as, *n.*, a weight let into a bowl which deflects it from running straight; prepossession; *v.t.*, to prejudice.

bi'as(s)ed, *p.p.*, bias.

bi'as(s)ing, *pr.p.*, bias.

biax'ial, *adj.*, having two axes.

bib, *n.*, a chin-cloth worn by a child to protect its clothes; *v.t.*, to tipple; to drink frequently.

biba'cious, *adj.*, addicted to drinking.

bibac'ity, *n.*, a fondness for drinking.

bib'ber, *n.*, a tippler.

bib'-cock, *n.*, a tap with an inverted nozzle.

bibelot, *n.*, a small curio or artistic trinket; a nicknack (*Fr.*).

bib'itory, *adj.*, tippling.

Bi'ble, *n.*, the scriptures comprising the Old and New Testaments.

bib'lical, *adj.*, pert. to the Bible.

bib'licist, *n.*, one skilled in the knowledge of the Bible.

bibliog'rapher, *n.*, one versed in bibliography.

bibliograph'ic, *adj.*, pert. to bibliography.

bibliograph'ical, *adj.*, *i.q.* bibliographic.

bibliog′raphy, *n.*, a history of the different editions of a book; a list of works on a given subject.

bibliol′atry, *n.*, an excessive reverence for any book.

bibliolog′ical, *adj.*, rel. to bibliology.

bibliol′ogy, *n.*, biblical literature.

bib′liomancy, *n.*, divination by means of a book, esp. the Bible.

biblioma′nia, *n.*, a passion for collecting books.

biblioma′niac, *n.*, one affected by bibliomania.

bibliomani′acal, *adj.*, pert. to bibliomania.

bibliom′anist, *n.*, *i.q.* bibliomaniac.

bibliop′egy, *n.*, the art of bookbinding.

bib′liophile, *n.*, a lover of books.

biblioph′ilist, *n.*, *i.q.* bibliopole.

biblioph′ily, *n.*, a love of books.

bibliopho′bia, *n.*, a dislike of books.

bib′liopole, *n.*, a bookseller.

bibliop′olism, *n.*, bookselling.

bibliop′olist, *n.*, *i.q.* bibliopole.

bibliop′oly, *n.*, *i.q.* bibliopolism.

bibliothe′ca, *n.*, a library (*Lat.*).

bib′ulous, *adj.*, addicted to drinking.

bical′carate, *adj.*, having two spurs.

bicam′eral, *adj.*, having two (legislative) chambers.

bicap′sular, *adj.*, having two capsules.

bicar′bonate, *n.*, a carbonate having two equivalents of carbon dioxide to one of a base.

bice, *n.*, a blue or green colour used by painters.

bicen′tenary, *n.*, two hundred years; the two-hundredth anniversary.

bicentenn′ial, *adj.* and *n.*, occurring every two hundred years; lasting this length of time.

biceph′alous, *adj.*, having two heads.

bi′ceps, *n.*, a muscle of the arm or thigh, having two heads or origins.

bichlor′ide, *n.*, a compound where double proportion of chlorine combines with metal, etc.

bichro′mate, *n.*, a salt with two parts of chromic acid to one of the other ingredients.

bicip′ital, *adj.*, two-headed; pert. to the biceps.

bicip′itous, *adj.*, *i.q.* bicipital.

bick′er, *v.i.*, to quarrel; *n.*, a quarrel, a brawl; a flash; a porringer.

bick′ered, *p.p.*, bicker.

bick′erer, *n.*, one who bickers.

bick′ering, *n.*, quarrelling; *pr.p.*, bicker.

bicon′jugate, *adj.*, in pairs; placed side by side.

bicon′vex, *adj.*, convex on both sides.

bi′corn, *adj.*, having two horns.

bicorn′ous, *adj.*, *i.q.* bicorn.

bicor′poral, *adj.*, double-bodied.

bicor′porate, *adj.*, *i.q.* bicorporal.

bicru′ral, *adj.*, having two legs.

bicus′pid, *adj.*, two-fanged.

bi′cycle, *n.*, a light, two-wheeled conveyance propelled by the rider.

bicyclette′, *n.*, a low-wheeled bicycle.

bi′cyclist, *n.*, a bicycle rider.

bid, *n.*, an offer of a price at an auction; *v.t.*, to command; to pray; to offer as a price at an auction.

bidd′able, *adj.*, obedient; able to be bid.

bid′den, *p.p.*, bid.

bid′der, *n.*, one who bids.

bid′ding, *pr.p.*, bid.

bidd′y, *n.*, a chicken (*dial.*).

bide, *v.i.*, to remain in a place; *v.t.*, to wait for.

bid′ed, *p.p.*, bide.

bidet′, *n.*, a soldier's baggage horse; a small bath.

bid′ing, *pr.p.*, bide.

bien′nial, *adj.*, happening once in two years; lasting for two years; a plant that springs from seed and vegetates one year and flowers the next.

bien′nially, *adv.*, once in two years.

bier, *n.*, a frame for conveying a corpse to the grave.

bifa′cial, *adj.*, two-faced.

bifa′rious, *adj.*, double; two-fold.

bif′erous, *adj.*, bearing twice a year.

biff, *n.* and *v.t.*, a smart blow; to strike a person (*slang*).

bif′fin, *n.*, a cooking-apple.

bi′fid, *adj.*, cleft; forked.

bi′fidate, *adj.*, *i.q.* bifid.

bi′fidated, *adj.*, *i.q.* bifid.

biflo′rous, *adj.*, bearing two flowers.

bifoc′al, *adj.*, with two different focal lengths.

bifoc′als, *n. pl.*, spectacles for far and near vision.

bi′fold, *adj.*, two-fold; double.

bifo′liate, *adj.*, having two leaves.

bi′forate, *adj.*, having two perforations.

bi′forine, *n.*, a two-doored cell on the leaves of certain plants.

bi′form, *adj.*, double-bodied; having two shapes.

bi′formed, *adj.*, *i.q.* biform.

bi′furcate, *adj.*, forked; *v.i.*, to fork.

bi′furcated, *p.p.*, bifurcate.

bi′furcating, *pr.p.*, bifurcate.

bifurca′tion, *n.*, a forking.

bifur′cous, *adj.*, *i.q.* bifurcate.

big, *adj.*, great; pregnant; full.

big′amist, *n.*, one who has committed bigamy.

big′amize, *v.i.*, to commit bigamy.

big′amous, *adj.*, rel. to bigamy.

big′amy, *n.*, the crime or state of having more than one husband or wife at the same time.

big′aroon, *n.*, a white-heart cherry.

big′arreau, *n.*, *i.q.*, bigaroon.

big′enous, *adj.*, inherited from both parents.

bigen'tial, *adj.*, rel. to two tribes.

bigg, big, *n.*, a kind of barley.

big'ger, *adj.*, *comp.*, big.

big'gest, *adj.*, *super.*, big.

big'gin, *n.*, a child's cap; a night-cap; a colt.

bight, *n.*, a bay, a loop.

big'ness, *n.*, the state of being big.

bigno'nia, *n.*, a climbing shrub.

big'ot, *n.*, a person blindly attached to any opinion or creed.

big'oted, *adj.*, having the character of a bigot.

big'otry, *n.*, unreasoning zeal; intolerance.

big'wig, *n.*, a person of importance (*colloq.*).

bijou', *n.*, something small and pretty; a jewel (*Fr.*).

bijou'terie, *n.*, *i.q.* bijoutry (*Fr.*).

bijou'try, *n.*, jewellery; trinkets (*Fr.*).

bi'jugate, *adj.*, having two pairs of leaflets.

bi'jugous, *adj.*, *i.q.* bijugate.

bike, *n.* and *v.i.*, the colloq. abbrev. for bicycle (*slang*).

bikin'i, *n.*, a two-part bathing dress.

bilab'ial, *adj.*, two-lipped; *n.*, a consonant produced by two lips.

bila'biate, *adj.*, having two lips; applied to the corolla of a flower.

bilam'ellate, *adj.*, formed of two plates.

bilam'ellated, *adj.*, *i.q.* bilamellate.

bil'ander, *n.*, a two-masted Dutch canal boat.

bilat'eral, *adj.*, two-sided.

bil'berry, *n.*, the whortleberry.

bil'bo, *n.*, a sword.

bil'boes, *n. pl.*, a bar with shackles for the feet.

bile, *n.*, a yellow bitter liquid separated from the blood by the liver; ill-nature.

bile'-duct, *n.*, the tube conducting the bile.

bilge, *n.*, the floor of a ship's bottom; worthless nonsense (*colloq.*); *v.i.*, to spring a leak in the bilge.

bilged, *p.p.*, bilge.

bilge'water, *n.*, the water

lying in a ship's bottom.

bilg'ing, *pr.p.*, bilge.

bilharz'ia, *n.*, a disease-carrying flat-worm parasite.

bilharziasis, *n.*, the disease caused by the bilharzia worm.

bil'iary, *adj.*, pert. to bile.

bilin'gual, *adj.*, expressed in two languages.

biling'ualism, *n.*, the ability to speak two languages.

bilin'guist, *n.*, one who speaks two languages.

bil'ious, *adj.*, suffering from an excess of bile.

bil'iousness, *n.*, the state of being bilious.

bilit'eral, *adj.*, consisting of two letters.

bilk, *v.t.*, to decamp without paying.

bilked, *p.p.*, bilk.

bilk'ing, *pr.p.*, bilk.

bill, *n.*, the beak of a bird; a pruning instrument; a note of charges with amount due; an advertisement sheet; an order to pay; a parliamentary proposal; *v.i.*, to join bills, as doves do.

bill'abong, *n.*, the branch of a river coming to a dead end (*Austral.*).

bill'book, *n.*, a book in which bills of exchange, etc., are noted.

bill'-broker, *n.*, a dealer in bills of exchange.

billed, *p.p.*, bill.

bil'let, *n.*, a note in writing; a soldier's lodging; a small fuel log; a Norman architectural ornament; *v.i.*, to lodge a soldier in a private house.

billet-doux', *n.*, a love-letter (*Fr.*).

bil'leted, *p.p.*, billet.

bil'leting, *pr.p.*, billet.

bill'hook, *n.*, a small hatchet with a hook.

bill'iard-room, *n.*, a room with a billiard table.

bill'iards, *n.*, a game played on a table with balls and cues.

bil'likin, *n.*, a billy-can (*colloq.*).

bil'ling, *pr.p.*, bill.

bil'lingsgate, *n.*, foul language.

bil'lion, *n.*, a million millions.

bill'on, *n.*, gold or silver alloy with a large amount of some base metal.

bil'lot, *n.*, bullion in bar or mass.

bil'low, *n.*, a great wave; *v.i.*, to swell.

bil'lowy, *adj.*, swelling into large waves.

bill'poster, *n.*, *i.q.* bill-sticker.

bill'sticker, *n.*, one who posts placards in public places.

bill'y, *n.*, a tin can used as a kettle (*Austral.*).

bill'yboy, *n.*, a river or coasting trading barge.

bill'ycock, *n.*, a bowler hat.

bill'y-goat, *n.*, a male goat.

bill'y-(h)o, *n.*, meaning intense (*colloq.*).

bilo'bate, *adj.*, divided into two lobes.

bi'lobed, *adj.*, *i.q.* bilobate.

biloc'ular, *adj.*, divided into two cells.

bil'tong, *n.*, strips of dried, lean meat.

Bim, *n.*, an inhabitant of Barbados (*colloq.*).

bimac'ulate, *adj.*, marked with two spots.

bim'ana, *n. pl.*, animals having two hands.

bi'mane, *n.*, one of the bimana.

bim'anous, *adj.*, having two hands.

biman'ual, *adj.*, performed with both hands.

bimbash'i, *n.*, a Turkish military captain.

bime'dial, *adj.*, applied to lines which can only be summed in powers, being otherwise incommensurable.

bimes'trial, *adj.*, continuing two months.

bimet'al(l)ism, *n.*, a system of currency recognizing coins of two metals as legal tender to any amount.

bimonth'ly, *adj.* and *adv.*, occurring every two months or half-monthly (*see* bi-weekly).

bin, *n.*, a sub-division of a wine-cellar for bottles; a receptacle, as dust-bin, etc.

bi'nac, *n.*, a type of electronic computer.

bi'nary, *adj.*, composed of two parts.

bi′nate, *adj.*, growing in pairs.

binaur′al, *adj.*, used with two ears.

bind, *v.t.*, to fasten, esp. with anything flexible; to join together; to restrain.

bind′er, *n.*, one who binds, esp. books, sheaves, etc.

bind′ery, *n.*, a book-binding workshop.

bind′ing, *n.*, the cover, etc., of a book; *pr.p.*, bind.

bind′weed, *n.*, the convolvulus.

bine, *n.*, a flexible shoot.

binerv′ate, *adj.*, two-nerved.

binge, *n.*, a drinking bout; a spree (*slang*).

bing′o, *n.*, a popular gambling game; housey-housey; brandy (*slang*).

binitar′ian, *adj.*, rel. to binitarianism; *n.*, one who believes in a Godhead of two persons only.

binitar′ianism, *n.*, the doctrine of the binitarians.

bin′nacle, *n.*, the ship's compass-box near the helm.

bin′ocle, *n.*, a fieldglass; a telescope with two tubes, one for each eye.

binoc′ular, *adj.*, having two eyes; suited for the use of both eyes at once; *n.*, *i.q.* binocle.

binoc′ulate, *adj.*, having two eyes.

bino′mial, *adj.* and *n.*, having two algebraic terms.

binom′inal, *adj.*, having two names.

binom′inous, *adj.*, *i.q.* binominal.

bi′nous, *adj.*, *i.q.* binate.

bioc′ellate, *adj.*, marked with two eye-like spots.

biochem′ical, *adj.*, rel. to biochemistry.

biochem′ist, *n.*, one versed in biochemistry.

biochem′istry, *n.*, the chemistry of living organisms.

biodynam′ics, *n.*, the doctrine of vital energy.

biogen′esis, *n.*, the doctrine that life can spring only from living organisms.

biogeog′raphy, *n.*, the study of the distribution of living things.

bi′ograph, *n.*, a kind of cinematograph.

biog′rapher, *n.*, one who writes a biography.

biograph′ic, *adj.*, pert. to biography.

biograph′ical, *adj.*, *i.q.* biographic.

biog′raphy, *n.*, a life history.

biolog′ical, *adj.*, pert. to biology.

biol′ogist, *n.*, one who studies biology.

biol′ogy, *n.*, the science that treats of the lives of animals and plants.

biolyt′ic, *adj.*, rel. to the destruction of life.

biomet′rics, *n. pl.*, the science of statistics relating to life expectancy.

biom′etry, *n.*, the calculation of expectation of life.

bionom′ics, *n. pl.*, the study of life in natural surroundings.

biophys′ics, *n.*, the interpretation of biological phenomena in terms of physics.

bi′oplasm, *n.*, germinal matter.

bi′opsy, *n.*, an examination of tissue taken from a living body.

bi′oscope, *n.*, a toy or an appliance showing pictures in movement.

bi′otaxy, *n.*, the scientific classification of animals and plants.

bip′arous, *adj.*, bearing twins.

bipart′ible, *adj.*, capable of being divided into two.

bipart′ient, *adj.*, bearing twins.

bipart′ile, *adj.*, *i.q.* bipartible.

bipartisan′, *adj.*, of or involving two political parties.

bipart′ite, *adj.*, having two corresponding parts.

biparti′tion, *n.*, the act of making bipartite.

bipec′tinate, *adj.*, having two toothed margins.

bi′ped, *n.*, an animal having two feet.

bi′pedal, *adj.*, having two feet.

bipel′tate, *adj.*, covered with a shell like a double shield.

bipen′nate, *adj.*, having two wings.

bipen′nated, *adj.*, *i.q.* bipennate.

bipet′alous, *adj.*, having two petals.

bipin′nate, *adj.*, doubly lobed.

bi′plane, *n.*, an aeroplane with an upper and a lower plane or carrying surface.

bipo′lar, *adj.*, doubly polar.

bipolar′ity, *n.*, the bipolar quality.

bi′pont, *adj.*, rel. to books printed at Deuxponts (Bipontium, now Zwelbrücken).

bipont′ine, *adj.*, *i.q.* bipont.

bipunct′ual, *adj.*, having two points.

biquad′rate, *n.*, the square of the square; the fourth power.

biquadrat′ic, *adj.*, of the fourth power.

bi-quart′erly, *adj.* and *adv.*, half-quarterly.

biquint′ile, *n.*, an astronomical term applied to the relative positions of two planets separated by 144 degrees.

bira′diate, *adj.*, having two rays.

bira′mous, *adj.*, consisting of two branches.

birch, *n.*, a graceful tree with small leaves and a whitish bark; an instrument of punishment; *v.t.*, to punish with the birch rod.

birched, *p.p.*, birch.

birch′en, *adj.*, consisting of birch.

birch′ing, *pr.p.*, birch.

birch′-rod, *n.*, a birch used for punishment.

bird, *n.*, a feathered winged animal producing young from eggs.

bird′-cage, *n.*, a cage for a song-bird.

bird′call, *n.*, an instrument used for imitating birds' notes.

bird′catcher, *n.*, one who catches birds.

bird′fan′cier, *n.*, a bird dealer.

bird′ie, *n.*, a hole played in one under par (*golf*).

bird′like, *adj.*, resembling a bird.

bird′lime, *n.*, a sticky substance for entangling birds.

bird's'-eye, *n.*, a species of primrose; a kind of tobacco.

bird's'-eye view, *n.*, the view seen from above.

bi'reme, *n.*, a Greek or Roman vessel with two tiers of oars.

biret'ta, *n.*, a square cap worn by ecclesiastics.

biros'trate, *adj.*, having a double beak.

biros'trated, *adj.*, *i.q.* birostrate.

birth, *n.*, the process of being born; lineage; origin.

birth'-control', *n.*, the artificial control of reproduction.

birth'day, *n.*, the day on which anyone is born, or its anniversary.

birth'mark, *n.*, a congenital mark.

birth'place, *n.*, the place of one's birth.

birth'rate, *n.*, the rate of births to population by the thousand.

birth'right, *n.*, a right to which a person is entitled by birth.

bis, *adv.*, repeat; over again (*mus.*).

Biscay'an, *adj.*, pert. to Biscay in Spain.

bis'cotin, *n.*, a confection made of flour, sugar, eggs and marmalade.

bis'cuit, *n.*, a confection of wheat flour made in great variety; unglazed porcelain after the first baking.

bise, *n.*, a keen, dry N.W. wind in Switzerland and on the Mediterranean.

bisect', *v.t.*, to cut into two parts, esp. into two equal parts.

bisect'ed, *p.p.*, bisect.

bisect'ing, *pr.p.*, bisect.

bisec'tion, *n.*, the act of bisecting.

bisec'tor, *n.*, that which separates in parts of equal proportion.

biseg'ment, *n.*, one of the parts of a bisected line.

bisen'sory, *adj.*, affecting two senses.

bise'rial, *adj.*, arranged in two series or rows.

biser'rate, *adj.*, doubly notched.

bise'tose, *adj.*, having two bristles.

bise'tous, *adj.*, *i.q.* bisetose.

bisex'ual, *adj.*, of both sexes.

bish'op, *n.*, a member of the highest order of the Christian ministry; a piece in the game of chess.

bish'opric, *n.*, the dignity of a bishop.

bisk, *n.*, a soup made of several sorts of meat.

Bis'ley, *n.*, a place in Surrey used for shooting competitions of the British National Rifle Association.

bis'muth, *n.*, a yellowish metal.

bis'muthal, *adj.*, composed of bismuth.

bi'sociation, *n.*, the immediate association of an article or thought with two normally unrelated areas.

bi'sociative, *adj.*, pert. or rel. to bisociation.

bi'son, *n.*, a wild American ox.

bisque, *n.*, unglazed white porcelain; a point conceded to a tennis-player which he can claim when he chooses (*Fr.*).

bissex'tile, *adj.*, pert. to leap-year.

bis'ter, *n.*, *i.q.* bistre.

bistip'uled, *adj.*, having two stipules.

bis'tort, *n.*, a plant with twisted roots; snakeweed or adder's-wort.

bis'toury, *n.*, a surgical instrument.

bis'tre, *n.*, a brown pigment (*Fr.*).

bisul'cate, *adj.*, cloven footed.

bisul'phate, *n.*, a metallic salt of sulphuric acid in which one-half the hydrogen remains.

bisul'phuret, *n.*, a sulphide with two atoms of sulphur in the molecule.

bit, *n.*, a small piece; a boring tool; the metal part of a horse's bridle; *p.p.*, bite.

bitch, *n.*, the female of canine animals, as the dog, fox, wolf.

bite, *n.*, a wound made by biting; a mouthful; *v.t.*, to cut or crush with the teeth.

bit'er, *n.*, one who bites.

bitern'ate, *adj.*, doubly ternate.

bit'ing, *adj.*, sharp, sarcastic; *pr.p.*, bite.

bitt, *n.*, a frame fastened to the deck of a vessel on which to secure

cables; *v.t.*, to put round the bitts.

bit'ted, *adj.*, having bitts; *p.p.*, bitt.

bit'ten, *p.p.*, bite.

bit'ter, *adj.*, acrid; keen; reproachful; sarcastic.

bit'terish, *adj.*, rather bitter.

bitt'erling, *n.*, a small, carp-like freshwater fish.

bit'terly, *adv.*, in a bitter manner.

bit'tern, *n.*, a wading-bird of the heron family.

bit'terness, *n.*, the quality of being bitter.

bit'ters, *n. pl.*, a liquor used as a stomachic, made of bitter herbs.

bit'tersweet, *n.*, the woody nightshade.

bit'terweed, *n.*, the yellow gentian.

bit'ting, *pr.p.*, bitt.

bitt'ock, *n.*, a little bit (*dial.*).

bitts, *n. pl.*, the short bifurcated posts used for securing a ship's cable.

bit'umen, *n.*, a mineral resin.

bitu'minate, *v.t.*, to impregnate with bitumen.

bit'uminated, *p.p.*, bituminate.

bitu'minating, *pr.p.*, bituminate.

bitu'minize, *v.t.*, *i.q.* bituminate.

bitu'minous, *adj.*, containing bitumen.

bi'valve, *n.*, a shellfish with two hinged valves.

bival'vous, *adj.*, *i.q.* bivalvular.

bival'vular, *adj.*, having two valves.

bivault'ed, *adj.*, having two arches.

biven'tral, *adj.*, having two bellies.

biv'ious, *adj.*, leading two ways.

biv'ouac, *n.*, an open-air encampment of soldiers without tents; *v.i.*, to encamp in bivouac.

biv'ouacked, *p.p.*, bivouac.

biv'ouacking, *pr.p.*, bivouac.

biweek'ly, *adj.* and *adv.*, occurring every two weeks; also half-weekly.

bizarre', *adj.*, odd, fantastic.

blab, *v.t.*, to let out secrets.

blabbed, *p.p.*, blab.

blab'ber, *n.*, one who blabs.

blab'bing, *pr.p.*, blab.

black, *adj.*, of the darkest colour; *v.t.*, to blacken.

black'amoor, *n.*, a dark-skinned person.

black' art, *n.*, magic.

black'avised, *adj.*, dark-complexioned.

black'ball, *v.t.*, to exclude or reject by vote.

black'balled, *p.p.*, blackball.

black'balling, *pr.p.*, blackball.

black'beetle, *n.*, a cockroach.

black'berry, *n.*, the berry of the bramble.

black'bird, *n.*, a songbird of the thrush family with black plumage.

black'board, *n.*, a board used for instruction to receive drawing or writing in chalk.

black'-book, *n.*, a record of offences and punishments.

black'-cap, *n.*, a bird of the warbler family.

black'-cattle, *n.*, oxen reared for slaughter, no matter what their colour may be.

Black' Death, *n.*, an Eastern plague (bubonic).

blacked, *p.p.*, black.

black'en, *v.t.*, to make black.

black'ened, *p.p.*, blacken.

black'ener, *n.*, a slanderer.

black'ening, *pr.p.*, blacken.

black'-eyed, *adj.*, having eyes with black or very dark irises.

black'fish, *n.*, a small whale.

black'-flag, *n.*, a pirate's flag.

Black'fri'ar, *n.*, a Dominican friar.

black'guard, *n.*, a fellow of low character; *v.t.*, to use abusive language to.

black'guardism, *n.*, the conduct of a blackguard.

black'head, *n.*, the seaduck of Iceland; a black spot.

black'ing, *n.*, a black polish for leather; *pr.p.*, black.

black'ish, *adj.*, rather black.

black'-jack, *n.*, a large leather jug.

black'lead, *n.*, graphite; plumbago; *v.t.*, to polish with blacklead.

black'leg, *n.*, a cheat; a strike breaker.

black'letter, *n.*, the Old English or Gothic type used in early printed books.

black'list, *n.*, a list of defaulters, etc.; *v.t.*, to put on the blacklist.

black'ly, *adv.*, in a black manner.

black'mail, *n.*, extortion by intimidation; *v.t.*, to levy blackmail on.

Black' Mari'a, *n.*, the name for a special type of police van used for the removal of prisoners (*colloq.*).

black' mark'et, *n.*, illegitimate traffic in goods or currencies.

black'ness, *n.*, the state of being black.

black'out, *n.*, complete darkness; sudden loss of consciousness.

Black' Rod, *n.*, the usher of the Order of the Garter; the usher of the Lords in Parliament.

black'shirt, *n.*, a Fascist.

black'smith, *n.*, an ironsmith.

black'thorn, *n.*, the sloe; a cudgel.

blad'der, *n.*, a thin membranous bag in the body of an animal containing the urine, the gall, etc.; any similar vesicle.

blade, *n.*, the cutting part of an instrument; a leaf of grass; the broad part of an oar; a rollicking fellow.

blade'-bone, *n.*, the shoulder-blade, the scapula.

blad'ed, *adj.*, having a blade.

blade'less, *adj.*, without a blade.

blain, *n.*, a blister.

blam'able, *adj.*, deserving of blame.

blame, *n.*, the imputation of a fault; *v.t.*, to censure or reproach.

blamed, *p.p.*, blame.

blame'ful, *adj.*, faulty; meriting blame.

blame'less, *adj.*, without fault.

blame'lessly, *adv.*, in a blameless way.

blame'lessness, *n.*, the state of being blameless.

blam'er, *n.*, one who blames.

blame'worthy, *adj.*, culpable.

blam'ing, *pr.p.*, blame.

blanch, *v.t.* and *i.*, to whiten.

blanched, *p.p.*, blanch.

blanchim'eter, *n.*, an instrument for measuring bleaching power.

blanch'ing, *pr.p.*, blanch.

blancmange', *n.*, a kind of jellylike pudding.

blan'co, *n.*, a colouring preparation for accoutrements.

bland, *adj.*, mild; gentle; suave.

blandil'oquence, *n.*, flattering speech.

bland'ish, *v.t.* and *i.*, to caress or flatter; to render alluring.

bland'ished, *p.p.*, blandish.

bland'isher, *n.*, a flatterer.

bland'ishing, *pr.p.*, blandish.

bland'ishment, *n.*, artful caresses; cajolery; endearment.

bland'ly, *adv.*, in a bland manner.

bland'ness, *n.*, the state of being bland.

blank, *adj.*, white; empty; vacant; *n.*, an empty paper or space on a paper; a void.

blank'et, *n.*, a soft, thick woollen cloth used as a bed-covering; *v.t.*, to stifle; to take wind from the sails of another ship.

blank'eted, *adj.*, covered with a blanket; *p.p.*, blanket.

blank'eting, *n.*, the material of which blankets are made; *pr.p.*, blanket.

blank'ly, *adv.*, expressionless.

blank'ness, *n.*, the state of being blank.

blank' verse', *n.*, verse without rhyme.

blanquette, *n.*, a white fricassee (*Fr.*, *cookery*).

blare, *n.*, a loud noise; *v.i.*, to make a loud trumpet-like noise; *v.t.*, to proclaim loudly.

blared, *p.p.*, blare.

bla'ring, *adj.*, harsh, loud; *pr.p.*, blare.

blar'ney, *n.*, gross flattery; deceitful talk; *v.t.*, to humbug with talk.

blar'neyed, *p.p.*, blarney.

blar'neying, *n.*, the act of blarneying; *pr.p.*, blarney.

blasé, *adj.*, sated with pleasure.

blaspheme', *v.t.*, to speak impiously of; *v.i.*, to utter blasphemy.

blasphemed', *p.p.*, blaspheme.

blasph'emer, *n.*, one who blasphemes.

blasphe'ming, *pr.p.*, blaspheme.

blas'phemous, *adj.*, impiously irreverent towards God.

blas'phemously, *adv.*, in a blasphemous way.

blas'phemy, *n.*, grossly irreverent or outrageous language.

blast, *n.*, a gust of wind, the sound of blowing a wind-instrument; a blight; a violent explosion; *v.t.*, to injure by a blast or blight; to split by an explosion.

blast'ed, *p.p.*, blast.

blaste'ma, *n.*, the axis of growth of an embryo plant.

blast'er, *n.*, one who blasts.

blast'-furnace, *n.*, a smelting-furnace.

blast'ing, *n.*, the operation of blasting; *pr.p.*, blast.

blastocar'pous, *adj.*, having the germ beginning to grow inside the fruit.

blas'toderm, *n.*, the outside of the embryo in its earliest condition.

blastogen'esis, *n.*, reproduction by budding.

blast'pipe, *n.*, the pipe of a locomotive which carries the waste steam up the chimney.

blat'ancy, *n.*, idle noise.

bla'tant, *adj.*, noisy, palpable, ostentatious, defiant.

bla'tantly, *adv.*, in a blatant manner.

blath'er, *v.i.*, i.q. blether.

blat'ter, *v.i.*, to make a senseless noise.

blay, *n.*, a small fish.

blaze, *n.*, a flame, a bursting out; a white spot on a horse's forehead; a white spot on a tree made by removing the bark; *v.i.*, to flame; *v.t.*, to proclaim; to mark trees to indicate a path.

blazed, *p.p.*, blaze.

blaz'er, *n.*, a light sports jacket.

blaz'ing, *pr.p.*, blaze.

bla'zon, *n.*, a heraldic figure, *v.t.*, to describe armorial bearings; to adorn; to proclaim.

bla'zoned, *p.p.*, blazon.

bla'zoner, *n.*, one who blazons; a herald; a scandalmonger.

bla'zoning, *pr.p.*, blazon.

bla'zonry, *n.*, the art of describing coats-of-arms.

bleach, *n.*, a whitening agent; *v.t.*, to whiten.

bleached, *p.p.*, bleach.

bleach'er, *n.*, one who, or that which, bleaches.

bleach'ery, *n.*, an establishment where cloth is bleached.

bleach'ing, *n.*, the act or art of making textile fabrics white; *pr.p.*, bleach.

bleak, *adj.*, cold; chill; dreary.

bleak'ish, *adj.*, rather bleak.

bleak'ly, *adv.*, in a bleak manner.

bleak'ness, *n.*, the state of being bleak.

blear, *adj.*, sore (of the eyes); *v.t.*, to make sore so that the sight is dimmed.

blear'-eyed, *adj.*, soreeyed; dim-sighted.

blear'y, *adj.*, i.q. blear.

bleat, *n.*, the cry of a sheep; *v.i.*, to utter the cry of a sheep.

bleat'ed, *p.p.*, bleat.

bleat'er, *n.*, one who bleats.

bleat'ing, *n.*, the cry of a sheep; *pr.p.*, bleat.

bleb, *n.*, a blister.

bled, *p.p.*, bleed.

bleed, *v.i.*, to lose blood; *v.t.*, to take blood from.

bleed'ing, *n.*, the operation of letting blood; *pr.p.*, bleed.

bleep, *n.*, a radio signal; *v.i.*, to transmit this signal.

blem'ish, *n.*, a defect; *v.t.*, to impair or sully.

blem'ished, *p.p.*, blemish.

blem'ishing, *pr.p.*, blemish.

blench, *v.i.*, to shrink; to flinch.

blenched, *p.p.*, blench.

blench'ing, *pr.p.*, blench.

blend, *n.*, a mixture; *v.t.*, to mingle; *v.i.*, to be mixed.

blende, *n.*, an ore of zinc.

blend'ed, *adj.*, mixed; *p.p.*, blend.

blend'er, *n.*, one who, or that which, blends.

blend'ing, *pr.p.*, blend.

Blen'heim, *adj.* and *n.*, a kind of spaniel; the variety of apple; the Duke of Marlborough's seat at Woodstock.

blen'ny, *n.*, a small fish found among rocks.

blent, *adj.*, i.q. blended.

blephari'tis, *n.*, inflammation of the eyelid.

bles'-bok, *n.*, a whitefaced South African antelope.

bless, *v.t.*, to invoke or bestow happiness on; to glorify for benefits received.

blessed, *p.p.*, bless.

bless'ed, *adj.*, favoured with blessings; sacred.

bless'edly, *adv.*, in a blessed manner.

bless'edness, *n.*, happiness; God's favour.

bless'er, *n.*, one who blesses.

bless'ing, *n.*, the act of one who blesses; any good thing falling to one's lot; *pr.p.*, bless.

blest, *adj.*, another form of *blessed*.

blet, *n.*, over-ripeness in fruit.

bleth'er, *v.i.*, to talk nonsense.

bleth'erskate, *n.*, a blethering person.

blet′onism, *n.*, the faculty of water divination.

blet′onist, *n.*, a water diviner.

blew, *p.p.*, blow.

blight, *n.*, something that nips or destroys plants; *v.t.*, to blast; to frustrate.

blight′ed, *adj.*, smitten with blight; blasted; *p.p.*, blight.

blight′er, *n.*, a scoundrel or other offensive person (*slang*).

blight′ing, *adj.*, destroying; *pr.p.*, blight.

blight′ingly, *adv.*, in a blighting manner.

blight′y, *n.*, soldiers' slang for home (the word is of Urdu origin, corrupted).

blimp, *n.*, a little scouting airship; a person of entrenched reactionary ideas.

blind, *adj.*, without sight; closed at one end; *n.*, something to hinder sight or to keep out light; the cover of a window; a pretext; a covert design; *v.t.*, to make blind.

blind′age, *n.*, a screen for troops in fortification.

blind′-all′ey, *adj.*, leading nowhere; *n.*, a cul de sac.

blind′ed, *p.p.*, blind.

blind′er, *n.*, one who blinds; a horse's blinker.

blind′fold, *adj.*, having the eyes bandaged; *v.t.*, to cover the eyes with a bandage.

blind′folded, *adj.*, *i.q.* blindfold; *p.p.*, blindfold.

blind′folding, *pr.p.*, blindfold.

blind′ing, *adj.*, making blind; dazzling; *pr.p.*, blind.

blind′ly, *adv.*, without sight or understanding; recklessly.

blind′man's-buff, *n.*, a child's game.

blind′ness, *n.*, the state of being blind.

blind′-side, *n.*, a weakness of character which allows one to be taken advantage of.

blind spot, *n.*, an insensitive spot on the retina; a point where radio reception is weak; a mental area of insensitivity.

blind′worm, *n.*, a legless lizard with small eyes.

blink, *n.*, a glance of the eye; a glimmer; *v.i.*, to wink; to glimmer; *v.t.*, to shut one's eyes to; to evade purposely.

blink′ard, *n.*, one who blinks.

blinked, *p.p.*, blink.

blink′er, *n.*, one who blinks; a leather flap placed on either side of a horse's head to prevent him from seeing sideways or backwards.

blink′ered, *adj.*, provided with blinkers (of horses).

blink′ing, *adj.*, slang for infernal, confounded; *pr.p.*, blink.

blip, *n.*, any sudden small occurrence of light or sound.

bliss, *n.*, supreme happiness.

bliss′ful, *adj.*, full of bliss.

bliss′fully, *adv.*, in a blissful way.

bliss′fulness, *n.*, extreme happiness.

blis′ter, *n.*, a thin vesicle on the skin containing watery matter; a protective hull below the water, defending a ship's inner hull; *v.t.*, to raise a blister on; *v.i.*, to become blistered.

blis′tered, *p.p.*, blister.

blis′tering, *adj.*, causing blisters; *pr.p.*, blister.

blis′tery, *adj.*, full of blisters.

blithe, *adj.*, gay, joyful, merry.

blithe′ful, *adj.*, *i.q.* blithe.

blithe′ly, *adv.*, in a blithe manner.

blith′er, *v.i.*, *i.q.* blether.

blith′ering, *adj.*, consummate; contemptible (*colloq.*); *pr.p.*, blither.

blithe′some, *adj.*, full of gaiety; cheerful.

blithe′someness, *n.*, gaiety.

blitz, *n.* and *v.t.*, the abbrev. of blitzkrieg, an intensive attack (esp. air); to attack fiercely (*colloq.*).

blitzed, *adj.*, severely damaged; *p.p.*, blitz.

blitz′krieg, *n.*, a lightning war.

bliz′zard, *n.*, a driving storm of sleet and snow.

bloat, *v.t.*, to make swollen; *v.i.*, to become swollen.

bloat′ed, *adj.*, swollen; unduly large; *p.p.*, bloat.

bloat′edness, *n.*, the state of being bloated.

bloat′er, *n.*, a smoke-dried herring.

bloat′ing, *pr.p.*, bloat.

blob, *n.*, a drop of liquid.

blob′ber, *n.*, *i.q.* blubber.

blob′ber-lipped, *adj.*, having thick lips.

bloc, *n.*, a political or similar group.

block, *n.*, a solid mass usually shaped with flat sides; an obstruction; a casing containing pulleys; a portion of a city enclosed by streets; a piece of wood or metal on which an engraving is cut; *v.t.*, to obstruct; to stop.

blockade′, *n.*, the prevention of ingress to a place by surrounding it with ships or troops; *v.t.*, to shut a place up in this way.

blockad′ed, *p.p.*, blockade.

blockad′ing, *pr.p.*, blockade.

block′-book, *n.*, a book printed from movable wooden blocks.

blocked, *p.p.*, block.

block′head, *n.*, a stupid fellow.

block′house, *n.*, a sort of fort.

block′ing, *pr.p.*, block.

block′ish, *adj.*, stupid.

block′-tin, *n.*, tin cast into ingots.

bloke, *n.*, man (*colloq.*), fellow (*slang*).

blond(e), *adj.*, of fair complexion.

blondinette′, *n.*, a breed of oriental pigeons.

blond′ity, *n.*, the state of being blond.

blood, *n.*, the fluid in the arteries and veins of the body; consanguinity; *v.t.*, to bleed; to give a taste of blood.

blood′-bath, *n.*, a massacre.

blood′ed, *p.p.*, blood.

blood'-group, n., one of the four groups distinguished in blood transfusions.

blood'-guiltiness, n., murder.

blood'-heat, n., the temperature of the human blood in health.

blood'hound, n., a large dog of acute powers of scent.

blood'ily, adv., in a bloody manner.

blood'iness, n., murderousness.

blood'ing, pr.p., blood.

blood'less, adj., empty of blood; without shedding blood.

blood'-lust, n., a craving for blood.

blood'-red, adj., as red as blood.

blood'-relation, n., one related by blood.

blood'root, n., the tormentil.

blood'shed, n., slaughter.

blood'shot, adj., red and with congested veins (said of the eyes).

blood'stained, adj., stained with blood.

blood'stock, n., thoroughbred horses.

blood'sucker, n., any animal that sucks blood; an extortioner.

blood'thirsty, adj., desirous to shed blood.

blood'-transfusion, n., the transfer of one person's blood to another.

blood'-vessel, n., a vein or artery.

blood'wort, n., the bloody-veined dock plant.

blood'y, adj., pert. to blood; bloodstained.

bloom, n., a blossom; fullness of life and vigour; a glow or flush; a wedge of smelted iron; the delicate powdery coating of certain fruits; v.i., to produce flowers; to show the beauty of youth.

bloom'ary, n., the first forge in which iron is smelted.

bloomed, p.p., bloom.

bloom'er, n., a costume for women including loose trousers; pl., the trousers alone; blunder (slang).

bloom'ery, n., i.q. bloomary.

bloom'ing, adj., glowing as with youth and health; pr.p., bloom.

bloom'ingly, adv., in a blooming manner.

Blooms'bury, n., a part of London containing the British Museum.

bloom'y, adj., full of bloom.

blos'som, n., the flower of a plant; v.i., to put forth blossoms.

blos'somed, adj., in bloom; p.p., blossom.

blos'soming, pr.p., blossom.

blos'somry, n., blossoms collectively.

blot, n., a spot or stain; v.t., to stain; to dry by means of blotting-paper, etc.

blotch, n., an irregular spot; v.t., to mark with blotches.

blotch'y, adj., full of blotches.

blote, v.t., to cure herrings.

blot'ted, p.p., blot.

blot'ter, n., one who, or that which, blots.

blottesque', adj. and n., painting done with heavy blots.

blot'ting, pr.p., blot.

blot'ting-pa'per, n., paper prepared to absorb ink.

blott'o, adj., fuddled with drink (slang).

blouse, n., a light, loose upper garment.

blow, n., a stroke with the hand or a weapon; a calamity; v.i., to make a current of air; to blossom; v.t., to drive a current of air upon or into.

blow'er, n., one who, or that which, blows.

blow'ing, pr.p., blow.

blow'lamp, n., a hand lamp used in soldering, etc.

blown, p.p., blow.

blow'-pipe, n., an instrument to produce intense heat; a tube through which savages blow poisoned darts.

blow'-torch, n., a hand torch used in welding.

blow'-valve, n., a snifting valve.

blow'y, adj., gusty.

blowzed, adj., fat and ruddy.

blowz'y, adj., i.q. blowzed.

blub, v.i., to shed tears—short for blubber (slang).

blub'ber, n., the fat of whales; v.i., to weep so as to disfigure the face.

blub'bered, p.p., blubber.

blub'bering, pr.p., blubber.

bluch'er, n., a strong, leather half-boot or high shoe.

blud'geon, n., a short stick with a heavy end used as a weapon; v.t., to strike with a bludgeon.

blue, adj., sky-coloured; n., the colour of clear sky or deep sea; v.t., to make blue; to squander money (slang).

Blue'beard, n., the husband of many wives.

blue'bell, n., the wild hyacinth or the harebell.

blue'berry, n., a plant or shrub of the heath kind, bearing edible blue berries.

blue'bird, n., the blue robin (U.S.A.).

blue'book, n., a British Government official report.

blue'bottle, n., a fly with a large blue belly.

blue'-chip, n., a fairly safe investment.

blue'-eyed, adj., having blue eyes.

blue'ing, n., the process of making blue.

blue'jacket, n., a British naval seaman.

blue'-light, n., a composition burning with a brilliant blue light, used as a flare.

blue'ness, n., the quality of being blue.

blue'-pen'cil, v.t., to censor.

blue'print, n., a photographic print, white upon blue; a working plan.

blu'er, adj., comp. of blue.

Blues, n., the Royal Horse Guards.

blues, n. pl., hypochondria; dejection.

blu'est, adj., super. of blue.

blue'stocking, n., a literary lady; a female pedant.

blue'stone, n., sulphate of copper.

bluette', *n.*, an oriental pigeon.

blu'ey, *adj.*, rather blue.

bluff, *adj.*, broad and full; frank and good-humoured; *n.*, a high bank with a steep front; bold words or acts meant to daunt an opponent; *v.t.*, to deceive with bluff.

bluffed, *p.p.*, bluff.

bluff'ing, *pr.p.*, bluff.

bluff'ness, *n.*, frankness; good-humour.

bluf'fy, *adj.*, having bold, projecting banks.

blu'ing, *n.*, *i.q.* blueing.

blu'ish, *adj.*, blue in a slight degree.

blu'ishly, *adv.*, in a bluish manner.

blun'der, *n.*, a stupid mistake; *v.i.*, to make a gross mistake; to stumble.

blun'derbuss, *n.*, a short gun or long pistol with a wide barrel.

blun'dered, *p.p.*, blunder.

blun'derer, *n.*, one who blunders.

blun'derhead, *n.*, a stupid fellow.

blun'dering, *pr.p.*, blunder.

blunge, *v.t.*, to mix clay, etc. with water by revolving machinery (pottery).

blunt, *adj.*, dull, not sharp; having a thick edge or point; unceremonious; *v.t.*, to impair the keenness of.

blunt'ed, *p.p.*, blunt.

blunt'ing, *pr.p.*, blunt.

blunt'ish, *adj.*, rather blunt.

blunt'ly, *adv.*, in a blunt manner.

blunt'ness, *n.*, the state of being blunt.

blur, *n.*, a blot; a confused appearance; *v.t.*, to render indistinct.

blurb, *n.*, a descriptive note on the jacket of a book.

blurred, *p.p.*, blur.

blur'ring, *pr.p.*, blur.

blurt, *v.t.*, to utter suddenly.

blurt'ed, *p.p.*, blurt.

blurt'ing, *pr.p.*, blurt.

blush, *n.*, the act of blushing; *v.i.*, to redden in the cheeks.

blushed, *p.p.*, blush.

blush'ing, *adj.*, exhibiting blushes; *pr.p.*, blush.

blush'ingly, *adv.*, with blushes.

blus'ter, *v.i.*, to roar; to bully.

blus'tered, *p.p.*, bluster.

blus'terer, *n.*, one who blusters.

blus'tering, *adj.*, noisy; swaggering; *pr.p.*, bluster.

blus'teringly, *adv.*, boisterously.

blus'terous, *adj.*, noisy; tempestuous.

blus'tery, *adj.*, *i.q.* blusterous.

blus'trous, *adj.*, *i.q.* blusterous.

bo, a cry used to startle (*interj.*).

bo'a, *n.*, a very large species of serpents; a lady's neck-wrap.

bo'a-constric'tor, *n.*, one of the largest serpents, often 30 ft. long.

Boaner'ges, *n.*, a vociferous preacher.

boar, *n.*, a male pig.

board, *n.*, a piece of timber sawed thin and of considerable length and breadth compared with the thickness; daily food; a committee; *v.t.*, to go on to a vessel; to supply with board; *v.i.*, to live as a boarder.

board'able, *adj.*, capable of being boarded (as a ship).

board'ed, *p.p.*, board.

board'er, *n.*, one who boards a ship in action; one who has his daily food for payment at another's table.

board'ing, *pr.p.*, board.

board'ing-house, *n.*, a house where board and lodging is provided.

board'ing-school, *n.*, a school in which the pupils are boarded.

board'-wages, *n.*, wages allowed to servants in lieu of victuals.

boar'ish, *adj.*, pert. to a boar; swinish; brutal.

boast, *n.*, a statement expressing vanity or pride; *v.i.*, to speak in high praise of oneself or one's belongings.

boast'ed, *p.p.*, boast.

boast'er, *n.*, one who boasts.

boast'ful, *adj.*, addicted to boasting.

boast'fully, *adv.*, in a boastful way.

boast'fulness, *n.*, the state of being boastful.

boast'ing, *n.*, the habit of being boastful; *pr.p.*, boast.

boast'ingly, *adv.*, in a boasting manner.

boat, *n.*, a small vessel usually propelled by rowing; *v.i.*, to row or sail.

boat'able, *adj.*, fit to sail or row a boat on.

boat'bill, *n.*, a South American bird.

boat'builder, *n.*, a man who builds boats.

boat'-deck, *n.*, the top deck of a ship.

boat'ed, *p.p.*, boat.

boat'er, *n.*, a flat-crowned straw hat.

boat'hook, *n.*, an iron hook for pulling or pushing a boat.

boat'house, *n.*, a waterside shed for boats.

boat'ing, *n.*, rowing or sailing; *pr.p.*, boat.

boat'man, *n.*, a man who manages a boat.

boat'swain, *n.*, a ship's officer who summons the crew to their duty.

bob, *n.*, any small round object at the end of a string, chain, etc.; *v.t.*, to move jerkily; *v.i.*, to drop a curtsey.

Bob'adil, *n.*, a braggart.

bobbed, *p.p.*, bob.

bobb'ery, *adj.* and *n.*, noisy; disturbance.

bob'bin, *n.*, a small drum of wood on which thread is wound.

bob'binet, *n.*, a machine-made cotton net.

bob'bing, *pr.p.*, bob.

bobb'ish, *adj.*, brisk, well (*slang*).

bob'ble, *n.*, a woolly ball used as a trimming.

bobb'y, *n.*, a policeman (*slang*).

bob'by-dazzler, *n.*, anything overwhelmingly striking, especially a woman.

bob′bysock, *n.*, an ankle sock (*slang*).

bobb′y-sox, *n. pl.*, short socks covering the ankle.

bob′bysoxer, *n.*, a fashion-conscious teenage girl.

bob′cat, *n.*, the American lynx.

bob′olink, *n.*, the rice-bird of .North America.

bob′sled, *n.*, *i.q.* bob-sleigh.

bob′sleigh, *n.*, a short sledge, or two smaller sledges coupled together.

bob′stay, *n.*, a rope or chain attached to the bowsprit.

bob′tail, *n.*, a short tail; the rabble.

bob′tailed, *adj.*, having a tail cut short.

bob′wig, *n.*, a short wig curled at the bottom.

boc′asin, *n.*, a woollen stuff or calamanco.

Boche, *n.*, a name invented for the Germans by the French in the Great War.

bock, *n.*, lager beer.

bocking, *n.*, a coarse, woollen fabric used as a floor-cloth.

bock′land, *n.*, a species of land-tenure.

bode, *p.p.*, bide; *v.i.*, to be ominous; *v.t.*, to portend.

bod′ed, *p.p.*, bode.

bode′ful, *adj.*, ominous.

bo′dega, *n.*, a wine shop; a shop (*Span.*).

bod′ice, *n.*, the body part of a woman's dress.

bod′ied, *adj.*, having a body; *p.p.*, body.

bod′iless, *adj.*, having no material form; incorporeal.

bod′ily, *adj.*, concerning the body; *adv.*, completely.

bod′ing, *adj.*, ominous; *pr.p.*, bode.

bod′kin, *n.*, a blunt needle for drawing cord through a slot; a hair-pin.

Bodlei′an, *adj.*, rel. to Bodley,. esp. describing the great university library at Oxford; *n.*, the library itself.

Bodo′ni, *n.*, a type-face used in printing.

bod′y, *n.*, any entity; a human being; a corporation; substance; strength; *v.i.*, to invest with a body.

bod′y-clothes, *n. pl.*, attire, dress.

bod′yguard, *n.*, a band of life-guards.

bod′ying, *pr.p.*, body.

bod′y-pol′itic, *n.*, the whole body of citizens.

Boeo′tian, *adj.*, pert. to Boeotia; stupid.

Boer, *n.*, a South African of Dutch descent.

boff′in, *n.*, a scientist (*slang*).

bo′fors, *n.*, a type of naval gun.

bog, *n.*, a quagmire or morass; *v.t.*, to overwhelm in mire.

bo′gey, *n.*, *i.q.* bogy; also a fixed score-value for the holes on a golf course.

bogg′ard, -art, *n.*, a spectre, a bogy, a bugbear (*dial.*).

bogged, *p.p.*, bog.

bog′gle, *v.i.*, to hesitate; to shilly-shally.

bog′gled, *p.p.*, boggle.

bog′gler, *n.*, a waverer; an inconstant person.

bog′gling, *pr.p.*, boggle.

bog′gy, *adj.*, marshy; miry.

bo′gie, *n.*, a four-wheeled truck supporting the front or hind part of a wagon or locomotive.

bog′-land, *n.*, marshy land.

bo′gle, *n.*, a phantom, a bogy.

bog′myrtle, *n.*, a bog shrub.

Bo′gomilism, *n.*, the 10th century Bulgarian doctrine that God had two sons, Christ and Satan.

bo′gus, *adj.*, spurious; counterfeit.

bo′gy, *n.*, a hobgoblin; a wicked spirit.

boh, *i.q.* bo (*interj.*).

Bohair′ic, *n.*, the classical form of Coptic spoken in the Nile delta.

bohea′, *n.*, an inferior black tea.

Bohe′mian, *adj.*, pert. to Bohemia (now part of Czechoslovakia).

bohe′mian, *n.*, a person who despises conventionalities.

bohem′ianism, *n.*, the life and manners of bohemians.

boil, *n.*, an inflamed, suppurating tumour; *v.i.*, to bubble by the action of heat; to be violently agitated; *v.t.*, to subject to the action of heat in a liquid.

boiled, *p.p.*, boil.

boil′er, *n.*, a vessel in which water is boiled or steam generated.

boil′er-plate, *n.*, an iron plate for making boilers of engines.

boil′ery, *n.*, a place for boiling.

boil′ing, *pr.p.*, boil.

boil′ing-point, *n.*, the temperature at which a liquid changes into a gas and vice versa.

bois′terous, *adj.*, violent; stormy; turbulent.

bois′terously, *adv.*, in a boisterous manner.

bok′o, *n.*, the nose (*slang*).

bo′lar, *adj.*, clayey.

bol′as, *n.* (*sing.* and *pl.*), a long rope with three balls used by S. Americans for bringing down animals.

bold, *adj.*, daring; executed with courage; impudent; conspicuous.

bold′er, *adj.*, *comp.* of bold.

bold′est, *adj.*, *super.* of bold.

bold′ly, *adv.*, in a bold manner.

bold′ness, *n.*, the state or quality of being bold.

bole, *n.*, a tree-stem; a kind of yellow or brown earth containing iron oxide.

bolec′tion, *adj.* and *n.*, (moulding) raised above panel, etc.

bole′ro, *n.*, a Spanish dance.

bol′ide, *n.*, a large meteor, a fire-ball.

bol′ivar, *n.*, the standard monetary unit of Venezuela.

bolivia′no, *n.*, a Bolivian dollar.

boll, *n.*, a Scottish dry measure containing about six bushels.

bol′lard, *n.*, a post or stanchion on a wharf or traffic island.

boll′-weev′il, *n.*, an insect pest that infests the cotton-boll.

Bolognese', *adj.*, pert. to Bologna.

Bolo'gnian, *adj.*, *i.q.* Bolognese; *n.*, an inhabitant of Bologna.

bolom'eter, *n.*, an instrument for measuring radiation.

bolon'ey, *n.*, nonsense, humbug (*slang*).

Bol'shevik, *n.*, one belonging to the Russian revolutionary party.

Bol'shevism, *n.*, the principles of Bolsheviks.

Bol'shevist, *n.*, a member of the Russian Leninist party of extremists, *i.q.* Bolshevik.

bol'ster, *n.*, a kind of long under-pillow; *v.t.*, to support unworthily.

bol'stered, *p.p.*, bolster.

bol'stering, *pr.p.*, bolster.

bolt, *n.*, an arrow; a stream of lightning; a stout metallic pin for fastening objects together; a bar; *v.t.*, to fasten with a bolt; to swallow hurriedly; to sift; *v.i.*, to start and run off.

bolt'ed, *p.p.*, bolt.

bolt'er, *n.*, a horse given to bolting; a sieve.

bolt'ing, *pr.p.*, bolt.

bolt'ing-cloth, *n.*, a sieve cloth.

bolt'upright, *adv.*, sitting very erect.

bo'lus, *n.*, a round mass of medicinal matter to be swallowed at a gulp, larger and softer than a pill.

bom'a, *n.*, the police or a military post (*Swahili*).

bomb, *n.*, a destructive projectile, hollow and filled with explosives; *v.t.*, to throw bombs at.

bom'bard, *n.*, a short, wide-mouthed cannon.

bombard', *v.t.*, to attack with projectiles.

bombard'ed, *p.p.*, bombard.

bombardier', *n.*, a soldier who throws bombs; a non-commissioned artillery officer (*Fr.*).

bombard'ing, *pr.p.*, bombard.

bombard'ment, *n.*, the act of bombarding.

bom'bardon, *n.*, a low-pitched, brass instrument.

bombasine', *n.*, a fabric partly worsted and partly silk or cotton.

bom'bast, *n.*, high-sounding words.

bombast'ic *adj.*, high sounding in words.

Bom'bay duck, *n.*, a small, salted fish eaten dried with curry.

bombazette', *n.*, a thin, woollen cloth.

bombazine', *n.*, *i.q.* bombasine.

bombe *n.*, a cone-shaped dish or confection (cookery) (*Fr.*).

bombed, *p.p.*, bomb.

bomb'er, *n.*, a soldier trained to bomb; an aircraft used for bombing.

bomb'ing, *pr.p.*, bomb.

bomb'proof, *adj.*, secure against the action of bombs.

bomb'shell, *n.*, a spherical bomb; a complete surprise (*colloq.*).

bom'byx, *n.*, a silkworm.

bon, *adj.*, good (*Fr.*).

bon'-accord', *n.*, goodwill (*Scot.*).

bo'na fi'de, *adj.*, and *adv.*, in good faith.

bo'na fi'des, *n.*, good faith; honesty of purpose (*Lat.*).

bonan'za, *n.*, a rich mine; an unexpected prize.

Bonapart'ean, *adj.*, rel. to Napolean Bonaparte.

Bo'napartism, *n.*, support of the Bonaparte family in their claim to the French throne.

Bo'napartist, *n.*, one who supported the Bonapartes.

bonas'sus, *n.*, *i.q.* bonasus.

bona'sus, *n.*, the European bison; the aurochs.

bon'-bon, *n.*, a sugar-plum (*Fr.*).

bonce, *n.*, a large playing-marble; the head (*slang*).

bond, *n.*, anything that binds; the state of being bonded.

bond'age, *n.*, slavery.

bond'ed, *adj.*, applied to a licensed warehouse in which goods liable to government duties are stored.

bond'holder, *n.*, one who holds a bond or binding deed.

bond'ing, *adj.*, pert. to a bond.

bond'maid, *n.*, a female slave.

bond'man, *n.*, a slave.

bond'servant, *n.*, a slave.

bonds'man, *n.*, *i.q.* bondman.

bond'stone, *n.*, a stone running through a wall.

Bond Street, *n.*, a London street in the fashion quarter.

bond'woman, *n.*, a woman slave.

bone, *n.*, one of the pieces of which the skeleton of an animal is composed; *v.t.*, to take the bones out of; to put whalebone into.

boned, *p.p.*, bone.

bone'head, *n.*, a dolt (*slang*).

bone'lace, *n.*, a linen lace.

bone'less, *adj.*, without bones; lacking stamina.

bone'meal, *n.*, a fertilizer of ground bones.

bone'set, *v.i.*, to set broken bones.

bone'setter, *n.*, one who sets broken or dislocated bones.

bone'setting, *n.*, the art of setting bones.

bone'shaker, *n.*, an obsolete or defective bicycle or motor-car.

bon'fire, *n.*, a large, open-air fire made to express public joy or resentment or to destroy rubbish.

bon'go, *n.*, a large, striped African antelope.

bonhomie', *n.*, good humour.

Bon'iface, *n.*, a sleek, jolly innkeeper.

bon'ing, *pr.p.*, bone.

bon'ism, *n.*, the doctrine that it is a good world, but not the best possible.

bonit'o, *n.*, striped tunny fish.

bonjour, good day (*Fr.*).

bon mot, *n.*, a witticism (*Fr.*).

bonne, *adj.*, good; *n.*, a nursemaid (*Fr.*).

bonne bouche, *n.*, a tit-bit (*Fr.*).

bonnes for'tunes, *n.*, ladies' favours to boast of (*Fr.*).

bon′net, *n.,* a covering for the head; one for the top of anything; *v.t.,* to force the hat over the eyes of.

bon′neted, *adj.,* wearing a bonnet; *p.p.,* bonnet.

bon′netting, *pr.p.,* bonnet.

bon′nily, *adv.,* in a bonny manner.

bon′ny, *adj.,* handsome; pretty; fine.

bonsoir, good evening (*Fr.*).

bon′spiel, *n.,* a curling match.

bon ton, *n.,* good manners and breeding (*Fr.*).

bo′nus, *n.,* an extra payment made out of profits.

bon vivant, *n.,* a gourmet (*Fr.*).

bon′y, *adj.,* having prominent bones.

bonze, *n.,* a Buddhist monk.

bon′zer, *adj.,* excellent; first-rate (*Aust. slang*).

bon′zoline, *n.,* an ivory substitute.

boo, a rude expression of contempt (*interj.*); *n.,* a hoot; *v.t.,* to insult with booing; *v.i.,* to hoot.

boo′by, *n.,* a stupid fellow; a bird of the pelican family.

boo′by-prize, *n.,* a prize for the lowest score.

boo′by-trap, *n.,* a form of practical joke; a harmless-looking explosive.

boo′dle, *n.,* money; profit (*Amer. slang*).

boo′gie-woo′gie, *n.,* a jazz rhythm.

boohoo′, *n.* and *v.i.,* (make) the sound of noisy weeping.

book, *n.,* a number of sheets of paper stitched together and bound in a cover; *v.t.,* to register in a book; to buy a ticket for a journey, theatre performance, etc.

book′able, *adj.,* able to be booked.

book′-account, *n.,* a statement of debts.

book′binder, *n.,* one who binds books.

book′bindery, *n.,* a place where books are bound.

book′binding, *n.,* the art of binding books.

book′case, *n.,* a case of shelves for holding books.

book′club, *n.,* a club in which members buy books to circulate among themselves; the means of selling books through the post.

book′-debt, *n.,* a debt against a person in an account-book.

booked, *p.p.,* book.

book′ie, *n.,* a professional betting man.

book′ing, *pr.p.,* book.

book′ish, *adj.,* studious; better acquainted with books than with the world.

book′ishly, *adv.,* in a bookish manner.

book′ishness, *n.,* fondness for study.

book′-keeper, *n.,* one who keeps accounts.

book′-keeping, *n.,* the art of keeping accounts.

book′-knowledge, *n.,* knowledge derived from books.

book′land, *n., i.q.* bockland.

book′let, *n.,* a little book.

book′maker, *n.,* a maker of books; a betting-man who wagers on the defeat of a specified horse; a layer of odds as opposed to a backer.

book′mark, *n.,* a slip or strip to put between the leaves of a book to mark a place.

book′plate, *n.,* a book label indicating ownership.

book′post, *n.,* the system of conveying books, etc., by post at a cheaper rate.

book′rack, *n.,* a rack for books.

book′seller, *n.,* one whose occupation is to sell books.

book′selling, *n.,* the business of selling books.

book′shelf, *n.,* a shelf to hold books.

book′stall, *n.,* a stall holding books offered for sale.

book′store, *n.,* a bookshop.

book′worm, *n.,* a worm or mite that eats holes in books; an overstudious person.

boom, *n.,* a long pole on which the bottom parts of sails are extended; a beam across a river which prevents ships from entering; a deep, hollow noise; *v.i.,* to advertise; to make a hollow noise.

boomed, *adj.,* having a boom; *p.p.,* boom.

boom′er, *n.,* a large, male kangaroo; a N. American rodent.

boom′erang, *n.,* an Australian missile which returns to the thrower if it misses its mark.

boom′ing, *pr.p.,* boom.

boom′let, *n.,* a small boom in the Stock Exchange.

boom′slang, *n.,* the tree snake of S. Africa.

boon, *n.,* a favour; an advantage.

boon′gary, *n.,* the tree kangaroo of N. Queensland.

boor, *n.,* a rustic; an ill-mannered person.

boor′ish, *adj.,* awkward in manners.

boor′ishly, *adv.,* in a boorish manner.

boose, *v.i., i.q.* booze.

boos′er, *n., i.q.* boozer.

boost, *n.,* a push; *v.t.,* to help forward.

boos′ter, *n.,* an auxiliary motor in a rocket; any device for increasing power or motion.

boos′y, *adj., i.q.* boozy.

boot, *n.,* a covering for the foot and part of the leg; profit; the luggage receptacle of a motor-car or coach; *v.t.,* to avail (*impers.*).

boot′ed, *adj.,* wearing boots; *p.p.,* boot.

bootee′, *n.,* a child's knitted boot, a lady's small boot.

booth, *n.,* a temporary house or shed in a fair or market.

boot′ikin, *n.,* a child's legging.

boot′jack, *n.,* an instrument for drawing off boots.

boot′legger, *n.,* a smuggler.

boot′less, *adj.,* unprofitable; unavailing.

boot′lessly, *adv.,* in a bootless manner.

boot′licker, *n.,* a toady.

boots, *n.,* the man at an hotel who cleans

boots, carries luggage etc.

boot'-tree, *n.*, a contrivance to stretch and keep a boot in shape.

boot'y, *n.*, plunder.

booze, *v.i.*, to drink heavily.

boozed, *p.p.*, booze.

booz'er, *n.*, a heavy drinker.

booz'ing, *pr.p.*, booze.

booz'y, *adj.*, fuddled.

bopeep', *n.*, a game among children.

bor'a, *n.*, the Adriatic N.E. wind; a Mohammedan trader.

borac'ic, *adj.*, produced from borax.

boracif'erous, *adj.*, containing or yielding borax.

bor'age, *n.*, a plant formerly infused in hot drinks, akin to the forget-me-not.

bo'rate, *n.*, a salt formed from boracic acid and a base.

bo'rax, *n.*, a crystalline compound of soda and boracic acid.

Bordeaux, *n.*, a place in S.W. France; wine from this place.

bordell'o, *n.*, a brothel (*It.*).

bor'der, *n.*, the outer edge of anything; a boundary; *v.i.*, to adjoin.

bor'dered, *p.p.*, border.

bor'derer, *n.*, one who dwells on or near the border of a country.

bor'dering, *pr.p.*, border.

bor'derland, *n.*, land forming a border or frontier.

bor'derline, *adj.*, marginal.

bor'dure, *n.*, in heraldry, the border of a shield.

bore, *n.*, the hole made by boring; the cavity of a tube; a dull person; a sudden tidal wave in a river; *p.p.*, bear; *v.t.*, to penetrate by piercing; to weary by dullness.

bo'real, *adj.*, northern.

Bo'reas, *n.*, the North Wind.

bore'cole, *n.*, a hardy winter cabbage.

bored, *p.p.*, bore.

bore'dom, *n.*, the state of being bored.

bor'er, *n.*, one who, or that which, bores.

bo'ric, *adj.*, *i.q.* boracic.

bo'ring, *adj.*, tedious, wearisome; *pr.p.*, bore.

born, *p.p.*, bear (to bring forth).

borne, *p.p.*, bear (to carry).

bor'né, *adj.*, narrow-minded (*Fr.*).

Bor'nean, *adj.*, bel. to Borneo, a native of Borneo.

born'ite, *n.*, a reddish-brown copper ore.

bo'ron, *n.*, the characteristic element contained in borax.

bor'ough, *n.*, a corporate town.

borough-*Eng'lish*, *n.*, the inheritance by which, in some parts of England, all lands fell to the youngest son.

bor'row, *v.t.*, to obtain on loan.

bor'rowed, *p.p.*, borrow.

bor'rower, *n.*, one who borrows.

bor'rowing, *pr.p.*, borrow.

borsch, *n.*, a Russian soup which includes beetroot.

borsel'la, *n.*, a glass-blowing instrument.

Bor'stal system, *n.*, a method of reclaiming young criminals.

bort, *n.*, a diamond dust, used as an abrasive.

borzo'i, *n.*, a long-haired, greyhound-like Russian wolf-hound (*Russ.*).

bos(s), *n.*, an ox (*Lat.*); *v.t.* and *i.*, to miss (of a shot).

bos'cage, *n.*, sylvan foliage.

bosh, *n.*, nonsense; the lower part of a blast-furnace shaft.

bosk'et, *n.*, a grove; a shrubbery.

bosk'y, *adj.*, covered with thickets; bushy.

bo's'n, *n.*, abbrev. for for boatswain (also bo'sun).

Bos'nian, *adj.*, rel. to Bosnia, a province of Jugoslavija; *n.*, a native of B.

bos'om, *adj.*, dear; *n.*, the human breast; *v.t.*, to embrace, to embosom.

bos'omed, *p.p.*, bosom.

bos'oming, *pr.p.*, bosom.

boss, *n.*, a knob, a protuberance; a master; *v.t.*, to order peremptorily.

bos'sage, *n.*, rustic work made of rough stones in building.

bossed, *adj.*, ornamented with bosses; *p.p.*, boss.

boss'ily, *adv.*, in a bossy way.

boss'ing, *pr.p.*, boss.

bos'sy, *adj.*, *i.q.* bossed; dictatorially.

Bos'ton, *n.*, a kind of whist; a kind of waltz.

Bos'well, *n.*, any biographer, after James Boswell.

botan'ic, *adj.*, rel. to plants or botany.

botan'ical, *adj.*, *i.q.* botanic.

botan'ically, *adv.*, in a botanic way.

bot'anist, *n.*, one skilled in botany.

bot'anize, *v.i.*, to study plants.

bot'anized, *p.p.*, botanize.

bot'anizing, *pr.p.*, botanize.

bot'any, *n.*, the science of plants.

botar'go, *n.*, the salted roes of the mullet or tunny.

botch, *n.*, a swelling or blotch on the skin; *v.t.*, to mend or patch clumsily.

botched, *p.p.*, botch.

botch'er, *n.*, a clumsy workman at mending.

botch'ery, *n.*, clumsy workmanship.

botch'ing, *pr.p.*, botch.

botch'y, *adj.*, marked with botches.

bote, *n.*, compensation (*leg.*).

bot'-fly, *n.*, a fly that produces bots.

both, *adj.*, *pron.*, *adv.* and *conj.*, the one and the other; the pair.

both'er, *n.*, a trouble; *v.t.*, to annoy.

bothera'tion, *int.* and *n.*, confound it! annoyance.

both'ered, *p.p.*, bother.

both'ering, *pr.p.*, bother.

both'ersome, *adj.*, annoying, troublesome.

both'ie, *n.*, a building used as a lodging by work-people (*Scot.*).

Both'nian, *adj.*, rel. to the Gulf of Bothnia, between Sweden and Finland.

Both'nic, *adj.*, *i.q.* Bothnian.

both'y, *n.*, *i.q.* bothie.

bo'-tree, *n.*, the Indian sacred tree.

bot'ryoid, *adj.*, shaped like a bunch of grapes.

botryoid'al, *adj.*, *i.q.* botryoid.

bot'ryolite, *n.*, a variety of datolite.

bots, *n. pl.*, the maggots of gadflies, causing a cattle disease.

bot'tine, *n.*, a halfboot; a surgical boot.

bot'tle, *n.*, a narrow-mouthed, hollow vessel for containing liquids; *v.t.*, to put into bottles.

bot'tled, *p.p.*, bottle.

bot'tlegreen, *adj.*, dark green.

bot'tleneck, *n.*, a constricted outlet.

bot'tlewa'sher, *n.*, an underling.

bot'tling, *pr.p.*, bottle.

bot'tom, *adj.*, lowest; *n.*, the lowest part of anything; the seat; the base; *v.t.*, to furnish with a bottom; to reach the bottom of.

bot'tomed, *adj.*, having a bottom; *p.p.*, bottom.

bot'toming, *pr.p.*, bottom.

bot'tomless, *adj.*, fathomless.

bot'tomry, *n.*, the act of borrowing money by mortgaging or pledging a ship.

botts, *n. pl.*, *i.q.* bots.

bot'ulism, *n.*, ptomaine poisoning.

bouche, *v.t.*, to drill a new mouth in a spiked gun (*Fr.*).

boudoir', *n.*, a small, private room belonging to a lady (*Fr.*).

bough, *n.*, a large branch of a tree.

bought, *p.p.*, buy.

bou'gie, *n.*, a wax taper; a surgical instrument for opening obstructed narrow passages.

bouil'li, *n.*, meat stewed with vegetables (*Fr.*).

bouil'lon, *n.*, broth, soup (*Fr.*).

boul'der, *n.*, a waterworn, rounded stone, larger than a pebble; an iceworn rock of large size found in clays and gravels of the Drift formation.

Boule, *n.*, a legislative council of ancient Greece; a kind of roulette; a popular French ball game.

boul'evard, *n.*, a wide street shaded with trees; properly, a walk on the bulwarks or ramparts of a town (*Fr.*).

boul'ter, *n.*, a long fishing line with many hooks.

bounce, *n.*, a heavy blow; boasting; *v.i.*, to make a sudden leap; to boast; *v.t.*, to recoil sharply from.

bounced, *p.p.*, bounce.

bounc'er, *n.*, one that bounces; a braggart.

bounc'ing, *adj.*, vigorous; stout; *pr.p.*, bounce.

bounc'ingly, *adv.*, in a bouncing manner.

bound, *adj.*, prepared; destined; restrained; *n.*, a limit; a leap; *v.t.*, to circumscribe; *v.i.*, to spring; *p.p.*, bind.

bound'ary, *n.*, a limit.

bound'ed, *adj.*, limited; *p.p.*, bound.

bound'en, *adj.*, obligatory.

bound'er, *n.*, one who, or that which, bounds; a pretentious, vulgar fellow.

bound'ing, *pr.p.*, bound.

bound'less, *adj.*, illimitable; infinite.

bound'lessly, *adv.*, in unlimited degree.

bound'lessness, *n.*, the state of being boundless.

boun'teous, *adj.*, generous.

boun'teously, *adv.*, liberally.

boun'teousness, *n.*, the quality of being bounteous.

boun'tiful, *adj.*, munificent.

boun'tifulness, *n.*, the quality of being bountiful.

boun'ty, *n.*, generosity; a favour; a premium.

bouquet', *n.*, a bunch of flowers; an agreeable aroma.

bouquetin, *n.*, the Alpine ibex (*Fr.*).

bour'bon, *n.*, a kind of whisky.

Bour'bonism, *n.*, support of the claims of the Bourbon family to the French throne.

Bour'bonist, *n.*, a French royalist.

bour'don, *n.*, a bass stop in an organ or harmonium.

bour'geois, *adj.*, mediocre in taste or manners; *n.*, a citizen, a man of middle rank (*Fr.*).

bourgeois', *n.*, small printing type, between brevier and long primer.

bourgeois'ie, *n.*, the middle class (*Fr.*).

bour'geon, *v.i.* and *n.*, *i.q.* burgeon.

bourn, *n.*, a brook or small river.

bourn(e), *n.*, a limit.

bou'rrée, *n.*, a brisk dance movement in duple time (*Fr.*).

bourse, *n.*, an exchange where merchants meet to transact business (*Fr.*).

bouse, *v.i.*, *i.q.* booze and bowse.

boustrophe'don, *n.*, writing running in lines alternately from left to right and from right to left.

bout, *n.*, a set-to; a contest; a debauch.

boutique', *n.*, a shop (*Fr.*).

boutonnière, *n.*, spray of flowers as a buttonhole (*Fr.*).

bouts-rimés', *n. pl.*, words that rhyme given as the ends of lines of a stanza, the other parts to be filled in as an exercise (*Fr.*).

bo'vine, *adj.*, pert. to oxen.

bo'vril, *n.*, a preparation of beef essences.

bov'rilize, *v.t.*, to condense, to abbreviate.

bow, *n.*, a rod for playing a violin; a weapon; a looped knot; an arch or curve.

bow, *n.*, the front part of a ship; *v.t.*, to make to bend; *v.i.*, to bend the body.

Bow bells, *n.*, bells in London symbolizing cockneydom.

bowd'lerize, *v.t.*, to alter a text by cutting out improprieties.

bowd'lerized, *p.p.*, bowdlerize.

bowd′lerizing, *pr.p.,* bowdlerize.

bowed, *p.p.,* bow.

bow′els, *n. pl.,* the intestines; compassion.

bow′er, *n.,* one who bows; one of two anchors at the bow of a ship; a boudoir; an arbour.

bow′ery, *adj.,* having bowers, arboured.

bow′ie-knife, *n.,* a strong knife used as a weapon in the United States.

bow′ing, *pr.p.,* bow.

bow′knot, *n.,* a slipknot.

bowl, *n.,* a hollow vessel, almost hemispherical; the hollow part of anything, as of a spoon or tobacco-pipe; a ball of wood used in a lawn game; *v.t.,* to deliver the ball at cricket; to roll a bowl.

bowled, *p.p.,* bowl.

bow′-leg, *n.,* a crooked leg.

bow′-legged, *adj.,* having crooked or bandy legs.

bowl′er, *n.,* one who plays at bowls; at cricket, the player who delivers or serves the ball to the batsman; a kind of hat.

bow′line, *n.,* a rope attached to a square sail and fastened so as to stretch the sail tight forward towards the bow.

bowl′ing, *pr.p.,* bowl.

bowl′ing-green, *n.,* a level lawn for bowling.

bow′man, *n.,* an archer.

bowse, *v.i.,* to pull or haul hard.

bow′sprit, *n.,* the large spar projecting over the bow of a vessel.

Bow′-street, *adj.* and *n.,* a street near Covent Garden in London which has in it the chief metropolitan police court.

bow′-string, *n.,* the string that bends a bow.

bow′-window, *n.,* a projecting window whose plan is a segment of a circle.

bow′-wow′, *n.,* the bark of a dog (*interj.*); *v.i.,* to bark.

bow′yer, *n.,* a maker or seller of bows.

box, *n.,* an evergreen shrub with hard wood; a case; a small room for spectators in a theatre; a shelter; the driver's seat on a carriage; a small house for sportsmen; *v.t.,* to enclose, as in a box; to fight with the fists.

Box and Cox, *n.,* two persons who are never at home at the same time.

box-calf′, *n.,* chrome-tanned calfskin.

box′-car, *n.,* a closed-in railway wagon.

boxed, *p.p.,* box.

box′er, *n.,* a pugilist.

box′-haul, *v.i.,* to turn a ship round on her keel owing to lack of room.

box′ing, *pr.p.,* box.

Box′ing-day, *n.,* the 26th December.

box′ing-glove, *n.,* a padded glove used in boxing.

box′-kite, *n.,* a kite made on a rectangular frame.

box′-office, *n.,* a place in a theatre for booking seats.

box′-resp′irator, *n.,* a gas mask of which a box containing chemicals is a part.

box′-room, *n.,* a storage room for trunks, etc.

box′-tree, *n.,* a hard-timbered, evergreen shrub.

box′wood, *n.,* the fine, hard-grained timber of the box-tree.

box′y, *adj.,* resembling a box.

boy, *n.,* a male child; a youth; a comrade.

boy′au, *n.,* a zig-zag trench in fortification (*Fr.*).

boy′cott, *n.,* ostracism; *v.t.,* to ostracize.

boy′cotted, *p.p.,* boycott.

boy′cotting, *pr.p.,* boycott.

boy′friend, *n.,* any woman's favourite male.

boy′hood, *n.,* the state of being a boy.

boy′ish, *adj.,* pert. to a boy; immature.

boy′ishly, *adv.,* in a boyish manner.

boy′ishness, *n.,* the quality of being boyish.

boy′s′-play, *n.,* child's play; anything easy to accomplish.

bra, *n.,* short for brassière.

brab′ble, *n.,* a noisy quarrel; *v.t.,* to wrangle noisily.

brac′cate, *adj.,* feathered as to the feet.

brace, *n.,* that which holds two or more things tight together; a couple; *v.t.,* to tie closely; to strengthen.

braced, *p.p.,* brace.

brace′let, *n.,* an ornament for the wrist.

bra′cer, *n.,* a guard for the wrist; a pick-me-up.

bra′ces, *n. pl.,* straps for supporting trousers.

brach, *n.,* a bitch hound.

brach′ial, *adj.,* rel. to the arm.

brach′iate, *adj.,* having branches in pairs, each pair at right angles to the next.

brach′iopod, *n.,* a marine mollusc with breathing appendages on either side of its mouth.

brachyg′rapher, *n.,* a shorthand writer.

brachyg′raphy, *n.,* shorthand; stenography.

brachyl′ogy, *n.,* conciseness of expression.

bra′cing, *adj.,* invigorating; *pr.p.,* brace.

brack′en, *n.,* fern.

brack′et, *n.,* a short support projecting from a vertical surface; a gas-pipe projecting from a wall; one of two marks used by printers to enclose an interpolation, etc.; space beyond and short of a target; *v.t.,* to furnish with a bracket; to enclose within brackets; *v.i.,* to shoot beyond and short of a target.

brack′eted, *p.p.,* bracket.

brack′eting, *pr.p.,* bracket.

brack′ish, *adj.,* rather salty.

brack′ishness, *n.,* the quality of being brackish.

bract, *n.,* a modified leaf on the peduncle near the flower.

brac′tea, *n.,* a thin plate of metal (*Lat.*).

bract'eal, *adj.*, having bracts.

bract'eate, *adj.*, *i.q.* bracteal; *n.*, a thin plate of metal.

brad, *n.*, a small-headed nail.

brad'awl, *n.*, an awl to make holes for brads.

brad'ded, *adj.*, furnished with brads.

Brad'shaw, *n.*, a railway time-table so named.

bradycar'dia, *n.*, slowness of pulse.

bradyphra'sia, *n.*, slowness of speech.

brad'ypod, *n.*, a sloth.

bradyseism', *n.*, the slow movements in the earth's crust.

brae, *n.*, a steep bank (*Scot.*).

brag, *n.*, a game of cards; *v.i.*, to boast.

braggado'cio, *n.*, a braggart; empty boasting.

brag'gart, *n.*, a boaster.

bragged, *p.p.*, brag.

brag'ger, *n.*, one who brags.

brag'ging, *pr.p.*, brag.

Brah'ma, *n.*, a Hindu god; the Creator.

brah'ma, *n.*, *i.q.* brahmaputra.

Brah'man, *n.*, a member of the Hindu sacred caste.

brahmaput'ra, *n.*, a kind of domestic fowl.

Brah'min, *n.*, *i.q.* Brahman.

Brahmin'ical, *adj.*, pert. to the Brahmins.

braid, *n.*, a narrow plaited band; *v.t.*, to plait; to intertwine.

braid'ed, *adj.*, plaited; *p.p.*, braid.

braid'ing, *n.*, a trimming; *pr.p.*, braid.

brail, *n.*, a rope attached to a fore-and-aft sail; *v.t.*, to haul in by means of the brails.

Braille, *n.*, a system of reading for the blind using raised letters.

brain, *n.*, the soft, greyish matter contained in the skull; the understanding; *v.t.*, to beat out the brains of.

brain'child, *n.*, an original idea.

brained, *adj.*, furnished with brains; *p.p.*, brain.

brain'ily, *adv.*, cleverly.

brain'ing, *pr.p.*, brain.

brain'less, *adj.*, without understanding; silly.

brain'pan, *n.*, the skull.

brain'storm, *n.*, a violent mental upset.

brain'wash, *n.*, a systematic mental pressure; *v.t.*, to apply mental pressure.

brain'wave, *n.*, a sudden inspiration (*colloq.*).

brain'y, *adj.*, possessing brains; intellectual.

braird, *v.i.* and *n.*, (to come up in) fresh shoots.

braise, *v.t.*, to stew with vegetables.

braised, *p.p.*, braise.

brais'ing, *pr.p.*, braise.

brake, *n.*, a thicket; an appliance to stop motion by friction; a heavy vehicle for breaking in young horses to harness; a wagonette; *v.t.*, to apply the brake to a train, car, etc.; to bruise flax by beating.

brake'man, *n.*, a man who attends to the brakes of a train.

brakes'man, *n.*, *i.q.* brakeman.

brak'ing, *n.*, the act of applying a brake; *pr.p.*, brake.

brak'y, *adj.*, full of brambles and shrubs.

bramantesque', *adj.*, Renaissance style.

bram'ble, *n.*, a prickly shrub; a blackberry.

bram'bling, *n.*, a British finch, larger than the chaffinch.

bram'bly, *adj.*, full of brambles.

bran, *n.*, the husk of grain.

bran'card, *n.*, a portable bed borne by horses.

branch, *n.*, a bough; an offshoot; a subdivision or department; *v.i.*, to send out branches; to diverge.

branched, *p.p.*, branch.

bran'chia, *n.*, a gill (of fish, etc.).

bran'chial, *adj.*, rel. to the branchiae.

bran'chiate, *adj.*, furnished with gills.

branch'ing, *pr.p.*, branch.

branch'iopod, *n.*, a crustacean whose gills are on the feet.

branch'less, *adj.*, without branches.

branch'ling, *n.*, a small branch.

branch'y, *adj.*, having wide-spreading branches.

brand, *n.*, a sword; a piece of burning wood; a mark made by burning; a trademark; a mark of infamy; *v.t.*, to mark; to stigmatize.

brand'ed, *p.p.*, brand.

brand'er, *n.*, one who brands.

bran'died, *adj.*, flavoured with brandy.

bran'dified, *adj.*, *i.q.* brandied.

brand'ing, *pr.p.*, brand.

bran'dish, *v.t.*, to wave; to flourish.

bran'dished, *p.p.*, brandish.

bran'dishing, *pr.p.*, brandish.

brand'ling, *n.*, the parr; a young salmon.

brand'-name, *n.*, a trademark.

brand'-new, *adj.*, absolutely new.

bran'dreth, *n.*, a wooden stand for cask, hayrick, etc.

bran'dy, *n.*, a spirituous liquor distilled from wine.

bran'dy-snap, *n.*, a gingerbread wafer.

bran'gle, *n.*, a squabble; *v.i.*, to wrangle.

bran'gled, *p.p.*, brangle.

bran'gler, *n.*, a squabbler.

bran'gling, *pr.p.*, brangle.

bran'lin, *n.*, a small, red worm used as bait.

bran'ny, *adj.*, resembling or consisting of bran.

brant, *adj.*, *i.q.* brent.

bran'-tub, *n.*, a tub of bran containing presents.

brash, *n.*, a heap of fragments; *adj.*, cheeky, saucy (*colloq.*).

brass, *n.*, an alloy of copper and zinc; a monumental plate; impudence; money (*slang*).

brass'age, *n.*, the mint-charge for coining money.

bras'sard, *n.*, an armlet.

bras'sart, *n.*, *i.q.* brassard.

brass'-band, *n.*, a company of musicians who perform on instruments of brass.

brasse, *n.*, a spotted fish resembling a perch.

brass'erie, *n.*, a beer-shop with restaurant (*Fr.*).

brass'hat, *n.*, a staff officer (*mil. slang*).

brass'ière, *n.*, a garment which supports the breasts (*Fr.*).

brass'iness, *n.*, the state of being brassy.

brass'y, *adj.*, resembling or composed of brass; impudent; *n.*, a golf club protected at the bottom by a brass plate.

brat, *n.*, a child; an apron (*Prov.*).

bratt'ice, *n.*, *i.q.* brettice.

brava'do, *n.*, a boast; needlessly daring behaviour.

brave, *adj.*, courageous; *n.*, a daring person; a North American Indian warrior; *v.t.*, to defy.

braved, *p.p.*, brave.

brave'ly, *adv.*, in a brave manner.

brave'ness, *n.*, the quality of being brave.

brav'er, *n.*, one who braves; *adj.*, *comp.* of brave.

brav'ery, *n.*, courage; splendour.

brav'est, *adj.*, *super.* of brave.

brav'ing, *pr.p.*, brave.

bra'vo, well done! (*interj.*); *n.*, a hired assassin.

bravu'ra, *adj.*, florid, elaborate (*mus.*).

brawl, *n.*, a noisy quarrel; *v.i.*, to quarrel noisily.

brawled, *p.p.*, brawl.

brawl'er, *n.*, one who brawls.

brawl'ing, *adj.*, quarrelsome; *pr.p.*, brawl.

brawn, *n.*, pig's cheek and ox feet, boiled and pickled, and pressed into a shape; muscular strength.

brawn'y, *adj.*, having large, strong muscles.

brax'y, *n.*, a disease of sheep.

bray, *n.*, the cry of an ass; *v.t.*, to pound or grind small; *v.i.*, to cry like an ass.

brayed, *p.p.*, bray.

bray'er, *n.*, one that brays like an ass.

bray'ing, *pr.p.*, bray.

braze, *v.t.*, to solder with a hard alloy of brass and zinc; to cover or ornament with brass.

brazed, *p.p.*, braze.

braze'less, *adj.*, unsoldered.

bra'zen, *adj.*, made of brass; impudent.

bra'zen-faced, *adj.*, impudent.

bra'zenness, *n.*, brassiness; impudence.

bra'zier, *n.*, an open pan for burning wood or coal; a worker in brass.

brazil', *n.*, a very heavy, red, tropical wood used in dyeing; a kind of edible nut.

Brazil'ian, *adj.*, pert. to Brazil, a republic of S. America; *n.*, a native of B.

braz'ing, *pr.p.*, braze.

breach, *n.*, the violation of a pledge; a gap, esp. in fortifications; a quarrel; *v.t.*, to make a breach in.

breached, *p.p.*, breach.

breach'ing, *pr.p.*, breach.

bread, *n.*, flour moistened, fermented and baked into a food.

bread'-corn, *n.*, corn or grain of which bread is made.

bread'fruit, *n.*, the fruit of a tree in Polynesia, used as a substitute for bread.

bread'stuff, *n.*, a collective name for all kinds of grain and flour.

breadth, *n.*, extent from side to side; width.

bread'winner, *n.*, one whose labour supports a family.

break, *n.*, a breach; a brake; *v.t.*, to divide by force; to train to obedience; to cashier or reduce in rank; to violate; to become broken; to become bankrupt.

break'able, *adj.*, capable of being broken.

break'age, *n.*, the act of breaking; allowance for accidental breaking.

break'away, *n.*, a severance.

break'down, *n.*, an overthrow; a failure; a lively, noisy, native dance.

break'er, *n.*, one who breaks; a wave broken into foam, near the shore; a small, flat watercask.

break' even, *v.i.*, to cover costs and no more.

break'fast, *n.*, the first meal of the day; *v.i.*, to eat breakfast.

break'fasted, *p.p.*, breakfast.

break'fasting, *pr.p.*, breakfast.

break'ing, *pr.p.*, break.

break'man, *n.*, *i.q.* brakeman.

break'neck, *adj.*, headlong.

break'up, *n.*, decay, collapse.

break'water, *n.*, a structure protecting a harbour by breaking the force of the waves.

bream, *n.*, a freshwater fish of the carp family; also a spiny sea-perch; *v.t.*, to clean a ship's bottom by fire.

breamed, *p.p.*, bream.

bream'ing, *pr.p.*, bream.

breast, *n.*, the forepart of the body between the neck and the belly; the seat of the affections and emotions; *v.t.*, to meet in front boldly; to oppose with the breast.

breast'bone, *n.*, the bone of the breast, also called the sternum.

breast'ed, *adj.*, having a breast; *p.p.*, breast.

breast'fast, *n.*, a cable used to fasten the midship part of a boat to a wharf.

breast'feed, *v.t.*, to suckle a child, as opposed to feeding with cow's milk, etc.

breast'ing, *pr.p.*, breast.

breast'knot, *n.*, a knot of ribbon worn on the breast.

breast'pin, *n.*, a fastening or ornament worn on the breast.

breast'plate, n., defensive armour covering the breast.

breast'-stroke, n., a style of swimming.

breast'summer, n., a lintel.

breast'wheel, n., a waterwheel which delivers the water about halfway between the top and the bottom.

breast'work, n., a breast-high parapet.

breath, n., the air inhaled and exhaled during respiration; air in gentle motion.

breath'able, adj., capable of being breathed.

breath'alyzer, n., a device for measuring the alcoholic content of the blood.

breathe, v.i., to take breath; to be alive; v.t., to inhale; to utter.

breathed, p.p., breathe.

breath'er, n., a sharp spell of exercise; a brief pause for rest.

breath'ing, n., respiration; in grammar, an aspirate; pr.p., breathe.

breath'less, adj., out of breath.

breath'me'ter, n., i.q. breathalyzer.

breath'y, adj., not clear-cut at the beginning of sound in singing.

brec'cia, n., a rock made of angular fragments united by a cement.

bred, p.p., breed.

breech, n., the hinder end of anything, esp. of a cannon; v.t., to put into breeches; to flog; to fasten with a breeching.

breeched, adj., having a breech or breeches; p.p., breech.

breech'es, n. pl., a garment worn by men to cover their hips and thighs.

breech'es-buoy, n., a life-saving device in which the person is enclosed.

breech'ing, n., a strong rope to minimize the recoil of a gun; the part of the harness round a horse's breech; pr.p., breech.

breech'less, adj., without breeches.

breech'loader, n., a firearm loaded at the

breech instead of the muzzle.

breech'loading, adj., pert. to a firearm loaded at the breech.

breed, n., a progeny from the same stock; v.t., to produce, to bring up, to rear; v.i., to bear a child.

breed'er, n., one who breeds young; one who takes care to raise a particular breed of animal.

breed'ing, n., the act of producing young, of rearing live stock; upbringing; deportment; good manners; pr.p., breed.

breeze, n., a light wind; a horse-fly.

breez'y, adj., fanned with light winds.

Bre'hon, n., an ancient Irish judge.

Bren, n., a lightweight machine gun.

brent, adj., pert. to a small, wild goose which breeds in the north.

bress'ummer, n., i.q. breastsummer.

bret, n., a kind of brill or turbot.

bretelle', n., an ornamental shoulder strap (Fr.).

breth'ren, n., pl. of brother.

Bret'on, adj. and n., a native of or rel. to Brittany.

bret'tice, n., a partition in mining shafts to assist ventilation; a fence put round dangerous machinery.

breve, n., a note four minims in length (mus.).

brev'et, adj., of temporary rank; n., a patent or warrant; an honorary rank in the army; v.t., to confer brevet rank upon.

brev'eted, p.p., brevet.

brev'eting, pr.p., brevet.

bre'viary, n., a service book, containing the daily offices of the Church.

brevier', n., a printing type between bourgeois and minion.

brev'iped, adj., having short legs.

brevipen'nate, adj., having short wings.

brev'ity, n., shortness; conciseness; fewness of words.

brew, n., the mixture formed by brewing; v.t., to prepare by steeping, boiling and fermentation; to mingle; to contrive.

brew'age, n., a mixed drink.

brewed, p.p., brew.

brew'er, n., one who brews.

brew'ery, n., a place where brewing is carried on.

brew'house, n., a house in which beer is brewed.

brew'ing, n., the process of making beer, etc.; the quantity brewed at one time; pr.p., brew.

brew'is, n., i.q. brewhouse; broth.

brew'ster, n., one who brews; a brewer, esp. a female brewer.

Brew'ster Se'ssions, n., Sessions for the issue of licences to trade in alcoholic liquors.

bri'ar, n., i.q. brier.

Bria'rean, adj., pert. to Briareus, a giant with a hundred hands.

bribe, n., a gift bestowed to corrupt the conduct; v.t., to gain over by a bribe; v.i., to practise bribery.

bribed, p.p., bribe.

brib'er, n., one who bribes.

brib'ery, n., the act of giving or receiving a bribe.

brib'ing, pr.p., bribe.

bric'-à-brac, n., articles having interest or value because of their rarity, antiquity, novelty, etc (Fr.).

brick, adj., made of brick; n., a kind of artificial stone made by burning moistened and moulded clay; v.t., to cover with brick.

brick'bat, n., a fragment of a brick.

brick'field, n., a place where bricks are made.

brick'-kiln, n., a furnace in which bricks are burned.

brick'layer, n., one who builds with bricks.

brick'maker, n., a maker of bricks.

brick'-tea, n., compressed tea.

brick'work, n., masonry made of bricks.

brick'y, adj., looking like bricks; composed only of bricks.

brick'yard, n., a yard in which bricks are stored for sale.

bric'ole, n., a particular kind of stroke in tennis and billiards (Fr.).

bri'dal, adj., pert. a wedding or a bride; n., a marriage.

bride, n., a woman newly married or about to be married.

bride'cake, n., the cake made for the guests at a wedding.

bride'chamber, n., a nuptial apartment.

bride'groom, n., a man newly married or about to be married.

bride'less, adj., without a bride.

brides'maid, n., a girl or woman who attends the bride at a wedding.

brides'man, n., a man who attends the bridegroom and bride at their marriage; a groomsman.

bride-to-be, n., a woman about to be married.

bride'well, n., a prison for disorderly persons.

bridge, n., a structure raised over a river or other depression to provide a suitable passage; a game of cards resembling whist; v.t., to build a bridge over.

bridge'able, adj., able to be bridged.

bridged, p.p., bridge.

bridge'head, n., a fortification at the head of a bridge.

bridg'ing, pr.p., bridge.

bri'dle, n., the headharness for a horse; a restraint; v.t., to restrain; v.i., to toss the head, expressing indignation.

bri'dled, p.p., bridle.

bri'dlepath, n., a horsetrack.

bri'dler, n., one who bridles.

bri'dling, pr.p., bridle.

bridoon', n., a light snaffle with a distinct rein.

Brie, n., a soft cheese made in northern France.

brief, adj., short; n., a summary of a case-at-law; a Papal letter; a circular appeal.

brief'case, n., a slim case for carrying documents.

brief'er, adj., comp. of brief; n., a solicitor who hands a brief to counsel.

brief'est, adj., super. of brief.

brief'less, adj., having received no briefs.

brief'ly, adv., concisely.

brief'ness, n., conciseness.

bri'er, n., a prickly shrub, esp. the wild rose.

bri'ered, adj., set with briers.

bri'ery, adj., full of briers; thorny.

brig, n., a square-rigged, two-masted vessel.

brigade', n., a number of battalions of troops.

brigadier', n., the general commanding a brigade.

brig'and, n., a robber, esp. one of those who live in bands in mountains.

brig'andage, n., robbery by brigands.

brig'andine, n., i.q. brigantine.

brig'andry, n., robbery on the highway.

brig'antine, n., a two-masted sailing vessel resembling a brig.

Brig'hamite, n., a follower of Brigham Young; a Mormon.

bright, adj., shining; clever; cheerful.

bright'en, v.t., to make bright or brighter; v.i., to grow bright or brighter.

bright'ened, p.p., brighten.

bright'ening, pr.p., brighten.

bright'er, adj., comp. of bright, more bright.

bright'est, adj., super. of bright.

bright'-eyed, adj., having bright eyes.

bright'ly, adv., in a bright manner.

bright'ness, n., the state of being bright.

Bright's' disease', n., a dangerous disease of the kidneys.

brigue, n., a cabal; a secret contrivance (Fr.).

brill, n., a flat-fish.

bril'liance, n., great brightness; splendour.

bril'liancy, n., i.q. brilliance.

bril'liant, adj., sparkling; glittering; shining; n., a finecut diamond.

bril'iantine, n., a hair cosmetic.

bril'liantly, adv., in a brilliant manner.

brim, n., a margin; a rim; v.t., to fill full; v.i., to be full to overflowing.

brim'ful, adj., full to the top.

brim'less, adj., having no brim.

brimmed, p.p., brim.

brim'mer, n., a glass full to the brim.

brim'ming, adj., full to the top; pr.p., brim.

brim'stone, n., sulphur.

brind'ed, adj., i.q. brindled.

brind'led, adj., grey or tawny streaked with a darker colour.

brine, n., salt water.

brine'pan, n., a pit in which salt is formed by the evaporation of brine.

bring, v.t., to fetch; to convey from a distant to a nearer place.

bring'er, n., one who brings.

bring'ing, pr.p., bring.

brin'ish, adj., rather salty.

brink, n., the edge of a steep place.

brink'manship, n., the diplomatic policy which risks but evades war.

brin'y, adj., consisting of brine; n., the sea (colloq.).

bri'o, n., vivacity (It.).

bri'que'tage, n., imitation brickwork (Fr.).

briquette', bri'quet, n., a brick of compressed fuel (Fr.).

bri'sance, n., a shattering explosion.

bri'sant, adj., shattering.

brisk, adj., lively; nimble; quick.

brisk'er, *adj.*, *comp.* of brisk.

brisk'est, *adj.*, *super.* of brisk.

brisk'et, *n.*, the breast of an animal.

brisk'ly, *adv.*, in a brisk manner.

brisk'ness, *n.*, the state of being brisk.

bris'(t)ling, *n.*, a sprat.

bris'tle, *n.*, a stiff hair; *v.i.*, to stand on end like bristles.

bris'tled, *p.p.*, bristle.

bris'tling, *pr.p.*, bristle.

bris'tly, *adj.*, thick set with hairs like bristles.

Bris'tol, *n.*, a smooth pasteboard; a type of aircraft; the city giving its name to B. cream, B. milk—types of sherry.

Bris'tol-diamond, *n.*, a rock crystal found near Bristol.

Bris'tol-fashion, *adj.*, ship-shape; in good order (*naut.*).

Brit'ain, *n.*, the island of which Scotland, England and Wales are parts.

Britan'nia, *n.*, the personification of Britain.

Britan'nic, *adj.*, pert. to Britain.

Brit'icism, *n.*, *i.q.* Britishism.

Brit'ish, *adj.*, pert. to Great Britain; sometimes applied specifically to the ancient Celtic inhabitants.

Brit'isher, *n.*, a vulgarism for Briton.

Britishism, *n.*, something peculiar to Great Britain.

Brit'on, *n.*, a member of the British race.

brit'tle, *adj.*, easily broken; fragile.

brit'tleness, *n.*, fragility.

britz'ka, *n.*, an open carriage with a folding top.

broach, *n.*, a spit; a spire; *v.t.*, to open for the first time.

broached, *p.p.*, broach.

broach'er, *n.*, one who broaches, opens or utters.

broach'ing, *pr.p.*, broach; introducing a topic of conversation.

broad, *adj.*, having extent from side to side; wide.

broad'-arrow, *n.*, a stamp resembling the head of an arrow marking government property.

broad'-axe, *n.*, a woodman's axe.

broad'cast, *adj.*, effected by casting the seed with the hand in sowing; *adv.*, far and wide; *v.t.*, to transmit from radio stations to listeners-in (*q.v.*).

broad'caster, *n.*, one who broadcasts.

broad'cloth, *n.*, a fine, woollen cloth.

broad'en, *v.t.*, to make broad or broader.

broad'ened, *p.p.*, broaden.

broad'ening, *pr.p.*, broaden.

broad'er, *adj.*, *comp.* of broad.

broad'est, *adj.*, *super.* of broad.

broad'ish, *adj.*, rather broad.

Broad'land, *n.*, the Broads, East Anglia.

broad'loom, *n.*, a method of carpet manufacturing.

broad'ly, *adv.*, widely; comprehensively.

broad'mind'ed, *adj.*, of tolerant opinions.

broad'mind'edness, *n.*, tolerance in thought.

Broad'moor, *n.*, an English asylum in Berkshire for criminal lunatics.

broad'ness, *n.*, breadth.

broad'sheet, *n.*, a small newspaper.

broad'side, *n.*, a simultaneous discharge of all the guns on one side of a ship; a sheet of paper printed on one side only, usually with popular matter.

broad'sword, *n.*, a sword with a broad blade and sharp edge, formerly the national weapon of the Highlanders.

Brobdingna'gian, *adj.*, rel. to the land of the Brobdingnags in *Gulliver's Travels;* gigantic.

brocade', *n.*, silk material richly embroidered.

brocad'ed, *adj.*, worked into a brocade; dressed in brocade.

broc'coli, *n.*, a cabbage resembling a cauliflower.

broch, *n.*, a Scottish prehistoric circular stone tower.

bro'ché, *adj.* and *n.*, embossed fabric.

brochette', *n.*, a bar for fixing medals (*Fr.*).

bro'chure, *n.*, a pamphlet (*Fr.*).

brock, *n.*, a badger.

brock'et, *n.*, a red deer, two years old.

broderie Anglaise, *n.*, open embroidery on white linen (*Fr.*).

brog, *n.*, a bradawl.

bro'gan, *n.*, *i.q.* brogue.

brogue, *n.*, a shoe of rough hide; dialectical peculiarity.

broid'er, *v.t.*, to adorn with needlework.

broid'ered, *p.p.*, broider.

broid'ering, *pr.p.*, broider.

broil, *n.*, a noisy quarrel; *v.t.*, to cook over a fire on a gridiron; *v.i.*, to sweat with heat.

broiled, *p.p.*, broil.

broil'er, *n.*, one who broils; a fowl fit only for broiling.

broil'ing, *pr.p.*, broil.

broke, *p.p.*, break.

bro'ken, *adj.*, interrupted; *p.p.*, break.

brok'enheart'ed, *adj.*, crushed with grief.

bro'kenly, *adv.*, in a broken manner.

bro'kenness, *n.*, the state of being broken.

bro'ker, *n.*, an agent who buys or sells on commission.

bro'kerage, *n.*, a broker's commission.

brok'ing, *n.*, the trade of a broker.

broll'y, *n.*, the abbrev. for umbrella (*slang*).

bro'ma, *n.*, a form of prepared cocoa.

bro'mal, *n.*, a colourless, oily liquid obtained by the action of bromine on alcohol.

bro'mate, *n.*, a salt of bromic acid.

bromatol'ogy, *n.*, the science of alimentation.

brom'ic, *adj.*, containing bromine in chem. combination.

bro'mide, *n.*, a compound of bromine and another element; any device to dull the sharpness of mind.

bro'mine, *n.*, a dark-reddish liquid element of strong odour.

bron'chi, *n. pl., i.q.* bronchia.

bron'chia, *n. pl.*, the air-tubes leading to the lungs.

bron'chial, *adj.*, pert. to the bronchia.

bronchi'ectasis, *n.*, dilation of the bronchi (*med.*).

bronchi'tis, *n.*, inflammation of the lining membrane of the bronchi or bronchia.

bron'choscope, *n.*, an instrument for inspecting the bronchi.

bron'chus, *n.*, one of the two bronchia.

bron'co, *n.*, a half-tamed horse (*Span.*).

brontosaur'us, *n.*, a huge dinosaurian reptile.

bronze, *n.*, an alloy of copper, tin and sometimes zinc; *v.t.*, to make to look like bronze; to brown; *v.i.*, to turn brown.

bronzed, *p.p.*, bronze.

bronz'ing, *pr.p.*, bronze.

brooch, *n.*, an ornamental clasp.

brood, *n.*, offspring; *v.i.*, to sit on eggs, as a hen; to dwell continuously on something with the mind.

brood'ed, *p.p.*, brood.

brood'ing, *adj.*, pondering; thinking deeply; *pr.p.*, brood.

brood'y, *adj.*, as a sitting hen.

brook, *n.*, a small stream of water; *v.t.*, to endure.

brooked, *p.p.*, brook.

brook'ing, *pr.p.*, brook.

brook'let, *n.*, a little brook.

broom, *n.*, a shrub with yellow flowers growing on heaths; a long-handled brush.

broom'stick, *n.*, the handle of a broom.

broom'y, *adj.*, full of broom.

brose, *n.*, a kind of Scotch broth or porridge.

broth, *n.*, liquor in which meat has been boiled, usu. with vegetables.

broth'el, *n.*, a place for the commercial exploitation of sexual desire.

broth'er, *n.*, the son of the same parents; a fellow-creature.

broth'erhood, *n.*, an association of men for any purpose.

broth'er-in-law, *n.*, the brother of one's husband or wife; a sister's husband.

broth'erliness, *n.*, the quality of being brotherly.

broth'erliwise, *adv.*, in brotherly fashion.

broth'erly, *adj.*, such as is natural for brothers.

brough'am, *n.*, a one-horse closed carriage.

brought, *p.p.*, bring.

brou'haha, *n.*, an uproar; a commotion.

brow, *n.*, the ridge over the eye; the forehead; the upper portion of a slope; a gangway (*naut.*).

brow'beat, *v.t.*, to bully.

brow'beaten, *adj.*, bullied; *p.p.*, browbeat.

brow'beating, *pr.p.*, browbeat.

brown, *adj.*, a dark colour inclining to red; *v.t.*, to make brown; *v.i.*, to turn brown.

browned, *p.p.*, brown.

brown'ie, *n.*, a kind of fairy; a junior girl guide.

Brown'ing, *n.*, a kind of automatic rifle; the poet Robert Browning.

brown'ing, *n.*, a preparation of burnt sugar, etc.; for colouring dishes; *pr.p.*, brown.

brown'ish, *adj.*, rather brown.

brown'stone, *n.*, dark sandstone much used for building.

brown' stud'y, *n.*, a reverie.

browse, *v.t.* and *i.*, to graze; to read casually.

browsed, *p.p.*, browse.

brows'er, *n.*, one who browses.

brows'ing, *pr.p.*, browse.

browze, *v.t.* and *i., i.q.* browse.

bru'in, *n.*, a name given to the bear.

bruise, *n.*, a contusion; *v.t.*, to injure by a blow without laceration.

bruised, *p.p.*, bruise.

bruis'er, *n.*, one that bruises; a pugilist.

bruis'ing, *pr.p.*, bruise.

bruit, *n.*, a rumour; *v.t.*, to noise abroad.

bruit'ed, *p.p.*, bruit.

bruit'ing, *pr.p.*, bruit.

bru'mal, *adj.*, rel. to the winter.

brumb'y, *n.*, an unbroken horse (*Aust. colloq.*).

brume, *n.*, mist, fog (*Fr.*).

Brumm'agem, *adj.*, cheap, showy (*from Birmingham*).

brum'ous, *adj.*, wintry, foggy.

brunch, *n.*, a single meal in lieu of breakfast and lunch.

brune, *n., i.q.* brunette.

brunette', *n.*, a woman of dark complexion.

brunt, *n.*, the heat or utmost violence of an onset.

brush, *n.*, an implement made of bristles used for various purposes; a thicket of small trees and shrubs; the tail of a fox; a skirmish; *v.t.*, to rub as with a brush.

brushed, *p.p.*, brush.

brush'er, *n.*, one who, or that which, brushes.

brush'ing, *pr.p.*, brush.

brush'let, *n.*, a small brush; hairs on the legs of certain insects.

brush'wood, *n.*, small trees forming a coppice.

brush'y, *adj.*, rough; shaggy.

brusque, *adj.*, abrupt in manner; offhand.

brusque'ly, *adv.*, in an abrupt manner.

brusque'ness, *n.*, an abrupt manner.

brus'querie, *n., i.q.* brusqueness; a blunt expression.

brus'sels sprouts', *n. pl.*, a variety of cabbage consisting of little clusters of leaves forming small heads.

brut, *adj.*, unsweetened (of wines) (*Fr.*).

bru'tal, *adj.*, savage; cruel.

brutalita'rian, *n.*, one who favours brutality.

brutal'ity, *n.*, gross cruelty.

bru'talize, *v.t.*, to degrade to the level of a brute.

bru'talized, *p.p.*, brutalize.

bru'talizing, *pr.p.*, brutalize.

bru'tally, *adv.*, in a brutal manner.

brute, *n.*, a beast; a savage in disposition or manners.

bru'tified, *p.p.*, brutify.

bru'tify, *v.t.*, to make a person a brute.

bru'tifying, *pr.p.*, brutify.

bru'tish, *adj.*, resembling a brute.

bru'tishly, *adv.*, in a brutish manner.

bru'tishness, *n.*, the state of being brutish.

Brut'us, *n.*, a 19th century wig; a Roman hero.

bryol'ogy, *n.*, the science of mosses.

bry'ony, *n.*, one of two British climbing plants, one called *white*, the other *black*.

bub'al, *n.*, a North-African antelope.

bub'ble, *n.*, a small vesicle of fluid containing air; *v.i.*, to rise in bubbles; *v.t.*, to cause to bubble.

bub'ble-car, *n.*, a midget motor car with a round, windowed top.

bub'bled, *p.p.*, bubble.

bub'ble-gum, *n.*, a kind of chewing gum.

bub'bling, *pr.p.*, bubble.

bub'bly, *adj.*, full of bubbles.

bu'bo, *n.*, an inflammatory tumour in the groin or armpit.

bubon'ic, *adj.*, characterized by buboes; of a particular plague.

bubon'ocele, *n.*, rupture of the groin.

buc'cal, *adj.*, pert. to the cheek.

buccaneer', *n.*, a pirate, esp. an English or French pirate in the Spanish Main.

buccaneer'ing, *n.*, piracy.

buc'cinal, *adj.*, trumpet-like.

buc'cina'tor, *n.*, a muscle in the cheek used in blowing a wind instrument (*anat.*).

bucen'taur, *n.*, the Doge's state-barge at Venice; a mythical monster, half man and half ox.

Buceph'alus, *n.*, a riding-horse.

bu'ceros, *n.*, a hornbill; a perching bird.

Buch'manism, *n.*, a religious system sometimes called the Oxford Group.

buck, *n.*, the male of various animals; a fop; a bleaching-lye; a frame on which wood is cross-cut; a basket for trapping eels; a dollar (*Amer. slang*); *v.t.*, to wash in bleaching-lye; *v.i.*, to shy, to jib (of a horse).

buck'-bean, *n.*, a water plant with pinkish racemes.

bucked, *p.p.*, buck.

buck'et, *n.*, a vessel, now usu. of plastic or metal, for holding liquid; *v.i.*, to spurt (*slang*).

buck'etful, *n.*, as much as a bucket will hold.

buck'et-shop, *n.*, the office of an unauthorized broker used for gambling in stocks, etc.

buck'ing, *pr.p.*, buck.

Buckingham Pal'ace, *n.*, the London residence of the British sovereign.

buck'ish, *adj.*, foppish.

buck'ishly, *adv.*, in a foppish way.

buc'kle, *n.*, an instrument, consisting of a rim, chape and tongue, for fastening; *v.t.*, to fasten with a buckle; *v.t.* and *i.*, to crumple in.

buc'kled, *p.p.*, buckle.

buck'ler, *n.*, a kind of shield.

buck'ling, *pr.p.*, buckle.

buck'o, *adj.* and *n.*, swaggering (fellow).

buck'ra, *adj.* and *n.*, rel. to the white man; a white man, the master (*native dial.*).

buck'-rabb'it, *n.*, a male rabbit; a Welsh rarebit with poached egg.

buck'ram, *n.*, a coarse, stiff linen cloth.

buck'shee, *n.*, *adj.* and *adv.*, extra rations (*army slang*); free.

buck'shot, *n.*, a large kind of shot.

buck'skin, *n.*, a soft yellowish or greyish leather, made of sheepskin.

buck'thorn, *n.*, a spiny British shrub of various species.

buck'wheat, *n.*, a herbaceous plant bearing small triangular seeds used for food.

bucol'ic, *adj.*, pastoral; *n.*, a pastoral poem.

bucol'ical, *adj.*, *i.q.* bucolic.

bud, *n.*, the early form of leaves or flowers before they expand; *v.i.*, to produce buds; *v.t.*, to graft into a leafbud instead of a shoot.

bud'ded, *p.p.*, bud.

Bud'dhism, *n.*, the chief religion of Asia.

Bud'dhist, *n.*, a worshipper of Buddha, the founder of Buddhism.

bud'ding, *pr.p.*, bud.

bud'dle, *n.*, a square frame used in washing metallic ore.

budd'leia, *n.*, a kind of shrub.

budd'y, *n.*, a chum, a mate (*colloq.*).

Bude'-light, *n.*, a brilliant light obtained by forcing oxygen into a coal or oil-gas flame.

budge, *v.i.*, to move away.

budged, *p.p.*, budge.

budg'er, *n.*, one who moves away.

budg'erigar, *n.*, a favourite cage bird, the grass or zebra parrakeet.

budg'et, *n.*, a little sack; a stock (of news, etc.); the Chancellor of the Exchequer's annual statement; a financial plan.

budg'eted, *p.p.*, budget.

budg'eting, *n.*, the act of drawing up a budget; *pr.p.*, budget.

budg'ing, *pr.p.*, budge.

bud'let, *n.*, a little bud springing from another bud.

buff, *n.*, a soft kind of leather; a light yellow colour.

buf'falo, *n.*, a large oriental draught-ox;

the bison of North America.

buf'fel, n., a small duck.

buf'fer, n., anything to deaden the impact between two bodies.

buf'fet, n., a refreshment room; informal refreshments (Fr.).

buf'fet, n., a blow; v.t., to beat.

buf'feted, p.p., buffet.

buf'feter, n., one who buffets.

buf'feting, n., the act of beating; pr.p., buffet.

buff'ish, adj., somewhat buff.

buf'flehead, n., an American wild duck.

buf'fo, n., an operatic cosmic singer.

buffoon', n., a jester.

buffoon'ery, n., ridiculous pranks.

buffoon'ing, n., i.q. buffoonery.

buf'fy, adj., buff-coloured.

bug, n., an insect of various kinds; esp. the domestic bug; a germ (colloq.).

bug'aboo, n., anything which frightens.

bug'bear, n., something that causes worry or annoyance.

bug'gy, adj., abounding with bugs; n., a light one-horse carriage.

bug'house, adj., crazy; n., an asylum; a dirty place (slang).

bu'gle, n., a hunting horn; a military, musical, brass wind instrument; a long, black bead.

bu'gler, n., one who plays a bugle.

bu'gloss, n., a weed with purple flowers.

buhl, n., an inlaid ornamentation of gold, mother-of-pearl, etc.

buhl'-work, n., cabinet work inlaid with buhl.

buhr'-stone, n., stone used for millstones.

build, v.t., to construct.

build'able, adj., capable of being built.

build'ed, p.p., build; (used poetically).

build'er, n., one who builds.

build'ing, n., the act of one who builds; the thing built; pr.p., build.

build'up, n., the preparatory work to reach a desired point or climax.

built, adj., shaped; p.p., build.

bulb, n., the rounded part of an onion or similar plant; any protuberance resembling a bulb.

bulbed, adj., having a bulb.

bulbif'erous, adj., producing bulbs.

bulb'il, n., a small bulb formed at the side of the old one.

bulb'let, n., a bulb which separates from the stem of a plant.

bulb'ous, adj., resembling a bulb in shape.

bul'bul, n., a nightingale (Persian).

bulb'ule, n., a small or immature bulb.

Bul'gar, n., a member of an ancient tribe that settled in Bulgaria.

Bulga'rian, adj., rel. to Bulgaria; n., a native of B.

bulge, n., a swelling out; v.i., to swell out.

bulged, p.p., bulge.

bul'ger, n., a wooden golf club with a convex face.

bulg'ing, pr.p., bulge.

bulim'ia, n., a voracious appetite.

bul'imy, n., i.q. bulimia.

bulk, n., size; the main mass; v.i., to swell.

bulked, p.p., bulk.

bulk'head, n., a partition in a ship.

bulk'iness, n., the quality of being bulky.

bulk'ing, pr.p., bulk.

bulk'y, n., large.

bull, adj., male; n., a deck game; a male ox; on the stock exchange, one who works for a rise in the price of stock; a papal edict; an inconsistency in language.

bul'la, n., a leaden seal.

bul'lace, n., a damson-like plum.

bul'late, adj., puffy, blistered-looking.

bull'dog, n., a muscular, courageous, determined species of dog.

bull'doze, v.t., to coerce by violence; to level

or clear by a bulldozer.

bull'dozer, n., one who bulldozes; a tractor for levelling and clearing land.

bul'let, n., a projectile, usually leaden, to be discharged from small arms.

bul'letin, n., an official report.

bul'let-proof, adj., able to resist bullets.

bull'fight, n., a ritual combat between armed men and bulls.

bull'finch, n., a British song-bird.

bull'frog, n., a large American frog with a loud bass voice.

bul'lied, p.p., bully.

bul'lion, n., uncoined gold or silver; a kind of heavy silk and metallic fringe.

bul'lionist, n., one who advocates an exclusive metallic currency.

bul'lock, n., a young bull; an ox.

bull'ring, n., a large open arena for bull-fights.

bull's'-eye, n., a circular opening in a building; a small lantern with a circular lens; the centre of a target, and the shot that hits it; a kind of sweet.

bull'-terrier, n., a cross between a terrier and a bulldog.

bul'ly, n., an arrogant, domineering fellow; v.t. and i., to act as a bully towards; to persecute, to oppress.

bull'y-beef, n., tinned beef.

bul'lying, pr.p., bully.

bul'rush, n., a large rush that grows in marshes.

bulse, n., in the East Indies, a bag for valuables.

bul'wark, n., a rampart; a kind of wall round the deck of a ship.

bum, n., a humming sound; the buttocks; v.i., to boom; v.t., to wheedle; to beg for.

bumbail'iff, n., an under-bailiff who serves writs for debt.

bum'ble, n., a beadle.

bum'ble-bee, n., a large kind of bee.

bum'ble-puppy, n., a racquet game with tennis ball tied to a post.

bum'bo, *n.*, cold rum-punch.

bum'boat, *n.*, a boat for carrying provisions to a ship.

bum'kin, *n.*, a short boom or spar.

bumm'alo, *n.*, a small South Asian fish.

bummaree', *n.*, a middle-man at Billingsgate fish-market; a licensed porter at Smithfield meat market.

bumm'er, *n.*, an idler, a loafer.

bum'ming, *n.*, a humming sound; *pr.p.*, bum.

bump, *n.*, a protuberance; a shock from a collision; *v.t.*, to strike; *v.i.*, to come into collision.

bumped, *p.p.*, bump.

bump'er, *n.*, a glass filled to the brim; the front and rear guard of a motor vehicle; a railway buffer (*Amer.*).

bump'ily, *adv.*, in a bumpy way.

bump'iness, *n.*, joltiness.

bump'ing, *pr.p.*, bump.

bump'kin, *n.*, an awkward, rustic lout; *i.q.* bumkin.

bump'tious, *adj.*, offensively self-assertive.

bump'tiously, *adv.*, in a bumptious way.

bump'tiousness, *n.*, the quality of being bumptious.

bum'py, *adj.*, full of bumps (road or air).

bun, *n.*, a little puffed cake; a chignon.

bunch, *n.*, a cluster; a protuberance; *v.t.*, to make into a bunch; *v.i.*, to cluster.

bunched, *p.p.*, bunch.

bunch'iness, *n.*, the state of being bunchy.

bunch'ing, *pr.p.*, bunch.

bunch'y, *adj.*, growing in a bunch.

bunc'o, *n.* and *v.t.*, (to) swindle by card-sharping.

bun'combe, *n.*, *i.q.* bunkum.

bund, *n.*, an Eastern waterside promenade; a league, an alliance (*Ger.*).

bun'der, *n.*, a landing-place, a harbour.

Bun'desrat(h), *n.*, in Germany and Switzerland, a federal council.

Bun'destag, *n.*, the lower legislative house of federal Germany.

bun'dle, *n.*, a package; *v.t.*, to fasten into a shapeless package.

bun'dled, *p.p.*, bundle.

bun'dling, *pr.p.*, bundle.

bung, *n.*, a large cork; *v.t.*, to close up.

bung'aloid, *adj.*, in bungalow style.

bun'galow, *n.*, a low verandahed house, common in India; a single-storeyed house.

bung'-hole, *n.*, the hole in a cask through which it is filled.

bun'gle, *v.t.* and *i.*, to perform inefficiently.

bun'gled, *p.p.*, bungle.

bun'gler, *n.*, an unskilful performer.

bun'gling, *adj.*, clumsy; *pr.p.*, bungle.

bun'glingly, *adv.*, clumsily.

bun'ion, *n.*, an inflammatory swelling of the great toe-joint.

bunk, *n.*, a sleeping-berth; *v.i.*, to run away.

bunk'er, *n.*, a large bin; a difficulty (*golf*); an underground shelter (*mil.*); *v.t.*, to make difficult.

bunk'ered, *p.p.*, bunker.

bunk'ering, *pr.p.*, bunker.

bun'kum, *n.*, talking for talking's sake; nonsense.

bunn'ia, *n.*, an Indian trader or shopkeeper.

bun'ny, *n.*, a pet name for a rabbit.

bun'sen, *adj.*, pert. to a burner invented by a German chemist (Bunsen); *n.*, a kind of gas heating device.

bunt, *n.*, the belly of a sail or net; a wheat disease; *v.i.*, to swell.

bunt'ing, *n.*, a bird akin to the finch; a woollen material for flags.

buoy, *n.*, a float used for various purposes; *v.t.*, to keep afloat.

buoy'age, *n.*, the providing of buoys; the course marked by buoys.

buoy'ancy, *n.*, the quality of being buoyant.

buoy'ant, *adj.*, floating; light; cheerful; easy.

buoy'antly, *adv.*, in a buoyant manner.

buoyed, *p.p.*, buoy.

bur, *n.*, *i.q.* burr.

Burb'erry, *n.*, the trade name for a distinctive cloth or clothing.

bur'ble, *v.i.*, to boil over with mirth or rage.

bur'bled, *p.p.*, burble.

bur'bling, *pr.p.*, burble.

bur'bot, *n.*, an English fresh-water cod, eel-shaped and bearded.

bur'den, *n.*, a load; the refrain of a song; *v.t.*, to load; to oppress.

bur'dened, *p.p.*, burden.

bur'dening, *pr.p.*, burden.

bur'densome, *adj.*, heavy; *or* grievous to be borne.

bur'densomeness, *n.*, op-*or* pressiveness; heaviness.

bur'dock, *n.*, a large, rough-leaved, perennial weed.

bureau', *n.*, a writing-table with drawers; a business office; a public department.

bureau'cracy, *n.*, the system of centralizing government, esp. when carried to excess.

bur'eaucraft, *n.*, *i.q.* bureaucracy.

bur'eaucrat, *n.*, one who supports bureaucracy.

bureaucrat'ic, *adj.*, rel. to bureaucracy.

bureaucrat'ical, *adj.*, *i.q.* bureaucratic.

bureaucrat'ically, *adv.*, in a bureaucratic way.

bureau'cratist, *n.*, *i.q.* bureaucrat.

bureau'cratize, *v.t.*, to govern bureaucratically.

bu'r(h)el, *n.*, Himalayan wild sheep.

burette', *n.*, a graduated pipette with a stop-cock (*Fr.*).

burg, *n.*, a borough.

burg'age, *n.*, a system of land tenure.

burgee', *n.*, a small pennant.

bur'geon, *n.*, a bud; *v.i.*, to sprout.

bur'geoned, *p.p.*, burgeon.

bur'geoning, *pr.p.*, burgeon.

bur'gess, *n.*, a citizen or a parliamentary representative of a borough.

burgh, *n.*, a corporate town; a borough.

burgh′er, n., an inhabitant of a burgh; a freeman.

burg′lar, n., a nocturnal housebreaker.

burgla′rious, adj., pert. to burglary.

burgla′riously, adv., with intent to commit burglary.

burg′lary, n., the crime of nocturnal housebreaking.

bur′gle, v.t. and v.i., to commit burglary; to enter burglariously.

burg′mote, n., a borough court held thrice yearly.

burg′omaster, n., a Dutch, Flemish or German mayor.

burg′onet, n., a visored helmet; a steel cap.

burgoo′, n., a kind of oatmeal porridge.

bur′goyne, n., a variety of trenching tool.

bur′grave, n., an hereditary governor of a castle or town.

Bur′gundy, n., a kind of wine.

bur′ial, n., interment.

bur′ial-place, n., a place of burial.

bur′ied, p.p., bury.

bur′ier, n., one who buries.

bu′rin, n., an engraver's style or needle; a graver.

burke, v.t., to smother; to shelve.

burked, p.p., burke.

burk′er, n., one who burks.

burk′ing, pr.p., burke.

burl, n., a small lump in thread or cloth; v.t., to finish cloth by picking out burls.

burl′ap, n., a coarse canvas used for packing.

burled, p.p., burl.

burl′er, n., one who picks burls out of cloth in finishing.

burlesque′, adj., ludicrous because of contrast between subject and manner of treatment; n., a dramatic or literary extravaganza; a travesty; a caricature; v.t., to turn into a burlesque.

burlesqued′, p.p., burlesque.

burlesqu′ing, pr.p., burlesque.

burlet′ta, n., a musical farce.

bur′liness, n., the quality of being burly.

burl′ing, pr.p., burl.

Burl′ington House, n., the London headquarters of the Royal Academy.

bur′ly, adj., great in bodily size.

Burm′an, adj. and n., i.q. Burmese.

Burmese′, adj., pert. to Burma; n., a native or the language of B.

bur′mite, n., a kind of amber.

burn, n., an injury caused by fire; a rivulet (Scot.); v.t., to consume or injure by fire; v.i., to flame.

burn′able, adj., capable of being burned.

burned, p.p., burn.

burn′er, n., one who, or that which, burns; the jet-piece of a lamp.

burn′et, n., variety of brown-flowered plant.

burn′ing, adj., flaming; causing ardour; pr.p., burn.

bur′nish, v.t., to polish and make shining.

bur′nished, p.p., burnish.

bur′nisher, n., one who, or that which, burnishes.

bur′nishing, pr.p., burnish.

burnous(e)′, n., a white, woollen hood and mantle worn by Arabs.

burnt, p.p., burn.

burnt′-offering, n., a sacrifice or atonement for sin burnt on an altar.

burp, n., a belch; v.i., to belch (slang).

burr, n., the rough, prickly covering of certain seeds; the burdock; a guttural pronunciation of the sound r.

bur′ral, n., i.q. burrel.

bur′rel, n., the red-butter pear.

burro, n., a Spanish name for a small donkey (colloq.).

bur′rock, n., a little weir or dam in a river.

bur′row, n., a hole in the ground in which certain animals shelter; v.t., to make a

burrow or tunnel in the ground.

bur′rowed, p.p., burrow.

bur′rower, n., one who, or that which, burrows.

bur′rowing, pr.p., burrow.

bur′ry, adj., covered with burrs.

burs′a, n., a saclike cavity to lessen friction (anat., zool.).

bur′sar, n., the treasurer of a college or monastery; a student to whom a bursary is paid.

bur′sary, n., a scholarship or exhibition (usually Scottish); the treasury of a college or monastery.

bursic′ulate, adj., resembling a purse.

bursi′form, adj., purse-shaped.

burst, n., a sudden explosion; p.p., burst; v.i., to explode; v.t., to break by violence.

burst′er, n., one who, or that which, bursts.

burst′ing, n., the act of exploding; pr.p., burst.

bur′then, n. and v.t., i.q. burden.

bur′ton, n., a small tackle with two pulleys used in ships.

bur′y, v.t., to cover with earth; to hide.

bur′ying, pr.p., bury.

bur′ying-ground, n., a cemetery.

bus, 'bus, n., a public conveyance (abbrev. of omnibus); aircraft, motorcar (slang).

bus′by, n., a military fur headdress.

bush, n., a shrub with branches; a district overgrown with shrubs; a hard lining let into the axle-socket of a carriage; v.i., to form a bush.

bush′bab′y, n., a small lemur; the South African night-ape.

bushed, p.p., bush.

bush′el, n., a dry measure of eight gallons.

bush′iness, n., the quality of being bushy.

bush′ing, pr.p., bush.

bush′man, n., a woodsman.

bush′master, n., a large and poisonous rattle-snake.

bush′ranger, *n.,* a robber in the bush country.

bushveld, *n.,* low country of the Transvaal.

bush′y, *adj.,* like a bush.

bus′ied, *p.p.,* busy.

bus′ier, *adj., comp.* of busy.

bus′iest, *adj., super.* of busy.

bus′ily, *adv.,* in a busy manner.

bus′iness, *n.,* employment; concern; affair.

bus′inesslike, *adj.,* systematic, well-ordered, efficient.

bus′inessman′, *n.,* one engaged in commercial transactions.

busk, *n.,* a support or stiffening in a woman's undergarment.

bus′ker, *n.,* an itinerant musician.

bus′ket, *n.,* a shrubbery.

bus′kin, *n.,* a high boot worn by ancient tragic actors.

bus′kined, *adj.,* wearing buskins; pert. to tragedy.

buss, *n.,* a kiss; a small vessel used in herring-fishing; *v.t.,* to kiss.

bust, *n.,* the figure down to just below the shoulders; the breasts.

bus′tard, *n.,* a large bird.

bus′tle, *n.,* activity with noise and agitation; a pad worn by women to stress the prominence of the buttocks; *v.i.,* to be active and stirring.

bus′tled, *p.p.,* bustle.

bus′tler, *n.,* an active, stirring person.

bus′tling, *adj.,* busy; stirring; *pr.p.,* bustle.

bus′y, *adj.,* employed with constant attention; *v.t.,* to make or keep busy.

bus′ybody, *n.,* one who officiously concerns himself with the affairs of others.

bus′ying, *pr.p.,* busy.

bus′yness, *n.,* the state or quality of being busy.

but, *adv., prep.,* and *conj.,* except, unless; only; on the contrary; however.

butadi′ene, *n.,* gas used in making synthetic rubber (*chem.*).

but′ane, *n.,* hydrocarbon of the methane series (*chem.*).

butch′er, *n.,* one who kills beasts for food; a purveyor of meat; one who slays barbarously; *v.t.,* to kill for food or lust of slaughter.

butch′ered, *p.p.,* butcher.

butch′ering, *pr.p.,* butcher.

butch′erly, *adj.,* murderous, brutal.

butch′ery, *n.,* the business of slaughtering; barbarous and extensive bloodshed.

but′ler, *n.,* a domestic servant who takes charge of the wines, plate, etc.; a head manservant.

but′lerage, *n.,* an ancient duty paid on imported wine.

but′lership, *n.,* the office of a butler.

but′lery, *n.,* a butler's pantry.

but′ment, *n.,* a buttress of an arch.

butt, *n.,* the larger end of a thing; a large cask; the object of aim or attack; a push with the head; *v.t.* and *i.,* to strike with the head.

but′te, *n.,* a ridge or plateau (*Fr.*).

butt′ed, *p.p.,* butt.

butt′-end, *n.,* the thicker end of anything.

but′ter, *n.,* an animal that butts; an oily substance obtained from cream or milk by churning; *v.t.,* to smear with butter; to flatter grossly.

but′terbean, *n.,* an American bean akin to the French bean.

but′tercup, *n.,* a yellow flower; the ranunculus.

but′tered, *p.p.,* butter.

but′terfingers, *n.,* one apt to let things slip or fall.

but′terfly, *n.,* a diurnal lepidopterous insect with four coloured wings.

but′terine, *n.,* an artificial butter made from animal fat; yolks of eggs, etc., churned with milk.

but′tering, *pr.p.,* butter.

butt′eris, *n.,* a farrier's tool for paring the hoof.

but′terknife, *n.,* a special knife used for cutting butter.

but′termilk, *n.,* the milk that remains after the butter is separated from it.

but′ter mus′lin, *n.,* a thin, loose-woven cloth.

but′ter-tooth, *n.,* a broad fore-tooth.

but′tery, *adj.,* resembling butter; *n.,* a storeroom for wines, provisions, etc.

butt′-hinge, *n.,* a door hinge.

but′ting, *pr.p.,* butt.

but′tock, *n.,* the rump.

but′ton, *n.,* a small round fastener for clothing; the disc at the end of a fencing foil; *v.t.,* to fasten with buttons.

but′ton-ball, *n., i.q.* button-wood.

but′toned, *p.p.,* button.

but′tonhole, *n.,* the hole or loop in which a button is fastened; a flower in a buttonhole; *v.t.,* to make buttonholes in; to detain.

but′toning, *pr.p.,* button.

but′tons, *n.,* a page in buttoned livery (*colloq.*).

but′ton-wood, *n.,* the American plane tree.

but′tony, *adj.,* with many buttons.

but′tress, *n.,* a projecting support of masonry built on to a wall; any support or prop; *v.t.,* to prop.

but′tressed, *p.p.,* buttress.

but′tressing, *pr.p.,* buttress.

butts, *n. pl.,* the end of a rifle range where the targets are placed.

but′ty, *n.,* a man who raises coal by contract at a stated price per ton, employing others to do the work.

butyra′ceous, *adj.,* resembling butter.

butyr′ic, *adj.,* derived from butter.

bu′tyrin, *n.,* a fat contained in milk which gives butter its peculiar flavour.

butyrom′eter, *n.,* an instrument for estimating the fat content in milk.

bux′eous, *adj.,* pert. to the box-tree.

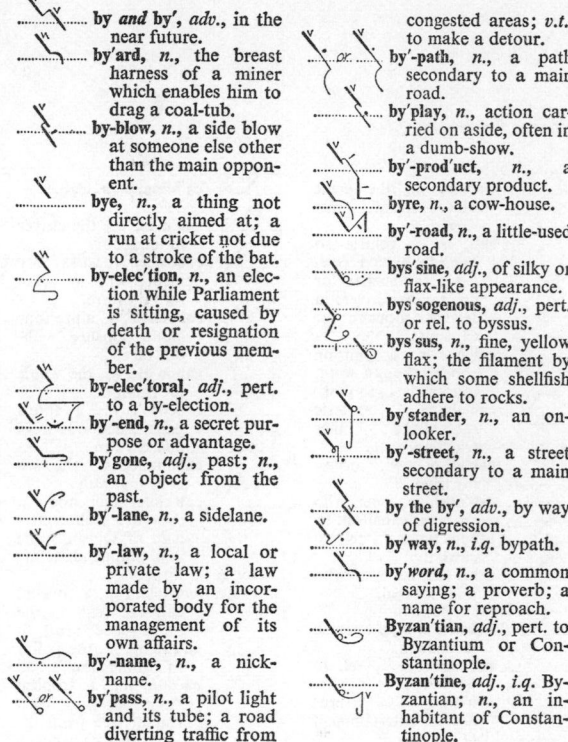

buxi'na, *n.*, an alkaloid obtained from the box-tree.

bux'ine, *n. i.q.* buxina.

bux'om, *adj.*, pliant; jolly; plump.

bux'omly, *adv.*, in a buxom manner.

bux'omness, *n.*, the quality of being buxom.

buy, *v.t.*, to acquire by paying a price to the seller.

buy'er, *n.*, one who buys.

buy'ing, *pr.p.*, buy.

buzz, *n.*, a low whispering hum; *v.i.*, to make a low hissing sound; *v.t.*, to transmit a telephone message in Morse; *v.t.*, to whisper.

buz'zard, *n.*, a large bird of the falcon family.

buzzed, *p.p.*, buzz.

buz'zer, *n.*, one who, or that which, buzzes; one who tells tales secretly.

buz'zing, *pr.p.*, buzz.

buz'zingly, *adv.*, with a low, humming sound.

by, *prep.*, near; through; *adv.*, near; aside.

by *and* by', *adv.*, in the near future.

by'ard, *n.*, the breast harness of a miner which enables him to drag a coal-tub.

by-blow, *n.*, a side blow at someone else other than the main opponent.

bye, *n.*, a thing not directly aimed at; a run at cricket not due to a stroke of the bat.

by-elec'tion, *n.*, an election while Parliament is sitting, caused by death or resignation of the previous member.

by-elec'toral, *adj.*, pert. to a by-election.

by'-end, *n.*, a secret purpose or advantage.

by'gone, *adj.*, past; *n.*, an object from the past.

by'-lane, *n.*, a sidelane.

by'-law, *n.*, a local or private law; a law made by an incorporated body for the management of its own affairs.

by'-name, *n.*, a nickname.

by'pass, *n.*, a pilot light and its tube; a road diverting traffic from

congested areas; *v.t.*, to make a detour.

by'-path, *n.*, a path secondary to a main road.

by'play, *n.*, action carried on aside, often in a dumb-show.

by'-prod'uct, *n.*, a secondary product.

byre, *n.*, a cow-house.

by'-road, *n.*, a little-used road.

bys'sine, *adj.*, of silky or flax-like appearance.

bys'sogenous, *adj.*, pert. or rel. to byssus.

bys'sus, *n.*, fine, yellow flax; the filament by which some shellfish adhere to rocks.

by'stander, *n.*, an onlooker.

by'-street, *n.*, a street secondary to a main street.

by the by', *adv.*, by way of digression.

by'way, *n.*, *i.q.* bypath.

by'word, *n.*, a common saying; a proverb; a name for reproach.

Byzan'tian, *adj.*, pert. to Byzantium or Constantinople.

Byzan'tine, *adj.*, *i.q.* Byzantian; *n.*, an inhabitant of Constantinople.

C

Ca'aba, n., the great Mecca shrine. (Also *Kaaba*).

cab, n., a vehicle so named; a taxi (*colloq.*); the shelter for an engine driver; a Jewish measure of capacity.

cabal', n., a plotting combination, a secret intrigue; v.i., to plot.

cab'ala, n., esoteric rabbinism; inner teaching.

cab'alism, n., occult doctrine.

cab'alist, n., one who practises cabalism.

cabalis'tic, adj., rel. to cabala.

cabal'ler, n., one who joins a cabal.

caballer'o, n., a Spanish gentleman.

cab'alline, adj., rel. to horses.

cab'aret, n., a tavern; an entertainment (*Fr.*).

cab'bage, n., the vegetable so named; the head of a palm-tree; v.t., to appropriate (*slang*).

cab'bala, n., i.q. cabala.

cabb'y, n., a cab driver (*colloq.*).

ca'ber, n., a spar of wood, tossed in a Highland game.

cab'in, n., a hut, small cottage or room; a room in a ship; v.t., to confine in close quarters.

cab'in-boy, n., a boy servant on board ship.

cab'ined, p.p., cabin.

cab'inet, n., a small room; a storage or display case; a select body of Ministers.

ca'ble, n., a large, strong chain or rope; a submarine telegraph line; v.t., to transmit a message by cable.

ca'bled, p.p., cable.

ca'blegram, n., a cable message.

ca'blet, n., a little cable; a tow-rope.

ca'bling, pr.p., cable.

cab'man, n., the driver of a cab.

cabob', n., roast savoury meat; v.t., to make into a cabob.

cabochon', n., a precious stone polished without facets.

caboo'dle, n., the whole lot (*slang*).

caboose', n., a ship's galley; a goods train guard's van.

cab'otage, n., the sea coasting trade.

cab'riole, adj. and n., curved leg characteristic of Queen Anne and Chippendale furniture.

cabriolet', n., a covered carriage (cab is the abbreviated form).

ca'can'ny, n., the policy of "going slow".

caca'o, n., a tropical American and West Indian tree from the seed of which cocoa is prepared.

cachaem'ia, n., a morbid blood condition.

cach'alot, n., the sperm whale.

cache, n., a hiding place (*Fr.*).

cachec'tic, adj., suffering from cachexy.

ca'chet, n., a seal, an impress; esteem.

cachex'ia, n., poor health, bad condition.

cachex'y, n., i.q. cachexia.

cach'innate, v.i., to laugh loudly.

cachinna'tion, n., loud laughter.

cach'olong, n., a pearl opal.

cachou', n., an aromatic breath-sweetening pill.

cachu'cha, n., a Spanish solo dance (*Span.*).

cacique', n., a tribal chief (W. Indian and S. American).

cack'le, v.i., to make the sound of a hen or goose; to prattle.

cack'led, p.p., cackle.

cack'ler, n., one who cackles.

cack'ling, pr.p., cackle.

cacochym'ic, adj., suffering from cacochymy.

cac'ochymy, n., a disordered condition of bodily fluids.

cacodem'on, n., an evil spirit; a demon.

cac'odyl, n., a stinking, poisonous compound of arsenic and methyl.

caco'epy, n., bad pronunciation.

cacoe'thes, n., a bad propensity (*Gr.*).

cacogen'ics, n., the study of race deterioration.

cacog'raphy, n., bad writing.

cacol'ogy, n., the faulty pronunciation or use of words.

cacoon', n., a large, flat, polished bean of a tropical shrub.

cacophon'ic, adj., discordant, ill-sounding.

cacoph'onous, adj., i.q. cacophonic.

cacoph'ony, n., a discordant noise.

cacta'ceous, adj., rel. to or resembling the cactus.

cac'tus, n., a flowering spiny and fleshy plant.

cacum'inal, adj., describing the sound produced with tip of tongue curled upwards towards hard palate.

cad, n., a low, mean fellow.

cadas'tral, adj., a survey map on a large scale.

cada'ver, n., a corpse.

cadaver'ic, adj., pert. to a cadaver or carcass.

cadav'erous, adj., corpse-like.

cadav'erously, adv., in a cadaverous way.

cadav'erousness, n., a cadaverous state.

cad'die, n., one who carries for a golf player.

cad'dis, n., the caddis-fly larva.

cad'dish, adj., like a cad.

cad'dy, n., a domestic box for holding tea.

cade, n., a cask of capacity to hold 500 herrings or 1,000 sprats.

ca'dence, n., the fall of the voice in speaking or reading; the close of a musical sentence.

ca'dency, n., the precedence of younger members and branches of a great family.

caden'za, n., an improvised or prepared addition before the close of a musical movement.

cadet', n., a younger son; a young military student.

cadge, v.i., to beg, to sponge.

cadged, p.p., cadge.

cadg'er, n., one who cadges.

cadg'ing, pr.p., cadge.

ca'di, n., a Mohammedan judge.

cadil'lac, n., a large kind of pear.

Cadme'an, adj., pert. to Cadmus of Thebes: Theban.

cad'mia, n., a zinc ointment.

cad'mium, n., a metallic element so named.

ca'dre, n., a regimental staff; any trained permanent nucleus of staff.

cadu'cean, adj., rel. to the caduceus.

cadu'ceus, n., Mercury's winged staff.

cadu'cous, adj., dropping before ripened.

cae'cal, adj., rel. to the caecum.

cae'cum, n., a sort of pouch, closed at one end and attached to the great intestine.

Ca'en-stone, n., a soft stone from Caen.

Caesar, n., the first Roman emperor and his successors.

Caesa'rean, adj., rel. to Caesar; delivered at birth by cutting the abdomen.

Caesa'reanist (ianist), n., one who advocates Caesarean births.

Cae'sarism, n., absolute rule; autocracy.

Caes'arist, n., a believer in autocracy.

caes'ious, adj., bluish or greyish green (bot.).

caes'ium, n., an alkalimetal (chem.).

caesu'ra, n., a break in a metrical foot, making a pause in the verse.

ca'fé, n., a coffee-house, a restaurant (Fr.).

café au lait, n., coffee with milk (Fr.).

cafeter'ia, n., a restaurant with self-service counter (Span.).

caffe'ic, adj., rel. to coffee.

caf'feine, n., a coffee-extract.

Caf'fre, n., a native of a S. African tribe so named.

caf'tan, n., a Turkish garment; a loose type of dress.

cage, n., an enclosure for birds or beasts; a contrivance for lowering and raising miners; v.t., to confine in a cage, to keep within narrow limits.

caged, p.p., cage.

cage'ling, n., a caged bird.

cage'work, n., open-work.

ca'gey, adj., shrewd, self-contained.

cag'ing, pr.p., cage.

ca'hier, n., loose sheets of paper collected together; a committee's report.

cahoot, n., a company; a partnership (slang).

Cain, n., a murderer.

caique', n., a light, Turkish skiff.

cairn, n., a monument composed of piled stones.

cairngorm', n., a species of rock-crystal.

cais'son, n., an ammunition chest; a box for explosives in blasting; a casing for building under water.

cai'tiff, adj., vile, despicable; n., a vile fellow.

cajole', v.t., to wheedle, to flatter.

cajoled', p.p., cajole.

cajole'ment, n., the act of cajoling.

cajo'ler, n., one who cajoles.

cajo'lery, n., i.q. cajolement.

cajo'ling, pr.p., cajole.

cajol'ingly, adv., in a cajoling way.

cake, n., a sweet confection, flour based; a hardened mass; v.t., to make into a cake; v.i., to harden.

caked, p.p., cake.

cake'let, n., a small cake.

cake'walk, n., a gliding kind of dance, of American origin.

cak'ing, pr.p., cake.

cak'y, adj., like a cake.

calabar' bean, n., a poisonous seed of an African climbing plant.

cal'abash, n., the fruit of a tropical tree, used for containing liquids.

cal'aber, -ar, n., fur of the Siberian grey squirrel.

calaboose', n., a common prison in the U.S.A. (slang).

Cala'brian, adj., pert. to Calabria.

calaman'co, n., a woollen material, brocaded or checkered.

calaman'der, n., a hard cabinet wood of Ceylon and India.

cal'amar, n., i.q. calamary.

cal'amary, n., a cuttlefish.

calamif'erous, adj., reedy.

cal'amine, n., a zinc silicate.

cal'amint, n., kinds of aromatic herb.

cal'amite, n., a species of tremolite.

calam'itous, adj., bringing calamity.

calam'itously, adv., in a calamitous way.

calam'itousness, n., the quality of calamity.

calam'ity, n., disaster, misfortune.

cal'amus, n., a cane-bearing palm; the sweet-flag.

calan'do, decreasing in speed and tone (mus.), (It.).

calash', n., a low-wheeled, hooded vehicle; a woman's hood.

cal'car, n., a spur or a spur-like figure; a calcinating oven in glass-works.

calca'reous, adj., rel. to limestone.

calca'reousness, n., the calcareous quality.

cal'ceated, adj., wearing shoes.

calceola'ria, n. pl., a botanical genus, popularly known as slipperworts.

cal'cic, adj., pert. or rel. to calcium.

calcic'olous, adj., growing upon limestone.

calcif'erous, adj., containing lime.

cal′cify, *v.i.*, to form lime.

cal′cimine, *n.* and *v.t.*, white or tinted wash for ceilings and walls.

calcin′able, *adj.*, able to be calcined.

calcina′tion, *n.*, the process of calcining.

calcin′atory, *adj.*, tending to calcination.

cal′cine, *v.t.*, to make friable by the application of heat; *v.i.*, to become friable.

cal′cined, *p.p.*, calcine.

cal′cining, *pr.p.*, calcine.

cal′cite, *n.*, native carbonate of lime.

cal′cium, *n.*, a metallic element so named.

calcog′raphy, *n.*, a drawing with pastels or chalks.

cal′culable, *adj.*, able to be calculated.

cal′culary, *n.*, concretions in fruit pulp.

cal′culate, *v.t.*, to reckon arithmetically; to estimate, plan, design.

cal′culated, *p.p.*, calculate.

cal′culating, *adj.*, designing; *pr.p.*, calculate.

calcula′tion, *n.*, the process of calculating; an arithmetical reckoning.

cal′culative, *adj.*, rel. to calculation.

cal′culator, *n.*, one who calculates; a calculating machine.

cal′culatory, *adj.*, rel. to calculation.

cal′culiform, *adj.*, pebble-shaped.

cal′culous, *adj.*, gritty.

cal′culus, *n.*, a stony growth in the body; a method of calculating by means of symbols.

cal′dron, *n.*, a large kettle.

Caledo′nian, *adj.*, rel. to Caledonia; Scottish.

calefa′cient, *adj.*, producing warmth or heat.

calefac′tion, *n.*, the process of producing warmth.

calefac′tor, *n.*, a small stove.

calefac′tory, *adj.*, warmth-producing; *n.*, a chamber in a monastery where a fire is allowed; a chafing-dish or hot water sphere.

cal′endar, *n.*, a system of reckoning years, months and days; an official list; *v.t.*, to put into a calendar, to index.

cal′ender, *n.*, a papermaking machine giving a glossy surface; a Turkish dervish; *v.t.*, to press in order to produce a glossy surface.

cal′endered, *p.p.*, calender.

cal′enderer, *n.*, one who calenders.

cal′endering, *pr.p.*, calender.

cal′ends, *n.*, the Latin name for the first day of the month. (Also *kalends*).

cal′enture, *n.*, a delirious fever; hallucination.

cales′cence, *n.*, the process of growing warm.

calf, *n.*, a cow's offspring; the back of the leg below the knee.

calf′-love, *n.*, a boy's or girl's transient attachment.

calf′s-foot, *n.*, the wake-robin.

Cal′iban, *n.*, a man of degraded bestial nature.

cal′ibrate, *v.t.*, to mark the correct settings on a scale.

calibra′tion, *n.*, the process of calibrating.

cal′ibre, cal′iber, *n.*, the bore of a tube; the size of bore; a standard of ability.

cal′icle, *n.*, a small, cup-like body (*biol.*).

cal′ico, *adj.*, made of calico; *n.*, cotton cloth, whether plain or printed on one side.

ca′lif, *n.*, *i.q.* caliph.

californ′ium, *n.*, a radioactive, transuranic element.

cal(l)igraph′ic, *adj.*, rel. to caligraphy.

cal(l)ig′raphy, *n.*, the art of penmanship.

caliol′ogy, *n.*, the study of birds' nests.

cal′ipash, *n.*, the green gelatinous part of a turtle's flesh.

calipee′, *n.*, the yellow gelatinous part of a turtle's flesh.

cal′(l)iper, *n.*, an instrument for measuring diameters.

cal′iph, *n.*, a Mohammedan ruler.

cal′iphate, *n.*, the office, and tenure of office, of a caliph.

calisay′a, *n.*, a species of Peruvian bark.

cal(l)isthen′ic, *adj.*, rel. to calisthenics.

cal(l)isthen′ics, *n. pl.*, easy gymnastic exercises, promoting gracefulness of body.

cal′ix, *n.*, a cavity in the shape of a cup.

ca(u)lk, *v.t.*, to plug with oakum or other soft substance or to close up the seams of a ship by hammering; to trace on transfer paper.

calked, *p.p.*, calk.

calk′er, *n.*, one who calks.

cal′kin, *n.*, the turned-down heel of a horseshoe; an iron guard on a boot or a shoe.

calk′ing, *pr.p.*, calk.

call, *n.*, a cry, a demand, a vocation, a short visit; *v.t.*, to summon, arouse, proclaim; deem or style; *v.i.*, to pay a short visit.

call′a, *n.*, a marsh plant of N. Europe.

call′able, *adj.*, able to be called.

called, *p.p.*, call.

call′er, *n.*, one who calls.

call′-girl, *n.*, a prostitute on call by telephone.

calligraphic, *adj.*, *i.q.* caligraphic.

calligraphy, *n.*, *i.q.* caligraphy.

call′ing, *pr.p.*, call.

Calli′ope, *n.*, the chief of the Muses, patroness of epic poetry; a humming bird so named.

callisthen′ic, *adj.*, *i.q.* calisthenic.

callisthen′ics, *n. pl.*, *i.q.* calisthenics.

callos′ity, *n.*, a thickening of the skin; the state of being hardened.

cal′lous, *adj.*, hardened, insensible, indifferent.

cal′lously, *adv.*, in a callous way.

cal′lousness, *n.*, insensibility, indifference.

cal′low, *adj.*, unfledged.

cal′lus, *n.*, a hardened part, a callosity.

calm, adj., quiet, still, serene; n., a state of smoothness or tranquility; v.t., to tranquillize, to soothe; v.i., to become tranquil.

calm'ative, adj, and n., calming (agent), a sedative.

calmed, p.p., calm.

calm'er, adj., comp. of calm; n., one who calms.

calm'est, adj., super. of calm.

calm'ing, pr.p., calm.

calm'ingly, adv., in a calming manner.

calm'ly, adv., with calmness.

calm'ness, n., a state of calm.

cal'omel, n., the purgative drug so named.

calores'cence, n., the generation of heat by reflection through a body partially transparent.

calor'ic, n., heat.

cal'orie, n., a unit of heat.

calorif'ic, adj., heat-producing, heat-carrying.

calorifica'tion, n., the causing of heat.

calorim'eter, n., a heat-measuring apparatus.

calotte', n., a skullcap, or other closefitting cap (Fr.).

cal'otype, n., a photograph produced by a now antiquated process.

calp, n., Irish dark-grey limestone.

cal'trop, n., a four-spiked iron ball thrown to maim cavalry horses; a kind of plant with spine-like flowers.

calum'ba, n., a bitter, vegetable tonic so named.

cal'umet, n., the long, reed-stemmed pipe of the N. American Indians.

calum'niate, v.t., to defame, to slander.

calum'niated, p.p., calumniate.

calum'niating, pr.p., calumniate.

calumnia'tion, n., the act of calumniating.

calum'niator, n., one who calumniates.

calum'niatory, adj., defamatory, slanderous.

calum'nious, adj., i.q. calumniatory.

calum'niously, adv., slanderously.

calum'niousness, n., a habit of slandering; the quality of being slanderous.

cal'umny, n., a slanderous report or charge.

Cal'vary, n., the place of Christ's crucifixion; an open-air erection representing the crucifixion.

calve, v.t., to give birth to a calf; to throw off a part of an iceberg.

calved, p.p., calve.

calves, n., pl. of calf.

calves'-foot, adj., made from the feet of a calf.

calv'ing, pr.p., calve.

Cal'vinism, n., the principles taught by John Calvin; the Calvinistic system.

Cal'vinist, n., a follower of Calvin.

Calvinis'tic, adj., rel. to Calvin or Calvinism.

Calvinis'tical, adj., i.q. Calvinistic.

calx, n., the residuum after calcination; chalk, lime; glass fragments for remelting.

cal'ycate, adj., provided with a calyx.

cal'ycine, adj., rel. to a calyx.

cal'ycle, n., a supplementary calyx.

calyp'so, n., a musical style of W. Indian origin.

cal'yx, n., the outer covering of a flower, composed of sepals.

cam, n., a revolving piece of machinery, giving a reciprocating motion.

cam'alote, n., a water-lily.

camaraderie, n., good fellowship (Fr.).

cam'aron, n., a species of freshwater shrimp (Span.).

cam'ber, n., a slight convexity; a harbour (obs.); v.t., to curve slightly upwards.

cam'bered, p.p., camber.

cam'bering, pr.p., camber.

Cam'berwell Beaut'y, n., a kind of butterfly.

cam'bial, n., rel. to commercial exchange, or to cambium.

cam'bist, n., an expert in exchange values; a book which shows the moneys, weights and measures of foreign countries, with their equivalents.

cam'bistry, n., the theory of commercial exchange.

cam'bium, n., the organic source of new tissues in certain plants; property exchange.

camboose', n., i.q. caboose.

cam'brel, n., bent wood or iron used by butchers.

Cam'brian, adj., rel. to Cambria or Wales.

cam'bric, n., a fine, white linen; also a cotton fabric made to look like linen.

Cam'bridge, n., a university town in England.

came, p.p., come.

cam'el, n., the well-known beast of burden, native to Arabia and Bactria.

cameleer', n., a camel-driver.

camel'lia, n., the flower named after G. J. Kamel.

cam'eloid, adj. and n., (a member) of the camel family.

camel'opard, n., another name for the giraffe.

cam'elry, n., troops on camels.

Cam'embert, n., a rich, soft cheese.

cam'eo, n., a stone or shell so cut as to throw one layer into relief in one colour, the rest forming a background in a different colour.

cam'era, n., the photographic box in which the image is received; a room, esp. a judge's private chamber.

cameralis'tic, adj., pert. to high finance.

cam'erate, adj., partitioned into rooms.

cam'erated, adj., i.q. camerate.

camera'tion, n., partition into rooms; a vaulting.

camerleng'o, n., i.q. camerlingo.

camerling'o, n., the Pope's chamberlain and financial secretary.

Camero'nian, adj., pert. to the teaching of

Richard Cameron; *n.*, a follower of C.

cam'ion, *n.*, a low, heavy motor lorry (*Fr.*).

Cam'isard, *n.*, a smock wearer; the nickname of the French Calvinists at the time of the revocation of the Edict of Nantes.

cam'let, *n.*, a material made from camel's hair.

camm'ock, *n.*, kinds of yellow-flowered plant.

cam'omile, *n.*, a bitter aromatic plant, much used in medicine.

Camor'ra, *n.*, an Italian secret organization.

cam'ouflage, *n.*, a disguise for the purpose of hiding; *v.t.*, to disguise.

camp, *n.*, an encampment, a place of encampment; *v.t.* and *i.*, to encamp.

campaign', *n.*, a series or a period of military operations; any organized course of action; *v.i.*, to try to arouse public opinion.

campaigned', *p.p.*, campaign.

campaign'er, *n.*, one engaged in a campaign.

campaign'ing, *n.*, the conducting of a campaign; *pr.p.*, campaign.

cam'pan, *n.*, a marble of which there are several varieties.

campani'le, *n.*, a bell-tower, a belfry.

campanol'ogy, *n.*, the science of bell-construction and bell-ringing.

campan'ula, *n.*, one of the bell-worts, as the Canterbury bell.

campan'ulate, *adj.*, bell-shaped (*zool. and bot.*).

camp'-bed, *n.*, a portable, folding bed.

camped, *p.p.*, camp.

camp'er, *n.*, one who camps.

cam'phene, *n.*, the oil of turpentine.

cam'phine, *n.*, *i.q.* camphene.

cam'phogen, *n.*, *i.q.* cymene.

cam'phor, *n.*, a medicinal, resinous compound.

cam'phorate, *adj.*, impregnated with camphor.

cam'phorated, *adj.*, *i.q.* camphorate.

campim'eter, *n.*, an instrument for testing the retina.

cam'ping, *pr.p.*, camp.

cam'pion, *n.*, a member of the pink family (*bot.*).

camp'shed, *n.*, a raised platform on which a craft may rest level when the tide ebbs.

camp'stool, *n.*, a light, folding stool.

cam'pus, *n.*, an agglomeration of university or college buildings and grounds (*Lat.*).

cam'shaft, *n.*, the shaft on which the cams are mounted.

cam'wood, *n.*, a hard, red W. African wood giving dye.

can, a defective verb used as an auxiliary = to be able; *v.t.*, to preserve in cans.

can, *n.*, a vessel, usually of metal.

Can'aan, *n.*, the land of promise, paradise.

Ca'naanite, *n.*, an inhabitant of Canaan.

Ca'naanitish, *adj.*, bel. to Canaan.

Cana'dian, *adj.*, bel. to Canada; *n.*, an inhabitant of C.

canaille', *n.*, the vulgar, the rabble (*Fr.*).

canal', *n.*, an artificial watercourse; a channel, a groove.

canalic'ulate, *adj.*, having canaliculi, *i.e.*, small ducts.

canaliza'tion, *n.*, conversion into a canal.

ca'nalize, *v.t.*, to convert into a canal.

Ca'nanites, *n.*, a sect of Jewish zealots.

can'apé, *n.*, a small, savoury delicacy (*Fr.*).

canard', *n.*, a made-up sensational statement; a literary hoax (*Fr.*).

cana'ry, *n.*, a song-bird originally found in the Canary Islands.

canas'ta, *n.*, a card game of S. American origin resembling rummy (*Span.*).

canas'ter, *n.*, a kind of tobacco (*Span.*).

can'can, *n.*, a high-kicking, indecorous dance (*Fr.*).

can'cel, *v.t.*, to annul, to cut out.

can'cellate, *adj.*, having a lattice-like appearance.

cancella'tion, *n.*, a lattice-like network; an excision; an annulment.

can'celled, *p.p.*, cancel.

can'celling, *pr.p.*, cancel.

Can'cer, *n.*, "The Crab" one of the signs of the Zodiac; a Tropic.

can'cer, *n.*, a malignant growth.

can'cerate, *v.i.*, to become cancerous.

cancera'tion, *n.*, a cancerous state.

can'cerous, *adj.*, of the nature of cancer.

can'cerously, *adv.*, in a cancerous manner.

can'cerousness, *n.*, a tendency to cancer.

can'criform, *adj.*, crab-like.

can'crine, *adj.*, rel. to crabs.

can'crinite, *n.*, a silicate so named.

canc'roid, *adj.*, crab- or cancer-like.

candela'bra, *n.*, pl. of candelabrum.

candela'brum, *n.*, a branched candlestick.

can'dent, *adj.*, glowing, at white heat.

candes'cent, *adj.*, glowing with white heat.

can'did, *adj.*, fair, frank.

can'didate, *n.*, an applicant for an office or situation.

can'didature, *n.*, a candidate's application.

can'didly, *adv.*, in a candid way.

can'didness, *n.*, a frank attitude.

can'died, *adj.*, made into candy; frosted; *p.p.*, candy.

can'dle, *n.*, a stick of wax or other preparation, with a central wick.

can'dlelight, *n.*, the light given by candles.

Can'dlemas, *n.*, the Feast of the Purification of Our Lady (2 Feb.), celebrated with the display of many candles.

can'dlestick, *n.*, a stand to hold a candle.

can'dour, can'dor, *n.*, fairness, frankness.

can'dy, *n.*, a confection of sugar; *v.t.*, to turn into sugar crystals; to frost preserved fruits with sugar.

can'dying, *pr.p.*, candy.

can′dytuft, *n.*, a plant of the mustard family.

cane, *n.*, a species of reed or grass; a walking-stick; *v.t.*, to strike with a cane.

cane′brake, *n.*, land covered with growing sugar canes.

caned, *p.p.*, cane.

can′gan, *n.*, a coarse, Chinese cloth.

cangue, cang, *n.*, a wooden yoke, used as a Chinese instrument of torture or punishment.

canic′ular, *adj.*, rel. to the dog-star.

can′ine, *adj.*, rel. to a dog; *n.*, a canine tooth.

ca′ning, *n.*, the act of caning; *pr.p.*, cane.

can′ister, *n.*, a box or case of metal.

canit′ies, *n.*, whiteness of the hair.

can′ker, *n.*, an eating and spreading ulcer; *v.t.*, to eat away, to corrode; *v.i.*, to be infected with canker.

can′kered, *p.p.*, canker.

can′kering, *pr.p.*, canker.

can′kerous, *adj.*, of the nature of canker.

can′ker-worm, *n.*, a destructive kind of caterpillar.

can′kery, *adj.*, affected with canker; cross, crabby.

cann′a, *n.*, a plant with bright yellow, red or orange flowers and ornamental leaves.

Cann′abis, *n.*, the hemp plant from which the narcotic drug marijuana (or hashish) is derived.

canned, *adj.*, intoxicated (*colloq.*); *p.p.*, can.

can′nel-coal, *n.*, a coal that burns very brightly.

can′nery, *n.*, a place where provisions are tinned.

can′nibal, *n.*, one who eats human flesh.

can′nibalism, *n.*, a cannibal's state of life; the eating of human flesh.

can′nibalize, *v.t.*, to mix parts from similar sources.

can′nikin, *n.*, a little can.

can′ning, *pr.p.*, can.

can′non, *n.*, a large gun; a smooth horse bit; a stroke at billiards; *v.i.*, to glance off; to rebound from another object.

cannonade′, *n.*, a sustained attack with cannon; *v.t.*, to make an attack with cannon.

cannona′ded, *p.p.*, cannonade.

cannona′ding, *pr.p.*, cannonade.

cannoneer′, cannonier′, *n.*, a man who serves a cannon.

can′non-proof, *adj.*, impenetrable to cannonshot.

can′non-shot, *n.*, a cannon-ball; the shooting of cannon; the range of a gun.

can′not, the negative of can.

can′nula, *n.*, a surgical tube for conveying away pus.

can′nular, *adj.*, hollow, tubular.

can′ny, *adj.*, cautious, sagacious, worldlywise.

canoe′, *n.*, a boat propelled by the paddle; *v.i.*, to paddle a boat.

canoe′able, *adj.*, navigable by canoe.

canoe′ing, *n.*, using a canoe; *pr.p.*, canoe.

canoe′ist, *n.*, one who paddles a canoe.

can′on, *n.*, a rule or standard; a member of a Collegiate or Cathedral Chapter; the more solemn part of the Mass; the Church's standard of selection in regard to the scriptures.

cañ′on, *n.*, a deep ravine.

can′oness, *n.*, a woman of rank in a conventual Chapter.

canon′ic, *adj.*, rel. to canons.

canon′ical, *adj.*, *i.q.* canonic; in accordance with rule.

canon′icals, *n. pl.*, the vestments or habits prescribed by the canons for the clergy.

can′onist, *n.*, an expert in canon law.

canoniza′tion, *n.*, the act or state of canonizing.

can′onize, *v.t.*, to raise to the rank of a saint in the Calendar.

can′onized, *p.p.*, canonize.

can′onizing, *pr.p.*, canonize.

can′onry, *n.*, the office and dignity of a canon.

canood′le, *v.t.* and *v.i.*, to cuddle (*slang*).

canoph′ilist, *n.*, a lover of dogs.

can′opied, *adj.*, having a canopy over.

can′opy, *n.*, an overhead covering; *v.t.*, to cover with a canopy.

cano′rous, *adj.*, tuneful, melodious.

canst, *v.*, a defective auxiliary verb, second person singular.

cant, *n.*, an inclination to one side; hypocritical talk; *v.t.*, to tip up, to bevel; *v.i.*, to tilt; to whine like a beggar; to talk hypocritically.

can′t, *v.*, an abbreviation for cannot (*colloq.*).

Can′tab, *n.*, a Cantabrigian (or Cambridge man).

cantab′ile, *adj.*, smoothly flowing; *n.*, a smooth-flowing style in music.

Canta′brian, *adj.*, pert. to Cantabria (northern Spain).

Cantabrig′ian, *adj.*, pert. to Cambridge.

can′taloup(e), *n.*, a variety of melon.

cantan′kerous, *adj.*, quarrelsome, crusty, contrary.

canta′ta, *n.*, the musical setting of a poem or a drama.

Canta′te, *n.*, the 98th Psalm used as a canticle.

canta′tion, *n.*, an incantation.

cantatri′ce, *n.*, a woman vocalist (*Fr.* and *It.*).

cant′ed, *p.p.*, cant.

canteen′, *n.*, a soldier's drinking-flask; a military stores for food; a place for the refreshment of workpeople.

can′tel, *n.*, *i.q.* cantle.

can′ter, *n.*, a gentle gallop; *v.t.*, to ride a horse at a canter; *v.i.*, to move at a canter.

can′terbury, *n.*, a stand with partitions for music, etc.

Can′terbury bell, *n.*, a kind of campanula.

can′tered, *p.p.*, canter.

can'tering, *pr.p.,* canter.

canthar'ides, *n. pl.,* dried Spanish fly.

canthar'idin, *n.,* a compound extracted from the Spanish fly and other insects.

can'thus, *n.,* the outer or inner corner of the eye where the lids meet.

can'ticle, *n.,* a religious prose song, such as the *Magnificat.*

can'tilever, *n.,* a long bracket supporting a bridge roadway, a balcony or other heavy structure.

can'tillate, *v.i.,* to chant.

cantilla'tion, *n.,* chanting.

cant'ing, *adj.,* leaning; hypocritical; *pr.p.,* cant.

can'tle, *n.,* a hunk of cheese or bread; the backbone of a saddle.

can'to, *n.,* a division in a long poem (*It.*).

can'to fer'mo, *n.,* the plainsong melody to which the counterpoint is added (*It., mus.*).

can'ton, *n.,* a division of a country; *v.t.,* to divide into districts.

can'tonal, *adj.,* rel. to cantons.

can'toned, *p.p.,* canton.

Can'tonese, *adj.,* rel. to Canton.

can'toning, *pr.p.,* canton.

canton'ment, *n.,* a military station, either temporary or permanent.

can'tor, *n.,* a precentor.

cantor'ial, *adj.,* of the precentor's side of the choir.

can'trip, *n.,* an incantation, a frolic.

Canuck', *adj.* and *n.,* French Canadian (*slang*).

can'vas, *adj.,* made of canvas; *n.,* a coarse cloth from which sails are made, or on which pictures are painted.

can'vass, *v.t.,* to examine closely; to solicit.

can'vassed, *p.p.,* canvass.

can'vasser, *n.,* one who canvasses.

can'vassing, *pr.p.,* canvass.

ca'ny, *adj.,* full of canes.

can'yon, *n.,* a deep ravine. (Also *cañon.*)

canzo'ne, *n.,* a Provençal type of madrigal.

canzonet', *n.,* a short song; a light operatic air.

caout'chouc, *n.,* india-rubber.

caout'choucin, *n.,* oil of caoutchouc.

cap, *n.,* a head covering; the top; anything like a cap; *v.t.,* to put a cap or cover on; to put a finishing touch to; to surpass; to salute.

capabil'ity, *n.,* skill, the ability to do things.

cap'able, *adj.,* skilful, able.

ca'pableness, *n.; i.q.* capability.

ca'pably, *adv.,* skilfully, ably.

capa'cious, *adj.,* roomy, wide, able to hold much.

capa'ciously, *adv.,* in a capacious way.

capa'ciousness, *n.,* the state of being capacious.

capac'itance, *n.,* electrostatic capacity.

capac'itate, *v.t.,* to qualify, to render capable.

capac'itated, *p.p.,* capacitate.

capac'itating, *pr.p.,* capacitate.

capac'itor, *n.,* an electrical condenser.

capac'ity, *n.,* the cubic content; ability, skill; the function or relation.

cap-à-pie', *adv.,* from head to foot (*Fr.*).

capar'ison, *n.,* horse-trappings; *v.t.,* to cover with trappings.

capar'isoned, *p.p.,* caparison.

capar'isoning, *pr.p.,* caparison.

cape, *n.,* a headland; a short, circular cloak.

cap'el(l)et, *n.,* a swelling on a horse's hock.

cap'(e)lin, *n.,* a small variety of smelt used for cod bait.

ca'per, *n.,* a frisky antic; a shrub with pungent flower-buds used for flavouring; *v.i.,* to dance, to leap about.

capercail'zie, *n.,* a large kind of grouse.

ca'pered, *p.p.,* caper.

ca'pering, *pr.p.,* caper.

cap'ias, *n.,* a writ authorizing the seizure of a person or goods.

capilla'ceous, *adj.,* hair-like.

capillaire', *n.,* a syrup, once made from the maidenhair fern.

capillar'ity, *n.,* capillary attraction.

cap'illary, *adj.,* rel. to the hair, hair-like; *n.,* a minute blood-vessel uniting the veins and arteries.

capil'liform, *adj.,* in the form of hair.

cap'ital, *adj.,* chief, rel. to the head; rel. to the death penalty; *n.,* the head of a column; the chief city in a State; stock, money.

cap'italism, *n.,* the economic system under which capital and labour are employed by private enterprise.

cap'italist, *n.,* one who possesses and employs capital.

capitalis'tic, *adj.,* rel. to capitalism.

capitaliza'tion, *n.,* the process of converting into capital.

cap'italize, *v.t.,* to convert into capital.

cap'italized, *p.p.,* capitalize.

cap'italizing, *pr.p.,* capitalize.

cap'itate, *adj.,* head-shaped; having a head.

capita'tion, *n.,* a grant made by heads.

Cap'itol, *n.,* the temple of Jupiter in Rome, called the Capitolium; the building at Washington in which the U.S. Congress meets.

Cap'itoline, *adj.,* rel. to the Capitolium.

capit'ular, *adj.,* pert. to a monastic or cathedral Chapter; *n.,* a collection of laws.

capit'ularly, *adv.,* in chapter form.

capit'ulary, *adj.* and *n., i.q.* capitular.

capit'ulate, *v.i.,* to surrender on terms.

capit'ulated, *p.p.,* capitulate.

capit'ulating, *pr.p.,* capitulate.

capitula'tion, *n.,* the act of capitulating.

capit'ulator, *n.,* one who capitulates.

capit'ulum, *n.,* a little head; a chapter.

capi′vi, *n.*, a S. American balsam; copaiba.

cap′lin, *n.*, the part of a flail handle through which the thongs pass.

cap′nomor, *n.*, a compound distilled from wood-tars.

ca′pon, *n.*, a young cock fattened for table.

caponier′, *n.*, a covered passage across the ditch of a fort.

cap′oral, *n.*, a French tobacco (*Fr.*).

capot′, *n.*, a term at piquet when all tricks are won by one player; *v.t.*, to do this against an opponent (*Fr.*).

capote′, *n.*, a cloak or coat with a hood; the hood of a vehicle.

Cappado′cian, *adj.*, rel. to Cappadocia; *n.*, a native of C.

capped, *p.p.*, cap.

cap′per, *n.*, one who, or that which, caps.

cap′ping, *pr.p.*, cap.

cappucci′no, *n.*, black coffee with a little milk.

cap′ric, *adj.*, obtained from butter, coconut oil, etc.

capric′cio, *n.*, a short, lively musical composition in free style (*It.*).

caprice′, *n.*, a whim, a sudden change of mind.

capri′cious, *adj.*, subject to whims.

capri′ciously, *adv.*, in a capricious way.

capri′ciousness, *n.*, the state of being subject to sudden changes of mind.

Cap′ricorn, *n.*, the tenth of the signs of the Zodiac; a Tropic.

Cap′ricorneans, *n.*, people born under the tenth sign of the Zodiac.

Cap′ricornus, *n.*, the Latin name for Capricorn = horned like a goat.

caprifica′tion, *n.*, artificial fertilization of the fig or date.

cap′riform, *adj.*, shaped like a goat.

cap′rine, *adj.*, goat-like.

cap′riole, *n.*, a leap, esp. of a trained horse.

cap′sicum, *n.*, the plant from which cayenne pepper comes.

capsize′, *v.t.* and *i.*, to overturn.

capsized′, *p.p.*, capsize.

capsi′zing, *pr.p.*, capsize.

cap′stan, *n.*, an upright drum used in raising an anchor and other heavy weights.

cap′sular, *adj.*, rel. to or resembling a capsule.

cap′sulary, *adj.*, i.q. capsular.

cap′sule, *n.*, a plant's seed-vessel; a gelatinous bag containing medicine.

cap′tain, *n.*, a head officer; a commander of a ship, a company of troops, a team or club; the head boy of a school.

cap′taincy, *n.*, a captain's rank or tenure of office.

cap′tained, *p.p.*, captain.

cap′tainship, *n.*, a captaincy; skill as a captain.

capta′tion, *n.*, the use of arguments or appeals.

cap′tion, *n.*, a title in a legal document; a chapter or section heading; an arrest.

cap′tious, *adj.*, making frivolous or vexatious objections.

cap′tiously, *adv.*, in a captious way.

cap′tiousness, *n.*, a tendency to be captious.

cap′tivate, *v.t.*, to make captive; to charm.

cap′tivated, *p.p.*, captivate.

cap′tivating, *pr.p.*, captivate.

captiva′tion, *n.*, the act of captivating; the state of being captivated.

cap′tive, *adj.*, taken prisoner; held in captivity or bondage; *n.*, a prisoner.

captiv′ity, *n.*, the state of a captive.

cap′tor, *n.*, one who takes captive.

cap′ture, *n.*, the act of capturing; *v.t.*, to catch by force, to arrest.

cap′tured, *p.p.*, capture.

cap′turing, *pr.p.*, capture.

Cap′uchin, *n.*, a monk of the Franciscan Order distinguished by his *capuche* or cowl.

cap′ulet, *n.*, a peasant woman's headgear worn in the S. of France.

car, *n.*, a generic name for many kinds of vehicles.

carabineer′, *n.*, a soldier armed with a carbine. (Also *carbineer*.)

car′acal, *n.*, a species of Asiatic or African lynx.

car′ack, *n.*, a large, armed Spanish or Portuguese trading vessel. (Also *carrack*.)

car′acole, *n.*, a quick half-turn made by a horseman; *v.i.*, to make sudden turns with horses (*Fr.*).

car′acoly, *n.*, an alloy of gold, silver and copper.

ca′racul, *n.*, a kind of astrakhan fur; cloth imitating this (*Russ.*).

carafe′, *n.*, a water-bottle for the table.

car′amel, *n.*, burnt sugar for colouring; a form of sweetmeat.

ca′rapace, *n.*, the thick, heavy shell of a tortoise.

car′at, *n.*, a unit of weight (= 4 grains) for precious stones; the one twenty-fourth part of gold purity.

car′avan, *n.*, an Oriental company of travellers for trade or other purposes; a house on wheels.

caravaneer′, *n.*, one who uses a caravan.

car′avanner, *n.*, i.q. caravaneer.

caravan′sary, *n.*, i.q. caravanserai.

caravan′serai, *n.*, an enclosed shelter for caravans; an inn.

car′avel, *n.*, a small ship, formerly used in Spain and Portugal. (Also *carvel.*)

car′away, *n.*, a plant, the seeds of which are used for flavouring.

car′bide, *n.*, a carbon compound generating acetylene.

car′bine, *n.*, a short rifle, used chiefly by cavalry.

carbineer′, *n.*, i.q. carabineer.

carbohy′drate, *n.*, a compound of carbon and water.

carbol′ic, *adj.*, produced from coal or coal-tar; *n.*, a disinfectant.

car′bolize, *v.t.*, to charge with carbolic.

car′bolized, *p.p.*, carbolize.

car′bolizing, *pr.p.*, carbolize.

car′bon, *n.*, a chemical element; pure charcoal.

carbona′ceous, *adj.*, producing carbon.

carbona′do, *n.*, a dark, opaque variety of diamond used in drilling, etc.

Carbona′ri, *n. pl.*, members of an Italian secret society.

car′bonate, *adj.*, charged with carbon; *n.*, a carbonic acid salt.

carbon′ic, *adj.*, produced from carbon.

carbonif′erous, *adj.*, yielding coal or carbon.

car′bonite, *n.*, an explosive.

carboniza′tion, *n.*, the process of converting into coal or carbon.

car′bonize, *v.t.*, to reduce to carbon.

car′bonized, *p.p.*, carbonize.

car′bonizer, *n.*, one who, or that which, carbonizes.

car′bonizing, *pr.p.*, carbonize.

carborun′dum, *n.*, a silicon carbide used for scouring and abrasion.

car′boy, *n.*, a large bottle, enclosed in wickerwork, for carrying acids.

car′buncle, *n.*, a precious stone of a deep red colour; an ulcer so named.

car′buncled, *adj.*, set with carbuncles.

carbun′cular, *adj.*, of the nature of a carbuncle.

car′burate, *v.t.*, *i.q.* carburet.

car′buret, *n.*, a compound of carbon; carbide; *v.t.*, to impregnate with carbon.

car′buretted, -ted, *p.p.*, carburet.

car′burettor, -ter, *n.*, an apparatus for carburetting.

car′burize, *v.t.*, *i.q.* carburet.

car′cajou, *n.*, the wolverine.

car′canet, *n.*, a jewelled chain or necklace.

car′cass, car′case, *n.*, a dead body; a framework.

carcin′ogen, *n.*, a substance that encourages cancer.

carcinogen′esis, *n.*, the spread of cancer in the body.

carcinogen′ic, *adj.*, cancer-producing.

carcinol′ogy, *n.*, the study of crustaceans.

carcino′ma, *n.*, a cancer (*Gr.*).

carcinomato′sis, *n.*, *i.q.* carcinogenesis.

carcino′matous, *adj.*, cancerous.

card, *n.*, a piece of pasteboard, intended for written or printed matter; *v.t.*, to comb wool or flax.

cardamine, *n.*, a perennial plant of the mustard family.

car′damom, *n.*, an aromatic East Indian and Chinese plant.

card′an, *adj.*, with universal joint at one or both ends (*eng.*).

card′board, *adj.*, made of cardboard; *n.*, thick card.

card′-case, *n.*, a case containing calling-cards.

card′ed, *p.p.*, card.

card′er, *n.*, one who cards.

car′diac, *adj.*, rel. to the heart; *n.*, a cordial.

cardi′acal, *adj.*, *i.q.* cardiac.

cardiag′raphy, *n.*, the process of recording the strength of the heart's movements.

cardial′gia, *n.*, heartburn.

cardial′gy, *n.*, *i.q.* cardialgia.

car′digan, *n.*, a knitted woollen jacket.

car′dinal, *adj.*, principal (*lit.*, that on which something hinges); of a red colour; *n.*, a member of the Sacred College at Rome.

car′dinalate, *n.*, the body of Cardinals, the rank of a cardinal, a cardinal's tenure of office.

car′dinally, *adv.*, preeminently.

card′-in′dex, n., an index with a separate card for each item; *v.t.*, to index on separate cards.

card′ing, *pr.p.*, card.

car′diogram, *n.*, the tracing from a cardiograph.

car′diograph, *n.*, an instrument for recording heart movements.

cardiog′raphy, *n.*, *i.q.* cardiagraphy.

car′dioid, *n.*, a heart-shaped curve.

cardiol′ogy, *n.*, the science of the heart and of the heart's anatomy.

cardi′tis, *n.*, inflammation of the heart.

cardoon′, *n.*, a perennial aster.

care, *n.*, a state of anxiety, solicitude; charge; the object of one's care; *v.i.*, to have regard; to be willing.

cared, *p.p.*, care.

careen′, *v.t.*, to overturn a ship for the purpose of repairs, etc.; *v.i.*, to heel over.

careen′age, *n.*, the fee for careening; a place for careening purposes.

careened′, *p.p.*, careen.

careen′ing, *pr.p.*, careen.

career′, *n.*, a vocation, a profession.

career′ist, *n.*, one intent on personal advancement.

care′free, *adj.*, free from anxiety.

care′ful, *adj.*, full of care; conscientious in action; prudent.

care′fully, *adv.*, with care.

care′fulness, *n.*, the habit or state of taking care.

care′less, *adj.*, not taking care, indifferent; free from care.

care′lessly, *adv.*, in a careless way.

care′lessness, *n.*, the habit or state of not caring.

caress′, *n.*, an embrace, a fondling; *v.t.*, to fondle, stroke, pet.

caressed′, *p.p.*, caress.

caress′ing, *pr.p.*, caress.

caress′ingly, *adv.*, in a caressing way.

car′et, *n.*, a printer's or writer's mark of omission.

care′taker, *n.*, one who looks after a building or house.

care′worn, *adj.*, worn out with care.

car′go, *n.*, a ship's lading.

car′goose, *n.*, the crested grebe.

Car′ib, *n.*, one of an almost extinct American race, the Caribs, inhabiting the islands of the Caribbean Sea.

Carib(b)e′an, *adj.*, rel. to the Caribs and to the sea containing their islands.

Car′ibee, *n.*, *i.q.* Carib.

caribou′, *n.*, the reindeer of N. America.

car′icature, *n.*, a likeness purposely distorted or exaggerated; *v.t.*, to represent in a ridiculous way.

car′icatured, *p.p.*, caricature.

car′icaturing, *pr.p.*, caricature.

car′icaturist, *n.*, one who caricatures.

car′icous, *adj.*, fig-shaped.

ca′ries, *n.*, the decay of teeth or bone.

car′illon, *n.*, a peal or chime of bells, acted upon by a performer or by mechanism.

cari′na, *n.*, a keel (*zool.* and *bot.*).

car′inate, *adj.*, keeled, keel-shaped.

car′inated, *adj.*, *i.q.* carinate.

car′ing, *pr.p.*, care.

car′iole, *n.*, a light, one-horse vehicle.

carios′ity, *n.*, a carious state.

ca′rious, *adj.*, rotten, decaying.

cark, *n.*, anxiety, worry; *v.t.*, to oppress with care.

cark′ing, *adj.*, worrying; *pr.p.*, cark.

car′line, *adj.*, rel. to the Carlina; *n.*, a plant of the Carlina family; the short timber that joins the deck beams of a ship.

carl′ing, *n.*, the dish of fried peas, once peculiar to Carling Sunday.

Carl′ism, *n.*, the support of Don Carlos rel. the Spanish throne.

Carl′ist, *n.*, a supporter of Don Carlos.

Carlovin′gian, *adj.*, rel. to the dynasty of Charlemagne; *n.*, a member of the family of C.

car′man, *n.*, the driver of a delivery vehicle.

Car′melite, *n.*, a member of the Order of Friars of Our Lady of Mount Carmel, known as the White Friars.

car′minate, *v.i.*, to emit internal wind.

car′minative, *adj.*, relieving flatulence.

car′mine, *n.*, a deep red colour made from cochineal.

car′nage, *n.*, great slaughter, butchery.

car′nal, *adj.*, rel. to the flesh, fleshly, sensual.

carnal′ity, *n.*, a sensual tendency or state.

car′nalize, *v.t.*, to make sensual.

car′nally, *adv.*, in a carnal way.

car′nal-mind′ed, *adj.*, disposed to sensuality.

carna′tion, *n.*, flesh-tint; the flowering plant so named.

carnau′ba, *n.*, the Brazilian wax palm.

carne′lian, *n.*, a red stone, much used for seals.

car′neous, *adj.*, fleshy.

car′ney, *n.*, a mouth disease in horses.

carnifica′tion, *n.*, a morbid conversion of tissue into fleshlike consistency.

car′nified, *p.p.*, carnify.

car′nify, *v.t.*, to convert into flesh *v.i.*, to suffer carnification.

car′nifying, *pr.p.*, carnify.

car′nival, *n.*, the feast that precedes the Lenten fast; any sort of revel.

carniv′ora, *n.*, pl. of carnivore.

carn′ivore, *n.*, a flesh-eating animal or plant.

carniv′orous, *adj.*, flesh-eating.

carnos′ity, *n.*, fleshiness.

car′nous, *adj.*, fleshy.

carn′y-ey, *v.t.*, to coax, to wheedle (*colloq.*).

car′ob, *n.*, the tree so named, bel. to the bean order.

car′ol, *n.*, a joyous song, esp. a joyous song of Christmas, Epiphany and Easter; *v.i.*, to sing cheerfully, to warble.

Ca′roline, *adj. n.*, of the time of Charles I and II of England; a girl's name.

car′ol(l)ed, *p.p.*, carol.

car′ol(l)ing, *pr.p.*, carol.

ca′rom, *n.*, a cannon at billiards.

carot′id, *adj.*, rel. to the carotids; *n.*, one of the great neck arteries.

carou′sal, *n.*, a revel, a drinking bout.

carouse′, *v.i.*, to revel, to hold a drinking-bout.

caroused′, *p.p.*, carouse.

car(r)ousel′, *n.*, a tournament; a round-about; a merry-go-round; any rotating device for holding objects.

carous′er, *n.*, one who carouses.

carous′ing, *pr.p.*, carouse.

carp, *n.*, a freshwater fish so named; *v.i.*, to cavil, to criticize censoriously.

car′pal, *adj.*, rel. to the wrist.

Carpa′thian, *adj.*, rel. to the Carpathian chain of mountains.

carped, *p.p.*, carp.

car′pel, *n.*, a simple pistil or seed-vessel.

car′pellary, *adj.*, resembling a carpel.

car′penter, *n.*, a skilled worker in timber; *v.i.*, to do carpentry.

car′pentry, *n.*, a carpenter's craft.

carp′er, *n.*, a caviller.

car′pet, *n.*, a woven floor-covering; *v.t.*, to cover with carpet.

car′pet-bag, *n.*, a travelling bag made of carpet.

car′pet-bagger, *n.*, an opportunist candidate in politics.

car′peted, *p.p.*, carpet.

car′peting, *n.*, carpet material, carpet goods; the act of carpeting; *pr.p.*, carpet.

car′pet-sweeper, *n.*, a device for sweeping carpet.

carphol′ogy, *n.*, delirious grasping at imaginary objects or fumbling with bedclothes, etc. (*med.*).

carp′ing, *pr.p.*, carp.

car′polite, *n.*, fruit fossilized.

carpol′ogist, *n.*, a student of carpology.

carpol′ogy, *n.*, the study of fruits.

car′pus, *n.*, the wrist.

car′rack, *n.*, *i.q.* carack.

carrageen, *n.*, edible seaweed.

car′raway, *n.*, *i.q.* caraway.

car′rel, *n.*, a recess in a library for a desk.

car′riage, *n.*, the act of carrying; the cost of freight; a vehicle; bearing, demeanour; a thing carried (*obs.*).

ca′rriageable, *adj.*, able to be carried; passable by carriages.

ca′rrick bend, *n.*, a kind of knot or splice (*naut.*).

car′ried, *p.p.*, carry.

car′rier, *n.*, one who carries; something that carries; one whose business it is to convey goods, parcels, etc.; part of a machine-gun.

car′riole, *n.*, a small, open carriage.

car′rion, *n.*, dead and putrefying flesh; any loathsome object.

carronade′, *n.*, a short, naval gun with a large bore.

car′rot, *n.*, an edible vegetable.

car′roty, *adj.*, like a carrot; reddish-yellow.

car′ry, *n.*, portage; the range of a gun or missile; *v.t.*, to convey, to bear; to capture (a fort); to involve, imply; to hold up; to act as a bearer of anything.

car′rying, *pr.p.*, carry.

car′ry-over, *n.*, a postponed payment.

cart, *n.*, a vehicle for carrying loads; *v.t.*, to carry in a cart, to convey.

cart′age, *n.*, the carrying in a cart; the cost of carting.

carte, *n.*, a card, a bill of fare; a term in fencing to denote a particular position.

carte blanche′, *n.*, full permission to act as one pleases (*Fr.*).

cart′ed, *p.p.*, cart.

carte-de-visite′, *n.*, a visiting card; a small, mounted photograph (*Fr.*).

car′tel, *n.*, a written agreement for the interchange of prisoners; a written

challenge; a consortium.

cart′er, *n.*, one who drives a cart.

Carte′sian, *adj.*, rel. to Descartes and his philosophy.

Carte′sianism, *n.*, the philosophical system of Descartes.

Carthagin′ian, *adj.*, rel. to Carthage or the Carthaginians.

car′thamin, *n.*, a red dye.

cart′horse, *n.*, a horse that draws a cart.

Carthu′sian, *adj.*, rel. to the Carthusians; *n.*, a monk of the Order of St. Bruno; a member of Charterhouse School.

car′tilage, *n.*, gristle.

cartilag′inous, *adj.*, gristly.

cart′ing, *pr.p.*, cart.

cart′-load, *n.*, the contents of a cart.

cartog′rapher, *n.*, a map-maker.

cartograph′ic, *adj.*, rel. to cartography.

cartog′raphy, *n.*, the art of map-making.

cartol′ogy, *n.*, the science of maps and charts.

cart′omancy, *n.*, fortune-telling by playing-cards.

car′ton, *n.*, a light, cardboard box.

cartoon′, *n.*, a large sketch for a picture; a picture representing, often comically, topical subjects.

cartoon′ing, *n.*, the drawing of cartoons.

cartoon′ist, *n.*, a drawer of cartoons.

cartoph′ilist, *n.*, a collector of cigarette cards.

cartoph′ily, *n.*, cigarette-card collecting.

cartouche′, *n.*, a cartridge box; an inscribed tablet.

car′tridge, *n.*, a case in which is held the charge of a firearm.

car′tulary, *n.*, a register of charters and other records.

cart′way, *n.*, a road fit for carting purposes.

cart′wheel, *n.*, the wheel of a cart; a somersault.

cart′wright, *n.*, one who makes or repairs carts.

car′ucate, *n.*, a measure of plough land; it

varied from 80 to 120 acres.

carun′cle, *n.*, a bird's wattles; the fleshy growth in the inner corner of the eye.

carun′cular, *adj.*, of the nature of a caruncle.

carun′culate, *adj.*, having caruncles.

carun′culated, *adj.*, *i.q.* carunculate.

carve, *v.t.*, to cut, to fashion.

carved, *p.p.*, carve.

car′vel, *n.*, *i.q.* caravel.

carv′er, *n.*, one who carves; a kind of knife used for carving.

carv′ers, *n. pl.*, a carving knife and fork.

carv′ing, *n.*, the art or act of carving; a piece of carved work; *pr.p.*, carve.

car′yate, *n.*, *i.q.* caryatid.

caryat′ic, *adj.*, rel. to caryatid.

caryat′id, *n.*, a female figure supporting (instead of a pillar) an entablature.

caryat′ides, *n.*, pl. of caryatid.

cas′cabel, *n.*, the loop at the breech of a cannon.

cascade′, *n.*, a waterfall.

cascal′ho, *n.*, a Brazilian name for detritus.

cascar′a, *n.*, bark; the medicine derived from the bark of the California buckthorn.

cascaril′la, *n.*, a diminutive of cascara—an aromatic bark.

case, *n.*, a covering, a sheath, a book cover; something that happens; a condition; anyone under medical treatment; a law-suit; a grammatical name for the various relations of a noun; *v.t.*, to enclose, to cover.

case′-book, *n.*, a doctor's record of his cases.

cased, *p.p.*, case.

case′harden, *v.t.*, to harden (iron) by making the surface into steel.

case′hardened, *p.p.*, caseharden.

case′hardening, *n.*, the act or state of casehardening; *pr.p.*, caseharden.

ca′seic, *adj.*, rel. to cheese or casein.

ca'sein, *n.*, milk curd.

case'-knife, *n.*, a knife enclosed in a case or sheath.

case'-law, *n.*, law as decided in previous cases.

case'mate, *n.*, a vaulted chamber in a fort; an armoured gun station in a ship.

case'mated, *adj.*, having casemates.

case'ment, *n.*, a hinged window, opening like a door.

case'mented, *adj.*, having casements.

ca'seous, *adj.*, like cheese.

casern', *n.*, a barrack.

case'work, *n.*, social work amongst individuals.

cash, *n.*, money of all kinds; a Chinese coin so named; *v.t.*, to change into money.

cash'able, *adj.*, capable of being cashed.

cash'-account, *n.*, a record of money received and paid.

cash'-book, *n.*, the book recording receipts and payments of cash.

cashed, *p.p.*, cash.

cashew', *n.*, a nut-bearing tree; the nut itself.

cashier', *n.*, one who looks after the money in a shop or bank; *v.t.*, to dismiss with ignominy.

cashiered', *p.p.*, cashier.

cashier'ing, *pr.p.*, cashier.

cash'ing, *pr.p.*, cash.

cash'keeper, *n.*, a cashier.

cash'mere, *n.*, a fine fabric made from the wool of a Cashmere goat.

cashoo', *n.*, *i.q.* catechu.

cash'-register, *n.*, a till that automatically records the amount received.

ca'sing, *n.*, a covering, a framing; *pr.p.*, case.

casi'no, *n.*, a building for public entertainments.

cask, *n.*, a round, hooped vessel; *v.t.*, to place in a cask.

cas'ket, *n.*, a small box; a jewel-case; a coffin.

Cas'lon, *n.*, old face type cut in the foundry of William Caslon.

casque, *n.*, a helmet (*hist.*, *poet.*).

cassa'da, *n.*, *i.q.* cassava.

Cassan'dra, *n.*, the Trojan princess, whose prophecies went unheeded.

cas'sareep, *n.*, a condiment made from cassava.

cassa'tion, *n.*, the reversal of a judicial sentence.

cassa'va, *n.*, the mandioc plant from which tapioca is derived.

cass'erole, *n.*, a stewpan; food prepared in a c.

cass'ette, *n.*, a small container.

cas'sia, *n.*, the plant from which senna is obtained.

cas'simere, *n.*, *i.q.* cashmere.

cassit'erite, *n.*, a tin dioxide.

cas'sock, *n.*, an ecclesiastical habit, close fitting and long.

cas'socked, *adj.*, wearing a cassock.

cassolette', *n.*, a censer.

cas'sowary, *n.*, a large, ostrich-like bird.

cast, *n.*, the act of throwing; the length of a throw; a squint; a type; a mould; the assignment of *dramatis personae*; *v.t.*, to throw, to throw off, to deposit; to mould; to reckon, calculate.

Casta'lian, *adj.*, rel. to Castalia, the spring sacred to the Muses.

cas'tanets, *n. pl.*, two wooden or ivory clappers, fastened to a dancer's thumb.

cast'away, *n.*, a person or ship that has been abandoned.

caste, *n.*, hereditary class; class distinction.

cas'tellan, *n.*, one in charge of a castle.

cas'tellany, *n.*, a castellan's jurisdiction.

cas'tellated, *adj.*, battlemented like a castle.

cas'ter, *n.*, one who casts; also *i.q.* castor.

cas'tigate, *v.t.*, to chastise, to criticize, to emend.

cas'tigated, *p.p.*, castigate.

cas'tigating, *pr.p.*, castigate.

castiga'tion, *n.*, the act of castigating.

cas'tigator, *n.*, one who castigates.

cas'tigatory, *adj.*, rel. to castigation.

Castile' soap, *n.*, a hard soap of olive oil and soda.

Castil'ian, *adj.*, rel. to Castile; *n.*, a native of Castile.

cast'ing, *n.*, the act or result of casting; *pr.p.*, cast.

cast'ing-net, *n.*, a net which is flung out and drawn back.

cast'ing-vote, *n.*, the chairman's extra vote when the sides are equal.

cast'-iron, *adj.*, made of or like cast-iron; *n.*, iron that has been melted.

cas'tle, *n.*, a fortress; a chess piece (rook); *v.t.*, to fortify; to exchange the places of the king and the castle at chess.

cas'tled, *adj.*, having a castle on it; *p.p.*, castle.

cas'tling, *pr.p.*, castle.

cast'-off, *n.*, anything thrown aside; an estimate of the amount of printing involved in copy; *v.t.* and *i.*, to untie (ship); to finish (knitting work).

Cas'tor, *n.*, the twin brother of Pollux; a star.

cas'tor, *n.*, a beaver; a tall hat; a utensil for sprinkling; a small wheel for furniture legs; a substance secreted by the beaver; a hard protuberance on a horse's leg.

cas'tor-oil, *n.*, a vegetable purgative.

castrameta'tion, *n.*, the act or method of measuring a camp.

cas'trate, *v.t.*, to emasculate; to cut off the testicles.

cas'trated, *p.p.*, castrate.

cas'trating, *pr.p.*, castrate.

castra'tion, *n.*, the act or process of castrating.

castra'to, *n.*, a male singer castrated to preserve a soprano or alto voice (*It.*).

cas'trel, *n.*, *i.q.* kestrel.

cas'ual, *adj.*, accidental, happening by chance; unmethodical and careless; *n.*, a tramp.

cas'ualism, *n.*, the doctrine that chance governs all things.

cas'ually, *adv.*, unmethodically, carelessly.

cas'uals, *n.*, slip-on, flat-heeled shoes.

cas'ualty, *n.*, an accident; loss through death or wounds.

casuarin'a, *n.*, a kind of tree with jointed leafless branches found in Australia and India.

cas'uist, *n.*, one who studies casuistry.

casuis'tic, *adj.*, rel. to casuistry.

casuis'tical, *adj.*, *i.q.* casuistic.

cas'uistry, *n.*, in moral science the study of cases of conscience; oversubtlety; sophistry.

cat, *n.*, a domestic feline; *v.t.*, to haul up.

catab'olism, *n.*, lit., a casting down; the change of protoplasm into other substances.

catachre'sis, *n.*, a misuse of metaphors.

catachres'tic, *adj.*, of the nature of catachresis.

cat'aclasm, *n.*, a violent break, a disruption.

cat'aclysm, *n.*, a flood, a deluge; any great upheaval.

cataclys'mic, *adj.*, rel. to cataclysms or to the cataclysmic theory.

cataclys'mist, *n.*, one who supports a particular view about cataclysms.

cat'acomb, *n.*, a subterranean cave-tomb.

catacous'tics, *n.*, the theory of reflected sound.

catadiop'tric, *adj.*, rel. to the reflection or refraction of light.

catad'romous, *adj.*, going to lower river or sea to spawn.

cat'afalque, *n.*, a temporary canopy over a corpse or coffin.

catagen'esis, *n.*, retrogressive evolution.

catagmat'ic, *adj.*, rel. to a fracture.

Cat'alan, *adj.*, rel. to Catalonia.

catalec'tic, *adj.*, lacking metrical completeness.

cat'alepsis, *n.*, *i.q.* catalepsy.

cat'alepsy, *n.*, a nervous affection characterized by unconsciousness and bodily rigidity.

catalep'tic, *adj.*, rel. or subject to catalepsy.

catallac'tics, *n.*, the theory of commercial exchange.

cat'aloguable, *adj.*, capable of being catalogued.

cat'alogue, *n.*, a list or detailed enumeration; *v.t.*, to make or to include in a list.

cat'alogued, *p.p.*, catalogue.

cat'aloguer, *n.*, one who prepares catalogues.

cat'aloguing, *pr.p.*, catalogue.

Catalo'nian, *adj.*, rel. to Catalonia; *n.*, a native of C.

catal'pa, *n.*, a genus of N. American trees.

catal'ysis, *n.*, a chemical process in which a stable agent changes a compound.

catalyt'ic, *adj.*, rel. to catalysis.

catamaran', *n.*, a boat with one or more outriggers; a quarrelsome woman.

catame'nia, *n. pl.*, the menses.

catame'nial, *adj.*, rel. to catamenia.

cat'amite, *n.*, a sodomite's minion.

cat'amount, *n.*, the panther.

catamoun'tain, *n.*, a wild, quarrelsome person.

catapet'alous, *adj.*, with petals at the base of a group of stamens.

cat'aphract, *n.*, plate or scale armour.

cat'aplasm, *n.*, a poultice.

cat'apult, *n.*, originally a Roman engine for discharging heavy missiles; a device for projecting small missiles, pebbles, shot.

catapult'ic, *adj.*, rel. to a catapult.

cat'aract, *n.*, a great waterfall or rush of water; a disease of the eye.

cat'aractal, *adj.*, *i.q.* cataractous.

catarac'tous, *adj.*, catar-act-like.

catarrh', *n.*, an affection of the mucous membrane; a cold in the head.

catarrh'al, *adj.*, of the nature of catarrh.

cat'a(r)rhine, *adj.* and *n.*, (a monkey) having nostrils close together (*zool.*).

catas'tasis, *n.*, the part in a Greek drama that next precedes the catastrophe.

catas'trophe, *n.*, in a drama = the *dénouement* or final conclusion; a disastrous ending, a calamity.

catastroph'ic, *adj.*, of the nature of a catastrophe.

Cataw'ba, *n.*, a U.S. grape and wine.

cat'bird, *n.*, the N. American mockingthrush.

cat'boat, *n.*, a single-masted sailing boat.

cat'-burg'lar, *n.*, a burglar who enters by climbing.

cat'call, *n.*, a derisive outcry; *v.i.*, to raise this cry.

catch, *n.*, anything that is caught; the act of catching; an impediment; a kind of part song (*mus.*); a fastening; *v.t.*, to lay hold of, to seize; to grasp the meaning; to hear sound; to overtake.

catch'er, *n.*, one who catches.

catch'fly, *n.*, a plant so named from its glutinous stem.

catch'ing, *pr.p.*, catch.

catch'ment, *n.*, drainage.

catch'penny, *adj.*, worthless; *n.*, a worthless article.

catch'-phrase, *n.*, a slogan.

catch'pole, *n.*, an instrument of medieval warfare for unhorsing an opponent.

catch'up, *n.*, *i.q.* catsup.

catch'word, *n.*, a word or phrase designed to arrest the popular fancy; the first word of a page repeated at the foot of the preceding page.

catch'y, *adj.*, attractive, pleasing.

cate, *n.*, choice food.

catechet'ic, *adj.*, of the nature of a catechism.

catechet'ical, *adj.*, *i.q.* catechetic.

cat′echism, n., instruction by question and answer.

cat′echist, n., one who catechizes; a teacher of catechumens.

catechist′ic, adj., rel. to catechizing.

catechiza′tion, n., the act of catechizing.

cat′echize, v.t., to teach by question and answer; to question closely.

cat′echized, p.p., catechize.

cat′echizer, n., one who catechizes.

cat′echizing, pr.p., catechize.

cat′echu, n., an astringent extract.

catechu′men, n., a person under religious instruction.

catechumen′ic, adj., in the relation of a catechumen.

catechumen′ical, adj., i.q. catechumenic.

categoremat′ic, adj., said of terms which are complete in themselves.

categor′ical, adj., positive, unequivocal.

cat′egorize, v.t., to classify.

cat′egory, n., a class; a general heading or grouping.

cate′na, n., a chain, a series.

catena′rian, adj., rel. to a catenary.

cate′nary, adj., i.q. catenarian; n., a mathematical curve so named.

cat′enate, v.t., to form into a chain or series.

cat′enated, p.p., catenate.

cat′enating, pr.p., catenate.

catena′tion, n., the act of catenating.

caten′ist, n., one who prepares a catena of authorities or evidence.

ca′ter, v.i., to provide food; to minister to any taste or desire.

cat′eran, n., a Highland name for a freebooter (Scot.).

cat′er-cousin, n., a person on intimate terms.

ca′tered, p.p., cater.

ca′terer, n., one who caters.

ca′teress, n., the fem. of caterer.

ca′tering, pr.p., cater.

cat′erpillar, n., a grub; the larva of some insects.

cat′erwaul, n., a hideous cry; v.i., to make the cry of a cat; to raise any hideous cry.

caterwaul′ing, n., a hideous crying noise.

cates, n. pl., eatables; dainty meats.

cat′fish, n., a large, American river fish so named from the purring sound it makes when caught.

cat′gut, n., strong cord made from animals' intestines.

Cath′ari, adj., a name corresponding to the Puritans.

cathar′sis, n., a purging.

cathar′tic, adj., purging, purifying.

cathar′tical, adj., i.q. cathartic.

Cathay′, n., a poetic name for China.

cat′head, n., the projecting piece of timber or iron from which a ship's anchor hangs.

cathe′dra, n., the Greek name for any seat; hence, the bishop's seat, stool or throne.

cathe′dral, adj., containing a cathedra or bishop's seat; n., a church in which the bishop has his seat.

catheret′ic, adj., destructive; erosive; n., a caustic.

cath′erine-wheel, n., a spiked wheel; a rose window; a rotating firework; a sidewise somersault.

cath′eter, n., a surgical instrument for insertion into passages.

cathex′is, n., mental concentration.

cath′ode, n., the negative pole or electrode of an electrical apparatus.

cathode ray, n., a beam of electrons from a cathode.

cathod′ic, adj., rel. to a cathode.

cathod′ograph, n., an x-ray photograph.

cath′olic, adj., universal; pert. to the whole world; [in religion, often limited in its application to the Roman Catholic faith]; n., one who believes the Roman Catholic faith.

Cathol′icism, n., the system and doctrines of the Catholic Church.

catholic′ity, n., the catholic character; widespread general applicability.

cathol′icize, v.t., to make catholic.

cathol′icon, n., a universal remedy; a comprehensive book.

Catilina′rian, adj., rel. to Catiline.

Cat′iline, n., a profligate conspirator.

cat′ion, n., Faraday's name for the element which in electrolysis makes its appearance at the cathode.

cat′kin, n., the spikes of flowers on the willow and other trees.

cat′-like, adj., like a cat.

cat′ling, n., a kitten; a surgical knife so named.

cat′mint, n., a kind of mint of which cats are fond.

cat′nap, n., a short sleep.

cat′-nip, n., i.q. cat-mint.

Cato, n., the Roman Censor.

Cato′nian, adj., rel. to Cato.

cat-o′-nine′-tails, n., an obsolete instrument of punishment. It consisted of nine knotted cords attached to a handle.

catop′tric, adj., reflecting.

cat′s′-eye, n., a vitreous variety of quartz; a reflector set in the road surface.

cat′s′-paw, n., anyone made to do another's unpleasant work.

cat′sup, n., a liquid aromatic condiment.

catt′ish, adj., spiteful.

cat′tle, n., domesticated live stock, particularly bovine.

cat′tle-grid, n., a grid covering a trench to restrict the movement of cattle.

cat′tle-show, n., an exhibition of cattle.

catt′y, adj., like a cat; spiteful; n., a Chinese weight (1⅓ lb.).

cat′-walk, n., a narrow access platform used in large industrial installations.

Cauca′sian, adj., rel. to the Caucasus region; n., a native of the C.

cau'cus, *n.*, a private association of political partisans.

cau'dal, *adj.*, rel. to the tail.

cau'date, *adj.*, tailed.

cau'dated, *adj.*, *i.q.* caudate.

caudillo, *n.*, a leader (*Span.*).

cau'dle, *n.*, a warm concoction of wine, spices, etc., for a sick person.

cauf, *n.*, a basket in which fish are kept under water.

caught, *p.p.*, catch.

caul, *n.*, a fold of the peritoneum; a membranous covering of some infants' heads at child-birth; a hairnet.

caul'dron, *n.*, a large boiler or kettle.

caules'cent, *adj.*, having a stem.

cau'licle, *n.*, a little stem.

cau'licolous, *adj.*, living on stalks.

caul'icule, *n.*, *i.q.* caulicle.

caulif'erous, *adj.*, having a stem.

cau'liflower, *n.*, a cabbage with edible flowers.

cau'liform, *adj.*, stemlike.

cau'line, *adj.*, growing on a stalk; *n.*, the colouring matter in red cabbage.

caulk, *v.t.*, *i.q.* calk.

caus'al, *adj.*, rel. to cause.

causal'ity, *n.*, the relation of cause and effect.

causa'tion, *n.*, *i.q.* causality; the act of causing.

caus'ative, *adj.*, producing effect from cause.

caus'atively, *adv.*, in a causative way.

cause, *n.*, the original source; the reason, motive; a suit at law; a movement or principle; *v.t.*, to produce an effect; to compel.

cause célèbre, *n.*, a lawsuit that excites much attention (*Fr.*).

caused, *p.p.*, cause.

cause'less, *adj.*, without any just cause.

cause'lessly, *adv.*, in a causeless way.

cause'lessness, *n.*, an unreasonable condition or state.

caus'er, *n.*, one who causes.

cause'rie, *n.*, a chat, a conversation (*Fr.*).

causeuse', *n.*, a seat for two people to chat on (*Fr.*).

cause'way, *n.*, a raised path.

cau'sey, *n.*, *i.q.* causeway.

cau'seyed, *adj.*, having a causeway.

causid'ical, *adj.*, rel. to advocacy.

caus'ing, *pr.p.*, cause.

caus'tic, *adj.*, burning; sarcastic; *n.*, a burning substance.

caustic'ity, *n.*, the quality of being caustic.

cau'tel, *n.*, caution; in ecclesiastical language, a precaution against defects or irregularities in saying Mass.

cau'ter, *n.*, a burning-iron.

cau'terant, *adj.*, of the character of a cautery.

cauteriza'tion, *n.*, the act of using a cautery.

cau'terize, *v.t.*, to burn with a cautery.

cau'terized, *p.p.*, cauterize.

cau'terizing, *pr.p.*, cauterize.

cau'tery, *n.*, burning with an acid or a hot iron; a searing iron or other similar implement.

cau'tion, *n.*, prudence, consideration, advice, admonition; *v.t.*, to admonish, to warn.

cau'tionary, *adj.*, of the nature of a warning.

cau'tioned, *p.p.*, caution.

cau'tioner, *n.*, one who cautions.

cau'tioning, *pr.p.*, caution.

cau'tious, *adj.*, wary, discreet.

cau'tiously, *adv.*, warily, discreetly.

cau'tiousness, *n.*, a wary, discreet characteristic.

cavalcade', *n.*, a train of horsemen.

cavalier', *adj.*, like a cavalier, gay, offhand; arrogant, abrupt; *n.*, an armed horseman; a lady's escort; a Royalist.

cavalier'ish, *adj.*, *i.q.* cavalier.

cavalier'ly, *adv.*, in free and easy, offhand fashion.

cavall'y, *n.*, a tropical fish; a horse-mackerel.

cav'alry, *adj.*, rel. to cavalry; *n.*, horse soldiers.

cavass', *n.*, a Turkish military guard.

cavati'na, *n.*, a short aria without a repeat.

cave, *n.*, a hollow subterranean place; *v.i.*, to fall in, to collapse.

ca'veat, *n.*, a legal process in delay of proceedings. (It. means "let him beware.")

ca'veat emptor, let the buyer beware or look after his own interests (*Lat.*).

ca'veator, *n.*, one who files a caveat.

caved, *adj.*, hollowed; *p.p.*, cave.

cav'endish, *n.*, moistened tobacco pressed into cakes.

cav'ern, *n.*, an underground cave; *v.t.*, to excavate; to enclose in a cavern.

cav'erned, *p.p.*, cavern.

cavernic'olous, *adj.*, cave-dwelling.

cav'ernous, *adj.*, like a cavern; caverned.

cav'es(s)on, *n.*, a strong nose-band used when breaking in troublesome horses.

cavet'to, *n.*, a grooved moulding.

caviar(e)', *n.*, sturgeon-roe prepared as a relish.

cav'icorn, *adj.*, with hollow horns.

cav'il, *n.*, a captious objection, needless criticism; *v.i.*, to find needless fault, to be captious.

cav'il(l)ed, *p.p.*, cavil.

cav'il(l)er, *n.*, one who cavils.

cav'il(l)ing, *pr.p.*, cavil.

cav'il(l)ingly, *adv.*, in a captious way.

cav'ing, *pr.p.*, cave.

cav'ity, *n.*, a hollow.

cavort', *v.i.*, to prance (*slang*).

ca'vy, *n.*, a burrowing rodent, such as the guinea pig.

caw, *n.*, the cry of the crow, rook, jackdaw or raven; *v.i.*, to make a sound like that cry.

cawed, p.p., caw.

caw'ing, pr.p., caw.

cawk, n. and v.i., i.q. caw.

cax'on, n., a chest.

Cax'ton, n., any book printed by William Caxton; a kind of printing type.

cay, n., a bank or reef of coral, sand, etc.

Cayenne', n., a town in French Guiana; (c-) a hot, red pepper, named from that place.

cay'man, n., an American alligator.

cayuse, n., an Indian pony (Amer.-Ind.).

cazique', n., i.q. cacique.

ceanoth'us, n., a flowering shrub (Gr.).

cease, n., the end, a pause; v.i. and t., to stop, to desist, to come to an end, to bring to an end.

ceased, p.p., cease.

cease'less, adj., without cease.

cease'lessly, adv., in a ceaseless way.

ceas'ing, pr.p., cease.

ce'city, n., blindness.

ce'dar, adj., made of cedar wood; n., a large tree of the pine and fir order.

ce'dared, adj., cedar-covered.

ce'darn, adj., made of cedar.

cede, v.t., to give up, to resign.

ce'ded, p.p., cede.

ce'der, n., one who cedes.

cedil'la, n., the sign (,) beneath the letter c, softening it before a, o, u.

ce'ding, pr.p., cede.

ce'drat, n., the citron.

ce'drate, n., i.q. cedrat.

ce'drin, n., the substance extracted from the cedronella, the bitter fruit of the cedar tree.

ce'drine, adj., pert. to cedar.

ceil, v.t., to cover with ceiling.

ceiled, p.p., ceil.

ceil'ing, n., the roof of a room; an upper limit; pr.p., ceil.

cel'adon, adj. and n., sea-green.

cel'andine, n., the swallow-wort, a kind of poppy.

Celanese', n., an artificial silk named after the makers.

cel'ature, n., the art of chasing and engraving.

cel'ebrant, n., one who celebrates; the officiating priest at a communion service.

cel'ebrate, v.t., to make famous; to observe with ceremonies; to commemorate; to officiate at the Mass.

cel'ebrated, adj., famous; p.p., celebrate.

cel'ebrating, pr.p., celebrate.

celebra'tion, n., the act of celebrating.

cel'ebrator, n., one who celebrates.

cel'ebret, n., a bishop's written permission to say mass.

celeb'rity, n., the state of being celebrated; a famous personage.

celer'iac, n., turnip-rooted celery.

celer'ity, n., speed, rapidity.

cel'ery, n., an edible vegetable.

celes'ta, n., a keyboard instrument with a bell-like sound.

celeste', adj., sky-blue; n., a stop on the organ.

celes'tial, adj., pert. or rel. to the sky or heavens.

ce'liac, adj., rel. to the abdomen.

cel'ibacy, n., the unmarried state; bachelorhood.

cel'ibate, adj., not married; abstaining from marriage; n., an unmarried person.

celidog'raphy, n., the study or description of the sun's spots.

cell, n., a small room (in a monastery or a prison); a cavity; a little mass of protoplasm enclosed in a sac; a division of an electric battery; a small revolutionary group.

cel'lar, n., an underground chamber for storage, especially wines.

cel'larage, n., a system or series of cellars; the capacity of a cellar; the charge for storing.

cel'larer, n., a person in charge of a wine cellar.

cel'laret, n., a cabinet for holding wine or spirit decanters.

celled, adj., containing cells.

'cell'ist, n., the abbreviation of violoncellist; one who plays the violoncello.

'cel'lo, n., the abbreviation for violoncello.

Cell'ophane, n., a transparent wrapping material.

cel'lular, adj., in cell formation.

cel'lulated, adj., formed into cells.

cel'lule, n., a little cell.

cellulif'erous, adj., producing cellules.

cel'luloid, n., a hard, plastic substance composed of camphor and gun-cotton.

cel'lulose, adj., full of little cells; made of cellulose; n., a natural polymer basic to wood and plant life [its derivatives are extensively used in industry].

Cel'sius, n., a thermometrical scale, named after the Swedish astronomer, Anders Celsius.

Celt, n., a member of the Celtic race; a pre-historic stone; an axe-like implement.

Celtibe'rian, adj., pert. to the Celtiberi, a mixed people partly Celts, partly Iberians (Basques).

Celt'ic, adj., rel. to the Celts.

Celt'icism, n., something characteristic of a Celt.

Celt'ish, adj., i.q. Celtic.

cem'balo, n., the abbreviation for clavicembalo; a keyed dulcimer, i.e. harpsichord.

cement', n., a substance making things adhere; a kind of mortar; (metaphorically a bond or union); v.t., to join, to unite closely.

cementa'tion, n., the process of cementing.

cement'atory, *adj.*, rel. to cement.

cement'ed, *p.p.*, cement.

cement'er, *n.*, one who cements.

cement'ing, *pr.p.*, cement.

cemen'tite, *n.*, iron carbide.

cementi'tious, *adj.*, tending to cement.

cem'etery, *n.*, a graveyard, a burial-ground.

cen'obite, *n.*, *i.q.*, coenobite.

cenobit'ical, *adj.*, rel. to a cenobite.

cenog'amy, *n.*, a community of wives or husbands.

cen'otaph, *n.*, a tomb not containing the body or bodies of a person or persons commemorated.

cense, *v.t.*, to offer incense to; to perfume.

censed, *p.p.*, cense.

cen'ser, *n.*, the vessel in which incense is burned.

cens'ing, *pr.p.*, cense.

cen'sor, *n.*, an ancient Roman official who looked after taxation and superintended the public morals; an official examiner of books, plays, etc.; one who criticizes with a moral purpose; *v.t.*, to reject after examination.

cen'sored, *p.p.*, censor.

censo'rial, *adj.*, rel. to a censor.

cen'soring, *pr.p.*, censor.

censo'rious, *adj.*, adversely critical.

censo'riously, *adv.*, in a censorious way.

censo'riousness, *n.*, the habit of criticizing.

cen'sorship, *n.*, the office of a censor; the tenure of his office.

cen'sual, *adj.*, rel. to the census.

cen'surable, *adj.*, fit to be censured.

cen'sure, *v.t.*, to blame, to reprove.

cen'sured, *p.p.*, censure.

cen'surer, *n.*, one who censures.

cen'suring, *pr.p.*, censure.

cen'sus, *n.*, a numbering of the people; the periodical collection and classification of statistics about the population.

cent, *n.*, a hundred, a hundredth of a dollar (*U.S.*, etc.).

cent'age, *n.*, *i.q.* percentage.

cen'tal, *n.*, a weight of 100 lb.

cen'taur, *n.*, a fabled creature, half man, half horse.

cen'taury, *n.*, a plant of the gentian family.

centa'vo, *n.*, a hundredth of an escudo (*Port.*).

centena'rian, *adj.*, rel. to a hundred years; *n.*, a person aged a hundred.

cen'tenary, *n.*, the hundredth anniversary.

centen'nial, *adj.*, rel. to a period of a hundred years.

center, *n.*, *v.t.* and *i.*, *i.q.* centre.

centered, *p.p.*, center.

cen'tering, *pr.p.*, center.

centes'imal, *adj.*, hundredth; *n.*, a hundredth part.

centesima'tion, *n.*, the act of taking one in every hundred.

cen'tibar, *n.*, a hundredth of a bar (*meteor.*).

centifo'lious, *adj.*, hundred-leaved.

cen'tigrade, *adj.*, of a hundred degrees.

cen'tigramme, *n.*, a hundredth of a gram.

cen'tilitre, -ter, *n.*, a hundredth of a litre.

centill'ion, *n.*, the hundredth power of a million (*i.e.* 1 with 600 ciphers); in Amer. and France, the hundredth power of a thousand.

centime', *n.*, a hundredth of a franc (*Fr.*).

cen'timetre, -ter, *n.*, a hundredth of a metre.

cen'timo, *n.*, a hundredth of a peseta (*Span.*).

cen'tipede, *n.*, a creature with a hundred (*i.e.* very many) feet.

cent'ner, *n.*, a German weight, about 1 cwt.

cen'to, *n.*, a selection, patchwork.

cen'tral, *adj.*, rel. to, or placed at, the centre.

cen'tralism, *n.*, a centralizing system.

cen'tralist, *n.*, the upholder of a centralizing system.

central'ity, *n.*, the state or relation of the central.

centraliza'tion, *n.*, the drawing to a centre; the concentration of authority or administration in a single body or office.

cen'tralize, *v.t.*, to draw to a centre; to concentrate authority or administration.

cen'tralized, *p.p.*, centralize.

cen'tralizing, *pr.p.*, centralize.

cen'trally, *adv.*, at or in the centre.

cen'tre, *n.*, the middle point of a circle; a point to which things converge; *v.t.*, to fix on a centre, to place at the centre; *v.i.*, to be at the centre.

cen'tre-bit, *n.*, a boring tool with a centre point.

cen'tred, *p.p.*, centre.

cen'tric, *adj.*, central.

cen'trical, *adj.*, *i.q.* centric.

centric'ity, *n.*, the centric relation.

centrif'ugal, *adj.*, flying off from the centre.

cen'trifuge, *n.*, a centrifugal machine rotating at very high speed.

cen'tring, *pr.p.*, centre.

centrip'etal, *adj.*, tending towards the centre.

cen'trosphere, *n.*, the barysphere.

cen'trum, *n.*, the place where an earthquake originates; the body of a vertebra.

centum'vir, *n.*, a Roman judge so named. (The centumviri numbered 105, and were presided over by a praetor.)

centum'virate, *n.*, the body of centumvirs; the office, and tenure of office, of the centumvirs.

cen'tuple, *adj.* and *n.*, a hundredfold; *v.t.*, to increase a hundredfold.

centup'licate, *adj.* and *n.*, of things of which a hundred copies are produced.

centu'rial, *adj.*, rel. to a century.

centu'rion, *n.*, a Roman military officer, commanding a hundred foot soldiers.

cen'tury, *n.*, a period of 100 years; a hundred in number; a Roman political division according to property.

cephalal'gia, *n.*, *i.q.* cephalalgy.

cephalal'gic, *adj.*, rel. to headache; *n.*, a remedy for headache.

ceph'alalgy, *n.*, a headache.

cephal'ic, *adj.*, rel. to the head.

cephali'tis, *n.*, inflammation of the brain.

ceph'alopod, *adj.*, rel. to the Cephalopods, molluscs with a sub-central head.

cephalothor'ax, *n.*, the coalesced head and thorax of the spider, crab etc.

ceph'alous, *adj.*, having a head.

cera'ceous, *adj.*, waxen.

ceram'ic, *adj.*, rel. to industrial and artistic ceramics.

ceram'ics, *n.*, the craft of producing solid products by heat and fusion (*orig. pottery*).

cer'asite, *n.*, a fossil resembling a cherry.

ceras'tes, *n.*, the horned viper, a poisonous snake of N. Africa.

ceras'tium, *n.*, a herb with horn-shaped capsules.

ce'rate, *adj.*, having a cere.

ce'rated, *adj.*, coated with wax.

cer'atin, *n.*, the essential element in the composition of horny tissue.

ceratosaur'us, *n.*, an extinct dinosaurian reptile.

Cerbe'rean, *adj.*, rel. to Cerberus.

Cerb'erus, *n.*, the three-headed watch-dog of Hades.

cere, *n.*, wax; the waxy membrane on a bird's beak; *v.t.*, to cover with wax or cerecloth.

ce'real, *adj.*, rel. to Ceres; rel to corn; *n.*, an edible product made from grain.

cerebel'lum, *n.*, the lower and back portion of the head.

cer'ebral, *adj.*, rel. to the brain.

cerebra'tion, *n.*, the action of the brain; thought processes.

cerebri'tis, *n.*, inflammation of the cerebrum.

cer'ebrum, *n.*, the brain.

cere'cloth, *n.*, a waxed-cloth.

cere'ment, *n.*, a wrapping, esp. one covered with wax.

ceremo'nial, *adj.*, rel. to ceremony; *n.*, an order of ceremonies; a book of ceremonies.

ceremo'nialism *n.*, a fondness for ceremonial practices.

ceremo'nious, *adj.*, formal; with dignified ritual.

ceremo'niously, *adv.*, in a ceremonious way.

cer'emony, *n.*, the formal acts illustrating a rite or other observance; a way of showing respect or civility; regard for etiquette.

ce'reous, *adj.*, waxen.

ce'ric, *adj.*, rel. to wax.

ce'rin, *n.*, a compound obtained from cork.

cer'iph, *n.*, *i.q.* serif.

cerise', *adj.*, cherry-coloured; *n.*, the cherry colour.

ce'rite, *n.*, a cerium silicate.

ce'rium, *n.*, a rare metal of a steel-grey colour.

cerne, *n.*, a circle; *v.t.*, to surround.

cerog'raphy, *n.*, writing on wax.

ce'romancy, *n.*, divination by means of wax.

ceroplas'tic, *adj.*, modelled in wax; rel. to wax moulding.

ceroplas'tics, *n.*, the art of modelling in wax.

cert, *n.*, an event or result certain to happen (*slang*).

cer'tain, *adj.*, sure, unquestionable, confident, convinced; appointed; one or some.

cer'tainly, *adv.*, truly, assuredly, inevitably.

cer'tainty, *n.*, the state or fact of being certain.

cer'tes, *adv.*, certainly (*obs.*).

cert'ifiable, *adj.*, capable of being certified (esp. as a lunatic).

certif'icate, *n.*, a testimonial to character or proficiency; *v.t.*, to give a certificate to.

certif'icated, *adj.*, holding a certificate.

certifica'tion, *n.*, the act of certifying; a guarantee.

cer'tified, *p.p.*, certify.

cer'tifier, *n.*, one who certifies.

cer'tify, *v.t.*, to guarantee, to make evident, to testify.

cer'tifying, *pr.p.*, certify.

certiora'ri, *n.*, a writ from a higher court requiring the records from a lower court (*Lat.*).

cer'titude, *n.*, assured belief; certainty.

ceru'lean, *adj.*, of a sky-blue colour.

ceru'men, *n.*, the wax in the ears.

ce'ruse, *n.*, white lead; *v.t.*, to paint with ceruse, a cosmetic made from white lead.

ce'rused, *p.p.*, ceruse.

ce'rusing, *pr.p.*, ceruse.

cer'vical, *adj.*, rel. to the neck.

cer'vine, *adj.*, rel. to deer.

cer'vix, *n.*, the neck of an organ.

Cesa'rean, *adj.*, rel. to Caesar. (Also *Caesarean*.)

Cesar'ewitch, *n.*, a classic, long-distance horse-race in England.

ces'pitous, *adj.*, turfy.

cess', *n.*, rate, tax; *v.t.*, to assess, to tax; *v.i.*, to surrender.

cessa'tion, *n.*, a leaving off.

ces'ser, *n.*, a ceasing to perform some duty.

ces'sion, *n.*, a yielding up, a surrender.

ces'sionary, *adj.*, giving up, surrendering.

ces'sor, *n.*, *i.q.* cesser.

cess'pit, *n.*, a pit for refuse.

cess'pool, *n.*, a covered well to receive the solid contents of a drain.

cest, *n.*, *i.q.* cestus.

ces'toid, *adj.*, ribbon-like; *n.*, tapeworm.

ces'tui, *n.*, an old French expression = he; the man who.

ces'tus, *n.*, a girdle; a pugilist's fistguard (*Lat.*).

cesu'ra, *n.*, a break or pause in a metrical

and rhythmic composition.

cesu'ral, *adj.*, rel. to, or of the nature of, cesura.

ceta'cea, *n. pl.*, marine animals, like the whale, the dolphin, etc.

ceta'cean, *adj.*, rel. to the cetacea; *n.*, one of these creatures.

ceta'ceous, *adj.*, *i.q.* cetacean.

cet'erach, *n.*, a kind of fern covered with scales.

ce'tic, *adj.*, rel. to the whale.

ce'tin, *n.*, a fatty compound containing spermacetti.

ce'tine, *n.*, *i.q.* cetin.

cetol'ogy, *n.*, the study of cetaceans.·

Ceylonese', *adj.* and *n.*, rel. to or a native of Ceylon.

Chab'lis, *n.*, a French white wine from Chablis.

cha'-cha', *n.*, a dance, originally from the West Indies.

chaconne', *n.*, a dance tune. in slow triple time.

chad, *n.*, otherwise the shad, a young seabream.

chafe, *v.t.*, to rub sore, to gall; to annoy; to restore warmth; *v.i.*, to be hot with anger, to fume.

chafed, *p.p.*, chafe.

cha'fer, *n.*, one who chafes; also a common name for the cockchafer; a chafingdish *q.v.*

cha'fery, *n.*, a forge for the making of iron bars.

chaff, *n.*, the husk of grain; cut straw or hay; banter; *v.t.*, to teaze, to make fun of.

chaff'cutter, *n.*, a machine for cutting chaff.

chaffed, *p.p.*, chaff.

chaf'fer, *n.*, bargaining; *v.i.*, to bargain, to haggle.

chaf'fered, *p.p.*, chaffer.

chaf'ferer, *n.*, one who chaffers.

chaf'fering, *pr.p.*, chaffer.

chaf'finch, *n.*, a small, British song-bird.

chaf'fing, *pr.p.*, chaff.

chaf'fy, *adj.*, like chaff, covered with chaff; disposed to banter.

cha'fing, *n.*, impatience, irritation; *pr.p.*, chafe.

cha'fing-dish, *n.*, a receptacle for keeping food hot.

Chagi'gah, *n.*, a Jewish sacrifice at the Passover.

chagreen', *n.*, *i.q.* shagreen.

chagrin', *n.*, disappointment; mortification; *v.t.*, to vex, to mortify.

chagrined', *p.p.*, chagrin.

chain, *n.*, a series of links for the purpose of binding; bond, slavery; a connected series; a measuring line; *v.t.*, to fasten with a chain, to fasten securely; to measure with a chain.

chained, *p.p.*, chain.

chain'ing, *pr.p.*, chain.

chain'let, *n.*, a small chain.

chain'-pump, *n.*, a pump with an endless chain to which buckets are attached.

chain'-shot, *n.*, cannon balls chained together.

chain'-stitch, *n.*, a loopstitch.

chair, *n.*, a single seat; an official seat; a sedan chair; *v.t.*, to place in a chair; to carry in a chair.

chaired, *p.p.*, chair.

chair'ing, *pr.p.*, chair.

chair'man, *n.*, the president of any assembly or company for whom a special chair is reserved.

chair'manship, *n.*, the function, or term of office, of a chairman.

chair'oplane, *n.*, a roundabout with suspended seats.

chaise, *n.*, a two-wheeled, light carriage.

chaise-longue, *n.*, a kind of sofa, open at one end (*Fr.*).

chalcedon'ic, *adj.*, rel. to, or resembling, the chalcedony.

chalced'ony, *n.*, a precious stone of the quartz kind.

chalcog'rapher, *n.*, one who engraves on copper.

chalcog'raphy, *n.*, copper engraving.

Chalcolith'ic, *adj.*, relating to the period when stone and bronze instruments were used concurrently.

chalcopyr'ite, *n.*, a copper ore.

Chalda'ic, *adj.*, pert. to the Chaldees.

Chalde'an, *adj.*, rel. to Chaldea or Babylon; *n.*, a Babylonian.

Chaldee', *adj.*, *i.q.* Chaldean; *n.*, a Chaldean.

chal'dron, *n.*, a coal and coke measure, of varying capacity according to the country.

cha'let, *n.*, a Swiss mountain dwelling; any small country house built in imitation (*Fr.*).

chal'ice, *n.*, a cup or bowl; pre-eminently the Eucharistic cup.

chal'iced, *adj.*, cup-like.

chalk, *n.*, a soft, white limestone; *v.t.*, to mark with chalk; to treat with chalk.

chalked, *p.p.*, chalk.

chalk'iness, *n.*, a chalky nature.

chalk'ing, *pr.p.*, chalk.

chalk'-pit, *n.*, a pit from which chalk is extracted.

chalk'-stone, *n.*, a chalky formation in the body.

chalk'y, *adj.*, like chalk, rel. to, or made of, chalk.

chal'lenge, *n.*, an invitation to a trial or contest; a calling to account; *v.t.*, to call out to combat, to defy; to demand proof; to take exception to.

chal'lengeable, *adj.*, able to be challenged.

chal'lenged, *p.p.*, challenge.

chal'lenger, *n.*, one who challenges.

chal'lenging, *pr.p.*, challenge.

chall'is, *n.*, a soft, delicate fabric used for ladies' garments.

chalyb'eate, *adj.*, impregnated with iron.

cham, *n.*, a Tartar or Mogul chief.

chamade', *n.*, the trumpet or drum appeal for a parley (*Fr.*).

chamar', *n.*, a tanner; a shoemaker.

cham'ber, *n.*, a room; an assembly; *v.t.*, to furnish with chambers; *v.i.*, to act wantonly.

cham'bered, *adj.*, provided with, or divided into, chambers; *p.p.*, chamber.

cham'bering, *n.*, wanton behaviour; *pr.p.*, chamber.

cham'berlain, *n.*, an officer in a royal or great household, who has charge of the chambers and the ceremonial.

cham'bermaid, *n.*, a domestic servant in charge of bedrooms.

cham'bray, *n.*, a kind of gingham.

chame'leon, *n.*, a kind of lizard, possessed of the power to change colour.

cham'fer, *v.t.*, to groove, to bevel; *n.*, a groove, a bevel.

cham'fered, *p.p.*, chamfer.

cham'fering, *pr.p.*, chamfer.

cham'ois, *n.*, a species of mountain goat; a soft leather.

cham'omile, *n.*, *i.q.* camomile.

chamotte', *n.*, powdered fragments of burnt fireclay.

champ, *n.*, the act of champing; *v.t.* and *i.*, to gnash, to crunch.

champagne', *n.*, a sparkling wine from the Champagne district of France.

cham'paign, *adj.*, open country; unenclosed; *n.*, a plain; open country.

champed, *p.p.*, champ.

cham'perty, *n.*, a bargain between two litigants, to carry on a suit and share in the property.

champ'ing, *pr.p.*, champ.

cham'pion, *n.*, a defender; *v.t.*, to act as a champion for, to defend a cause.

cham'pioned, *p.p.*, champion.

cham'pioning, *pr.p.*, champion.

cham'pionship, *n.*, a contest to discover a champion.

champlevé, *adj.*, of inlaid enamel; *n.*, work in inlaid enamel (*Fr.*).

chance, *n.*, that which happens unexpectedly; an opportunity; a possibility; *v.t.* and *i.*, to take the risk of; to happen by chance.

chanced, *p.p.*, chance.

chan'cel, *n.*, the eastern section of a church.

chan'cellery, *n.*, the office of a chancellor; a court; a department of a legation.

chan'cellor, *n.*, an official who keeps the Great Seal; the head of a university; a cathedral dignitary so named; a diocesan judge.

chan'cellorship, *n.*, the office, and tenure of office, of a chancellor.

chan'cellory, *n.*, *i.q.* chancellery.

chan'cery, *n.*, a court of equity, now one of the divisions of the High Court.

chanc'ing, *pr.p.*, chance.

chan'cre, *n.*, an ulcer.

chan'crous, *adj.*, ulcerous.

chan'cy, *adj.*, uncertain, risky.

chandelier', *n.*, a branched, suspended frame for holding lights.

chand'ler, *n.*, originally a maker of and dealer in candles; now a general dealer.

chand'lery, *n.*, a chandler's shop; a chandler's goods.

chan'frin, *n.*, the forehead of a horse.

change, *n.*, an alteration, an exchange; smaller money for larger; *v.t.* and *i.*, to alter, to make or become different; to exchange.

changeabil'ity, *n.*, a tendency to change.

change'able, *adj.*, prone to change.

change'ableness, *n.*, *i.q.* changeability.

change'ably, *adv.*, in a changeable way.

changed, *p.p.*, change.

change'ful, *adj.*, full of changes.

change'less, *adj.*, unchanging.

change'ling, *n.*, a substituted child.

change'o'ver, *n.*, a transition from one system, etc. to another.

chan'ger, *n.*, one who changes, esp. money.

chan'ging, *pr.p.*, change.

chan'nel, *n.*, the bed of a stream; a strait, an estuary; a means or passage; a line of action; *v.t.*, to divide with channels; to groove.

chan'nelled, *adj.*, having channels; channellike; *p.p.*, channel.

chan'nelling, *pr.p.*, channel.

chan'son, *n.*, a song or ballad (*Fr.*).

chansonette', *n.*, a short ballad (*Fr.*).

chant, *n.*, a melody to which psalms and other non-metrical words are sung; *v.t.* and *i.*, to sing; to celebrate with praise.

chant'ed, *p.p.*, chant.

chant'er, *n.*, one who chants, a singer, a precentor; the fingerpipe on a bagpipe.

chanterelle', *n.*, a yellow edible fungus (*Fr.*).

chant'ey, *n.*, a rhythmical song sung by sailors when at work. (Also *shanty*).

chan'ticleer, *n.*, a cock.

chant'ing, *pr.p.*, chant.

chant'ress, *n.*, the fem. of chanter.

chant'ry, *n.*, an endowment for prayers to be said for a founder or benefactor; an endowed chapel.

chant'y, *n.*, *i.q.* chantey.

cha'os, *n.*, a formless and disordered state; utter confusion.

chaot'ic, *adj.*, like chaos, in utter confusion.

chap, *n.*, a split or crack in the skin; any fissure; a man or boy (*colloq.*); a dealer; a jaw; *v.t.* and *i.*, to split, to crack.

chaparejos, *n. pl.*, leather or sheepskin overalls used by cowboys to protect their legs (*abbrev.* chaps).

chaparral', *n.*, the dwarf evergreen oak.

chap'book, *n.*, popular literature formerly hawked by chapmen.

chape, *n.*, the tip of a scabbard; the part of a rein that goes into the buckle.

chapeau', *n.*, a hat (*Fr.*).

chap'el, *n.*, a small church or part of a church; the collective journeymen in a printing works.

chap'elry, *n.*, a district in the jurisdiction of a chapel.

chap'eron, *n.*, one who attends upon a lady; *v.t.*, to attend as a guardian.

chap'eronage, *n.*, the act or state of chaperoning.

chap'eroned, *p.p.*, chap'eron.

chaperoning, *pr.p.*, chaperon.

chap'fallen, *adj.*, with drooping jaw; dejected.

chap'iter, *n.*, a pillar capital.

chap'lain, *n.*, a priest attached to a chapel, the forces, a ship, an institution or company.

chap'laincy, *n.*, a chaplain's office or tenure of office.

chap'lainship, *n.*, *i.q.* chaplaincy.

chap'let, *n.*, a garland for the head; a part of a rosary.

chap'man, *n.*, a dealer in small wares.

chapped, *p.p.*, chap.

chap'pie, *n.*, a little chap (*colloq.*).

chap'ping, *pr.p.*, chap.

chap'py, *n.*, *i.q.* chappie.

chaps, *n.*, abbrev. of chaparejos.

chap'ter, *n.*, a chief division of a book; the collective name for the clergy of a cathedral or collegiate church; a local branch of a society.

chap'ter-house, *n.*, the building in which a chapter assembles.

chap'trel, *n.*, an impost.

char, *n.*, an odd job; a salmon-like fish; *v.t.*, to scorch; *v.i.*, to do household chores. (Also *chare*.)

char'abanc, *n.*, an old type of horsedrawn coach or motorcoach.

char'acter, *n.*, a distinctive quality or set of qualities; a letter of the alphabet; reputation; *v.t.*, to impress, to engrave; to characterize.

char'acterful, *adj.*, strongly expressive of character.

characterist'ic, *adj.*, distinctive, peculiarly marked; *n.*, a distinctive mark or quality.

characterist'ically, *adv.*, in a characteristic way.

characteriza'tion, *n.*, the act or effect of characterizing; the description.

char'acterize, *v.t.*, to make distinguishable; to describe.

char'acterized, *p.p.*, characterize.

char'acterizing, *pr.p.*, characterize.

char'acterless, *adj.*, without character, not distinctive.

characterol'ogy, *n.*, the science that deals with the study of character.

charade', *n.*, a riddle, a word-puzzle; a play consisting of a word-puzzle.

char'coal, *n.*, charred wood; a drawing-pencil made of charcoal dust; a drawing in charcoal.

chard, *n.*, the white leaves or stalks of certain plants.

chare, *n.*, *v.i.* and *t.*, *i.q.* char.

charge, *n.*, something imposed or put on; a command; an accusation; a demand of a price; an attack; *v.t.*, to impose, to lay upon; to command; to fill; to accuse; to debit, to fix a price for; to attack.

chargeabil'ity, *n.*, a chargeable state.

charge'able, *adj.*, able to be charged.

charge'ably, *adv.*, expensively.

charged, *p.p.*, charge.

chargé d'affaires', *n.*, a diplomatic official in charge of affairs, in place, or during the absence of, an ambassador (*Fr.*).

char'ger, *n.*, one who charges; a war-horse; a large dish; a case for the charge of a machine gun.

charg'ing, *pr.p.*, charge.

cha'rily, *adv.*, in a chary way.

cha'riness, *n.*, a state of being chary.

char'iot, *n.*, a two-wheeled carriage, used in war and races; a state carriage.

charioteer', *n.*, the driver of a chariot.

char'ism, *n.*, a grace or power bestowed by the Holy Ghost.

charismat'ic, *adj.*, of the nature of a spiritual gift.

char'itable, *adj.*, apt at bestowing charity; benevolent.

char'itableness, *n.*, a charitable temper.

chari'tably, *adv.*, in a charitable way.

char'ity, *n.*, love, esp. to one's neighbour; lenity of judgment.

chariva'ri, *n.*, a wild sort of serenade with a medley of noises (*Fr.*).

chark'a, *n.*, a country-made, Indian spinning-wheel.

char'lady, *n.*, a charwoman.

char'latan, *n.*, an impostor, a quack.

charlatan'ic, *adj.*, resembling a charlatan.

char'latanism, *n.*, the act or state of a charlatan.

char'latanry, *n.*, *i.q.* charlatanism.

Charles'ton, *n.*, an American jazz dance; *v.i.*, to Charleston.

char'lock, *n.*, the wild mustard.

charl'otte, *n.*, a kind of pudding (*Fr.*).

charm, *n.*, attractiveness, fascination, a spell; *v.t.*, to enchant; to cast a spell on, to delight.

char'mante, *n.*, a silk fabric with a satin face and crêpe back.

charmed, *p.p.*, charm.

char'melaine, *n.*, a dress material of artificial silk and wool.

charm'er, *n.*, one who charms.

char'meuse, *n.*, a soft, smooth, silk fabric (*Fr.*).

charm'ing, *adj.*, delightful; *pr.p.*, charm.

charm'ingly, *adv.,* delightfully.

char'nel, *adj.,* rel. to a corpse, ghastly; *n.,* a charnel-house.

char'nel-house, *n.,* a mortuary, a depository for bones.

char'pie, *n.,* lint.

char'poy, *n.,* a Hindu bed.

charred, *p.p.,* char.

char'ring, *pr.p.,* char.

char'ry, *adj.,* like charcoal.

chart, *n.,* a map of land, sea or sky; a tabular sheet; *v.t.,* to lay out on a chart.

char'ta, *n.,* a parchment, writing.

charta'ceous, *adj.,* like paper.

char'ter, *n.,* a grant of titles, privileges, etc.; *v.i.,* to hire, to engage.

char'terage, *n.,* charges for chartering ships.

char'tered, *adj.,* authorized by charter; *p.p.,* charter.

char'terer, *n.,* one who charters.

Char'terhouse, *n.,* a Carthusian monastery; an English public-school.

char'tering, *pr.p.,* charter.

char'ter-party, *n.,* an agreement for hiring a ship or a part of a ship.

char'tism, *n.,* the principles of chartists.

char'tist, *n.,* an advocate of the so-called People's Charter.

chartog'rapher, *n.,* one who draws charts or maps.

chartog'raphy, *n.,* the art and practice of map-drawing.

chartom'eter, *n.,* an instrument for measuring distances on maps.

Chartreuse, *n.,* a Carthusian monastery; a liqueur distilled at La Grande Chartreuse in Grenoble (*Fr.*).

Char'treux, *n.,* a Charterhouse (*Fr.*).

char'tulary, *n.,* a record of property of a religious community.

char'woman, *n.,* a woman who does chores, usually menial household tasks.

cha'ry, *adj.,* careful, cautious.

chas(e)'able, *adj.,* able to be chased.

chase, *n.,* hunting, pursuit; the part of a gun next to, and in front of, the trunnions; *v.t.,* to hunt, to pursue, to drive off; to ornament metal by indenting.

chased, *p.p.,* chase.

chas'er, *n.,* one who chases.

chas'ing, *pr.p.,* chase.

chasm, *n.,* a gap in the earth's surface; any great breach or severance.

chasse, *n.,* liqueur after coffee etc. (*Fr.*).

chassé, *n.* and *v.i.,* (to make) a gliding step in dancing (*Fr.*).

chasse'pot, *n.,* the French needle-gun, now out of date.

chasseur', *n.,* a French, light-armed soldier.

chas'sis, *n.,* the lower frame of a motor-car; a type of gun-carriage; any framework (*Fr.*).

chaste, *adj.,* pure, clean, refined.

chaste'ly, *adv.,* in a chaste way.

chast'en, *v.t.,* to purify, to punish.

chast'ened, *p.p.,* chasten.

chast'ener, *n.,* one who chastens.

chast'ening, *n.,* punishment; *pr.p.,* chasten.

chastis'able, *adj.,* capable or deserving of punishment.

chastise', *v.t.,* to punish.

chastised', *p.p.,* chastise.

chas'tisement, *n.,* punishment.

chastis'er, *n.,* one who chastises.

chastis'ing, *pr.p.,* chastise.

chas'tity, *n.,* the quality of being chaste.

chas'uble, *n.,* the vestment of the celebrant at Mass.

chat, *n.,* informal talk, gossip; *v.i.,* to talk informally, to gossip.

château', *n.,* a French castle.

chat'elaine, *n.,* the lady of a castle; a lady's chain to which are attached a variety of trinkets, keys, etc. (*Fr.*).

chat'ted, *p.p.,* chat.

chat'tel, *n.,* a movable article of property.

chat'ter, *n.,* informal talking; *v.i.,* to prattle, to talk uselessly; to shiver with cold (said of the teeth).

chat'terbox, *n.,* a garrulous person.

chat'tered, *p.p.,* chatter.

chat'terer, *n.,* one who chatters.

chat'tering, *pr.p.,* chatter.

chat'tily, *adv.,* in a chatty fashion.

chat'ting, *pr.p.,* chat.

chat'ty, *adj.,* agreeably talkative, gossiping.

chat'wood, *n.,* twigs for burning.

Chauce'rian, *adj.,* rel. to the poet Chaucer.

Chau'cerism, *n.,* a Chaucerian idiom or peculiarity.

chauff'er, *n.,* a metal basket holding fire.

chauf'feur, *n.,* a person employed as a motor-car driver (*Fr.*).

chauf'feuse, *n.,* the fem. of chauffeur (*Fr.*).

chaulmoo'gra, *n.,* an East-Indian tree.

Chau'tauqua, *n.,* a mutual improvement union (*Amer.*).

chau'vinism, *n.,* the principles of a chauvinist.

chau'vinist, *n.,* one who says "My country, right or wrong" and despises every foreign country.

chaw, *n.,* a quid of tobacco.

Chazzan', *n.,* a Jewish precentor.

cheap, *adj.,* of low price, of little value, common, poor.

cheap'en, *v.t.,* to make cheap, to lower the value; *v.i.,* to fall in price.

cheap'ened, *p.p.,* cheapen.

cheap'ener, *n.,* one who, or that which, cheapens.

cheap'ening, *pr.p.,* cheapen.

cheap'er, *adj.,* comp. of cheap.

cheap'est, *adj.,* super. of cheap.

cheap'ly, *adv.,* at a cheap rate.

cheap'ness, *n.,* the state or quality of being cheap.

cheat, *n.*, a fraudulent person, an act of cheating; *v.t.*, to deceive, to defraud, to mislead.

cheat′able, *adj.*, liable to be cheated.

cheat′ed, *p.p.*, cheat.

cheat′er, *n.*, one who cheats.

cheat′ing, *n.*, the act or practice of a cheat; *pr.p.*, cheat.

ché′chia, *n.*, a cylindrical, tufted fez.

check, *n.*, a sudden stoppage; something that stops; the American equivalent of English *cheque;* a crossed pattern in weaving; an identifying ticket or disc; *v.t.*, to bring to a sudden stop; to moderate; to verify; to threaten a king in chess.

check′book, *n.*, *i.q.* cheque-book.

checked, *p.p.*, check.

check′er, *n.*, one who checks; *v.t.*, to mark with a cross pattern; to fill with changes of fortune.

check′er-board, *n.*, *i.q.* chequer-board.

check′ered, *adj.*, full of vicissitudes; *p.p.*, checker.

check′ering, *pr.p.*, checker.

check′ers, *n. pl.*, the game of draughts.

check′erwork, *n.*, work on a checkered pattern.

check′ing, *pr.p.*, check.

check′mate, *n.*, defeat, thwarting; *v.t.*, to beat at chess; to thwart, to overcome.

check′mated, *p.p.*, checkmate.

check′mating, *pr.p.*, checkmate.

check′out, *n.*, a pay-desk in a self-service store.

check′-up, *n.*, a detailed examination.

Ched′ar, *n.*, a Hebrew school.

Chedd′ar, *n.*, a kind of cheese; a place in Somerset (England).

chedd′ite, *n.*, a high explosive.

chee′-chee, *n.*, an Eurasian; an Eurasian's speech.

cheek, *n.*, the lower part of the side-face;

impudence (*slang*); *v.t.*, to treat impudently.

cheek′-tooth, *n.*, a molar.

cheek′y, *adj.*, saucy.

cheep, *n.*, a chick's shrill note; *v.i.*, to chirp feebly.

cheer, *n.*, a cry of applause, good entertainment, an expression of countenance; *v.t.*, to put heart into, to inspirit, to applaud.

cheered, *p.p.*, cheer.

cheer′er, *n.*, one who cheers.

cheer′ful, *adj.*, hearty, gay.

cheer′fully, *adv.*, in a cheerful manner.

cheer′fulness, *n.*, the state of being cheerful.

cheer′ily, *adv.*, brightly, gaily.

cheer′iness, *n.*, the state of being cheery.

cheer′ing, *adj.*, encouraging; *n.*, applause; *pr.p.*, cheer.

cheer′ingly, *adv.*, encouragingly.

cheer′io, *interj.*, an informal farewell.

cheer′less, *adj.*, gloomy, depressing.

cheer′lessly, *adv.*, gloomily.

cheer′lessness, *n.*, gloominess.

cheer′y, *adj.*, bright, gay.

cheese, *n.*, the curd of milk compacted and dried into an edible protein.

cheese′cake, *n.*, a sweet made of curd, sugar and butter.

cheese′cutter, *n.*, an instrument for cutting cheese.

cheese′monger, *n.*, a dealer in cheeses.

cheese′paring, *adj.*, parsimonious.

cheese′-press, *n.*, a press used in making cheeses.

chees′er, *n.*, a cheesing-frame operative.

cheese′-straw, *n.*, a straw-like, cheese-flavoured biscuit.

cheese′wood, *n.*, a pale yellow, Australian timber.

chees′ing, *n.*, winding yarn on cheese-shaped bobbins.

chee′sy, *adj.*, like cheese, or containing cheese.

chee′tah, *n.*, a kind of leopard.

chef, *n.*, the head or chief; a male head cook (*Fr.*).

chef-d′œuvre′, *n.*, a masterpiece (*Fr.*).

cheiro-, *prefix*, *i.q.* chiro-.

cheirop′tera, *n. pl.*, bats.

cheirop′terous, *adj.*, having wings like hands.

Chell′ean, *adj.*, rel. to the earliest palaeolithic period of Europe (from Chelles, France).

Chel′sea, *adj. and n.*, the artistic quarter of London; a kind of currant-bun; a kind of porcelain; a kind of old-age pensioner.

Chelton′ian, *adj.*, of Cheltenham College; *n.*, a member of C.C.

chem′ic, *n.*, chloride of lime; an alchemist; *v.t.*, to apply chloride of lime.

chem′ical, *adj.*, rel. to chemistry; *n.*, a chemical substance.

chemig′raphy, *n.*, an engraving process depending upon chemical action.

chemise′, *n.*, a woman's under-garment, a shift.

chemisette′, *n.*, an under-bodice of feminine wear.

chem′ist, *n.*, one who is practised in chemistry.

chem′istry, *n.*, the science dealing with the composition of matter.

chem′itype, *n.*, a stereotype obtained from an engraved plate by chemical process; the process itself.

chemopsychi′atry, *n.*, the use of drugs in mental illness.

chemothe′rapy, *n.*, the treatment of disease by chemical means.

chem′urgy, *n.*, the use of raw materials in ways to produce new products.

chenille′, *n.*, a velvety cord trimming (*Fr.*).

cheque, *n.*, an order on a bank for payment of a named sum.

cheque′-book, *n.*, a book containing cheques.

cheq′uer, *v.t.*, *i.q.* checker.

cheq′uerboard, *n.*, the board with which chequers is played.

cheq′uers, *n. pl.*, *i.q.* checkers.

cher'alite, n., a radio-active mineral.

cher'ish, v.t., to treat with affection; to retain in the memory.

cher'ished, p.p., cherish.

cher'isher, n., one who cherishes.

cher'ishing, pr.p., cherish.

cheroot', n., a form of cigar.

cher'ry, adj., cherry-coloured; n., the fruit of the cherry tree.

cher'ry-bran'dy, n., a liqueur of thick, sweetened brandy in which cherries have been steeped.

cher'sonese, n., a peninsula, but esp. the Crimea or Jutland.

chert, n., hornstone.

cher'ty, adj., consisting of or like chert.

cher'ub, n., an angel ranking next below a seraph; a beautiful child.

cheru'bic, adj., cherublike.

cher'ubim, n., pl. of cherub.

cher'vil, n., a potherb so named.

Chesh'ire, adj., a kind of cheese; n., an English county.

chess, n., the game so named.

chess'board, n., the board on which chess is played; it has 64 squares.

chess'el, n., a cheesemaking mould.

chess'man, n., one of the pieces used on a chessboard.

chest, n., a box; the capacity of a chest; the thorax.

chest'ed, adj., having a chest.

ches'terfield, n., a kind of overcoat; a kind of couch.

ches(t)'nut, adj., of chestnut colour; n., the nut of the castanea; the tree so named; a reddish brown; a horse of chestnut colour; a venerable jest or story.

cheval'-glass, n., a tall, swinging mirror.

chevalier', n., a knight, a horseman (Fr.).

chevaux'-de-frise', n., a low spiked fence (Fr.).

chev'iot, adj. and n., a short-woolled sheep, named from hills in Northumberland.

chev'ron, n., an heraldic term; the V-shaped badge of a non-commissioned officer.

chev'ronal, n., a narrow chevron.

chev'ronel, n., a narrow chevron (aero.).

chev'rotain, n., a small, musk deer (Fr.).

chev'rotin, n., i.q. chevrotain.

chev'y, v.t., to chase.

chew, v.t., to masticate, to crush with the teeth.

chewed, p.p., chew.

chew'ing, pr.p., chew.

Chianti, n., a red, Italian wine.

chiaroscu'ro, adj., rel. to light and shade; n., light and shade in painting (It.).

chib'bal, chib'ol, n., i.q. cibol.

chibouk', chibouque', n., a Turkish pipe.

chic, adj., in the mode, stylish; n., stylishness, smartness.

chicane', n., sophistry, a cunning way of hiding the truth; the holding of no trumps at cards (Fr.).

chica'nery, n., the employment of chicane.

chich, adj., niggardly.

chichi, adj. and n., a frilly (thing); a fussy or effeminate (person) (Fr.).

chich'ling, n., i.q. chickling.

chick, n., a young bird.

chick'abiddy, n., a term of endearment for a child.

chick'en, n., a domestic fowl.

chick'en-pox, n., a childhood, eruptive disorder.

chick'ling, n., a small chick.

chick'pea, n., a leguminous plant with nutritious, edible seeds.

chick'weed, n., a wild flower so named.

chi'cle, n., the milky juice of the sapodilla, the basis of chewing-gum.

chic'ory, n., a perennial which, when roasted, is mixed with coffee.

chid, p.p., chide.

chid'den, p.p., chide.

chide, v.t., to reprove.

chid'ed, p.p., chide.

chid'er, n., one who chides.

chid'ing, pr.p., chide.

chief, adj., principal, foremost; n., a leader.

chief'ly, adv., principally, firstly.

chief'ness, n., superiority.

chief'tain, n., a leader, the head of a clan.

chief'tainship, n., the office or rank of chieftain.

chiel, n., a youth.

chield, n., i.q. chief.

chiff'-chaff, n., a variety of British warbler; a warbling bird.

chiffon, n., a gauzy fabric.

chiffon(n)ier', n., a ragcollector; a kind of sideboard (Fr.).

chi'gnon, n., a mode of dressing the back hair over a pad (Fr.).

chig'oe, n., a tropical flea.

Chihua'hua, n., a very small breed of dog, originating in Mexico.

chil'blain, n., a sore produced by poor blood circulation; v.t., to cause chilblains.

chil'blained, adj., suffering from chilblains.

child, n., a son or daughter, the human young; a person under age.

child'bed, n., the time and place of delivery of a child.

child'birth, n., the delivery of a child.

childe, n., a son, not yet knighted, of a great house.

Chil'dermas, n., the Feast of Holy Innocents, Dec. 28.

child'hood, n., the childish period of life.

child'ish, adj., like a child, puerile, silly.

child'ishly, adv., like a child, sillily.

child'ishness, n., puerility.

child'less, adj., without a child.

child'like, adj., like a child, innocent.

child'ling, n., a little child.

chil'dren, n., pl. of child.

Chil'ean, adj., rel. to Chile; n., a native of C.

chil'iad, n., a group of 1,000; a thousand years.

chil'iagon, n., a thousand-sided figure.

chil'iarch, n., a commander of a thousand men.

chil'iasm, n., the doctrine rel. to Christ's reign on earth for a thousand years.

chil'iast, n., one who believes in chiliasm.

chil'iastic, adj., rel. to chiliasm.

chill, adj., feeling cold, discouraging; n., a feeling of sudden cold; discouragement; v.t., to make cold; to discourage; to harden by cooling.

chilled, p.p., chill.

chil'li, n., dried capsicum-pod.

chil'liness, n., the sensation or cause of chill.

chil'ling, adj., depressing; pr.p., chill.

chil'ly, adj., i.q. chill.

chi'lopod, adj., having 1,000 feet.

Chil'tern Hun'dreds, n., Crown lands in Bucks, the stewardship of which, being a Crown appointment, vacates the holder's seat in Parliament.

chime, n., the sound of chiming bells; the chimed bells collectively; harmony; v.t. and i., to make music with bells, to accord.

chimed, p.p., chime.

chi'mer, n., a person or apparatus that chimes.

chime'ra, n., a strange creation of the fancy.

chimere', n., a sort of cape, with armholes, worn over robes.

chimer'ical, adj., fantastic, impossible.

chi'ming, pr.p., chime.

chim'ney, n., a smoke vent; the tube of a lamp.

chim'ney-board, n., a fireboard.

chim'neypiece, n., the outer frame of a chimney-opening.

chim'neypot, n., a tubular added top to

a chimney; a tall silk hat (colloq.).

chim'ney-sweep, n., one who sweeps chimneys.

chimpan'zee, n., an anthropoid ape.

chin, n., the face below the lips.

chi'na, adj., made of china; n., a fine porcelain.

chi'na-as'ter, n., the aster of China.

chi'na-clay, n., a fine kind of clay.

chin'capin, n., an American shrub, bearing edible nuts.

chinchil'la, adj., made of chinchilla; n., a small furry rodent; the fur of the chinchilla.

chin'-cough, n., the whooping-cough.

chin'-deep, adj., deeply immersed.

Chin'dit, n., a commando (in Burma during the second world war).

chine, n., an animal's backbone; a cliff fissure; v.t., to cut through the backbone; v.i., to fissure.

chined, adj., having a chine; p.p., chine.

Chinese', adj., rel. to China; n., a native of C.

Chinese' lan'tern, n., a paper lantern.

chin'ing, pr.p., chine.

chink, n., the sound of rattled money; money (slang); a narrow opening; a Chinese (slang); v.t. and i., to rattle with a metallic sound.

chinked, p.p., chink.

chink'ing, pr.p., chink.

chink'y, adj., having chinks.

chinned, adj., having a chin.

chinook', n., a warm, dry wind which blows over the Rockies (native name).

chinse, v.t., to stop a ship's seams with oakum.

chintz, adj., of chintz material; n., a glazed cotton cloth.

chin'wag, n., a chat, a talk (slang).

chip, adj., made of chip; n., a little piece; a kind of straw; a sliced and fried potato; v.t., to cut into little pieces; v.i., to fly into little pieces.

chip'muck, n., a North-American squirrel.

chip'munk, n., i.q. chipmuck.

chipolata, adj., a kind of sausage.

chipped, p.p., chip.

Chip'pendale, adj., in the style invented by Chippendale; n., a piece of Chippendale furniture.

chip'per, adj., pert, smart (Amer.).

chip'ping, pr.p., chip.

chip'py, adj., having chips, dry.

chirag'ra, n., gout in the hand.

chirog'nomy, n., the judging of character from the hand.

chi'rograph, n., a piece of handwriting, a deed.

chirog'rapher n., an engrosser.

chirograph'ic, adj., written by the hand.

chirog'raphist, n., an expert in handwriting, a copyist.

chirog'raphy, n., handwriting.

chirolog'ical, adj., rel. to chirology.

chirol'ogy, n., the art of sign-speech; the study of the hand.

chi'romancy, n., palmistry; telling fortunes by reading the hands.

chiroman'tic, adj., rel. to palmistry.

chiron'omy, n., gesticulation.

chi'roplast, n., an apparatus for making the fingers supple.

chirop'odist, n., one who doctors the feet and hands.

chirop'odous, adj., having feet like hands.

chirop'ody, n., the treatment of the feet.

chiroprac'tic, n., healing by manipulation of the spine.

chiroprac'tor, n., one who practises chiropractic.

chirop'tera, n. pl., bats.

chirop'terous, adj., having wings like hands.

chiros'ophy, n., palmistry.

chirp, n., a bird's short, shrill note; v.i., to make the short, shrill sound of a bird.

chirped, p.p., chirp.

chirp'er, n., one who chirps.

chirp'ing, *pr.p.,* chirp.

chirp'y, *adj.,* lively.

chirr, *n.* and *v.i.,* (to make) a prolonged trilling sound (as) of grass-hopper.

chir'rup, *v.i., i.q.* chirp.

chir'ruped, *p.p.,* chirrup.

chir'ruping, *pr.p.,* chirrup.

chis'el, *n.,* a bevel-edged tool used for cutting wood, stone or iron; *v.t.,* to carve, to cut with a chisel.

chis'el(l)ed, *adj.,* finely outlined; edged with a chisel; *p.p.,* chisel.

chis'el(l)er, *n.,* one who chisels.

chis'el(l)ing, *pr.p.,* chisel.

chiselly, *adj.,* gritty, gravelly.

Chis'leu, *n.,* a month in the Jewish calendar.

chit, *n.,* a sprout; a child; a note; a voucher; *v.i.,* to sprout.

chi'tal, *n.,* the Indian, spotted deer.

chit'-chat, *n.,* prattling talk, gossip.

chit'in, *n.,* the horny substance of certain beetles' shells.

chi'ton, *n.,* a Greek slave's tunic.

chi'tosan, *n.,* a substance obtained from chitin.

chitt'ack, *n.,* an Indian weight corresponding to the ounce.

chit'tagong, *n.,* an Indian fowl.

chit'terlings, *n. pl.,* a pig's small intestines.

chit'ty, *adj.,* with sprouts, pimpled; *n., i.q.* chit.

chiv'alric, *adj.,* rel. to chivalry.

chiv'alrous, *adj.,* rel. to chivalry.

chiv'alry, *n.,* the system of knighthood; gallant behaviour; courtesy.

chive, *n.,* a garden herb allied to the leek or onion; a piece cut off.

chlo'ral, *n.,* an oily liquid used to promote sleep.

chlo'rate, *n.,* a chloric acid salt.

chlo'ric, *adj.,* rel. to chlorine.

chlo'rid, *n.,* chlorine compounded with some other element.

chlo'ridate, *v.t.,* to combine with a chlorid.

chlo'ride, *n., i.q.* chlorid.

chlor'idize, *v.t., i.q.* chloridate.

chlor'inate, *v.t.,* to treat with chlorine.

chlor'inated, *p.p.,* chlorinate.

chlor'inating, *pr.p.,* chlorinate.

chlorina'tion, *n.,* the act of chlorinating.

chlo'rine, *n.,* a chemical, gaseous element.

chlo'rinize, *v.t., i.q.* chlorinate.

chlo'rite, *n.,* a common appellation of several green stones.

chlorit'ic, *adj.,* containing chlorite.

chlo'rodyne, *n.,* an anodyne so named.

chlo'roform, *n.,* an anaesthetic so named; *v.t.,* to treat a patient with chloroform.

chlorom'eter, *n.,* an instrument for measuring the degree of chlorine.

chlorom'etry, *n.,* the process of using a chlorometer.

chloromy'cetin, *n.,* an antibiotic.

chlo'rophyl(l), *n.,* the green colouring matter in plants.

chloro'sis, *n.,* a kind of anaemia, marked by a greenish pallor.

chlo'rous, *adj.,* combined with chlorine.

cho'ate, *adj.,* complete.

chock, *n.,* a block or wedge of wood, to plug a hole or prevent something from slipping; *v.t.,* to fasten with a chock.

chockful, *adj.,* quite full.

choc'olate, *adj.,* of a dark reddish brown colour; *n.,* a beverage or sweet from the cacao.

choice, *adj.,* worthy to be chosen, select, precious; *n.,* the act or power of choosing, a thing chosen, determination.

choi'cer, *adj.,* comp. of choice.

choi'cest, *adj.,* super. of choice.

choir, *n.,* a company of singers; the part of a church occupied by the singers; *v.i.,* to sing in chorus.

choir'-organ, *n.,* the part of an organ containing the soft stops.

choir'-screen, *n.,* the screen separating the choir and nave.

choke, *n.,* the inner part of the artichoke; that part of the carburettor of an internal combustion engine which temporarily restricts air intake; *v.t.,* to stop the breath, to throttle, to block up; *v.i.,* to be suffocated, to become stopped up.

choke'-bore, *n.,* a gun-bore narrowed at the muzzle.

choked, *p.p.,* choke.

choke'-damp, *n.,* the poisonous, carbonic acid gas often found in mines, wells and quarries.

chok'er, *n.,* one who chokes; a crushing rejoinder; a large cravat.

chok'iness, *n.,* a choky condition.

chok'ing, *pr.p.,* choke.

chok'y, *adj.,* like choking, suffocating.

chol'er, *n.,* anger, passion.

chol'era, *n.,* a dangerous, epidemic, bilious disease.

cholera'ic, *adj.,* rel. to cholera.

chol'era mor'bus, *n., i.q.* cholera.

chol'eric, *adj.,* passionate, hasty-tempered.

chol'erine, *n.,* summer cholera.

ch'olesterol, *n.,* a crystalline deposit found in various organs of the human body.

chondri'tis, *n.,* inflammation of the cartilage.

chondrom'eter, *n.,* a grain-weighing apparatus.

choose, *v.t.,* to make a choice; to select; to have a preference for.

choos'er, *n.,* one who chooses.

choos'ing, *pr.p.,* choose.

chop, *v.t.,* to cut into pieces; to bargain over; *v.i.,* to shift or change suddenly; *n.,* a small piece cut off; a jaw, a chap.

chop'-chop', *adv.* and *interj.,* quick, quickly.

chop'-house, *n.,* a restaurant.

chop'in, *n.*, an earthenware drinking-vessel; a liquid measure.

chopine', *n.*, a high clog.

chopped, *p.p.*, chop.

chop'per, *n.*, one who chops; a chopping instrument.

chop'ping, *pr.p.*, chop.

chop'py, *adj.*, breaking in short waves.

chops, *n. pl.*, the cheeks or chaps.

chop'sticks, *n. pl.*, thin wooden or ivory sticks used by the Chinese at meals.

chop-su'ey, *n.*, a dish of fried or stewed meat or chicken served in Chinese restaurants.

chorag'ic, *adj.*, belonging to a choragus.

chora'gus, *n.*, the leader or furnisher of a chorus.

cho'ral, *adj.*, rel. to a choir or chorus; *n.*, a harmonized hymn tune of German type.

chorale', *n.*, *i.q.* choral.

cho'ralist, *n.*, one who makes or sings chorals.

chord, *n.*, the string of a musical instrument; a combination of musical notes; a straight line joining the ends of an arc or apse; *v.t.*, to string; *v.i.*, to accord.

chord'al, *adj.*, of, like, etc. a chord.

chord'ed, *p.p.*, chord.

chord'ing, *pr.p.*, chord.

chore, *n.*, a small domestic job; a monotonous job.

chore'a, *n.*, a nervous twitching. St. Vitus's dance (*Lat.*).

choree', *n.*, a trochee.

cho'reograph, *n.*, *i.q.* choreographer.

choreog'rapher, *n.*, the designer of a ballet.

choreog'raphy, *n.*, the art of dancing, esp. ballet.

cho'riamb, *n.*, *i.q.* choriambus.

choriam'bic, *adj.*, rel. to a choriambus.

choriam'bus, *n.*, a metrical foot of four syllables, viz., a trochee followed by an iambus.

chor'ic, *adj.*, of, like, a chorus in a Greek play.

cho'rion, *n.*, an enveloping membrane of the fetus.

chor'ist, *n.*, a singer in a chorus.

chor'ister, *n.*, a member of a choir.

chorog'rapher, *n.*, a surveyor.

chorograph'ic, *adj.*, rel. to surveys.

chorog'raphy, *n.*, the art or practice of regional surveying.

cho'roid, *adj.*, resembling the chorion.

chorol'ogy, *n.*, the local distribution of species, etc.

chor'tle, *v.i.*, to chuckle.

cho'rus, *n.*, a choir of singers; united song; *v.t.*, to sing the chorus of, to celebrate in concert.

cho'rus(s)ed, *p.p.*, chorus.

cho'rus(s)ing, *pr.p.*, chorus.

chose, *p.p.*, choose.

chos'en, *p.p.*, choose.

chou, *n.*, an ornamental knot of ribbon, etc.

chough, *n.*, a kind of jackdaw.

chouse, *n.*, a swindle; *v.t.*, to swindle.

choused, *p.p.*, chouse.

chous'ing, *pr.p.*, chouse.

chow', *n.*, *abbrev.* of chow-chow; *abbrev.* of chowder (*slang*).

chow'-chow', *adj.*, mixed up, miscellaneous; *n.*, a mixture of food; a breed of dogs.

chow'der, *n.*, a mixed dish; a picnic.

chrematis'tic, *adj.*, pert. or rel. to the acquisition of wealth.

chrestom'athy, *n.*, a collection of useful extracts.

chrism, *n.*, the consecrated oil used in religious ceremonies.

chris'mal, *n.*, a vessel containing chrism.

chris'matory, *adj.*, rel. to chrism or unction; *n.*, a case to carry the chrism vessels.

chris'mon, *n.*, the sacred monogram consisting of two Greek letters rep. Christ.

chris'om, *n.*, a baptismal robe.

chris'om-child, *n.*, a child dying in its first month and buried in its chrisom.

Christ, *n.*, the Saviour in the Christian Faith; the Messiah.

chris'ten, *v.t.*, to baptize, to admit to the Christian family.

Chris'tendom, *n.*, all Christian peoples collectively.

chris'tened, *p.p.*, christen.

chris'tening, *n.*, the baptismal ceremony; *pr.p.*, christen.

Chris'tian, *adj.*, rel. to Christ's followers; *n.*, one of the baptized, a follower of Christ.

Christian'ia, *n.*, a turn in skiing.

Christian'ity, *n.*, the practice or doctrines of the Christian faith.

Christianiza'tion, *n.*, the act or state of Christianizing.

Christ'ianize, *v.t.*, to convert to Christianity.

Christ'ianized, *p.p.*, Christianize.

Christ'ianizing, *pr.p.*, Christianize.

Christ'ianly, *adv.*, in a Christian way.

Christie's, *n.*, a famous auction room in London.

Christ'mas, *n.*, the season of Christ's birth.

Christ'mas-box, *n.*, a Christmas gift.

Christ'mas-day', *n.*, the celebration of the birth of Christ (25 Dec.).

Christ'massy, *adj.*, savouring of Christmas.

Christol'ogy, *n.*, the study of the attributes and person of Christ.

chro'mate, *n.*, a chromic acid salt.

chromat'ic, *adj.*, rel. to colour; proceeding by semitones; *n.*, a note modified by an accidental.

chromat'ics, *n.*, pl. of chromatic; the science of colour.

chrom'atin, *n.*, tissue that can be stained (*biol.*).

chromatog'raphy, *n.*, the study of work in colour.

chro'matoid, *adj.*, able to be stained.

chromatol'ogy, *n.*, the scientific study of colour.

chromatom'eter, *n.*, a colour-measuring scale.

chrom'atrope, *n.*, a lantern slide giving kaleidoscopic movement of colours.

chrome, *n.*, a yellow pigment.

chro'mic, *adj.*, rel. to chromium.

chro'mium, *n.*, a whitish, metallic element so named.

chro'mogram, *n.*, a photograph in colours.

chromolith'ograph, *n.*, a colour-printed lithograph.

chromolithog'raphy, *n.*, the art of making chromolithographs.

chromoplas'tic, *n.*, modelling in colours.

chrom'osome, *n.*, the part of a cell-nucleus, thought to be an agent in hereditary transmission.

chro'mosphere, *n.*, a layer of glowing hydrogen through which the light of the sun has to pass.

chro'motype, *n.*, a photographic colour-process.

chro'mo-typog'raphy, *n.*, colour-printing.

chron'ic, *adj.*, lasting for a long time; firmly established.

chron'icle, *n.*, a record of events in order of time; *v.t.*, to record in order of time.

chron'icled, *p.p.*, chronicle.

chron'icler, *n.*, one who chronicles.

Chron'icles, *n.*, one of the books of the Old Testament.

chron'icling, *pr.p.*, chronicle.

chron'ogram, *n.*, an inscription in which a date can be read by the numeral letters (M. D. V. and the like) contained in the words.

chronogrammat'ic, *adj.*, in the style of a chronogram.

chron'ograph, *n.*, an accurate stopwatch; an instrument determining the muzzle velocity of a shot.

chronog'rapher, *n.*, a chronicler; a chronologist.

chronog'raphy, *n.*, the inquiry into dates and past history.

chronol'oger, *n.*, one versed in the study of dates and events.

chronolog'ic, *adj.*, in order of time.

chronolog'ical, *adj.*, in order of time.

chronolog'ically, *adv.*, in chronological order.

chronol'ogist, *n.*, one who studies dates and events.

chronol'ogy, *n.*, the study of events and dates.

chronom'eter, *n.*, a specially accurate timekeeper.

chronomet'ric, *adj.*, rel. to the chronometer.

chronom'etry, *n.*, time-measurement.

chron'opher, *n.*, an electric apparatus for transmitting time-indications.

chron'oscope, *n.*, an instrument for ascertaining precise length of minute intervals of time.

chrys'alid, *adj.*, like a chrysalis.

chrys'alis, *n.*, a butterfly or moth in the grub state.

Chrysan'themum, *n.*, the common name for a genus of flower of the aster type; the flower so named.

chrysobe'ryl, *n.*, a precious stone of yellowish-green colour.

chrysog'raphy, *n.*, illuminating in gold.

chrys'olite, *n.*, a yellow topaz.

chrysol'ogy, *n.*, the science of wealth.

chry'soprase, *n.*, *i.q.* chrysoprasus.

chrysop'rasus, *n.*, a precious stone of apple-green colour.

chrys'otype, *n.*, a photographic proof in which gold chlorid is used.

chub, *n.*, a little river fish.

chubbed, *adj.*, *i.q.* chubby.

chub'by, *adj.*, plump, round.

chuck, *n.*, an upward pat, a throw; a part of a machine tool for holding in position; *v.t.*, to throw, to tip up; to call by clucking.

chucked, *p.p.*, chuck.

chuck'ing, *pr.p.*, chuck.

chuck'le, *v.i.*, to laugh to oneself.

chuck'led, *p.p.*, chuckle.

chuck'ling, *pr.p.*, chuckle.

chud'dar, *n.*, an Indian, fine, wool shawl.

chuff, *adj.*, churlish; chubby.

chuf'fily, *adv.*, churlishly.

chuf'finess, *n.*, surliness.

chuf'fy, *adj.*, *i.q.* chuff.

chug, *n.*, the characteristic sound of an engine when running slowly.

chukk'a, *n.*, each of the periods into which a game of polo is divided.

chukk'er, *n.*, *i.q.* chukka.

chum, *n.*, a close friend; *v.i.*, to share rooms with.

chump, *n.*, a small block of wood; the thick end of a joint; a fool (*colloq.*); *v.t.*, to munch.

chu'nam, *n.*, a plaster of lime and sea sand; *v.t.*, to plaster with chunam.

chunk, *n.*, a short, thick piece.

chunk'y, *adj.*, like a chunk; solidly built.

church, *n.*, a building for religious services; the whole collection of believers in a religion; *v.t.*, to say the Office for the churching of women.

churched, *p.p.*, church.

church'ing, *n.*, the thanksgiving after childbirth; *pr.p.*, church.

church'man, *n.*, a member of the church; an ecclesiastic.

church'manship, *n.*, the status of a churchman.

church'-rate, *n.*, a rate levied for the maintenance of the church.

church'warden, *n.*, an officer who has the charge of a church and its property.

church'yard, *n.*, the area in which a church stands.

churl, *n.*, a rude rustic, a clown.

churl'ish, *adj.*, like a churl, ill-bred.

churl'ishly, *adv.*, rudely.

churl'ishness, *n.*, rudeness, ill-breeding.

churn, *n.*, a vessel in which butter is produced by agitating cream; *v.t.*, to stir cream into butter.

churned, *p.p.*, churn.

churn'ing, *pr.p.*, churn.

churr, *n.* and *v.i.*, (to make) a deep trill as of the night-jar.

chute, *n.*, a rapid fall in a river; an inclined trough.

chut'ney, *n.*, an Indian condiment of mixed ingredients.

chyla'ceous, *adj.*, of like nature with chyle.

chyle, *n.*, a milky fluid in the intestine.

chylifac'tive, *adj.*, rel. to chylification.

chylif'erous, *adj.*, chyle-carrying.

chylifica'tion, *n.*, the formation of chyle.

chy'lous, *adj.*, rel. to chyle.

chyme, *n.*, the pulp in the stomach resulting from the first act of digestion.

chymifica'tion, *n.*, the formation of chyme.

chym'ify, *v.i.*, and *i.*, to turn into chyme.

ciba'rious, *adj.*, edible.

cib'ol, *n.*, the shallot.

cibo'rium, *n.*, a large covered cup; a receptacle for a pyx; a canopy over an altar.

cic'ad, *n.*, *i.q.* cicada.

cica'da, *n.*, the harvest-fly, cricket, locust.

cic'atrice, *n.*, the scar of a healed wound. (Also *cicatrix*.)

cicatri'sive, *adj.*, tending to form a cicatrix.

cica'trix, *n.*, *i.q.* cicatrice (*Lat.*).

cicatriza'tion, *n.*, the forming of a cicatrix.

cic'atrize, *v.i.*, to form a cicatrix.

cic'atrized, *p.p.*, cicatrize.

cic'atrizing, *pr.p.*, cicatrize.

cic'ely, *n.*, a species of parsley.

cicero'ne, *n.*, a guide to the sights of a place.

Cicero'nian, *adj.*, in the style of Cicero (Roman orator).

cichora'ceous, *adj.*, rel. to chicory.

Cid, *n.*, a leader, a chief.

cid'aris, *n.*, a Persian tiara; a low-crowned mitre.

ci'der, *n.*, a drink from pressed apple juice.

ci'devant', *adj.*, previous, former (*Fr.*).

cierge, *n.*, a wax taper (*Fr.*).

cigar', *n.*, a roll of tobacco leaves for smoking.

cigarette', *n.*, a cylindrical shape of packed tobacco rolled in paper for smoking.

cil'ia, *n. pl.*, the hair-like growth on cells.

cil'iary, *adj.*, rel. to the eyelashes or to cilia.

cil'iate, *adj.*, having cilia.

cil'iated, *adj.*, *i.q.* ciliate.

cil'ice, *n.*, a hair-shirt.

Cili'cian, *adj.*, bel. to Cilicia, in Asia Minor.

cili'cious, *adj.*, made of hair.

cil'iform, *adj.*, *i.q.* ciliate.

cil'iograde, *adj.*, moving by means of cilia.

cil'ium, *n.*, the sing. of cilia.

ci'ma, *i.q.* cyma.

Cim'bric, *adj.*, rel. to the Cimbri (or Cymri); Welsh.

Cimme'rian, *adj.*, rel. to the Cimmerii (people in perpetual darkness); very dark.

cim'olite, *n.*, an aluminium silicate.

cinch, *n.*, a broad saddle-girth; a certainty (*Amer.*); *v.t.*, to get a grip on, to compel.

cincho'na, *n.*, the name of the tree from which quinine is produced.

cincho'nic, *adj.*, rel. to cinchona.

cin'chonine, *n.*, an alkaloid so named.

cinct'ure, *n.*, a girdle, anything that encircles; *v.t.*, to girdle, to surround.

cinct'ured, *p.p.*, cincture.

cinct'uring, *pr.p.*, cincture.

cin'der, *n.*, the refuse of burnt coal.

Cinderell'a, *n.*, a person or subject of unrecognized merit or beauty.

cin'derous, *adj.*, like a cinder.

cin'dery, *adj.*, like, or abounding in, cinders.

cin'e-, abbrev. of cinema used in compounds, as cine-camera.

cine-cam'era, *n.*, a camera for taking moving pictures.

cinefac'tion, *n.*, the reduction to cinders.

cin'ema, *n.*, an apparatus for showing films; the place where such films are shown.

cinemat'ic, *adj.*, rel. to the cinematograph.

cinemat'ograph, *n.*, a moving picture.

cinematog'rapher, *n.*, one who takes moving pictures.

cinematograph'ic, *adj.*, *i.q.* cinematic.

cinematog'raphy, *n.*, the art of making moving pictures.

cinemat'oscope, *n.*, a form of cinematograph.

cine-microg'raphy, *n.*, the recording of microscopic changes by cinematograph.

cinera'ceous, *adj.*, ashy-coloured.

cinerama, *n.*, three-dimensional film direction.

cinera'ria, *n.*, the family name for a variety of flowering shrubs.

cinerar'ium, *n.*, the recess in which a cinerary urn is placed.

cin'erary, *adj.*, rel. to ashes, holding ashes.

cinera'tion, *n.*, the reduction to ashes.

ciner'eous, *adj.*, ashen-grey (esp. of birds' plumage).

cine'rious, *adj.*, ashy-grey.

Cingalese', *adj.*, rel. to the Cingalese or Ceylon. (Also *Sinhalese*.)

cin'nabar, *n.*, vermilion.

cin'nabarine, *adj.*, like cinnabar.

cin'namon, *n.*, the spicy inner bark of the cinnamon tree.

cinnamon'ic, *adj.*, consisting of cinnamon.

cinq', cinque, *adj.*, five (at dice and cards).

cinque'foil, *adj.*, having cinquefoils; *n.*, a five-cusped architectural ornament.

Cinque' Ports, *n.*, five English seaports charged with the defence of the realm.

ci′pher, *n.*, the figure 0, the sign of zero; anything unimportant; a cryptic way of writing; *v.t.*, to calculate arithmetically; *v.i.*, to continue sounding (said of an organpipe).

ci′phered, *p.p.*, cipher.

ci′phering, *pr.p.*, cipher.

cip′olin, *n.*, an Italian marble.

cir′ca, *prep.*, around, about (*Lat.*).

Circas′sian, *adj.*, rel. to Circassia; *n.*, a native of C., a province of Russia.

Circe′an, *adj.*, rel. to Circe (an enchantress); bewitching.

circen′sian, *adj.*, rel. to the (Roman) circus.

cir′cinal, *adj.*, circled back, coiled back on itself.

cir′cinate, *adj.*, coiled inward.

cir′cle, *n.*, a plane figure consisting of a continuous line equidistant at all points from a centre; a round figure, a ring; an assemblage of people sharing the same ideas or being of the same rank; *v.t.* and *i.*, to move circularly; to encircle.

cir′cled, *p.p.*, circle.

cir′clet, *n.*, a little circle.

cir′cling, *pr.p.*, circle.

cir′cuit, *n.*, a going round; the extent of a circumference; a defined district; the passage of an electric current; *v.i.*, to circulate.

cir′cuited, *p.p.*, circuit.

cir′cuiting, *pr.p.*, circuit.

circu′itous, *adj.*, roundabout.

circu′itously, *adv.*, in a roundabout way.

circu′ity, *n.*, a roundabout method.

cir′culable, *adj.*, able to be circulated.

cir′cular, *adj.*, round; of the nature of a circle; *n.*, a notice sent round.

cir′cularism, *n.*, the circular theory of the universe.

circular′ity, *n.*, the character of being circular.

circulariza′tion, *n.*, the sending of circulars.

cir′cularize, *v.t.*, to address a circular notice to: to make circular.

cir′cularized, *p.p.*, circularize.

cir′cularizing, *pr.p.*, circularize.

cir′cularly, *adv.*, in a circular way.

cir′culate, *v.t.*, to send round, to spread about; *v.i.*, to be spread about, to go round.

cir′culated, *p.p.*, circulate.

cir′culating, *pr.p.*, circulate.

circula′tion, *n.*, the act of circulating; something circulated.

cir′culative, *adj.*, causing circulation.

circ′ulator, *n.*, one who circulates news, etc.

cir′culatory, *adj.*, rel. to circulation.

circumam′bient, *adj.*, surrounding.

circumam′bulate, *v.i.*, to walk right round.

circumben′dibus, *n.*, i.q. circumlocution.

cir′cumcise, *v.t.*, to perform circumcision on.

cir′cumcised, *p.p.*, circumcise.

cir′cumciser, *n.*, one who circumcises.

cir′cumcising, *pr.p.*, circumcise.

circumci′sion, *n.*, the removal of the foreskin from the penis.

circumduct′, *v.t.*, to lead round.

circum′ference, *n.*, the boundary line of a circle; the distance round.

circumferen′tial, *adj.*, in, or rel. to, the circumference.

circum′ferentor, *n.*, an instrument for measuring circumferences.

cir′cumflect, *v.t.*, to bend round.

cir′cumflex, *n.*, an accent mark, combined of the acute and the grave; *v.t.*, to accent with the circumflex.

cir′cumflexed, *p.p.*, circumflex.

circumflex′ing, *pr.p.*, circumflex.

circumflex′ion, *n.*, the act of circumflexing.

circum′fluence, *n.*, a flowing round.

circum′fluent, *adj.*, flowing round.

circum′fluous, *adj.*, i.q. circumfluent.

circumfuse′, *v.t.*, to pour or spread round, to surround.

circumfused′, *p.p.*, circumfuse.

circumfu′sile, *adj.*, able to be circumfused.

circumfu′sing, *pr.p.*, circumfuse.

circumfu′sion, *n.*, the act of circumfusing.

circumgy′rate, *v.i.*, to revolve.

circumgy′rated, *p.p.*, circumgyrate.

circumgyra′ting, *pr.p.*, circumgyrate.

circumgyra′tion, *n.*, the act of revolving.

circumja′cence, *n.*, the relation of lying around.

circumja′cent, *adj.*, lying around, closely bordering.

circumlitt′oral, *adj.*, bordering the shore.

circumlocu′tion, *n.*, a roundabout way of speaking; a redundant phrase.

circumloc′utory, *adj.*, redundant, roundabout.

circumnav′igable, *adj.*, able to be sailed round.

circumnav′igate, *v.t.*, to sail round.

circumnav′igated, *p.p.*, circumnavigate.

circumnav′igating, *pr.p.*, circumnavigate.

circumnaviga′tion, *n.*, the act of sailing round.

circumnav′igator, *n.*, one who circumnavigates.

circumpo′lar, *adj.*, round the pole.

circumro′tary, *adj.*, revolving on an axis.

circumrota′tion, *n.*, the act of revolving on an axis.

circumro′tatory, *adj.*, i.q. circumrotary.

circumscrib′able, *adj.*, able to be circumscribed.

circumscribe′, *v.t.*, to confine within boundaries, to limit.

circumscribed′, *p.p.*, circumscribe.

circumscrib′er, *n.*, one who circumscribes.

circumscrib′ing, *pr.p.*, circumscribe.

circumscrip′tion, *n.*, the act of circumscribing; the state of being circumscribed.

circumscrip′tive, *adj.*, tending to circumscribe.

circumsol'ar, *adj.*, revolving round, being near, the sun.

cir'cumspect, *adj.*, wary, discreet.

circumspec'tion, *n.*, wariness, discretion, vigilance.

circumspec'tive, *adj.*, watchful.

circumspec'tively, *adv.*, *i.q.* circumspectly.

cir'cumspectly, *adv.*, warily, discreetly.

cir'cumspectness, *n.*, the habit of being circumspect.

cir'cumstance, *n.*, an incident; an event; an attendant condition; *v.t.*, to place in particular circumstances.

cir'cumstanced, *p.p.*, circumstance.

circumstan'tial, *adj.*, containing full details; matter of fact.

circumstantial'ity, *n.*, the circumstantial character.

circumstan'tially, *adv.*, in a circumstantial manner.

circumstan'tiate, *v.t.*, to confirm with facts or details.

circumstan'tiated, *p.p.*, circumstantiate.

circumstan'tiating, *pr.p.*, circumstantiate.

circumval'late, *v.t.*, to make a trench round, to fortify.

circumvalla'ted, *p.p.*, circumvallate.

circumvalla'ting, *pr.p.*, circumvallate.

circumvalla'tion, *n.*, the act of circumvallating; a rampart and trench.

circumvent', *v.t.*, to outwit, to get the better of; to go round.

circumvent'ed, *p.p.*, circumvent.

circumvent'ing, *pr.p.*, circumvent.

circumven'tion, *n.*, the act of circumventing.

circumven'tive, *adj.*, able to circumvent.

circumven'tively, *adv.*, in a circumventive way.

circumvola'tion, *n.*, the act of flying round.

circum'volute, *v.t.*, to wrap round.

circum'voluted, *p.p.*, circumvolute.

circum'voluting, *pr.p.*, circumvolute.

circumvolu'tion, *n.*, the act of wrapping round.

circumvolve, *v.i.*, to roll round.

circumvolved, *p.p.*, circumvolve.

circumvolv'ing, *pr.p.*, circumvolve.

cir'cus, *n.*, a circular-ended race-course; a traditional show with clowns and animal performances; a hippodrome; a row of houses forming a circle or part of a circle.

cir'cus(s)y, *adj.*, like a circus.

cirque, *n.*, an arena, a natural amphitheatre (*Fr.*).

cirrho'sis, *n.*, a morbid condition of tissue.

cir'ri, *n.*, pl. of cirrus.

cirrif'erous, *adj.*, having cirri.

cir'riform, *adj.*, like a cirrus.

cirrig'erous, *adj.*, carrying cirri.

cir'riped, *adj.*, having cirrus-like feet.

cirro-cu'mulus, *n.*, a pile of small clouds, part cirrus, part cumulus.

cir'rose, *adj.*, having cirri.

cirro-stra'tus, *n.*, a mass of clouds terminating in cirri.

cir'rus, *n.*, a cloud-shape resembling a wisp of hair; a tendril.

cir'socele, *n.*, a varicocele.

cisal'pine, *adj.*, on this (the Roman) side of the Alps.

cisatlan'tic, *adj.*, on this side of the Atlantic.

cise'leur, *n.*, a metal-carver (*Fr.*).

cise'lure, *n.*, metal carving.

cismon'tane, *adj.*, on this side of the mountains.

cispon'tine, *adj.*, on this side of the bridges.

cis'soid, *adj.*, within two intersecting curves; *n.*, a variety of curve so named.

ciss'y, *n.*, an effeminate person (*slang*).

cist, *n.*, a case or chest; an ancient tomb made of stones; a non-malignant swelling. (Also *cyst.*)

Cister'cian, *adj.*, rel. to the Cistercian Order; *n.*, a C. monk.

cis'tern, *n.*, a receptacle for holding liquid.

cis'tic, *adj.*, *i.q.* cystic.

cis'tus, *n.*, an ornamental shrub bearing large white or red flowers.

cit, *n.*, a Hindu name for the Universal Spirit; a city man (*colloq.*).

ci'table, *adj.*, able to be cited.

cit'adel, *n.*, a fortress within or defending a city.

cita'tion, *n.*, the act of citing, or quoting; a quotation; a summons.

ci'tatory, *adj.*, of the nature of a citation.

cite, *v.t.*, to call, to quote, to summon.

ci'ted, *p.p.*, cite.

ci'ter, *n.*, one who cites.

cith'ara, *n.*, the Greek lyre.

cith'er, *n.*, a zither.

cith'ern, *n.*, *i.q.* cither.

cit'ified, *adj.*, having city airs.

cit'igrade, *adj.*, fast-running.

ci'ting, *pr.p.*, cite.

cit'izen, *n.*, the dweller in a city or country.

cit'izenship, *n.*, the status of a citizen.

cit'rate, *n.*, citric acid salt (*chem.*).

cit'rene, *n.*, a volatile oil so named.

cit'ric, *adj.*, consisting of fruit of the citron.

cit'ril, *n.*, a little bird so named.

cit'rin, *n.*, a flavone glucoside, known as vitamin P, first found in lemon and orange juice.

cit'rine, *adj.*, lemon-coloured.

citrom'eter, *n.*, an instrument for testing lemon juice.

cit'ron, *n.*, the fruit of the citron tree.

citronell'a, *n.*, fragrant ethereal oil used for keeping away insects.

Cit'rus, *n.*, the genus incl. the citron, lemon, orange, etc.

cit'tern, *n.*, *i.q.* cithern.

cit'y, *n.*, a community of citizens; a place where citizens live; a large town made a city by charter and having a mayor and corporation.

civ'et, *n.*, a perfume so named; the civet-cat; a culinary sauce.

civ'et-cat, n., a small, carnivorous animal found in N. Africa and Asia.

civ'ic, adj., rel. to a city or citizenship.

civ'ics, n., the study of civil government.

civ(v)'ies, n. pl., civilian clothes (slang) (abbrev.).

civ'il, adj., rel. to a city or state; polite, well-mannered.

civ'il engineer', n., an engineer of roads, bridges, etc., for civil (not military) purposes.

civil'ian, n., one engaged in civil (not military) occupations.

civil'ity, n., good manners, courteous treatment.

civ'ilizable, adj., capable of civilization.

civiliza'tion, n., the state of being civilized; the act of civilizing.

civ'ilize, v.t., to bring under refining and progressive influences.

civ'ilized, p.p., civilize.

civ'ilizer, n., one who civilizes.

civ'ilizing, adj., refining, progressive; pr.p., civilize.

civ'illy, adv., courteously; in rel. to the State.

civ'ism, n., the profession of devotion to the community.

Civv'y Street, n., civilian life (slang) (abbrev.).

clab'ber, v.i., to curdle.

clab'bered, p.p., clabber.

clabb'ering, pr.p., clabber.

clack, v.i., to rattle, to babble; n., a sudden noise, rattle or prattle.

clacked, p.p., clack.

clack'er, n., anything that clacks.

clack'ing, pr.p., clack.

clad, p.p., clothe.

claim, n., an assertion of a right; anything claimed; v.t., to assert a right; to affirm.

claim'able, adj., able to be claimed.

claim'ant, n., one who claims.

claimed, p.p., claim.

claim'ing, pr.p., claim.

clairau'dience, n., the power of supranormal hearing.

clairau'dient, adj., able to hear supranormally.

clair-de-lune', adj., moonlight-colour; pale blue-grey (Fr.).

clair-obscure', i.q. chiaroscuro.

clairvoy'ance, n., the power of seeing absent persons and objects.

clairvoy'ant, n., one who has clairvoyance.

clam, n., a bivalve shellfish; v.t., to starve (colloq.).

cla'mant, adj., loud, urgent.

clam'atory, adj., clamorous.

clam'ber, n., the act of clambering; v.i., to climb with the hands and feet.

clam'bered, p.p., clamber.

clam'bering, pr.p., clamber.

clammed, adj., starved of food; p.p., clam.

clam'miness, n., a state or feeling of damp and cold.

clam'ming, pr.p., clam.

clam'my, adj., damp, cold and sticky.

clam'orous, adj., making a vociferous outcry.

clam'orously, adv., vociferously.

clam'our, n., an outcry, a vociferation; v.i., to raise an outcry.

clam'oured, p.p., clamour.

clam'ourer, n., one who clamours.

clam'ouring, pr.p., clamour.

clamp, n., a stiff fastening; the name of a variety of tool; v.t., to fasten tightly, to secure.

clamped, p.p., clamp.

clamp'ing, pr.p., clamp.

clan, n., a group with strong ties of family and traditional loyalties.

clandes'tine, adj., secret, underhand.

clandes'tinely, adv., secretly.

clang, n., a ringing, metallic sound; v.i., to make a ringing noise.

clanged, p.p., clang.

clang'er, n., an ill-timed remark (Amer.).

clang'ing, pr.p., clang.

clan'gorous, adj., noisily sounding.

clan'gorously, adv., in a clangorous way.

clan'gour, n., a clanking sound.

clank, n., a metallic sort of sound; v.t., to make something clank; v.i., to resound.

clanked, p.p., clank.

clank'ing, pr.p., clank.

clan'nish, adj., rel. to a clan; exclusive; united.

clan'nishly, adv., in a clannish fashion.

clan'ship, n., the rights of a member of a clan.

clans'man, n., a member of a clan.

clans'woman, n., the fem. of clansman.

clap, n., a sudden, sharp noise; v.t. and i., to strike together; to strike suddenly; to applaud.

clap'board, n., a weather board; v.t., to protect with a clap-board.

clap'boarded, p.p., clapboard.

clap'board'ing, pr.p., clapboard.

clapped, p.p., clap.

clap'per, n., anything that claps; a bell's tongue.

clap'per-claw, n., a back-scratcher; v.t., to scratch and slap.

clap'ping, pr.p., clap.

clap'trap, n., balderdash, cheap talk.

claque, n., a hired body of supporters (Fr.).

claqueur', n., a hired applauder (Fr.).

clarabel'la, n., a sweet, soft organ-stop.

Clar'enc(i)eux, n., the higher of the two provincial Kings-of-Arms. His province is South of the River Trent.

clar'endon, n., a heavy-faced printing type.

clare-obscure', n., i.q. clair-obscure.

clar'et, adj., claret-coloured; n., a light red Bordeaux wine.

clarifica'tion, n., the process of clarifying.

clar'ified, p.p., clarify.

clar'ifier, n., anything that clarifies.

clar'ify, v.t., to make clear, to purify.

clar'ifying, *pr.p.*, clarify.

clar'inet, *n.*, a keyed, wooden, wind instrument.

clar'ion, *adj.*, loud; *n.*, a form of trumpet.

clarionet', *n.*, *i.q.* clarinet.

cla'rity, *n.*, clearness.

clark'ia, *n.*, a flowering plant of that name.

clar'y, *n.*, a kind of pot-herb.

clash, *n.*, a noise of things striking together; *v.t.*, to strike together; *v.i.*, to collide.

clashed, *p.p.*, clash.

clash'ing, *pr.p.*, clash.

clasp, *n.*, an embrace, a fastening; *v.t.*, to embrace, to fasten close.

clasped, *p.p.*, clasp.

clasp'er, *n.*, anything that clasps.

clasp'ing, *pr.p.*, clasp.

clasp'-knife, *n.*, a knife, the blade of which shuts into the handle.

class, *adj.*, rel. to class distinction; *n.*, a rank, group or division; *v.t.*, to group together, to rank.

class'able, *adj.*, able to be classed.

classed, *p.p.*, class.

clas'sic, *adj.*, of the first rank; rel. to the Greek or Latin classics; *n.*, a standard work or author.

clas'sical, *adj.*, *i.q.* classic.

classical'ity, *n.*, the classic quality.

clas'sicism, *n.*, the style of the classics; an idiom of the classics.

clas'sicist, *n.*, one who favours or studies the ancient classical styles.

class'icize, -se, *v.t.* and *i.*, to make classic.

classifi'able, *adj.*, cap. of classification.

classifica'tion, *n.*, the act of classifying; a classified system.

clas'sified, *p.p.*, classify.

clas'sifier, *n.*, one who classifies.

clas'sify, *v.t.*, to group in classes.

clas'sifying, *pr.p.*, classify.

class'ing, *pr.p.*, class.

clas'sis, *n.*, a division into a class.

class'ism, *n.*, class distinction.

class'man, *n.*, a member of a class; one who obtains university honours.

class'mate, *n.*, a fellow-member of a class.

class'room, *n.*, a room where lessons are taught.

class'-war', *n.*, hostility between social groups.

class'y, *adj.*, superior; stylish (*slang*).

clas'tic, *adj.*, relating to anything that may be broken or taken apart.

clat'ter, *n.*, a confused noise, prattle; *v.t.* and *i.*, to rattle; to prate.

clat'tered, *p.p.*, clatter.

clat'terer, *n.*, one who clatters.

clat'tering, *pr.p.*, clatter.

clause, *n.*, a group of words containing a finite verb; an article in a contract, will or parliamentary bill.

claus'tral, *adj.*, rel. to a cloister; secluded.

claustrophob'ia, *n.*, a dread of closed spaces.

claustrophob'ic, *adj.*, rel. to claustrophobia.

clau'sular, *adj.*, containing clauses.

cla'vate, *adj.*, club-like.

cla'vated, *adj.*, *i.q.* clavate.

clave, *p.p.*, cleave.

clav'ecin, *n.*, an alternative name for a harpsichord (*Fr.*).

clav'iary, *n.*, *i.q.* clavier.

clavicem'balo, *n.*, *i.q.* cembalo.

clav'ichord, *n.*, an early, stringed instrument with a keyboard.

clav'icle, *n.*, the collar-bone.

clavic'ular, *adj.*, rel. to the collar bone.

clavier', *n.*, a keyboard.

clav'iform, *adj.*, club-shaped.

clavig'erous, *adj.*, key-bearing.

cla'vis, *n.*, a key; a clue.

claw, *n.*, a hooked nail, the head of a hammer; *v.t.*, to seize, tear or scratch.

clawed, *p.p.*, claw.

claw'-hamm'er, *n.*, a hammer with a partly-clawed head.

claw'ing, *pr.p.*, claw.

clay, *n.*, stiff, damp soil; *v.t.*, to cover with clay.

clayed, *p.p.*, clay.

clay'ey, *adj.*, like clay, abounding in clay.

clay'eyness, *n.*, a clayey condition.

clay'ing, *pr.p.*, clay.

clay'ish, *adj.*, slightly clayey.

clay'more, *n.*, a Highlander's two-edged sword.

clead'ing, *n.*, a wooden lining.

clean, *adj.*, purified, free from dirt, smooth, morally pure; *adv.*, wholly, quite; *v.t.*, to purify, to cleanse.

cleaned, *p.p.*, clean.

clean'er, *adj.*, *comp.* of clean; *n.*, one who, or that which, cleans.

clean'est, *adj.*, *super.* of clean.

clean'ing, *pr.p.*, clean.

clean'lily, *adv.*, *i.q.* cleanly.

clean'liness, *n.*, the clean quality or habit.

clean'ly, *adj.*, habitually clean.

clean'ly, *adv.*, in a clean way.

clean'ness, *n.*, the state of being clean.

cleanse, *v.t.*, to make clean, to remove defilement.

cleansed, *p.p.*, cleanse.

cleans'er, *n.*, anything that cleanses.

cleans'ible, *adj.*, able to be cleansed.

cleans'ing, *n.*, the act of cleaning; *pr.p.*, cleanse.

clear, *adj.*, bright, pellucid, unobstructed, net, plainly manifest; *v.t.*, to make bright; to free from blame; to remove; to gain; *v.i.*, to become brighter.

clear'able, *adj.*, able to be cleared.

clear'age, *n.*, a clearing.

clear'ance, *n.*, the act of setting free; a cleared space; a permit.

clear'cole, *n.*, size and white-lead used as first coat when painting a house; *v.t.*, to paint with this.

clear-cut, *adj.*, outlined sharply and clearly.

cleared, *p.p.*, clear.

clear'er, *adj.*, *comp.* of clear; *n.*, anything that clears.

clear'est, *adj.*, *super.* of clear.

clear'ing, *n.*, a cleared space; the settlement of bank balances; *pr.p.*, clear.

clear'ing-house, *n.*, an office where bankers' balances are adjusted.

clear'ly, *adv.*, plainly, evidently.

clear'ness, *n.*, the state or quality of being clear.

clear'-sighted, *adj.*, having clear vision.

clear'way, *n.*, a stretch of road on which vehicles may not stop.

cleat, *n.*, a strip nailed across something to prevent slipping; *v.t.*, to supply with a cleat.

cleav'able, *adj.*, able to be cleft.

cleav'age, *n.*, the act of cleaving, a cleft; the depth of gap between a woman's breasts.

cleave, *v.t.*, to split, to divide; *v.i.*, to cling to.

cleaved, *p.p.*, cleave.

cleav'er, *n.*, one who cleaves, a chopper.

cleav'ers, *n.*, goose-grass, a prickly plant.

cleav'ing, *pr.p.*, cleave.

cledge, *n.*, clay.

cledg'y, *adj.*, clayey.

cleek, *n.*, a golf club with an iron head.

clef, *n.*, a musical sign to indicate pitch.

cleft, *n.*, a fissue; *p.p.*, cleave.

cleg, *n.*, a horse-fly.

clem'atis, *n.*, a climbing plant so named.

clem'ency, *n.*, the quality of gentleness, compassion, mercy.

clem'ent, *adj.*, gentle, compassionate, mild.

Clem'entine, *adj.*, rel. to St. Clement.

clench, *v.t.*, to grasp, to double up, to brace.

clenched, *p.p.*, clench.

clen'cher, *n.*, anything that clenches.

clench'ing, *pr.p.*, clench.

Cleopat'ra's Nee'dle, *n.*, the Egyptian obelisk on the Thames Embankment in London.

clep'sydra, *n.*, a Greek water-clock.

clere'story, *n.*, the upper range of windows in a church.

cler'gy, *n.*, the collective name for clergymen as a body; the clerical status.

cler'gyman, *n.*, a member of the clergy.

cler'gywoman, *n.*, a woman pastor.

cler'ic, *n.*, a clerk or clergyman.

cler'ical, *adj.*, rel. to the clergy or to a clerk.

cle'rihew, *n.*, short, witty nonsensical verse.

clerk, *n.*, a cleric; a writer in an office; a scholar.

clerk'ess, *n.*, a female clerk.

clerk'ly, *adj.*, scholarly; rel. to a clerk.

clerk'ship, *n.*, a clerk's office or function.

cleroden'dron, *n.*, a climbing shrub with campanulate flowers.

cle'romancy, *n.*, divination by lots.

clev'er, *adj.*, skilful, capable.

clev'erish, *adj.*, somewhat clever.

clev'erly, *adv.*, in a clever way.

clev'erness, *n.*, the quality of being clever.

clev'is, *n.*, an iron loop round a plough beam.

clew, *n.*, a ball of thread; a guide to a mystery; the lower corner of a sail; *v.t.*, to roll up.

cliché, *n.*, an electrotype or stereotype plate; a hackneyed literary phrase (*Fr.*).

click, *n.*, a short, sharp sound; *v.t.*, to make to click; *v.i.*, to give a click.

clicked, *p.p.*, click.

click'er, *n.*, anything that clicks; a foreman shoemaker.

click'et, *n.*, a latch.

click'ing, *pr.p.*, click.

cli'ent, *n.*, a dependent, a customer; one who consults a lawyer.

cli'entage, *n. pl.*, a number of clients.

clientele', *n. pl.*, a body of clients, followers, etc. (*Fr.*).

cliff, *n.*, a high, steep rock.

cliff-hang'er, *n.*, a climacteric situation (*colloq.*).

clift, *n.*, *i.q.* cleft.

climac'teric, *adj.*, rel. to a climax; *n.*, a critical period in life.

cli'mate, *n.*, the local atmospheric conditions.

climat'ic, *adj.*, rel. to climate.

climat'ical, *adj.*, *i.q.* climatic.

cli'matize, *v.t.*, to accustom to a climate.

cli'matized, *p.p.*, climatize.

cli'matizing, *pr.p.*, climatize.

climatog'raphy, *n.*, a description of climate.

climatol'ogist, *n.*, an expert in climate.

climatol'ogy, *n.*, the study of climatic conditions.

climatothe'rapy, *n.*, the climatic treatment of disease.

cli'max, *n.*, an ascending scale; the highest point; the acme; a turning point.

climb, *v.t.*, to ascend, to mount.

climb'able, *adj.*, able to be climbed.

climbed, *p.p.*, climb.

climb'er, *n.*, one who, or that which, climbs.

climb'ing, *pr.p.*, climb.

clime, *n.*, a region, climate.

clinch, *n.*, a clinched bolt; a particular knot in a rope; *v.t.*, to grasp, to fasten tightly, to set the teeth, to settle.

clinched, *p.p.*, clinch.

clinch'er, *n.*, a settler.

clinch'ing, *pr.p.*, clinch.

cling, *v.i.*, to hold on to, to adhere to.

cling'er, *n.*, one who, or that which, clings.

cling'ing, *pr.p.*, cling.

cling'stone, *adj.*, descriptive of a peach of which the pulp adheres to the stone.

cling'y, *adj.*, adhesive.

clin'ic, *adj.*, rel. to a bed; *n.*, a patient in bed; bedside teaching; a session of consultation of doctors by patients; a place designed for medical consultation.

clin'ical, *adj.*, *i.q.* clinic.

clin'ically, *adv.*, in a clinical way.

clinic'ian, *n.*, a doctor in charge of a clinic.

clink, *n.*, a sound as of metal on metal; *v.t.*, to produce a tinkling sound; *v.i.*, to tinkle.

clinked, *p.p.*, clink.

clink'er, *n.*, one who clinks; a slag; *v.i.*, to form clinkers.

clink'ered, *p.p.*, clinker.

clink'ering, *pr.p.*, clinker.

clink'ing, *pr.p.*, clink.

clinoceph'aly, *n.*, a flattening of the cranium.

cli'noid, *adj.*, like a bed.

clinom'eter, *n.*, an instrument for measuring angles of elevation and depression.

clinomet'ric, *adj.*, rel. to a clinometer.

clinomet'rical, *adj.*, *i.q.* clinometric.

clin'quant, *adj.*, tinselled.

clip, *n.*, the act or result of clipping; a device for holding things fast; the holder for the charge of a magazine rifle; *v.t.*, to cut off, to crop, to shear; to embrace.

clipped, *p.p.*, clip.

clip'per, *n.*, one who clips; an instrument for clipping; a fast sailing ship.

clip'ping, *pr.p.*, clip.

clique, *n.*, a small closely-united party (*Fr.*).

cli'quish, *adj.*, exclusive, clannish.

cli'quishness, *n.*, *i.q.* cliquism.

cli'quism, *n.*, an exclusive tendency.

cli'quy, *adj.*, *i.q.* cliquish.

clish-ma-cla'ver, *n.*, gossip (*Scot.*).

clit'oris, *n.*, the internal part of the female genitals analogous to the male penis.

cliv'ers, *n. pl.*, grass-tufts.

cloa'ca, *n.*, a sewer (*Lat.*).

cloa'cal, *adj.*, rel. to a sewer.

cloak, *n.*, a loose, outer garment; an excuse, a disguise; *v.t.*, to cover with a cloak, to hide.

cloaked, *p.p.*, cloak.

cloak'ing, *pr.p.*, cloak.

cloak'room, *n.*, a room where coats, hats, parcels, luggage, etc., may be deposited for a time.

clob'ber, *n.*, a black paste; clothes, gear (*slang*); *v.t.*, to patch up.

cloche, *n.*, a bell-glass; a woman's bell-shaped hat (*Fr.*); a glass protection for garden plants.

clo'cher, *n.*, a belfry (*Fr.*).

clock, *n.*, a time-measuring instrument.

clock'-golf, *n.*, a putting game, with holes numbered and arranged like a clock face.

clock'-maker, *n.*, a maker of clocks.

clock'wise, *adj.*, moving in a left-to-right curve.

clock'work, *adj.*, regular, accurate; *n.*, a clock's mechanism.

clod, *n.*, a lump of earth or turf; a bumpkin; *v.t.*, to pelt with clods; to make clods of; *v.i.*, to form into clods.

clod'ded, *p.p.*, clod.

clod'ding, *pr.p.*, clod.

clod'dy, *adj.*, full of clods.

clod'hopper, *n.*, a rustic, a yokel.

clod'hopping, *adj.*, loutish.

clod'pate, *n.*, a blockhead.

clod'pated, *adj.*, stupid.

clod'poll, *n.*, a stupid fellow.

cloff, *n.*, a small deduction of weight.

clog, *n.*, an impediment; a shoe with a wooden sole; *v.t.*, to choke up, to impede; *v.i.*, to become clogged.

clogged, *p.p.*, clog.

clog'giness, *n.*, a tendency to clog.

clog'ging, *pr.p.*, clog.

clog'gy, *adj.*, apt to clog; lumpy; sticky.

cloisonné', *n.*, a kind of enamel ware (*Fr.*).

clois'ter, *n.*, a covered walk, partly or wholly enclosed; a monastery; *v.t.*, to enclose in a monastery.

clois'tered, *p.p.*, cloister.

clois'terer, *n.*, one who lives in a cloister.

clois'tering, *pr.p.*, cloister.

clois'tral, *adj.*, rel. to a cloister.

clon'ic, *adj.*, rel. to a spasm.

clo'nus, *n.*, a spasm.

cloop, *n.*, the sound as of a cork being drawn; *v.i.*, to make this sound.

close, *v.t.*, to shut up, to fill up; *v.i.*, to come near, to come together.

close, *adj.*, near, attentive, confined, stifling, stingy; *adv.*, fast shut up, nearly, near; *n.*, an enclosure; an end.

close'-bodied, *adj.*, close-fitting.

closed, *p.p.*, close.

close'ly, *adv.*, in a close way; attentively; compactly.

close'ness, *n.*, the state of being close; the proximity; stinginess.

clo'ser, *adj.*, *comp.* of close.

clos'est, *adj.*, *super.* of close.

clos'et, *n.*, a closed chamber, a private room, *v.t.*, to shut in a closet.

clos'eted, *p.p.*, closet.

clos'eting, *pr.p.*, closet.

clos'et-play, *n.*, a play for reading rather than acting.

close'up, *n.*, a short-range picture.

clos'ing, *pr.p.*, close.

clos'ish, *adj.*, rather close.

clo'sure, *n.*, the sudden ending of a debate; *v.t.*, to put the closure on.

clot, *n.,* a thick, coagulated mass of liquid matter; *v.t.,* to make into clots; *v.i.,* to become clotted.

clot'-bur, *n.,* the cocklebur.

cloth, *n.,* woven material.

clothe, *v.t.,* to cover with a garment; to invest.

clothed, *p.p.,* clothe.

clothes, *n. pl.,* dress, garments.

clothes'-basket, *n.,* a basket for holding clothes.

clothes'-brush, *n.,* a brush for clothes.

clothes'-horse, *n.,* a rail (or rails) to hang clothes on.

clothes'-line, *n.,* a line to hang clothes on.

clothes'-peg, *n.,* a device used for securing clothes on a line.

cloth'ier, *n.,* a seller, or maker of, clothes.

cloth'ing, *n.,* garments; *pr.p.,* clothe.

clot'ted, *p.p.,* clot.

clot'ting, *pr.p.,* clot.

clot'ty, *adj.,* full of clots.

clou, *n.,* a central idea; a point of great interest (*Fr.*).

cloud, *n.,* vapour floating in the air; a dimmed effect; a soft wrap for the head; *v.t.,* to darken, to overshadow.

cloud'-burst, *n.,* a torrential downpour of rain.

cloud'-capt, cloud'-capped, *adj.,* having clouds on the summit.

cloud'ed, *p.p.,* cloud.

cloud'ily, *adv.,* in a cloudy way.

cloud'iness, *n.,* the state of being cloudy.

cloud'ing, *pr.p.,* cloud.

cloud'less, *adj.,* without a cloud.

cloud'y, *adj.,* covered with clouds, lowering, not clear.

clough, *n.,* a sluice; a ravine.

clout, *n.,* a piece of cloth, a rag; a blow; *v.t.,* to patch; to cuff.

clout'ed, *p.p.,* clout.

clout'ing, *pr.p.,* clout.

clout-nàĭl, *n.,* a short nail used by cobblers.

clove, *n.,* a spice from the bud of the clove tree; *p.p.,* cleave.

clovehitch, *n.,* a knot used to secure a rope to any object which it crosses at right angles.

clo'ven, *adj.,* divided; *p.p.,* cleave.

clo'ven-footed, *adj.,* having the foot divided.

clo'ver, *n.,* a trefoil plant used as fodder.

clo'vered, *adj.,* planted with clover.

clo'verleaf, *n.,* a flyover with connecting roads shaped like a four-leaved clover.

clown, *n.,* a rustic, a boor, a buffoon.

clown'ish, *adj.,* like a clown.

clown'ishly, *adv.,* in a clown-like way.

clown'ishness, *n.,* the quality of a clown.

cloy, *v.t.,* to fill to excess.

cloyed, *p.p.,* cloy.

cloy'ing, *pr.p.,* cloy.

club, *n.,* a heavy stick; an association; *v.t.,* to strike with a club; to use as a club; to contribute.

club'bable, *adj.,* sociable.

clubbed, *p.p.,* club.

club'bing, *pr.p.,* club.

club'bist, *n.,* one who favours clubs.

club'footed, *adj.,* having deformed feet.

club'haul, *v.t.,* to tack by anchoring and cutting cable when short of room.

club'-house, *n.,* a house in which a club meets.

club'-law, *n.,* rule by violence.

club'room, *n.,* a room for a club's meetings.

cluck, *n.,* the sound made by a hen; *v.i.,* to make the sound of a hen.

clucked, *p.p.,* cluck.

cluck'er, *n.,* an incessant talker.

cluck'ing, *pr.p.,* cluck.

clue, *n.,* a guide, a means to solving a problem.

clum'ber, *n.,* a variety of spaniel.

clump, *n.,* a cluster, a mass; a thick bootsole; *v.t.,* to group; *v.i.,* to tramp.

clumped, *p.p.,* clump.

clump'ing, *pr.p.,* clump.

clum'sily, *adv.,* in a clumsy way.

clum'siness, *n.,* the quality of being clumsy.

clum'sy, *adj.,* awkward, unwieldy.

clunch, *adj.,* stumpy; *n.,* indurated clay.

clung, *p.p.,* cling.

Clu'niac, *adj.,* rel. to the Cluniac Order; *n.,* a monk of Cluny.

clus'ter, *n.,* a bunch, a group; *v.t.,* to gather into clusters; *v.i.,* to grow in clusters, to form into clusters.

clus'tered, *p.p.,* cluster.

clus'tering, *pr.p.,* cluster.

clus'tery, *adj.,* having clusters.

clutch, *n.,* a grasp, a seizure; a mechanical device for putting parts into or out of action; a batch of eggs; *v.t.,* to grasp.

clutched, *p.p.,* clutch.

clutch'ing, *pr.p.,* clutch.

clut'ter, *n.,* a heap of confusion; *v.t.,* to disorder; *v.i.,* to make a noise.

clut'tered, *p.p.,* clutter.

clut'tering, *pr.p.,* clutter.

Clydes'dale, *adj.* and *n.,* a district in Scotland; a breed of heavy draught-horses.

clys'mic, *adj.,* rel. to a deluge.

clys'ter, *n.,* an enema.

coacerva'tion, *n.,* a heaping together, a pile.

coach, *n.,* a large carriage, a railway carriage; a motor-driven conveyance for long distance transport; a tutor; *v.i.,* to travel by coach; to work under a tutor; *v.t.,* to tutor.

coach'-horse, *n.,* a carriage horse.

coach'-house, *n.,* a building where a carriage is kept.

coach'man, *n.,* the driver of a carriage.

coach'work, *n.,* the body of a vehicle.

coac'tion, n., joint action.

coac'tive, adj., acting conjointly.

coac'tively, adv., in a coactive way.

coadjust', v.t., to accommodate mutually.

coad'jutant, adj., co-operating.

coadju'tor, n., an assistant colleague.

coadju'trix, n., the fem. of coadjutor.

coad'unate, adj., congenitally united.

coadven'ture, n., an adventure in company; v.i., to share in an adventure.

coag'ulable, adj., able to coagulate.

coag'ulant, adj., causing coagulation; n., something that causes coagulation.

coag'ulate, v.t., to curdle, to thicken; v.i., to become curdled.

coag'ulated, p.p., coagulate.

coag'ulating, pr.p., coagulate.

coagula'tion, n., the act or state of coagulating.

coag'ulative, adj., tending to coagulate.

coag'ulator, n., something that causes coagulation.

coag'ulatory, adj., i.q. coagulative.

coag'ulum, n., i.q. coagulant.

co'-aid, n., mutual or joint help.

coai'ta, n., the red-faced spider-monkey.

coal, n., a black mineral used for fuel; v.t., to furnish with coal; v.i., to take in coal.

coal'-bed, n., a stratum of coal.

coal'-bunker, n., storage space for coal.

coal'-cellar, n., a cellar for storing coal.

coaled, p.p., coal.

coalesce', v.i., to grow together, to combine.

coalesced', p.p., coalesce.

coales'cence, n., the act or state of coalescing.

coales'cent, adj., growing together.

coalesc'ing, pr.p., coalesce.

coal'face, n., the exposed surface of a coal seam.

coal'field, n., a coal-bearing district.

coal'-gas, n., gas from coal distillation.

coal'-hole, n., a place for storing coal (slang).

coal'ing, pr.p., coal.

coal'ite, n., a smokeless fuel.

coali'tion, n., the act of combining; a union of parties (pol.).

coali'tionist, n., one who believes in coalition.

co-ally', n., a joint ally.

coal'-mine, n., a mine from which coal is hewn.

coal'mouse, n., a small, dark-coloured bird.

coal'-pit, n., a pit from which coal is drawn.

coal'-tar, n., tar obtained from bituminous coal.

coal'-trimm'er, n., one who stores coal in ships.

coal'y, adj., like, or containing, coal.

coam'ing, n., the raised border of a hatchway, cockpit, etc., to keep out water (naut.).

coapta'tion, n., the fitting together of parts (of a broken bone).

coarc'tate, adj., pressed together.

coarcta'tion, n., stricture, contraction.

coarse, adj., rough, of poor quality, unrefined.

coarse'ly, adv., in a coarse way.

coars'en, v.t. and i., to make or become coarse.

coarsened, p.p., coarsen.

coarse'ness, n., the quality of being coarse.

coarse'ning, pr.p., coarsen.

coars'er, adj., comp. of coarse.

coars'est, adj., super. of coarse.

coast, n., border, the edge of land by the sea; v.i., to travel or sail along; to move along by momentum or gravity only.

coast'al, adj., relating to the coast.

coast'ed, p.p., coast.

coas'ter, n., a vessel sailing from port to port on the same coast.

coast'guard, n., a government officer for coast duties and protection.

coast'ing, n., the travelling by momentum or gravity only; pr.p., coast.

coast'line, n., the line showing on a map the coast of a country.

coast'wise, adj. and adv., along the coast.

coat, n., an outer covering; a layer; v.t., to apply a coating to; to cover with a coat.

coat'ed, p.p., coat.

coatee', n., a short coat. (Also coatie.)

coa'ti, n., an American carnivorous mammal with a long, flexible snout.

coatie', n., i.q. coatee.

coat'ing, n., an outer layer; material for a coat; pr.p., coat.

coax, v.t., to wheedle, to persuade.

coaxed, p.p., coax.

coax'er, n., one who coaxes.

coax'ial, adj., having the same axis.

coax'ing, adj., wheedling, fondling; n., the act of one who coaxes; pr.p., coax.

coax'ingly, adv., in a coaxing way.

cob, n., a roundish hump; a small sturdy horse; a head of wheat; a blow on the buttocks; a break-water; v.t., to beat.

co'balt, n., a mineral so named; a pigment made from the same.

cobalt'ic, adj., rel. to cobalt.

cobb'er, n., a chum, a pal, (Austral. slang).

cob'bing, adj., vulgarly ostentatious; n., copper-impregnated rubble.

cob'ble, n., a variety of fishing-boat; a large, round paving-stone; v.t., to patch up; to lay cobble-stones on.

cob'bled, p.p., cobble.

cob'bler, n., one who cobbles, a shoe-mender; a summer beverage so named.

cob'blestone, n., a cobble for paving.

cob'bling, pr.p., cobble.

cob'bly, adj., paved with cobblestones.

cob'by, adj., headstrong; ardent.

Cob′denism, n., the doctrine of Cobden, i.e., Free Trade.

Cob′denite, n., a Free Trader.

co′ble, n., kinds of fishing-boat in Scotland and N. E. England.

cob′nut, n., a variety of hazel-nut.

co′bol, n., a computer language.

cob′ra, n., an Indian snake, exceedingly venomous.

cob′web, n., a spider's web; v.t., to cover with a cobweb.

cob′webbed, adj., covered with cobwebs.

cob′webby, adj., i.q. cob-webbed.

co′ca, n., the dried leaf of a Peruvian shrub.

coc′a-col′a, n., an aerated non-alcoholic drink.

co′caine, n., an anaesthetic, produced from the coca plant.

coca′inism, n., the effect of cocaine poisoning.

coca′inist, n., a cocaine addict.

coc′cagee, n., a cider apple; cider from it.

coccinel′la, n., a lady-bird.

coc′culus, n., a tropical plant bearing berries of a narcotic character.

coc′cyx, n., the lower end of the spine.

coch′ineal, n., a bright red dye, made from cochineal insects dried.

coch′lea, n., one of the ear passages.

coch′lear, adj., like a spoon; n., the communion-spoon of the Greek Church.

cochlear′iform, adj., spoon-shaped.

coch′leate, adj., spiral, like a snail-shell.

cock, n., a male bird; a hay-pile; a jaunty tip; v.t., to set up on one side; to raise the hammer of a gun.

cockabon′dy, n., a kind of fishing-fly.

cockade′, n., a knot of ribbons or other badge attached to a cap or hat.

cocka′ded, adj., decorated with a cockade.

cock-a-hoop′, adj. and adv., exultantly.

Cockaigne′, n., an imaginary country; London, the home of cockneys.

cockalor′um, n., a self-important little man (colloq.).

cock′amaroo, n., a form of bagatelle.

cockatoo′, n., a variety of parrot.

cock′atrice, n., a fabulous snake-like creature, hatched from a cock's egg.

cock′bill, v.t., to hang (an anchor) from the cathead; to raise the sign of mourning (naut.).

cock′boat, n., a little rowing boat.

cock′chafer, n., a winged beetle.

cock′-crow, n., the early morning.

cock′-crowing, n., i.q. cock-crow.

cocked, p.p., cock.

Cock′er, n., the famous teacher of arithmetic. ("According to Cocker" = necessarily correct.)

cock′er, adj., exact, correct; n., a breed of spaniels; v.t., to pamper, to indulge.

cock′erel, n., a young cock.

cock′et, n., a seal of the custom house.

cock′eyed, adj., squinting.

cock′fight, n., a fight between cocks.

cock′horse, n., a hobby horse; anything across which a child can straddle.

cock′ing, pr.p., cock.

cock′le, n., a weed growing amid corn; a bivalve so named; v.i., to wrinkle.

cock′led, p.p., cockle.

cock′ling, pr.p., cockle.

cock′ling, n., i.q. cockerel.

cock′loft, n., a loft next to the roof.

cock′ney, n., a Londoner.

cock′neyfied, p.p., cockneyfy.

cock′neyfy, v.t., to change to a Londoner.

cock′neyism, n., the London manner and idiom.

cock′pit, n., a ring for cock-fights; the pilot's compartment in an aircraft.

cock′roach, n., a black beetle.

cocks′comb, n., i.q. coxcomb.

cock′sparrow, n., a male sparrow.

cock′spur, n., a spur on a cock's legs.

cock′sure, adj., self-confident, dogmatic.

cock′swain, n., i.q. coxswain.

cock′sy, adj., i.q. cocky.

cock′tail, n., a mixed alcoholic drink as an aperitif, or drunk at a party.

cock′-up, n., an initial letter much taller than the others; a failure (colloq.).

cock′y, adj., conceited, pert.

cocky-leek′y, n., a cock boiled with leeks to make Scotch soup.

co′co(a), n., the palm tree; the seeds of the cacao tree.

co′coa-nib, n., the roasted cacao seeds.

co′co(a)nut, n., the fruit of the coco-palm.

cocoon′, n., an envelope spun by caterpillars.

cocoon′ery, n., a place where silk is spun.

cocotte′, n., a fashionable prostitute (Fr.).

coc′tion, n., the process of boiling.

cod, n., an abundant edible fish.

co′da, n., an additional ending to a piece of music; the finale of a fugue or sonata.

cod′dle, n., one that is pampered; v.t., to pamper.

cod′dled, p.p., coddle.

cod′dling, pr.p., coddle.

code, n., a body of law; a system of signs for conveying messages briefly or in cipher.

co′declina′tion, n., the complement of the declination in astronomy.

co′deine, n., an analgesic alkaloid so named.

co′dex, n., a manuscript volume.

cod′fish, n., a cod.

codg′er, n., an eccentric, old person.

codices, n., pl. of codex.

cod′icil, n., a later note modifying or explaining a will.

codicil′lary, adj., rel. to a codicil.

codifica'tion, *n.,* the systematizing of laws already in existence.

cod'ified, *p.p.,* codify.

cod'ifier, *n.,* one who codifies.

cod'ify, *v.t.,* to reduce existing enactments to a code.

cod'ifying, *pr.p.,* codify.

codil'la, *n.,* part of the flax or hemp.

codille', *n.,* a term used in the game of ombre.

cod'ling, *n.,* a young cod; a cooking apple.

cod'liver-oil, *n.,* medicinal oil obtained from the liver of cod.

co'don, *n.,* a bell; the mouth of a trumpet.

cod'piece, *n.,* the bagged appendage to the front of men's breeches.

co'ed, *n.,* a female co-educational student (*colloq.*).

co'ed'ucate, *v.t.,* to educate both sexes together.

coeduca'tion, *n.,* the education of both sexes together.

co'educa'tional, *adj.,* rel. to coeducation.

co'educa'tionalism, *n.,* the system of co-education.

co'educa'tionist, *n.,* one who favours coeducation.

co-effi'ciency, *n.,* combined efficiency.

coeffi'cient, *adj.,* co-operative, working with another; *n.,* a number placed commonly before another to multiply it.

coel'acanth, *adj.* and *n.,* (a fish) having a hollow spine.

coe'liac, *adj.,* rel. to the abdomen.

coe'liostat, *n.,* a clock-driven reflector used in astronomy.

coeliot'omy, *n.,* an operation on the abdomen.

coemp'tion, *n.,* an old form of marriage by mutual purchase.

coen'obite, *n.,* one who lives a communal life, a monk, a nun. (Also *cenobite.*)

coenobit'ical, *adj.,* rel. to a coenobite.

coenog'amy, *n.,* a community of wives and husbands.

coe'qual, *adj.,* jointly equal.

coequal'ity, *n.,* the state of being coequal.

coerce', *v.t.,* to compel, to force.

coerced', *p.p.,* coerce.

coer'cible, *adj.,* able to be coerced.

coer'cibleness, *n.,* the state of being coercible.

coer'cibly, *adv.,* in a coercible way.

coerc'ing, *pr.p.,* coerce.

coer'cion, *n.,* the act of coercing.

coer'cive, *adj.,* producing coercion.

coer'cively, *adv.,* in a coercive way; by restraint.

coessen'tial, *adj.,* having the same essence.

coessential'ity, *n.,* the quality or state of being coessential.

coeter'nal, *adj.,* equally eternal.

coeter'nity, *n.,* equal eternity.

coe'val, *adj.,* of the same generation, contemporary.

co-exec'utor, *n.,* a joint executor.

co-exec'utrix, *n.,* i.q. co-executor (*fem.*).

coexist', *v.i.,* to exist together.

coexist'ed, *p.p.,* co-exist.

coexist'ence, *n.,* the state or fact of co-existing.

coexist'ent, *adj.,* i.q. co-existing.

coexist'ing, *adj.,* existing together; *pr.p.,* co-exist.

coextend', *v.i.,* to be equally extensive.

coextend'ed, *p.p.,* co-extend.

coextend'ing, *adj.,* equally extensive; *pr.p.,* co-extend.

coexten'sion, *n.,* the act or state of coextending.

coexten'sive, *adj.,* i.q. co-extending.

cof'fee, *n.,* the seeds of the coffee plant; the beverage made from them.

cof'fee-house, *n.,* a place of refreshment selling coffee.

cof'fee-mill, *n.,* a machine for grinding coffee beans.

cof'feepot, *n.,* a pot from which coffee is served.

cof'fer, *n.,* a chest; a sunk panel; *v.t.,* to shut in a chest.

cof'fer-dam, *n.,* a temporary dam.

cof'fered, *adj.,* having coffers; *p.p.,* coffer.

cof'ferer, *n.,* a treasurer.

cof'fin, *n.,* a chest to hold a dead body; *v.t.,* to place in a coffin.

cof'fined, *p.p.,* coffin.

cof'finite, *n.,* a uranium-yielding ore.

coff'le, *n.,* a train of beasts, slaves, etc., fastened together.

cof'fret, *n.,* a small casket.

cog, *n.,* a tooth on a wheel's surface; a projecting catch; a trick; a small fishing vessel; *v.t.,* to supply with cogs; to load (dice); to cheat.

co'gency, *n.,* the state or quality of being cogent.

co'gent, *adj.,* compelling, convincing.

co'gently, *adv.,* in a cogent way.

cogged, *adj.,* having cogs; *p.p.,* cog.

cog'ger, *n.,* one who builds with mine-props.

cog'ging, *pr.p.,* cog.

cog'itable, *adj.,* able to be cogitated.

cog'itate, *v.t.,* to think over; *v.i.,* to reflect, to meditate.

cog'itated, *p.p.,* cogitate.

cog'itating, *pr.p.,* cogitate.

cogita'tion, *n.,* the act or state of cogitating.

cog'itative, *adj.,* given to reflecting.

co'gnac, *n.,* a fine French brandy.

cog'nate, *adj.,* of the same family or kind; allied.

cog'nateness, *n.,* the quality of being cognate.

cogna'tion, *n.,* a family relationship.

cogni'tion, *n.* clear apprehension, knowledge.

cog'nitive, *adj.,* rel. to cognition.

cog'nitum, *n.,* an object of cognition.

cog'nizable, *adj.,* able to be apprehended.

cog'nizance, *n.,* knowledge, recognition; an heraldic badge.

cog'nizant, *adj.,* perceiving, taking notice.

cog'nize, *v.t.,* to perceive, to recognize.

cog'nized, *p.p.,* cognize.

cognizee', n., one accepting the acknowledgment of a fine of lands.

cog'nizing, pr.p., cognize.

cog'nizor, n., one acknowledging a fine of lands.

cogno'men, n., a surname, a nickname.

cognom'inal, adj., rel. to a cognomen; of the same name.

cognoscente, n., a connoisseur (It.).

cognos'cible, adj., capable of being known.

cog-wheel, n., a cogged or toothed wheel.

cohab'it, v.i., to live together as married.

cohab'itant, n., one who lives in the same place with another.

cohabita'tion, n., the act or state of cohabiting.

cohab'ited, p.p., cohabit.

cohab'iter, n., i.q. cohabitant.

cohab'iting, pr.p., cohabit.

coheir', n., a joint heir.

coheir'ess, n., the fem. of coheir.

cohere', v.i., to stick together.

cohered', p.p., cohere.

coher'ence, n., the act or state of cohering.

coher'ency, n., a tendency to cohere; consistency.

coher'ent, adj., sticking together; logically consistent.

coher'ently, adv., in a coherent way.

coher'er, n., an instrument for detecting electric waves.

coher'ing, pr.p., cohere.

cohesibil'ity, n., the state of being cohesible.

cohe'sible, adj., able to cohere.

cohe'sion, n., the act or state of cohering.

cohe'sive, adj., holding together well.

cohe'siveness, n., the state of being cohesive.

cohib'it, v.t., to restrain.

cohib'ited, p.p., cohibit.

cohib'iting, pr.p., cohibit.

cohibi'tion, n., the act or effect of cohibiting.

co'hobate, v.t., to redistil.

co'hort, n., the tenth part of a Roman legion.

coif, n., a form of headgear, particularly as worn by serjeants-at-law and by women.

coifed, adj., wearing a coif.

coiffeur', n., a hairdresser (Fr.).

coiffeuse', n., a female hairdresser (Fr.).

coiffure', n., a headdressing; the mode of dressing the hair (Fr.).

coif'fured, adj., arranged in a coiffure.

coign(e), n., a corner; a corner-stone.

coil, n., a rope gathered into a ring; a stir, a noise; an electrical apparatus; v.i. and t., to wind round.

coiled, p.p., coil.

coil'ing, pr.p., coil.

coin, n., stamped money; v.t., to stamp metal as money; to invent.

coin'age, n., the process of stamping money; the money stamped; an invention.

coincide', v.i., to occur simultaneously; to agree exactly; to lie on the same line or point.

coincid'ed, p.p., coincide.

coin'cidence, n., the act of coinciding; an unforeseen, simultaneous occurrence.

coin'cident, adj., simultaneously occurring.

coinciden'tal, adj., of the nature of (a) coincidence.

coin'cidentally, adv., i.q. coincidently.

coin'cidently, adv., simultaneously.

coincid'ing, pr.p., coincide.

coindica'tion, n., a supplementary indication.

coined, p.p., coin.

coin'er, n., one who makes coins, esp. spurious ones.

co-inhab'itant, n., a fellow-dweller.

co-inhe'ritor, n., a joint heir.

coin'ing, pr.p., coin.

coinstantan'eous, adj., exactly at the same moment.

co-insure', v., to insure jointly.

coir, n., coconut fibre.

coit, n., i.q. quoit.

coi'tion, n., copulation, conjunction.

coju'ror, n., a fellow-juryman.

coke, n., coal residue after the withdrawal of the gas; v.t., to turn into coke.

coked, p.p., coke.

co'kernut, n., the popular form of the name coconut.

co'kery, n., a coke furnace.

cok'ing, pr.p., coke.

co'ky, adj., resembling coke.

col, n., a depression in a mountain-chain.

col'a, k-, n., a West African tree.

col'ander, n., a domestic strainer.

co-lat'itude, n., a complement of latitude; the difference between it and 90°.

colcann'on, n., an Irish dish of cabbage and potatoes.

col'chicum, n., the meadow saffron.

col'cothar, n., an iron peroxide.

cold, adj., without heat; passionless; of a bluish tone; n., the absence of heat; the sensation of chill; a virus infection of the respiratory and muscular systems.

cold'-blooded, adj., having blood of a low temperature; cruel.

cold'-chisel, n., a highly-tempered chisel for cutting cold metal.

cold'er, adj., comp. of cold.

cold'est, adj., super. of cold.

cold'-frame', n., an unheated, plant frame.

cold'hearted, adj., without natural affection, cruel.

cold'ish, adj., somewhat cold.

cold'ly, adv., in a cold way.

cold'ness, n., the state of being cold; indifference.

cold-short, adj., liable to crack or break when cold; brittle.

cold'-shoulder, v.t., to neglect; to treat coldly.

cold-war, *n.,* an intense struggle for supremacy short of actual war; brinkmanship.

cole, *n.,* a general name for cabbage-plants.

cole'mouse, *n., i.q.* coalmouse.

Coleop'tera, *n. pl.,* insects with sheathed wings; beetles.

coleop'terist, *n.,* a collector of Coleoptera.

coleop'terous, *adj.,* having sheathed wings.

cole'seed, *n.,* rape-seed.

cole'slaw, *n.,* salad made of sliced cabbage.

col'et, *n.,* an acolyte.

cole'wort, *n.,* a young cabbage.

col'ic, *adj.,* rel. to the bowels; *n.,* violent pain of the bowels.

col'icky, *adj.,* rel. to colic.

col'in, *n.,* a variety of quail.

Colise'um, *n.,* the great Flavian amphitheatre in Rome. (Also *Colosseum.*)

colit'is, *n.,* inflammation of the colon lining.

collab'orate, *v.t.,* to join with someone in a piece of work.

collab'orated, *p.p.,* collaborate.

collab'orating, *pr.p.,* collaborate.

collabora'tion, *n.,* the act of collaborating.

collab'orator, *n.,* one who collaborates.

collae'mia, *n.,* a glutinous blood condition.

collage', *n.,* a picture made from pasted scraps (*Fr.*).

collaps'able, *adj., i.q.* collapsible.

collapse', *n.,* a breakdown, a falling down; failure; *v.i.,* to fall down, to break down, to fail.

collapsed, *p.p.,* collapse.

collaps'ible, *adj.,* constructed so that collapse is possible. (Also *collapsable.*)

collaps'ing, *pr.p.,* collapse.

col'lar, *n.,* something worn round the neck; *v.t.,* to seize by the neck.

col'lared, *p.p.,* collar.

col'laret(te), *n.,* a fichu; an ornamental collar.

col'laring, *pr.p.,* collar.

colla'table, *adj.,* able to be collated.

collate', *v.t.,* to compare a text or texts critically; to gather separate pieces of a whole in the right order.

colla'ted, *p.p.,* collate.

collat'eral, *adj.,* side by side; subsidiary; not in direct descent; *n.,* assets pledged as security.

collat'erally, *adv.,* in a parallel manner.

collat'eralness, *n.,* the state of being collateral.

collat'ing, *pr.p.,* collate.

colla'tion, *n.,* the act of collating; a light repast.

colla'tive, *adj.,* pert. to collation.

colla'tor, *n.,* one who collates.

col'league, *n.,* an associate in an office, employment or undertaking.

col'lect, *n.,* a short, liturgical prayer.

collect', *v.i.,* to assemble together; *v.t.,* to gather together, to assemble.

collect'able, *adj.,* able to be collected. (Also *collectible.*)

collecta'nea, *n. pl.,* selected passages from books.

collecta'neous, *adj.,* selected.

collect'ed, *adj.,* self-possessed; *p.p.,* collect.

collect'edly, *adv.,* with self-possession.

collect'edness, *n.,* a self-possessed attitude.

collect'ible, *adj., i.q.* collectable.

collect'ing, *pr.p.,* collect.

collec'tion, *n.,* the act or state of collecting; a number of things collected together; a crowd; the gathering of alms; a college examination.

collect'ive, *adj.,* taken as a whole or in bulk.

collect'ively, *adv.,* altogether.

collect'iveness, *n.,* the state of being collective.

collect'ivism, *n.,* the political theory of

collective ownership by the state.

collectiviza'tion, *n.,* the organization and establishment in accordance with the principles of collectivism.

collect'ivize, *v.t.,* to establish collectivism.

collect'or, *n.,* one who collects.

collect'orate, *n.,* a collector's district.

collect'orship, *n.,* the office of a collector.

col'leen, *n.,* a girl (*Irish*).

col'lege, *n.,* a society, a community; its hall or house of residence.

coll'eger, *n.,* one of seventy foundation scholars at Eton.

colle'gial, *adj.,* rel. to a college.

colle'gian, *n.,* the member of a college.

colle'giate, *adj.,* rel. to a college; corporately established.

col'let, *n.,* the part of a ring in which the stone is set.

collide', *v.i.,* to strike up against.

colli'ded, *p.p.,* collide.

colli'ding, *pr.p.,* collide.

col'lie, *n.,* a sheep-dog. (Also *colly.*)

col'lier, *n.,* one who hews coal; a coaling vessel.

col'liery, *n.,* a coal mine.

col'ligate, *v.t.,* to fasten together.

col'ligated, *p.p.,* colligate.

col'ligating, *pr.p.,* colligate.

colliga'tion, *n.,* the act of fastening together.

col'limate, *v.t.,* to make parallel.

col'limated, *p.p.,* collimate.

col'limating, *pr.p.,* collimate.

collima'tion, *n.,* the act of collimating.

coll'imator, *n.,* a small attached telescope for collimating an instrument.

collin'ear, *adj.,* in the same straight line.

collinea'tion, *n.,* the act or state of bringing into line.

colliq'uative, *adj.,* marked by excessive purging.

colli'sion, *n.,* the act of colliding, concussion.

col'locate, *v.t.*, to place or arrange together.

col'located, *p.p.*, collocate.

col'locating, *pr.p.*, collocate.

colloca'tion, *n.*, the act or state of collocating.

collocu'tion, *n.*, the act of making a colloquy.

coll'ocutor, *n.*, a talker in a dialogue.

collo'dion, *n.*, soluble gun-cotton treated with ether.

collo'dionize, *v.t.*, to treat with collodion.

collog'raphy, *n.*, printing from gelatine, esp. by heliotypy or collotypy.

collogue', *v.i.*, to talk in secret; to conspire.

col'loid, *adj.*, glue-like; *n.*, a glue-like substance.

col'lop, *n.*, a slice (of meat).

collo'quial, *adj.*, in the ordinary style of speech; rel. to conversation.

collo'quialism, *n.*, a colloquial expression.

col'loquist, *n.*, one who engages in a colloquy.

col'loquy, *n.*, a conversation.

col'lotype, *n.*, a photograph produced on gelatine; the collotype process; *v.t.*, to reproduce in collotype.

col'lotypy, *n.*, the collotype process.

collude', *v.i.*, to be a partner to a collusion.

collu'ded, *p.p.*, collude.

collu'der, *n.*, one who colludes.

collu'ding, *pr.p.*, collude.

collu'sion, *n.*, a secret agreement to deceive.

collu'sive, *adj.*, fraudulently agreed, deceitful.

collu'sively, *adv.*, with collusion.

col'ly, *n.*, *i.q.* collie.

colly'ria, *n.*, pl. of collyrium.

colly'rium, *n.*, eye lotion; a suppository.

coll'ywobbles, *n. pl.*, a nervous stomachache (*colloq.*).

col'ocynth, *n.*, a purgative medicine.

colocyn'thin, *adj.*, rel. to colocynth.

co'lon, *n.*, the large intestine; a punctuation mark (:).

colon'ate, *n.*, the serf system in the later Roman Empire.

col'onel, *n.*, the head of a regiment.

col'onelcy, *n.*, a colonel's rank and office.

colonelship, *n.*, the office of being a colonel.

colo'nial, *adj.*, rel. to a colony.

colon'ialism, *n.*, the establishment of colonies.

col'onist, *n.*, a settler in a colony.

coloniza'tion, *n.*, the act or effect of colonizing.

coloniza'tionist, *n.*, an advocate of colonizing.

col'onize, *v.t.*, to form into a colony.

col'onized, *p.p.*, colonize.

col'onizer, *n.*, one who establishes a colony; a colonist.

col'onizing, *pr.p.*, colonize.

colonnade', *n.*, a row of columns.

col'ony, *n.*, a region controlled and exploited by another country.

col'ophon, *n.*, a device to mark the end of, or a break in, a book.

coloph'ony, *n.*, a dark resin produced from turpentine.

Colora'do beetle, *n.*, a yellow black-striped beetle which destroys potatoes.

colo(u)ra'tion, *n.*, the act or state of colouring.

coloratu'ra, *n.*, florid ornaments in vocal music; a singer in this style.

col'orature, *n.*, colour in music.

colorif'ic, *adj.*, producing colour.

colorim'eter, *n.*, an instrument for comparing colour.

colos'sal, *adj.*, gigantic, huge.

Colosse'um, *n.*, *i.q.* Coliseum.

Colos'sian, *adj.*, pert. to the Greek city of Colosse; pert. to a colossus.

Colos'sus, *n.*, the gigantic statue at Rhodes.

colot'omy, *n.*, an incision to open the colon.

col'our, *n.*, a tint, a tinge, a dye; a pretext; a flag; *v.t.*, to tint, to impart colour to; *v.i.*, to show colour.

col'ourable, *adj.*, plausible, resembling.

col'ourableness, *n.*, the quality of being colourable.

col'ourably, *adv.*, in a colourable way.

col'our-blind, *adj.*, unable to distinguish colours.

col'our-cast, *n.*, a television broadcast in colour.

col'oured, *adj.*, having colour; dark-complexioned; *p.p.*, colour.

col'ourful, *adj.*, full of colour.

col'ouring, *n.*, the act or art of applying colour; the colour applied; *pr.p.*, colour.

col'ourist, *n.*, an artist skilled in colouring.

col'ourless, *adj.*, without colour, pale, white.

col'oury, *adj.*, having the colour that goes with good quality of hops, coffee, etc.

col'portage, *n.*, the distribution of books.

col'porteur, *n.*, one who distributes books.

Colt, *n.*, a revolver; an automatic gun or pistol.

colt, *n.*, a young male horse; an untrained youth; *v.t.*, to punish with a colt or rope's end.

colt'ish, *adj.*, like a colt, untamed.

colt'er, *i.q.* coulter.

colts'foot, *n.*, a medicinal plant.

col'uber, *n.*, a serpent (*Lat.*).

col'ubrine, *adj.*, rel. to serpents.

colum'ba, *n.*, a pigeon; a dove.

columba'rium, *n.*, a pigeon-house; dovecot; a set of niches for cinerary urns.

col'umbary, *n.*, *i.q.* columbarium.

Colum'bian, *adj.*, pert. to Columbus, Columbia or the U.S.A.

colum'bic, *adj.*, pert. to columbium.

colum'bine, *n.*, a female pantomime dancer; a perennial plant.

colum'bium, *n.*, a dark grey metallic element.

columel'la, *n.*, a central column.

col'umn, *n.*, a cylindrical pillar; a large body of troops; a vertical row of figures; a division of a page.

colum'nar, adj., rel. to columns.

col'umned, adj., having columns.

columnia'tion, n., the arrangement of colums.

col'umnist, n., one who conducts a column in a newspaper.

colure', n., the name of the two great circles in the celestial sphere.

col'za-oil, n., oil from the seeds of a certain cabbage.

co'ma, n., complete insensibility.

co'mate, n., hairy; (written co-mate it means companion).

co'matose, adj., in a stupor, insensible.

comb, n., an instrument for adjusting the hair; a cock's crest; v.t., to arrange the hair with a comb.

com'bat, n., a fight, a contest; v.t., to fight against.

com'batable, adj., able to be combated.

com'batant, n., one who combats.

com'bated, p.p., combat.

com'bater, n., i.q. combatant.

com'bating, pr.p., combat.

com'bative, adj., pugnacious, fond of fighting.

com'bativeness, n., pugnacity.

combe, n., i.q. coomb.

combed, p.p., comb.

comb'er, n., anything that combs; a rolling breaker.

combin'able, adj., able to be combined.

combina'tion, n., the act or effect of combining; a union.

combina'tions, n. pl., a single undergarment for the body, the arms and the legs.

com'bine, n., an association of business firms.

combine', v.t., to join or associate together; v.i., to unite, to agree.

combined', p.p., combine.

combi'ner, n., one who combines.

comb'ing, pr.p., comb.

comb'ings, n., combed off hairs.

combin'ing, pr.p., combine.

comb'less, adj., lacking a comb.

combust', adj., burnt.

combustibil'ity, n., the state or quality of being combustible.

combus'tible, adj., inflammable; n., anything inflammable.

combus'tibleness, n., i.q. combustibility.

combus'tion, n., the act of burning; the condition of being burnt.

combus'tive, adj., inflammatory.

come, v.i., to draw near, to arrive, to happen; v.t., to play the part of.

come-at'-able, adj., accessible.

come'back, n., a revival.

come'dian, n., a writer or player of comedies.

comédienne', n., a comedy actress (Fr.).

comediet'ta, n., a short comedy.

com'edist, n., a writer of comedies.

come'down, n., a fall, a drop.

com'edy, n., a comic drama.

come'lier, adj., comp. of comely.

come'liest, adj., super. of comely.

come'lily, adv., in a comely way.

come'liness, n., beauty, grace.

comely, adj., beautiful, graceful.

com'er, n., one who comes.

comes'tible, adj., eatable; n., an article of food.

com'et, n., a solar satellite with a luminous trail.

cometa'rium, n., an instrument to measure a comet's motion.

com'etary, adj., rel. to a comet.

comet'ic, adj., i.q. cometary.

cometog'raphy, n., the study of comets.

com'fit, n., a dry, sweetmeat.

com'fiture, n., i.q. comfit.

com'fort, n., solace, support, warmth; v.t., to cheer, to warm, to solace.

com'fortable, adj., imparting comfort, in a state of ease.

com'fortableness, n., the quality of being comfortable.

com'fortably, adv., in a comfortable way.

com'forted, p.p., comfort.

com'forter, n., one who, or anything that, comforts; a neckwrap, a padded quilt.

com'forting, pr.p., comfort.

com'fortless, adj., without comfort, dreary.

com'frey, n., a hairy plant.

com'fy, adj., comfortable (colloq.) (abbrev.).

com'ic, adj., ludicrous, exciting mirth.

com'ical, adj., i.q. comic.

comical'ity, n., ludicrousness, funniness.

com'ically, adv., in a comical way.

com'icalness, n., i.q. comicality.

Com'inform, n., the Communist Information Bureau, replacing the Comintern in 1947.

com'ing, n., an arrival; pr.p., come.

Com'intern, n., the Communist International, or Third International.

com'ity, n., courtesy, civility.

com'ma, n., a punctuation mark (,). In music, a very small interval.

command', n., an order; a superior position, an advantage; the charge of a naval or military force; v.t., to order, to lead.

commandant', n., an officer in command.

command'atory, adj., mandatory.

command'ed, p.p., command.

commandeer', v.t., to seize under military law.

commandeered', p.p., commandeer.

commandeer'ing, pr.p., commandeer.

command'er, n., one who commands; a naval officer so named.

command'ery, n., a commander's office or sphere of jurisdiction; the rank of a Knight Commander; the name of a branch house of the Knights Templars.

_...or_ command'ing, *adj.*, in a position of superiority, authoritative; *pr.p.*, command.

_...or_ command'ingly, *adv.*, in a commanding way.

_...or_ command'ment, *n.*, a command, a precept, a law.

_...or_ comman'do, *n.*, a specialized military force.

commat'ic, *adj.*, terse, concise.

com'matism, *n.*, terseness, conciseness.

commeas'urable, *adj.*, commensurate.

comme il faut, *adj.*, well-bred (*Fr.*).

commem'orable, *adj.*, worthy of commemoration.

commem'orate, *v.t.*, to celebrate the memory of.

commem'orated, *p.p.*, commemorate.

commem'orating, *pr.p.*, commemorate.

commemora'tion, *n.*, the act of commemorating.

commem'orative, *adj.*, celebrating the memory of.

commem'orator, *n.*, one who commemorates.

commem'oratory, *adj.*, *i.q.* commemorative.

commence', *v.t.* and *i.*, to begin.

commenced', *p.p.*, commence.

commence'ment, *n.*, a beginning; a university ceremony of granting degrees.

commenc'ing, *pr.p.*, commence.

commend', *v.t.*, to recommend, to entrust.

commend'able, *adj.*, worthy to be commended.

commend'ably, *adv.*, in a commendable way.

commen'dam, *n.*, a trust.

commenda'tion, *n.*, the act of commending, approval.

commen'datory, *adj.*, laudatory, approving.

commend'ed, *p.p.*, commend.

commend'ing, *pr.p.*, commend.

commen'sal, *adj.*, sharing the same table.

commensurabil'ity, *n.*, the quality of being commensurable.

commen'surable, *adj.*,

reducible to the same measure.

commen'surate, *adj.*, equal, proportionate.

commensura'tion, *n.*, the act of reducing to a common measure.

com'ment, *n.*, an annotation, an explanation; *v.i.*, to remark on, to make notes on.

com'mentary, *n.*, an exposition.

com'mentate, *v.i.*, to make comments; to review.

commenta'tion, *n.*, the act of commenting.

com'mentator, *n.*, an expositor, an annotator.

com'mented, *p.p.*, comment.

com'menter, *n.*, one who comments.

com'menting, *pr.p.*, comment.

commenti'tious, *adj.*, of the nature of a commentary.

com'merce, *n.*, trade, dealing, intercourse; *v.i.*, to have business intercourse.

commer'cial, *adj.*, rel. to trade and commerce.

commercialese', *n.*, commercial jargon.

commer'cialism, *n.*, commercial ways, the commercial spirit.

commer'cialize, *v.t.*, to make commercial.

commer'cialized, *p.p.*, commercialize.

commer'cializing, *pr.p.*, commercialize.

commer'cially, *adv.*, in the way of trade.

commère', *n.*, the fem. of compère (*Fr.*).

Comm'ie, *n.*, a Communist (*colloq.*) (*abbrev.*).

commina'tion, *n.*, a denunciation of sins and offences.

com'minatory, *adj.*, condemnatory.

commin'gle, *v.t.* and *i.*, to mingle together.

commin'gled, *p.p.*, commingle.

commin'gling, *pr.p.*, commingle.

com'minute, *adj.*, ground small; *v.t.*, to grind small, to pulverize.

com'minuted, *p.p.*, comminute.

com'minuting, *pr.p.*, comminute.

comminu'tion, *n.*, the act or state of comminuting.

commis'erate, *v.t.*, to

pity, to express sympathy.

commis'erated, *p.p.*, commiserate.

commis'erating, *pr.p.*, commiserate.

commisera'tion, *n.*, the act of commiserating.

commis'erative, *adj.*, pitiful, compassionate.

commis'erator, *n.*, one who commiserates.

commissar', *n.*, the head of a Soviet Government Department.

com'missa'rial, *adj.*, rel. to a commissary.

commissa'riat, *n.*, the supply department of an organization.

com'missary, *n.*, a person charged with a commission, a delegate; an ordnance officer with honorary rank.

com'missary-gen'eral, *n.*, the head of the commissariat.

commis'sion, *n.*, a charge, trust; the act of commissioning; a warrant; an appointment in the navy or the army; a body of commissioned persons; *v.t.*, to charge; to entrust.

commissionaire, *n.*, a light porter or messenger (*Fr.*).

commis'sioned, *p.p.*, commission.

commis'sioner, *n.*, a member of a commission.

commis'sionership, *n.*, the office of a commissioner.

commis'sioning, *pr.p.*, commission.

com'missure, *n.*, a seam, a point of union.

commit', *v.t.*, to entrust, to consign, to perpetrate, to send to gaol or trial.

commit'ment, *n.*, *i.q.* committal; an engagement, a pledge.

commit'tal, *n.*, the act of committing.

commit'ted, *p.p.*, commit.

commit'tee, *n.*, a body of persons dealing with a particular business.

committee', *n.*, a person appointed to the guardianship of another's property.

commit'ter, *n.*, one who commits.

commit'ting, *pr.p.*, commit.

commit'tor, *n.*, *i.q.* committer.

commix', *v.t.* and *i.*, to intermingle.

commixed', *p.p.*, commix.

commix'ing, *pr.p.*, commix.

commix'ture, *n.*, the act or result of intermingling or mixing together.

com'modate, *n.*, a form of loan, free of charge on return of loan undamaged.

commode', *n.*, a piece of furniture; a nightstool.

commo'dious, *adj.*, roomy, convenient, useful.

commo'diously, *adv.*, in a commodious way.

commo'diousness, *n.*, the quality of being commodious.

commod'ity, *n.*, something of use, an article of commerce; in *pl.*, goods, wares.

com'modore, *n.*, the commander of a naval squadron.

com'mon, *adj.*, belonging to two or more persons; vulgar; *n.*, an open space that is common property.

com'monable, *adj.*, having common pasturage rights.

com'monage, *n.*, pasturage rights.

com'monalty, *n.*, the collective people.

com'mon coun'cil, *n.*, the municipal body.

com'moner, *adj.*, *comp.* of common; *n.*, anyone not a peer; a M.P.; one who has joint rights in common lands; academically one who is admitted to commons but is not on the foundation.

com'monest, *adj.*, *super.* of common.

comm'oney, *n.*, an inferior playing-marble.

com'mon law, *n.*, English unwritten law.

com'monly, *adv.*, generally, usually, in common.

com'monness, *n.*, the quality of being common.

com'monplace, *adj.*, ordinary; *n.*, an obvious saying; anything ordinary.

com'monplace-book, *n.*, a book in which memorable quotations or extracts are recorded.

com'mons, *n.*, the name for food in the Oxford colleges; the common people of England; the House of Commons.

com'monsense, *adj.*, marked by ordinary good sense; *n.*, sound sense, judgment.

com'monweal, *n.*, the well-being of the community; the commonwealth.

Commonwealth, *n.*, the group of nations having ties with the United Kingdom and common interests in world affairs.

com'monwealth, *n.*, a body politic.

com'morancy, *n.*, residence.

commo'tion, *n.*, tumult, disturbance.

commove', *v.t.*, to move violently; to excite.

commoved', *p.p.*, commove.

commov'ing, *pr.p.*, commove.

com'munal, *adj.*, rel. to a commune; for common use.

comm'unalism, *n.*, the theory of government by local autonomy.

com'munalize, *v.t.*, to make into a commune.

com'munalized, *p.p.*, communalize.

com'munalizing, *pr.p.*, communalize.

com'mune, *n.*, a self-governing community.

commune', *v.i.*, to hold intercourse.

communed', *p.p.*, commune.

communicabil'ity, *n.*, the state of being communicable.

commu'nicable, *adj.*, able to be communicated.

commu'nicant, *adj.*, one who imparts information; *n.*, a receiver of Holy Communion.

commu'nicate, *v.t.*, to impart, to reveal; *v.i.*, to share; to receive the Sacrament.

commu'nicated, *p.p.*, communicate.

commu'nicating, *pr.p.*, communicate.

communica'tion, *n.*, the act of communicating; the means of getting from place to place; news.

commu'nicative, *adj.*, able and ready to impart information.

commu'nicator, *n.*, anything, or anyone, that communicates.

commu'nicatory, *adj.*, imparting information; connecting.

commu'ning, *pr.p.*, commune.

commun'ion, *n.*, intercourse, fellowship, a religious body; the common name for the eucharistic service.

commun'ionist, *n.*, an adherent of close, open communion.

commu'niqué, *n.*, an official report (*Fr.*).

com'munism, *n.*, political doctrine and practice of total socialism.

com'munist, *n.*, an upholder of communism.

communis'tic, *adj.*, rel. to communism.

communitar'ian, *n.*, a member of a communistic community.

commu'nity, *n.*, a sharing; a common society; a religious corporation.

com'munize, *v.t.*, to make property public.

commutabil'ity, *n.*, the quality of being commutable.

commu'table, *adj.*, able to be commuted.

commuta'tion, *n.*, the act of commuting.

commu'tative, *adj.*, rel. to commutation.

com'mutator, *n.*, a contrivance for altering the course of an electrical current.

commute', *v.t.*, to exchange, to buy off an obligation; to hold a season ticket.

commu'ted, *p.p.*, commute.

commu'ter, *n.*, one who commutes.

commu'ting, *pr.p.*, commute.

comose', *adj.*, hairy; downy.

comp., *n.*, a compositor (*colloq.*) (*abbrev.*).

compact', *adj.*, pressed close, solid; *v.t.*, to pack tightly, to press closely.

com'pact, *n.*, an agreement; a small, flat vanity case.

compact'ed, *p.p.*, compact.

compact'edly, *adv.*, compactly.

compact'ing, *pr.p.*, compact.

compac'tion, *n.,* the state of being compacted.

compact'ly, *adv.,* closely, solidly.

compact'ness, *n.,* the quality of being compact.

compa'ges, *n.,* a structure of united parts; a joint (*Lat.*).

compag'inate, *v.t.,* to knit together.

compag'inated, *p.p.,* compaginate.

compag'inating, *pr.p.,* compaginate.

compagina'tion, *n.,* the state of being compaginated.

compan'ion, *adj.,* attendant; *n.,* an associate, a comrade; the shelter over the ship's ladder; *v.t.,* to accompany.

compan'ionable, *adj.,* sociable, agreeable.

compan'ionless, *adj.,* without a companion.

compan'ionship, *n.,* the society of a comrade.

companion-way, *n.,* a communicating stairway and passage in a ship.

com'pany, *n.,* an assembly, a society, fellowship; a trading firm, a crew, part of a regiment; *v.i.,* to associate with.

com'parability, *n.,* the ability to be compared.

com'parable, *adj.,* able to be compared.

compar'ative, *adj.,* judged or measured by comparison; not positive; *n.,* the comparative degree.

compar'atively, *adv.,* by comparison; not positively.

compare', *n.,* comparison; *v.t.,* to estimate one thing by reference to another; to examine; to form the degrees of comparison.

compared', *p.p.,* compare.

compar'er, *n.,* one who compares.

compar'ing, *pr.p.,* compare.

compar'ison, *n.,* the act of comparing; a comparative estimate.

compart', *v.t.,* to subdivide.

compart'ed, *p.p.,* compart.

compart'ing, *pr.p.,* compart.

compart'ment, *n.,* a subdivision; a section of a railway carriage.

com'pass, *n.,* a circuit; an enclosed space; capacity; a magnetic instrument determining the north; in *pl.,* instruments for drawing and dividing circles; *v.t.,* to achieve, to effect, to encircle.

com'passable, *adj.,* able to be compassed.

com'passed, *p.p.,* compass.

com'passes, *n. pl., i.q.* compass.

com'passing, *pr.p.,* compass.

compas'sion, *n.,* pity, sympathy.

compas'sionate, *adj.,* pitiful, sympathetic.

compas'sionate, *v.t.,* to feel pity for.

compas'sionated, *p.p.,* compassionate.

compas'sionately, *adv.,* with compassion.

compas'sionateness, *n.,* the quality of being compassionate.

compas'sionating, *pr.p.,* compassionate.

compatibil'ity, *n.,* the quality of being compatible.

compat'ible, *adj.,* consistent with, suitable.

compat'ibleness, *n., i.q.* compatibility.

compat'ibly, *adv.,* consistently, agreeably.

compat'riot, *n.,* a fellow-countryman.

compat'riotism, *n.,* the quality of fellow-countrymanship.

compeer', *n.,* an equal; a comrade; an associate.

compel', *v.i.,* to force, to drive.

compel'lable, *adj.,* able to be compelled.

compella'tion, *n.,* the act of addressing; a form of address.

compelled', *p.p.,* compel.

compel'ler, *n.,* anything, or anyone, that compels.

compel'ling, *pr.p.,* compel.

com'pend, *n.,* an abridgment.

compen'dious, *adj.,* summarized, abridged.

compen'diously, *adv.,* succinctly.

compen'diousness, *n.,* the quality of being compendious.

compen'dium, *n.,* an abridgment, a summary; an assembly of related objects or tropics.

com'pensate, *v.t.,* to remunerate, to make amends for; *v.i.,* to make compensation.

com'pensated, *p.p.,* compensate.

com'pensating, *pr.p.,* compensate.

compensa'tion, *n.,* recompense, a setoff.

compen'sative, *adj.,* bringing recompense.

com'pensator, *n.,* one who compensates.

compen'satory, *adj., i.q.* compensative.

com'père, *n.,* one who acts as a liaison in an entertainment; *v.t.,* to act as compère (*Fr.*).

compete', *v.i.,* to contend in rivalry.

compet'ed, *p.p.,* compete.

com'petence, *n.,* ability, sufficiency.

com'petency, *n., i.q.* competence.

com'petent, *n.,* sufficient, qualified.

com'petently, *adv.,* in a competent way.

compet'ing, *pr.p.,* compete.

competi'tion, *n.,* the act of competing, rivalry.

compet'itive, *adj.,* rel. to competition.

compet'itor, *n.,* one who competes.

compila'tion, *n.,* the act or result of compiling.

compile', *v.t.,* to bring together materials.

compiled', *p.p.,* compile.

compi'ler, *n.,* one who compiles.

compi'ling, *pr.p.,* compile.

compla'cence, *n.,* civility, affableness, self-satisfaction.

compla'cency, *n., i.q.* complacence.

compla'cent, *adj.,* civil, affable; accepting without question.

compla'cently, *adv.,* in a complacent way.

complain', *v.i.,* to murmur, to grumble, to lament.

complain'ant, *n.,* a plaintiff.

complained', *p.p.,* complain.

complain'er, *n.,* one who complains.

complain'ing, *pr.p.,* complain.

complaint', *n.*, an accusation, a lament; an ailment.

complais'ance, *n.*, courtesy.

complais'ant, *adj.*, courteous, agreeable.

complais'antly, *adv.*, in a complaisant way.

com'plement, *n.*, the completion of a quantity or number; *v.t.*, to complete a number or quantity.

complemen'tal, *adj.*, *i.q.* complementary.

complemen'tary, *adj.*, completing a quantity or number.

complete', *adj.*, perfected, finished; *v.t.*, to perfect, to finish.

comple'ted, *p.p.*, complete.

complete'ly, *adv.*, entirely, wholly.

complete'ness, *n.*, the quality or state of being complete.

complet'ing, *pr.p.*, complete.

comple'tion, *n.*, the act or result of completing.

comple'tive, *adj.*, tending to completion.

comple'tory, *adj.*, *i.q.* completive.

com'plex, *adj.*, not simple, of many parts; *n.*, a number of buildings, objects or topics having a common purpose, different but interconnected.

complex'ion, *n.*, colour of the skin; an aspect.

complex'ional, *adj.*, rel. to the complexion.

complex'ioned, *adj.*, having a complexion.

complex'ity, *n.*, the state or quality of being complex.

com'plexness, *n.*, *i.q.* complexity.

complex'us, *n.*, the large muscle in the neck.

compli'able, *adj.*, *i.q.* compliant.

compli'ance, *n.*, an act of yielding; acquiescence.

compli'ant, *adj.*, ready to yield or acquiesce.

compli'antly, *adv.*, in a compliant way.

com'plicacy, *n.*, the state of being complicated.

com'plicate, *v.t.*, to involve, to entangle.

com'plicated, *adj.*, intricate; *p.p.*, complicate.

com'plicating, *pr.p.*, complicate.

complica'tion, *n.*, the act or result of complicating.

complic'ity, *n.*, the state of being an accomplice; an involvement.

complied', *p.p.*, comply.

compli'er, *n.*, one who complies.

com'pliment, *n.*, praise, flattery; *v.t.*, to praise, to flatter.

compliment'al, *adj.*, *i.q.* complimentary.

compliment'ary, *adj.*, flattering.

com'plimented, *p.p.*, compliment.

com'plimenter, *n.*, one who pays compliments.

com'plimenting, *pr.p.*, compliment.

com'plin, *n.*, the last religious office of the day.

com'pline, *n.*, *i.q.* complin.

complot, *n.*, a joint plot; *v.i.*, to join in a plot.

complot'ted, *p.p.*, complot.

complot'ter, *n.*, one who complots.

complot'ting, *pr.p.*, complot.

comply', *v.i.*, to yield, to acquiesce.

comply'ing, *pr.p.*, comply.

com'po, *n.*, a sort of concrete; a material used in printing.

compo'nent, *adj.*, forming a part; *n.*, an ingredient.

comport', *v.t.*, to conduct, to bear oneself; *v.i.*, to agree with.

comport'ed, *p.p.*, comport.

comport'ing, *pr.p.*, comport.

compose', *v.t.*, to put together, to write; to quiet; to arrange type.

composed', *adj.*, calm, self-possessed; *p.p.*, compose.

compo'sedly, *adv.*, calmly.

compo'sedness, *n.*, calmness, self-possession.

compo'ser, *n.*, one who composes a book or a piece of music.

compo'sing, *pr.p.*, compose.

com'posite, *adj.*, compound, made up of parts.

composi'tion, *n.*, the act or result of composing; an agreement, esp. for the acceptance

by one's creditors of a smaller amount than the debt.

compos'itive, *adj.*, compound.

compos'itively, *adv.*, in a compositive way.

compos'itor, *n.*, a typesetter.

compos mentis, sound of mind; quite sane (*Lat.*).

composs'ible, *adj.*, able to coexist (with).

com'post, *n.*, a land-fertilizing material of organic origin.

compo'sure, *n.*, calmness, sedateness.

compota'tion, *n.*, drinking in company.

com'potator, *n.*, a drinker in company.

com'pote, *n.*, stewed fruit.

compound', *v.t.*, to mix together; to settle; to condone; *v.i.*, to come to terms.

com'pound, *adj.*, containing a mixture; *n.*, a mixture; the grounds of an Indian house.

compound'able, *adj.*, able to be compounded.

compound'ed, *p.p.*, compound.

compound'er, *n.*, one who compounds.

compound'ing, *pr.p.*, compound.

comprador', *n.*, (in China) the chief agent in a European business house.

compreca'tion, *n.*, a sharing in prayer; praying together.

comprehend', *v.t.*, to comprise; to understand.

comprehend'ed, *p.p.*, comprehend.

comprehend'er, *n.*, one who comprehends.

comprehend'ing, *pr.p.*, comprehend.

comprehensibil'ity, *n.*, the state or quality of being comprehensible.

comprehen'sible, *adj.*, able to be understood.

comprehen'sibly, *adv.*, in a comprehensible way.

comprehen'sion, *n.*, the act or state of understanding.

comprehen'sive, *adj.*, embracing, full; inclusive of everything essential.

comprehen'sively, *adv.*, in a comprehensive way; fully.

comprehen'siveness, *n.*, the quality of being comprehensive.

compress', *v.t.*, to press together.

com'press, *n.*, a surgical pad.

compressed', *p.p.*, compress.

compressibil'ity, *n.*, the quality of being compressible.

compress'ible, *adj.*, able to be compressed.

compress'ibleness, *n.*, *i.q.* compressibility.

compress'ing, *pr.p.*, compress.

compres'sion, *n.*, the act or result of compressing.

compress'ive, *adj.*, compressing.

compress'or, *n.*, anything that compresses; a machine for producing power from compressed air.

compress'ure, *n.*, *i.q.* compression.

comprimar'ia, *n.*, a singer ranking with a prima donna.

compris'al, *n.*, the act of comprising.

comprise', *v.t.*, to contain, to include.

comprised', *p.p.*, comprise.

compris'ing, *pr.p.*, comprise.

com'promise, *n.*, a settlement by mutual concessions; *v.t.*, to involve in risk; to settle by mutual concessions; *v.i.*, to make a compromise.

com'promised, *p.p.*, compromise.

com'promiser, *n.*, one who compromises.

com'promising, *pr.p.*, compromise.

compromit', *v.t.*, to imperil, to compromise.

compromit'ted, *p.p.*, compromit.

compromit'ting, *pr.p.*, compromit.

comprovin'cial, *adj.*, belonging to the same province or archiepiscopal jurisdiction; *n.*, a person, esp. a bishop, of the same archiepiscopal province.

compt'ograph, *n.*, a machine for adding up figures.

comptoir', *n.*, a counting-house, a factory (*Fr.*).

comptom'eter, *n.*, an adding machine.

comptrol'ler, *n.*, an examiner of public accounts. (Also *controller*.)

compul'satory, *adj.*, for-, cible.

compul'sion, *n.*, the act of compelling; force.

compul'sionist, *n.*, a supporter of compulsory military service.

compul'sive, *adj.*, compelling.

compul'sively, *adv.*, with compulsion.

compul'siveness, *n.*, the quality of being compulsive.

compul'sorily, *adv.*, by compulsion.

compul'sory, *adj.*, using compulsion, obligatory.

compunc'tion, *n.*, remorse, contrition.

compunc'tious, *adj.*, feeling compunction.

compurga'tion, *n.*, a joint testimony to clear an accused person.

com'purgator, *n.*, one who testifies with others to clear an accused person.

compu'table, *adj.*, able to be computed.

computa'tion, *n.*, an estimate, a reckoning.

comput'ative, *adj.*, given to computation.

compute', *v.t.*, to estimate, to reckon.

compu'ted, *p.p.*, compute.

compu'ter, *n.*, one who computes; an electronic and mechanical device for numerical and other types of calculations.

compu'terize, *v.t.*, to record, or to calculate by computer.

compu'terized, *p.p.*, computerize.

compu'terizing, *pr.p.*, computerize.

compu'ters, *n.*, pl. of computer.

compu'ting, *pr.p.*, compute.

com'rade, *n.*, a companion.

com'radeship, *n.*, companionship.

Com'stockery, *n.*, prudery in art.

Com'tist, *adj.*, rel. to Comte and the positive philosophy; *n.*, a

follower of Comte, a positivist.

con, *v.t.*, to pursue, to study; *prep.*, short for Lat. *contra*, against; Italian word = with.

con'acre, *n.*, the letting of small pieces of crop land in Ireland.

con amor'e, *adv.*, zealously (*It.*).

cona'tion, *n.*, endeavour.

cona'tive, *adj.*, endeavouring.

cona'tus, *n.*, an attempt (*Lat.*).

conax'ial, *adj.*, having the same axis.

concam'erate, *v.t.*, to divide into chambers.

concat'enate, *v.t.*, to link together.

concat'enated, *p.p.*, concatenate.

concat'enating, *pr.p.*, concatenate.

concatena'tion, *n.*, the act of concatenating; a series.

con'cave, *adj.*, with a curved hollow.

con'caved, *adj.*, *i.q.* concave.

con'cavely, *adv.*, in a concave way.

con'caveness, *n.*, the quality or state of being concave.

concav'ity, *n.*, *i.q.*, concaveness.

conca'vo-con'vex, *adj.*, concave one side, convex the other.

conceal', *v.t.*, to hide, to cover.

conceal'able, *adj.*, able to be concealed.

concealed', *p.p.*, conceal.

conceal'er, *n.*, one who conceals.

conceal'ing, *pr.p.*, conceal.

conceal'ment, *n.*, the act of concealing; a hiding-place.

concede', *v.t.*, to grant, to give up.

conce'ded, *p.p.*, concede.

conce'ding, *pr.p.*, concede.

conceit', *n.*, a notion; a quaint idea; vanity.

conceit'ed, *adj.*, vain.

conceit'edly, *adv.*, in a vain way.

conceit'edness, *n.*, the quality of being conceited.

conceivabil'ity, *n.*, *i.q.* conceivableness.

conceiv'able, *adj.*, able to be conceived.

conceiv′ableness, *n.*, the quality of being conceivable.

conceiv′ably, *adv.*, in a conceivable way.

conceive′, *v.t.*, to think, to understand, to form in the mind or in the womb; *v.i.*, to think; to become pregnant.

conceived′, *p.p.*, conceive.

conceiv′er, *n.*, one who conceives.

conceiv′ing, *pr.p.*, conceive.

concel′ebrate, *v.i.*, to celebrate mass with ordaining bishop.

concel′ebra′tion, *n.*, the celebration of mass with ordaining bishop.

concent′, *n.*, a song in harmony.

concen′ter, *v.t.* and *i.*, *i.q.* concentre.

con′centrate, *v.t.*, to bring to a common centre; to apply fixedly; to condense; *v.i.*, to fix all one's attention.

con′centrated, *p.p.*, concentrate.

con′centrating, *pr.p.*, concentrate.

concentra′tion, *n.*, the act or quality of concentrating or being concentrated.

concen′trative, *adj.*, fixing (the mind) on one object.

concen′trativeness, *n.*, the quality of being concentrative.

con′centrator, *n.*, an apparatus for separating ore; an arrangement for narrowing the muzzle of a shot-gun.

concen′tre, *v.t.* and *i.*, to bring, or come, to the same centre.

concen′tric, *adj.*, having a common centre.

concen′trical, *adj.*, *i.q.* concentric.

concentric′ity, *n.*, the quality of being concentric.

con′cept, *n.*, an abstract conception.

concep′tacle, *n.*, that which contains; a follicle.

concep′tion, *n.*, the act of conceiving in the womb or in the mind; an idea.

concep′tive, *adj.*, capable of conception.

concep′tual, *adj.*, rel. to mental conceptions.

concep′tualism, *n.*, a theory that the mind is able to form for itself general ideas of persons and objects.

concep′tualize, *v.t.*, to form a concept of.

concep′tualized, *p.p.*, conceptualize.

concep′tualizing, *pr.p.*, conceptualize.

concern′, *n.*, business, solicitude; *v.t.*, to relate to, to interest, to perturb.

concerned′, *p.p.*, concern.

concern′edly, *adv.*, anxiously.

concern′ing, *pr.p.*, concern; *prep.*, with reference to.

concern′ment, *n.*, solicitude, business.

concert′, *v.t.*, to arrange in association with someone.

con′cert, *n.*, a musical entertainment; concord; union.

concertan′te, *adj.*, containing parts for solo instruments (*mus.*, *It.*).

concert′ed, *p.p.*, concert.

concerti′na, *n.*, a musical instrument with reeds activated by air.

concert′ing, *pr.p.*, concert.

concer′to, *n.*, a musical work for orchestra and solo instrument or instruments.

con′cert-pitch, *n.*, the standard musical pitch for concerts which is at least half a tone higher than generally.

conces′sion, *n.*, the act of conceding; something conceded; territorial and other rights conceded by a government to a foreigner.

concession(n)aire′, *n.*, the holder of a concession, grant, monopoly, etc.

conces′sionary, *adj.*, rel. to concession.

conces′sionist, *n.*, one who favours concession.

conces′sive, *adj.*, conceding.

conces′sory, *adj.*, *i.q.* concessive.

concett′ism, *n.*, the use of fanciful turns in literature.

conch, *n.*, a sea-shell.

con′cha, *n.*, the outer ear.

con′chate, *adj.*, shell-shaped.

Conchif′era, *n.* *pl.*, the class name of bivalve molluscs.

conchif′erous, *adj.*, pert. to the Conchifera.

con′chiform, *adj.*, *i.q.* conchate.

con′chite, *n.*, a fossil shell.

conchi′tis, *n.*, inflammation of the concha.

con′choid, *adj.*, curved like a shell; *n.*, a curve like a shell.

conchoi′dal, *adj.*, *i.q.* conchoid.

conecholog′ical, *adj.*, rel. to conchology.

conchol′ogist, *n.*, a student of conchology.

conchol′ogy, *n.*, the science of molluscs and shells.

conchom′eter, *n.*, an instrument for measuring shells.

con′chy, *n.*, a conscientious objector (abbrev.). (Also *conshie.*)

concierge′, *n.*, a doorkeeper (*Fr.*).

concil′iar, *adj.*, pert. to ecclesiastical councils.

concil′iate, *v.t.*, to win over, to reconcile.

concil′iated, *p.p.*, conciliate.

concil′iating, *pr.p.*, conciliate.

concilia′tion, *n.*, the act of conciliating.

concil′iator, *n.*, one who conciliates.

concil′iatory, *adj.*, tending to conciliation.

concin′nity, *n.*, agreeableness, elegance.

concise′, *adj.*, terse, brief.

concise′ly, *adv.*, tersely, briefly.

concise′ness, *n.*, terseness, brevity.

conci′sion, *n.*, a cutting; an abbreviation.

con′clave, *n.*, a private assembly.

conclude′, *v.t.*, to close, to end; to infer; to settle.

conclu′ded, *p.p.*, conclude.

conclud′er, *n.*, one who concludes.

conclu′ding, *pr.p.*, conclude.

conclu′sion, *n.*, the act of ending; an end; an inference.

conclu′sive, *adj.*, final, decisive.

conclu′sively, *adv.*, decisively; finally.

conclu'siveness, *n.*, the quality of being conclusive.

conclu'sory, *adj.*, *i.q.* conclusive.

concoct', *v.t.*, to mix with ingredients; to plot; to devise.

concoct'ed, *p.p.*, concoct.

concoct'er, *n.*, one who concocts.

concoct'ing, *pr.p.*, concoct.

concoc'tion, *n.*, the act or result of concocting.

concoc'tive, *adj.*, pert. to concocting; having the ability to digest.

concol'orous, *adj.*, of uniform colour.

concom'itance, *n.*, the state of being concomitant.

concom'itant, *adj.*, associated with, following, attendant; *n.*, an attendant circumstance.

con'cord, *n.*, harmony, agreement.

concord'ance, *n.*, an agreement; a dictionary of words and passages with reference marks.

concord'ant, *adj.*, agreeable to, in harmony.

concord'antly, *adv.*, agreeably, harmoniously.

concord'at, *n.*, a formal agreement between the Holy See and a secular power.

con'course, *n.*, an arrival together, a gathering, a crowd; a place designed for general assembly.

concres'cence, *n.*, a growing together.

concres'cent, *adj.*, growing together.

concres'cible, *adj.*, able to grow together.

con'crete, *adj.*, solid, real; *n.*, material for forming durable surfaces or packing of powdered chalk, sand and aggregate; *v.t.*, to solidify.

concre'ted, *adj.*, laid down with concrete; *p.p.*, concrete.

con'cretely, *adv.*, not abstractly.

concreteness, *n.*, the quality of being concrete.

concre'ting, *pr.p.*, concrete.

concre'tion, *n.*, the act of concreting; a solidified mass.

concre'tional, *adj.*, rel. to concretion.

concre'tionary, *adj.*, marked by concretions.

concre'tive, *adj.*, tending to concretion.

concre'tor, *n.*, an apparatus for solidifying cane-juice.

concu'binage, *n.*, cohabitation without marriage.

concu'binary, *adj.*, rel. to concubinage.

con'cubine, *n.*, an unmarried woman cohabiting with a man.

concu'bitancy, *n.*, the custom of obligatory marriage.

concu'bitant, *adj.*, rel. to concubitancy; *n.*, one subject to concubitancy.

concu'piscence, *n.*, the lust for sexual intercourse.

concu'piscent, *adj.*, having a strong desire for sexual intercourse.

concur', *v.i.*, to agree with, to coincide.

concurred', *p.p.*, concur.

concur'rence, *n.*, the act or result of concurring.

concur'rent, *adj.*, coincident, simultaneous, acting in conjunction.

concur'rently, *adv.*, simultaneously, jointly.

concur'ring, *pr.p.*, concur.

concuss', *v.t.*, to shake violently.

concus'sion, *n.*, a physical shock; the result of such a shock.

concus'sive, *adj.*, causing concussion.

condemn', *v.t.*, to find guilty, to censure.

condem'nable, *adj.*, worthy of condemnation.

condemna'tion, *n.*, the act of condemning; censure.

condem'natory, *adj.*, expressing condemnation.

condemned', *p.p.*, condemn.

condemn'er, *n.*, one who condemns.

condemn'ing, *pr.p.*, condemn.

condensabil'ity, *n.*, the state or quality of being condensable.

condens'able, *adj.*, able to be condensed.

condens'ate, *v.t.*, to compress.

condens'ated, *p.p.*, condensate.

condens'ating, *pr.p.*, condensate.

condensa'tion, *n.*, the act or result of condensing.

condens'ative, *adj.*, producing condensation.

condense', *v.t.*, to compress; to reduce by evaporation; *v.i.*, to become dense.

condensed', *p.p.*, condense.

condens'er, *n.*, an apparatus for condensing gases; a storer of electricity; a concentrating lens.

condens'ing, *pr.p.*, condense.

condescend', *v.i.*, to come down, to stoop, to deign.

condescend'ed, *p.p.*, condescend.

condescend'ing, *pr.p.*, condescend.

condescend'ingly, *adv.*, with condescension.

condescen'sion, *n.*, the act or state of condescending.

condign, *adj.*, thoroughly deserved.

condign'ly, *adv.*, deservedly.

condign'ness, *n.*, the quality of being condign.

con'diment, *n.*, a seasoning for food.

condi'tion, *n.*, a stipulation, a limiting circumstance, state, etc.; *v.t.*, to stipulate, to impose limitations, to predispose; to make fit.

condi'tional, *adj.*, depending on conditions.

condi'tionalism, *n.*, the doctrine of conditional survival after death.

condi'tionalist, *n.*, a believer in conditionalism.

condi'tionally, *adv.*, with limitations.

condi'tioned, *p.p.*, condition.

condi'tioner, *n.*, that which conditions.

condi'tioning, *adj.*, predisposing; *pr.p.*, condition.

condo'latory, *adj.*, conveying condolence.

condole', *v.i.*, to express sympathy with one in distress.

condoled', *p.p.*, condole.

condole'ment, *n.*, *i.q.* condolence.

condo'lence, *n.*, the act of condoling.

condo'ler, *n.*, one who condoles.

condo'ling, *pr.p.*, condole.

con'dom, *n.*, a contraceptive sheath.

condomin'ium, *n.*, the joint control of a state by other states.

condona'tion, *n.*, the act of condoning.

condone', *v.t.*, to pardon, to overlook.

condoned', *p.p.*, condone.

condon'ing, *pr.p.*, condone.

con'dor, *n.*, the great vulture of the Andes.

condottie're, *n.*, an Italian mercenary soldier.

conduce', *v.i.*, to promote an end, to contribute to.

conduced', *p.p.*, conduce.

conducibil'ity, *n.*, the quality of being conducible.

condu'cible, *adj.*, tending to promote, contributory.

condu'cing, *pr.p.*, conduce.

condu'cive, *adj.*, *i.q.* conducible.

conduct', *v.t.*, to lead, to direct; to behave; to transmit.

con'duct, *n.*, behaviour; management; a right of passage.

conduct'ed, *p.p.*, conduct.

conductibil'ity, *n.*, the quality of being conductible.

conduct'ible, *adj.*, able to be conducted.

conduct'ing, *pr.p.*, conduct.

conduc'tion, *n.*, transmission by a conductor.

conduct'ive, *adj.*, having the quality of directing or transmitting.

conductiv'ity, *n.*, the quality of being conductive.

conduct'or, *n.*, one who, or that which, conducts; a guide, an attendant on an omnibus; a transmitting medium.

conduct'ress, *n.*, the fem. of conductor.

con'duit, *n.*, a waterpipe, a canal for bringing water.

condu'plicate, *adj.*, doubled together.

con'dyle, *n.*, the round end of a bone.

con'dyloid, *adj.*, like, or rel. to, a condyle.

Con'dy's fluid, *n.*, a solution of potassium (per)manganate used as disinfectant.

cone, *n.*, a solid body circular at one end and coming to a point at the other; the fruit of certain trees, as the pine; a storm or danger signal.

cones, *n.*, a fine flour.

co'ney, *n.*, a rabbit.

confab'ulate, *v.i.*, to chat together.

confab'ulated, *p.p.*, confabulate.

confab'ulating, *pr.p.*, confabulate.

confabula'tion, *n.*, a chat.

confec'tion, *n.*, a sweet; something compounded with sugar; any object put together to give pleasure.

confec'tionary, *adj.*, rel. to confections.

confec'tioner, *n.*, one who makes and sells sweets.

confec'tionery, *n.*, sweetmeats, cakes, etc.

con'federacy, *n.*, a league of any description.

confed'erate, *v.t.* and *i.*, to unite in a league.

confed'erate, *adj.*, united in a league; *n.*, a member of a confederation; an accomplice.

confed'erated, *p.p.*, confederate.

confed'erating, *pr.p.*, confederate.

confedera'tion, *n.*, the act of confederating; a league; an association of once independent states.

confed'erative, *adj.*, leading to confederation.

confer', *v.t.*, to bestow; *v.i.*, to consult with; to hold conversation.

con'ference, *n.*, the act of conferring; a gathering for discussion; a lecture.

confer'ment, *n.*, a bestowal.

confer'rable, *adj.*, able to be conferred.

conferred', *p.p.*, confer.

confer'rer, *n.*, one who confers.

confer'ring, *pr.p.*, confer.

confess', *v.t.*, to own, to admit; to hear confession; to make confession.

confess'ant, *n.*, one who confesses.

confessed', *p.p.*, confess.

confes'sedly, *adv.*, admittedly.

confess'ing, *pr.p.*, confess.

confes'sion, *n.*, the act of confessing; an avowal.

confes'sional, *adj.*, rel. to confession; *n.*, the place where confessions are heard; the system of confession.

confes'sionary, *adj.*, rel. to confession.

confes'sionist, *n.*, one who professes a particular faith.

confes'sor, *n.*, one who confesses; one who avows his faith; a priest who hears confessions.

confet'ti, *n. pl.*, comfits; pellets, small round pieces of coloured paper showered on newly-weds.

confidant(e)', *n.*, the sharer of one's secrets.

confide', *v.t.*, to entrust; *v.i.*, to repose trust in.

confi'ded, *p.p.*, confide.

con'fidence, *n.*, a feeling of trust; reliance.

con'fident, *adj.*, trustful, reliant; very sure.

confiden'tial, *adj.*, worthy of trust; said or done in confidence or secret.

confiden'tially, *adv.*, in a confidential way.

con'fidently, *adv.*, with confidence.

confi'der, *n.*, one who confides.

confi'ding, *pr.p.*, confide.

config'urate, *v.t.*, to shape, to fashion.

config'urated, *p.p.*, configurate.

config'urating, *pr.p.*, configurate.

configura'tion, *n.*, the outward shape; the relative position.

config'ure, *v.t.*, to shape to a pattern.

config'ured, *p.p.*, configure.

con'figuring, *pr.p.*, configure.

confi'nable, *adj.*, able to be confined.

confine', *v.t.*, to place within limits; to imprison. In the passive, to be brought to child-bed.

con'fine, *n.*, a frontier.

confined', *p.p.*, confine.

confine'ment, *n.*, the act of confining; the state of being confined; the period of childbirth with reference to the woman who is being delivered.

confi'ner, *n.*, one who confines.

confi'ning, *pr.p.*, confine.

confirm', *v.t.*, to strengthen, to support, to ratify; to administer the Sacrament of Confirmation.

confirm'able, *adj.*, able to be confirmed.

confirma'tion, *n.*, the act of confirming; a further proof; a religious ceremony.

confirm'ative, *adj.*, attesting.

confirm'atively, *adv.*, in a confirmative way.

confirm'atory, *adj.*, *i.q.* confirmative.

confirmed', *p.p.*, confirm.

confirm'edly, *adv.*, with confirmation.

confirmee', *n.*, a person confirmed or to whom something is confirmed.

confirm'er, *n.*, one who confirms.

confirm'ing, *pr.p.*, confirm.

confis'cable, *adj.*, able to be confiscated.

con'fiscate, *v.t.*, to appropriate to other than for private use.

con'fiscated, *p.p.*, confiscate.

con'fiscating, *pr.p.*, confiscate.

confisca'tion, *n.*, the act or result of confiscating.

con'fiscator, *n.*, one who confiscates.

confis'catory, *adj.*, in the nature of confiscation.

conflagra'tion, *n.*, a fire on a great scale.

confla'tion, *n.*, the fusing together of two texts or readings into one.

conflict', *v.i.*, to fight, to be inconsistent with.

con'flict, *n.*, a fight.

conflict'ed, *p.p.*, conflict.

conflict'ing, *pr.p.*, conflict.

conflic'tion, *n.*, a struggle; a contest.

conflict'ive, *adj.*, conflicting.

con'fluence, *n.*, a meeting; the junction of two streams.

con'fluent, *adj.*, flowing to the same point; *n.*, a tributary stream.

con'flux, *n.*, the junction of streams; a meeting.

conform', *v.t.*, to make alike, to adapt; *v.i.*, to comply with.

conformabil'ity, *n.*, the state or quality of being conformable.

conform'able, *adj.*, compliant, corresponding.

conform'ably, *adv.*, correspondingly, compliantly.

conforma'tion, *n.*, structure.

conformed', *p.p.*, conform.

conform'ing, *pr.p.*, conform.

conform'ist, *n.*, one who conforms.

conform'ity, *n.*, compliance, resemblance.

confound', *v.t.*, to mix together; to amaze; to confuse.

confound'ed, *p.p.*, confound.

confound'er, *n.*, one who confounds.

confound'ing, *pr.p.*, confound.

confrater'nity, *n.*, a brotherhood.

confrère', *n.*, a colleague, an associate (*Fr.*).

confront', *v.t.*, to face, to oppose.

confronta'tion, *n.*, the meeting face to face.

confront'ed, *p.p.*, confront.

confront'er, *n.*, one who confronts.

confront'ing, *pr.p.*, confront.

Confu'cian, *adj.*, rel. to Confucius, the Chinese philosopher, and his philosophy.

Confu'cianism, *n.*, the teachings of Confucius, accepted as the basis of Chinese law and education.

Confu'cianist, *n.*, a follower of, and believer in, Confucianism.

confuse', *v.t.*, to blend, or jumble together; to perplex, to muddle.

confused', *adj.*, bewildered; *p.p.*, confuse.

confu'sedly, *adv.*, in a confused way.

confu'sedness, *n.*, the state of being confused.

confu'sing, *pr.p.*, confuse.

confu'sion, *n.*, the act of confusing; tumult, disorder.

confu'sional, *adj.*, rel. to confusion.

confu'table, *adj.*, able to be confuted.

confuta'tion, *n.*, the act or result of confuting.

confute', *v.t.*, to convict of error; to rebut.

confu'ted, *p.p.*, confute.

confu'ter, *n.*, one who confutes.

confu'ting, *pr.p.*, confute.

congé, *n.*, a bow, leave-taking permission (*Fr.*).

congeal', *v.t.* and *i.*, to freeze, to harden.

congeal'able, *adj.*, able to be congealed.

congealed', *p.p.*, congeal.

congeal'ing, *pr.p.*, congeal.

congeal'ment, *n.*, the act or effect of congealing.

con'gee, *n.*, boiled rice, rice-water.

congela'tion, *n.*, the act of congealing.

con'gener, *n.*, one of the same stock.

congener'ic, *adj.*, of the same stock.

congen'erous, *adj.*, *i.q.* congeneric.

conge'nial, *adj.*, of the same nature; agreeable, affable.

congenial'ity, *n.*, the quality of being congenial.

congen'ially, *adv.*, in a congenial manner.

conge'nialness, *n.*, *i.q.* congeniality.

congen'ital, *adj.*, existing at, or from, birth.

con'ger, *n.*, a sea-eel.

con'ger-eel', *n.*, *i.q.* conger.

conge'ries, *n.*, a mass of particles (*Lat.*).

congest', *v.t.*, to block, crowd or obstruct.

congest'ed, *adj.*, crowded, blocked; with an undue accumulation; *p.p.*, congest.

congest'ible, *adj.*, able to be congested.

conges'tion, n., over-crowding, a stoppage.

congest'ive, adj., causing congestion.

con'globate, adj., spherical.

congloba'tion, n., the act or effect of making spherical.

conglob'ulate, adj., made spherical.

conglom'erate, adj., gathered into a round mass; n., a rock consisting of rounded and water-worn stones; v.t. and i., to gather into a round mass.

conglom'erated, p.p., conglomerate.

conglom'erating, pr.p., conglomerate.

conglomera'tion, n., the act or effect of conglomerating; a mixture.

conglu'tinant, adj., cementing together.

conglu'tinate, v.t., to cement together; to form into a single mass.

conglu'tinated, p.p., conglutinate.

conglu'tinating, pr.p., conglutinate.

conglutina'tion, n., the act or effect of conglutinating.

conglu'tinative, adj., causing conglutination.

Congo'ese, n., i.q. Congolese.

Congolese', n. and adj., a native of, or rel. to the Congolese Republic or the Congo (Brazzaville).

con'gou, n., a species of black China tea.

congrat'ulant, adj., i.q. congratulatory.

congrat'ulate, v.t., to felicitate, to wish joy to.

congrat'ulated, p.p., congratulate.

congrat'ulating, pr.p., congratulate.

congratula'tion, n., the act of congratulating.

congrat'ulator, n., one who congratulates.

congrat'ulatory, adj., expressing congratulation.

con'gregate, v.t., to bring together; v.i., to meet together.

con'gregated, p.p., congregate.

con'gregating, pr.p., congregate.

congrega'tion, n., the act of congregating; an assembly.

congrega'tional, adj., rel. to congregation.

Congrega'tionalism, n., the Congregational religious belief.

Congrega'tionalist, n., one who adheres to Congregationalism.

con'gress, n., a meeting, a legislative assembly.

congres'sional, adj., rel. to congress.

congres'sionist, n., one who supports a congress.

con'greve, n., a rocket.

con'gruence, n., the state or quality of being congruent.

con'gruent, adj., accordant, suited.

congru'ity, n., fitness, agreement.

con'gruous, adj., i.q. congruent.

con'gruously, adv., agreeably, in accordance.

con'gruousness, n., i.q. congruity.

con'ic, adj., cone-shaped, rel. to a cone.

con'ical, adj., i.q. conic.

con'ically, adv., in the form of a cone.

con'ic sec'tions, n., the department of mathematics rel. to ellipses, parabolas and hyperbolas.

co'nifer, n., a cone-bearing plant.

Conif'erae, n., the family of conifers.

conif'erous, adj., cone-bearing.

co'niform, adj., cone-shaped.

con'ine, n., the poisonous alkaloid of hemlock.

co'niine, n., i.q. conine.

conjec'turable, adj., able to be conjectured.

conjec'tural, adj., dubious; guessed.

conjec'turally, adv., without proof or knowledge.

conjec'ture, n., a guess, a surmise; v.t., to guess, to surmise.

conjec'tured, p.p., conjecture.

conjec'turer, n., one who conjectures.

conjec'turing, pr.p., conjecture.

con'jee, n., rice-water.

conjoin', v.t., to join together.

conjoined', p.p., conjoin.

conjoin'ing, pr.p., conjoin.

conjoint', adj., united in combination.

conjoint'ly, adv., together.

conjoint'ness, n., the state of being conjoint.

con'jugal, adj., rel. to marriage.

conjugal'ity, n., the state of marriage.

con'jugate, adj., of kindred meaning; v.t., to join; to inflect a verb.

con'jugated, p.p., conjugate.

con'jugating, pr.p., conjugate.

conjuga'tion, n., a union; the inflection of a verb.

conjuga'tional, adj., rel. to conjugation.

conjunct', adj., united, in association.

conjunc'tion, n., the act or result of conjoining; a part of speech denoting a word that connects words and sentences.

conjunc'tional, adj., rel. to a conjunction.

conjuncti'va, n., the mucous membrane within the eyelid.

conjunc'tive, adj., uniting; connected; n., the grammatical mood so named.

conjunc'tively, adv., in union.

conjunctivi'tis, n., inflammation of the conjunctiva.

conjunc'ture, n., a point of time at which various circumstances or causes meet.

conjura'tion, n., the act of conjuring; an incantation.

con'jure, v.i., to practise a conjurer's arts; to imagine without reason.

conjure', v.t., to bind by an oath; to exhort solemnly.

con'jured, p.p., conjure.

conjured', p.p., conjure.

con'jurer, n., one who does tricks of sleight of hand.

conjur'er, n., one who conjures'.

con'juring, pr.p., conjure.

conjur'ing, pr.p., conjure'.

conjur'or, *n.*, one who takes an oath.

conk, *n.*, the nose (*slang*); *v.i.*, to break down (*slang*).

con'ker, *n.*, a horse-chestnut (*slang*).

conk'ers, *n. pl.*, the game played with horse-chestnuts.

connas'cent, *adj.*, having a common origin.

con'nate, *adj.*, united in the same body.

connat'ural, *adj.*, sharing the same nature.

connat'uralize, *v.t.*, to make of similar nature.

connect', *v.t.*, to join, to bind.

connect'ed, *adj.*, coherent; *p.p.*, connect.

connect'edly, *adv.*, in a connected way.

connect'ing, *pr.p.*, connect.

connec'tion, *n.*, the act or result of connecting; intercourse; an association; a religious body.

connect'ive, *adj.*, connecting; *n.*, that which connects.

connect'ively, *adv.*, in a connective way.

connect'or, *n.*, that which connects.

conned, *p.p.*, con.

con'ner, *n.*, one who cons.

connex'ion, *n.*, i.q. connection.

con'ning, *n.*, the act of directing a steersman; *pr.p.*, con.

con'ning-tower, *n.*, the pilot-house in an armoured ship, esp. submarines.

connip'tion, *n.*, a fit of rage or hysteria (*slang*).

conni'vance, *n.*, assumed ignorance of a plan; winking at a fault.

connive', *v.i.*, to wink at; to share secretly in a plan.

connived', *p.p.*, connive.

conniv'ent, *adj.*, gradually convergent.

conni'ver, *n.*, one who connives.

conni'ving, *pr.p.*, connive.

connoisseur', *n.*, an expert judge in the fine arts (*Fr.*).

connota'tion, *n.*, the implication of qualities.

connota'tive, *adj.*, rel. to connotation.

connota'tively, *adv.*, implying connotation.

connote', *v.t.*, to imply qualities or attributes.

conno'ted, *p.p.*, connote.

conno'ting, *pr.p.*, connote.

connu'bial, *adj.*, rel. to married life.

connubial'ity, *n.*, the connubial state.

connumera'tion, *n.*, the act of numbering together.

co'noid, *adj.*, cone-like; *n.*, anything cone-like.

conoi'dal, *adj.*, i.q. conoid.

conoi'dic, *adj.*, i.q. conoid.

co'noscope, *n.*, an instrument for examining crystals.

con'quer, *v.t.*, to overcome; *v.i.*, to win a victory.

con'querable, *adj.*, able to be conquered.

con'quered, *p.p.*, conquer.

con'quering, *pr.p.*, conquer.

con'queror, *n.*, one who conquers.

con'quest, *n.*, the act of conquering; a victory.

conquist'ador, *n.*, a conqueror (*Span.*).

consanguin'eal, *adj.*, i.q. consanguineous.

consanguin'eous, *adj.*, related in blood.

consanguin'ity, *n.*, relationship in blood.

con'science, *n.*, a sense of right and wrong.

conscien'tious, *adj.*, having a conscience; scrupulous.

conscien'tiously, *adv.*, scrupulously, exactly.

conscien'tiousness, *n.*, the quality of being conscientious.

con'scionable, *adj.*, in accordance with conscience; reasonable.

con'scious, *adj.*, aware; in possession of one's faculties.

con'sciously, *adv.*, with full knowledge.

con'sciousness, *n.*, the state or quality of being conscious.

conscript', *v.t.*, to enroll for military service.

con'script, *adj.*, enlisted; *n.*, one enlisted by conscription.

conscript'ed, *p.p.*, conscript'.

conscript'ing, *pr.p.*, conscript'.

conscrip'tion, *n.*, the act of conscripting; compulsory service.

conscrip'tionist, *n.*, an advocate of conscription.

conscrip'tive, *adj.*, involving conscription.

con'secrate, *adj.*, set apart; *v.t.*, to set apart for a sacred purpose.

con'secrated, *p.p.*, consecrate.

con'secrating, *pr.p.*, consecrate.

consecra'tion, *n.*, the act of consecrating.

con'secrator, *n.*, one who consecrates.

consec'tary, *adj.*, logically following; *n.*, a corollary.

consecu'tion, *n.*, a consequence.

consec'utive, *adj.*, following in order.

consec'utively, *adv.*, in a consecutive way.

consec'utiveness, *n.*, the state or quality of being consecutive.

consenes'cence, *n.*, decay through ageing.

consen'sual, *adj.*, rel. to agreement of opinion.

consen'sus, *n.*, an agreement of opinion.

consent', *n.*, acquiescence, concurrence; *v.t.*, to be of one mind; to comply.

consenta'neous, *adj.*, accordant.

consent'ed, *p.p.*, consent.

consent'er, *n.*, one who consents.

consen'tient, *adj.*, agreeing in opinion.

consent'ing, *pr.p.*, consent.

con'sequence, *n.*, a result, an effect; importance.

con'sequent, *adj.*, resulting, following.

consequen'tial, *adj.*, following as a consequence.

consequen'tially, *adv.*, in a consequential way.

con'sequently, *adv.*, naturally, as a consequence.

conserv'able, *adj.*, able to be conserved.

conserv'ancy, *n.*, preservation.

conserva'tion, *n.*, the act of preserving.

conserva'tionist, *n.*, one who conserves.

conserv'atism, *n.*, the political principle of

preserving what is good in old institutions.

Conserv'ative, *n.*, a member of the Conservative English political party.

conserv'ative, *adj.*, preserving; politically opposed to rapid change; cautious; *n.*, one who professes conservatism.

conserv'atively, *adv.*, in a conservative mood.

conserv'ativeness, *n.*, moderation; caution.

conserv'atoire, *n.*, a music-teaching institution (*Fr.*).

con'servator, *n.*, a preserver; an official custodian of parks, museums, etc.

conserv'atory, *n.*, a greenhouse; a school of music.

conserve', *v.t.*, to save, to preserve.

conserved', *p.p.*, conserve.

conserv'ing, *pr.p.*, conserve.

con'shie, *n.*, *i.q.* conchy (*colloq.*).

consid'er, *v.t.*, to think over, to deliberate, to deem.

consid'erable, *adj.*, worthy of consideration; valuable; more than a little.

consid'erably, *adv.*, more than a little.

consid'erate, *adj.*, thoughtful for others.

consid'erately, *adv.*, with thought for others.

consid'erateness, *n.*, the state or quality of being considerate.

considera'tion, *n.*, deliberation; respect for a person's claims; a *quid pro quo.*

consid'ered, *p.p.*, consider.

consid'erer, *n.*, one who considers.

consid'ering, *pr.p.*, consider.

consign', *v.t.*, to entrust; to hand over.

consign'able, *adj.*, able to be consigned.

consigna'tion, *n.*, the formal payment of money to a person legally appointed.

consigned', *p.p.*, consign.

consignee', *n.*, one to whom anything is consigned.

consign'er, *n.*, one who consigns.

consign'ing, *pr.p.*, consign.

consign'ment, *n.*, the act of consigning; goods consigned.

consignor', *n.*, *i.q.* consigner.

consil'ient, *adj.*, accordant.

consist', *v.i.*, to be composed of; to coexist; to agree.

consist'ed, *p.p.*, consist.

consist'ence, *n.*, the degree of density; agreement.

consist'ency, *n.*, *i.q.* consistence; conformity with; uniformity (of texture or make-up).

consist'ent, *adj.*, solid; in conformity with; firm in principle.

consist'ently, *adv.*, conformably; in a consistent manner.

consist'ing, *pr.p.*, consist.

consisto'rial, *adj.*, rel. to a consistory.

consis'tory, *n.*, an assembly; the meeting of Cardinals; the court of a diocesan bishop.

conso'ciate, *v.t.*, to take into one's society; *v.i.*, to be in company.

conso'ciated, *p.p.*, consociate.

conso'ciating, *pr.p.*, consociate.

consocia'tion, *n.*, the act of consociating.

consol'able, *adj.*, willing to be consoled.

consola'tion, *n.*, comfort, the alleviation of sorrow or disappointment.

consol'atory, *adj.*, offering consolation, comforting.

console', *v.t.*, to comfort, to cheer.

con'sole, *n.*, an ornamental bracket under a cornice; a control panel for electrical or mechanical installation.

consoled', *p.p.*, console.

conso'ler, *n.*, one who consoles.

consol'idate, *v.t.*, to make solid, to combine; *v.i.*, to become solid.

consol'idated, *p.p.*, consolidate.

consol'idating, *pr.p.*, consolidate.

consolida'tion, *n.*, the act or result of consolidating.

consol'idator, *n.*, anything that consolidates.

consol'idatory, *adj.*, tending to consolidate.

consol'ing, *adj.*, comforting; *pr.p.*, console.

consols', *n. pl.*, consolidated government stocks.

consommé', *n.*, clear soup (*Fr.*).

con'sonance, *n.*, concord, harmony.

con'sonancy, *n.*, *i.q.* consonance.

con'sonant, *adj.*, in harmony, accordant; *n.*, a speech sound produced without vocalization.

consonan'tal, *adj.*, rel. to consonants.

con'sonantly, *adv.*, agreeably, harmoniously.

con'sonous, *adj.*, *i.q.* consonant.

consort', *v.i.*, to join company with.

con'sort, *n.*, a wife or husband; an attendant ship.

consort'ed, *p.p.*, consort.

consort'ing, *pr.p.*, consort.

consor'tium, *n.*, a temporary association of persons or groups for a common purpose (*Lat.*).

conspec'tus, *n.*, a general view, an abstract.

conspic'uous, *adj.*, plainly seen, eminent.

conspic'uously, *adv.*, visibly, eminently.

conspic'uousness, *n.*, the state or quality of being conspicuous.

conspir'acy, *n.*, a combined plot.

conspira'tion, *n.*, the act of conspiring.

conspir'ator, *n.*, one who joins a conspiracy.

conspire', *v.i.*, to join in a conspiracy; to plot.

conspired', *p.p.*, conspire.

conspir'er, *n.*, one who conspires.

conspir'ing, *pr.p.*, conspire.

con'stable, *n.*, a high official (as Constable of the Tower); a police officer.

constab'ulary, *n.*, a police force.

con'stancy, *n.*, firmness, stability.

con'stant, *adj.*, firm, unvarying; *n.*, an invariable quantity.

con'stantly, *adv.*, regularly, without variation.

con'stellate, *v.t.*, to arrange in constellations; to cover with constellations.

constella'tion, *n.*, a group of fixed stars.

con'sternate, *v.t.*, to dismay.

con'sternated, *p.p.*, consternate.

con'sternating, *pr.p.*, consternate.

consterna'tion, *n.*, alarm, amazement.

con'stipate, *v.t.*, to bind, to make costive.

con'stipated, *adj.*, costive; *p.p.*, constipate.

con'stipating, *pr.p.*, constipate.

constipa'tion, *n.*, costiveness.

constit'uency, *n.*, a body of electors; an electoral division.

constit'uent, *adj.*, elemental, essential; *n.*, a member of a constituency.

con'stitute, *v.t.*, to form, to compose; to appoint, to establish.

con'stituted, *p.p.*, constitute.

con'stituting, *pr.p.*, constitute.

constitu'tion, *n.*, the act of constituting; that which is constituted; the fundamental laws of a nation; the bodily condition.

constitu'tional, *adj.*, rel. to the constitution; fundamental; *n.*, a walk for exercise (*colloq.*).

constitu'tionalism, *n.*, loyalty to the constitution.

constitu'tionalist, *n.*, an upholder of the constitution.

constitu'tionalize, *v.t.*, to make constitutional; to take a constitutional.

constitu'tionalized, *p.p.*, constitutionalize.

constitu'tionalizing, *pr.p.*, constitutionalize.

constitu'tionally, *adv.*, in accordance with the constitution.

constitu'tionist, *n.*, *i.q.* constitutionalist.

con'stitutive, *adj.*, essential, component.

con'stitutively, *adv.*, essentially.

con'stitutor, *n.*, one who,

or that which, constitutes.

constrain', *v.t.*, to compel, to coerce.

constrain'able, *adj.*, able to be constrained.

constrained', *p.p.*, constrain.

constrain'er, *n.*, one who constrains.

constrain'ing, *pr.p.*, constrain.

constraint', *n.*, the act or effect of constraining; confinement.

constrict', *v.t.*, to narrow, to cramp.

constrict'ed, *p.p.*, constrict.

constrict'ing, *pr.p.*, constrict.

constric'tion, *n.*, the act or effect of constricting.

constrict'ive, *adj.*, cramping, binding.

constrict'or, *n.*, that which constricts; the boa-constrictor.

constringe', *v.t.*, to contract, to bind.

constringed', *p.p.*, constringe.

constrin'gency, *n.*, the constringent quality.

constrin'gent, *adj.*, binding, contracting.

constrin'gently, *adv.*, bindingly.

constrin'ging, *pr.p.*, constringe.

construct', *v.t.*, to put together, to build, to compose.

construct'ed, *p.p.*, construct.

construct'er, *n.*, one who constructs.

construc'ting, *pr.p.*, construct.

construc'tion, *n.*, the act or result of constructing; an interpretation; the syntactical formation of a sentence.

construc'tional, *adj.*, rel. to construction.

construc'tionist, *n.*, one skilled in constructing.

construct'ive, *adj.*, with a capacity for constructing; inferred.

construct'ively, *adv.*, in a constructive way.

construct'iveness, *n.*, the capacity for constructing.

construct'or, *n.*, one who constructs; a builder.

construct'ure, *n.*, that which is formed or built; a building.

con'strue, *v.t.*, to interpret, to translate.

con'strued, *p.p.*, construe.

con'struing, *pr.p.*, construe.

consubstan'tial, *adj.*, of one substance or nature with.

consubstan'tialist, *n.*, a believer in consubstantiation.

consubstantial'ity, *n.*, the quality of being consubstantial.

consubstan'tially, *adv.*, in a consubstantial manner.

consubstan'tiate, *v.t.*, to form into one substance with.

consubstan'tiated, *p.p.*, consubstantiate.

consubstan'tiating, *pr.p.*, consubstantiate.

consubstantia'tion, *n.*, the process by which, according to the Lutherans, the Body and Blood of Christ are consubstantiated with the elements of Bread and Wine.

con'suetude, *n.*, custom; intercourse.

consuetu'dinal, *adj.*, customary.

consuetu'dinary, *adj.*, *i.q.* consuetudinal.

con'sul, *n.*, a chief magistrate at Rome; the legal representative of a foreign State in another country.

con'sulage, *n.*, the period of a consul's service.

con'sular, *adj.*, rel. to a consul.

con'sulate, *n.*, the office of a consul; a consul's official home.

con'sulship, *n.*, the office of a Roman consul.

consult', *v.t.*, to seek advice from, to deliberate with; to regard.

consult'ant, *n.*, one who is consulted.

consulta'tion, *n.*, the act of consulting; the deliberation of two or more persons together.

consul'tative, *adj.*, deliberative.

consul'tatory, *adj.*, *i.q.* consultative.

consult'ed, *p.p.*, consult.

consult'er, *n.*, one who consults.

consult'ing, *pr.p.*, consult.

consu'mable, *adj.*, able to be consumed.

consume', *v.t.*, to destroy, to devour; *v.i.*, to waste away.

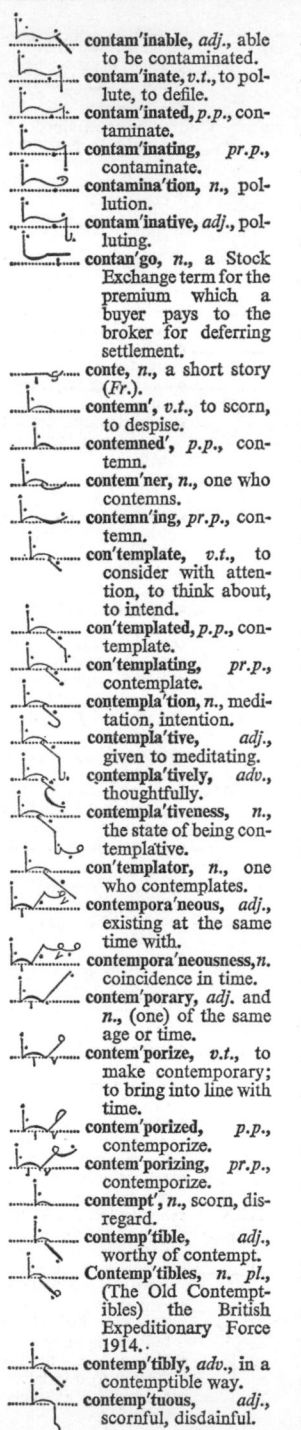

consumed', *p.p.*, consume.

consum'edly, *adv.*, excessively.

consu'mer, *n.*, one who consumes.

consu'ming, *pr.p.*, consume.

con'summate, *v.t.*, to accomplish, to complete.

consum'mate, *adj.*, complete; excellent.

con'summated, *p.p.*, consummate.

consum'mately, *adv.*, completely, utterly.

con'summating, *pr.p.*, consummate.

consumma'tion, *n.*, the act or result of consummating; the completion.

con'summator, *n.*, one who consummates.

consump'tion, *n.*, the act of consuming; the decline.

consump'tive, *adj.*, causing consumption; suffering from phthisis.

consump'tively, *adv.*, in a consumptive way.

consump'tiveness, *n.*, the tendency to phthisis.

contabes'cence, *n.*, sterile pollen (*bot.*); wasting away.

con'tact, *n.*, close touch, close union; *v.t.* and *i.*, to communicate with (*colloq.*).

contadi'no, *n.*, an Italian peasant (*It.*).

conta'gion, *n.*, contact conveying a disease.

conta'gionist, *n.*, one who thinks a disease contagious.

conta'gious, *adj.*, conveyed by contact.

conta'giously, *adv.*, in a contagious way.

conta'giousness, *n.*, the state of being contagious.

contain', *v.t.*, to hold within it, to hold up, to keep within bounds; *v.i.*, to live continently.

contain'able, *adj.*, able to be contained.

contained', *p.p.*, contain.

contain'er, *n.*, that which contains; a receptacle for transporting goods.

containeriza'tion, *n.*, the putting into containers.

contain'erize, *v.t.*, to put into containers.

contain'ing, *pr.p.*, contain.

contam'inable, *adj.*, able to be contaminated.

contam'inate, *v.t.*, to pollute, to defile.

contam'inated, *p.p.*, contaminate.

contam'inating, *pr.p.*, contaminate.

contamina'tion, *n.*, pollution.

contam'inative, *adj.*, polluting.

contan'go, *n.*, a Stock Exchange term for the premium which a buyer pays to the broker for deferring settlement.

conte, *n.*, a short story (*Fr.*).

contemn', *v.t.*, to scorn, to despise.

contemned', *p.p.*, contemn.

contem'ner, *n.*, one who contemns.

contemn'ing, *pr.p.*, contemn.

con'template, *v.t.*, to consider with attention, to think about, to intend.

con'templated, *p.p.*, contemplate.

con'templating, *pr.p.*, contemplate.

contempla'tion, *n.*, meditation, intention.

con'templative, *adj.*, given to meditating.

contempla'tively, *adv.*, thoughtfully.

contempla'tiveness, *n.*, the state of being contemplative.

con'templator, *n.*, one who contemplates.

contempora'neous, *adj.*, existing at the same time with.

contempora'neousness, *n.*, coincidence in time.

contem'porary, *adj.* and *n.*, (one) of the same age or time.

contem'porize, *v.t.*, to make contemporary; to bring into line with time.

contem'porized, *p.p.*, contemporize.

contem'porizing, *pr.p.*, contemporize.

contempt', *n.*, scorn, disregard.

contemp'tible, *adj.*, worthy of contempt.

Contemp'tibles, *n. pl.*, (The Old Contemptibles) the British Expeditionary Force 1914.

contemp'tibly, *adv.*, in a contemptible way.

contemp'tuous, *adj.*, scornful, disdainful.

contemp'tuously, *adv.*, with contempt.

contemp'tuousness, *n.*, the state of being contemptuous.

contend', *v.i.*, to dispute, to strive; to affirm.

contend'ed, *p.p.*, contend.

contend'er, *n.*, one who contends.

contend'ing, *pr.p.*, contend.

content', *adj.*, satisfied; *n.*, a contented state; *v.t.*, to gratify.

con'tent, *n.*, that which is contained.

content'ed, *adj.*, satisfied; *p.p.*, content.

content'edly, *adv.*, in a contented way.

content'edness, *n.*, the state of being contented.

content'ing, *pr.p.*, content.

conten'tion, *n.*, strife, argument.

conten'tious, *adj.*, leading to contention, quarrelsome.

conten'tiously, *adv.*, in a contentious way.

conten'tiousness, *n.*, the state or quality of being contentious.

content'ment, *n.*, a contented state.

con'tents, *n.*, the pl. of content.

conter'minable, *adj.*, able to be made conterminous.

conter'minal, *adj.*, i.q. conterminous.

conter'minous, *adj.*, bordering upon, contiguous.

contest', *v.t.* and *i.*, to dispute, to litigate.

con'test, *n.*, a fight, a struggle.

contest'able, *adj.*, debatable.

contest'ant, *n.*, one who contests.

contesta'tion, *n.*, a disputation, emulation.

contest'ed, *p.p.*, contest.

contest'ing, *pr.p.*, contest.

con'text, *n.*, the whole from which a passage is quoted.

context'ual, *adj.*, rel. to context.

context'ural, *adj.*, rel. to contexture.

contex'ture, *n.*, structure.

contigu'ity, *n.*, actual contact, close proximity.

contig'uous, *adj.,* closely adjacent.

contig'uously, *adv.,* adjacently.

con'tinence, *n.,* self-restraint, chastity.

con'tinency, *n., i.q.* continence.

con'tinent, *adj.,* chaste; *n.,* the largest geographical division of land.

continen'tal, *adj.,* rel. to a continent.

con'tinently, *adv.,* chastely.

contin'gence, *n., i.q.* contingency.

contin'gency, *n.,* chance, that which may happen.

contin'gent, *adj.,* accidental, conditional; *n.,* something depending on chance; a body of troops.

contin'gently, *adv.,* conditionally.

contin'uable, *adj.,* able to be continued.

contin'ual, *adj.,* continuing, lasting.

contin'ually, *adv.,* lastingly; happening repeatedly.

contin'uance, *n.,* permanence, duration.

contin'uant, *adj.,* continuing.

continua'tion, *n.,* the act or state of continuing; that which is continued.

contin'native, *adj.,* continuing.

contin'uator, *n.,* one who continues.

contin'ue, *v.t.,* to carry on; *v.i.,* to persist, to abide.

contin'ued, *p.p.,* continue.

contin'uer, *n.,* one who continues.

contin'uing, *pr.p.,* continue.

continu'ity, *n.,* the state of being continuous.

contin'uo, *n.,* the abbrev. for basso continuo; an accompaniment improvised upon a bass (*mus.*).

contin'uous, *adj.,* uninterrupted, without a break.

contin'uously, *adv.,* uninterruptedly; happening all the time.

contin'uousness, *n.,* the state or quality of being continuous.

contin'uum, *n.,* an unbroken mass or sequence.

cont'-line, *n.,* a spiral interval between strands of rope; the space between casks placed side by side.

contorn'iate, *adj. and n.,* (medal) with deep furrow round disc inside edge.

contort', *v.t.,* to twist.

contort'ed, *p.p.,* contort.

contort'ing, *pr.p.,* contort.

contor'tion, *n.,* a twisting, a writhing.

contor'tionist, *n.,* a variety of acrobat.

con'tour, *n.,* an outline; a line on a map joining places of equal height; *v.t.,* to draw an outline.

con'tra, *prep.,* against (*Lat.*).

con'traband, *adj.,* illegal, prohibited; *n.,* smuggled goods.

con'trabandist, *n.,* a smuggler.

con'tra-bass, *n.,* the double-bass or bass viol.

con'tra-bassoon', *n.,* a double bassoon.

contracep'tion, *n.,* the prevention of uterine conception.

contracep'tive, *adj.,* rel. to contraception; *n.,* a means of contraception.

contract', *v.t.,* to draw together, to narrow, to shorten; *v.i.,* to become shorter, to make an agreement.

con'tract, *n.,* an agreement.

contract'able, *adj.,* able to be contracted.

contract'ed, *p.p.,* contract.

contract'edly, *adv.,* in a contracted way.

contract'edness, *n.,* the state of being contracted.

contractibil'ity, *n.,* the state or quality of being contractible.

contract'ible, *adj., i.q.* contractable.

contract'ile, *adj.,* having the power of contraction.

contractil'ity, *n.,* the state or quality of being contractile.

contract'ing, *pr.p.,* contract.

contrac'tion, *n.,* a reduction in size or scope; an abbreviation.

contrac'tive, *adj.,* able to be contracted.

contract'or, *n.,* one who makes a contract.

contrac'tual, *adj.,* of the nature of a contract.

contrac'ture, *n.,* chronic shortening or stiffening.

con'tra-dance, *n.,* a country-dance in which the partners face one another. (Also *contre-danse*.)

contradict', *v.t.,* to gainsay, to say the opposite to.

contradic'table, *adj.,* able to be contradicted.

contradict'ed, *p.p.,* contradict.

contradict'ing, *pr.p.,* contradict.

contradic'tion, *n.,* the act of contradicting; a denial.

contradic'tious, *adj.,* apt to contradict.

contradict'ive, *adj., i.q.* contradictious.

contradic'tor, *n.,* one who contradicts.

contradict'orily, *adv.,* in a contradictory way.

contradict'ory, *adj.,* saying the opposite, giving the lie to, inconsistent with.

contradistinct', *adj.,* distinguished by opposite qualities.

contradistinc'tion, *n.,* a separation by opposite qualities.

contradistinc'tive, *adj.,* distinguishing by opposite qualities.

contradistin'guish, *v.t.,* to distinguish by opposite qualities.

contradistin'guished, *p.p.,* contradistinguish.

contradistin'guishing, *pr.p.,* contradistinguish.

con'trail, *n.,* the vapour trail of an aircraft.

contral'to, *n.,* the vocal range between soprano and tenor; a contralto singer.

contraposi'tion, *n.,* opposition; contrast.

con'traprop, *n.,* an oppositely rotating airscrew.

contrap'tion, *n.,* a queer contrivance.

contrapun'tal, *adj.,* rel. to counterpoint (*mus.*).

contrapun'tist, *n.,* a person skilled in counterpoint.

contrar'iant, *adj.,* opposed (to).

con'traries, *n. pl.*, opposites.

contrari'ety, *n.*, opposition, disagreement.

con'trarily, *adv.*, in a contrary direction.

con'trariness, *n.*, *i.q.* contrariety.

contrar'ious, *adj.*, opposed; perverse.

con'trariwise, *adv.*, on the contrary, conversely.

con'trary, *adj.*, opposed, in an opposite direction; perverse; *n.*, something the opposite to others.

contrast', *v.t.*, to place in opposition or dissimilitude.

con'trast, *n.*, opposition, dissimilitude.

contrast'ed, *p.p.*, contrast.

contrast'ing, *adj.*, having striking difference; *pr.p.*, contrast.

contrast'ive, *adj.*, conveying a contrast.

contravalla'tion, *n.*, a military defence-work made by the besiegers of a town.

contravene', *v.t.*, to transgress; to offend against.

contravened', *p.p.*, contravene.

contrave'ner, *n.*, one who contravenes.

contrave'ning, *pr.p.*, contravene.

contraven'tion, *n.*, the act of contravening.

con'tre-danse, *n.*, *i.q.* contra-dance (*Fr.*).

con'tretemps, *n.*, a mishap, a hitch (*Fr.*).

contrib'ute, *v.t.*, to give to a common object or stock; *v.i.*, to lend support.

contrib'uted, *p.p.*, contribute.

contrib'uting, *pr.p.*, contribute.

contribu'tion, *n.*, the act of contributing; a share; a subscription; a writing in a review or paper.

contrib'utive, *adj.*, contributing.

contrib'utor, *n.*, one who contributes.

contrib'utory, *adj.*, *i.q.* contributive.

con'trite, *adj.*, repentant, sorry.

con'tritely, *adv.*, penitently.

contri'tion, *n.*, penitence, remorse.

contri'vable, *adj.*, able to be contrived.

contri'vance, *n.*, the act of contriving; a device, apparatus.

contrive', *v.t.*, to devise, to plan out, to effect.

contrived', *p.p.*, contrive.

contri'ver, *n.*, one who contrives.

contri'ving, *pr.p.*, contrive.

control', *n.*, restraint, superintendence; *v.t.*, to check, to guide, to govern.

controllabil'ity, *n.*, the state or quality of being controllable.

control'lable, *adj.*, subject to control.

controlled', *p.p.*, control.

control'ler, *n.*, one who controls; a device regulating the speed of an electric motor; a public official of accounts. (Also *comptroller*.)

control'lership, *n.*, the office of a controller.

control'ling, *pr.p.*, control.

control'ment, *n.*, the effect of controlling.

controver'sial, *adj.*, rel. to controversy; disputatious.

controver'sialist, *n.*, one who engages in controversy.

con'troversy, *n.*, disputation.

controvert', *v.t.*, to oppose a statement; to refute.

controvert'ed, *p.p.*, controvert.

controvert'ible, *adj.*, refutable.

controvert'ing, *pr.p.*, controvert.

contuma'cious, *adj.*, perversely wilful, disobedient.

contuma'ciously, *adv.*, in a contumacious way.

contuma'ciousness, *n.*, the state of being contumacious.

con'tumacy, *n.*, wilfulness, disobedience to law.

contume'lious, *adj.*, contemptuously insolent.

con'tumely, *n.*, arrogant abuse.

contuse', *v.t.*, to crush, to bruise.

contused', *p.p.*, contuse.

contu'sing, *pr.p.*, contuse.

contu'sion, *n.*, a bruise, the act of bruising.

con'ular, *adj.*, cone-shaped.

conun'drum, *n.*, a riddle.

conurba'tion, *n.*, an aggregation of urban districts.

convalesce', *v.i.*, to recover from sickness.

convalesced', *p.p.*, convalesce.

convales'cence, *n.*, the state of recovering one's health.

convales'cency, *n.*, *i.q.* convalescence.

convales'cent, *adj.*, rel. to convalescence; recovering health.

convales'cing, *pr.p.*, convalesce.

convec'tion, *n.*, transmission; diffusion; the transfer of heat by circulation.

convec'tive, *adj.*, conveying.

convec'tor, *n.*, an apparatus that heats by convection.

conve'nable, *adj.*, capable of being convened.

con'venances, *n. pl.*, social proprieties (*Fr.*).

convene', *v.t.*, to summon together; *v.i.*, to come together.

convened', *p.p.*, convene.

conve'ner, *n.*, one who convenes.

conve'nience, *n.*, fitness, accommodation; a water-closet.

conve'niency, *n.*, *i.q.* convenience.

conve'nient, *adj.*, fit, suitable; giving accommodation.

conve'niently, *adv.*, in a convenient way.

conve'ning, *pr.p.*, convene.

con'vent, *n.*, a community of religious males or females; a nunnery or a monastery.

conven'ticle, *n.*, an irregular or schismatic assembly.

conven'ticler, *n.*, a frequenter of conventicles.

conven'tion, *n.*, an assembly, a contract; common usage.

conven'tional, *adj.*, rel. to convention; ordinary; orthodox.

conven'tionalism, *n.*, the tendency to be conventional.

conven'tionalist, n., one who is conventional.

conventional'ity, n., the state or quality of being conventional.

conven'tionalize, v.t., to make conventional.

conven'tionalized, p.p., conventionalize.

conven'tionalizing pr.p., conventionalize.

conven'tionary, adj. and n., (tenant, tenure) on terms fixed by contract, not by custom.

conven'tionist, n., one who makes a convention.

conven'tual, adj., rel. to a convent.

converge', v.i., to incline towards the same point.

converged', p.p., converge.

conver'gence, n., a tendency towards the same point.

conver'gent, adj., inclining to the same point.

conver'ging, pr.p., converge.

convers'able, adj., fond of conversing.

convers'ableness, n., the state or quality of being conversable.

con'versance, n., familiarity with.

con'versant, adj., familiar with, thoroughly informed about.

conversa'tion, n., talk, discourse.

conversa'tional, adj., colloquial.

conversa'tionalist, n., one with high powers of conversation.

conversa'tionist, n., i.q. conversationalist.

convers'ative, adj., social.

conversazio'ne, n., a meeting for friendly talk (It.).

converse', v.i., to talk, to join in conversation.

con'verse, adj., opposite; n., talk.

conversed', p.p., converse.

con'versely, adv., from the opposite point of view.

convers'er, n., one who converses.

convers'ible, adj., i.q. convertible.

convers'ing, pr.p., converse.

conver'sion, n., the act or result of converting.

convers'ive, adj., leading to conversion.

convert', v.t., to change, to transmute; to bring over to a change of belief or opinion; to apply to some use.

con'vert, n., one who is converted.

convert'ed, p.p., convert.

convert'er, n., one who converts.

convertibil'ity, n., the state or quality of being convertible.

convert'ible, adj., able to be converted.

convert'ing, pr.p., convert.

converti-plane, n., an aircraft equipped for both a horizontal and vertical take-off.

con'vex, adj., with a curved bulge.

con'vexed, adj., i.q. convex.

convex'ity, n., the quality or state of being convex.

con'vexly, adv., in a convex way.

convex'o-con'cave, adj., convex on one side, concave on the other.

convex'o-con'vex, adj., convex on both sides.

convey', v.t., to carry; to impart; to transfer (property).

convey'able, adj., able to be conveyed.

convey'ance, n., the act of conveying; a deed of transfer; a vehicle.

convey'ancer, n., one who negotiates the transfer of property.

convey'ancing, n., the profession of a conveyancer.

conveyed', p.p., convey.

convey'er, n., one who, or that which, conveys.

convey'ing, pr.p., convey.

convey'or, n., a conveyancer; a mechanism for continuous transport.

convict', v.t., to prove guilty.

con'vict, n., one undergoing sentence.

convict'ed, p.p., convict.

convict'ing, pr.p., convict.

convic'tion, n., the act of convicting; the state of being convicted; a firm belief.

convict'ive, adj., tending to conviction.

convince', v.t., to bring over to one's side by argument; to persuade.

convinced', p.p., convince.

convince'ment, n., the state of being convinced.

convin'cer, n., one who convinces.

convin'cible, adj., open to conviction.

convin'cing, adj., persuasive; pr.p., convince.

convin'cingly, adv., persuasively.

conviv'ial, adj., sociable, fond of good fellowship; lively.

conviv'ialist, n., a convivial person.

convivial'ity, n., good fellowship.

con'vocate, v.t., to call together.

con'vocated, p.p., convocate.

con'vocating, pr.p., convocate.

convoca'tion, n., the act of convocating; the assembly of the English clergy, and of certain universities.

convoca'tional, adj., rel. to convocation.

convoke', v.t., to summon together.

convoked', p.p., convoke.

convo'king, pr.p., convoke.

con'volute, adj., twisted.

con'voluted, adj., i.q. convolute.

convolu'tion, n., a twisting.

convolve', v.t., to roll together.

convolved', p.p., convolve.

convolv'ing, pr.p., convolve.

convol'vulus, n., the twining plant so named.

convoy', v.t., to protect while travelling by land or sea.

con'voy, n., an escort; a group of ships or conveyances travelling together.

convoyed', p.p., convoy.

convoy'ing, pr.p., convoy.

convulse', v.t., to shake violently.

convulsed', p.p., convulse.

convuls'ing, pr.p., convulse.

convul'sion, *n.,* violent agitation; a sort of fit.

convul'sionary, *adj.,* causing convulsion.

convuls'ive, *adj.,* violently agitated.

convuls'ively, *adv.,* with violent agitation.

co'n(e)y, *n.,* a rabbit.

coo, *n.,* the sound a pigeon makes; *v.i.,* to produce the note of a pigeon; to speak wooingly.

cooed, *p.p.,* coo.

coo'ee, *n.* and *v.i.,* (to make) the signal call of Australian natives.

coo'ey, *n.* and *v.i., i.q.* cooee.

coo'ing, *n.,* the call of the dove; *pr.p.,* coo.

cook, *n.,* a person proficient in cooking; *v.t.,* to prepare food for eating by applying heat.

cooked, *p.p.,* cook.

cook'er, *n.,* an apparatus for cooking; fruit that cooks well.

cook'ery, *n.,* the art and practice of cooking.

cook'ing, *n., i.q.* cookery; *pr.p.,* cook.

cook'y, *n.,* a flat cake.

cool, *adj.,* slightly cold, calm, calculating; *n.,* a state of moderate temperature; *v.t.,* to reduce the temperature; to make cool; *v.i.,* to become cool.

cool'ant, *n.,* a cooling agent.

cooled, *p.p.,* cool.

cool'er, *n.,* comp. of cool; *n.,* a cooling receptacle.

cool'est, *adj., super.* of cool.

cool'-headed, *adj.,* deliberate, calculating.

coo'lie, *n.,* a porter in India.

cool'ing, *pr.p.,* cool.

cool'ish, *adj.,* somewhat cool.

cool'ly, *adv.,* in a cool way.

cool'ness, *n.,* the state of being cool.

coolth, *n.,* coolness (*colloq.*).

coom, *n.,* an old measure of capacity = 4 bushels.

coomb, *n., i.q.* coom; a small valley. (Also *combe.*)

coon, *n.,* a cunning person.

coon'can', *n.,* a simple, two-handed card-game.

co-op', *n.,* the abbrev. for co-operative society or store (*colloq.*).

coop, *n.,* a cage, a pen; *v.t.,* to cage, to pen up.

cooped, *p.p.,* coop.

coop'er, *n.,* one who makes barrels; a malt liquor so named; a North Sea refreshment-selling vessel.

coop'erage, *n.,* a cooper's trade; payment for coopers' work.

co-op'erant, *adj.,* co-operating.

co-op'erate, *v.i.,* to work together.

co-op'erated, *p.p.,* co-operate.

co-op'erating, *pr.p.,* co-operate.

co-opera'tion, *n.,* the act of co-operating.

co-op'erative, *adj.,* associated, working in combination.

co-op'erator, *n.,* one who co-operates.

coop'ering, *n.,* a cooper's business.

coop'ery, *n.,* a cooper's trade.

coop'ing, *pr.p.,* coop.

co-opt', *v.t.,* to elect on to a committee (by the existing members).

co-op'tate, *v.t., i.q.* co-opt.

co-op'ted, *p.p.,* co-opt.

co-op'ting, *pr.p.,* co-opt.

co-op'tion, *n.,* the act or result of co-opting.

co-or'dinance, *n.,* joint regulation.

co-or'dinate, *adj.,* of the same order or class; *n.,* an equal in rank; one of the geometrical elements defining the position of a point.

co-or'dinate, *v.t.,* to range or class together; to combine.

co-or'dinately, *adv.,* of the same order.

co-or'dinateness, *n.,* the state or quality of being co-ordinate.

co-ordina'tion, *n.,* the act or result of co-ordinating.

co-ord'inator, *n.,* one who co-ordinates.

coot, *n.,* a British aquatic bird.

coot'ie, *n.,* a body-louse (*army slang*).

cop, *n.,* a conical ball of thread; the top; a policeman (*slang*); to be punished (*slang*).

copai'ba, *n.,* a S. American drug. (Also *copivi.*)

copai'va, *n., i.q.* copaiba.

copai'vic, *adj.,* rel. to copaiba.

co'pal, *n.,* a resinous, transparent substance used in varnishes.

copar'cenary, *n.,* an estate held by coheirs.

copar'cener, *n.,* a joint holder of an estate.

copart'ner, *n.,* a joint partner.

copart'nership, *n.,* the state of a copartner.

copart'nery, *n., i.q.* copartnership.

copas'torate, *n.,* a joint pastorate.

cope, *n.,* an ecclesiastical and academical hooded mantle; *v.i.,* to strive, to contend successfully; *v.t.,* to add a coping to.

co'peck, *n.,* a Russian coin of low value.

coped, *adj.,* wearing a cope; *p.p.,* cope.

cop'er, *n.,* a horse-dealer; a floating grog-shop for North Sea fishers.

Coper'nican, *adj.,* rel. to Copernicus (the Greek astronomer) and the Copernican system.

cope'-stone, *n., i.q.* coping-stone.

cop'iable, *adj.,* able to be copied.

cop'ied, *p.p.,* copy.

cop'ier, *n.,* one who copies.

co'-pi'lot, *n.,* a fellow pilot.

co'ping, *n.,* the topmost course of a wall; *pr.p.,* cope.

co'ping-stone, *n.,* the topmost course, or a stone in the topmost course, of a wall.

co'pious, *adj.,* abundant, plentiful.

co'piously, *adv.,* abundantly.

co'piousness, *n.,* the state of being copious.

copi'vi, *n., i.q.* copaiba.

cop'land, *n.,* a headland; a piece of land which ends in a point.

copol'ymer, *n.*, a compound analogous to a polymer, but with more than one kind of unit.

cop'per, *n.*, a ductile metal of reddish colour; a copper coin; a boiler; a policeman (*slang*); *v.t.*, to overlay with copper.

cop'peras, *n.*, green vitriol.

cop'pered, *p.p.*, copper.

cop'per-faced, *adj.*, faced with copper.

cop'perhead, *n.*, a poisonous, N. American snake.

cop'pering, *pr.p.*, copper.

cop'perish, *adj.*, like copper.

cop'perize, *v.t.*, to treat like copper.

cop'perized, *p.p.*, copperize.

cop'perizing, *pr.p.*, copperize.

cop'perplate, *adj.*, printed on copperplate; *n.*, a plate of copper for engraving or etching; a formal, exact style of handwriting.

cop'persmith, *n.*, a worker in copper.

cop'pery, *adj.*, *i.q.* copperish.

cop'pice, *n.*, a wood of low trees.

cop'ra, *n.*, dried coconut kernels.

co-pres'ence, *n.*, presence together.

cop'rolite, *n.*, petrified dung of extinct animals.

cop'rolith, *n.*, *i.q.* coprolite.

coprolit'ic, *adj.*, rel. to coprolite.

coproph'agous, *adj.*, dung eating.

copse, *n.*, *i.q.* coppice.

cops'y, *adj.*, covered with copses; copselike.

Copt, *n.*, one of the original Egyptian stock.

Cop'tic, *adj.*, rel. to the Copts.

cop'ula, *n.*, the word expressing the relation of predicate to subject.

cop'ulate, *v.i.*, to unite; to have sexual intercourse with.

cop'ulated, *p.p.*, copulate.

cop'ulating, *pr.p.*, copulate.

copula'tion, *n.*, sexual interocurse.

cop'ulative, *adj.*, having the effect of joining; rel. to copulation.

cop'ulatively, *adv.*, with the effect of joining.

cop'ulatory, *adj.*, serving for copulation.

cop'y, *n.*, an exact reproduction, a transcription; one of a set of volumes; writing to be reproduced; *v.t.*, to imitate, to reproduce exactly, to transcribe.

cop'y-book, *n.*, a book containing writing to be imitated.

cop'y-cat, *n.*, an imitator (*colloq.*).

cop'ygraph, *n.*, a duplicator of scripts or drawings.

cop'yhold, *n.*, the holding of land on the strength of a copy of the court roll.

cop'yholder, *n.*, an owner of copyhold; a proof-reader's assistant; an appliance for holding copy.

cop'ying, *pr.p.*, copy.

cop'ying-press, *n.*, a press for making copies.

cop'yist, *n.*, one who transcribes, or imitates.

cop'yright, *n.*, the exclusive publishing rights.

cop'y-writ'er, *n.*, one who prepares copy, esp. advertisements, etc. for the press.

coque, *n.*, a small loop of ribbon; trimming feathers (*Fr.*).

coquet', *v.i.*, to flirt, to trifle.

co'quetry, *n.*, the arts of a coquette.

coquette', *n.*, a woman who coquets; a crested humming-bird.

coquet'ted, *p.p.*, coquet.

coquet'ting, *pr.p.*, coquet.

coquet'tish, *adj.*, given to coquetry.

coquet'tishly, *adv.*, in a coquettish way.

coqui'to, *n.*, the Chilian palm-tree giving palm-honey.

cor'acle, *n.*, a wicker, leather-covered boat.

cor'acoid, *adj.*, like a crow's beak; rel. to the c. bone; *n.*, a hook-like formation.

cor'al, *adj.*, consisting of coral; *n.*, a hard structure in the sea composed of the skeletons of zoophytes; a child's coral toy.

coralla'ceous, *adj.*, made of coral.

corallif'erous, *adj.*, coral-producing.

coral'liform, *adj.*, branching like coral.

cor'alline, *adj.*, of, or like, coral; *n.*, a dye.

cor'allite, *n.*, fossilized coral.

coralloid'al, *adj.*, like coral.

cor'am, *prep.*, in the presence of.

cor anglais, *n.*, the tenor oboe (*Fr.*).

cor'ban, *n.*, an offering.

cor'be(i)l, *n.*, a little basket used in siege work.

cor'bel, *n.*, a projection or bracket.

corb'ie, *n.*, the carrion crow; the raven (*Scot.*).

cord, *v.t.*, to fasten; *n.*, a string, a wood measure.

cord'age, *n.*, a mass or collection of ropes.

cor'date, *adj.*, heart-shaped.

cord'ed, *adj.*, having cords; *p.p.*, cord.

cordelier', *n.*, a Franciscan (*Fr.*).

cordelle', *n.*, a tassel.

cor'dial, *adj.*, hearty, genial; *n.*, an invigorating medicine or liqueur.

cordial'ity, *n.*, a cordial manner, geniality.

cor'dially, *adv.*, genially, heartily.

cor'diform, *adj.*, heart-shaped.

cordille'ra, *n.*, a mountain-chain (*Span.*).

cord'ing, *n.*, a ribbed surface; *pr.p.*, cord.

cor'dite, *n.*, smokeless, explosive powder.

cor'don, *n.*, a ribbon, a line (*Fr.*).

cor'don bleu, *n.*, the top of a profession (*Fr.*).

cor'dovan, *n.*, Spanish leather.

cor'duroy, *adj.*, made of corduroy; *n.*, a ribbed material of cotton or fustian; *v.t.*, to make a corduroy road (tree-trunks across a swamp).

cord'wain, *n.*, Spanish leather formerly used for shoes.

cord'wainer, n., a leather-worker, a shoe-maker.

core, n., the heart or inmost part; v.t., to extract the core from.

cored, adj., having a core; p.p., core.

co-re'gent, n., a joint regent or ruler.

co-relig'ionist, n., a professor of the same religion.

Coreop'sis, n., a genus of composite plants; a yellow-flowering plant.

cor'er, n., a device for coring fruit.

co-respond'ent, n., a joint respondent in a divorce suit (leg.).

corf, n., a coal-heaving basket.

corg'i -y, n., a small Welsh dog.

coria'ceous, adj., leathery.

corian'der, n., a seed-bearing plant.

corian'drol, n., a colourless liquid from the coriander.

cor'ing, pr.p., core.

Corin'thian, adj., pert. or rel. to Corinth; n., a native of C.

cork, adj., made of cork; n., the outer part of a cork-tree's bark; a stopper; v.t., to stop with a cork.

cork'age, n., a hotel-keeper's charge for serving wine to guests.

corked, adj., stopped with a cork; tasting of the cork; p.p., cork.

cork'er, n., something astonishing (slang).

cork'ing, pr.p., cork.

cork'screw, n., a cork-extractor.

cork'tree, n., the tree from which cork is stripped.

cork'y, adj., of, or like, cork.

corm, n., a short, bulbous stem.

cor'morant, n., a fish-eating bird so named; a greedy person.

corn, n., grain of several varieties; a horny growth on the foot or toe; v.t., to cure or preserve.

corn'brash, n., coarse, calcareous sandstone.

corn'chandler, n., a retailer of corn.

corn'cob, n., the spike on the ear of maize.

corn'cockle, n., a weed that grows in corn.

corn'crake, n., the land-rail bird.

cor'nea, n., the horny membrane of the eye-ball.

corned, adj., preserved, cured; p.p., corn.

cor'nel, n., a wild sort of cherry.

corne'lian, adj., made of cornelian; n., a sort of chalcedony.

cor'neous, adj., horny.

cor'ner, n., an angle, a recess; a monopolizing ring; v.t., to drive into a corner or difficulty; to set up a monopoly.

cor'nered, adj., having corners; p.p., corner.

cor'nering, pr.p., corner.

cor'nerstone, n., the principal stone.

cor'net, n., a trumpet-like instrument; a junior cavalry officer; the white head-dress of a Sister of Charity; a conical wafer for holding icecream.

cor'net-à-pis'tons, n., a cornet on which the notes are produced by pistons (Fr.).

cor'netcy, n., the rank of a cornet.

corn'eum, n., the horny layer of the skin.

corn'field, n., a field for corn.

corn'flour, n., fine meal from corn.

corn'flower, n., the plant Centaurea cyanus, found wild in corn-fields and cultivated in gardens.

cor'nice, n., a projection from the top of a wall or range of columns; overhanging snow.

cor'nicle, n., a little horn-like process (e.g. of a snail).

cornic'ulate, adj., having horns.

cornif'erous, adj., producing or containing hornstone; horn-bearing.

cor'niform, adj., horn-shaped.

corn'ing, n., meat-curing; pr.p., corn.

Cor'nish, adj., pert. or rel. to Cornwall, a county in England.

cor'nist, n., a player on the cornet.

corn'land, n., corn-growing land.

corn'-laws, n. pl., laws rel. to the import and export of corn.

cor'no, n., a horn.

corno'pean, n., a musical instrument; an organ stop so named.

corn'plaster, n., a plaster for relieving corns.

corn'stone, n., mottled red and green lime-stone.

cornuco'pia, n., the horn of plenty.

cornute', adj., horned.

cornu'ted, adj., i.q. cornute.

corn'y, adj., horny; corn-producing; out-of-date.

cor'ocore, n., a Malay form of boat.

cor'ody, n., i.q. corrody.

corol'la, n., a flower's inner envelope.

corolla'ceous, adj., like a corolla.

corol'lary, n., a further inference.

cor'ollate, adj., having a corolla.

cor'ollated, adj., i.q. corollate.

coro'na, n., a crown; a halo; a brand of Havana cigar (Span.).

cor'onach, n., a dirge.

cor'onal, adj., rel. to the corona; n., a garland.

cor'onary, adj., rel. to a crown; encircling; rel. to the heart arteries.

cor'onated, adj., having a corona.

corona'tion, n., the ceremony of crowning.

cor'oner, n., a Crown officer who holds inquests.

cor'onet, n., a little or lesser crown.

cor'oneted, adj., having a coronet.

coro'niform, adj., crown-shaped.

cor'onoid, adj., crown-like.

coro'nule, n., the tuft of a seed.

coroz'o, n., a S. American type of palm-tree.

cor'poral, adj., pert. to the body; n., a white, linen cloth used at the altar; a non-commissioned officer.

corporal'ity, *n.*, the state of being corporal (*i.e.*, unspiritual).

cor'porally, *adv.*, bodily.

cor'poralship, *n.*, the office of corporal.

cor'porate, *adj.*, collective.

cor'porately, *adv.*, collectively.

cor'porateness, *n.*, the state of being united in a body.

corpora'tion, *n.*, an authorized body, with powers to act as a single unit; a potbelly (*slang*).

cor'porative, *adj.*, corporate.

cor'porator, *n.*, a member, or cofounder, of a corporation.

corpo'real, *adj.*, having a body.

corporeal'ity, *n.*, the state of being corporeal.

corpo'really, *adv.*, in bodily form.

corpo'realness, *n.*, *i.q.* corporeality.

corpore'ity, *n.*, physical existence.

cor'posant, *n.*, the fireball seen on ships' masts in stormy weather.

corps, *n.*, a body, a company (*Fr.*).

corpse, *n.*, a dead, human body.

cor'pulence, *n.*, excessive stoutness.

cor'pulency, *n.*, *i.q.* corpulence.

cor'pulent, *adj.*, excessively stout.

cor'pus, *n.*, a body; a whole (*Lat.*).

Corpus Chris'ti, *n.*, the festival of the Eucharist (*Lat.*).

cor'puscle, *n.*, a diminutive body, a particle.

corpus'cular, *adj.*, consisting of corpuscles.

corpuscula'rian, *adj.*, rel. to corpuscles.

corral', *n.*, an enclosure for cattle, or for capturing wild elephants; *v.t.*, to enclose in a corral.

corralled', *p.p.*, corral.

corral'ling, *pr.p.*, corral.

correct', *adj.*, strictly accurate, right, proper; *v.t.*, to put right; to punish.

correct'able, *adj.*, able to be corrected.

correct'ed, *p.p.*, correct.

correct'ing, *pr.p.*, correct.

correc'tion, *n.*, the process of correcting, the amending of an error; punishment.

correc'tional, *adj.*, with a correcting purpose.

correc'titude, *n.*, correctness of conduct.

correct'ive, *adj.*, tending to correction; *n.*, an antidote.

correct'ively, *adv.*, in a corrective way.

correct'ly, *adv.*, rightly, properly, accurately.

correct'ness, *n.*, the state or habit of being correct.

correct'or, *n.*, one who corrects.

cor'relate, *v.t.*, to bring into reciprocal relation.

cor'related, *adj.*, reciprocally relative; *p.p.*, correlate.

cor'relating, *pr.p.*, correlate.

correla'tion, *n.*, the state of reciprocal relation.

correl'ative, *adj.*, *i.q.* correlated; *n.*, the antecedent to a relative pronoun.

correl'atively, *adv.*, in reciprocal relation.

correl'ativeness, *n.*, the state or quality of reciprocal relation.

correl'ativism, *n.*, the doctrine based on the correlative nature of ideas.

correspond', *v.i.*, to answer, to agree, to be equal to; to write letters to.

correspond'ed, *p.p.*, correspond.

correspond'ence, *n.*, the act of corresponding; agreement; communications in writing.

correspond'ent, *adj.*, equal, in agreement; *n.*, one who corresponds.

correspond'ing, *pr.p.*, correspond.

corri'da, *n.*, a bull-fight (*Span.*).

cor'ridor, *n.*, an open gallery or passage.

co'rrie, *n.*, a circular hollow on a mountain side (*Scot.*).

corrigen'da, *n.*, the pl. of corrigendum (*Lat.*).

corrigen'dum, *n.*, a point to be corrected (*Lat.*).

corrigibil'ity, *n.*, the state of being corrigible.

cor'rigible, *adj.*, capable of reform or correction.

cor'rigibleness, *n.*, a willingness to be corrected.

corrob'orant, *adj.*, verifying, confirming.

corrob'orate, *v.t.*, to confirm, to verify, to establish.

corrob'orated, *p.p.*, corroborate.

corrob'orating, *pr.p.*, corroborate.

corrobora'tion, *n.*, the act of corroborating; a verification.

corrob'orative, *adj.*, confirming, supporting.

corrob'orator, *n.*, one who corroborates.

corrob'oratory, *adj.*, *i.q.* corroborative.

corroboree', *n.*, an Australian aboriginal tribal dance.

corrode', *v.t.*, to eat away, to rust; *v.i.*, to rust.

corro'ded, *p.p.*, corrode.

corro'dible, *adj.*, liable to corrosion.

corro'ding, *pr.p.*, corrode.

cor'rody, *n.*, a founder's right of subsistence in his own monastery; provision.

corro'sible, *adj.*, *i.q.* corrodible.

corro'sibleness, *n.*, the state of being corrosible.

corro'sion, *n.*, the process of corroding.

corro'sive, *adj.*, tending to corrode.

corro'sively, *adv.*, in a corrosive way.

corro'siveness, *n.*, the corrosive power.

cor'roval, *n.*, a S. American arrow-poison.

cor'rugant, *adj.*, wrinkling.

cor'rugate, *v.t.*, to wrinkle, or make folds in.

cor'rugated, *adj.*, wrinkled; *p.p.*, corrugate.

cor'rugating, *pr.p.*, corrugate.

corruga'tion, *n.*, the act of corrugating; a wrinkle.

cor'rugator, *n.*, something that corrugates.

corrupt', *adj.*, tainted, depraved, full of errors; *v.t.*, to make putrescent; to taint, to spoil, to make impure, to deprave; *v.i.*, to become impure.

corrupt'ed, *p.p.*, corrupt.

corrupt'er, *n.*, one who corrupts.

corruptibil'ity, *n.*, the state of being corruptible.

corrupt'ible, *adj.*, able to be corrupted; tending to decay.

corrupt'ibleness, *n.*, the state of being corruptible.

corrupt'ibly, *adv.*, in a corruptible way.

corrupt'ing, *pr.p.*, corrupt.

corrup'tion, *n.*, the process of corrupting; decay; dissolution.

corrupt'ive, *adj.*, with a corrupting tendency.

corrupt'ly, *adv.*, wrongly, in error, depravedly.

corrupt'ness, *n.*, the state or quality of being corrupt.

cors'ac, -ak, *n.*, a Tartar fox (*zool.*).

cor'sage, *n.*, a bodice (*Fr.*).

cor'sair, *n.*, a pirate.

corse, *n.*, a dead body.

corse'let, *n.*, light armour for the body.

cor'set, *n.*, a body support, stays.

cors'etier, *n.*, a corsetmaker or -fitter.

cors'etière, *n.*, *i.q.* corsetier (*Fr.*).

Cor'sican, *adj.*, pert. or rel. to Corsica; *n.*, a native of C.

cors'let, *n.*, a light, body armour.

cors'ned, *n.*, a piece of bread used as the test of guilt or innocence.

cortège', *n.*, a train, a procession, esp. funeral (*Fr.*).

Cor'tes, *n.*, the Parliament of Spain or Portugal.

cor'tex, *n.*, bark.

cor'tical, *adj.*, of, or like; bark; external.

cor'ticate, *adj.*, covered with bark.

cor'ticated, *adj.*, *i.q.* corticate.

corticif'erous, *adj.*, bearing bark.

cort'isone, *n.*, a preparation used against arthritis.

corun'dum, *n.*, a hard mineral.

corus'cant, *adj.*, glittering, sparkling.

cor'uscate, *v.i.*, to sparkle, to glitter.

cor'uscated, *p.p.*, çoruscate.

cor'uscating, *pr.p.*, coruscate.

corusca'tion, *n.*, a flash, a sparkle.

corvée', *n.*, the forced labour of feudalism (*Fr.*).

corvette', *n.*, a sloop (*Fr.*).

cor'vine, *adj.*, like, or pert. to a crow.

cor'vus, *n.*, a crow.

Cor'ybant, *n.*, a priest of Cybele.

Coryban'tic, *adj.*, rel. to the Corybants; wild, frenzied.

cor'yl, *n.*, a local anaesthetic.

coryphae'us, *n.*, the leader of a Greek dramatic chorus.

coryphée', *n.*, a ballet dancer (*Fr.*).

cor'yphene, *n.*, a dolphin.

coryphe'us, *n.*, *i.q.* coryphaeus.

cory'za, *n.*, a cold in the head.

cos, *n.*, a long-leaved lettuce.

coscoro'ba, *n.*, a South-American duck.

cose'cant, *n.*, the secant of the complement of any angle.

coseis'mal, *adj.* and *n.*, (a connecting line or curve) of simultaneous shock from an earthquake wave.

cosh, *n.*, a bludgeon (*slang*); *v.t.*, to strike with a cosh.

cosh'er, *v.t.*, to pamper; *v.i.*, to cheat.

co'sier, *adj.*, *comp.* of cosy.

co'siest, *adj.*, *super.* of cosy.

co-'sig'natory, *adj.* and *n.*, (a person) signing jointly with others.

co'sily, *adv.*, in a cosy fashion.

co'sine, *n.*, the sine of a complement of an angle or arc.

cosmet'ic, *adj.*, adorning; heightening beauty; *n.*, a dye, wash, or special preparation for adornment.

cosmetol'ogist, *n.*, one who studies the science of cosmetics.

cosmetol'ogy, *n.*, the science of cosmetics.

cos'mic, *adj.*, rel. to the cosmos or kosmos.

cos'mical, *adj.*, *i.q.* cosmic.

cos'mically, *adv.*, in the manner of the cosmos.

cos'mism, *n.*, seeing of the cosmos as a self-acting whole.

cosmog'onal, *adj.*, rel. to cosmogony.

cosmog'onist, *n.*, a student of cosmogonies.

cosmog'ony, *n.*, a work on the origin of the cosmos.

cosmog'rapher, *n.*, a student of cosmography.

cosmograph'ic, *adj.*, rel. to cosmography.

cosmog'raphy, *n.*, the science of the cosmos.

cos'molabe, *n.*, an astrolabe.

cosmol'atry, *n.*, worship of the cosmos.

cosmolog'ical, *adj.*, rel. to cosmology.

cosmol'ogist, *n.*, a student of cosmology.

cosmol'ogy, *n.*, the study of the origin of the cosmos.

cos'monaut, *n.*, one who travels in space.

cosmoplas'tic, *adj.*, rel. to the structure of the cosmos.

cosmop'olis, *n.*, a cosmopolitan city.

cosmopol'itan, *adj.*, claiming the citizenship of the world; *n.*, a citizen of the world.

cosmopol'itanism, *n.*, the claim to be a citizen of the world.

cosmop'olite, *n.*, *i.q.* cosmopolitan.

cosmopolit'ical, *adj.*, rel. to universal policy.

cosmora'ma, *n.*, a realistic representation of parts of the universe.

cosmoram'ic, *adj.*, of the nature of cosmorama.

cos'mos, *n.*, order; the universe, the world; the system of worlds, galaxies, etc. making up the universe.

cos'mosphere, *n.*, an apparatus showing the relative positions of the earth and stars.

cosmothe'ism, *n.*, pantheism.

cos'motron, *n.*, an apparatus producing nuclear energy.

Cos'sack, *adj.*, rel. to the Cossacks; *n.*, a South Russian horseman.

cos'set, *n.*, a pet lamb; a comforting drink; *v.t.*, to; pamper, to fuss over.

cost, *n.*, an amount to be paid, a charge; *v.t.*, to be valued at; to inflict.

cost'al, *adj.*, rel. to the ribs.

cos'tard, *n.*, a variety of apple.

cos'tate, *adj.*, ribbed.

cos'tated, *adj.*, *i.q.* costate.

cost'-book, *n.*, a list of partners in a mine; a book showing the cost of materials, etc. used in manufacture.

costean', -een, *v.i.*, to sink pits down to rock to find lode.

cos'ter, *n.*, the abbrev. for costermonger.

cos'terdom, *n.*, costers collectively.

cos'termonger, *n.*, a hawker of goods (originally apples).

cost'ing, *pr.p.*, cost.

cos'tive, *adj.*, constipated.

cos'tively, *adv.*, in a costive way.

cos'tiveness, *n.*,. constipation.

cost'liness, *n.*, a high price.

cost'ly, *adj.*, costing much, high-priced.

cost'mary, *n.*, a fragrant plant.

cost-plus, *n.*, the cost plus an agreed· percentage.

cos'tume, *n.*, dress, mode of dress; *v.t.*, to put into costume.

costu'mer, *n.*, one who makes or provides costumes.

costu'mier, *n.*, *i.q.* costumer (*Fr.*).

co'sy, *adj.*, snug, comfortable; *n.*, a cover for a teapot.

cot, *n.*, a cottage; a child's bed.

cotan'gent, *n.*, the tangent of the complement of an angle or arc.

cote, *n.*, a hut, a sheepfold.

cotempora'neous, *adj.*, *i.q.* contemporaneous.

cotem'porary, *adj.* and *n.*, *i.q.* contemporary.

co-ten'ant, *n.*, a joint tenant.

co'terie, *n.*, a company, a party (*Fr.*).

coter'minous,. *adj.*, *i.q.* conterminous.

cothurn'ate, *adj.*, wearing cothurni or buskins; pert. to tragedy.

cothur'nus, *n.*, a buskin, worn by Greek tragic actors; tragedy.

co-tid'al, *adj.*, showing an equality in the tides in different places.

cotil'l(i)on, *n.*, a variety of dance or dance-music; a black and white woollen fabric (*Fr.*).

co'tinine, *n.*, a product of nicotine.

cotoneas'ter, *n.*, a kind of small tree or shrub bearing red berries.

co-trustee', *n.*, a joint trustee.

cot'ta, *n.*, a truncated surplice.

cot'tage, *n.*, a small, country house.

cot'tager, *n.*, the occupant of a cottage, a rustic.

cot'tar, *n.*, *i.q.* cottager.

cott'er, *n.*, a wedge, a pin.

cot'tier, *n.*, *i.q.* cottar.

cot'tolene, *n.*, a lard substitute.

cot'ton, *adj.*, made of cotton; *n.*, a textile; white fluffy material of the plant from which yarn is spun.

cot'ton-gin, *n.*, a machine for cleansing cotton.

cottonoc'racy, *n.*, the magnates of the cotton trade.

Cottonop'olis, *n.*, Manchester.

cot'tonwool', *n.*, raw cotton prepared for wadding.

cot'tony, *adj.*, cotton-like.

cotyle'don, *n.*, a seed lobe.

cotyle'donous, *adj.*, like a cotyledon.

cotyl'iform, *adj.*, cup-shaped.

cot'yloid, *adj.*, like a cup.

couch, *v.t.*, to hide; to express in terms; to operate for cataract; *v.i.*, to lie down; *n.*, a kind of sofa or divan.

couch'ant, *adj.*, lying, crouching (*her.*).

couché, *adj.*, partly lying (*her.*, *Fr.*).

couched, *p.p.*, couch.

couch'er, *n.*, one who couches.

couch'-grass, *n.*, a species of rapidly growing grass.

couch'ing, *n.*, an operation for cataract; *pr.p.*, couch.

cou'eism, *n.*, systematic auto-suggestion, advocated by Emile Coue.

cou'gar, *n.*, a panther.

cough, *n.*, a violent expulsion of air from the· lungs; *v.i.*, to expel air from the lungs with violence.

coughed, *p.p.*, cough.

cough'er, *n.*, one who coughs.

cough'ing, *pr.p.*, cough.

could, *p.p.*, can.

couldn't, *abbrev.* of could not (*colloq.*).

coulisse', *n.*, a portcullis; a side-scene of a stage (*Fr.*).

cou'loir, *n.*, a steep gorge (*Fr.*).

coulomb, *n.*, the unit to measure current electricity, quantitatively.

coul'ter, *n.*, a ploughshare.

coum'arin, *n.*, a fragrant, white crystalline substance obtained from the Tonka bean, etc.

coun'cil, *n.*, a conference, an assembly of councillors.

coun'cil-board, *n.*, the table at which councillors meet, a council meeting.

coun'cil(l)or, *n.*, a member of a council.

coun'sel, *n.*, advice, deliberation; a barrister; *v.t.*, to give advice to.

coun'sel(l)ed, *p.p.*, counsel.

coun'sel(l)ing, *pr.p.*, counsel.

coun'sel(l)or, *n.*, one who gives counsel.

coun'sel(l)orship, *n.*, a counsellor's office or function.

count, *n.*, reckoning; a particular charge; the title of a grade of nobility; *v.t.*, to reckon up, to esteem; *v.i.*, to rely upon.

count'able, *adj.*, able to be counted.

count'ed, *p.p.*, count.

coun'tenance, *n.*, the face, the appearance, the support; *v.t.*, to approve, to support.

coun'tenanced, *p.p.*, countenance.

coun'tenancer, *n.*, one who countenances.

coun'tenancing, *pr.p.*, countenance.

count'er, *adj.*, adverse, contrary; *n.*, one who counts; part of a horse's breast; part of a ship's stern; a shop table; a piece in a game; *v.t.*, to parry, to oppose.

counteract', *v.t.*, to defeat, to neutralize.

counterac'ted, *p.p.*, counteract.

counteract'ing, *pr.p.*, counteract.

counterac'tion, *n.*, the act of counteracting.

counteract'ive, *adj.*, tending to counteract.

counteract'ively, *adv.*, with counteracting effect.

counter-a'gent, *n.*, a counteracting agent or force.

coun'ter-approach, *n.*, trenches dug in front of a besieged place.

coun'ter-attack', *n.*, an attack in reply to an enemy attack; *v.t.* and *i.*, to make this attack.

counter-attrac'tion, *n.*, attraction in an opposite direction.

counterbal'ance, *v.t.*, to weigh against.

counterbal'anced, *p.p.*, counterbalance.

counterbal'ancing, *pr.p.*, counterbalance.

coun'terblast, *n.*, an energetic denunciation.

count'erbrace, *n.*, a device to relieve the stress on a mainbrace; *v.t.*, to brace in opposite directions.

counterchange', *n.*, an exchange, a substitution; *v.t.* and *i.*, to exchange, to substitute.

count'ercharge, *n.*, an opposing charge; *v.t.*, to charge in opposition.

count'ercharm, *n.*, a counteractive charm.

count'ercheck, *n.*, a check in opposition.

count'erclaim, *n.*, a claim against a claim.

counter-clock'wise, *adj.* and *adv.*, opposite to the movement of the hands of a clock.

coun'ter-es'pionage, *n.*, spying directed against the enemy's spy system.

count'erfeit, *adj.*, spurious, feigned; *n.*, an imitation, forgery; *v.t.*, to feign, to imitate; to forge.

count'erfeited, *p.p.*, counterfeit.

count'erfeiter, *n.*, one who counterfeits.

count'erfeiting, *pr.p.*, counterfeit.

count'erfoil, *n.*, the part of a document retained by the originator.

coun'terfort, *n.*, a buttress built to support a wall or terrace.

count'erguard, *n.*, a guard against a guard.

count'er-ir'ritant, *adj.*, producing counter-irritation; *n.*, an irritant to relieve pain in one part by causing it in another.

count'er-jumper, *n.*, a shop assistant.

countermand', *n.*, the cancelling of an order; *v.t.*, to cancel an order.

countermand'ed, *p.p.*, countermand.

countermand'ing, *pr.p.*, countermand.

count'ermarch, *n.*, a march back; *v.i.*, to march back.

count'ermark, *n.*, an additional mark; *v.t.*, to put a countermark on.

count'ermine, *n.*, a mine against a mine; *v.t.*, to engineer a countermine; to thwart.

count'er-motion, *n.*, a motion in opposition.

count'ermure, *n.*, a strengthening wall.

count'erpane, *n.*, a bedcover.

count'erpart, *n.*, a duplicate.

count'er-plea, *n.*, a plea in opposition.

count'erplot, *n.*, a plot against a plot; *v.i.*, to plot against a plot.

count'erplotted, *p.p.*, counterplot.

count'erplotting, *pr.p.*, counterplot.

count'erpoint, *n.*, a branch of musical science.

count'erpoise, *n.*, balance; *v.t.*, to balance.

count'erpoised, *p.p.*, counterpoise.

count'erpoising, *pr.p.*, counterpoise.

coun'ter-punch, *n.*, a die.

coun'ter-reforma'tion, *n.*, reformation running counter to another.

coun'ter-revolu'tion, *n.*, a revolution opposed to a former one or reversing its results.

count'erscarp, *n.*, the slope of a ditch opposite to the scarp.

coun'tershaft, *n.*, a shaft from a main driving shaft, to give motion to certain parts of a system of machinery.

count'ersign, *n.*, an additional signature; a sign corresponding to a sign; *v.t.*, to put an authenticating additional signature.

count'ersigned, *p.p.*, countersign.

count'ersigning, *pr.p.*, countersign.

count'ersink, *v.t.*, to prepare a bed for the head of a screw or bolt.

count'er-stroke, *n.*, a stroke against a stroke.

count'er-tenor, *n.*, the voice part above the tenor.

countervail', *v.t.*, to counterbalance, to compensate.

countervailed', *p.p.*, countervail.

countervail'ing, *pr.p.*, countervail.

countervalla'tion, *n.*, the act of opposing with a rampart; the rampart itself.

count'erview, *n.*, a contrary view.

count'erweigh, *v.t.*, to balance.

count'erweighed, *p.p.*, counterweigh.

count'erweighing, *pr.p.*, counterweigh.

count'erweight, *n.*, a balance.

count'erwork, *n.*, a work against a work; work done at a counter.

count'ess, *n.*, the fem. of earl or count.

count'ing, *pr.p.*, count.

count'ing-house, *n.*, a department of an office in which the accounts are kept.

count'less, *adj.*, innumerable.

count'rified, *adj.*, rustic (*colloq.*); *p.p.*, countrify.

count'rify, *v.t.*, to make rustic.

count'rifying, *pr.p.,* countrify.

count'ry, *n.,* a region, the rustic districts, a political division of territory.

count'ry-dance, *n.,* *i.q.* contre-danse.

count'ryman, *n.,* a native of a country; a rustic.

count'ry-seat, *n.,* a house or estate in the country.

count'ryside, *n.,* a rural area.

count'y, *n.,* a local division for political or administrative purposes.

count'y-court, *n.,* a court for small, civil lawsuits; *v.t.,* to sue.

coup, *n.,* a sudden stroke (*Fr.*).

coup de grâce, *n.,* a final stroke (*Fr.*).

coup de main', *n.,* a sudden exercise of force (*Fr.*).

coup d'état', *n.,* a political sudden exercise of force (*Fr.*).

coupé', *n.,* the front part of a stage-coach; the end of a railway carriage; a four-wheeled carriage for two (*Fr.*).

coupee', *n.,* the salute in a dance (*Fr.*).

coup'élet, *n.,* a motor car with a partially folding hood (*Fr.*).

coup'er, *n.,* a lever on a loom.

coup'le, *n.,* a pair, two of the same kind, a man and his wife; *v.t.,* to link, to join; *v.i.,* to be joined.

coup'led, *p.p.,* couple.

coup'ler, *n.,* one who couples, a thing that couples; an apparatus on an organ for linking keyboards.

coup'let, *n.,* two successive rhyming lines of verse.

coup'ling, *n.,* a link; *pr.p.,* couple.

cou'pon, *n.,* a certificate; a ticket.

cour'age, *n.,* bravery, fortitude.

coura'geous, *adj.,* brave, spirited.

coura'geously, *adv.,* bravely.

coura'geousness, *n.,* courageous character.

cour'ant, *adj.,* running (*her.*); *n.,* a newssheet.

cour'bash, *n.,* a whip made of hippopotamus hide.

cour'ier, *n.,* a messenger; an attendant (*Fr.*).

cour'lan, *n.,* a long-billed wading bird of tropical America, famous for its dismal cry (*Fr.*).

course, *n.,* a race; a racing-track; direction, a line of movement, a stage in a meal; a level of masonry; *v.t.,* to chase with greyhounds.

coursed, *p.p.,* course.

cours'er, *n.,* one who courses; a swift horse.

cours'ing, *n.,* chasing hares; *pr.p.,* course.

court, *n.,* an enclosed space; a palace, a king's household; a place of justice, the judge; *v.t.,* to solicit, to flatter, to pay devotion to.

court'-bar'on, *n.,* a manorial court.

court'-chaplain, *n.,* the chaplain of a sovereign.

court'ed, *p.p.,* court.

Courtelle', *n.,* a synthetic fibre or fabric.

court'eous, *adj.,* polite, considerate.

court'eously, *adv.,* politely.

court'eousness, *n.,* the exercise of courtesy.

court'er, *n.,* one who courts.

court'esan, *n.,* a prostitute.

court'esy, *n.,* politeness, considerateness, civility.

court'-hand, *n.,* an old style of handwriting.

court'-house, *n.,* a building in which a court is held.

court'ier, *n.,* one who is attached to a court; a person of courtly manners; one who seeks favours.

court'ing, *n.,* wooing; *pr.p.,* court.

court'-lands, *n.,* the land of a lord of the manor.

court'-leet, *n.,* an old court of record.

court'liness, *n.,* the habit of dignified courtesy.

court'ly, *adj.,* courteous, refined.

court-mar'tial, *n.,* a naval or military court of discipline.

court'-plaster, *n.,* a superior sticking-plaster.

courtroom, *n.,* a room in which law court proceedings take place.

court'ship, *n.,* the act or period of courting.

court'yard, *n.,* an open yard enclosed wholly or partly by buildings.

cous'in, *n.,* an uncle's or aunt's son or daughter.

cous'in ger'man, *n.,* a first-cousin.

Cousteau', *n.,* a breathing apparatus for frogmen (after its inventor).

couteau, *n.,* a knife or dagger (*Fr.*).

couture', *n.,* dressmaking (*Fr.*).

couturier', *n.,* a dressmaker (*Fr.*).

couturiere', *n.,* the fem. of couturier; a modiste (*Fr.*).

couvade', *n.,* a primitive practice of putting to bed the father of a newly born infant and conveying to him sympathetic felicitations.

cove, *n.,* a creek, a small bay; a quiet corner; a hollowed moulding; *v.t.,* to arch.

coved, *adj.,* arched; *p.p.,* cove.

cov'enant, *n.,* a written agreement; a common pledge; *v.i.,* to make a covenant.

cov'enanted, *adj.,* under agreement; *p.p.,* covenant.

covenantee', *n.,* one with whom a contract is made.

cov'enanter, *n.,* one who makes an agreement. (Also *covenantor.*)

cov'enanting, *pr.p.,* covenant.

cov'enantor, *n.,* *i.q.* covenanter.

Cov'ent Gard'en, *n.,* the famous fruit and vegetable market in London, England. Also the Royal Opera House (*colloq.*).

cov'er, *n.,* something spread over; a shelter; a covert; a furnished place for each guest at table; *v.t.,* to lay something over, to hide.

cov'erage, *n.,* the extent covered.

cov'er-charge, *n.,* a service charge.

cov′ered, *p.p.*, cover.

cov′erer, *n.*, one who covers.

cov′er-girl, *n.*, a girl pictured on the cover of a magazine, etc.

cov′ering, *n.*, something that covers; *pr.p.*, cover.

cov′erlet, *n.*, a bed-quilt.

cov′er-point, *n.*, a fieldsman deeper than point in cricket.

cov′ert, *adj.*, concealed, secret, underhand; protected; *n.*, a shelter, a thicket, the hiding-place of wild animals.

cov′ertly, *adv.*, secretly.

cov′erture, *n.*, shelter; the protected state of a married woman.

cov′et, *v.t.*, to desire what is not one's own.

cov′etable, *adj.*, able to be coveted.

cov′eted, *p.p.*, covet.

cov′eter, *n.*, one who covets.

cov′eting, *pr.p.*, covet.

cov′etous, *adj.*, ardently desirous, avaricious.

cov′etously, *adv.*, in a covetous way.

cov′etousness, *n.*, the habit of coveting.

cov′ey, *n.*, a brood of birds, particularly partridges.

cov′in, *n.*, a collusion in a fraud.

co′ving, *n.*, the projection of a higher over a lower storey; *pr.p.*, cove.

cov′inous, *adj.*, fraudulent.

cow, *n.*, the female ox; *v.t.*, to quell by fear.

cow′age, *n.*, a tropical plant used as a vermifuge.

cow′an, *n.*, an unapprenticed workman (*Scot.*).

cow′ard, *n.*, one who lacks courage, a poltroon.

cow′ardice, *n.*, conduct showing fear, or lack of courage.

cow′ardliness, *n.*, *i.q.* cowardice.

cow′ardly, *adj.* and *adv.*, without courage, fearful.

cow′boy, *n.*, a boy in charge of cows; a ranchman.

cow′-calf, *n.*, a female calf.

cow′catcher, *n.*, an apparatus in front of a locomotive for clearing away obstructions.

cowed, *p.p.*, cow.

cow′er, *v.i.*, to shudder, to crouch in fear.

cow′ered, *p.p.*, cower.

cow′ering, *pr.p.*, cower.

cow′gate, *n.*, the right to pasture cattle.

cow′hage, *n.*, a vermifuge.

cow′heel, *n.*, gelatine made from a cow's foot.

cow′herd, *n.*, one who has charge of cows.

cow′hide, *adj.*, made of cowhide; *n.*, leather made of cow's skin; a whip made of hide.

cow′ing, *pr.p.*, cow.

cowl, *n.*, a monk's hooded robe; a revolving top to a chimney pot.

cowled, *adj.*, wearing a cowl.

cowl′ing, *n.*, the casing of an engine.

co-work′er, *n.*, a colleague, a collaborator.

cow′pox, *n.*, a disease affecting a cow's udders.

cow′rie, cow′ry, *n.*, shell money.

co-wri′ter, *n.*, a joint author.

cow′slip, *n.*, a yellow flower.

cox′comb, *n.*, a conceited fellow.

coxcom(b)′ical, *adj.*, conceited, foppish.

cox′combry, *n.*, the act or nature of a coxcomb.

cox′swain, *n.*, one who steers a boat.

cox′y, *adj.*, *i.q.* cocky.

coy, *adj.*, bashful, demure.

coy′ish, *adj.*, playfully demure.

coy′ly, *adv.*, demurely, modestly.

coy′ness, *n.*, demureness.

coyo′te, *n.*, the prairie wolf.

coypu, *n.*, a South American, aquatic, beaver-like rodent.

coz′en, *v.t.*, to cheat.

coz′enage, *n.*, cheating, trickery.

coz′ened, *p.p.*, cozen.

coz′ener, *n.*, one who cozens.

coz′ening, *pr.p.*, cozen.

co′zily, *adv.*, *i.q.* cosily.

co′zy, *adj.*, *i.q.* cosy.

crab, *n.*, a crustacean; *v.t.*, to catch crabs; to beat; to irritate.

crab′-apple, *n.*, a small, very sour kind of apple.

crab′bed, *adj.*, sour, morose; difficult to read; *p.p.*, crab.

crab′bedly, *adv.*, morosely.

crab′bedness, *n.*, morosity.

crab′ber, *n.*, a faultfinder.

crab′bing, *pr.p.*, crab.

crab′by, *adj.*, morose.

crab′stick, *n.*, a cudgel; a morose fellow.

crab′-tree, *n.*, a tree growing crab apples.

crab′-yaws, *n. pl.*, ulcers on the sole.

crack, *adj.*, first-class (*colloq.*); *v.t.*, to make a fissure in, to break open; *v.i.*, to split open; *n.*, a fissure, a fracture, a sharp sound (as of a whip, etc.); a witty sarcastic comment (*colloq.*); an attempt (*colloq.*).

crack′ajack, *n.* and *adj.*, *i.q.* crackerjack.

crack′brained, *adj.*, silly.

cracked, *adj.*, broken, imperfect; out of one's mind (*colloq.*); *p.p.*, crack.

crack′er, *n.*, anything that cracks; a variety of biscuit; a firework.

crack′erjack, *n.* and *adj.*, (a person or thing) of supreme excellence.

crack′ing, *pr.p.*, crack.

crack′le, *n.*, a cracking sound repeated; *v.i.*, to make a slight explosion; *v.t.*, to cover with cracks.

crack′led, *p.p.*, crackle.

crack′ling, *n.*, a continued sound of slight explosion; the rind of roast pig; *pr.p.*, crackle.

crack′nel, *n.*, a variety of biscuit.

crack′pot, *n.*, a crazy person (*colloq.*).

cracks'man, *n.*, a burglar.

crack'y, *adj.*, full of cracks; liable to crack; crazy (*colloq.*).

cra'dle, *n.*, a babe's bed; a native place; a timber-frame for launching vessels; a gold-washing apparatus; *v.t.*, to put into a cradle; to protect.

cra'dled, *p.p.*, cradle.

cra'dling, *pr.p.*, cradle.

craft, *n.*, skill of hand, cunning.

craft'ily, *adv.*, cunningly.

craft'iness, *n.*, the act or quality of being crafty.

crafts'man, *n.*, a skilled worker, a member of a trade.

craft'y, *adj.*, cunning.

crag, *n.*, a steep, rough rock.

crag'ged, *adj.*, having crags.

crag'giness, *n.*, the quality of being craggy.

crag'gy, *adj.*, precipitous, rugged.

crags'man, *n.*, an expert crag-climber.

crake, *n.*, the corn-crake.

cram, *n.*, a falsehood (*slang*); preparation for an examination; *v.t.*, to stuff, to fill to overflowing; to prepare intensively for examination; to tell a falsehood to.

cram'bo, *n.*, a family game of rhyming.

crammed, *p.p.*, cram.

cram'mer, *n.*, one who crams.

cram'ming, *pr.p.*, cram.

cramp, *n.*, a muscular spasm; a kind of tool; *v.t.*, to confine, to narrow; to cause a muscular spasm.

cramped, *p.p.*, cramp.

cramp'-fish, *n.*, the torpedo, a fish that gives an electric shock.

cramp'ing, *pr.p.*, cramp.

cramp'-iron, *n.*, a piece of iron, bent at the ends, to hold masonry in place.

cram'pon, *n.*, a piece of iron fastened to a climber's shoes; the aerial root of a climbing plant.

crampoon', *n.*, a weight-lifting apparatus.

cran, *n.*, a measure of fresh herrings which is approx. 37½ gallons (*Scot.*).

cra'nage, *n.*, the right or cost of loading or unloading.

cran'berry, *n.*, a variety of whortleberry.

crane, *n.*, a tall wading bird; a weight-lifting machine; *v.i.*, to stretch.

crane'-fly, *n.*, the daddy-long-legs.

cranes'bill, *n.*, a variety of geranium.

cra'nial, *adj.*, rel. to the skull.

craniog'nomy, *n.*, the science of skulls.

craniolog'ical, *adj.*, rel. to craniology.

craniol'ogist, *n.*, an expert in skulls.

craniol'ogy, *n.*, the study of skulls.

craniom'eter, *n.*, a skull-measuring instrument.

craniomet'rical, *adj.*, rel. to craniometry.

craniom'etry, *n.*, the scientific measurement of skulls.

cranios'copy, *n.*, the scientific study of skull formation.

cra'nium, *n.*, the skull.

crank, *adj.*, easily overturned; *n.*, a turn; an instrument for turning an axis; a monomaniac.

crank'le, *v.t.* and *i.*, to bend.

crank'led, *p.p.*, crankle.

crank'ling, *pr.p.*, crankle.

crank'y, *adj.*, shaky, loose, crotchety.

cran'nied, *adj.*, chinky.

crann'og, *n.*, an ancient lake-dwelling in Scotland or Ireland.

cran'ny, *n.*, a chink.

crape, *n.*, a thin, gauzy material; *v.t.*, to cover with crape.

craps, *n. pl.*, a game of chance played with dice.

crap'ulence, *n.*, sickness after a debauch.

crap'ulent, *adj.*, drunken.

crap'ulous, *adj.*, *i.q.* crapulent.

crash, *n.*, a loud, alarming noise; coarse linen; *v.t.*, to dash; *v.i.*, to make a loud noise; to be involved in a transport accident.

crash'-dive, *n.*, a steep and sudden dive (submarine).

crashed, *p.p.*, crash.

crash'ing, *pr.p.*, crash.

crash'-lan'ding, *n.*, a forced landing (aircraft).

cra'sis, *n.*, the formation of a long vowel or diphthong from two vowels.

crass, *adj.*, coarse, stupid; unsubtle.

crass'ier, *n.*, a dump (*Fr.*).

crass'itude, *n.*, stupidity.

cratch, *n.*, a crib, a rack.

cratch'es, *n. pl.*, a swelling on a horse's pastern or beneath the hoof.

crate, *n.*, a hamper, a packing-frame.

cra'ter, *n.*, the hollow of a volcano.

crater'iform, *adj.*, cup-shaped.

craunch, *v.t.* and *i.*, *i.q.* crunch.

craunched, *p.p.*, craunch.

craunch'ing, *pr.p.*, craunch.

cravat', *n.*, a neck-tie.

crave, *v.t.*, to beg humbly, to yearn for.

craved, *p.p.*, crave.

cra'ven, *adj.*, cowardly, dastardly.

cra'ver, *n.*, one who craves.

cra'ving, *pr.p.*, crave.

cra'vingly, *adv.*, with great yearning.

craw, *n.*, a bird's crop.

craw'fish, *n.*, *i.q.* crayfish.

crawk, *v.i.*, to squawk.

crawl, *n.*, a slow, difficult walk on hands and knees; *v.i.*, to creep, to move with difficulty.

crawled, *p.p.*, crawl.

crawl'er, *n.*, one who, or that which, crawls.

crawl'ing, *pr.p.*, crawl.

cray'fish, *n.*, a fresh-water crustacean. (A corruption of the French *écrevisse*.)

cray'on, *adj.*, drawn in chalks; *n.*, a drawing chalk; a drawing in chalks; a carbon point.

cray'onist, *n.*, an artist in chalks.

craze, *n.*, a besetting whim, an obsession; a crack; *v.i.*, to lose one's senses; *v.t.*, to drive out of one's wit; to produce fissures in a smooth surface.

crazed, *p.p.*, craze.

cra'zily, *adv.*, in a crazy fashion.

cra'ziness, *n.*, a crazy condition.

cra'zing, *pr.p.*, craze.

cra'zy, *adj.*, demented; unsafe.

creak, *n.*, a grating noise; *v.i.*, to make a sound of grating.

creaked, *p.p.*, creak.

creak'ing, *pr.p.*, creak.

creak'y, *adj.*, producing creaks.

cream, *n.*, the oily element of milk; the choicest part; *v.t.*, to skim; *v.i.*, to form cream.

cream'-cheese', *n.*, a cheese made from cream.

creamed, *p.p.*, cream.

cream'er, *n.*, a machine for separating cream; a flat dish for skimming cream off milk.

cream'ery, *n.*, a shop where cream and butter are sold.

cream'ing, *pr.p.*, cream.

cream'-laid, *adj.*, cream-coloured with a laid watermark.

cream'y, *adj.*, yielding cream; cream-like.

crease, *n.*, a wrinkle; a demarcation line in cricket; *v.t.* and *i.*, to wrinkle.

creased, *p.p.*, crease.

creas'er, *n.*, anything that creases.

creas'ing, *pr.p.*, crease.

crea'table, *adj.*, able to be created.

create', *v.t.*, to bring into being, to make, to originate, to appoint.

crea'ted, *p.p.*, create.

cre'atine, *n.*, an organic base found in flesh juice.

crea'ting, *pr.p.*, create.

crea'tion, *n.*, the act of creating; all created things; a masterpiece; an elevation to rank.

crea'tionism, *n.*, the theory that a soul is specifically created for every human being at birth.

crea'tive, *adj.*, with the faculty of creating.

crea'tiveness, *n.*, the faculty of creating.

creativ'ity, *n.*, *i.q.* creativeness.

crea'tor, *n.*, one who creates.

crea'tural, *adj.*, rel. to creatures.

crea'ture, *n.*, a created being; the tool of another.

crea'turely, *adj.*, of creatures.

crèche, *n.*, a public nursery (*Fr.*).

cre'dence, *n.*, belief; a side sanctuary table.

creden'da, *n.*, the pl. of credendum (*Lat.*).

creden'dum, *n.*, an article for belief (*Lat.*).

cre'dent, *adj.*, believing.

creden'tial, *n.*, a testimonial or proof of identity and status.

credibil'ity, *n.*, the state of being credible.

cred'ible, *adj.*, worthy of belief; believable.

cred'ibleness, *n.*, *i.q.* credibility.

cred'ibly, *adv.*, believably.

cred'it, *n.*, belief; honour, permission to defer payment; *v.t.*, to believe, to trust; to acknowledge as owning.

cred'itable, *adj.*, with honour.

cred'itably, *adv.*, to one's honour.

cred'ited, *p.p.*, credit.

cred'iting, *pr.p.*, credit.

cred'itor, *n.*, one to whom a debt is due.

cred'o, *n.*, the musical setting of the Nicene Creed.

credu'lity, *n.*, the state of being credulous.

cred'ulous, *adj.*, believing anything that is said.

cred'ulously, *adv.*, with credulity.

cred'ulousness, *n.*, *i.q.* credulity.

creed, *n.*, an accepted belief; articles of faith.

creek, *n.*, a small inlet of the sea.

creek'let, *n.*, a small stream.

creel, *n.*, a fishing-basket; *v.t.*, to place in a creel.

creep, *v.i.*, to crawl; to move painfully; to grow along the ground.

creep'age, *n.*, gradual movement.

creep'er, *n.*, anything that creeps; a clinging plant; a sycophant.

creep'ing, *pr.p.*, creep.

creep'ingly, *adv.*, in a creeping way.

creep'y, *adj.*, mysterious; fearful.

creese, *n.*, a Malayan knife.

cremate', *v.t.*, to burn a corpse.

crema'ted, *p.p.*, cremate.

crema'ting, *pr.p.*, cremate.

crema'tion, *n.*, the act of cremating.

cremat'or, *n.*, a person or furnace cremating corpses or rubbish.

cremato'rium, *n.*, a place for cremation.

crème, *n.*, cream; the élite (*Fr.*).

crème de menthe, *n.*, a peppermint liqueur (*Fr.*).

cremnophob'ia, *n.*, a morbid dread of heights.

Cremo'na, *n.*, a city in Italy; a violin by one of the great Cremona makers.

cre'nate, *adj.*, with notches.

cren'ature, *n.*, a notching.

cren'el, *n.*, *i.q.* crenelle.

cren'el(l)ate, *v.t.*, to embattle; to decorate with indented mouldings.

cren'el(l)ated, *p.p.*, crenellate.

cren'el(l)ating, *pr.p.*, crenellate.

crenella'tion, *n.*, a decoration with indented mouldings.

crenelle′, *n.*, an embrasure of a battlement.

cren′ulate, *adj.*, notched.

cre′ole, *adj.*, rel. to Creoles; *n.*, a European born in the W. Indies or Span. America; in Louisiana a native of French or Spanish origin; one born there.

cre′osote, *n.*, an antiseptic product of wood-tar.

cre′pance, *n.*, a wound in a horse's hind leg produced by the other leg striking against it.

crêpe, *n.*, a crape-like fabric (*Fr.*).

crêpe de chine, *n.*, a strong, glossy crape (*Fr.*).

crêpe′line, *n.*, a light dress material (*Fr.*).

crep′itant, *adj.*, making a cracking or grinding sound.

crep′itate, *v.i.*, to make a cracking or grinding sound.

crep′itated, *p.p.*, crepitate.

crep′itating, *pr.p.*, crepitate.

crepita′tion, *n.*, the act or sound of cracking or grinding.

crep′on, *n.*, a crape-like material (*Fr.*).

crept, *p.p.*, creep.

crep′uscle, *n.*, *i.q.* crepuscule.

crepus′cular, *adj.*, dim; twilight.

crepus′cule, *n.*, twilight.

crepus′culous, *adj.*, *i.q.* crepuscular.

crescen′do, *adv.*, with increasing volume; *n.*, a growing volume of sound.

cres′cent, *adj.*, growing; *n.*, a new moon; a moon-shaped emblem; the Moslem Empire.

cresco′graph, *n.*, an instrument for recording plant growth.

cress, *n.*, the name for a variety of cruciferous plants.

cres′set, *n.*, a beacon-light; a stand for the light.

crest, *n.*, a top, a ridge, a plume; the emblem surmounting a helmet; *v.t.*, to top, to surmount.

crest′ed, *adj.*, having a crest; *p.p.*, crest.

crest′fallen, *adj.*, dejected through disappointment.

crest′ing, *n.*, a surmounting ornament; *pr.p.*, crest.

creta′ceous, *adj.*, chalky.

Cre′tan, *adj.*, bel. or pert. to Crete; *n.*, a native of C.

cret′ic, *n.*, a metrical foot.

cre′tin, *n.*, one suffering from cretinism.

cre′tinism, *n.*, a disease producing deformity and idiocy.

cret′inoid, *adj.*, like a cretin.

cretonne′, *n.*, a printed, cotton fabric used for curtains and coverings (*Fr.*).

crevasse′, *n.*, a cleft in a glacier (*Fr.*).

crev′et, *n.*, a pot for melting gold.

crevette′, *adj.*, shrimp-pink.

crev′ice, *n.*, a fissure.

crew, *n.*, the men of a ship or boat; *p.p.*, crow.

crew-cut, *n.*, a male hair style.

crew′el, *n.*, a material used for fancy work.

crib, *n.*, a manger; a child's bed; a translation; *v.t.*, to confine; to appropriate.

crib′bage, *n.*, a card game.

cribbed, *p.p.*, crib.

crib′bing, *pr.p.*, crib.

crib′ble, *n.*, a riddle; a coarse meal; *v.t.*, to riddle.

crib′bled, *adj.*, dotted or punctured; *p.p.*, cribble.

crib′bling, *pr.p.*, cribble.

crib′riform, *adj.*, like a sieve.

crick, *n.*, a muscular twisting of the neck; *v.t.*, to twist.

crick′et, *n.*, a field game played with bats, ball and stumps; a grass-hopper-like insect.

crick′eter, *n.*, one who plays cricket.

crick′le, *v.i.*, to make a sharp, thin sound.

cri′coid, *adj.*, like a ring.

cri de coeur, *n.*, a passionate cry; an appeal (*Fr.*).

cried, *p.p.*, cry.

cri′er, *n.*, one who cries; an official who proclaims publicly.

crik′ey, *int.*, an exclamation of surprise (*slang*).

crime, *n.*, an offence.

crim′inal, *adj.*, pert. or rel. to crime; *n.*, one guilty of crime.

criminal′ity, *n.*, the state or quality of a criminal.

crim′inally, *adv.*, in a criminal way.

crim′inaloid, *n.*, one with criminal tendencies; a first offender.

crim′inate, *v.t.*, to accuse, to incriminate.

crim′inated, *p.p.*, criminate.

crim′inating, *pr.p.*, criminate.

crimina′tion, *n.*, the act of criminating.

crim′inative, *adj.*, tending to criminate.

crim′inatory, *adj.*, *i.q.* criminative.

criminol′ogy, *n.*, the study of crime and criminals.

crim′inous, *adj.*, guilty of crime (only in the phrase *criminous clerk*, i.e. priest).

crimp, *n.*, one who crimps soldiers or sailors; the keeper of a low class of seamen's lodgings; *v.t.*, to make wavy; to contract; to enlist by foul means; to nip together by bending.

crimped, *p.p.*, crimp.

crimp′ing, *pr.p.*, crimp.

crimp′ing-iron, *n.*, an iron for crimping.

crim′ple, *n.*, a wrinkle; *v.t.*, to crimp.

crim′pled, *p.p.*, crimple.

Crim′plene, *n.*, a crease-resistant material.

crim′pling, *pr.p.*, crimple.

crim′py, *adj.*, frizzy.

crim′son, *adj.*, of deep red colour; *n.*, a deep red; *v.t.*, to stain deep red; *v.i.*, to blush.

crim′soned, *p.p.*, crimson.

crim′soning, *pr.p.*, crimson.

cri′nal, *adj.*, rel. to hair.

cri′nate, *adj.*, having hairs.

cri'natory, adj., i.q. cri-nal.

cringe, n., servile self-abasement; v.i., to bend down servilely.

cringed, p.p., cringe.

crin'ger, n., one who cringes.

crin'ging, pr.p., cringe.

crin'gingly, adv., in a cringing way.

crin'gle, n., a.loop.

crinicul'tural, adj., concerning the cultivation of hair.

crinig'erous, adj., producing hair.

cri'nite, adj., hairy.

crin'kle, n., a wrinkle; v.t. and i., to wrinkle.

crin'kled, p.p., crinkle.

crin'kling, pr.p., crinkle.

crin'kum-cran'kum, n., a zig-zag.

crin'oid, n., a sea-lily.

crinol'dal, adj., rel. to a crinoid.

crinolette', n., a contrivance for distending the back of a woman's skirt.

crin'oline, n., a hoop skirt.

crip'ple, n., one who is crippled; v.t., to maim, to hamper.

crip'pled, p.p., cripple.

crip'pling, pr.p., cripple.

cri'sis, n., a turning-point; an extremity of danger.

crisp, adj., wavy, brittle, bright; v.t., to make wavy.

cris'pated, adj., curled.

crispa'tion, n., curling.

crisped, p.p., crisp.

crisp'er, n., anything that crisps.

Cris'pin, n., the patron saint of shoemakers.

crisp'ing, pr.p., crisp.

crisp'ly, adv., in a crisp way.

crisp'ness, n., the crisp state or quality.

crisp'y, adj., somewhat crisp.

criss'-cross, adj., backwards and forwards; n., an intersection.

cris'tate, adj., crested.

cris'tated, adj., i.q. cristate.

crite'ria, n., the pl. of criterion.

crite'rion, n., a test, a proof; a standard of attainment.

crit'ic, n., a critical person; a professional reviewer.

crit'ical, adj., exact; judging; censorious; at a crisis.

crit'ically, adv., in a critical way.

crit'icalness, n., the critical habit or quality.

crit'icism, n., judgment, censure.

crit'icize, v.t., to pass judgment on; to review; to censure.

crit'icized, p.p., criticize.

crit'icizer, n., one who criticizes.

crit'icizing, pr.p., criticize.

critique', n., a review of literary or artistic work (Fr.).

criz'zle, v.i., to become wrinkled.

criz'zled, p.p., crizzle.

crizz'ling, pr.p., crizzle.

croak, n., a hoarse noise or cry; v.i., to make a hoarse noise; to grumble; to die (colloq.).

croaked, p.p., croak.

croak'er, n., one who croaks; a grumbler.

croak'ing, pr.p., croak.

Cro'at, n., a native of Croatia.

Croa'tian, adj., pert. or rel. to Croatia.

cro'ceate, adj., saffron, saffron-coloured.

croche, n., the top of an antler.

cro'chet, n., a form of working a textile yarn into patterned garments; v.t., to work at crochet (Fr.).

cro'cheted, p.p., crochet.

cro'cheting, pr.p., crochet.

cro'cidolite, n., a yellow mineral used for ornament.

crock, n., an earthenware pot; soot on a pot; v.t., to overlay with soot.

crock'ery, n., earthenware.

crock'et, n., a projecting ornament on spires and canopy work.

croc'odile, n., a large, carnivorous amphibian.

crocodil'ian, adj., rel. to the crocodile.

cro'cus, n., a spring flower.

Croe'sus, n., a wealthy man (orig. the rich king of Lydia).

croft, n., a small field enclosure; a small farm holding; v.t., to bleach.

croft'ed, p.p., croft.

croft'er, n., one who cultivates a croft.

croft'ing, pr.p., croft.

crois'ant, adj., crescent.

crois'sant, n., a crescent-shaped bread roll (Fr.).

cro'ma, n., a quaver (mus.).

crom'lech, n., a prehistoric, stone circle.

cromor'na, n., an organ reed-stop.

Cromwellian, adj., rel. to Oliver Cromwell, Lord Protector of England, Scotland and Ireland, 1653.

crone, n., an old woman.

cro'ny, n., a very intimate friend.

crook, n., a staff with a bent end; a sharper; a criminal; v.t., to bend; v.i., to be bent.

crooked, p.p., crook.

crook'ed, adj., not straight; unprincipled.

crook'edly, adv., in a crooked way.

crook'edness, n., the crooked state or quality.

crook'ing, pr.p., crook.

croon, n., a low hum; v.t. and i., to sing softly.

crooned, p.p., croon.

croon'er, n., one who sings sentimentally.

croon'ing, pr.p., croon.

crop, n., the result of cropping; a bird's craw; a close cut of hair; a hunting-whip; v.t., to cut close, to reap; v.i., to sprout, to appear suddenly.

cropped, p.p., crop.

crop'per, n., a cropping implement; one who crops; a bad fall (slang).

crop'ping, pr.p., crop.

cropp'y, *n.*, a person with short, cropped hair, esp. an Irish rebel in 1798.

cro'quet, *n.*, a game with balls, mallets and hoops (*Fr.*); *v.t.*, to drive away an opponent's ball.

croquette', *n.*, a fried ball of minced meat, potatoes, fish, etc. (*Fr.*).

crore, *n.*, a sum of Indian money = 100 lakhs.

cro'sier, *n.*, a bishop's staff or crook. (Also *crozier.*)

cro'siered, *adj.*, having a crosier.

cros'let, *n.*, *i.q.* crosslet.

cross, *n.*, an upright line crossed by another at right angles; the Christian emblem; a great trial; a cross-breed; *v.t.*, to place across; to pass over; to mark crosswise; to hinder.

cross'-action, *n.*, a counter-suit.

cross'-armed, *adj.*, with crossed arms.

cross'bar, *n.*, the horizontal part of a football goal; *v.t.*, to draw a bar across.

cross'barred, *p.p.*, crossbar.

cross'bearer, *n.*, the bearer of a cross.

cross'belt, *n.*, a belt for cartridges, etc., hanging from the shoulder to the opposite hip.

cross'bill, *n.*, a bird with a cruciform bill.

cross'-bones, *n. pl.*, crossed thigh bones under a skull as the emblem of death.

cross'bow, *n.*, an old cross-shaped bow.

cross'-breed, *n.*, an animal of mixed breed.

cross'-butt'ock, *n.* and *v.t.*, (to) throw over the hip, in wrestling.

cross'-coun'ter, *n.*, a cross blow at the head, in boxing.

cross'-cut, *n.*, a diagonal cut, path, etc.; *v.t.*, to intersect.

crosse, *n.*, a long racquet used in the game of lacrosse (*Fr.*).

crossect', *v.t.*, to divide transversely.

crossed, *p.p.*, cross.

cross-examina'tion, *n.*, the examination of a

witness on behalf of the opposing party.

cross-exam'ine, *v.t.*, to examine a witness on behalf of the opposing party. (Also *cross-question.*)

cross-exam'ined, *p.p.*, cross-examine.

cross-exam'ining, *pr.p.*, cross-examine.

cross'-eyed, *adj.*, squinting.

cross'-garnet, *n.*, a T-shaped hinge, fixed to a door, etc. by the long shank.

cross'-grain, *n.*, a grain running across the regular grain.

cross'-grained, *adj.*, with irregular grain; of difficult temper.

cross'-hatch, *v.t.*, to engrave with intersecting parallel lines.

cross'-head, *n.*, a beam crossing the top; a contents heading across the column in a newspaper. (Also *cross-heading.*)

cross'-heading, *n.*, *i.q.* cross-head (second meaning).

cross'ing, *n.*, the act of crossing; a way over; a thwarting; *pr.p.*, cross.

cross'-legged, *adj.*, with the legs crossed.

cross'let, *n.*, a crucible. (Also *croslet.*)

cross'-light, *n.*, a light which crosses another; the illustration of a subject from another viewpoint.

cross'ly, *adv.*, in a cross way.

cross'ness, *n.*, the cross quality; bad temper.

cross'ov'er, *n.*, a woman's dress or wrap, one part of which crosses another; one road over another.

cross'patch, *n.*, an ill-tempered person (*colloq.*).

cross'-pur'pose, *n.*, a contrary purpose.

cross'-ques'tion, *v.t.*, *i.q.* cross-examine.

cross'-ques'tioned, *p.p.*, cross-question.

cross'-ques'tioning, *pr.p.*, cross-question.

cross'-ref'erence, *n.*, a reference to another part.

cross'road, *n.*, a road meeting or crossing another.

cross'ruff, *n.* and *v.i.*,

(to) alternate trumping by partners in whist or bridge.

cross'-sec'tion, *n.*, a transverse section; a representative sample.

cross'-stitch, *n.*, in needlework, two stitches crossing each other.

cross'-tie, *n.*, a railway sleeper.

cross'-tree, *n.*, a cross-piece at the mast-head (*naut.*).

cross'ways, *n.*, a meeting-place of several roads.

cross'wise, *adv.*, across; like a cross.

cross'word, *n.*, a puzzle with crossed words for completion.

crotch, *n.*, a hook.

crotched, *adj.*, hooked.

crotch'et, *n.*, a hook-shaped musical note; a foolish whim.

crotch'eted, *adj.*, consisting of crotchets.

crotch'ety, *adj.*, possessed by whims; odd.

cro'ton, *n.*, an E. Indian plant yielding a purgative oil.

croton'ic, *adj.*, rel. to croton.

cro'ton-oil, *n.*, the oil from the seeds of the croton.

crouch, *v.i.*, to bend down, to stoop.

crouched, *p.p.*, crouch.

crouch'ing, *adj.*, bent; *pr.p.*, crouch.

croup, *n.*, an affection of the trachea and larynx.

croupade', *n.*, a horse's leap in which the hind legs are drawn up.

crou'pier, *n.*, the man who handles the money at a gaming-table (*Fr.*).

croustade', *n.*, a dish with a crust of bread (*Fr.*).

croute, *n.*, a toasted bread crust (*Fr.*).

crouton', *n.*, a diced, quick-fried bread added to soups (*Fr.*).

crow, *n.*, the sound of a cock; a large, black, croaking bird; *v.i.*, to make the sound of a cock; to exult over.

crow'bar, *n.*, an iron lever.

crowd, *n.*, a gathering of people or things; a Welsh, stringed, musical instrument; *v.t.*,

to press together; to oppress with numbers; *v.i.*, to assemble in great numbers.

crowd′ed, *adj.*, very busy with people; *p.p.*, crowd.

crowd′er, *n.*, one who crowds; a player to a crowd.

crowd′ie, *n.*, a thick gruel (*Scot.*).

crowd′ing, *pr.p.*, crowd.

crowd′y, *n.*, thick gruel.

crowed, *p.p.*, crow.

crow′foot, *n.*, *i.q.* crow's-foot.

crow′ing, *pr.p.*, crow.

crown, *n.*, a king's head-covering; royal power; a wreath; the summit; formerly a five-shilling piece; one of the sizes of paper and books; *v.t.*, to place a crown on; to surmount; to complete.

crown-agent, *n.*, the representative of the government of a monarchy.

crown-colony, *n.*, a colony under the control of a home government.

crowned, *p.p.*, crown.

crown′er, *n.*, one who crowns.

crown′-glass, *n.*, the best window glass.

crown′ing, *adj.*, completing; supreme; *pr.p.*, crown.

crown′ lawyer, *n.*, the Crown's legal adviser.

crown′less, *adj.*, without a crown.

crown′ post, *n.*, a king-post.

crown′ prince, *n.*, the heir apparent.

crown′-wheel, *n.*, a variety of cog-wheel.

crow's′-foot, *n.*, the ranunculus; a wrinkling of the skin at the side of the eyes.

crow's′-nest, *n.*, a look-out on a mast.

cro′zier, *n.*, *i.q.* crosier.

cro′ziered, *adj.*, *i.q.* crosiered.

cru′cial, *adj.*, rel. to a crux or cross; transverse; severe; vital, critical.

cru′cian, -sian, *n.*, a yellow fish allied to the carp.

cru′ciate, *adj.*, cross-shaped (*bot.* and *zool.*).

cru′cible, *n.*, a melting-pot.

cru′cifer, *n.*, a processional cross-bearer.

crucif′erous, *adj.*, with petals arranged in the form of a cross.

cru′cified, *p.p.*, crucify.

cru′cifier, *n.*, one who crucifies.

cru′cifix, *n.*, a cross with Christ's figure on it.

crucifix′ion, *n.*, the act of crucifying; terrible suffering.

cru′ciform, *adj.*, cross-shaped.

cru′cify, *v.t.*, to fasten to a cross; to torture; to subdue.

cru′cifying, *pr.p.*, crucify.

crude, *adj.*, raw, coarse, uncultured.

crude′ly, *adv.*, in a crude way.

crude′ness, *n.*, the crude quality.

cru′dity, *n.*, *i.q.* crudeness.

cru′el, *adj.*, pitiless, fond of inflicting pain, severe.

cru′elly, *adv.*, in a cruel way.

cru′elty, *n.*, a cruel act.

cru′et, *n.*, a small vial; a condiments container.

cruise, *n.*, a voyage; *v.i.*, to sail about or along.

cruised, *p.p.*, cruise.

cruis′er, *n.*, a fast, large, naval vessel; a boat designed for cruising; a weight range in boxing.

cruis′ing, *pr.p.*, cruise.

cruive, *n.*, a wicker salmon-trap (*Scot.*).

crull′er, *n.*, a small Dutch cake twisted or curled and fried in fat.

crumb, *n.*, a small fragment; *v.t.*, to spread crumbs on.

crumb′-cloth, *n.*, a cloth to protect against crumbs.

crumb′ing, *pr.p.*, crumb.

crum′ble, *v.t.*, to break up into crumbs; to shatter to pieces; *v.i.*, to go to pieces.

crum′bled, *p.p.*, crumble.

crum′bling, *n.*, a breaking away into small pieces; *pr.p.*, crumble.

crum′bly, *adj.*, full of

crumbs; apt to crumble or break.

crum′my, *adj.*, full of crumbs; soft.

crump, *adj.*, crisp; *n.*, a hard hit (esp. a cricket ball); a heavy fall or shell burst; *v.t.*, to hit hard.

crum′pet, *n.*, a variety of tea-cake.

crum′ple, *v.t.*, to rumple, to squeeze into folds; *v.i.*, to become crumpled.

crum′pled, *p.p.*, crumple.

crum′pling, *pr.p.*, crumple.

crunch, *n.*, the act of crunching; a crucial moment or situation (*colloq.*); *v.t.*, to crush with the teeth; *v.i.*, to make a crunching noise.

crunched, *p.p.*, crunch.

crunch′ing, *pr.p.*, crunch.

crup′per, *n.*, a horse's buttocks; the leather loop passed under a horse's tail.

cru′ral, *adj.*, rel. to the thigh.

crusade′, *n.*, an expedition of crusaders; any vigorous concerted action; *v.i.*, to go on crusade; to achieve a moral or ethical objective.

crusa′ded, *p.p.*, crusade.

crusa′der, *n.*, a soldier under the emblem of the Cross fighting for the recovery of the Holy Land; a person dedicated to a cause.

crusa′ding, *pr.p.*, crusade.

crusad′o, *n.*, an old Portuguese coin marked with a cross.

cruse, *n.*, a vessel, dish.

crush, *n.*, a press, crowd; *v.t.*, to press to break; to put down; *v.i.*, to go out of shape or into a smaller space.

crushed, *p.p.*, crush.

crush′er, *n.*, anything that crushes; a conclusive argument.

crush′ing, *pr.p.*, crush.

crust, *n.*, a hard, outer layer or surface; *v.t.*, to overlay with crust; *v.i.*, to form a crust

Crusta′cea, *n. pl.,* the generic name of shell-fish.

crusta′cean, *adj.,* rel. to the Crustacea; *n.,* one of the C.

crustaceol′ogy, *n.,* the study of Crustacea.

crusta′ceous, *adj.,* shell-covered.

crusta′ceousness, *n.,* the quality or state of being crustaceous.

crusta′ted, *adj., i.q.* crustaceous.

crusta′tion, *adj.,* the act of forming a crust.

crust′ed, *adj.,* having a crust; *p.p.,* crust.

crust′ily, *adv.,* in a crusty way.

crust′iness, *n.,* surliness.

crust′ing, *pr.p.,* crust.

crust′y, *adj.,* crustlike, surly.

crutch, *n.,* a support for lameness; part of a lady's saddle.

crutched, *adj.,* having a crutch.

Crutch′ed Fri′ars, *n.,* members of an Order wearing a cross on their habits.

crux, *n.,* a cross; a trial; the crucial point.

cruzeiro, *n.,* the monetary unit of Brazil.

cry, *n.,* a loud utterance, an attack of weeping, a party watchword, the noise of a pack of hounds on the chase; *v.t.,* to call out, to proclaim; *v.i.,* to utter a cry, to exclaim, to weep.

cry′ing, *pr.p.,* cry.

cryo′biologic, *adj.,* rel. to cryobiology.

cryo′biology, *n.,* the study of life at low temperature.

cry′ogen, *n.,* a freezing mixture.

cry′olite, *n.,* valuable, lustrous mineral found in Greenland.

crypt, *n.,* an underground vault.

cryptaesthes′ia, *n.,* super-normal knowledge, telepathic or clairvoyant.

crypt′ic, *adj.,* dark, mysterious.

crypt′ical, *adj., i.q.* cryptic.

cryptically, *adv.,* in a cryptic way.

cryp′to, *n.,* a person owing secret allegiance to a political creed, etc. (*colloq.*).

cryp′togam, *n.,* one of the cryptogamous plants.

Cryptoga′mia, *n.,* a genus of flowerless plants.

cryptogam′ic, *adj.,* rel. to Cryptogamia.

cryptog′amist, *n.,* a student of cryptogams.

cryptog′amous, *adj.,* pert. to the cryptogams.

cryptog′amy, *n.,* the cryptogamous state.

cryp′togram, *n.,* a writing in cipher.

cryp′tograph, *n.,* a piece of writing in cipher.

cryptog′rapher, *n.,* one who writes in cipher.

cryptograph′ic, *adj.,* rel. to cryptography.

cryptograph′ical, *adj., i.q.* cryptographic.

cryptographically, *adv.,* in a cryptographic way.

cryptog′raphy, *n.,* the art of writing in cipher.

cryptomer′ia, *n.,* a cypress type of evergreen tree; the Japanese cedar.

crys′tal, *adj.,* made of crystal; transparent; *n.,* a definitely shaped, light refracting piece of inorganic matter; very clear glass.

crys′talline, *adj.,* like crystal, transparent.

crys′tallite, *n.,* a spurious crystal formation.

crys′tallizable, *adj.,* able to be crystallized.

crystalliza′tion, *n.,* the act or state of crystallizing.

crys′tallize, *v.t.,* to turn into crystal; to give a permanent definite shape to; *v.i.,* to become crystal; to take definite shape.

crys′tallized, *p.p.,* crystallize.

crys′tallizing, *pr.p.,* crystallize.

crystallog′rapher, *n.,* an expert in the science of crystals.

crystallograph′ic, *adj.,* rel. to crystallography.

crystallog′raphy, *n.,* the science of crystal structure.

crys′talloid, *adj.,* like a crystal; *n.,* a protein crystal.

crystallol′ogy, *n.,* the science of crystals.

crys′tallotype, *n.,* a picture taken on glass or some transparent material.

cte′noid, *adj.,* having combs; *n.,* a fish with comb-like scales.

cub, *n.,* the young of a wild beast; *v.t.,* to produce cubs.

cu′bage, *n.,* the act of estimating cubic content; the measure of cubic content.

Cu′ban, *adj.,* pert. or rel. to Cuba; *n.,* a native of C.

cuba′tion, *n.,* the act or period of lying.

cu′bature, *n.,* the cubic content; the process of ascertaining it.

cubbed, *p.p.,* cub.

cub′bing, *n.,* pert. to the chase of young foxes; *pr.p.,* cub.

cubb′ish, *adj.,* ill-mannered; boorish.

cubb′y, *n.,* a snug place, usually a cubby-hole.

cub′by-hole, *n.,* a snug hiding place.

cube, *n.,* a solid body with six equal square faces; the multiple of the square of a quantity by the quantity itself; *v.t.,* to raise to the power of a cube.

cu′beb, *n.,* Java pepper.

cubed, *p.p.,* cube.

cu′bic, *adj.,* rel. to a cube.

cu′bicle, *n.,* a bedroom; a division of a room.

cu′biform, *adj.,* cube-shaped.

cub′ism, *n.,* art based on geometrical figures.

cub′ist, *n.,* a cubistic artist.

cubist′ic, *adj.,* rel. to geometrical figures.

cu′bit, *n.,* a measure roughly corresponding to the length of the forearm.

cu′bital, *adj.,* rel. to the cubit.

cu′boid, *adj.,* cubelike.

cuboi′dal, *adj., i.q.* cuboid.

cuck′ing-stool, *n.,* a chair in which disorderly women, etc. were ducked under water as punishment.

cuck′old, *n.,* a man whose wife is an adulteress; *v.t.,* to seduce a man's wife.

cuck′oo, *n.,* a migratory bird which lays its eggs in the nests of other birds; a simpleton (*colloq.*).

cuck′oo-clock, *n.,* a clock which strikes the hours by a cuckoo's note.

cu′cullate, *adj.,* hooded, hood-shaped.

cu′cullated, *adj., i.q.* cucullate.

cu′cumber, *n.,* a creeping plant bearing long, green, fleshy fruit used as a vegetable or in salads.

Cucur′bit, *n.,* a generic name for pumpkins, melons, etc.; a gourd-shaped vessel.

cud, *n.,* food returned from a ruminant's first stomach.

cud′bear, *n.,* a dye made from a cudbear lichen.

cud′dle, *n.,* an embrace; *v.t.,* to clasp closely; *v.i.,* to snuggle up.

cud′dled, *p.p.,* cuddle.

cud′dlesome, *adj.,* inviting cuddling.

cud′dling, *pr.p.,* cuddle.

cud′dly, *adj., i.q.* cuddlesome.

cud′dy, *n.,* a ship's galley; a fool; a donkey; an ass.

cudg′el, *n.,* a short, thick stick; *v.t.,* to strike with a cudgel.

cudg′el(l)ed, *p.p.,* cudgel.

cudg′el(l)er, *n.,* one who cudgels.

cudg′el(l)ing, *pr.p.,* cudgel.

cud′weed, *n.,* a plant with chaffy scales, given to cattle to replace lost cud.

cue, *n.,* a tail; words that prompt an actor; a hint; a stick for driving a billiard ball.

cue′ist, *n.,* a billiards-player.

cuff, *n.,* a blow with the hand; a wristband; *v.t.,* to slap.

cuffed, *p.p.,* cuff.

cuff′ing, *pr.p.,* cuff.

Cu′fic, *adj.,* pert. to the old Arabic written character.

cuirass′, *n.,* a breastplate (*Fr.*).

cuirassier′, *n.,* a horse soldier wearing a cuirass (*Fr.*).

cuish, *n., i.q.* cuisse.

cuisine′, *n.,* a kitchen; cookery (*Fr.*).

cuisse, *n.,* armour for the thigh (*Fr.*).

Cul′dees, *n. pl.,* an early religious Order.

cul-de-sac′, *n.,* a passage with one outlet; a street which is open at one end only; a situation from which one cannot retreat (*Fr.*).

culic′iform, *adj.,* shaped like a gnat.

cu′licine, *adj.,* rel. to gnats.

cu′linary, *adj.,* pert. or rel. to the kitchen.

cull, *v.t.,* to pick out, to gather.

culled, *p.p.,* cull.

cul′lender, *n., i.q.* colander.

cull′et, *n.,* broken glass.

cull′ing, *pr.p.,* cull.

cul′lion, *n.,* an orchid; a low, mean person.

cul′lis, *n.,* a roof-gutter; a groove; *i.q.,* coulisse.

cul′ly, *n.,* a dupe; *v.t.,* to trick.

culm, *n.,* a grass-stem; a poor kind of anthracite.

culmif′erous, *adj.,* having stems.

cul′minant, *adj.,* culminating.

cul′minate, *v.i.,* to reach the highest point.

cul′minated, *p.p.,* culminate.

cul′minating, *pr.p.,* culminate.

culmina′tion, *n.,* the act of culminating; the highest point attained.

culottes′, *n. pl.,* a divided skirt (*Fr.*).

culpabil′ity, *n.,* the state or quality of being culpable.

cul′pable, *adj.,* blameworthy, guilty.

cul′pableness, *n., i.q.* culpability.

cul′pably, *adv.,* in a culpable way.

cul′prit, *n.,* a guilty person.

cult, *n.,* a system of worship; a particular devotion.

cul′tivable, *adj.,* able to be cultivated.

cul′tivatable, *adj., i.q.* cultivable.

cul′tivate, *v.t.,* to prepare soil and raise crops from it; to seek the society of.

cul′tivated, *p.p.,* cultivate.

cul′tivating, *pr.p.,* cultivate.

cultiva′tion, *n.,* the act of cultivating; a cultivated state; refinement.

cul′tivator, *n.,* anything that cultivates.

cul′trate, *adj.,* like a knife.

cul′trated, *adj.,* made like a knife.

cul′triform, *adj.,* knife-like.

cul′tural, *adj.,* tending or pert. to culture.

cul′turally, *adv.,* in a cultural manner.

cul′ture, *n.,* tillage; intellectual improvement; a refined, intellectual state; the growing of bacteria.

cul′tured, *adj.,* cultivated, refined.

cul′tus, *n.,* a system of worship; a cult.

cul′ver, *n.,* a wood-pigeon.

cul′verin, *n.,* an obsolete type of cannon.

cul′vert, *n.,* a subterranean drain.

cum′bent, *adj.,* reclining.

cum′ber, *v.t.,* to oppress, to burden.

cum′bered, *p.p.,* cumber.

cum′berer, *n.,* one who cumbers.

cum′bering, *pr.p.,* cumber.

cum′bersome, *adj.,* troublesome, embarrassing.

cum′bersomely, *adv.,* in a cumbersome way.

cum′bersomeness, *n.,* the state or quality of being cumbersome.

Cum′brian, *adj.,* pert. or rel. to the English County of Cumberland; *n.,* a native of C.

cum′brous, *adj.,* troublesome, heavy.

cum′brously, *adv.,* in a cumbrous way.

cum′brousness, *n.,* the state or quality of being cumbrous.

cum′(m)in, *n.,* an aromatic plant with seeds which remedy flatulence.

cumm′er, *n.,* a female companion (*Scot.*). (Also *kimmer.*)

cum′merbund, *n.,* a sash or waistband.

cum′quat, *n.,* an orange-like fruit used in preserves.

cum′shaw, *n.,* a present; a tip in the East (*pidgin-Eng.*).

cu′mulate, *v.t.,* to pile up.

cu'mulated, *p.p.*, cumulate.

cu'mulating, *pr.p.*, cumulate.

cumula'tion, *n.*, the act of cumulating.

cu'mulative, *adj.*, increasing by addition.

cumulatively, *adv.*, in a cumulative way.

cu'mulet, *n.*, a high-flying pigeon.

cu'muli, *n. pl.*, the pl. of cumulus.

cumulo-cirro-stra'tus, *n.*, a composite cloud-formation consisting of cumulus and cirro-stratus.

cumulo-nimbus, a rain-cloud.

cu'mulose, *adj.*, composed of cumuli.

cumulo-stra'tus, *n.*, a cloud, half cumulus, half stratus.

cu'mulus, *n.*, a pile; a mass of round, woolly clouds.

Cunard'er, *n.*, a ship of the Cunard line.

cu'neal, *adj.*, rel. to a wedge.

cu'neate, *adj.*, wedge-like.

cu'neated, *adj.*, *i.q.* cuneate.

cune'iform, *n.*, the ancient wedgeshaped Assyrian and Persian script.

cunette', *n.*, a trench for draining at the foot of a dry ditch (*Fr.*).

cun'ning, *adj.*, sly, underhand, designing; *n.*, skill, craftiness.

cun'ningly, *adv.*, in a cunning way.

cun'ningness, *n.*, cunning conduct.

cup, *n.*, a vessel for drinking; anything shaped like a cup; a vessel used in surgical bleeding; *v.t.*, to bleed by cupping.

cup'bearer, *n.*, one who hands round a cup.

cup'board, *n.*, an enclosed construction for storage within buildings.

cu'pel, *n.*, a refining vessel.

cupella'tion, *n.*, the act of refining.

cup'ful, *n.*, the quantity contained in a cup.

Cu'pid, *n.*, the Roman god of love.

cupid'ity, *n.*, covetousness.

cu'pola, *n.*, a small, domical lantern surmounting a building;

a hemispherical roof; a domical, shot-proof ship's turret.

cupped, *p.p.*, cup.

cup'per, *n.*, one who cups.

cup'ping, *pr.p.*, cup.

cu'preous, *adj.*, coppery.

cup'ric, *adj.*, containing divalent copper.

cuprif'erous, *adj.*, yielding copper.

cu'prite, *n.*, red copper oxide.

cup'ro-nick'el, *n.*, copper-nickel alloy.

cup'-tie, *n.*, a game in a contest for a cup.

cu'pule, *n.*, a small cup.

cupulif'erous, *adj.*, producing small cups.

cur, *n.*, a mongrel; a debased person.

curabil'ity, *n.*, a curable state.

cur'able, *adj.*, able to be cured.

cur'ableness, *n.*, *i.q.* curability.

curaçao',   curaçoa' (*erron.*), *n.*, a liqueur flavoured with orange-peel.

cu'racy, *n.*, a curate's office or sphere of work.

cura're, *n.*, a S. American poison used for smearing arrows.

curas'sow, *n.*, a S. American turkey-like bird.

cu'rate, *n.*, the parish priest; an assistant to a vicar.

cur'ative, *adj.*, having a curing effect.

cura'tor, *n.*, an officer in charge of a gallery, museum or library.

cura'trix, *n.*, the female of curator.

curb, *n.*, anything that checks; a bit; *v.t.*, to restrain, to hold.

curbed, *p.p.*, curb.

curb'ing, *pr.p.*, curb.

curb'-roof, *n.*, a roof with two sets of rafters.

curb'stone, *n.*, *i.q.* kerbstone.

curcu'lio, *n.*, a weevil.

curc'uma, *n.*, a substance used in curry powder.

curd, *n.*, the separated solid part of milk; *v.t.*, to make into curd; *v.i.*, to form curd.

curd'ed, *p.p.*, curd.

curd'iness, *n.*, the state or quality of curd.

curd'ing, *pr.p.*, curd.

cur'dle, *v.t.*, to make into curd; *v.i.*, to become curd; (of a liquid) to become partly solid.

cur'dled, *p.p.*, curdle.

cur'dling, *pr.p.*, curdle.

curd'y, *adj.*, curd-like, curding.

cure, *n.*, healing; spiritual charge; a benefice; *v.t.*, to heal, to remedy, to preserve; to salt.

curé, *n.*, a French, parish priest.

cure'-all, *n.*, a panacea.

cured, *p.p.*, cure.

cure'less, *adj.*, past healing; without a cure.

cur'er, *n.*, one who cures; a fish-drier.

curett'age, *n.*, the scraping away of diseased matter (*surg.*, *Fr.*).

curette', *n.*, a small, scoop-like surgical instrument (*Fr.*).

cur'few, *n.*, an old edict for the extinction of house fires at a fixed hour; the bell rung at curfew time; a restriction on movement.

cu'ria, *n.*, an assembly, a senate-house; the papal court.

cu'rial, *adj.*, rel. to a curia.

cu'rie, *n.*, a unit of radium emanation.

curiethe'rapy, *n.*, radium treatment.

cur'ing, *pr.p.*, cure.

cu'rio, *n.*, a curiosity, bric-à-brac.

curios'ity, *n.*, the act or character of the curious.

curio'so, *n.*, a person skilled in an art or the arts.

cu'rious, *adj.*, inquisitive, exact, strange.

cu'riously, *adv.*, in a curious way.

cu'riousness, *n.*, the character of the curious.

cur'ium, *n.*, a radioactive, transuranic element.

curl, *n.*, a ringlet of hair; *v.t.*, to twist, to bend; *v.i.*, to move

spirally; to become curled; to play at curling (*Scot.*).

curled, *p.p.*, curl.

curl'er, *n.*, one who curls; a player at curling.

cur'lew, *n.*, a marsh-dwelling bird.

curl'icue, *n.*, any queer, twisted thing.

cur'liness, *n.*, a tendency to curl.

curl'ing, *n.*, the Scottish, winter game similar to bowls but played on ice; *pr.p.*, curl.

curl'y, *adj.*, in curls; full of curls.

curmudg'eon, *n.*, a stingy person.

cu'rrach, *n.*, a coracle.

cur'rant, *n.*, a small dried grape; the shrub and fruit of the Ribes specie.

cur'rency, *n.*, circulation; the monetary system.

cur'rent, *adj.*, running; of the present time; common; *n.*, a flow, a stream, the set of a stream.

cur'rently, *adv.*, commonly; in the general opinion at the time.

cur'ricle, *n.*, an old-fashioned, two-wheeled, two-horsed vehicle.

curric'ula, *n.*, the pl. of curriculum.

curric'ulum, *n.*, a prescribed course of studies (*Lat.*).

cur'ried, *p.p.*, curry.

cur'rier, *n.*, a leather-dresser.

cur'rish, *adj.*, cur-like.

curr'ishness, *n.*, a currish nature.

cur'ry, *n.*, an Indian sauce powder; *v.t.*, to dress tanned leather; to clean a horse; to flavour with curry; to flatter.

cur'ry-comb, *n.*, a comb for grooming horses; *v.t.*, to groom a horse.

cur'rying, *pr.p.*, curry.

curse, *n.*, an imprecation against; a cause of trouble; *v.t.*, to invoke evil against, to imprecate; *v.i.*, to use bad language.

cursed, *adj.*, afflicted; *p.p.*, curse.

curs'edness, *n.*, the state of being cursed.

curs'er, *n.*, one who curses.

curs'ing, *pr.p.*, curse.

cur'sitor, *n.*, once a clerk of the Chancery Court.

cur'sive, *adj.*, running (of handwriting).

curs'ively, *adv.*, in a flowing style.

curs'or, *n.*, the sliding part of an instrument.

cursor'ial, *adj.*, having limbs fitted for running or walking.

cur'sorily, *adv.*, in a cursory way.

cur'soriness, *n.*, the quality of being cursory.

cur'sory, *adj.*, superficial.

curs'us, *n.*, a racecourse; a curriculum; a stated order of daily prayer (*Lat.*).

curt, *adj.*, short, abrupt.

curtail', *v.t.*, to shorten at the end; to reduce.

curtailed, *p.p.*, curtail.

curtail'er, *n.*, one who curtails.

curtail'ing, *pr.p.*, curtail.

curtail'ment, *n.*, the act or effect of curtailing.

curt'ail-step, *n.*, the lowest step of a stair, with rounded outer end.

cur'tain, *n.*, a screen; a castle wall between the towers; a soft furnishing for windows, etc.; *v.t.*, to enclose with a curtain.

cur'tained, *p.p.*, curtain.

cur'tain-fire, *n.*, *i.q.* barrage.

cur'taining, *n.*, the material used for curtains; *pr.p.*, curtain.

curta'na, *n.*, a pointless sword (*Lat.*).

cur'tate, *adj.*, shortened in orthographic projection.

curta'tion, *n.*, the difference between the curtate and the real distance of a planet from the sun.

cur'tilage, *n.*, the ground immediately connected with a house (*leg.*).

curt'ly, *adv.*, in a curt way.

curt'ness, *n.*, the act or state of being curt.

curtsied, *p.p.*, curtsy.

curt'sy, *n.*, a respectful dropping of the knees by women; *v.i.*, to drop a curtsy.

curt'sying, *pr.p.*, curtsy.

cu'rule, *adj.*, magisterial.

curv'ate, *adj.*, curved.

curv'ated, *adj.*, *i.q.* curvate.

curva'tion, *n.*, the act of curving.

curv'ature, *n.*, the act of bending; a bent state.

curve, *n.*, a bent line, a bend; *v.t.*, to bend; *v.i.*, to move in a curve.

curved, *p.p.*, curve.

cur'vet, *n.*, a horse's prance; *v.i.*, to prance.

cur'veted, *p.p.*, curvet.

cur'veting, *pr.p.*, curvet.

cur'viculate, *adj.*, slightly curved.

cur'viform, *adj.*, curved.

curvilin'eal, *adj.*, having curved lines.

curvilin'ear, *adj.*, *i.q.* curvilineal.

curv'ing, *pr.p.*, curve.

curv'ity, *n.*, the state of being curved.

curvom'eter, *n.*, an instrument for measuring curves.

cus'cus, *n.*, an aromatic Indian grass root, used for fans etc.

cu'sec, *n.*, the abbrev. for cubic feet per second.

cush'at, *n.*, a ring-dove.

cush'ion, *n.*, a sort of pillow; the elastic padding round a billiards table; *v.t.*, to put on a cushion, to furnish with cushions, *v.i.*, to go off the cushion at billiards; to diminish the impact; to protect from.

cush'ioned, *p.p.*, cushion.

cush'ionet, *n.*, a small cushion.

cush'ioning, *pr.p.*, cushion.

cush'iony, *adj.*, cushion-like, comfortable.

cush'y, *adj.*, easy, pleasant (*slang*).

cusp, *n.*, a sharp point; an architectural, spear-shaped ornament.

cusped, *adj.*, having cusps.

cus'pid, *n.*, a canine tooth.

cus'pidal, *adj.*, rel. to, or of the nature of, a cusp.

cus'pidated, *adj.*, sharpened to a cusp.

cus'pidor, *n.*, a spittoon.

cuss'edness, *n.*, perversity, obstinacy.

cus'tard, *n.*, a confection of milk, eggs and sugar, baked or served as a liquid sauce.

custo'dial, *adj.*, rel. to custody.

custo'dian, *n.*, one who has custody.

cus'tody, *n.*, guard, confinement, care, charge.

cus'tom, *n.*, what is usual; habit, wont; purchasing.

cus'tomable, *adj.*, liable to duty.

cus'tomarily, *adv.*, in a customary way.

cus'tomary, *adj.*, usual, according to custom.

cus'tomed, *adj.*, accustomed.

cus'tomer, *n.*, a buyer; a person with some peculiarity (*colloq.*).

cus'tom-house, *n.*, the place where customs duties are collected.

cus'toms, *n. pl.*, the taxes on goods imported or exported.

cus'tos, *n.*, a guardian, a warden; a mark at the end of a musical line, showing the first note on the following line (*Lat.*).

cut, *v.t.*, to cleave, to divide, to make an incision; to refuse to recognize; to put a spin on a ball; to hit a ball to the off side; *n.*, an incision, a gash; a stroke at cricket; a ditch; style; an engraving; a direct way; a spin on a ball; a snub.

cuta'neous, *adj.*, rel. to the skin.

cut'away, *adj.* and *n.*, (a coat) with the skirt cut back from the waist.

cutch'a, *adj.*, of poor quality; makeshift; (of bricks) dried in the sun.

cutche'r(r)y, *n.*, an Indian court of justice.

cute, *adj.*, sharp, cunning; attractively novel.

cute'ness, *n.*, the quality of being cute.

cuth'bert, *n.*, the holder of a government post to escape military service.

cu'ticle, *n.*, the outer skin.

cutic'ular, *adj.*, rel. to the cuticle.

cu'tis, *n.*, the true skin.

cut'lass, *n.*, a short, heavy sort of sword, slightly curved.

cut'ler, *n.*, one who makes or sells cutlery.

cut'lery, *n.*, a cutler's trade; cutting implements.

cut'let, *n.*, a slice of meat or fish for broiling.

cut'-out, *n.*, a switch to cut off an electric circuit when the current exceeds a certain strength.

cut'purse, *n.*, one who steals purses; a thief.

cut'ter, *n.*, anything that cuts; a small single-masted vessel; a small steamer used in the revenue service.

cut'throat, *n.*, an assassin.

cut'ting, *adj.*, sharp-edged; *n.*, the act of cutting; an extract, a clipping; the excavation for a railway or road; *pr.p.*, cut.

cutt'ingly, *adv.*, in a cutting way, dividingly.

cut'tle-fish, *n.*, the marine creature which ejects black fluid when chased or disturbed.

cut'ty, *adj.*, short; *n.*, a short thing, as a pipe, etc.

cut'-water, *n.*, the front part of a ship or boat.

cut'worm, *n.*, a caterpillar that eats off young plants level with the ground; any worm that destroys plants.

cuvette, *n.*, a spoon-shaped, surgical instrument; a clay crucible (*Fr.*).

cy'anate, *n.*, a cyanic acid salt.

cyan'ic, *adj.*, rel. to blue or to cyanogen.

cy'anid, *n.*, a compound formed with cyanogen.

cy'anide, *n.*, *i.q.* cyanid.

cy'anite, *n.*, an aluminium silicate.

cyan'ogen, *n.*, a gas compounded of carbon and nitrogen.

cyanom'eter, *n.*, an apparatus for measuring the intensity of blue.

cyanos'is, *n.*, a blue discoloration of the skin in certain diseases and following death.

cyan'uret, *n.*, *i.q.* cyanid.

cyanu'ric, *adj.*, pert. to cyanogen and urea.

cybernet'ics, *n.*, the study of control mechanisms.

cy'cad, *n.*, a kind of palm-like plant (*bot.*).

cyc'lamen, *n.*, a bulbous, early-flowering plant.

cycle, *n.*, a recurring period; a series; a bicycle or motorcycle; *v.i.*, to move in a cycle; to bicycle.

cy'cled, *p.p.*, cycle.

cyc'lic, *adj.*, moving in a fixed order, recurring in cycles; bel. to the epic cycle.

cyc'lical, *adj.*, *i.q.* cyclic.

cy'cling, *n.*, the act of cycling; *pr.p.*, cycle.

cy'clist, *n.*, a bicyclist or motor-cyclist.

cy'clograph, *n.*, an apparatus for drawing arcs.

cy'cloid, *adj.*, like a circle; approaching the circular.

cycloi'dal, *adj.*, *i.q.* cycloid.

cyclom'eter, *n.*, an instrument that records a wheel's rotations.

cyclom'etry, *n.*, the art of measuring circles.

cy'clone, *n.*, a storm moving in a circle.

cyclope'an, *adj.*, rel. to the Cyclopes (giants with one eye); gigantic.

cyclop(a)e'dia, *n.*, a dictionary of general knowledge, or of a special subject.

cyclope'dic, *adj.*, like a cyclopedia.

cyclope'dical, *adj.*, *i.q.* cyclopedic.

cyclop'ic, *adj.*, *i.q.* cyclopean.

Cy'clops, *n.*, one of the Cyclopes, fabulous one-eyed giants.

cyclora'ma, *n.*, a circular panorama.

cy'clostyle, *n.*, a machine for multiplying copies from sheets prepared by a well-pointed stylus; *v.t.*, to reproduce with this.

cy'clotron, *n.*, an apparatus used in nuclear disintegration, etc.

cyd'er, *n.*, *i.q.* cider.

cyg'net, *n.*, a young swan.

cyl'inder, *n.*, a solid, roll-like figure; a hollow cylinder-like vessel.

cyl'indered, *adj.*, made cylinder-shaped.

cylin'dric, *adj.*, pert. to a cylinder.

cylin'drical, *adj.*, *i.q.* cylindric.

cylin'driform, *adj.*, shaped like a cylinder.

cyl'indroid, *adj.*, like a cylinder.

cylindromet'ric, *adj.*, pert. to the measuring of cylinders.

cy'ma, *n.*, a curved moulding.

cymar', *n.*, a woman's undergarment; a chemise.

cym'bal, *n.*, one of a pair of brass plates clashed together for musical purposes.

cym'balo, *n.*, a dulcimer.

cym'balon, *n.*, *i.q.* cymbalo.

cym'biform, *adj.*, boat-shaped.

cyme, *n.*, a form of inflorescence (*bot.*).

cy'mene, *n.*, an oily, liquid compound obtained by the distillation of camphor with phosphoric anhydrid.

cymom'eter, *n.*, an instrument for measuring wave-length, etc.

cy'moscope, *n.*, a wave-detector.

cy'mose, *adj.*, of the nature of a cyme.

Cym'ric, *adj.*, rel. to the Cymri or Welsh.

cynan'che, *n.*, inflammation of the throat.

cynan'thropy, *n.*, the mental delusion of a man who believes himself to be a dog.

cyn'ic, *adj.*, rel. to Diogenes and the Cynics; *n.*, a sneering, captious person, incredulous of good intentions or of situations as represented.

cyn'ical, *adj.*, sneering, captious.

cyn'ically, *adv.*, in a cynical way.

cyn'icism, *n.*, the act or character of a cynic.

cynoceph'alus, *n.*, the fabulous dog-headed man; a dog-faced baboon (*zool.*).

cyn'osure, *n.*, the Little Bear constellation; a centre of attraction.

cy'pher, *n.*, *i.q.* cipher.

cy'press, *n.*, a large, dark evergreen.

Cyp'rian, *adj.*, pert. or rel. to Cyprus and Venus; *n.*, a native of C.

cyp'rine, *adj.*, pert. to the cypress.

Cyp'riot(e), *n.*, a native of Cyprus.

Cyrena'ic, *adj.*, pert. or rel. to Cyrene.

Cyre'nian, *adj.*, *i.q.* Cyrenaic.

cyriolog'ic, *adj.*, rel. to hieroglyphics and capital letters.

cyst, *n.*, a sac of morbid matter in an animal body.

cyst'ic, *adj.*, rel. to cysts.

cysti'tis, *n.*, inflammation of the bladder.

cys'tocele, *n.*, a form of hernia.

cystot'omy, *n.*, an operation for cyst.

Cythere'an, *adj.*, concerned with physical love (from *Cytherea*, *i.e.*, *Aphrodite, Venus*).

cyti'tis, *n.*, dermatitis.

cytol'ogist, *n.*, a person who studies cells.

cytol'ogy, *n.*, the study of cells.

Czar, *n.*, the Slav title for a king or emperor.

Czar'evitch, *n.*, a Czar's heir apparent.

Czarev'na, *n.*, a Czarevitch's consort.

Czari'na, *n.*, a Czar's consort.

Czech, *n.*, a Bohemian Slav; a native of Czechoslovakia.

Czech'oslovak, *adj.* and *n.*, (a native) of the State of Czechoslovakia.

D

dab, *n.*, a gentle blow; a piece of something soft; a small edible sea fish; *v.t.*, to strike gently, or with something soft or moist; to deface.

dabbed, *p.p.*, dab.

dab'bling, *pr.p.*, dab.

dab'ble, *v.t.* and *i.*, to wet by dips or strokes; to work or take part in, but not in earnest.

dab'bled, *p.p.*, dabble.

dab'bler, *n.*, one who dabbles.

dab'bling, *pr.p.*, dabble.

dab'chick, *n.*, a small swimming bird.

dab'ster, *n.*, an adept; a proficient.

dace, *n.*, a small river fish.

dachs'hund, *n.*, a badger dog; a small, short-legged, long-bodied, dog (*Germ.*).

Da'cian, *adj.*, rel. to the Roman province of Dacia in S. Eastern Europe; *n.*, a native of D.

dacoit', *n.*, an East Indian brigand.

dacoit'y, *n.*, (act of) gang-robbery.

Da'cron, *n.*, a synthetic, man-made fibre.

dac'tyl, *n.*, in poetry, a foot containing one long and two short syllables.

dac'tylar, *adj.*, pert. to a finger, toe, or claw; dactylic.

dactyl'ic, *adj.*, consisting of dactyls.

dactyliog'raphy, *n.*, the study of finger-rings or gem engraving.

dactyl'ion, *n.*, the adhesion of two fingers.

dac'tylogram, *n.*, a fingerprint.

dactylog'raphy, *n.*, typewriting.

dactylol'ogy, *n.*, the finger-language used by deaf mutes.

dactylos'copy, *n.*, the examination of fingerprints.

dad, *n.*, a family name for father.

dad'dy, *n.*, a longer form of dad.

dadd'y-long'-legs, *n.*, the crane-fly.

da'do, *n.*, the lower part of a wall when ornamented differently from the rest.

dae'dal, *adj.*, ingenious; intricate.

Daed'alus, *n.*, the builder of the Cretan Labyrinth.

daff, *v.t.*, to put off.

daffed, *p.p.*, daff.

daff'ing, *pr.p.*, daff.

daf'fodil, *n.*, a kind of lily.

daft, *adj.*, crazy (*Scot.*).

dag'ger, *n.*, a short sword for stabbing.

dag'gle, *v.t.* and *i.*, to draggle.

Da'gon, *n.*, the Philistine god.

daguer'rean, *adj.*, rel. to Daguerre or the daguerreotype.

daguerre'otype, *n.*, an early kind of photograph.

dahabee'yah, *n.*, a Nile passenger-boat.

dah'lia, *n.*, a flowering plant, native of Mexico.

Dail Ei'reann, *n.*, the lower house of the Eire parliament.

dai'ly, *adj.* and *adv.*, day by day.

dain'tily, *adv.*, in a dainty manner.

dain'tiness, *n.*, fineness of taste; refinement; fastidiousness.

dain'ty, *adj.*, delicious; fastidious; elegant; trim; *n.*, something pleasant to the taste.

daiquiri, *n.*, a kind of rum-based cocktail.

dai'ry, *n.*, a place for selling milk and making butter and cheese.

dai'rymaid, *n.*, a female servant doing dairy work.

da'is, *n.*, the raised end of a hall.

dais'ied, *adj.*, adorned with daisies.

dai'sy, *n.*, a small, white flower with a yellow centre.

dak, *n.*, a relay of letter carriers, etc.; the post.

Da'lai La'ma, *n.*, the head of the Buddhist religion in Tibet.

dale, *n.*, a hollow between hills.

dall, *n.*, a slab of marble.

dal'liance, *n.*, a trifling; the giving and receiving of caresses.

dal'lied, *p.p.*, dally.

dal'lier, *n.*, one who dallies.

dal'ly, *v.i.*, to put off by doing little or nothing; to trifle.

dal'lying, *pr.p.*, dally.

Dalma'tian, *n.*, a breed of black-spotted dog.

dalmat'ic, *n.*, a religious vestment.

Dalto'nian, *n.*, one suffering from colour-blindness (after John Dalton).

dal'tonism, *n.*, colour-blindness.

dam, *n.*, a bank to keep back water; a mother of four-footed animals; *v.t.*, to confine water by a bank.

dam'age, *n.*, harm; loss; *v.t.*, to injure.

dam'ageable, *adj.*, capable of being damaged.

dam'aged, *p.p.*, damage.

dam'aging, *adj.*, injurious; *pr.p.*, damage.

dam'ascene, *n.*, a damson; *v.t.*, *i.q.* damaskeen.

dam'ask, *adj.*, of a deep rose colour; *n.*, cloth with woven figures on it; *v.t.*, to ornament.

dam'asked, *p.p.*, damask.

damaskeen', *v.t.*, to ornament metals with inlaid gold or silver.

damaskeened', *p.p.*, damaskeen.

damaskeen'ing, *pr.p.*, damaskeen.

dam'asking, *pr.p.,* damask.

dam'assin, *n.,* damask with gold and silver flowers woven in.

dame, *n.,* a lady; a knight's or baronet's wife; an honorific title.

damm'ar, *n.,* a pine resin obtained from certain Indian and Australasian coniferous trees.

dammed, *p.p.,* dam.

dam'ming, *pr.p.,* dam.

damn, *v.t.,* to give over to everlasting punishment; to condemn.

damnabil'ity, *n.,* the quality of being damnable.

dam'nable, *adj.,* odious; detestable.

dam'nableness, *n.,* the state of being damnable.

dam'nably, *adv.,* in a damnable manner.

damna'tion, *n.,* the eternal punishment of the wicked.

dam'natory, *adj.,* condemnatory.

damned, *adj.,* detestable; *p.p.,* damn.

dam'nified, *p.p.,* damnify.

dam'nify, *v.t.,* to cause loss to.

dam'nifying, *pr.p.,* damnify.

dam'ning, *adj.,* convicting; *pr.p.,* damn.

Dam'ocles, *n.,* the Greek who was feasted with a sword suspended above him, held only by a hair.

damp, *adj.,* feeling wet; *n.,* slight wetness; noxious gas in a coalmine; *v.t.,* to make slightly wet; to depress.

damped, *p.p.,* damp.

damp'en, *v.t.,* to make damp.

damp'ened, *p.p.,* dampen.

damp'ening, *pr.p.,* dampen.

damp'er, *n.,* a plate in a chimney to regulate draught; a means of reducing sound in a musical instrument; *adj., comp.* of damp.

damp'est, *adj., super.* of damp.

damp'ing, *adj.,* depressing; *pr.p.,* damp.

damp'ish, *adj.,* rather damp.

damp'ness, *n.,* slight wetness.

dam'sel, *n.,* a girl.

dam'son, *n.,* a kind of plum.

dan, *n.,* an old title = master.

dance, *n.,* physical movements in time with music; *v.i.,* to move on foot to music.

danced, *p.p.,* dance.

dan'cer, *n.,* one who dances.

dancette', *n.,* a chevron moulding (*archit.*).

dan'cing, *n.,* the act of dancing; *pr.p.,* dance.

dan'delion, *n.,* a herb with a yellow flower.

dan'der, *n.,* temper; a feeling of anger (*colloq.*).

Dan'die Din'mont, *n.,* a breed of rough-haired Scottish terrier.

dan'dified, *p.p.,* dandify.

dan'dify, *v.t.,* to dress out like a dandy.

dan'difying, *pr.p.,* dandify.

dan'dle, *v.t.,* to toss up and down gently.

dan'dled, *p.p.,* dandle.

dan'dler, *n.,* one who dandles.

dan'dling, *pr.p.,* dandle.

dan'druff, *n.,* scurf on the scalp.

dan'dy, *n.,* a fop.

dan'dyish, *adj.,* like a dandy.

dan'dyism, *n.,* foppishness.

Dane, *n.,* a native of Denmark.

Dane'geld, *n.,* the Danish exaction on Saxon kings.

Dane'gelt, *n., i.q.* Danegeld.

dane'wort, *n.,* the dwarf elder.

dan'ger, *n.,* a state in which harm may happen; a hazard.

dan'gerous, *adj.,* bringing or involving danger.

dan'gerously, *adv.,* in a dangerous manner.

dan'gerousness, *n.,* the state of being dangerous.

dan'gle, *v.t.* and *i.,* to hang loosely.

dan'gled, *p.p.,* dangle.

dan'gler, *n.,* one who hangs about women.

dan'gling, *pr.p.,* dangle.

Dan'iel, *n.,* an infallible judge.

Da'nish, *adj.,* pert. or rel. to Denmark.

dank, *adj.,* damp.

dan'sant, *adj.,* dancing (*Fr.*).

danseuse', *n.,* a female stage-dancer (*Fr.*).

Dante', a famous Italian poet.

Dante'an, *adj.* and *n.,* in the style of Dante.

Danu'bian, *adj.,* rel. to the R. Danube.

dap, *v.i.,* to let bait fall gently into the water.

daph'ne, *n.,* a laurel (*Gr.*).

dap'per, *adj.,* little and active; smart in dress.

dap'perling, *n.,* a little fellow; a dwarf.

dap'ple, *adj.,* spotted; *v.t.,* to mark with spots.

dap'pled, *adj.,* variegated; *p.p.,* dapple.

dap'pling, *pr.p.,* dapple.

dar, *n.,* the European black tern.

darb'ies, *n. pl.,* handcuffs (*slang*).

dar'by, *n.,* a tool for plastering ceilings.

dare, *n.,* a dace; *v.i.,* to be bold enough; *v.t.,* to defy; to challenge.

dared, *p.p.,* dare.

dare'devil, *n.,* a reckless intrepid person.

dar'er, *n.,* one who dares.

dare'say, *v.i.,* to be ready to believe; to hold as probable (often used ironically).

dar'ic, *n.,* a Persian gold or silver coin.

dar'ing, *adj.,* bold; *n.,* courage; *pr.p.,* dare.

dar'ingly, *adv.,* in a daring manner.

dark, *adj.,* wanting light; *n.,* a want of light.

dark'en, *v.t.,* to make dark; *v.i.,* to grow dark.

dark'ened, *p.p.,* darken.

dark'ener, *n.,* one who or that which, darkens.

dark'ening, *pr.p.,* darken.

dark'er, *adj., comp.* dark.

dark'est, *adj., super.* dark.

dark'-eyed, *adj.,* having dark eyes.

dark'fall, *n.,* dusk.

dark'ish, *adj.,* dusky.

dark'le, *v.i.,* to lie concealed; to grow dark.

dark'ling, *adj.,* black-looking; groping; *adv.,* in the dark.

dark'ly, *adv.,* in a dark manner.

dark'ness, *n.* the state of being dark.

dark'some, *adj.* dark.

dar'ling, *adj.,* dearly loved; *n.,* one much beloved.

darn, *n.,* a darned place; *v.t.,* to mend a hole in a textile material.

darned, *p.p.,* darn.

dar'nel, *n.,* a troublesome weed in corn.

darn'er, *n.,* one who darns.

darn'ing, *n.,* the act of darning; *pr.p.,* darn.

dart, *n.,* a pointed hand-missile; a sudden spring; *v.t.,* to throw suddenly; *v.i.,* to shoot out.

dart'ed, *p.p.,* dart.

dart'er, *n.,* one who darts; a tropical swimming bird.

dart'ing, *pr.p.,* dart.

dar'tle, *v.t.* and *i.,* to keep on darting.

Dart'moor, *n.,* the site of a prison in England.

Dart'mouth, *n.,* the site of a Royal Naval College in England.

dar'tre, *n.,* all kinds of skin disease, esp. herpes.

Dar'winism, *n.,* the biological doctrines of Charles Darwin.

dash, *n.,* a sudden rush; a mark (—) in printing or writing; *v.t.,* to strike strongly against; *v.i.,* to rush.

dash'board, *n.,* a mud-catching board; the instrument-board of a motor-car.

dashed, *p.p.,* dash.

dash'er, *n.,* one who, or that which, dashes.

dash'ing, *adj.,* showy; impetuous; *pr.p.,* dash.

das'tard, *n.,* a coward.

das'tardliness, *n.,* cowardliness.

das'tardly, *adj.,* cowardly.

das'tardy, *n.,* mean timorousness.

da'ta, *n. pl.,* facts given from which others may be inferred.

da't(e)able, *adj.,* capable of being dated.

dat'aller, *n.,* a workman engaged and paid by the day. (Also *daytaler.*)

Data'ria, *n.,* an office in the papal court.

da'tary, *n.,* an officer having charge of the Dataria.

date, *n.,* the fruit of a kind of palm; a fixed point of time; *v.t.,* to note the time of; to make an appointment with a member of the opposite sex.

da'ted, *p.p.,* date.

date'less, *adj.,* undated; of extreme antiquity; eternal.

date'-line, *n.,* the meridian east and west of which the date differs.

da'ting, *pr.p.,* date.

da'tive, *adj.,* describing one of the cases of a noun; *n.,* the case expressing movement or attitude towards.

da'tum, *n.,* the sing. of data.

Datu'ra, *n.,* a strong, narcotic plant.

datu'rin(e), *n.,* atropin.

daub, *n.,* a coarse painting; *v.t.,* to smear with something soft.

daubed, *p.p.,* daub.

daub'er, *n.,* one who daubs; an indifferent painter.

daub'ing, *pr.p.,* daub.

daub'y, *adj.,* slimy; viscous.

daugh'ter, *n.,* a female child.

daugh'ter-in-law, *n.,* a son's wife.

daugh'terly, *adj.,* dutiful; becoming a daughter.

daunt, *v.t.,* to intimidate.

daunt'ed, *p.p.,* daunt.

daunt'er, *n.,* one who daunts.

daunt'ing, *pr.p.,* daunt.

daunt'less, *adj.,* fearless.

daunt'lessly, *adv.,* in a bold, fearless manner.

daunt'lessness, *n.,* fearlessness.

Dau'phin, *n.,* the French heir apparent.

dau'phiness, *n.,* the Dauphin's wife.

dav'enport, *n.,* a small writing-table.

dav'it, *n.,* one of the two wooden or iron arms for hoisting or lowering a boat.

da'vy, *n.,* a miner's safety lamp.

daw, *n.,* a jackdaw.

daw'dle, *v.i.,* to waste time; to saunter.

daw'dled, *p.p.,* dawdle.

daw'dler, *n.,* a waster of time.

daw'dling, *n.,* the act or habit of sauntering; *pr.p.,* dawdle.

dawn, *n.,* the break of day; *v.i.,* to begin to show light.

dawned, *p.p.,* dawn.

dawn'ing, *n.,* the growing light in the morning; *pr.p.,* dawn.

day, *n.,* a period of 24 hours; the time of light between sunrise and sunset.

day'book, *n.,* a book recording daily transactions or events.

day'break, *n.,* the beginning of the dawn.

day'dream, *n.,* a reverie.

day'-labourer, *n.,* a worker for a daily wage.

day'light, *n.,* the light of the day; natural light.

day'-long, *adj.,* lasting all day.

day'spring, *n.,* the dawn.

day'star, *n.,* the star or planet that remains visible some time after dawn.

day'-taler, *n., i.q.* dataller.

day'time, *n.,* the time of daylight.

day'-work, *n.,* work for a day's wage.

daze, *v.t.,* to make stupid or fuddled.

dazed, *p.p.,* daze.

daz'edly, *adv.,* in a dazed manner.

da'zing, *pr.p.,* daze.

daz'zle, *v.t.,* to dim the eyes by too strong light.

daz'zled, *p.p.,* dazzle.

daz'zling, *adj.,* excessively brilliant; *pr.p.,* dazzle.

D'-day, *n.*, the Allied invasion of Europe (6th June, 1944); any critical day of action.

dea'con, *n.*, a member of the third order of the clergy; a Presbyterian secular office-bearer.

dea'coness, *n.*, a female deacon, but not in Holy Orders.

dea'conry, *n.*, the office of a deacon.

de'activate, *v.t.*, to render inactive.

deactiva'tion, *n.*, the process of rendering inactive.

dead, *adj.*, without life; *adv.*, completely; *n.*, stillest time; *pl.*, those who are dead.

dead-and-alive', *adj.*, dull, monotonous.

dead'beat, *adj.*, exhausted; *n.*, an idler without hope or ambition.

dead'en, *v.t.*, to remove feeling; to soften.

dead'ened, *p.p.*, deaden.

dead'ening, *adj.*, depressing; *pr.p.*, deaden.

dead'eye, *n.*, a block pierced with three holes used on ships.

dead' freight, *n.*, the payment for empty space in a ship.

dead'head, *n.*, one who is admitted free to a theatre, etc.

dead'heat, *n.*, the result of a competition in which the winners tie.

dead'-letter, *n.*, a law no longer enforced; a letter returned by the P.O.

dead'lier, *adj.*, *comp.* of deadly.

deadliest, *adj.*, *super.* of deadly.

dead'lift, *n.*, a direct lift of a dead-weight; an extreme emergency.

dead'light, *n.*, a shutter over a cabin window.

dead'line, *n.*, a line that may not be passed; a time limit.

dead'liness, *n.*, the quality of being deadly.

dead'lock, *n.*, a complete standstill.

dead'ly, *adj.*, causing death.

dead'-march, *n.*, a funeral march.

dead'ness, *n.*, lifelessness.

dead'pan, *n.*, an expressionless face (*slang*).

dead' reck'oning, *n.*, the calculation of a ship's position by log-book and compass.

dead'-weight, *n.*, an oppressive burden.

deaf, *adj.*, unable to hear.

deaf'-aid, *n.*, a hearing aid.

deaf'en, *v.t.*, to make deaf.

deaf'ened, *p.p.*, deafen.

deaf'ening, *adj.*, extremely loud; *pr.p.*, deafen.

deaf'-mute, *n.*, a deaf and dumb person.

deaf'ness, *n.*, want of hearing.

deal, *n.*, a division; a thin cutting of wood; *v.t.*, to give out in parts; to carry on business; to distribute cards.

deal'er, *n.*, one who deals; a trader.

deal'ing, *n.*, conduct; intercourse of business; *pr.p.*, deal.

dealt, *p.p.*, deal.

deambula'tion, *n.*, walking.

deambula'tory, *adj.*, walking.

dean, *n.*, the chief dignitary in a cathedral or collegiate church; the disciplinary official of a college; the president of an academic faculty.

dean'ery, *n.*, the charge of a dean; also his house; the area of a rural dean's authority.

dear, *adj.*, greatly beloved; costly.

dear'er, *adj.*, *comp.* of dear.

dear'est, *adj.*, *super.* of dear.

dear'ly, *adv.*, with great love; at a high price.

dear'ness, *n.*, a high price; preciousness.

dearth, *n.*, scarcity.

dear'y, **dear'ie**, *n.*, a word of endearment.

dea'sil, *n.*, motion from east to west, as of the sun (*Scot.*).

death, *n.*, loss of life.

death'bed, *n.*, the bed on which one dies.

death'less, *adj.*, cannot die.

death'lessly, *adv.*, immortally.

death'lessness, *n.*, immortality.

death'like, *i.q.* deathly.

death'ly, *adj.*, resembling death.

death'-mask, *n.*, a plaster-cast of a dead person's face.

death'-rate, *n.*, the proportion of deaths in a specified area.

death'-rat'tle, *n.*, the gurgling sound of a dying person.

death's'-head, *n.*, a human skull; a type of moth.

death-trap, *n.*, a highly dangerous place.

death'-warrant, *n.*, an order for execution.

débâc'le, *n.*, the sudden collapse of a situation; a confused rout; a sudden breaking up of ice in a river (*Fr.*).

debag', *v.t.*, to remove the "bags" or trousers (*slang*).

debar', *v.t.*, to shut out; to hinder.

debark', *v.t.* and *i.*, to land from a ship.

debarka'tion, *n.*, the act of landing.

debarked', *p.p.*, debark.

debark'ing, *pr.p.*, debark.

debarred', *p.p.*, debar.

debar'ring, *pr.p.*, debar.

debase', *v.t.*, to make of less value.

debased', *p.p.*, debase.

debase'ment, *n.*, the act of debasing.

deba'ser, *n.*, one who debases.

deba'sing, *pr.p.*, debase.

deba'table, *adj.*, can be debated.

debate', *n.*, a contention in words; *v.t.*, to discuss.

deba'ted, *p.p.*, debate.

deba'ter, *n.*, one who debates.

deba'ting, *pr.p.*, debate.

debauch', *n.*, a course of intemperance or impurity; an excess in eating or drinking; *v.t.*, to lead away from virtue.

debauched', *adj.*, vitiated in morals; *p.p.*, debauch.

debauchee', *n.*, a person given over to intemperance.

debauch'er, *n.*, one who debauches.

debauch'ery, *n.*, sensual indulgence.

debauch'ing, *pr.p.*, debauch.

deben'ture, *n.,* a document charging property with the repayment of a loan.

deben'tured, *adj.,* secured by debenture.

debil'itate, *v.t.,* to make weak.

debil'itated, *p.p.,* debilitate.

debil'itating, *adj.,* tending to weaken; *pr.p.,* debilitate.

debilita'tion, *n.,* the act of weakening.

debil'ity, *n.,* bodily weakness.

deb'it, *n.,* something recorded as owed; *v.t.,* to mark as due.

deb'itable, *adj.,* able to be debited.

deb'ited, *p.p.,* debit.

deb'iting, *pr.p.,* debit.

debonair', *adj.,* accomplished; well-bred; courteous; affable.

debonair'ly, *adv.,* in a debonair way.

debouch', *v.i.,* to emerge into open ground.

débris, *n.,* broken pieces of anything; wreckage (*Fr.*).

debt, *n.,* what one owes.

debt'less, *adj.,* free of debt.

debt'or, *n.,* one who owes.

debunk', *v.t.,* to expose as false (*colloq.*).

debus', *v.t.* and *i.,* to unload or alight from motor vehicles.

début', *n.,* a first appearance (*Fr.*).

débutant, *n.,* one who makes his début (*Fr.*).

débutante, *n.,* the fem. of débutant (*Fr.*).

dec'achord, *n.,* a Greek, ten-stringed, musical instrument.

dec'adal, *adj.,* pert. to, or consisting of, tens.

dec'ade, *n.,* ten years; any group of ten.

dec'adence, *n.,* a growing worse.

dec'adency, *n., i.q.* decadence.

dec'adent, *adj.* and *n.,* declining; falling away; morally degenerate.

dec'agon, *n.,* a plane figure with ten sides.

decag'onal, *adj.,* having ten sides and angles.

dec'agram, *n.,* a weight of ten grammes.

Decagyn'ia, *n. pl.,* plants having ten pistils.

decag'ynous, *adj.,* having ten pistils.

decahe'dral, *adj.,* having ten plane faces.

decahe'dron, *n.,* a solid figure with ten faces.

decal'cify, *v.t.,* to deprive (bone etc.) of its lime.

dec'alitre, dec'aliter, *n.,* a French measure of capacity.

Dec'alogue, *n.,* the Ten Commandments.

Decam'eron, *n.,* the Boccaccio collection of tales.

dec'ametre, dec'ameter, *n.,* a French measure of length.

decamp', *v.i.,* to go away secretly.

decamped', *p.p.,* decamp.

decamp'ing, *pr.p.,* decamp.

decamp'ment, *n.,* a marching off.

deca'nal, *adj.,* rel. to a dean.

Decan'dria, *n. pl.,* plants having ten stamens.

decan'drian, *adj.,* having ten stamens.

decan'drous, *adj., i.q.* decandrian.

decan'gular, *adj.,* having ten angles.

deca'ni, *n., lit.,* the Dean's side of the choir (a direction in ecclesiastical music) (*Lat.*).

decant', *v.t.,* to pour from one vessel to another.

decant'ed, *p.p.,* decant.

decant'er, *n.,* a glass bottle for wine or spirits.

decant'ing, *pr.p.,* decant.

decaphyl'lous, *adj.,* having ten leaves (*bot.*).

decap'itate, *v.t.,* to behead.

decap'itated, *p.p.,* decapitate.

decap'itating, *pr.p.,* decapitate.

decapita'tion, *n.,* the act of beheading.

dec'apod, *n.,* a crustacean with ten feet (crab, etc.).

decap'odous, *adj.,* having ten feet.

decar'bonate, *v.t.,* to deprive of carbon dioxide.

decar'bonated, *p.p.,* decarbonate.

decar'bonating, *pr.p.,* decarbonate.

decarboniza'tion, *n.,* the act of decarbonizing.

decar'bonize, *v.t.,* to deprive of carbon.

decar'bonized, *p.p.,* decarbonize.

decar'bonizing, *pr.p.,* decarbonize.

decarteliza'tion, *n.,* the abolition of controlling or restricting agreements.

dec'astich, *n.,* a ten-line poem.

dec'astyle, *n.,* a portico of ten columns.

deca'sualize, *v.t.,* to dispense with casual employment.

decasyllab'ic, *adj.,* having ten syllables.

decay', *n.,* a growing weak; withering; *v.i.,* to waste away.

decayed', *p.p.,* decay.

decay'ing, *pr.p.,* decay.

decease, *n.,* death; *v.i.,* to die.

deceased', *p.p.,* decease.

deceas'ing, *pr.p.,* decease.

deceit', *n.,* misrepresentation; trickery.

deceit'ful, *adj.,* addicted to deceit.

deceit'fully, *adv.,* in a deceitful way.

deceit'fulness, *n.,* a tendency to deceive.

deceit'less, *adj.,* free of deceit.

deceiv'able, *adj.,* liable to be deceived.

deceive', *v.t.,* to mislead; to practise deceit on; to disappoint.

deceived', *p.p.,* deceive.

deceiv'er, *n.,* one who deceives.

deceiv'ing, *pr.p.,* deceive.

decel'erate, *v.t.* and *i.,* to diminish speed.

decelera'tion, *n.,* the reduction of speed.

decel'erator, *n.,* an apparatus for reducing speed.

Decem'ber, *n.,* the twelfth (last) month of the year.

decem'fid, *adj.,* divided into ten parts.

decem'vir, *n.,* one of ten magistrates in ancient Rome (*Lat.*).

decem'viral, *adj.,* pert. to the decemvirs.

decem'virate, *n.,* the decemvirs collectively.

de′cency, n., propriety, delicacy, becomingness.

decen′nary, adj., pert. to a ten year period; n., a period of ten years.

decen′nial, adj., happening every ten years.

decen′nium, n., i.q. decennary (Lat.).

de′cent, adj., acting in a proper way; becoming; morally acceptable.

de′cently, adv., in a decent manner.

decen′tralist, n., one who favours decentralization.

decentraliza′tion, n., the act or result of dispersing from the centre; the transfer of administration from central to local government.

decen′tralize, v.t., to distribute what has been centralized.

decen′tralized, p.p., decentralize.

decen′tralizing, pr.p., decentralize.

decep′tion, n., the act of deceiving.

decep′tive, adj., tending to deceive.

decep′tively, adv., in a manner to deceive.

decep′tiveness, n., a tendency to deceive.

decern′, v.t. and i., to pass judgment (Scots law).

dechristianiz′ation, n., the divesting of Christianity.

dechris′tianize, v.t., to divest of Christianity.

dechris′tianized, p.p., dechristianize.

dechris′tianizing, pr.p., dechristianize.

dec′ibar, n., one-tenth of a bar (meteorol.).

de′cibel, n., one-tenth of a bel, a measurement of intensity of sound.

deci′dable, adj., able to be decided.

decide′, v.t., to determine; v.i., to resolve.

deci′ded, adj., with one's mind made up; unmistakable; p.p., decide.

deci′dedly, adv., in a decided way; certainly.

deci′der, n., one who decides; a last game to resolve an undecided issue.

deci′ding, pr.p., decide.

decid′uous, adj., shedding leaves periodically.

decid′uousness, n., the quality of being deciduous.

dec′igram, n., a measure of weight.

dec′ilitre, dec′iliter, n., a measure of capacity.

decil′lion, n., a number consisting of 1 followed by sixty ciphers.

decil′lionth, n., one of a decillion equal parts.

dec′imal, adj., counted by tens; n., a fraction having some power of 10 as denominator.

decimaliza′tion, n., the act of decimalizing; the state of being decimal.

dec′imalize, v.t., to turn into a decimal.

deci′malized, p.p., decimalize.

dec′imalizing, pr.p., decimalize.

dec′imate, v.t., to kill every tenth man.

dec′imated, p.p., decimate.

dec′imating, pr.p., decimate.

decima′tion, n., the act of decimating.

dec′imetre, dec′imeter, n., a measure of length.

deci′pher, v.t., to read a cipher; to solve a difficulty in writing.

deci′pherable, adj., able to be deciphered.

deci′phered, p.p., decipher.

deci′pherer, n., one who deciphers.

deci′phering, pr.p., decipher.

deci′sion, n., determination; a judgment.

deci′sive, adj., ending dispute; quick in deciding.

deci′sively, adv., in a decisive manner.

deci′siveness, n., the quality of being decisive.

deciviliza′tion, n., the diverting of civilization.

deciv′ilize, v.t., to divest of civilization.

deciv′ilized, p.p., decivilize.

decivilizing, pr.p., decivilize.

deck, n., a platform of a ship; a pack of cards; v.t., to cover; to adorn.

deck′-carg′o, n., cargo stowed on deck.

deck′-chair, n., a light, folding chair.

decked, adj., adorned; furnished with a deck; p.p., deck.

deck′er, n., a vessel with a deck or decks; one who decks.

deck′-hand, n., a sailor employed on a ship's deck for cleaning and odd jobs.

deck′ing, n., the act of adorning; pr.p., deck.

deck′le, n., a machine that fixes the width of paper in paper-making.

deck′steward, n., a ship's steward employed to look after the passengers whilst on deck.

declaim′, v.i. and t., to make a set speech.

declaimed′, p.p., declaim.

declaim′er, n., one who speaks for effect.

declaim′ing, pr.p., declaim.

declama′tion, n., an impassioned speech; the art of declaiming.

declam′atory, adj., rel. to declamation.

declar′able, adj., able to be declared.

declar′ant, n., a person who makes a legal declaration.

declara′tion, n., the act of declaring.

declar′ative, adj., making declaration.

declar′atively, adv., in a declarative manner.

declar′atory, adj., distinctly expressive of opinions.

declare′, v.t., to affirm; to state fully.

declared′, p.p., declare.

declar′er, n., one who declares.

declar′ing, pr.p., declare.

declass′, v.t., to remove from one's class.

declassifica′tion, n., a removal from one's class.

declass′ified, p.p., declassify.

declass′ify, v.t., to take off the security list.

declass′ifying, pr.p., declassify.

declen′sion, n., a falling off; a deterioration; case-inflection; a noun-class.

decli′nable, *adj.*, having case inflections.

declina′tion, *n.*, deviation; one of the co-ordinates of a heavenly body; the deviation of the magnetic needle from the true north.

dec′linator, *n.*, an instrument for observing declination.

decli′natory, *adj.*, characterized by declining.

decline′, *n.*, a deterioration; tuberculosis; *v.i.*, to sink or stoop to a lower level; to decay; *v.t.*, to refuse; to inflect so as to form the oblique cases.

declined′, *p.p.*, decline.

decli′ner, *n.*, one who declines.

decli′ning, *pr.p.*, decline.

declinom′eter, *n.*, an instrument for measuring the declination of the magnetic needle.

decli′nous, *adj.*, bending downwards (applied to stamens of a flower) (*bot.*).

decliv′itous, *adj.*, steep.

decliv′ity, *n.*, a slope downward.

decli′vous, *adj.*, sloping downward.

declutch′, *v.i.*, to release the clutch.

declutched′, *p.p.*, declutch.

declutching, *pr.p.*, declutch.

decoct′, *v.t.*, to prepare by boiling.

decoct′ed, *p.p.*, decoct,

decoct′ible, *adj.*, able to be boiled.

decoct′ing, *pr.p.*, decoct.

decoc′tion, *n.*, the water in which a substance has been boiled; the act of boiling.

decoc′tive, *adj.*, having a tendency to decoct.

decode′, *v.t.*, to translate from code.

decod′ed, *p.p.*, decode.

decod′ing, *pr.p.*, decode.

decohe′rer, *n.*, a separator (of electric waves).

decoke′, *n.*, a decarbonization; *v.t.*, to decarbonize.

decol′late, *v.t.*, to behead.

decolla′ted, *adj.*, beheaded; truncated; *p.p.*, decollate.

decolla′ting, *pr.p.*, decollate.

decolla′tion, *n.*, the act of beheading.

decol′letage, *n.*, a low-cut neck of a dress.

décolleté′, *adj.*, having the neck and part of the bust exposed (*Fr.*).

decol′orant, *n.*, a substance that bleaches.

decolora′tion, *n.*, the removal of colour.

decol′orize, *v.t.*, *i.q.* decolour.

decol′orized, *p.p.*, decolorize.

decol′orizing, *pr.p.*, decolorize.

decol′o(u)r, *v.t.*, to deprive of colour; to bleach.

decol′o(u)red, *p.p.*, decolour.

decol′o(u)ring, *pr.p.*, decolour.

de′complex, *adj.*, having complex parts.

decompo′sable, *adj.*, able to be decomposed.

decompose′, *v.t.*, to resolve into original elements; *v.i.*, to decay.

decomposed′, *p.p.*, decompose.

decompo′sing, *pr.p.*, decompose.

decom′posite, *adj.*, compounded a second time.

decomposi′tion, *n.*, an analysis; a disintegration; decay.

decompound′, *adj.*, *i.q.* decomposite; *v.t.* to compound with things already compounded.

decompound′ed, *p.p.*, decompound.

decompound′ing, *pr.p.*, decompound.

decompress′, *v.t.*, to release from pressure.

decompressed′, *p.p.*, decompress.

decompress′ing, *pr.p.*, decompress.

decompre′ssion, *n.*, the relief from pressure.

decompre′ssor, *n.*, a contrivance for relieving the pressure in a motor engine.

decon′secrate, *v.t.*, to unconsecrate; to secularize.

deconsecra′ted, *p.p.*, deconsecrate.

deconsecra′ting, *pr.p.*, deconsecrate.

deconsecra′tion, *n.*, secularization.

decontam′inate, *v.t.*, to free from contamination.

decontamina′ted, *p.p.*, decontaminate.

decontamina′ting, *pr.p.*, decontaminate.

decontamina′tion, *n.*, the freeing from contamination.

decontrol′, *n.*, the removal of control; *v.t.*, to remove control.

decontrolled′, *p.p.*, decontrol.

decontroll′ing, *n.*, *i.q.* decontrol; *pr.p.*, decontrol.

décor′, *n.*, the decorative and artistic ensemble; the general aesthetic arrangement of objects (*Fr.*).

dec′orate, *v.t.*, to adorn.

dec′orated, *p.p.*, decorate.

dec′orating, *pr.p.*, decorate.

decora′tion, *n.*, ornamentation; a badge of honour.

dec′orative, *adj.*, adorning.

dec′orativeness, *n.*, the quality of being decorative.

dec′orator, *n.*, one who decorates.

deco′rous, *adj.*, seemly; befitting.

deco′rously, *adv.*, in a becoming manner.

deco′rousness, *n.*, the propriety of behaviour.

decor′ticate, *v.t.*, to strip the bark from.

decor′ticated, *p.p.*, decorticate.

decort′icating, *pr.p.*, decorticate.

decortica′tion, *n.*, the act of decorticating.

deco′rum, *n.*, decency of behaviour.

de′coy, *n.*, a lure; a snare; *v.t.*, to entrap by deceit.

de′coy-duck, *n.*, a duck used to ensnare other ducks.

decoyed′, *p.p.*, decoy.

decoy′ing, *pr.p.*, decoy.

decrease′, *n.*, a diminution; *v.t.* and *i.*, to diminish.

decreased′, *p.p.*, decrease.

decreas′ing, *pr.p.*, decrease.

decreas′ingly, *adv.*, by diminishing.

decree′, *n.*, an edict; a judicial decision; *v.t.*, to determine judicially or legislatively.

decreed', *p.p.*, decree.

decree'ing, *pr.p.*, decree.

decree'nis'i, *n.*, a Divorce Court Order.

decre'er, *n.*, one who decrees.

dec'rement, *n.*, the small quantity by which a variable becomes less and less.

decrep'it, *adj.*, weakened with age.

decrep'itate, *v.i.*, to crackle when roasting.

decrep'itated, *p.p.*, decrepitate.

decrep'itating, *pr.p.*, decrepitate.

decrepita'tion, *n.*, the act of flying asunder with a crackling noise when strongly heated.

decrep'itude, *n.*, the state of being decrepit.

decres'cent, *adj.*, decreasing.

decre'tal, *n.*, a papal letter settling a point of ecclesiastical law.

decre'tist, *n.*, one who is skilled in knowledge of decretals or common law.

decre'tive, *adj.*, pert. to a decree.

decre'tory, *adj.*, established by a decree.

decri'al, *n.*, the act of decrying.

decried', *p.p.*, decry.

decrusta'tion, *n.*, the removal of a crust.

decry', *v.t.*, to discredit by fault-finding.

decry'ing, *pr.p.*, decry.

dec'uman, *adj.*, especially large or powerful.

decum'bence, *n.*, the state of being decumbent.

decum'bency, *n.*, *i.q.* decumbence.

decum'bent, *adj.*, reclining; prostrate.

dec'uple, *adj.*, tenfold; *n.*, a number ten times repeated; *v.t.*, to multiply by 10.

dec'upled, *p.p.*, decuple.

dec'upling, *pr.p.*, decuple.

decu'rion, *n.*, a Roman officer over ten soldiers.

decur'rent, *adj.*, the base extended downwards along the stem (*bot.*).

decur'sive, *adj.*, running down; decurrent.

decurve', *v.t.*, to make to curve downward.

decurved', *p.p.*, decurve.

decurv'ing, *pr.p.*, decurve.

decus'sate, *adj.*, *i.q.* decussated; *v.t.*, to intersect in a crosswise manner.

decus'sated, *adj.*, crossed; *p.p.*, decussate.

decus'sately, *adv.*, crosswise.

decus'sating, *pr.p.*, decussate.

decussa'tion, *n.*, the act of crossing at right angles.

decus'satively, *adv.*, crosswise.

de'dal, *adj.*, *i.q.* daedal.

deda'lian, *adj.*, *i.q.* daedal.

ded'alous, *adj.*, having a margin with intricate windings (*bot.*).

dedans, *n.*, the gallery of a tennis-court (*Fr.*).

ded'icate, *v.t.*, to set apart, to devote; to inscribe to somebody.

ded'icated, *adj.*, devoted to a cause; *p.p.*, dedicate.

ded'icating, *pr.p.*, dedicate.

dedica'tion, *n.*, devotion; a setting apart for a use; an address prefixed to a book.

ded'icator, *n.*, one who dedicates.

ded'icatory, *adj.*, serving as a dedication.

dedi'tion, *n.*, a surrender.

deduce', *v.t.*, to infer; to trace the descent of.

deduced', *p.p.*, deduce.

deduce'ment, *n.*, deduction.

deducibil'ity, *n.*, the quality of being deducible.

dedu'cible, *adj.*, able to be deduced.

deduc'ing, *pr.p.*, deduce.

deduct', *v.t.*, to subtract.

deduct'ed, *p.p.*, deduct.

deduct'ible, *adj.*, able to be deducted.

deduct'ing, *pr.p.*, deduct.

deduc'tion, *n.*, an inference from general to particular; a subtraction.

deduc'tive, *adj.*, deducible; rel. to deduction.

deduc'tively, *adv.*, in a deductive way.

dee, *n.*, the letter D; a D-shaped ring.

deed, *n.*, an act; a legal instrument.

deed'less, *adj.*, inactive.

deed'-poll, *n.*; a deed executed by one party.

deem, *v.t.*, to believe; to judge; *v.i.*, to suppose.

deemed, *p.p.*, deem.

deem'ing, *pr.p.*, deem.

deem'ster, *n.*, one of two Manx (Isle of Man) justices.

deep, *adj.*, descending far downward; *n.*, the open sea.

deep'en, *v.t.*, to make deep or deeper; *v.i.*, to become deeper.

deep'ened, *p.p.*, deepen.

deep'ening, *pr.p.*, deepen.

deep'er, *adj.*, *comp.* of deep.

deep'est, *adj.*, *super.* of deep.

deep'freeze, *n.*; a storage at low temperature.

deep'ing, *n.*, a section of a fishing-net one fathom deep.

deep'ish, *adj.*, rather deep.

deep'ly, *adv.*, far below the surface; profoundly.

deep'ness, *n.*, depth.

deep'rooted, *adj.*, *i.q.* deepseated.

deep'seated, *adj.*, deep down; firmly established.

deer, *n.*, a ruminant quadruped with branching horns.

deer'skin, *n.*, the skin of a deer.

deer'stalker, *n.*, one who stalks deer; a type of hat.

deface', *v.t.*, to disfigure.

defaced', *adj.*, injured on the surface; *p.p.*, deface.

deface'ment, *n.*, an injury to the surface.

defa'cer, *n.*, one who defaces.

defa'cing, *pr.p.*, deface.

de fac'to, phrase = actual (*Lat.*).

defal'cate, *v.t.*, to misappropriate money.

defal'cated, *p.p.*, defalcate.

defal'cating, *pr.p.*, defalcate.

defalca'tion, *n.*, a fraudulent deficiency in money matters.

de'falcator, *n.*, an embezzler.

defama'tion, *n.*, slander; calumny.

defam'atory, *adj.*, slanderous; calumnious.

defame', *v.t.*, to slander; to libel.

defamed', *p.p.*, defame.

defa'mer, *n.*, a slanderer.

defa'ming, *pr.p.*, defame.

defatt'ed, *adj.*, deprived of its fat.

default', *n.*, an omission of a duty; *v.i.*, to neglect an engagement.

default'ed, *p.p.*, default.

default'er, *n.*, one who makes default.

default'ing, *pr.p.*, default.

defea'sance, *n.*, a rendering null and void (*leg.*).

defeasibil'ity, *n.*, *i.q.* defeasibleness.

defea'sible, *adj.*, able to be annulled.

defea'sibleness, *n.*, the state of being defeasible.

defeat', *n.*, a frustration; an overthrow; *v.t.*, to overcome; to resist with success.

defeat'ed, *p.p.*, defeat.

defeat'ing, *pr.p.*, defeat.

defeat'ism, *n.*, a disposition to accept defeat.

defeat'ist, *n.*, one disposed to accept defeat.

def'ecate, *v.t.*, to purge of extraneous matter; *v.i.*, to excrete.

def'ecated, *p.p.*, defecate.

def'ecating, *pr.p.*, defecate.

defeca'tion, *n.*, the act of purifying.

def'ecator, *n.*, one who, or that which, defecates.

defect', *n.*, a fault; something lacking; a shortcoming.

defect'ible, *adj.*, deficient.

defec'tion, *n.*, abandonment; apostasy.

defect'ive, *adj.*, imperfect.

defect'ively, *adv.*, imperfectly.

defect'iveness, *n.*, faultiness.

defence', *n.*, the act of defending; a protection; a vindication.

defenced', *adj.*, provided with a defence.

defence'less, *adj.*, without defence.

defence'lessness, *n.*, the state of being defenceless.

defend', *v.t.*, to protect against attack.

defend'able, *adj.*, able to be defended.

defend'ant, *n.*, one who opposes a charge or complaint.

defend'ed, *p.p.*, defend.

defend'er, *n.*, a champion; an advocate.

defend'ing, *pr.p.*, defend.

defenestra'tion, *n.*, the action of throwing out of a window.

defensibil'ity, *n.*, the quality of being defensible.

defen'sible, *adj.*, able to be defended.

defen'sive, *adj.*, serving to defend.

defen'sively, *adv.*, in a defensive manner.

defens'ory, *adj.*, *i.q.* defensive.

defer', *v.t.*, to postpone; *v.i.*, to yield to another's opinion.

def'erence, *n.*, respect; courteous consideration.

def'erent, *n.*, an imaginary circle employed by Ptolemy in his system of astronomy.

deferen'tial, *adj.*, expressing deference.

deferen'tially, *adv.*, respectfully.

defer'ment, *n.*, a postponement.

deferred', *p.p.*, defer.

defer'rer, *n.*, one who defers.

defer'ring, *pr.p.*, defer.

defeu'dalize, *v.t.*, to deprive of feudal character.

defi'ance, *n.*, a challenging to fight; opposition to authority.

defi'ant, *adj.*, insolent, bold, disobedient.

defi'antly, *adv.*, in a defiant way.

defi'ciency, *n.*, want; something less than is necessary.

defi'cient, *adj.*, wanting, imperfect.

defi'ciently, *adv.*, in a defective manner.

def'icit, *n.*, a deficiency (in money).

defied', *p.p.*, defy.

defi'er, *n.*, one who defies.

defilade', *n.*, a fortification against enfilading fire; *v.t.*, to fortify against enfilading fire.

defile', *v.t.*, to make unclean; *v.i.*, to march off in a line.

de'file, *n.*, a long, narrow pass.

defiled', *p.p.*, defile.

defile'ment, *n.*, the effect of defiling.

defi'ler, *n.*, one who defiles.

defi'ling, *pr.p.*, defile.

defi'nable, *adj.*, able to be defined.

define', *v.t.*, to determine the limits or meaning of.

defined', *p.p.*, define.

defi'ner, *n.*, one who defines.

defi'ning, *pr.p.*, define.

def'inite, *adj.*, certain; precise.

def'initely, *adv.*, in a definite manner.

def'initeness, *n.*, the state or character of being definite.

defini'tion, *n.*, a brief and exact description of a thing by its properties; clearness of outline.

defin'itive, *adj.*, determinate; conclusive.

defin'itively, *adv.*, conclusively; unconditionally.

deflagrabil'ity, *n.*, combustibility.

def'lagrable, *adj.*, combustible.

def'lagrate, *v.t.* and *i.*, to burn rapidly.

def'lagrated, *p.p.*, deflagrate.

def'lagrating, *pr.p.*, deflagrate.

deflagra'tion, *n.*, the rapid combustion of a mixture.

def'lagrator, *n.*, an electrical instrument for producing intense heat for combustion.

deflate', *v.t.*, to withdraw the air from.

defla'ted, *p.p.*, deflate.

defla'ting, *pr.p.*, deflate.

defla'tion, *n.*, the act or effect of deflating; an artificial depression of prices.

defla'tionary, *adj.*, rel. to, or tending towards, deflation.

defla'tionist, *n.*, one who favours deflation.

deflect', *v.t.* and *i.*, to cause to turn from a straight line or set course.

deflect'ed, *p.p.*, deflect.

deflect'ing, *pr.p.*, deflect.

deflec'tion, **deflex'ion**, *n.*, deviation.

deflect'or, *n.*, a diaphragm in a lamp or stove by means of which air and gas are mingled and made to burn completely.

deflo'rate, *adj.*, of plants, having shed their pollen on their flowers.

deflora'tion, *n.*, the act of deflowering; rape.

deflow'er, *v.t.*, to violate; to ravish.

deflow'ered, *p.p.*, deflower.

deflow'erer, *n.*, one who deflowers.

deflow'ering, *pr.p.*, deflower.

de'fluent, *adj.* and *n.*, down-flowing.

deflux'ion, *n.*, a catarrhal discharge.

defo'liate, *adj.*, without leaves.

defolia'tion, *n.*, the dropping of leaves.

defor'est, *v.t.*, to remove the trees from.

deforesta'tion, *n.*, the act or practice of deforesting.

defor'ested, *p.p.*, deforest.

defor'esting, *pr.p.*, deforest.

deform', *v.t.*, to disfigure.

deforma'tion, *n.*, malformation; an alteration of shape.

deformed', *adj.*, misshapen; *p.p.*, deform.

deform'er, *n.*, one who deforms.

deform'ing, *pr.p.*, deform.

deform'ity, *n.*, the state of being deformed; any misshapen part of the body.

defraud', *v.t.*, to cheat.

defraud'ed, *p.p.*, defraud.

defraud'er, *n.*, one who defrauds.

defraud'ing, *pr.p.*, defraud.

defray', *v.t.*, to discharge; to settle.

defrayed', *p.p.*, defray.

defray'er, *n.*, one who pays expenses.

defray'ing, *pr.p.*, defray.

defrost', *v.t.*, to unfreeze.

defrosted', *p.p.*, defrost.

defrost'ing, *pr.p.*, defrost.

deft, *adj.*, dexterous.

deft'ly, *adv.*, neatly; dexterously.

deft'ness, *n.*, dexterity.

defunct', *adj.*, dead.

defy', *v.t.*, to challenge; to set at naught.

defy'ing, *pr.p.*, defy.

degauss', *v.t.*, to neutralize a ship's magnetization (as protection from mines).

degen'eracy, *n.*, a state of deterioration.

degen'erate, *adj.*, base; mean; having declined in natural or moral worth; *n.*, a creature that has so declined.

de'generate, *v.i.*, to become of a lower type, physically or morally.

degen'erated, *p.p.*, degenerate.

degen'erately, *adv.*, in a degenerate manner.

degen'erateness, *n.*, a degenerate state.

degen'erating, *pr.p.*, degenerate.

degenera'tion, *n.*, *i.q.* degeneracy.

degen'erative, *adj.*, causing degeneration.

deglu'tinate, *v.t.*, to unglue; to separate from adhesion.

deglu'tinated, *p.p.*, deglutinate.

deglu'tinating, *pr.p.*, deglutinate.

degluti'tion, *n.*, the act or power of swallowing.

degrada'tion, *n.*, debasement; the act of degrading.

degrade', *v.t.*, to debase; to reduce from a higher to a lower rank; *v.i.*, to degenerate.

degra'ded, *adj.*, sunk to a vile state; *p.p.*, degrade.

degra'ding, *adj.*, dishonouring; *pr.p.*, degrade.

degra'dingly, *adv.*, in a degrading manner.

degree', *n.*, rank; station; extent; the 360th part of the circumference of a circle; a division marked on a scientific instrument; an academic title of distinction.

degres'sion, *n.*, graduated reduction in taxation.

dehisce', *v.i.*, to open, as the seed-vessels of plants (*bot.*); to gape.

dehis'cence, *n.*, the opening or splitting of certain organs in plants (*bot.*).

dehis'cent, *adj.*, gaping open.

dehort', *v.t.*, to give contrary advice.

dehorta'tion, *n.*, dissuasion.

dehort'ative, *adj.*, dissuasive.

dehort'atory, *adj.*, *i.q.* dehortative.

dehum'anize, *v.t.*, to divest of human qualities.

dehum'anized, *p.p.*, dehumanize.

dehum'anizing, *pr.p.*, dehumanize.

dehyd'rate, *v.t.*, to deprive of water (*chem.*).

dehyd'rated, *p.p.*, dehydrate.

dehyd'rating, *pr.p.*, dehydrate.

dehydra'tion, *n.*, a deprivation of water.

dehyp'notize, *v.t.*, to cause to waken from an hypnotic state.

de-ice', *v.t.*, to remove ice from surfaces.

de-i'cer, *n.*, a device used to prevent the formation of ice.

de'icide, *n.*, the act of putting Jesus Christ to death; one of Christ's murderers.

de-ic'ing, *n.*, the freeing from ice; *pr.p.*, de-ice.

deic'tic, *adj.*, pointing, demonstrative.

deif'ic, *adj.*, making divine.

deifica'tion, *n.*, the act of deifying.

de'ified, *p.p.*, deify.

de'ifier, *n.*, one that deifies.

de'iform, *adj.*, of godlike form.

de'ify, *v.t.*, to make a god of.

de'ifying, *pr.p.*, deify.

deign, *v.i.*, to condescend.

deigned, *p.p.*, deign.

deign'ing, *pr.p.*, deign.

de'i gra'tia, *adv.*, by God's grace (*Lat.*).

deil, *n.*, the devil (*Scot.*).

deipnos'ophist, *n.*, a philosopher who cultivates learned conversation at meals.

de'ism, *n.*, the creed of a deist.

de'ist, *n.*, one who believes in a supreme being but denies revealed religion.

deis'tic, *adj.*, pert. to deism.

deis'tical, *adj.*, *i.q.* deistic.

de'ity, *n.*, divinity; Godhead; God; a fabulous god or goddess.

deject', *v.t.*, to cast down; to dispirit.

deject'ed, *adj.*, downcast; sorrowful; *p.p.*, deject.

deject'edly, *adv.*, sadly; heavily.

deject'edness, *n.*, dejection.

deject'er, *n.*, one who dejects.

deject'ing, *n.*, the casting down; *pr.p.*, deject.

dejec'tion, *n.*, lowness of spirits.

deject'ory, *adj.*, promoting the action of the bowels.

déjeuner, *n.*, breakfast; luncheon (*Fr.*).

de ju're, *adv.* and *adj.*, by right; rightful (*Lat.*).

dekk'o, *n.*, a look (*slang*).

delaine', *n.*, a muslin made of cotton and wool, used chiefly as a printing cloth.

delasse'ment, *n.*, relaxation (*Fr.*).

delate', *v.t.*, to accuse.

dela'ted, *p.p.*, delate.

delat'ing, *pr.p.*, delate.

dela'tion, *n.*, an accusation.

dela'tor, *n.*, one who accuses or informs against.

delay', *n.*, a lingering or deferring; *v.t.*, to retard; to hinder; *v.i.*, to linger.

delayed', *p.p.*, delay.

delay'er, *n.*, one who delays.

delay'ing, *pr.p.*, delay.

del cred'ere, *adj.*, applied to an agent who guarantees the buyer's solvency (*It.*).

de'le, *v.t.*, to blot out; to erase; to remove (*Lat.*).

delec'table, *adj.*, highly pleasing.

delecta'tion, *n.*, a giving of delight; delight.

delec'tified, *p.p.*, delectify.

delec'tify, *v.t.*, to delight.

delec'tifying, *pr.p.*, delectify.

delec'tus, *n.*, a school reading-book of selected passages from the classics.

del'egacy, *n.*, the system of delegating; a delegate appointment; a body of delegates.

del'egate, *adj.*, representative; *n.*, a representative; a deputy.

dele'gate, *v.t.*, to entrust to another's care and management.

del'egated, *p.p.*, delegate.

del'egating, *pr.p.*, delegate.

delega'tion, *n.*, an appointment to act as deputy; a person or body of persons deputed to act for another or others.

delen'da, *n. pl.*, words to be struck out (*Lat.*).

delete', *v.t.*, to erase; to strike out with a pen or pencil.

dele'ted, *p.p.*, delete.

delete'rious, *adj.*, noxious.

delet'ing, *pr.p.*, delete.

dele'tion, *n.*, the act of deleting; a passage deleted.

delf(t), *n.*, glazed earthenware dishes made at Delft in Holland.

De'lian, *adj.*, rel. to the Aegian island of Delos or to Apollo, the Greek god of poetry.

del'ibate, *v.t.*, to sip or taste.

delib'erate, *adj.*, carefully considering probable consequences; not hasty; slow.

delib'erate, *v.i.*, to ponder; to reflect.

delib'erated, *p.p.*, deliberate.

delib'erately, *adv.*, in a deliberate manner.

delib'erateness, *n.*, the state or quality of being deliberate.

delib'erating, *pr.p.*, deliberate.

delibera'tion, *n.*, careful consideration; the discussion and examination of pros and cons.

delib'erative, *adj.*, pert. to deliberation.

delib'eratively, *adv.*, *i.q.* deliberately.

delib'erator, *n.*, one who deliberates.

del'ible, *adj.*, able to be deleted.

del'icacy, *n.*, the quality of being delicate; a dainty morsel.

del'icate, *adj.*, dainty; easily injured; in weak health.

del'icately, *adv.*, daintily; tenderly.

del'icateness, *n.*, the state of being delicate.

delicatesse', *n.*, a delicacy (*Fr.*).

delicates'en, *n.*, a shop that sells a range of cooked meats, savouries and delicacies (*Ger.*).

deli'cious, *adj.*, highly pleasing to the taste or smell.

deli'ciously, *adv.*, in a delicious manner.

deli'ciousness, *n.*, the quality of being delicious.

delict', *n.*, a violation of law; an offence.

delic'tual, *adj.*, law-breaking; offensive.

deliga'tion, *n.*, bandaging.

delight', *n.*, joy; the cause of joy; *v.t.*, to please highly; *v.i.*, to be greatly pleased.

delight'ed, *adj.*, overjoyed; *p.p.*, delight.

delight'ful, *adj.*, charming.

delight'fully, *adv.*, in a delightful way.

delight'fulness, *n.*, the quality of being delightful.

delight'ing, *pr.p.*, delight.

delight'some, *adj.*, *i.q.* delightful.

Deli'lah, *n.*, a temptress.

delim'it, *v.t.*, to fix boundaries of.

delimita'tion, *n.*, the fixing of boundaries.

delim'ited, *p.p.*, delimit.

delim'iting, *pr.p.*, delimit.

delin'eament, *n.*, a portrayal either pictorially or in words.

delin'eate, v.t., to depict or describe.

delin'eated, p.p., delineate.

delin'eating, pr.p., delineate.

delinea'tion, n., the process of delineating.

delin'eator, n., one who delineates.

delin'eatory, adj., rel. to delineation.

delin'quency, n., a misdeed; a failure in duty.

delin'quent, n., one who fails to perform his duty.

del'iquate, v.i., to be dissolved; v.t., to melt.

del'iquated, p.p., deliquate.

del'iquating, pr.p., deliquate.

deliqua'tion, n., a melting.

deliquesce', v.i., to become liquid by absorbing moisture from the air.

deliquesced', p.p., deliquesce.

deliques'cence, n., a gradual melting by absorption of moisture from the atmosphere.

deliques'cent, adj., liquefying in the air.

deliques'cing, pr.p., deliquesce.

delir'ious, adj., affected with delirium.

delir'iously, adv., in a delirious manner.

delir'ium, n., a temporary disorder of the mind.

delir'ium tre'mens, n., an affection of the brain caused by alcoholic excess.

delites'cence, n., a latent state.

delites'cent, adj., latent.

deliv'er, v.t., to rescue; to hand over; to resign; to utter; to help a woman during childbirth.

deliv'erable, adj., capable of being delivered.

deliv'erance, n., release; a verdict; a delivered opinion.

deliv'ered, p.p., deliver.

deliv'erer, n., one who delivers.

deliv'ering, pr.p., deliver.

deliv'ery, n., a giving up; an utterance; a manner of speaking; childbirth.

dell, n., a small, narrow valley.

Della-Crus'can, adj., pert. to the Academia della Crusca in Florence; applied to a class of affected English writers.

delouse', v.t., to free from lice.

deloused', p.p., delouse.

delous'ing, pr.p., delouse.

Del'phian, adj., rel. to Delphi; oracular.

Del'phic, adj., i.q. Delphian.

Del'phin, adj., pert. to the Dauphin of France, in particular the Delphin classics.

del'phine, adj., deep blue.

del'phinine, n., a poisonous alkaloid used in medicine.

Delphin'ium, n., a plant genus comprising larkspurs.

del'phinoid, n. and adj., (member) of the dolphin family.

del'ta, n., the fourth letter of the Greek alphabet; an alluvial tract at the mouth of a river.

del'ta-wing, n., a jet aircraft with triangular wings.

del'toid, adj., triangular; in anatomy, applied to a muscle of the shoulder.

delude', v.t., to mislead.

delu'ded, p.p., delude.

delu'der, n., a deceiver.

delu'ding, pr.p., delude.

del'uge, n., a flood; v.t., to inundate.

del'uged, p.p., deluge.

del'uging, pr.p., deluge.

delu'sion, n., a misleading of the mind; a false belief.

delu'sive, adj., deceptive.

delu'sively, adv., in a delusive manner.

delu'sory, adj., apt to deceive.

de luxe, adj. and adv., luxurious(ly), sumptuous(ly); superior.

delve, v.i. and t., to dig.

delved, p.p., delve.

delv'er, n., one who delves.

delv'ing, pr.p., delve.

demag'netiza'tion, n., the deprivation of magnetic quality.

demag'netize, v.t., to deprive of magnetic influence.

demag'netized, p.p., demagnetize.

demag'netizing, pr.p., demagnetize.

demagog'ic, adj., rel. to a demagogue.

dem'agogism, n., demagogic principles.

dem'agogue, n., one who gains influence by playing on prejudices.

demand', n., a request with authority; v.t., to ask; to claim; to necessitate; v.i., to inquire.

demand'able, adj., liable to demand.

demand'ant, n., a plaintiff; a demander.

demand'ed, p.p., demand.

demand'er, n., one who demands.

demand'ing, pr.p., demand.

de'marcate, v.t., to mark the boundaries of.

demarcated, p.p., demarcate.

demarcating, pr.p., demarcate.

demarca'tion, n., the process of marking off boundaries; a separation.

démarche, n., a policy or plan of action; an ultimatum; an approach towards a policy. (Fr.).

demater'ialize, v.t. and i., to make nonmaterial; to make spiritual.

demater'ialized, p.p., dematerialize.

demater'ializing, pr.p., dematerialize.

deme, n., the township of ancient Attica (Greece).

demean', v.t., to behave.

demeaned', p.p., demean.

demean'ing, pr.p., demean.

demean'our, n., behaviour; attitude.

dement', v.t., to drive mad.

dement'ed, *adj.*, insane.

demen'tedly, *adv.*, in a demented manner.

démen'ti, *n.*, the official denial of rumour etc. (*Fr.*).

demen'tia, *n.*, a form of insanity.

demerar'a, *n.*, a brownish, cane sugar.

demer'it, *n.*, that which is blamable in moral conduct.

deme'ritor'ious, *adj.*, having faults or defects.

demersed', *adj.*, growing under water.

demer'sion, *n.*, the act of plunging into a liquid.

demesne', *n.*, land adjacent to a manor house.

dem'i, *prefix*, half.

dem'igod, *n.*, an inferior deity; one partly human, partly divine.

dem'ijohn, *n.*, a glass bottle with a large body and small neck, enclosed in wickerwork.

demil'itarize, *v.t.*, to remove the military organization from (frontier, zone, etc.).

demil'itarized, *p.p.*, demilitarize.

demil'itarizing, *pr.p.*, demilitarize.

dem'ilune, *n.*, an outwork in fortification, protecting a bastion.

dem'i-monde, *n.*, women of doubtful character living as ladies of position (*Fr.*).

dem'iquaver, *n.*, *i.q.* semiquaver.

dem'i-rep, *n.*, a woman of doubtful chastity.

demisabil'ity, *n.*, the capability of being demised.

demi'sable, *adj.*, able to be demised.

demise', *n.*, the death of a person of distinction; the conveyance of an estate in law; *v.t.*, to transfer, convey or bequeath.

demised', *p.p.*, demise.

dem'isemiqua'ver, *n.*, the half of a semiquaver.

demi'sing, *pr.p.*, demise.

demis'sion, *n.*, a laying down of office; a resignation.

demit', *v.t.*, to resign.

---

dem'itone, *n.*, *i.q.* semitone.

dem'iurge, *n.*, the Creator of the world.

demiur'gic, *adj.*, rel. to demiurge.

demob', *v.t.*, the abbrev. of demobilize (*colloq.*).

demo'bilize, *v.t.*, to disband troops.

demo'bilized, *p.p.*, demobilize.

demo'bilizing, *pr.p.*, demobilize.

democ'racy, *n.*, government by the people; the people as rulers.

dem'ocrat, *n.*, one who adheres to democracy.

democrat'ic, *adj.*, pert. to democracy.

democrat'ical, *adj.*, *i.q.* democratic.

democratiza'tion, *n.*, the act of making democratic.

democ'ratize, *v.t.*, to make democratic.

democ'ratized, *p.p.*, democratize.

democ'ratizing, *pr.p.*, democratize.

Democ'rite'an, *adj.*, of Democritus (Greek philosopher), his humour or his theory of atoms.

démo'dé, *adj.*, out of fashion (*Fr.*).

demod'ed, *adj.*, *i.q.* démodé.

Demogorg'on, *n.*, a mysterious and terrible deity of the infernal regions.

demog'rapher, *n.*, one who deals in demography.

demograph'ic, *adj.*, rel. to demography.

demo'graphy, *n.*, statistics, etc., rel. to population.

demoiselle', *n.*, a young lady; the Numidian crane (*Fr.*).

demol'ish, *v.t.*, to destroy.

demol'ished, *p.p.*, demolish.

demol'isher, *n.*, one who demolishes.

demol'ishing, *pr.p.*, demolish.

demoli'tion, *n.*, destruction.

demoli'tionist, *n.*, one who pulls down buildings.

d(a)e'mon, *n.*, a malignant spirit.

demonetiza'tion, *n.*, the act of demonetizing.

demon'etize, *v.t.*, to deprive of standard

---

value as money; to withdraw from circulation.

demon'etized, *p.p.*, demonetize.

demon'etizing, *pr.p.*, demonetize.

demo'niac, *adj.*, influenced by demons; *n.*, a human being possessed by a demon.

demoni'acal, *adj.*, *i.q.* demoniac.

demon'ic, *adj.*, rel. to a demon.

de'monism, *n.*, the belief in demons.

de'monist, *n.*, a believer in demons.

de'monize, *v.t.*, to render diabolical.

de'monized, *p.p.*, demonize.

de'monizing, *pr.p.*, demonize.

demonol'atry, *n.*, devilworship.

demonol'ogy, *n.*, knowledge regarding evil spirits.

demonstrabil'ity, *n.*, the state of being demonstrable.

demon'strable, *adj.*, capable of being demonstrated.

demon'strate, *v.t.*, to prove beyond doubt; to make evident; to show.

demon'strated, *p.p.*, demonstrate.

demon'strating, *pr.p.*, demonstrate.

demon'stration, *n.*, a logical proof; a manifestation; a military operation intended to deceive the enemy; an assembly for protest.

demon'strative, *adj.*, proving by certain evidence; outwardly expressive of the emotions; pointing out.

demon'stratively, *adv.*, in a demonstrative manner.

dem'onstrator, *n.*, one who demonstrates.

demoraliza'tion, *n.*, the act of demoralizing; the state of being demoralized.

demor'alize, *v.t.*, to corrupt the morals of; to deprive (troops) of courage and self-reliance.

demor'alized, *p.p.*, demoralize.

demor'alizing, *pr.p.*, demoralize.

de'mos, *n.*, the common people.

Demosthen'ic, *adj.*, resembling Demosthenes; eloquent.

demote', *v.t.*, to reduce in rank.

demot'ed, *p.p.*, demote.

demot'ic, *adj.*, popular; said of the ordinary alphabet of ancient Egypt.

demot'ing, *pr.p.*, demote.

demo'tion, *n.*, a reduction in rank.

demount'able, *adj.*, able to be taken to pieces for convenience of transport.

demp'ster, *n.*, *i.q.* deemster.

demul'cent, *adj.*, mollifying; *n.*, a medicine which reduces the effects of irritation.

demul'sion, *n.*, the act of soothing.

demur', *n.*, hesitation; an objection; *v.i.*, to object hesitatingly.

demure', *adj.*, affectedly modest; consciously reserved.

demure'ly, *adv.*, In a demure manner.

demure'ness, *n.*, the state of being demure.

demur'rable, *adj.*, open to objection (esp. legal).

demur'rage, *n.*, time of detention of a vessel by the freighter beyond his agreement; corresponding compensation.

demurred', *p.p.*, demur.

demur'rer, *n.*, one who demurs; in law, a stop at some point in the pleadings and dependence on that point for the decision of the cause.

demur'ring, *pr.p.*, demur.

demus'ter, *v.t.*, to disband.

demus'tered, *p.p.*, demuster.

demus'tering, *pr.p.*, demuster.

demy', *n.*, a particular size of paper, about 22½ in. by 17½ in.; a scholar of Magdalen College, Oxford.

den, *n.*, a cave or pit used for shelter.

denar'cotize, *v.t.*, to deprive of narcotine.

denar'cotized, *p.p.*, denarcotize.

denar'cotizing, *pr.p.*, denarcotize.

dena'rius, *n.*, a Roman silver coin of low value.

den'ary, *adj.*, proceeding by tens.

denationaliza'tion, *n.*, the act of denationalizing.

dena'tionalize, *v.t.*, to remove from national control; to divest of national character.

dena'tionalized, *p.p.*, denationalize.

dena'tionalizing, *pr.p.*, denationalize.

denaturaliza'tion, *n.*, the act of denaturalizing.

dena'turalize, *v.t.*, to change the nature of; to make unnatural.

dena'turalized, *p.p.*, denaturalize.

dena'turalizing, *pr.p.*, denaturalize.

dena'turant, *n.*, a substance used in denaturing.

dena'ture, *v.t.*, to change the essential qualities of.

dena'turing, *pr.p.*, denature.

dena'zifica'tion, *n.*, the removal of Nazism.

dena'zify, *v.t.*, to remove Nazism and its influence.

den'driform, *adj.*, shaped like a tree.

den'drite, *n.*, a mineral on which or in which are figures resembling trees or mosses, the result of crystallization.

dendrit'ic, *adj.*, tree-like.

dendrit'ical, *adj.*, *i.q.* dendritic.

den'droid, *adj.*, resembling a small tree.

dendrol'ogist, *n.*, one acquainted with dendrology.

dendrol'ogy, *n.*, the natural history of trees.

dene, *n.*, a low sandhill by the sea.

denega'tion, *n.*, a denial.

dene-hole, *n.*, *i.q.* dane-hole.

den'gue, *n.*, a W. Indian epidemic fever resembling scarlet fever with rheumatism.

deni'able, *adj.*, capable of being denied.

deni'al, *n.*, contradiction; disownment.

denied', *p.p.*, deny.

deni'er, *n.*, one who denies.

denier', *n.*, a very small sum or coin; a unit of weight for estimating fineness of silk, etc.

den'igrate, *v.t.*, to blacken thoroughly.

den'igrated, *p.p.*, denigrate.

den'igrating, *pr.p.*, denigrate.

den'igra'tion, *n.*, *i.q.* defamation.

den'igrator, *n.*, one who denigrates.

de'nim, *n.*, a twilled, cotton fabric.

denit'rate, *v.t.*, to free of nitric or nitrous acid or nitrates.

denit'rify, *i.q.* denitrate.

deniza'tion, *n.*, the act of making one a denizen.

den'izen, *n.*, an inhabitant; a naturalized alien.

denom'inate, *v.t.*, to give a name to.

denom'inated, *p.p.*, denominate.

denom'inating, *pr.p.*, denominate.

denomina'tion, *n.*, a collection of individuals called by the same name; a religious sect; a level of value.

denomina'tional, *adj.*, pert. to particular, esp. religious, denominations.

denomina'tionalism, *n.*, the system of dividing into sects.

denom'inative, *adj.*, conferring a distinct appellation.

denom'inator, *n.*, the number below the line in a vulgar fraction; one who, or that which, gives a name.

deno'table, *adj.*, that may be denoted.

denota'tion, *n.*, the act of denoting; what a word or sign denotes.

denot'ative, *adj.*, indicative of.

denote', *v.t.*, to be the name of; to indicate.

deno'ted, *p.p.*, denote.

deno'ting, *pr.p.*, denote.

dénoue'ment, *n.*, the unravelling of a plot; the solution of a mystery; the issue of any course of conduct (*Fr.*).

denounce', *v.t.*, to accuse; to terminate.

denounced', *p.p.*, denounce.

denounce'ment, *n.*, *i.q.* denunciation.

denounc'er, *n.*, one who denounces.

denounc'ing, *pr.p.*, denounce.

de nouveau, *adv.*, afresh; starting afresh (*Fr.*).

dense, *adj.*, compact; thick; stupid.

dense'ly, *adv.*, compactly; stupidly.

dense'ness, *n.*, density; stupidity.

den'ser, *adj.*, *comp.* of dense.

den'sest, *adj.*, *super.* of dense.

den'sity, *n.* closeness of constituent parts.

dent, *n.* a depression made by a blow; *v.t.* to make a dent in.

den'tal, *adj.*, rel. to the teeth; *n.*, a dental sound, as *d, t, th.*

den'talize, *v.t.*, to convert to a dental letter.

den'tate, *adj.*, toothed.

den'tated, *adj.*, *i.q.* dentate.

denta'tion, *n.*, a toothed form.

dent'ed, *p.p.*, dent.

dentelle', *n.*, lace (*Fr.*).

den'ticle, *n.*, a small tooth or projecting point.

dentic'ulate, *adj.*, having small teeth.

dentic'ulated, *adj.*, *i.q.* denticulate.

denticula'tion, *n.*, the state of being denticulate.

den'tiform, *adj.*, toothlike.

den'tifrice, *n.*, a powder for cleaning the teeth.

den'til, *n.*, a little square block cut on a Greek cornice (*archit.*).

den'tine, *n.*, the hard structure in teeth.

dent'ing, *pr.p.*, dent.

den'tist, *n.*, one who extracts, cleans, repairs and supplies teeth.

dentis'tic, *adj.*, rel. to dentistry.

den'tistry, *n.*, the profession or art of a dentist.

denti'tion, *n.*, the cutting of teeth in infancy; the system of teeth peculiar to an animal.

den'toid, *adj.*, shaped like a tooth.

den'ture, *n.*, a dentist's name for one or more artificial teeth.

den'udate, *adj.*, denuded; *v.t.*, *i.q.* denude.

den'udated, *adj.*, *i.q.* denudate; *p.p.*, denudate.

den'udating, *pr.p.*, denudate.

denuda'tion, *n.*, the act of denuding.

denud'ative, *adj.*, having a baring effect.

denude', *v.t.*, to make bare.

denu'ded, *p.p.*, denude.

denu'ding, *pr.p.*, denude.

denun'ciate, *v.t.*, to denounce.

denun'ciated, *p.p.*, denunciate.

denun'ciating, *pr.p.*, denunciate.

denuncia'tion, *n.*, a public menace or accusation. (Also *denouncement.*)

denun'ciative, *adj.*, implying denunciation.

denun'ciator, *n.*, one who denounces.

denun'ciatory, *adj.*, *i.q.* denunciative.

deny', *v.t.*, to declare not to be true; to refuse; *v.i.*, to answer in the negative.

deny'ing, *pr.p.*, deny.

deobstruct', *v.t.*, to remove obstructions from.

deobstruc'ted, *p.p.*, deobstruct.

deobstruc'ting, *pr.p.*, deobstruct.

deob'struent, *adj.*, that which opens the natural ducts and pores of the body.

deoc'ulate, *v.t.*, to make blind.

deoc'ulated, *p.p.*, deoculate.

deoc'ulating, *pr.p.*, deoculate.

deocula'tion, *n.*, the act of making blind.

de'odand, *n.*, a chattel which, having caused the death of a person, was formerly confiscated by the king and devoted to religious uses.

de'odar, *n.*, the Indian-cedar tree.

de'odorant, *n.*, a preventative against odour (partic. perspiration).

deodoriza'tion, *n.*, the act of deodorizing.

deo'dorize, *v.t.*, to deprive of smell, esp. of obnoxious smell.

deo'dorized, *p.p.*, deodorize.

deo'dorizer, *n.*, a substance which destroys fetid effluvia.

deo'dorizing, *pr.p.*, deodorize.

deontol'ogy, *n.*, the science of duty; ethics.

De'o volen'te, *adv.*, God willing (*Lat.*, abbrev. D.V.).

deox'idate, *v.t.*, to deprive of oxygen.

deox'idated, *p.p.*, deoxidate.

deox'idating, *pr.p.*, deoxidate.

deoxida'tion, *n.*, the process of reducing an oxide.

deox'idize, *v.t.*, *i.q.* deoxidate.

deox'idized, *p.p.*, deoxidize.

deox'idizing, *pr.p.*, deoxidize.

deox'ygenate, *v.t.*, *i.q.* deoxidate.

deox'ygenize, *v.t.*, *i.q.* deoxidate.

depart', *v.i.*, to go elsewhere.

depart'ed, *adj.*, gone; dead; *p.p.*, depart.

depart'er, *n.*, one who departs.

depart'ing, *pr.p.*, depart.

depart'ment, *n.*, a separate branch of business, science, etc.; a division of territory.

department'al, *adj.*, pert. to a department.

department'ally, *adv.*, in or by means of departments.

depar'ture, *n.*, the act of departing; deviation from a custom or plan.

depas'ture, *v.t.*, to put out to graze.

depatria'tion, *n.*, the removal from one's country.

depau'perate, *v.t.*, to impoverish.

depau'perize, *v.t.*, to free from pauperism.

depend', *v.t.*, to be sustained by being attached to something above; to hang down; to be contingent (on); to rely (upon).

dependabil'ity, *n.*, reliability.

depend'able, *adj.*, trustworthy.

depend'ably, *adv.*, in a trustworthy way.

depend'ant, *n.*, one who relies upon another.

depend'ed, *p.p.*, depend.

depend'ence, *n.*, the state of being dependent; confidence.

depend'ency, *n.*, a territory remote from the state by which it is governed.

depend'ent, *adj.*, hanging down; at the disposal of; relying for support.

depend'ently, *adj.*, in a dependent manner.

depend'ing, *pr.p.*, depend.

dephos'phorize, *v.t.*, to remove phosphorus from.

dephos'phorized, *p.p.*, dephosphorize.

dephos'phorizing, *pr.p.*, dephosphorize.

depict', *v.t.*, to portray in colours or words; to describe.

depict'ed, *p.p.*, depict.

depict'er, *n.*, one who depicts.

depict'ing, *pr.p.*, depict.

depic'tion, *n.*, the act of depicting.

depic'tive, *adj.*, represented in a colourful way.

depic'ture, *v.t.*, to depict; to picture.

depic'tured, *p.p.*, depicture.

depic'turing, *pr.p.*, depicture.

dep'ilate, *v.t.*, to strip of hair.

dep'ilated, *p.p.*, depilate.

dep'ilating, *pr.p.*, depilate.

depila'tion, *n.*, the removal of hair.

depi'lator, *n.*, that which removes hair.

depil'atory, *n.*, a cosmetic used to remove superfluous hairs.

deplete', *v.t.*, to exhaust by draining away.

deple'ted, *p.p.*, deplete.

deple'ting, *pr.p.*, deplete.

deple'tion, *n.*, the act of depleting.

deple'tory, *adj.*, causing depletion.

deplorabil'ity, *n.*, *i.q.* deplorableness.

deplor'able, *adj.*, lamentable; contemptible.

deplor'ableness, *n.*, the state of being deplorable.

deplor'ably, *adv.*, lamentably.

deplora'tion, *n.*, lamentation.

deplore', *v.t.*; to grieve for.

deplored', *p.p.*, deplore.

deplor'er, *n.*, one who deplores.

deplor'ing, *pr.p.*, deplore.

deplor'ingly, *adv.*, in a deploring manner.

deploy', *v.t.*, to extend in a line of small depth; *v.i.*, to form a more extended front; to set out or display.

deployed', *p.p.*, deploy.

deploy'ing, *pr.p.*, deploy.

deploy'ment, *n.*, the act of deploying.

deplume', *v.t.*, to strip of feathers.

deplumed', *p.p.*, deplume.

deplum'ing, *n.*, the act of stripping of feathers; *pr.p.*, deplume.

depo'larize, *v.t.*, to deprive of polarity.

depo'larized, *p.p.*, depolarize.

depo'larizing, *pr.p.*, depolarize.

depo'nent, *adj.*, laying down; *n.*, one who makes a deposition; a deponent verb, *i.e.*, a verb passive in form but active in meaning.

depop'ularize, *v.t.*, to make unpopular.

depop'ulate, *v.t.*, to deprive of inhabitants.

depop'ulated, *p.p.*, depopulate.

depop'ulating, *pr.p.*, depopulate.

depopula'tion, *n.*, the act of depopulating.

depop'ulator, *n.*, one who depopulates.

deport', *v.t.*, to banish; *refl.*, to behave.

deporta'tion, *n.*, banishment.

deport'ed, *p.p.*, deport.

deportee', *n.*, a deported person.

deport'ing, *pr.p.*, deport.

deport'ment, *n.*, demeanour; conduct.

depo'sable, *adj.*, that may be deposed.

depose', *v.t.*, to remove from a throne or other high station; to bear witness in a court of law.

deposed', *p.p.*, depose.

depo'ser, *n.*, one who deposes.

depo'sing, *pr.p.*, depose.

depos'it, *n.*, that which is laid down; a pledge; a sum of money lodged in a bank; *v.t.*, to lay down; to entrust; to put in a place for preservation.

depos'itary, *n.*, a person holding a deposit in trust.

depos'ited, *p.p.*, deposit.

depos'iting, *pr.p.*, deposit.

deposi'tion, *n.*, the act of giving sworn evidence; the attested written testimony of a witness; the dethroning of a king; the act of depositing; something deposited.

depos'itor, *n.*, one who makes a deposit.

depos'itory, *n.*, a place where anything is lodged for preservation.

dep'ot, *n.*, a building where goods are stored; the headquarters of a regiment (*Fr.*); a railway-station (*Amer.*).

deprava'tion, *n.*, the act of corrupting; deterioration.

deprave', *v.t.*, to corrupt.

depraved', *adj.*, vitiated; vicious; *p.p.*, deprave.

depra'ver, *n.*, one who depraves.

depra'ving, *pr.p.*, deprave.

deprav'ity, *n.*, a state of corrupted morals; wickedness.

dep'recate, *v.t.*, to argue against; to express disapproval of.

dep'recated, *p.p.*, deprecate.

dep'recating, *pr.p.*, deprecate.

dep'recatingly, *adv.*, in a deprecating manner.

depreca'tion, *n.*, disapproval.

dep'recative, *adj.*, *i.q.* deprecatory.

dep'recatory, *adj.*, serving to deprecate.

depre'ciate, *v.t.*, to reduce the value of; *v.i.*, to fall in value.

depre'ciated, *p.p.*, depreciate.

depre'ciating, *pr.p.*, depreciate.

deprecia'tion, *n.*, a reduction in value.

depre'ciative, *adj.*, *i.q.* depreciatory.

depre'ciator, *n.*, one who, or that which, depreciates.

depre'ciatory, *adj.*, tending to depreciate.

dep'redate, *v.t.*, to plunder.

dep'redated, *p.p.*, depredate.

dep'redating, *pr.p.*, depredate.

depreda'tion, *n.*, a robbing.

dep'redator, *n.*, a spoiler; a robber.

depred'atory, *adj.*, rel. to pillaging.

depress', *v.t.*, to press down; to lower; to make sad.

depress'ant, *adj.*, lowering; *n.*, a sedative.

depressed', *adj.*, dispirited; sad, flattened in shape; *p.p.*, depress.

depress'ing, *adj.*, sad; *pr.p.*, depress.

depress'ingly, *adv.*, in a depressing manner.

depres'sion, *n.*, the act of depressing; a hollow; dejection; a state of commercial dulness.

depress'ive, *adj.*, tending to depress.

depress'or, *n.*, that which depresses.

depri'vable, *adj.*, able to be deprived.

depriva'tion, *n.*, the act of depriving; a state of being deprived; want; the taking of a preferment from a clergyman.

deprive', *v.t.*, to dispossess.

deprived', *p.p.*, deprive.

depri'ver, *n.*, one who deprives.

depri'ving, *pr.p.*, deprive.

depth, *n.*, the distance from top to bottom, or from front to back, of a thing; profoundness; intensity.

depth'-charge, *n.*, a high explosive dropped into the sea for destroying.

depth'less, *adj.*, unfathomable.

depul'sion, *n.*, a thrusting away.

dep'urate, *v.t.*, to purify; *v.i.*, to turn pure.

dep'urated, *p.p.*, depurate.

dep'urating, *pr.p.*, depurate.

depura'tion, *n.*, the cleansing of a wound.

dep'urator, *n.*, one who, or that which, depurates.

depu'ratory, *adj.*, purifying the blood.

deputa'tion, *n.*, the person or persons deputed to transact business for another or others; the act of deputing.

depute', *v.t.*, to appoint as a substitute or representative.

depu'ted, *p.p.*, depute.

depu'ting, *pr.p.*, depute.

dep'utize, *v.t.*, to act as a deputy.

dep'utized, *p.p.*, deputize.

deputi'zing, *pr.p.*, deputize.

dep'uty, *n.*, a representative or substitute.

dera'cinate, *v.t.*, to uproot.

derail', *v.t.*, to cause to leave the rails.

derailed', *p.p.*, derail.

derail'ing, *pr.p.*, derail.

derail'ment, *n.*, the state of being derailed.

derange', *v.t.*, to disorder.

derange'able, *adj.*, able to be deranged.

deranged', *p.p.*, derange.

derange'ment, *n.*, confusion; mental disorder.

derang'ing, *pr.p.*, derange.

derate', *v.t.*, to relieve from rates.

dera'ted, *p.p.*, derate.

derat'ing, *n.*, the reducing or abolishing of rates; *pr.p.*, derate.

de-ra'tion, *v.t.*, to free from rationing.

der'by, *n.*, an important contest, particularly in horse-racing.

Derbyshire, *adj.*, pert. or rel. the English county of that name.

dere'gister, *v.t.*, to remove a name from a register.

dere'gistered, *p.p.*, deregister.

dere'gistering, *pr.p.*, deregister.

deregistra'tion, *n.*, the removal of a name from a register.

der'elict, *adj.*, abandoned, esp. at sea; *n.*, an article abandoned by the owner, esp. a vessel at sea.

derelic'tion, *n.*, abandonment.

derequisi'tion, *n.*, the freeing of requisitioned property; *v.t.*, to free requisitioned property.

derequisi'tioned, *p.p.*, derequisition.

derequisi'tioning, *pr.p.*, derequisition.

deride', *v.t.*, to ridicule; to mock.

deri'ded, *p.p.*, deride.

deri'der, *n.*, a mocker.

deri'ding, *pr.p.*, deride.

deri'dingly, *adv.*, mockingly.

de rigueur', *adj.*, indispensable; required by etiquette (*Fr.*).

deris'ible, *adj.*, ridiculous insultingly laughable.

deri'sion, *n.*, mockery; scorn.

deri'sive, *adj.*, mocking.

deri'sively, *adv.*, with mockery.

deri'siveness, *n.*, the state of being derisive.

deri'sory, *adj.*, *i.q.* derisive.

deri'vable, *adj.*, capable of being derived.

deriva'tion, *n.*, the act of deriving; etymology.

deriva'tional, *adj.*, rel. to derivation.

deriv'ative, *adj.*, taken from something preceding.

deriv'atively, *adv.*, by derivation.

derive', *v.t.*, to receive from a source; to trace the etymology of; *v.i.*, to trace the origin from.

derived', *p.p.*, derive.

deri'ver, *n.*, one who derives.

deri'ving, *pr.p.*, derive.

derm, *n.*, the true skin lying beneath the cuticle.

der'mal, *adj.*, pert. to, or consisting of, skin.

dermat'ic, *adj.*, pert. to the skin.

dermatit'is, *n.,* an inflammation of the skin.

dermatog'raphy, *n., i.q.* dermography.

der'matoid, *adj.,* resembling skin.

dermatol'ogy, *n.,* the science of the skin and its diseases.

der'mic, *adj.,* rel. to the skin.

dermog'raphy, *n.,* a scientific description of the skin.

der'moid, *adj.,* resembling skin.

dermot'omy, *n.,* dissection of the skin.

der'nier, *adj.,* last (*Fr.*).

der'ogate, *v.t.,* to disparage; *v.i.,* to lessen by taking away a part.

der'ogated, *p.p.,* derogate.

der'ogating, *pr.p.,* derogate.

deroga'tion, *n.,* disparagement.

derog'atory, *adj.,* lessening the effect or value.

der'rick, *n.,* a kind of crane for lifting weights.

de'rring-do', *n.,* desperate courage; daredevilry.

der'ringer, *n.,* a short-barrelled pistol of large calibre.

der'ris, *n.,* kinds of tall, tropical, woody climbers; an insecticide made from these.

derv', *n.,* diesel oil.

der'vish, *n.,* a Mohammedan friar or monk; a person of wild uninhibited behaviour.

de'scala'tion, *n.,* the act of descaling.

de'scale, *v.t.,* to remove scaly deposit.

de'scaled, *p.p.,* descale.

de'scaling, *pr.p.,* descale.

des'cant, *n.,* a melody, a song; a contrapuntal ornamenting of a melody.

descant', *v.t.,* to discourse freely; to add a part to a melody.

descant'ed, *p.p.,* descant.

descant'er, *n.,* one who descants.

descant'ing, *pr.p.,* descant.

descend', *v.i.,* to move downward; *v.t.,* to pass from the top to the bottom of.

descend'ant, *n.,* an individual proceeding from an ancestor in any degree.

descend'ed, *p.p.,* descend.

descend'ent, *adj., i.q.* descending.

descend'er, *n.,* one who descends; part of a letter that goes below the writing line.

descendibil'ity, *n.,* the quality of being descendible.

descend'ible, -able, *adj.,* able to be passed down.

descend'ing, *adj.,* moving downwards; *pr.p.,* descend.

descen'sion, *n.,* a descent; a degradation.

descen'sional, *adj.,* pert. to descension.

descen'sive, *adj.,* tending downward.

descent', *n.,* the act of descending; declivity; an invasion; transmission by inheritance; lineage.

descri'bable, *adj.,* able to be described.

describe', *v.t.,* to trace out; to depict in words.

described', *p.p.,* describe.

descri'ber, *n.,* one who describes.

descri'bing, *pr.p.,* describe.

descried', *p.p.,* descry.

descri'er, *n.,* one who descries.

descrip'tion, *n.,* the act of describing; delineation in words; variety or kind.

descrip'tions, *n.,* the pl. of description.

descrip'tive, *adj.,* containing description.

descrip'tively, *adv.,* in a descriptive manner.

descry', *v.t.,* to espy; to see at a distance.

descry'ing, *pr.p.,* descry.

des'ecrate, *v.t.,* to profane.

des'ecrated, *p.p.,* desecrate.

des'ecrating, *pr.p.,* desecrate.

desecra'tion, *n.,* profanation.

deseg'regate, *v.t.,* to abolish racial segregation.

deseg'regated, *p.p.,* desegregate.

deseg'regating, *pr.p.,* desegregate.

desegrega'tion, *n.,* the abolishment of racial segregation.

desen'sitize, *v.t.,* to reduce or destroy sensitiveness.

des'ert, *adj.,* lying waste, uncultivated and uninhabited; *n.,* a wilderness; a solitude; a vast sandy waste, almost destitute of vegetation.

desert', *n.,* reward or punishment merited; *v.t.,* to abandon; *v.i.,* to quit a post or service without permission.

desert'ed, *p.p.,* desert.

desert'er, *n.,* one who deserts, esp. a soldier or sailor.

desert'ing, *pr.p.,* desert.

deser'tion, *n.,* the act of deserting.

desert'less, *adj.,* undeserving.

deserve', *v.t. and i.,* to merit.

deserved', *p.p.,* deserve.

deserv'edly, *adv.,* justly.

deserv'er, *n.,* one who deserves.

deserv'ing, *adj.,* meritorious; *pr.p.,* deserve.

deserv'ingly, *adv.,* meritoriously.

desex'ualize, *v.t.,* to deprive of sexual qualities.

déshabille', *n.,* the state of not being fully or properly dressed (*Fr.*).

des'iccate, *v.t.,* to exhaust of moisture; *v.i.,* to become dry.

des'iccated, *p.p.,* desiccate.

des'iccating, *pr.p.,* desiccate.

desicca'tion, *n.,* the act of making dry.

des'iccative, *adj.,* drying; *n.,* an application that dries a sore.

des'iccator, *n.,* that which desiccates.

desid'erate, *v.t.,* to feel the want of; to desire.

desid'erated, *p.p.,* desiderate.

desid'erating, *pr.p.,* desiderate.

desid'erative, *adj.,* expressing desire; *n.,* a verb formed from another and expressing a desire of doing what the primitive verb implies.

desidera'tum, *n.*, something much wanted (*pl.* desiderata, *Lat.*).

design', *n.*, a sketch; a scheme; an intention; *v.t.*, to sketch; to plan; to purpose.

design'able, *adj.*, able to be designed.

des'ignate, *adj.*, marked out for office; *v.t.*, to mark out by description; to select for a purpose.

des'ignated, *p.p.*, designate.

des'ignating, *pr.p.*, designate.

designa'tion, *n.*, the act of designating; a distinctive appellation.

des'ignator, *n.*, one who designates.

designed', *p.p.*, design.

design'edly, *adv.*, intentionally.

design'er, *n.*, one who designs.

design'ing, *adj.*, artful; *pr.p.*, design.

design'ingly, *adv.*, artfully.

design'less, *adj.*, without intention.

design'lessly, *adv.*, inadvertently.

desip'ience, *n.*, a trifling; silliness.

desip'ient, *adj.*, silly; foolish.

desirabil'ity, *n.*, the quality of being desirable.

desir'able, *adj.*, worthy of desire.

desir'ableness, *n.*, *i.q.* desirability.

desire', *n.*, a craving to obtain something; that which is desired; *v.t.*, to covet; to request.

desired', *p.p.*, desire.

desir'er, *n.*, one who desires.

desir'ing, *pr.p.*, desire.

desir'ous, *adj.*, wishful.

desist', *v.i.*, to discontinue.

desist'ance, *n.*, a ceasing to act.

desist'ed, *p.p.*, desist.

desist'ing, *pr.p.*, desist.

desi'tion, *n.*, an end or ending.

desk, *n.*, a kind of table for the use of writers and readers, often with a sloping upper surface.

des'man, *n.*, a musk-rat of Russia and the Pyrenees.

desmol'ogy, *n.*, the anatomical study of sinews and ligaments.

des'olate, *adj.*, uninhabited; forlorn; laid waste.

des'olate, *v.t.*, to lay waste; to ruin.

des'olated, *p.p.*, desolate.

des'olateness, *n.*, a state of being desolate.

des'olating, *pr.p.*, desolate.

desola'tion, *n.*, ruin; melancholy.

des'olator, *n.*, one who desolates.

despair', *n.*, hopelessness; *v.i.*, to give up hope.

despaired', *p.p.*, despair.

despair'ing, *adj.*, prone to despair; *pr.p.*, despair.

despair'ingly, *adv.*, in a despairing manner.

despatch', *n.*, dismissal; speed; a letter on public business; *v.t.*, to send; to hasten; to kill. (Also *dispatch*.)

despatched', *p.p.*, despatch.

despatch'ing, *pr.p.*, despatch.

despera'do, *n.*, a desperate fellow; a reckless ruffian.

des'perate, *adj.*, beyond hope; reckless.

des'perately, *adv.*, in a desperate manner.

despera'tion, *n.*, the state of being desperate.

des'picable, *adj.*, contemptible.

des'picableness, *n.*, the quality of being despicable.

des'picably, *adv.*, vilely.

despi'sable, *adj.*, worthy of contempt.

despise', *v.t.*, to look down on; to scorn.

despised', *p.p.*, despise.

despi'ser, *n.*, one who despises.

despi'sing, *pr.p.*, despise.

despite', *n.*, extreme malice; contemptuous defiance; *prep.*, notwithstanding.

despite'ful, *adj.*, malicious; malignant.

despite'fully, *adv.*, vindictively.

despoil', *v.t.*, to rob; to strip.

despoiled', *p.p.*, despoil.

despoil'er, *n.*, a plunderer.

despoil'ing, *pr.p.*, despoil.

despoil'ment, *n.*, *i.q.* despoliation.

despolia'tion, *n.*, the act of despoiling.

despond', *v.i.*, to feel dejected; to lose heart.

despond'ed, *p.p.*, despond.

despond'ence, *n.*, *i.q.* despondency.

despond'ency, *n.*, the state of being despondent.

despond'ent, *adj.*, sinking into dejection.

despon'dently, *adv.*, pessimistically.

despond'ing, *adj.*, *i.q.* despondent; *pr.p.*, despond.

des'pot, *n.*, an absolute monarch; a tyrant.

despot'ic, *adj.*, arbitrary; tyrannical.

despot'ical, *adj.*, *i.q.* despotic.

despot'ically, *adv.*, tyrannically.

des'potism, *n.*, autocracy; tyranny.

des'potize, *v.i.*, to act as a despot.

des'pumate, *v.t.* and *i.*, to remove or throw off scum.

des'pumated, *p.p.*, despumate.

des'pumating, *pr.p.*, despumate.

despuma'tion, *n.*, the act of despumating.

des'quamate, *v.i.*, to peel off an outer skin or tegument.

des'quamated, *p.p.*, desquamate.

des'quamating, *pr.p.*, desquamate.

desquama'tion, *n.*, a scaling off.

dessert', *n.*, a sweet course at the end of a meal.

dessertspoonful, *n.*, as much as fills a dessertspoon.

dessous', *n.*, underwear (*Fr.*).

destina'tion, *n.*, the appointed end of a journey or voyage.

des'tine, *v.t.*, to fix unalterably; to doom.

des'tined, *p.p.*, destine.

des'tining, *pr.p.*, destine.

des'tiny, n., fortune; doom; fate.

des'titute, adj., devoid; in abject poverty.

destitu'tion, n., a state of utter want.

des'trier, n., a hand-led war-horse.

destroy', v.t., to demolish; to put an end to.

destroyed', p.p., destroy.

destroy'er, n., anything that destroys; a swift armed naval vessel.

destroy'ing, pr.p., destroy.

destructibil'ity, n., the state of being destructible.

destruc'tible, adj., liable to destruction.

destruc'tion, n., the act of destroying; the state of being destroyed.

destruc'tive, adj., causing destruction.

destruc'tively, adv., in a destructive manner.

destruc'tiveness, n., a propensity to destroy.

destruc'tor, n., a refuse-burner.

desuda'tion, n., a profuse sweating.

des'uetude, n., a discontinuance of a practice or custom.

desulphuriza'tion, n., the freeing from sulphur.

desul'phurize, v.t., to free from sulphur.

des'ultorily, adv., without method.

des'ultoriness, n., the character of being desultory.

des'ultory, adj., rambling; inconstant; unmethodical.

desynon'ymize, v.t., to differentiate in sense (synonymous words).

detach', v.t., to separate.

detach'able, adj., able to be detached.

detached', adj., standing apart; p.p., detach.

detach'edly, adv., in a detached manner.

detach'edness, n., the ability to be detached.

detach'ing, pr.p., detach.

detach'ment, n., a state of being detached; troops taken from the main army for some special service; impartiality.

detail', v.t., to recite the particulars of; to appoint to a special duty.

de'tail, n., a fact; a minute part; an item; a detachment.

detailed', adj., exact; particular; p.p., detail.

detail'ing, pr.p., detail.

detain', v.t., to keep back; to hold in custody.

detained', p.p., detain.

detainee', n., a person who is detained.

detain'er, n., one who detains; in law, a keeping of what belongs to another.

detain'ing, pr.p., detain.

detain'ment, n., detention.

detect', v.t., to discover.

detect'able, -ible, adj., able to be detected.

detect'ed, p.p., detect.

detect'er, -or, n., one who, or that which, detects.

detect'ing, pr.p., detect.

detec'tion, n., discovery.

detec'tive, adj., pert. to detection; n., a police officer whose special duty it is to detect crimes and apprehend criminals.

detent', n., a click or pawl in a clock, watch or lock.

détente', n., a relaxation of tension, esp. political (Fr.).

deten'tion, n., the act of detaining; confinement; delay.

détenu, n., a person held in custody (Fr.).

deter', v.t., to prevent; to dissuade.

deterge', v.t., to cleanse (a sore).

deterged', p.p., deterge.

deter'gent, adj., cleansing; n., anything with cleansing power.

deter'ging, pr.p., deterge.

dete'riorate, v.i., to grow worse; v.t., to make worse.

dete'riorated, p.p., deteriorate.

dete'riorating, pr.p., deteriorate.

deteriora'tion, n., the process or state of growing worse.

deter'ment, n., that which deters.

deter'minable, adj., capable of being determined.

deter'minant, adj., i.q. determinative; n., in mathematics, an algebraical expression formed according to certain laws.

deter'minate, adj., definite; conclusive.

deter'minately, adv., precisely; in a determinate manner.

determina'tion, n., decision; settled purpose; resoluteness.

deter'minative, adj., having power to direct to a definite end.

deter'mine, v.t., to fix or establish; to cause to come to a conclusion; v.i., to resolve; to terminate.

deter'mined, adj., resolute; p.p., determine.

deter'minedly, adv., in a determined manner.

deter'miner, n., one who determines.

deter'mining, pr.p., determine.

deter'minism, n., the philosophical denial of free will.

deterred', p.p., deter.

deter'rence, n., i.q. deterrent.

deter'rent, adj., deterring; n., that which deters.

deter'ring, pr.p., deter.

deter'sion, n., the act of cleansing.

deter'sive, adj., i.q. detergent.

detest', v.t., to hate extremely.

detest'able, adj., very odious.

detestably, adv., in a detestable way.

detesta'tion, n., loathing.

detest'ed, p.p., detest.

detest'er, n., one who detests.

detest'ing, pr.p., detest.

dethrone', v.t., to depose.

dethroned', p.p., dethrone.

dethrone'ment, n., deposition.

dethro'ner, n., one who dethrones.

dethro'ning, pr.p., dethrone.

det'inue, n., a thing or person detained; legal action for recovery.

det'onate, v.t. and i., to explode, or cause to explode.

det'onated, p.p., detonate.

det'onating, adj., explosive; pr.p., detonate.

detona'tion, n., an explosion.

det'onator, n., a capsule filled with some fulminating substance to fire a high explosive.

detona'tion, n., the act of exploding.

det'onize, v.t., i.q. detonate.

det'onized, p.p., detonize.

det'onizing, pr.p., detonize.

detor'sion, n., a wresting away from true shape; a perversion.

detort', v.t., to distort; to pervert.

detor'ted, p.p., detort.

detor'ting, pr.p., detort.

detour', n., a roundabout way (Fr.).

detract', v.t., to take away from a whole; v.i., to take away reputation.

detract'ed, p.p., detract.

detract'ing, pr.p., detract.

detrac'tion, n., malicious depreciation.

detract'ive, adj., having the power to take away.

detract'or, n., one who detracts.

detract'ory, adj., depreciatory.

detrain', v.t., to remove troops from a train; v.i., to alight.

detrained', p.p., detrain.

detrain'ing, pr.p., detrain.

detrain'ment, n., the action of detraining.

detrib'alize, v.t., to break away from the tribe; to break up tribal influences.

det'riment, n., harm.

detrimen'tal, adj., injurious.

detri'tal, adj., pert. or rel. to detritus.

detri'tion, n., the wearing down or weathering of rocks.

detri'tus, n., the disintegrated materials of rocks.

de trop', adj., superfluous; unwelcome (Fr.).

detrude', v.t., to thrust down.

detrud'ed, p.p., detrude.

detrud'ing, pr.p., detude.

detrun'cate, v.t., to lop.

detrun'cated, p.p., detruncate.

detrun'cating, pr.p., detruncate.

detrunca'tion, n., the act of detruncating.

detru'sion, n., the act of detruding.

deuce, n., a playing card or die with two spots; the devil.

deuterag'onist, n., a person of next importance to a protagonist.

deuter'ium, n., heavy hydrogen.

deuterog'amist, n., one who marries a second time.

deuterog'amy, n., a second marriage; the marriage of a widow or widower.

deu'teron, n., a nucleus of the deuterium atom.

Deuteron'omist, n., the author of Deuteronomy.

Deuteron'omy, n., the fifth book of the Pentateuch, containing a second version of Israelite law.

deuterop'athy, n., the sympathetic affection of one part with another (med.).

deutox'ide, n., dioxide; binoxide.

deut'zia, n., a white-flowered shrub.

deux-temps, n., a quick waltz (Fr.).

deval'orize, v.t., i.q. devalue.

deval'uate, v.t., i.q. devalue.

deval'uated, p.p., devaluate.

devalua'ting, pr.p., devaluate.

devalua'tion, n., the process or result of devaluing.

deval'ue, v.t., to reduce the value of; to stabilize currency at a lower level.

devapora'tion, n., the change of vapour into water.

dev'astate, v.t., to ravage.

dev'astated, p.p., devastate.

dev'astating, pr.p., devastate.

devasta'tion, n., havoc; destruction.

dev'astator, n., a person or thing which devastates.

devel'op, v.t., to unfold gradually; to make photographic positives from negatives; v.i., to advance from stage to stage.

devel'oped, p.p., develop.

devel'oper, n., one who, or that which, develops.

devel'oping, pr.p., develop.

devel'opment, n., a gradual growth through progressive changes.

developmen'tal, adj., incidental to growth.

dever'bative, n., a word formed from a verb.

devest', v.t., to divest; to alienate.

de'viable, adj., capable of being deflected.

de'viate, v.i., to diverge; to vary from a uniform state.

de'viated, p.p., deviate.

de'viating, pr.p., deviate.

devia'tion, n., a turning aside.

devia'tionist, n., one who departs from the strict communist doctrine.

de'viator, n., a person who deviates.

device, n., a design; a scheme; an ornamental design; an emblem.

dev'il, n., an evil spirit; the Evil One; a lawyer's, printer's or author's assistant; v.t., to pepper copiously and grill; v.i., to work as devil for a printer, etc.

dev'il-box, n., an electronic computer (from digital electronic universal computing engine) (colloq.).

dev'il(l)ed, p.p., devil.

dev'il(l)ing, pr.p., devil.

dev'ilish, adj., pert. to the devil; very evil.

dev'ilishly, adv., in a devilish manner.

dev'ilishness, n., the qualities of the devil.

dev'ilism, n., the worship of the devil; devilish quality or behaviour.

dev'il-may-care, adj., happy - go - lucky (slang).

dev'ilment, n., mischief.

dev'ilry, *n.,* wicked mischief.

de'vious, *adj.,* rambling; straying; circuitous.

de'viously, *adv.,* in a devious manner.

de'viousness, *n.,* the state of being devious.

devi'sable, *adj.,* able to be devised.

devise', *n.,* a share of a bequeathed estate; *v.t.,* to invent or contrive; to bequeath; *v.i.,* to form a scheme.

devised', *p.p.,* devise.

devisee', *n.,* the person to whom a devise is made.

devi'ser, *n.,* one who devises; a contriver.

devi'sing, *pr.p.,* devise.

devi'sor, *n.,* one who gives by a will.

devitaliza'tion, *n.,* the act of devitalizing.

devi'talize, *v.t.,* to deprive of vitality.

devi'talized, *p.p.,* devitalize.

devi'talizing, *pr.p.,* devitalize.

devitrifica'tion, *n.,* the act of devitrifying.

devit'rified, *p.p.,* devitrify.

devit'rify, *v.t.,* to deprive of the character of glass.

devit'rifying, *pr.p.,* devitrify.

devocaliza'tion, *n.,* the act of making voiceless.

devo'calize, *v.t.,* to make toneless.

devo'calized, *p.p.,* devocalize.

devo'calizing, *pr.p.,* devocalize.

devoid', *adj.,* not possessing.

devoir', *n.,* service or duty; respect due to another (*Fr.*).

dev'olute, *v.t.,* to degenerate; to transfer.

devolu'ted, *p.p.,* devolute.

devolu'ting, *pr.p.,* devolute.

devolu'tion, *n.,* the act of devolving.

devolve', *v.t.* and *i.,* to pass, or make to pass, from one person to another; to transfer.

devolved', *p.p.,* devolve.

devolv'ing, *pr.p.,* devolve.

Devo'nian, *adj.,* pert. or rel. to Devonshire; rel. to Old Red Sandstone; *n.,* a native of Devonshire.

dev'onport, *n.,* a small writing table fitted with drawers; a sofa.

Dev'onshire, *adj.,* pert. or rel. to the English county of that name.

devote', *v.t.,* to set apart; to consecrate; to direct the attention entirely.

devo'ted, *adj.,* zealous; *p.p.,* devote.

devo'tedly, *adv.,* in a devoted way.

devo'tedness, *n.,* the state of being devoted.

devotee', *n.,* an enthusiast, a devout adherent; a fanatic.

devo'ter, *n.,* one who devotes.

devo'ting, *pr.p.,* devote.

devo'tion, *n.,* ardent attachment; earnestness; a religious exercise.

devo'tional, *adj.,* pert. to devotion.

devo'tionalism, *n.,* excessive piousness.

devo'tionally, *adv.,* in a devotional way.

devour', *v.t.,* to eat up; to consume.

devoured', *p.p.,* devour.

devour'er, *n.,* one who devours.

devour'ing, *adj.,* consuming; destroying; *pr.p.,* devour.

devout', *adj.,* pious; religious; earnest.

devout'ly, *adv.,* in a devout manner.

devout'ness, *n.,* the state of being devout.

dew, *n.,* condensed atmospheric vapour.

dewan', *n.,* an Indian state treasurer.

dew'drop, *n.,* a drop of dew.

dew'iness, *n.,* a state of being dewy.

dew'lap, *n.,* a fold of skin hanging from the neck, esp. of cows.

dew'-point, *n.,* the temperature at which dew begins to form.

dew'y, *adj.,* partaking of the nature or appearance of dew.

dex'ter, *adj.,* situated on the right hand.

dexter'ity, *n.,* skill; expertness.

dex'tral, *adj.,* right (as opposed to left).

dextral'ity, *n.,* right-handedness.

dex'trin(e), *n.,* the gummy matter into which the interior of starch globules is convertible.

dextrors'al, *adj.,* rising from left to right (as a climbing plant).

dex'trose, *n.,* grape-sugar.

dex't(e)rous, *adj.,* skilful; adroit; expert.

dex't(e)rously, *adv.,* with dexterity.

Dey, *n.,* the title of the old governors of Algiers and Tripoli under the Sultan of Turkey.

dhal, *n.,* a common foodstuff in India.

dhar'ma, *n.,* the Buddhist law.

dharmsala, *n.,* a travellers' rest-house in India.

dho'bi, *n.,* an Indian washerman.

dho'ti, *n.,* a Hindoo's loincloth.

dhow, *n.,* an Arab vessel, 150–250 tons burden, usually one-masted.

dhur'rie, *n.,* an Indian, fringed, cotton carpet.

diabe'tes, *n.,* a urinary disease.

diabe'tic, *adj.,* pert. to diabetes.

dia'blerie, *n.,* devilry; witchcraft.

diabol'ic, *adj.,* devilish; infernal; atrocious.

diabol'ical, *adj., i.q.* diabolic.

diabol'ically, *adv.,* in a devilish way.

diab'olism, *n.,* possession by the devil.

diab'olize, *v.t.,* to make into or represent a devil.

diab'olo, *n.,* a game of skill played with two sticks and a reel.

diacaus'tic, *adj.,* rel. to a class of caustic curves formed by refraction.

diachron'ic, *adj.,* historical.

diach'ylon, *n.,* a medical plaster made of olive oil and powdered litharge.

diac'onal, *adj.,* rel. to a deacon.

diac'onate, *n.,* the office or dignity of a deacon.

diacous'tic, *adj.,* rel. to the refraction of sound.

diacrit'ic, *adj.,* distinguishing; distinctive.

diacrit'ical, *adj.*, *i.q.* diacritic.

diactin'ic, *adj.*, able to transmit the sun's actinic rays.

diadel'phous, *adj.*, having stamens united in two bodies (*bot.*).

di'adem, *n.*, a crown; a coronet.

diaer'esis, *n.*, the mark (``) over the latter of two vowels, making them two syllables. (Also *dieresis*.)

diagnose', *v.t.*, to identify from symptoms.

diagnosed', *p.p.*, diagnose.

diagnos'ing, *pr.p.*, diagnose.

diagno'sis, *n.*, the discrimination of diseases by their symptoms.

diagnos'tic, *adj.*, indicating the nature of a disease.

diag'onal, *adj.*, from angle to angle; *n.*, a straight line joining opposite corners of a figure.

diag'onally, *adv.*, in a diagonal direction.

di'agram, *n.*, an illustrative outline drawing.

diagrammat'ic, *adj.*, pert. to a diagram.

di'agraph, *n.*, an instrument which enables one to reproduce objects before one without requiring skill in drawing, a kind of *camera lucida*.

diagraph'ic, *adj.*, pert. to the diagraph.

di'al, *n.*, the face of a watch or other timekeeper; any similar face over which a pointer moves; *v.t.*, to measure with a dial; to operate a telephone number selector.

di'alect, *n.*, a local idiom differing from the standard speech.

dialec'tic, *adj.*, pert. to a dialect or to dialectics; *n.*, reasoning.

dialec'tical, *adj.*, *i.q.* dialectic.

dialecti'cian, *n.*, a reasoner; a logician.

dialec'tics, *n.*, the art of discussing.

di'al(l)ing, *n.*, the art of constructing dials; the theory of the sundial; *pr.p.*, dial.

di'alist, *n.*, a maker or user of dials.

di'allage, *n.*, a foliated mineral akin to augite.

di'alled, *p.p.*, dial.

dialo'gic, *adj.*, in, or of, dialogue.

dial'ogism, *n.*, oblique narration; dialogue in the third person.

dial'ogist, *n.*, a writer of dialogue; a speaker in a dialogue.

dialogis'tic, *adj.*, having the form of a dialogue.

dial'ogize, *v.i.*, to discourse in dialogue.

di'alogue, *n.*, a conversation between two or more persons, esp. in a stage-play.

di'al-plate, *n.*, the plate of a dial.

dial'ysis, *n.*, the separation of the crystalloid from the colloid elements of a body; debility; a solution of continuity.

dialyt'ic, *adj.*, of, or by, dialysis.

diamagnet'ic, *adj.*, showing the peculiarity of pointing east and west under magnetic influence.

diamag'netism, *n.*, a diamagnetic tendency.

diamanté, *n.*, a scintillating fabric; paste brilliants (*Fr.*).

diamantif'erous, *adj.*, diamond-yielding.

diam'eter, *n.*, a straight-line through the centre of a body; thickness; the maximum distance across a circle from circumference to circumference.

diam'etral, *adj.*, *i.q.* diametric.

diamet'ric, *adj.*, pert. to a diameter.

diamet'rical, *adj.*, *i.q.* diametric.

diamet'rically, *adv.*, like a diameter; entirely; directly.

di'amond, *n.*, a very hard precious stone; a very small kind of printing type; a lozenge or rhombus.

di'amondif'erous, *adj.*, made of, or set with, diamonds.

Dian'a, *n.*, the goddess of hunting.

Dian'dria, *n. pl.*, plants with two stamens (*bot.*).

dian'drian, *adj.*, having two stamens (*bot.*).

Dian'thus, *n.*, a genus of plants including the pink and carnation.

diapa'son, *n.*, an octave; the compass of a voice or instrument; an organ stop.

di'aper, *n.*, a linen or cotton fabric with a figured pattern; a baby's napkin; *v.t.*, to variegate with figures.

di'aphane, *n.*, a silk fabric with transparent figures.

diaphane'ity, *n.*, the quality of being diaphanous.

diaphanom'eter, *n.*, an instrument for measuring the transparency of the air.

diaph'anous, *adj.*, partly transparent; allowing the passage of some light.

diaphon'ic, *adj.*, diacoustic; rel. to sound-refraction.

diaphore'sis, *n.*, excessive perspiration.

diaphoret'ic, *adj.*, having the power to increase perspiration; *n.*, a sudorific.

di'aphragm, *n.*, the midriff; a partition.

diaphragmat'ic, *adj.*, rel. to the diaphragm.

diaph'ysis, *n.*, the shaft of a long bone.

di'archy, *n.*, dual government.

dia'rian, *adj.*, rel. to a diary.

di'arist, *n.*, one who keeps a diary.

di'arize, *v.i.* and *t.*, to keep, or enter in, a diary.

di'arized, *p.p.*, diarize.

diarizing, *pr.p.*, diarize.

diarrh(o)e'a, *n.*, an ailment of the intestines; excessive looseness of the bowels.

diarrhoe'ic, *adj.*, rel. to diarrhoea.

diarrhoet'ic, *adj.*, producing diarrhoea.

diarthro'sis, *n.*, a joint capable of revolving in all directions, as the shoulder-joint.

di'ary, *n.*, a journal of daily transactions.

Dias'pora, *n.*, the dispersion of the Jews.

di'astase, *n.*, a substance in barley and oats after germination, which turns starch into sugar at 150° F.

dias'tole, *n.*, the dilatation of the heart; the lengthening of a short

syllable; (*opp.* systole).

di'astyle, *n.*, an arrangement of columns in classical architecture in which intercolumniation is equal to three diameters.

diates'saron, *n.*, a harmony of the four gospels; an electuary or medicine containing four drugs; a musical interval.

diather'mal, *adj.*, penetrable by heat.

diatherm'ancy, *n.*, the quality of transmitting radiant heat.

diather'manous, *adj.*, letting radiant heat pass through.

diatherm'ic, *adj.*, *i.q.* diathermanous.

di'athermy, *n.*, heat treatment of the deeper body tissues.

diath'esis, *n.*, habit of body; a predisposition to certain diseases.

Diatoma'ceae, *n. pl.*, a family of minute, unicellular algae, or primitive plant forms.

diatom'ic, *adj.*, consisting of two atoms.

diaton'ic, *adj.*, pert. to the major and minor scales in music.

di'atribe, *n.*, a long invective.

dib, *n.*, a small bone in a sheep's knee.

dibas'ic, *adj.*, having two bases or two atoms of a base.

dibb'er, *n.*, *i.q.* dibble.

dib'ble, *n.*, a pointed tool used in gardening, *v.t.*, to dig with a dibble.

dib'bled, *p.p.*, dibble.

dib'bler, *n.*, one who dibbles.

dib'bling, *pr.p.*, dibble.

dibs, *n. pl.*, a child's game; counters at cards; money (*slang*).

dib'stone, *n.*, a pebble used in a child's game (called *dibstones*).

dic'ast, *n.*, (a member of) an Athenian jury.

dicas'tery, *n.*, *i.q.* dicast.

dice, *n.*, the pl. of die; *v.i.*, to play with dice; *v.t.*, to cut up into dicelike portions.

dice'-box, *n.*, a box from which dice are thrown.

diced, *p.p.*, dice.

diceph'alous, *adj.*, having two heads.

di'cer, *n.*, a player at dice.

dichlor'ide, *n.*, a chemical form of bichloride.

dichog'amous, *adj.*, unable to self-fertilize because stamens and pistils mature at different times.

di'chord, *n.*, the two-stringed lyre.

dichot'omize, *v.i.*, to become dichotomous.

dichot'omous, *adj.*, regularly dividing by pairs from top to bottom.

dichot'omously, *adv.*, in a dichotomous way.

dichot'omy, *n.*, the distribution of ideas by pairs; branching by continual forking.

dichro'ic, *adj.*, showing two colours.

dichrom'ate, *n.*, a chemical form of bichromate.

dichromat'ic, *adj.*, having two colours.

dichrom'ic, *adj.*, seeing only two colours in colour-blindness.

di'cing, *n.*, the practice or act of dicing; *pr.p.*, dice.

dick, *n.*, an affirmation; a detective (*slang*).

dick'ens, *n.*, the devil; deuce (*slang*).

Dick'ensian, *adj.*, rel. or pert. to the period of Charles Dickens or his writings.

dick'er, *n.*, ten hides or skins; *v.i.*, to trade by barter, to haggle.

dick'(e)y, *adj.*, unsound, shaky (*slang*); *n.*, a false shirt-front; the driver's seat; a seat at the back of a carriage.

dicotyle'don, *n.*, a plant whose seeds contain a pair of seed-leaves.

dicotyle'donous, *adj.*, having two seed-leaves.

dic'ta, *n. pl.*, sayings.

dictate', *v.t.*, to deliver a command; to speak what is to be written.

dic'tate, *n.*, a rule suggested to the mind.

dicta'ted, *p.p.*, dictate.

dicta'ting, *pr.p.*, dictate.

dicta'tion, *n.*, the act of dictating.

dicta'tor, *n.*, one invested with absolute authority; one who dictates.

dictato'rial, *adj.*, overbearing.

dicta'torship, *n.*, the office of a dictator.

dic'tion, *n.*, the choice of words; the mode of expression; the act of speaking.

dic'tionary, *n.*, a book containing the words of a language arranged alphabetically, with meanings, etc.

dic'tograph, *n.*, an instrument reproducing in one room sounds made in another; a loud-speaking, internal telephone.

dic'tum, *n.*, an authoritative saying.

did, *p.p.*, do.

didac'tic, *adj.*, intended to instruct.

didac'tical, *adj.*, *i.q.* didactic.

didac'tically, *adv.*, in an instructive way.

didac'tyl, *adj.*, two-toed; *n.*, a two-toed animal.

didac'tylous, *adj.*, two-toed or two-fingered.

did'apper, *n.*, a small, diving water-fowl.

did'dle, *v.t.*, to cheat; to dandle.

did'dled, *p.p.*, diddle.

did'dling, *n.*, cheating; *pr.p.*, diddle.

didecahe'dral, *adj.*, having ten planes at either extremity.

didgeridoo', -ydoo', *n.*, a tubular, musical instrument of the Australian aboriginals.

didn't, *abbrev.* of did not (*colloq.*).

did'o, *n.*, an antic; a caper; a prank (*colloq.*).

didst, *p.p.*, 2nd pers. sing., do.

didym'ium, *n.*, a rare metal.

did'ymous, *adj.*, twin; growing double.

didyna'mian, *adj.*, *i.q.* didynamous.

didyn'amous, *adj.*, having four stamens in pairs, one pair longer than the other.

die, *v.i.*, to cease to live; *n.*, a small cube used in gaming; a square body; a stamp used in coining, etc.

died, *p.p.*, die.

die'hard, *n.*, a brave man who fights to the death; a person of entrenched views.

dielec'tric, *adj.*, insulating; *n.*, a non-conductor.

dieresis, *n.*, *i.q.* diaeresis.

die'sel, *n.*, a compression-ignition oil engine.

die'-sinker, *n.*, an engraver of dies for embossing.

di'esis, *n.*, a very small interval in music.

di'et, *n.*, regular food and drink; a prescribed regimen of selected food and drink; a legislative session; a German or Austrian parliament; *v.t.*, to prescribe a diet; *v.i.*, to conform to feeding rules.

di'etary, *adj.*, rel. to diet; *n.*, a system of diet.

di'eted, *p.p.*, diet.

di'eter, *n.*, one who prescribes rules for eating.

dietet'ic, *adj.*, pert. to a regulated diet.

dietet'ical, *adj.*, *i.q.* dietetic.

dietet'ically, *adv.*, in a dietetic way.

dietet'ics, *n.*, rules for dieting.

dietet'ist, *n.*, *i.q.* dietician.

dieti'cian, *n.*, a person versed in dietetics.

di'etine, *n.*, a local assembly or diet.

di'eting, *pr.p.*, diet.

di'etist, *n.*, *i.q.* dietician.

dif'fer, *v.i.*, to be unlike; to be of another opinion; to quarrel.

dif'fered, *p.p.*, differ.

dif'ference, *n.*, dissimilarity; a dispute; the remainder after arithmetical subtraction; *v.t.*, to cause a difference in; to discriminate.

dif'ferenced, *p.p.*, difference.

dif'ferencing, *pr.p.*, difference.

dif'ferent, *adj.*, distinct; separate; unlike.

differen'tia, *n.*, the characteristic attribute of a species.

differen'tial, *adj.*, making a difference; discriminating; *n.*, a mathematical epithet applied to the infinitesimal difference between two values of a variable; part of the transmission mechanism of a motor vehicle.

differen'tiate, *v.t.*, to distinguish by a difference; in mathematics, to obtain the differential coefficient of.

differen'tiated, *p.p.*, differentiate.

differen'tiating, *pr.p.*, differentiate.

differentia'tion, *n.*, the act of differentiating.

dif'ferently, *adv.*, in a different manner.

diff'icile, *adj.*, unaccommodating; hard to deal with (*Fr.*).

dif'ficult, *adj.*, not easy; hard to do or to understand.

dif'ficulty, *n.*, the hardness to be done; a problem; an embarrassment of affairs; a quarrel.

diff'idence, *n.*, want of confidence; self-distrust.

dif'fident, *adj.*, not confident; bashful.

dif'fidently, *adv.*, bashfully.

diff'luence, *n.*, a flowing apart, becoming fluid; deliquescence.

diff'luent, *adj.*, deliquescent.

dif'form, *adj.*, irregular in form; anomalous.

diffract', *v.t.*, to bend from a straight line.

diffract'ed, *p.p.*, diffract.

diffract'ing, *pr.p.*, diffract.

diffrac'tion, *n.*, deflection of light.

diffrac'tive, *adj.*, deflecting light.

diffrac'tively, *adv.*, in a diffractive manner.

diffuse', *adj.*, verbose; wanting in conciseness; scattered; *v.t.*, to send out in all directions.

diffused', *adj.*, spread; dispersed; *p.p.*, diffuse.

diffuse'ly, *adv.*, extensively; with too many words.

diffu'ser, *n.*, one who, or that which, diffuses.

diffusibil'ity, *n.*, the quality of being diffusible.

diffu'sible, *adj.*, capable of being spread in all directions.

diffu'sing, *pr.p.*, diffuse.

diffu'sion, *n.*, a spreading abroad, propagation.

diffu'sive, *adj.*, widely reaching.

diffu'sively, *adv.*, extensively; widely.

diffu'siveness, *n.*, the character of being diffusive.

dig, *v.t.*, to open and turn up with a spade; *v.i.*, to work with a spade or similar implement.

dig'amist, *n.*, a person second time married.

digam'ma, *n.*, a lost Greek letter, probably equivalent to *v* or *f*.

dig'amy, *n.*, a second marriage.

digas'tric, *adj.*, double bellied.

di'gest, *n.*, a collection of Roman laws, arranged by the Emperor Justinian; any similar collection of summarized material.

digest', *v.t.*, to arrange methodically for study; to dissolve in the stomach.

digest'ed, *p.p.*, digest.

digest'er, *n.*, one who arranges in order; that which assists the digestion of food; a vessel in which substances in water are exposed to great heat so as to extract their essences.

digestibil'ity, *n.*, the quality of being digestible.

digest'ible, *adj.*, capable of being digested.

digest'ing, *pr.p.*, digest.

diges'tion, *n.*, the act of methodizing; the process which food undergoes in the stomach.

digest'ive, *adj.*, having the power to promote digestion; *n.*, a stomachic.

di'gestively, *adv.*, in a digestive way.

dig'ger, *n.*, one who digs, esp. for gold.

dig'ging, *n.*, the act of digging; *pr.p.*, dig.

dig'gings, *n. pl.*, lodgings (*slang*).

dight, *adj.*, adorned; *adv.*, finely; *v.t.*, to make ready.

dig'it, *n.*, a finger; any whole number less than ten.

dig′ital, adj., pert. or rel. to the fingers; n., a piano or organ key.

Digita′lis, n., a genus of plants including the foxglove; a medicine obtained from them.

dig′itate, adj., branched out into divisions like fingers.

dig′itated, adj., i.q. digitate.

digita′tion, n., division into finger-like processes.

dig′itigrade, n., an animal that walks on its toes.

digitor′ium, n., a dumb piano-keyboard.

di′glyph, n., a projecting face with two channels sunk in it (arch.).

dig′nified, adj., stately in deportment; p.p., dignify.

dig′nify, v.t., to invest with dignity or high rank; to honour.

dig′nifying, pr.p., dignify.

dig′nitary, n., a person of exalted rank or office.

dig′nity, n., nobleness of mind; an elevated office.

di′graph, n., a union of two letters signifying one sound.

digress′, v.i., to wander from a theme.

digressed′, p.p., digress.

digress′ing, pr.p., digress.

digres′sion, n., a departure from a main subject.

digres′sional, adj., consisting in digression.

digres′sive, adj., i.q. digressional.

digres′sively, adv., in a digressive way.

digs, n., the abbrev. of diggings (slang).

digyn′ian, adj., having two pistils (bot.).

dig′ynous, adj., i.q. digynian.

dihe′dral, adj., having two plane faces, as a crystal.

dihe′dral an′gle, n., the inclination to each other of an aeroplane's wings.

dihe′dron, n., a figure with two plane sides.

diju′dicate, v.i., to judge or adjudicate between two.

diju′dicated, p.p., dijudicate.

diju′dicating, pr.p., dijudicate.

dijudica′tion, n., the act of adjudicating between two.

dike, n., a ditch; a bank; v.t., to surround with a dike; to secure by a bank. (Also dyke.)

diked, p.p., dike.

dike′let, n., a small or low dike.

di′king, pr.p., dike.

dilac′erate, v.t., to rend asunder.

dilac′erated, p.p., dilacerate.

dilac′erating, pr.p., dilacerate.

dilacera′tion, n., the act of tearing asunder; the state of being torn to pieces.

dilap′idate, v.i., to fall to ruin; v.t., to allow buildings to become ruinous by neglect.

dilap′idated, adj., in a ruinous state; p.p., dilapidate.

dilap′idating, pr.p., dilapidate.

dilapida′tion, n., the state of being dilapidated; such a state of disrepair as has to be made good.

dilap′idator, n., one who dilapidates.

dilatabil′ity, n., the quality of being dilatable.

dila′table, adj., elastic; able to be dilated.

dilata′tion, n., the act of expanding; the state of being distended.

dilate′, v.t. and i., to expand; to distend; to enlarge on.

dila′ted, p.p., dilate.

dila′ting, pr.p., dilate.

dila′tion, n., i.q. dilatation.

dilat′or, n., a muscle that dilates an organ.

dil′atorily, adv., in a dilatory manner.

dil′atoriness, n., tardiness.

dil′atory, adj., procrastinating, delaying.

dildo(e), n., a tree or shrub; a cylindrical glass tube; an artificial penis.

dilem′ma, n., a logical argument which catches an adversary between two fatal alternatives; an awkward situation.

dilem′matic, adj., rel. to dilemma.

dilettan′te, n., an amateur; one who cultivates an art for amusement.

dilettan′tism, n., the character of a dilettante.

dil′igence, n., industry; a four-wheeled stagecoach.

dil′igent, adj., industrious; attentive.

dil′igently, adv., in a diligent manner.

dill, n., a European medicinal plant.

dill′y-dally, v.i., to procrastinate (colloq.).

dil′uent, n., that which dilutes; a medicine to make the blood more fluid.

dilute′, adj., weakened by adding water; washed-out; faded.

dilute′, v.t., to weaken by mixing with water; v.i., to become thin or diluted.

dilu′ted, adj., watered down; p.p., dilute.

dilu′ter, n., one who, or that which, dilutes.

dilu′ting, pr.p., dilute.

dilu′tion, n., the act of diluting; the weakened mixture.

dilu′vial, adj., pert. or rel. to a deluge, esp. to the Noachian Deluge.

dilu′vian, adj., i.q. diluvial.

dilu′vium, n., a deluge; a deposit caused by the extraordinary action of water.

dim, adj., not seeing clearly; not clearly seen; obscure; v.t., to obscure; to reduce light.

dime, n., an American silver coin, the tenth of a dollar; ten cents.

dimen′sion, n., extension in a single direction.

dim′erous, adj., with two parts.

dim′eter, n., a verse of two measures.

dimid′iate, adj., halved.

dimin′ish, v.t. and i., to lessen.

dimin′ished, adj., lessened in size or importance; p.p., diminish.

dimin′ishing, n., a lessening; pr.p., diminish.

diminuen'do, *adv.,* diminishingly; *n.,* a lessening in volume of sound (*It.*).

diminu'tion, *n.,* the act of diminishing; the making smaller or becoming less.

dimin'utive, *adj.,* smaller than the normal size; *n.,* a word formed from another to express a little thing of the same kind.

dimin'utively, *adv.,* in a diminutive way.

dimis'sory, *adj.,* dismissing to another jurisdiction.

dim'ity, *n.,* a stout cotton fabric.

dim'ly, *adv.,* in a dim manner.

dimmed, *p.p.,* dim.

dim'ming, *n.,* a lessening of light; *pr.p.,* dim.

dim'mish, *adj.,* somewhat dim.

dim'ness, *n.,* the state of being dim.

dimorph'ic, *adj.,* i.q. dimorphous.

dimor'phism, *n.,* the property of having two distinct forms, exhibited by some crystalline minerals.

dimor'phous, *adj.,* exhibiting dimorphism.

dim'ple, *n.,* a small depression, esp. on the face; *v.i.,* to form dimples; *v.t.,* to mark with dimples.

dim'pled, *adj.,* having a surface marked by dimples; *p.p.,* dimple.

dim'pling, *pr.p.,* dimple.

dim'ply, *adj.,* full of dimples.

din, *n.,* a loud, long-continued noise; *v.t.,* to stun with noise.

dinar', *n.,* the unit of currency in Iraq and Yugoslavia.

dine, *v.i.,* to take dinner; *v.t.,* to give a dinner to.

dined, *p.p.,* dine.

di'ner, *n.,* one who dines.

ding, *v.t.,* to dash, to strike.

ding'-dong, *adv.,* with alternating success; *n.,* the sound of bells.

dinged, *p.p.,* ding.

din'gey, *n.,* a ship's small boat; a small, open sailing craft.

din'giness, *n.,* the state of being dingy.

ding'ing, *pr.p.,* ding.

din'gle, *n.,* a little wooded valley.

din'go, *n.,* a wild, Australian dog.

din'gy, *adj.,* soiled; dirty white.

di'ning, *pr.p.,* dine.

din'ing-car, *n.,* a railway restaurant car.

din'ing-hall, *n.,* a hall used for dining (esp. Universities).

di'ning-room, *n.,* a room to dine in.

din'ing-table, *n.,* a table for dining.

Din'ka, *n.,* a native of the Nile area; the language of that area.

dink'um, *adj.,* genuine, real; *n.,* work, toil, (*Austral. dial. or slang*).

dink'y, *adj.,* dainty (*colloq.*).

dinned, *p.p.,* din.

din'ner, *n.,* the principal meal of the day.

din'nerless, *adj.,* having no dinner.

din'ning, *pr.p.,* din.

dino'ceras, *n.,* a large, extinct, horned mammal.

dinorn'is, *n.,* an extinct ostrich-sized bird.

din'osaur, *n.,* a huge extinct reptile.

din'othere, *n.,* a huge extinct elephant.

dinothe'rium, *n.,* i.q. dinothere.

dint, *n.,* the mark made by a blow; a dent; *v.t.,* to dent.

dint'ed, *p.p.,* dint.

dint'ing, *pr.p.,* dint.

dioc'esan, *adj.,* rel. to a diocese; *n.,* a bishop as related to his own diocese; one in a diocese in relation to the bishop.

di'ocese, *n.,* the extent of a bishop's jurisdiction.

di'ode, *n.,* a two-electrode valve.

Dioe'cia, *n. pl.,* a genus of plants, some being male and some female.

dioe'cian, *adj.,* having individuals of either sex (*zool.*).

dioe'cious, *adj.,* with the male and female organs borne by different individuals (*zool.*).

Dionys'iac, *adj.,* i.q. Dionysian.

Dionys'ian, *adj.,* of Dionysos, the Greek god of wine; roisterous.

diop'ter, *n.,* an optical instrument for taking altitudes.

diop'tric, *adj.,* pert. or rel. to dioptrics; that branch of optics which deals with refraction, esp. through lenses.

diop'trical, *adj.,* i.q. dioptric.

diora'ma, *n.,* a scenic spectacle produced by transmission and reflection of light.

diora'mic, *adj.,* pert. or rel. to diorama.

diortho'sis, *n.,* the correction of a deformity; a critical revision of a text.

diox'ide, *n.,* an oxide containing two atoms of oxygen and one of another element.

dip, *n.,* an immersion, an inclination; a rude kind of candle; a wash; *v.t.,* to put into a fluid and withdraw; *v.i.,* to sink; to slope.

dipet'alous, *adj.,* two-petalled (*bot.*).

di'phone, *n.,* a phonographic sign representing two consecutive vowels, which are pronounced separately.

diphon'ic, *adj.,* rel. to a diphone.

diphthe'ria, *n.,* an acute, infectious disease of the throat.

diph'thong, *n.,* a union of two vowel-sounds to form a single sound.

diphthon'gal, *adj.,* rel. to a diphthong.

diphylet'ic, *adj.,* having two sets of ancestors.

dipleg'ia, *n.,* a paralysis of corresponding parts on both sides of the body.

diple'gic, *adj.,* rel. to diplegia.

diplod'ocus, *n.,* a gigantic extinct N. American herbivorous reptile.

dip'loe, *n.,* the soft substance between the plates of the skull.

diplo'ma, *n.,* a written document conferring a privilege or honour.

diplo'macy, *n.,* the art of conducting negotiations between people.

dip'lomat, *n., i.q.* diplomatist.

diplomat'ic, *adj.,* rel. to diplomacy; tactful.

diplomat'ically, *adv.,* in a diplomatic manner; tactfully.

diplo'matist, *n.,* a person skilled in diplomacy (esp. between nations).

diplom'atize, *v.i.,* to act as a diplomatist; to use diplomatic arts.

dip'lon, *n.,* another name for deuteron.

dip'noan, *adj.* and *n.,* (a fish) having both gills and lungs.

di'pode, *n.,* a lizard with only two fully-developed feet.

dipol'ar, *adj.,* having two poles.

di'pole, *n.,* an object with two poles; a type of television aerial.

dipped, *p.p.,* dip.

dip'per, *n.,* one who, or that which, dips; an American Baptist; a water-ousel.

dip'ping, *pr.p.,* dip.

dipp'y, *adj.,* crazy (*slang*).

dipsoma'nia, *n.,* an uncontrollable mania for drinking alcoholic drinks.

Dip'tera, *n. pl.,* the class of animals having two wings only.

dip'teral, *adj.,* having two wings.

dip'terous, *adj.,* two-winged.

dip'tote, *n.,* a noun with only two cases.

dip'tych, *n.,* a carving or painting on two folding tablets.

diradia'tion, *n.,* the emission and diffusion of light.

dire, *adj.,* dreadful; dismal.

direct', *adj.,* straight; *v.t.,* to point in a straight line; to order; to address correspondence.

direct'ed, *p.p.,* direct.

direct'ing, *pr.p.,* direct.

direc'tion, *n.,* the act of directing; a course; management.

direc'tional, *adj.,* rel. to direction in space.

direct'ive, *adj.,* having the power of directing; *n.,* a memorandum of instruction or a guide to conduct.

direct'ly, *adv.,* in a direct manner; immediately.

direct'ness, *n.,* the quality of being direct.

Direc'toire, *adj.,* rel. to the fashions of the Directory period in France (1796–99); *n.,* a hat of this style (*Fr.*).

direct'or, *n.,* one who directs, esp. a company; a spiritual adviser.

direct'orate, *n.,* a body of directors.

directo'rial, *adj.,* pert. or rel. to a director,

direct'orship, *n.,* the office of a director.

direct'ory, *n.,* a book containing an alphabetical list of persons, addresses, etc.

direct'ress, *n.,* a woman who directs.

direct'rix, *n.,* a straight line of importance in the theory of conic sections.

dire'ful, *adj., i.q.* dire.

dire'fulness, *n.,* the state of being dire.

dir'er, *adj., comp.* of dire.

dir'est, *adj., super.* of dire.

dirge, *n.,* a song expressing mourning.

dir'igible, *adj.,* able to be directed; *n.,* an airship capable of being steered.

dirigisme', *n.,* the state direction and control of policy in economic and social matters.

di'riment, *adj.,* making void; *n.,* an impediment that nullifies marriage.

dirk, *n.,* a dagger.

dirn'dl, *n.,* an Alpine peasant's costume, with tight bodice and full skirt.

dirt, *n.,* any foul or filthy substance.

dirt'ied, *p.p.,* dirty.

dirt'ier, *adj., comp.* of dirty.

dirt'iest, *adj., super.* of dirty.

dirt'ily, *adv.,* in a dirty manner.

dirt'iness, *n.,* foulness; nastiness.

dirt'-track, *n.,* a racing track of soft earth.

dirt'y, *adj.,* not clean; impure; *v.t.,* to defile, to soil.

dirt'ying, *pr.p.,* dirty.

dirz'i, *n.,* an Indian, native tailor (*Anglo-Ind.*).

Dis, *n.,* the god Pluto.

disabil'ity, *n.,* incapacity.

disa'ble, *v.t.,* to render incapable.

disa'bled, *p.p.,* disable.

disa'blement, *n.,* an incapacitation through being disabled.

disa'bling, *pr.p.,* disable.

disabuse', *v.t.,* to undeceive.

disabused', *p.p.,* disabuse.

disabus'ing, *pr.p.,* disabuse.

disaccord', *n.,* a disagreement; *n.,* to be at a variance with.

disadvan'tage, *n.,* an injury, harm; damage; *v.t.,* to affect injuriously.

disadvan'taged, *p.p.,* disadvantage.

disadvanta'geous, *adj.,* unfavourable to success.

disadvanta'geously, *adv.,* in a disadvantageous manner.

disadvan'taging, *pr.p.,* disadvantage.

disaffect', *v.t.,* to make unfriendly.

disaffect'ed, *adj.,* unfriendly, disloyal; *p.p.,* disaffect.

disaffect'ing, *pr.p.,* disaffect.

disaffec'tion, *n.,* an alienation of goodwill.

disaffil'iate, *v.t.,* to dissociate.

disaffil'iated, *p.p.,* disaffiliate.

disaffil'iating, *pr.p.,* disaffiliate.

disaffilia'tion, *n.,* a dissociation.

disaffirm', *v.t.,* to repudiate.

disaffirm'ance, *n., i.q.* disaffirmation.

disaffirma'tion, *n.,* a denial.

disaffirmed', *p.p.,* disaffirm.

disaffirm'ing, *pr.p.,* disaffirm.

disaffor'est, *v.t.,* to divest of forest laws.

disaffor'resta'tion, *n.,* the reduction from forest to ordinary land.

disaffor'ested, *p.p.,* disafforest.

disaffor'esting, *pr.p.,* disafforest.

disagree', *v.i.,* to differ; to quarrel.

disagree'able, *adj.,* unpleasing.

disagree'ableness, *n.,* the quality of being disagreeable.

disagree'ably, *adv.,* unpleasantly.

disagreed', *p.p.,* disagree.

disagree'ing, *pr.p.,* disagree.

disagree'ment, *n.,* a difference; a quarrel.

disallow', *v.t.,* to refuse permission for; to reject.

disallow'able, *adj.,* not to be permitted.

disallow'ance, *n.,* prohibition.

disallowed', *p.p.,* disallow.

disallow'ing, *pr.p.,* disallow.

disannul', *v.t.,* to cancel.

disannulled', *p.p.,* disannul.

disannul'ling, *pr.p.,* disannul.

disappear', *v.i.,* to vanish.

disappear'ance, *n.,* the removal from sight.

disappeared', *p.p.,* disappear.

disappear'ing, *pr.p.,* disappear.

disappoint', *v.t.,* to belie expectation or hopes.

disappoint'ed, *p.p.,* disappoint.

disappoint'ing, *adj.,* contrary to hope; *pr.p.,* disappoint.

disappoint'ment, *n.,* a failure of expectation.

disapproba'tion, *n.,* disapproval; censure.

disap'probatory, *adj.,* conveying disapprobation.

disappro'priate, *v.t.,* to release from individual ownership.

disapprov'al, *n.,* disapprobation; dislike.

disapprove', *v.t.,* to censure; *v.i.,* to express disapproval.

disapproved', *p.p.,* disapprove.

disapprov'ing, *pr.p.,* disapprove.

disapprov'ingly, *adv.,* in a disapproving manner.

disarm', *v.t.,* to take the arms from; to render harmless.

disarm'ament, *n.,* the act of disarming.

disarmed', *p.p.,* disarm.

disarm'ing, *pr.p.,* disarm.

disarrange', *v.t.,* to put out of order.

disarranged', *p.p.,* disarrange.

disarrange'ment, *n.,* disorder.

disarrang'ing, *pr.p.,* disarrange.

disarray', *n.,* disorder; confusion; *v.t.,* to undress; to throw into disorder.

disarrayed', *p.p.,* disarray.

disarray'ing, *pr.p.,* disarray.

disartic'ulate, *v.t.,* to separate; to take to pieces.

disassem'ble, *v.t.,* to take apart.

disassimila'tion, *n.,* the conversion of assimilated substances into simpler forms.

disassocia'tion, *n.,* dissociation (*Psych.*).

disas'ter, *n.,* a great misfortune or calamity.

disas'trous, *adj.,* causing or accompanied by disaster.

disas'trously, *adv.,* in a disastrous manner.

disavow', *v.t.,* to repudiate; to disown.

disavow'al, *n.,* a denial; repudiation.

disavowed', *p.p.,* disavow.

disavow'ing, *pr.p.,* disavow.

disband', *v.t. and i.,* to dismiss; to break up as a band of men.

disband'ed, *p.p.,* disband.

disband'ing, *pr.p.,* disband.

disband'ment, *n.,* the act of disbanding.

disbar', *v.t.,* to deprive of the status of a barrister.

disbar'ment, *n.,* the expulsion of a barrister from the bar.

disbelief', *n.,* the denial of belief.

disbelieve', *v.t.,* to hold not to be true; *v.i.,* to refuse to believe.

disbelieved', *p.p.,* disbelieve.

disbeliev'er, *n.,* an unbeliever.

disbeliev'ing, *pr.p.,* disbelieve.

disbench', *v.t.,* to deprive of the status of a bencher.

disbranch', *v.t.,* to strip of branches.

disbud', *v.t.,* to remove buds from.

disbud'ded, *p.p.,* disbud.

disbudd'ing, *pr.p.,* disbud.

disbur'den, *v.t.,* to remove a burden from.

disbur'dened, *p.p.,* disburden.

disbur'dening, *pr.p.,* disburden.

disburs'al, *i.q.* disbursement.

disburse', *v.t.,* to expend.

disbursed', *p.p.,* disburse.

disburse'ment, *n.,* a sum paid out; a paying out.

disburs'er, *n.,* one who disburses.

disburs'ing, *pr.p.,* disburse.

disc, *n.,* a flat, circular plate.

discal'ceate, *adj.,* barefoot or only sandalled; *n.,* a barefoot or sandalled religious.

discal'ceated, *adj.,* barefoot or sandalled.

discalced', *adj., i.q.* discalceated.

discard', *v.t. and i.,* to throw out of the hand cards not wanted in the game; to cast off.

discard'ed, *p.p.,* discard.

discard'ing, *pr.p.,* discard.

discarn'ate, *adj.,* stripped of flesh; disembodied.

discern', *v.t.,* to discriminate by the eye or intellect.

discerned', *p.p.,* discern.

discern'er, *n.,* a clearsighted observer.

discern'ible, *adj.,* able to be discerned.

discern'ing, *adj.,* sharpsighted; acute of understanding; *pr.p.,* discern.

discern'ingly, *adv.,* in a discerning manner.

discern'ment, *n.,* acuteness of judgment, penetration.

discerp', *v.t.*, to tear or pluck apart.

discerped', *p.p.*, discerp.

discerp'ing, *pr.p.*, discerp.

discerp'tible, *adj.*, that may be plucked apart.

discerp'tion, *n.*, the pulling apart; the severed piece.

discharge', *n.*, a release; a dismissal; payment; *v.t.*, to free from a burden; to fire off; to pay (a debt); to dismiss.

discharge'able, *adj.*, able to be discharged.

discharged', *p.p.*, discharge.

dischar'ger, *n.*, one who, or that which, discharges.

discharg'ing, *pr.p.*, discharge.

dis'ciform, *adj.*, disc-shaped.

disci'ple, *n.*, a pupil; a follower.

disci'pleship, *n.*, the state of being a disciple.

disciplina'rian, *n.*, one who enforces rigid discipline; a martinet.

dis'ciplinary, *adj.*, promoting discipline.

dis'cipline, *n.*, firm regulation by rule; training; correction; chastisement; *v.t.*, to subject to discipline.

dis'ciplined, *p.p.*, discipline.

dis'ciplining, *pr.p.*, discipline.

discip'ular, *adj.*, rel. or pert. to a disciple.

disc'-jock'ey, *n.*, the compère of a record-playing session.

disclaim', *v.t.*, to disavow.

disclaimed', *p.p.*, disclaim.

disclaim'er, *n.*, one who disclaims; an act of disclaiming.

disclaim'ing, *pr.p.*, disclaim.

disclose', *v.t.*, to reveal.

disclosed', *p.p.*, disclose.

disclo'ser, *n.*, one who discloses.

disclo'sing, *pr.p.*, disclose.

disclo'sure, *n.*, the act of revealing; the thing revealed.

discob'olus, *n.*, a quoit or discus thrower.

discog'raphy, *n.*, the cataloguing, etc. of gramophone records.

dis'coid, *adj.*, resembling a disc.

discoi'dal, *adj.*, *i.q.* discoid.

discolo(u)ra'tion, *n.*, the act of discolouring.

discol'our, *v.t.*, to stain.

discol'oured, *adj.*, having lost, or differing in, colour; *p.p.*, discolour.

discol'ouring, *pr.p.*, discolour.

discom'fit, *v.t.*, to vanquish; to disconcert.

discom'fited, *p.p.*, discomfit.

discom'fiter, *n.*, one who discomfits.

discom'fiting, *pr.p.*, discomfit.

discom'fiture, *n.*, defeat; disappointment; a sudden failure of plans or hopes.

discom'fort, *n.*, an absence of comfort; a disturbance of peace; *v.t.*, to make uneasy.

discom'forted, *p.p.*, discomfort.

discom'forting, *pr.p.*, discomfort.

discommode', *v.t.*, to put to inconvenience.

discommo'ded, *p.p.*, discommode.

discommo'ding, *adj.*, inconvenient; *pr.p.*, discommode.

discomm'on, *v.t.*, to prevent a tradesman from serving undergraduates; to make common land private.

discomm'ons, *v.t.*, to deprive (member of college) of commons.

discompose', *v.t.*, to disturb; to vex.

discomposed', *p.p.*, discompose.

discompo'sing, *pr.p.*, discompose.

discompo'sure, *n.*, an agitation of mind.

disconcert', *v.t.*, to frustrate; to confuse; to thwart unexpectedly.

disconcert'ed, *p.p.*, disconcert.

disconcert'ing, *adj.*, upsetting; *pr.p.*, disconcert.

disconnect', *v.t.*, to detach.

disconnect'ed, *p.p.*, disconnect.

disconnect'ing, *pr.p.*, disconnect.

disconnec'tion, *n.*, a separation.

discon'solate, *adj.*, hopeless; sad.

discon'solately, *adv.*, sadly.

discontent', *n.*, dissatisfaction.

discontent'ed, *adj.*, dissatisfied.

discontent'edly, *adv.*, in a discontented manner.

discontent'edness, *n.*, *i.q.* discontent.

discontent'ing, *adj.*, causing discontent.

discontent'ment, *n.*, *i.q.* discontent.

discontig'uous, *adj.*, having parts not in contact.

discontin'uance, *n.*, cessation.

discontinua'tion, *n.*, *i.q.* discontinuance.

discontin'ue, *v.t.*, to put an end to; *v.i.*, to cease.

discontin'ued, *p.p.*, discontinue.

discontin'uing, *pr.p.*, discontinue.

discontinu'ity, *n.*, a want of continuity.

discontin'uous, *adj.*, interrupted.

dis'cord, *n.*, a disagreement; strife; a union of musical sounds disagreeable to the ear.

discord', *v.i.*, to be out of harmony or agreement with.

discord'ance, *n.*, an offence against harmony; a state of discord.

discord'ancy, *n.*, *i.q.* discordance.

discord'ant, *adj.*, disagreeing; not harmonious.

discord'antly, *adv.*, in a discordant manner.

discos'tate, *adj.*, having ribs diverging radiately.

dis'cotheque, *n.*, a place for the playing of popular gramophone records and dancing.

dis'count, *n.*, a deduction from a price or other sum of money to cover interest or for prompt payment.

discount', *v.t.*, to deduct discount from; to discredit; to express a lack of reliance on.

discount'able, *adj.*, capable of being discounted.

discount'ed, *p.p.*, discount.

discoun'tenance, *v.t.*, to discourage by disapproval.

discoun'tenanced, *p.p.*, discountenance.

discoun'tenancing, *pr.p.,* discountenance.

dis'counter, *n.,* one who discounts bills, etc.

discount'ing, *pr.p.,* discount.

discour'age, *v.t.,* to dishearten; to dissuade.

discour'aged, *p.p.,* discourage.

discour'agement, *n.,* the act of discouraging; that which discourages.

discour'ager, *n.,* one who discourages.

discour'aging, *adj.,* disheartening; *pr.p.,* discourage.

discou'ragingly, *adv.,* in a discouraging manner.

dis'course, *n.,* a conversation; a treatise; a sermon.

discourse', *v.i.,* to communicate thoughts in a formal manner.

discoursed', *p.p.,* discourse.

discours'er, *n.,* one who discourses.

discours'ing, *pr.p.,* discourse.

discour'teous, *adj.,* uncivil.

discour'teously, *adv.,* uncivilly.

discour'tesy, *n.,* the want of courtesy.

dis'cous, *adj.,* discshaped.

discov'er, *v.t.,* to have the first sight of; to find.

discov'erable, *adj.,* able to be discovered.

discov'ered, *p.p.,* discover.

discov'erer, *n.,* one who discovers.

discov'ering, *pr.p.,* discover.

disco'vert, *n.,* an unmarried or widowed woman (*leg.*).

discov'erture, *n.,* in law, the release of a woman from the coverture of her husband.

discov'ery, *n.,* a finding out; a revealing; that which is discovered.

discred'it, *n.,* disrepute; disbelief; *v.t.,* to disbelieve; to cast doubt on.

discred'itable, *adj.,* disgraceful; reflecting no credit on.

discred'ited, *p.p.,* discredit.

discred'iting, *pr.p.,* discredit.

discreet', *adj.,* prudent; cautious.

discreet'ly, *adv.,* prudently.

discreet'ness, *n.,* the quality of being discreet.

discrep'ance, *n.,* *i.q.* discrepancy.

discrep'ancy, *n.,* an inconsistency among facts.

discrep'ant, *adj.,* differing; inconsistent.

discrete', *adj.,* separate; distinct.

discrete'ness, *n.,* *i.q.* disjunctiveness.

discre'tion, *n.,* discreetness; sound judgment; the liberty of acting according to one's own judgment.

discre'tional, *adj.,* *i.q.* discretionary.

discre'tionary, *adj.,* left to one's own discretion.

discre'tive, *adj.,* denoting a separation or opposition.

discrim'inate, *adj.,* having the power of noting minute distinctions.

discrim'inate, *v.t.,* to distinguish by observing differences; to select; *v.i.,* to note differences.

discrim'inated, *p.p.,* discriminate.

discrim'inately, *adv.,* with minute distinction.

discrim'inating, *adj.,* able to make nice distinctions; *pr.p.,* discriminate.

discrimina'tion, *n.,* the faculty of discriminating.

discrim'inative, *adj.,* characteristic; *i.q.* discriminating.

discrim'inator, *n.,* one who discriminates.

discrim'inatory, *adj.,* *i.q.* discriminative.

discrown', *v.t.,* to deprive of a crown.

discrowned', *p.p.,* discrown.

discrown'ing, *pr.p.,* discrown.

discur'sion, *n.,* the act of ranging from thought to thought.

discur'sive, *adj.,* passing rapidly from one subject to another.

discur'sively, *adv.,* in a discursive manner.

discur'sory, *adj.,* argumentative.

dis'cus, *n.,* a kind of ancient quoit; a disc.

discuss', *v.t.,* to debate; to argue.

discussed', *p.p.,* discuss.

discuss'er, *n.,* one who discusses.

discus'sing, *pr.p.,* discuss.

discus'sion, *n.,* a debate; the act of discussing.

discuss'ive, *adj.,* having the power to discuss.

discu'tient, *n.,* a medicine or application which disperses a tumour.

disdain', *n.,* haughtiness; contempt; *v.t.,* to scorn.

disdained', *p.p.,* disdain.

disdain'ful, *adj.,* contemptuous; haughty.

disdain'fully, *adv.,* in a disdainful manner.

disdain'ing, *pr.p.,* disdain.

disease', *n.,* any morbid state of the body.

diseased', *adj.,* affected with disease.

disembark', *v.t.* and *i.,* to land from a ship.

disembarka'tion, *n.,* the act of disembarking.

disembarked', *p.p.,* disembark.

disembark'ing, *pr.p.,* disembark.

disembar'rass, *v.t.,* to free from embarrassment.

disembar'rassed, *p.p.,* disembarrass.

disembar'rassing, *pr.p.,* disembarrass.

disembar'rassment, *n.,* the act of disembarrassing.

disembod'ied, *p.p.,* disembody.

disembod'iment, *n.,* the act of disembodying.

disembod'y, *v.t.,* to disband (troops); to divest of the body.

disembod'ying, *pr.p.,* disembody.

disembogue', *v.i.,* to discharge water (as a stream) into the sea or a lake.

disembos'om, *v.t.* and *i.,* to disclose; to reveal.

disembow'el, *v.t.,* to deprive of the viscera; to gut.

disembow'el(l)ed, *p.p.,* disembowel.

disembow'el(l)ing, *pr.p.,* disembowel.

disembroil', *v.t.,* to extricate from confusion.

disembroiled', *p.p.,* disembroil.

disembroil'ing, *pr.p.,* disembroil.

disena'ble, *v.t.,* to disqualify.

disena'bled, p.p., disenable.

disena'bling, pr.p., disenable.

disenchant', v.t., to free from fascination or pleasing delusion.

disenchant'ed, p.p., disenchant.

disenchant'er, n., one who disenchants.

disenchant'ing, pr.p., disenchant.

disenchant'ment, n., the act of disenchanting.

disencum'ber, v.t., to free from encumbrance.

disencum'bered, p.p., disencumber.

disencum'bering, pr.p., disencumber.

disencum'brance, n., the deliverance from encumbrance.

disendow', v.t., to rob or deprive of endowments.

disendowed', p.p., disendow.

disendow'ing, pr.p., disendow.

disendow'ment, n., the act of taking away an endowment.

disenfran'chise, v.t., i.q. disfranchise.

disengage', v.t., to disentangle; to free; to set free from an engagement.

disengaged', adj., at leisure; not occupied; p.p., disengage.

disengage'ment, n., the state or action of being disengaged.

disengag'ing, pr.p., disengage.

disentail', v.t., to free from entail (leg.).

disentan'gle, v.t., to unravel; to free from entanglements.

disentan'gled, p.p., disentangle.

disentan'glement, n., the setting free from tangle.

disentan'gling, pr.p., disentangle.

disenthrall', v.t., to rescue from slavery or oppression.

disenthralled', p.p., disenthrall.

disenthrall'ing, pr.p., disenthrall.

disenti'tle, v.t., to deprive of a title or right.

disenti'tlement, n., the deprivation of a title or right.

disentomb', v.t., to take out of a tomb; to unearth; to find by research.

disequilib'rium, n., the loss of equilibrium; instability.

disestab'lish, v.t., to cause to cease to be established.

disestab'lished, p.p., disestablish.

disestab'lishing, pr.p., disestablish.

disestab'lishment, n., the act of disestablishing.

disestab'lishmentar'ianism, n., the theory of disestablishment.

disesteem', n., the want of esteem; v.t., to dislike slightly.

disesteemed', p.p., disesteem.

disesteem'ing, pr.p., disesteem.

di'seur, n., a monologuist (Fr.).

di'seuse, n., the fem. of diseur (Fr.).

disfa'vour, n., slight displeasure; a disobliging act; v.t., to withdraw favour from.

disfa'voured, p.p., disfavour.

disfa'vouring, pr.p., disfavour.

disfea'ture, v.t., i.q. disfigure.

disfigura'tion, n., the act of disfiguring; a disfigurement.

disfig'ure, v.t., to injure the beauty of.

disfig'ured, p.p., disfigure.

disfig'urement, n., harm to physical appearance (esp. the face); that which disfigures.

disfig'urer, n., one who disfigures.

disfig'uring, pr.p., disfigure.

disfo'rest, v.t., i.q. disafforest.

disfran'chise, v.t., to deprive of the rights of citizenship, esp. of the vote.

disfran'chised, p.p., disfranchise.

disfran'chisement, n., the state or act of being disfranchised.

disfran'chising, pr.p., disfranchise.

disfrock', v.t., to deprive of clerical garb and status.

disgorge', v.t., to vomit; to surrender.

disgorged', p.p., disgorge.

disgorge'ment, n., the act of disgorging.

disgorg'ing, pr.p., disgorge.

disgrace', n., disfavour; shame; a cause of shame; v.t., to put out of favour; to dishonour.

disgraced', p.p., disgrace.

disgrace'ful, adj., shameful; infamous.

disgrace'fully, adv., in a disgraceful manner.

disgrac'ing, pr.p., disgrace.

disgrun'tled, adj., discontented; not satisfied.

disgrun'tlement, n., discontentedness.

disguise', v.t., to conceal the ordinary appearance of; n., a dress intended to conceal identity.

disguised', p.p., disguise.

disgui'ser, n., one who disguises.

disgui'sing, pr.p., disguise.

disgust', n., strong dislike; v.t., to stir up loathing in.

disgust'ed, p.p., disgust.

disgust'ful, adj., exciting disgust.

disgust'ing, adj., loathsome; nasty; pr.p., disgust.

disgust'ingly, adv., in a disgusting manner.

dish, n., a broad, open vessel for serving or cooking food; v.t., to put in a dish; to ruin (slang).

dishabille', n., i.q. deshabille.

dishabit'uate, v.t., to make a person unaccustomed.

disharmo'nious, adj., discordant.

disharmo'niously, adv., in a discordant manner.

disharm'onize, v.t., to put out of harmony; to make discordant.

dishar'mony, n., a lack of harmony.

dish'cloth, n., a cloth for washing dishes.

disheart'en, v.t., to discourage; to dispirit.

disheart'ened, p.p., dishearten.

disheart'ening, pr.p., dishearten.

disheart'enment, n., discouragement.

dished, p.p., dish.

dishe'rison, n., the act of disinheriting.

dishev'el, v.t., to cause to appear in an unkempt state.

dishev'el(l)ed, adj., unkempt; disarranged; p.p., dishevel.

dishev'el(l)ing, pr.p., dishevel.

dishev'elment, n., disarrangement.

dish'ful, n., the amount a dish will hold.

dish'ing, pr.p., dish.

dishon'est, adj., not honest.

dishon'estly, adv., fraudulently.

dishon'esty, n., fraud; treachery.

dishon'our, n., want of honour; disgrace; v.t., to disgrace; to treat with indignity; to refuse to accept or pay (a cheque).

dishon'ourable, adj., disgraceful.

dishon'oured, p.p., dishonour.

dishon'ourer, n., one who dishonours.

dishon'ouring, pr.p., dishonour.

dishorn', v.t., to deprive of horns.

disillu'sion, n., disenchantment; v.t., to free from illusion.

disillu'sioned, p.p., disillusion.

disillu'sioning, pr.p., disillusion.

disillu'sionize, v.t., to free from illusions.

disillu'sionment, n., freedom from illusions.

disincen'tive, n., a discouragement to any effort.

disinclina'tion, n., unwillingness.

disincline', v.t., to make unwilling.

disinclined', p.p., disincline.

disincli'ning, pr.p., disincline.

disincor'porate, v.t., to deprive of corporate powers.

disincor'porated, p.p., disincorporate.

disincor'porating, pr.p., disincorporate.

disincorpora'tion, n., the act of disincorporating.

disinfect', v.t., to purify from infectious matter.

disinfect'ant, n., a substance that disinfects.

disinfect'ed, p.p., disinfect.

disinfect'ing, pr.p., disinfect.

disinfec'tion, n., the purification from infecting matter.

disinfect'or, n., one who, or that which, disinfects.

disinfla'tion, n., i.q. deflation.

disinfla'tionary, adj., rel. to disinflation.

disingen'uous, adj., insincere; appearing to be artless but not so.

disingen'uously, adv., in a disingenuous manner.

disingen'uousness, n., insincerity; apparent artlessness.

disinher'it, v.t., to deprive of the right to an inheritance.

disinher'itance, n., the act of disinheriting.

disinher'ited, p.p., disinherit.

disinher'iting, pr.p., disinherit.

disin'tegrable, adj., that can be disintegrated.

disin'tegrate, v.t., to reduce to fragments; v.i., to fall apart.

disin'tegrated, p.p., disintegrate.

disin'tegrating, pr.p., disintegrate.

disintegra'tion, n., the act of disintegrating.

disin'tegrator, n., one who, or that which, disintegrates.

disinter', v.t., to take out of the earth.

disin'terested, adj., unselfish; without personal motive.

disin'terestedly, adv., in a disinterested manner.

disin'terestedness, n., the state of being disinterested.

disinter'ment, n., exhumation.

disinterred', p.p., disinter.

disinter'ring, pr.p., disinter.

disinvest'ment, n., the realization of a country's assets.

disjec'ta mem'bra, n. pl., fragments; scattered remains (Lat.).

disjoin', v.t., to separate; v.i., to part.

disjoined', p.p., disjoin.

disjoin'ing, pr.p., disjoin.

disjoint', v.t., to separate at the joints; to render incoherent.

disjoint'ed, adj., incoherent; out of order; p.p., disjoint.

disjoint'ing, pr.p., disjoint.

disjunct', adj., separated.

disjunc'tion, n., disunion; separation.

disjunct'ive, adj., tending to separate; marking opposition.

disjunct'ively, adv., in a disjunctive manner.

disjunctiveness, n., i.q. disjunction.

disk, n., i.q. disc.

disli'kable, adj., exciting dislike.

dislike', n., antipathy; aversion; v.t., to feel dislike towards.

disliked', p.p., dislike.

disli'king, pr.p., dislike.

dis'locate, v.t., to displace; to put out of joint.

dis'located, p.p., dislocate.

dis'locating, pr.p., dislocate.

disloca'tion, n., the act of dislocating or displacing.

dislodge', v.t., to drive from the place occupied.

dislodged', p.p., dislodge.

dislodg'ing, pr.p., dislodge.

dislodg'ment, n., the act of dislodging.

disloy'al, adj., faithless; treacherous.

disloy'ally, adv., in a disloyal manner.

disloy'alty, n., infidelity.

dis'mal, adj., gloomy.

dis'mally, adv., in a dismal manner.

disman'tle, v.t., to strip of equipments; to take apart.

disman'tled, p.p., dismantle.

disman'tling, pr.p., dismantle.

dismast', v.t., to deprive of masts.

dismast'ed, p.p., dismast.

dismast'ing, pr.p., dismast.

dismay', n., a loss of courage; a feeling of apprehension and helplessness; v.t., to discourage.

dismayed', *p.p.*, dismay.

dismay'ing, *pr.p.*, dismay.

disme, *n.*, a tenth part; the number ten.

dismem'ber, *v.t.*, to divide limb from limb.

dismem'bered, *p.p.*, dismember.

dismem'bering, *pr.p.*, dismember.

dismem'berment, *n.*, the act of dismembering.

dismiss', *v.t.*, to send away.

dismiss'al, *n.*, discharge.

dismissed', *p.p.*, dismiss.

dismiss'ing, *pr.p.*, dismiss.

dismis'sion, *n.*, the act of dismissing.

dismiss'ive, *adj.*, giving dismission.

dismiss'ory, *adj.*, granting permission to depart.

dismount', *v.i.*, to alight from an animal or a cycle.

dismount'able, *adj.*, capable of being dismounted.

dismount'ed, *p.p.*, dismount.

dismount'ing, *pr.p.*, dismount.

disobe'dience, *n.*, neglect or refusal to obey.

disobe'dient, *adj.*, guilty of disobedience.

disobe'diently, *adv.*, in a disobedient manner.

disobey', *v.t.*, to neglect or refuse to obey.

disobeyed', *p.p.*, disobey.

disobey'er, *n.*, one who disobeys.

disobey'ing, *pr.p.*, disobey.

disoblige', *v.t.*, to offend by failing to oblige.

disobliged', *p.p.*, disoblige.

disobli'ging, *adj.*, unaccommodating; *pr.p.*, disoblige.

disor'der, *n.*, a want of order; confusion; sickness; *v.t.*, to throw into confusion.

disor'dered, *adj.*, irregular; deranged; *p.p.*, disorder.

disor'dering, *pr.p.*, disorder.

disor'derliness, *n.*, the state of being disorderly.

disor'derly, *adj.*, marked by disorder; unruly.

disorganiza'tion, *n.*, the state of being disorganized.

disor'ganize, *v.t.*, to throw into confusion.

disor'ganized, *p.p.*, disorganize.

disor'ganizer, *n.*, one who disorganizes.

disor'ganizing, *pr.p.*, disorganize.

diso'rientate, *v.t.*, to place a church with the chancel not directly eastwards; to confuse a person as to his bearings.

diso'rientated, *p.p.*, disorientate.

disorienta'tion, *n.*, a loss of direction or bearings.

disown', *v.t.*, to refuse to acknowledge.

disowned', *p.p.*, disown.

disown'ing, *pr.p.*, disown.

dispar'age, *v.t.*, to depreciate; to detract from.

dispar'aged, *p.p.*, disparage.

dispar'agement, *n.*, detraction; dishonour.

dispar'ager, *n.*, one who disparages.

dispar'aging, *pr.p.*, disparage.

dispar'agingly, *adv.*, in a belittling manner.

dis'parate, *adj.*, dissimilar.

dispar'ity, *n.*, inequality.

dispark', *v.t.*, to turn (parkland) to some other use.

dispart', *n.*, the difference between half the diameter of the base ring and the muzzle of a gun; a muzzle sight; *v.t.*, to sever; *v.i.*, to open.

dispart'ed, *p.p.*, dispart.

dispart'ing, *pr.p.*, dispart.

dispas'sion, *n.*, freedom from passion; equanimity.

dispas'sionate, *adj.*, unmoved by feelings; impartial.

dispas'sionately, *adv.*, impartially; without feeling.

dispatch', *v.t.* and *n.*, *i.q.* despatch.

dispel', *v.t.*, to disperse.

dispelled', *p.p.*, dispel.

dispel'ling, *pr.p.*, dispel.

dispen'sable, *adj.*, able to be dispensed with.

dispen'sary, *n.*, a place for the preparation and issue of medicines.

dispensa'tion, *n.*, the act of dispensing; a system of religion and morals; the setting free from an obligation.

dispen'satory, *adj.*, having power to grant dispensations; *n.*, a pharmacopoeia.

dispense', *v.t.*, to distribute; to administer; to excuse from an obligation; to compound.

dispensed', *p.p.*, dispense.

dispen'ser, *n.*, one who dispenses.

dispen'sing, *adj.*, granting dispensation; *n.*, the act or practice of dispensing; *pr.p.*, dispense.

dispeo'ple, *v.t.*, to empty of inhabitants.

dispeo'pled, *p.p.*, dispeople.

disper'mous, *adj.*, two-seeded (*bot.*).

dispers'al, *n.*, *i.q.* dispersion.

disperse', *v.t.* and *i.*, to scatter.

dispersed', *adj.*, scattered; *p.p.*, disperse.

dispers'er, *n.*, one who, or that which, disperses.

dispers'ing, *pr.p.*, disperse.

disper'sion, *n.*, the state of being scattered.

dispers'ive, *adj.*, tending to scatter.

dispir'it, *v.t.*, to dishearten.

dispir'ited, *adj.*, depressed in spirits; *p.p.*, dispirit.

dispir'itedly, *adv.*, in a dispirited manner.

dispir'iting, *adj.*, depressing; *pr.p.*, dispirit.

dispit'eous, *adj.*, without pity; cruel.

dispit'eously, *adv.*, in a cruel manner.

displace', *v.t.*, to remove from its place.

displaced', *p.p.*, displace.

displace'ment, *n.*, removal; the quantity of water displaced by a floating body.

displac'ing, *pr.p.*, displace.

displant', *v.t.*, to pluck up what is planted.

displant'ed, *p.p.*, displant.

displant'ing, *pr.p.,* displant.

display', *n.,* an exhibition; an ostentatious show; *v.t.,* to spread before the view.

displayed', *p.p.,* display.

display'er, *n.,* one who displays.

display'ing, *pr.p.,* display.

displease', *v.t.,* to offend; to make slightly angry.

displeased', *p.p.,* displease.

displeas'er, *n.,* one who displeases.

displeas'ing, *adj.,* disagreeable; *pr.p.,* displease.

displeas'ure, *n.,* vexation; annoyance.

displume', *v.t.,* to strip of feathers.

displumed', *p.p.,* displume.

displum'ing, *pr.p.,* displume.

dispone', *v.t.,* in Scots law, to convey (property) to another formally.

disponed', *p.p.,* dispone.

dispo'ner, *n.,* one who dispones.

dispon'ing, *pr.p.,* dispone.

disport', *n.,* a sport; a pastime; *v.i.,* to play; to sport.

disport'ed, *p.p.,* disport.

disport'ing, *pr.p.,* disport.

dispo'sable, *adj.,* free to be used when required; able to be discarded after use.

dispo'sal, *n.,* arrangement; the power of bestowing; the act of selling or parting with.

dispose', *v.t.,* to arrange; to incline; to apply to a particular purpose.

disposed', *adj.,* inclined; minded; *p.p.,* dispose.

dispo'ser, *n.,* one who disposes.

dispo'sing, *pr.p.,* dispose.

disposi'tion, *n.,* a manner of arrangement; the natural constitution of the mind; propensity.

dispossess', *v.t.,* to deprive of ownership or occupancy.

dispossessed', *p.p.,* dispossess.

dispossess'ing, *pr.p.,* dispossess.

dispossess'sion, *n.,* the act of dispossessing.

dispossess'or, *n.,* one who dispossesses.

dispraise', *n.,* blame; *v.t.,* to censure.

dispraised', *p.p.,* dispraise.

disprais'ing, *pr.p.,* dispraise.

disproof', *n.,* a proving to be false or erroneous.

dispropor'tion, *n.,* the want of proportion or symmetry; inequality.

dispropor'tionable, *adj.,* not having due proportion; unequal; inadequate.

dispropor'tional, *adj., i.q.* disproportionable.

dispropor'tionate, *adj., i.q.* disproportionable.

dispropor'tioned, *adj.,* wanting in symmetry.

disprov'able, *adj.,* capable of being disproved.

disprov'al, *n.,* the act of disproving.

disprove', *v.t.,* to prove to be false or erroneous.

disproved', *p.p.,* disprove.

disprov'er, *n.,* one who disproves.

disprov'ing, *pr.p.,* disprove.

disput'able, *adj.,* controvertible.

dis'putant, *n.,* one who disputes or argues.

disputa'tion, *n.,* the act of disputing; controversy.

disputa'tious, *adj.,* inclined to dispute.

dispute', *n.,* a controversy; strife; *v.i.,* to contend in argument; to wrangle; *v.t.,* to attempt to disprove; to call in question; to contest.

dispu'ted, *p.p.,* dispute.

dispu'ter, *n.,* one who disputes.

dispu'ting, *pr.p.,* dispute.

disqualifica'tion, *n.,* a disability; that which disqualifies.

disqual'ified, *p.p.,* disqualify.

disqual'ify, *v.t.,* to incapacitate; to reject as not meeting conditions.

disqual'ifying, *pr.p.,* disqualify.

disqui'et, *n.,* uneasiness; anxiety; *v.t.,* to make uneasy; to harass.

disqui'eted, *p.p.,* disquiet.

disqui'eting, *adj.,* disturbing the mind; *pr.p.,* disquiet.

disqui'etness, *n.,* anxiety; unrest.

disqui'etude, *n.,* the want of tranquillity; disquiet.

disquisi'tion, *n.,* a dissertation, essay or treatise; an argumentative inquiry.

disquisi'tional, *adj.,* pert. or rel. to a disquisition.

disrate', *v.t.,* to reduce in rank (*naut.*).

disregard', *n.,* neglect; *v.t.,* to pay no heed to.

disregard'ed, *p.p.,* disregard.

disregard'ful, *adj.,* neglectful.

disregard'ing, *pr.p.,* disregard.

disrel'ish, *n.,* distaste; *v.t.,* to dislike the taste of.

disrel'ished, *p.p.,* disrelish.

disrel'ishing, *pr.p.,* disrelish.

disremem'ber, *v.t.,* to forget.

disrepair', *n.,* a state of requiring to be repaired.

disrep'utable, *adj.,* dishonourable; low.

disrepute', *n.,* the loss or want of reputation.

disrespect', *n.,* the want of respect, rudeness.

disrespect'ful, *adj.,* wanting in respect.

disrespect'fully, *adv.,* in a disrespectful manner.

disrespect'fulness, *n.,* the lack of respect.

disrobe', *v.t. and i.,* to undress; to divest of a garment.

disrobed', *p.p.,* disrobe.

disro'ber, *n.,* one who disrobes.

disro'bing, *pr.p.,* disrobe.

disroot', *v.t.,* to uproot; to dislodge.

disrupt', *v.t. and i.,* to break up; to shatter.

disrupted, *p.p.,* disrupt.

disrupting, *pr.p.,* disrupt.

disrup'tion, *n.,* the act of bursting and separating.

disrup'tive, *adj.,* causing or following disruption.

disrup'ture, *n.*, a rending asunder.

dis'satisfac'tion, *n.*, discontent.

dissatisfac'tory, *adj.*, causing dissatisfaction.

dissat'isfied, *adj.*, discontented; *p.p.*, dissatisfy.

dissat'isfy, *v.t.*, to fail to satisfy; to render discontented.

dissat'isfying, *pr.p.*, dissatisfy.

dissave', *v.i.*, to spend one's savings.

disseat', *v.t.*, to unseat.

dissect', *v.t.*, to divide with a cutting instrument; to analyse.

dissect'ed, *p.p.*, dissect.

dissect'ible, *adj.*, capable of being dissected.

dissect'ing, *adj.*, used in dissection; *pr.p.*, dissect.

dissec'tion, *n.*, the act or art of dissecting.

dissect'or, *n.*, one who dissects.

disseize', *v.t.*, to dispossess wrongfully.

disseized', *p.p.*, disseize.

disseizee', *n.*, one who is disseized.

disseiz'in, *n.*, the act of disseizing.

disseiz'ing, *pr.p.*, disseize.

disseiz'or, *n.*, one who dispossesses another.

dissem'blance, *n.*, concealment by false pretences.

dissem'ble, *v.t.*, to hide by false pretences; *v.i.*, to put on an assumed manner.

dissem'bled, *p.p.*, dissemble.

dissem'bler, *n.*, one who dissembles.

dissem'bling *pr.p.*, dissemble.,

dissem'inate, *v.t.*, to diffuse; to spread by dispersion.

dissem'inated, *p.p.*, disseminate.

dissem'inating, *pr.p.*, disseminate.

dissemina'tion, *n.*, the act of disseminating.

dissem'inator, *n.*, one who disseminates.

dissen'sion, *n.*, strife, quarrel; a breach of friendship.

dissent', *n.*, a difference of opinion; separation from the Church in England; *v.i.*, to disagree in opinion.

dissent'ed, *p.p.*, dissent.

dissent'er, *n.*, one who dissents; a separatist.

dissen'tient, *adj.*, declaring dissent; voting differently; *n.*, a person expressing disagreement.

dissent'ing, *adj.*, disagreeing in opinion; bel. to a body of dissenters; *pr.p.*, dissent.

dissep'iment, *n.*, a partition; a septum.

dissert', *v.i.*, to give an exposition; to argue.

disser'tate, *v.i.*, *i.q.* dissert.

disserta'tion, *n.*, a treatise; a formal discourse.

disserve', *v.t.*, to do an ill-service to.

disserved', *p.p.*, disserve.

disserv'ice, *n.*, an ill turn; an injury.

disserv'iceable, *adj.*, injurious.

disserv'ing, *pr.p.*, disserve.

dissev'er, *v.t.*, to part in two; to separate.

dissev'erance, *n.*, the act of dissevering.

dissevera'tion, *n.*, *i.q.* disseverance.

dissev'ered, *p.p.*, dissever.

dissev'ering, *pr.p.*, dissever.

dis'sidence, *n.*, dissent.

dis'sident, *adj.*, dissenting; *n.*, a dissenter.

dissil'ient, *adj.*, bursting (as the dry pod of a plant) (*bot.*).

dissim'ilar, *adj.*, unlike.

dissimilar'ity, *n.*, unlikeness.

dissim'ilarly, *adv.*, in a dissimilar manner.

dissimila'tion, *n.*, the act of rendering dissimilar, esp. with reference to sounds in orthoepy.

dissimil'itude, *n.*, unlikeness; the want of resemblance.

dissim'ulate, *v.i.*, to feign; to make pretence.

dissim'ulated, *p.p.*, dissimulate.

dissim'ulating, *pr.p.*, dissimulate.

dissimula'tion, *n.*, a concealment of fact; hypocrisy.

dissim'ulator, *n.*, one who acts hypocritically.

dis'sipate, *v.t.*, to scatter; to drive away; to waste; *v.i.*, to vanish.

dis'sipated, *adj.*, extravagant; dissolute; *p.p.*, dissipate.

dis'sipating, *pr.p.*, dissipate.

dissipa'tion, *n.*, the act of dissipating; dissolute conduct.

disso'ciable, *adj.*, incongruous; not reconcilable.

disso'cialize, *v.t.*, to make unsocial; to disincline towards society.

disso'ciate, *v.t.*, to disunite; to part.

disso'ciated, *p.p.*, dissociate.

disso'ciating, *pr.p.*, dissociate.

dissocia'tion, *n.*, disunion; a chemical decomposition.

dissolubil'ity, *n.*, the quality of being dissoluble.

dis'soluble, *adj.*, susceptible of decomposition.

dis'solute, *adj.*, debauched; given to vice or profligacy.

dis'solutely, *adv.*, in a dissolute manner.

dis'soluteness, *n.*, viciousness, dissipation.

dissolu'tion, *n.*, decomposition; death; the putting an end to the existence of an assembly.

dissolvabil'ity, *n.*, capability of being dissolved.

dissolv'able, *adj.*, able to be dissolved.

dissolve', *v.t.*, to melt; to liquefy; to disband any connected system or body; *v.i.*, to melt; to break up.

dissolved', *p.p.*, dissolve.

dissolv'ent, *n.*, anything that dissolves.

dissolv'er, *n.*, one who, or that which, dissolves.

dissolv'ing, *pr.p.*, dissolve.

dis'sonance, *n.*, discord.

dis'sonancy, *n.*, *i.q.* dissonance.

dis'sonant, *adj.*, harsh sounding; incongruous.

dissuade', *v.t.*, to advise against; to turn from

a purpose by argument.

dissua'ded, *p.p.*, dissuade.

dissua'der, *n.*, one who dissuades.

dissua'ding, *pr.p.*, dissuade.

dissua'sion, *n.*, advice in opposition to something.

dissua'sive, *adj.*, tending to dissuade; *n.*, an argument against.

dissua'sively, *adv.*, in a dissuasive way.

dissymmet'rical, *adj.*, symmetrical in opposite directions.

dissymm'etry, *n.*, symmetry in opposite directions.

dis'taff, *n.*, a staff holding textile raw material from which thread is spun; distaff side = female side.

distain', *v.t.*, to stain.

distained', *p.p.*, distain.

distain'ing, *pr.p.*, distain.

dis'tal, *adj.*, furthest away from the centre or joining point (*anat.*, *bot.*).

dis'tance, *n.*, an interval of space or time; remoteness; *v.t.*, to outstrip.

dis'tanced, *p.p.*, distance.

dis'tancing, *pr.p.*, distance.

dis'tant, *adj.*, remote in place or time; not intimate.

dis'tantly, *adv.*, at a distance; with reserve.

distaste', *n.*, disrelish; disinclination.

distaste'ful, *adj.*, disagreeable.

distaste'fully, *adv.*, disagreeably.

distem'per, *n.*, a malady; a disease of young dogs; a paint used for stage scenery and walls; tempera, *v.t.*, to paint in tempera.

distem'perature, *n.*, confusion.

distem'pered, *adj.*, diseased in body or mind; *p.p.*, distemper.

distem'pering, *pr.p.*, distemper.

distend', *v.t.*, to swell; *v.i.*, to become inflated.

distend'ed, *p.p.*, distend.

distend'ing, *pr.p.*, distend.

distensibil'ity, *n.*, the quality of being distensible.

disten'sible, *adj.*, capable of being distended.

disten'sile, *adj.*, able to cause distension.

disten'sion, *n.*, the act of distending; the state of being distended.

disten'sive, *adj.*, *i.q.* distensible.

dis'tich, *n.*, a couplet.

dis'tichous, *adj.*, having fruit arranged in two vertical lines on the opposite sides of a stem (*bot.*).

distil(l'), *v.t.*, to yield in drops; to extract by distillation.

distil'lable, *adj.*, fit for distillation.

distil'late, *n.*, a distilled fluid.

distilla'tion, *n.*, the operation of extracting spirit from a substance by volatilization and condensation.

distil'latory, *adj.*, used in distillation; *n.*, a still.

distilled', *p.p.*, distil.

distil'ler, *n.*, one whose occupation is to extract spirit by distillation.

distil'lery, *n.*, the works where distilling is carried on.

distil'ling, *n.*, the act or business of distilling; *pr.p.*, distil.

distinct', *adj.*, well-defined; different; obvious.

distinc'tion, *n.*, a distinguishing quality; superiority; an honour of some kind.

distinct'ive, *adj.*, indicating difference.

distinct'ively, *adv.*, in a distinctive manner.

distinct'iveness, *n.*, the quality of being distinctive.

distinct'ly, *adv.*, clearly; obviously.

distinct'ness, *n.*, clearness; precision.

distin'gué, *adj.*, of distinguished appearance, manners, etc. (*Fr.*).

distin'guish, *v.t.*, to recognize the individuality of; to mark out from others by some point of

difference; to confer an honour on.

distin'guishable, *adj.*, capable of being distinguished.

distin'guished, *adj.*, eminent; *p.p.*, distinguish.

distin'guisher, *n.*, one who, or that which, distinguishes.

distin'guishing, *adj.*, characteristic; *pr.p.*, distinguish.

distort', *v.t.*, to twist out of natural shape.

distort'ed, *adj.*, shaped abnormally; mis-shapen; *p.p.*, distort.

distort'edly, *adv.*, in a distorted manner.

distort'ing, *pr.p.*, distort.

distor'tion, *n.*, a twisting out of natural shape or meaning.

distor'tional, *adj.*, able to be distorted.

distor'tionist, *n.*, a caricaturist; an acrobat who distorts his body.

distort'ive, *adj.*, causing distortion.

distract', *v.t.*, to cause to turn from any object; to perplex; to render insane; to shift interest from one topic to another.

distract'ed, *adj.*, perplexed; crazy; *p.p.*, distract.

distract'ing, *pr.p.*, distract.

distrac'tion, *n.*, confusion of the mind; diversion.

distract'ive, *adj.*, causing perplexity.

distrain', *v.t.*, to seize for debt.

distrain'able, *adj.*, liable to be distrained.

distrained', *p.p.*, distrain.

distrain'er, *n.*, one who distrains.

distrain'ing, *pr.p.*, distrain.

distraint', *n.*, the legal seizure of goods.

distrait', *adj.*, absent-minded; upset (*Fr.*).

distraught', *adj.*, distracted.

distress', *n.*, anguish of mind or body; misery; seizure for debt; *v.t.*, to make miserable.

distressed', *adj.*, suffering distress; *p.p.*, distress.

distress'ful, *adj.*, inflicting or indicating distress.

distress'fully, *adv.*, in a distressful way.

distress'ing, *adj.*, very afflicting; *pr.p.*, distress.

distrib'utary, *adj.*, *i.q.* distributive.

distrib'ute, *v.t.*, to divide among a number of recipients.

distrib'uted, *p.p.*, distribute.

distrib'uter, *n.*, one who, or that which distributes.

distrib'uting, *pr.p.*, distribute.

distribu'tion, *n.*, the act of separating into distinct parts; a division among recipients.

distrib'utism, *n.*, the theory of the "distributive state," or private ownership.

distrib'utive, *adj.*, serving to distribute.

distrib'utively, *adv.*, separately.

distrib'utor, *n.*, *i.q.* distributer; a device for distributing electric current to the sparking plugs of a motor, or the compressed air of a self starter to the cylinders.

dis'trict, *n.*, a region, locality or quarter.

distrin'gas, *n.*, a writ authorizing distraint (*leg.*).

dis'trix, *n.*, a disease of the hair in which individual hairs split.

distrust', *n.*, doubt; suspicion; *v.t.*, to have no confidence in; to suspect.

distrust'ed, *p.p.*, distrust.

distrust'er, *n.*, one who distrusts.

distrust'ful, *adj.*, suspicious; wanting confidence.

distrust'fully, *adv.*, in a distrustful way.

distrust'ing, *pr.p.*, distrust.

disturb', *v.t.*, to agitate; to disquiet; to interfere with.

disturb'ance, *n.*, an interruption of a settled state of things; confusion; a tumult.

disturbed', *p.p.*, disturb.

disturb'er, *n.*, one who, or that which, disturbs.

disturb'ing, *adj.*, causing anxiety; *pr.p.*, disturb.

---

dis'tyle, *n.*, a portico with two columns (*archit.*).

disul'phate, *n.*, an acid salt of sulphuric acid.

disul'phide, *n.*, a sulphide containing two atoms of sulphur in the molecule.

disul'phuret, *n.*, a binary compound of sulphur.

disulphu'ric, *adj.*, applied to an acid containing two atoms of sulphur in each molecule.

disu'nion, *n.*, separation; dissension.

disu'nionist, *n.*, an advocate of disunion.

disunite', *v.t.*, to separate; to set at variance; *v.i.*, to fall asunder.

disunit'ed, *adj.*, separated; *p.p.*, disunite.

disuni'ter, *n.*, anything that disjoins.

disuni'ting, *pr.p.*, disunite.

disu'nity, *n.*, a want of unity.

disu'sage, *n.*, the gradual cessation of use, custom or practice.

disuse', *n.*, *i.q.* disusage.

disuse', *v.t.*, to cease to use.

disused', *p.p.*, disuse.

disus'ing, *pr.p.*, disuse.

disutil'ity, *n.*, a disadvantage.

disyllab'ic, *adj.*, consisting of two syllables only.

disyl'lable, *n.*, a word of two syllables.

ditch, *n.*, a trench; *v.i.*, to dig a ditch; to drain by a ditch; to abandon; (of an aircraft) to descend into water.

ditched', *p.p.*, ditch.

ditch'er, *n.*, one who digs ditches.

ditch'ing, *pr.p.*, ditch.

ditch'water, *n.*, water contained in a ditch; a simile for dullness.

di'theism, *n.*, the doctrine of the existence of good and evil principles in nature.

di'theist, *n.*, one who believes in ditheism.

ditheis'tic, *adj.*, rel. to ditheism.

dith'er, *n.*, a trembling; *v.i.*, to tremble; to waver.

---

dith'ering, *adj.* and *n.*, (a) shaking; (a) quivering.

dith'yramb, *n.*, a Bacchic hymn; an irregular poem of impetuous character.

dithyram'bic, *adj.*, resembling a dithyramb; enthusiastic; *n.*, *i.q.* dithyramb.

di'tone, *n.*, a musical interval measuring two tones.

dit'tany, *n.*, a plant of Southern Europe yielding a fragrant oil.

dit'to, *adj.*, same as aforesaid; (*abbrev.* do).

dittograph'ic, *adj.*, rel. or pert. to dittography.

dittog'raphy, *n.*, a letter, word or phrase repeated in error by a copyist.

dit'ty, *n.*, a song; a little lyric poem.

ditt'y-bag, *n.*, a sailor's or fisherman's box or bag for keeping odds and ends.

ditt'y-box, *n.*, *i.q.* dittybag.

diure'sis, *n.*, an excessive flow of urine.

diuret'ic, *adj.*, tending to excite the secretion of urine, *n.*, a medicine to stimulate the bladder or kidneys.

diur'nal, *adj.*, pert. or rel. to the daytime; daily.

div, *n.*, an evil spirit in Persian mythology.

di'va, *n.*, a great female singer; a prima donna.

div'agate, *v.i.*, to stray; to wander; to digress.

divaga'tion, *n.*, a digression.

di'valent, *adj.*, having two combining equivalents.

divan', *n.*, an oriental court of justice, council or council-chamber; a cushioned seat against a wall; a sofa or bed; a café.

divar'icate, *v.t.* and *i.*, to branch, esp. at an obtuse angle.

divar'icated, *p.p.*, divaricate.

divar'icating, *pr.p.*, divaricate.

divarica'tion, *n.*, a forking.

dive, n., a plunge; the act of diving; a saloon for drinking (colloq.); v.i., to plunge into water head first.

dived, p.p., dive.

di'ver, n., one who dives; a marine swimming bird.

diverge', v.i., to proceed in different directions from one point; to deviate; to differ or vary.

diverged', p.p., diverge.

diver'gence, n., the act of diverging; a deviation from the normal way or standard state.

diver'gency, n., i.q. divergence.

diver'gent, adj., diverging, as lines separating from one another, proceeding from the same point.

diver'gently, adv., in a divergent manner.

diver'ging, pr.p., diverge.

di'vers, adj., different; several.

diverse', adj., unlike.

diverse'ly, adv., in different directions.

diversifica'tion, n., the act of diversifying.

diver'sified, adj., characterized by a variety of forms or objects; p.p., diversify.

diver'siform, adj., of various forms.

diver'sify, v.t., to give variety to; to change and increase the activities carried on.

diver'sifying, pr.p., diversify.

diver'sion, n., the act of diverting; an amusement; a pastime; a feint to mislead an enemy.

diver'sity, n., unlikeness; variety.

divert', v.t., to turn aside; to amuse.

divert'ed, p.p., divert.

divert'er, n., one who, or that which, diverts.

diverticulo'sis, n., the inflammation of a saccule in the colon.

divertic'ulum, n., a pocket-like branch (anat.).

divertimen'to, n., a light, instrumental piece of music (It.).

divert'ing, adj., entertaining; pr.p., divert.

divert'ingly, adv., in a diverting way.

divertisse'ment, n., music or other entertainment during an interlude (Fr.).

divert'ive, adj., amusing; interesting.

Div'es, n., rel. to costs at a higher rate (leg.).

divest', v.t., to deprive; to strip.

divest'ed, p.p., divest.

divest'ing, pr.p., divest.

divest'iture, n., the deprivation or surrender of rights, property, etc.

div'i, n., dividend (abbrev., slang).

divi'dable, adj., capable of division.

divide', n., a water-shed; v.t., to part; to set at variance; to split up among a number; v.i., to become separated; to open; to vote by a division into two parts.

divi'ded, adj., separated; at variance; p.p., divide.

div'idend, n., a number to be divided; the profit made by a company, divided among the shareholders.

divi'der, n., one who, or that which, divides.

divi'ding, pr.p., divide.

div'i-div'i, n., the curved pods of a small, tropical American tree, used in tanning.

divid'ual, adj., separate; separable.

divid'ually, adv., in a separate manner.

divina'tion, n., the act of divining; an omen.

divine', adj., rel. to God, or to a heathen deity; godlike; holy; n., a priest; a theologian; v.t., to prognosticate; to guess; v.i., to practise divination.

divined', p.p., divine.

divine'ly, adv., by the agency of God; in a supreme degree.

divi'ner, n., a soothsayer; a guesser.

di'ving, n., the art of descending into water to work at the bottom; an aquatic sport; pr.p., dive.

di'ving-bell, n., an apparatus used in professional diving.

divi'ning, pr.p., divine.

divin'ity, n., a godhead; divine nature; God; a celestial being; sacredness; the science of theology.

divisibil'ity, n., the quality of being divisible.

divis'ible, adj., capable of division.

divis'ibleness, n., i.q. divisibility.

divi'sion, n., a partition; a distinct segment or portion; a certain portion of an organized whole, as of an army; variance; one of the four fundamental rules of arithmetic.

divi'sional, adj., rel. to division, or to a division or district.

divi'sionism, n., the practice of painting with pure colours.

divi'sive, adj., tending to divide.

divi'sively, adv., in a divisive manner.

divi'sor, n., the number by which the dividend is divided.

divor'cable, adj., eligible to be divorced.

divorce', n., a severance, sundering; a legal separation of married persons involving termination of the marriage; v.t., to divorce.

divorced', p.p., divorce.

divorcee', n., a divorced person.

divorce'ment, n., i.q. divorce.

divor'cer, n., one who divorces.

divor'cing, pr.p., divorce.

div'ot, n., a sod or turf used in some places for roofing; the piece of turf a golf player displaces.

divulga'tion, n., a revealing.

divulge', v.t., to reveal a secret.

divulged', p.p., divulge.

divulge'ment, n., i.q. divulgation.

divul'gence, n., i.q. divulgation.

divul'ger, *n.*, one who divulges.

divul'ging, *pr.p.*, divulge.

divul'sion, *n.*, a rending asunder; a laceration.

Dix'ie, *n.*, the former southern slave states of the U.S.A.

dix'y, -ie, *n.*, a field-service kettle or pot.

di'zen, *v.t.*, to dress gaudily; to bedizen.

dizz'ily, *adv.*, in a dizzy manner.

diz'ziness, *n.*, giddiness; vertigo.

diz'zy, *adj.*, giddy, heedless; causing giddiness.

do, *v.t.* and *auxil.*, to effect; to cause to be, to cheat; to prepare.

doat, *v.t.*, *i.q.* dote.

dob'bin, *n.*, sea gravel mixed with sand; an old horse.

dob'erman(n), *n.*, a large, smooth-coated, German terrier.

do'cent, *n.*, a tutor.

Docet'ic, *adj.*, of the belief that Christ's body was spiritual rather than real.

Docet'ism, *n.*, the theory that Christ's body was spiritual rather than real.

Docet'ist, *n.*, one who believes in Docetism.

doch'-an-do'ris, *n.*, a last drink (*Scot.*).

doch'miac, *adj.* and *n.*, a five-syllabled metrical foot, consisting of a short, two longs, a short and a long.

do'cile, *adj.*, teachable; tractable; easy to control.

docil'ity, *n.*, the state of being docile.

docimas'tic, *adj.*, proving by experiments or tests; metallurgic.

doc'imasy, *n.*, metallurgy; the art of assaying metals.

docimol'ogy, *n.*, a treatise on the art of testing.

dock, *n.*, a weed with broad leaves; the place where a prisoner stands in court; an artificial basin for ships; *v.t.*, to bring into a dock; to shorten.

dock'age, *n.*, charges for the use of docks.

docked, *p.p.*, dock.

docker, *n.*, a dock labourer.

dock'et, *n.*, a summary; any small written paper; *v.t.*, to mark the contents of a paper on the back.

dock'eted, *p.p.*, docket.

dock'eting, *pr.p.*, docket.

dock'ing, *pr.p.*, dock.

dock'land, *n.*, the district surrounding a dock area.

dock'yard, *n.*, an enclosure containing docks.

doc'tor, *n.*, a university graduate of the highest degree in any faculty; a physician; a teacher; *v.t.*, to treat medically; to falsify.

doc'toral, *adj.*, rel. to a doctor's degree.

doc'torand, *n.*, a candidate for a doctor's degree.

doc'torate, *n.*, the degree of doctor.

doc'tored, *p.p.*, doctor.

doc'toring, *pr.p.*, doctor.

doctrinaire', *n.*, a theorist who ignores practical considerations (*Fr.*).

doc'trinal, *adj.*, pert. or rel. to doctrine.

doc'trine, *n.*, a principle; a set of opinions or beliefs; teaching.

doc'ument, *n.*, an official or authoritative paper containing instructions or proof; any formal written or printed paper.

documen'tal, *adj.*, *i.q.* documentary.

documen'tary, *adj.*, consisting of documents.

documenta'tion, *n.*, the use of documentary evidence; the listing of documents; a group of documents related to a subject.

doc'umented, *adj.*, illustrated with documentary proofs.

dod'der, *n.*, a leafless parasitic plant; *v.i.*, to shake or tremble.

dod'dered, *adj.*, overgrown with dodder; *p.p.*, dodder.

dodd'erer, *n.*, a feeble person.

dod'dering, *adj.*, feeble; having impaired faculties.

dodd'eringly, *adv.*, in a doddering way.

dodd'ery, *adj.*, skaky; feeble; frail.

dodec'agon, *n.*, a regular polygon having twelve equal sides and angles.

dodecagyn'ian, *adj.*, having twelve styles.

dodecahe'dron, *n.*, a solid having twelve equal faces, each a regular pentagon.

dodecan'drian, *adj.*, having twelve stamens (*bot.*).

dodecan'drous, *adj.*, *i.q.* dodecandrian.

dodecasyl'lable, *n.*, a word of twelve syllables.

dodge, *n.*, a trick; *v.i.*, to start suddenly aside; *v.t.*, to evade; to baffle.

dodged, *p.p.*, dodge.

dodg'er, *n.*, one who dodges.

dodg'ing, *pr.p.*, dodge.

dodg'y, *adj.*, tricky (*slang*).

do'do, *n.*, an extinct bird of Mauritius.

doe, *n.*, the female of a buck.

do'er, *n.*, one who does or performs.

does, *v.t.* and *auxil.*, 3rd pers. sing. *pres.* *of* to do.

doe'skin, *adj.*, made of doeskin; *n.*, the skin of a doe; a twilled woollen cloth.

does'n't, *abbrev.* of *does not* (*colloq.*).

doff, *v.t.*, to take off; *v.i.*, to take off the hat.

doffed, *p.p.*, doff.

doff'ing, *pr.p.*, doff.

dog, *n.*, a domesticated, canine quadruped; a term of contempt; a gay fellow (*colloq.*); *v.t.*, to follow closely.

dog'ate, *n.*, the office of a doge.

dog'berry, *n.*, the berry of the dogwood.

dog'-cart, *n.*, a gig, the rear occupants facing backwards.

dog'-coll'ar, *n.*, a dog's collar; a stiff collar; a clerical collar.

dog'-days, *n. pl.*, the days from about 3 July to 11 August; days of great heat.

doge, *n.*, the chief magistrate of the old republics of Venice and Genoa.

dog'-eared, *adj.*, having the corners turned down and crumpled.

dog'fight, *n.*, a shindy; a mêlèe; an aerial combat.

dog'fish, *n.*, a kind of small shark.

dogged, *p.p.*, dog.

dog'ged, *adj.*, obstinate; sullen.

dog'gedly, *adv.*, in a dogged manner.

dog'gedness, *n.*, the quality of being dogged.

dog'ger, *n.*, a Dutch, two-masted, fishing boat.

dog'gerel, *adj.*, defective in sense and rhythm; *n.*, extremely poor verses.

dog'ging, *pr.p.*, dog.

dog'gish, *adj.*, brutal; snappish.

dogg'o, *adv.*, motionless (*slang*).

dogg'y, *adj.*, devoted to dogs.

dog'ma, *n.*, a doctrine received on authority.

dogmat'ic, *adj.*, pert. or rel. to dogmas; dictatorial.

dogmat'ical, *adj.*, *i.q.* dogmatic.

dogmat'ically, *adv.*, in a dictatorial way.

dogmat'icalness, *n.*, the quality of being dogmatic.

dogmat'ics, *n. pl.*, doctrinal theology.

dog'matism, *n.*, arrogant assertion.

dog'matist, *n.*, one who is dogmatic.

dog'matize, *v.i.*, to assert authoritatively.

dog'matized, *p.p.*, dogmatize.

dog'matizer, *n.*, one who dogmatizes.

dog'matizing, *pr.p.*, dogmatize.

do'-good'er, *n.*, an idealistic person; a would-be reformer.

dog'-rose, *n.*, the British wild rose.

dog's'-ear, *n.*, the corner of a leaf turned down by careless handling of a book; *v.t.*, to turn down and disfigure in this way.

dog's'-eared, *adj.*, with the corners crumpled.

dog's'-meat, *n.*, meat for, or only fit for, dogs.

dog'-star, *n.*, the star Sirius, of the first magnitude.

dog-tired', *adj.*, over-fatigued.

dog'tooth, *n.*, a canine tooth; an ornament characteristic of Early English architecture.

dog'-trot, *n.*, a gentle trot.

dog'-watch, *n.*, a watch of two turns on board ship.

dog'-weary, *adj.*, *i.q.* dog-tired.

dog'wood, *n.*, a British hedgerow shrub; the cornel.

doh, *n.*, the first key-note of a tonic solfa scale.

dohl, *n.*, a kind of pulse like dried pease.

doi'ly, *n.*, a small ornamental table- or plate-mat. (Also *doyley*.)

do'ing, *pr.p.*, do.

do'ings, *n. pl.*, things done; performances; conduct.

doit, *n.*, a small Dutch copper coin; the old Scottish penny; any small coin.

doit'ed, *adj.*, crazed, esp. with age.

dolab'riform, *adj.*, in the shape of an axe or hatchet.

dol'ce, *adj. or adv.*, soft and sweet, in music (*It.*).

dol'drums, *n. pl.*, the equatorial belt of calms; low spirits.

dole, *n.*, a gratuity or allowance; grief; *v.t.*, to deal out in small quantities.

doled, *p.p.*, dole.

dole'ful, *adj.*, mournful.

dole'fully, *adv.*, mournfully.

dole'fulness, *n.*, the state of being doleful.

dol'erite, *n.*, coarse, basaltic rock.

dole'some, *adj.*, *i.q.* doleful.

dole'somely, *adv.*, *i.q.* dolefully.

dol'ichocephal'ic, *adj.*, long-headed.

do'ling, *pr.p.*, dole.

do'-little, *n.*, an idler.

doll, *n.*, a toy baby or puppet used as a plaything.

dol'lar, *n.*, a silver coin of varying value; the unit of currency used in the U.S.A., etc.

doll'ish, *adj.*, like a doll.

doll'ishly, *adv.*, in a dollish manner.

doll'ishness, *n.*, dressing-up.

doll'op, *n.*, a lump of food, etc. (*colloq.*).

dolly, *n.*, a little doll.

dol'man, *n.*, a kind of Turkish robe; a lady's wide jacket.

dol'men, *n.*, a large, unhewn stone resting on two or more upright stones; a cromlech; a stone circle.

dol'omite, *n.*, a rock, composed of the carbonates of lime and magnesia.

dolomit'ic, *adj.*, of the nature of dolomite.

dolorif'ic, *adj.*, causing grief.

doloro'so, *adj.*, plaintive, pathetic (*mus., It.*).

dol'orous, *adj.*, sorrowful.

dol'orously, *adv.*, in a dolorous manner.

dolose', *adj.*, having criminal intentions; wilfully deceitful.

do'lour, *n.*, sorrow.

dol'phin, *n.*, the name of several species of cetaceans; the grampus; a mooring buoy or post.

dolt, *n.*, a blockhead.

dolt'ish, *adj.*, stupid.

dolt'ishly, *adv.*, in a stupid way.

dolt'ishness, *n.*, stupidity.

domain', *n.*, a dominion; a landed estate; a demesne.

dome, *n.*, the hemispherical roof of a building; the rounded top of any building or chamber.

domed, *adj.*, provided with a dome.

Domes'day, *adj.*, rel. or pert. to the survey and census of William the Conqueror.

domes'tic, *adj.*, rel. to the home; tame; rel. to one's own country; *n.*, a household servant.

domes'ticate, *v.t.*, to make domestic; to tame; to reduce from a wild to a cultivated condition.

domes'ticated, *p.p.,* domesticate.

domes'ticating, *pr.p.,* domesticate.

domestica'tion, *n.,* the state of being domesticated.

domestic'ity, *n.,* the state of being domestic.

dom'ett, *n.,* wool and cotton fabric used for shrouds, etc.

dom'ical, *adj.,* dome-like.

dom'icile, *n.,* a place of residence; a permanent abode; *v.t.,* to establish in a fixed residence.

dom'iciled, *p.p.,* domicile.

domicil'iary, *adj.,* rel. to a domicile.

domicil'iate, *v.t., i.q.* domicile.

domicil'iated, *p.p.,* domiciliate.

domicil'iating, *pr.p.,* domiciliate.

domicilia'tion, *n.,* a permanent residence.

dom'iciling, *pr.p.,* domicile.

dom'inance, *n.,* ascendancy.

dom'inant, *adj.,* prevailing; predominant; *n.,* the fifth tone of the diatonic scale.

dom'inate, *v.t.,* to have power over; to govern.

dom'inated, *p.p.,* dominate.

dom'inating, *pr.p.,* dominate.

domina'tion, *n.,* government; tyranny.

dom'inative, *adj.,* governing; imperious.

dom'inator, *n.,* one who, or that which dominates.

domineer', *v.i.* and *t.,* to rule or command insolently.

domineered', *p.p.,* domineer.

domineer'ing, *adj.,* overbearing; *pr.p.,* domineer.

domineer'ingly, *adv.,* in a domineering manner.

Domin'ical, *adj.,* rel. to Sunday or the Lord's Day; *n.,* one of seven letters used in calendars.

Domin'ican, *adj.,* rel. or pert. to St. Dominic or his religious Order of Preachers; *n.,* a member of this Order; a Black Friar.

dom'inie, *n.,* a Scottish schoolmaster.

domin'ion, *n.,* supreme authority; territory under a government; *pl.,* an order of angels.

dom'ino, *n.,* a masquerade dress; a half-mask; a dotted tablet used in a game.

dom'inoes, *n. pl.,* a game played with dotted oblong tablets.

dom'inus, *n.,* a lord or master; an owner (*Lat.*).

don, *n.,* a Spanish title of courtesy; a university dignitary; *v.t.,* to put on; to assume.

do'na(h), *n.,* the fem. of don; a sweetheart (*slang*).

donate', *v.i.* and *t.,* to give; to bestow.

dona'ted, *p.p.,* donate.

dona'ting, *pr.p.,* donate.

dona'tion, *n.,* a gratuity; a gift.

Don'atism, *n.,* the doctrines of Donatus.

Don'atist, *n.,* a follower of Donatus.

don'ative, *n.,* a gift; in law, a benefice bestowed by a patron without the intervention of a bishop.

don'ator, *n.,* one who gives.

don'atory, *n.,* the recipient of a donation.

Dona'tus, *n.,* the founder of a sect in N. Africa in the fourth century who believed that saintliness was essential to belong to the Church of Christ.

done, *interj.,* agreed; *p.p.,* do.

donee', *n.,* the recipient of a grant or gift.

don'ga, *n.,* a gully; a ravine (*S. Africa*).

don'jon, *n.,* the principal tower of a castle; a keep.

don'key, *n.,* an ass.

don'key-engine, *n.,* a small, subsidiary steam engine.

don'na, *n.,* an Italian, Spanish or Portuguese lady.

donned, *p.p.,* don.

don'ning, *pr.p.,* don.

donn'ish, *adj.,* like a don.

donn'ishness, *n.,* the characteristic behaviour of a don.

Donn'ybrook, *n.,* a fair; a scene of uproar; a free fight.

do'nor, *n.,* a giver.

don't, *n.,* prohibition; the abbrev. of *do not* (*colloq.*).

doo'dle, *n.,* a scrawly drawing; *v.i.,* to scrawl or to draw absent-mindedly.

doo'dlebug, *n.,* a flying-bomb (*colloq.*); a device for locating minerals.

doo'lie, doo'ly, *n.,* a palanquin.

doom, *n.,* final judgment; fate; ruin; *v.t.,* to condemn.

doomed, *p.p.,* doom.

doom'ing, *pr.p.,* doom.

dooms'day, *n.,* the day of judgment.

door, *n.,* a device of wood or other material which closes the access to a room or building, and is designed to hinge, slide, or revolve on a central, vertical pivot.

door'bell, *n.,* a bell on a door for ringing within the building.

door'keeper, *n.,* a porter.

door'mat, *n.,* a mat placed at a door for rubbing mud from shoes.

door'nail, *n.,* the nail on which a door-knocker strikes.

door'step, *n.,* the stone at a threshold.

door'way, *n.,* the entrance into a room or building.

dop, *n.,* a cheap, S. African brandy; a dram of liquor.

dope, *n.,* a thick liquid used as a lubricant, etc.; a narcotic; *v.t.* and *i.* to drug.

dop'per, *n.,* an Anabaptist.

dor(r), *n.,* a British beetle.

Dor'a, *n.,* an acronym for *Defence of the Realm Act.*

dora'do, *n.,* a splendidly coloured sea-fish; a dolphin, a southern constellation of six stars.

Dor'cas, *adj.*, pert. or rel. to a society of ladies who make garments for the poor.

do'ree, *n.*, *i.q.* dory (the fish).

Do'rian, *adj.*, pert. or rel. to the Dorians, a people of Ancient Greece.

Dor'ic, *adj.*, *i.q.* Dorian; naming one of the ancient Greek orders or architecture; *n.*, a rustic dialect.

Dor'icism, *n.*, a peculiarity of the Doric dialect.

dor'mancy, *n.*, the state of being dormant.

dor'mant, *adj.*, sleeping; not in action; not claimed.

dor'mer, *n.*, a window in a roof.

dor'mitive, *adj.*, tending to cause sleep; *n.*, a soporific.

dor'mitory, *n.*, a building or room to sleep in.

dor'mobile, *n.*, a motorized caravan.

dor'mouse, *n.*, a small rodent, torpid in the winter.

dor'my, *adj.*, a golf term implying that a person is up by as many holes as remain to play.

dorp, *n.*, a village; a small township (*Dutch*).

dor'sal, *adj.*, rel. to the back.

dor'sel, *n.*, a pannier; a hanging of rich material at the back of a throne or altar.

dor'sigerous, *adj.*, carrying the young on the back.

dor'sum, *n.*, a ridge; the back of an animal (*Lat.*).

dort'our, -ter, *n.*, a bedroom, a dormitory, esp. in a monastery.

do'ry, *n.*, a yellow European food-fish; a small boat.

do'sage, *n.*, the process of improving wine by additions of other substances; the prescribed frequency and amount of medicine.

dose, *n.*, the quantity of medicine to be taken at one time; *v.t.*, to physic.

dosed, *p.p.*, dose.

do'sing, *pr.p.*, dose.

doss, *n.*, a bed in a dosshouse (*slang*); *v.i.*, to sleep.

dos'sal, *n.*, *i.q.* dorsel.

doss'er, *n.*, one who lodges in a dosshouse.

doss'-house, *n.*, a cheap lodging-house.

dossier', *n.*, a collection of all the papers rel. to some matter (*Fr.*); a brief.

dos'sil, *n.*, a plug of lint for a wound.

dost, *v.t.* and *auxil.*, 2nd pers. sing. *pres. of* to do.

dot, *n.*, a speck; a small spot; *v.t.*, to mark with dots.

do'tage, *n.*, the childishness of old age.

do'tard, *n.*, a man whose mind is enfeebled by age.

dota'tion, *n.*, the bestowal of a dowry; an endowment.

dote, *v.i.*, to be senile; to love to excess.

do'ted, *p.p.*, dote.

do'tel, *n.*, a dotard; a silly fellow.

do'ter, *n.*, one who dotes.

doth, *v.t.* and *auxil.*, 3rd pers. sing. *pres. of* to do.

do'ting, *pr.p.*, dote.

do'tingly, *adv.*, with excessive fondness.

dot'tard, *n.*, an old, decayed tree.

dot'ted, *p.p.*, dot.

dot'ter, *n.*, a device for elevating a naval gun in accordance with the ship's roll.

dot'terel, *n.*, a kind of plover.

dot'ting, *pr.p.*, dot.

dot'tle, -tel, *n.*, a small piece of tobacco left unsmoked in a pipe.

dott'y, *adj.*, marked with dots; feeble-minded; half-witted (*colloq.*).

Dou'ai, -ay, *adj.*, (name describing) the Roman Catholic Bible in English; *n.*, a place in France.

douane', *n.*, a custom-house (*Fr.*).

doub'le, *adj.*, twofold; twice as much; deceitful; *n.*, a duplicate; a quick step in marching; *v.t.*, to make double; to pass round; *v.i.*, to run.

doub'le-bar'rel(l)ed, *adj.*, having two barrels.

doub'le-bass', *n.*, a large viol with deep tones.

doub'lecross', *n.*, a betrayal of both sides; *v.t.* (loosely) to cheat; to betray (*slang*).

doub'led, *p.p.*, double.

doub'le-deal'ing, *adj.*, deceitful; *n.*, duplicity.

double entente, *n.*, a double meaning (*Fr.*).

doub'le-face, *n.*, double dealing; hypocrisy.

doub'le-faced, *adj.*, hypocritical.

doub'leness, *n.*, the state of being double.

doub'let, *n.*, a kind of waistcoat; one of two words really the same but differing in form.

dou'bleton, *n.*, two cards only of a suit (dealt to a player).

doub'ling, *pr.p.*, double.

doubloon', *n.*, a Spanish gold coin.

doublure', *n.*, an ornamental, leather lining inside a book-cover.

doub'ly, *adv.*, to twice the extent.

doubt, *n.*, uncertainty of mind; want of belief; suspicion; *v.i.*, to be uncertain; *v.i.*, to distrust.

doubt'able, *adj.*, liable to be doubted.

doubt'ed, *p.p.*, doubt.

doubt'er, *n.*, one who doubts.

doubt'ers, *n.*, the pl. of doubter.

doubt'ful, *adj.*, undetermined; not certain.

doubt'fully, *adv.*, in a doubtful manner.

doubt'fulness, *n.*, the state of being doubtful.

doubt'ing, *adj.*, unsure; *pr.p.*, doubt.

doubt'ingly, *adv.*, in a doubting manner.

doubt'less, *adv.*, unquestionably.

doubts, *n.*, the pl. of doubt.

douce, *adj.*, sober; gentle (*Scot.*).

douceur', *n.*, a gratuity; a bribe (*Fr.*).

douche, *n.*, a kind of bath in which a jet of water or vapour is directed upon some part of the body (*Fr.*).

dough, *n.*, paste of bread; money (*slang*).

dough'boy, *n.*, a boiled dumpling.

dough'nut, *n.*, a small round cake, usually with some preserve in the centre.

dough'tily, *adv.*, with doughtiness.

dough'tiness, *n.,* bravery; valour.

dough'ty, *adj.*, valiant; noble.

dough'y, *adj.*, like dough; flabby and pale.

Dou'khobors, *n. pl.*, a religious sect similar to Quakers.

doum, *n.*, an Egyptian palm-tree.

dour, *adj.*, stubborn; grim (*Scot.*).

dour'ly, *adv.*, in a dour manner.

douse, *v.t.*, to plunge into water; to extinguish. (Also *dowse*.)

doused, *p.p.*, douse.

dous'ing, *pr.p.*, douse.

dove, *n.*, a kind of pigeon.

dove'cot(e), *n.*, a house for doves.

dove'like, *adj.*, like a dove; gentle.

dove'tail, *n.*, a method of fastening boards at right angles; *v.t.* and *i.*, to unite in this way; to fit exactly.

dove'tailed, *p.p.*, dovetail.

dove'tailing, *n.*, the state of being dovetailed; *pr.p.*, dovetail.

dow, *i.q.* dhow.

dow'able, *adj.*, entitled to dower.

dow'ager, *n.*, the widow of a person of rank whose heir has a wife.

dow'diness, *n.*, the state of being dowdy; shabbiness.

dow'dy, *adj.*, illdressed.

dow'dyish, *adj.*, rather dowdy.

dow'el, *n.*, a wooden or iron pin used in fastening pieces of wood, etc., edgewise; *v.t.*, to fasten with dowels.

dow'el(l)ed, *p.p.*, dowel.

dow'el(l)ing, *pr.p.*, dowel.

dow'er, *n.*, a wife's portion; a widow's third; *v.t.*, *i.q.* endow.

dow'ered, *p.p.*, dower.

dow'erless, *adj.*, without dower.

dow'las, *n.*, a coarse, linen cloth.

down, *n.*, rising ground; a rounded, grassy hill; the soft covering of birds under the feathers; *prep.* and *adv.*, from a higher to a lower position; *v.t.*, to bring down; to swallow.

down'cast, *adj.*, cast downward; dejected; *n.*, the ventilating shaft down which air passes into a mine.

down'fall, *n.*, a falling down; loss of fortune or fame; ruin.

down'grade, *n.*, a downward course; *v.t.*, to lower in status.

down'graded, *p.p.*, downgrade.

down'grading, *n.*, a lowering; *pr.p.*, downgrade.

down'haul, *n.*, a rope to haul down a sail.

down'hearted, *adj.*, dejected.

down'heartedness, *n.*, depression.

down'hill, *adj.*, sloping downwards; *adv.*, down a slope.

down'iness, *n.*, the quality of being downy.

Down'ing Street, *n.*, place of the British Prime Minister's official residence in London.

down'land, *adj.* and *n.*, (rel. to) undulating areas of a countryside.

down'pour, *n.*, a continuous fall of rain.

down'right, *adj.*, plain; blunt; unceremonious; *adv.*, in plain terms; thoroughly.

down'-shaft, *n.*, *i.q.* downcast.

down'sitting, *n.*, the act of sitting down.

down'stairs, *adj.*, rel. or pert. to the lower part of a house; *adv.*, below; down the stairs.

down'stream, *adv.*, with the current.

down'stroke, *n.*, a downward blow; the thick stroke of a letter.

down'throw, *n.*, a depression of strata on one side of a fault (*geol.*).

down'trodden, *adj.*, trampled upon; oppressed.

down'ward, *adj.* and *adv.*, in a descending course.

down'wards, *adj.* and *adv.*, *i.q.* downward.

down'y, *adj.*, covered with down; soothing; knowing (*slang*).

dow'ry, *n.*, a wife's property at marriage.

dowse, *v.t.*, *i.q.* douse.

dows'er, *n.*, one who searches for hidden water with a divining-rod.

dows'ing, *n.*, finding hidden water or a mineral with a divining-rod; a soaking (*slang*).

doxol'ogy, *n.*, a short hymn glorifying God.

dox'y, *n.*, a theological opinion.

doyen', *n.*, a dean; the senior member (*Fr.*).

doyl'ey, *n.*, *i.q.* doily.

doze, *n.*, a light sleep; *v.i.*, to sleep lightly.

dozed, *p.p.*, doze.

doz'en, *n.*, a collection of twelve, or about twelve, things or persons.

do'zer, *n.*, one who dozes.

do'ziness, *n.*, drowsiness.

do'zing, *pr.p.*, doze.

do'zy, *adj.*, sleepy.

drab, *adj.*, dull-brown; featureless; *n.*, a slut; a thick, dull-brown, woollen cloth; a dull-brown colour.

drabb'et, *n.*, a coarse, drab linen made in Yorkshire.

drab'ble, *v.t.*, to draggle; to wet and dirty.

drab'bled, *p.p.*, drabble.

drab'bling, *pr.p.*, drabble.

drab'ly, *adv.*, in a drab manner; dully.

Dracaen'a, *n.*, a kind of liliaceous tree, including the dragon tree.

drachm, *n.*, a dram; three scruples.

drach'ma, *n.*, a Greek coin and weight.

Dracon'ian, *adj.*, *i.q.* Draconic.

Dracon'ic, *adj.*, rel. or pert. to Draco, the Athenian law-giver; extremely severe.

dracon'iform, *adj.*, dragon-shaped.

draff, *n.*, refuse; hogswash.

draff'y, *adj.*, consisting of draff; worthless.

draft, *n.*, a body of men drawn from a larger body; an order

for payment; a document in outline; a sketch; *v.t.*, to make a sketch or outline of.

draft'ed, *p.p.*, draft.

draft'ing, *pr.p.*, draft.

drafts'man, *n.*, *i.q.* draughtsman.

drag, *n.*, a kind of grapnel for recovering articles lost in the water; an obstacle; a long, open carriage; costume of the opposite sex (*colloq.*); *v.t.*, to pull; to draw along the ground; *v.i.*, to be drawn along; to proceed slowly.

drag'ée, *n.*, a sweetmeat enclosing a nut, etc. (*Fr.*).

dragged, *p.p.*, drag.

drag'ging, *pr.p.*, drag.

drag'gle, *v.t.* and *i.*, to wet and dirty by drawing along the ground.

drag'gled, *p.p.*, draggle.

drag'gling, *pr.p.*, draggle.

drag'net, *n.*, a fishing-net to be drawn along the bottom of a river or pond.

drag'oman, *n.*, an interpreter, esp. one attached to an embassy or consulate in the East.

drag'on, *n.*, a fabulous monster, a sort of winged reptile.

drag'onet, *n.*, a small fish; a little goby.

drag'onfly, *n.*, a large brilliantly coloured insect, found near water.

drag'onish, *adj.*, like a dragon.

dragonnade', *n.*, a Protestant persecution under Louis XIV; *v.t.*, to use the military against citizens.

dragoon', *n.*, a cavalry soldier; *v.t.*, to compel by violence.

dragooned', *p.p.*, dragoon.

dragoon'ing, *pr.p.*, dragoon.

drail, *n.*, a lead-weighted fish-hook and line used for deep dragging through water.

drain, *n.*, a trench to convey water from wet land; a continuous outflow; *v.t.*, to

exhaust; (of a liquid) to deprive by drawing off gradually; *v.i.*, to flow off gradually;

drain'able, *adj.*, capable of being drained.

drain'age, *n.*, a system of drains; the manner in which the waters of a country pass off by rivers.

drained, *p.p.*, drain.

drain'er, *n.*, one who, or that which, drains; a colander.

drain'ing, *pr.p.*, drain.

drain'less, *adj.*, without drains.

drain'pipe, *n.*, a pipe to carry away sewage or waste water.

drain'-trap, *n.*, a device which prevents foul air from escaping from drains.

drake, *n.*, a male duck; a kind of fly used in fishing.

dram, *n.*, the sixteenth part of an ounce avoirdupois; a drink of spirituous liquor.

dra'ma, *n.*, a stage-play; theatrical composition and representation; an emotive event.

dramat'ic, *adj.*, pert. or rel. to drama; theatrical.

dramat'ical, *adj.*, *i.q.* dramatic.

dramat'ically, *adv.*, in a dramatic manner.

dram'atis person'ae, *n. pl.*, (list of) characters in a play (*Lat.*).

dram'atist, *n.*, a playwright.

dram'atize, *v.t.*, to make into a play.

dram'atized, *p.p.*, dramatize.

dram'atizing, *pr.p.*, dramatize.

dram'aturge, *n.*, *i.q.* dramatist.

dramatur'gic, *adj.*, relating to a playwright.

dramatur'gist, *n.*, *i.q.* dramaturge.

dram'aturgy, *n.*, a dramatic composition.

dram'-shop, *n.*, a shop where spirits are sold in small quantities.

drank, *p.p.*, drink.

drape, *v.t.*, to cover with drapery.

draped, *p.p.*, drape.

dra'per, *n.*, a dealer in cloths.

dra'pery, *n.*, the business of a draper; hangings.

dra'ping, *pr.p.*, drape.

dras'tic, *adj.*, powerful; efficacious; harsh.

dras'tically, *adv.*, in a drastic manner.

drat, *v.t.*, to curse; to bother (*vulg.*).

draught, *n.*, the act of drawing; the act of drinking; a drink; a drawing or sketch; the depth a laden ship sinks in water; a current of air; *v.t.*, to sketch roughly.

draught'board, *n.*, a checkered board for the game of draughts.

draught'-engine, *n.*, a mining engine used for pumping, etc.

draught'-horse, *n.*, a horse used for drawing vehicles.

draught'iness, *n.*, the state of being draughty.

draughts, *n. pl.*, a game played with round pieces on a checkered board.

draughts'man, *n.*, one who draws designs and plans. (Also *draftsman*.)

draughts'woman, *n.*, the fem. of draughtsman.

draught'y, *adj.*, exposed to draughts.

Dravid'ian, *adj.*, pert. or rel. to a family of languages spoken in southern India and Ceylon; *n.*, a native race of Ceylon and southern India.

draw, *n.*, a contest in which both parties are equally successful; a lottery; *v.t.*, to pull; to lead; to form a picture; to form a writing.

draw'back, *n.*, a disadvantage; customs duties repaid.

draw'bridge, *n.*, a bridge that may be drawn up or aside.

drawcan'sir, *adj.* and *n.*, (a person) formidable both to friend and foe; a fierce swashbuckler.

drawee', *n.*, the person on whom a bill of exchange is drawn.

draw'er, *n.*, one who draws; a sliding box in a table or other piece of furniture.

draw'ers, *n. pl.*, a garment to cover the lower part of the body and the upper legs.

draw'ing, *n.*, the act of one who draws; a pictorial representation; *pr.p.*, draw.

draw'ing-master, *n.*, one who teaches the art of drawing.

draw'ing-pen, *n.*, a pen for drawing lines.

draw'ing-pin, *n.*, a short pin with a large flat head.

draw'ing-room, *n.*, a reception room.

drawl, *v.i.*, to speak with drawn out utterance.

drawled, *p.p.*, drawl.

drawl'er, *n.*, one who drawls.

drawl'ing, *pr.p.*, drawl.

drawl'ingly, *adv.*, in a drawling manner.

drawn, *p.p.*, draw.

draw'-net, *n.*, a net for catching birds.

draw'-well, *n.*, a deep well with a rope and bucket.

dray, *n.*, a low cart on heavy wheels.

dray'-cart, *n.*, *i.q.* dray.

dray'-horse, *n.*, a horse used in a dray.

dray'man, *n.*, a dray driver or attendant.

dread, *adj.*, terrible; *n.*, a great fear; *v.t.* and *i.*, to fear greatly.

dread'ed, *p.p.*, dread.

dread'ful, *adj.*, terrible.

dread'fully, *adv.*, in a manner to be dreaded.

dread'fulness, *n.*, the quality of being dreadful.

dread'ing, *pr.p.*, dread.

dread'less, *adj.*, intrepid.

dread'lessness, *n.*, fearlessness.

dread'nought, *n.*, a thick, rainproof cloth or garment; formerly an armed ship.

dream, *n.*, the series of thoughts of a sleeping person; *v.i.*, to have images in the mind when asleep; *v.t.*, to see in a dream.

dreamed, *p.p.*, dream.

dream'er, *n.*, one who dreams; a visionary.

dream'-hole, *n.*, a small window in a tower for letting in light and air.

dream'ily, *adv.*, in a dreamy way.

dream'iness, *n.*, the state of being dreamy.

dream'ing, *pr.p.*, dream.

dream'ingly, *adv.*, as though dreaming.

dream'land, *n.*, a world of dreams or fancies.

dream'less, *adj.*, free from dreams.

dreamt', *p.p.*, dream.

dream'y, *adj.*, full of dreams; dream-like.

drear, *adj.*, gloomy; cheerless.

drear'ily, *adv.*, dismally.

drear'iness, *n.*, the state of being dreary.

drear'y, *adj.*, dismal; oppressively monotonous.

dredge, *n.*, an apparatus for clearing the bed of a channel; a dragnet; *v.t.*, to use a dredge; to sprinkle flour on meat to be roasted.

dredged, *p.p.*, dredge.

dredg'er, *n.*, one who, or that which, dredges; a caster for sugar, flour, etc.

dredg'ing, *pr.p.*, dredge.

dredg'ing-box, *n.*, a utensil for dredging flour.

dree, *v.t.*, to submit to one's lot; to endure (*Scot.*).

dreg'gy, *adj.*, consisting of dregs; muddy.

dregs, *n. pl.*, the sediment of liquors; lees; the most worthless of human beings.

drench, *n.*, a purgative for an animal; *v.t.*, to wet thoroughly; to purge with a strong aperient medicine.

drenched, *p.p.*, drench.

dren'cher, *n.*, a drenching shower.

drench'ing, *pr.p.*, drench.

Dres'den, *adj.*, pert. or rel. to china made near Dresden; *n.*, a town of Saxony; porcelain made near there.

dress, *v.t.*, to put clothes on; to prepare, in a general sense; *v.i.*, to clothe oneself; to arrange oneself in a line with others; *n.*, garments; a woman's gown.

dress'age, *n.*, the training of horses in obedience and deportment (*Fr.*).

dress'coat, *n.*, a coat with narrow pointed tails worn at ceremonies.

dressed, *p.p.*, dress.

dress'er, *n.*, one who dresses; a hospital attendant; a kind of sideboard and low cupboard.

dress'ing, *n.*, an application to a wound; manure for land; the preparation of food for cooking; a sauce or cream for a salad; *pr.p.*, dress.

dres'sing-case, *n.*, a case of toilet requisites.

dres'sing-gown, *n.*, a flowing coat worn to cover night attire.

dres'sing-room, *n.*, a room in which one dresses oneself; a room for changing costumes in a theatre.

dres'sing-table, *n.*, a toilet table.

dress'maker, *n.*, a maker of women's garments.

dress'y, *adj.*, wearing showy dress (*colloq.*).

drew, *p.p.*, draw.

drey, *n.*, a squirrel's nest.

drib'ble, *n.*, a trickle; *v.t.*, to let fall in drops; to work a football forward with the feet; *v.i.*, to fall in a quick succession of drops; just to roll (into).

drib'bled, *p.p.*, dribble.

drib'bling, *pr.p.*, dribble.

drib'let, *n.*, a small part doled out as one of a series.

dried, *p.p.*, dry.

dri'er, *n.*, *comp.* of dry; *n.*, one who dries.

dri'est, *adj.*, *super.* of dry.

drift, *adj.*, drifted by wind or water; *n.*, a heap of matter driven together by wind or water; a tendency; an intention; a slow, uncontrolled movement in air or water; *v.i.*, to be driven along by a current.

drift'ed, *p.p.*, drift.

drif'ter, n., a fishing boat.

drift'ing, pr.p., drift.

drift'wood, n., wood drifted by water.

drill, n., a pointed instrument for boring holes; the exercises by which persons are trained; a coarse linen; a kind of baboon; v.t., to bore; to train by exercises.

drilled, p.p., drill.

drill'ing, n., a coarse linen or cotton cloth; pr.p., drill.

drill'-plough, n., a plough for sowing grain in drills or straight rows.

drill'-sergeant, n., a sergeant who drills soldiers.

dri'ly, adv., in a dry manner.

drink, n., liquids to be swallowed; v.i., to swallow liquor; to absorb; to be an habitual drinker; v.t., to imbibe.

drink'able, adj., fit for drink.

drink'er, n., one who drinks.

drink'ing, pr.p., drink.

drink'-offering, n., a Jewish offering of wine.

drip, n., the fall; a boring person (slang); v.i., to fall in drops.

dripped, p.p., drip.

drip'ping, n., the fat which falls from roasting meat; pr.p., drip.

drip'ping-pan, n., a pan to catch dripping.

drip'pings, n. pl., that which drips from anything.

drip'-stone, n., a projecting moulding over a doorway, etc. (archit.).

drive, n., a road prepared for driving; a sweeping blow; v.t., to urge forward; to control a mechanically propelled vehicle; v.i., to travel in a carriage.

driv'el, n., silly, meaningless talk; v.i., to salver; to be foolish.

driv'el(l)ed, p.p., drivel.

driv'el(l)er, n., one who drivels; a fool.

driv'el(l)ing, n., i.q. drivel; pr.p., drivel.

driv'en, p.p., drive.

dri'ver, n., one who, or that which, drives; a wooden golf-club.

drive'way, n., the approach to a building, for vehicles.

dri'ving, adj., supplying power or impetus; pr.p., drive.

dri'ving-shaft, n., a shaft from a driving-wheel setting a machine in motion.

driv'ing-wheel, n., the wheel of a locomotive to which the power is applied.

driz'zle, n., a fine rain; v.i., to rain in small drops.

driz'zled, p.p., drizzle.

driz'zling, pr.p., drizzle.

driz'zly, adj., shedding fine rain.

dro'gher, n., a clumsy sailing vessel used for coasting work.

drogue, n., a floating sea-anchor; a windsock.

droit, n., a right; a legal claim of ownership.

droll, adj., laughable; n., a jester.

droll'ery, n., comicalness.

drol'ly, adv., in a funny or amusing way.

drome, n., the abbrev. for aerodrome (colloq.).

drom'edary, n., the Arabian or single-humped camel.

dro'mograph, n., a device for measuring the speed of blood flowing through the body.

drom'ond, n., a large, medieval ship.

dromophob'ia, n., a morbid fear of crossing streets.

drone, n., the male of the honey-bee; an idler; a humming sound; a bag-pipe's bass note; v.i., to hum, v.t., to speak in a dull manner.

droned, p.p., drone.

dro'ning, pr.p., drone.

dro'nish, adj., lazy; sluggish.

dron'ishly, adv., sluggishly.

drool, v.i., to drivel or slobber.

drooled, p.p., drool.

drool'ing, pr.p., drool.

droop, n., a drooping position; v.i., to bend downward as from weakness; to sag.

drooped, p.p., droop.

droop'ing, pr.p., droop.

droop'ingly, adv., in a drooping manner.

drop, n., a small portion of a liquid falling or about to fall; anything that hangs in the form of a drop; v.t., to let fall; v.i., to fall.

drop'let, n., a little drop.

drop'-out, n., a social misfit.

dropped, p.p., drop.

drop'per, n., a glass rod or tube for letting a liquid fall drop by drop.

drop'ping, pr.p., drop.

dropp'ings, n. pl., that which falls or has fallen in drops, e.g. candle-wax; the dung of beasts or birds.

drop'-scene, n., a scenic picture suspended by pulleys which falls in front of the other scenery in theatres.

drop'sical, adj., diseased with, inclined to, or resembling dropsy.

drop'sy, n., an unnatural collection of fluid in any cavity or in the tissues of the body.

dros'ky, n., a light, four-wheeled carriage used in Russia.

drosom'eter, n., an instrument for measuring dew.

Drosoph'ila, n., a common fruit-fly.

dross, n., waste or worthless matter; the refuse of metals.

dross'iness, n., the quality of being drossy.

dross'y, adj., worthless; impure; pert. to dross.

drought, n., want of rain; aridness.

drought'y, adj., full of drought.

drouth, n., drought; thirst.

drove, n., a number of animals driven in a body; p.p., drive.

dro'ver, n., one who drives cattle or sheep.

drown, v.t., to kill by immersion in water; v.i., to perish by suffocation in water.

drowned, p.p., drown.

drown'ing, pr.p., drown.

drowse, *v.i.*, to sleep imperfectly; *v.t.*, to make dull or stupid.

drowsed, *p.p.*, drowse.

drow′sily, *adv.*, in a drowsy manner.

drow′siness, *n.*, the state of being drowsy.

drows′ing, *pr.p.*, drowse.

drow′sy, *adj.*, sleepy; lulling.

drub, *v.t.*, to cudgel.

drubbed, *p.p.*, drub.

drub′bing, *n.*, a sound beating; *pr.p.*, drub.

drudge, *n.*, one who works hard and without pleasure; *v.i.*, to work hard.

drudged, *p.p.*, drudge.

drudg′er, *n.*, one who drudges; a taskmaster.

drudg′ery, *n.*, ignoble toil; menial, unsatisfying work.

drudg′ing, *pr.p.*, drudge.

drudg′ingly, *adv.*, laboriously.

drug, *n.*, any substance used alone in the preparation of medicines; an article of slow sale; *v.t.*, to administer narcotics to and to stupefy.

drugged, *p.p.*, drug.

drug′get, *n.*, a woollen cloth for temporarily covering carpets or for use as a carpet.

drug′ging, *pr.p.*, drug.

drug′gist, *n.*, one who deals in drugs.

dru′id, *n.*, an ancient Celtic priest.

dru′idess, *n.*, a female druid.

druid′ic, *adj.*, pert. or rel. to the druids.

druid′ical, *adj.*, *i.q.* druidic.

dru′idism, *n.*, the doctrines and rites of the druids.

drum, *n.*, an instrument of music in the form of a hollow cylinder with ends covered with vellum; anything of the shape of a drum; a long, oval mound of drift or diluvial formation; *v.i.*, to beat a drum.

drum′head, *n.*, the head of a drum.

drum′lin, *n.*, *i.q.* drum.

drum′-major, *n.*, the chief drummer of a regiment.

drummed, *p.p.*, drum.

drum′mer, *n.*, one who drums.

drum′ming, *pr.p.*, drum.

Drumm′ond light, *n.*, a limelight or an oxy-hydrogen light.

drum′stick, *n.*, the stick of a drum; the upper part of the leg of a cooked bird.

drunk, *adj.*, intoxicated by alcoholic liquor; *p.p.*, drink.

drunk′ard, *n.*, one given to over-indulgence in strong liquor.

drunk′en, *adj.*, *i.q.* drunk; proceeding from intoxication.

drunk′enly, *adv.*, in a drunken manner.

drunk′enness, *n.*, the state of being drunk; inebriety.

drupa′ceous, *adj.*, like a drupe.

drupe, *n.*, a stone fruit.

drup′el, *n.*, a small drupe in compound fruit, as in the blackberry.

drupe′let, *n.*, *i.q.* drupel.

Druse, *n.*, one of a Syrian people and religious sect.

druse, *n.*, a cavity in a rock having its interior surface studded with crystals.

dry, *adj.*, destitute of moisture; uninteresting; quietly sarcastic; *v.t.*, to make dry; *v.i.*, to grow dry.

dry′ad, *n.*, a nymph of the woods.

dry′asdust, *adj.*, extremely uninteresting.

dry′clean, *v.t.*, to clean with spirit, etc.

dry′-dock, *n.*, a graving dock from which the water is emptied in order that a vessel may be repaired.

dry′er, *n.*, one who, or that which, dries.

dry′-goods, *n. pl.*, textiles; non-liquid groceries and canned goods.

dry′ing, *pr.p.*, dry.

dry′ly, *adv.*, without moisture, affection or interest; sarcastically. (Also *drily*.)

dry′ness, *n.*, the state or quality of being dry.

dry′-nurse, *n.*, a nurse who tends but does

not suckle; *v.t.*, to bring up in this way.

dry′-rot, *n.*, a disease of timber which reduces it to powder.

dry′salt, *v.t.*, to cure by salting and drying.

dry′salter, *n.*, a dealer in chemicals.

dry′shod, *adv.*, without wetting the feet.

du′ad, *n.*, a pair; a combination of two.

du′al, *adj.*, twofold; *n.*, the grammatical form used in some languages when two things are referred to.

du′alin, *n.*, a powerful explosive of nitre, nitroglycerin and sawdust.

du′alism, *n.*, the belief in two antagonistic principles governing human life.

du′alist, *n.*, a believer in dualism.

du′alis′tically, *adv.*, in a dualistic manner.

dual′ity, *n.*, the state of being dual.

dub, *n.*, a deep pool in northern streams; a puddle (*slang*); *v.t.*, to strike with a sword and make a knight; to give a new name to; to rub (leather) with grease; to make another recording of a sound-track of film; to add sound effects or music to a film, radio or television production (abbrev. of double).

du′bash, *n.*, a native Indian interpreter or commissionaire.

dubbed, *p.p.*, dub.

dub′ber, *n.*, one who dubs.

dubb′in, *n.*, *i.q.* dubbing.

dub′bing, *n.*, grease used for smoothing and rendering leather watertight; *pr.p.*, dub.

dubi′ety, *n.*, doubtfulness.

du′bious, *adj.*, doubtful.

du′biously, *adv.*, in a dubious manner.

du′biousness, *n.*, the state of being dubious.

du′bitable, *adj.*, liable to be doubted.

dubita′tion, *n.*, the act of doubting or hesitating.

dub′itative, *adj.*, expressing or inclined to doubt or hesitation.

du′cal, *adj.*, pert. or rel. to a duke.

duc′at, *n.*, a gold or silver coin, formerly used in many European countries.

ducatoon′, *n.*, a silver coin once common on the Continent.

Du′ce, *n.*, the title assumed by Mussolini, an Italian dictator.

duch′ess, *n.*, the wife of a duke.

duchesse′, *n.*, a kind of satin (*Fr.*).

duch′y, *n.*, a dukedom.

duck, *n.*, a coarse cloth, usually white; a water-fowl; a bend of the head; an amphibious landing-craft; *v.t.*, to dip in water and suddenly withdraw; *v.i.*, to stoop; to bow; to evade.

duck′board, *n.*, a slatted timber path.

ducked, *p.p.*, duck.

duck′er, *n.*, one who ducks; a bathing-pond; a kind of diving bird; a breeder of ducks.

duck′ing, *pr.p.*, duck.

duck′ling, *n.*, a young duck.

duck′weed, *n.*, an aquatic plant that floats on the surface of still or gently running water.

duct, *n.*, a tube by which a fluid is conveyed.

duc′tile, *adj.*, capable of being drawn out into a thread.

ductil′ity, *n.*, the quality of being ductile.

dud, *adj.*, useless; *n.*, a defective thing (*colloq.*).

dud′der, *v.i.*, to shiver; to tremble.

dude, *n.*, a fop (*Amer.*).

dud(h)een′, *n.*, a short clay pipe (*Irish*).

dudg′eon, *n.*, angry resentment.

dud′ish, *adj.*, foppish (*slang*).

due, *adj.*, demanding payment or performance; *n.*, a toll, tax or tribute.

du′el, *n.*, a single combat.

du′el(l)er, *n.*, *i.q.* duellist.

du′el(l)ing, *n.*, the act or practice of engaging in duels.

du′el(l)ist, *n.*, one who engages in duels.

duel′lo, *n.*, a duel; the code of laws regulating duels.

duen′na, *n.*, an elderly woman who takes charge of a younger one (*Span.*).

duet(t)′, *n.*, a musical composition for two voices or instruments.

duett′ist, *n.*, one who plays duets.

duet′to, *n.*; *i.q.* duet (*It.*).

duff, *n.*, a stiff, flour pudding containing dried fruit, boiled in a cloth.

duf′fel, duf′fle, *n.*, frieze; a coarse woollen cloth.

duf′fer, *n.*, a stupid person; a cheat.

dug, *n.*, the pap or nipple of an animal; *p.p.*, dig.

dug′ong, *n.*, a large, herbivorous mammal of Indian seas.

dug′out, *n.*, a shelter dug in the ground or in trenches; a canoe hollowed out of a tree-trunk.

duik′er, *n.*, a small, S. African antelope.

duke, *n.*, a nobleman of highest rank; a sovereign prince.

duke′dom, *n.*, the territory or rank of a duke.

Duk′eries, *n. pl.*, an English rural district in Nottinghamshire containing several ducal estates.

Dul′ag, *n.*, a camp for prisoners of war in transit (*Ger.*).

dul′cet, *adj.*, melodious.

dul′cified, *p.p.*, dulcify.

dul′cify, *v.t.*, to render agreeable to the taste.

dul′cifying, *pr.p.*, dulcify.

dul′cimer, *n.*, a stringed musical instrument, played by being struck by two hammers.

dul′cin, *n.*, a sweet substance used in diabetes.

Dulcine′a, *n.*, a sweetheart; the girl beloved by Don Quixote.

dul′citone, *n.*, a keyboard instrument sounding similar to a celesta.

dull′a, *n.*, veneration paid to saints or angels.

dull, *adj.*, without life or spirit; cheerless; dim; blunt; *v.t.*, to make dull.

dull′ard, *n.*, a blockhead.

dulled, *p.p.*, dull.

dull′er, *adj.*, comp. of dull.

dull′est, *adj.*, super. of dull.

dull′ing, *pr.p.*, dull.

dul′ly, *adv.*, in a dull manner.

dul(l)ness, *n.*, the character of being dull.

dulse, *n.*, an edible seaweed.

du′ly, *adv.*, properly.

Du′ma, *n.*, the Russian parliament 1905–17.

dumb, *adj.*, unable to utter any articulate sounds; silent.

dumb′-bell, *n.*, a free-standing piece of gymnastic apparatus, grasped, and used for strengthening hand and arm.

dumbfound′, *v.t.*, to strike dumb; to confuse.

dumbfound′ed, *p.p.*, dumbfound.

dumbfound′ing, *pr.p.*, dumbfound.

dum′bledor(e), *n.*, a bumble-bee; a cockchafer (*dial.*).

dumb′ly, *adv.*, without speech.

dumb′ness, *n.*, the state of being dumb.

dumb′show, *n.*, gesture without words.

dumb′wait′er, *n.*, a stand with (usu. revolving) shelves.

dum′dum, *n.*, a soft-cored bullet.

dum′my, *adj.*, fictitious; *n.*, the exposed hand at bridge; any sham object; a lay-figure.

du′mose, *adj.*, bushy; resembling a bush in growth and habit (*bot.*).

dump, *n.*, a place for rubbish; *v.t.*, to deposit carelessly; to sell cheaply in a foreign country owing to protection at home.

dumped, *p.p.*, dump.

dump′ing, *pr.p.*, dump.

dump′ish, *adj.*, melancholy.

dump′ling, *n.*, a spherical comestible made from flour and suet.

dumps, *n. pl.,* low spirits.

dump'y, *adj.,* short and thick.

dun, *adj.,* dull brown; *n.,* one who duns; a maund; *v.t.,* to demand a debt in a pressing manner from (*colloq.*); to importune.

dunce, *n.,* an ignoramus.

dun'der, *n.,* the dregs of sugar-cane juice used in distilling rum.

dun'derhead, *n.,* a blockhead; a stupid person.

dun'derheaded, *adj.,* stupid.

Dundrear'y, *n.,* long side whiskers worn without a beard.

dune, *n.,* a low sandhill on the coast.

dun'fish, *n.,* cured codfish.

dung, *n.,* the excrement of animals; *v.t.,* to manure with dung; *v.i.,* to void excrement.

dungaree', *n.,* a coarse calico used in overalls as a working dress.

dunged, *p.p.,* dung.

dun'geon, *n.,* a deep, dark prison; a donjon or keep.

dung'hill, *n.,* a heap of dung; a mean abode.

dung'ing, *pr.p.,* dung.

dung'y, *adj.,* full of dung.

dung'-yard, *n.,* a yard in which dung is collected.

duniwas'sal, *n.,* a cadet of a Highland family of rank (*Scot.*).

dunk, *v.t. and i.,* to dip (bread, cake, etc.) into soup or a beverage while eating.

Dunkirk', *n.,* (scene of) the evacuation of a defeated army by sea, e.g. the British from Dunkirk in May 1940; a port in France.

dun'lin, *n.,* a redbacked sandpiper.

Dunlop', *n.,* a cheese made at Dunlop in Ayrshire; a make of rubber tyre for a motor-car, etc.

dun'nage, *n.,* material laid in the hold of a ship to keep the cargo out of the bilge-water.

dunned, *p.p.,* dun.

dun'ner, *n.,* a debt-collector.

dun'ning, *pr.p.,* dun.

dun'nish, *adj.,* somewhat dun.

dunn'ock, *n.,* a hedgesparrow.

dunt, *n.,* a dull blow.

du'o, *n.,* a duet.

duodecen'nial, *adj.,* consisting of twelve years.

duodec'imal, *adj.,* reckoning by twelves.

duodec'imo, *adj.,* consisting of twelve leaves to a sheet; *n.,* a book made of sheets folded in this way.

duodec'uple, *adj.,* consisting of twelve.

duoden'al, *adj.,* rel. or pert. to the duodenum.

duoden'ary, *adj.,* rel. to the number twelve; increasing by twelves.

duode'num, *n.,* the first portion of the small intestine.

duolit'eral, *adj.,* consisting of two letters only.

du'ologue, *n.,* a dialogue between two.

duom'o, *n.,* an Italian cathedral (*It.*).

dupabil'ity, *n.,* the ability to be duped.

du'pable, *adj.,* gullible.

dupe, *n.,* a person easily led astray by his credulity; *v.t.,* to make a dupe of.

duped, *p.p.,* dupe.

du'pery, *n.,* the practice of duping.

du'ping, *pr.p.,* dupe.

du'ple, *adj.,* double.

du'plex, *adj.,* twofold; *n.,* a kind of flat (*Amer.*).

duplexity, *n.,* the state of being twofold.

du'plicate, *adj.,* double; expressing proportion between squares; *n.,* a second thing of the same kind.

du'plicate, *v.t.,* to double; to make copies of.

du'plicated, *p.p.,* duplicate.

du'plicating, *pr.p.,* duplicate.

duplica'tion, *n.,* the act of doubling.

du'plicative, *adj.,* having the quality of doubling.

du'plicator, *n.,* one who, or that which, duplicates; a copying machine.

du'plicature, *n.,* a doubling; a fold.

duplic'ity, *n.,* doubledealing; deceit.

durabil'ity, *n.,* the quality of being durable.

du'rable, *adj.,* not perishable.

du'rableness, *n., i.q.* durability.

dural'umin, *n.,* a tough aluminium used esp. for aircraft.

duralumin'ium, *n., i.q.* duralumin.

du'ra ma'ter, *n.,* the outer membrane of the brain.

duram'en, *n.,* the heartwood of an exogenous tree.

du'rance, *n.,* imprisonment.

durate', *adj.,* harsh sounding (*mus.*).

dura'tion, *n.,* continuance in time.

dur'bar, *n.,* an Indian state levee; an audience room in an Indian palace.

duress(e)', *n.,* the restraint of liberty; constraint by threats.

dur'ian, *n.,* an E. Indian fruit which has an offensive smell and a delicious taste.

dur'ing, *prep.,* throughout the course of.

durm'ast, *n.,* a kind of oak.

d(h)u'rra, *n.,* an Indian millet.

du'rrie, *n., i.q.* dhurrie.

durst, *p.p.,* dare.

dusk, *adj.,* tending to darkness; *n.,* twilight.

dusk'ily, *adv.,* in a dusky manner.

dusk'iness, *n.,* the state of being dusky.

dusk'ish, *adj.,* rather dusky.

dusk'ishness, *n.,* the state of being duskish.

dusk'y, *adj.,* darkcoloured; not bright.

dust, *n.,* fine, dry particles of matter; *v.t.,* to free from dust.

dust'bin, *n.,* a bin used for rubbish.

dust'bin'ful, *n.,* the amount a dustbin holds when full.

dust'cart, *n.,* a cart for refuse.

dust'ed, *p.p.,* dust.

dust'er, *n.,* a cloth for dusting; a flag (*colloq.*).

dust'-hole, *n.,* a place for rubbish.

dust′iness, *n.*, the state of being dusty.

dust′ing, *pr.p.*, dust.

dust′-jack′et, *n.*, the dust-cover of a book.

dust′man, *n.*, one whose business is to remove rubbish.

dust′pan, *n.*, a pan to hold swept up dust.

dust′y, *adj.*, covered with dust; dust-coloured.

Dutch, *adj.*, pert. or rel. to Holland.

Dutch′man, *n.*, a native of Holland.

du′teous, *adj.*, dutiful; obedient.

du′teously, *adv.*, in a duteous manner.

du′teousness, *n.*, the quality of being duteous.

du′tiable, *adj.*, subject to the imposition of duty or customs.

du′tiful, *adj.*, performing one's duty.

du′tifully, *adv.*, in a dutiful manner.

du′tifulness, *n.*, the character of being dutiful.

du′ty, *n.*, a moral obligation; a sum of money exacted by the government in the course of trade.

duum′vir, *n.*, one of two Roman magistrates who performed the same duties.

duum′viral, *adj.*, pert. or rel. to the duumviri.

duum′virate, *n.*, the union of two men in the same office; control by two persons.

duvet, *n.*, an eiderdown quilt (*Fr.*).

dux, *n.*, the head of a class or school (*Scot.*).

duyk′er, *n.*, *i.q.* duiker.

dwale, *n.*, the deadly nightshade.

dwarf, *n.*, a diminutive man or woman; anything much smaller than the ordinary size; *v.t.*, to stunt; to cause to look small or insignificant.

dwarfed, *p.p.*, dwarf.

dwarf′ing, *pr.p.*, dwarf.

dwarf′ingly, *adv.*, in a dwarfing way.

dwarf′ish, *adj.*, below the common size or height.

dwarf′ishly, *adv.*, in a dwarfish way.

dwarf′ish′ness, *n.*, extreme smallness.

dwell, *v.i.*, to live in a place.

dwelled, *p.p.*, dwell.

dwell′er, *n.*, an inhabitant.

dwell′ing, *n.*, a place of residence; *pr.p.*, dwell.

dwell′ing-house, *n.*, a house intended as a residence.

dwell′ing-place, *n.*, a place of residence.

dwelt, *p.p.*, dwell.

dwin′dle, *v.i.*, to diminish gradually.

dwin′dled, *adj.*, diminished in size; *p.p.*, dwindle.

dwin′dling, *pr.p.*, dwindle.

dy′ad, *n.*, the number two; a couple; an element with the combining power of two hydrogen atoms (*chem.*).

Dy′ak, *n.*, an aboriginal inhabitant of Borneo.

dyarchy, *n.*, *i.q.* diarchy.

dye, *n.*, a stain; *v.t.*, to colour.

dyed, *p.p.*, dye.

dye′-house, *n.*, a building in which dyeing is carried on.

dye′ing, *pr.p.*, dye.

dy′er, *n.*, one who dyes cloth.

dye′stuff, *n.*, materials used in dyeing.

dye′-wood, *n.*, wood from which dye is extracted.

dy′ing, *adj.*, associated with death *pr.p.*, die.

dyke, *n.*, *i.q.* dike.

dynam′eter, *n.*, an instrument for determining the magnifying power of telescopes.

dynamet′rical, *adj.*, pert. or rel. to a dynameter.

dynam′ic, *adj.*, pert. or rel. to force as a moving agency.

dynam′ical, *adj.*, *i.q.* dynamic.

dynam′ically, *adv.*, in a dynamic way.

dynam′ics, *n. pl.*, the science which deals with the nature and action of force.

dyn′amism, *n.*, an energizing or motive force.

dyn′amist, *n.*, one who studies dynamics.

dy′namite, *n.*, an explosive prepared from nitro-glycerine.

dyn′amiter, *n.*, one who uses dynamite.

dynamit′ic, *adj.*, rel. or pert. to dynamite.

dyn′amitism, *n.*, the use of dynamite to destroy for revolutionary purposes.

dyn′amitist, *n.*, *i.q.* dynamiter.

dy′namo, *n.*, a machine in which electric current is produced by power.

dynamom′eter, *n.*, an instrument for measuring force.

dy′namotor, *n.*, a combined electrical motor and generator.

dyn′ast, *n.*, a ruler; a prince.

dynast′ic, *adj.*, rel. or pert. to a dynasty.

dynas′tically, *adv.*, in a dynastic manner.

dyn′asty, *n.*, a line of kings of common ancestry.

dyne, *n.*, a unit for measuring force.

dysenter′ic, *adj.*, pert. or rel. to dysentery.

dys′entery, *n.*, inflammation of the mucous membrane of the large intestine.

dysgen′ic, *adj.*, causing a detrimental effect on the race.

dyslogis′tic, *adj.*, disapproving; shameful.

dyslogis′tically, *adv.*, in a dyslogistic way.

dysmenorrhoe′a, *n.*, difficult menstruation.

dyspep′sia, *n.*, indigestion.

dyspep′sy, *n.*, *i.q.* dyspepsia.

dyspep′tic, *adj.*, afflicted with dyspepsia; *n.*, a person who suffers from dyspepsia.

dyspep′tical, *adj.*, *i.q.* dyspeptic.

dyspha′gia, *n.*, difficulty in swallowing.

dyspho′nia, *n.*, difficulty of speech.

dys′phony, *n.*, difficulty of speaking distinctly.

dyspnoe′a, *n.*, difficulty in breathing.

dyspros′ium, *n.*, an element of a rare-earth group (*chem.*).

dysthe′sia, *n.*, a morbid feeling of discomfort.

dysthet′ic, *adj.*, pert. or rel. to dysthesia.

dysur′ia, *n.*, *i.q.* dysury.

dys′ury, *n.*, difficulty and pain in discharging urine.

E

each, *pron.*, every one (separately).

ea'ger, *adj.*, keen, earnest; ardently desirous; *n.*, *i.q.* eagre.

ea'gerly, *adv.*, with eagerness.

ea'gerness, *n.*, a state of ardent desire.

ea'gle, *n.*, a large bird of prey.

ea'gle-eyed, *adj.*, with the eyes of an eagle; keen-sighted.

ea'glet, *n.*, a young eagle.

ea'gre, *n.*, a tidal wave. (Also *eager*.)

ear, *n.*, the organ of hearing; an ear-like projection; fine perception; a corn-spike; *v.t.*, to plough.

ear'ache, *n.*, internal pain of the ear; otalgia.

ear'drum, *n.*, the tympanum.

eared, *adj.*, having ears; *p.p.*, ear.

ear'ing, *n.*, the growth of an ear of corn; a small line for fastening (*naut.*); *pr.p.*, ear.

earl, *n.*, the third highest rank of nobility.

earl'dom, *n.*, an earl's rank and territory.

ear'less, *adj.*, without ears.

ear'let, *n.*, a tragus, esp. in some bats.

ear'lier, *adj.*, *comp.* of early.

ear'liest, *adj.*, *super.* of early.

ear'liness, *n.*, the state of being early.

Earl Mar'shal, *n.*, an English state officer; head of the College of Arms.

ear'ly, *adj.*, and *adv.*, near the beginning; in good time; betimes; before time.

ear'mark, *n.*, an owner's mark on an animal; a mark of identification or appropriation; *v.t.*, to mark specially.

earn, *v.t.*, to gain by service; to merit.

earned, *p.p.*, earn.

earn'er, *n.*, one who earns.

ear'nest, *adj.*, serious, determined; *n.*, seriousness, zeal; a pledge or promise.

ear'nestly, *adv.*, in earnest.

ear'nest-money, *n.*, money paid to bind a bargain.

ear'nestness, *n.*, the state of being earnest.

earn'ing, *pr.p.*, earn.

earn'ings, *n. pl.*, wages, payment for service.

ear'-phone, *n.*, a listening device applied to the ear.

ear'ring, *n.*, a ring hung from, clipped to or pierced through the ear.

ear'shot, *n.*, a distance to which the hearing reaches.

earth, *n.*, the ground, the globe on which we live; soil; a burrowing animal's hole; *v.t.*, to place in the earth, to drive into the earth; to mound up; to conduct (electricity) to earth.

earth'born, *adj.*, of earthly birth.

earthed, *p.p.*, earth.

earth'en, *adj.*, made of earth.

earth'enware, *n.*, domestic utensils made of burnt clay.

earth'ing, *pr.p.*, earth.

earth'liness, *n.*, the state or quality of being earthly.

earth'ling, *n.*, a worldling.

earth'ly, *adj.*, rel. or pert. to earth; gross; carnal.

earth'quake, *n.*, a disturbance of the earth's surface.

earth'work, *n.*, a rampart of earth.

earth'worm, *n.*, the common worm.

earth'y, *adj.*, rel. to or like, the earth; gross.

ear'-trumpet, *n.*, an instrument assisting the deaf to hear.

ear'wax, *n.*, cerumen; wax in the ear.

ear'wig, *n.*, a small insect erroneously believed to crawl into the ear.

ear'-witness, *n.*, one who testifies what he has heard.

ease, *n.*, freedom from pain or trouble; comfort, rest; *v.t.*, to lighten, to make looser.

eased, *p.p.*, ease.

ease'ful, *adj.*, full of ease.

ea'sel, *n.*, a stand for a picture, portfolio, etc.

ease'less, *adj.*, without ease.

ease'ment, *n.*, a right apart from ownership of the soil; relief.

eas'ier, *adj.*, *comp.* of easy.

eas'iest, *adj.*, *super.* of easy.

eas'ily, *adv.*, with ease.

eas'iness, *n.*, the state of being easy.

eas'ing, *pr.p.*, ease.

East, *adj.*, rel. or pert. to the East; *n.*, one of the cardinal points; an Eastern region.

East'er, *n.*, the greatest of the Christian Festivals, commemorating Christ's Resurrection.

Eas'terling, *n.*, a native of an Eastern country; formerly the English name for the Hanseatic traders.

east'erly, *adj.*, eastward; coming from the East.

east'ern, *adj.*, rel. or pert. to the East.

eas'ternmost, *adj.*, furthest east.

eas'ting, *n.*, a ship's course to the east (*naut.*); the first map reference on the grid system.

east'ward, *adj.* and *adv.*, toward the East.

east'wards, *adv.*, *i.q.* eastward.

eas'y, *adj.*, not difficult; comfortable, free from pain or trouble; unaffected.

eas'ychair, n., an armchair made to be especially comfortable.

eas'y-going, adj., casual, good-natured.

eat, v.t., to consume with the teeth; to wear away; v.i., to take food; to taste.

eat'able, adj., fit to eat; n., anything edible.

eat'en, p.p., eat.

eat'er, n., one who, or that which, eats.

eat'ing, n., food; pr.p., eat.

eat'ing-house, n., a restaurant.

eats, n. pl., food (slang).

eau-de-Cologne', n., a perfume first made at Cologne.

eau-de-nil', n., a greenish colour (Fr.).

eau-de-vie', n., brandy (Fr.).

eaves, n. pl., the overhanging part of a roof.

eaves'drop, v.i., to listen secretly.

eaves'dropper, n., one who listens secretly.

ebb, n., the back flow of the tide; a decline; v.i., to flow back, to subside; to decline.

ebbed, p.p., ebb.

ebb'ing, pr.p., ebb.

ebb'tide, n., low tide.

eb'on, adj., made of ebony; black; n., ebony.

eb'onite', n., vulcanite.

eb'onize, v.t., to make look like ebony.

eb'ony, adj., made of ebony; n., a hard, black wood.

ebri'ety, n., a state of drunkenness.

eb'rious, adj., drunk; given to drunkenness.

ebul'lience, n., i.q. ebulliency.

ebul'liency, n., the state of being ebullient.

ebul'lient, adj., bubbling over; excessively enthusiastic.

ebulli'tion, n., the act of bubbling over; an outburst of enthusiasm.

écar'té, n., a card game for two (Fr.).

ec'bole, n., a digression (Gr.).

Ec'ce Ho'mo, n., a picture of Christ wearing a crown of thorns; "behold the man" (Lat.).

eccen'tric, adj., not in the centre; peculiar; n., a device for alternating circular with rectilinear motion; a queer person.

eccen'trical, adj., i.q. eccentric.

eccentric'ity, n., the state or quality of being eccentric.

eccle'sia, n., an assembly; the church.

eccle'siarch, n., a church ruler.

eccle'siast, n., a member of an ecclesia; a churchman.

Ecclesias'tes, n., the name of one of the canonical scriptures = the preacher.

ecclesias'tic, adj., rel. or pert. to the church; n., a churchman (i.e. in the sense of a person in holy orders).

ecclesias'tical, adj., i.q. ecclesiastic.

ecclesias'tically, adv., in an ecclesiastic way.

ecclesias'ticism, n., devotion to the church; the ecclesiastical system.

Ecclesias'ticus, n., one of the deuterocanonical scriptures.

ecclesiolog'ical, adj., rel. or pert. to ecclesiology.

ecclesiol'ogist, n., a student of ecclesiology.

ecclesiol'ogy, n., the study of church antiquities and church architecture.

ec'dysis, n., a casting off, esp. the skin of serpents.

ech'elon, n., an arrangement of troops in a succession of receding lines, each to the right or left of the first; v.t., to dispose in echelon; v.i., to take up a position in echelon.

echid'na, n., an Australian, toothless, burrowing animal similar to the hedgehog.

ech'inate, adj., prickly, bristly.

ech'inite, n., a fossil sea-urchin.

echin'oderm, n., a prickly-skinned sea-urchin.

echi'nus, n., the sea-urchin; a hedgehog.

ech'o, n., a reflection of sound; an exact imitation; v.t., to reflect back (a sound); v.i., to resound.

ech'oed, p.p., echo.

ech'ogram, n., a record made in calculating distance from sound.

ech'oic, adj., like an echo.

ech'oing, p.p., echo.

ech'oism, n., the construction of words to imitate sounds.

echom'eter, n., an instrument for measuring sound-distance.

echom'etry, n., the art of measuring sound-distance.

ech'urin, n., a yellow dye.

éc'lair, n., a small, finger-shaped, iced cake filled with cream (Fr.).

éclaircissement, n., a clearing up; an explanation (of conduct, etc.), (Fr.).

eclamp'sia, n., a kind of epileptic convulsion.

éclat', n., brilliant effect, applause, distinction (Fr.).

eclec'tic, adj., selecting; picking and choosing; n., one who is eclectic.

eclec'tical, adj., i.q. eclectic.

eclec'ticism, n., the eclectic spirit; the selection from a variety of opinions.

eclipse', n., an obscuration of a heavenly body; v.t., to put under an eclipse; to obscure, to throw into the shade.

eclipsed', p.p., eclipse.

eclips'ing, pr.p., eclipse.

eclip'tic, adj., rel. or pert. to eclipses, or to the ecliptic; n., the sun's apparent path.

ec'logue, n., a simple, rustic poem.

ecmne'sia, n., temporary amnesia.

ecol'ogy, oec-, n., the branch of biology which deals with animals and plants in relation to their natural surroundings.

econom'ic, *adj.*, pert. or rel. to economy; concerned with the study of economics.

econom'ical, *adj.*, careful of expenditure; thrifty.

econom'ically, *adv.*, thriftily.

econom'ics, *n. pl.*, the science of wealth in relation to the state and the people; the political economy.

econ'omist, *n.*, a student of economics.

economiza'tion, *n.*, the practice of economy.

econ'omize, *v.i.*, to be thrifty; *v.t.*, to husband, to use thriftily.

econ'omized, *p.p.*, economize.

écon'omizing, *pr.p.*, economize.

econ'omy, *n.*, domestic management, saving; the adjustment of means to ends; a system of government.

écraseur', *n.*, a surgical instrument so named (*Fr.*).

é'crin, *n.*, a jewel box (*Fr.*).

écritoire', *n.*, *i.q.* escritoire.

ecru', *adj.*, like unbleached linen; *n.*, coarse linen.

ec'stasis, *n.*, a trance.

ec'stasize, *v.t. and i.*, to go into ecstasies.

ec'stasy, *n.*, a rapturous, exalted state.

ecstat'ic, *adj.*, exalted, rapturous, entrancing.

ecstat'ical, *adj.*, *i.q.* ecstatic.

ecstat'ically, *adv.*, rapturously.

ec'toderm, *n.*, the outer cellular membrane covering a multicellular animal.

ec'toplasm, *n.*, the outer protoplasm of a cell; a substance supposed to emanate from a spiritualistic medium during trance, taking human shape.

ectro'sis, *n.*, arrestive treatment (*med.*).

écu, *n.*, an ancient coin (*Fr.*).

ecumen'ical, *adj.*, pert. or rel. to the whole world; general. (Also *oecumenical*.)

ec'zema, *n.*, an inflamed state of the skin.

eczem'atous, *adj.*, of the nature of eczema.

eda'cious, *adj.*, voracious, destructive.

edac'ity, *n.*, voracity, greediness.

Ed'am, *n.*, a spherical, Dutch cheese.

Ed'da, *n.*, the name of either of the two series of ancient Icelandic books.

ed'der, *n.*, a hedge; the binding for a hedge; *v.t.*, to bind with osiers.

ed'died, *p.p.*, eddy.

ed'dy, *n.*, a whirling current; *v.i.*, to whirl round and round.

ed'dying, *pr.p.*, eddy.

ed'elweiss, *n.*, a small, white Alpine flower.

ede'ma, *n.*, *i.q.* oedema.

edem'atous, *adj.*, *i.q.* oedematous.

E'den, *n.*, Paradise.

eden'tate, *adj.*, without teeth.

eden'tated, *adj.*, deprived of teeth.

edge, *n.*, the sharp side of a blade; a sharp border; the brink; a fringe; *v.t.*, to put an edge to; to incite; *v.i.*, to sidle, to come up slowly.

edged, *p.p.*, edge.

edge'less, *adj.*, without an edge.

edge'rail, *n.*, a rail on the edge of which wheels run.

edge'-tool, *n.*, a cutting-tool.

edge'ways, *adv.*, *i.q.* edgewise.

edge'wise, *adv.*, sideways.

edg'ily, *adv.*, irritably.

edg'ing, *n.*, a border; *pr.p.*, edge.

edg'y, *adj.*, sharp-edged; with nerves on edge.

edibil'ity, *n.*, the quality of being edible.

ed'ible, *adj.*, eatable.

e'dict, *n.*, a proclamation by authority.

edic'tal, *adj.*, able to be proclaimed by authority.

edifica'tion, *n.*, the act or effect of edifying.

ed'ifice, *n.*, a building or structure.

ed'ified, *p.p.*, edify.

ed'ify, *v.t.*, to build up; to instruct; to improve.

ed'ifying, *pr.p.*, edify.

e'dile, *n.*, *i.q.* aedile.

ed'it, *v.t.*, to look after the publication of a book; to prepare a book for publication.

ed'ited, *p.p.*, edit.

ed'iting, *pr.p.*, edit.

edi'tion, *n.*, the issue of a book to the public; the number of copies printed at one time.

edi'tion de luxe, *n.*, a handsome edition.

edi'tio prin'ceps, *n.*, the first printed edition of a book (*Lat.*).

ed'itor, *n.*, one who edits either a book or a newspaper, magazine, etc.

edito'rial, *adj.*, rel. or pert. to an editor.

ed'itorship, *n.*, the office of an editor.

ed'itress, *n.*, the fem. of editor.

ed'ucable, *adj.*, capable of education.

educand', *n.*, one to be educated.

ed'ucatable, *adj.*, *i.q.* educable.

ed'ucate, *v.t.*, to train, to develop the mind and character.

ed'ucated, *p.p.*, educate.

ed'ucating, *pr.p.*, educate.

educa'tion, *n.*, the process or effect of educating.

educa'tional, *adj.*, rel. to education; instructive.

educa'tionalist, *n.*, *i.q.* educationist.

educa'tionally, *adv.*, in respect of education.

educa'tionist, *n.*, one who professes a knowledge of education and its working.

ed'ucative, *adj.*, *i.q.* educational.

ed'ucator, *n.*, one who educates.

educe', *v.t.*, to draw out; to make an inference.

educed', *p.p.*, educe.

edu'cible, *adj.*, able to be educed.

edu'cing, *pr.p.*, educe.

ed'uct, *n.*, a disengaged body (*chem.*); an inference.

educ'tion, *n.*, the act or result of educing.

educ'tor, *n.*, anything that educes.

edul'corant, *adj.*, sweetening.

edul'corate, *v.t.*, to sweeten by reducing acidity.

edulcora'tion, *n.*, sweetness.

edul'corator, *n.*, anything that edulcorates.

Edward'ian, *adj.* and *n.*, characteristic of Edward VII's reign; a person of this period.

eel, *n.*, a snake-like fish.

e'en, *adv.* and *n.*, *i.q.*, even.

e'er, *adv. i.q.*, ever.

ee'rie, **ee'ry**, *adj.*, fear-inspiring; causing a feeling of loneliness.

efface', *v.t.*, to destroy the face of, to blot out, to remove from notice.

efface'able, *adj.*, able to be effaced.

effaced', *p.p.*, efface.

efface'ment, *n.*, the act of effacing.

effa'cing, *pr.p.*, efface.

effect', *n.*, a result, an accomplishment; *v.t.*, to bring to pass, to accomplish.

effect'ed, *p.p.*, effect.

effect'ible, *adj.*, able to be effected.

effect'ing, *pr.p.*, effect.

effect'ive, *adj.*, effect-producing, successful.

effect'ively, *adv.*, in an effective way.

effect'iveness, *n.*, the quality of being effective.

effect'or, *n.*, one who, or that which, effects.

effects', *n. pl.*, belongings, chattels; simulators.

effec'tual, *adj.*, producing intended effect.

effec'tually, *adv.*, in an effectual way.

effec'tuate, *v.i.*, to accomplish.

effec'tuated, *p.p.*, effectuate.

effec'tuating, *pr.p.*, effectuate.

effectua'tion, *n.*, the act or result of effectuating.

effem'inacy, *n.*, womanish character, unmanliness.

effem'inate, *adj.*, woman-like, unmanly.

effem'inate, *v.t.*, to weaken, to render womanly.

effem'inated, *p.p.*, effeminate.

effem'inately, *adv.*, in an effeminate way.

effem'inateness, *n.*, the quality of being effeminate.

effem'inating, *pr.p.*, effeminate.

effen'di, *n.*, a Turkish courtesy title.

ef'ferent, *adj.*, discharging.

effervesce', *v.i.*, to bubble up, to froth up.

effervesced', *p.p.*, effervesce.

efferves'cence, *n.*, the act or process of effervescing.

efferves'cent, *adj.*, *i.q.* effervescing.

efferves'cing, *adj.*, rising and bubbling; *pr.p.*, effervesce.

effete', *adj.*, worn out by age.

effica'cious, *adj.*, able to produce intended result.

effica'ciously, *adv.*, in an efficacious way.

effica'ciousness, *n.*, the state or quality of being efficacious.

ef'ficacy, *n.*, *i.q.* efficaciousness.

effi'ciency, *n.*, the state or quality of being efficient.

effi'cient, *adj.*, able to produce intended effect; capable; vigorous.

effi'ciently, *adv.*, in an efficient way.

ef'figy, *n.*, a figure, an image.

effloresce', *v.i.*, to blossom forth, to flower.

effloresced', *p.p.*, effloresce.

efflores'cence, *n.*, the state or period of efflorescing.

efflores'cency, *n.*, the state or quality of being efflorescent.

efflores'cent, *adj.*, blossoming forth; flowering.

efflores'cing, *pr.p.*, effloresce.

ef'fluence, *n.*, a flowing out; that which flows out.

ef'fluent, *adj.*, flowing out; *n.*, an outlet or outflow.

efflu'via, *n.*, the pl. of effluvium (*Lat.*).

efflu'vium, *n.*, an invisible vapour, generally from decaying matter; an offensive smell.

ef'flux, *n.*, the act or process of outflowing.

efflux'ion, *n.*, a lapse; an issue.

ef'fort, *n.*, an exertion of strength; an attempt; an achievement.

ef'fortful, *adj.*, exhibiting or requiring effort.

ef'fortless, *adj.*, without effort.

effort'lessly, *adv.*, in an effortless way.

effort'lessness, *n.*, the quality of being effortless.

effront'ery, *n.*, impudence, barefacedness.

efful'gence, *n.*, brightness, lustre.

efful'gent, *adj.*, shining forth, splendid.

efful'gently, *adv.*, in an effulgent manner.

effuse', *v.t.*, to pour forth.

effused', *p.p.*, effuse.

effu'sing, *pr.p.*, effuse.

effu'sion, *n.*, the act or result of effusing.

effu'sive, *adj.*, exuberant in sentiment; gushing.

effu'sively, *adv.*, in an effusive way.

effu'siveness, *n.*, gush; an embarrassing excess of attention.

eft, *n.*, a newt.

egalitar'ian, *adj.*, holding the principle of the equality of mankind; *n.*, one who asserts the equality of mankind.

egal'ity, *n.*, *i.q.* equality.

eges'tion, *n.*, excretion.

egg, *n.*, the rounded body containing the substance of the creature to be born from it; *v.t.*, to incite, to goad on.

egged, *p.p.*, egg.

egg'er, *n.*, a large moth common in Great Britain.

egg'ery, *n.*, an egg-producing establishment.

egg'ing, *pr.p.*, egg.

egg'shell, *n.*, the shell of the egg.

e′gis, *n.*, *i.q.* aegis.

eg′lantine, *n.*, the sweet-briar; (possibly) the honeysuckle.

eg′o, *n.*, the "I" or self; that which is conscious and thinks (*psych.*).

egocen′tric, *adj.*, self-centred, egoistic.

eg′oism, *n.*, the self-regarding theory of morals.

eg′oist, *n.*, a continuously selfish person.

egois′tic, *adj.*, selfish.

egois′tically, *adv.*, in an egoistic way.

egoman′ia, *n.*, morbid egoism.

egoman′iac, *n.*, a sufferer from egomania.

eg′otism, *n.*, a fondness for saying "I"; self-praise.

eg′otist, *n.*, a person too much concerned with himself and his own interests; a self-centred person.

egotis′tic, *adj.*, self-centred; inordinately self-regarding.

egotis′tical, *adj.*, *i.q.* egotistic.

egotis′tically, *adv.*, in an egotistic way.

eg′otize, *v.t.*, to indulge in egotism.

egre′gious, *adj.*, remarkable; standing out of the crowd, (often used disparagingly).

egre′giously, *adv.*, in an egregious way.

e′gress, *n.*, an exit, a going out.

egres′sion, *n.*, an exit.

eg′ret, *n.*, a variety of heron; a tuft of heron's feathers.

Egyp′tian, *adj.*, rel. or pert. to Egypt; *n.*, a native of E.; the language of E.; a kind of printing type.

Egyptol′ogy, *n.*, the study of Egyptian history and antiquities.

eh, *interj.*, what?

ei′con, *n.*, a sacred picture or image. (Also *icon* and *eikon*.)

ei′der, *n.*, a large sea-duck.

ei′derdown, *n.*, the breast feathers of the eider; a bed-quilt.

ei′der-duck, *n.*, *i.q.* eider.

ei′dograph, *n.*, an apparatus for copying drawings.

eido′lon, *n.*, a spectre; a phantom, (*Gr.*).

eight, *adj.*, one of the cardinal numbers.

eighteen, *adj.* and *n.*, one of the cardinal numbers, eight and ten.

eighteenth, *adj.*, the ordinal of eighteen.

eight′fold, *adj.* and *adv.*, eight times repeated.

eighth, *adj.*, the ordinal of eight.

eighth′ly, *adv.*, in the eighth place.

eight′ieth, *adj.*, the ordinal of eighty.

eight′pence, *n.*, the amount of eight pence.

eight′penny, *adj.*, costing eight pence.

eight′score, *adj.* and *n.*, eight times twenty.

eight′some, *adj.* and *n.*, a lively Scottish reel for eight dancers.

eight′y, *adj.* a cardinal number.

eigne, *adj.*, the eldest or elder (*leg.*).

eik′on, *n.*, *i.q.* icon.

Einstein′ium, *n.*, the element of the atomic number 99.

eire′nicon, *n.*, an attempt (usually written) to bring about a reconciliation.

Eistedd′fod, *n.*, a Welsh bardic assembly.

eiswool, *n.*, a very fine, glossy, worsted wool of two-thread thickness. (Also *ice wool*.)

ei′ther, *conj.*, in one of two cases; *pron.*, one or the other of two.

ejac′ulate, *v.t.*, to jerk out words; to speak in short sentences; to issue in spurts.

ejac′ulated, *p.p.*, ejaculate.

ejac′ulating, *pr.p.*, ejaculate.

ejacula′tion, *n.*, the act of ejaculating; a short, sharp exclamation.

ejac′ulatory, *adj.*, rel. or pert. to ejaculation.

eject′, *n.*, something inferred.

eject′, *v.t.*, to throw out, to dismiss, to banish.

eject′ed, *p.p.*, eject.

eject′ing, *pr.p.*, eject.

ejec′tion, *n.*, the act of ejecting.

eject′ive, *adj.*, tending to eject.

eject′ively, *adv.*, in an ejective manner.

eject′ment, *n.*, removal (by law); dispossession.

eject′or, *n.*, one who ejects.

eke, *adv.*, equally; *v.t.*, to make to suffice.

eked, *p.p.*, eke.

e′king, *pr.p.*, eke.

ekk′a, *n.*, a small cart drawn by a horse or bullock.

elab′orate, *adj.*, made with much toil; highly finished.

elab′orate, *v.t.*, to work out with much pains; to add improvements to.

elab′orated, *p.p.*, elaborate.

elab′orately, *adv.*, in an elaborate way.

elab′orating, *pr.p.*, elaborate.

elabora′tion, *n.*, the act or process of elaborating.

elab′orative, *adj.*, tending to elaboration.

elab′orator, *n.*, one who elaborates.

ela′in, *n.*, an oily liquid compound. (Also *olein*.)

élan, *n.*, dash, ardour (*Fr.*).

e′land, *n.*, a S. African antelope.

elapse′, *v.i.*, to pass away; to end.

elapsed′, *p.p.*, elapse.

elaps′ing, *pr.p.*, elapse.

elas′tic, *adj.*, having the power of returning to the state from which it has been disturbed by pressure, pulling or distortion; *n.*, a strip or band of rubber.

elas′tically, *adv.*, in an elastic way.

elastic′ity, *n.*, the elastic property.

elate′, *v.t.*, to exalt, to elevate, to make proud.

ela′ted, *p.p.*, elate.

ela′ting, *pr.p.*, elate.

ela′tion, *n.*, a state produced by elating.

el′bow, *n.*, the joint at the middle of the arm; any elbow-like bend; *v.t.*, to push aside, to jostle.

el′bow-*chair*, *n.*, a chair with rests for the elbow.

el'bowed, *adj.*, elbow-shaped; *p.p.*, elbow.

el'bow-grease, *n.*, energetic rubbing; hard work.

el'bowing, *pr.p.*, elbow.

el'bow-room, *n.*, space to turn round in.

el'chee, *n.*, an ambassador (*Turk.*).

eld, *n.*, old age (*dial.*).

el'der, *adj.*, older; *n.*, an old person; a functionary; a shrub.

el'derberry, *n.*, the fruit of the elder tree.

eld'erly, *adj.*, becoming old; rather aged.

eld'est, *adj.*, *super.* of elder.

El Dora'do, *n.*, a fabulous country rich in gold.

el'dritch, *adj.*, weird, hideous (*Scot.*).

Eleat'ic, *adj.*, rel. or pert. to Elea, an ancient Greek city in S.W. Italy; the school of philosphers in E.

elecampane', *n.*, a variety of aster.

elect', *adj.*, chosen; *n.*, one chosen; *v.t.*, to choose, to select (by vote).

elect'ed, *p.p.*, elect.

elect'ing, *pr.p.*, elect.

elec'tion, *n.*, the act, result or occasion of electing.

electioneer', *n.*, one who organizes an election; *v.t.*, to organize an election.

electioneered', *p.p.*, electioneer.

electioneer'ing, *pr.p.*, electioneer.

elec'tive, *adj.*, pert. or rel. to election.

elec'tively, *adv.*, in an elective manner.

elect'or, *n.*, one who has the right of electing.

elect'oral, *adj.*, rel. to an elector or election.

elect'orate, *n.*, the collective body of electors.

elec'torial, *adj.*, *i.q.* electoral.

elec'torship, *n.*, the right to share in election.

elec'tric, *adj.*, rel. or pert. to electricity; magnetic.

elec'trical, *adj.*, *i.q.* electric.

elec'trically, *adv.*, by means of electricity.

electri'cian, *n.*, an expert in electrics.

electric'ity, *n.*, a force produced in nature or by man, and the conduction of this force through wires and cables for its application in light, heat, or power.

elec'trics, *n. pl.*, the science of electricity.

elec'trifiable, *adj.*, able to be electrified.

electrifica'tion, *n.*, the process or result of electrifying.

elec'trified, *p.p.*, electrify.

elec'trify, *v.t.*, to charge with electricity; to amaze.

elec'trifying, *pr.p.*, electrify.

elec'triza'tion, *n.*, *i.q.* electrification.

elec'trize, *v.t.*, *i.q.* electrify.

elec'tro, *n.*, electroplate, an electrotype.

elec'trocute, *v.t.*, to execute by means of electricity.

electrocu'tion, *n.* death or execution, by electricity.

elec'trode, *n.*, either of the poles or terminals of a galvanic battery or dynamo.

electrolier', *n.*, a holder of electric lamps.

electrol'ogy, *n.*, the science of electric phenomena.

electrol'ysis, *n.*, decomposition by means of electricity.

elec'trolyte, *n.*, a substance decomposable by electricity.

elec'trolyzable, *adj.*, able to be electrolyzed.

elec'trolyze, *v.t.*, to decompose by means of electricity.

elec'trolyzed, *p.p.*, electrolyze.

elec'trolyzing, *pr.p.*, electrolyze.

electro-mag'net, *n.*, a magnetized piece of soft metal.

electro-mag'netism, *n.*, the science dealing with the development of magnetism by electric currents.

electrom'eter, *n.*, an instrument for measuring the strength of an electric current.

electromot'ive, *adj.*, motivated by electricity; pert. or rel. to the motion of electricity.

electromo'tor, *n.*, a machine applying electricity as a motive power.

elec'tron, *n.*, an elementary particle, normally forming part of an atom and charged with negative electricity.

electron'ic, *adj.*, rel. or pert. to electrons.

electron'ics, *n.*, the science and technology of the conduction of electricity in vacua, gases and semi-conductors.

electrop'athy, *n.*, the treatment of disease with electricity.

electroph'orus, *n.*, an apparatus generating static electricity by induction.

elec'troplate, *n.*, a piece of ware coated with metal by electricity; *v.t.*, to cover with metal by means of electricity.

elec'troplated, *p.p.*, electroplate.

elec'troplating, *pr.p.*, electroplate.

elec'troscope, *n.*, an instrument detecting the presence of electricity.

electrostat'ics, *n.*, the study of electricity at rest.

electrotech'nics, *n.*, the technology of electricity.

electrothana'sia, *n.*, death by electricity.

electrotherapeut'ics, *n.*, *i.q.* electropathy.

electrothe'rapy, *n.*, *i.q.* electropathy.

elec'trotype, *n.*, a reproduction in copper by means of electricity; *v.t.*, to make an electrotype of.

elec'trotyped, *p.p.*, electrotype.

elec'trotyper, *n.*, a maker of electrotypes.

elec'trotyping, *pr.p.*, electrotype.

elec'trum, *n.*, amber.

elec'tuary, *n.*, a medicine prepared as a confection.

eleemos'ynary, *adj.*, rel. or pert. to almsgiving; given from charity.

el'egance, *n.*, gracefulness, daintiness.

el'egancy, *n.*, *i.q.* elegance.

el'egant, *adj.*, graceful, refined.

el'egantly, *adv.*, with elegance.

elegi'ac, *adj.*, pert. or rel. to elegy and elegiacs; *n.*, elegiac verse.

elegi'acal, *adj.*, *i.q.* elegiac.

el'egist, *n.*, one who writes elegies.

el'egize, *v.i.* and *t.*, to write an elegy.

el'egy, *n.*, a death-poem, a funeral song.

el'eme, *adj.*, handpicked, choice (*Turk.*).

el'ement, *n.*, one of the simplest parts; an unanalysable substance; a first principle; an ingredient; a natural environment.

elemen'tal, *adj.*, rel. or pert. to the elements.

elemen'tary, *adj.*, primary, simple.

el'ements, *n.*, the pl. of element; the rudiments of learning; the matter (bread and wine) of the eucharist; the forces of nature.

el'emi, *n.*, a general name for gum resins.

elen'chus, *n.*, a refuting argument.

elenc'tic, *adj.*, given to refutation or cross-examination.

el'ephant, *n.*, a large pachydermous quadruped of the tropics; a size of paper.

elephanti'asis, *n.*, a disease which makes the skin hard, rough and thick.

elephan'tine, *adj.*, rel. or pert. to or like an elephant.

elephan'toid, *adj.*, *i.q.* elephantine.

Eleusin'ian, *adj.*, rel. or pert. to Eleusis (an ancient, Greek city near Athens) and the Eleusinian mysteries.

el'evate, *adj.*, *i.q.* elevated; *v.t.*, to raise up, to exalt, improve or cheer.

el'evated, *adj.*, exalted; intoxicated; *p.p.*, elevate.

el'evating, *pr.p.*, elevate.

eleva'tion, *n.*, the act or result of elevating; exaltation; raised ground.

el'evator, *n.*, anything that elevates; a lift; a limb-raising muscle; a horizontal plane, fore and aft, for steering an aeroplane upwards or downwards.

elev'en, *n.*, one more than ten. The complement of a cricket or football team.

elev'enses, *n. pl.*, morning coffee, snack, etc., taken at about eleven o'clock (*colloq.*).

elev'enth, *adj.*, the ordinal of eleven.

elf, *n.*, a small spirit, a fairy.

elf'in, *adj.*, rel. or pert. to elves; *n.*, an elf, a playful child.

elf'ish, *adj.*, like an elf.

elf'ishness, *n.*, the state of being elfish.

elic'it, *v.t.*, to draw forth, to educe.

elic'ited, *p.p.*, elicit.

elic'iting, *pr.p.*, elicit.

elide', *v.t.*, to strike out, to erase.

eli'ded, *p.p.*, elide.

eli'ding, *pr.p.*, elide.

eligibil'ity, *n.*, the state of being eligible.

el'igible, *adj.*, worthy of choice; desirable; qualified.

elim'inate, *v.t.*, to cast out or aside; to obtain by separation.

elim'inated, *p.p.*, eliminate.

elim'inating, *pr.p.*, eliminate.

elimina'tion, *n.*, the act or effect of eliminating.

elimina'tor, *n.*, that which eliminates.

el'iquate, *v.t.*, to melt out.

el'iquated, *p.p.*, eliquate.

el'iquating, *pr.p.*, eliquate.

eliqua'tion, *n.*, the process or effect of eliquating.

eli'sion, *n.*, the act or result of eliding.

élite', *adj.*, choice, select; *n.*, the pick (*Fr.*).

elix'ir, *n.*, a liquor brewed by alchemists for preserving life indefinitely, or for converting baser metals into gold; an enlivening drink.

Elizabe'than, *adj.*, rel. or pert. to the first Queen Elizabeth and the Elizabethan period or architectural style.

elk, *n.*, the largest kind of deer.

ell, *n.*, an old cloth measure of varying lengths.

ellipse', *n.*, an oval-shaped figure.

ellip'sis, *n.*, the leaving out of words needed for completion of the sense.

ellip'soid, *n.*, a solid figure of which every plane section is an ellipse.

ellipsoi'dal, *adj.*, in the form of an ellipse.

ellip'tic, *adj.*, like an ellipse.

ellip'tical, *adj.*, *i.q.* elliptic; tersely or obliquely expressed.

ellip'tically, *adv.*, in an elliptic or elliptical way.

ellipticity, *n.*, the state of being elliptic.

ellip'toid, *adj.*, *i.q.* elliptic.

elm, *n.*, a common tree of the temperate zones.

elm'en, *adj.*, rel. or pert. to elms.

elm'y, *adj.*, covered with elms.

elocu'tion, *n.*, the art of speaking with correct and clear articulation.

elocu'tionary, *adj.*, rel. or pert. to elocution.

elocu'tionist, *n.*, one who professes elocution.

éloge', *n.*, a panegyric, an encomium (*Fr.*).

el'ogy, *n.*, *i.q.* éloge.

e'longate, *v.t.*, to draw out, to make longer.

e'longated, *p.p.*, elongate.

e'longating, *pr.p.*, elongate.

elonga'tion, *n.*, the process or result of elongating.

elope', *v.i.*, to run away clandestinely with a partner of the opposite sex.

eloped', *p.p.*, elope.

elope'ment, *n.*, the act of eloping.

elo'ping, *pr.p.*, elope.

el'oquence, *n.*, the power of fine speech.

el'oquent, *adj.*, gifted with eloquence.

el'oquently, *adv.*, in an eloquent way.

else, *adv.*, in addition, also, instead.

else'where, *adv.*, in some other place.

elu'cidate, *v.t.*, to make clear, to explain.

elu'cidated, *p.p.*, elucidate.

elu'cidating, *pr.p.*, elucidate.

elucida'tion, *n.*, the act or result of elucidating.

elu'cidative, *adj.*, explanatory, throwing light on.

elu'cidator, *n.*, one who elucidates.

elu'cidatory, *adj.*, *i.q.* elucidative.

elude', *v.t.*, to baffle, to avoid by artifice, to escape.

elu'ded, *p.p.*, elude.

elu'dible, *adj.*, able to be eluded.

elu'ding, *pr.p.*, elude.

Elul', *n.*, the twelfth month of the Jewish civil year.

elu'sion, *n.*, the act of eluding.

elu'sive, *adj.*, baffling, hard to grasp.

elu'sively, *adv.*, in an elusive way.

elu'siveness, *n.*, the quality of being elusive.

elu'soriness, *n.*, the quality of being elusory.

elu'sory, *adj.*, *i.q.* elusive.

el'van, *n.*, a broad vein of hard rock caused by a volcano; *adj.*, relating to elves.

el'ver, *n.*, a young eel.

elves, *n.*, the pl. of elf.

el'vish, *adj.*, *i.q.* elfish.

Élysée, *n.*, the official residence of the French President.

Elys'ian, *adj.*, rel. or pert. to Elysium (the paradise of Greek heroes after death); delightful, blessed.

Elys'ium, *n.*, the blissful place of the dead, the classic Paradise.

el'ytron, *n.*, a sheath; the hard, outer case covering the real wings of certain insects.

El'zevir, *adj.*, pert. or rel. to the Elzevirs, the famous 17th cent. Dutch publishers.

em, *n.*, a printer's unit of measurement.

ema'ciate, *v.t.*, to make thin, to reduce to

leanness; *v.i.*, to become lean.

ema'ciated, *p.p.*, emaciate.

ema'ciating, *pr.p.*, emaciate.

emacia'tion, *n.*, the state of being emaciated; extreme leanness.

em'anant, *adj.*, flowing from a source.

em'anate, *v.i.*, to flow from, to proceed from.

em'anated, *p.p.*, emanate.

em'anating, *pr.p.*, emanate.

emana'tion, *n.*, the act of emanating; something that emanates.

em'anative, *adj.*, tending to emanate.

eman'cipate, *v.t.*, to set free from slavery or any oppression or bad influence.

eman'cipated, *p.p.*, emancipate.

eman'cipating, *pr.p.*, emancipate.

emancipa'tion, *n.*, the act or result of emancipating.

emancipa'tionist, *n.*, a supporter of the emancipation of slaves.

eman'cipator, *n.*, one who emancipates.

eman'cipatory, *adj.*, able to be emancipated.

eman'cipist, *n.*, an ex-convict who has served his term.

emas'culate, *v.t.*, to deprive of male strength; to take out the vigour.

emas'culated, *p.p.*, emasculate.

emas'culating, *pr.p.*, emasculate.

emascula'tion, *n.*, the act of emasculating.

embale', *v.t.*, to make a bale of.

embaled', *p.p.*, embale.

embal'ing, *pr.p.*, embale.

embalm', *v.t.*, to preserve a corpse with spices and drugs.

embalmed', *p.p.*, embalm.

embalm'er, *n.*, one who embalms.

embalm'ing, *pr.p.*, embalm.

embalm'ment, *n.*, the preservation of a corpse with spices and drugs.

embank', *v.t.*, to build a bank around or against.

embanked', *p.p.*, embank.

embank'ing, *pr.p.*, embank.

embank'ment, *n.*, the act or result of embanking.

embarca'tion, *n.*, *i.q.*, embarkation.

embar'go, *n.*, an order forbidding a ship to leave a port; a ban; *v.t.*, to lay an embargo on.

embar'goed, *p.p.*, embargo.

embark', *v.t.*, to place on board; *v.i.*, to go on board; to begin an enterprise.

embarka'tion, *n.*, the act of embarking. (Also *embarcation*.)

embarked', *p.p.*, embark.

embark'ing, *pr.p.*, embark.

embar'rass, *v.t.*, to hamper, trouble or perplex.

embar'rassed, *p.p.*, embarrass.

embar'rassing, *adj.*, awkward, troublesome; *pr.p.*, embarrass.

embar'rassment, *n.*, perturbation, perplexity, money trouble.

embas'sador, *n.*, *i.q.*, ambassador.

em'bassy, *n.*, an ambassador's mission; an ambassador's residence and the officials.

embat'tle, *v.t.*, to draw up in battle array.

embat'tled, *adj.*, having battlements; prepared for battle; *p.p.*, embattle.

embat'tling, *pr.p.*, embattle.

embay', *v.t.*, to place in a bay.

embayed', *p.p.*, embay.

embay'ing, *pr.p.*, embay.

embay'ment, *n.*, the enclosing in a bay.

embed', *v.t.*, to lay in a bed.

embed'ded, *p.p.*, embed.

embed'ding, *pr.p.*, embed.

embel'lish, *v.t.*, to adorn, to beautify.

embel'lished, *p.p.*, embellish.

embel'lisher, *n.*, one who embellishes.

embel'lishing, *pr.p.*, embellish.

embel'lishment, n., the act or result of embellishing; an ornament.

em'ber, n., a live coal; a remnant of a fire; an Orkney sea-fowl.

Em'ber-Days, n., the three fast days (Wed., Fri. and Sat.) in Ember-Week.

Em'ber-Week, n., a week of the ecclesiastical year set aside for fasting and prayer.

embez'zle, v.t., to steal something entrusted to one's care.

embez'zled, p.p., embezzle.

embez'zlement, n., the act of embezzling.

embez'zler, n., one who embezzles.

embez'zling, pr.p., embezzle.

embit'ter, v.t., to impart bitterness to; to intensify.

embit'tered, p.p., embitter.

embit'tering, pr.p., embitter.

embit'terment, n., the making bitter; exasperation.

emblaze', v.t., to embellish, to emblazon.

emblazed', p.p., emblaze.

emblazing, pr.p., emblaze.

embla'zon, v.t., to adorn with heraldic figures, or with bright colours.

embla'zoned, p.p., emblazon.

embla'zoner, n., one who emblazons.

embla'zoning, pr.p., emblazon.

embla'zonment, n., i.q. emblazonry.

embla'zonry, n., the act or art of emblazoning.

em'blem, n., a type, figure or symbol.

emblemat'ic, adj., typical, symbolical.

emblemat'ical, adj., i.q. emblematic.

emblemat'ically, adv., symbolically.

emblem'atist, n., one who makes emblems or allegories.

emblem'atize, v.t., i.q. emblemize.

em'blements, n. pl., profits on crops (leg.).

em'blemize, v.t., to represent emblematically.

embod'ied, p.p., embody.

embod'ier, n., that which embodies.

embod'iment, n., the act or result of embodying; a complete representation.

embod'y, v.t., to form into a body; to give concrete expression to; to contain within it.

embod'ying, pr.p., embody.

embog', v.t., to plunge into.

embold'en, v.t., to make bold, to encourage or hearten.

embold'ened, p.p., embolden.

embold'ening, pr.p., embolden.

em'bolism, n., the periodic intercalation of days or years; an obstruction caused by a clot of blood.

embolis'mal, adj., rel. or pert. to an embolism.

embolis'mic, adj., i.q. embolismal.

em'bolus, n., an insertion; a blood-clot.

embonpoint', adj., plump, well nourished; n., plumpness, from en bon point (Fr.).

embos'om, v.t., to receive into the bosom; to embrace or envelop.

embos'omed, p.p., embosom.

embos'oming, pr.p., embosom.

emboss', v.t., to ornament with raised work.

embossed', p.p., emboss.

emboss'ing, pr.p., emboss.

emboss'ment, n., the act or result of embossing.

embot'tle, v.t., to put in a bottle.

embouchure', n., a rivermouth; the mouthpiece of a wind instrument (Fr.).

embow'el, v.t., to remove the entrails of; to bury.

embow'el(l)ed, p.p., embowel.

embow'el(l)er, n., one who embowels.

embowel(l)ing, pr.p., embowel.

embow'elment, n., the act or result of embowelling.

embow'er, v.t., to cover with a bower, to shelter with trees.

embow'ered, p.p., embower.

embow'ering, pr.p., embower.

embrace', n., the act of embracing; a clasping in the arms; v.t., to clasp lovingly with the arms; to adopt; to include.

embrace'able, adj., able to be embraced.

embraced', p.p., embrace.

embrace'ment, n., i.q. embrace.

embra'cer, n., one who, or that which, embraces.

embra'cery, n., a tampering with a jury.

embra'cing, pr.p., embrace.

embranch'ment, n., a branching out; a tributary of a river.

embrang'le, v.t., to entangle; to complicate.

embra'sure, n., an opening in a wall, with its sides bevelled, so that the opening widens inwards; a loophole.

em'brocate, v.t., to apply a liquid medicine to the body.

em'brocated, p.p., embrocate.

em'brocating, pr.p., embrocate.

embroca'tion, n., the act of embrocating; a liniment.

embro'glio, n., i.q., imbroglio (It.).

embroid'er, v.t., to ornament with needlework designs; to variegate.

embroid'ered, p.p., embroider.

embroid'erer, n., one who embroiders.

embroid'ering, pr.p., embroider.

embroid'ery, n., the art or act of embroidering; a piece of embroidered work.

embroil', v.t., to involve in a quarrel.

embroiled', p.p., embroil.

embroil'ing, pr.p., embroil.

embroil'ment, n., the act or result of embroiling.

embrown, v.t., to make brown.

embrute', v.t. and i., i.q. imbrute.

em'bryo, n., a rudimentary form; the vitalized germ in the first stage of development.

embryog'raphy, n., a treatise on embryos.

embryol'ogy, n., the study of embryos and the development of organisms.

em'bryonate, adj., rel. or pert. to embryos.

em'bryonated, adj., i.q. embryonate.

embryon'ic, adj., in the state of an embryo; rel. or pert. to an embryo.

embryot'ic, adj., i.q. embryonic.

embryot'omy, n., the cutting or dissection of a foetus.

embus', v.t. and v.i., to put into a motor vehicle; to mount a motor vehicle.

Emeer', n., i.q. Emir.

emend', v.t., to correct.

emend'able, adj., able to be emended.

emen'dals, n. pl., money reserved for emergencies.

emenda'tion, n., the act or result of emending; a correction.

em'endator, n., one who emends.

emend'atory, adj., correcting.

emend'ed, p.p., emend.

emend'ing, pr.p., emend.

em'erald, adj., green like an emerald; n., a green gem or colour; a printing type.

emerge', v.i., to rise out of; to come into view; to result.

emerged', p.p., emerge.

emer'gence, n., the act of emerging.

emer'gency, n., a sudden occurrence requiring instant action.

emer'gent, adj., i.q. emerging.

emer'ging, pr.p., emerge.

emer'iti, adj., the pl. of emeritus (Lat.).

emer'itus, adj., retired from office (Lat.).

emer'itus-profes'sor, n., an ex-professor.

em'erods, n. pl., hemorrhoids.

em'eroids, n., i.q. hemorrhoids.

emersed', adj., standing out of the water; protruding.

emer'sion, n., the act of emerging.

em'ery, n., a hard mineral used in polishing.

em'esis, n., vomiting.

emet'ic, adj., producing vomiting; n., a medicine that causes vomiting.

emet'ical, adj., i.q. emetic.

e'meu, n., i.q. emu.

émeute', n., a riot, an outbreak (Fr.).

em'igrant, adj., migrating; n., one who emigrates.

em'igrate, v.i., to leave one's country in order to settle in another.

em'igrated, p.p., emigrate.

em'igrating, pr.p., emigrate.

emigra'tion, n., the act of emigrating.

emigra'tory, adj., the state of being an emigrant.

ém'igré, n., a French emigrant, (Fr.).

em'inence, n., height, distinction; a title bestowed on cardinals.

eminence grise, n., a confidential agent; a powerful supporter in secret (Fr.).

em'inency, n., i.q. eminence.

em'inent, adj., towering above, exalted, distinguished.

em'inently, adv., markedly, conspicuously.

Emir', n., a Turkish or Arabic tribal ruler.

em'issary, adj., rel. or pert. to a spy or an emissary; n., one sent on a mission, a spy.

emis'sion, n., the act or result of emitting.

emis'sive, adj., leading to emission.

em'issory, adj., i.q. emissive.

emit', v.t., to send forth, to put forth.

emit'ted, p.p., emit.

emit'ting, pr.p., emit.

em'met, n., an ant.

emolles'cence, n., the act or process of softening.

emol'liate, v.t., to soften.

emol'liated, p.p., emolliate.

emol'liating, pr.p., emolliate.

emol'lient, adj., softening in its effect; n., an emollient substance.

emol'ument, n., pay, reward.

emo'tion, n., mental excitement, deep feeling.

emo'tionable, adj., i.q. emotional.

emo'tional, adj., rel. or pert. to the emotions; excitable.

emo'tionalism, n., a tendency to be emotional.

emo'tionally, adv., in an emotional way.

emo'tionless, adj., without emotion.

emo'tive, adj., causing emotion.

empale', v.t., i.q., impale.

empaled', p.p., empale.

empale'ment, n., the act of empaling.

empa'ling, pr.p., empale.

empan'el, v.i., i.q., impanel.

empan'el(l)ed, p.p., empanel.

empan'el(l)ing, pr.p., empanel.

empa'radise, v.t., i.q. imparadise.

empark', v.i., i.q. impark.

em'pathy, n., the power of feeling the experiences and emotions of others.

empen'nage, n., the tail unit of an aircraft.

em'peror, n., the ruler of an empire.

em'phasis, n., stress, intensity.

em'phasize, v.t., to lay stress on; to call special attention to.

em'phasized, p.p., emphasize.

em'phasizing, pr.p., emphasize.

emphat'ic, adj., laying stress, urgent.

emphat'ical, adj., i.q. emphatic.

emphat'ically, adv., with emphasis.

emphysem'a, n., an unnatural swelling; a disease of the lungs characterized by enlarged air vesicles (med.).

em'pire, n., rule; the rule of an emperor; the territory of an empire; the nations composing an imperial whole.

empir'ic, adj., rel. or pert. to experience; based on experience or observation only.

empir'ical, *adj.*, *i.q.* empiric.

empir'ically, *adv.*, in an empirical way.

empir'icism, *n.*, the empirical method and characteristics.

empir'icist, *n.*, one who professes empiricism.

emplace'ment, *n.*, the act of placing; a gun-platform.

emplane, *v.t.* and *i.*, to board an aircraft.

emplas'tic, *adj.*, adhesive; *n.*, a glutinous, adhesive substance.

empleoman'ia, *n.*, a mania for holding public office.

employ', *v.t.*, to engage in labour; *n.*, the state of being employed.

employabil'ity, *n.*, the quality of being employable.

employ'able, *adj.*, capable of being employed.

employé, *n.*, a male employed person (*Fr.*).

employed, *p.p.*, employ.

employée, *n.*, a female employed person (*Fr.*).

employee', *n.*, an employed person of either sex.

employ'er, *n.*, one who engages employees.

employ'ing, *pr.p.*, employ.

employ'ment, *n.*, the state of being employed; the act of employing; an occupation for gain.

empo'rium, *n.*, a large store.

empow'er, *v.t.*, to authorize, to entrust with power.

empow'ered, *p.p.*, empower.

empow'ering, *pr.p.*, empower.

em'press, *n.*, the fem. of emperor.

empres'sé, *adj.*, eager; zealous (*Fr.*).

empresse'ment, *n.*, a display of cordiality (*Fr.*).

emprise', *n.*, an adventurous undertaking.

emp'tied, *p.p.*, empty.

emp'tier, *adj.*, *comp.* of empty; *n.*, anything that empties.

emp'tiest, *adj.*, *super.* of empty.

emp'tiness, *n.*, the state of being empty.

emp'ty, *adj.*, containing nothing; unsubstantial; unintelligent; vain; *v.t.* and *i.*, to remove the contents of.

emp'tying, *pr.p.*, empty.

emp'tyings, *n. pl.*, lees; sediment.

empur'ple, *v.t.*, to stain with purple.

empye'ma, *n.*, suppuration.

empyr'eal, *adj.* and *n.*, *i.q.* empyrean.

empyre'an, *adj.*, pert. or rel. to the highest heaven; *n.*, the highest heaven.

empyreu'ma, *n.*, the smell of burning organic matter.

empyreumat'ic, *adj.*, rel. or pert. to empyreuma.

empyreumat'ical, *adj.*, *i.q.* empyreumatic.

empyr'ical, *adj.*, pert. or rel. to combustion.

empyro'sis, *n.*, a fire; a conflagration.

e'mu, *n.*, the Australian ostrich.

em'ulate, *v.t.*, to vie with, to rival.

em'ulated, *p.p.*, emulate.

em'ulating, *pr.p.*, emulate.

emula'tion, *n.*, the act of emulating; rivalry.

em'ulative, *adj.*, inclined to emulating.

em'ulator, *n.*, one who emulates.

emul'gent, *adj.*, straining out.

em'ulous, *adj.*, trying to surpass or equal.

em'ulousness, *n.*, the state or quality of being emulous.

emulsifica'tion, *n.*, the act or effect of emulsifying.

emul'sified, *p.p.*, emulsify.

emul'sifier, *n.*, an emulsifying agent.

emul'sify, *v.t.*, to convert into an emulsion.

emul'sifying, *pr.p.*, emulsify.

emul'sion, *n.*, a mixture of two liquids that do not normally mix.

emul'sive, *adj.*, producing emulsion.

emunc'tory, *adj.*, excretory.

en, *n.*, a printer's unit of measurement, smaller than an em.

ena'ble, *v.t.*, to give power to; to make able.

ena'bled, *p.p.*, enable.

ena'bling, *pr. p.*, enable.

enact', *v.t.*, to give Parliamentary sanction to; to perform.

enact'ed, *p.p.*, enact.

enact'ing, *pr.p.*, enact.

enac'tion, *n.*, *i.q.* enactment.

enact'ive, *adj.*, enacting.

enact'ment, *n.*, the act or result of enacting; a statute.

enact'or, *n.*, one who enacts.

enam'el, *n.*, a smooth, glossy material for laying over surfaces; the hard coating of teeth; *v.t.*, to cover with enamel.

enam'el(l)ed, *p.p.*, enamel.

enam'el(l)ing, *n.*, a covering with enamel; *pr.p.*, enamel.

enam'el(l)er, *n.*, one who enamels.

enam'our, *v.t.* and *i.*, to captivate, to inspire with passion.

enam'oured, *p.p.*, enamour.

enam'ouring, *pr.p.*, enamour.

enan'tiomorph, *n.*, a mirror image.

enantiop'athy, *n.*, *i.q.* allopathy.

enarmed, *adj.*, armed.

enarthro'sis, *n.*, a ball-and-socket joint formation.

e'nate, *n.*, a relative on the maternal side.

en bloc, *adv.*, in a lump; wholesale (*Fr.*).

encae'nia, *n. pl.*, a dedication festival. At Oxford, the encaenia are the yearly commemoration of founders and benefactors. (Also *encenia*.)

encage', *v.t.*, to confine in a cage.

encaged', *p.p.*, encage.

encag'ing, *pr.p.*, encage.

encamp', *v.i.*, to place in a camp; *v.i.*, to pitch a camp'

encamped', *p.p.*, encamp.

encamp'ing, *pr.p.*, encamp.

encamp'ment, *n.*, the act or place of encamping.

encan'this, *n.*, a tumour in the eye.

encar'pus, *n.*, a festoon of fruit and flowers.

encase', *v.t.*, to put into a case.

encased', *p.p.*, encase.

encase'ment, *n.*, the act or result of encasing.

encash', *v.t.*, to cash.

encash'ment, *n.*, conversion into cash.

enca'sing, *pr.p.*, encase.

encaus'tic, *adj.*, burnt in; *n.*, encaustic work.

encave', *v.t.*, to shut into a cave.

enceinte', *adj.*, pregnant; *n.*, a surrounding wall; an enclosure (*Fr.*).

ence'nia, *n.*, *i.q.* encaenia.

encephal'ic, *adj.*, rel. or pert. to the encephalos.

encephalit'is, *n.*, inflammation of the brain.

encephalo'gram, *n.*, a recording of the electric currents generated in the brain.

enceph'alon, *n.*, the brain (*Gr.*).

enceph'alos, *n.*, *i.q.* encephalon.

enchain', *v.t.*, to bind with a chain.

enchained', *p.p.*, enchain.

enchain'ing, *pr.p.*, enchain.

enchain'ment, *n.*, chaining up; fettering.

enchant', *v.t.*, to cast a spell on; to charm or delight.

enchant'ed, *p.p.*, enchant.

enchant'er, *n.*, one who enchants.

enchant'ing, *adj.*, charming, delightful; *pr.p.*, enchant.

enchant'ingly, *adv.*, charmingly.

enchant'ment, *n.*, the act of enchanting; the state of being enchanted.

enchant'ress, *n.*, the fem. of enchanter.

enchase', *v.t.*, to enclose in a border; to set in ornamental work; to ornament; to chase.

enchased', *p.p.*, enchase.

encha'sing, *pr.p.*, enchase.

enchirid'ion, *n.*, a small handbook (*Gr.*).

encho'rial, *adj.*, rel. or pert. to a country; indigenous.

encir'cle, *v.t.*, to surround.

encir'cled, *p.p.*, encircle.

encir'clement, *n.*, an enclosure in a circle.

encir'cling, *pr.p.*, encircle.

enclasp, *v.t.*, to embrace.

enclasped, *p.p.*, enclasp.

enclasping, *pr.p.*, enclasp.

enclave', *n.*, a piece of territory in a foreign country.

enclit'ic, *adj.*, unaccented and attached to the final syllable of a preceding word; *n.*, a particle so attached.

enclit'ical, *adj.*, *i.q.* enclitic.

enclit'ically, *adv.*, in an enclitic way.

enclose', *v.t.*, to shut in, to confine or frame. (Also *inclose.*)

enclosed', *p.p.*, enclose.

enclo'sing, *pr.p.*, enclose.

enclo'sure, *n.*, the act of enclosing; an enclosed space.

enclothe', *v.t.*, to clothe.

encloud', *v.t.*, to envelop in cloud.

encode', *v.t.*, to put a message into a code or cipher.

enco'miast, *n.*, one who pronounces an encomium; a flatterer.

encomias'tic, *adj.*, laudatory.

encomias'tical, *adj.*, *i.q.* encomiastic.

enco'mium, *n.*, an eulogy, praise.

encom'pass, *v.t.*, to encircle, to surround.

encom'passed, *p.p.*, encompass.

encom'passing, *pr.p.*, encompass.

encom'passment, *n.*, an encirclement.

encore', *adv.*, again; *n.*, a call for a repetition; *v.t.*, to demand a repetition of (*Fr.*).

encored', *p.p.*, encore.

encor'ing, *pr.p.*, encore.

encoun'ter, *n.*, a meeting; *v.t.*, to meet, to engage with, to experience.

encoun'tered, *p.p.*, encounter.

encoun'tering, *pr.p.*, encounter.

encour'age, *v.t.*, to cheer, to hearten, to incite.

encour'aged, *p.p.*, encourage.

encour'agement, *n.*, the act of encouraging, the state of being encouraged.

encour'ager, *n.*, one who encourages.

encour'aging, *adj.*, promising success, favourable; *pr.p.*, encourage.

encour'agingly, *adv.*, in an encouraging way.

En'cratite, *n.*, a member of an early Christian heretical sect which abstained from meat, wine and marriage.

encrim'son, *v.t.*, to make crimson.

encroach', *v.i.*, to trespass, to invade.

encroached', *p.p.*, encroach.

encroach'er, *n.*, one who encroaches.

encroach'ing, *pr.p.*, encroach.

encroach'ment, *n.*, the act or result of encroaching.

encrust', *v.i.*, *i.q.* incrust.

encrust'ed, *p.p.*, encrust.

encrust'ing, *pr.p.*, encrust.

encum'ber, *v.t.*, to burden, to hamper.

encum'bered, *p.p.*, encumber.

encum'bering, *pr.p.*, encumber.

encum'berment, *n.*, *i.q.* encumbrance.

encum'brance, *n.*, a hindrance; a mortgage on property.

encum'brancer, *n.*, one who has an encumbrance on another's estate (*leg.*).

ency'clical, *adj.*, put into general circulation; *n.*, a papal letter.

encyclop(a)e'dia, *n.*, a dictionary of general information.

encyclop(a)e'dian, *adj.*, rel. or pert. to an encyclopedia.

encyclop(a)e'dic, *adj.*, *i.q.* encyclopedian.

encyclop(a)e'dist, *n.*, one who compiles an encyclopedia; a man of great knowledge.

encyst', *v.t.*, to surround with a cyst; *v.i.*, to be surrounded with a cyst.

encysta'tion, n., the enclosing in a cyst.

encyst'ed, p.p., encyst.

encyst'ing, pr.p., encyst.

encyst'ment, n., i.q. encystation.

end, n., the finish of anything, the termination; an object in view; v.t., to bring to an end, to terminate; v.i., to finish.

en'danger, v.t., to involve in danger.

en'dangered, p.p., endanger.

endan'gering, pr.p., endanger.

endear, v.t., to make dear.

endeared', p.p., endear.

endear'ing, adj., making dear; p.p., endear.

endear'ingly, adv., in an endearing way.

endear'ment, n., the act of endearing; affectionate speech or behaviour.

endeav'our, n., an attempt; v.t., to try, to attempt.

endeav'oured, p.p., endeavour.

endeav'ouring, pr.p., endeavour.

end'ed, p.p., end.

endem'ic, adj., peculiar to a people or country; occurring in a region; n., a disease constantly prevailing in a locality.

endem'ical, adj., i.q. endemic.

endem'ically, adv., in an endemic way.

endemi'city, n., the state of being endemic.

ender'mic, adj., through the skin.

end'ing, pr.p., end.

en'dive, n., a garden herb, used in salads.

end'less, adj., without end.

end'lessly, adv., without end.

end'lessness, n., the state of being endless.

end'long, adv., lengthwise.

endocri'nal, adj., i.q. endocrine.

en'docrine, adj., secreting internally; n., a ductless gland.

endo'crinology, n., the branch of biology which deals with glands.

en'dogen, n., a plant growing from within.

endog'enous, adj., growing from within.

endors'able, adj., able to be endorsed.

endorse', v.t., to write one's name on the back of; to confirm, to approve. (Also indorse.)

endorsed', p.p., endorse.

en'dorsee', n., one in whose favour an endorsement is made.

endorse'ment, n., the act of endorsing, a signature, a confirmation.

endors'er, n., one who endorses.

endors'ing, pr.p., endorse.

en'dosperm, n., the albumen in a seed.

endos'mose, n., the passage inward of liquid through the pores of a septum.

endow', v.t., to furnish with a dowry, to give money; to enrich.

endowed', p.p., endow.

endow'er, n., one who endows.

endow'ing, pr.p., endow.

endow'ment, n., the act of endowing; money given for the permanent income of a foundation; talent, grace.

Endozo'a, n. pl., parasites.

endue', v.t., to clothe, vest or endow. (Also indue.)

endued', p.p., endue.

endu'ing, pr.p., endue.

endur'able, adj., able to be endured.

endur'ance, n., the faculty of enduring.

endure', v.t., to bear, to sustain; v.i., to last, to continue.

endured', p.p., endure.

endur'ing, pr.p., endure.

endur'ingly, adv., in an enduring way.

end'ways, adv., i.q. endwise.

end'wise, adv., end first or uppermost.

Ene'id, n., i.q. Aeneid.

en'ema, n., an injection into the rectum.

en'emy, n., a foe, an unfriendly person or people.

energet'ic, adj., full of energy, active.

energet'ical, adj., i.q. energetic.

energet'ically, adv., in an energetic way.

energet'ics, n. pl., the science of energy in physics.

ener'gic, adj., rare, precious.

ener'gico, adv., with energy, forcefully (It., mus.).

en'ergize, v.t., to make active or forceful; v.i., to display energy.

en'ergized, p.p., energize.

en'ergizer, n., anything that energizes.

en'ergizing, pr.p., energize.

energum'en, n., an enthusiast; a fanatic.

en'ergy, n., activity, force.

en'ervate, adj., wanting in vigour; v.t., to enfeeble; to deprive of nerve or strength.

en'ervated, p.p., enervate.

en'ervating, pr.p., enervate.

enerva'tion, n., the act or effect of enervating.

enface', v.t., to write on the front of a document.

enfaced', p.p., enface.

enfac'ing, pr.p., enface.

en famille, adv., at home; among one's family, (Fr.).

enfant terrible, n., a child who asks embarrassing questions or repeats what he has heard (Fr.).

enfee'ble, v.t., to reduce to weakness.

enfee'bled, p.p., enfeeble.

enfee'blement, n., the act or result of enfeebling.

enfee'bling, pr.p., enfeeble.

enfeoff', v.t., to convey (lands), to transfer.

enfeoffed', p.p., enfeoff.

enfeoff'ing, pr.p., enfeoff.

enfeoff'ment, n., the act of enfeoffing; the legal instrument of transference.

enfett'er, v.t., to bind in fetters; to enslave.

enfilade', n., a line; gun fire from the flank; v.t., to rake with shot.

enfila'ded, p.p., enfilade.

enfila'ding, *pr.p.*, enfilade.

enfold', *v.t.*, to wrap up,
to clasp. (Also *infold*.)

enfold'ed, *p.p.*, enfold.

enfold'ing, *pr.p.*, enfold.

enforce', *v.t.*, to compel,
to give force to, to
put into practice.

enforce'able, *adj.*, able
to be enforced.

enforced', *p.p.*, enforce.

enforc'edly, *adv.*, in an
enforced way.

enforce'ment, *n.*, the act
or result of enforcing.

enforc'er, *n.*, one who
enforces.

enforc'ing, *pr.p.*, en-
force.

enframe', *v.t.*, to set
pictures in frames;
to serve as a frame to.

enfran'chise, *v.t.*, to set
free; to bestow the
vote on.

enfran'chised, *p.p.*, en-
franchise.

enfran'chisement, *n.*, the
act or result of en-
franchising.

enfran'chising, *pr.p.*, en-
franchise.

engage', *v.t.*, to bind
by promise; to em-
ploy; to entangle; *v.i.*,
to promise; to under-
take; to busy one-
self; to join in.

engaged', *p.p.*, engage.

engage'ment, *n.*, an un-
dertaking in words;
a contract; a battle; a
promise.

enga'ging, *adj.*, pleasing,
attractive; *p.p.*, en-
gage.

enga'gingly, *adv.*, plea-
singly, attractively.

engarl'and, *v.t.*, to place
a garland upon; to
wreathe with flowers,
etc.

engen'der, *v.t.*, to beget,
to cause; to bring
about.

engen'dered, *p.p.*, en-
gender.

engen'dering, *pr.p.*, engender.

en'gine, *n.*, a power-
producing machine;
an instrument or de-
vice.

engineer', *n.*, one who
makes, repairs, uses
or drives engines; one
who practises the art
and science of engine-
ering; *v.t.*, to organ-
ize; to manage; to
carry through.

engineered', *p.p.*, engineer.

engineer'ing, *n.*, the science and art of con-
struction; *pr.p.*, en-
gineer.

en'ginery, *n.*, engines
collectively; the art
of working engines.

engird', *v.t.*, to encircle
with a belt; to sur-
round.

engird'ed, *p.p.*, engird.

engird'ing, *pr.p.*, engird.

engir'dle, *v.t.*, *i.q.* engird.

Eng'lander, *n.*, someone
opposed to imperial
policy.

Eng'lish, *adj.*, rel. or
pert. to England and
the English; *n.*, the
English language;
English literature.

Eng'lishism, *n.*, an English idiom.

Eng'lishman, *n.*, a
native of England.

Eng'lishwoman, *n.*, a
woman native of Eng-
land.

engorge', *v.t.*, to fill up,
to congest; to con-
sume voraciously.

engorged', *p.p.*, engorge.

engorge'ment, *n.*, the act
or result of engorg-
ing.

engorg'ing, *pr.p.*, en-
gorge.

engraft', *v.t.*, to graft,
to impress upon the
mind. (Also *ingraft*.)

engraft'ed, *p.p.*, engraft.

engraft'ing, *pr.p.*, en-
graft.

engrail', *v.t.*, to indent.

engrailed', *p.p.*, engrail.

engrail'ing, *pr.p.*, en-
grail.

engrail'ment, *n.*, the arrangement of dots
at the rim of a coin.

engrain', *v.t.*, *i.q.* ingrain.

engrave', *v.t.*, to cut a
design or picture into
metal or wood.

engraved', *p.p.*, engrave.

engra'ver, *n.*, one who
engraves.

engra'ving, *n.*, a picture
produced from an en-
graved plate; *pr.p.*,
engrave.

engross', *v.t.*, to pre-
occupy, to completely
occupy; to write in a
large, clear hand.

engrossed', *p.p.*, engross.

engross'er, *n.*, one who
writes out documents
in a large, clear hand.

engross'ing, *adj.*, absorbing, enthralling; *n.*,
the transcript of a
document in a large
hand; *pr.p.*, engross.

engross'ment, *n.*, the act
of engrossing; an
engrossed document;
mental absorption.

engulf', *v.t.*, to over-
whelm, to completely
swallow up. (Also *in-
gulf*.)

engulfed', *p.p.*, engulf.

engulf'ing, *pr.p.*, engulf.

enhance', *v.t.*, to increase
in value, to heighten.

enhanced', *p.p.*, enhance.

enhance'ment, *n.*, the act
or result of enhanc-
ing.

enhan'cing, *pr.p.*, en-
hance.

enharmon'ic, *adj.*, with
musical intervals
smaller than a semi-
tone.

enharmon'ical, *adj.*, *i.q.*
enharmonic.

enharmon'ically, *adv.*, in
an enharmonic way.

enheart'en, *v.t.*, to cheer
up, to inspirit.

enheartened, *p.p.*, en-
hearten.

enheart'ening, *pr.p.*, en-
hearten.

En'iac, *n.*, an acronym,
from *electronic num*-
erical *integrator and
calculator*.

enig'ma, *n.*, a riddle or
word-puzzle.

enigmat'ic, *adj.*, puzz-
ling, obscure.

enigmat'ical, *adj.*, *i.q.*
enigmatic.

enigmat'ically, *adv.*, ob-
scurely; puzzlingly.

enig'matist, *n.*, one who
makes or solves enig-
mas.

enig'matize, *v.t.*, to
speak in enigmas.

enisle', *v.t.*, to make into
an isle; to isolate.
(Also *inisle*.)

enjamb'(e)ment, *n.*, the
continuing of a sen-
tence from one line to
the next (esp. in verse).

enjoin', *v.t.*, to com-
mand, to lay a charge
upon.

enjoined', *p.p.*, enjoin.

enjoin'ing, *pr.p.*, enjoin.

enjoy, v.t., to take pleasure in; to have possession of.

enjoy'able, adj., delightful, causing enjoyment.

enjoy'ableness, n., i.q. enjoyment.

enjoy'ably, adv., in an enjoyable way.

enjoyed', p.p., enjoy.

enjoy'ing, pr.p., enjoy.

enjoy'ment, n., the act or state of enjoying; delight.

enkin'dle, v.t., to set fire to; to rouse.

enkin'dled, p.p., enkindle.

enkin'dling, pr.p., enkindle.

enlace', v.t., to encircle; to entwine; to ornament with lace.

enlaced', p.p., enlace.

enlace'ment, n., an ornamentation of lace; a twining with lace.

enlac'ing, pr.p., enlace.

enlarge', v.t., to make larger, to increase; to set at liberty; v.i., to expatiate at length; to exaggerate.

enlarged', p.p., enlarge.

enlarge'ment, n., the act of enlarging; being set free.

enlar'ger, n., one who enlarges.

enlar'ging, pr.p., enlarge.

enlight'en, v.t., to illuminate; to bring understanding to; to give light to; to throw light off.

enlight'ened, p.p., enlighten.

enlight'ener, n., one who enlightens.

enlight'ening, pr.p., enlighten.

enlight'enment, n., the act or result of enlightening.

enlink', v.t., to link together; to connect closely.

enlinked, p.p., enlink.

enlinking, pr.p., enlink.

enlist', v.t., to put on a list or roll, to recruit; to win to one's side; v.i., to join the colours.

enlist'ed, p.p., enlist.

enlist'ing, pr.p., enlist.

enlist'ment, n., the act of enlisting.

enli'ven, v.t., to put life into, to add brightness to.

enli'vened, p.p., enliven.

enli'vener, n., one who enlivens.

enli'vening, pr.p., enliven.

en masse, adv., all together (Fr.).

enmesh', v.t., to entangle, to snare.

enmesh'ment, n., an entanglement.

en'mity, n., hostility, unfriendliness.

enn'ead, n., the number nine; any set or series of nine.

en'neagon, n., a nine-sided figure.

Ennean'dria, n. pl., one of Linnaeus's grouping of plants. It contains flowers with nine stamens.

enno'ble, v.t., to make noble, either morally or in rank.

enno'bled, p.p., enoble.

enno'blement, n., the act of ennobling; the state of being ennobled.

enno'bling, pr.p., enoble.

ennui, n., boredom, lassitude (Fr.).

enor'mity, n., the state of being enormous; a monstrous offence.

enor'mous, adj., excessively large, huge.

enor'mously, adv., to an enormous degree.

enor'mousness, n., the quality of being enormous.

en'osis, n., union; (e.g. of Cyprus with Greece) (Gr.).

enough', adj., sufficient.

enounce', v.t., to state, to declare, to enunciate.

enounced', p.p., enounce.

enounce'ment, n., the enunciation of words.

enoun'cing, pr.p., enounce.

en pass'ant, adv., by the way (Fr.).

enquire', v.i., i.q. inquire.

enquired', p.p., enquire.

enquir'er, n., i.q. inquirer.

enquir'ing, pr.p., enquire.

enquir'y, n., i.q. inquiry.

enrage', v.t., to put into a rage, to infuriate.

enraged', p.p., enrage.

enra'ging, pr.p., enrage.

en rapport, adv., in touch (with) (Fr.).

enrap'ture, v.t., to fill with rapture.

enrap'tured, p.p., enrapture.

enrap'turing, pr.p., enrapture.

enrav'ish, v.t., i.q. ravish.

enrav'ishment, n., i.q. ravishment.

enre'giment, v.t., to form men into a regiment; to discipline.

en règle, adv., in due form (Fr.).

enrich', v.t., to make wealthy; to add worth to; to ornament.

enriched', p.p., enrich.

enrich'er, n., one who enriches.

enrich'ing, pr.p., enrich.

enrich'ment, n., the act or result of enriching; ornamentation.

enrobe', v.t., to deck with a robe.

enrobed', p.p., enrobe.

enrob'ing, pr.p., enrobe.

enrol(l)', v.t., to place on a roll, to enlist.

enrolled', p.p., enrol.

enroll'er, n., one who enrols.

enroll'ing, pr.p., enrol.

enrol'ment, n., the act or result of enrolling.

enroot', v.t., to cause to take root.

enroot'ed, p.p., enroot.

enroot'ing, pr.p., enroot.

en route, adv., on the way (Fr.).

ens, n., an entity, an existing thing.

En'sa, n., an acronym from Entertainments National Service Association.

ensam'ple', n., i.q. example.

ensan'guine, v.t., to stain with blood.

ensang'uined, adj., bloodstained; p.p., ensanguine.

ensconce', v.t., to hide with safety; to instal in a place of security.

ensconced', p.p., ensconce.

ensconc'ing, pr.p., ensconce.

enseal', v.t., to seal up.

ensealed', p.p., enseal.

enseal'ing, pr.p., enseal.

enseam', v.t., to scar; to sew up.

ensem'ble, n., the whole; the general effect (Fr.).

enshield', v.t., to cover with a shield.

enshrine', v.t., to set in a shrine; to cherish with affection.

enshrined', p.p., enshrine.

enshrin'ing, pr.p., enshrine.

enshroud', v.t., to wrap up in a shroud, to envelop.

enshroud'ed, p.p., enshroud.

enshroud'ing, pr.p., enshroud.

en'siform, adj., sword-shaped.

en'sign, n., a standard, a flag; a military officer who bore the flag of his regiment.

en'signcy, n., the rank and office of an ensign.

en'silage, n., the storage of green fodder in a silo.

ensile', v.t., to put fodder into a silo.

enslave', v.t., to make a slave of; to captivate.

enslaved', p.p., enslave.

enslave'ment, n., the act or result of enslaving.

ensla'ver, n., one who enslaves.

enslav'ing, pr.p., enslave.

ensnare', v.t., to entrap, to entangle.

ensnared', p.p., ensnare.

ensnar'er, n., one who ensnares.

ensnar'ing, pr.p., ensnare.

ensoul', v.t., to infuse a soul into.

ensphere', v.t., to place within a sphere.

ensphered', p.p., ensphere.

enspher'ing, pr.p., ensphere.

enstamp', v.t., to stamp.

enstamped', p.p., enstamp.

enstamp'ing, pr.p., enstamp.

ensue', v.t. and i., to follow.

ensued', p.p., ensue.

ensu'ing, pr.p., ensue.

ensure', v.t., to make sure of, to guarantee. (Also insure.)

ensured', p.p., ensure.

ensur'ing, pr.p., ensure.

enswathe', v.t., to bind or wrap in a bandage.

entab'lature, n., the topmost member (in a classical building) that rests upon the capitals of the pillars.

enta'blement, n., a platform used to support a statue.

entail', n., settlement of an estate upon a named succession of inheritors; v.t., to settle in tail; to involve as a consequence.

entailed', p.p., entail.

entail'ing, pr.p., entail.

entail'ment, n., the act or result of entailing.

entan'gle, v.t., to twist together, to involve.

entan'gled, p.p., entangle.

entan'glement, n., the act or result of entangling; a military obstruction of barbed wire, etc.

entan'gling, pr.p., entangle.

en'tasis, n., a slight convexity in the shaft of a column; a spasm.

entel'echy, n., a term in Greek philosophy meaning that which converts the potential into the actual.

entell'us, n., the sacred bearded monkey of the Hindus.

entente', n., an understanding, an agreement (Fr.).

entente' cordiale', n., the alliance formed in 1904 between Great Britain and France (Fr.).

en'ter, v.t. and i., to come into; to make a record of; to name for a contest.

enterable, adj., able to be entered.

en'tered, p.p., enter.

en'terer, n., one who enters.

enter'ic, adj., rel. or pert. to the intestines.

en'tering, pr.p., enter.

enteri'tis, n., inflammation of the small intestine.

entero'colitis, n., inflammation of the upper colon.

enterol'ogy, n., the science of the intestines.

en'teron, n., the alimentary canal or gut.

en'terprise, n., a bold attempt; an undertaking; v.t., to attempt.

en'terprised, p.p., enterprise.

en'terpriser, n., one who is enterprising.

en'terprising, adj., bold, adventurous; pr.p., enterprise.

en'terprisingly, n., in an enterprising way.

entertain', v.t., to receive hospitably; to admit to one's thoughts; to amuse.

entertained', p.p., entertain.

entertain'er, n., one who entertains.

entertain'ing, adj., amusing; pr.p., entertain.

entertain'ment, n., the act or result of entertaining.

enthral', v.t., to captivate, to charm.

enthralled', p.p., enthral.

enthrall'ing, pr.p., enthral.

enthral'ment; n., charmed enslavement.

enthrone', v.t., to place on a throne.

enthroned', p.p., enthrone.

enthrone'ment, n., the act or result of enthroning.

enthro'ning, pr.p., enthrone.

enthroniza'tion, n., the ceremony of enthroning.

enthuse', v.t., to show enthusiasm; to gush.

enthused', p.p., enthuse.

enthu'siasm, n., a state or feeling of intense zeal or gratification.

enthu'siast, n., one who shows himself enthusiastic.

enthusias'tic, adj., full of enthusiasm; very zealous.

enthusias'tical, adj., i.q. enthusiastic.

enthusias'tically, *adv.*, with enthusiasm.

enthus'ing, *pr.p.*, enthuse.

en'thymeme, *n.*, an elliptical argument.

entice', *v.t.*, to allure, to draw on.

enticed', *p.p.*, entice.

entice'ment, *n.*, the act of enticing; a snare.

enti'cer, *n.*, one who entices.

enti'cing, *adj.*, attractive; *pr.p.*, entice.

enti'cingly, *adv.*, attractively, alluringly.

entire', *adj.*, whole, complete.

entire'ly, *adv.*, wholly, completely.

entire'ness, *n.*, the quality of being entire.

entire'ty, *n.*, completeness.

en'titative, *adj.*, having existence; rel. or pert. to existence.

enti'tle, *v.t.*, to give a title or right to; to name.

enti'tled, *p.p.*, entitle.

entitle'ment, *n.*, a claim.

enti'tling, *pr.p.*, entitle.

en'tity, *n.*, any individual existing thing; existence, essence.

entomb', *v.t.*, to place in a tomb.

entombed', *p.p.*, entomb.

entomb'ing, *pr.p.*, entomb.

entomb'ment, *n.*, the act or result of entombing.

entom'ic, *adj.*, rel. or pert. to insects.

entom'ical, *adj.*, i.q. entomic.

en'tomoid, *adj.*, insect-like.

entomolog'ical, *adj.*, rel. or pert. to entomology.

entomol'ogist, *n.*, one who studies entomology.

entomol'ogy, *n.*, the branch of natural history that relates to insects.

entomoph'agous, *adj.*, insect-eating.

enton'ic, *adj.*, at high tension.

entourage', *n.*, surroundings; followers (*Fr.*).

en-tout-cas, *n.*, a type of hard tennis-court (*Fr.*).

Entozo'a, *n. pl.*, internal parasites.

entozo'on, *n.*, the sing. of entozoa.

en'tr'acte, *n.*, the interval between the acts; the music played in that interval (*Fr.*).

en'trails, *n. pl.*, intestines, bowels.

entrain, *v.t.*, to put into a train; *v.i.*, to board a train.

entrained', *p.p.*, entrain.

entrain'ing, *pr.p.*, entrain.

entrain'ment, *n.*, the act or fact of entraining.

entram'mel, *v.t.*, i.q. trammel.

entram'mel(l)ed, *p.p.*, entrammel.

entram'mel(l)ing, *pr.p.*, entrammel.

entrance', *v.t.*, to throw into a trance, to charm.

en'trance, *n.*, the act of entering, admission, an opening into.

entranced', *p.p.*, entrance.

entrance'ment, *n.*, a trance.

entranc'ing, *adj.*, charming; *pr.p.*, entrance.

en'trant *adj.*, entering. *n.*, a novice; one entered for an event.

entrap', *v.t.*, to catch in a trap.

entrapped', *p.p.*, entrap.

entrap'ping, *pr.p.*, entrap.

entreat', *v.t.*, to implore, to beseech.

entreat'ed, *p.p.*, entreat.

entreat'er, *n.*, one who entreats.

entreat'ing, *pr.p.*, entreat.

entreat'ingly, *adv.*, pleadingly, beseechingly.

entreat'y, *n.*, an earnest request or prayer.

entrechat, *n.*, a striking together of the heels several times in the air when dancing (*Fr.*).

en'trecôte, *n.*, a steak from the ribs (*Fr.*).

en'tredeux, *n.*, an insertion (of lace, etc.) (*Fr.*).

entrée', *n.*, an entrance, the privilege of entering; a dish served at dinner before the main course (*Fr.*).

entremets', *n. pl.*, the viands that follow the

pièce de résistance at a meal (*Fr.*).

entrench', *v.t.*, to dig a trench; to fortify with a trench; *v.i.*, to encroach.

entrenched', *p.p.*, entrench.

entrench'ing, *pr.p.*, entrench.

entrench'ment, *n.*, the act or result of entrenching.

entre nous, *adv.*, confidentially (*Fr.*).

en'trepôt, *n.*, a warehouse; a trade-distributing centre (*Fr.*).

entrepreneur', *n.*, one who undertakes a business enterprise (*Fr.*).

en'tresol, *n.*, a low storey between two higher ones; a mezzanine (*Fr.*).

en'tropy, *n.*, the gain or loss of heat in thermodynamics (*phys.*).

entrust', *v.t.*, to put into the care of; to charge with.

entrust'ed, *p.p.*, entrust.

entrust'ing, *pr.p.*, entrust.

en'try, *n.*, the act of entering; the place of entering; the act of entering in a ledger, register, etc.

entwine', *v.t.*, to interlace twice round.

entwined', *p.p.*, entwine.

entwin'ing, *pr.p.*, entwine.

entwist', *v.t.*, to twist. (Also *intwist*.)

entwist'ed, *p.p.*, entwist.

entwist'ing, *pr.p.*, entwist.

enu'cleate, *v.t.*, to extract; to explain.

enu'cleated, *p.p.*, enucleate.

enu'cleating, *pr.p.*, enucleate.

enuclea'tion, *n.*, the act of enucleating; the extraction of a tumour.

enu'merate, *v.t.*, to reckon, to count up, to mention severally.

enu'merated, *p.p.*, enumerate.

enu'merating, *pr.p.*, enumerate.

enumera'tion, *n.*, the act of enumerating; a list.

enu'merative, *adj.*, enumerating.

enu'merator, *n.*, one who enumerates.

enun'ciate, *v.t.*, to utter, to declare, to pronounce articulately.

enun'ciated, *p.p.*, enunciate.

enun'ciating, *pr.p.*, enunciate.

enuncia'tion, *n.*, the act of enunciating; clear articulation; the formal statement of a proposition.

enun'ciative, *adj.*, declaratory; rel. or pert. to enunciation.

enun'ciator, *n.*, one who declares a formal statement; one who articulates words very distinctly.

enun'ciatory, *adj.*, *i.q.* enunciative.

enure', *v.t.* and *i.*, *i.q.* inure; to take effect; to operate (*leg.*).

enured', *p.p.*, enure.

enure'sis, *n.*, incontinence of urine.

enur'ing, *pr.p.*, enure.

envel'op, *v.t.* to wrap round; to surround.

en'velope, *n.*, a covering; the cover of a letter.

envel'oped, *p.p.*, envelop.

envel'oping, *pr.p.*, envelop.

envel'opment, *n.*, the act of enveloping; a covering.

enven'om, *v.t.*, to poison; to put venom into.

enven'omed, *p.p.*, envenom.

enven'oming, *pr.p.*, envenom.

en'viable, *adj.*, worthy of envy.

en'viably, *adv.*, in a way to be envied.

en'vied, *p.p.*, envy.

en'vier, *n.*, one who envies.

en'vious, *adj.*, feeling envy, jealous.

en'viously, *adv.*, with envy, jealously.

envi'ron, *v.t.*, to surround.

envi'roned, *p.p.*, environ.

envi'roning, *pr.p.*, environ.

envi'ronment, *n.*, surroundings; the external circumstances conditioning existence.

envi'rons, *n. pl.*, the surrounding neighbourhood, suburbs.

envis'age, *v.t.*, to face; to contemplate.

envis'aged, *p.p.*, envisage.

envisage'ment, *n.*, a contemplation.

envis'aging, *pr.p.*, envisage.

en'voy, *n.*, a special messenger; the concluding lines of a poem. (Also *envoi*.)

en'voyship, *n.*, the office of an envoy.

en'vy, *n.*, the feeling of jealousy of another's situation; *v.t.*, to be jealous of another's good fortune.

en'vying, *pr.p.*, envy.

enwind', *v.t.* to coil or wind around.

enwomb', *v.t.*, to conceal in a gulf, pit etc.; to enclose in the womb.

enwrap', *v.t.*, to wrap closely. (Also *inwrap*.)

enwreathe, *v.t.*, *i.q.* wreathe.

enzoot'ic, *adj.*, regularly affecting animals in a particular place or at a particular time; *n.*, a disease occurring predictably in time and place.

en'zyme, *n.*, the active principle of a ferment (*chem.*).

E'ocene, *adj.*, the lowest of the four sub-divisions of the Tertiary formation (*geol.*).

Eo'ka, *n.*, a combatant organization contending for the union of Cyprus with Greece.

Eo'lian, *adj.*, *i.q.* Aeolian.

e'olith, *n.*, a pre-Palaeolithic stone implement.

eolith'ic, *adj.*, rel. or pert. to the earliest period of the Stone Age.

e'on, *n.*, *i.q.* aeon.

e'osin, *n.*, a red dye used in colour-photography.

Eozo'ic, *adj.*, pert. or rel. to the Eozoic or Upper Archaean rocks.

eozo'on, *n.*, a formituferous fossil.

ep'act, *n.*, the amount by which the solar exceeds the lunar year.

ep'arch, *n.*, a Greek or Russian ruler of an eparchy; a Russian metropolitan.

ep'archy, *n.*, a province.

epaule'ment, *n.*, a protective parapet.

ep'aulet, *or* -ette, *n.*, a shoulder ornament (*Fr.*).

ép'ée, *n.*, a duelling sword; a fencing sword (*Fr.*).

epeirogen'esis, *n.*, the process of making continents (*geol.*).

epen'thesis, *n.*, the addition of a syllable or a letter (*Gr.*).

epenthet'ic, *adj.*, rel. or pert. to epenthesis.

épergne', *n.*, a fruit or flower stand (*Fr.*).

epexeges'is, *n.*, something added to make a meaning clear.

epexeget'ical, *adj.*, rel. or pert. to epexegesis.

epexeget'ically, *adv.*, in an epexegetical way.

e'phah, *n.*, a Hebrew measure of capacity.

ephebe', *n.*, a youth between 18 and 20 (*Gr.*).

ephem'era, *n. pl.*, the May-fly; a genus of short-lived insects.

ephem'eral, *adj.*, lasting for a day; short-lived.

ephem'eris, *n.*, a day-by-day calculation of the motions of the heavenly bodies.

ephem'eron, *n.*, a May-fly.

Ephe'sian, *adj.*, rel. or pert. to Ephesus (a city of the classical Ionic Confederation) and the Ephesians.

eph'od, *n.*, a linen vestment of the Jewish ceremonial.

eph'or, *n.*, one of the five magistrates of Sparta.

ep'iblast, *n.*, the outermost layer of blastoderm.

ep'ic, *adj.*, rel. or pert. to an heroic story; *n.*, a literary work on grand heroic themes.

epican'thus, *n.*, a fold of skin in the corner of the eye.

ep'icarp, *n.*, the outer layer of a pericarp.

epiced'ium, *n.*, a funeral ode.

ep'icene, *adj.*, common to both sexes.

epicen'tre, *n.*, the point on the earth's surface immediately above the epicentrum.

epicen'trum, *n.*, the point where an earthquake starts.

epicles'is, n., an invocation of the Holy Spirit to consecrate the eucharistic elements.

epicra'nium, n., the covering of the skull.

Epicte'tian, adj., bel. or pert. to Epictetus, a philosopher of Hierapolis in Phrygia.

ep'icure, n., a person expert in good eating.

epicure'an, adj., rel. or pert. to Epicurus; concerned with the philosophy of pleasure as the aim of life.

epicure'anism, n., the practices of the Epicureans.

ep'icurism, n., the practices of an epicure.

Epicur'us, n., an Athenian philosopher of refined and cultivated taste.

ep'icycle, n., a circle centred on the circumference of another circle.

epicyc'lic, adj., rel. or pert. to epicycle.

epicy'cloid, n., the formation of an epicycle.

epideic'tic, adj., intended for display.

epidem'ic, adj., spreading among the people, n., a communal outbreak of disease.

epidem'ical, adj., rel. or pert. to epidemics.

epidem'ically, adv., to an epidemical degree.

epidemiolog'ical, adj., rel. or pert. to epidemiology.

epidemiol'ogist, n., one who studies epidemic diseases.

epidemiol'ogy, n., the study of epidemic diseases.

epider'mal, adj., rel. or pert. to epidermis.

epider'mis, n., the outer skin, the scarf-skin.

epidermoid'al, adj., i.q. epidermal.

epidi'ascope, n., a lantern projecting images of both opaque and transparent objects.

epifoc'al, adj., above the focus of an earthquake.

epigas'tric, adj., pert. or rel. to the abdomen.

epigas'trium, n., the part of the abdomen which lies immediately over the stomach.

ep'igene, adj., produced or originating on the surface of the earth.

epigen'esis, n., the creation of an organic germ as a new product.

epiglot'tic, adj., pert. or rel. to the epiglottis.

epiglot'tis, n., the cartilage at the tongue's root, partly closing the larynx.

ep'igon(e), n., one of a later (and less distinguished) generation.

ep'igram, n., a terse pithy saying, a short verse composition, satirical, antithetic or complimentary.

epigrammat'ic, adj., rel. to or like an epigram.

epigrammat'ical, adj., i.q. epigrammatic.

epigrammat'ically, adv., in an epigrammatic way.

epigram'matist, n., a writer of epigrams.

epigramm'atize, v.t. and i., to write epigrams.

ep'igraph, n., an inscription.

epigraph'ic, adj., rel. or pert. to epigraph.

epig'raphist, n., a writer of epigraphs.

epig'raphy, n., a motto.

ep'ilepsy, n., the "falling sickness," a nervous disorder accompanied by convulsive fits.

epilep'tic, adj., rel. to, or suffering from, epilepsy; n., one who suffers from epilepsy.

epil'ogist, n., a writer or speaker of an epilogue.

ep'ilogue, n., a speech at the end of a play; the conclusion of a discourse.

epinos'ic, adj., unwholesome; unhealthy.

Epiph'any, n., the Feast of Christ's Manifestation, Jan 6.

epiphenom'enon, n., a secondary symptom.

epiphyt'al, adj., rel. or pert. to epiphyte.

ep'iphyte, n., a parasitical plant.

epiphyt'ic, adj., i.q. epiphytal.

Epir'ot, n., an inhabitant of Epirus (Gr.).

epis'copacy, n., the principles or system of episcopal rule.

epis'copal, adj., rel. or pert. to a bishop.

episcopa'lia, n. pl., episcopal belongings.

episcopa'lian, adj., rel. to episcopacy.

episcopa'lianism, n., the doctrine of episcopal rule.

epis'copate, n., a bishop's incumbency of his office; the collective bishops.

ep'isodal, adj., of the nature of an episode.

ep'isode, n., a separate story or incident in a book or speech; any incident.

episod'ic, adj., i.q. episodal.

episod'ical, adj., i.q. episodal.

episod'ically, adv., in an episodal way.

epispas'tic, adj., blistering, n., a plaster, a drawing substance.

ep'isperm, n., a seed's outer covering.

epistemol'ogy, n., the study of knowledge.

epis'tle, n., a letter; pl., certain books of the New Testament.

epis'tolary, adj., of the nature of a letter.

epis'toler, n., one who reads the Epistle.

epis'trophe, n., an ending of several clauses or sentences with the same word.

ep'itaph, n., an inscription on a tomb; a composition in honour of a dead person.

epithala'mium, n., a wedding song.

epithe'lium, n., the coating of the internal parts and organs of the body.

ep'ithet, n., a word, usu. an adj., describing some quality of a person or thing.

epithet'ic, adj., of the nature of an epithet.

epithet'ical, adj., i.q. epithetic.

epithet'ically, adv., in an epithetical way.

epit'ome, n., an abbreviation; an abstract.

epit'omist, n., one who makes an epitome.

epit'omize, v.t., to reduce to an epitome.

epit'omized, p.p., epitomize.

epit'omizer, n., one who epitomizes.

epit'omizing, pr.p., epitomize.

ep'itrite, n., a metric foot containing one short and three long syllables variously arranged.

epizo'a, n. pl., external parasites.

epizo'an, adj., rel. or pert. to epizoa.

epizo'ic, adj., i.q. epizoan.

epizo'on, n., an external parasite or a commensal animal or plant.

epizoot'ic, adj., spreading among animals.

ep'och, n., a fixed point in time; an era.

ep'ochal, adj., rel. or pert. to an epoch.

ep'ode, n., the third number of a lyric ode; a kind of ode in which a long verse is followed by a shorter one.

epod'ic, adj., rel. or pert. to an epode.

ep'onym, n., the supposed or actual founder of a city named after him.

epon'ymous, adj., giving a name to.

ep'opee, n., an epic poem or poetry.

ep'os, n., early epic poetry, usually recited, not written.

epsil'on, n., the Greek letter E/ε, the fifth letter of the Greek alphabet.

Ep'som, adj., a kind of salts; n., a town in the English county of Surrey; a famous racecourse.

equabil'ity, n., the quality of being equable.

e'quable, adj., of even temper, calm.

e'quably, adv., in an equable way.

e'qual, adj., the same in size, amount and quality; v.t., to make equal; to be equal to.

equalitar'ian, n., one who favours equality.

equal'ity, n., the state of being equal.

equaliza'tion, n., the act or effect of equalizing.

e'qualize, v.t., to make equal.

e'qualized, p.p., equalize.

e'qualizer, n., a device for giving lateral stability to an aircraft.

e'qualizing, pr.p., equalize.

e'qual(l)ed, p.p., equal.

e'qual(l)ing, pr.p., equal.

e'qually, adv., in the same degree.

equan'gular, adj., i.q. equiangular.

equanim'ity, n., evenness of temper; calmness.

equate', v.t., to form an equation with.

equa'ted, p.p., equate.

equa'ting, pr.p., equate.

equa'tion, n., a proposition indicating equality between two quantities.

equa'tor, n., an imaginary line round the earth along the points equidistant from the poles.

equato'rial, adj., rel. or pert. to the equator.

eq'uerry, n., a court official under the Master of the Horse.

eques'trian, adj., rel. or pert. to horsemanship; n., a rider on horseback.

eques'trianism, n., horsemanship.

equestrienne', n., a horsewoman; a female circus-rider (Fr.).

equian'gular, adj., having equal angles.

equidis'tant, adj., at an equal distance.

equilat'eral, adj., having equal sides.

equili'brate, v.t. and i., to balance equally.

equili'brated, p.p., equilibrate.

equili'brating, pr.p., equilibrate.

equilibra'tion, n., the act of balancing; a state of equal balance.

equil'ibrator, n., a device for maintaining equilibrium.

equilib'rious, adj., in equilibrium.

equil'ibrist, n., a balancer or tight-rope walker.

equilib'rity, n., the state of equilibrium.

equilib'rium, n., equal balance, equipoise.

equimul'tiple, n., a number that has a common factor with another.

e'quine, adj., pert. or rel. to a horse.

equinoc'tial, adj., rel. to the time; rel. to the equinoxes.

e'quinox, n., one of the two periods when day and night are equal at a point not on the equator.

equip', v.t., to fit out, to furnish, to arm.

eq'uipage, n., equipment; a train of attendants.

equip'ment, n., the state of being equipped; materials for equipping; outfit.

e'quipoise, n., equality of weight; perfect balance.

equipol'lence, n., equality of skill or influence.

equipol'lency, n., i.q. equipollence.

equipol'lent, adj., equally skilful or influential.

equipon'derance, n., the state of being equal in weight.

equipon'derant, adj., equal in weight.

equipon'derate, v.t., to counterbalance; to equal in weight.

equipoten'tial, adj., having equal influence or power (phys.).

equipped', p.p., equip.

equip'ping, pr.p., equip.

equiso'nance, n., the concord of an octave.

equiso'nant, adj., sounding in concord of an octave.

eq'uitable, adj., just, fair.

eq'uitableness, n., justice.

eq'uitably, adv., justly, fairly.

eq'uitant, adj., on horseback; overlapping (bot.).

equita'tion, n., the art of horsemanship.

eq'uites, n. pl., the knights or members of the Roman equestrian order.

Eq'uity, n., the actors' trade-union.

eq'uity, n., fairness, impartiality. In the legal sense, it is the correction of what is defective in the broad statements of the law.

equiv'alence, n., the state of being equivalent.

equiv'alency, n., i.q. equivalence.

equiv'alent, adj., of equal value to; n., something of equal value.

equiv'ocal, adj., having more than one meaning; questionable.

equiv'ocally, adv., in an equivocal way.

equiv'ocate, v.i., to use intentionally misleading words.

equiv'ocated, p.p., equivocate.

equiv'ocating, pr.p., equivocate.

equivoca'tion, n., the act of equivocating; prevarication.

equiv'ocator, n., one who equivocates.

e'quivoque, -oke, n., an ambiguous expression; a pun.

equiv'orous, adj., eating horseflesh.

e'ra, n., a period of time.

era'diate, v.t., to shed as rays; v.i., to radiate.

era'diated, p.p., eradiate.

era'diating, pr.p., eradiate.

eradia'tion, n., the act or effect of radiating.

erad'icable, adj., able to be eradicated.

erad'icate, v.t., to remove by the roots; to destroy.

erad'icated, p.p., eradicate.

erad'icating, pr.p., eradicate.

eradica'tion, n., the act or effect of eradicating.

erad'icative, adj., utterly destructive.

era'sable, adj., able to be erased.

erase', v.t., to rub or cross out.

erased', p.p., erase.

erase'ment, n., an erasure.

era'ser, n., anything that erases.

era'sing, pr.p., erase.

era'sion, n., the act of erasing, an erasure.

Eras'tian, adj., rel. or pert. to Erastus and his teaching.

Eras'tianism, n., the tenets of Erastus and his followers.

era'sure, n., the act or effect of erasing; an obliteration.

E'rato, n., the Muse of amatory poetry.

ere, prep. and conj., sooner than, before.

Er'ebus, n., in mythology, an intermediate place of the dead.

erect', adj., upright; v.t., to set upright, to build.

erect'able, adj., able to be erected.

erect'ed, p.p., erect.

erect'ile, adj., with power to erect.

erectil'ity, n., the quality or state of being erectile.

erect'ing, pr.p., erect.

erec'tion, n., the act or result of erecting; a building; a tumescence of the penis from sexual desire.

erect'ly, adv., straight upright.

erect'ness, n., the quality of being erect.

erect'or, n., anything that, or anyone who, erects.

ere'long, adv., shortly.

er'emite, n., a hermit (lit., a dweller in the desert).

eremit'ic, adj., rel. or pert. to hermits.

eremit'ical, adj., i.q. eremitic.

er'ethism, n., excessive excitability.

erg, n., a unitary measure of energy. (Also ergon.)

ergatoc'racy, n., the rule of the workers.

er'go, adv., therefore (Lat.).

erg'ograph, n., an instrument for recording muscular work.

ergom'eter, n., an instrument for measuring work or energy.

erg'on, n., i.q. erg.

ergonom'ics, n., the study of man in relation to his working environment.

ergopho'bia, n., a fear of work.

er'got, n., a fungus on rye; a growth on a horse's fetlock.

er'gotism, n., the growth of ergot; the effect of ergot as a medicine.

Eri'ca, n., a genus of heath plants.

erica'ceous, adj., belonging to the heath genus.

erig'eron, n., a flowering perennial.

E'rin, n., Ireland.

eri'naceous, adj., rel. or pert. to hedgehogs.

eriom'eter, n., a measuring apparatus used in the textile industry.

eris'tic, adj., aiming at victory rather than truth; n., the art of argument.

erl'-king', n., a malicious spirit in Norse folklore who lures children to the land of death.

er'mine, adj., made of ermine; n., a small furry animal; its fur worn by kings, peers and judges; v.t., to invest with the ermine.

er'mined, adj., decorated with ermine; p.p., ermine.

erne, n., a sea eagle.

Ern'ie, n., an acronym of Electronic Random Number Indicator Equipment, a device for drawing prizewinning numbers of premium bonds.

erode', v.t., to eat away.

ero'ded, p.p., erode.

ero'dent, adj., producing erosion.

ero'ding, pr.p., erode.

Er'os, n., the god of love; Cupid (Gr.).

ero'sion, n., the act or result of eroding.

ero'sive, adj., eating away, wearing away.

erot'ic, adj., pert. or rel. to love; passionate.

e'rotism, n., sexual desire or excitement.

erot'oman'ia, n., morbid sexual love.

erpetol'ogy, n., i.q. herpetology.

err, v.i., to go astray, to do wrong, to make a mistake.

er'rancy, n., a roaming in quest of adventure.

er'rand, n., a journey on someone's business, a commission.

er'rant, adj., roving.

er'rantry, n., a knight errant's service.

erra'ta, n. pl., mistakes (Lat.).

errat'ic, adj., roving, uncertain, irregular.

errat'ical, adj., i.q. erratic.

errat'ically, adv., in an erratic way.

erra'tum, n., the sing. of errata (Lat.).

erred, p.p., err.

er'rhine, adj., causing sneezing; n., a medicine which causes a mucus discharge.

er'ring, pr.p., err.

erro'neous, adj., in error, mistaken.

erro'neously, adv., incorrectly.

érro'neousness, *n.*, the state or quality of being erroneous.

er'ror, *n.*, a mistake, a blunder, a false belief.

ersatz', *adj.* and *n.* (a) substitute (*Ger.*).

Erse, *adj.*, rel. or pert. to Ireland and the Irish; *n.*, the native speech of Ireland.

erst, *adv.*, formerly, in the beginning.

erst'while, *adj.*, former; *adv.*, formerly.

erubes'cence, *n.*, a reddening, blushing.

erubes'cent, *adj.*, reddening, blushing.

eruct'ate, *v.t.*, to belch forth; *v.i.*, to belch.

eructa'tion, *n.*, the act of belching.

er'udite, *adj.*, learned, cultivated.

er'uditely, *adv.*, in an erudite way.

er'uditeness, *n.*, the state of being erudite.

erudi'tion, *n.*, learning; scholarship.

eru'ginous, *adj.*, rel. or pert. to verdigris.

erupt', *v.t.*, to cause to burst forth; *v.i.*, to burst forth.

erupt'ed, *p.p.*, erupt.

erupt'ing, *pr.p.*, erupt.

erup'tion, *n.*, the act or effect of erupting; an outbreak on the skin.

erup'tive, *adj.*, causing eruption.

eruptiv'ity, *n.*, the state of being eruptive.

erysip'elas, *n.*, a disease usually in the face or head, attended with inflammation and fever.

erysipel'atous, *adj.*, suffering from erysipelas.

erythe'ma, *n.*, excessive redness; a skin disease attended by redness.

escalade', *n.*, an attack by means of ladders; *v.t.*, to attack by means of ladders.

escala'ded, *p.p.*, escalade.

escala'ding, *pr.p.*, escalade.

es'calate, *v.i.*, to rise, to increase.

escala'ted, *p.p.*, escalate.

escala'ting, *pr.p.*, escalate.

escala'tion, *n.*, a rising; an increase.

es'calator, *n.*, a moving staircase.

escallon'ia, *n. pl.*, a group of S. American flowering shrubs.

escal'lop, *n.*, *i.q.* scallop.

escal'loped, *adj.*, charged with scallops (*her.*).

escapade, *n.*, a frolic, an adventure.

escape', *n.*, a flight, deliverance; *v.t.*, to get clear from, to avoid; *v.i.*, to get away safely.

escaped', *p.p.*, escape.

escapee', *n.*, an escaped person.

escape'ment, *n.*, a part of the works of a watch, clock or typewriter.

escap'ing, *pr.p.*, escape.

escap'ism, *n.*, the seeking of freedom from trouble or difficulty by ignoring them, or resorting to distractions.

escap'ist, *n.*, one who practises, or believes in, escapism.

escarp', *n.*, the side of a ditch nearest to the rampart; *v.t.*, to form a steep slope.

escarped', *p.p.*, escarp.

escarpes'cent, *adj.*, sloping steeply.

escarp'ing, *pr.p.*, escarp.

escarp'ment, *n.*, a steep side of a rock, hill or rampart.

eschalot', *n.*, *i.q.* shallot.

es'char, *n.*, a slough; a scab.

eschatolo'gical, *adj.*, rel. or pert. to eschatology.

eschatol'ogy, *n.*, the department of theology that deals with the last things of death, judgment, etc.

escheat', *n.*, the reversion by forfeiture or failure of heirs; *v.t.*, to take over forfeited property; *v.i.*, to revert by forfeiture or failure of heirs.

escheat'able, *adj.*, liable to escheat.

escheat'ed, *p.p.*, escheat.

escheat'ing, *pr.p.*, escheat.

escheat'or, *n.*, an official who superintends escheating.

eschew', *v.t.*, to avoid.

eschewed', *p.p.*, eschew.

eschew'ing, *pr.p.*, eschew.

eschscholt'zia, *n.*, a Californian yellow poppy.

esclandre, *n.*, a scandal; a disturbance (*Fr.*).

Esco'rial, *n.*, the royal palace near Madrid. (Also *Escurial.*)

es'cort, *n.*, a guard of armed men, protection; a guide, an attendant.

escort', *v.t.*, to accompany for protection.

escor'tage, *n.*, the action of escorting.

escort'ed, *p.p.*, escort.

escort'ing, *pr.p.*, escort.

escribe', *v.t.*, to describe a circle so as to touch one side of a triangle on the outside and the productions of the other two (*math.*).

escritoire', *n.*, a writing-desk. (Also *écritoire* and *secretaire* (*Fr.*).

escrow', *n.*, a conditional deed in the hands of a third party (*leg.*).

escud'o, *n.*, a Spanish and Portuguese silver coin; the monetary unit of Portugal.

Escula'pian, *adj.*, rel. or pert. to Aesculapius (*med.*). (Also *Aesculapian.*)

es'culent, *adj.*, eatable, fit for food; *n.*, anything eatable.

Escu'rial, *n.*, *i.q.* Escorial.

escutch'eon, *n.*, an heraldic shield; a plate round a keyhole.

escutch'eoned, *adj.*, furnished with an escutcheon.

es'kar, *n.*, a ridge of glacial gravel formed in river valleys. (Also *esker*) (*geol.*).

Es'kimo, *adj.*, the name of an indigenous people in Arctic regions; *n.*, one of the race.

esoph'agus, *n.*, the gullet, conveying food and drink into the stomach (properly written *oesophagus*).

esoter'ic, *adj.*, inner, secret, mysterious; *n.*, a person initiated in esoteric principles.

esote'rical, *adj.*, *i.q.* esoteric.

esote'rically, *adv.*, in an esoterical way.

espa'da, n., a matador (Span.).

es'padon, n., a long Spanish sword for two hands (Span.).

espadrille', n., a rope-soled shoe.

espagnolette', n., the fastening of a French window (Fr.).

espal'ier, n., a trellis on which trees are trained; a tree so trained.

espar'to, n., a strong variety of grass used in paper making.

espe'cial, adj., special, particular, pre-eminent.

espe'cially, adv., pre-eminently, particularly.

Esperant'ist, n., a student of Esperanto.

Esperan'to, n., an invented universal language.

espi'al, n., the act of spying, or keeping secret watch.

espied', p.p., espy.

espièglerie, n., roguishness (Fr.).

es'pionage, n., the practice of a spy (Fr.).

esplanade', n., an open space for promenading; the level space between a citadel and a town.

espou'sal, adj., rel. or pert. to a betrothal or marriage; n., the act of espousing, a betrothal.

espouse', v.t., to take as a spouse, to betroth; to adopt a cause.

espoused', p.p., espouse.

espous'er, n., one who espouses.

espous'ing, pr.p., espouse.

espressiv'o, adv., with expression (mus., It.).

espress'o, n., a machine for making coffee under pressure (It.).

esprit de corps, n., the animating spirit of a collective body (Fr.).

espy', v.t., to catch sight of.

espy'ing, pr.p., espy.

Es'quimau, adj. and n., i.q. Eskimo.

esquire', n., a shield-bearer; one entitled to arms; now a general title of respect.

ess, n., anything which is S-shaped.

essay', v.t., to attempt.

es'say, n., an endeavour; a short dissertation.

essayed', p.p., essay.

essay'er, n., one who essays.

essay'ing, pr.p., essay.

es'sayist, n., a writer of essays.

ess'e, n., the essential being or nature (Lat.).

es'sence, n., the true distinctive quality of anything; being in the abstract; a perfume; v.t., to perfume.

es'senced, p.p., essence.

es'sencing, pr.p., essence.

Essene', n., a member of a Jewish ascetic party.

essen'tial, adj., rel. or pert. to the essence; necessary; n., something necessary.

essential'ity, n., the quality of being essential.

essen'tialize, v.t., to raise to essential character.

essen'tially, adv., necessarily.

ess-hook, n., an S-shaped hook.

estab'lish, v.t., to settle, to make firm or stable; to institute; to ratify; to prove.

estab'lished, p.p., establish.

estab'lisher, n., anything that establishes.

estab'lishing, pr.p., establish.

estab'lishment, n., the act of establishing; that which is established; an institution; a business or household.

establishmentar'ian, adj., adhering to the principle of an established church; n., a supporter of the established church.

estafette', n., a mounted, military courier.

estam'inet, n., a café (Fr.).

estate', n., condition, state, property.

estat'ed, adj., landed (property).

esteem', n., a favourable opinion, respect; v.t., to value, to prize.

esteem'able, adj., i.q. estimable.

esteemed', p.p., esteem.

esteem'ing, pr.p., esteem.

es'ter, n., a compound formed by replacing the hydrogen of an acid by a hydrocarbon radical of the ethyl type (chem.).

esthet'ic, adj., i.q. aesthetic.

Esthon'ian, adj., rel. or pert. to Esthonia; n., a native of Esthonia.

es'timable, adj., worthy of esteem or respect.

es'timate, n., a valuation.

es'timate, v.t., to judge the value, height, weight, etc., of.

es'timated, p.p., estimate.

es'timating, pr.p., estimate.

estima'tion, n., the act or result of estimating; esteem.

estimative, adj., rel. or pert. to estimate.

es'timator, n., one who makes an estimate.

est'ival, adj., rel. or pert. to summer. (Also aestival.)

estiva'tion, n., the act of spending the summer; dormancy in summer.

estop', v.t., to bar, to prevent, to dam.

estop'page, n., i.q. estoppel.

estopped', p.p., estop.

estop'pel, n., a prohibition (leg.).

estop'ping, pr.p., estop.

esto'vers, n. pl., necessaries allowed as such by law.

estrade, n., a low platform.

estrange', v.t., to make strange, to alienate.

estranged', p.p., estrange.

estrange'ment, n., the act of estranging; the state of being estranged.

estran'ging, pr.p., estrange.

estrapade', n., a horse's kicking.

estray', n., an unclaimed horse or ox.

estreat', n., a correct copy of the record under which a fine is levied; v.t., to levy a fine under an estreat (leg.).

estreat'ed, p.p., estreat.

estreat'ing, *pr.p.*, estreat.

estrepe'ment, *n.*, waste committed on another man's lands, as by a tenant on his landlord's property (*leg.*).

es'tuarine, *adj.*, rel. or pert. to estuary.

es'tuary, *n.*, the wide, tidal mouth of a river.

es'tuate, *v.i.*, to boil up.

es'tuated, *p.p.*, estuate.

es'tuating, *pr.p.*, estuate.

estua'tion, *n.*, the act of boiling up.

esurience, *n.*, hunger.

esur'ient, *adj.*, hungry; greedy.

esurine, *adj.*, causing hunger; helping the appetite.

et'a, *n.*, the Greek letter H, η (*Gr.*).

et'acism, *n.*, the pronunciation of the Greek ē as the English ā.

état-major, *n.*, staff, staff-office (*mil., Fr.*).

et cet'era, phrase = and the rest (*Lat.*) (*Abbrev.* etc.).

etch, *v.t.*, to engrave with the use of a corrosive acid; to scratch lines with a sharp, needle-like instrument.

etched, *p.p.*, etch.

etch'er, *n.*, one who etches.

etch'ing, *n.*, the process of etching; a printed impression; *pr.p.*, etch.

eter'nal, *adj.*, without beginning or end; everlasting.

eter'nalize, *v.t.*, *i.q.* eternize.

eter'nally, *adv.*, without end.

eter'nity, *n.*, infinite being or existence.

eter'nized, *p.p.*, eternize.

eter'nizing, *pr.p.*, eternize.

ete'sian, *adj.*, annual.

eth'al, *n.*, cetyl alcohol.

eth'ane, *n.*, ethyl hydride, a colourless and odourless gas.

e'ther, *n.*, the clear sky; the impalpable, invisible medium that fills all space; a mobile, colourless fluid; an anaesthetic.

ethe'real, *adj.*, rel. or pert. to the sky; light airy. (Also *etherial*.)

etherealiza'tion, *n.*, the act or result of etherealizing.

ethe'realize, *v.t.*, to make ethereal.

ethe'realized, *p.p.*, etherealize.

ethe'realizing, *pr.p.*, etherealize.

e'theriform, *adj.*, of like nature with ether.

e'therism, *n.*, the effect of inhaling ether.

etheriza'tion, *n.*, the act or result of etherizing.

e'therize, *v.t.*, to bring under the influence of ether.

e'therized, *p.p.*, etherize.

e'therizing, *pr.p.*, etherize.

eth'ic, *adj.*, *i.q.* ethical.

eth'ical, *adj.*, moral.

eth'ically, *adv.*, morally.

eth'icism, *n.*, a devotion to ethical ideals.

eth'ics, *n.*, the science of morals and duties.

E'thiop, *n.*, an Ethiopian.

Ethio'pian, *adj.*, rel. or pert. to Ethiopia and the Ethiopians; *n.*, a native of Ethiopia.

Ethiop'ic, *adj.*, *i.q.* Ethiopian.

eth'moid, *adj.*, sieve-like.

ethmoi'dal, *adj.*, *i.q.* ethmoid.

eth'nic, *adj.*, rel. or pert. to race; *n.*, a heathen.

eth'nical, *adj.*, *i.q.* ethnic.

eth'nicalism, *n.*, paganism.

eth'nically, *adv.*, in an ethnic way.

ethnog'rapher, *n.*, one who describes races and peoples.

ethnograph'ic, *adj.*, rel. or pert. to ethnography.

ethnograph'ical, *adj.*, *i.q.* ethnographic.

ethnograph'ically, *adv.*, in an ethnographical way.

ethnog'raphy, *n.*, the description of races and peoples.

ethnolog'ic, *adj.*, rel. or pert. to ethnology.

ethnolog'ical, *adj.*, *i.q.* ethnologic.

ethnol'ogist, *n.*, one who studies ethnology.

ethnol'ogy, *n.*, the science rel. to races and peoples.

etholog'ic, *adj.*, rel. or pert. to ethology.

etholog'ical, *adj.*, *i.q.* ethologic.

ethol'ogist, *n.*, one who studies ethology.

ethol'ogy, *n.*, the science of human character.

eth'os, *n.*, habitual character and disposition.

eth'yl, *n.*, the base of alcohol and ether, etc.

eth'ylene, *n.*, a hydrocarbon.

e'tiolate, *v.t.*, to blanch; to make sickly-looking; *v.i.*, to become pale.

etiola'tion, *n.*, a whitening; blanching.

etiol'ogy, *n.*, the science of causes. (Also *aetiology*.)

et'iquette, *n.*, social formalities and rules.

etiquett'ical, *adj.*, rel. or pert. to etiquette.

Et'na, *n.*, a volcanic mountain on the island of Sicily.

et'na, *n.*, a small spirit stove for heating liquid.

Etne'an, *adj.*, pert. or rel. to Etna. (Also *Aetnean*.)

Et'on, *n.*, a famous English public school.

Eto'nian, *adj.*, pert. or rel. to Eton; *n.*, a past or present Eton schoolboy.

Etrus'can, *adj.*, pert. or rel. to Etruria and the Etruscans; *n.*, a native of Etruria, an ancient country in central Italy; the language of the Etruscans.

étude', *n.*, a short musical piece (*Fr.*).

etui', *n.*, a lady's case for carrying small useful articles (*Fr.*).

etymol'oger, *n.*, *i.q.* etymologist.

etymolog'ic, *adj.*, rel. or pert. to etymology.

etymolog'ical, *adj.*, *i.q.* etymologic.

etymolog'ically, *adv.*, according to etymology.

etymol'ogist, *n.*, a student of etymology.

etymol'ogize, *v.t.* and *i.*, to suggest the etymology for; to study etymology.

etymol'ogy, *n.*, the science and history of word-growth and word-formation.

et'ymon, *n.*, the root form of a word.

eucalyp'tol, *n.*, a liquid found in eucalyptus oil.

eucalyp'tus, *n.*, the gum-tree of Australia.

eu'charis, *n.*, a S. American lily bearing white, bell-shaped flowers.

Eu'charist, *n.*, the Roman Catholic sacrament of the mass; (also used for the Anglican communion service).

eucharis'tic, *adj.*, rel. to the Eucharist.

eucharis'tical, *adj.*, *i.q.* eucharistic.

eu'chre, *n.*, a card-game.

Euclid, *n.*, the Alexandrian geometer, the treatise which he wrote on geometry.

Euclid'ian, *adj.*, rel. or pert. to Euclid.

eu'crasy, *n.*, sound health.

eudaem'onism, *n.*, the moral obligation to produce happiness.

eudaem'onist, *n.*, a believer in eudaemonism.

eudiom'eter, *n.*, a vessel employed in the volumetric analysis of gases.

eudiomet'ric, *adj.*, rel. or pert. to eudiometry.

eudiomet'rical *adj.*, *i.q.* eudiometric.

eudiomet'rically, *adv.*, in an eudiometrical way.

eudiom'etry, *n.*, the use of the eudiometer.

eugen'ic, *adj.*, rel. or pert. to eugenics.

eugen'ics, *n.*, the study of means for the physical improvement of the human race.

eu'genist, *n.*, a student or advocate of eugenics.

euhem'erism, *n.*, the teaching that myths and gods were based on historical events.

euhem'erist, *n.*, one who studies or believes in euhemerism.

euhemeris'tic, *adj.*, rel. or pert. to euhemerism.

eu'logist, *n.*, one who pronounces a eulogy.

eulogis'tic, *adj.*, laudatory.

eulogis'tically, *adv.*, in a laudatory manner.

eulo'gium, *n.*, a laudation.

eu'logize, *v.t.*, to praise highly.

eu'logized, *p.p.*, eulogize.

eu'logizing, *pr.p.*, eulogize.

eu'logy, *n.*, a laudation.

Eumen'ides, *n. pl.*, the euphemistic name for Furies (*Gr.*).

eu'nomy, *n.*, law and order; a well-ordered constitution.

eu'nuch, *n.*, the guardian of a harem; a castrated male.

Euon'ymus, *n.*, a genus of European and American shrub, including the spindle-tree.

eupep'sia, *n.*, good digestion.

eupep'sy, *n.*, *i.q.* eupepsia.

eupep'tic, *adj.*, promoting a good digestion.

eu'phemism, *n.*, a word or expression used to mask or soften the harshness of the correct one.

eu'phemist, *n.*, one who uses euphemism.

euphemist'ic, *adj.*, of the nature of euphemism.

euphemis'tically, *adv.*, in an euphemistic way.

eu'phemize, *v.t.*, to describe euphemistically; *v.i.*, to speak euphemistically.

euphon'ic, *adj.*, sounding pleasantly.

euphon'ically, *adv.*, in a euphonic way.

eupho'nious, *adj.*, *i.q.* euphonic.

euphon'iously, *adv.*, *i.q.* euphonically.

eu'phonism, *n.*, a concord of sweet sounds.

euphon'ium, *n.*, the bass saxhorn.

euph'onize, *v.t.*, to make pleasing or easy pronunciation.

eu'phony, *n.*, pleasant sound; the avoidance of harsh-sounding words in written or spoken composition.

euphor'bia, *n.*, a shrubby, thorny plant of the spurge family.

euphor'ia, *n.*, a feeling of well-being. (Also *euphory*.)

eupho'ric, *adj.*, feeling well; inducing a sensation of well-being.

euph'ory, *n.*, *i.q.* euphoria.

eu'phrasy, *n.*, eyebright.

Euphros'yne, *n.*, one of the Graces (*Gr.*).

eu'phuism, *n.*, affected speech (in the manner of Lyly's *Euphues*).

eu'phuist, *n.*, one who speaks affectedly.

euphuis'tic, *adj.*, rel. or pert. to, or marked by, euphuism.

euphuis'tically, *adv.*, in an euphuistic way.

euplast'ic, *adj.*, easily moulded.

Eura'sian, *adj.*, rel. or pert. to Eurasia; (*i.e.*, Europe and Asia combined); half-caste.

eure'ka, *n.*, a Greek word = "I have found," the exclamation of Archimedes on making a scientific discovery.

eurhyth'mic, *adj.*, in harmonious proportion (*arch.*).

eurhyth'mics, *n. pl.*, a system of rhythmic movements for physical improvement.

eurhyth'my, *n.*, harmony, proportion.

euri'pus, *n.*, any arm of the sea like the original Euripus in Greece.

Euroc'lydon, *n.*, the N.E. wind.

Eur'omart, *n.*, the European Common Market.

Europe'an, *adj.*, rel. or pert. to Europe; *n.*, a native of Europe.

europ'ium, *n.*, a rare-earth metallic element (*chem.*).

Eur'ovision, *n.*, the European range of television.

eur'yscope, *n.*, a wide-angle lens.

eu'sol, *n.*, an acronym of Edinburgh University Solution of Lime; an antiseptic and bactericide prepared from bleaching powder.

eusta'chian, *adj.*, rel. or pert. to the Italian 16th cent. anatomist, Eustachius.

eu'style, *adj.*, having good pillars—a term used with reference to intercolumniation.

eutec'tic, *adj.*, fusing at a low temperature.

Euterp'e, *n.*, the muse of music.

Euter'pean, *adj.*, rel. or pert. to music.

euthana'sia, *n.*, an easy death; death induced by painless means.

evac'uant, *adj.*, purgative; *n.*, a purging

medicine; the safety-valve in organ bellows.

evac′uate, v.t., to void, to excrete; to withdraw from.

evac′uated, p.p., evacuate.

evac′uating, pr.p., evacuate.

evacua′tion, n., the act of evacuating.

evac′uative, adj., causing evacuation.

evac′uator, n., that which evacuates.

evac′uee, n., one moved in an evacuation.

evad′able, adj., able to be evaded. (Also evasible.)

evade′, v.t., to get out of the way of; to elude.

eva′ded, p.p., evade.

eva′der, n., one who evades.

eva′ding, pr.p., evade.

eva′ginate, v.t., to turn inside out (physiol.).

evagina′tion, n., the turning inside out (physiol.).

eval′uate, v.t., to determine the value of.

evalua′ted, p.p., evaluate.

evalua′ting, pr.p., evaluate.

evalua′tion, n., the act or result of evaluating.

evanesce′, v.i., to vanish; to disappear.

evanes′cence, n., a vanishing, or passing away.

evanes′cent, adj., vanishing, passing away.

evanes′cently, adv., in an evanescent way.

evan′gel, n., good tidings, the gospel.

evangel′ic, adj., rel. or pert. to the gospel.

evangel′ical, adj., i.q. evangelic; concerned with the supposed true teaching and interpretation of the gospels.

evan′gelism, n., the propagation of the gospel.

evan′gelist, n., a preacher of the gospel, esp. applied to the writers of the four gospels.

evangelis′tic, adj., of the four evangelists; rel. or pert. to the preachers of the gospel.

evangeliza′tion, n., the act or process of evangelizing.

evan′gelize, v.t., to instruct in the gospel.

evan′gelized, p.p., evangelize.

evan′gelizing, pr.p., evangelize.

evan′ish, v.i., to vanish.

evap′orable, adj., able to be evaporated.

evap′orate, v.t., to vaporize; v.i., to become vapour and pass away.

evap′orated, p.p., evaporate.

evap′orating, pr.p., evaporate.

evapora′tion, n., the process of evaporating.

evap′orative, adj., causing evaporation.

evap′orator, n., an apparatus for dissipating moisture.

evap′orometer, n., a device for testing the rate of evaporation of a liquid.

eva′sible, adj., i.q. evadable.

eva′sion, n., the act of evading; illegal avoidance; a sophistical excuse.

eva′sive, adj., shifty, not straightforward.

eva′sively, adv., shiftily.

eva′siveness, n., the act or quality of evading.

Eve, n., the first woman.

eve, n., evening; the day preceding a feast; the time immediately preceding an event.

evec′tion, n., an inequality in the moon's motion.

e′ven, adv., quite; to the same degree; n., evening; v.t., to level, to make equal; v.i., to be even; adj., equal, not odd, level, uniform.

e′vened, p.p., even.

e′vening, pr.p., even.

eve′ning, n., the end of day and beginning of night.

e′venly, adv., equally, levelly, smoothly.

e′venness, n., the state or quality of being even.

e′vensong, n., the evening office of the English Church; vespers.

event′, n., something that happened; an incident; an issue or result; an item in a programme.

event′ful, adj., full of incident, momentous.

event′fully, adv., in an eventful way.

event′fulness, n., the state or quality of being eventful.

e′ventide, n., the evening.

even′tual, adj., following as a consequence.

eventual′ity, n., a contingency, an event, an occurrence.

even′tualize, v.t., to take place.

even′tually, adv., ultimately.

even′tuate, v.i., to have an issue.

ev′er, adv., at any time, at all times.

ev′erglade, n., a marshy tract of land covered with clumps of tall grass and trees.

ev′ergreen, adj., always green; n., a tree always in leaf.

everlast′ing, adj., always lasting.

everlast′ingly, adv., without end.

everlast′ingness, n., eternity.

everliv′ing, adj., living for ever.

evermore′, adv., unendingly.

ever′sion, n., a turning backward or inside out.

evert′, v.t., to turn inside out.

evert′ed, p.p., evert.

evert′ing, pr.p., evert.

ev′ery, adj., each one of all; very special.

ev′erybody, n., each person; the whole world.

ev′eryday, adj., suitable for each day.

ev′eryman, n., the average person.

ev′eryone, n., everybody.

ev′erything, n., each one of all things.

ev′erywhere, adv., in every place.

evict′, v.t., to dispossess, to expel.

evict′ed, p.p., evict.

evict′ing, pr.p., evict.

evic′tion, n., the act or result of evicting; an ejectment.

evic′tor, n., one who evicts.

ev′idence, n., testimony, a clear sign; v.t., to prove, to show clearly.

ev′idenced, *p.p.*, evidence.

ev′idencing, *pr.p.*, evidence.

ev′ident, *adj.*, clear, manifest.

eviden′tial, *adj.*, rel. or pert. to evidence; furnishing evidence.

eviden′tially, *adv.*, in an evidential way.

eviden′tiary, *adj.*, *i.q.* evidential.

ev′idently, *adv.*, manifestly, clearly.

e′vil, *adj.*, bad, wicked; *n.*, badness, wickedness; affliction, harm.

e′vildoer, *n.*, one who commits evil deeds.

e′vil-eyed, *adj.*, possessing the evil eye.

e′villy, *adv.*, in an evil way.

evince′, *v.t.*, to prove clearly; to show plainly.

evinced′, *p.p.*, evince.

evin′cible, *adj.*, capable of proof.

evinc′ing, *pr.p.*, evince.

evin′cive, *adj.*, capable of evincing or proving.

ev′irate, *v.t.*, to castrate the male; to deprive of manly qualities.

evira′tion, *n.*, castration; emasculation.

evis′cerate, *v.t.*, to take the entrails out of; to disembowel.

evis′cerated, *p.p.*, eviscerate.

evis′cerating, *pr.p.*, eviscerate.

eviscera′tion, *n.*, the act or process of eviscerating.

ev′itable, *adj.*, avoidable.

evoca′tion, *n.*, a calling forth; a summoning.

evoc′ative, *adj.*, able to be evoked; having power to bring back memories.

evoc′atory, *adj.*, *i.q.* evocative.

evoke′, *v.t.*, to call forth.

evoked′, *p.p.*, evoke.

evo′king, *pr.p.*, evoke.

ev′olute, *n.*, a form of curve.

evolu′tion, *n.*, the act or result of evolving; development; ordered movement.

evolu′tional, *adj.*, *i.q.* evolutionary.

evolu′tionary, *adj.*, rel. or pert. to evolution.

evolu′tionist, *adj.*, *i.q.* evolution; *n.*, one who holds the doctrine of evolution, or who is skilled in the ordering of ships, soldiers, etc.

ev′olutive, *adj.*, tending to evolution.

evolve′, *v.t.*, to unroll, unfold or develop; *v.i.*, to open or develop.

evolved′, *p.p.*, evolve.

evolve′ment, *n.*, *i.q.* evolution.

evolv′ing, *pr.p.*, evolve.

evul′sion, *n.*, a plucking out; forcible extraction.

ewe, *n.*, a female sheep.

ew′er, *n.*, a large jug or pitcher.

ew′ery, *n.*, the room where ewers and napkins are kept.

ew′ry, *n.* *i.q.* ewery.

ex-, *adj.*, hyphenated prefix = former.

exac′erbate, *v.t.*, to embitter; to irritate; to increase the sharpness of.

exac′erbated, *p.p.*, exacerbate.

exac′erbating, *pr.p.*, exacerbate.

exacerba′tion, *n.*, the act of exacerbating; the exacerbated state.

exact′, *adj.*, precise, accurate; *v.t.*, to require, enforce or impose.

exact′able, *adj.*, able to be exacted.

exact′ed, *p.p.*, exact.

exact′er, *n.*, one who exacts. (Also *exactor*.)

exact′ing, *adj.*, unreasonable in one's demands; demanding much work and care; *pr.p.*, exact.

exac′tion, *n.*, the act of exacting; that which is unreasonably demanded.

exact′itude, *n.*, the state or quality of being exact.

exact′ly, *adv.*, precisely, accurately.

exact′ness, *n.*, *i.q.* exactitude.

exact′or, *n.*, *i.q.* exacter.

exag′gerate, *v.t.*, to make more of anything than it really is; to make a false representation.

exag′gerated, *p.p.*, exaggerate.

exag′gerating, *pr.p.*, exaggerate.

exaggera′tion, *n.*, the act of exaggerating; a false statement.

exag′gerator, *n.*, one who exaggerates.

exalt′, *v.t.*, to elevate, to raise.

exalta′tion, *n.*, the act of exalting; the state of being exalted.

exalt′ed, *p.p.*, exalt.

exalt′edness, *n.*, the state of being exalted.

exalt′ing, *pr.p.*, exalt.

exam′, *n.*, the abbrev. for examination (*colloq.*).

exam′inable, *adj.*, able to be examined.

examina′tion, *n.*, the act of examining; formal testing according to regulations.

exam′ine, *v.t.*, to look into carefully, to survey or test.

exam′ined, *p.p.*, examine.

examinee′, *n.*, one who is examined.

exam′iner, *n.*, one who examines.

exam′ining, *pr.p.*, examine.

exam′ple, *n.*, a sample, pattern, model of conduct or instance; *v.t.*, to illustrate with instances.

exan′imate, *adj.*, dead; spiritless.

ex an′imo, *adj.* and *adv.*, heartily; sincere(ly) (*Lat.*).

exanthe′ma, *n.*, a rash, an eruption.

exanthem′atous, *adj.*, subject to exanthema.

exanthe′sis, *n.*, *i.q.* exanthema.

ex′arch, *n.*, a Byzantine provincial ruler; the ecclesiastical title in the East for a prelate next in rank below a patriarch.

ex′archate, *n.*, the office, or term or sphere of office, of an exarch.

exas′perate, *v.t.*, to ruffle the temper, to provoke.

exas′perated, *p.p.*, exasperate.

exas′perating, *adj.*, provoking; *pr.p.*, exasperate.

exas′peratingly, *adv.*, in an exasperating way.

exaspera′tion, *n.*, the act of exasperating; the state of being exasperated.

ex′calate, *v.t.*, to remove from a series.

ex′calated, *p.p.*, excalate.

ex′calating, *pr.p.*, excalate.

excandes′cent, *adj.*, at a white heat.

ex cathed′ra, *adv.* and *adj.*, phrase, meaning "from the chair," *i.e.* with authority (*Lat.*).

ex′cavate, *v.t.*, to hollow out, to dig.

ex′cavated, *p.p.*, excavate.

ex′cavating, *pr.p.*, excavate.

excava′tion, *n.*, the act of excavating; a cavity made by digging.

ex′cavator, *n.*, one who excavates; a mobile machine for digging.

exceed′, *v.t.*, to go beyond, to surpass; *v.i.*, to go beyond bounds.

exceed′ed, *p.p.*, exceed.

exceed′ing, *adj.*, very great; *pr.p.*, exceed.

exceed′ingly, *adv.*, very greatly.

excel′, *v.t.*, to go beyond, to outdo; *v.i.*, to be superior.

excelled′, *p.p.*, excel.

ex′cellence, *n.*, the state or quality of excelling; superiority.

ex′cellency, *n.*, *i.q.* excellence; an honorific title.

ex′cellent, *adj.*, surpassing, very great or good.

ex′cellently, *adv.*, surpassingly, very greatly, very well.

excel′ling, *pr.p.*, excel.

excel′sior, *n.*, a variety of printing fount.

except′, *prep.*, leaving out, but; *v.t.*, to leave out, to withdraw; *v.i.*, to raise objection.

except′ed, *p.p.*, except.

except′ing, *pr.p.*, except.

excep′tion, *n.*, the act of excepting, the state of being excepted, an omission, a special case or objection.

excep′tionable, *adj.*, open to objection.

excep′tional, *adj.*, special, uncommon.

excep′tionally, *adv.*, in an exceptional way.

except′ive, *adj.*, rel. or pert. to an exception; captious.

except′or, *n.*, one who excepts.

excerpt′, *v.t.*, to extract.

ex′cerpt, *n.*, an extract.

excerp′ta, *n. pl.*, extracts (*Lat.*).

excerp′tion, *n.*, the act or process of excerpting; an excerpted passage.

excess′, *n.*, the act of going beyond, overdoing, over-indulgence; the sum by which an amount exceeds the normal or the expected.

excess′ive, *adj.*, going to excess, passing the limit.

excess′ively, *adv.*, in an excessive degree.

excess′iveness, *n.*, the state or quality of being excessive.

exchange′, *n.*, barter; the system of trading by means of credit, etc.; the passing from one state to another; a place where trading takes place; *v.t.*, to give or take an equivalent; *v.t.*, to pass from one thing to another.

exchangeabil′ity, *n.*, the state or quality of being exchangeable.

exchange′able, *adj.*, able to be exchanged.

exchanged′, *p.p.*, exchange.

exchan′ger, *n.*, one who exchanges.

exchan′ging, *pr.p.*, exchange.

excheq′uer, *n.*, the public treasury; any private resources.

exci′sable, *adj.*, able to be excised, dutiable.

excise′, *n.*, a duty on certain commodities; *v.t.*, to cut out; to levy duty on.

excised′, *p.p.*, excise.

excise′man, *n.*, an official who collects excise.

exci′sing, *pr.p.*, excise.

exci′sion, *n.*, the act or result of excising.

excitabil′ity, *n.*, the state of being excitable.

exci′table, *adj.*, able to be excited, prone to excitement.

exci′tant, *adj.*, conducive to excitement.

excita′tion, *n.*, the act or state of excitement.

exci′tative, *adj.*, *i.q.* excitant.

exci′tatory, *adj.*, *i.q.* excitant.

excite′, *v.t.*, to arouse, to stimulate.

exci′ted, *p.p.*, excite.

excit′edly, *adv.*, in an excited way.

excite′ment, *n.*, the act of exciting; the state of being excited; that which excites.

exci′ter, *n.*, one who excites.

exci′ting, *adj.*, stirring, rousing; *pr.p.*, excite.

exci′tingly, *adv.*, stirringly.

exclaim′, *v.t. and i.*, to call out.

exclaimed′, *p.p.*, exclaim.

exclaim′ing, *pr.p.*, exclaim.

exclama′tion, *n.*, the act of exclaiming; that which is exclaimed.

exclam′ative, *adj.*, expressing exclamation.

exclam′atory, *adj.*, *i.q.* exclamative.

exclo′sure, *n.*, an area shut off.

exclude′, *v.t.*, to shut out, bar or reject.

exclu′ded, *p.p.*, exclude.

exclu′der, *n.*, one who, or that which, excludes.

exclu′ding, *pr.p.*, exclude.

exclu′sion, *n.*, the act of excluding; the state of being excluded.

exclu′sionist, *n.*, one who favours exclusion.

exclu′sive, *adj.*, with a tendency to exclude; exceptional; preferential; arrogant.

exclu′sively, *adv.*, specially, preferentially.

exclu′siveness, *n.*, the state of being exclusive.

exclu′sivism, *n.*, *i.q.* exclusiveness.

excog′itate, *v.t.*, to think out, to plan.

excog′itated, *p.p.*, excogitate.

excog′itating, *pr.p.*, excogitate.

excogita′tion, *n.*, the act or result of excogitating.

excog′itative, *adj.*, able to be thought out.

excommu′nicable, *adj.*, worthy to be excommunicated.

excommu'nicate, *n.,* a person expelled from church communion; *v.t.,* to expel from church communion.

excommu'nicated, *p.p.,* excommunicate.

excommu'nicating, *pr.p.,* excommunicate.

excommunica'tion, *n.,* the act of excommunicating; the state of being excommunicated.

excommu'nicative, *adj.,* i.q. excommunicable.

excommu'nicator, *n.,* one who excommunicates.

excommu'nicatory, *adj.,* i.q. excommunicable.

exco'riate, *v.t.,* to flay, to abrade.

exco'riated, *p.p.,* excoriate.

exco'riating, *pr.p.,* excoriate.

excoria'tion, *n.,* the act or result of excoriating.

excor'ticate, *v.t.,* to strip the bark from.

excortica'tion, *n.,* the act of excorticating.

ex'crement, *n.,* an animal discharge; the faeces.

excremen'tal, *adj.,* discharged as excrement.

excremi'tious, *adj.,* i.q. excremental.

excres'cence, *n.,* a superfluous growth.

excres'cent, *adj.,* growing superfluously.

excrescen'tial, *adj.,* i.q. excrescent.

excre'ta, *n. pl.,* matter eliminated from the body.

excrete', *v.t.,* to eliminate waste matter.

excre'ted, *p.p.,* excrete.

excre'ting, *pr.p.,* excrete.

excre'tion, *n.,* the act or result of excreting.

excre'tive, *adj.,* conducive to excretion.

excre'tory, *adj.,* i.q. excretive.

excru'ciate, *v.t.,* to torture, to agonize.

excru'ciated, *p.p.,* excruciate.

excru'ciating, *adj.,* agonizing; *pr.p.,* excruciate.

excru'ciatingly, *adv.,* in an excruciating way.

excrucia'tion, *n.,* agony.

excul'pable, *adj.,* able or worthy to be exculpated.

ex'culpate, *v.t.,* to acquit from blame.

ex'culpated, *p.p.,* exculpate.

ex'culpating, *pr.p.,* exculpate.

exculpa'tion, *n.,* the act of exculpating; the state of being exculpated.

excul'patory, *adj.,* leading to exculpation.

excu'rrent, *adj.,* running or passing out.

excur'sion, *n.,* a journey; a departure from the ordinary.

excur'sionist, *n.,* one who goes on an excursion.

excur'sive, *adj.,* wandering, disconnected.

excur'sively, *adv.,* in a wandering way.

excur'sus, *n.,* a supplementary treatise.

excu'sable, *adj.,* capable of excuse.

excu'sably, *adv.,* in an excusable way.

excu'satory, *adj.,* apologetic.

excuse', *v.t.,* to acquit of blame, to pardon; *n.,* an exonerating plea; a justification; a reason for doing something; a purported reason to evade blame.

excused', *p.p.,* excuse.

excuse'less, *adj.,* without excuse.

excu'ser, *n.,* one who excuses.

excu'sing, *pr.p.,* excuse.

ex'eat, *n.,* leave of absence (*Lat.,* = let him depart).

ex'ecrable, *adj.,* deserving execration; detestable; abominable.

ex'ecrably, *adv.,* outrageously, detestably.

ex'ecrate, *v.t.,* to invoke curses on.

ex'ecrated, *p.p.,* execrate.

ex'ecrating, *pr.p.,* execrate.

execra'tion, *n.,* the act of execrating; a curse or malediction.

ex'ecrative, *adj.,* i.q. execratory.

ex'ecratory, *adj.,* of the nature of a curse.

exec'utant, *n.,* a performer on an instrument.

ex'ecute, *v.t.,* to perform, to finish; to put to death.

ex'ecuted, *p.p.,* execute.

ex'ecuting, *pr.p.,* execute.

execu'tion, *n.,* the act of executing; a performance; a dispatch.

execu'tioner, *n.,* one who executes, the headsman or the hangman.

exec'utive, *adj.,* rel. or pert. to execution; carrying into effect; *n.,* an official or officials charged with the duty of getting things done.

exec'utor, *n.,* one who carries out another's testamentary instructions.

executo'rial, *adj.,* rel. or pert. to an executor.

exec'utorship, *n.,* the office and duty of an executor.

exec'utory, *adj.,* administrative; rel. or pert. to the execution of the law.

exec'utrix, *n.,* the fem. of executor.

exege'sis, *n.,* an interpretation, an exposition.

exeget'ic, *adj.,* interpretative, expository.

exeget'ical, *adj.,* i.q. exegetic.

exeget'ically, *adv.,* in an exegetical way.

exem'plar, *n.,* a pattern, or model.

exem'plarily, *adv.,* in an exemplary way.

exem'plariness, *n.,* the state of being exemplary.

exem'plary, *adj.,* appearing as a model or typical.

exemplifica'tion, *n.,* the act or result of illustrating by example.

exem'plified, *p.p.,* exemplify.

exem'plifier, *n.,* one who exemplifies.

exem'plify, *n.,* to show by example, to illustrate.

exem'plifying, *pr.p.,* exemplify.

exempli gratia, phrase, meaning by way of example (abbrev. *e.g.*) (*Lat.*).

exempt', *adj.,* released, not liable; *v.t.,* to except, to set free.

exempt'ed, *p.p.,* exempt.

exempt'ing, *pr.p.,* exempt.

exemp'tion, *n.,* the act and result of exempting.

exen'terate, *v.t.,* to disembowel.

exentera'tion, *n.,* disemboweling.

exequa'tur, n., an official warrant (Lat.).

ex'equies, n. pl., funeral ceremonies.

ex'ercisable, adj., able to be exercised.

ex'ercise, n., practising; training; work by way of training; v.t., to practise, to put forth; v.i., to take exercise.

ex'ercised, p.p., exercise.

ex'erciser, n., one who exercises.

ex'ercising, pr.p., exercise.

exercita'tion, n., i.q. exercise.

exerg'ual, adj., rel. or pert. to exergue.

exergue', n., the place on the reverse of a coin where the date, etc., is shown.

exert', v.t., to put forth; to employ.

exert'ed, p.p., exert.

exert'ing, pr.p., exert.

exer'tion, n., effort, toil.

exes, n. pl., expenses (abbrev., colloq.).

ex'eunt, v.i., stage direction, meaning to (they) go out (Lat.).

exfo'liate, v.t. and i., to scale.

exfo'liated, p.p., exfoliate.

exfo'liating, pr.p., exfoliate.

exfolia'tion, n., a scaling or peeling.

exfo'liative, adj., causing exfoliation.

ex gra'tia, phrase, meaning as an act of grace (Lat.).

exha'lable, adj., able to be exhaled.

exha'lant, adj., exhaling.

exhala'tion, n., the process of breathing out; that which is exhaled or given off.

exhale', v.t., to breathe out, to give off.

exhaled', p.p., exhale.

exhale'ment, n., i.q. exhalation.

exha'ling, pr.p., exhale.

exhaust', n., waste gases from an internal combustion machine; v.t. and i., to draw completely off, to drain, to overcome with weariness.

exhaust'ed, p.p., exhaust.

exhaust'ible, adj., able to be exhausted.

exhaust'ing, adj., causing exhaustion; pr.p., exhaust.

exhaustion, n., the act or result of exhausting; extreme fatigue.

exhaust'ive, adj., thorough; complete.

exhaust'ively, adv., in an exhaustive way.

exhaust'iveness, n., i.q. exhaustion.

exhaust'less, adj., inexhaustible.

exhib'it, n., something exhibited; v.t., to show.

exhib'ited, p.p., exhibit.

exhib'iting, pr.p., exhibit.

exhibi'tion, n., the act of exhibiting; a public show; an academic endowment.

exhibi'tioner, n., the holder of a college or university exhibition.

exhibi'tionism, n., an extravagant display; indecent exposure (psych.).

exhibi'tionist, n., one given to exhibitionism.

exhib'itive, adj., exhibiting.

exhib'itor, n., one who shows exhibits.

exhib'itory, adj., i.q. exhibitive.

exhil'arant, adj., exhilarating; n., that which exhilarates.

exhil'arate, v.t., to cheer, to gladden.

exhil'arated, p.p., exhilarate.

exhil'arating, adj., cheerful, gladdening; pr.p., exhilarate.

exhilara'tion, n., the act of exhilarating; the state of being exhilarated.

exhil'arative, adj., i.q. exhilarating.

exhort', v.t., to admonish, entreat or incite.

exhorta'tion, n., the act of exhorting; a hortatory address.

exhort'ative, adj., exhorting.

exhort'atory, adj., i.q. exhortative.

exhort'ed, p.p., exhort.

exhort'er, n., one who exhorts.

exhort'ing, pr.p., exhort.

exhuma'tion, n., the act of exhuming.

exhume', v.t., to disinter.

exhumed', p.p., exhume.

exhu'ming, pr.p., exhume.

exigeant, adj., exacting (Fr.).

ex'igency, n., urgency, a pressing necessity.

ex'igent, adj., exacting, urgent.

ex'igently, adv., urgently.

ex'igible, adj., able to be exacted.

exigu'ity, n., scantiness; smallness.

exig'uous, adj., small, insignificant.

exig'uousness, n., the condition of exiguity.

ex'ile, n., one banished from a country; the state of being exiled; v.t., to banish from a country.

ex'iled, p.p., exile.

exil'ian, adj., rel. or pert. to the Jews' exile in Babylon.

exil'ic, adj., i.q. exilian.

ex'iling, pr.p., exile.

exil'ity, n., thinness; subtlety (pedant.).

exinani'tion, n., the act of emptying; the state of being emptied.

exist', v.i., to be, or to go on being.

exist'ed, p.p., exist.

exist'ence, n., the state or continuance of being.

exist'ent, adj., existing.

existen'tial, adj., of, or rel. to, existence.

existen'tialism, n., an anti-intellectualist and anti-historical philosophy of life.

existen'tialist, n., one who believes in existentialism.

existibil'ity, n., the state or quality of being existible.

exist'ible, adj., able to exist.

exist'ing, pr.p., exist.

ex'it, n., a going out, a passage out; v.i., to go off stage (stage direction).

ex-lib'ris, n., a bookplate, the words meaning "from the library of" (Lat.).

ex'ode, n., the part of a Greek tragedy following the last choral ode; a farce in the Roman drama.

exo'dium, *n.*, *i.q.* exode.

Ex'odus, *n.*, the second book of the Old Testament, describing the escape of the Israelites.

ex'odus, *n.*, a general departure; a migration.

ex offi'cio, *adv.* and *adj.*, in virtue of his office (*Lat.*).

exog'amous, *adj.*, rel. or pert. to exogamy; marrying outside the tribe.

exog'amy, *n.*, marriage outside one's own tribe.

ex'ogen, *n.*, a plant that grows by the addition of concentric rings beneath the bark.

exog'enous, *adj.*, of the nature of an exogen.

ex'on, *n.*, one of four officers of the Yeoman of the Guard.

exon'erate, *v.t.*, to acquit, to free from blame.

exon'erated, *p.p.*, exonerate.

exon'erating, *pr.p.*, exonerate.

exonera'tion, *n.*, the act of exonerating; acquittal.

exon'erative, *adj.*, exonerating, freeing from blame.

exon'erator, *n.*, one who exonerates.

Exo'nian, *n.*, a native of Exeter.

exophthal'mic, *adj.*, of the nature of, or accompanied by, exophthalmus.

exophthal'mos, *n.*, *i.q.* exophthalmus.

exophthal'mus, *n.*, the protrusion of an eyeball.

ex'orable, *adj.*, able to be entreated, relenting.

exor'bitance, *n.*, extravagance, excessive cost.

exor'bitancy, *n.*, *i.q.* exorbitance.

exor'bitant, *adj.*, extravagant, excessive.

exor'bitantly, *adv.*, extravagantly.

exor'cism, *n.*, the act of exorcizing; a formula of exorcizing.

exor'cist, *n.*, one who exorcizes; one of the minor orders of the Church.

ex'orcize, *v.t.*, to allay (an evil spirit); *v.i.*, to practise exorcism.

ex'orcized, *p.p.*, exorcize.

ex'orcizer, *n.*, one who exorcizes.

ex'orcizing, *pr.p.*, exorcize.

exor'dial, *adj.*, pert. or rel. to an exordium.

exor'dium, *n.*, an opening or beginning of a speech (*Lat.*).

exoter'ic, *adj.*, pert. or rel. to those outside the mysteries (*i.e.*, the uninitiated); of a popular character.

exoter'ical, *adj.*, *i.q.* exoteric.

exoter'ically, *adv.*, in an exoterical way.

exot'ic, *adj.*, foreign; very unusual; not native; *n.*, anything from another country.

exot'icism, *n.*, exotic nature.

expand', *v.i.*, to open out, to spread out; *v.i.*, to become broader; to increase in size.

expand'ed, *p.p.*, expand.

expand'er, *n.*, that which expands.

expand'ing, *pr.p.*, expand.

expanse', *n.*, something spread out; a stretch.

expansibil'ity, *n.*, the state or quality of being expansible.

expan'sible, *adj.*, able to be expanded.

expan'sibly, *adv.*, in an expansible way.

expan'sile, *adj.*, (capable) of expansion.

expan'sion, *n.*, the act or result of expanding.

expan'sionist, *n.*, one who believes in expansion.

expan'sive, *adj.*, causing expansion; broadminded; wide-ranging.

expan'sively, *adv.*, in an expansive way.

expan'siveness, *n.*, largeness.

expansiv'ity, *n.*, *i.q.* expansiveness.

ex part'e, *adv.* and *adj.*, one sided; from one side only (*Lat.*).

expa'tiate, *v.i.*, to discourse at length, to enlarge upon.

expa'tiated, *p.p.*, expatiate.

expa'tiating, *pr.p.*, expatiate.

expatia'tion, *n.*, the act of expatiating.

expat'iative, *adj.*, *i.q.* expatiatory.

expa'tiator, *n.*, one who expatiates.

expa'tiatory, *adj.*, inclined to expatiation.

expat'riate, *adj.* and *n.*, expatriated (person); *v.t.*, to banish from one's country.

expat'riated, *p.p.*, expatriate.

expat'riating, *pr.p.*, expatriate.

expatria'tion, *n.*, the act or result of expatriating; exile.

expect', *v.t.*, to await, to look for; to suppose.

expect'ance, *n.*, *i.q.* expectancy.

expect'ancy, *n.*, a state of suspense and waiting.

expect'ant, *adj.*, in a state of expecting; (of women) pregnant.

expect'antly, *adv.*, in an expectant way.

expecta'tion, *n.*, the state of expecting.

expec'tative, *adj.*, reversionary.

expect'ed, *p.p.*, expect.

expect'ing, *pr.p.*, expect.

expec'torant, *adj.*, promoting expectoration; *n.*, a medicine that promotes expectoration.

expec'torate, *v.t.*, to cough or spit out; *v.i.*, to discharge phlegm.

expec'torated, *p.p.*, expectorate.

expec'torating, *pr.p.*, expectorate.

expectora'tion, *n.*, the act or result of expectorating.

expe'dience, *n.*, *i.q.* expediency.

expe'diency, *n.*, advantageousness, policy.

expe'dient, *adj.*, advantageous, politic.

expe'diently, *adv.*, with advantage.

ex'pedite, *adj.*, prompt; *v.t.*, to hasten, to facilitate, to send forth.

ex'pedited, *p.p.*, expedite.

ex'peditely, *adv.*, promptly.

ex'pediting, *pr.p.*, expedite.

expedi'tion, *n.*, a journey (usually of a number of persons); speed, promptness.

expedi′tionary, adj., pert. or rel. to an expedition.

expedi′tionist, n., one who goes on expeditions.

expedi′tious, adj., prompt, speedy.

expedi′tiously, adv., promptly.

expedi′tiousness, n., speed; promptitude.

expel′, v.t., to drive forth, to banish.

expel′lable, adj., able to be expelled.

expelled′, p.p., expel.

expel′lent, adj., i.q. expellable.

expel′ler, n., one who expels.

expel′ling, pr.p., expel.

expend′, v.t., to spend, lay out or use up.

expend′able, adj., that which may be expended.

expend′ed, p.p., expend.

expend′ing, pr.p., expend.

expend′iture, n., the act of expending; that which is expended.

expense′, n., cost, outlay.

expen′sive, adj., costly, dear.

expen′sively, adv., in an expensive way.

expen′siveness, n., the state of being expensive.

expe′rience, n., knowledge gained from personal trial; v.t., to make personal trial of, to undergo.

expe′rienced, adj., practised, skilful; p.p., experience.

expe′riencing, pr.p., experience.

experien′tial, adj., pert. or rel. to experience; empirical.

experien′tialism, n., the theory which believes that all our ideas come from experience, and which tests all knowledge from experience.

experien′tialist, n., one who believes in experientialism.

experien′tially, adv., with experience.

exper′iment, n., a trial for the purpose of discovery; v.i., to make a test or trial.

experimen′tal, adj., of the nature of an experiment.

experimen′talist, n., one who makes experiments.

experimen′talize, v.i., to make experiments.

experimen′tally, adv., in an experimental way.

exper′imented, p.p., experiment.

exper′imenter, n., one who experiments.

exper′imenting, pr.p., experiment.

exper′imentist, n., i.q. experimentalist.

ex′pert, adj., adept, clever; n., one known for his special knowledge or skill.

expertise′, n., expert knowledge and skill.

expert′ly, adv., in an expert way.

expert′ness, n., skill.

expert′o cred′e, you may take my word for it because I have tried (Lat. = believe one who has tried).

ex′piable, adj., able to be expiated.

ex′piate, v.t., to atone for; to make reparation for.

ex′piated, p.p., expiate.

ex′piating, pr.p., expiate.

expia′tion, n., the act of expiating; reparation.

ex′piator, n., one who expiates.

ex′piatory, adj., making reparation.

expira′tion, n., the act of breathing out; the coming to an end.

expir′atory, adj., pert. or rel. to expiration.

expire′, v.t., to breathe out; v.i., to die; to come to an end.

expired′, p.p., expire.

expir′ing, pr.p., expire.

expi′ry, n., an end, a termination.

expis′cate, v.t., to fish out; to find by cunning means (Scot.).

explain′, v.t., to make plain or clear.

explain′able, adj., able to be explained.

explained′, p.p., explain.

explain′er, n., one who explains.

explain′ing, pr.p., explain.

explana′tion, n., the act or result of explaining.

explan′atorily, adv., in an explanatory way.

explan′atory, adj., explaining.

ex′pletive, adj., filling out, superfluous; n., a superfluous word; an oath.

ex′pletory, adj., superfluous.

ex′plicable, adj., able to be explained.

explicand′, n., something to be explained.

ex′plicate, v.t., to explain, to unfold.

ex′plicated, p.p., explicate.

ex′plicating, pr.p., explicate.

explica′tion, n., the act or result of explicating.

ex′plicative, adj., explanatory.

ex′plicatory, adj., i.q. explicative.

ex′plicit, n., a word sometimes used to mark the end of a book.

explic′it, adj., distinct, outspoken.

explic′itly, adv., in an explicit way.

explic′itness, n., distinctness, outspokenness.

explode′, v.t., to cause to burst with a loud noise; v.i., to burst with a loud noise.

explo′ded, adj., extinct; p.p., explode.

explo′dent, n., an explosive sound (phonet.).

explo′der, n., anything that explodes.

explo′ding, pr.p., explode.

exploit′, n., a brave deed, a great feat; v.t., to put to one's own use, to employ for one's own ends.

exploit′able, adj., able to be exploitable.

exploita′tion, n., the act of exploiting; the development of a country's resources.

explora′tion, n., the act of exploring.

explor′ative, adj., i.q. exploratory.

explor′atory, adj., exploring.

explore′, v.t., to search carefully, to examine; to travel to find out.

explored′, p.p., explore.

explor′er, n., one who explores.

explor′ing, pr.p., explore.

explo′sion, n., the act of exploding; a bursting forth.

explo'sive, *adj.*, causing explosion; *n.*, that which explodes.

explo'sively, *adv.*, in an explosive way.

explo'siveness, *n.*, the state of being explosive.

expo'nent, *adj.*, explaining, making clear; *n.*, one who explains or argues in favour of; an algebraical symbol indicating the power of a quantity.

exponen'tial, *adj.*, pert. or rel. to exponents.

export', *v.t.*, to send out of the country.

ex'port, *n.*, that which is exported.

export'able, *adj.*, able or fit to be exported.

exporta'tion, *n.*, the act of exporting; an export.

export'ed, *p.p.*, export.

export'er, *n.*, one who exports.

export'ing, *pr.p.*, export.

expose', *v.t.*, to exhibit; to lay open to view; to place in danger.

exposé', *n.*, an exposure; an embarrassing disclosure; an explanation (*Fr.*).

exposed', *p.p.*, expose.

expo'ser, *n.*, one who exposes.

expo'sing, *pr.p.*, expose.

exposi'tion, *n.*, the act of exposing or expounding; an explanation or commentary; the working out of a climax.

expos'itive, *adj.*, pert. or rel. to exposition.

expos'itor, *n.*, one who expounds.

expos'itory, *adj.*, i.q. expositive.

expos'tulate, *v.i.*, to reason seriously with a person at fault.

expos'tulated, *p.p.*, expostulate.

expos'tulating, *pr.p.*, expostulate.

expostula'tion, *n.*, the act of expostulating.

expos'tulator, *n.*, one who expostulates.

expos'tulatory, *adj.*, in the nature of expostulation.

expo'sure, *n.*, the act or effect of exposing; revelation of the truth; subjection to extreme weather; one picture in a camera film.

expound', *v.t.*, to explain or interpret.

expound'ed, *p.p.*, expound.

expound'er, *n.*, one who expounds.

expound'ing, *pr.p.*, expound.

express', *adj.*, exact, emphatic, with despatch; *n.*, a fast train; an express message or messenger; *v.t.*, to press out; to make known; to send by quick despatch.

express'age, *n.*, the charge for expressing.

expressed', *p.p.*, express.

express'ible, *adj.*, able to be expressed.

express'ing, *pr.p.*, express.

expres'sion, *n.*, the act of expressing; what is said, a form of speech; the outward aspect of features; the power of giving the spirit of a musical piece.

expres'sional, *adj.*, of verbal, facial or artistic expression.

expres'sionism, *n.*, the trend among painters, dramatic authors, musicians, etc., to discard rules and conventions, and so obtain complete freedom for the artist's self-expression.

expres'sionist, *n.*, the execution that expresses the feeling of a passage (*mus.*).

expres'sionless, *adj.*, lacking expression.

express'ive, *adj.*, showing a power of expression.

express'ively, *adv.*, with emphasis.

express'iveness, *n.*, the state or quality of being expressive.

express'ly, *adv.*, intentionally, emphatically, directly.

exprobra'tion, *n.*, reproach, censure.

expro'priate, *v.t.*, to dispossess, to put out of one's possession.

expro'priated, *p.p.*, expropriate.

expro'priating, *pr.p.*, expropriate.

expropria'tion, *n.*, the act or result of expropriating.

expul'sion, *n.*, the act or result of expelling.

expul'sive, *adj.*, producing expulsion.

expunc'tion, *n.*, erasion.

expunge', *v.t.*, to erase.

expunged', *p.p.*, expunge.

expun'ging, *pr.p.*, expunge.

ex'purgate, *v.t.*, to cleanse from filth, to purify.

ex'purgated, *p.p.*, expurgate.

ex'purgating, *pr.p.*, expurgate.

expurga'tion, *n.*, the act of expurgating; anything expurgated.

ex'purgator, *n.*, one who expurgates.

expur'gatory, *adj.*, making expurgation.

ex'quisite, *adj.*, choice, refined, fastidious, intense; *n.*, a fop.

ex'quisitely, *adv.*, in an exquisite way.

ex'quisiteness, *n.*, the state or quality of being exquisite.

exsang'uinate, *v.t.*, to drain of blood.

exsang'uine, *adj.*, lacking blood.

exscind', *v.t.*, to cut out, to sever.

exscind'ed, *p.p.*, exscind.

exscind'ing, *pr.p.*, exscind.

exsert', *v.t.*, to put forth (*biol.*).

exsertile, *adj.*, that may be exserted.

ex-serv'ice, *adj.*, formerly in a fighting service.

exsic'cant, *adj.*, drying up.

ex'siccate, *v.t.*, to dry up.

ex'siccated, *p.p.*, exsiccate.

ex'siccating, *pr.p.*, exsiccate.

exsicca'tion, *n.*, the act or result of exsiccating.

exsuc'tion, *n.*, a sucking out.

ex'tant, *adj.*, still existing.

ex'tasy, *n.*, i.q. ecstasy.

extempora'neous, *adj.*, or done at the moment, without preparation.

extempora'neously, *adv.*, off-handedly.

extempora'neousness, *n.*, off-handedness.

extem'porary, *adj.*, i.q. extemporaneous.

extem'pore, *adj.*, i.q. extemporaneous; *adv.*, at the moment (*Lat.*).

extemporiza'tion, *n.,* the act of extemporizing; that which is extemporized.

extem'porize, *v.t.,* to make without preparation; *v.i.,* to speak or to perform without preparation.

extem'porized, *p.p.,* extemporize.

extem'porizer, *n.,* one who extemporizes.

extem'porizing, *pr.p.,* extemporize.

extend', *v.t.,* to stretch, enlarge or prolong; *v.i.,* to stretch out, to be prolonged.

extend'able, *adj.,* capable of extension or expansion.

extend'ed, *p.p.,* extend.

extend'er, *n.,* one who extends.

extend'ible, *adj.,* i.q. extensible.

extend'ing, *pr.p.,* extend.

extensibil'ity, *n.,* the state or quality of being extensible.

exten'sible, *adj.,* capable of extension or expansion.

exten'sile, *adj.,* capable of extending.

exten'sion, *n.,* the act of extending; the state of being extended; a logical term denoting, collectively, all the things of which a particular term can be predicated.

exten'sive, *adj.,* wide, comprehensive.

exten'sively, *adv.,* widely, comprehensively.

exten'siveness, *n.,* the quality or state of being extensive.

exten'sor, *n.,* a muscle that causes extension.

extent', *n.,* the measure of extension; size, compass.

exten'uate, *v.t.,* to lessen, weaken or tone down.

exten'uated, *p.p.,* extenuate.

exten'uating, *pr.p.,* extenuate.

extenua'tion, *n.,* the act of extenuating, palliation.

exten'uator, *n.,* a plea in extenuation.

exte'rior, *adj.,* outward, external; *n.,* the outside of anything.

exterior'ity, *n.,* outwardness.

exte'riorize, *v.t.,* to conceive in outward form.

exte'riorly, *adv.,* outwardly.

exter'minate, *v.t.,* to expel; to destroy completely.

exter'minated, *p.p.,* exterminate.

exter'minating, *pr.p.,* exterminate.

extermina'tion, *n.,* the act or result of exterminating.

exter'minator, *n.,* that which exterminates.

exter'minatory, *adj.,* causing extermination.

extern', *adj.,* external; *n.,* a day scholar.

exter'nal, *adj.,* on the outside of; foreign; on the surface.

exter'nalism, *n.,* a liking for externals in religion.

external'ity, *n.,* the quality of being external.

exter'nalize, *v.t.,* to make objective.

exter'nally, *adv.,* outwardly.

exterritorial, *adj.,* i.q. extraterritorial.

exter'sion, *n.,* erasion.

extinct', *adj.,* extinguished, dead.

extinc'teur, *n.,* a fire-extinguisher (Fr.).

extinc'tion, *n.,* the act of extinguishing; death; annihilation.

extin'guish, *v.t.,* to put out, destroy or annihilate.

extin'guishable, *adj.,* able to be extinguished.

extin'guished, *p.p.,* extinguish.

extin'guisher, *n.,* anything that extinguishes.

extin'guishing, *pr.p.,* extinguish.

extin'guishment, *n.,* i.q. extinction.

ex'tirpate, *v.t.,* to root out, to destroy.

ex'tirpated, *p.p.,* extirpate.

ex'tirpating, *pr.p.,* extirpate.

extirpa'tion, *n.,* the act or effect of extirpating.

ex'tirpator, *n.,* one who extirpates.

extol', *v.t.,* to praise highly.

extolled', *p.p.,* extol.

extol'ler, *n.,* one who extols.

extol'ling, *pr.p.,* extol.

extor'sive, *adj.,* producing extortion.

extort', *v.t.,* to wring from a person by threat or force.

extort'ed, *p.p.,* extort.

extort'er, *n.,* one who extorts.

extort'ing, *pr.p.,* extort.

extor'tion, *n.,* an act of extorting; an overcharge.

extor'tionary, *adj.,* i.q. extortionate.

extor'tionate, *adj.,* oppressive; greatly overcharged.

extor'tioner, *n.,* one who practises extortion.

extor'tive, *adj.,* able to be extorted.

ex'tra, *adj.,* additional; *n.,* something additional.

extract', *v.t.,* to draw out; to obtain by chemical means.

ex'tract, *n.,* something extracted; an essence.

extract'able, *adj.,* able to be extracted.

extract'ed, *p.p.,* extract.

extract'ing, *pr.p.,* extract.

extrac'tion, *n.,* the act of extracting.

extrac'tive, *adj.,* causing or pert. to extraction; *n.,* a thing of the nature of an extract.

extrac'tor, *n.,* that which extracts; a device for extracting unexploded cartridges from a gun, etc.

extradit'able, *adj.,* liable to extradition.

ex'tradite, *v.t.,* to deliver up to another State.

ex'tradited, *p.p.,* extradite.

ex'traditing, *pr.p.,* extradite.

extradi'tion, *n.,* the act of surrendering the custody of a person to another State.

extra'dos, *n.,* the outer curve of an arch.

extrajudi'cial, *adj.,* outside the proper court.

extramun'dane, *adj.,* outside the world.

extramu'ral, *adj.,* outside the boundaries of a place; in addition to the ordinary.

extra'neous, *adj.,* external, not essential.

extra'neously, *adv.,* in an extraneous way.

extraor'dinarily, *adv.*, in an extraordinary degree.

extraor'dinary, *adj.*, out of the common order; strange, exceptional, amazing.

extrap'olate, *v.t. and i.*, to calculate from known terms other terms which are outside the range of the known terms (*math.*).

extrapola'tion, *n.*, the mathematical calculation from known terms.

extraterritor'ial, *adj.*, free from the jurisdiction of a country (of ambassadors, etc.) (Also *exterritorial.*)

extrav'agance, *n.*, reckless spending; the exceeding of limits.

extrav'agant, *adj.*, exceeding limits, wastefully lavish.

extrav'agantly, *adv.*, in an extravagant way.

extravagan'za, *n.*, a fantastic composition (*It.*).

extrav'agate, *v.i.*, to wander beyond ordinary limits.

extrav'asate, *v.t.*, to let out of the proper (blood) vessels; *v.i.*, to exude from the blood vessels.

extrav'asated, *p.p.*, extravasate.

extrav'asating, *pr.p.*, extravasate.

extravasa'tion, *n.*, the state of being extravasated.

ex'travascular, *adj.*, outside the system of arteries and veins (the vascular system) (*med.*).

ex'travert, *n.*, *i.q.* extrovert.

extreme', *adj.*, at the utmost point, on the edge, furthest.

extreme'ly, *adv.*, in the highest degree.

extrem'ism, *n.*, the policy or doctrine which advocates extreme action.

extre'mist, *n.*, one who holds extreme views.

extrem'ity, *n.*, the very end; dire misfortune.

ex'tricable, *adj.*, able to be extricated.

ex'tricate, *v.t.*, to liberate; to disentangle.

ex'tricated, *p.p.*, extricate.

ex'tricating, *pr.p.*, extricate.

extrica'tion, *n.*, the act of extricating.

extrin'sic, *adj.*, not essential or inherent.

extrin'sical, *adj.*, *i.q.* extrinsic.

extrin'sically, *adv.*, in an extrinsic way.

extrorse', *adj.*, turned outwards (of anthers, *bot.*).

extrover'sion, *n.*, an outward-looking temperament.

ex'trovert, *n.*, a person of outward-looking temperament. (Also *extravert.*)

extrude', *v.t.*, to thrust out.

extru'ded, *p.p.*, extrude.

extru'ding, *pr.p.*, extrude.

extru'sion, *n.*, the act of extruding.

extrus'ive, *adj.*, thrusting out.

exu'berance, *n.*, the state of being exuberant.

exu'berant, *adj.*, abounding to excess; overflowing.

exu'berantly, *adv.*, in an exuberant way.

exu'berate, *v.i.*, to abound; to overflow.

exu'berated, *p.p.*, exuberate.

exu'berating, *pr.p.*, exuberate.

exuda'tion, *n.*, the act or state of exuding; that which has exuded.

exud'ative, *adj.*, able to be exuded.

exude', *v.t.*, to give out through pores; *v.i.*, to sweat or ooze slowly.

exud'ed, *p.p.*, exude.

exud'ing, *pr.p.*, exude.

exul'cerate, *v.t.*, to produce an ulcer; *v.i.*, to become ulcerated.

exul'cerated, *p.p.*, exulcerate.

exul'cerating, *pr.p.*, exulcerate.

exulcera'tion, *n.*, the act of forming an ulcer; the ulcerated state.

exult', *v.i.*, to feel great joy; to triumph.

exult'ancy, *n.*, *i.q.* exultation.

exult'ant, *adj.*, triumphing.

exult'antly, *adv.*, in an exultant way.

exulta'tion, *n.*, a state of great joy.

exult'ed, *p.p.*, exult.

exult'ing, *pr.p.*, exult.

exult'ingly, *adv.*, in an exulting way.

exu'viae, *n. pl.*, the cast-off skins of animals (*Lat.*).

exu'vial, *adj.*, pert. or rel. to exuviae.

exu'viate, *v.t. and i.*, to cast or shed an animal's skin.

exuvia'tion, *n.*, the casting off of an animal's skin.

eyas, *n.*, an unfledged hawk.

eye, *n.*, the organ of sight; a small hole; a catch for a hook; a bud; *v.t.*, to look fixedly at; to make an eye-like hole in.

eye'ball, *n.*, the ball or apple of the eye.

eye'bath, *n.*, a small vessel shaped to facilitate bathing the eyes.

eye'-bolt, *n.*, a bolt or bar eyed to receive a hook, etc.

eye'bright, *n.*, a plant formerly used for eye diseases.

eye'brow, *n.*, the hairy growth above the eyes.

eye'-catching, *adj.*, unusually attracting or attractive.

eyed, *adj.*, having eyes; *p.p.*, eye.

eye'glass, *n.*, a single lens.

eye'ing, *pr.p.*, eye.

eye'lash, *n.*, one of the hairs growing from the eyelids.

eye'less, *adj.*, without eyes, blind.

eye'let, *n.*, a small hole for laces, etc.

eye'let-hole, *n.*, *i.q.* eyelet.

eye'lid, *n.*, the outer covering of the eye.

eye'mark, *n.*, an object of vision.

eye'-op'ener, *n.*, anything that causes surprise; an early drink (U.S.A.).

eye'piece, *n.*, the part of a microscope or telescope nearest to the eye and containing the focussing lenses.

eye'pit, *n.*, the eyesocket.

eyes, *n.*, pl. of eye.

eye'-salve, *n.*, an eye-ointment.

eye'-servant, *n.*, one who works only when under observation.

eye'-serve, *v.i.*, to work only under the master's eye.

eye'-server, *n.*, *i.q.* eye-servant.

eye'-service, *n.*, working only under the master's eye.

*eye'*shot, *n.*, the range of vision.

*eye'*sight, *n.*, vision.

*eye'*sore, *n.*, an affection of the eye; anything offensive to the sight.

*eye'*spot, *n.*, the rudimentary eye.

*eye'*strain, *n.*, a condition of the eyes resulting from excessive use.

*eye'*string, *n.*, the muscle holding the eye.

*eye'*tooth, *n.*, one of the two canines in the upper jaw.

*eye'*wash, *n.*, an eye lotion; humbug, deception (*slang*).

eye'-water, *n.*, eye-wash.

eye'-witness, *n.*, one who testifies to what he has actually seen; *v.i.*, to bear such witness.

eye'-witnessed, *p.p.*, eye-witness.

eye'-witnessing, *pr.p.*, eye-witness.

eyot, *n.*, a small river-island. (Also *ait*.)

eyre, *n.*, a circuit (*leg.*).

ey'rie, ey'ry, *n.*, the nest of an eagle or other bird of prey.

F

fa, n., the fourth ascending note in the tonic solfa musical scale.

Fa'bian, adj., pert. or rel. to Fabius; of the "wait and see" policy; n., a member of the Fabian society.

Fa'bianism, n., the cautious policy of Fabius; the principles of the Fabian Society concerned entirely with moral force.

Fa'bius, n., a Roman general who practised delay and dilatory tactics.

fa'ble, n., a moral story; an impossible tale; v.t., to speak untruthfully.

fa'bled, p.p., fable.

fa'bler, n., an inventor of fables.

fab'liau, n., a short metrical tale of early French poetry (Fr.).

fa'bling, pr.p., fable.

fab'ric, n., a building; a woven material.

fab'ricate, v.t., to construct; to invent falsely.

fab'ricated, p.p., fabricate.

fab'ricating, pr.p., fabricate.

fabrica'tion, n., a made-up story.

fab'ricator, n., one who fabricates.

fab'ulist, n., a writer of fables.

fabulos'ity, n., incredibility.

fab'ulous, adj., fictitious.

fab'ulously, adv., in a fabulous way.

fab'ulousness, n., i.q. fabulosity.

fab'urden, n., a form of counterpoint, an undersong (mus.).

façade', n., the front elevation of a building; a pretence concealing the true situation (Fr.).

face, n., the visage; a surface; v.t., to confront, to oppose; to turn up with facings.

faced, adj., with the surface covered or dressed; p.p., face.

fa'cer, n., a blow in the face; a sudden difficulty.

fac'et, n., a small surface, one of the planes of a cut gem; one aspect of a situation; v.t., to cut (a gem) with facets.

fac'eted, adj., having facets; p.p., facet.

face'tiae, n. pl., amusing, witty sayings; books containing coarse but witty sayings.

face'tious, adj., witty, jocular.

face'tiously, adv., jocularly.

face'tiousness, n., the quality of being facetious.

fa'cia, n., the name plate on a shop front; a fillet or band; any plate or board containing scales, dials, lettering and the like. (Also fascia.)

fa'cial, adj., pert. or rel. to the face.

fac'ile, adj., easy, pliant.

fa'cile prin'ceps, pred. adj., easily first (Lat.).

facil'itate, v.t., to make easy.

facil'itated, p.p., facilitate.

facil'itating, pr.p., facilitate.

facilita'tion, n., the act of making easy.

facil'ity, n., easiness, dexterity, freedom.

fa'cing, pr.p., face.

fa'cings, n. pl., the trimmings on clothes.

facsim'ile, n., an exact copy.

fact, n., something done or that has happened; reality.

fac'tion, n., a political party; dissension.

fac'tional, adj., i.q. factious.

fac'tious, adj., promoting dissension, disorderly; contentious.

fac'tiously, adv., in a factious way.

fac'tiousness, n., a tendency to faction.

facti'tious, adj., artificial.

facti'tiously, adv., artificially.

facti'tiousness, n., artificiality.

fac'titive, adj., causative.

fac'tor, n., a business agent; an estate steward; one of the elements in an arithmetical product; a cause, agency or constituent part; v.t., to resolve into factors.

fac'torage, n., a factor's commission.

facto'rial, adj., pert. or rel. to an arithmetical factor.

fac'torize, v.t., to resolve into factors.

fac'tory, n., a place where goods are manufactured.

facto'tum, n., one who does all manner of work (Lat.).

fac'tual, adj., concerned with fact.

fac'tually, adv., in a factual way.

fac'tum, n., a deed; a statement of facts (Lat.).

fac'ula, n., a bright spot on the sun (astron.).

fac'ultative, adj., permissive.

fac'ulty, n., ability; a learned profession; an academic department, as theology, law, etc.

fad, n., a foolish whim, a craze.

fad'diness, n., the state of being faddy.

fad'dish, adj., displaying fads.

fad'dishness, n., i.q. faddiness.

fad'dism, n., i.q. faddiness.

fad'dist, n., one who cherishes fads.

fad'dle, v.i., to act in a trifling way.

fad'dy, adj., i.q. faddish.

fade, v.i., to lose colour; to wither; to become indistinct.

fa'ded, p.p., fade.

fade'less, adj., unfading.

fade'lessly, adv., in an unfading way.

fade'-out', n., a gradual disappearance.

fa'ding, pr.p., fade.

fa'dingly, adv., in a fading way.

fae'cal, adj., pert. or rel. to faeces.

fae'ces, n. pl., excrement (Lat.).

faec'ula, n., powdery matter from plants; starch; chlorophyll. (Also fecula.)

fa'erie(ry), adj. and n., like fairies; fairyland.

fag, n., a drudge; a boy who does menial work for a senior boy; drudgery; a cheap cigarette (slang); v.t., to overwork; to compel to work; v.i., to drudge, to grow weary.

fag'-end, n., the refuse or worthless part.

fagged, p.p., fag.

fag'ging, pr.p., fag.

fag(g)'ot, n., a bound up bundle of sticks.

fagot'to, n., a bassoon (It.).

Fah'renheit, n., a thermometrical scale, with 32 deg. as its freezing point and 212 deg. its boiling point.

faience', n., glazed, decorated earthenware (Fr.). (Also fayence.)

fail, n., a failure in an examination; v.i., to be deficient; to waste away; to become insolvent; to fall short of one's goal; v.t., to desert, to be wanting to.

failed, p.p., fail.

fail'ing, n., a fault, a weakness; pr.p., fail.

faille, n., a soft kind of silk (Fr.).

fail'ure, n., the act of failing, deficiency, omission, bankruptcy; an unsuccessful person or thing.

fain, adj., willing; adv., gladly.

fainéant', adj., idle, feeble; n., an idler (Fr.).

faint, adj., losing strength, weak, indistinct; n., a swoon; v.i., to swoon; to lose consciousness temporarily.

faint'ed, p.p., faint.

faint'er, adj., comp. of faint.

faint'est, adj., super. of faint.

faintheart'ed, adj., wanting in courage or zeal.

faintheart'edly, adv., in a faint-hearted way.

faint'heart'edness, n., cowardice.

faint'ing, pr.p., faint.

faint'ish, adj., somewhat faint.

faint'ly, adv., weakly, dimly.

faint'ness, n., a faint feeling.

faints, n. pl., an impure spirit given off when distillation begins and ends.

fair, adj., beautiful, comely; light; just, reasonable; moderately good; n., a market at stated times; an assembly of amusements and pastimes.

fair'er, adj., comp. of fair.

fair'est, adj., super. of fair.

fair'-haired, adj., having fair hair.

fair'ily, adv., in a fairy-like way.

fair'ing, n., a present from the fair; a piece of the surface structure of any conveyance, designed to improve its streamlining and reduce its friction.

Fair Isle, adj., describing a knitting pattern invented on the Shetland Islands; n., one of the Shetlands.

fair'ly, adv., justly, moderately.

fair'-minded, adj., acting honestly and fairly.

fair'ness, n., just conduct.

fair'-play, n., just treatment; justice.

fair'-sized, adj., somewhat large.

fair'-spoken, adj., plausible, courteous.

fair'way, n., a navigable channel; the smooth turf between a tee and a putting-green.

fair'weath'er, adj., only fit for fine weather; unreliable.

fair'y, adj., pert. or rel. to fairies; n., a sprite or elf.

fair'yhood, n., the state of being a fairy.

fair'y-lamp, n., a small coloured lamp used for decorative illuminations.

fair'yland, n., the imaginary realm of the fairies.

fair'ylike, adj., resembling fairies.

fairyol'ogy, n., the study of fairies.

fair'y-rings, n. pl., circles in grass caused by fungus but thought to be the haunt of fairies.

fair'y-tale, n., a romance; an untruth.

fait accompli, n., a thing done and past altering (Fr.).

faith, n., belief, trust, fidelity.

faith'ful, adj., loyal, honest; n. pl., members of the Church.

faith'fully, adv., with loyalty.

faith'fulness, n., the quality of being faithful.

faith'less, adj., disloyal; unbelieving.

faith'lessly, adv., in a faithless way; unbelievingly.

faith'lessness, n., deceptiveness; disloyalty.

fake, n., a coil; a made-up thing; a sham; v.t., to fold; to fabricate; to cheat; to steal (colloq.).

faked, p.p., fake.

fa'king, pr.p., fake.

fakir', n., an Indian mendicant.

Falang'e, n., a Spanish Fascist group.

Falan'gist, n., a member of a Spanish Fascist group.

fal'bala, n., a flounce, a trimming (Fr.).

fal'cade, n., the quick curvet of a horse on its haunches.

fal'cate, adj., sickle-shaped.

fal'cated, adj., i.q. falcate (of moon, etc.) (astron.).

falca'tion, n., a sickle-shape formation.

fal'chion, n., a short sword with a curved point.

fal'ciform, adj., sickle-shaped (anat.).

fal'con, n., a bird of prey, trained for sport.

fal'coner, n., one who manages or hunts with falcons.

fal'conet, n., a small 15th cent. cannon.

fal′conry, *n.*, the sport of hunting with falcons.

falderal′, *n.*, a bauble, a trifle.

fald′stool, *n.*, a bishop's folding chair.

Faler′nian, *adj.*, pert. or rel. to Mt. Falernus; *n.*, Falernian wine.

fall, *n.*, a downfall, a cascade; a drop in value; a veil; the autumn (*Amer.*); *v.i.*, to drop, to decline or ebb.

falla′cious, *adj.*, deceptive, misleading.

falla′ciously, *adv.*, in a fallacious way.

falla′ciousness, *n.*, the quality of being fallacious.

fal′lacy, *n.*, a deceitful argument; logically defective reasoning; a sophism; a mistaken belief.

fal′lal′, *n.*, a piece of finery.

fallal(l)′ery, *n.*, *i.q.* falderal.

fall′en, *p.p.*, fall.

fallibil′ity, *n.*, the liability to error.

fal′lible, *adj.*, liable to error.

fall′ing, *pr.p.*, fall.

falling-star, *n.*, a shooting star (*meteorol.*).

Fallo′pian, *adj.*, pert. or rel. to the Fallopian ducts connecting the womb to the ovaries.

fall′-out, *n.*, a deposit of radioactive particles.

fal′low, *adj.*, untilled, unsown; *n.*, unsown land; *v.t.*, to make fallow.

fal′low-deer, *n.*, a variety of deer.

fal′lowed, *p.p.*, fallow.

fal′lowing, *pr.p.*, fallow.

false, *adj.*, untrue, dishonest, treacherous.

false′hearted, *adj.*, treacherous.

false′hood, *n.*, a lie, an untruth.

false′ly, *adv.*, treacherously; in error.

false′ness, *n.*, the character of being false.

fal′ser, *adj.*, *comp.* of false.

fal′sest, *adj.*, *super.* of false.

falset′to, *n.*, an artificial voice above the natural compass (*It.*).

falsi′fiable, *adj.*, that may be made false or imitated.

falsifica′tion, *n.*, the act or result of falsifying.

fal′sified, *p.p.*, falsify.

fal′sifier, *n.*, one who falsifies.

fal′sify, *v.t.*, to make or prove to be false; to forge.

fal′sifying, *pr.p.*, falsify.

fal′sity, *n.*, the quality of being false; a lie.

Falstaff′ian, *adj.*, like or characteristic of Falstaff, one of Shakespeare's characters; fat, jovial and humorous.

fal′ter, *v.i.*, to waver, to hesitate.

fal′tered, *p.p.*, falter.

fal′tering, *pr.p.*, falter.

fal′teringly, *adv.*, in a wavering manner.

fame, *n.*, celebrity, reputation, rumour.

famed, *adj.*, famous, renowned, rumoured.

famil′ial, *adj.*, characteristic of a family.

famil′iar, *adj.*, intimate; domestic; unceremonious; accustomed; *n.*, an attendant spirit.

familiar′ity, *n.*, intimacy, acquaintance with; easy intercourse; an impertinence.

familiariza′tion, *n.*, the act of familiarizing.

famil′iarize, *v.t.*, to make familiar.

famil′iarized, *p.p.*, familiarize.

famil′iarizing, *pr.p.*, familiarize.

famil′iarly, *adv.*, in a familiar way.

fam′ily, *n.*, a household; the children of a house, a race; high descent; a group of animals or plants.

fam′ine, *n.*, dearth, hunger; scarcity of food.

fam′ish, *v.t.*, to reduce to starvation, *v.i.*, to be starving.

fam′ished, *p.p.*, famish.

fam′ishing, *pr.p.*, famish.

fa′mous, *adj.*, celebrated; capital.

fa′mously, *adv.*, in a famous way; capitally.

fam′ulus, *n.*, a magician's assistant (*Lat.*).

fan, *n.*, an instrument to agitate the air; a propeller; a devotee of a specified person or amusement (*slang*, abbrev. for *fanatic*); *v.t.*, to cool with a fan; to ventilate; to winnow.

fanat′ic, *adj.*, *i.q.* fanatical; *n.*, a wild enthusiast.

fanat′ical, *adj.*, wild, mad.

fanat′ically, *adv.*, wildly, madly.

fanat′icism, *n.*, mad enthusiasm.

fan′cied, *p.p.*, fancy.

fan′cier, *n.*, a breeder of birds and animals.

fan′ciful, *adj.*, full of fancies, crotchety; fantastic.

fan′cifully, *adv.*, in a fanciful way.

fan′cifulness, *n.*, the quality of being fanciful.

fan′cy, *adj.*, not plain, ornamental; *interj.*, expressing surprise; *n.*, imagination; a liking; *v.t.*, to conceive in the mind; to imagine; to conceive a liking for.

fan′cying, *pr.p.*, fancy.

fandan′gle, *n.*, a fantastic ornament; tomfoolery.

fandan′go, *n.*, a Spanish dance for two with castanets.

fane, *n.*, a temple, a church.

fan′fare, *n.*, a flourish of trumpets.

fanfaronade′, *n.*, blustering language; *v.i.*, to boast or brag.

fang, *n.*, a long tusk or tooth; *v.t.*, to prime a pump by pouring liquid in to start it.

fanged, *adj.*, having fangs; *p.p.*, fang.

fang′ing, *pr.p.*, fang.

fan′gled, *adj.*, showy.

fang′less, *adj.*, without fangs.

fan′light, *n.*, a window over a door, orig. fanshaped.

fanned, *p.p.*, fan.

fan′ner, *n.*, a ventilating apparatus; a winnowing machine.

fan′ning, *pr.p.*, fan.

fan′tail, *n.*, a variety of pigeons.

fan′-tan′, *n.*, a Chinese gambling game.

fanta'sia, *n.*, a musical reverie (*It.*).

fan'tasm, *n.*, *i.q.* phantasm.

fan'tast, *n.*, a dreamer. (Also *phantast.*)

fantas'tic, *adj.*, fanciful, whimsical; exotically imaginative.

fantas'tical, *adj.*, *i.q.* fantastic.

fantas'tically, *adv.*, in a fantastic way.

fan'tasy, *n.*, fancy, imagination. (Also *phantasy.*)

Fan'tee, *n.*, a member or the language of a people living in Ghana. (Also *Fanti.*)

fantocci'ni, *n. pl.*, mechanically worked puppets; a marionette show (*It.*).

fan'tom, *n.*, *i.q.* phantom.

faquir', *n.*, *i.q.* fakir (*Arab.*).

far, *adj.*, distant, remote; *adv.*, remotely; by many degrees.

far'ad, *n.*, a unit of electrical capacity.

farada'ic, *adj.*, applied to inductive electricity.

faradiza'tion, *n.*, the excitation of a nerve with a magneto-electric current.

far'away, *adj.*, remote; dreamy.

farce, *n.*, a short comical play; a ridiculous, futile proceeding; *v.t.*, to season, to spice or stuff.

farceur', *n.*, a wag (*Fr.*).

far'cical, *adj.*, of the nature of a farce.

farcical'ity, *n.*, *i.q.* farce.

far'cically, *adv.*, in a farcical way.

far'cin, *n.*, *i.q.* farcy.

farc'ing, *n.*, mixed stuffing; forcemeat.

far'cy, *n.*, an indisposition of horses.

far'del, *n.*, a bundle.

fare, *n.*, food; the price for conveyance; a passenger; *v.i.*, to go, to succeed, to be fed.

fared, *p.p.*, fare.

farewell', *interj.*, goodbye; *n.*, leave-taking; an adieu.

far'fetched, *adj.*, exaggerated; forced.

far'-flung, *adj.*, distant.

fari'na, *n.*, meal, flour, starch.

farina'ceous, *adj.*, mealy, containing farina.

farina'ceously, *adv.*, in a farinaceous or mealy manner.

far'ing, *pr.p.*, fare.

far'inose, *adj.*, producing farina.

farl, *n.*, a thin oatmeal cake (*Scot.*).

farm, *n.*, a tract of cultivated land; *v.t.*, to cultivate land; to let out for a sum.

farmed, *p.p.*, farm.

farm'er, *n.*, one who cultivates a farm; a collector of taxes who pays a fixed sum and collects what he can.

farm'ery, *n.*, a farm and its buildings.

farm'hand, *n.*, a worker on a farm.

farm'house, *n.*, a farmer's dwelling.

farm'ing, *n.*, the cultivation of land; the leasing of taxes; *pr.p.*, farm.

farm'-labourer, *n.*, *i.q.* farmhand.

farm'stead, *n.*, a farm with buildings on it.

farm'yard, *n.*, the yard of a farmhouse.

fa'ro, *n.*, a gambling card game.

farouche', *adj.*, sullen, wild (*Fr.*).

farra'ginous, *adj.*, jumbled.

farra'go, *n.*, a medley; a rigmarole.

far'-reaching, *adj.*, widely applicable; having many consequences.

far'rier, *n.*, a shoer of horses; a horse doctor.

far'riery, *n.*, the trade of shoeing horses.

far'row, *n.*, not calving; *n.*, a litter of pigs; *v.i.*, to give birth to (pigs).

far'sighted, *adj.*, sagacious.

far'-sightedness, *n.*, shrewdness; sagacity.

far'ther, *adj.* and *adv.*, *comp.* of far.

far'thermost, *adj.*, the most advanced.

far'thest, *adj.* and *adv.*, *super.* of far.

far'thing, *n.*, an old English coin, formerly the fourth part of a penny.

far'thingale, *n.*, a hooped skirt.

fart'lek, *n.*, a method of training for running athletes.

fas'ces, *n.*, the emblem of the Roman magistrates; a bundle of rods with an axe in the middle.

fas'cia, *n.*, *i.q.* facia.

fas'ciated, *adj.*, compressed; growing into one; striped.

fascia'tion, *n.*, the act of bandaging diseased parts; the compressions of stems or branches (*bot.*).

fas'cicle, *n.*, a small bundle; a division of a book. (Also *fascicule* and *fasciculus.*)

fas'cicled, *adj.*, clustered.

fascic'ular, *adj.*, rel. to a cluster.

fascic'ulate, *adj.*, growing in clusters.

fascic'ulated, *adj.*, *i.q.* fasciculate.

fascicula'tion, *n.*, one part of a book published by instalments.

fas'cicule, *n.*, *i.q.* fascicle.

fas'ciculus, *n.*, *i.q.* fascicle.

fas'cinate, *v.t.*, to charm, to bewitch.

fas'cinated, *p.p.*, fascinate.

fas'cinating, *adj.*, charming; *pr.p.*, fascinate.

fas'cinatingly, *adv.*, in a fascinating way.

fascina'tion, *n.*, a charm, a spell; intense interest.

fascina'tor, *n.*, one who, or that which, fascinates.

fascine', *n.*, a brushwood faggot used for lining trenches, etc. (*mil.*).

Fa'scism, *n.*, Fascist principles.

Fa'scist, *n.*, a supporter of a form of dictatorship.

fash, *n.*, an inconvenience; *v.t.*, to annoy, to bother (*Scot.*).

fash'ion, *n.*, style, shape; society; *v.t.*, to shape, to mould.

fash'ionable, *adj.*, in the mode, stylish.

fash'ionableness, *n.*, the state of being in fashion.

fash'ionably, *adv.*, stylishly.

fash'ioned, *p.p.*, fashion.

fash'ioner, *n.*, one who fashions.

fash'ioning, *pr.p.,* fashion.

fast, *adj.,* quick, firm, dissipated; *adv.,* firmly, securely; *n.,* abstinence from food; *v.i.,* to abstain from food.

fast'-day, *n.,* a day of fasting.

fast'ed, *p.p.,* fast.

fast'en, *v.t.,* to make secure, to cement.

fas'tened, *p.p.,* fasten.

fast'ener, *n.,* a clip; that which holds or secures things together.

fast'ening, *n.,* a bolt or clasp; *pr.p.,* fasten.

fast'er, *adj.,* *comp.* of fast.

fast'est, *adj.,* *super.* of fast.

fas'ti, *n. pl.,* a calendar (*Lat.*).

fastid'ious, *adj.,* critical; hard to please.

fastid'iously, *adv.,* critically; with care and delicacy over personal matters.

fastid'iousness, *n.,* squeamishness; delicacy.

fasti'giate, *adj.,* narrowing to a point; like a pyramid; *v.t.,* to make pointed.

fast'ing, *pr.p.,* fast.

fast'ness, *n.,* firmness; a stronghold.

fat, *adj.,* fleshy, corpulent; greasy, affluent; *n.,* adipose matter; the unctuous part of animal flesh; *v.t.,* to fatten.

fa'tal, *adj.,* fateful, destined, deadly; causing death.

fa'talism, *n.,* the doctrine of the inevitability of fate.

fa'talist, *n.,* one who believes in fatalism.

fatalist'ic, *adj.,* leaning towards fatalism.

fatalist'ically, *adv.,* in a fatalistic way.

fatal'ity, *n.,* destiny; a death.

fa'talize, *v.t.* and *i.,* to lean towards fatalism.

fa'tally, *adv.,* in a fatal manner.

fate, *n.,* destiny, doom.

fa'ted, *adj.,* destined.

fate'ful, *adj.,* pregnant with destiny.

Fates, *n. pl.,* the three mythical dispensers of the future.

fa'ther, *n.,* a male parent; an ancestor; *v.t.,* to adopt, to ascribe.

fa'thered, *p.p.,* father.

fa'therhood, *n.,* paternity.

fa'thering, *pr.p.,* father.

fa'ther-in-law, *n.,* the father of one's husband or wife.

fa'therland, *n.,* one's own country.

fa'therless, *adj.,* without a father.

fa'therlike, *adj.,* like a father.

fa'therliness, *n.,* the fatherly character.

fa'therly, *adj.* and *adv.,* like a father; pert. or rel. to a father.

fath'om, *n.,* a measure of depth equal to 6 ft.; *v.t.,* to sound, to plumb; to assess.

fath'omable, *adj.,* capable of being sounded.

fath'omed, *p.p.,* fathom.

fathom'eter, *n.,* an instrument for measuring the sea depth by sound-waves.

fath'oming, *pr.p.,* fathom.

fath'omless, *adj.,* bottomless.

fath'omlessly, *adv.,* in a fathomless way.

fatid'ic, *adj.,* prophetic. (Also *fatidical.*)

fatid'ical, *adj.,* *i.q.* fatidic.

fatid'ically, *adv.,* in a prophetic way.

fatigue', *n.,* weariness; toil; an assigned duty; *v.t.,* to weary.

fatigued', *p.p.,* fatigue.

fatigue'less, *adj.,* tireless.

fatigu'ing, *adj.,* inducing fatigue; *pr.p.,* fatigue.

fat'ling, *n.,* a young animal fattened for slaughter.

fat'ly, *adv.,* in a fat manner.

fat'ness, *n.,* plumpness; oiliness; fertility.

fat'ted, *adj.,* fattened for slaughter; *p.p.,* fat.

fat'ten, *v.t.,* to make fat; *v.i.,* to grow fat.

fat'tened, *p.p.,* fatten.

fat'tener, *n.,* one who, or that which, fattens.

fat'tening, *pr.p.,* fatten.

fat'ter, *adj.,* *comp.* of fat.

fat'test, *adj.,* *super.* of fat.

fat'tiness, *n.,* greasiness.

fat'ting, *pr.p.,* fat.

fat'tish, *adj.,* somewhat fat.

fat'ty, *adj.,* oily; composed of fat; *n.,* a fat person (*colloq.*).

fatu'ity, *n.,* foolishness.

fat'uous, *adj.,* foolish.

fat'uously, *adv.,* foolishly.

fau'bourg, *n.,* a suburb; an urban district formerly a suburb (*Fr.*).

fauc'al, *adj.,* of the throat; *n.,* a deep, guttural sound. (Also *faucial.*)

fau'ces, *n. pl.,* the windpipe (*Lat.*).

fau'cet, *n.,* a spigot; a tap; a pipe for drawing liquor from a cask (*U.S.A.*).

fau'cial, *adj.,* *i.q.* faucal.

fauci'tis, *n.,* inflammation of the throat (*med.*).

faugh, *interj.,* an exclamation of disgust.

fault, *n.,* a slight offence; a defect; a lost scent (in hunting); a dislocation of geological strata.

fault'finder, *n.,* a censorious person.

fault'finding, *adj.,* capable of finding fault; *n.,* the finding of fault.

fault'ily, *adv.,* in a faulty manner.

fault'iness, *n.,* the state of being faulty.

fault'less, *adj.,* without fault; perfect.

fault'lessly, *adv.,* in a faultless manner.

fault'lessness, *n.,* freedom from faults.

fault'y, *adj.,* defective; blamable.

faun, *n.,* a Roman rural deity, a deer-like deity, having a tail and horns.

fau'na, *n.,* a collective term for the animals peculiar to a region or period.

fau'nal, *adj.,* like fauna.

fau'nist, *n.,* one who describes the fauna of a district.

faun'ology, *n.,* the study of fauna.

fausse-braye, n., an earth mound in front of a rampart.

fauteuil', n., an armchair, a theatre stall (Fr.).

fauvette', n., a family of warblers (Fr.).

faux pas, n., a false step; a breach of manners or morals (Fr.).

fav'eolate, adj., like a honeycomb.

fav'illous, adj., like ashes.

favon'ian, adj., pert. or rel. to the west wind; propitious.

fav'osites, n. pl., a fossil which has a honeycomb formation.

fa'vour, n., a friendly disposition; an act of good-will; a token; a knot of ribbon; v.t., to regard with kindness; to render easy, to show more consideration to one than to another; to use less (as of an injured limb).

fa'vourable, adj., friendly, advantageous.

fa'vourably, adv., in a favourable manner.

fa'voured, adj., regarded with favour; featured; p.p., favour.

fa'vourer, n., one who favours.

fa'vouring, pr.p., favour.

fa'vourite, adj., regarded with preference; n., one greatly beloved; one unduly favoured.

fa'vouritism, n., the disposition to promote the interest of one person to the neglect of others with equal claims.

fa'vus, n., a contagious scalp disease causing baldness.

fawn, n., a young deer; v.i., to cringe and bow to gain favour.

fawned, p.p., fawn.

fawn'er, n., one who fawns.

fawn'ing, adj., flattering, servile; pr.p., fawn.

fawn'ingly, adv., in a servile manner.

fay, n., a fairy; v.t., to fit two pieces of wood closely together.

fayal'ite, n., a black silicate of iron.

fay'ence, n., i.q. faience.

faze, v.t., to roughhandle; to ill-treat.

fea'berry, n., the gooseberry.

feal, adj., faithful.

fe'alty, n., fidelity.

fear, n., apprehension of danger; a strong emotion of impending harm or evil; reverence; v.t., to be afraid of; to venerate; v.i., to be afraid.

feared, p.p., fear.

fear'ful, adj., afraid; timorous; terrible.

fear'fully, adv., terribly; with fear; extremely (colloq.).

fear'fulness, n., the quality of being fearful.

fear'ing, pr.p., fear.

fear'less, adj., courageous.

fear'lessly, adv., in a fearless manner.

fear'lessness, n., the state or quality of being fearless.

fear'nought, n., a stout woollen cloth used for protection at sea.

fear'some, adj., exciting fear.

feasibil'ity, n., practicability.

fea'sible, adj., practicable.

fea'sibleness, n., i.q. feasibility.

fea'sibly, adv., possibly.

feast, n., a banquet; a festival; v.i., to take a sumptuous meal; v.t., to entertain with sumptuous food.

feast'-day, n., a day of celebration of a festival.

feast'ed, p.p., feast.

feast'er, n., one who feasts.

feast'ing, pr.p., feast.

feat, adj., neat; skilful (arch.); n., an exploit.

feath'er, n., a plume; v.t., to fit or cover with feathers; to skim the blade of an oar horizontally along the surface.

feath'erbed, n., a bed stuffed with feathers; v.t., to make circumstances unwarrantably easy.

feath'erbrained, adj., frivolous.

feath'er-duster, n., a duster made of feathers.

feath'ered, adj., covered or fitted with feathers; winged; p.p., feather.

feath'er-edge, n., the thinner edge of a plank.

feath'er-grass, n., a kind of perennial grass.

feath'erheaded, adj., lacking in serious thought and attitudes.

feath'ering, n., in Gothic architecture, an ornament consisting of small arcs separated by cusps; the act of turning an oar-blade; pr.p., feather.

feath'erstitch, n., zigzag stitches in needlework.

feath'erweight, n., a very light thing; a boxer weighing below nine stones.

feath'ery, adj., covered with or resembling feathers.

feat'ly, adv., deftly, smartly (arch.).

fea'ture, n., a lineament of the face; a prominent part; v.t., to resemble in the face; to give prominence to.

fea'tured, adj., having a certain cast of features; p.p., feature.

fea'tureless, adj., without features; lacking characteristics.

fea'turing, pr.p., feature.

feaze, v.t., to unravel; to untie, string, rope, etc.

febricula, n., a passing fever.

febrifa'cient, adj., causing fever.

febrif'ugal, adj., capable of reducing or curing fever.

feb'rifuge, n., a medicine that removes fever.

feb'rile, adj., indicating fever.

febril'ity, n., feverishness.

Feb'ruary, n., the second month of the year.

fe'cal, adj., i.q. faecal.

fe'ces, n. pl., i.q. faeces.

feck'less, adj., feeble, ineffective.

fec'ula, n., i.q. faecula.

fec'ulence, n., sediment; dregs.

fec'ulent, adj., muddy; turbid; foul.

fec'und, *adj.*, prolific.

fec'undate, *v.t.*, to make fruitful.

fecunda'tion, *n.*, the act of fecundating.

fecun'dity, *n.*, fertility; richness of invention.

fed, *p.p.*, feed.

fed'eral, *adj.*, pert. or rel. to a league; founded on alliance between States otherwise independent; *n.*, a member of the Northern party in the American Civil War, 1861-5.

fed'eralism, *n.*, the principles of federal government.

fed'eralist, *n.*, one who supports federalism; a federal.

federaliza'tion, *n.*, *i.q.* federalism.

fed'eralize, *v.t.* and *i.*, to unite in a federal compact.

fed'eralized, *p.p.*, federalize.

fed'eralizing, *pr.p.*, federalize.

fed'erate, *adj.*, leagued; *v.t.* and *i.*, to band together; to organize as a federal association.

federa'tion, *n.*, a league; a federal government.

fed'erative, *adj.*, forming a confederacy.

fed'eratively, *adv.*, in a federative way.

fee, *n.*, a reward for services; a fief; *v.t.*, to give a fee to.

fee'ble, *adj.*, weak.

fee'bleness, *n.*, weakness.

fee'bler, *adj.*, comp. of feeble.

fee'blest, *adj.*, super. of feeble.

fee'bly, *adv.*, in a feeble manner.

feed, *n.*, food; fodder; an allowance of food; *p.p.*, fee; *v.t.*, to give food to; *v.i.*, to eat.

feed'back, *n.*, the carrying back of something to its source, or a preceding stage, to strengthen or modify it.

feed'er, *n.*, one who feeds; that which supplies something.

feed'ing, *n.*, food; that which furnishes food for animals; *pr.p.*, feed.

feed'-pipe, *n.*, a pipe which supplies a boiler with water.

fee'-farm, *n.*, an estate in fee simple, subject to a perpetual rent.

fee'ing, *pr.p.*, fee.

feel, *n.*, the sensation on being touched; *v.t.*, to perceive by touch; to experience; *v.i.*, to have the sensibility excited.

feel'er, *n.*, an organ of touch; a device to find out another's feelings or plans.

feel'ing, *adj.*, affecting; tender; *n.*, the sense of touch; tenderness of heart; sensitiveness; an emotion.

feel'ingly, *adv.*, tenderly; keenly.

fee-sim'ple, *n.*, an absolute entitlement to landed property; freehold.

feet, *n.*, pl. of foot.

fee' tail, *n.*, an estate limited to a man and the heirs of his body.

feeze, *v.t.*, to twist; to tighten a screw etc.; to scare.

feign, *v.t.*, to counterfeit; to pretend.

feigned, *adj.*, simulated; *p.p.*, feign.

feign'edly, *adv.*, in a feigned manner.

feign'edness, *n.*, pretence; simulation.

feigner, *n.*, one who pretends.

feign'ing, *pr.p.*, feign.

feign'ingly, *adv.*, with pretence.

feint, *n.*, a pretence; a mock attack; *v.i.*, to make a mock attack; *i.q.* faint (lines).

feld'spar, *n.*, *i.q.* felspar.

feldspath'ic, *adj.*, *i.q.* felspathic.

fel'icide, *n.*, the killing of cats.

felicif'ic, *adj.*, leading to happiness (*eth.*).

felic'itate, *v.t.*, to congratulate.

felic'itated, *p.p.*, felicitate.

felic'itating, *pr.p.*, felicitate.

felicita'tion, *n.*, congratulation.

felic'itous, *adj.*, happy; extremely appropriate.

felic'itously, *adv.*, in a felicitous manner.

felic'itousness, *n.*, *i.q.* felicity.

felic'ity, *n.*, blissfulness; appropriateness.

fe'lid, *n.*, a member of the Felidae or cat-tribe.

fe'line, *adj.*, pert. or rel. to cats.

fell, *adj.*, cruel; *n.*, a skin or hide; a seam or hem; a barren hill; *p.p.*, of fall; *v.t.*, to sew a seam level with the cloth; to cause to fall; to hew or knock down.

fel'lah, *n.*, an Egyptian peasant.

fellaheen', *n.*, pl. of fellah.

fella'tio, *n.*, sexual satisfaction in a man produced by oral stimulation by a woman (*It.*).

felled, *p.p.*, fell.

fell'er, *n.*, one who fells.

fell'ic, *adj.*, formed in the bile.

fell'ing, *pr.p.*, fell.

fell'monger, *n.*, a dealer in hides.

fel'loe, *n.*, *i.q.* felly.

fel'low, *n.*, a companion; an equal; one of a pair; a member of a college or incorporated society; familiar for individual.

fel'low-cit'izen, *n.*, one who lives in the same city.

fel'low-coun'tryman, *n.*, one born or living in the same country.

fel'low-crea'ture, *n.*, one made by the same Creator.

fel'low-feel'ing, *n.*, sympathy.

fel'low-heir, *n.*, a joint inheritor.

fel'lowship, *n.*, companionship; a brotherhood; an establishment in a college entitling the holder to a share of its revenues.

fel'low-trav'eller, *n.*, a travelling companion; a sympathizer (esp. Communist).

fel'ly, *n.*, the circular rim of a wheel, or one of the parts thereof. (Also *felloe*.)

fe'lo-de-se, *n.*, suicide.

fel'on, *adj.*, wicked; *n.*, a criminal; a whitlow.

felo'nious, *adj.*, deliberately criminal.

felo'niously, *adv.*, in a felonious manner.

fel'onry, *n.*, the class of felons.

fel'ony, *n.*, a serious crime.

fel'spar, *n.*, a mineral—a constituent of granite, gneiss, etc. (Also *feldspar.*)

felspath'ic, *adj.*, containing felspar. (Also *feldspathic.*)

fel'stone, *n.*, rock masses of quartz and felspar.

felt, *n.*, wool compacted by rolling, beating, etc.; *p.p.*, feel; *v.t.*, to make into felt.

felt'ed, *p.p.*, felt.

felt'er, *n.*, one who makes or covers with felt; *v.t.*, to mat together.

fel'teric, *n.*, a horse-disease.

felt'ing, *n.*, the process by which, or the materials of which, felt is made; *pr.p.*, felt.

felt'y, *adj.*, like felt.

feluc'ca, *n.*, a long, narrow Mediterranean vessel with two large lateen sails.

fe'male, *adj.*, rel. to the sex which reproduces the race; *b.*, an animal or plant that belongs to the sex which reproduces young or fruit.

feme, *n.*, a woman (*leg.*).

feme co'vert, *n.*, a married woman (*leg.*).

feme sole, *n.*, a spinster, widow or married woman entirely independent of her husband regarding property (*leg.*).

feminal'ity, *n.*, *i.q.* femininity.

femine'ity, *n.*, womanliness.

fem'inine, *adj.*, pert. or rel. to the female sex; characteristic of women.

feminin'ity, *n.*, the quality of being feminine.

fem'inism, *n.*, the advocacy of woman's improved status.

fem'inist, *n.*, one who supports feminism.

femin'ity, *n.*, *i.q.* femininity.

fem'inize, *v.t.*, to make feminine; to give feminine qualities to.

femme de chambre, *n.*, a chambermaid (*Fr.*).

fem'oral, *adj.*, rel. to the thigh.

fe'mur, *n.*, the thigh-bone.

fen, *n.*, low land covered partly with water; a marsh.

fence, *n.*, a boundary; the art of fencing; skill in repartee; a receiver of stolen goods; *v.t.*, to enclose with a fence; to hedge in; *v.i.*, to use a sword in order to learn attack and defence with it; to prevaricate.

fenced, *adj.*, inclosed with a fence; *p.p.*, fence.

fence'less, *adj.*, uninclosed; open.

fen'cer, *n.*, one who teaches or practises fencing with a sword or foil.

fen'cible, *n.*, a soldier for home defence only.

fen'cing, *n.*, the art of using a sword; material for making fences; *pr.p.*, fence.

fend, *v.t.*, to ward off; *v.i.*, to provide for.

fend'ed, *p.p.*, fend.

fend'er, *n.*, a device to keep live coals from rolling on to the floor; a contrivance hung over the side of a ship to protect it from injury by rubbing.

fend'ing, *pr.p.*, fend.

fenestell'a, *n.*, a niche on the south side of an altar (*archit.*).

fenes'tra, *n.*, a small hole in a bone in the inner ear (*Lat.*).

fenes'tral, *adj.*, pert. or rel. to a window.

fenes'trate, *adj.*, having windows or interstices; *v.t.*, to arrange windows in.

fenes'trated, *adj.*, furnished with windows; perforated; *p.p.*, fenestrate.

fenes'trating, *pr.p.*, fenestrate.

fenestra'tion, *n.*, the arrangement of windows in a building.

fen'gite, *n.*, a transparent alabaster used in windows.

Fe'nian, *adj.*, of the Fenians; *n.*, a member of an Irish republican secret society.

Fe'nianism, *n.*, the principles of the Fenians.

fenks, *n. pl.*, the fibrous parts of a whale's blubber, the remainder of blubber when melted.

fenn'ec, *n.*, a small N. African fox notable for its very large pointed ears (*Arab.*).

fen'nel, *n.*, a fragrant plant.

fen'ny, *adj.*, marshy; boggy.

fent, *n.*, an opening or a slit in a garment.

fen'ugreek, *n.*, a leguminous plant with bitter, mucilaginous seeds.

feoff, *n.*, *i.q.* fief or fee.

feoffee', *n.*, the holder of land in fee.

feoff'er, *n.*, one who grants a fee. (Also *feoffor.*)

feoff'ment, *n.*, the transference of a freehold estate; the deed by which a freehold is conveyed.

feoff'or, *n.*, *i.q.* feoffer.

fera'cious, *adj.*, fruitful.

ferac'ity, *n.*, fruitfulness.

fe'rae, *n. pl.*, carnivorous mammals (*Lat.*).

fe'rae natur'ae, *adj.*, living in a wild state, not domesticated (*Lat.*).

fe'ral, *adj.*, wild, untamed; funereal.

fer-de-lance, *n.*, the large, venomous pit-viper of Brazil (*Fr.*).

fe'retory, *n.*, a shrine for the relics of saints, a chapel which contains shrines.

fe'rial, *adj.*, pert. or rel. to holidays; ordinary.

fe'rine, *adj.*, pert. or rel. to a wild beast; savage.

fer'ment, *n.*, any substance which produces the peculiar decomposition called fermentation; agitation; confused opinions.

ferment', *v.t.*, to cause fermentation; to excite; *v.i.*, to undergo fermentation; to work; to be agitated.

fermentabil'ity, *n.*, capability of being fermented.

ferment'able, *adj.*, capable of fermentation.

fermenta'tion, *n.,* the process by which grape juice is converted into wine, or a sweet infusion of malt into beer; any similar process; agitation; excitement.

ferment'ative, *adj.,* causing or produced by fermentation.

ferment'ed, *p.p.,* ferment.

ferment'ing, *pr.p.,* ferment.

fern, *n.,* a cryptogamous plant.

fern'ery, *n.,* a place where ferns are artificially grown.

fern'y, *adj.,* overgrown with fern.

fero'cious, *adj.,* fierce; savage.

fero'ciously, *adv.,* with savage cruelty.

fero'ciousness, *n.,* the state of being ferocious.

feroc'ity, *n., i.q.* ferociousness.

fe'rox, *n.,* the great lake trout.

ferra'ra, *n.,* a broadsword.

fer'rate, *n.,* a salt of ferric acid.

fer'rel, *n., i.q.* ferrule.

fer'reous, *adj.,* made of, or rel. to, iron.

fer'ret, *n.,* a domesticated sort of polecat, yellow, with red eyes; stout cotton or silk tape; *v.t.,* to hunt with ferrets; to search out cunningly.

fer'reted, *p.p.,* ferret.

fer'reter, *n.,* one who, or that which, ferrets.

fer'reting, *n.,* hunting with ferrets; *pr.p.,* ferret.

fer'riage, *n.,* the fare paid at a ferry.

fer'ric, *adj.,* pert. to, or extracted from, iron.

fer'ried, *p.p.,* ferry.

ferrif'erous, *adj.,* yielding iron.

Fer'ris wheel, *n.,* a giant, revolving, vertical wheel carrying passengers at fairs, etc.

ferrocon'crete, *n.,* reinforced concrete.

ferro-magnet'ic, *adj.,* magnetic as opposed to diamagnetic.

fer'rotype, *n.,* a positive photograph taken on thin iron plate.

fer'rous, *adj.,* obtained from or containing iron.

ferru'ginated, *adj.,* having the colour or properties of iron-rust.

ferru'ginous, *adj.,* of the colour of iron-rust.

fer'rule, *n.,* a ring of metal put round anything to prevent splitting. (Also *ferrel.*)

fer'ruled, *adj.,* having a strengthening band.

fer'ry, *n.,* the place where passengers are carried over a narrow piece of water; a ferry-boat; *v.t.,* to carry in a boat or raft over a river or other piece of water.

fer'ry-boat, *n.,* a boat that plies at a ferry.

fer'ry-bridge, *n.,* a large train-carrying ferry.

fer'rying, *pr.p.,* ferry.

fer'ryman, *n.,* one who keeps a ferry.

fer'tile, *adj.,* fruitful.

fertil'ity, *n.,* fruitfulness.

fer'tilizable, *adj.,* capable of being fertilized.

fertiliza'tion, *n.,* the process of rendering fertile.

fer'tilize, *v.t.,* to make fertile.

fer'tilized, *p.p.,* fertilize.

fer'tilizer, *n.,* one who, or that which, fertilizes.

fer'tilizing, *pr.p.,* fertilize.

fer'ula, *n.,* a rod or cane with which light punishment was inflicted (*Lat.*).

ferula'ceous, *adj.,* having a stalk like a reed.

fer'ule, *n., i.q.* ferula; *v.t.,* to punish with a ferula.

fer'vency, *n.,* ardour; warmth of devotion.

fer'vent, *adj.,* hot; ardent; earnest.

fer'vently, *adv.,* earnestly.

ferves'cent, *adj.,* becoming hot.

fer'vid, *adj.,* very hot; fervent; strongly passionate.

fer'vidly, *adv.,* with glowing warmth.

fer'vour, *n.,* ardour; extreme earnestness.

fes'cennine, *adj.,* licentious.

fes'cue, *n.,* a kind of grass; a small stick.

fesse, *n.,* a broad horizontal band across a shield (*her.*).

fes'tal, *adj.,* festive; pert. or rel. to a feast.

fes'tally, *adv.,* in a festal way.

fes'ter, *n.,* an inflamed sore which suppurates; *v.i.,* to suppurate; to rankle.

fes'tered, *p.p.,* fester.

fes'tering, *pr.p.,* fester.

festina lente, *adv. phr.,* hasten slowly (*Lat.*).

fes'tival, *n.,* a time of feasting; an anniversary.

fes'tive, *adj.,* joyous; gay.

fes'tively, *adv.,* in a festive manner.

festiv'ity, *n.,* a festal celebration; social exhilaration.

festoon', *n.,* a garland; *v.t.,* to adorn with festoons.

festooned', *p.p.,* festoon.

festoon'ing, *pr.p.,* festoon.

fe'tal, *adj.,* pert. or rel. to a fetus. (Also *foetal.*)

fetch, *n.,* a stratagem; the apparition of a living person; *v.t.,* to bring.

fetched, *p.p.,* fetch.

fetch'ing, *adj.,* attractive; *pr.p.,* fetch.

fête, *n.,* a holiday; a festival day; *v.t.,* to honour with a festive entertainment (*Fr.*).

fet'id, *adj.,* stinking. (Also *foetid.*)

fet'idly, *adv.,* in a fetid way.

fet'idness, *n.,* the state of being fetid.

fetif'erous, *adj.,* producing young.

fe'tish, fe'tich(e), *n.,* any object regarded with awe or pleasure, stimulating strong feelling, and irrationally reverenced.

fetish'ism, *n.,* the worship of a fetish.

fetishis'tic, *adj.,* like a fetish.

fet'lock, *n.,* a tuft of hair behind the pastern joint of a horse; the joint itself.

fe'tor, *n.,* a stench (*Lat.* Also *foetor.*)

fet'ter, *n.,* a chain for the feet; a restraint; *v.t.,* to bind; to restrain.

fet'tered, *p.p.,* fetter.

fet'tering, *pr.p.,* fetter.

fetter'less, *adj.,* without fetters.

fet'tle, *n.,* condition, vigorous health; *v.t.,* to put right.

fet'tled, *p.p.,* fettle.

fet'tling, *pr.p.,* fettle.

fe'tus, *n.,* the perfectly formed young of an animal before it is born or hatched. (Also *foetus.*)

fet'wa, *n.,* a decision, esp. written, given by a Mohammedan judge (*Arab.*).

feu, *n.,* a small piece of ground granted in perpetuity on payment of annual rent (*Scots law*).

feud, *n.,* a fief; hostility.

feu'dal, *adj.,* pert. or rel. to the system of holding lands by military services and defined duties.

feu'dalism, *n.,* the feudal system.

feudalis'tic, *adj., i.q.* feudal.

feudal'ity, *n.,* the feudal system, or its principles.

feuda'liza'tion, *n.,* the act of feudalizing.

feu'dalize, *v.t.,* to reduce to a feudal tenure.

feu'dalized, *p.p.,* feudalize.

feu'dalizing, *pr.p.,* feudalize.

feu'dally, *adv.,* in a feudal way.

feu'dary, *n.,* a feudatory; a vassal.

feu'datory, *adj.,* holding by feudal tenure; *n.,* a feudal tenant or vassal.

feu de joie, *n.,* a salute of guns (*Fr.*).

feuds, *n.,* pl. of feud; a state of hostility; land held in fee.

feuilleton', *n.,* that part of a French newspaper occupied by light literature; a serial story in a newspaper (*Fr.*).

fe'ver, *n.,* a condition of increased body temperature, pulse rate and mental clouding accompanying some maladies.

fe'vered, *adj.,* taken with fever.

fe'verfew, *n.,* a plant with much-divided leaves and a white flower.

fe'verish, *adj.,* slightly affected with fever; indicating fever.

fe'verishly, *adv.,* in a feverish manner.

fe'verishness, *n.,* the state of being feverish; anxious excitement.

fe'verous, *adj.,* tending to cause fever.

fe'verously, *adv.,* in a feverous way.

few, *adj.,* not many.

few'er, *adj., comp.* of few.

few'est, *adj., super.* of few.

few'ness, *n.,* the state of being few.

fey, *adj.,* about to die; irrational in behaviour.

fez, *n.,* a flowerpot-shaped hat worn in the Middle East.

fiacre, *n.,* a hackney cab with four wheels (*Fr.*).

fiancé(e), *n.,* a betrothed person.

Fianna Fail, *n.,* an Irish Political Party.

fias'co, *n.,* an ignominious failure (*It.*).

fi'at, *n.,* a command (*Lat.*).

fib, *n.,* a falsehood; a blow; *v.i.,* to tell an untruth.

fibbed, *p.p.,* fib.

fib'ber, *n.,* one who tells fibs.

fib'bing, *pr.p.,* fib.

fi'bre, *n.,* a thread or filament.

fi'breboard, *n.,* a building-board of compacted fibres.

fi'bred, *adj.,* made of fibres.

fi'breglass, *n.,* a synthetic fibre of very fine filaments of molten glass.

fi'briform, *adj.,* fibre-like.

fi'bril, *n.,* a small fibre.

fi'brilated, *adj.,* having small fibres.

fi'brila'tion, *n.,* the state of having fibrils.

fi'bril'iform, *adj., i.q.* fibrilated.

fibril'la, *n.,* a hair on the root of a young plant.

fi'brillose, *adj.,* with fibres.

fi'brillous, *adj.,* fibril-shaped.

fi'brin, *n.,* a substance contained in blood, causing it to clot.

fi'brinous, *adj.,* having the nature of fibrin.

fi'broid, *adj.,* made up of fibres.

fi'broin, *n.,* the chemical substance of silk and cobwebs.

fibrom'a, *n.,* a fibrous tumour.

fibro'sis, *n.,* a growth of fibrous tissue.

fibrosit'is, *n.,* muscular rheumatism.

fi'brous, *adj.,* consisting of fibres.

fib'ula, *n.,* a brooch or buckle; the smaller bone of the lower leg; a needle for sewing up wounds.

ficelle', *adj.,* string-coloured (*Fr.*).

fi'chu, *n.,* a light kind of shawl (*Fr.*).

fick'le, *adj.,* inconstant; changeable.

fick'leness, *n.,* inconstancy.

fi'co, *n.,* a fig; an insignificant trifle.

fic'tile, *adj.,* moulded by art; manufactured by a potter.

fictil'ia, *n. pl.,* ornamental moulded articles (*Lat.*).

fic'tion, *n.,* romances, novels, tales, etc.

fic'tional, *adj.,* pert. or rel. to fiction.

fictioneer', *n., i.q.* fictionist.

fic'tionist, *n.,* a writer of fiction.

ficti'tious, *adj.,* imaginary; false.

ficti'tiously, *adv.,* in a fictitious manner.

ficti'tiousness, *n.,* the quality of being fictitious.

fic'tive, *adj.,* creating or created by imagination.

fic'tor, *n.,* a clay modeller.

Fi'cus, *n.,* a genus of trees and shrubs including the fig.

fid, *n.,* a block or pin of wood, used as a support.

fid'dle, *n.,* a violin; *v.i.,* to play on a fiddle; to trifle; *v.t.,* to attain or obtain by underhand or illegal means.

fid'dled, *p.p.,* fiddle.

fid'dle-fad'dle, *n.,* small talk; *v.i.,* to be fussy and waste time over trivialities.

fid′dler, *n.,* one who plays on a fiddle; a small crab.

fid′dlestick, *interj.,* (in pl.) nonsense!; *n.,* a fiddle-bow.

fid′dley, *n.,* the iron framework surrounding a stoke-hole (*naut.*).

fid′dling, *adj.,* trivial; fussy; *n.,* playing the fiddle; *pr.p.,* fiddle.

fidel′ity, *n.,* faithfulness.

fidg′et, *n.,* restlessness; a worrier; *v.i.,* to be restless.

fidg′eted, *p.p.,* fidget.

fidg′etiness, *n.,* the state of being fidgety.

fidg′eting, *pr.p.,* fidget.

fidg′ety, *adj.,* restless; uneasy.

fid′ibus, *n.,* a paper spill (*slang*).

Fi′do, *n.,* an acronym for Fog Investigation Dispersal Operation, a device to help aircraft to land in fog.

fidu′cial, *adj.,* undoubting; fiduciary.

fidu′ciary, *adj.,* trustful; held in trust; *n.,* a trustee.

fid′us Achat′es, *n.,* a devoted follower, a henchman (*Lat.*).

fie, *interj.,* denoting impatience or contempt.

fief, *n.,* an estate held on feudal tenure. (Also *feoff*.)

fie′-fie, *adj.,* improper, scandalous.

field, *n.,* cleared or cultivated land; open country; a battle; the scene of military operations; scope; cricketers collectively; all the horses in a race; *v.i.,* to watch and recover the ball at cricket.

field′-book, *n.,* a surveyor's notebook.

field′-day, *n.,* a day of excitement or of unusual success.

field′ed, *p.p.,* field.

field′er, *n.,* a player who fields at cricket.

field′fare, *n.,* a bird of the thrush family.

field′-glass, *n.,* a binocular glass for looking at distant objects.

field′-hos′pital, *n.,* a hospital in immediate touch with an army.

field′ing, *pr.p.,* field.

field′-marsh′al, *n.,* a military officer of the highest rank.

field′mouse, *n.,* a mouse which lives in the fields.

field′-of′ficer, *n.,* a military officer above the rank of captain and below that of general.

field′-piece, *n.,* a gun used on the field of battle.

fiend, *n.,* a devil; a wicked person.

fiend′ish, *adj.,* devilish.

fiend′ishly, *adv.,* in a fiendish way.

fiend′ishness, *n.,* devilishness; wickedness.

fiend′like, *adj.,* like a fiend; devilish.

fierce, *adj.,* violent; savage.

fierce′ly, *adv.,* furiously, savagely.

fierce′ness, *n.,* violence; fury, ferocity.

fierc′er, *adj., comp.* of fierce.

fierc′est, *adj., super.* of fierce.

fi′eri-fa′cias, *n.,* a writ authorizing a sheriff to distrain.

fi′erily, *adv.,* in a fiery way.

fi′eriness, *n.,* the state of being fiery.

fi′ery, *adj.,* consisting of fire; blazing; impetuous; bright.

fies′ta, *n.,* a festivity, a holiday (*Span.*).

fife, *n.,* a small kind of flute; *v.i.,* to play on a fife.

fifed, *p.p.,* fife.

fi′fer, *n.,* one who plays on a fife.

fife′-rail, *n.,* a rail running round the foot of a mast for securing running tackle.

fifteen, *adj.,* five and ten.

fifteenth, *adj.,* the fifth in order after the tenth; *n.,* one of fifteen equal parts into which a whole is divided.

fifth, *adj.,* next after the fourth; *n.,* one of five equal parts into which a whole is divided.

fifth-col′umnist, *n.,* an enemy sympathizer; a person secretly undermining one's efforts.

fifth′ly, *adv.,* in the fifth place.

fif′tieth, *adj.,* next in order after the fortyninth; *n.,* one of fifty equal parts into which a whole is divided.

fif′ty, *adj.,* five times ten.

fif′tyfold, *adj.,* fifty times as much or great.

fig, *n.,* a fruit; something of very small value; dress, equipment (*colloq.*).

fight, *n.,* a contest; a battle; *v.i.,* to contend; to strive; *v.t.,* to war against.

fight′er, *n.,* a combatant.

fight′ing, *adj.,* trained for war; *pr.p.,* fight.

fig′-leaf, *n.,* a leaf of a fig-tree.

fig′ment, *n.,* something feigned or imagined.

fig′-tree, *n.,* a tree that bears figs.

figurabil′ity, *n.,* the quality of being figurable.

fig′urable, *adj.,* capable of being figured.

fig′ural, *adj.,* pert. or rel. to figures.

fig′urant, *n.,* a male ballet-dancer (*Fr.*).

fig′urante, *n.,* a female ballet-dancer (*It.*).

fig′urate, *adj.,* of a certain definite shape.

fig′urated, *adj.,* of definite form.

figura′tion, *n.,* the act of giving definite form.

fig′urative, *adj.,* symbolical; not literal.

fig′uratively, *adv.,* metaphorically.

fig′urativeness, *n.,* in the state of being figurative.

fig′ure, *n.,* form; shape; a character denoting a number; a rhetorical device, a trope; *v.t.,* to represent; to imagine; *v.i.,* to cipher.

fig′ured, *p.p.,* figure.

fig′urehead, *n.,* the ornamental figure on a ship under the bowsprit; a person who is nominally but not actually a head.

figurine′, *n.,* a statuette (*Fr.*).

fig′uring, *pr.p.,* figure.

Fiji′an, *adj.,* pert. or rel. to Fiji, a Pacific island; *n.,* a native of F.

fila′ceous, *adj.,* consisting of threads.

fil′acer, *n.*, a former official of the Common Pleas, who made out and filed writs.

fil′agree, *n.*, *i.q.* filigree.

fil′ament, *n.*, a fine thread.

filamen′tous, *adj.*, like a thread; bearing filaments.

fil′ander, *n.*, a New Guinea kangaroo.

filar′ia, *n.*, a parasitic worm brought into the blood by certain flies and mosquitoes.

filar′ial, *adj.*, pert. or rel. to filaria.

filari′asis, *n.*, the disease caused by a filaria.

fil′atory, *n.*, a machine for spinning threads.

fil′ature, *n.*, *i.q.* filatory; the reeling off of silk from cocoons.

fil′bert, *n.*, the fruit of a cultivated hazel tree.

filch, *v.t.*, to pilfer.

filched, *p.p.*, filch.

filch′er, *n.*, one who filches.

filch′ing, *adj.*, thievish; *n.*, thieving; *pr.p.*, filch.

file, *n.*, a collection of papers arranged for reference; a row of soldiers one behind another; a steel instrument for cutting or smoothing; *v.t.*, to place in a file; to cut with a file; *v.i.*, to march one by one.

filed, *p.p.*, file.

fil′emot, *adj.*, having the colour of a dead leaf.

fi′ler, *n.*, one who files.

filet, *n.*, a kind of net with a square mesh (*Fr.*).

fil′ial, *adj.*, becoming a child in relation to his parents; pert. or rel. to a son or daughter.

filia′tion, *n.*, adoption; the fixing of paternity.

fil′ibeg, *n.*, a Scottish kilt.

fil′ibuster, *n.*, a buccaneer; an adventurer; a continuous oration designed as a delaying tactic; *v.i.*, to act as a filibuster.

fil′ibustering, *n.*, buccaneering; *pr.p.*, filibuster.

fil′ibusterism, *n.*, the practice of filibustering.

fil′icoid, *adj.*, having the form of a fern.

fil′igree, *n.*, ornamental wire-work. (Also *filagree*.)

fil′igreed, *adj.*, ornamented with filigree.

fi′ling, *n.*, a particle rubbed off by a file; *pr.p.*, file.

Filipi′no, *n.*, a native of the Philippines.

fi′lite, *n.*, an Italian smokeless combustible powder.

fill, *n.*, as much as fills; *v.t.*, to occupy the whole space of; *v.i.*, to become full.

fille, *n.*, a chambermaid (*Fr.*).

filled, *p.p.*, fill.

fill′er, *n.*, that which, or one who, fills.

fil′let, *n.*, a narrow strip or band; meat rolled and tied round; *v.t.*, to bind with a fillet; to remove the bones from.

fil′leted, *p.p.*, fillet.

fil′leting, *n.*, material of which fillets are made; *pr.p.*, fillet.

fill′ing, *adj.*, able to fill or satisfy; *n.*, materials for stopping up a hole; *pr.p.*, fill.

fill′ing-sta′tion, *n.*, a petrol station.

fil′lip, *n.*, a smart blow; a stimulus; *v.t.*, to strike smartly.

fil′liped, *p.p.*, fillip.

fil′liping, *pr.p.*, fillip.

fil′lister, *n.*, a rabbeting-plane.

fil′ly, *n.*, a young mare; a young, lively girl (*colloq.*).

film, *n.*, a thin skin; a thin layer for receiving a photographic negative; a cinematographic ribbon; a motion picture; *v.t.*, to photograph for the cinematograph; *v.i.*, to cover with a film.

film′ily, *adv.*, in a filmy way; mistily.

film′iness, *n.*, the state of being filmy.

film′star, *n.*, an eminent actor or actress of the cinema.

film′y, *adj.*, like a film.

fil′oplume, *n.*, a hair-like feather.

fi′lose, *adj.*, ending in a thread-like process.

fil′oselle, *n.*, floss silk.

fils, *n.*, the son, the junior (attached to a name to distinguish between the father and son of the same names) (*Fr.*).

fil′ter, *n.*, a strainer; *v.t.*, to purify by passing through a filter; *v.i.*, to percolate.

fil′tered, *p.p.*, filter.

fil′tering, *pr.p.*, filter.

filth, *n.*, dirt; foul matter.

filth′ily, *adv.*, in a filthy manner.

filth′iness, *n.*, the state of being filthy; impurity.

filth′y, *adj.*, foul; morally impure.

fil′trate, *n.*, liquid passed through a filter; *v.t.*, to filter.

fil′trated, *p.p.*, filtrate.

fil′trating, *pr.p.*, filtrate.

filtra′tion, *n.*, the process of filtering.

fim′briate, *adj.*, fringed; *v.t.*, to hem; to fringe.

fim′briated, *p.p.*, fimbriate.

fim′briating, *pr.p.*, fimbriate.

fin, *n.*, a projecting wing-like organ or limb of a fish.

fi′nable, *adj.*, capable of being refined; admitting of a fine.

fi′nal, *adj.*, last, conclusive.

fina′le, *n.*, the last part of a musical composition; the last scene (*mus.*, *It.*).

fi′nalist, *n.*, one who reaches the final; a teleologist.

final′ity, *n.*, the state of being final; a philosophical doctrine that everything exists for a determinate end.

fi′nalize, *v.t.*, to complete.

fi′nalized, *p.p.*, finalize.

fi′nalizing, *pr.p.*, finalize.

fi′nally, *adv.*, lastly.

finance′, *n.*, the science of revenue and expenditure, both public and private; *v.i.*, to conduct financial operations; *v.t.*, to support with pecuniary assistance.

financed', *p.p.*, finance.

finan'cial, *adj.*, pert. or rel. to money matters.

finan'cially, *adj.*, pert. or rel. to finance.

finan'cier, *n.*, one skilled in finance.

finan'cing, *pr.p.*, finance.

finch, *n.*, a small singing bird.

find, *n.*, discovery of anything valuable; something found; *v.t.*, to discover.

find'er, *n.*, one who, or that which, finds; a small telescope attached to a larger one to locate the object to be observed.

fin de siècle, *adj.*, marking the end of the 19th century, modern; decadent (*Fr.*).

find'ing, *n.*, discovery; a verdict; *pr.p.*, find.

fine, *adj.*, slender; very small; elegant; pure, free from clouds; *n.*, a payment in money imposed as a punishment; *v.t.*, to refine, to punish by fine.

fine champagne, *n.*, liqueur brandy (*Fr.*).

fined, *p.p.*, fine.

fine'draw, *v.t.*, to sew up so as to conceal a rent.

fine'drawer, *n.*, one who finedraws.

fine'drawing, *pr.p.*, finedraw.

fine'drawn, *adj.*, drawn out too finely or subtly; *p.p.*, finedraw.

fine'ly, *adv.*, delicately; admirably.

fine'ness, *n.*, the state of being fine.

fi'ner, *adj.*, *comp.* of fine; *n.*, one who refines or fines.

fi'nery, *n.*, ornament, showy decoration; a forge in an ironworks.

fine'spun, *adj.*, drawn to a fine thread; over-elaborated.

finesse', *n.*, artifice; subtlety of contrivance; *v.i.*, to use finesse; to play a card in the hope of capturing one of higher rank (*Fr.*).

finessed', *p.p.*, finesse.

finess'ing, *pr.p.*, finesse.

fi'nest, *adj.*, *super.* of fine.

fine'-still, *v.t.*, to distil spirit from molasses.

fin'ger, *n.*, one of the five extreme members of the hand; an index; *v.t.*, to touch with the fingers.

fin'gered, *adj.*, having fingers; *p.p.*, finger.

fin'gering, *n.*, the management of the fingers in playing on a musical instrument; the marking of the notes of a piece of music to guide the fingers in playing it; a kind of knitting worsted; *pr.p.*, finger.

fin'gerling, *n.*, a young salmon.

fin'ger-mark, *n.*, a mark left on some substances after being touched by a finger.

fin'ger-nail, *n.*, the horny growth at the tip of the finger.

fin'gerprint, *n.*, a mark left by the finger used for identification or the detection of criminals.

fin'ger-ring, *n.*, a ring worn on a finger.

fin'gerstall, *n.*, a leather protection for a wounded or sore finger.

fin'gerstone, *n.*, a fossil stone which tapers to a point.

fin'ial, *n.*, the ornamental termination of a pinnacle or gable.

fin'ical, *adj.*, particular about trifles.

finical'ity, *n.*, the state of being finical.

fin'ically, *adv.*, in a finical way.

fin'icalness, *n.*, *i.q.* finicality.

fin'icking, *adj.*, *i.q.* finical.

fin'icky, *adj.*, *i.q.* finical.

fin'ikin, *adj.*, *i.q.* finical.

fi'ning, *n.*, the process of refining or clarifying; the preparation used in clarifying; *pr.p.*, fine.

fi'nis, *n.*, conclusion (*Lat.*).

fin'ish, *n.*, careful elaboration; *v.t.*, to bring to an end; *v.i.*, to come to an end.

fin'ished, *adj.*, perfectly polished; complete; *p.p.*, finish.

fin'isher, *n.*, one who finishes; that which gives the finishing touch.

fin'ishing, *pr.p.*, finish.

fi'nite, *adj.*, limited; quantifiable.

fi'nitely, *adv.*, in a finite manner.

fi'niteness, *n.*, the state of being finite.

fin'itude, *n.*, limitation; *i.q.* finiteness.

fin'less, *adj.*, destitute of fins.

Finn, *n.*, a native of Finland.

finn'an, *n.*, smoked haddock.

finned, *adj.*, possessing fins.

fin'ner, *n.*, a kind of whale having a dorsal fin.

Finn'ic, *adj.*, pert. or rel. to the Finns.

Finn'ish, *adj.*, *i.q.* Finnic; *n.*, the language of Finland.

Finn'o-Ug'ric, *adj.*, rel. to the family of Ural-Altaic languages.

fin'ny, *adj.*, furnished with fins.

fin'-toed, *adj.*, having toes connected by a membrane.

fiord, *n.*, a long, narrow arm of the sea, common on the coast of Norway. (Also *fjord*.)

fi'orin, *n.*, a kind of grass.

fir, *n.*, a coniferous tree; a pine.

fire, *n.*, heat and light produced by burning; a conflagration; vehemence; *v.t.*, to set on fire; to discharge a firearm.

fire'-alarm, *n.*, an apparatus for raising the alarm of fire.

fire'arm, *n.*, a weapon discharged by the combustion of powder.

fire'back, *n.*, the rear wall of a fireplace; a kind of pheasant.

fire'-bas'ket, *n.*, a portable fire-grate.

fire'brand, *n.*, a piece of kindled wood; one who causes strife.

fire'brick, *n.*, a clay brick capable of withstanding intense heat.

fire'-brigade, *n.*, an organized body for extinguishing fires.

fire'clay, *n.*, a kind of clay capable of withstanding intense heat.

fire'-control, *n.*, the method of controlling from one place the firing of a group of guns.

fire′cracker, *n.*, a small paper cylinder containing explosive.

fire′crest, *n.*, the golden-crested wren.

fired, *p.p.*, fire.

fire′-damp, *n.*, a highly explosive gas found in mines.

fire′dog, *n.*, the bar which supports a log on a wood fire.

fire′-drill, *n.*, the exercises practised periodically by firemen, ships' crews, schools and commercial organizations to combat fire and save life.

fire′eater, *n.*, a juggler who pretends to eat fire; a person ready for an argument or dissension.

fire′-engine, *n.*, an engine for extinguishing fires.

fire′-escape, *n.*, the apparatus used for saving people from burning buildings.

fire′-extinguisher, *n.*, a portable apparatus containing special liquid for putting out a fire in its early stages.

fire′fly, *n.*, a luminous winged insect.

fire′guard, *n.*, a metal protection placed in front of a fireplace.

fire′hose, *n.*, a hose-pipe used to convey water for extinguishing fires.

fire′-insurance, *n.*, insurance against loss caused by fire.

fire′light, *n.*, the light coming from a fire.

fire′lighter, *n.*, chemically prepared kindling-fuel.

fire′lock, *n.*, a musket with a flint-and-steel lock.

fire′man, *n.*, one whose work is to extinguish fires; a man who tends the fire of a steam-engine.

fire′place, *n.*, a hearth.

fire′plug, *n.*, a plug of a water-main.

fire′-policy, *n.*, a certificate issued by an insurance company guaranteeing compensation in case of fire.

fire′proof, *adj.*, rendered incombustible.

fir′er, *n.*, one who, or that which, fires.

fire′ship, *n.*, a vessel filled with combustibles to be set on fire so as to burn an enemy's ships.

fire′-shovel, *n.*, a shovel for putting fuel on a fire.

fire′side, *n.*, the hearth; the home.

fire′stone, *n.*, any stone that resists the action of fire.

fire′wood, *n.*, wood for fuel.

fire′work, *n.*, a preparation of gun-powder used for making a show.

fir′ing, *n.*, the act of discharging; fuel; *pr.p.*, fire.

fir′kin, *n.*, a small wooden cask containing 9 gals. of liquid or 56 lb. of butter.

firm, *adj.*, compact; solid; steady; not easily moved; *n.*, a commercial house.

fir′mament, *n.*, the heavens.

firmamen′tal, *adj.*, pert. or rel. to the firmament.

fir′man, *n.*, a decree or licence of an Eastern monarch.

firm′er, *adj.*, *comp.*, of firm.

firm′est, *adj.*, *super.* of firm.

firm′ly, *adv.*, in a firm manner.

firm′ness, *n.*, solidity; resolution.

firr′y, *adj.*, like a fir.

first, *adj.* and *adv.*, preceding all others; foremost.

first′-aid, *n.*, medicaments and materials for giving immediate help to an injured person; the special skill needed for this.

first′-born, *adj.* and *n.*, eldest; first brought forth.

first′-class, *adj.*, of the highest excellence.

first′floor, *n.*, the floor above the ground floor.

first′-foot, *n.*, a Scottish New Year superstition that prosperity will be affected by the first person to cross the threshold.

first′-fruits, *n.* *pl.*, the first produce; profits or effects.

first′-hand, *adj.*, direct from the source.

first′ling, *n.*, the first-born of an animal.

first′ly, *adv.*, in the first place.

first′-rate, *adj.*, *i.q.* first-class.

firth, *n.*, a Scottish river-estuary, or arm or channel of the sea.

fir′-tree, *n.*, a coniferous tree; a pine-tree.

fisc, *n.*, a state treasury. (Also *fisk*.)

fis′cal, *adj.*, pert. or rel. to the public revenue.

fis′calism, *n.*, the fiscal policy.

fis′cally, *adv.*, in a fiscal way.

fish, *n.*, an animal that lives in water, having gills and cold blood; a strengthening beam or joint (*naut.*); a counter used in games; *v.i.*, to catch fish.

fished, *p.p.*, fish.

fish′er, *n.*, one who fishes.

fish′erman, *n.*, one whose occupation is to catch fish.

fish′ery, *n.*, a place where fish are regularly bred and/or caught.

fish′gig, *n.*, a kind of harpoon. (Also *fiz-gig*.)

fish′-hook, *n.*, a hook for catching fish.

fish′ily, *adv.*, in a fishy way.

fish′iness, *n.*, the state of being fishy.

fish′ing, *adj.*, used in fishing; *n.*, the art of catching fish; *pr.p.*, fish.

fish′ing-boat, *n.*, a boat used for catching fish.

fish′ing-line, *n.*, a line for catching fish.

fish′ing-net, *n.*, a net of twine or cord used for catching fish.

fish′ing-rod, *n.*, a rod with an attached line used for angling.

fish′-market, *n.*, a market where fish is sold.

fish′monger, *n.*, a seller of fish.

fish′-plate, *n.*, an iron plate joining railway rails.

fish′-pond, *n.*, a pond stocked with fresh-water fish.

fish′-shop, *n.*, a shop where fish is sold.

fish′-slice, *n.*, a fish-carver, a knife for serving fish.

fish'-tackle, n., rods, lines, hooks, nets, etc., for fishing.

fish'wife, n., a woman who retails fish.

fish'y, adj., having the qualities of fish; worn out, as by dissipation; suspiciously unsafe or treacherous.

fisk, n., i.q. fisc.

fis'sile, adj., readily splitting into flakes.

fissil'ity, n., the quality of being fissile.

fis'sion, n., the act of splitting.

fis'sionable, adj., able to be split.

fissip'arous, adj., reproducing by fission or spontaneous division.

fis'siped, adj., having the toes separated.

fis'sure, n., a cleft, crack or narrow chasm; v.i. and i., to crack or fracture.

fis'sured, p.p., fissure.

fis'suring, pr.p., fissure.

fist, n., the clenched hand.

fist'ed, adj., having fists.

fist'ic, adj., pugilistic.

fist'ical, adj., i.q. fistic.

fist'icuffs, n. pl., a combat with fists.

fis'tula, n., a morbid channel from an internal part of the surface of the skin; a musical pipe.

fis'tular, adj., hollow; like a pipe or reed.

fis'tulary, adj., i.q. fistular.

fis'tulous, adj., formed like a fistula.

fit, adj., suitable; n., a sudden violent attack of disease; a paroxysm; a sudden activity followed by relaxation; conformity to requirement; v.t., to adapt; to suit; v.i., to be adjusted to shape.

fitch, n., a vetch; a kind of bearded wheat; a polecat.

fitch'et, n., a polecat.

fitch'ew, n., a polecat.

fit'ful, adj., spasmodic.

fit'fully, adv., in a fitful way.

fit'fulness, n., the state of being fitful.

fit'ly, adv., suitably.

fit'ment, n., a piece of furniture; a fixture or fitting.

fit'ness, n., suitableness.

fit'ted, p.p., fit.

fit'ter, adj., comp. of fit; n., one who fits; one who puts the parts of machinery together.

fit'test, adj., super. of fit.

fit'ting, adj., appropriate; n., something fitted to another thing as an accessory; pr.p., fit.

fit'tingly, adv., suitably.

fit'ting-out, n., equipment (esp. of a ship).

fit'tings, n., pl. of fitting.

fit'ting-up, n., the act of furnishing with suitable requirements.

fit'-up, n., a temporary stage and fittings.

fitz, adj., a prefix meaning "son of" used to form a patronymic surname.

five, adj., four and one added.

five'fold, adj., five times repeated.

five'pence, n., the amount or value of five pence.

five'penny, adj., worth or costing five pence.

fiv'er, n., a five-pound note (colloq.).

fives', n., a kind of wall-tennis.

five'score, adj., one hundred.

fives'-court, n., a court in which the game of fives is played.

fix, n., a dilemma; a dose of a drug (colloq.); v.t., to make firm; to fasten.

fix'able, adj., capable of being fixed.

fixa'tion, n., the act of fixing; arrested mental development.

fix'ative, n., gum or glue.

fix'ature, n., a gummy preparation for fixing the hair.

fixed, adj., established; fast; not volatile; p.p., fix.

fix'edly, adv., in a fixed manner.

fix'edness, n., the state of being fixed.

fix'ing, pr.p., fix.

fix'ings, n. pl., accessories; equipment.

fix'ity, n., fixed character; stability.

fix'ture, n., anything fixed in position; part of the furniture of a house fixed to it with nails, screws, etc.

fiz'gig, n., i.q. fishgig.

fizz, n., a sparkling, effervescent wine (slang); v.i., to make a hissing sound.

fizzed, p.p., fizz.

fizz'ing, pr.p., fizz.

fiz'zle, v.i., i.q. fizz.

fiz'zled, p.p., fizzle.

fiz'zling, pr.p., fizzle.

fjeld, n., a high, barren Norwegian plateau.

fjord, n., i.q. fiord.

flab'bergast, v.t., to astound.

flab'bergasted, p.p., flabbergast.

flab'bergasting, pr.p., flabbergast.

flab'biness, n., the state of being flabby.

flab'by, adj., soft and yielding to the touch; hanging loose by its own weight.

flabel'late, adj., fan-shaped (bot. and zool.).

flabella'tion, n., fanning to keep fractured limbs and wounds cool.

flabell'iform, adj., i.q. flabellate.

flac'cid, adj., lax; drooping.

flaccid'ity, n., i.q. flaccidness.

flac'cidly, adv., in a flaccid manner.

flac'cidness, n., the state of being flaccid.

flag, n., a banner; a flat paving-stone; a kind of iris, having sword-shaped leaves; v.i., to droop; to grow languid.

flag'-captain, n., the captain of a flag-ship.

flagell'ant, n., a fanatic who scourges himself.

flag'ellate, adj., whip-like; v.t., to scourge.

flag′ellated, *p.p.*, flagellate.

flag′ellating, *pr.p.*, flagellate.

flagella′tion, *n.*, a flogging; the discipline of the scourge.

flag′ellator, *n.*, one who flagellates.

flag′ellatory, *adj.*, pert. or rel. to flagellate.

flagell′iform, *adj.*, *i.q.* flagellate.

flagell′um, *n.*, a runner (*bot.*); a whiplike appendage (*biol.*).

flageolet′, *n.*, a small wind instrument resembling a flute; a sort of kidney-bean.

flagged, *p.p.*, flag.

flag′ging, *pr.p.*, flag.

flagi′tious, *adj.*, grossly wicked.

flagi′tiously, *adv.*, in a villainous way.

flagi′tiousness, *n.*, gross wickedness.

flag′-lieutenant, *n.*, a lieutenant in attendance on an admiral in the navy.

flag′man, *n.*, one who signals with a flag.

flag′-officer, *n.*, an admiral.

flag′on, *n.*, a narrow-mouthed vessel for holding liquors.

fla′grance, *n.*, *i.q.* flagrancy.

fla′grancy, *n.*, heinousness; enormity.

fla′grant, *adj.*, glaring; notorious; openly wicked.

fla′grantly, *adv.*, in a flagrant manner.

flag′-ship, *n.*, the ship of a flag-officer.

flag′staff, *n.*, the pole on which a flag is displayed.

flag′stone, *n.*, fissile sandstone; a large, flat paving-stone.

flail, *n.*, an instrument for threshing grain from the ear.

flair, *n.*, an intuitive perception; a power of scent.

flak, *n.*, anti-aircraft fire.

flake, *n.*, a scale; a small fleecy particle; a rack for storing; a stage for drying; *v.i.*, to peel off in particles.

flaked, *p.p.*, flake.

flake′-white, *n.*, a fine white pigment.

fla′kiness, *n.*, the state of being flaky.

fla′king, *pr.p.*, flake.

fla′ky, *adj.*, lying in flakes or thin layers.

flam, *n.*, a falsehood.

flam′beau, *n.*, a torch (*Fr.*).

flamboy′ant, *adj.*, a term applied to Gothic architecture, the chief feature of which is a wavy, flame-like tracery in the mouldings; extravagant; boldly ostentatious.

flame, *n.*, a blaze; one beloved; *v.i.*, to blaze; to break out into violent passion.

flamed, *p.p.*, flame.

fla′men, *n.*, an ancient Roman priest (*Lat.*).

flame′thrower, *n.*, a device for discharging liquid fire.

fla′ming, *pr.p.*, flame.

flamin′go, *n.*, a long-legged, web-footed, tropical bird with some pink plumage.

Flamin′ian, *adj.*, pert. or rel. to C. Flaminius, a Roman censor.

flammabil′ity, *n.*, inflammability.

flam′mable, *adj.*, inflammable.

flam′menwerfer, *n.*, a flamethrower (*Ger.*).

flam′meous, *adj.*, pert. or rel. to flame.

flammi′ferous, *adj.*, producing flame.

fla′my, *adj.*, consisting of flame.

flan, *n.*, an open tart (*Fr.*).

flanch, *n.*, *i.q.* flange.

fla′neur, *n.*, an idler, a loafer (*Fr.*).

flange, *n.*, a projecting rim; *v.t.*, to make a flange on.

flank, *n.*, the side; *v.t.*, to be at the side of.

flanked, *p.p.*, flank.

flank′er, *n.*, one who, or that which, flanks; a trick, a deception (*colloq.*).

flank′ing, *pr.p.*, flank.

flan′nel, *n.*, a soft, woollen cloth; deception (*slang*).

flan′nel(l)ed, *adj.*, covered with flannel.

flannelette′, *n.*, a cotton cloth like flannel.

flap, *n.*, a loose, flat appendage hanging by the end or side and easily moved; the motion of anything broad and loose; a stroke; *v.t.*, to move or beat as with a flap; *v.i.*, to flutter; to become panicky (*colloq.*).

flapdoo′dle, *n.*, nonsense.

flap′dragon, *n.*, *i.q.* snapdragon.

flap′jack, *n.*, a pancake or apple puff; a small flat case for a lady's powder and puff.

flapped, *p.p.*, flap.

flap′per, *n.*, a young wild duck; one who, or that which, flaps; a young woman (*slang*).

flap′ping, *pr.p.*, flap.

flare, *n.*, a bright, unsteady light; a luminous device for attracting attention; *v.i.*, to burn brightly but waveringly.

flared, *p.p.*, flare.

flar′ing, *pr.p.*, flare.

flash, *adj.*, gaudy; counterfeit; *n.*, momentary brightness; an instant; *v.i.*, to give out a flash; to dart; *v.t.*, to convey instantaneously.

flashed, *p.p.*, flash.

flash′er, *n.*, one who, or that which, flashes.

flash′-house, *n.*, a brothel.

flash′ily, *adv.*, in a flashy manner.

flash′ing, *pr.p.*, flash.

flash′light, *n.*, a light used for signalling and photography; an electric torch.

flash′point, *n.*, the temperature at which a vapour ignites.

flash′y, *adj.*, tawdry.

flask, *n.*, a narrow-necked, globular glass bottle; a pocket spirit-bottle; a sportsman's gunpowder holder.

flas′ket, *n.*, a long, shallow basket.

flat, *adj.*, having a level surface; stale; dull; *n.*, a plain; a musical sign (♭); a floor; a simpleton; a barge;

housing accommodation that is part of a larger unit; *v.t.*, to flatten.

flat'-boat, *n.*, a canal boat or barge.

flat'-bott'omed, *adj.*, having a flat bottom.

flat'fish, *n.*, a fish with a flattened body.

flat'head, *adj.*, having a flat head produced artificially; *n.*, a Chinook Indian.

flat'iron, *n.*, a smoothing iron used in laundries.

flat'ly, *adv.*, positively.

flat'ness, *n.*, the quality of being flat.

flat'ted, *p.p.*, flat.

flat'ten, *v.t.*, to make flat.

flat'tened, *p.p.*, flatten.

flat'tening, *pr.p.*, flatten.

flat'ter, *adj.*, *comp.* of flat; *v.t.*, to gratify; to inspire with false hopes; to praise unduly or hypocritically.

flat'tered, *p.p.*, flatter.

flat'terer, *n.*, one who flatters.

flat'tering, *n.*, *i.q.* flattery; *pr.p.*, flatter.

flat'teringly, *adv.*, in a flattering way.

flat'tery, *n.*, insincere praise; adulation.

flat'test, *adj.*, *super.* of flat.

flat'ting, *n.*, a kind of house-painting.

flat'tish, *adj.*, somewhat flat.

flat'ulence, *n.*, the state of being flatulent.

flat'ulency, *n.*, *i.q.* flatulence.

flat'ulent, *adj.*, windy; affected with wind in the stomach.

flat'ulently, *adv.*, in a flatulent way.

fla'tus, *n.*, wind in the stomach or bowels.

flaunt, *v.t.*, to act ostentatiously; to show off defiantly; *v.t.*, to display.

flaunt'ed, *p.p.*, flaunt.

flaunt'er, *n.*, one who flaunts.

flaunt'ing, *adj.*, ostentatious; *pr.p.*, flaunt.

flaunt'ingly, *adv.*, in a flaunting way.

flaunt'y, *adj.*, *i.q.* flaunting.

flaut'ist, *n.*, a player on the flute.

flaves'cent, *adj.*, yellowish.

flav'in, *n.*, a yellow dye; an antiseptic.

flav'o-prot'ein, *n.*, one of a group of proteins constituting the yellow oxidizable enzymes.

fla'vorous, *adj.*, having a rich flavour.

fla'vour, *n.*, taste; relish; *v.t.*, to season.

fla'voured, *adj.*, affecting the taste or smell; having some taste added to it; *p.p.*, flavour.

fla'vouring, *n.*, something that gives flavour to another thing; *pr.p.*, flavour.

fla'vourless, *adj.*, tasteless.

flaw, *n.*, a crack; a defect; a sudden, short gust of wind; *v.t.*, to produce a flaw in.

flaw'less, *adj.*, without defect.

flaw'lessly, *adv.*, in a flawless way.

flaw'lessness, *n.*, the state of being flawless.

flawn, *n.*, a kind of custard (*arch.*).

flaw'y, *adj.*, faulty; full of flaws; subject to sudden gusts.

flax, *n.*, a plant of which the fibres are made into linen threads; the fibre prepared for spinning.

flax'en, *adj.*, made of flax; of the colour of flax; fair.

flax'seed, *n.*, the seed of flax; linseed.

flax'y, *adj.*, like flax.

flay, *v.t.*, to skin.

flayed, *p.p.*, flay.

flay'er, *n.*, one who flays.

flay'ing, *pr.p.*, flay.

flea, *n.*, an agile insect with an irritating bite.

flea'bane, *n.*, a plant with a supposed power of driving away fleas.

flea'bite, *n.*, the bite of a flea; a trifling inconvenience; a trifle.

flea'bitten, *adj.*, bitten by fleas.

fleam, *n.*, a farrier's lancet.

flea'some, *adj.*, full of fleas.

flea'wort, *n.*, a medicinal herb with seeds shaped like fleas.

flèche, *n.*, a slender spire (*Fr.*).

fleck, *n.*, a spot; *v.t.*, to dapple.

flecked, *p.p.*, fleck.

fleck'er, *v.t.*, *i.q.* fleck.

fleck'ing, *pr.p.*, fleck.

fleck'less, *adj.*, spotless.

flec'tion, *n.*, the act of bending.

flec'tor, *n.*, a muscle that produces bending.

fled, *p.p.*, flee.

fledge, *v.t.*, to furnish with feathers; to initiate.

fledged, *p.p.*, fledge.

fledg'ing, *pr.p.*, fledge.

fledg(e)'ling, *n.*, a young bird just fledged.

flee, *v.i.*, to run away from; to seek shelter.

fleece, *n.*, the woollen coat of a sheep, *v.t.*, to rob pitilessly.

fleeced, *p.p.*, fleece.

flee'cer, *n.*, one who fleeces or robs of money.

flee'ciness, *n.*, woolliness.

flee'cing, *pr.p.*, fleece.

flee'cy, *adj.*, woolly.

flee'ing, *pr.p.*, flee.

fle'er, *n.*, one who flees.

fleer, *n.*, the act of mocking; *v.i.*, to sneer.

fleered, *p.p.*, fleer.

fleer'er, *n.*, a sneerer.

fleer'ing, *pr.p.*, fleer.

fleet, *adj.*, swift; *n.*, a number of ships in company; a creek, an inlet; *v.i.*, to flit; to move swiftly.

fleet'er, *adj.*, *comp.* of fleet.

fleet'est, *adj.*, *super.* of fleet.

fleet'ing, *adj.*, transient; *pr.p.*, fleet.

fleet'ingly, *adv.*, in a fleeting way.

fleet'ly, *adv.*, swiftly.

fleet'ness, *n.*, rapidity.

Flem'ing, *n.*, a native of Flanders.

Flem'ish, *adj.*, pert. or rel. to Flanders; *n.*, the language of the Flemings; *pl.*, the people of Flanders.

flense, *v.t.*, to cut up and remove blubber from a whale.

flensed, *p.p.*, flense.

flens'ing, *pr.p.*, flense.

flesh, *n.*, the softer, solid part of the body of an animal; meat; mankind; carnal desire; the pulp of fruit; *v.t.*, to give the first taste of blood to; to use for the first time.

flesh'-colour, *n.*, the colour of flesh.

fleshed, *adj.*, having flesh of a particular kind; *p.p.*, flesh.

flesh'er, *n.*, a butcher (*Scot.*).

flesh'iness, *n.*, corpulence.

flesh'ing, *pr.p.*, flesh.

flesh'ings, *n. pl.*, tight garments worn on stage, coloured to resemble the skin.

flesh'liness, *n.*, carnal appetites.

flesh'ly, *adj.*, carnal; not spiritual.

flesh'monger, *n.*, a slave-dealer.

flesh'y, *adj.*, corpulent.

fletch, *v.t.*, to feather an arrow.

fleur-de-lis', *n.*, an heraldic lily; the iris (*Fr.*). (Also *flower-de-luce.*)

fleur'et, *n.*, an ornament in the shape of a small flower (*Fr.*).

fleuron, *n.*, a flower-shaped ornament in architecture or printing (*Fr.*).

fleur'y, *adj.*, decorated with the fleurs-de-lis.

flew, *p.p.*, fly.

flews, *n. pl.*, the hanging lips of a blood-hound, etc.

flex, *n.*, flexible insulated wire; *v.t.* and *i.*, to bend.

flexed, *p.p.*, flex.

flexibil'ity, *n.*, pliancy, readiness to comply.

flex'ible, *adj.*, pliant; yielding to pressure.

flex'ibly, *adv.*, in a flexible manner.

flex'ile, *adj.*, *i.q.* flexible; pliable.

flexil'ity, *n.*, the state of being flexile.

flex'ing, *pr.p.*, flex.

flex'ion, *n.*, the act of bending; a bent part; an inflection.

flex'or, *n.*, a muscle that produces flexion.

flexuos'ity, *n.*, the state of being flexuous.

flex'uous, *adj.*, having turns or windings.

flex'ure, *n.*, a bend; a bent part.

flib'bertigib'bet, *n.*, a restless, flighty person; a busy imp.

flick, *n.*, a light, sudden stroke, as with a whip; *v.t.*, to flip.

flick'er, *n.*, a wavering gleam; *v.i.*, to waver; to flutter; to show a small uncertain light.

flick'ered, *p.p.*, flicker.

flick'ering, *pr.p.*, flicker.

flick'eringly, *adv.*, in a flickering way.

flick'-knife, *n.*, a spring-bladed knife.

flicks, *n.*, the cinema (*slang*).

fli'er, *n.*, one who flies. (Also *flyer.*)

flies, 3rd per. sing., *pres.*, fly; pl. of fly.

flight, *n.*, the act of fleeing or flying; a volley; a journey by air.

flight'-comman'der, *n.*, an R.A.F. officer senior to flight-lieutenant.

flight'-deck, *n.*, the top deck of an aircraft-carrier; the control deck of an aircraft.

flight'iness, *n.*, volatility; an irresponsible lack of seriousness.

flight'-lieuten'ant, *n.*, an R.A.F. officer.

flight'y, *adj.*, volatile; giddy; fickle.

flim'-flam, *n.*, a trifle; nonsense.

flim'sily, *adv.*, in a flimsy manner.

flim'siness, *n.*, the quality of being flimsy.

flim'sy, *adj.*, unsubstantial; *n.*, a thin sort of paper.

flinch, *v.i.*, to shrink, to wince.

flinched, *p.p.*, flinch.

flinch'ing, *pr.p.*, flinch.

flin'ders, *n. pl.*, splinters, fragments.

fling, *n.*, a Scottish dance; full enjoyment of pleasure; *v.t.*, to throw.

fling'er, *n.*, one who flings.

fling'ing, *pr.p.*, fling.

flint, *n.*, a very hard stone, a kind of quartz.

flint'iness, *n.*, the quality of being flinty or very hard.

flint'y, *adj.*, containing flints; like flint; very hard; cruel.

flip, *n.*, a flick; a short, quick, turning movement; a drink made of beer and spirits heated; a quick trip in an aircraft (*colloq.*); *v.t.*, to flick.

flip'pancy, *n.*, the quality of being flippant.

flip'pant, *adj.*, pert; displaying levity.

flip'pantly, *adv.*, in a flippant manner.

flip'pantness, *n.*, *i.q.* flippancy.

flip'per, *n.*, the paddle of a turtle; the arm of a seal; a paddle-shaped shoe to increase swimming speed.

flip'perty-flop'perty, *adj.*, hanging or dangling loosely.

flirt, *n.*, one who flirts or plays at love; *v.t.*, to throw with a jerk; to play at courtship.

flirta'tion, *n.*, playing at courtship.

flirta'tious, *adj.*, disposed to flirting.

flirt'ed, *p.p.*, flirt.

flirt'ing, *pr.p.*, flirt.

flit, *v.i.*, to fly away quickly; to flutter; to migrate.

flitch, *n.*, a side of bacon.

flit'ted, *p.p.*, flit.

flit'ter, *n.*, a rag; a tatter; *v.t.* and *i.*, to flutter.

flit'ting, *pr.p.*, flit.

fliv'ver, *n.*, a cheap motor-car (*slang*).

flix, *n.*, fur; beaver down.

float, *n.*, that which floats on the surface of a fluid; a buoy; the cork or plastic bubble on an angler's line; a raft; *v.i.*, to be supported by a fluid; *v.t.*, to cause to float; to launch a company or scheme.

float'able, *adj.*, able to float.

float'age, *n.*, anything floating on water.

floata'tion, *n.*, *i.q.* flotation.

float'ed, *p.p.*, float.

float'er, *n.*, one who, or that which, floats.

float'ing, *adj.*, resting on a fluid; not invested; unsettled; *pr.p.*, float.

float'-plane, n., an aircraft designed to float.

floccilla'tion, n., the picking of bedclothes by a sick person in delirium.

floc'cose, adj., tufted (bot.).

floc'cule, n., a small piece of matter resembling a flock of wool.

floc'culence, n., the state of being flocculent.

floc'culent, adj., adhering in flakes or flocks.

floc'culose, adj., i.q. flocculent.

floc'culous, adj., i.q. flocculent.

floc'culus, n., a small lobe under the surface of the cerebellum (Lat., anat.).

floc'cus, n., a tuft of hair or feathers (Lat.).

flock, n., a lock of wool or hair; woollen refuse used for stuffing mattresses; a company of living creatures; v.i., to crowd together.

flock'-bed, n., a bed stuffed with flocks of wool or shredded cloth.

flocked, p.p., flock.

flock'ing, pr.p., flock.

flock'y, adj., abounding with flocks.

floe, n., a large mass of floating ice.

flog, v.t., to beat or whip.

flogged, p.p., flog.

flog'ger, n., one who flogs.

flog'ging, n., a beating; pr.p., flog.

flong, n., papier-mâché for stereotyping.

flood, n., a great flow or overflow of water; the flowing in of the tide; abundance; v.t., to overflow.

flood'ed, p.p., flood.

flood'gate, n., a gate to be opened to let water flow, or shut to prevent it.

flood'ing, n., the act of overflowing; pr.p., flood.

flood'light, n., the copious illumination of a building exterior; a bright light for photography; v.t., to illuminate with floodlight.

flood'lit, adj., illuminated by floodlight.

floo'kan, n., soft, clayey matter surrounding a vein of ore.

flook'ing, n., i.q. flookan.

floor, n., that part of a room on which we walk; a storey in a building; v.t., to furnish with a floor; to knock down; to render incapable of response.

floor'age, n., an area of floor.

floor'board, n., timber used for flooring.

floor'cloth, n., linoleum, etc. for covering floors; a cloth for washing floors.

floored, p.p., floor.

floor'er, n., a knockdown blow; a difficult task (colloq.).

floor'ing, n., materials for floors; pr.p., floor.

flop, n., a sudden sinking to the ground; a total failure; v.i., to fall down suddenly; to relax; to fail utterly.

flopped, p.p., flop.

flop'ping, pr.p., flop.

flop'py, adj., falling loosely.

Flo'ra, n., the goddess of flowers; a collective term for the plants indigenous to a region.

flo'ral, adj., pert. or rel. to flowers.

flo'rally, adv., like or with flowers.

Flor'entine, adj., pert. or rel. to Florence; n., a native of F.; a kind of silk cloth.

flores'cence, n., a bursting into flower.

flores'cent, adj., flowering.

flo'ret, n., a single small flower in an inflorescence. (Also floscule.)

flo'riate, v.t., to decorate with floral designs, etc.

floricul'tural, adj., pert. or rel. to floriculture.

flo'riculture, n., the cultivation of flowers.

floricul'turist, n., one who cultivates flowers.

flor'id, adj., flushed with red; profusely ornamented; copious and dashing in style.

florid'ity, n., i.q. floridness.

flor'idly, adv., in a florid manner.

flor'idness, n., the state of being florid.

florif'erous, adj., producing flowers.

flo'riform, adj., in the form of a flower.

flor'in, n., formerly a two-shilling piece; a gold or silver coin of various countries, periods and values.

flor'ist, n., a dealer in, or cultivator of, flowers.

flor'uit, n., the approximate period during which a person was alive (Lat.).

flory, adj., i.q. fleury.

flos'cular, adj., inflorescent.

flos'cule, n., i.q. floret.

flos'culous, adj., i.q. floscular.

flos'culus, n., a floweret (Lat.).

floss, n., a silky substance; a small stream.

flo'ta, n., an old Spanish treasure-fleet.

flota'tion, n., the state of being afloat; the science dealing with floating bodies; the act of launching a company. (Also floatation.)

flotil'la, n., a little fleet; a fleet of small vessels.

flot'sam, n., portions of a wreck that remain afloat.

flounce, n., a jerking motion of the body indicating displeasure; a horizontal strip attached to a frock; v.i., to move the body in jerks to show displeasure.

flounced, p.p., flounce.

flounc'ing, pr.p., flounce.

floun'cy, adj., with flounces.

floun'der, n., a flatfish; v.i., to roll or tumble about without control; to wallow.

floun'dered, p.p., flounder.

floun'derer, n., one who makes mistakes.

floun'dering, pr.p., flounder.

flour, n., finely ground meal of grain; v.t., to sprinkle with flour.

floured, *p.p.*, flour.

flour'ing, *pr.p.*, flour.

flour'ish, *n.*, an embellishment; a waving of something held in the hand; a fanfare; *v.i.*, to increase; to prosper; to make ornamental strokes; *v.t.*, to brandish.

flour'ished, *p.p.*, flourish.

flour'isher, *n.*, one who flourishes.

flour'ishing, *adj.*, thriving; *pr.p.*, flourish.

flour'ishingly, *adv.*, in a flourishing manner.

flour'y, *adj.*, covered with flour.

flout, *v.t.*, to treat with contempt; to defy deliberately.

flout'ed, *p.p.*, flout.

flout'er, *n.*, one who flouts.

flout'ing, *pr.p.*, flout.

flow, *n.*, a current; the rise of the tide; even movement; *v.i.*, to run smoothly, like water; to rise, as the tide.

flow'chart, *n.*, a sheet showing successive stages or operations in a business or industrial procedure or process. (Also *flow-sheet*.)

flowed, *p.p.*, flow.

flow'er, *n.*, a blossom; youthful vigour; *v.i.*, to blossom; to flourish.

flower-de-luce', *n.*, *i.q.* fleur-de-lis.

flow'ered, *adj.*, ornamented with flowers; *p.p.*, flower.

flow'erer, *n.*, a plant that flowers at a specified time.

flow'eret, *n.*, a small flower.

flow'eriness, *n.*, the state of being flowery; figurative and unduly ornate language.

flow'ering, *adj.*, producing flowers; *pr.p.*, flower.

flow'erless, *adj.*, having no flowers.

flow'ery, *adj.*, florid; full of flowers.

flow'ing, *adj.*, fluent; smooth; *pr.p.*, flow.

flow'ingly, *adv.*, in a flowing manner.

flown, *p.p.*, fly.

flow'sheet, *n.*, *i.q.* flow-chart.

'flu, *n.*, the abbrev. for influenza (*colloq.*).

flu'c(c)an, *n.*, *i.q.* flookan.

fluctif'erous, *adj.*, tending to produce waves.

fluc'tuate, *v.i.*, to move backward and forward; to rise and fall.

fluc'tuated, *p.p.*, fluctuate.

fluc'tuating, *adj.*, wavering; changeable; *pr.p.*, fluctuate.

fluctua'tion, *n.*, a rising and falling; unsteadiness.

flue, *n.*, a smoke-passage in a chimney; fluff; a kind of fishing net; *v.i.* and *t.*, to splay.

flu'ency, *n.*, readiness of expression, oral or written.

flu'ent, *adj.*, flowing; voluble; smooth.

flu'ently, *adv.*, in a fluent manner.

fluff, *n.*, down or nap, generally loose.

fluff'iness, *n.*, the state of being fluffy.

fluff'y, *adj.*, downy; giving off fluff.

flu'id, *adj.*, liquid or gaseous; *n.*, a liquid.

fluid'ify, *v.t.*, to convert into a fluid.

fluid'ity, *n.*, the state of being fluid; the level of the availability of money.

flu'idize, *v.t.*, to convert into a fluid.

flu'idness, *n.*, *i.q.* fluidity.

fluke, *n.*, the part of an anchor which catches in the ground; a flounder; a parasite in sheep's liver; a variety of potato; an accidental success; *v.i.*, to make a fluke.

fluk'ily, *adv.*, in a fluky way.

fluk'iness, *n.*, the state of being fluky.

flu'ky, *adj.*, accidentally lucky; (of wind) uncertain.

flume, *n.*, an artificial channel for water to drive a mill, mine gold or transport logs.

flu'minous, *adj.*, abounding in streams.

flum'mery, *n.*, a sort of jelly made from flour or meal; an empty compliment.

flum'mox, *v.t.*, to embarrass, to perplex.

flump, *v.i.* and *t.*, to fall or move heavily.

flung, *p.p.*, fling.

flunk'ey, *n.*, a male servant in livery; a toady.

flunk'eyism, *n.*, servility.

flu'or, *n.*, a beautiful transparent mineral.

fluores'cence, *n.*, the coloured luminosity produced in a transparent body by the direct action of light; the even dispersion of light.

fluores'cent, *adj.*, possessing fluorescence.

fluor'ic, *adj.*, pert. or rel. to fluor.

flu'oride, *n.*, a compound of fluorine and another element.

flu'orine, *n.*, a halogen element occurring naturally in fluorspar.

flu'orspar, *n.*, Derbyshire Spar; *i.q.* fluor.

flur'ried, *adj.*, agitated; *p.p.*, flurry.

flur'ry, *n.*, agitation; a gust of wind; *v.t.*, to agitate.

flur'rying, *pr.p.*, flurry.

flush, *adj.*, having the surface level with the adjacent surface; well supplied with money; *n.*, any warm colouring; a run of cards of the same suit; *v.i.*, to blush; *v.t.*, to cause to redden suddenly; to elate; to wash out with water; to bring into the open.

flushed, *p.p.*, flush.

flush'er, *n.*, one who, or that which, flushes.

flush'ing, *pr.p.*, flush.

flus'ter, *n.*, agitation of mind; *v.t.*, to confuse. (Also *flutter*.)

flus'tered, *p.p.*, fluster.

flus'tering, *pr.p.*, fluster.

flus'tra, *n.*, a polyzoic species resembling seaweed.

flute, *n.*, a small musical wind instrument; a perpendicular furrow on the shaft of a column; *v.t.*, to make flutes or channels in.

flu'ted, *adj.*, channelled; *p.p.*, flute.

flu'ter, *n.*, one who makes grooves; a flautist.

flu'ting, *n.*, fluted work; *pr.p.*, flute.

flu'tist, n., a flute-player (more correctly *flau-tist*).

flut'ter, n., i.q. fluster; v.i., to move with quick vibrations or undulations; v.t., to throw into confusion.

flut'tered, p.p., flutter.

flut'tering, pr.p., flutter.

flu'ty, adj., soft and clear in tone.

flu'vial, adj., pert. or rel. to rivers.

flu'vialist, n., one who explains geological phenomena by the action of streams.

flu'viatile, adj., growing in a river.

flux, n., the act of flowing; a discharge; a liquid state due to heat; v.t., to fuse.

fluxa'tion, n., a passing away.

fluxibil'ity, n., the state of being fluxible.

flux'ible, adj., capable of being fused.

flux'ion, n., an excessive flowing or discharge; (in mathematics) a differential.

flux'ional, adj., variable.

flux'ionary, adj., i.q. fluxional.

flux'ionist, n., one skilled in fluxions or the differential calculus.

fly, adj., wide-awake (slang); n., a winged insect; a hackney coach; the sides of a theatre stage; a flap on clothing to conceal buttons or a zip-fastener; v.i., to move through the air; to flee.

fly'blow, n., the egg of a fly.

fly'blown, adj., infected with flies eggs.

fly'catcher, n., that which catches flies; a kind of bird.

fly'er, n., one who, or that which, flies; part of a printing machine.

fly'ing, pr.p., fly.

fly'ing-fish, n., a fish that can fly through the air for a time by using its fins as planes.

fly'-leaf, n., a blank leaf at the beginning or end of a book.

fly'over, n., a processional flight of aircraft; an intersecting road carried over another.

fly'past, n., a processional flight of aircraft past a given spot.

fly'shuttle, n., the shuttle impelled by the weaver.

fly'-trap, n., an American sensitive plant, the leaves of which close upon and capture insects.

fly-*under*, n., an intersecting road carried under another.

fly'weight, n., a boxer weighing eight stones or less.

fly'wheel, n., a heavy wheel which regulates the motion of an engine.

foal, n., a young horse or mare; v.i., to bring forth young, said of a mare or ass.

foaled, p.p., foal.

foal'ing, pr.p., foal.

foam, n., froth; v.i., to froth; to be angry.

foamed, p.p., foam.

foam'ing, pr.p., foam.

foam'y, adj., frothy.

fob, n., a small pocket; v.t., to trick.

fobbed, p.p., fob.

fob'bing, pr.p., fob.

fo'cal, adj., pert. or rel. to a focus.

focaliza'tion, n., the bringing to a focus.

foc'alize, v.t., to bring to a focus.

foc'alized, p.p., focalize.

foc'alizing, pr.p., focalize.

fo'ci, n., pl. of focus; the points of convergence. (Also *focuses*.)

focim'eter, n., an instrument for finding the focus of a lens.

fo''c'sle, n., i.q. forecastle.

fo'cus, n., a point of concentration; v.t., to bring to a focus.

fo'cus(s)ed, p.p., focus.

fo'cus(s)es, n. pl., i.q. foci.

fo'cus(s)ing, pr.p., focus.

fod'der, n., food for cattle; v.t., to feed with fodder.

fod'dered, p.p., fodder.

fod'dering, pr.p., fodder.

fod'derless, adj., without cattle food.

foe, n., an enemy.

foe'man, n., an enemy in war; a personal antagonist.

foe'tal, adj., i.q. fetal.

foe'tid, adj., i.q. fetid.

foe'tor, n., i.q. fetor.

foe'tus, n., i.q. fetus.

fog, n., a dense, watery vapour darkening the atmosphere; v.t., to envelop with fog; to bemuse.

fog'-bank, n., a bank of fog at sea.

fogged, adj., bewildered; p.p., fog.

fog'gily, adv., in a foggy manner.

fog'giness, n., the state of being foggy.

fog'ging, pr.p., fog.

fog'gy, adj., abounding with fog; misty.

fog'-horn, n., a warning in foggy weather.

fo'gle, n., a silk handkerchief (slang).

fog'-signal, n., a warning instrument to ships at sea during foggy weather; a detonator used on the railway during fog.

fo'g(e)y, n., an old-fashioned person.

fog'yish, adj., behind the times; old-fashioned.

Foh, foh, interj., an exclamation of impatience or dislike.

Föhn, n., a warm southerly wind in the Alps.

foi'ble, n., the weak part of a sword; a slight moral weakness; an eccentricity.

foil, n., a blunt sword for fencing; leaf metal; something enhancing beauty or interest by contrast; (in architecture) having hollow curves; v.t., to frustrate.

foiled, adj., having arcs or hollow curves, said of a Gothic window; p.p., foil.

foil'er, n., one who foils.

foil'ing, pr.p., foil.

fois'on, n., plenty (arch.).

foist, v.t., to pass off as genuine.

foist'ed, p.p., foist.

foist'er, n., one who foists.

foist'ing, *pr.p.*, foist.

fold, *n.*, the doubling of cloth; an enclosure for sheep; *v.t.*, to lay one part over another; to enfold; to confine in a fold.

fold'age, *n.*, a manorial privilege rel. to sheepfolds.

fold'ed, *p.p.*, fold.

fold'er, *n.*, one who or that which, folds; a container for papers.

fold'ing, *pr.p.*, fold.

folia'ceous, *adj.*, leafy.

fo'liage, *n.*, leaves collectively.

fo'liaged, *adj.*, ornamented with leaves.

fo'liar, *adj.*, of leaves.

fo'liate, *adj.*, furnished with leaves; *v.t.*, to beat into a thin plate; to cover with foil.

fo'liated, *adj.*, consisting of plates or laminae; in architecture, containing foils.

folia'tion, *n.*, the leafing of plants; the property in some rocks of splitting into laminae; the foils, cusps, etc., in a Gothic window.

fo'liature, *n.*, *i.q.* foliage.

fo'lier, *n.*, goldsmith's foil.

folif'erous, *adj.*, producing leaves.

fo'lio, *n.*, a book of the largest size; an opening of an account-book; a sheet of typescript or manuscript.

fo'liole, *n.*, a leaflet; a division of a compound leaf.

fo'liomort, *adj.*, having the colour of a dead leaf.

fo'lious, *adj.*, thin, like a leaf.

folk, *n.*, people in general.

folk'dance, *n.*, a traditional country dance.

folk'land, *n.*, public land held in common by the people in ancient England.

folk'lore, *n.*, rural superstitions, tales, traditions, etc.

folk'lorist, *n.*, a student of folklore.

folk'moot, *n.*, an assembly of the people in ancient England for legislative purposes.

folk'mote, *n.*, *i.q.* folkmoot.

folk'right, *n.*, the old common law of England.

folk'song, *n.*, a traditional song.

fol'licle, *n.*, a dry seedvessel opening on one side only; a vesicle, a gland.

follic'ular, *adj.*, pert. or rel. to follicles.

follic'ulated, *adj.*, having follicles.

follic'ulous, *adj.*, *i.q.* follicular.

fol'low, *v.t.*, to move behind in the same direction.

fol'lowed, *p.p.*, follow.

fol'lower, *n.*, one who, or that which, follows; an adherent.

fol'lowing, *adj.*, being next after; *n.*, a body of followers; *pr.p.*, follow.

fol'ly, *n.*, foolish, weak conduct. (Also *foolery*.)

foment', *v.t.*, to apply warm lotions to; to abet; to aggravate.

fomenta'tion, *n.*, the act of fomenting; encouragement; a warm lotion.

foment'ed, *p.p.*, foment.

foment'er, *n.*, one who foments.

foment'ing, *pr.p.*, foment.

fond, *adj.*, foolish; loving ardently.

fon'dant, *n.*, a soft, moulded, sweet confection.

fond'er, *adj.*, *comp.* fond.

fond'est, *adj.* *super.* fond.

fond'le, *v.t.*, to caress.

fond'led, *p.p.*, fondle.

fond'ler, *n.*, one who fondles.

fond'ling, *n.*, a person or thing fondled; *pr.p.*, fondle.

fond'ly, *adv.*, affectionately; tenderly.

fond'ness, *n.*, great affection; liking.

font, *n.*, an ecclesiastical vessel used in baptism; a complete assortment of printing types of one size.

font'al, *adj.*, pert. or rel. to a fount or source.

fontanelle', *n.*, a membranous interval between the bones of a child's skull.

food, *n.*, nutriment.

food'-card, *n.*, a ration card used during a war or emergency.

food'less, *adj.*, not having food.

food'stuff, *n.*, any edible material.

fool, *n.*, an idiot; a professional jester; *v.t.*, to deceive.

fooled, *p.p.*, fool.

fool'ery, *n.*, *i.q.* folly.

fool'hardiness, *n.*, mad rashness.

fool'hardy, *adj.*, daring without judgment.

fool'ing, *pr.p.*, fool.

fool'ish, *adj.*, unwise; silly.

fool'ishly, *adv.*, in a foolish manner.

fool'ishness, *n.*, stupidity, folly.

fool'proof, *adj.*, infallible; safe against human error.

fools'cap, *n.*, a dunce's cap; long folio printing paper; writing paper, normally 8 in. × 13 in.

foot, *n.*, the lower extremity of an animal's leg; the bottom; infantry; a length of 12 in.; a measure of a verse; *v.t.*, to add up; to pay; *v.i.*, to walk or dance.

foot'ball, *n.*, an inflated leather ball used in association and rugby football and other games.

foot'baller, *n.*, one who plays the game of football.

foot'board, *n.*, a treadle; a foot-rest.

foot'boy, *n.*, a page.

foot'bridge, *n.*, a narrow bridge for foot passengers.

foot'-can'dle, *n.*, illumination from a standard candle at a distance of one foot.

foot'ed, *adj.*, provided with a foot or feet; *p.p.*, foot.

foot'er, *n.*, football (*slang*).

foot'fall, *n.*, the sound of a footstep.

foot'-gear, *n.*, *i.q.* footwear.

foot'-guards, *n. pl.*, household infantry.

foot'hill, *n.*, a hill at the base of a mountain.

foot'hold, *n.*, a firm standing; a place secured from which to proceed farther.

foot'ing, *n.*, a permanent settlement; a foundation; also *i.q.* foothold; *pr.p.*, foot.

foo'tle, *v.i.*, to trifle (*colloq.*).

foot'lights, *n. pl.*, a row of lights on the front of a theatre stage.

foot'ling, *adj.*, trifling; drivelling.

foot'loose, *adj.*, free to wander.

foot'man, *n.*, a man-servant.

foot'mark, *n.*, the mark of a foot.

foot'-muff, *n.*, a muff for keeping the feet warm.

foot'note, *n.*, a comment at the foot of a page.

foot'-pace, *n.*, a slow step.

foot'pad, *n.*, a highwayman on foot.

foot'path, *n.*, a narrow path for pedestrians only.

foot'plate, *n.*, the driver's platform on a locomotive.

foot'-pound, *n.*, the amount of energy needed to lift 1 lb. 1 ft.

foot'print, *n.*, the mark of a foot.

foot'-slog, *n.*, a march; *v.i.*, to tramp.

foot'-soldier, *n.*, an infantryman.

foot'sore, *adj.*, having feet made tender by much walking.

foot'stalk, *n.*, a petiole; a peduncle.

foot'step, *n.*, a footprint; a footfall; the sound of a footfall.

foot'stool, *n.*, a stool for the feet.

foot'-warmer, *n.*, a contrivance for warming the feet.

foot'way, *n.*, a path for walkers.

foot'wear, *n.*, clothing for the feet.

foo'zle, *n.*, a bad shot; *v.t.*, to play a shot badly at golf; to miss a chance.

fop, *n.*, a dandy.

fop'ling, *n.*, a petty fop.

fop'pery, *n.*, dandyism.

fop'pish, *adj.*, vain of dress; affected in manners.

fop'pishly, *adv.*, in a foppish manner.

fop'pishness, *n.*, the state of being foppish.

for, *conj.*, because; *prep.*, instead of; for the sake of; with a view to, etc.

for'age, *n.*, food for horses and cattle; *v.i.*, to search for forage.

for'aged, *p.p.*, forage.

for'ager, *n.*, one who forages.

for'aging, *pr.p.*, forage.

fora'men, *n.*, a small natural opening in animals and plants.

fora'minated, *adj.*, having foramina or little holes.

Foraminif'era, *n. pl.*, an order of minute animals having a perforated skull.

foraminif'erous, *adj.*, pert. or rel. to the Foraminifera.

forasmuch', *conj.*, seeing that; since.

for'ay, *n.*, a predatory excursion; *v.i.*, to pillage.

forbad'(e), *p.p.*, forbid.

forbear', *v.i.*, to refrain. (Also *forebear*.)

for'bear, *n.*, an ancestor.

forbear'ance, *n.*, long-suffering; lenity.

forbear'ing, *adj.*, having forbearance; *pr.p.*, forbear.

forbear'ingly, *adv.*, leniently.

forbid, *v.t.*, to prohibit.

forbid'den, *adj.*, prohibited; *p.p.*, forbid.

forbid'der, *n.*, one who forbids.

forbid'ding, *adj.*, repulsive; *pr.p.*, forbid.

forbid'dingly, *adv.*, repulsively.

forbid'dingness, *n.*, the state of forbidding.

forbore', *p.p.*, forbear.

forborne', *p.p.*, forbear.

forby(e)', *adv.* and *prep.*, besides; not to mention; close to (*Scot.*).

force, *n.*, power; strength; a body of troops or other organized body of men; a waterfall; *v.t.*, to compel; to stuff.

forced, *adj.*, constrained, unnatural; *p.p.*, force.

force'ful, *adj.*, powerful.

force'fully, *adv.*, in a forceful manner.

force'fulness, *n.*, determination.

force'less, *adj.*, feeble.

force'lessness, *n.*, feebleness.

force'meat, *n.*, stuffing used in cookery.

for'ceps, *n.*, a two-bladed instrument like tongs, used by surgeons, jewellers, etc.

force'-pump, *n.*, a pump which delivers the water by means of pressure.

for'cer, *n.*, one who, or that which, forces.

for'cible, *adj.*, powerful; violent.

for'cibleness, *n.*, the state of being forcible.

for'cibly, *adv.*, in a forcible manner.

for'cing, *n.*, the art of raising plants earlier than their natural season; *pr.p.*, force.

for'cipate, *adj.*, like a pair of pincers.

for'cipated, *adj.*, formed like forceps.

forcipa'tion, *n.*, torture by pinching with a forceps.

for'cite, *n.*, a kind of dynamite.

ford, *n.*, a shallow river-crossing; *v.t.*, to wade through.

ford'able, *adj.*, capable of being forded.

ford'ed, *p.p.*, ford.

ford'ing, *pr.p.*, ford.

fordo', *adj.*, exhausted; *v.t.*, to kill, destroy or spoil.

fore, *adj.*, in front; *interj.*, a warning cry in the game of golf.

fore'arm, *n.*, that part of the arm between the elbow and the wrist.

forearm', *v.t.*, to arm before the time of need.

fore'bear, *n.*, *i.q.* forebear.

forebode', *v.t.*, to presage.

forebo'ded, *p.p.*, forebode.

forebo'der, *n.*, one who forebodes.

forebo'ding, *n.,* a feeling of apprehension; *pr.p.,* forebode.

forebo'dingly, *adv.,* in a foreboding way.

fore'brace, *n.,* a rope fastened to the fore yard-arm.

fore'-cabin, *n.,* a cabin in the fore part of a ship, usually for second-class passengers.

forecast', *v.t.,* to calculate beforehand; to predict.

fore'cast, *n.,* a guess or estimate of the future.

fore'casted, *p.p.,* forecast.

forecast'ing, *pr.p.,* forecast.

fore'castle, *n.,* the fore part of a vessel.

fore'chains, *n. pl.,* a contrivance to carry the lower shrouds of a foremast outside the ship's side.

foreclose', *v.t.,* to prevent; to compel a mortgagor to pay the money borrowed or forfeit his estate.

foreclosed', *p.p.,* foreclose.

foreclo'sing, *pr.p.,* foreclose.

foreclo'sure, *n.,* the act of foreclosing.

fore'court, *n.,* an outer court.

foredate', *v.t.,* to antedate.

foredat'ed, *p.p.,* foredate.

foredat'ing, *pr.p.,* foredate.

fore'deck, *n.,* the forepart of the deck of a ship.

foredoom', *v.t.,* to predestinate.

fore'edge, *n.,* the outer or front edge of a leaf or book.

fore'father, *n.,* an ancestor.

fore'finger, *n.,* the first or index finger.

fore'foot, *n.,* a front foot.

fore'front, *n.,* the foremost part.

foregath'er, *v.t., i.q.* foregather.

fore'gift, *n.,* a premium for a lease (*leg.*).

forego', *v.t.,* to precede.

forego'er, *n.,* a predecessor.

forego'ing, *adj.,* preceding; *pr.p.,* forego.

foregone', *adj.,* predetermined; *p.p.,* forego.

fore'ground, *n.,* the front part of the scene in a picture.

fore'hand, *adj.,* done beforehand; of a stroke, executed in some games (as tennis) with the arm extended away from the body; *n.,* the front position; that part of a horse in front of the saddle.

fore'handed, *adj.,* beforehand; seasonable.

fore'hander, *n.,* a forehand stroke.

fore'head, *n.,* the brow.

fore'hold, *n.,* a ship's foremost hold.

for'eign, *adj.,* alien; irrelevant.

for'eigner, *n.,* an alien.

for'eignness, *n.,* the quality of being foreign.

forejudge', *v.t.,* to prejudge.

forejudged', *p.p.,* forejudge.

forejudg'ing, *pr.p.,* forejudge.

foreknew', *p.p.,* foreknow.

foreknow', *v.t.,* to have previous knowledge of.

foreknow'er, *n.,* one who foreknows.

foreknow'ing, *pr.p.,* foreknow.

foreknowl'edge, *n.,* prescience.

foreknown', *p.p.,* foreknow.

fo'r(r)el, *n.,* thin, vellumlike parchment.

fore'land, *n.,* a promontory.

fore'leg, *n.,* a beast's front leg.

fore'lock, *n.,* the lock of hair that grows above the forehead.

fore'man, *n.,* a chief workman; the chief man of a jury.

fore'mast, *n.,* the front mast of a ship.

fore'most, *adj.,* first; most advanced.

fore'name, *n.,* a personal name preceding the surname.

fore'named, *adj.,* mentioned before.

fore'noon, *n.,* morning between sunrise and midday.

foren'sic, *adj.,* medical science pert. or rel. to courts of justice and the law.

foren'sically, *adv.,* in a forensic way.

foreordain', *v.t.,* to appoint beforehand.

foreordained', *p.p.,* foreordain.

foreordain'ing, *pr.p.,* foreordain.

foreordina'tion, *n.,* predetermination; predestination.

fore'part, *n.,* the first part in time or place.

fore'peak, *n.,* the part of a ship immediately behind the bows (*naut.*).

fore'plane, *n.,* the first plane used after the saw or axe.

fore'rank, *n.,* the front.

fore'reach', *v.i.* and *t.,* to shoot ahead; to overtake.

fore'reached', *p.p.,* forereach.

fore'reach'ing, *adj.,* over-taking; *pr.p.,* fore-reach.

forerun', *v.t.,* to run before.

forerun'ner, *n.,* a harbinger.

forerun'ning, *pr.p.,* forerun.

fore'said, *adj.,* mentioned before.

fore'sail, *n.,* the sail nearest the bars on the foremast.

foresee', *v.t.,* to see beforehand.

foresee'able, *adj.,* able to be foreseen.

foresee'ing, *pr.p.,* foresee.

foresee'ingly, *adv.,* in a foreseeing way.

foreseen', *p.p.,* foresee.

forese'er, *n.,* one who foresees.

foreshad'ow, *v.t.,* to typify or adumbrate beforehand.

foreshad'owed, *p.p.,* foreshadow.

foreshad'owing, *pr.p.,* foreshadow.

fore'sheet, *n.,* the rope with which the foresail is set.

fore'shore, *n.,* the shore between high- and low-water mark.

foreshort'en, *v.t.,* to depict an object directed towards the spectator with the due expression of its length and relative position.

foreshort'ened, *p.p.,* foreshorten.

foreshort'ening, *pr.p.,* foreshorten.

foreshow', *v.t.,* to exhibit beforehand; to foretell.

foreshowed', *p.p.,* foreshow.

foreshow'ing, *pr.p.,* foreshow.

fore'side, *n.,* the front side.

fore'sight, *n.,* provident care for the future; the sight on the muzzle of a gun.

fore'skin, *n.,* the prepuce; the folds of skin covering the tip of the penis.

for'est, *adj.,* pert. or rel. to a forest; *n.,* a large tract of land covered with trees; a district devoted to the chase; *v.t.,* to plant with trees.

forestall', *v.t.,* to anticipate; to prevent.

forestalled', *p.p.,* forestall.

forestall'er, *n.,* one who forestalls.

forestall'ing, *pr.p.,* forestall.

fore'stay, *n.,* a foremast support.

for'ester, *n.,* one who has charge of a forest, or of the timber on an estate.

for'estry, *n.,* the art of managing growing trees.

foret', *n.,* a drill for making vents in ordnance.

fore'taste, *n.,* enjoyment in advance.

foretaste', *v.t.,* to taste before possession.

foretast'ed, *p.p.,* foretaste.

foretast'ing, *pr.p.,* foretaste.

foretell', *v.t.,* to predict.

foretell'er, *n.,* one who foretells.

foretell'ing, *pr.p.,* foretell.

fore'thought, *n.,* provident care.

fore'time, *n.,* the past, the olden times.

foreto'ken, *n.,* a sign of something to come; *v.t.,* to foreshow.

foretold', *p.p.,* foretell.

fore'top, *n.,* the platform at the top of a foremast.

forev'er, *adv.,* permanently.

forewarn', *v.t.,* to give previous notice to.

forewarned', *p.p.,* forewarn.

forewarn'ing, *pr.p.,* forewarn.

fore'wind, *n.,* a following wind.

fore'woman, *n.,* a woman who superintends others.

fore'word, *n.,* a preface.

fore'yard, *n.,* the lowest yard on the foremast.

for'feit, *adj.,* forfeited; *n.,* the act of forfeiting; that which is forfeited; a penalty; *v.t.,* to lose the right to.

for'feitable, *adj.,* subject to forfeiture.

for'feited, *p.p.,* forfeit.

for'feiter, *n.,* one who forfeits.

for'feiting, *pr.p.,* forfeit.

for'feiture, *n.,* the losing of some right by an offence or omission; the thing forfeited.

forfend', *v.t.,* to avert.

forfend'ed, *p.p.,* forfend.

forfend'ing, *pr.p.,* forfend.

for'fex, *n.,* a pair of shears (*Lat.*)

for'ficate, *adj.,* like scissors (*zool.*).

forgath'er, *v.i.,* to meet; to convene. (Also *foregather*.)

forgath'ered, *p.p.,* forgather.

forgath'ering, *n.,* a meeting; *pr.p.,* forgather.

forgave', *p.p.,* forgive.

forge, *n.,* a smithy; *v.t.,* to work metal into shape in a forge; to counterfeit a signature, etc.; *v.i.,* to commit forgery; to move on slowly.

forge'able, *adj.,* capable of being forged.

forged, *p.p.,* forge.

forge'man, *n.,* a man employed at a forge.

for'ger, *n.,* one who commits forgery.

for'gery, *n.,* the crime of counterfeiting handwriting, etc.; that which is forged.

forget', *v.t.* and *i.,* to let go from the memory.

forget'ful, *adj.,* apt to forget.

forget'fully, *adv.,* in a forgetful way.

forget'fulness, *n.,* the quality of being forgetful; oblivion.

forget'-me-not, *n.,* a small, bright-blue flower with a yellow eye.

forget'table, *adj.,* capable of being forgotten; of no merit.

forget'ter, *n.,* one who forgets.

forget'ting, *pr.p.,* forget.

for'ging, *n.,* an article of metal forged; *pr.p.,* forge.

forgiv'able, *adj.,* pardonable.

forgive', *v.t.,* to pardon.

forgiv'en, *p.p.,* forgive.

forgive'ness, *n.,* pardon; willingness to forgive.

for'giver, *n.,* one who forgives.

forgiv'ing, *adj.,* inclined to overlook offences; *pr.p.,* forgive.

forgiv'ingly, *adv.,* in a forgiving manner.

forgiv'ingness, *n.,* the state of being forgiven.

forgo', *v.t.,* to give up; to resign.

forgo'ing, *pr.p.,* forgo.

for'gone, *p.p.,* forgo.

forgot', *p.p.,* forget.

forgot'ten, *p.p.,* forget.

fo'rint, *n.,* the principal monetary unit of Hungary.

forjudge', *v.t.,* to prejudge; to expel from court.

fork, *n.,* an instrument with prongs or tines for lifting something; one of the parts into which any thing is bifurcated; *v.i.,* to divide into branches; *v.t.,* to dig or raise with a fork.

forked, *adj.,* having prongs or divisions like a fork; *p.p.,* fork.

fork'edness, *n.,* the quality of being forked.

fork'ing, *pr.p.,* fork.

fork'y, *adj., i.q.* forked.

forlorn', *adj.,* abandoned; wretched.

forlorn'ly, *adv.,* in a forlorn way.

forlorn'ness, *n.,* the state of being forlorn.

form, *n.,* shape; a long seat; the bed of a hare; *v.t.,* to shape.

form′al, *adj.*, ceremonious; conventional.

formal′dehyde, *n.*, a colourless, volatile liquid, chemically intermediate between formic acid and methyl alcohol.

form′alin, *n.*, an aqueous solution of formaldehyde, used as an antiseptic.

form′alism, *n.*, strict adherence to form.

form′alist, *n.*, one given to formalism.

formal′ity, *n.*, a rule of proceeding; conventionality.

formaliza′tion, *n.*, the state of being formal.

form′alize, *v.t.*, to render formal.

form′alized, *p.p.*, formalize.

form′alizing, *pr.p.*, formalize.

form′ally, *adv.*, in a formal manner; stiffly.

for′mat, *n.*, the size of a book or other printed production.

for′mate, *n.*, a salt of formic acid.

forma′tion, *n.*, production; arrangement.

form′ative, *adj.*, giving form.

form′atively, *adv.*, in a formative way.

formato′re, *n.*, a modeller in wax or plaster (*It.*).

forme, *n.*, type or plates fixed in a frame ready for printing.

formed, *p.p.*, form.

for′mer, *adj.*, preceding; earlier.

form′er, *n.*, one who forms.

for′merly, *adv.*, before the present time.

for′mic, *adj.*, pert. to, or produced by, ants.

for′micate, *adj.*, pert. or rel. to an ant.

formica′tion, *n.*, a sensation like that of ants creeping on the skin.

for′midable, *adj.*, exciting fear or dread.

for′midably, *adv.*, in a formidable manner.

form′ing, *pr.p.*, form.

form′less, *adj.*, shapeless.

for′mula, *n.*, a prescribed form of words, doctrines, figures or symbols expressing a rule or other statement.

formulariza′tion, *n.*, that which is formularized; the act of formularizing.

for′mularize, *v.t.*, to formulate.

for′mularized, *p.p.*, formularize.

for′mularizing, *pr.p.*, formularize.

for′mulary, *n.*, a book containing prescribed forms.

for′mulate, *v.t.*, to express in a formula; to state precisely.

for′mulated, *p.p.*, formulate.

for′mulating, *pr.p.*, formulate.

formula′tion, *n.*, the act of formulating.

form′ulism, *n.*, the study or use of formulas.

form′ulist, *n.*, one who studies or uses formulas.

formulis′tic, *adj.*, according to form.

form′ulized, *adj.*, expressed in formula.

for′nicate, *adj.*, arched or vaulted; *v.i.*, to have illicit sexual intercourse.

for′nicated, *p.p.*, fornicate.

for′nicating, *pr.p.*, fornicate.

fornica′tion, *n.*, illicit sexual intercourse.

for′nicator, *n.*, one guilty of fornication.

for′nix, *n.*, the vault of the cranium (*Lat.*).

forpined′, *adj.*, wasted by torture, hunger, etc.

forrader, *adj. comp.*, further forward.

forsake′, *v.t.*, to abandon.

forsa′ken, *p.p.*, forsake.

forsa′ker, *n.*, one who forsakes.

forsa′king, *pr.p.*, forsake.

forsook′, *p.p.*, forsake.

forsooth′, *adv.*, in truth (often ironical).

forspent′, *adj.*, worn out, exhausted.

forswear′, *v.t.*, to reject on oath; *v.i.*, to swear falsely.

forswear′er, *n.*, one who forswears; a perjurer.

forswear′ing, *pr.p.*, forswear.

forswore′, *p.p.*, forswear.

forsworn′, *p.p.*, forswear.

forsyth′ia, *n.*, a flowering shrub.

fort, *n.*, a small fortified place.

fort′alice, *n.*, a small outwork of a fortification.

for′te, *adv.*, loudly (*mus.*, *It.*).

forte, *n.*, the strong part of a sword-blade; chief excellence.

fortepia′no, *adj.* and *adv.*, loud(ly) and then immediately soft(ly) (*mus.*, *It.*).

forth, *adv.*, onward in time, place or order.

forth′coming, *adj.*, ready to appear.

forth′right, *adj.*, outspoken; *adv.*, straightforward.

forthwith′, *adv.*, immediately.

for′tieth, *adj.*, next after the thirtyninth; *n.*, one of forty equal parts into which a whole is divided.

for′tifiable, *adj.*, capable of being fortified.

fortifica′tion, *n.*, the art of strengthening military positions for defensive purposes; a fortified place.

for′tified, *p.p.*, fortify.

for′tifier, *n.*, one who fortifies.

for′tify, *v.t.*, to strengthen in any way.

for′tifying, *pr.p.*, fortify.

fortis′simo, *adv.*, very loudly (*mus.*, *It.*).

for′titude, *n.*, passive courage.

fort′night, *n.*, two weeks.

fort′nightly, *adj.* and *adv.*, once a fortnight.

for′tran, *n.*, a computer language.

for′tress, *n.*, a large fortified place.

fortu′itism, *n.*, belief in chance and not design.

fortu′itist, *n.*, a believer in chance.

fortu′itous, *adj.*, accidental.

fortu′itously, *adv.*, by chance.

fortu′itousness, *n.*, accident, chance.

fortu′ity, *n.*, *i.q.* fortuitousness.

for′tunate, *adj.*, lucky, successful.

for′tunately, *adv.*, luckily; happily.

for′tune, *n.*, chance; good luck; prosperity; great possessions.

for'tune-hunter, n., a man who seeks to marry a rich woman.

for'tuneless, adj., without success.

for'tune-teller, n., one who tells people their fortune in life.

for'ty, adj., four times ten.

for'tyfold, adj., forty times over.

fo'rum, n., a court, a tribunal (Lat.).

for'ward, adj., being at the front, ready; pert; adv., onward; v.t., to promote; to send on.

for'warded, p.p., forward.

for'warder, n., one who forwards.

for'warding, pr.p., forward.

for'wardly, adv., precociously.

for'wardness, n., the quality of being to the front; officiousness.

for'wards, adv., forward; to the front.

forzan'do, adv., with emphasis (mus., It.).

fosse, n., a moat or ditch.

fossette', n., a small depression or dimple (Fr.).

fosse'way, n., one of the great Roman roads of England.

fos'sick, v.i., to work waste heaps in hopes of finding gold; to rummage about for profit.

fos'sicker, n., a miner who fossicks.

fos'sil, n., a specimen of petrified remains of animals and plants found in rocks.

fos'silate, v.t. and i., i.q., fossilize.

fossila'tion, n., i.q. fossilization.

fossilif'erous, adj., containing fossils.

fossilifica'tion, n., the act of fossilizing or becoming fossil.

fos'silist, n., one versed in fossils.

fossiliza'tion, n., the state of being fossilized.

fos'silize, v.t., to convert into a fossil; v.i., to become a fossil.

fos'silized, p.p., fossilize.

fos'silizing, pr.p., fossilize.

fossilol'ogy, n., palaeontology.

fosso'rial, adj., pert. or rel. to animals that dig in the ground for food and to make dwellings.

foss'way, n., i.q. fosseway.

fos'ter, v.t., to nourish; to encourage.

fos'terage, n., the care of a foster-child.

fos'ter-brother, n., a male child brought up with another of different parentage.

fos'ter-child, n., a child nurtured by one who is not its father or mother.

fos'ter-daugh'ter, n., an adopted daughter.

fos'tered, p.p., foster.

fos'terer, n., one who fosters.

fos'ter-father, n., a man who adopts a child and performs the duties of a father.

fos'tering, pr.p., foster.

fos'terling, n., a foster-child.

fos'ter-mother, n., a woman who adopts a child and performs the duties of a mother; an apparatus for rearing chickens.

fos'ter-parent, n., one who brings up and looks after a child in place of its parent.

fos'ter-sister, n., a girl or woman, not a sister, but brought up by the same person.

fos'ter-son, n., an adopted son.

foth'er, n., a weight for lead (19½ cwt.); v.t., to stop a leak.

foth'ered, p.p., fother.

foth'ering, pr.p., fother.

fougasse, n., improvised mortar (Fr.).

fought, p.p., fight.

foul, adj., filthy; obscene; unfair; entangled; contrary; adv., in an irregular way; n., a collision, an infringement of rules; v.t., to make foul; v.i., to come into collision.

foulard', n., a thin silk fabric (Fr.).

foulé, n., a light, woollen dress material with a glossy surface (Fr.).

fouled, p.p., foul.

foul'ing, pr.p., foul.

foul'ly, adv., in a foul manner; shamefully.

foul'-mouthed, adj., using obscene or abusive language.

foul'ness, n., filthiness.

foul'-play, n., unfair action, dishonest dealing.

foul'-spo'ken, adj., i.q. foul-mouthed.

fou'mart, n., a polecat.

found, p.p., find; v.t., to lay the basis of; to form by melting a metal and pouring into a mould.

founda'tion, n., the act of founding; a basis; an endowed institution.

founda'tional, adj., pert. or rel. to a foundation.

founda'tioner, n., one who derives support from the endowment of a school or college.

founda'tion-stone, n., a stone of a public building laid in public with some ceremony.

found'ed, p.p., found.

foun'der, n., one who founds; v.i., to fill and sink; to go lame; to miscarry.

foun'dered, p.p., founder.

foun'dering, pr.p., founder.

foun'der-member, n., an original member of an institution, etc.

foun'derous, adj., difficult to travel (of a road).

foun'dership, n., the original membership of an institution, etc.

foun'dery, n., i.q. foundry.

found'ing, pr.p., found.

found'ling, n., a child found without known parents.

found'ress, n., a female founder.

foun'dry, n., a place where metals are cast.

foun'dryman, n., a workman in a foundry.

fount, n., a spring of water; printing-type of the same kind.

foun'tain, n., a spring of water; an artificial jet of water; a basin kept filled with water; origin or source.

foun'tain-head, n., origin; primary source.

foun'tain-pen, n., a pen which has a reservoir for ink.

fount'ful, adj., having plenty of springs.

four, adj., three and one.

fourchette', n., the frog of a horse's hoof; part of the fingers of a glove; a fork (Fr.).

four'-cor'nered, adj., having four corners.

four'fold, adj. and adv., four times over.

four'-footed, adj., having four feet.

four'gon, n., a luggage-van (Fr.).

Fou'rierism, n., a socialistic system or form of communism.

four'-in-hand, n., a vehicle with four horses and one driver.

four'-legged, adj., having four legs.

four'pence, n., the amount or value of four pence.

four'penny, adj., worth or costing four pence.

four'poster, n., a large, curtained bed with four pillars at the corners and a canopy.

four'score, adj., eighty.

four'-seat'er, n., a vehicle accommodating four persons.

four'some, n., a match in which four people (two on either side) engage.

four'-square, adj., square; solidly based.

fourteen, adj., four and ten.

fourteenth, adj., the ordinal of fourteen; n., one of fourteen equal parts into which a whole is divided.

fourth, adj., the ordinal of four; n., one of four equal parts into which a whole is divided.

fourth'ly, adv., in the fourth place.

four'-wheeler, n., a four-wheeled vehicle.

fo'vea, n., a little depression or pit.

fo'veate, adj., pitted.

fo'veola, n., a small fovea.

fo'veolate, adj., i.q. foveate.

fo'veolated, adj., i.q. foveolate.

fovil'la, n., the powder in a pollen grain that causes fertilization.

fowl, n., a bird; a domestic cock or hen.

fowl'er, n., a sportsman who pursues wild fowl.

fowl'-house, n., a shed, sometimes portable, for sheltering fowls.

fowl'ing, n., the practice of pursuing wild fowl.

fowl'ing-piece, n., a light gun for shooting birds.

fowl'-run, n., an enclosed area for fowls.

fox, n., a wild animal of the dog kind that preys on chickens and other small animals; a cunning fellow; v.i., to turn sour; to become discoloured; to outwit.

fox'aline, n., imitation fox fur.

fox'-case, n., the skin of a fox.

fox'-chase, n., the hunting of a fox with hounds and horses.

foxed, adj., marked with brownish spots, as paper; outwitted.

fox'glove, n., a plant with a spike of drooping flowers.

fox'hole, n., a fox's burrow; a small entrenchment.

fox'hound, n., a hound for chasing foxes.

fox'hunter, n., one who follows the fox-hounds.

fox'hunting, n., the sport of hunting a fox with hounds.

fox'iness, n., cunning.

fox'like, adj., resembling a fox.

fox'-sleep, n., feigned sleep.

fox'tail, n., a grass with a close, cylindrical panicle of flowers resembling a fox's brush.

fox'terrier, n., a short-haired terrier used for unearthing foxes.

fox'trap, n., a snare set to catch foxes.

fox'trot, n., short steps taken by a horse when changing its pace; a ballroom dance.

fox'y, adj., cunning; sour (of beer, wine, etc.).

foyer', n., the entrance hall of a public building (Fr.).

or fracas, n., a disturbance (U.S.) (Fr.).

frac'tion, n., a fragment; a part.

frac'tional, adj., pert. or rel. to fractions.

frac'tionalist, n., one who breaks up political unity.

frac'tionally, adv., insignificantly.

frac'tionary, adj., i.q. fractional.

frac'tionate, v.t., to separate a mixture into different properties by distillation, etc.

frac'tionated, p.p., fractionate.

frac'tionating, pr.p., fractionate.

fractiona'tion, n., the act of fractionating.

frac'tionator, n., one who, or that which, fractionates.

frac'tionize, v.t., to break up into portions or fractions (math.).

frac'tious, adj., peevish.

frac'tiously, adv., snappishly.

frac'tiousness, n., a fractious temper.

frac'ture, n., a breakage; a crack; v.t., to cause to break.

frac'tured, p.p., fracture.

frac'turing, pr.p., fracture.

fraen'um, n., a ligament (Lat.). (Also frenum.)

frag'ile, adj., easily broken; frail.

frag'ilely, adv., in a fragile manner.

fragil'ity, n., the quality of being fragile.

frag'ment, n., a part broken off; anything left unfinished.

frag'mentary, adj., composed of fragments; incomplete.

fragmenta'tion, n., the breaking into fragments.

fra'grance, n., pleasing scent.

fra'grancy, n., i.q. fragrance.

fra'grant, adj., sweet-smelling.

fra'grantly, adv., with a sweet scent.

frail, adj., fragile; perishable; not strong against temptation; weak; n., a basket made of rushes.

frail'ness, n., the condition of being frail.

frail'ty, n., frailness; infirmity; a fault proceeding from weakness.

fraise, *n.*, a down-sloping palisade of pointed stakes; a tool for cutting teeth in watch wheels (*Fr.*).

fram'able, *adj.*, capable of being framed.

framboes'ia, *n.*, a contagious tropical disease causing raspberry-like swellings.

frame, *n.*, structure; a case for enclosing a picture, etc.; disposition of the mind; *v.t.*, to invent; to surround with a frame; to put a person into a position of risk.

framed, *p.p.*, frame.

frame'less, *adj.*, without a frame.

fram'er, *n.*, one who frames.

frame'up, *n.*, a conspiracy.

frame'work, *n.*, a structure acting as a support or pattern.

fram'ing, *n.*, a system of frames; *pr.p.*, frame.

franc, *n.*, the French unit of currency.

fran'chise, *n.*, the right of voting at a parliamentary election; a saleable right to operate.

fran'chisement, *n.*, *i.q.* enfranchisement.

Francis'can, *adj.* and *n.*, (a person) of the Order of St. Francis of Assisi.

fran'cium, *n.*, a radioactive metallic element.

franc'olin, *n.*, a kind of partridge resembling a pheasant.

francoma'nia, *n.*, a craze for imitating French ways.

francopho'bia, *n.*, a morbid dislike of anything French.

franctireur', *n.*, an irregular sharpshooter or sniper, employed in guerrilla warfare.

frangibil'ity, *n.*, the quality of being frangible.

fran'gible, *adj.*, brittle.

fran'gipane, *n.*, pastry containing cream and almonds; a perfume (*Fr.*).

frangipa'ni, *n.*, a tropical flower; scent with the odour of this flower.

Frank, *n.*, one of the ancient German race of Franks.

frank, *adj.*, candid; *v.t.*, to transmit free of cost.

franked, *p.p.*, frank.

frank'furter, *n.*, a highly seasoned German sausage.

frank'incense, *n.*, a gum obtained from an Indian tree resembling the sumach, which is aromatic when burned.

frank'ing, *pr.p.*, frank.

frank'lin, *n.*, a yeoman; a freeholder.

frank'ly, *adv.*, candidly.

frank'ness, *n.*, the quality of being frank.

frank'-pledge, *n.*, the relation between members of a Government; a system in tithing where each member was responsible for every other (*hist.*).

fran'tic, *adj.*, mad; furious; distracted.

fran'tically, *adv.*, in a frantic manner.

fran'ticness, *n.*, the state of being frantic.

frap, *v.t.*, to make fast by binding (*naut.*).

frap'pé, *adj.*, iced, cooled with crushed ice (*Fr.*).

frass, *n.*, the excrement of larvae.

frat'e, *n.*, a friar (*It.*).

frat'er, *n.*, a refectory (*hist.*).

frater'nal, *adj.*, brotherly.

frater'nally, *adv.*, in a brotherly way.

frater'nity, *n.*, a brotherhood; a society.

fraterniza'tion, *n.*, the act of fraternizing.

frat'ernize, *v.i.*, to hold sympathetic intercourse.

frat'ernized, *p.p.*, fraternize.

frat'ernizer, *n.*, one who fraternizes.

frat'ernizing, *pr.p.*, fraternize.

frat'ricidal, *adj.*, pert. or rel. to fratricide.

frat'ricide, *n.*, the crime of murdering a brother; one who commits such a murder.

Frau, *n.*, a married woman; Mrs. (*Ger.*).

fraud, *n.*, an act of deceit to gain unfair advantage.

fraud'ful, *adj.*, characterized by fraud.

fraud'ulence, *n.*, the quality of being fraudulent.

fraud'ulency, *n.*, *i.q.* fraudulence.

fraud'ulent, *adj.*, using fraud; founded on fraud.

fraud'ulently, *adv.*, in a fraudulent manner.

fraught, *adj.*, freighted; filled; abounding.

Fräul'ein, *n.*, a spinster; Miss (*Ger.*).

fraxinell'a, *n.*, a kind of garden herb.

fray, *n.*, an affray; *v.t.*, to rub away the surface of.

frayed, *p.p.*, fray.

fray'ing, *pr.p.*, fray.

frazil', *n.*, anchor ice (*Canada* and *U.S.*).

fraz'zle, *n.*, complete exhaustion; a thing frayed; *v.t.* and *i.*, to fray.

freak, *n.*, a whim or fancy; an odd, irregular thing.

freaked, *adj.*, oddly streaked; dappled.

freak'ish, *adj.*, whimsical; capricious.

freak'ishly, *adv.*, in a freakish way.

freak'ishness, *n.*, the state of being freakish.

freak'out, *n.*, a period of abandonment of everyday life.

freck'le, *n.*, a small yellowish spot in the skin; *v.t.* and *i.*, to mark or become marked with freckles.

freck'led, *adj.*, marked with freckles; *p.p.*, freckle.

freck'ling, *pr.p.*, freckle.

freck'ly, *adj.*, covered with freckles.

free, *adj.*, at liberty; liberal; gratuitous; exempt; *v.t.*, to set at liberty.

free'-bench, *n.*, a widow's right in copyhold; a kind of dower.

free'booter, *n.*, a plunderer.

free'-born, *adj.*, born free.

freed, *p.p.*, free.

freed'man, *n.*, a manumitted slave.

free'dom, *n.*, the state of being free; independence; particular privileges.

free-enter'prise, *n.*, privately controlled business.

free'hand, *adj.,* done without the use of instruments; drawn without artificial aid.

free'handed, *adj.,* open-handed, liberal.

free'hand'edness, *n.,* liberality.

free-heart'ed, *adj.,* generous.

free-heart'edness, *n.,* generosity.

free'hold, *n.,* an estate, the tenant of which owes no duty except to the crown; the tenure of such an estate.

free'holder, *n.,* the possessor of a freehold.

free'ing, *pr.p.,* free.

free'lance, *adj.,* unattached to an employer; *n.,* a medieval mercenary; one who works for himself.

free'-liver, *n.,* one who indulges his appetite freely.

free'-love, *n.,* the doctrine of unrestrained sexual intercourse outside marriage.

free'ly, *adv.,* in a free manner.

free'man, *n.,* a man who is free.

free'martin, *n.,* an imperfect female calf, born with a male.

free'mason, *n.,* a member of a lodge of a society.

free'masonry, *n.,* the system of the society into which freemasons are initiated.

free'-minded, *adj.,* unperplexed; free from care.

free'ness, *n.,* the state of being free.

free'port, *n.,* a port free of customs.

fre'er, *adj., comp.* of free; *n.,* one who frees.

frees'ia, *n.,* a highly scented South African flowering plant.

free'-spoken, *adj.,* accustomed to speak without reserve.

fre'est, *adj., super.* of free.

free'stone, *n.,* sandstone.

free'thinker, *n.,* a sceptic; a deist.

freethink'ing, *adj.,* holding the principles of a freethinker.

free-trade, *n.,* trade free from imposts on imported articles.

free-tra'der, *n.,* an advocate of free-trade.

free'wheel, *n.,* a wheel which can be released from the driving gear so as to run freely.

freewill', *adj.,* voluntary; *n.,* voluntariness.

freeze, *v.i.,* to change from a liquid to a solid; *v.t.,* to harden into ice.

freez'er, *n.,* a refrigerator.

freez'ing, *pr.p.,* freeze.

freez'ingly, *adv.,* in a freezing way.

freez'ing-point, *n.,* the temperature at which water becomes ice or at which a liquid becomes solid.

freight, *n.,* cargo; the charge for transport of goods; *v.t.,* to load a ship or aircraft.

freight'age, *n.,* money paid for freight.

freight'ed, *p.p.,* freight.

freight'er, *n.,* one who freights; a ship or aircraft that carries goods.

freight'ing, *pr.p.,* freight.

fremes'cent, *adj.,* noisy.

French, *adj.,* pert. or rel. to France; *n.,* the language of France; the French people.

French' bean, *n.,* the common kidney bean.

French bread', *n.,* a kind of crusty bread.

Frenchchalk', *n.,* soapstone used for marking, particularly cloth, or for smoothing a surface.

French' horn, *n.,* a musical instrument of brass with many curves.

French'ified, *p.p.,* Frenchify.

French'ify, *v.t.,* to make French; to infect with French manners.

frenchleave', *n.,* absence without permission.

French'less, *adj.,* having no knowledge of French.

french letter, *n.,* a contraceptive sheath.

French'man, *n.,* a man of the French nation.

French'ness, *n.,* the state of being French.

french pol'ish, *n.,* a spirit furniture polish.

french pol'isher, *n.,* one skilled in the use of French polish.

french win'dow, *n.,* a tall window divided vertically to serve as doors.

French'woman, *n.,* a woman native of France.

Fren'chy, *adj.,* pert. or rel. to France; *n.,* a French man or woman (*slang*).

frenet'ic, *adj.,* frenzied; frantic.

fren'ulum, *n.,* a little frenum or restraining band.

fre'num, *n., i.q.* fraenum.

fren'zied, *adj.,* maddened; frantic.

fren'ziedly, *adv.,* distractedly.

fren'zy, *n.,* madness; delirium, distraction; *v.t.,* to drive to frenzy.

fre'quency, *n.,* the state of being frequent; the rate of occurrence.

fre'quent, *adj.,* occurring often.

frequent', *v.t.,* to visit often.

frequent'able, *adj.,* that which may be easily visited.

frequenta'tion, *n.,* the habit of going to a place frequently.

frequent'ative, *adj.,* expressing repeated action; *n.,* a verb expressing frequent action (*gram.*).

frequent'ed, *p.p.,* frequent.

frequent'er, *n.,* one who frequents.

frequent'ing, *pr.p.,* frequent.

fre'quently, *adv.,* often.

fre'quentness, *n., i.q.* frequency.

fres'cade, *n.,* a cool walk.

fres'co, *n.,* a method of painting on walls; *v.t.,* to paint on walls (*It.*).

fres'coed, *p.p.,* fresco.

fresh, *adj.,* lively; bright; in good condition; health-giving; pure and cool; new; not salt; reinvigorated.

fresh'-blown, *adj.,* newly come to blossom.

fresh'en, *v.t.,* to make fresh; *v.i.,* to grow fresh.

fresh'ened, *p.p.,* freshen.

fresh'ener, *adj.,* that which freshens.

fresh'ening, *pr.p.,* freshen.

fresh′er, *adj.*, *comp.* of fresh; *n.*, a freshman (*slang*).

fresh′est, *adj.*, *super.* of fresh.

fresh′et, *n.*, a small flood in a river.

fresh′-looking, *adj.*, healthy-looking.

fresh′ly, *adv.*, newly; recently.

fresh′man, *n.*, a first-year university student.

fresh′ness, *n.*, the state of being fresh.

fresh′water, *adj.*, living in or pert. to fresh water.

fret, *n.*, vexation; a kind of ornament of interlacing bands; *v.t.*, to eat into; to chafe; to irritate; *v.i.*, to be peevish.

fret′ful, *adj.*, ill-humoured.

fret′fully, *adv.*, peevishly.

fret′fulness, *n.*, peevishness.

fret′saw, *n.*, a saw used for fretwork.

fret′ted, *adj.*, adorned with fretwork; *p.p.*, fret.

fret′ter, *n.*, one who, or that which, frets.

fret′ting, *pr.p.*, fret.

fret′ty, *adj.*, adorned with fretwork.

fret′work, *n.*, ornamental work consisting of designs cut through thin wood.

Freud′ian, *adj.*, pert. or rel. to Freud, the psychologist, and his teaching; *n.*, an adherent of Freud.

friabil′ity, *n.*, the quality of being easily pulverized.

fri′able, *adj.*, easily crumbled.

fri′ableness, *n.*, *i.q.* friability.

fri′ar, *n.*, a member of a mendicant religious order.

friar′s-bal′sam, *n.*, a compound tincture of benzoin, used for healing.

friar′s-cowl, *n.*, a plant shaped like a cowl.

fri′ary, *n.*, a convent of friars.

fria′tion, *n.*, the act of pulverizing.

frib′ble, *n.*, a frivolous, contemptible fellow; *v.i.*, to trifle.

frib′bler, *n.*, a trifler.

frib′bling, *adj.*, frivolous; trifling.

fricandeau′, *n.*, a fricassee of veal (*Fr.*).

fricassee′, *n.*, a dish made by cutting meat into small fragments and cooking them with sauce or stock in a stew-pan over heat; *v.t.*, to cook in this way (*Fr.*).

fricasseed′, *p.p.*, fricassee.

fricassee′ing, *pr.p.*, fricassee.

fric′ative, *adj.*, a term applied to certain sounds (e.g., *s, z, f, v*) in which air passes through a narrow passage.

fric′tion, *n.*, the rubbing of the surface of one body against that of another; the resistance a moving body experiences for this reason.

fric′tional, *adj.*, pert. or rel. to friction.

fric′tionally, *adv.*, in a frictional way.

fric′tionless, *adj.*, having no friction.

Fri′day, *n.*, the sixth day of the week.

fridge, *n.*, the abbrev. for refrigerator (*colloq.*).

fried, *p.p.*, fry.

friend, *n.*, one attached to another by affection.

friend′less, *adj.*, destitute of friends.

friend′lessness, *n.*, the state of being without friends.

friend′lier, *adj.*, *comp.* of friendly.

friend′liest, *adj.*, *super.* of friendly.

friend′liness, *n.*, goodwill; kindliness.

friend′ly, *adj.*, kind; not hostile; well disposed.

friend′ship, *n.*, the feeling of mutual attachment that binds friends together.

frier, *n.*, *i.q.* fryer.

Fries′ian, *adj.*, pert. or rel. to Friesland, a province of the Netherlands; a breed of cattle. (Also *Frisian.*)

frieze, *n.*, a coarse, woollen cloth with a shaggy nap; in architecture, an upper surface for ornament.

frig′ate, *n.*, a small, fast fighting ship.

fright, *n.*, sudden fear; *v.t.*, to scare.

fright′en, *v.t.*, to terrify.

fright′ened, *p.p.*, frighten.

fright′ening, *pr.p.*, frighten.

fright′ful, *adj.*, causing fright; dire, tragic.

fright′fully, *adv.*, terribly; shockingly.

fright′fulness, *n.*, dreadfulness.

frig′id, *adj.*, cold; sexually unresponsive.

frigida′rium, *n.*, the cooling room of a Roman bath (*Lat.*).

frigid′ity, *n.*, coldness; sexual impotence, esp. in women.

frig′idly, *adv.*, in a frigid manner.

frig′idness, *n.*, the state of being frigid.

fri′go, *n.*, frozen meat (*slang*).

frigorif′ic, *adj.*, causing cold.

frill, *n.*, a ruffle or ornamental edging; *v.t.*, to decorate with a frill.

frilled, *p.p.*, frill.

frill′ies, *n. pl.*, frilled underwear (*colloq.*).

frill′ing, *n.*, frill; ruffles; *pr.p.*, frill.

fril′ly, *adj.*, with lots of frills.

fringe, *n.*, a border consisting of loose threads attached at one end; a margin; *v.t.*, to border with a fringe.

fringed, *adj.*, bordered with a fringe; *p.p.*, fringe.

fring′ing, *pr.p.*, fringe.

fringe′less, *adj.*, without a fringe.

frip′pery, *adj.*, contemptible; *n.*, useless things.

frisette′, *n.*, a frizz of artificial hair worn as a band at the front (*Fr.*).

friseur′, *n.*, a hairdresser (*Fr.*).

Fris′ian, *adj.*, *i.q.* Friesian.

frisk, *n.*, a frolic; *v.i.*, to gambol; to search a person for hidden arms, etc.

frisked, *p.p.*, frisk.

frisk′er, *n.*, one who frisks.

frisk′et, *n.*, a light frame hinged to the tympan in printing.

frisk'ily, *adv.*, in a frisky manner.

frisk'iness, *n.*, the state of being frisky.

frisk'ing, *pr.p.*, frisk.

frisk'y, *adj.*, frolicsome.

frit, *n.*, calcined material for glass-making.

frit'-fly, *n.*, a small fly which destroys wheat.

frith, *n.*, *i.q.* firth.

fritill'ary, *n.*, a herbaceous plant; a British butterfly.

frit'ter, *n.*, a small piece of foodstuff encased in a batter and fried; *v.t.*, to break into small pieces; to waste on vain pursuits.

frit'tered, *p.p.*, fritter.

frit'tering, *pr.p.*, fritter.

Fritz, *n.*, a nickname for a German.

friv'ol, *v.i.* and *t.*, to act foolishly.

frivol'ity, *n.*, levity of mind or disposition; an insignificant trifle.

friv'olous, *adj.*, trifling; trivial; of no importance.

friv'olously, *adv.*, in a frivolous manner.

friv'olousness, *n.*, the quality of being frivolous.

frizz, *n.*, that which is frizzed; *v.t.*, to curl or crisp.

frizzed, *p.p.*, frizz.

friz'zle, *n.*, a curl; a lock of hair crisped; *v.t.* and *i.*, to curl or crisp; to fry with a spluttering noise.

friz'zled, *p.p.*, frizzle.

friz'zler, *n.*, one who, or that which, frizzles.

friz'zling, *pr.p.*, frizzle.

friz'zly, *adj.*, curly.

friz'zy, *adj.*, curly or crispy.

fro, *adv.*, from; away; back.

frock, *n.*, a gown.

frock'coat, *n.*, a man's coat with full skirts reaching to the knees.

frocked, *adj.*, clothed in a frock.

froe, *n.*, a cleaving tool with the handle set at right angles to the blade. (Also *frow.*)

Froebel'ian, *adj.*, pert. or rel. to the kindergarten system of education; *n.*, a kindergarten teacher.

Froe'belism, *n.*, the kindergarten system of education originated by Froebel, the German educationalist.

frog, *n.*, an amphibious animal with great powers of leaping; a tender horn in a horse's hoof; a fastening for a coat in the form of a tassel or loop; *v.t.*, to ornament with frogs.

frog'gy, *adj.*, like a frog, abounding in frogs; *n.*, a Frenchman (*slang*).

frog'hopper, *n.*, a small leaping insect.

frog'man, *n.*, a person equipped for underwater operations.

frog'march, *n.*, the method of carrying a resisting person by holding each limb; *v.t.*, to conduct a person in this fashion.

frol'ic, *adj.*, full of mirth; *n.*, a merry-making; *v.i.*, to gambol; to play merry tricks.

frol'icked, *p.p.*, frolic.

frol'icking, *pr.p.*, frolic.

frol'icsome, *adj.*, sportive.

frol'icsomely, *adv.*, playfully.

frol'icsomeness, *n.*, sportiveness.

from, *prep.*, out of; by reason of.

frond, *n.*, a fern-leaf.

fron'dage, *n.*, fronds collectively.

Fronde, *n.*, violent opposition, esp. in politics (from a 17th Cent. political movement in France).

frondesce', *v.i.*, to become leafy.

frondes'cence, *n.*, the act of bursting into leaf.

frondose', *adj.*, covered with leaves.

fron'dous, *adj.*, producing leaves and flowers on the same part.

front, *adj.*, pert or rel. to the front; *n.*, the part of anything directed forward; the foremost part; *v.t.*, to face; to confront; to adorn in front.

front'age, *n.*, the whole extent of the front.

front'ager, *n.*, one who owns land abutting on a road.

fron'tal, *adj.*, pert. or rel. to the forehead; directed towards the front; *n.*, a fillet for the forehead; a frontlet.

front'ate, *adj.*, growing broader and broader.

front'ed, *p.p.*, front.

fron'tier, *n.*, the border of a country where it adjoins another.

Fron'tignac, *n.*, a muscat wine (*Fr.*).

front'ing, *pr.p.*, front.

fron'tispiece, *n.*, an ornamental figure or picture at the beginning of a book.

front'less, *adj.*, wanting modesty; unblushing.

front'let, *n.*, a band worn on the forehead.

fron'ton, *n.*, a pediment (*Fr.*).

front'ward, *adv.*, towards the front.

frore, *adj.*, frosty, frozen (*poet.*).

frost, *n.*, freezing weather; frozen dew; coldness; *v.t.*, to cover with anything resembling hoar-frost, such as white sugar.

frost'bite, *n.*, a state of arrested circulation in any part of the body, due to exposure to frost.

frost'bitten, *adj.*, affected with frostbite.

frost'ed, *p.p.*, frost.

frost'ily, *adv.*, in a frosty manner; coldly.

frost'iness, *n.*, the quality of being frosty.

frost'ing, *n.*, a covering resembling frost, esp. on a cake; *pr.p.*, frost.

frost'work, *n.*, the beautiful covering of hoar-frost deposited on trees, etc.

frost'y, *adj.*, attended with frost; coldhearted.

froth, *n.*, foam; bubbly liquid; *v.i.*, to foam.

frothed, *p.p.*, froth.

froth'ily, *adv.*, in a frothy manner.

froth'iness, *n.*, the state of being frothy.

froth'ing, *pr.p.*, froth.

froth'y, *adj.*, foamy; given to empty display.

frou'-frou, n., a rustling, as of silk (Fr.).

frounce, n., a curl, plait or flounce; a disease of hawks and horses; v.t., to adorn with fringes, plaits, etc.

frounced, p.p., frounce.

froun'cing, pr.p., frounce.

frou'zy, adj., i.q. frowzy.

frow, n., i.q. froe.

frow, n., a Dutchwoman.

fro'ward, adj., perverse; disobedient; peevish.

fro'wardly, adv., perversely; disobediently.

fro'wardness, n., the quality of being froward.

frown, n., a contraction or wrinkling of the brow, expressing displeasure; v.i., to knit the brow.

frowned, p.p., frown.

frown'ing, pr.p., frown.

frown'ingly, adv., in a frowning manner.

frowst, n., fusty heat (colloq.).

frow'sty, adj., hot and stuffy.

frow'ziness, n., the state of being frowzy.

frow'zy, adj., musty; dingy; slovenly. (Also frouzy.)

froze, p.p., freeze.

fro'zen, p.p., freeze.

fructes'cence, n., the fruiting season.

fructif'erous, adj., producing fruit.

fructifica'tion, n., the act of forming fruit; fecundation.

fruc'tified, p.p., fructify.

fruc'tify, v.i., to produce fruit; to come to success; v.t., to fertilize.

fruc'tifying, pr.p., fructify.

fruc'tose, n., fruit sugar.

fruc'tuous, adj., full of fruit.

fru'gal, adj., thrifty; sparing.

frugal'ity, n., a prudent and sparing use of anything.

fru'gally, adv., in a frugal manner.

frugif'erous, adj., producing fruit or crops.

frugiv'orous, adj., feeding on fruit or seeds.

fruit, n., the succulent edible product of certain plants, usually containing the seeds; seed; produce; result; v.i., to bear fruit; v.t., to cause to bear fruit.

fruit'age, n., fruit collectively; produce.

fruit'arian, n., one who lives on fruit.

fruit'-cake, n., a cake containing currants, raisins, etc.

fruit'ed, adj., abounding in fruit; p.p., fruit.

fruit'er, n., a fruit-ship; a fruit-bearing tree; a fruit grower.

fruit'erer, n., a seller of fruits.

fruit'ery, n., a repository for fruit.

fruit'ful, adj., prolific; fertile; productive.

fruit'fully, adv., in a fruitful way.

fruit'fulness, n., productiveness; fertility.

fruit'-grower, n., one who grows fruit.

fruit'ing, n., the process of forming fruit; pr.p., fruit.

frui'tion, n., the use of anything, accompanied with pleasure; a successful outcome.

fruit'-knife, n., a special knife for cutting fruit, usually with an acid-resisting blade.

fruit'less, adj., devoid of fruit; vain.

fruit'lessly, adv., in a fruitless manner.

fruit'lessness, n., unprofitableness.

fruit'let, n., a drupel (bot.); fruit in which a stone is enclosed.

fruit'-pigeon, n., a pigeon that feeds on fruit.

fruit'salad, n., a mixture of sliced fruits.

fruit'-tree, n., a tree specially cultivated for its fruit.

fruit'y, adj., resembling fruit; having the taste of fruit.

frumenta'ceous, adj., resembling wheat or some other cereal.

fru'menty, n., i.q. furmenty.

frump, n., a bad-tempered, old-fashioned, dowdy woman.

frump'iness, n., dowdiness.

frump'ish, adj., old-fashioned, dowdy (colloq.).

frump'ishly, adv., in a frumpish way.

frump'ishness, n., i.q. frumpiness.

frump'y, adj., i.q. frumpish.

frush, adj., brittle.

frus'trate, v.t., to defeat; to balk.

frus'trated, p.p., frustrate.

frus'trating, pr.p., frustrate.

frustra'tion, n., the act of frustrating.

frus'tule, n., a two-valved shell of a diatom.

frus'tum, n., the part of a solid left after cutting off the top by a plane.

frutes'cence, n., the quality of being shrublike.

frutes'cent, adj., shrubby.

frut'ex, n., a shrub.

fru'ticose, adj., pert. or rel. to shrubs.

fru'ticous, adj., i.q. fruticose.

frutic'ulose, adj., branching like a shrub.

fry, n., anything fried; the young of fishes; v.t., to cook with oil or fat in a pan over heat.

fry'er, n., one who, or that which, fries. (Also frier.)

fry'ing, pr.p., fry.

fry'ing-pan, n., a long-handled pan used for frying.

fu'ar, n., one who holds a feu.

fub, n., a young, plump person.

fub'sy, adj., fat or squat.

fu'cate, adj., painted; disguised with paint.

fu'cated, adj., i.q. fucate.

fuch'sia, n., a flowering shrub with beautiful funnel-shaped, deciduous blossoms.

fuch'sine, n., the salt of rosaniline giving a deep red dye.

fuciv'orous, adj., subsisting on seaweed.

fu'coid, adj., pert. or rel. to seaweed.

fucoi'dal, adj., i.q. fucoid.

fu'cus, n., a tough, leathery, brownish-green seaweed.

fud'dle, v.i., to drink to excess; to addle the brain; v.t., to make tipsy.

fud'dled, p.p., fuddle.

fud'dler, n., a drunkard.

fud'dling, pr.p., fuddle.

fud'dy-duddy, adj., old-fashioned; n., an old fogy.

fudge, n., a made-up story; nonsense; a sweetmeat; v.t., to make up or fabricate.

Fue'gian, n., a native of Tierra del Fuego.

fueh'rer, n., a leader (Ger.). (Also führer.)

fu'el, n., that which is used to feed fire or provide a driving force; v.t., to feed fire.

fu'elled, p.p., fuel.

fuel'ling, n., the act of providing fuel; pr.p., fuel.

fug, n., a stuffy atmosphere (colloq.).

fuga'cious, adj., fleeting.

fugac'ity, n., transitoriness.

fug'al, adj., pert. or rel. to a fugue, containing repetitions or imitations of a given musical theme.

fug'ally, adv., in a fugal way.

fuga'to, adv., in fugue style (mus., It.).

fugg'y, adj., stuffy (colloq.).

fu'gitive, adj., fleeting; not fixed or durable; fleeing from danger, duty, etc.; n., one who flees.

fu'gitively, adv., in a fugitive manner.

fu'gitiveness, n., the state of being a fugitive.

fu'gleman, n., a file-leader; any one who sets an example for others to follow.

fugue, n., a musical composition in parts which follow each other regularly.

fu'guist, n., a composer of fugues.

führer, n., i.q. fuehrer.

ful'crate, adj., having a fulcrum.

ful'crum, n., a support; the point about which a lever turns.

fulfil', v.t., to accomplish; to perform; to complete.

fulfilled', p.p., fulfil.

fulfil'ler, n., one who fulfils.

fulfil'ling, pr.p., fulfil.

fulfil'ment, n., completion; performance.

ful'gency, n., splendour.

ful'gent, adj., dazzlingly bright.

ful'gently, adv., very brightly.

ful'gural, adj., flashing like lightning.

ful'gurite, n., an explosive.

ful'ham, n., weighted, and hence unfair, dice.

fuli'ginous, adj., sooty; dusky.

full, adj., having all it can contain; entire; adv., quite; n., the utmost extent; v.t., to thicken woollen fibres; to cleanse or bleach.

full'-aged, adj., mature.

full'-blood'ed, adj., thoroughbred; with maximum effort.

full'-blown, adj., fully developed.

full'-dress, n., dress worn at formal, social gatherings; the military uniform for ceremonial parades.

fulled, p.p., full.

full'er, adj., comp. of full; n., one who fulls cloth; one who bleaches.

full'er's earth', n., a kind of clay useful in cleansing cloth.

full'ery, n., a fulling-works.

full'est, adj., super. of full.

full'-faced, adj., with a full face; directly from the front.

full'grown, adj., mature.

full'-heart'ed, adj., full of courage or sympathy.

full'ing, n., the business of a fuller; pr.p., full.

full'ing-mill, n., a mill for fulling cloth.

full'-length, adj., extending for the whole length.

full'ness, n., i.q. fulness.

full'-pitch, n., a ball that pitches inside the crease in cricket.

full'-sized, adj., of full size.

full'-stop, n., a period used in punctuation; the end.

full'-swing, adv., with zest and impetuosity.

full'-time, adj., all the time, as opposed to half-time or part-time.

full'y, adv., completely.

full'y-fashioned, adj., well-shaped; completely shaped (esp. for the legs).

ful'mar, n., a marine swimming bird.

ful'minant, adj., thundering; making a loud noise.

ful'minate, n., an explosive compound; an unstable chemical; v.i., to thunder; to explode with a loud noise; to threaten or denounce; to declaim loudly against.

ful'minated, p.p., fulminate.

ful'minating, adj., thundering; exploding; detonating; pr.p., fulminate.

fulmina'tion, n., the act of fulminating; a menace; a censure.

ful'minatory, adj., sending forth thunders.

ful'mine, v.t. and i., to send forth lightning or thunder (poet.).

fulmin'ic, adj., pert. or rel. to the hypothetical parent of the fulminates (chem.).

ful'ness, n., the state of being full or filled.

ful'some, adj., offensive from excessive praise; nauseous.

ful'somely, adv., in a fulsome way.

ful'someness, n., the state of being fulsome.

fulves'cent, adj., i.q. fulvous.

ful'vid, adj., i.q. fulvous.

ful'vous, adj., tawny yellow.

fumade', n., a smoked pilchard (Span.).

fum'arole, n., a smoke-hole in a volcanic region (Fr.).

fumato'rium, n., a place for fumigating plants or other objects.

fum'atory, adj., i.q. fumitory.

fum'ble, v.i., to grope about; to use the hands awkwardly.

fum'bled, p.p., fumble.

fum'bler, n., one who fumbles.

fum'bling, pr.p., fumble.

fum'blingly, adv., in a fumbling way.

fume, *n.*, a smoky, volatile matter, usually narcotic; mental agitation; *v.i.*, to pass off in a vapour; to be in a rage; *v.t.*, to fumigate.

fumed, *p.p.*, fume.

fu′mer, *n.*, one who, or that which, fumes.

fu′met, *n.*, the excrement of deer.

fu′mette, *n.*, the smell of high game cooking.

fumif′erous, *adj.*, producing smoke.

fu′migate, *v.t.*, to apply smoke to; to render free from infestation by smoking.

fu′migated, *p.p.*, fumigate.

fu′migating, *pr.p.*, fumigate.

fumiga′tion, *n.*, the act of fumigating.

fu′migator, *n.*, one who, or that which, fumigates.

fu′ming, *pr.p.*, fume.

fu′mingly, *adv.*, excitedly; angrily.

fu′mitory, *n.*, a common plant with purple flowers. (Also *fumatory*.)

fu′mous, *adj.*, *i.q.* fumy.

fu′my, *adj.*, producing fumes; apt to fume or fret.

fun, *n.*, frolicsome amusement.

funam′bulate, *v.i.*, to walk on a rope.

funambula′tion, *n.*, the art of walking on a rope.

funam′bulatory, *adj.*, pert. or rel. to rope walking.

funam′bulist, *n.*, a rope-walker.

func′tion, *n.*, office; duty; business; a formal ceremony; a purpose; a mathematical quantity depending on another; *v.i.*, to operate or work correctly.

func′tional, *adj.*, pert. or rel. to a function or functions.

func′tionalism, *n.*, the design of anything with primary regard to its purpose.

func′tionally, *adv.*, in a functional way.

func′tionary, *n.*, one who has special duties to perform.

func′tionate, *v.i.*, *i.q.* function.

func′tioned, *p.p.*, function.

func′tioning, *pr.p.*, function.

fund, *n.*, money used as capital; part of the national debt; a store; a supply; *v.t.*, to put into the form of bonds or stock bearing interest.

fun′dament, *n.*, a foundation; the anus.

fundamen′tal, *adj.*, essential; at the foundation of something; *n.*, a leading principle or rule.

fundamen′talism, *n.*, belief in the literal truth of the Bible against evolution, etc.

fundamen′talist, *n.*, one who professes fundamentalism.

fundamen′tally, *adv.*, essentially.

fund′ed, *p.p.*, fund.

fund′-holder, *n.*, one who has property in the public funds.

fund′ing, *pr.p.*, fund.

fun′dus, *n.*, the base of any hollow anatomical organ.

funeb′rial, *adj.*, of a funeral.

fu′neral, *adj.*, used at the interment of the dead; *n.*, the procedure and ceremony attendant upon the disposal of a corpse.

fun′erary, *adj.*, *i.q.* funebrial.

fune′real, *adj.*, dismal; gloomy.

fune′really, *adv.*, in a funereal way.

fu′nest, *adj.*, causing death; sad.

fun′gi, *n. pl.*, cryptogamous plants, including mushrooms, moulds, etc.

Fun′gia, *n.*, a genus of corals with radiating plants like the gills of a mushroom.

fun′gible, *adj.*, that can serve for, or be replaced by, something else answering the same definition (*leg.*).

fun′gic, *adj.*, pert. or rel. to fungi.

fun′gicide, *n.*, a fungus-destroying substance.

fun′giform, *adj.*, having the form of a fungus.

fun′goid, *adj.*, like a fungus.

fun′gous, *adj.*, *i.q.* fungoid; growing quickly but not durable.

fun′gus, *n.*, a vegetable parasite, usually spongy.

fungusiv′orous, *adj.*, *i.q.* fungoid.

fu′nicle, *n.*, a little ligament attached to a seed.

funic′ular, *adj.*, depending on the tension of a cord; worked by a cable.

funic′ulus, *n.*, *i.q.* funicle, funis.

fu′nis, *n.*, the umbilical cord.

funk, *n.*, fear (*slang*); *v.i.*, to flinch; to be frightened; *v.t.*, to evade.

funk′-hole, *n.*, any place or position of shelter from danger.

funk′y, *adj.*, cowardly (*colloq.*).

fun′nel, *n.*, a hollow cone with a pipe leading from its apex; the chimney of a powered ship; *v.i.*, to converge.

fun′nelled, *adj.*, like a funnel; *p.p.*, funnel.

fun′nelling, *pr.p.*, funnel.

fun′nier, *adj.*, *comp.* of funny.

fun′niest, *adj.*, *super.* of funny.

fun′nily, *adv.*, in a funny way.

fun′niment, *n.*, a joke, drollery.

fun′ny, *adj.*, comical.

fun′ny-bone, *n.*, the bony projection of the elbow.

fur, *adj.*, made of fur; *n.*, the short, soft hair growing on the skin of certain animals; *v.t.* and *i.*, to cover with fur.

fu′racious, *adj.*, thievish.

fur′below, *n.*, a kind of flounce or plaited border to a gown or petticoat; a kind of seaweed.

fur′bish, *v.t.*, to brighten; to polish up.

fur′bishable, *adj.*, that may be furbished.

fur′bished, *p.p.*, furbish.

fur′bisher, *n.*, one who or that which, furbishes.

fur′bishing, *pr.p.*, furbish.

fur′cal, *adj.*, *i.q.* furcate.

fur'cate, *adj.*, forked.

fur'cated, *adj.*, *i.q.* furcate.

furca'tion, *n.*, a forking or branching.

fur'cula, *n.*, the wishbone.

fur'cular, *adj.*, pert. or rel. to the furcula.

fur'fur, *n.*, scurf.

furfura'ceous, *adj.*, scurfy; covered with bran-like scales (*bot.*).

furibon'do, *adv.*, with energy (*mus.*, *It.*).

furios'ity, *n.*, a raving fury.

furio'so, *adv.*, with great energy (*mus.*, *It.*).

fu'rious, *adj.*, raging; frenzied; violent.

fu'riously, *adv.*, in a furious manner.

fu'riousness, *n.*, the state of being furious.

furl, *v.t.*, to wrap (a sail) close and fasten.

furled, *p.p.*, furl.

furl'ing, *pr.p.*, furl.

fur'long, *n.*, the eighth part of a mile.

fur'lough, *n.*, leave of absence given to a soldier.

fur'menty, *n.*, a dish made of hulled wheat boiled in milk and seasoned. (Also *frumenty*.)

fur'nace, *n.*, a structure containing a very hot fire.

fur'nish, *v.t.*, to equip; to supply.

fur'nished, *p.p.*, furnish.

fur'nisher, *n.*, one who furnishes.

furn'ishing, *pr.p.*, furnish.

fur'nishment, *n.*, a furnishing; a supply.

furn'iture, *n.*, equipment, esp. chairs, tables and fittings for domestic purposes.

fu'ror, *n.*, rage; mania.

furo're, *n.*, great excitement; enthusiasm (*It.*).

furred, *p.p.*, fur.

fur'rier, *n.*, a dealer in furs.

fur'riery, *n.*, the trade of a furrier.

fur'ring, *pr.p.*, fur.

fur'row, *n.*, a groove; a wrinkle; *v.t.*, to plough; to mark with wrinkles.

fur'rowed, *adj.*, having grooves or furrows; *p.p.*, furrow.

fur'rowing, *pr.p.*, furrow.

fur'rowless, *adj.*, without furrows.

fur'row-weed, *n.*, a weed which grows on the furrows of ploughed land.

fur'rowy, *adj.*, marked with furrows.

fur'ry, *adj.*, covered with, or resembling, fur.

fur'ther, *adj.*, additional, another; *adv.*, moreover; in addition; *v.t.*, to promote.

fur'therance, *n.*, the act of furthering.

fur'thered, *p.p.*, further.

fur'therer, *n.*, a promoter.

fur'thering, *pr.p.*, further.

fur'thermore, *adv.*, moreover.

fur'thermost, *adj.*, furthest; most remote; (more correctly *farthermost*).

fur'thest, *adj.* and *adv.*, most distant; (more correctly *farthest*).

fur'tive, *adj.*, stealthy.

fur'tively, *adv.*, stealthily.

fur'tiveness, *n.*, stealth.

fur'uncle, *n.*, a boil, a tumour.

fur'uncular, *adj.*, pert. or rel. to a boil or tumour.

fur'unculous, *adj.*, *i.q.* furuncular.

fu'ry, *n.*, rage; madness.

furze, *n.*, gorse.

furze'chat, *n.*, the whinchat.

furz'y, *adj.*, overgrown with furze.

fu'sain, *n.*, fine charcoal crayon or a drawing done with it.

fusca'tion, *n.*, obscurity; darkening.

fus'cous, *adj.*, brown; dark-coloured.

fuse, *n.*, a tube filled with combustibles, used in discharging a shell and in blasting; a protective device in an electrical circuit; *v.t.*, to liquefy by heat; to unite as if melted together by heat. (Also *fuze*.)

fused, *p.p.*, fuse.

fusee', *n.*, a small musket; a kind of match; a fuse; the conical piece in a watch or clock round which the chain or cord is wound.

fu'selage, *n.*, the framework of an aircraft.

fu'sel-oil, *n.*, an acrid oil in spirits distilled from barley, potatoes, etc.

fusibil'ity, *n.*, the quality of being fusible.

fu'sible, *adj.*, capable of being fused or melted.

fu'siform, *adj.*, spindle-shaped.

fu'sil, *n.*, a light musket formerly used.

fusilier', *n.*, an infantry soldier; a rifleman.

fusillade', *n.*, a volley of shots.

fu'sing, *pr.p.*, fuse.

fu'sion, *n.*, melting by heat; uniting as if melted together; complete union.

fu'sionist, *n.*, one who, or that which, fuses.

fuss, *n.*, unnecessary trouble; *v.i.*, to make much ado about nothing.

fussed, *p.p.*, fuss.

fuss'ily, *adv.*, in a fussy manner.

fuss'iness, *n.*, the character or state of being fussy.

fuss'ing, *pr.p.*, fuss.

fuss'-pot, *n.*, a fussy person (*colloq.*).

fuss'y, *adj.*, bustling; making a fuss.

fust, *n.*, a musty smell; *v.i.*, to become musty.

fustanell'a, *n.*, a Greek's white kilt.

fus'tian, *n.*, a coarse cotton cloth with a pile like velvet, but shorter; inflated writing; bombast.

fus'tianist, *n.*, one who writes in a pompous style.

fus'tic, *n.*, the wood of a West Indian tree used in dyeing yellow.

fus'tigate, *v.t.*, to club or cudgel.

fustiga'tion, *n.*, a cudgelling.

fust'iness, *n.*, the state of being fusty.

fust'y, *adj.*, musty; ill-smelling.

fut, *n.*, *i.q.* phut.

futch'el(l), *n.*, a timber supporting pole, axlebar or shafts of a carriage.

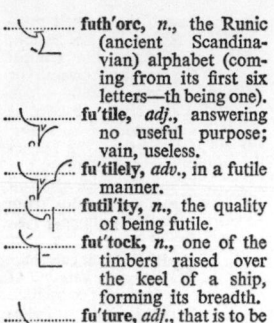

futh'orc, *n.,* the Runic (ancient Scandinavian) alphabet (coming from its first six letters—th being one).

fu'tile, *adj.,* answering no useful purpose; vain, useless.

fu'tilely, *adv.,* in a futile manner.

futil'ity, *n.,* the quality of being futile.

fut'tock, *n.,* one of the timbers raised over the keel of a ship, forming its breadth.

fu'ture, *adj.,* that is to be hereafter; *n.,* time to come.

fu'tureless, *adj.,* without prospects.

fu'turism, *n.,* the doctrines of futurist art.

fu'turist, *n.,* one who believes that the Old Testament prophecies are yet to be fulfilled; an impressionist painter, sculptor or poet who claims that his art is the art of the future.

futuris'tic, *adj.,* pert. or rel. to futurism.

futu'rity, *n.,* time yet to come.

fuze, *n.* and *v.t.,* *i.q.* fuse.

fuzz, *n.,* fine, light particles; fine matted hair.

fuzz'-ball, *n.,* a sort of fungus full of fine powder.

fuzz'ily, *adv.,* in a fuzzy manner.

fuzz'iness, *n.,* the state of being fuzzy.

fuzz'le, *v.t.,* to intoxicate (*colloq.*).

fuzz'y, *adj.,* light and spongy; shaggy.

fy (fie), *interj.,* expressing impatience or disapproval.

fyl'fot, *n.,* a swastika, esp. one turned counter-clockwise.

G

gab, *n.*, foolish chatter; a hook on a lever which forms a temporary connection; the abbrev. of gaberdine; *v.i.*, to talk a lot about nothing.

gab'ardine, *n.*, a corded cloth used chiefly for raincoats.

gab'ble, *n.*, rapid talk; *v.i.*, to chatter without meaning; *v.t.*, to read hurriedly without attention to sense.

gab'bled, *p.p.*, gabble.

gab'bler, *n.*, one who gabbles.

gab'bling, *pr.p.*, gabble.

gab'bro, *n.*, an igneous rock composed mainly of felspar and resembling dolerite.

ga'bel(le), *n.*, a tax on salt (*Fr.*).

gab'erdine, *n.*, a fine cloth frock; see also gabardine.

gaberlun'zie, *n.*, a wandering beggar (*Scot.*).

ga'bion, *n.*, a wickerwork cylinder containing earth.

gabionade', *n.*, a defensive work consisting of gabions.

ga'ble, *n.*, a triangular elevation in a building.

ga'bled, *adj.*, having gables.

ga'ble-end, *n.*, the outside wall of a building having a gable.

ga'blet, *n.*, a little gable.

ga'ble-win'dow, *n.*, a window in a gable or with a gable above it.

ga'by, *n.*, a fool (*colloq.*).

gad, *interj.*, surprise; *n.*, a pointed tool; *v.i.*, to ramble purposelessly.

gad'about, *n.*, *i.q.* gadder.

gad'ded, *p.p.*, gad.

gad'der, *n.*, one who gads.

gad'ding, *pr.p.*, gad.

gad'fly, *n.*, a fly that stings cattle.

gad(d)i, *n.*, the cushioned throne of an Indian ruler; the regal position.

gadg'et, *n.*, any small ingenious device.

Gadhel'ic, *adj.* and *n.*, Gaelic in its wider sense (*lit.*).

gad'oid, *adj.*, of the cod family; *n.*, a fish of the cod family.

gadroon', *n.*, a moulding consisting of a series of convex curves (*archit.*).

gad'wall, *n.*, a large, freshwater migratory duck of America and N. Europe.

Gael, *n.*, one of Gaelic stock.

Gael'ic, *adj.*, pert. or rel. to the Gaels; *n.*, the Gaelic language.

gaff, *n.*, an iron-hooked stick; a low-class theatre; *v.t.*, to land a fish with the gaff.

gaffe, *n.*, a blunder; an indiscreet remark or action (*Fr.*).

gaffed, *p.p.*, gaff.

gaf'fer, *n.*, a grandfather; a foreman.

gaf'fing, *pr.p.*, gaff.

gag, *n.*, something stuffed into the mouth; *v.t.*, to stop the mouth.

ga'ga, *adj.*, fatuous, senile, (*slang, Fr.*).

gage, *n.*, a pledge, a challenge; a kind of plum; *v.t.*, to wager, pledge, guarantee.

gaged, *p.p.*, gage.

ga'ger, *n.*, one who gages.

gagged, *p.p.*, gag.

gag'ger, *n.*, one who gags.

gag'ging, *n.*, a regurgitation in revulsion; *pr.p.*, gag.

gag'gle, *n.*, a flock of geese; *v.i.*, to cackle.

gag'gled, *p.p.*, gaggle.

gag'gling, *pr.p.*, gaggle.

ga'ging, *pr.p.*, gage.

gaie'ment, *adv.*, briskly, in a lively style (*mus., Fr.*).

gai'ety, *n.*, mirth, cheerfulness, finery. (Also *gayety*.)

gai'ly, *adv.*, merrily, cheerfully, finely. (Also *gayly*.)

gain, *n.*, profit, advantage; a notch; *v.t.*, to acquire, to obtain.

gain'able, *adj.*, able to be gained.

gained, *p.p.*, gain.

gain'er, *n.*, one who gains.

gain'ful, *adj.*, profitable.

gain'fully, *adv.*, profitably.

gain'fulness, *n.*, the state of being gainful.

gain'ing, *pr.p.*, gain.

gain'less, *adj.*, without profit.

gain'ly, *adj.*, comely.

gain'said, *p.p.*, gainsay.

gain'say, *v.t.*, to contradict, to oppose.

gain'sayer, *n.*, one who gainsays.

gain'saying, *pr.p.*, gainsay.

gair'ish, *adj.*, *i.q.* garish.

gair'ishly, *adv.*, *i.q.* garishly.

gair'ishness, *n.*, *i.q.* garishness.

gait, *n.*, the manner of walking, bearing.

gait'er, *n.*, an anklecovering.

ga'la, *n.*, a show, festivity.

galac'tic, *adj.*, pert. or rel. to milk or to a galaxy.

galactom'eter, *n.*, an instrument for testing the purity of milk. (Also *lactometer*.)

galac'tose, *n.*, a sweet, crystalline glucose obtained from milksugar.

gal'antine, *n.*, a quantity of white meat, boned, compressed and served cold.

galan'ty show, *n.*, a pantomime on a screen made by puppet shadows.

galate′a, n., a superior blue and white cotton fabric.

Gala′tian, adj., pert. or rel. to Galatia, a region of Asia Minor; n., a native of G.

gal′axy, n., the Milky Way; a system of stars; a notable assembly.

gal′banum, n., a gum resin.

gale, n., a violent windstorm; a periodic payment of rent; bogmyrtle.

ga′lea, n., a helmet (Lat.).

ga′leate, adj., helmeted; helmet-like.

ga′leated, adj., i.q. galeate.

galeen′y, n., a guineafowl.

gale′na, n., the principal ore of lead.

galen′ic, adj., pert. or rel. to Galen (the Greek writer on medicine).

galen′ical, adj., i.q. Galenic.

ga′lenism, n., the teaching of Galen.

ga′lenist, n., a disciple of Galen.

Gali′cian, adj., pert. or rel. to Galicia, a province of north-west Spain; n., a native of G.

Galile′an, adj., pert. or rel. to Galilee in Palestine or to Galileo, the astronomer; n., a native of G.

gal′ilee, n., a porch at a church entrance.

gal′ingale, n., the aromatic root of E. Indian plants used in cookery and medicine; a kind of sedge of southern Britain.

gal′(l)iot, n., a variety of trading vessel.

gal′ipot, n., a juice exuded from pine trees (Fr.).

gall, n., bile; rancour, malignity; v.t., to fret, to chafe.

gal′lant, adj., brave, spirited, chivalrous; n., a fashionable person, a beau.

gallant′, adj., deferential to women; chivalrous; v.t., to pay court to.

gallant′ed, p.p., gallant.

gallant′ing, pr.p., gallant.

gal′lantly, adv., bravely, chivalrously.

gallant′ly, adv., politely.

gallant′ness, n., the state or quality of being gallant.

gal′lantry, n., bravery, chivalrousness.

galled, p.p., gall.

gal′leon, n., a Spanish three-decker ship.

gal′lery, n., a corridor; a long room leading to others; a balcony. in or round a room; a place for exhibiting works of art; spectators; the highest tier of seats in a theatre.

gal′ley, n., a low, flat, oar-propelled vessel; a ship's kitchen; a frame for holding printing type.

gal′ley-proof, n., an impression from a printer's galley, sent for correction before being made up into page form, etc.

gal′ley-slave, n., a slave who rowed a galley.

galliam′bic, n., a classical metre.

gal′liard, n., a gayspirited person; a quick, Spanish dance.

Gal′lic, adj., pert. or rel. to Gaul (France).

Gal′lican, adj., i.q. Gallic.

Gal′licanism, n., the system or principles of French Catholics who favoured the restriction of Papal interference.

gal′licanist, n., a follower of Gallicanism.

gal′lice, adv., in French (used in giving the French for an English phrase, etc.).

Gal′licism, n., a French idiom.

Gal′licize, v.t., to make conformable to French.

galligas′kins, n., leggings.

gallimau′fry, n., a medley.

gallina′ceous, adj., pert. or rel. to domestic birds, pheasants, etc.

gallina′zo, n., an American vulture.

gall′ing, adj., irritating, vexing; pr.p., gall.

gal′linipper, n., a species of mosquito.

gal′linule, n., an American moor-hen bird.

gal′lio, n., one who refuses to interfere outside his province.

gal′lipot, n., a glazed earthenware pot.

gal′lium, n., a soft, bluish-white metal.

gallivant′, v.i., to go about pleasure-seeking.

gallivant′ed, p.p., gallivant.

gallivant′ing, pr.p., gallivant.

gal′liwasp, n., a W. Indian lizard.

gall′nut, n., a round excrescence on the oak.

Galloman′ia, n., a craze for French fashions, manners, literature, etc.

gal′lon, n., a liquid measure of four quarts.

galloon′, n., a lace made of gold, silver or silk.

gallooned′, adj., decorated with galloon.

gal′lop, n., a horse's gait at speed; a ride at full speed; v.i., to run full speed.

gallopade′, n., a rapid dance.

gal′loped, p.p., gallop.

gal′loper, n., one who gallops; a light fieldgun used by cavalry.

gal′loping, pr.p., gallop.

Gallovid′ian, adj., pert. or rel. to Galloway; n., a native of G.

gal′loway, n., a small horse of the Galloway breed.

gal′lows, n., an erection for hanging criminals.

gall′stone, n., a formation in the gall bladder.

Gal′lup poll, n., a test of how a representative sample of the public will vote, used esp. for forecasting the result.

galoot′, n., a clumsy lout (colloq.).

gal′op, n., a fast dance.

galore′, adj., abundant, in plenty.

galosh′, n., a rubber over-shoe. (Also golosh.)

galumph′, v.i., to prance about triumphantly.

galvan′ic, adj., pert. or rel. to galvanism.

gal′vanism, n., a species of electricity.

gal′vanist, *n.*, one who uses galvanism medically.

gal′vanize, *v t*, to shock or stimulate; to coat with a metal (by electrolysis or not).

gal′vanized, *p.p.*, galvanize. (Applied to iron = coated with zinc.)

gal′vanizer, *n.*, anything that galvanizes.

gal′vanizing, *pr.p.*, galvanize.

galvanog′raphy, *n.*, an electrotype process of reproduction.

galvanol′ogist, *n.*, an expert in galvanology.

galvanol′ogy, *n.*, the study of galvanic phenomena.

galvanom′eter, *n.*, an instrument to measure the intensity of electric currents.

galvan′oscope, *n.*, a delicate instrument to measure electric currents.

Galwe′gian, *adj.*, pert. or rel. to Galway; *n.*, a native of G.

gam, *n.*, a complimentary visit; a school of whales; *v.t.*, to pay a call to (naut.); *v.i.*, to gather together in schools (a whaling term).

gama grass, *n.*, a tall, very productive fodder grass of southern U.S.A.

gam′ba, *n.*, an organstop; otherwise the *viol de Gamba.*

gambade′, *n.*, a flourish.

gamba′do, *n.*, *i.q.* gambade.

gam′bier, *n.*, the astringent extract of an oriental plant used in tanning, etc.

gam′bit, *n.*, one of the openings in chess; any initial move.

gam′ble, *n.*, a game of chance; a speculation; *v.i.*, to play for money; *v.t.*, to play away; to throw away.

gam′bled, *p.p.*, gamble.

gam′bler, *n.*, one who gambles.

gam′bling, *pr.p.*, gamble.

gamboge′, *adj.*, of gamboge colour; *n.*, a yellow gum-resin.

gambo′gian, *adj.*, pert. or rel. to gamboge.

gam′bol, *n.*, a frisking, a frolic; *v.i.*, to frisk or frolic.

gam′bol(l)ed, *p.p.*, gambol.

gam′bol(l)ing, *pr.p.*, gambol.

gam′brel, *n.*, a horse's hock; a bent stick.

gam′brel-roof, *n.*, a double-pitched roof.

gambroon′, *n.*, twilled linen used for linings.

game, *adj.*, sporting, plucky; *n.*, a sport or contest, play; wild animals pursued in sport; *v.i.*, to play for a stake.

game′-cock, *n.*, a fighting cock.

gamed, *p.p.*, game.

game′-fowl, *n. pl.*, birds trained to fight.

game′ful, *adj.*, sportive.

game′fully, *adv.*, sportively.

game′keeper, *n.*, one who looks after game.

game′ly, *adv.*, pluckily.

game′-preserve, *n.*, land strictly preserved for game for the sport and profit of the owner.

game′some, *adj.*, *i.q.* gameful.

game′somely, *adv.*, sportively.

game′someness, *n.*, playfulness, merriment.

game′ster, *n.*, a gambler.

gamete′, *n.*, a sexual protoplasmic cell that unites with another for reproduction.

gametogen′esis, *n.*, an abnormal form of fertilization caused by more than one of spermatozoa entering the ovum.

ga′min, *n.*, a street urchin (Fr.).

gam′ing, *pr.p.*, game.

ga′ming-house, *n.*, a house where gambling is carried on.

gam′ing-table, *n.*, a table used for gambling games.

gam′ma, *n.*, the Greek letter G.

gammad′ion, *n.*, the swastika or fylfot.

gam′ma-rays, *n. pl.*, short-wave rays emitted by radioactive material.

gam′mer, *n.*, grandmother.

gam′mon, *interj.*, nonsense; *v.t.*, to humbug or cheat; *n.*, smoked ham; a hoax.

gam′moned, *p.p.*, gammon.

gam′moning, *pr.p.*, gammon.

gamogen′esis, *n.*, sexual reproduction.

gamopet′alous, *adj.*, with petals united at the base (*bot.*).

gamosep′alous, *adj.*, with sepals cohering at the edges (*bot.*).

gamp, *n.*, a baggy umbrella (*colloq.*).

ga′mut, *n.*, the musical scale; an entire range.

gam′y, *adj.*, highflavoured; like game.

ganch, *v.t.*, to let fall on to sharp spikes.

ganched, *p.p.*, ganch.

ganch′ing, *pr.p.*, ganch.

gan′der, *n.*, the male of the goose.

gang, *n.*, a company, a band; *v.i.*, to go (*Scot.*).

gang′er, *n.*, a foreman worker or railway platelayer..

Ganget′ic, *adj.*, pert. or rel. to the River Ganges,

gang′liac, *adj.*, pert. or rel. to ganglions.

gang′liform, *adj.*, ganglion-shaped.

gang′ling, *adj.*, straggling, loosely formed.

gang′lioform, *adj.*, *i.q.* gangliform.

gang′lion, *n.*, a collection of nerves or nervecells.

gang′lionary, *adj.*, pert. or rel. to ganglion.

gang′lionated, *adj.*, *i.q.* gangliac.

ganglion′ic, *adj.*, *i.q.* ganglionary.

gang′renate, *adj.*, *i.q.* gangrenous.

gang′rene, *n.*, mortification of part of the body; *v.i.*, to mortify.

gang′rened, *p.p.*, gangrene.

gang′rening, *pr.p.*, gangrene.

gang′renous, *adj.*, mortifying.

gang′ster, *n.*, a member of a criminal gang.

gang′sterdom, *n.*, the area of jurisdiction of gangsters.

gang′sterism, *n.*, rough or criminal behaviour.

gangue, *n.*, a kind of earth containing ore.

gang'way, *n.,* a passage way; a way from ship to shore.

gan'ister, *n.,* a hard clay-rock found in Yorkshire and used for furnace linings, etc.

gan'net, *n.,* a species of sea-bird.

gan'oid, *adj.,* pert. or rel. to the Ganoidel (the class of fish, like the sturgeon, having shiny bony scales).

gant'let, *n., i.q.* gauntlet.

gan'try, *n.,* a barrel-stand; a platform for a moving crane.

Gan'ymede, *n.,* a cup-bearer, a waiter; the largest satellite of Jupiter (*astron.*).

gaol, *n.,* a prison; *v.t.,* to put into prison. (Also *jail.*)

gaol'bird, *n.,* one who has been in gaol. (Also *jailbird.*)

gaoled, *p.p.,* gaol.

gaol'ing, *pr.p.,* gaol.

gaol'er, *n.,* a prison-keeper; a warder. (Also *jailer.*)

gap, *n.,* an opening, a breach; *v.i.,* to yawn open.

gape, *v.i.,* to open the mouth wide, to yawn, to stare in amazement.

gaped, *p.p.,* gape.

ga'per, *n.,* one who gapes.

ga'ping, *pr.p.,* gape.

ga'pingly, *adv.,* in amazement.

gar, *v.t.,* to make, to cause (*Scot.*).

garage, *n.,* a place for storing or repairing automobiles.

garb, *n.,* dress, fashion of dress; *v.t.,* to clothe.

gar'bage, *n.,* refuse, offal.

garbed, *p.p.,* garb.

garb'ing, *pr.p.,* garb.

gar'ble, *v.t.,* to mix ready for selection at random; to confuse or misinterpret.

gar'bled, *adj.,* mixed, confused; *p.p.,* garble.

gar'bler, *n.,* one who garbles.

gar'bling, *pr.p.,* garble.

gar'board, *n.,* the planks on a ship's bottom next to the keel.

garçon', a boy, a waiter (*Fr.*).

gar'dant, *adj.,* on guard, confronting (*her.*).

gar'den, *n.,* cultivated ground for pleasure or for growing vegetables, or fruit and flowers; *v.i.,* to cultivate a garden.

gar'dened, *p.p.,* garden.

gar'dener, *n.,* one who gardens.

gar'den-frame, *n.,* a glass frame for forcing plants.

garde'nia, *n.,* a tropical plant with yellow or white flowers.

gar'dening, *n.,* the care of a garden; *pr.p.,* garden.

garden-par'ty, *n.,* a party held in private grounds or a garden.

gare, *n.,* the coarse wool on a sheep's leg.

gare'fowl, *n.,* the great auk.

gar'fish, *n.,* a long sea-fish with a sharp snout.

gar'ganey, *n.,* a kind of teal.

gargan'tuan, *adj.,* monstrous, enormous.

gar'garism, *n.,* gargling.

gar'garize, *v.i.,* to gargle.

gar'get, *n.,* a species of cattle-disease.

gar'gil, *n.,* a disease of geese.

gar'gle, *n.,* a wash for the inside of the throat; *v.t.* and *i.,* to wash and sterilize the inside of the throat.

gar'gled, *p.p.,* gargle.

gar'gling, *pr.p.,* gargle.

gar'goyle, *n.,* a projecting water-spout (*archit.*).

garibal'di, *n.,* a woman's or child's loose blouse, orig. bright red; a biscuit containing currants (*It.*).

gar'ish, *adj.,* gaudy, showy, but of no artistic merit.

gar'ishly, *adv.,* gaudily.

gar'ishness, *n.,* the state or quality of being garish.

gar'land, *n.,* a wreath of flowers; *v.t.,* to wreathe.

gar'lic, *n.,* a species of onion used to flavour dishes.

gar'ment, *n.,* an article of clothing.

gar'ner, *n.,* a granary; *v.t.,* to store, to gather up.

gar'nered, *p.p.,* garner.

gar'nering, *pr.p.,* garner.

gar'net, *n.,* a crystallized gem of reddish colour.

gar'nish, *v.t.,* to decorate, to embellish.

gar'nished, *p.p.,* garnish.

garnishee', *n.,* the temporary holder of property pending the settlement of a third party's claim; *v.t.,* to secure by garnishment.

garnisheed', *p.p.,* garnishee.

garnishee'ing, *pr.p.,* garnishee.

gar'nisher, *n.,* one who garnishes.

gar'nishing, *n.,* decorations for a dish at table; *pr.p.,* garnish.

gar'nishment, *n.,* decoration, embellishment; a warning.

gar'niture, *n.,* decoration.

garotte', *n., i.q.* garrotte.

ga'rous, *adj.,* pert. or rel. to garum.

gar'ret, *n.,* a small room at the top of a house; *v.t.,* to insert small pieces of stone in the joints of rough masonry (*archit.*).

gar'rison, *n.,* soldiers stationed in a fortified place; *v.t.,* to furnish a fortified place with soldiers.

gar'risoned, *p.p.,* garrison.

gar'risoning, *pr.p.,* garrison.

gar'ron, *n.,* a small inferior horse bred in Ireland and Scotland.

gar'rot, *n.,* a kind of sea duck (*Fr.*); a tourniquet which checks haemorrhage of an amputated limb.

garrotte', *n.,* a Spanish mode of execution by strangling; *v.t.,* to strangle; to strangle and rob.

garrot'ted, *p.p.,* garrotte.

garrot'ter, *n.,* one who garrottes.

garrot'ting, *pr.p.,* garrotte.

garru'lity, *n.,* talkativeness.

gar'rulous, *adj.*, talkative.

gar'rulously, *adv.*, talkatively.

gar'rulousness, *n.*, *i.q.* garrulity.

gar'ter, *n.*, a band round a stocking; *v.t.*, to fasten with a garter; to invest with the Order of the Garter.

gar'tered, *p.p.*, garter.

gar'tering, *pr.p.*, garter.

gar'ter-snake, *n.*, a nonvenomous, striped, grass snake of the U.S.A.

garth, *n.*, an enclosure.

ga'rum, *n.*, pickled fish.

gar'vie, *n.*, the sprat (*Scot.*). (Also *garvock*.)

gar'vock, *n.*, *i.q.* garvie.

gas, *n.*, the abbrev. of gasoline (*Amer.*); the common term for coal-gas and natural gas used for domestic heating; highly rarefied matter; matter in a non-solid, nonliquid form; *v.t.*, to supply, or apply, gas to; to poison with gas; *v.i.*, to talk boastfully, to talk volubly (*colloq.*).

gas'bag, *n.*, a bag for stopping an escape of gas from the main; a talkative person (*fig.*).

gas'-bracket, *n.*, a pipe projecting from a wall which holds one or more gas-burners.

gas'-burner, *n.*, the jet where gas issues and is lit.

gas'-coal, *n.*, coal from which gas is extracted; anthracite.

Gas'con, *n.*, a native of Gascony.

gasconade', *n.*, boastfulness, bravado; *v.i.*, to talk big.

gascona'ded, *p.p.*, gasconade.

gascona'der, *n.*, a braggart.

gascona'ding, *pr.p.*, gasconade.

gas'-cooker, *n.*, a stove which uses gas for cooking.

gaselier', *n.*, a frame for holding gas burners.

gas'eous, *adj.*, of the nature of gas.

gas'-fire, *n.*, a fire which heats space by means of gas.

gas'fired, *adj.*, deriving heat from gas.

gas'fitter, *n.*, one who attends to gas fittings.

gas'fitting, *n.*, the trade of a gasfitter; in pl. gas heating appliances.

gash, *adj.*, spare, extra (*naut. slang*); *n.*, a deep cut; *v.t.*, to cut deep.

gashed, *p.p.*, gash.

gash'ing, *pr.p.*, gash.

gas'holder, *n.*, a container for storing gas.

gasifica'tion, *n.*, the production of gas in a confined area by natural means; the supplying of gas.

gas'ified, *p.p.*, gasify.

gas'iform, *adj.*, like gas.

gas'ify, *v.t.*, to bring under gas.

gas'ifying, *pr.p.*, gasify.

gas'-jet, *n.*, a gas burner.

gas'ket, *n.*, a piece of rope for binding a furled sail; gas-tight packing and fittings for boiler-heads, cylinder blocks, etc.

gas'king, *n.*, hemp-packing.

gas'less, *adj.*, without gas.

gas'light, *n.*, the light of gas; a gas lamp.

gas'mask, *n.*, a mask for protection against poisonous gas.

gas'-meter, *n.*, an instrument for measuring gas consumption.

gas'ogen, *n.*, an apparatus for making aerated water. (Also *gazogene*.)

gas'ogene, *n.*, *i.q.* gasogen.

gas'olene, *n.*, a product of petroleum. (Also *gasoline*.)

gasom'eter, *n.*, a gas reservoir.

gasom'etry, *n.*, the system of measuring gas.

gas'-oven, *n.*, an oven which derives its heat from gas.

gasp, *n.*, painful, convulsive breathing; *v.i.*, to catch the breath, to pant.

gasped, *p.p.*, gasp.

gasp'er, *n.*, one who gasps; a cheap cigarette (*slang*).

gasp'ing, *pr.p.*, gasp.

gasp'ingly, *adv.*, in a gasping way.

gas'-ring, *n.*, a metal ring perforated with holes through which gas passes, used for cooking.

gassed, *p.p.*, gas, meaning poisoned with noxious gas.

gas'sing, *n.*, boastful talk (*colloq.*); *pr.p.*, gas.

gas'-stove, *n.*, a cooking-stove which derives its heat from gas.

gas'sy, *adj.*, like gas, filled with gas.

gas'teropod, *n.*, one of the gasteropoda. (Also *gastropod*.)

gasterop'oda, *n. pl.*, molluscs having a foot beneath the belly. (Also *gastropoda*.)

gasterop'odous, *adj.*, characteristic of the gasteropoda. (Also *gastropodous*.)

gastrae'a, *n.*, a primitive sac-like animal consisting of two layers of cells (*Lat.*).

gastral'gia, *n.*, stomach-ache.

gas'tric, *adj.*, pert. or rel. to the stomach.

gastril'oquist, *n.*, a ventriloquist.

gastril'oquy, *n.*, ventriloquism.

gastri'tis, *n.*, inflammation of the stomach.

gas'trocele, *n.*, stomach-hernia.

gastrol'oger, *n.*, one who studies the science of cookery.

gastrol'ogist, *n.*, *i.q.* gastrologer.

gastrol'ogy, *n.*, the art and science of cookery.

gas'tronome, *n.*, an epicure (*Fr.*).

gastron'omer, *n.*, *i.q.* gastronome.

gastronom'ic, *adj.*, pert. or rel. to gastronomy.

gastronom'ical, *adj.*, *i.q.* gastronomic.

gastronom'ically, *adv.*, in a gastronomic way.

gastron'omist, *n.*, *i.q.* gastronome.

gastron'omy, *n.*; the science of good eating.

gas'tropod, *n.*, *i.q.* gasteropod.

gastrop′oda, *n.*, *i.q.* gasteropoda.

gastrop′odous, *adj.*, *i.q.* gasteropodous.

gas′troscope, *n.*, an instrument for inspecting the interior of the stomach.

gastrot′omy, *n.*, the opening of the abdomen by cutting.

gas′works, *n.*, a gas factory.

gat, *n.*, a gun, a revolver (*slang*); the abbrev. of gatling; a narrow opening between cliffs; a strait, a channel.

gate, *n.*, a hinged or movable fence closing an entrance or passage; a street (*Scot.*); *v.t.*, to punish (in colleges) by confining to a defined area.

gâ′teau, *n.*, a cake (*Fr.*).

gate′crasher, *n.*, one who attends a function uninvited (*colloq.*).

gate′house, *n.*, the outer entrance to a castle, monastery, etc.

gate′keeper, *n.*, a person in charge of an entrance; one who collects tolls at a tollgate.

gate′less, *adj.*, without a gate.

gate′man, *n.*, the man in charge of a gate.

gate′-money, *n.*, the money takings for entrance to a sports meeting, public exhibition, etc.

gate′post, *n.*, a post on which a gate is hinged, or against which it swings.

gate′way, *n.*, the entrance through a gate.

gath′er, *n.*, a pleat or pucker; *v.i.*, to assemble; to form pus; *v.t.*, to collect, to pluck; to infer.

gath′ered, *p.p.*, gather.

gath′erer, *n.*, one who gathers.

gath′ering, *n.*, an assembly; an abscess; *pr.p.*, gather.

gath′ers, *n. pl.*, part of a garment that is gathered or drawn in.

gat′ling, *n.*, a machine gun with clustered barrels (named after the inventor).

gauche, *adj.*, awkward; the left (*Fr.*).

gaucherie′, *n.*, awkwardness (*Fr.*).

gau′cho, *n.*, a S. American cowboy.

gaud, *n.*, a piece of finery. (Also *gawd*.)

gaudea′mus, *n.*, a rejoicing (*Lat.*).

gaud′ily, *adv.*, in a gaudy way.

gaud′iness, *n.*, the state or quality of being gaudy.

gaud′y, *adj.*, showy.

gauf′fer, *n.*, *i.q.* goffer and gopher.

gauf′fering, *n.*, *i.q.* goffering.

gaufre, *n.*, *i.q.* gofer.

gauge, *n.*, a measure of capacity; a standard; a measuring instrument; a carpenter's tool to mark parallel lines; *v.t.*, to measure capacity, to estimate.

gauge′able, *adj.*, capable of being gauged.

gauged, *p.p.*, gauge.

gau′ger, *n.*, an excise officer who measures the contents of casks.

gau′ging, *pr.p.*, gauge.

Gaul, *n.*, the country now called France; a native of G.

Gau′leiter, *n.*, a local Nazi leader (*Ger.*).

Gaul′ish, *adj.*, pert. or rel. to Gaul.

gault, *n.*, a clay stratum.

gaum′, *v.t.*, to smear.

gaum′y, *adj.*, smeary.

gaunt, *adj.*, thin, lean.

gaunt′let, *n.*, a long glove. (Also *gantlet*.)

gaunt′leted, *adj.*, wearing gauntlets.

gaunt′ly, *adv.*, with a pinched look.

gaunt′ness, *n.*, the state of being gaunt.

gaunt′ry, *n.*, *i.q.* gantry.

gaur, *n.*, a wild ox of the Indian mountain jungles.

gauss, *n.*, a unit of magnetic induction.

gauze, *n.*, a thin, transparent fabric.

gauz′iness, *n.*, the state or quality of being gauzy.

gauz′y, *adj.*, like gauze, transparent.

gave, *p.p.*, give.

gav′el, *n.*, a chairman's or auctioneer's hammer.

gav′elkind, *n.*, a form of land tenure under which, in a case of intestacy, all the sons share equally in the father's estate.

gavotte′, *n.*, a lively dance.

gawd, *n.*, *i.q.* gaud.

gawk, *n.*, a lout; a cuckoo.

gawk′y, *adj.*, ungainly.

gay, *adj.*, sprightly, merry.

gayal′ *n.*, the domesticated ox of Bengal.

gay′er, *adj.*, *comp.* of gay.

gay′est, *adj.*, *super.* of gay.

gay′ety, *n.*, *i.q.* gaiety.

gay′ly, *adv.*, *i.q.* gaily.

gaze, *n.*, an intent look; *v.i.*, to look intently.

gaze′bo, *n.*, an elevated structure commanding a wide view.

gazed, *p.p.*, gaze.

gaze′hound, *n.*, a hound which hunts by sight rather than by scent.

gazelle′, *n.*, a small, graceful antelope.

ga′zer, *n.*, one who gazes.

gazette′, *n.*, an official or any other newspaper; *v.t.*, to announce officially.

gazet′ted, *p.p.*, gazette.

gazetteer′, *n.*, a geographical dictionary.

gazet′ting, *pr.p.*, gazette.

ga′zing, *pr.p.*, gaze.

ga′zing-stock, *n.*, an object of scorn and criticism.

gaz′ogene, *n.*, *i.q.* gasogene.

gean, *n.*, the wild cherry tree and fruit.

gear, *n.*, tackle; toothed wheels; harness; dress; *v.t.*, to put gear on.

geared, *p.p.*, gear.

gear′ing, *n.*, toothed wheels working into each other; *pr.p.*, gear.

gear′wheel, *n.*, a cogged wheel.

gec′ko, *n.*, the walllizard.

ged, *n.*, a pike.

ged′da, *n.*, an inferior gum arabic.

gee, *v.i.*, to go on, to move faster.

gee'-gee, *n.*, childish language for a horse.

geese, *n.*, the pl. of goose.

gee-whizz', *interj.*, an exclamation of surprise.

geez'er, *n.*, an eccentric person (*slang*).

Gehen'na, *n.*, the valley of Hinnom; hell.

gei'ger coun'ter, *n.*, a device for detecting and registering the intensity of radioactivity.

gei'sha, *n.*, a dancing-girl; a social hostess (*Jap.*).

Geiss'ler tube, *n.*, a sealed tube filled with gas that becomes white with heat when electricity passes through it.

geist, *n.*, intellectuality; a tendency towards mental activity.

gel, *n.*, a semi-solid colloidal solution; *v.i.*, to form this solution.

gelat'inate, *v.i.*, to become jelly; *v.t.*, to turn into jelly.

gelat'inated, *p.p.*, gelatinate.

gelat'inating, *pr.p.*, gelatinate.

gelatina'tion, *n.*, the act or effect of gelatinating.

gel'atin(e), *n.*, animal jelly.

gelat'inous, *adj.*, like gelatine.

gela'tion, *n.*, solidification with cold.

geld, *v.t.*, to castrate; to deprive of essentials.

geld'ed, *p.p.*, geld.

geld'er, *n.*, one who gelds.

geld'ing, *n.*, castration; a young horse that has been castrated; *pr.p.*, geld.

gel'id, *adj.*, cold; freezing.

gelid'ity, *n.*, the state of being gelid.

gel'idly, *adv.*, icily.

gel'idness, *n.*, *i.q.* gelidity.

gel'ignite, *n.*, a nitroglycerine explosive.

gem, *n.*, a precious stone; anything very choice; *v.t.*, to adorn with jewels.

Gema'ra, *n.*, the part of the Talmud following the Mishnah, on which it is a commentary.

gemar'ic, *adj.*, pert. or rel. to the Gemara.

gem'el, *n.*, one of a pair of bars (*her.*).

gem'inate, *adj.*, arranged in pairs; *v.t.*, to double.

gemina'tion, *n.*, a doubling.

gem'inative, *adj.*, *i.q.* geminate.

Gem'ini, *n. pl.*, the Zodiacal sign of the Twins (Castor and Pollux).

gem'inous, *adj.*, double, in pairs.

gem'ma, *n.*, a bud.

gem'mary, *adj.*, pert. or rel. to gems.

gem'mate, *adj.*, having buds.

gem'mated, *adj.*, *i.q.* gemmate.

gemma'tion, *n.*, the formation of buds.

gemmed, *adj.*, adorned with gems; *p.p.*, gem.

gem'meous, *adj.*, *i.q.* gemmary.

gemmif'erous, *adj.*, bearing buds.

gem'ming, *pr.p.*, gem.

gemmipar'ity, *n.*, the state of producing gems or buds.

gemmip'arous, *adj.*, producing buds or precious stones.

gemmipa'rously, *adv.*, in a gemmiparous way.

gemmol'ogist, *n.*, one who studies gems.

gemmol'ogy, *n.*, the science of gems.

gem'mule, *n.*, a small bud.

gem'my, *adj.*, set with gems; gem-like.

gemot', *n.*, a meeting in Anglo-Saxon times.

gems'bok, *n.*, the antelope of S. Africa.

gen, *n.*, information (*slang*).

genappe', *n.*, a smooth kind of worsted cloth (from Genappe in Belgium).

gendarme', *n.*, a policeman (*Fr.*).

gendar'merie, *n.*, the police force (*Fr.*).

gendarm'ery, *n.*, *i.q.* gendarmerie.

gen'der, *n.*, a kind, sort, sex; *v.t.*, to engender (*poet.*).

gen'derless, *adj.*, without gender.

gene, *n.*, a physiological unit causing transmission of parental characteristics (*biol.*).

genealog'ical, *adj.*, pert. or rel. to genealogy.

genealog'ically, *adv.*, by descent.

geneal'ogist, *n.*, one who studies pedigrees.

geneal'ogize, *v.t.* and *i.*, to trace the genealogy of; to write up genealogies.

geneal'ogy, *n.*, pedigree; the science of tracing pedigrees.

gen'era, *n.*, the pl. of genus.

gen'eral, *adj.*, generic, rel. to the whole of a genus, class or order; *n.*, the whole; a military commander of high rank.

generalis'simo, *n.*, a commander-in-chief.

general'ity, *n.*, the main body; the bulk.

generaliza'tion, *n.*, the act of generalizing; an induction.

gen'eralize, *v.t.* and *i.*, to extend from particulars to universals; to reduce to a genus.

gen'eralized, *p.p.*, generalize.

gen'eralizing, *pr.p.*, generalize.

gen'erally, *adv.*, universally, as a whole, commonly.

gen'eralship, *n.*, a general's rank or office; strategical skill.

gen'erant, *adj.*, generating.

gen'erate, *v.t.*, to produce or form.

gen'erated, *p.p.*, generate.

gen'erating, *pr.p.*, generate.

genera'tion, *n.*, the act of generating; offspring; a period (usually of 25 years).

gen'erative, *adj.*, producing, forming.

gen'erator, *n.*, one who, or that which, generates; an apparatus for generating gas, electricity, steam.

genera'trix, *n.*, the fem. of generator.

gener'ic, *adj.*, pert. or rel. to genus or kind.

gener'ical, *adj.*, *i.q.* generic.

generosity, *n.*, the quality of being generous; kindness, liberality.

gen′erous, *adj.*, kind, noble, liberal.

gen′erously, *adv.*, kindly, liberally.

Gen′esis, *n.*, the first book of the Bible (Old Testament).

gen′esis, *n.*, creation, origin.

gen′et, *n.*, a small Spanish horse.

genet′, *n.*, a civet cat; its fur.

geneth′liac, *adj.*, pert. or rel. to nativities; *n.*, a birthday ode.

genet′ic, *adj.*, pert. or rel. to genesis.

genet′ically, *adv.*, in a genetic way.

genet′icist, *n.*, a student of genetics.

genet′ics, *n. pl.*, the science of heredity.

genev′a, *n.*, a strong alcoholic liquor flavoured with juniper berries and made in Holland.

Gene′van, *adj.*, pert. or rel. to Geneva and to Calvinism; *n.*, a native of G.

Gene′vanism, *n.*, the Calvinistic system.

Genevese′, *adj.*, pert. or rel. to Geneva; *n.*, a native of G.

ge′nial, *adj.*, cheerful, kindly; situated near, or rel. to, the chin.

genial′ity, *n.*, cheeriness, kindliness.

ge′nialize, *v.t.*, to make genial.

ge′nialized, *p.p.*, genialize.

ge′nializing, *pr.p.*, genialize.

ge′nially, *adv.*, in a genial way.

genic′ulate, *adj.*, having knee-like joints.

genic′ulated, *adj.*, *i.q.* geniculate.

genicula′tion, *n.*, the state of knottiness; having joints like a knee.

ge′nie, *n.*, a jinn; a spirit.

ge′nii, *n. pl.*, the pl. of genie.

gen′ipap, *n.*, the fruit of the jagua, a W. Indian tree.

genis′ta, *n.*, the broom (*Lat.*).

gen′ital, *adj.*, pert. or rel. to reproduction.

genita′lia, *n. pl.*, *i.q.* genitals.

gen′itals, *n. pl.*, the reproductive organs.

genitiv′al, *adj.*, pert. or rel. to the genitive.

gen′itive, *n.*, the grammatical case of relation, origin and possession.

gen′itor, *n.*, a father.

gen′iture, *n.*, birth.

ge′nius, *n.*, a guardian spirit; mental talent; spirit; aptitude; a person of great natural gifts.

geni′zah, *n.*, a synagogue store-room.

geni′zoth, *n. pl.*, genizah.

gen′ocide, *n.*, race extermination.

Genoese′, *adj.*, pert. or rel. to Genoa; *n.*, a native of G.

gen′otype, *n.*, the type-species of a genus.

genre, *n.*, common life as represented in art; a kind (*Fr.*).

gen′ro, *n. pl.*, elder statesmen (*Jap.*).

gens, *n.*, a clan, a house (*Lat.*).

gent, *n.*, the abbrev. of gentleman.

genteel′, *adj.*, polite, well-bred.

genteel′ism, *n.*, a word used as a polite substitute.

genteel′ly, *adv.*, politely.

gen′tian, *n.*, a bitter medicinal herb.

Gen′tile, *adj.*, non-Jewish; *n.*, a heathen.

Gen′tilism, *n.*, heathenism.

gentili′tial, *adj.*, pert. or rel. to a nation or family.

gentil′ity, *n.*, the quality of good breeding.

gen′tle, *adj.*, well-born, mild-mannered, kindly, easy; *n.*, the larva of the flesh-fly.

gen′tlefolk, *n. pl.*, persons of good birth and breeding.

gen′tlehood, *n.*, the character or position rel. to gentle birth.

gen′tleman, *n.*, one of good birth and breeding.

gen′tleman-at-arms, *n.*, one of the sovereign's bodyguard on ceremonial occasions.

gen′tleman-farm′er, *n.*, a wealthy man who farms his own land.

gen′tlemanlike, *adj.*, *i.q.* gentlemanly.

gen′tlemanly, *adj.*, having the manners of a gentleman.

gen′tleman-ush′er, *n.*, a gentleman acting as usher to a person of high rank.

gen′tlemen, *n.*, the pl. of gentleman.

gen′tleness, *n.*, the quality of being gentle.

gen′tler, *adj.*, *comp.* of gentle.

gen′tlest, *adj.*, *super.* of gentle.

gen′tlewoman, *n.*, the fem. of gentleman.

gen′tly, *adv.*, in a gentle way.

gen′try, *n.*, *i.q.* gentlefolk.

ge′nu, *n.*, the knee (*Lat.*).

gen′ual, *adj.*, pert. or rel. to the knee.

gen′uflect, *v.i.*, to bend the knee (in worship).

gen′uflected, *p.p.*, genuflect.

gen′uflecting, *pr.p.*, genuflect.

gen′uflector, *n.*, one who genuflects.

gen′uflectory, *adj.*, bending in worship or as a token of respect.

genuflex′ion, *n.*, the act of genuflecting.

gen′uine, *adj.*, unadulterated, real, sincere.

gen′uinely, *adv.*, sincerely, really.

gen′uineness, *n.*, the quality of being genuine.

ge′nus, *n.*, a distinct class, group or order.

geocen′tric, *adj.*, with the earth as centre.

geocen′trical, *adj.*, *i.q.* geocentric.

geochronol′ogy, *n.*, the science of measuring geological time.

geocyc′lic, *adj.*, pert. or rel. to the earth's revolutions.

ge′ode, *n.*, a concretionary stone with a crystal-lined cavity.

geodes′ic, *adj.*, pert or rel. to geodesy.

geodes′ical, *adj.*, *i.q.* geodesic.

geod′esy, *n.*, the science of land-measurement.

geodet′ic, *adj.*, *i.q.* geodesic.

geodet′ical, *adj.*, *i.q.* geodetic.

geodet′ically, *adv.*, in a geodetic way.

geod′ic, *adj.*, pert. or rel. to a geode.

geodif′erous, *adj.*, producing geodes.

geodynam'ic, *adj.*, pert. or rel. to the latent forces of the earth.

geodynam'ics, *n. pl.*, the study of the latent forces of the earth.

geognos'tic, *adj.*, pert. or rel. to geognosy.

geognos'tical, *adj.*, *i.q.* geognostic.

geog'nosy, *n.*, knowledge of the earth.

geogon'ic, *adj.*, pert. or rel. to geogony.

geog'ony, *n.*, the study of the earth's formation.

geog'rapher, *n.*, a student of geography.

geograph'ic, *adj.*, pert. or rel. to geography.

geograph'ical, *adj.*, *i.q.* geographic.

geograph'ically, *adv.*, in a geographic way.

geog'raphy, *n.*, the study of the earth, its flora and fauna in all physical, political and economic aspects.

geolog'ical, *adj.*, pert. or rel. to geology.

geolog'ically, *adv.*, in a geological way.

geol'ogist, *n.*, an expert in geology.

geol'ogize, *v.i.*, to study geology.

geol'ogy, *n.*, the science of the earth's structure.

ge'omancer, *n.*, one who practises geomancy.

ge'omancy, *n.*, divination by broken earth thrown down, or by lines or figures drawn from dots made at random.

geoman'tic, *adj.*, pert. or rel. to geomancy.

geom'eter, *n.*, a geometrician; a kind of caterpillar and moth.

geomet'ric, *adj.*, pert. or rel. to geometry.

geomet'rical, *adj.*, *i.q.* geometric.

geomet'rically, *adv.*, in accordance with geometry.

geometri'cian, *n.*, *i.q.* geometer.

geomet'rist, *n.*, *i.q.* geometer.

geom'etrize, *v.i.* and *t.*, to form, or work, by geometrical methods.

geom'etry, *n.*, the science which treats of the properties and relations of magnitudes, lines, planes and figures in two or three dimensions.

geomorphol'ogy, *n.*, the study of the physical features of the earth's crust.

geon'omy, *n.*, the study of the laws relating to the earth's structure.

geoph'agist, *n.*, one who practises geophagy.

geoph'agy, *n.*, earth-eating done by some primitive tribes.

geophys'ical, *adj.*, pert. or rel. to geophysics.

geophys'icist, *n.*, one skilled in geophysics.

geophys'ics, *n.*, the physics of the earth.

geopol'itics, *n.*, politics as determined by geography.

geopon'ic, *adj.*, agricultural.

geopon'ics, *n. pl.*, the science or art of agriculture.

geop'ony, *n.*, *i.q.* geoponics.

geora'ma, *n.*, a hollow globe showing a view of the earth's inner surface.

Geor'die, *n.*, a native of Tyneside in the north of England (*colloq.*).

George, *n.*, the jewel of a Knight of the Garter's collar.

georgette', *n.*, a fine, silk crepe.

Geor'gian, *adj.*, pert. or rel. to the reigns of the Georges; also to Georgia in Europe and the U.S.A.

geor'gic, *adj.*, pert. or rel. to rustic affairs; *n.*, a poem on agriculture.

Geor'gium Si'dus, *n.*, the planet Uranus, named after George III.

geos'copy, *n.*, observation of the earth's surface-matter.

geostat'ic, *adj.*, able to stand the earth's pressure on all sides (*archit.*).

geostroph'ic, *adj.*, depending on the earth's rotation (*meteorol.*).

geotherm'ic, *adj.*, pert. or rel. to the earth's internal heat.

geothermom'eter, *n.*, an instrument for taking the earth's temperature.

geotro'pic, *adj.*, pert. or rel. to geotropism.

geotrop'ically, *adv.*, in a geotropic way.

geot'ropism, *n.*, the tendency of plants to grow towards the centre of the earth.

ge'rah, *n.*, a Jewish weight and coin.

Gera'nium, *n.*, a genus of flowering plants.

geratol'ogy, *n.*, the study of decadence, esp. of animals approaching extinction.

ge'rent, *n.*, a governing force; a manager.

ger'enuk, *n.*, an E. African antelope.

ger'falcon, *n.*, a large kind of falcon.

geriat'ric, *adj.*, pert. or rel. to geriatrics.

geriatri'cian, *n.*, one skilled in geriatrics.

geriat'rics, *n. pl.*, the branch of medicine which deals with old age and its diseases.

geriat'rist, *n.*, *i.q.* geriatrician.

geri'atry, *n.*, the care of the old.

germ, *n.*, a sprout; origin; first principle; microbe.

Ger'man, *adj.*, pert. or rel. to Germany; *n.*, a native of G.; the German language.

ger'man, *adj.*, of the same family.

german'der, *n.*, a wild plant.

germane', *adj.*, near, akin; closely allied; relevant.

German'ic, *adj.*, pert. or rel. to Germany and the Germans.

Ger'manism, *n.*, a German idiom.

german'ium, *n.*, a brittle, white, rare, extremely hard, metallic element.

Germaniza'tion, *n.*, the adoption of German ways.

Ger'manize, *v.i.*, to adopt German ways; *v.t.*, to make German.

Ger'manized, *p.p.*, Germanize.

Ger'manizing, *pr.p.*, Germanize.

ger'man-silver, *n.*, an alloy of zinc, copper and nickel.

germ-carrier, *n.*, that which, or one who, carries germs; an elementary principle from which something may spring; an origin.

ger'men, *n.*, the ovary of a plant.

germicid'al, *adj.*, *i.q.* germicide.

ger'micide, *adj.*, destructive of germs; *n.*, a substance for destroying germs.

germig'enous, *adj.*, pert. or rel. to a germen.

ger'minal, *adj.*, pert. or rel. to germs; productive.

ger'minant, *adj.*, sprouting.

ger'minate, *v.i.*, to sprout.

ger'minated, *p.p.*, germinate.

ger'minating, *pr.p.*, germinate.

germina'tion, *n.*, the act of germinating.

ger'minative, *adj.*, causing germination.

ger'minator, *n.*, that which germinates or produces germination.

ger'mon, *n.*, a long-finned tunny fish (*Fr.*).

ger'mule, *n.*, a diminutive germ.

geroc'omy, *n.*, the science of the treatment of old people.

geron'tic, *adj.*, pert. or rel. to old age, senile.

gerontoc'racy, *n.*, governing by, or a government of, old men.

gerontol'ogy, *n.*, the scientific study of old age.

gerry'man'der, *v.t.*, to tinker with the arrangement of constituencies.

ger'und, *n.*, a verbal noun which is one of the parts of a verb.

gerun'dial, *adj.*, rel. to a gerund.

gerundiv'al, *adj.*, *i.q.* gerundive.

gerun'dive, *adj.*, *i.q.* gerundial; *n.*, a verbal adjective.

ges'so, *n.*, a plaster (gypsum) used for painting, etc.

gestalt', *n.*, an organized whole of individual parts affecting each other, the whole totalling more than its parts (*psych.*).

Gesta'po, *n.*, the German Nazi secret police.

gesta'tion, *n.*, pregnancy.

gestator'ial, *adj.*, pregnant; used to describe a chair for carrying the Pope on certain occasions.

ges'tatory, *adj.*, pert. or rel. to gestation.

gestic'ulate, *v.i.*, to accompany speech with gesture; to gesture.

gestic'ulated, *p.p.*, gesticulate.

gestic'ulating, *pr.p.*, gesticulate.

gesticula'tion, *n.*, the act of gesticulating.

gestic'ulative, *adj.*, *i.q.* gesticulatory.

gestic'ulator, *n.*, one who gesticulates.

gestic'ulatory, *adj.*, pert. or rel. to gesticulation.

ges'ture, *n.*, gesticulation; movement expressing a meaning or an attitude; *v.i.*, *i.q.* gesticulate.

get, *n.*, offspring; *v.i.*, to arrive; to go; *v.t.*, to obtain; to acquire; to meet with.

get-at'-able, *adj.*, easily accessible.

get'away, *n.*, an escape.

get'ter, *n.*, one who gets.

get'ting, *pr.p.*, get.

get-*together*, *n.*, an informal gathering of people.

get-up', *n.*, equipment; style, appearance, etc. (*colloq.*).

ge'um, *n.*, a kind of rosaceous plant.

gew'-gaw, *n.*, a bauble, toy or showy trifle.

gey, *adv.*, very, considerably (*Scot.*).

gey'ser, *n.*, an intermittent hot spring; an apparatus for heating water.

ghaf'fir, *n.*, an Egyptian policeman.

Ghanai'an, *adj.*, pert. or rel. to Ghana; *n.*, a native of G.

ghar'ry, *n.*, an Indian native cart.

ghast'ily, *adv.*, in a ghastly way.

ghast'lier, *adj.*, *comp.* of ghastly.

ghast'liest, *adj.*, *super.* of ghastly.

ghast'liness, *n.*, the state of being ghastly.

ghast'ly, *adj.*, deadly pale, cadaverous, horrible.

gha(u)t, *n.*, a mountain pass; a wharf at a riverside (*Ind.*).

ghazee'yeh, *n.*, an Egyptian dancing girl.

Gha'zi, *n.*, a Turkish high commander.

ghee, *n.*, clarified butter.

gher'kin, *n.*, a small cucumber.

ghet'to, *n.*, the Jewish quarter of a town; any segregated area.

ghoont', *n.*, a Himalayan pony.

Ghoor'ka, *n.*, *i.q.* Gurkha.

ghost, *n.*, a spirit, a phantom; the immaterial apparition of a dead person.

ghost'like, *adj.*, like a ghost.

ghost'liness, *n.*, the state of being ghostly.

ghost'ly, *adj.*, *i.q.* ghostlike; spiritual.

ghost'-moth, *n.*, a nocturnal British moth.

ghoul, *n.*, an imaginary creature that feeds on human flesh.

ghoul'ish, *adj.*, pert. or rel. to a ghoul.

ghoul'ishly, *adv.*, in a ghoulish way.

Ghur'ka, *n.*, *i.q.* Gurkha.

ghur'ry, *n.*, an Indian division of time.

ghyll, *n.*, a ravine.

gial'lo anti'co, *n.*, rich yellow marble found in ruins in Italy (*It.*).

gi'ant, *adj.*, very large; *n.*, a being of monstrous size; an abnormally big and tall man.

giantesque', *adj.*, *i.q.* gigantic.

gi'antess, *n.*, the fem. of giant.

gi'antlike, *adj.*, gigantic, monstrous.

gi'ant-powder, *n.*, a kind of dynamite.

giaour, *n.*, the Mohammedan name for an unbeliever.

gib, *n.*, a piece of metal for holding another in place; *v.t.*, to fasten or furnish with a gib.

gib'ber, *n.*, fast speech; *v.t.*, to talk unintelligibly.

gib'berish, *n.*, unintelligible talk.

gib'bet, *n.*, the gallows; *v.t.*, to hang on gallows; to ridicule.

gib'beted, *p.p.*, gibbet.

gib'beting, *pr.p.*, gibbet.

gib'bon, *n.*, a long-armed ape.

gib'bose, *adj.*, *i.q.* gibbous.

gibbos'ity, n., protuberance.

gib'bous, adj., humped, protuberant.

gibe, n., a sarcastic jest; v.t. and i., to scoff at, to mock; v.t., to change direction of a sailing craft; v.i., to swing over; also jibe in these two senses.

gibed, p.p., gibe.

gi'ber, n., one who gibes.

gi'bing, pr.p., gibe.

gi'bingly, adv., jeeringly.

gib'lets, n., the edible viscera of poultry.

gib'staff, n., a boat pole.

gib'us, n., an opera hat.

gid, n., a disease in sheep.

gid'dier, adj., comp. of giddy.

gid'diest, adj., super. of giddy.

gid'dily, adv., in a giddy way.

gid'diness, n., the state of being giddy.

gid'dy, adj., dizzy; thoughtless.

gift, n., anything given; a present; mental endowment.

gift'ed, adj., talented.

gig, n., a two-wheeled one-horse trap; a contrivance for raising nap on woollen cloth; a ship's boat; a racing boat; a fish spear.

gigantesque', adj., i.q. gigantic.

gigan'tic, adj., huge, of abnormal size.

gigan'tically, adv., in a gigantic way.

gigantol'ogy, n., the scientific study of the unusually large.

gig'gle, n., a foolish laugh; v.i., to titter, to laugh foolishly.

gig'gled, p.p., giggle.

gig'gler, n., one wno giggles.

gig'gling, pr.p., giggle.

gig'-lamps, n. pl., spectacles (colloq.).

gig'let, n., a giddy girl.

gig'lot, n., i.q. giglet.

gigman'ity, n., respectability.

gig-mill, n., a contrivance for raising nap on cloth; the works in which these stand.

gig'olo, n., a professional male dancing-partner (Fr.).

gig'ot, n., a leg (Fr.).

gigue, n., a jig (Fr.).

gila mon'ster, n., a large, American, venomous lizard.

Gilber'tian, adj., pert. or rel. to Gilbert; serio-comic.

Gil'bertine, adj., pert. or rel. to St. Gilbert of Sempringham and to his Order.

gild, n., i.q. guild; v.t., to overlay with gold; to make to appear bright.

gild'ed, p.p., gild.

gild'er, n., one who gilds.

gild'ing, n., the art of overlaying with gold; gold leaf; pr.p., gild.

gill, n., the respiratory organ in a fish; a deep, wooded ravine; a swift-flowing, mountain stream.

gill, n., the fourth part of a pint; a young girl.

gillaroo', n., Irish trout.

gil'lie, n., a Highland attendant on a shooting party (Scot.).

gil'lyflower, n., a flower with a clove-like smell.

gil'py, n., one who is frolicsome.

gilt, adj., gilded; n., a gilding; a young sow.

gilt'-edged, adj., of the highest class.

gim'bal, n., a ring for suspending objects aboard ship to steady them against the motion of the ship.

gim'bri, n., a Moorish guitar.

gim'crack, adj., worthless; n., a trumpery thing.

gim'let, n., a small boring tool.

gim'mer, n., a young ewe (dial.); a woman (derog.).

gim'mick, n., any ingenious device or ploy to secure attention.

gimp, n., edging made of silk cord. (Also gymp.)

gin, n., a trap; a snare; an alcoholic liquor; a machine used in the preparation of cotton; an Australian aboriginal woman; v.t., to snare or trap.

gin'gal(l), n., a swivel gun; a Chinese or Indian light rest-musket. (Also jingal.)

gin'ger, n., the spicy root of an Indian plant.

gingerade', n., a mineral water flavoured with ginger.

ginger-beer', n., an effervescent drink flavoured with ginger.

gin'gerbread, n., a cake flavoured with ginger.

gin'gerly, adv., cautiously, delicately.

gin'ger-pop, n., a popular name for ginger-beer.

gin'gery, adj., rel. to, or resembling, ginger.

ging'ham, n., a kind of cotton or linen cloth; an umbrella.

gin'gili, n., an East Indian plant, the sweet oil obtained from it.

gingi'val, adj., pert. or rel. to the gums.

gingivi'tis, n., inflamation of the gums.

gin'gles, n., i.q. shingles.

gin'glymus, n., a hinge-like body joint which can only move in two directions, e.g. the elbow (anat.).

gink, n., a queer fellow (slang).

gink'go, n., a Chinese and Japanese tree with dark green fan-shaped leaves.

ginned', p.p., gin.

gin'ning, n., the process of separating cotton from its seeds; pr.p., gin.

gin'ny-carriage, n., a small, strong railway van.

gin'seng, n., a Chinese aromatic root.

gip, v.t., to remove the entrails of herrings.

gipp'o, n., soup, gravy (slang).

gipp'y, adj., Egyptian; n., the abbrev. for an Egyptian soldier (slang).

gip'sy, n., one of the wandering race; any swarthy person. (Also gypsy.)

gip'syfied, adj., pert. or rel. to gipsies.

gip'syism, n., a gipsy expression.

gip'sy-van, n., the caravan in which gipsies live and move from place to place.

giraffe', n., the camel-opard.

gir'andole, n., a branched candlestick.

gir'asol(e), n., the fire-opal.

gird, n., a sudden spasm of pain; v.i., to gibe; v.t., to bind round, to encircle.

gird'ed, p.p., gird.

gird'er, n., the principal beam in a floor, bridge, etc.

gird'ing, pr.p., gird.

gir'dle, n., a band for the waist; any girdle-like enclosure; a gri-diron; v.t., to bind with a girdle; to en-close.

gir'dled, adj., wearing a girdle; p.p., girdle.

gir'dler, n., a girdle-maker.

gir'dling, pr.p., girdle.

girl, n., a female child; a young woman.

girl'hood, n., the state of being a girl.

girl'ish, adj., like a girl, youthful.

girl'ishly, adv., in a girl-ish way.

girl'ishness, n., the state or quality of being girlish.

giro, n., a current ac-count banking ser-vice based on credit transfers and con-ducted by banks and the Post Office.

Giron'dists, n. pl., a moderate Republican group in the French Assembly, 1791-3.

girouette', n., a weather-cock.

girt, p.p., gird.

girth, n., a saddle-belt; the circumference.

gist, n., the main point of a question or action.

gite, n., a lodging place (Fr.).

git'tern, n., a cithern.

gius'to, adj., steady (mus., It.).

give, n., elasticity; v.t., to bestow, to confer without reward, to concede.

give'able, adj., able to be given.

giv'en, p.p., give.

giv'er, n., one who gives.

giv'ing, pr.p., give.

giz'zard, n., a fowl's muscular stomach.

gla'brous, adj., smooth, bald.

glacé, adj., cooled, iced; n., a thin, shiny, silk material.

gla'cial, adj., consisting of, or rel. to, ice.

gla'cialist, n., one who believes that certain geological pheno-mena have their ori-gin in ice action.

gla'ciated, adj., marked by ice-action; covered with glaciers.

glacia'tion, n., the act of covering with glaciers.

glac'ier, n., accumulated mountain-ice and snow with a slow stream-like flow.

glac'ière, n., an ice-cave (Fr.).

glacieret', n., a small glacier.

glaciol'ogy, n., that branch of geology which deals with gla-ciers.

gla'cis, n., the sloping outer branch of a fortified ditch (Fr.).

glad, adj., delighted, cheery; v.t., i.q. glad-den.

glad'den, v.t., to make glad.

glad'dened, p.p., glad-den.

glad'dening, pr.p., glad-den.

glade, n., an open green space in a wood.

gla'diate, adj., sword-like.

glad'iator, n., a Roman fighter in the arena.

gladiato'rial, adj., pert. or rel. to gladiators and the arena.

glad'iole, n., i.q. gladio-lus.

gladi'olus, n., the sword-lily.

glad'ly, adv., cheerily, willingly.

glad'ness, n., the state of being glad.

glad'some, adj., joyous, cheerful.

glad'someness, n., joy-ousness.

glad'stone-bag, n., a light, leather travel-ling bag.

Gladsto'nian, adj., rel. to or resembling Gladstone, the Eng-lish statesman.

glair, n., the white of egg; viscous matter; v.t., to smear with glair.

glaired, p.p., glair.

glair'ing, pr.p., glair.

glair'y, adj., gluey.

glais'tig, n., a she-devil of goat form.

glaive, n., a sort of halberd.

glam'orous, adj., be-witching, fascinating.

glam'orously, adv., in a glamorous way.

glamour, n., charm, witchery.

glance, n., a rapid view; a look; a lustrous ore of any metal; v.i., to shoot obliquely; to take a rapid view.

glanced, p.p., glance.

glan'cing, pr.p., glance.

glan'cingly, adv., in a glancing way.

gland, n., a secreting organ of the body; a sleeve used for pack-ing on a piston.

glan'dered, adj., affected with glanders.

glan'ders, n. pl., a con-tagious disease in horses.

glandif'erous, adj., acorn-bearing.

gland'iform, adj., acorn-shaped.

glan'dular, adj., pert. to, or resembling, glands.

glandula'tion, n., glandu-lar structure.

glan'dule, n., a little gland.

glandulif'erous, adj., i.q. glandular.

glandulos'ity, n., the qua-lity of being glandu-lous.

glan'dulous, adj., i.q. glandular.

glare, n., a dazzling light, lustre; a fierce look; v.i., to give a dazzling light, to look fiercely.

glared, p.p., glare.

glar'eous, adj., gravelly.

glar'iness, n., brilliance.

glar'ing, adj., dazzling, gaudy; conspicuous; pr.p., glare.

glar'ingly, adv., conspi-cuously.

glar'ingness, n., strong, fierce light.

glar'y, adj., bright, dazz-ling.

glass, adj., vitreous, made of glass; n., a transparent, brittle substance; a vessel

made of glass; *v.t.*, to reflect; to fit with glass, to glaze.

glass'blower, *n.*, one who blows molten glass into desired shapes.

glass'cloth, *n.*, a linen cloth specially for drying and polishing glasses.

glass'cutter, *n.*, one who, or that which, cuts glass.

glass'es, *n. pl.*, spectacles (*colloq.*); the plural of glass (vessels).

glass'ful, *n.*, as much as a glass holds.

glass'house, *n.*, a building where glass is made; a greenhouse or a conservatory; a military prison (*colloq.*).

glas'sichord, *n.*, a glass-vibrating musical instrument.

glass'ily, *adv.*, in a glassy way.

glass'iness, *n.*, the state or quality of being glassy.

glass'paper, *n.*, powdered glass glued on paper and used for abrasive purposes.

glass'ware, *n.*, glass articles.

glass'works, *n.*, a glass-making factory.

glass'wort, *n.*, a plant used in glass-making.

glass'y, *adj.*, glass-like, slippery.

Glas'tonbury thorn, *n.*, a variety of hawthorn flowering about Christmas.

Glaswe'gian, *adj.*, pert. or rel. to Glasgow; *n.*, a native of G.

glau'ber-salt, *n.*, sulphate of soda, a powerful purgative named after a German chemist, J. R. Glauber.

glau'cine, *n.*, an alkaloid in the horse-poppy.

glauco'ma, *n.*, a disease of the eye.

glauco'matous, *adj.*, of the nature of glaucoma.

glauco'sis, *n.*, *i.q.* glaucoma.

glau'cous, *adj.*, sea-green; covered with a white bloom.

glaze, *n.*, vitreous coating; *v.t.*, to fit with

glass; *v.i.*, to become glassy.

glazed, *p.p.*, glaze.

gla'zer, *n.*, that which gives a glaze.

gla'zier, *n.*, one who sets glass.

gla'ziery, *n.*, a glazier's trade.

gla'zing, *n.*, the act of setting glass; an enamel; window panes; *pr.p.*, glaze.

gla'zy, *adj.*, covered with a glaze.

gleam, *n.*, a sudden emission of light; *v.i.*, to send out rays.

gleamed, *p.p.*, gleam.

gleam'ing, *pr.p.*, gleam.

glean, *v.i.*, to pick up information; *v.t.*, to gather the leavings of reapers; to collect.

gleaned, *p.p.*, glean.

glean'er, *n.*, one who gleans.

glean'ing, *n.*, the act of gleaning; that which is gathered; *pr.p.*, glean.

glebe, *n.*, clod, soil, landed property of the church.

gle'by, *adj.*, pert. or rel. to glebe.

glee, *n.*, joyousness; a variety of part-song.

glee'ful, *adj.*, full of glee.

glee'fully, *adv.*, in a gleeful way.

gleep, *n.*, an atomic pile; the acronym from Graphite Low Energy Experimental Pile.

glee'some, *adj.*, *i.q.* gleeful.

gleet, *n.*, a mucous discharge.

gleet'y, *adj.*, slimy.

gleg, *adj.*, quick, alert (*Scot.*).

glen, *n.*, a narrow valley.

glen'doveer, *n.*, a beautiful sprite in Hindu myths.

gle'ne, *n.*, the eye-pupil.

glengar'ry, *n.*, a Scottish bonnet.

glenliv'et, *n.*, a kind of malt whisky.

gle'noid, *adj.*, having a cavity (*anat.*).

gley, *adj.*, askew; *v.i.*, to have a cast in the eye.

glib, *adj.*, smooth; ready of tongue; flippant.

glib'ly, *adv.*, in a glib way.

glib'ness, *n.*, the quality of being glib.

glid'dery, *adj.*, slippery.

glide, *n.*, a smooth, sliding movement; *v.i.*, to flow gently; to fly in an unpowered aircraft; to slide.

gli'ded, *p.p.*, glide.

gli'der, *n.*, one who glides; an aircraft using only air currents for its powers of flight.

gli'ding, *pr.p.*, glide.

gli'dingly, *adv.*, in a gliding manner.

glim, *n.*, a light, a candle (*slang*).

glim'mer, *n.*, a faint light; *v.i.*, to give a faint light.

glim'mered, *p.p.*, glimmer.

glim'mering, *n.*, a faint perception; *pr.p.*, glimmer.

glimpse, *n.*, a sudden flash; a faint idea; *v.i.*, to appear momentarily; *v.t.*, to catch a sudden sight of.

glimpsed, *p.p.*, glimpse.

glimps'ing, *pr.p.*, glimpse.

glint, *n.*, a short gleam; *v.i.*, to flash; *v.t.*, to reflect.

glissade', *n.*, the act of sliding down; *v.i.*, to slide downward.

glissan'do, *adv.*, with a sliding movement (*mus.*, It.).

glissé, *n.*, a sliding step in dancing (*Fr.*).

glis'ten, *n.*, a shining brightness; *v.i.*, to shine, to sparkle.

glis'tened, *p.p.*, glisten.

glis'tening, *pr.p.*, glisten.

glis'ter, *v.i.*, *i.q.* glisten.

glis'tered, *p.p.*, glister.

glis'tering, *adj.*, bright; *pr.p.*, glister.

glit'ter, *v.i.*, to sparkle with quick flashes of light, to make a show.

glit'tered, *p.p.*, glitter.

glit'tering, *pr.p.*, glitter.

glit'teringly, *adv.*, brilliantly.

gloam'ing, *n.*, twilight, dusk.

gloat, *v.i.*, to stare admiringly or exultingly.

gloat'ed, *p.p.*, gloat.

gloat'ing, *pr.p.*, gloat.

gloat'ingly, *adv.*, in a gloating way.

glo'bal, *adj.*, spherical; world-wide; all-embracing.

glo'bate, *adj.*, *i.q.* globose.

glo'bated, *adj.*, *i.q.* globate.

globe, *n.*, a sphere, a ball, the world; a model of the world or the heavens.

globe'-fish, *n.*, a fish which inflates itself to the shape of a globe.

globe'trotter, *n.*, a person who is constantly moving about the world.

glob'oid, *adj.*, like a globe; *n.*, a global shaped object.

glo'bose, *adj.*, globe-shaped.

globos'ity, *n.*, the state or quality of being globose.

glo'bous, *adj.*, *i.q.* globular.

glob'ular, *adj.*, spherical.

glob'ularity, *n.*, the state of being globular.

glob'ularly, *adv.*, in a globular way.

glob'ule, *n.*, a small globe; a homoeopathic pill.

glob'ulin, *n.*, an albuminous particle found in blood and plants.

glob'ulous, *adj.*, *i.q.* globular.

glochid'iate, *adj.*, barbèd at the tip (*bot.*).

glock'enspiel, *n.*, a musical instrument consisting of suspended metal bars (*Ger.*).

glome, *n.*, part of the frog in a horse's foot; a roundish head of flowers.

glom'erate, *adj.*, gathered into a mass.

glomera'tion, *n.*, a cluster.

glom'erule, *n.*, a clustered flower-head; a cluster of blood-vessels, etc.

gloom, *n.*, partial darkness, sadness; *v.i.*, to be or look gloomy; *v.t.*, to sadden.

gloom'ier, *adj.*, *comp.* of gloomy.

gloom'iest, *adj.*, *super.* of gloomy.

gloom'ily, *adv.*, in a gloomy way.

gloom'iness, *n.*, the state or quality of being gloomy.

gloom'ing, *pr.p.*, gloom.

gloom'y, *adj.*, partially dark, dismal.

Glo'ria, *n.*, the doxology (*Lat.*).

glo'ried, *p.p.*, glory.

glorifica'tion, *n.*, the act or effect of glorifying.

glo'rified, *p.p.*, glorify.

glo'rify, *v.t.*, to make glorious, to magnify.

glo'rifying, *pr.p.*, glorify.

glo'riole, *n.*, a halo.

glo'rious, *adj.*, illustrious; celebrated; winning glory.

glo'riously, *adv.*, in a glorious way.

glo'riousness, *n.*, the state of being glorious.

glo'ry, *n.*, splendour, honour, fame; *v.i.*, to exult, to take pride in.

glo'ry-hole, *n.*, an opening in the wall of a blast-furnace; a place where odds and ends are kept (*colloq.*).

glo'rying, *pr.p.*, glory.

glo'ryingly, *adv.*, in a glorying way.

gloss, *n.*, false lustre, comment; *v.t.*, to excuse plausibly; to make notes on; to make lustrous.

gloss'al, *adj.*, pert. or rel. to the tongue; lingual.

glossal'gia, *n.*, pain in the tongue.

glossa'rial, *adj.*, pert. or rel. to a glossary.

glos'sarist, *n.*, the compiler of a glossary.

glos'sary, *n.*, a dictionary of special terms.

glossat'or, *n.*, a commentator.

glossed, *p.p.*, gloss.

gloss'er, *n.*, one who glosses; a polisher.

gloss'ier, *adj.*, *comp.* of glossy.

gloss'iest, *adj.*, *super.* of glossy.

gloss'ily, *adv.*, in a glossy way.

gloss'iness, *n.*, the state or quality of being glossy.

gloss'ing, *pr.p.*, gloss.

glossi'tis, *n.*, inflammation of the tongue.

glossog'rapher, *n.*, one skilled in glossography.

glossograph'ical, *adj.*, pert. or rel. to glossography.

glossog'raphy, *n.*, the scientific study of the tongue and its diseases.

glossolog'ical, *adj.*, pert. or rel. to glossology.

glossol'ogist, *n.*, one skilled in glossology.

glossol'ogy, *n.*, the science of languages.

gloss'y, *adj.*, having a gloss; shiny; *n.*, a periodical printed on shiny paper (*colloq.*).

glot'tal, *adj.*, pert. or rel. to the glottis.

glot'tic, *adj.*, *i.q.* glottal.

glot'tis, *n.*, the opening of the larynx.

glottol'ogy, *n.*, *i.q.* glossology.

glove, *n.*, a covering for the hand, usually separately fitted for the fingers; *v.t.*, to cover with a glove.

gloved, *adj.*, covered with a glove; *p.p.*, glove.

glov'er, *n.*, a maker or seller of gloves.

glow, *n.*, intense, shining heat; brightness; emotional warmth; *v.i.*, to shine with intense heat; to become animated.

glowed, *p.p.*, glow.

glow'er, *v.i.*, to glare; to look angry.

glow'ered, *p.p.*, glower.

glower'ing, *pr.p.*, glower.

glower'ingly, *adv.*, glaringly.

glow'ing, *pr.p.*, glow.

glow'ingly, *adv.*, in a glowing way.

glow'-worm, *n.*, a kind of beetle, the female having the ability to emit a phosphoric light.

gloxin'ia, *n.*, a tropical plant.

gloze, *v.t.*, to gloss over.

glozed, *p.p.*, gloze.

glo'zer, *n.*, one who glozes.

glo'zing, *pr.p.*, gloze.

glo'zingly, *adv.*, in a glozing way.

glu'cic, *adj.*, sugary.

gluci'na, *n.*, glucinum oxide.

glu'cine, *adj.*, pert. or rel. to glucinum.

gluci'num, *n.*, a white metal derived from beryl.

glu'cose, *n.*, a sugar preparation obtained from corn, grapes, etc.

glucos'ic, *adj.*, pert. or rel. to glucose.

glu'coside, *n.*, a vegetable substance yielding glucose.

glucosu'ria, *n.*, a kind of sugar diabetes, affecting the urine (*path.*). (Also glycosuria.)

glue, *n.*, a viscous adhesive; *v.t.*, to cement with glue.

glued, *p.p.*, glue.

glue'-pot, *n.*, a double pot for melting glue, the outer one containing water.

glu'er, *n.*, anything that glues.

glu'ey, *adj.*, like glue.

glu'ing, *pr.p.*, glue.

glum, *adj.*, doleful, sullen.

gluma'ceous, *adj.*, pert. or rel. to glumes.

glume, *n.*, the husk of grasses and grain.

glum'ly, *adv.*, dolefully.

glum'ness, *n.*, the state of being glum.

glumose', *adj.*, *i.q.* glumaceous.

glu'mous, *adj.*, having glumes.

glut, *n.*, an over-supply; *v.t.*, to fill to satiety; to over-fill.

glute'al, *adj.*, pert. or rel. to the buttocks.

glu'ten, *n.*, a viscid, elastic substance found in grain.

glu't(a)eus, *n.*, one of the three muscles of the buttocks.

glu'tinate, *v.t.*, to cement.

glu'tinated, *p.p.*, glutinate.

glu'tinating, *pr.p.*, glutinate.

glu'tinize, *v.t.*, to make sticky.

glutinos'ity, *n.*, the state of being glutinous.

glu'tinous, *adj.*, viscous, gluey.

glu'tinously, *adv.*, in a sticky way.

glut'ted, *p.p.*, glut.

glut'ting, *pr.p.*, glut.

glut'ton, *n.*, one who gluts himself with food; a voracious weasel-like carnivore.

glut'tonize, *v.i.*, to play the glutton.

glut'tonous, *adj.*, greedy over food.

glut'tonously, *adv.*, in a very greedy way.

glut'tony, *n.*, excess in eating.

gly'ceric, *adj.*, pert. or rel. to glycerine (*chem.*).

gly'cerinate, *v.t.*, to treat with glycerine.

gly'cerine, *n.*, a liquid extract from fatty matter used as a solvent, emulsifier and a saponaceous moistener.

gly'cerol, *n.*, the scientific name for glycerine.

gly'cogen, *n.*, the substance which produces glucose in animal tissues (*chem.*).

glycogen'esis, *n.*, the process by which glucose is formed in the liver and other animal organs.

glycogen'ic, *adj.*, producing glucose in animal tissues (*chem.*).

gly'col, *n.*, a compound between glycerine and alcohol giving a thick, colourless fluid.

glycol(l)'ic, *adj.*, pert. or rel. to glycol.

glyco'nian, *adj.*, *i.q.* glyconic.

glycon'ic, *adj.*, pert. or rel. to a particular metre in Greek and Latin poetry; *n.*, a line in the glyconic metre.

glycosur'ia, *n.*, *i.q.* glucosuria.

glyph, *n.*, upright fluting.

glyph'ic, *adj.*, pert. or rel. to sculpture.

glyph'ograph, *n.*, a reproduction in relief.

glyphog'rapher, *n.*, one skilled in glyphography.

glyphograph'ic, *adj.*, pert. or rel. to glyphography.

glyphog'raphy, *n.*, an electrotype process giving a raised copy of an engraved plate.

glyp'tic, *adj.*, pert. or rel. to glyptography.

glyp'todon, *n.*, an extinct S. American quadruped with fluted teeth.

glyptog'raphy, *n.*, the art of engraving gems.

glyptothe'ca, *n.*, a museum of sculptures.

G'-man, *n.*, a Federal Bureau Investigation agent (*Amer.*).

gnarl, *n.*, a knot on a tree; *v.t.*, to make knotty.

gnarled, *adj.*, knotty; *p.p.*, gnarl.

gnarl'ing, *pr.p.*, gnarl.

gnarl'y, *adj.*, having gnarls.

gnash, *v.i.*, to grind the teeth; *v.t.*, to strike together.

gnashed, *p.p.*, gnash.

gnash'ing, *pr.p.*, gnash.

gnash'ingly, *adv.*, in a gnashing manner.

gnat, *n.*, a small, winged, stinging insect.

gnath'ic, *adj.*, of the jaws.

gnathi'tis, *n.*, inflammation of the upper jaw or cheek.

gnaw, *v.t.*, to eat away, bite or fret.

gnawed, *p.p.*, gnaw.

gnaw'er, *n.*, one who, or that which, gnaws.

gnaw'ing, *pr.p.*, gnaw.

gnaw'ingly, *adv.*, in a gnawing way.

gneiss, *n.*, a crystalline rock.

gneiss'ose, *adj.*, of the nature of gneiss.

gnome, *n.*, an imaginary earthy sprite; a sententious saying.

gno'mic, *adj.*, sententious, didactic and brief.

gno'mish, *adj.*, dwarfish.

gno'mon, *n.*, the rod, pillar or pin of a sundial; what is left of a parallelogram when a smaller parallelogram has been taken out of it.

gnomon'ic, *adj.*, pert. or rel. to dials.

gnomon'ical, *adj.*, *i.q.* gnomonic.

gnomon'ics, *n. pl.*, the science and art of constructing dials.

gnomonol'ogy, *n.*, the science of dialling.

gnosiol'ogy, *n.*, the theory of knowledge.

gno'sis, n., higher knowledge.

gnos'tic, adj., pert. or rel. to the gnostics and gnosticism.

gnos'ticism, n., a religious and philosophical system, partly Christian, partly pagan, prevalent in the first six centuries.

gnu, n., a S. African ruminant of the antelope family, with a buffalo-like head.

go, n., the mode; mettle; zeal; v.i., to walk, move or travel.

go'a, n., a Tibetan antelope.

goad, n., a pointed stick for driving oxen; v.t., to prick with a goad; to incite.

goad'ed, p.p., goad.

goad'ing, pr.p., goad.

goads'man, n., one who uses a goad to drive oxen.

goaf, n., a worked out section of a coalmine; waste.

go'-ahead, adj., advanced, progressive; n., the ability to, or the signal to, proceed.

goal, n., the winning-post in a race; the structure of posts between which the ball has to be driven in some ball games; a score in some ball games.

goal'ie, n., a goal-keeper (colloq.).

goal'keeper, n., a footballer who guards the goal.

goal'-line, n., the line parallel with the goal-posts at each end of the field.

goal'-posts, n. pl., the uprights supporting the goal crossbar.

goan'na, n., any large lizard. (Also iguana.)

goat, n., a horned, long-haired quadruped.

goatee', n., a short beard.

goat'herd, n., one who tends goats.

goat'ish, adj., goat-like; lascivious.

goat'ishly, adv., in a goatish way.

goat'ishness, n., the state of being goatish.

goat'ling, n., a goat which is under two years of age.

goat's'-beard, n., meadowsweet.

goat'skin, adj., made of goatskin; n., the skin of a goat; leather made from the skin.

goat'sucker, n., an insectivorous bird.

gob, n., spittle (vulg.); a sailor; the mouth (slang); v.t., to spit (vulg.).

gobang', n., a game played with counters.

gobbed, p.p., gob.

gob'bet, n., a lump; a mouthful.

gob'bing, n., refuse; pr.p., gob.

gob'ble, n., a turkey's crop; v.i., to make the cry of a turkey; v.t., to swallow greedily.

gob'bled, p.p., gobble.

gob'bledegook, -dygook, n., official jargon.

gob'bler, n., one who gobbles.

gob'bling, pr.p., gobble.

gob'elin, n., tapestry made at, or copied from, the Gobelins works in France.

gobe'mouche, n., a credulous newsmonger (Fr.).

go'-between, n., that which links up two things; an intermediary; an agent.

gob'let, n., a drinking vessel without a handle.

gob'lin, n., an evil spirit; an elf; a fairy.

go'by, n., a small, sea fish.

go'-by, n., avoidance.

go'-cart, n., a child's cart.

God, n., the Supreme Deity.

god, n., an image, animal or other object worshipped as a divine power; the supreme deity of a religion not one's own; an idol.

god'child, n., one for whom godparents are sponsors in Holy Baptism.

god'daughter, n., a female godchild.

god'dess, n., a pagan female deity; a supremely beautiful woman.

go'det, n., a triangular piece of material inserted in a dress or glove, etc. (Fr.).

gode'tia, n., a flowering, annual plant.

god'father, n., a male godparent.

God'fearing, adj., reverencing God.

God'-forsaken, adj., depraved; abandoned.

God'head, n., the divine nature; divinity.

god'less, adj., ungodly.

god'lessly, adv., in an ungodly way.

god'lessness, n., the state of being ungodly.

god'like, adj., resembling a god.

god'liness, n., the state or quality of being godly.

god'ly, adj., pious, holy, highly virtuous.

god'mother, n., a female godparent.

godown', n., an E. Indian warehouse.

god'parent, n., a child's sponsor at its baptism.

god'send, n., a piece of providential good fortune.

god'son, n., a male godchild.

god'speed, interj. and n., good success.

god'ward, adv., towards God.

god'wit, n., a marsh bird, similar to the curlew but with an upturned bill.

go'er, n., one who goes; a very active person.

goes, pr.p., go.

Goethe, n., a German poet and philosopher.

Goeth'ian, adj., pert. or rel. to Goethe; n., a follower of Goethe or his works.

gof'er, n., a cake made of thin batter stamped in a honeycomb pattern from the baking irons. (Also gaufre.)

gof'(f)er, v.t., to crimp. (Also gopher and gaufer.)

gof'fered, p.p., goffer.

gof'fering, n., fluting; an ornamental edging to a book. (Also gauffering); pr.p., goffer.

go'-get'ter, n., a pushing person; one determined to secure what he wants (colloq.).

gog'gle, n., a rolling of the eyes; an amazed look; v.i., to roll the eyes; to look in amazement.

gog'gled, *adj.*, wearing goggles; *p.p.*, goggle.

gog'gle-eyed, *adj.*, having big, rolling eyes; amazed.

gog'gles, *n. pl.*, big spectacles.

gog'gling, *pr.p.*, goggle.

gog'let, *n.*, an Indian water-cooler. (Also *gugglet*.)

go'ing, *pr.p.*, go.

goi'tre, *n.*, a tumour or swelling in the throat.

goi'tred, *adj.*, pert. or rel. to the goitre.

goi'trous, *adj.*, affected with goitre.

golcon'da, *n.*, a rich gold-mine.

gold, *n.*, the chief precious metal.

gold'beater, *n.*, one who beats out gold-leaf.

gold'crest, *n.*, a very small bird with a golden crest.

gold'-digger, *n.*, one who digs for gold; a woman who wants men for their money (*colloq.*).

gold'en, *adj.*, made of gold, like gold.

gold'field, *n.*, an auriferous district.

gold'finch, *n.*, a yellow singing-bird.

gold'fish, *n.*, a reddish carp-like fish.

gold'-foil, *n.*, gold, beaten thin.

gold'hammer, *n.*, the yellow-hammer bird.

gold'ilocks, *n.*, a name for the butter-cup and other yellow flowers.

gold'-lace, *n.*, lace with a gold thread in it.

gold'-leaf, *n.*, gold, beaten extremely thin.

gold'mine, *n.*, a mine which produces gold; a source of wealth.

gold'plate, *n.*, gold vessels collectively.

gold'-size, *n.*, a size used in laying on gold-leaf.

gold'smith, *n.*, a worker in gold.

gold'-stick, *n.*, a Court official.

gold'thread, *n.*, an evergreen.

golf, *n.*, a ball game played over links; *v.i.*, to play the game of golf.

golf'-club, *n.*, the implement used to strike a golf ball; a society of golf players.

golf'er, *n.*, one who plays the game of golf.

golf'-links, *n. pl.*, land planned out for the playing of golf.

Goli'ath, *n.*, the Philistine giant; any huge person or object.

goll'iwog, *n.*, a grotesque, black doll.

goll'y, *interj.* by God; *n.*, the abbrev. for golliwog.

golosh', *n.*, *i.q.* galosh.

golup'tious, *adj.*, delightful, luscious (*colloq.*).

gombeen', *n.*, money-lending.

gombroon', *n.*, *i.q.* gomroon.

gomphi'asis, *n.*, looseness of the teeth.

gompho'sis, *n.*, socketing.

gomroon', *n.*, pottery, originally from Persia. (Also *gombroon*.)

gomu'ti, *n.*, a variety of fibre.

go'nad, *n.*, a germ-gland which acts both as ovary and spermary.

gon'dola, *n.*, a Venetian boat.

gondolier', *n.*, one who propels a gondola.

gone, *p.p.*, go.

gon'falon, *n.*, an ensign, a standard.

gonfalonier', *n.*, a chief standard-bearer.

gong, *n.*, a tambourine-like bell struck with a padded stick.

gon'gorism, *n.*, a particular kind of Spanish literary style.

goniom'eter, *n.*, an instrument for measuring angles.

goniomet'ric, *adj.*, pert. or rel. to goniometry.

goniomet'rical, *adj.*, *i.q.* goniometric.

goniom'etry, *n.*, the science of measuring angles.

gonorrhoe'a, *n.*, a contagious venereal disease.

good, *adj.*, excellent, beneficial, pious, kind; *n.*, benefit, advantage, prosperity.

good-bye', *interj.*, farewell; *n.*, a farewell (God be with ye).

good-day', *interj.*, a salutation at meeting or parting.

good-hu'moured, *adj.*, good-tempered.

good-hu'mouredly, *adv.*, cheerfully.

good'iness, *n.*, the quality of being goody.

good'ish, *adj.*, rather good.

good'lier, *adj.*, *comp.* of goodly.

good'liest, *adj.*, *super.* of goodly.

good'liness, *n.*, the quality of being goodly.

good'ly, *adj.*, pleasing to behold; noble.

good'man, *n.*, the master of a household.

goodna'ture, *n.*, a kind disposition.

goodna'tured, *adj.*, kindly disposed.

goodna'turedly, *adv.*, in a goodnatured way.

good'ness, *n.*, the quality of being good; kindness; piety.

good-night', an exclamation; *n.*, a parting salutation at night.

goods, *n. pl.*, property; chattels, commodities.

good'-sized, *adj.*, of a fair or moderate size.

goods'-train, *n.*, a freight train.

good-tem'pered, *adj.*, not easily vexed.

good-tem'peredly, *adv.*, *i.q.* goodnaturedly.

good'wife, *n.*, the mistress of a household.

goodwill', *n.*, kindliness; additional value; the intangible asset of trust and confidence in business; payment for goodwill.

Good'wins, *n. pl.*, the Goodwin sands in the Strait of Dover.

Good'wood, *n.*, a racecourse in Sussex, England.

good'y, *adj.*, feebly pious; namby-pamby; *n.*, a sweetmeat.

goof, *n.*, a stupid person.

goof'y, *adj.*, silly.

goog'ly, *n.*, a deceptive break-ball (*cricket*).

goon, *n.*, a stupid person; a person hired to terrorize workers.

Goor'kha, *n.*, *i.q.* Gurkha.

goosan'der, *n.*, a waterfowl.

goose, *n.*, a domestic, web-footed waterfowl; a tailor's iron; a foolish person (*colloq.*).

goose'berry, *n.*, a prickly shrub; its fruit.

goose'-flesh, *n.*, a roughness of the human skin caused by cold or fear.

goose′gog, *n.,* a gooseberry (*slang*).

goose′neck, *n.,* a piece of bent iron at the end of a boom or yard (*naut.*).

goos′ery, *n.,* a place for geese.

goose′step, *n.,* the German military way of marching.

go′pher, *n.,* a variety of wood; a N. American rodent; *v.t., i.q.* goffer and gauffer.

gor′al, *n.,* the Himalayan antelope.

gor′cock, *n.,* the male of the red grouse.

Gor′dian, *adj.,* pert. or rel. to Gordius, the Phrygian king.

Gor′dian knot, *n.,* Gordius's knot which Alexander cut with his sword; a complex problem.

gore, *n.,* blood, clotted blood; a triangular piece of cloth; a strip of land; *v.t.,* to pierce with a horn; to make gores in a garment.

gored, *p.p.,* gore.

gorge, *n.,* the throat; a narrow mountain pass; *v.t.,* to eat to excess; to satiate.

gorged, *p.p.,* gorge.

gor′geous, *adj.,* splendid, glittering.

gor′geously, *adv.,* in a gorgeous way.

gor′geousness, *n.,* the quality of being gorgeous.

gor′get, *n.,* throatarmour.

gor′ging, *pr.p.,* gorge.

Gor′gon, *n.,* one of the three mythological sisters, the sight of whom turned the beholder to stone.

gorgon′ia, *n.,* a sea-fan.

gorgon′ian, *adj.,* pert. or rel. to the Gorgons.

gorg′onize, *v.t.,* to petrify.

gorgonzo′la, *n.,* a variety of cheese.

goril′la, *n.,* the largest of the apes.

gorill′ine, *adj.,* like a gorilla.

gor′ily, *adv.,* in a gory way.

gor′ing, *pr.p.,* gore.

gor′mand, *n.,* a glutton. (Also *gourmand.*)

gor′mandism, *n.,* gluttony.

gor′mandize, *v.i.,* to play the glutton.

gor′mandized, *p.p.,* gormandize.

gor′mandizer, *n.,* one who gormandizes.

gor′mandizing, *pr.p.,* gormandize.

gorm′less, *adj.,* foolish, lacking in sense (*colloq.*).

gorm′lessness, *n.,* foolishness (*colloq.*).

gorse, *n.,* the furze.

Gors′edd, *n.,* the preliminary meeting of Welsh bards and druids prior to the Eisteddfod.

gors′y, *adj.,* covered with gorse.

gor′y, *adj.,* bloody.

gosh, *interj.,* by God.

gos′hawk, *n.,* a large short-winged hawk.

Gosh′en, *n.,* a place of plenty.

gos′ling, *n.,* a young goose.

gos′pel, *n.,* good tidings; the story of Jesus Christ as related by the four evangelists; truth; faith.

gos′peller, *n.,* the English name for the deacon at mass.

gos′samer, *n.,* a fine spider's web; any filmy substance.

gos′samery, *adj.,* filmy.

gos′sip, *n.,* a busy talker about other people's business; *v.i.,* to tattle, to chat.

gos′siped, *p.p.,* gossip.

gos′siper, *n.,* one who gossips.

gossip′ing, *pr.p.,* gossip.

gossoon′, *n.,* a lad.

got, *p.p.,* get.

Goth, *n.,* one of an ancient Teutonic race.

Go′tham, *n.,* a town in Nottinghamshire; New York City (*colloq.*).

Go′thamite, *n.,* one of the men of Gotham.

Goth′ic, *adj.,* like a Goth, barbarous; pert. or rel. to Gothic architecture; *n.,* the pointed style in European architecture; black-letter type.

goth′ically, *adv.,* in a Gothic way.

Goth′icism, *n.,* the principles or idiom of the Gothic style.

Goth′icize, *v.t.,* to convert into Gothic.

got′ten, *p.p.,* get; *i.q.* got.

gouache, *n.,* a way of painting in opaque colours mixed with gum, water and honey (*Fr.*).

Goud′a, *n.,* a Dutch cheese.

gouge, *n.,* a chisel with a rounded edge; *v.i.,* to force out the eye; *v.t.,* to scoop out with a gouge.

gouged, *p.p.,* gouge.

gou′ging, *pr.p.,* gouge.

gou′lash, *n.,* a highly-seasoned stew; a special deal when the cards are thrown in at contract bridge.

gourd, *n.,* a large plant with bottle-shaped fruit; a drinking vessel.

gourd′y, *adj.,* having swollen legs.

gour′mand, *n., i.q.* gormand.

gour′mandize, *n., i.q.* gormandize.

gourmet′, *n.,* an epicure; a person with refined taste in food and drink (*Fr.*).

gout, *n.,* a disease of the joints accompanied by much swelling and pain.

goût, *n.,* taste, relish (*Fr.*).

gout′ily, *adv.,* in a gouty way.

gout′iness, *n.,* a tendency to gout.

gout′y, *adj.,* affected with gout.

gov′ern, *v.t.,* to control or rule over.

governabil′ity, *n.,* the state of being governable.

gov′ernable, *adj.,* subject to control.

gov′ernance, *n., i.q.* government.

gov′ernante, *n.,* a governess, a duenna (*Fr.*).

gov′erned, *p.p.,* govern.

gov′erness, *n.,* an instructress.

gov′erning, *pr.p.,* govern.

gov′ernment, *n.,* the act of governing; rule; the Ministry.

*govern*men′tal, *adj.*, pert. or rel. to government.

gov′ernor, *n.*, one who governs; a tutor; a regulating appliance on an engine or other machine.

gov′ernorate, *n.*, a governor's province.

gov′ernor-*general*, *n.*, the ruler of a province.

gov′ernorship, *n.*, the office of a governor.

gow′an, *n.*, the daisy.

gowk, *n.*, a cuckoo, a half-witted person (*dial.*).

gown, *n.*, a long, loose garment especially of university students and teachers; a woman's dress.

gowned, *adj.*, wearing a gown; dressed.

gown′man, *n.*, *i.q.* gownsman.

gowns′man, *n.*, one who wears a gown.

goy, *n.*, Yiddish for Gentile.

goy′a, *n.*, a deep pink.

grab, *n.*, the act of grabbing; a mechanical device for shifting rough bulk materials; *v.t.*, to seize with violence, to snatch greedily.

grabbed, *p.p.*, grab.

grab′ber, *n.*, one who, or that which, grabs.

grab′bing, *pr.p.*, grab.

grab′ble, *v.i.*, to grope.

grab′bled, *p.p.*, grabble.

grab′bling, *pr.p.*, grabble.

gra′ben, *n.*, a rift-valley.

grace, *n.*, a favour, charm or divine influence; a giving of thanks; an academic decree of permission; *v.t.*, to adorn, to honour.

graced, *p.p.*, grace.

grace′ful, *adj.*, elegant, charming; aesthetically pleasing.

grace′fully, *adv.*, charmingly.

grace′fulness, *n.*, the quality of being graceful.

grace′less, *adj.*, void of grace, abandoned.

grace′lessness, *n.*, the quality of being graceless.

grace′-note, *n.*, an extra ornamental note (*mus.*).

Gra′ces, *n. pl.*, the three attendant nymphs of Venus.

gra′cile, *adj.*, slender.

gracil′ity, *n.*, slenderness.

gra′cing, *pr.p.*, grace.

gra′cious, *adj.*, elegant, kindly.

gra′ciously, *adv.*, in a gracious way.

gra′ciousness, *n.*, the quality of being gracious.

grac′kle, *n.*, a bird like a jackdaw.

gradate′, *v.t.*, to blend in grades. (Also *graduate*.)

grada′ted, *p.p.*, gradate.

grada′ting, *pr.p.*, gradate.

grada′tion, *n.*, a step in a series, gradual blending.

grada′tional *adj.*, in gradation.

grada′tionally, *adv.*, in a gradational way.

grada′tory, *adj.*, *i.q.* gradational.

grade, *n.*, degree or rank; *v.t.*, to rank in order.

gra′ded, *p.p.*, grade.

grade′ly, *adj.*, fine, decent; *adv.*, well (*Lancs.*).

grad′grind, *n.*, a person who does not allow for sentiment or the individual, as his theories are wholly statistically based.

gra′dient, *n.*, the topographical angle of incline from the horizontal.

gradin(e)′, *n.*, one in a range of steps or of seats in tiers; a ledge over an altar.

gra′ding, *pr.p.*, grade.

grad′ual, *adj.*, advancing by steps, slow; *n.*, a prose anthem sung between the epistle and gospel.

grad′ually, *adv.*, slowly, regularly.

grad′ualness, *n.*, the state of being gradual.

grad′uand, *n.*, someone about to receive an academic degree (*Scot.*).

grad′uate, *n.*, the holder of a degree; *v.i.*, *i.q.* gradate; to take an academic degree; to qualify.

grad′uated, *p.p.*, graduate.

grad′uating, *pr.p.*, graduate.

gradua′tion, *n.*, admission to a degree or diploma; regular progression.

grad′uator, *n.*, an apparatus for the minute division of lines; an electromagnet.

gra′dus, *n.*, a dictionary of prosody (*Lat.*).

graffi′ti, *n. pl.*, rough wall-sketches and writings (*It.*).

graffi′to, *n.*, the sing. of graffiti (*It.*).

graft, *n.*, a grafted shoot; a bribe (*Amer.*); a spadeful of earth; *v.i.*, to take a bribe; to work hard; *v.t.*, to insert a shoot into another tree; to transfer tissue. (Also *graf*.)

graft′ed, *p.p.*, graft.

graft′er, *n.*, one who grafts; a hard worker.

graft′ing, *pr.p.*, graft.

grail, *n.*, a chalice; a dish; a comb-maker's file.

grain, *n.*, a seed of corn; corn in general; a small unit of weight; the pattern of growth in cut wood; *v.t.*, to granulate; to paint in imitation of wood or marble.

grained, *p.p.*, grain.

grain′er, *n.*, one who grains.

grain′ing, *n.*, the act of imitating in paint the grain of wood or marble; *pr.p.*, grain.

grains, *n.*, a forked fish-spear, a harpoon.

grain′y, *adj.*, like grains; patterned.

graip, *n.*, a three-or four-pronged fork.

grallator′ial, *adj.*, pert. or rel. to the *Grallatores* or long-legged wading birds (*zool.*).

gral′lic, *adj.*, pert. or rel. to the *Grallae* or waders.

gral′loch, *n.*, a deer's viscera; *v.t.*, to disembowel.

gram, *n.*, a metric unit of weight (about 15½ grains troy weight). (Also *gramme*.)

gram(m)′a, *n.*, low-lying grasslands used for pasturage in America.

gram′arye, *n.*, witchcraft, magic.

gramer′cy, *interj.*, thank you (*arch.*).

gramina′ceous, *adj.*, *i.q.* gramineous.

gramin′eal, *adj.*, pert. or rel. to grass.

gramin′eous, *adj.*, consisting of grass.

graminif′erous, *adj.*, producing grass.

graminiv′orous, *adj.*, eating grass.

gram′malogue, *n.*, a word represented by a single shorthand sign.

gram′mar, *n.*, the conventions of correct speech or writing.

gramma′rian, *n.*, the writer of grammar; an expert in grammar.

grammat′ic, *adj.*, pert. or rel. to grammar.

grammat′ical, *adj.*, *i.q.* grammatic; correct in expression.

grammat′ically, *adv.*, according to grammatical rule.

gram′matist, *n.*, *i.q.* grammarian.

gramme, *n.*, *i.q.* gram.

gram′ophone, *n.*, an apparatus for reproducing recorded sounds; a record-player.

gramophon′ic, *adj.*, pert. or rel. to the gramophone.

gram′pus, *n.*, a porpoise-like cetacean.

granadill′a, *n.*, a kind of passion-flower or its fruit (*Span.*). (Also *grenadilla*.)

gran′am, *n.*, *i.q.* grannom.

gran′ary, *n.*, a store for grain.

grand, *adj.*, large, magnificent, exalted; *n.*, one thousand dollars (*Amer. colloq.*).

gran′dad, *n.*, the childish or affectionate name for grandfather. (Also *granddad*.)

gran′dam(e), *n.*, a grandmother.

grand′child, *n.*, a son's or daughter's child.

grandchil′dren, *n. pl.*, the pl. of grandchild.

grand′dad, *n.*, *i.q.* grandad.

grand′-daughter, *n.*, the daughter of a son or daughter.

grandee′, *n.*, one of the highest rank.

grand′er, *adj.*, *comp.* of grand.

grand′est, *adj.*, *super.* of grand.

gran′deur, *n.*, greatness, splendour.

grand′father, *n.*, a parent's father.

grandil′oquence, *n.*, bombastic talk.

grandil′oquent, *adj.*, bombastic.

grandil′oquently, *adv.*, bombastically.

gran′diose, *adj.*, affectedly grand.

gran′diosely, *adv.*, in a grandiose way.

grandios′ity, *n.*, the state of being grandiose.

grandison′ian, *adj.*, characterized by stately courtesy and great chivalry.

grand-ju′ror, *n.*, a member of a grand jury.

grand-ju′ry, *n.*, a jury to whom cases are referred from a court of first instance.

grand′ly, *adv.*, in a grand way.

grand′mother, *n.*, a parent's mother.

grand′parent, *n.*, a parent of a parent.

grand′sire, *n.*, a grandfather.

grand′son, *n.*, the son of a son or daughter.

grange, *n.*, a farmstead.

gran′ger, *n.*, a farmer.

gran′gerism, *n.*, the practice of illustrating a book with pictures lifted from other books.

gran′gerize, *v.t.*, to illustrate (books) with lifted pictures.

gran′gerized, *p.p.*, grangerize.

gran′gerizer, *n.*, one who grangerizes.

gran′gerizing, *pr.p.*, grangerize.

granif′erous, *adj.*, grain-producing.

gran′iform, *adj.*, like a grain.

gran′ite, *n.*, a hard igneous rock formation.

granit′ic, *adj.*, pert. or rel. to granite.

gran′itoid, *adj.*, like granite.

graniv′orous, *adj.*, grain-eating.

gran′nom, *n.*, a kind of water-fly or its imitation used for fly-fishing. (Also *granam*.)

gran′ny, *n.*, an old woman; a grandmother.

gran′ny-knot, *n.*, a reef-knot crossed the wrong way.

granolith′ic, *adj.*, composed of cement and granite chips.

grant, *n.*, a gift; a conveyance of property; an allowance of money for a defined purpose; *v.t.*, to concede, give or bestow.

grant′able, *adj.*, able to be granted.

grant′ed, *p.p.*, grant.

grantee′, *n.*, the recipient of a grant.

grant′er, *n.*, one who grants.

grant-in-aid, *n.*, a monetary grant.

grant′ing, *pr.p.*, grant.

grant′or, *n.*, one who conveys property.

gran′ular, *adj.*, consisting of, or resembling, grains.

granula′rity, *n.*, the state of being granular.

gran′ularly, *adv.*, in a granular way.

gran′ulate, *adj.*, *i.q.* granular; *v.t.*, to form into grains.

gran′ulated, *p.p.*, granulate.

gran′ulating, *pr.p.*, granulate.

granula′tion, *n.*, the act or effect of granulating.

gran′ulator, *n.*, that which granulates.

gran′ule, *n.*, a little grain.

gran′ulose, *n.*, an ingredient in starch convertible into sugar.

gran′ulous, *adj.*, *i.q.* granular.

grape, *n.*, the fruit of the vine; grape-shot.

grape′fruit, *n.*, a citrous, sub-tropical fruit.

gra′pery, *n.*, a vinery.

grape′-shot, *n.*, shot arranged in clusters.

grape′-sugar, *n.*, glucose.

grape′-vine, *n.*, the vine that yields the grape.

graph, *n.*, a diagram showing, by various visual means, relationships and chronologically arranged facts.

graph'ic, *adj.*, pert. or rel. to writing or drawing; highly descriptive.

graph'ical, *adj.*, i.q. graphic.

graph'ically, *adv.*, in a graphic way.

graph'ite, *n.*, blacklead.

graph'ium, *n.*, a pencil; a stylus.

graph'iure, *n.*, a S. African rodent.

graph'olite, *adj.*, pert. or rel. to graphite.

grapholog'ic, *adj.*, pert. or rel. to graphology.

grapholog'ical, *adj.*, i.q. graphologic.

graphol'ogy, *n.*, the art of judging character from handwriting.

graphom'eter, *n.*, an instrument that measures angular degrees.

graphomet'ric, *adj.*, pert. or rel. to a graphometer.

graphomet'rical, *adj.*, i.q. graphometric.

graph'otype, *n.*, a printing process for producing relief blocks.

grap'nel, *n.*, a small anchor; large tongs; a hook for attaching one thing to another.

grap'ple, *n.*, a fight, a seizure; *v.i.*, to struggle; to contend with; *v.t.*, to seize.

grap'pled, *p.p.*, grapple.

grap'pling, *pr.p.*, grapple.

grap'pling-iron, *n.*, a hook; a grapnel.

grap'y, *adj.*, of, or like, grapes.

grasp, *n.*, a seizure, hold, intellectual apprehension or scope; *v.t.*, to seize with the hand; to perceive meaning.

grasp'able, *adj.*, able to be grasped.

grasped, *p.p.*, grasp.

grasp'er, *n.*, one who grasps.

grasp'ing, *adj.*, avaricious; *pr.p.*, grasp.

grasp'ingly, *adv.*, in a grasping way.

grasp'ingness, *n.*, avariciousness.

grass, *n.*, the common herbage of the field; *v.t.*, to cover with grass; to betray by giving information to the police (*slang*).

grass'-blade, *n.*, a blade of grass.

grass'-cutter, *n.*, one who, or that which, cuts grass.

grassed, *p.p.*, grass.

grass'-green, *adj.*, of the colour of grass; *n.*, the colour of grass.

grass'hopper, *n.*, a locust-like, jumping insect.

grass'iness, *n.*, the state of being grassy.

grass'ing, *pr.p.*, grass.

grass'land, *n.*, land which is kept under grass.

grass'-plot, *n.*, a grass-covered plot of ground.

grass'-snake, *n.*, a common, non-venomous English snake.

grass'-wid'ow, *n.*, a wife temporarily separated from her husband.

grass'-wid'ower, *n.*, a husband temporarily separated from his wife.

grass'-wrack, *n.*, a kind of seaweed.

grass'y, *adj.*, covered with grass; grass-like.

grate, *n.*, a frame for holding fuel; *v.i.*, to make a grinding noise; to jar; *v.t.*, to rub; to break into small pieces.

gra'ted, *p.p.*, grate.

grate'ful, *adj.*, full of gratitude, thankful.

grate'fully, *adv.*, in a grateful way.

grate'fulness, *n.*, gratitude.

gra'ter, *n.*, a utensil on which substances can be grated.

gra'ticulate, *v.t.*, to divide into squares.

gra'ticule, *n.*, the ruled grid on a map; a scale in the eye-piece of a telescope, etc.

gratifica'tion, *n.*, the act of gratifying; pleasure, reward.

grat'ified, *p.p.*, gratify.

grat'ifier, *n.*, one who gratifies.

grat'ify, *v.t.*, to give satisfaction or pleasure.

grat'ifying, *adj.*, agreeable; *pr.p.*, gratify.

grat'ifyingly, *adv.*, rewardingly.

grat'in, *n.*, a light crust of breadcrumbs or grated cheese (*Fr.*).

gra'ting, *adj.*, harsh; *n.*, open bars; *pr.p.*, grate.

gra'tingly, *adv.*, in a grating way.

gra'tis, *adv.*, without pay (*Lat.*).

grat'itude, *n.*, the feeling of thankfulness.

gratu'itous, *adj.*; without pay; unprovoked.

gratu'itously, *adv.*, without pay or provocation.

gratu'ity, *n.*, a free gift.

grat'ulant, *adj.*, congratulating.

grat'ulate, *v.t.*, i.q. congratulate.

grat'ulated, *p.p.*, gratulate.

grat'ulating, *pr.p.*, gratulate.

gratula'tion, *n.*, i.q. congratulation.

grat'ulatory, *adj.*, i.q. congratulatory.

grava'men, *n.*, a complaint; substance, weight (*Lat.*).

grava'mina, *n. pl.*, the pl. of gravamen (*Lat.*).

grave, *adj.*, heavy, serious, of low musical pitch; *n.*, a burial-place in the ground; *v.t.*, to carve, to engrave.

graved, *p.p.*, grave.

grave'digger, *n.*, one who · digs graves; a kind of insect that buries the bodies of other insects, etc. to use as food for its larvae.

grav'el, *n.*, small stones, usually mixed with sand; a disease of the kidneys and bladder; *v.t.*, to lay gravel on; to embarrass.

grav'el-blind, *adj.*, half-blind.

grav'el(l)ed, *p.p.*, gravel.

grav'el'less, *adj.*, unburied.

grav'el(l)ing, *pr.p.*, gravel.

grav'elly, *adj.*, composed, or full of, gravel.

grav'el-pit, *n.*, a pit out of which gravel is dug.

grav'el-voiced, *adj.*, hoarse-voiced.

grave'ly, *adv.*, seriously.

gra'ven, *adj.*, carved; *p.p.*, grave.

grave′ness, n., the quality of being grave.

grave′olence, n., a rank, disagreeable smell.

grave′olent, adj., having a strong, unpleasant smell.

gra′ver, adj., comp. of grave; n., an engraver; a burin.

Graves, n., light, white wine produced in the Graves area of France (Fr.).

gra′vest, adj., super. of grave.

grave′stone, n., a stone over, or at the head of, a grave.

grave′yard, n., a cemetery or churchyard.

grav′id, adj., pregnant.

grav′igrade, adj., walking heavily.

gravim′eter, n., an instrument for finding the specific gravity of bodies.

gra′ving, n., the act of engraving; the act of cleaning a ship's bottom; pr.p., grave.

gra′ving-dock, n., a dock where a ship's bottom is cleaned.

grav′itate, v.i., to tend towards.

grav′itated, p.p., gravitate.

grav′itating, pr.p., gravitate.

gravita′tion, n., the process of gravitating; the force by which particles of matter tend to be drawn toward each other.

gravita′tional, adj., with a natural tendency.

grav′itative, adj., causing or tending to gravitate.

grav′ity, n., weightiness; seriousness; importance; the force drawing all bodies towards the earth's centre.

gravure′, n., an engraving; the abbrev. for photogravure.

gra′vy, n., the juice of roast meat.

gray, adj., i.q. grey.

gray′beard, n., i.q. greybeard.

gray′ish, adj., i.q. greyish.

gray′ling, n., a freshwater fish.

gray′wacke, n., a palaeozoic sandstone. (Also greywacke.)

graze, n., a slight rub; a minor abrasion;

v.i., to eat grass; v.t., to use as pasture; to touch or rub very lightly.

grazed, p.p., graze.

gra′zer, n., anything that grazes.

gra′zier, n., a cattlebreeder.

gra′ziery, n., the place where cattle are fed for market.

gra′zing, pr.p., graze.

grease, n., animal fat; a disease of horses' heels; v.t., to smear with grease; to bribe.

greased, p.p., grease.

greas′er, n., a lubricator.

greas′ier, adj., comp. of greasy.

greas′iest, adj., super. of greasy.

greas′ily, adv., in a greasy way.

greas′iness, n., the state of being greasy.

greas′ing, pr.p., grease.

greas′y, adj., like grease; smeared.

great, adj., large, exalted, pregnant.

great′coat, n., an overcoat.

great′er, adj., comp. of great.

great′est, adj., super. of great.

great′-hearted, adj., generous; high-minded.

great′-heart′edness, n., magnanimity.

great′ly, adv., much.

great′ness, n., the quality of being great.

greats, n. pl., the final honours school at Oxford.

greave, n., ancient leg armour.

greaves, n. pl., armour for the ankles; fibrous scraps and tallow refuse used for dog food and fish-bait.

grebe, n., a diving-bird.

Gre′cian, adj., Greek, pert. or rel. to Greece; n., a Greek scholar; a sixth-form boy at Christ's Hospital.

Gr(a)e′cism, n., a Greek idiom.

Gr(a)e′cize, v.t. and i., to emulate the Greeks in spirit, ideas, ways, etc.

greed, n., avarice.

greed′ily, adv., in a greedy way.

greed′iness, n., the state or quality of being greedy.

greed′y, adj., avaricious, gluttonous.

Greek, adj., i.q. Grecian; n., a native of Hellas; the Greek language.

greek′-fire, n., an inflammable substance said to be inextinguishable.

green, adj., of the colour of grass; new, fresh; n., the colour of growing grass; a grassy space.

green′back, n., American paper money.

green′er, adj., comp. of green.

green′ery, n., green things, vegetables.

green′est, adj., super. of green.

green′-eyed, adj., jealous.

green′finch, n., a yellow and green British song-bird.

green′fing′ers, n., gardening skill (colloq.).

green′fly, n., a kind of aphis.

green′gage, n., a variety of plum.

green′grocer, n., one who sells fruit, flowers and vegetables.

green′horn, n., a simpleton.

green′house, n., a conservatory; a glass house for the protection of young or tender plants.

green′ing, n., the act of becoming green; an apple which is green when ripe.

green′ish, adj., almost green.

green′let, n., a small, American songbird.

green′ness, n., verdure, inexperience.

green′-room, n., the actors' room behind the scenes.

greens, n. pl., vegetables.

green′sand, n., a greenish sandstone.

green′shank, n., a European sandpiper.

green′stick, n., a type of bone-fracture, esp. in children.

green′sward, n., turf covered with green grass.

Green′wich, n., a district of London famous as the place of 0° longitude.

green'wood, n., a wood in leaf.

greet, v.i., to weep (Scot.); v.t., to welcome, to accost.

greet'ed, p.p., greet.

greet'er, n., one who greets.

greet'ing, n., a salute, a welcome; weeping (Scot.); pr.p., greet.

greff'ier, n., a registrar, esp. in the Channel Islands (Fr.).

grega'rious, adj., living in flocks; fond of company; growing in clusters (bot.).

grega'riously, adv., in a gregarious way.

grega'riousness, n., living gregariously.

Grego'rian, adj., pert. or rel. to Pope Gregory I.

Grego'rian chant, n., plainsong choral music arranged by Pope Gregory I.

greg'ory-powd'er, n., a mild aperient powder of magnesia, ginger and rhubarb.

grem'ial, n., a silk apron worn by a bishop at some ceremonies.

grem'lin, n., a mischievous sprite believed to cause accidents (R.A.F. slang).

grenade', n., a hollow shell filled with explosives; a fire-extinguisher.

grenadier', n., a soldier in the British Grenadier Guards; a S. African weaver-bird.

grenadill'a, n., i.q. granadilla.

gren'adine, n., a thin gauzy, dress fabric; a dish of larded and glazed fillets of veal or poultry (Fr.).

gren'adine, n., a black-currant syrup (Fr.).

gresso'rial, adj., capable of walking (zool.).

grew, p.p., grow.

grey, adj., of a colour—white and black mixed. (Also gray.)

grey'beard, n., an old man. (Also gray-beard.)

grey'cing, n., the abbrev. for greyhound-racing (colloq.).

grey'hound, n., a slender, swift type of hound.

grey'hound-rac'ing, n., a modern sport in which greyhounds course a mechanical

hare for betting purposes.

grey'ish, adj., somewhat grey. (Also grayish.)

grey'lag, n., the common European wild goose, being the original of the domestic goose.

grey'ness, n., the state of being grey.

grey'wacke, n., i.q. gray-wacke.

grice, n., a small, sucking pig.

grid, n., a grating, a gridiron; a system of power-transmission lines; numbered squares on a map.

grid'dle, n., an iron plate; i.q. girdle.

grid'dle-cake, n., a cake baked on a griddle.

gride, v.t., to jar.

gri'ded, p.p., gride.

grid'elin, n., a grey-violet colour.

gri'ding, pr.p., gride.

grid'iron, n., an iron grated cooking-utensil.

grief, n., sorrow, compunction.

griev'ance, n., a sense of injustice; a complaint.

grieve, n., a farm-bailiff (Scot.); v.i., to feel grief, to mourn; v.t., to cause grief.

grieved, p.p., grieve.

griev'er, n., one who grieves.

griev'ing, pr.p., grieve.

griev'ingly, adv., sadly, sorrowfully.

griev'ous, adj., causing grief; distressing; vexatious; severe.

griev'ously, adv., in a grievous way.

griev'ousness, n., the quality of being grievous.

grif'fin, n., a fabulous beast with eagle's wings and a lion's body; a novice. (Also griffon and gryphon.)

grif'fon, n., a coarse-haired terrier-type dog.

grig, n., a small eel; a cricket or grasshopper.

grill, n., a gridiron; a device in a cooker for grilling meat; meat grilled; a grating; v.t., to broil; to question closely, severely.

grill(e), n., an opening through bars.

grillade', n., the act of grilling; grilled meat.

grill'age, n., timber foundations laid in marshy ground.

grilled, p.p., grill.

grill'ing, adj., scorching hot; pr.p., grill.

grill'-room, n., the part of a restaurant where meat is grilled and served as ordered.

grilse, n., a young Scotch salmon.

grim, adj., forbidding, stern, hideous.

grimace', n., a distortion of the countenance; v.i., to make faces.

grimaced', p.p., grimace.

grimac'er, n., one who grimaces.

grimac'ing, pr.p., grimace.

grimal'kin, n., an old cat; a jealous old woman.

grime, n., dirt, mud, especially ingrained; v.t., to make grimy.

grimed, adj., pitted with dirt; p.p., grime.

gri'mier, adj., comp. of grimy.

gri'miest, adj., super. of grimy.

gri'mily, adv., in a grimy way.

gri'miness, n., the state or quality of being grimy.

gri'ming, pr.p., grime.

grim'ly, adv., in a grim way.

grim'mer, adj., comp. of grim.

grim'mest, adj., super. of grim.

grim'ness, n., the quality of being grim.

grimoire', n., a magician's manual (Fr.).

gri'my, adj., muddy, dirty.

grin, n., a forced or sneering smile; v.i., to set the teeth together and withdraw the lips in anger or mirth.

grind, v.t., to sharpen; to reduce to powder; to oppress.

grind'er, n., anything that grinds; a molar tooth.

grind'ery, n., a place for grinding; material in the leather trade.

grind'ing, *n.,* the grinder's trade; *pr.p.,* grind.

grind'stone, *n.,* a stone for sharpening tools.

grin'go, *n.,* an Englishman or Anglo-American in Latin America.

grinned, *p.p.,* grin.

grin'ner, *n.,* one who grins.

grin'ning, *pr.p.,* grin.

grin'ningly, *adv.,* in a grinning manner.

grip, *n.,* a grasp, pressure; part of a golf-club shaft held by the player; a capacious bag (*U.S.A.*). (Also **gripsack**) *v.t.,* to clutch or hold tightly.

gripe, *n.,* a grasp; colic pain; *v.t.,* to hold in a clutch; to squeeze.

griped, *p.p.,* gripe.

gri'per, *n.,* anything that gripes.

grip'ing, *pr.p.,* gripe.

grippe, *n.,* influenza (*Fr.*).

gripped, *p.p.,* grip.

grip'per, *n.,* anything that grips.

grip'ping, *pr.p.,* grip.

grip'sack, *n.,* a traveller's handbag (*U.S.A.*).

grisaille', *n.,* a mode of painting in grey.

gris'eous, *adj.,* bluish-grey (*bot.,* *zool.*).

grisette', *n.,* a shop-girl; a smartly dressed working-girl (*Fr.*).

gris'kin, *n.,* the spine of pork.

gris'liness, *n.,* the quality of being grisly.

gris'ly, *adj.,* rather grey; hideous; horrific in appearance.

gris'on, *n.,* a weasel-like animal.

Grisons', *n. pl.,* Swiss cantons (*Fr.*).

grist, *n.,* corn for grinding; supply.

gris'tle, *n.,* cartilage.

gris'tly, *adj.,* cartilaginous.

grit, *n.,* the coarse part of meal, sand or gravel; endurance.

grits, *n. pl.,* coarsely ground grain.

grit'stone, *n.,* coarse sandstone.

grit'tiness, *n.,* the state or quality of being gritty.

grit'ty, *adj.,* full of grit.

griz'zle, *v.i.,* to complain whiningly (*slang*).

griz'zled, *adj.,* growing grey; *p.p.,* grizzle.

griz'zler, *n.,* one who frets or grumbles.

griz'zling, *pr.p.,* grizzle.

griz'zly, *adj.,* greyish; *n.,* a grizzly bear.

groan', *n.,* a low sound of pain; *v.i.,* to utter a low sound of pain.

groaned, *p.p.,* groan.

groan'er, *n.,* one who groans.

groan'ing, *pr.p.,* groan.

groan'ingly, *adv.,* in a groaning way.

groat, *n.,* an old English coin.

groats, *n. pl.,* oats or wheat hulled.

grob'ian, *n.,* a clumsy, awkward, slovenly person.

gro'cer, *n.,* a dealer in tea, sugar, spice, etc.

gro'cery, *n.,* a grocer's shop; grocer's goods.

grocete'ria, *n.,* a self-service grocery store (*colloq.*).

grog, *n.,* a mixture of spirits and water.

grog'gery, *n.,* a grog-shop (*Amer.*).

grog'gily, *adv.,* shakily.

grog'giness, *n.,* the state of being groggy.

grog'gy, *adj.,* intoxicated; unsteady.

gro'gram, *n.,* a coarse fabric of silk, mohair, etc.

groin, *n.,* the depressed part of the thigh; the line where two vaults intersect (*arch.*); *v.t.,* to construct groins.

groined, *adj.,* having groins; *p.p.,* groin.

groin'ing, *pr.p.,* groin.

Gro'lier, *n.,* a highly ornate style of binding.

Gro'lieresque, *adj.,* in the Grolier style of binding.

grom'(m)et, *n.,* a rope-bound ring; a cannon-wad. (Also **grummet.**)

grom'well, *n.,* a plant with stony seeds, previously used in medicine.

groom, *n.,* one who has the care of a horse; a bridegroom; *v.t.,* to look after a horse.

groomed, *p.p.,* groom.

groom'ing, *pr.p.,* groom.

grooms'man, *n.,* a bridegroom's supporter.

groove, *n.,* a channel or furrow; *v.t.,* to cut into channels.

grooved, *p.p.,* groove.

groov'er, *n.,* anything that grooves.

groov'iness, *n.,* routine; the state of being cut in furrows.

groov'ing, *pr.p.,* groove.

groov'y, *adj.,* cut in furrows; trendy (*colloq.*).

grope, *v.i.,* to feel about in the dark.

groped, *p.p.,* grope.

gro'per, *n.,* one who gropes; a kind of fish.

gro'ping, *pr.p.,* grope.

gro'pingly, *adv.,* in a groping way.

gros'beak, *n.,* a kind of finch, with a large, strong bill.

gro'schen, *n.,* a small bronze Austrian coin (*Ger.*).

gros de Naples, *n.,* heavy silk fabric with a dull finish (*Fr.*).

gros'grain, *n.,* a variety of strong corded fabric (*Fr.*).

gross, *adj.,* coarse, big; *n.,* the bulk; twelve dozen.

gross'er, *adj.,* *comp.* of gross.

gross'est, *adj.,* *super.* of gross.

grossifica'tion, *n.,* the act of making, or the state of being, thick or gross; the swelling of the ovary after being fertilized (*bot.*).

gross'ly, *adv.,* in a gross way.

gross'ness, *n.,* coarseness; unrefined animal behaviour.

grossula'ceous, *adj.,* pert. or rel. to the gooseberry and currant plants.

gross'ular, *adj.,* pert. or rel. to the gooseberry; *n.,* a kind of garnet found in Siberia.

grot, *n.,* *i.q.* grotto.

grotesque', *adj.,* odd, fantastic.

grotesque'ly, *adv.,* oddly, ludicrously.

grotesque'ness, *n.,* the quality of being grotesque.

grotes′querie, *n.*, ludicrous incongruity.

grot′to, *n.*, a cavern. (Also *grot*.)

grouch, *n.*, a sulky fit; a discontented mood or person; *v.i.*, to grumble or grouse (*colloq.*).

ground, *adj.*, fundamental; *n.*, the earth's surface; a basis; *p.p.*, grind; *v.i.*, to run aground; *v.t.*, to fix or base; to instruct in elements.

ground′age, *n.*, a port duty.

ground′-ash, *n.*, a young ash.

ground′-control′, *n.*, the radar control of aircraft landings.

ground′ed, *p.p.*, ground.

ground′-floor, *n.*, the storey on street level or the next one above the basement.

ground′hog, *n.*, a N. American marmot.

ground′ing, *n.*, elementary instruction; *pr.p.*, ground.

ground′-ivy, *n.*, a creeping plant with bluish-purple flowers and pungent leaves.

ground′-landlord, *n.*, the owner of land on a building lease.

ground′less, *adj.*, lacking proof, foundation or certainty; unreasonable.

ground′lessly, *adv.*, in an unreasonable way.

ground′lessness, *n.*, the quality of being groundless.

ground′ling, *n.*, an uneducated person; a kind of fish; a dwarf or creeping plant.

ground′-nut, *n.*, the peanut or monkey-nut.

ground′-oak, *n.*, an oak sapling.

ground′-plan, *n.*, a drawing in flat of the divisions of a building on the ground level.

ground′-plot, *n.*, a plot of ground; *n.*, *i.q.* ground-plan.

ground′-rent, *n.*, rent paid to a freeholder.

ground′sel, *n.*, a weed with yellow flowers; *i.q.* groundsill.

ground′sill, *n.*, the lowest timber in a wooden framework. (Also *groundsel*.)

grounds′man, *n.*, a man in charge of a sports ground; an aerodrome mechanic.

ground′-swell, *n.*, a deep, heavy sea swell due to a storm or an earthquake.

ground′work, *n.*, the elements of a subject.

group, *n.*, an assemblage, a cluster; a number of people associated for a common purpose; *v.t.* and *i.*, to collect together, to form into a group or cluster.

group′age, *n.*, *i.q.* grouping.

Group′ Captain, *n.*, an R.A.F. officer corresponding to the Army rank of Colonel.

grouped, *p.p.*, group.

group′er, *n.*, a kind of W. Indian and Australian fish.

group′ing, *n.*, a collecting together; *pr.p.*, group.

grouse, *n.*, a game bird; *v.i.*, to complain (*slang*).

groused, *p.p.*, grouse.

grous′er, *n.*, one who is always complaining.

grouse′-shooting, *n.*, the shooting of driven grouse, which begins on 12th August.

grous′ing, *pr.p.*, grouse.

grout, *n.*, a coarse mortar; *v.t.*, to fill in the spaces between stone.

grout′ed, *p.p.*, grout.

grout′ing, *pr.p.*, grout.

grove, *n.*, a wood; a shady avenue.

groved, *adj.*, wooded.

grov′el, *v.i.*, to lie prone, to be low or mean; to adopt an abject manner.

grov′el(l)ed, *p.p.*, grovel.

grov′el(l)er, *n.*, one who grovels.

grove′less, *adj.*, without groves.

grov′el(l)ing, *pr.p.*, grovel.

grov′el(l)ingly, *adv.*, abjectly.

grov′y, *adj.*, *i.q.* groved.

grow, *v.i.*, to increase; (of a plant) to develop and become larger; *v.t.*, to cultivate.

grow′able, *adj.*, able to be grown.

grow′er, *n.*, a cultivator; one who grows.

grow′ing, *pr.p.*, grow.

grow′ingly, *adv.*, in a growing way.

growl, *n.*, a dog's angry snarl; *v.i.*, to snarl like a dog.

growled, *p.p.*, growl.

growl′er, *n.*, one who, or that which, growls; a four-wheeled cab (*old slang*).

growl′ery, *n.*, a place to growl in; a private room or den.

growl′ing, *pr.p.*, growl.

growl′ingly, *adv.*, in a growling way.

grown, *p.p.*, grow.

grown-up′, *adj.*, mature; *n.*, an adult.

growth, *n.*, the act of growing; increase; result, effect.

groyne, *n.*, a breakwater.

grub, *n.*, the larva of an insect; a dirty-looking sloven; food (*slang*); *v.i.*, to do dirty work; *v.t.*, to dig or root up.

grubbed, *p.p.*, grub.

grub′ber, *n.*, one who grubs.

grub′biness, *n.*, the state of being grubby or dirty; the state of being full of grubs.

grub′bing, *pr.p.*, grub.

grub′bing-hoe, *n.*, a tool used for uprooting shrubs, trees, etc.

grub′by, *adj.*, grub-infested; dirty.

Grub′-street, *adj.*, low, mean, of little value; *n.*, a street in London (now Milton Street) once occupied by needy authors and booksellers' hacks.

grudge, *n.*, ill-will, envy; an old-standing offence; *v.t.*, to give or take reluctantly.

grudged, *p.p.*, grudge.

grudg′er, *n.*, one who grudges.

grudg′ing, *pr.p.*, grudge.

grudg′ingly, *adv.*, in a grudging way.

gru′el, *n.*, meal boiled in milk or water.

gru′elling, *adj.*, exacting; *n.*, rough treatment.

grue′some, adj., horrible.

grue′somely, adv., in a gruesome way.

grue′someness, n., the state of being gruesome.

gruff, adj., rough, harsh, hoarse.

gruff′ish, adj., i.q. gruff.

gruff′ly, adv., roughly, hoarsely.

gruff′ness, n., the quality of being gruff.

grum, adj., surly, morose.

grum′ble, v.i., to complain, to find fault.

grum′bled, p.p., grumble.

grum′bler, n., one who grumbles.

grum′bling, pr.p., grumble.

grum′blingly, adv., in a grumbling way.

grume, n., a bloodclot.

grum′met, n., i.q. grommet.

gru′mous, adj., clotted, concreted.

grump, n., a grumpy person.

grump′ily, adv., in a grumpy way.

grump′iness, n., ill-temper.

grump′ish, adj., i.q. grumpy.

grump′y, adj., surly, cross.

grun′del, n., a kind of fish.

grun′dyism, n., conventional prudery.

grunt, n., a pig's natural noise; an American edible fish; v.i., to make the sound of a pig.

grunt′ed, p.p., grunt.

grunt′er, n., a pig; a kind of fish.

grunt′ing, pr.p., grunt.

grunt′ingly, adv., in a grunting manner.

Gruyère′, n., a variety of cheese.

gry′phon, n., i.q. griffin.

grypo′sis, n., the abnormal inward-growing of a nail.

grys′bok, n., a small, grey-speckled antelope of S. Africa.

guacha′ro, n., a S. American bird valued for its oil.

gua′co, n., a South American tropical plant whose sap is said to cure snakebites.

guai′acum, n., a resinous shrub.

guan, n., a S. American gallinaceous bird allied to the curassow.

gua′na, n., i.q. iguana.

guana′co, n., a wild llama.

guanif′erous, adj., producing guano.

gua′no, n., a fertilizer made from sea-fowls' dung.

guara′cha, n., a lively Spanish dance in which the dancer accompanies himself on the guitar (Span.).

guara′na, n., an Indian food made from the powdered seeds of a Brazilian shrub (also used in medicine).

guarantee′, n., a surety; one to whom a guaranty is given; v.t., to warrant, insure, be surety for.

guaranteed′, adj., warranted; p.p., guarantee.

guarantee′ing, pr.p., guarantee.

guarantor′, n., one who guarantees.

guaranty, n., a legal guarantee.

guard, n., defence, an attitude of defence; one in charge of a coach or train; soldiers on guard; a person whose duty it is to protect people or property; v.t., to protect or defend.

guard′ant, adj., on guard, confronting (her.).

guard′-boat, n., an official harbour-boat for the safety of those under way.

guard′ed, adj., cautious; p.p., guard.

guard′edly, adv., cautiously, with reserve.

guard′edness, n., cautiousness, circumspection.

guard′er, n., one who guards.

guard′house, n., a building for military guards or for prisoners.

guard′ian, adj., guarding; n., one who guards; a warden.

guard′ianship, n., the office of a guardian.

guard′ing, pr.p., guard.

guard′less, adj., without guard.

guard′-rail, n., a rail to prevent falling, etc.

guard′-ring, n., a ring worn to protect another.

guard′room, n., i.q. guardhouse.

guard′ship, n., a warship used for defending a port or harbour.

guards′man, n., a soldier, esp. an officer in a regiment of the Guards.

Guatema′lan, adj., pert. or rel. to Guatemala; n., a native of G.

gua′va, n., a S. American tree with pear-shaped fruit.

guayule′, n., an aster-like Mexican plant whose sap produces a rubber substitute.

gubernato′rial, adj., pert. or rel. to a governor.

gud′dle, v.t. and i., to tickle fish; to catch fish with the hands (Scot.).

gudg′eon, n., a freshwater fish; a silly person (colloq.).

gudg′eon-pin, n., a pin which holds a piston-rod and a connecting-rod together.

Guebre, n., a fire-worshipper.

guel′der-rose, n., the snowball tree.

Guelph, n., one of the great Italian party of Guelphs.

Guelph′ic, adj., pert. or rel. to the Guelphs.

guer′don, n., reward.

guer′donless, adj., without reward.

guere′za, n., a black, long-haired Abyssinian monkey.

guer(r)il′la, adj., pert. or rel. to irregular warfare; n., irregular warfare (Span.).

Guern′sey, adj., a kind of cow from the Channel Islands which produces very rich milk; n., one of the English Channel Islands.

guern′sey, n., a close-fitting knitted woollen garment.

guess, n., a conjecture or surmise; v.t., to conjecture, to surmise.

guess′able, adj., able to be guessed.

guessed, p.p., guess.

guess′er, n., one who guesses.

guess'ing, *pr.p.*, guess.

guess'ingly, *adv.*, surmisingly.

guess'work, *n.*, guessing at random.

guest, *n.*, a visitor being entertained.

guest'house, *n.*, a boarding-house.

guest'-night, *n.*, a night set aside for the entertainment of guests at a club, mess, etc.

guest'-rope, *n.*, a rope to fasten a boat to a vessel; an additional tow-rope used for steadying.

guest'wise, *adv.*, like a guest or stranger.

guff, *n.*, empty, useless talk (*slang*).

guffaw', *n.*, a rude laugh; *v.i.*, to laugh rudely.

guffawed, *p.p.*, guffaw.

guffaw'ing, *pr.p.*, guffaw.

guggle, *n.* and *v.i.*, *i.q.* gurgle.

gugg'let, *n.*, *i.q.* goglet.

guhr, *n.*, an earthy deposit from water in rocks.

guib, *n.*, a W. African antelope.

gui'chet, *n.*, a ticket-office window; a hatch (*Fr.*).

guid'able, *adj.*, willing or able to be guided.

guid'age, *n.*, *i.q.* guidance.

guid'ance, *n.*, leading, direction.

guide, *n.*, one who leads the way; a guide-book; *v.t.*, to lead or direct.

guide'-book, *n.*, a book directing the traveller.

guid'ed, *p.p.*, guide.

guide'less, *n.*, without a guide.

guide'-post, *n.*, a sign-post.

guid'er, *n.*, anything that guides.

guide'-rope, *n.*, a small, steadying rope.

guid'ing, *pr.p.*, guide.

guid'on, *n.*, a pennant.

guild, *n.*, a fraternity, an association. (Also gild.)

guild'er, *n.*, the Dutch florin.

guild'hall, *n.*, the hall where a guild or corporation meets.

guile, *n.*, deceit, cunning.

guile'ful, *adj.*, deceitful, cunning.

guile'fully, *adv.*, deceitfully.

guile'fulness, *n.*, the quality of being guileful.

guile'less, *adj.*, innocent of guile; ingenuous.

guile'lessly, *adv.*, in a guileless way.

guile'lessness, *n.*, freedom from guile.

guil'lemot, *n.*, a kind of auk.

guilloche', *n.*, a twisted ornament (*archit.*).

guillotine', *n.*, an instrument for beheading, cutting and trimming; *v.t.*, to behead with the guillotine.

guillotined', *p.p.*, guillotine.

guillotin'ing, *pr.p.*, guillotine.

guilt, *n.*, sin, crime.

guilt'ier, *adj.*, *comp.* of guilty.

guilt'iest, *adj.*, *super.* of guilty.

guilt'ily, *adv.*, in a guilty way.

guilt'iness, *n.*, the state or quality of being guilty.

guilt'less, *adj.*, innocent.

guilt'lessly, *adv.*, in a guiltless way.

guilt'lessness, *n.*, the state of being guiltless.

guilt'y, *adj.*, sinful, criminal.

guim'bard, *n.*, a jew's-harp.

guimpe, *n.*, an under-blouse for wear with a low-necked dress (*Fr.*).

Guin'ea, *n.*, an African and S. American place-name.

guin'ea, *n.*, an old English coin.

guin'ea-fowl, *n.*, a bird found in the African Guinea.

Guin'ean, *adj.*, pert. or rel. to Guinea; *n.*, a native of G.

guin'ea-pig, *n.*, a little rodent of S. America.

guipure, *n.*, a kind of lace, sometimes used in a guimpe (*Fr.*).

guise, *n.*, manner, appearance, semblance.

guitar', *n.*, a stringed instrument.

guitar'ist, *n.*, a guitar-player.

Gujara'ti, *n.*, a language of N.W. India.

gulch, *n.*, a rocky valley.

gul'den, *n.*, a dutch silver coin; also the florin of Austria and Hungary.

gules, *adj.* and *n.*, heraldic for the colour red.

gulf, *n.*, a large bay; an abyss.

Gulf'-stream, *n.*, a current of warm water coming from the Gulf of Mexico across the Atlantic towards Europe.

gulf'-weed, *n.*, seaweed found in tropical waters.

gulf'y, *adj.*, full of whirl-pools.

gull, *n.*, a trick; a person easily tricked; a sea-bird; *v.t.*, to trick, to cheat.

gulled, *p.p.*, gull.

gull'ery, *n.*, the habitation of gulls.

gull'et, *n.*, the food passage; a water channel; a river mouth.

gul'ley, *n.*, a water-worn channel; a drain; a large knife; a fielding position in cricket.

gullibil'ity, *n.*, the quality of being gullible.

gul'lible, *adj.*, easily tricked.

gul'lied, *adj.*, channelled.

gul'ling, *pr.p.*, gull.

gul'lish, *adj.*, *i.q.* gullible.

gul'ly-hole, *n.*, the opening from the street into a drain or sewer.

gulos'ity, *n.*, greediness, gluttony.

gulp, *n.*, the act of gulping; *v.t.*, to swallow eagerly; to suck down.

gulped, *p.p.*, gulp.

gulp'ing, *pr.p.*, gulp.

gulp'ingly, *adv.*, in a gulping way.

gum, *n.*, a resinous exudation; the fleshy socket of the teeth; *v.t.*, to stick with gum.

gum-ar'abic, *n.*, gum derived from the acacia.

gum'bo, *n.*, a soup thickened with the pods of the okra plant.

gum'boil, *n.*, a boil on the gums.

gum'boot', *n.*, a rubber boot.

gum'lah, *n.*, a large, Indian, earthenware water-pot.

gumm′a, *n.*, a syphilitic tumour.

gummed, *p.p.*, gum.

gummif′erous, *adj.*, yielding gum.

gum′miness, *n.*, the state or quality of being gummy.

gum′ming, *pr.p.*, gum.

gum′mous, *adj.*, *i.q.* gummy.

gum′my, *adj.*, sticky, like gum.

gump′tion, *n.*, intelligent perception (*colloq.*).

gum′-tree, *n.*, a gum-producing tree, esp. the eucalyptus.

gun, *n.*, a fire-arm.

gun′-barrel, *n.*, the barrel of a gun.

gun′boat, *n.*, a light warship with heavy guns.

gun′-carriage, *n.*, a carriage on which a gun is mounted.

gun′-cotton, *n.*, a high explosive.

gun′fire, *n.*, the sound of guns firing.

gun′layer, *n.*, a gunner who sights and elevates a gun.

gun′man, *n.*, a ruffian armed with a revolver.

gun′-metal, *n.*, a copper and tin or zinc alloy.

gun′nel, *n.*, *i.q.* gunwale.

gun′ner, *n.*, an artilleryman; a naval warrant officer with charge of the ordnance.

gunn′era, *n.*, the prickly rhubarb, an ornamental plant having large leaves.

gun′nery, *n.*, the science of artillery.

gun′ning, *n.*, game-shooting (*Amer.*).

gun′ny, *n.*, a coarse kind of sackcloth.

gun′powder, *n.*, an explosive powder.

gun′-room, *n.*, the junior officers' compartment in a ship.

gun′shot, *n.*, the range of a gun's fire.

gun′smith, *n.*, a manufacturer of guns.

gun′-stock, *n.*, the stock of a gun.

gun′ter, *n.*, a flat 2 ft. rule with logarithms, etc. for solving surveying and navigational problems; a special arrangement of top mast and rigging of a sailing craft.

gun′wale, *n.*, the upper edge of a ship's side. (Also *gunnel.*)

gun′yah, *n.*, a native Australian hut.

gup, *n.*, gossip (*Hind.*).

gurgita′tion, *n.*, a surging or bubbling sound.

gur′gle, *n.*, the sound of gurgling; *v.i.*, to flow with a bubbling noise. (Also *guggle.*)

gur′gled, *p.p.*, gurgle.

gur′gling, *pr.p.*, gurgle.

gur′jun, *n.*, a large tree of the East Indies used for building and canoe-making; a fluid balsam obtained from this tree used in medicine and varnishes.

Gur′kha, one of the most predominant race of Nepal. (Also *Ghurka, Ghoorka* and *Goorkha.*)

gurl′y, *adj.*, stormy; bad-tempered.

gur′nard, *n.*, *i.q.* gurnet.

gur′net, *n.*, a sea-fish.

gu′rrah, *n.*, a kind of coarse East Indian muslin; a common Indian earthen vessel.

gu′rry, *n.*, a small native Indian fort.

guru, *n.*, a spiritual, religious Hindu instructor; any dignified person.

gush, *n.*, a violent outflow; effusive sentiment; *v.i.*, to stream out forcefully; to overflow with sentiment.

gushed, *p.p.*, gush.

gush′er, *n.*, one who, or that which, gushes; an automatic well for discharging oil forcibly.

gush′ily, *adv.*, *i.q.* gushingly.

gush′ing, *adj.*, effusive; *pr.p.*, gush.

gush′ingly, *adv.*, in a gushing way.

gush′y, *adj.*, *i.q.* gushing.

gus′set, *n.*, a three-cornered inset of cloth.

gust, *n.*, a sudden blast of wind; a sense of taste.

gust′able, *adj.*, that may be tasted; relished by taste.

gusta′tion, *n.*, the act or power of taste.

gus′tative, *adj.*, *i.q.* gustatory.

gus′tatory, *adj.*, pert. or rel. to taste.

gus′tily, *adv.*, in a gusty way.

gus′to, *n.*, relish (*It.*).

gust′y, *adj.*, coming in blasts.

gut, *n.*, the intestinal canal; a strait; *v.t.*, to eviscerate; to empty.

gut′ta, *n.*, a drop, in Doric architecture (*pl.* ae).

gut′ta-per′cha, *n.*, a gum-resin.

gut′tate, *adj.*, spotted (*bot.* and *zool.*).

gut′ted, *p.p.*, gut.

gut′ter, *n.*, a water-channel; *v.i.*, to run in drops; *v.t.*, to form into channels.

gut′ter-bird, *n.*, a sparrow; a mean person.

gut′tered, *p.p.*, gutter.

gut′tering, *pr.p.*, gutter.

gut′tersnipe, *n.*, a neglected child; a street arab.

gut′ter-spout, *n.*, a pipe for water from eaves, troughs, gutters, etc.

guttif′erous, *adj.*, yielding gum.

gutt′iform, *adj.*, drop-shaped.

gut′ting, *pr.p.*, gut.

gut′tle, *v.i.* and *t.*, to eat or drink greedily; to guzzle.

gutt′ler, *n.*, one who guttles.

gut′tural, *adj.*, pert. or rel. to the throat; sounding deep in the throat; *n.*, a consonant pronounced in the throat.

gut′turally, *adv.*, in a guttural way.

gut′turalness, *n.*, the guttural quality.

gut′ty, *n.*, a golf-ball made of gutta-percha.

guy, *n.*, a steadying rope; a grotesque effigy; an odd-looking, or queerly-dressed, person.

Guy′s, *n.*, the abbrev. for Guy's Hospital in London, England.

guz′zle, *n.*, a debauch; *v.i.*, to drink to excess.

guz′zled, *p.p.*, guzzle.

guz′zler, *n.*, one who guzzles.

guz'zling, *pr.p.*, guzzle.

gwyn'iad, *n.*, a white-fleshed lake fish like the salmon (*Welsh*).

gybe, *v.i.*, to swing a sailing craft from one direction to another with, instead of into, the wind; *v.t.*, to shift a sail from one side of a ship to the other.

gybed, *p.p.*, gybe.

gyb'ing, *pr.p.*, gybe.

gyle, *n.*, a quantity of beer brewed at the same time; fermenting wort.

gym, *n.*, the abbrev. for gymnasium, gymnastics, (*colloq.*).

gymkha'na, *n.*, a sports entertainment (*Ind.*).

gymnade'nia, *n.*, an orchid.

gymna'sia, *n. pl.*, gymnasium.

gymna'sial, *adj.*, pert. or rel. to gymnasium.

gymna'siarch, *n.*, the superintendent of gymnasia.

gymna'sium, *n.*, a place for exercise; a continental school of high grade.

gym'nast, *n.*, one skilled in gymnastics.

gymnas'tic, *adj.*, pert. or rel. to gymnastics.

gymnas'tical, *adj.*, *i.q.* gymnastic.

gymnas'tically, *adv.*, in a gymnastic way.

gymnas'tics, *n. pl.*, highly skilled physical exercises.

gymnos'ophist, *n.*, a Hindu philosopher.

gym'nosperm, *n.*, a plant having seeds unprotected by seed-vessels.

gymnosperm'ous, *adj.*, pert. or rel. to gymnosperms.

gym'note, *n.*, an electric eel.

gymnot'us, *n.*, *i.q.* gymnote.

gymp, *n.*, *i.q.* gimp.

gynaece'um, *n.*, the women's quarters in an ancient Greek or Roman house.

gynaecol'ogist, *n.*, one who studies gynaecology.

gynaecol'ogy, *n.*, the science of women's diseases and functions.

Gynan'dria, *n. pl.*, plants whose stamens are jointed with the pistil, as in orchids (*bot.*).

gynan'drian, *adj.*, *i.q.* gynandrous.

gynan'drous, *adj.*, having stamens and pistils united, as in orchids (*bot.*).

gyn'archy, *n.*, female government.

gyne'cian, *adj.*, rel. to women.

gyn(a)ecoc'racy, *n.*, female rule.

gyniat'rics, *n.*, the treatment of women's diseases.

gyno'cracy, *n.*, *i.q.* gynaecocracy.

gyp, *n.*, a college servant at Cambridge and Durham; a scolding, (*colloq.*); *v.t.*, to cheat or swindle (*slang*).

gyp'seous, *adj.*, containing gypsum.

gypsif'erous, *adj.*, yielding gypsum.

gypsoph'ila, *n.*, a white flowering plant.

gyp'sum, *n.*, hydrous sulphate of lime.

gypsumog'raphy, *n.*, the use of gypsum as manure.

gyp'sy, *n.*, *i.q.* gipsy.

gy'ral, *adj.*, *i.q.* gyratory.

gy'rate, *adj.*, convoluted.

gyrate', *v.i.*, to revolve.

gyra'ted, *p.p.*, gyrate.

gyra'ting, *pr.p.*, gyrate.

gyra'tion, *n.*, the act of gyrating.

gy'ratory, *adj.*, revolving.

gyre, *n.*, a gyration; *v.i.*, to rotate.

gy'romancy, *n.*, divination by walking round and round in circles until dizziness is caused.

gy'roplane, *n.*, an aeroplane with rotating overhead vanes.

gy'roscope, *n.*, an instrument demonstrating the laws of circular motion.

gyroscop'ic, *adj.*, pert. or rel. to gyroscope.

gy'rose, *adj.*, wavy (*bot.*).

gyrosta'bilizer, *n.*, a device for countering the roll of a ship, etc.

gy'rostat, *n.*, a modified gyroscope illustrating the dynamics of rotating bodies.

gyrostat'ics, *n.*, the science of rotating bodies.

gyttja, *n.*, a post-glacial deposit, usually covered by peat, in Sweden (*geol.*).

gyve, *n.*, a fetter; *v.t.*, to fetter (*poet.*).

gyved, *p.p.*, gyve.

gyv'ing, *pr.p.*, gyve.

H

ha, *interj.*, expressing surprise, welcome, suspicion, etc.

haaf, *n.*, a fishing ground off the Orkneys or Shetlands.

haar, *n.*, mist or fog with a cold east wind.

ha'beas cor'pus, *Lat.* phrase (= you must have the body); a writ issued to a gaoler, requiring him to bring a prisoner into court.

habend'um, *n.*, a conveyance clause defining what estate or interest is granted by it (*Lat.*, *leg.*).

hab'erdasher, *n.*, a dealer in small wares connected with dress.

hab'erdashery, *n.*, the wares sold by a haberdasher.

hab'ergeon, *n.*, a coat of mail, without sleeves.

hab'ile, *adj.*, dextrous; skilful (*lit.*).

habil'iment, *n.*, dress, attire.

habil'itate, *v.t.*, to supply capital to.

habil'itated, *p.p.*, habilitate.

habil'itating, *pr.p.*, habilitate.

habilita'tion, *n.*, the supplying of capital to.

hab'it, *n.*, usage; a fixed course of conduct; an ingrained behaviour pattern; the constitution of body or mind; dress (chiefly ecclesiastical or academic); *v.t.*, to dress.

habitabil'ity, *n.*, the state of being habitable.

hab'itable, *adj.*, fit to be lived in.

hab'itableness, *n.*, *i.q.* habitability.

hab'itably, *adv.*, in a habitable way.

hab'itant, *n.*, an inhabitant; a Canadian of French descent.

hab'itat, *n.*, the natural home of plants, etc.

habita'tion, *n.*, the act of inhabiting; abode.

hab'ited, *p.p.*, habit.

hab'iting, *pr.p.*, habit.

habit'ual, *adj.*, customary, usual.

habit'ually, *adv.*, customarily.

habit'uate, *v.t.*, to accustom.

habit'uated, *p.p.*, habituate.

habit'uating, *pr.p.*, habituate.

habitua'tion, *n.*, the act or effect of habituating.

hab'itude, *n.*, the constitution of body or mind; custom; usual behaviour.

habitué', *n.*, one who is a habitual visitor or frequenter (*Fr.*).

habutai', *n.*, a fine Japanese silk.

hachures, *n. pl.*, shading or lines to indicate elevations or shadows.

hacien'da, *n.*, a Spanish-American homestead (*Span.*).

hack, *n.*, a hired horse; a drudge; a mattock; a cut on the shins; *v.i.*, to ride in an ordinary way; to cough in a dry way; *v.t.*, to hew; to kick on the shins; to cut irregularly.

hack'berry, *n.*, a N. American tree.

hacked, *p.p.*, hack.

hackee, *n.*, the N. American chipmuck or ground-squirrel.

hack'er, *n.*, one who hacks.

hack'ery, *n.*, an Indian bullock-cart.

hack'ing, *adj.*, dry, short, intermittent (a cough); *pr.p.*, hack.

hack'le, *n.*, a comb for parting flax; a cock's neck feathers; a stickleback; *v.t.*, to dress flax or hemp.

hack'led, *p.p.*, hackle.

hack'ler, *n.*, a flax-dresser.

hack'ling, *pr.p.*, hackle.

hack'ly, *adj.*, rough, jagged.

hack'-matack, *n.*, a larch (*Amer.*).

hack'ney, *n.*, a horse for general use; a hireling; *v.t.*, to make common.

hack'ney-coach, *n.*, a vehicle legally plying for hire.

hack'neyed, *adj.*, commonplace; over-used; *p.p.*, hackney.

hack'neying, *pr.p.*, hackney.

hack'saw, *n.*, a saw for metals.

had, *p.p.*, have.

had'dock, *n.*, a sea-fish of the cod family.

Ha'des, *n.*, the underworld in Greek mythology.

hadj, *n.*, the pilgrimage to Mecca.

hadj'i, *n.*, a pilgrim to Mecca.

had'n't, abbrev. of *had not*.

haecce'ity, *n.*, individuality; thisness (*philos.*).

hae'mal, *adj.*, pert. or rel. to blood. (Also *hemal*.)

haemat'ic, *adj.*, pert. or rel. to blood; *n.*, a medicine acting on the blood. (Also *hematic*.)

hae'matin, *n.*, a blue-black substance contained in haemoglobin. (Also *hematin*.)

hae'matite, *n.*, a red iron ore. (Also *hematite*.)

haemati'tic, *adj.*, pert. or rel. to haematite. (Also *hematitic*.)

haematol'ogy, *n.*, the study of blood. (Also *hematology*.)

haematur'ia, *n.*, the presence of blood in the urine. (Also *haematuria*.)

haemoglo'bin, *n.*, the colouring matter of the red corpuscles. (Also *hemoglobin*.)

haemophil'ia, *n.*, an hereditary tendency to continuous bleeding (*med.*). (Also *hemophilia*.)

haemophil'iac, *n.*, a sufferer from haemophilia. (Also *hemophiliac*.)

haem′orrhage, *n.*, bleeding from a blood-vessel. (Also *hemorrhage*.)

haemorrhoi′dal, *adj.*, of the nature of haemorrhoids. (Also *hemorrhoidal*.)

haem′orrhoids, *n.. pl.*, piles; a varicose condition of the rectal veins. (Also *emeroids* and *hemorrhoids*.)

haem′ostat, *n.*, an anti-bleeding agent. (Also *hemostat*.)

haemostat′ic, *adj.*, able to stop haemorrhage; styptic. (Also *hemostatic*.)

haff′ets, *n. pl.*, the sides of the head; the temples.

haf′nium, *n.*, a metallic element found in 1923 (*chem.*).

haft, *n.*, a handle.

haft′ed, *adj.*, having a handle.

hag, *n.*, a witch, an ugly old woman; soft ground in a moor; firm ground in a bog.

hag′gard, *adj.*, wild-looking, worried; *n.*, a young hawk.

hag′gis, *n.*, a Scottish pudding, made of sheep's entrails and oatmeal boiled in a maw.

hag′gish, *adj.*, hag-like.

hag′gishly, *adv.*, in a haggish way.

hag′gle, *n.*, wrangling; *v.i.*, to wrangle, to dispute; to argue about a price.

hag′gled, *p.p.*, haggle.

hag′gler, *n.*, one who haggles.

hag′gling, *pr.p.*, haggle.

hag′iarchy, *n.*, the rule or order of saints.

ha′giograph, *n.*, a sacred writing.

Hagiog′rapha, *n. pl.*, books of the Hebrew Scriptures other than the Law and the Prophets.

hagiog′rapher, *n.*, a writer on sacred things or of sacred books.

hagiog′raphy, *n.*, the writing of sacred books.

hagiol′ogist, *n.*, a writer about the saints.

hagiol′ogy, *n.*, knowledge about the saints.

hag′ioscope, *n.*, an oblique opening in a church wall affording a view of the high altar; a squint.

hah, *interj.*, *i.q.* ha.

ha ha, *interj.*, rep. laughter.

ha′ha, *n.*, a sunk fence (*Fr.*).

hai(c)k, *n.*, an Arabian outer wrapper of wool or cotton for the head and upper part of the body.

hail, *interj.*, of greeting; *n.*, a precipitation of ice; *v.i.*, to come down violently as hail; *v.t.*, to greet, to call to; to rain down (blows).

hailed, *p.p.*, hail.

hail′ing, *pr.p.*, hail.

hail′stone, *n.*, a pellet of hail.

hail′storm, *n.*, a storm accompanied by hail.

hail′y, *adj.*, mixed with hail.

hair, *n.*, the filament growing out of the skin.

hair′bell, *n.*, the blue-bell of Scotland. (Also *harebell*); a wild hyacinth.

hair′brush, *n.*, a brush for the hair.

hair′cloth, *n.*, cloth made of hairs.

hair′do, *n.*, a washing, trimming and styling of the hair (*colloq.*).

hair′dresser, *n.*, one who cuts and dresses hair.

hair′dressing, *n.*, the business of cutting and styling hair.

haired, *adj.*, covered with hair.

hair′iness, *n.*, the state of being hairy.

hair′less, *adj.*, bald.

hair′like, *adj.*, resembling a hair.

hair′-pencil, *n.*, a very fine hair brush for painting.

hair′piece, *n.*, a partial wig.

hair′pin, *n.*, a pin to fasten up the hair.

hair′s′-breadth, *n.*, a very small distance.

hair′-splitting, *adj.*, quibbling; *n.*, the practice of making very minute distinctions.

hair′spring, *n.*, a fine watch-spring.

hair′style, *n.*, a manner of dressing and arranging the hair.

hair′stylist, *n.*, *i.q.* hairdresser.

hair′trigger, *n.*, a secondary trigger.

hair′-wave, *n.*, a wave-like hair-style.

hair′y, *adj.*, covered with hairs, hirsute.

Hai′tian, *adj.*, pert. or rel. to Haiti in the Caribbean; *n.*, a native of H.

hake, *n.*, a cod-like fish; a drying framework made of wood.

hala′tion, *n.*, the spreading of light beyond its proper boundary in a negative, causing a halo (*photog.*).

hal′berd, *n.*, an antique battle-axe on a long shaft.

halberdier′, *n.*, a soldier using a halberd.

hal′cyon, *adj.*, calm and delightful; *n.*, a fabulous bird.

hale, *adj.*, robust, fresh-looking; *v.t.*, to drag, to draw.

haled, *p.p.*, hale.

half, *n.*, in value equal to a half; *adv.*, to the degree of a half; *n.*, one of the two equal divisions of anything.

half′back, *n.*, the position of a footballer immediately behind the forwards.

half′blood, *adj.*, of mixed race, in the relation of persons having only one common parent; *n.*, a half-caste.

half′-bred, *adj.*, of mixed breed; lacking refinement.

half′-brother, *n.*, a brother by one parent only.

half′-caste, *n.*, one who has a European father and an Indian mother.

half′-cock, *n.*, the position of a gun's hammer when drawn back to the first notch.

half′-dead, *adj.*, exhausted; almost dead.

half′-dozen, *n.*, six or half of a dozen.

halfheart′ed, *adj.*, without enthusiasm; lacking courage.

half′-hol′iday, *n.*, a half-day for recreation.

half′-length, *adj.*, half the length of a piece of material or garment.

half′mast, *adj.*, half-way up a mast esp. to denote the position of a lowered flag, as a sign of mourning.

half'moon, *adj.* and *n.*, (a) crescent-shaped (object).

half-nel'son, *n.*, an arm and neck hold in wrestling.

half'-note, *n.*, a semitone, a minim (*mus.*).

half'-pay, *n.*, pay at half the normal rate.

half'pence, *n.*, the plural of halfpenny.

half'penny, *n.*, the half of a penny.

half'price, *n.* and *adj.*, a reduced charge; half the usual price.

half'-sis'ter, *n.*, a sister by one parent only.

half'-sized, *adj.*, of half size.

half'-time, *n.*, half the usual or full time esp. for work; halfway through a game.

half'-tone, *adj.*, light and shade rep. by dots; a semi-tone.

half'-truth, *n.*, only half or part of the truth.

half'way, *adj.*, midway.

half'wit, *n.*, a simpleton.

half'witted, *adj.*, nearly imbecile.

half'-year', *n.*, the period of half the year.

half'-year'ly, *adj.*, recurring each half-year.

hal'ibut, *n.*, a large flat fish.

hal'idom, *n.*, holiness; a sacred object.

halieu'tic, *adj.*, pert. or rel. to fishing.

hal'ing, *pr.p.*, hale.

hal'ite, *n.*, rock-salt.

halitos'is, *n.*, foul breath (*med.*).

halit'uous, *adj.*, vaporous.

hal'itus, *n.*, a vapour.

hall, *n.*, a large room or building; a manorhouse; a corridor.

hall'-door, *n.*, the door leading to a hall.

hallelu'jah, *interj.*, *i.q.* alleluia.

hal'liard, *n.*, *i.q.* halyard.

hall'mark, *n.*, the goldsmiths' stamp on gold and silver; any standard of excellence.

halloo', *interj.*, calling someone's attention; urging hounds on; *v.i.*, to shout halloo.

hallooed', *p.p.*, halloo.

halloo'ing, *pr.p.*, halloo.

hal'low, *v.t.*, to make holy, to venerate.

hal'lowed, *p.p.*, hallow.

Hallow-e'en', *n.*, the eve of All Saints' or AllHallows' Day. (Also *Halloween*.)

hal'lowing, *pr.p.*, hallow.

Hal'lowmas, *n.*, the feast of All-Hallows, 1st Nov.

hallu'cinate, *v.t.*, to affect with hallucination.

hallu'cinated, *p.p.*, hallucinate.

hallu'cinating, *pr.p.*, hallucinate.

hallucina'tion, *n.*, illusion.

hallu'cinatory, *adj.*, illusory.

hallucino'sis, *n.*, the mental condition of being subject to hallucinations.

hall'ux, *n.*, the great toe in mammals; the hind or inner toe in birds.

halm, *n.*, *i.q.* haulm.

hal'ma, *n.*, a game played by two persons, each with 19 pieces, on a board of 256 squares.

ha'lo, *n.*, a luminous circle; the nimbus of a saint.

hal'ogen, *n.*, any one of the elements fluorine, chlorine, bromine, iodine, combining simply with metals (*chem.*).

halog'enous, *adj.*, pert. or rel. to halogen.

hal'oid, *adj.*, like common salt (*chem.*).

halt, *adj.*, limping, lame; *n.*, a stop; a limp; *v.i.*, to walk lamely; to hesitate; *v.t.* and *i.*, to stop.

halt'ed, *p.p.*, halt.

halt'er, *n.*, a band round a horse's neck and head; a hangman's rope; *v.t.*, to secure with a halter.

halt'ered, *p.p.*, halter.

halt'ering, *pr.p.*, halter.

halt'ing, *adj.*, hesitating; *pr.p.*, halt.

halt'ingly, *adv.*, in a halting way.

halve, *v.t.*, to share equally with another; to divide in two.

halved, *p.p.*, halve.

halves, *n.*, pl. of half.

halv'ing, *pr.p.*, halve.

hal'yard, *n.*, tackle for raising sails, etc. (Also *halliard*.)

ham, *n.*, the back of the thigh; the buttock; a small village.

hamadry'ad, *n.*, a wood nymph who dies with the tree she inhabits.

ha'mate, *adj.*, hooked. (Also *hamous*.)

ha'mated, *adj.*, furnished with hooks; hooked.

ham'ble, *v.t.*, to mutilate (dogs).

ham'burger, *n.*, fried chopped meat; a large sausage.

Ham'burgh, *n.*, a black variety of hothouse grape; a small domestic fowl.

hames, *n. pl.*, the bars of metal attached to a horse's collar, and having the traces fastened to them.

ham'hand'ed, *adj.*, clumsy (*slang*).

Hamilt'onian, *adj.*, pert. or rel. to Hamilton Academy (Scotland).

Ham'ite, *n.*, a descendant of Ham (the youngest son of Noah); an Etheopian.

Hamit'ic, *adj.*, descended from Ham; African.

ham'let, *n.*, a little village, usually without a church.

hammam, *n.*, an Oriental bathing establishment; a Turkish bath.

ham'mer, *n.*, a tool for driving, striking or breaking; *v.t.*, to drive in with a hammer; to strike hard, to drive; to announce as insolvent (Stock Exchange).

ham'merable, *adj.*, able to be hammered.

ham'mercloth, *n.*, the cloth and hangings of a coach-box.

ham'mered, *p.p.*, hammer.

ham'merer, *n.*, one who hammers.

ham'mering, *pr.p.*, hammer.

ham'merman, *n.*, one who uses a hammer in metal-work.

ham'mock, *n.*, a canvas or network couch or bed, slung at the ends.

ha'mous, adj., i.q. hamate.

ham'per, n., rigging; a large wicker basket; v.t., to obstruct or hinder.

ham'pered, p.p., hamper.

ham'pering, pr.p., hamper.

Hamp'ton Court, n., an English palace, now partly occupied and partly open for public visiting.

ham'shackle, v.t., to shackle a horse with a rope from the head to the foreleg.

ham'ster, n., a rat-like rodent with pouched cheeks, kept as a pet.

ham'string, n., a tendon at the back of the knee; v.t., to disable by cutting the hamstring.

ham'stringed, p.p., hamstring. (Also hamstrung.)

ham'stringing, pr.p., hamstring.

ham'strung, p.p., hamstring.

ham'ulus, n., a small hook or hook-like process (bot., zool., anat.).

han'aper, n., a basket; a department of the Court of Chancery where certain documents were kept in a hanaper.

hand, n., the terminate part of the forearm; anything like a hand; a hand-worker; one of a ship's crew; help; a share in an enterprise; cards dealt to a player; a height measurement for a horse; v.t., to deliver; to help with the hand or arm.

hand'bag, n., a small bag carried by women.

hand'bill, n., a small printed notice or advertisement.

hand'book, n., a manual; a guide-book.

hand'breadth, n., a space the breadth of the hand. (Also handsbreadth.)

hand'cart, n., a cart drawn or driven by hand.

hand'cuff, v.t., to secure with handcuffs.

hand'cuffed, p.p., handcuff.

hand'cuffing, pr.p., handcuff.

hand'cuffs, n. pl., steel manacles joined by a short chain.

hand'ed, p.p., hand.

Hande'lian, adj., pert. or rel. to Handel or his music.

hand'ful, n., a quantity filling the hand.

hand'gallop, n., an easy gallop.

hand'-grenade, n., an explosive shell small enough to be thrown by hand.

hand'icap, n., a condition imposed on competitors to equalize their chances; a race where there is such handicap; a limitation on a person's capacity; v.t., to impose a handicap; to impede.

hand'icapped, p.p., handicap.

hand'icapper, n., one who decides the handicap.

hand'icapping, pr.p., handicap.

hand'icraft, n., manual skill; a manual art.

hand'icraftsman, n., one who practises a handicraft.

hand'ier, adj., comp. of handy.

hand'iest, adj., super. of handy.

hand'ily, adv., cleverly with the hands.

hand'iness, n., cleverness with the hand.

hand'ing, pr.p., hand.

hand'iwork, n., something made, or done, with the hands.

hand'kerchief, n., a square of material, carried in the pocket, used to wipe away the excretions of nose, eyes or mouth.

hand'le, n., the part by which anything is held; something that can be grasped; v.t., to touch with the hands; to manage; to treat; to train.

hand'lebar, n., a steering bar, esp. of a cycle.

hand'led, p.p., handle.

hand'ler, n., one who handles, e.g. dogs.

hand'ling, pr.p., handle.

hand'made, adj., made with the hand.

hand'maid, n., a maidservant.

hand'maiden, n., i.q. handmaid.

hand'out, n., information officially released; literature handed out at the beginning of a lecture or demonstration.

hand'rail, n., a rail to support the hand.

hand'saw, n., a carpenter's saw.

hands'breadth, n., i.q. handbreadth.

hand'screw, n., a jackscrew.

hand'sel, n., a gift at the New Year; earnest money; v.t., to be the first to use; to use for the first time. (Also hansel.)

hand'sel(l)ed, p.p., handsel.

hand'sel(l)ing, pr.p., handsel.

hand'some, adj., fine to the sight; generous.

hand'somely, adv., generously.

hand'someness, n., the state or quality of being handsome.

hand'spike, n., a kind of lever.

hand'spun, adj., spun or woven by hand.

hand'work, n., work not done by machinery.

hand'writing, n., a person's autograph; a style of penmanship.

hand'written, adj., describing writing done by hand.

hand'y, adj., deft; ready to hand.

hang, v.i., to depend, to lag; v.t., to suspend, to execute on the gallows; to let droop.

hang'ar, n., a protective structure for aircraft.

hang'bird, n., any bird that builds a hanging nest.

hang'dog, adj., sneakish; n., a sneak.

hanged, p.p., hang (said of one who is executed).

hang'er, n., anything by which something is hung; one who hangs (bells, etc.); a short sword; wood on a hill-slope.

hang'er-on, n., a parasite, a follower.

hang'ing, n., a curtain; a small drape; pr.p., hang.

hang'man, n., an executioner.

hang'nail, n., torn skin at the root of a finger nail.

hang'over, n., the aftereffects of dissipation.

hank, n., a skein of yarn; a fastening; v.t., to form into hanks.

hank'er, v.t., to crave for (followed by after).

hank'ered, p.p., hanker.

hank'ering, n., a craving; pr.p., hanker.

hank'eringly, adv., in a hankering way; longingly.

hank'y, n., the abbrev. for handkerchief (colloq.).

hank'y-pank'y, n., jugglery; trickery.

Han'over, n., the House of Hanover—British sovereigns from George I to Queen Victoria.

Hanove'rian, adj., pert. or rel. to Hanover.

Hans, n., a nickname for a German or a Dutchman.

Han'sard, n., the printed record of Parliamentary proceedings.

Hanse, n., the Germanic league of trading cities.

Hanseat'ic, adj., pert. or rel. to the Hanse.

han'sel, n. and v.t., i.q. handsel.

han'som, n., a two-wheeled, one-horsed cab.

hap, n., an occurrence, chance; v.i., to happen.

haphaz'ard, adj., accidental; adv., at random; n., mere chance.

haphaz'ardly, adv., in a haphazard way.

hap'less, adj., unlucky.

haplog'raphy, n., the unintentional omission of a syllable from a word in which it should be repeated.

hap'ly, adv., perchance, perhaps.

hap'pen, v.i., to occur; to fall out by chance.

hap'pened, p.p., happen.

hap'pening, n., an event; pr.p., happen.

hap'pier, adj., comp. of happy.

hap'piest, adj., super. of happy.

hap'pily, adv., in a happy way, cheerfully, felicitously.

hap'piness, n., the state of being happy.

hap'py, adj., glad, cheerful, felicitous.

happ'y-go-luck'y, adj., easy-going.

hara-ki'ri, n., ceremonious Japanese suicide.

harangue', v.i., to make a speech; v.t., to address in a speech.

harangued', p.p., harangue.

harang'uer, n., one who harangues.

harang'uing, pr.p., harangue.

har'ass, v.t., to vex, annoy or worry.

har'assed, p.p., harass.

har'assing, pr.p., harass.

ha'rassment, n., the act of harassing; the state of being harassed.

or har'binger, n., one who announces a coming person or thing; v.t., to proclaim or announce.

har'bour, n., a haven, a place of shelter; v.i., to seek shelter; v.t., to shelter, to cherish.

har'bourage, n., a place of shelter.

har'boured, p.p., harbour.

har'bourer, n., one who harbours.

har'bouring, pr.p., harbour.

har'bourless, adj., without a harbour.

harbour-mas'ter, n., the officer who supervises the mooring, etc. of harbour vessels; the chief of the harbour police.

hard, adj., solid, firm; difficult; severe, exacting; enduring; adv., strenuously, tightly, nearly.

hardbitten, adj., stubborn; self-willed; tough in character.

hard'board, n., a compressed fibreboard.

hard'-earned, adj., earned with difficulty.

hard'en, v.i., to become hard; v.t., to make hard.

hard'ened, p.p., harden.

hard'ener, n., anything that hardens.

hard'ening, pr.p., harden.

hard'er, adj., comp. of hard.

hard'est, adj., super. of hard.

hard'faced, adj., stern.

hard'-fought, adj., fiercely fought.

hard'head, n., a large round stone.

hard'head'ed, adj., shrewd.

hard'-hearted, adj., unkind, unfeeling.

hard'-heartedly, adv., cruelly, mercilessly.

hard'-heartedness, n., cruelty.

hard'ier, adj., comp. of hardy.

hard'iest, adj., super. of hardy.

hard'ihood, n., boldness, audacity.

hard'ily, adv., in a hardy way.

hard'iness, n., the state of being hardy.

hard'ly, adv., harshly, severely, with difficulty; scarcely, barely.

hard'met'al, n., sintered tungsten carbide, used for cutting tools.

hard'ness, n., the quality of being hard.

hards, n. pl., the refuse of flax or wool.

hard'ship, n., hardness of circumstances; injustice, suffering.

hard'ware, n., metal manufactured articles.

hard'wareman, n., one who makes or deals in hardware.

hard'wood, n., wood from deciduous trees.

hard'y, adj., tough, capable of enduring, brave; n., part of an anvil, a bar for cutting on.

hare, n., a four-footed rodent with long ears and cleft upper lip.

hare'bell, n., a bell-flower with round leaves. (Also hairbell).

hare'brained, adj., giddy, rash.

hare'foot, n., a foot like a hare's.

hare'lip, n., a malformation of the upper lip.

hare'lipped, adj., having a harelip.

ha'rem, n., the women's quarter in a Turkish house; the women of the harem.

hare'wood, n., stained sycamore, used in cabinet-making.

har'icot, n., a ragoût; a floury bean.

hari-ka'ri, n., an incorrect form of hara-kiri.

hark, n., the cry "Hark!"; v.i., to listen, to hearken.

hark'en, *v.i.*, *i.q.* hearken.

harl, *n.*, flaxen or hempen filament.

Harlei'an, *adj.*, pert. or rel. to Robert and Edward Harley, and the Harleian MSS.

har'lequin, *adj.*, fantastic; *n.*, a buffoon in mask and multi-coloured costume appearing in mime.

harlequinade', *n.*, the part after a pantomime in which a harlequin appears.

Harl'ey Street, *n.*, a street and area in London where medical consultants practise.

har'lot, *n.*, a prostitute.

har'lotry, *n.*, a harlot's trade; lewdness.

harm, *n.*, hurt, injury, mischief; *v.t.*, to hurt, to injure.

harmattan', *n.*, a dry W. African wind.

harmed, *p.p.*, harm.

harm'ful, *adj.*, hurtful, mischievous.

harm'fully, *adv.*, hurtfully, mischievously.

harm'fulness, *n.*, the quality or state of being harmful.

harm'ing, *pr.p.*, harm.

harm'less, *adj.*, free from offence; incapable of injury.

harm'lessly, *adv.*, in a harmless way.

harm'lessness, *n.*, the state or quality of being harmless.

harmon'ic, *adj.*, pert. or rel. to harmony; harmonious.

harmon'ica, *n.*, a small, musical, wind instrument; a mouth-organ.

harmon'ical, *adj.*, *i.q.* harmonic.

harmon'ically, *adv.*, harmoniously.

harmon'icon, *n.*, a mouth-organ.

harmon'ics, *n. pl.*, the science of musical sounds; additional notes faintly heard when one musical note on an instrument is played.

harmo'nious, *adj.*, in harmony, concordant, symmetrical.

harmo'niously, *adv.*, in harmony, accordantly.

harmo'niousness, *n.*, the quality of being harmonious.

har'monist, *n.*, an expert in harmony; a writer on the agreements of writings, particularly the Sacred Scriptures.

harmonis'tic, *adj.*, pert. or rel. to harmony.

harmo'nium, *n.*, a small, old-fashioned reed-organ.

harmoniza'tion, *n.*, the act or quality of harmonizing.

har'monize, *v.t.*, to bring into agreement; to arrange in harmony; *v.i.*, to agree, to accord with; to sing or play with a pleasant combination of sounds.

har'monized, *p.p.*, harmonize.

har'monizer, *n.*, one who harmonizes.

har'monizing, *pr.p.*, harmonize.

harmonom'eter, *n.*, an apparatus for measuring harmonic sound relations.

har'mony, *n.*, agreement; agreeable effect of arrangement; sound produced in chords.

har'most, *n.*, a Lacedaemonian provincial governor in the Greek islands.

har'ness, *n.*, the gear of a draught horse; armour; working equipment; *v.t.*, to put harness on; to control the power of.

har'nessed, *p.p.*, harness.

har'nesser, *n.*, one who harnesses.

har'nessing, *pr.p.*, harness.

harp, *n.*, a musical stringed instrument; *v.i.*, to play on the harp; to repeat tediously (*colloq.*).

harped, *p.p.*, harp.

harp'er, *n.*, *i.q.* harpist.

harp'ing, *n.*, tedious dwelling on a theme; the act of playing the harp; *pr.p.*, harp.

harp'ist, *n.*, the player on a harp.

harpoon', *n.*, a missile attached to a line used by whalers; *v.t.*, to strike with a harpoon.

harpooned', *p.p.*, harpoon.

harpoon'er, *n.*, one who harpoons.

harpoon'ing, *pr.p.*, harpoon.

harp'sichord, *n.*, an old musical instrument, the strings of which were plucked with quills set in motion from a finger-board.

har'py, *n.*, a rapacious monster; a grasping person.

har'quebus, *n.*, an antique gun. (Also *arquebuse*.)

har'ridan, *n.*, an old jade.

har'ried, *p.p.*, harry.

har'rier, *n.*, one who harries; a hound used for coursing hares; a cross-country runner.

Ha'rris tweed, *n.*, a kind of tweed made in Harris in the Hebrides in Scotland.

Harro'vian, *n.*, one who is educated at Harrow School, England.

har'row, *n.*, an agricultural implement for turning or breaking clods; *v.t.*, to draw the harrow over; to torment, to lacerate the feelings of; to spoil.

har'rowed, *p.p.*, harrow.

har'rower, *n.*, one who harrows.

har'rowing, *adj.*, distressing; *pr.p.*, harrow.

har'ry, *v.t.*, to ravage, to harass.

har'rying, *pr.p.*, harry.

harsh, *adj.*, rough (in any sense), severe.

har'shen, *v.t.*, to make harsh.

har'shened, *p.p.*, harshen.

har'shening, *pr.p.*, harshen.

harsh'er, *adj.*, *comp.* of harsh.

harsh'est, *adj.*, *super.* of harsh.

harsh'ly, *adv.*, in a harsh way.

harsh'ness, *n.*, the quality or state of being harsh.

hars'let, *n.*, *i.q.* haslet.

hart, *n.*, a male deer.

hart'al, *n.*, a kind of boycott in India.

hart'bees, *n.*, a S. African antelope.

harts'horn, *n.*, a preparation of ammonia (formerly distilled from a hart's horn).

hart's'-tongue, *n.*, a kind of fern.

har'um-scar'um, *adj.*, wild, reckless; *n.*, such a person.

harus'pex, *n.*, a diviner (*Lat.*).

harus'pice, *n.*, *i.q.* haruspex.

harus'picy, *n.*, divination by inspection of animals' entrails.

har'vest, *n.*, the ingathering; the gathered crops; the time of ingathering; any reward of labour; *v.t.*, to gather in and store.

har'vested, *p.p.*, harvest.

har'vester, *n.*, a harvest labourer; a reaping machine.

harvest festival, *n.*, a thanksgiving service for the gathering of the harvest.

har'vesting, *pr.p.*, harvest.

harvestman, *n.*, a kind of insect common during harvest time.

has, *v.t.*, 3rd pers. sing., *pres.* of have.

has'-been, *n.*, a person who, or thing which, has lost qualities or proficiency (*slang*).

hash, *n.*, a dish of meat chopped small; a medley; a failure (*colloq.*); *v.t.*, to chop small.

Hash'emite, *adj.*, pert. or rel. to the Kingdom of Jordan; a native of this area.

hash'ish, *n.*, the tops and tender sprouts of hemp used as a drug.

has'let, *n.*, pig's fry. (Also *harslet.*)

Hasmone'an, *adj.*, *i.q.* Asmonean.

has'n't, abbrev. of *has not.*

hasp, *n.*, a door or lid fastening; a skein of yarn; *v.t.*, to fasten with a hasp.

hasped, *p.p.*, hasp.

hasp'ing, *pr.p.*, hasp.

has'sock, *n.*, a kneeling-or foot-cushion; a tussock of grass.

hast, *v.t.*, 2nd pers. sing., *pres.* of have.

has'tate, *adj.*, spear-shaped (chiefly *bot.*).

hast'ated, *adj.*, *i.q.* hastate.

haste, *n.*, hurry, celerity; *v.i.*, to hurry, to hasten.

ha'sted, *p.p.*, haste.

ha'sten, *v.i.*, to be quick; *v.t.*, to urge forward, to hurry.

ha'stened, *p.p.*, hasten.

ha'stener, *n.*, one who, or that which, urges; an old-fashioned screen round meat roasting before a fire.

ha'stening, *pr.p.*, hasten.

ha'stier, *adj.*, *comp.* of hasty.

ha'stiest, *adj.*, *super.* of hasty.

has'tiform, *adj.*, *i.q.* hastate.

ha'stily, *adv.*, in haste.

ha'stiness, *n.*, the quality of being hasty.

ha'sting, *pr.p.*, haste.

ha'sty, *adj.*, quick-tempered; speedy, over-quick.

ha'sty-pud'ding, *n.*, a pudding made with flour batter.

hat, *n.*, a head covering.

hat'band, *n.*, a band for a hat.

hat'box, *n.*, a box for a hat.

hatch, *n.*, engraved line; a half-door or wicket; a deck-opening; *v.i.*, to come out of the egg; *v.t.*, to produce young birds; to develop; to close with a hatch; to score with lines.

hatched, *p.p.*, hatch.

hatch'el, *n.*, a sort of comb for cleaning flax, etc.; *v.t.*, to hackle.

hatch'el(l)ed, *p.p.*, hatchel.

hatch'el(l)ing, *pr.p.*, hatchel.

hatch'er, *n.*, a bird that breeds; any thing or person that hatches.

hatch'ery, *n.*, a place where the eggs of poultry and the ova of fish are hatched artificially.

hatch'es, *n. pl.*, the openings to a ship's hold.

hatch'et, *n.*, a short axe.

hatch'ing, *n.*, the act of marking with incised lines; *pr.p.*, hatch.

hatch'ment, *n.*, an escutcheon used in memorials (*her.*).

hatch'way, *n.*, a hatch.

hate, *n.*, strong dislike, malice; *v.t.*, to dislike strongly.

hate'able, *adj.*, odious.

ha'ted, *p.p.*, hate.

hate'ful, *adj.*, detestable, odious.

hate'fully, *adv.*, detestably.

hate'fulness, *n.*, the quality of being hateful.

ha'ter, *n.*, one who hates.

hate'worthy, *adj.*, deserving hate.

hath, *v.t.*, 3rd pers. sing., *pres.* of have.

ha'ting, *pr.p.*, hate.

ha'tred, *n.*, the feeling of hate.

hat'ter, *n.*, one who sells or makes hats.

hatti-sherif', *n.*, a Turkish command countersigned by the Sultan.

hat'-trick, *n.*, taking three wickets by consecutive balls in cricket.

hau'berk, *n.*, a coat of steel armour.

haugh, *n.*, a water-meadow.

haught'ier, *adj.*, *comp.* of haughty.

haught'iest, *adj.*, *super.* of haughty.

haught'ily, *adv.*, in a haughty manner.

haugh'tiness, *n.*, arrogance, pride. (Also *hauteur.*)

haugh'ty, *adj.*, proud, arrogant.

haul, *n.*, a pull; the material results of a lucky discovery; a catch of fish; *v.t.*, to pull or drag; to change a ship's course.

haul'age, *n.*, the act of hauling; the charge for hauling; the heavy transport industry.

hauled, *p.p.*, haul.

haul'er, *n.*, one who, or that which, hauls.

haul'ier, *n.*, one who hauls, esp. tubs in a coal mine; one engaged in road haulage.

haul'ing, *pr.p.*, haul.

haulm, *n.*, a stalk, a stem. (Also *halm.*)

haunch, *n.*, the part between the ribs and the thigh; the side of an arch between the crown and the piers (*archit.*).

haunched, *adj.*, having haunches.

haunt, *n.*, a place of frequent resort; a favourite spot; *v.t.*, to frequent.

haunt'ed, *adj.*, visited by ghosts; *p.p.*, haunt.

haunt'er, *n.*, one who haunts.

haunt'ing, *adj.*, strongly evocative; *pr.p.*, haunt.

haut'boy, *n.*, a kind of strawberry; a woodwind instrument of reedy quality; an organ stop. (Also *oboe* and *hoboy*.)

haute, *adj.*, superior; excellent (*Fr.*).

haute couture, *n.*, superior dressmaking or dress designing (*Fr.*).

haute cuisine, *n.*, superior cooking (*Fr.*).

haute école, *n.*, the more difficult horsemanship feats (*Fr.*).

haut'eur, *n.*, *i.q.* haughtiness (*Fr.*).

haut-goût, *n.*, seasoning, taint (*Fr.*).

Havan'a, *n.*, a cigar imported from Havana or Cuba.

have, *n.*, a swindle (*slang*); *v.t.*, to hold, to possess.

have'lock, *n.*, a cap cover with neck-flap.

ha'ven, *n.*, a harbour or shelter.

have'n't, abbrev. of *have not*.

hav'er, *n.*, foolish talk; nonsense; oats; *v.i.*, to babble (*Scot.*).

hav'ersack, *n.*, a soldier's sack for rations.

hav'ildar, *n.*, a sepoy sergeant.

hav'ing, *pr.p.*, have.

hav'oc, *n.*, damage, devastation.

haw, *n.*, the fruit of a hawthorn; the sloe; an enclosure; the third eyelid or nictitating membrane.

Hawai'ian, *adj.*, pert. or rel. to the island of Hawaii; *n.*, a native of H.

haw'buck, *n.*, a country bumpkin.

haw-haw', *v.i.*, to guffaw.

hawk, *n.*, a clearing of the throat; a bird of prey; a mortar-board; *v.i.*, to clear the throat of phlegm; to practise falconry or hawking; *v.t.*, to cry for sale.

hawked, *p.p.*, hawk.

hawk'er, *n.*, a street trader; one who practises hawking.

hawk'ey, *n.*, a way of spelling *hockey*.

hawk'eyed, *adj.*, with exceptional powers of sight and observation.

hawk'ing, *n.*, a hawker's trade; *pr.p.*, hawk.

hawk'weed, *n.*, a kind of aster; a species of groundsel.

hawse, *n.*, the part of a ship's bows where the hawse-holes are made; *v.t.*, to hoist.

hawse'-holes, *n. pl.*, holes for a cable to pass through.

haws'er, *n.*, a thick rope.

haw'thorn, *n.*, a thorny shrub.

hay, *n.*, cut and dried grass; a figure in a country dance; *v.i.*, to make hay; *v.t.*, to make into hay; to feed with hay.

hay'cock, *n.*, a pile of hay in a field.

hay'field, *n.*, a field where grass for hay is grown.

hay'ing, *n.*, the work of making hay; the haymaking season; *pr.p.*, hay.

hay'loft, *n.*, a loft for storing hay.

hay'maker, *n.*, one who makes hay; a very successful ploy.

hay'mow, *n.*, stored hay.

hay'rick, *n.*, *i.q.* haystack.

hay'stack, *n.*, a pile of stacked hay.

hay'ward, *n.*, an officer of the parish, etc. appointed to look after fences, commons, etc. and to impound stray cattle.

hay'wire, *adj.* and *adv.*, crazy (*slang*); *n.*, anything tangled.

haz'ard, *n.*, exposure to risk; a game of chance; the pocketing stroke at billiards; a difficulty on a golf-course; a possible source of danger; *v.t.*, to risk, imperil or venture.

haz'arded, *p.p.*, hazard.

haz'arding, *pr.p.*, hazard.

haz'ardous, *adj.*, risky.

haz'ardously, *adv.*, riskily.

haz'ardousness, *n.*, the state of being hazardous.

haze, *n.*, a dimming of the atmosphere; indistinctness; *v.i.*, to become hazy; *v.t.*, to bully, to harass.

hazed, *p.p.*, haze.

haz'el, *adj.*, made of hazel-wood; *n.*, a bush bearing the hazel-nut.

ha'zel-nut, *n.*, the fruit of the hazel bush.

haz'ily, *adv.*, in a hazy way.

ha'ziness, *n.*, the state of being hazy.

ha'zing, *pr.p.*, haze.

ha'zy, *adj.*, misty; vague; partly intoxicated.

H'-bomb, *n.*, the hydrogen bomb.

he, *pers. pron.*, the male referred to.

head, *n.*, the upper part of an animal's body containing the brain; the top of anything; a single unit; a measure of stored force (as a head of water); a subject in a writing; *v.t.*, to lead, to stand at the head of; to intercept; to place at the top of; to move in a direction; to form a head; to lop off.

head'ache, *n.*, a pain in the head.

head'band, *n.*, a band round the head; an ornamental band at the top or bottom of a bound book.

head'board, *n.*, a board at the top end of an object, esp. a board forming the upper end of a bedstead.

head'-dress, *n.*, an ornamental head-covering.

head'ed, *p.p.*, head.

head'er, *n.*, one who puts in heads (of barrels); a stone or brick laid endwise across the thickness of a wall; a plunge.

head'-gear, *n.*, anything worn on the head.

head'ily, *adv.*, in a heady way.

head'iness, *n.*, the state or quality of being heady.

head'ing, n., a caption, title or entry; pr.p., head.

head'land, n., a projecting cliff.

head'less, adj., wanting a head.

head'light, n., a white light at the masthead; the front light of a locomotive or motor-car.

head'line, n., a line over a written or printed passage.

head'long, adj., precipitate; adv., precipitately, impetuously.

head'man, n., a chief; a leader.

headmast'er, n., the chief master in a school.

headmist'ress, n., the fem. of headmaster.

head'most, adj., foremost.

head'-on', adj. and adv., full-front; directly opposed.

head'phone, n., a telephone receiver worn on a headband; a plaited hair-coil covering the ear.

headquart'ers, n. pl., a position where a command or group of officials is centred.

head'-rest, n., a support for the head.

heads'man, n., an executioner.

head'stall, n., the bridle straps that pass round a horse's head.

head'stone, n., a gravestone at the head of a grave.

head'strong, adj., perverse, self-willed.

head'way, n., forward movement; progress.

head'wind, n., an opposing wind.

head'work, n., brainwork.

head'y, adj., impetuous, violent; intoxicating, exciting.

heal, v.i., to become well; v.t., to restore to health; to cure.

heal'able, adj., curable.

healed, p.p., heal.

heal'er, n., a physician; one who heals.

heal'ing, n., cure; pr.p., heal.

health, n., the state of being whole or well.

health'ful, adj., healthgiving.

health'fully, adv., in a healthful way.

health'fulness, n., the quality or state of being healthful.

health'ier, adj., comp. of healthy.

health'iest, adj., super. of healthy.

health'ily, adv., in a healthy way.

health'iness, n., the state or quality of being healthy.

health'y, adj., well, sound, in good condition; conducive to health.

heap, n., a pile, a mass of piled things; a large quantity or number; v.t., to pile, to load, to accumulate.

heaped, p.p., heap.

heap'ing, pr.p., heap.

heap'y, adj., in heaps.

hear, v.t., to perceive with the ear; to listen to; to obey.

hear'able, adj., that can be heard.

heard, p.p., hear.

hear'er, n., one who hears.

hear'ing, n., the sense of hearing; consideration; pr.p., hear.

hear'ing-aid, n., a device to assist hearing.

heark'en, v.i., to listen. (Also harken.)

heark'ened, p.p., hearken.

heark'ener, n., one who listens or attends.

heark'ening, pr.p., hearken.

hear'say, n., gossip, rumour.

hearse, n., a carriage for coffins; a latticework canopy over a tomb, often stuck with tapers or herse lights. (Also herse.)

heart, n., the organ that maintains the circulation of the blood; the seat of the affections; courage; pity; the centre or core.

heart'ache, n., sorrow.

heart'broken, adj., crushed with grief.

heart'burn, n., a burning feeling in the lower part of the chest.

heart'en, v.t., to cheer, to encourage.

heart'ened, p.p., hearten.

heart'ening, adj., encouraging; pr.p., hearten.

heart'felt, adj., sincere.

hearth, n., the floor of a fireplace.

hearth'-rug, n., a rug placed in front of the fireplace.

hearth'stone, n., the slab forming the hearth; a soft stone for scouring purposes; v.t., to scour with a hearthstone.

heart'ier, adj., comp. of hearty.

heart'iest, adj., super. of hearty.

heart'ily, adv., in a hearty way.

heart'iness, n., geniality, relish.

heart'less, adj., unfeeling, cruel.

heart'lessly, adv., cruelly.

heart'lessness, n., cruelty, want of heart.

heart'rending, adj., distressing; emotionally grievous.

hearts'ease, n., the pansy.

heart'sick, adj., sick at heart.

heart'sickness, n., depression.

heart'some, adj., cheerful, lively.

heart'strings, n. pl., deepest feelings; strongest affections.

heart'whole, adj., of good courage.

heart'y, adj., genial, cordial, relishing.

heat, n., hotness, high temperature, flush, fury, excitement; a division of a race; lust; the sexual excitement of animals during the breeding season; v.i., to become hot; v.t., to make hot, to inflame, to excite.

heat'ed, adj., hot; excited; p.p., heat.

heated'ly, adv., excitedly.

heat'er, n., anything that heats.

heath, n., an open tract of uncultivated land overgrown with heath; a shrub of the Erica genus.

heath'en, n., a pagan, a Gentile; an unenlightened person.

heath'endom, n., heathens collectively; heathenism.

heath′enish, adj., in the state of a heathen.

heath′enishly, adv., in a heathenish way.

heath′enishness, n., the state of being heathen.

heath′enism, n., the state of being a heathen.

heath′enize, v.t., to make heathen.

heath′enized, p.p., heathenize.

heath′enizing, pr.p., heathenize.

heath′er, n., the Erica plant, a moorland growth.

hea′ther-mixture, n., a speckled tweed fabric resembling the colour of heather.

heath′ery, adj., like, or covered with, heather.

heath′y, adj., like, or covered with, heath.

heat′ing, n., the act or process of imparting heat; pr.p., heat.

heat′-spot, n., a freckle; a small postule characterizing a slight rash in hot weather.

heat′-stroke, n., prostration caused by excessive heat.

heat′wave, n., a period of excessively hot weather.

heave, n., displacement; v.i., to rise and fall; to retch; a strong pull; v.t., to lift, to pull, to utter.

heaved, p.p., heave.

heav′en, n., the sky or firmament; the abode of God.

heav′enliness, n., the state of being heavenly.

heav′enly, adj., pert. or rel. to heaven; blissful.

heav′enward, adv., towards heaven.

heav′enwards, adv., i.q. heavenward.

heav′er, n., one who heaves.

heaves, n. pl., broken wind (in horses).

heav′ier, adj., comp. of heavy.

heav′iest, adj., super. of heavy.

heav′ily, adv., with weight, oppressively.

heav′iness, n., weight; depression of spirit.

heav′ing, pr.p., heave.

Hea′viside lay′er, n., an atmospheric layer that reflects back radio waves causing them to follow the contour of the earth.

heav′y, adj., weighty, ponderous, sad, overcast (of sky).

heav′y-hand′ed, adj., awkward, clumsy.

heav′y-heart′ed, adj., depressed, doleful.

heav′y-la′den, adj., overburdened.

heav′yweight, n., a boxer over 12 st. 7 lb.

heb′domad, n., a week.

hebdom′adal, adj., weekly.

Heb′e, n., the Greek goddess of youth; a waitress or barmaid (colloq.).

heb′etate, v.i., to become dull; v.t., to dull.

heb′etude, n., dullness; stupidity.

Hebra′ic, adj., pert. or rel. to Hebrew or the Hebrews.

Hebra′ically, adv., in a Hebraic way.

He′braism, n., Hebrew idiom or attribute.

He′braist, n., a Hebrew scholar; one who favours Hebrew religious thought.

Hebraist′ic, adj., pert. or rel. to Hebrew religion or language.

Hebraist′ically, adv., in a Hebraistic way.

He′braize, v.i., to conform to Hebraism; v.t., to make Hebrew.

He′braized, p.p., Hebraize.

He′braizing, pr.p., Hebraize.

He′brew, adj., Israelitish, Jewish; n., an Israelite, a Jew; the Jewish language.

Hebrid′ean, adj., pert. or rel. to the Hebrides, islands off the west coast of Scotland; n., a native of the H.

hec′atomb, n., a large public sacrifice.

heck, n., a device for stopping fish on a river.

heck′le, v.t., to dress flax; to badger with questions.

heck′led, p.p., heckle.

heck′lephone, n., a baritone oboe.

heck′ler, n., one who heckles, esp. at political meetings.

heck′ling, pr.p., heckle.

hec′ogenin, n., a synthetic form of cortisone.

hec′tare, n., a metric unit of the French land measure.

hec′tic, adj., constitutional; consumptive; flushed; wild, exciting (slang); n., a fever accompanying consumption; a flush.

hec′tical, adj., i.q. hectic.

hec′tically, adv., with feverish activity.

hec′togramme, n., the weight of 100 grammes (Fr.).

hec′tograph, n., a multiplying gelatine pad, an early form of duplicator; v.t., to copy with a hectograph.

hectograph′ic, adj., able to be hectographed.

hectog′raphy, n., the use of the hectograph.

hec′tolitre, -ter, n., 100 litres (Fr.).

hec′tometre, -ter, n., 100 metres (Fr.).

hec′tor, n., a bully; v.i., to bluster, to play the bully; v.t., to bully.

hec′tored, p.p., hector.

hec′toring, pr.p., hector.

hec′torism, n., bullying conduct.

hed′dles, n. pl., fine vertical wires or cords in a loom.

hedera′ceous, adj., ivy-like.

hed′eral, adj., pert. or rel. to ivy.

hederif′erous, adj., ivy-growing.

hedge, n., a fence of bushes or low trees; v.i., to avoid loss by betting on both sides; to avoid committing oneself; v.t., to fence round; to make or trim a hedge.

hedge′bill, n., a long-handled, curved instrument used for cutting hedges.

hedged, p.p., hedge.

hedge′hog, n., an insect-eating mammal armed with spines.

hedg′er, n., one who makes or trims hedges; one who hedges.

hedge′row, n., a line of shrubs planted as a fence.

hedge'sparrow, *n.*, a small, brown, common, British and European hedge bird belonging to the warblers.

hedg'ing, *pr.p.*, hedge.

hedon'ic, *adj.*, pert. or rel. to pleasure.

hed'onism, *n.*, the pursuit of pleasure as the chief good.

hed'onist, *n.*, one who cultivates the pleasures of life.

hedonis'tic, *adj.*, pleasure-seeking.

heed, *n.*, attention, notice; *v.t.*, to notice, to pay attention to, to care about.

heed'ed, *p.p.*, heed.

heed'ful, *adj.*, attentive, considerate.

heed'fully, *adv.*, in a heedful way.

heed'fulness, *n.*, carefulness; attentiveness.

heed'ing, *pr.p.*, heed.

heed'less, *adj.*, not heeding.

heed'lessly, *adv.*, carelessly.

heed'lessness, *n.*, want of thought.

hee'-haw, *n.*, an ass's bray; *v.i.*, to bray, as a donkey.

heel, *n.*, the hinder part of the foot, or of a boot; anything like a heel; *v.i.*, to turn over on its side (of a ship); *v.t.*, to put a heel to; to strike with the heel of a golf club.

heeled, *p.p.*, heel.

heel'ing, *pr.p.*, heel.

heel'tap, *n.*, a thickness of leather added to a heel; liquor left at the bottom of a glass; *v.t.*, to add thicknesses of leather to a heel.

heft, *v.t.*, to lift, to judge weight.

hef'ty, *adj.*, able to lift weights; strong.

Hegel'ian, *adj.*, pert. or rel. to the German philosopher Hegel; *n.*, a follower of this philosophy.

hegemon'ic, *adj.*, having dominion; supreme.

he'gemony, *n.*, supreme rule, leadership.

Heg'ira, *n.*, Mohammed's flight from Mecca; any momentous flight. (Also *Hejira*.)

heif'er, *n.*, a young cow.

heigh'-ho, *interj.*, expressing disappointment.

height, *n.*, elevation from a base; the distance from top to bottom; eminence; rising ground.

height'en, *v.i.*, to rise; *v.t.*, to make higher, to intensify, to advance.

height'ened, *p.p.*, heighten.

height'ening, *pr.p.*, heighten.

hei'nous, *adj.*, atrocious, odious, wicked.

hei'nously, *adv.*, atrociously, wickedly.

hei'nousness, *n.*, the quality of being heinous.

heir, *n.*, one entitled to succeed to another's estate; one who inherits anything.

heir-appa'rent, *n.*, one who may in due course become the heir.

heir'dom, *n.*, the state of being an heir.

heir'ess, *n.*, the fem. of heir.

heir'less, *adj.*, without an heir.

heir'loom, *n.*, a chattel that comes to the heir; personal property that has been in a family for a long time.

heir'-presump'tive, *n.*, one whose claim may be superseded by a nearer heir.

heir'ship, *n.*, the right of inheritance.

Hej'ira, *n.*, *i.q.* Hegira.

held, *p.p.*, hold.

hele, *v.t.*, to set a plant and cover it in; to cover, to hide (*dial.*).

heli'acal, *adj.*, pert. or rel. to the sun (*astron.*).

Helian'themum, *n.*, a genus of spreading evergreen shrubs with showy flowers.

Helian'thus, *n.*, a large genus of plants of the aster family, including the sunflower (*Gr.*).

hel'ical, *adj.*, spiral.

hel'ically, *adv.*, spirally.

hel'icite, *n.*, a spiral fossil.

hel'icoid, *adj.*, spiral, like a snail shell; *n.*, a spiral surface.

helicoid'al, *adj.*, *i.q.* helicoid.

Hel'icon, *n.*, the Boeotian mountain, abode of the Muses.

Helico'nian, *adj.*, pert. or rel. to Helicon and the Muses.

hel'icopter, *n.*, a heavier-than-air machine, able to rise vertically under its own power by means of rotor blades. (Also *hoverplane*.)

heliocen'tric, *adj.*, having the sun as centre (*astron.*).

he'liochrome, *n.*, a photograph in colours from nature.

he'liogram, *n.*, a message transmitted by the heliograph.

he'liograph, *n.*, an apparatus for photographing the sun; a photograph obtained from exposure; a signalling instrument using the sun's rays.

heliograph'ic, *adj.*, pert. or rel. to heliography.

heliog'raphy, *n.*, the use of a heliograph; a description of the sun's surface.

he'liogravure, *n.*, photoengraving.

heliol'ater, *n.*, a sun-worshipper.

heliol'atry, *n.*, sun-worship.

heliolith'ic, *adj.*, pert. or rel. to the civilization characterized by megaliths and sun-worship.

heliom'eter, *n.*, an instrument for ascertaining the angular distance between stars.

helior'nis, *n.*, the sun-bird of Central and S. America.

he'lioscope, *n.*, a protected telescope for examining the sun.

helios'is, *n.*, sunstroke; spots on leaves caused by the sun's rays concentrated through glass, etc. (*bot.*).

he'liostat, *n.*, a mirror reflecting the sun.

heliothe'rapy, *n.*, the sun-ray treatment of disease.

he'liotrope, *n.*, a flowering shrub with clustered flowers; the heliotrope colour; the blood-stone.

heliotro'pic, *adj.*, turning toward the light.

he'liotype, *n.*, a picture from gelatine exposed to light.

he'liotypy, *n.*, the heliotype process.

hel'iport, *n.*, a helicopter station.

he'liscoop, *n.*, a helicopter rescue-net.

helispher'ic, *adj.*, spherically spiral.

he'lium, *n.*, the lightest gaseous element.

hel'ix, *n.*, a spiral; a spiral ornament; the border of the external ear; a screw-thread.

hell, *n.*, the lower world; the place of evil spirits.

hell'-cat, *n.*, a witch, a hag.

hel'lebore, *n.*, anciently a flower that cured madness; the Christmas rose and other species, *e.g.* bearsfoot.

hel'leborine, *n.*, a plant of the orchid family.

Hell'ene, *n.*, a Greek.

Helle'nian, *adj.*, Greek or Grecian.

Helle'nic, *adj.*, *i.q.* Hellenian.

Hel'lenism, *n.*, the Greek idiom; Greek culture.

Hel'lenist, *n.*, a Greek-speaking alien; a Greek scholar.

Hellenis'tic, *adj.*, pert. or rel. to Hellenists.

Hel'lenize, *v.i.*, to adopt Greek ideas; *v.t.*, to make Greek.

Hel'lenized, *p.p.*, Hellenize.

Hel'lenizing, *pr.p.*, Hellenize.

Hellespon'tine, *adj.*, pert. or rel. to the Hellespont or the Dardanelles (Çanakkale Boğazi), the narrow strait connecting the Aegean Sea and the Sea of Marmora.

hell'hound, *n.*, a fiend.

hell'ish, *adj.*, hell-like, diabolical.

hell'ishly, *adv.*, diabolically.

hell'ishness, *n.*, the state of being hellish.

hello', *n.*, a friendly greeting.

hell'ward, *adv.*, toward hell.

helm, *n.*, a tiller; the wheel by which the rudder is moved; a helmet; *v.t.*, to steer.

helm'et, *n.*, defensive headgear.

helm'eted, *adj.*, wearing a helmet.

hel'minth, *n.*, a worm, usually intestinal.

helmin'thagogue, *n.*, any drug which expels intestinal worms.

helminthi'asis, *n.*, a disease characterized by the presence of helminths in the body.

helmin'thic, *adj.*, pert. or rel. to worms.

helmin'thoid, *adj.*, vermiform.

helminthol'ogy, *n.*, the study of parasitic worms (*med.*).

helms'man, *n.*, the man at the helm.

Heloder'ma, *n.*, a genus of venomous lizards.

hel'ot, *n.*, a Spartan serf.

hel'otism, *n.*, the system of serfdom in ancient Sparta.

help, *n.*, aid, assistance; *v.t.*, to aid or assist.

helped, *p.p.*, help.

help'er, *n.*, one who helps.

help'ful, *adj.*, of assistance.

help'fully, *adv.*, usefully.

help'fulness, *n.*, usefulness.

help'ing, *n.*, a portion; *pr.p.*, help.

help'less, *adj.*, incapable of self-help; without resource.

help'lessly, *adv.*, in a helpless way.

help'lessness, *n.*, the state of being helpless.

help'mate, *n.*, a helping partner.

help'meet, *n.*, *i.q.* help-mate.

hel'ter-skel'ter, *adv.*, in disordered hurry; *n.*, a helical slide.

helve, *n.*, a handle; *v.t.*, to fit with a handle.

helved, *p.p.*, helve.

Helve'tian, *adj.*, Swiss.

Helvet'ic, *adj.*, *i.q.* Helvetian.

helv'ing, *pr.p.*, helve.

hem, *n.*, a border turned down and sewn over; an interjection; the sound of clearing the throat; *v.i.*, to clear the throat; to express hesitation; *v.t.*, to sew a turned-down border; to enclose.

hem'achate, *n.*, a species of agate.

hem'adynamom'eter, *n.*, an instrument for measuring arterial blood-pressure (*med.*).

hem'al, *adj.*, *i.q.* haemal.

hemat'ic, *adj.* and *n.*, *i.q.* haematic.

hem'atin, *n.*, *i.q.* haematin.

hem'atite, *n.*, iron ore.

hematit'ic, *adj.*, *i.q.* haematitic.

hematology, *n.*, *i.q.* haematology.

hematuria, *n.*, *i.q.* haematuria.

hemianop'sia, *n.*, half-blindness.

hemicra'nia, *n.*, pain on one side of the head; imperfect development of one side of the head.

hem'icycle, *n.*, a semicircular arrangement of seating.

hemihe'dral, *adj.*, having half its complement of planes.

hemino'pia, *n.*, *i.q.* hemianopsia.

hemiop'sy, *n.*, half-blindness.

hemiple'gia, *n.*, paralysis of one side (*med.*).

hemiple'gic, *adj.*, half-paralysed.

hem'iplegy, *n.*, *i.q.* hemiplegia.

Hemip'tera, *n.*, an order of insects with wings half leathery, half membranous.

hemip'teral, *adj.*, pert. or rel. to the hemiptera.

hemip'terous, *adj.*, *i.q.* hemipteral.

hem'isphere, *n.*, a half sphere; half the globe's surface.

hemispher'ic, *adj.*, like a half sphere.

hemispher'ical, *adj.*, *i.q.* hemispheric.

hemispher'oid, *n.*, a half-spheroid.

hemispheroid'al, *adj.*, like a hemispheroid.

hem'istich, *n.*, a half-line of verse.

hem'itrope, *adj.*, half inverted; *n.*, a twin crystal.

hem'-line, *n.*, the bottom edge of a dress.

hem'lock, *n.*, an umbelliferous plant, poisonous and sedative.

hemmed, *p.p.*, hem.

hem'ming, *n.*, hems; the stitching of hems; *pr.p.*, hem.

hemoglo'bin, n., i.q. haemoglobin.

hemophil'ia, n., i.q. haemophilia.

hemophil'iac, n., i.q. haemophiliac.

hem'orrhage, n., i.q. haemorrhage.

hemorrhoid'al, n., i.q. haemorrhoidal.

hem'orrhoids, n. pl., i.q. haemorrhoids and emeroids.

hem'ostat, n., i.q. haemostat.

hemostat'ic, adj., i.q. haemostatic.

hemp, n., an Indian, annual, fibre-producing plant.

hemp'en, adj., made of hemp.

hemp'seed, n., the seed of hemp.

hem'stitch, n., ornamental stitching in a hem; v.t., to embroider with hemstitch.

hem'stitched, p.p., hemstitch.

hem'stitching, pr.p., hemstitch.

hen, n., a female bird, esp. the domestic fowl.

hen'bane, n., a poisonous, narcotic plant.

hence, adv., from here; away.

henceforth', adv., from this time onward.

hencefor'ward, adv., i.q. henceforth.

hench'man, n., a squire, attendant or supporter.

hen'coop, n., a pen for fowls.

hendec'agon, n., an eleven-sided, plane, rectilineal figure.

hendecasyll'able, n., a verse of eleven syllables.

hen'-harrier, n., the blue hawk.

hen'house, n., a place for fowls to live and roost in.

Hen'ley, n., a place on the River Thames, England, where an annual regatta takes place.

hen'na, n., the Egyptian privet.

henn'y, adj., henlike; n., a hen-like cock.

hen'otheism, n., belief in one God; monotheism.

hen'peck, v.t., to nag at; to harass.

hepat'ic, adj., pert. or rel. to the liver.

hepat'ica, n., an anemone with leaves resembling the liver.

hepat'ical, adj., i.q. hepatic.

hepatit'is, n., inflammation of the liver.

hepatiza'tion, n., change of tissue into liver substance.

hepatol'ogy, n., the study of the liver.

hep'-cat, n., a jazz fiend or player (colloq.).

Hep'plewhite, n., a delicate kind of furniture.

hep'tachord, n., a seven-stringed instrument; the major seventh (mus.).

hep'tad, n., a set or group of seven (Gr.).

hep'tagon, n., a figure with seven angles and sides.

heptag'onal, adj., seven-sided.

heptagyn'ia, n., an order of plants with seven distinct styles.

heptahe'dron, n., a seven-faced solid.

heptan'drian, adj., having seven stamens.

heptan'gular, adj., having seven angles.

hep'tarch, n., the ruler of one of the kingdoms in a heptarchy.

hep'tarchy, n., the rule of seven princes; a group of seven kingdoms.

her, pers. pron., objective case of she; possess. pron., bel. to her.

her'ald, n., an officer who carries messages from state to state; one who makes public proclamations; one who determines questions of precedence, etc.; one who is expert in the blazoning of arms; v.t., to announce, to proclaim the advent.

her'alded, p.p., herald.

heral'dic, adj., pert. or rel. to heraldry.

her'alding, pr.p., herald.

her'aldry, n., the science of a herald; heraldic symbolism, as represented on coats of arms.

herb, n., a plant with a non-persistent, non-woody stem.

herba'ceous, adj., of the nature of herbs.

herb'age, n., herbs collectively; pasturage.

herb'al, adj., pert. or rel. to herbs; n., a botany book.

herb'alism, n., the knowledge of herbs.

herb'alist, n., one skilled in herb-lore.

herb'alistic, adj., pert. or rel. to herbs.

herba'rium, n., any collection of dried plants.

Herbart, n., a German philosopher and educationist.

Herbar'tian, adj., pert. or rel. to Herbart or his teaching.

her'bary, n., a herb garden.

herb'-beer, n., a drink made from herbs.

herbes'cent, adj., becoming herb-like.

herbif'erous, adj., herb-producing.

Herbiv'ora, n. pl., creatures that feed on herbs.

herbiv'orous, adj., feeding on herbs.

herboriza'tion, n., botanical study.

her'borize, v.i., to botanize.

her'borized, p.p., herborize.

her'borizing, pr.p., herborize.

herb'y, adj., abounding in, or resembling, herbs.

Hercu'lean, adj., pert. or rel. to Hercules; immensely strong; extremely arduous.

Her'cules, n., the national hero of ancient Greece.

herd, n., a group or flock of animals; a crowd of people; a herdsman; v.i., to go in a herd; v.t., to tend, to gather into a herd.

herd'ed, p.p., herd.

herd'er, n., a herdsman.

herd'ing, pr.p., herd.

herds'man, n., the keeper of a herd.

here, adv., in this place; present.

here'about, adv., somewhere near here.

here'abouts', adv., i.q. hereabout.

hereaf'ter, adv., in the future.

hereat', adv., at this spot.

hereby', adv., near here; by this means.

hereditabil'ity, *n.,* the state of being inherited.

hered'itable, *adj.,* that may be inherited.

heredit'ament, *n.,* heritable property.

hereditar'ian, *n.,* one who believes in heredity.

hered'itary, *adj.,* inherited, transmitted by descent.

hered'ity, *n.,* transmission of qualities, etc., by descent.

He'reford, *n.,* a breed of cattle originating in the English county of Herefordshire.

herein', *adv.,* in this place, book, etc.

hereinaf'ter, *adv.,* below (in a document, etc.); from now on.

hereof', *adv.,* of this.

hereon', *adv.,* on this.

hereout', *adv.,* out of this.

Herer'o, *n. pl.,* natives of S.W. Africa; their language.

her'esiarch, *n.,* the leader of a heresy.

heresiol'ogist, *n.,* one who writes about heresies.

heresiol'ogy, *n.,* the study of heresy.

her'esy, *n.,* the doctrine opposed to orthodox beliefs.

her'etic, *n.,* one who holds heretical opinions.

heret'ical, *adj.,* of the nature of heresy.

hereto', *adv.,* to this point or matter.

heretofore', *adv.,* up to this time.

hereun'der, *adv.,* below.

hereunto', *adv.,* up to here or now.

hereupon', *adv.,* following on this.

herewith', *adv.,* with this.

her'iot, *n.,* a payment to a lord on the death of a tenant.

her'iotable, *adj.,* liable to heriot.

her'isson, *n.,* a spiked revolving beam defending a gate.

her'itable, *adj.,* that can be inherited.

her'itably, *adv.,* in a heritable way.

her'itage, *n.,* inherited property; share; transmitted quality.

her'itor, *n.,* one who inherits.

her'itrix, *n.,* the fem. of heritor.

hermaph'rodite, *adj.,* bisexual; *n.,* a bisexual being.

hermaphrodit'ic, *adj.,* pert. or rel. to a hermaphrodite.

hermeneut'ic, *adj., i.q.* hermeneutical.

hermeneu'tical, *adj.,* interpretative.

hermeneu'tics, *n. pl.,* (the study of) interpretation.

Herm'es, *n.,* in Greek mythology, the messenger of the gods.

hermet'ic, *adj.,* pert. or rel. to alchemy; impervious to air.

hermet'ical, *adj., i.q.* hermetic.

hermet'ically, *adv.,* by fusion.

her'mit, *n.,* a dweller apart, a recluse.

her'mitage, *n.,* a hermit's shelter; a French wine.

her'mitary, *n.,* a hermit's cell.

hermit'ical, *adj.,* pert. or rel. to a hermit.

her'nia, *n.,* a rupture.

her'nial, *adj.,* pert. or rel. to hernia.

hern'iary, *adj., i.q.* hernial.

herniot'omy, *n.,* the operation for the relief of strangulated hernia.

hern'shaw, *n.,* a young heron.

he'ro, *n.,* a demigod; a man of great valour; the principal character in a story.

Hero'dian, *adj.,* pert. or rel. to Herod the tetrarch.

hero'ic, *adj.,* rel. to, or like, a hero.

hero'ical, *adj., i.q.* heroic.

hero'ically, *adv.,* with heroism.

heroi-com'ic, *adj.,* consisting of the heroic and the ludicrous.

hero'ics, *n. pl.,* high-flown language.

hero'ify, *v.t.,* to make a hero of.

her'oin, *n.,* a morphia drug.

her'oine, *n.,* the fem. of hero.

her'oism, *n.,* courage, fortitude.

hero'ize, *v.t.* and *i.,* to make heroic; to play the hero.

hero'ized, *p.p.,* heroize.

hero'izing, *pr.p.,* heroize.

her'on, *n.,* a wading bird.

her'onry, *n.,* a heron's breeding-place.

he'ro-worship, *n.,* the worship of great men.

her'pes, *n.,* a vesicula skin-disease.

herpet'ic, *adj.,* of the nature of herpes.

herpetol'ogist, *n.,* a student of herpetology.

herpetol'ogy, *n.,* the zoology of reptiles.

Herr, *n.,* the German equivalent of Mr.; a German gentleman.

her'ring, *n.,* a common, sea-water fish.

her'ring-bone, *adj.,* arranged slantingly in opposite directions (brick-laying, stitching, weaving, etc.).

hers, *possess. adj.,* the absolute form of *her;* used predicatively.

herse, *n.,* a portcullis; an heraldic charge like a harrow. (Also *hearse.*)

herself', *pron.,* the emphatic and reflexive substitute for *she* and *her.*

Hert'zian, *adj.,* pert. or rel. to the German physicist, H. R. Hertz.

Heshvan', *n.,* the second month of the Jewish civil year.

hes'itance, *n., i.q.* hesitancy.

hes'itancy, *n.,* hesitation, vacillation.

hes'itant, *adj.,* hesitating, vacillating.

hes'itantly, *adv.,* in a hesitant way.

hes'itate, *v.i.,* to be undecided, doubtful or slow; to stammer.

hes'itated, *p.p.,* hesitate.

hes'itating, *adj.,* wavering; *pr.p.,* hesitate.

hes'itatingly, *adv.,* in a hesitating way.

hesita'tion, *n.,* uncertainty, indecision.

hes'itative, *adj., i.q.* hesitating.

hes'itatively, *adv., i.q.* hesitatingly.

hes'ped, *n.,* a Jewish funeral oration.

Hes'per, *n.,* the evening star.

Hespe′ria, *n.,* Italy (to the Greeks), Spain (to the Romans).

Hespe′rian, *adj.,* pert. or rel. to Hesperia; Western.

Hes′peris, *n.,* a genus of cruciferous herbs.

Hesperorn′is, *n.,* an extinct American genus of gigantic fossil birds.

Hes′perus, *n., i.q.* Hesper.

Hes′sian, *adj.,* pert. or rel. to Hesse in Germany; *n.,* a native of H.

hes′sian, *n.,* a strong, coarse cloth of jute or hemp.

hest, *n., i.q.* behest.

het, *adj.,* excited (*slang*).

hetae′ra, *n.,* a Greek courtezan.

hetae′ria, *n.,* a Greek club or association.

hetaer′ism, *n.,* tribal communal marriage.

heterocar′pous, *adj.,* bearing more than one kind of fruit.

heterochro′mous, *adj.,* of more than one colour.

het′eroclite, *adj.,* irregularly declined; *n.,* an irregular noun.

heteroclit′ic, *adj., i.q.* heteroclite.

heterodac′tyl, *adj.,* with the second toe irregular.

het′erodont, *adj.,* having teeth of different types.

het′erodox, *adj.,* not orthodox; taking different viewpoints.

het′erodoxy, *n.,* unorthodox opinion.

het′erodyne, *n.,* a device for converting a high-frequency radio wave to one of audible frequency.

heterog′amous, *adj.,* bearing bi-sexual flowers.

heterogene′ity, *n.,* the state of being heterogeneous.

heteroge′neous, *adj.,* not alike in character; not uniform in composition.

heteroge′neously, *adv.,* in a heterogeneous way.

heteroge′neousness, *n., i.q.* heterogeneity.

heterogen′esis, *n.,* spontaneous generation.

heterogenet′ic, *adj.,* pert. or rel. to heterogenesis.

het′erography, *n.,* incorrect or inconsistent spelling.

heterol′ogy, *n.,* abnormality.

heteromor′phic, *adj.,* of irregular form.

heteromor′phous, *adj., i.q.* heteromorphic.

heteron′omy, *n.,* the opposite of autonomy; subjection to another's rule.

het′eronym, *n.,* a word spelt like another but pronounced differently.

heteropath′ic, *adj.,* pert. or rel. to heteropathy; of different effect.

heterop′athy, *n.,* allopathy.

heteropha′sia, *n.,* confusion of speech.

het′erophyll′ous, *adj.,* bearing leaves of different kinds on the same plant.

heterosex′ual, *adj.,* normally sexual; having sexual feeling for the opposite sex.

het′erotaxy, *n.,* the abnormal disposition of parts or organs.

heterozy′gote, *n.,* a zygote resulting from the fusion of dissimilar gametes.

heterozygo′teous, *adj.,* pert. or rel. to heterozygote.

het′man, *n.,* a Cossack military commander (*Pol.*).

heur′ism, *n.,* the heuristic method in education.

heuris′tic, *adj.,* helping discovery; learning by finding out.

He′vea, *n.,* a genus of tropical American trees.

hew, *v.t.,* to cut (with an axe or sword); to fashion.

hewed, *p.p.,* hew.

hew′er, *n.,* one who hews.

hew′ing, *pr.p.,* hew.

hewn, *p.p.,* hew.

hex′achord, *n.,* a diatonic group of notes with a semitone between the third and the fourth (*mus.*); a six-stringed musical instrument.

hex′ad, *adj.,* of sixfold value.

hexadac′tylous, *adj.,* with six fingers or toes.

hexae′meron, *n.,* the space of six days.

hex′agon, *n.,* a six-sided and six-angled figure.

hexag′onal, *adj.,* having six sides.

hexag′onally, *adv.,* in a hexagonal way.

hexagyn′ial, *adj.,* having six styles.

hexag′ynous, *adj., i.q.* hexagynial.

hexahe′dral, *adj.,* having six faces.

hexahe′dron, *n.,* a six-faced figure.

hexam′eter, *n.,* a line having six metrical feet.

hexamet′ric, *adj.,* pert. or rel. to hexameters.

hexamet′rical, *adj., i.q.* hexametric.

hexam′etrist, *n.,* one who studies hexametric verse.

hexan′dria, *n.,* flowers having six stamens.

hexan′drous, *adj.,* having six stamens.

hexan′gular, *adj.,* having six angles.

hexapet′alous, *adj.,* six-petalled.

hexaphyl′lous, *adj.,* six-leaved.

hex′apla, *n.,* a sixfold text in parallel columns (esp. of Old or New Testament).

hex′aplar, *adj.,* six-fold.

hex′apod, *adj.,* having six feet.

hex′astich, *n.,* a six-lined stanza.

hex′astyle, *adj.,* having six pillars.

Hex′ateuch, *n.,* the first six books of the Old Testament.

hey, *interj.,* expressing joy, surprise and question; also calling attention.

hey′day, *interj.,* expressing joy, surprise, etc.; *n.,* the time of youth, prosperity, etc.

hey′duck, *n.,* a Polish liveried retainer (*Pol.*).

hey-pres′to, *interj.,* an exclamation used by conjurers to attract or divert attention.

hi, *interj., i.q.* hey.

hia′tus, *n.,* a gap (*Lat.*).

hiber′nal, *adj.,* wintry.

hib′ernant, *adj.,* an animal which hibernates.

hi′bernate, *v.i.,* to spend the winter (in torpor or inactivity).

hi'bernated, *p.p.*, hibernate.

hi'bernating, *pr.p.*, hibernate.

hiberna'tion, *n.*, the state or period of hibernating.

hi'bernator, *n.*, that which hibernates.

Hiber'nian, *adj.*, Irish.

Hiber'nianism, *n.*, Irish idiom.

Hiber'nicism, *n.*, *i.q.* Hibernianism.

Hibern'icize, *v.t.*, to make Irish.

hibis'cus, *n.*, a cultivated malvaceous plant or shrub with big, showy flowers, grown mostly in tropical countries.

hic'cough, *n.*, *i.q.* hiccup.

hic'cup, *n.*, an involuntary spasm of the breathing organs; *v.i.*, to make a hiccup; *v.t.*, to utter with hiccups.

hic'cuped, *p.p.*, hiccup.

hic'cuping, *pr.p.*, hiccup.

hic ja'cet, *n.*, an epitaph = here lies (*Lat.*).

hick, *n.*, a countryman or farmer (*colloq.*).

hick'boo, *n.*, an air-raid (*slang*).

hick'ory, *n.*, a N. American tree allied to the walnut.

hick'wall, *n.*, a woodpecker.

hid, *p.p.*, hide.

hi'dage, *n.*, a tax on hides of land.

hidal'go, *n.*, a Spanish gentleman.

hid'den, *p.p.*, hide.

hid'denly, *adv.*, covertly.

hide, *n.*, an animal's skin; a measure of land; *v.i.*, to seek shelter, to be concealed; *v.t.*, to conceal, to shelter; to flog.

hide'bound, *adj.*, prejudiced, uncompromising; unduly restricted by tradition or rules.

hid'eous, *adj.*, frightful, extremely ugly.

hid'eously, *adv.*, in a hideous way.

hid'eousness, *n.*, the state of being hideous.

hide'out, *n.*, a retreat.

hi'der, *n.*, one who hides.

hi'ding, *n.*, the act of hiding; concealment; a flogging (*colloq.*); *pr.p.*, hide.

hidro'sis, *n.*, sweat (*med.*).

hidro'tic, *adj.*, tending to cause sweating.

hie, *v.i.*, to hasten; *v.t.*, to incite, to urge on.

hied, *p.p.*, hie.

hie'ing, *pr.p.*, hie.

hi'emal, *adj.*, pert. or rel. to winter.

hiema'tion, *n.*, the act of spending the winter in a particular way or place.

hi'erarch, *n.*, a chief priest.

hierarch'al, *adj.*, *i.q.* hierarchical.

hierarch'ical, *adj.*, pert. or rel. to hierarchy.

hi'erarchism, *n.*, hierarchical principles.

hi'erarchy, *n.*, a body of ecclesiastical rulers; government by an organized body of such rulers; a defined order of precedence.

hierat'ic, *adj.*, sacerdotal.

hierat'ical, *adj.*, *i.q.* hieratic.

hieroc'racy, *n.*, ecclesiastical rule.

hierocrat'ic, *adj.*, pert. or rel. to hierocracy.

hierod'ule, *n.*, a slave kept in the temple to serve a god.

hi'eroglyph, *n.*, picture writing.

hieroglyph'ic, *adj.*, represented by picture-signs; *n.*, *i.q.* hieroglyph.

hieroglyph'ical, *adj.*, *i.q.* hieroglyphic.

hieroglyph'ically, *adv.*, in a hieroglyphic way.

hi'erogram, *n.*, a sacred symbol.

hierogram'matist, *n.*, a writer of hierograms.

hierolog'ic, *adj.*, pert. or rel. to hierology.

hierol'ogist, *n.*, an expert in hierology.

hierol'ogy, *n.*, the study of ancient sacred writings.

hi'erophant, *n.*, a teacher of religious mysteries.

hierophan'tic, *adj.*, pert. or rel. to hierophant.

hi-fi, *adj.*, high-fidelity (sound reproduction).

hig'gle, *v.i.*, to dispute, to haggle.

hig'gled, *p.p.*, higgle.

hig'gledy-pig'gledy, *adv.*, in a muddled state.

hig'gler, *n.*, one who higgles.

hig'gling, *pr.p.*, higgle.

high, *adj.*, elevated, lofty; exalted; strong; tainted.

high'ball, *n.*, a whisky and soda (*U.S.A.*).

high'-born, *adj.*, of exalted birth.

high'-bred, *adj.*, of good pedigree.

high'brow, *adj.*, intellectually superior; *n.*, an intellectual.

high'-class, *adj.*, of superior order.

high court, *n.*, a supreme court; the High Court of Justice.

high'er, *adj.*, comp. of high.

high'est, *adj.*, super. of high.

high-falu'tin, *adj.*, bombastic; unduly exalted; *n.*, bombast.

high-falu'ting, *adj.* and *n.*, *i.q.* high-falutin.

high'-flown, *adj.*, proud, extravagant.

high'-flyer, *n.*, an ambitious person; one of superior attainment.

high'-freq'uency, *adj.* and *n.*, (any frequency) of alternating current above the audible range.

high'-grade, *adj.*, *i.q.* high-class.

high-hand'ed, *adj.*, arbitrary.

high'-heeled, *adj.*, having high heels.

high'-jinks, *n.*, merry-making, revelry (*colloq.*).

high'land, *n.*, a hilly or mountainous range.

High'lander, *n.*, a native of the Highlands; a soldier in a Highland regiment.

Highlands, *n. pl.*, the north-west hills of Scotland.

high'light, *n.*, the brightest part; an outstanding feature; *v.t.*, to emphasize.

high'lighted, *p.p.*, highlight.

high'lighting, *pr.p.*, highlight.

high'lows, *n. pl.*, ankle boots.

high'ly, *adv.*, greatly.

high'-minded, *adj.*, proud, arrogant; upright; of strict principles of conduct.

high'ness, n., the state of being high; a princely title.

high'-pitched, adj., steep; of high tone (mus.).

high'-pressure, adj., having high steam pressure; intensive.

high'-priest, n., a chief priest.

high'road, n., a main road.

high'-seas, n., the open sea.

high'-sound'ing, adj., pompous; ostentatious.

high'-spirited, adj., impetuous, unrestrained.

high'-stepper, n., a horse that lifts his feet high; a person of stately walk or bearing (colloq.).

high'-strung, adj., very sensitive; tense.

hight, v.i., to be called or named (passive).

high'-tea, n., a late afternoon tea at which fish, meat, etc. are served.

high'-tide, n., high water; full tide; a festival; the peak of achievement.

high'-toned, adj., honourable; high of pitch.

high'-treas'on, n., treason against the state.

high'ty-tigh'ty, interj., i.q. hoity-toity.

high'-up, n., one in a high position.

high'water, n., the state of the tide when the water is highest.

high'way, n., the public main road.

High'way Code, n., the official code of directions and rules for road users in Great Britain, first issued in 1930.

high'wayman, n., a highway robber.

high'wrought, adj., elaborate; agitated.

hi'jack, v.t. and i., to rob or blackmail; to seize by force.

hi'jacked, p.p., hijack.

hi'jacker, n., a highwayman; one who seizes by force.

hi'jacking, pr.p., hijack.

hike, n., a long, country walk; v.i., to ramble; v.t., to hoist or jerk.

hiked, p.p., hike.

hi'ker, n., one who hikes.

hi'king, pr.p., hike.

hi'lar, adj., pert. or rel. to the hilum.

hilar'ious, adj., loudly cheerful, festive; highly amusing.

hilar'iously, adv., cheerfully, festively.

hilar'iousness, n., i.q. hilarity.

hilar'ity, n., cheerfulness, merriment.

Hil'ary, n., St. Hilary of Poitiers; a period of the legal year.

hill, n., ground elevated above the surrounding area; a heap; v.t., to bank up.

hill'iness, n., the state of being hilly.

hill'ock, n., a little hill.

hill'side, n., the slope of a hill.

hill'y, adj., steep; abounding in hills.

hilt, n., a sword handle.

hilt'ed, adj., having a hilt.

hi'lum, n., the point where a seed is attached to a seed-vessel.

him, pron., the objective case of he.

Hima'layan, adj., pert. or rel. to the Himalayas.

Hima'layas, n., a vast mountain range on the northern frontier of India.

himself', pron., the reflexive of he.

hind, adj., in the rear; posterior; n., a female deer; a farm servant.

hind'er, adj., farther back.

hin'der, v.t., to prevent, to retard; to obstruct.

hin'dered, p.p., hinder.

hin'derer, n., one who hinders.

hin'dering, pr.p., hinder.

hind'ermost, adj., rearmost, farthest back.

Hin'di, n., an Aryan language, officially spoken in India.

hind'most, adj., i.q. hindermost.

hin'drance, n., a bar, impediment or check.

hind'sight, n., wisdom after the event.

Hin'du, adj., pert. or rel. to the Hindus; n., a native of India following the Hindu religion.

Hin'duism, n., the polytheistic religion of Hindus.

Hin'duize, v.t., to make Hindu in custom, religion, etc.

Hindusta'ni, adj., pert. or rel. to Hindustan, orig. that part of India north of the Vindhya Mountains; n., a native of H.

hinge, n., a device to secure one object which moves to another which is stationary; v.i., to turn on a hinge; v.t., to fix with a hinge; to make to turn on a hinge.

hinged, p.p., hinge.

hinge'less, adj., without a hinge.

hing'ing, pr.p., hinge.

hin'ny, n., a Scottish term of endearment; v.i., to neigh.

hint, n., a slight suggestion; v.i., to give a hint of; v.t., to suggest slightly.

hint'ed, p.p., hint.

hin'terland, n., the region lying behind a coast or another defined geographical feature (Ger.).

hint'ing, pr.p., hint.

hint'ingly, adv., in an indirect way.

hip, n., the part of the body between the pelvis and the upper part of the thigh; the fruit of a rose; the blues (also hyp.); interj., (of acclamation) hip, hip, hurrah!; v.t., to depress.

hipbone, n., the bone of the hip.

hipe, n., a method of throwing in wrestling.

hipped, adj., depressed; put out; p.p., hip.

hipp'ic, adj., pert. or rel. to horses.

hip'ping, pr.p., hip.

hipp'o, n., the abbrev. of hippopotamus (colloq.).

hippocam'pus, n., a sea-horse.

hippocen'taur, n., a fabulous monster, half horse and half man (often as centaur).

hip'pocras, n., spiced wine.

Hippo′crates, *n.,* a Greek physician of the fifth century B.C.

Hippocrat′ic, *adj.,* pert. or rel. to Hippocrates and applied to the professional oath of the medical profession.

Hippoc′ratism, *n.,* the study of the philosophy of Hippocrates.

Hipp′ocrene, *n.,* a sacred fountain on Mount Helicon.

hippocre′pian, *adj.,* shaped like a horseshoe.

hip′podrome, *n.,* a circus; a horse show; a theatre.

hip′pogriff, *n.,* a fabulous beast, part griffin, part horse.

hippoph′agy, *n.,* the eating of horseflesh.

hippopot′amus, *n.,* the river-horse, an African pachyderm.

hippu′ric, *adj.,* pert. or rel. to an acid in a horse's urine.

Hippur′is, *n.,* a genus of aquatic herbs.

hip′py, *n.,* a drug addict (*colloq.*).

hip′-roof, *n.,* a roof that rises direct from the wall-plate.

hip′shot, *adj.,* lame.

hip′ster, *n.,* a jazz enthusiast.

hip′wort, *n.,* a common British weed.

hir′able, *adj.,* that can be hired.

hir′cine, *adj.,* pert. or rel. to goats; goatlike; *n.,* a fetid, oily product of goat's fat.

hir′cus, *n.,* a goat (*Lat.*).

hire, *n.,* pay, bribe; *v.t.,* to engage for temporary service for pay; to bribe.

hired, *p.p.,* hire.

hire′ling, *n.,* a mercenary; a paid servant.

hire′-pur′chase, *n.,* a system of paying for goods by instalments, the goods becoming the property of the hirer when the last payment is made.

hir′er, *n.,* one who hires.

hir′ing, *pr.p.,* hire.

hirondelle′, *n.,* a swallow (*Fr., her.*).

hir′rient, *adj.,* trilling.

hir′sute, *adj.,* shaggy, hairy.

hir′suteness, *n.,* shagginess, hairiness.

hi′rudine, *adj.,* pert. or rel. to leeches; like a leech.

hirun′dine, *adj.,* pert. or rel. to, or like, a swallow.

his, *possess. adj.,* of he.

Hispan′ia, *n.,* a name for Spain (*Lat.*).

Hispan′ic, *adj.,* pert. or rel. to Spain or its people.

Hispan′icism, *n.,* a Spanish custom, saying, etc.

his′pid, *adj.,* bristly.

hiss, *n.,* a sibilant sound; *v.i.,* to make the sound of a goose or snake; *v.t.,* to show disapproval of.

hissed, *p.p.,* hiss.

hiss′er, *n.,* one who, or that which, hisses.

hiss′ing, *pr.p.,* hiss.

hist, *interj.,* hark! silence!

hist′amine, *n.,* a base used in medicine; a body substance which plays a part in inflammation and allergy.

hist′ogram, *n.,* a statistical graph consisting of rectangles proportional to the statistics represented.

histog′raphy, *n.,* a description of tissues.

histolog′ical, *adj.,* pert. or rel. to histology.

histol′ogist, *n.,* an expert in histology.

histol′ogy, *n.,* the science of minute structure of organisms.

histor′ian, *adj.,* a writer or student of history.

histor′iated, *adj.,* decorated with figures of men and beasts representing history, etc.

histor′ic, *adj.,* pert. or rel. to, or famous in, history.

histor′ical, *adj., i.q.* historic.

histor′ically, *adv.,* in an historical way

historic′ity, *n.,* truth to history; historical basis.

historiog′rapher, *n.,* an official writer of history.

historiog′raphy, *n.,* the writing of history.

historiol′ogy, *n.,* historical science.

hist′ory, *n.,* the narration of past events; the record of the past.

his′trion, *n.,* a stage-player.

histrion′ic, *adj.,* theatrical; pert. or rel. to actors; showy, gesticulatory.

histrion′ically, *adv.,* theatrically.

hist′rionism, *n.,* acting; affected acting.

hit, *n.,* a blow; a lucky stroke; a success; *v.t.,* to strike, to reach, to suit.

hitch, *n.,* a catch, an impediment; *v.t.,* to hook, catch or fasten.

hitched, *p.p.,* hitch.

hitch′hike, *n.,* the moving from place to place by begging lifts from passing vehicles; *v.i.,* to travel in this way.

hitch′ing, *pr.p.,* hitch.

hithe, *n., i.q.* hythe.

hith′er, *adj.,* on this nearest side; *adv.,* to this place.

hith′ermost, *adj.,* the nearest in this direction.

hitherto′, *adv.,* up to this point (of time or place).

hith′erward, *adv.,* in this direction.

Hit′lerism, *n.,* the policy, aims or methods of the German Nazi dictator, Adolf Hitler (1889–1945).

Hit′lerite, *adj.,* pert. or rel. to Adolf Hitler; *n.,* a follower or supporter of Hitler.

hit′ter, *n.,* one who hits.

hit′ting, *pr.p.,* hit.

Hitt′ite, *adj.,* pert. or rel. to the Hittites, an ancient people of Turkey and Syria; *n.,* a member of this race or its language.

hive, *n.,* a bee-house; a swarm; a busy company; *v.i.,* to assemble in a hive; *v.t.,* to place in a hive.

hived, *p.p.,* hive.

hives, *n. pl.,* nettlerash.

hiv′ing, *pr.p.,* hive.

ho, *interj.,* stop there!

hoar, *adj.*, gray-white; ancient.

hoard, *n.*, a secret store or pile; *v.t.*, to store secretly; to amass.

hoard'ed, *p.p.*, hoard.

hoard'er, *n.*, one who hoards.

hoard'ing, *n.*, a fence of boards for the display of notices; *pr.p.*, hoard.

hoar'frost, *n.*, white frost.

hoar'hound, *n.*, *i.q.* horehound.

hoar'iness, *n.*, the state or quality of being hoary.

hoarse, *adj.*, harsh-sounding; rough-voiced.

hoarse'ly, *adv.*, in a hoarse way.

hoars'en, *v.t.* and *i.*, to make hoarse.

hoarse'ness, *n.*, harshness of voice.

hoar'stone, *n.*, a landmark or boundary stone.

hoar'y, *adj.*, white with age or frost.

hoast, *n.*, a cough, hoarseness.

hoax, *n.*, a practical joke; *v.t.*, to play a trick upon.

hoaxed, *p.p.*, hoax.

hoax'er, *n.*, one who plays a hoax.

hoax'ing, *pr.p.*, hoax.

hob, *n.*, part of a grate for placing things upon; a sprite.

Hobbe'sian, *adj.*, pert. or rel. to Thomas Hobbes, an English philosopher, or his doctrines.

Hob'bism, *n.*, the teaching and philosophy of Hobbes.

Hob'bist, *n.*, a follower of Hobbes.

hob'ble, *n.*, a limp; a loop to restrict the movements of a horse; *v.i.*, to limp; *v.t.*, to shackle.

hob'bled, *p.p.*, hobble.

hob'bledehoy, *n.*, a youth between a man and a boy; a raw youth.

hob'bler, *n.*, one who hobbles.

hob'ble-skirt, *n.*, a close-fitting, old-fashioned skirt which made walking difficult.

hob'bling, *pr.p.*, hobble.

hob'by, *n.*, a favourite recreational pursuit; a breed of falcon.

hob'byhorse, *n.*, a child's toy (a stick with a horse's head); a favourite topic of conversation.

hobgob'lin, *n.*, a mischievous imp.

hob'nail, *n.*, a thick, roundheaded nail; a rustic.

hob'nailed, *adj.*, studded with hobnails.

hob'nob, *v.i.*, to associate with familiarly.

hob'o, *n.*, a tramp or vagrant (*U.S.A.*).

Hob'son's choice, *n.*, only one offer (no choice, in fact).

hock, *n.*, the joint at the lower extremity of the tibia; a Rhine wine.

hock'ey, *n.*, a team ball game played with curved sticks.

hock'eystick, *n.*, a hooked stick for playing hockey.

Hock'-tide, *n.*, an old festival formerly kept on the second Monday and Tuesday after Easter.

ho'cus, *v.t.*, to take in; to trick.

ho'cuspo'cus, *n.*, a cheat; deceptive behaviour.

hod, *n.*, a bricklayer's trough for bricks or mortar.

hod'den-grey, *n.*, a coarse cloth made of natural wool (*Scot.*).

hodge, *n.*, a rustic.

hodge'-podge', *n.*, a mixed mass; a medley.

hodiern'al, *adj.*, of to-day; modern.

hod'man, *n.*, the carrier of a hod.

hod'mandod, *n.*, a snail.

hodom'eter, *n.*, *i.q.* odometer.

hodomet'rical, *adj.*, pert. or rel. to hodometry.

hodom'etry, *n.*, the measurement of distance travelled.

hoe, *n.*, a garden tool for weeding; *v.t.*, to clean with a hoe.

hoed, *p.p.*, hoe.

hoe'ing, *pr.p.*, hoe.

ho'er, *adj.*, one who, or that which, hoes.

hog, *n.*, a swine; a young sheep newly shorn; a swinish person; *v.i.*, to dip at both ends; *v.t.*, to clip the hair short.

Hogar'thian, *adj.*, in the manner of William Hogarth, the English satirical painter.

hog'back, *n.*, a very steep hill-ridge, with a rising crest.

hog'-deer, *n.*, the spotted deer of southern Asia.

hogged, *p.p.*, hog.

hog'gery, *n.*, a piggery.

hogg'et, *n.*, a yearling sheep.

hogg'in, *n.*, sifted gravel.

hog'ging, *pr.p.*, hog.

hog'gish, *adj.*, swinish.

hogg'ishly, *adv.*, in a hoggish way.

hogg'ishness, *n.*, the state of being hoggish.

hog'like, *adj.*, like a hog.

Hogmanay', *n.*, New Year's Eve (*Scot.*).

hogs'head, *n.*, a measure of capacity; a large cask holding 52½ gallons.

hoicks, *interj.*, used to incite hounds.

hoi'den, *adj.*, illmannered; *n.*, a rude, rough girl; *v.i.*, to romp. (Also *hoyden*.)

hoi(c)k, *v.t.* and *i.*, to force an aircraft to turn upwards abruptly.

hoi'poll'oi, *n. pl.*, the ordinary people (*Gr.*).

hoist, *n.*, a hoisting apparatus; a lift; *v.t.*, to lift up, to heave.

hoist'ed, *p.p.*, hoist.

hoist'ing, *pr.p.*, hoist.

hoi'ty-toi'ty, *n.*, *interj.*, expressing surprise, reproof, etc.

ho'key-po'key, *n.*, a cheap ice-cream of coloured layers; a kind of dance.

hok'um, *n.*, film scenario designed to appeal to the uncritical; bunkum.

hold, *n.*, a support, a clutch; the lowest part of a ship; a fortress; *v.t.*, to grasp, keep, consider, esteem or celebrate.

hold'all, *n.*, a traveller's bag.

hold'en, *p.p.*, hold.

hold'er, *n.*, anyone or anything that holds; a handle.

hold'fast, *adj.*, tenacious; *n.*, a catch, a hook.

hold'ing, *n.*, anything held; a tenure; influence; *pr.p.*, hold.

hold'up, *n.*, a delay; armed robbery; an assault; a stoppage.

hole, *n.*, a cavity, a perforation; a mean dwelling (*slang*); *v.i.*, to go into a hole; to drive a ball into a hole in golf; *v.t.*, to make a hole.

holed, *p.p.*, hole.

hol'ey, *adj.*, full of holes.

hol'iday, *n.*, a holy day; a time of rest from labour; a festival.

ho'lier, *adj.*, *comp.* of holy.

ho'liest, *adj.*, *super.* of holy.

ho'lily, *adv.*, in a holy way.

ho'liness, *n.*, the quality or state of being holy; sanctity.

hol'ing, *pr.p.*, hole.

hol'la, *n.*, a shout; *v.i.*, to shout to someone far off.

hol'laed, *p.p.*, holla.

hol'laing, *pr.p.*, holla.

hol'land, *n.*, a variety of unbleached, coarse linen.

Hol'lander, *n.*, a native of Holland.

hol'lands, *n.*, Dutch gin.

hol'loa, *n.* and *v.i.*, *i.q.* holla.

hol'low, *adj.*, empty inside; sunken; vain; *n.*, a cavity; *v.t.*, to scoop, to excavate.

Holl'oway, *n.*, an English prison for women.

hol'lowed, *p.p.*, hollow.

hol'lowing, *pr.p.*, hollow.

hol'lowness, *n.*, the state or quality of being hollow.

hol'ly, *n.*, an evergreen tree or shrub.

holl'yhock, *n.*, the rosemallow.

Holl'ywood, *n.*, the American film-making centre in California.

holm(e), *n.*, an evergreen oak; a river island.

hol'ocaust, *n.*, a burnt sacrifice; a completely destructive fire.

hol'ograph, *n.*, a document entirely in the author's handwriting.

holom'eter, *n.*, an instrument of various applications for measurements.

holothur'ian, *adj.* and *n.*, (animal) of the Holothuria genus; a seaslug.

hol'ster, *n.*, a pistol case attached to a saddle.

hol'stered, *adj.*, furnished with holsters.

holt, *n.*, a wood, a copse; an animal's lair.

hol'us-bol'us, *adv.*, altogether in a lump.

ho'ly, *adj.*, sacred, pure, devout.

ho'ly-day, *n.*, *i.q.* holiday.

ho'ly-rood, *n.*, the Sacred Cross.

ho'lystone, *n.*, a stone used for scrubbing a deck; *v.t.*, to scrub with holystone.

Ho'ly-Week, *n.*, the week before Easter.

Ho'ly-Writ, *n.*, the sacred writings, esp. the Bible.

hom', *n.*, the sacred palm tree of the ancient Persians; a sacrificial drink made from its juice.

hom'age, *n.*, reverence, fealty, respect.

hombre, *n.*, a man (*Span.*).

Hom'burg, *n.*, a soft, felt hat.

home, *adj.*, domestic; *n.*, one's own dwelling-place; one's country.

home'bred, *adj.*, bred at home.

home'brewed, *adj.*, brewed at home.

home'coming, *n.*, the arrival home.

Home'-Guard, *n.*, the British citizen army formed in 1940; a home-defence volunteer.

home'land, *n.*, one's native land.

home'less, *adj.*, without a home.

home'lessness, *n.*, the state of being homeless.

home'lier, *adj.*, *comp.* of homely.

home'liest, *adj.*, *super.* of homely.

home'like, *adj.*, like a home.

home'liness, *n.*, the quality of being homely.

home'ly, *adj.*, domestic, plain of feature, uncultivated, simple.

home'-made, *adj.*, made at home.

hom'er, *n.*, a homing pigeon.

Homer'ic, *adj.*, pert. or rel. to Homer, the great epic poet of early Greece.

home'sick, *adj.*, pining for home.

home'sickness, *n.*, depression caused by separation from home; a longing for home.

home'spun, *adj.*, plain, coarse; *n.*, homespun material.

home'stead, *n.*, a house and land.

home'ward, *adj.* and *adv.*, in the direction of home.

home'wards, *adv.*, *i.q.* homeward.

home'work, *n.*, work, esp. lessons, to be done at home.

homici'dal, *adj.*, pert. or rel. to homicide.

hom'icide, *n.*, the killing of a man; a man-killer.

homilet'ic, *adj.*, of the nature of a homily.

homilet'ics, *n. pl.*, literature relating to preaching.

hom'ilist, *n.*, a preacher.

hom'ily, *n.*, a sermon; a discourse of moral instruction.

ho'ming, *adj.*, returning home.

hom'iny, *n.*, maize hulled and broken.

hom'mock, *n.*, *i.q.* hummock.

homocen'tric, *adj.*, concentric.

homochro'mous, *adj.*, of the same colour.

hom'oeopath, *n.*, *i.q.* homoeopathist.

homoeopath'ic, *adj.*, pert. or rel. to homoeopathy.

homoeop'athist, *n.*, one who favours or practises homoeopathy.

homoeop'athy, *n.*, a medical system based on the doctrine that like cures like; simple, natural medical treatment (often by distillations of herbs).

homog'amous, *adj.*, having only one kind of flower.

homog'amy, *n.*, the simultaneous ripening of the stamens and pistils in a flower.

homogene'ity, *n.*, identity of nature.

homoge'neous, *adj.*, of the same kind or nature.

homo'genize, *v.t.*, to make milk more digestible by breaking up the droplets of fat into smaller particles.

hom'ograph, *n.*, a word which is spelt like another, but which has a different meaning.

homol'ogate, *v.t.*, to confirm, to allow.

homolog'ical, *adj.*, pert. or rel. to homology.

homol'ogize, *v.i.* and *t.*, to be homologous; to correspond.

homol'ogous, *adj.*, identical in relative proportion, value or structure.

hom'ologue, *n.*, an organ or part common to various animals but differing in function.

homol'ogy, *n.*, structural similarity.

hom'onym, *n.*, a word of similar sound to another but of different meaning.

homonym'ic, *adj.*, of the nature of a homonym.

homon'ymous, *adj.*, sounding alike.

homon'ymy, *n.*, the state of sounding alike.

hom'ophone, *n.*, a letter, or group of letters, standing for the same sound as another.

homoph'onous, *adj.*, having the same sound.

homoph'ony, *n.*, the state of being homophonous.

homosex'ual, *adj.*, sexually attracted by one's own sex; *n.*, one who has a sexual propensity to one's own sex.

homosex'ualist, *n.*, *i.q.* homosexual.

homosexual'ity, *n.*, the quality or state of being homosexual.

homot'ropal, *adj.*, turned in the same direction.

hom'otype, *n.*, a corresponding part.

homunc'ule, *n.*, an undersized man; a dwarf.

hom'y, *adj.*, home-like; comfortable (*colloq.*).

hone, *n.*, a whetstone; *v.t.*, to sharpen.

honed, *p.p.*, hone.

hon'est, *adj.*, upright, trustworthy, frank, truthful.

hon'estly, *adv.*, in an honest way.

hon'esty, *n.*, the quality of being honest; a plant with purple flowers.

hon'ey, *n.*, the flower-product collected and produced by bees; an endearing term; *v.t.*, to sweeten, to make agreeable.

hon'eybear, *n.*, a small, carnivorous honey-eating animal of S. America.

hon'ey-bee, *n.*, a honey-making bee.

hon'eycomb, *n.*, the system of cells in a hive; *v.t.*, to riddle with holes.

hon'eydew, *n.*, a saccharine secretion; a variety of tobacco.

hon'eyed, *adj.*, sweet, cajoling; *p.p.*, honey.

hon'eying, *pr.p.*, honey.

hon'eymoon, *n.*, the first month of married life; a holiday spent together by a newly married couple.

hon'eysuckle, *n.*, a climbing fragrant plant.

hong, *n.*, a trading-place (*Chinese*); a foreign factory.

hon'ied, *adj.*, *i.q.* honeyed.

hon'ing, *pr.p.*, hone.

hon'iton, *n.*, a kind of lace originally made in England at Honiton in Devon.

honk, *n.*, the cry of the wild goose; the sound of a motor horn; *v.i.*, to emit this sound.

honora'rium, *n.*, a fee; a complimentary gift.

hon'orary, *adj.*, done or held as a mark of honour.

honorif'ic, *adj.*, conferring honour and respect.

honor'is caus'a, *adv.*, a phrase meaning "as a mark of esteem" (*Lat.*).

hon'our, *n.*, respect, reverence, integrity, glory; *v.t.*, to respect, to revere, to accept and pay.

hon'ourable, *adj.*, worthy to be honoured; conferring honour; upright; with a sense of honour.

hon'ourably, *adv.*, in an honourable way.

hon'oured, *p.p.*, honour.

hon'ourer, *n.*, one who honours or confers honour.

hon'ouring, *pr.p.*, honour.

hon'ours, *n. pl.*, in universities, advanced or specialized work; civilities.

hon'oursman, *n.*, one who attains academic honours.

hooch, *n.*, alcoholic liquor (*slang*).

hood, *n.*, a covering for the head; a carriage cover; part of the academic costume; a suffix denoting state or quality.

hood'ed, *adj.*, having a hood.

hood'lum, *n.*, a bully; a gangster (*Amer.*).

hoo'doo, *n.*, bad luck, *v.t.*, to bewitch.

hood'wink, *v.t.*, to impose on; to deceive.

hoo'ey, *n.*, nonsense (*slang*).

hoof, *n.*, the hard part of a quadruped's foot.

hoofed, *adj.*, having a hoof.

hook, *n.*, anything bent so as to hold on; that which is to be bent; to catch on; *v.t.*, to catch with a hook.

hook'ah, *n.*, a tobacco pipe, in which the smoke passes through water.

hooked, *adj.*, bent like a hook; attracted to (*slang*); *p.p.*, hook.

hook'er, *n.*, anything that hooks; a fishing craft.

hook'ing, *pr.p.*, hook.

hook'worm, *n.*, a parasite infesting men and animals.

hook'y, *adj.*, full of hooks; hooked; *n.*, truant (*slang*).

hoo'ligan, *adj.*, rowdy; *n.*, a street rowdy.

hoop, *n.*, a band round a cask; a circular band; a child's toy; *v.t.*, to bind round with hoops.

hooped, *p.p.*, hoop.

hoop'er, *n.*, a cooper.

hoop'ing, *pr.p.*, hoop.

hoop'ing-cough, *n.*, *i.q.* whooping-cough.

hoop'-la, *n.*, a game played with rings at fairs, etc.

hoo'poe, *n.*, a large-crested bird with variegated plumage.

hoosh, *n.*, a stew prepared on Arctic journeys (*slang*).

Hoo'sier, *n.*, the nickname for a native of the State of Indiana (*U.S.A.*).

hoot, *n.*, a derisive shout; *v.i.*, to make a hooting noise; *v.t.*, to drive with shouts.

hoot'ed, *p.p.*, hoot.

hoot'er, *n.*, a warning horn; a factory siren.

hoot'ing, *pr.p.*, hoot.

hoots, *interj.*, an expression of impatience or dissatisfaction (*Scot.*).

hoove, *n.*, a cattle disease, attended with inflation of the stomach.

Hoo'ver, *n.*, a make of electric cleaner.

hoo'ver, *v.t.*, to clean with a Hoover cleaner.

hoo'vered, *p.p.*, hoover.

hoo'vering, *pr.p.*, hoover.

hop, *n.*, a spring; a dance; a climbing perennial; *v.i.*, to jump on one foot (or simultaneously with both or all).

hop'-bine, *n.*, the climbing stem of the hop.

hope, *n.*, expectant desire; confidence; a belief in a successful or happy outcome; *v.i.*, to be expectant; *v.t.*, to desire with expectation.

hoped, *p.p.*, hope.

hope'ful, *adj.*, confident, full of hope.

hope'fully, *adv.*, in a hopeful way.

hope'fulness, *n.*, the state of being hopeful.

hope'less, *adj.*, without hope, past hope.

hope'lessly, *adv.*, in a hopeless way.

hope'lessness, *n.*, the state of being hopeless.

hop'ing, *pr.p.*, hope.

hop'lite, *n.*, a heavily-armed soldier of ancient Greece.

hopped, *p.p.*, hop.

hop'per, *n.*, a hop-picker; one who hops; a funnel through which grain is passed; a hopping insect, e.g. the flea; a vessel for conveying dredged mud to the sea.

hop'-picker, *n.*, a picker of hops; a hopper.

hop'ping, *pr.p.*, hop.

hop'ple, *n.*, a leg-shackle; *i.q.* hobble; *v.t.*, to fetter the legs.

hop'scotch, *n.*, a child's game of hopping and at the same time kicking a stone over lines scotched on the ground.

ho'ral, *adj.*, hourly.

ho'rary, *adj.*, of the hours; hourly; *n.*, a time-recorder.

Hora'tian, *adj.*, pert. or rel. to Horace, the Latin poet; *n.*, a student of Horace.

horde, *n.*, a troop, a gang; *v.i.*, to be in a horde.

hordea'ceous, *adj.*, pert. or rel. to barley.

hord'ed, *p.p.*, horde.

horde'in, *n.*, a starchy substance obtained from barley (*chem.*).

hord'ing, *pr.p.*, horde.

hore'hound, *n.*, an aromatic, bitter-tasting herb, used medicinally for colds and coughs. (Also hoarhound.)

hori'zon, *n.*, the boundary line of earth and sky; the farthest limit.

horizon'tal, *adj.*, of the horizon; parallel to the horizon.

horizon'tally, *adv.*, levelly.

hor'mone, *n.*, a gland secretion which may act as a stimulant.

horn, *n.*, the hard excrescence on an animal's head; a musical wind-instrument; a flask made of horn; *v.t.*, to supply with horns; to gore; to adjust a ship's frame at right angles to line of keel.

horn'beam, *n.*, a small British tree of the birch family.

horn'bill, *n.*, a large tropical bird, with a horn-like growth on the beak.

horn'blende, *n.*, a mineral, composed of silica, magnesia, etc.

horn'book, *n.*, a child's book mounted on a wooden tablet under a thin plate of transparent horn (*hist.*).

horned, *adj.*, having horns; *p.p.*, horn.

horn'er, *n.*, a horn-blower.

horn'et, *n.*, a large wasp-like insect.

horn'ing, *pr.p.*, horn.

horn'less, *adj.*, lacking horns.

horn'pipe, *n.*, an old wind-instrument; a lively sailors' dance.

horn'rimmed, *adj.*, having rims made of horn (of spectacles).

horn'y, *adj.*, hard, like horn.

horog'raphy, *n.*, the art of making clock dials.

hor'ologe, *n.*, a time-piece.

horol'oger, *n.*, *i.q.* horologist.

horolog'ical, *adj.*, pert. or rel. to horology.

horologiog'raphy, *n.*, a description of time-pieces; the clock-maker's art described.

horol'ogist, *n.*, a maker or seller of time-pieces.

horol'ogy, *n.*, the science of time-measuring and clock-making.

horom'eter, *n.*, a time-measuring instrument.

horom'etry, *n.*, the art of time-measuring.

horop'ter, *n.*, in optics, a straight line through the junction of the optic axes parallel to one joining the centres of the two pupils.

hor'oscope, *n.*, the disposition of heavenly bodies at a given date; a prediction based on this information.

hor'oscopic, *adj.*, pert. or rel. to horoscope.

horoscop'ical, *adj.*, pert. or rel. to horoscopy.

horos'copy, *n.*, the art of casting a horoscope.

horren'dous, *adj.*, fearsome; inspiring fear.

hor'rent, *adj.*, bristling.

hor'rible, *adj.*, horrifying, shocking, hideous.

hor'ribleness, *n.*, the quality or state of being horrible.

hor'ribly, *adv.*, in a horrible way.

hor'rid, *adj.*, frightful; rough, bristling.

hor'ridly, *adv.*, in a horrid way.

hor'ridness, *n.*, the state of being horrid.

horrif'ic, *adj.*, causing horror.

horrifica'tion, *n.*, the state of being horrified.

hor'rified, *adj.*, shocked with fear or revulsion; *p.p.*, horrify.

hor'rify, *v.t.*, to move with horror, to scandalize.

hor'rifying, *pr.p.*, horrify.

horripila'tion, *n.*, a bristling of the hair, caused by fear, cold, etc.; goose-flesh.

horrison'ant, *adj.*, having a dreadful or horrible sound.

hor'ror, *n.*, a shuddering; extreme dislike; fear and revulsion.

hors, *adv.* and *prep.*, outside (*Fr.*).

hors concours, *adv. phr.*, in a class by itself (*Fr.*).

hors de combat, *adv.phr.*, disabled; out of action (*Fr.*).

hors-d'oeuvres, *n. pl.*, appetizing dishes served at the beginning of a meal (*sing.* hors-doeuvre) (*Fr.*).

horse, *n.*, a quadruped, solid-hoofed, and used for burden and draught or for riding; *v.t.*, to provide horses for; to mount on one's back; to punish.

horse'back, *adv.*, on a horse's back; *n.*, the back of a horse.

horse'-box, *n.*, a closed vehicle for transporting horses by rail or road or for slinging horses on board ship.

horse'-boy, *n.*, a stable-boy.

horse'breaker, *n.*, one who breaks horses in.

horse'-chestnut, *n.*, a large tree with clustering white or pink flowers.

horse'-cloth, *n.*, a cloth covering for a horse.

horse'-coper, *n.*, a horse dealer.

horse'flesh, *n.*, the collective term for the flesh of horses.

horse'fly, *n.*, a large winged insect which stings horses.

Horse' Guards, *n.*, the cavalry; household troops usually attendant on royalty; their headquarters.

horse'hair, *n.*, the hair of horses; a fabric made of the same.

horse'-laugh, *n.*, a loud, coarse laugh.

horse'-leech, *n.*, a large kind of leech; a greedy person.

horse'less, *adj.*, without a horse.

horse'-litter, *n.*, a horse-drawn palanquin.

horse'man, *n.*, a rider; a clever rider.

horse'manship, *n.*, the craft of riding a horse.

horse'play, *n.*, rough and tumble play.

horse'-power, *n.*, a standard unit of measure of work (550 foot-pounds per second).

horse'-race, *n.*, a race run by mounted horses.

horse'-racing, *n.*, the sport of racing mounted horses.

horse'-radish, *n.*, a garden herb whose pungent root is used as a condiment.

horse'-sense, *n.*, plain commonsense (*colloq.*).

horse'shoe, *n.*, the iron shoe of a horse; anything shaped like it.

horse'tail, *n.*, a Turkish ensign.

horse'-trainer, *n.*, one who trains horses for races.

horse'whip, *n.*, a whip for horses; *v.t.*, to flog with a horsewhip.

horse'whipped, *p.p.*, horsewhip.

horse'whipping, *pr.p.*, horsewhip.

horse'woman, *n.*, the fem. of horseman.

hors'ily, *adv.*, in a horsy way.

hors'iness, *n.*, the state of being horsy.

hors'ing, *n.*, a grinder's seat in a factory; punishment by mounting on someone's back.

hors'y, *adj.*, addicted to the turf; aping the dress and manners of a jockey.

hort'ative, *adj.*, conveying exhortation.

hort'atory, *adj.*, *i.q.* hortative.

horten'sial, *adj.*, pert. or rel. to a garden.

hort'icultor, *n.*, the cultivator of a garden.

horticul'tural, *adj.*, pert. or rel. to horticulture.

hort'iculture, *n.*, the cultivation of gardens.

horticul'turist, *n.*, one skilled in horticulture.

hor'tus sic'cus, *n.*, collected dried plants; a mass of uninteresting facts (*Lat.*).

Hor'us, *n.*, an Egyptian deity rep. by a falcon.

hosan'na, *n.*, (save, pray) a cry of adoration.

hose, *n.*, a flexible pipe for watering purposes; textile garments for the legs; *v.t.*, to sprinkle with a hose.

hosed, *p.p.*, hose.

Ho'sier, *n.*, *i.q.* Hoosier.

ho'sier, *n.*, one who sells hose and underwear.

ho'siery, *n.*, a hosier's wares.

hos'ing, *pr.p.*, hose.

hos'pice, *n.*, a traveller's shelter; a home for sick or destitute people.

hos'pitable, *adj.*, ready to entertain; hearty, sociable.

hos'pitably, *adv.*, in a hospitable way.

hos'pital, *n.*, a charitable institution of various types; a centre for skilled medical treatment.

hos'pital(l)er, *n.*, one of the Knights Hospitallers; the chaplain in some London hospitals.

hos'pitalism, *n.*, the hospital system.

hospital'ity, *n.*, entertaining; a readiness to welcome visitors.

hospitaliza'tion, *n.*, the state of being hospitalized.

hos'pitalize, *v.t.*, to accommodate in hospital.

hos'pitalized, *p.p.*, hospitalize.

hospitaliz'ing, *pr.p.*, hospitalize.

hos'podar, *n.*, a lord.

host, *n.*, a victim; the consecrated wafer in the Eucharist; a large number'; an army; one who entertains guests, an innkeeper; a plant or animal upon which another lives (*biol.*).

hos'tage, *n.*, a person taken as a security; a human pledge.

hos'tel, *n.*, an inn; a students' hall of residence.

hos'teller, *n.*, the guest-master in a monastery.

hos'telry, *n.*, an inn.

host'ess, *n.*, a lady who entertains guests; the mistress of an inn.

hos'tile, *adj.*, of an enemy; showing ill-will; antagonistic.

hos'tilely, *adv.*, in a hostile way.

hostil'ities, *n. pl.*, acts of warfare; warlike measures.

hostil'ity, *n.*, ill-will, antagonism; in pl., acts of war.

hos'tler, *n.*, *i.q.* ostler.

hot, *adj.*, heated; at a high temperature; fierce.

hot'bed, *n.*, a bed for forcing plants; a favourable condition or place for developing anything, usually bad.

hot'blooded, *adj.*, passionate.

hotch'pot, *n.*, the aggregation of property for division (*leg.*); a dish of several ingredients = hotch-potch; an ill-assorted mixture.

hotch'potch, *n.*, a cooked dish with many ingredients.

hot'-cock'les, *n. pl.*, an old game like blindman's buff.

hot'dog, *n.*, a hot sausage sandwich (*colloq.*).

hotel', *n.*, a place offering accommodation for travellers.

hotel'ier, *n.*, a hotelkeeper (*Fr.*).

hot'foot, *adv.*, with haste.

hot'head, *n.*, a fiery person.

hot'headed, *adj.*, fiery, impetuous.

hot'house, *n.*, a forcinghouse.

hot'ly, *adv.*, with heat.

hot'ness, *n.*, the state of being hot.

hot'pot, *n.*, beef or mutton stewed in a covered pot with vegetables.

hot'press, *n.*, a press for bringing hot metal plates on to the surface of paper or other fabric; *v.i.*, to press paper for smoothing purposes.

hot'pressed, *p.p.*, hotpress.

hot'pressing, *pr.p.*, hotpress.

hot'spur, *n.*, an impetuous person.

hot'tempered, *adj.*, having a violent or quick temper.

Hot'tentot, *n.*, a member of an indigenous people once occupying the Cape region of South Africa.

hot'ter, *adj.*, *comp.* of hot.

hot'test, *adj.*, *super.* of hot.

hough, *n.*, the posterior part of the knee-joint in man; the part of the hind-leg between the knee and the fetlock in an animal; *v.t.*, to hamstring.

houghed, *p.p.*, hough.

hough'ing, *pr.p.*, hough.

hound, *n.*, a dog for the chase; a worthless person; *v.t.*, to chase; to incite; to pursue with ill-will.

hound'ed, *p.p.*, hound.

hound'ing, *pr.p.*, hound.

hound'ish, *adj.*, like a hound.

hour, *n.*, the one-twenty-fourth part of a day; an appointed time.

hour'glass, *n.*, a sandglass marking the duration of an hour.

hour'-hand, *n.*, the pointer that shows the hours on a dial.

hou'ri, *n.*, a nymph of the Mohammedan Paradise.

hour'ly, *adj.*, occurring every hour; often.

house, *n.*, a building to dwell in; any place giving shelter from the elements; an assembly; a business firm; *v.i.*, to seek shelter; *v.t.*, to give shelter to; to place securely.

house'-agent, *n.*, one who lets, sells or collects the rents of houses.

house'boat, *n.*, a boat fitted up like a house.

house'breaker, *n.*, one who breaks into a house with ill intent; one whose occupation is the breaking up of old houses.

house'breaking, *n.*, the occupation of a housebreaker.

housed, *p.p.*, house.

house'dog, *n.*, a watchdog.

house'fly, *n.*, the common fly that frequents dwelling houses.

house'ful, *n.*, the full capacity of a house.

house'hold, *n.*, the inmates of a house; a domestic establishment.

house'holder, *n.*, the occupier of a house.

house'keeper, *n.*, one who manages the affairs of a household; one in charge of an office, business premises, hotel, etc.

house'keeping, *n.*, the general management of domestic affairs.

house'leek, *n.*, a herb with pink flowers, growing on walls and roofs.

house'less, *adj.*, without a house.

house'maid, *n.*, a servant in charge of the rooms of a house.

house'master, *n.*, a master in charge of boarders in a public school.

house'-physician, *n.*, a physician attached to a hospital and in residence there.

house'proud, *adj.*, concerned with the care and beautification of the home.

house'sparrow, *n.*, the common British sparrow.

house'-surgeon, *n.*, a resident hospital surgeon.

house'top, *n.*, the uppermost floor, or roof of a house.

house'tops, *adj.*, publicly.

house'-trained, *adj.*, trained to be clean in the house (domestic animals).

house'warming, *n.*, hospitality given when a family enters a new house.

house'wife, *n.*, a mistress of a family; *i.q.* hussif.

house'wifely, *adj.*, like a housewife.

house'wifery, *n.*, domestic economy.

house'work, *n.*, the work arising from living in a house.

hous'ing, *n.*, a covering for horses, usually ornamental; the problem of providing adequate living accommodation; *pr.p.*, house.

Hov'a, *n.*, a native of the ruling tribe in Madagascar a large island off the S.E. coast of Africa; the dialect of this tribe.

hove, *p.p.*, heave.

hov'el, *n.*, a shed; a wretched dwelling.

hov'eller, *n.*, an unlicensed pilot or boatman.

hov'er, *v.i.*, to hang in the air; to loiter about.

hov'ercraft, *n.*, a transport craft designed to travel over land or water on a cushion of air.

hov'ered, *p.p.*, hover.

hov'ering, *adj.*, suspended in the air on wings; *pr.p.*, hover.

hov'eringly, *adv.*, in a hovering way.

hov'erplane, *n.*, *i.q.* helicopter.

how, *adv.*, in what manner or way; to what extent.

how, *n.*, a low hill.

howbe'it, *conj.*, nevertheless, although.

how'dah, *n.*, a canopied seat on an elephant's back.

how'die, *n.*, a midwife (*Scot.*).

how'el, *n.*, a plane used to smooth the interior of barrels.

howev'er, *adv.*, in whatever way; to whatsoever extent; *conj.*, nevertheless.

how'itzer, *n.*, a short gun firing heavy projectiles at a high elevation and slow trajectory.

howk, *v.t.*, to excavate or dig out.

howl, *n.*, a loud inarticulate cry of pain, rage, etc.; *v.i.*, to make a sound of pain, rage, etc.

howled, *p.p.*, howl.

howl'er, *n.*, one who howls; a type of monkey; an egregious blunder (*colloq.*).

howl'et, *n.*, an owlet.

howl'ing, *pr.p.*, howl.

howsoev'er, *adv.*, in whatsoever way or degree.

hoy, *interj.*, hallo!; *n.*, a small coasting vessel.

Hoy'a, *n.*, a genus of tropical climbing shrubs; the wax plant, named after Thomas Hoy, an English gardener.

hoy'den, *n.*, *i.q.* hoiden.

hoy'denish, *adj.*, like a hoyden.

hub, *n.*, the central part of a wheel from which the spokes radiate; any central point.

hub'ble-bubble, *n.*, an Eastern tobacco pipe, in which the smoke passes through water, making bubbling noises.

hub'bub, *n.*, a stir, confusion or riot; a loud noise of many voices.

hubb'y, *n.*, the abbrev. of husband (*colloq.*).

hub'ris, *n.*, insolent pride or security (*Gr.*).

hubris'tic, *adj.*, overweeningly insolent.

huck'aback, *n.*, a coarse, rough linen used for towelling.

huck'le, *n.*, the hip or haunch.

huck'lebacked, *adj.*, round-shouldered.

huck'leberry, *n.*, a N. American shrub bearing berries.

huck'ster, *n.*, a pedlar; a venal person; *v.t.* and *i.*, to sell; to haggle.

huck'stered, *p.p.*, huckster.

huck'stering   *pr.p.*, ·huckster.

huck'stress, *n.*, the fem. of huckster.

hud'dle, *n.*, a confused heap or crowd; *v.i.*, to crowd promiscuously; a close gathering together of persons; *v.t.*, to crowd together disorderly.

hud'dled, *p.p.*, huddle.

hud'dler, *n.*, one who huddles.

hud'dling, *pr.p.*, huddle.

Hudibras'tic, *adj.*, in the style of Hudibras, a famous mock-heroic poem.

hue, *n.*, colour, shade or tint; a cry in pursuit.

hued, *adj.*, having a particular colour.

hue'less, *adj.*, without a colour.

huff, *n.*, a sudden taking of offence; the act of huffing; *v.i.*, to swell up; to be puffed up; *v.t.*, to bully; to remove a piece from a chess-board or draughts-board.

huffed, *p.p.*, huff.

huff'iness, *n.*, the quality or state of being huffy.

huff'ing, *pr.p.*, huff.

huff'ish, *adj.*, petulant.

huff'ishly, *adv.*, in a huffish way.

huff'ishness, *n.*, the state of being huffish.

huf'fy, *adj.*, touchy.

hug, *n.*, a tight embrace; *v.t.*, to clasp tightly with the arms; to cherish; to keep near to.

huge, *adj.*, big, bulky.

huge'ly, *adv.*, very greatly.

huge'ness, *n.*, immensity.

hugged, *p.p.*, hug.

hug'ger-mug'ger, *adj.*, secret, confused; *n.*, secrecy; confusion; *v.t.* and *i.*, to hide.

hugg'ery, *n.*, the practice of a barrister of courting an attorney, etc. for employment (*leg.*).

hug'ging, *pr.p.*, hug.

hug'-me-tight, *n.*, a close-fitting, knitted garment.

Hu'guenot, *n.*, a French Protestant.

hul'a, *n.*, a large, New Zealand bird, prized for its feathers; an Hawaiian woman's dance.

hul'a-hoop, *n.*, a light hoop used for hip-swinging.

hulk, *n.*, the body of a wrecked ship; anything big and clumsy; *v.t.*, to remove before blasting.

hulked, *p.p.*, hulk.

hul'king, *adj.*, bulky, clumsy; *pr.p.*, hulk.

hull, *n.*, the outer covering of fruit or nuts; a ship's frame; *v.t.*, to remove the hull from; to pierce a ship's hull.

hullabaloo', *n.*, an uproar or hurly-burly.

hulled, *p.p.*, hull.

hul'ling, *pr.p.*, hull.

hullo', *interj.*, an exclamation to attract attention or signify presence.

hum, *n.*, a low, inarticulate sound or murmur; *v.t.* and *i.*, to make the sound of bees; to sing inarticulately.

hu'man, *adj.*, pert. or rel. to man.

humane', *adj.*, kind, compassionate.

humane'ly, *adv.*, in a humane way.

humane'ness, *n.*, the state or quality of being humane.

hu'manism, *n.*, literary culture; a system in which human affairs are the chief interest and as opposed to formal religion.

hu'manist, *n.*, a student of polite learning or human affairs.

humanis'tic, *adj.*, pert. or rel. to classical studies.

humanita'rian, *adj.*, pert. or rel. to humanitarianism; *n.*, a philanthropist.

humanita'rianism, *n.*, the principles of humanitarians or philanthropists.

human'ities, *n.*, polite learning, esp. the Latin and Greek classics.

human'ity, *n.*, human nature; the human race; philanthropy; mankind collectively.

humaniza'tion, *n.*, the act of humanizing; the humanized state.

hu'manize, *v.t.*, to make human, to civilize.

hu'manized, *p.p.*, humanize.

hu'manizer, *n.*, one who humanizes.

hu'manizing, *pr.p.*, humanize.

hu'mankind, *n.*, mankind.

hu'manly, *adv.*, in a human way.

hu'manness, *n.*, the state or quality of being human.

hu'manoid, *adj.*, of human form.

hum'ble, *adj.*, lowly in mind or station; *v.t.*, to bring low, to abase.

hum'ble-bee, *n.*, the bumble-bee.

hum'bled, *p.p.*, humble.

hum'bleness, *n.*, the state of being humble; humility.

hum'ble-pie, *n.*, a pie made from the umbles of deer; humiliation (*fig.*).

hum'bler, *adj.*, *comp.* of humble.

hum'blest, *adj.*, *super.* of humble.

hum'bling, *pr.p.*, humble.

hum'bly, *adv.*, in a humble way.

hum'bug, *n.*, sham, fraud; *v.t.*, to trick, to impose upon.

hum'bugged, *p.p.*, humbug.

hum'bugging, *pr.p.*, humbug.

humding'er, *n.*, an excellent person or thing (*colloq.*).

hum'drum, *adj.*, monotonous, commonplace; *n.*, sameness, commonplaceness.

hum'drumness, *n.*, the state of being humdrum.

humec'tant, *n.*, a diluent, esp. of the blood (*med.*).

humecta'tion, *n.*, a making wet.

humec'tive, *adj.*, having the power to moisten.

hu'mefy, *v.t.*, to soften with water; to make moist.

hu'meral, *adj.*, pert. or rel. to the humerus or to the shoulder; *n.*, a kind of veil worn over the shoulders by a priest.

hu'merus, *n.*, the bone of the upper arm.

hum'hum, *n.*, a coarse Indian cotton cloth.

hu'mic, *adj.*, pert. or rel. to vegetable mould. (Also *humous*.)

hu'mid, *adj.*, damp, moist and warm.

humid'ify, *v.t.*, to moisten.

humid'ity, *n.*, dampness, moisture.

hu'midness, *n.*, *i.q.* humidity.

hu'midor, *n.*, a contrivance for keeping things moist.

humifica'tion, *n.*, the turning into mould.

hu'mify, *v.t.*, to turn into mould.

humil'iate, *v.t.*, to abase, to put to shame.

humil'iated, *p.p.*, humiliate.

humil'iating, *pr.p.*, humiliate.

humilia'tion, *n.*, the act or effect of humiliating.

humil'ity, *n.*, *i.q.* humbleness.

hummed, *p.p.*, hum.

humm'el, *adj.*, hornless (of cattle and stags) (*Scot.*).

hum'mer, *n.*, one who hums.

hum'ming, *pr.p.*, hum.

hum'ming-bird, *n.*, a bird whose vibrating wings make a humming sound.

hum'ming-top, *n.*, a top which hums when it spins.

hum'mock, *n.*, a hillock, a knoll.

hu'moral, *adj.*, pert. or rel. to the fluids of the body.

humoresque', *n.*, a musical caprice (*Fr.*).

hu'morist, *n.*, a humorous person.

humoris'tic, *adj.*, pert. or rel. to humour.

hu'morous, *adj.*, displaying humour; with a sense of humour.

hu'morously, *adv.*, in a humorous way.

hu'mour, *n.*, mental disposition; mood; drollery, comicality; a sense of what inspires laughter or merriment; droll imaginativeness, distinguished from wit by being kindlier, but less intellectual; *v.t.*, to indulge the caprices of; to manage.

hu'moured, *p.p.*, humour.

hu'mouring, *pr.p.*, humour.

hu'mourless, *adj.*, lacking humour.

hu'moursome, *adj.,* crotchety, capricious.

hu'moursomeness, *n.,* the state of being humoursome.

hu'mous, *adj., i.q.* humic.

hump, *n.,* a protuberance; a rounded boss of earth; ill-temper (*slang*); *v.t.,* to round or bend.

hump'back, *n.,* a crooked back; one with a bent back.

hump'backed, *adj.,* having a humped back.

humped, *p.p.,* hump.

humph, *interj.,* expressing doubt or dissatisfaction.

hump'ing, *pr.p.,* hump.

hump'ty-dump'ty, *adj.,* of stunted growth; *n.,* a dumpy person.

hum'py, *adj.,* a native hut in Australia.

hu'mulin, *n.,* a hop-extract.

hu'mus, *n.,* mould.

Hun, *n.,* a member of a wandering, ravaging race of Asiatic barbarians; anyone with like qualities.

hunch, *n.,* a hump; a thick piece; a hunk; an idea (*colloq.*); *v.t.,* to crook.

hunch'back, *n., i.q.* humpback.

hunched, *p.p.,* hunch.

hunch'ing, *pr.p.,* hunch.

hun'dred, *adj.,* a cardinal number = 10 × 10; *n.,* five score collectively; a county subdivision.

hun'dredfold, *n.,* a hundred times as many or much.

hun'dredth, *adj.,* the ordinal numeral of a hundred.

hun'dredweight, *n.,* 112 lb. avoirdupois.

hung, *p.p.,* hang.

Hunga'rian, *adj.,* pert. or rel. to Hungary, a country of Central Europe; *n.,* a native of H.

hun'ger, *n.,* the craving for food; eager desire; *v.i.,* to be hungry; to crave; to desire eagerly.

hun'gered, *p.p.,* hunger.

hun'gering, *pr.p.,* hunger.

hun'ger-strike, *n.,* a refusal to take food until demands have been granted; *v.i.,* to call a hunger-strike.

hun'grily, *adv.,* in a hungry way.

hun'griness, *n.,* the state of being hungry.

hun'gry, *adj.,* craving food; ardently desiring.

hunk, *n.,* a thick piece; a hunch.

hunk'ers, *n. pl.,* the hams.

hunks, *n.,* a miser.

hun'ky-dor'y, *adj.,* splendid, excellent (*slang*).

Hunn'ish, *adj.,* pert., rel. or like a Hun.

hunt, *n.,* a chase; a search; a company of huntsmen; a hunting district; *v.t.,* to chase, to pursue.

hunt'ed, *p.p.,* hunt.

hunt'er, *n.,* one who hunts; a huntsman; a horse for hunting; a pocket watch.

hunt'ing, *n.,* the practice of the chase; *pr.p.,* hunt.

hun'tress, *n.,* the fem. of hunter.

hunts'man, *n.,* one who hunts; one in charge of a pack.

hunts'manship, *n.,* the art of hunting.

hur'dle, *n.,* a movable framework of wood, strengthened with bars or withies; *v.t.,* to enclose or mark off with hurdles; to surmount an obstacle.

hur'dled, *p.p.,* hurdle.

hurd'ler, *n.,* one who makes hurdles or competes in a hurdle-race.

hurd'le-race, *n.,* a race by horses or athletes over hurdles.

hurd'ling, *pr.p.,* hurdle.

hur'dy-gur'dy, *n.,* a stringed musical instrument, actuated by means of a revolving wheel, or played with the fingers of one hand.

hurl, *v.t.,* to fling, to throw with force.

hurl'bat, *n.,* a cudgel.

hurl'bone, *n., i.q.* whirlbone.

hurled, *p.p.,* hurl.

hurl'er, *n.,* one who hurls.

hurl'ey, *n., i.q.* hurling.

hurl'ing, *n.,* Irish hockey; *pr.p.,* hurl.

Hurl'ingham, *n.,* the headquarters of the English polo club.

hurl'y-bur'ly, *n.,* tumult, uproar.

hurrah', *interj.,* expressing joy, triumph or approval; *v.t.* and *i.,* to encourage by shouting hurrah!

hur'ricane, *n.,* a tempest; a violent cyclone.

hur'ried, *p.p.,* hurry.

hur'riedly, *adv.,* in a hurried way.

hur'riedness, *n.,* the state of being in a hurry.

hur'rier, *n.,* one who hurries.

hur'ry, *n.,* excessive haste; eagerness; *v.i.,* to move hastily; *v.t.,* to urge on; to drive.

hur'rying, *pr.p.,* hurry.

hur'ry-skur'ry, *adj.,* disorderly, confused; *n.,* disordered movement; bustle.

hurst, *n.,* a small hill; a sandbank in the sea or in a river; a thicket.

hurt, *n.,* pain, harm, injury; *v.i.,* to experience pain or distress; *v.t.,* to cause pain to; to injure.

hurt'er, *n.,* one who hurts.

hurt'ful, *adj.,* injurious, harmful.

hurt'fully, *adv.,* in a hurtful way.

hurt'fulness, *n.,* the quality of being hurtful.

hur'tle, *v.i.,* to move with a clattering sound; to move swiftly through the air; *v.t.,* to hurl; to push with violence.

hur'tleberry, *n.,* the whortleberry.

hur'tled, *p.p.,* hurtle.

hurt'less, *adj.,* causing no harm.

hurt'lessly, *adv.,* in a harmless way.

hurt'lessness, *n.,* the state of being harmless.

hurt'ling, *pr.p.,* hurtle.

hus'band, *n.,* a man in relation to his wife; *v.t.,* to manage economically; to till.

hus'banded, *p.p.,* husband.

hus'banding, *pr.p.,* husband.

hus'bandman, *n.*, a far-mer.

hus'bandry, *n.*, farming; good management.

hush, *n.*, stillness, silence; *v.i.*, to become silent; *v.t.*, to silence.

hushed, *p.p.*, hush.

hush'-hush, *adj.*, secret (*slang*).

hush'ing, *pr.p.*, hush.

hush'-money, *n.*, a bribe for silence.

husk, *n.*, the outer covering of fruits or seeds; *v.t.*, to take the husks from.

husked, *p.p.*, husk.

husk'ier, *adj.*, *comp.* of husky.

husk'iest, *adj.*, *super.* of husky.

husk'ily, *adv.*, in a husky way.

husk'iness, *n.*, the quality or state of being husky.

husk'ing, *pr.p.*, husk.

hus'ky, *adj.*, hoarse; harsh-voiced; like husk; strong, robust; *n.*, an Eskimo dog.

hussar, *n.*, a light cavalry soldier.

huss'if, *n.*, a small sewing case. (Also *housewife*.)

Huss'ite, *adj.*, pert. or rel. to John Huss, a Bohemian religious reformer of the 15th century; *n.*, a follower of H.

hus'sy, *n.*, a mischievous woman trading on her feminine wiles and attractions.

hust'ings, *n.*, a court of council; a stand on which Parliamentary candidates stood to speak.

hus'tle, *v.i.*, to show alacrity; *v.t.*, to push violently; to jostle.

hus'tled, *p.p.*, hustle.

hus'tler, *n.*, one who hustles.

hus'tling, *pr.p.*, hustle.

hut, *n.*, a small house or cabin; *v.t.*, to lodge in huts.

hutch, *n.*, a chest, cupboard or pen; a trough; *v.t.*, to place in a hutch; to wash ore in a hutch.

hutched, *p.p.*, hutch.

hutch'ing, *pr.p.*, hutch.

hut'ment, *n.*, an encampment of huts.

hut'ted, *p.p.*, hut.

hut'ting, *pr.p.*, hut.

Huzoor', *n.*, an Indian title of respect.

huzza', *interj.*, *v.t.* and *i.*; *i.q.* hurrah.

huzzaed', *p.p.*, huzza.

huzza'ing, *pr.p.*, huzza.

hy'acinth, *n.*, a bulbous fragrant plant.

hyacinth'ine, *adj.*, handsome, lovely.

Hy'ades, *n. pl.*, five stars in Taurus, said to bring rain at certain times.

Hy'ads, *n.*, *i.q.* Hyades.

hyae'na, *n.*, a carnivorous, dog-like beast.

hy'aline, *adj.*, glassy, crystalline, clear.

hy'alite, *n.*, a transparent colourless opal.

hy'aloid, *adj.*, glassy; *n.*, a thin transparent membrane.

hy'brid, *adj.*, mongrel, of different species; *n.*, a mongrel; a word of mixed composition.

hy'bridism, *n.*, the state of being hybrid; cross-breeding.

hy'bridizable, *adj.*, able to be hybridized.

hybridiza'tion, *n.*, the act or effect of hybridizing.

hy'bridize, *v.t.*, to produce a hybrid.

hy'bridized, *p.p.*, hybridize.

hy'bridizing, *pr.p.*, hybridize.

hy'datid, *n.*, a bladder enclosing a tapeworm's larvae.

hy'datism, *n.*, the sound produced by fluid in a body cavity.

Hyde Park, *n.*, a famous London Park, often the scene of political, etc., demonstrations.

hy'dra, *n.*, a mythical, multi-headed water-serpent (*Gr. myth.*).

hydrac'id, *n.*, an acid containing hydrogen.

hydraem'ia, *n.*, the condition where the blood contains an excess of water (*med.*).

hy'dragogue, *n.*, a drug that promotes the secretion of water.

hy'dra-headed, *adj.*, having many heads.

Hydran'gea, *n.*, a genus of shrub producing a fine, clustering flower.

hy'drant, *n.*, a pipe for discharging water.

hydrar'gyrum, *n.*, quicksilver.

hy'drate, *n.*, a compound containing a definite proportion of water after crystallization (*chem.*); *v.t.*, to make into a hydrate.

hy'drated, *p.p.*, hydrate.

hy'drating, *pr.p.*, hydrate.

hydra'tion, *n.*, the act of impregnating with water.

hydraul'ic, *adj.*, pert. or rel. to moving fluids and the pressures they exert.

hydraul'ically, *adv.*, in a hydraulic way.

hydraulic'ity, *n.*, the quality of being hydraulic.

hydraul'ics, *n. pl.*, the science of fluids in motion.

hyd'ric, *adj.*, pert. or rel. to, or containing, hydrogen (*chem.*).

hy'dride, *n.*, the combination of hydrogen with another element.

hy'dro, *n.*, a hydropathic establishment (*colloq.*).

hydrobro'mic, *adj.*, containing bromine and hydrogen.

hydrocar'bon, *n.*, a compound of hydrogen and carbon.

hydrocar'bonate, *adj.*, containing carbon and hydrogen.

hy'drocele, *n.*, serous matter in the scrotum.

hydroceph'alous, *adj.*, suffering from water on the brain.

hydroceph'alus, *n.*, water in the head.

hydrochlo'rate, *n.*, a salt of hydrochloric acid.

hydrochlo'ric, *adj.*, containing hydrogen and chlorine.

hydrocy'anate, *n.*, a salt of hydrocyanic acid.

hydrocy'anic, *adj.*, pert. or rel., or composed of, cyanogen and hydrogen.

hydrodynam'ics, *n. pl.*, the science of motion in fluids.

hydro'elec'tric, *adj.*, producing electricity by friction of steam or water.

hydrofluor'ic, *adj.*, composed of fluorine and hydrogen.

hy'drofoil, *n.*, a device on speedboats and seaplanes for improving their performance against friction.

hydro-galvan'ic, *adj.*, pert. or rel. to galvanic currents produced by liquids.

hy'drogen, *n.*, a colourless, tasteless gas, lighter than air, which, combined with oxygen, makes water.

hydro'genate, *v.t.*, to charge with hydrogen.

hydro'genated, *p.p.*, hydrogenate.

hydro'genating, *pr.p.*, hydrogenate.

hydrogena'tion, *n.*, the state of being hydrogenated.

hydrog'enize, *v.t.*, to make to combine with hydrogen.

hydrog'enized, *p.p.*, hydrogenize.

hydrog'enizing, *pr.p.*, hydrogenize.

hydrog'enous, *adj.*, pert. or rel. to hydrogen.

hydrog'rapher, *n.*, an expert in hydrography.

hydrograph'ic, *adj.*, pert. or rel. to hydrography.

hydrograph'ical, *adj.*, *i.q.* hydrographic.

hydrog'raphy, *n.*, the art of measuring and describing lakes, seas, etc.

hy'droid, *n.*, a hydralike creature.

hydrolog'ical, *adj.*, pert. or rel. to hydrology.

hydrol'ogist, *n.*, an expert in hydrology.

hydrol'ogy, *n.*, the science of the phenomena and laws of water.

hydrol'ysis, *n.*, the decomposition of water where the two components are fixed in distinct compounds.

hy'dromel, *n.*, honey and water mixed.

hydrom'eter, *n.*, an instrument for measuring the specific gravity, etc., of fluids.

hydromet'ric, *adj.*, pert. or rel. to hydrometry.

hydrom'etry, *n.*, the measurement of the specific gravity, etc., of fluids.

hydropath'ic, *adj.*, pert. or rel. to hydropathy.

hydrop'athist, *n.*, one who practises hydropathy.

hydrop'athy, *n.*, the treatment of disease with water.

hy'drophane, *n.*, an opal which, when wet, loses its opacity.

hydroph'anous, *adj.*, translucent when wet.

hydropho'bia, *n.*, the fear of water; madness caused by the bite of a dog, wolf or fox.

hydropho'bic, *adj.*, pert. or rel. to hydrophobia.

hy'drophone, *n.*, an instrument for detecting sound in water.

hy'drophyte, *n.*, a waterplant.

hydrop'ic, *adj.*, dropsical.

hy'droplane, *n.*, a waterplane.

hydropon'ics, *n.*, the growing of plants in water containing chemicals.

hy'dropsy, *n.*, *i.q.* dropsy.

hydrop'tic, *adj.*, insatiably thirsty.

hy'drosalt, *n.*, a salt containing hydrogen.

hy'droscope, *n.*, an apparatus for detecting the presence of water in the air.

hy'drostat, *n.*, a contrivance for detecting and regulating the presence of water.

hydrostat'ic, *adj.*, pert. or rel. to hydrostatics.

hydrostat'ical, *adj.*, *i.q.* hydrostatic.

hydrostat'ically, *adv.*, in a hydrostatical way.

hydrostat'ics, *n. pl.*, the science rel. to fluids at rest.

hydrothe'rapy, *n.*, a treatment of disease by water.

hydrot'ic, *adj.*, promoting a discharge of water.

hy'drous, *adj.*, containing water.

hy'drovane, *n.*, a rudder working horizontally in depressing or raising a submarine.

hydrox'ide, *n.*, a compound containing hydroxyl.

hydrox'yl, *n.*, a compound radical occurring in alcohol, etc.

hy'dyne, *n.*, a rocket-launching fuel.

hy'emal, *adj.*, wintry. (Also *hiemal*.)

hye'na, *n.*, *i.q.* hyaena.

hy'etal, *adj.*, pert. or rel. to rain or rainfall.

hyetom'eter, *n.*, a rain gauge.

Hygei'a, *n.*, the goddess of health.

hygei'an, *adj.*, pert. or rel. to health.

hy'giene, *n.*, the science treating of the prevention of disease and the preservation of health.

hygien'ic, *adj.*, health-preserving.

hygien'ical, *adj.*, pert. or rel. to hygiene.

hygien'ically, *adv.*, in a hygienic way.

hygienist, *n.*, one who studies hygiene.

hygrol'ogy, *n.*, the science rel. to the presence of moisture in the air.

hygrom'eter, *n.*, an apparatus for measuring the extent of moisture in the air.

hygromet'ric, *adj.*, pert. or rel. to hygrometry.

hygrom'etry, *n.*, the measurement of the extent of water in the air.

hy'groscope, *n.*, an apparatus recording visually the moisture in the air.

Hyk'sos, *n.pl.*, the shepherd kings of Egypt (*circa* 2,000 B.C.).

hy'la, *n.*, the tree-toad.

hyl'ic, *adj.*, pert. or rel. to matter; material.

Hy'lobate, *n.*, a genus of apes.

hy'loist, *n.*, a materialist.

hy'lotheism, *n.*, pantheism.

hylozo'ic, *adj.*, pert. or rel. to hylozoism.

hylozo'ism, *n.*, materialism.

Hy'men, *n.*, the god of marriage.

hy'men, *n.*, a semi-lunar membrane before the vaginal entrance; the pellicle enclosing a flower inside the bud.

hymene'al, *adj.*, pert. or rel. to marriage.

hymene'ally, *adv.*, in a hymeneal way.

hymene'an, *adj.*, *i.q.* hymeneal.

Hymenop'tera, *n. pl.*, insects with fine membranous wings, as bees, etc.

hymenop'teral, *adj.,* pert. or rel. to the Hymenoptera.

hymn, *n.,* a song of praise or adoration; *v.t.,* to praise with song.

hym'nal, *n., i.q.* hymnbook.

hym'nary, *n., i.q.* hymnbook.

hymn'-book, *n.,* a collection of hymns.

hymned, *p.p.,* hymn.

hym'nic, *adj.,* lyrical.

hymn'ing, *pr.p.,* hymn.

hym'nist, *n.,* one who sings or studies hymns.

hym'nody, *n.,* hymns and hymn-writing.

hymnog'rapher, *n.,* one who writes hymns.

hymnolo'gic, *adj.,* pert. or rel. to hymnology.

hymnol'ogist, *n.,* an expert in hymnology.

hymnol'ogy, *n.,* the study of hymn literature.

hy'oid, *n.,* the cartilaginous arch beneath the tongue.

hyoscine, *n., i.q.* hyoscyamine.

hyoscy'amine, *n.,* a highly poisonous alkaloid obtained from certain plant seeds and used in medicine.

Hyoscy'amus, *n.,* one of the nightshade group of plants.

hyp, *n.,* hypochondria; depression. (Also *hip.*)

hypaeth'ral, *adj.,* roofless, open to the sky. (Also *hypethral.*)

hypall'age, *n.,* a figure of speech where there is an interchange of terms in a sentence or proposition, the natural relationship being reversed (*gram.*).

hyperaesthes'ia, *n.,* excessive sensitiveness of nerves and nerve centres (*med.*).

hyperbat'ic, *adj.,* transposed.

hyper'baton, *n.,* the transposition of words.

hyper'bola, *n.,* one of the conic sections, having identical infinite curves.

hyper'bole, *n.,* an exaggeration for the sake of effect.

hyperbol'ic, *adj.,* pert. or rel. to a hyperbola; exaggerated.

hyperbol'ical, *adj., i.q.* hyperbolic.

hyperbol'ically, *adv.,* with exaggeration.

hyper'bolism, *n.,* a tendency to exaggeration.

hyper'bolist, *n.,* one given to exaggeration.

hyper'bolize, *v.i.,* to use hyperbole.

hyper'boloid, *n.,* a special kind of hyperbola.

hyperbo'rean, *in the far north; arctically cold; n.,* one who lives in northern climes.

hypercar'buretted, *adj.,* having an excessive quantity of gaseous hydrocarbons.

hypercatalec'tic, *adj.,* having an extra final syllable.

hypercrit'ic, *n.,* a severely critical person.

hypercrit'ical, *adj.,* unduly critical.

hypercrit'ically, *adv.,* in a severely critical way.

hypercrit'icism, *n.,* undue criticism.

hypercrit'icize, *v.t.,* to criticize unreasonably.

Hype'rion, *n.,* one of the Titan deities of Greek legend.

hyper'meter, *n.,* a metrically redundant verse.

hypermet'ric, *adj., i.q.* hypermetrical.

hypermet'rical, *adj.,* pert. or rel. to a hypermeter.

hypermetrop'ia, *n.,* morbidly long sight.

hypermetrop'ic, *adj.,* pert. or rel. to hypermetropia.

hy'peron, *n.,* any particle with mass greater than that of a neutron.

hyperphys'ical, *adj.,* supernatural.

hyperphys'ically, *adv.,* supernaturally.

hyperphys'ics, *n.pl.,* the science of the supernatural.

hyperson'ic, *adj.,* ten to twenty times the speed of sound.

hyp'ersthene, *n.,* a greenish-black, lustrous mineral.

hyperten'sion, *n.,* abnormally high blood pressure.

hypertroph'ic, *adj.,* pert. or rel. to hypertrophy.

hypertroph'ied, *adj., i.q.* hypertrophic.

hyper'trophy, *n.,* excessive physical development.

hypeth'ral, *adj., i.q.* hypaethral.

hy'phen, *n.,* a stroke (-) joining syllables or words; *v.t.,* to join with a hyphen.

hy'phenate, *v.t.,* to hyphen.

hy'phenated, *adj.,* joined with a hyphen; *p.p.,* hyphenate.

hy'phenating, *pr.p.,* hyphenate.

hyphena'tion, *n.,* the state of being hyphenated.

hypno'anaesthes'ia, *n.,* hypnotic sleep.

hypnogen'esis, *n.,* the induction of the hypnotic condition.

hypnol'ogist, *n.,* an expert in hypnology.

hypnol'ogy, *n.,* the study of the phenomena of sleep.

Hyp'nos, *n.,* the Greek god of sleep.

hypnos'is, *n.,* artificial sleep.

hypnothe'rapy, *n.,* the treatment of illness by hypnotism.

hypnot'ic, *adj.,* pert. or rel. to hypnotism.

hyp'notism, *n.,* an impressionable sleepy state produced by suggestion.

hyp'notist, *n.,* one who practises hypnotism.

hypnotiza'tion, *n.,* the state or condition of being hypnotized.

hyp'notize, *v.t.,* to send into a trance-like sleep.

hyp'notized, *p.p.,* hypnotize.

hyp'notizer, *n., i.q.* hypnotist.

hyp'notizing, *pr.p.,* hypnotize.

hy'po-, a prefix = under; *n.,* a salt used for fixing in photography.

hyp'ocaust, *n.,* a heating arrangement beneath a building.

hypochon'dria, *n.,* a morbid state of low spirits.

hypochon'driac, *n.,* one suffering from hypochondria.

hypochondri'acal, *adj.,* morbidly low-spirited.

hypochondri'acally, *adv.,* in a hypochondriacal way.

hypochondri'asis, *n., i.q.* hypochondria.

hy′pocist, *n.*, a medicinal plant with astringent properties.

hypocoris′tic, *adj.*, like a pet-name (*gram.*).

hypoc′risy, *n.*, false profession; dissimulation.

hyp′ocrite, *n.*, a false pretender.

hypocrit′ical, *adj.*, dissimulating, false.

hypocrit′ically, *adv.*, in a hypocritical way.

hypoder′mic, *adj.*, injected beneath the skin; *n.*, the device used for this (*med.*).

hypoderm′ically, *adv.*, in a hypodermic way (*med.*).

hypoder′mis, *n.*, the tissue next under the epidermis.

hypogas′tric, *adj.*, pert. or rel. to the lowest part of the abdomen.

hyp′ogene, *adj.*, pert. or rel. to subterranean rock formation.

hypoge′um, *n.*, an underground chamber.

hypogloss′al, *adj.*, under the tongue.

hypoman′ia, *n.*, over-excitability.

hypophos′phate, *n.*, an acid salt.

hy′poscope, *n.*, a kind of periscope.

hypos′tasis, *n.*, an underlying principle; basic substance.

hypostat′ic, *adj.*, essential, fundamental.

hypostat′ical, *adj.*, *i.q.* hypostatic.

hypostat′ically, *adv.*, essentially, fundamentally.

hy′postyle, *n.*, a covered colonnade.

hypoten′sion, *n.*, low blood pressure.

hypot′enuse, *n.*, the side of a right-angled triangle subtending the right angle.

hypoth′ec, *n.*, a pledge.

hypoth′ecary, *adj.*, pert. or rel. to hypothec.

hypoth′ecate, *v.t.*, to pledge, to mortgage.

hypoth′ecated, *p.p.*, hypothecate.

hypoth′ecating, *pr.p.*, hypothecate.

hypotheca′tion, *n.*, the act of hypothecating.

hypother′mia, *n.*, subnormal body temperature.

hypoth′esis, *n.*, an assumption, a supposition.

hypoth′esize, *v.t.* and *i.*, to assume; to frame a hypothesis.

hypothet′ic, *adj.*, conjectural, founded on assumption.

hypothet′ical, *adj.*, *i.q.* hypothetic.

hypothet′ically, *adv.*, by hypothesis.

hypsom′eter, *n.*, an apparatus for determining heights by the variation in the boiling point of water.

Hyr′ax, *n.*, a genus of small quadrupeds, including the Syrian rock-rabbit.

hy′son, *n.*, a green (China) tea.

hys′sop, *n.*, an aromatic plant.

hysteran′thus, *adj.*, describing plants where the flowers come before the leaves.

hysterec′tomy, *n.*, the operation of removal of the womb.

hysteres′is, *n.*, a lag of magnetization behind the magnetizing force. (*phys.*).

hyste′ria, *n.*, a disorder of the nerves; unhealthy excitement (*med.*).

hyster′ic, *adj.*, pert. or rel. to hysteria.

hyster′ical, *adj.*, *i.q.* hysteric.

hyster′ically, *adv.*, in a hysterical way.

hyster′ics, *n. pl.*, *i.q.* hysteria.

hys′teron prot′eron, *n.*, a figure of speech where the last is put first (*gram.*); an inversion of the natural or logical order of things (*Gr.*).

hyste′rophyte, *n.*, a fungus growing on organic matter (*bot.*).

hysterot′omy, *n.*, the operation of cutting into the uterus.

hythe, *n.*, a small marine haven. (Also *hithe.*)

I

I, *pers. pron.*, myself.

i'amb, *n.*, *i.q.* iambus.

iam'bic, *adj.*, rel. to the iambus.

iam'bus, *n.*, a metrical foot, consisting of a short syllable followed by a long one.

Ibe'rian, *adj.*, rel. to Iberia; *n.*, a native of Spain.

i'bex, *n.*, a variety of wild goat.

ib'id, *abbrev.*, *i.q.* ibidem.

ibi'dem, *adv.*, in the same place (*Lat.*).

i'bis, *n.*, a large wading-bird.

Ib'senism, *n.*, the teaching of Henrik Ibsen.

Ica'rian, *adj.*, rel. to Icarus; rash, presumptuous.

ice, *v.t.*, to cover with ice; to refrigerate; to decorate a cake with icing sugar; *n.*, frozen water.

ice'-age, *n.*, the glacial period.

ice'berg, *n.*, a great mass of floating ice.

ice'boat, *n.*, a boat built specially strong to force its way through ice.

ice'bound, *adj.*, frozen in.

ice'-box, *n.*, a refrigerator.

ice'-break'er, *n.*, a ship or device used to break up ice concentrations.

ice'-cream, *n.*, a cold confection that has undergone freezing.

iced, *p.p.*, ice; *adj.*, coated with sugar.

ice'-floe, *n.*, a fragment of floating ice.

ice'-hockey, *n.*, a game played on ice.

ice'-house, *n.*, a building for storing ice.

Ice'lander, *n.*, a native of Iceland.

Icelan'dic, *adj.*, rel. to Iceland.

ichneu'mon, *n.*, an Egyptian quadruped.

ich'nograph, *n.*, a ground-plan.

ichnograph'ic, *adj.*, rel. to ichnography.

ichnograph'ical, *adj.*, *i.q.* ichnographic.

ichnog'raphy, *n.*, the art of drawing plans, etc.

ichnolog'ical, *adj.*, rel. to ichnology.

ichno'logy, *n.*, the study of fossil foot-tracks.

i'chor, *n.*, the blood (or its equivalent) of the gods; the discharge from an ulcer.

i'chorous, *adj.*, pert. to ichor.

ichthyog'raphy, *n.*, a work on fishes.

ich'thyoid, *adj.*, fish-like, *n.*, a vertebrate of fish type.

ichthyol'ogist, *n.*, one interested in ichthyology.

ichthyol'ogy, *n.*, the study of fishes.

ichthyoph'agy, *n.*, the practice of fish-eating.

ichthyosau'rus, *n.*, a fossil marine creature.

ichthyos'is, *n.*, a skin disease (*med.*).

i'cicle, *n.*, a hanging piece of ice.

i'ciness, *n.*, the state of being icy.

i'cing, *pr.p.*, ice; *n.*, a coating of sugar.

i'con, *n.*, a picture, an image.

icon'ic, *adj.*, like an image or statue.

icon'oclasm, *n.*, the breaking of images.

icon'oclast, *n.*, a breaker of images.

iconoclast'ic, *adj.*, destructive of images; generally destructive.

iconograph'ic, *adj.*, rel. to iconography.

iconog'raphy, *n.*, the science of describing statues, pictures, likenesses, etc.

iconol'ater, *n.*, a worshipper of images.

iconol'atry, *n.*, the worship of images.

iconol'ogy, *n.*, the study of pictorial representation.

iconom'eter, *n.*, an optical measuring instrument used in surveying; a type of viewfinder used in photography.

icosahe'dral, *adj.*, having twenty faces.

icosahe'dron, *n.*, a solid figure with twenty faces.

icosan'dria, *n. pl.*, plants with twenty or more unconnected stamens.

icosan'drous, *adj.*, rel. to icosandria.

icter'ic, *adj.*, suffering from jaundice.

icter'ical, *adj.*, *i.q.* icteric.

icteri'tious, *adj.*, jaundiced, yellow.

ic'tus, *n.*, a stroke, a blow; a musical beat.

i'cy, *adj.*, like ice; extremely cold.

ide'a, *n.*, a fancy, a thought intention.

ide'al, *adj.*, according to an idea; perfect; *n.*, a standard of perfection.

ide'alism, *n.*, the tendency to form ideals; the philosophical system which explains phenomena as modes of thought.

ide'alist, *n.*, one who forms ideals; an idealist philosopher.

idealis'tic, *adj.*, pert. to idealism.

ideal'ity, *n.*, the character of being ideal or unreal.

idealiza'tion, *n.*, the tendency to idealize.

ide'alize, *v.t.*, to refer things to an imaginary standard.

ide'alized, *p.p.*, idealize.

ide'alizing, *pr.p.*, idealize.

ide'ally, *adv.*, conceived as perfect.

idea'tion, *n.*, the shaping of ideas.

idée-fixe, *n.*, monomania; an obsession (*Fr.*).

i'dem, *pron.*, the same man (*Lat.*).

id'em, *pron.*, the same thing (*Lat.*).

iden'tical, *adj.*, exactly the same.

iden'tically, *n.*, in an identical way.

iden'tifiable, *adj.*, able to be identified.

identifica'tion, *n.*, the act or result of identifying.

iden'tified, *p.p.*, identify.

iden'tify, *v.t.*, to prove to be the same; to recognize.

iden'tifying, *pr.p.*, identify.

iden'tikit, *n.*, the system of making up pictorial facial resemblances from standard parts.

iden'tity, *n.*, the state of being identical.

i'deograph, *n.*, a picture or symbol.

ideograph'ic, *adj.*, rel. to ideography.

ideograph'ical, *adj.*, *i.q.* ideographic.

ideog'raphy, *n.*, the pictorial representation of things or ideas.

ideolog'ical, *adj.*, rel. to ideology.

ideol'ogist, *n.*, one interested in ideology.

ideol'ogy, *n.*, the science and study of ideas.

ides, *n. pl.*, one of the fixed dates in the Roman month. In March, May, July, October, the Ides fell on 15th; in the other months, on 13th.

idioc'rasy, *n.*, *i.q.* idiosyncrasy.

idiocrat'ic, *adj.*, *i.q.* idiosyncratic.

id'iocy, *n.*, the state of being an idiot.

id'iograph, *n.*, a private signature; a trade mark.

idiograph'ic, *adj.*, rel. to an idiograph.

id'iom, *n.*, a usage peculiar to a particular language.

idiomat'ic, *adj.*, containing idiom; peculiar to a given language.

idiomat'ically, *adv.*, in an idiomatic way.

idiopath'ic, *adj.*, rel. to idiopathy.

idiop'athy, *n.*, a primary disease.

id'ioplasm, *n.*, a portion of protoplasm which establishes the nature of an organism.

idiosyn'crasy, *n.*, a personal peculiarity of mind.

idiosyncrat'ic, *adj.*, peculiar to an individual.

id'iot, *n.*, a person of undeveloped intellect.

idiot'ic, *adj.*, idiot-like, imbecile.

idiot'ical, *adj.*, *i.q.* idiotic.

idiot'ically, *adv.*, in an idiotic way.

idiot'icon, *n.*, a glossary of provincialisms.

id'iotism, *n.*, barbarism; individual peculiarity of expression.

i'dle, *adj.*, doing nothing, lazy, vain, useless; *v.t.*, to spend in idleness; *v.i.*, to do nothing.

i'dled, *p.p.*, idle.

i'dleness, *n.*, the state of being idle.

i'dler, *n.*, one who idles; a sluggard.

i'dling, *pr.p.*, idle.

i'dly, *adv.*, lazily, vainly.

Id'o, *n.*, an artificial universal language like Esperanto.

i'dol, *n.*, an image; a false appearance.

idol'ater, *n.*, an idol-worshipper.

idol'atress, *n.*, fem. of idolater.

idol'atrize, *v.t.*, to idolize; *v.i.*, to play the idolater.

idol'atrous, *adj.*, rel. to idolatry; loving to a morbid excess.

idol'atrously, *adv.*, in an idolatrous way.

idol'atry, *n.*, image-worship; excessive fondness.

i'dolize, *v.t.*, to make an idol of; to love excessively.

i'dolized, *p.p.*, idolize.

i'dolizer, *n.*, one who idolizes.

i'dolizing, *pr.p.*, idolize.

idol'um, *n.*, a mental image or idea, a fallacy.

i'dyll, *n.*, a short, simple, descriptive poem; a descriptive pastoral poem.

idyl'lic, *adj.*, rel. to idylls; resembling pastoral poetry.

if, *conj.*, implying condition or supposition.

ig'loo, *n.*, a snow-built dome-shaped hut used by Eskimos.

ig'neous, *adj.*, fiery; caused by fire.

ignes'cent, *adj.*, scintillating.

ignif'erous, *adj.*, fire-producing.

ig'nis fat'uus, *n.*, a phosphorent gleam seen in marshy places: the will-o'-the-wisp (*Lat.*).

igni'table, *adj.*, able to be ignited.

ignite', *v.t.*, to kindle, to cause to flame; *v.i.*, to take fire.

igni'ted, *p.p.*, ignite.

igni'tible, *adj.*, *i.q.* ignitable.

igni'ting, *pr.p.*, ignite.

igni'tion, *n.*, the act of igniting.

igno'ble, *adj.*, not noble; base, mean.

igno'bly, *adv.*, basely, meanly.

ignomin'ious, *adj.*, bringing disgrace, shameful.

ignomin'iously, *adv.*, with ignominy.

ig'nominy, *n.*, shame, disgrace, infamy.

ignora'mus, *n.*, an ignorant person; a pretender to knowledge he does not possess.

ig'norance, *n.*, the state of being ignorant or uninformed.

ig'norant, *adj.*, without knowledge, uninformed, unaware.

ig'norantly, *adv.*, in an ignorant way.

ignore', *v.t.*, to regard as non-existent; to leave out of consideration.

ignored', *p.p.*, ignore.

ignor'ing, *pr.p.*, ignore.

igua'na, *n.*, a large lizard of tropical America.

igua'nodon, *n.*, a fossil reptile, resembling the iguana.

ilei'tis, *n.*, inflammation of part of the ileum.

il'eum, *n.*, the lower portion of the small intestine.

il'eus, *n.*, colic.

i'lex, *n.*, the holly; holm oak.

il'iac, *adj.*, rel. to the ilium.

Il'iad, *n.*, the Homeric Epic of the fall of Ilium or Troy.

il'ium, *n.*, the upper portion of the hip-bone.

ilk, *adj.* and *n.*, the same.

ill, *adj.*, evil, disordered, sick; *adv.*, badly, poorly; *n.*, a wrong, an injury, a misfortune, a pain.

illa'tion, *n.*, the act of drawing an inference; the inference when made.

illa'tive, *adj.*, inferential.

ill'-bred, *adj.*, badly brought up, rude.

ill-condi'tioned, *adj.*, badly disposed.

ill-disposed', *adj.*, disposed to evil; malevolent.

ille'gal, *adj.*, not legal, contrary to law.

illegal'ity, *n.*, the state or quality of being illegal.

ille'galize, *v.t.*, to make illegal.

ille'gally, *adv.*, in an illegal way.

illegibil'ity, *n.*, the quality of being illegible.

illeg'ible, *adj.*, not able to be deciphered.

illeg'ibly, *adv.*, in an undecipherable way.

illegit'imacy, *n.*, the state of being illegitimate.

illegi'timate, *adj.*, not in accordance with legal requirements; bastard; contrary to logic.

illegit'imate, *v.t.*, to pronounce illegitimate, to bastardize.

illev'iable, *adj.*, unable to be levied.

ill-fa'voured, *adj.*, evil-looking, repulsive.

ill-gott'en, *adj.*, gained by evil means.

ill-hu'mour, *n.*, bad temper.

ill-hu'moured, *adj.*, bad-tempered.

illib'eral, *adj.*, not liberal.

illiberal'ity, *n.*, the state of being illiberal.

illib'erally, *adv.*, in an illiberal way.

illic'it, *adj.*, unlawful.

illic'itly, *adv.*, unlawfully.

illic'itness, *n.*, the state of being illicit.

illimitabil'ity, *n.*, the quality of being illimitable.

illim'itable, *adj.*, not able to be limited; boundless.

illim'ited, *adj.*, not limited, boundless.

ill-in'formed, *adj.*, badly informed.

illini'tion, *n.*, the act of rubbing in.

illiq'uid, *adj.*, (of assets) not easily realizable.

illi'sion, *n.*, the act of striking against.

illit'eracy, *n.*, the state of being illiterate.

illit'erate, *adj.*, unlettered, uneducated.

illit'erateness, *n.*, *i.q.* illiteracy.

ill-judged', *adj.*, unwise.

ill-man'nered, *adj.*, having bad manners.

ill-na'ture, *n.*, bad temper, peevishness.

ill-na'tured, *adj.*, bad-tempered, peevish.

ill'ness, *n.*, the state of being ill.

illog'ical, *adj.*, not logical.

illog'icality, *n.*, the quality or state of being illogical.

illog'ically, *adv.*, in an illogical way.

ill-o'mened, *adj.*, of evil omen, inauspicious.

ill-starred', *adj.*, born under an unlucky star; unfortunate.

ill-timed', *adj.*, untimely, unseasonable.

ill-treat', *v.t.*, to treat evilly; to be cruel to.

ill-treat'ed, *p.p.*, ill-treat.

ill-treat'ing, *pr.p.*, ill-treat.

illude', *v.t.*, to deceive, to impose on.

illud'ed, *p.p.*, illude.

illud'ing, *pr.p.*, illude.

illu'minable, *adj.*, able to be illuminated.

illu'minant, *n.*, something that gives light.

illu'minate, *v.t.*, to throw light on, to enlighten; to embellish.

illu'minated, *p.p.*, illuminate.

illumina'ti, *n. pl.*, "The Enlightened" (*i.e.*, members of certain secret societies; any who claim to possess superior knowledge.

illu'minating, *pr.p.*, illuminate.

illumina'tion, *n.*, the act or effect of illuminating.

illu'minative, *adj.*, illuminating.

illu'minator, *n.*, one who embellishes.

illu'mine, *v.t.*, to throw light on, to light up.

illu'mined, *p.p.*, illumine.

illu'mining, *pr.p.*, illumine.

illu'minism, *n.*, the doctrines of the illuminati; illumination.

illu'minize, *v.t.*, to make one of the illuminati.

ill-use', *v.t.*, to treat badly.

ill'-used, *adj.*, badly treated.

ill'using, *pr.p.*, ill-use.

illu'sion, *n.*, the act of illuding; a deception of the senses; a false show.

illu'sional, *adj.*, prone to illusion.

illu'sionism, *n.*, jugglery.

illu'sionist, *n.*, a dreamer; one who practises illusions (*e.g.*, as a conjuror).

illu'sive, *adj.*, producing illusion.

illu'sively, *adv.*, in an illusive way.

illu'siveness, *n.*, the state or quality of being illusive.

illu'sory, *adj.*, producing illusion.

ill'ustrate, *v.t.*, to explain by examples; to embellish with pictures.

ill'ustrated, *p.p.*, illustrate.

ill'ustrating, *pr.p.*, illustrate.

illustra'tion, *n.*, the act of illustrating; a pictorial embellishment; an example.

illus'trative, *adj.*, tending to illustrate; explanatory.

illus'tratively, *adv.*, in an illustrative way.

ill'ustrator, **ill'ustrater**, *n.*, one who illustrates.

illus'trious, *adj.*, distinguished, glorious.

illus'triously, *adv.*, in an illustrious way.

illus'triousness, *n.*, the quality of being illustrious.

ill-will', *n.*, bad feeling, spite.

ill-wish'er, *n.*, one who wishes ill.

im'age, *v.t.*, to form an image of, to represent, to reflect; *n.*, a representation, a statue, a sculpture, a mental picture.

im'ageable, *adj.*, imaginable.

im'aged, *p.p.*, image.

im'agery, *n.*, images in general; figurative writing or speech.

imag'inable, *adj.*, able to be imagined.

imag'inably, *adv.*, in an imaginable way.

imag'inary, *adj.*, not real, fancied.

imagina'tion, *n.*, the act or power of imagining.

imag'inative, *adj.*, given to imagining.

imag'ine, v.t., to conceive mentally, to form an idea; to fancy.

imag'ined, p.p., imagine.

imag'iner, n., one who imagines.

im'aging, pr.p., image.

imag'ining, pr.p., imagine.

ima'go, n., a winged insect, fully developed.

ima(u)m', n., a Mohammedan minister.

imbal'ance, n., a lack of balance.

im'becile, adj., mentally defective; physically and mentally weak; n., an intellectually weak person.

imbecil'ic, adj., of a feeble nature.

imbecil'ity, n., the state or quality of being imbecile.

imbed', v.t., to lay in a mass of matter.

imbibe', v.t., to drink in; to take into the mind.

imbibed', p.p., imbibe.

imbi'ber, n., one who imbibes.

imbi'bing, pr.p., imbibe.

imbibi'tion, n., the act of imbibing.

imbo'som, see embosom.

im'bricate, v.t., to lay so as to overlap; adj., overlapping like tiles.

im'bricated, p.p., imbricate; adj., i.q. imbricate.

im'bricating, pr.p., imbricate.

imbrica'tion, n., a pattern that overlaps at the edges.

imbro'glio, n., a complicated misunderstanding; an elaborate plot.

imbrue', v.t., to wet, to moisten, to soak.

imbrued', p.p., imbrue.

imbru'ing, pr.p., imbrue.

imbrute', v.t., to brutalize.

imbru'ted, p.p., imbrute.

imbru'ting, pr.p., imbrute.

imbue', v.t., to impregnate, to tinge; to instruct.

imbued', p.p., imbue.

imbu'ing, pr.p., imbue.

imitabil'ity, n., the quality of being imitable.

im'itable, adj., capable of imitation.

im'itate, v.t., to copy, to emulate, to mimic.

im'itated, p.p., imitate.

im'itating, pr.p., imitate.

imita'tion, n., the act of imitating; a copy.

im'itative, adj., copying, mimicking; following a pattern.

im'itator, n., one who imitates.

immac'ulate, adj., spotless, absolutely pure.

immac'ulately, adv., in an immaculate fashion.

immac'ulateness, n., the state or quality of being immaculate.

im'manence, n., the state of being immanent.

im'manency, n., i.q. immanence.

im'manent, adj., remaining in; inherent, present.

immate'rial, adj., not material, incorporeal; of no importance.

immate'rialism, n., the doctrine of the immaterial.

immate'rialist, n., a believer in immaterialism.

immaterial'ity, n., the quality of being immaterial.

immate'rially, adv., in an immaterial way.

immature', adj., not mature, unripe, undeveloped.

immatured', adj., i.q. immature.

immature'ly, adj., in an immature way.

immatur'ity, n., the state of being immature.

immeas'urable, adj., incapable of being measured.

immeas'urably, adv., without measure.

im'mediacy, n., the state of being immediate; directness.

imme'diate, adj., instant, very close; direct, without external agency.

imme'diately, adv., instantly, at once.

immed'icable, adj., incurable.

immem'orable, adj., unworthy of remembrance.

immemo'rial, adj., old beyond record.

immense', adj., boundless, illimitable, vast.

immense'ly, adv., very greatly.

immense'ness, n., the state or quality of the immense.

immen'sity, n., i.q. immenseness; limitless space.

immensurabil'ity, n., the state or quality of the immeasurable.

immen'surable, adj., incapable of measurement.

immerge', v.t., to immerse; v.i., to vanish.

immerged', p.p., immerge.

immer'ging, pr.p., immerge.

immer'sal, n., i.q. immersion; an act of involvement in thought, etc.; the process of dipping or plunging into a liquid.

immerse', v.t., to dip or plunge into water; to engross.

immersed', p.p., immerse.

immers'ing, pr.p., immerse.

immer'sion, n., the act of dipping; absorption.

immer'sion-heat'er, n., an electrical appliance for heating water.

immer'sionist, n., a supporter of the practice of baptizing with immersion.

immethod'ical, adj., unmethodical, untidy.

im'migrant, n., one who immigrates; adj., coming to live in a foreign country.

im'migrate, v.t., to come into a country to live in it.

im'migrated, p.p., immigrate.

im'migrating, pr.p., immigrate.

immigra'tion, n., the act of immigrating.

im'minence, n., the state or quality of being imminent.

im'minent, adj., impending, close at hand, threatening.

im'minently, adv., in an imminent way.

immin'gle, v.t., to mix together.

immin'gled, p.p., immingle.

immin'gling, pr.p., immingle.

immiscibil'ity, n., the state or quality of being immiscible.

immis'cible, *adj.*, incapable of mixture.

immis'sion, *n.*, the act of sending in; something injected.

immit'igable, *adj.*, unable to be mitigated.

immix', *v.t.*, to mix in.

immix'ture, *n.*, a mixing together; an involvement.

immo'bile, *adj.*, not mobile, immovable.

immobil'ity, *n.*, the state or quality of being immobile.

immobiliza'tion, *n.*, *i.q.* immobility.

immo'bilize, *v.t.*, to make immovable.

immo'bilized, *p.p.*, immobilize.

immo'bilizing, *pr.p.*, immobilize.

immod'erate, *adj.*, excessive, inordinate.

immod'erately, *adv.*, excessively.

immod'est, *adj.*, not modest, conceited, unreserved, impure.

immod'estly, *adv.*, in an immodest way.

immod'esty, *n.*, the lack of modesty; impurity.

im'molate, *v.t.*, to sacrifice.

im'molated, *p.p.*, immolate.

im'molating, *pr.p.*, immolate.

immola'tion, *n.*, the act of immolating.

im'molator, *n.*, a sacrificer.

immor'al, *adj.*, offending the divine or moral law; unscrupulous; unchaste.

immoral'ity, *n.*, the state or quality of being immoral.

immor'ally, *adv.*, in an immoral way.

immor'tal, *adj.*, not mortal, undying.

immortal'ity, *n.*, the state or quality of being immortal.

immortaliza'tion, *n.*, the state of being immortalized.

immor'talize, *v.t.*, to render immortal.

immor'talized, *p.p.*, immortalize.

immor'talizing, *pr.p.*, immortalize.

immor'tally, *adv.*, eternally.

immortelle', *n.*, an everlasting flower (*Fr.*).

immovabil'ity, *n.*, the state or quality of being immovable.

immov'able, *adj.*, unable to be moved.

immov'ably, *adv.*, in an immovable way.

immune'; *adj.*, free or exempt from, proof against.

immu'nity, *n.*, the state of being immune.

immuniza'tion, *n.*, the act or effect of rendering immune.

im'munize, *v.t.*, to render immune.

im'munized, *p.p.*, immunize.

im'munizing, *pr.p.*, immunize.

immure', *v.t.*, to wall up, to imprison.

immured', *p.p.*, immure.

immur'ing, *pr.p.*, immure.

immutabil'ity, *n.*, the state or quality of being immutable.

immu'table, *adj.*, unchangeable.

immu'tably, *adv.*, unchangeably.

imp, *v.t.*, to help out; *n.*, a child; a mischievous sprite.

impact', *v.t.*, to press together.

im'pact, *n.*, the act of striking or colliding.

impact'ed, *p.p.*, impact.

impact'ing, *pr.p.*, impact.

impac'tion, *n.*, the wedging together of the broken ends of bones (*surg.*).

impair', *v.t.*, to damage, to lessen in value.

impaired', *p.p.*, impair.

impair'er, *n.*, one who impairs.

impair'ing, *pr.p.*, impair.

impair'ment, *n.*, weakness, damage.

impa'la, *n.*, a large species of S. African antelope.

impale', *v.t.*, to run a stake through; to fasten on a stake; to fence round; to place two coats of arms on one shield, side by side.

impaled', *p.p.*, impale.

impale'ment, *n.*, the act of impaling; a space enclosed; the union of two coats of arms.

impa'ling, *pr.p.*, impale.

impalpabil'ity, *n.*, the state or quality of being impalpable.

impal'pable, *adj.*, not

able to be felt or touched; unreal.

impal'udism, *n.*, a malarial-type disease.

impan'ate, *adj.*, embodied in the bread after consecration.

impana'tion, *n.*, the embodiment in bread.

impan'el, *v.t.*, to enter names on a list; to form a jury. (Also *empanel*.)

impan'el(l)ed, *p.p.*, impanel.

impan'el(l)ing, *pr.p.*, impanel.

imparisyllab'ic, *adj.*, not having the same number of syllables.

impar'ity, *n.*, inequality.

impark', *v.t.*, to enclose with a fence.

imparl'ance, *n.*, the postponement of a suit.

impart', *v.t.*, to give a share of, to communicate.

impart'ed, *p.p.*, impart.

impart'er, *n.*, one who imparts.

impar'tial, *adj.*, not partial; fair, equitable.

impartial'ity, *n.*, the state or quality of being fair.

impar'tially, *adv.*, equitably, fairly.

impar'tialness, *n.*, *i.q.* impartiality.

impartibil'ity, *n.*, the quality of being impartible.

impart'ible, *adj.*, incapable of partition.

impart'ing, *pr.p.*, impart.

impart'ment, *n.*, the act of imparting.

impas'sable, *adj.*, unable to be passed over or through.

impasse', *n.*, an insuperable obstacle (*Fr.*).

impassibil'ity, *n.*, the state or quality of being impassible.

impas'sible, *adj.*, incapable of feeling; apathetic.

impas'sibly, *adv.*, apathetically.

impas'sion, *v.t.*, to fill with passion.

impas'sionate, *adj.*, impassioned.

impas'sioned, *p.p.*, impassion.

impas'sioning, *pr.p.*, impassion.

impas'sive, *adj.*, *i.q.* impassible.

impas'sively, *adv.*, in an impassive way.

impas'siveness, *n.*, *i.q.* impassivity.

impassiv'ity, *n.*, the state or quality of being impassive.

impasta'tion, *n.*, the act of turning into paste.

impaste', *v.t.*, to make into · paste; to lay colours on thickly.

impa'sted, *p.p.*, impaste.

impa'sting, *pr.p.*, impaste.

impas'to, *n.*, the art of laying on paint thickly (*It.*).

impas'toed, *adj.*, covered thickly with paste.

impa'tience, *n.*, inability to endure pain or delay; restlessness.

impa'tient, *adj.*, unable to bear discomfort, pain, or delay; restless; opposed to restraint.

impa'tiently, *adv.*, with impatience.

impawn', *v.t.*, to place in pawn; to pledge.

impawned', *p.p.*, impawn.

impawn'ing, *pr.p.*, impawn.

impeach', *v.t.*, to charge, to accuse; to throw doubt on.

impeach'able, *adj.*, able to be impeached.

impeached', *p.p.*, impeach.

impeach'er, *n.*, one who impeaches.

impeach'ing, *pr.p.*, impeach.

impeach'ment, *n.*, the act of impeaching; a charge laid.

impeccabil'ity, *n.*, the state of being impeccable.

impec'cable, *adj.*, incapable of error or sinning.

impec'cably, *adv.*, faultlessly.

impec'cancy, *n.*, sinlessness.

impec'cant, *adj.*, sinless.

impecunios'ity, *n.*, the state of being impecunious.

impecu'nious, *adj.*, without money.

imped'ance, *n.*, a term relating to electrical resistance.

impede', *v.t.*, to hamper, to stop.

impe'ded, *p.p.*, impede.

impe'dient, *adj.*, hindering.

imped'iment, *n.*, a hindrance, an obstacle.

impedimen'ta, *n. pl.*, baggage (*Lat.*).

impedimen'tal, *adj.*, obstructing.

impe'ding, *pr.p.*, impede.

impel', *v.t.*, to drive forward, to encourage.

impelled', *p.p.*, impel.

impel'lent, *adj.*, impelling.

impel'ler, *n.*, one who impels.

impel'ling, *pr.p.*, impel.

impen', *v.t.*, to enclose in a pen or fold.

impend', *v.i.*, to hang over, to threaten, to be imminent.

impend'ed, *p.p.*, impend.

impend'ence, *n.*, the state of being impendent.

impend'ent, *adj.*, imminent, hanging over.

impend'ing, *pr.p.*, impend.

impenetrabil'ity, *n.*, the state or quality of being impenetrable.

impen'etrable, *adj.*, unable to be penetrated or passed through.

impen'itence, *n.*, the state of being impenitent.

impen'itency, *n.*, *i.q.* impenitence.

impen'itent, *adj.*, unrepentant, stubborn.

impen'itently, *adv.*, in an impenitent way.

impen'nate, *adj.*, short-winged.

impen'nous, *adj.*, wingless.

imperati'val, *adj.*, rel. to the imperative mood.

imper'ative, *adj.*, commanding; having authority; necessary; obligatory; *n.*, the imperative mood.

imper'atively, *adv.*, urgently, with authority.

impera'tor, *n.*, a commander-in-chief.

imperato'rial, *adj.*, rel. to an imperator.

imper'atory, *adj.*, *i.q.* imperatorial.

imperceptibil'ity, *n.*, the quality or state of being imperceptible.

impercep'tible, *adj.*, unable to be perceived; invisible.

impercep'tibleness, · *n.*, *i.q.* imperceptibility.

impercep'tibly, *adv.*, in an imperceptible way.

imper'ception, *n.*, the state of being imperceptive.

imper'fect, *adj.*, not perfect, incomplete.

imper'fection, *n.*, incompleteness, a blemish.

imper'fectly, *adv.*, in an imperfect way.

imper'fectness, *n.*, *i.q.* imperfection.

imper'forable, *adj.*, unable to be perforated.

imper'forate, *adj.*, without perforations.

imper'forated, *adj.*, *i.q.* imperforate.

imperfora'tion, *n.*, the state of being imperforate.

impe'rial, *adj.*, rel. to an emperor or empire; descriptive of scale of measures; sovereign; *n.*, a size of paper.

impe'rialism, *n.*, the principles or the system of Imperial Government.

impe'rialist, *n.*, one who professes imperialism.

impe'rialistic, *adj.*, pert. to imperialism.

impe'rialize, *v.t.*, to make imperial.

impe'rially, *adv.*, in an imperial way.

imper'il, *v.t.*, to bring into danger.

imper'illed, *p.p.*, imperil.

imper'illing, *pr.p.*, imperil.

impe'rious, *adj.*, dictatorial, commanding.

impe'riously, *adv.*, in an imperious way.

impe'riousness, *n.*, the state of being imperious.

imperishabil'ity, *n.*, *i.q.* imperishableness.

imper'ishable, *adj.*, never perishing, everlasting.

imper'ishableness, *n.*, the state or quality of being imperishable.

imper'ishably, *adv.*, everlastingly.

imper'manence, *n.*, the want of permanence.

imper'manent, *adj.*, without permanence.

impermeabil'ity, *n.*, the quality of being impermeable.

imper'meable, *adj.*, impenetrable.

impermis'sible, *adj.*, not permitted.

imper'sonal, *adj.*, not relating to any particular person.

impersonal'ity, *n.*, the quality of being impersonal.

imper'sonally, *adv.*, in an impersonal way.

imper'sonate, *v.t.*, to assume the part of some-

one; to represent; *adj.*, embodied in someone.

imper'sonated, *p.p.*, impersonate.

imper'sonating, *pr.p.*, impersonate.

impersona'tion, *n.*, the act of impersonating.

imper'sonator, *n.*, one who impersonates.

imper'tinence, *n.*, rudeness; uncivil behaviour; effrontery.

imper'tinency, *n.*, *i.q.* impertinence.

imper'tinent, *adj.*, presuming, rude; irrelevant.

imper'tinently, *adv.*, rudely, impudently.

imperturbabil'ity, *n.*, the quality of being imperturbable.

imperturb'able, *adj.*, unable to be ruffled.

imperturb'ably, *adv.*, calmly.

imperturba'tion, *n.*, calmness.

imperviabil'ity, *n.*, *i.q.* imperviousness.

imper'viable, *adj.*, *i.q.* impervious.

imper'vious, *adj.*, unable to be passed through.

imper'viousness, *n.*, the quality of being impervious.

impeti'go, *n.*, a skin disease.

im'petrate, *v.t.*, to gain by entreating.

impetra'tion, *n.*, the act of impetrating.

im'petratory, *adj.*, expressing entreaty.

impetuos'ity, *n.*, vehemence, rash energy.

impet'uous, *adj.*, vehement, rashly energetic.

impet'uously, *adv.*, in an impetuous way.

impet'uousness, *n.*, *i.q.* impetuosity.

im'petus, *n.*, the momentum.

im'peyan, *n.*, an East-Indian pheasant.

im'pi, *n.*, a small body of African warriors.

impi'ety, *n.*, the state or quality of being impious.

impinge', *v.i.*, to strike against, to collide, to touch upon.

impinged', *p.p.*, impinge.

impinge'ment, *n.*, the act of impinging.

imping'ing, *pr.p.*, impinge.

im'pious, *adj.*, profane, irreverent.

im'piously, *adv.*, irreverently, profanely.

im'piousness, *n.*, *i.q.* impiety.

imp'ish, *adj.*, imp-like.

imp'ishly, *adv.*, in an impish way.

implacabil'ity, *n.*, the quality or state of being implacable.

impla'cable, *adj.*, unable to be appeased; unforgiving.

impla'cably, *adv.*, in an implacable way.

implacen'tal, *adj.*, with no placenta.

implant', *v.t.*, to plant into; to inculcate.

implanta'tion, *n.*, the act of implanting.

implant'ed, *p.p.*, implant.

implant'ing, *pr.p.*, implant.

implausibil'ity, *n.*, the quality of being implausible.

implau'sible, *adj.*, not readily believed or accepted.

implead', *v.t.*, to bring an action against.

implead'ed, *p.p.*, implead.

implead'er, *n.*, one who impleads.

implead'ing, *pr.p.*, implead.

im'pledge, *v.t.*, to put in pledge, to pawn.

implement, *n.*, a tool or instrument; *v.t.*, to apply (a regulation); to fulfil (a contract).

implement'al, *adj.*, pert. to implement.

implementa'tion, *n.*, the act of implementing.

implemented, *p.p.*, to implement (*v.t.*).

implementing, *pr.p.*, implement (*v.t.*).

imple'tion, *n.*, the act of filling; the state of being full.

im'plicate, *v.t.*, to entangle, to involve; *n.*, that which is involved.

im'plicated, *p.p.*, implicate.

im'plicating, *pr.p.*, implicate.

implica'tion, *n.*, a deduction; that which is implied.

im'plicative, *adj.*, of the nature of implication.

implic'it, *adj.*, implied; unquestioning.

implic'itly, *adv.*, inferentially; absolutely.

implic'itness, *n.*, the state of being implicit.

implied', *p.p.*, imply.

implied'ly, *adv.*, by implication.

im'plode, *v.t.*, to produce a stop consonant without audibly breathing out after the sound is made.

implora'tion, *n.*, the act of imploring.

implore', *v.t.*, to pray earnestly for, to entreat.

implored', *p.p.*, implore.

implor'er, *n.*, one who implores.

implor'ing, *pr.p.*, implore.

implor'ingly, *adv.*, with earnest prayer.

implo'sion, *n.*, the act of imploding.

imply', *v.t.*, to signify, to mean, to convey.

imply'ing, *pr.p.*, imply.

impold'er, *v.t.*, to reclaim from the sea.

impol'icy, *n.*, an inexpediency.

impolite', *adj.*, rude, unpolished.

impolite'ly, *adv.*, rudely.

impolite'ness, *n.*, the state of being impolite.

impol'itic, *adj.*, an inexpedient, not prudent.

impol'iticly, *adv.*, indiscreetly.

imponderabil'ity, *n.*, the state or quality of being imponderable.

impon'derable, *adj.*, without perceptible weight; not to be thought out; uncertain; *n.*, something not appreciably heavy.

impon'derous, *adj.*, *i.q.* imponderable.

impo'nent, *adj.*, imposing.

imporos'ity, *n.*, solidity.

impo'rous, *adj.*, solid, without pores.

import', *v.t.*, to carry in; to signify.

im'port, *n.*, something imported; a meaning; what is implied.

import'able, *adj.*, able to be imported.

impor'tance, *n.*, the quality of being important; the significance.

impor'tant, *adj.*, significant, weighty, of much consequence.

impor'tantly, *adv.*, in an important way.

importa'tion, *n.*, the act of importing; that which is imported

import'ed, *p.p.*, import.

importee', *n.*, a person brought from abroad.

import′er, *n.*, one who imports.

import′ing, *pr.p.*, import.

impor′tunacy, *n.*, urgent pleading.

impor′tunate, *adj.*, pressing, urgent, insistent.

impor′tunately, *adv.*, in an importunate way.

importune′, *v.t.*, to solicit earnestly; to press.

importuned′, *p.p.*, importune.

importu′ner, *n.*, one who importunes.

importu′ning, *pr.p.*, importune.

importu′nity, *n.*, the act of importuning; an incessant entreaty.

impo′sable, *adj.*, able to be imposed.

impose′, *v.t.*, to lay upon; *v.i.*, to practise deceit.

imposed′, *p.p.*, impose.

impo′ser, *n.*, one who imposes.

impo′sing, *pr.p.*, impose; *adj.*, specious, showy, commanding.

impo′singly, *adv.*, in an imposing way.

impo′sing-stone, *n.*, a slab used by printers for imposing formes.

imposi′tion, *n.*, a laying on (as in Ordination and Confirmation); deceit; a punishment-task.

impossibil′ity, *n.*, the state or quality of being impossible; something that is impossible.

impos′sible, *adj.*, not possible; unable to be done or thought.

impos′sibly, *adv.*, in an impossible way.

im′post, *n.*, that which is imposed, as a tax; the resting (place) of an arch on its support.

imposthuma′tion, *n.*, the formation of an abscess.

impos′thume, *n.*, an abscess.

impos′tor, *n.*, a deceiver.

impos′ture, *n.*, a false pretence, a fraud.

impos′tured, *adj.*, of the nature of fraud.

im′potence, *n.*, want of strength, feebleness.

im′potency, *n.*, *i.q.* impotence.

im′potent, *adj.*, without strength; without self-control; having no sexual power.

im′potently, *adv.*, feebly.

impound′, *v.t.*, to shut into a pound; to take legal possession of.

impound′ed, *p.p.*, impound.

impound′er, *n.*, one who impounds.

impound′ing, *pr.p.*, impound.

impov′erish, *v.t.*, to reduce to poverty; to exhaust.

impov′erished, *p.p.*, impoverish.

impov′erisher, *n.*, one who impoverishes.

impov′erishing, *pr.p.*, impoverish.

impov′erishment, *n.*, the act of impoverishing; the impoverished state.

impracticabil′ity, *n.*, the state or quality of being impracticable.

imprac′ticable, *adj.*, not practicable; unable to be done; stubborn.

imprac′tical, *adj.*, not of a practical nature

impractical′ity, *n.*, that which is not practical.

im′precate, *v.t.*, to curse.

im′precated, *p.p.*, imprecate.

im′precating, *pr.p.*, imprecate.

impreca′tion, *n.*, the act of imprecating; a curse.

im′precatory, *adj.*, expressing a curse.

impregnabil′ity, *n.*, the state of being impregnable.

impreg′nable, *adj.*, not to be taken by assault; capable of impregnation.

impreg′nably, *adv.*, in an impregnable way.

impreg′nate, *v.t.*, to make pregnant; to infuse qualities or particles; *adj.*, pregnant; filled with.

impreg′nated, *p.p.*, impregnate.

impreg′nating, *pr.p.*, impregnate.

impregna′tion, *n.*, the act of impregnating; the state of being impregnated.

impresa′rio, *n.*, a manager or conductor of a troupe of singers or actors.

imprescrip′tible, *adj.*, independent of prescription.

impress′, *v.t.*, to stamp, to fix deeply in, to influence.

im′press, *n.*, a mark, a stamp.

impressed′, *p.p.*, impress.

impressibil′ity, *n.*, the state or quality of being impressible.

impress′ible, *adj.*, able to be impressed.

impress′ing, *pr.p.*, impress.

impres′sion, *n.*, the act or effect of impressing; an indistinct recollection; a faint notion; a printing.

impres′sionable, *adj.*, susceptible to impressions.

impres′sionism, *n.*, an artistic doctrine that a picture should convey a general impression, without particular regard to details.

impres′sionist, *n.*, one who practises impressionism.

impressionis′tic, *adj.*, pert. to a type of modern art; characterized by impression.

impress′ive, *adj.*, impressing, striking, solemn.

impress′ively, *adv.*, in an impressive way.

impress′ment, *n.*, the act of pressing men for service; the state of being impressed.

impress′ure, *n.*, *i.q.* impression.

im′prest, *n.*, money on account, or in advance.

imprima′tur, *n.*, the official permission to print a book (*Lat.*).

impri′mis, *adv.*, in the first place (*Lat.*).

imprint′, *v.t.*, to print in; to stamp in the mind.

im′print, *n.*, a stamp, an impression; the name and address of a publisher at the foot of a title page; a printer's name.

imprint′ed, *p.p.*, imprint.

imprint′ing, *pr.p.*, imprint.

impris′on, *v.t.*, to confine in prison; to shut in.

impris′oned, *p.p.*, imprison.

impris′oning, *pr.p.*, imprison.

impris′onment, *n.*, the act of imprisoning.

the state of being imprisoned.

improbabil'ity, *n.,* the state or quality of being improbable.

improb'able, *adj.,* not probable, unlikely.

improb'ably, *adv.,* not probably.

improb'ity, *n.,* dishonesty.

impromp'tu, *adj.,* unpremeditated; *adv.,* offhand; *n.,* something said or done on the spur of the moment.

improp'er, *adj.,* not proper, indecorous.

improp'erly, *adv.,* not properly.

impro'priate, *v.t.,* to take to private use—said of a layman or lay body holding Church property.

impro'priated, *p.p.,* impropriate.

impro'priating, *pr.p.,* impropriate.

impropria'tion, *n.,* the act of impropriating; that which is impropriated.

impro'priator, *n.,* one who holds impropriated property.

impropri'ety, *n.,* the state or quality of being improper; an improper act.

improvabil'ity, *n.,* the state or quality of being improvable.

improv'able, *adj.,* capable of improvement.

improv'ableness, *n., i.q.* improvability.

improve', *v.t.,* to make better, to reform; *v.i.,* to become better.

improved', *p.p.,* improve.

improve'ment, *n.,* the act or effect of improving.

improv'er, *n.,* anything or anyone that improves.

improv'idence, *n.,* the quality of being improvident; wastefulness.

improv'ident, *adj.,* wasteful, careless of the future.

improv'idently, *adv.,* in an improvident way.

improv'ing, *pr.p.,* improve.

improv'ingly, *adv.,* in an improving way.

improvisa'tion, *n.,* the act of improvising.

improvis'ator, *n.,* an extempore creator of poetry, music, etc.; an improviser.

improvisato're, *n.,* one who improvises (*It.*).

improvise', *v.t.,* to compose without preparation; to make something on the spur of the moment.

improvised', *p.p.,* improvise.

improvi'ser, *n.,* one who improvises.

improvi'sing, *pr.p.,* improvise.

impru'dence, *n.,* want of sagacity or thought; an indiscretion.

impru'dent, *adj.,* lacking thought or sagacity; incautious.

impru'dently, *adv.,* in an imprudent way.

im'pudence, *n.,* shamelessness, audacity.

im'pudent, *adj.,* shameless, audacious.

im'pudently, *adv.,* in an impudent way.

impudic'ity, *n.,* immodesty.

impugn', *v.t.,* to attack, to contradict.

impugned', *p.p.,* impugn.

impugn'er, *n.,* one who impugns.

impugn'ing, *pr.p.,* impugn.

impu'issant, *adj.,* impotent, weak (*Fr.*).

im'pulse, *n.,* an impelling force; a sudden motive.

impul'sion, *n.,* a sudden impetus; the act of impelling, the state of being impelled.

impul'sive, *adj.,* acting without waiting to reflect.

impul'sively, *adv.,* in an impulsive way.

impul'siveness, *n.,* the state or quality of being impulsive.

impu'nity, *n.,* freedom from punishment or injury.

impure', *adj.,* not pure, unclean, unchaste.

impure'ly, *adv.,* in an impure way.

impure'ness, *n.,* the state or quality of being impure.

impu'rity, *n.,* impureness; anything impure.

impur'ple, *v.t.,* to stain purple.

impu'table, *adj.,* able to be imputed.

imputa'tion, *n.,* the act of imputing; a charge or accusation.

impu'tative, *adj.,* imputed; able to be imputed.

impute', *v.t.,* to attribute, to ascribe, to place to one's account.

impu'ted, *p.p.,* impute.

impu'ter, *n.,* one who imputes.

impu'ting, *pr.p.,* impute.

imputres'cible, *adj.,* not liable to putrescence.

in, *prep.* and *adv.,* within; into.

inabil'ity, *n.,* the state of being unable.

inaccessibil'ity, *n.,* the state of being inaccessible.

inaccess'ible, *adj.,* unable to be approached.

inaccess'ibly, *adv.,* unapproachably.

inac'curacy, *n.,* the state or quality of being inaccurate; an error.

inac'curate, *adj.,* not exact, careless.

inac'curately, *adv.,* in an inaccurate way.

inac'tion, *n.,* a state of not acting.

inac'tivate, *v.t.,* to prevent action; to render inert.

inact'ive, *adj.,* not acting, idle.

inact'ively, *adv.,* idly.

inactiv'ity, *n.,* the quality of being inactive.

inad'equacy, *n.,* the state or quality of being inadequate.

inad'equate, *adj.,* insufficient, not competent.

inad'equately, *adv.,* insufficiently.

inadmissibil'ity, *n.,* the state or quality of being inadmissible.

inadmis'sible, *adj.,* unable to be admitted.

inadvert'ence, *n.,* heedlessness, carelessness, an act of carelessness.

inadvert'ent, *adj.,* not paying attention, careless.

inadvert'ently, *adv.,* carelessly.

inadvis'able, *adj.,* not advisable.

ina'lienable, *adj.,* unable to be alienated.

inamora'ta, *n.,* a woman one is in love with (*It.*).

inamora'to, *n.,* a man one is in love with (*It.*).

inane', *adj.,* empty, foolish.

inane'ly, *adv.,* foolishly.

inan'imate, *adj.,* lifeless.

inan'imately, *adv.,* lifelessly.

inan'imated, *adj.*, rendered spiritless.

inani'tion, *n.*, a state of emptiness.

inan'ity, *n.*, the state of being inane or empty; silliness.

inap'petence, *n.*, a lack of desire.

inap'petency, *n.*, *i.q.* inappetence.

inapplicabil'ity, *n.*, the state or quality of being inapplicable.

inap'plicable, *adj.*, unable to be applied; irrelevant.

inapplica'tion, *n.*, indolence.

inap'posite, *adj.*, irrelevant, unsuited.

inappre'ciable, *adj.*, not appreciable.

inapprecia'tion, *n.*, a lack of appreciation.

inappre'ciative, *adj.*, not appreciative.

inapprehen'sible, *adj.*, cannot be understood by mind or senses.

inappro'priate, *adj.*, not appropriate, unsuited.

inappro'priately, *adv.*, unsuitably.

inapt', *adj.*, not fit or apt.

inapt'itude, *n.*, the state of being inapt.

inapt'ly, *adv.*, in an inapt way.

inapt'ness, *n.*, *i.q.* inaptitude.

inarch', *v.t.*, to graft by drawing the branch of one tree to the stock of another.

in'arm, *v.t.*, to embrace.

inartic'ulacy, *n.*, a speech deficiency, a lack of coherence in speech.

inartic'ulate, *adj.*, not jointed; unable to speak distinctly.

inartic'ulately, *adv.*, indistinctly.

inartic'ulateness, *n.*, the state of being inarticulate.

inarticula'tion, *n.*, *i.q.* inarticulateness.

inartis'tic, *adj.*, not artistic.

inartis'tically, *adv.*, in an inartistic way.

inasmuch', *adv.*, seeing that, considering.

inatten'tion, *n.*, the want of attention, carelessness.

inatten'tive, *adj.*, not attentive, careless.

inatten'tively, *adv.*, carelessly.

inatten'tiveness, *n.*, the state of being inat-

tentive.

inaudibil'ity, *n.*, the state or quality of being inaudible.

inaud'ible, *adj.*, unable to be heard.

inaud'ibly, *adv.*, in an inaudible way.

inau'gural, *adj.*, rel. to inauguration.

inau'gurate, *v.t.*, to open with formality.

inau'gurated, *p.p.*, inaugurate.

inau'gurating, *pr.p.*, inaugurate.

inaugura'tion, *n.*, the act of inaugurating; ceremonial commencement.

inau'gurator, *n.*, one who inaugurates.

inauspi'cious, *adj.*, not auspicious, unlucky, ill-omened.

inauspi'ciously, *adv.*, unluckily, with ill-omen.

in'born, *adj.*, innate.

inbreathe', *v.t.*, to inspire; to draw in breath.

in'bred, *adj.*, bred in; natural.

in'breeding, *n.*, breeding between species closely related.

in'ca, *n.*, a Peruvian chief or emperor.

incage', *v.t.*, to shut in a cage.

incal'culable, *adj.*, unable to be calculated.

incales'cence, *n.*, the state or quality of being incalescent.

incales'cent, *adj.*, growing warm.

incandesce', *v.t.* and *i.*, to glow, to cause to glow.

incandes'cence, *n.*, the state or quality of being incandescent.

incandes'cent, *adj.*, glowing white.

incanta'tion, *n.*, a magical formula; an enchantment.

incan'tatory, *adj.*, enchanting.

incapabil'ity, *n.*, the state of being incapable.

inca'pable, *adj.*, not capable, lacking power or fitness.

incapac'itate, *v.t.*, to render incapable; to disqualify.

incapac'itated, *p.p.*, incapacitate.

incapac'itating, *pr.p.*, incapacitate.

incapac'ity, *n.*, the want of power or fitness.

incar'cerate, *v.t.*, to imprison.

incar'cerated, *p.p.*, incarcerate.

incar'cerating, *pr.p.*, incarcerate.

incarcera'tion, *n.*, imprisonment.

incar'nadine, *v.t.*, to dye crimson.

incar'nate', *v.t.*, to embody in flesh.

incar'nate, *adj.*, united with humanity; embodied.

incarnat'ed, *p.p.*, incarnate.

incarnat'ing, *pr.p.*, incarnate.

incarna'tion, *n.*, the act of incarnating.

incase', *v.t.*, to shut in a case, to surround.

incased', *p.p.*, incase.

incas'ing, *pr.p.*, incase.

incau'tious, *adj.*, not cautious, unwary.

incau'tiously, *adv.*, without caution.

incau'tiousness, *n.*, the want of caution.

in'cavated, *adj.*, hollowed.

incava'tion, *n.*, the act or effect of hollowing.

incen'diarism, *n.*, the act of setting fire.

incen'diary, *n.*, one who, or that which, sets property on fire.

incendiv'ity, *n.*, the tendency to burn or glow.

in'cense, *n.*, a preparation of aromatic gums, spices, etc., producing, when burnt, a fragrant fume.

incense', *v.t.*, to kindle rage; to bless with incense.

incensed', *p.p.*, incense; *adj.*, angry, enraged.

incens'ing, *pr.p.*, incense.

incen'sive, *adj.*, provoking.

in'censory, *n.*, a vessel used for burning incense.

incen'tive, *adj.*, stimulating; *n.*, a stimulus.

incep'tion, *n.*, a beginning.

incep'tive, *adj.*, initial.

incer'titude, *n.*, the state of uncertainty.

inces'sancy, *n.*, the state of not ceasing.

inces'sant, *adj.*, not ceasing, continual.

inces'santly, *adv.*, unceasingly.

in'cest, *n.*, sexual intercourse within the

prohibited degrees of relationship.

inces'tuous, *adj.*, of the nature of incest.

inch, *v.t.*, to mark with lines at intervals of an inch; *v.i.*, to move a little at a time; *n.*, the one-twelfth part of a foot; an island.

inch'meal, *adv.*, by inches.

in'choate, *adj.*, begun, not nearly complete; formless.

in'choately, *adv.*, incompletely, initially.

inchoa'tion, *n.*, the act of beginning.

incho'ative, *adj.*, initial.

in'cidence, *n.*, a falling; an occurrence.

in'cident, *adj.*, falling upon, happening; *n.*, something that happens.

inciden'tal, *adj.*, casual, happening.

inciden'tally, *adv.*, in an incidental way.

incin'erate, *v.t.*, to burn to ashes.

incin'erated, *p.p.*, incinerate.

incin'erating, *pr.p.*, incinerate.

incinera'tion, *n.*, the act of cremating.

incin'erator, *n.*, a device for burning by fire.

incip'ience, *n.*, *i.q.* incipiency.

incip'iency, *n.*, the initial stage, the beginning.

incip'ient, *adj.*, beginning.

incip'iently, *adv.*, initially.

incise', *v.t.*, to cut in, to engrave.

incised', *p.p.*, incise.

inci'sing, *pr.p.*, incise.

inci'sion, *n.*, the act or effect of incising.

inci'sive, *adj.*, cutting in; penetrating; trenchant.

inci'sor, *adj.*, rel. to the incisors; *n.*, one of the front or cutting teeth.

inci'sory, *adj.*, *i.q.* incisive.

incis'ure, *n.*, *i.q.* incision.

incita'tion, *n.*, the act of inciting; an incentive.

incite', *v.t.*, to arouse, to urge on.

inci'ted, *p.p.*, incite.

incite'ment, *n.*, *i.q.* incitation.

inci'ter, *n.*, anything or anyone that incites.

inci'ting, *pr.p.*, incite.

incivil'ity, *n.*, the lack of civility; rudeness.

inclasp', *v.t.*, to clasp.

inclasped', *p.p.*, inclasp.

inclasp'ing, *pr.p.*, inclasp.

in'-clearing, *n.*, cheques which have been received for settlement.

inclem'ency, *n.*, harshness, severity.

inclem'ent, *adj.*, harsh, severe.

incli'nable, *adj.*, able to be inclined.

inclina'tion, *n.*, the act of inclining; a preference, leaning, liking.

incli'natory, *adj.*, leaning.

incline', *v.t.*, to cause to lean; *v.i.*, to lean, to give approval to.

in'cline, *n.*, a slope.

inclined', *p.p.*, incline; *adj.*, disposed to.

incli'ner, *n.*, anything that inclines.

incli'ning, *pr.p.*, incline.

inclinom'eter, *n.*, an apparatus for measuring slope.

inclose', *v.t.*, to shut in, to fence round. Also enclose.

inclosed', *p.p.*, inclose.

inclo'sing, *pr.p.*, inclose.

inclo'sure, *n.*, the act of inclosing; an inclosed space.

include', *v.t.*, to shut in, to contain, to embrace.

inclu'ded, *p.p.*, include.

inclu'ding, *pr.p.*, include.

inclu'sion, *n.*, the act or effect of including.

inclu'sive, *adj.*, including.

inclu'sively, *adv.*, so as to include.

incoer'cible, *adj.*, not able to be coerced.

incog', *abbrev.* for *incognito.*

incog'nita, *n.*, fem. of incognito.

incog'nito, *adj.*, unknown; in an assumed character; *adv.*, in disguise; *n.*, an assumed character (*It.*).

incog'nizable, *adj.*, not cognizable.

incog'nizance, *n.*, the inability to understand.

incog'nizant, *adj.*, failing to understand.

incoher'ence, *n.*, confusion, want of connexion.

incoher'ency, *n.*, *i.q.* incoherence.

incoher'ent, *adj.*, not cohering, loose, rambling.

incoher'ently, *adv.*, without connexion.

incohe'sive, *adj.*, not cohesive.

incombustibil'ity, *n.*, the state or quality of being incombustible.

incombus'tible, *adj.*, unable to be burned.

in'come, *n.*, the means of living; money coming in.

in'comer, *n.*, one who comes in, an immigrant, intruder, successor.

in'come-tax, *n.*, the tax levied on incomes.

in'coming, *n.*, an entrance; *adj.*, coming in.

incom'ing, *adj.*, succeeding; accruing; immigrating.

incommensurabil'ity, *n.*, the quality of being incommensurable.

incommen'surable, *adj.*, having no common measure.

incommen'surate, *adj.*, *i.q.* incommensurable.

incommode', *v.t.*, to inconvenience, to worry.

incommo'ded, *p.p.*, incommode.

incommo'ding, *pr.p.*, incommode.

incommo'dious, *adj.*, not commodious, inconvient, too small.

incommunicabil'ity, *n.*, the quality of being incommunicable.

incommu'nicable, *adj.*, unable to be imparted.

incommunica'do, *adj.*, lacking means of communication (*Span.*).

incommu'nicative, *adj.*, not communicative; reserved.

incommu'table, *adj.*, not commutable.

incompact', *adj.*, not compact.

incom'parable, *adj.*, above comparison; unequalled.

incom'parably, *adv.*, in an incomparable way.

incompatibil'ity, *n.*, the state or quality of being incompatible.

incompat'ible, *adj.*, not compatible; inconsistent with.

incom'petence, *n.*, a state of being not competent.

incom'petency, *n.*, *i.q.* incompetence.

incom'petent, *adj.*, not competent; unqualified, unable.

incom'petently, *adv.*, in an incompetent way.

incomplete', *adj.*, not complete, unfinished, imperfect.

incomplete'ly, *adv.*, in an incomplete way.

incomplete'ness, *n.*, the state of being incomplete.

incom'posite, *adj.*, not composite.

incomprehensibil'ity, *n.*, the quality of being incomprehensible.

incomprehen'sible, *adj.*, unintelligible; not capable of being understood.

incomprehen'sion, *n.*, a failure to comprehend.

incomprehen'sive, *adj.*, limited.

incompressibil'ity, *n.*, the state or quality of being incompressible.

incompress'ible, *adj.*, not able to be compressed.

incompu'table, *adj.*, not to be computed.

inconceiv'able, *adj.*, beyond conception; not to be believed.

inconclu'sive, *adj.*, leading to no decision.

inconclu'sively, *adv.*, without finality.

incondens'able, *adj.*, not able to be condensed.

incon'dite, *adj.*, badly constructed, lacking polish (as applied to written composition).

inconform'ity, *n.*, dissimilarity, the want of conformity.

incon'gruent, *adj.*, incongruous.

incongru'ity, *n.*, the want of harmony with; inconsistency; anything incongruous.

incon'gruous, *adj.*, incompatible with, inconsistent; odd.

incon'gruously, *adv.*, in an incongruous way.

inconsec'utive, *adj.*, wanting in sequence.

incon'sequence, *n.*, illogicality, inconsistency.

incon'sequent, *adj.*, illogical, inconsistent.

inconsequen'tial, *adj.*, *i.q.* inconsequent.

inconsid'erable, *adj.*, not to be considered; quite unimportant.

inconsid'erate, *adj.*, wanting in consideration; thoughtless.

inconsid'erately, *adv.*, without consideration.

inconsidera'tion, *n.*, want of forethought; thoughtlessness.

inconsist'ency, *n.*, the state or quality of being inconsistent; the disagreement of two things.

inconsist'ent, *adj.*, not logically or morally consistent.

inconsist'ently, *adv.*, not consistently.

inconsol'able, *adj.*, unable to be consoled.

incon'sonance, *n.*, the want of consonance.

inconspic'uous, *adj.*, not conspicuous.

inconspic'uously, *adv.*, not noticeably.

incon'stancy, *n.*, the want of constancy or firmness.

incon'stant, *adj.*, not constant; unstable; wanting uniformity.

incon'stantly, *adv.*, in an inconstant way.

inconsum'able, *adj.*, unable to be consumed.

incontest'able, *adj.*, indisputable.

incon'tinence, *n.*, a lack of self-restraint; the loss of power to retain.

incon'tinent, *adj.*, without self-restraint; unceasing; unable to retain.

incon'tinently, *adv.*, without restraint; straightway.

incontrol'lable, *adj.*, uncontrollable.

incontrovertibil'ity, *n.*, the state or quality of being incontrovertible.

incontrovert'ible, *adj.*, unable to be controverted or disproved.

inconve'nience, *v.t.*, to give trouble to; *n.*, the state or quality of being inconvenient.

inconve'nienced, *p.p.*, inconvenience.

inconve'niencing, *pr.p.*, inconvenience.

inconve'nient, *adj.*, not convenient, unsuitable, causing trouble.

inconven'iently, *adv.*, un-

favourably, awkwardly.

inconvertibil'ity, *n.*, state of being inconvertible.

inconvert'ible, *adj.*, not exchangeable; incapable of being (logically) converted.

inconvin'cible, *adj.*, not to be convinced.

inco-or'dinate, *adj.*, not co-ordinate.

inco-ordina'tion, *n.*, the state of being inco-ordinate.

incor'porate, *adj.*, formed into one body; embodied; not material.

incor'porate, *v.t.*, to form into one body; to admit to a society; *v.i.*, to join a body or society.

incor'porated, *p.p.*, incorporate.

incor'porating, *pr.p.*, incorporate.

incorpora'tion, *n.*, the act of incorporating; an association.

incorpo'real, *adj.*, having no body; immaterial.

incorpore'ity, *n.*, the quality of being incorporeal.

incorrect', *adj.*, not correct, irregular.

incorrect'ly, *adv.*, erroneously.

incorrect'ness, *n.*, the state or quality of being incorrect.

incorrigibil'ity, *n.*, the state of being incorrigible.

incor'rigible, *adj.*, not submitting to correction; hopelessly bad.

incor'rigibleness, *n.*, *i.q.* incorrigibility.

incor'rigibly, *adv.*, in an incorrigible way.

incorro'dible, *adj.*, unable to be corroded.

incorrupt', *adj.*, pure, sound, undecayed.

incorruptibil'ity, *n.*, the state or quality of being incorruptible.

incorrupt'ible, *adj.*, not able to be corrupted.

incorrup'tion, *n.*, the state of being incorrupt.

incorrupt'ness, *n.*, *i.q.* incorruption.

incras'sate, *adj.*, thickened (*bot.*, *zool.*).

incrassate', *v.t.*, to make thicker; *v.i.*, to become thick.

incrassa'tion, *n.*, the state of being incrassate.

incras'sative, *adj.*, causing a thickening.

in'crease, n., growth of all kinds.

increase', v.t., to make greater in any way; v.i., to become greater.

increased', p.p., increase.

increas'er, n., that which increases.

increas'ing, pr.p., increase.

increas'ingly, adv., in an increasing degree.

incredibil'ity, n., the quality of being incredible.

incred'ible, adj., beyond belief.

incred'ibly, adv., in an incredible way.

incredu'lity, n., the state of being incredulous.

incred'ulous, adj., not credulous; unwilling to believe; sceptical.

incred'ulousness, n., i.q. incredulity.

in'crement, n., an increase, an augmentation; increased value.

incremen'tal, adj., rel. to augmentation.

incrim'inate, v.t., to accuse, to involve in a charge.

incrim'inated, p.p., incriminate.

incrim'inating, pr.p., incriminate.

incrim'inatory, adj., incriminating.

incrust', v.t., to cover with a crust or coating; to apply decorative materials.

incrust'ate, adj., incrusted.

incrusta'tion, n., an outer coating or crust.

incrust'ed, p.p., incrust.

incrust'ing, pr.p., incrust.

in'cubate, v.t., to sit on eggs for hatching; to meditate on; v.i., to brood.

in'cubated, p.p., incubate.

in'cubating, pr.p., incubate.

in'cubation, n., the act of incubating.

in'cubator, n., a contrivance for hatching chickens or for rearing abnormally delicate children.

in'cubus, n., an oppressive weight (Lat.).

in'culcate, v.t., to impress upon the mind, to teach.

in'culcated, p.p., inculcate.

in'culcating, pr.p., inculcate.

inculca'tion, n., the act of inculcating.

incul'pable, adj., blameless.

incul'pate, v.t., to accuse; to blame.

incul'pated, p.p., inculpate.

incul'pating, pr.p., inculpate.

inculpa'tion, n., the act or effect of inculpating.

incul'patory, adj., attributing or involving blame.

incum'bency, n., the office of an incumbent; the period of an incumbent's tenure.

incum'bent, adj., leaning or resting on; obligatory; n., the holder of an official position, ecclesiastical, legal, etc.

incur', v.t., to become liable to; to run into.

incurabil'ity, n., the state of being incurable.

incur'able, adj., past cure or remedy.

incur'ably, adv., in an incurable way.

incu'rious, adj., not curious; indifferent.

incu'riously, adv., indifferently.

incurred', p.p., incur.

incur'ring, pr.p., incur.

incur'sion, n., an invasion, a raid.

incur'sive, adj., invading, aggressive.

incurv'ate, adj., curved inward; v.t., to curve, to bend.

incurv'ated, p.p., incurvate.

incurv'ating, pr.p., incurvate.

incurva'tion, n., the state of being bent inwards or curved.

incurve', v.t. and i., to bend or curve inwards.

incurved', p.p., incurve.

incurv'ing, pr.p., incurve.

incuse', v.t., to impress by stamping, n., an impression hammered or stamped in.

indebt'ed, adj., under debt or obligation.

indebt'edness, n., the state of being indebted.

inde'cency, n., unseemliness, indelicacy.

inde'cent, adj., unbecoming, unseemly, immoral.

inde'cently, adv., in an indecent way.

indecid'uous, adj., not deciduous; perennial.

indeci'pherable, adj., unable to be deciphered.

indeci'sion, n., the lack of decision; a hesitation.

indeci'sive, adj., uncertain, not final.

indeci'sively, adv., in an indecisive way.

indecli'nable, adj., not able to be declined.

indeco'rous, adj., not decorous; unseemly.

indeco'rousness, n., unseemliness.

indeco'rum, n., impropriety.

indeed', adv., truly, really; interj., expressing surprise or doubt.

indefatigabil'ity, n., the quality of being untiring.

indefat'igable, adj., untiring.

indefat'igably, adv., untiringly.

indefeasibil'ity, n., the state or quality of being indefeasible.

indefea'sible, adj., unable to be made void or defeated.

indefec'tible, adj., not liable to defect or decay, faultless.

indefensibil'ity, n., the quality of being indefensible.

indefen'sible, adj., not to be defended.

indefen'sibly, adv., in an indefensible way.

indefin'able, adj., not able to be defined.

indefin'ably, adv., in a way not to be defined.

indef'inite, adj., not defined, indistinct, vague.

indef'initely, adv., in an indefinite way.

indef'initeness, n., the state or quality of being indefinite.

indelibil'ity, n., the quality of being indelible.

indel'ible, adj., unable to be erased or blotted out.

indel'ibly, adv., in an indelible way.

indel'icacy, n., want of delicacy or refinement.

indel'icate, adj., unrefined, improper.

indel'icately, adv., in an indelicate way.

indemnifica'tion, n., the act of indemnifying.

indem'nified, *p.p.*, indemnify.

indem'nify, *v.t.*, to give compensation or security.

indem'nifying, *pr.p.*, indemnify.

indem'nity, *n.*, compensation; security; the legal exemption from liability.

indemon'strable, *adj.*, that cannot be shown or proved.

indent', *v.t.*, to notch; to begin a printed line short by the space of a word; to apprentice.

in'dent, *n.*, an order for goods; a notch, cut.

indenta'tion, *n.*, a small depression.

indent'ed, *adj.*, notched; apprenticed; *p.p.*, indent.

indent'ing, *pr.p.*, indent.

inden'tion, *n.*, the indenting of a line in printing.

inden'ture, *n.*, a contract in writing; apprenticeship.

independ'able, *adj.*, not to be depended upon.

independ'ence, *n.*, freedom of action; state without ties or commitments.

independ'ent, *adj.*, not depending on; free; in easy circumstances.

independ'ently, *adv.*, separately.

or indescri'bable, *adj.*, unable to be described.

or indescri'bably, *adv.*, beyond description.

indestructibil'ity, *n.*, the quality of being indestructible.

indestruc'tible, *adj.*, not able to be destroyed.

indeter'minable, *adj.*, not able to be determined or classified.

indeter'minate, *adj.*, not determined; not precise.

indeter'minately, *adv.*, not precisely.

indetermina'tion, *n.*, hesitation, want of decision.

indeterm'inism, *n.*, the theory of unmotivated action.

indevout', *adj.*, not devout.

in'dex, *v.t.*, to furnish with an index; *n.*, a pointer, sign, forefinger; an alphabetic table of entries.

in'dexed, *p.p.*, index.

in'dexer, *n.*, one who, or that which, indexes.

in'dexes, *n.*, pl. of index.

index'ical, *adj.*, rel. to an index.

in'dexing, *pr.p.*, index.

indexter'ity, *n.*, a lack of dexterity.

In'diaman, *n.*, a ship that traded with India.

In'dian, *adj.*, rel. to India; *n.*, a native of India.

In'dianesque, *adj.*, of Indian style.

Indianol'ogist, *n.*, one who studies American Indians.

in'dia-rub'ber, *n.*, caoutchouc.

in'dicate, *v.t.*, to point out, to show.

in'dicated, *p.p.*, indicate.

in'dicating, *pr.p.*, indicate.

indica'tion, *n.*, the act or result of indicating; a sign.

indic'ative, *adj.*, indicating, showing; *n.*, the indicative mood.

indic'atively, *adv.*, significantly.

in'dicator, *n.*, anything that indicates.

in'dicatory, *adj.*, showing.

ind'ices, *n. pl.*, figures indicating the power of a number.

indict', *v.t.*, to lay a charge against.

indict'able, *adj.*, liable to a charge.

indict'ed, *p.p.*, indict.

indict'er, *n.*, one who indicts.

indict'ing, *pr.p.*, indict.

indic'tion, *n.*, a period of fifteen years; a proclamation.

indict'ment, *n.*, a charge, an accusation.

indif'ference, *n.*, impartiality; unconcern.

indif'ferent, *adj.*, impartial; unconcerned, not interested; passable.

indif'ferentism, *n.*, the view that all religions are of equal merit.

indif'ferently, *adv.*, impartially; passably.

in'digence, *n.*, the state of being indigent.

in'digene, *n.*, a native.

indig'enous, *adj.*, native to the soil.

in'digent, *adj.*, poor, needy.

indigest'ed, *adj.*, not digested.

indigestibil'ity, *n.*, the quality of being indigestible.

indigest'ible, *adj.*, not easy to be digested.

indiges'tion, *n.*, dyspepsia; the inability to digest.

indig'nant, *adj.*, scornfully angry.

indig'nantly, *adv.*, angrily.

indigna'tion, *n.*, scornful anger.

indig'nity, *n.*, an undeserved slight; an insult.

in'digo, *adj.*, of the colour of indigo; *n.*, a vegetable dye; violetblue.

indigom'eter, *n.*, an appliance for testing the strength of an indigo solution.

in'digotin, *n.*, the pure indigo.

indirect', *adj.*, not direct, misleading.

indirec'tion, *n.*, *i.q.* indirectness.

indirect'ly, *adv.*, not directly; through some other's intervention.

indirect'ness, *n.*, the state of being indirect.

indiscern'ible, *adj.*, not discernible, imperceptible.

indiscern'ibly, *adv.*, imperceptibly.

indiscerp'tible, *adj.*, incapable of destruction by dissolution of parts.

indis'cipline, *n.*, the lack of discipline.

indiscreet', *adj.*, foolish, wanting in forethought.

indiscreet'ly, *adv.*, injudiciously.

indiscrete', *adj.*, not separate.

indiscre'tion, *n.*, want of forethought, imprudence; an act of imprudence.

indiscrim'inate, *adj.*, without distinction; promiscuous.

indiscrim'inately, *adv.*, promiscuously.

indiscrimina'tion, *n.*, want of discriminating power.

indispen'sable, *adj.*, unable to be done without; completely necessary.

indispen'sably, *adv.*, necessarily.

indispose', *v.t.*, to turn

one against; to dis-
incline; to make un-
well.

indisposed', *p.p.*, indispose; *adj.*, unwell.

indisposi'tion, *n.*, a disinclination; a slight
illness.

indispu'table, *adj.*, beyond dispute.

indispu'tably, *adv.*, in an
indisputable way.

indissolubil'ity, *n.*, the
quality of being in-
dissoluble.

indissol'uble, *adj.*, not
able to be dissolved
or broken.

indissol'ubly, *adv.*, in an
indissoluble way.

indissol'vable, *adj.*, *i.q.*
indissoluble.

indistinct', *adj.*, not distinct, obscure.

indistinct'ly, *adv.*, not
distinctly.

indistinct'ness, *n.*, obscurity, faintness.

indistin'guishable, *adj.*,
not to be distin-
guished.

indite', *v.t.*, to write,
to compose.

indi'ted, *p.p.*, indite.

indite'ment, *n.*, a com-
position.

indi'ter, *n.*, one who in-
dites.

indi'ting, *pr.p.*, indite.

indivert'ible, *adj.*, cannot be turned aside.

individ'ual, *adj.*, single,
not divided, distinct;
n., a single object or
person.

individ'ualism, *n.*, the
political theory that
the individual's rights
are paramount; per-
sonal freedom.

individ'ualist, *n.*, one
who prefers to act
alone.

individualis'tic, *adj.*,
acting as an indivi-
dualist; active, apart
from a group.

individual'ity, *n.*, a separate existence; a dis-
tinctive character.

individualiza'tion, *n.*,
the act of individualiz-
ing.

individ'ualize, *v.t.*, to distinguish from other
persons or things.

individ'ualized, *p.p.*, in-
dividualize.

individ'ualizing, *pr.p.*, in-
dividualize.

individ'ually, *adv.*, separately, one by one.

individ'uate, *v.t.*, to indi-
vidualize, to form into
an individual.

indivisibil'ity, *n.*, the
quality of being in-
divisible.

indivis'ible, *adj.*, not able
to be divided.

indo'cile, *adj.*, unteach-
able.

indocil'ity, *n.*, unteach-
ableness.

or indoc'trinate, *v.t.*, to instruct, to acquaint.

or indoc'trinated, *p.p.*, indoctrinate.

or indoc'trinating, *pr.p.*, indoctrinate.

or indoctrina'tion, *n.*, instruction.

in'dolence, *n.*, laziness,
idleness.

in'dolent, *adj.*, lazy, idle.

in'dolently, *adv.*, lazily.

indom'itable, *adj.*, not
to be subdued.

Indo'nesian, *adj.*, pert. or
rel. to Indonesia; a
native of I.

in'door, *adj.*, at home,
within doors.

indoors', *adv.*, in or into
a building.

indors'able, *adj.*, able to
be indorsed.

indorse', *v.t.*, to sign on
the back; to approve,
to sanction. Also *en-
dorse*.

indorsed', *p.p.*, indorse.

indorsee', *n.*, one in
whose favour indorse-
ment is made.

indorse'ment, *n.*, the
signing on the back of
a document; sanc-
tion, approval.

indors'er, *n.*, one who
indorses.

indors'ing, *pr.p.*, indorse.

or in'draught, *n.*, an inward flow of air,
water, etc.

in'drawn, *adj.*, drawn in.

indu'bitable, *adj.*, be-
yond doubt, certain.

indu'bitably, *adv.*, certainly.

induce', *v.t.*, to lead on,
to persuade, to cause.

induced', *p.p.*, induce.

induce'ment, *n.*, that
which induces.

indu'cer, *n.*, one who induces.

indu'cible, *adj.*, able to
be induced.

indu'cing, *pr.p.*, induce.

induct', *v.t.*, to put in
possession; to intro-

duce into a new place
or new mode of life.

induc'tance, *n.*, the capacity for induction
(*elec.*).

induct'ed, *p.p.*, induct.

induct'ile, *adj.*, not ductile.

inductil'ity, *n.*, the quality of being inductile.

induct'ing, *pr.p.*, induct.

induc'tion, *n.*, the ceremony of inducting; the
reasoning from parti-
culars to general con-
clusions; a conclusion
so arrived at; the
bringing about of an
electrical state by the
proximity without
contact of another ele-
ctrically charged body.

induc'tive, *adj.*, rel. to
induction.

induc'tively, *adv.*, by induction.

inductom'eter, *n.*, an apparatus measuring
electric inductance.

induct'or, *n.*, one who,
or that which, inducts.

indue', *v.t.*, to endow;
to clothe. Also *endue*.

indued', *p.p.*, indue.

indu'ing, *pr.p.*, indue.

indulge', *v.t.*, to humour,
to gratify; *v.i.*, to yield
to.

indulged', *p.p.*, indulge.

indul'gence, *n.*, the act of
indulging; a favour
granted; the remission
of temporal punish-
ment.

indul'gent, *adj.*, exceed-
ingly· kind; readily
yielding.

indul'gently, *adv.*, in an
indulgent way.

indul'ging, *pr.p.*, indulge.

in'durate, *v.t.*, to harden; *v.i.*, to become
hard.

in'durated, *p.p.*, in-
durate.

in'durating, *pr.p.*, indu-
rate.

indura'tion, *n.*, hardening.

indus'trial, *adj.*, rel. to
industry.

indus'trialism, *n.*, the
policy or science of
planning industry.

indus'trialist, *n.*, one engaged in the develop-
ment of industry;
a manufacturer.

industrializa'tion, *n.*, expanding and develop-
ing industry.

indus'trialize, *v.t.*, to set up industries.

indus'trialized, *p.p.*, industrialize.

indus'trializing, *pr.p.*, industrialize.

indus'trious, *adj.*, diligent, hard-working.

indus'triously, *adv.*, diligently.

in'dustry, *n.*, steady, hard work; productive employment generally.

in'dwelling, *adj.*, abiding or residing in.

ine'briant, *adj.*, intoxicating; *n.*, an intoxicant.

ine'briate, *v.t.*, to make drunk; *adj.*, drunken, *n.*, a drunkard.

ine'briated, *p.p.*, inebriate.

ine'briating, *pr.p.*, inebriate.

inebria'tion, *n.*, the state of being drunk.

inebri'ety, *n.*, drunkenness.

ined'ible, *adj.*, unfit to be eaten.

ined'ita, *n. pl.*, that which is not edited; something unpublished (*Lat.*).

ined'ited, *adj.*, not published; unrevised.

ineducabil'ity, *n.*, the state of being ineducable.

ined'ucable, *adj.*, incapable of being educated.

inef'fable, *adj.*, unspeakable, inexpressible.

inef'fableness, *n.*, the quality of being ineffable.

inef'fably, *adv.*, unspeakably.

ineffface'able, *adj.*, not to be effaced.

ineffec'tive, *adj.*, not effective.

ineffec'tively, *adv.*, in an ineffective manner.

ineffect'ual, *adj.*, not effective, unavailing.

ineffect'ually, *adv.*, without effect.

ineffica'cious, *adj.*, not efficacious.

inef'ficacy, *n.*, the state of being inefficacious.

ineffi'ciency, *n.*, the state of being inefficient.

ineffi'cient, *adj.*, lacking ability; not achieving an object.

ineffi'ciently, *adv.*, in an inefficient way.

inelas'tic, *adj.*, not elastic.

inelastic'ity, *n.*, the want of elasticity.

inel'egance, *n.*, the want of elegance or refinement.

inel'egant, *adj.*, wanting in elegance.

inel'egantly, *adv.*, in an inelegant way.

ineligibil'ity, *n.*, the quality of being ineligible.

inel'igible, *adj.*, not eligible; not qualified.

ineluc'table, *adj.*, that cannot be escaped.

inept', *adj.*, unfit, foolish, inexpert.

inept'itude, *n.*, unfitness, foolishness.

inept'ly, *adv.*, in an inept way.

inept'ness, *n.*, *i.q.* ineptitude.

inequal'ity, *n.*, the want of equality; unevenness; injustice.

inequilat'eral, *adj.*, with unequal sides.

ineq'uitable, *adj.*, not equitable; unjust.

ine'quity, *n.*, unfairness.

inerad'icable, *adj.*, not to be eradicated.

inerrabil'ity, *n.*, the quality of being infallible.

inerr'able, *adj.*, incapable of error; infallible.

iner'rancy, *n.*, the quality of being inerrant.

iner'rant, *n.*, not erring; infallible.

inert', *adj.*, inactive, apathetic.

iner'tia, *n.*, sluggishness, inactivity.

inert'ly, *adv.*, sluggishly, inactively.

inert'ness, *n.*, the state of being inert.

inesca'pable, *adj.*, from which there is no escape; inevitable.

inessen'tial, *adj.*, not essential. Also *unessential*.

ines'timable, *adj.*, beyond estimating.

ines'timably, *adv.*, in an inestimable way.

inev'itable, *adv.*, not to be avoided.

inev'itably, *adv.*, unavoidably.

inexact', *adj.*, not exact, inaccurate.

inexac'titude, *n.*, being inexact; inexactness.

inexact'ness, *n.*, the state of being inexact.

inexcus'able, *adj.*, without excuse.

inexcu'sableness, *n.*, the state or quality of being inexcusable.

inexcu'sably, *adv.*, in an inexcusable way.

inexec'utable, *adj.*, that cannot be executed.

inexhaust'ible, *adj.*, not to be exhausted.

inexhaust'ibly, *adv.*, in an inexhaustible way.

inex'orable, *adj.*, not to be won by entreaty; relentless.

inex'orably, *adv.*, relentlessly.

inexpe'diency, *n.*, unfitness, unadvisability.

inexpe'dient, *adj.*, unadvisable, unfit.

inexpen'sive, *adj.*, not costly.

inexpen'sively, *adv.*, in an inexpensive way.

inexpens'iveness, *n.*, the quality of being inexpensive.

inexpe'rience, *n.*, the lack of experience.

inexpe'rienced, *adj.*, without experience.

inexpert', *adj.*, not expert, unskilful.

inex'piable, *adj.*, past atoning for.

inex'plicable, *adj.*, not to be explained; past explanation.

inex'plicably, *adv.*, in an inexplicable way.

inexplic'it, *adj.*, not distinctly expressed.

inexpress'ible, *adj.*, not to be told or uttered; beyond telling.

inexpress'ibly, *adv.*, in an inexpressible way.

inexpress'ive, *adj.*, without significance.

inexpug'nable, *adj.*, not to be controverted.

in exten'so, *adj.*, unabridged (*Lat.*).

inextin'guishable, *adj.*, unquenchable.

in extre'mis, *adj.*, in the last stage (*Lat.*).

inex'tricable, *adj.*, unable to be disentangled; beyond disentangling.

inex'tricably, *adv.*, in an inextricable way.

infallibil'ity, *n.*, the exemption from error.

infal'lible, *adj.*, incapable of error.

infal'libly, *adv.*, with absolute certainty.

in'famize, *v.t.*, to render infamous.

in'famous, *adj.*, notoriously bad.

in'famously, *adv.*, disgracefully.

in'famy, *n.*, public disgrace, ignominy.

in'fancy, *n.*, the period of childhood; the beginning.

in'fant, n., a babe; one under the legal full age of 18 years.

infan'ta, n., the fem. of infante.

infan'te, n., a Spanish or Portuguese prince.

in'fanticide, n., child-murder.

in'fantile, adj., childlike, rel. to children.

infan'tilism, n., the state of being mentally or physically infantile.

in'fantine, adj., i.q. infantile.

in'fantry, n., foot-soldiers.

infat'uate, v.t., to affect with folly or passion.

infat'uated, p.p., infatuate.

infat'uating, pr.p., infatuate.

infatua'tion, n., the state of being infatuated.

infect', v.t., to taint, to corrupt.

infect'ed, p.p., infect.

infect'ing, pr.p., infect.

infec'tion, n., the act of infecting; pollution; the communication of disease.

infec'tious, adj., spreading infection.

infec'tiously, adv., in an infectious way.

infec'tiousness, n., the character of being infectious.

infecun'dity, n., barrenness.

infeft'ment, n., the symbolical transfer of property.

infelic'itous, adj., not felicitous, unfortunate.

infelic'ity, n., misfortune, inappropriateness.

infer', v.t., to draw a conclusion.

infer'able, adj., capable of being inferred.

infer'ably, adv., by way of regular inference.

in'ference, n., a deduction or conclusion.

inferen'tial, adj., of the nature of an inference.

inferen'tially, adv., in an inferential way.

infe'rior, adj., lower (in any relation).

inferior'ity, n., the state of being inferior; subordination.

infer'nal, adj., pert. to hell.

infer'nally, adv., outrageously.

infer'no, n., the place or state of torment.

inferred', p.p., infer.

infer'ring, pr.p., infer.

infer'tile, adj., not fertile.

infertil'ity, n., barrenness.

infest', v.t., to harass, to overrun.

infesta'tion, n., the act of infesting or overrunning.

infest'ed, p.p., infest.

infest'er, n., an invader.

infest'ing, pr.p., infest.

in'fidel, n., an unbeliever; an enemy to the Christian faith; adj., unbelieving.

infidel'ity, n., unfaithfulness; disbelief.

infil'trate, v.t., to penetrate through pores.

infil'trated, p.p., infiltrate.

infil'trating, pr.p., infiltrate.

infiltra'tion, n., the act of infiltrating; something that infiltrates.

in'finite, adj., not bounded by space or time.

in'finitely, adv., without limit.

in'finiteness, n., the state of the infinite; immensity.

infinites'imal, adj., infinitely minute; n., a quantity infinitesimally small.

infinites'imally, adv., in infinitesimal degree.

infin'itive, n., the infinitive mood.

infin'itude, n., i.q. infinity.

infin'ity, n., the state of being infinite; an infinite quantity.

infirm', adj., weak, shaky.

infir'mary, n., a house for the sick and infirm.

infir'mity, n., the state of being infirm; a complaint; a fault.

infirm'ly, adj., weakly.

infix', v.t., to fix in; to insert.

inflame', v.t., to set on fire, kindle, excite.

inflamed', p.p., inflame.

inflam'er, n., one who, or that which, inflames.

infla'ming, pr.p., inflame.

inflammabil'ity, n., the quality of being inflammable.

inflam'mable, adj., capable of being set on fire.

inflamma'tion, n., the heated action of the blood, causing swelling, redness and pain.

inflam'matory, adj., producing inflammation; tending to passion, sedition, etc.

infla'table, adj., able to be inflated.

inflate', v.t., to fill with wind or breath; to elate; to raise prices artificially.

infla'ted, p.p., inflate.

infla'ter, n., anything that inflates.

infla'ting, pr.p., inflate.

infla'tion, n., the act or effect of inflating; price rises.

infla'tionary, adj., producing inflation.

infla'tionism, n., the process of currency inflation.

infla'tionist, n., one who causes or advocates inflation.

inflect', v.t., to bend; to vary a noun or verb; to modulate the voice.

inflect'ed, p.p., inflect.

inflec'tion, inflex'ion, n., a bending; a modulation of the voice; the variations of the noun or verb.

inflec'tional, adj., rel. to inflection.

inflec'tive, adj., capable of bending.

inflexed', adj., bent.

inflexibil'ity, n., firmness, stiffness.

inflex'ible, adj., unable to be bent, stiff; immovable.

inflex'ibly, adv., firmly.

inflex'ional, adj., pertaining to inflexion.

inflict', v.t., to impose.

inflict'ed, p.p., inflict.

inflict'ing, pr.p., inflict.

inflic'tion, n., the act of inflicting; a calamity.

inflores'cence, n., the general arrangement of blossoms.

in'flow, n., a flowing in.

in'fluence, v.t., to affect, to modify, to bias; n., a favour, authority, sway.

in'fluenced, p.p., influence.

in'fluencing, *pr.p.*, influence.

in'fluential, *adj.*, having influence or power.

influen'tially, *adv.*, in an influential way.

influen'za, *n.*, a respiratory disease.

in'flux, *n.*, a flowing into; infusion.

infold', *v.t.*, to envelop, to clasp.

infold'ed, *p.p.*, infold.

infold'ing, *pr.p.*, infold.

inform', *v.t.*, to instruct; to acquaint.

inform'al, *adj.*, unofficial, unceremonious.

informal'ity, *n.*, an absence of formality.

inform'ally, *adv.*, in an informal way.

inform'ant, *n.*, one who gives information.

informa'tion, *n.*, intelligence given; instruction.

inform'ative, *adj.*, giving information, instructive.

inform'atory, *adj.*, *i.q.* informative.

informed', *p.p.*, inform.

inform'er, *n.*, one who lays an information before a magistrate; a spy.

inform'ing, *pr.p.*, inform; *adj.*, instructive.

in'fra, *adv.*, lower down, further on; (prefix), below or underneath.

infract', *v.t.*, to make a breach in.

infrac'tion, *n.*, a breach, violation, infringement.

infran'gible, *adj.*, unbreakable; inviolable.

infra'-red, *adj.*, beyond the red end of the visible spectrum.

infra'structure, *n.*, a substructure.

infre'quence, *n.*, rareness.

infre'quency, *n.*, *i.q.* infrequence.

infre'quent, *adj.*, rare, uncommon.

infre'quently, *adv.*, not often.

infringe', *v.t.*, to break in upon, to violate.

infringed', *p.p.*, infringe.

infringe'ment, *n.*, the act of infringing; a breach.

infrin'ger, *n.*, one who infringes.

infrin'ging, *pr.p.*, infringe.

infruc'tuous, *adj.*, unfruitful.

infu'riate, *v.t.*, to rouse to fury; *adj.*, mad, raging.

infu'riated, *p.p.*, infuriate.

infu'riating, *pr.p.*, infuriate.

infuse', *v.t.*, to pour in, to instil, to make an infusion of.

infused', *p.p.*, infuse.

infu'ser, *n.*, one who, or that which, infuses.

infusibil'ity, *n.*, the state of being able to be infused.

infu'sible, *adj.*, capable of being infused.

infu'sing, *pr.p.*, infuse.

infu'sion, *n.*, the act of infusing; an extract made by steeping in liquid without boiling.

Infuso'ria, *n. pl.*, microscopic beings developed in infusions.

infuso'rial, *adj.*, rel. to Infusoria.

infu'sory, *adj.*, *i.q.* infusorial.

in'gather, *v.t.*, to harvest, to gather in.

in'gathering, *pr.p.*, ingather; *n.*, the harvest.

ingem'inate, *v.t.*, to repeat; to reiterate.

inge'nious, *adj.*, clever, inventive.

inge'niously, *adv.*, cleverly.

inge'niousness, *n.*, cleverness, ingenuity.

ingen'ium, *n.*, natural character, or disposition.

ingénue', *n.*, an artless girl (*Fr.*).

ingenu'ity, *n.*, cleverness, inventiveness.

ingen'uous, *adj.*, natural, open, sincere.

ingen'uously, *adv.*, frankly, sincerely.

ingen'uousness, *n.*, frankness, naturalness.

ingest', *v.t.*, to take into the stomach.

inges'ta, *n. pl.*, food; things taken into the stomach (*Lat.*).

inges'tion, *n.*, the act of taking in food.

in'gle, *n.*, the fireside.

ing'le-nook, *n.*, a cosy chimney corner.

inglo'rious, *adj.*, ignominious.

inglo'riously, *adv.*, ignominiously.

in'going, *adj.*, going in; *n.*, the money paid by an incoming tenant.

in'got, *n.*, a mass of cast metal.

ingraft', *v.t.*, to propagate by incision.

ingraft'ed, *p.p.*, ingraft.

ingraft'ing, *pr.p.*, ingraft.

ingraft'ment, *n.*, the act of ingrafting.

ingrain', *v.t.*, to dye deeply; to infix deeply.

ingrained', *p.p.*, ingrain.

ingrain'ing, *pr.p.*, ingrain.

in'grate, *n.*, a thankless person.

ingra'tiate, *v.t.*, to secure favour with someone.

ingra'tiated, *p.p.*, ingratiate.

ingra'tiating, *pr.p.*, ingratiate.

ingrat'itude, *n.*, unthankfulness.

ingre'dient, *n.*, a part of a mixture.

in'gress, *n.*, an entrance.

in'-group, *n.*, a group of people sharing common interests.

in'growing, *adj.*, growing inwards.

in'growth, *n.*, the act of growing inwards.

in'guinal, *adj.*, rel. to the groin.

ingulf', *v.t.*, to swallow up. Also *engulf*.

ingulfed', *p.p.*, ingulf.

ingulf'ing, *pr.p.*, ingulf.

ingur'gitate, *v.t.*, to swallow down; to guzzle.

ingurgita'tion, *n.*, a swallowing down, an engulfing.

inhab'it, *v.t.*, to live in; to occupy.

inhab'itable, *adj.*, fit to be lived in.

inhab'itancy, *n.*, a residence, an occupancy.

inhab'itant, *n.*, one who inhabits; a resident.

inhabita'tion, *n.*, a permanent residence.

inhab'ited, *p.p.*, inhabit.

inhab'iter, *n.*, one who inhabits.

inhab'iting, *pr.p.*, inhabit.

inhab'itiveness, *n.*, the love of home and country.

inhal'ant, *n.*, that which is inhaled; a medicinal nasal spray; *adj.*, for inhaling.

inhala′tion, *n.*, the act of inhaling; an inspiration.

inhalato′rium, *n.*, a place for treatment of respiratory complaints.

inhale′, *v.t.*, to draw into the lungs.

inhaled′, *p.p.*, inhale.

inha′ler, *n.*, an instrument for inhaling.

inha′ling, *pr.p.*, inhale.

inharmon′ic, *adj.*, discordant.

inharmo′nious, *adj.*, *i.q.* inharmonic.

inharmo′niously, *adv.*, discordantly.

inharmo′niousness, *n.*, unmusicalness, discordance.

inhere′, *v.i.*, to be fixed or incorporated in.

inhered′, *p.p.*, inhere.

inher′ence, *n.*, the state of inhering.

inher′ency, *n.*, *i.q.* inherence.

inher′ent, *adj.*, innate; naturally a part of.

inher′ently, *adv.*, innately.

inher′ing, *pr.p.*, inhere.

inher′it, *v.t.*, to receive by descent or birth or legacy.

inher′itable, *adj.*, capable of being inherited.

inher′itance, *n.*, the act of inheriting; something inherited.

inher′ited, *p.p.*, inherit.

inher′iting, *pr.p.*, inherit.

inher′itor, *n.*, one who inherits.

inher′itrix, *n.*, the fem. of inheritor.

inhib′it, *v.t.*, to restrain, to hinder.

inhib′ited, *p.p.*, inhibit.

inhib′iting, *pr.p.*, inhibit.

inhibi′tion, *n.*, the act of inhibiting; a mental block.

inhib′itory, *adj.*, forbidding, restraining.

inhomogen′eous, *adj.*, not homogeneous.

inhos′pitable, *adj.*, not hospitable, unfriendly.

inhos′pitably, *adv.*, in an inhospitable manner.

inhospital′ity, *n.*, the lack of hospitality.

inhu′man, *adj.*, lacking humanity, cruel.

inhumane′, *adj.*, *i.q.* inhuman.

inhuman′ity, *n.*, the lack of humanity; cruelty.

inhu′manly, *adv.*, cruelly.

inhuma′tion, *n.*, the act of burying.

inhume′, *v.t.*, to bury, to inter.

inhumed′, *p.p.*, inhume.

inhu′ming, *pr.p.*, inhume.

inim′ical, *adj.*, unfriendly, hostile.

inim′ically, *adv.*, in an unfriendly way.

inim′itable, *adj.*, not to be imitated; unequalled.

inim′itably, *adv.*, in an inimitable way.

iniq′uitous, *adj.*, unjust, wicked.

iniq′uity, *n.*, injustice, wickedness.

ini′tial, *adj.*, beginning, inceptive; *n.*, a letter beginning a word; *v.t.*, to write one's initials on.

ini′tialled, *p.p.*, initial.

ini′tialling, *pr.p.*, initial.

ini′tially, *adv.*, at the beginning.

ini′tiand, *n.*, a candidate for initiation.

ini′tiate, *n.*, a novice; *v.t.*, to begin; to instruct.

ini′tiated, *p.p.*, initiate.

ini′tiating, *pr.p.*, initiate.

initia′tion, *n.*, the act of initiating; the first admission.

ini′tiative, *adj.*, beginning; *n.*, a beginning; the capacity for taking the first step.

init′iator, *n.*, one who initiates.

ini′tiatory, *adj.*, introducing.

ini′tis, *n.*, the inflammation of muscular tissue.

inject′, *v.t.*, to throw or force into.

inject′ed, *p.p.*, inject.

inject′ing, *pr.p.*, inject.

injec′tion, *n.*, the act of injecting; something injected.

inject′or, *n.*, anything which injects.

injudi′cious, *adj.*, indiscreet, unwise.

injudi′ciously, *adv.*, unwisely.

injunc′tion, *n.*, a command, a behest; a restraining writ.

in′jure, *v.t.*, to hurt, to do harm to.

in′jured, *p.p.*, injure.

in′jurer, *n.*, one who injures.

inju′ria, *n.*, a legal wrong (*Lat.*).

inju′rious, *adj.*, causing injury.

inju′riously, *adv.*, harmfully.

in′jury, *n.*, a mischief; a hurt.

injus′tice, *n.*, a violation of right.

ink, *v.t.*, to smear with ink.

inked, *p.p.*, ink.

ink′er, *n.*, an inking roller.

ink′ily, *adv.*, like ink.

ink′iness, *n.*, the state of being inky.

inking, *pr.p.*, ink.

ink′ling, *n.*, a hint.

ink′stand, *n.*, a stand for ink-bottles.

inkwell, *n.*, a container for ink fitted into a hole in a desk.

ink′y, *adj.*, smeared with ink; black.

inlace′, *v.t.*, to lace; to ornament with lace.

inlaced′, *p.p.*, inlace.

inla′cing, *pr.p.*, inlace.

inlaid, *adj.*, decorated with inserted ornamentation; *p.p.*, inlay.

in′land, *adj.*, and *adv.*, interior; away from the sea; *n.*, the interior of a country.

in′lander, *n.*, an inland inhabitant.

in-law, *n.*, a relative by marriage (*colloq.*).

inlay′, *v.t.*, to decorate with wood, ivory, etc.

in′lay, *n.*, inlaying material; a decoration with wood, ivory, etc.

in′layer, *n.*, one who inlays.

inlay′ing, *pr.p.*, inlay; *n.*, the art of inlaying.

inlet′, *v.t.*, to insert.

in′let, *n.*, a small bay; a creek.

in loco parentis, *adj.*, in the place of a parent (*Lat.*).

in′ly, *adv.*, inwardly (*poet.*).

in′lying, *adj.*, lying inside.

in′mate, *n.*, a lodger; a dweller in.

in′most, *adj.*, deepest within; innermost.

inn, *n.*, a place for

entertaining travellers; a legal society.

in'nards, n. pl., inner or interior parts or organs; the insides (colloq.).

innate', adj., inborn, inbred.

innate'ly, adv., naturally, inherently.

innate'ness, n., the quality of being innate.

innav'igable, adj., inaccessible to ships.

in'ner, adj., interior.

in'nermost, adj., inmost, deepest within.

innerv'ate, v.t., to give nervous stimulation to.

innerva'tion, n., the disposition of the nervous system; a nervous stimulus.

innerve', v.t., to invigorate; to give nervous stimulus to.

innerved', p.p., innerve.

innerv'ing, pr.p., innerve.

in'nings, n., a period of play in a game.

inn'keeper, n., the keeper of an inn.

in'nocence, n., harmlessness, guiltlessness, simplicity.

in'nocency, n., i.q. innocence.

in'nocent, adj., harmless, guiltless, simple.

in'nocently, adv., in an innocent way.

innoc'uous, adj., not hurtful.

innoc'uously, adv., harmlessly.

innom'inate, adj., nameless.

in'novate, v.i., to introduce a change.

in'novated, p.p., innovate.

in'novating, pr.p., innovate.

innova'tion, n., a novelty.

in'novator, n., one who innovates.

innox'ious, adj., harmless, safe.

innox'iously, adv., harmlessly.

innuen'do, n., an insinuation.

innu'merable, adj., countless.

innu'merably, adv., without number.

innu'merous, adj., i.q. innumerable.

innutri'tion, n., the state of being innutritious.

innutri'tious, adj., not nourishing.

innu'tritive, adj., i.q. innutritious.

inobserv'ance, n., inattention.

inobtru'sive, adj., unobtrusive.

inobtru'sively, adv., unobtrusively.

inobtru'siveness, n., unobtrusiveness.

inoc'ulate, v.t., to propagate by grafting; to inject (med.).

inoc'ulated, p.p., inoculate.

inoc'ulating, pr.p., inoculate.

inocula'tion, n., the act of inoculating; an injection (med.).

inoc'ulator, n., one who inoculates.

ino'dorous, adj., scentless, without smell.

inoffen'sive, adj., harmless.

inoffen'sively, adv., harmlessly.

inoffi'cious, adj., without office or function.

inop'erable, adj., that cannot be operated on.

inop'erative, adj., not working; without effect.

inopex'ia, n., a thickening of the blood.

inopportune', adj., untimely; inconvenient.

inopportune'ly, adv., in an inopportune way.

inor'dinate, adj., irregular, immoderate.

inor'dinately, adv., excessively.

inorgan'ic, adj., not organic; without organs.

inorganiza'tion, n., a lack of organization.

inos'culate, v.t., to unite by contact.

inoscula'tion, n., the act or effect of inosculating.

in'-patient, n., a patient confined to hospital.

in'put, n., that which is fed into or taken in.

in'quest, n., a judicial inquiry.

inqui'etude, n., uneasiness, a disturbed state.

in'quiline, adj. and n., (animal) living in the home of another.

inquire', v.i. and t., to ask, to make investigation. Also enquire.

inquired', p.p., inquire.

inquiren'do, n., the power to hold an inquiry (leg.).

inquir'er, n., one who inquires.

inquir'ing, pr.p., inquire.

in'quiringly, adv., in an inquiring way.

inquir'y, n., an examination, investigation.

inquisi'tion, n., a judicial examination; an inspection.

inquisi'tional, adj., rel. to an inquisition.

inquis'itive, adj., curious, prying.

inquis'itively, adv., curiously, in a prying way.

inquis'itiveness, n., prying curiosity.

inquis'itor, n., one who holds an inquisition.

inquisito'rial, adj., in the manner of an inquisitor.

inquisito'rially, adv., in an inquisitorial manner.

in'road, n., an incursion, a breach.

in'rush, n., a rushing in.

insaliva'tion, n., the action of saliva.

insalu'brious, adj., unhealthy.

insalu'brity, n., unhealthiness.

insal'utary, adj., not salutary; not beneficial.

insane', adj., out of the mind, mad.

insane'ly, adv., like a madman.

insan'itary, adj., unhealthy, likely to cause disease.

insan'ity, n., madness.

insatiabil'ity, n., the quality of being insatiable.

insa'tiable, adj., never satisfied, greedy.

insa'tiableness, n.. i.q. insatiability.

insa'tiably, adv., in an insatiable way.

insa'tiate, adj., i.q. insatiable.

inscribe', v.t., to write on; to dedicate.

inscribed', p.p., inscribe.

inscri'ber, n., one who inscribes.

inscri'bing, pr.p., inscribe.

inscript', n., i.q. inscription.

inscrip'tion, n., that which is inscribed.

inscrip'tive, adj., inscribed.

inscroll', *v.t.*, to enter on a scroll.

inscrutabil'ity, *n.*, the quality of being inscrutable.

inscru'table, *adj.*, mysterious; impenetrable.

inseam', *v.t.*, to mark with a seam.

in'sect, *n.*, a small creeping or flying creature.

insecta'rium, *n.*, a collection of insects for observation.

insec'ticide, *n.*, a poison for insects.

in'sectile, *adj.*, rel. to insects.

insec'tion, *n.*, an incision.

insectiv'orous, *adj.*, devouring insects.

insectol'ogy, *n.*, the science of insects.

insecure', *adj.*, not secure, unsafe.

insecure'ly, *adv.*, unsafely.

insecu'rity, *n.*, danger.

insem'inate, *v.t.*, to impregnate.

insemina'tion, *n.*, impregnation.

insen'sate, *adj.*, lacking perception, mad.

insensibil'ity, *n.*, apathy; the state of being insensible.

insen'sible, *adj.*, incapable of feeling; senseless.

insen'sibly, *adv.*, in an insensible way.

insen'sitive, *adj.*, not sensitive to touch, sight, light, mental or moral impressions.

insen'tient, *adj.*, not sentient.

inseparabil'ity, *n.*, the state of being inseparable.

insep'arable, *adj.*, that cannot be separated.

insep'arableness, *n.*, *i.q.* inseparability.

insep'arably, *adv.*, in an inseparable way.

insert', *v.t.*, to set or place in or among.

insert'ed, *p.p.*, insert.

insert'ing, *pr.p.*, insert.

inser'tion, *n.*, the act of inserting; something inserted.

Insesso'res, *n. pl.*, percher-birds (*Lat.*).

insesso'rial, *adj.*, perching.

in'set, *n.*, additional matter put into a book; a piece let into a dress.

inset', *v.t.*, to set in.

in'shore, *adj.* and *adv.*, near or towards shore.

insicca'tion, *n.*, the act of drying in.

in'side, *adj.*, *prep.* and *adv.*, within; *n.*, the interior.

insi'der, *n.*, one who is inside.

insid'ious, *adj.*, lying in wait, treacherous, sly.

insid'iously, *adv.*, in an insidious way.

in'sight, *n.*, clear perception.

insig'nia, *n. pl.*, emblems of office (*Lat.*).

insignif'icance, *n.*, the want of meaning, unimportance.

insignif'icant, *adj.*, without meaning, unimportant.

insignif'icantly, *adv.*, in an insignificant way.

insincere', *adj.*, not sincere, false.

insincere'ly, *adv.*, without sincerity.

insincer'ity, *n.*, want of sincerity, falseness.

insin'uate, *v.t.*, to hint indirectly, to intimate; *v.i.*, to ingratiate oneself.

insin'uated, *p.p.*, insinuate.

insin'uating, *pr.p.*, insinuate.

insin'uatingly, *adv.*, in an insinuating way.

insinua'tion, *n.*, the act of insinuating; an artful, indirect hint.

insin'uative, *adj.*, conveying an insinuation.

insip'id, *adj.*, tasteless, flat, vapid.

insipid'ity, *n.*, the absence of savour; vapidity.

insip'idly, *adv.*, in an insipid way.

insip'idness, *n.*, tastelessness, dullness.

insip'ience, *n.*, the want of wisdom.

insip'ient, *adj.*, wanting wisdom, foolish.

insist', *v.i.*, to press a command, to persist.

insist'ed, *p.p.*, insist.

insist'ence, *n.*, the act of insisting.

insist'ency, *n.*, *i.q.* insistence.

insist'ent, *adj.*, urgent, imperative; persisting.

insist'ently, *adv.*, in an insistent way.

insist'ing, *pr.p.*, insist.

insi'tion, *n.*, ingrafting.

in si'tu, *adverbial phrase* = in position (*Lat.*).

insobri'ety, *n.*, intemperance.

in'solate, *v.t.*, to dry in the sun.

in'solated, *p.p.*, insolate.

in'solating, *pr.p.*, insolate.

insola'tion, *n.*, sun-drying.

in'solence, *n.*, arrogance; offensive rudeness.

in'solent, *adj.*, arrogant; rude.

in'solently, *adv.*, in an insolent way.

insolid'ity, *n.*, the quality of being not solid.

insolubil'ity, *n.*, the quality of being insoluble.

insol'uble, *adj.*, that which cannot be solved or dissolved.

insol'ubly, *adv.*, in an insoluble way.

insolv'ency, *n.*, the inability to meet one's creditors.

insolv'ent, *adj.*, unable to pay one's debts; *n.*, a bankrupt.

insom'nia, *n.*, the inability to sleep.

insomuch', *adv.*, so, to such a degree.

insouciance', *n.*, indifference, carelessness (*Fr.*).

inspan', *v.t.*, to yoke up, to harness.

inspect', *v.t.*, to view, to superintend.

inspect'ed, *p.p.*, inspect.

inspect'ing, *pr.p.*, inspect.

inspec'tion, *n.*, a close scrutiny, superintendence.

inspec'tor, *n.*, one who inspects.

inspec'torate, *n.*, the office of an inspector; a body of inspectors.

inspec'tor-gen'eral, *n.*, or an inspector of the highest rank.

inspec'torship, *n.*, the office of inspector.

inspi'rable, *adj.*, able to be inspired.

inspira'tion, *n.*, the act of inspiring.

inspira'tor, *n.*, apparatus used for the intake of air.

inspir'atory, *adj.*, rel. to inspiration.

inspire', *v.t.* and *i.*, to draw in breath; to breathe into; to influence the mind; to give official information to.

inspired', *p.p.*, inspire.

inspi'rer, *n.*, one who inspires.

inspi'ring, *pr.p.*, inspire; *adj.*, stimulating to the mind.

inspir'it, *v.t.*, to hearten, to encourage.

inspir'ited, *p.p.*, inspirit.

inspir'iting, *pr.p.*, inspirit.

inspis'sate, *v.t.*, to thicken.

inspis'sated, *p.p.*, inspissate.

inspis'sating, *pr.p.*, inspissate.

inspissa'tion, *n.*, the act or effect of inspissating.

instabil'ity, *n.*, the want of stability; inconstancy.

install', *v.t.*, to put into an official place or office; to fit into place.

installa'tion, *n.*, the act of installing; the fitting into place of plant, machinery or services.

installed', *p.p.*, instal.

install'ing, *pr.p.*, instal.

instal'ment, *n.*, the act of installing; part payment.

in'stance, *v.t.*, to quote an example; *n.*, an example; a request.

in'stanced, *p.p.*, instance.

in'stancing, *pr.p.*, instance.

in'stancy, *n.*, insistency, the urgency.

in'stant, *adj.*, insistent, earnest, immediate; *n.*, a particular point of time.

instanta'neous, *adj.*, occurring in an instant.

instanta'neously, *adv.*, at the moment.

instan'ter, *adv.*, immediately (*Lat.*).

in'stantly, *adv.*, at once.

instate', *v.t.*, to place in a particular rank.

instead', *prep.* and *adv.*, in the place of.

in'step, *n.*, the upper side of the foot.

in'stigate, *v.t.*, to urge on, to prompt.

in'stigated, *p.p.*, instigate.

in'stigating, *pr.p.*, instigate.

instiga'tion, *n.*, the act of instigating; encouragement.

in'stigator, *n.*, one who instigates.

instil', **instill'**, *v.t.*, to infuse by dropping in; to pour slowly in.

instilla'tion, *n.*, the act or effect of instilling.

instilled', *p.p.*, instil.

instil'ler, *n.*, one who instils.

instil'ling, *pr.p.*, instil.

instinct', *adj.*, animated by, stimulated.

in'stinct, *n.*, a natural impulse.

instinc'tive, *adj.*, in accordance with natural impulse.

instinc'tively, *adv.*, in an instinctive way.

in'stitute, *v.t.*, to establish, to found; to commence; *n.*, a maxim, a principle; a society or building devoted to art, science, etc.

in'stituted, *p.p.*, institute.

in'stituting, *pr.p.*, institute.

institu'tion, *n.*, an establishment or society; a building used for philanthropic, scientific, or other purposes.

institu'tional, *adj.*, rel. to institutions.

institu'tionalize, *v.*, to confine to an institution.

institu'tionary, *adj.*, *i.q.* institutional.

in'stitutive, *adj.*, tending to establish.

in'stitutor, *n.*, a founder.

instruct', *v.t.*, to inform, to teach, to give orders.

instruct'ed, *p.p.*, instruct.

instruct'ing, *pr.p.*, instruct.

instruc'tion, *n.*, teaching, information, orders.

instruc'tional, *adj.*, instructive.

instruc'tive, *adj.*, teaching, informing.

instruc'tively, *adv.*, in an instructive manner.

instructive'ness, *n.*, the quality of being instructive.

instruc'tor, *n.*, a teacher.

instruc'tress, *n.*, the fem. of instructor.

in'strument, *n.*, that by which anything is effected; a tool; a contrivance for producing musical sounds; a deed (*leg.*).

instrumen'tal, *adj.*, conducing as a means to an end; rel. to musical instruments.

instrument'alist, *n.*, a player on an instrument.

instrumental'ity, *n.*, agency.

instrument'ally, *adv.*, by means; played on an instrument.

instrumenta'tion, *n.*, the disposition and character of instrumental music.

insubjec'tion, *n.*, the state of not being subject.

insubor'dinate, *adj.*, unruly.

insubordina'tion, *n.*, unruliness.

insubstan'tial, *adj.*, not substantial.

insubstantial'ity, *n.*, the quality of being insubstantial.

insubstan'tially, *adv.*, in an insubstantial way.

insuf'ferable, *adj.*, unendurable, intolerable.

insuf'ferably, *adv.*, intolerably.

insuffi'ciency, *n.*, a lack of sufficiency; inadequacy.

insuffi'cient, *adj.*, inadequate.

insuffi'ciently, *adv.*, inadequately.

insuf'flate, *v.t.*, to breathe into or upon.

insuffla'tion, *n.*, the act of insufflating.

in'sufflator, *n.*, a blowing instrument.

in'sular, *adj.*, rel. to an island; narrow.

in'sularism, *n.*, the state or quality of being insular.

insular'ity, *n.*, *i.q.* insularism; narrowness of mind.

in'sulate, *v.t.*, to detach; to prevent the escape of electricity.

in'sulated, *p.p.*, insulate.

in'sulating, *pr.p.*, insulate.

insula'tion, *n.*, the act or effect of insulating.

in'sulator, *n.*, anything that insulates; a nonconductor.

in'sulin, *n.*, a hormone produced by the pancreas and used for treating diabetes.

insult', *v.t.*, to affront, to outrage.

in'sult, *n.*, an affront, an outrage.

insult'ed, *p.p.*, insult.

insult'er, *n.*, one who insults.

insult'ing, *pr.p.*, insult; *adj.*, abusive.

insult'ingly, *adv.*, in an insulting way.

insuperabil'ity, *n.*, the quality of being insuperable.

insu'perable, *adj.*, not to be overcome, insurmountable.

insu'perably, *adv.*, insurmountably.

insupport'able, *adj.*, not to be supported, unendurable.

insupport'ably, *adv.*, unendurably.

insuppres'sible, *adj.*, not to be suppressed.

insur'able, *adj.*, able to be insured.

insur'ance, *n.*, security against loss.

insur'ant, *n.*, a person to whom an insurance policy is issued.

insure', *v.t.*, to make sure or secure; to provide insurance.

insured', *p.p.*, insure.

insur'er, *n.*, one who insures.

insur'gent, *adj.*, rebellious; *n.*, a rebel.

insur'ing, *pr.p.*, insure.

insurmount'able, *adj.*, not to be surmounted or overcome.

insurmount'ably, *adv.*, in an insurmountable way.

insurrec'tion, *n.*, an act of rebellion.

insurrec'tionary, *adj.*, seditious.

insurrec'tionist, *n.*, one who takes part in insurrection.

insusceptibil'ity, *n.*, the state of being insusceptible.

insuscep'tible, *adj.*, not susceptible, not readily affected.

in'swept, *adj.*, narrowed.

intact', *adj.*, untouched, uninjured.

inta'gliated, *adj.*, carved on the surface.

inta'glio, *n.*, a figure cut in a hard surface (*Lat.*).

in'take, *n.*, anything taken in; a narrowing-point; an inflow.

intangibil'ity, *n.*, the state of being intangible.

intan'gible, *adj.*, not perceptible to the touch; vague.

in'teger, *n.*, a whole number.

in'tegral, *adj.*, whole, entire; forming a whole.

in'tegrant, *adj.*, forming part of a whole.

in'tegrate, *v.t.* and *i.*, to combine the parts.

in'tegrated, *p.p.*, integrate.

in'tegrating, *pr.p.*, integrate.

integra'tion, *n.*, the act or effect of integrating.

integ'rity, *n.*, uprightness.

integ'ument, *n.*, a covering or membrane.

integumen'tary, *adj.*, pert; to an integument.

in'tellect, *n.*, the understanding; mental powers.

intellec'tion, *n.*, the action or process of understanding.

intellec'tual, *adj.*, rel. to the intellect; endowed with intellect.

intellec'tualism, *n.*, the doctrine of pure reason.

intellec'tualist, *n.*, one who. professes intellectualism.

intellectual'ity, *n.*, the quality of being intellectual.

intellec'tually, *adv.*, on the score of intellect.

intel'ligence, *n.*, understanding; information.

intel'ligencer, *n.*, one who conveys news.

intel'ligent, *adj.*, understanding, mentally alert; having mental powers.

intelligen'tial, *adj.*, rel. to intelligence.

intel'ligently, *adv.*, with intelligence.

intelligent'sia, *n.*, the intellectual or cultured classes (*Russ.*).

intelligibil'ity, *n.*, the quality of being intelligible.

intel'ligible, *adj.*, capable of being understood.

intel'ligibly, *adv.*, in a way to be understood.

intem'perance, *n.*, want of self-control, violence; drunkenness.

intem'perate, *adj.*, violent, excessive; given to drink.

intem'perately, *adv.*, in an intemperate way.

intem'perateness, *n.*, *i.q.* intemperance.

intend', *v.t.*, to purpose, to design.

intend'ancy, *n.*, superintendence.

intend'ant, *n.*, a superintendent.

intend'ed, *p.p.*, intend.

intend'ing, *pr.p.*, intend.

intense', *adj.*, strained, vehement, earnest.

intense'ly, *adv.*, earnestly, strongly.

intense'ness, *n.*, the state of being intense.

intensifica'tion, *n.*, the act or effect of intensifying.

inten'sified, *p.p.*, intensify.

inten'sifier, *n.*, anything that intensifies.

inten'sify, *v.t.*, to render intense; to strengthen.

inten'sifying, *pr.p.*, intensify.

inten'sion, *n.*, connotation, logical context; exertion.

inten'sity, *n.*, density, force, vehemence.

inten'sive, *adj.*, tending to intensify; intense.

inten'sively, *adv.*, in an intensive way.

intent', *adj.*, concentrated on; eager; *n.*, the purpose, the meaning.

inten'tion, *n.*, the design or purpose.

inten'tional, *adj.*, intended.

inten'tionally, *adv.*, on purpose.

inten'tioned, *adj.*, having intention, designed.

intent'ly, *adv.*, fixedly, earnestly.

intent'ness, *n.*, the state of being intent.

inter', *v.t.*, to bury.

in'ter-, prefix, between (*Lat.*).

interact', *v.i.*, to have mutual influence.

interac'tion, *n.*, reciprocal action.

interac'tive, *adj.*, active in a reciprocal way.

inter alia, *prep. phrase*, among other things (*Lat.*).

interblend', *v.t.* and *i.*, to mingle, to blend with each other.

interbred', *p.p.*, interbreed.

interbreed', *v.t.* and *i.*, to breed in, to crossbreed.

interbreed'ing, *pr.p.*, interbreed.

inter'calar, *adj.*, *i.q.* intercalary.

inter'calary, *adj.*, inserted, esp. in the calendar.

inter'calate, *v.t.*, to put between.

inter'calated, *p.p.*, intercalate.

inter'calating, *pr.p.*, intercalate.

intercala'tion, *n.*, the act of intercalating; an intercalated date.

intercede', *v.i.*, to intervene for; to plead in favour of.

interce'ded, *p.p.*, intercede.

interce'der, *n.*, one who intercedes.

interce'ding, *pr.p.*, intercede.

intercept', *v.t.*, to cut off, to stop, to obstruct.

intercept'ed, *p.p.*, intercept.

intercept'er, *n.*, one who intercepts.

intercept'ing, *pr.p.*, intercept.

intercep'tion, *n.*, the act of intercepting.

intercep'tor, *n.*, one who intercepts; a swift aeroplane for pursuit.

interces'sion, *n.*, the act of interceding; a prayer on behalf of; mediation.

interces'sional, *adj.*, rel. to intercession.

interces'sor, *n.*, one who intercedes.

interces'sory, *adj.*, interceding.

interchange', *v.t.*, to exchange reciprocally.

in'terchange, *n.*, a mutual exchange, commerce.

interchangeabil'ity, *n.*, the quality of being interchangeable.

interchange'able, *adj.*, able to be interchanged.

interchange'ableness, *n.*, *i.q.* interchangeability.

interchange'ably, *adv.*, reciprocally.

interchanged', *p.p.*, interchange.

interchang'ing, *pr.p.*, interchange.

intercolo'nial, *adj.*, pert. to colonial intercourse.

intercolum'nar, *adj.*, between columns.

intercolumnia'tion, *n.*, the architectural spacing between columns.

in'tercom, *n.*, a system of intercommunication.

intercommu'nicate, *v.i.*, to practise intercommunion.

intercommu'nion, *n.*, a sharing in communion.

intercommu'nity, *n.*, reciprocity.

intercos'tal, *adj.*, situated between the ribs.

in'tercourse, *n.*, fellowship; conversation; sexual connection.

intercur'rent, *adj.*, happening between.

interdepartmen'tal, *adj.*, between departments.

interdepend'ence, *n.*, the state of being interdependent.

interdepend'ent, *adj.*, mutually dependent.

interdepend'ently, *adv.*, in an interdependent way.

interdict', *v.t.*, to prohibit.

in'terdict, *n.*, a decree withholding the Sacraments.

interdict'ed, *p.p.*, interdict.

interdict'ing, *pr.p.*, interdict.

interdic'tion, *n.*, the act or result of interdicting.

interdict'ive, *adj.*, *i.q.* interdictory.

interdict'ory, *adj.*, interdicting, prohibitive.

in'terest, *v.t.*, to engage attention, to entertain; *n.*, concern, entertainment, advantage; premium for money loan.

in'terested, *p.p.*, interest.

in'teresting, *pr.p.*, interest; *adj.*, engaging, entertaining.

in'terestingly, *adv.*, in an interesting manner.

interfa'cial, *adj.*, between the faces of a many-sided figure.

interfere', *v.i.*, to meddle; to intervene.

interfered', *p.p.*, interfere.

interfer'ence, *n.*, meddling.

interfer'er, *n.*, one who interferes.

interfer'ing, *pr.p.*, interfere; *adj.*, meddlesome.

interfer'ingly, *adv.*, in an interfering way.

interferom'eter, *n.*, an instrument for measuring light waves.

interfuse', *v.t.* and *i.*, to spread between.

in'terim, *n.*, the meantime; *adj.*, for part of a longer period (*Lat.*).

inte'rior, *adj.*, inner; *n.*, the inside.

interja'cent, *adj.*, lying between.

interject', *v.t.*, to throw in, to put between.

interject'ed, *p.p.*, interject.

interject'ing, *pr.p.*, interject.

interjec'tion, *n.*, a word thrown in; an exclamation.

interjec'tional, *adj.*, exclamatory.

interlace', *v.t.* and *i.*, to twine.

interlaced', *p.p.*, interlace.

interla'cing, *pr.p.*, interlace.

interlard', *v.t.*, to diversify with mixture.

interlard'ed, *p.p.*, interlard.

interlard'ing, *pr.p.*, interlard.

interleave', *v.t.*, to introduce blank leaves in.

interleaved', *p.p.*, interleave.

interleav'ing, *pr.p.*, interleave.

interline', *v.t.*, to write between the lines.

interlin'eal, *adj.*, written between the lines.

interlin'ear, *adj.*, *i.q.* interlineal.

interlinea'tion, *n.*, writing between the lines.

interlined', *p.p.*, interline.

interling'ual, *adj.*, able to speak an international language based on Latin.

interlin'ing, *pr.p.*, interline.

interlink', *v.t.*, to connect with links.

interlock', *v.t.*, to lock into one another.

interlocked', *p.p.*, interlock.

interlock'ing, *pr.p.*, interlock.

interlocu'tion, *n.*, a conversation, a dialogue interchange of speech.

interloc'utor, *n.*, a questioner.

interloc'utory, *adj.*, questioning.

in'terloper, *n.*, an intruder.

interlu'cent, *adj.*, shining between.

in'terlude, *n.*, an interval in a performance; music played in the interval.

interlu'nar, *adj.*, rel. to the period of the moon's invisibility.

interlu'nary, adj., i.q. interlunar.

intermar'riage, n., marriage with a member of the same tribe or family; also marriage between different tribes.

intermar'ried, p.p., intermarry.

intermar'ry, v.i., to marry with a member of the same tribe or family.

intermar'rying, pr.p., intermarry.

intermed'dle, v.i., to interfere.

intermed'dled, p.p., intermeddle.

intermed'dler, n., one who intermeddles.

intermed'dling, pr.p., intermeddle.

interme'dial, adj., intervening.

interme'diary, adj., i.q. intermedial; n., a go-between.

interme'diate, v.i., to act as a go-between; adj., lying between; intervening.

intermedia'tion, n., the act of intermediating.

intermed'ium, n., an intermediate thing, a medium.

inter'ment, n., a burial.

intermez'zo, n., an interlude; a short musical movement (It.).

intermigra'tion, n., reciprocal migration.

inter'minable, adj., endless, unlimited.

inter'minableness, n., endlessness, boundlessness.

inter'minably, adv., endlessly.

intermin'gle, v.t. and i., to mix together.

intermin'gled, p.p., intermingle.

intermin'gling, pr.p., intermingle.

intermis'sion, n., a temporary cessation, a pause.

intermis'sive, adj., pausing for a space.

intermit', v.i., to leave off for a space.

intermit'ted, p.p., intermit.

intermit'tent, adj., coming and going at intervals.

intermit'tently, adv., in an intermittent way.

intermit'ting, pr.p., intermit.

intermix', v.t. and i., to intermingle.

intermixed', p.p., intermix.

intermix'ing, pr.p., intermix.

intermix'ture, n., a mixed mass.

intramu'ral, adj., between walls.

intern', v.t., to impose residence within defined limits.

inter'nal, adj., inner; domestic; not foreign.

inter'nally, adv., inwardly.

interna'tional, adj., rel. to intercourse between nations.

internationale', n., an international communist song (Fr.).

interna'tionalism, n., the principle of a common interest among nations.

interna'tionalist, n., one who advocates internationalism.

interna'tionalize, v.t., to make international.

interna'tionally, adv., by nations as a whole.

interne'cine, adj., mutually destructive.

interned', p.p., intern.

internee', n., one who suffers internment.

intern'ing, pr.p., intern.

intern'ment, n., the placing under confinement.

internun'cial, adj., rel. to an internuncio.

internun'cio, n., an ambassador.

interocean'ic, adj., lying between oceans.

interos'culate, v.i., to intermingle.

interpage', v.t., to insert on intermediate pages.

interpari'etal, adj., lying between the parietal bones.

interpel'late, v.i., to question.

interpel'lated, p.p., interpellate.

interpella'ting, pr.p., interpellate.

interpella'tion, n., a question.

interpen'etrate, v.t. and i., to penetrate thoroughly, to pervade reciprocally.

interplan'etary, adj., between planets.

in'terplay, n., reciprocal play; an exchange of viewpoints and attitudes.

interplead', v.i., to discuss an incidental question at law.

interplead'ed, p.p., interplead.

interplead'er, n., one who interpleads.

interplead'ing, pr.p., interplead.

In'terpol, n., the International Police Commission.

inter'polate, v.t., to insert new or alien matter in a writing.

inter'polated, p.p., interpolate.

inter'polater, n., one who interpolates.

inter'polating, pr.p., interpolate.

interpola'tion, n., the act of interpolating; an interpolated passage.

interpose', v.t. and i., to place between; to interfere, to mediate.

interposed', p.p., interpose.

interpo'ser, n., one who interposes.

interpo'sing, pr.p., interpose.

interposi'tion, n., an intervention.

inter'pret, v.t., to explain, to translate.

inter'pretable, adj., capable of explanation.

interpreta'tion, n., an explanation, an exposition.

inter'preted, p.p., interpret.

inter'preter, n., one who interprets.

inter'preting, pr.p., interpret.

inter'pretive, adj., explanatory.

interred', p.p., inter.

interreg'num, n., the suspension of government; a period between two reigns.

interrela'tion, n., mutual relation.

interrela'tionship, n., mutual relationship.

inter'ring, pr.p., inter.

inter'rogate, v.t., to question.

inter'rogated, p.p., interrogate.

interroga'tion, n., a question.

interrog'ative, adj., questioning.

inter'rogator, n., a questioner.

interrog'atory, adj., i.q. interrogative.

interrupt', v.t., to break off, to hinder.

interrupt'ed, p.p., interrupt.

interrupt'er, n., one who interrupts.

interrupt'ing, pr.p., interrupt.

interrup'tion, n., an act of interrupting; a breaking off; an obstruction.

interscap'ular, adj., between the shoulderblades.

interse'cant, adj., cutting across; intersecting.

intersect', v.t., to cut mutually; v.i., to meet and cross each other.

intersect'ed, p.p., intersect.

intersect'ing, pr.p., intersect.

intersec'tion, n., the point where lines cross each other.

intersec'tional, adj., crossing and cutting.

in'tersex, n., an organism with intermediate sex characteristics.

intersex'ual, adj., relationship between the sexes.

in'terspace, n., an intervening space.

intersperse', v.t., to scatter among.

interspersed', p.p., intersperse.

interspers'ing, pr.p., intersperse.

intersper'sion, n., the act of interspersing.

interstel'lar, adj., between or amid stars.

interstel'lary, adj., i.q. interstellar.

inter'stice, n., a narrow chink, a crevice.

intersti'tial, adj., having interstices.

intertex'ture, n., interwoven texture.

in'tertrade, n., reciprocal trade.

intertri'bal, adj., pert. to the relations between tribes.

intertrop'ical, adj., between the tropics.

intertwine', v.t. and i., to twist together.

intertwined', p.p., intertwine.

intertwi'ning, pr.p., intertwine.

intertwi'ningly, adv., interlacing.

intertwist', v.t., to twist together.

intertwist'ed, p.p., intertwist.

intertwist'ing, pr.p., intertwist.

in'terval, n., an intervening space.

intervene', v.i., to come between; to interfere.

intervened', p.p., intervene.

interve'ner, n., one who intervenes.

interve'nient, adj., intervening.

interve'ning, pr.p., intervene.

interven'tion, n., the act of intervening; an interference.

in'terview, v.t., to hold an interview with; n., a meeting to elicit views or information by question and answer.

in'terviewed, p.p., interview.

in'terviewer, n., one who interviews.

in'terviewing, pr.p., interview.

intervolve', v.t., to wind, to roll up things within each other.

interweave', v.t., to weave together.

interweaved', p.p., interweave.

interweav'ing, pr.p., interweave.

interwind', v.t., to wind together.

interwov'en, p.p., interweave.

interzon'al, adj., between zones.

intes'table, adj., not qualified to make a will.

intes'tacy, n., the state of an intestate.

intes'tate, adj., not having made a proper will; not legally bequeathed; n., one who leaves no will.

intes'tinal, adj., rel. to the intestines.

intes'tine, adj., internal, domestic; n., the alimentary canal. In pl., the internal organs.

in'timacy, n., the state of being intimate; familiarity.

in'timate, adj., closely associated; innermost; n., a familiar friend and confidant.

in'timate, v.t., to hint, to make known indirectly.

in'timated, p.p., intimate.

in'timately, adv., closely, familiarly.

in'timating, pr.p., intimate.

intima'tion, n., an indirect hint, a suggestion.

intim'idate, v.t., to cause to be afraid; to terrorize.

intim'idated, p.p., intimidate.

intim'idating, pr.p., intimidate.

intimida'tion, n., terrorism.

intim'ity, n., inwardness, privacy.

intit'uled, adj., entitled.

in'to, prep., moving to and remaining in.

intoed, adj., having toes turned inwards.

intol'erable, adj., not to be tolerated; unendurable.

intol'erably, adv., insufferably.

intol'erance, n., the want of forbearance.

intol'erant, adj., not tolerant, bigoted.

intol'erantly, adv., with intolerance.

in'tonate, v.t., to intone, to sound the notes of a scale.

in'tonated, p.p., intonate.

in'tonating, pr.p., intonate.

intona'tion, n., voice-modulation; the act of intoning.

in'tonator, n., a monochord accurately divided into parts.

intone', v.t. and i., to recite musically.

intoned', p.p., intone.

inton'ing, pr.p., intone.

intox'icant, n., an alcoholic drink; anything that causes high excitement.

intox'icate, v.t., to make drunk; to elate greatly.

intox'icated, p.p., intoxicate.

intox'icating, adj., causing great elation; pr.p., intoxicate.

intoxica'tion, n., the state of drunkenness.

intractabil'ity, n., the quality of being intractable.

intrac'table, adj., unmanageable; obstinate.

intrac'tably, adv., in an intractable way.

in tra'da, n., an introduction (mus.).

intra'dos, n., a soffit.

intramu'ral, adj., within walls.

intra'mus'cular, adj., between muscles.

intranquil'lity, n., restlessness.

intran'sigence, n., obstinacy, stubbornness, irreconcilability. Also **intransigeance.**

intran'sigent, adj., irreconcilable. Also *intransigeant*.

intran'sitive, adj., not passing over to an object.

intransmis'sible, adj., not able to be transmitted.

intranspar'ent, adj., opaque.

in'trant, n., one who enters a college or office.

intraven'ous, adj., within the veins; put into the veins by injection.

intrench', v.t., to dig a trench; to fortify with a trench. Also *entrench*.

intrench'ed, p.p., intrench.

intrench'ing, pr.p., intrench.

intrench'ment, n., the act of intrenching; an intrenched position.

intrep'id, adj., fearless, dauntless.

intrepid'ity, n., fearlessness.

intrep'idly, adv., fearlessly.

in'tricacy, n., an entanglement, complexity.

in'tricate, adj., involved, entangled.

in'tricately, adv., in an intricate way.

intrigue', v.i., to plot, to scheme; n., a plot, an underhand scheme.

intrigued', p.p., intrigue.

intrigu'er, n., one who intrigues.

intrigu'ing, pr.p., intrigue.

intrin'sic, adj., inherent; in itself; essential.

intrin'sically, adv., essentially; in itself.

introces'sion, n., a depression.

introduce', v.t., to bring in; to make known.

introduced', p.p., introduce.

introdu'cer, n., one who introduces.

introdu'cing, pr.p., introduce.

introd'uction, n., the act of introducing; something leading up, as the Introduction before a book.

introduc'tive, adj., leading up to, beginning.

introduc'tory, adj., i.q. introductive.

intro'it, n., the anthem preceding the Mass.

introjec'tion, n., mental identification with another person or object.

intromis'sion, n., an insertion; an introduction.

intromit', v.t., to insert, to place within.

intromit'ted, p.p., intromit.

intromit'ting, pr.p., intromit.

introrse', adj., turned inwards.

introspect', v.t., to look into; to examine.

introspec'tion, n., self-examination.

introspec'tive, adj., self-examining.

introver'sion, n., the act of turning inward.

introvert', v.t., to turn inward; n., one who is introspective.

introvert'ed, p.p., introvert.

introvert'ing, pr.p., introvert.

intrude', v.t., to push in without permission; v.i., to force oneself upon.

intru'ded, p.p., intrude.

intru'der, n., one who intrudes.

intru'ding, pr.p., intrude.

intru'sion, n., the act of intruding; an encroachment.

intru'sive, adj., coming in uninvited.

intrusive'ly, adv., in an intrusive way.

intrust', see entrust.

intuba'tion, n., the process of inserting a tube.

in'tuit, v.t. and i., to know by intuition.

intui'tion, n., immediate perception; instinctive knowledge.

intui'tional, adj., having immediate apprehension or insight.

intu'itive, adj., immediately perceptive; having knowledge gained without conscious reasoning.

intu'itively, adv., in an intuitive way.

intumesce', v.i., to swell.

intumesced', p.p., intumesce.

intumes'cence, n., a swelling.

intumes'cing, pr.p., intumesce.

intussuscep'tion, n., the state of being received within; a partial displacement of the intestine.

intwine', see entwine.

intwist', see entwist.

in'undate, v.t., to flood, to submerge, to overwhelm.

in'undated, p.p., inundate.

in'undating, pr.p., inundate.

inunda'tion, n., a deluge, an overflow.

inur'bane, adj., not urbane, discourteous.

inure', v.t., to accustom, to harden.

inured', p.p., inure.

inure'ment, n., the act of inuring.

inur'ing, pr.p., inure.

inurn', v.t., to enclose in an urn.

inurned', p.p., inurn.

inurn'ing, pr.p., inurn.

inu'tile, adj., useless.

inutil'ity, n., uselessness.

invade', v.t., to come into, to attack, to encroach upon.

inva'ded, p.p., invade.

inva'der, n., one who invades.

inva'ding, pr.p., invade.

invag'inate, v.t., to sheath.

invagina'tion, n., i.q. intussusception.

in'valid, n., a sick person; adj., sick, weakly.

inval'id, adj., not valid; without authority or legal force.

inval'idate, v.t., to render invalid.

inval'idated, p.p., invalidate.

inval'idating, pr.p., invalidate.

invalid'ity, n., the state of being null and void.

inval'uable, adj., priceless; of the greatest value.

in'var, n., a nickel and steel alloy.

invariabil'ity, n., the quality of being invariable.

inva'riable, adj., not subject to variation; always the same.

inva'riableness, n., i.q. invariability.

inva'riably, adv., constantly.

inva'sion, n., the act of invading; an attack.

inva'sive, adj., making invasion.

invec'tive, *adj.*, abusive; *n.*, vituperation, railing.

inveigh', *v.i.*, to rail against; to speak in denunciation.

inveighed', *p.p.*, inveigh.

inveigh'er, *n.*, one who inveighs.

inveigh'ing, *pr.p.*, inveigh.

invei'gle, *v.t.*, to entice, to lead astray.

invei'gled, *p.p.*, inveigle.

invei'gler, *n.*, one who inveigles.

invei'gling, *pr.p.*, inveigle.

invent', *v.t.*, to find out, to originate, to contrive.

invent'ed, *p.p.*, invent.

invent'ing, *pr.p.*, invent.

inven'tion, *n.*, the act of inventing; something invented.

invent'ive, *adj.*, able to invent; rel. to invention.

invent'or, *n.*, one who invents.

in'ventory, *n.*, a list or schedule of household or other effects.

invera'city, *n.*, untruthfulness.

inverse', *adj.*, contrary, indirect.

inverse'ly, *adv.*, in an inverted order or degree.

inver'sion, *n.*, the act of inverting; the state of being inverted; a change of order or position.

invert', *v.t.*, to place upside down; to change the order of; to turn inside out, *n.*, an inverted arch; a person with inverted sex instinct.

invert'ant, *adj.*, reversed (*her.*).

inver'tebral, *adj.*, *i.q.* invertebrate.

inver'tebrate, *adj.*, backboneless, irresolute; *n.*, an animal without a backbone.

inver'tebrated, *adj.*, *i.q.* invertebrate.

invert'ed, *p.p.*, invert.

invert'edly, *adv.*, in an inverted way.

invert'ing, *pr.p.*, invert.

invest', *v.t.*, to lay out; to clothe with official garb and so to give

authority; to besiege closely; to lay out money on; to put money into stocks, etc.

invest'ed, *p.p.*, invest.

inves'tigable, *adj.*, able to be investigated.

inves'tigate, *v.t.*, to track out, to search into.

inves'tigated, *p.p.*, investigate.

inves'tigating, *pr.p.*, investigate.

investiga'tion, *n.*, a careful search.

inves'tigative, *adj.*, making search.

inves'tigator, *n.*, one who investigates.

inves'tigatory, *adj.*, *i.q.* investigative.

invest'ing, *pr.p.*, invest.

invest'iture, *n.*, the act or ceremony of conferring authority, esp. of delivering the ring and staff to a bishop.

invest'ment, *n.*, the laying out of money; money invested; the object on which money is laid out; a close siege.

invest'or, *n.*, one who invests.

invet'eracy, *n.*, the state of being inveterate.

invet'erate, *adj.*, deep-rooted; of long standing.

invi'able, *adj.*, incapable of surviving.

invid'ious, *adj.*, exciting dislike or envy; offensive.

invid'iously, *adv.*, in an invidious way.

invi'gilate, *v.i.*, to supervise (esp. examinations).

invigila'tion, *n.*, supervising.

invi'gilator, *n.*, a supervisor.

invig'orate, *v.t.*, to strengthen, to brace.

invig'orated, *p.p.*, invigorate.

invig'orating, *pr.p.*, invigorate.

invigora'tion, *n.*, the effect of invigorating.

invincibil'ity, *n.*, the state of being invincible.

invin'cible, *adj.*, unconquerable.

invin'cibly, *adv.*, unconquerably.

inviolabil'ity, *n.*, the state of being inviolable.

invi'olable, *adj.*, not to be violated, or broken, or profaned.

invi'olably, *adv.*, in an inviolable way.

invi'olate, *adj.*, not violated, uninjured.

invisibil'ity, *n.*, the state of being invisible.

invis'ible, *adj.*, that cannot be seen.

invis'ibly, *adv.*, in an invisible way.

invita'tion, *n.*, the act of inviting.

invi'tatory, *adj.*, of the nature of an invitation; *n.*, a psalm inviting to worship (as Ps. xcv).

invite', *v.t.*, to bid, to summon, to ask to come.

invi'ted, *p.p.*, invite.

invi'ter, *n.*, one who invites.

invi'ting, *pr.p.*, invite; *adj.*, enticing, alluring.

invi'tingly, *adv.*, enticingly.

invit'rifiable, *adj.*, that cannot be vitrified.

in'vocate, *v.t.*, to call upon, to address in prayer.

invoca'tion, *n.*, the act of invoking; an incantation.

invoc'atory, *adj.*, invoking.

in'voice, *v.t.*, to make a bill of; *n.*, a list of the items of a bill.

in'voiced, *p.p.*, invoice.

in'voicing, *pr.p.*, invoice.

invoke', *v.t.*, to call upon, to supplicate.

invoked', *p.p.*, invoke.

invo'king, *pr.p.*, invoke.

invol'ucel, *n.*, a diminutive involucre (*bot.*).

involucel'late, *adj.*, furnished with involucels.

involu'cral, *adj.*, having an involucre.

involu'crate, *adj.*, *i.q.* involucral.

in'volucre, *n.*, a whorl surrounding a flower.

in'volucred, *adj.*, having an involucre.

involu'cret, *n.*, *i.q.* involucel.

involu'crum, *n.*, *i.q.* involucre.

invol'untarily, *adv.*, in an involuntary way.

invol'untary, *adj.*, unintentioned; not of one's own will.

in'volute, *adj.*, twisted, turned inwards.

in'voluted, *adj.*, *i.q.* involute.

involu'tion, *n.*, a complication; the state of being involved.

involve', *v.t.*, to wrap round; to include; to entangle; to become concerned in.

involved', *p.p.*, involve.

involve'ment, *n.*, concern in; engagement in; a complicated affair.

involv'ing, *pr.p.*, involve.

invulnerabil'ity, *n.*, the state or quality of being invulnerable.

invul'nerable, *adj.*, that cannot be wounded.

in'ward, *adj.*, internal, inner; *adv.*, towards the interior.

in'wardly, *adv.*, internally.

in'wardness, *n.*, the true, inner meaning.

in'wards, *adv.*, *i.q.* inward.

inweave', *v.t.*, to entwine; to weave into.

inweav'ing, *pr.p.*, inweave.

in'working, *n.*, an operation from within.

inwove', *p.p.*, inweave.

inwo'ven, *p.p.*, inweave.

inwrap', *v.t.*, to envelop.

inwrapped', *p.p.*, inwrap.

inwrap'ping, *pr.p.*, inwrap.

inwrought', *adj.*, worked in (as in metal work).

i'odate, *n.*, an iodic acid salt.

iod'ic, *adj.*, containing iodine.

i'odide, *n.*, a compound of iodine.

i'odine, *n.*, a nonmetallic chemical element.

i'odize, *v.t.*, to treat with iodine.

i'odized, *p.p.*, iodize.

i'odizing, *pr.p.*, iodize.

io'doform, *n.*, a compound of iodine, with antiseptic properties.

i'olite, *n.*, a violet-coloured gem.

i'on, *n.*, a component part of a substance after electrolytic decomposition.

Io'nian, *adj.*, rel. to Ionia; *n.*, a native of I.

Ion'ic, *adj.*, *i.q.* Ionian; also the architectural term for one of the classical orders; *n.*, a dialect of Greek.

ion'ium, *n.*, a radioactive isotope of thorium.

ioniza'tion, *n.*, the process of ionizing.

i'onize, *v.t.*, to convert or split into ions.

ion'osphere, *n.*, the Heaviside Layer, or layer above the earth's surface where ionization takes place.

io'ta, *n.*, the ninth letter of the Greek alphabet; a very small part, a jot.

ipecacuan'ha, *n.*, a S. American shrub; the emetic made from its root.

ip'se dix'it, *n.*, a substantive phrase = he himself has said; a dictum (*Lat.*).

ip'so fac'to, adverbial phrase = in very fact; by that means (*Lat.*).

Ira'nian, *adj.*, pert. or rel. to Iran (Persia); *n.*, a native of I.

Iraqi, Iraki, *adj.*, pert. or rel. to Iraq; *n.*, a native of I.

irascibil'ity, *n.*, irritability, hot temper.

iras'cible, *adj.*, hot-tempered.

iras'cibleness, *n.*, *i.q.* irascibility.

iras'cibly, *adv.*, irritably.

irate', *adj.*, angry.

ire, *n.*, anger, wrath.

ire'ful, *adj.*, very angry.

ire'fully, *adv.*, very angrily.

iren'ical, *adj.*, rel. to an irenicon.

ire'nicon, *n.*, a proposal of peace. Also *Eire*-*nicon*.

i'rid, *n.*, one of the iris family.

irida'ceous, *adj.*, like an iris.

i'rides, *n.*, pl. of iris.

irides'cence, *n.*, the state of being iridescent.

irides'cent, *adj.*, shining with the colours of the rainbow.

irid'ium, *n.*, a hard white metallic element.

iridos'mine, *n.*, an alloy mixture of osmium and iridium.

i'ris, *n.*, the rainbow; the coloured part of the eye showing through the pupil; a plant family so named.

i'risated, *adj.*, iridescent.

i'riscope, *n.*, a plate for showing the prismatic colours.

i'rises, *n.*, the English pl. of iris.

I'rish, *adj.*, pert. to Ireland and the Irish; *n.*, the Irish language.

I'rishism, *n.*, an Irish idiom.

I'rishman, *n.*, a native of Ireland.

I'rishry, *n.*, the Irish people collectively.

iri'tis, *n.*, inflammation of the iris.

irk, *v.t.*, to annoy.

irk'some, *adj.*, disagreeable, annoying.

irk'someness, *n.*, troublesomeness.

i'ron, *v.t.*, to smooth with a hot iron; to fetter; *adj.*, made of iron, resembling iron; *n.*, the common metal so named; any iron weapon or implement; a golf club.

i'roned, *p.p.*, iron.

i'roner, *n.*, anything that irons.

iron'ic, *adj.*, *i.q.* ironical.

iron'ical, *adj.*, of the nature of irony; meaning the opposite of what is said.

iron'ically, *adv.*, in an ironical way.

i'roning, *pr.p.*, iron.

i'ronmaster, *n.*, an iron manufacturer.

i'ronmonger, *n.*, a dealer in goods made of iron.

i'ronmongery, *n.*, goods made of iron.

i'ron-mould, *n.*, a stain of iron rust.

i'ronside, *n.*, a man of sturdy, resolute character.

i'ronwork, *n.*, anything made of iron.

i'rony, *n.*, saying something that means more than appears on the surface, and conceals contempt, ridicule, etc.

Iro'quois, *n.*, a tribe of N. American Indians.

irra'diance, *n.*, the act or state of irradiating.

irra'diancy, *n.*, *i.q.* irradiance.

irra'diant, *adj.*, illuminating.

irra'diate, *v.t.*, to illuminate.

irra'diated, *p.p.*, irradiate.

irra'diating, *pr.p.*, irradiate.

irradia'tion, *n.*, illumination.

irra'tional, *adj.*, not rational, unreasoning, absurd.

irrational'ity, *n.*, the quality of being irrational.

irra'tionally, *adv.*, in an irrational way.

irreclaim'able, *adj.*, unable to be reclaimed.

irreclaim'ably, *adv.*, in an irreclaimable way.

irreconci'lable, *adj.*, not to be reconciled.

irreconci'lably, *adv.*, beyond reconciling.

irrec'onciled, *adj.*, unreconciled.

irrecov'erable, *adj.*, unable to be recovered.

irrecov'erably, *adv.*, beyond recovery.

irrecus'able, *adj.*, not to be refused.

irredeem'able, *adj.*, unable to be redeemed; not to be converted into cash.

irredeem'ably, *adv.*, past redemption.

irredu'cible, *adj.*, unable to be reduced.

irrefragabil'ity, *n.*, the quality of being irrefragable.

irref'ragable, *adj.*, that cannot be broken; irrefutable.

irrefu'table, *adj.*, that cannot be refuted or disproved.

irreg'ular, *adj.*, not regular, not straight, not honourable.

irregular'ity, *n.*, a departure from the rule; improper conduct.

irreg'ularly, *adv.*, in an irregular way.

irrel'ative, *adj.*, unrelated, unconnected.

irrel'evance, *n.*, something that is not pertinent.

irrel'evancy, *n.*, *i.q.* irrelevance.

irrel'evant, *adj.*, not pertinent; off the point.

irrel'evantly, *adv.*, in an irrelevant way.

irrelig'ion, *n.*, ungodliness, unbelief.

irrelig'ious, *adj.*, destitute of religion.

irrelig'iously, *adv.*, in an irreligious way.

irreme'diable, *adj.*, past remedy.

irreme'diably, *adv.*, in an irremediable way.

irremiss'ible, *adj.*, not remissible.

irremov'able, *adj.*, that cannot be removed.

irremov'ably, *adv.*, fixedly.

irreparabil'ity, *n.*, the quality of being irreparable.

irrep'arable, *adj.*, not to be repaired or made good.

irrep'arably, *adv.*, in an irreparable way.

irrepealabil'ity, *n.*, the state of being irrepealable.

irrepeal'able, *adj.*, irrevocable, not to be repealed.

irrepeal'ably, *adv.*, irrevocably.

irreplace'able, *adj.*, that cannot be replaced.

irreprehen'sible, *adj.*, blameless.

irrepres'sible, *adj.*, not to be repressed or kept down.

irreproach'able, *adj.*, beyond reproach.

irreproach'ably, *adv.*, in an irreproachable way.

irreprov'able, *adj.*, not to be reproved.

irresistibil'ity, *n.*, the quality of being irresistible.

irresist'ible, *adj.*, that cannot be resisted.

irresist'ibly, *adv.*, in an irresistible way.

irres'oluble, *adj.*, that cannot be resolved.

irres'olute, *adj.*, hesitating, weak in purpose.

irresolu'tion, *n.*, weakness of purpose, hesitation.

irresolvabil'ity, *n.*, the quality of being irresolvable.

irresolv'able, *adj.*, *i.q.* irresoluble.

irrespec'tive, *adj.*, not having regard to.

irrespec'tively, *adv.*, without regard to.

irresponsibil'ities, *n.*, pl. of irresponsibility.

irresponsibil'ity, *n.*, the state or quality of being irresponsible.

irrespon'sible, *adj.*, not answerable; incapable of fulfilling obligations.

irrespon'sibly, *adv.*, in an irresponsible way.

irreten'tive, *adj.*, not retentive.

irretriev'able, *adj.*, that cannot be retrieved.

irretriev'ably, *adv.*, in an irretrievable way.

irrev'erence, *n.*, the want of reverence.

irrev'erent, *adj.*, wanting in reverence or respect.

irrev'erently, *adv.*, in an irreverent way.

irrevers'ible, *adj.*, that cannot be reversed.

irrevocabil'ity, *n.*, the state of being irrevocable.

irrev'ocable, *adj.*, beyond recall.

irrev'ocably, *adv.*, in an irrevocable way.

irrifran'gible, *adj.*, unbreakable, incapable of refraction.

ir'rigable, *adj.*, capable of being irrigated.

ir'rigant, *adj.*, serving to irrigate; *n.*, a ditch.

ir'rigate, *v.t.*, to supply land with water.

ir'rigated, *p.p.*, irrigate.

ir'rigating, *pr.p.*, irrigate.

irriga'tion, *n.*, the act or system of irrigating.

irrig'uous, *adj.*, watersupplying.

irritabil'ity, *n.*, the state of being irritable.

ir'ritable, *adj.*, easily provoked; ill-tempered.

ir'ritancy, *n.*, making, being, null and void; irritation, annoyance.

ir'ritant, *adj.*, causing irritation; *n.*, anything that causes irritation.

ir'ritate, *v.t.*, to vex, to annoy, to inflame.

ir'ritated, *p.p.*, irritate.

ir'ritating, *adj.*, annoying; *pr.p.*, irritate.

irrita'tion, *n.*, vexation, annoyance, inflammation.

ir'ritative, *adj.*, *i.q.* irritant.

ir'ritatory, *adj.*, *i.q.* irritant.

irrora'tion, *n.*, a small colour-marking.

irrup'tion, *n.*, a bursting in; an invasion.

irrup'tive, *adj.*, bursting in.

is, *v.*, the third pers. sing., pres. tense of the verb *to be*.

isabell'a, *adj.*, greyish yellow; *n.*, a kind of grape and peach.

isagog'ics, *n. pl.*, introductory writings.

ischiad'ic, *adj.*, sciatic.

is'chiagra, n., sciatic gout.

ischiat'ic, adj., rel. to the hip.

ischuret'ic, adj., relieving ischuria; n., a remedy for ischuria.

ischu'ria, n., the retention of urine.

is'chury, n., i.q. ischuria.

Ish'maelite, n., a descendant of Ishmael; an outcast.

i'singlass, n., a gelatinous product from the viscera of certain fish.

Is'lam, n., the religion of Mohammed; the Mohammedan world.

Is'lamism, n., Mohammedanism.

Is'lamite, n., a Mohammedan.

Islamit'ic, adj., rel. to Mohammedanism.

is'land, n., land surrounded by water.

is'lander, n., a dweller on an island.

isle, n., an island; v.t. and i., to place or to live on an island.

is'let, n., a little island.

ism, n., a set of doctrines.

isn't, abbrev. of is not (colloq.).

i'sobar, n., a line drawn or supposed to be drawn through a number of places where the barometric pressure is the same.

isobar'ic, adj., showing equal pressure.

isobaromet'ric, adj., i.q. isobaric.

isochromat'ic, adj., of the same colour.

isoch'ronal, adj., of equal lengths of time.

isoch'ronism, n., the quality of being isochronal.

isoch'ronous, adj., i.q. isochronal.

iso'cynate, n., of the group of cyanic acid and cyanates.

isog'onal, adj., having equal angles.

isogon'ic, adj., descriptive of lines on a map (isogonic lines) indicating equal magnetic variation at any time.

i'solate, v.t., to insulate; to place in a detached position; to separate; n., a person who prefers to be alone.

i'solated, p.p., isolate.

i'solating, pr.p., isolate.

isola'tion, n., the state of being isolated.

isola'tionism, n., the policy of non-involvement with other nations.

isola'tionist, n., one who advocates isolationism.

isomer'ic, adj., composed of the same elements in the same proportions.

isom'erism, n., the state of being isomeric.

isomet'ric, adj., of equal measure.

isomet'rical, adj., i.q. isometric.

isomor'phic, adj., of similar groups, superficially alike.

isomor'phism, n., the state of being isomorphous.

isomor'phous, adj., identical in construction; like in form.

isonom'ic, adj., having equal rights.

ison'omy, n., the equality of civil rights.

i'sopod, n., one of the Isopoda.

I'sopoda, n. pl., a group of crustaceans, having seven pairs of legs.

isop'odous, adj., rel. to the Isopoda.

isos'celes, adj., having two equal sides.

isostem'onous, adj., having as many stamens as petals and sepals.

isoth'eral, adj., rel. to isothere.

i'sothere, n., a line joining points where the same mean summer temperatures are shown.

i'sotherm, n., a line joining places which have the same temperature.

isother'mal, adj., rel. to an isotherm.

iso'tone, n., an atomic particle distinguished by the number of protons.

isoton'ic, adj., with equal tones; rel. to an isotone.

is'otope, n., an element distinguished by the nuclear mass of its atoms.

isotop'ic, adj., from other forms of the same element.

isot'opy n., the study of isotopes.

is'otron, n., an instrument for separating uranium isotopes.

isotrop'ic, adj., exhibiting the same properties in every direction.

iso'type, n., a plant or animal common to two or more regions. A form of graphical statistical presentation.

Is'raeli, adj., pert. or rel. to Israel; n., a native of I.

Is'raelite, n., a descendant of Jacob; a Hebrew.

Is'raelitic, adj., i.q. Israelitish.

Is'raelitish, adj., rel. to Israel.

is'suable, adj., able to be issued, or to have a legal issue upon it.

is'sue, v.i., to come out; to arise; to result; v.t., to put forth, to publish; n., anything that issues; an offspring; an end or result; a point of discussion or at law.

is'sued, p.p., issue.

is'suer, n., one who issues.

is'suing, pr.p., issue.

isth'mus, n., a narrow strip of land connecting two larger areas.

it, pron., neuter of he; the thing referred to.

Ital'ian, adj., pert. to Italy and the Italians; n., a native of I; the language of I.

Ital'ianize, v.t., to make Italian; v.i., to become Italian.

ital'ic, adj., rel. to Italy; in the italic type; n., a peculiar kind of printing type.

ital'icize, v.t., to print in italic.

ital'icized, p.p., italicize.

ital'icizing, pr.p., italicize.

ital'ics, n. pl., letters with specific style or slope used for emphasis or distinction.

itch, v.i., to suffer from skin irritation; to have a great desire for; n., a distressing skin disease; a feeling of skin irritation.

itched, p.p., itch.

itch'ing, pr.p., itch.

itch'y, adj., having the itch.

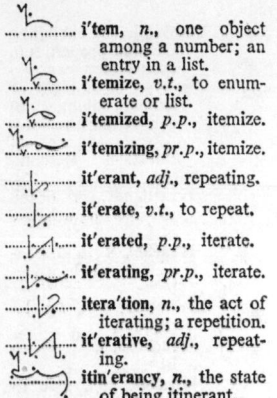

i'tem, *n.*, one object among a number; an entry in a list.

i'temize, *v.t.*, to enumerate or list.

i'temized, *p.p.*, itemize.

i'temizing, *pr.p.*, itemize.

it'erant, *adj.*, repeating.

it'erate, *v.t.*, to repeat.

it'erated, *p.p.*, iterate.

it'erating, *pr.p.*, iterate.

itera'tion, *n.*, the act of iterating; a repetition.

it'erative, *adj.*, repeating.

itin'erancy, *n.*, the state of being itinerant.

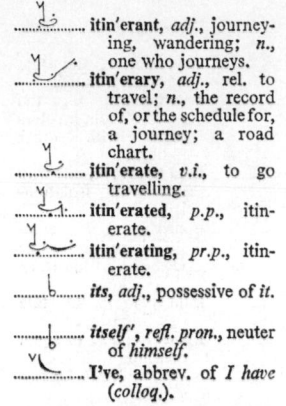

itin'erant, *adj.*, journeying, wandering; *n.*, one who journeys.

itin'erary, *adj.*, rel. to travel; *n.*, the record of, or the schedule for, a journey; a road chart.

itin'erate, *v.i.*, to go travelling.

itin'erated, *p.p.*, itinerate.

itin'erating, *pr.p.*, itinerate.

its, *adj.*, possessive of *it*.

itself', *refl. pron.*, neuter of *himself*.

I've, abbrev. of *I have* (*colloq.*).

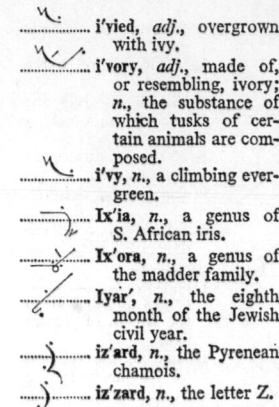

i'vied, *adj.*, overgrown with ivy.

i'vory, *adj.*, made of, or resembling, ivory; *n.*, the substance of which tusks of certain animals are composed.

i'vy, *n.*, a climbing evergreen.

Ix'ia, *n.*, a genus of S. African iris.

Ix'ora, *n.*, a genus of the madder family.

Iyar', *n.*, the eighth month of the Jewish civil year.

iz'ard, *n.*, the Pyrenean chamois.

iz'zard, *n.*, the letter Z.

J

jab, v.t., to give a sharp thrust or poke; n., an abrupt blow; a sudden thrust; an injection (med., slang).

jab'ber, v.i., to talk rapidly and indistinctly; v.t., to utter rapidly; n., rapid, indistinct talk.

jab'bered, p.p., jabber.

jab'berer, n., one who jabbers.

jab'bering, pr.p., jabber.

jab'iru, n., a large tropical South American bird of the stork family.

jaboran'di, n., dried leaflets of a Brazilian plant.

jabot', n., an ornamental frill (Fr.).

jac'amar, n., a tropical American climbing bird.

jac'ana, n., a small tropical wading bird.

jacaran'da, n., hard wood trees found in America.

jac'inth, n., the gem, also called hyacinth.

jack, n., a contrivance for raising weights, turning a spit, pulling off boots, etc.; the knave of a suit of cards; a flag; a pike (fish); a leather pitcher; a small bowl (the game of bowls); v.t., to hoist with a jack.

jack'al, n., a carnivorous wild animal akin to the dog and the wolf.

jack'anapes, n., an impertinent fellow.

jack'ass, n., a male ass; a stupid fellow.

jack'-block, n., a block fixed high in a ship, and used for raising light spars, etc.

jack'boot, n., a large boot reaching above the knee.

jack'daw, n., a small species of crow.

jack'et, n., a short coat; a cover of many kinds; v.t., to provide with a jacket; to beat.

jack'eted, adj., furnished with a jacket; p.p., jacket.

jack'eting, pr.p., jacket; n., a beating.

jack'knife, n., a large pocket clasp-knife.

jack'plane, n., a large joiner's plane.

jack'pot, n., an accumulating pool, a lottery prize.

jack'-pudding, n., a buffoon.

jack'screw, n., a jack for lifting heavy weights.

Jack-tar', n., a sailor.

jack'wood, n., a heavy, fine-grained, yellow wood used in cabinet-making.

Jacobe'an, adj., a term specially applied to early 17th cent. architecture.

Jac'obin, n., a violent republican.

Jacobin'ic, adj., resembling the French Jacobins of 1789.

Jacobin'ical, adj., i.q. Jacobinic.

Jac'obinism, n., the principles of Jacobins.

Jac'obite, n., an adherent of James II of England and his descendants.

Jacobit'ical, adj., rel. to the Jacobites.

Jac'obitism, n., the principles of the Jacobites.

Ja'cob's-lad'der, n., a cottage-garden flower; a ship's rope-ladder with wooden rungs.

jac'onet, n., a light, soft muslin of open texture.

Jacquard', adj., a term descriptive of a loom for weaving figured goods.

jacta'tion, n., an agitation of the body; morbid restlessness.

jactita'tion, n., a false assertion; a frequent tossing about of the body.

jac'ulator, n., the archer fish.

jade, n., a hard greenish stone with an oily-looking surface; a mean woman, a hussy; v.t., to fatigue.

ja'ded, adj., very weary; p.p., jade.

ja'ding, pr.p., jade.

Jaeg'er, n., a kind of woollen clothing material.

Jaff'a, n., a kind of dessert orange.

jag, v.t., to notch; n., a notch; a sharp protuberance.

jäg'er, n., a member of the German rifle corps.

jagged, p.p., jag.

jag'ged, adj., having notches or teeth.

jag'gedness, n., the state of being jagged.

jag'ger, n., one who, or that which, jags.

jagg'ery, n., coarse brown Indian sugar.

jag'gy, adj., i.q. jagged.

jag'uar, n., the American tiger.

jail, n., i.q. gaol.

jail'bird, n., i.q. gaolbird.

jailed, p.p., i.q. gaoled.

jail'er, n., i.q. gaoler.

Jain, n., one of a Hindu religious sect whose creed resembles Buddhism.

Jain'ism, n., the doctrines of the Jains.

jal'ap, n., a purgative medicine.

jalop(p)'y, n., a dilapidated motor car.

jalousie', n., a kind of outside venetian blind (Fr.).

jam, n., a preserve of fruit boiled with sugar and water; a press of people; v.t., to wedge in; to squeeze tight; to render immovable.

Jamai'can, adj., pert. or rel. to Jamaica; n., a native of J.

jamb, n., the vertical side-piece of an opening in a wall.

jamboree', n., a rally of scouts or girl guides; a celebration; a hand in euchre.

jammed, *p.p.*, jam.

jam'ming, *pr.p.*, jam.

jam'my, *adj.*, sticky with jam; lucky (*slang*).

jan'gle, *n.*, a discordant sound; *v.t.*, to cause to sound harshly; *v.i.*, to sound inharmoniously; to quarrel in words.

jan'gled, *p.p.*, jangle.

jan'gler, *n.*, a babbler.

jan'gling, *pr.p.*, jangle.

jani'form, *adj.*, two-faced; having face on two sides; double-headed.

jan'itor, *n.*, a door-keeper.

janiza'rian, *adj.*, rel. to the janizaries.

jan'izary, *n.*, a soldier of the Turkish foot-guards.

Jan'senism, *n.*, the doctrine of the Jansenists.

Jan'senist, *n.*, a follower of Bishop Jansen of Ypres.

Jan'uary, *n.*, the first month of the year.

Jan'us, *n.*, an ancient Italian and Tuscan God.

japan', *n.*, work varnished and figured as in Japan; a lacquer; *v.t.*, to varnish with japan-lacquer.

Japanese', *adj.*, pert. to Japan; *n.*, a native of Japan; the language of Japan.

Japanes'ery, *n.*, Japanese conduct, art, etc.

japanned', *p.p.*, japan.

japan'ner, *n.*, one who japans.

japan'ning, *pr.p.*, japan.

jape, *n.*, a coarse joke.

Japhet'ic, *adj.*, pert. to Japheth, ·one of the sons of Noah.

japon'ic, *adj.*, Japanese.

japon'ica, *n.*, an ornamental variety of a Japanese plant.

jar, *v.i.*, to sound discordantly; *v.t.*, to cause to shake; *n.*, a harsh sound; a clash of opinion; a vessel of earthenware or glass.

jarara'ca, *n.*, a small poisonous Brazilian snake.

jarde, *n.*, a hard tumour on the leg of a horse.

jardinière', *n.*, a pot or stand for displaying plants indoors; a vegetable soup (*Fr.*).

jar'don, *n.*, a tumour peculiar to horses' legs.

jar'gon, *n.*, gibberish; professional slang; *i.q.* jargoon.

jargonelle', *n.*, a variety of early pear.

jargoon', *n.*, a kind of zircon found in Ceylon.

jar'rah, *n.*, an Australian timber-tree.

jarred, *p.p.*, jar.

jar'ring, *pr.p.*, jar.

jar'ringly, *adv.*, in a jarring manner.

jar'vey, *n.*, a coach or cab driver (*colloq.*).

jas'hawk, *n.*, a young hawk.

jas'min(e), *n.*, a shrub with white or yellow sweet-smelling flowers. Also *jessamin*.

jas'per, *n.*, a coloured opaque quartz.

jas'perated, *adj.*, containing particles of jasper.

jas'pery, *adj.*, resembling or mixed with jasper.

jaspid'ean, *adj.*, resembling, containing, or consisting of, jasper.

Jat, *n.*, a tribe or sect, esp. N.W. India.

ja'to, *n.*, a jet assisted take-off.

jaun'dice, *n.*, a disease of the liver causing yellowness of the skin; an emotion affecting the judgment; *v.t.*, to affect with prejudice.

jaun'diced, *adj.*, affected with prejudice.

jaunt, *v.i.*, to ramble; *n.*, a short journey; an excursion.

jaun'ted, *p.p.*, jaunt.

jaun'tily, *adv.*, briskly; in a sprightly way.

jaunt'ing, *pr.p.*, jaunt.

jaun'ty, *adj.*, sprightly.

Ja'van, *adj.*, *i.q.* Javanese.

Javanese', *adj.*, rel. to Java; *n.*, a native, or the language, of Java.

jav'elin, *n.*, a light spear thrown from the hand.

jaw, *n.*, the bones of the mouth; *v.i.*, to gossip; to scold; *v.t.*, to lecture severely.

jaw'bone, *n.*, the bone of the jaw.

jawed, *adj.*, having jaws; *p.p.*, jaw.

jaw'ing, *pr.p.*, jaw; *n.*, a lecturing (*slang*).

jaw'y, *adj.*, rel. to the jaws.

jay, *n.*, a bird of the crow family.

jay'wa'lker, *n.*, a person who aimlessly crosses the road.

jazz, *n.*, a form of popular music or dance; *adj.*, having a resemblance to jazz; *v.t.*, to dance, to play jazz.

jazz'y, *adj.*, flashy, gawdy; resembling jazz.

jeal'ous, *adj.*, suspicious in love; anxiously careful.

jeal'ously, *adv.*, in a jealous manner.

jeal'ousy, *n.*, the state of being jealous.

jean, *n.*, a denim cotton cloth.

jeans, *n. pl.*, casual trousers of denim cotton.

jeep, *n.*, a small utility motor vehicle.

jeer, *v.t.* and *i.*, to mock; to deride; *n.*, a gibe.

jeered, *p.p.*, jeer.

jeer'er, *n.*, one who jeers.

jeer'ing, *pr.p.*, jeer.

jeeringly, *adv.*, mockingly.

Jeho'vah, *n.*, a name of God.

Jeho'vist, *adj.*, pert. to the Jehovistic portions of the Old Testament.

je'hu, *n.*, a furious driver.

jejune', *adj.*, dry; uninteresting; barren.

jejune'ness, *n.*, the state of being jejune.

jel'lied, *adj.*, of the consistency of jelly.

jel'lify, *v.t.*, to make into, or like, jelly.

jel'ly, *n.*, a viscous, glutinous, transparent substance; *v.t.* and *i.*, to congeal.

jel'lyfish, *n.*, a marine animal of jelly-like appearance.

jem'my, *n.*, a short, stout crowbar.

jen'net, *n.*, a small, Spanish horse. Also *genet*.

jen'neting, *n.*, an early apple.

jen'ny, *n.*, a textile spinning machine.

jeof'ail, *n.*, an oversight in pleading, and its acknowledgement.

jeop'ardize, *v.t.*, to expose to loss or injury.

jeop'ardized, *p.p.*, jeopardize.

jeop'ardizing, *pr.p.*, jeopardize.

jeop'ardous, *adj.,* hazardous.

jeo'pardy, *n.,* peril.

jerbo'a, *n.,* a small kind of rat with very long hind legs.

jeremi'ad, *n.,* a lamentation.

Jeremi'ah, *n.,* a doleful person, a kill-joy.

jer'falcon, *n.,* a bold and handsome kind of falcon.

jerk, *v.t.,* to give a sudden pull or push to; to cut (beef) into long strips and dry in the sun; *n.,* a sudden pull or push.

jerked, *p.p.,* jerk.

jerked'-beef, *n.,* beef cut into strips and dried in the sun.

jerk'er, *n.,* one who jerks; an officer who searches ships for contraband.

jer'kin, *n.,* a jacket; a close waistcoat.

jerk'ing, *pr.p.,* jerk.

jerque', *v.t.,* to search, to examine (a ship).

jer'ry, *adj.,* trashy; flimsy.

jer'rybuilder, *n.,* a builder of cheap and poorly constructed houses.

jer'sey, *n.,* a close-fitting, woollen upper shirt.

jess, *n.,* a short strap fastened round a hawk's leg.

jes'samin(e), *n.,* *i.q.* jasmine.

Jes'se, *n.,* an artistic genealogical representation of Christ's family tree; a large brass candlestick with many branches used in churches.

jest, *n.,* a joke; *v.i.,* to talk jokingly.

jest'ed, *p.p.,* jest.

jest'er, *n.,* a buffoon; a person formerly retained by men of rank to make sport for them.

jest'ing, *pr.p.,* jest.

jest'ingly, *adj.,* in a jesting manner; not in earnest.

Jes'uit, *n.,* a member of the Society of Jesus; a religious Order.

Jesuit'ic, *adj.,* pert. to, or resembling, the Jesuits.

Jesuit'ical, *adj.,* *i.q.* Jesuitic.

Jes'uitism, *n.,* the principles and practices of the Jesuits.

jet, *n.,* a hard, black mineral used for ornaments; a shooting forth; a pipe out of which a stream of fluid or gas is forced; that which flows out of an orifice in a small stream; an aircraft propelled by jet; *v.i.,* to issue in a jet; to jut; *v.t.,* to spout forth.

jet d'eau', *n.,* an ornamental fountain (*Fr.*).

jet'-engine, *n.,* an engine that derives power from backward thrust.

jet'-propelled', *adj.,* propelled by jet engine.

jet'sam, *n.,* goods thrown overboard to lighten a ship.

jet'tison, *n.,* *i.q.* jetsam; *v.t.,* to throw overboard; to discard.

jett'on, *n.,* a counter with stamped or engraved device.

jet'ty, *adj.,* made of, or black as, jet; *n.,* a pier used for discharging or loading ships.

jeu d'esprit', *n.,* an elegant witty trifle (*Fr.*).

jeune, *adj.,* young (*Fr.*).

Jew, *n.,* an Israelite.

jew'el, *n.,* a precious stone; an ornament of great value; *v.t.,* to adorn with jewels.

jew'el(l)ed, *p.p.,* jewel.

jew'el(l)er, *n.,* one who deals in jewels.

jew'el(l)ing, *pr.p.,* jewel.

jew'ellery, *n.,* the art or trade of a jeweller; jewels in general.

Jew'ess, *n.,* a female Jew.

jew'ing, *n.,* a pigeon's wattles.

Jew'ish, *adj.,* rel. or pert. to the Jews.

Jew'ishly, *adv.,* in a Jewish way.

Jew'ry, *n.,* Jewish people; a ghetto.

jew's'-ear, *n.,* a kind of fungus.

jew's'-harp, *n.,* a musical instrument held in the teeth and played by having a metal tongue struck or plucked.

jez'ebel, *n.,* an unscrupulous, vicious woman.

jib, *n.,* a sail in front of the foremast; *v.t.,* to shift a sail from one side to the other; *v.i.,*
to react against; to pull against the bit.

jibbed, *p.p.,* jib.

jib'ber, *n.,* a horse that jibs.

jib'bing, *pr.p.,* jib.

jib'-boom, *n.,* a spar serving as a continuation of the bowsprit.

jib'-door, *n.,* a door flush with the wall.

jibe, *v.t.* and *i.,* *i.q.* jib; to jeer.

jif'fy, *n.,* a moment.

jig, *n.,* a lively tune or dance; *v.i.,* to dance a jig.

jigged, *p.p.,* jig.

jig'ger, *n.,* the chigoe; a kind of light tackle used in ships; a potter's wheel; a short rest for a billiard cue.

jigg'ered, *adj.,* confounded (*colloq.*).

jigg'ery-pok'ery, *n.,* underhand scheming, humbug, trickery.

jig'ging, *pr.p.,* jig.

jig'gle, *v.t.,* to rock or jerk lightly.

jig'gled, *p.p.,* jiggle.

jiggling, *pr.p.,* jiggle.

jig'saw, *n.,* a type of machine saw; a puzzle.

jill, *n.,* a sweetheart.

jilt, *n.,* a person who abandons a lover; *v.t.,* to abandon a lover.

jilt'ed, *p.p.,* jilt.

jilt'ing, *pr.p.,* jilt.

jim'my, *n.,* *i.q.* jemmy.

jimp, *adj.,* neat; elegant.

jin'gal, *n.,* a small portable cannon; *i.q.* gingal.

jin'gle, *v.i.* and *t.,* to sound like small bells; *n.,* a clinking sound; a correspondence of sound in words; a short rhyme to music.

jin'gled, *p.p.,* jingle.

jin'gling, *pr.p.,* jingle.

jin'go, *n.,* a mild oath; a person clamorous for war.

jin'goism, *n.,* the advocacy of war.

jink, *n.,* the act of turning quickly.

jinn, *n.,* pl. of jinnee.

jin'nee, *n.,* a Mohammedan spirit, usually a demon.

jinrick'sha, *n.,* a light Eastern chaise drawn by a man.

jinx, *n.*, someone or something that brings bad luck (*slang*).

jip'po, *n.*, a kind of corset.

jitt'er, *v.i.*, to act nervously; to fluster (*slang*).

jitt'erbug, *n.*, someone addicted to dancing to jazz music; a nervous person; a scaremonger.

jitt'ers, *n. pl.*, nerves; extreme nervousness.

jitt'ery, *adj.*, jumpy, nervy.

jiu-jit'su, *n.*, the Japanese art of wrestling (Judo).

jive, *n.*, a kind of jazz music or dance; *v.i.*, to play or dance to jive.

job, *n.*, a piece of work; public work bringing gain to a private person; *v.i.*, to buy and sell stocks; *v.t.*, to let out on hire; to stab or peck.

joba'tion, *n.*, a long tedious reprimand (*colloq.*).

jobbed, *p.p.*, job.

job'ber, *n.*, one who jobs; one who lets out vehicles; a stockjobber.

job'bery, *n.*, underhand dealing.

job'bing, *adj.*, a term applied to a person who works by the job; *pr.p.*, job.

Job's-com'forter, *n.*, one who seems to comfort, but makes things worse.

jock'ey, *n.*, one who rides horses in races; a horse-dealer; one who deals unfairly in business; *v.t.*, to jostle in riding; to treat unfairly; *v.i.*, to get into a favourable position.

jock'eyed, *p.p.*, jockey.

jock'eying, *pr.p.*, jockey.

jock'eyism, *n.*, the practice of jockeys.

jock'eyship, *n.*, the art of riding horses.

jocose', *adj.*, full of jokes or fun.

jocose'ly, *adv.*, in a jocose manner.

jocose'ness, *n.*, the quality of being jocose.

jocos'ity, *n.*, *i.q.* jocoseness.

joc'ular, *adj.*, fond of making jokes.

jocular'ity, *n.*, merriment; a fondness for jokes.

joc'ularly, *adv.*, in a jocular manner.

joc'und, *adj.*, cheerful; lighthearted.

jocund'ity, *n.*, the state of being jocund.

jod'el, *v.i.*, to yodel; *n.*, a Swiss manner of singing.

jodhpurs', *n. pl.*, riding breeches.

jog, *n.*, a push; a slight shake; *v.t.*, to push slightly; *v.i.*, to move along slowly with shakes and jolts.

jogged, *p.p.*, jog.

jog'ger, *n.*, one who jogs.

jog'ging, *pr.p.*, jog.

jog'gle, *v.t.*, to push slightly; *v.i.*, to totter; *n.*, a carpenter's joint made by means of notches.

jog'gled, *p.p.*, joggle.

jog'gling, *pr.p.*, joggle.

johan'nes, *n.*, a Portuguese gold coin.

joie de vivre, *n.*, the joy of living (*Fr.*).

join, *v.t.*, to bring or fix together; to engage in.

join'der, *n.*, a joining of parties as plaintiffs or defendants in a suit.

joined, *p.p.*, join.

join'er, *n.*, a worker in wood.

join'ery, *n.*, carpentry.

join'-hand, *n.*, writing in which the letters of a word are joined together.

join'ing, *n.*, a joint; *pr.p.*, join.

joint, *n.*, the place where two things are joined; a piece of meat cut; *v.t.*, to fix by joints; to divide by joints; *adj.*, shared in common.

joint'ed, *adj.*, provided with joints; formed with knots; *p.p.*, joint.

joint'er, *n.*, one who, or that which, joints.

joint'ing, *pr.p.*, joint.

joint'less, *adj.*, without joints or seams.

joint'ly, *adv.*, together.

joint'ress, *n.*, a woman who has a jointure.

joint-ten'ant, *n.*, one who holds an estate with another and, if the other dies, takes the whole.

join'ture, *n.*, property settled on a woman at marriage; *v.t.*, to settle a jointure upon.

join'tured, *p.p.*, jointure.

join'turing, *pr.p.*, jointure.

joist, *n.*, one of the beams upon which the boards of a floor or the laths of a ceiling are nailed; *v.t.*, to fit with joists.

joist'ed, *adj.*, having joists; *p.p.*, joist.

joist'ing, *pr.p.*, joist.

joke, *n.*, a jest; *v.i.*, to jest; *v.t.*, to rally.

joked, *p.p.*, joke.

jo'ker, *n.*, a merry fellow; one of the cards in certain card games.

jo'king, *pr.p.*, joke.

jo'kingly, *adv.*, in a joking manner.

jole, *n.*, the jowl; the head.

jollifica'tion, *n.*, a merrymaking.

joll'ify, *v.t.* and *i.*; to make merry, to make jolly.

jol'lily, *adv.*, in a jolly manner.

jol'lity, *n.*, mirth; joviality.

jol'ly, *adj.*, jovial; looking and feeling well; *n.*, a marine.

jol'ly-boat, *n.*, a ship's boat.

jolt, *v.i.* and *t.*, to shake with sudden jerks; *n.*, a sudden shock or jerk.

jolt'ed, *p.p.*, jolt.

jolt'er, *n.*, one who, or that which, jolts.

jolt'ing, *pr.p.*, jolt.

jolt'ingly, *adv.*, in a jolting manner.

jon'quil, *n.*, a species of narcissus or daffodil.

jo'rum, *n.*, a drinking vessel; the liquor in it.

joss, *n.*, a Chinese idol.

joss'-house, *n.*, a Chinese temple.

joss'-stick, *n.*, a stick of fragrant incense.

jos'tle, *v.t.*, to elbow; to hustle; *v.i.*, to shove about as in a crowd.

jos'tled, *p.p.*, jostle.

jos'tling, *pr.p.*, jostle.

jot, *n.*, an iota; the least possible quantity; *v.t.*, to make a memorandum of.

jot'ted, *p.p.*, jot.

jot'ter, n., a notebook for brief notes.

jot'ting, n., a short note; pr.p., jot.

joule, n., a unit of work equal to ten million ergs.

jounce, v.t. and i., to jolt; n., a jolt.

jour'nal, n., an account of a day's proceedings, or the paper in which they are recorded; a daily newspaper; that part of an axle which rests in the bearings.

journalese', n., a poor journalistic style of writing; the jargon of bad journalism.

jour'nalism, n., the occupation of publishing, writing in, or conducting a journal.

jour'nalist, n., a newspaper editor or contributor.

journalis'tic, adj., rel. to journalism.

jour'nalize, v.t., to enter in a journal.

jour'nalized, p.p., journalize.

jour'nalizing, pr.p., journalize.

jour'ney, n., the travelling from one place to another; v.i., to travel.

jour'neyed, p.p., journey.

jour'neyer, n., one who journeys.

jour'neying, pr.p., journey.

jour'neyman, n., a mechanic or workman who has learned his special trade.

jour'ney-work, n., work done by a journeyman.

joust, n., an encounter with spears on horseback as a trial of skill; v.i., to tilt.

joust'ed, p.p., joust.

joust'er, n., one who jousts.

joust'ing, pr.p., joust.

jo'vial, adj., gay.

jovial'ity, n., the quality of being jovial.

jo'vially, adv., in a jovial manner.

jowl, n., the cheek or jaw.

jowl'er, n., a dog with large jowls; a beagle.

joy, n., gladness; v.i., to rejoice.

joyed, p.p., joy.

joy'ful, adj., full of joy.

joy'fully, adv., in a joyful manner.

joy'fulness, n., the state of being joyful.

joy'ing, pr.p., joy.

joy'less, adj., destitute of joy.

joy'lessly, adv., in a joyless manner.

joy'lessness, n., the state of being joyless.

joy'ous, adj., joyful.

joy'ously, adv., in a joyous manner.

joy'ousness, n., the state of being joyous.

joy'ride, n., a pleasure ride in a motor, etc. (slang).

joy'stick, n., the control lever of an aircraft.

ju'bilance, n., the state of being jubilant.

ju'bilant, adj., shouting or singing with joy.

ju'bilantly, adv., in a joyful way.

ju'bilate, v.i., to rejoice; to triumph.

Jubila'te, the 100th Psalm.

ju'bilate, n., a cry of triumph.

jubila'tion, n., exultation.

ju'bilee, n., a rejoicing on the fiftieth anniversary of any event.

Juda'ic, adj., pert. to the Jews.

Juda'ical, adj., i.q. Judaic.

Ju'daism, n., the Jewish system.

Judaiza'tion, n., the act of Judaizing.

Ju'daize, v.t., to convert to Judaism; v.i., to practise Judaism.

Ju'daized, p.p., Judaize.

Ju'daizer, n., one who Judaizes.

Ju'daizing, pr.p., Judaize.

ju'das, n., a treacherous person; a hole for peeping into a room furtively.

jud'der, v.i., to shake, to wobble; n., a shaking, a wobbling.

jud'dered, p.p., judder.

jud'dering, pr.p., judder.

Jude'an, adj., pert. or rel. to Judea; a native of J.

judge, n., one who examines and decides; v.t. and i., to examine and determine; to estimate; to criticize.

judged, p.p., judge.

judg'er, n., one who judges.

judge'ship, n., the office of a judge.

judg'ing, pr.p., judge.

judg'ment, n., the power of judging; the decision come to; a sentence passed on a prisoner.

ju'dicative, adj., having power to judge.

ju'dicatory, adj., bel. to a judge; n., a court of justice.

ju'dicature, n., the duties of a judge; the extent of a court's power; the body of judges.

judi'cial, adj., bel. to a judge or a court; used in or enforced by a court; fitted for judging.

judi'cially, adv., in a judicial manner.

judi'ciary, adj., bel. to courts of justice; n., the judges as a body.

judi'cious, adj., wise; sound in judgment.

judi'ciously, adv., in a judicious manner.

ju'do, n., now used for jiu-jitsu.

jug, n., a vessel with a narrow mouth and swelling body, and usually a handle and a lip; v.t., to stew or boil in a jug or jar.

ju'gal, adj., in the region of the cheek-bone.

jug'ate, adj., coupled together; having small leaves in pairs (bot.).

ju'gated, adj., coupled together, as a pair of small leaves in a compound leaf.

jug'ful, n., the maximum quantity a jug will hold.

jug'gernaut, n., a triumphal car in India, underneath which people used to throw themselves as a sacrifice.

jug'gle, v.i., to play tricks by sleight-of-hand.

jug'gled, p.p., juggle.

jug'gler, n., one who deceives by quickness of hand.

jug'glery, n., the skill and tricks of a juggler.

jug'gling, pr.p., juggle.

ju'gular, adj., pert. to the neck or throat; n., a large vein on each side of the neck.

jug'ulate, *v.t.*, to kill, to destroy; to cut the throat; to strangle.

jugula'tion, *n.*, the act of slitting a throat.

juice, *n.*, the watery part of vegetables, fruits and animal substances; petrol or electricity (*colloq.*).

juice'less, *adj.*, destitute of juice.

jui'ciness, *n.*, the state of being juicy.

jui'cy, *adj.*, full of juice.

ju'jube, *n.*, a sweetmeat of gum and sugar; the fruit of a shrub of Southern Europe.

juke'-box, *n.*, a machine used to play gramophone records when coins are inserted.

ju'lep, *n.*, a sweet liquid in which disagreeable medicines are taken; an American cocktail.

Ju'lian, *adj.*, derived from Julius Caesar; a term applied to the calendar arranged by him.

julienne', *n.*, a soup containing vegetables cut into very small pieces (*Fr.*).

July', *n.*, the seventh month of the year.

ju'mart, *n.*, the supposed offspring of a bull and a mare.

jum'bal, *n.*, a crisp, sweet cake.

jum'ble, *v.t.*, to put together without order; *n.*, a mass without order; *i.q.* jumbal.

jum'bled, *p.p.*, jumble.

jum'bler, *n.*, one who jumbles.

jum'ble-sale, *n.*, a sale of oddments.

jum'bling, *pr.p.*, jumble.

jum'bo, *n.*, any large person or object.

jumelle', *adj.*, twin; paired; a term applied to binocular glasses, etc. (*Fr.*).

jump, *v.i.*, to leap; to accord; *v.t.*, to leap over; *n.*, a leap.

jumped, *p.p.*, jump.

jump'er, *n.*, one who jumps; a sailor's outer jacket; a silk or wool pullover.

jump'ing, *pr.p.*, jump.

jump'y, *adj.*, nervous, excitable (*colloq.*).

junc'tion, *n.*, the line or point where two things come together.

junc'ture, *n.*, an important point of time.

June, *n.*, the sixth month of the year.

jun'gle, *n.*, land covered with coarse, rank vegetation.

ju'nior, *adj.*, younger; lower in standing.

ju'niorate, *n.*, a state, or period, of probation in the Jesuit Order.

junior'ity, *n.*, the state of being junior.

ju'niorship, *n.*, the office of a junior.

ju'niper, *n.*, a shrub, the berries of which are used in making gin.

junk, *n.*, pieces of old rope; salt beef; a Chinese ship; worthless material.

junk'er, *n.*, a Prussian aristocrat; a young German nobleman.

jun'ket, *n.*, curds and cream; *v.i.*, to feast.

jun'keted, *p.p.*, junket.

jun'keting, *n.*, feasting; *pr.p.*, junket.

junk'ie, *n.*, one addicted to drugs (*slang*).

Ju'no, *n.*, a Roman goddess (*Lat.*).

junoesque', *adj.*, tall and amply proportioned (of a woman).

jun'ta, *n.*, a council; a grand council of a state in Spain.

jun'to, *n.*, a secret council; a faction, a cabal.

ju'pati, *n.*, a tall Brazilian palm.

jupe, *n.*, *i.q.* jupon.

Ju'piter, *n.*, a Roman god; one of the superior planets (*Lat.*).

ju'pon, *n.*, a tight-fitting garment worn over armour; a petticoat (*Fr.*).

Juras'sic, *adj.*, a geological term applied to certain limestone rocks.

ju'rat, *n.*, a kind of magistrate.

ju'ratory, *adj.*, rel. to an oath.

jurid'ical, *adj.*, bel. to a judge or a court of law.

jurid'ically, *adv.*, in a juridical manner.

jurisconsult', *n.*, anyone learned in jurisprudence.

jurisdic'tion, *n.*, legal authority and its extent.

jurisdic'tional, *adj.*, pert. to jurisdiction.

jurisdic'tive, *adj.*, having jurisdiction.

jurispru'dence, *n.*, knowledge of law and its principles.

jurispru'dent, *adj.*, understanding law; *n.*, a jurist.

ju'rist, *n.*, a man learned in the civil law.

ju'ror, *n.*, a member of a jury.

ju'ry, *n.*, a body of persons on oath, who judge the facts stated at a trial.

ju'ryman, *n.*, a juror.

ju'ry-mast, *n.*, a mast to replace temporarily a broken one.

juss'ive, *adj.*, expressing a command (*gram.*).

just, *v.i.*, *i.q.* joust; *adj.*, according to what is right; doing right; *adv.*, exactly; barely; a little while ago.

jus'tice, *n.*, justness; fairness; a judge or magistrate.

justi'ciable, *adj.*, subject to jurisdiction.

justi'ciary, *n.*, a chief-justice.

jus'tifiable, *adj.*, defensible; excusable.

jus'tifiably, *adv.*, excusably.

justifica'tion, *n.*, the act of justifying.

justifica'tive, *adj.*, justifying.

justifica'tory, *adj.*, vindicatory.

jus'tified, *p.p.*, justify.

jus'tifier, *n.*, one who justifies.

jus'tify, *v.t.*, to make just, to prove to be right; to free from blame; to equalize a right-hand margin in printing.

jus'tifying, *pr.p.*, justify.

jus'tle, *v.t.*, *i.q.* jostle.

jus'tled, *p.p.*, justle.

just'ling, *pr.p.*, justle.

just'ly, *adv.*, in a just manner.

just'ness, *n.*, the quality of being just.

jut, *v.i.*, to project.

jute, *n.*, a fibrous material for sacks, mats, etc.

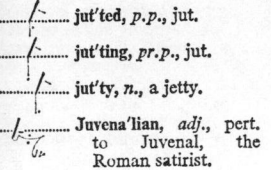

jut′ted, *p.p.*, jut.

jut′ting, *pr.p.*, jut.

jut′ty, *n.*, a jetty.

Juvena′lian, *adj.*, pert. to Juvenal, the Roman satirist.

juvenes′cence, *n.*, the state of being juvenescent.

juvenes′cent, *adj.*, becoming young.

ju′venile, *adj.*, youthful; *n.*, a young person.

juvenil′ia, *n. pl.*, youth-ful writings and actions (*Lat.*).

juvenil′ity, *n.*, youthfulness.

juxtapose′, *v.t.*, to place side by side.

juxtaposi′tion, *n.*, the placing near to or side by side; proximity.

K

Ka'aba, n., the shrine at Mecca.

kaba'ka, n., (title of) the ruler of Buganda.

kabb'ala(h), n., i.q. cabala.

kabuki', n., Japanese drama with music.

Kabyle', n., a native of the highlands of Algeria.

kack'le, v.t., to secure an end of a rope.

kad'dish, n., a form of prayer used in the synagogue.

kadi', n., i.q. cadi; a Turkish or Arabian civil judge.

Kaf'fir, n., one of the S. African Bantu people; the language of the Bantus.

kaff'irs, n., South African mine shares.

ka'go, n., a Japanese palanquin.

kail, kale, n., a kind of cabbage; broth made from cabbage.

kain'it(e), n., a fertiliser.

Kai'ser, n., the German title of an emperor.

ka'ka, n., a New Zealand parrot.

kakemon'o, n., a Japanese wall-picture.

kaleid'ophone, n., an instrument for making sound waves visible.

kalei'doscope, n., a tube containing bits of coloured glass, which, being shaken and reflected in mirrors, produce symmetrical patterns.

kaleidoscop'ic, adj., rel. to a kaleidoscope; constantly changing.

Kal'ends, n., see Calends.

ka'li, n., the saltwort.

Kal'muck, n., a Mongol race.

ka'mi, n., a Japanese ruler, a native god.

kamika'ze, n., a suicidal act of warfare (Japanese).

kampong', n., an enclosed space; a Malayan village.

kamptu'licon, n., a cork carpet.

kam'sin, n., a hot wind in Egypt. Also khamsin.

kan'aka, n., a South Sea Islander.

kangaroo', n., a marsupial quadruped of Australasia.

Kant'ian, adj., rel. to Kant, a German philosopher.

Kant'ism, n., Kant's critical philosophy.

Kant'ist, n., a disciple of Kant.

ka'olin, n., fine white clay, from which porcelain is made; also used for poultices.

ka'pok, n., a fine fibre for stuffing pillows, cushions, etc.

kaput', adj., done for, smashed (slang).

kar'ma, n., an act and its effects; destiny.

kar(r)oo', n., a plateau covered with low scrub.

kaross', n., an African garment; a skincoat.

Kash'miri, n., a native of Kashmir (India); the language of K.

katabat'ic, adj., rel. to downward air currents, windy (meteorol.).

katab'olism, n., destructive metabolism.

katathermom'eter, n., a thermometer indicating the cooling power of air.

kath'ode, n., the negative pole of a magnetic battery. Also cathode.

ka'tydid, n., a long-horned insect.

kau'ri, n., a New Zealand pine.

ka'va, n., a strong intoxicant made from the kava root.

kavass', n., a Turkish guard or courier.

kay'ak, n., an Esquimo canoe.

ke'a, n., a New Zealand parrot.

Keats'ian, aaj., pert. or rel. to the English poet, John Keats.

keb, v.i., to give birth to a lamb prematurely; n., a ewe that has given birth prematurely.

keck, v.i., to make the sound of vomiting; n., the hollow stalk of a plant.

keck'le, v.i., i.q. kackle.

keck'led, p.p., keckle.

keck'ling, pr.p., keckle.

keck'y, adj., like a keck.

kedge, v.t., to move (a ship) by pulling on a grounded anchor; v.i., to move in this way (said of the ship); n., a light anchor.

kedged, p.p., kedge.

kedg'er, n., a fisherman, a cadger.

kedg'eree, n., a stew of various ingredients, as fish, rice, eggs, etc.

kedg'ing, pr.p., kedge.

keek, v.i. and n., to peep; a peep.

keel, v.t., to supply with a keel; v.i., to turn keel upwards; n., the lowest part of a ship's framework.

keel'age, n., the payment for anchoring a vessel in port.

keeled, p.p., keel.

keel'er, n., a bargeman.

keel'haul, v.t., to haul under the keel as a punishment.

keel'hauled, p.p., keelhaul.

keel'hauling, pr.p., keelhaul; n., a former punishment in the navy.

keel'ing, pr.p., keel.

keel'man, n., a labourer on a barge.

keel'son, n., a beam running longitudinally along the bottom of a ship.

keen, v.t., to bewail; v.i., to moan, to wail; n., an Irish dirge; adj., sharp-pointed, intense, vigorous, intellectually alert.

keen'er, n., one who keens; adj., comp. of keen.

keen'est, adj., super. of keen.

keen'ly, adv., in a keen way.

keen'ness, n., sharpness, vigour, acumen.

keep, v.t., to retain, to guard, to employ, to have habitually, to have charge of, to maintain; n., a fortress; maintenance.

keep'er, n., one who keeps; an attendant; a guardring.

keep'ing, pr.p., keep.

keep'sake, n., a souvenir.

keeve, n., a large tub or vat.

kef, n., the state of drowsiness induced by smoking hemp, etc.; Indian hemp (smoked).

keg, n., a small barrel.

ke'lis, n., a skin-disease.

kelp, n., a large seaweed.

kel'pie, kel'py, n., a water-sprite.

kel'son, n., i.q. keelson; a set of timbers securing a ship's floor timbers to the keel.

kelt, n., a spent salmon after spawning; a foul fish.

kemp, n., knotty hair.

ken, v.t., to recognize, to know; n., the range of sight or understanding; a view; a low place of resort (slang).

ken'nel, v.t., to house in a kennel; v.i., to go to kennel; n., a shelter for dogs; a mean dwelling; the gutter.

ken'nelled, p.p., kennel.

ken'nelling, pr.p., kennel.

kenogen'esis, n., the development of fresh characteristics.

keno'sis, n., a renunciation of godly nature (as of Christ).

Kent'ish, adj., pert. to the English county of Kent.

kent'ledge, n., permanent ballast of pig-iron (naut.).

Ken'yan, n., a native of Kenya.

ke'nyte, n., black volcanic rock.

kep'i, n., a French military cap with horizontal peak (Fr.).

kept, p.p., keep.

ke'ratin, n., the chief constituent in horns, nails, etc.

ker'atose, adj., horny; n., a horny substance.

keraun'ograph, n., an instrument for recording thunderstorms.

kerb, n., a pavement-edging; a raised pathway.

kerb'stone, n., the stone of the kerb.

ker'chief, n., a head-covering; a handkerchief.

ker'chiefed, adj., wearing a kerchief.

kerf, n., the groove made by a saw.

ker'mes, n., an insect found on certain oaks; a red dye prepared from dead kermes.

kern(e), n., an Irish footsoldier; a boor.

ker'nel, n., the inner edible part of a nut or fruit-stone; the nucleus of a seed.

ker'nel(l)ed, adj., having a kernel.

ker'nel(l)y, adj., full of kernels.

ker'osene, n., hydro-carbon lamp-oil; paraffin.

ker'ril, n., an E. Indian sea-snake.

ker'ry, n., a breed of terrier.

ker'sey, adj., homespun; n., a cloth, smooth-faced and soft-napped.

ker'seymere, n., a variety of cashmere.

kes'trel, n., a variety of hawk.

ketch, n., a two-masted sailing ship.

ketch'up, n., a sauce prepared from mushroom or tomato juice.

ket'one, n., an organic compound.

ket'tle, n., a vessel for boiling or stewing.

ket'tledrum, n., a drum made hemispherical and having a parchment head.

ket'tleholder, n., a piece of cloth for protection from the heat of the kettle handle.

kev'el, n., a cleat (naut.).

kex, n., a weed; a husk.

key, v.t., to wedge, to

bolt; to regulate musical pitch of an instrument; n., an instrument for working a lock; a solution of a problem; a series of related musical notes; a reef.

key'board, n., a range of levers or keys pressed by the fingers.

keyed, p.p., key.

key'hole, n., the hole into which the key is inserted.

key'less, adj., having no key.

key'nes'ian, adj., rel. to the theories of Keynes, the economist.

key'note, n., the tonic note of a key.

key'stone, n., the topmost stone of an arch.

key'word, n., a word used as the basis of a system or code.

khadd'ar, n., Indian cloth.

kha'ki, adj., dust-coloured; made of khaki-coloured material; n., a dust-coloured cloth.

khal'iph, n., i.q. caliph.

kham'sin, n., i.q. kamsin.

khan, n., a Tartar, Turkish, and Mongolian sovereign; an official or gentleman in Afghanistan and India.

khan'ate, n., a Tartar or Mongolian principality.

kib'ble, n., a bucket for hoisting; v.t., to grind.

kib'bled, p.p., kibble.

kib'bler, n., one who kibbles stones.

kib'bling, pr.p., kibble.

kibbutz', n., an Israeli communal farming centre (pl. Kibbutzim).

kibe, n., an ulcerous chilblain.

kibed, adj., chapped.

kibit'ka, n., a Russian sledge; a Tartar's tent.

kib'lah, n., the temple at Mecca towards which a Mohammedan prays.

ki'bosh, n., nonsense; end; v.t., to dispose of; to end (slang).

ki'by, adj., i.q. kibed.

kick, v.t. and i., to strike with the foot; n., a blow with the foot; a

gun's recoil; the depression in the bottom of a bottle.

kicked, *p.p.*, kick.

kick'er, *n.*, one who kicks.

kick'ing, *pr.p.*, kick; *n.*, the act of a kicker.

kick'shaw, *n.*, a fancy dish; an unconsidered trifle.

kid, *v.t.* and *i.*, to bring forth a kid; to hoax (*slang*); *n.*, the young of a goat; leather made of kid's skin; a child (*slang*).

kid'der, *n.*, a forestaller; a hoaxer.

Kid'derminster, *n.*, a manufacture of carpet named after the town.

kid'dle, *n.*, a fish-trap set in a weir.

kid'dow, *n.*, the guillemot.

kid'ling, *n.*, a young kid.

kid'nap, *v.t.*, to steal a child; to abduct.

kid'napped, *p.p.*, kidnap.

kid'napper, *n.*, one who kidnaps.

kid'napping, *pr.p.*, kidnap; *n.*, abduction.

kid'ney, *n.*, a urine-secreting organ.

kie-kie, *n.*, a New Zealand climbing plant.

kier, *n.*, a bleaching vat.

kie'selguhr, *n.*, a substance used in making dynamite (*Ger.*).

Kiku'yu, *n.*, an East African Bantu-speaking tribe.

kil'derkin, *n.*, a large cask holding some 18 gallons.

kill, *v.t.*, to destroy the life of; to slay; to neutralize; to consume; *n.*, the act of killing; that which is killed.

kill'dee, *n.*, the N. American plover.

killed, *p.p.*, kill.

kill'er, *n.*, that which, or someone who, kills.

kill'ick, *n.*, a small anchor.

kill'ing, *pr.p.*, kill; *adj.*, destructive, overpowering; extremely laughable (*slang*).

kill'joy, *n.*, a spoilsport.

kilmar'nock, *n.*, a kind of tam-o'-shanter (*Scot.*).

kiln, *v.t.*, to burn in a kiln; *n.*, an oven or furnace.

kiln'-dried, *adj.*, dried in a kiln; *p.p.*, kiln-dry.

kiln'-dry, *v.t.*, to dry in a kiln.

kiln'-drying, *pr.p.*, kiln-dry; *n.*, the act of kiln-drying.

ki'lo, *prefix.*, a thousand (e.g. kilowatt—1,000 watts).

kil'ocurie, *n.*, a unit of radio-activity.

kil'ogramme, kil'ogram, *n.*, a weight of 1,000 grammes.

kilogramme'tre, *n.*, a unit of energy that raises one kilogramme to the height of one metre.

kil'olitre, *n.*, a measure of 1,000 litres.

kil'ometre, kil'ometer, *n.*, a measure of 1,000 metres.

kil'ovolt, *n.*, 1,000 volts.

kil'owatt, *n.*, 1,000 watts.

kilt, *v.t.*, to tuck up; to gather vertically in pleats; *n.*, a Scottish skirt.

kilt'ed, *p.p.*, kilt; *adj.*, wearing the kilt.

kil'ter, *n.*, good working order.

kilt'ing, *pr.p.*, kilt.

kil'ty, *n.*, the wearer of a kilt.

kim'bo, *v.t.*, to crook; *adv.*, akimbo (astride).

kim'mer, *n.*, *i.q.* cummer.

kimon'o, *n.*, a loose Japanese robe with wide sleeves.

kin, *n.*, the consanguinity or affinity; kindred.

kinaesthe'sia, *n.*, a sense of movement or muscular effort.

kinaesthe'sis, *n.*, the perception of muscular movement or effort.

kinaesthet'ic, *adj.*, pert. to kinaesthesia.

kin'chin, *n.*, a child.

kin'cob, *n.*, an Indian embroidered cloth.

kind, *adj.*, considerate, benevolent, gentle; *n.*, the sort, a distinctive group.

kind'er, *adj.*, *comp.* of kind.

kin'dergarten, *n.*, a school for infants.

kind'est, *adj.*, *super.* of kind.

kind'hearted, *adj.*, benevolent.

kind'heartedly, *adv.*, in a kindhearted way.

kin'dle, *v.t.*, to ignite, to inflame, to inspire; *v.i.*, to burst into flames.

kin'dled, *p.p.*, kindle.

kin'dler, *n.*, that which kindles.

kind'lier, *adj.*, *comp.* of kindly.

kind'liest, *adj.*, *super.* of kindly.

kind'liness, *n.*, benevolence.

kin'dling, *pr.p.*, kindle; *n.*, the material for a fire.

kind'ly, *adj.*, good-natured, genial; natural; *adv.*, in a kind manner.

kind'ness, *n.*, *i.q.* kindliness.

kin'dred, *n.*, blood relationship; *adj.*, of like nature, congenial.

kine, *n.*, pl. of cow.

kinem'a, *n.*, *i.q.* cinema.

kinemat'ic, *adj.*, rel. to motion.

kinemat'ical, *adj.*, *i.q.* kinematic.

kinemat'ics, *n. pl.*, the science of pure motion.

kinemat'ograph, *n.*, a contrivance showing on a screen a number of scenes in rapid succession, giving the semblance of motion. Also *cinematograph*.

kinet'ic, *adj.*, rel. to, or depending on, motion.

kinet'ics, *n. pl.*, the science of the relation of forces to the motions of bodies.

kinet'oscope, *n.*, an early form of cinematograph.

king, *v.t.*, to crown, to enthrone; *v.i.*, to play the king; *n.*, a male sovereign.

king'-bird, *n.*, a bird of Paradise.

king'-crab, *n.*, a large crustacean.

king'craft, *n.*, the art of ruling as a king.

king'cup, *n.*, a buttercup.

king'dom, *n.*, a king's dominion; a monarchy; any separate sphere of authority.

king'fisher, *n.*, a small bird with beautiful plumage.

king'let, *n.,* a petty sovereign.

king'like, *adj.,* regal; like a king.

king'liness, *n.,* the quality of being kingly.

king'ling, *n.,* a petty king; a golden-crested wren.

king'ly, *adj., i.q.* kinglike.

king'-pin, *n.,* a pin or bolt used in the steering mechanism of motor vehicles; the centre pin in ninepins; the most important person.

king'-post, *n.,* a vertical post between a tie-beam and the apex of a roof.

king's e'vil, *n.,* scrofula.

king'ship, *n.,* the royal state.

kink, *v.t.,* to make to kink; *v.i.,* to form a kink; *n.,* a twist or curl; a queer mental twist.

kin'kajou, *n.,* a nocturnal carnivorous, arboreal animal.

kinn'ikinic, *n.,* a substitute for tobacco.

ki'no, *n.,* an astringent gum.

kins'folk, *n.,* one's relatives.

kin'ship, *n.,* the status of a relative.

kins'man, *n.,* a relative.

kins'woman, *n.,* the fem. of kinsman.

kiosk', *n.,* a small outdoor structure for retailing or entertainment.

kip, *n.,* untanned calfskin; a slight incline; a lodging (*slang*); *v.i.,* to sleep (*slang*).

kip'per, *v.t.,* to cure; *n.,* a cured salmon; a herring smoked or dried in a special way.

kirk, *n.,* a church (*Scot.*).

kirsch'wasser, *n.,* a spirit distilled from cherries (*Ger.*).

kir'tle, *v.t.,* to dress in a kirtle; *n.,* a petticoat, a tunic.

kir'tled, *p.p.,* kirtle.

Kislev', *n.,* the third month of the Jewish civil year.

kis'met, *n.,* fate (*Turk.*).

kiss, *v.t.,* to salute or caress with the lips; *n.,* a caress or salutation with the lips.

kissed, *p.p.,* kiss.

kiss'ing, *pr.p.,* kiss; *n.,* the act of kissing.

kit, *n.,* a wooden tub; a packing case or its contents; a small fiddle with three strings; an assembly of articles for a special purpose.

kit'bag, *n.,* a bag for equipment especially used by the armed forces.

kit'cat, *n.,* a portrait, showing about half length, with the hands.

kitch'en, *n.,* a room for cooking.

kitch'ener, *n.,* a cooking-range.

kitchenette', *n.,* a small kitchen or scullery.

kite, *n.,* a falcon-like bird; a flying toy.

kite'-mark, *n.,* the trademark of the British Standards Institution.

kith, *n.,* an acquaintance; kindred.

kit'ling, *n.,* a kitten.

kit'ten, *n.,* a young cat.

kit'tenish, *adj.,* kittenlike, playful.

kitti'wake, *n.,* a species of seagull.

kit'tle, *adj.,* ticklish, difficult to deal with; *v.i.,* to have kittens.

kittul', *n.,* a kind of palm.

kitt'y, *n.,* a kitten; a pool in gambling; a common fund.

ki'wi, *n.,* an apteryx.

klax'on, *n.,* a powerful electric motor horn.

kleptoma'nia, *n.,* a form of mental imbalance marked by the impulse to steal.

kloof, *n.,* a ravine valley.

knack, *n.,* dexterity, a trick.

knack'er, *n.,* a horse-slaughterer.

knag, *n.,* a knob.

knag'gy, *adj.,* full of knots.

knap'sack, *n.,* a travelling-bag strapped to the back.

knap'weed, *n.,* a common European weed.

knar, *n.,* a knot in wood.

knarled, *see* gnarled.

knarred, *adj.,* having knots.

knave, *n.,* a rogue, a servant.

kna'very, *n.,* roguishness; unethical conduct.

kna'vish, *adj.,* roguish.

kna'vishly, *adv.,* roguishly.

kna'vishness, *n.,* the conduct of a rogue.

knead, *v.t.,* to work up into a mass; to massage.

knead'ed, *p.p.,* knead.

knead'er, *n.,* one who kneads.

knead'ing, *pr.p.,* knead.

knee, *v.t.,* to touch with the knee; to fasten with the knees; *n.,* the joint between the thigh and the lower leg; an angular beam or piece of iron.

knee'cap, *n.,* the patella; a covering for the knee.

kneed, *p.p.,* knee; *adj.,* gone at the knees.

knee'deep, *adj.,* and *adv.,* up to the knees.

knee'joint, *n.,* the joint of the knee.

kneel, *v.i.,* to fall on the knees; to bend the knee.

kneeled, *p.p.,* kneel.

kneel'er, *n.,* one who kneels; a mat to kneel on.

kneel'ing, *pr.p.,* kneel.

knee'pan, *n.,* the patella.

knell, *v.t.* and *i.,* to toll; to give a sad sound; *n.,* the tolling; the last warning; a death omen.

knelt, *p.p.,* kneel.

Knes'set, *n.,* the Israeli parliament.

knew, *p.p.,* know.

knick'erbockers, *n., pl.,* loose-fitting breeches.

knick'ers, *n.,* women's underclothing; breeches.

knick'nack, *n.,* a gimcrack; a light decorative article of furniture.

knife, *v.t.,* to stab, to cut; *n.,* a cutting-blade set in a handle.

knife'board, *n.,* a board for knife-cleaning; formerly, the longitudinal seat on an omnibus.

knife'-cleaner, *n.,* an apparatus for knife cleaning.

knife'-edge, n., a fine, metal edge on which scientific instruments balance.

knife'grinder, n., a grinder of knives.

knight, v.t., to confer knighthood on; n., a person of rank so honoured for services rendered.

knight'age, n., a record of knights; knights as a whole.

knight'ed, p.p., knight.

knight'-errant, n., a knight wandering about for adventures; a quixotic person.

knight'-errantry, n., the conduct of a knight errant.

knight'hood, n., the dignity of a knight; chivalry; the whole body of knights.

knight'liness, n., the quality of being knightly.

knight'ly, adj., chivalrous.

knit, v.t., to make a close texture with looped yarn; to contract; to make compact.

knitt'ed, p.p., knit; adj., interlooped by knitting; wrinkled (as of brows).

knit'ter, n., one who knits; a knitting-machine.

knit'ting, pr.p., knit; n., the process or work of knitting.

knit'ting-nee'dle, n., a long thin rod used in knitting.

knit'tle, n., a small line made of twisted yarns.

knit'wear, n., knitted articles.

knives, n., pl. of knife.

knob, v.t., to put knobs on; v.i., to bulge out; n., a round protuberance; a round handle; a lump.

knobbed, p.p., knob; adj., having knobs.

knob'biness, n., the quality of being knobby.

knob'bing, pr.p., knob.

knob'ble, n., a small knob.

knob'bly, adj., lumpy.

knob'by, adj., having knobs.

knob'stick, n., a knobbed stick; a blackleg (slang).

knock, v.t., to strike, to beat; n., a stroke, a rap.

knocked, p.p., knock.

knock'er, n., one who knocks; a striker attached to a door.

knock'ing, pr.p., knock.

knock'-kneed, adj., weak in the knees.

knock'out, n., a finishing blow; an auction ring; a funny fellow (slang).

knoll, v.t., to toll, to ring; v.i., to sound out; n., a low hill or mound.

knolled, p.p., knoll.

knoll'ing, pr.p., knoll.

knop, n., a knob; a bud.

knot, v.t., to tie in a knot; v.i., to form into knots; n., an intertwining of parts of a cord or rope; an ornamental tied bow; a nautical measure of length; an excrescence; a hard formation in wood; a small wading bird.

knot'berry, n., the cloudberry.

knot'-grass, n., a trailing weed.

knot'ted, p.p., knot.

knot'tiness, n., the quality of being knotty.

knot'ting, pr.p., knot.

knot'ty, adj., knotted; full of knots.

knout, v.t., to flog with the knout; n., a scourge formerly used in Russia.

know, v.t., to recognize with certainty; to be on intimate terms with; to understand.

know'able, adj., able to be known.

know'how, n., practical knowledge.

know'ing, pr.p., know; adj., wideawake, smart.

know'ingly, adv., in a wideawake way.

knowl'edge, n., knowing; the result of knowing; mental apprehension.

knowl'edgeable, adj., well-informed.

known, p.p., know.

knuck'le, v.t., to press with the knuckles;

v.i., to give in; n., the bone of the finger-joint; a tarsal joint.

knuck'led, p.p., knuckle.

knuck'leduster, n., a metal protection for the knuckles.

knuck'ling, pr.p., knuckle.

knur(r)', n., a knot, a wooden ball.

knurl, n., a knot, a protuberance.

knurled, adj., knobbed.

knur'ly, adj., having knots or knobs.

ko'a, n., an acacia tree.

koa'la, n., an Australian bear.

Ko'dak, n., a portable photographic camera; v.t., to photograph with a Kodak.

ko'el, n. pl., Indian and Australian cuckoos.

koh'-i-noor, n., a famous Indian diamond.

kohl, n., a powder for darkening the eyes.

kohl'rabi, n., a variety of cabbage.

kolin'ski, n., the fur of Siberian mink.

kolkhoz', n., a Russian collective farm.

koo'doo, n., a S. African antelope.

kooka'burr'a, n., the laughing jackass.

koo'lah, n., an Australian sloth-like mammal.

ko'pec(k), see copeck.

kopj'e, n., a little hill.

Ko'ran, n., the Mohammedan sacred book.

Kore'an, adj., pert. or rel. to Korea; n., a native of K.

korf'ball, n., a kind of basketball.

ko'sher, adj., clean, pure, legally correct.

kotow', v.i., to perform the kotow; n., touching the ground with one's forehead in obeisance.

kou'miss, n., fermented mare's milk.

kour'bash, n., a hide whip.

kow'-tow', v.i., to be servile, to submit.

kraal, n., a group of native huts.

kraft, n., a kind of strong brown paper.

krait', n., a venomous Indian snake.

kra'ken, n., a mythical sea monster.

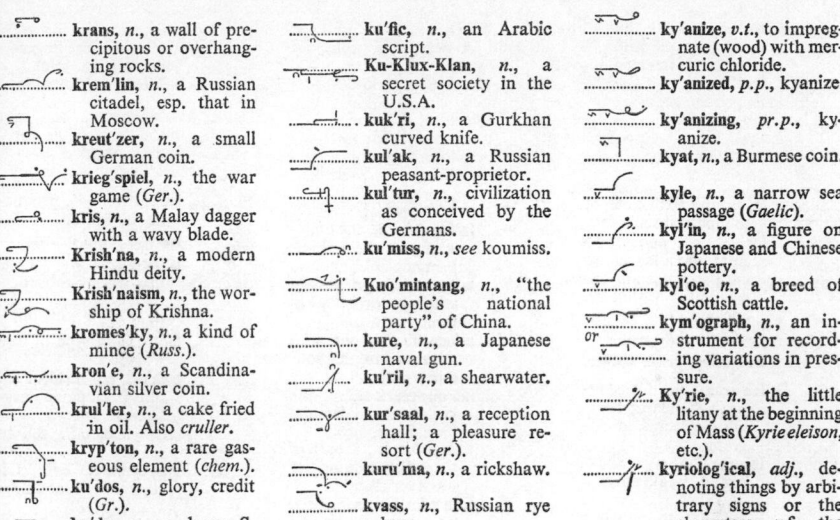

krans, *n.,* a wall of precipitous or overhanging rocks.

krem′lin, *n.,* a Russian citadel, esp. that in Moscow.

kreut′zer, *n.,* a small German coin.

krieg′spiel, *n.,* the war game (*Ger.*).

kris, *n.,* a Malay dagger with a wavy blade.

Krish′na, *n.,* a modern Hindu deity.

Krish′naism, *n.,* the worship of Krishna.

kromes′ky, *n.,* a kind of mince (*Russ.*).

kron′e, *n.,* a Scandinavian silver coin.

krul′ler, *n.,* a cake fried in oil. Also *cruller.*

kryp′ton, *n.,* a rare gaseous element (*chem.*).

ku′dos, *n.,* glory, credit (*Gr.*).

ku′du, *n.,* a large S. African antelope.

ku′fic, *n.,* an Arabic script.

Ku-Klux-Klan, *n.,* a secret society in the U.S.A.

kuk′ri, *n.,* a Gurkhan curved knife.

kul′ak, *n.,* a Russian peasant-proprietor.

kul′tur, *n.,* civilization as conceived by the Germans.

ku′miss, *n., see* koumiss.

Kuo′mintang, *n.,* "the people's national party" of China.

kure, *n.,* a Japanese naval gun.

ku′ril, *n.,* a shearwater.

kur′saal, *n.,* a reception hall; a pleasure resort (*Ger.*).

kuru′ma, *n.,* a rickshaw.

kvass, *n.,* Russian rye beer.

ky′anite, *n., i.q.* cyanite.

ky′anize, *v.t.,* to impregnate (wood) with mercuric chloride.

ky′anized, *p.p.,* kyanize.

ky′anizing, *pr.p.,* kyanize.

kyat, *n.,* a Burmese coin.

kyle, *n.,* a narrow sea passage (*Gaelic*).

kyl′in, *n.,* a figure on Japanese and Chinese pottery.

kyl′oe, *n.,* a breed of Scottish cattle.

kym′ograph, *n.,* an instrument for recording variations in pressure.

Ky′rie, *n.,* the little litany at the beginning of Mass (*Kyrie eleison,* etc.).

kyriolog′ical, *adj.,* denoting things by arbitrary signs or the characters of the alphabet.

L

la, *n.*, the sixth note of the musical scale.

laa'ger, *v.t.* and *i.*, to form into a laager; to encamp; *n.*, an encampment within an enclosure of wagons.

laa'gered, *p.p.*, laager.

laa'gering, *pr.p.*, laager.

lab'arum, *n.*, Constantine's standard, bearing the sacred monogram.

labefac'tion, *n.*, a shaking, a weakening, a downfall.

la'bel, *v.t.*, to attach a label to; to classify; *n.*, a slip of some material, used for naming.

la'belled, *p.p.*, label.

la'belling, *pr.p.*, label.

label'lum, *n.*, a lower petal (*bot.*).

la'bent, *adj.*, gliding.

la'bial, *adj.*, rel. to, or produced by, the lips; *n.*, a sound produced by the lips.

la'biate, *adj.*, lipped.

lab'ile, *adj.*, unstable, liable to displacement or change (*chem.*).

lab'ilize, *v.t.*, to make unstable, to change, to displace.

labioden'tal, *adj.*, labial and dental.

lab'ium, *n.*, the lip of the female pudendum (*Lat., anat.*).

lab'oratory, *n.*, a scientific workshop.

labo'rious, *adj.*, hard-working, difficult.

labo'riously, *adv.*, in a laborious way.

la'bour, *v.i.*, to work hard, to strive, to move with difficulty; *v.t.*, to elaborate, to work out; *n.*, toil, hard work, difficulty; child-birth; working people collectively.

la'boured, *p.p.*, labour; *adj.*, done with labour; not spontaneous.

la'bourer, *n.*, one who labours.

la'bouring, *pr.p.*, labour.

la'bourism, *n.*, the philosophy of the Labour Party.

la'bourist, *n.*, a person who supports the Labour Party.

la'bourite, *n.*, one who adheres to Labour Party policy.

lab'our-mark'et, *n.*, the supply of and demand for labour.

Lab'rador, *n.*, a part of Canada; a kind of retriever dog.

Labrador'ian, *adj.*, pert. or rel. to Labrador; *n.*, a native of L.

Lab'radorite, *n.*, a variety of feldspar.

la'bret, *n.*, an ornament inserted in the lip.

la'brose, *adj.*, thick-lipped.

labur'num, *n.*, a tree with clustering yellow flowers.

lab'yrinth, *n.*, a maze; an arrangement of tortuous passages.

labyrin'thian, *adj.*, like a labyrinth.

labyrin'thine, *adj.*, *i.q.* labyrinthian.

labyrin'thodon, *n. pl.*, large amphibious fossils.

labyrin'thodont, *n.*, *i.q.* labrynthodon.

lac, *n.*, a dark-red resin; a hundred thousand (*Anglo-Ind.*); milk (*Lat.*).

lac'cic, *adj.*, rel. to lac.

lac'cin, *n.*, a compound contained in shellac.

lace, *v.t.*, to fasten, to flavour; *v.i.*, to compress the waist; *n.*, string, cord, braid, fabric.

laced, *p.p.*, lace.

la'cer, *n.*, a tool for lacing footballs; a liquor used for flavouring.

lac'erable, *adj.*, able to be lacerated.

lac'erate, *v.t.*, to tear, to mangle, to distress.

lac'erated, *p.p.*, lacerate.

lac'erating, *pr.p.*, lacerate.

lacera'tion, *n.*, the act of lacerating.

lac'erative, *adj.*, producing laceration.

lacer'ta, *n.*, a lizard.

lacer'tian, *adj.*, lizard-like.

lacer'tine, *adj.*, *i.q.* lacertian.

lacet', *n.*, a type of lace work.

lach'es, *n.*, neglect of duty; culpable negligence.

lach'rymal, *adj.*, rel. to tears.

lach'rymary, *adj.*, rel. to, or containing, tears.

lach'rymating, *adj.*, *i.q.* lachrymatory.

lachryma'tion, *n.*, the flow of tears.

lach'rymatory, *adj.*, causing tears; *n.*, a tear-vessel.

lach'rymose, *adj.*, tearful, given to weeping.

la'ciness, *adj.*, having the appearance or structure of lace.

la'cing, *pr.p.*, lace; *n.*, the flavouring added to a drink.

lacin'iate, *adj.*, jagged, segmented.

lacin'iated, *adj.*, *i.q.* laciniate.

lack, *v.t.*, to be without; *v.i.*, to be wanting; *n.*, a want, a deficiency.

lackadai'sical, *adj.*, languishing, half-hearted, indolent.

lack'adaisy, *adj.*, *i.q.* lackadaisical.

lack'-a-day, *interj.*, sorrow or pained surprise.

lacked, *p.p.*, lack.

lack'ey, *v.t.*, to attend upon; to be servile to; *n.*, a footman; a servile follower.

lack'eyed, *p.p.*, lackey.

lack'eying, *pr.p.*, lackey.

lack'ing, *pr.p.*, lack.

lacon'ic, *adj.*, brief, terse.

lacon'ical, *adj.*, *i.q.* laconic.

lacon'ically, *adv.*, briefly, tersely.

lacon'icism, *n.*, brevity in expression.

la'conism, *n., i.q.* laconicism; a brief saying.

lac'quer, *v.t.*, to varnish with lacquer; *n.*, a gold-coloured varnish.

lac'quered, *p.p.*, lacquer.

lac'quering, *pr.p.*, lacquer; *n.*, the art of varnishing like lacquer; lacquer work.

lac'rimose, *adj., i.q.* lachrymose.

lacrosse', *n.*, an American ball game, played with a long, loosely-strung racquet.

lactalbum'en, *n.*, the albumen of milk.

lac'tarene, lac'tarine, *n.*, a preparation from milk curd, used in calico printing.

lac'tate, *v.t.*, to make into, or like, milk; *v.i.*, to secrete milk.

lacta'ted, *p.p.*, lactate; *adj.*, secreted milk, suckled; combined with a milk substance.

lacta'ting, *pr.p.*, lactate.

lacta'tion, *n.*, the act of secreting milk; suckling.

lacta'tional, *adj.*, pertaining to lactation, in milk.

lac'teal, *adj.*, rel. to milk; conveying a milk-like fluid.

lac'tean, *adj., i.q.* lacteal.

lac'teous, *adj.*, milky.

lactes'cence, *n.*, milkiness; milky juice.

lactes'cent, *n.*, milky; conveying milky juice.

lac'tic, *adj.*, rel. to milk.

lactif'erous, *adj.*, milk producing.

lactom'eter, *n.*, an instrument for testing the purity of milk.

lactose', *n.*, milk sugar.

lacu'na, *n.*, a gap, a blank, a cavity (*Lat.*).

lacu'nar, *adj.*, pert. to a lacuna.

lac'unose, *adj.*, full of lacunae.

lacus'tral, *adj., i.q.* lacustrine.

lacus'trine, *adj.*, rel. to or growing in lakes.

la'cy, *adj.*, like lace.

lad, *n.*, a boy, a youth.

lad'anum, *n.*, a species of resin.

lad'der, *n.*, a contrivance for climbing; a series of steps or rungs between two uprights.

lad'die, *n.*, the Scottish for lad.

lad'dish, *adj.*, boy-like, youthful.

lade, *v.t.*, to fill with cargo; to load.

la'ded, *adj., i.q.* laden; *p.p.*, lade.

la'den, *adj.*, loaded.

la-di-da', *n.*, a pretentious person, a swaggerer; *adj.*, given to pretence in manners and speech.

la'ding, *pr.p.*, lade; *n.*, the act of lading; a cargo.

la'dle, *v.t.*, to remove in a ladle; *n.*, a long-handled spoon with a large bowl.

la'dled, *p.p.*, ladle.

la'dleful, *n.*, the quantity a ladle contains.

la'dling, *pr.p.*, ladle.

la'dy, *n.*, a gentlewoman; a woman of rank; a wife.

la'dybird, *n.*, a small, winged insect.

La'dy-chap'el, *n.*, a small chapel attached to a cathedral or large church and dedicated to the Virgin Mary.

La'dy Day, *n.*, the Feast of the Annunciation (March 25).

lad'y-killer, *n.*, a man who sets out to impress women; a flirt.

la'dylike, *adj.*, like a lady, refined.

la'dylove, *n.*, a sweetheart.

la'dy's-fin'ger, *n.*, the kidney vetch.

la'dyship, *n.*, being a lady; title of a lady of rank.

la'dy's-maid, *n.*, a personal attendant on a lady.

la'dy's-slipper, *n.*, a plant with yellow slipper-shaped flowers.

lag, *v.i.*, to go very slowly; to be left behind; *n.*, retardation.

la'ger, *n.*, a light German-type beer.

lag'gard, *n.*, one who lags.

lagged, *p.p.*, lag.

lag'ger, *n., i.q.* laggard.

lag'ging, *pr.p.*, lag.

lagoon', *n.*, a salt-water lake separated by a sandbank from the sea; the water within an atoll.

lagrimo'so, *adv.*, plaintively (*mus.*).

la'ic, *adj.*, the opposite to clerical; *n.*, a layman.

la'ical, *adj.*, non-clerical.

laiciza'tion, *n.*, the act of laicizing.

la'icize, *v.t.*, to make lay; to open to the laity.

laid, *p.p.*, lay.

lain, *p.p.*, lie.

lair, *n.*, a hiding-place, a den; a shelter for cattle.

laird, *n.*, a Scottish landowner.

laiss'ez-aller, *n.*, unrestricted freedom (*Fr.*).

laiss'ez-faire, *n.*, freedom from interference (esp. commerce) (*Fr.*).

la'ity, *n.*, lay folk collectively.

lake, *n.*, a large expanse of landlocked water; a crimson pigment.

lake'let, *n.*, a diminutive lake.

lakh, *n.*, a hundred thousand (*see* lac); a resinous secretion used for making dyes.

la'lang, *n.*, a coarse grass.

lalla'tion, *n.*, a tendency to pronounce the letter *r* as *l*.

lam, *v.t.* and *i.*, to thrash, to hit.

la'ma, *n.*, a Mongolian or Tibetan high priest.

La'maism, *n.*, the religion of Tibet.

la'maist, *n.*, a professor of Lamaism.

lama'sery, *n.*, a monastery of lamas.

lamb, *n.*, a young sheep.

lambaste', *v.t.*, to beat, to thrash (*dial.*).

lamb'dacism, *n., i.q.* lallation.

lamb'doid, *adj.*, in the form of the Greek lambda.

lamb'doidal, *adj., i.q.* lambdoid.

lam'bency, *n.*, brilliance.

lam'bent, *adj.*, playing over a surface, like a flame; soft, liquid.

lamb'ing, *n.*, the birth of lambs.

lamb'kin, *n.*, a little lamb.

lamb'-like, *adj.*, gentle.

lamb'skin, *adj.*, made of lambskin; *n.*, the skin of a lamb.

lamb's'-wool, *n.*, the wool of lambs.

lame, *v.t.*, to cripple; *adj.*, crippled, halting, inadequate.

lamé, *n.* and *adj.*, a dress material with gold and silver thread interwoven.

lamed, *p.p.*, lame.

lamel'la, *n.*, a thin plate or film (*Lat.*).

lamel'lar, *adj.*, scalelike; forming a thin plate.

lam'ellate, *adj.*, composed of lamellae.

lam'ellated, *adj.*, *i.q.* lamellate.

lamel'liform, *adj.*, scalelike.

lamel'loid, *adj.*, structured in layers, like a lamella.

lame'ly, *adv.*, in a lame way.

lame'ness, *n.*, the state of being lame.

lament', *v.t.*, to grieve for; *v.i.*, to utter grief; *n.*, a passionate utterance of grief; a dirge.

lam'entable, *adj.*, mournful, deplorable.

lam'entably, *adv.*, in a lamentable way.

lamenta'tion, *n.*, the act of lamenting; a lament.

lament'ed, *p.p.*, lament.

lament'er, *n.*, one who laments.

lament'ing, *pr.p.*, lament.

lam'ia, *n.*, a sorceress, a witch.

lam'ina, *n.*, a thin plate or layer.

laminabil'ity, *n.*, the state of being laminable.

lam'inable, *adj.*, able to be hammered or rolled fine.

lam'inar, *adj.*, arranged in thin plates.

lam'inary, *adj.*, *i.q.* laminar.

lam'inate, *v.t.*, to roll or beat thin; *v.i.*, to become thin.

lam'inated, *p.p.*, laminate; *adj.*, in thin layers.

lam'inating, *pr.p.*, laminate.

lamina'tion, *n.*, the state of being laminated.

la'ming, *pr.p.*, lame.

laminif'erous, *adj.*, composed of laminae.

la'mish, *adj.*, somewhat lame.

Lam'mas, *n.*, Loafmass (the name for 1 Aug.).

lam'mergeyer, *n.*, the bearded vulture.

lamp, *n.*, a device for giving artificial light.

lam'pas, *n.*, a mouth disease in horses; a Chinese flowered silk.

lamp'black, *n.*, the pigment from soot.

lam'per-eel, *n.*, a lamprey.

lamp'ic, *adj.*, rel. to a lamp or flame.

lamp'light, *n.*, the light from a lamp.

lamp'lighter, *n.*, one who lights lamps.

lampoon', *v.t.*, to satirize; *n.*, an abusive piece of satire.

lampooned', *p.p.*, lampoon.

lampoon'er, *n.*, a writer of a lampoon.

lampoon'ing, *pr.p.*, lampoon.

lampoon'ry, *n.*, the practice of lampooning.

lamp'-post, *n.*, the pillar which holds a street lamp.

lam'prey, *n.*, an eel-like fish.

la'nary, *n.*, a wool-store.

la'nate, *adj.*, woolly.

la'nated, *adj.*, *i.q.* lanate.

Lancas'trian, *adj.*, rel. to Lancaster; *n.*, a native of the county of L.

lance, *v.t.*, to cut or open with a lancet; *n.*, a long spearheaded shaft.

lance'-corporal, *n.*, a private with the temporary rank of corporal.

lanced, *p.p.*, lance.

lance'let, *n.*, a small fishlike animal.

lan'ceolar, *adj.*, shaped like a spearhead.

lan'ceolate, *adj.*, *i.q.* lanceolar.

lan'ceolated, *adj.*, *i.q.* lanceolar.

lan'cer, *n.*, a cavalry soldier armed with the lance.

lan'cers, *n. pl.*, soldiers of the cavalry; an oldtime dance.

lan'cet, *n.*, a surgical instrument for lancing; a high, narrow, pointed window.

lance'wood, *n.*, a W. Indian wood used for fishing-rods, etc.

lan'ciform, *adj.*, spearlike.

lan'cinate, *v.t.*, to pierce.

lan'cinated, *p.p.*, lancinate.

lan'cinating, *pr.p.*, lancinate; *adj.*, (of pain) acute, shooting.

lancina'tion, *n.*, an acute shooting pain.

lan'cing, *pr.p.*, lance.

land, *v.t.*, to bring to land, to put on land; *v.i.*, to go ashore; *n.*, the solid earth, landed estate.

lan'damman, *n.*, the President of the Diet in Switzerland.

lan'dau, *n.*, a fourwheeled carriage, the top of which can be opened and laid back.

landaulet', *n.*, a small single-seated landau.

land'ed, *p.p.*, land; *adj.*, possessing land.

land'girl, *n.*, a girl engaged in farmwork.

land'grave, *n.*, a German title, resembling that of a marquis.

landgra'viate, *n.*, the area of a landgrave's jurisdiction.

land'gravine, *n.*, the fem. of landgrave.

land'holder, *n.*, one who holds land as an owner or tenant.

land'ing, *pr.p.*, land; *n.*, the act of going ashore; a wharf; a stage on a stairway; the touchdown of an aircraft.

land'ing-chas'sis, *n.*, the under-body of an aircraft.

land'ing-craft, *n.*, a naval vessel designed to put forces ashore.

land'lady, *n.*, the mistress of an inn; a woman who has tenants.

land'less, *adj.*, without lands.

land'locked, *adj.*, shut in by land.

land'loper, *n.*, a tramp.

land'lord, *n.*, the keeper of an inn or lodgings; one who has tenants.

land'lordism, *n.*, the attitude of landlords.

land'lubber, *n.*, one unused to the sea; a raw sailor.

land'mark, *n.*, a boundary mark.

land'mine, *n.*, an explosive mine laid in the ground.

landoc'racy, *n.*, the land-owning class.

land'ocrat, *n.*, a land owner.

land'owner, *n.*, an owner of landed property.

land'owning, *n.*, the ownership of land.

land'rail, *n.*, the corn crake.

land'reeve, *n.*, a farm bailiff.

land'-rover, *n.*, a motor vehicle constructed for use over difficult country.

land'scape, *n.*, a prospect of country; *v.t.* and *i.*, to improve a garden or land by giving it the appearance of a landscape.

land'slide, *n.*, the fall of a mass of a cliff or mountain.

land'slip, *n.*, *i.q.* landslide.

lands'man, *n.*, a person having no liking for, or knowledge of, the sea or the air.

lands'woman, *n.*, a woman who works or lives on the land.

land'ward, *adv.*, toward land.

lane, *n.*, a narrow road.

lan'grage, *n.*, case-shot.

lan'grel, *n.*, *i.q.* langrage.

langsyne', *adv.*, in the old days; *n.*, the old days.

lan'guage, *n.*, speech, tongue.

Languedoc, *n.*, an old French province.

lan'guid, *adj.*, inert, spiritless, faint.

lan'guidly, *adv.*, faintly, weakly.

lan'guish, *v.i.*, to become feeble, to pine, to be sentimentally tender.

lan'guished, *p.p.*, languish.

lan'guisher, *n.*, one who languishes.

lan'guishing, *pr.p.*, languish.

lan'guishment, *n.*, the state of being languid.

lan'guor, *n.*, faintness, weariness, dullness; heavy stillness.

lan'guorous, *adj.*, showing or causing languor.

lan'guorously, *adv.*, in a languorous way.

lanif'erous, *adj.*, fleecy, wool-bearing.

lanig'erous, *adj.*, *i.q.* laniferous.

lank, *adj.*, spare, long and lean, limp.

lank'ness, *n.*, the state of being lank.

lank'y, *adj.*, excessively lank; tall (*colloq.*).

lan'ner, *n.*, a species of falcon.

lann'eret, *n.*, a male falcon.

lan'olin, *n.*, oil from wool; the basis of ointments.

lan'oline, *n.*, *i.q.* lanolin.

lans'quenet, *n.*, a game of cards.

lan'tern, *n.*, a case shielding a flame; the luminous chamber of a lighthouse; a cupola with glazed openings; a lamp.

lan'thanum, *n.*, a rare metal (*chem.*).

lan'thorn, *n.*, *i.q.* lantern.

lanu'ginous, *adj.*, downy.

lan'yard, *n.*, a short rope or line for securing; a cord attached to a breech mechanism for firing a gun; a cord round the neck or shoulder to secure a knife or whistle.

Laodice'an, *adj.*, rel. to Laodicea; indifferent.

lap, *v.t.*, to fold, to encircle, to drink with the tongue; *v.i.*, to make a lapping sound, to break gently on the shore; *n.*, an overhanging flap; the waist to the knees of a seated person; the clothing of that part; overlapping; a single circuit of a running-track; an act of lapping.

lap'dog, *n.*, a pet dog.

lapel', *n.*, the reversed part of a coat-breast.

lap'ful, *n.*, the amount held in the lap.

lapida'rian, *adj.*, rel. to stones or stone-work; monumental.

lap'idary, *adj.*, *i.q.* lapidarian; *n.*, a cutter of gems.

lap'idate, *v.t.*, to stone; to cut and polish.

lapida'tion, *n.*, stoning.

lapidif'ic, *adj.*, petrifying.

lapid'ified, *adj.*, petrified.

lapid'ify, *v.t.*, to turn to stone, to petrify.

la'pis, *n.*, a way of calico printing.

lap'is-laz'uli, *n.*, a blue mixture of minerals.

Lap'lander, *n.*, a native of Lapland.

Lapp, *n.*, *i.q.* Laplander.

lapped, *p.p.*, lap.

lap'per, *n.*, anything that laps.

lap'pet, *n.*, an overlapping piece.

lap'ping, *pr.p.*, lap.

lapse, *v.i.*, to fall back or away; to become void; to revert; to glide; *n.*, a fall, a slip, a slight error; flow; passage.

lapsed, *p.p.*, lapse.

laps'ing, *pr.p.*, lapse.

lap'sus, *n.*, a slip (*Lat.*).

Lapu'tan, *adj.*, rel. to Laputa; chimerical; *n.*, a native of Laputa.

lap'wing, *n.*, the peewit.

lar, *n.*, a Roman household god.

lar'board, *n.*, the port side of a vessel (*naut.*).

lar'ceny, *n.*, theft.

larch, *n.*, a coniferous tree.

lard, *v.t.*, to lace with strips of bacon; to embellish with foreign words; *n.*, the half-solid oil of hog's fat.

larda'ceous, *adj.*, like lard.

lard'ed, *p.p.*, lard.

lard'er, *n.*, a storeroom for foodstuffs.

lard'ing, *pr.p.*, lard.

lard'on, *n.*, pork or bacon strips for larding meat.

lardoon', *n.*, *i.q.* lardon.

la'res, *n.*, pl. of lar.

large, *adj.*, great, broad, generous; *n.*, used in phrase "at large" (*i.e.*, at liberty).

large'-hearted, *adj.*, magnanimous.

large'ly, *adv.*, in a large way; to a great extent.

large'ness, *n.*, the quality of being large.

larg'er, *adj.*, comp. of large.

large'-sized, adj., above normal size.

larg'ess(e), n., a free gift.

larg'est, adj., super. of large.

larghet'to, adj., slow musical time; n., a slow movement (It.).

larg'ish, adj., fairly large.

lar'go, n., a slower time than larghetto; a largo movement; adj., slow (It.).

lar'iat, n., a lasso.

lark, n., a singing-bird; a frolic; v.i., to frolic.

lark'spur, n., one of the Delphinia.

lar'rikin, n., a young hooligan.

la'rrup, v.t., to thrash (colloq.).

lar'um, n., i.q. alarum.

lar'va, n., a grub.

lar'vae, n., pl. of larva.

lar'val, adj., rel. to larvae.

lar'vated, adj., covered with a mask.

laryn'geal, adj., rel. to the larynx.

laryn'gean, adj., i.q. laryngeal.

laryngi'tis, n., inflammation of the larynx.

laryn'goscope, n., a mirror for examining the larynx.

laryngoscop'ic, adj., rel. to a laryngoscope.

laryngot'omy, n., a cutting into the larynx.

lar'ynx, n., the seat of the vocal chords.

las'car, n., an Asiatic seaman.

lasciv'ious, adj., wanton, lustful.

lasciv'iously, adv., lustfully.

lasciv'iousness, n., wantonness, lustfulness.

la'ser, n., a gum resin; an amplification of light by radiation.

la'ser-beam, n., a high-powered directional penetrating beam of light.

lash, v.t., to flog, to whip; to move suddenly; to satirize; to tie securely; n., a stroke with a whip; the flexible end of a whip; an eyelash.

lashed, p.p., lash.

lash'er, n., a weir.

lash'ing, pr.p., lash.

lash'ings, n. pl., an abundance (Scot.).

las'pring, n., a young salmon.

lasque, n., an inferior diamond.

lass, n., a girl, sweetheart.

las'sie, n., the Scottish form of "lass."

las'situde, n., weariness, an incapacity for exertion.

las'so, v.t., to catch with a lasso; n., a noosed rope.

last, v.i., to endure, to continue; v.t., to suffice; adj. and adv., at the end; after the rest; n., a shoemaker's model; a measure.

last'ed, p.p., last.

last'ing, pr.p., last; adj., permanent, durable.

last'ingly, adv., permanently.

last'ingness, n., durability, endurance.

last'ly, adv., finally.

lataki'a, n., a variety of Turkish tobacco.

latch, v.t., to fasten with a latch; n., the fastening of a door or gate.

latched, p.p., latch.

latch'et, n., a shoe fastening.

latch'ing, pr.p., latch.

latch'key, n., a pocket door key.

late, adj., behind time, backward; far on in point of time; dead; recent; adv., behind time; far on in time; hitherto.

lateen', adj., of the lateen type (i.e., triangular), on a long, tapering yard and a short mast; n., a sail so rigged.

late'ly, adv., recently.

la'tency, n., the state of being latent.

late'ness, n., the state of being late.

la'tent, adj., secret, dormant.

la'tently, adv., in a latent way.

la'ter, adj., comp. of late.

lat'eral, adj., rel. to the side; n., a sprout.

lateral'ity, n., physical one-sidedness.

lat'erally, adv., in a lateral position; sideways.

Lat'eran, adj., rel. to the Lateran; n., the cathedral church (St. John Lateran) of Rome.

laterifo'lious, adj., by the side of a leaf.

lateri'tious, adj., of brick, or brick-like.

la'test, adj., super. of late.

la'tex, n., a milky fluid of the rubber plant.

lath, v.t., to overlay with laths; n., a narrow strip of wood.

lathe, n., a machine for turning wood, metal, etc.

lathed, p.p., lath.

lath'er, n. the froth of soap and water; froth-like sweat; v.t., to spread lather on; to thrash; v.i., to form into a lather; to sweat.

lath'ered, p.p., lather.

lath'ering, pr.p., lather; n., a thrashing.

lath'i, n., an Indian weapon.

lath'ing, pr.p., lath.

lath'y, adj., slender, like a lath.

laticos'tate, adj., broad-ribbed.

latiden'tate, adj., broad-toothed.

latifo'lious, adj., broad-leaved.

latifun'dia, n. pl., large estates (Lat.).

Lat'in, adj., pert to Latium and the Latins; n., the L. language.

Latinesque', adj., like Latin.

Lat'inism, n., the Latin idiom.

Lat'inist, n., an accomplished Latin scholar.

Latin'ity, n., the style in which one writes Latin; the Latin quality.

Lat'inize, v.t., to turn into Latin; v.i., to adopt Latin ways.

Lat'inized, p.p., Latinize.

Lat'inizing, pr.p., Latinize.

la'tish, adj., somewhat late.

lat'itude, n., breadth, scope; the distance from the equator.

latitu'dinal, adj., rel. to latitude.

latitudina'rian, *adj.*, unorthodox.

latitudina'rianism, *n.*, unorthodoxy.

latitu'dinous, *adj.*, having width or scope.

la'trant, *adj.*, barking.

latri'a, *n.*, worship.

latrine', *n.*, a lavatory in a camp or barrack.

lat'ten, *adj.*, made of latten; *n.*, a mixed, brass-like metal.

lat'ter, *adj.*, of more recent date; *n.*, the second of two things.

lat'terly, *adv.*, recently, of late.

lat'tice, *n.*, a screen or door made of laths crossed and showing interstices; *v.t.*, to supply with a lattice.

lat'ticed, *p.p.*, lattice.

lat'ticing, *pr.p.*, lattice.

laud, *v.t.*, to praise, to extol.

laud'able, *adj.*, praiseworthy.

laud'ableness, *n.*, praiseworthiness.

laud'ably, *adv.*, praiseworthily.

laud'anum, *n.*, the tincture of opium.

lauda'tion, *n.*, praise.

laud'atory, *adj.*, in praise, flattering.

laud'ed, *p.p.*, laud.

laud'ing, *pr.p.*, laud.

laugh, *v.i.*, to give vocal expression to amusement; *n.*, an expression of joy, gaiety, pleasure, scorn.

laugh'able, *adj.*, ludicrous.

laugh'ably, *adv.*, ludicrously.

laughed, *p.p.*, laugh.

laugh'er, *n.*, one who laughs.

laugh'ing, *pr.p.*, laugh.

laugh'ingly, *adv.*, in a laughing way.

laugh'ter, *n.*, laughing, gaiety, merriment.

launch, *v.t.*, to hurl; to set afloat; to send off; *v.i.*, to begin an enterprise; *n.*, the act of launching; a warship's large open boat; an electric or steam boat.

launched, *p.p.*, launch.

launch'ers, *n.*, devices used for launching rockets, etc.

launch'ing, *pr.p.*, launch.

launch'ing-pad, *n.*, a construction from which rockets are launched.

laun'der, *v.t.*, to wash, iron, and fold (linen); *n.*, a trough.

laun'dered, *p.p.*, launder; *adj.*, washed (as applied to linen and clothes).

laun'dering, *pr.p.*, launder; *n.*, the process of washing linen and clothes.

laun'derette, *n.*, a do-it-yourself laundry.

laun'dry, *n.*, a place where clothes are washed, etc.

lau'reate, *adj.*, wreathed with laurel; *n.*, a poet laureate.

lau'reated, *adj.*, *i.q.* laureate.

lau'reateship, *n.*, the office of laureate.

laurea'tion, *n.*, the act of conferring the laurel.

lau'rel, *n.*, an evergreen shrub.

lau'rel(l)ed, *adj.*, laurel-crowned; laureate.

lau'rustine, *n.*, an evergreen shrub.

laurusti'nus, *n.*, *i.q.* laurustine.

la'va, *n.*, the molten rock thrown up by a volcano.

lava'bo, *n.*, the ceremony of hand-washing in the Mass; the vessel for the water.

lava'tion, *n.*, washing.

lav'atory, *n.*, a vessel for washing; a room for the purpose; a water-closet.

lave, *v.t.*, to bathe, to wash.

laved, *p.p.*, lave.

lave'ment, *n.*, an injection, an enema (*med.*).

lav'ender, *v.t.*, to lay up in lavender; *n.*, a perfumed shrub.

la'ver, *n.*, an edible seaweed.

la'ving, *pr.p.*, lave.

lav'ish, *v.t.*, to give in profusion, to expend; *adj.*, profuse, prodigal.

lav'ished, *p.p.*, lavish.

lav'isher, *n.*, one who lavishes.

lav'ishing, *pr.p.*, lavish.

lav'ishly, *adv.*, profusely.

lavol'ta, *n.*, an old dance.

law, *n.*, a set of rules; an enactment, a precedent; rule of invariable sequence.

law'ful, *adj.*, in accordance with law; legal; allowable.

law'fully, *adv.*, in a lawful way.

law'fulness, *n.*, the quality of being lawful.

law'giver, *n.*, one who makes laws.

law'less, *adj.*, lacking laws; regardless of law, wild.

law'lessly, *adv.*, in a lawless way.

law'lessness, *n.*, the quality of being lawless.

lawn, *n.*, a glade; a surface of mown grass; a fine variety of linen.

lawn-mow'er, *n.*, a machine for cutting grass.

lawn-ten'nis, *n.*, *i.q.* tennis.

law'suit, *n.*, an action, in a court of law.

law'yer, *n.*, a practitioner in the law; one versed in law.

law'yerish, *adj.*, lawyer-like.

lax, *adj.*, loose, flabby; easygoing.

laxa'tion, *n.*, the act or effect of loosening.

lax'ative, *adj.*, purgative; *n.*, a purgative medicine.

lax'ity, *n.*, the quality of being lax.

lax'ly, *adv.*, loosely.

lay, *v.t.*, to place, to cause to lie; to arrange in order; to deposit; *adj.*, non-clerical; non-professional, not expert; *n.*, a song.

lay'about, *n.*, an habitual loafer or tramp.

lay'by, *n.*, a section of widened road for the parking of vehicles; a railway siding.

lay'er, *n.*, one who lays; a stratum; the thickness of something spread; a shoot not severed from its stem, and fastened into the ground; *v.t.*, to treat a plant thus.

lay'ered, *p.p.*, layer.

lay'ering, *pr.p.*, layer.

layette', *n.*, a newly-born infant's outfit.

lay-fig'ure, *n.*, a model.

lay'ing, *pr.p.,* lay.

lay'man, *n.,* not a clergyman nor one skilled in a particular profession referred to.

lay'-off, *n.,* temporary unemployment, a slack season.

lay'out, *n.,* a plan for the arrangement of land; printed matter or display material.

lay'stall, *n.,* a refuse heap.

lay'woman, *n.,* a non-professional woman.

laz'ar, *n.,* a leper.

lazaret', *n.,* a leper hospital; a quarantine hospital.

lazaret'to, *n., i.q.* lazaret.

laze, *v.i.,* to be lazy (*colloq.*).

la'zier, *adj., comp.* of lazy.

la'ziest, *adj., super.* of lazy.

la'zily, *adv.,* in a lazy way.

la'ziness, *n.,* the state or quality of being lazy.

laz'uli, *n.,* see lapis-lazuli.

la'zy, *adj.,* slothful, idle.

lazzaro'ne, *n.,* a Neapolitan street-idler.

lea, *n.,* grassland; a yarn measure.

leach, *v.t.,* to wash by draining; *v.i.,* to percolate; *n.,* leached material; the edge of a ship's sail.

leached, *p.p.,* leach.

leach'ing, *pr.p.,* leach.

lead, *n.,* a heavy, ductile metal; a thin strip of metal used to widen spaces in printer's type; *v.t.,* to insert metal strips.

lead, *v.t.,* to bring along, to guide, to go in front of; to give direction and command; *n.,* direction given, an example set; a water channel; the right to play first in a round of cards; the card or suit first played; an electric cable; a string of leather or chain for controlling an animal.

lead'ed, *adj.,* widened with leads; *p.p.,* lead.

lead'en, *adj.,* made of, or like lead; heavy.

lead'er, *n.,* one who leads; a leading article in a journal.

lead'ered, *adj.,* treated in a leading article.

leaderette', *n.,* a short editorial.

lead'erless, *adj.,* without a leader.

lead'ership, *n.,* the function of a leader; guidance.

lead'-in, *n.,* a point of entrance; wire connecting aerial to a radio or television receiver.

lead'ing, *pr.p.,* lead (metal).

lead'ing, *pr.p.,* lead; *n.,* guidance; a large type editorial; *adj.,* influential; foremost.

lead'ing-strings, *n. pl.,* supports for infants learning to walk.

lead-pen'cil, *n.,* a pencil of wood encasing a graphite writing stem.

leads'man, *n.,* a sailor who heaves the lead.

leaf, *n.,* an expansion from the side or root of a plant stem; a petal; a single thickness of paper; a thin foil; the flap of a door, shutter or table.

leaf'age, *n.,* foliage.

leafed, *adj.,* having leaves.

leaf'iness, *n.,* the quality of being leafy.

leaf'less, *adj.,* without leaves.

leaf'let, *n.,* a little leaf; a small printed leaf.

leaf'y, *adj.,* full of leaves.

league, *v.t.,* to combine in a league; *v.i.,* to form a league; *n.,* an alliance, a compact; a measure of three miles.

leagued, *p.p.,* league.

lea'guing, *pr.p.,* league.

leak, *v.t.,* to allow to escape or pass through; *v.i.,* to pass out or through; to escape (of liquid, gas or information); *n.,* a hole letting water in or out.

leak'age, *n.,* the act of leaking; the quantity that has leaked out.

leaked, *p.p.,* leak.

leak'iness, *n.,* the state or quality of being leaky.

leak'ing, *pr.p.,* leak.

leak'y, *adj.,* having a leak or leaks; unable to keep a secret.

leal, *adj.,* loyal.

lean, *v.t.,* to incline, to support; *v.i.,* to incline oneself; to be inclined; to droop; *adj.,* thin, slender, meagre; *n.,* the non-fat part of meat.

leaned, *p.p.,* lean.

lean'er, *adj., comp.* of lean.

lean'est, *adj., super.* of lean.

lean'ing, *pr.p.,* lean.

lean'ness, *n.,* the quality of being lean.

leant, *i.q.* leaned.

lean'-to, *n.,* a shed, hut or greenhouse built against an outer wall.

leap, *v.i.,* to jump, to spring; *n.,* a jump, a spring.

leaped, *p.p.,* leap.

leap'er, *n.,* one who leaps.

leap'frog, *n.,* a game of leaping.

leap'ing, *pr.p.,* leap.

leapt, *i.q.* leaped; *adj.,* jumped, vaulted.

leap'-year, *n.,* every fourth year, to which is added the intercalary day, Feb. 29.

learn, *v.t.,* to come to know; to know by heart; *v.i.,* to become instructed.

learned, *p.p.,* learn.

learn'ed, *adj.,* instructed, erudite, deeply versed.

learn'edly, *adv.,* in a learned way.

learn'er, *n.,* one who learns.

learn'ing, *pr.p.,* learn; *n.,* erudition, acquired knowledge, instruction.

learnt, *i.q.* learned.

leas'able, *adj.,* able to be leased.

lease, *v.t.,* to convey to a tenant for a fixed time and rent; *n.,* the contract by which such conveyance is made; any terminable period; the crossing of warp-threads.

leased, *p.p.,* lease.

lease'hold, *n.,* a tenure under lease.

lease'holder, *n.,* one who holds a lease.

leash, *v.t.,* to fasten in a leash; *n.,* a thong holding one or more hounds.

leashed, *p.p.,* leash.

leas'ing, *pr.p.*, lease; *n.*, lying (*biblical*).

least, *adj.* and *adv.*, smallest, slightest.

least'ways, *adv.*, or at least, or rather.

leat, *n.*, an open watercourse.

leath'er, *v.t.*, to cover with leather; to beat with a thong; *n.*, dressed hide.

leatherette', *n.*, an imitation leather made of paper or cloth.

lea'ther-jacket, *n.*, the larva of the crane-fly (daddy-long-legs).

leath'ern, *adj.*, made of leather.

lea'theroid, *n.*, an imitation hide made from cotton paper.

leath'ery, *adj.*, like leather.

leave, *v.t.*, to allow to remain; to depart from, to quit; to go away without; to deliver; *n.*, permission; a departure.

leaved, *adj.*, having leaves.

leav'en, *v.t.*, to cause to ferment; to influence imperceptibly; *n.*, something added to dough to cause fermentation; subtle influence.

leav'ened, *p.p.*, leaven.

leav'ening, *pr.p.*, leaven.

leav'er, *n.*, one who leaves.

leaves, *n.*, pl. of leaf.

leav'ing, *pr.p.*, leave.

leav'ings, *n. pl.*, remnants, residue.

Lebanese', *adj.*, rel. to Lebanon; *n.*, a native of L.

leb'ensraum, *n.*, the living space believed to be necessary for the natural development of a nation (*Ger.*).

lech'er, *n.*, a debauchee; a fornicator.

lech'erous, *adj.*, debauched.

lech'erously, *adv.*, in a lecherous way.

lech'ery, *n.*, debauchery; fornication.

lec'tern, *n.*, a raised desk for readers aloud and lecturers.

lec'tion, *n.*, a portion read; a difference in text; a lesson.

lec'tor, *n.*, a reader (one of the minor orders of the Church).

lec'ture, *v.t.*, to admon-

ish, to reprove; *v.i.*, to deliver a discourse; *n.*, a discourse; an admonition, a reproof.

lec'tured, *p.p.*, lecture.

lec'turer, *n.*, one who lectures.

lec'tureship, *n.*, the office of a lecturer.

lecturette', *n.*, a short lecture.

lec'turing, *pr.p.*, lecture.

led, *p.p.*, lead.

ledge, *n.*, a shelf or shelf-like projection; a ridge.

ledg'er, *n.*, the chief account book in a business establishment; a horizontal piece of wood used in scaffolding; *adj.*, in the phrase "ledger line", *i.e.*, an additional line above or below the musical stave.

led'-horse, *n.*, a horse without a rider and led.

lee, *n.*, shelter; side away from the wind.

leech, *v.t.*, to doctor; *n.*, a doctor; a bloodsucking worm; the sloping side of a sail.

leech'craft, *n.*, the art of healing.

leeched, *p.p.*, leech.

leech'ing, *pr.p.*, leech.

leek, *n.*, a culinary herb, like the onion.

leer, *v.i.*, to glance slyly or malignantly; *n.*, a lascivious or sly glance; an annealing chamber in a glassworks.

leered, *p.p.*, leer.

leer'ing, *pr.p.*, leer; *adj.*, glancing slyly.

leer'ingly, *adv.*, with a leer.

leer'y, *adj.*, sly.

lees, *n. pl.*, deposit in a wine-glass; refuse.

lee shore, *n.*, the shore on the leeward side.

leet, *n.*, an old kind of English court.

lee'ward, *adj.* and *adv.*, on the lee side, *i.e.*, opposite to the windward side; *n.*, the leeward direction.

lee'wardly, *adj.*, inclined to drift to leeward.

lee'way, *n.*, a drift to leeward; any falling off.

left, *p.p.*, leave; *adj.*, the side opposed to

the right; *n.*, the left side; *adv.*, on or by the left.

left'handed, *adj.*, using the left hand rather than the right; double-edged.

left'hander, *n.*, a left-handed person.

left'ism, *n.*, the principles of the political left.

left'ist, *n.*, a follower of the policies of the left.

left'-off, *adj.*, disused.

left'ward, *adj.*, on the left.

left'wards, *adv.*, towards the left.

leg, *v.i.*, to run (in the phrase, *leg it*); *n.*, a supporting and locomotive limb; any support or leg-like thing.

leg'acy, *n.*, a gift under a will; anything inherited.

le'gal, *adj.*, in accordance with, having the sanction of, law; rel. to law.

le'galism, *n.*, a theological preference of the Law to the Gospel.

le'galist, *n.*, a professor of legalism.

legal'ity, *n.*, lawfulness.

legaliza'tion, *n.*, the act or result of legalizing.

le'galize, *v.t.*, to make legal; to give the force of law to.

le'galized, *p.p.*, legalize.

le'galizing, *pr.p.*, legalize.

le'gally, *adv.*, in a legal way.

leg'ate, *n.*, an accredited envoy.

legate', *v.t.*, to bequeath.

legatee', *n.*, the recipient of a legacy.

lega'tion, *n.*, an embassy; an ambassador's residence.

lega'to, *adv.*, smoothly; without breaks (*mus.*).

lega'tor, *n.*, one who bequeaths; a testator.

leg'end, *n.*, a traditional story; an inscription.

leg'endary, *adj.*, of a mythical character.

leg'erdemain, *n.*, sleight of hand.

legged, *p.p.*, leg.

leg'giness, *n.*, lanky-leggedness.

legginette', *n.*, a short gaiter or leg covering.

leg'ging, *pr.p.*, leg; *n.*, an outer covering for the lower leg.

leg'gy, *adj.*, lanky; all leg.

leghorn', *adj.*, made of leghorn straw; *n.*, a straw plait.

legibil'ity, *n.*, the quality of being legible.

leg'ible, *adj.*, readable, decipherable.

leg'ibly, *adv.*, clearly, decipherably.

le'gion, *n.*, a large division of the Roman army; a multitude.

le'gionary, *adj.*, rel. to legions; *n.*, a soldier of a legion.

legionnaire', *n.*. a member of a legion (soldier).

leg'islate, *v.i.*, to pass laws.

leg'islated, *p.p.*, legislate.

leg'islating, *pr.p.*, legislate.

legisla'tion, *n.*, the enacting of laws.

leg'islative, *adj.*, that which enacts laws; law-making; *n.*, the authority that makes laws.

leg'islator, *n.*, a law maker; a member of the legislature.

leg'islature, *n.*, the legislative body.

le'gist, *n.*, a person versed in law.

legit'imacy, *n.*, the state or quality of being legitimate.

legit'imate, *adj.*, lawful, regular; lawfully begotten.

legitimate', *v.t.*, to make legitimate by law or proof; to justify.

legit'imated, *p.p.*, legitimate.

legit'imately, *adv.*, lawfully.

legit'imating, *pr.p.*, legitimate.

legitima'tion, *n.*, the act of legitimating.

legit'imatize, *v.t.*, i.q. legitimate.

legit'imism, *n.*, the doctrine of succession by direct descent.

legit'imist, *n.*, an adherent of legitimism.

leg'ume, *n.*, the eatable part of a leguminous plant.

legu'men, *n.*, i.q. legume.

legu'min, *n.*, vegetable casein.

legu'minous, *adj.*, of the order of pulse (*bot.*).

lei, *n.*, a garland of flowers.

leis'ter, *n.*, a pronged salmon spear; *v.t.*, to spear with a leister.

lei'surable, *adj.*, vacant, idle.

lei'sure, *n.*, free time; spare time; freedom from fixed occupation.

lei'sured, *adj.*, disengaged; free to do as one likes.

lei'surely, *adj.*, deliberate, slow; *adv.*, deliberately, slowly.

lem'ma, *n.*, a theme for argument; a literary subject named in a heading.

lem'ming, *n.*, a kind of field mouse.

lem'on, *n.*, a pale yellow citrus fruit.

lemonade', *n.*, a drink made from the lemon.

lem'on-cheese, *n.*, a mixture of lemon, eggs and butter.

lem'on-sole, *n.*, a kind of plaice.

le'mur, *n.*, a monkeylike nocturnal mammal.

lend, *v.t.*, to give for temporary use; to let out on interest; to afford.

lend'able, *adj.*, able to be lent.

lend'er, *n.*, one who lends.

lend'ing, *pr.p.*, lend.

length, *n.*, a longitudinal measurement; the distance from end to end; the degree or extent.

length'en, *v.t.*, to make longer; *v.i.*, to grow longer.

length'ened, *p.p.*, lengthen.

length'ening, *pr.p.*, lengthen.

length'ily, *adv.*, in a lengthy way.

length'iness, *n.*, prolixity.

length'ways, *adv.*, in a longitudinal way.

length'wise, *adv.*, as measured in length.

length'y, *adj.*, prolix, wearisome.

len'ience, *n.*, i.q. leniency.

le'niency, *n.*, gentleness, mildness.

le'nient, *adj.*, mild, gentle.

le'niently, *adv.*, gently.

Len'inism, *n.*, the political philosophy of Lenin, the Russian revolutionary.

Len'inist, *n.*, a professor of Leninism.

len'itive, *adj.*, soothing, palliating; *n.*, an assuaging remedy.

len'ity, *n.*, gentleness, mildness.

le'no, *n.*, a kind of gauze.

lens, *n.*, a piece of glass or transparent material, so shaped as to concentrate or disperse light rays.

len'ses, *n.*, pl. of lens.

Lent, *n.*, the forty days from Ash Wednesday to Easter Eve.

lent, *p.p.*, lend.

lent'en, *adj.*, rel. to Lent.

lentic'ular, *adj.*, lentilshaped; like a doubleconvex lens.

len'tiform, *adj.*, i.q. lenticular.

lentig'inous, *adj.*, dusty.

lenti'go, *n.*, freckles.

len'til, *n.*, a leguminous plant.

lent'isk, *n.*, the mastic tree.

len'titude, *n.*, sluggishness.

len'to, *adv.*, slowly (*It.*, *mus.*).

Le'o, *n.*, the Lion, one of the signs of the Zodiac.

le'onid, *n.*, a meteor from the Leo quarter of the heavens.

le'onine, *adj.*, like a lion, fierce; *n.*, a hexameter or pentameter line rhyming internally.

leop'ard, *n.*, a carnivorous, feline mammal.

le'otard, *n.*, a tight garment worn by stage performers.

lep'er, *n.*, one afflicted with leprosy.

lep'idolite, *n.*, a scaly silicate.

Lepidop'tera, *n. pl.*, insects with scaly wings.

lepidop'terous, *adj.*, rel. to Lepidoptera.

lepido'sis, *n.*, a mild skin disease.

lep'idote, *adj.*, scurfy.

lep'orine, *adj.*, hare-like.

lep'rechaun, *n.*, an Irish sprite.

lepros'ery, *n.*, a leperhouse.

lep'rosy, *n.*, a fearful wasting disease, accompanied by scales.

lep'rous, *adj.*, rel. to leprosy.

leptodac'tyl, *adj.*, having long slender toes.

lep'ton, *n.*, a hundredth of a drachma; a small electron.

Les'bian, *adj.*, rel. to Lesbos; *n.*, a female homosexual.

lese-maj'esty, *n.*, treason; an offence against a monarch.

le'sion, *n.*, hurt, damage; a morbid derangement of tissue or organ.

less, *adj.* and *adv.*, smaller; not so much.

lessee', *n.*, one to whom property is leased.

les'sen, *v.t.* and *i.*, to diminish.

les'sened, *p.p.*, lessen.

les'sening, *pr.p.*, lessen.

les'ser, *adj.*, *i.q.* less.

les'son, *v.t.*, to instruct, to admonish; *n.*, a passage for reading; a lection; teaching; a rebuke, a punishment.

lessor', *n.*, one who leases out a property.

lest, *conj.*, for fear that; in order to prevent.

let, *v.t.*, to hinder; to grant use for rent; to permit, to allow; *n.*, a hindrance; the letting of a house; the house let.

le'thal, *adj.*, deadly.

lethar'gic, *adj.*, apathetic, drowsy.

leth'argy, *n.*, drowsiness, apathy.

Le'the, *n.*, a river in Hades; oblivion.

Lethe'an, *adj.*, rel. to Lethe.

lethif'erous, *adj.*, deadly.

let'-off, *n.*, a chance missed; a penalty remitted.

Lett, *n.*, a Lithuanian.

let'ter, *n.*, an alphabetical sign; a written communication; *v.t.*, to put lettering on.

let'terbox, *n.*, a receptacle for letters.

let'tered, *p.p.*, letter; *adj.*, learned, literary.

let'terhead, *n.*, the printing at the top of letter paper.

let'tering, *pr.p.*, letter; *n.*, an inscription.

let'terpress, *n.*, printed matter.

let'ters, *n. pl.*, literature, learning.

let'ting, *pr.p.*, let.

let'tuce, *n.*, a garden herb used for salads.

let'-up, *v.t.* and *i.*, to be less severe, to take off the pressure; *n.*, a reduction in impetus or activity.

leu'cocyte, *n.*, a white blood corpuscle.

leucorrhoe'a, *n.*, a mucous discharge.

leucot'omy, *n.*, an incision into the front lobe of the brain.

leukaem'ia, *n.*, a blood disease in which there is an excess of white corpuscles.

lev, *n.*, a Bulgarian monetary unit.

Levant', *n.*, the Eastern Mediterranean; a variety of morocco.

levant', *v.i.*, to abscond.

levant'ed, *p.p.*, levant.

levant'er, *n.*, an absconder; a dweller in the Levant.

Levant'ine, *adj.*, rel. to the Levant.

levant'ing, *pr.p.*, levant.

leva'tor, *n.*, a lifting muscle.

lev'ee, *n.*, a reception; a court function.

lev'el, *v.t.*, to make level, flat, or even; to make even with the ground; to point (a gun); *adj.*, horizontal; on an equality, even, uniform; *n.*, an instrument showing horizontality; a horizontal plane.

lev'elled, lev'eled, *p.p.*, level.

lev'eller, lev'eler, *n.*, one who would abolish inequalities.

lev'elling, lev'eling, *pr.p.*, level.

le'ver, *v.t.*, to lift or move with a lever; *n.*, a bar turning on a fulcrum and used for lifting up a weight.

le'verage, *n.*, the power gained by levering; the action of a lever; added power.

le'vered, *p.p.*, lever.

lev'eret, *n.*, a young hare.

le'vering, *pr.p.*, lever.

lev'iable, *adj.*, able to be levied upon.

levi'athan, *n.*, a huge sea-monster; anything immensely large.

lev'ied, *p.p.*, levy.

lev'igate, *v.t.*, to grind to powder; to make smooth, to polish.

lev'igated, *p.p.*, levigate.

lev'igating, *pr.p.*, levigate.

leviga'tion, *n.*, the act of levigating.

lev'in, *n.*, lightning.

le'virate, *n.*, the Jewish practice which required a dead man's brother or nearest kinsman to marry his wife.

lev'itate, *v.t.*, to make to float in the air; *v.i.*, to float in the air.

levita'tion, *n.*, the act of levitating.

Le'vite, *n.*, one of the priestly tribe of Levi.

Levit'ical, *adj.*, rel. to Levites and Leviticus.

Levit'icus, *n.*, one of the books of the Pentateuch.

lev'ity, *n.*, lightness; frivolity, trifling behaviour.

lev'ulose, *n.*, fruit sugar (*chem.*).

lev'y, *v.t.*, to collect tax; to enrol men for war; to proceed to take; *n.*, the collection or assessment of tax; the enrolment.

lev'ying, *pr.p.*, levy.

lewd, *adj.*, obscene, lascivious.

lewd'ly, *adv.*, in a lewd way.

lewd'ness, *n.*, obscenity, indecency.

lew'is, *n.*, an iron device for hoisting heavy stones.

Lew'is gun, *n.*, a light machine-gun.

lew'isite, *n.*, blister gas.

lex, *n.*, law (*Lat.*).

lex'ical, *adj.*, rel. to words or to a lexicon.

lexicog'rapher, *n.*, the compiler of a lexicon.

lexicograph'ic, *adj.*, rel. to lexicography.

lexicograph'ical, *adj.*, *i.q.* lexicographic.

lexicog'raphy, *n.*, dictionary-making.

lexicol'ogy, *n.*, the study of words in a language.

lex'icon, *n.*, a dictionary.

lexigraph'ic, *adj.*, rel. to lexigraphy.

lexig'raphy, *n.*, the system of representing words by single signs.

ley, *n.*, a pasture.

Ley'den, *n.*, a city of Holland; a Leyden jar is a condenser.

liabil'ity, *n.*, the state of being liable.

li'able, *adj.*, exposed or subject to some obligation or debt.

li'ableness, *n.*, *i.q.* liability.

liaise', *v.i.*, to establish or maintain a relationship between individuals or groups.

liais'on, *n.*, an illicit sexual relationship; connection. In French it is the sounding of an ordinarily silent consonant before a vowel or *h* mute.

liais'on-officer, *n.*, one who acts as a go-between.

lia'na, *n.*, a variety of rope-like climbing tropical forest plant.

lia'nae, *n.*, pl. of liana.

li'ar, *n.*, one who lies.

li'as, *n.*, a blue lime rock.

liba'tion, *n.*, an offering of wine.

li'bel, *v.t.*, to defame with a libel; to falsely accuse; *n.*, written and published slander; a declaration in writing.

li'bel(l)ant, *n.*, the instituter of an Admiralty suit.

li'bel(l)ed, *p.p.*, libel.

li'bel(l)er, *n.*, one guilty of libel.

li'bel(l)ing, *pr.p.*, libel.

lib'elist, *n.*, a victim of libel.

li'bel(l)ous, *adj.*, of the nature of libel.

lib'el(l)ously, *adv.*, in a libelous manner.

lib'er, *n.*, a book (*Lat.*); bark (*Lat.*).

lib'eral, *adj.*, generous; unstinted; wide in scope; unprejudiced; rel. to liberalism; *n.*, a professor of liberalism.

lib'eralism, *n.*, the profession of liberal opinions or policy.

lib'eralist, *n.*, a person who advocates liberalism.

lib'eralistic, *adj.*, *i.q.* liberal.

liberal'ity, *n.*, generosity, bounty.

liberaliza'tion, *n.*, the act of liberalizing; the condition of being liberalized.

lib'eralize, *v.t.*, to make liberal.

lib'eralized, *p.p.*, liberalize.

lib'eralizing, *pr.p.*, liberalize.

lib'erally, *adv.*, generously.

lib'erate, *v.t.*, to set free.

lib'erated, *p.p.*, liberate.

lib'erating, *pr.p.*, liberate.

libera'tion, *n.*, deliverance; the setting free.

lib'erator, *n.*, one who liberates.

liberta'rian, *adj.*, rel. to the freewill doctrine.

liber'ticide, *n.*, the destruction of liberty; a destroyer of liberty.

lib'ertine, *adj.*, regardless of morals, dissolute; *n.*, a dissolute person.

lib'ertinism, *n.*, dissoluteness.

lib'erty, *n.*, freedom, exemption, immunity.

libid'inal, *adj.*, lustful, lewd.

libid'inous, *adj.*, lustful.

libid'o, *n.*, the craving for sexual experience.

Li'bra, *n.*, the Balance, one of the signs of the Zodiac; the pound.

libra'rian, *n.*, the custodian of a library.

libra'rianship, *n.*, a librarian's office.

li'brary, *n.*, a collection of books; a bookroom.

li'brate, *v.i.*, to balance; to poise.

li'brated, *p.p.*, librate.

li'brating, *pr.p.*, librate.

libra'tion, *n.*, the act of balancing.

li'bratory, *adj.*, balancing.

libret'tist, *n.*, the writer of a libretto.

libret'to, *n.*, the words of an opera or oratorio (*It.*).

Lib'yan, *adj.*, rel. to Libya; *n.*, a native of L.

lice, *n.*, pl. of louse.

li'cence, *n.*, an official permission; an excessive liberty; an irregularity; a certificate to do or possess something.

li'cense, *v.t.*, to grant permission.

li'censed, *p.p.*, license.

licensee', *n.*, the holder of a licence.

li'censer, *n.*, the granter of a licence.

li'censing, *pr.p.*, license.

licen'tiate, *n.*, the holder of an academic licence.

licen'tious, *adj.*, irregular, lewd.

licen'tiously, *adv.*, in a licentious way.

licen'tiousness, *n.*, lewd behaviour.

lich, *n.*, a corpse.

li'chen, *n.*, a parasitic fungus.

lichenog'raphy, *n.*, the description of lichens.

lichenol'ogy, *n.*, the study of lichens (fungoid plants).

lich'-gate, *n.*, the covered gateway at the entrance of a churchyard.

lic'it, *adj.*, lawful.

lic'itly, *adv.*, lawfully.

lick, *v.t.*, to smooth with the tongue; to pass the tongue over; to overcome (*slang*); *n.*, the act of licking.

licked, *p.p.*, lick.

lick'er, *n.*, one who licks.

lick'erish, *adj.*, greedy; lecherous.

lick'ing, *pr.p.*, lick.

lick'spittle, *adj.*, toadying; *n.*, a toady.

lic'orice, *n.*, *see* liquorice.

lic'tor, *n.*, an ancient Roman official (*Lat.*).

lid, *n.*, a cover, a top.

lid'less, *adj.*, without a lid.

lid'o, *n.*, an open-air bathing place.

lie, *v.t.*, to be in a horizontal position, to be situated; to tell a falsehood; *n.*, a falsehood; a position; in golf, the place or manner in which a ball happens to lie.

lied, *p.p.*, lie, in the sense of telling a falsehood.

lied, *n.*, a German song or ballad.

lief, *adv.*, willingly.

lief'er, *adv.*, sooner, rather.

liege, *adj.*, bound to service; claiming allegiance; *n.*, a vassal; a lord.

li'en, *n.*, a legal claim to hold property as security.

li'entery, *n.*, a form of diarrhoea.

lierne', *n.*, a cross-rib in vaulting (*archit.*).

lieu, *n.*, place, stead.

lieuten'ancy, *n.,* the rank or office of lieutenant.

lieuten'ant, *n.,* a deputy, a substitute; an officer in the navy and the army.

lieuten'ant-col'onel, *n.,* a military officer next in rank below a colonel.

life, *n.,* the state of being alive; animation; existence; the living form; living things collectively.

life'assurance, *n.,* an insurance on the chances of living or against the risk of dying at a particular time.

life'belt, *n.,* a life-preserving belt.

life'blood, *n.,* that which is essential to life.

life'boat, *n.,* a life-saving boat.

life'buoy, *n.,* a buoyant device for keeping a person afloat.

life'giving, *adj.,* in-spiriting, animating.

life'guard, *n.,* a body-guard of soldiers.

life'less, *adj.,* dead, spiritless.

life'lessly, *adv.,* in a lifeless way.

life'lessness, *n.,* the state of being lifeless.

life'like, *adj.,* true to reality.

life'line, *n.,* a rope for saving life, attached to a buoy or ship; a line fired by a rocket from shore to ship.

life'long, *adj.,* lasting through life.

life'manship, *n.,* behaviour causing others to feel inferior.

life'-preserver, *n.,* a loaded short stick.

life' saver, *n.,* someone who, or something that, saves or protects human life.

life'-size, *adj.,* of natural size.

life'time, *n.,* the period of a life.

lift, *v.t.,* to raise, to hoist, to steal; *v.i.,* to dispense, to rise; *n.,* the act of lifting; the extent of a rise; an elevator or hoist.

lift'ed, *p.p.,* lift.

lift'er, *n.,* anything or anyone that lifts.

lift'ing, *pr.p.,* lift.

lig'ament, *n.,* a tie; a binding membrane.

ligamen'tal, *adj.,* binding.

ligamen'tous, *adj., i.q.* ligamental.

li'gate, *v.t.,* to bind.

liga'tion, *n.,* the act of tying arteries, etc.

lig'ature, *n., i.q.* ligation; that which unites or binds; a slur or tie in music.

lig'er, *n.,* the offspring of a lion and a tigress.

light, *v.t.,* to set fire to, to illumine; *v.i.,* to take fire, to brighten; *adj.,* luminous, not dark; pale of hue; not heavy; elegant; easy to digest; trivial, thoughtless; *n.,* radiant energy acting on the sight; brightness; illuminant; illumination; a section of a window; a match or spill; understanding.

light'ed, *p.p.,* light.

light'en, *v.t.,* to make light; *v.i.,* to grow light; to emit lightning.

light'ened, *p.p.,* lighten.

light'ening, *pr.p.,* lighten.

light'er, *n.,* a boat for loading and unloading a ship; an appliance for lighting; *adj., comp.* of light.

light'erage, *n.,* the charge for unloading a ship; the craft of working, or the mooring place for, lighters.

light'erman, *n.,* one employed on a lighter.

light'est, *adj., super.* of light.

light'fingered, *adj.,* thievish, pilfering.

light'footed, *adj.,* nimble.

light'-handed, *adj.,* needing help; having little to carry.

light'headed, *adj.,* delirious.

light'hearted, *adj.,* cheerful.

light'heartedly, *adv.,* cheerfully.

light'heartedness, *n.,* the state of being light-hearted.

light'house, *n.,* a lofty tower containing powerful lamps to guide mariners.

light'houseman, *n.,* a lightkeeper in a lighthouse.

light'-in'fantry, *n.,* light-armed infantry.

light'ing, *pr.p.,* light; *n.,* artificial illumination.

light'ish, *adj.,* somewhat light.

light'ly, *adv.,* in a light way.

light'minded, *adj.,* frivolous.

light'ness, *n.,* the state or quality of being light.

light'ning, *n.,* an electric discharge between clouds, or between the clouds and the earth.

lights, *n. pl.,* lungs.

light'ship, *n.,* a ship carrying a warning light.

light'some, *adj.,* luminous, bright.

light'-spir'ited, *adj.,* cheerful.

light'weight, *adj. and n.,* (one) below average weight.

light'-wood, *n.,* wood that burns brightly.

lign-al'oes, *n.,* aloes wood.

lig'neous, *adj.,* woody.

lignifica'tion, *n.,* the state of being lignified.

lig'nified, *p.p.,* lignify.

lig'niform, *adj.,* like wood.

lig'nify, *v.t.,* to turn into wood; *v.i.,* to become wood.

lig'nifying, *pr.p.,* lignify.

lig'nin, *n.,* xylogen.

lig'nite, *n.,* brown coal.

lignit'ic, *adj.,* rel. to lignite.

lig'num vi'tae, *n.,* a tree producing very hard wood (*Lat.*).

lig'ula, *n.,* a fillet; a tongue-like lobe (*Lat.*).

lig'ulate, *adj.,* having a ligula.

lig'ure, *n.,* amber.

like, *v.t.,* to take a fancy to; to find agreeable; *v.i.,* to desire; *adj.,* resembling; equal; *prep.,* in the manner of; *n.,* anything equivalent.

like'able, *adj.,* attractive.

liked, *p.p.,* like.

like'lihood, *n.,* a probability.

like'liness, *n., i.q.* likelihood.

like'ly, *adj.,* probable, reasonable, capable-looking; *adv.,* probably.

like′minded, *adj.*, in agreement.

li′ken, *v.t.*, to make like; to compare.

li′kened, *p.p.*, liken.

like′ness, *n.*, a resemblance; a portrait.

li′kening, *pr.p.*, liken.

like′wise, *adv.*, in the same way; moreover.

li′king, *pr.p.*, like; *n.*, a fondness for; a personal taste.

li′lac, *adj.*, lilac-coloured; *n.*, a flowering shrub; a pale purple colour.

lilia′ceous, *adj.*, pert. to lilies.

lil′ied, *adj.*, full of lilies.

lillibulle′ro, *n.*, an old English political song.

Lillipu′tian, *adj.*, rel. to the kingdom of Lilliput; tiny.

lilt, *v.t.*, to sing with a rhythm; *n.*, a rhythmical, gay song.

lilt′ed, *p.p.*, lilt.

lilt′ing, *adj.*, pleasantly rhythmical; *pr.p.*, lilt.

lil′y, *n.*, a plant of the genus Lilium.

lima′ceous, *adj.*, sluglike.

li′mature, *n.*, polishing, filings.

limb, *n.*, a member (arm, leg, branch); an edge; *v.t.*, to disable.

lim′bate, *adj.*, (flowers) having an edge of a different colour (*bot.*).

limbed, *p.p.*, limb; *adj.*, having limbs.

lim′ber, *v.t.*, to fasten limber to a gun; *n.*, the front part of a gun-carriage; *adj.*, pliant, nimble.

lim′bered, *p.p.*, limber.

lim′bering, *pr.p.*, limber.

lim′berness, *n.*, pliancy, nimbleness.

limb′ing, *pr.p.*, limb.

limb′less, *adj.*, without limbs.

lim′bo, *n.*, a shadowy region on the border of hell; prison; oblivion.

lim′burger, *n.*, the Tibeto-Burmese language; a kind of cheese.

lim′bus, *n.*, an edge or border (*Lat.*).

lime, *v.t.*, to catch (birds) with a sticky substance; to manure with lime; to treat with lime and water;

n., calcium oxide obtained from burnt limestone; a small fruit like the lemon.

lime′kiln, *n.*, a kiln for burning lime.

lime′light, *n.*, calcium light; admiring attention.

lim′en, *n.*, the dividing line between the conscious and subconscious (*psych.*).

lim′erick, *n.*, a form of nonsense-verse.

lime′stone, *n.*, rock containing calcium carbonate.

lime′wash, *v.t.*, to whitewash.

lime′water, *n.*, an aqueous solution containing calcium hydrate.

lime′wort, *n.*, the plant brooklime.

lim′inal, *adj.*, on the threshold.

li′miness, *n.*, the state of being limy.

lim′it, *v.t.*, to put bounds to; to restrict; *n.*, a boundary, a terminal point.

lim′itable, *adj.*, able to be limited.

limitar′ian, *n.*, one who believes only the chosen can be saved.

lim′itary, *adj.*, limiting, subject to restriction.

limita′tion, *n.*, the act of limiting; a disabled or limited condition; a defect.

lim′ited, *p.p.*, limit.

lim′iting, *pr.p.*, limit.

lim′itless, *adj.*, without limit.

lim′itrophe, *adj.*, situated on or near a frontier.

limnol′ogy, *n.*, the study of fresh waters, lakes and ponds (*chem.* and *biol.*).

lim′ousine, *n.*, a large motor car, with a permanently enclosed body.

limp, *v.i.*, to walk lamely; *n.*, a lame walk; *adj.*, not stiff; lacking energy.

limped, *p.p.*, limp.

lim′pet, *n.*, a mollusc that clings to rocks.

lim′pid, *adj.*, clear.

limpid′ity, *n.*, the quality of clearness.

lim′pidness, *n.*, *i.q.* limpidity.

limp′ing, *pr.p.*, limp.

limp′ingly, *adv.*, in a limping way.

limp′kin, *n.*, kinds of bird between cranes and rails.

li′my, *adj.*, covered with, or resembling, lime.

lin, *n.*, a pool, esp. under a waterfall.

linch, *n.*, a ridge marking a boundary.

linch′pin, *n.*, the pin of an axle keeping the wheel on.

lincrus′ta, *n.*, a type of heavy paper used in decorating.

linc′tus, *n.*, a cough syrup.

lin′den, *n.*, the lime tree.

line, *v.t.*, to mark with lines; to draw up a line; to put a lining to; *v.i.*, to form up in line; *n.*, a fine, long flax; a cord; a long mark; a streak; a series or row; a metrical verse; troops deployed for action; a railway track; a department of business; lineage.

lin′eage, *n.*, lineal descent.

lin′eal, *adj.*, in direct succession.

lineal′ity, *n.*, the state of being lineal.

lin′eally, *adv.*, by descent in line.

lin′eament, *n.*, a feature.

lin′ear, *adj.*, rel. to line.

linear′ity, *n.*, the quality of being linear (*i.e.*, measured in one dimension).

linea′tion, *n.*, the marking with lines.

lined, *p.p.*, line.

lin′en, *adj.*, made of flax; *n.*, cloth made from flax.

lin′en-draper, *n.*, one who deals in linen and calico goods.

li′ner, *n.*, a vessel bel. to a line of passenger ships.

li′nesman, *n.*, a member of a line regiment; an official in a game who watches the marked lines.

ling, *n.*, an edible seafish; heather.

lin′ger, *v.i.*, to delay starting; to dally, to drag on.

lin′gered, *p.p.*, linger.

ling′erer, *n.*, one who lingers.

lin′gerie, *n.*, underwear (*Fr.*).

lin'gering, *adj.*, loitering; *pr.p.*, linger.

lin'go, *n.*, a foreign tongue (a contemptuous expression).

ling'ua franc'a, *n.*, the international language of the Levant.

lin'gual, *adj.*, rel. to the tongue; *n.*, a letter pronounced by the tongue.

lin'guiform, *adj.*, tongue-shaped.

lin'guist, *n.*, an expert in languages.

linguis'tic, *adj.*, rel. to language.

linguis'tical, *adj.*, *i.q.* linguistic.

linguis'tics, *n. pl.*, the study of language.

ling'ulate, *adj.*, tongue shaped.

linguoden'tal, *adj.*, made with tongue and teeth.

lin'hay, *n.*, an open-fronted farm shed.

lin'iment, *n.*, a liquid ointment.

li'niness, *n.*, liny technique (*art*).

li'ning, *pr.p.*, line; *n.*, an inner covering.

link, *v.t.*, to join; *v.i.*, to become joined; *n.*, a ring in a chain; a part of a connected series; a torch.

link'boy, *n.*, a torch-bearer.

linked, *p.p.*, link.

link'ing, *pr.p.*, link.

links, *n.pl.*, sandy ground near the sea, with turf and bents; a golf course.

linn, *n.*, *i.q.* lin.

Linne'an, *adj.*, pert. to Linnaeus, the 18th cent. botanist.

lin'net, *n.*, a singing-bird.

linn(e)y, *n.*, *i.q.* linhay.

li'no, *n.*, linoleum, a floor covering.

li'nocut, *n.*, a relief design cut on a block of lino; a print from this.

lino'leum, *n.*, a floor-cloth or oilcloth.

li'notype, *n.*, a machine producing a line of type cast in one piece.

li'notyper, *n.*, a linotype setting machine operator.

li'notypist, *n.*, *i.q.* linotyper.

lin'sang, *n.*, a Borneo civet cat.

lin'seed, *n.*, flax seed.

lin'sey-wool'sey, *adj.*, made of linen and wool, or of cotton and linen with wool; *n.*, a dress made of the material.

lin'stock, *n.*, an iron-shod pike used in firing a gun.

lint, *n.*, ravelled linen used for dressing wounds.

lin'tel, *n.*, the horizontal top of a doorway or window.

lin'y, *adj.*, lined, wrinkled; using line too much (*art*).

li'on, *n.*, a large carnivorous beast.

li'oness, *n.*, the fem. of lion.

li'onhearted, *adj.*, courageous.

li'onize, *v.t.*, to show famous persons and places; *v.i.*, to visit show places.

li'onized, *p.p.*, lionize.

li'onizing, *pr.p.*, lionize.

lip, *v.t.*, to touch with the lip; to touch the edge of; to murmur; *n.*, the upper or lower edge of the mouth's opening.

lipog'raphy, *n.*, the omission of letters or words, in writing.

lipped, *p.p.*, lip.

lip'per, *n.*, a slight ripple or ruffling motion; the surface roughness of the sea (*naut.*).

lip'pitude, *n.*, ophthalmia.

lip'-read, *v.t.*, to interpret speech by watching lip movements.

lip'salve, *n.*, an ointment for sore lips.

lip'stick, *n.*, a lip colouring cosmetic.

liq'uable, *adj.*, able to be melted.

liqua'tion, *n.*, the act or effect of melting.

liquefac'tion, *n.*, *i.q.* liquation.

liquefi'able, *adj.*, able to be liquefied.

liq'uefied, *p.p.*, liquefy.

liq'uefier, *n.*, anything that liquefies.

liq'uefy, *v.t.*, to reduce to a liquid state; *v.i.*, to be melted.

liq'uefying, *pr.p.*, liquefy.

liques'cency, *n.*, the state of being liquescent.

liques'cent, *adj.*, in the act of becoming liquid.

liqueur', *n.*, a sweetened alcoholic cordial.

liq'uid, *adj.*, flowing; not solid, not gaseous; *n.*, a liquid substance.

liq'uidate, *v.t.*, to settle, to pay off; to wind up a bankrupt's affairs.

liq'uidated, *p.p.*, liquidate.

liq'uidating, *pr.p.*, liquidate.

liquida'tion, *n.*, the act of liquidating; bankruptcy.

liq'uidator, *n.*, one who winds up a debtor's liabilities.

liquid'ity, *n.*, the state or quality of being liquid.

liq'uidize, *v.t.*, to render liquid.

liq'uidized, *p.p.*, liquidize.

liq'uidizing, *pr.p.*, liquidize.

liq'uor, *n.*, a fluid; a solution of dye; alcoholic drink.

liq'uorice, *n.*, the plant so named; a substance made from the *glycyrrhiza glabra*.

li'ra, *n.*, the Italian monetary unit.

li're, *n.*, pl. of lira.

Lis'bon, *n.*, a wine named after the place.

lisle, *n.*, a fine, hard thread.

lisp, *v.t.*, to pronounce with a lisp; to utter imperfectly; *v.i.*, to pronounce sibilants as *th*; *n.*, a speech defect.

lisped, *p.p.*, lisp.

lisp'er, *n.*, one who lisps.

lisp'ing, *pr.p.*, lisp.

lis'som, *adj.*, lithe, agile.

list, *v.t.*, to register; to cover with a list; to hear; to give heed to; to cause to careen; *v.i.*, to careen; to enlist; to listen; *n.*, a register or catalogue; selvage; the careening of a ship; a position at an angle from the normal.

list'ed, *p.p.*, list.

lis'tel, *n.*, a fillet.

lis'ten, *v.i.*, to try to hear; to harken.

lis'tened, *p.p.*, listen.

lis'tener, *n.*, one who listens.

lis'tener-*in*, *n.*, one who listens in.

lis'ten-*in*, *v.i.*, to listen to radio; to tap telephone communications.

lis'tening, *pr.p.*, listen.

lis'tening-*in*, *pr.p.*, listening in.

lis'terine, *n.*, an antiseptic solution.

Lis'terism, *n.*, antiseptic surgery.

lis'terize, *v.t.*, to treat with antiseptic.

list'ing, *pr.p.*, list; *n.*, the act of listing.

list'less, *adj.*, apathetic, without interest.

list'lessly, *adv.*, in a listless way.

list'lessness, *n.*, apathy, a lack of interest.

lists, *n. pl.*, the palisades round a tournament ground.

lit, *p.p.*, light.

lit'any, *n.*, a supplication, esp. petitions sung by priests and people in procession.

litchi, *n.*, a Chinese fruit.

lit'eracy, *n.*, the ability to read and write.

lit'eral, *adj.*, in accordance with the letter; exact; expressed in letters.

lit'eralism, *n.*, the understanding of words in their simplest sense.

lit'eralist, *n.*, a matter-of-fact person.

lit'erally, *adv.*, in a literal way.

lit'erary, *adj.*, rel. to, or engaged in, learning or literature.

lit'erate, *adj.*, able to read and write; *n.*, a person acquainted with learning.

litera'ti, *n. pl.*, learned people (*Lat.*).

litera'tim, *adv.*, letter for letter (*Lat.*).

lit'erature, *n.*, the collective written works of all human minds; the profession of letters; the higher kind of writing; what has been written about a given subject.

lith'arge, *n.*, the protoxide of lead.

lithe, *adj.*, supple, active.

lithe'ness, *n.*, suppleness.

lithe'some, *adj.*, *i.q.* lissom.

lith'ia, *n.*, lithium oxide.

lith'ic, *adj.*, rel. to stone or to lithium.

lith'ium, *n.*, a metallic element, soft and white.

lith'oglyph, *n.*, a carving on a gem; a carved gem.

lithoglyph'ic, *adj.*, rel. to a lithoglyph.

lith'ograph, *v.t.*, to reproduce on stone by lithography; *n.*, a picture so reproduced.

lith'ographed, *p.p.*, lithograph; *adj.*, printed on stone.

lithog'rapher, *n.*, one who lithographs.

lithograph'ic, *adj.*, rel. to lithography.

lithograph'ically, *adv.*, by lithography.

lith'ographing, *pr.p.*, lithograph.

lithog'raphy, *n.*, the art of printing on stone.

lith'oid, *adj.*, resembling stone.

lithoi'dal, *adj.*, *i.q.* lithoid.

litholog'ic, *adj.*, rel. to lithology.

litholog'ical, *adj.*, *i.q.* lithologic.

litholog'ically, *adv.*, in a lithological sense.

lithol'ogy, *n.*, the science of rock-structure and composition.

lithontrip'tic, *adj.*, a remedial for calculi in the bladder; *n.*, a solvent of calculi.

lithoph'agous, *adj.*, eating or boring stone.

lith'ophane, *n.*, a transparency.

lith'ophyte, *n.*, a calcareous polyp; a plant that grows in stone.

litho'sis, *n.*, a lung disease caused by stone dust.

litho'sphere, *n.*, the earth's rocky crust.

lith'otome, *n.*, a mineral resembling cut stone.

lithot'omist, *n.*, one skilled in lithotomy.

lithot'omy, *n.*, the cutting for stone in the bladder.

lithot'rity, *n.*, a crushing stone in the bladder.

lit'igant, *adj.*, engaged in litigation; *n.*, a party to a suit.

lit'igate, *v.t.*, to contest at law; *v.i.*, to go to law.

lit'igated, *p.p.*, litigate.

lit'igating, *pr.p.*, litigate.

litiga'tion, *n.*, the act of going to law.

liti'gious, *adj.*, addicted to litigation; legally disputable.

lit'mus, *n.*, a blue dye-stuff.

lit'otes, *n.*, an ironical way of saying less than is intended, as *no little* for *much*.

litram'eter, *n.*, a device for ascertaining the specific gravity of liquids.

li'tre, *n.*, a metrical unit of capacity.

lit'ter, *v.t.*, to bring forth young; to make untidy with things scattered about; to provide a bed for cattle; *v.i.*, to bring forth a litter; *n.*, a palanquin; waste materials thrown about in disorder; the young of animals brought forth at one birth.

littérateur', *n.*, a literary person (*Fr.*).

lit'tered, *p.p.*, litter.

lit'tering, *pr.p.*, litter.

lit'tery, *adj.*, strewn with litter, untidy.

lit'tle, *adj.*, small, mean.

lit'tleness, *n.*, smallness, meanness.

lit'toral, *adj.*, rel. to the shore; *n.*, the country along the shore.

litur'gic, *adj.*, rel. to liturgy.

litur'gical, *adj.*, *i.q.* liturgic.

lit'urgy, *n.*, a eucharistic religious service; the whole of formal religious ritual.

liv'able, *adj.*, endurable; worth living; fit to live in or with.

live, *v.i.*, to be alive; to have life; to exist, to subsist; *v.t.*, to spend, to pass; to act up to.

live, *adj.*, alive; burning.

live'-bait, *n.*, living fish for bait.

lived, *p.p.*, live; *adj.*, having a life.

live'lier, *adj.*, *comp.* of lively.

live'liest, *adj.*, *super.* of lively.

live'lihood, *n.*, a means of living.

live'liness, *n.*, brightness, briskness.

live'long, *adj.*, whole, entire.

live′ly, *adj.*, quick, brisk, vivid.

liv′en, *v.t.* and *i.*, to brighten, to cheer.

liv′er, *n.*, one who lives or dwells; **a** large glandular bile-secreting organ.

liv′eried, *adj.*, wearing livery.

liv′erish, *adj.*, suffering from a liver upset, bilious; irritable.

liv′erwort, *n.*, a lichen.

liv′ery, *n.*, the provision of food or clothing for dependants; the care and stabling of horses and carriages for payment; the legal delivery of property to a ward; the membership of a City Guild; the members collectively.

liv′eryman, *n.*, a member of a Livery Company.

lives, *n.*, pl. of life.

live′stock, *n.*, animals for use or sale.

live′wire, *n.*, a quick, energetic person.

liv′id, *adj.*, lead-coloured; discoloured as though bruised.

livid′ity, *n.*, the quality of being livid.

liv′ing, *pr.p.*, live; *adj.*, not dead; still alive; *n.*, a livelihood, a parochial benefice.

liv′ing-room, *n.*, a sitting-room.

li′vre, *n.*, an old French coin = a franc.

lixiv′ial, *adj.*, of the nature of lixivium.

lixiv′iate, *v.t.*, to dissolve by lixiviation; to leach; *adj.*, leached.

lixiv′iated, *p.p.*, lixiviate.

lixiv′iating, *pr.p.*, lixiviate.

lixivia′tion, *n.*, the act of extracting soluble from insoluble matter by means of washing; leaching.

lixiv′ium, *n.*, any mixture that has been leached.

liz′ard, *n.*, a scaly reptile.

lla′ma, *n.*, a small kind of camel found in S. America; also its wool.

lla′no, *n.*, a S. American barren plain.

Lloyd′s, *n.*, the British corporation of marine underwriters in London.

lo, *interj.*, see there! look!

loach, *n.*, an edible fresh water fish.

load, *v.t.*, to heap upon; to lay a burden on; to fill with ammunition; *n.*, a burden; a unit of weight or measure.

load′ed, *p.p.*, load.

load′er, *n.*, a person who is employed loading; one who loads guns; a loading machine.

load′ing, *pr.p.*, load; *n.*, something added to give weight.

load′-line, *n.*, a ship's Plimsoll mark (*naut.*).

load′star, *n.*, *i.q.* lodestar.

load′stone, *n.*, *i.q.* lodestone.

loaf, *v.i.*, to loiter idly; *n.*, a mass of bread or cake; a lump.

loafed, *p.p.*, loaf.

loaf′er, *n.*, an idle lounger.

loaf′ing, *pr.p.*, loaf.

loaf′sugar, *n.*, refined, crystallized sugar in the form of a cube.

loam, *v.t.*, to cover with loam; *n.*, a mixture of sand and clay.

loam′y, *adj.*, like loam.

loan, *n.*, something lent; the act of lending.

loan′able, *adj.*, able to be lent.

loanee′, *n.*, the receiver of a loan.

loan′er, *n.*, one who grants a loan.

loan′-office, *n.*, a pawnbroker's shop.

loath, loth, *adj.*, unwilling, reluctant.

loathe, *v.t.*, to detest, to abominate.

loathed, *p.p.*, loathe.

loath′ing, *pr.p.*, loathe; *n.*, disgust, nausea.

loath′some, *adj.*, detestable, disgusting.

loath′someness, *n.*, the quality of being loathsome.

loaves, *n.*, pl. of loaf.

lob, *v.t.*, to bowl a slow or high-pitched ball; *v.i.*, to move clumsily; *n.*, a ball bowled underhand or struck high with a racket.

lo′bate, *adj.*, having lobes.

lo′bated, *adj.*, *i.q.* lobate.

loba′tion, *n.*, the state of having lobes.

lob′by, *v.t.*, to try to get a measure passed; *v.i.*, to use one's influence in the lobby; to attempt to persuade to a point of view; *n.*, a corridor or entrance hall.

lob′byist, *n.*, one who regularly practises lobbying.

lobe, *n.*, the projecting part of an ear; a subdivision of the liver or the lungs.

lobec′tomy, *n.*, a surgical operation on a lobe (*med.*).

lobe′lia, *n.*, a herbaceous plant.

lob′lolly, *n.*, gruel.

lob′lolly boy, *n.*, a ship doctor's assistant.

lobot′omy, *n.*, *i.q.* leucotomy (*med.*).

lob′scouse, *n.*, a mess of salt meat, vegetables, and ship's biscuits.

lob′ster, *n.*, an edible crustacean.

lob′ster-pot, *n.*, a wicker trap for catching lobsters.

lob′ular, *adj.*, having small lobes.

lob′ule, *n.*, a small lobe.

lob′worm, *n.*, a large earthworm.

lo′cal, *adj.*, related to a place.

local(e)′, *n.*, the place where the action occurs (*Fr.*).

lo′calism, *n.*, a fondness for a place; a narrowness of outlook; a local idiom.

local′ity, *n.*, position; an aptitude for remembering places.

loc′alizable, *adj.*, capable of being localized.

localiza′tion, *n.*, the act or result of localizing.

lo′calize, *v.t.*, to make local; to fix the position of.

lo′calized, *p.p.*, localize.

lo′calizing, *pr.p.*, localize.

lo′cally, *adv.*, with reference to a place.

locate′, *v.t.*, to establish in a place; to fix the place of.

loca′ted, *p.p.*, locate.

loca′ter, *n.*, one that locates; a fixing device.

loca′ting, *pr.p.*, locate.

loca'tion, n., the act of locating; the exact position; a plot of ground defined by boundaries.

loc'ative, adj., denoting the place where; indicating the place in a series; n., an old case-ending that related to a place.

loch, n., a Scottish lake or land-locked arm of the sea.

lock, v.t., to fasten with a lock; to encircle; v.i., to become locked, to be held tight; n., a fastening; a contrivance for exploding a firearm; a portion of hair from the head; an arrangement for raising and lowering the levels of navigable water.

lock'age, n., a toll for the passage through a lock; the difference of the level of locks.

locked, p.p., lock.

lock'er, n., one who locks; a small cupboard; a sailor's clothes-chest.

lock'et, n., a small metal case for a miniature or a lock of hair, usually on a chain worn round the neck.

lock'ing, pr.p., lock.

Lock'ist, adj., rel. to John Locke and his metaphysical teaching.

lock'jaw, n., trismus; a spasmodic permanent closure of the lower jaw.

lock'out, n., the shutting out of employees from a workplace.

lock'smith, n., one who makes or repairs locks.

lock'-up, n., a house of temporary detention; the act or time of locking up.

lo'co, n., a locomotive engine (abbrev.); a poisonous leguminous plant; adj., mad (colloq.).

lo'co cita'to, adv. phr., in the passage already quoted (Lat.).

lo'como'tion, n., the movement from place to place.

lo'como'tive, adj., rel. to locomotion; n., an engine for drawing trains.

lo'comotor, n., a locomotive person or thing; adj., rel. to locomotion.

lo'comotory, adj., of, having, locomotion.

loc'ulament, n., i.q. loculus.

loc'ular, adj., rel. to a loculus.

loc'ulus, n., a small cavity or cell.

lo'cum-te'nens, n., a substitute or deputy (Lat.).

lo'cus, n., the locality, the situation; a path traced by points under specific conditions.

lo'cust, n., an edible insect; a N. American variety of bean.

locu'tion, n., a mode of speech; a phrase..

loc'utory, n., a monastic parlour; a grille.

lode, n., a watercourse; a vein of metal.

lode'star, n., a guiding star; the pole-star.

lode'stone, n., magnetic iron ore.

lodge, v.t., to give shelter to; to put in; v.i., to reside temporarily; to rest in or upon; n., a small house; a gate-keeper's house; the residence of the Master of a College; an association of Freemasons.

lodged, p.p., lodge.

lodg'er, n., one who lives in lodgings.

lodg'ing, pr.p., lodge; n., a hired room or rooms; an abode.

lodg'ing-house, n., a house where lodgings may be had.

lodg'ment, n., a foothold; the act of lodging; that which has lodged.

lo'ess, n., an alluvial deposit of calcareous loam.

loft, v.t., to hit (a golf ball) up into the air; to provide with a loft; n., a room next to the roof; a raised floor or gallery; the tilt back of a golf-club's head.

loft'ier, adj., comp. of lofty.

loft'iest, adj., super. of lofty.

loft'ily, adv., in a lofty way.

loft'iness, n., height.

loft'y, adj., high, towering, noble.

log, v.t., to record in a log-book; to cut into logs; n., a piece of felled timber; a float showing speed of a ship; a record of daily progress.

log'anberry, n., a hybrid between a blackberry and a raspberry.

logaoed'ic, adj. and n., combining (combination of) prose and poetry.

log'arithm, n., the index of the power of a fixed number (called the base) which must be raised to produce a given number.

logarith'mic, adj., rel. to logarithms.

log'book, n., i.q. log.

log'-cabin, n., a hut made of rough logs.

logged, p.p., log; adj., waterlogged.

log'gerhead, n., a fool. (The phrase "at loggerheads" = quarrelling or disputing.)

log'gia, n., a gallery or arcade having one side open (It.).

log'ging, pr.p., log.

log'house, n., a building of logs.

log'hut, n., a wooden hut.

log'ic, n., the science of correct thinking; the correct use of argument.

log'ical, adj., in accordance with correct reasoning; rel. to logic.

log'ically, adv., according to the rules of logic.

logi'cian, n., an expert in logic.

logis'tic, adj., rel. to calculation or logistics.

logis'tical, adj., i.q. logistic.

logis'tics, n. pl., the science of moving and storing.

log'line, n., a line used for paying out the log.

log'ogram, n., a shorthand sign representing a whole word.

log'ograph, n., i.q. logotype.

logograph'ic, adj., rel. to logography.

logog'raphy, n., the use of logotypes in printing.

logom'achist, n., one who disputes about mere words (lit.).

logom'achy, n., controversy over words.

logom'eter, n., a logarithmic scale.

logomet'ric, adj., rel. to a logometer.

Log'os, n., the name in St. John i. for the Divine Word; the Second Person of the Blessed Trinity (theol.).

log'otype, n., several letters or a word cast in one piece for printing.

log'wood, n., an American wood used in dyeing.

loin, n., the part between the lower rib and the hip bone.

loi'ter, v.i., to hang about, to dawdle.

loi'tered, p.p., loiter.

loi'terer, n., one who loiters.

loi'tering, pr.p., loiter.

loll, v.t., to hang (the tongue) out; v.i., to recline lazily, to sit idly about.

Lol'lard, n., one of Wyclif's followers.

Lol'lardism, n., the doctrines of Wyclif.

lolled, p.p., loll.

loll'ing, pr.p., loll.

lol'lipop, n., a sugarplum; any confection on a stick; lolly (colloq.).

Lom'bard, n. and adj., (a) native to Lombardy.

Lombar'dic, adj., rel. to Lombardy, its people, and its school of artists; n., a peculiar kind of script.

lo'ment, n., a variety of pod.

Lon'doner, n., an inhabitant or native of London.

lone, adj., lonely, alone, unfrequented.

lone'lier, adj., comp. of lonely.

lone'liest, adj., super. of lonely.

lone'liness, n., solitariness.

lone'ly, adj., solitary, unfrequented.

lone'some, adj., i.q. lonely.

lone'someness, n., the state of being lonesome.

long, v.i., to desire earnestly; adj., great in measurement from end to end; tedious;

delaying; adv., for a long time.

longanim'ity, n., long suffering, forbearance.

long'-boat, n., the large boat of a ship.

long'-bow, n., a hand bow.

long'-cloth, n., a superior cotton cloth.

longed, p.p., long.

long'er, n., one who longs.

lon'ger, adj., comp. of long.

lon'geron, n., the longitudinal members of an aircraft's fuselage.

lon'gest, adj., super. of long.

longe'val, adj., longlived.

longev'ity, n., long life.

longe'vous, adj., i.q. longeval.

long'hand, n., ordinary writing, as distinct from shorthand.

long'-headed, adj., shrewd.

longim'anous, adj., longhanded.

long'ing, pr.p., long; n., a yearning.

long'ingly, adv., yearningly.

long'ish, adj., somewhat long.

lon'gitude, n., the distance E. or W. from an agreed meridian.

longitu'dinal, adj., rel. to length; lengthwise.

long'last'ing, adj., lasting a long time.

long'lived, adj., living for a long time.

long' run, phrase = the final issue.

long'shore, adj., along the water-side.

long'shore'man, n., a landsman working on the shore; a stevedore.

long'sighted, adj., far-sighted.

longsight'edness, n., the state of being far-sighted.

long'stop, v.i., to be the longstop; n., the man behind the wicketkeeper.

long'suffering, adj., patient; n., patience.

long'-term, n., matures or takes place over a long period.

longue haleine, n., work requiring persistent effort (Fr.).

longueur, n., a tedious part of a story (Fr.).

long'winded, adj., prolix.

long'wise, adv., and adj., lengthwise.

loo, v.t., to penalize at loo; n., a round game at cards; a water closet (colloq.).

loo'by, n., a stupid fellow; a lubber.

loo'fah, n., a vegetable sponge.

look, v.i., to use the eyes; to direct the gaze; to seem; to watch; n., the act of looking or watching; appearance.

looked, p.p., look.

look'er, n., one who looks.

look'er-in, n., a television viewer.

look'-in, v.i., to chance; to watch television; n., a short visit.

look'ing, pr.p., look.

look'ing-glass, n., a mirror.

look'out, n., a place for observation; the observer.

loom, v.i., to appear indistinctly; n., an apparatus for weaving; the inboard portion of an oar; a guillemot.

loomed, p.p., loom.

loom'ing, pr.p., loom.

loon, n., a dolt; a grebe.

loon'y, n., a lunatic (colloq.).

loony'bin, n., a mental home (colloq.).

loop, v.t., to bind into a loop; to fasten; v.i., to move in loops; n., a fold or doubling of a cord, etc.; a curved shape for a handle.

looped, p.p., loop.

loop'er, n., a caterpillar that loops itself.

loop'hole, n., a narrow opening in a wall for archers or look-outs; a means of evasion; v.t., to make loopholes in.

loop'holed, p.p., loophole.

loop'holing, pr.p., loophole.

loop'ing, pr.p., loop.

loop'y, adj., crazy (slang).

loose, v.t., to set free, to release; adj., free, not attached; lax.

loose'ly, adv., in a loose way.

loos'en, v.t., to make loose, to detach; v.i., to come detached.

loos'ened, p.p., loosen.

loose'ness, n., the state or quality of being loose.

loos'ening, pr.p., loosen.

loos'er, adj., comp. of loose.

loos'est, adj., super. of loose.

loose'strife, n., an herbaceous plant.

loot, v.t., to plunder; to carry off as spoil; n., plunder.

lop, v.t., to cut at the top; to allow to hang down; v.i., to hang down; to break in short waves; n., something lopped; the lumpy break of a wave.

lopped, p.p., lop.

lop'per, n., one who, or that which, lops.

lop'ping, pr.p., lop.

lop'sided, adj., uneven, one-sided.

lopsid'edly, adv., in a lopsided manner.

lopsid'edness, n., the state of being lopsided.

loqua'cious, adj., talkative, garrulous.

loqua'ciously, adv., talkatively.

loquac'ity, n., talkativeness.

loquat, n., a Chinese and Japanese fruit.

lor'cha, n., a ship, European in build, but with Chinese rig.

lord, v.t., to ennoble; v.i., to be a ruler; n., a nobleman, a ruler.

lord'ed, p.p., lord.

lord'ing, pr.p., lord.

lord'like, adj., like a lord.

lord'liness, n., the quality of being lordly.

lord'ling, n., a little lord.

lord'ly, adj., i.q., lordlike.

lordo'sis, n., curvature of the spine.

Lord's, n., the London headquarters of English cricket.

lord'ship, n., rule, ownership; a manor; the status or person of a lord.

lore, n., teaching, erudition; the space between the eye and the beak of a bird.

lorgnette', n., an opera-glass (Fr.).

lor'icate, adj., covered with armour.

lor'icated, adj., i.q. loricate.

lorica'tion, n., the state of being loricated; defensive armour.

lo'rikeet, n., a small Polynesian parrot.

lor'is, n., a small nocturnal mammal.

lorn, adj., desolate, forlorn.

lor'ry, n., a long wagon; a motorized truck.

lo'ry, n., a variety of parrot.

lose, v.t., to be parted from, to miss, to fail to gain; v.i., to be unsuccessful.

lo'sel, n., a wastrel.

los'er, n., one who loses.

los'ing, pr.p., lose.

loss, n., the act of losing or being lost; anything lost; a misfortune; a bereavement.

loss'leader, n., an article sold at a loss to attract other custom.

lost, p.p., lose.

lot, v.t., to divide into lots; n., a die; a fortune; a graduated portion of land; an item in a sale at an auction; a number of collected things.

lo'ta, **lo'tah**, n., an Indian round pot.

lote'-tree, n., the lotus.

loth, adj., i.q. loath.

lotha'rio, n., a rake.

lo'tion, n., a liquid medicine externally applied.

lot'tery, n., a scheme for distributing prizes by lot to ticket-holders.

lot'to, n., an indoor game of chance (It.).

lo'tus, n., a plant of the water-lily family.

loud, adj., having a great intensity of sound; noisy; flashy; adv., = loudly.

loud'er, adj., comp. of loud.

loud'est, adj., super. of loud.

loud'ly, adv., sonorously, very audibly.

loud'ness, n., the quality of being loud.

loud'speak'er, n., an instrument for magnifying sound.

lough, n., a lake, or arm of the sea (Ir.).

lou'is, n., a French gold piece = 20 francs.

lou'is d'or', n., i.q. louis.

lounge, v.i., to saunter; to loll; to idle; n., a room for relaxation.

lounged, p.p., lounge.

loung'er, n., one who lounges.

loung'ing, pr.p., lounge.

lour, v.i., to frown, to threaten; n., a scowl.

loured', p.p., lour.

lour'ing, adj., threatening; pr.p., lour.

lour'ingly, adv., in a threatening way.

louse, n., a small parasitic insect.

lous'iness, n., the state of being lousy.

lou'sy, adj., infected with lice; bad (colloq.).

lout, n., a bumpkin; v.i., to bow.

lout'ish, adj., awkward, clownish.

lout'ishly, adv., like a lout.

lout'ishness, n., the state of being loutish.

lou'ver, n., a protected vent; a lantern with cupola; an overlapping slat. Also louvre.

lou'ver-boards, n. pl., openings in a window-space to admit air but not rain.

lou'vre, n., i.q. louver.

lov'able, adj., worthy of love.

lov'age, n., the herb Levisticum.

love, v.t., to have affection or regard for; to cherish; to delight in; n., affection, a strong attachment, devotion; (in games) nothing, no score.

love'-apple, n., the tomato.

love'bird, n., a small breed of parrot.

loved, p.p., love.

love'-feast, n., the ancient Christian Agapé, a common meal taken in brotherly love.

love'-knot, n., a ribbon tied in a knot to signify love.

love'less, adj., without love.

love'-letter, n., a letter from or to a sweetheart.

love'lier, adj., comp. of lovely.

love'liest, *adj.*, *super.* of lovely.

love'liness, *n.*, the quality of being lovely.

love'lorn, *adj.*, pining for a lover.

love'ly, *adj.*, attracting by its beauty, delightful.

lov'er, *n.*, one who loves; a sweetheart.

love'sick, *adj.*, pining with love.

lov'ing, *pr.p.*, love; *adj.*, affectionate.

loving-kind'ness, *n.*, tenderness, compassion.

lov'ingly, *adv.*, tenderly.

lo'vingness, *n.*, the quality of being loving.

low, *v.i.*, to make the cry of a cow; *n.*, a cow's cry; *adj.*, not high; deep, depressed; deep in pitch; mean, base.

low'born, *adj.*, of humble birth.

low'bred, *adj.*, illbred.

low'brow, *n.*, a person who is not highly intellectual (*colloq.*); *adj.*, not cultural.

low'-church, *adj.*, regarding as non-essential the three-fold order of ministry, apostolic succession, and high views on the sacraments.

lowed, *p.p.*, low.

low'er, *adj.*, *comp.* of low; *v.t.*, to let down, to decrease.

low'er, *v.i.*, to be gloomy and threatening.

low'ered, *p.p.*, lower.

low'ering, *pr.p.*, lower.

low'ering, *adj.*, threatening.

lower'most, *adj.* and *adv.*, lowest.

low'ery, *adj.*, *i.q.* lowering.

low'est, *adj.*, *super.* of low.

low'ing, *n.*, a cow's cry; *pr.p.*, low.

low'land, *adj.*, of the low or level country; *n.* In pl. less elevated country.

Low'lander, *n.*, a native of the Lowlands.

low'lier, *adj.*, *comp.* of lowly.

low'liest, *adj.*, *super.* of lowly.

low'lily, *adv.*, in a lowly way.

low'liness, *n.*, humility.

low'ly, *adj.*, humble, unpretentious.

low'-minded, *adj.*, base, vulgar.

low'-mindedness, *n.*, baseness, vulgarity.

low'ness, *n.*, the quality or state of being low.

low'-spirited, *adj.*, depressed, melancholy.

low'-wines, *n.*, weak spirit after distillation of alcoholic substances.

lox', *n.*, liquid oxygen; smoked salmon; a rocket propellant.

loxodrom'ic, *adj.*, rel. to oblique sailing.

loy'al,' *adj.*, faithful in allegiance.

loy'alist, *n.*, one who supports the lawful government.

loy'ally, *adv.*, in a loyal way.

loy'alty, *n.*, fidelity, constancy in allegiance.

loz'enge, *n.*, a rhombus, a diamond figure; a small tablet, either a sweet or a medicine.

lub'ber, *n.*, a lout; a raw sailor.

lubb'erliness, *n.*, the quality of being lubberly.

lub'berly, *adj.*, loutish.

lu'bricant, *adj.*, lubricating; *n.*, anything that lubricates.

lu'bricate, *v.t.*, to make slippery by greasing.

lu'bricated, *p.p.*, lubricate.

lu'bricating, *pr.p.*, lubricate.

lubrica'tion, *n.*, the act of lubricating.

lu'bricator, *n.*, *i.q.* lubricant.

lubric'ity, *n.*, slipperiness, smoothness; lewdness.

lu'bricous, *adj.*, smooth, slippery.

luce, *n.*, a pike.

lu'cent, *adj.*, shining.

lucer'nal, *adj.*, rel. to a lamp.

lucerne', *n.*, a plant like clover, used for fodder.

lucian'ic, *adj.*, witty, scoffing.

lu'cid, *adj.*, clear.

lucid'ity, *n.*, clearness.

lu'cidly, *adv.*, clearly.

lu'cidness, *n.*, *i.q.* lucidity.

lu'cifer, *n.*, the morning star; a friction match.

lucif'erous, *adj.*, light-bringing.

lucif'ic, *adj.*, light-producing.

lu'ciform, *adj.*, like a light.

lucim'eter, *n.*, an apparatus for gauging the intensity of light.

luck, *n.*, chance, fortune.

luck'ier, *adj.*, *comp.* of lucky.

luck'iest, *adj.*, *super.* of lucky.

luck'ily, *adv.*, by good luck.

luck'iness, *n.*, the quality of being lucky.

luck'less, *adj.*, unfortunate.

luck'y, *adj.*, fortunate.

lu'crative, *adj.*, bringing gain, profitable.

lu'cre, *n.*, pecuniary gain; money (*contemptuous*).

Lucre'tia, *n.*, a model of feminine chastity.

lu'cubrate, *v.t.*, to spend the midnight oil on; to write.

lucubra'tion, *n.*, the act of lucubrating; a literary product.

lu'culent, *adj.*, *i.q.* lucid.

lud'dite, *n.*, a rioter against technological innovation.

lu'dicrous, *adj.*, ridiculous.

lu'dicrously, *adv.*, ridiculously.

lud'o, *n.*, a game with dice and counters.

lues, *n.*, a contagious disease, a plague.

luff, *v.t.* and *i.*, to bring (a ship) into the wind; *n.*, a sail's foremost edge; the carved part of a ship's bow.

luffed, *p.p.*, luff.

luff'er, *n.*, *i.q.* louver; a louver-board.

luff'ing, *pr.p.*, luff.

Luft'waffe, *n.*, the German Air Force.

lug, *v.t.*, to pull, to haul; *v.i.*, to pull hard at; *n.*, a pull; an ear; a square sail.

lug'-chair, *n.*, an easy chair with side head rests.

lug'gage, *n.*, baggage.

lugged, *p.p.*, lug.

lug'ger, *n.*, a small ship with lug sails.

lug'ging, *pr.p.*, lug.

lug'sail, n., a sail set fore and aft and slung at a third or quarter of its length from one end.

lugu'brious, adj., doleful.

lugu'briously, adv., in a doleful way.

luke'warm, adj., neither hot nor cold; indifferent.

luke'warmness, n., indifference.

lull, v.t., to appease, to make quiet; v.i., to grow quiet; n., a period of calm.

lull'aby, n., a cradle song.

lulled, p.p., lull.

lull'ing, pr.p., lull.

lumachel'la, n., limestone containing fossils.

lu'machelle, n., i.q. lumachella.

lumba'ginous, adj., rel. to lumbago.

lumba'go, n., rheumatic pain in the loins.

lum'bar, adj., rel. to the loins.

lum'ber, v.t., to fill with lumber; to encumber; v.i., to trade in lumber; to go clumsily along; n., litter, rubbish; cut and prepared timber; superfluous weight.

lum'bered, p.p., lumber.

lum'bering, pr.p., lumber; adj., clumsy, moving heavily.

lum'beringly, adv., in a clumsy, blundering manner.

lum'ber-jack, n., a man who cuts and prepares trees for use as timber.

lum'ber-jacket, n., an anorak-type jacket, sometimes belted.

lum'berman, n., a person engaged in the lumber trade.

lum'ber-room, n., a room for useless articles.

lumbri'cal, n., a muscle in the hand or foot.

lu'men, n., a unit of light.

lu'minary, n., a light-giving body.

luminif'erous, adj., light-producing.

luminos'ity, n., the state or quality of being luminous.

lu'minous, adj., yielding light.

lumm'e, interj., of surprise or emphasis (vulg.).

lump, v.t., to make into a lump; to put up with (colloq.); v.i., to grow lumpy; n., a mass; the aggregate; a protuberance; a dull person.

lumped, p.p., lump.

lump'er, n., one who lumps.

lump'ing, pr.p., lump.

lump'ish, adj., dull, stupid.

lump'ishly, adv., stupidly.

lum'pishness, n., the quality of being lumpish.

lump'y, adj., having lumps.

Lu'na, n., the Moon-goddess (Lat.).

lu'nacy, n., madness.

lu'nar, adj., pert. to the moon or month.

luna'rian, n., a dweller on the moon; an expert in knowledge about the moon.

lu'nary, adj., i.q. lunar.

lu'nate, adj., crescent-shaped.

lu'nated, adj., i.q. lunate.

lu'natic, adj., insane; n., a madman.

luna'tion, n., the interval between one new moon and another.

lunch, v.i., to take lunch; n., a midday meal.

lunched, p.p., lunch.

lunch'eon, n., i.q. lunch.

lunch'ing, pr.p., lunch.

lune, n., a figure bounded by two arcs of circles.

lunette', n., a moon-shaped opening, or a space in a dome or ceiling; a crescent-shaped holder in a monstrance.

lung, n., a breathing organ.

lunge, v.t., to break in with a lunge; v.i., to make a thrust; n., a long rope; a sudden thrust or hit out.

lunged, p.p., lunge.

lun'geing, pr.p., lunge.

lung'wort, n., a borage-like herb.

lu'niform, adj., crescent-shaped.

luniso'lar, adj., caused by sun and moon combined.

lunk'ah, n., a kind of Indian cheroot.

lunok'hod, n., a moon vehicle (Russ.).

lu'nular, adj., like a small crescent.

lu'nulate, adj., almost crescent-shaped.

lu'nulated, adj., i.q. lunulate.

Lu'percal, adj., rel. to Lupercus, the protector of shepherds.

lu'pine, adj., wolfish, ravenous; rel. to wolves.

lu'pine, lu'pin, n., a lupinus plant.

lu'pulin, n., an alkaloid found in hops.

lu'pus, n., an ulcerous skin disease (Lat.).

lurch, v.i., to swing, to sway to one side; n., a roll to one side; a stagger, an embarrassing position (as at cribbage).

lurched, p.p., lurch.

lurch'er, n., a poacher, a swindler; a cross-breed of dogs.

lurch'ing, pr.p., lurch.

lure, v.t., to entice; to recall (a hawk); n., a falconer's device for recalling a hawk with bait.

lured, p.p., lure.

lu'rid, adj., ghastly, stormy, dull red.

lu'ring, pr.p., lure.

lu'ringly, adv., enticingly, temptingly.

lurk, v.i., to wait about in hiding; to be unnoticed.

lurked, p.p., lurk.

lurk'er, n., one who lurks.

lurk'ing, pr.p., lurk.

lus'cious, adj., rich and sweet; succulent.

lus'ciously, adv., with a luscious flavour.

lus'ciousness, n., a luscious flavour.

lush, adj., luxuriant; n., drink (slang); v.i., to indulge in wine; to ply with drink (slang)

lush'y, adj., drunk (slang).

Lu'siad, n., a Portuguese epic.

lust, v.i., to desire inordinately; n., an inordinate desire.

lust'ed, p.p., lust.

lust'ful, adj., passionate sensual.

lust'fully, adv., in a lustful way.

lust'fulness, n., the state of being lustful.

lust'ier, *adj.*, *comp.* of lusty.

lust'iest, *adj.*, *super.* of lusty.

lust'ily, *adv.*, vigorously.

lust'iness, *n.*, sturdiness.

lust'ing, *pr.p.*, lust.

lus'tral, *adj.*, purifying.

lus'trate, *v.t.*, to purify ceremonially.

lustra'tion, *n.*, the act of lustrating.

lus'tre, *v.t.*, to put a gloss on; *n.*, a gloss, a sheen, glory; a dress material; a candelabrum with glass pendants; china or earthenware lustred; *i.q.* lustrum.

lus'treless, *adj.*, without lustre.

lus'trine, *n.*, a glossy silk fabric.

lus'tring, *n.*, *i.q.* lustrine.

lus'trous, *adj.*, shining, splendid.

lus'trously, *adv.*, in a lustrous way.

lus'trum, *n.*, a quinquennium; a period of five years (*Lat.*). Also *lustre*.

lust'y, *adj.*, stout, vigorous.

lu'tanist, *n.*, a lute player.

luta'tion, *n.*, the process of luting.

lute, *v.t.*, to stop a hole with clay; to apply lute to; *n.*, a stopping, a stringed instrument like the guitar; also *v.i.*, to play on the lute.

lut'ed, *p.p.*, lute.

lu'teous, *adj.*, golden-yellow coloured.

lute'string, *n.*, a glossy silk fabric.

Lute'tian, *adj.*, Parisian.

Lu'theran, *adj.*. bel. to Luther; *n.*, a follower of Luther.

Lu'theranism, *n.*, the doctrines of the Augsburg Confession.

lut'ing, *pr.p.*, lute.

lu'tose, *adj.*, muddy.

lu'tulent, *adj.*, muddy.

lux'ate, *v.t.*, to dislocate, to displace.

lux'ated, *p.p.*, luxate.

lux'ating, *pr.p.*, luxate.

luxa'tion, *n.*, the act or result of luxating.

luxu'riance, *n.*, profuse growth, rankness.

luxu'riancy, *n.*, *i.q.* luxuriance.

luxu'riant, *adj.*, growing in profusion, rank.

luxu'riantly, *adv.*, profusely.

luxu'riate, *v.t.*, to grow in profusion; to take extreme pleasure or delight.

luxu'riated, *p.p.*, luxuriate.

luxu'riating, *pr.p.*, luxuriate.

luxu'rious, *adj.*, given to luxury.

luxu'riously, *adv.*, in a luxurious way.

lux'ury, *n.*, an excessive indulgence in costly things; enjoyment; a thing desired but not necessary; extravagance.

lycan'thropy, *n.*, the supposed power of changing from a man into a wolf.

ly'cée, *n.*, a State secondary school in France.

lyce'um, *n.*, a literary institution or meeting-place.

lych'-gate, *n.*, *i.q.* lich-gate.

Lych'nis, *n.*, a genus of plants of the pink family.

lyc'opod, *n.*, clubmoss.

lyc'opodium, *n.*, the yellow powder from the spores of clubmoss.

lyd'dite, *n.*, a high explosive containing picric acid.

Lyd'ian, *adj.*, rel. to Lydia in Asia Minor.

lye, *n.*, a leached solution from ashes; an alkaline solution used in various industries.

ly'ing, *pr.p.*, lie; *n.*, telling falsehoods; *adj.*, mendacious.

ly'ing-in', *n.*, childbirth.

lyke'wake, *n.*, a night watch over the dead.

lyme'grass, *n.*, a coarse grass planted on sand to stop it shifting.

lymph, *n.*, water; the colourless alkaline fluid in the bodily tissues; the virus of a disease.

lymphat'ic, *adj.*, rel. to or secreting lymph; of a phlegmatic temperament.

lynch, *v.t.*, to execute by mob law.

lynched, *p.p.*, lynch.

lynch'er, *n.*, one who lynches.

lynch'ing, *pr.p.*, lynch.

lynx, *n.*, a cat-like animal, possessed of very keen sight.

lynx'-eyed, *n.*, keen-sighted.

Ly'ra, *n.*, one of the signs of the Zodiac.

ly'rate, *adj.*, lyre-shaped.

lyre, *n.*, an ancient kind of harp.

lyr'ic, *adj.*, to be sung to a lyre accompaniment; expressing emotion in verse; *n.*, a poem expressing the poet's own emotions and experiences; the words of a popular song.

lyr'ical, *adj.*, *i.q.* lyric.

lyr'icism, *n.*, a lyric expression.

ly'ricist, *n.*, one who writes lyrics.

lyr'ist, *n.*, a player on the lyre; a lyric poet.

lysim'eter, *n.*, an instrument for measuring rain absorption by the soil.

ly'sol, *n.*, a coal-tar-based disinfectant.

lyte'rian, *adj.*, showing the end.

M

ma, *n.*, abbrev., mamma (*colloq.*).

or. ma'am, *n.*, abbrev. of madam, esp. in addressing royalty.

Mab, *n.*, the queen of the fairies.

maca'bre, *adj.*, gruesome; unnatural, horrible.

macac'o, *n.*, a monkey of the genus Macacus; a kind of lemur.

macad'am, *adj.*, (of roads) made as advocated by J. L. McAdam (d. 1836), in stone layers; *n.*, such material.

macadamiza'tion, *n.*, the act or effect of macadamizing.

macad'amize, *v.t.*, to cover with broken stone.

macad'amized, *p.p.*, macadamize.

macad'amizing, *pr.p.*, macadamize.

macaro'ni, *n.*, long, slender tubes made of wheat flour; a crested penguin.

macaron'ic, *adj.*, composed of Latin or Greek and a vernacular language given Latin or Greek forms; *n.*, a verse in macaronic.

macaroon', *n.*, a biscuit containing flour, eggs, almonds and sugar.

macass'ar, *n.* and *adj.*, a kind of hair oil.

macaw', *n.*, a large kind of parrot.

Maccabe'an, *adj.*, rel. to the Maccabees (Jewish princes).

mac'caboy, *n.*, a variety of snuff.

mace, *n.*, an emblem of power; a spice; a bagatelle cue; a spiked club.

mace'-bearer, *n.*, an officer who carries the mace.

mace'doine, *n.*, a mixture of diced fruit or vegetables (*Fr.*).

Macedo'nian, *adj.*, rel. to Macedonia; a native of M.

mac'erate, *v.t.*, to soften with fluid.

mac'erated, *p.p.*, macerate.

mac'erating, *pr.p.*, macerate.

macera'tion, *n.*, the act of macerating.

mach (number), *n.*, the ratio of the speed of a body to the speed of sound in the surrounding atmosphere.

machan', *n.*, a platform used in tiger shooting.

Machiavel'lian, *adj.*, rel. to Machiavelli; crafty.

Machiavel'lianism, *n.*, crafty policy.

Machiavel'lism, *n.*, *i.q.* Machiavellianism.

machic'olate, *v.t.*, to make machicolations on.

machicola'tion, *n.*, an addition to the top of a fortress.

machi'coulis, *n.*, *i.q.* machicolation.

mach'inate, *v.t.*, to plan, to contrive.

mach'inated, *p.p.*, machinate.

mach'inating, *pr.p.*, machinate.

machina'tion, *n.*, a plot, a contrivance.

machine', *v.t.*, to apply a machine; *n.*, any mechanical contrivance.

machined', *p.p.*, machine.

machine'-gun, *n.*, a small rapid-firing gun.

machin'ery, *n.*, machines collectively; any contrivance by which action is maintained.

machine'-shop, *n.*, a workshop where machines are made or used.

machine'-tool, *n.*, a machine for working, cutting or shaping tools.

machin'ing, *pr.p.*, machine.

machin'ist, *n.*, a machine operator; one skilled in machinery.

mack'erel, *n.*, a sea fish.

mac(k)'intosh, *n.*, a waterproof overcoat.

mack'le, *n.*, a blur.

ma'cle, *n.*, twin-crystal.

Mâcon', *n.*, a French wine so named.

macra'me, *n.*, a fringe a trimming of knotted thread work.

macra'mi, *n.*, *i.q.* macrame.

macrobiol'ics, *n.*, the science of prolonging life.

macrocephal'ic, *adj.*, long-headed.

mac'rocosm, *n.*, the universe.

macrom'eter, *n.*, an instrument for measuring distance.

mac'ron, *n.*, a mark placed over a vowel to indicate it has a long sound, e.g. ā.

mac'ropod, *n.*, a long footed animal; the spider crab.

macroscop'ic, *adj.*, visible to the naked eye.

mac'ula, *n.*, a spot (*Lat.*)

mac'ulate, *v.t.*, to spot.

mac'ulated, *p.p.*, maculate.

mac'ulating, *pr.p.*, maculate.

macula'tion, *n.*, the act or effect of maculating.

mad, *adj.*, angry, insane.

madam, *n.*, the title or address for a married or mature woman.

madaro'sis, *n.*, loss of hair, esp. the eyelashes.

mad'cap, *n.*, a rash thoughtless person.

mad'den, *v.t.*, to infuriate.

mad'dened, *p.p.*, madden.

mad'dening, *pr.p.*, madden; *adj.*, infuriating.

mad'der, *adj.*, *comp.* of mad; *n.*, a plant yielding a red dye.

mad'dest, *adj.*, *super.* of mad.

mad'ding, *adj.*, *i.q.* maddening.

made, *p.p.*, make.

Madei'ra, *n.*, an island in the Atlantic; the wine of M; a kind of sponge cake.

mad'house, *n.*, a lunatic asylum.

mad'ia, *n.*, a plant allied to the sunflower.

madia'-oil, *n.*, oil from crushed madia seeds.

mad'ly, *adv.*, insanely.

mad'man, *n.*, a lunatic; an angry person.

mad'ness, *n.*, rage, fury, insanity.

madon'na, *n.*, an image of the Virgin Mary.

mad'repore, *n.*, coral.

mad'rigal, *n.*, a choral song of special form.

madrigal'esque, *adj.*, having the characteristics of a madrigal.

madu'ro, *adj.*, full-flavoured (cigars) (*Span.*).

mael'strom, *n.*, a whirlpool off Norway.

mae'nad, *n.*, a Bacchante.

maesto'so, *adv.*, majestically (*It.*, *mus.*).

maes'tro, *n.*, a great musician, composer or conductor (*It.*).

Mae' West, *n.*, an airman's life-jacket.

maff'ick, *v.i.*, to exult riotously.

Mafi'a, *n.*, a Sicilian secret society.

mag, *n.*, short for magneto (*slang*).

magazine', *n.*, a storehouse; a periodical publication.

mag'dalen, *n.*, a penitent.

mag'dalene, *n.*, *i.q.* magdalen.

mage, *n.*, a magician, a learned person.

magen'ta, *n.*, a red dye.

mag'got, *n.*, a worm or grub; a whim.

mag'goty, *adj.*, full of maggots; whimsical.

Ma'gi, *n. pl.*, the Wise Men of the East.

Ma'gian, *adj.*, rel. to the Magi.

mag'ic, *adj.*, rel. to magic; *n.*, sorcery, enchantment, witchcraft; illusion.

mag'ical, *adj.*, *i.q.* magic.

mag'ically, *adv.*, in a magical way.

magi'cian, *n.*, a sorcerer; one skilled in magic.

magilp', *n.*, linseed oil and mastic varnish.

magiste'rial, *adj.*, rel. to a teacher or a magistrate; authoritative.

magiste'rially, *adv.*, authoritatively.

mag'istracy, *n.*, the office of a magistrate; magistrates collectively.

magis'tral, *adj.*, rel. to a master; *n.*, a special remedy made up to suit a particular patient (*med.*).

mag'istrate, *n.*, a public civil officer.

mag'ma, *n.*, a composite paste; a dough-like mass (*geol.*).

Mag'na C(h)ar'ta, *n.*, the Great Charter of England.

magnal'ium, *n.*, an alloy of aluminium and magnesium.

magnanim'ity, *n.*, generosity; a greatness of mind.

magnan'imous, *adj.*, great-minded, very generous.

magnan'imously, *adv.*, with magnanimity.

mag'nate, *n.*, a grandee; one of the highest rank.

magne'sia, *n.*, a white powder, the oxide of magnesium.

magne'sian, *adj.*, rel. to magnesium.

magne'sium, *n.*, the metallic base of magnesia.

mag'net, *n.*, a steel bar having the properties of a lodestone.

magnet'ic, *adj.*, rel. to magnetism.

magnet'ically, *adv.*, in magnetic fashion.

mag'netism, *n.*, the properties of attracting and repelling; the science of magnetic phenomena; the personal power to attract.

mag'netist, *n.*, one learned in magnetism.

mag'netite, *n.*, magnetic iron oxide.

magnetiza'tion, *n.*, the act of magnetizing; the state of being magnetized.

mag'netize, *v.t.*, to imbue with magnetic properties.

mag'netized, *p.p.*, magnetize.

mag'netizer, *n.*, anything that magnetizes.

mag'netizing, *pr.p.*, magnetize.

magnet'o, *n.*, an electrical generator; an igniting apparatus for a motor vehicle engine.

magne'to-elec'tric, *adj.*, rel. to magneto-electricity.

magne'to-electric'ity, *n.*, the electricity produced by magnetism.

magnetom'eter, *n.*, an apparatus measuring magnetic force.

magnetomet'ric, *adj.*, rel. to a magnetometer.

mag'netron, *n.*, a device for generating very high frequency oscillations (*phys.*).

magnif'ic, *adj.*, *i.q.* magnificent.

magnif'ical, *adj.*, *i.q.* magnificent.

Magnif'icat, *n.*, the song of the Virgin Mary.

magnifica'tion, *n.*, magnifying.

magnif'icence, *n.*, splendour, grandeur.

magnif'icent, *adj.*, splendid, grand.

magnif'icently, *adv.*, splendidly.

magnif'ico, *n.*, a Venetian magnate; a grandee.

mag'nified, *p.p.*, magnify.

mag'nifier, *n.*, anything that magnifies.

mag'nify, *v.t.*, to enlarge, to exaggerate, to extol.

mag'nifying, *pr.p.*, magnify.

magnil'oquence, *n.*, pompous or lofty language.

magnil'oquent, *adj.*, talking big.

magnil'oquently, *adv.*, pompously.

mag'nitude, *n.*, size, greatness.

Magno'lia, *n.*, a flowering shrub genus.

mag'num, *n.*, a large size of bottle (*Lat.*).

mag'pie, *n.*, a bird; a chatterer (*colloq.*).

Mag'yar, *n.*, a native of, or the language of, Hungary; *adj.*, rel. to Hungary; a type of sleeve.

Mahara'ja, Mahara'jah, *n.*, a title of some Indian princes.

Maharan'ee, *n.*, the wife or widow of a Maharaja.

Mahat'ma, *n.*, a professor of esoteric Buddhism.

Mah'di, *n.*, a Mohammedan religious leader.

mah-jong(g)', *n.*, a Chinese game.

mahl'stick, *n.*, a painter's hand-rest.

mahog'any, *adj.*, made of mahogany; *n.*, a reddish-brown wood.

Mahom'etan, *adj.*, rel. to Mahomet (Mohammed). Also *Mohammedan*.

Mahom'etanism, n., the Mahometan religion.

mahout', n., an elephant driver.

Mahratt'a, n., a member of a warlike Indian race.

mah'seer, n., an Indian freshwater fish.

maid, n., an unmarried woman; a female servant.

maid'en, adj., new, untried; n., a virgin, a girl; an over in cricket producing no runs.

maid'enhair, n., a variety of fern.

maid'enhood, n., the state of being a maiden.

maid'enish, adj., girlish.

maid'en-like, adj., modest, gentle.

maid'enly, adj., i.q. maiden-like.

Maid Ma'rian, n., a May Queen.

maid'servant, n., a female domestic.

maieut'ic, adj., rel. to childbirth; n., the Socratic technique for stimulating a person's mind.

mail, v.t., to arm with mail; to send by post; n., armour; the conveyance of letters; a batch of letters; a tribute.

mail'able, adj., ready for posting.

mailed, p.p., mail.

mail'ing, pr.p., mail.

mail'van, n., a van for carrying mail.

maim, v.t., to injure, to cripple.

maimed, p.p., maim.

maim'ing, pr.p., maim.

main, adj., chief, leading; n., the ocean; a chief sewer, gas-, or water-pipe; a match in cock-fighting; a throw of dice.

main'brace, n., the rope attached to the mainyard (naut.).

main'land, n., the land as distinguished from the sea or an island.

main'ly, adv., chiefly.

main'mast, n., the principal mast.

main'sail, n., the sail on the mainmast or bent to the mainyard.

main'spring, n., the principal spring; a source of power.

main'stay, n., a chief support; the stay stretching from the foot of the foremast to the maintop.

maintain', v.t., to keep, to defend, to affirm.

maintain'able, adj., able to be maintained.

maintained', p.p., maintain.

maintain'er, n., one who maintains.

maintain'ing, pr.p., maintain.

main'tenance, n., support, livelihood.

main'top, n., the top of a mainmast.

main'yard, n., the yard on which the mainsail is extended.

maisonette', n., a part of a house converted into a flat.

maître d'hôtel', n., the hotel staff controller.

maize, n., Indian corn.

majes'tic, adj., stately, regal.

majes'tically, adv., in a majestic way.

maj'esty, n., dignity, sovereignty, sublimity.

Majlis', n., the Persian parliament.

majol'ica, n., fine painted earthenware.

ma'jor, adj., greater; n., a military officer, next above a captain.

ma'jor-do'mo, n., a chief house-steward.

maj'or-gen'eral, n., a military officer, next below a lieutenant-general.

major'ity, n., the greater number; the full legal age.

majus'cule, n., a capital letter.

make, v.t., to create, to produce, to cause; n., a form, a structure.

make'believe, n., a pretence; adj., unreal.

ma'ker, n., one who makes.

make'shift, n., an extemporized substitute; adj., extemporized.

make'-up, n., composition; an actor's disguise; cosmetics applied.

make'weight, n., something added to make up weight.

ma'king, pr.p., make.

mak'ings, n. pl., profits; earnings; essential qualities.

mal'achite, n., a carbonate of copper.

malacol'ogy, n., the study of molluscs.

maladjust'ment, n., a faulty adjustment.

maladministra'tion, n., mismanagement.

maladroit', adj., clumsy.

mal'adroitly, adv., clumsily.

mal'adroitness, n., the state of being clumsy.

mal'ady, n., a disease.

mal'a fid'e, adj. and adv., in bad faith (Lat.).

Mal'aga, n., a kind of wine from M. in S. Spain.

mal'aise, n., bodily discomfort; the state of feeling unwell (Fr.).

mal'amute, n., an Eskimo dog.

mal'anders, n., a scurfy complaint in horses.

mal'apert, adj., saucy.

mal'aprop, n., i.q. malapropism.

mal'apropism, n., a misapplication of words.

malapropos', adj., inopportune (Fr.).

ma'lar, adj., rel. to the cheek.

mala'ria, n., exhalations from swampy ground; a mosquito-borne disease.

mala'rial, adj., rel. to malaria.

malariol'ogy, n., the study of malaria.

mala'rious, adj., producing malaria.

malassimila'tion, n., imperfect assimilation.

Malay', adj., i.q. Malayan; n., a Malayan native.

Malay'an, adj., rel. to the Malays.

mal'content, adj., discontented.

mal'de mer', n., seasickness (Fr.).

male, adj., not female; of the begetting sex; n., one of the male sex.

maledic'tion, n., a curse.

malefac'tion, n., an evil.

mal'efactor, n., a criminal.

mal'efactress, n., the fem. of malefactor.

malef'ic, adj., baneful, evil.

malef'icence, n., evil; crime.

malef'icent, adj., hurtful (to); criminal.

malev'olence, *n.*, ill-will, spite.

malev'olent, *adj.*, spiteful, bearing ill-will.

malev'olently, *adv.*, spitefully.

malfea'sance, *n.*, an illegality.

malforma'tion, *n.*, mis-shapenness.

ma'lic, *adj.*, rel. to fruit—to apples particularly.

mal'ice, *n.*, spite, evil intent.

mali'cious, *adj.*, spiteful.

mali'ciously, *adv.*, spitefully.

mali'ciousness, *n.*, spitefulness, cruel intent.

malign', *v.t.*, to slander; *adj.*, hurtful.

malig'nancy, *n.*, the state of being malignant.

malig'nant, *adj.*, malicious, injurious; diseased.

malig'nantly, *adv.*, in a malignant manner.

maligned', *p.p.*, malign.

malign'er, *n.*, one who maligns.

malign'ing, *pr.p.*, malign.

malig'nity, *n.*, malice, cruelty.

malign'ly, *adv.*, in a malign way.

malin'ger, *v.i.*, to shirk duty on pretence of illness.

malin'gered, *p.p.*, malinger.

malin'gerer, *n.*, one who malingers.

malin'gering, *pr.p.*, malinger.

mal'ism, *n.*, a doctrine based on a belief that the world is bad.

mal'ison, *n.*, a curse.

mal'kin, *n.*, a cat, a mop, a scarecrow, a drab.

mall, *n.*, a mallet.

mall, *n.*, the place where pall-mall was played; a public walk.

mal'lard, *n.*, a wild duck.

malleabil'ity, *n.*, the quality of being malleable.

mal'leable, *adj.*, able to be hammered out.

mal'leate, *v.t.*, to hammer (metal).

mallea'tion, *n.*, the act of hammering.

mall'emuck, *n.*, a fulmar, petrel or similar bird.

mall'enders, *n.*, *i.q.* malanders.

malle'olar, *adj.*, rel. to the ankle.

mal'let, *n.*, a wooden hammer.

mall'eus, *n.*, the bone of the middle ear (*Lat.*).

mal'low, *n.*, a plant of the Malva genus.

mal'lows, *n.*, *i.q.* mallow.

malm, *n.*, the loam used in brickmaking.

malmais'on, *n.*, a variety of carnation and rose.

malm'sey, *n.*, a species of grape; a wine made from the same.

mal'nutri'tion, *n.*, insufficient feeding.

malod'orous, *adj.*, evil-smelling.

malprac'tice, *n.*, evil.

malt, *v.t.*, to make into malt; *v.i.*, to become malt; *adj.*, made with malt; *n.*, grain fermented for brewing.

malt'ed, *p.p.*, malt.

Maltese', *adj.*, rel. to Malta; *n.*, a native of Malta.

mal'tha, *n.*, a sort of pitch.

Malthu'sian, *adj.*, rel. to Malthus and his population theory.

malt'ing, *pr.p.*, malt.

mal'tose, *n.*, the sugar produced from starch by fermentation.

maltreat', *v.t.*, to treat ill or cruelly.

maltreat'ed, *p.p.*, maltreat.

maltreat'ing, *pr.p.*, maltreat.

maltreat'ment, *n.*, cruel treatment.

malt'ster, *n.*, one who makes malt.

malt'y, *adj.*, like or containing malt.

Malva'ceae, *n.* *pl.*, an order of plants containing the mallows.

malva'ceous, *adj.*, rel. to Malvaceae.

malversa'tion, *n.*, the fraudulent abuse of trust.

mama', *n.*, *i.q.* mamma.

mam'ba, *n.*, a venomous African snake.

mam'bo, *n.*, a voodoo priestess; a West Indian dance and music.

mam'elon, *n.*, a mound.

mam'eluke, *n.*, one of the Egyptian cavalry.

mam'iform, *adj.*, breast-shaped.

mamill'a, *n.*, a nipple; a protuberance.

mam'illary, *adj.*, rel. to the breast.

mam'illated, *adj.*, having breasts; protuberant.

mamma', *n.*, a familiar name for mother.

mam'mal, *n.*, an animal that suckles its young.

mamma'lia, *n.*, pl. of mammal.

mamma'lian, *adj.*, rel. to mammals.

mammal'ogist, *adj.*, one who studies mammalogy.

mammal'ogy, *n.*, the study of mammals.

mam'mary, *adj.*, rel. to the breasts.

mammee', *n.*, a tropical American tree.

mammif'erous, *adj.*, having breasts.

Mam'mon, *n.*, the god of worldly riches.

mam'monist, *n.*, a worshipper of Mammon.

mam'moth, *adj.*, huge; *n.*, a huge extinct elephant.

man, *v.t.*, to furnish with men, to guard; *n.*, mankind collectively, a human being, a male.

man'acle, *v.t.*, to handcuff, to fasten the hands; *n.*, a shackle for the hands.

man'acled, *p.p.*, manacle; *adj.*, handcuffed.

man'acling, *pr.p.*, manacle.

man'age, *v.t.*, to conduct, to govern, to contrive.

man'ageable, *adj.*, able to be managed.

man'aged, *p.p.*, manage.

man'agement, *n.*, superintendence, contrivance.

man'ager, *n.*, one who manages.

man'ageress, *n.*, the fem. of manager.

manage'rial, *adj.*, rel. to management.

manager'ship, *n.*, the office of manager.

man'aging, *pr.p.*, manage.

man'akin, *n.*, a dwarf.

manatee', *n.*, the sea-cow.

manchineel', *n.*, a tropical W. Indian tree; a poisonous fruit from the tree.

Manchu', *n.*, one of the Manchus, the early conquerors of China.

man'ciple, *n.*, a steward.

Man'cunian, *adj.*, pert.

or rel. to Manchester; *n.*, a native of M.

manda′mus, *n.*, a writ from a higher to a lower court, or to a person.

man′darin, *n.*, a Chinese magistrate; a kind of orange; a liqueur.

man′datary, *n.*, one to whom a mandate is issued.

man′date, *n.*, a command, a precept.

man′datory, *adj.*, directing, ordering.

man′dible, *n.*, the upper jaw of an insect, the lower of vertebrates.

mandib′ular, *adj.*, rel. to mandibles.

mandib′ulate, *adj.*, possessing mandibles.

Mandin′go, *n.*, the name of a S. African negro tribe.

mandol′a, *n.*, a kind of mandolin or lute.

man′dolin, *n.*, a kind of guitar.

man′drake, *n.*, a narcotic plant.

man′drel, *n.*, a revolving shank in a lathe.

man′dril, *n.*, *i.q.* mandrel.

man′drill, *n.*, a large and ferocious baboon.

man′ducate, *v.t.*, to eat, to chew.

manduca′tion, *n.*, the act of eating.

mane, *n.*, the hair on the neck of a horse, lion, etc.

man′-eater, *n.*, a tiger that has tasted human flesh.

manège′, *n.*, horsemanship (*Fr.*).

ma′nes, *n. pl.*, the shades of the departed (*Lat.*).

man′ful, *adj.*, manly, courageous.

man′fully, *adv.*, courageously; in a manly way.

man′fulness, *n.*, courage, manliness.

man′gabey, *n.*, one of the monkey tribes.

man′ganese, *n.*, a hard and brittle grey metal.

mangane′sian, *adj.*, rel. to manganese.

mangan′ic, *adj.*, produced from manganese.

mange, *n.*, a skin disease in dogs and cattle.

man′gel-wur′zel, *n.*, a kind of beet.

man′ger, *n.*, a trough for cattle food.

man′giness, *n.*, the state of being mangy.

man′gle, *v.t.*, to lacerate, to mutilate; to smooth linen; *n.*, a rolling press for smoothing linen.

man′gled, *p.p.*, mangle.

man′gling, *pr.p.*, mangle.

man′go, *n.*, a fruit-bearing tree.

mang′osteen, *n.*, an East Indian tree.

man′grove, *n.*, an Indian fruit-bearing tree.

man′gy, *adj.*, suffering from mange.

man′handle, *v.t.*, to move by force of man alone; to handle roughly (*colloq.*).

man*hand***′led**, *p.p.*, manhandle.

man*hand***′ling**, *pr.p.*, manhandle.

manhatt′an, *n.*, a kind of cocktail.

man′hole, *n.*, an opening by which a sewer, etc., can be entered.

man′hood, *n.*, human nature; the state of being a man; courage.

ma′nia, *n.*, violent madness; an insane desire.

ma′niac, *n.*, one suffering from mania.

mani′acal, *adj.*, suffering from mania.

mani′acally, *adv.*, in a maniacal way.

Manichae′an, *adj.*, rel. to the Manichees.

Man′ichaeism, *n.*, the doctrine of the Manichees, or the dualistic theory of deity.

Manichee′, *n.*, a believer in two Supreme Powers.

man′icure, *v.t.*, to care for the hands and nails; *n.*, the special treatment of the nails, etc.

man′icurist, *n.*, one who practises manicuring.

man′ifest, *v.t.*, to show, to exhibit, to reveal, to give proof of; *adj.*, evident, plain, obvious; *n.*, an invoice of cargo.

man′ifestable, *adj.*, able to be manifested.

manifesta′tion, *n.*, the discovery, display, proof.

man′ifested, *p.p.*, manifest.

man′ifesting, *pr.p.*, manifest.

man′ifestly, *adv.*, plainly, obviously.

manifes′to, *n.*, a public declaration (*It.*).

man′ifold, *adj.*, multi-

plied many times; various; many; *adv.*, many times; *v.t.*, to duplicate.

man′ifolder, *n.*, a duplicating machine.

man′ikin, *n.*, a little man; a model of the human form.

manil′la, *n.*, a variety of hemp; a cheroot.

manille′, *n.*, the second best trump or honour in some card games.

man′ioc, *n.*, a plant from which tapioca is made.

man′iple, *n.*, a division of the Roman legion; a stole-like band worn round the left wrist in celebrating Mass.

manip′ular, *adj.*, rel. to handling.

manip′ulate, *v.t.*, to work with the hands, to control, to falsify.

manip′ulated, *p.p.*, manipulate.

manip′ulating, *pr.p.*, manipulate.

manipula′tion, *n.*, the act of manipulating; manual skill; falsification.

manip′ulative, *adj.*, done by manipulating.

manip′ulator, *n.*, one who manipulates.

Ma′nis, *n.*, a genus of mammals including ant-eaters.

man′itou, *n.*, the Great Spirit (N. Amer. Indian).

mankind′, *n.*, human beings collectively, the human race.

man′lier, *adj.*, comp. of manly.

man′liest, *adj.*, super. of manly.

man′like, *adj.*, manly.

man′liness, *n.*, manly qualities.

man′ly, *adj.*, brave, noble.

man′na, *n.*, the Israelites' food in the wilderness; a saccharine substance obtained from a species of ash.

manned, *p.p.*, man.

mann′equin, *n.*, a person who models clothes.

man′ner, *n.*, form, custom, habit. In pl., morals; conduct.

man′nered, *adj.*, behaved.

man′nerism, *n.*, an eccentricity of manner; an affected style.

man′nerist, *n.*, one who shows mannerism.

man'nerliness, *n.*, politeness, courtesy.

man'nerly, *adj.*, polite, courteous.

man'ning, *pr.p.*, man.

man'nish, *adj.*, aping the masculine.

mann'ite, *n.*, a substance obtained from manna.

mann'itose, *n.*, *i.q.* mannite.

manoeu'vrable, *adj.*, capable of being manoeuvred.

manoeu'vre, *v.t.*, to cause to perform manoeuvres; *v.i.*, to conduct military operations; to scheme; to contrive; *n.*, a skilful movement, esp. in naval and military operations.

manoeu'vred, *p.p.*, manoeuvre.

manoeu'vrer, *n.*, one who manoeuvres.

manoeu'vring, *pr.p.*, manoeuvre.

man'-of-war', *n.*, a warship; a type of jellyfish.

manom'eter, *n.*, an instrument for measuring the rarefaction of elastic fluids.

manomet'rical, *adj.*, rel. to a manometer.

man'or, *n.*, a district under the jurisdiction of a lord; a lord's landed estate.

man'or-house, *n.*, the manorial lord's residence.

mano'rial, *adj.*, rel. to a manor.

man'power, *n.*, the number of people available for military or other services.

man'sard, *n.*, a roof, an attic (*Fr.*).

manse, *n.*, the house of a minister of religion (*Scot.*).

man'sion, *n.*, a large house.

man'slaughter, *n.*, the killing of a human being without malice.

man'suetude, *n.*, gentleness.

man'tel, *n.*, a shelf over a fireplace.

man'telet, *n.*, a movable shelter for soldiers. Also *mantlet*.

man'telpiece, *n.*, *i.q.* mantel; a chimneypiece.

man'tic, *adj.*, rel. to divination.

mantil'la, *n.*, a Spanish veil or cloak.

man'tis, *n.*, the praying-insect.

mantis'sa, *n.*, the decimal part of a logarithm.

man'tle, *v.t.*, to cover with a mantle, to conceal; *v.i.*, to spread over; *n.*, a cloak.

man'tled, *p.p.*, mantle.

man'tling, *pr.p.*, mantle; *n.*, the heraldic drapery round a shield.

man'trap, *n.*, a gin.

man'tua, *n.*, a loose gown.

man'ual, *adj.*, rel. to, or done with, the hands; *n.*, a handbook; an organ finger-board.

man'ually, *adv.*, in a manual way.

manufact'ory, *n.*, a workshop.

manufac'ture, *v.t.* and *i.*, to make by machinery on a large scale; to fabricate a story (*colloq.*); *n.*, a branch of such industry.

manufac'tured, *p.p.*, manufacture.

manufac'turer, *n.*, one engaged in manufacture.

manufac'turing, *pr.p.*, manufacture.

manumis'sion, *n.*, the act of setting free.

manumit', *v.t.*, to set free.

manumit'ted, *adj.*, freed; *p.p.*, manumit.

manumit'ting, *pr.p.*, manumit.

manumo'tor, *n.*, a hand-driven carriage.

manure', *v.t.*, to fertilize with dung or other substances; *n.*, fertilizing substances.

manured', *p.p.*, manure.

manu'rial, *adj.*, rel. to manure.

manur'ing, *pr.p.*, manure.

man'uscript, *adj.*, hand-written; *n.*, a written paper or book.

man'ward, *adj.*, tending, directed, towards man.

Manx, *adj.*, rel. to the Isle of Man; *n.*, the language of I. of M.

Manx'man, *n.*, a native of the I. of M.

man'y, *adj.*, not few; composed of a great number.

Ma'ori, *adj.*, rel. to the Maoris; *n.*, an original native of New Zealand.

map, *v.t.*, to delineate geographically; to set out; *n.*, a delineation of a surface of the earth.

ma'ple, *n.*, a tree of the genus *Acer*.

mapped, *p.p.*, map.

map'ping, *pr.p.*, map.

mar, *v.t.*, to spoil, to damage, to deface.

mar'abou, *n.*, a species of stork.

mar'about, *n.*, a Mohammedan saint.

mara'ca, *n.*, a rattle-like instrument (*mus.*).

marana'tha, a Syriac phrase = the Lord is at hand; *see* I Cor. xvi.

maraschi'no, *n.*, a liqueur distilled from the cherry.

maras'mus, *n.*, atrophy.

ma'rathon, *n.*, a strenuous, long-distance race (around 26 miles).

maraud', *v.i.*, to raid.

maraud'ed, *p.p.*, maraud.

maraud'er, *n.*, a raider.

maraud'ing, *pr.p.*, maraud.

marave'di, *n.*, an old Spanish coin.

mar'ble, *v.t.*, to vein like marble; *adj.*, made of marble; cold, hard; *n.*, a calcareous stone, a compact stone.

mar'bled, *p.p.*, marble.

mar'bler, *n.*, one who marbles.

mar'blette, *n.*, imitation marble.

mar'bling, *pr.p.*, marble.

marb'ly, *adj.*, like marble.

marc, *n.*, fruit refuse after crushing (*Fr.*).

mar'casite, *n.*, white pyrites.

marca'to, *adj.*, strongly accentuated (*mus.*); *adv.*, in a strongly stressed way.

marcel', *n.*, artificial waves in the hair; *v.t.*, to wave the hair.

marces'cent, *adj.*, fading.

March, *n.*, the third month of the year.

march, *v.i.*, to move by steps, or in military form; to border; *n.*, a military walk; an advance; a frontier; music for marching.

marched, *p.p.*, march.

march'ing, *pr.p.*, march.

mar'chioness, n., the fem. of marquess or marquis.

march'pane, n., i.q. marzipan.

marco'nigram, n., a radio message.

Mar'di gras', n., Shrove Tuesday (Fr.).

mare, n., the fem. of horse.

mar'e claus'um, n. pl., territorial waters (Lat.).

mar'e lib'erum, n., sea open to all (Lat.).

maremm'a, n., the low marshy unhealthy country by the seashore, esp. in Italy.

mare's'-nest, n., a fruitless discovery.

mare's'-tail, n., a waterplant; a variety of cloud.

mar'garine, n., imitation butter made from fats or nut oil.

mar'garite, n., pearl mica.

marg'ay, n., a S. American tiger-cat.

marge, n., margarine (colloq.).

mar'gin, n., an edge, a border, the brink; something over.

mar'ginal, adj., rel. to a margin.

margina'lia, n., marginal notes (Lat.).

mar'ginally, adv., in a marginal way.

mar'grave, n., a German marquis.

mar'gravine, n., the fem. of margrave.

mar'guerite, n., the daisy.

Ma'rian, adj., rel. to Mary; n., a girl's name.

ma'rid, n., powerful Jinn.

mar'igold, n., a yellow flower.

marihua'na, n., dried Indian hemp; a narcotic. Also marijuana.

marim'ba, n., a sort of xylophone.

mari'na, n., a harbour for yachts and small craft.

marinade', n., a sort of pickle; v.t., to pickle in oil and vinegar.

marine', adj., rel. to the sea.

mar'iner, n., a seaman.

marionette', n., a puppet.

marionet'tist, n., a person who manipulates, or exhibits, puppets.

mar'ish, n., a marsh; adj., marshy (poet.).

mar'ital, adj., rel. to the wedded state.

mar'itime, adj., rel. to the sea; nautical.

mar'joram, n., an aromatic herb.

mark, v.t., to notify by a stamp; to notice; n., a stamp, an impression, a sign.

marked, p.p., mark.

mark'edly, adv., plainly, evidently.

mark'er, n., one who marks; a scorer.

mar'ket, v.t., to dispose of wares; v.i., to go to market; n., a space for buying and selling.

mar'ketable, adj., saleable.

mar'keted, p.p., market.

mar'ket-gar'den, n., a garden producing for the market.

mar'ket-gar'dener, n., the keeper of a market-garden.

mar'keting, pr.p., market.

mar'ketplace, n., the place where a market is held.

mar'khor, n., a N. Indian wild goat.

mark'ing, pr.p., mark; n., a mark; the arrangement of colouring.

marks'man, n., a skilled shot.

marks'manship, n., skill at shooting.

marks'woman, n., a skilled riflewoman.

marl, v.t., to spread with marl; to wind with a marline; n., earth containing carbonate of lime, etc.

marla'ceous, adj., composed of marl.

marled, p.p., marl.

mar'line, n., a cord used in splicing (naut.).

mar'line-spike, n., a piece of iron used in splicing (naut.).

mar'ling, pr.p., marl.

marl'ite, n., a kind of marl.

mar'ly, n., containing, or resembling, marl.

mar'malade, n., a preserve, usually of oranges.

marm'ite, n., a stew pot; an extract made from brewer's yeast; a high explosive shell.

marm'olite, n., a pale green laminated serpentine.

marmora'ceous, adj., containing marble.

marmo'real, adj., rel. to marble (poet.).

mar'moset, n., a small monkey.

mar'mot, n., a variety of rat.

ma'rocain, n., a dress fabric.

Mar'onite, n., one of an early Christian sect.

maroon', v.t., to leave on a desert island; n., a runaway slave; a reddish brown colour; an explosive rocket used as a warning.

mar'plot, n., one who spoils another's plan.

marque, n., a licence to a private vessel to take reprisal.

marquee', n., a large tent.

mar'quess, n., a nobleman next in rank to a duke.

mar'queterie, n., inlaid work.

mar'quetry, n., i.q. marqueterie.

mar'quis, n., i.q. marquess.

mar'quisate, n., the lordship of a marquis.

marquise', n., a marchioness; the fem. of marquis (Fr.); a kind of finger ring.

mar'quois, n., an apparatus for drawing equidistant parallel lines.

ma'rram, n., a shore grass that binds sand.

marred, p.p., mar.

mar'riage, n., a wedding, matrimony.

mar'riageable, adj., fit to be married.

mar'ried, p.p., marry.

mar'ring, pr.p., mar.

marron glacé', n., a sugar-iced chestnut, a sweetmeat (Fr.).

mar'row, n., the oleaginous substance in bones; a vegetable.

mar'rowbone, n., a bone containing marrow.

mar'rowfat, n., a variety of pea.

mar'rowy, adj., containing marrow.

mar'ry, v.t., to take to wife or husband; to perform the ceremony of a marriage; v.i., to take a wife or a husband; to wed.

mar'rying, pr.p., marry.

Mars, *n.,* the Roman war god; the planet Mars.

Marsa'la, *n.,* a kind of sherry.

Marseillaise', *n.,* rel. to Marseilles, a seaport in S. France; *n.,* the French national song.

marsh, *n.,* a watery tract of land.

mar'shal, *v.t.,* to arrange, to rank in order; *n.,* a director of ceremonies; a military officer of the highest rank.

mar'shalcy, *n.,* the status of a marshal.

mar'shal(l)ed, *p.p.,* marshal.

mar'shal(l)ing, *pr.p.,* marshal.

marsh'iness, *n.,* the quality of being marshy.

marsh'land, *n.,* low, wet land.

marsh'mallow, *n.,* a herb found in the salt marshes; a sweetmeat made of it.

marsh'-marigold, *n.,* a plant growing in damp meadows.

marsh'y, *adj.,* fenny, swampy.

marsu'pial, *adj.* and *n.,* (animal) having an external pouch.

marsu'pium, *n.,* the external pouch of kangaroos and opossums.

mart, *n.,* a market; a public sale.

martel'lo-tow'er, *n.,* an old type of coast defence.

mar'ten, *n.,* a furred animal, like the sable.

mar'tenot, *n.,* a melodic electrophone.

mar'tial, *adj.,* warlike, rel. to warfare.

mar'tially, *adv.,* in a warlike way.

Mar'tian, *adj.,* rel. to Mars.

mar'tin, *n.,* a bird like a swallow.

martinet', *n.,* a severe disciplinarian.

mar'tingale, *n.,* a strap passing between a horse's forelegs, from the nose-band to the girth to prevent rearing, etc.

marti'ni, *n.,* a make of rifle; a cocktail containing gin, vermouth, etc.

Mar'tinmas, *n.,* the Feast of St. Martin (Nov. 11).

mart'let, *n.,* an heraldic bird.

mar'tyr, *n.,* one who dies for his belief or cause; *v.t.,* to put to a martyr's death.

mar'tyrdom, *n.,* a martyr's death or suffering.

mar'tyred, *p.p.,* martyr.

mar'tyring, *pr.p.,* martyr.

martyrolog'ical, *adj.,* rel. to martyrology.

martyrol'ogist, *n.,* a writer on martyrology.

martyrol'ogy, *n.,* the history of martyrs.

mart'yry, *n.,* a monument, a church, erected in honour of a martyr.

mar'vel, *v.i.,* to wonder, to be astonished; *n.,* something astonishing.

mar'vel(l)ed, *p.p.,* marvel.

mar'vel(l)ing, *pr.p.,* marvel.

mar'vel(l)ous, *adj.,* wonderful, astonishing.

mar'vel(l)ously, *adv.,* wonderfully.

Marx'ian, *adj.,* rel. to Karl Marx.

Marx'ism, *n.,* the teaching of Karl Marx, the State socialist.

Marx'ist, *n.,* a believer in Marxism.

mar'zipan, *n.,* a confection of almonds, sugar, and the white of egg.

mascar'a, *n.,* a preparation for cosmetic use on the eyelashes.

mas'cle, *n.,* an heraldic perforated lozenge.

mas'cot, *n.,* something supposed to bring good luck; a charm.

mas'cotry, *n.,* pert. to mascots.

mas'culine, *adj.,* male, manly.

ma'ser, *n.,* an acronym from *M*icrowave *A*mplification by *St*imulated *E*mission of *R*adiation.

mash, *v.t.,* to reduce to a pulpy state; to mix; *n.,* a blend of ingredients.

mashed, *p.p.,* mash.

mash'er, *n.,* a mashing machine.

mash'ie, *n.,* a light, iron golf-club so named.

mash'ing, *pr.p.,* mash.

ma'sjid, *n.,* a mosque.

mask, *v.t.,* to disguise with a mask; to conceal; *n.,* a face-cover.

masked, *p.p.,* mask; *adj.,* wearing a mask.

mask'er, *n.,* a masquerader.

mask'ing, *pr.p.,* mask.

maskinon'ge, *n.,* a large pike (N. American).

mas'ochism, *n.,* the sexual behaviour of a masochist.

mas'ochist, *n.,* one who welcomes pain and humiliation as sexually satisfying.

ma'son, *n.,* one who builds with stone; a freemason.

mason'ic, *adj.,* rel. to masons and masonry.

ma'sonry, *n.,* the work of a mason; freemasonry.

Mas(s)o'ra(h), *n.,* a body of Aramaic notes on the Old Testament.

Masoret'ic, *adj.,* rel. to the Masora.

Mas'orite, *n.,* one of the contributors to the Masora.

masque, *n.,* amateur entertainment, the performers being masked.

masquerade', *v.i.,* to assemble in masks; to pose; *n.,* a ball.

masquera'ded, *p.p.,* masquerade.

masquera'der, *n.,* one who masquerades.

masquera'ding, *pr.p.,* masquerade.

Mass, *n.,* the Holy Eucharist.

mass, *n.,* a large quantity; a lump; *v.t.* and *i.,* to collect together.

mas'sacre, *v.t.,* to slay indiscriminately; *n.,* an indiscriminate slaughter.

mas'sacred, *p.p.,* massacre.

mas'sacring, *pr.p.,* massacre.

massage', *n.,* medical rubbing or kneading; *v.t.,* to rub or knead.

masse'ter, *n.,* a muscle used in chewing.

masseur', *n.,* one who massages (*Fr.*).

masseuse', *n.,* the fem. of masseur (*Fr.*).

mass'if, *n.,* mountain heights forming compact group.

mass'iness, *n.,* the quality of being massy.

mass'ive, *adj.,* bulky, weighty.

mass'ively, *adv.,* weightily, bulkily.

mass′iveness, *n.*, the quality of being massive.

mass′-meeting, *n.*, a large public gathering.

mass′y, *adj.*, *i.q.* massive.

mast, *n.*, an upright pole or tall structure rigged for various uses (esp. on ships); the fruit of the beech and the oak.

mas′taba, *n.*, an Ancient Egyptian tomb.

mas′tectomy, *n.*, the removal by operation of the female breast (*med.*).

mast′ed, *adj.*, having a mast.

mas′ter, *v.t.*, to conquer, to overcome, to excel; *n.*, a governor, an owner, a teacher, the captain of a merchantman, the head of a house.

mas′tered, *p.p.*, master.

mas′terful, *adj.*, superior, domineering.

ma′sterfully, *adv.*, in a masterful manner.

ma′sterfulness, *n.*, the quality of being masterful.

mas′tering, *pr.p.*, master.

mas′ter-key, *n.*, a key that fits many different locks.

mas′terless, *adj.*, without a master.

mas′terly, *adj.*, supremely skilful.

mas′terpiece, *n.*, a *chef-d′oeuvre*; a consummate piece of work.

mas′tership, *n.*, the office of a master.

mas′ter-stroke, *n.*, a consummate achievement.

mas′tery, *n.*, victory, a conquest, the upper hand.

mast′head, *v.t.*, to send up to the masthead (for punishment); *n.*, the top of a mast.

mas′tic, *n.*, a gum used for varnish.

mas′ticate, *v.t.*, to chew with the teeth.

mas′ticated, *p.p.*, masticate.

mas′ticating, *pr.p.*, masticate.

mastica′tion, *n.*, the act of chewing.

mas′ticator, *n.*, anything that masticates; a mincing machine.

mas′ticatory, *adj.*, fit for, or rel. to, chewing.

mas′tiff, *n.*, a large breed of bulldog.

mastit′is, *n.*, inflammation of the breast.

mas′todon, *n.*, an extinct animal.

mas′toid, *adj.*, breast-like; *n.*, an ear abscess (*colloq.*).

mas′turbate, *v.i.*, to obtain sexual satisfaction by self-excitation.

masturba′tion, *n.*, sexual satisfaction by self-excitation.

mat, *v.t.* and *i.*, to interweave, to entangle; *n.*, a texture used for the floor or other protective covering.

mat′ador, *n.*, a bull-fighter; a card in the games of ombre and quadrille.

match, *v.t.*, to oppose as equal or alike; to equal; *v.i.*, to arrange a marriage with; *n.*, a contest, a completed game, an equal, a marriageable party, a matrimonial engagement, a lucifer.

match′able, *n.*, able to be matched.

match′board, *n.*, a type of tongued and grooved boarding.

matched, *p.p.*, match.

match′er, *n.*, one who, or that which, matches.

match′et, *n.*, a broad, heavy knife.

match′ing, *pr.p.*, match.

match′less, *adj.*, inimitable.

match′lock, *n.*, an obsolete musket.

match′maker, *n.*, one interested in getting people married.

match′making, *adj.*, of the character of a matchmaker; *n.*, the practice of a matchmaker.

match′wood, *n.*, wood suitable for matchmaking; smashed up wood.

mate, *v.i.*, to match, to marry; *n.*, a companion; the final move in chess; a ship's officer.

ma′té, *n.*, a Brazilian tea.

ma′ted, *p.p.*, mate.

mate′less, *adj.*, lonely; without a mate.

mat′elot, *n.*, a sailor (*Fr.*).

ma′telote, *n.*, a dish made of various fish (*Fr.*).

ma′ter, *n.*, a membrane of the brain; mother (*Lat.*).

mate′rial, *adj.*, rel. to matter, corporeal, essential, that matters; *n.*, that of which a thing is made.

mate′rialism, *n.*, the denial of the spiritual in the world and man.

mate′rialist, *n.*, one who believes in materialism.

materialis′tic, *adj.*, rel. to materialism.

mater′ialistically, *adv.*, *i.q.* materially.

material′ity, *n.*, the material existence.

mate′rialize, *v.t.*, to make material; *v.i.*, to become material.

mate′rialized, *p.p.*, materialize.

mate′rializing, *pr.p.*, materialize.

mate′rially, *adv.*, substantially; seriously.

mate′ria med′ica, *n.*, the substances used in medicine (*Lat.*, *med.*).

mater′nal, *adj.*, motherly; rel. to a mother.

mater′nally, *adv.*, in a motherly way.

mater′nity, *n.*, the relation of a mother; motherhood.

mathemat′ic, *adj.*, *i.q.* mathematical.

mathemat′ical, *adj.*, rel. to mathematics.

mathemat′ically, *adv.*, according to mathematics.

mathemati′cian, *n.*, one skilled in mathematics.

mathemat′ics, *n. pl.*, the science of numbers and space.

mathe′sis, *n.*, learning.

mathe′tic, *adj.*, pert. to learning by a cued response-stimulus method.

mat′in, *adj.*, rel. to the morning.

mat′inée, *n.*, an afternoon musical or theatrical performance (*Fr.*).

ma′tiness, *n.*, friendliness.

ma′ting, *pr.p.*, mate.

mat′ins, *n. pl.*, morning prayer in the Church of England.

mat′rass, *n.*, a distilling vessel.

mat′riarch, *n.,* a woman corresponding in status to patriarch.

matriarch′al, *adj.,* rel. to a matriarch or to matriarchy.

mat′riarchy, *n.,* the social predominance of women.

ma′trice, *n., i.q.* matrix.

mat′ricidal, *adj.,* rel. to matricide.

mat′ricide, *n.,* the murder of a mother.

matric′ulate, *v.t.,* to enter a university; *v.i.,* to be entered at a university.

matric′ulated, *p.p.,* matriculate.

matric′ulating, *pr.p.,* matriculate.

matricula′tion, *n.,* the act of matriculating.

matrimo′nial, *adj.,* rel. to matrimony.

matrimo′nially, *adv.,* by matrimony.

mat′rimony, *n.,* the married state.

ma′trix, *n.,* a mould; the womb; the bed in which brasses are let into stone; the five basal colours in dyeing; a pattern.

ma′tron, *n.,* a married woman; the woman head of an establishment.

ma′tronage, *n.,* matrons as a body.

ma′tronal, *adj.,* rel. to matrons.

ma′tronhood, *n.,* the state of being matronly.

ma′tronly, *adj.,* matronlike, elderly.

matronym′ic, *n.,* a name derived from a mother.

matt′amore, *n.,* a subterranean dwelling or storehouse.

mat′ted, *p.p.,* mat.

mat′ter, *v.i.,* to signify, to be important; *n.,* substance, a thing treated of.

mat′tered, *p.p.,* matter.

mat′ter-of-fact, *adj.,* adhering to facts; commonplace; prosaic.

mat′ting, *pr.p.,* mat; *n.,* mats as a whole; material used for mats.

mat′tock, *n.,* a pickaxe with one end flat.

matt′oid, *n.,* an erratically minded person.

mat′tress, *n.,* originally a case stuffed with straw or hair and used for bedding; now often a spring contrivance.

mat′urate, *v.t.,* to hasten on (as of a boil, pimple or cataract, *med.*).

matura′tion, *n.,* ripening.

matu′rative, *adj.,* with a ripening effect.

mature′, *v.t.* and *i.,* to ripen; *adj.,* ripe, completed.

matured′, *p.p.,* mature.

mature′ly, *adv.,* in a mature way.

mature′ness, *n.,* ripeness.

matures′cence, *n.,* the process of ripening.

matu′ring, *pr.p.,* mature.

matu′rity, *n.,* the mature state, ripeness, completion.

matutin′al, *adj.,* early; of the morning.

mat′utine, *adj., i.q.* matutinal.

ma′t(e)y, *adj., adv.,* sociable, friendly (*colloq.*).

mat′zo, *n.,* unleavened bread.

maud, *n.,* a grey plaid.

maud′lin, *adj.,* fuddled, silly.

mau′gre, *prep.,* in spite of (*old Fr.*).

maul, *v.t.,* to bruise and beat; to handle roughly; *n.,* a large wooden hammer.

mauled, *p.p.,* maul.

maul′ing, *pr.p.,* maul.

maul′stick, *n., i.q.* mahlstick.

maund, *n.,* a basket; an Indian weight.

maund′er, *v.i.,* to ramble in speech.

maun′dered, *p.p.,* maunder.

maun′dering, *pr.p.,* maunder.

maun′dy, *n.,* a ceremonial washing of the feet of the poor; the distribution of royal alms (Maundy money).

Maun′dy Thurs′day, *n.,* the Thursday in Holy Week.

Mauri′tian, *adj.,* pert. or rel. to the island of Mauritius; *n.,* a native of M.

Mau′ser, *n.,* a make of breech-loading magazine rifle.

mausole′um, *n.,* a magnificent tomb.

mauve, *n.,* a purple colour.

ma′vis, *n.,* the thrush (*poet.*).

maw, *n.,* an animal's stomach; a bird's craw.

mawk′ish, *adj.,* nauseous; sentimental.

maw′seed, *n.,* the seed of the opium poppy.

maw′worm, *n.,* a worm in the intestines.

maxil′la, *n.,* the jawbone.

max′illar, *adj.,* rel. to the maxilla.

maxil′lary, *adj., i.q.* maxillar.

maxil′liform, *adj.,* like a jawbone.

max′im, *n.,* an accepted principle; an adage; a variety of gun.

max′imalist, *n., i.q.* communist.

max′imize, *v.t.,* to increase to the uttermost.

max′imum, *n.,* the greatest degree possible.

May, *n.,* the fifth month; a girl's name.

may, *v.i.,* to be permitted; *n.,* hawthorn.

may′be, phrase = perhaps.

May′day, *n.,* the 1st of May.

may′day, *n.,* the international radiotelephone distress signal (from *m′aider* (*Fr.*) help me).

May′flower, *n.,* the ship that bore the Pilgrim Fathers.

may′fly, *n.,* an ephemeral insect.

may′hap, phrase = perhaps.

may′hem, *n.,* injury by violence.

may′ing, *n.,* keeping the Mayday festival.

mayonnaise′, *n.,* a sauce or dressing (*Fr.*).

may′or, *n.,* the chief magistrate of a town.

may′oral, *adj.,* rel. to a mayor.

may′oralty, *n.,* a mayor's office, or period of office.

may′oress, *n.,* the fem. of mayor.

may′pole, *n.,* a pole danced round on Mayday.

maz′ard, *n.,* a variety of cherry.

mazarine′, *adj.,* of mazarine colour; *n.,* a deep blue.

maze, *n.,* a labyrinth; confusion of thought; *v.t.,* to bewilder.

mazed, *p.p.,* maze.

maz'er, *n.,* a wooden, silver mounted drinking bowl.

ma'zily, *adv.,* winding about.

ma'ziness, *n.,* the state of being mazy.

ma'zing, *pr.p.,* maze.

mazur'ka, *n.,* a gay, Polish dance.

ma'zy, *adj.,* intricate, winding.

me, *pron. pers.,* obj. case of "I."

mead, *n.,* a drink of fermented honey; a meadow.

mead'ow, *n.,* pasture land.

mead'owsweet, *n.,* one of the Spiraea.

mead'owy, *adj.,* like meadows; abounding in meadows.

mea'gre, *adj.,* lean, scanty.

mea'grely, *adv.,* scantily.

mea'greness, *n.,* leanness, scantiness.

meal, *n.,* a repast; the edible part of corn.

meal'ie, *n.,* an ear of Indian corn.

meal'iness, *n.,* the quality of being mealy.

meal'y, *adj.,* having the taste or quality of a meal.

meal'y-mouthed, *adj.,* soft-tongued, hypocritical.

mean, *v.t.,* to purpose, to design, to signify; *adj.,* worthless, contemptible, base; not generous; *n.,* a middle state; a statistical average.

mean'der, *v.i.,* to run in windings; to be intricate.

mean'dered, *p.p.,* meander.

mean'dering, *pr.p.,* meander.

mean'er, *adj.,* comp. of mean.

mean'est, *adj., super.* of mean.

mean'ing, *pr.p.,* mean; *adj.,* significant; *n.,* the sense, the significance.

mean'ingless, *adj.,* without meaning.

mean'ly, *adv.,* in a mean way.

mean'ness, *n.,* a want of dignity; baseness, stinginess.

means, *n. pl.,* resources, wealth, instruments.

meant, *p.p.,* mean.

mean'time, *adv.,* in the intervening time; *n.,* the intervening time.

mean'while, *adv.* and *n., i.q.* meantime.

mea'sled, *adj.,* suffering from measles.

mea'sles, *n.,* a contagious febrile disease.

mea'sly, *adj.,* affected with measles; shabby (*slang*).

meas'urable, *adj.* able to be measured.

meas'urably, *adv.,* in a measurable degree.

meas'ure, *v.t.,* to ascertain by measuring; to mark out; to compare with a standard; *n.,* a standard, a rule, a proportion, a metre, a Bill or Act of Parliament.

meas'ured, *p.p.,* measure.

meas'ureless, *adj.,* immeasurable.

meas'urement, *n.,* the act of measuring; a dimension.

meas'urer, *n.,* one who, that which, measures.

meas'uring, *pr.p.,* measure.

meat, *n.,* food from animal flesh.

meat'less, *adj.,* without meat.

meat'us, *n.,* a channel, a passage in the body.

meat'y, *adj.,* meat-like, fleshy.

Mecc'a, *n.,* Mohammed's birthplace; a desired goal.

Meccan'o, *n.,* the trade name of a make of metal parts for model making.

mechan'ic, *adj., i.q.* mechanical; *n.,* one who practises a mechanical art.

mechan'ical, *adj.,* rel. to mechanics and machines; automatic.

mechan'ically, *adv.,* automatically.

mechani'cian, *n.,* one skilled in mechanics and machinery.

mechan'ics, *n. pl.,* the science of the action of forces on bodies; the science of machinery.

mech'anism, *n.,* the mechanical construction.

mech'anist, *n.,* a designer of machines.

mechaniza'tion, *n.,* the substitution of machines for manual labour.

mech'anize, *v.t.,* to make mechanical.

mech'anized, *p.p.,* mechanize.

mech'anizing, *pr.p.,* mechanize.

Mech'lin, *n.,* a Belgian lace.

mecom'eter, *n.,* an instrument for measuring the length of a newly-born child.

meco'nium, *n.,* opium; the bowel discharge of a new-born infant.

med'al, *n.,* a piece of metal, struck and stamped with a device.

medal'lic, *adj.,* rel. to medals.

medal'lion, *n.,* a large medal; a round or oval tablet.

med'allist, *n.,* the winner of a medal; a medal engraver.

med'allurgy, *n.,* the art of making medals.

med'dle, *v.i.,* to interfere.

med'dled, *p.p.,* meddle.

med'dler, *n.,* a busybody.

med'dlesome, *adj.,* officiously interfering.

med'dling, *pr.p.,* meddle.

me'dia, *n.,* the middle membrane of an artery or vessel (*anat.*); *n. pl.,* medium; means of communication.

mediae'val, *adj.,* rel. to the Middle Ages.

mediae'valism, *n.,* the characteristics of the Middle Ages.

me'dial, *adj.,* denoting an average or mean.

me'dian, *adj.,* rel. to the middle; *n.,* a statistical average.

me'diant, *n.,* the third note in the musical scale.

mediasti'num, *n.,* the intervening septum between the two chief parts of an organ (*anat.*).

me'diate, *v.i.,* to interpose between two parties; *adj.,* indirectly connected.

me'diated, *p.p.,* mediate.

me'diately, *adv.,* by means.

me'diating, *pr.p.,* mediate.

media'tion, *n.,* the act of mediating; the agency.

me'diatize, *v.t.,* to make a sovereign state a subject one, leaving

to the ruler his title and some power.

me′diatized, *p.p.*, mediatize.

me′diatizing, *pr.p.*, mediatize.

me′diator, *n.*, one who mediates; an intercessor.

mediato′rial, *adj.*, rel. to a mediator; intercessory.

media′trix, *n.*, the fem. of mediator.

med′icable, *adj.*, curable.

med′ical, *adj.*, rel. to medicine.

med′ically, *adv.*, according to medicine.

medic′ament, *n.*, a healing drug.

med′icaster, *n.*, a quack-doctor.

med′icate, *v.t.*, to tincture with anything medicinal.

med′icated, *p.p.*, medicate.

med′icating, *pr.p.*, medicate.

medica′tion, *n.*, the act or the result of medicating.

med′icative, *adj.*, pert. or rel. to medication.

medic′inal, *adj.*, rel. to physic or medicine.

medic′inally, *adv.*, medically.

med′icine, *n.*, a drug used as a remedy; the art and science of health; the profession of a doctor.

med′ico-le′gal, *adj.*, rel. to law in connexion with medicine.

medie′val, *adj.*, *i.q.* mediaeval.

medie′valism, *n.*, *i.q.* mediaevalism.

me′diocre, *adj.*, moderate, ordinary.

medioc′rity, *n.*, the middle state or degree; a person of merely ordinary ability.

med′itate, *v.t.*, to plan, to contrive, to think about; *v.i.*, to ponder.

med′itated, *p.p.*, meditate.

med′itating, *pr.p.*, meditate.

medita′tion, *n.*, reflection, deep thought.

med′itative, *adj.*, reflecting; given to meditation.

med′itatively, *adv.*, in a meditative way.

mediterra′nean, *adj.*, in-land; lying between lands; *n.*, the Mediterranean Sea.

me′dium, *n.*, a mean; the middle place; an agency; the space in which bodies move; a spiritualistic agent.

mediumis′tic, *adj.*, rel. to spiritualistic mediums.

med′lar, *n.*, a fruit tree.

med′ley, *n.*, a mixture.

Médoc′, *n.*, a French claret.

medul′la, *n.*, the marrow, pith (*Lat.*).

med′ullary, *adj.*, rel. to the medulla.

medul′lin, *n.*, pith, cellulose.

medu′sa, *n.*, a sea-nettle.

meed, *n.*, reward, desert.

meek, *adj.*, humble, mild.

meek′en, *v.t.*, to make meek.

meek′ly, *adv.*, with meekness.

meek′ness, *n.*, humility, mildness.

meer′kat, *n.*, a small S. African mammal.

meer′schaum, *n.*, a silicated soft magnesian clay; a pipe made of it.

meet, *v.t.*, to encounter; to satisfy; *v.i.*, to come together; *adj.*, fitting; *n.*, a gathering of huntsmen.

meet′ing, *pr.p.*, meet; *n.*, an assembly, an interview.

meet′ing-house, *n.*, a conventicle; a place for a meeting.

meet′ly, *adv.*, in a meet way.

meg′alith, *n.*, a large ancient stone.

megalith′ic, *adj.*, composed of megaliths.

megaloman′ia, *n.*, a form of insanity in which the sufferer believes in his own greatness or genius.

megalosau′rus, *n.*, a huge, extinct lizard.

meg′aphone, *n.*, a large speaking-trumpet.

megass(e)′, *n.*, the fibrous residue from sugar cane after the extraction of sugar.

megathe′rium, *n.*, a huge, extinct monster.

meg′aton, *n.*, a million tons.

megg′er, *n.*, an apparatus for measuring insulation resistance (*elec.*).

megilp′, *n.*, a vehicle for oil colours (e.g., turpentine-oil).

meg′ohm, *n.*, a unit of resistance (one million ohms).

meg′rim, *n.*, a smooth sole or similar flat fish; a sick headache.

meio′sis, *n.*, a lessening; saying less than is meant (as "no small" for "great").

meis′tersinger, *n. pl.* or *sing.*, German lyric poet(s) and musician(s).

mekom′eter, *n.*, a portable military range finder.

melancho′lia, *n.*, insanity accompanied by depression.

melanchol′ic, *adj.*, depressed.

mel′ancholy, *adj.*, depressed, sad; *n.*, a depression of the spirit, *i.q.* melancholia.

Melane′sian, *adj.*, rel. to the M. islands.

mélange′, *n.*, a mixture, a medley (*Fr.*).

mel′anism, *n.*, an excessive colouring in the skin.

mel′anite, *n.*, a black garnet; a high explosive.

mela′no, *n.*, a man or beast with abnormally dark skin and hair.

melanoch′roi, *n. pl.*, smooth-haired men with dark hair and pale complexion.

melano′sis, *n.*, a kind of black cancer.

melas′ma, *n.*, a liver-patch on the skin.

meld, *v.t.* and *i.*, to merge; to declare for a score (card games); *n.*, the act of so declaring.

meldom′eter, *n.*, a device for showing fusing points.

mêlée′, *n.*, a scuffle, an affray (*Fr.*).

mel′ic, *adj.*, (lyric) meant to be sung.

mel′ilot, *n.*, a variety of clover.

mel′inite, *n.*, an explosive.

mel′iorant, *n.*, that which brings about an improvement or an amendment.

me′liorate, *v.t.*, to improve, to ameliorate.

meliora′tion, *n.*, an improvement.

mel'iorism, n., the doctrine that human effort must improve the world.

melis'ma, n., a musical term connected with singing.

melismat'ic, adj., florid in melody.

mell'ay, n., i.q. mêlée (arch.).

mellif'erous, adj., honey-producing.

mellif'ic, adj., i.q. melliferous.

mellif'luence, n., smoothness (of voice or words).

mellif'luent, adj., smooth, flowing like honey.

mellif'luous, adj., sweet as honey.

mel'lite, n., honey stone.

mellit'ic, adj., rel. to mellite.

mel'low, v.t., to make mellow, to soften; v.i., to ripen; adj., soft with ripeness; semi-intoxicated.

mel'lowed, p.p., mellow.

mel'lowing, pr.p., mellow.

mel'lowness, n., ripeness.

melo'deon, n., a small reed-organ; a kind of accordion. Also melodion.

melod'ic, adj., of or rel. to melody.

melo'dious, adj., tuneful, having a melody.

melo'diously, adv., tunefully.

melo'diousness, n., tunefulness.

mel'odist, n., a maker of melody.

melod'ium, n., i.q. melodeon.

mel'odize, v.t., to compose a melody.

mel'odrama, n., a sensational play.

melodramat'ic, adj., rel. to melodrama.

melodramat'ical, adj., i.q. melodramatic.

melodramat'ically, adv., in a melodramatic way.

melodram'atist, n., a writer of melodrama.

mel'ody, n., a tune, an air.

meloma'nia, n., an excessive liking for melody or music.

mel'on, n., an edible fruit of the gourd kind.

melt, v.t., to reduce to a liquid state, to dissolve, to soften; v.t., to be liquefied or softened.

melt'ed, p.p., melt.

melt'ing, pr.p., melt.

melt'ingly, adv., softly.

mel'ton, n., a kind of cloth.

mem'ber, n., a limb, a part; one of a society.

mem'bered, adj., having members or limbs.

mem'bership, n., the state of being a member.

membrana'ceous, adj., rel. to membrane.

mem'brane, n., a layer of tissue.

membranif'erous, adj., producing membrane.

membra'niform, adj., like membrane.

mem'branous, adj., consisting of, or. like, membrane.

memen'to, n., a souvenir.

mem'o, n., abbrev. of memorandum (colloq.).

mem'oir, n., a record of personal history or scientific discovery.

memorabil'ia, n. pl., things worth recording (Lat.).

memorabil'ity, n., the quality of being memorable.

mem'orable, adj., worthy to be recorded or remembered.

mem'orably, adv., in a memorable way.

memoran'da, n. pl., memorandums (Lat.).

memoran'dum, n., a written communication (Lat.).

memo'rial, adj., commemorative; rel. to memory; n., a monument or tablet, or other emblem; a petition.

memo'rialist, n., one who presents a petition.

memo'rialize, v.t., to petition with a memorial.

memo'rialized, p.p., memorialize.

memo'rializing, pr.p., memorialize.

memor'ia tech'nica, n., a memory aid (Lat.).

memoriza'tion, n., the act of memorizing.

mem'orize, v.t., to fix in the memory.

mem'orized, p.p., memorize.

mem'orizing, pr.p., memorize.

mem'ory, n., the power of remembering; remembrance.

Mem'phian, adj., rel. to Memphis.

mem'sah'ib, n., a European married woman (Ind.).

men, n., pl. of man.

men'ace, v.t., to threaten; n., a threat.

men'aced, p.p., menace.

men'acing, pr.p., menace; adj., threatening.

men'acingly, adv., threateningly.

ménage', n., a system, management (Fr.).

menag'erie, n., a wild beast collection.

mend, v.t., to put together again, to repair, to reform; v.i., to grow better; n., a repair.

mend'able, adj., not past mending.

menda'cious, adj., lying.

menda'ciously, adv., with a lie.

menda'ciousness, n., habitual lying.

mendac'ity, n., i.q. mendaciousness.

mend'ed, p.p., mend.

Men'delism, n., the study of the inheritance of parental characteristics.

mend'er, n., one who mends.

men'dicancy, n., begging.

men'dicant, n., a beggar; adj., begging.

mendic'ity, n., i.q. mendicancy.

mend'ing, pr.p., mend.

men'folk, n., men, especially of a family or group.

menhad'en, n., a herring used in making manure.

men'hir, n., a prehistoric monolith.

me'nial, adj., servile, mean; n., an inferior servant.

menin'geal, adj., rel. to the meninges.

menin'ges, n. pl., the membranes round the brain and spinal cord.

meningi'tis, n., inflammation of the meninges.

menis'cal, adj., rel. to a meniscus.

menis'coid, adj., like a meniscus.

menis′cus, *n.*, a crescent; a lens with one surface convex, the other concave.

menol′ogy, *n.*, a calendar (*Gr.*).

men′opause, *n.*, the natural cessation of menstruation.

men′ses, *n. pl.*, the monthly discharge of blood from the female uterus.

Men′shevism, *n.*, a moderate form of Russian socialism.

Men′shevist, *adj.*, rel. to Menshevism.

men′strual, *adj.*, rel. to the menses.

men′struate, *v.i.*, to discharge the menses.

men′struated, *p.p.*, menstruate.

men′struating, *pr.p.*, menstruate.

menstrua′tion, *n.*, the act of menstruating.

men′struous, *adj.*, rel. to the menses.

men′struum, *n.*, a solvent.

mensurabil′ity, *n.*, the quality of being mensurable.

men′surable, *adj.*, measurable.

men′sural, *adj.*, rel. to measurement.

mensura′tion, *n.*, the art of measuring.

men′tal, *adj.*, rel. to the mind.

mental′ity, *n.*, mental characteristics.

men′tally, *adv.*, in relation to the mind.

menta′tion, *n.*, a state of mind.

men′thol, *n.*, a crystalline preparation from peppermint.

men′tion, *v.t.*, to notice, to name; *n.*, the act of mentioning.

men′tionable, *adj.*, fit to be mentioned.

men′tioned, *p.p.*, mention.

men′tioning, *pr.p.*, mention.

men′tor, *n.*, a wise counsellor.

mento′rial, *adj.*, giving advice.

mento′rially, *adv.*, in an advisory way.

men′u, *n.*, a bill of fare.

mep′acrine, *n.*, an antimalarial chemical.

mephistophe′lian, *adj.*, like Mephistopheles; fiendishly cynical.

mephit′ic, *adj.*, noxious, poisonous (*Lat.*).

mephit′ical, *adj.*, i.q. mephitic.

mephi′tis, *n.*, noxious fumes.

mer′cantile, *adj.*, commercial.

mer′cenarily, *adv.*, in a mercenary spirit.

mer′cenary, *adj.*, with an eye to gain; *n.*, a hired soldier.

mer′cer, *n.*, a trader in textiles.

mer′cerize, *v.t.*, to make cotton fabric look like silk.

mer′cerized, *p.p.*, mercerize.

mer′cerizing, *pr.p.*, mercerize.

mer′cery, *n.*, a mercer's wares.

mer′chandise, *n.*, goods bought and sold.

mer′chant, *n.*, one who trades.

mer′chantable, *adj.*, fit for trading with.

mer′chantman, *n.*, a trading-ship.

mer′ciful, *adj.*, kind, pitiful.

mer′cifully, *adv.*, in a merciful way.

mer′ciless, *adj.*, pitiless, cruel.

mer′cilessly, *adv.*, pitilessly.

mercu′rial, *adj.*, volatile, flighty; rel. to mercury.

mercu′rialize, *v.t.*, to salivate.

mercur′ic, *adj.*, of or containing mercury.

Mer′cury, *n.*, a Roman god; the planet nearest to the sun.

mer′cury, *n.*, the chemical element quicksilver.

mer′cy, *n.*, pity, compassion.

mere, *adj.*, simple, absolute; *n.*, a lake.

mere′ly, *adv.*, simply, absolutely.

mer′est, *adj.*, super. of mere.

meretri′cious, *adj.*, rel. to prostitutes; showily alluring; tawdry.

morgan′ser, *n.*, a diving fish-eating duck.

merge, *v.t.*, to swallow up; *v.i.*, to be swallowed up; to sink.

merged, *p.p.*, merge.

mer′ger, *n.*, the merging or combining.

merg′ing, *pr.p.*, merge.

merid′ian, *adj.*, rel. to midday; *n.*, midday; noon; the great circle

on the earth's surface at right angles to the equator.

merid′ional, *adj.*, rel. to the meridian; southern.

meringue′, *n.*, a confection of sugar and the white of egg (*Fr.*).

meri′no, *adj.*, made of merino wool; *n.*, a finewooled sheep; cloth made of the wool; a variety of potato.

mer′it, *v.t.*, to deserve; *n.*, desert, excellence.

mer′ited, *p.p.*, merit.

mer′iting, *pr.p.*, merit.

merito′rious, *adj.*, praiseworthy, creditable.

merle, *n.*, the blackbird (*Scot.*).

mer′lin, *n.*, a small falcon.

mer′ling, *n.*, the whiting.

mer′lon, *n.*, the space between embrasures.

mer′maid, *n.*, a fabulous creature, half woman, half fish.

mer′man, *n.*, the masc. of mermaid.

merop′idan, *adj.*, rel. to the Meropidae or beeeaters.

Merovin′gian, *adj.*, rel. to the Merovingian dynasty.

mer′rier, *adj.*, comp. of merry.

mer′riest, *adj.*, super. of merry.

mer′rily, *adv.*, gaily.

mer′riment, *n.*, gaiety, joyousness, mirth.

mer′ry, *adj.*, gay, joyous, mirthful.

merry-an′drew, *n.*, a buffoon.

mer′rymaking, *n.*, festivity.

mer′rythought, *n.*, the front bone in a fowl's breast.

me′sa, *n.*, a high table land (*Span.*).

mésall′iance, *n.*, a marriage with someone of inferior social position (*Fr.*).

mesdames′, *n.*, pl. of madame (*Fr.*).

mesdemoiselles′, *n.*, pl. of mademoiselle (*Fr.*).

meseems′, phrase = methinks; it seems to me.

Mesembrian′themum, *n.*, a genus of succulent flowering plants.

mesenter′ic, *adj.*, rel. to the mesentery.

mesenteri′tis, *n.*, inflammation of the mesentery.

mes'entery, n., the membrane that keeps the intestines in their place.

mesh, n., an interstice in a net; network; v.t., to entangle.

meshed, p.p., mesh.

mesh'ing, p.p., mesh.

mesh'y, adj., entangling.

mes'ial, adj., of, or in the direction of the middle line of a body.

mesmer'ic, adj., rel. to mesmerism.

mes'merism, n., animal magnetism.

mes'merist, n., one who mesmerizes.

mesmeriza'tion, n., the act of mesmerizing.

mes'merize, v.t., to throw into a trance.

mes'merized, p.p., mesmerize.

mes'merizer, n., one who mesmerizes.

mes'merizing, pr.p., mesmerize.

mesne, adj., intervening.

mesoco'lon, n., a continuation of the mesentery.

mesolith'ic, adj., intermediate between palaeolithic and neolithic.

mes'on, n., a fundamental particle whose mass is between that of an electron and a proton.

mes'osperm, n., a seed's second membrane.

mesotho'rax, n., the middle ring of an insect's thorax.

Mesozo'ic, adj., rel to the Secondary era (geol.).

mes'quit(e), n., a N. American leguminous tree.

mess, v.t., to dirty, to muddle; to feed; v.i., to share food; n., a state of dirt or muddle; a common meal.

mes'sage, n., an errand, a communication (verbal or written).

messed, p.p., mess.

mes'senger, n., one who takes a message.

Messi'ah, n., the predestined liberator of the oppressed.

Messi'ahship, n., the office of the Messiah.

Messian'ic, adj., rel. to the Messiah.

mes'sieurs, n., pl. of monsieur (Fr.).

mess'ing, pr.p., mess.

mess'mate, n., a sharer of one's table.

Messrs., n. pl., abbrev. of Messieurs; gentlemen.

mes'suage, n., a dwelling-house and land (leg.).

mestee', n., one born of a white person and a quadroon.

mesti'zo, n., one born of a Spaniard or Creole and an Indian.

met, p.p., meet.

metab'asis, n., transition.

Metab'ola, n. pl., insects that undergo transformation.

metabo'lian, adj., rel. to Metabola.

metabol'ic, adj., subject to change or transformation.

metab'olism, n., the process of chemical change; living matter.

metab'olon, n., a radioactive atom.

metacar'pal, adj., rel. to the metacarpus.

metacar'pus, n., the part of the hand between the wrist and the fingers.

metach'ronism, n., an error in dating an event.

metagal'axy, n., the whole universe.

me'tage, n., a measurement; a toll.

metagen'esis, n., the alternation between sexual and asexual reproduction.

me'tal, v.t., to cover with broken stone; to macadamize; n., an insoluble body, fusible by heat; small stone cubes.

met'alled, p.p., metal.

metal'lic; adj., rel. to metal; hard.

metallif'erous, adj., metal-producing.

metal'liform, adj., metal-like.

met'alline, met'aline, adj., i.q. metallic.

met'allist, met'alist, n., a worker in metal.

met'allize, v.t., to make into a metal.

metallog'raphy, n., the science of metals; a description of metals.

met'alloid, adj., like metal; n., an elementary, nonmetallic substance.

metalloid'al, adj., i.q. metalloid.

metallur'gic, adj., rel. to metallurgy.

metallur'gical, adj., i.q. metallurgic.

metall'urgist, n., one skilled in metallurgy.

metall'urgy, n., working in metals.

met'al-man, n., a worker in metals.

met'amere, n., one of like segments of a body (zool.).

metamer'ic, adj., rel. to a metamere.

metamor'phic, adj., rel. to metamorphism.

metamor'phism, n., the process of change in form or structure.

metamor'phose, v.t., to transform.

metamor'phosed, p.p., metamorphose.

metamor'phosing, pr.p., metamorphose.

metamor'phosis, n., a transformation.

met'aphor, n., a condensed simile; an implied comparison of unlikes.

metaphor'ic, adj., figurative; of the nature of a metaphor.

metaphor'ical, adj., i.q. metaphoric.

metaphor'ically, adv., not literally; figuratively.

met'aphrase, n., a close translation.

met'aphrast, n., a literal translator.

metaphras'tic, adj., literally translating.

metaphys'ic, adj., rel. to metaphysics.

metaphys'ical, adj., i.q. metaphysic.

metaphysi'cian, n., a student of metaphysical philosophy.

metaphys'ics, n. pl., mental philosophy; the science of what is beyond the physical.

met'aplasm, n., the part of protoplasm that contains formative material (biol.).

metapol'itics, n. pl., abstract political science.

metapsychol'ogy, n., the study of the intimate nature of the mind.

metapto'sis, n., change in a disease.

metas'tasis, n., change; the removal of a disease from one part or organ of the body to another.

metastat'ic, adj., rel. to metastasis.

metatar'sus, *n.*, the part of the foot between the tarsus and the toes.

metath'esis, *n.*, a transposition.

metathet'ical, *adj.*, transposing.

metatho'rax, *n.*, the hindmost thoracic segment.

métayage, *n.*, a land tenure in which the tenant pays part of his rent in produce, the owner providing the seed (*Fr.*).

métayer, *n.*, a tenant who gives to his landlord part of the produce in return for stock, seed, etc., (*Fr.*).

mete, *v.t.*, to measure, to allot.

me'ted, *p.p.*, mete.

metempi'ric, *n.*, the philosophy of that which lies beyond experience.

metempi'rical, *adj.*, rel. to metempiric.

metempi'ricist, *n.*, a believer in metempiric philosophy.

metempsycho'sis, *n.*, the transmigration of souls.

metempto'sis, *n.*, the solar equation used to keep the lunar calendar in agreement with time.

me'teor, *n.*, a flying luminous body; a shooting star.

meteo'rette', *n.*, a small meteor.

meteor'ic, *adj.*, rel. to meteors.

me'teorite, *n.*, a meteoric stone.

me'teorogram, *n.*, a record made by a meteorograph.

meteor'ograph, *n.*, an apparatus recording meteorological phenomena.

meteorograph'ic, *adj.*, rel. to meteorography.

meteorog'raphy, *n.*, the record of meteorological phenomena.

me'teoroid, *n.*, a body which becomes a meteor when it reaches the atmosphere.

me'teorolite, *n.*, a meteoric stone.

meteorolog'ical, *adj.*, rel. to meteorology.

meteorol'ogist, *n.*, an expert in meteorology.

meteorol'ogy, *n.*, the science of the atmosphere; weather forecasting.

meteorom'eter, *n.*, an instrument that transmits meteorological records.

me'ter, *n.*, a measuring apparatus.

meth'ane, *n.*, hydro-carbon gas; marsh gas, fire damp.

metheg'lin, *n.*, a beverage made of honey.

meth'ene, *n.*, marsh gas.

meth'ide, *n.*, a compound of methyl and an element.

methinks', *v.*, *impers.*, I think; it seems to me.

meth'od, *n.*, rule, system, order.

method'ic, *adj.*, systematic, regular.

method'ical, *adj.*, *i.q.* methodic.

method'ically, *adv.*, systematically.

Meth'odism, *n.*, the principles of the Methodists.

Meth'odist, *n.*, a follower of Wesley and his method or rule of life.

methodis'tic, *adj.*, rel. to the Methodists.

methodis'tical, *adj.*, *i.q.* methodistic.

meth'odize, *v.t.*, to reduce to system.

meth'odized, *p.p.*, methodize.

meth'odizing, *pr.p.*, methodize.

methought', *v. impers.*, *p.p.*, methinks.

meth'yl, *n.*, wood spirit.

meth'ylated, *adj.*, containing methyl.

meth'ylene, *n.*, an inflammable liquid.

methyl'ic, *adj.*, *i.q.* methylated.

metic'ulous, *adj.*, very careful about details; extremely fussy.

metic'ulously, *adv.*, in a meticulous manner.

metic'ulousness, *n.*, the practice of being meticulous.

métier', *n.*, a business, trade or profession (*Fr.*).

me'ting, *pr.p.*, mete.

me'tis, *n.*, an offspring of a white and American Indian.

Meton'ic, *adj.*, rel. to Meton, the astronomer.

metonym'ic, *adj.*, rel. to metonymy.

meton'ymy, *n.*, the use of one word to symbolize another.

met'ope, *n.*, the space between triglyphs.

met'opon, *n.*, the opium drug.

met'opryl, *n.*, an anaesthetic.

me'tre, *n.*, a rhythmic grouping of syllables; a unit of decimal measurement.

met'ric, *adj.*, rel. to decimal measurement.

met'rical, *adj.*, rel. to poetical or decimal metre.

met'rically, *adv.*, in a metrical way.

met'rochrome, *n.*, a colour-measuring apparatus.

met'rograph, *n.*, an apparatus for gauging mileage.

metrol'ogy, *n.*, the science of measures and weights.

met'ronome, *n.*, an instrument measuring musical time.

metronom'ic, *adj.*, rel. to the metronome.

metronom'ical, *adj.*, *i.q.* metronomic.

metron'omy, *n.*, the art of measuring musical time.

metronym'ic, *n.*, a name bestowed after one's mother.

metrop'olis, *n.*, a mother city or state; the seat of an archbishop.

metropol'itan, *adj.*, rel. to a metropolis; *n.*, the archbishop or chief bishop of a province.

met'tle, *n.*, ardour, spirit.

met'tled, *adj.*, *i.q.* mettlesome.

met'tlesome, *adj.*, high-spirited.

mew, *v.t.*, to shut up, to confine; *v.i.*, to cry as a cat; *n.*, a seagull; a cage for hawks; the cry of a cat.

mewed, *p.p.*, mew.

mew'ing, *pr.p.*, mew.

mewl, *v.t.*, to cry as an infant; *n.*, an infant's cry.

mewled, *p.p.*, mewl.

mewl'er, *n.*, one who mewls.

mewl'ing, *pr.p.*, mewl.

mews, *n. pl.*, stables for carriage horses (*orig.* a place where hawks were kept).

Mex'ican, *adj.*, rel. to Mexico; *n.*, a native of Mexico.

mez'zanine, *n.*, a low storey between higher ones.

mez'zo, *adj.*, half, middle (*It.*).

mez'zo-sopra'no, *n.*, a singing voice between soprano and contralto.

mez'zotint, *n.*, a method of engraving on copper or steel; a print.

miaow', *n.*, a cry or mew like a cat; *v.i.*, to cry or mew like a cat.

miaowed', *p.p.*, miaow.

miaow'ing, *pr.p.*, miaow.

mias'ma, *n.*, a noxious exhalation; malaria.

mias'mal, *adj.*, malarious.

miasmat'ic, *adj.*, rel. to miasma.

miasmat'ical, *adj.*, *i.q.* miasmatic.

mias'matist, *n.*, one who studies malarious disorders.

miaul', *v.i.*, *i.q.* miaow.

mi'ca, *n.*, a mineral divisible into transparent flakes.

mica'ceous, *adj.*, containing, or like, mica.

Micaw'berism, *n.*, the idle belief that something good will "turn up." [Dickens's *David Copperfield*.]

mice, *n.*, pl. of mouse.

Mich'aelmas, *n.*, the Feast of St. Michael (Sep. 29).

mick'le, *adj.*, much, great; *n.*, a large amount (*Scot.*).

micracous'tic, *adj.*, making faint sounds audible.

mi'crobar, *n.*, a unit of pressure used in acoustics and meteorology; one-millionth of a bar (of pressure).

mi'crobe, *n.*, a microscopic organism, such as bacteria, etc.

microb'iol'ogy, *n.*, the study of microbes or bacteria.

microceph'alous, *adj.*, small-skulled.

microcop'ying, *n.*, copying on microfilm.

mi'crocosm, *n.*, a miniature world.

microcos'mic, *adj.*, like a microcosm.

microcos'mical, *adj.*, *i.q.* microcosmic.

mi'cro-dot, *n.*, a photo-graph reduced to a dot.

mi'crofilm, *n.*, a minute photographic film.

mi'crograph, *n.*, a microphotograph (very small); a pantograph for minute engraving.

micrograph'ophone, *n.*, an instrument recording the most delicate sounds.

microg'raphy, *n.*, the description of microscopic objects.

mi'crogroove, *n.*, a microscopic groove (as on gramophone records).

mi'crolith, *n.*, a very small stone particle.

microl'ogy, *n.*, the science of microscopic objects.

microm'eter, *n.*, an apparatus for measuring minute distances.

micromet'ric, *adj.*, rel. to the micrometer.

micronom'eter, *n.*, an instrument recording minute time-divisions.

mi'cro-or'ganism, *n.*, a microscopic organism.

mi'crophone, *n.*, an instrument for receiving sound which is then amplified and transmitted or recorded.

microphon'ics, *n. pl.*, the study of minute sounds.

microph'onous, *adj.*, producing minute sounds.

mi'croscope, *n.*, an apparatus for magnifying minute objects.

microscop'ic, *adj.*, rel. to the microscope; infinitely small.

microscop'ical, *adj.*, *i.q.* microscopic.

micros'copist, *n.*, one who uses a microscope.

micros'copy, *n.*, the use of the microscope.

mi'croseismom'eter, *n.*, a small seismometer for recording earth tremors.

mi'crowave, *n.*, an ultra-short wireless wave.

microzo'on, *n.*, a microscopic creature.

micturi'tion, *n.*, the voiding of urine.

mid, *adj.*, middle; *prep.*, amid.

mid'day, *n.*, noon.

mid'den, *n.*, a dung-hill.

mid'dle, *adj.*, intermediate; equally distant; *n.*, a middle point or part.

mid'dle-aged, *adj.*, neither young nor old.

mid'dlebrow, *adj.*, *n.*, between highbrow and lowbrow.

mid'dle-class, *adj.*, of the class between the highest and the lowest.

mid'dleman, *n.*, a trader between the producer and the consumer.

mid'dlemost, *adj.*, nearest the middle.

mid'dling, *adj.*, moderate; ordinary.

mid'dy, *n.*, a midshipman.

midge, *n.*, a gnat.

midg'et, *n.*, a dwarf.

mid'land, *adj.*, in the interior of a country.

mid'most, *adj.*, nearest the middle.

mid'night, *n.*, the last moment of the day.

mid'rib, *n.*, a leaf's central rib.

mid'riff, *n.*, the diaphragm.

mid'ship, *n.*, *adj.*, *adv.*, (in) the middle of a ship.

mid'shipman, *n.*, a junior naval officer.

midst, *n.*, the middle.

mid'stream, *adv.* and *n.*, (in) the middle of a stream.

mid'summer, *n.* and *adj.*, (the) height of summer.

mid'way, *adj.* and *adv.*, halfway between one point and another.

mid'wicket', *n.*, an on-side fielding position in cricket.

mid'wife, *v.t.*, to assist in childbirth; *n.*, a woman who assists in childbirth.

mid'wifery, *n.*, obstetrics.

mien, *n.*, air, aspect, appearance (*lit.*).

miff, *v.t.*, to vex slightly; *adj.*, somewhat annoyed; *n.*, a display of vexation (*colloq.*).

might, *n.*, power, strength; *p.p.*, may.

might'ier, *adj.*, *comp.* of mighty.

might'iest, *adj.*, *super.* of mighty.

might'ily, *adv.*, in a mighty degree; with much strength or vehemence.

might'iness, *n.*, the quality of being mighty.

might'y, *adj.*, powerful, exalted.

mign'on, *adj.*, small and delicately shaped (*Fr.*).

mignonette', *n.*, a fragrant plant.

migraine', *n.*, a severe headache. Also *megrim*.

mi'grant, *adj.*, moving from one region to another; *n.*, one who migrates.

mi'grate, *v.i.*, to leave one region for another.

migra'ted, *p.p.*, migrate.

migra'ting, *pr.p.*, migrate.

migra'tion, *n.*, a movement from one region to another.

mi'gratory, *adj.*, wandering.

Mika'do, *n.*, the Japanese Emperor.

mike, *n.*, a microphone (*colloq.*); *v.i.*, to shirk work, to idle; *n.*, idleness (*slang*).

mil, *n.*, a thousand.

mil'(e)age, *n.*, a record of miles travelled; a reckoning in miles.

Milanese', *adj.*, rel. to Milan; *n.*, a native of Milan.

milch, *adj.*, giving milk.

mild, *adj.*, gentle, indulgent.

mild'er, *adj.*, *comp.* of mild.

mild'est, *adj.*, *super.* of mild.

mil'dew, *v.t.*, to affect with mildew; *v.i.*, to be mildewed; *n.*, a plant disease; dampproduced spots on paper, leather, etc.

mil'dewed, *p.p.*, mildew.

mil'dewing, *pr.p.*, mildew.

mild'ly, *adv.*, gently.

mild'ness, *n.*, gentleness, kindness.

mile, *n.*, a measure of distance (1,760 yards).

mil'er, *n.*, a person or a horse able to run a mile (*colloq.*).

Mile'sian, *adj.*, rel. to Milesius.

Mile'sius, *n.*, a fabulous Spanish king whose sons are supposed to have conquered Ireland.

mile'stone, *n.*, a stone marking the distance in miles; a climacteric point.

mil'foil, *n.*, a plant.

mil'iary, *adj.*, like millet.

mil'ieu, *n.*, environment; surroundings (*Fr.*).

mil'itant, *adj.*, warring; forcefully active in pursuing some goal.

mil'itantly, *adv.*, in a militant fashion.

mil'itarism, *n.*, the military principle or system.

mil'itarist, *n.*, an advocate of militarism; a specialist in military matters.

militaris'tic, *adj.*, advocating organized force.

mil'itary, *adj.*, rel. to soldiers; *n.*, soldiery.

mil'itate, *v.i.*, to conflict; to act against.

mil'itated, *p.p.*, militate.

mili'tating, *pr.p.*, militate.

mili'tia, *n.*, an armed force for home service.

milk, *v.t.*, to draw milk; *n.*, a white secretion in female mammals.

milked, *p.p.*, milk.

milk'er, *n.*, a cow that gives milk.

milk'ier, *adj.*, *comp.* of milky.

milk'iest, *adj.*, *super.* of milky.

milk'iness, *n.*, the quality of being milky.

milk'ing, *pr.p.*, milk.

milk'maid, *n.*, a woman who milks cows.

milk'man, *n.*, a man who supplies milk.

milk'sop, *n.*, an effeminate or weak-minded person.

milk'tooth, *n.*, one of the first growth of teeth.

milk'warm, *adj.*, warm as new milk.

milk'-white, *adj.*, white as milk.

milk'wort, *n.*, one of the plants of the Polygala genus.

milk'y, *adj.*, like milk.

milky'-way, *n.*, a galaxy of numberless fixed stars.

mill, *v.t.*, to grind; to indent the edge of a coin; to roll (metal); *n.*, a machine for grinding; a place where grinding is done; a factory; a prize-fight (*slang*).

mill'board, *n.*, strong pasteboard.

mill'-dam, *n.*, a dam in a mill-stream.

milled, *p.p.*, mill.

millena'rian, *adj.*, of a

thousand years; rel. to the millennium.

mil'lenary, *n.*, the space of a thousand years; *adj.*, *i.q.* millenarian.

millen'nial, *adj.*, rel. to a millennium.

millen'nialism, *n.*, the doctrine or belief in the millennium.

millen'nialist, *n.*, one who believes in the coming of a thousand years of peace.

millen'nium, *n.*, a period of a thousand years; a thousand years of peace.

mil'lepede, *n.*, a manyfooted insect.

mil'lepore, *n.*, a coral with many pores.

mill'er, *n.*, one who works a mill or who works in a mill.

mill'er's-thumb, *n.*, a small fish.

milles'imal, *adj.*, having a thousand parts.

mil'let, *n.*, a hardy grass or grain.

mill'head, *n.*, a head of water for a mill.

mil'liard, *n.*, one thousand millions.

milliardaire', *n.*, a person possessing a milliard of money.

mil'liary, *adj.*, rel. to a Roman mile.

mill'ibar, *n.*, a unit of barometric pressure.

milli'gramme, milli'gram, *n.*, the thousandth part of a gramme.

milli'litre, *n.*, the thousandth part of a litre.

mill'imetre, *n.*, the thousandth part of a metre.

mil'liner, *n.*, one who deals in women's hats.

mil'linery, *n.*, a milliner's wares.

mill'ing, *pr.p.*, mill; *n.*, the raised impression on the edge of a coin; the process of fulling cloth; the act of milling.

mil'lion, *n.*, a thousand thousands.

millionaire', *n.*, a person with a million of money; a very wealthy person.

mill'ionary, *adj.*, rel. to millions.

mil'lionth, *adj.*, *n.*, the ordinal of a million.

mill'ipede, *n.*, *i.q.* millepede.

mill'pond, *n.*, a pond supplying waterpower to a mill.

mill'race, n., the rush of water that drives a mill.

mill'stone, n., a stone for grinding corn.

mill'wheel, n., the wheel of a mill.

milor(d), n., a lord or gentleman (Fr.).

mil'reis, n., a Portuguese unit of currency.

milt, n., the spleen; a fish's soft roe; v.t., to impregnate.

mil'ter, n., the male fish in spawning time.

Mil'ton, n., John, a famous poet.

Milton'ic, adj., rel. to Milton.

mil'vine, adj., rel. to kites.

mil'vus, n., a kite (Lat.).

mime, n., a type of drama ridiculing persons and things; an actor in a mime; v.i., to act with mimic gesture, usu. in silence.

mimed, p.p., mime.

mim'eograph, n., a copying machine.

mimet'ic, adj., imitative.

mimet'ically, adv., imitatively.

mim'ic, v.t., to imitate; adj., imitative; n., one who imitates.

mim'ical, adj., i.q. mimic.

mim'icked, p.p., mimic.

mim'icker, n., one who mimics.

mim'icking, pr.p., mimic.

mim'icry, n., the act of imitating.

mim'ing, pr.p., mime.

mimog'rapher, n., a writer of mimes.

mimo'sa, n., a leguminous plant.

mim'ulus, n. pl., flowering plants.

mina'cious, adj., threatening.

mina'ciously, adv., threateningly.

minac'ity, n., a threatening.

minar', n., a lighthouse; a turret.

min'aret, n., the turret of a mosque.

min'atory, adj., i.q. minacious.

mince, v.t., to chop small; v.i., to speak affectedly; n., a dish of finely-chopped meat.

minced, p.p., mince.

mince'meat, n., meat chopped small and mixed with various ingredients; a mixture of suet, raisins, currants, peel, etc. finely minced.

mincepie', n., a small Christmas pie containing mincemeat (second meaning).

min'cer, n., a device for mincing (e.g. meat, etc.).

min'cing, pr.p., mince; adj., affectedly graceful.

min'cingly, adv., in a mincing manner.

mind, v.t., to mark, to attend, to heed; v.i., to care; n., the intellectual faculty; memory, intention.

mind'ed, p.p., mind; adj., disposed in mind.

mind'er, n., one who keeps watch.

mind'ful, adj., remembering, attentive.

mind'fully, adv., attentively.

mind'ing, pr.p., mind.

mind'less, adj., lacking intelligence.

mine, v.t., to sap, to undermine; v.i., to do mining operations; n., a deep excavation for minerals; adj. possess., bel. to me.

mine'-crater, n., a crater made by the explosion of a landmine.

mined, p.p., mine.

mine'field, n., an area of land or sea in which mines have been laid.

mine'layer, n., a vessel or aircraft specially equipped for laying mines.

mi'ner, n., a worker in a mine.

min'eral, adj., rel. to minerals; n., any inorganic body.

min'eralist, n., a collector of minerals.

mineraliza'tion, n., the act or result of mineralizing.

min'eralize, v.t., to turn into a mineral; to impregnate minerally.

min'eralized, p.p., mineralize.

min'eralizer, n., that which mineralizes.

min'eralizing, pr.p., mineralize.

mineralog'ic, adj., rel. to mineralogy.

mineralog'ical, adj., i.q. mineralogic.

mineral'ogist, n., an expert in mineralogy.

mineral'ogy, n., the science of minerals.

Miner'va, n., the goddess of wisdom.

mine'sweeper, n., a vessel for removing floating mines.

min'ever, n., a kind of fur. Also miniver.

min'gle, v.t., to mix, to blend; v.i., to join in.

min'gled, p.p., mingle.

min'gling, pr.p., mingle.

min'gy, adj., mean, stingy (colloq.).

min'i, adj. and n., very small (applied in compound words and standing alone).

min'iate, adj., vermilion-coloured; v.t., to paint with vermilion.

min'iature, adj., on a small scale; n., a small portrait on ivory, etc.

min'iaturist, n., an artist in miniatures.

min'icab, n., a small taxi.

Min'ie, n., a bullet or rifle invented by a French musketry instructor, Capt. Minié.

minifica'tion, n., a reduction in size.

min'ify, v.t., to reduce in size.

min'ikin, n., any very small thing.

min'im, n., half a semibreve; one-sixtieth of a dram.

min'imal, adj., very minute; n., the least possible.

min'imalist, n., a person willing to accept a provisional minimum.

min'imize, v.t., to reduce to a minimum.

min'imized, p.p., minimize.

min'imizing, pr.p., minimize.

min'imum, n., the smallest possible amount.

mi'ning, pr.p., mine; adj., rel. to a mine; n., the mining industry.

min'ion, n., an obsequious dependant; a small printing type.

min'ish, v.t. and i., to diminish; to reduce in power, etc.

min'ister, v.t., to supply, to afford, to administister; v.i., to act as a minister or helper; n., an assistant, an agent; an administrator; an ambassador; a clergyman.

min'istered, *p.p.*, minister.

ministe'rial, *adj.*, rel. to a minister or ministry.

ministe'rialist, *n.*, a supporter of the Government party.

ministe'rially, *adv.*, in a ministerial capacity.

min'istering, *pr.p.*, minister.

min'istrant, *adj.*, acting as a minister.

ministra'tion, *n.*, the service or act of a minister.

min'istry, *n.*, the office of a minister; a department of Government.

min'isub, *n.*, a miniature submarine.

min'ium, *n.*, the red oxide of lead.

min'iver, *n.*, *i.q.* minever.

mink, *n.*, a weasel-like, fur-bearing mammal; the valuable fur itself.

min'nesinger, *n.*, one of the lyric poets and singers of mediaeval Germany.

min'now, *n.*, a small freshwater fish.

mi'nor, *adj.*, smaller, less, subordinate; *n.*, one under age.

Mi'norite, *n.*, a Franciscan brother.

minor'ity, *n.*, the status of a minor; the underage period; the smaller number.

Min'otaur, *n.*, a fabulous monster, half bull, half man.

min'ster, *n.*, a monastery; sometimes applied to a cathedral or other very large church.

min'strel, *n.*, a travelling poet or singer.

min'strelsy, *n.*, the minstrel's art; minstrels as a whole; ballad poetry.

mint, *v.t.*, to coin; to stamp money, to invent; *n.*, a place where money is coined; an aromatic plant.

mint'age, *n.*, the production of a mint; the duty paid for coining.

mint'ed, *p.p.*, mint.

mint'er, *n.*, one who mints.

mint'ing, *pr.p.*, mint.

min'uend, *n.*, a number from which the subtrahend is taken.

minuet', *n.*, a stately dance; its music.

mi'nus, a Latin adverb = less, used prepositionally in the sense of "without"; *n.*, the sign (–) of subtraction.

min'uscule, *adj.*, small; *n.*, a lower case letter.

min'ute, *v.t.*, to make a memorandum of; *n.*, a memorandum or entry of record; the sixtieth part of an hour; the exact point of time.

minute', *adj.*, very small, exact.

min'ute-book, *n.*, a memorandum book; a book to record the minutes of a meeting.

min'uted, *p.p.*, minute.

min'ute-glass, *n.*, a sandglass.

min'ute-gun, *n.*, a gun fired at intervals of a minute.

min'ute-hand, *n.*, a watch or clock hand pointing to the minutes.

min'utely, *adj.*, occurring every minute.

minute'ly, *adv.*, exactly; on a very small scale.

minute'ness, *n.*, exactness; the quality of being minute.

min'utes, *n. pl.*, a brief summary of an assembly or committee proceedings.

minu'tiae, *n. pl.*, small details.

min'uting, *pr.p.*, minute.

minutis'simic, *adj.*, exceedingly minute.

minx, *n.*, *i.q.* mink; also a pert girl.

minx'ish, *adj.*, saucy; forward; hussyish.

Mi'ocene, *adj.*, less recent; rel. to the middle period of the Tertiary geological formation.

mir, *n.*, a Russian village community (*Russ.*).

mir'acle, *n.*, a wonderful occurrence.

mirac'ulous, *adj.*, marvellous; of the nature of a miracle.

mirac'ulously, *adv.*, as by a miracle.

mirac'ulousness, *n.*, the state of being miraculous.

mirage', *v.t.*, to reflect as in a mirror; *n.*, an atmospheric optical illusion.

mire, *v.t.*, to stain with mud; to plunge into mud; *v.i.*, to sink in mud; *n.*, mud; dirt mixed with water.

mired, *p.p.*, mire.

mirif'ic, *adj.*, wondrous.

mi'riness, *n.*, the state or quality of being miry.

mir'ror, *v.t.*, to reflect in a mirror, or as in a mirror; *n.*, a lookingglass, a pattern.

mir'rored, *p.p.*, mirror.

mirth, *n.*, gaiety, merriment.

mirth'ful, *adj.*, gay, merry.

mirth'fully, *adv.*, gaily, merrily.

mirth'fulness, *n.*, the quality of being mirthful.

mirth'less, *adj.*, without mirth.

mir'y, *adj.*, full of, or smothered in, mire.

mir'za, *n.*, a Persian prince (*Pers.*).

misadven'ture, *n.*, a mischance.

misadven'turous, *adj.*, unfortunate.

misadvised', *adj.*, illadvised.

misalli'ance, *n.*, an illassorted marriage.

misallied', *adj.*, illassorted.

mis'anthrope, *n.*, a hater of mankind.

misanthrop'ic, *adj.*, antisocial.

misanthrop'ical, *adj.*, *i.q.* misanthropic.

misan'thropist, *n.*, *i.q.* misanthrope.

misan'thropy, *n.*, hatred of mankind.

misapplica'tion, *n.*, an incorrect application.

misapplied', *p.p.*, misapply.

misapply', *v.t.*, to apply incorrectly.

misapply'ing, *pr.p.*, misapply.

misapprehend', *v.t.*, to misunderstand.

misapprehend'ed, *p.p.*, misapprehend.

misapprehend'ing, *pr.p.*, misapprehend.

misapprehen'sion, *n.*, a misunderstanding.

misappro'priate, *v.t.*, to apply wrongly.

misappro'priated, *p.p.*, misappropriate.

misappro'priating, *pr.p.*, misappropriate.

misappropria'tion, *n.*, a wrong application.

misbecome'. *v.t.*, to suit ill.

misbecom'ing, *pr.p.*, misbecome; *adj.*, unfitting.

misbegot'ten, *adj.*, illegitimate; contemptible.

misbehave', *v.t.*, to behave badly.

misbehaved', *p.p.*, misbehave.

misbeha'ving, *pr.p.*, misbehave.

misbeha'viour, *n.*, illconduct.

misbelief', *n.*, a false belief.

misbelieve', *v.t.*, to believe erroneously.

misbelieved', *p.p.*, misbelieve.

misbeliev'er, *n.*, one who misbelieves.

misbeliev'ing, *pr.p.*, misbelieve.

misbeseem', *v.t.*, *i.q.* misbecome.

miscal'culate, *v.t.*, to calculate wrongly.

miscal'culated, *p.p.*, miscalculate.

miscal'culating, *pr.p.*, miscalculate.

miscalcula'tion, *n.*, a wrong calculation.

miscall', *v.t.*, to call by a wrong name.

miscalled', *p.p.*, miscall.

miscall'ing, *pr.p.*, miscall.

miscar'riage, *n.*, a failure; a premature parturition.

miscar'ried, *p.p.*, miscarry.

miscar'ry, *v.i.*, to fail; to be delivered prematurely.

miscar'rying, *pr.p.*, miscarry.

mis'cast', *n.*, a wrong addition (of accounts); *v.t.* and *i.*, to cast wrongly (of actors).

miscas'ting, *n.*, *i.q.* miscast; *pr.p.*, miscast.

miscegena'tion, *n.*, a mixture of races.

miscellana'rian, *adj.*, rel. to miscellanies.

miscella'nea, *n. pl.*, a miscellaneous collection.

miscella'neous, *adj.*, composed of a variety of things; promiscuous.

miscella'neously, *adv.*, promiscuously.

miscel'lanist, *n.*, a writer of miscellany.

miscel'lany, *n.*, a mixture; a book on a variety of subjects.

mischance', *n.*, ill-luck.

mis'chief, *n.*, harm; intentional injury.

mis'chiefmaker, *n.*, a busybody.

mis'chievous, *adj.*, harmful, pernicious; impish.

mis'chievously, *adv.*, harmfully; impishly.

misch'metall, *n.*, a metal alloy (*Ger.*).

mischoose', *v.t.*, to make a wrong choice.

mis'cible, *adj.*, able to be mixed.

miscomputa'tion, *n.*, a wrong reckoning.

miscompute', *v.t.*, to reckon wrongly.

misconceive', *v.t.*, to have a false notion of.

misconceived', *p.p.*, misconceive.

misconceiv'ing, *pr.p.*, misconceive.

misconcep'tion, *n.*, a false notion; a misunderstanding.

misconduct', *v. reflex.*, to behave oneself badly.

miscon'duct, *n.*, bad behaviour.

misconjec'ture, *n.*, a false conjecture.

misconstruc'tion, *n.*, a false construction.

miscon'strue, *v.t.*, to interpret wrongly.

miscon'strued, *p.p.*, misconstrue.

miscon'struing, *pr.p.*, misconstrue.

miscount', *v.t.*, to count wrongly; *n.*, an error in counting.

mis'creant, *n.*, a base wretch.

miscreat'ed, *adj.*, ill-formed.

miscue', *v.i.*, to make a miscue; *n.*, a slip with a billiard cue.

misdate', *v.t.*, to date wrongly.

misdat'ed, *p.p.*, misdate.

misdat'ing, *pr.p.*, misdate.

misdeal', *v.t.*, to deal cards wrongly; *n.*, a false deal.

mis'deed, *n.*, a wicked action.

misdemean', *v. reflex.*, to behave oneself ill.

misdemean'ant, *n.*, one guilty of a misdemeanour.

misdemean'our, *n.*, a petty crime; ill-behaviour.

misdirect', *v.t.*, to direct wrongly.

misdirect'ed, *p.p.*, misdirect.

misdirect'ing, *pr.p.*, misdirect.

misdirec'tion, *n.*, the act or result of misdirecting.

misdo', *v.t.*, to do amiss.

misdo'er, *n.*, one guilty of misdeeds.

misdo'ing, *pr.p.*, misdo; *n.*, evil conduct.

misdoubt', *n.*, a suspicion, a misgiving; *v.t.*, to doubt, to suspect.

mise, *n.*, expenses; a settlement on terms.

misemploy', *v.t.*, to employ wrongly.

misemployed', *p.p.*, misemploy.

misemploy'ing, *pr.p.*, misemploy.

misemploy'ment, *n.*, the state of being misemployed; putting to a wrong use.

mi'ser, *n.*, one who hoards his money and lives miserably; a boring tool to sink wells.

mis'erabilism, *n.*, a philosophy of pessimism.

mis'erable, *adj.*, wretched, worthless.

mis'erably, *adv.*, in a miserable way.

misere're, *n.*, the 51st Psalm, and its musical setting.

miser'icord, *n.*, a projecting bracket beneath the folding seat of a choir stall; a room in a monastery where discipline was somewhat relaxed.

mi'serly, *adj.*, like a miser.

mis'ery, *n.*, wretchedness.

misfea'sance, *n.*, a wrong performance; a trespass.

misfire', *v.i.*, to fail to go off (said of a firearm); to not work as planned; *n.*, a failing to go off.

mis'fired, *p.p.*, misfire.

mis'firing, *pr.p.*, misfire.

misfit', *v.t.*, to fit badly; *n.*, a badly made garment; a badly adjusted person.

misform', *v.t.*, to shape badly.

misformed', *p.p.*, misform; *adj.*, badly formed.

mis'forming, *pr.p.*, misform.

misfor'tune, *n.*, bad luck, ill-fortune.

misgave', *p.p.*, misgive.

misgive', v.t., to arouse doubt; v.i., to be apprehensive.

misgiv'en, p.p., misgive.

misgiv'ing, pr.p., misgive; n., a feeling of doubt.

misgot'ten, adj.; ill-got.

misgov'ern, v.t., to govern badly.

misgov'erned, p.p., misgovern.

misgov'erning, pr.p., misgovern.

misgov'ernment, n., bad government.

misguid'ance, n., bad guidance, delusion.

misguide', v.t., to delude, to guide wrongly.

misguid'ed, p.p., misguide; adj., deluded, ill-advised.

misguid'ing, pr.p., misguide.

mishan'dle, v.t., to ill-treat, to handle wrongly.

mis'han'dling, pr.p., mishandle; n., handling wrongly.

mis'hap, n., an unfortunate occurrence.

mishear', v.t., to hear amiss.

misheard', p.p., mishear.

mis'hearing, pr.p., mishear.

mis'hit, n., a faulty hit; v.t., to hit faultily.

mish'-mash, n., a hotchpotch.

Mish'nah, n., the Talmud text.

misinform', v.t., to inform falsely.

misinforma'tion, n., false information.

misinformed', p.p., misinform.

misinform'ing, pr.p., misinform.

misinter'pret, v.t., to understand or interpret wrongly.

misinterpreta'tion, n., a wrong construction.

misinter'preted, p.p., misinterpret.

misinter'preter, n., one who misinterprets.

misinter'preting, pr.p., misinterpret.

misjoin'der, n., the joining of things or parties that should not be joined.

misjudge', v.t., to judge wrongly, to mistake.

misjudged', p.p., misjudge.

misjudg'ing, pr.p., misjudge.

misjudg'ment, n., a wrong determination.

mislaid', p.p., mislay.

mislay', v.t., to lay in a wrong place; to lose.

mislay'ing, pr.p., mislay.

mislead', v.t., to lead astray.

mislead'er, n., one who misleads.

mislead'ing, pr.p., mislead; adj., deceptive.

mislead'ingly, adv., in a misleading way.

misled', p.p., mislead.

misman'age, v.t., to manage badly.

misman'aged, p.p., mismanage.

misman'agement, n., bad management.

misman'ager, n., one who mismanages.

misman'aging, pr.p., mismanage.

misname', v.t., to name wrongly.

misnamed', p.p., misname.

misnam'ing, pr.p., misname.

misno'mer, n., a wrong name.

misog'amist, n., a hater of marriage.

misog'amy, n., hatred of marriage.

misog'ynist, n., a woman-hater.

misog'yny, n., hatred of women.

mis'pickel, n., an arsenopyrite.

misplace', v.t., to put in the wrong place; to bestow wrongly.

misplaced', p.p., misplace.

misplace'ment, n., putting in the wrong place.

misplac'ing, pr.p., misplace.

misplead', v.t., to plead wrongly.

misplead'ed, p.p., misplead.

misplead'ing, pr.p., misplead.

misprint', v.t., to make a printer's error; n., a printer's error.

misprint'ed, p.p., misprint.

misprint'ing, pr.p., misprint.

mispri'sion, n., the concealment of a felony or treason.

misprize', v.t., to despise; to fail to appreciate.

mispronounce', v.t., to pronounce wrongly.

mispronounced', p.p., mispronounce.

mispronounc'ing, pr.p., mispronounce.

mispronuncia'tion, n., the act of mispronouncing; a word improperly pronounced.

mispropor'tion, v.t., to proportion badly.

mispropor'tioned, p.p., misproportion.

mispropor'tioning, pr.p., misproportion.

misquota'tion, n., the act of misquoting; a passage misquoted.

misquote', v.t., to quote incorrectly.

misquot'ed, p.p., misquote.

misquot'ing, pr.p., misquote.

misread', v.t., to read incorrectly.

misread', p.p., misread.

misread'ing, pr.p., misread; n., an error in a text.

misreck'on, v.t., to reckon inaccurately.

misreck'oned, p.p., misreckon.

misreck'oning, pr.p., misreckon; n., an incorrect reckoning.

misremem'ber, v.t., to remember wrongly.

misremem'bered, p.p., misremember.

misremem'bering, pr.p., misremember.

misreport', v.t., to report incorrectly.

misreport'ed, p.p., misreport.

misreport'ing, pr.p., misreport.

misrepresent', v.t., to falsify, to mis-state.

misrepresenta'tion, n., the act or effect of misrepresenting.

misrepresent'ed, p.p., misrepresent.

misrepresent'ing, pr.p., misrepresent.

misrule', n., tumult, confusion, bad government.

miss, v.t., to fail of hitting, finding, or obtaining; to feel the loss of; v.i., to miss the mark; n., a loss; an unmarried woman.

mis'sal, n., a book of prayer.

missed', p.p., miss.

mis'sel-thrush, n., a thrush that eats mistletoe berries.

miss'es, n. pl., miss.

mis'shape', *v.t.*, to shape badly; *n.*, a badly shaped article.

mis-shaped', *p.p.*, mis-shape.

mis'sha'pen, *adj.*, deformed, ugly.

mis'sile, *n.*, a weapon or thing thrown or projected.

miss'ing, *adj.*, lost, wanting; *pr.p.*, miss.

mis'sion, *n.*, an errand, an embassy; the act of sending or state of being sent on some high business; a missionary station; a series of religious services.

mis'sionary, *n.*, one sent abroad to preach religion; *adj.*, rel. to missionaries.

mis'sioner, *n.*, the conductor of a mission.

miss'ionist, *n.*, *i.q.* missioner.

mis'sis, *n.*, the courtesy title of a married woman (represented in writing as *Mrs*, abbrev. of mistress); wife (*slang*).

mis'sive, *n.*, a letter despatched, a message.

mis-spell', *v.t.*, to spell incorrectly.

mis-spelled', *p.p.*, mis-spell.

mis'spell'ing, *pr.p.*, mis-spell; *n.*, an error in spelling.

mis-spelt', *p.p.*, mis-spell.

mis-spend', *v.t.*, to spend foolishly; to waste.

mis-spend'ing, *pr.p.*, mis-spend.

mis-spent', *adj.*, wasted; *p.p.*, mis-spend.

mis-state', *v.t.*, to state wrongly; to falsify.

mis-sta'ted, *p.p.*, mis-state.

mis'state'ment, *n.*, an erroneous statement.

mis-sta'ting, *pr.p.*, mis-state.

mist, *n.*, small, thin rain; light fog.

mista'kable, *adj.*, capable of being mistaken.

mistake', *v.t.*, to take one thing for another; *v.i.*, to err in judgment or opinion; *n.*, an error in judgment or opinion; a blunder; an oversight.

mista'ken, *p.p.*, mistake; *adj.*, misunderstood; erroneous; ill-judged.

mistak'enly, *adv.*, erroneously.

mista'king, *pr.p.*, mistake.

mistaught', *p.p.*, mis-teach.

misteach', *v.t.*, to teach wrongly.

misteach'ing, *pr.p.*, mis-teach; *n.*, false teaching.

mis'ter, *n.*, the courtesy title of a man (represented in writing as *Mr.*).

mis'tigris, *n.*, a blank playing card used in the poker game.

mis'time, *v.t.*, to time wrongly.

mistimed', *p.p.*, mistime; *adj.*, inopportune, badly timed.

mis'timing, *pr.p.*, mistime; *n.*, a badly judged time.

mist'iness, *n.*, the state of being misty.

mis'tletoe, *n.*, a parasitic evergreen plant.

mist'-like, *adj.*, like mist.

mis'took, *p.p.*, mistake.

mis'tral, *n.*, a N.W. wind that blows in the French Mediterranean provinces.

mistranslate', *v.t.*, to translate incorrectly.

mistransla'ted, *p.p.*, mis-translate.

mistransla'ting, *pr.p.*, mistranslate.

mistransla'tion, *n.*, an error in translating.

mistreat', *v.t.*, to treat badly.

mis'tress, *n.*, a woman who governs; a female head of a house; a female teacher in a school or of a special subject; a skilled woman; a female lover, a concubine.

mistri'al, *n.*, a trial rendered void by an error in proceedings.

mistrust', *v.t.*, to suspect, to doubt; *n.*, a doubt, a suspicion.

mistrust'ed, *p.p.*, mistrust.

mistrust'ful, *adj.*, suspicious.

mistrust'fully, *adv.*, suspiciously.

mistrust'ing, *pr.p.*, mistrust.

mist'y, *adj.*, covered with mist; cloudy; dim.

misunderstand', *v.t.*, to mistake, to misconceive.

misunderstand'ing, *pr.p.*, misunderstand; *n.*, taking in a wrong sense.

misunder'stood, *p.p.*, misunderstand.

misu'sage, *n.*, a wrong usage.

misuse', *v.t.*, to make a wrong use of; to treat improperly.

misuse', *n.*, a wrong use.

misused', *p.p.*, misuse.

misu'ser, *n.*, one who misuses.

misu'sing, *pr.p.*, misuse.

mite, *n.*, a very small insect; the smallest coin; anything tiny.

mi'ter, *v.t.*, *i.q.* mitre.

mithridat'ic, *adj.*, rel. to mithridatize.

mithrid'atize, *v.t.*, to immunize against poison by gradually increasing the dosage.

mit'igable, *adj.*, able to be assuaged.

mit'igant, *adj.*, assuaging.

mit'igate, *v.t.*, to assuage; to render less severe.

mit'igated, *p.p.*, mitigate.

mit'igating, *pr.p.*, mitigate.

mitiga'tion, *n.*, the abatement of anything painful or harsh.

mit'igative, *adj.*, causing mitigation.

mit'igator, *n.*, anything that mitigates.

mit'igatory, *adj.*, *i.q.* mitigative.

mito'sis, *n.*, cell division (*biol.*).

mitrailleuse', *n.*, a machine gun (*Fr.*).

mi'tral, *adj.*, rel. to, or like, a mitre.

mi'tre, *v.t.*, to cover with a mitre; to join two boards at an angle of 45°; *n.*, a headdress of the Jewish high priest, a bishop, archbishop, or abbot.

mi'tred, *p.p.*, mitre; *adj.*, wearing the mitre; joined mitre-fashion.

mi'triform, *adj.*, mitre-shaped, conical.

mi'tring, *pr.p.*, mitre.

mitt, *n.*, *i.q.* mitten.

mit'ten, *n.*, a fingerless glove.

mit'timus, *n.*, a warrant committing to prison, or transferring from one court to another.

mix, *v.t.*, to mingle, to blend, to confuse; *v.i.*, to combine; *n.*, a confusion (*colloq.*).

mix'able, *adj.*, able to be mixed.

mixed, *p.p.*, mix.

mix'edly, *adv.*, confusedly.

mix'en, *n.*, a dunghill.

mix'er, *n.*, a bowl; a sociable person.

mix'ing, *pr.p.*, mix.

mixtilin'eal, *adj.*, combining straight and curved lines.

mixtilin'ear, *adj.*, *i.q.* mixtilineal.

mix'tion, *n.*, a mixture for fixing gold leaf.

mix'ture, *n.*, a mass formed by mixing.

miz'en, miz'zen, *n.*, the hindmost of the fore-and-aft sails.

miz'en-mast, *n.*, the mast abaft the mainmast.

miz'zle, *v.i.*, to rain in small drops; to disappear (*slang*); *n.*, fine rain.

miz'zled, *p.p.*, mizzle.

miz'zling, *pr.p.*, mizzle.

miz'zly, *adj.*, drizzling.

mnemon'ic, *adj.*, memory-aiding; *n.*, a memory aid.

mnemon'ical, *adj.*, *i.q.* mnemonic.

mnemon'ics, *n. pl.*, the cultivation of the memory.

mnem'otechny, *n.*, the art of memory.

moan, *v.i.*, to make a moaning sound; *n.*, a low sound of pain or grief.

moaned, *p.p.*, moan.

moan'ing, *pr.p.*, moan; *n.*, the act of moaning.

moat, *v.t.*, to surround with a moat; *n.*, a ditch round a castle or house.

moat'ed, *adj.*, having a moat; *p.p.*, moat.

mob, *v.t.*, to attack in a disorderly way; to crowd round; *n.*, a disorderly crowd.

mobbed, *p.p.*, mob; *adj.*, surrounded and overwhelmed by a crowd.

mob'bing, *pr.p.*, mob.

mobbish, *adj.*, pert. or rel. to a mob.

mo'bile, *adj.*, moved or moving easily; changeable.

mobil'ity, *n.*, the state of being mobile.

mobiliza'tion, *n.*, the calling up for service.

mo'bilize, *v.t.*, to call up for service; to get the troops ready.

mo'bilized, *p.p.*, mobilize.

mo'bilizing, *pr.p.*, mobilize.

mob'-law, *n.*, anarchy; the rule of the populace.

moboc'racy, *n.*, the rule of the mob or the populace.

moc'casin, *n.*, a N. American shoe of deerskin.

mo'cha, *n.*, a particular kind of coffee.

mock, *v.t.*, to mimic, to deride; *adj.*, false, counterfeit; *n.*, derision.

mocked, *p.p.*, mock.

mock'er, *n.*, one who mocks.

mock'ery, *n.*, derision, scorn.

mock'-hero'ic, *adj.*, pseudo-heroic.

mock'ing, *pr.p.*, mock.

mock'ing-bird, *n.*, a bird that mimics other birds.

mock'-orange, *n.*, the syringa.

mock'-turtle, *n.*, veal made into soup, resembling turtle soup.

mo'co, *n.*, a kind of burrowing rodent. Also *cavy*.

mo'dal, *adj.*, rel. to mode or form; bel. to one of the modes (*mus.*).

modal'ity, *n.*, the difference in mode.

mode, *n.*, form, custom, manner; a musical scale.

mod'el, *v.t.*, to shape, to mould; *v.i.*, to do modelling; *n.*, a pattern, a mould, a standard, an example; *adj.*, serving as a pattern.

mod'el(l)ed, *p.p.*, model.

mod'el(l)er, *n.*, one who models.

mod'el(l)ing, *pr.p.*, model; *n.*, the art of modelling.

mod'ena, *n.* and *adj.*, (a) deep purple (colour).

mod'erate, *adj.*, temperate, reasonable, mild.

moderate', *v.t.*, to temper, to abate, to regulate; *v.i.*, to act as a moderator; to abate in violence.

mod'erated, *p.p.*, moderate.

mod'erately, *adv.*, in a moderate degree.

mod'erating, *pr.p.*, moderate.

modera'tion, *n.*, the act of moderating; the state or quality of being moderate; restraint.

Modera'tions, *n. pl.*, the first public examination at Oxford (Mods).

mod'eratism, *n.*, the principles of the Moderate party.

modera'to, *adj.* and *adv.*, at moderate speed (*It.*, *mus.*).

mod'erator, *n.*, one who, or that which, moderates; the president of an assembly; an Oxford examiner; a Cambridge superintendent at examinations.

mod'ern, *adj.*, rel. to recent or present times.

mod'ernism, *n.*, a theological system which dispenses with the historical basis of Christian doctrines.

mod'ernist, *n.*, one who accepts modernism; a supporter of modern doctrines.

modernis'tic, *adj.*, *i.q.* modern.

moder'nity, *n.*, the quality or state of being modern.

moderniza'tion, *n.*, the act or result of modernizing.

mod'ernize, *v.t.*, to make modern.

mod'ernized, *p.p.*, modernize.

mod'ernizer, *n.*, one who modernizes.

mod'ernizing, *pr.p.*, modernize.

mod'ernness, *n.*, *i.q.* modernity.

mod'est, *adj.*, not self-assertive; chaste, simple.

mod'estly, *adv.*, in a modest way.

mod'esty, *n.*, unassuming, self-deprecating, shy or chaste behaviour.

mod'icum, *n.*, a small portion; a pittance (*Lat.*).

modifiabil'ity, *n.*, the quality of being modifiable.

mod'ifiable, *adj.*, able to be modified.

modifica'tion, *n.*, the act of modifying; a modified state or form.

mod'ified, *p.p.*, modify.

mod'ifier, *n.*, one who, or that which, modifies.

mod'ify, *v.t.*, to change the form of; to qualify; to tone down.

mod'ifying, *pr.p.*, modify.

modil'lion, *n.*, a bracket under a cornice.

mo'dish, *adj.*, affecting the fashions; fashionable.

mo'dishly, *adv.*, in a modish way.

mo'dist, *n.*, a follower of the fashions.

modiste', *n.*, a woman who makes fashionable dresses or a milliner (*Fr.*).

modis'tic, *adj.*, rel. to fashions.

mod'ular, *adj.*, pert. to, or made of, modules.

mod'ulate, *v.t.*, to regulate or adjust; to vary the tone and pitch; *v.i.*, to make a key-change (*mus.*).

mod'ulated, *p.p.*, modulate.

mod'ulating, *pr.p.*, modulate.

modula'tion, *n.*, the act of modulating; the passage from one key to another (*mus.*).

mod'ulator, *n.*, a chart showing the musical scales.

mod'ule, *n.*, a unit for proportionate measurement; a self-contained unit in an instructional programme.

mo'dus, *n.*, the manner, the means (*Lat.*).

mofus'sil, *n.*, the country districts of India.

Mogul', *adj.*, rel. to the Moguls; *n.*, the Great M. (emperor of Delhi); a Mongol.

mo'hair, *n.*, a fabric made from the hair of the Angora goat.

Moham'med, *n.*, the founder of the Moslem religion.

Moham'medan, *adj.*, rel. to Mohammed and his followers.

Moham'medanism, *n.*, the religion of Mohammed.

Moham'medanize, *v.t.*, to convert to Mohammedanism; *v.i.*, to turn Mohammedan.

Mo'hawk, *n.*, one of the N. American tribes.

mo'hock, *n.*, an 18th century London street rowdy (*hist.*).

mo'hole, *n.*, a deep boring to reach the earth's substructure.

moid'er, *v.t.*, to perplex, to worry, to confuse.

moi'dore, *n.*, a Portuguese gold piece.

moi'ety, *n.*, a half.

moil, *v.i.*, to toil.

moiled, *p.p.*, moil.

moil'ing, *pr.p.*, moil.

moi'neau, *n.*, a small bastion.

moire, *n.*, watered silk; *adj.*, like watered silk.

moir'é, *adj.* and *n.*, i.q. moire (*Fr.*).

moist, *adj.*, damp.

mois'ten, *v.t.*, to make moist.

mois'tened, *p.p.*, moisten.

mois'tening, *n.*, a dampening; *pr.p.*, moisten.

moist'ness, *n.*, dampness.

mois'ture, *n.*, dampness, moderate wetness.

mois'turize, *v.t.*, i.q. moisten.

mois'turized, *p.p.*, moisturize.

mois'turizing, *pr.p.*, moisturize.

moke, *n.*, a donkey (*slang*).

mok'o, *n.*, the Maori system of tattooing.

mol'ar, *adj.*, grinding; pert. to mass; *n.*, a grinding tooth.

molas'ses, *n. pl.*, treacle.

mole, *n.*, a pier; a natural spot on the skin; a small burrowing quadruped.

molec'ular, *adj.*, rel. to molecules.

molecular'ity, *n.*, the quality of being molecular.

mol'ecule, *n.*, a minute particle of matter.

mole'-eyed, *adj.*, blind.

mole'hill, *n.*, the soil upturned by a mole.

mole'skin, *adj.*, made of moleskin; *n.*, a cloth resembling a mole's skin.

molest', *v.t.*, to annoy, disturb.

molesta'tion, *n.*, the act of molesting.

molest'ed, *p.p.*, molest.

molest'er, *n.*, one who molests.

molest'ing, *pr.p.*, molest.

molest'ive, *adj.*, tending to annoy.

moll, *n.*, a prostitute; a gangster's mistress.

mol'lient, *adj.*, softening.

mol'lifiable, *adj.*, able to be mollified.

mollifica'tion, *n.*, the act or effect of mollifying.

mol'lified, *p.p.*, mollify.

mol'lifier, *n.*, one who, or that which, mollifies.

mol'lify, *v.t.*, to soften, to assuage.

mol'lifying, *pr.p.*, mollify.

mol'lusc, *n.*, one of the Mollusca.

Mollus'ca, *n. pl.*, invertebrates with soft bodies and a shelly covering.

mollus'can, *adj.*, rel. to the Mollusca.

mollus'cous, *adj.*, i.q. molluscan.

mol'lusk, *n.*, i.q. mollusc.

Mo'loch, *n.*, the god of fire.

molos'sus, *n.*, a foot of three long syllables (*Gr.*).

mol'ten, *p.p.*, melt; *adj.*, made of molten metal.

mol'to, *adv.*, very (*It.*, *mus*).

mo'ly, *n.*, the Homeric herb that availed against Circe's spells.

molyb'denous, *adj.*, rel. to molybdenum.

molyb'denum, *n.*, a rare metal, combined with steel for toolmaking.

mo'ment, *n.*, an instant; importance.

mo'mentarily, *adv.*, in a moment of time.

mo'mentary, *adj.*, lasting for, or done in, a moment.

momen'tive, *adj.*, rel. to momentum.

mo'mently, *adv.*, each moment.

momen'tous, *adj.*, of great importance.

momen'tum, *n.*, the force of matter in motion (*Lat.*).

Mo'mus, *n.*, the Greek god of ridicule; the spirit of mockery.

mon'achal, *adj.*, rel. to monks.

mon'achism, *n.*, the monastic system.

mon'ad, *n.*, a primary constituent of matter; a simple, minute organism; a molecule.

monadel'phia, *n. pl.*, plants having their stamens united.

monadelph'ian, *adj.*, rel. to monadelphia.

monadelph'ous, *adj.*, i.q. monadelphian.

monad'ic, *adj.*, rel. to monads.

monad'ical, *adj.*, *i.q.* monadic.

monan'drian, *adj.*, having only one stamen (*bot.*).

monan'drous, *adj.*, *i.q.* monandrian.

monan'dry, *n.*, marriage to only one husband at a time.

mon'arch, *n.*, one who rules alone; a sovereign.

monar'chic, *adj.*, rel. to monarchy.

monar'chical, *adj.*, *i.q.* monarchic.

mon'archism, *n.*, the principles of monarchy.

mon'archist, *n.*, a supporter of monarchy.

mon'archy, *n.*, the government of a single ruler.

monaste'rial, *adj.*, rel. to a monastery.

mon'astery, *n.*, a house of religious men (monks).

monas'tic, *adj.*, rel. to monks and monasteries.

monas'tical, *adj.*, *i.q.* monastic.

monas'tically, *adv.*, in a monastic way.

monas'ticism, *n.*, the monastic system.

monas'ticon, *n.*, a book about monasteries.

monau'ral, *adj.*, affecting only one ear.

mondaine', *n.*, a woman of fashion; a worldly woman (*Fr.*).

Mon'day, *n.*, the second day of the week.

mon'dial, *adj.*, worldwide.

mon'etary, *adj.*, rel. to money.

mon'etize, *v.t.*, to change into money; to standardize the value of.

mon'ey, *n.*, currency; metal coined; bank notes.

mon'eyed, *adj.*, wealthy.

mon'eyer, *n.*, a coiner.

mon'ey-len'der, *n.*, one who lends money at interest.

mon'eyless, *adj.*, without money.

mon'ger, *n.*, a dealer.

Mong'ol, *adj.*, rel. to Mongolia; *n.*, a native of Mongolia; an idiot.

Mongo'lian, *adj.*, *i.q.* Mongol.

mong'olism, *n.*, a type of idiocy.

mong'oose, *n.*, a snake-destroying ichneumon.

mon'grel, *adj.*, of mixed breed; hybrid; *n.*, a hybrid.

mon'ial, *n.*, mullion.

monil'iform, *adj.*, like a necklace.

mon'ism, *n.*, the theory that mind and matter are identical.

mon'ist, *n.*, a believer in monism.

monist'ic, *adj.*, rel. to monism.

moni'tion, *n.*, a warning, an instruction.

mon'itor, *n.*, one who warns; an elder boy who instructs the juniors; an old type of man-of-war (warship).

monito'rial, *adj.*, rel. to a monitor.

mon'itory, *adj.*, warning, giving notice.

mon'itress, *n.*, the fem. of monitor.

monk, *n.*, a man who lives the monastic life.

mon'key, *n.*, a quadrumanous mammal.

monk'hood, *n.*, the monastic character.

monk'ish, *adj.*, rel. to monks.

monk's'-hood, *n.*, an aconite.

monocar'pous, *adj.*, bearing fruit only once.

monoceph'alous, *adj.*, having only one head.

monoc'eros, *adj.*, having one horn.

mon'ochord, *adj.*, having one string.

monochro'masy, *n.*, a form of colour blindness.

monochromat'ic, *adj.*, having only one colour.

mon'ochrome, *adj.*, *i.q.* monochromatic; *n.*, a painting in a single colour.

monochro'mic, *adj.*, in one colour.

mon'ocle, *n.*, a single eyeglass.

monoclin'al, *adj.*, dipping in one direction.

monocli'nous, *adj.*, *i.q.* monoclinal.

monocotyle'don, *n.*, a plant having only one cotyledon.

mono'cracy, *n.*, autocracy.

mon'ocrat, *n.*, an autocrat.

monoc'ular, *adj.*, for use with one eye; having a single eye.

mon'ocule, *n.*, a creature with a single eye.

monoc'ulous, *adj.*, *i.q.* monocular.

monodac'tylous, *adj.*, having one finger or toe.

mon'odist, *n.*, a writer or singer of monodies.

mon'odont, *adj.*, one-toothed.

mon'odrama, *n.*, a play for a single actor.

monodramat'ic, *adj.*, rel. to monodrama.

mon'ody, *n.*, a mournful song for a single voice.

monog'amist, *n.*, an advocate of monogamy.

monog'amous, *adj.*, having only one wife.

monog'amy, *n.*, marriage with one wife only.

monogen'esis, *n.*, reproduction from a single cell.

monogenet'ic, *adj.*, rel. to monogenesis.

monog'enism, *n.*, the theory that all men derive from one ancestor.

monog'enist, *n.*, a believer in monogenism.

monogenist'ic, *adj.*, rel. to monogenism.

mon'ogram, *n.*, two or more letters forming a cipher.

mon'ograph, *n.*, a treatise on a single subject.

monog'rapher, *n.*, the writer of a monograph.

monograph'ic, *adj.*, rel. to a monograph.

mon'olith, *n.*, an upright, single stone.

monolith'ic, *adj.*, rel. to a monolith.

mon'ologue, *n.*, a soliloquy.

monoma'nia, *n.*, insanity on one particular subject.

monoma'niac, *n.*, one suffering from monomania.

mon'omark, *n.*, a registered identification mark.

monometal'lic, *adj.*, rel. to monometallism.

monomet'allism, *n.*, a single currency arrangement.

monomet'allist, *n.*, an advocate of monometallism.

monom'eter, *adj.,* containing a single foot.

monomet'ric, *adj., i.q.* monometer.

mono'mial, *adj.,* consisting of a single term.

monopet'alous, *adj.,* having a single petal.

mono'phase, *adj.,* having only one phase (*elec.*).

monoph'onous, *adj.,* giving only one sound.

mon'ophthong, *n.,* a single vowel sound.

monophthon'gal, *adj.,* rel. to a monophthong.

monophyl'lous, *adj.,* single-leaved.

mon'oplane, *n.,* an aeroplane of the single plane type.

monop'olism, *n.,* the practice of monopoly.

monop'olist, *n.,* one who monopolizes or favours monopoly.

monop'olize, *v.t.,* to obtain exclusive sale of; to engross entirely.

monop'olized, *p.p.,* monopolize.

monop'olizer, *n.,* one who monopolizes.

monop'olizing, *pr.p.,* monopolize.

monop'oly, *n.,* an exclusive sale, or possession.

monop'teral, *adj.,* having only one wing.

mon'orail, *n.,* a railway running on a single rail.

mon'orhyme, *n.,* a verse with a single rhyme.

monosep'alous, *adj.,* having united sepals.

monosper'mous, *adj.,* one-seeded.

monospher'ical, *adj.,* rel. to a single sphere.

mon'ostich, *n.,* a one-versed composition.

monostroph'ic, *adj.,* having a single strophe.

monosyllab'ic, *adj.,* having a single syllable.

mon'osyllable, *n.,* a word of a single syllable.

monotech'nic, *adj.,* having a single purpose; dealing with one predominating theme.

mon'otheism, *n.,* the worship of one God.

mon'otheist, *n.,* a worshipper of one God.

monotheis'tic, *adj.,* rel. to monotheism.

monothema'tic, *adj.,* having one dominating theme.

mon'otone, *n.,* singing or speaking at a uniform pitch; *v.t.* and *i.,* to recite on one note.

monot'onous, *adj.,* without variety; wearisome.

monot'onously, *adv.,* wearisomely.

monot'ony, *n.,* wearisomeness, sameness.

mon'otype, *n.,* a composing machine that casts and sets up type.

monotyp'ic, *adj.,* rel. to monotype.

monox'ide, *n.,* an oxide with only one atom of oxygen in each molecule.

monseigneur', *n.,* a title of rank in France.

monsieur', *n.,* the French equivalent of Mister.

monsoon', *n.,* a periodical wind in the Indian Ocean.

mon'ster, *n.,* something out of the common order; *adj.,* huge.

mon'strance, *n.,* a transparent pyx used for religious purposes.

monstros'ity, *n.,* the quality of being monstrous or unnatural.

mon'strous, *adj.,* unnatural, shocking, huge.

mon'strously, *adv.,* hugely; in a shocking way.

mon'tage, *n.,* the editing and final arrangement of photographic film (*Fr.*).

montan'ic, *adj.,* rel. to mountains.

mon'tant, *adj.,* mounting, increasing.

montbre'tia, *n.,* an iridaceous plant.

mon'te, *n.,* a Spanish gambling game.

Montessor'ian, *adj.,* rel. to the education system of Dr. Maria Montessori of Rome.

month, *n.,* the twelfth part of the year; four weeks.

month'ly, *adj.,* happening every month.

mon'ument, *n.,* a memorial.

monumen'tal, *adj.,* memorial; rel. to a monument; enormous.

monumen'talism, *n.,* the monumental style.

monumentalize, *v.t.,* to commemorate with a monument.

monumen'tally, *adv.,* as a memorial; hugely.

moo, *v.i.,* to make the noise of a cow; *n.,* a cow's lowing.

mooch, mouch, *v.i.,* to loiter, to idle about; *v.t.,* to steal.

mood, *n.,* the temper of the mind; the change in a verb; the logical form of a syllogism.

mood'ily, *adv.,* in a moody way.

mood'iness, *n.,* a liability to strange moods.

mood'y, *adj.,* abstracted, gloomy; out of humour.

mooed, *p.p.,* moo.

moo'ing, *pr.p.,* moo.

moon, *n.,* the earth's satellite; a month; any satellite of a planet; *v.i.,* to roam or gaze around in an abstracted way.

moon'beam, *n.,* a shaft of moonlight.

moon'calf, *n.,* a dolt.

moon'less, *adj.,* without a moon.

moon'light, *n.,* the light of the moon.

moon'lighter, *n.,* formerly one engaged in agrarian outrages in Ireland.

moon'lit, *adj.,* lit by the moon.

moon'raker, *n.,* one who pursues foolish fancies.

moon'raking, *n.,* the pursuit of foolish fancies.

moon'shee, *n.,* a Mohammedan scribe.

moon'shine, *n.,* moonlight; sheer nonsense; smuggled spirits.

moon'shiner, *n.,* a distiller of illicit whiskey.

moon'stone, *n.,* a yellowish white stone.

moon'struck, *adj.,* lunatic.

moon'wort, *n.,* a fern.

moon'y, *adj.,* crescent-shaped; sentimental; listless, dreamy.

moor, *v.t.,* to secure a ship with an anchor or cable; *v.i.,* to be so secured; *n.,* a native of Morocco; a large heathy tract.

moor'age, *n.,* a place for mooring.

moor'cock, *n.,* a red grouse.

moored, *p.p.,* moor.

moor'fowl, *n., i.q.* moorcock.

moor'grass, *n.,* a grass found on moors.

moor'hen, *n.,* a waterfowl.

moor'ing, pr.p., moor; n., the act of mooring; in pl., the place of mooring.

Moor'ish, adj., rel. to the Moors.

moor'land, n., heathery land.

moor'stone, n., Cornish granite.

moose, n. a large animal allied to the elk.

moose'wood, n., leatherwood.

moot, v.t., to start a discussion; to debate; n., a discussion; adj., disputable.

moot'able, adj., able to be mooted.

moot'-case, n., a case for discussion.

moot'ed, p.p., moot.

moot'ing, pr.p., moot.

mop, v.t., to rub with a mop; n., a cloth broom for cleaning floors; thick, unruly hair.

mope, v.i., to be spiritless or silent.

moped, p.p., mope.

mo'ped, n., a motorized pedal cycle.

mo'per, n., one who mopes.

mo'ping, pr.p., mope.

mo'pish, adj., inclined to mope.

mo'pishness, n., the state of being mopish.

mopped, p.p., mop.

mop'pet, n., a rag doll.

mop'ping, pr.p., mop.

moquette', n., a carpet and upholstery fabric.

moraine', n., a line of stones and gravel at the edge of a glacier.

mor'al, adj., rel. to morality; virtuous; probable; according to the highest standards of behaviour; n., the significance of a story.

morale', n., a state of attitudes; temperament or mental condition.

mo'ralism, n., i.q. morality.

mor'alist, n., one who moralizes or makes moral reflections.

moral'ity, n., the practice of moral duties; ethics; virtue; an allegorical play.

moraliza'tion, n., the act or effect of moralizing.

mor'alize, v.t., to give a moral meaning to;

v.i., to make moral reflections.

mor'alized, p.p., moralize.

mor'alizer, n., one who moralizes.

mor'alizing, pr.p., moralize.

mor'ally, adv., according to the moral law; practically.

mor'als, n. pl., ethics, moral conduct; code of behaviour.

morass', n., a swamp, a bog (lit.).

morass'y, adj., swampy.

morato'rial, adj., pert. to a moratorium.

morato'rium, n., an agreed or imposed period of delay in meeting obligations.

Mora'vian, adj., rel. to Moravia; n., a native of Moravia (now part of Czechoslovakia).

Mora'vianism, n., the religious system of the followers of John Huss.

mor'bid, adj., diseased, sickly, unhealthy.

morbid'ity, n., a diseased condition.

mor'bidly, adv., in a morbid way.

mor'bidness, n., a morbid tendency.

morbif'ic, adj., causing disease.

morbil'lous, adj., rel. to measles.

mor'bus, n., a disease, as cholera morbus (Lat.).

morceau', n., a small piece (Fr.).

morda'cious, adj., biting.

mordac'ity, n., a tendency to bite.

mor'dant, adj., biting; fixing colour; sarcastic.

more, adj., greater in quantity or number; added; adv., in greater degree; a second time.

moreen', n., a strong woollen or cotton fabric.

morel', n., an edible fungus; a variety of nightshade.

morel'lo, n., a dark, bitter cherry (It.).

moren'do, adj., adv., dying away (mus.).

moreo'ver, adv., further, besides.

mor'es, n. pl., conventions regarded as essential to a social group (Lat.).

morganat'ic, adj., rel. to a marriage in which the wife legally renounces her children's rights in succession, rank and property.

morgue, n., a mortuary.

mor'ibund, adj., in a dying condition.

moril'lon, n., a choice, dark grape.

mo'rion, n., a visorless helmet.

Moris'co, adj., Moresque; n., a Moorish dance.

Mor'mon, n., an adherent of the Mormon sect; adj., rel. to Mormonism.

Mor'monism, n., the principles of the Mormons; polygamy.

morn, n., i.q. morning.

morn'ing, n., the earliest part of the day.

morn'ing-star, n., Venus.

moroc'co, n., a fine leather from Morocco.

mor'on, n., an adult with a child's mentality; a fool.

morone', n., a dark crimson.

moron'ic, adj., pert. or rel. to a moron.

morose', adj., surly, sullen.

morose'ly, adv., surlily.

morose'ness, n., surliness.

Mor'pheus, n., the god of sleep (Lat.).

mor'phia, n., the narcotic principle of opium.

mor'phine, n., i.q. morphia.

mor'phinism, n., the morphine habit.

morpholog'ic, adj., pert. to morphology.

morpholog'ical, adj., i.q. morphologic.

morpholog'ically, adv., in a morphological sense.

morphol'ogy, n., the science of plant and animal forms (biol.).

mor'ris, n., a rustic (orig. Moorish) dance.

mor'ris-dance, n., i.q. morris.

mo'rris tube, n., a tube inserted in a rifle to reduce its bore.

mor'row, n., morning; the day after today.

Morse, adj., the morse-code system of telegraphy invented by S. F. B. Morse in 1872.

morse, *n.*, a clasp or brooch; the walrus.

mor'sel, *n.*, a small portion or bite.

mort, *n.*, the huntsman's note sounded when a deer is killed; a salmon in its third year.

mor'tal, *adj.*, subject to death, deadly; *n.*, a human being.

mortal'ity, *n.*, the state of being mortal; death.

mor'tally, *adv.*, to a mortal degree.

mor'tar, *v.t.*, to cement with mortar; *n.*, a vessel for pounding; a piece of ordnance; cement.

mor'tarboard, *n.*, a small flat board for holding mortar; a kind of college cap.

mort'gage, *v.t.*, to make over to a creditor as security; *n.*, a grant or deed of property as security.

mort'gaged, *p.p.*, mortgage.

mortgagee', *n.*, one to whom a mortgage is given.

mort'gager, *n.*, one who gives a mortgage.

mort'gaging, *pr.p.*, mortgage.

mort'gagor, *n.*, *i.q.* mortgager.

morti'cian, *n.*, an undertaker.

mortif'erous, *adj.*, deadly.

mortifica'tion, *n.*, the effect of mortifying; gangrene; chagrin; humiliation.

mor'tified, *p.p.*, mortify.

mor'tify, *v.t.*, to humiliate; *v.i.*, to gangrene or decay.

mor'tifying, *pr.p.*, mortify; *adj.*, humiliating.

mor'tise, *v.t.*, to make a mortise in; *n.*, a hole in timber for the reception of a tenon or a lock.

mor'tised, *p.p.*, mortise.

mor'tising, *pr.p.*, mortise.

mort'main, *n.*, an inalienable tenure; the state in which inalienable property is held (*Fr.*, *leg.*).

mor'tuary, *n.*, a temporary resting place for dead bodies.

mo'rus, *n.*, the mulberry (*Lat.*).

Mosa'ic, *adj.*, rel. to Moses.

mosa'ic, *n.*, inlaid work of coloured glass or stones.

mosasaur'us, *n.*, an extinct marine reptile.

moschatel', *n.*, a plant with a musk-like scent.

Moselle', *n.*, a river in Germany; a white wine.

Mos'lem, *n.*, a Mussulman; *adj.*, Mohammedan. Also *Muslim*.

mosque, *n.*, a Mohammedan temple.

mosqui'to, *n.*, a variety of gnat.

moss, *n.*, a lichen; a morass.

moss'clad, *adj.*, overgrown with moss.

moss'iness, *n.*, the state of being mossy.

moss'trooper, *n.*, a freebooter of the Scottish border.

moss'y, *adj.*, covered with moss; like moss.

most, *adj.*, the greatest in quantity or number; *adv.*, the sign of the superlative degree; in the highest degree.

most'ly, *adv.*, for the most part.

mot, *n.*, a witticism (*Fr.*).

mote, *n.*, a small speck; a council.

motel', *n.*, a drive-in hotel for motorists.

motet', *n.*, unaccompanied choral music.

moth, *n.*, a genus of nocturnal insects.

moth'eaten, *adj.*, eaten by moths; decayed.

moth'er, *v.t.*, to be a mother to; *adj.*, in the relation of a mother; *n.*, a female parent.

moth'er-coun'try, *n.*, *i.q.* motherland.

mo'thercraft, *n.*, the skill in the handling and treatment of children.

moth'ered, *p.p.*, mother.

moth'erhood, *n.*, a mother's office; maternity.

moth'ering, *pr.p.*, mother; *n.*, acting as a mother; celebrating Mothering Sunday.

moth'er-in-law, *n.*, a wife's or husband's mother.

moth'erland, *n.*, one's own native country.

moth'erless, *adj.*, without a mother.

mother'ly, *adj.*, like a mother; affectionate, gentle.

moth'er-of-pearl, *n.*, a hard internal layer in shells.

moth'er tongue, *n.*, native speech; the vernacular.

moth'er-wit, *n.*, natural intelligence; common sense.

moth'y, *adj.*, infested with moths.

motif, *n.*, a musical subject; a basic decorative design; a theme (*Fr.*).

mot'ile, *adj.*, capable of motion (*zool.*, *bot.*).

motil'ity, *n.*, the ability to move (*zool.*, *bot.*).

mo'tion, *v.i.*, to make a sign with the head or hand; *n.*, movement, a proposal, an action; a course.

mo'tioned, *p.p.*, motion.

mo'tioning, *pr.p.*, motion.

mo'tionless, *adj.*, without movement.

mot'ivate, *v.t.*, to provide a motive for; to induce.

mot'ivated, *p.p.*, motivate.

mot'ivating, *pr.p.*, motivate.

motiva'tion, *n.*, the act or result of motivating.

mo'tive, *adj.*, causing movement; *n.*, that which is actuated; an actuating purpose.

motiv'ity, *n.*, the quality of being motive.

mot'ley, *adj.*, of mixed colours; heterogeneous; *n.*, a coat of mixed colours, as worn by a jester.

mot'mot, *n.*, a S. American bird.

mo'tor, *n.*, a machine actuated by applied power; *v.t.* and *i.*, to travel, or to convey, in a motor-car.

mo'torable, *adj.*, suitable for a motor vehicle.

mo'tor-boat, *n.*, a boat propelled by a motor.

mo'tor-bus, *n.*, an omnibus run with a motor.

mot'orcade, *n.*, a procession of motor-cars.

mo'tor-car, *n.*, a car run with a motor.

mo'tor-coach, *n.*, a single-decked motor vehicle carrying a large number of passengers.

mo'tor-cy'cle, *n.*, a cycle run with a motor.

mo'tored, *p.p.*, motor.

moto'rial, *adj.*, rel. to motors.

motor'ing, *pr.p.*, motor.

mot'orism, *n.*, the use or prevalence of motor-cars.

mo'torist, *n.*, a motor-car driver.

mot'orize, *v.t.*, to equip with motor transport.

mot'orized, *p.p.*, motorize.

mot'orizing, *pr.p.* motorize.

motorpho'bia, *n.*, a morbid fear of motor vehicles.

mot'orway, *n.*, a dual-track road for fast-moving traffic.

mot'tle, *v.t.*, to mark with mottles; *n.*, an arrangement of various colours; a blotch.

mot'tled, *adj.*, speckled, blotched; *p.p.*, mottle.

mot'tling, *pr.p.*, mottle.

mot'to, *n.*, a maxim; a sentence or quotation appended to a coat of arms.

mouf'flon, *n.*, a wild mountain sheep.

mould, *v.t.*, to fashion, to shape, to model; *n.*, a matrix, shape; a spot; loose earth; fine surface soil; a fungus growth.

mould'able, *adj.*, able to be moulded.

mould'ed, *p.p.*, mould.

mould'er, *n.*, one who, or that which, moulds; *v.i.*, to crumble away.

mould'ered, *p.p.*, moulder.

mould'ering, *pr.p.*, moulder.

mould'iness, *n.*, the quality of being mouldy.

mould'ing, *pr.p.*, mould; *n.*, a term denoting the form of moulded objects.

mould'y, *adj.*, decaying with mould.

moult, *v.i.*, to shed feathers or hair.

moult'ed, *p.p.*, moult.

moult'ing, *pr.p.*, moult; *n.*, the act or period of moulting.

mound, *v.t.*, to bank up; *n.*, an artificial bank.

mount, *v.t.*, to climb, to ascend, to get up on; to lend a horse to; to set up; *n.*, a mountain or hill; that on which something (e.g., a picture) is mounted; a horse for riding.

mount'able, *adj.*, able to be mounted.

moun'tain, *n.*, a large hill.

moun'tain-ash, *n.*, a tree with red berries.

mountaineer', *v.i.*, to climb mountains; *n.*, a mountain climber; a dweller in mountains.

moun'tainous, *adj.*, pert. to a mountain; full of mountains; formidable.

mountain'side, *n.*, the side of a mountain.

mount'ebank, *n.*, a quack, an impostor.

mount'ed, *p.p.*, mount.

mount'er, *n.*, one who mounts.

mount'ing, *pr.p.*, mount; *n.*, the setting of a picture, etc.

mourn, *v.t.*, to grieve for; *v.i.*, to be sorrowful.

mourned, *p.p.*, mourn.

mourn'er, *n.*, one who mourns.

mourn'ful, *adj.*, sad, sorrowful.

mourn'fully, *adv.*, sadly.

mourn'fulness, *n.*, the state of being mournful.

mourn'ing, *pr.p.*, mourn; *n.*, a state of sorrow; funeral dress.

mourn'ing-ring, *n.*, a ring worn to commemorate a dead person.

mouse, *v.i.*, to catch mice; *n.*, a small rodent.

moused, *p.p.*, mouse.

mouse'-ear, *n.*, hawkweed.

mouse'hole, *n.*, a hole by which a mouse passes to and fro.

mous'er, *n.*, a cat good at catching mice.

mouse'trap, *n.*, a trap for catching mice.

mous'ing, *pr.p.*, mouse.

mousse, *n.*, a dish of flavoured whipped cream (*Fr.*).

moustache', *n.*, hair on the human upper lip.

mous'y, *adj.*, mouse-like; infested with mice.

mouth, *n.*, the orifice in a head through which food and speech pass; any orifice or opening, as the mouth of a river, etc.

mouth, *v.t.*, to speak words pompously or distinctly; to take food with the mouth; *v.i.*, to grimace.

mouthed, *p.p.*, mouth.

mouth'er, *n.*, one who mouths.

mouth'ful, *n.*, the quantity that will fill a mouth.

mouth'ing, *pr.p.*, mouth.

mouth'piece, *n.*, that part of an instrument, pipe, etc., that is put into the mouth; one who speaks for another.

mouth'y, *adj.*, bombastic; ranting.

mov'able, **move'able**, *adj.*, able to be moved.

mov'ables, *n. pl.*, furniture, belongings.

move, *v.t.*, to put in motion; to change the position of; to agitate; to put a resolution; *v.i.*, to change one's position; to propose; *n.*, an act of moving; the moving of a piece in some games; a scheme.

moved, *p.p.*, move.

move'less, *adj.*, motionless.

move'ment, *n.*, the act of moving; the motional part in a machine; a tendency or fashion in thought; a division of a musical work; any kind of activity.

mov'er, *n.*, one who moves.

mo'vies, *n. pl.*, motion films (*slang*).

mov'ing, *pr.p.*, move; *adj.*, affecting emotion.

mov'ingly, *adv.*, in a pitiful way.

mow, *n.*, a stack of barley, hay, etc.; a store for these; *v.t.*, to cut down.

mow, *v.i.*, to grimace.

mow'er, *n.*, one who, or that which, mows.

mow'ing, *pr.p.*, mow.

mown, *p.p.*, mow.

moy'a, *n.*, volcanic mud.

mozet'ta, *n.*, a short cape worn by papal dignitaries.

Mr., *n.*, the ordinary title prefixed to a man's name. A corruption of *Master*.

Mrs., *n.*, the ordinary title of a married woman. Abbreviated from *Mistress*.

much, *adj.* and *adv.*, in great quantity or degree.

much′ness, *n.*, greatness of degree or quantity.

mu′cid, *adj.*, slimy.

mu′ciform, *adj.*, like mucus.

mu′cilage, *n.*, a gummy extract; gum.

mucilag′inous, *adj.*, of the nature of mucilage.

mucip′arous, *adj.*, producing mucus.

muck, *v.t.*, to dirty; *n.*, wet dung; dirt.

muck′heap, *n.*, a dunghill.

muckle, *n.*, *i.q.* mickle.

muck′worm, *n.*, a larva found in dungheaps.

muck′y, *adj.*, dirty.

mu′coid, *adj.*, like mucus.

mucos′ity, *n.*, the state of being mucous.

mu′cous, *adj.*, rel. to mucus.

mu′cronate, *adj.*, pointed.

mu′culent, *adj.*, slimy.

mu′cus, *n.*, a slimy secretion.

mud, *n.*, soft, wet earth; mire.

mudar′, *n.*, an East Indian shrub.

mud′dily, *adv.*, in a muddy way.

mud′diness, *n.*, the state of being muddy.

mud′dle, *v.t.*, to confuse; to mix up; *v.i.*, to do things in an ineffectual way.

mud′dled, *p.p.*, muddle.

mud′dler, *n.*, one who muddles.

mud′dling, *pr.p.*, muddle; *adj.*, confusing, perplexing.

mud′dy, *adj.*, stained with mud; in a state of mud; confused; dark; *v.t.*, to cover with mud.

mud′flat, *n.*, an area of mud usu. covered at high tide.

mud′guard, *n.*, a protection against mud thrown up by a wheel.

mud′lark, *n.*, one who plays in mud; a muddy game.

muez′zin, *n.*, the Mohammedan who calls the hours of prayer.

muff, *n.*, a covering for the hands to keep them warm; a dull, clumsy person; a bungler; *v.t.*, to bungle.

muffetee′, *n.*, a worsted cuff for the wrist.

muf′fin, *n.*, a kind of spongy tea-cake.

muffineer′, *n.*, a sugar or salt castor for sprinkling on muffins.

muf′fle, *v.t.*, to wrap or cover up; to deaden (sound); *n.*, the upper lip of certain animals; a leather glove; a compartment in a pottery kiln.

muf′fled, *p.p.*, muffle.

muf′fler, *n.*, a wrap for the throat or mouth; anything that muffles.

muf′fling, *pr.p.*, muffle.

muf′ti, *n.*, a Mohammedan teacher of the law; the civilian dress worn by members of armed forces.

mug, *n.*, a vessel for drinking; a silly person; the face (*slang*); *v.i.*, to work hard at a subject; *v.t.*, to study hard (*slang*).

mug′ger, *n.*, an Indian crocodile so named.

mug′get, *n.*, the lily-of-the-valley (*Fr.*).

mugg′ins, *n.*, a simpleton; a mug; a game of dominoes or cards.

mug′gy, *adj.*, close, damp and warm.

mug′wump, *n.*, a man who holds himself superior to party politics.

mulat′to, *n.*, the offspring of black and white parents.

mulat′tress, *n.*, fem. of mulatto.

mul′berry, *n.*, a fruit-bearing tree whose leaves are used for feeding silkworms; the fruit of the same.

mulch, *n.*, decayed vegetable matter often used to protect plant roots.

mulched, *adj.*, having mulch spread.

mulct, *v.t.*, to fine; to take away from; *n.*, a fine.

mulct′ed, *p.p.*, mulct.

mulct′ing, *pr.p.*, mulct.

mulc′tuary, *adj.*, mulcting.

mule, *n.*, the offspring of a horse and an ass; any hybrid creature; a spinning machine.

muleteer′, *n.*, a mule driver.

mulieb′rity, *n.*, the womanish state or quality.

mu′lish, *adj.*, mulelike, stubborn.

mu′lishly, *adv.*, in a stubborn way.

mu′lishness, *n.*, stubbornness.

mull, *n.*, a thin muslin; a muddle; a promontory (*Scot.*); *v.t.*, to concoct with sugar, spice, etc., into a drink; *v.i.*, to consider, to pore over.

mull′ah, *n.*, a teacher of the Mohammedan religion and law.

mulled, *p.p.*, mull.

mull′ein, *n.*, an herbaceous plant.

mull′er, *n.*, a sort of pestle.

mull′et, *n.*, a fish.

mulligataw′ny, *n.*, an E. Indian soup.

mull′igrubs, *n.pl.*, a depression of the spirits; a stomach-ache.

mull′ing, *pr.p.*, mull.

mul′lion, *n.*, a vertical division in a window.

mull′ock, *n.*, a rock from which gold has been extracted.

multan′gular, *adj.*, having many angles.

multe′ity, *n.*, the quality of being numerous.

multiartic′ulate, *adj.*, many-jointed.

multicap′sular, *adj.*, many-capsuled.

mul′ticoloured, *adj.*, having many colours.

multiden′tate, *adj.*, many-toothed.

multifa′rious, *adj.*, very various.

multifa′riously, *adv.*, in a variety of ways.

mul′tifid, *adj.*, with many clefts.

multiflo′rous, *adj.*, having more than three flowers.

mul′tiform, *adj.*, having many shapes.

multiform′ity, *n.*, the state of being multiform.

mul′tigraph, *n.*, a letterpress copying machine; *v.t.*, to print with such a machine.

multilat′eral, *adj.*, many-sided.

multilin′eal, *adj.*, having many lines.

mul′tilith, *n.*, a lithograph copying machine; *v.t.*, to print with such a machine.

multil′oquence, *n.*, a flow of speech.

multil'oquent, *adj.,* speaking much.

multino'mial, *adj.,* having more than two terms in algebra.

multip'arous, *adj.,* bearing many at a birth.

multipar'tite, *adj.,* having many parts.

mul'tiped, *adj.,* many-footed.

mul'tiphase, *adj.,* having many phases (*elec.*).

mul'tiplane, *adj.,* having many planes.

mul'tiple, *adj.,* composed of many parts, etc.; *n.,* a quantity which exactly contains another so many times.

mul'tiplex, *adj.,* mani-fold.

mul'tipliable, *adj.,* able to be multiplied.

multiplicand', *n.,* a quantity to be multiplied.

mul'tiplicate, *adj.,* many-folded; composed of more than one.

multiplica'tion, *n.,* multi-plying.

mul'tiplicative, *adj.,* multiplying.

mul'tiplicator, *n.,* the multiplying number.

multiplic'ity, *n.,* a great variety.

mul'tiplied, *p.p.,* multi-ply.

mul'tiplier, *n.,* one who, or that which, multi-plies.

mul'tiply, *v.t.,* to increase the number of; *v.i.,* to grow in number.

mul'tiplying, *pr.p.,* multi-ply.

multip'otent, *adj.,* very powerful.

multira'cial, *adj.,* composed of many races.

multira'diate, *adj.,* having many rays.

multis'onous, *adj.,* loud-sounding; giving forth many sounds.

multispi'ral, *adj.,* with many rings.

mul'titude, *n.,* a large number; a crowd; the mob.

multitu'dinary, *adj.,* numerous.

multitud'inism, *n.,* the putting of interests of multitudes before those of individuals.

multitu'dinous, *adj., i.q.* multitudinary.

mul'tivalve, *adj.,* many-valved.

multival'vular, *adj., i.q.* multivalve.

Multo'ca, *n.,* the Mohammedan legal code.

multoc'ular, *adj.,* many-eyed.

mum, *adj.,* silent; *v.i.,* to be silent; to play a mummer's part.

mum'ble, *v.t.* and *i.,* to utter indistinctly; to chew toothlessly.

mum'bled, *p.p.,* mumble.

mum'bler, *n.,* one who mumbles.

mum'bling, *pr.p.,* mum-ble.

mum'blingly, *adv.,* in a mumbling way.

mum'bo-jum'bo, *n.,* a venerated idol; pre-tentious nonsense.

mummed, *p.p.,* mum.

mum'mer, *n.,* a play-actor; a buffoon.

mum'mery, *n.,* play-acting by mummers (esp. morality plays); buffoonery.

mummifica'tion, *n.,* the act or effect of mum-mifying.

mum'mified, *p.p.,* mum-mify.

mum'miform, *adj.,* like a mummy.

mum'mify, *v.t.,* to embalm as a mummy.

mum'ming, *pr.p.,* mum; *n., i.q.* mummery.

mum'my, *n.,* an embalmed human body; a brown pigment; a child's pet name for mother.

mump, *v.i.,* to be sul-lenly silent; to be a beggar.

mumped, *p.p.,* mump.

mump'er, *n.,* one who mumps.

mump'ing, *pr.p.,* mump.

mump'ish, *adj.,* inclined to sulk.

mumps, *n. pl.,* a glandu-lar disease of the neck (parotitis, *med.*); the sulks.

munch, *v.t.,* to chew.

munched, *p.p.,* munch.

munch'er, *n.,* one who munches.

munch'ing, *pr.p.,* munch.

mun'dane, *adj.,* rel. to the world; worldly.

mun'datory, *adj.,* purify-ing; *n.,* a purificator for cleansing a chalice.

mundifica'tion, *n.,* cleansing.

mundif'icative, *adj.,* cleansing.

mun'go, *n.,* an inferior sort of shoddy cloth.

mung'oose, *n., i.q.* mon-goose.

munic'ipal, *adj.,* bel. to a city or borough.

municipal'ity, *n.,* a self-governing town.

munif'icence, *n.,* splen-did liberality.

munif'icent, *adj.,* giving generously.

munif'icently, *adv.,* with munificence.

mu'niment, *n.,* support; defence; a document.

mu'niment-room, *n.,* a place where docu-ments are carefully kept.

muni'tion, *n.,* war ma-terial; *v.t.,* to supply with munitions.

munjeet', *n.,* an E. Indian dye.

mun'nion, *n., i.q.* mul-lion.

muntz, *n.,* an alloy of copper and zinc.

mu'ral, *adj.,* rel. to a wall; *n.,* a picture painted on a wall.

mur'der, *v.t.,* to kill with malice prepense; to slay; to spoil bad-ly (*fig.*); *n.,* the act of murdering in all senses.

mur'dered, *p.p.,* murder.

mur'derer, *n.,* one who murders.

mur'deress, *n.,* the fem. of murderer.

mur'dering, *pr.p.,* mur-der.

mur'derous, *adj.,* with intent to murder; of the nature of murder.

mur'derously, *adv.,* in a murderous way.

mure, *v.t.,* to confine as in prison; to shut up.

mu'rex, *n.,* a kind of shell fish giving a purple dye (*Lat.*).

mu'riate, *n.,* chloride.

mu'riated, *adj.,* pickled; treated with chloride.

muriat'ic, *adj.,* of the nature of brine.

mu'ricate, *adj.,* rough-surfaced.

mu'ricated, *adj., i.q.* muricate.

mu'riform, *adj.,* mouse-like.

mu'rine, *adj.,* rel. to mice.

murk, *n.,* foggy, smoky darkness.

murk'ily, *adv.,* in a murky way.

murk'y, *adj.,* dark, gloomy.

mur'mur, *v.i.* and *t.,* to make a low sound; to

mutter; *n.*, a continued complaint; a softly spoken word.

mur'mured, *p.p.*, murmur.

mur'murer, *n.*, one who murmurs.

mur'muring, *pr.p.*, murmur.

mur'murous, *adj.*, murmur-like.

mur'phy, *n.*, a potato (*slang*).

mur'rain, *n.*, an infectious cattle disease.

mur'rey, *adj.* and *n.*, purple-red; the mulberry colour.

mur'rhine, *adj.*, made of fine glass.

mur'za, *n.*, a lower rank of Tartar nobility.

muscadel', *n.*, *i.q.* muscatel.

mus'cadine, *n.*, a grape with musklike flavour.

muscar'dine, *n.*, a disease of silkworms (*Fr.*).

Muscari, *n.*, a genus of bulbous plants, esp. the grape hyacinth.

mus'cat, *n.*, a variety of grape; a wine made from muscadines.

muscatel', *n.*, the muscadine raisin.

mus'cle, *n.*, the fleshy contractile fibre in animals, providing movement and power.

mus'cled, *adj.*, having muscles.

mus'coid, *adj.*, like moss.

muscol'ogy, *n.*, the science of mosses.

mus'cose, *adj.*, mossy.

muscos'ity, *n.*, mossiness.

muscova'do, *n.*, unrefined sugar.

Mus'covite, *adj.* and *n.*, Russian.

mus'cular, *adj.*, strong; rel. to muscles.

muscular'ity, *n.*, strength of muscle.

mus'culature, *n.*, the muscular system.

mus'culous, *adj.*, *i.q.* muscular.

muse, *v.i.*, to meditate; to be pensive; *n.*, one of the nine nymphs who inspired the arts.

mused, *p.p.*, muse.

muse'ful, *adj.*, silently thoughtful.

muse'fully, *adv.*, in a museful way.

mu'ser, *n.*, one who muses.

musette', *n.*, a small bagpipe; a simple tune for this.

muse'um, *n.*, a repository of objects relating to the history and activities of mankind.

muse'um-piece, *n.*, a remarkable specimen of art, etc., worthy of a museum.

mush, *n.*, soft pulp; a food of maize meal.

mush'room, *n.*, an edible fungus; anything of rapid growth; *v.i.*, to go gathering mushrooms.

mu'sic, *n.*, the art and science of beautiful sound; melodious or harmonious sound.

mu'sical, *adj.*, rel. to music; melodious or harmonious.

musicale', *n.*, a musical party (*Fr.*).

mu'sically, *adv.*, in a melodious way.

mu'sic-hall, *n.*, a theatre where variety shows take place.

musi'cian, *n.*, one who composes or performs music.

mu'sic-master, *n.*, a teacher of music.

musicolog'ical, *adj.*, rel. to the study of music.

musicol'ogist, *n.*, a student of musicology.

musicol'ogy, *n.*, the scientific study of music.

mu'sic-stool, *n.*, a seat for a player of music.

mu'sing, *pr.p.*, muse.

musk, *n.*, a strong-scented substance secreted by the musk-deer.

musk'-deer, *n.*, a small hornless deer.

mus'ket, *n.*, an infantryman's gun.

musketeer', *n:*, one armed with a musket.

musketoon', *n.*, an old type of cavalry musket.

mus'ketry, *n.*, muskets collectively; the art of shooting.

musk'iness, *n.*, the quality of being musky.

musk'rat, *n.*, a N. American rodent.

musk'y, *adj.*, smelling of musk.

Muslim, *n.*, *i.q.* Moslem.

mus'lin, *n.*, a fine, cotton cloth; *adj.*, made of muslin.

muslinet(te)', *n.*, a thick muslin.

mus'quash, *n.*, *i.q.* muskrat; fur from this source.

muss, *n.*, a mess; a squabble; *v.t.*, to disarrange (*Amer.*).

mus'sel, *n.*, a species of edible bivalve.

muss'uck, *n.*, a leather water-bag.

Mus'sulman, *adj.* and *n.*, Mohammedan.

must, *n.*, mouldiness; new unfermented wine; *v. aux.*, to be obliged to, or to be impelled by duty.

mus'tang, *n.*, a wild Californian or Mexican horse.

mus'tard, *n.*, a plant so named and its seed, used for various purposes; a table condiment.

mus'teline, *adj.*, rel. to weasels.

mus'ter, *v.t.* and *i.*, to assemble; to summon; *n.*, an assembling.

mus'tered, *p.p.*, muster.

mus'tering, *pr.p.*, muster.

mus'ter-roll, *n.*, a list of forces.

mus'tily, *adv.*, in a musty way.

mus'tiness, *n.*, the state of being musty.

mustn't, abbrev. of *must not*.

mus'ty, *adj.*, affected with mould; spoiled by damp or age.

mutabil'ity, *n.*, a liability to change.

mu'table, *adj.*, changeable.

mu'tably, *adv.*, in a mutable way.

mu'tage, *n.*, an arresting process in wine-fermentation.

mu'tant, *adj.*, resulting from change; *n.*, a new type of organism produced by mutation.

mutate', *v.t.* and *i.*, to alter, to change.

muta'ted, *p.p.*, mutate.

muta'tion, *n.*, a biological change; the process of changing.

muta'tional, *adj.*, rel. to change.

mutatis mutandis, *adv.*, with the necessary changes (*Lat.*).

mutch, *n.*, a linen cap (*Scot.*).

mute, *adj.*, dumb, silent; *n.*, one who is dumb; a hired mourner; a contrivance for reducing the sound of musical instruments.

mute'ly, *adv.*, silently.

mute'ness, *n.*, speechlessness.

mu'tilate, *v.t.*, to deprive of a limb; to damage by cutting, etc.

mu'tilated, *p.p.*, mutilate.

mu'tilating, *pr.p.*, mutilate.

mutila'tion, *n.*, the act or effect of mutilating.

mu'tilator, *n.*, one who mutilates.

mutineer', *n.*, one who mutinies.

mu'tinied, *p.p.*, mutiny.

mu'tinous, *adj.*, guilty of, or inclined to, mutiny.

mu'tinously, *adv.*, in a mutinous way.

mu'tiny, *v.i.*, to rise against authority, esp. of armed forces; *n.*, a revolt of sailors or soldiers.

mu'tinying, *pr.p.*, mutiny.

mu'tism, *n.*, dumbness.

mutt, *n.*, an incompetent fool.

mut'ter, *v.t.* and *i.*, to speak under one's breath; to grumble; *n.*, muttered words.

mut'tered, *p.p.*, mutter.

mut'terer, *n.*, one who mutters.

mut'tering, *pr.p.*, mutter.

mut'ton, *n.*, the flesh of sheep.

mu'tual, *adj.*, reciprocal; in relation to one another.

mut'ualism, *n.*, the doctrine of mutual dependence.

mutual'ity, *n.*, the quality of being mutual.

mu'tually, *adv.*, reciprocally.

mu'tule, *n.*, a detail of a Doric cornice.

muzz, *v.t.*, to make muzzy.

muz'zle, *v.t.*, to fasten the mouth; to silence (a person); *n.*, an animal's mouth; a fastening for the mouth.

muz'zled, *p.p.*, muzzle.

muz'zle-loader, *n.*, a gun loaded from the muzzle end.

muz'zling, *pr.p.*, muzzle.

muzz'y, *adj.*, dull, spiritless, stupid from drinking.

my, *possess. adj.*, of, or belonging to, me.

myal'gia, *n.*, muscular rheumatism.

my'all-wood, *n.*, a kind of acacia-wood.

mycel'ium, *n.*, the spawn of fungi (*bot.*).

mycetom'a, *n.*, the fungoid disease of feet and hands.

mycolog'ic, *adj.*, rel. to mycology.

mycol'ogist, *n.*, a student of mycology.

mycol'ogy, *n.*, the study of fungi.

myelit'is, *n.*, inflammation of the spinal cord (*med.*).

myog'raphy, *n.*, the scientific description of muscles.

myolog'ic, *adj.*, rel. to myology.

myolog'ical, *adj.*, *i.q.* myologic.

myol'ogist, *n.*, a student of myology.

myol'ogy, *n.*, the science of the muscles.

my'ope, *n.*, a short-sighted person.

myo'pia, *n.*, short-sightedness.

myo'pic, *adj.*, short-sighted.

my'opy, *n.*, *i.q.* myopia.

my'osin, *n.*, a substance in muscular tissue.

myo'sis, *n.*, contraction of the pupil.

myosit'ic, *adj.*, pert. to myosis.

my'osote, *n.*, the flower forget-me-not.

Myosot'is, *n.*, a genus of small flowering plants including the forget-me-not.

myot'omy, *n.*, the dissection of muscles.

myr'iad, *adj.* and *n.*, ten thousand; a number indefinitely large.

myr'iagram(me), *n.*, a weight of 10,000 grams.

myr'ialitre, *n.*, a measure of 10,000 litres.

myr'iametre, *n.*, a measure of 10,000 metres.

myr'iapod, *n.* and *adj.*, a many-legged animal; many-legged (*zool.*).

myringo'tomy, *n.*, perforation of the membrana tympani (*med.*).

myriora'ma, *n.*, a succession of views or pictures.

myr'ioscope, *n.*, a sort of kaleidoscope.

myrmecol'ogist, *n.*, a specialist in the study of ants.

myrmecol'ogy, *n.*, the study of ants.

myr'midon, *n.*, a rough soldier; a hired ruffian.

myrob'alan, *n.*, a sort of plum used by tanners and dyers.

myrrh, *n.*, an inspissated sap variously used.

myr'rhine, *adj.*, rel. to myrrh.

myr'tiform, *adj.*, like myrtle.

myr'tle, *n.*, a shrub.

myself', *pron.*, *refl.* rel. to the first person singular.

mys'tagogue, *n.*, one who teaches mysteries.

myste'rious, *adj.*, full of mystery; obscure.

myste'riously, *adv.*, in a mysterious way.

mys'tery, *n.*, a sacrament; an esoteric truth; a deep religious rite; a secret; a handicraft (*arch.*).

mys'tic, *adj.*, rel. to mystery; *n.*, one who seeks communion with God in contemplation.

mys'tical, *adj.*, *i.q.* mystic; mysterious; secret.

mys'tically, *adv.*, in a mystical way.

mys'ticism, *n.*, the practice of the mystics.

mystifica'tion, *n.*, the act or result of mystifying.

mys'tified, *p.p.*, mystify.

mys'tify, *v.t.*, to render obscure or perplexing; to puzzle.

mys'tifying, *pr.p.*, mystify.

mystique', *n.*, an atmosphere of mystery; a skill or technique which mystifies.

myth, *n.*, a fictitious story; a fable.

myth'ic, *adj.*, rel. to a myth.

myth'ical, *adj.*, *i.q.* mythic.

myth'ically, *adv.*, in a mythical way.

myth'icize, *v.t.*, to treat as a myth; to interpret mythically.

mythog'rapher, *n.*, a myth-writer.

mythog'raphy, *n.*, the writing of myths.

mythol'oger, *n.*, an expert in mythology.

mytholog'ic, *adj.*, pert. to mythology.

mytholog'ical, *adj., i.q.* mythologic.

mytholog'ically, *adv.,* in a mythological way.

mythol'ogist, *n., i.q.* mythologer.

mythol'ogize, *v.t.,* to turn into a myth; *v.i.,* to explain a myth.

mythologized, *p.p.,* mythologize.

mythol'ogizing, *pr.p.,* mythologize.

mythol'ogy, *n.,* the study of myths; myths collectively.

myth'oplasm, *n.,* the earliest source of myth.

my'thus, *n.,* a myth (*Lat.*).

myxoede'ma, *n.,* a disease of the thyroid gland.

myxo'ma, *n.,* a kind of tumour.

myxomato'sis, *n.,* a virus; a disease in rabbits.

N

Naaf'i, *n.*, an acronym for Navy, Army and Airforce Institute.

nab, *v.t.*, to arrest (*slang*).

nabbed, *p.p.*, nab.

nab'bing, *pr.p.*, nab.

na'bob, *n.*, a Mogul governor; a wealthy retired Anglo-Indian.

nac'arat, *n.*, an orange-red colour.

nacelle', *n.*, an aircraft body or housing for an engine (*Fr.*).

na'cre, *n.*, mother-of-pearl.

na'creous, *adj.*, rel. to nacre.

na'dir, *n.*, the lowest point in the sky (the opposite to the zenith); any lowest point.

nae'vose, *adj.*, freckled.

nag, *v.i.*, to scold incessantly; *n.*, a small riding horse; a horse.

naga'na, *n.*, a cattle disease caused by the tsetse fly.

nagged, *p.p.*, nag.

nag'ging, *pr.p.*, nag; *n.*, incessant fault-finding.

na'gor, *n.*, a Senegal antelope.

nai'ad, *n.*, a water-nymph.

nail, *v.t.*, to fasten with a nail, to secure; *n.*, the horny growth on the finger-ends; a piece of metal driven in with a hammer.

nail'brush, *n.*, a brush for the finger-nails.

nailed, *p.p.*, nail.

nail'er, *n.*, a nail-maker; a consummately clever person (*slang*).

nail'ery, *n.*, a nail factory.

nail'ing, *pr.p.*, nail; *adj.*, excellent; supremely skilful (*slang*).

nail'-scissors, *n. pl.*, scissors for trimming the finger-nails.

nain'sook, *n.*, a fine cotton material.

naïve', *adj.*, simple, artless (*Fr.*).

naïve'ly, *adv.*, artlessly.

naïve'té, *n.*, artlessness, simplicity (*Fr.*).

na'ked, *adj.*, bare, unclothed, plain.

na'kedly, *adv.*, in a naked way.

na'kedness, *n.*, the state of being naked.

nak'er, *n.*, a kettledrum.

na'm(e)able, *adj.*, fit to be named.

nam'by-pam'by, *adj.*, affected, insipid, soft; *n.*, sentimental, affected talk.

name, *v.t.*, to give a name to; to call by a name; to quote, to specify; to appoint; *n.*, an identifying word or title; a reputation; a virtually non-existent thing.

named, *p.p.*, name.

name'less, *adj.*, without a name; inglorious; unnamable.

name'ly, *adv.*, that is to say.

na'mer, *n.*, one who names.

name'sake, *n.*, one called by one's own name.

na'ming, *pr.p.*, name.

nan'cy, *n.*, a homosexual; an effeminate man; *adj.*, effeminate.

nankeen', *n.*, a yellow cotton fabric; a pale buff colour.

nann'y, *n.*, a child's nurse; abbrev. of nanny-goat (*colloq.*).

Nantes, *n.*, brandy. Also *Nantz.*

nap, *v.i.*, to take a short, light sleep; to doze; *v.t.*, to put a nap on (cloth); *n.*, a short sleep; a raised surface; a card-game.

nap'alm, *n.*, a product from naphthalene and coconut oil; a jellied petrol used as a war weapon.

nape, *n.*, the back of the neck.

na'pery, *n.*, table linen.

naph'tha, *n.*, an inflammable oil.

naphthal'ic, *adj.*, rel. to naphtha.

naph'thalene, *n.*, a solid crystalline hydrocarbon.

na'piform, *adj.*, turnip-like (*bot.*).

nap'kin, *n.*, a square of linen; a small towel.

nap'les yell'ow, *n.*, a bright yellow pigment.

napo'leon, *n.*, a French coin = 20 francs.

Napoleon'ic, *adj.*, rel. to, or resembling, Napoleon I.

napoo', *adj.*, no good, hopeless, done for (*slang*).

napped, *p.p.*, nap.

nap'piness, *n.*, the quality of being nappy.

nap'ping, *pr.p.*, nap.

nap'py, *adj.*, foaming, heady; *n.*, abbrev. of baby's napkin.

napu, *n.*, the musk-deer of Java.

nar'ceine, *n.*, a substitute for morphine.

narcis'ine, *n.*, one who suffers from morbid self-admiration.

narcis'ism, *n.*, *i.q.* narcissine.

Narcis'sus, *n.*, the son of Cephisus, the classical river god. The prototype of self-admiration and self-absorption; a kind of bulbous plant.

narc'olepsy, *n.*, a disease causing drowsy fits.

narco'sis, *n.*, the result of using a narcotic.

narcot'ic, *adj.*, inducing sleep or torpor; *n.*, a narcotic drug.

narcot'ical, *adj.*, *i.q.* narcotic.

narcot'ically, *adv.*, in a narcotic way.

nar'cotine, *n.*, a drug used in fevers.

nar'cotism, *n.*, the narcotized state.

nar'cotize, *v.t.*, to bring under narcotic influence.

nar'cotized, *p.p.*, narcotize.

nar'cotizing, *pr.p.*, narcotize.

nard, *n.*, ointment; spikenard.

nard'ine, *adj.*, rel. to nard.

na'res, *n.*, the nostrils (*Lat.*).

nar'ghile, *n.*, an Eastern tobacco pipe; a hookah.

nark, *n.*, a police decoy or informer (*slang*).

narrate', *v.t.*, to relate, to recite.

narra'ted, *p.p.*, narrate.

narra'ting, *pr.p.*, narrate.

narra'tion, *n.*, the act of narrating.

nar'rative, *n.*, a story, history; *adj.*, in the form of narration.

narra'tor, *n.*, a storyteller.

nar'row, *v.t.*, to reduce in width; *v.i.*, to be so reduced; *adj.*, small in width; cramped; illiberal; scrutinizing closely; *n.*, a strait.

nar'rowed, *p.p.*, narrow.

nar'rower, *adj.*, *comp.* of narrow.

nar'rowest, *adj.*, *super.* of narrow.

nar'rowing, *pr.p.*, narrow.

nar'rowly, *adv.*, with small breadth; parsimoniously; with close scrutiny.

nar'row-minded, *adj.*, illiberal, bigoted.

nar'row-mind'edness, *n.*, bigotry, illiberality.

nar'rowness, *n.*, a lack of breadth.

nar'thex, *n.*, a vestibule; the part of a Christian basilica near the entrance.

nar'whal, *n.*, an Arctic cetacean, with two teeth formed into one long tusk.

na'sal, *adj.*, rel. to the nose; *n.*, a nasal letter or sound (*i.e.*, pronounced through the nose).

nasal'ity, *n.*, the nasal quality.

nasaliza'tion, *n.*, the giving of a nasal sound.

na'salize, *v.t.*, to give a nasal sound to.

na'salized, *p.p.*, nasalize.

na'salizing, *pr.p.*, nasalize.

na'sally, *adv.*, through the nose.

nas'cent, *adj.*, beginning to be born.

nas'cently, *adv.*, incipiently.

nase'berry, *n.*, the sapodilla plum tree.

na'sicornous, *adj.*, having a horn on the nose.

na'siform, *adj.*, in the form of a nose.

nasol'ogy, *n.*, the study of the nose.

nas'tier, *adj.*, *comp.* of nasty.

nas'tiest, *adj.*, *super.* of nasty.

nas'tily, *adv.*, in a nasty way.

nas'tiness, *n.*, the state of being nasty.

nastur'tium, *n.*, a plant of the watercress type; a garden plant with spurred flowers.

nas'ty, *adj.*, disgusting, dirty, illnatured.

na'tal, *adj.*, rel. to birth.

natal'ity, *n.*, birth rate.

na'tant, *adj.*, floating.

nata'tion, *n.*, swimming.

Natato'res, *n. pl.*, webfooted birds (*Lat.*).

natato'rial, *adj.*, rel. to the Natatores or to swimming.

na'tatory, *adj.*, *i.q.* natatorial.

nat'es, *n. pl.*, buttocks; a pair of optic lobes in the brain (*Lat.*).

nath(e)'less, *adv.*, nevertheless (*arch.*).

na'tion, *n.*, an individual people or race, of common origin, customs and language.

na'tional, *adj.*, rel. to a nation; *n.*, a member of a nation.

na'tionalism, *n.*, patriotism; the policy of national independence.

na'tionalist, *n.*, a patriot, a supporter of nationalism.

national'ity, *n.*, the quality of being national; membership of a nation; an independent people.

nationaliza'tion, *n.*, the act of nationalizing.

na'tionalize, *v.t.*, to make national; to make into a nation; to subject to the nation's control.

na'tionalized, *p.p.*, nationalize.

na'tionalizing, *pr.p.*, nationalize.

na'tionally, *n.*, by the nation collectively.

na'tionhood, *n.*, the condition of being a nation.

nation'wide, *adj.*, *adv.*, throughout the entire nation.

na'tive, *adj.*, born in a given place; indigenous; inherited; *n.*, one born in a place named; the cultivated oyster.

na'tivism, *n.*, the doctrine of innate ideas.

nativ'ity, *n.*, birth; a representation in art of Christ's birth; a horoscope (*astrol.*).

na'tron, *n.*, sesquicarbonate of soda occurring naturally.

nat'ter, *v.i.*, to chatter idly, to grumble (*colloq.*).

nat'terjack, *n.*, a British variety of toad.

nat'tier blue, *n.*, a soft shade of blue.

nat'tily, *adv.*, in a natty way.

nat'ty, *adj.*, trim, dainty.

nat'ural, *adj.*, according to nature; instinctive; unaffected; simple; not artificial; not sharped or flatted; *n.*, a note not marked as a sharp or flat; a white note on a keyboard; a born idiot; an expert.

nat'uralism, *n.*, conduct based on natural instincts; religious and philosophic theories opposed to supernaturalism.

nat'uralist, *n.*, a student of flora and fauna.

naturalis'tic, *adj.*, rel. to naturalism or to natural history.

naturaliza'tion, *n.*, the act or result of naturalizing.

nat'uralize, *v.t.*, to admit an alien to citizenship; to make natural; *v.i.*, to pursue natural history.

nat'uralized, *p.p.*, naturalize.

nat'uralizing, *pr.p.*, naturalize.

nat'urally, *adv.*, in a natural way; of course; certainly.

nat'uralness, *n.*, the quality of being natural; freedom from artificiality.

na'ture, *n.*, the collective phenomena of the material universe; the collective forces underlying these phenomena; the essential qualities of a

thing; the unregenerate state of man.

na'turism, n., nudism.

na'turist, n., a nudist.

naught, adj., of no value; n., nothing, a cipher.

naugh'tier, adj., comp. of naughty.

naugh'tiest, adj., super. of naughty.

naugh'tily, adv., in a naughty way.

naugh'tiness, n., disobedience, wilfulness, depravity.

naugh'ty, adj., disobedient, wicked.

nau'sea, n., a feeling of qualm; a loathing.

nau'seant, adj., nauseating.

nau'seate, v.t., to produce nausea; v.i., to turn sick.

nau'seated, p.p., nauseate.

nau'seating, adj., sickening; pr.p., nauseate.

nausea'tion, n., the state of being nauseated.

nau'seous, adj., causing nausea; nasty.

nautch, n., an Indian dancing entertainment.

nautch'-girl, n., an Indian dancing-girl.

nau'tical, adj., rel. to sailors and navigation.

nau'tically, adv., in a nautical way.

nau'tilite, n., a fossil like the nautilus.

nau'tilus, n., a cephalopod.

na'val, adj., rel. to a navy or ships.

na'varchy, n., an admiral's office; skill in naval command.

nave, n., the hub of a wheel; the body of a church.

na'vel, n., the scar on the abdomen where the umbilical cord was cut.

navette', n., an incenseboat (Fr.).

nav'icert, n., a certificate that a ship's cargo is not contraband.

navic'ular, adj., boatshaped.

navigabil'ity, n., the state of being navigable.

nav'igable, adj., admitting navigation.

nav'igate, v.t., to sail, to manage, to steer; v.i., to sail a ship, to make a voyage.

nav'igated, p.p., navigate.

nav'igating, pr.p., navigate.

naviga'tion, n., the act or science of navigating.

nav'igator, n., one who navigates, or is skilled in navigating; an explorer.

nav'vy, n., a labourer.

navy, n., the ships and the whole naval service bel. to a State.

nawab', n., an Indian nobleman.

nay, adv., no; n., a denial or refusal; a negative vote or voter.

Nazarene', adj., rel. to Nazareth; n., a native of Nazareth.

Naz'arite, n., a Hebrew ascetic, wearing long hair and abstaining from wine.

Naz'aritism, n., the vows or practices of a Nazarite.

naze, n., a headland.

Nazi, adj. and n., (a) German National Socialist.

né (masc.) or née (fem.), adj., born (Fr.).

Nean'derthal, adj., rel. to primeval man.

neap, v.i., to tend towards neap; v.t., to leave a ship aground till the next high tide; adj., low, lowest; n., a neap tide, the lowest ebb.

Neapol'itan, adj., rel. to Naples.

neap'tide, n., i.q. neap.

near, v.t., to approach; v.i., to draw near; adj., not far off, not distant; closely related; intimate; closely following; stingy; adv., close by, nigh, closely; prep., close by, not far from.

near'by, adj., adv., adjacent; near to.

neared, p.p., near.

near'er, adj., comp. of near.

near'est, adj., super. of near.

near'ing, pr.p., near.

near'ly, adv., almost, not quite, closely.

near'ness, n., proximity; the state of being near.

near'sighted, adj., shortsighted; myopic.

neat, adj., nice, elegantly simple, trim, tidy; clever; net, undiluted; adj., bovine; n., any kind of ox.

neat'-cattle, n., bovine cattle.

neat'er, adj., comp. of neat.

neat'est, adj., super. of neat.

neath, prep., beneath (poet.).

neat'herd, n., a cowherd.

neat'ly, adv., in a neat way.

neat'ness, n., the quality of being neat.

neb, n., a beak, nose, tip.

neb'ula, n., a star-cluster; a speck on the cornea (Lat.).

neb'ular, adj., rel. to nebulae.

neb'ule, n., an architectural moulding.

nebul'ium, n., a hypothetical element detected in certain nebulae.

nebulos'ity, n., the quality of being nebulous.

neb'ulous, adj., confused, hazy, nebular.

necessa'rian, adj. and n., i.q. necessitarian.

nec'essarily, adv., of necessity, inevitably.

nec'essariness, n., the quality of being necessary.

nec'essary, adj., indispensable, requisite, compulsory, inevitably resulting; n., an indispensable thing.

necessita'rian, adj., denying the doctrine of free will; n., one who asserts that everything results from antecedent causes and denies free will.

neces'sitate, v.t., to render necessary or inevitable.

neces'sitated, p.p., necessitate.

neces'sitating, pr.p., necessitate.

neces'sitous, adj., needy, in straitened circumstances.

neces'sity, n., the quality of being necessary; an inevitability; a compulsion, want, hardship; an urgent need.

neck, n., the part connecting a head with a trunk; anything resembling a neck, as a neck of land; the neck of a bottle, etc.

neck'cloth, n., a cravat, a necktie.

neck'erchief, n., a kerchief for the neck.

neck'lace, n., precious stones, or beads, worn round the neck.

neck'let, n., an ornament or covering for the neck.

neck'line, n., the extent of the opening of the neckband of a garment.

neck'tie, n., a cravat.

neck'wear, n., wear worn round the neck.

necrol'atry, n., ancestor-worship.

necrolog'ic, adj., rel. to necrology.

necrolog'ical, adj., i.q. necrologic.

necrol'ogist, n., one who records the names of the dead.

necrol'ogy, n., a list of the names of the dead.

nec'romancer, n., one who practises necromancy.

nec'romancy, n., magic, divination through communication with the dead.

nec'romantic, adj., rel. to necromancy.

necrop'olis, n., a cemetery.

necro'scopy, n., an autopsy; a post-mortem examination.

necro'sis, n., mortification, gangrene.

necrot'omy, n., dissection of dead bodies.

nec'tar, n., the drink of the gods; any delicious drink; the honey of plants.

necta'real, adj., rel. to nectar; deliciously sweet.

necta'rean, adj., i.q. nectareal.

necta'reous, adj., i.q. nectareal.

nectarif'erous, adj., honey-producing.

nec'tarine, n., a variety of peach with a smooth skin.

nec'tarize, v.t., to sweeten.

nec'tary, n., a plant's organ that secretes honey.

Ned'dy, n., a donkey.

née, adj., denotes married woman's maiden name.

need, v.t., to require, to be in need of; v.i., to be under the necessity of; n., a lack, a want, an emergency, a thing needed.

need'ed, p.p., need.

need'ful, adj., needed, requisite.

need'fully, adv., in a needful way.

need'ier, adj., comp. of needy.

need'iest, adj., super. of needy.

need'ily, adv., in a needy way.

need'iness, n., the quality of being needy.

need'ing, pr.p., need.

nee'dle, v.t., to sew; to form needle-like crystals; v.i., to sew, to crystallize; n., a pointed instrument used for sewing, knitting, etc.; a piece of magnetized steel used as the indicator of a compass, or magnetic or electric apparatus.

nee'dle-book, n., a needle-case like a book.

nee'dleful, n., as much thread as can well be used at once.

nee'dle-gun, n., a gun fired by a blow from a spring-needle.

nee'dle-shaped, adj., long, narrow and sharp-pointed.

need'less, adj., unnecessary.

need'lessly, adv., unnecessarily.

need'lessness, n., the quality of being needless.

nee'dlewoman, n., a seamstress.

nee'dlework, n., work done with a needle.

needs, adv., of necessity; n. pl., wants.

need'y, adj., in want; necessitous.

ne'er, adv., never.

nefa'rious, adj., wicked, heinous.

nefa'riously, adv., wickedly.

negate', v.t., to nullify; to deny.

negat'ed, p.p., negate.

negat'ing, pr.p., negate.

nega'tion, n., the act of denying; a denial; the absence of something positive.

neg'ationist, n., one who believes in the denial of ideas.

neg'ative, v.t., to veto, to contradict, to disprove; adj., not positive; expressing negation or subtraction; n., a negative expression; the right of veto; a photographic picture where the lights and shades are reversed.

neg'atived, p.p., negative.

neg'atively, adv., in a negative way or sense.

neg'ativism, n., the attitude of a negationist.

neg'atron, n., a four-electrode thermionic tube (radio); a negative-charge electron (atomic physics).

neglect', v.t., to slight; to not do; n., negligence.

neglect'ed, p.p., neglect.

neglect'er, n., one who neglects.

neglect'ful, adj., remiss, careless.

neglect'fully, adv., in a neglectful way.

neglect'ing, pr.p., neglect.

négligé', n., unceremonious dress; a loose gown (Fr.).

neg'ligence, n., carelessness, remissness, disregard.

neg'ligent, adj., careless, remiss.

neg'ligently, adv., carelessly.

negligibil'ity, n., the state of being negligible.

neg'ligible, adj., able to be disregarded.

negotiabil'ity, n., the quality of being negotiable.

nego'tiable, adj., able to be negotiated, arranged.

nego'tiate, v.t., to arrange, to bring about, to convert into cash; v.i., to transact business.

nego'tiated, p.p., negotiate.

nego'tiating, pr.p., negotiate.

negotia'tion, n., a business transaction; a discussion with the object of reaching agreement.

nego'tiator, n., one who negotiates.

nego'tiatory, adj., rel. to negotiation.

ne'gress, n., a negroid woman.

negrill'o, n., a pygmy.

negrit'ic, adj., rel. to negroes.

negri'to, n., a Malayo-Polynesian pygmy.

ne'gro, adj., of the negro type; n., a black-skinned man.

ne'groid, adj., negro-like.

ne'grophil, n., a friend of negroes.

ne'grophobe, n., one who dislikes negroes.

negropho'bia, n., a dislike of negroes.

Ne'gus, n., the Emperor of Abyssinia.

ne'gus, n., wine and water, hot and sweetened.

neigh, v.i., to make a horse's cry.

neigh'bour, v.t. and i., to adjoin, to border upon; n., one who lives near; a person next to another.

neighboured, adj., having neighbours or particular surroundings.

neigh'bourhood, n., the vicinity; the people of the vicinity; neighbourliness; nearness.
or

neigh'bouring, pr.p., neighbour; adj., adjacent.

neigh'bourliness, n., kindliness.

neigh'bourly, adj., kindly, sociable; adv., in a neighbourly spirit.

neighed, p.p., neigh.

neigh'ing, pr.p., neigh.

nei'ther, adj., and pron.,
or
not either; not the one or the other; adv., not either, not on the one hand nor on the other; conj., nor yet.

nek'ton, n., forms of free-swimming organism (biol.).

nematode, adj., pertaining to the nematoda class of worms, e.g. the common roundworm; n., a worm.

Neme'an, adj., rel. to Nemea and the games held there.

neme'sia, n., a colourful garden flower.

Nem'esis, n., the goddess of retribution.

nen'uphar, n., a waterlily.

Ne'ocene, adj., rel. to the later Tertiary.

neog'raphy, n., a new system of writing.

neolith'ic, adj., rel. to the later Stone Age.

neolo'gian, adj., rel. to neology.

neolog'ical, adj., i.q. neologian.

neol'ogism, n., the coining of new words; adopting new and rationalistic opinions.

neol'ogist, n., one who coins new words, or preaches new doctrines.

neol'ogize, v.i., to coin new words or to preach new doctrines.

neol'ogy, n., the introducing of new words or doctrines.

neomy'cin, n., an antibiotic drug.

ne'on, n., a gaseous element; a kind of light.

ne'ophron, n., the white Egyptian vulture.

ne'ophyte, n., a novice; one lately converted.

neoplas'ticism, n., an art form based on geometrical patterns.

neoplaton'ic, adj., pert. to neoplatonism.

neoplat'onism, n., a blend of Judaism and Christianity with Greek philosophy and the mysticism of the East.

neoplaton'ist, n., one of the neoplatonic school.

neoter'ic, adj., recent; n., a modern person.

neozo'ic, adj., pert. to the later rock series.

nepen'the, n., the pitcher plant, narcotic in its effect. Also nepenthes.

neph'ew, n., a sister's or brother's son.

nephol'ogy, n., the study of the clouds.

neph'oscope, n., an apparatus for observing cloud phenomena.

nephral'gia, n., kidney neuralgia.

nephral'gy, n., i.q. nephralgia.

neph'rite, n., the kidney stone.

nephrit'ic, adj., rel. to nephritis.

nephri'tis, n., inflammation of the kidneys.

nephrol'ogy, n., the study of kidney pathology.

nephrot'omy, n., the cutting operation for stone in the kidneys.

nep'otal, adj., rel. to nephews.

nep'otism, n., favouritism towards relatives.

nep'otist, n., one who practises nepotism.

Nep'tune, n., the Roman god of the sea; the planet so named.

Neptu'nian, adj., rel. to Neptune.

Nep'tunist, n., a believer in the aqueous formation of certain rocks.

neptun'ium, n., a radioactive element.

ne'reid, n., a sea-nymph.

ne'roli, n., an orange essence.

Nero'nian, adj., pert. or rel. to the Roman Emperor, Nero; cruel, tyrannical.

nerv'ate, adj., (of leaves) having ribs.

nerva'tion, n., the distribution of the nerves.

nerve, v.t., to inspirit; to impart vigour to; n., a fibre conveying physical sensations; courage.

nerved, p.p., nerve.

nerve'less, adj., without courage or vigour.

ner'vine, n., a nerve-medicine.

nerv'ing, pr.p., nerve.

ner'vous, adj., rel. to the nerves; having nerve-force; easily perturbed.

nerv'ously, adv., in a nervous way.

nerv'ousness, n., the state of being nervous.

ner'vure, n., a nerve or rib in architecture, or in botany.

ner'vy, adj., in a nervous state.

nes'cience, n., ignorance; agnosticism.

nes'cient, adj., ignorant; agnostic.

ness, n., a promontory.

nest, v.t. and i., to place in a nest; to occupy a nest; n., a place or structure where a bird lays its eggs or tends its young.

nest'ed, p.p., nest.

nest'-egg, n., an egg, natural or artificial, placed in a nest to induce a hen to lay; a financial security for the future.

nest'ing, pr.p., nest.

nes'tle, v.t., to cuddle; v.i., to lie comfortably as in a nest.

nes'tled, p.p., nestle.

nes'tling, pr.p., nestle; n., a very young bird.

Nes'tor, n., a wise old man.

net, v.t., to catch; to protect with a net; to make into network; to gain clear; v.i., to make nets,

to do netting; *adj.*, made of netting; clear after deduction of costs; not subject to discount; *n.*, a meshed fabric of cord, hair, etc.

net′ball, *n.*, an outdoor ball game.

neth′er, *adj.*, lower.

neth′ermost, *adj.*, *super.* of nether.

net′suke, *n.*, a kind of Japanese brooch.

net′ted, *p.p.*, net.

net′ting, *pr.p.*, net; *n.*, network.

net′tle, *v.t.*, to sting; to annoy; *n.*, the common stinging plant.

net′tled, *p.p.*, nettle.

net′tle-rash, *n.*, urticaria, a skin eruption.

net′tlewort, *n.*, one of the urticaceae.

net′tling, *adj.*, provoking; *pr.p.*, nettle.

net′work, *n.*, woven meshes.

neum(e), *n.*, a group of musical notes in plainsong notation.

neu′ral, *adj.*, rel. to the nerves.

neural′gia, *n.*, a painful affection of the nerves.

neural′gic, *adj.*, rel. to neuralgia.

neurasthe′nia, *n.*, nervous debility.

neurasthen′ic, *adj.*, rel. to neurasthenia.

neura′tion, *adj.*, the arrangement of nerves in a leaf or on an insect's wings, etc.

neuri′tis, *n.*, inflammation of a nerve.

neurological, *adj.*, rel. to the nervous system.

neurol′ogist, *n.*, a student of neurology.

neurol′ogy, *n.*, the study of the nervous system.

neurom′a, *n.*, a tumour upon or in a nerve.

Neurop′tera, *n. pl.*, insects with membranous wings.

neurop′teran, *adj.*, rel. to Neuroptera.

neuro′sis, *n.*, an affection of the nerves, as epilepsy.

neurot′ic, *adj.*, nervous; abnormally sensitive; *n.*, a drug affecting the nerves.

neurot′omy, *n.*, the cutting of a nerve.

neu′ter, *adj.*, bel. to neither sex; *n.*, a sexless, sterile organism.

neu′tral, *adj.*, bel. to neither side; indifferent; not distinctly coloured; *n.*, a state that takes no side in a war.

neutral′ity, *n.*, the state of being neutral.

neutraliza′tion, *n.*, the act or effect of neutralizing.

neu′tralize, *v.t.*, to counteract; to exclude from an area of hostilities.

neu′tralized, *p.p.*, neutralize.

neu′tralizer, *n.*, anything that neutralizes.

neu′tralizing, *pr.p.*, neutralize.

neu′trally, *adv.*, not taking sides.

neut′ron, *n.*, a particle consisting of an electron and a proton (*chem.*).

névé, *n.*, granular snow that feeds a glacier.

nev′er, *adv.*, at no time; not ever.

nev′ermore, *adv.*, not again.

nevertheless′, *adv.*, and *conj.*, notwithstanding.

new, *adj.*, fresh, recent, strange.

new′born, *adj.*, lately born.

new′comer, *n.*, one who has lately come.

new′el, *n.*, the central pillar of a winding staircase; the top or bottom post of a stair handrail.

new′er, *adj.*, *comp.* of new.

new′est, *adj.*, *super.* of new.

newfan′gled, *adj.*, strange; of new fashion.

new-fash′ioned, *adj.*, of new fashion.

new′ish, *adj.*, somewhat new.

new′laid, *adj.*, freshly laid.

new′ly, *adv.*, recently, lately.

new′-made, *adj.*, recently made.

new′ness, *n.*, the state of being new; a novelty.

news, *n. pl.*, tidings; fresh information.

news′agent, *n.*, a seller of newspapers.

news′boy, *n.*, a boy who sells newspapers.

news′cast, *n.*, a radio or T.V. broadcast of news.

news′caster, *n.*, one who prepares news for broadcasting.

news′man, *n.*, one who reports news, or sells or delivers newspapers.

news′monger, *n.*, a gossip.

news′paper, *n.*, a public journal.

news′print, *n.*, the printing-paper for newspapers.

news′reel, *n.*, a cinema news-film.

news′room, *n.*, a place where papers may be read.

news′vendor, *n.*, a seller of newspapers.

news′y, *adj.*, full of information (*slang*).

newt, *n.*, a small amphibian; an eft.

Newto′nian, *adj.*, rel. to Sir Isaac Newton and his philosophy.

next, *adj.*, nearest; immediately following; *adv.*, immediately following; *prep.*, adjoining, nearest to.

nex′us, *n.*, a bond; a connexion. In plain song, a melodic movement by intervals (*Lat.*).

niac′in, *n.*, nicotinic acid.

nib, *v.t.*, to point (a pen); *n.*, a penpoint; *pl.*, crushed cacao beans; a naturally humorous person (*slang*).

nibbed, *p.p.*, nib.

nib′ble, *v.t.* and *i.*, to take small bites of; to bite cautiously at; *n.*, the act of nibbling; a small bite.

nib′bled, *p.p.*, nibble.

nib′bler, *n.*, one who nibbles.

nib′lick, *n.*, a type of golf club.

nib′bling, *pr.p.*, nibble.

nibs, *n.*, a form of title for His Grace (*slang*).

nice, *adj.*, fastidious, particular, discerning, agreeable.

nice′ly, *adv.*, neatly, agreeably.

Ni′cene, *adj.*, rel. to Nicáea and the Nicene Councils (A.D. 325 and 787).

nice′ness, *n.*, the state of being nice.

ni'cer, *adj.*, *comp.* of nice.

ni'cest, *adj.*, *super.* of nice.

ni'cety, *n.*, *i.q.* niceness; a subtle quality; a minute distinction.

niche, *n.*, a recess in a wall; any special place; *v.t.*, to put in a niche.

niched, *p.p.*, niche.

nich'ing, *pr.p.*, niche.

nick, *v.t.*, to indent; to notch; to fit exactly; *n.*, a small cut at the edge; a notch.

nicked, *p.p.*, nick.

nick'el, *v.t.*, to nickel-plate; *adj.*, made of nickel; *n.*, a malleable and ductile white metal; a nickel coin.

nick'ing, *pr.p.*, nick.

nick'nack, *n.*, *i.q.* knickknack.

nick'name, *v.t.*, to call by a substituted name; *n.*, a familiar substitute for a person's real name.

nick'named, *p.p.*, nick-name.

nick'naming, *pr.p.*, nickname.

nico'tian, *adj.*, rel. to tobacco.

nico'tianin, *n.*, a compound distilled from tobacco.

nic'otine, *n.*, a poisonous alkaloid in tobacco and other plants.

nic'otinism, *n.*, tobacco poisoning.

nic'tate, *v.i.*, to wink the eyes.

nic'tated, *p.p.*, nictate.

nic'tating, *pr.p.*, nictate.

nicta'tion, *n.*, the act of nictating.

nic'titate, *v.i.*, *i.q.* nictate.

nictita'tion, *n.*, *i.q.* nictation.

nidamen'tal, *adj.*, rel. to nests or their construction.

nid'dering, *n.* and *adj.*, a coward; cowardly.

nide, *n.*, a brood of pheasants.

nid'get, *n.*, an idiot.

nid'ificate, *v.i.*, to build a nest.

nidifica'tion, *n.*, the act of nest-building.

nid'ify, *v.i.*, *i.q.* nidifi-cate.

nid'ulant, *adj.*, lying free; nestling.

ni'dus, *n.*, a nest or breeding-place; a place where a disease is bred (*Lat.*).

niece, *n.*, the daughter of a brother or sister.

niel'lo, *n.*, a filling for engraved lines in metal; a piece of work so treated.

nif'ty, *adj.*, smart, stylish (*slang*).

Nigerian, *adj.*, pert. or rel. to Nigeria; *n.*, a native of N.

nig'gard, *n.*, a stingy fellow; *adj.*, stingy; in mean quantity.

nig'gardliness, *n.*, stinginess.

nig'gardly, *adj.*, *i.q.* niggard; *adv.*, sparingly.

nig'ger, *n.*, a negro (*derog.*).

nig'gle, *v.i.*, to be over-exact; to worry over details.

nig'gled, *p.p.*, niggle.

nig'gler, *n.*, one who niggles.

nig'gling, *pr.p.*, niggle; *adj.*, petty, trifling.

nigg'ly, *adj.*, *i.q.* niggling.

nigh, *adj.*, *n.* and *adv.*, near.

nigh'ness, *n.*, nearness.

night, *n.*, the period of darkness between sunset and sunrise.

night'cap, *n.*, a cap once used for sleeping in; the last drink before going to bed.

night'clothes, *n. pl.*, garments worn in bed.

night'club, *n.*, *i.q.* night-spot.

night'dress, *n.*, a loose garment worn in bed.

night'fall, *n.*, the approach of night.

night'gown, *n.*, *i.q.* night-dress.

night'ingale, *n.*, a migratory songster that sings by night as well as in the day.

night'jar, *n.*, a nocturnal bird.

night'light, *n.*, a candle or lamp burnt through the night.

night'long, *adj.* and *adv.*, lasting all night.

night'ly, *adj.* and *adv.*, each night.

night'man, *n.*, one who guards, or works, at night.

night'mare, *n.*, an oppressive or terrifying dream; an incubus.

night'marish, *adj.*, like a nightmare.

night'-piece, *n.*, a picture of a nightly scene.

night'-porter, *n.*, a porter on duty at night.

night'school, *n.*, a school which provides evening instruction.

night'shade, *n.*, the name of several poisonous plants, as belladonna.

night'shift, *n.*, a spell of work done at night; men employed on night work.

night'shirt, *n.*, a shirt worn in bed.

night'spot, *n.*, a night-club or nocturnal entertainment place.

night'stool, *n.*, a commode.

night'-time, *n.*, the period of night.

night'-walker, *n.*, one who walks in sleep.

night'-walking, *n.*, the act of walking in sleep.

night'-watch, *n.*, the act of watching by night; a body of night-watchers.

night'-watchman, *n.*, one keeping night-watch.

nigres'cence, *n.*, the state of growing black.

nigres'cent, *adj.*, turning black.

nig'ritude, *n.*, blackness.

ni'hilism, *n.*, an absolutely destructive scepticism.

ni'hilist, *n.*, a person whose philosophy is the rejection of all current beliefs.

nihilis'tic, *adj.*, rel. to nihilism.

nihil'ity, *n.*, nothingness.

nil, *n.*, nothing; no number (*Lat.*).

nil'gai, *n.*, an Indian antelope.

nilom'eter, *n.*, a measured pillar marking the rise of the Nile.

nilot'ic, *adj.*, pert. to the Nile.

nimbif'erous, *adj.*, cloud-bringing.

nim'ble, *adj.*, active, quick.

nim'bleness, *n.*, the quality of being nimble.

nim'bler, *adj.*, *comp.* of nimble.

nim'blest, *adj.*, *super.* of nimble.

nim'bly, *adv.*, actively, quickly.

nim'bus, *n.*, a cloud; a halo round the head of a deity or a saint.

nimi′ety, *n.*, an excess; too much.

nim′iny-piminy, *adj.*, prim; full of affectation.

nincompoop, *n.*, an affected fool (*colloq.*).

nine, *adj.*, the cardinal number next above eight; *n.*, the number 9; a card with nine pips.

nine′fold, *adj.*, nine times repeated.

nine′pence, *n.*, the amount of nine pence.

nine′penny, *adj.*, costing nine pence.

nine′pins, *n.*, a game resembling skittles.

nine′score, *adj.*, 9 × 20.

nineteen′, *adj.*, one short of twenty.

nineteenth′, *adj.*, the ordinal of nineteen.

nine′tieth, *adj.*, the ordinal of ninety.

nine′ty, *adj.*, nine times ten; *n.*, the number 90.

nin′ny, a simpleton (*colloq.*).

ninon, *n.*, light-weight silk.

ninth, *adj.*, the ordinal of nine.

ninth′ly, *adv.*, in the ninth place.

niob′ium, *n.*, a metallic element (*chem.*).

nip, *v.t.*, to pinch, to pinch off, to take a small drink of; *n.*, a pinch; a bite; a nipping air; a small draught of spirits.

nipped, *p.p.*, nip.

nip′per, *n.*, one who nips; a small boy.

nip′perkin, *n.*, a little cup.

nip′pers, *n. pl.*, small forceps.

nip′ping, *pr.p.*, nip; *adj.*, keen, biting.

nip′ple, *n.*, the protuberant termination of the mammary duct; anything resembling this.

nip′py, *adj.*, keen, biting; nimble (*slang*).

nirva′na, *n.*, the highest state of Buddhist perfection.

Ni′san, *n.*, the seventh month of the Jewish civil year.

ni′si pri′us, *n.*, a writ beginning with these two Latin words = "unless before"; a hearing of civil cases at the Assizes.

nit, *n.*, a small insect's egg; a stupid person (*slang*).

nit′on, *n.*, *i.q.* radon.

ni′trate, *n.*, a salt having nitric acid as its base.

nitrate′, *v.t.*, to impregnate with nitric acid.

ni′tre, *n.*, potassium nitrate.

ni′tric, *adj.*, of nitre.

nitrifica′tion, *n.*, the act of nitrifying.

ni′trified, *p.p.*, nitrify.

ni′trify, *v.t.*, to turn into nitre; *v.i.*, to become nitrous.

ni′trifying, *pr.p.*, nitrify.

ni′trite, *n.*, a nitrous acid salt.

ni′trogen, *n.*, a gas without colour, scent or taste.

nitrog′enous, *adj.*, pert. to nitrogen.

nitrog′enize, *v.t.*, to impregnate with nitrogen.

nitro-glyc′erine, *n.*, a high-explosive liquid, produced by the action of nitric acid.

nitromuriat′ic, *adj.*, rel. to nitric and hydrochloric acid.

ni′trous, *adj.*, pert. to nitre.

nit′ty, *adj.*, full of nits.

nit′wit, *n.*, a person of little intelligence; a fool.

nit′witted, *adj.*, lacking intelligence.

niv′eous, *adj.*, like snow.

nix, *n.*, a water-elf.

Nizam′, *n.*, the ruler of Hyderabad; a regular Turkish soldier.

no, *adj.*, not any; none; *adv.* and *neg. particle* of denial.

Noa′chian, *adj.*, rel. to Noah.

nob, *n.*, a knob, a head; a superior person (*slang*).

nob′ble, *v.t.*, to influence fraudulently (*slang*).

nobel′ium, *n.*, an element artificially produced in 1957 at the Nobel Institute.

nobil′iary, *adj.*, pert. to the nobility; *n.*, the nobility.

nobil′ity, *n.*, the quality of being noble; the noble class.

no′ble, *adj.*, illustrious, of high birth, generous, magnificent; *n.*, one of the noble class.

no′bleman, *n.*, a peer.

no′bleness, *n.*, the quality of being noble.

noblesse′, *n.*, the nobility; the class of nobles (*Fr.*).

no′bly, *adv.*, in a noble way.

no′body, *n.*, no one; an insignificant person.

noctambula′tion, *n.*, the practice of night-walking.

noctam′bulism, *n.*, the tendency to night-walking.

noctam′bulist, *n.*, a night-walker.

noctilu′cous, *adj.*, phosphorescent.

noctiv′agant, *adj.*, night-wandering.

noctivaga′tion, *n.*, the act of night-wandering.

noc′tograph, *n.*, an apparatus enabling the blind to write.

noc′tule, *n.*, a large bat.

noc′turn, *n.*, a section of the office of Matins.

noctur′nal, *adj.*, nightly, by night.

noc′turnally, *adv.*, in a nocturnal way.

noc′turne, *n.*, a musical reverie; a night-scene.

noc′uous, *adj.*, harmful.

noc′uously, *adv.*, harmfully.

nod, *v.t.*, to shake the head, to assent, to order; *v.i.*, to drop off to sleep; to decline from the perpendicular.

no′dal, *adj.*, rel. to nodes.

nod′ded, *p.p.*, nod.

nod′der, *n.*, one who nods.

nod′ding, *pr.p.*, nod.

nod′dle, *n.*, the head (*colloq.*).

nod′dy, *n.*, a fool; a sea-bird (*colloq.*).

node, *n.*, a knot in timber; the point from which a leaf springs, or where a planet's orbit intersects the ecliptic.

nodose′, *adj.*, knotty.

nodos′ity, *n.*, knottiness.

no′dous, *adj.*, *i.q.* nodose.

nod′ular, *adj.*, rel. to a nodule.

nodula′tion, *n.*, the formation of nodules.

nod′ule, *n.*, a little rounded lump; a small node.

nod′uled, *adj.*, having nodules.

noegen′esis, *n.*, the gaining of knowledge from experience.

No′el, *n.*, Christmas; the expression of joy at Christmas (*interj.*).

noet′ic, *adj.*, rel. to intellect; abstract; speculative.

nog, *n.*, a tree-snag; a wooden pin or peg.

nog′gin, *n.*, a small mug; a small liquid measure.

nog′ging, *n.*, a partition of scantling with a brick filling.

no′how, *adv.*, in no way.

noise, *n.*, excessive sound, clamour; *v.t.*, to publish abroad.

noised, *p.p.*, noise.

noise′less, *adj.*, silent.

noise′lessly, *adv.*, silently.

noise′lessness, *n.*, the absence of sound.

noisette′, *n.*, a small portion of meat cooked in a special way; a variety of rose (*Fr.*).

nois′ier, *adj.*, *comp.* of noisy.

nois′iest, *adj.*, *super.* of noisy.

nois′ily, *adv.*, loudly, with noise.

nois′iness, *n.*, the quality of being noisy.

nois′ing, *pr.p.*, noise.

noi′some, *adj.*, offensive, harmful.

noi′someness, *n.*, the quality of being noisome.

nois′y, *adj.*, making a noise; turbulent, loud.

noll, *n.*, the crown of the head.

nom′ad, *adj.*, *i.q.* nomadic; *n.*, a wanderer.

nomad′ic, *adj.*, wandering hither and thither; migratory.

nom′adism, *n.*, the nomadic tendency.

nom′adize, *v.i.*, to become a nomad.

nom′adized, *p.p.*, nomadize.

nom′adizing, *pr.p.*, nomadize.

nom de guerre′, *n.*, a pseudonym (*Fr.*).

nom de plume′, *n.*, a penname; an assumed name (*Fr.*).

nome, *n.*, an ancient Greek and Egyptian territorial area.

no′menclator, *n.*, in ancient Rome a person who assigned the guests their places at a banquet; one who names things.

no′menclature, *n.*, the system of naming used in an activity.

nom′ic, *adj.*, usual.

nom′inal, *adj.*, rel. to a noun or a name; existing in name only; of no significance.

nom′inalism, *n.*, the philosophic doctrine that abstract ideas are merely names.

nom′inalist, *n.*, a believer in nominalism.

nominalist′ic, *adj.*, pert. to nominalism.

nom′inally, *adv.*, in name only.

nom′inate, *v.t.*, to mention by name; to appoint; to propose for election.

nom′inated, *p.p.*, nominate.

nom′inating, *pr.p.*, nominate.

nomina′tion, *n.*, the act or right of nominating.

nominati′val, *adj.*, rel. to nominative; appointed by nomination.

nom′inative, *adj.*, rel. to the nominative case; *n.*, the case of the grammatical subject.

nom′inator, *n.*, one who nominates.

nominee′, *n.*, a person nominated.

nomolog′ical, *adj.*, pert. to nomology.

nomol′ogy, *n.*, the science of laws.

non-accept′ance, *n.*, a refusal to accept.

non′age, *n.*, minority; immaturity.

nonagena′rian, *n.*, a person between ninety and one hundred years of age.

nonages′imal, *adj.*, rel. to ninety or a nonagesimal; *n.*, the highest point of the ecliptic above the horizon.

non′agon, *n.*, a nine-sided and nine-angled plane figure.

non-appear′ance, *n.*, a failure to appear.

non-arri′val, *n.*, a failure to arrive.

non′ary, *adj.*, based on nine.

non-attend′ance, *n.*, a failure to attend.

non′-belli′gerent, *n.*, *adj.*, a neutral; taking no active part in war.

nonce, *n.*, the time being.

nonce′-word, *n.*, a word coined for the occasion.

non′chalance, *n.*, calm indifference.

non′chalant, *adj.*, calmly indifferent.

non′chalantly, *adv.*, in a nonchalant way.

non-com′batant, *adj.*, non-fighting; *n.*, a civilian in war-time; a surgeon or a chaplain in the forces.

non-commis′sioned, *adj.*, not having commission in the armed forces.

non-commis′sioned offi′cer, *n.*, an officer of non-commissioned rank.

non-commit′tal, *adj.*, avoiding the taking of a side or committing oneself.

non-conduct′or, *n.*, a substance that resists the passage of heat or electricity.

nonconform′ist, *adj.*, not subscribing to accepted beliefs; *n.*, a follower of a religious sect dissenting from the Church of England.

nonconform′ity, *n.*, the rejection of accepted beliefs in religion, morals or politics.

non-content′, *adj.*, opposed to a motion; *n.*, one who votes against.

non-cum′ulative, *adj.*, not accumulating.

non-deliv′ery, *n.*, a failure to deliver.

non′descript, *adj.*, odd, neither one thing nor the other; *n.*, a person or thing hard to classify.

none, *adj.*, not any or one; *n.* and *pron.*, no one.

non-effect′ive, *adj.*, ineffective, disabled; *n.*, a disabled or unfit person.

non-effi′cient, *adj.*, incompetent; *n.*, one who is not qualified.

nonen'tity, *n.*, non-existence; a person of no account.

nones, *n. pl.*, the ninth day before the Roman Ides.

non-essen'tial, *adj.*, not essential.

none'such, *n.*, a paragon.

nonet', *n.*, a musical composition for nine players or singers.

none'-the-less', *adv.*, *i.q.* nevertheless.

non-exist'ence, *n.*, the state of not being.

non-exis'tent, *adj.*, not existing.

non'-feas'ance, *n.*, failing to carry out that which ought to have been done (*leg.*).

nonil'lion, *n.*, the ninth power of a million (in English reckoning); the tenth power of a thousand (in French reckoning).

non'-interven'tion, *n.*, non-interference.

non'ius, *n.*, an early type of vernier.

nonju'ring, *adj.*, refusing to take the oath of allegiance.

nonju'ror, *n.*, one who refused allegiance to William III.

non-nat'ural, *adj.*, un-natural.

non-obe'dience, *n.*, the failure to obey.

non-observ'ance, *n.*, the failure to observe.

no'noh, *n.*, a kind of Japanese musical drama.

non'-op'erable, *adj.*, unable to operate or be operated upon.

nonpareil', *adj.*, unique; *n.*, a paragon; a variety of printers' type; a variety of bird, apple, wheat (*Fr.*).

non-par'ty, *adj.*, not attached to any particular party.

nonpay'ment, *n.*, an omission to pay.

non-perform'ance, *n.*, the failure to perform.

non'plus, *v.t.*, to puzzle, to perplex; *n.*, a perplexed condition.

non'plussed, *p.p.*, nonplus.

non'plussing, *pr.p.*, nonplus.

non-produc'tion, *n.*, the failure to produce.

non-res'idence, *n.*, the fact of not residing; absenteeism.

non-res'ident, *adj.*, not residing; not permanently settled.

non-resist'ance, *n.*, a passive attitude.

non'sense, *n.*, anything meaningless or ridiculous; *interj.*, ridiculous!

nonsen'sical, *adj.*, having no sense.

nonsen'sically, *adv.*, absurdly.

non-se'quitur, *n.*, the fallacy of a conclusion not warranted by the premises (*Lat.* = it follows not).

non'-skid', *adj.*, safe against skidding.

non'-smo'ker, *n.*, a person who does not smoke; a railway compartment for non-smokers.

non'-star'ter, *n.*, one destined to fail; a race-horse which does not compete.

non'-stop, *adj.*, not stopping.

non'such, *n.*, a paragon; a variety of lucerne; *i.q.* nonesuch.

non'suit, *v.t.*, to subject to a nonsuit; *n.*, the judicial stopping of a suit where there is no proper case.

non'suited, *p.p.*, nonsuit.

non'suiting, *pr.p.*, nonsuit.

noo'dle, *n.*, a simpleton; a small shape of dough used in soups.

nook, *n.*, a corner; a recess.

noolog'ical, *adj.*, rel. to noology.

nool'ogist, *n.*, a student of noology.

nool'ogy, *n.*, the science of mental phenomena.

noon, *n.*, midday.

noon'day, *adj.*, rel. to midday; *n.*, *i.q.* noon.

no-one, *pron.*, not a single person, nobody.

noon'tide, *adj.* and *n.*, *i.q.* noonday.

noose, *v.t.*, to catch with a noose; *n.*, a loop with a running knot; a lasso.

noosed, *p.p.*, noose.

noos'ing, *pr.p.*, noose.

no'pal, *n.*, a variety of cactus.

nor, *conj.*, and not; and not either.

Nor'dic, *adj.*, from N.W. Europe.

norl'and, *n.*, a northern region.

norm, *n.*, a pattern; a standard.

nor'mal, *adj.*, according to type, regular; *n.*, the ordinary state.

normal'ity, *n.*, the normal state, condition or quality.

nor'malize, *v.t.*, to make conform to a standard.

nor'mally, *adv.*, ordinarily, regularly.

Nor'man, *adj.*, rel. to the Normans; the N. style of architecture; *n.*, a native of Normandy.

norn, *n.*, one of the Scandinavian Fates.

Nor'roy, *n.*, the title of the heraldic King of Arms, whose jurisdiction lies north of the Trent.

Norse, *adj.*, Scandinavian; *n.*, the Scandinavian language.

Norse'man, *n.*, a Scandinavian.

north, *adj.*, in the north or northward; *n.*, the point opposite to the south.

north-east', *n.*, a point between N. and E.

north-east'er, *n.*, a N.E. wind.

north-east'erly, *adj.*, in, or from, a N.E. direction.

north-east'ern, *adj.*, rel. to the N.E.

north'-east'ward, *adv.*, towards the N.E.

north'erly, *adj.*, toward the N.; from the N.

north'ern, *adj.*, in, or toward, the N.

north'erner, *n.*, a native of the north country.

north'ernmost, *adj.*, furthest N.

north'ing, *n.*, the progress or drift northwards.

Northum'brian, *adj.*, pert. to Northumbria or Northumberland; *n.*, a native of N.

north'ward, *adj.* and *adv.*, toward the N.

north'wardly, *adv.*, toward the N.

north'wards, *adv.*, *i.q.* northward.

north-west', *n.*, a point between N. and W.

north-west'er, *n.*, a N.-Westerly wind.

north-west'erly, *adj.*, from, or towards, the N.W.

north-west′ern, *adj.*, rel. to the N.W.

Norwe′gian, *adj.*, rel. to Norway and the Norwegians; *n.*, a native of N.

nor′-west′er, *n.*, a north-west wind; an oilskin coat.

nose, *v.t.*, to smell or to scent; *n.*, the organ of smell; a snout.

nose′bag, *n.*, a bag for fodder hung round a horse's neck.

nosed, *p.p.*, nose.

nose′dive, *n.*, a downward plunge; a plung nose first.

nose′gay, *n.*, a bouquet of flowers.

nos′er, *n.*, a strong head wind.

no′sing, *pr.p.*, nose.

nosog′raphy, *n.*, the scientific description of diseases.

nosolog′ical, *adj.*, rel. to nosology.

nosol′ogist, *n.*, a student of nosology.

nosol′ogy, *n.*, the classification of diseases.

nosopho′bia, *n.*, a fear of disease.

nostal′gia, *n.*, homesickness.

nostal′gic, *adj.*, pert. to nostalgia.

nos′toc, *n.*, blue-green algae.

nostoma′nia, *n.*, *i.q.* nostalgia.

nostop′athy, *n.*, a fear of returning to familiar places.

nos′tril, *n.*, one of the openings of the nose.

nos′trum, *n.*, a quack medicine; a pet project (*Lat.*).

nos′y, *adj.*, large-nosed; inquisitive; an inquisitive person (*slang*).

not, *adv.* of negation.

no′ta be′ne, *n.*, mark well or note specially (*Lat.*).

notabil′ia, *n. pl.*, things worthy of notice.

notabil′ity, *n.*, the quality of being notable; a notable person.

no′table, *adj.*, worthy of note, remarkable; *n.*, a person of distinction.

no′tably, *adv.*, in a way worthy of remark or note.

notal′gia, *n.*, backache.

nota′rial, *adj.*, rel. to a notary.

no′tary, *n.*, an official who attests writings.

nota′tion, *n.*, the act or system of noting by marks, figures or characters.

notch, *v.t.*, to nick or to cut into small hollows; *n.*, a cut so made, *i.q.* nick.

notched, *p.p.*, notch.

notch′ing, *pr.p.*, notch.

note, *v.t.*, to set down, to observe closely; *n.*, a mark; a short writing; a musical sound or character; a written acknowledgment of a debt with promise of payment.

note′book, *n.*, a book for notes.

note′case, *n.*, a case for holding notes or bank-notes.

no′ted, *p.p.*, note; *adj.*, celebrated.

note′worthy, *adj.*, worthy to be noted.

noth′ing, *n.*, not anything; a cipher.

noth′ingness, *n.*, non-existence, worthlessness.

no′tice, *v.t.*, to remark, to observe, to see; *n.*, remark, regard; a printed or written sheet giving information.

no′ticeable, *adj.*, worthy of observation.

no′ticeably, *adv.*, in a noticeable way.

no′tice-board, *n.*, a board on which notices are fixed.

no′ticed, *p.p.*, notice.

no′ticing, *pr.p.*, notice.

not′ifiable, *adj.*, requiring to be reported.

notifica′tion, *n.*, the act of giving notice; notice given.

no′tified, *p.p.*, notify.

no′tify, *v.t.*, to inform; to make known to.

no′tifying, *pr.p.*, notify.

no′ting, *pr.p.*, note.

no′tion, *n.*, an idea, a conception, an opinion.

no′tional, *adj.*, rel. to notions; imaginary.

notionally, *adv.*, in a notional way.

notori′ety, *n.*, the state of being notorious; publicity.

noto′rious, *adj.*, publicly known (commonly in a bad sense).

noto′riously, *adv.*, publicly, openly.

notwithstand′ing, *prep.*, in spite of; *adv.*, nevertheless; *conj.*, usu. with *that* = despite the fact that.

nougat′, *n.*, a confection of sugar, nuts, etc.

nought, *adj.*, *i.q.* naught; *n.*, the figure 0.

nou′menal, *adj.*, pert. to noumena.

nou′menon, *n.*, something conceived in the mind, apart from external phenomena (*pl.* noumena).

noun, *n.*, a name of anything.

nour′ish, *v.t.*, to feed, to bring up.

nour′ishable, *adj.*, able to be nourished.

nour′ished, *p.p.*, nourish.

nour′isher, *n.*, one who nourishes.

nour′ishing, *pr.p.*, nourish; *adj.*, nutritious.

nour′ishment, *n.*, food.

nous, *n.*, the mind; intelligence; enlightened common sense (*Gr.*).

nouveau, *adj.*, new (*Fr.*).

nouveau riche, *n.*, one who has recently become rich; *pl.* nouveaux riches (*Fr.*).

nov′el, *adj.*, new; strange; *n.*, a tale of fiction.

novelette′, *n.*, a short novel.

nov′elist, *n.*, a novel-writer.

nov′elize, *v.t.*, to convert into a novel.

nov′elty, *n.*, newness; a new thing.

Novem′ber, *n.*, the eleventh month of the year.

nove′na, *n.*, a religious devotion observed for a period of nine days.

nov′enary, *adj.*, pert. to a novena; also to the number nine; *n.*, a group of nine units.

noven′nial, *adj.*, happening every ninth year.

noverc′al, *adj.*, stepmotherly.

nov′ice, *n.*, a beginner; an initiate.

novi′ciate, *n.*, a novice's period of probation; the novices' quarters in a religious house.

novilu'nar, *adj.*, rel. to the new moon.

novi'tiate, *n.*, *i.q.* noviciate.

nov'ocaine, *n.*, a regional anaesthetic (*pharm.*).

now, *adv.*, at the present time (used also without reference to time, in the sense of "It follows, then", "Beware", "Please do," etc.).

now'adays, *adv.*, in these times.

no'way, *adv.*, in no way; not at all.

now'el, *interj.*, expressing Christmas joy (Also *Noel*); *n.*, the inner part of a large mould.

no'where, *adv.*, in no place.

no'wise, *adv.*, in no way.

nox'ious, *adj.*, harmful, deadly.

nox'iously, *adv.*, in a noxious way.

nox'iousness, *n.*, harmfulness.

noyau', *n.*, a liqueur flavoured with bitter almonds or peach kernels (*Fr.*).

noz'zle, *n.*, a spout; the end of a hose.

nuance', *n.*, a fine shade of meaning, colour, expression, etc. (*Fr.*).

nub, *n.*, a small lump or knob; the point or gist.

Nu'bian, *adj.*, rel. to Nubia, N.E. Africa; *n.*, a native of N.

nubif'erous, *adj.*, cloud-bearing.

nu'bile, *adj.*, marriageable.

nu'chal, *adj.*, rel. to the nape of the neck.

nucif'erous, *adj.*, nut-bearing.

nu'ciform, *adj.*, nut-shaped.

nu'cleal, *adj.*, rel. to a nucleus.

nu'clear, *adj.*, *i.q.* nucleal.

nu'cleate, *adj.*, *i.q.* nucleated; *v.t.* and *i.*, to form into a nucleus.

nu'cleated, *adj.*, having a nucleus; *p.p.*, nucleate.

nucleating, *pr.p.*, nucleate.

nuclea'tor, *n.*, a nuclei-producing agent.

nu'clei, *n.*, the pl. of nucleus.

nucle'ic, *adj.*, pert. or rel. to a class of organic acids.

nu'cleiform, *adj.*, like a nucleus.

nuc'leole, *n.*, a body within a nucleus (*biol.*).

nucleon'ics, *n.*, nuclear physics.

nu'cleus, *n.*, a central mass round which other matter accumulates; the body of a comet.

nu'clide, *n.*, any atom in respect of its neutron and proton composition.

nuda'tion, *n.*, the act of making bare.

nude, *adj.*, naked, bare.

nude'ly, *adv.*, nakedly.

nude'ness, *n.*, the nude state.

nudge, *n.*, a slight push; *v.t.*, to jog with the elbow; to give a hint to.

nudged, *p.p.*, nudge.

nudg'ing, *pr.p.*, nudge.

nu'dism, *n.*, the cult of the nude.

nu'dist, *n.*, an adherent to nakedness.

nu'dity, *n.*, *i.q.* nudeness.

nu'gae, *n. pl.*, trifles, profitless minutiae (*Lat.*).

nu'gatory, *adj.*, of no force, trifling, futile.

nug'get, *n.*, a lump of metal or ore.

nui'sance, *n.*, that which, or anyone who, annoys or offends.

null, *adj.*, void; of no force.

nul'lah, *n.*, a ravine with a watercourse.

nullifica'tion, *n.*, the act of nullifying.

nullifid'ian, *adj.*, with no religious belief.

nul'lified, *p.p.*, nullify.

nul'lifier, *n.*, one who nullifies.

nul'lify, *v.t.*, to make void, to cancel.

nul'lifying, *pr.p.*, nullify.

null'ipore, *n.*, a kind of marine vegetation.

nul'lity, *n.*, invalidity, the state of being null; a nonentity.

numb, *adj.*, without feeling; *v.t.*, to deprive of feeling.

numbed, *p.p.*, numb.

num'ber, *n.*, a single unit; a total of units; a measure; one of a series; a metre or verse; *v.t.*, to count; to reckon; to mark numerically.

num'bered, *p.p.*, number.

num'bering, *pr.p.*, number.

num'berless, *adj.*, innumerable.

Num'bers, *n. pl.*, one of the books of the Pentateuch; poetry, metre.

numb'ing, *pr.p.*, numb.

numb'ly, *adv.*, without feeling.

numb'ness, *n.*, a loss of sensation.

nu'merable, *adj.*, able to be reckoned.

nu'meral, *adj.*, rel. to number; *n.*, a numerical symbol.

nu'merary, *adj.*, rel. to a number.

nu'merate, *v.t.*, to count; to read or point as a numerical expression.

nu'merated, *p.p.*, numerate.

nu'merating, *pr.p.*, numerate.

numera'tion, *n.*, the act or method of numbering.

nu'merator, *n.*, one who numbers; the figure or figures above the line of a fraction showing how many times the denominator is taken.

nume'ric, *n.*, that which concerns numbers.

numer'ical, *adj.*, denoting numbers.

numer'ically, *adv.*, in number; by means of numbers.

nu'merous, *adj.*, composed of a number; many.

nu'merously, *adv.*, in number.

num'inous, *adj.*, pert. to a reverence for religion.

numismat'ics, *n. pl.*, the science of coins and medals.

numis'matist, *n.*, one skilled in numismatics.

numismatol'ogy, *n.*, *i.q.* numismatics.

num'mary, *adj.*, rel. to coins.

numm'et, *n.*, lunch (*dial.*).

num'mular, *adj.*, rel. to coins.

num'mulary, *adj.*, *i.q.* nummular.

numm'ulite, *n.*, a fossil shell of the Tertiary strata.

num'nah, *n.*, a saddle cloth; a pad for under a saddle.

num'skull, *n.*, a blockhead (*colloq.*).

nun, *n.*, a cloistered woman-religious; a variety of pigeon; a blue titmouse.

nun'atak, *n.*, rock that projects above the surface of the ice.

nun'buoy, *n.*, a buoy which is circular in the middle and tapering at each end.

nun'cheon, *n.*, *i.q.* luncheon.

nun'ciature, *n.*, a nuncio's office.

nun'cio, *n.*, a papal envoy (*It.*).

nunc'upate, *v.t.*, to declare orally.

nunc'upated, *p.p.*, nuncupate.

nunc'upating, *pr.p.*, nuncupate.

nuncupa'tion, *n.*, a verbal declaration (will, testament, etc.).

nun'cupative, *adj.*, oral, verbal.

nuncupa'tory, *adj.*, *i.q.* nuncupative.

nun'dinal, *adj.*, rel. to markets.

nunna'tion, *n.*, the adding of the letter "n" to the endings of words.

nun'nery, *n.*, a religious house of nuns.

nup'tial, *adj.*, rel. to marriage.

nup'tials, *n. pl.*, the marriage ceremony.

nurse, *n.*, one who tends a child or sick patient; *v.t.*, to suckle or tend; to bring up; to tend a sick person; to cherish; to manage economically.

nursed, *p.p.*, nurse.

nurse'maid, *n.*, a servant in charge of a child.

nurs'ery, *n.*, a room for children; a plantation for young trees.

nurs'eryman, *n.*, the keeper of a nursery for young trees.

nurs'ing, *n.*, the business of a nurse; *pr.p.*, nurse.

nurs'ling, *n.*, an infant.

nur'ture, *n.*, that which nurtures; education; *v.t.*, to feed; to educate.

nur'tured, *p.p.*, nurture.

nur'turing, *pr.p.*, nurture.

nut, *n.*, a fruit consisting of a shell and a kernel; a metal block for securing a bolt; the tightener on a fiddle bow; a silly youth with affectations of dress, etc. (*slang*); *v.i.*, to go nutting.

nu'tant, *adj.*, drooping.

nut'ate, *v.t.*, to nod, to droop.

nuta'tion, *n.*, nodding; the apparent vibratory motion of the earth's axis (*astron.*).

nut'brown, *adj.*, brown as a nut.

nut'crackers, *n. pl.*, an instrument for cracking nuts.

nut'gall, *n.*, an excrescence on the oak.

nut'hatch, *n.*, a small bird that feeds on nuts.

nut'hook, *n.*, a hook used in gathering nuts.

nut'meg, *n.*, the kernel of an aromatic nut found in E. India.

nut'-oil, *n.*, oil obtained from nuts.

nut'ria, *n.*, fur of the coypu.

nu'trient, *adj.*, nutritious.

nu'triment, *n.*, nutritious food.

nutri'tion, *n.*, nourishment, food.

nutri'tional, *adj.*, rel. to nutrition.

nutri'tionist, *n.*, an expert in nutrition.

nutri'tious, *adj.*, nourishing.

nu'tritive, *adj.*, having the quality of nourishment.

nu'tritively, *adv.*, in a nourishing way.

nu'tritiveness, *n.*, the quality of being nourishing.

nut'shell, *n.*, the hard outside of a nut; something of small compass or capacity.

nut'ted, *p.p.*, nut.

nut'ting, *pr.p.*, nut.

nutt'y, *adj.*, rich in nuts; dandy-like; amorous (*slang*).

nut'-wrench, *n.*, a spanner.

nux, *n.*, a nut (*Lat.*).

nux vom'ica, *n.*, an Indian fruit yielding strychnine (*Lat.*).

nuz'zle, *v.t.*, to nose, to burrow with the snout; *v.i.*, to nestle, to lie close.

nuz'zled, *p.p.*, nuzzle.

nuz'zling, *pr.p.*, nuzzle.

nyan'za, *n.*, a lake, a marsh (*African*).

nyct'alope, *n.*, one affected by nyctalopia.

nyctalo'pia, *n.*, night-blindness.

nyc'talopy, *n.*, *i.q.* nyctalopia.

nyctitrop'ic, *adj.*, changing position by night.

nyctophob'ia, *n.*, a fear of darkness.

nye, *n.*, a brood of pheasants.

nyl'ghau, *n.*, a variety of Indian antelope.

ny'lon, *n.*, a strong, synthetic, plastic material.

nymph, *n.*, a semidivine maiden dwelling in woods, streams, mountains, etc.; a young and lovely woman.

nym'pha, *n.*, a pupa or chrysalis.

Nymphæa, *n.*, a genus of water plants.

nym'phal, *adj.*, rel. to nymphs.

nymphe'an, *adj.*, *i.q.* nymphal.

nymph'olepsy, *n.*, a state of ecstasy.

nym'pholept, *n.*, one who experiences nympholepsy.

nympholep'tic, *adj.*, in a state of ecstasy.

nymphoman'ia, *n.*, an over-sexed state in women.

nystag'mus, *n.*, an eye-disease common among miners.

O

O, *interj.*, with vocative case, or expressing wonder, pain, etc. The other form is "Oh".

oaf, *n.*, a changeling, a lout.

oaf'ish, *adj.*, loutish.

oak, *n.*, a tree of the genus Quercus; oak timber.

oak'-apple, *n.*, an excrescence on the oak.

oak'en, *adj.*, made of oak.

oak'um, *n.*, old rope untwisted.

oar, *n.*, a pole broadened at one end into a blade for propelling a boat; *v.t.*, to propel by rowing.

oar'age, *n.*, oars collectively.

oared, *adj.*, having oars; *p.p.*, oar.

oar'ing, *pr.p.*, oar.

oars'man, *n.*, a rower.

oars'manship, *n.*, the skill of using oars.

oars'woman, *n.*, the fem. of oarsman.

oa'sis, *n.*, a fertile spot in a desert.

oast, *n.*, a kiln for hop-drying.

oast'house, *n.*, the building containing an oast.

oat, *n.*, a cereal plant; the seed of the same; a shepherd's pipe.

oat'cake, *n.*, a cake made of oatmeal.

oat'en, *adj.*, made of, or pert. to, oats.

oath, *n.*, a solemn affirmation calling God to witness.

oat'meal, *n.*, meal made from oats.

ob(b)liga'to, *adj.*, indispensable to a musical composition; *n.*, an additional accompaniment (*It.*).

obcor'date, *adj.*, inversely heart-shaped.

ob'duracy, *n.*, stubbornness, hardheartedness.

ob'durate, *adj.*, inflexibly hard.

ob'durately, *adv.*, in an obdurate way.

ob'durateness, *n.*, *i.q.* obduracy.

o'beah, *n.*, a form of sorcery among W. Indians.

obe'dience, *n.*, submission to authority; compliance with command.

obe'dient, *adj.*, submissive, compliant.

obe'diently, *adv.*, submissively.

obei'sance, *n.*, an act of reverence; a bow.

obei'sant, *adj.*, reverential.

obelis'coid, *adj.*, obelisk-shaped.

ob'elisk, *n.*, a rectangular tapering pillar; an old manuscript mark (†) denoting corruptness of text.

ob'elize, *v.t.*, to mark with an obelus or obelisk.

ob'elus, *n.*, a critical sign, as the obelisk (†); or + as marking a passage for omission; or (—).

obese', *adj.*, fat.

obes'ity, *n.*, fatness, corpulence.

obey', *v.t.*, to comply with; to perform a command.

obeyed', *p.p.*, obey.

obey'er, *n.*, one who obeys.

obey'ing, *pr.p.*, obey.

ob'fuscate, *v.t.*, to darken, obscure or bewilder.

ob'fuscated, *p.p.*, obfuscate.

ob'fuscating, *pr.p.*, obfuscate.

obfusca'tion, *n.*, darkening; confusion.

o'bi, *n.*, *i.q.* obeah.

ob'it, *n.*, death; the anniversary memorial of the dead, especially of a founder or benefactor (*Lat.*).

ob'iter, *adv.*, by the way, incidentally (*Lat.*).

obit'ual, *adj.*, rel. to obit.

obit'uary, *adj.*, rel. to a person's death; *n.*, a written notice of a person's death.

object', *v.t.*, to urge in opposition; *v.i.*, to express disapproval.

ob'ject, *n.*, anything visible or presented to the mind or senses; an aim or purpose.

object'ed, *p.p.*, object.

objec'tify, *v.t.*, to present facts objectively.

object'ing, *pr.p.*, object.

objec'tion, *n.*, an adverse reason.

objec'tionable, *adj.*, liable to objection; offensive.

objec'tionably, *adv.*, in an objectionable way.

objec'tive, *adj.*, pert. to an object; external to the mind; *n.*, the accusative case; a goal.

objec'tively, *adv.*, in an objective sense; externally to the mind.

objec'tivism, *n.*, the doctrine that the knowledge of the non-ego or external world comes before, and is more important than the ego; an artist's or poet's power to give reality to what he is depicting.

objectiv'ist, *adj.*, rel. to objectivism.

objectiv'ity, *n.*, the quality of being objective.

ob'jectless, *n.*, without a purpose.

object'or, *n.*, one who objects.

ob'jurgate, *v.t.*, to reprove, to scold.

ob'jurgated, *p.p.*, objurgate.

ob'jurgating, *pr.p.*, objurgate.

objurga'tion, *n.*, a reproof.

objur'gatory, *adj.*, reproving, scolding.

ob'late, *adj.*, broad, flattened out at the poles of a sphere; *n.*, a secular person who has devoted himself to the service of a monastery; a member of the Order of Oblates.

obla'tion, *n.*, an offering, a sacrifice.

ob'ligate, *v.t.*, to hold (a person) to performance; to put a person under some debt of service or duty.

ob'ligated, *p.p.*, obligate.

ob'ligating, *pr.p.*, obligate.

obliga'tion, *n.*, the binding force of a vow, law or pledge; a bond; indebtedness for a favour.

ob'ligatorily, *adv.*, in a binding way.

ob'ligatory, *adj.*, compulsory, binding.

oblige', *v.t.*, to constrain, to bind; to gratify.

obliged', *p.p.*, oblige.

obligee', *n.*, one to whom a bond is executed.

obli'ger, *n.*, one who obliges.

obli'ging, *adj.*, accommodating, polite; *pr.p.*, oblige.

obli'gingly, *adv.*, courteously.

ob'ligor, *n.*, one who gives a bond (*leg.*).

oblique', *adj.*, slanting; deviating from a right line.

oblique'ly, *adv.*, slantingly, not straightforward.

obliq'uity, *n.*, the divergence from a straight line, or from the moral standard.

oblit'erate, *v.t.*, to blot out, to efface.

oblit'erated, *p.p.*, obliterate.

oblit'erating, *pr.p.*, obliterate.

oblitera'tion, *n.*, effacement, extinction.

obliv'ion, *n.*, the state of forgetfulness or of being forgotten.

obliv'ious, *adj.*, forgetful, disregarding.

obliv'iously, *adv.*, with forgetfulness.

oblivis'cence, *n.*, forgetfulness.

oblivis'cible, *adj.*, likely to be forgotten.

ob'long, *adj.*, longer than broad; *n.*, a rectangular figure longer than broad.

ob'loquy, *n.*, slander, calumnious language.

obmutes'cence, *n.*, taciturnity.

obnox'ious, *adj.*, liable; or offensive.

obnox'iously, *adv.*, offensively.

obnox'ity, *n.*, an object of aversion.

o'boe, *n.*, a wood reed instrument; an organ stop (hautboy).

o'boist, *n.*, an oboe player.

ob'olus, *n.*, an old Greek coin.

obo'vate, *adj.*, inversely ovate.

obscene', *adj.*, filthy, grossly indecent.

obscene'ly, *adv.*, in an obscene way.

obscene'ness, *n.*, filthiness.

obscen'ity, *n.*, *i.q.* obsceneness.

obscur'ant, *n.*, one who opposes enlightenment.

obscur'antism, *n.*, resistance to enlightenment.

obscur'antist, *n.*, *i.q.* obscurant.

obscura'tion, *n.*, the act of darkening.

obscure', *adj.*, dark; difficult to understand; humble; *v.t.*, to hide from view, to darken, to dim.

obscured', *p.p.*, obscure.

obscure'ly, *adv.*, dimly, darkly.

obscure'ness, *n.*, the state of being obscure.

obscur'ing, *pr.p.*, obscure.

obscu'rity, *n.*, the state of being obscure; a humble position.

obsecrate, *v.t.*, to entreat; to implore.

obsecra'tion, *n.*, a strong entreaty.

ob'sequies, *n. pl.*, funeral rites.

obse'quious, *adj.*, servilely compliant.

obse'quiously, *adv.*, in an obsequious way.

obse'quiousness, *n.*, fawning, compliance; servility.

observ'able, *adj.*, worthy to be observed, remarkable.

observ'ably, *adv.*, in a remarkable way.

observ'ance, *n.*, the act of observing; the performance of a rite, custom or rule.

observ'ant, *adj.*, attentive, regardful.

observ'antly, *adv.*, in an observant way.

observa'tion, *n.*, the act of observing; attention; a remark; a notice.

observa'tional, *adj.*, pert. to observation.

observ'atory, *n.*, a place for astronomical observations.

observe', *v.t.*, to perform a rite, duty, etc.; to mark, watch, note; to say; *v.i.*, to make a remark.

observed', *p.p.*, observe.

observ'er, *n.*, one who observes, esp. an astronomer.

observ'ing, *pr.p.*, observe.

observ'ingly, *adv.*, attentively.

obsess', *v.t.*, to haunt, to take complete possession of.

obsessed', *p.p.*, obsess.

obsess'ing, *pr.p.*, obsess.

obses'sion, *n.*, the state of being obsessed; a fixed idea; a delusion.

obsess'ionist, *n.*, one preoccupied with fixed ideas.

obsid'ian, *n.*, dark, glassy stone from lava.

obsid'ional, *adj.*, pert. to a siege.

obsoles'cence, *n.*, the state of becoming obsolete.

obsoles'cent, *adj.*, growing obsolete.

ob'solete, *adj.*, gone out of use, antiquated; less developed than formerly.

ob'stacle, *n.*, a hindrance or bar.

obstet'ric, *adj.*, rel. to midwifery.

obstetri'cian, *adj.*, one skilled in midwifery.

obstet'rics, *n. pl.*, the branch of medicine concerned with childbirth.

ob'stinacy, *n.*, stubbornness.

ob'stinate, *adj.*, stubborn, refractory.

ob'stinately, *adv.*, stubbornly.

obstrep'erous, *adj.*, noisy, unruly.

obstrep'erously, *adv.*, noisily.

obstruct', *v.t.*, to impede, to block.

obstruct'ed, *p.p.*, obstruct.

obstruct'er, *n.*, one who, or that which, obstructs.

obstruct'ing, *pr.p.*, obstruct.

obstruc'tion, *n.*, the act of obstructing; a barrier or impediment.

obstruc'tionist, *n.*, one who hinders public business.

obstruc'tive, *adj.*, hindering.

obstruc'tively, *adv.*, in an obstructive way.

ob'struent, *adj.*, i.q. obstructive; *n.*, an obstructive medicine.

obtain', *v.t.*, to get possession of; to get; *v.i.*, to prevail, to be in vogue.

obtain'able, *adj.*, able to be obtained.

obtained', *p.p.*, obtain.

obtain'er, *n.*, one who obtains.

obtain'ing, *pr.p.*, obtain.

obtain'ment, *n.*, an acquisition.

obtect, *v.t.*, to enclose or encase the pupae of certain insects.

obtest', *v.t.* and *i.*, to beseech, to adjure.

obtesta'tion, *n.*, the act of obtesting.

obtest'ed, *p.p.*, obtest.

obtest'ing, *pr.p.*, obtest.

obtrude', *v.t.*, to force upon; *v.i.*, to enter unbidden.

obtru'ded, *p.p.*, obtrude.

obtru'der, *n.*, one who obtrudes.

obtru'ding, *pr.p.*, obtrude.

obtru'sion, *n.*, the act of obtruding.

obtru'sive, *adj.*, apt to obtrude; thrusting upon the attention.

obtru'sively, *adv.*, in an obtrusive way.

obtru'siveness, *n.*, a tendency to obtrude.

obtund', *v.t.*, to blunt.

obtund'ed, *p.p.*, obtund.

obtund'ing, *pr.p.*, obtund.

ob'turator, *n.*, that which closes up.

obtuse', *adj.*, blunt in form; (of angles) greater than 90°; stupid, thickheaded.

obtuse'-angled, *adj.*, containing an obtuse angle.

obtuse'-angular, *adj.*, forming an obtuse angle.

obtuse'ly, *adv.*, in an obtuse way.

obtuse'ness, *n.*, dulness, stupidity.

obtu'sion, *n.*, the act of blunting.

obverse', *adj.*, narrower at the bottom than at the top.

ob'verse, *n.*, the side of a coin stamped with the head; the opposite.

obverse'ly, *adv.*, in a contrary way.

obver'sion, *n.*, a turning toward; the logical inference by change of quality of proposition.

obvert', *v.t.*, to turn toward; to infer (logically) by obversion.

obvert'ed, *p.p.*, obvert.

obvert'ing, *pr.p.*, obvert.

ob'viate, *v.t.*, to meet, prevent or remove; to turn aside the risk of.

ob'viated, *p.p.*, obviate.

ob'viating, *pr.p.*, obviate.

ob'vious, *adj.*, evident, palpable.

ob'viously, *adv.*, evidently, palpably.

ob'volute, *adj.*, covered over.

ocari'na, *n.*, a flute-like, musical instrument.

occa'sion, *n.*, cause, need, an opportunity, an event; *v.t.*, to cause.

occa'sional, *adj.*, occurring at one time or another.

occa'sionalism, *n.*, a philosophical doctrine of the interaction of soul and body.

occa'sionally, *adv.*, now and again.

occa'sioned, *p.p.*, occasion.

occa'sioning, *pr.p.*, occasion.

occa'sive, *adj.*, western.

oc'cident, *n.*, the western world; the west.

occiden'tal, *adj.*, pert. or rel. to the west.

occip'ital, *adj.*, pert. to the occiput.

oc'ciput, *n.*, the hinder part of the head.

occlude', *v.t.*, to close; to shut off from; to absorb (gases).

occlud'ed, *p.p.*, occlude.

occlud'ing, *pr.p.*, occlude.

occlu'sion, *n.*, the act or effect of occluding.

occult', *adj.*, secret, mysterious; *v.i.*, to cut off from view (as of navigation lights).

occulta'tion, *n.*, the act or effect of occulting.

occult'ed, *p.p.*, occult.

occult'ing, *pr.p.*, occult.

occult'ism, *n.*, esoteric teaching.

occult'ly, *adv.*, in an occult way.

occult'ness, *n.*, secrecy.

oc'cupancy, *n.*, the act of taking possession; the being in possession of.

oc'cupant, *n.*, one in possession.

occupa'tion, *n.*, business, possession.

occupa'tional, *adj.*, incident to, or arising from, an occupation.

oc'cupied, *adj.*, busy; *p.p.*, occupy.

oc'cupier, *n.*, one who occupies.

oc'cupy, *v.t.*, to take possession of; to be in possession of; to fill; to employ; to use in business (*obs.*).

oc'cupying, *pr.p.*, occupy.

occur', *v.i.*, to happen; to present itself to the mind or eye.

occurred', *p.p.*, occur.

occur'rence, *n.*, the act of occurring; something that has happened.

occur'rent, *adj.*, happening.

occur'ring, *pr.p.*, occur.

o'cean, *n.*, the great water area of the earth's surface.

oceanau'tics, *n.*, the art and science of shipping.

Ocea'nia, *n.*, the islands between S. America and S.E. Asia.

Ocea'nian, *adj.*, pert. or rel. to Oceania and its islanders.

ocean'ic, *adj.*, rel. to the ocean.

oceanog'raphist, *n.*, one who studies the science of oceanography.

oceanog'raphy, *n.,* the scientific study of the ocean.

o'ceanward, *adj.,* and *adv.,* toward the ocean.

o'cellate, *adj.,* having eye-like spots (*zool.*); having a spot of one colour surrounded by a spot of another colour (*bot.*).

o'cellated, *adj., i.q.* ocellate.

o'celot, *n.,* an American wild cat.

ochloc'racy, *n.,* mob rule.

ochra'ceous, *adj.,* ochre-coloured.

o'chre, *n.,* a clay used as a pigment.

o'chreous, *adj.,* containing ochre.

o'chry, *adj.,* like ochre.

oc'tachord, *n.,* an eight-stringed instrument.

oc'tad, *n.,* a series of eight.

oc'tagon, *n.,* a figure of eight angles and sides.

octag'onal, *adj.,* having eight angles and sides.

octahe'dral, *adj.,* with eight equal plane faces.

octahe'dron, *n.,* a solid figure with eight plane faces.

octan'dria, *n. pl.,* flowers with eight stamens.

octan'drous, *adj.,* pert. to octandria.

oc'tane, *n.,* hydrocarbon of the paraffin series.

oct'angle, *n.,* a plane figure with eight sides and angles.

octan'gular, *adj.,* having eight angles.

oc'tant, *n.,* the eighth part of a circle.

oc'tarch, *n.,* one of eight rulers in an octarchy.

oc'tarchy, *n.,* a government of eight; a country with eight governments.

oc'tastyle, *adj.,* with eight columns; *n.,* a building with eight columns. (Also *octostyle.*)

oc'tateuch, *n.,* a group of eight books.

octa'val, *adj.,* pert. to an octave.

oc'tave, *n.,* an eighth in music; the interval between a note and the eighth above or below it; these two notes sounded together; the eighth day after a feast day; the

period (inclusive) from the one day to the other; a liquid measure = one-eighth of a pipe of wine.

octav'ic, *adj.,* of the eighth degree.

octa'vo, *adj.,* with eight leaves to a sheet when folded; *n.,* a book or pamphlet with eight leaves to a sheet.

octen'nial, *adj.,* occurring every eighth year; lasting eight years.

octen'nially, *adv.,* in an octennial way.

octet(te)', *n.,* a musical piece of eight parts or voices; a group of eight verses.

octil'lion, *n.,* the eighth power of a million. (In French reckoning, it is the ninth power of a thousand.)

octingenten'ary, *n.,* an 800th anniversary.

Octo'ber, *n.,* the tenth month; ale brewed in October.

octodec'imo, *n.,* a book-size, eighteen leaves to the sheet.

octoden'tate, *adj.,* with eight teeth.

octogena'rian, *adj.,* aged eighty; *n.,* one aged eighty.

oc'tonal, *adj.,* divided into groups of eight.

oc'tonary, *n.,* a group of eight; an eight-line stanza.

octopet'alous, *adj.,* having eight petals.

oct'opod, *n.,* one of the octopoda.

Octop'oda, *n. pl.,* creatures with eight suckered arms.

oc'topus, *n.,* an octopod cuttle fish.

octoroon', *n.,* the progeny of a quadroon and a white; a person one-eighth coloured and seven-eighths white.

octosper'mous, *adj.,* eight-seeded.

oc'tostyle, *n., i.q.* octastyle.

octosyllab'ic, *adj.,* composed of eight syllables; *n.,* an eight-syllabled line.

octosyl'lable, *n.,* a word of eight syllables.

octroi', *n.,* a duty levied at the entrance to a city on trade wares; the station where the duty is levied (*Fr.*).

oc'tuple, *adj.,* eight-fold; *n.,* the product of

multiplying eight times; *v.t.,* to multiply by eight.

oc'ular, *adj.,* pert. or rel. to the eyes; *n.,* the eye-piece of an optical instrument.

oc'ularist, *n.,* a maker of artificial eyes.

oc'ularly, *adv.,* by means of the eyes.

oc'ulate, *adj.,* having eyes.

oc'ulated, *adj., i.q.* oculate.

oc'uliform, *adj.,* in the form of an eye.

oc'ulist, *n.,* an expert in eye-treatment.

od, *n.,* an assumed all-pervading force in nature. (Also *odyl.*)

o'dal, *n.,* a form of land tenure in Shetland and the Orkneys.

o'dalisque, *n.,* a female slave in a harem.

odd, *adj.,* not even in number; not matching; strange; remaining over.

Odd'fellows, *n. pl.,* members of a friendly society.

odd'ity, *n.,* the quality of being odd; a queer, eccentric person.

odd'ly, *adv.,* strangely.

odd'ment, *n.,* something over and above, or casual.

odd'ments, *n. pl.,* odds and ends.

odd'ness, *n.,* singularity.

odds, *n. pl.,* inequality; excess; advantage; variance.

ode, *n.,* a song; a poem for singing.

o'deon, *n.,* a Greek or Roman hall for musical performances; a theatre or cinema.

o'deum, *n., i.q.* odeon.

od'ic, *adj.,* rel. to od.

O'din, *n.,* the chief of the Scandinavian gods. (Also *Woden.*)

o'dious, *adj.,* hateful, detestable.

o'diously, *adv.,* hatefully.

o'dium, *n.,* hatred, unpopularity.

odom'eter, *n.,* a contrivance for measuring distance travelled.

odomet'rical, *adj.,* pert. to odometry.

odom'etry, *n.,* the measurement of distance travelled.

odontal'gia, n., toothache.

odontal'gic, adj., rel. to toothache; n., a cure for toothache.

odontal'gy, n., i.q. odontalgia.

odon'to-, a form derived from the Greek word for *tooth*, and used in combination with many English scientific words.

odontolog'ical, adj., pert. to odontology.

odontol'ogy, n., the science of dentistry.

o'dorant, adj., i.q. odorous.

odorif'erent, adj., fragrant, scented.

odorif'erous, adj., smelling, scented.

odorif'erously, adj., fragrantly.

o'dorous, adj., having an odour; fragrant.

o'dorously, adv., fragrantly.

o'dour, n., smell, scent, fragrance.

o'dourless, adj., without odour.

o'dyl, n., i.q. od.

Od'yssey, n., the great Greek epic (attributed to Homer) describing the wanderings of Odysseus.

oe'cist, n., the founder of a colony.

oecumen'ic, adj., pert. or rel. to the universal Church or Christian world.

oecumen'ical, adj., i.q. oecumenic.

oedem'a, n., swollen tissue due to fluid; local dropsy.

oedem'atous, adj., relating to oedema; swollen.

oenom'eter, n., an apparatus for testing the alcoholic strength of wine.

o''er, adv. and prep., i.q. over.

oer'sted, n., a unit of magnetic force.

oesoph'agus, n., the gullet.

oes'trogen, n., a female sex-hormone.

oes'trum, n., the sexual impulse of animals.

oes'trus, n., i.q. oestrum.

of, prep., denoting various relations of one word with another (e.g., possession, origin, cause, partition, separation, privation, etc.).

off, adj., far; adv., away, at, or to, a distance; prep., from, away from, distant from; interj., away with you!; n., the off-side at cricket.

off'al, n., food refuse, dregs.

off'chance, n., a remote chance.

offence', n., the act of offending; a cause of stumbling; a sin, a transgression; displeasure or a cause of displeasure; an assault or attack.

offence'less, adj., harmless.

offend', v.t., to cause to stumble; to transgress; to cause anger or displeasure; v.i., to stumble; to be an offender.

offend'ed, p.p., offend.

offend'er, n., one who offends.

offend'ing, pr.p., offend.

offen'sive, adj., giving offence; repulsive; aggressive; insulting; n., the military operations of attack.

offen'sively, adv., in an offensive way.

offen'siveness, n., the quality of being offensive.

of'fer, n., an expressed willingness to do or give something; a price proposed by a seller or a buyer; v.t., to present, to sacrifice; to attempt; to show for sale; v.i., to be ready; to present itself.

of'fered, p.p., offer.

of'ferer, n., one who offers.

of'fering, n., anything offered, a sacrifice or a gift; pr.p., offer.

of'fertory, n., the part of a religious service at which the oblations are made; money collected at a religious service.

off'hand, adj., unpremeditated, extempore, casual; adv., without premeditation; casually.

of'fice, n., service, duty, function, a position of trust or authority; a ritual service; a place of business; a department of Government administration.

of'fice-bearer, n., one who holds office.

of'ficer, n., one who holds any office; esp. in the navy or army; v.t., to furnish with officers; to take the command of.

of'ficered, adj., staffed; p.p., officer.

of'ficering, pr.p., officer.

off'ices, n. pl., services, duties; business premises, subsidiary apartments of a house.

offi'cial, adj., pert. to office; authoritative; n., any office-holder; an officer of the ecclesiastical courts.

offi'cialdom, n., the holding of a public office; officialism.

offi'cialese, n., official jargon.

offi'cialism, n., officeholding; red-tapeism; perfunctoriness.

offi'cially, adv., in an official capacity; by authority.

offi'ciant, n., a priest officiating.

offi'ciate, v.i., to perform an office of the Church; to act in some official capacity.

offi'ciated, p.p., officiate.

offi'ciating, pr.p., officiate.

offi'ciator, n., one who officiates.

offic'inal, adj., used in the arts and medicine; on sale at a druggist's; n., a drug prepared according to the pharmacopoeia.

offi'cious, adj., fussy, intrusive; meddlesome.

offi'ciously, adv., intrusively.

offi'ciousness, n., fussiness; informal intervention; unnecessary intrusion.

off'ing, n., the distance seaward; a position away from the shore.

offish, adj., aloof in manner (colloq.).

off-licence, n., a licence for the sale of beer, wine or spirits for consumption off the premises.

off'scourings, n. pl., anything scoured away; refuse, dregs.

off'scum, *n.*, refuse.

off'set, *v.t.*, to balance; to set over against.

off'set, *n.*, an equivalent; an off-shoot, the spur of a mountain; a line drawn from a main to a subsidiary line for the purpose of surveying; a method of printing.

off'shoot, *n.*, a branch; a side issue.

off'shore, *n.*, a short way out to sea.

off'side, *adj.* or *adv.*, on the wrong side; *n.*, the side away from the roadside in riding and driving.

off'spring, *n.*, an issue; a child.

oft, *adv.*, poetical for often.

oft'en, *adv.*, repeatedly, frequently, many times.

oft'entimes, *adv.*, *i.q.* often.

oft'times, *adv.*, *i.q.* often.

og'(h)am, *n.*, an ancient British and Irish alphabet of twenty letters, found in inscriptions.

og'doad, *n.*, the number, a set of, eight.

ogee', *adj.*, characterized by the ogee curve; *n.*, a moulding which, seen in cross section, resembles the letter S.

ogi'val, *adj.*, rel. to the ogive; descriptive of architecture in which the ogee occurs.

o'give, *n.*, a diagonal vaulting rib; a statistical curve, concave in lower numbers, convex in higher, or vice versa.

o'gle, *v.t.* and *i.*, to look amorously at; to cast a side glance; *n.*, a side glance.

o'gled, *p.p.*, ogle.

o'gler, *n.*, one who ogles.

o'gling, *pr.p.*, ogle.

o'gre, *n.*, a monster in a fairy-tale that devours human beings.

o'gress, *n.*, the fem. of ogre.

ug'rish, *adj.*, like an ogre.

Ogyg'ian, *adj.*, prehistoric.

oh, *interj.*, expressing pain, pleasure, surprise, etc.

ohm, *n.*, the unit of electrical resistance.

ohm'meter, *n.*, an instrument for measuring resistance.

oho', *interj.*, expressing astonishment.

oil, *v.t.*, to smear or anoint with oil; *n.*, a liquid, unctuous substance obtained from various sources—animal, vegetable and mineral.

oil'-bomb, *n.*, an incendiary bomb filled with inflammable oil.

oil'cake, *n.*, a cattle-food made of substances from which oil has been expressed.

oilcan, *n.*, a long-nozzled can for oiling machinery.

oil'cloth, *n.*, a cloth coated with a preparation of oil.

oil'-colour, *n.*, an oil-based paint.

oiled, *p.p.*, oil.

oil'er, *n.*, one who oils; an oiling appliance.

oil'-field, *n.*, an area producing mineral oil.

oil'-fired, *adj.*, burning oil as fuel.

oil'iness, *n.*, the state or quality of being oily.

oil'ing, *pr.p.*, oil.

oil'man, *n.*, a dealer in oils.

oil'-painting, *n.*, a painting in oil colours.

oil'-rig, *n.*, a device for oil-well drilling, esp. at sea.

oil'-shop, *n.*, a shop where oil is sold.

oil'skin, *n.*, a waterproof cloth; a garment of that material.

oil'stone, *n.*, a fine kind of stone; *v.t.*, to polish or sharpen with oilstone.

oil'-tanker, *n.*, a ship built for carrying bulk oil.

oil'-well, *n.*, a drilling into the earth for mineral oil.

oil'y, *adj.*, full of oil, smeared with oil, like oil, unctuous.

oint'ment, *n.*, any soft unctuous matter.

Oir'eachtas, *n.*, the legislature of Eire.

Ojib'way, *n.*, a Chippeway Indian.

oka'pi, *n.*, a Central African ruminant.

o'konite, *n.*, an insulating material.

ok'ra, *n.*, an edible herb.

old, *adj.*, aged; having lived or been in use a long time; antiquated; of long standing.

old'en, *adj.*, old, ancient; *v.t.* and *i.*, to make or grow feeble.

old'er, *adj.*, *comp.* of old.

old'est, *adj.*, *super.* of old.

old-fash'ioned, *adj.*, antiquated; of the mode of an older day.

old'ish, *adj.*, rather old.

old'ness, *n.*, the state of being old.

old'ster, *n.*, one approaching middle age.

old'-style, *adj.*, of an earlier mode or style.

old'-time, *adj.*, pert. or rel. to the past.

old'wife, *n.*, an old woman who babbles; a kind of duck or fish.

oleag'inous, *adj.*, oily.

olean'der, *n.*, a flowering, evergreen shrub.

oleas'ter, *n.*, the wild olive.

o'leate, *n.*, an oleic acid salt.

ole'fiant, *adj.*, oil-yielding (*chem.*).

ole'ic, *adj.*, pert. to oil.

oleif'erous, *adj.*, *i.q.* olefiant.

o'lein, *n.*, an oleaginous, liquid compound.

o'lent, *adj.*, emitting fragrance or perfume.

o'leo-, a prefix meaning *oil* or *oily*.

o'leograph, *n.*, a coloured lithograph imitating an oil painting.

oleomar'garine, *n.*, an artificial butter made of various ingredients.

oleom'eter, *n.*, an apparatus for finding the purity and density of oil.

o'leoresin, *n.*, a preparation of oil with resin.

o'leous, *adj.*, oily.

olera'ceous, *adj.*, rel. to cooking herbs.

olfac'tion, *n.*, the sense of smell; the act of smelling.

olfactom'eter, *n.*, an instrument for measuring smells, or the sense of smell.

olfac'tory, *adj.*, pert. or rel. to smelling.

olib'anum, *n.*, frankincense.

ol'id, *adj.*, foul-smelling.

ol'igarch, n., one of the members of a government by the few.

oligarch'ic, adj., rel. to oligarchy.

oligarch'ical, adj., i.q. oligarchic.

ol'igarchy, n., government by the few.

o'lio, n., a medley.

ol'itory, adj., pert. or rel. to potherbs; n., a potherb.

oliva'ceous, adj., pert. to the olive; olive-coloured.

ol'ivary, adj., oval-shaped.

ol'ive, adj., olive coloured; n., a tree producing oil.

ol'ive-branch, n., the emblem of peace.

ol'iver, n., an olive grove; a kind of hammer used in metalwork.

ol'ivine, n., a chrysolite.

ol'la, n., a cooking-pot; an earthen jar.

Olym'piad, n., the period of four years between the holding of one Olympic festival and the next. The Greeks reckoned dates in Olympiads.

Olym'pian, adj., rel. to Mt. Olympus; n., any one of the twelve chief Greek deities.

Olym'pic, adj., i.q. Olympian; also pert. to Olympia in Elis, where the Olympic games were held.

om'bre, n., a Spanish gambling game with cards.

ombrom'eter, n., a rain-gauge.

ombuds'man, n., an officer appointed by the Government to investigate certain individual complaints against public or institutional services.

o'mega, n., the long Greek O, the last letter in the Greek alphabet.

om'elet(te), n., a fritter of eggs with or without other ingredients (Fr.).

o'men, n., a sign, favourable or the reverse; a prognostication; v.t., to portend.

omen'tum, n., a fold of the peritoneum. (anat.).

o'mer, n., a Biblical measure of capacity (Heb.).

om'inous, adj., foreboding ill.

om'inously, adv., in an ominous way.

om'inousness, n., the quality of being ominous.

omis'sible, adj., that may be omitted.

omis'sion, n., the act of omitting; something omitted.

omis'sive, adj., omitting.

omit', v.t., to leave out; to pass over; to overlook.

omit'ted, p.p., omit.

omit'ting, pr.p., omit.

om'nibus, adj., all-embracing; covering many subjects; n., a large public vehicle.

omnifa'rious, adj., miscellaneous.

omnif'erous, adj., producing every variety.

omnif'ic, adj., all-creating.

om'niform, adj., assuming every form.

omniform'ity, n., the power of being omniform.

omnig'en(o)us, adj., containing all kinds.

omnipar'ity, n., equality all round.

omnip'otence, n., power without limit; almighty power.

omnip'otent, adj., possessing all power.

omnip'otently, adv., all-powerfully.

omnipres'ence, n., presence everywhere.

omnipres'ent, adj., present everywhere.

omnis'cience, n., unlimited knowledge.

omnis'cient, adj., knowing everything.

om'nium, n., the total value of the stocks of an English public loan.

omniv'ora, n. pl., omnivorous creatures.

omniv'orous, adj., eating indiscriminately; all-devouring.

omophag'ic, adj., living on raw flesh.

om'oplate, n., the shoulder-blade or scapula.

omphal'ic, adj., rel. to the navel.

om'phalism, n., the centralization.

om'phalocele, n., a rupture near the navel.

om'phalos, n., the navel (Gr.).

omphalot'omy, n., the cutting of the navel.

on, adv., forward, onward; prep., upon, at, near.

on'ager, n., a wild ass.

on'anism, n., self-abuse, masturbation.

once, adv., at a single time; formerly; ever.

oncol'ogy, n., the study of tumourous or cancerous growths.

on'coming, adj., approaching, coming on; n., an approach.

on'cost, n., overhead expenses.

oncot'omy, n., the cutting of a tumour or abscess.

on'dine, n., i.q. undine.

one, adj., single; any; a certain; n., a single unit; the figure 1; an indefinite person.

one'-eyed, adj., having only one eye.

one'-horse, adj., drawn by a single horse; insignificant.

oneirocrit'ic, adj., pert. to the power of interpreting dreams.

oneirol'ogy, n., the study of dream phenomena.

onei'romancy, n., divination by dreams.

oneiros'copy, n., the interpretation of dreams.

one'ness, n., unity; the quality of being one.

on'erous, adj., burdensome, heavy.

on'erously, adv., heavily, burdensomely.

oneself', pron., the reflexive of one; one's self.

one'sided, adj., partial; imperfect; unbalanced.

onesid'edness, n., unfairness; partiality.

one'step, adj., in one direction only; n., a form of dance.

one'-way, adj., in one direction only.

on'ion, n., an edible bulb.

on'looker, n., a spectator.

on'looking, adj., in the position of a spectator.

on'ly, adj., alone, single; adv., singly, alone, merely.

onol'atry, *n.*, ass-worship.

on'omancy, *n.*, divination by means of names.

onomas'tic, *adj.*, pert. to a name.

onomas'ticon, *n.*, a dictionary (of names especially).

onomatol'ogy, *n.*, the study of names; nomenclature.

on'omatop, *n.*, an onomatopoeic word.

onomatopoe'ia, *n.*, the representation of natural sounds by words which imitate them.

onomatopoe'ic, *adj.*, pert. or rel. to onomatopoeia.

on'rush, *n.*, *i.q.* onset.

on'set, *n.*, a dash forward, an attack.

on'slaught, *n.*, a murderous onset.

ontolog'ical, *adj.*, rel. to ontology; metaphysical.

ontol'ogism,*n.*,a theological doctrine attributing to the human mind an immediate consciousness of the Deity.

ontol'ogist, *n.*, one learned in ontology.

ontol'ogy, *n.*, the science of being.

o'nus, *n.*, a burden, a responsibility (*Lat.*).

on'ward, *adj.*, progressive, advancing; *adv.*, forward, ahead. (Also *onwards.*)

on'wards, *adv.*, *i.q.* onward.

on'ymous, *adj.*, not anonymous; having a name.

on'yx, *n.*, a quartz stone, much used for cameos.

o'o-, o-, a prefix to many compound words; it means *egg.*

oo'dle, *n.*, a super-abundance (*colloq.*).

oof', *n.*, money, cash (*slang*).

o'olite, *n.*, a variety of limestone.

oolit'ic, *adj.*, of oolite; pert. or rel. to oolite.

oolog'ical, *adj.*, pert. to oology.

ool'ogist, *n.*, one who makes a study of birds' eggs.

ool'ogy, *n.*, the study of birds' eggs and nidification.

oo'long, *n.*, a kind of Chinese tea.

oom, *n.*, uncle.

Oo'pak, *n.*, a black tea.

ooze, *v.i.* and *t.*, to flow or distil gently *n.*, soft mud.

oozed, *p.p.*, ooze.

oo'zing, *pr.p.*, ooze.

oo'zy, *adj.*, spongy and wet.

opac'ity, *n.*, the quality of being opaque.

o'pah, *n.*, a brightly coloured fish.

o'pal, *n.*, a precious stone.

opalesce', *v.i.*, to be iridescent like the opal.

opales'cence, *n.*, the iridescence of an opal.

opales'cent, *adj.*, iridescent like the opal.

o'paline, *adj.*, pert. or rel. to the opal; *n.*, a variety of glass or porcelain.

o'palize, *v.t.*, to change to opal.

o'palized, *p.p.*, opalize.

o'palizing, *pr.p.*, opalize.

opaque', *adj.*, not transparent; resisting the passage of light.

ope, poetical for *open.*

o'pen, *adj.*, unshut, free, frank, accessible; *n.*, any unenclosed area; *v.t.* and *i.*, to unclose, to expand, to unfold.

open-air', *adj.*, out of doors.

op'en'cast, *n.*, surface excavation.

o'pened, *p.p.*, open.

o'pener, *n.*, anything that opens.

op'en'-eyed', *adj.*, alert, with eyes open; vigilant.

o'pen-handed, *adj.*, generous, liberal.

o'pen-hearted, *adj.*, frank, sincere.

o'pening, *n.*, the act of opening; a hole, an aperture, a breach; a beginning; an opportunity; *pr.p.*, open.

o'penly, *adv.*, in an open way; publicly.

o'pen-mouthed, *adj.*, eagerly expecting; gaping with surprise.

o'penness, *n.*, the quality of being open.

o'pen-work, *n.*, work with openings in it.

op'era, *n.*, a musical drama.

op'erable, *adj.*, allowing operation.

op'era bouffe, *n.*, comic opera.

operam'eter, *n.*, a speed-indicator.

op'erant, *adj.*, acting, effective.

op'erate, *v.t.*, to make active, to set working; *v.i.*, to work, to act; to perform a surgical operation.

op'erated, *p.p.*, operate.

operat'ic, *adj.*, pert. or rel. to opera.

operat'ically, *adv.*, in the manner of an opera.

op'erating, *pr.p.*, operate.

opera'tion, *n.*, the process of operating; action; agency; a surgeon's act with the knife or other instrument.

opera'tional, *adj.*, pert. or rel. to operations; ready for action.

opera'tionally, *adv.*, in an operational way.

opera'tions, *n. pl.*, military or naval movements.

op'erative, *adj.*, active, effective;*n.*, an artisan.

operatively, *adv.*, in an operative way.

op'eratize, *v.t.*, to put into operatic form.

op'erator, *n.*, one who operates in any sense.

oper'cular, *adj.*, having, or forming, a lid.

oper'culate, *adj.*, having a lid.

oper'culated, *adj.*, *i.q.* operculate.

oper'culum, *n.*, a small cover, a little lid (*Lat.*).

operet'ta, *n.*, a short, light opera, usually of one act.

op'erose, *adj.*, laborious.

oph'icleide, *n.*, a large, brass instrument (*mus.*).

ophid'ian, *adj.*, rel. to snakes.

ophiol'ogist, *n.*, a student of ophiology.

ophiol'ogy, *n.*, the study of snakes and serpents.

oph'ite, *n.*, serpentine, serpentine marble.

Ophiu'chus, *n.*, the snake-bearer constellation.

ophthal'mia, *n.*, inflammation of the eye.

ophthal'mic, *adj.*, pert. or rel. to the eye.

ophthalmolo'gist, *n.*, an eye specialist.

ophthal'moscope, *n.*, an instrument used in examining the eye.

o'piate, *adj.*, containing opium; narcotic; *n.*, a narcotic; *v.t.*, to drug, to narcotize.

opine', *v.t.* and *i.*, to think; to hold an opinion.

opined', *p.p.*, opine.

opi'ning, *pr.p.*, opine.

opin'ion, *n.*, mental judgment; a notion; a conjecture; judicial decision.

opin'ionated, *adj.*, fond of expressing an opinion; conceited.

opin'ionative, *adj.*, *i.q.* opinionated.

opisom'eter, *n.*, an instrument for measuring the length of irregular lines.

opis'thograph, *n.*, a writing on both sides of a leaf or a slab.

o'pium, *n.*, the inspissated juice of the poppy.

o'pium-eater, *n.*, one who habitually consumes opium.

opodel'doc, *n.*, a saponaceous, camphorated liniment.

opop'anax, *n.*, a gum resin; a herb.

opos'sum, *n.*, an American quadruped.

op'pidan, *adj.*, pert. or rel. to a town; *n.*, an Eton boy who is not a foundationer.

opp'ilate, *v.t.*, to block-up, to obstruct (*med.*).

oppo'nency, *n.*, the position of an opponent in an academic dispute.

oppo'nent, *adj.*, opposing, opposite; *n.*, one who opposes; an antagonist.

opportune', *adj.*, timely, well-seasoned, fitting.

opportune'ly, *adv.*, at a fitting moment.

opportune'ness, *n.*, the quality of being opportune.

opportu'nism, *n.*, a readiness to take advantage of the moment, often at the cost of consistency and principle.

opportu'nist, *n.*, one who practises opportunism.

opportu'nity, *n.*, a seasonable moment; a favourable chance.

oppo'sable, *adj.*, able to be opposed.

oppose', *v.t.*, to resist, to withstand, to dispute; to set up in opposition; *v.i.*, to offer resistance.

opposed', *p.p.*, oppose.

oppose'less, *adj.*, irresistible.

oppo'ser, *n.*, one who opposes.

oppo'sing, *pr.p.*, oppose.

op'posite, *adj.*, facing, confronting, contrary to, antagonistic.

op'positely, *adv.*, adversely.

opposi'tion, *n.*, the act of opposing; an obstacle; the political groups opposed to the Government.

opposi'tionist, *n.*, one belonging to the opposition.

oppos'itive, *adj.*, contrasting.

oppress', *v.t.*, to burden, to press down, to harass, to tyrannize over.

oppressed', *p.p.*, oppress.

oppress'ing, *pr.p.*, oppress.

oppres'sion, *n.*, the act of oppressing; tyranny; a languid feeling.

oppress'ive, *adj.*, causing oppression; tyrannical; overpowering.

oppress'ively, *adv.*, in an oppressive way.

oppres'siveness, *n.*, the state of being oppressive.

oppress'or, *n.*, a tyrant.

oppro'brious, *adj.*, contumelious; contemptuously abusive.

oppro'briously, *adv.*, with opprobrium.

oppro'brium, *n.*, contemptuous abuse; infamy.

oppugn', *v.t.*, to contradict, to attack, to conflict with.

oppug'nancy, *n.*, opposition.

oppug'nant, *adj.*, opposing.

oppugned', *p.p.*, oppugn.

oppugn'er, *n.*, one who oppugns.

oppugn'ing, *pr.p.*, oppugn.

op'simath, *n.*, one who learns late in life.

opsiom'eter, *n.*, *i.q.* optometer.

opson'ic, *adj.*, pert. or rel. to opsonin.

op'sonin, *n.*, the injection of dead bacteria cultures of a disease, to give immunization against it.

opt', *v.i.*, to choose.

opt'ant, *n.*, one who opts.

op'tative, *adj.*, pert. or rel. to wishing; *n.*, the optative or wishing mood.

opta'tively, *adv.*, in an optative way.

op'ted, *p.p.*, opt.

op'tic, *adj.*, rel. to the eye and vision; *n.*, an eye.

op'tical, *adj.*, *i.q.* optic.

op'tically, *adv.*, in an optic way.

opti'cian, *n.*, a maker of optical instruments or glasses.

op'tics, *n. pl.*, the science of the nature and laws of vision.

op'tigraph, *n.*, an apparatus for copying a landscape.

op'timacy, *n.*, aristocracy.

optima'tes, *n. pl.*, the upper classes.

op'time, *adv.*, in high degree (a university term).

op'timism, *n.*, a tendency to look always at the bright side of things; the belief that everything is for the best.

op'timist, *n.*, one who practises optimism.

optimis'tic, *adj.*, practising optimism.

optimis'tically, *adv.*, in an optimistic way.

op'timize, *v.t.*, to reckon as best; to make the best of; *v.i.*, to be an optimist.

op'timum, *n.*, the most favourable conditions; the best (*Lat.*).

op'ting, *pr.p.*, opt.

op'tion, *n.*, choice; the liberty to choose.

op'tional, *adj.*, at one's discretion; left to choice.

op'tionally, *adv.*, in an optional way.

optom'eter, *n.*, an apparatus for measuring the eye's focal range.

op'tophone, n., an instrument converting light into sound.

op'ulence, n., wealth, abundance, luxuriance.

op'ulent, adj., wealthy, rich.

op'ulently, adv., richly.

op'us, n., a work or composition (Lat.).

opus'cule, n., a trifling musical or literary work

opus'culum, n., i.q. opuscule (Lat.).

or, prep. and conj., before, ere; conj., uniting alternatives, as "this or that"; otherwise, else; n., in heraldry, it represents the Fr. or = gold.

o'rach(e), n., wild plants of the goosefoot family.

or'acle, n., a sacred place from which a deity was said to deliver prophetic utterances; a prophecy so delivered; any solemn communication; an unusually wise person.

orac'ular, adj., pert. to, or resembling, an oracle.

orac'ularly, adv., in an oracular way.

ora'culum, n., i.q. oracle (Lat.).

o'ral, adj., pert. to the mouth; verbal (Lat.).

o'rally, adv., verbally, by word of mouth.

or'ange, adj., of the colour of an orange; bel. to the Orange political society; n., the tree and fruit of the Citrus genus.

orangeade', n., a pleasant drink made from oranges.

or'ange-bloss'om, n., white flowers of the orange, often worn by brides.

Or'angeism, n., the principles of the Orange Society, named after William of Orange (Ir.).

Or'angeman, n., a member of the Orange political party (Ir.).

or'angery, n., a garden or greenhouse containing orange trees.

orang'-outang', n., a large ape with long reddish-brown hair.

orate, v.i., to make a speech; to harangue.

ora'tion, n., a speech, a harangue; a formal public address to a large audience.

or'ator, n., an eloquent speaker.

orato'rial, adj., rel. to oratory.

orator'ical, adj., in the manner of oratory.

orator'ically, adv., in the manner of an orator.

orato'rio, n., a quasi-dramatic religious cantata.

or'atory, n., the art of speaking; rhetoric; a small church or chapel, esp. in a house.

orb, n., once a circular disc, now a sphere; an eyeball; one of the regalia—a sphere surmounted by a cross; v.t., to gather into an orb.

or'bate, adj., fatherless.

orbed, p.p., orb.

or'bic, adj., circular.

or'bical, adj., i.q. orbic.

orbic'ular, adj., circular, spherical.

orbic'ulate, adj., i.q. orbicular.

orb'ing, pr.p., orb.

or'bit, n., an eye socket; the course described by one body in space round another.

or'bital, adj., pert. or rel. to an orbit.

orc, n., a variety of sea monster.

Orca'dian, adj., pert. or rel. to the Orkneys; n., a native of the O.

or'chard, n., an enclosure for fruit-growing trees.

or'charding, n., the care of an orchard.

or'chardist, n., one who cultivates an orchard.

orche'sis, n., the art of dancing.

orches'tic, adj., pert. or rel. to orchesis.

or'chestra, n., a combination of instrumental players; the platform on which they play; originally, the semicircular area in front of a Greek stage.

orches'tral, adj., pert. or rel. to an orchestra; set for a number of instruments.

or'chestrate, v.t. and i., to compose, to arrange, to score for an orchestra.

or'chestrated, p.p., orchestrate.

or'chestrating, pr.p., orchestrate.

orchestra'tion, n., the art of composing for, or adapting to, an orchestra; instrumentation.

orchestra'tor, n., a composer or arranger of orchestral music.

orchestri'na, n., a kind of barrel-organ.

or'chid, n., a perennial, herbaceous plant with tuberous roots.

orchida'ceous, adj., pert. or rel. to the orchis.

orch'idist, n., an expert grower of orchids.

or'chil, n., a red or purple dyestuff derived from a lichen.

Or'chis, n., the name given to a genus of plants bel. to the orchid family.

orchi'tis, n., inflammation of the testicles.

or'cin, n., a substance obtained from lichen and used for dyeing.

ordain, v.t., to appoint, to destine; to command; to admit to Holy Orders.

ordained', p.p., ordain.

ordain'er, n., one who ordains.

ordain'ing, pr.p., ordain.

or'deal, n., a severe trial, as by fire, water, etc.; any trying experience.

or'der, v.t., to put in order; to draw up in array; to regulate; to command; n., a systematic arrangement; an array; rank; class; sequence; a command; a fraternity or community under one rule; a type of architecture, as the Corinthian Order, etc.

or'dered, p.p., order.

or'derer, n., one who orders.

or'dering, pr.p., order.

or'derliness, n., the quality of being orderly; tidiness; method·

or'derly, adj., methodical, tidy, well regulated; rel. to the carrying out or execution of military orders; n., a soldier whose duty it is to carry orders.

or'ders, n. pl., clerical grades in the Christian ministry.

ordinaire', *n.*, ordinary wine; a common person (*Fr.*).

or'dinal, *n.*, a numeral marking order or succession, as fifth, seventh, etc.; a pontifical containing the Ordination rites; a book of directions for saying Mass.

or'dinance, *n.*, an authoritative order, a decree; a sacred rite.

or'dinand, *n.*, one selected for Holy Orders.

or'dinant, *n.*, an ordaining bishop.

or'dinarily, *adv.*, usually.

or'dinary, *adj.*, usual, customary, without rank; commonplace; *n.*, a bishop or his deputy in a judicial capacity; in heraldry, any of the common charges; a table d'hôte.

or'dinate, *adj.*, regular; *n.*, one of two elements defining the position of a point in a plane.

ordina'tion, *n.*, the act of ordaining; that which is ordained; an arrangement.

ordinee', *n.*, a newly ordained deacon.

ord'nance, *n.*, cannon; the department concerned with military stores and equipments.

or'donnance, *n.*, correct arrangement; an ordinance (*Fr.*).

or'dure, *n.*, excrement, filth.

ore, *n.*, a metal-bearing, mineral substance.

or'ead, *n.*, a mountain nymph.

orec'tic, *adj.*, appetitive.

orfe, *n.*, a goldfish species.

or'gan, *n.*, an instrument of action or motion; a means of expressing opinion, as in a newspaper, review, etc.; a musical wind instrument containing pipes of various kinds— flue and reed.

org'andie, *n.*, a stiff kind of muslin.

organ'ic, *adj.*, pert. or rel. to the bodily organs; having organs (as distinguished from inorganic); systematized; containing carbon; having life.

organ'ical, *adj.*, *i.q.* organic.

organ'ically, *adv.*, in an organic way.

organ'icism, *n.*, the conception that everything in nature has an organic basis.

or'ganism, *n.*, an organic structure; any living entity.

or'ganist, *n.*, an organplayer.

or'ganizable, *adj.*, able to be organized.

organiza'tion, *n.*, the act or result of organizing; an organized system.

or'ganize, *v.t.* and *i.*, to form with organs, to make organic; to put into order, to make arrangements for; to unite in a body or force; to arrange for a purpose with system and method.

or'ganized, *p.p*, organize

or'ganizer, *n.*, one who organizes.

or'ganizing, *pr.p.*, organize.

organog'raphist, *n.*, an expert in organography.

organog'raphy, *n.*, the description of organs.

organol'ogy, *n.*, the study of organs and structures.

or'ganon, *n.*, *i.q.* organum (*Gr.*).

org'anothe'rapy, *n.*, medical treatment by organic extracts.

or'ganum, *n.*, an instrument of thought; a system of logic (*Lat.*).

or'ganzine, *n.*, a variety of silk thread; the material made from it.

or'gasm, *n.*, violent excitement; the climax of sexual arousal.

or'geat, *n.*, a drink made of barley or almonds and flavoured with orange water.

orgias'tic, *adj.*, rel. to an orgy.

or'gies, *n.*, the pl. of orgy.

orguinette', *n.*, a reed organ played through perforated paper.

or'gy, *n.*, a revel, a debauch; any social occasion when normal restraints and values are discarded.

o'riel, *n.*, a projecting, overhanging window or recess.

or'ielled, *adj.*, built with oriels.

o'rient, *adj.*, eastern, oriental; rising; *n.*, the East; the Eastern world.

orien'tal, *adj.*, eastern.

orien'talism, *n.*, the characteristics of the Eastern world; the study of Eastern matters.

orien'talist, *n.*, one learned in Eastern matters.

orien'talize, *v.t.*, to make oriental.

orien'tate, *v.t.*, to set pointing eastward; *reflex.*, to determine one's position in regard to surroundings or circumstances.

orienta'ted, *p.p.*, orientate.

orienta'ting, *pr.p.*, orientate.

orienta'tion, *n.*, the eastward lie of the axis of a building; the situation in regard to the points of the compass; the act of discovering, direction; a determination of one's position in regard to opinions, beliefs, etc.

or'ifice, *n.*, an opening, a vent.

orifi'cial, *adj.*, rel. to an orifice.

or'iflamme, *n.*, the banner of St. Denis of France; the French royal ensign; any splendid symbol.

or'igan, *n.*, *i.q.* origanum.

orig'anum, *n.*, the wild marjoram.

Or'igenism, *n.*, the doctrines of Origen of Alexandria.

Or'igenist, *n.*, a disciple of Origen.

or'igin, *n.*, the source, the beginning, the extraction.

orig'inal, *adj.*, first, primitive, novel; *n.*, a model or pattern; the first example of anything; an independent thinker.

original'ity, *n.*, the quality of being original; inventiveness.

orig'inally, *adv.*, at first, in the beginning.

orig'inate, *v.t.*, to initiate; *v.i.*, to have origin.

orig'inated, *p.p.*, originate.

orig'inating, *pr.p.*, originate.

origina'tion, *n.*, the act of originating; a beginning.

orig'inative, *adj.*, initiative; causing a beginning.

orig'inator, *n.*, one who originates.

orinas'al, *adj.*, sounded with mouth and nose; *n.*, a nasal-sounded word.

o'riole, *n.*, the golden thrush.

Ori'on, *n.*, a brilliant constellation of seven conspicuous stars.

ori'onid, *n.*, one of the meteor-system, with the radiant point in the Orion (*astron.*).

or'ison, *n.*, a prayer.

orle, *n.*, a bearing; a bordure (*her.*).

or'lide, *n.*, imitation gold.

or'lop, *n.*, a ship's lower deck.

orm'er, *n.*, the ear-shell.

or'molu, *n.*, brass or copper gilt; an alloy of copper, zinc and tin; ormolu ware.

or'nament, *n.*, a decoration, an adornment; *v.t.*, to adorn, to decorate, to beautify.

ornamen'tal, *adj.*, of the nature of an ornament.

ornament'ally, *adv.*, in an ornamental way.

ornamenta'tion, *n.*, adornment.

or'namented, *p.p.*, ornament.

or'namenting, *pr.p.*, ornament.

ornate', *adj.*, splendid, highly ornamented.

ornate'ly, *adv.*, in ornate fashion.

ornate'ness, *n.*, the state of being ornate.

ornith'olite, *n.*, a bird-fossil.

ornithol'ogist, *n.*, one who makes a study of birds.

ornithol'ogy, *n.*, the study of birds.

orni'thomancy, *n.*, divination by the flight of birds.

ornithop'ter, *n.*, an aeroplane with flapping wings; a species of butterfly.

ornithorhyn'cus, *n.*, the duck-billed platypus of Australia.

orogen'esis, *n.*, the process of making mountains.

orog'eny, *n.*, the formation of mountains.

orog'raphy, *n.*, that department of geography which deals with mountains.

o'rohip'pus, *n.*, a fossilized form of ancestral horse.

or'oide, *n.*, an alloy of copper and zinc.

orol'ogy, *n.*, the study of mountains.

orom'eter, *n.*, an instrument for measuring mountain heights.

orom'etry, *n.*, the measurement of reliefs.

orope'sa, *n.*, a mine-sweeping device.

o'rotund, *adj.*, resonant, full.

or'phan, *adj.*, bereft of parents; *n.*, a person bereft of parents; *v.t.*, to bereave of parents.

or'phanage, *n.*, a home for orphans.

or'phaned, *p.p.*, orphan.

or'phaning, *pr.p.*, orphan.

Orphe'an, *adj.*, rel. or pert. to Orpheus; melodious.

Or'phic, *adj.*, pert. to Orpheus and the Orphic mystical sect; mysterious.

or'phrey, *n.*, the embroidered border on an ecclesiastical vestment, etc.

or'piment, *n.*, a yellow, mineral dye.

or'pin(e), *n.*, a variety of stonecrop.

Orp'ington, *n.*, a breed of poultry.

o'rra, *adj.*, odd, not matched, occasional (*Scot.*).

or'rery, *n.*, a mechanical apparatus showing the motions of planets.

or'ris, *n.*, a variety of the Iris; a gold and silver lace.

or'tanique, *n.*, a cross between an orange and a tangerine.

orthocaine', *n.*, a white, crystalline, local anaesthetic.

orthochromat'ic, *adj.*, reproducing true colour values.

orthodon'tic, *adj.*, in need of dental correction.

orthodon'tics, *n.*, the correction of teeth irregularities.

or'thodox, *adj.*, holding an accepted belief.

or'thodoxy, *n.*, a soundness in belief and doctrine.

orthodrom'ic, *adj.*, pert. to orthodromy.

orthod'romy, *n.*, sailing in a great circle.

orthoep'ic, *adj.*, pronouncing correctly.

orthoep'ical, *adj.*, *i.q.* orthoepic.

or'thoepist, *n.*, one who is skilled in pronunciation.

or'thoepy, *n.*, the art of correct pronunciation.

orthog'rapher, *n.*, one who has studied spelling.

orthograph'ic, *adj.*, pert. to the right spelling; rightly spelt.

orthograph'ical, *adj.*, *i.q.* orthographic.

orthog'raphist, *n.*, *i.q.* orthographer.

orthog'raphy, *n.*, correct spelling; the study of correct spelling; correct perspective or architectural drawing.

orthomet'ric, *adj.*, rel. to orthometry.

orthom'etry, *n.*, correct versification.

ortho'mor'phic, *adj.*, pert. or rel. to a map projection in which small areas retain correct shape and distances.

orthopae'dic, *adj.*, rel. to orthopaedy.

or'thopaedy, *n.*, the correction of physical deformities and irregularities.

orthop'ter, *n.*, one of the Orthoptera.

Orthop'tera, *n. pl.*, straight-winged creatures.

orthop'teran, *adj.*, pert. or rel. to Orthoptera.

orthop'terous, *adj.*, *i.q.* orthopteran.

or'tive, *adj.*, rising.

or'tolan, *n.*, the garden bunting esteemed as a table delicacy.

orts, *n. pl.*, refuse, scraps.

oryctog'raphy, *n.*, the description of fossils.

oryctol'ogy, *n.*, the study of fossils.

O'ryx, *n.*, the genus of the large, African antelope.

Os'car, *n.*, a special Motion Picture Academy award for the best acting or directing.

os'cheocele, *n.*, scrotal dropsy.

os'cillate, *v.t.* and *i.*, to sway to and fro; to vibrate.

os'cillated, *p.p.*, oscillate.

os'cillating, *pr.p.*, oscillate.

oscilla'tion, *n.*, a swaying to and fro.

os'cillatory, *adj.*, swinging like a pendulum.

os'cillograph, *n.*, the apparatus for recording oscillations.

os'cillom'eter, *n.*, an instrument for measuring the roll of a ship, or to measure oscillations of blood pressure.

os'citancy, *n.*, a tendency to yawning.

os'citant, *adj.*, yawning.

oscita'tion, *n.*, the act of yawning; negligence.

os'culant, *adj.*, kissing; clinging closely together; adherent.

os'cular, *adj.*, rel. to kissing; of the mouth.

os'culate, *v.t.* and *i.*, to kiss; to touch closely; to have closely resembling characters.

os'culated, *p.p.*, osculate.

os'culating, *pr.p.*, osculate.

oscula'tion, *n.*, kissing; contact.

os'culatory, *adj.*, kissing.

os'cule, *n.*, a vent.

o'sier, *adj.*, made from osier; *n.*, a kind of willow used in basketwork.

o'siered, *adj.*, abounding in osiers.

Osi'ris, *n.*, an Egyptian god.

os'mic, *adj.*, rel. to osmium.

os'mium, *n.*, a metallic element having the highest density.

osmom'eter, *n.*, an apparatus for gauging the power of smell.

os'mose, *n.*, the mixture of liquids percolating through membranes.

osmos'is, *n.*, *i.q.* osmose.

osmot'ic, *adj.*, pert. or rel. to osmose.

os'munda, *n.*, a flowering fern.

Osmun'da, *n.*, a genus of ferns.

os'prey, *n.*, a bird of prey. (Also *ossifrage*.)

os'seous, *adj.*, bony, ossified.

Ossian'ic, *adj.*, rel. to Ossian, the Gaelic poet.

os'sicle, *n.*, a small bone, or piece of bone.

ossif'erous, *adj.*, containing bone.

ossif'ic, *adj.*, bonemaking.

ossifica'tion, *n.*, the process of turning into bone.

os'sified, *p.p.*, ossify.

os'sifrage, *n.*, *i.q.* osprey.

os'sify, *v.t.* and *i.*, to change into bone.

os'sifying, *pr.p.*, ossify.

ossiv'orous, *adj.*, boneeating.

os'suary, *n.*, a bone-urn; a charnel house.

ostensibil'ity, *n.*, the quality of being ostensible.

osten'sible, *adj.*, not real but pretended; seeming.

osten'sibly, *adv.*, seemingly.

osten'sive, *adj.*, showing.

osten'sively, *adv.*, apparently.

osten'sory, *n.*, a monstrance.

ostenta'tion, *n.*, display, vanity.

ostenta'tious, *adj.*, pretentious; vulgarly displaying.

ostenta'tiously, *adv.*, in an ostentatious way.

osteo'arthrit'is, *n.*, a form of arthritis in a bone or joint.

os'teocele, *n.*, a form of hernia.

osteog'raphy, *n.*, a scientific description of the bones.

osteol'oger, *n.*, *i.q.* osteologist.

osteol'ogist, *n.*, one skilled in bone-anatomy.

osteol'ogy, *n.*, the science of bone-anatomy.

osteomyelit'is, *n.*, inflammation of bone marrow.

os'teopath, *n.*, one who practises osteopathy.

osteop'athy, *n.*, manipulative surgery.

os'teophone, *n.*, an instrument helping the deaf to hear.

osteot'omy, *n.*, the dissection or dividing of a bone.

ostia'rius, *n.*, a doorkeeper.

os'tiary, *n.*, *i.q.* ostiarius.

os'tler, *n.*, a man in charge of horses and stables. (Also *hostler*.)

os'tracism, *n.*, the act of ostracizing.

os'tracize, *v.t.*, to banish by vote; to exclude from society.

os'tracized, *p.p.*, ostracize.

os'tracizing, *pr.p.*, ostracize.

os'treiculture, *n.*, the artificial breeding of oysters.

os'trich, *n.*, a large, flightless bird, once valued for its feathers.

Os'trogoth, *n.*, one of the Eastern Goths who invaded Italy in the fifth century.

otacous'tic, *adj.*, aiding the hearing; *n.*, an ear-trumpet.

otal'gia, *n.*, earache.

otal'gic, *adj.*, pert. or rel. to otalgia.

otal'gy, *n.*, *i.q.* otalgia.

oth'er, *adj.*, *adv.*, *pron.*, not the same; different.

o'therness, *n.*, the quality of being distinct from; the things known to common experience.

oth'erwise, *adv.*, else, differently.

otherworld'liness, *n.*, the character of living as for the future life.

ot'ic, *adj.*, rel. to the ear.

o'tiose, *adj.*, idle, futile; with no practical purpose.

oti'tis, *n.*, inflammation of the ear.

otograph'ic, *adj.*, pert. or rel. to otography.

otog'raphy, *n.*, the scientific description of the ear.

otol'ogy, *n.*, the science of the ear.

otop'athy, *n.*, a pathological condition of the ear.

o'toscope, *n.*, an instrument for examining the ear.

otot'omy, *n.*, dissection of the ear.

ot'ter, *n.*, an aquatic mammal.

ot'to, *n.*, *i.q.* attar.

ot'toman, *n.*, a cushioned seat.

Ot'toman, *adj.,* pert. or rel. to Turkey; *n.,* a Turk.

oubliette', *n.,* a secret dungeon (*Fr.*).

ouch, *n.,* the setting of a gem; a clasp; *interj.,* expressing pain.

ought, *aux. v.,* to be bound to do or be.

ouija, *n.,* a lettered board used in spiritualism.

ounce, *n.,* a unit of weight; a lynx.

our, *adj. possess.,* bel. to us.

ouranog'raphy, *n.,* the scientific description of the sky.

ourol'ogy, *n., i.q.* urology.

ouros'copy, *n., i.q.* uroscopy.

ours, *pron., possess.* and *adj.,* bel. to us.

ourself', *reflex. pron.,* we ourselves.

ourselves', *reflex. pron.,* we or us in particular; not others.

oust, *v.t.,* to push aside, to eject.

oust'ed, *p.p.,* oust.

oust'er, *n.,* one who ousts.

oust'ing, *pr.p.,* oust.

out, *adj.,* away from home; *adv.,* the opposite to in; *n.,* in the pl., the Outs = the party not in office; *v.t.,* to turn out; *v.i.,* to come out.

outbal'ance, *v.t.,* to outweigh.

outbid, *v.t.,* to make a larger bid than.

outblown', *adj.,* inflated.

out'board, *adj.,* outside a boat or ship.

outbound', *adj.,* outward bound.

out'break, *n.,* an outburst.

out'build'ing, *n.,* an outside building; an outhouse.

out'burst, *n.,* a violent outbreak.

out'cast, *adj.,* forlorn; ejected from society; *n.,* one who is cast out.

outclass', *v.t.,* to surpass in quality or skill.

outclassed', *adj.,* completely surpassed in skill or quality; *p.p.,* outclass.

outclass'ing, *pr.p.,* outclass.

out'come, *n.,* a result; an issue.

out'crop, *n.,* appearance above ground; an exposed rock.

out'cry, *n.,* a loud cry; an auction; an expression of public disapproval.

out'date', *v.t.,* to put out of date.

out'dated', *adj.,* out of date; *p.p.,* outdate.

out'dat'ing, *pr.p.,* outdate.

outdo', *v.t.,* to surpass, to excel.

outdo'ing, *pr.p.,* outdo.

outdone', *p.p.,* outdo.

out'door, *adj.,* in the open air.

outdoors', *adv., i.q.* outdoor.

out'ed, *p.p.,* out.

out'er, *adj.,* external; away from the inside.

out'ermost, *adj.,* furthest outward; on the extreme part.

outface', *v.t.,* to stare out of countenance; to defy.

outfaced', *p.p.,* outface.

outfa'cing, *pr.p.,* outface.

out'fall, *n.,* a river or sewer outlet.

out'fit, *n.,* complete gear for a purpose; complete clothing.

out'fitter, *n.,* one who supplies outfit.

outflank', *v.t.,* to cut off on the flank.

outflanked', *p.p.,* outflank.

outflank'ing, *pr.p.,* outflank.

outgen'eral, *v.t.,* to surpass in generalship.

outgo', *v.t.,* to surpass.

out'going, *adj.,* going outward; *n.,* the act of going out; *pr.p.,* outgo.

out'goings, *n. pl.,* expenditure.

outgrow', *v.t.,* to surpass in growth; to become too large or old for.

outgrow'ing, *pr.p.,* outgrow.

outgrown', *p.p.,* outgrow.

out'growth, *n.,* that which grows out from something.

out'house, *n.,* a detached building bel. to a larger building.

out'ing, *n.,* a holiday jaunt; an airing; *pr.p.,* out.

out'lander, *n.,* a foreigner.

outland'ish, *adj.,* foreign; barbarous.

outlast', *v.t.,* to survive.

outlast'ed, *p.p.,* outlast.

outlast'ing, *pr.p.,* outlast.

out'law, *n.,* a felon; a person proscribed; *v.t.,* to deny the protection of the law.

out'lawed, *p.p.,* outlaw.

out'lawing, *pr.p.,* outlaw.

out'lawry, *n.,* the state of being an outlaw.

out'lay, *n.,* expenditure, disbursement.

out'let, *n.,* a passage outward, an exit.

outlie', *v.t.,* to surpass in lying; *v.i.,* to encamp under canvas.

out'lier, *n.,* something external to the main body.

out'line, *n.,* a sketch, rough plan or contour; *v.t.,* to sketch; to draw in outline.

outlined, *p.p.,* outline.

out'lining, *n.,* sketching; *pr.p.,* outline.

outlive', *v.t.,* to live longer than.

outlived', *p.p.,* outlive.

outliv'ing, *pr.p.,* outlive.

out'look, *n.,* a prospect; a view.

out'lying, *adj.,* situated apart; distant; *pr.p.,* outlie.

out'mod'ed, *adj.,* out of fashion.

out'most, *adj.,* outermost.

outnum'ber, *v.t.,* to be greater in number than.

outnum'bered, *p.p.,* outnumber.

outnum'bering, *pr.p.,* outnumber.

out-of-date, *adj.* and *adv.,* antiquated; behind the times.

out-of-doors', *adj.* and *adv.,* in the open air.

outpatient, *n.,* a hospital patient who is not an inmate.

out'point', *v.t.,* to defeat on points.

out'post, *n.,* an advanced or detached position.

out'pour, *n.,* an outpouring; *v.t.* and *i.,* to pour out.

out'pouring, *n.,* a flowing out; *pr.p.,* outpour.

out′put, *n.*, the quantity put out or produced.

out′rage, *n.*, violence, an insult; *v.t.*, to insult; to do violence to.

out′raged, *p.p.*, outrage.

outra′geous, *adj.*, violent; grossly cruel; flagrant; immoderate.

outra′geously, *adv.*, in an outrageous way.

out′raging, *pr.p.*, outrage.

outrange′, *v.t.*, to surpass in range (said of a gun).

outré, *adj.*, odd, extravagant (*Fr.*).

outreach′, *v.t.*, to go beyond, to overreach.

outride′, *v.t.*, to outstrip in riding.

out′rider, *n.*, an attendant on a carriage, mounted on horseback.

out′rigged, *adj.*, having outriggers.

out′rigger, *n.*, a projection from a boat's side, such as the bracket supporting the external rowlocks.

out′right, *adj.* and *adv.*, downright, absolutely.

outrun′, *v.t.*, to outstrip in a race.

outsail′, *v.t.*, to outstrip in sailing.

outsell′, *v.t.*, to sell at a better price than another.

out′set, *n.*, a start, a beginning.

outshine′, *v.t.*, to eclipse; *v.i.*, to shine out.

outside′, *adj.*, external; *n.*, the exterior; *prep.*, external to; beyond the limits of.

outsi′der, *n.*, one who is excluded from any society, etc.; a layman; a person of no account; a horse not thought to have a chance of a place.

out′size, *adj.*, over normal size.

out′skirt, *n.*, the outer borders of a place.

out′skirts, *n. pl.*, a suburb; the borders of a thing; a town fringe.

out′span, *n.*, the act of outspanning; the encampment; *v.t.* and *i.*, to release the horses or oxen for the purpose of encamping.

out′spoken, *adj.*, bold, frank.

outspread′, *adj.*, spread out, extended; *v.t.* and *i.*, to spread out.

outstand′ing, *adj.*, still remaining; prominent, leading.

outstand′ingly, *adv.*, in an outstanding way.

out′station, *n.*, a station away from headquarters.

outstretch′, *v.t.*, to extend.

outstretched′, *p.p.*, outstretch.

outstretch′ing, *pr.p.*, outstretch.

outstrip′, *v.t.*, to surpass in anything.

outstripped′, *p.p.*, outstrip.

outstrip′ping, *pr.p.*, outstrip.

out′talk′, *v.t.*, to talk a person down.

out′-turn, *n.*, output.

outvote′, *v.t.*, to defeat by a majority of votes.

outvo′ted, *p.p.*, outvote.

out′voter, *n.*, one who lives in one constituency and votes in another.

outvo′ting, *pr.p.*, outvote.

outwalk′, *v.t.*, to walk faster than.

out′ward, *adj.*, outer, external; *adv.*, toward the exterior; *n.*, the exterior.

out′ward-bound, *adj.*, starting on a voyage.

out′wardly, *adv.*, externally; on the exterior or surface.

out′wardness, *n.*, externality; objectivity.

out′wards, *adv.*, *i.q.* outward.

outwear′, *v.t.*, to last longer than.

outweigh′, *v.t.*, to exceed the weight of.

outweighed′, *p.p.*, outweigh.

outweigh′ing, *pr.p.*, outweigh.

outwit′, *v.t.*, to get the better of with cunning.

outwit′ted, *p.p.*, outwit.

outwit′ting, *pr.p.*, outwit.

outwork′, *v.t.*, to exceed in work.

out′work, *n.*, an advanced defence.

ou′zel, *n.*, the name of sundry small birds.

o′va, *n.*, the pl. of ovum.

o′val, *adj.*, egg-shaped, ellipsoidal; *n.*, anything of oval shape.

ovalbu′men, *n.*, *i.q.* ovalbumin.

oval′bumin, *n.*, eggalbumin.

ova′rian, *adj.*, rel. to ovaries.

o′vary, *n.*, an organ in the female which produces ova.

o′vate, *adj.*, *i.q.* oval.

o′vate-oblong, *adj.*, combining the oval with the oblong.

ova′tion, *n.*, a secondary kind of triumph in ancient Rome; now used to mean a spontaneous acclamation, a joyous reception.

ov′en, *n.*, a cooking-chamber or box.

oven′ette′, *n.*, a small oven.

o′ver, *adj.*, upper; *adv.*, above, across, from one to another, from end to end, in excess, in addition, at an end; *n.*, in cricket, a spell of bowling; *prep.*, above, in command of, on the outside of, across, in excess of, extending over, beyond.

overabun′dance, *n.*, excessive abundance.

overact′, *v.t.*, to overdo.

overact′ed, *p.p.*, overact.

overact′ing, *pr.p.*, overact.

o′ver-age, *adj.*, too old.

o′verall, *adj.*, complete; *n.*, a protective outer garment.

o′veralled, *adj.*, covered with an overall.

o′veralls, *n. pl.*, a workman's cover to protect his clothes.

over-anxi′ety, *n.*, anxiety in excess.

o′ver-anx′ious, *adj.*, too anxious.

o′ver-anx′iously, *adv.*, in an over-anxious way.

overarch′, *v.t.* and *i.*, to make an arch over.

o′verarm, *adj.*, with the arm raised.

overawe′, *v.t.*, to fill with excessive awe.

overawed′, *p.p.*, overawe.

overaw′ing, *pr.p.*, overawe.

overbal′ance, *v.t.*, to outbalance; to lose balance.

overbal′anced, *p.p.*, overbalance.

overbal′ancing, *pr.p.*, overbalance.

overbear', *v.t.*, to domineer over; to overpower.

overbear'ing, *adj.*, domineering; *pr.p.*, overbear.

overbear'ingly, *adv.*, domineeringly.

overbear'ingness, *n.*, the state of being overbearing.

overbid', *v.t.*, to bid higher or in excess.

overbid'der, *n.*, one who overbids.

overbid'ding, *pr.p.*, overbid.

overblown', *adj.*, withered; beyond the best point in development.

o'verboard, *adv.*, from off a ship into the water.

overboil', *v.t.* and *i.*, to boil to excess.

overboiled', *p.p.*, overboil.

overboil'ing, *pr.p.*, overboil.

overborne', *p.p.*, overbear.

overbought', *p.p.*, overbuy.

overbur'den, *n.*, an excessive load; *v.t.*, to load too heavily.

overbur'dened, *adj.*, overloaded; *p.p.*, overburden.

overburden'ing, *pr.p.*, overburden.

overbur'densome, *adj.*, excessively loading.

overbuy', *v.t.*, to buy in excess.

overbuy'ing, *pr.p.*, overbuy.

overcall', *v.t.*, (in bridge) to bid above; to call too high.

overcalled', *p.p.*, overcall.

overcall'ing, *pr.p.*, overcall.

overcame', *p.p.*, overcome.

overcapitaliza'tion, *n.*, the use of excessive capital.

overcap'italize, *v.t.*, to invest excessive capital.

overcap'italized, *p.p.*, overcapitalize.

overcap'italizing, *pr.p.*, overcapitalize.

overcare'ful, *adj.*, excessively cautious.

o'vercast, *adj.*, cloudy, with no sky visible; *v.t.*, to cover over.

o'vercasting, *n.*, an overstated sum; *pr.p.*, overcast.

overcharge', *v.t.*, to charge too high a price.

o'vercharge, *n.*, an excessive charge.

overcharged', *p.p.*, overcharge.

overcharg'ing, *pr.p.*, overcharge.

overclothed', *adj.*, covered or dressed to excess.

overcloud', *v.t.*, to darken with clouds.

overcloud'ed, *p.p.*, overcloud.

overcloud'ing, *pr.p.*, overcloud.

o'vercoat, *n.*, a greatcoat, a topcoat.

overcome', *v.t.*, to conquer, to surmount.

overcom'ing, *pr.p.*, overcome.

overcom'pensate, *v.t.*, to make excessive allowance.

overcom'pensated, *p.p.*, overcompensate.

overcom'pensating, *pr.p.*, overcompensate.

overcompensa'tion, *n.*, an excessive allowance.

overcompensa'tory, *adj.*, pert. or rel. to overcompensation.

over-con'fidence, *n.*, excessive confidence.

over-con'fident, *adj.*, with excessive confidence.

over-con'fidently, *adv.*, in an over-confident way.

overcrowd', *v.t.*, to crowd to overflowing.

overcrowd'ed, *p.p.*, overcrowd.

overcrowd'ing, *pr.p.*, overcrowd.

overdar'ing, *adj.*, excessively daring.

overdevel'op, *v.t.* and *i.*, to develop to excess.

overdevel'oped, *p.p.*, overdevelop.

overdevel'oping, *pr.p.*, overdevelop.

overdevelop'ment, *n.*, excessive development.

overdo', *v.t.*, to do to excess; to carry too far.

overdo'ing, *pr.p.*, overdo.

overdone', *adj.*, done to excess; *p.p.*, overdo.

overdos'age, *n.*, *i.q.* overdose.

overdose', *v.t.*, to administer an overdose to.

o'verdose, *n.*, an excessive dose.

overdosed', *p.p.*, overdose.

overdos'ing, *pr.p.*, overdose.

o'verdraft, *n.*, a permission to withdraw from an account more than the actual credit balance.

overdraw', *v.t.*, to draw upon one's banker in excess of one's credit balance.

overdraw'ing, *pr.p.*, overdraw.

overdrawn', *p.p.*, overdraw.

over'dress', *v.t.*, to dress ostentatiously.

over'dressed, *adj.*, ostentatiously dressed; *p.p.*, overdress.

over'dress'ing, *pr.p.*, overdress.

overdrive', *n.*, a device for increasing an engine's speed performance; *v.t.*, to drive too hard.

overdriv'en, *p.p.*, overdrive.

overdriv'ing, *pr.p.*, overdrive.

overdue', *adj.*, past the date when due.

overeat, *v.i.*, to eat too much.

overeat'en, *p.p.*, overeat.

overeat'ing, *pr.p.*, overeat.

overes'timate, *v.t.*, to value above worth.

over'estimate, *n.*, an excessive estimate.

over'estimated, *p.p.*, overestimate.

over'estimating, *pr.p.*, overestimate.

over'estimation, *n.*, *i.q.* overestimate.

overexcite', *v.t.*, to excite to excess.

overexci'ted, *p.p.*, overexcite.

overexcit'ing, *adj.*, exciting to excess; *pr.p.*, overexcite.

overexert', *v.t.*, to exert to excess.

overexert'ed, *p.p.*, overexert.

overexert'ing, *pr.p.*, overexert.

overexer'tion, *n.*, excessive exertion.

overexpose', *v.t.*, to expose to excess.

overexposed', *adj.*, exposed to excess; *p.p.*, overexpose.

overexpos'ing, *pr.p.*, overexpose.

overexpos'ure, *n.*, too great an exposure.

over'fed, *adj.*, fed to excess; *p.p.*, overfeed.

over'feed, *v.t.*, to feed to excess.

over'feeding, *pr.p.*, overfeed.

overfill', _v.t._, to fill beyond capacity.

over'filled, _adj._, filled to excess; _p.p._, overfill.

over'filling, _pr.p._, overfill.

overflow', _v.t._ and _i._, to flow over.

o'verflow, _n._, an overflowing; a flood; a super-abundance.

overflowed', _p.p._, overflow.

overflow'ing, _pr.p._, overflow.

overfond', _adj._, too fond.

overfull', _adj._, satiated, too full.

overground', _adj._, above the ground.

overgrow', _v.t._, to grow all over; _v.i._, to grow too fast or too much.

overgrow'ing, _pr.p._, overgrow.

overgrown', _adj._, beyond normal size; _p.p._, overgrow.

o'vergrowth, _n._, the state of being overgrown; the growth itself.

overhand', _adv._, with the hand above; _i.q._ overarm.

overhang', _v.t._, to impend over; _v.i._, to jut out.

o'verhang, _n._, the extent to which a thing juts out.

overhang'ing, _adj._, projecting over; _pr.p._, overhang.

o'verhas'ty, _adj._, too hasty.

overhaul', _v.t._, to catch up with; to make a search in; to recondition.

o'verhaul, _n._, a thorough examination; _v.t._, to inspect thoroughly; to overtake.

overhauled', _p.p._, overhaul.

overhaul'ing, _pr.p._, overhaul.

overhead', _adj._ and _adv._, above one's head.

o'verheads, _n. pl._, general expenses.

overhear', _v.t._, to hear by listening unseen.

overheard', _p.p._, overhear.

overhear'ing, _pr.p._, overhear.

overheat', _v.t._, to heat excessively.

overheat'ed, _adj._, heated to excess; _p.p._, overheat.

overheat'ing, _pr.p._, overheat.

overhung', _adj._, suspended; _p.p._, overhang.

overindul'gent, _adj._, too indulgent.

overinsur'ance, _n._, the act of overinsuring.

overinsure', _v.t._, to insure in excess of the real value.

overinsured', _p.p._, overinsure.

overinsur'ing, _pr.p._, overinsure.

overjoyed', _adj._, rejoicing exceedingly.

overkind, _adj._, too kind.

overla'den, _adj._, _i.q._ overloaded.

overlaid', _p.p._, overlay.

o'verland, _adj._ and _adv._, by land.

overlap', _v.t._, to extend over and beyond.

o'verlap, _n._, an overlapping part; the extent of overlapping.

overlapped', _p.p._, overlap.

overlapp'ing, _pr.p._, overlap.

overlay', _p.p._, overlie; _v.t._, to lay over a surface.

o'verlay, _n._, something laid over; a coverlet.

overlay'ing, _pr.p._, overlay.

over'leaf', _adv._, on the next page; on the other side.

overleap', _v.t._, to leap over.

overlie', _v.t._, to lie on; to suffocate by lying on.

overload', _v.t._, to load to excess.

o'verload, _n._, an excessive load.

overload'ed, _p.p._, overload.

overload'ing, _pr.p._, overload.

overlook', _v.t._, to superintend; to ignore; to forgive.

overlooked', _p.p._, overlook.

overlook'ing, _pr.p._, overlook.

o'verlord, _n._, a superior lord.

overly'ing, _adj._, lying above; _pr.p._, overlie.

o'verman', _n._, a mining overseer.

overman', _v.t._, to supply too much labour.

overmanned', _p.p._, overman.

overmann'ing, _pr.p._, overman.

o'vermantel, _n._, ornamental shelves above a chimneypiece.

overmas'ter, _v.t._, to ove[r]power.

overmatch', _v.t._, to b[e] more than a match fo[r]

o'vermuch', _adj._ an[d] _adv._, to an excessiv[e] degree or amount.

overnice', _adj._, too pa[r]ticular.

overnight', _adj._, for th[e] night-time; _adv._, du[r]ing the previous nigh[t]

overpaid', _p.p._, overpa[id]

overpass', _v.t._, to cros[s] to pass through.

o'verpass', _n._, a canal; [a] road or railway cros[s]ing another road, et[c]

overpassed', _p.p._, ove[r]pass.

overpass'ing, _pr.p._, ove[r]pass.

overpay', _v.t._, to pa[y] more than is due.

o'verpay, _n._, a paymen[t] in excess.

overpay'ing, _pr.p._, ove[r]pay.

o'verpay'ment, _n._, a pa[y]ment in excess.

overpersuade', _v.t._, [to] persuade against a pe[r]son's inclination.

overpersuad'ed, _p.p._ overpersuade.

overpersuad'ing, _pr.p[.]_ overpersuade.

overplay', _v.t._, to exa[g]gerate; to play to e[x]cess.

overplayed', _adj._, exa[g]gerated; _p.p._, ove[r]play.

overplay'ing, _pr.p._, ove[r]play.

o'verplus, _n._, a surplu[s] an excess.

overpop'ulate, _v.t._, t[o] overfill with inhab[i]tants.

over'populated, _adj[.]_ overfilled with inhab[i]tants; _p.p._, ove[r]populate.

overpopulat'ing, _pr.p[.]_ overpopulate.

overpopula'tion, _n._, [a]n overfilling with in[habitants].

overpow'er, _v.t._, to sub[due], to overcome.

overpow'ered, _p.p._, ove[r]power.

overpow'ering, _pr.p[.]_ overpower.

overpow'eringly, _adv[.]_ very intensely.

overpraise', _n._, excessiv[e] praise; _v.t._, to prais[e] to excess.

overpraised', _p.p._, ove[r]praise.

overprais'ing, n., i.q. overpraise; pr.p., overpraise.

overprint', v.t., to print too many; to print on pre-printed material.

overprint'ed, p.p., overprint.

overprint'ing, pr.p., overprint.

o'verproduc'tion, n., production exceeding demand.

o'verproof', adj., above proof in rel. to alcoholic content.

overran', p.p., overrun.

overrash', adj., too rash.

overrash'ly, adv., in an overrash way.

overrash'ness, n., excessive rashness.

overrate', v.t., to rate too highly.

overra'ted, p.p., overrate.

overra'ting, pr.p., overrate.

overreach', v.t., to gain advantage over; to go beyond; to extend over; to exceed one's power or authority.

overreached', p.p., overreach.

overreach'ing, pr.p., overreach.

o'verridden, p.p., override.

o'verride', v.t., to supersede, to disregard; to trample on; v.i., to tire from.

o'verrid'ing, adj., superior, predominant; pr.p., override.

overripe', adj., too ripe.

overrip'en, v.t., to ripen to excess.

overrip'ened, p.p., overripe.

overripen'ing, pr.p., overripe.

overrule', v.t., to control, to influence.

overruled', p.p., overrule.

overru'ling, pr.p., overrule.

overrun', p.p., overrun; v.t., to run over; to pass; to alter the setting of printer's type by removing words from one line into another line, column or page.

overrun'ning, pr.p., overrun.

o'versea, adj., beyond the sea; foreign.

o'verseas', adj. and adv., coming from abroad.

oversee', v.t., to superintend.

o'verseer, n., a manager, a superintendent.

oversell', v.t., to sell at too high a price; to sell beyond availability.

oversell'ing, pr.p., oversell.

overset', v.t., to upset; to set too much printer's type.

o'verset, n., too much printed type.

oversew', v.t., to sew with an overhand stitch.

oversewed', p.p., oversew.

oversew'ing, n., the sewing with an overhand stitch; pr.p., oversew.

oversewn', adj., sewn with an overhand stitch; p.p., oversew.

oversexed', adj., having excessive sexual emotion.

overshade', v.t., to cast a shade over.

overshad'ow, v.t., i.q. overshade; to throw into insignificance.

oversha'dowed, p.p., overshadow.

oversha'dowing, pr.p., overshadow.

o'vershoe, adj. and adv., above shoe-tops; n., a golosh.

overshoot', v.t., to shoot beyond the mark.

overshoot'ing, pr.p., overshoot.

overshot', p.p., overshoot.

o'vershot', adj., turned as by a waterwheel.

o'versight, n., neglect, an omission.

oversimplifica'tion, n., excessive simplification.

oversim'plified, p.p., oversimplify.

oversim'plify, v.t., to make too simple.

oversim'plifying, pr.p., oversimplify.

oversized', adj., above standard size.

oversleep', v.i., to oversleep oneself (i.e., to sleep beyond the proper time).

oversleep'ing, pr.p., oversleep.

overslept', p.p., oversleep.

oversold', p.p., oversell.

oversow', v.t., to sow (seed) in addition to other seed in the same land at the same time.

oversow'ing, pr.p., oversow.

oversown', p.p., oversow.

overspec'ialization, n., excessive specialization.

overspec'ialize, v.i., to specialize too much.

overspec'ialized, p.p., overspecialize.

overspec'ializing, pr.p., overspecialize.

overspend', v.t., to spend too much; to exhaust.

overspend'ing, pr.p., overspend.

overspent', adj., wearied out; spent beyond one's means; p.p., overspend.

o'verspill, n., the amount by which the population exceeds local capacity.

over'spread', p.p., overspread; v.t., to spread over.

o'verstaff, v.t., to employ an excess of staff.

o'verstaffed', adj., employing too many staff; p.p., overstaff.

overstaff'ing, pr.p., overstaff.

overstate', v.t., to exaggerate.

overstat'ed, p.p., overstate.

overstate'ment, n., an exaggeration.

overstat'ing, pr.p., overstate.

overstay', v.t., to wait or stay too long.

overstayed', p.p., overstay.

overstay'ing, pr.p., overstay.

overstep', v.t., to transgress.

overstepped', p.p., overstep.

overstep'ping, pr.p., overstep.

overstock', v.t., to put in too much stock.

o'verstock, n., too much stock.

overstocked', p.p., overstock.

overstock'ing, pr.p., overstock.

overstrain', v.t., to strain unduly.

o'verstrain, n., excessive strain.

overstrained', adj., unduly strained; p.p., overstrain.

overstrain'ing, pr.p., overstrain.

overstress', v.t., to stress too much.

o'verstress, n., an excessive stress.

overstressed', *p.p.*, overstress.

overstress'ing, *pr.p.*, overstress.

overstrew', *v.t.*, to strew over.

overstrewn', *p.p.*, overstrew.

overstrung', *adj.*, too tensely strung; with the strings crossing obliquely.

overstud'ied, *p.p.*, overstudy.

overstud'ious, *adv.*, too studious.

overstud'y, *v.t.*, to study too much.

overstudy'ing, *pr.p.*, overstudy.

oversubscribe', *v.t.*, to subscribe too much.

oversubscribed', *p.p.*, oversubscribe.

oversubscrib'ing, *pr.p.*, oversubscribe.

oversubscrip'tion, *n.*, an excessive subscription.

o'vert, *adj.*, open; without concealment.

overtake', *v.t.*, to catch up.

overta'ken, *adj.*, intoxicated; confused; *p.p.*, overtake.

over'taking, *pr.p.*, overtake.

overtask', *v.t.*, to task unduly.

overtax', *v.t.*, to tax excessively.

o'vertax, *n.*, tax in excess.

overtaxed', *p.p.*, overtax.

overtax'ing, *pr.p.*, overtax.

overthrew', *p.p.*, overthrow.

overthrow', *v.t.*, to throw down; to destroy.

o'verthrow, *n.*, demolition, defeat; a ball thrown in past the player to whom it was directed.

overthrow'ing, *pr.p.*, overthrow.

overthrown', *p.p.*, overthrow.

o'vertime, *adj.* and *adv.*, beyond the stipulated hours; *n.*, time in excess.

o'vertly, *adv.*, openly.

o'vertone', *n.*, an harmonic; a subtlety not superficially noticeable; *v.t.*, to print in too deep a tone.

overtook', *p.p.*, overtake.

overtop', *v.t.*, to surmount; to tower above.

overtrade', *v.i.*, to do business beyond one's means.

overtrad'ed, *p.p.*, overtrade.

overtrad'ing, *n.*, trading beyond one's capital; *pr.p.*, overtrade.

overtrain', *v.t.*, to train harmfully to excess.

overtrained', *p.p.*, overtrain.

overtrain'ing, *pr.p.*, overtrain.

o'vertrick, *n.*, (in bridge) a trick more than contracted for.

overtrump', *v.t.*, (in card games) to play a higher trump.

overtrumped', *p.p.*, overtrump.

overtrump'ing, *pr.p.*, overtrump.

o'verture, *n.*, an offer, a proposal; the introduction to an opera, oratorio, etc.

overturn', *v.t.*, to upset, to destroy; *v.i.*, to capsize.

overturned', *p.p.*, overturn.

overturn'ing, *pr.p.*, *n.*, overturn.

overval'ue, *v.t.*, to value too highly.

overval'ued, *adj.*, valued too highly; *p.p.*, overvalue.

overvalu'ing, *pr.p.*, overvalue.

overvi'olent, *adj.*, excessively violent.

overvi'olently, *adv.*, in an overviolent way.

overwear', *v.t.*, to wear out.

overwear'ied, *adj.*, exhausted with fatigue; *p.p.*, overweary.

overwear'ing, *pr.p.*, overwear.

overwear'y, *v.t.*, to exhaust with fatigue.

overweary'ing, *pr.p.*, overweary.

overween'ing, *adj.*, arrogant.

over'weeningly, *adv.*, in an overweening way.

overweight', *v.t.*, to put too much weight on to.

o'verweight, *adj.* and *n.*, excess weight.

overwhelm', *v.t.*, to cover, to spread over, to subdue, to overcome.

overwhelmed', *p.p.*, overwhelm.

overwhelm'ing, *adj.*, crushing, overpowering; *pr.p.*, overwhelm.

overwhelm'ingly, *adv.*, overpoweringly.

overwind', *v.t.*, to wind too much.

overwind'ing, *pr.p.*, overwind.

o'verwise', *adj.*, excessively wise.

overwise'ly, *adv.*, in an overwise way.

overwork', *v.t.*, to exact too much work from; to elaborate to excess.

o'verwork, *n.*, excessive labour.

overworked', *p.p.*, overwork.

overwork'ing, *pr.p.*, overwork.

overworn', *adj.*, worn out or spoiled; *p.p.*, overwear.

overwound', *adj.*, wound too much; *p.p.*, overwind.

o'verwrought', *adj.*, worked too hard; overstrained.

o'vibos, *n.*, the musk-ox.

ovic'ular, *adj.*, pert. to an egg.

Ovid'ian, *adj.*, pert. to, or in the style of, the Latin poet, Ovid.

o'viduct, *n.*, the passage for the ova.

ovif'erous, *adj.*, eggholding. (Also *ovigerous*.)

o'viform, *adj.*, eggshaped. (Also *ovoid*.)

ovig'erous, *adj.*, *i.q.* oviferous.

o'vine, *adj.*, pert. or rel. to sheep; like a sheep.

ovip'arous, *adj.*, eggproducing.

ovipos'itor, *n.*, the eggdepositing organ of insects.

o'void, *adj.*, *i.q.* oviform.

ovoi'dal, *adj.*, *i.q.* ovoid.

o'volo, *n.*, a convex moulding found in Greek and Roman architecture.

ovo-vivip'arous, *adj.*, describes animals which hatch their eggs within their bodies.

o'vular, *adj.*, rel. to an ovule.

o'vule, *n.*, a rudimentary seed; an unfertilized ovum.

o'vum, *n.*, an egg; an animal female cell (*Lat.*).

owe, *v.t.*, to be under a debt for; *v.i.*, to be in debt.

owed, *p.p.*, owe.

ow'elty, *n.*, equality (*leg.*).

Ow'enite, *n.*, a follower of Robert Owen, the socialist.

owes, *pr.p.*, owe.

ow'ing, *adj.*, due; *pr.p.*, owe.

owl, *n.*, a raptorial and nocturnal bird.

owl'et, *n.*, a young owl.

owl'ing, *n.*, the illegal export of wool (*obs.*).

owl'ish, *adj.*, owl-like, stupid.

owl'-like, *adj.*, *i.q.* owl-ish.

own, *adj.*, bel. to one-self; not another's; *v.t.*, to possess; to claim possession of; to admit, to confess.

owned, *p.p.*, own.

own'er, *n.*, one who owns.

own'er-driv'er, *n.*, one who drives his own car.

own'erless, *adj.*, without an owner; unclaimed.

own'ership, *n.*, posses-sion.

own'ing, *pr.p.*, own.

ox, *n.*, any bovine animal, esp. the domesticated and castrated male ox.

ox'alate, *n.*, an oxalic acid salt.

oxal'ic, *adj.*, derived from wood-sorrel (oxalis).

o'xcart, *n.*, an ox-drawn cart.

ox'en, *n.*, the pl. of ox.

ox'eye, *n.*, the name of several genera of the aster.

ox'-eyed, *adj.*, having large, gentle eyes.

oxidabil'ity, *n.*, the qua-lity of being oxidable.

ox'idable, *adj.*, able to be converted into an oxide.

ox'idate, *v.t.*, to oxidize.

ox'idated, *p.p.*, oxidate.

ox'idating, *pr.p.*, oxi-date.

oxida'tion, *n.*, the state or result of oxidating.

ox'idator, *n.*, an oxygen-generator.

ox'ide, *n.*, oxygen com-pounded with another element or with an or-ganic radical.

ox'idizable, *adj.*, able to be oxidized.

oxidiza'tion, *n.*, the state or process of being oxidized.

ox'idize, *v.t.*, to make to combine with oxygen; to rust; *v.i.*, to rust.

ox'idized, *p.p.*, oxidize.

ox'idizement, *n.*, *i.q.* oxi-dation.

ox'idizing, *pr.p.*, oxidize.

oxim'eter, *n.*, a meter for registering oxygen in the blood.

ox'lip, *n.*, a type of primrose.

Oxo'nian, *adj.*, rel. or pert. to Oxford; *n.*, a member of Oxford University.

ox'-tongue, *n.*, an ox's tongue; several kinds of plants.

oxy'-acet'ylene, *adj.*, pert. or rel. to the welding process using this gas; *n.*, a mixture of oxygen and acety-lene gas.

oxyac'id, *n.*, an acid containing oxygen.

ox'ygen, *n.*, a colour-less, tasteless, scent-less, atmospheric gas essential to life and combustion.

ox'ygenate, *v.t.*, to treat with oxygen.

ox'ygenated, *p.p.*, oxy-genate.

ox'ygenating, *pr.p.*, oxy-genate.

oxygena'tion, *n.*, the effect of oxygenating.

oxyg'enator, *n.*, an oxy-gen-generating appar-atus.

oxygen'ic, *adj.*, pert. or rel. to oxygen.

ox'ygenizable, *adj.*, able to be oxygenized.

ox'ygenize, *v.t.*, *i.q.* oxy-genate.

ox'ygenized, *p.p.*, oxy-genize.

ox'ygenizement, *n.*, *i.q.* oxidation.

ox'ygenizing, *pr.p.*, oxy-genize.

oxyg'enous, *adj.*, *i.q.* oxy-genic.

ox'ygon, *n.*, a triangle with three acute angles.

oxyg'onal, *adj.*, acute-angled.

oxyhy'drogen, *adj.* and *n.*, (rel. to) a combina-tion of oxygen with hydrogen.

ox'ymel, *n.*, a syrup made from vinegar and honey.

oxymor'on, *n.*, a figure of speech.

oxymu'riate, *n.*, a chlo-ride.

oxymuriat'ic, *adj.*, rel. to oxygen and mu-riatic acid.

ox'yopy, *n.*, abnormally acute sight.

oxyph'ony, *n.*, shrillness.

oxyrhyn'cous, *adj.*, with a pointed snout or beak.

ox'ytone, *adj.*, with the last syllable accented; *n.*, the accent so placed.

oy'er, *n.*, a criminal trial by court of *oyer* and *terminer.*

oyes', oyez', *interj.*, the crier's demand for at-tention.

oys'ter, *n.*, an edible bivalve.

oys'ter-bed, *n.*, a bed where oysters are cul-tivated.

oys'ter-catcher, *n.*, a bird which eats oysters, snails, etc. between the tides.

oys'ter-knife, *n.*, a knife for opening oysters.

oys'ter-shell, *n.*, the shell of an oyster.

oze'na, *n.*, an ulcer on the nostrils.

ozo'cerite, *n.*, a wax-like, fossil resin used for making candles, etc.

ozona'tion, *n.*, the effect of treating with ozone.

o'zone, *n.*, oxygen of different molecular structure; an ex-hilarating colourless gas.

ozonif'erous, *adj.*, charged with ozone.

ozonifica'tion, *n.*, the act of treating with ozone.

o'zonize, *v.t.*, to treat with ozone.

o'zonized, *p.p.*, ozonize.

o'zonizer, *n.*, an appara-tus for converting oxygen into ozone.

o'zonizing, *pr.p.*, ozo-nize.

ozonom'eter, *n.*, an ap-paratus measuring the quantity of ozone.

ozonomet'ric, *adj.*, pert. or rel. to ozonometry.

ozonom'etry, *n.*, the pro-cess of testing for the presence of ozone.

P

pa, *n.*, a childish form of *Papa*.

pab'ular, *adj.*, pert. or rel. to food.

pabula'tion, *n.*, the act of providing food.

pab'ulous, *adj.*, *i.q.* pabular.

pab'ulum, *n.*, food (*Lat.*).

pac'a, *n.*, a large S. American rodent animal used for food.

pace, *n.*, a step; the speed of travelling; *v.i.*, to walk with measured steps; *v.t.*, to measure by steps.

paced, *p.p.*, pace.

pace'maker, *n.*, one who encourages a rider or a runner by setting the pace.

pa'cer, *n.*, one who paces; a horse well-trained in pacing.

pacha', *n.*, *i.q.* pasha.

pacha'lic, *n.*, *i.q.* pashalic.

pachydac'tylous, *adj.*, thick-toed.

pach'yderm, *adj.*, pert. or rel. to thick-skinned animals; *n.*, an elephant, etc.

pachyder'mal, *adj.*, thick-skinned.

Pachyder'mata, *n. pl.*, an order of hoofed mammals.

pachyder'matous, *adj.*, pert. or rel. to thick-skinned animals; not sensitive.

Pacific, *n.*, the largest of the oceans.

pacif'ic, *adj.*, making peace; at peace.

pacifica'tion, *n.*, the act of pacifying.

pacif'icator, *n.*, a peacemaker.

pacif'icatory, *adj.*, conciliatory.

pacif'icism, *n.*, *i.q.* pacifism.

pacif'icist, *n.*, *i.q.* pacifist.

pac'ified, *p.p.*, pacify.

pac'ifier, *n.*, one who pacifies.

pacif'ism, *n.*, the policy of peace at any price. (Also *pacificism*.)

pacif'ist, *adj.*, advocating a peace policy; *n.*, one who advocates a peace policy. (Also *pacificist*.)

pac'ify, *v.t.*, to calm.

pac'ifying, *pr.p.*, pacify.

pa'cing, *pr.p.*, pace.

pack, *n.*, that which is bound up to be carried; a set of cards; a number of hounds; a mass of floating ice; *v.t.*, to press into narrow space.

pack'age, *n.*, something packed.

packed, *p.p.*, pack.

pack'er, *n.*, one who packs.

pack'et, *n.*, a little package; a packet-boat.

pack'et-boat, *n.*, a vessel carrying mail, passengers and goods on regular days of starting.

pack'et-ship, *n.*, *i.q.* packet-boat.

pack'horse, *n.*, a horse used for carrying packs of goods.

pack'ing, *n.*, the act of tying into a bundle; stuffing; material used to make the joints of machinery close; *pr.p.*, pack.

pack'ing-case, *n.*, a box for stowing and protecting goods.

pack'ing-needle, *n.*, a strong needle for sewing packages.

pack'man, *n.*, a man who carries a pack; a pedlar.

pack'thread, *n.*, a strong thread for sewing up packages.

pack'wax, *n.*, *i.q.* paxwax.

pa'co, *n.*, the alpaca.

pa'cos, *n.*, *i.q.* paco.

pact, *n.*, something agreed upon; a bargain.

pac'tion, *n.*, *i.q.* pact.

pac'tional, *adj.*, by way of agreement.

pad, *n.*, a soft bag or cushion; a number of leaves of paper or of textile materials laid together; an easy-going horse; a measure of fruit, etc.; a leg-guard used in cricket; an animal's foot; *v.i.*, to walk slowly; *v.t.*, to stuff with something soft.

pad'ded, *p.p.*, pad.

pad'ding, *n.*, the soft stuffing of a cushion; matter of small value put into a book to extend it; *pr.p.*, pad.

pad'dle, *n.*, a broad-bladed oar; *v.i.* and *t.*, to row with a paddle; *v.i.*, to play in water with hands or feet.

pad'dle-box, *n.*, the covering of a paddle-wheel.

pad'dled, *p.p.*, paddle.

pad'dler, *n.*, one who paddles.

pad'dle-wheel, *n.*, a wheel with flat blades used in driving a ship.

pad'dling, *pr.p.*, paddle.

pad'dock, *n.*, a toad or frog; a small grass park.

Padd'y, *n.*, the nickname for an Irishman.

padd'y, *n.*, rice in the husk; a fit of temper (*colloq.*).

Pa'dishah, *n.*, a title of the Shah of Persia and formerly of the Sultan of Turkey and the Emperor of India.

pad'lock, *n.*, a hanging lock with a clasp; *v.t.*, to fasten or provide with a padlock.

pad'locked, *p.p.*, padlock.

pad'locking, *pr.p.*, padlock.

padouk', *n.*, a Burmese tree.

pa'dre, *n.*, father; a priest; a clergyman (*colloq.*, It., *Span.*).

padro'ne, *n.*, a master; an employer of labour (*It.*).

pad′uasoy, *n.*, a kind of silk stuff formerly made in Padua.

pae′an, *n.*, a hymn of triumph. (Also *pean*.)

paed′erast, *n.*, a sodomite. (Also *pederast*.)

paed′erasty, *n.*, sodomy with a boy. (Also *pederasty*.)

paediat′ric, *adj.*, pert. or rel. to child diseases. (Also *pediatric*.)

paediat′rics, *n. pl.*, the treatment of childhood diseases. (Also *pediatrics*.)

paedobap′tism, *n.*, the baptism of infants. (Also *pedobaptism*.)

paedobap′tist, *n.*, one who holds to infant baptism. (Also *pedobaptist*.)

paedol′ogist, *n.*, a student of paedology. (Also *pedologist*.)

paedol′ogy, *n.*, the scientific study of children. (Also *pedology*.)

pae′on, *n.*, a metrical four-syllabled foot, with one syllable long.

pa′gan, *adj.*, pert. or rel. to false gods; *n.*, a heathen.

pa′ganish, *adj.*, heathenish.

pa′ganism, *n.*, the state of being a pagan.

pa′ganize, *v.t.*, to render heathenish.

pa′ganized, *p.p.*, paganize.

pa′ganizing, *pr.p.*, paganize.

page, *n.*, a boy trained as a servant; a youth waiting on a person of rank; one side of a leaf; *v.t.*, to number pages.

pag′eant, *n.*, any great show; a stage on wheels; a picturesque play.

pag′eantry, *n.*, great display; a showy exhibition.

page′-boy, *n.*, a uniformed boy or attendant.

paged, *p.p.*, page.

page′-proof, *n.*, a proof set up in page.

pag′inal, *adj.*, consisting of pages.

pag′inate, *v.t.*, to indicate the pages of a book.

pag′inated, *p.p.*, paginate.

pag′inating, *pr.p.*, paginate.

pagina′tion, *n.*, the figures indicating the number of pages.

pa′ging, *pr.p.*, page.

pago′da, *n.*, a Buddhist temple; a coin formerly used in India.

pagu′rian, *n.*, a hermit-crab.

pah, *interj.*, an exclamation of disgust; *n.*, a fortified Maori camp.

paid, *p.p.*, pay.

pail, *n.*, a vessel, now usu. of metal or plastic, for holding liquid.

pail′ful, *n.*, as much as a pail will hold.

paillasse′, *n.*, a straw mattress. (Also *palliasse*.)

paillette, *n.*, a spangle (*Fr.*).

pain, *n.*, suffering; *v.t.*, to give pain to.

pained, *p.p.*, pain.

pain′ful, *adj.*, giving pain; requiring labour; careful.

pain′fully, *adv.*, in a painful manner.

pain′ing, *pr.p.*, pain.

pain′-killer, *n.*, anything that alleviates pain.

pain′less, *adj.*, free from pain.

pain′lessly, *adv.*, in a painless manner.

pain′lessness, *n.*, the state of being painless.

pains, *n. pl.*, close application in working; penalties.

pains′taker, *n.*, one who takes pains.

pains′taking, *adj.*, laborious and careful; *n.*, careful labour.

paint, *n.*, a pigment for artistic, decorative or protective use; *v.i.*, to practise painting; *v.t.*, to colour; to depict.

paint′-box, *n.*, a colour-box.

paint′brush, *n.*, a brush used in painting.

paint′ed, *p.p.*, paint.

paint′er, *n.*, one who paints; an artist in colour; a rope used to fasten a boat.

paint′ing, *n.*, the act or art of laying on colours; a painted picture; *pr.p.*, paint.

paint′work, *n.*, the art of painting; anything painted.

pair, *n.*, a couple; *v.i.*, to join in pairs; *v.t.*, to assort in twos.

paired, *p.p.*, pair.

pair′-horse, *adj.*, drawn by two horses.

pair′ing, *pr.p.*, pair.

pair′ing-off, *n.*, the act of departing from a company in couples.

pair′ing-time, *n.*, the time when birds couple.

pair-royal, *n.*, three similar things, e.g. three cards of the same sort (kings, queens, etc.) in some games. (Also *pairial* or *prial*.)

paja′mas, *n. pl.*, *i.q.* pyjamas.

Pakista′ni, *adj.*, pert. or rel. to Pakistan; *n.*, a native of P.

pal, *n.*, a partner; a chum (*slang*).

pal′ace, *n.*, the house in which a king, queen or other distinguished person lives; a bishop's official residence; a stately mansion.

pal′adin, *n.*, a knight attached to a sovereign's court; a hero.

palaeanthrop′ic, *adj.*, pert. or rel. to earliest man.

pal′aeograph, *n.*, an ancient manuscript.

palaeog′rapher, *n.*, one skilled in palaeography. (Also *paleographer*.)

palaeograph′ic, *adj.*, pert. or rel. to palaeography. (Also *paleographic*.)

palaeog′raphist, *n.*, *i.q.* palaeographer. (Also *paleographist*.)

palaeog′raphy, *n.*, the art of deciphering ancient writings. (Also *paleography*.)

palaeolith′ic, *adj.*, bel. to the earlier stone period of prehistoric time. (Also *paleolithic*.)

palaeolog′ical, *adj.*, pert. to palaeology. (Also *paleological*.)

palaeol′ogist, *n.*, one conversant with palaeology. (Also *paleologist*.)

palaeol′ogy, *n.*, archaeology. (Also *paleology*.)

palaeontol′ogy, *n.*, that branch of biology which deals with organic fossil remains. (Also *paleontology*.)

palaeothe′rium, *n.*, an extinct pachyderm found fossilized.

palaeozo'ic, *adj.*, a term applied to the lowest division of stratified rocks. (Also *paleozoic*.)

palae'stra, *n.*, *i.q.* palestra.

palae'stric, *adj.*, *i.q.* palestric.

pal'afitte, *n.*, a prehistoric Swiss lake dwelling.

palais de danse, *n.*, a dance hall (*Fr.*).

palankeen', *n.*, a covered conveyance for one person, carried on poles on the shoulders of bearers.

palanquin, *n.*, *i.q.* palankeen.

pal'atable, *adj.*, agreeable to the taste.

pal'atal, *adj.*, pert. or rel. to the palate; *n.*, a sound pronounced with the aid of the palate.

pal'ate, *n.*, the roof of the mouth; taste.

pala'tial, *adj.*, magnificent; like a palace.

palat'inate, *n.*, the seignory of a palatine.

pal'atine, *adj.*, possessing royal privileges; *n.*, a count palatine.

pal'atogram, *n.*, a record of palate sounds.

pala'ver, *n.*, a conference among some savage races; idle talk (*slang*); *v.i.*, to talk idly; to hold a palaver.

pala'vered, *p.p.*, palaver.

pala'vering, *pr.p.*, palaver.

pale, *adj.*, whitish; dim; *n.*, a pointed stake used in fencing; an enclosure; a district; in heraldry, a vertical stripe on a shield; *v.i.*, to lose colour.

palea'ceous, *adj.*, consisting of chaff-like scales.

paled, *p.p.*, pale.

pale'-eyed, *adj.*, having pale eyes.

pale'face, *n.*, a name among Red Indians for a white person.

pale'-faced, *adj.*, having a pale face; wan.

pale'ness, *n.*, the condition of being pale.

pal'eograph, *n.*, *i.q.* palaeograph. *or*

pal'eographer, *n.*, *i.q.* palaeographer.

pal'eographic, *adj.*, *i.q.* palaeographic.

pal'eography, *n.*, *i.q.* palaeography.

pal'eolithic, *adj.*, *i.q.* palaeolithic.

pal'eological, *adj.*, *i.q.* palaeological.

pal'eologist, *n.*, *i.q.* palaeologist.

pal'eology, *n.*, *i.q.* palaeology.

pal'eontology, *n.*, *i.q.* palaeontology.

pal'eozoic, *adj.*, *i.q.* palaeozoic.

Palestin'ian, *adj.*, pert. or rel. to Palestine; *n.*, a native of P.

pales'tra, *n.*, a place for wrestling; wrestling.

pales'tric, *adj.*, pert. or rel. to (the) palestra.

pal'etot, *n.*, an overcoat; a loose coat or long jacket (*Fr.*).

pal'ette, *n.*, a thin board on which a painter lays his pigments. (Also *pallet*.)

pal'ette-knife, *n.*, a thin, flat blade used for mixing colours and for culinary purposes.

pal'frey, *n.*, a small riding horse.

Pa'li, *n.*, the sacred language of the Buddhists.

palil'logy, *n.*, the repetition of words to produce emphasis.

pal'impsest, *n.*, a parchment from which one writing, still faintly visible, has been removed to make room for another.

pal'indrome, *n.*, a word or sentence which reads the same backwards as forwards (*e.g.*, "madam").

pa'ling, *n.*, a fence formed with pales; *pr.p.*, pale.

palingene'sia, *n.*, *i.q.* palingenesis.

palingen'esis, *n.*, a metamorphosis; a great geological change.

pal'inode, *n.*, a recantation.

palisade', *n.*, a fence made of stakes; *v.t.*, to enclose or fortify with a palisade.

palisa'ded, *p.p.*, palisade.

palisa'ding, *n.*, *i.q.* palisade; *pr.p.*, palisade.

pa'lish, *adj.*, somewhat pale.

pall, *n.*, a mantle; an ecclesiastical vestment worn by archbishops; a large cloth to cover a coffin; *v.i.*, to become insipid; to lose charm.

Palla'dian, *adj.*, pert. or rel. to Palladio, a famous Italian architect, or to his style.

palla'dium, *n.*, a sacred image of Pallas; a guarantee of safety; a rare metal.

Pall'as, *n.*, the Greek goddess of wisdom.

pall'bearer, *n.*, one of the mourners at a funeral who hold the corners of the pall.

palled, *p.p.*, pall.

pal'let, *n.*, a small crude bed of straw; a palette; a wooden instrument used by potters and goldbeaters; part of the mechanism of a clock; a flat structure for lifting and stowing goods.

pal'lial, *adj.*, pert. or rel. to a pallium.

palliasse', *n.*, *i.q.* paillasse.

pal'liate, *v.t.*, to mitigate; to extenuate.

pal'liated, *p.p.*, palliate.

pal'liating, *pr.p.*, palliate.

pallia'tion, *n.*, alleviation; extenuation.

pal'liative, *adj.*, serving to palliate; *n.*, that which palliates.

pal'liatory, *adj.*, *i.q.* palliative.

pal'lid, *adj.*, pale; deficient in colour.

pal'lidness, *n.*, paleness.

pall'ing, *pr.p.*, pall.

pal'lium, *n.*, the mantle of a mollusc; an archbishop's pall (*Lat.*).

pall-mall', *n.*, an ancient game played with balls and mallets.

pal'lor, *n.*, paleness.

pall'y, *adj.*, friendly, chummy (*colloq.*).

palm, *n.*, the inside of the hand; a tropical tree of many species; a symbol of triumph; *v.t.*, to conceal in the palm of the hand; to impose by fraud.

palma'ceous, *adj.*, rel. to the palm-tree family.

Pal'ma Chris'ti, *n.*, the castor-oil plant (*Lat.*).

pal'mar, *adj.*, rel. to the palm of the hand.

pal'mary, *adj.*, worthy of receiving the palm.

pal'mate, *adj.*, having the toes webbed; having the shape of the hand.

pal'mate, *n.*, a salt of palmic acid.

pal'mated, *adj.*, *i.q.* palmate.

palmed, *p.p.*, palm.

palm'er, *n.*, a pilgrim to the Holy Land.

palmet'to, *n.*, the W. Indian cabbage-palm.

palm'ier, *adj.*, *comp.* of palmy.

palm'iest, *adj.*, *super.* of palmy.

pal'min, *n.*, ricinelaidin; a white fatty compound of castor-oil and nitric peroxide.

palm'ing, *pr.p.*, palm.

pal'miped, *adj.*, web-footed; *n.*, a bird with webbed feet.

palm'ist, *n.*, a fortune teller.

pal'mister, *n.*, one that practises palmistry.

pal'mistry, *n.*, the art of telling fortunes by the lines on the hand.

palm'-leaf, *n.*, the leaf of a palm.

palm'-oil, *n.*, a fatty substance resembling butter, obtained from the fruit of certain palms; a bribe (*slang*).

palm'-tree, *n.*, *i.q.* palm (a tree).

palm'y, *adj.*, flourishing.

palp, *n.*, a feeler on the head of an insect.

palpabil'ity, *n.*, obviousness.

pal'pable, *adj.*, perceptible; obvious; noticeable to the touch.

pal'pably, *adv.*, obviously.

pal'pate, *v.t.*, to examine by touch.

palpa'tion, *n.*, the act of feeling; a medical examination by touch.

pal'pebral, *adj.*, pert. or rel. to the eyelid or eyebrow.

pal'pebrous, *adj.*, having heavy eyebrows.

pal'piform, *adj.*, having the form of palps or feelers.

palpig'erous, *adj.*, bearing palps.

pal'pitate, *v.i.*, to throb; to tremble.

pal'pitated, *p.p.*, palpitate.

pal'pitating, *pr.p.*, palpitate.

palpita'tion, *n.*, an abnormal pulsation of the heart.

pals'grave, *n.*, a count palatine.

pal'sied, *adj.*, affected with palsy; *p.p.*, palsy.

pal'stave, *n.*, a prehistoric bronze or stone implement.

pal'sy, *n.*, paralysis; *v.t.*, to paralyse.

pal'sying, *pr.p.*, palsy.

pal'ter, *v.i.*, to equivocate.

pal'tered, *p.p.*, palter.

pal'terer, *n.*, an insincere dealer.

pal'tering, *pr.p.*, palter.

pal'trier, *adj.*, *comp.* of paltry.

pal'triest, *adj.*, *super.* of paltry.

pal'trily, *adv.*, in a paltry manner.

pal'triness, *n.*, the state of being paltry.

pal'try, *adj.*, worthless; contemptible.

palu'dal, *adj.*, pert. or rel. to a swamp; fenny.

palu'dinous, *adj.*, inhabiting marshes.

pa'ly, *adj.*, wanting colour; divided palewise (*her.*).

pam, *n.*, the knave of clubs in the game of loo.

pam'pas, *n. pl.*, the grassy, treeless plains of south-east S. America.

pam'pas-grass, *n.*, a gigantic variety of ornamental grass.

pam'per, *v.t.*, to indulge to excess.

pam'pered, *adj.*, spoiled by indulgence or luxurious feeding; *p.p.*, pamper.

pam'perer, *n.*, one who pampers.

pam'pering, *pr.p.*, pamper.

pamper'o, *n.*, a cold S.W. wind from the Andes to the Atlantic.

pam'phlet, *n.*, a small book, stitched but not bound; a short treatise.

pamphleteer', *n.*, a writer of pamphlets; *v.i.*, to write pamphlets.

pamphleteer'ing, *n.*, the writing of pamphlets; *pr.p.*, pamphleteer.

pam'pre, *n.*, an architectural ornament consisting of vine-leaves and grapes.

Pan, *n.*, a Greek god of pastures, woods, etc.

pan, *n.*, a broad, shallow dish; *v.i.*, to turn out well; *v.t.*, to cook in a pan; to obtain in any way.

panace'a, *n.*, a universal remedy.

panace'an, *adj.*, of the nature of a panacea.

panache', *n.*, a decorative head-dress; swagger, stylish display (*fig.*).

pana'da, *n.*, breadsop.

panama', *n.*, a thin, light, flexible hat made of fine straw or grass.

Panama Canal, *n.*, the waterway through the isthmus which joins N. and S. America.

pan'atrope, *n.*, a type of record player.

pan'cake, *n.*, a thin cake of batter cooked in a pan.

panchayat, *n.*, an Indian village council.

panchromat'ic, *adj.*, equally sensitive to all colours.

pancra'tium, *n.*, an ancient Greek gymnastic contest, consisting of boxing and wrestling.

pan'creas, *n.*, a large gland lying between the base of the stomach and the vertebrae; the sweetbread.

pancreat'ic, *adj.*, pert. or rel. to the pancreas.

pan'da, *n.*, the Himalayan bear-cat.

Pande'an, *adj.*, pert. or rel. to Pan.

pan'dect, *n.*, a complete scientific treatise; in the pl., the digest of Roman civil law made by order of the emperor, Justinian.

pandem'ic, *adj.*, *i.q.* epidemic.

pandemo'nium, *n.*, a lawless, disorderly place or assemblage; a volume of loud confused sound.

pan'der, *n.*, one who ministers to any of the baser passions; *v.i.*, to act as agent for the unworthy desires of others.

pan'dered, *p.p.,* pander.

pan'dering, *pr.p.,* pander.

pandicula'tion, *n.,* the act of stretching oneself.

Pando'ra, *n.,* the name of the first woman on whom all the gods bestowed gifts (*myth.*).

pando'ra, *n.,* an Eastern stringed instrument.

pandore', *n., i.q.* pandora; a variety of oyster.

pan'dour, *n.,* a savage Austrian foot soldier.

pan'dy, *n.,* a blow on the hand with a cane or strap; *v.t.,* to slap (*colloq.*).

pane, *n.,* a sunken panel surrounded by a border; a plate of glass inserted in a window; *v.t.,* to make up in coloured strips.

paned, *adj.,* provided with, or composed of, panes.

panegyr'ic, *adj.,* eulogistic; *n.,* an elaborate encomium.

pan'egyrist, *n.,* a eulogist.

pan'egyrize, *v.t.,* to write or pronounce a eulogy on.

pan'el, *n.,* a compartment of a surface more or less distinct from the rest; a document containing the names of a jury; *v.t.,* to form with panels.

pan'el()ed, *p.p.,* panel.

pan'el()ing, *n.,* panelled work; *pr.p.,* panel.

pan'ful, *n.,* the amount a pan will hold.

pang, *n.,* a sudden, sharp pain or excess of emotion.

pan'ga, *n.,* a broad African knife.

pangen'esis, *n.,* a hypothesis to explain the phenomena of organic development.

Pan-Ger'man, *adj.,* pert. or rel. to the union of all the German peoples in one State.

Pan-Ger'manism, *n.,* the Pan-German theory.

pango'lin, *n.,* an anteater.

pan'handle, *n.,* a narrow land corridor.

Panhellen'ic, *adj.,* pert. or rel. to all Greeks.

Panhel'lenism, *n.,* the union of all the Greeks into one political body.

Panhel'lenist, *n.,* one who advocates Panhellenism.

pan'ic, *adj.,* fearfully excessive; *n.,* a sudden fright; conduct dictated by fear; a kind of grass; *v.i.,* to act according to the dictates of fear.

pan'icked, *p.p.,* panic.

pan'icking, *pr.p.,* panic.

pan'icky, *adj.,* prompted by fear.

pan'icle, *n.,* a branching inflorescence, as in lilac.

pan'ic-stricken, *adj.,* struck with sudden fear.

pan'ic-struck, *adj., i.q.* panic-stricken.

panifica'tion, *n.,* bread making.

Panislam'ic, *adj.,* pert. or rel. to a confederation of all the Mohammedan nations.

Panis'lamism, *n.,* the doctrine of the union of all the Mohammedan nations.

paniv'orous, *adj.,* breadeating.

panjan'drum, *n.,* a high and mighty personage (a mock title).

pan'nage, *n.,* the food of swine in the woods; beech-mast, acorns, etc.; the money paid for this.

panne, *n.,* a type of cloth (*Fr.*).

pan'nel, *n.,* the accused in a criminal trial (*Scots law*).

pan'nier, *n.,* one of two baskets slung across a beast of burden or a cycle; part of a lady's dress attached to the back of the skirt; a robed waiter in the Inner Temple, London (*colloq.*).

pan'nikin, *n.,* a small cup; its contents.

pan'oplied, *adj.,* having a full suit of armour.

pan'oply, *n.,* a full suit of armour.

panop'ticon, *n.,* Bentham's model prison; an exhibition of novelties.

panora'ma, *n.,* a picture in which all the objects visible from a point are represented on the inside of a cylinder; a broad general view.

panoram'ic, *adj.,* pert. or rel. to a panorama or complete view.

panoram'ically, *adv.,* in a panoramic way.

pan'-pipe, *n.,* a musical wind-instrument made of reeds of different lengths, tied together.

pan-sex'ualism, *n.,* the theory that the sex instinct determines behaviour.

Panslav'ic, *adj.,* pert. or rel. to all the Slavic races.

Panslav'ism, *n.,* a confederation of all the Slavic peoples.

Panslav'ist, *n.,* one who favours Panslavism.

pansoph'ical, *adj.,* pretending to universal knowledge.

pan'sophy, *n.,* Comenius's scheme of universal knowledge.

pantereora'ma, *n.,* a model in relief of a town or country.

pan'sy, *n.,* a garden violet; heartsease.

pant, *n.,* a gasp; *v.i.,* to breathe quickly.

pan'tagraph, *n., i.q.* pantograph.

pantagru'elism, *n.,* Rabelasian humour.

pantalet(t)es', *n. pl.,* loose short trousers.

pantaloon', *n.,* in modern pantomimes, a fatuous old man; *pl.,* a pair of trousers.

pantech'nicon, *n.,* a place where manufactured articles are exposed for sale; a large van for removing furniture.

pant'ed, *p.p.,* pant.

pant'er, *n.,* one who pants.

pan'theism, *n.,* the doctrine that the universe is God; *i.q.* cosmotheism.

pan'theist, *n.,* one who believes in pantheism.

pantheist'ic, *adj.,* pert. or rel. to pantheism.

pan'thenol, *n.,* vitamin B.

pantheol'ogy, *n.,* a system of theology comprehending all religions.

Panthe'on, *n.,* a temple dedicated to all the gods.

pan'ther, *n.,* a fierce kind of leopard.

pan'ties, *n. pl.,* children's and women's undergarment (*colloq.*).

pan'tile, *n.,* a tile with a cross section resembling the letter S.

pant'ing, *pr.p.,* pant.

pantisoc'racy, *n.,* an ideal state where all are equal.

pan'tler, *n.,* a servant in charge of the pantry.

pan'tofle, *n.,* a slipper.

pan'tograph, *n.,* an instrument for copying drawings to any scale; the arm conducting current from overhead wires for an electric train. (Also *pantagraph* and *pentagraph*.)

pantograph'ic, *adj.,* pert. or rel. to a pantograph.

pantog'raphy, *n.,* copying by means of a pantograph.

pantolog'ic, *adj.,* pert. or rel. to pantology.

pantol'ogist, *n.,* one who aims at systematizing all branches of knowledge.

pantol'ogy, *n.,* universal knowledge.

pantom'eter, *n.,* an instrument for producing portraits in profile; an instrument for measuring angles.

pantom'etry, *n.,* the use of the pantometer.

pan'tomime, *n.,* a dumb show; a Christmas theatrical entertainment of gorgeous scenery and costume and popular music.

pantomim'ic, *adj.,* pert. or rel. to pantomime.

pan'tomimist, *n.,* one who acts in pantomime.

pantomor'phic, *adj.,* assuming any shape.

pan'ton, *n.,* a kind of horse-shoe.

pantoph'agist, *n.,* one who eats anything edible.

pantoph'agy, *n.,* miscellaneous diet.

pan'try, *n.,* a room where provisions are kept or where plate is cleaned.

pants, *n. pl.,* womens' knickers; mens' undertrousers (*colloq.*).

pan'zer, *n.,* a unit of German armoured troops.

pap, *n.,* soft food; a teat.

papa', *n.,* a child's word for father; the Latin name of the Pope.

pa'pacy, *n.,* the popedom.

pa'pal, *adj.,* pert. or rel. to the Pope.

papav'erous, *adj.,* pert. or rel. to the poppy family.

papaw', *n.,* a tropical tree. (Also *pawpaw*.)

pa'per, *adj.,* made of paper; *n.,* a substance for writing and printing on, wrapping or covering; a newspaper; an essay; a document; *v.t.,* to cover with paper.

pa'perchase, *n.,* a cross-country run with a paper trail.

pa'per-cutter, *n.,* a paper-knife; a machine for cutting paper; a "guillotine."

pa'pered, *p.p.,* paper.

pa'perhanger, *n.,* a wallpaperer.

pa'pering, *pr.p.,* paper.

pa'per-maker, *n.,* one who manufactures paper.

pa'per-mus'lin, *n.,* a glazed muslin.

pa'perweight, *n.,* a small heavy object to prevent loose papers from blowing about.

pa'perwork, *n.,* dealing with documents; clerical work.

pa'pery, *adj.,* like paper.

Pa'phian, *adj.,* pert. or rel. to Venus or her rites.

pa'pier-mâ'ché, *n.,* pulped paper moulded and varnished (*Fr.*).

papiliona'ceous, *adj.,* resembling a butterfly.

papil'la, *n.,* a small pap or nipple; a little eminence on the skin; in pl., papillae.

pap'illary, *adj.,* pert. or rel. to, or resembling, the nipple.

pap'illate, *adj.,* covered with papillae; *v.t.,* to grow into a nipple.

pap'illose, *adj., i.q.* papillary.

pa'pist, *n.,* a Roman Catholic; an adherent of the papacy.

papis'tical, *adj.,* pert. or rel. to papists.

papoose', *n.,* a Red Indian baby or child.

pappes'cent, *adj.,* gradually becoming covered with down.

pappose', *adj.,* downy (*bot.*).

pap'pus, *n.,* a downy appendage on dandelions, etc. (*bot.*).

pap'py, *adj.,* soft, like pap.

pap'rika, *n.,* Hungarian red pepper.

Pap'uan, *adj.,* bel. to Papua or New Guinea; *n.,* a native of P. or N. G.

pap'ula, *n.,* a pimple.

pap'ular, *adj.,* covered with pimples.

pap'ulous, *adj., i.q.* papular.

papyra'ceous, *adj.,* made of papyrus.

papy'rograph, *n.,* a copying apparatus; a mimeograph.

papyrog'raphy, *n.,* the use of a papyrograph.

papy'rus, *n.,* a kind of sedge common in the Nile valley; a sort of paper made from its stems; a written scroll made of this material.

pa'quined, *adj.,* fashionably dressed.

par, *n.,* the state of equality; *i.q.* parr.

para., *n.,* the abbrev. of paragraph.

parab'asis, *n.,* a chorus sung to the audience (*Gk.*).

parabel'lum, *n.,* an automatic pistol.

par'able, *n.,* a similitude; a fable or allegory with a moral.

parab'ola, *n.,* a plane figure formed when a cone intersects with a plane parallel to its side.

parabol'ic, *adj.,* pert. or rel. to a parabola or to a parable.

parabol'iform, *adj.,* having the shape of a parabola.

parab'olist, *n.,* a maker of parables.

parab'oloid, *n.,* the solid figure generated by the revolution of a parabola about its axis.

Paracel'sian, *adj.,* pert. or rel. to the doctrines of Paracelsus, the famous 16th cent. philosopher; *n.,* a follower of P.

parach'ronism, *n.,* a mistake in chronology which places an event later than its real date. (The opposite to an anachronism.)

par'achute, n., a hemispherical device, made of strong lightweight material, to which a harness is attached, used for safe descent to the ground.

par'achutist, n., one who uses a parachute.

par'aclete, n., one called to aid; the Holy Spirit.

paracros'tic, n., a poem in which the first verse contains, in order, the initial letters of all verses that follow.

parade', n., a display; the place where troops are drawn up for inspection; a public walk; v.t. and i., to assemble in order.

para'ded, p.p., parade.

par'adigm, n., a word displayed with all its inflections.

para'ding, pr.p., parade.

paradisa'ical, adj., pert. or rel. to Paradise.

par'adisal, adj., i.q. paradisaical.

Par'adise, n., the Garden of Eden; the abode of the blessed.

par'ados, n., a parapet in the rear of a fortification.

par'adox, n., a true statement which seems contrary to common sense.

paradox'ical, adj., pert. or rel. to a paradox.

par'adoxically, adv., in a paradoxical way.

paradox'ure, n., a palm-cat.

par'affin, n., a distillation from petroleum.

paragen'esis, n., the origin of two things side by side.

parago'ge, n., the addition of a letter or syllable to a word.

paragog'ic, adj., lengthening a word by an affix.

par'agon, n., a model of excellence.

par'agram, n., a pun.

paragram'matist, n., a punster.

par'agraph, n., a portion of a writing dealing with one particular word.

paragraph'ic, adj., pert. or rel. to a paragraph.

paragraph'ically, adv., by means of paragraphs.

Paraguay'an, adj., pert. or rel. to Paraguay; n., a native of P.

paraheliot'ropism, n., the turning of leaves to light.

par'akeet, n., i.q. parrakeet.

par'akite, n., a kite-like parachute.

paral'dehyde, n., a colourless liquid hypnotic.

paralipom'ena, n. pl., a supplement containing omissions; the Books of Chronicles in the Bible.

paralip'sis, n., a rhetorical figure involving a pretended omission.

parallac'tic, adj., pert. or rel. to parallax.

par'allax, n., an apparent change of position due to the change of a point of view; the angular difference between direction of a heavenly body as viewed from the surface and the centre of the earth or sun.

par'allel, adj., lying in the same direction and equidistant throughout; exactly similar; n., one of such a pair of lines; a circle on a globe entirely equidistant from its equator; a likeness; a comparison; v.t., to compare; to equal.

par'alleled, p.p., parallel.

parallelep'iped, n., a solid shaped like a brick.

parallelepip'edon, n., i.q. parallelepiped.

par'allelism, n., the state of being parallel.

parallel'ogram, n., a four-sided figure with its opposite sides parallel.

paral'ogism, n., a piece of false reasoning.

paral'ogize, v.i., to reason falsely.

paralysa'tion, n., the action of paralysis.

par'alyse, v.t., to affect with paralysis.

par'alysed, p.p., paralyse.

par'alysing, pr.p., paralyse.

paral'ysis, n., a nervous disease producing loss of power or sensation.

paralyt'ic, adj., pert. or rel. to paralysis; n., a person affected with paralysis.

paramagnet'ic, adj., capable of being attracted by poles of a magnet.

paramat'ta, n., a light merino and cotton dress fabric.

param'eter, n., a constant in the equation of a curve or in the facts of a situation.

paramil'itary, adj., on military lines.

par'amount, adj., superior to all others; n., the chief.

par'amour, n., an illicit lover.

par'ang, n., a Malayan sheath knife.

paranoi'a, n., mental derangement marked by delusions.

par'anoid, adj., resembling paranoia.

paranoid'al, adj., i.q. paranoid.

par'anymph, n., a bridesmaid or bridesman.

par'apegm, n., a brass tablet for proclamations fixed to a pillar.

par'apet, n., a breastwork; a wall placed at the edge of a bridge or platform to prevent people from falling over.

par'apeted, adj., provided with a parapet.

par'aph, n., a flourish under a signature.

parapherna'lia, n. pl., appendages; trappings; formerly, a bride's private possessions.

par'aphrase, n., a restatement in other and clearer terms; v.t. and t., to explain fully; to make a paraphrase of.

par'aphrased, p.p., paraphrase.

par'aphrasing, pr.p., paraphrase.

par'aphrast, n., one who paraphrases.

paraphras'tic, adj., having the nature of a paraphrase.

paraphre'nia, n., a form of mental illness.

paraple'gia, n., paralysis of the lower limbs.

paraple'gic, adj., affected with paraplegia; n., a person so paralysed.

par'aplegy, n., i.q. paraplegia.

parapsychol'ogy, n., the study of psychic phenomena.

par'asang, n., an ancient Persian measure of length.

par'ascene, n., i.q. parascenium.

parasce′nium, *n.,* one of the projecting wings of a Greek theatre.

parasce′ve, *n.,* preparation for the Sabbath; Good Friday.

parasele′ne, *n.,* a mock moon; a luminous ring round the moon.

par′asite, *n.,* a sycophant; a plant or animal that lives on, or in, other plants or animals and feeds upon their juices.

parasit′ic, *adj.,* having the nature of a parasite.

parasit′ical, *adj., i.q.* parasitic.

parasit′icide, *n.,* an agent that destroys parasites.

par′asitism, *n.,* the state of being a parasite.

parasitol′ogy, *n.,* the study of parasites.

parasito′sis, *n.,* the infestation by parasites.

parasol′, *n.,* a small umbrella or sunshade.

parasyn′thesis, *n.,* derivation from a compound.

paratax′is, *n.,* the joining of successive clauses without grammatical links.

parath′esis, *n.,* grammatical apposition.

pa′ratrooper, *n.,* a member of a parachute force.

pa′ratroops, *n. pl.,* airborne troops dropped by parachute.

paratyph′oid, *n.,* mild typhoid fever.

paravail′, *adj.,* inferior; lowest (a feudal term).

pa′ravane, *n.,* a submerged marine mine remover.

par′boil, *v.t.,* to boil partly.

par′boiled, *p.p.,* parboil.

par′boiling, *pr.p.,* parboil.

par′buckle, *n.,* a single rope used in hoisting.

par′cel, *n.,* a package; a collection or group; a divided portion; *v.t.,* to divide into portions.

par′cel(l)ed, *p.p.,* parcel.

par′cel(l)ing, *pr.p.,* parcel.

par′cenary, *n., i.q.* coparcenary.

par′cener, *n.,* a coheir.

parch, *v.i.,* to grow very dry; *v.t.,* to dry extremely.

parched, *p.p.,* parch.

parching, *adj.,* causing extreme dryness or thirst; *pr.p.,* parch.

parch′ment, *n.,* the skin of a young animal prepared for writing on.

pard, *n.,* a leopard or panther.

par′don, *n.,* forgiveness; *v.t.,* to forgive.

par′donable, *adj.,* excusable.

par′doned, *p.p.,* pardon.

par′doner, *n.,* one who pardons; one licensed to sell indulgences.

par′doning, *pr.p.,* pardon.

pare, *v.t.,* to trim or shave off the surface of.

pared, *p.p.,* pare.

paregor′ic, *n.,* a medicine assuaging pain; a tincture of opium.

pareir′a, *n.,* a drug for the treatment of urinary disorders.

parem′bole, *n.,* an explanatory phrase thrown into a sentence.

paren′chyma, *n.,* the spongy and fibrous tissue of plants or animals.

parenchym′atous, *adj.,* of the nature of parenchyma.

parenet′ic, *adj.,* persuasive.

pa′rent, *n.,* a father or mother.

pa′rentage, *n.,* birth; origin.

paren′tal, *adj.,* characteristic of parents.

paren′thesis, *n.,* a detached explanatory passage inserted into a sentence and enclosed by brackets, dashes or commas.

parenthet′ic, *adj.,* of the nature of a parenthesis.

parenthet′ical, *adj., i.q.* parenthetic.

paren′ticide, *n.,* the killing of a parent.

pa′rentless, *adj.,* without parents; orphaned.

pa′rer, *n.,* one who, or that which, pares.

parerg′on, *n.,* part-time work.

par excellence, *adv.,* superior (*Fr.*).

par′gasite, *n.,* a kind of hornblende.

par′get, *n.,* ornamental plaster; *v.t.* and *i.,* to

ornament with plasterwork.

par′geted, *p.p.,* parget.

par′geter, *n.,* an ornamental plasterer.

par′geting, *n.,* ornamental plasterwork; *pr.p.,* parget.

parhe′lic, *adj.,* pert. or rel. to parhelia.

parhe′lion, *n.,* a mock sun (*pl.,* parhelia).

pa′riah, *n.,* an outcast; one of the lowest class of Hindus.

pari′al, *n., i.q.* pair royal.

Pa′rian, *adj.,* pert. or rel. to the island of Paros and its marble.

pari′etal, *adj.,* pert. or rel. to a wall.

pari′etary, *n.,* the wall-pellitory.

pari mut′uel, *n.,* a form of betting; a totalisator.

pa′ring, *n.,* what is pared off; the rind; *pr.p.,* pare.

par′i pass′u, *adv.,* with equal pace; simultaneously and equally (*Lat.*).

par′ish, *adj.,* pert. or rel. to a parish; *n.,* an ecclesiastical, administrative district under a parson.

parish′ioner, *n.,* one bel. to a parish.

Paris′ian, *adj.,* pert. or rel. to Paris; *n.,* a native or inhabitant of Paris.

parisol′ogy, *n.,* the use of ambiguous language.

parisyllab′ic, *adj.,* having equal syllables.

par′ity, *n.,* equality; analogy.

park, *n.,* a large piece of pasture and woodland ground surrounding a mansion; a public pleasure garden; a train of artillery; *v.t.* and *i.,* to station a vehicle in a position where it may be left temporarily.

park′a, *n.,* an eskimo skin jacket.

parked, *p.p.,* park.

park′in, *n.,* a biscuit of oatmeal, ginger and treacle.

par′king, *pr.p.,* park.

par′king-meter, *n.,* a coin-operated meter imposing a time limit for the parking of a vehicle.

park'y, *adj.,* chilly (*slang*).

par'lance, *n.,* conversation; talk; a manner of oral expression.

par'ley, *n.,* a conference with an enemy; *v.i.,* to confer with an enemy.

par'leyed, *p.p.,* parley.

par'leying, *pr.p.,* parley.

par'liament, *n.,* the supreme national council.

parliamenta'rian, *n.,* one of those who served the Parliament against Charles I; a person skilled in the procedures of a parliament.

parliamen'tary, *adj.,* pert. or rel. to parliament.

par'lour, *n.,* a sitting-room.

par'lous, *adj.,* risky; shocking; sorry.

par'lousness, *n.,* riskiness.

Parmesan', *adj.,* pert. or rel. to Parma in Italy and its cheese.

par'mo, *n.,* a treeless plateau.

Parnas'sian, *adj.,* pert. or rel. to Mount Parnassus and the Muses.

paro'chial, *adj.,* rel. to a parish.

parod'ic, *adj.,* pert. or rel. to parody.

par'odied, *p.p.,* parody.

par'odist, *n.,* one who writes a parody.

par'ody, *n.,* a burlesque imitation of a serious composition; *v.t.,* to turn into a parody.

par'odying, *pr.p.,* parody.

parole', *n.,* word of honour (*Fr.*).

paronomas'ia, *n.,* a word play, a pun.

par'onym, *n.,* a paronymous word.

paron'ymous, *adj.,* having the same sound but differing in spelling.

paron'ymy, *n.,* the quality of being paronymous.

par'oquet, *n.,* i.q. parrakeet.

parot'id, *n.,* a salivary gland on either side of the face.

paroti'tis, *n.,* mumps, a glandular disease.

parou'sia, *n.,* the second coming of Christ.

par'oxysm, *n.,* a convulsion; a fit.

paroxys'mal, *adj.,* marked by a paroxysm.

parox'ytone, *adj.* and *n.,* acutely accented on the penultimate syllable.

parp'en, *n.,* a binding stone for walls.

par'quet, *adj.,* of inlaid woodwork; *n.,* that part of the floor of a theatre between the pit and the orchestra; *v.t.,* to ornament with parquetry.

par'quetry, *n.,* inlaid woodwork used for floors.

parr, *n.,* a young salmon. (Also *par.*)

par'rakeet, *n.,* a small eastern parrot with a long tail. (Also *parakeet, paroquet* and *perroquet.*)

par'resis, *n.,* partial muscular paralysis (*med.*).

parrici'dal, *adj.,* tending towards parricide.

par'ricide, *n.,* the murder, or murderer, of a father.

par'ried, *p.p.,* parry.

par'rot, *n.,* a climbing bird with a hooked beak, sometimes able to imitate the human voice.

par'ry, *n.,* the act of parrying; *v.t.,* to ward off.

par'rying, *pr.p.,* parry.

parse, *v.t.,* to analyse a word grammatically.

pars'ec, *n.,* a unit for measuring the distance of stars.

parsed, *p.p.,* parse.

Parsee', *n.,* an Indian fire-worshipper.

Par'seeism, *n.,* the religion of the Parsees.

pars'er, *n.,* one who parses.

parsimo'nious, *adj.,* niggardly.

parsimo'niously, *adv.,* in a parsimonious manner.

parsimo'niousness, *n.,* the quality of being parsimonious.

par'simony, *n.,* niggardliness.

pars'ing, *n.,* the act of analysing a word grammatically; *pr.p.,* parse.

pars'ley, *n.,* a garden herb.

pars'nip, *n.,* a plant with a white, edible root.

par'son, *n.,* the priest of a parish; the curate.

par'sonage, *n.,* the house of a parson; a benefice.

part, *n.,* a portion; *v.t.* and *i.,* to divide; to separate. (To take one's part = to defend; to take part = to participate.)

partake', *v.i.,* to participate; to eat or drink some (of).

parta'ken, *p.p.,* partake.

parta'ker, *n.,* a sharer.

parta'king, *pr.p.,* partake.

part'an, *n.,* a crab.

part'ed, *p.p.,* part.

part'er, *n.,* one who parts.

parterre', *n.,* a system of flower-beds; the pit of a theatre (*Fr.*).

parthen'ic, *adj.,* belonging to, or of the nature of, a virgin.

parthenogen'esis, *n.,* non-sexual reproduction (*biol.*).

Par'thenon, *n.,* the temple of Athena on the Acropolis at Athens.

Parthen'ope, *n.,* one of the Sirens of Sicily, who was buried at Naples; (hence) the city of Naples (*myth.*).

Parthenope'an, *adj.,* pert. or rel. to Parthenope.

par'tial, *adj.,* affecting a part only; inclined to favour; *n.,* a harmonic (*mus.*).

par'tialism, *n.,* the doctrine of the partialists.

par'tialist, *n.,* one who holds the doctrine that the Atonement was made for a part only of mankind.

partial'ity, *n.,* undue favour; fondness.

par'tially, *adv.,* in part; with undue bias.

part'ible, *adj.,* divisible.

partic'ipant, *n.,* i.q. partaker; one who takes part in.

partic'ipate, *v.i.,* to have a share.

partic'ipated, *p.p.,* participate.

partic'ipating, *pr.p.,* participate.

participa'tion, *n.,* the state of sharing in common with others; the taking part in.

partic'ipative, *adj.*, capable of participating.

partic'ipator, *n.*, one who participates.

particip'ial, *adj.*, having the nature of a participle.

par'ticiple, *n.*, a form of the verb which possesses some of the characteristics of an adjective or of a noun.

par'ticle, *n.*, any very small portion; a word incapable of being inflected.

part'icoloured, *adj.*, mixed in colour.

partic'ular, *adj.*, individual; special; circumstantial; precise; *n.*, a detail; a single instance.

partic'ularism, *n.*, the theological doctrine of particular election.

partic'ularist, *n.*, one who holds the doctrine of particularism.

particular'ity, *n.*, that which is particular; the state of being particular.

partic'ularize, *v.t.*, to specify precisely.

partic'ularized, *p.p.*, particularize.

partic'ularizing, *pr.p.*, particularize.

partic'ularly, *adv.*, in a particular manner; specifically.

part'ing, *adj.*, separating; *n.*, a division; a leave taking; *pr.p.*, part.

par'tisan, *adj.*, biased; *n.*, a kind of halbert or pike; an adherent of a party.

par'tisanship, *n.*, the state of being a partisan.

par'tite, *adj.*, divided to the base.

parti'tion, *n.*, a division; a wall of separation; *v.t.*, to divide.

parti'tioned, *p.p.*, partition.

parti'tioning, *pr.p.*, partition.

parti'tionist, *n.*, one who advocates partition.

par'titive, *adj.*, expressing the relation of a part to the whole.

part'let, *n.*, a 16th cent. garment; a hen; a middle-aged woman.

part'ly, *adv.*, in part.

part'ner, *n.*, one who shares with another in a business, dance, etc.; a husband or wife.

part'nership, *n.*, the state of being a partner.

partook', *p.p.*, partake.

part'-own'er, *n.*, one who shares ownership with others.

par'tridge, *n.*, a bird of the grouse family.

parts, *n.*, the pl. of part; talent, ability.

part'-song, *n.*, a song with three or more voice parts.

part'-time, *adj.*, requiring to be done part-time only; *adv.*, for only part of the time.

partu'rient, *adj.*, bringing forth young.

parturi'tion, *n.*, the act of bringing forth young.

par'ty, *adj.*, divided into differently tinctured parts (*her.*); separating; *n.*, a number of persons united for a common purpose.

par'ty-coloured, *adj.*, coloured differently in different parts.

par'ty-line, *n.*, a party policy; a shared telephone line; a boundary.

par'ty-politics, *n. pl.*, politics from a particular party's standpoint.

par'ty-spirit, *n.*, the spirit that unites members of a party.

par'ty-wall, *n.*, a jointly-owned dividing wall.

parure', *n.*, a set of ornaments; personal jewellery, etc. (*Fr.*).

par'venu, *n.*, an upstart; one newly risen (*Fr.*).

parv'is, *n.*, the enclosed space in front of a church.

pas, *n.*, a step; precedence (*Fr.*).

Pasch, *n.*, the Passover; Easter.

pas'chal, *adj.*, pert. or rel. to the Passover or to Easter.

pas'chaltide, *n.*, Easter.

pash, *v.t.*, to strike violently.

pasha', *n.*, a Turkish officer of high rank.

pa'shm, *n.*, the underfur from Tibetan goats.

pa'shalic, *n.*, a province governed by a pasha.

pasigraph'ic, *adj.*, pert. or rel. to pasigraphy.

pasig'raphy, *n.*, a system of universal writing.

pasque'-flower, *n.*, the Easter anemone with large purple flowers.

pas'quin, *n.*, *i.q.* pasquinade.

pasquinade', *n.*, a lampoon; *v.t.* and *i.*, to satirize in writing.

pass, *n.*, a defile between two mountains; a ticket of free admission or passage; attainment of the qualifying standard in an examination; an incomplete action; *v.t.* and *i.*, to proceed; to vanish; to go beyond or by; to succeed in an examination.

pass'able, *adj.*, current; receivable; tolerable.

pass'ably, *adv.*, tolerably.

passade', *n.*, a thrust in fencing (*Fr.*).

pas'sage, *n.*, transit; a way or corridor through which one may pass; a portion of a quoted book or poem.

pas'sant, *adj.*, an heraldic term describing an animal which appears to be walking.

pass'-book, *n.*, a bank book.

passed, *p.p.*, pass.

passé(e), *adj.*, faded; past the prime (*Fr.*).

pas'senger, *n.*, a traveller in a conveyance of any kind.

passe'-partout', *n.*, a master key; gummed framing tape; a picture so framed (*Fr.*).

pass'er, *n.*, one that passes.

passer-by', *n.*, one who goes by.

pas'serine, *adj.*, pert. or rel. to the order of birds called Passeres.

passibil'ity, *n.*, the quality of being passible.

pass'ible, *adj.*, impressionable.

pas'sim, *adv.*, here and there; in many places in a book (*Lat.*).

passim'eter, *n.*, a ticket-issuing machine.

pass'ing, *adv.*, exceedingly; *pr.p.*, pass.

pass'ing-bell, *n.*, a bell rung when a parishioner is dying.

pas'sion, n., the last suffering of Christ; a strong emotion; anger; ardour; sexual desire; v.i., to express passion.

pas'sional, n., a book describing the sufferings of saints and martyrs.

pas'sionate, adj., vehement; strongly emotional.

pas'sionately, adv., ardently; angrily.

pas'sion-flower, n., a plant with flowers supposed to symbolize the Passion.

pas'sionless, adj., void of passion.

Pas'sion-play, n., a miracle play representing scenes in the Passion.

Pas'sion Week, n., the week before Holy Week and following Passion Sunday, the fifth Sunday in Lent.

pas'sive, adj., unresisting; inert.

pas'sively, adv., without action or resistance.

pas'siveness, n., the quality of being passive.

passiv'ity, n., i.q. passiveness.

pass'key, n., a master key.

Pass'over, n., a Jewish religious commemoration.

pass'port, n., a safe-conduct document granted to travellers abroad.

pass'way, n., a means of passing.

pass'word, n., a secret word used to establish identity.

past, adj., existing no more; adv., by; n., a bygone time; prep., after; beyond; by.

paste, n., a soft mass; a kind of cement; a composition of which imitation precious stones are made; an adhesive; v.t., to cement with paste.

paste'board, n., cardboard.

pa'sted, p.p., paste.

pas'tel, adj., soft, subdued in colour; n., a coloured crayon.

pas'tern, n., that part of the leg of a horse between the hoof and the next joint; a shackle for horses while grazing.

past'eurism, n., a method of inoculation practised by Louis Pasteur.

past'eurize, v.t., to render a liquid free from harmful bacteria by Pasteur's method.

pastic'cio, n., a picture painted by a master in imitation of the style of another artist; a medley or miscellany.

pastiche', n., i.q. pasticcio.

pas'til, n., i.q. pastille.

pastille', n., a little roll of paste which gives a fragrant smell when burned; a sweetmeat.

pas'time, n., an amusement; sport.

pa'sting, pr.p., paste.

past'mas'ter, n., an expert; one who has been a master.

pas'tor, n., a bishop; a minister of religion.

pas'toral, adj., rural; pert. or rel. to a pastor; n., a bucolic poem.

pastora'le, n., a melody or symphony in rustic style.

pas'torate, n., the office of pastor.

pa'stry, n., food made chiefly of flour paste.

pa'strycook, n., one who makes and sells pastry.

pas'turable, adj., fit for pasture.

pas'turage, n., growing grass on which cattle are fed.

pas'ture, n., a grazing ground; v.t., to feed on growing grass.

pas'tured, p.p., pasture.

pas'turing, pr.p., pasture.

pa'sty, n., a meat-pie covered with a crust.

pas'ty, adj., like paste; having a pale complexion.

pat, adj., apt; adv., fitly; n., a light blow; a small shaped piece of butter; v.t., to tap with the fingers.

Patago'nian, adj., pert. or rel. to Patagonia; n., a native of P.

patch, n., a piece of cloth sewn on a garment to repair it; a small plot of ground; v.t., to mend by patching.

patched, p.p., patch.

patch'er, n., one who patches.

patch'ing, pr.p., patch.

patchou'li, n., an Eastern perfume.

patch'work, n., pieces of material of various shapes and colours sewn together.

patch'y, adj., full of patches; uneven.

pate, n., the head; the top of the head.

pâté, n., a little pie; a luxurious paste (Fr.).

patel'la, n., a small dish; the knee-cap.

patel'liform, adj., saucer-shaped.

pat'en, n., a metal plate in which the bread is placed in the Eucharist.

patent, adj., evident; clear for all to see.

pat'ent, adj., secured by law as an exclusive privilege; n., a privilege conferring a limited monopoly; v.t., to secure by a patent.

pat'entable, adj., capable of being patented.

pat'ented, p.p., patent.

patentee', n., one who possesses patent-rights.

pat'enting, pr.p., patent.

pat'ently, adv., in an obvious manner.

patentor', n., one who grants a patent.

pat'er, n., father (colloq., Lat.).

paterfamil'ias, n., the father or head of a family (Lat.).

pater'nal, adj., fatherly; on the father's side.

pater'nally, adv., in a fatherly way.

pater'nity, n., the relation of a father to his offspring.

pat'ernoster, n., the Lord's Prayer; every tenth bead in a rosary; a rosary itself.

path, n., a way.

Pathan', n., an Afghan; an Indian of Afghan descent.

pathet'ic, adj., exciting tender emotion.

pathet'ically, *adj.*, in a pathetic manner.

path'finder, *n.*, one who goes ahead to explore the territory or objective; an aircraft used for target marking.

path'ic, *n.*, catamite.

path'less, *adj.*, untrodden; having no beaten way.

pathogen'esis, *n.*, the development of a disease.

pathogen'ic, *adj.*, disease producing.

pathog'eny, *n.*, the science of the origin and development of disease.

pathognomon'ic, *adj.*, characteristic of a particular disease.

pathog'nomy, *n.*, the science of the expression of the passions.

patholog'ic, *adj.*, *i.q.* pathological.

patholog'ical, *adj.*, pert. or rel. to pathology.

patholog'ically, *adv.*, in a pathological manner.

pathol'ogist, *n.*, one skilled in pathology.

pathol'ogy, *n.*, the science of the causes and symptoms of diseases.

pa'thos, *n.*, the quality that awakens the tender emotions.

paths, *n. pl.* of path.

path'way, *n.*, a path; a narrow way for foot-passengers.

pa'tience, *n.*, forbearance; sustained restraint.

pa'tient, *adj.*, suffering in silence; calmly diligent; *n.*, a person under medical treatment.

pa'tiently, *adv.*, uncomplainingly.

pat'ina, *n.*, the fine green rust of copper or bronze; any even or smooth surface.

patina'ted, *adj.*, pert. or rel. to patina.

pa'tio, *n.*, an inner courtyard; an open quadrangle.

pat'ly, *adv.*, fitly.

patois', *n.*, a rustic or provincial mode of speech (*Fr.*).

pa'trial, *adj.*, pert. or rel. to one's native land.

pa'triarch, *n.*, the father and ruler of a family; an aged venerable man; a bishop of the highest rank.

patriar'chal, *adj.*, rel. to a patriarch.

pat'riarchate, *n.*, the jurisdiction of a patriarch.

patriar'chic, *adj.*, *i.q.* patriarchal.

pa'triarchy, *n.*, *i.q.* patriarchate.

patri'cian, *n.*, of noble birth; bel. to the senatorial order in ancient Rome; *n.*, a person of noble birth.

patri'ciate, *n.*, the patrician order.

pat'ricidal, *adj.*, pert. or rel. to patricide.

pat'ricide, *n.*, the murder, or murderer, of a father.

patrilin'eal, *adj.*, of male descent.

patrimo'nial, *adj.*, inherited from ancestors.

pat'rimony, *n.*, a right or estate inherited from ancestors.

pat'riot, *n.*, a person who loves his country and zealously supports and defends it.

patriot'ic, *adj.*, having the feelings of a patriot.

patriot'ically, *adv.*, in a patriotic manner.

pat'riotism, *n.*, the love of one's country.

Patripas'sian, *n.*, one of a sect of the early Christian Church who taught that God the Father shared the sufferings of Christ.

patris'tic, *adj.*, pert. or rel. to the fathers of the early Christian Church.

patrol', *n.*, the marching round of a military or police guard; a constable with a regular beat; *v.i.* and *t.*, to go the rounds.

patrolled', *p.p.*, patrol.

patrol'ling, *pr.p.*, patrol.

pa'tron, *n.*, a man of position who assists one less well endowed; one who has the gift of an ecclesiastical benefice.

pat'ronage, *n.*, the act of patronizing; the right of presentation to an ecclesiastical benefice.

pat'ronal, *adj.*, acting as a patron; bel. to a patron saint.

pa'troness, *n.*, a woman patron.

pat'ronize, *v.t.*, to act as, or to assume the air of, a patron; to act condescendingly.

pat'ronized, *p.p.*, patronize.

pat'ronizer, *n.*, one who patronizes.

pat'ronizing, *adj.*, condescending; *pr.p.*, patronize.

pat'ronizingly, *adv.*, in a patronizing way.

patronym'ic, *n.*, a personal name derived from that of a parent or ancestor; a surname.

patroon', *n.*, the proprietor of a manor in the State of New York.

pat'ten, *n.*, a wooden shoe standing on a ring, worn to keep the feet above the mud.

pat'ter, *n.*, thieves' slang; rapid talk; quick amusing talk to accompany a stage act; *v.i.*, to make a quick succession of small sounds; to mutter.

pat'tered, *p.p.*, patter.

pat'tering, *pr.p.*, patter.

pat'tern, *n.*, a model; an ornamental design on a woven fabric.

pat'tress, *n.*, a wall block for supporting brackets, switches, etc.

pat'ty, *n.*, a little pie.

pat'ty-pan, *n.*, a pan to bake patties in.

pat'ulous, *adj.*, opening widely.

pau'city, *n.*, fewness.

Paul'ine, *adj.*, pert. or rel. to St. Paul.

Paul'ist, *n.*, a member of the American Congregation of the Missionary Priests of St. Paul the Apostle.

paunch, *n.*, the belly, esp. if large.

pau'per, *n.*, a poor person, esp. one supported by law or charity.

pau'perism, *n.*, indigence.

pauperiza'tion, *n.*, the act of pauperizing.

pau'perize, *v.t.*, to reduce to the state of a pauper.

pau'perized, *p.p.*, pauperize.

pau'perizing, *pr.p.*, pauperize.

pause, *n.*, a temporary cessation; *v.i.*, to make a short stop.

paused, *p.p.*, pause.

paus'er, *n.*, one who pauses.

paus'ing, *pr.p.*, pause.

pav'age, *n.*, a toll paid for paving streets; laying pavements.

pave, *v.t.*, to floor with stone, wood, brick, etc.

pavé', *n.*, a street pavement (*Fr.*).

paved, *p.p.*, pave.

pave'ment, *n.*, a paved path for pedestrians.

pa'ver, *n.*, *i.q.* paviour.

pavil'ion, *n.*, a tent; a canopy.

pa'ving, *n.*, the laying of pavement; *pr.p.*, pave.

pa'vio(u)r, *n.*, one whose occupation is to pave.

Pa'vo, *n.*, the Peacock—a constellation.

pavona'zzo, *adj.* and *n.*, with peacock-coloured markings (marble) (*It.*).

pav'onine, *adj.*, bel. to a peacock; iridescent.

paw, *n.*, the foot of a quadruped; *v.i.*, to draw the forefoot along the ground.

pawed, *adj.*, having paws; *p.p.*, paw.

paw'ing, *pr.p.*, paw.

pawk'y, *adj.*, humorous in an ironic way.

pawl, *n.*, a click which falls into the teeth of a ratchet-wheel to prevent its movement.

pawn, *n.*, a piece of the lowest value at chess; a pledge; *v.t.*, to pledge with a pawnbroker.

pawn'broker, *n.*, a person licensed to lend money on goods deposited with him.

pawned, *p.p.*, pawn.

pawnee', *n.*, one with whom a pledge is deposited as security.

pawn'er, *n.*, one who pawns.

pawn'ing, *pr.p.*, pawn.

pawn'shop, *n.*, the place of business of a pawnbroker.

pawn'-ticket, *n.*, a ticket or receipt given by a pawnbroker to the pawner.

pawpaw', *n.*, *i.q.* papaw.

pax, *n.*, a small tablet engraved with sacred emblems.

pax'wax, *n.*, a tendon in the neck of an animal.

pay, *n.*, the remuneration for goods purchased, services rendered, etc.; *v.i.*, to be remunerative; *v.t.*, to discharge a debt.

pay'able, *adj.*, suitable to be paid; due.

pay'-day, *n.*, the day for paying wages.

payee', *n.*, one to whom money is to be paid.

pay'er, *n.*, one who pays.

pay'ing, *adj.*, advantageous; *pr.p.*, pay.

pay'load, *n.*, part of a load; the load that earns revenue.

pay'master, *n.*, an officer in the armed services who pays the men.

pay'ment, *n.*, the discharge of a debt.

pay'nim, *n.*, a pagan.

pay'-off, *n.*, the time of reckoning; the outcome.

pay'-roll, *n.*, a list of persons entitled to payment of wages, etc.

paysage', *n.*, landscape (*Fr.*).

pea, *n.*, an edible vegetable; one of its seeds.

peace, *n.*, a state of tranquillity.

peace'able, *adj.*, disposed to peace.

peace'ably, *adv.*, in a peaceable manner.

peace'ful, *adj.*, possessing peace.

peace'fully, *adv.*, tranquilly.

peace'fulness, *n.*, the state or quality of being peaceful.

peace'maker, *n.*, one who reconciles parties in disagreement.

peace'-offering, *n.*, a propitiatory offering.

peace'-officer, *n.*, a civil officer to preserve the public peace.

peach, *n.*, a delicious fleshy fruit containing a stone; *v.i.*, to turn informer.

pea'-chick, *n.*, a young peafowl.

peach'-tree, *n.*, a tree bearing peaches.

peach'y, *adj.*, resembling a peach, esp. in colour and texture.

pea'cock, *n.*, a large gallinaceous bird of beautiful plumage.

pea'fowl, *n.*, the peacock or peahen.

pea'hen, *n.*, the female of the peacock.

pea'-jacket, *n.*, a thick, loose, woollen jacket worn by seamen.

peak, *n.*, the top of a hill that ends in a point; any projection, esp. of a cap; *v.i.*, to look thin and ill.

peaked, *adj.*, pointed; *p.p.*, peak.

peak'ish, *adj.*, thin-faced and sickly-looking.

peak'y, *adj.*, sickly, puny.

peak'y-faced, *adj.*, sickly-looking.

peal, *n.*, a succession of loud sounds; sea trout; *v.i.*, to utter a peal; *v.t.*, to cause to ring or sound. (Also *peel*.)

pealed, *p.p.*, peal.

peal'ing, *n.*, ringing; *pr.p.*, peal.

pean, *n.*, *i.q.* paean.

pea'nut, *n.*, the groundnut or earth-nut.

pear, *n.*, a common fruit of temperate regions.

pearl, *n.*, a silvery, hard, smooth, round or oval body produced by certain molluscs in their shells; an affection of the eye, also called cataract; a small printing type; *v.i.*, to form into pearls; to dive for pearls; *v.t.*, to set with pearls; to make like pearls.

pearl'-ash, *n.*, commercial potassium carbonate.

pearled, *adj.*, adorned with pearls; *p.p.*, pearl.

pear'lies, *n. pl.*, pearl buttons; a costermonger's dress decorated with pearl buttons.

pearl'ing, *pr.p.*, pearl.

pearl'-stitch, *n.*, a seam-stitch in knitting.

pearl'y, *adj.*, containing or resembling pearls.

pear'main, *n.*, a kind of apple.

pear'-shaped, *adj.*, shaped like a pear.

pear'-tree, *n.*, a fruit-tree yielding pears.

peas'ant, *n.*, a countryman.

peas'antry, *n.*, country people collectively.

peas'cod, *n.*, the pod or shell of a pea. (Also *peasecod*.)

pease, *n. pl.*, peas collectively.

pease'cod, *n.*, *i.q.* peascod.

pease'-pudding, *n.*, a pudding made chiefly of peas.

pea'shooter, *n.*, a tube through which peas are blown as missiles.

pea'-soup, *n.*, soup made from peas.

pea-soup'er, *n.*, a thick yellow fog.

peat, *n.*, a kind of turf used as fuel.

peat'-moss, *n.*, a moss producing peat.

peat'y, *adj.*, resembling, composed of, or abounding in, peat.

peb'ble, *n.*, a small rounded stone; agate; colourless, transparent rock-crystal.

peb'bled, *adj.*, abounding with pebbles.

peb'ble-stone, *n.*, a pebble.

peb'bly, *adj.*, full of pebbles.

pebrine, *n.*, a disease of silkworms.

pecan', *n.*, a kind of hickory.

peccabil'ity, *n.*, the state of being peccable.

pec'cable, *adj.*, liable to sin.

peccadil'lo, *n.*, a slight offence.

pec'cancy, *n.*, the state of being peccant.

pec'cant, *adj.*, sinning; corrupt.

pec'cantly, *adv.*, corruptly, defectively.

pec'cary, *n.*, a pachydermatous American hog.

pecca'vi, *interj.*, an acknowledgment of fault = I have sinned (*Lat.*).

pêche Mel'ba, *n.*, an ice-cream and peach confection.

peck, *n.*, a quarter of a bushel; *v.t.*, to strike or pick up with the beak, or with a pointed instrument.

pecked, *p.p.*, peck.

peck'er, *n.*, one who, or that which, pecks.

peck'ing, *pr.p.*, peck.

peck'ish, *adj.*, hungry (*colloq.*).

pec'ten, *n.*, a marine bivalve, the shells of which have diverging ribs and furrows.

pec'tin, *n.*, the basis of vegetable jelly (*chem.*).

pec'tinal, *adj.*, resembling a comb.

pec'tinate, *adj.*, toothed like a comb.

pec'tinated, *adj.*, *i.q.* pectinate.

pectina'tion, *n.*, the state of being pectinated.

pec'tolite, *n.*, a whitish sodium-calcium silicate.

pec'toral, *adj.*, pert. or rel. to the breast; *n.*, a breastplate.

pec'tose, *n.*, an insoluble substance in fruit (*chem.*).

pec'ulate, *v.i.*, to embezzle.

pec'ulated, *p.p.*, peculate.

pec'ulating, *pr.p.*, peculate.

pecula'tion, *n.*, embezzlement.

pec'ulator, *n.*, one who peculates.

pecu'liar, *adj.*, one's own; specially belonging; eccentric.

peculiar'ity, *n.*, a special characteristic; the state of being peculiar.

pecu'liarize, *v.t.*, to set apart; to appropriate.

pecu'liarly, *adv.*, in a manner not common to others.

pecu'niarily, *adv.*, in a pecuniary manner.

pecu'niary, *adj.*, pert. or rel. to money.

pedagog'ic, *adj.*, pert. or rel. to pedagogy.

pedagog'ically, *adv.*, in the manner of a teacher.

ped'agog(u)ism, *n.*, the business or manners of a pedagogue.

ped'agogue, *n.*, a schoolmaster (usually in a slighting sense).

ped'agogy, *n.*, the science of the principles of teaching.

ped'al, *adj.*, pert. or rel. to a foot or to a pedal; *n.*, a lever to be pressed down by the foot.

peda'lian, *adj.*, pert. or rel. to metrical feet.

pedal'ity, *n.*, measurement by paces.

ped'ant, *n.*, one who vainly displays his learning; a formalist.

pedan'tic, *adj.*, pert. or rel. to a pedant.

ped'antry, *n.*, a boastful display of learning; an obstinate adherence to rules.

ped'ate, *adj.*, having divisions like toes; divided into lobes.

ped'dle, *v.i.*, to retail small wares; to trifle; *v.t.* to sell in small quantities while travelling about the country.

ped'dled, *p.p.*, peddle.

ped'dling, *pr.p.*, peddle.

ped'erast, *n.*, *i.q.* paederast.

ped'erasty, *n.*, *i.q.* paederasty.

ped'estal, *n.*, a basement or support for a statue, etc.

pedes'trial, *adj.*, rel. to the feet.

pedes'trian, *adj.*, going on foot; *n.*, a walker.

pedes'trianism, *n.*, the practice of walking.

pedes'trianize, *v.i.*, to tour on foot.

ped'iatric, *adj.*, *i.q.* paediatric.

ped'iatrics, *n. pl.*, *i.q.* paediatrics.

ped'icel, *n.*, the stalk of a single flower or leaf; the footstalk of a zoophyte.

ped'icel(l)ate, *adj.*, having a pedicel.

ped'icel(l)ed, *adj.*, *i.q.* pedicellate.

ped'icle, *n.*, *i.q.* pedicel.

pedic'ular, *adj.*, lousy.

pedicula'tion, *n.*, lousiness.

pedic'ulous, *adj.*, *i.q.* pedicular.

ped'icure, *n.*, the care and lesser surgery of the feet.

ped'icurist, *n.*, a chiropodist.

pedig'erous, *adj.*, having feet or legs.

ped'igree, *n.*, lineage; a genealogical tree.

ped'iment, *n.*, a gable in Greek architecture.

ped'imented, *adj.*, having a pediment.

ped'ipalp, *n.*, an arachnid; an appendage of a male spider.

pedi'tis, *n.*, a disease of horses' feet.

ped'lar, *n.*, a travelling chapman.

ped'lary, *n.*, pedlar's wares; the employment of a pedlar.

pedobap'tism, *n.*, *i.q.* paedobaptism.

pedobap'tist, *n.*, *i.q.* paedobaptist.

pedolog'ical, *adj.*, pert. or rel. to pedology.

pedol'ogist, *n.,* *i.q.* paedologist.

pedol'ogy, *n.,* *i.q.* paedology.

pedom'eter, *n.,* an instrument for numbering paces and so ascertaining distances travelled on foot.

pedomet'ric, *adj.,* pert. or rel. to a pedometer.

ped'oscope, *n.,* an X-ray apparatus for examining the fit of a shoe.

ped'rail, *n.,* a wheel device for assisting heavy vehicles over rough ground.

pedun'cle, *n.,* the stalk of a flower or fruit; the stem of a brachiopod.

pedun'cular, *adj.,* pert. or rel. to a peduncle.

pedun'culate, *adj.,* having a peduncle; growing on one.

peek, *n.,* *i.q.* peep; *v.i.,* to peep.

peel, *n.,* the rind of anything; a baker's shovel; a fortified tower; sea-trout; *v.i.,* to lose the skin or rind; *v.t.,* to strip the rind or bark from.

peeled, *p.p.,* peel.

peel'er, *n.,* one who peels; a policeman (*slang*).

peel'ing, *n.,* the act of removing a rind; the rind removed; *pr.p.,* peel.

peen, *n.,* the end of a hammer-head opposite the face.

peep, *n.,* a sly look; *v.i.,* to cry as a chicken; to look through a crevice; to look slyly.

peeped, *p.p.,* peep.

peep'er, *n.,* one who peeps.

peep'-hole, *n.,* a hole to peep through unseen.

peep'ing, *pr.p.,* peep.

peep'-show, *n.,* an exhibition of objects viewed through a lens.

peep'-toe, *n.,* a shoe or sandal cut away at the toe-cap.

peep'ul, *n.,* the sacred, Indian fig-tree. (Also *pipal*.)

peer, *n.,* an equal; a nobleman; *v.i.,* to look hard and fixedly.

peer'age, *n.,* the body of peers collectively; the rank of a peer.

peered, *p.p.,* peer.

peer'ess, *n.,* the consort of a peer; a noblewoman holding a title in her own right.

peer'ing, *pr.p.,* peer.

peer'less, *adj.,* unequalled.

peer'lessness, *n.,* the state of being without an equal.

peeved, *adj.,* annoyed, irritated.

pee'vish, *adj.,* fretful.

pee'vishly, *adv.,* in a peevish manner.

pee'vishness, *n.,* fretfulness.

pee'wit, *n.,* the lapwing. (Also *pewit.*)

peg, *n.,* a wooden pin; a pin on which to hang anything; a drink (*slang*); a degree in position or estimation (*colloq.*); *v.t.,* to fasten or mark with pegs; to stabilize.

Peg'asus, *n.,* a winged horse; the horse of the Muses, and, hence, connected with poetry.

pegged, *adj.,* fastened with pegs; *p.p.,* peg.

peg'ger, *n.,* one who pegs.

peg'ging, *pr.p.,* peg.

peg'-top, *n.,* a toy made to spin by a string.

peignoir, *n.,* a loose dressing-gown (*Fr.*).

peiram'eter, *n.,* an instrument to measure the resistance a road offers to a wheeled vehicle.

peiras'tic, *adj.,* tentative.

pejor'atist, *n.,* a pessimist.

pej'orative, *adj.,* depreciating.

pek'an, *n.,* a North American marten.

Pekin(g)ese', *n.,* a breed of small dog.

Pekingman, *n.,* the prehistoric remains of man found in Peking.

pek'oe, *n.,* a fine, black tea.

pel'age, *n.,* the fur covering of a mammal.

Pela'gian, *adj.,* pert. or rel. to Pelagianism; *n.,* a follower of Pelagius, a British monk who denied the doctrine of original sin.

Pela'gianism, *n.,* the Pelagian heresy.

pela'gic, *adj.,* of, in, or on the open sea.

pelargo'nium, *n.,* a type of geranium or stork's-bill.

pel'erine, *n.,* a lady's long cape or tippet.

pelf, *n.,* money; filthy lucre.

pel'ican, *n.,* a large webfooted bird with a great pouched bill.

Pe'lion, *n.,* a mountain of Thessaly.

pelisse', *n.,* a heavy robe of silk for outdoor use.

pell, *n.,* a skin; a roll of parchment.

pel'lage, *n.,* a duty on hides or leather.

pella'gra, *n.,* a skin disease akin to leprosy.

pel'let, *n.,* a little ball.

pel'licle, *n.,* a thin skin; the outer covering of plants.

pellic'ular, *adj.,* pert. or rel. to a pellicle.

pel'litory, *n.,* a British plant with a pungent flavoured root.

pell-mell', *adv.,* in utter confusion.

pellu'cid, *adj.,* translucent; very clear.

pellucid'ity, *n.,* the quality of being pellucid.

Pel'manism, *n.,* a system of memory training.

pel'met, *n.,* a valance or pendant for hiding curtain rails.

Peloponne'sian, *adj.,* bel. to the southern peninsula of Greece.

pelor'us, *n.,* a device for sighting bearings on a ship's compass.

pelot'a, *n.,* a Basque ball-game.

pelt, *n.,* a raw hide; *v.i.,* to drive; to come down with violence (as rain, hail, etc.); *v.t.,* to throw something at.

pel'tate, *adj.,* shield-shaped.

pel'tated, *adj.,* *i.q.* peltate.

pelt'ed, *p.p.,* pelt.

pelt'ing, *adj.,* driving; violent; *pr.p.,* pelt.

pelt'ry, *n. pl.,* pelts collectively.

pel'vic, *adj.,* pert. or rel. to the pelvis.

pel'vis, *n.,* the bony framework of the lower part of the abdomen.

pem'mican, *n.*, lean venison or beef, dried, pounded into paste, and pressed into cakes.

pem'phigus, *n.*, a form of skin eruption.

pen, *n.*, an instrument used for writing; a small enclosure for animals or fowls; a female swan; *v.t.*, to write; to encage.

pe'nal, *adj.*, pert. or rel. to, or entailing, punishment.

penaliza'tion, *n.*, the act of penalizing.

pe'nalize, *v.t.*, to subject to a penalty.

pe'nalized, *p.p.*, penalize.

pe'nalizing, *pr.p.*, penalize.

pe'nally, *adv.*, in a penal way.

pen'alty, *n.*, a punishment; a forfeiture.

pen'ance, *n.*, a punishment imposed for sin.

penann'ular, *adj.*, almost ring-like.

Pena'tes, *n. pl.*, household gods; *i.q.* Larés.

pence, *n.*, the pl. of penny.

pen'chant', *n.*, a liking; a trend towards (*Fr.*).

pen'cil, *n.*, an implement formed of graphite, crayon, etc., for marking on paper; a collection of rays of light; *v.t.* and *i.*, to write with a pencil.

pen'cil(l)ed, *adj.*, delicately marked, as with a pencil; *p.p.*, pencil.

pen'cil(l)ing, *pr.p.*, pencil.

pend'ant, *n.*, a suspended ornament; a flag borne at a mast-head; a hanging chandelier.

pend'ence, *n.*, *i.q.* pendency.

pend'ency, *n.*, the state of being pendent.

pend'ent, *adj.*, hanging.

penden'tive, *n.*, the support for a dome or cupola.

pen'dicle, *n.*, a croft or farm.

pend'ing, *adj.*, not terminated; temporarily postponed; *prep.*, during.

pendrag'on, *n.*, a chief leader among the ancient British.

pen'dulate, *v.i.*, to swing like a pendulum.

pen'duline, *adj.*, suspended.

pendulos'ity, *n.*, the state of being pendulous.

pen'dulous, *adj.*, hanging loosely.

pen'dulously, *adv.*, in a pendulous way.

pen'dulum, *n.*, the swinging piece in a clock.

pen'eplain, *n.*, geographically, almost a plain.

penetrabil'ity, *n.*, the state of being penetrable.

pen'etrable, *adj.*, capable of being penetrated.

penetra'lia, *n. pl.*, a sanctuary; the inmost parts (*Lat.*).

pen'etrant, *adj.*, having the power to penetrate.

pen'etrate, *v.t.*, to enter into or pierce.

pen'etrated, *p.p.*, penetrate.

pen'etrating, *adj.*, acute; discerning; *pr.p.*, penetrate.

pen'etratingly, *adv.*, in a penetrating way.

penetra'tion, *n.*, the act of penetrating; mental acuteness.

pen'etrative, *adj.*, sharp; subtle.

pen'etratively, *adv.*, sharply.

pen'-friend, *n.*, one who sustains friendship through correspondence.

pen'guin, *n.*, an Antarctic swimming bird with rudimentary wings.

pen'holder, *n.*, the stalk for holding a pen-nib.

pen'ial, *adj.*, pert. or rel. to the penis.

pen'icil, *n.*, a wad of lint for applying to wounds; a small tuft of hair.

penicil'late, *adj.*, consisting of a bundle of short, compact fibres or hairs.

penicill'in, *n.*, a therapeutic, antibiotic drug.

penin'sula, *n.*, a portion of land almost surrounded by water.

penin'sular, *adj.*, pert. or rel. to a peninsula.

penin'sulate, *v.t.*, to form into a peninsula.

penin'sulated, *p.p.*, peninsulate.

penin'sulating, *pr.p.*, peninsulate.

pe'nis, *n.*, the male sex organ.

pen'itence, *n.*, repentance.

pen'itencer, *n.*, a priest who hears confession, esp. in reserved cases.

pen'itency, *n.*, *i.q.* penitence.

pen'itent, *adj.*, contrite; *n.*, one who is contrite.

peniten'tial, *adj.*, expressing penitence.

peniten'tially, *adv.*, in a penitential way.

peniten'tiary, *adj.*, pert. or rel. to penance; *n.*, a place of discipline; a prison.

pen'itently, *adv.*, in a penitent manner.

pen'knife, *n.*, a pocketknife.

pen'man, *n.*, a writer.

pen'manship, *n.*, the skilled use of the pen.

pen'nant, *n.*, *i.q.* pennon; a small flag.

pen'nate, *adj.*, formed like a feather (*bot.*).

penned, *p.p.*, pen.

pen'-nib, *n.*, the writing part of a pen.

pen'niform, *adj.*, resembling the barbs of a feather.

pennig'erous, *adj.*, bearing feathers or quills.

pen'niless, *adj.*, destitute of money.

penn'ill, *n.*, improvised verse sung to the harp.

pen'ning, *pr.p.*, pen.

pen'non, *n.*, a small pointed flag borne on a lance. (Also *pennant*.)

pen'noned, *adj.*, displaying a pennon.

pen'ny, *n.*, a British unit of currency, a coin one hundredth part of a £; a cent (*U.S.A.*).

penny-a-li'ner, *n.*, a poor writer for hire.

penn'yfarth'ing, *n.*, an old-fashioned bicycle having one big and one small wheel.

pennyroy'al, *n.*, a plant of the mint family.

pen'nyweight, *n.*, a weight equal to 24 grains.

pen'nywise, *adj.*, saving on small things, but losing on large ones.

pen'nyworth, *n.*, as much as costs a penny.

penol'ogy, *n.*, the science and philosophy of public punishments.

pen'sile, *adj.*, hanging.

pen'sion, n., an allowance made for past services; v.t., to grant a pension to.

pension, n., a Continental boarding-house or boarding-school (Fr.).

pen'sionable, adj., entitled to a pension.

pen'sionary, adj., receiving or consisting in a pension.

pen'sioned, p.p., pension.

pen'sioner, n., one who receives a pension; one who pays for his board and lodging.

pen'sioning, pr.p., pension.

pen'sive, adj., thoughtful and a little melancholy.

pen'sively, adv., in a pensive manner.

pen'siveness, n., the state of being pensive.

pen'stock, n., a floodgate.

pent, adj., penned; closely confined.

pen'tachord, n., a five-stringed instrument of music; a scale of five diatonic intervals.

pen'tacle, n., a five-pointed star.

pentacros'tic, adj., containing five acrostics of the same word.

pen'tad, n., the number five; a group of five.

pentadac'tyl, adj., five-fingered; five-toed.

pen'tagon, n., a five-sided figure.

pentag'onal, adj., having five angles.

pen'tagram, n., i.q. pentacle.

pen'tagraph, n., i.q. pantograph.

pentagyn'ia, n. pl., plants with flowers having five styles.

pentahe'dral, adj., having five equal faces.

pentahe'dron, n., a solid with five equal faces.

pentam'eter, n., a verse containing five feet.

pentan'dria, n. pl., plants having flowers with five stamens.

pen'tane, n., paraffin hydrocarbon having five carbon atoms.

pentan'gular, adj., having five angles.

pentapet'alous, adj., having five petals.

pentaphyl'lous, adj., having five leaves.

pen'tarchy, · n., government by five persons.

pentasper'mous, adj., containing five seeds.

pen'tastich, n., a poem of five verses.

pen'tastyle, adj., having five columns in front.

Pen'tateuch, n., the first five books of the Old Testament.

pentath'lon, n., an athletic contest of five events.

pentaton'ic, adj., consisting of five tones.

Pen'tecost, n., Whitsuntide; a solemn festival of the Jews coming fifty days after the Passover.

Pen'tecostal, adj., pert. or rel. to Pentecost.

pent'house, n., a shed sloping from another building; a luxurious flat.

pen'tode, adj., (of radio valves) having five electrodes.

Pentste'mon, n., a genus of plants with bright red or blue flowers.

penult', n., the last syllable but one of a word.

penul'tima, n., i.q. penult.

penul'timate, adj., the last but one; n., i.q. penult.

penum'bra, n., a partial shadow outside of the total shadow.

penum'bral, adj., pert. or rel. to a penumbra.

penu'rious, adj., parsimonious.

penu'riously, adv., in a penurious manner.

penu'riousness, n., niggardliness.

pen'ury, n., extreme poverty.

pe'on, n., a South or Central American day-labourer or peasant.

pe'onage, n., the condition of a peon.

pe'ony, n., a ranunculaceous garden-plant with gaudy flowers.

peo'ple, n., the body of persons composing a nation or race; persons indefinitely; v.t., to stock with inhabitants.

peo'pled, p.p., people.

peo'pling, pr.p., people.

pep, n., vigour, energy, (colloq.).

peperi'no, n., porous volcanic rock.

pep'per, n., a plant and its fruit, the latter having a hot, pungent taste and used, when ground, as a condiment; v.t., to sprinkle with pepper; to pelt.

pep'percorn, n., the berry of the pepper; an insignificant amount.

pep'pered, p.p., pepper.

pep'pergrass, n., a garden salad; the pillwort.

pep'pering, n., a pelting; pr.p., pepper.

pep'permint, n., a plant of the mint family having a pungent taste; a confection of this characteristic.

pep'pery, adj., hot; irritable.

pep'sin, n., the active principle of gastric juice.

pep'tic, adj., digestive.

pep'toid, adj., pert. or rel. to digestion.

pep'tone, n., the substance into which the food is changed by the gastric juice.

per, prep., through; by; by means of (Lat.).

peradven'ture, adv., perhaps.

perai', n., a voracious, American freshwater fish.

peram'bulate, v.t., to walk through or over.

peram'bulated, p.p., perambulate.

peram'bulating, pr.p., perambulate.

perambula'tion, n., a travelling survey.

peram'bulator, n., a baby-carriage (abbrev. pram); one who perambulates.

per an'num, adv., annually (Lat. phrase).

percale', n., a closely woven cotton fabric.

perceiv'able, adj., i.q. perceptible.

perceiv'ably, adv., in a perceivable way.

perceive', v.t., to see; to understand; to observe.

perceived', p.p., perceive.

perceiv'er, n., one who perceives.

perceiv'ing, pr.p., perceive.

per cent', *adv.*, the abbrev. of *per centum* (*Lat.*).

percent'age, *n.*, the rate of units on a hundred.

per cen'tum, *adv.*, for or of each hundred (*Lat.*).

per'cept, *n.*, that which is perceived.

perceptibil'ity, *n.*, the quality of being perceptible; the power of perceiving.

percep'tible, *adj.*, capable of being perceived.

percep'tibly, *adv.*, in a perceptible manner.

percep'tion, *n.*, the act or faculty of perceiving.

percep'tive, *adj.*, having the faculty of perception; observant.

percep'tively, *adv.*, in a perceptive manner.

percep'tivity, *n.*, the power of perception.

percep'tual, *adj.*, pert. or rel. to perception.

perch, *n.*, a fresh-water fish; a measure of length of 5½ yds.; a roost; *v.i.*, to roost; *v.t.*, to place on a perch.

perchance', *adv.*, perhaps.

perched, *p.p.*, perch.

perch'er, *n.*, one that perches; an insessorial bird.

percheron, *n.*, a French bred, draught horse.

perch'ing, *pr.p.*, perch.

perchlo'rate, *n.*, a salt of perchloric acid.

perchlo'ric, *adj.*, a term applied to an explosive acid.

perchlo'ride, *n.*, a chloride with the largest proportion of chlorine.

percip'ience, *n.*, *i.q.*, perception.

percip'iency, *n.*, *i.q.* percipience.

percip'ient, *adj.*, having the power of perception; *n.*, one who perceives.

per'coid, *adj.*, bel. to the perch family.

per'colate, *v.i.*, to pass through pores or small interstices; *v.t.*, to filter.

per'colated, *p.p.*, percolate.

per'colating, *pr.p.*, percolate.

percola'tion, *n.*, the act of percolating.

per'colator, *n.*, a filter; a coffee pot in which boiling water is strained through the coffee.

percuss', *v.t.*, to give a shock to; to strike against.

percussed', *p.p.*, percuss.

percuss'ing, *pr.p.*, percuss.

percus'sion, *n.*, forcible collision; a section of musical instruments requiring striking.

percus'sion-cap, *n.*, a small copper cup containing fulminating powder, used to explode gunpowder.

percus'sive, *adj.*, acting by percussion.

percu'tient, *n.*, that which strikes.

perdi'tion, *n.*, utter destruction.

perdu(e)', *adj.*, hid; in concealment (*Fr.*).

perdur'able, *n.*, permanent; eternal; durable.

per'egrin(e), *adj.*, foreign; *n.*, a kind of falcon.

per'egrinate, *v.i.*, to travel.

peregrina'tion, *n.*, a journey.

per'egrinator, *n.*, a traveller.

per'emptorily, *adv.*, in a peremptory manner.

per'emptoriness, *n.*, the state of being peremptory.

per'emptory, *adj.*, brusquely authoritative; decisive; imperious.

peren'nial, *adj.*, lasting throughout the year; unceasing; *n.*, a plant whose roots remain alive longer than two years but whose stems wither annually.

peren'nially, *adv.*, every year.

per'fect, *adj.*, finished; faultless; *v.t.*, to complete.

per'fected, *p.p.*, perfect.

per'fecter, *n.*, one who perfects.

perfectibil'ity, *n.*, the capacity of being made perfect.

perfect'ible, *adj.*, capable of being made perfect.

per'fecting, *pr.p.*, perfect.

perfec'tion, *n.*, the highest degree of excellence.

perfec'tionism, *n.*, the doctrine of the Perfectionists; the state or quality of being perfect.

Perfec'tionist, *n.*, a member of the American sect of Bible Communists.

perfec'tionist, *n.*, one who believes that moral or religious perfection can be attained during life; one who aims at perfection in everything.

perfect'ive, *adj.*, tending to make perfect.

per'fectly, *adv.*, thoroughly, faultlessly.

per'fectness, *n.*, the quality of being perfect.

perfect'or, *n.*, one who perfects; a press that prints on both sides at once.

perfer'vid, *adj.*, very fervid.

perfi'cient, *adj.*, thorough.

perfid'ious, *adj.*, treacherous.

perfid'iously, *adv.*, in a perfidious manner.

perfid'iousness, *n.*, the quality of being perfidious.

per'fidy, *n.*, treachery.

perfo'liate, *adj.*, (applied to) a leaf whose base surrounds the stem.

per'forate, *v.t.*, to pierce.

per'forated, *p.p.*, perforate.

per'forating, *pr.p.*, perforate.

perfora'tion, *n.*, the act of perforating; a pierced hole; a series of closeset holes to make detachment easy.

per'forative, *adj.*, having the power of piercing.

per'forator, *n.*, that which pierces.

perforce', *adv.*, of necessity.

perform', *v.i.*, to act a part or play on a musical instrument; *v.t.*, to accomplish.

perform'able, *adj.*, capable of being performed.

perform'ance, *n.*, a thing done; an entertainment; the act of performing.

performed', *p.p.*, perform.

perform'er, *n.*, one who performs; an actor, musician, etc.

perform'ing, *pr.p.*, perform.

perfume', v.t., to scent.

per'fume, n., a sweet odour; a scent.

perfumed', p.p., perfume.

perfu'mer, n., one who makes or sells perfumes.

perfu'mery, n., perfumes collectively.

perfu'ming, pr.p., perfume.

perfunc'torily, adv., in a perfunctory manner; carelessly.

perfunc'toriness, n., the state of being perfunctory.

perfunc'tory, adj., halfhearted; negligent.

perfuse', v.t., to suffuse.

perfu'sive, adj., adapted to perfuse.

pergame'neous, adj., resembling parchment.

per'gola, n., an arbour or bower on which plants may grow.

pergunn'ah, n., a group of Indian villages.

perhaps', adv., possibly; maybe.

pe'ri, n., a fallen angel; a kind of fairy (Persian myth.).

peri'agua, n., i.q. piragua.

per'ianth, n., a combination of calyx and corolla in a flower.

per'iapt, n., a charm.

pericar'diac, adj., pert. or rel. to the pericardium.

pericar'dial, adj., i.q. pericardiac.

pericar'dian, adj., i.q. pericardiac.

pericar'dic, adj., i.q. pericardiac.

pericardi'tis, n., inflammation of the pericardium.

pericar'dium, n., the membrane enclosing the heart.

per'icarp, n., the seedvessel of a plant.

pericar'pial, adj., pert. or rel. to a pericarp.

per'iclase, n., a transparent green magnesium oxide.

peric'ope, n., an arrangement of the Epistles and Gospels to the needs of Sundays and festivals.

pericra'nium, n., the membrane surrounding the skull.

per'iderm, n., a sort of outer layer or skin; the outer layer of bark.

per'idot, n., green olivine; a chrysolite stone.

per'idrome, n., an ambulatory.

per'igee, n., the point where the moon is nearest the earth.

perigraph'ic, adj., having a circumference.

perihe'lion, n., a point nearest the sun in the orbit of a planet.

perihexahe'dral', adj., having six equal faces.

per'il, n., danger; v.t., to risk.

per'il(l)ed, p.p., peril.

per'il(l)ing, pr.p., peril.

per'ilous, adj., dangerous.

per'ilously, adv., in a perilous manner.

per'ilousness, n., the state of being perilous.

perim'eter, n., the boundary of a figure, or the sum of its sides; the outer boundary of a camp, etc.; an instrument for measuring the field of vision.

perine'um, n., the region of the body between the anus and the genitals.

pe'riod, n., an indefinite time; the conclusion; a complete sentence; a full-stop or point; the time of menstruation.

period'ic, adj., performed in a regular revolution; published at regular intervals.

period'ical, adj., recurring or happening regularly; n., a periodical publication.

period'ically, adv., at stated periods.

periodic'ity, n., the quality or state of being periodical.

period'ogram, n., a diagram showing periodic phenomena.

perios'teum, n., a vascular membrane surrounding a bone.

peripatet'ic, adj., itinerant; Aristotelian.

peripetei'a, n., a sudden change of fortune.

periph'eral, adj., pert. or rel. to a periphery.

peripher'ic, adj., i.q. peripheral.

periph'ery, n., the circumference; the outside edge.

per'iphrase, n., i.q. periphrasis.

periph'rasis, n., a circumlocution; a meaning stated in different words.

periphras'tic, adj., characterized by periphrasis.

peripneumo'nia, n., i.q. pneumonia.

peripneumon'ic, adj., i.q. pneumonic.

peripneu'mony, n., i.q. peripneumonia.

perip'teral, adj., surrounded by a row of columns.

perip'terous, adj., i.q. peripteral.

perip'tery, n., a surrounding row of columns.

perique', n., a dark tobacco from Louisiana, U.S.A.

per'iscope, n., an optical instrument used by submarines and elsewhere, enabling objects above the level of the viewer to be surveyed.

periscop'ic, adj., viewing on all sides.

per'ish, v.i., to die; to be destroyed.

per'ishable, adj., subject to decay.

per'ishables, n. pl., things (esp. food) liable to decay.

per'ished, p.p., perish.

per'ishing, adj., word used colloquially as a condemnatory expletive; pr.p., perish.

per'isperm, n., the external skin of a seed.

perispher'ic, adj., globular.

perispom'enon, adj., marked with a circumflex; n., a circumflex accent on the last syllable.

perissol'ogy, n., a superfluity of words.

peris'talith, n., a series of stones around burial ground.

peristal'tic, adj., contracting all round in successive circles (describing the movement of the intestines forcing their contents downwards).

peristreph'ic, adj., rotatory. (Also peritropal.)

per'istyle, n., a row of surrounding columns.

perisys'tole, n., the interval between the contraction and the dilatation of the heart.

perit'omous, *adj.*, cleaving in more directions than one.

peritone'um, *n.*, the membranous lining of the abdomen.

peritoni'tis, *n.*, inflammation of the peritoneum.

perit'ropal, *adj.*, *i.q.* peristrephic.

perityphli'tis, *n.*, inflammation of the caecum or blind gut.

per'iwig, *n.*, a small wig.

per'iwinkle, *n.*, a British herbaceous plant with blue, white or purple flowers and evergreen leaves; a small mollusc.

per'jure, *v.i.*, to forswear.

per'jured, *adj.*, guilty of perjury; *p.p.*, perjure.

per'jurer, *n.*, one who takes a false oath.

per'juring, *pr.p.*, perjure.

per'jury, *n.*, violation of an oath.

perk, *v.i.*, to hold up the head pertly.

perked, *p.p.*, perk.

per'kin, *n.*, weak perry.

perk'ing, *pr.p.*, perk.

perk'y, *adj.*, saucy.

perl'ite, *n.*, a kind of vitreous rock.

per'mafrost, *n.*, a condition of continuous deep freezing (as of polar sub-sail). (Also *permofrost*.)

perm'alloy, *n.*, an alloy of nickel and iron.

per'manence, *n.*, the state or quality of being permanent.

per'manency, *n.*, *i.q.* permanence.

per'manent, *adj.*, remaining unaltered; lasting all the time.

per'manently, *adv.*, in a permanent manner.

perman'ganate, *n.*, a salt of permanganic acid.

permangan'ic, *adj.*, acid obtained from manganese (*chem.*).

permeabil'ity, *n.*, the quality of being permeable.

per'meable, *adj.*, capable of being permeated.

per'meate, *v.t.*, to pass through the pores of.

per'meated, *p.p.*, permeate.

per'meating, *pr.p.*, permeate.

permea'tion, *n.*, the act of permeating.

perm'ian, *n.*, a kind of rock (*geol.*).

permissibil'ity, *n.*, the quality of being permissible.

permis'sible, *adj.*, allowable.

permis'sion, *n.*, authorization; leave.

permis'sive, *adj.*, permitting; socially unregulated.

permis'sively, *adv.*, without prohibition.

permis'sory, *adj.*, *i.q.* permissive.

permit', *v.t.* and *i.*, to allow.

per'mit, *n.*, a written permission.

permit'ted, *p.p.*, permit.

permit'ter, *n.*, one who permits.

permit'ting, *pr.p.*, permit.

per'mofrost, *n.*, *i.q.* permafrost.

permu'table, *adj.*, exchangeable.

per'mutate, *v.i.*, to alter the order of, to subject to permutation.

permuta'tion, *n.*, interchange; a systematic change of arrangement.

permute', *v.t.*, to alter the order of.

pern, *n.*, the honeybuzzard.

per'nancy, *n.*, in law, the taking or receiving of something.

perni'cious, *adj.*, destructive.

perni'ciously, *adv.*, in a pernicious manner.

perni'ciousness, *n.*, the state of being pernicious.

pernick'e(t)ty, *adj.* fastidious, ticklish; requiring careful handling; over-demanding in small matters (*colloq.*).

pernocta'tion, *n.*, the act of passing the night.

per'one, *n.*, the fibula.

perone'al, *adj.*, pert. or rel. to the fibula.

per'orate, *v.i.*, to sum up in a speech.

perora'tion, *n.*, the concluding part of a speech.

per'orative, *adj.*, suggesting peroration.

perox'ide, *n.*, an oxide containing the greatest possible quantity of oxygen.

perpend', *v.t.*, to consider attentively.

perpendic'ular, *adj.*, perfectly vertical; at right angles to.

perpendicular'ity, *n.*, the state of being perpendicular.

perpendic'ularly, *adv.*, in a perpendicular manner; vertically.

per'petrate, *v.t.*, to commit; to be guilty of.

per'petrated, *p.p.*, perpetrate.

per'petrating, *pr.p.*, perpetrate.

perpetra'tion, *n.*, the act of perpetrating.

per'petrator, *n.*, one who perpetrates.

perpet'ual, *adj.*, lasting for ever.

perpet'ually, *adv.*, for ever.

perpet'uate, *v.t.*, to make perpetual.

perpet'uated, *p.p.*, perpetuate.

perpet'uating, *pr.p.*, perpetuate.

perpetua'tion, *n.*, the act of making perpetual.

perpetu'ity, *n.*, the state or quality of being perpetual.

perphos'phate, *n.*, a phosphate formed by combining a peroxide with phosphoric acid.

perplex', *v.t.*, to puzzle.

perplexed', *adj.*, puzzled; *p.p.*, perplex.

perplex'ing, *adj.*, embarrassing, difficult; *pr.p.*, perplex.

perplex'ity, *n.*, the state of being puzzled, or of being intricate.

per'quisite, *n.*, some sort of addition to wages or salary.

perquisi'tion, *n.*, a thorough inquiry.

per'ron, *n.*, an outside staircase leading to the main entrance of a building.

perroquet', *n.*, *i.q.* parrakeet.

per'ry, *n.*, a fermented drink made from the juice of pears.

perscruta'tion, *n.*, a minute inquiry or search.

per se', considered by itself (*Lat.*).

perse, *adj.* and *n.*, bluishgrey.

per'secute, *v.t.*, to harass or afflict persistently.

per'secuted, *p.p.*, persecute.

per'secuting, *adj.*, addicted to persecution; *pr.p.*, persecute.

persecu'tion, *n.*, the act or practice of persecuting; the state of being persecuted.

per'secutor, *n.*, one who persecutes.

persecu'trix, *n.*, a female persecutor.

persever'ance, *n.*, persistence in any undertaking.

persev'erate, *v.i.*, the negative power to switch from one activity to another (*psych.*).

persevera'tion, *n.*, the unnecessary persistence of a repetitive activity (*psych.*).

persevere', *v.i.*, to continue resolutely any course begun.

persevered', *p.p.*, persevere.

perseve'ring, *adj.*, steadfast in purpose; *pr.p.*, persevere.

perseve'ringly, *adv.*, in a persevering manner.

Per'sian, *adj.*, pert. or rel. to Persia; *n.*, a native of, or the language of, P. (Also *Iranian*.)

Per'sic, *adj.*, *i.q.* Persian.

persiennes, *n. pl.*, lath-type outside blinds (*Fr.*).

persiflage', *n.*, idle banter (*Fr.*).

persimm'on, *n.*, the American date-plum.

persist', *v.i.*, to continue steadily in the face of opposition.

persist'ed, *p.p.*, persist.

persist'ence, *n.*, steady continuance in a course.

persist'ency, *n.*, *i.q.* persistence.

persist'ent, *adj.*, tenacious of purpose. (Also *persistive*.)

persist'ently, *adv.*, in a persistent manner.

persist'ing, *pr.p.*, persist.

persist'ingly, *adv.*, in a persisting manner.

persist'ive, *adj.*, *i.q.* persistent.

per'son, *n.*, an individual human being; a body; in grammar, the relation of a noun or pronoun to the act of speaking, doing, etc.

person'a, *n.*, a person considered from the viewpoint of aura and temperament (*Lat.*).

per'sonable, *adj.*, handsome.

per'sonage, *n.*, a person of distinction.

per'sonal, *adj.*, peculiar to an individual; disparaging a person; private.

persona'lia, *n.*, notes relating to persons, personal matters, etc.

personal'ity, *n.*, the state of being personal; the characteristics of an individual; a disparaging remark.

pers'onalize, *v.t.*, to personify.

per'sonally, *adv.*, in person; as regards one's individuality.

per'sonalty, *n.*, personal property.

per'sonate, *v.t.*, to assume the character and appearance of.

per'sonated, *p.p.*, personate.

per'sonating, *pr.p.*, personate.

persona'tion, *n.*, the act of counterfeiting the person or character of another.

per'sonator, *n.*, one who personates.

personifica'tion, *n.*, the act of personifying; figuratively, the attribution of personal qualities to objects or abstractions.

person'ified, *p.p.*, personify.

person'ify, *v.t.*, to treat as a person; to impersonate.

person'ifying, *pr.p.*, personify.

personnel', *n.*, the body of persons employed in any occupation.

perspec'tive, *n.*, the act of drawing objects so that they appear to have their natural positions, sizes and three-dimensional relationships; a vista.

perspec'tograph, *n.*, an instrument to aid in perspective drawing.

perspectog'raphy, *n.*, the science or art of perspective.

pers'pex, *n.*, tough plastic material, sometimes substituted for glass.

perspica'cious, *adj.*, quick of understanding.

perspica'ciously, *adv.*, keenly, astutely.

perspicac'ity, *n.*, penetration; acuteness of discernment.

perspicu'ity, *n.*, easiness of being understood.

perspic'uous, *adj.*, clear to the understanding.

perspirabil'ity, *n.*, the quality of being perspirable.

perspi'rable, *adj.*, capable of being perspired.

perspira'tion, *n.*, the act of perspiring; sweat.

perspir'atory, *adj.*, pert. or rel. to perspiration.

perspire', *v.i.*, to sweat.

perspired', *p.p.*, perspire.

perspi'ring, *pr.p.*, perspire.

persua'dable, *adj.*, capable of being persuaded. (Also *persuasible*.)

persuade', *v.t.*, to advise; to convince by argument.

persua'ded, *p.p.*, persuade.

persuad'er, *n.*, one who persuades.

persua'ding, *pr.p.*, persuade.

persua'sible, *adj.*, *i.q.* persuadable.

persua'sion, *n.*, the act of persuading; a creed; a sect adhering to a creed.

persua'sive, *adj.*, having the power of persuasion. (Also *persuasory*.)

persua'sively, *adv.*, in a persuasive manner.

persua'siveness, *n.*, the quality of being persuasive.

persua'sory, *adj.*, *i.q.* persuasive.

persul'phate, *n.*, a sulphate of a metal containing as much. of the acid as possible.

persulta'tion, *n.*, bloody sweat; the exudation of blood through the skin.

pert, *adj.*, saucy; indecorously free.

pertain', *v.i.*, to belong.

pertained', *p.p.*, pertain.

pertain'ing, *pr.p.*, pertain.

pertina'cious, *adj.*, obstinate.

pertina'ciously, *adv.*, obstinately.

pertinac'ity, *n.*, obstinacy; resolution.

per'tinence, *n.*, fitness; appositeness; relevance. (Also *pertinency*.)

per'tinency, *n.*, *i.q.* pertinence.

per'tinent, *adj.*, apposite.

per'tinently, *adv.*, to the purpose.

pert'ly, *adv.*, in a pert manner.

pert'ness, *n.*, sauciness; forwardness.

perturb', *v.t.*, to agitate.

perturb'ance, *n.*, *i.q.* perturbation.

per'turbate, *v.t.*, *i.q.* perturb.

perturba'tion, *n.*, disquiet of mind; disorder.

perturb'ative, *adj.*, in a state of agitation, anxious, upset.

perturbed', *adj.*, *i.q.* perturbative; *p.p.*, perturb.

perturb'ing, *pr.p.*, perturb.

peruke', *n.*, a periwig.

peru'sal, *n.*, the act of perusing.

peruse', *v.t.*, to read with attention.

perused', *p.p.*, peruse.

peru'ser, *n.*, one who peruses.

peru'sing, *pr.p.*, peruse.

Peru'vian, *adj.*, pert. or rel. to Peru; *n.*, a native of P.

pervade', *v.t.*, to diffuse throughout.

perva'ded, *p.p.*, pervade.

perva'ding, *pr.p.*, pervade.

perva'sion, *n.*, the act of pervading.

perva'sive, *adj.*, having the characteristic of pervading.

perverse', *adj.*, turned to evil; stubborn; untoward.

perverse'ly, *adv.*, obstinately in the wrong.

perverse'ness, *n.*, a disposition to thwart.

perver'sion, *n.*, the act of perverting; a change to something worse; abnormal and unusual sexual behaviour.

perver'sity, *n.*, the state or quality of being perverse.

perver'sive, *adj.*, tending to pervert.

pervert', *v.t.*, to turn from the right.

per'vert, *n.*, one who has been turned from one religion to another regarded as inferior; one in whom unusual sexual behaviour has become dominant.

pervert'ed, *p.p.*, pervert.

pervert'er, *n.*, one that perverts, distorts or misapplies.

pervert'ible, *adj.*, capable of being perverted.

pervert'ing, *pr.p.*, pervert.

per'vious, *adj.*, penetrable.

per'viousness, *n.*, the quality of being pervious.

pesade', *n.*, the rearing of a horse (*Fr.*).

pese'ta, *n.*, a Spanish coin and unit of currency.

pesky, *adj.*, annoying (*colloq.*).

pe'so, *n.*, a South American coin and unit of currency in Argentina.

pes'sary, *n.*, an instrument for the treatment of *prolapsus uteri*; a contraceptive inserted into the vagina.

pes'simism, *n.*, the opinion or doctrine that the present state of things tends to evil; looking on the dark side of things.

pes'simist, *n.*, one who holds pessimistic opinions.

pessimis'tic, *adj.*, pert. or rel. to pessimism.

pessimis'tically, *adv.*, in a pessimistic way.

pest, *n.*, a plague; anything or anybody noxious.

Pestaloz'zian, *adj.*, pert. or rel. to the system of elementary education devised by Johann Pestalozzi.

pes'ter, *v.t.*, to annoy with vexatious trifles.

pes'tered, *p.p.*, pester.

pes'terer, *n.*, one who pesters.

pes'tering, *pr.p.*, pester.

pest'-house, *n.*, a hospital for plague patients.

pest'icide, *n.*, anything which destroys a pest.

pestif'erous, *adj.*, pestilential; malignant.

pestif'erously, *adv.*, in a pestilential way.

pes'tilence, *n.*, an epidemic, malignant, contagious disease.

pes'tilent, *adj.*, noxious to morals or health.

pestilen'tial, *adj.*, producing a pestilence; noxious.

pes'tle, *n.*, an instrument for pounding substances in a mortar.

pestol'ogy, *n.*, the study of pests.

pet, *adj.*, favourite; *n.*, a fit of peevishness; a term of endearment; a fondling; a tame and well-loved animal; *v.t.*, to fondle; to indulge.

pet'al, *n.*, a flower-leaf.

pet'al(l)ed, *adj.*, having petals. (Also *petalous*.)

petalif'erous, *adj.*, bearing petals.

petal'iform, *adj.*, shaped like a petal.

pet'aline, *adj.*, pert. or rel. to a petal.

pet'alite, *n.*, a mineral of foliated structure.

pet'alless, *adj.*, devoid of petals.

pet'aloid, *adj.*, resembling petals.

pet'alon, *n.*, gold decoration on a Jewish high priest's mitre.

pet'alous, *adj.*, *i.q.* petalled.

petard', *n.*, a container for explosive, fixed to a door or a barricade so as to break it down by explosion.

pet'asus, *n.*, Mercury's winged cap.

Petaur'ist, *n.*, a genus of mammals equipped with a pouch to carry their young and the ability to take flying leaps.

pete'chiae, *n. pl.*, purple spots due to malignant fever.

pe'ter, *v.i.*, to give out, to end (usually with "out").

pe'tered, *adj.*, given out, ended; *p.p.*, peter.

pe'tering, *pr.p.*, peter.

pe'tersham, *n.*, a thick, ribbed or corded silk ribbon.

pe'ter-wort, *n.*, (St. Peter's-wort), a plant of the genus Ascyrum.

peth'idine, *n.*, a pain-killing drug.

pet'iolar, *adj.*, proceeding from a leaf-stalk.

pet'iolate, *adj.,* having a petiole.

pet'iole, *n.,* a leaf-stalk.

petiol'ule, *n.,* a small or partial petiole.

petit', *adj.,* small in figure (*Fr.*).

petite', *adj.,* the fem. of petit (*Fr.*).

peti'tion, *n.,* a supplication; *v.t.,* to address a petition to.

peti'tionary, *adj.,* offering or containing a petition.

peti'tioned, *p.p.,* petition.

peti'tioner, *n.,* one who presents a petition.

peti'tioning, *pr.p.,* petition.

petit mai'tre, *n.,* a fop (*Fr.*).

petre'an, *adj.,* pert. or rel. to rock or stone.

pet'rel, *n.,* a web-footed sea-bird, found far from land.

petres'cence, *n.,* the process of changing into stone.

petres'cent, *adj.,* changing into stony hardness.

petrifac'tion, *n.,* the process of converting into stone; a fossil.

petrifac'tive, *adj.,* having power to petrify.

petrif'ic, *adj., i.q.* petrifactive.

pet'rified, *p.p.,* petrify.

pet'rify, *v.t.,* to convert into stone; to stupefy with fear or amazement.

pet'rifying, *pr.p.,* petrify.

Pe'trine, *adj.,* pert. or rel. to St. Peter.

petrogen'esis, *n.,* the formation of rocks.

pet'roglyph, *n.,* rock carving.

pet'rol, *n.,* petroleum spirit, the chief fuel of motor-cars.

petro'leum, *n.,* mineral oil.

petrol'ic, *adj.,* pert. or rel. to petrol or petroleum.

pet'rolin, *n.,* a hydrocarbon akin to paraffin, found in Burmese petroleum.

petrolog'ical, *adj.,* pert. or rel. to petrology.

petrolog'ically, *adv.,* in a petrological manner.

petrol'ogist, *n.,* one versed in petrology.

petrol'ogy, *n.,* the chemical study of rocks.

pet'ronel, *n.,* a kind of carbine.

petronel'la, *n.,* a Scottish country dance.

petrosi'lex, *n.,* rock flint.

petrosili'cious, *adj.,* consisting of petrosilex.

pet'rous, *adj.,* like stone; hard.

pet'ted, *p.p.,* pet.

pet'tichaps, *n. pl.,* a name applied to several British warblers.

pet'ticoat, *n.,* a loose undergarment formerly worn by women.

pet'ticoat-gov'ernment, *n.,* women's rule.

pet'tier, *n., comp.* of petty.

pet'tiest, *adj., super.* of petty.

pet'tifog, *v.i.,* to indulge in disreputable trickery.

pet'tifogger, *n.,* an inferior lawyer.

pet'tifoggery, *n.,* the practice of a pettifogger; mean tricks.

pet'tifogging, *adj.,* given to pettifoggery; trifling, worthless (*colloq.*).

pet'tily, *adv.,* in a petty manner.

pet'tiness, *n.,* smallness.

pet'ting, *pr.p.,* pet.

pet'tish, *adj.,* proceeding from peevishness.

pet'tishly, *adv.,* in a pettish manner.

pet'tishness, *n.,* fretfulness. (Also *petulance.*)

pet'titoes, *n. pl.,* the feet of a pig cooked for food.

pet'to, *n.,* the breast (*Ital., in petto* = with reserve).

pet'ty, *adj.,* small; inferior; insignificant.

pet'ulance, *n., i.q.* pettishness.

pet'ulancy, *n., i.q.* petulance.

pet'ulant, *adj.,* capricious; fretful.

pet'ulantly, *adv.,* in a petulant manner.

Petu'nia, *n.,* a genus of American herbaceous plants with beautiful multi-coloured flowers.

petunt'se, *n.,* Chinese fine clay.

pew, *n.,* a fixed seat in a church; *v.t.,* to provide with pews.

pewed, *adj.,* furnished with pews; *p.p.,* pew.

pe(e)'wit, *n., i.q.* peewit.

pew'ter, *n.,* an alloy of tin and lead; vessels made of pewter.

pew'terer, *n.,* one who makes vessels of pewter.

pew'tery, *adj.,* resembling pewter.

pfen'nig, *n.,* a small German coin, one hundredth of a mark.

phac'oid, *adj.,* like a lentil; lenticular.

phacoid'al, *adj.,* lens- or lentil-shaped.

phaenog'amous, *adj., i.q.* phanerogamous.

pha'eton, *n.,* an open four-wheeled carriage; an open touring motor-car.

phagede'na, *n.,* a spreading ulcer.

phageden'ic, *adj.,* pert. or rel. to phagedena.

phag'ocyte, *n.,* an infection-destroying leucocyte.

phal'ange, *n.,* one of the small bones of the fingers and toes.

phalan'geal, *adj.,* bel. to the phalanges.

phalan'ger, *n.,* an Australian pouched animal living in trees.

phalan'ges, *n.,* pl. of phalanx and phalange.

phalan'gian, *adj., i.q.* phalangeal.

phalangi'tis, *n.,* inflammation of the phalanges.

phalanste'rian, *adj.,* pert. or rel. to a phalanstery; *n.,* a dweller in a phalanstery.

phal'anstery, *n.,* a socialistic community, as proposed by the French philosopher, Charles Fourier.

phal'anx, *n.,* a body of troops in close array; a phalange.

phal'arope, *n.,* a small water-fowl.

phal'lic, *adj.,* pert. or rel. to the phallus.

phal'lical, *adj., i.q.* phallic.

phal'lus, *n.,* the penis-like emblem of the generative principle in nature carried in the Bacchic rites of ancient Greece, and of frequent occurrence in all cultures.

phan'erogam, *n.,* a flowering plant.

phanerog'amous, adj., bearing conspicuous flowers. (Also phaenogamous and phenogamous.)

phan'tascope, n., an optical contrivance for making fixed objects seem to be in motion.

phan'tasm, n., a creation of the fancy: a phantom.

phantas'ma, n., i.q. phantasm; a daydream.

phantasmago'ria, n., illusive images; a succession of fantastic appearances.

phantasmagor'ic, adj., pert. or rel. to phantasmagoria.

phantas'mal, adj., spectral; resembling a phantasm.

phantas'mascope, n., i.q. phantascope.

phan'tast, n., i.q. fantast.

phan'tasy, n., i.q. fantasy.

phan'tom, n., a ghost; something unreal. (Also fantom.)

Pharaon'ic, adj., pert. or rel. to the Pharaohs, ancient Egyptian kings.

phare, n., a lighthouse.

Pharisa'ic. adj., pert. or rel. to, or resembling, the Pharisees.

Pharisa'ical, adj., i.q. Pharisaic.

Phar'isaism, n., the doctrines and conduct of the Pharisees; the scrupulous observance of the forms of religion.

Pharise'an, adj., i.q. Pharisaic.

Phar'isee, n., one of a sect among the Jews; a formalist.

Phar'iseeism, n., i.q. Pharisaism.

pharmaceu'tic, adj., pert. or rel. to pharmacy.

pharmaceu'tical, adj., i.q. pharmaceutic.

pharmaceu'tist, n., an apothecary; a chemist in medicine.

phar'macist, n., one skilled in pharmacy.

phar'macolite, n., a white mineral containing lime and arsenic.

pharmacol'ogist, n., one skilled in pharmacology.

pharmacol'ogy, n., the art of preparing medicines.

pharmacopoe'ia, n., a book of directions for preparing medicines; an official list of drugs and medicaments of the Materia Medica.

phar'macy, n., the art of dispensing medicines; the occupation of a chemist; a store for medical supplies.

pha'ro, n., i.q. faro.

pha'ros, n., a lighthouse or beacon.

pharyn'gal, adj., i.q. pharyngeal.

pharyn'geal, adj., pert. or rel. to the pharynx.

pharyngi'tis, n., inflammation of the pharynx.

pharyngot'omy, n., the operation of cutting into the pharynx to remove an obstruction.

phar'ynx, n., that part of the throat lying between the mouth and the oesophagus.

phase, n., one of the appearances of the moon in respect of quantity of illumination of its disc; an aspect.

pha'sis, n., a phase, in astronomy.

pheas'ant, n., a gallinaceous game-bird.

pheas'antry, n., a place for breeding pheasants.

phee'sy, adj., fretful.

phena'cetin, n., a drug used for overcoming fever (chem., med.).

phen'gite, n., colourless, translucent, glucinum silicate.

phen'icin, n., a brown dye.

phe'nix, n., i.q. phoenix.

phenobar'bitone, n., a sedative drug (med.).

phenoga'mian, adj., having flowers.

phenog'amous, adj., i.q. phanerogamous.

phe'nol, n., carbolic acid.

phenol'ogist, n., one versed in phenology.

phenol'ogy, n., the science of the distribution of plant and animal life according to climate.

phenom'ena, n., the pl. of phenomenon.

phenom'enal, adj., pert. or rel. to phenomena; most extraordinary.

phenom'enon, n., a visible manifestation, fact or occurrence; an unusual occurrence.

phe'on, n., the barbed head of a dart (her.).

phew, an interj. of impatience or disgust.

phi'al, n., a small glass bottle.

Philadel'phian, adj., pert. or rel. to Philadelphia; n., a native of P.; one of a 17th cent. sect of mystics.

philan'der, v.i., to flirt.

philan'dered, p.p., philander.

philan'derer, n., a male flirt.

philan'dering, pr.p., philander.

phil'anthrope, n., i.q. philanthropist.

philanthrop'ic, adj., benevolent.

philan'thropist, n., one who does good to his fellow-men.

philan'thropize, v.i. and t., to practise philanthropy.

philan'thropy, n., universal benevolence.

philatel'ic, adj., pert. or rel. to philately.

philat'elist, n., a stamp-collector.

philat'ely, n., the science of collecting postage stamps.

philharmon'ic, adj., fond of music; n., a musical society.

phil'hellene, n., a friend of Greece.

philhellen'ic, adj., loving and supporting the Greeks.

philhel'lenism, n., the principles of the philhellenists.

philhelle'nist, n., one who supports the interests of the Greeks.

phil'ibeg, n., the Highland kilt (Scot.).

Philip'pian, adj., pert. or rel. to Philippi, a city of Thrace; n., a native of P.

philip'pic, n., a speech attacking someone acrimoniously.

Phil'ippine, adj., pert. or rel. to the Philippine Islands; n., a native of the P.I.

Phil'istine, n., a native of Philistia in Syria.

phil'istine, n., a person of narrow views, deficient in culture and taste.

phil'istinism, n., the characteristics of the Philistines.

phillum'enist, n., a collector of match-box labels.

phillum'eny, n., the collecting of match-box labels.

philog'ynist, n., a lover of women.

philog'yny, n., love of women.

philol'oger, n., i.q. philologist.

philolog'ic, adj., i.q. philological.

philolog'ical, adj., pert. or rel. to philology.

philol'ogist, n., one versed in philology.

philol'ogy, n., the study of language and literature; the historical science of language.

phil'omath, n., a lover of learning.

philomath'ic, adj., pert. or rel. to the love of learning.

philom'athy, n., the love of learning.

phil'omel, n., the nightingale.

Philome'la, n., the daughter of Pandion, king of Athens, who was changed into a nightingale; the nightingale.

philop(o)e'na, n., a game in which two persons eat the twin kernels of an almond and one pays a forfeit.

philopolem'ical, adj., disputatious.

philoprogen'itiveness, n., the love of offspring.

philos'opher, n., one versed in philosophy; one who lives according to the rules of practical wisdom.

philosoph'ic, adj., pert. or rel. to philosophy; calm; based on practical wisdom.

philosoph'ical, adj., i.q. philosophic.

philosoph'ically, adv., in a philosophical manner.

philos'ophism, n., the affectation of philosophy.

philos'ophist, n., a would-be philosopher.

philos'ophize, v.i., to reason like a philosopher.

philos'ophized, p.p., philosophize.

philos'ophizing, pr.p., philosophize.

philos'ophy, n., the science which seeks to explain all things by ultimate causes; the endeavour to systematize knowledge and behaviour into a coherent and logical structure; the calmness of the wise man.

philotech'nic, adj., fond of the arts.

phil'ter, n., i.q. philtre.

phil'tre, n., a love potion.

phiz, n., a humorous name for the face.

phlebi'tis, n., inflammation of a vein.

phlebol'ogy, n., that part of the anatomy dealing with the veins.

phlebot'omist, n., one who opens a vein to let blood.

phlebot'omize, v.i. and t., to practise phlebotomy; to bleed.

phlebot'omy, n., the practice of letting blood.

phlegm, n., bronchial mucus; sluggishness.

phlegmat'ic, adj., sluggish in temperament; not easily disturbed.

phleg'mon, n., an inflammation.

phleme, n., a fleam; a farrier's lancet.

phlo'em, n., the fibrous bark of a tree, esp. lime.

phlogis'tic, adj., pert. or rel. to phlogiston.

phlogis'ton, n., the hypothetical principle of inflammability, according to an obsolete theory.

Phlox, n., a genus of garden plants with red, white or purple flowers.

phob'ia, n., fear, hatred, especially of a morbid kind.

pho'bism, n., i.q. phobia.

pho'ca, n., a seal (Lat.).

pho'cine, adj., pert. or rel. to seals.

Phoe'bus, n., Apollo; the sun (poet.).

Phoeni'cian, adj., pert. or rel. to Phoenicia, part of Syria; n., a native of P.

phoe'nix, n., a mythical bird; a paragon. (Also phenix.)

phon, n., a unit of sound measurement (phys.).

phon'ate, v.i., to utter vocal sounds.

phonaut'ograph, n., an apparatus for recording sound vibrations.

phone, n. and v.t., the abbrev. of telephone (colloq.); a simple vowel or consonant sound.

phon'eme, n., a unit of significant sound in a given language.

phonen'doscope, n., a sound amplifier.

phonet'ic, adj., pert. or rel. to the voice; representing vocal sounds.

phonet'ically, adv., in a phonetic manner.

phoneti'cian, n., an expert in phonetics.

phonet'icist, n., one who advocates phonetic spelling.

phonet'icize, v.t. and i., to write phonetically.

phonet'ics, n. pl., the science of vocal sounds and their representation.

phon'etist, n., a person versed in phonetics.

phonetiza'tion, n., the act of representing vocal sounds phonetically.

phon'ey, adj., bogus, sham, fictitious. (Also phony.)

pho'nic, adj., pert. or rel. to sound.

pho'nics, n. pl., the science of sounds; phonetics.

phon'ofilm, n., a sound film.

phon'ogram, n., a symbol representing a spoken sound.

phon'ograph, n., an instrument to register and reproduce sounds.

phonog'rapher, n., one skilled in phonography.

phonograph'ic, adj., pert. or rel. to phonography or to the phonograph.

phonog'raphy, n., a system of representing sounds in writing.

pho'nolite, n., clinkstone.

phonolo'gic, adj., pert. or rel. to phonology.

phonol'ogist, n., one versed in phonology.

phonol'ogy, n., the study of the science of vocal sounds.

phonom'eter, *n.*, an instrument for measuring the number, in a given time, of vibrations that produce a given sound.

pho'notype, *n.*, a character used in phonetic printing.

phonotyp'ic, *adj.*, pert. or rel. to phonotypy.

pho'notypist, *n.*, one who uses or advocates phonotypy.

pho'notypy, *n.*, phonetic printing.

phon'y, *n.*, *i.q.* phoney.

phorm'ium, *n.*, a liliaceous plant; New Zealand flax.

phos'gene, *n.*, a suffocating gas produced by the action of light on chlorine and carbon dioxide.

phos'phate, *n.*, a salt of phosphoric acid.

phos'phene, *n.*, the spectrum or luminous image made by pressing the eye-ball.

phos'phide, *n.*, a combination of phosphorus and one other element (*chem.*).

phos'phine, *n.*, a foul-smelling gas.

phos'phite, *n.*, a salt of phosphorus acid.

phos'phor, *n.*, the morning star; phosphorus.

phos'phorate, *v.t.*, to impregnate with phosphorus.

phos'phorated, *p.p.*, phosphorate.

phos'phorating, *pr.p.*, phosphorate.

phos'phor-bronze, *n.*, a tough bronze alloy.

phosphoresce', *v.i.*, to give out phosphoric light.

phosphores'cence, *n.*, luminosity without combustion.

phosphores'cent, *adj.*, luminous without sensible heat.

phosphor'ic, *adj.*, pert. or rel. to phosphorus.

phos'phorite, *n.*, a phosphate of lime.

phos'phorous, *adj.*, obtained from phosphorus.

phos'phorus, *n.*, a solid non-metallic element found in bones.

phos'phuret(t)ed, *adj.*, combined with phosphorus.

phossy, *adj.*, *i.q.* phosphorous.

pho'tism, *n.*, an hallucinatory sensation or vision of light.

pho'to, *n.* and *v.t.*, the abbrev. of photograph.

photo'copied, *adj.*, copied by the photocopying process; *p.p.*, photocopy.

photo'copier, *n.*, a machine for taking a copy of an original document.

photo'copy', *n.*, a copy of an original document, etc., taken by a photocopying process; *v.t.*, to make such a copy.

photo'copy'ing, *n.*, a photographic process for making a copy of an original document, etc.; *pr.p.*, photocopy.

photo'-finish, *n.*, the photograph of a close finish in a race.

photogen'ic, *adj.*, suitable for photographing.

photog'eny, *n.*, *i.q.* photography.

pho'togram, *n.*, a facsimile sent by telegraph; a silhouette photograph.

pho'tograph, *n.*, a picture obtained by photography; *v.t.*, to produce a picture by photography.

photog'rapher, *n.*, one who photographs.

photograph'ic, *adj.*, pert. or rel. to photography.

photog'raphy, *n.*, the art of obtaining representations of objects or persons by means of the action of light on certain chemicals.

photogravure', *n.*, a plate etched from a photograph; this process; the picture printed from the plate. (Also gravure.)

photo-lithog'raphy, *n.*, a mode of lithographing in which a photograph is transferred to a prepared stone.

photolog'ic, *adj.*, pert. or rel. to photology.

photol'ogy, *n.*, the science of light.

photom'eter, *n.*, an instrument measuring the intensity of light.

photomet'ric, *adj.*, pert. or rel. to a photometer.

photom'etry, *n.*, the measurement of the intensity of light.

pho'ton, *n.*, a quantum of light.

photopho'bia, *n.*, an intense dislike of light.

pho'tophone, *n.*, an apparatus for transmitting sound by light.

photop'sia, *n.*, a morbid affection of the sight, in which sparks and flashes of light seem to play before the eyes.

pho'topsy, *n.*, *i.q.* photopsia.

photora'diogram, *n.*, a photogram sent by radio; *v.t.*, to photograph by x-rays.

pho'tosphere, *n.*, the luminous envelope of the sun.

pho'tostat, *n.*, a reproduction made by photo-copying apparatus.

pho'totype, *n.*, a plate on which a photograph has been etched with certain acids and used for printing copies from.

phototypog'raphy, *n.*, a photo-mechanical process of engraving which produces a plate that can be used on a printing machine.

photo-zincog'raphy, *n.*, the process of printing from a zinc plate on which a photograph has been etched.

phrase, *n.*, a short expression consisting of two or more words; *v.t.*, to express in words.

phrased, *p.p.*, phrase.

phra'seogram, *n.*, a combination of shorthand characters representing a phrase.

phra'seograph, *n.*, *i.q.* phraseogram.

phraseog'raphy, *n.*, the representation of phrases by means of shorthand signs.

phraseol'ogist, *n.*, a phrase-maker.

phraseol'ogy, *n.*, a way of expression; diction.

phra'sing, *pr.p.*, phrase.

phra'try, *n.*, the Greek family unit; a tribal division among primitive races.

phrenet'ic, *adj.*, disordered in mind; fevered in behaviour.

phren'ic, *adj.*, pert. or rel. to the diaphragm.

phreni'tis, *n.*, inflammation of the brain; frenzy.

phrenolog'ical, *adj.*, pert. or rel. to phrenology.

phrenol'ogist, *n.*, one versed in phrenology.

phrenol'ogy, *n.*, the science connecting different parts of the brain with different faculties of the mind.

phren'sy, *n.*, *i.q.* frenzy.

Phryg'ian, *adj.*, pert. or rel. to Phrygia, an ancient country in Asia Minor; *n.*, a native of P.

phthis'ic, *n.*, consumption; a consumptive patient.

phthis'ical, *adj.*, suffering from phthisis or from asthma.

phthis'icky, *adj.*, asthmatic.

phthisiol'ogy, *n.*, the study of phthisis.

phthi'sis, *n.*, a wasting away of the lungs.

phur'nacite, *n.*, a smokeless fuel.

phut, *adv.*, break down, collapse; *n.*, a collapsing sound (bladder); a breaking down. (Also *fut.*)

phylac'tery, *n.*, an amulet or charm worn by the ancient Jews.

phylet'ic, *adj.*, pert. or rel. to a tribe; racial (*biol.*).

phyllo'dium, *n.*, a leafstalk flattened and resembling a leaf.

phyl'lopod, *n.*, a crustacean with swimming limbs resembling leaves.

phylloxe'ra, *n.*, an insect-borne disease of grape vines.

phyl'um, *n.*, a division or group of related animals or plants (*biol.*).

phys'ic, *n.*, the art of healing; the science of medicine; a medicine; *v.t.*, to give medicine to.

phys'ical, *adj.*, pert. or rel. to the nature of the material and sensible; pert. or rel. to the science of physics.

phys'ically, *adv.*, in a physical manner.

physi'cian, *n.*, one skilled in the art of healing.

phys'icist, *n.*, one skilled in physics.

phys'icked, *p.p.*, physic.

phys'icking, *pr.p.*, physic.

phys'icky, *adj.*, suggestive of physic.

physico-log'ical, *adj.*, pert. or rel. to logic illustrated by physics.

physico-theol'ogy, *n.*, theology illustrated by physics.

phys'ics, *n. pl.*, the science of the laws and properties of matter.

physiognom'ic, *adj.*, pert. or rel. to physiognomy.

physiogn'omist, *n.*, one skilled in physiognomy.

physiogn'omy, *n.*, the art of reading character from the features; the face.

physiog'raphy, *n.*, a description of the natural features of the earth.

physiolog'ic, *adj.*, pert. or rel. to physiology.

physiolog'ical, *adj.*, *i.q.* physiologic.

physiolog'ically, *adv.*, according to the principles of physiology.

physiol'ogist, *n.*, one versed in physiology.

physiol'ogy, *n.*, the science of the phenomena of life.

physiotherapeut'ic, *adj.*, pert. or rel. to physiotherapy.

physiothe'rapist, *n.*, one skilled in physiotherapy, a masseur.

physiothe'rapy, *n.*, cure by physical means (massage, heat, etc.).

physique', *n.*, a person's bodily structure or constitution (*Fr.*).

phytiv'orous, *adj.*, eating plants.

phytog'eny, *n.*, the science of the generation of plants.

phytog'raphy, *n.*, a branch of botany dealing with the naming and description of plants.

phytolog'ical, *adj.*, pert. or rel. to phytology.

phytol'ogist, *n.*, a botanist.

phytol'ogy, *n.*, botany.

phyton'omy, *n.*, the science of the life of plants.

phytoph'agous, *adj.*, plant-eating.

phytot'omy, *n.*, the anatomy of plants.

Phytozo'a, *n. pl.*, zoophytes — plant-like animals, as sponges, etc.

phytozo'on, *n.*, a zoophyte.

pi, *n.*, the Greek letter *p*; a mathematical constant.

piac'ular, *adj.*, making atonement.

piaffe', *v.i.*, to trot slowly (of a horse).

piaff'er, *n.*, the movement of piaffing.

piaff'ing, *pr.p.*, piaffe.

pi'a ma'ter, *n.*, the membrane surrounding the brain (*Lat.*, *anat.*).

pian'ino, *n.*, a small upright piano (*It.*).

pianiss'imo, *adv.*, very softly (*It.*, *mus.*).

pi'anist, *n.*, a player on the piano.

pi'aniste, *n.*, a female pianist.

pian'o, *adv.*, softly (*It.*, *mus.*); *n.*, a pianoforte.

pianofor'te, *n.*, a musical instrument with metal strings struck by hammers set in motion from a keyboard.

pianol'a, *n.*, a mechanical piano.

pian'o-org'an, *n.*, a mechanical piano, like a barrel organ.

pias'saba, *n.*, a strong fibre obtained from the stem of the plant Attaleafunifera.

pias'sava, *n.*, *i.q.* piassaba.

pias'ter, *n.*, *i.q.* piastre.

pias'tre, *n.*, a coin used in some Mediterranean countries.

piaz'za, *n.*, a rectangular open space; a colonnade (*It.*).

pi'broch, *n.*, a Highland march played on the bagpipe.

pi'ca, *n.*, a large printing type; the magpie.

picador', *n.*, a Spanish horseman, armed with a lance, who takes part in a bullfight.

pic'amar, *n.*, an oily liquid contained in wood tar.

Pic'ard, *n.*, an inhabitant of Picardy, in North France.

picaroon', *n.*, a rogue; an adventurer; a robber; *v.i.*, to rob.

picayune', *adj.*, mean; *n.*, a coin in Florida and Louisiana (U.S.A.), sixteen of which made a dollar; an insignificant thing or person.

Pic'cadilly, *n.*, a street in London, England; a collar or ruff.

pic'calilli, *n.*, a pungent pickle made of various vegetables.

pic'caninny, *n.*, a coloured infant.

pic'colo, *n.*, a small or octave flute.

pice, *n.*, a Pakistani coin.

pick, *v.t.*, to strike with anything pointed; to choose; to steal; *v.i.*, to eat by morsels; *n.*, a sharp-pointed tool for loosening earth, cleaning teeth, etc.; the best selection.

pick'aback, *adv.*, on the back like a pack.

pick'axe, *n.*, a long-handled instrument with a head consisting of a pick pointed at one end and bladed at the other.

picked, *p.p.*, pick.

pick'elhaube, *n.*, a German spiked helmet.

pick'er, *n.*, one who picks or collects.

pick'erel, *n.*, a small freshwater fish.

pick'et, *n.*, a peg for fastening a horse; a small body of soldiers; a body of men posted to encourage observance of a strike; one of such a body; a metal peg to support a rope for an enclosure; *v.t.*, to fasten to a peg; to post a guard or picket.

pick'eted, *p.p.*, picket.

pick'eting, *pr.p.*, picket.

pick'ing, *pr.p.*, pick.

pick'ings, *n. pl.*, odds and ends; perquisites.

pick'le, *n.*, brine or vinegar for preserving food; food so preserved; a plight (*colloq.*); a troublesome child (*colloq.*); *v.t.*, to preserve in pickle.

pick'led, *p.p.*, pickle.

pick'ling, *pr.p.*, pickle.

pick'lock, *n.*, an instrument for picking a lock.

pick'-me-up, *n.*, a drug or dram to revive one's energies.

pick'pocket, *n.*, one who steals from the pocket.

pick'thank, *n.*, a parasite; a toady.

pick'-up, *n.*, an electric device used on a gramophone arm for tracking records.

Pickwick'ian, *adj.*, pert. or rel. to Pickwick.

pic'nic, *n.*, an open-air pleasure party; an easy undertaking (*colloq.*); *v.i.*, to go on a picnic.

pic'nicked, *p.p.*, picnic.

pic'nicker, *n.*, one who picnics.

pic'nicking, *pr.p.*, picnic.

picotee', *n.*, a hardy variety of the carnation or pink.

pic'ric, *adj.*, having a bitter taste.

picric-ac'id, *n.*, a yellow and bitter compound, used in dyeing and the making of explosives.

pic'rolite, *n.*, a fibrous or columnar kind of serpentine.

pic'romel, *n.*, a constituent of bile.

picrotox'in, *n.*, the bitter, poisonous principle of the plant species, *Cocculus indicus*.

Pict, *n.*, a former inhabitant of north-east Scotland.

Pict'ish, *adj.*, pert. or rel. to the Picts.

pic'togram, *n.*, a prehistoric symbolic drawing in caves.

pic'tograph, *n.*, a picture representing an idea.

picto'rial, *adj.*, pert. or rel. to pictures.

picto'rially, *adv.*, by means of pictures.

pic'ture, *n.*, a painted likeness; a work of art in which delineation and/or colour are used; any likeness; *v.t.*, to paint; to describe clearly.

pic'ture-book, *n.*, a book for children containing many pictures.

pic'tured, *p.p.*, picture.

pic'turedrome, *n.*, *i.q.* cinema.

pic'ture-frame, *n.*, a border surrounding a picture.

pic'ture-gallery, *n.*, a large room in which pictures are exhibited.

pic'ture-hat, *n.*, a lady's wide-brimmed hat.

picturesque', *adj.*, suitable to form a pleasing picture; graphically written.

picturesque'ly, *adv.*, in a picturesque way.

picturesque'ness, *n.*, the quality of being picturesque.

pic'turing, *pr.p.*, picture.

pic'ul, *n.*, a Chinese weight exceeding 1 cwt.

pid'dle, *v.i.*, to attend to trivialities.

pid'dled, *p.p.*, piddle.

pid'dler, *n.*, one who piddles or pettifogs.

pid'dling, *pr.p.*, piddle.

pidd'ock, *n.*, a kind of bait.

pid'gin, *n.*, a jargon of English expressed in a foreign idiom.

pie, *n.*, the magpie; paste cooked with something in it; disordered printing type.

pie'bald, *adj.*, having white spots all over the body.

piece, *n.*, a bit of anything; a composition; a gun; a coin; *v.t.*, to patch; to join.

pièce de résistance, *n.* the main dish at a meal; a word or action which cannot be countered (*Fr.*).

pieced, *p.p.*, piece.

piece'-goods, *n.*, textile fabrics of standard length.

piece'meal, *adv.*, bit by bit.

piece'ner, *n.*, one who feeds the slubbing-machine in a woollen mill.

pie'cer, *n.*, one who joins threads in spinning; connecting evidence, a story, etc.

piece'-work, *n.*, a method of payment for the quantity of work done.

piece'-work'er, *n.*, one who is paid piece-work rates.

piec'ing, *pr.p.*, piece.

pied, *adj.*, parti-coloured.

pied à terre, *n.*, a foothold; somewhere to stay.

pier, *n.*, the stonework supporting one side of an arch; a jetty or mole stretching into the sea.

pier′age, *n.*, the toll paid for using a pier.

pierce, *v.t.*, to bore; to penetrate; to perforate.

pierce′able, *adj.*, capable of being pierced.

pierced, *p.p.*, pierce.

pier′cer, *n.*, an instrument, organ or person that pierces.

pier′cing, *pr.p.*, pierce.

pier′-glass, *n.*, a large mirror between windows.

pier′-head, *n.*, the seaward end of a pier.

Pie′rian, *adj.*, bel. to the Pierides or Muses.

pi′errot, *n.*, a buffoon or comic artist dressed in a loose white costume trimmed with black (*Fr.*).

pierrot′ic, *adj.*, clownish, of pantomimic character.

pier′-table, *n.*, a table between windows.

pieta, *n.*, a picture or sculpture of the Virgin Mary holding the dead body of Christ (*It.*).

pi′etism, *n.*, the practice or principles of the pietists.

pi′etist, *n.*, one of a religious party in Germany who sought to quicken piety in the Protestants; one who makes a display of religious feeling.

pietist′ic, *adj.*, pert. or rel. to pietists.

pi′ety, *n.*, a sense of duty to God, parents, country, etc.

piezom′eter, *n.*, an instrument for measuring compressibility.

pif′fle, *n.*, nonsense, twaddle (*slang*).

pig, *n.*, a swine; an oblong mass of unforged metal; *v.t.*, to farrow; *v.i.*, to live like pigs.

pig′eon, *n.*, a dove; a simpleton.

pig′eon-breasted, *adj.*, having a deformed chest with a protuberant breast-bone.

pig′eon-chested, *adj.*, *i.q.* pigeon-breasted.

pig′eon-hearted, *adj.*, timid; cowardly.

pig′eonhole, *n.*, a compartment or nest in a case for papers; *v.t.*, to place or deposit in a pigeon-hole

pig′eonholed, *p.p.*, pigeonhole.

pig′eon-house, *n.*, a dovecot.

pig′eonry, *n.*, a place for keeping pigeons.

pig′eon-toed, *adj.*, having the toes turning inwards.

pig′gery, *n.*, a collection of pigsties.

pig′gin, *n.*, a small wooden vessel with an erect handle.

pig′gish, *adj.*, like pigs.

pig′gishly, *adv.*, in a piggish way.

pig′gy, *n.*, a little pig.

pig′headed, *adj.*, stupidly obstinate.

pig′iron, *n.*, iron in rough bars or pigs.

pig′-lead, *n.*, lead in pig form (second meaning).

pigme′an, *adj.*, dwarfish.

pig′ment, *n.*, colouring matter; paint.

pigmen′tal, *adj.*, pert. or rel. to pigments.

pig′mentary, *adj.*, secreting pigment.

pigmenta′tion, *n.*, the degeneration of tissues with discoloration; the coloration of tissues.

pig′my, *n.*, a small human being.

pignora′tion, *n.*, the practice or act of pawning; a pledge.

pig′-nut, *n.*, the earth nut.

pig′skin, *n.*, the skin of a pig tanned into leather.

pig′sty, *n.*, a pen for pigs.

pig′tail, *n.*, the hair of the head tied into a tail; tobacco twisted into a rope.

pike, *n.*, a sharp-pointed weapon with a long shaft; a freshwater fish with a long-pointed snout; a toll.

piked, *adj.*, furnished with a pike.

pike′let, *n.*, a kind of teacake; a crumpet.

pike′man, *n.*, a soldier armed with a pike.

pik′er, *n.*, a cautious gambler (*colloq.*).

pike′staff, *n.*, the shaft of a pike.

pilaff, *n.*, *i.q.* pilau.

pilas′ter, *n.*, a square pillar, partly projecting from, partly engaged in, a wall.

pilas′tered, *adj.*, furnished with pilasters.

pilau′, *n.*, an Oriental dish of rice cooked with butter or meat. (Also *pilaff*.).

pilaw, *n.*, *i.q.* pilau.

pilch, *n.*, a flannel cloth for an infant.

pil′chard, *n.*, a fish like a small herring.

pil′corn, *n.*, a kind of oat.

pile, *n.*, a heap; a mass of buildings; a beam driven into soft earth to form a foundation; the nap of cloth or carpet; *v.i.*, to heap up.

pi′leate, *adj.*, having the form of a cap for the head.

pi′leated, *adj.*, *i.q.* pileate.

piled, *p.p.*, pile.

pile′driver, *n.*, a machine for driving piles.

pi′ler, *n.*, one who piles.

piles, *n. pl.*, haemorrhoids; inflammation of the anal orifice or the rectum.

pil′fer, *v.t.* and *i.*, to steal by petty theft.

pil′ferage, *n.*, petty theft.

pil′fered, *p.p.*, pilfer.

pil′ferer, *n.*, one who pilfers.

pil′fering, *n.*, petty theft; *pr.p.*, pilfer.

pilgar′lick, *n.*, a person made bald by disease; a scurvy fellow.

pil′grim, *n.*, a traveller, esp. to holy places.

pil′grimage, *n.*, a journey undertaken by a pilgrim.

pilig′erous, *adj.*, bearing hairs, as a leaf.

pi′ling, *pr.p.*, pile.

pill, *n.*, a little ball of medicine to be swallowed whole.

pil′lage, *n.*, plunder; *v.t.*, to plunder.

pil′laged, *p.p.*, pillage.

pil′lager, *n.*, one who pillages.

pil′laging, *pr.p.*, pillage.

pil′lar, *n.*, a column; a support.

pil'lar-box, *n.*, a receptacle for letters to be sent by post.

pil'lared, *adj.*, having pillars.

pil'larist, *n.*, a stylite.

pill'-box, *n.*, a box for holding pills; a small fortified defensive position.

pil'lion, *n.*, a seat immediately behind a horse-rider or motorcyclist.

pil'lionist, *n.*, a pillion rider.

pil'liwinks, *n.*, an instrument of torture for squeezing the fingers.

pil'loried, *p.p.*, pillory.

pil'lory, *n.*, a wooden frame in which offenders were fastened and exhibited in public; *v.t.*, to punish in the pillory; to ridicule publicly.

pil'low, *n.*, a bedcushion; *v.t.*, to rest on for support.

pil'lowcase, *n.*, a washable case for covering a pillow.

pil'lowed, *adj.*, provided with pillows; *p.p.*, pillow.

pil'lowing, *pr.p.*, pillow.

pil'lowslip, *n.*, *i.q.* pillowcase.

pil'lowy, *adj.*, soft; yielding.

pill'wort, *n.*, a plant of the genus Pilularia.

pi'lose, *adj.*, covered with hairs.

pilos'ity, *n.*, hairiness.

pi'lot, *n.*, a man who guides a vessel into a harbour or along a coast; a person qualified to operate the flying controls of an aircraft; *v.t.*, to act as pilot to.

pi'lotage, *n.*, the remuneration or the guidance of a pilot.

pi'loted, *p.p.*, pilot.

pi'lot-fish, *n.*, a fish which attends sharks at sea.

pi'loting, *pr.p.*, pilot.

pi'lous, *adj.*, *i.q.* pilose.

Pil'sener, *n.*, a kind of light German beer.

pil'ular, *adj.*, pert. or rel. to pills.

pil(l)ule, *n.*, a small pill.

pi'lum, *n.*, a Roman javelin (*Lat.*).

pim'elite, *n.*, a variety of steatite, apple-green in colour.

pimen'ta, *n.*, allspice.

pimen'to, *n.*, *i.q.* pimenta.

pimp, *n.*, a procurer; *v.i.*, to pander.

pimped, *p.p.*, pimp.

pim'pernel, *n.*, a little red-flowered plant common in cornfields.

pimp'ing, *pr.p.*, pimp.

pim'ple, *n.*, a little swelling on the skin.

pim'pled, *adj.*, having pimples on the skin.

pim'ply, *adj.*, full of pimples.

pin, *n.*, a fastener usually consisting of a short piece of pointed wire with a rounded head; *v.t.*, to fasten with a pin.

pin'afore, *n.*, a sort of apron to keep the front of a dress clean.

pinas'ter, *n.*, a kind of pine found in S. Europe.

pin'ball, *n.*, a game played on a pin-table.

pin'-board, *n.*, *i.q.* pin-table.

pin'-case, *n.*, a case for holding pins.

pince'-nez, *n. pl.*, a pair of eyeglasses supported by the bridge of the nose (*Fr.*).

pin'cers, *n. pl.*, an instrument for gripping and drawing out nails.

pincette', *n.*, small pincers (*Fr.*).

pinch, *n.*, a compression, as with the finger and thumb; distress; *v.t.*, to grip with the fingers; *v.i.*, to be niggardly; to sail very close up into the wind.

pinch'beck, *adj.*, sham; *n.*, a yellow alloy of copper and zinc.

pinched, *p.p.*, pinch.

pinch'er, *n.*, one who pinches.

pinch'ing, *pr.p.*, pinch.

pin'cushion, *n.*, a pad in which pins are stuck to store them.

pindar'ic, *adj.*, pert. or rel. to Pindar, the Greek lyric poet; *n.*, an irregular ode.

pin'darism, *n.*, a style of writing in imitation of Pindar.

pin'darist, *n.*, one who practises pindarism.

pine, *n.*, a cone-bearing tree; *v.i.*, to waste away.

pin'eal, *adj.*, shaped like a pine-cone (applied to a gland in the brain which Descartes considered the seat of the soul).

pine'apple, *n.*, a tropical fruit.

pined, *p.p.*, pine.

pi'nery, *n.*, a hot-house for pineapples; a plantation of pine-trees.

pine'-tree, *n.*, an evergreen, cone-bearing, timber tree.

pine'-wood', *n.*, wood from pine trees.

pi'ney, *adj.*, pert. or rel. to, or abounding in, pines. (Also *piny*.)

pin'fold, *n.*, a pound for stray animals; *v.t.*, to confine to this.

ping, *n.*, the sound made by a small missile passing through the air.

ping'er, *n.*, an acoustic transmitter; that which makes a sharp ringing or whistling sound.

ping'-pong, *n.*, amateurish table-tennis.

ping'uid, *adj.*, fat, oily.

ping'uin, *n.*, a W. Indian plant and fruit.

pin'head, *adj.*, minute, rounded; *n.*, a minute object.

pin'hole, *n.*, the puncture made by a pin; a very small hole.

pi'nic, *adj.*, derived from the pine-tree.

pi'ning, *pr.p.*, pine.

pin'ion, *n.*, a wing; the joint of a wing; a small toothed wheel; *v.t.*, to bind the arms of.

pin'ioned, *p.p.*, pinion.

pin'ioning, *pr.p.*, pinion.

pin'ite, *n.*, impure muscovite (mica).

pink, *adj.*, coloured like the pink; *n.*, a garden flower—the carnation; a narrow-sterned vessel; a young salmon; perfect condition; *v.t.*, to ornament with holes and scollops; to stab; *v.i.*, to fire incorrectly (of an internal combustion engine).

pinked, *p.p.*, pink.

pink'er, *n.*, one who, or that which, pinks.

pink'ing, *n.*, the process of decorating with holes and scollops; *pr.p.*, pink.

pin'-money, *n.*, an allowance made to a wife for her own use.

pin'nace, *n.*, an eight-oared sea-boat; a small schooner-rigged vessel.

pin'nacle, *n.*, a pointed summit.

pin'nate, *adj.*, feather-shaped.

pin'nated, *adj.*, *i.q.* pinnate.

pinned, *p.p.*, pin.

pin'ner, *n.*, one who, or that which, pins; an 18th cent. female head-dress.

pin'ning, *pr.p.*, pin.

pin'niped, *n.*, a fin-footed animal.

pin'nock, *n.*, a hedge-sparrow; a titmouse.

pinn'othere, *n.*, kinds of small crabs.

pin'nular, *adj.*, pert. or rel. to a pinnule.

pin'nule, *n.*, the barb of a feather; a leaflet (*bot.*).

pinn'y, *n.*, the abbrev. for pinafore.

pinol'e, *n.*, a kind of corn-flower and sugar dish.

pin'point, *n.*, a very small object; *v.t.*, to locate accurately.

pin'pointed, *p.p.*, pin-point.

pin'pointing, *pr.p.*, pin-point.

pin'prick, *n.*, a trifling injury or annoyance.

pin'stripe, *n.*, a narrow, feint stripe in cloth.

pint, *n.*, a liquid measure of one-eighth of a gallon.

pin'table, *n.*, a gaming board studded with pins for obstacles.

pinta'do, *n.*, the guinea-fowl; a kestrel.

pin'tail, *n.*, a duck with a pointed tail.

pin'tle, *n.*, a pin or bolt, to prevent the recoil of a cannon, to hang a rudder to, to fasten a wheel to its axle, etc.

pin'-up, *adj.*, favourite; *n.*, a picture of a favourite person.

pi'ny, *adj.*, *i.q.* piney.

piolet, *n.*, an alpinist's ice-axe (*Fr.*).

pioneer', *n.*, a soldier who goes before to clear the way; one who opens up new regions or new ideas; *v.i.*, to clear the way.

pioneered', *p.p.*, pioneer.

pioneer'ing, *pr.p.*, pioneer.

pi'ous, *adj.*, dutiful; doing the will of God.

pi'ously, *adv.*, in a pious manner.

pip, *n.*, a short high-pitched sound; a disease of fowls; the seed of a fruit; a symbol on a playing card; *v.t.*, to black-ball; to defeat; to hit with shot (*colloq.*).

pi'pal, *n.*, *i.q.* peepul.

pipe, *n.*, a musical instrument formed of a long tube; any long tube; tube with a bowl for smoking tobacco, etc.; a large cask; *v.i.*, to play on a pipe.

pipe'-case, *n.*, a case for a tobacco-pipe.

pipe'clay, *n.*, white clay; *v.t.*, to whiten with pipeclay.

piped, *adj.*, tubular; *p.p.*, pipe.

pipe'dream, *n.*, a pleasant notion incapable of realization.

pipe'-fish, *n.*, a long, slender fish.

pipe'ful, *n.*, sufficient tobacco to fill the bowl of a pipe.

pipe'-laying, *n.*, the laying down of pipes.

pipe'less, *adj.*, without pipes.

pipe'line, *n.*, a continuous line of pipes; what is planned for the future.

pip-emm'a, *adv.*, afternoon (p.m.) (*colloq.*).

pi'per, *n.*, one who plays on the pipes.

pip'erine, *n.*, a crystalline extract of pepper.

pipette', *n.*, a tube used by chemists for transferring liquids.

pi'ping, *adj.*, hissing with heat; *n.*, pipes collectively; *pr.p.*, pipe.

pipistrel(le'), *n.*, the common bat.

pip'it, *n.*, a bird allied to the lark.

pip'kin, *n.*, a small earthen pot.

pip'pin, *n.*, a type of apple.

pip'squeak, *n.*, a kind of shell; an insignificant person or thing (*slang*).

pi'quancy, *n.*, pungency (*Fr.*).

pi'quant, *adj.*, stimulating to the taste; lively; sparkling (*Fr.*).

pi'quantly, *adv.*, in a piquant way (*Fr.*).

piqué', *n.*, a heavy figured cotton fabric (*Fr.*).

pique, *n.*, wounded pride; a particular scoring manoeuvre in a card game; *v.t.*, to wound the pride of; to score a pique against (*Fr.*).

piqued, *p.p.*, pique.

piquet', *n.*, a card game for two (*Fr.*).

piqu'ing, *pr.p.*, pique.

pi'racy, *n.*, robbery at sea; literary theft.

pira'gua, *n.*, a canoe made by hollowing out a log (*Span.*).

pi'rate, *n.*, a sea-robber; a stealer of copyright; *v.i.* and *t.*, to act as a pirate.

pi'rated, *p.p.*, pirate.

pirat'ical, *adj.*, acting as a pirate.

pirat'ically, *adv.*, in a piratical way.

pi'rating, *pr.p.*, pirate.

pira'ya, *n.*, *i.q.* perai.

pirn, *n.*, a reel or bobbin.

pir'nie, *n.*, a woollen nightcap (*Scot.*).

pirogue', *n.*, *i.q.* piragua.

pirouette', *n.*, a quick turn on the toes; *v.i.*, to whirl as a dancer (*Fr.*).

pis aller, *n.*, the best course to take (*Fr.*).

pis'cary, *n.*, fishing rights.

piscato'rial, *adj.*, pert. or rel. to fish.

pis'catory, *adj.*, *i.q.* piscatorial.

Pis'ces, *n. pl.*, the constellation called The Fishes and the twelfth zodiacal sign (*Lat.*).

piscicul'ture, *n.*, the rearing of fish.

piscicul'turist, *n.*, one who practises pisciculture.

pis'ciform, *adj.*, fish-shaped.

pisci'na, n., a small basin and drain near the altar in a church; a Roman fish-pond (Lat.).

pis'cinal, adj., pert. or rel. to a fish-pond or to a piscina.

pis'cine, adj., pert. or rel. to fishes.

pisciv'orous, adj., feeding on fish.

pisé', n., stiff clay rammed into moulds and used in building walls (Fr.).

pish, interj., a word expressing contempt.

pishogue', n., sorcery; a charm; a spell (Ir.).

pis'iform, adj., pea-shaped; having a structure resembling peas.

pis'mire, n., an ant.

pis'olite, n., carbonate of lime of pisiform structure.

pista'chio, n., a small southern tree and its nut.

pistareen', n., an old Spanish silver coin.

pis'til, n., the seed-bearing part of a flower.

pistilla'ceous, adj., pert. or rel. to a pistil.

pis'tillary, adj., pert. or rel. to a pistil.

pis'tillate, adj., having a pistil.

pistillif'erous, adj., having a pistil and no stamens.

pistil'liform, adj., pistil-like in form.

pis'tol, n., a small gun held in one hand.

pistole', n., a Spanish gold coin.

pis'tolet, n., a small pistol; a breakfast bread roll.

pis'ton, n., a rod or solid cylinder fitted to move up and down in the hollow cylinder of an engine.

pit, n., a hole in the earth; a mine; the floor of a theatre; v.t., to mark with small hollows; to put into opposition.

pit'-a-pat, adv., in a flutter.

pitch, n., a black, sticky substance, prepared from tar; a throw; the height of a note; the slope of a roof; v.i., to rise and fall, as a ship; v.t., to cover with pitch; to throw; to fix on to the ground.

pitch'-black, adj., as black or dark as pitch.

pitch'blende, n., a mineral containing radium, etc.

pitch'-dark, adj., very dark.

pitched, p.p., pitch.

pitch'er, n., a vessel for holding water or other liquid; a ball thrower (baseball); a street vendor; a stone used for paving.

pitch'er-plant, n., a plant with pitcher-shaped leaves.

pitch'fork, n., a fork with a long handle for pitching hay, etc.; a tuning-fork.

pitch'ing, pr.p., pitch.

pitch'-pine, n., a resinous pine from which pitch is produced.

pitch'-pipe, n., a pipe for tuning.

pitch'y, adj., black like pitch.

pit'eous, adj., causing pity; showing pity.

pit'eously, adv., in a piteous manner.

pit'fall, n., a hidden pit; a snare.

pith, n., the soft middle of a stem; the lining of rind; life and strength.

pithecan'thrope, n., an ape-man.

pithec'oid, adj., ape-like.

pith'ily, adv., in a pithy manner.

pith'iness, n., the quality of being pithy.

pith'less, adj., without force and energy.

pith'-hole, n., a pock-mark.

pith'y, adj., full of force and energy; witty.

pit'iable, adj., deserving pity.

pit'iably, adv., in a pitiable way.

pit'ied, p.p., pity.

pit'ier, n., one who pities.

pit'iful, adj., tender-hearted; causing pity; contemptible.

pit'ifully, adv., in a pitiful manner.

pit'ifulness, n., the state of being pitiful.

pit'iless, adj., having no pity.

pit'ilessly, adv., in a pitiless way.

pit'ilessness, n., the state of being pitiless.

pit'man, n., one who works in a pit; a collier.

pit'-pan, n., a central American dug-out boat.

pit'-saw, n., a large saw worked by two men, one standing below in a pit.

pit'tacal, n., a dark-blue substance distilled from wood-tar.

pit'tance, n., a small portion of money or food.

pit'ted, adj., having little pits on the surface; p.p., pit.

pit'ting, pr.p., pit.

pit'tite, n., a person sitting in a theatre pit.

pitu'itary, adj., (of) the gland which influences body growth.

pit'uite, n., mucus; phlegm.

pitu'itous, adj., resembling, or consisting of, mucus.

pit'y, n., a tender feeling for suffering; a reason for feeling pity; v.i., to feel tenderness for.

pit'ying, pr.p., pity.

pit'yingly, adv., compassionately.

pityri'asis, n., a skin disease producing fine scales.

pit'yroid, adj., resembling bran.

piu, adv., more (It.).

piv'ot, n., a pin or shaft on which something turns; v.i., to turn on a pivot.

piv'otal, adj., pert. or rel. to a pivot.

pix, n., i.q. pyx.

pixie, n., i.q. pixy.

pix'ing, v.t., i.q. pyxing.

pix'y, n., a fairy.

piz'za, n., an open tart of bread, containing cheese, meat, etc. (It.).

pizzicato, adj. and adv., by plucking (rather than bowing) strings; n., a passage or note so played (It., mus.).

placabil'ity, n., the quality of being placable.

pla'cable, adj., easily pacified.

pla'cableness, n., i.q. placability.

plac′ard, n., a written or printed paper stuck on a wall.

placard′, v.t., to stick up a placard.

placard′ed, p.p., placard.

placard′ing, pr.p., placard.

placate′, v.t., to appease.

placat′ed, p.p., placate.

placat′ing, pr.p., placate.

place, n., a location; a broad, open space; rank; a passage in a book; v.t., to fix or settle.

place′bo, n., the first antiphon of the vespers for the dead; a medicine to humour or soothe; a non-medical replacement for a medicine (Lat.).

placed, p.p., place.

place′man, n., an office-bearer.

place′ment, n., the action of placing, arranging.

placen′ta, n., the spongy substance connecting a mother with her unborn young.

placen′tal, adj., pert. or rel. to, or possessing, a placenta.

placenta′tion, n., the disposition of the placenta.

pla′cer, n., one who places; a place where gold-dust is found in the soil.

pla′cet, n., a vote of assent (Lat.).

plac′id, adj., peaceful.

placid′ity, n., calmness.

plac′idly, adv., calmly.

plac′idness, n., calmness, mildness.

pla′cing, pr.p., place.

plac′itory, adj., pert. or rel. to pleading in courts of law.

plack′et, n., the opening or slit in a skirt.

plac′oid, adj., having scales like detached plates (applied to fishes).

placoi′dian, n., a placoid fish, as the shark.

plafond′, n., a richly painted ceiling; a soffit (Fr.).

pla′gal, adj., applied in music to a cadence in which the tonic chord follows that of the subdominant.

plage, n., a sea beach (Fr.).

pla′giarism, n., literary theft; that which is plagiarized.

pla′giarist, n., one who plagiarizes.

pla′giarize, v.t. and i., to steal the writings of another.

pla′giarized, p.p., plagiarize.

pla′giarizing, pr.p., plagiarize.

pla′giary, n., i.q. plagiarist.

plagihe′dral, adj., having oblique faces arranged spirally.

plague, n., a deadly sickness; a troublesome person or thing; v.t., to trouble.

plagued, p.p., plague.

pla′guer, n., one who, or that which, plagues.

pla′guily, adv., vexatiously.

pla′guing, pr.p., plague.

pla′guy, adj., vexatious.

plaice, n., an edible flat fish.

plaid, n., an outer woollen garment worn by Scottish Highlanders.

plaid′ing, n., a coarse twilled woollen cloth.

plain, adj., flat; simple; unadorned; n., a flat stretch of country.

plain′-chant, n., i.q. plain-song.

plain′-clothes, n., civilian dress.

plain′-dealing, adj., honest; n., honest speaking and acting.

plain′er, n., comp. of plain.

plain′est, n., super. of plain.

plain′ly, adv., in a plain manner.

plain′ness, n., the state or quality of being plain.

plain′-song, n., vocal music in the old ecclesiastical modes, unmeasured in rhythm and sung in unison. (Also plain-chant.)

plain′-speaking, n., straightforwardness of speech.

plain′-spoken, adj., speaking what one thinks.

plaint, n., an expression of sorrow; the written statement of a plaintiff in a court of law.

plain′tiff, n., one who brings an action into court.

plain′tive, adj., mournful; complaining.

plain′tively, adv., in a plaintive manner.

plain′tiveness, n., the quality or state of being plaintive.

plait, n., a fold of twisted hair, wool, etc.; v.t., to fold, to weave hairs, etc.

plait′ed, adj., braided; interwoven; p.p., plait.

plait′er, n., one who plaits.

plait′ing, pr.p., plait.

plan, n., a sketch or design; the shape of anything on a flat surface; v.t., to design.

pla′nary, adj., pert. or rel. to a plane.

planch, n., a flat slab generally made of fireclay; v.t., to cover with planks.

plan′chet, n., a flat piece of metal to be stamped into a coin.

planchette′, n., a little tablet of wood running on wheels and provided with a lead-pencil, used as a kind of oracle (Fr.).

plane, adj., flat; n., a flat surface; a surface such that parallel straight lines in any direction would lie on it; a tall, spreading tree; a tool for making wood smooth; v.t., to make level or smooth; v.i., to sail on speed on the surface of the water.

planed, p.p., plane.

pla′ner, n., a wooden block to smooth a forme of type; a planing machine.

plan′et, n., a heavenly body moving round the sun.

planeta′rium, n., an installation representing the planets moving in their orbits.

plan′etary, adj., pert. or rel. to the planets.

plan′etoid, n., a very small planet.

planetol′ogy, n., the study of the planets.

plane′-tree, n., a tree used for lining avenues, possessing a straight stem and palmate leaves.

plan'etule, *n.*, a little planet.

plan'gent, *adj.*, beating or dashing, like a wave.

planim'eter, *n.*, an instrument for measuring areas.

planimet'ric, *adj.*, pert. or rel. to planimetry.

planim'etry, *n.*, the mensuration of plane figures.

pla'ning, *pr.p.*, plane.

pla'ning-mill, *n.*, a machine with a revolving cutter for planing wood.

planipet'alous, *adj.*, having petals lying in the same plane.

plan'ish, *v.t.*, to make smooth.

plan'ished, *p.p.*, planish.

plan'ishing, *pr.p.*, planish.

plan'isphere, *n.*, a map showing the circles of the sphere.

plank, *n.*, a long, narrow, flat piece of wood; *v.t.*, to cover with planks.

planked, *p.p.*, plank.

plank'ing, *n.*, planks collectively; *pr.p.*, plank.

plank'ton, *n.*, a form of aquatic organic life (*biol.*).

planned, *p.p.*, plan.

plan'ner, *n.*, one who plans.

plan'ning, *pr.p.*, plan.

plano-con'cave, *adj.*, plane on one side and concave on the other.

plano-con'ical, *adj.*, plane on one side and conical on the other.

plano-con'vex, *adj.*, plane on one side and convex on the other.

plano'graphy, *n.*, offset-printing; print from a level surface.

plant, *n.*, a vegetable with roots, stem and leaves; the machines and equipment for industry; a trick to deceive over the possession of an object (*colloq.*); *v.t.*, to put in the ground for growth; to set.

plant'able, *adj.*, capable of being planted.

plan'tain, *n.*, a plant with broad leaves and a long flower-spike;

a fruit akin to the banana.

plan'tar, *adj.*, pert. or rel. to the sole of the foot (*anat.*).

planta'tion, *n.*, a place planted with young trees; a colony.

plant'ed, *p.p.*, plant.

plant'er, *n.*, the owner of a plantation; one who, or that which, plants.

plant'icle, *n.*, an embryo plant.

plan'tigrade, *adj.*, walking on the sole, not on the toes; *n.*, an animal that walks on its soles, e.g., the bear.

plant'ing, *pr.p.*, plant.

plant'let, *n.*, a little rudimentary plant.

plant'ule, *n.*, a plant embryo.

planx'ty, *n.*, a lively harp tune.

plaque, *n.*, an ornamental plate (*Fr.*).

plaquette', *n.*, a small plaque (*Fr.*).

plash, *n.*, a small, shallow pool; a dash of water; *v.i.*, to dabble in water.

plashed, *p.p.*, plash.

plash'ing, *pr.p.*, plash.

plash'y, *adj.*, watery; marshy.

plasm, *n.*, a mould or matrix; *i.q.* plasma.

plas'ma, *n.*, a green mineral; formless elementary matter; protoplasm; the part of blood which coagulates.

plasmat'ic, *adj.*, pert. or rel. to plasma.

plasmod'ium, *n.*, a mass of protoplasm (*biol.*).

plasmol'ysis, *n.*, the loss of liquid from vegetation by immersion in a strong solution.

plas'ter, *n.*, a mixture of lime, sand and water for covering walls; a cloth spread with ointment; *v.t.*, to cover with plaster.

plas'tered, *p.p.*, plaster.

plas'terer, *n.*, one who plasters.

plas'tering, *n.*, plasterwork; *pr.p.*, plaster.

plas'tery, *adj.*, resembling or containing plaster.

plas'tic, *adj.*, easily moulded; made of a plastic material.

Plas'ticine, *n.*, the brand name of a substance used for teaching modelling.

plas'ticism, *n.*, the theory of plastic art.

plastic'ity, *n.*, the state of being plastic.

plas'ticizer, *n.*, a chemical for inducing plasticity.

plas'tics, *n. pl.*, synthetic chemical substances capable of moulding or extrusion into any desired form; the science and technology of manufacturing plastic substances.

plastog'raphy, *n.*, the art of moulding or modelling; forgery of handwriting.

plas'tron, *n.*, a leather breast-plate used in fencing.

plat, *n.*, a piece of ground laid out with some sort of design; *v.t.*, to plait.

plat, *n.*, a dish of food (*Fr.*).

plat'an, *n.*, the plane-tree.

plat'band, *n.*, a flower border in a garden; a flat rectangular moulding.

plate, *n.*, a thin piece of metal; a nearly flat dish; a piece of household crockery; household articles of gold or silver; *v.t.*, to cover with a thin coat of metal.

plateau', *n.*, a tableland (*Fr.*).

pla'ted, *p.p.*, plate.

plate'ful, *n.*, as much as fills a plate.

plate'-glass, *n.*, thick glass used for windows, mirrors, etc.

plate'lay'er, *n.*, a workman engaged on laying and maintaining railway lines.

plat'en, *n.*, the flat part of a printing-press; the hard cylinder against which the type of a typewriter strikes.

pla'ter, *n.*, one who coats articles with gold or silver.

plate'-rack, *n.*, a frame where plates are kept or drained.

plate'-warmer, *n.*, a shelved case in which plates are warmed.

plat'form, *n.,* an elevated floor or flat surface; a foundation; an agreed set of principles.

plat'ina, *n., i.q.* platinum.

pla'ting, *n.,* a thin covering; *pr.p.,* plate.

platinif'erous, *adj.,* producing platinum.

plat'inite, *n.,* an alloy of steel and nickel.

plat'inize, *v.t.,* to combine or cover with platinum.

plat'inized, *p.p.,* platinize.

plat'inizing, *pr.p.,* platinize.

plat'inode, *n.,* a cathode.

plat'inoid, *n.,* a name given to any metal with which platinum is associated.

plat'inotype, *n.,* a permanent photograph in platinum black.

plat'inous, *adj.,* containing or consisting of platinum.

plat'inum, *n.,* a valuable metal like dim silver but very heavy. (Also *platina*.)

plat'itude, *n.,* a commonplace, obvious remark.

platitudinar'ian, *adj., i.q.* platitudinous; *n.,* one who has a reputation for using platitudes.

platitud'inist, *n.,* one who indulges in platitudes.

platitud'inize, *v.i.,* to talk in platitudes.

platitud'inous, *adj.,* characterized by platitudes.

platom'eter, *n., i.q.* planimeter.

Platon'ic, *adj.,* pert. or rel. to Plato, the Greek philosopher, or his philosophy; passionless.

Platon'ically, *adv.,* in a Platonic way.

Pla'tonism, *n.,* the philosophy of Plato.

Pla'tonist, *n.,* a follower of Plato.

Pla'tonize, *v.i.,* to adopt the philosophy of Plato.

Pla'tonized, *p.p.,* platonize.

Pla'tonizing, *pr.p.,* platonize.

platoon', *n.,* a firing party; a sub-division of a company of soldiers (*mil.*).

plat'ted, *p.p.,* plat.

plat'ter, *n.,* a large flat dish.

plat'ting, *n.,* woven or plaited strips of straw for hats; *pr.p.,* plat.

plat'ypus, *n.,* a small Australasian mammal.

plau'dit, *n.,* an expression of praise.

plau'ditory, *adj.,* applauding.

plausibil'ity, *n.,* superficial reasonableness.

plau'sible, *adj.,* appearing reasonable.

plau'sibly, *adv.,* speciously.

plau'sive, *adj.,* manifesting praise.

play, *n.,* amusement; a scene or story for acting; scope; *v.t.,* to join in a game; to act; to make music; to keep in action.

play'able, *adj.,* able to be played.

play'actor, *n.,* a theatrical performer.

play'bill, *n.,* a programme of a play in the form of a placard.

played, *p.p.,* play.

play'er, *n.,* one who plays; an actor; a gambler.

play'fellow, *n.,* a playmate.

play'ful, *adj.,* fond of play or fun.

play'fully, *adv.,* in a playful manner.

play'fulness, *n.,* sportiveness.

play'goer, *n.,* one who frequents the theatre.

play'ground, *n.,* a piece of ground for recreation.

play'house, *n.,* a theatre.

play'ing, *pr.p.,* play.

play'mate, *n.,* one who plays along with another.

play'pen, *n.,* a pen in which a child can play safely.

play'thing, *n.,* a toy.

play'time, *n.,* a time set apart for play.

play'wright, *n.,* a maker of plays.

play'writer, *n., i.q.* playwright.

pla'za, *n.,* a market place (*Span.*).

plea, *n.,* a lawsuit; an answer to a charge; an urgent prayer.

pleach, *v.t.,* to entwine or interlace.

plead, *v.t. and i.,* to use as a plea; to entreat.

plead'able, *adj.,* capable of being alleged in proof or defence.

plead'ed, *p.p.,* plead.

plead'er, *n.,* an advocate.

plead'ing, *adj.,* imploring; *n.,* advocacy; the statement of a litigant; *pr.p.,* plead.

plead'ingly, *adv.,* by pleading.

plead'ings, *n. pl.,* statements in a lawsuit.

plea'sance, *n.,* a pleasure garden; pleasure; pleasantry.

pleas'ant, *adj.,* giving pleasure; cheerful.

pleas'anter, *adj., comp.* of pleasant.

pleas'antest, *adj., super.* of pleasant.

pleas'antly, *adv.,* cheerfully.

pleas'antness, *n.,* the state of being pleasant.

pleas'antry, *n.,* lively talk; a jest.

please, *v.t. and t.,* to give satisfaction.

pleased, *adj.,* delighted; *p.p.,* please.

pleas'ing, *adj.,* delightful; *pr.p.,* please.

pleas'ingly, *adv.,* in a pleasing way.

pleas'urable, *adj.,* giving pleasure.

pleas'urably, *adv.,* happily.

pleas'ure, *n.,* delight; amusement; *v.t.,* to gratify.

pleas'ure-boat, *n.,* a boat used for excursions and amusement.

pleas'ured, *p.p.,* pleasure.

pleas'uring, *pr.p.,* pleasure.

pleat, *n.,* a fold; *v.t., i.q.* plait.

plea'ted, *p.p.,* pleat.

pleat'ing, *n.,* folding; *pr.p.,* pleat.

pleb, *n., i.q.* plebeian (*colloq.*).

plebe, *n.,* a junior member of a military academy (*colloq.*).

plebe'ian, *adj.,* pert. or rel. to the common people; *n.,* one of the common people.

plebe'ianism, *n.,* vulgarity.

pleb'iscite, *n.,* a decision by the votes of the whole of the people.

plec'trum, n., a sort of comb for striking the strings of a lyre or other stringed instrument (Lat.).

pled, p.p., plead.

pledge, n., a promise; a security; v.t., to promise; to pawn; to drink a health.

pledged, p.p., pledge.

pledgee', n., the person to whom anything is pledged.

pled'ger, n., one who pledges.

pledg'et, n., a compress laid on a wound.

pledg'ing, pr.p., pledge.

Plei'ad, n., one of the Pleiades.

Plei'ades, n. pl., a group of seven stars.

plei'ocene, adj., more recent (geol.). (Also pliocene.)

pleiosau'rus, n., an extinct saurian of great size. (Also pliosaurus.)

pleis'tocene, adj., postpliocene; most recent (geol.).

ple'narily, adv., in a plenary manner.

plena'rium, n., a set of sacred writings.

ple'narty, n., the state of an ecclesiastical benefice when occupied.

ple'nary, adj., complete.

plenilu'nar, adj., pert. or rel. to the full moon.

plenip'otence, n., completeness of power.

plenip'otent, adj., possessing full power.

plenipoten'tiary, n., a person who has full power to act for another; an ambassador with absolute power to make treaties, etc.

ple'nist, n., one who believes that every portion of space is filled with matter.

plen'itude, n., completeness.

plen'teous, adj., abundant.

plen'teously, adv., in a plenteous manner.

plen'tiful, adj., i.q. plenteous.

plen'tifully, adv., abundantly.

plen'tifulness, n., a state of plenty.

plen'ty, n., a full supply; abundance.

ple'num, n., that state of things in which every part of space is supposed to be full of matter (Lat.).

ple'onasm, n., the redundancy of words.

pleonas'tic, adj., redundant.

plesiomor'phism, n., a state of crystallization which produces substances resembling one another closely, though they are not identical.

ple'siosaur, n., an extinct gigantic long-necked saurian.

plesiosau'rus, n., i.q. plesiosaur.

pleth'ora, n., overfulness; too much blood.

plethor'ic, adj., having too much blood.

pleu'ra, n., the covering membrane of the lungs.

pleu'risy, n., inflammation of the pleura.

pleurit'ic, adj., pert. or rel. to pleurisy.

pleuro-pneumo'nia, n., inflammation of the lungs and pleura.

plex'iform, adj., formed like network.

plexim'eter, n., a little instrument used in diagnosing disease by percussion of the body (med.).

plex'or, n., a hammer used with a pleximeter (med.).

plex'ure, n., an interweaving; a texture.

plex'us, n., a network, as of nerves, fibres, etc. (anat., Lat.).

pliabil'ity, n., flexibility.

pli'able, adj., easily bent or persuaded.

pli'ancy, n., an easiness to be bent or influenced.

pli'ant, adj., i.q. pliable.

pli'antly, adv., in a pliant manner.

pli'ca, n., a disease of the hair and skin.

pli'cate, adj., folded like a fan; plaited.

pli'cated, adj., i.q. plicate.

plica'tion, n., a fold; a folding.

plic'ature, n., i.q. plication.

plied, p.p., ply.

pli'er, n., one who plies; pl., an instrument for bending wire.

pli'form, adj., having the form of a ply or fold.

plight, n., condition; a state of risk; v.t., to give as a pledge.

plight'ed, p.p., plight.

plight'er, n., one who plights.

plight'ing, pr.p., plight.

plim, v.t. and i., to make or grow plump.

Plim'soll line, n., line painted on a ship's side to indicate the loading capacity.

plim'solls, n. pl., rubber-soled canvas shoes.

plinth, n., the lowest part of the base of a column; a thin course of masonry projecting near the base of a wall.

plin'thite, n., a kind of brick-red clay.

pli'ocene, adj., i.q. pleiocene.

pliosau'rus, n., i.q. pleiosaurus.

plod, v.i., to go on slowly but without stopping.

plod'ded, p.p., plod.

plod'der, n., a slow, hard-working person.

plod'ding, adj., patiently laborious; pr.p., plod.

plom'bé, adj., officially lead-sealed (Fr.).

plonge, v.t., to cleanse a drain by stirring up the sediment.

plot, n., a piece of ground; a secret plan or conspiracy; the story of a novel or play; v.i., to plan mischief; v.t., to represent in graphs; to map out or chart.

plot'ted, p.p., plot.

plot'ter, n., one who plots.

plot'ting, pr.p., plot.

plough, n., an instrument for turning up the soil; v.t. and i., to turn up the soil with a plough; to fail an exam (colloq.).

plough'able, adj., arable.

ploughed, p.p., plough.

plough'er, n., one who ploughs.

plough'ing, pr.p., plough.

plough'land, n., land suitable for cultivation by ploughing.

plough'man, n., a man who guides a plough.

plough'share, *n.,* the blade of a plough.

plough'-tail, *n.,* the handle of a plough.

plov'er, *n.,* a common wading-bird.

ploy, *n.,* a job, an expedition; a planned action with an outcome intended (*colloq.*).

pluck, *n.,* courage; the heart, liver, etc., of an animal; *v.t.,* to strip off; to gather.

plucked, *p.p.,* pluck.

pluck'er, *n.,* one who plucks.

pluck'ier, *adj., comp.* of plucky.

pluck'iest, *adj., super.* of plucky.

pluck'ily, *adv.,* in a plucky manner.

pluck'iness, *n.,* the quality of being plucky.

pluck'ing, *pr.p.,* pluck.

pluck'y, *adj.,* courageous.

plug, *n.,* a stopper for a hole; a piece of advertising; *v.t.,* to stop with a plug.

plugged, *p.p.,* plug.

plug'ging, *pr.p.,* plug.

plum, *n.,* a fleshy fruit containing a stone; £100,000; a handsome fortune (*slang*).

plu'mage, *n.,* the feathers of a bird.

plumassier', *n.,* a preparer of, or dealer in, ornamental feathers (*Fr.*).

plumb, *adj.,* perpendicular; *n.,* a leaden weight hung on a string; *v.t.,* to test with a plumb.

plumbag'inous, *adj.,* resembling, or consisting of, plumbago.

plumba'go, *n.,* blacklead; graphite.

plumb'-bob, *n.,* a bob or weight attached to a plumb-line.

plum'bean, *adj.,* leaden.

plum'beous, *adj., i.q.* plumbean.

plumb'er, *n.,* a worker in lead; a craftsman in domestic water installations.

plumb'ery, *n.,* works or manufactures of lead.

plum'bic, *adj.,* pert. or rel. to lead.

plumbif'erous, *adj.,* producing lead.

plumb'ing, *n.,* the art of working in lead; the apparatus for conveying water or gas throughout a building.

plumb'-line, *n.,* a line with a plumb attached.

plumb'-rule, *n.,* a bricklayer's or carpenter's straight-edge with a plumb-line attached.

plum'-cake, *n.,* a raisin cake.

plume, *n.,* a crest, a feather; *v.t.,* to adorn with feathers; to boast.

plumed, *adj.,* having plumes; *p.p.,* plume.

plume'let, *n.,* a little plume.

plumig'erous, *adj.,* having plumes.

plu'miliform, *adj.,* in the form of a feather.

plu'ming, *pr.p.,* plume.

plu'miped, *adj.,* with feathered feet; *n.,* a bird with feathered feet.

plu'mist, *n.,* a featherdresser.

plum'mer-block, *n.,* a metal cover for shaft bearings.

plum'met, *n.,* a leaden weight on a line for sounding; *v.t.,* to sound with a lead.

plum'my, *adj.,* good, desirable; abounding in plums.

plu'mose, *adj.,* having feathers.

plu'mous, *adj., i.q.* plumose.

plump, *adj.,* round, sleek, fat; in good condition; *v.i.,* to give all one's support.

plumped, *p.p.,* plump.

plump'er, *n., comp.* of plump; *n.,* one who plumps; a barefaced lie (*slang*).

plump'est, *adj., super.,* of plump.

plump'ish, *adj.,* rather plump.

plump'ness, *n.,* the quality of being plump.

plum'-pudding, *n.,* a pudding made with raisins, currants, eggs, spices, suet, flour, etc., and generally eaten at Christmas time.

plum'-tree, *n.,* a tree bearing plums.

plu'mule, *n.,* a downfeather; a rudimentary bud of an embryo plant.

plu'my, *adj.,* feathery.

plun'der, *n.,* pillage, spoil; *v.t.,* to pillage, to rob.

plun'derage, *n.,* the embezzlement of goods on board a ship.

plun'dered, *p.p.,* plunder.

plun'derer, *n.,* a pillager, a robber.

plun'dering, *pr.p.,* plunder.

plunge, *n.,* the act of plunging; a sudden drop; *v.t.,* to immerse; *v.i.,* to jump down; to gamble.

plunged, *p.p.,* plunge.

plun'ger, *n.,* one who plunges; a piece of mechanism with plunging action.

plun'ging, *pr.p.,* plunge.

plunk, *n.,* plucking sounds; *v.t.* and *i.,* to throw fiercely.

pluper'fect, *adj.,* denoting time previous to time already past; *n.,* the tense so named.

plu'ral, *adj.,* more than one; *n.,* the plural number.

plu'ralism, *n.,* the holding simultaneously of several offices.

plu'ralist, *n.,* one who holds several offices at once.

plural'ity, *n.,* more than one.

plu'ralize, *v.t.,* to make plural, or express in the plural.

plu'ralized, *p.p.,* pluralize.

plu'ralizing, *pr.p.,* pluralize.

pluranim'ity, *n.,* a diversity of opinions.

pluren'nial, *adj.,* occurring once in several years; lasting several years.

pluri'literal, *adj.* and *n.,* (a word) consisting of more than one letter.

plus, *adv.,* more; *n.,* the sign (+); a positive quantity; *prep.* with the addition of.

plus'-fours, *n. pl.,* baggy, wide knickerbockers.

plush, *adj.,* made of plush; luxurious; *n.,* a fabric with a long, soft nap.

plu'tarchy, *n.,* government by the rich.

Plu'to, *n.,* a remote planet; god of the underworld.

plutoc′racy, n., i.q. plut-archy; a wealthy ruling class.

plu′tocrat, n., one who exerts the power of wealth.

plutocrat′ic, adj., pert. or rel. to plutocracy.

pluto′-democ′racy, n., democracy based on wealth.

plutol′atry, n., the worship of wealth.

Pluto′nian, adj., pert. or rel. to Pluto and Hades; igneous.

Pluton′ic, adj., i.q. Plutonian.

Plu′tonism, n., the Plutonists' theory that rock-structure is chiefly the result of igneous action.

Plu′tonist, n., an adherent to Plutonism.

pluton′ium, n., a radioactive element produced from uranium (chem.).

pluton′omy, n., political economy.

plu′vial, adj., rainy; pert. or rel. to rain.

pluviom′eter, n., a rain-gauge.

plu′vious, adj., i.q. pluvial.

ply, n., a layer or fold of cloth, a strand of rope, etc.; v.i., to go backwards and forwards; v.t., to practise diligently; to wield; to assail (as with arguments).

ply′ing, pr.p., ply.

ply′wood, n., a strong, thin, laminated board.

pneumat′ic, adj., pert. or rel. to air.

pneumat′ics, n. pl., the science of airs and gases.

pneumatol′ogy, n., the science of spiritual existence (embracing theology, demonology and psychology).

pneumatom′eter, n., a contrivance for measuring the amount of breath taken in at one inspiration.

pneumogas′tric, adj., pert. or rel. to the lungs or stomach.

pneumo′nia, n., inflammation of the lungs.

pneumon′ic, adj., pert. or rel. to the lungs.

pneumoni′tis, n., i.q. pneumonia.

Pnyx, n., the Athenian place of meeting.

Po′a, n., large grass.

poach, v.i., to trespass; v.t., to steal game; to boil (an egg) without the shell; to trample into holes; to seethe.

poached, p.p., poach.

poach′er, n., one who poaches.

poach′ing, n., stealing game and trespassing; pr.p., poach.

poach′y, adj., sodden from trampling.

poch′ard, n., a European diving-bird.

pochette′, n., kit; a hand-bag; a pocket-wallet.

pock, n., a mark left by certain diseases; v.t., to score with pockmarks.

pock′et, n., a bag in the material of a coat, etc., or on a billiard table; a cavity in a rock or in the air; v.t., to put in one's pocket; to submit to.

pock′etable, adj., able to be pocketed.

pock′et-book, n., a note-book for the pocket.

pock′et-compass, n., a compass for the pocket.

pock′eted, p.p., pocket.

pock′etful, n., as much as a pocket will hold when full.

pocket-hand′kerchief, n., a handkerchief for the pocket.

pock′eting, pr.p., pocket.

pock′et-knife, n., a knife for the pocket.

pock′etless, adj., without a pocket.

pock′et-money, n., money for small expenses.

pock′-mark, n., the scar left by disease.

pock′y, adj., pock-marked.

po′co, adv., slightly (mus.).

pococuran′te, adj. and n., indifferent (person) (It.).

poc′uliform, adj., cup-shaped.

pod, n., the seed-vessel of peas, beans, etc.; a small flock of seals; v.i., to form pods; v.t., to drive (seals) into a pod.

pod′agra, n., gout in the foot (med.).

pod′agral, adj., pert. or rel. to gout.

podag′ric, adj., i.q. podagral.

pod′ded, adj., having pods; p.p., pod.

pod′ding, pr.p., pod.

podesta′, n., a magistrate (It.).

po′dex, n., the rump (Lat.).

podge, n., a short, fat person (colloq.).

podg′iness, n., a podgy state.

podg′y, adj., soft and fat.

po′dium, n., a base or plinth; a continuous bench round a room.

podophyl′lin, n., a purgative medicine made from the wild mandrake (chem.).

pod′osperm, n., a seed's stalk.

po′e-bird, n., the parson bird of New Zealand.

poecilit′ic, adj., variegated, mottled.

po′em, n., a poetical composition.

po′esy, n., the art of poetry; verse-making.

po′et, n., a writer of poetry.

poetas′ter, n., an indifferent poet.

po′etess, n., the fem. of poet.

poet′ic, adj., pert. or rel. to poetry.

poet′ical, adj., i.q. poetic.

poet′ically, adv., in a poetic manner.

poet′icize, v.t., to make poetic.

poet′ics, n. pl., the study of the art of poetry.

po′etize, v.t. and i., to write as a poet.

po′et-lau′reate, n., the official state poet.

po′etry, n., verse; poems in general.

pog′gy, n., a small whale.

pogo, n., a toy-like stilt.

pogrom′, n., a planned massacre.

poign′ancy, n., sharpness, acuteness.

poign′ant, adj., sharp, acute.

poign′antly, adv., acutely.

poikilit′ic, adj., i.q. poecilitic.

poilu′, n., a French soldier (slang).

poinset′tia, n., a Mexican flower with large, scarlet, showy bracts and small yellow flowers.

point, *n.*, a sharp end; a headland; a punctuation mark; a subject in an argument; the true bearing of an argument; a fielding position in cricket; *v.t.*, to sharpen; to aim; to punctuate; to cement the joints of brickwork on the face; to indicate by gesture.

point'blank, *adj.*, and *adv.*, in direct line; flatly.

point-device', *adj.* and *adv.*, extremely neat.

point'ed, *adj.*, sharpended; *p.p.*, point.

point'el, *n.*, a stilus.

poin'tillism, *n.*, the method of producing light effects using coloured dots instead of pigments.

poin'tillist, *n.*, one who practises pointillism.

point'ing, *n.*, the act of pointing in any sense; *pr.p.*, point.

point'er, *n.*, one who points; a variety of sporting dog; a stick for pointing with; one of the two stars in the Great Bear.

point'less, *adj.*, without point.

point'lessly, *adv.*, in a pointless way.

point'lessness, *n.*, the state of being pointless.

points'man, *n.*, one on point duty.

poise, *n.*, weight, balance; *v.t.*, to weigh, balance.

poised, *p.p.*, poise.

pois'ing, *pr.p.*, poise.

poi'son, *n.*, a deadly drug; venom; *v.t.*, to kill by poison; to taint.

poi'soned, *p.p.*, poison.

poi'soner, *n.*, one who administers poison.

poi'son-gas, *n.*, an injurious chemical gas used in warfare.

poi'soning, *pr.p.*, poison.

poi'sonous, *adj.*, containing poison; venomous.

poi'sonously, *adv.*, in a poisonous way.

poi'trel, *n.*, a horse's breastplate.

poke, *n.*, a push; a prod; a bag or pouch; *v.t.*, to thrust forward; to push.

poked, *p.p.*, poke.

po'ker, *n.*, a bar for poking the fire; a card game.

poke'weed, *n.*, a perennial herb.

po'king, *pr.p.*, poke.

po'ky, *adj.*, small, confined.

polac'ca, *n.*, a three-masted Mediterranean merchant vessel.

pola'cre, *n.*, *i.q.* polacca.

po'lar, *adj.*, pert. or rel. to a pole or poles.

polarim'eter, *n.*, an apparatus for measuring the polarization of light. (Also *polariscope*.)

polarim'etry, *n.*, the measuring of polarization.

Polar'is, *n.*, a class of nuclear submarine.

polar'iscope, *n.*, *i.q.* polarimeter.

polar'ity, *n.*, the quality of having opposed poles; tendency towards the earth's magnetic poles; the quality of being attracted and repelled; modification of light and heat vibrations, so that the ray shows different qualities in different directions.

polariza'tion, *n.*, the effect of polarizing.

po'larize, *v.t.*, to give polarity to.

po'larized, *p.p.*, polarize.

po'larizer, *n.*, that which polarizes.

po'larizing, *pr.p.*, polarize.

polatouche', *n.*, a small flying squirrel.

pol'der, *n.*, reclaimed marsh land.

Pole, *n.*, a native of Poland.

pole, *n.*, a rod or shaft; a measure of length (5½ yds.); the North or the South Pole; *v.t.*, to propel with a pole.

pole'axe, *n.*, an axe on the end of a pole; *v.t.*, to strike down with sudden violence.

pole'cat, *n.*, a wild cat.

poled, *p.p.*, pole.

pol'emarch, *n.*, an ancient Greek military commander.

polem'ic, *adj.*, controversial; *n.*, a controversialist.

polem'ical, *adj.*, *i.q.* polemic.

polem'ically, *adv.*, controversially.

polem'ics, *n. pl.*, controversial writings.

polen'ta, *n.*, Italian porridge made of barley, maize and chestnut meal, etc.

pole'-star, *n.*, the North Star.

polewards, *adv.*, towards the pole.

polianthus, *n.*, a plant of the Amaryllis family.

police', *n.*, a civil force to uphold the law; *v.t.*, to guard with a police force.

police'-court, *n.*, a court of summary jurisdiction presided over by a magistrate.

policed', *p.p.*, police.

police'man, *n.*, a member of the police force.

police'-officer, *n.*, *i.q.* policeman.

police'-station, *n.*, the headquarters of the local police; a police office.

police'woman, *n.*, a female member of the police force.

policlin'ic, *n.*, medical treatment given in private houses; the out-patients' department in a hospital.

pol'icy, *n.*, a scheme of governing; any course of action; an insurance contract; the pleasure-grounds of an estate (*Scot.*).

pol'icy-holder, *n.*, a holder of an insurance or assurance policy.

po'ling, *n.*, a scaffolding; propelling by poles; *pr.p.*, pole.

pol'io, *n.* (*abbrev.*), poliomyelitis.

pol'iomyelit'is, *n.*, infantile paralysis; a spinal disease.

Po'lish, *adj.*, pert. or rel. to Poland and the Poles; the language of P.

pol'ish, *n.*, the result of polishing; a material for giving a smooth, glossy surface; refinement of manners; *v.t.*, to make bright by rubbing.

pol'ishable, *adj.*, that will take a polish.

pol'ished, *adj.*, refined; *p.p.*, polish.

pol'isher, *n.*, one who, or anything that, polishes.

pol'ishing, *pr.p.*, polish.

pol'itarch, *n.*, an Oriental governor (*hist.*).

polit'buro, *n.*, a policy-making body of the U.S.S.R.

polite', *adj.*, gentle, courteous.

polite'ly, *adv.*, courteously.

polite'ness, *n.*, courteousness.

politesse', *n.*, good breeding (*Fr.*).

pol'itic, *adj.*, sagacious; well advised.

polit'ical, *adj.*, pert. or rel. to the state and to politics.

polit'ically, *adv.*, in regard to politics and the State.

politi'cian, *n.*, one who makes politics his business.

polit'icize, *v.i.* and *t.*, to engage in politics.

pol'itics, *n. pl.*, the art or science of governing.

pol'ity, *n.*, civil constitution.

polk, *v.i.*, to dance the polka.

pol'ka, *n.*, a Bohemian dance.

Poll (Polly), *n.*, a pet name for a parrot.

poll, *n.*, the back of the head; votes taken and registered; *v.i.*, to give a vote; *v.t.*, to crop the hair of; to take the votes of; to lop.

pol'lack, *n.*, a kind of cod-fish.

pol'lan, *n.*, Irish fresh-water fish.

pol'lard, *n.*, a lopped tree; an animal that has lost its horns; *v.t.*, to lop trees.

polled, *p.p.*, poll.

pol'len, *n.*, the dust of a flower.

poll'er, *n.*, one who polls.

pollicita'tion, *n.*, a revocable promise (*leg.*).

pol'linate, *v.t.*, to fertilise with pollen.

pol'linated, *p.p.*, pollinate.

pol'linating, *pr.p.*, pollinate.

pollina'tion, *n.*, the fertilisation with pollen.

pol'linator, *n.*, an agent for pollinating (insect, etc.).

poll'ing, *pr.p.*, poll.

pollinif'erous, *adj.*, producing pollen.

pol'linose, *adj.*, covered with a pollen-like substance.

pol'lock, *n.*, i.q. pollack.

poll'oi, *n. pl.*, the majority (*Gk.*).

poll'-tax, *n.*, a tax on each member of a community.

pollute', *v.t.*, to defile, to contaminate.

pollu'ted, *p.p.*, pollute.

pollu'ter, *n.*, one who, or that which, pollutes.

pollu'ting, *pr.p.*, pollute.

pollu'tion, *n.*, contamination.

Pol'lux, *n.*, the twin-brother of Castor in the Twin constellation.

po'lo, *n.*, a ball game played by horsemen.

polonaise', *n.*, a Polish dance; a feminine dress.

polon'ium, *n.*, a radio-active metallic element.

polo'ny, *n.*, a variety of sausage.

polo'-stick, *n.*, a long-handled mallet used in the game of polo.

pol'tergeist, *n.*, a noisy, mischievous spirit.

polt'foot, *n. adj.*, club foot(ed).

poltroon', *n.*, an arrant coward; a dastard.

poltroon'ery, *n.*, dastardliness.

polyacous'tic, *adj.*, sound increasing.

Polyadel'phia, *n. pl.*, a class of plants with stamens joined in bundles.

polyan'dry, *n.*, the social system under which a woman has several husbands.

polyan'thus, *n.*, a flowering plant of the primrose variety.

pol'yarchy, *n.*, government by many.

polyatomic, *adj.*, having more than one replaceable atom (*chem.*).

polyba'sic, *adj.*, having more than two bases.

polycar'pic, *adj.*, fruiting more than once in a season.

polycar'pous, *adj.*, having several carpels.

pol'ychord, *n.*, a ten-stringed musical instrument.

pol'ychroite, *n.*, safranin; the colouring matter of saffron.

polychromat'ic, *adj.*, many-coloured.

pol'ychrome, *adj.*, multi-coloured; *n.*, a substance obtained from chestnut wood.

pol'ychromy, *n.*, a many-coloured picture.

polyclin'ic, *n.*, a general clinic.

polycotyle'don, *n.*, a plant with many cotyledons.

polydac'tyl, *adj.*, with an abnormal number of fingers.

polydip'sia, *n.*, an excessive craving for drink.

poly'gala, *n.*, a plant of the Milk-wort genus.

polyg'amist, *n.*, the husband of several wives.

polyg'amous, *adj.*, having a plurality of wives.

polyg'amy, *n.*, the plurality of wives.

polygas'tric, *adj.*, having many stomachs.

polyg'enous, *adj.*, heterogeneous.

pol'yglot, *adj.*, written in many languages; *n.*, a version in many languages; a person who speaks many tongues.

pol'ygon, *n.*, a many-sided figure.

polyg'onal, *adj.*, with many sides or angles.

polyg'onous, *adj.*, i.q. polygonal.

Polyg'onum, *n.*, a plant genus (knot-grass).

polyg'ony, *n.*, a plant of the Polygonum genus.

pol'ygram, *n.*, a many-lined figure.

pol'ygraph, *n.*, a device for multiplying a writing.

polygraph'ic, *adj.*, pert. or rel. to polygraph.

polygraph'ical, *adj.*, i.q. polygraphic.

polyg'raphy, *n.*, multiplying by means of a polygraph.

pol'ygyn, *n.*, a plant of the Polygynia order.

Polygyn'ia, *n. pl.,* an order of plants having many styles.

polyg'yny, *n.,* the plurality of wives.

polyhe'dral, *adj.,* with many sides.

polyhe'dric, *adj., i.q.* polyhedral.

polyhe'dron, *n.,* a many-sided solid.

polyhe'drous, *adj., i.q.* polyhedral.

polyhis'tor, *n.,* a scholar.

Polyhym'nia, *n.,* the Muse of sacred song.

pol'ymath, *n.,* a very learned person.

polymath'ic, *adj.,* pert. or rel. to polymathy.

polym'athy, *n.,* much learning.

pol'ymer, *n.,* a compound differing from another in molecular weight only (*chem.*).

polymor'phism, *n.,* the assumption of many forms.

polymor'phous, *adj.,* assuming many forms.

pol'yneme, *n.,* a thread fish.

Polyne'sian, *adj.,* pert. or rel. to Polynesia; *n.,* a native of P., the language of P.

polyn'ia, *n.,* a lake in the midst of ice (in Arctic seas).

polyno'mial, *n.,* an algebraic expression of more than two terms.

polyon'ymous, *adj.,* having many names.

polyon'ymy, *n.,* the multiplicity of names.

pol'yp(e), *n.,* an eight- or ten-armed cephalopod; one of a colony of organisms.

pol'ypary, *n.,* the structure supporting a cluster of polyps.

polyp'ean, *adj.,* pert. or rel. to a polyp.

polypet'alous, *adj.,* with many petals.

polyph'agous, *adj.,* eating many kinds of food.

polyphar'macy, *n.,* the blending of many medicinal drugs.

Polyphe'mus, *n.,* the one-eyed mythical Cyclops.

pol'yphone, *n.,* a written sign standing for more than one word.

polyphon'ic, *adj.,* with many sounds; with several melodies.

pol'yphonist, *n.,* a contrapuntist.

polyph'ony, *n.,* the blending of several strains.

polyphyl'lous, *adj.* many-leaved.

pol'ypi, *n.,* the pl. of polypus.

pol'ypidom, *n., i.q.* polypary.

pol'ypite, *n.,* an individual polyp.

pol'ypod, *adj.,* having many feet; *n.,* a many-footed creature.

Pol'ypody, *n.,* a genus of ferns.

pol'ypoid, *adj.,* like a polyp or polypus.

pol'ypous, *adj.,* pert. or rel. to a polypus.

polyprismat'ic, *adj.,* showing many prisms.

pol'ypus, *n.,* a tumour.

polysep'alous, *adj.,* with many sepals.

pol'ysperm, *n.,* a tree of which the fruit has many seeds.

polysper'mous, *adj.,* having many seeds.

pol'ystyle, *adj.,* having many styles.

polysty'rene, *n.,* a hydrocarbon polymer used in the plastics industry.

polysyllab'ic, *adj.,* many-syllabled.

polysyl'lable, *n.,* a word of many syllables.

polytech'nic, *adj.,* comprising many arts; *n.,* an institution where many arts are taught.

pol'ytheism, *n.,* the worship of many gods.

pol'ytheist, *n.,* a worshipper of many gods.

polytheis'tic, *adj.,* pert. or rel. to polytheism.

polytheis'tical, *adj., i.q.* polytheistic.

pol'ythene, *n.,* a thermoplastic material.

poly'urethane, *n.,* a kind of plastic-based varnish and paint.

polyzo'a, *n. pl.,* the lowest grade of the Molluscs.

polyzo'nal, *adj.,* with many zones.

polyzo'on, *n.,* one of the polyzoa, or compound invertebrates.

pom, *n.,* the Pomeranian dog.

pom'ace, *n.,* the substance of apples and kindred fruit.

poma'ceous, *adj.,* pert. or rel. to pomace.

pomade', *n.,* a scented preparation for the hair.

poman'der, *n.,* a ball for carrying perfume.

poma'tum, *n., i.q.* pomade.

pom'be, *n.,* an intoxicating African drink.

pome, *n.,* a hollow metal sphere holding hot water to keep the hands warm; an apple-like fruit.

pomegran'ate, *n.,* a tropical fruit with many seeds and a thick skin.

pom'elo, *n.,* grapefruit.

Pomeran'ian, *adj.,* pert. or rel. to Pomerania, one of the Baltic provinces; *n.,* a native of P.; a variety of pet dog.

pom'fret, *n.,* edible fish.

pom'fret-cake, *n.,* a liquorice cake made at Pontefract in Yorkshire, England.

pom'iculture, *n.,* fruit growing.

pomif'erous, *adj.,* pome-producing.

pom'mel, *n.,* the knob of a saddle-bow, or at the end of a sword-hilt; *v.t.,* to thump with the fists. (Also *pummel.*)

pom'mel(l)ed, *p.p.,* pommel.

pom'mel(l)ing, *pr.p.,* pommel; *n.,* the act of pommelling, a thrashing.

pomm'y, *n.,* a British immigrant to Australia or New Zealand (*slang*).

pomolog'ical, *adj.,* pert. or rel. to pomology.

pomol'ogist, *n.,* an expert in pomology.

pomol'ogy, *n.,* the science of fruit culture.

Pomo'na, *n.,* the goddess of fruits (*Lat.*).

pomp, *n.,* show, display, pageantry.

pom'padour, *n.,* a style of coiffure; a mode of corsage; a shade of red.

pom'pano, *n.,* a kind of W. Indian and N. American fish.

Pompe'ian, *adj.,* pert. or rel. to Pompey and Pompeii.

pom'pier, *adj.,* scaling (ladder).

pom'-pom, *n.,* a quick-firing, automatic gun.

pom'pon, *n.,* ornamental head gear; a coloured ball of wool.

pompos'ity, *n.*, an inflated manner.

pom'pous, *adj.*, inflated; affecting the grand.

pom'pously, *adv.*, in a pompous way.

ponce, *n.*, a man who lives on a prostitute's earnings (*slang*).

pon'ceau, *n.*, bright red (*Fr.*).

pon'cho, *n.*, a Latin-American cloak.

pond, *n.*, a body of stagnant water.

pond'age, *n.*, the capacity of a pond; a storage of water.

pon'der, *v.t.*, to meditate on; to think over.

ponderabil'ity, *n.*, the quality of being ponderable.

pon'derable, *adj.*, able to be weighed.

pon'deration, *n.*, weighing, balancing.

pon'dered, *p.p.*, ponder.

pon'derer, *n.*, one who ponders.

pon'dering, *pr.p.*, ponder.

ponderos'ity, *n.*, the quality of being ponderous.

pon'derous, *adj.*, heavy, weighty, important.

pon'derously, *adv.*, in a ponderous way.

pon'derousness, *n.*, *i.q.* ponderosity.

pond'-lil'y, *n.*, a kind of water-lily; an aquatic flowering plant.

pond'weed, *n.*, a general name of weeds growing in still water.

pon'e, *n.*, a leader's partner in some card games.

pone, *n.*, Indian maize bread.

po'nent, *adj.*, occidental.

pongee', *n.*, Chinese silk.

pon'go, *n.*, an African ape.

pon'iard, *n.*, a kind of dagger; *v.t.*, to stab with a poniard.

pon'tage, *n.*, a bridge-toll.

Pon'tic, *adj.*, pert. or rel. to the Pontus or Euxine (the Black Sea).

pon'tifex, *n.*, a member of the college of priests in Rome.

pon'tiff, *n.*, a priest; a bishop; the Supreme Pontiff = the Pope.

pontif'ic, *adj.*, pert. or rel. to, or like, a pontiff.

pontif'ical, *adj.*, *i.q.* pontific; *n.*, a bishop's service book. In pl. = a bishop's vestments and insignia.

pontifical'ia, *n.* *pl.*, pontificals (*Lat.*).

pontif'ically, *adv.*, in the character of a pontiff.

pontif'icate, *n.*, a pontiff's office, or term of office.

pontif'icate, *v.i.*, to celebrate, or assist at, Mass pontifically; to discourse with an air of high authority.

pon'tify, *v.i.*, to play the pontiff; to assume an air of infallibility.

pont-lev'is, *n.*, a drawbridge (*Fr.*).

pontoneer', (-ier) *n.*, a supervisor of bridge building; a soldier with charge of a pontoon or pontoon bridge.

pontoon', *n.*, a boat forming, with others, a floating bridge; an air-filled container for the support of weight on water; a card game.

po'ny, *n.*, a little horse; £25 (*slang*).

pon'y-tail, *n.*, a hair style resembling a pony's tail.

pood, *n.*, a Russian weight.

poo'dle, *n.*, a breed of dog.

poo'die-faker, *n.*, a young man who too often frequents women's society.

pooh, *n.*, an exclamation of contempt or derision.

pooh-pooh', *v.t.*, to treat with contempt and as of no importance.

pooh-poohed', *p.p.*, pooh-pooh.

pooh-pooh'ing, *pr.p.*, pooh-pooh.

poo'koo', *n.*, an African red antelope.

pool, *n.*, a pond; a common fund; a billiard game; *v.t.*, to share collectively.

pooled, *p.p.*, pool.

pool'er, *n.*, one who pools.

pool'ing, *pr.p.*, pool.

poon, *n.*, an E.-Indian tree.

poop, *n.*, the hinder part of a ship; a foolish person (*slang*); *v.t.*, to break over a ship's stern.

pooped, *p.p.*, poop.

poop'ing, *pr.p.*, poop.

poor, *adj.*, not rich, needy; barren, unproductive.

poor'-box, *n.*, an almsbox.

poor'er, *adj.*, *comp.* of poor.

poor'est, *adj.*, *super.* of poor.

poor'house, *n.*, the workhouse.

poor'-law, *n.*, the law rel. to the relief of the poor.

poor'ly, *adj.*, somewhat unwell; *adv.*, indifferently.

poor'ness, *n.*, poverty.

poor'-relief, *n.*, the aid from public funds to the poor.

poort, *n.*, a narrow pass (*S. Afr.*).

pop, *n.*, a small, quick explosion; ginger beer; a popular concert; popular music; *v.t.*, to put suddenly; to make a small explosion (*colloq.*).

Pope, *n.*, the chief dignitary of the Roman Catholic church.

pope, *n.*, a Russian priest.

pope'dom, *n.*, the rule of popes.

pope'-joan, *n.*, an antiquated card game.

pope'ling, *n.*, a little pope.

po'pery, *n.*, a name given to the beliefs and practices of the Roman Church and to anything assumed to resemble them.

pope's'-eye, *n.*, a gland in a sheep's or ox's thigh.

pop'gun, *n.*, a child's toy that goes off with a pop.

pop'injay, *n.*, a parrot; a babbling fool; a bird used as an archery mark.

po'pish, *adj.*, pert. or rel. to popery.

pop'lar, *n.*, a tall, slender tree.

pop'lin, *n.*, a dress fabric.

poplit'eal, *adj.*, pert. or rel. to the upper part of the leg near the knee.

poplit'ic, *adj.*, pert. or rel. to the part behind the knee.

popped, *p.p.*, pop.

pop'pet, *n.*, a word of endearment; a short piece of timber.

pop'ping, *n.*, the act of popping; *pr.p.*, pop.

pop'ple, *n.*, small short waves on water; *v.i.*, to ripple, to bubble, to toss up and down.

pop'py, *n.*, a plant from which opium is made.

pop'pycock, *n.*, nonsense (*slang*).

pop'py-head, *n.*, a poppy's seed capsule; the carved end of a stall or seat.

pop'shop, *n.*, a pawnbroker's shop (*colloq.*).

pop'sy(-wopsy), *n.*, a girl (*colloq.*).

pop'ulace, *n.*, the multitude.

pop'ular, *adj.*, pert. or rel. to the people; generally esteemed.

popular'ity, *n.*, general esteem.

populariza'tion, *n.*, the act of popularizing.

pop'ularize, *v.t.*, to make known to and adopted by the multitude.

pop'ularized, *p.p.*, popularize.

pop'ularizing, *pr.p.*, popularize.

pop'ularly, *adv.*, in a popular way.

pop'ulate, *v.t.*, to fill with inhabitants.

pop'ulated, *p.p.*, populate.

pop'ulating, *pr.p.*, populate.

popula'tion, *n.*, inhabitants; the number of inhabitants.

pop'ulin, *n.*, a compound obtained from the aspen.

pop'ulist, *n.*, an advocate of collectivism.

pop'ulous, *adj.*, with a numerous population.

pop'ulousness, *n.*, the state of being populous.

por'beagle, *n.*, mackerelshark.

por'cate, *adj.*, furrowed and ridged.

por'cated, *adj.*, i.q. porcate.

porce'lain, *n.*, the finest kind of earthenware.

porce'lainize, *v.t.*, to turn into porcelain.

porch, *n.*, the covered entrance to a building.

por'cine, *adj.*, pert. or rel. to pigs.

por'cupine, *n.*, a creature

with a bristly hide and long quills.

pore, *n.*, a passage through the skin; *v.i.*, to gaze attentively.

pored, *p.p.*, pore.

porge, *v.t.*, to make clean by the ceremonial removal of sinews.

porg'y, *n.*, a saltwater fish.

po'riform, *adj.*, like pores.

po'ring, *pr.p.*, pore.

por'ism, *n.*, pert. or rel. to mathematics.

pork, *n.*, swine's flesh.

pork'-butcher, *n.*, a dealer in pork.

pork'er, *n.*, a wild pig.

pork'et, *n.*, a little hog.

pork'ling, *n.*, a little pig.

pork'y, *adj.*, like pork.

pornograph'ic, *adj.*, obscene.

pornograph'ically, *adv.*, obscenely.

pornog'raphy, *n.*, indecent literature or art.

por'oplastic, *adj.*, both porous and plastic.

poros'ity, *n.*, the state of being porous.

porot'ic, *adj.*, producing callus-formation.

po'rous, *adj.*, full of pores.

porphyrit'ic, *adj.*, pert. or rel. to porphyry.

por'phyry, *n.*, a hard rock, containing white and red crystals.

por'poise, *n.*, a cetaceous creature with a short, rounded snout.

porra'ceous, *adj.*, leek-coloured.

porrect', *adj.*, stretched out; *v.t.*, to stretch forth; to submit (a document).

porrec'tion, *n.*, an extension forward.

por'ridge, *n.*, cooked oatmeal.

porri'go, *n.*, a skin disease of the head.

por'ringer, *n.*, a porridge bowl.

port, *n.*, a harbour; the left side of a ship; the wine of Oporto; a gateway; deportment; an aperture for the escape of steam, etc.; *v.t.*, to lay a ship over to the left side; to carry aslant.

portabil'ity, *n.*, the quality of being portable.

port'able, *adj.*, able to be carried.

port'age, *n.*, carriage; the hire of transport; the conveyance from one lake or river to another; *v.t.*, to convey in this way.

port'al, *n.*, a gate; a gateway.

portamen'to, *adv.*, sustaining the sound (*mus., It.*).

portcray'on, *n.*, a pencil holder.

portcul'lis, *n.*, an openwork barrier drawn up and down in a castle gateway.

Porte, *n.*, the Ottoman court at Constantinople.

porte-cochére, *n.*, a protective porch for vehicles outside an entrance door (*Fr.*).

porte-monnaie, *n.*, a purse (*Fr.*).

portend', *v.t.*, to foretoken, to presage.

portend'ed, *p.p.*, portend.

portend'ing, *pr.p.*, portend.

por'tent, *n.*, a presage, sign or omen.

porten'tous, *adj.*, ominous, alarming.

porten'tously, *adv.*, ominously.

port'er, *n.*, one who carries for hire; a malt liquor; a gate-keeper.

port'erage, *n.*, a porter's hire.

port'fire, *n.*, a slowmatch.

portfo'lio, *n.*, a case for loose papers, prints, etc.

port'hole, *n.*, a ship's window.

port'ico, *n.*, a colonnade; a porch.

port'ière, *n.*, a doorway curtain (*Fr.*).

por'tion, *n.*, a part; a dowry; *v.t.*, to parcel; to endow.

por'tioned, *p.p.*, portion.

por'tioning, *pr.p.*, portion.

por'tionist, *n.*, one who enjoys a portion; a joint incumbent.

por'tionless, *adj.*, without a portion.

port'liness, *n.*, the quality of being portly.

port'ly, *adj.*, large, dignified of mien.

portman'teau, *n.*, a travelling case (*Fr.*).

portola'no, n., a book of sailing directions (It.).

por'trait, n., a person's picture.

port'raitist, n., a painter or photographer who creates portraits.

por'traiture, n., the art of making portraits; vivid word-painting.

portray', v.t., to represent; to describe in a picture or as in a picture.

portray'al, n., the act of portraying.

portrayed', p.p., portray.

portray'er, n., one who portrays.

portray'ing, pr.p., portray.

port'reeve, n., formerly the highest municipal officer.

port'ress, n., a woman gatekeeper.

port'-toll, n., a harbour toll.

port'-town, n., a harbour town.

Portuguese', adj., pert. or rel. to Portugal; a native of P.; the language of P.

port-ward'en, n., a harbour-master.

port wine', n., the wine of Oporto.

posa'da, n., a Spanish inn.

pose, v.i., to assume a character or attitude; v.t., to puzzle; to state.

posed, p.p., pose.

po'ser, n., a difficult problem.

poseur', n., an affected person (Fr.).

posh, adj., smart (slang).

po'sing, pr.p., pose.

pos'it, v.t., to place; to assume as fact.

pos'ited, p.p., posit.

pos'iting, pr.p., posit.

posi'tion, n., situation; posture; place.

posi'tional, adj., pert. or rel. to position.

pos'itive, adj., real, explicit; assertive.

pos'itively, adv., in a positive way; really.

pos'itiveness, n., a tendency to make statements dogmatically.

pos'itivism, n., Comte's philosophical system of the co-ordination of the sciences.

pos'itivist, n., an adherent of positivism.

pos'itron, n., a positive electron.

pos'net, n., a small basin.

posolog'ical, adj., pert. or rel. to posology.

posol'ogy, n., the science of quantity.

posse, n., an armed force; potentiality.

possess', v.t., to own; to be master of; to seize.

possessed', adj., under the influence of an evil spirit; p.p., possess.

possess'ing, pr.p., possess.

posses'sion, n., ownership; a thing owned; demoniacal control.

possess'ive, adj., having or denoting possession; n., the genitive case.

possess'ively, adv., in a possessive way.

possess'or, n., an owner, a master.

possess'ory, adj., pert. or rel. to possession.

pos'set, n., a warm drink of milk curdled with wine, etc.

possibil'ity, n., the quality of being possible.

pos'sible, adj., that may exist or be done.

possib'ilist, n., a practical person.

pos'sibly, adv., within the limits of possibility.

poss'um, n., a small tree mammal.

post, n., a courier; the postal service; an upright piece of timber; an office or situation; the prefix meaning after; v.t., to despatch a letter.

post'able, adj., able to be posted.

post'age, n., the fee for posting an item of mail.

post'age-stamp, n., a printed stamp indicating payment of postage.

post'al, adj., pert. or rel. to the post.

post'card, n., a card that can be stamped for postage.

post'code, n., an alpha-numeral area designation; v.t., to designate a postal address.

post'coded, p.p., postcode.

post'coding, pr.p., postcode.

post'date, v.t., to name, on a document, etc.,

a later than the actual date.

post'dated, p.p., postdate.

post'dating, pr.p., post date.

pos'tea, n., the proceedings in a lawsuit between the joining of issue and the verdict.

post'ed, p.p., post.

posteen', n., an Afghan sheepskin greatcoat.

post'-entry, n., a late or subsequent entry.

post'er, n., an advertisement for posting up.

poste restante', n., the branch of a post office where letters are kept to be called for (Fr.).

poste'rior, adj., subsequent in time or place; n., the hinder parts.

posterior'ity, n., the state of being posterior.

poste'riorly, adv., subsequently.

poste'riors, n. pl., the hinder parts.

poster'ity, n., succeeding generations.

pos'tern, adj., in the rear; private; n., a small or secret gate or entrance.

post'-free, adj., free of postage.

post'-graduate, adj., rel. to study after graduation.

post-haste', adv., at a rapid speed; in haste.

post'humous, adj., born after a parent's death; published after the author's death; awarded after death.

post'humously, adv., in a posthumous way.

postiche', adj., counterfeit, artificial; n., an addition after work is completed.

postic'ous, adj., posterior, hinder (bot.).

pos'til, n., a marginal note; v.t., to make a marginal note or commentary on.

postil'(l)ion, n., an outrider.

post'-impres'sionism, n., an attitude to art as a reaction against impressionism.

post'ing, pr.p., post.

postlim'iny, n., a right to national status.

post'man, n., a letter carrier.

post'mark, n., the mark showing the office at which a letter was posted or through which it has passed.

post'master, n., the head of a post-office; a junior member of the foundation of Merton College, Oxford.

postmerid'ian, adj., after mid-day.

post merid'iem, a Latin phrase = after mid-day.

post'mistress, n., a woman in charge of a post-office.

post-mor'tem, n., an autopsy after death.

postnup'tial, adj., after marriage.

post-ob'it, n., an agreement to repay a loan on the death of someone named in the bond.

post'-office, n., a place for receiving and distributing letters, parcels, etc.

post'paid, adj., having the postage prepaid.

postpone', v.t., to put off; to delay for a while.

postponed', p.p., postpone.

postpone'ment, n., the act of putting off; a temporary delay.

postpon'ing, pr.p., postpone.

postposi'tion, n., a word placed after another.

postposi'tional, adj., behind.

postpran'dial, adj., after dinner.

postsce'nium, n., the part of a theatre behind the scenes.

post'script, n., something added to a letter.

post'-town, n., a town with a regional post-office.

pos'tulant, n., a candidate for admission to an order.

pos'tulate, n., a self-evident proposition; something accepted as not needing proof.

pos'tulate, v.t. and i., to assume without proof.

pos'tulated, p.p., postulate.

pos'tulating, pr.p., postulate.

postula'tion, n., the act of postulating.

pos'tulator, n., one who postulates.

pos'tulatory, adj., assuming as self-evident.

pos'tural, adj., pert. or rel. to posture.

pos'ture, n., an attitude or state; v.i., to pose.

post'-war, adj., after a war.

po'sy, n., a nosegay; a motto.

pot, n., a vessel of metal or earthenware; a size of paper; the drug, cannabis (colloq.); v.t., to put into pots; to preserve; to shoot.

po'table, adj., drinkable.

potage', n., soup (Fr.).

potam'ic, adj., pert. or rel. to rivers.

potamog'raphy, n., a description of river systems.

potamol'ogy, n., the study of river systems.

pot'ash, n., an alkali from wood ashes.

potas'sium, n., a metallic element.

pota'tion, n., drinking; a large draught.

pota'to, n., a round or oblong tuber widely used as food.

pot'boiler, n., a piece of literary or artistic work done quickly to make a little money.

pot'-bound, adj., having massed roots restricting growth.

potch, v.t., to bleach.

potched, p.p., potch.

potch'ing, pr.p., potch.

poteen', n., Irish whisky. (Also potheen.)

po'tency, n., the quality of being potent.

po'tent, adj., powerful; intoxicating.

po'tentate, n., a sovereign; an exalted person.

poten'tial, adj., possible (but not real); latent; powerful; indicating power; n., a state of electricity; power existing, as yet undeveloped.

potential'ity, n., the possibility.

poten'tialize, v.t., to make potential.

poten'tialized, p.p., potentialize.

poten'tializing, pr.p., potentialize.

poten'tially, n., possibly (but not really).

poten'tiate, v.t., to endow with power; to make possible.

potentiom'eter, n., an instrument for measuring electrical potential.

po'tently, adv., powerfully.

pot'ful, n., the quantity held by a pot.

potheen', n., i.q. poteen.

poth'er, n., fuss, confusion; v.i., to make a fuss; v.t., to confuse.

pot'herb, n., a vegetable for cooking.

poth'ered, p.p., pother.

poth'ering, pr.p., pother.

pot'hole, n., a hollow worn in the bed of a stream; a hole found in limestone rock.

pot'holing, n., the exploration of potholes.

pot'hook, n., a hook for hanging pots; one of the first signs learnt in writing.

pot'house, n., a low tavern.

pot'hunter, n., one who plays games for the sake of prizes.

po'tion, n., a draught or dose.

pot'latch, n., a N. American Indian feast.

potluck', n., any food that is going; chance.

pot'man, n., a serving man in a public-house.

potpourri', n., a literary or musical medley; a mixture of herbs, spices, etc. (Fr.).

pot'sherd, n., a piece of a broken pot.

pot'tage, n., a stew.

pot'ted, p.p., pot.

pot'ter, n., a maker of pottery; v.i., to dawdle.

pot'tered, p.p., potter.

pot'tering, pr.p., potter.

pot'tery, n., all kinds of earthenware; the potter's workshop.

pot'ting, pr.p., pot.

pot'tle, n., a liquid measure = 2 qts.; a kind of fruit basket.

pott'o, n., a W. African lemur.

pott'y, adj., crazy, trivial (colloq.).

pouch, *n.*, a small bag; a sack; a container for tobacco; *v.i.*, to swell; *v.t.*, to pocket.

pouched, *p.p.*, pouch.

pouch'ing, *pr.p.*, pouch.

pouchong', *n.*, a Chinese tea.

poudrette, *n.*, a kind of manure.

pouf(fe), *n.*, a pad of woman's hair; a large stuffed cushion or seat (*Fr.*); a homosexual (*slang*).

poulp(e), *n.*, an octopus.

poult, *n.*, a young fowl, turkey, pheasant, etc.

poul'terer, *n.*, a vendor of poultry.

poul'tice, *n.*, a soft application of bread, linseed, etc. mixed with boiling water, applied to sores or inflamed parts of the body; *v.t.*, to apply a poultice to.

poul'ticed, *p.p.*, poultice.

poul'ticing, *pr.p.*, poultice.

poul'try, *n.*, domestic fowls.

poul'try-yard, *n.*, a yard for poultry.

pounce, *n.*, powder once used for drying ink; a bird of prey's talon; *v.i.*, to swoop down; *v.t.*, to sprinkle with powder.

pounce'-box, *n.*, a box for holding pounce.

pounced, *p.p.*, pounce.

poun'cet-box, *n.*, *i.q.* pounce-box.

pounc'ing, *pr.p.*, pounce.

pound, *v.t.*, to grind; to shut in a pound; *n.*, a standard weight; the British sterling unit of currency = 100 pence; an enclosure for stray animals.

pound'age, *n.*, an allowance or charge of so much on the pound.

pound'ed, *p.p.*, pound.

pound'er, *n.*, one who pounds.

pound'ing, *pr.p.*, pound.

pour, *v.i.*, to stream forth; *v.t.*, to empty from a vessel; to emit; to utter.

pourboire', *n.*, a tip (*Fr.*).

poured, *p.p.*, pour.

pour'er, *n.*, one who, or that which, pours.

pour'ing, *pr.p.*, pour.

pour'parler', *n.*, an informal, preliminary discussion before negotiation (*Fr.*).

poussette', *n.*, one of the figures in a country dance (*Fr.*).

pout, *n.*, an expression of sullenness by thrusting out the lips; a kind of fish; *v.i.*, to thrust out the lips; to look sullen.

pout'ed, *p.p.*, pout.

pout'er, *n.*, one who pouts; a breed of pigeons.

pout'ing, *pr.p.*, pout.

pout'ingly, *adv.*, sullenly.

pov'erty, *n.*, the state of being poor.

pow'der, *n.*, a pulverized substance; gunpowder; *v.t.*, to pulverize; to grind small; to sprinkle, as with dust.

pow'dered, *p.p.*, powder.

pow'der-house, *n.*, place where gunpowder is stored.

pow'deriness, *n.*, the state of being powdery.

pow'dering, *pr.p.*, powder.

pow'der-magazine, *n.*, a store for gunpowder.

pow'der-mill, *n.*, a manufactory of gunpowder.

pow'der-puff, *n.*, a puff-like pad used for applying powder to the face or body.

pow'der-room, *n.*, a ladies' cloakroom.

pow'dery, *adj.*, like powder.

pow'er, *n.*, strength of body or mind; authority.

pow'erful, *adj.*, strong, influential.

pow'erfully, *adv.*, in a powerful way.

pow'er-house, *n.*, a place where power is generated.

pow'erless, *adj.*, wanting power.

pow'erlessly, *adv.*, in a powerless way.

pow'er-point, *n.*, a place or device providing connection to an electricity supply.

pow'wow, *n.*, a N. American Indian conjuror; incantation rites; an unofficial conference; *v.i.*, to conjure.

pox, *n.*, an eruption of the skin.

poy, *n.*, a pole.

pozzola'na, *n.*, volcanic ash used in making mortar (*It.*).

pozz'y, *adj.*, soldiers' jam or marmalade, (*From Urdu*).

praam, **(pram)**, *n.*, a Dutch and Baltic lighter.

practicabil'ity, *n.*, the quality of being practicable.

prac'ticable, *adj.*, able to be put into practice; feasible.

prac'ticably, *adv.*, feasibly.

prac'tical, *adj.*, pert. or rel. to practice or use; able to do.

practical'ity, *n.*, the quality of being practical; feasibility.

prac'tically, *adv.*, in effect; in practice.

prac'tice, *n.*, habitual action; acquired skill; action; one of the arithmetical rules.

practi'cian, *n.*, a worker, a practitioner.

prac'tise, *v.i.*, to acquire a habit; to be a practitioner; *v.t.*, to do habitually; to do repeatedly; to exercise.

prac'tised, *adj.*, skilled; *p.p.*, practise.

prac'tiser, *n.*, one who practises.

prac'tising, *pr.p.*, practise.

practi'tioner, *n.*, one who exercises a profession.

prae'cipe, *n.*, a legal writ demanding that a thing shall be done, or why it has not been performed.

praeco'cial, *adj.*, (of birds) able to feed themselves on hatching.

praecor'dia, *n. pl.*, the region of the heart.

praemuni're, *n.*, an offence against the royal prerogative; the writ against one so offending (*Lat.*).

praeno'men, *n.*, a name preceding the family name (*Lat.*).

praetex'ta, *n.*, a white toga edged with purple stripes, the dress of priests, magistrates, and free-born youths in ancient Rome (*Lat.*).

prae'tor, *n.*, one of the high magistrates in ancient Rome (*Lat.*).

praeto'rial, *adj.*, *i.q.* praetorian.

praeto'rian, *adj.*, pert. or rel. to praetors.

praeto'rium, *n.*, a governor's residence (*Lat.*).

pragmat'ic, *adj.*, officious; busy; concerned with the practical applications of philosophy.

pragmat'ical, *adj.*, *i.q.* pragmatic.

pragmat'ically, *adv.*, in a pragmatic way.

prag'matism, *n.*, a philosophic system which regards belief merely in its relation to human interests.

prag'matist, *n.*, one who adopts pragmatism.

prag'matize, *v.t.*, to treat as real.

prag'matized, *p.p.*, pragmatize.

prag'matizing, *pr.p.*, pragmatize.

prai'rie, *n.*, a vast tract of grass-covered land.

prai'rie-dog, *n.*, a small rodent found in prairies.

prai'rie-wolf, *n.*, the coyote.

praise, *n.*, high approval, laudation, worship; *v.t.*, to laud; to express approval of; to glorify.

praised, *p.p.*, praise.

prais'er, *n.*, one who praises.

praise'worthiness, *n.*, the state of being praiseworthy.

praise'worthy, *adj.*, deserving of praise.

prais'ing, *pr.p.*, praise.

pra'line, *n.*, a kind of sweet.

pram, *n.*, the abbrev. of perambulator; a small service dinghy.

prance, *n.*, a bound; *v.i.*, to bound; to strut.

pranced, *p.p.*, prance.

pranc'ing, *pr.p.*, prance.

pran'dial, *adj.*, pert. or rel. to dinner.

prang, *n.*, a crash; *v.t.*, to crash; to bomb (*slang*).

prank, *n.*, a frolic or trick; *v.t.*, to dress out.

pranked, *p.p.*, prank.

prank'ing, *pr.p.*, prank.

prank'ish, *adj.*, full of tricks.

prase, *n.*, a light green quartz.

pras'inous, *n.*, of the colour of grass.

prate, *n.*, idle talk; *v.i.*, to talk foolishly.

pra'ted, *p.p.*, prate.

pra'ter, *n.*, one who prates.

pra'ties, *n. pl.*, potatoes (*Ir.*, *colloq.*).

prat'incole, *n.*, a kind of sandpiper.

pra'ting, *n.*, loquacity; *pr.p.*, prate.

prat'ique, *n.*, a licence to a ship to communicate or trade after quarantine (*Fr.*).

prat'tle, *v.i.*, to chatter; to talk childishly.

prat'tled, *p.p.*, prattle.

prat'tler, *n.*, one who prattles.

prat'tling, *pr.p.*, prattle.

prav'ity, *n.*, wickedness, depravity.

prawn, *n.*, a large shrimp; *v.i.*, to fish for prawns.

prax'is, *n.*, materials for exercise (*Gr.*).

pray, *v.t. and i.*, to entreat; to offer prayer.

prayed, *p.p.*, pray.

prayer, *n.*, a petition, an entreaty.

pray'er, *n.*, one who prays.

prayer'-book, *n.*, a book of prayers or devotions.

prayer'ful, *adj.*, strong in prayer.

prayer'fully, *adv.*, in a prayerful way.

prayer'fulness, *n.*, the quality of being prayerful.

prayer'less, *adj.*, not praying; without a prayer.

prayer'lessness, *n.*, the state of being prayerless.

prayer'-meeting, *n.*, a gathering for prayer.

pray'ing, *pr.p.*, pray.

preach, *v.i.*, to deliver a sermon; to give advice; *v.t.*, to utter.

preached, *p.p.*, preach.

preach'er, *n.*, one who preaches.

preach'ify, *v.i.*, to moralize; to bore an audience.

preach'ing, *n.*, the delivery of sermons; *pr.p.*, preach.

preach'ment, *n.*, a sermon; a solemn harangue.

preach'y, *adj.*, fond of preaching (*colloq.*).

pre-acquaint', *v.t.*, to make acquainted in advance.

pre-acquaint'ance, *n.*, knowledge in advance.

pre-acquaint'ed, *p.p.*, pre-acquaint.

pre-acquaint'ing, *pr.p.*, pre-acquaint.

pre-adam'ic, *adj.*, *i.q.* pre-adamite.

pre-ad'amite, *adj.*, previous to the birth of Adam.

preadmon'ish, *v.t.*, to admonish beforehand.

preadmon'ished, *p.p.*, preadmonish.

preadmon'ishing, *pr.p.*, preadmonish.

preadmoni'tion, *n.*, the act of preadmonishing; a previous warning.

pream'ble, *n.*, a preface; the introductory or explanatory part of a statute or document.

prearrange', *v.t.*, to arrange beforehand.

prearranged', *p.p.*, prearrange.

prearrang'ing, *pr.p.*, prearrange.

preassu'rance, *n.*, assurance beforehand.

preb'end, *n.*, a manor or estate attached to a canon of a cathedral or collegiate church.

preb'endal, *adj.*, pert. or rel. to a prebend or a prebendary.

preb'endary, *n.*, the holder of a prebend.

preca'rious, *adj.*, risky, uncertain, dubious.

preca'riously, *adv.*, riskily, uncertainly.

preca'riousness, *n.*, uncertainty.

pre'cast, *adj.*, cast before use; (pre-cast concrete).

prec'ative, *adj.*, *i.q.* precatory.

prec'atory, *adj.*, suppliant.

precau'tion, *n.*, previous care; preventive measures.

precau'tionary, *adj.*, guarding in advance.

precede', *v.t. and i.*, to go before in time or rank.

prece'ded, *p.p.*, precede.

pre'cedence, *n.*, priority; superiority of rank.

prece′dency, *n.*, *i.q.* precedence.

prece′dent, *adj.*, going before.

prec′edent, *n.*, an example or rule; an earlier parallel.

prec′edented, *adj.*, having a precedent.

prece′ding, *pr.p.*, precede.

precent′, *v.i.* and *t.*, to act as precentor; to lead in a choir.

precen′tor, *n.*, a cathedral or collegiate dignitary who rules the choir; one who leads the singers.

precen′torship, *n.*, a precentor's office.

pre′cept, *n.*, an instruction, command or maxim.

precep′tive, *adj.*, pert. or rel. to precepts; didactic.

precep′tor, *n.*, a teacher.

precepto′rial, *adj.*, pert. or rel. to a preceptor.

precep′tory, *adj.*, didactic; *n.*, a subsidiary house of the Knights Templars.

precep′tress, *n.*, a woman teacher.

preces′sion, *n.*, a going forward, esp. of the equinoxes.

pre′cinct, *n.*, an enclosure; a territorial division.

precios′ity, *n.*, affectation; over-fastidiousness.

pre′cious, *adj.*, of high price, valuable; affectedly superior.

pre′ciously, *adv.*, in a precious way.

pre′ciousness, *n.*, value.

prec′ipice, *n.*, a steep place; an abrupt descent.

precip′itance, *n.*, *i.q.* precipitancy.

precip′itancy, *n.*, overhaste.

precip′itant, *adj.*, headlong, hasty; *n.*, in chemistry, an agent that solidifies a substance held in solution.

precip′itantly, *adv.*, rashly.

precip′itate, *adj.*, hasty, rash; *n.*, a precipitated substance.

precip′itate, *v.t.*, to urge on with haste; to bring about before the time; to cause to sink to the bottom of a solution.

precip′itated, *p.p.*, precipitate.

precip′itating, *pr.p.*, precipitate.

precipita′tion, *n.*, the act of precipitating; extreme haste; rainfall (*meteorol.*).

precip′itous, *adj.*, abruptly steep.

precip′itously, *adv.*, steeply.

pré′cis, *n.*, a concise summary or abstract (*Fr.*).

precise′, *adj.*, exact, formal.

precise′ly, *adv.*, exactly, formally.

precise′ness, *n.*, formality, exactness, punctiliousness.

precis′ian, *n.*, a stickler for exactness; a purist.

precis′ion, *n.*, accuracy, exactness.

preci′sive, *adj.*, lopping, pruning.

preclude′, *v.t.*, to make impossible.

preclu′ded, *p.p.*, preclude.

preclu′ding, *pr.p.*, preclude.

preclu′sion, *n.*, prevention.

preclu′sive, *adj.*, preventive.

preclu′sively, *adv.*, in a preventive way.

preco′cious, *adj.*, prematurely developed.

preco′ciously, *adv.*, in a precocious way.

preco′ciousness, *n.*, *i.q.* precocity.

precoc′ity, *n.*, premature development, esp. of the mind.

precogni′tion, *n.*, previous knowledge; a preliminary examination of witnesses.

preconceive′, *v.t.*, to conceive in anticipation.

preconceived′, *p.p.*, preconceive.

preconceiv′ing, *pr.p.*, preconceive.

preconcep′tion, *n.*, the act of preconceiving; something preconceived.

preconcert′, *v.t.*, to concert or arrange beforehand.

preconcert′ed, *p.p.*, preconcert.

preconcert′ing, *pr.p.*, preconcert.

pre′conize, *v.t.*, to proclaim, to summon by name; to give official approval to the appointment of a bishop.

precontract′, *v.t.* and *i.*, to contract beforehand.

precon′tract, *n.*, a contract beforehand.

precontract′ed, *p.p.*, precontract.

precontract′ing, *pr.p.*, precontract.

precord′ial, *adj.*, pert. or rel. to the parts in front of the heart.

precurs′ive, *adj.*, going before.

precurs′or, *n.*, a forerunner.

precurs′ory, *adj.*, forerunning, anticipatory.

preda′cious, *adj.*, apt to plunder or to prey; predatory.

predate′, *v.t.*, to antedate.

pred′ative, *adj.*, *i.q.* predatory.

pred′ator, *n.*, a predatory creature.

pred′atorily, *adv.*, in a predatory way.

pred′atory, *adj.*, preying, plundering.

predecease′, *n.*, the death of a person before another; *v.t.*, to die before another.

predeceased′, *p.p.*, predecease.

predeceas′ing, *pr.p.*, predecease.

predeces′sor, *n.*, one who has held a position before another.

predell′a, *n.*, painting on altar-steps; a raised shelf at the back of an altar.

predestina′rian, *adj.*, pert. or rel. to predestination.

predes′tinate, *adj.*, foreordained.

predes′tinate, *v.t.*, to foreordain.

predes′tinated, *p.p.*, predestinate.

predes′tinating, *pr.p.*, predestinate.

predestina′tion, *n.*, foreordaining.

predes′tinator, *n.*, one who predestinates.

predes′tine, *v.t.*, *i.q.* predestinate.

predes′tined, *p.p.*, predestine.

predes′tining, *pr.p.*, predestine.

predeterm′inate, *adj.*, decreed beforehand.

predetermina′tion, *n.*, a decree or decision beforehand.

predeterm′ine, *v.t.* and *i.*, to decree or decide beforehand.

predeterm'ined, *p.p.,* predetermine.

predeterm'ining, *pr.p.,* predetermine.

pre'dial, *adj.,* pert. or rel. to landed estates, agrarian; *n.,* a slave.

predicabil'ity, *n.,* the quality of being predicable.

pred'icable, *adj.,* able to be predicted or affirmed.

predic'ament, *n.,* something predicated; a category; an awkward position, a fix.

pred'icant, *adj.,* preaching; *n.,* a preaching friar.

pred'icate, *n.,* that which is affirmed or denied; an attribute.

pred'icate, *v.t.,* to affirm or assert one thing or another.

pred'icated, *p.p.,* predicate.

pred'icating, *pr.p.,* predicate.

predica'tion, *n.,* an affirmation concerning anything.

predic'ative, *adj.,* affirming.

pred'icatory, *adj., i.q.* predicative.

predict', *v.t.,* to foretell.

predict'able, *adj.,* that which may be predicted or foretold.

predict'ed, *p.p.,* predict.

predict'ing, *pr.p.,* predict.

predic'tion, *n.,* a foretelling.

predict'ive, *adj.,* predicting.

predic'tor, *n.,* one who predicts; a device for predicting the position of aircraft.

predilec'tion, *n.,* a preference; a bent.

predispose', *v.t.,* to make liable or inclined.

predisposed', *p.p.,* predispose.

predispos'ing, *pr.p.,* predispose.

predisposi'tion, *n.,* a mental or physical condition of being liable or inclined.

predom'inance, *n.,* sway, preponderance; a leading position.

predom'inancy, *n., i.q.* predominance.

predom'inant, *adj.,* having superiority or preponderance.

predom'inantly, *adv.,* in a predominant fashion.

predom'inate, *v.i.,* to have preponderance or superiority.

predom'inated, *p.p.,* predominate.

predom'inating, *pr.p.,* predominate.

predomina'tion, *n.,* preponderance, superiority, control.

predoom', *v.t.,* to destine, to foredoom.

predoomed', *p.p.,* predoom.

predoom'ing, *pr.p.,* predoom.

pre-elect', *adj.,* forechosen; predestinate.

pre-elect'ed, *adj., i.q.* pre-elect.

pre-elec'tion, *n.,* choice beforehand.

pre-em'inence, *n.,* high superiority or excellence.

pre-em'inent, *adj.,* highly superior or excellent.

pre-em'inently, *adv.,* in a pre-eminent manner.

pre-empt', *v.t.,* to get by pre-emption.

pre-emp'tion, *n.,* the purchase, or the right to purchase or hold, before any other person.

preen, *v.t.,* to trim with the beak; *reflex.* to trim oneself.

preened, *p.p.,* preen.

pre-engage', *v.t. and i.,* to engage beforehand.

pre-engaged', *p.p.,* pre-engage.

pre-engage'ment, *n.,* a previous engagement.

pre-engag'ing, *pr.p.,* pre-engage.

preen'ing, *pr.p.,* preen.

pre-*estab'lish*, *v.t.,* to establish before.

pre-*estab'lished*, *p.p.,* pre-establish.

pre-*estab'lishing*, *pr.p.,* pre-establish.

pre-exam'ine, *v.t.,* to examine beforehand.

pre-exam'ined, *p.p.,* pre-examine.

pre-exam'ining, *pr.p.,* pre-examine.

pre-exist', *v.i.,* to exist previously.

pre-exist'ed, *p.p.,* pre-exist.

pre-exist'ence, *n.,* previous existence.

pre-exist'ent, *adj.,* existing before.

pre-exist'ing, *pr.p.,* pre-exist.

pre'fab, *n.,* the abbrev. for a prefabricated building (*colloq.*).

prefab'ricate, *v.t.,* to manufacture in parts prior to assembly.

prefab'ricated, *adj.,* manufactured in parts; composed of sections; *p.p.,* prefabricate.

prefab'ricating, *pr.p.,* prefabricate.

prefabrica'tion, *n.,* prior manufacture.

pref'ace, *n.,* an introduction to a book; a prefatory note or remark; *v.t.,* to introduce with a written or spoken word.

pref'aced, *p.p.,* preface.

pref'acer, *n.,* one who prefaces.

pref'acing, *pr.p.,* preface.

prefato'rial, *adj.,* pert. or rel. to a preface.

pref'atory, *adj.,* introductory.

pre'fect, *n.,* a Roman officer of high civil or military rank; the head of a French administrative department; a student given authority in a school.

pre'fecture, *n.,* a prefect's term of office, official residence, area of jurisdiction.

prefer', *v.i.,* to be more willing; *v.t.,* to choose in preference; to promote; to bring forward.

pref'erable, *adj.,* more desirable than another.

pref'erably, *adv.,* for choice.

pref'erence, *n.,* the liking of one thing more than another; a thing preferred; a special favour; the right to be paid before others.

preferen'tial, *adj.,* giving or receiving preference.

preferen'tially, *adv.,* in a preferential way.

prefer'ment, *n.,* promotion to office.

preferred', *p.p.,* prefer.

prefer'rer, *n.,* one who prefers.

prefer'ring, *pr.p.,* prefer.

prefigura'tion, *n.,* representation through a type.

prefig'urative, *adj.,* representing by type.

prefig'ure, *v.t.,* to represent beforehand by type; to imagine the details of.

prefig'ured, *p.p.*, prefigure.

prefig'uring, *pr.p.*, prefigure.

prefix', *v.t.*, to place before; to add to in front.

pre'fix, *n.*, something prefixed, as a word or particle joined to the front of another word (as *re*-place); a title.

prefixed', *p.p.*, prefix.

prefix'ing, *pr.p.*, prefix.

pre'form, *v.t.*, to form beforehand.

preforma'tion, *n.*, previous formation.

preform'ative, *adj.*, forming beforehand, *n.*, a prefix.

preformed', *p.p.*, preform.

preforming, *pr.p.*, preform.

preg'nable, *adj.*, open to attack; able to be captured.

preg'nancy, *n.*, the state of being pregnant; the fullness of meaning.

preg'nant, *adj.*, being with young; gravid; full of meaning.

prehen'sible, *adj.*, able to be grasped.

prehen'sile, *adj.*, capable of grasping (*zool.*).

prehensil'ity, *n.*, the ability to grasp by tail or limb (*zool.*).

prehen'sion, *n.*, grasping, seizing, whether with the hand or with the mind.

prehistor'ic, *adj.*, antecedent to historic record.

prehistor'ically, *adv.*, in a prehistoric way.

prehis'tory, *n.*, prehistoric times or matters.

pre-igni'tion, *n.*, the premature firing of an engine, etc.

prejudge', *v.t.*, to judge beforehand or prematurely.

prejudged', *p.p.*, prejudge.

prejudg'ing, *pr.p.*, prejudge.

prejudg'ment, *n.*, a judgment formed prematurely.

prejudica'tion, *n.*, *i.q.* prejudgment.

pre'judice, *n.*, bias; preconception; detriment; *v.t.*, to influence the mind of; to injure the validity of a case or claim.

pre'judiced, *adj.*, biassed; *p.p.*, prejudice.

prejudi'cial, *adj.*, detrimental.

prejudi'cially, *adv.*, detrimentally.

pre'judicing, *pr.p.*, prejudice.

prel'acy, *n.*, the office or status of a prelate; prelatic government. (Also *prelatism*.)

prel'ate, *n.*, one holding high rank in the Church—an archbishop, a cardinal, a bishop, an abbot, etc.

prel'atess, *n.*, an abbess or prioress.

prelat'ic, *adj.*, pert. or rel. to prelates and prelacy.

prelat'ical, *adj.*, *i.q.* prelatic.

prelat'ically, *adv.*, in the manner of a prelate.

prel'atism, *n.*, *i.q.* prelacy; the advocacy of church hierarchy.

prel'atist, *n.*, an advocate of prelacy.

prel'atize, *v.t.*, to bring under church control.

prel'ature, *n.*, the office of prelate.

prelect', *v.i.*, to lecture, to discourse.

prelect'ed, *p.p.*, prelect.

prelect'ing, *pr.p.*, prelect.

prelec'tion, *n.*, a discourse or lecture.

prelec'tor, *n.*, a lecturer.

preliba'tion, *n.*, a foretaste.

prelim', *n.*, a preliminary (examination) (*colloq.*).

prelim'inarily, *adv.*, by way of a beginning.

prelim'inary, *adj.*, introductory; *n.*, a first step.

pre'lims, *n. pl.*, in printing, the pages preceding the text (*abbrev.*).

prel'ude, *n.*, something introductory; an opening (musical) movement; *v.t.* and *i.*, to preface; to introduce; to open with a (musical) prelude.

prel'uded, *p.p.*, prelude.

prelud'ial, *adj.*, pert. or rel. to a prelude.

prel'uding, *pr.p.*, prelude.

prelu'sion, *n.*, a premonition.

prelu'sive, *adj.*, of the nature of a prelude; foreshadowing.

prelu'sively, *adv.*, in a prelusive way.

prelu'sory, *adj.*, *i.q.* prelusive.

premature', *adj.*, ripe before the time; occurring too soon, hasty.

premature'ly, *adv.*, too soon.

premature'ness, *n.*, *i.q.* prematurity.

prematur'ity, *n.*, the state of being premature.

premed'itate, *v.t.* and *i.*, to plan, to think out, beforehand.

premed'itated, *adj.*, conceived beforehand; *p.p.*, premeditate.

premed'itatedly, *adv.*, with premeditation.

premed'itating, *pr.p.*, premeditate.

premedita'tion, *n.*, deliberate purpose; previous consideration.

prem'ier, *adj.*, first; of the first importance; *n.*, a Prime Minister.

première', *n.*, the first performance of a show (*Fr.*).

prem'iership, *n.*, the office of Prime Minister.

premillen'nial, *adj.*, before the millennium.

prem'ise, *n.*, a proposition from which another is inferred, as the major and minor premises in logic; the foregoing.

premise', *v.t.*, to state in introduction; to lay down premises.

premised', *p.p.*, premise.

prem'ises, *n. pl.*, a building and its adjuncts.

premi'sing, *pr.p.*, premise.

prem'iss, *n.*, *i.q.* premise.

pre'mium, *n.*, a prize; a price paid; a value above par; the excess value of one currency over another.

premol'ar, *n.*, a tooth between the canines and the molars.

premon'ish, *v.t.*, to warn.

premon'ished, *p.p.*, premonish.

premon'ishing, *pr.p.*, premonish.

premoni'tion, *n.*, a warning; a presage.

premon'itor, *n.*, one who premonishes.

premon'itory, adj., conveying a warning.

Premonstraten'sian, adj., pert. or rel. to the Order of Canons Regular; n., a member of the Order.

premorse', adj., having the end truncated.

premuni'tion, n., a defensive state.

pre-nat'al, adj., before birth.

preno'men, n., i.q. praenomen; the first name.

prenom'inal, adj., pert. or rel. to the prenomen.

pren'tice, n., and v.t., i.q. apprentice.

preoc'cupancy, n., the right or state of occupying beforehand.

preoccupa'tion, n., preoccupancy; business more important than other matters; the state of being mentally engrossed.

preoc'cupied, adj., not concerned with the immediate environment; p.p., preoccupy.

preoc'cupy, v.t., to engross (the mind).

preoc'cupying, pr.p., preoccupy.

pre-ordain', v.t., to foreordain.

pre-ordained', p.p., preordain.

pre-ordain'ing, pr.p., pre-ordain.

pre-ordina'tion, n., the act of preordaining.

prep, n., abbrev. of preparation (school slang)

prepaid', p.p., prepay.

prep'arable, adj., able to be prepared.

prepara'tion, n., the state of preparing; something done in readiness; anything prepared, as food or medicine; preliminary study of school lessons.

prepar'ative, adj., i.q. preparatory.

prepar'atorily, adv., in a preparatory way.

prepar'atory, adj., introductory; serving to prepare.

prepare', v.t. and i., to make ready; to get ready.

prepared', adj., ready; p.p., prepare.

prepar'edly, adv., in a state of readiness.

prepar'edness, n., a state of readiness.

prepar'ing, pr.p., prepare.

prepay, v.t., to pay in advance.

prepay'able, adj., on which a charge is to be prepaid.

prepay'ing, pr.p., prepay.

prepay'ment, n., a payment in advance.

prepense', adj., premeditated, deliberate.

prepense'ly, adv., deliberately.

prepol'lence, n., eminence, superiority.

prepol'lency, n., i.q. prepollence.

prepol'lent, adj., eminent, superior.

prepon'derance, n., superiority in weight, force, number, etc.

prepon'derancy, n., i.q. preponderance.

prepon'derant, adj., preponderating.

prepon'derate, v.i., to be superior in weight, force, number, etc.

prepon'derated, p.p., preponderate.

prepon'derating, pr.p., preponderate.

prepondera'tion, n., i.q. preponderance.

preposi'tion, n., a word which, placed before another, expresses its relation to some other word, as in, by, from.

preposi'tional, adj., with the force of a preposition.

prepos'itive, adj., that may be prefixed.

prepos'itor, n., a school monitor or prefect.

prepossess', v.t., to inspire; to prejudice; to bias.

prepossessed', p.p., prepossess.

prepossess'ing, adj., engaging; charming; pr.p., prepossess.

prepossession, n., something preconceived; an antecedent bias in favour of some person or thing.

prepos'terous, adj., contrary to nature, reason or common sense; outrageously absurd.

prepos'terously, adv., in a preposterous way.

prepo'tency, n., a predominating influence.

prepo'tent, adj., with stronger influence.

prepran'dial, adj., before dinner.

pre'puce, n., the foreskin.

Pre-Raph'aelite, adj., pert. or rel. to the Pre-Raphaelite movement in favour of returning to simplicity in art; n., one of the Pre-Raphaelite brotherhood.

Pre-Raph'aelitism, n., the Pre-Raphaelite principles.

pre-record'ed, adj., recorded in advance.

prereq'uisite, adj., antecedently required; n., a preliminary condition or requirement.

prerog'ative, adj., with the right of voting first; privileged; n., a peculiar right or privilege.

pres'age, n., a portent, an omen; a presentiment.

presage', v.t., to portend, betoken or forebode.

presaged', p.p., presage.

presa'ging, pr.p., presage.

pres'byope, n., a sufferer from presbyopia.

presbyo'pia, n., the long sight of old age.

pres'byter, n., an elder; a priest.

presbyt'eral, adj., pert. or rel. to presbyters.

presbyt'erate, n., a presbyter's office, or term of service.

Presbyte'rian, adj., pert. or rel. to the Presbyterian system; n., a member of the Presbyterian body.

Presbyte'rianism, n., the system of belief and polity adopted by Presbyterians.

pres'bytery, n., the part of a church east of the choir; the place where the clergy sit or officiate; the whole body of presbyters; a priest's house.

pre'science, n., foreknowledge.

pre'scient, adj., foreknowing.

pre'sciently, adv., in a foreknowing way.

prescind', v.t., to cut off, to abstract.

prescribe', v.i., to give directions of any kind; v.t., to lay down with authority; to impose; to recommend (a medicine).

prescribed', p.p., prescribe.

prescri'ber, n., one who prescribes.

prescri'bing, pr.p., prescribe.

pre'script, n., a direction, an ordinance.

prescriptibil'ity, n., the fitness to be prescribed.

prescript'ible, adj., fit to be prescribed.

prescrip'tion, n.; the act of prescribing; a doctor's recipe; direction; a right acquired by long, undisputed possession.

prescript'ive, adj., prescribing; based on prescription.

preselec'tive, n., that which can be selected in advance.

preselec'tor, n., any device for engaging or choosing something in advance.

pres'ence, n., the being present; vicinity; aspect.

pres'ence-chamber, n., a room where a sovereign receives visitors.

presen'sion, n., a former perception.

present', n., the act of presenting arms (in rifle drill); v.t., to introduce; to bestow; to offer; to level a weapon; to offer for judicial inquiry; to accuse.

pres'ent, adj., in company; being now or here; n., a gift; the present time.

present'able, adj., fit to be presented; fit for society.

presenta'tion, n., the act of presenting in any sense; a dramatic exhibition; the statement of a case.

presenta'tionism, n., immediate cognition.

present'ative, adj., serving to present; pert. or rel. to the right of an ecclesiastical patron to present to a benefice.

present'ed, p.p., present.

presentee', n., a churchman presented to a benefice; a person recommended for office, presented at court or receiving a present.

present'er, n., one who presents.

present'ient, adj., having a presentiment;

sensing an occurrence before it happens.

present'iment, n., a foreboding.

present'ing, pr.p., present.

present'ive, adj., presenting to the mind.

pres'ently, adv., soon, shortly. (In former times it often meant "at once; at the present time.")

present'ment, n., the act of presenting in various senses; a grand jury's report; charges officially laid before the ecclesiastical authorities.

preserv'able, adj., able to be preserved.

preserva'tion, n., the act of preserving; the state of being preserved.

preserv'ative, adj., aiding preservation; n., anything that preserves.

preserv'atory, adj., i.q. preservative.

preserve', n., jam; ground reserved for the protection of game, etc.; v.t., to keep safe; to secure the life of; to treat (fruit, meat, etc.) so as to keep them from decomposing.

preserved', p.p., preserve.

preserv'er, n., one who preserves.

preserv'ing, pr.p., preserve.

preside', v.i., to occupy the chief seat.

presi'ded, p.p., preside.

pres'idency, n., the status, jurisdiction, term of office and area of authority of a president.

pres'ident, n., one who presides over a state, a college, a society, etc.

presiden'tial, adj., pert. or rel. to a president.

presiden'tially, adv., in a presidential way.

pres'identship, n., a president's function or office.

presi'der, n., one who presides.

presid'ial, adj., pert. or rel. to a garrison.

presid'iary, adj., i.q. presidial.

presi'ding, pr.p., preside.

presid'io, n., a garrison town (Span.).

presid'ium, n., a standing committee in the Soviet system.

presignifica'tion, n., a presage.

presig'nified, p.p., presignify.

presig'nify, v.t., to foreshadow.

presig'nifying, pr.p., presignify.

press, n., a crowding; a hurry; a cupboard with or without shelves; the art or practice of printing; a machine for printing; journalism and journalists collectively; v.i., to bear weightily; to hurry on; to crowd; to importune; v.t., to bring weight or force to bear upon or against; to impress; to squeeze or crush; to flatten; to follow closely; to push (an argument).

pressed, p.p., press.

press'er, n., one who, or that which, presses.

press'-gang, n., men who were used to press others into the navy.

press'ing, adj., urgent, weighty; pr.p., press.

press'ingly, adv., urgently.

press'man, n., a journalist.

press'mark, n., a mark in a book showing its exact place in the library shelves.

press'room, n., the room where printers work.

pres'sure, n., the exertion of force or influence; embarrassment; urgency.

pres'sure-cooker, n., an apparatus for cooking at high temperature and high pressure.

pres'sure-gauge, n., an instrument for showing pressure.

pres'sure-group, n., a group which exerts pressure for its own purpose.

pres'surize, v.t., to construct for the control of air pressure, etc.; to exert too much strain on.

pres'surized, adj., overworked; p.p., pressurize.

pres'surizing, pr.p., pressurize.

press'-work, n., the output of a printing-press.

prest, adj., ready.

prestidigita'tion, n., sleight of hand.

prestidig'itator, n., a conjuror.

prestige', n., influence; importance, glamour.

prest'imony, n., a fund, privately administered, for the maintenance of a priest.

prestis'simo, adj. and adv., very fast; n., a very rapid musical piece (mus., It.).

pres'to, adj. and adv., fast; n., a fast movement (mus., It.).

presu'mable, adj., able to be presumed.

presu'mably, adv., on reasonable assumption.

presume', v.i., to take a liberty; v.t., to take for granted.

presumed', p.p., presume.

presu'ming, pr.p., presume.

presump'tion, n., the act of presuming; taking for granted; a reason for assuming; an assurance; an effrontery.

presump'tive, adj., with reasonable grounds for presuming.

presump'tuous, adj., arrogant, forward.

presump'tuously, adv., in a presumptuous way.

presump'tuousness, n., the state of being presumptuous.

presuppose', v.t., to suppose before obtaining evidence; to take for granted.

presupposed', p.p., presuppose.

presuppos'ing, pr.p., presuppose.

presupposi'tion, n., an act of presupposing; something previously assumed.

pretence', n., a claim; a pretext; a sham.

pretend', v.i., to make believe; v.t., to feign; to make a false show of; to make a false statement.

pretend'ed, p.p., pretend.

pretend'er, n., one who makes a false claim.

pretend'ing, pr.p., pretend.

preten'sion, n., the assertion of a claim; affectation.

preten'tious, adj., making a false claim; showy, ostentatious.

preten'tiously, adv., in a pretentious way.

preten'tiousness, n., ostentation.

preterhu'man, adj., more than human.

preterimper'fect, n., the imperfect tense in which an uncompleted action in the past is mentioned.

pret'erite, adj., past; n., a past tense.

preteri'tion, n., omission, disregard, passing over of the non-elect (theol.).

pretermis'sion, n., neglect, omission.

pretermit', v.t., to neglect to do or mention.

pretermit'ted, p.p., pretermit.

pretermit'ting, pr.p., pretermit.

preternat'ural, adj., beyond the natural order.

preterper'fect, n., a past tense denoting an action completed.

preterpluper'fect, n., a past tense denoting an action completed before a given point of time.

pre'text, n., an excuse, a pretence.

pretext', v.t., to advance as a pretext.

pret'one, n., the sound immediately preceding the stressed syllable.

pre'tor, n., the consul as head of the Roman army; a civil magistrate. (Also praetor.)

preto'rial, adj., pert. or rel. to a pretor.

preto'rian, adj., bel. to a pretor or the pretorium; n., a soldier of the Pretorian Guard.

preto'rium, n., a general's headquarters; a provincial governor's residence (Lat.).

pret'tier, adj., comp. of pretty.

pret'tiest, adj., super. of pretty.

pret'tify, v.t., to make pretty.

pret'tily, adv., in a pretty way.

pret'tiness, n., the quality or state of being pretty.

pret'ty, adj., visually pleasing, dainty; moderate, sufficient; affected; adv., fairly moderately.

pret'zel, n., a salty biscuit (Ger.).

prevail', v.i., to be victorious; to predominate; to exist.

prevailed', p.p., prevail.

prevail'ing, adj., in general use or occurrence; pr.p., prevail.

prev'alence, n., the state of being prevalent; vogue.

prev'alency, n., i.q. prevalence.

prev'alent, adj., prevailing, commonly occurring.

prev'alently, adv., commonly, generally.

prevar'icate, v.i., to speak or act evasively; to lie.

prevar'icated, p.p., prevaricate.

prevar'icating, pr.p., prevaricate.

prevarica'tion, n., evasion, quibble; lie.

prevar'icator, n., one who prevaricates.

preve'nient, adj., going before, preceding, preventing.

prevent', v.t., to stop, to hinder; an early meaning was "to go before in aid," as in the Collect—"Prevent us, O Lord, in all our doings."

prevent'able, adj., able to be prevented.

prevent'ably, adv., in a preventable way.

prevent'ative, adj. and n., i.q. preventive.

prevent'ed, p.p., prevent.

prevent'er, n., one who prevents.

prevent'ing, pr.p., prevent.

preven'tion, n., the act or effect of preventing; a hindrance; a precaution.

preven'tional, adj., of a preventive nature.

prevent'ive, adj., preventing; staving off; n., a protective medicine or agent; a contraceptive.

pre'view, n., the act of previewing; a view or examination of a film, book, etc. before seen by the general public; v.t., to view beforehand.

pre'viewed, p.p., preview.

pre'viewing, pr.p., preview.

pre'vious, adj., former, preceding.

pre'viously, *adv.*, before in time.

previse', *v.t.*, to foresee.

previ'sed', *p.p.*, previse.

previs'ing, *pr.p.*, previse.

previ'sion, *n.*, foresight.

previ'sional, *adj.*, foreseeing.

previ'sionally, *adv.*, in a foreseeing way.

pre'-war, *adj.*, before a war.

pre-warn', *v.t.*, to warn in advance.

pre-warned', *p.p.*, prewarn.

pre-warn'ing, *n.*, an advance warning; *pr.p.*, pre-warn.

prey, *n.*, an animal seized by another for food; plunder; a victim; *v.i.*, to seize food by violence; to exert a baneful influence on.

preyed, *p.p.*, prey.

prey'er, *n.*, a waster or plunderer.

prey'ing, *pr.p.*, prey.

pri'al, *n.*, *i.q.* parial or pair royal.

pri'apism, *n.*, sensuality.

price, *n.*, the equivalent value in exchange; the sum demanded or paid; *v.t.*, to estimate the value of; to ask the price of.

price'-current, *n.*, the ruling price.

priced, *p.p.*, price.

price'less, *adj.*, beyond price, invaluable; very amusing (*slang*).

price'lessness, *n.*, the state of being priceless.

price'-list, *n.*, a list of prices of goods for sale.

pric'ing, *pr.p.*, price.

prick, *n.*, the act or effect of pricking; a puncture; a point; a goad; *v.t.*, to pierce slightly; to puncture; to sting.

pricked, *p.p.*, prick.

prick'er, *n.*, one who, or that which, pricks; a pricking implement.

prick'et, *n.*, a two-year old buck; a spiked candlestick.

prick'ing, *pr.p.*, prick.

prick'le, *n.*, a small, sharp point; a make

of wicker basket; *v.i.*, to have a pricking sensation; *v.t.*, to cause a pricking sensation.

prick'leback, *n.*, the stickleback.

prick'led, *p.p.*, prickle.

prick'liness, *n.*, the quality of being prickly.

prick'ling, *pr.p.*, prickle.

prick'ly, *adj.*, furnished with prickles; prickling.

prick'ly-heat, *n.*, a skin disease with pricking and itching sensations.

prick'ly-pear, *n.*, a pear-shaped fruit, grown on a plant bearing clusters of spines.

pride, *n.*, an overweening estimate of self; arrogance; something to be proud of; the acme; a family of lions; *v. reflex.*, to be proud.

pri'ded, *p.p.*, pride.

pride'less, *adj.*, without pride.

prid'ing, *pr.p.*, pride.

pried, *p.p.*, pry.

prie-dieu, *n.*, a prayer-desk (*Fr.*).

pri'er, *n.*, one who pries.

priest, *n.*, one who offers sacrifice; a member of the clergy between a bishop and a deacon.

priest'craft, *n.*, priestly skill.

priest'ess, *n.*, a woman priest.

priest'hood, *n.*, the office or order of priests.

priest'like, *adj.*, like a priest; priestly.

priest'liness, *n.*, the quality of being priestly.

priest'ly, *adj.*, pert. or rel. to a priest.

priest'ridden, *adj.*, too much under priestly influence.

prig, *n.*, a dull person, precise in manner and affectedly superior.

prig'gery, *n.*, *i.q.* priggishness.

prig'gish, *adj.*, pert. or rel. to a prig.

prig'gishly, *adv.*, in a priggish way.

prig'gishness, *n.*, the assumption of superiority.

prig'gism, *n.*, the quality of a prig.

prill, *n.*, a choice piece of ore.

prim, *adj.*, formal and precise in appearance and manner; *v.i.*, to appear prim; *v.t.*, to make to appear prim.

pri'ma, *adj.*, first (*Lat.*).

pri'macy, *n.*, the chief place; the office of a primate.

pri'ma don'na, *n.*, the leading woman singer in opera (*It.*).

primae'val, *adj.*, *i.q.* primeval.

pri'ma fa'cie, *adj.* and *adv.*, at first sight; on the first impression (*Lat.*).

pri'mage, *n.*, an additional percentage paid for freight on board ship; water loss from rising steam (esp. from a boiler).

pri'mal, *adj.*, early, primeval, fundamental.

pri'marily, *adv.*, originally, fundamentally.

pri'mary, *adj.*, original, fundamental, first in order.

pri'mate, *n.*, the head of an ecclesiastical province; an archbishop.

primat'es, *n. pl.*, the highest order of mammals (*zool.*).

prima'tial, *adj.*, pert. or rel. to a primate.

primat'ical, *adj.*, *i.q.* primatial.

prime, *adj.*, chief, choice; *n.*, the early time (of day or life); the time of perfection; a Catholic service; the golden number; a position in fencing; *v.t.*, to make ready, to prepare; to charge a gun; to put on a first coat of paint.

primed, *p.p.*, prime.

prime'ly, *adv.*, originally; highly.

prime'ness, *n.*, the quality of being prime.

pri'mer, *n.*, a reading book; a book of prayers and instruction; a size of type; that which, or one who, primes, esp. in regard to a gun.

prime'val, *adj.*, primitive; bel. to the earliest ages. (Also *primaeval*.)

prime'vally, *adv.*, primitively.

prim'ing, *n.*, a gun-charge; *pr.p.*, prime.

primip'arous, *adj.*, bearing young for the first time.

primi'tiae, *n. pl.*, first fruits; the first fluid discharge at parturition (*Lat.*).

primi'tial, *adj.*, pert. or rel. to primitiae.

prim'itive, *adj.*, ancient, early, primary; rude, rough, lacking in civilized amenity; *n.*, a radical, underived word.

prim'itively, *adv.*, in a primitive way.

prim'itiveness, *n.*, the state of being primitive.

prim'ness, *n.*, the quality or state of being prim.

pri'mo, *n.*, the upper part in a duet, etc. (*It.*).

prim'o, *adv.*, in the first place (*Lat.*).

primogen'itive, *adj.*, pert. or rel. to primogeniture.

primogen'itor, *n.*, the remotest ancestor.

primogen'iture, *n.*, priority of birth; the status of the first-born.

primord'ial, *adj.*, *i.q.* primeval.

primp, *v.i.*, to put on airs; *v.t.*, to make oneself tidy.

prim'rose, *n.*, an early spring perennial, bearing yellow flowers.

Prim'ula, *n.*, a herbaceous multi-coloured perennial; a genus of plants to which the primrose belongs.

pri'mum mo'bile, *n.*, the assumed outermost sphere in the universe; any source of movement (*Lat.*).

pri'mus, *n.*, the title of the presiding bishop of the Scottish Church; a kind of oil stove.

prince, *n.*, a sovereign; the son of a king; a member of the highest ranks of nobility.

prince'dom, *n.*, a prince's sphere of authority.

prince'let, *n.*, a petty prince.

prince'ling, *n.*, *i.q.* princelet.

prince'ly, *adj.*, princelike; magnificent, sumptuous.

prin'cess, *n.*, the fem. of prince.

prin'cipal, *adj.*, chief in importance or station; leading; *n.*, one who takes the lead; a chief player; an employer; the head of a college, school, etc.; a soloist; an organ stop so named; the capital; a main rafter.

principal'ity, *n.*, the jurisdiction of a prince; a State governed by a prince.

prin'cipally, *adv.*, chiefly.

prin'cipate, *n.*, *i.q.* principality.

princip'ia, *n. pl.*, first principles (*Lat.*).

prin'ciple, *n.*, an original source; a fundamental truth; a law of morals or of nature; a theoretical basis.

prin'cipled, *adj.*, having principles.

prink, *v.t.* and *i.*, to dress for display.

prinked, *p.p.*, prink.

prink'ing, *pr.p.*, prink.

print, *n.*, an impress, printed type; a picture produced from the negative; a printed cotton fabric; a newspaper (*Amer.*); *v.i.*, to be a printer; *v.t.*, to impress; to put into type; to produce a photographic picture.

print'able, *adj.*, suitable to be printed, worthy of being printed.

print'ed, *p.p.*, print.

print'er, *n.*, one who prints.

print'ing, *n.*, a printer's art or trade; *pr.p.*, print.

print'ing-office, *n.*, an office where books, newspapers, etc., are printed.

print'ing-press, *n.*, a machine for printing.

print'-out, *n.*, a computer-printed record of electronically stored information.

pri'or, *adj.*, preceding, earlier; *n.*, a monastic officer ranking below an abbot.

pri'orate, *n.*, the office, or tenure of office, of a prior.

pri'oress, *n.*, the fem. of prior.

prior'ity, *n.*, precedence in time or position.

pri'ory, *n.*, a religious house governed by a prior or prioress.

prism, *n.*, a solid figure, having sides which are parallelograms and ends which are equal, similar and parallel rectilineal figures.

prismat'ic, *adj.*, pert. or rel. to a prism.

prismat'ical, *adj.*, *i.q.* prismatic.

prismat'ically, *adv.*, in a prismatic way.

pris'moid, *n.*; a prism-like body, but differing from a prism in regard to its ends.

prismoid'al, *adj.*, pert. or rel. to a prismoid.

pris'on, *n.*, a place of confinement; *v.t.*, to place in captivity or confinement.

pris'oner, *n.*, one kept in prison.

pris'oner's bars, *n.*, *i.q.* prisoner's base.

pris'oner's base, *n.*, a schoolboy game, in which each opposing party starts from a distinct base.

pris'on-van, *n.*, the van in which prisoners are conveyed from prison to court, and vice versa.

pris'tine, *adj.*, former, ancient.

prith'ee, *interj.* = I pray thee; please.

pri'vacy, *n.*, the state of being in private.

pri'vate, *adj.*, unobserved; withdrawn from public; unofficial; reticent; special; *n.*, a soldier of the lowest army rank.

privateer', *n.*, an armed ship in private ownership and commissioned (by letters of marque) by a Government to act against an enemy nation.

privateer'ing, *n.*, the act of cruising in a privateer.

pri'vate-eye, *n.*, a private detective.

pri'vately, *adv.*, in a private manner.

pri'vateness, *n.*, *i.q.* privacy.

priva'tion, *n.*, the act of depriving; the state of being deprived; loss, want.

priv'ative, *adj.*, denoting the loss or absence of; in grammar, it indicates a negative quality.

priv′et, *n*., an evergreen shrub used for hedges.

priv′ilege, *n*., a special right, advantage or immunity; *v.t.*, to bestow a privilege on.

priv′ileged, *p.p.*, privilege.

priv′ileging, *pr.p.*, privilege.

priv′ily, *adv.*, secretly, privately.

priv′ity, *n*., secrecy, privacy.

priv′y, *adj.*, secret, private, personal; informed of; *n*., a person concerned in an action or matter.

Priv′y Coun′cil, *n*., the private council of a sovereign.

prize, *n*., a reward; a thing much valued; leverage; *v.t.*, to value greatly; to capture as a prize (of war); to force by leverage.

prized, *p.p.*, prize.

prize′fight, *n*., a pugilistic contest for a prize.

prize′fighter, *n*., one who engages in a prizefight.

prize′fighting, *n*., *i.q.* prizefight.

prize′man, *n*., the winner of a prize.

prize′-money, *n*., money paid for the proceeds of a maritime prize.

priz′ing, *pr.p.*, prize.

pro, *prep.*, for (*Lat.*).

pro′a, *n*., a Malay sailing-boat.

proam′bient, *adj.*, in front of; before; moving before.

probabil′iorism, *n*., the doctrine that where evidence preponderates, that side should be followed.

prob′abilism, *n*., the doctrine that a belief may be held on a probable basis.

prob′abilist, *n*., a believer in probabilism.

probabil′ity, *n*., the quality of being probable; likelihood.

prob′able, *adj.*, likely.

prob′ably, *adv.*, presumably; in all probability.

pro′bang, *n*., a surgical implement for removing obstructions of the throat or oesophagus.

pro′bate, *adj.*, pert. or rel. to making proof; *n*., the official certifying of a will; a certified copy of a will.

proba′tion, *n*., the act of testing; the state of being tested; a novitiate; the state of legal surveillance while at liberty.

proba′tional, *adj.*, under probation.

proba′tionary, *adj.*, done as a probation; concerned with probation.

proba′tioner, *n*., a person on approval, as a novice, or as a convicted person not imprisoned.

pro′bative, *adj.*, evidential.

pro′batory, *adj.*, serving for a test.

probe, *n*., a surgical instrument for exploring wounds; *v.t.*, to penetrate; to examine with a probe; to discover the facts.

probed, *p.p.*, probe.

prob′ing, *pr.p.*, probe.

prob′ity, *n*., uprightness.

prob′lem, *n*., a question for solution; a difficult matter.

problemat′ic, *adj.*, doubtful; calling for solution.

problemat′ical, *adj.*, *i.q.* problematic.

problemat′ically, *adv.*, doubtfully.

prob′lematist, *n*., *i.q.* problemist.

prob′lemist, *n*., one who studies or creates problems.

proboscid′ean, *adj.*, pert. or rel. to proboscis.

probos′cis, *n*., an elephant's or tapir's trunk; the extended mouth of some insects.

proced′ural, *adj.*, pert. or rel. to procedure.

proce′dure, *n*., a proceeding; a method.

proceed′, *v.i.*, to advance, go on or come from.

proceed′ed, *p.p.*, proceed.

proceed′ing, *n*., an action; conduct. In *pl.* = an action at law; *pr.p.*, proceed.

pro′ceeds, *n. pl.*, results; a resulting sum of money.

procella′rian, *adj.*, pert. or rel. to petrels; *n*., a stormy petrel.

pro′cess, *n*., progress, a course of operation; a series of movements; a legal writ, action at law; *v.t.*, to subject to a process (as in photography), etc.

process′, *v.i.*, to walk in procession (*colloq.*).

pro′cessed, *adj.*, treated by a special process; prepared for eating; *p.p.*, process.

processed′, *p.p.*, process.

pro′cessing, *n*., the preparatory treatment of foodstuffs; a systematic treatment of documents, etc.; *pr.p.*, process.

process′ing, *pr.p.*, process.

proces′sion, *n*., a movement in orderly array; the act of proceeding or emanating.

proces′sional, *adj.*, pert. or rel. to processions; *n*., a service-book for processional use.

proces′sionist, *n*., one who joins in a procession.

procès verbal, *n*., a written record of proceedings (*Fr.*).

pro′chronism, *n*., the giving of an earlier than the true date; antedating.

proclaim′, *v.t.*, to announce publicly or officially; to declare officially; to place under legal disqualifications.

proclaimed′, *p.p.*, proclaim.

proclaim′er, *n*., one who proclaims.

proclaim′ing, *pr.p.*, proclaim.

proclama′tion, *n*., the act of proclaiming; an announcement.

proclit′ic, *adj.* and *n*., (a word) prefixed to another word and having itself no accent.

procliv′ity, *n*., a tendency.

procon′sul, *n*., a provincial or colonial governor.

procon′sular, *adj.*, pert. or rel. to a proconsul.

procon′sulary, *adj.*, *i.q.* proconsular.

procon′sulate, *n*., a proconsul's office or tenure of office.

procon'sulship, *n.*, *i.q.* proconsulate.

procras'tinate, *v.i.*, to put off or delay doing.

procras'tinated, *p.p.*, procrastinate.

procras'tinating, *pr.p.*, procrastinate.

procrastina'tion, *n.*, the act or habit of putting off.

procras'tinator, *n.*, one who procrastinates.

procras'tinatory, *adj.*, delaying, dilatory.

pro'creant, *adj.*, procreating.

pro'create, *v.t.*, to generate, to beget.

pro'created, *p.p.*, procreate.

pro'creating, *pr.p.*, procreate.

procrea'tion, *n.*, the act or process of procreating.

pro'creative, *adj.*, generative, begetting.

pro'creator, *n.*, one who procreates.

Procrust'ean, *adj.*, pert. or rel. to Procrustes, the legendary robber who stretched or mutilated robbers to fit the bed he supplied for them; hence = enforcing rigid uniformity.

procryp'sis, *n.*, the protective colouring of insects (*biol.*).

proc'tor, *n.*, the equivalent of the Lat. *procurator;* an agent, an attorney; a university disciplinary official; a clerical representative in the Convocations of Canterbury and York; one practising in the ecclesiastical courts.

procto'rial, *adj.*, bel. to a proctor.

proc'torize, *v.t.*, to summon (said of a proctor who summons an undergraduate before him).

proc'torized, *p.p.*, proctorize.

proc'torizing, *pr.p.*, proctorize.

procum'bent, *adj.*, prostrate.

procur'able, *adj.*, able to be procured.

procura'tion, *n.*, obtaining, bringing about; the power of attorney; the provision of entertainment for a visiting bishop or official; a fee.

proc'urator, *n.*, a Roman imperial treasurer; an agent, a proctor.

proc'uratory, *n.*, the power of attorney.

proc'uratrix, *n.*, the administrative inmate of a nunnery.

procure', *v.t.*, to acquire; to bring about; to act as a procurer or procuress.

procured', *p.p.*, procure.

procure'ment, *n.*, an attainment.

procur'er, *n.*, one who procures, esp. a man or woman who procures women for sexual intercourse.

procur'ess, *n.*, the fem. of procurer.

procur'ing, *pr.p.*, procure.

prod, *n.*, a poke; *v.t.*, to poke.

prod'ded, *p.p.*, prod.

prod'ding, *pr.p.*, prod.

prodeli'sion, *n.*, the elision of an initial vowel.

prod'igal, *adj.*, lavish, wasteful; *n.*, a wastrel.

prodigal'ity, *n.*, lavishness, wastefulness.

prod'igalize, *v.t.*, to spend lavishly.

prod'igally, *adv.*, lavishly.

prodig'ious, *adj.*, portentous, marvellous.

prodig'iously, *adv.*, marvellously.

prodig'iousness, *n.*, the state of being prodigious.

prod'igy, *n.*, a marvel, a portent; an astonishingly clever person.

prodrom'ata, *n. pl.*, premonitory symptoms.

prod'rome, *n.*, a preliminary publication; a premonitory symptom.

prod'romus, *n.*, a premonitory symptom.

prod'uce, *n.*, that which is produced; a yield.

produce', *v.t.*, to bring forth; to call into existence; to exhibit; to manufacture; to yield; to lengthen (a line).

produced', *p.p.*, produce.

produ'cer, *n.*, one who produces.

produ'cible, *adj.*, capable of being produced.

produ'cing, *pr.p.*, produce.

prod'uct, *n.*, something produced or yielded.

produc'tile, *adj.*, extensible.

produc'tion, *n.*, the act of producing; that which is produced; (in Scots law) an evidential document.

produc'tive, *adj.*, yielding results; producing.

produc'tively, *adv.*, in a productive way.

produc'tiveness, *n.*, the quality of being productive.

productiv'ity, *n.*, productiveness, the capacity to produce.

pro'em, *n.*, an introduction, preface or preamble.

proe'mial, *adj.*, introductory.

profana'tion, *n.*, the act of profaning.

profane', *adj.*, irreverent, secular; *v.t.*, to desecrate, to treat with irreverence.

profaned', *p.p.*, profane.

profane'ly, *adv.*, irreverently.

profane'ness, *n.*, the quality of being profane.

profan'er, *n.*, one who profanes.

profan'ing, *pr.p.*, profane.

profan'ity, *n.*, a profane act; irreverence; foul language.

profess', *v.i.*, to be a teacher or professor of a subject; *v.t.*, to avow openly; to pretend; to teach.

professed', *adj.*, avowed; alleged; *p.p.*, profess.

profess'edly, *adv.*, avowedly; by pretence.

profess'ing, *pr.p.*, profess.

profes'sion, *n.*, the act of professing; a declaration; a vocation, esp. a learned one.

profes'sional, *adj.*, the opposite to amateur; bel. to a profession; expert in knowledge and skill.

profes'sionalism, *n.*, the character or habits of the professional person.

profes'sionally, *adv.*, in a professional capacity.

profes'sor, *n.*, one who professes in any sense; a university teacher.

professo'rial, *adj.*, pert. or rel. to a professor.

professo'riate, *n.*, professors collectively; professorship.

profes'sorship, *n.*, the office of a professor.

prof'fer, *v.t.*, to propose, to offer.

prof'fered, *p.p.*, proffer.

prof'ferer, *n.*, one who proffers.

prof'fering, *pr.p.*, proffer.

profi'ciency, *n.*, skill, aptitude.

profi'cient, *adj.*, skilful, apt.

profi'ciently, *adv.*, skilfully.

pro'file, *n.*, the side face; a side view; a complete summarized statement; *v.t.*, to make a drawing of in profile.

pro'filist, *n.*, one who draws profiles.

prof'it, *n.*, advantage, gain, help; monetary value secured from work or investment; *v.i.*, to reap advantage; *v.t.*, to be of advantage to; to help.

profitabil'ity, *n.*, lucrativeness; the assessment of profit.

prof'itable, *adj.*, advantageous; lucrative.

prof'itably, *adv.*, with gain or profit.

prof'ited, *p.p.* profit.

profiteer', *n.*, one who profiteers; *v.i.*, to make profits, usually unscrupulously.

profiteered', *p.p.*, profiteer.

profiteer'ing, *n.*, the making of unreasonable or excessive profits; *pr.p.*, profiteer.

prof'iting, *pr.p.*, profit.

prof'itless, *adj.*, unprofitable.

prof'ligacy, *n.*, licentiousness; reckless wastefulness.

prof'ligate, *adj.*, licentious, recklessly wasteful; *n.*, a profligate person.

prof'ligately, *adv.*, licentiously.

pro form'a, *adv.*, done for form's sake; *n.*, a form sent on account or instead of.

profound', *adj.*, deep; intense; showing great insight; *n.*, an abyss.

profound'er, *adj.*, *comp.* of profound.

profound'est, *adj.*, *super.* of profound.

profound'ly, *adv.*, deeply.

profun'dity, *n.*, depth (in various senses).

profuse', *adj.*, lavish, abundant.

profuse'ly, *adv.*, lavishly, abundantly.

profuse'ness, *n.*, the quality of being profuse.

profu'sion, *n.*, abundance; exuberance.

prog, *v.t.*, to prod; *n.*, victuals (*slang*); a university proctor (*slang*).

progen'itive, *adj.*, pert. or rel. to the generation of offspring.

progen'itor, *n.*, an ancestor; a predecessor.

progen'iture, *n.*, procreation.

prog'eny, *n.*, an offspring.

proges'terone, *n.*, a steroid hormone affecting pregnancy.

proglott'is, *n.*, a segment of the tapeworm.

prognath'ic, *adj.*, with projecting jaw.

prog'nathous, *adj.*, *i.q.* prognathic.

progno'sis, *n.*, *i.q.* prognostication; an assessment of the probable course of events.

prognos'tic, *adj.*, forecasting, predicting; *n.*, an omen.

prognos'ticable, *adj.*, able to be prognosticated.

prognos'ticate, *v.t.*, to foretell, to forecast.

prognos'ticated, *p.p.*, prognosticate.

prognos'ticating, *pr.p.*, prognosticate.

prognostica'tion, *n.*, the act of prognosticating; a prediction.

prognos'ticator, *n.*, one who prognosticates.

prognos'ticatory, *adj.*, of the nature of prognostication.

pro'gramme, *n.*, a list of items or events; a detailed plan of arrangements; *v.t.*, to make such a list or plan.

pro'grammed, *p.p.*, programme.

pro'grammer, *n.*, one who programmes.

prog'ramming, *pr.p.*, programme.

pro'gress, *n.*, an advance; action leading to improvement; a royal or official tour.

progress', *v.i.*, to move onward; to advance.

progressed', *p.p.*, progress.

progres'sing, *pr.p.*, progress.

progres'sion, *n.*, progress; an arithmetical or geometrical series; in music, the passing of a note or chord to another note or chord.

progres'sional, *adj.*, pert. or rel. to progress.

progres'sionist, *n.*, one who advocates progress.

progres'sive, *adj.*, tending to advance; moving forward; enlightened; *n.*, a supporter of progressive principles.

progres'sively, *adv.*, step by step; making advance.

progres'siveness, *n.*, the state of being progressive.

progres'sivism, *n.*, progressive principles.

prohib'it, *v.t.*, to forbid, to prevent.

prohib'ited, *p.p.*, prohibit.

prohib'iter, *n.*, one who prohibits.

prohib'iting, *pr.p.*, prohibit.

prohibi'tion, *n.*, the act of forbidding; a forbidding decree or law.

prohibi'tionary, *adj.*, forbidding.

prohibi'tionist, *n.*, one who favours the prohibition of alcoholic liquor.

prohib'itive, *adj.*, forbidding, preventing.

prohib'itively, *adv.*, in a prohibitive sense.

prohib'itory, *adj.*, *i.q.* prohibitive.

proj'ect, *n.*, a scheme, a plan.

project', *v.i.*, to jut out; to form plans; *v.t.*, to plan, to contrive; to throw, to cast.

project'ed, *p.p.*, project.

project'ile, *adj.*, able to be shot forth or to impel; *n.*, a missile.

project'ing, *pr.p.*, project.

projec'tion, *n.*, casting; a jutting out; in geometry, the representation of a thing obtained by throwing its chief points forward upon a plane from a given point of sight. (Also *projecture*.)

projec'tive, *adj.,* characterized by projection.

projec'tively, *adv.,* in a projective way.

project'or, *n.,* one who forms a project, esp. one who starts a new company venture; an apparatus for projecting light rays or an image on to a screen.

project'ure, *n., i.q.* projection.

projet, *n.,* a plan or scheme (*Fr.*).

prolapse', *n., i.q.* prolapsus; *v.i.,* to slip forward.

prolap'sus, *n.,* a falling forward or down of a body organ or part of an organ (*Lat.*).

pro'late, *adj.,* elongated.

pro'lately, *adv.,* in an elongated way.

prola'tion, *n.,* the act of delaying; an utterance; the subdivision of a semibreve (*mus.*).

prola'tive, *adj.,* completing the predication of a sentence.

prolegom'ena, *n. pl.,* the preliminary statements introducing the subject of a treatise.

prolegom'enary, *adj.,* introductory; pert. or rel. to prolegomena.

prolegom'enon, *n.,* the sing. of prolegomena.

prolep'sis, *n.,* anticipation, esp. the use of an adjective or noun with a predicative force, as "they shot him *dead*," *i.e.,* so that he died.

prolep'tic, *adj.,* anticipatory.

prolep'tically, *adv.,* in an anticipatory way.

proleta'rian, *adj.,* pert. or rel. to the proletariat; *n.,* one of the people.

proleta'rianism, *n.,* the status or the principles of the people.

proleta'riat(e), *n.,* the people; the working class.

pro'letary, *adj., i.q.* proletarian.

pro'licide, *n.,* the murder of offspring before or immediately after birth.

prolif'erate, *v.t. and i.,* to increase rapidly.

prolife'rated, *p.p.,* proliferate.

prolife'rating, *pr.p.,* proliferate.

prolifera'tion, *n.,* reproduction by budding or by the multiplication of elementary parts (*bot.*).

prolif'erous, *adj.,* productive of offspring; in botany, producing an excessive number of parts.

prolif'ic, *adj.,* fruitful; producing abundantly.

prolifica'tion, *n.,* generation; in botany, the excessive production of parts.

proli'gerous, *adj.,* producing offspring; generative.

pro'lix, *adj.,* long-winded, wordy.

prolix'ity, *n.,* wordiness, long-windedness.

pro'locutor, *n.,* a spokesman.

pro'logue, *n.,* an introduction, esp. to a play; an introductory event; *v.t.,* to furnish with a prologue.

prolong', *v.t.,* to lengthen, to continue.

prolonga'tion, *n.,* a lengthening.

prolonge', *n.,* a rope for drawing a gun-carriage (*Fr.*).

prolonged', *p.p.,* prolong.

prolong'ing, *pr.p.,* prolong.

prolu'sion, *n.,* a preliminary essay; a prelude.

promenade', *n.,* a walk or ride; a place for promenading (esp. by the sea); *v.t.,* to walk or ride, esp. as a social proceeding.

promena'ded, *p.p.,* promenade.

promena'der, *n.,* one who promenades.

promenad'ing, *pr.p.,* promenade.

pro'metal, *n.,* a heat resisting cast-iron.

Prome'thean, *adj.,* pert. or rel. to Prometheus and his Olympian fire.

prom'inence, *n.,* a jutting out; conspicuousness; distinction.

prom'inency, *n., i.q.* prominence.

prom'inent, *adj.,* jutting out; conspicuous; distinguished.

prom'inently, *adv.,* in a prominent way.

promiscu'ity, *n.,* the condition or state of being promiscuous.

promis'cuous, *adj.,* mixed in confusion; without distinction; casual; having casual intercourse outside marriage.

promis'cuously, *adv.,* in a promiscuous way; casually.

prom'ise, *n.,* a pledge, an assurance; ground for expectation; *v.t.,* to covenant, to pledge; to give ground for expectation.

prom'ised, *p.p.,* promise.

promisee', *n.,* one to whom something is promised.

prom'iser, *n.,* one who promises.

prom'ising, *adj.,* giving ground for expectation; *pr.p.,* promise.

prom'isor, *n., i.q.* promiser.

prom'issorily, *adv.,* by way of a promise.

prom'issory, *adj.,* of the nature of a promise or engagement.

prom'ontory, *n.,* a headland.

promote', *v.t.,* to advance; to raise; to forward.

promo'ted, *p.p.,* promote.

promo'ter, *n.,* one who promotes.

promo'ting, *pr.p.,* promote.

promo'tion, *n.,* the act of promoting; advancement.

promo'tive, *adj.,* causing advance; forwarding.

prompt, *adj.,* ready, quick, alert; *n.,* a help given by a prompter; *v.t.,* to instigate; to suggest; to help the memory of; to remind.

prompt'-book, *n.,* the prompter's copy of a play.

prompt'ed, *p.p.,* prompt.

prompt'er, *n.,* one who prompts, esp. one who helps an actor's memory on the stage.

prompt'ing, *pr.p.,* prompt.

prompt'itude, *n.,* readiness, alertness.

prompt'ly, *adv.,* readily, punctually.

prompt'ness, *n.,* readiness, being to time.

prom'ulgate, *v.t.*, to publish or proclaim.

prom'ulgated, *p.p.*, promulgate.

prom'ulgating, *pr.p.*, promulgate.

promulga'tion, *n.*, a publication or proclamation.

prom'ulgator, *n.*, one who promulgates.

promulge', *v.t.*, *i.q.* promulgate.

promulged', *p.p.*, promulge.

promulg'er, *n.*, one who promulges.

promulg'ing, *pr.p.*, promulge.

pro'nate, *v.t.*, to lay prone (*physiol.*).

pro'nated, *p.p.*, pronate.

pro'nating, *pr.p.*, pronate.

prona'tion, *n.*, the act of pronating.

prona'tor, *n.*, a muscle used in pronating.

prone, *adj.*, face downwards; disposed, inclined towards.

prone'ness, *n.*, a disposition towards; a leaning.

proneur', *n.*, a eulogist (*Fr.*).

prong, *n.*, a forked implement; the tine of a forked implement; *v.t.*, to use a prong upon.

pronged, *adj.*, having prongs; *p.p.*, prong.

prong'ing, *pr.p.*, prong.

pronom'inal, *adj.*, pert. or rel. to a pronoun.

pro'noun, *n.*, a part of speech used instead of a proper noun.

pronounce', *v.t.*, to utter, to declare formally, to deliver, to articulate.

pronounce'able, *adj.*, able to be pronounced.

pronounced', *adj.*, marked, decided; *p.p.*, pronounce.

pronoun'cedly, *adv.*, in a pronounced way.

pronounce'ment, *n.*, the act of pronouncing; a delivered judgment or statement.

pronounc'er, *n.*, one who pronounces.

pronounc'ing, *pr.p.*, pronounce.

pron'to, *adv.*, promptly, quickly (*slang*, *Span.*).

pronunciamen'to, *n.*, a manifesto; a public proclamation (*Span.*).

pronuncia'tion, *n.*, the act of pronouncing; the way in which words are pronounced.

pronunc'iatory, *adj.*, of the nature of a pronouncement.

proof, *adj.*, able to resist, impenetrable; pert. or rel. to a printer's proof; *n.*, clear evidence of fact; a trial, a test; impenetrability; a standard of quality or strength; a printer's or engraver's trial impression; a perfect impression of an engraved plate; *v.t.*, to make impenetrable.

proofed, *p.p.*, proof.

proof'ing, *pr.p.*, proof.

proof'reader, *n.*, one who goes through a printer's proof to correct it.

proof'-sheet, *n.*, widemargined paper on which a printer's proof is printed.

prop, *n.*, a support; stage property (*abbrev.*); an aircraft propeller (*abbrev.*, *colloq.*); *v.t.*, to support by leaning against something, or by putting something underneath.

propaedeut'ic, *adj.*, preparatory (esp. study), *n. pl.*, preliminary learning.

propagand', *v.i.*, to organize or conduct propaganda.

propagan'da, *n.*, any means for the propagation of certain doctrines or principles (*Lat.*).

propagan'dism, *n.*, the spirit or methods of a propagandist.

propagan'dist, *adj.*, pert. or rel. to propaganda; *n.*, one who is zealous in propagating a certain set of principles.

propagan'dize, *v.i.*, to spread propaganda.

prop'agate, *v.t.*, to breed, to cause to multiply by generation; to diffuse, to disseminate; to transmit.

prop'agated, *p.p.*, propagate.

prop'agating, *pr.p.*, propagate.

propaga'tion, *n.*, the act of propagating.

prop'agative, *adj.*, able to propagate.

prop'agator, *n.*, one who propagates; a small greenhouse, heated from below.

proparox'ytone, *adj.* and *n.*, (a word) having an accent on the third syllable from the end.

propel', *v.t.*, to push forward; to cause to move forward.

propelled', *p.p.*, propel.

propell'ent, *adj.*, propelling; *n.*, an explosive propelling bullet.

propel'ler, *n.*, one who, or that which, propels, esp. the driving screw of a ship or aircraft (a bladed shaft revolving with a screw motion).

propel'ling, *pr.p.*, propel.

propend', *v.i.*, to incline or lean forward.

propend'ed, *p.p.*, propend.

propend'ent, *adj.*, inclining forward.

propend'ing, *pr.p.*, propend.

propense', *adj.*, inclined, disposed.

propen'sion, *n.*, *i.q.* propensity.

propen'sity, *n.*, inclination, disposition, tendency.

prop'er, *adj.*, own; special; correct; natural; goodly; according to accepted standards.

proper'din, *n.*, an immunizing substance in the blood.

prop'erly, *adv.*, in a proper way; correctly.

prop'erty, *n.*, something peculiarly one's own; possessions; a characteristic quality or function.

prop'erty-man, *n.*, a man in charge of stage props.

proph'ecy, *n.*, the power of prophesying; a prophetic utterance.

proph'esied, *p.p.*, prophesy.

proph'esier, *n.*, one who prophesies.

proph'esy, *v.t.*, to preach, to proclaim; to speak as a prophet; to foretell; to forecast.

proph'esying, *pr.p.*, prophesy.

proph'et, *n.*, one who speaks forth as a preacher or inspired teacher; one who predicts.

proph'etess, *n.,* the fem. of prophet.

prophet'ic, *adj.,* pert. or rel. to prophecy and prophets; foretelling.

prophet'ical, *adj.,* i.q. prophetic.

prophet'ically, *adv.,* in a prophetic way.

prophylac'tic, *adj.,* protective; *n.,* a medicine for warding off a disease.

prophylax'is, *n.,* preventative treatment.

propin'quity, *n.,* nearness, adjacency.

propi'tiable, *adj.,* able to be propitiated.

propi'tiate, *v.t.,* to appease; to make favourable.

propi'tiated, *p.p.,* propitiate.

propi'tiating, *pr.p.,* propitiate.

propitia'tion, *n.,* atonement; conciliation.

propi'tiator, *n.,* one who propitiates.

propi'tiatory, *adj.,* pert. or rel. to propitiation.

propi'tious, *adj.,* favourable; auspicious.

propi'tiously, *adv.,* in a propitious way.

prop'-jet, *adj.,* having a turbine-driven propeller (of an aircraft).

pro'plasm, *n.,* a matrix.

prop'olis, *n.,* bee-glue.

propone', *v.t.,* i.q. propose.

propo'nent, *adj.,* proposing.

propor'tion, *n.,* the relation of a part to the whole; a comparative part; a share; *v.t.,* to make proportionate.

propor'tionable, *adj.,* able to be proportioned.

propor'tional, *adj.,* in proportion; pert. or rel. to proportion.

propor'tionalist, *n.,* pert. or rel. to proportional.

propor'tionally, *adv.,* in due proportion.

propor'tionate, *adj.,* in due proportion; according to a ratio.

propor'tionately, *adv.,* in proportion.

propor'tioned, *p.p.,* proportion.

propor'tioning, *pr.p.,* proportion.

propor'tionment, *n.,* the act of proportioning.

propo'sal, *n.,* an offer of something to be done, accepted or discussed; an offer of marriage.

propose', *v.i.,* to intend; to offer marriage; *v.t.,* to offer for acceptance, deliberation, etc. (Also *propone.*)

proposed', *p.p.,* propose.

propos'er, *n.,* one who proposes.

propos'ing, *pr.p.,* propose.

proposi'tion, *n.,* a proposed scheme; a subject offered for discussion; a judgment in words (logic); in mathematics, the statement of a problem or a theorem.

proposi'tional, *adj.,* pert. or rel. to a proposition.

propound', *v.t.,* to put forth for argument; to produce (a will).

propound'ed, *p.p.,* propound.

propound'er, *n.,* one who propounds.

propound'ing, *pr.p.,* propound.

propped, *p.p.,* prop.

prop'ping, *pr.p.,* prop.

proprae'tor, *n.,* a magistrate in ancient Rome.

propri'etary, *adj.,* pert. or rel. to a proprietor; *n.,* proprietorship.

propri'etor, *n.,* one with an exclusive right in anything; an owner.

propri'etorship, *n.,* ownership.

propri'etress, *n.,* a female proprietor.

propri'ety, *n.,* correctness, fitness.

pro-proc'tor, *n.,* a proctor's deputy.

propto'sis, *n.,* a prolapse (*path.*).

propul'sion, *n.,* the act or effect of propelling.

propul'sive, *adj.,* having propelling force.

propylae'um, *n.,* an entrance to a temple.

prop'ylite, *n.,* a kind of volcanic rock.

prop'ylon, *n.,* i.q. propylaeum.

pro ra'ta, Lat. phrase = proportionately.

pro'rate, *v.t.,* to distribute or assess at a proportionate rate.

pro'rated, *p.p.,* prorate.

pro'rating, *pr.p.,* prorate.

prorec'tor, *n.,* a rector's deputy.

prorec'torate, *n.,* the office of a prorector.

proroga'tion, *n.,* the act of proroguing; an adjournment.

prorogue', *v.t.,* to postpone or adjourn; to suspend (meetings of Parliament or Convocation).

prorogued', *p.p.,* prorogue.

prorogu'ing, *pr.p.,* prorogue.

prosa'ic, *adj.,* prosy; like prose; unromantic; everyday.

prosa'ical, *adj.,* i.q. prosaic.

prosa'ically, *adv.,* in a prosaic way.

pro'saism, *n.,* prose style.

pro'saist, *n.,* a prose writer; a prosy person.

prosce'nium, *n.,* a Greek stage, now the space in front of a drop scene in a theatre.

proscribe', *v.t.,* to condemn as outside the protection of the law; to denounce.

proscribed', *p.p.,* proscribe.

proscrib'er, *n.,* one who proscribes.

proscrib'ing, *pr.p.,* proscribe.

proscrip'tion, *n.,* the act of proscribing; outlawry.

proscrip'tive, *adj.,* pert. or rel. to proscription.

prose, *adj.,* non-metrical; *n.,* non-metrical writing or speech; *v.i.* and *t.,* to write dully.

prosec'tor, *n.,* one who dissects for the purpose of an anatomical demonstration by a lecturer.

pros'ecute, *v.t.,* to accuse; to take proceedings at law against; to follow up, to pursue.

pros'ecuted, *p.p.,* prosecute.

pros'ecuting, *pr.p.,* prosecute.

prosecu'tion, *n.,* the act of prosecuting; the prosecuting party at law.

pros'ecutor, *n.,* one who prosecutes.

pros'ecutrix, *n.,* the fem. of prosecutor.

prosed, *p.p.,* prose.

pros'elyte, *n.*, a new convert; *v.t.*, *i.q.* proselytize.

pros'elyted, *p.p.*, proselyte.

pros'elyting, *pr.p.*, proselyte.

pros'elytism, *n.*, the proselytizing spirit.

pros'elytize, *v.t.*, to endeavour to make converts.

pros'elytized, *p.p.*, proselytize.

pros'elytizing, *pr.p.*, proselytize.

prosen'chyma, *n.*, elongated cell tissue.

pro'ser, *n.*, a dull talker; a bore.

pros'ified, *p.p.*, prosify.

pros'ify, *v.t. and i.*, to turn into prose.

pros'ifying, *pr.p.*, prosify.

pro'sily, *adv.*, in a dull, prosy fashion.

pro'siness, *n.*, dulness; tediousness.

pro'sing, *pr.p.*, prose.

pros'it, *interj.*, a good wish used in drinking a person's health ("may it be to your benefit").

pro-sla'very, *n.*, the advocacy of slavery.

prosodi'acal, *adj.*, pert. or rel. to prosody.

proso'dial, *adj.*, *i.q.* prosodiacal.

proso'dian, *n.*, *i.q.* prosodist.

pros'odist, *n.*, an authority on prosody.

pros'ody, *n.*, the science of form in poetry.

prosopopoe'ia, *n.*, the introduction of a pretended speaker into a dialogue; personification.

prospect', *v.i.*, to give promise; *v.t.*, to survey a country for mining purposes.

pros'pect, *n.*, an outlook; a wide view; the future; promise.

prospec'ted, *p.p.*, prospect.

prospec'ting, *pr.p.*, prospect.

prospec'tion, *n.*, prudence; foresight.

prospec'tive, *adj.*, pert. or rel. to the future; expected.

prospec'tively, *adv.*, with reference to the future.

prospec'tor, *n.*, one who prospects.

prospec'tus, *n.*, a published statement of objects or of any undertaking.

pros'per, *v.i.*, to be successful; to do well; *v.t.*, to forward; to make successful.

pros'pered, *p.p.*, prosper.

pros'pering, *pr.p.*, prosper.

prosper'ity, *n.*, success; good fortune.

pros'perous, *adj.*, successful; thriving.

pros'perously, *adv.*, successfully.

pros'tate, *n.*, a large gland between the bladder and urethra.

prostat'ic, *adj.*, pert. or rel. to the prostate.

prostatit'is, *n.*, inflammation of the prostate gland.

pros'thesis, *n.*, the adding of a letter or letters to the beginning of a word.

prosthet'ic, *adj.*, pert. or rel. to prosthesis.

pros'titute, *n.*, a woman who offers sexual intercourse with herself for gain; *v.t.*, to use for wrong purposes; to debase.

pros'tituted, *p.p.*, prostitute.

pros'tituting, *pr.p.*, prostitute.

prostitu'tion, *n.*, the practice of prostituting in any sense.

pros'trate, *adj.*, prone; thrown down.

prostrate', *v.t.*, to throw down; to bring to ruin or exhaustion.

prostra'ted, *p.p.*, prostrate.

prostra'ting, *pr.p.*, prostrate.

prostra'tion, *n.*, the state of being prostrate.

pro'style, *n.*, a front portico.

pro'sy, *adj.*, dull, tedious.

prosyl'logism, *n.*, a syllogism proving a premise of another.

protag'onism, *n.*, support of a cause.

protag'onist, *n.*, the chief actor; a leader or champion; one who is active in support of a cause.

prot'asis, *n.*, an antecedent clause, usu. conditional, leading up to the apodosis.

protat'ic, *adj.*, introductory.

pro'tean, *adj.*, rapidly changing; assuming many forms.

protect', *v.t.*, to guard, to keep; to support.

protect'ed, *adj.*, guarded; *p.p.*, protect.

protect'ing, *pr.p.*, protect.

protec'tion, *n.*, the act of protecting; safety; the economic policy of protecting home industries against foreign competition.

protec'tionism, *n.*, an economic policy of protecting home industries.

protec'tionist, *n.*, one who favours protectionism.

protect'ive, *adj.*, sheltering; defensive; *n.*, something that protects; a condom.

protect'ively, *adv.*, in a protective way.

protect'or, *n.*, one who protects.

protect'oral, *adj.*, pert. or rel. to a protector.

protect'orate, *n.*, the office or jurisdiction of a protector; a region under the control of another country.

protecto'rial, *adj.*, *i.q.* protectoral.

protec'tory, *n.*, an institution for children.

pro'tégé, *n.*, a protected person (*Fr.*).

pro'tégée, *n.*, the fem. of protégé (*Fr.*).

pro'teid, *n.*, *i.q.* protein.

pro'teiform, *adj.*, very changeable in form.

pro'tein, *n.*, albuminoid (*chem.*).

proteis'tic, *adj.*, pert. or rel. to protein.

pro tem'pore, Lat. phrase = for the time being. Often written *pro tem*.

pro'test, *n.*, the utterance of an objection or disagreement; a strong declaration; a notary's certificate of a bill's having been refused for acceptance.

protest', *v.t. and i.*, to affirm solemnly; to make a protest.

Pro'testant, *adj.*, professing, or rel. to, Protestantism; *n.*, one who professes Protestantism.

Prot'estantism, *n.*, the

Protestant Christian religion.

protesta′tion, *n.*, a solemn declaration.

protest′ed, *p.p.*, protest.

protest′er, *n.*, one who protests.

protest′ing, *pr.p.*, protest.

protest′ingly, *adv.*, in the manner of one protesting.

Pro′teus, *n.*, a Greek sea-god; any person or thing that changes capriciously; a variety of bacteria; a tailed amphibian.

proth′esis, *n.*, in religious observance, the preparation for the offertory.

protho′rax, *n.*, the anterior section of the thorax.

protis′ta, *n. pl.*, creatures not like plants or animals.

pro′tium, *n.*, hydrogen (*chem.*).

pro′tocol, *n.*, the rough, original draft of a document, despatch, etc.; the recognized order of precedence and behaviour on formal occasions; *v.t.* and *i.*, to draw up in protocol.

pro′togine, *n.*, an Alpine granite.

protomar′tyr, *n.*, the first of the martyrs, St. Stephen.

pro′ton, *n.*, an elementary particle charged with positive electricity, forming part (or in hydrogen, the whole) of the nucleus of the atom.

proton′ic, *adj.*, pert. or rel. to proton.

protono′tary, *n.*, a chief clerk or notary.

pro′toplasm, *n.*, the chief substance found in animal and vegetable cells.

protoplas′mic, *adj.*, pert. or rel. to protoplasm.

pro′toplast, *n.*, the earliest created man.

protoplas′tic, *adj.*, pert. or rel. to protoplasm.

pro′totype, *n.*, the original type or model.

protox′ide, *n.*, an oxide in which there is only one atom of oxygen.

protox′idize, *v.t.*, to form a protoxide by combining oxygen.

protox′idized, *p.p.*, protoxidize.

protox′idizing, *pr.p.*, protoxidize.

Protozo′a, *n. pl.*, animals of the simplest form.

protozo′ic, *adj.*, pert. or rel. to Protozoa.

protozo′on, *n.*, the sing. of Protozoa.

protract′, *v.t.*, to lengthen out; to continue to great length.

protract′ed, *adj.*, prolonged; *p.p.*, protract.

protrac′tedly, *adv.*, in a protracted way.

protract′ile, *adj.*, able to be lengthened.

protract′ing, *pr.p.*, protract.

protrac′tion, *n.*, the act or effect of protracting.

protract′ive, *adj.*, causing protraction.

protract′or, *n.*, an angle-measuring instrument; a muscle so named.

protrude′, *v.t.* and *i.*, to thrust forward; to stick out.

protrud′ed, *p.p.*, protrude.

protrud′ing, *pr.p.*, protrude.

protru′sile, *adj.*, able to be thrust out.

protru′sion, *n.*, the act of protruding; a projection.

protru′sive, *adj.*, tending to protrude.

protru′sively, *adv.*, in a protrusive way.

protu′berance, *n.*, a bulging out; that which bulges out.

protu′berant, *adj.*, bulging out.

protu′berantly, *adv.*, in a protuberant way.

protu′berate, *v.i.*, to bulge out.

protu′berated, *p.p.*, protuberate.

protu′berating, *pr.p.*, protuberate.

prot′yle, *n.*, original undifferentiated matter (*chem.*).

proud, *adj.*, haughty; vain; over-valuing self; highly gratified; splendid; inflamed (of skin).

proud′er, *adj.*, *comp.* of proud.

proud′est, *adj.*, *super.* of proud.

proud′ly, *adv.*, with pride.

proud′ness, *n.*, the state of being proud; pride.

prov′able, *adj.*, capable of proof.

prov′ably, *adv.*, in a way that can be proved.

prove, *v.t.*, to test; to demonstrate; *v.i.*, to turn out to be.

proved, *p.p.*, prove.

proved′itor, *n.*, *i.q.* provedore.

provedore′, *n.*, a caterer; an officer of the Venetian Republic.

prov′en, *adj.*, proved; *p.p.*, prove.

prov′enance, *n.*, source, origin (esp. of documents and information).

Proven′çal, *adj.*, pert. or rel. to Provence; *n.*, a native of P. (*Fr.*)

prov′ender, *n.*, fodder.

proven′ience, *n.*, *i.q.* provenance.

prov′er, *n.*, one who proves.

prov′erb, *n.*, an adage; a saw; a short, wise saying in frequent use.

prover′bial, *adj.*, pert or rel. to proverbs; commonly known.

prover′bialism, *n.*, a proverbial expression.

prover′bially, *adv.*, notoriously; in the manner of proverbs.

prov′iant, *n.*, food supply (esp. army).

provide′, *v.t.*, to prepare for or against; to supply; to stipulate; to appoint.

provi′ded, *conj.*, on condition that; *p.p.*, provide.

prov′idence, *n.*, foresight; care; thriftiness; divine care.

prov′ident, *adj.*, foreseeing; thrifty.

providen′tial, *adj.*, pert. or rel. to divine care; lucky.

providen′tialism, *n.*, the belief in God′s providence.

providen′tially, *adv.*, in a providential way.

prov′idently, *adv.*, in a provident way.

provi′der, *n.*, one who provides.

provi′ding, *conj.*, on condition that; *pr.p.*, provide.

prov′ince, *n.*, originally foreign territory

under a Roman governor; a chief territorial division; a function; in pl. the country, not the capital.

provin'cial, *adj.*, pert. or rel. to a province; narrow, unpolished; *n.*, a dweller in the provinces; the ecclesiastical ruler of an order for a whole province.

provin'cialism, *n.*, the manners and speech of the provinces.

provincial'ity, *n.*, the manners and attitudes of a provincial.

provin'cially, *adv.*, in a provincial way.

prov'ing, *pr.p.*, prove.

provi'sion, *n.*, the providing for; the supply of anything; esp. in pl., the supply of food, drink, etc.; a clause in a Bill or legal statement; *v.t.*, to supply with food, etc.

provi'sional, *adj.*, temporary.

provi'sionally, *adv.*, temporarily.

provi'sioned, *p.p.*, provision.

provi'sioning, *n.*, the act of supplying provisions; *pr.p.*, provision.

provi'so, *n.*, a stipulation or limiting clause.

provi'sor, *n.*, the holder of a provision; a vicar-general.

provi'sory, *adj.*, conditional.

provoca'tion, *n.*, the act of provoking; irritation goading into a reaction.

provoc'ative, *adj.*, challenging, irritating; designed to produce a reaction.

provoc'atively, *adv.*, in a provocative way.

provoc'ator, *n.*, one who provokes or challenges.

provok'able, *adj.*, easy to provoke.

provoke', *v.t.*, to challenge; to instigate; to irritate; to cause to goad into reaction.

provoked', *p.p.*, provoke.

provo'ker, *n.*, one who provokes.

provo'king, *adj.*, irritating; *pr.p.*, provoke.

provo'kingly, *adv.*, in a provoking way.

prov'ost, *n.*, the title of the head of certain colleges, Scottish cathedrals and municipal corporations.

prow, *n.*, the front part of a ship's stem.

prow'ess, *n.*, bravery, gallantry.

prowl, *v.i.*, to go about for prey; to wander about aimlessly.

prowled, *p.p.*, prowl.

prowl'er, *n.*, one who, or that which, prowls.

prowl'ing, *pr.p.*, prowl.

prox'imal, *adj.*, in biology, situated near the middle of the body or point of attachment.

prox'imate, *adj.*, nearest in time, place, etc.

prox'imately, *adv.*, very nearly or closely.

proxim'ity, *n.*, nearness.

prox'imo, *adv.*, in the next month (*obs.*).

prox'y, *n.*, an agency; a deputy.

prude, *n.*, an excessively proper person in speech and manners.

pru'dence, *n.*, foresight; sagacity; caution.

pru'dent, *adj.*, sagacious; foreseeing; cautious.

pruden'tial, *adj.*, showing prudence or sagacity.

pruden'tially, *adv.*, in a prudent way.

pru'dently, *adv.*, with prudence.

pru'dery, *n.*, the quality of a prude.

pru'dish, *adj.*, like a prude.

pru'dishly, *adv.*, in a prudish way.

pru'dishness, *n.*, *i.q.* prudery.

pru'inose, *adj.*, frost-like.

prune, *n.*, a dried plum; the colour of a prune; *v.t.*, to trim (trees, etc.); to remove anything superfluous.

pruned, *p.p.*, prune.

prunell'a, *n.*, strong silk or worsted cloth formerly used for barristers' gowns, etc.; a febrile disease of the throat.

prunel'lo, *n.*, a choice sort of prune.

pru'ner, *n.*, one who, or that which, prunes.

prunif'erous, *adj.*, plum-bearing.

pru'ning, *pr.p.*, prune.

pru'ning-hook, *n.*, an instrument for pruning.

prunt, *n.*, ornamental glass; a tool for making this.

pru'rience, *n.*, a curiosity about lewd things.

pru'riency, *n.*, *i.q.* prurience.

pru'rient, *adj.*, curious about lewd things.

pru'riently, *adv.*, in a prurient way.

prurig'inous, *adj.*, pert. or rel. to prurigo.

pruri'go, *n.*, itching.

Prus'sian, *adj.*, rel. to Prussia; *n.*, a native of P.

Prus'sianism, *n.*, the spirit of Prussia; military arrogance.

prus'siate, *n.*, a cyanide.

prus'sic, *adj.*, obtained from Prussian blue.

pry, *v.i.*, to look curiously and discourteously into.

pry'ing, *pr.p.*, pry.

pry'ingly, *adv.*, in a prying way.

prytane'um, *n.*, a Greek town hall.

pryt'anis, *n.*, the president of an ancient Greek State; one of the members of the Senate.

pryt'any, *n.*, presidency.

psalm, *n.*, a song to the music of the harp; a sacred song.

psalm'-book, *n.*, a book containing psalms and hymns.

psalm'ist, *n.*, a writer of psalms.

psalmod'ic, *adj.*, pert. or rel. to psalmody.

psalm'odist, *n.*, *i.q.* psalmist.

psalm'ody, *n.*, the art or practice of psalm-singing.

psalt'er, *n.*, a book of psalms; the Book of Psalms.

psalt'ery, *n.*, an ancient, musical, stringed instrument.

pseph'ism, *n.*, decree by vote (*Gr.*).

psephol'ogist, *n.*, one who studies psephology.

psephol'ogy, *n.*, the study of elections and voting. (Also *psyphology*.)

pseud'echis, *n.*, a kind of venomous snake.

pseu'do, *prefix* = false; seeming.

pseu'dograph, *n.*, a forgery.

pseudog'raphy, *n.*, false writing.

pseudol'oger, *n.*, a systematic liar.

pseudol'ogist, *n.*, a liar.

pseudol'ogy, *n.*, lying.

pseud'omorph, *n.*, a mineral deceptively like another mineral.

pseudomor'phous, *adj.*, pert. or rel. to a pseudomorph.

pseud'onym, *n.*, an assumed or false name.

pseudon'ymous, *adj.*, under a pseudonym.

pseudon'ymously, *adv.*, in a pseudonymous way.

pseud'oscope, *n.*, an optical instrument which makes the convex appear concave or the concave appear convex.

pseudoscop'ic, *adj.*, pert. or rel. to a pseudoscope.

pshaw, *interj.*, expressing impatience or contempt.

psilan'thropism, *n.*, the doctrine that Christ was only a man.

psilan'thropist, *n.*, one who affirms the humanity of Christ.

psilos'is, *n.*, a stripping bare.

psitt'acine, *adj.*, parrotlike; pert. or rel. to parrots.

psittacos'is, *n.*, a disease of parrots able to be caught by humans.

pso'ra, *n.*, the itch.

psori'asis, *n.*, an irritating skin disease.

psor'ic, *adj.*, pert. or rel. to psora.

Psych'e, *n.*, a genus of moths.

psych'e, *n.*, the soul, mind or spirit.

psychiat'ric, *adj.*, pert. or rel. to mental illness.

psychi'atrist, *n.*, a specialist in psychiatry.

psychi'atry, *n.*, the treatment of mental illness.

psych'ic, *adj.*, pert. or rel. to the mind.

psych'ical, *adj.*, i.q. psychic.

psycho'-an'alyse, *v.t.*, to investigate the mental processes.

psycho'-anal'ysis, *n.*, an investigation into the mental processes.

psycho'-an'alyst, *n.*, one who practises psychoanalysis.

psy'chogram, *n.*, writing supposed to come from the spirit world.

psy'chograph, *n.*, an instrument for spiritwriting.

psychog'raphy, *n.*, spiritwriting.

psycholog'ic, *adj.*, pert. or rel. to psychology.

psycholog'ical, *adj.*, i.q. psychologic.

psycholog'ically, *adv.*, in a psychological way.

psychol'ogist, *n.*, a student of psychology.

psychol'ogy, *n.*, the study of the human mind and behaviour.

psy'chopath, *n.*, a mentally deranged person.

psychop'athist, *n.*, one who treats mental illness.

psycho'sis, *n.*, mental or nervous derangement.

psychothcrapeut'ics, *n. pl.*, i.q. psychotherapy.

psychother'apist, *n.*, one who practises psychotherapy.

psychothe'rapy, *n.*, the treatment for mental disease by hypnosis.

psycho'tropic, *adj.*, affecting the state of mind.

psychrom'eter, *n.*, a thermometer with a wet and a dry bulb.

psychrom'etry, *n.*, the measurement of the air's humidity.

psychol'ogy, *n.*, i.q. psephology.

ptar'migan, *n.*, a type of grouse.

pteridol'ogist, *n.*, one who studies ferns.

pteridol'ogy, *n.*, the study of ferns.

pter'o, a *prefix* denoting wing, plume.

pterodac'tyl, *n.*, an extinct winged creature.

pter'opod, *n.*, having feet expanded into lobes like wings; *n.*, a creature so formed.

pter'opus, *n.*, the flying fox.

pter'ygoid, *adj.*, wing shaped.

ptis'an, *n.*, a decoction such as barley-water; a weak drink for a sick person. (Also *tisane.*)

Ptolema'ic, *adj.*, pert. or rel. to Ptolemy (the Alexandrian astronomer) and his system.

pto'maine, *n.*, a poison resulting from putrefaction.

ptos'is, *n.*, a drooping of the upper eyelid.

pty'alin, *n.*, a constituent of saliva.

pty'alism, *n.*, salivation.

pu'berty, *n.*, the age at which sexual and adult characteristics develop.

pubesc'ence, *n.*, the state of being pubescent.

pubesc'ent, *adj.*, arriving at puberty; covered with down.

pu'bic, *adj.*, pert. or rel. to the pelvic area.

pub'lic, *adj.*, pert. or rel. to the people; open to all; *n.*, the collective people; a public-house.

pub'lican, *n.*, a Roman farmer of taxes; a public-house keeper.

publica'tion, *n.*, the act of publishing; something published.

public-house, *n.*, a house of entertainment where refreshments, particularly alcoholic drinks, are served.

pub'licist, *n.*, one acquainted with international law; a newspaper writer; a person who acts to make a topic better known.

public'ity, *n.*, the state of being made public; advertising; the propagation of information.

pub'licize, *v.t.*, to make public.

pub'licized, *p.p.*, publicize.

pub'licizing, *pr.p.*, publicize.

pub'licly, *adv.*, in a public way.

pub'lic-relations, *n. pl.*, relations with the general public.

pub'lic-spirited, *adj.*, animated by zeal for the common welfare.

pub'lish, *v.t.*, to make openly known; to proclaim; to circulate; to issue (books, newspapers, etc.) for sale or free distribution.

pub'lishable, *adj.*, able to be published.

pub'lished, *p.p.*, publish.

pub'lisher, *n.*, one who publishes, esp. books.

pub'lishing, *n.*, a publisher's business; *pr.p.*, publish.

puccoon', *n.*, a N. American plant yielding red or orange dye.

puce, *adj.*, of purplish brown colour.

puck, *n.*, any hobgoblin, esp. Robin Goodfellow; a rubber disc used in ice-hockey.

puck'a, *adj.*, best of its kind, excellent, genuine. (Also *pukka*.)

puck'er, *n.*, a wrinkling or contraction; *v.t.* and *i.*, to contract into wrinkles.

puck'ered, *p.p.*, pucker.

puck'ering, *n.*, a wrinkling; *pr.p.*, pucker.

puck'ery, *adj.*, wrinkled; astringent.

puck'ish, *adj.*, impish.

pud, *n.*, a child's hand; the forefoot of some animals.

pud'der, *n.*, bother; *v.t.* and *i.*, to bother.

pud'dered, *p.p.*, pudder.

pud'dering, *pr.p.*, pudder.

pud'ding, *n.*, an edible mixture of various ingredients, sometimes enclosed in a soft paste, or a skin.

pud'ding-stone, *n.*, a composite rock containing rounded pebbles.

pud'dingy, *adj.*, like pudding.

pud'dle, *n.*, a little, dirty pool; a mess; puddled clay for lining embankments; *v.i.*, to dabble; *v.t.*, to make into wrought iron.

pud'dled, *p.p.*, puddle.

pud'dler, *n.*, one who puddles; a worker at puddling.

pud'dling, *n.*, the work of making molten iron malleable; *pr.p.*, puddle.

pud'dly, *adv.*, full of puddles.

pu'dency, *n.*, modesty.

puden'dal, *adj.*, pert. or rel. to the pudenda.

puden'dum, *n.*, the sexual organ; *pl.*, pudenda (*Lat.*).

pu'dent, *adj.*, modest.

pudge, *n.*, a stumpy person, animal or thing.

pud'ic, *adj.*, *i.q.* pudendal.

pudic'ity, *n.*, chasteness; delicacy.

pud'sy, *adj.*, plump.

pue'blo, *n.*, a Spanish town or village.

pu'erile, *adj.*, boyish, silly.

pueril'ity, *n.*, boyishness; silliness.

puer'peral, *adj.*, pert. or rel. to childbirth.

puer'perous, *adj.*, parturient.

puff, *n.*, a short breath or pant; a piece of advertisement; something fluffy; a light pastry; *v.i.*, to emit short breaths; to swell; *v.t.*, to blow out; to inflate; to praise excessively; to smoke (a pipe, etc.).

puff'-adder, *n.*, a poisonous snake.

puff'-ball, *n.*, a ball-shaped fungus.

puffed, *p.p.*, puff.

puff'er, *n.*, an advertiser; a kind of fish.

puff'ery, *n.*, advertising.

puff'et, *n.*, a kind of light pastry.

puf'fily, *adv.*, in a puffy manner.

puff'in, *n.*, a N. Atlantic sea-bird.

puff'iness, *n.*, the state of being puffy.

puff'ing, *pr.p.*, puff.

puff'y, *adj.*, gusty; inflated; panting; inflamed.

pug, *n.*, a pug-dog; a goblin; clay worked with water; the footprint of a beast; the abbrev. for pugilist (*slang*); *v.t.*, to puddle (clay); to deaden (sound).

pug'-dog, *n.*, a breed of dog with a short, snub nose.

pugged, *p.p.*, pug.

pug'ging, *pr.p.*, pug.

pug'g(a)ree, *n.*, a turban; a muslin scarf wound round a hat.

pu'gil, *n.*, a boxer (*Lat.*).

pu'gilism, *n.*, the practice of boxing.

pu'gilist, *n.*, a boxer; a prizefighter.

pugilis'tic, *adj.*, pert. or rel. to boxing.

pug'-mill, *n.*, a mill for brickmaking from clay.

pugna'cious, *adj.*, fond of fighting; aggressive.

pugna'ciously, *adv.*, in a pugnacious way.

pugnac'ity, *n.*, a readiness to fight.

pug'-nose, *n.*, a snub nose.

pug'nosed, *adj.*, having a pug-nose.

puis'ne, *adj.*, junior; subsequent; *n.*, a junior or inferior judge.

pu'issance, *n.*, power, influence.

pu'issant, *adj.*, powerful; influential.

pu'issantly, *adv.*, powerfully.

pu'ja, *n.*, Hindu religious rites.

puke, *v.i.* and *t.*, to vomit.

puked, *p.p.*, puke.

pu'king, *pr.p.*, puke.

pukk'a, *adj.*, *i.q.* pucka.

pul'chritude, *n.*, beauty, grace.

pule, *v.i.*, to whine feebly.

puled, *p.p.*, pule.

pu'ler, *n.*, a weakling.

pu'ling, *n.*, a feeble cry; *pr.p.*, pule.

pul'kha, *n.*, a Lapland sledge.

pull, *n.*, the act of pulling; a tug; something pulled; the act of rowing; a printer's proof; *v.i.*, to row; to drag; *v.t.*, to draw; to drag; to extract; to sunder; to row; to take off a printer's proof.

pull'-back, *n.*, a restraint; a drawback.

pulled, *p.p.*, pull.

pull'er, *n.*, one who, or that which, pulls.

pull'et, *n.*, a young hen.

pull'ey, *n.*, a wheel grooved for a cord or chain to pass over.

pull'-in, *n.*, a stopping place; a refreshment house.

pull'ing, *pr.p.*, pull.

pull'man-car, *n.*, a saloon car.

pull'-out, *n.*, a page that unfolds.

pull'over, *n.*, a sweater, a woollen jersey.

pull'ulate, *v.i.*, to sprout; to develop.

pull'ulated, *p.p.*, pullulate.

pull'ulating, *pr.p.*, pullulate.

pullula'tion, *n.*, sprouting, germination.

pul'monary, *adj.*, pert. or rel. to the lungs.

pul'monate, *adj.*, subject to, or affected by, lung disease.

pulmon'ic, *adj.*, *i.q.* pulmonary.

pul'motor, *n.*, an appliance used in artificial respiration.

pulp, *n.*, a soft, moist mass; *v.i.*, to turn to pulp; *v.t.*, to reduce to pulp; to remove pulp.

pulped, *p.p.*, pulp.

pulp'iness, *n.*, the state or quality of being pulpy.

pulp'ing, *pr.p.*, pulp.

pul'pit, *n.*, a raised platform for preaching; a protective rail at the prow of a boat.

pulpiteer', *n.*, a preacher, *v.i.*, to preach.

pulpiteer'ing, *n.*, preaching; *pr.p.*, pulpiteer.

pul'pitum, *n.*, a double choir-screen with a gallery over the intervening space.

pulp'y, *adj.*, consisting of pulp.

pulque, *n.*, a Mexican drink.

puls'ate, *v.i.*, to beat or move rhythmically.

puls'ated, *p.p.*, pulsate.

puls'atile, *adj.*, able to pulsate; actuated by percussion.

pulsatill'a, *n.*, the pasque flower.

pulsa'ting, *pr.p.*, pulsate.

pulsa'tion, *n.*, the act of pulsating.

puls'ative, *adj.*, pulsating; causing pulsation.

puls'atory, *adj.*, pert. or rel. to pulsation; throbbing.

pulse, *n.*, the rhythmic beating of arteries; any rhythmical repetition; the edible seeds of legumens; *v.i.*, to beat in rhythm.

pulsed, *p.p.*, pulse.

pulse'less, *adj.*, without a pulse.

pulsif'ic, *adj.*, causing pulsation.

pulsim'eter, *n.*, an apparatus for measuring pulsations.

puls'ing, *pr.p.*, pulse.

pulsom'eter, *n.*, a vacuum pump.

pulta'ceous, *adj.*, pappy, pulpy.

pulv'erable, *adj.*, able to be pulverized.

pulvera'ceous, *adj.*, with a powdery surface.

pulv'erine, *n.*, ashes from the alkaline marine plant, barilla.

pulveriza'tion, *n.*, the act or effect of pulverizing.

pulv'erize, *v.t.*, to reduce to powder or spray; to demolish.

pulv'erized, *p.p.*, pulverize.

pulv'erizer, *n.*, anything that pulverizes.

pulv'erizing, *pr.p.*, pulverize.

pulv'erous, *adj.*, dusty; dust-like.

pulver'ulent, *adj.*, powdery; powdered.

pulv'inated, *adj.*, swelling out like a cushion.

pulv'is, *n.*, dust (*Lat.*).

pu'ma, *n.*, a large American carnivore.

pum'ice, *n.*, a light lava, used for cleaning or polishing; *v.t.*, to clean with pumice.

pum'mel, *v.t.*, *i.q.* pommel.

pum'melled, *p.p.*, pummel.

pum'melling, *n.*, the act of pummelling; *pr.p.*, pummel.

pump, *v.t.*, to draw up with a pump; to pour forth; to question for information, *n.*, a machine for raising water and for shifting or compressing gases or liquids; a light shoe.

pump'age, *n.*, the amount of water lifted by a pump.

pumped, *p.p.*, pump.

pump'er, *n.*, one who, or that which, pumps.

pump'ernickel, *n.*, rye bread.

pump'-handle, *n.*, the handle of a pump; *v.t.*, to shake another's hand vigorously.

pump'ing, *pr.p.*, pump.

pump'ion, *n.*, *i.q.* pumpkin.

pump'kin, *n.*, a trailing plant, and its large, round, yellow fruit.

pump'-room, *n.*, a building where a pump is worked; a room at a spa where medicinal water is drunk.

pun, *n.*, a play on words; paronomasia; *v.i.*, to

play on words; *v.t.*, to ram.

pu'na, *n.*, a high plateau in the Andes.

punch, *n.*, a blow with the fist; a tool for perforating, etc.; a hot beverage with mixed ingredients; a variety of draught horse; *v.t.*, to hit with the fist; to pierce a hole.

punch'-card, *n.*, a card pierced with holes to record information.

punch'-drunk, *adj.*, dazed from repeated punching.

punched, *p.p.*, punch.

punch'eon, *n.*, a large cask; a prop in a coal mine.

punch'er, *n.*, one who, or that which, punches.

punchinel'lo, *n.*, the principal character in a puppet-show; Punch (the prototype puppet) (*It.*).

punch'ing, *pr.p.*, punch.

punch'-up, *n.*, a fight with fists.

punct'ate, *adj.*, having points or dots.

punct'ated, *adj.*, *i.q.* punctate.

punct'iform, *adj.*, like a point or dot.

punctil'io, *n.*, a fine point of ceremony or behaviour.

punctil'ious, *adj.*, scrupulously exact in conduct.

punctil'iously, *adv.*, in a punctilious way.

punctil'iousness, *n.*, the state of being punctilious.

punct'ual, *adj.*, exact in point of time; pert. or rel. to a punctum or point.

punctual'ity, *n.*, the quality of always being on time.

punct'ually, *adv.*, to the precise moment.

punct'uate, *v.t.*, to mark with the necessary stops or points; to emphasize.

punct'uated, *p.p.*, punctuate.

punct'uating, *pr.p.*, punctuate.

punctua'tion, *n.*, the act of punctuating; the insertion of stops or points.

punct'uator, *n.*, one skilled in punctuating.

punc'tum, *n.*, a dot or spot; a depression (*Lat.*).

punct'ure, *n.*, a prick; a hole made by a prick; *v.t.* and *i.*, to pierce; to make a hole.

punct'ured, *p.p.*, puncture.

punct'uring, *pr.p.*, puncture.

pun'dit, *n.*, a Brahmin scholar; a learned person.

pung, *n.*, a low, one-horse sled.

pun'gence, *n.*, the quality of being pungent.

pun'gency, *n.*, *i.q.* pungence.

pun'gent, *adj.*, pointed; biting; caustic; exciting to the taste, smell, etc.

pun'gently, *adv.*, in a pungent way.

Pu'nic, *adj.*, Carthaginian.

pu'nier, *adj.*, *comp.* of puny.

pu'niest, *adj.*, *super.* of puny.

pu'niness, *n.*, smallness; weakness.

pun'ish, *v.t.*, to chastise; to impose a penalty on; to strike with severe blows.

pun'ishable, *adj.*, that can, or ought to be, punished.

pun'ished, *p.p.*, punish.

pun'isher, *n.*, one who punishes.

pun'ishing, *pr.p.*, punish.

pun'ishment, *n.*, the act or effect of punishing.

pu'nitive, *adj.*, of the nature, or with the purpose of, punishment.

pu'nitory, *adj.*, *i.q.* punitive.

punk, *adj.*, worthless (*colloq.*); *n.*, rotting wood used for tinder; rubbish; a prostitute (*colloq.*).

pun'ka(h), *n.*, an E. Indian fan; an arrangement for keeping a place cool.

punned, *p.p.*, pun.

pun'ner, *n.*, a ramming implement.

pun'net, *n.*, a small fruit-basket.

pun'ning, *n.*, the practice of making puns; *pr.p.*, pun.

pun'ster, *n.*, a maker of puns.

punt, *n.*, a flat-bottomed, square-ended boat, propelled by poling or paddling; *v.i.*, to gamble; *v.t.* and *i.*, to propel a punt; to kick a dropping football.

punt'er, *n.*, one who punts; a gambler.

punt'ing, *n.*, the art or practice of propelling a punt.

pun'ty, *n.*, a glass-blowing tool.

pu'ny, *adj.*, undersized, feeble.

pup, *n.*, a whelp; *v.i.*, to bring forth.

pu'pa, *n.*, a chrysalis.

pu'pate, *v.i.*, to become a pupa.

pu'pil, *n.*, a young scholar; a minor under a guardian; the central part of an eye.

pu'pilage, *n.*, the condition of being a pupil.

pu'pil(l)ary, *adj.*, pert. or rel. to a pupil.

pupip'arous, *adj.*, bringing forth in the pupa state.

pupiv'orous, *adj.*, feeding on pupae.

pupped, *p.p.*, pup.

pup'pet, *n.*, a small figure moved by wires; one whose actions, etc., are controlled by another.

pup'petry, *n.*, the craft of operating puppets.

pup'pet-show, *n.*, a dramatic exhibition of puppets.

pup'ping, *pr.p.*, pup.

pup'py, *n.*, *dim.* of pup; a coxcomb.

pura'na, *n.*, one of the sacred Sanskrit poems.

puran'ic, *adj.*, pert. or rel. to puranas.

pur'beck, *n.*, hard limestone.

pur'blind, *adj.*, partially blind.

pur'chasable, *adj.*, for sale.

pur'chase, *n.*, buying; something bought; leverage; *v.t.*, to buy; gain or acquire; to haul up.

pur'chased, *p.p.*, purchase.

pur'chase-money, *n.*, payment for property acquired.

pur'chaser, *n.*, a buyer.

pur'chasing, *pr.p.*, purchase.

pur'chase-tax, *n.*, a tax levied on the wholesale price of goods.

pur'dah, *n.*, a curtain (used in India) to hide women from sight; the state of being cut off from other people.

pure, *adj.*, unadulterated, clean, simple, sheer.

pur'ée, *n.*, mashed meat and vegetables, etc., pulped and sieved (*Fr.*).

pure'ly, *adv.*, in a pure way; absolutely, simply.

pure'ness, *n.*, the state of being pure.

pur'er, *adj.*, *comp.* of pure.

pur'est, *adj.*, *super.* of pure.

pur'fle, *n.*, an ornament on the edge; *v.t.*, to embroider or adorn the edge of; to beautify.

purga'tion, *n.*, the act of purging or cleansing; the old method of clearing oneself by ordeal or sworn word.

pur'gative, *adj.*, having a purging quality; *n.*, a purging draught.

purgato'rial, *adj.*, pert. or rel. to purgatory.

pur'gatory, *adj.*, cleansing; *n.*, the place where departed souls are freed from sin.

purge, *n.*, a cathartic medicine; *v.t.*, to make clean; to clear out cathartically.

purged, *p.p.*, purge.

pur'ger, *n.*, one who, or that which, purges.

pur'ging, *n.*, diarrhoea; *pr p.*, purge.

purifica'tion, *n.*, the act of purifying; ritual cleansing.

pur'ificative, *adj.*, producing purification.

pur'ificator, *n.*, a napkin used by the celebrant at Mass.

pur'ificatory, *adj.*, *i.q.* purificative.

pur'ified, *p.p.*, purify.

pur'ifier, *n.*, one who, or that which, purifies.

pur'iform, *adj.*, like pus.

pur'ify, *v.t.*, to make pure; to cleanse.

pur'ifying, *pr.p.*, purify.

Pur'im, *n.*, an annual Jewish festival in

memory of the failure of Haman's attempt to massacre the Jews.

pur'ism, *n.*, the pedantic insistence on purity of language.

pur'ist, *n.*, an advocate of purism.

Pur'itan, *adj.*, pert. or rel. to Puritans and Puritanism; *n.*, one of the 16th and 17th cent. professors of pure religion as they conceived it.

puritan'ic, *adj.*, pert. or rel. to the Puritans; strait-laced.

puritan'ical, *adj.*, *i.q.* puritanic.

Pur'itanism, *n.*, the principles of the Puritans.

pur'ity, *n.*, cleanness, pureness.

purl, *n.*, an embroidered edge; a backward stitch; a rippling sound; hot beer with sundry ingredients; a fall (*colloq.*); *v.i.*, to make a rippling sound; to upset; *v.t.*, to purfle.

purled, *p.p.*, purl.

purl'er, *n.* a violent fall (*colloq.*).

pur'lieu, *n.*, outskirts (usually in pl.).

pur'lin, *n.*, a horizontal roof timber supporting rafters or boards.

purl'ing, *pr.p.*, purl.

purloin', *v.t.*, to pilfer.

purloined', *p.p.*, purloin.

purloin'er, *n.*, one who pilfers.

purloin'ing, *pr.p.*, purloin.

purpar'ty, *n.*, a share (*leg.*).

pur'ple, *adj.*, of purple colour; *n.*, a colour mixed of red and blue in various proportions; (formerly) crimson. Because emperors, kings, cardinals affected purple robes, the word *purple* stands for their rank; *v.t.*, to make purple.

pur'pled, *p.p.*, purple.

pur'ples, *n. pl.*, a disease of wheat.

pur'pling, *pr.p.*, purple.

pur'plish, *adj.*, inclining to purple.

purpoint, *n.*, a stuffed and quilted doublet.

purport', *v.t.*, to mean, to signify.

pur'port, *n.*, meaning, signification.

purport'ed, *p.p.*, purport.

purport'ing, *pr.p.*, purport.

pur'pose, *n.*, an intention; an object; *v.t.* and *i.*, to intend, to design.

pur'posed, *p.p.*, purpose.

pur'poseful, *adj.*, full of determination.

pur'posefully, *adv.*, in a purposeful way.

pur'poseless, *adj.*, without any object.

pur'posely, *adv.*, with intention.

pur'poser, *n.*, one who purposes.

pur'posing, *pr.p.*, purpose.

pur'posive, *adj.*, directed towards an end.

purpres'ture, *n.*, an encroachment on the highway.

pur'pura, *n.*, a disease indicated by purple spots on the skin.

pur'pure, *n.*, purple (*her.*).

purpu'real, *adj.*, purple.

purpur'ic, *adj.*, pert. or rel. to purpura.

pur'purin, *n.*, red colouring matter.

purr, *n.*, the sound a cat makes when pleased; *v.i.*, to make the sound of purring; *v.t.*, to speak words as if purring; to run smoothly (of a motor); to show contentment.

purred, *p.p.*, purr.

pur'ree, *n.*, yellow colouring matter.

pur'ring, *n.*, the act of purring; *pr.p.*, purr.

purse, *n.*, a pouch or bag for money; *v.t.* and *i.*, to contract, to wrinkle.

pursed, *p.p.*, purse.

purse'ful, *n.*, the contents of a full purse.

purse'-net, *n.*, a net with a mouth closing like a purse.

purse'-pride, *n.*, the pride of wealth.

purse'-proud, *adj.*, proud of one's wealth.

purs'er, *n.*, a ship's officer with charge of the accounts and provisions.

purse-strings, *n.*, the strings of an old-fashioned purse; the control of expenditure.

purs'ing, *pr.p.* purse.

purs'lane, *n.* a succulent pot-herb.

pursu'able, *adj.* able to be pursued.

pursu'al, *n.* pursuit.

pursu'ance, *n.* the act of pursuing or following out.

pursu'ant, *adj.*, following out; *adv.*, in consequence.

pursue', *v.i.*, to continue; *v.t.*, to follow up; to chase or hunt; to seek; to prosecute (*Scots law*).

pursued', *p.p.*, pursue.

pursu'er, *n.*, one who pursues; a prosecutor.

pursu'ing, *pr.p.*, pursue.

pursuit', *n.*, the act of pursuing; an occupation or recreation.

pur'suivant, *n.*, an attendant; an official at the Heralds' College, next in rank to the heralds.

purs'y, *adj.*, fat and short of breath; puckered.

pur'tenance, *n.*, an appendage; something accessory to the principal thing.

pur'ulence, *n.*, suppuration.

pur'ulency, *n.*, *i.q.* purulence.

pur'ulent, *adj.*, suppurating.

purvey', *v.t.*, to provide; to supply.

purvey'ance, *n.*, supply; the act of purveying; the state's right to demand supplies.

purveyed', *p.p.*, purvey.

purvey'ing, *pr.p.*, purvey.

purvey'or, *n.*, one who purveys; a supplier of provisions on a large scale.

pur'view, *n.*, purport, scope; visual range; the active parts of a statute as distinct from defining clauses.

pus, *n.*, morbid suppurating matter.

Pu'seyism, *n.*, a polemical term denoting the principles of the Tractarians.

Pu'seyite, n., a Tractarian; a disciple of Dr. E. B. Pusey.

push, n., a thrust; an advance; additional effort; self-interested activity; v.i., to be pushing for one's own ends; v.t., to thrust; to cause to move away; to advance; to distribute.

push-bike, n., a bicycle operated by pedals.

pushed, p.p., push.

push'er, n., one who pushes (in any sense).

push'ful, adj., bent on getting on (slang).

push'fulness, n., determination; self assertiveness.

push'ing, adj., pushful; pr.p., push.

push'over, n., a simple task.

Push'too (tu), n., the Afghan language.

pusillanim'ity, n., faintheartedness; poorspiritedness.

pusillan'imous, adj., poor-spirited; fainthearted.

puss, n., a cat; a hare; a girl (colloq.).

pus'sy, n., a cat.

pussyfoot, n., a prohibitionist; v.i., to move or act cautiously.

pus'tular, adj., pert. or rel. to pustules.

pus'tulate, adj., having pustules.

pus'tulate, v.i. and t., to form pustules.

pus'tulated, p.p., pustulate.

pus'tulating, pr.p., pustulate.

pustula'tion, n., the formation of pustules.

pus'tule, n., a pimple; excrescence.

pus'tulous, adj., i.q. pustulate.

put, n., a cast or throw; v.t. and i., to lay; to set; to place; to propose (an argument); to start; p.p., put.

putt, n., the shot for the hole (in golf); v.t. and i., to send a golf ball towards the putting-hole using a putter.

puta'men, n., the shell of the stone of a fruit.

pu'tative, adj., reputed; imagined; hypothetically intended.

pu'teal, n., the fencing of a well.

pu'tid, adj., stinking.

put'log, n., one of the short timbers supporting a scaffold.

put'-off, n., an evasive excuse; a delay.

putrefac'tion, n., the process of putrefying.

putrefac'tive, adj., putrefying.

pu'trefied, p.p., putrefy.

pu'trefy, v.i., to become putrid; v.t., to make putrid; to cause to decay.

pu'trefying, pr.p., putrefy.

putres'cence, n., the process of rotting.

putres'cent, adj., in a rotting state.

putres'cible, adj., liable to becoming rotten.

pu'trid, adj., rotten; stinking.

putrid'ity, n., the state or quality of being putrid.

putsch, n., a resolute attack; a rising; a revolt.

put'ted, p.p., putt.

put'tee, n., (usu. in pl.), a strip of cloth wound round and round the leg.

put'ter, n., a golf-club used for putting.

put'tied, p.p., putty.

put'ting, pr.p., putt.

put'ting, pr.p., put.

put'ting-green, n., a small golf green on which the entire game consists of putting.

putt'oo, n., patterned fabric from Cashmere.

put'ty, n., a plaster for fixing glass, polishing jewels, or stopping cracks; v.t., to fasten with putty.

put'tying, pr.p., putty.

put'up', adj., pre-arranged with intention to deceive.

puy, n., a small volcanic cone (Fr.).

puz'zle, n., a thing difficult to understand; an enigma; a toy, the object of which is to solve a problem; v.i., to try to solve; v.t., to perplex, mystify.

puz'zled, p.p., puzzle.

puz'zledom, n., bewilderment.

puz'zle-headed, adj., bewildered; stupid.

puz'zler, n., that which puzzles.

puz'zling, adj., bewildering; pr.p., puzzle.

puz'zlingly, adv., in a puzzling way.

puzzola'no, n., volcanic ash from Pozzuoli in Italy, used for making mortar.

pyae'mia, n., blood-poisoning.

pyc'nite, n., a variety of topaz.

pyc'nostyle, adj., having pillars set closely; n., a close arrangement of pillars.

pye, n., a magpie.

pye'dog, n., an ownerless mongrel of the East.

py'garg, n., the osprey.

pygm(a)e'an, adj., pert. or rel. to pygmies; dwarfish.

pyg'my, adj., diminutive, dwarfish; n., one of the race of small people called pygmies; any dwarf. (Also pigmy.)

pyja'mas, n., loose trousers; a sleeping-suit. (Also pajamas.)

pyk'nic, n., a short, thick-necked corpulent person.

pyl'on, n., a lofty, tapering structure carrying overhead cables; a gateway flanked big towers as in Egyptian temples; a guiding stake at an airfield.

pylo'ric, adj., pert. or rel. to the pylorus.

pylo'rus, n., the opening from the stomach to the smaller intestine (anat.).

pyonephrit'is, n., inflammation of the kidney (med.).

pyorrhoe'a, n., a disease of the gums.

py'racanth, n., an evergreen thorn.

pyr'amid, n., a solid structure, square at base, with triangular sides mounting to an apex.

pyram'idal, adj., pert. or rel. to, or resembling, a pyramid.

pyramid'ical, *adj.*, *i.q.* pyramidal.

py'ramidist, *n.*, one who studies pyramids.

pyre, *n.*, a funeral pile.

Pyrene'an, *adj.*, pert. or rel. to the Pyrenees, the mountain range separating France from Spain; *n.*, a native of the P.

Pyre'thrum, *n.*, a genus of plants to which the feverfew belongs.

pyret'ic, *adj.*, febrile; *n.*, a febrifuge.

pyretol'ogy, *n.*, the science of the study of fevers.

Py'rex, *n.*, a kind of heat-resisting glassware.

pyrex'ia, *n.*, fever.

pyrex'ial, *adj.*, pert. or rel. to fever.

pyr'gom, *n.*, a mineral.

pyrheliom'eter, *n.*, an instrument for measuring solar radiation.

pyr'idine, *n.*, a liquid alkaloid, used in asthma cases.

py'riform, *adj.*, pear-shaped.

pyrita'ceous, *adj.*, pyritic.

pyri'tes, *n.*, one of the metallic sulphides of iron or copper.

pyrit'ic, *adj.*, pert. or rel. to pyrites.

pyro-ac'id, *n.*, a reducing agent used in photography, etc. Abbrev. of pyrogallic acid.

py'ro-elec'tric, *adj.*, pert. or rel. to pyro-electricity.

py'ro-electric'ity, *n.*, electrification produced by heating or cooling.

pyrog'enous, *adj.*, igneous.

pyrol'atry, *n.*, fire-worship.

pyrolig'neous, *adj.*, in a state produced by fire on wood.

pyrolith'ic, *adj.*, cyanuric.

pyrol'ogist, *n.*, a student of pyrology.

pyrol'ogy, *n.*, the science of examination by means of heat.

py'romancy, *n.*, divination by fire.

pyroman'tic, *adj.*, pert. or rel. to pyromancy.

pyrom'eter, *n.*, an apparatus for measuring high degrees of heat.

pyromet'ric, *adj.*, pert. or rel. to pyrometry.

pyrom'etry, *n.*, the science of measuring high temperatures.

pyromorph'ous, *adj.*, crystallizing by means of fire.

py'rope, *n.*, a kind of garnet.

pyroph'orous, *adj.*, yielding fire.

pyroph'orus, *n.*, a spontaneously combustible compound.

pyrophot'ograph, *n.*, a photograph burnt in on glass or porcelain.

py'roscope, *n.*, an instrument for measuring the intensity of heat radiation.

pyro'sis, *n.*, a catarrhal state of the stomach.

pyrotech'nic, *adj.*, pert. or rel. to fireworks; dashing, brilliant.

pyrotech'nics, *n. pl.*, fireworks; the manufacture of them.

pyrotech'nist, *n.*, one who makes fireworks.

py'rotechny, *n.*, the art of making fireworks.

pyr'oxene, *n.*, a group of common minerals of variable composition but of the same chemical type, mainly subdivided into non-aluminous and aluminous.

pyroxyl'ic, *adj.*, produced, by distillation, from wood.

pyrox'ylin, *n.*, any explosive made from vegetable fibre to which nitric acid is applied.

Pyr'rhic, *adj.*, pert. or rel. to Pyrrhus, king of Epirus; costly, the losses exceeding the gain; *n.*, an ancient Greek war dance.

pyr'rhonism, *n.*, scepticism. (The word is derived from Pyrrho, an ancient Greek sceptical teacher.)

pyr'rhonist, *n.*, a follower of Pyrrho; a sceptic.

Pythagore'an, *adj.*, pert. or rel. to Pythagoras, who taught the doctrine of the transmigration of souls.

Pythag'orism, *n.*, the doctrines of Pythagoras.

Pyth'ian, *adj.*, pert. or rel. to the Delphic oracle of the Greek god, Apollo.

py'thon, *n.*, a large snake that kills by crushing; a soothsayer, an oracle.

python'ic, *adj.*, pert. or rel. to python.

py'thonism, *n.*, soothsaying; ventriloquism.

pyx, *n.*, a box, esp. that in which the Host or consecrated bread is kept; the box at the Royal Mint in which sample coins are kept.

pyxid'ium, *n.*, a lidded capsule or seed vessel (*bot.*).

pyx'is, *n.*, a casket or small box; a southern constellation, part of Argo.

Q

Q'-ship, n., a disguised naval vessel.

qua, conj., as; in the character or position of (Lat.).

quab, n., a kind of fish.

quack, n., an ignorant exponent of surgery or medicine; a charlatan; a duck's sound; v.i., to make a duck's sound; to prate.

quacked, p.p., quack.

quack'ery, n., the tricks of a quack.

quack'ing, pr.p., quack.

quack'ish, adj., like a quack.

quack'salver, n., i.q. quack (in the sense of a charlatan).

quad, n., i.q. quadrat; also i.q. quadrangle (of which words it is an abbreviation).

quad'ra, n., the border of a square panel; a fillet on an Ionic base; a plinth.

quad'rable, adj., capable of being represented by an equivalent square or expressed in finite numbers of algebraic terms.

quadragenar'ian, adj., forty-year old; n., a person forty years old.

Quadrages'ima, n., the first Sunday in Lent; the forty days of Lent.

quadrages'imal, adj., lasting forty days; Lent.

quad'rangle, n., a right-angled figure with four sides; a court enclosed by four sides.

quadran'gular, adj., having four sides.

quadran'gularly, adv., in a quadrangular way.

quad'rans, n., the fourth part of an as, a Roman weight, coin or measure (Lat.).

quad'rant, n., a quarter circumference of a circle; the figure contained between an arc and two radii at a right angle.

quadran'tal, adj., pert. or rel. to quadrant.

quad'rat, n., a little block

used in the spacing of type.

quad'rate, adj., rectangular, square; n., a bone in the lower jaw.

quadrate', v.t. and i., to square, or to make square; to conform with; to make conform with.

quadrat'ic, adj., involving a second and no higher mathematical power; n., a quadratic equation.

quadrat'ics, n. pl., the branch of algebra which deals with quadratic equations.

quad'rature, n., the process of expressing in terms of square measure the dimensions of any area.

quad'rel, n., a square brick, stone or tile; a square of turf.

quadren'nial, adj., in every four years; lasting four years.

quadren'nially, adv., every four years.

quadren'nium, n., a four-year period.

quad'rible, adj., able to be squared.

quad'ric, adj. and n., of the second degree.

quadricap'sular, adj., with four capsules.

quad'ricorn, adj., with four horns.

quadriden'tate, adj., with four rows of teeth.

quad'rifid, adj., with four lobes or divisions.

quad'rifoil, adj., with four foliations.

quad'riform, adj., four-fold.

quadri'ga, n., a four-horse chariot (Lat.).

quadrilat'eral, adj., having four sides; n., a figure with four sides.

quadriling'ual, adj., able to use four languages.

quadrilit'eral, adj., having four letters.

quadrille', n., a square dance; an old card game for four hands.

quadril'lion, n., a million to the fourth power.

quadrilo'bate, adj., having four lobes.

quad'rilobed, adj., i.q. quadrilobate.

quadriloc'ular, adj., four-chambered.

quadrino'mial, adj., having four algebraical terms.

quadripart'ite, adj., having four parts.

quadriphyl'lous, adj., with four leaves.

quad'rireme, n., a galley with four banks of rowers.

quadrisyllab'ic, adj., composed of four syllables.

quadrisyl'lable, n., a word with four syllables.

quad'rivalve, adj., having four valves.

quadrivalv'ular, adj., i.q. quadrivalve.

quadriv'ial, adj., pert or rel. to the quadrivium.

quadriv'ium, n., the mediaeval course of four studies.

quadroon', n., a person whose descent is three parts of one race and one of another.

Quadru'mana, n. pl., mammals having feet like hands.

quad'rumane, n., one of the Quadrumana.

quadru'manous, adj., four-handed; pert. or rel. to Quadrumana.

quad'rune, n., a gritstone.

quad'ruped, adj., having four feet; n., a four-footed animal.

quad'ruple, adj., multiplied by four; n., a quantity four times that of one given; v.t., to multiply by four.

quad'rupled, p.p., quadruple.

quad'ruplet, n., one of four at birth.

quadru'plicate, adj., fourfold; four times over.

quadru'plicate, v.t., to multiply by four; to quadruple.

quadru'plicated, p.p., quadruplicate.

quadru'plicating, pr.p., quadruplicate.

quadruplica'tion, n., a making fourfold.

quadrupli'city, *n.*, the characteristics of four-fold.

quad'rupling, *pr.p.*, quadruple.

quaere, *n.*, a question; *v.t.*, to inquire (*Lat.*).

quaest'or, *n.*, a Roman financial magistrate (*Lat.*). (Also *questor.*)

quaff, *v.t.*, to take a draught of (*Ir.*).

quaffed, *p.p.*, quaff.

quaff'er, *n.*, one who quaffs.

quaff'ing, *pr.p.*, quaff.

quag, *n.*, *i.q.* quagmire.

quag'ga, *n.*, a sort of zebra.

quag'gy, *adj.*, boggy.

quag'mire, *n.*, a bog or morass.

quaich(gh), *n.*, a double-handled cup (*Scot.*).

Quai d'Orsay, *n.*, (used for) the French Foreign Office.

quail, *n.*, a small partridge-like bird; *v.i.*, to shrink, to cower; *v.t.*, to cast down; to subdue or terrify.

quailed, *p.p.*, quail.

quail'ing, *pr.p.*, quail.

quaint, *adj.*, odd, whimsical, antique.

quaint'er, *adj.*, *comp.* of quaint.

quaint'est, *adj.*, *super.* of quaint.

quaint'ly, *adv.*, in a quaint way.

quaint'ness, *n.*, the state or quality of being quaint.

quake, *n.*, the act of quaking; *v.i.*, to tremble, shake or vibrate.

quaked, *p.p.*, quake.

qua'ker, *n.*, one who quakes; a person professing the beliefs and practices of the Society of Friends.

qua'keress, *n.*, the fem. of quaker.

qua'kerish, *adj.*, like the quakers.

qua'kerism, *n.*, the religious principles and system of the Society of Friends.

qua'king, *pr.p.*, quake.

qua'kingly, *adv.*, in a quaking way.

qual'ifiable, *adj.*, able to be qualified.

qualifica'tion, *n.*, a limiting or conditioning circumstance; a proof of fitness.

qual'ificative, *adj.*, qualifying.

qual'ificator, *n.*, an ecclesiastical official, charged with the duty of preparing disputed cases with theological precision.

qual'ified, *p.p.*, qualify.

qual'ifier, *n.*, one who, or that which, qualifies.

qual'ify, *v.i.*, to come up to standard; *v.t.*, to fit; to modify, to moderate.

qual'ifying, *pr.p.*, qualify.

qual'itative, *adj.*, pert. or rel. to quality.

quality, *n.*, kind, nature, a standard of excellence.

qualm, *n.*, a momentary sickness; a twinge of conscience; hesitancy.

qualm'ish, *adj.*, inclined to sickness.

qualm'ishly, *adv.*, in a qualmish way.

quan'dary, *n.*, a state of perplexity; a fix.

quant, *n.*, a punting-pole, *v.t.* and *i.*, to propel by a quant.

quan'tic, *n.*, a rational function of variables.

quantifica'tion, *n.*, the act of quantifying.

quan'tify, *v.t.*, to stipulate the quantity or extent of, to measure; to provide specific dimensions of.

quan'titative, *adj.*, pert. or rel. to quantity.

quan'tity, *n.*, the measure of how much, whether size, weight, amount, extent or number.

quantiv'alence, *n.*, the power of an atom to hold other atoms in combination (chem.).

quan'tum, *n.*, a share; a sufficient amount.

quaquavers'al, *adj.*, pointing in every direction (geol.).

qua'rantine, *n.*, the state, or period, of being quarantined; *v.t.*, to isolate travellers who are sick or considered capable of spreading infection.

qua'rantined, *p.p.*, quarantine.

qua'rantining, *pr.p.*, quarantine.

qua'renden, *n.*, a kind of apple.

quar'rel, *n.*, a complaint; a falling out, a dispute; a crossbow bolt; *v.i.*, to complain against; to fall out, to contend.

quar'rel(l)ed, *p.p.*, quarrel.

quar'rel(l)er, *n.*, one who quarrels.

quar'rel(l)ing, *pr.p.*, quarrel.

quar'relsome, *adj.*, ready to quarrel; touchy.

quar'relsomely, *adv.*, in a quarrelsome way.

quar'relsomeness, *n.*, the state of being quarrelsome.

quar'ried, *p.p.*, quarry.

quar'rier, *n.*, one who quarries.

quar'ry, *n.*, a place whence minerals (esp. stone) are extracted; prey; *v.t.* and *i.*, to take solid minerals from the earth; to do research work.

quar'rying, *n.*, the act of quarrying; *pr.p.*, quarry.

quart, *n.*, a quarter of a gallon; two pints.

quar'tan, *adj.*, recurring after every three days; *n.*, a quartan fever.

quarta'tion, *n.*, the addition of one part gold to three parts silver in assaying.

quar'ter, *adj.*, one-fourth in measure; *n.*, a fourth part; a district; (in *pl.*), the haunches; the side of a ship between the main chains and the stern; mercy to a fallen enemy; (in *pl.*), billets; *v.i.*, to be in billets; to avoid ruts in a road; *v.t.*, to divide into four parts; to billet; to range over.

quar'terage, *n.*, payment at quarter day; a quarter's allowance.

quar'ter-day, *n.*, one of the four statutory days on which payments are due.

quar'terdeck, *n.*, the part of a ship's deck reserved for officers.

quar'tered, *p.p.*, quarter.

quar'terfoil, *n.*, *i.q.* quatrefoil.

quar'tering, *n.*, the division of a shield to enable the addition of other arms (her.); *pr.p.*, quarter.

quar'terly, *adj.* and *adv.*, every quarter; in the four quarters or the diagonally opposite quarters of a shield (*her.*); *n.*, a periodical issued every three months.

quar'termaster, *n.*, a staff officer whose duty is to assign quarters, see to rations, etc.; a senior rating of the deck watch (*naut.*).

quar'tern, *n.*, a measure of capacity of differing values; a four-pound loaf.

quarteroon', *n.*, *i.q.* quadroon.

quar'ters, *n. pl.*, billets.

quar'ter-ses'sions, *n.*, a quarterly criminal court.

quar'terstaff, *n.*, a heavy pole used for defence or sport.

quartet', -ette', *n.*, a combination of four performers or instruments; a composition for four performers; any group of four.

quar'tile, *adj.*, pert. or rel. to the aspect of the planets which are 90° distant from each other (*astrol.*); *n.*, one quarter of the total number of items in a statistical sample arranged in order.

quar'to, *n.*, a size of paper resulting from two foldings; a page or book of this size.

quar'tole, *n.*, a series of four notes to be played in the time of three or six (*mus.*).

quartz, *n.*, a name for minerals consisting of silicon dioxide.

quartzif'erous, *adj.*, producing quartz.

quartz'ose, *adj.*, containing quartz.

quartz'y, *adj.*, *i.q.* quartzose.

quash, *v.t.*, to annul, to cancel.

quashed, *p.p.*, quash.

Quash'ee, *n.*, a W. Indian coloured person.

quash'ing, *pr.p.*, quash.

qua'si, *conj.* and *prefix*, as if; seemingly; almost (*Lat.*).

quass, *n.*, a weak Russian beer.

quassa'tion, *n.*, the act of shaking; concussion.

quas'sia, *n.*, a bitter wood.

quas'sin, *n.*, the bitter principle of quassia.

quat'er-centen'ary, *adj.*, pert. or rel. to 400 years; *n.*, a four-hundredth anniversary.

quater'nary, *adj.*, consisting of four parts; pert. or rel. to the number four.

quater'nion, *n.*, a body of four soldiers; a set of four.

quater'nity, *n.*, a group of four.

quat'orzain, *n.*, a fourteen-line sonnet.

quat'rain, *n.*, a four-line stanza (*Fr.*).

quat'refoil, *n.*, an architectural form with four cusps.

quattrocen'tism, *n.*, the study of the 15th century period of Italian art.

quattrocen'tist, *adj.* and *n.*, of the quattrocento.

quattrocen'to, *n.*, the 15th century as period in Italian art.

qua'ver, *n.*, a trilly, shaky speech; a note of the value of half a crotchet (*mus.*); *v.i.*, to shake, tremble, vibrate or trill.

qua'vered, *p.p.*, quaver.

qua'verer, *n.*, one who quavers.

qua'vering, *adj.*, shaking; *pr.p.*, quaver.

quay, *n.*, a wharf; a landing-stage.

quay'age, *n.*, wharfage.

quay'side, *n.*, wharfside, a landing place.

queach'y, *adj.*, quaking (as a bog).

quean, *n.*, an immoral woman.

quea'siness, *n.*, the state of being queasy.

quea'sy, *adj.*, nauseated; qualmish.

quebra'cho, *n.*, a S. American tree.

queen, *n.*, a king's consort; a female sovereign; a piece in chess; a fully developed female bee or ant; *v.i.*, to play a queen's part; *v.t.*, to make queen; to convert a pawn into a queen.

queened, *p.p.*, queen.

queen'ing, *n.*, a variety of apple; *pr.p.*, queen.

queen'like, *adj.*, *i.q.* queenly.

queen'liness, *n.*, the state or quality of being queenly.

queen'ly, *adj.*, resembling a queen.

queen'post, *n.*, one of two upright posts in a roof-truss.

queer, *adj.*, odd, strange; of doubtful character; feeling faint (*colloq.*); *v.t.*, to interfere with or spoil (*colloq.*).

queer'ish, *adj.*, rather queer.

queer'ly, *adv.*, in a queer way.

queer'ness, *n.*, strangeness; the quality of being queer.

quelch, *v.t.*, to make a sound as of water in one's boots.

quelched, *p.p.*, quelch.

quelch'ing, *pr.p.*, quelch.

quell, *v.t.*, to put down; to silence; to suppress.

quelled, *p.p.*, quell.

quell'er, *n.*, one who quells.

quell'ing, *pr.p.*, quell.

quench, *v.t.*, to extinguish; to cool; to suppress.

quench'able, *adj.*, able to be quenched.

quenched, *p.p.*, quench.

quench'er, *n.*, one who, or that which, quenches.

quench'ing, *pr.p.*, quench.

quench'less, *adj.*, unquenchable.

quenelle', *n.*, a meat or fish ball (*Fr.*).

quer'cine, *adj.*, pert. or rel. to oaks.

quer'citron, *n.*, the black oak; a dye made from this.

que'ried, *p.p.*, query.

querimo'nious, *adj.*, full of grievances.

que'rist, *n.*, a questioner.

quern, *n.*, a hand-mill; *v.t.* and *i.*, to grind.

quer'ulous, *adj.*, full of complaints; peevish.

quer'ulously, *adv.*, peevishly.

quer'ulousness, *n.*, the state of being querulous.

que'ry, *n.*, a question; an objection; *v.t.* and *i.*, to question.

que'rying, *pr.p.*, query.

quest, *n.*, a search or inquiry; a mission;

v.t. and *i.*, to go on quest (for).

ques'ted, *p.p.*, quest.

ques'ting, *pr.p.*, quest.

ques'tion, *n.*, an interrogation; a subject for discussion; torture; *v.t.*, to interrogate; to express disbelief in or doubt about.

ques'tionable, *adj.*, open to doubt or objection; of doubtful propriety.

ques'tionableness, *n.*, the quality of being questionable.

ques'tionably, *adv.*, in a questionable way.

ques'tioned, *p.p.*, question.

ques'tioner, *n.*, one who questions.

ques'tioning, *adj.*, inquiring; *pr.p.*, question.

ques'tioningly, *adv.*, inquiringly.

ques'tionist, *n.*, a candidate for a degree.

ques'tionless, *adj.*, unquestioning; *adv.*, without doubt.

ques'tion-mark, *n.*, the point of interrogation.

ques'tion-mas'ter, *n.*, a person who puts questions in a question session.

questionnaire', *n.*, a list of questions.

quest'man, *n.*, an inspector; a sidesman.

ques'tor, *n.*, *i.q.* quaestor.

quet'zal, *n.*, a Central-American bird.

queue, *n.*, a pig-tail; a file of people; *v.i.*, to join a file of people.

queued, *p.p.*, queue.

queue'ing, *pr.p.*, queue.

quib'ble, *n.*, an evasion of the point by playing with words; *v.i.*, to evade an argument; to shuffle.

quib'bled, *p.p.*, quibble.

quib'bler, *n.*, one who quibbles.

quib'bling, *n.*, an evasion of the point of an argument; *pr.p.*, quibble.

quick, *adj.*, alive; living; alert; fast; pregnant; *n.*, the living part; a vital, sensitive part.

quick'en, *v.i.*, to come to life; *v.t.*, to give life to; to animate; to stimulate.

quick'ened, *p.p.*, quicken.

quick'ener, *n.*, one who, or that which, quickens.

quick'ening, *pr.p.*, quicken.

quick'er, *adj.* and *adv.*, *comp.* of quick.

quick'est, *adj.*, *super.* of quick.

quick'-grass, *n.*, couch grass.

quick'lime, *n.*, a result of expelling, by means of heat, the carbon dioxide from limestone, etc.

quick'ly, *adv.*, with speed, rapidly.

quick'ness, *n.*, celerity.

quick'sand, *n.*, loose, moving sand.

quick'set, *adj.*, made of living shrubs; *n.*, a hedge so formed.

quick'-sighted, *adj.*, having quick sight.

quick'silver, *n.*, mercury; *v.t.*, to coat with quicksilver.

quick'step, *n.*, a quick marching step; a kind of dance.

quick'witted, *adj.*, with nimble wits.

quid, *n.*, a lump of tobacco for chewing; a something; a pound sterling (*slang*).

qui'dam, *n.*, somebody; a person not definitely known (*Lat.*).

quid'dity, *n.*, the essential nature of a thing; cavilling.

quid'dle, *v.i.*, to quiver (*Amer.*).

quid'nunc, *n.*, a gossip; a newsmonger (*Lat.*).

quid pro quo', substantival phrase = a set off, compensation (*Lat.*).

quiesce', *v.i.*, to become silent (*Lat.*).

quies'cence, *n.*, the state of becoming or being silent.

quies'cency, *n.*, *i.q.* quiescence.

quies'cent, *adj.*, silent, inert.

quies'cently, *adv.*, in a quiet way.

qui'et, *adj.*, calm, peaceful, silent, unobtrusive; *n.*, calmness, stillness, soundlessness; *v.i.*, to become quiet; *v.t.*, to calm, to appease.

qui'eted, *p.p.*, quiet.

qui'eten, *v.t.*, to make quiet.

qui'etened, *p.p.*, quieten.

quiet'ening, *pr.p.*, quieten.

qui'eter, *adj.*, *comp.* of quiet.

qui'etest, *adj.*, *super.* of quiet.

qui'eting, *pr.p.*, quiet.

qui'etism, *n.*, the principle of passivity; mysticism; quiet devotional contemplation.

qui'etist, *n.*, one who practises quietism.

quietist'ic, *adj.*, pert. or rel. to quietism.

qui'etly, *adv.*, in a quiet way.

qui'etness, *n.*, the state of being quiet.

qui'etude, *n.*, rest; tranquillity.

quie'tus, *n.*, a final blow; an acquittance (*Lat.*).

quiff, *n.*, a curl or tuft of hair over the forehead.

quill, *n.*, a large wing or tail feather; a pen made of this; a plectrum; one of a porcupine's spines; a musical pipe; *v.t.* and *i.*, to goffer.

quill'-driver, *n.*, a writer.

quilled, *adj.*, having quills; *p.p.*, quill.

quil'let, *n.*, a quibble.

quill'ing, *n.*, goffering; fluted muslin or lace; *pr.p.*, quill.

quill'wort, *n.*, a variety of aquatic plant.

quilt, *n.*, a bedcover; a quilted garment; *v.t.*, to line or cover with padded material.

quilt'ed, *p.p.*, quilt.

quilt'er, *n.*, one who quilts.

quilt'ing, *n.*, quilted work; material to be quilted; *pr.p.*, quilt.

qui'nary, *adj.*, pert. or rel. to five; containing five (*zool.*).

qui'nate, *adj.*, having five leaflets from one point (*bot.*).

quince, *n.*, a hard, acid, yellowish fruit.

quincenten'ary, *adj.*, pert. or rel. to 500 years; *n.*, a 500th anniversary.

quince'-tree, *n.*, the shrub that bears quinces.

quincun'cial, *adj.*, arranged in quincunx form.

quin'cunx, *n.,* an arrangement of five things in a square in the manner of the five on dice or playing cards.

quindec'agon, *n.,* a figure with fifteen angles and sides.

quingenten'ary, *n., i.q.* quincentenary.

quin'ia, *n., i.q.* quinine.

quinine', *n.,* an anti-malarial medicine made from Peruvian bark.

quinquagenar'ian, *adj.,* pert. or rel. to 50 years; *n.,* a 50th anniversary.

Quinquages'ima, *n.,* the Sunday before Lent (*Lat.*).

quinquan'gular, *adj.,* five-angled.

quinquefo'liate, *adj.,* five-leaved.

quinquelit'eral, *adj.,* five-lettered.

quinquen'nial, *adj.,* recurring every five years; lasting five years.

quinquen'nially, *adv.,* every five years.

quinquen'nium, *n.,* a period of five years.

quinquepar'tite, *adj.,* divided into five parts.

quin'quereme, *n.,* a galley with five banks of oars.

quinquesyll'able, *n.,* a five-syllable word.

quin'quevalve, *adj.,* having five valves.

quin'quifid, *adj.,* cleft in five.

quinqui'na, *n.,* Peruvian bark.

quin'sy, *n.,* inflammation of the tonsils.

quint, *n.,* a fifth (in *mus.*); an organ stop sounding the fifth; in piquet, a sequence of five cards of one suit.

quin'tain, *n.,* an old tilting sport (*hist.*).

quin'tal, *n.,* a hundred-weight.

quin'tan, *adj.,* returning every fifth day.

quinte, *n.,* the fifth fencing thrust.

quintess'ence, *n.,* concentrated essence; orig. the fifth substance in addition to the four elements.

quintessen'tial, *adj.,* pert. or rel. to quintessence.

quintet', -ette', *n.,* a combination of five voices or instruments (*mus.*); a musical composition for five performers; any group of five.

quintil'lion, *n.,* a million to the fifth power. In U.S., a thousand to the sixth power.

quin'tuple, *adj.,* five-fold; *n.,* a five-fold amount; *v.t.,* to multiply by five.

quintu'plicate, *adj.,* pert. or rel. to five separate parts; *n.,* fivefold.

quintu'plicate, *v.t.,* to make five times the original amount.

quintu'plication, *n.,* the state of being fivefold.

quin'zaine, *n.,* a composition containing fifteen lines.

quip, *n.,* a gibe or quibble; *v.t.* and *i.,* to gibe.

qui'ppu, *n.,* the old Peruvian substitute for writing. It consisted of knotted threads of various colours.

quire, *n.,* the one-twentieth of a ream; a book; *v.t.,* to fold in quires; to mark the quires.

Quir'inal, *n.,* a royal palace on the Quirinal Hill in Rome.

quirk, *n.,* a trick; in architecture, a groove; *v.t.,* to hollow out.

quirked, *p.p.,* quirk.

quirk'ing, *pr.p.,* quirk.

quirt, *n.,* a riding whip peculiar to S. America.

quis'ling, *n.,* one who openly collaborates with an enemy; a traitor.

quit, *v.t.,* to acquit; to conduct (*reflex.*); to desist from; to let go; to leave; to repay; *adj.,* clear, released from obligation.

quitch'-grass, *n.,* couch-grass.

quit'claim, *n.,* a renouncement of claim; a release in full.

quite, *adv.,* totally; without reservation, completely.

quit-rent, *n.,* the rent paid by a copy-holder, who was thus released from service.

quits, *adj.,* even; repaid.

quit'table, *adj.,* able to be quitted.

quit'tance, *n.,* release; requital.

quit'ted, *p.p.,* quit.

quit'ter, *n.,* one who quits.

quit'ting, *pr.p.,* quit.

quiv'er, *n.,* an arrow-holder; vibration, shaking; *v.i.,* to be agitated; to shake; to vibrate.

quiv'ered, *adj.,* having a quiver; *p.p.,* quiver.

quiv'erful, *n.,* the contents of a quiver.

quiv'ering, *pr.p.,* quiver.

quiv'eringly, *adv.,* in a quivering way.

qui vive', *n. phr.,* the alert (*Fr.*).

quixot'ic, *adj.,* pert. or rel. to Don Quixote; like Q. in being visionary, chivalrous and unpractical.

quixot'ically, *adv.,* in a quixotic fashion.

quix'otism, *n.,* quixotic ideals.

quix'otry, *n., i.q.* quixotism.

quiz, *n.,* a ridiculous person; one given to quizzing; a hoax, chaff; a series of questions; *v.t.,* to make fun of; to gibe; to stare at; to question.

quizzed, *p.p.,* quiz.

quiz'zer, *n.,* one who quizzes.

quiz'zical, *adj.,* mocking, chaffing.

quiz'zically, *adv.,* in a quizzical way.

quiz'zing, *pr.p.,* quiz.

quo'ad, *prep.,* as regards (*Lat.*).

quod, *n.,* prison (*slang*).

quod'libet, *n.,* a subject for argument; a subtle point.

quoin, *n.,* the outer angle of a building; a corner-stone; a wedge for the type in a forme, or for raising a gun's level; *v.t.,* to bind with a quoin.

quoit, *n.,* an iron disc open in the middle and thrown by the player to encircle a peg.

quon'dam, *adv.,* used as an *adj.* = sometime, former (*Lat.*).

quo′rum, *n.*, a specified required number for transacting business (*Lat.*).

quo′ta, *n.*, an individual share or contribution to a whole; a fixed permitted amount.

quo′table, *adj.*, able, or fit, to be quoted.

quota′tion, *n.*, the act of quoting; a passage quoted; a statement of price.

quota′tion-marks, *n. pl.*, *or* inverted commas and apostrophes used to mark the beginning and end of a quotation.

quot′ative, *adj.*, of quoting; given to quotation.

quote, *n.*, that which is quoted; a borrowed passage from a book, etc.; a price; *v.t.*, to repeat someone's written or spoken words; to adduce authority from a writer; to state a price.

quo′ted, *p.p.*, quote.

quo′ter, *n.*, one who quotes.

quoth, *v.t.*, an old past tense of an obsolete verb = I, he, she said.

quo′tha, *interj.*, an old word = says he, she, it.

quotid′ian, *adj.*, daily; ordinary.

quo′tient, *n.*, the figure that shows how many times one number is contained in another.

quo′ting, *pr.p.*, quote.

quo vadis, *interrog.*, "where are you going?" (*Lat.*).

Qurân′, *n.*, *i.q.* Koran.

R

Ra, *n.,* the Egyptian sun-god.

rab, *n.,* a mason's rod for mixing hair with mortar.

raban'a, *n.,* a raffia fabric.

rab'bet, *n.,* a groove cut on the end of a board so that another may fit into it; *v.t.,* to cut a board in this way.

rab'beted, *p.p.,* rabbet.

rab'beting, *pr.p.,* rabbet.

rab'bi, *n.,* a Jewish doctor or teacher.

rab'bin, *n., i.q.* rabbi.

rab'binate, *adj.,* pert. or rel. to rabbin.

Rabbin'ic, *n.,* a dialect of Hebrew; later Hebrew.

rabbin'ic, *adj.,* pert. or rel. to the rabbis, or to the non-canonical Hebrew writings.

rabbin'ical, *adj., i.q.* rabbinic.

rab'binism, *n.,* a rabbinic expression or phrase.

rab'binist, *n.,* a Jew who adheres to the Talmud and rabbinic traditions.

rab'bit, *n.,* a rodent mammal that burrows in the earth.

rab'ble, *n.,* a disorderly crowd; people actuated by base motives.

rab'blement, *n.,* a tumultuous crowd of people.

rabdol'ogy, *n.,* the art of computing by means of a set of ivory or bone rods called "Napier's Rods" after the inventor, Baron Napier, the mathematician. (Also *rhabdology.*)

rabelai'sian, *adj.,* like, pert. or rel. to the satirist, Rabelais, and his style; grotesque and earthy in humour.

rab'id, *adj.,* mad with rage; intolerant.

rab'idly, *adv.,* in a rabid manner.

rab'idness, *n.,* the state of being rabid.

ra'bies, *n.,* a disease of dogs and related animals, causing savage behaviour.

rab'innate, *n.,* the office of a rabbi; a body of rabbis.

ra'ca, *adj.,* a Syriac epithet of contempt, meaning worthless.

raccoon', *n.,* a N. American animal with valuable fur.

race, *n.,* a speed contest; a millstream; a rapid current in the sea; people related by descent; a breed or stock; a root; the channel in which a rotary device turns; *v.i.,* to run swiftly; to contend in a race.

race'course, *n.,* the ground on which horse-races are run.

raced, *p.p.,* race.

race'horse, *n.,* a horse kept for racing.

raceme', *n.,* a cluster of flowers growing out of a common slender axis.

ra'cer, *n.,* one who, or that which, races; a racehorse.

race'track, *n.,* the ground on which races are run.

rachil'la, *n.,* the zig-zag axis on a grass-spikelet along which the florets are arranged.

ra'chis, *n.,* the vertebral column; the shaft of a feather; the stalk of a fern-frond.

rachit'is, *n., i.q.* rickets.

ra'cial, *adj.,* pert. or rel. to a race of people.

ra'cialism, *n.,* the adherence to racial feeling or antagonism.

ra'cialist, *n.,* one who inspires racialism.

ra'cially, *adv.,* in a racial way.

ra'cier, *adj., comp.* of racy.

ra'ciest, *adj., super.* of racy.

ra'cily, *adv.,* in a racy manner.

ra'ciness, *n.,* the quality of being racy.

ra'cing, *adj.,* pert. or rel. to races; *n.,* the pastime of attending horse-races; *pr.p.,* race.

raciol'ogy, *n.,* the study of races.

rack, *n.,* a framework; an instrument of torture; a bar with a toothed edge working in the teeth of a wheel; thin flying clouds; destruction; a horse's gait; abbrev. of arrack; *v.i.,* to trot, to canter (esp. horse); *v.t.,* to strain vehemently; to torture; to draw pure liquor off from its sediment.

racked, *p.p.,* rack.

rack'et, *n.,* clamour; a battledore used in such games as tennis, racquets, etc.; an unscrupulous money-making activity; *v.i.,* to make a confused noise; to frolic.

rack'eted, *p.p.,* racket.

racketeer', *n.,* one who practises extortion.

rack'eting, *pr.p.,* racket.

rack'ets, *n.,* an old form of tennis; extortionist practices.

rack'ety, *adj.,* making a tumultuous noise.

rack'ing, *pr.p.,* rack.

rack'rent, *n.,* the full annual rent of a property equalling the market value; *v.t.,* to impose rackrent upon.

rack'renter, *n.,* a landlord who rackrents his tenants.

raconteur, *n.,* a good story-teller (*Fr.*).

raconteuse, *n.,* the fem. of raconteur (*Fr.*).

racoon', *n., i.q.* raccoon.

racqu'et, *n., i.q.* racket.

racqu'ets, *n., i.q.* rackets.

ra'cy, *adj.,* having a strong, piquant flavour; spirited.

rad, *adj.,* afraid (*Scot.*); abbrev. of radical in politics; *n.,* a unit of radiation dosage.

ra'dar, *n.,* a system of radio-detection or location.

rad'dle, *n.,* an interwoven or pleached hedge; a red pigment; *v.t.,* to interweave; to paint with raddle.

rad'dled, *adj.*, lined and timeworn of face.

ra'dial, *adj.*, pert. or rel. to a radius.

ra'dian, *n.*, a unit of circular measure.

ra'diance, *n.*, vivid brightness.

ra'diancy, *n.*, *i.q.* radiance.

ra'diant, *adj.*, brilliant; giving out rays.

ra'diantly, *adv.*, in a radiant manner.

ra'diary, *n.*, a radiate.

Radia'ta, *n. pl.*, a division of the animal kingdom introduced by Cuvier in 1812.

ra'diate, *adj.*, having rays; *n.*, a member of the Radiata; *v.i.*, to proceed in rays from a point or surface; *v.t.*, to emit in direct lines from a point or surface.

ra'diated, *p.p.*, radiate.

ra'diating, *pr.p.*, radiate.

radia'tion, *n.*, the act of radiating.

ra'diator, *n.*, that which radiates; the heat dispersal part of a heating apparatus.

rad'ical, *adj.*, pert. or rel. to the root; fundamental; thoroughgoing; *n.*, one who advocates thorough social or political reform; a root word.

rad'icalism, *n.*, the doctrines of the radicals or advanced liberals.

radical'ity, *n.*, the quality of being radical.

rad'ically, *adv.*, fundamentally.

rad'icant, *adj.*, taking root on or above the ground.

rad'icate, *adj.*, deeply rooted; *v.t.*, to plant deeply; to cause to take root.

rad'icated, *adj.*, *i.q.* radicate; *p.p.*, radicate.

rad'icating, *pr.p.*, radicate.

radica'tion, *n.*, the process of taking root deeply.

rad'icle, *n.*, that part of a seed which becomes the root; the fibrous parts of a root.

radic'ular, *adj.*, pert. or rel. to a radicle.

radif'erous, *adj.*, radium-producing.

ra'dii, *n.*, the pl. of radius.

ra'dio, *adj.*, pert. or rel. to radio; *n.*, a wireless set; wireless communication; *v.t.* and *i.*, to communicate by wireless.

radioac'tive, *adj.*, emitting invisible rays that penetrate solid and opaque bodies, producing electrical and physical effects; exercising radiation.

radioactiv'ity, *n.*, the property of emitting invisible rays that penetrate solid and opaque bodies.

radiobiol'ogy, *n.*, the study of effects of radiation on humans and animals.

radiogenet'ics, *n.*, the study of the effects of radiation on inheritance.

ra'diogram, *n.*, a radiogramophone; an x-ray photograph; a telegram sent by radio.

ra'diograph, *n.*, an instrument for recording radiation; an x-ray photograph.

ra'diographer, *n.*, one who practises radiography.

radiog'raphy, *n.*, x-ray photography; the study of radioactivity.

radio'location, *n.*, the use of wireless-wave reflection to locate objects (esp. aircraft).

radiolog'ical, *adj.*, pert. or rel. to radiology.

radiol'ogist, *n.*, a specialist in radiology.

radiol'ogy, *n.*, the study of radiation, and its use in medicine.

radiom'eter, *n.*, an instrument for measuring radiant energy.

ra'diophone, *n.*, an instrument for producing sound by radiated energy.

ra'dio-tele'gram, *n.*, a telegram sent or received by radio.

ra'diotele'graph, *n.*, *i.q.* radiotelegraphy.

ra'dioteleg'raphy, *n.*, telegraphy by radio.

ra'diotel'ephone, *n.*, a telephone system which uses radio.

ra'dio-therapeut'ics, *n.*, the study of medical treatment using radiation.

ra'dio-ther'apy, *n.*, the treatment of diseases by radiation.

rad'ish, *n.*, a cruciferous plant with an edible root.

ra'dium, *n.*, a radioactive element found in pitchblende.

ra'dius, *n.*, the shortest distance from the centre of a circle to the circumference; the smaller bone of the forearm.

ra'dix, *n.*, a root; a mathematical base.

ra'dome, *n.*, aircraft radar protection.

ra'don, *n.*, a radio-active element.

raff, *n.*, riff-raff.

raf'fia, *n.*, a fibre used in basketry, etc.

raf'fish, *adj.*, dissipated; worthless.

raf'fle, *n.*, a kind of lottery; rubbish, debris; *v.t.*, to dispose of by means of a raffle.

raf'fled, *p.p.*, raffle.

raf'fler, *n.*, one who raffles.

raf'fling, *pr.p.*, raffle.

raft, *n.*, a float made of planks, barrels, etc.; *v.t.*, to carry on a raft.

raft'er, *n.*, one of the sloping timbers of a roof; a man who rafts timber; *v.t.*, to provide with rafters.

raft'ered, *adj.*, furnished with rafters; *p.p.*, rafter.

raft'ing, *pr.p.*, raft.

rafts'man, *n.*, a man who manages a raft.

rag, *n.*, a shred of cloth; a tatter; a kind of hard, rough stone; *v.t.* and *i.*, to tease; to indulge in horse-play (*slang*).

rag'amuffin, *n.*, a ragged or worthless fellow.

rage, *n.*, furious anger; something eagerly sought after; *v.i.*, to act violently.

raged, *p.p.*, rage.

rag(g)ee', *n.*, coarse millet.

ra'ger, *n.*, one who rages.

rag'ged, *adj.*, tattered.

ragged, *p.p.*, rag.

rag'gedness, *n.*, the state of being ragged.

rag'ging, *pr.p.*, rag.

ra'ging, *adj.*, furious; *pr.p.*, rage.

ra'gingly, *adv.*, in a raging way.

rag'lan, *n.*, a loose overcoat with wide sleeves.

rag'man, *n.*, a collector of, and dealer in, rags.

ragout', *n.*, a highly seasoned stew (*Fr.*).

rag'stone, *n.*, a siliceous rock with a rough texture.

rag'-time, *n.*, syncopated music.

rag'wort, *n.*, a coarse weed with ragged leaves and a yellow flower.

raid, *n.*, a hostile attack; *v.t.*, to invade, esp. for plunder.

raided, *p.p.*, raid.

raid'er, *n.*, an attacker.

raid'ing, *pr.p.*, raid.

rail, *n.*, a bar of wood or iron; one of the metals of a railway; a kind of bird; *v.i.*, to use reproachful words; *v.t.*, to fence off with rails.

rail'age, *n.*, carriage charges for goods by rail.

railed, *p.p.*, rail.

rail'er, *n.*, one who rails.

rail'head, *n.*, the starting place of a railway system.

rail'ing, *adj.*, reproachful and insulting; *n.*, a fence made of posts and rails; abuse; *pr.p.*, rail.

rail'lery, *n.*, banter.

rail'road, *n.*, a railway.

rail'way, *n.*, a road with rails on which the wheels of vehicles run.

rai'ment, *n.*, clothing.

rain, *n.*, water dropping from the clouds; *v.i.*, to fall in drops from the clouds; to fall like rain.

rain'bow, *n.*, an arc of a circle, coloured prismatically, produced by the sun shining through rain.

rain'coat, *n.*, a waterproof coat.

rain'drop, *n.*, a drop of rain.

rained, *p.p.*, rain.

rain'fall, *n.*, the amount of rain that falls in a certain time.

rain'-gauge, *n.*, an instrument for measuring rainfall.

rain'ier, *adj.*, *comp.* of rainy.

rain'iest, *adj.*, *super.* of rainy.

rain'iness, *n.*, the state of being rainy.

rain'ing, *pr.p.*, rain.

rain'less, *adj.*, without rain.

rainproof, *adj.*, impermeable by rain.

rain'storm, *n.*, a heavy downpour of rain.

rain'-water, *n.*, water fallen from the clouds as rain.

rain'y, *adj.*, showery; abounding with rain.

rais'able, *adj.*, capable of being raised.

raise, *v.t.*, to elevate.

raised, *p.p.*, raise.

rais'er, *n.*, one who, or that which, raises.

rai'sin, *n.*, a dried grape.

rais'ing, *pr.p.*, raise.

ra'ja(h), *n.*, a Hindu chief or prince.

Rajpoot', *n.*, an inhabitant of Rajputana, in India.

rake, *n.*, a toothed gardening and farming tool; a dissolute fellow; a slope or inclination; *v.i.*, to lead a dissolute life; to slope; *v.t.*, to apply a rake to.

raked, *p.p.*, rake.

rakee', *n.*, an Oriental spirituous liquor.

rake'-hell, *n.*, a dissolute fellow; a profligate.

ra'ker, *n.*, one who, or that which, rakes.

ra'king, *adj.*, inclined; enfilading; scouring or cannonading along a line; *pr.p.*, rake.

ra'kish, *adj.*, dissolute; having a rake or inclination of the masts forward or aft.

ra'kishly, *adv.*, in a rakish way.

ra'kishness, *n.*, the quality of being rakish.

râle, *n.*, a noise made by air passing through mucus in the lungs (*Fr.*).

rallentan'do, *adv.*, becoming slower (*mus.*); *n.*, a slowing down (*mus. It.*).

ral'lied, *p.p.*, rally.

ral'lier, *n.*, one who rallies.

ral'ly, *n.*, a stand made by retreating troops; *v.i.*, to reform in order; to restore to health; *v.t.*, to reunite; to tease.

ral'lying, *pr.p.*, rally.

ram, *n.*, the male of the sheep; a battering-ram; the piston of a hydraulic press; *v.t.*, to strike with a ram; to force in.

Ramadan', *n.*, the ninth month of the Mohammedan year; the great annual Mohammedan fast.

ram'ble, *n.*, a roving or aimless excursion; *v.i.*, to wander; to think or talk incoherently.

ram'bled, *p.p.*, ramble.

ram'bler, *n.*, one who rambles; a plant which grows without restraint; a climbing rose or other plant.

ram'bling, *adj.*, straggling; confused in language or ideas; *n.*, a ramble; *pr.p.*, ramble.

rambut'an, *n.*, a red fruit.

ram'ekin, *n.*, a mixture of eggs and cheese, etc., cooked and served on bread.

ra'meous, *adj.*, rel. to, or growing on, a branch.

ram'ie, *n.*, a strong fine fibre.

ramifica'tion, *n.*, the act of ramifying; a subordinate branch; a branching-off into other directions.

ram'ified, *p.p.*, ramify.

ram'iform, *adj.*, shaped like a branch.

ram'ify, *v.i.*, to branch out; to be subdivided.

ram'ifying, *pr.p.*, ramify.

rammed, *p.p.*, ram.

ram'mer, *n.*, one who, or that which, rams; a ramrod.

ram'ming, *pr.p.*, ram.

ram'mish, *adj.*, ramlike; stinking; lascivious.

ram'my, *adj.*, *i.q.* rammish.

ramose, *adj.,* branched, branching.

ra′mous, *adj., i.q.* ramose.

ramp, *n.,* a boat's length overall (*naut.*); a slope from one level to another; a swindle or racket; *v.i.,* to climb, as a plant; to rear on the hind-legs; to rage.

rampa′cious, *adj.,* boisterous.

rampage′, *n.,* a state of passion or excitement; *v.i.,* to prance about furiously.

rampaged′, *p.p.,* rampage.

rampage′ous, *adj.,* violent; boisterous.

rampage′ously, *adv.,* violently, boisterously.

rampageousness, *n.,* the state of being rampageous.

rampa′ging, *pr.p.,* rampage.

ram′pancy, *n.,* the state of being rampant.

ram′pant, *adj.,* rank in growth; standing on one hind-leg, as if attacking (*her.*); in a state of vigorous growth.

ram′pantly, *adv.,* in a rampant way.

ram′part, *n.,* a bulwark or defence; a raised fortification round a place.

ramped, *p.p.,* ramp.

ramp′ing, *pr.p.,* ramp.

ram′pion, *n.,* a perennial bell-flower.

ram′rod, *n.,* a rod for ramming down the charge of a firearm.

ram′shackle, *adj.,* rickety; ill-made.

ram′sons, *n. pl.,* wild garlic.

ram′ulous, *adj.,* having many small branches.

ran, *n.,* a certain length of twine; *p.p.,* run.

rance, *n.,* a veined, red marble.

rances′cent, *adj.,* becoming rancid or sour.

ranch, *n.,* a large open livestock farm.

ranch′ing, *n.,* stock-raising on a ranch.

ranch′man, *n.,* a man employed on a ranch.

ran′cho, *n., i.q.* ranch.

ran′cid, *adj.,* having a rank smell and taste (said of oils and fats).

rancid′ity, *n.,* the quality of being rancid.

ran′cidness, *n., i.q.* rancidity.

ran′co(u)r, *n.,* spite; malice; malignant hatred.

ran′corous, *adj.,* full of rancour.

ran′corously, *adv.,* in a rancorous manner.

rand, *n.,* a sort of beefsteak; a thin inner sole for a shoe; highlands; a unit of S. African currency.

randan′, *n.,* a four-oared boat with three rowers, the middle rower pulling two oars; a spree (*colloq.*).

ran′dem, *adv.,* harnessed tandem fashion (esp. horses); *n.,* a team of three horses harnessed tandem.

ran′dom, *adj.,* fortuitous; without design; unplanned.

ran′dy, *adj.,* lustful; boisterous.

ra′nee, *n.,* an Indian princess, wife of a rajah.

rang, *p.p.,* ring.

range, *n.,* a row; extent; a kitchen grate; a place for rifle practice; the open region of a ranch; *v.i.,* to rank; *v.t.,* to set in a row or rows; to pass over.

ranged, *p.p.,* range.

range′fin′der, *n.,* an instrument for finding distances.

ran′ger, *n.,* one who ranges; the keeper of a royal park or forest.

ran′gership, *n.,* the office of a ranger.

ran′ging, *pr.p.,* range.

ran′iform, *adj.,* frog-shaped.

ra′nine, *adj.,* pert. or rel. to frogs.

rank, *adj.,* luxuriant; strong-scented; gross; *n.,* a row; a line of soldiers; a social class or order; high social position; *v.t.,* to classify.

ranked, *p.p.,* rank.

rank′er, *n.,* a private soldier; one raised from the ranks.

rank′ing, *pr.p.,* rank.

ran′kle, *v.i.,* to fester; to cause bitterness or irritation.

ran′kled, *p.p.,* rankle.

ran′kling, *n.,* deep irritation; *pr.p.,* rankle.

rank′ly, *adv.,* with vigorous growth; coarsely; grossly.

rank′ness, *n.,* the state of being rank.

ran′sack, *v.t.,* to rummage; to search thoroughly; to strip by plundering.

ran′sacked, *p.p.,* ransack.

ran′sacker, *n.,* one who ransacks.

ran′sacking, *pr.p.,* ransack.

ran′som, *n.,* a price of freedom from captivity; redemption; *v.t.,* to pay a ransom for.

ran′somed, *p.p.,* ransom.

ran′somer, *n.,* one who ransoms.

ran′soming, *pr.p.,* ransom.

ran′somless, *adj.,* free from ransom.

rant, *n.,* bombast; *v.i.,* to use extravagant language; to declaim.

rant′ed, *p.p.,* rant.

rant′er, *n.,* one who rants; a noisy preacher.

rant′ing, *pr.p.,* rant.

rant′y, *adj.,* boisterous.

ranuncula′ceous, *adj.,* of the ranunculus family (crow's-foot).

Ranun′culus, *n.,* one of the crow's-foot genus of plants.

rap, *n.,* a quick, smart knock; a small thing of little value; *v.i.,* to knock; *v.t.,* to give a knock to.

rapa′cious, *adj.,* wont to seize property violently; grasping.

rapa′ciously, *adv.,* in a rapacious manner.

rapa′ciousness, *n.,* a disposition to plunder or oppress.

rapac′ity, *n.,* the quality of being rapacious.

rape, *n.,* snatching by force; sexual intercourse procured by violence; refuse skins of raisins; a plant of the cabbage family; a division of the county of Sussex; a vessel used to make vinegar; *v.t.,* to seize or carry off.

Raphaelesque', *adj.*, in the style of Raphael, the Italian artist.

Raph'aelism, *n.*, the methods and principles of Raphael.

Raph'aelite, *n.*, an artist who adopts the methods and principles of Raphael.

Raph'aelitism, *n.*, *i.q.* Raphaelism.

ra'phe, *n.*, a suture or line of junction, in botany and zoology.

raph'ides, *n. pl.*, needle-shaped crystals occurring in plant cells.

raph'igraph, *n.*, an obsolete typewriter for the blind.

rap'id, *adj.*, very swift; *n.*, a swift current in a river where the bed slopes down steeply.

rapid'ity, *n.*, swiftness.

rap'idly, *adv.*, with swiftness.

ra'pier, *n.*, a sword without a cutting edge used only for thrusting.

rap'ine, *n.*, the act of plundering.

rapparee', *n.*, a wild Irish robber (*hist.*).

rapped, *p.p.*, rap.

rappee', *n.*, a strong kind of snuff.

rap'per, *n.*, one who raps; a door-knocker.

rap'ping, *pr.p.*, rap.

rapport', *n.*, correspondence; an established sympathy and understanding; harmony (*Fr.*).

rapporteur, *n.*, a reporter.

rapprochement, *n.*, a reconciliation (*Fr.*).

rapscal'lion, *n.*, a low, mean fellow. (Also *rascallion*.)

rapt, *adj.*, in an ecstasy.

rap'tor, *n.*, one of the Raptores or birds of prey.

rapto'rial, *adj.*, living by rapine; pert. or rel. to the Raptores or birds of prey.

rapto'rious, *adj.*, *i.q.* raptorial.

rap'ture, *n.*, extreme joy.

rap'tured, *adj.*, in ecstasy.

rap'turous, *adj.*, ecstatic; extremely delighted.

rap'turously, *adv.*, in a rapturous way.

ra'ra a'vis, *n.*, a rare bird = a very uncommon thing or person (*Lat.*).

rare, *adj.*, uncommon; sparse; excellent; only lightly cooked.

rare'bit, *n.*, a dish of toasted cheese; Welsh rarebit; a dainty morsel.

rar'ee-show, *n.*, a peep show.

rarefac'tion, *n.*, expansion by separation of constituent particles.

rar'efiable, *adj.*, capable of being rarefied.

rar'efied, *p.p.*, rarefy.

rar'efy, *v.i.*, to become less dense; *v.t.*, to make less dense.

rar'efying, *pr.p.*, rarefy.

rare'ly, *adv.*, seldom; in a rare manner or degree.

rare'ness, *n.*, uncommonness; tenuity; value due to scarcity.

rar'er, *adj.*, *comp.* of rare.

rar'est, *adj.*, *super.* of rare.

rar'ity, *n.*, the quality of being rare; a thing valued for its excellence or scarcity.

ras, *n.*, a head or promontory; an Abyssinian prince.

ras'cal, *n.*, a scoundrel; a rogue; a lean deer.

rascal'ity, *n.*, mean trickiness; dishonesty.

rascal'lion, *n.*, *i.q.* rapscallion.

ras'cally, *adj.* and *adv.*, like a rascal; vile.

rase, *v.t.*, *i.q.* raze.

rash, *adj.*, precipitate; acting without caution; *n.*, an eruption of red spots or patches on the skin.

rash'er, *adj.*, *comp.* of rash; *n.*, a slice of bacon.

rash'ly, *adv.*, in a rash manner.

rash'ness, *n.*, precipitation; a rash act.

raso'rial, *adj.*, pert. or rel. to the Rasores or gallinaceous birds (scratchers).

rasp, *n.*, a coarse kind of file; *v.t.*, to rub with something rough; to vex.

rasp'atory, *n.*, a surgeon's rasp.

rasp'berry, *n.*, an edible soft fruit.

rasped, *p.p.*, rasp.

rasp'er, *n.*, a scraper; one who, or that which, rasps; a high, difficult fence in hunting; a difficult person.

rasp'ing, *pr.p.*, rasp.

rasp'ingly, *adv.*, in a rasping way.

rasse, *n.*, a kind of civet cat.

ras'ter, *n.*, a patch of light on a television screen.

ra'sure, *n.*, the act of scraping or erasing.

rat, *n.*, a small rodent mammal; a political deserter; *v.i.*, to catch rats; to desert a party from selfish motives.

ra'ta, *n.*, a New Zealand flowering tree.

rat(e)abil'ity, *n.*, the quality of being rateable.

rat(e)'able, *adj.*, liable to taxation; reckoned according to a certain rate.

rat(e)'ably, *adv.*, by rate or proportion.

ratafi'a, *n.*, a spirit flavoured with the kernels of cherries, peaches, etc.

rat'al, *n.*, the basis of rate assessment.

ratan', *n.*, *i.q.* rattan.

rat'any, *n.*, a Peruvian shrub used in medicine.

rataplan', *n.*, a drumming sound; *v.t.* and *i.*, to play on a drum (*Fr.*).

ratch, *n.*, a rack-bar with teeth in which a pawl falls, used to prevent the motion of a machine from being reversed.

ratch'et, *n.*, a little bar which catches in the teeth of a toothed wheel and holds it; a pawl.

ratch'il, *n.*, gravelly stone.

rate, *n.*, a proportion or standard; a degree of speed or other variable; a local tax; *v.t.*, to fix the value of; to scold.

ra'ted, *p.p.*, rate.

rat'el, *n.*, a nocturnal mammal.

rate'payer, *n.*, one who pays rates.

rate'payers, n., the pl. of ratepayer.

ra'ter, n., one who rates; a racing yacht of specified tonnage.

rath, n., a prehistoric Irish hillfort; a mound.

rathe, adj., early flowering.

rath'er, adv., sooner; more readily or properly; somewhat.

ratifica'tion, n., the act of ratifying; authorization.

rat'ified, p.p., ratify.

rat'ifier, n., one who ratifies.

rat'ify, v.t., to confirm; to make valid.

rat'ifying, pr.p., ratify.

ratine', n., i.q. ratteen.

ra'ting, n., the act of estimating; rank, esp. of men and ships in the Navy; pr.p., rate.

ra'tio, n., the measure of a quantity in terms of another, often expressed as a fraction.

ratioc'inate, v.i., to reason; to argue.

ratiocina'tion, n., the process of deductive reasoning.

ratiocina'tive, adj., characterized by ratiocination.

ra'tion, n., a serviceman's daily allowance of food; a legally authorized portion; v.t., to supply with rations; to impose legal apportionment.

ra'tional, adj., endowed with reason; agreeable to reason; n., an algebraical or arithmetical quantity expressible in finite terms.

rational'e, n., a statement of reasons or principles.

ra'tionalism, n., a system of religious opinions which denies inspiration or revelation.

ra'tionalist, n., one who adheres to rationalism.

rationalist'ic, adj., pert. or rel. to rationalism.

rational'ity, n., reasonableness.

rationaliza'tion, n., the act or result of rationalizing; the reduction of a pattern of behaviour to causes acceptable to reason.

ra'tionalize, v.i., to act as a rationalist; v.t., to bring into line with reason; to interpret as a rationalist.

ra'tionalized, p.p., rationalize.

ra'tionalizing, pr.p., rationalize.

ra'tionally, adv., reasonably; sensibly.

ra'tioned, p.p., ration.

ra'tioning, n., apportionment; pr.p., ration.

rat'ite, adj., pert. or rel. to a group of flightless birds (emu, etc.).

rat'lin, n., a small rope used in rope-ladders in the rigging of a ship.

rat'line, n., i.q. ratlin.

ratoon', n., a sprout from the root of a cut sugar-cane.

rats'bane, n., poison for rats.

rat'snake, n., a Ceylon snake which preys on rats.

rat'-tail, n., a disease of horses affecting the hair of the tail.

rattan', n., a cane or walking-stick made of the flexible stem of a tropical palm; the continuous roll of a drum. (Also *ratan*.)

rat'tat', n., a rapping sound; a quick series of raps.

rat'ted, p.p., rat.

ratteen', n., a thick twilled woollen stuff. (Also *ratine*.)

rat'ten, v.t., to destroy or take away maliciously tools or machinery.

rat'ter, n., one who catches rats; a terrier.

rat'ting, n., the hunting of rats; the desertion of one's political party; pr.p., rat.

rat'tle, n., a rapid succession of sharp sounds; an instrument for producing a rattling sound; a child's toy of this type; a chatterer; v.i., to make a rapid series of sharp sounds.

rat'tled, p.p., rattle.

rat'tler, n., a babbler; a rattlesnake.

rat'tlesnake, n., a venomous American snake with a rattling tail.

rat'tling, adj., excellent (slang); pr.p., rattle.

rat'ty, adj., rat-infested; snappy, touchy (slang).

rau'city, n., hoarseness; harshness of sound.

rau'cous, adj., hoarse; harsh.

rau'cously, adv., in a raucous way.

raughty, adj., i.q. rorty.

rav'age, n., devastation; v.t. and i., to lay waste by force.

rav'aged, p.p., ravage.

rav'ager, n., one who ravages.

rav'aging, pr.p., ravage.

rave, v.i., to be delirious; to speak enthusiastically.

raved, p.p., rave.

rav'el, v.t., to unweave; to entangle; to confuse; to make intricate.

rav'el(l)ed, p.p., ravel.

rave'lin, n., a separate work in fortification, triangular in plan.

rav'el(l)ing, n., a thread detached in the process of untwisting; pr.p., ravel.

rav'elment, n., perplexity; entanglement.

rav'en, adj., black; n., a large black bird of the crow family.

rav'en, n., prey; v.i., to prey with rapacity; v.t., to devour. (Also *ravin*.)

rav'ened, p.p., raven.

rav'ener, n., one who ravens, a plunderer.

rav'ening, adj., plundering, devouring; pr.p., raven.

rav'enous, adj., extremely hungry.

rav'enously, adv., in a ravenous manner.

ra'ver, n., one who raves.

rav'in, n. and v., i.q. rav'en.

ravine', n., a deep, narrow gorge; a gully.

ra'ving, adj., mad; n., incoherent talk; pr.p., rave.

rav'ish, v.t., to seize and carry away by force; to commit a rape upon; to enrapture.

rav'ished, p.p., ravish.

rav'isher, n., one who ravishes.

rav'ishing, adj., very delightful; pr.p., ravish.

rav'ishingly, *adv.*, very delightfully.

rav'ishment, *n.*, ecstasy.

raw, *adj.*, uncooked; not manufactured; not diluted; inexperienced; cold and damp.

raw'-boned, *adj.*, lean; gaunt.

raw'-head, *n.*, a spectre to frighten children with; a death's head.

raw'hide, *n.*, untanned leather; a heavy rope or whip of this.

raw'ish, *adj.*, somewhat raw.

raw'ness, *n.*, the state of being raw.

ray, *n.*, a line of light; a diverging radius; a radiating spine in the fin of a fish; one of a genus of fishes to which the skate belongs.

ra'yah, *n.*, in Turkey, a non-Mohammedan who pays the poll-tax.

rayed, *adj.*, adorned with rays.

ray'less, *adj.*, dark.

Ray'on, *n.*, artificial silk made from cellulose.

raze, *v.t.*, to graze; to level with the ground; to erase. (Also *rase*.)

razed, *p.p.*, raze.

razee', *n.*, a ship of war cut down to a smaller size (*hist.*).

ra'zing, *pr.p.*, raze.

ra'zor, *n.*, a keen knife used in shaving.

ra'zorbill, *n.*, the common auk.

razz'ia, *n.*, a hostile raid, (esp. of mohammedans).

raz'zle-daz'zle, *n.*, a spree or jollification (*slang*).

reabsorb', *v.t.*, to absorb again.

reabsorbed', *p.p.*, reabsorb.

reabsorb'ing, *pr.p.*, reabsorb.

reabsorp'tion, *n.*, the act of reabsorbing.

reach, *n.*, the distance one can reach; scope; a straight portion of a river between bends; *v.i.*, to extend; *i.q.* retch; *v.t.*, to touch by stretching towards; to arrive at; to give with the hand.

reach'able, *adj.*, within reach.

reached, *p.p.*, reach.

reach'er, *n.*, one who reaches.

reach'ing, *pr.p.*, reach.

react', *v.i.*, to resist action by an opposing force; to act mutually upon each other; to respond to a stimulus.

reac'tance, *n.*, an electrical resistance or inductance.

reac'tion, *n.*, the resistance made by a body to anything tending to change its state; the mutual action of chemical agents on each other; a retrograde tendency; depression after excitement; response to a stimulus.

reac'tionary, *adj.*, pert. or rel. to reaction; resistant to change.

reac'tivate, *v.t.*, to restore to activity.

reac'tivated, *p.p.*, reactivate.

reactivat'ing, *pr.p.*, reactivate.

react'ive, *adj.*, able to react.

reactiv'ity, *n.*, the state of being reactive.

reac'tor, *n.*, a nuclear reactor; an atomic pile (*chem.*).

read, *v.i.*, to follow visually and mentally written or printed matter; *v.t.*, to peruse; to understand; to study; to explain.

read, *p.p.*, read.

readabi'lity, *n.*, the quality of being readable.

read'able, *adj.*, worth reading; legible.

readdress', *v.t.*, to address again; to correct a wrong address.

readdressed', *p.p.*, readdress.

readdress'ing, *pr.p.*, readdress.

read'er, *n.*, one who reads; a reading-book; a corrector of the press; one who reads lessons, lectures, etc.

rea'dership, *n.*, the office of a reader or lecturer; the readers of a newspaper or periodical.

read'ier, *adj.*, *comp.* of ready.

read'iest, *adj.*, *super.* of ready.

read'ily, *adv.*, quickly; willingly.

read'iness, *n.*, the state of being ready; due preparation.

read'ing, *adj.*, given to the study of books; *n.*, the act of one who reads; a particular version of a passage; the recital of a Bill in Parliament; *pr.p.*, read.

read'ing-book, *n.*, a school-book containing exercises in reading.

read'ing-room, *n.*, a room appropriated to books, newspapers, etc., for readers.

readjust', *v.t.*, to adjust again.

readjust'ed, *p.p.*, readjust.

readjust'ing, *pr.p.*, readjust.

readjust'ment, *n.*, the act of readjusting.

readmis'sion, *n.*, the act of admitting again.

readmit', *v.t.*, to admit again.

readmit'tance, *n.*, *i.q.* readmission.

readmit'ted, *p.p.*, readmit.

readmit'ting, *pr.p.*, readmit.

read'y, *adj.*, prepared; prompt; willing.

read'ymade, *adj.*, kept in stock ready for use; not made to measure or to order.

read'y-reck'oner, *n.*, a volume of precalculated commercial tables.

reaffirm', *v.t.*, to affirm again.

reaffirma'tion, *n.*, a second affirmation.

reaffirmed', *p.p.*, reaffirm.

reaffirm'ing, *pr.p.*, reaffirm.

reaffor'est, *v.t.*, to convert again into a forest.

reaffor'ested, *p.p.*, afforest.

reaffor'esting, *pr.p.*, afforest.

rea'gency, *n.*, reactive power or operation.

rea'gent, *n.*, anything that produces a reaction.

re'al, *adj.*, actual; not imaginary; pert. or rel. to things that are permanent and immovable, as lands and tenements (*leg.*).

real'gar, *n.*, red orpiment; a brilliant red pigment.

re'alism, *n.*, the principles of a realist.

re'alist, n., in meta-physics, one who holds that external objects exist apart from our conceptions of them; in art and letters, one who re-produces nature or describes real life ex-actly as it appears to him.

realist'ic, adj., pert. or rel. to realism.

real'ity, n., the quality of being real; truth; fact.

re'alizable, adj., capable of being realized.

realiza'tion, n., the act of realizing.

re'alize, v.t., to make real; to accomplish; to gain; to convert into money.

re'alized, p.p., realize.

re'alizing, pr.p., realize.

re'ally, adv., actually; in truth.

realm, n., a kingdom, region or sphere.

re'al-politik', n., the theory and practice of national self-in-terest in international politics (Gr.).

re'altor, n., an estate agent.

re'alty, n., a real prop-erty; lands, tene-ments, etc.

ream, n., a package of paper, containing 20 quires; v.t., to enlarge the bore, as of a tobacco pipe.

rean'imate, v.t., to re-suscitate.

rean'imated, p.p., reani-mate.

rean'imating, pr.p., re-animate.

reanima'tion, n., the act of reanimating.

reannex', v.t., to annex again.

reannexa'tion, n., the act of annexing again.

reap, v.t., to cut down and gather, as wheat, etc.; to receive as a reward.

reaped, p.p., reap.

reap'er, n., one who reaps; a reaping-machine.

reap'ing, pr.p., reap.

reap'ing-hook, n., a sickle.

reappear', v.i., to appear again.

reappear'ance, n., a new appearance.

reappeared, p.p., reap-pear.

reappear'ing, pr.p., re-appear.

reappoint', v.t., to ap-point again.

reappoint'ed, p.p., re-appoint.

reappoint'ing, pr.p., re-appoint.

reappoint'ment, n., a re-newed appointment.

reappor'tion, v.t., to ap-portion again.

reappor'tioned, p.p., re-apportion.

reappor'tioning, pr.p., reapportion.

reappor'tionment, n., the act of reapportioning.

rear, adj., in the rear; hinder-most; n., the part behind; the back-ground; v.i., to rise on the hind legs; v.t., to erect; to educate; to breed.

rear-ad'miral, n., an ad-miral of the third degree or rank.

rear'-arch, n., the inner arch of a window or porch.

reared, p.p., rear.

rear'er, n., one who, or that which, rears.

rear'guard, n., that part of an army which fol-lows the main body to protect it.

rear'ing, n., the act of one who, or that which, rears; pr.p., rear.

rearm', v.t., to furnish with new and up-to-date armament.

rearm'ament, n., the act of re-arming.

rearmed', p.p., rearm.

rearm'ing, pr.p., rearm.

rear'mouse, n., the lea-ther-winged bat.

re-arrange', v.i., to ar-range again.

re-arranged', p.p., re-arrange.

re-arrange'ment, n., a second arrangement.

re-arrang'ing, pr.p., re-arrange.

rear'-vault, n., a vault between an arched window or door head and an arch in the inner face of a wall.

rear'ward, adj. and adv., towards the rear; n., the rearguard.

reascend', v.i., to ascend again.

reascend'ed, p.p., re-ascend.

reascend'ing, pr.p., re-ascend.

reascen'sion, n., the act of reascending.

rea'son, n., a cause act-ing on the mind; an explanation; a faculty of the mind; fairness; v.i., to argue logically; v.t., to examine argu-mentatively.

rea'sonable, adj., rational; agreeable to rea-son; equitable; mode-rate.

rea'sonableness, n., the quality of being rea-sonable.

rea'sonably, adv., in a reasonable manner; moderately.

rea'soned, p.p., reason.

rea'soner, n., one who reasons or argues.

rea'soning, n., the act of exercising the reason; arguments, proofs or reasons; pr.p., rea-son.

reassem'blage, n., a new collection or gather-ing together again.

reassem'ble, v.i., to meet together again; v.t., to collect again.

reassem'bled, p.p., re-assemble.

reassem'bling, pr.p., re-assemble.

reassert', v.t., to assert again.

reassert'ed, p.p., reas-sert.

reassert'ing, pr.p., re-assert.

reasser'tion, n., a re-newed assertion.

re-assess', v.t., to assess again.

re-assessed', p.p., re-assess.

re'assess'ing, pr.p., re-assess.

re'assess'ment, n., a re-newed assessment.

reassign', v.t., to assign again.

reassigned', p.p., reas-sign.

reassign'ing, pr.p., re-assign.

reassign'ment, n., a re-newed assignment.

reassume', v.t., to re-sume; to take again.

reassumed', p.p., reas-sume.

reassum'ing, pr.p., re-assume.

reassump'tion, n., a new assumption.

reassu'rance, n., con-firmation repeated; reinsurance.

reassure', v.t., to restore courage to; to rein-sure.

reassured', *p.p.*, reassure.

reassur'ing, *pr.p.*, reassure.

reast'y, *adj.*, rusty and rancid (salt meat).

re-attempt', *v.t.*, to try again.

re-attempt'ed, *p.p.*, re-attempt.

re-attempt'ing, *pr.p.*, re-attempt.

rebap'tism, *n.*, the act of rebaptizing.

rebaptize', *v.t.*, to baptize a second time.

rebaptized', *p.p.*, rebaptize.

rebaptiz'ing, *pr.p.*, rebaptize.

rebate', *v.i.*, to make a discount or deduction from; to blunt.

re'bate, *n.*, *i.q.* rebatement; the return of some part of a sum of money.

reba'ted, *p.p.*, rebate.

rebate'ment, *n.*, a diminution in price.

reba'ting, *pr.p.*, rebate.

re'beck, *n.*, a medieval, stringed instrument.

reb'el, *adj.*, rebellious; *n.*, one who revolts.

rebel', *v.t.*, to revolt; to refuse to obey.

rebelled', *p.p.*, rebel.

rebel'ling, *pr.p.*, rebel.

rebell'ion, *n.*, the act of rebelling; a refusal to obey lawful authority or government.

rebell'ious, *adj.*, characterized by rebellion.

rebell'iously, *adv.*, in a rebellious way.

rebell'ow, *v.t. and i.*, to re-echo loudly.

re-bind', *v.t.*, to bind anew.

re-bind'ing, *pr.p.*, re-bind.

re'-birth, *n.*, a fresh birth (*fig.*).

re'bite, *v.t.*, to re-acid an engraving.

reb'oant, *adj.*, resounding, re-echoing(*poet.*).

rebound', *n.*, resilience; a spring back; emotional reaction.

rebound', *v.i.*, to spring back.

re-bound', *adj.*, bound again; *p.p.*, re-bind.

rebound'ed, *p.p.*, rebound.

rebound'ing, *pr.p.*, rebound.

rebuff', *n.*, a repulse; *v.t.*, to repel the advances of.

rebuffed', *p.p.*, rebuff.

rebuff'ing, *pr.p.*, rebuff.

rebuild', *v.t.*, to build again.

rebuild'ing, *pr.p.*, rebuild.

rebuilt', *p.p.*, rebuild.

rebuke', *n.*, a reproof; *v.t.*, to reprimand.

rebuked', *p.p.*, rebuke.

rebu'ker, *n.*, one who rebukes.

rebu'king, *pr.p.*, rebuke.

re'bus, *n.*, a puzzle of words partly expressed by figures or pictures.

rebut', *v.t.*, to refute.

rebut'tal, *n.*, the act of rebutting; confutation.

rebut'ted, *p.p.*, rebut.

rebut'ter, *n.*, the answer of a defendant to the surrejoinder of a plaintiff.

rebut'ting, *pr.p.*, rebut.

recal'citrant, *adj.*, refractory; insubordinate.

recal'citrate, *v.i.*, to be refractory.

recal'citrated, *p.p.*, recalcitrate.

recal'citrating, *pr.p.*, recalcitrate.

recalcitra'tion, *n.*, the act of recalcitrating; refractoriness.

recalesce', *v.i.*, to grow warm again.

recalesced', *p.p.*, recalesce.

recales'cence, *n.*, renewed warmth.

recalesc'ing, *pr.p.*, recalesce.

recall', *n.*, a calling back; *v.t.*, to call back; to revoke; to bring back to memory.

recall'able, *adj.*, able to be recalled.

recalled', *p.p.*, recall.

recall'ing, *pr.p.*, recall.

recant', *v.t. and i.*, to unsay; to retract.

recanta'tion, *n.*, a declaration contradicting a previous one.

recant'ed, *p.p.*, recant.

recant'er, *n.*, one who recants.

recant'ing, *pr.p.*, recant.

re'cap, *n.*, recapitulation; *v.t.*, to recapitulate (*abbrev.*).

recapit'ulate, *v.t.*, to repeat or summarize.

recapit'ulated, *p.p.*, recapitulate.

recapit'ulating, *pr.p.*, recapitulate.

recapitula'tion, *n.*, the act of recapitulating; a summary.

recapit'ulatory, *adj.*, containing recapitulation.

recap'tion, *n.*, the re-taking, without force or violence, of one's own property.

recap'ture, *n.*, the act of re-taking; *v.t.*, to re-take.

recap'tured, *p.p.*, recapture.

recap'turing, *pr.p.*, recapture.

recast', *v.t.*, to mould anew; *p.p.*, recast.

recast'ing, *n.*, a re-moulding; *pr.p.*, recast.

recce, *n.*, reconnaissance (*abbrev., mil. slang*).

recede', *v.i.*, to move back; to become more distant; *v.t.*, to yield to a former possessor.

rece'ded, *p.p.*, recede.

rece'ding, *pr.p.*, recede.

receipt', *n.*, the act of receiving; a recipe; a plan or scheme; a written acknowledgement of something received; *v.t.*, to give a receipt for.

receipt'-book, *n.*, a book containing receipt-forms.

receipt'ed, *p.p.*, receipt.

receipt'ing, *pr.p.*, receipt.

receiv'able, *adj.*, such as may be received.

receive', *v.t.*, to accept; to contain; to take from a thief, knowing the thing received to have been stolen.

received', *p.p.*, receive.

receiv'er, *n.*, one who receives; a person appointed to receive rents, profits, etc.; a person who takes stolen goods from a thief; a vessel for receiving liquids or gases; a telephone earpiece; a wireless receiving-set.

receiv'ership, *n.*, the office of a receiver.

receiv′ing, *pr.p.*, receive.

re′cency, *n.*, *i.q.* recentness; nearness in time.

recen′sion, *n.*, a critical revision of a text.

re′cent, *adj.*, of late origin; modern; fresh.

re′cently, *adv.*, lately; not long since.

re′centness, *n.*, the state of being recent.

recep′tacle, *n.*, a repository; an object designed to receive.

receptac′ular, *adj.*, pert. or rel. to a receptacle.

receptibil′ity, *n.*, receivableness; the state of being receptible.

recep′tible, *adj.*, capable of being received.

recep′tion, *n.*, a receiving; a welcome; an entertainment.

recep′tionist, *n.*, a person employed to receive people; a receiver of information.

recep′tive, *adj.*, able to take in or contain.

recep′tively, *adv.*, in a receptive way.

recep′tiveness, *n.*, *i.q.* receptivity.

receptiv′ity, *n.*, the quality or state of being receptive.

recess′, *n.*, a moving back; a public holiday; a temporary suspension of business.

re′cess, *n.*, a niche; an alcove; *v.t.*, to make a recess in.

recessed′, *adj.*, having a recess or recesses; *p.p.*, recess.

reces′sion, *n.*, the act of receding; a falling off in business.

reces′sional, *adj.*, pert. or rel. to recession; *n.*, a hymn or anthem sung while the clergy and choir withdraw after service.

recess′ive, *adj.*, *i.q.* recessional.

Rech′abite, *n.*, a member of a friendly society of total abstainers.

re′charge′, *v.t.*, to charge again.

re′charged′, *p.p.*, recharge.

re′charg′ing, *pr.p.*, recharge.

réchauffé, *n.*, a warmed-up dish; a concoction of old materials (*Fr.*).

recheat′, *n.*, a call to hounds on a huntsman's horn.

recherché, *adj.*, exquisite; choice (*Fr.*).

rechoose′, *v.t.*, to choose again; to make a second choice.

rechri′sten, *v.t.*, to give a fresh name to.

recid′ivism, *n.*, the relapsing into crime.

recid′ivist, *n.*, a relapsed criminal; any person lapsing into former ways.

rec′ipe, *n.*, a prescription or receipt for making any mixture.

recip′iency, *n.*, the act or capacity of receiving.

recip′ient, *adj.*, receiving; *n.*, one who receives.

recip′rocal, *adj.*, mutual; inverse; *n.*, a quantity which results from dividing unity by another, to which it is said to be reciprocal.

reciprocal′ity, *n.*, the quality of being reciprocal.

recip′rocally, *adv.*, mutually; inversely.

recip′rocate, *v.i.*, to alternate; *v.t.*, to give and return mutually; to respond to an action by a similar one.

recip′rocated, *p.p.*, reciprocate.

recip′rocating, *adj.*, moving backwards and forwards alternately; *pr.p.*, reciprocate.

reciproca′tion, *n.*, an interchange of acts; alternation.

recip′rocator, *n.*, one who acts in a reciprocal manner; a double acting engine.

reciproc′ity, *n.*, the character of being reciprocal; equal rights mutually yielded and enjoyed, esp. commercial privileges.

reci′sion, *n.*, the act of cutting off.

reci′tal, *n.*, the act of reciting; that which is recited; a narrative; a musical entertainment given by a single performer.

recita′tion, *n.*, the act of reciting; a composition learned by heart and delivered before an audience.

recitative′, *n.*, a musical recitation or declamatory piece.

reci′tatively, *adv.*, in a recitative way.

recitati′vo, *n.*, *i.q.* recitative (*It.*).

recite′, *v.i.*, to rehearse a composition committed to memory; *v.t.*, to repeat from memory; to narrate.

reci′ted, *p.p.*, recite.

reci′ter, *n.*, one who recites; a narrator.

reci′ting, *pr.p.*, recite.

reciv′ilize, *v.t.*, to refine again.

reciv′ilized, *p.p.*, recivilize.

reciv′ilizing, *pr.p.*, recivilize.

reck, *v.i.*, to heed.

recked, *p.p.*, reck.

reck′ing, *pr.p.*, reck.

reck′less, *adj.*, heedless of consequences.

reck′lessly, *adv.*, in a reckless manner.

reck′lessness, *n.*, the quality of being reckless.

reck′on, *v.i.*, to compute; to suppose; *v.t.*, to count; to calculate.

reck′oned, *p.p.*, reckon.

reck′oner, *n.*, one who reckons; a help in reckoning.

reck′oning, *n.*, a calculation; charges; *pr.p.*, reckon.

reclaim′, *v.t.*, to claim back; to bring under cultivation; to reform.

reclaim′able, *adj.*, capable of being reclaimed.

reclaim′ant, *n.*, one who opposes or contradicts.

reclaimed′, *p.p.*, reclaim.

reclaim′ing, *pr.p.*, reclaim.

reclama′tion, *n.*, the act of reclaiming.

réclame, *n.*, self-advertisement; a considerable effect (*Fr.*).

rec′linate, *adj.*, (of a leaf) bent downward (*bot.*).

reclina′tion, *n.*, a surgical operation in the treatment of cataract.

recline′, *v.i.*, to repose in a recumbent position; *v.t.*, to lay down to rest.

reclined′, *p.p.*, recline.

recli′ner, *n.*, one who reclines.

recli′ning, *adj.*, leaning back or sideways; *pr.p.*, recline.

re'close, *v.t.*, to close again.

re'clothe, *v.t.*, to cover afresh, to re-invest.

re'clothed, *p.p.*, re-clothe.

re'cloth'ing, *pr.p.*, re-clothe.

recluse', *n.*, a person who lives in seclusion; a hermit.

reclu'sion, *n.*, retirement from the world.

reclu'sive, *adj.*, affording retirement.

re'coat, *v.t.*, to put a new coat of paint on.

recogni'tion, *n.*, the act of recognizing; acknowledgment.

rec'ognizable, *adj.*, capable of being recognized.

recog'nizance, *n.*, a personal legal obligation entered into under a penalty; a token.
or

recog'nizant, *adj.*, displaying recognition.

rec'ognize, *v.t.*, to perceive the identity of; to acknowledge.

rec'ognized, *p.p.*, recognize.

rec'ognizer, *n.*, one who recognizes.

rec'ognizing, *pr.p.*, recognize.

rec'ognizor, *n.*, one who gives recognizances.

re'coil, *n.*, a rebound.

recoil', *v.i.*, to fall back after an advance or forward impetus.

recoiled', *p.p.*, recoil.

recoil'er, *n.*, one who recoils.

recoil'ing, *n.*, i.q. recoilment; *pr.p.*, recoil.

recoil'ment, *n.*, the act of recoiling.

recoin', *v.t.*, to melt and mint anew.

recoin'age, *n.*, the act of recoining.

recollect', *v.t.*, to bring back to the mind; to remember.

re'-collect', *v.t.*, to collect what has been scattered.

recollect'ed, *p.p.*, recollect.

re'-collect'ed, *p.p.*, re-collect.

recollect'ing, *pr.p.*, recollect.

re'-collect'ing, *pr.p.*, re-collect.

recollec'tion, *n.*, remembrance.

re'-collec'tion, *n.*, the act of collecting what has been scattered.

recollect'ive, *adj.*, having the power of recollection.

recol'onize, *v.t.*, to colonize afresh.

recol'our, *v.t.*, to colour again.

recombina'tion, *n.*, combination for the second time.

recombine', *v.t.*, to combine again.

recommence', *v.t.*, to begin again.

recommenced', *p.p.*, recommence.

recommence'ment, *n.*, a new beginning.

recommenc'ing, *pr.p.*, recommence.

recommend', *v.t.*, to put favourably before another.

recommend'able, *adj.*, worthy of recommendation.

recommenda'tion, *n.*, a favourable representation; that which recommends.

recommend'atory, *adj.*, serving to recommend.

recommend'ed, *adj.*, favourably represented; *p.p.*, recommend.

recommend'er, one who recommends.

recommend'ing, *pr.p.*, recommend.

recommis'sion, *v.t.*, to commission, or put into commission again (*mil.* and *navy*).

recommit', *v.t.*, to commit again (to prison); to refer again (to a committee).

recommit'ment, *n.*, a second commitment.

recommit'tal, *n.*, i.q. recommitment.

recommit'ted, *p.p.*, recommit.

recommit'ting, *pr.p.*, recommit.

rec'ompense, *n.*, a reward; a compensation; *v.t.*, to reward; to compensate.

rec'ompensed, *p.p.*, recompense.

rec'ompensing, *pr.p.*, recompense.

recompose', *v.t.*, to compose again.

recomposed', *p.p.*, recompose.

recompos'ing, *pr.p.*, recompose.

recomposi'tion, *n.*, the act of bringing separated elements together again.

re'compound', *v.t.*, to remix.

rec'oncilable, *adj.*, capable of being brought again to friendly feelings, or made to agree.

rec'oncilably, *adv.*, harmoniously; consistently.

rec'oncile, *v.t.*, to restore to friendship after estrangement; to harmonize.

rec'onciled, *p.p.*, reconcile.

rec'oncilement, *n.*, renewal of friendship.

rec'onciler, *n.*, one who reconciles.

reconcilia'tion, *n.*, the act of reconciling enemies; the act of making consistent.

reconcil'iatory, *adj.*, tending to reconcile.

rec'onciling, *pr.p.*, reconcile.

rec'ondite, *adj.*, abstruse; learned.

recondi'tion, *v.t.*, to overhaul, to renovate.

recondi'tioned, *adj.*, overhauled; *p.p.*, recondition.

recondi'tioning, *n.*, an overhauling; *pr.p.*, recondition.

reconduct', *v.t.*, to conduct back.

recon'naissance, *n.*, a preliminary survey of an enemy's position (*Fr.*).

reconnoi'tre, *v.t.*, to make a preliminary military survey of (*Fr.*).

reconnoi'tred, *p.p.*, reconnoitre.

reconnoi'tring, *pr.p.*, reconnoitre.

recon'quer, *v.t.*, to conquer again; to recover.

reconsid'er, *v.t.*, to consider again.

reconsidera'tion, *n.*, the act of reconsidering.

reconsid'ered, *p.p.*, reconsider.

reconsid'ering, *pr.p.*, reconsider.

recon'stitute, *v.t.*, to constitute afresh.

recon'stituted, *p.p.*, reconstitute.

reconstitu'ting, *pr.p.*, reconstitute.

reconstitu'tion, *n.*, the act of reconstituting afresh.

reconstruct', *v.t.*, to construct again.

reconstruct'ed, *p.p.*, reconstruct.

reconstruct'ing, *pr.p.*, reconstruct.

reconstruc'tion, n., the act of constructing again.

reconver'sion, n., the act of reconverting.

reconvert', v.t., to convert again.

reconvert'ed, p.p., reconvert.

reconvert'ing, pr.p., reconvert.

reconvey', v.t., to transfer to a former owner or place.

reconvey'ance, n., the act of reconveying.

reconveyed', p.p., reconvey.

reconvey'ing, pr.p., reconvey.

recop'ied, p.p., recopy.

recop'y, v.t., to copy again.

recop'ying, pr.p., recopy.

record', v.t., to write down or represent in permanent form.

rec'ord, n., something written down to preserve the memory of anything; a public document; a highest achievement; recorded sound for playback.

record'ed, p.p., record.

record'er, n., one who records; a borough or city chief judge; an old musical wind instrument; a registering apparatus.

record'ing, adj., registering; n., the process of registering sound for subsequent reproduction; pr.p., record.

record'ist, n., one who records sound for reproduction.

rec'ord-player, n., a gramophone; an electrical instrument for playing back from a recorded disc.

recount', v.t., to narrate.

re'-count', n., a counting over again; v.t., to count again.

recount'ed, p.p., recount.

re'-counted, p.p., recount.

recount'ing, pr.p., recount.

re'-counting, pr.p., recount.

recoup', v.t., to keep back; to indemnify.

recouped', p.p., recoup.

recoup'ing, pr.p., recoup.

recoup'ment, n., the act of recouping.

recourse', n., a going to, as for protection or help.

recov'er, v.i., to grow well again; to regain a former condition; v.t., to regain.

re'-cover, v.t., to cover again.

recov'erable, adj., capable of being recovered.

recov'ered, p.p., recover.

re'-covered, p.p., recover.

recov'erer, n., one who recovers.

recov'ering, pr.p., recover.

re'-covering, pr.p., recover.

recov'ery, n., the act or power of getting again; the restoration from sickness or any low condition.

rec'reancy, n., cowardice.

rec'reant, adj., cowardly; false; n., one who yields basely.

rec'reantly, adv., in a cowardly way.

rec'reate, v.i., to take recreation; v.t., to reanimate; to amuse.

re'-create', v.t., to form anew.

rec'reated, p.p., recreate.

re'-crea'ted, p.p., recreate.

rec'reating, pr.p., recreate.

re'-crea'ting, pr.p., recreate.

recrea'tion, n., a refreshment of strength and spirits after labour; amusement.

re'-crea'tion, n., the act of forming anew.

rec'reative, adj., tending to recreate; diverting.

rec'rement, n., superfluous matter separated from that which is useful; dross.

recremen'tal, adj., drossy.

recrementi'tial, adj., i.q. recremental.

recrementi'tious, adj., i.q. recremental.

recrim'inate, v.i., to make a counter-accusation.

recrim'inated, p.p., recriminate.

recrim'inating, pr.p., recriminate.

recrimina'tion, n., a counter-accusation.

recrim'inative, adj., accusatory retorting.

recross', v.t. and i., to cross again.

recrossed', p.p., recross.

recros'sing, pr.p., recross.

recrudes'cence, n., growing raw, sore or painful again; the increased severity of a disease after temporary remission; a breaking out afresh.

recrudes'cent, adj., breaking out afresh.

recruit', n., a newly enlisted soldier; v.t., to repair by fresh supplies; to refresh; to supply with new men.

recruit'ed, p.p., recruit.

recruit'er, n., one who recruits.

recruit'ing, n., the act of enlisting new soldiers; pr.p., recruit.

recruit'ment, n., the business of recruiting.

rec'tal, adj., pert. or rel. to the rectum.

rect'angle, n., a right-angled parallelogram.

rect'angled, adj., having right angles.

rectan'gular, adj., right-angled.

rectangular'ity, n., the state of being rectangular.

rectang'ularly, adv., in a rectangular way.

rec'tifiable, adj., capable of being rectified.

rectifica'tion, n., the operation of rectifying; the process of purifying.

rec'tified, p.p., rectify.

rec'tifier, n., one who rectifies; a radio device for transforming an alternating to a direct current.

rec'tify, v.t., to put right; to refine by distillation.

rec'tifying, pr.p., rectify.

rec'tigrade, adj., walking in a straight line; n., a kind of spider which walks in a straight line.

rectilin'eal, adj., bounded by, or consisting of, straight lines.

rectilin'ear, adj., i.q. rectilineal.

recti'tis, n., inflammation of the rectum (med.).

rec'titude, n., honesty; uprightness; rightness of principle.

rec'to, n., the right-hand page of an open book; front of leaf (Lat.).

rec'tor, n., a clergyman who possesses parsonage and predial tithes; the head of a college or university.

rec'torate, n., the office or rank of a rector.

recto'rial, adj., pert. or rel. to a rector or rectory.

rec'tory, n., a rector's benefice or dwelling.

rec'tum, n., the part of the large intestine leading to the anus.

recum'bence, n., the state of being recumbent.

recum'bency, n., i.q. recumbence.

recum'bent, adj., reclining; lying down.

recum'bently, adv., in a recumbent way.

recu'perate, v.i., to recover.

recu'perated, adj., recovered; p.p., recuperate.

recu'perating, pr.p., recuperate.

recupera'tion, n., recovery.

recu'perative, adj., tending to recovery.

recu'perator, n., that which revives or restores vigour.

recur', v.i., to return; to occur again.

recurred', p.p., recur.

recur'rence, n., the act of recurring; return.

recur'rent, adj., returning from time to time.

recur'rently, adv., in a recurrent way.

recur'ring, adj., returning again; circulating; pr.p., recur.

recurv'ate, adj., curved backward or outward.

recurv'ature, n., a bending backwards.

recurve, v.t. and i., to bend backwards.

recurved', p.p., recurve.

recurv'ing, pr.p., recurve.

recurv'ous, adj., bent backward.

rec'usancy, n., the state of being a recusant; nonconformity.

rec'usant, adj., refusing to acknowledge authority; n., one who will not conform.

recusa'tion, n., a refusal; an appeal (leg.).

red, adj., of the colour of blood; n., one of the primary colours.

redact', v.t., to prepare for publication.

redac'tion, n., the preparation for publication; an editorial staff.

redac'tor, n., an editor.

red-ad'miral, n., the British butterfly, vanessa atalanta.

redan', n., a simple field fortification with a salient angle (mil.).

red'breast, n., a bird commonly called the robin.

red'cap, n., the goldfinch; a kind of spectre haunting Scottish castles; slang for a military policeman.

red'coat, n., a soldier (18th and 19th cent.).

redd, v.t., to tidy-up; to put right (Scot.).

red'den, v.t., to make red; v.i., to become red.

redden'dum, n., a particular clause in a lease (Lat.).

red'dened, p.p., redden.

red'dening, pr.p., redden.

red'dish, adj., somewhat red.

redd'ishness, n., the state of being red.

red'dle, n., red chalk; a pigment used to mark sheep with.

rede, v.t., to counsel or advise.

re'dec'orate, v.t., to decorate again.

re'dec'orated, p.p., redecorate.

re'decorat'ing, pr.p., redecorate.

re'decora'tion, n., a decorating anew.

redeem', v.t., to buy back; to ransom; to rescue; to atone for.

redeem'able, adj., capable of being redeemed.

redeemed', p.p., redeem.

redeem'er, n., one who redeems.

redeem'ing, pr.p., redeem.

rede'less, adj., unwise.

redeliv'er, v.t., to deliver again; to restore.

redeliv'ered, p.p., redeliver.

redeliv'ering, pr.p., redeliver.

redemp'tible, adj., i.q. redeemable.

redemp'tion, n., the act of redeeming; the state of being redeemed.

redemp'tionary, n., one who may be redeemed.

redemp'tive, adj., serving to redeem.

Redemp'torist, n., one of a religious congregation which devotes itself to education.

redemp'tory, adj., paid for ransom.

redeploy', v.t., to rearrange staff or equipment to increase output.

redeployed', p.p., redeploy.

redeploy'ing, pr.p., redeploy.

redeploy'ment, n., an improving arrangement of men and equipment to increase output.

redescend', v.i. and t., to descend again.

re'develop', v.t., to develop anew.

re'developed', p.p., redevelop.

redevelop'ing, pr.p., redevelop.

re'develop'ment, n., the process of developing afresh.

red'-eye, n., the red-eyed vireo or greenlet; an American singing-bird; a small, freshwater fish.

red'-gum, n., an infantile eruptive skin disease; the red Eucalyptus tree.

red'handed, adj., at the moment of the act.

red'head, n., a person with red hair; an American duck; the red-headed woodpecker; a kind of milkweed.

redhibi'tion, n., the annulling of a sale and return of the purchase on account of some defect.

redhib'itory, adj., pert. or rel. to redhibition.

red'hot, adj., heated to redness; extreme (fig.)

red'ingote, n., a long, plain, double-breasted overcoat.

redin'tegrate, v.t., to make whole again.

redin'tegrated, p.p., redintegrate.

redin'tegrating, pr.p., redintegrate.

redintegra'tion, n., the restoration to a sound state.

redirect', v.t., to re-address a letter, etc., to send on.

redirect'ed, *p.p.*, redirect.

redirect'ing, *pr.p.*, redirect.

re'direction, *n.*, a new direction.

redisco'ver, *v.t.*, to discover anew.

redisco'vered, *p.p.*, rediscover.

redisco'vering, *pr.p.*, rediscover.

redisco'very, *n.*, a renewed discovery.

redispose', *v.t.*, to dispose again.

redistrib'ute, *v.t.*, to distribute again.

redistrib'uted, *p.p.*, redistribute.

redistrib'uting, *pr.p.*, redistribute.

redistribu'tion, *n.*, a new distribution.

redivide', *v.t.*, to divide anew.

redivid'ed, *p.p.*, redivide.

redivid'ing, *pr.p.*, redivide.

redivi'sion, *n.*, a dividing anew.

red'-letter, *adj.*, marked by red letters; fortunate.

red'ness, *n.*, the quality of being red.

red'olence, *n.*, fragrance.

red'olent, *adj.*, fragrant.

re'double, *v.i.*, to become twice as much; *v.t.*, to increase by repeated additions.

re'doubled, *p.p.*, redouble.

re'doubling, *pr.p.*, redouble.

redoubt', *n.*, a small, military fieldwork.

redoubt'able, *adj.*, formidable, valiant.

redoubt'ed, *adj.*, *i.q.* redoubtable.

redound', *v.i.*, to flow back as a wave; to contribute.

redound', *p.p.*, redound.

redound'ing, *pr.p.*, redound.

redraft', *n.*, a second copy; *v.i.*, to draw up a second time.

redraft'ed, *p.p.*, redraft.

redraft'ing, *pr.p.*, redraft.

redraw', *v.i.*, to draw a new bill of exchange; *v.t.*, to draw again.

redress', *n.*, a reparation; *v.t.*, to remedy; to compensate.

re'-dress', *v.t.* and *i.*, to dress again; to dress differently.

redress'able, *adj.*, capable of being redressed.

redressed', *p.p.*, redress.

re'-dressed', *p.p.*, redress.

redress'ing, *pr.p.*, redress.

re'-dress'ing, *pr.p.*, redress.

redress'ive, *adj.*, affording redress.

red'root, *n.*, a species of American plants with red roots.

red'shank, *n.*, a long-legged bird like a snipe.

red'skin, *n.*, a North American Indian.

red'-spider, *n.*, a mite which attacks plums, wines and greenhouse plants.

red'start, *n.*, a singing bird akin to the robin.

red'-streak, *n.*, a sort of apple.

red'-tape', *n.*, excessive regard to routine.

red-ta'pism, *n.*, excessive officialism.

red'top, *n.*, a valuable pasture grass grown in the U.S.A.

reduce', *v.t.*, to bring to any state or condition; to make less or lower; to subdue; to separate metal from dross.

reduced', *p.p.*, reduce.

redu'cent, *adj.*, tending to reduce.

redu'cible, *adj.*, capable of being reduced; convertible.

redu'cing, *pr.p.*, reduce.

reduc'tion, *n.*, the conversion into another state or denomination; a diminution; subjugation.

reduc'tive, *adj.*, tending to reduce.

reduit, *n.*, a place to retreat to (*Fr.*).

redun'dance, *n.*, superfluity; that which is redundant.

redun'dancy, *n.*, *i.q.* redundance; superfluity of labour for the employment available.

redun'dant, *adj.*, superfluous.

redun'dantly, *adv.*, superfluously.

redu'plicate, *v.t.*, to double; to multiply; to repeat.

redu'plicated, *p.p.*, reduplicate.

redu'plicating, *pr.p.*, reduplicate.

reduplica'tion *n.*, the act of reduplicating; the repetition of a root, prefix or initial syllable.

redu'plicative, *adj.*, tending to reduplicate.

red'wing, *n.*, a kind of thrush passing through Britain in winter.

reeb'ok, *n.*, a small S. African antelope.

re-ech'o, *n.*, the echo of an echo; *v.i.* and *t.*, to reverberate again.

re-ech'oed, *p.p.*, re-echo.

re-ech'oing, *pr.p.*, re-echo.

reed, *n.*, a tall, broad-leaved plant with a hollow stem; a musical instrument made from a reed; a little tube in a wind instrument; part of a loom; *v.t.*, to thatch.

reed'ed, *adj.*, covered with reeds; *p.p.*, reed.

re'ed'ify, *v.t.*, to rebuild.

reed'iness, *n.*, the state of being reedy.

reed'ing, *n.*, a small, convex, architectural moulding; the milling on the edge of a coin.

re-ed'it, *v.t.*, to edit afresh.

re-ed'ited, *p.p.*, re-edit.

re-ed'iting, *pr.p.*, re-edit.

reed'less, *adj.*, destitute of reeds.

reed'ling, *n.*, a bird, the bearded tit.

reed'y, *adj.*, abounding with reeds; resembling a reed; having a thin, harsh tone.

reef, *n.*, a mass of rocks in the sea near the surface; a gold-bearing vein of quartz; part of a sail capable of being drawn together; *v.t.*, to reduce the size of a sail by folding part of it.

reefed, *p.p.*, reef.

reef'er, *n.*, a thick, short jacket; a narcotic cigarette.

reef'ing, *pr.p.*, reef.

reef'y, *adj.*, abounding in reefs.

reek, *n.*, smoke; vapour; *v.i.*, to smoke; to emit vapour; to smell strongly.

reeked, *p.p.*, reek.

reek'ing, *adj.*, emitting vapour; smelling strongly; *pr.p.*, reek.

reek'y, *adj.*, smoky.

reel, *n.*, a bobbin; a frame on which a line may be wound; a dance (*Scot.*); a staggering motion; *v.i.*, to dance a reel; to stagger in walking.

re-elect', *v.t.*, to elect again.

re-elect'ed, *p.p.*, re-elect.

re-elect'ing, *pr.p.*, re-elect.

re'-elec'tion, *n.*, a second election.

reeled, *p.p.*, reel.

re-el'igible, *adj.*, qualified for re-election.

reel'ing, *adj.*, staggering; *pr.p.*, reel.

re-embark', *v.i.* and *t.*, to embark again.

re-embarka'tion, *n.*, a new embarkation.

re-embarked', *p.p.*, re-embark.

re-embark'ing, *pr.p.*, re-embark.

re-emerge', *v.i.*, to emerge again, to reappear.

re-emerged', *p.p.*, re-emerge.

re-emerg'ing, *pr.p.*, re-emerge.

re-enact', *v.t.*, to enact again.

re-enact'ed, *p.p.*, re-enact.

re-enact'ing, *pr.p.*, re-enact.

re-enact'ment, *n.*, the passing of a law a second time.

re-enforce', *v.t.*, to enforce anew.

re-enforced', *p.p.*, re-enforce.

re-enforce'ment, *n.*, the act of re-enforcing.

re-enforc'ing, *pr.p.*, re-enforce.

re-engage', *v.t.* and *i.*, to engage a second time.

re-engaged', *p.p.*, re-engage.

re-engage'ment, *n.*, a second engagement.

re-engag'ing, *pr.p.*, re-engage.

re-en'ter, *v.t.*, to enter again; to cut incisions deeper.

re-en'tered, *p.p.*, re-enter.

re-en'tering, *adj.*, (of an angle) pointing inwards; *pr.p.*, re-enter.

re-en'trance, *n.*, the act of entering again.

re-en'trant, *adj.*, (*angle*) that points inwards; *n.*, a re-entrant angle; a valley between two salients.

re-en'try, *n.*, an entry made again.

re-estab'lish, *v.t.*, to establish anew.

re-estab'lished, *p.p.*, re-establish.

re-estab'lishing, *pr.p.*, re-establish.

re-estab'lishment, *n.*, the act of re-establishing.

reeve, *n.*, a bailiff; a steward; a bird, the female of the ruff; *v.t.* and *i.*, to pass a rope through a hole.

reeved, *p.p.*, reeve.

reev'ing, *pr.p.*, reeve.

re'-examina'tion, *n.*, a renewed examination.

re-exam'ine, *v.t.*, to examine anew.

re-exam'ined, *p.p.*, re-examine.

re-exam'ining, *pr.p.*, re-examine.

re-exist', *v.i.*, to exist again.

re-export', *v.t.*, to export after having imported.

re-ex'port, *n.*, any commodity re-exported.

ref, *n.*, a football referee (*collog.*); the abbrev. for reference.

reface', *v.t.*, to put a new facing on.

refaced', *p.p.*, reface.

refac'ing, *pr.p.*, reface.

refash'ion, *v.t.*, to form into shape a second time.

refash'ioned, *p.p.*, refashion.

refash'ioning, *pr.p.*, refashion.

refec'tion, *n.*, refreshment; a repast.

refec'tive, *adj.*, refreshing.

refec'tory, *n.*, a dining-room, esp. in convents, colleges, etc.

refer, *v.i.*, to allude; to direct the attention; *v.t.*, to assign; to trace back; to impute.

ref'erable, *adj.*, considered as belonging.

referee', *n.*, an arbitrator.

ref'erence, *n.*, the act of referring; a note in a book which refers a reader elsewhere.

referen'dary, *adj.*, pert. to a referendum.

referen'dum, *n.*, a reference to the people of a measure passed by their representatives, for final approval.

referen'tial, *adj.*, having reference.

referred', *p.p.*, refer.

refer'rer, *n.*, one who refers.

refer'ring, *pr.p.*, refer.

re'fill, *n.*, a filling again.

refill', *v.t.* and *i.*, to fill again.

refilled', *p.p.*, refill.

refill'ing, *pr.p.*, refill.

refine', *v.t.*, to purify; to separate from other metals or dross; to give culture to; to polish (the manners).

refined', *adj.*, elegant in character; *p.p.*, refine.

refi'nedly, *adv.*, in a refined manner.

refine'ment, *n.*, the act of refining; elegance of manners, language, etc.; over-nicety.

refi'ner, *n.*, one who refines liquors, metals, sugar, etc.

refi'nery, *n.*, a place for refining metals, sugar, oil, etc.

refi'ning, *pr.p.*, refine.

refit', *v.t.*, to restore after damage or wear.

refit'ted, *p.p.*, refit.

refit'ting, *pr.p.*, refit.

refla'tion, *n.*, the process of correcting deflation.

refla'tionary, *adj.*, moving towards inflation.

reflect', *v.i.*, to return rays (of light, heat, sound, etc.); to consider seriously; to bring reproach; *v.t.*, to direct back after striking a surface; to give back an image.

reflect'ed, *p.p.*, reflect.

reflect'ible, *adj.*, capable of being reflected.

reflect'ing, *adj.*, throwing back light as a mirror; meditative; *pr.p.*, reflect.

reflect'ingly, *adv.*, *i.q.* reflectively.

reflec'tion, *n.*, the act of reflecting or the state of being reflected; an image formed by a reflecting surface; continued meditation; a reproach. (Also *reflexion*.)

reflect'ive, *adj.,* throwing back rays; exercising reflection; reflexive.

reflect'ively, *adv.,* in a reflective way.

reflect'or, *n.,* one who, or that which, reflects; a reflecting telescope.

reflet', *n.,* lustre, iridescence, esp. on pottery (*Fr.*).

re'flex, *adj.,* having a backward direction; performed involuntarily; *n.,* an image produced by reflection.

reflex', *v.t.,* to bend back.

reflexed', *adj.,* bent back; *p.p.,* reflex.

reflexibil'ity, *n.,* the quality of being reflexible.

reflex'ible, *adj.,* capable of being reflected or reflexed.

reflex'ing, *pr.p.,* reflex.

reflex'ion, *n.,* *i.q.* reflection.

reflex'ive, *adj.,* (of a verb) having as its direct object a pronoun standing for the subject (also applied to pronouns of this type).

refloat', *v.t.* and *i.,* to float again (as a ship).

refloat'ed, *p.p.,* refloat.

refloat'ing, *pr.p.,* refloat.

reflores'cence, *n.,* a second blossoming.

ref'luence, *n.,* a flowing back.

ref'luent, *adj.,* flowing back; ebbing.

re'flux, *adj.,* flowing back; *n.,* a flowing back; the ebb.

refoot', *v.t.,* to provide (a sock or stocking) with a new foot.

refoot'ed, *p.p.,* refoot.

refoot'ing, *pr.p.,* refoot.

refo'rest, *v.t.,* to turn into a forest again.

refo'rested, *p.p.,* reforest.

refo'resting, *pr.p.,* reforest.

reform', *n.,* the amendment of what is defective or bad; a change in the regulations affecting parliamentary representation; *v.i.,* to amend one's behaviour; *v.t.,* to amend.

re'-form, *v.t.,* to give another arrangement to.

reform'able, *adj.,* capable of being reformed.

Reforma'tion, *n.,* the religious revolution of the sixteenth century.

reforma'tion, *n.,* an amendment of life, manners, etc.

re-forma'tion, *n.,* the act of forming again; a second, and different, formation.

reform'ative, *adj.,* tending to reform.

reform'atory, *adj.,* *i.q.* reformative.

reformed', *adj.,* amended; changed; *p.p.,* reform.

re'-formed, *p.p.,* reform.

reform'er, *n.,* one who reforms; one who promotes political reform; one of those who brought about the Reformation.

reform'ing, *pr.p.,* reform.

re'-forming, *pr.p.,* reform.

reform'ism, *n.,* political or social reform.

reform'ist, *n.,* a political reformer.

refract', *v.t.,* to deflect light on passing from one medium to another.

refract'ed, *adj.,* turned from a direct course; *p.p.,* refract.

refract'ing, *adj.,* serving to refract; *pr.p.,* refract.

refrac'tion, *n.,* the act of refracting or the state of being refracted.

refract'ive, *adj.,* pert. or rel. to refraction.

refractom'eter, *n.,* an apparatus for measuring the angle of refraction.

refrac'tor, *n.,* a refracting medium; a lens or telescope (of this type).

refrac'torily, *adv.,* in a refractory manner.

refrac'toriness, *n.,* the quality or state of being refractory.

refrac'tory, *adj.,* stubborn and unmanageable.

re-frac'ture, *n.,* a second fracture of the same thing.

ref'ragable, *adj.,* capable of being resisted or refuted.

refrain', *n.,* the burden of a song; a kind of musical repetition; *v.i.,* to forbear; to abstain; *v.t.,* to restrain.

refrained', *p.p.,* refrain.

refrain'ing, *pr.p.,* refrain.

refrangibil'ity, *n.,* the quality of being refrangible.

refran'gible, *adj.,* subject to, or capable of, refraction.

refreeze', *v.t.,* to freeze again.

refreez'ing, *pr.p.,* refreeze.

refresh', *v.t.,* to give new strength to; to freshen.

refreshed', *p.p.,* refresh.

refresh'er, *n.,* one who, or that which, refreshes; an additional fee paid to counsel (*leg.*).

refresh'ing, *adj.,* invigorating; *pr.p.,* refresh.

refresh'ingly, *adv.,* in a refreshing way.

refresh'ment, *n.,* the act of refreshing; that which refreshes or reinvigorates.

refrig'erant, *adj.* and *n.,* *i.q.* refrigerative.

refrig'erate, *v.t.,* to cool.

refrig'erated, *p.p.,* refrigerate.

refrig'erating, *pr.p.,* refrigerate.

refrigera'tion, *n.,* the act of refrigerating.

refrig'erative, *adj.,* cooling; *n.,* a cooling medicine.

refrig'erator, *n.,* that which keeps cool or refrigerates; a machine for making ice; a cold chest.

refrig'eratory, *adj.,* cooling.

refroze', *p.p.,* refroze.

refu'el, *v.t.,* to supply again with fuel.

refu'elled, *p.p.,* refuel.

refu'elling, *pr.p.,* refuel.

ref'uge, *n.,* shelter from distress; an expedient to secure protection.

refugee', *n.,* one who flees for refuge.

reful'gence, *n.,* splendour; brilliancy.

reful'gent, *adj.,* shining; splendid.

refund', *n.,* a repayment; *v.t.,* to pay back.

refund'ed, *p.p.,* refund.

refund'ing, *pr.p.,* refund.

refurb'ish, v.t., to do up again; to restore to former condition.

refurb'ished, p.p., refurbish.

refurb'ishing, pr.p., refurbish.

refurn'ish, v.t. and i., to furnish afresh.

refurn'ished, adj., furnished again; p.p., refurnish.

refurn'ishing, pr.p., refurnish.

refu'sable, adj., capable of being refused.

refu'sal, n., the denial of a request; an option or pre-emption.

refuse', v.i., not to comply; to decline; v.t., to deny the request of.

ref'use, adj., left as worthless; n., waste matter; garbage.

refused', p.p., refuse.

refu'ser, n., one who refuses.

refu'sing, pr.p., refuse.

refu'table, adj., capable of being refuted.

refu'tably, adv., in a refutable way.

refuta'tion, n., an overthrow by argument.

refute', v.t., to disprove; to prove to be false.

refu'ted, p.p., refute.

refu'ting, pr.p., refute.

regain', v.t., to recover something lost.

regained', p.p., regain.

regain'ing, pr.p., regain.

re'gal, adj., royal.

regale', v.i., to fare sumptuously; v.t., to entertain sumptuously; to gratify.

regaled', p.p., regale.

regale'ment, n., entertainment; gratification.

rega'lia, n. pl., the symbols of royalty; the insignia of a society.

rega'ling, pr.p., regale.

reg'alism, n., the doctrine of royal supremacy.

regal'ity, n., kingship; a Scottish territorial jurisdiction.

re'gally, adv., in a regal manner.

regard', n., attention; esteem; reference; v.t., to look upon; to observe; to pay attention to; to respect or esteem; to view in the light of.

regard'ant, adj., watching, applied to an animal looking backward (her.).

regard'ed, p.p., regard.

regard'ful, adj., paying regard.

regard'ing, prep., in reference to; pr.p., regard.

regard'less, adj., heedless, without consideration.

regard'lessly, adv., heedlessly.

regard'lessness, n., the state of being heedless.

regat'ta, n., a meeting at which aquatic sports take place (It.).

regelate', v.i., to refreeze after a slight thaw.

regela'tion, n., the freezing together of two pieces of ice during a slight thaw.

re'gency, n., the office or jurisdiction of a regent.

regen'eracy, n., the state of being regenerated.

regen'erate, adj., reproduced; changed spiritually; n., a convert; one changed spiritually.

regen'erate, v.t., to reproduce; to change the affections from indifference to love; to create new force in.

regen'erated, p.p., regenerate.

regen'erating, pr.p., regenerate.

regenera'tion, n., the act of regenerating.

regen'erative, adj., producing regeneration.

regen'erator, n., one who regenerates; an apparatus to maintain and conserve heat in engines, furnaces, etc.

regen'eratory, adj., i.q. regenerative.

regen'esis, n., rebirth; reproduction.

re'gent, adj., exercising vicarious authority; n., one who rules during the minority or disability of a king.

regerm'inate, v.i., to sprout afresh.

regermina'tion, n., a second germination or vegetation.

reg'icidal, adj., pert. or rel. to regicide.

reg'icide, n., one who kills a king; the murder of a king.

régie, n., the state monopoly of tobacco, salt, etc. (Fr.).

regild', v.t., to gild afresh.

régime', n., a system of government or administration (Fr.).

reg'imen, n., orderly government; the regulation of diet, habits, etc.

reg'iment, n., a body of soldiers commanded by a colonel.

regimen'tal, adj., rel. to a regiment.

regimen'tally, adv., uniformly.

regimenta'tion, n., a strict ordering.

regin'a, n., a reigning queen (Lat.).

regin'al, adj., queenly.

re'gion, n., a tract of land of indefinite but considerable extent; a division of the body.

re'gional, adj., pert. or rel. to a particular region.

re'gionally, adv., in a regional way.

reg'ister, n., a record; a list; a contrivance for regulating combustion in a stove or range; the compass of a voice or musical instrument; a set of pipes in an organ; v.i., to correspond exactly, in colour-printing; v.t., to enter in a register.

reg'istered, adj., enrolled; entered in a list; p.p., register.

reg'istering, pr.p., register.

register office, n., a place where marriages are formally and legally conducted.

reg'istrar, n., a keeper of records.

reg'istrarship, n., the office of a registrar.

reg'istrary, n., i.q. registrar (a term used by Cambridge University).

registra'tion, n., the act of inserting in a register.

registra'tor, n., one concerned with registration.

reg'istry, n., the place where a register is kept.

reg'istry office, n., i.q. register office.

re'gius, adj., royal (Lat.).

re'gius profes'sor, n., one of certain professors at older universities appointed by the Crown.

reg'let, n., a strip used in printing to separate pages in the chase; a flat, narrow moulding between panels.

reg'nal, adj., pert. or rel. to the reign of a monarch.

reg'nancy, n., sovereignty; rule.

reg'nant, adj., reigning as sovereign; prevalent.

regorge', v.t., to swallow again; to vomit up.

regorged', p.p., regorge.

regorg'ing, pr.p., regorge.

regrant', n., a new grant; v.t., to grant back.

regrant'ed, p.p., regrant.

regrant'ing, pr.p., regrant.

regrate', v.t., to buy and sell again in (or near) the same market; to corner locally.

regra'ted, p.p., regrate.

regra'ter, n., one who buys provisions and sells them in the same market.

regra'ting, pr.p., regrate.

re'gress, n., the power of returning.

regress', v.i., to move backwards.

regressed', p.p., regress.

regress'ing, pr.p., regress.

regres'sion, n., the act of passing back.

regress'ive, adj., passing back.

regress'ively, adv., in a regressive way.

regress'iveness, n., i.q. regression.

regret', n., sorrowful longing; remorse; v.t., to look back at with sorrowful longing.

regret'ful, adj., full of regret.

regret'fully, adv., with regret.

regret'table, adj., to be regretted.

regret'tably, adv., in a regrettable way.

regret'ted, p.p., regret.

regret'ting, pr.p., regret.

regroup', v.t. and i., to form anew into a group; to re-form.

regrouped', p.p., regroup.

regroup'ing, pr.p., regroup.

reg'ular, adj., in accordance with rule; methodical; uniform; symmetrical; n., a soldier of a permanent army.

regular'ity, n., the quality of being regular.

reg'ularize, v.t., to make regular or conformable to rule.

re'gularized, p.p., regularize.

reg'ularizing, pr.p., regularize.

reg'ularly, adv., in a regular manner.

reg'ulate, v.t., to adjust by rule; to direct; to cause to act properly.

reg'ulated, p.p., regulate.

reg'ulating, pr.p., regulate.

regula'tion, n., the act of regulating; a rule.

reg'ulative, adj., tending to regulate.

reg'ulator, n., one who, or that which, regulates.

reg'ulus, n., an old name for antimony; a petty king.

regur'gitate, v.i., to surge back; to bring back some part of the contents of the stomach; v.t., to cause to surge back.

regur'gitated, p.p., regurgitate.

regur'gitating, pr.p., regurgitate.

regurgita'tion, n., the act of regurgitating; the rising into the mouth of part of the contents of the stomach.

rehabil'itate, v.t., to reinstate; to re-establish in the esteem of others; to retrain for everyday life.

rehabil'itated, p.p., rehabilitate.

rehabilitat'ing, pr.p., rehabilitate.

rehabilita'tion, n., the act of rehabilitating.

rehan'dle, v.t., to handle afresh.

rehan'dled, p.p., rehandle.

rehan'dling, pr.p., rehandle.

rehang', v.t., to hang again.

rehang'ing, pr.p., rehang.

rehash', n., old material newly made up; v.t., to work up old material in a new form.

rehear', v.t., to hear again; to try (a case) a second time.

reheard', p.p., rehear.

rehear'ing, n., a further trial; pr.p., rehear.

rehears'al, n., a trial performance; the act of rehearsing.

rehearse', v.t., to recite; to repeat experimentally before actually performing.

rehearsed', p.p., rehearse.

rehears'er, n., one who rehearses.

rehears'ing, pr.p., rehearse.

reheat', v.t., to heat again.

reheat'ed, adj., heated again; p.p., reheat.

reheater', n., that which reheats.

reheat'ing, pr.p., reheat.

rehouse', v.t., to provide new dwellings for.

rehoused', p.p., rehouse.

rehous'ing, n., the provision of new dwellings; pr.p., rehouse.

rehung', p.p., rehang.

Reich, n., the German state.

reign, n., sovereignty; the time during which a sovereign reigns; v.i., to exercise sovereign power.

reigned', p.p., reign.

reign'ing, pr.p., reign.

reignite', v.t. and i., to rekindle.

reignit'ed, p.p., reignite.

reignit'ing, pr.p., reignite.

reimburse', v.t., to refund; to pay back to.

reimbursed', p.p., reimburse.

reimburse'ment, n., a repayment.

reimburs'ing, pr.p., reimburse.

reim'port, v.t., to import (same goods) after exporting.

re'import, n., an item imported after having been exported.

reim'ported, p.p., reimport.

reim'porting, pr.p., reimport.

reimpose', v.t., to impose again; to re-arrange pages for printing.

reimposed', p.p., reimpose.

reimpos'ing, *pr.p.*, re-impose.

reimposi'tion, *n.*, a re-arrangement of pages for printing.

reimprint', *v.t.*, to im-print or print again.

reimprint'ed, *p.p.*, re-imprint.

reimprint'ing, *pr.p.*, re-imprint.

rein, *n.*, the strap of a bridle by which a horse is controlled; restraint; *v.t.*, to guide; to control.

reincarn'ate, *adj.*, re-em-bodied; *v.t. and i.*, to appear again in bod-ily form.

reincarn'ated, *p.p.*, re-incarnate.

reincarnat'ing, *pr.p.*, re-incarnate.

reincarna'tion, *n.*, the act of taking a human body as residence by a spirit for a second time; metempsycho-sis.

reincorp'orate, *v.t.*, to incorporate afresh.

reincorp'orated, *p.p.*, re-incorporate.

reincorp'orating, *pr.p.*, reincorporate.

reincorpora'tion, *n.*, a fresh incorporation.

rein'deer, *n.*, a deer of Northern Europe used as a domestic animal.

reined, *p.p.*, rein.

reinforce', *v.t.*, to streng-then, esp. with more troops, ships, etc.

reinforced', *p.p.*, rein-force.

reinforce'ment, *n.*, addi-tional forces to streng-then an army or fleet; a strengthening.

reinforc'ing, *pr.p.*, rein-force.

rein'ing, *pr.p.*, rein.

re-ink', *v.t.*, to ink again.

re-inked', *p.p.*, re-ink.

re-ink'ing, *pr.p.*, re-ink.

rein'less, *adj.*, without reins; uncontrolled.

reins, *n. pl.*, the kidneys; the loins; formerly the supposed seat of the affections and pas-sions; the pl. of rein.

reinsert', *v.t.*, to insert a second time.

reinsert'ed, *p.p.*, rein-sert.

reinsert'ing, *pr.p.*, re-insert.

reinser'tion, *n.*, a second insertion.

reinspect', *v.t.*, to inspect again.

reinspect'ed, *p.p.*, rein-spect.

reinspect'ing, *pr.p.*, re-inspect.

reinspec'tion, *n.*, the act of inspecting a second time.

reinstall', *v.t.*, to install again.

reinstalla'tion, *n.*, a second installation.

reinstalled', *p.p.*, rein-stall.

reinstall'ing, *pr.p.*, re-install.

reinstate', *v.t.*, to place again in a former state.

reinstat'ed, *p.p.*, rein-state.

reinstate'ment, *n.*, re-establishment.

reinstat'ing, *pr.p.*, rein-state.

reinsur'ance, *n.*, a re-newed or second in-surance; an insurance to cover risks under-taken by a first in-surance.

reinsure', *v.t.*, to insure again.

reinsured', *p.p.*, rein-sure.

reinsur'ing, *pr.p.*, rein-sure.

reinter', *v.t.*, to bury again.

reinter'ment, *n.*, a second burial.

reinterred', *p.p.*, reinter.

reinterr'ing, *pr.p.*, re-inter.

reintroduce', *v.t.*, to in-troduce again.

reintroduced', *p.p.*, re-introduce.

reintroduc'ing, *pr.p.*, re-introduce.

reintroduc'tion, *n.*, a second introduction.

reinvest', *v.t.*, to invest anew.

reinvest'ed, *p.p.*, rein-vest.

reinvest'ing, *pr.p.*, re-invest.

reinvest'ment, *n.*, the act of reinvesting the pro-ceeds of a realized in-vestment.

reinvig'orate, *v.t.*, to give fresh vigour to, to brace up.

reinvig'orated, *p.p.*, re-invigorate.

reinvig'orating, *pr.p.*, re-invigorate.

reis'sue, *n.*, a second or renewed issue; *v.i.*, to go forth again; *v.t.*, to issue a second time.

reis'sued, *p.p.*, reissue.

reis'suing, *pr.p.*, reissue.

reit'erate, *v.t.*, to repeat again and again.

reit'erated, *p.p.*, reiter-ate.

reit'erating, *pr.p.*, re-iterate.

reitera'tion, *n.*, repeti-tion.

reit'erative, *n.*, a word signifying repeated or intense action; a part of a word repeated so as to form a re-duplicated word.

reject', *v.t.*, to discard; to refuse to receive or grant.

re'ject, *n.*, somebody or something that has been rejected.

reject'able, *adj.*, capable of being rejected.

reject'ed, *p.p.*, reject.

reject'er, *n.*, one who rejects.

reject'ing, *pr.p.*, reject.

rejec'tion, *n.*, the act of rejecting; a refusal to grant or accept.

reject'ive, *adj.*, tending to reject.

reject'ment, *n.*, the act of rejecting.

reject'or, *n.*, one who, or that which, rejects.

rejoice', *v.i.*, to be joy-ful; *v.t.*, to gladden.

rejoiced', *p.p.*, rejoice.

rejoic'ing, *n.*, joy, glad-ness; *pr.p.*, rejoice.

rejoin', *v.i.*, to answer to a reply; *v.t.*, to join again; to reply.

rejoin'der, *n.*, an answer to a reply.

rejoined', *p.p.*, rejoin.

rejoin'ing, *pr.p.*, rejoin.

reju'venate, *v.t.*, to make young again.

reju'venated, *p.p.*, re-juvenate.

reju'venating, *pr.p.*, re-juvenate.

rejuvena'tion, *n.*, restora-tion of youth.

rejuv'enator, *n.*, that which restores youth.

rejuvenes'cence, *n.*, a re-newal of youth.

rejuvenes'cent, *adj.*, be-coming young again.

rejuveniza'tion, *n.*, a becoming, or making, young again.

reju'venize, *v.t.*, to make young again; to re-juvenate.

rejuv'enized, *p.p.*, re-juvenize.

reju'venizing, *pr.p.*, re-juvenize.

rekin'dle, *v.t.*, to kindle again.

rekin'dled, *p.p.*, rekindle.

rekin'dling, *pr.p.*, rekindle.

relab'el, *v.t.*, to rename; to fix a fresh label to.

relabel(l)ed, *p.p.*, relabel.

relabel(l)ing, *pr.p.*, relabel.

relaid', *p.p.*, relay (to lay again).

relais', *n.*, a narrow ledge between the foot of a rampart and the scarp of the ditch.

relapse', *n.*, a falling back into a former bad state; *v.i.*, to backslide.

relapsed', *p.p.*, relapse.

relaps'er, *n.*, one who relapses.

relaps'ing, *pr.p.*, relapse.

relate', *v.i.*, to have reference (to); *v.t.*, to tell; to narrate; to ally by kindred or connections.

rela'ted, *adj.*, connected by blood or alliance; standing in some relation; *p.p.*, relate.

rela'ting, *pr.p.*, relate.

rela'tion, *n.*, the act of relating; narrative; a connection between one thing and another; a kinsman or kinswoman.

rela'tional, *adj.*, indicating some relation.

rela'tionally, *adv.*, in a relational way.

rela'tionship, *n.*, kinship.

rel'ative, *adj.*, pertinent; not absolute; comparative; *n.*, a kinsman or kinswoman; a word which relates to another, or refers to a preceding statement.

rel'atively, *adv.*, in relation to; comparatively.

rel'ativism, *n.*, the belief that knowledge is of relations only.

relativ'ity, *n.*, Einstein's theory of all motion being relative.

rela'tor, *n.*, one who relates.

relax', *v.t.* and *i.*, to slacken; to become less severe; to relieve.

relaxa'tion, *n.*, the act of relaxing; recreation; an occupation to relieve after toil.

relax'ative, *adj.*, laxative; *n.*, a laxative medicine.

relaxed', *p.p.*, relax.

relax'ing, *adj.*, enervating; causing languor; *pr.p.*, relax.

relay', *n.*, a supply of horses on the road to relieve others; a number of men who work at stated intervals; a device for operating or stopping an electrical circuit; *v.t.*, to pass anything from one place to another; to transmit; to lay again.

re'layed, *p.p.*, relay.

re'laying, *pr.p.*, relay (all meanings).

releas'able, *adj.*, capable of being released.

release', *n.*, a liberation from bondage or obligation; *v.t.*, to liberate.

released', *p.p.*, release.

release'ment, *n.*, the act of releasing.

releas'er, *n.*, one who releases.

releas'ing, *pr.p.*, release.

rel'egate, *v.t.*, to send out of the way; to banish; to send to a position of less importance or status.

rel'egated, *p.p.*, relegate.

rel'egating, *pr.p.*, relegate.

relega'tion, *n.*, the act of relegating; banishment.

relent', *v.i.*, to become more mild; to yield.

relent'ed, *p.p.*, relent.

relent'ing, *adj.*, yielding; *pr.p.*, relent.

relent'less, *adj.*, implacable; pitiless.

relent'lessly, *adv.*, without pity.

relet', *p.p.*, relet; *v.t.*, to let again (as a house).

relet'ting, *n.*, the act of letting the house again; *pr.p.*, relet.

rel'evance, *n.*, pertinence.

rel'evancy, *n.*, *i.q.* relevance.

rel'evant, *adj.*, pertinent; applicable.

rel'evantly, *adv.*, pertinently.

reliabil'ity, *n.*, the quality of being reliable.

reli'able, *adj.*, to be depended on.

reli'ably, *adv.*, in a reliable way.

reli'ance, *n.*, trust; confidence.

reli'ant, *adj.*, having reliance; self-relying.

rel'ic, *n.*, a remaining fragment; a memento. (Also *relique*.)

rel'ict, *n.*, a widow (*leg.*).

relied', *p.p.*, rely.

relief', *n.*, succour; that which mitigates some evil; help given to the impoverished or distressed; in painting, an appearance of solidity; in sculpture and architecture, prominence above the ground or plane on which a figure is formed; the surface elevations of a country.

reli'er, *n.*, one who relies.

reliev'able, *adj.*, capable of being relieved.

relieve', *v.t.*, to alleviate pain, etc.; to help the poor, etc.; to set off by contrast; to give an appearance of solidity to; to release from duty by substituting another person.

relieved', *p.p.*, relieve.

reliev'ing, *adj.*, serving to relieve; *pr.p.*, relieve.

relie'vo, *n.*, the prominence of a figure above the ground on which it is formed—in sculpture and architecture.

relight', *v.t.*, to rekindle.

relight'ing, *pr.p.*, relight.

relig'ion, *n.*, piety; any system of belief and worship.

reli'gioner, *n.*, a member of a monastic order; someone zealous for religion.

relig'ionism, *n.*, affected religion.

relig'ionist, *n.*, a religious bigot; one who deals much in religious discourse.

relig'ionize, *v.t.* and *i.*, to convert to a religion; to exhibit religious zeal.

relig'iose, *adj.*, morbidly religious.

religios'ity, n., a morbidly religious state.

relig'ious, adj., pert. or rel. to religion; pious; devoted by vows to the service of God; scrupulously faithful; n., a member of a religious order; a monk or nun.

relig'iously, adv., piously; reverently; conscientiously.

reline, v.t., to provide with a new lining.

relined, p.p., reline.

relin'ing, n., a new lining; pr.p., reline.

relin'quish, v.t., to abandon; to desist from; to renounce a claim to.

relin'quished, p.p., relinquish.

relin'quishing, pr.p., relinquish.

relin'quishment, n., the act of relinquishing.

rel'lquary, n., a casket in which relics are kept.

relique, n., i.q. relic (Fr.).

rel'ish, n., savour; taste; liking; something taken with food to give it a flavour; v.i., to have a pleasing flavour; v.t., to like the flavour of; to find pleasure in.

rel'ishable, adj., capable of being relished.

rel'ished, p.p., relish.

rel'ishing, pr.p., relish.

relit', p.p., relight.

relive', v.i., to live again.

relived', p.p., relive.

reliv'ing, pr.p., relive.

reload', v.t. and i., to load again.

reloaded', p.p., reload.

reload'ing, pr.p., reload.

reloan', n., a repeated loan.

relu'cent, adj., luminous.

reluct', v.i., to show reluctance.

reluc'tance, n., unwillingness.

reluc'tant, adj., unwilling.

reluc'tantly, adv., unwillingly.

relume', v.t., to light again.

rely', v.i., to trust; to have confidence.

rely'ing, pr.p., rely.

rem, n., a rad in biological application.

remade', p.p., remake.

remain', v.i., to stay.

remain'der, n., that which remains.

remained', p.p., remain.

remain'ing, pr.p., remain.

remains', n. pl., a dead body; the literary works of a dead author; anything that is left.

remake', v.t., to make over again.

re'make, n., anything re-made.

remak'ing, pr.p., remake.

remand', n., the state of being remanded; v.t., to send (an accused person) back to jail till further evidence is forthcoming.

remand'ed, p.p., remand.

remand'ing, pr.p., remand.

remand'ment, n., a remand.

rem'anent, adj., remaining.

rem'anet, n., a postponed case for trial (leg.).

remar'gin, v.t., to provide with fresh margin(s).

remark', n., an observation; a comment; v.t., to observe; to utter as a comment.

re'-mark', v.t., to mark a second time.

remark'able, adj., worthy of notice; extraordinary; conspicuous.

remark'ably, adv., surprisingly; in a remarkable manner.

remarked', p.p., remark.

re'-marked', p.p., re-mark.

remark'ing, pr.p., remark.

re'-mark'ing, pr.p., re-mark.

remarque', n., a marginal sketch on an engraving (Fr.).

remar'riage, n., a second marriage.

remar'ried, p.p., remarry.

remar'ry, v.i., to be married again; v.t., to marry again.

remar'rying, pr.p., remarry.

remast', v.t., to provide with new mast(s).

remblai, n., earth, etc. used for railway embankments and ramparts (Fr.).

reme'diable, adj., capable of being remedied.

reme'dial, adj., affording a remedy.

reme'dially, adv., in a remedial way.

rem'edied, p.p., remedy.

rem'ediless, adj., incurable; irreparable.

rem'edy, n., a cure; redress; v.t., to cure; to redress.

rem'edying, pr.p., remedy.

remem'ber, v.i., to bear in mind; v.t., to keep in the mind; to recollect.

remem'bered, p.p., remember.

remem'bering, pr.p., remember.

remem'brance, n., the power of remembering; what is remembered; a keepsake.

remem'brancer, n., an officer in the Exchequer who makes records and processes; a recorder; an officer of the Corporation of London.

rem'iform, adj., oar-shaped.

rem'igate, v.i., to row.

remiga'tory, adj., pert. or rel. to rowing.

remi'grate, v.i., to migrate again.

remind', v.t., to cause to remember.

remind'ed, p.p., remind.

remind'er, n., one who, or that which, reminds.

remind'ful, adj., tending to remind.

remind'ing, pr.p., remind.

reminis'cence, n., recollection; a narration of what is recollected.

reminis'cent, adj., calling to mind; having remembrance.

reminis'cently, adv., in a reminiscent way.

remint', v.t., to mint coins afresh.

rem'iped, n., an aquatic animal that uses its feet as oars.

remise', n., a surrender or release (of a claim); a covered fly or carriage; a coach-house.

remise', v.t., to resign or surrender by deed (leg.).

remised', p.p., remise.

remis'ing, pr.p., remise.

remiss', adj., negligent.

remissibil'ity, n., the capability of being remitted.

remiss'ible, adj., capable of being remitted.

remis'sion, n., the act of remitting; abatement; forgiveness.

remiss'ive, adj., relaxing; pardoning.

remiss'ly, adv., carelessly.

remiss'ness, n., the quality of being remiss.

remiss'ory, adj., pert. or rel. to remission; tending to remit.

remit', v.i., to become less intense; v.t., to abate; to forgive; to send (back); to transmit money, etc.

remit'tal, n., a surrender; the remission of a case to another court.

remit'tance, n., the act of sending money as a payment; the sum so sent.

remit'ted, p.p., remit.

remit'tent, adj., ceasing temporarily.

remit'ter, n., one who remits.

remit'ting, pr.p., remit.

rem'nant, n., that which remains after the removal of the rest; esp. a piece of cloth remaining after the rest has been sold; a fragment.

remod'el, v.t., to model again.

remod'el(l)ed, p.p., remodel.

remod'el(l)ing, pr.p., remodel.

remon'etize, v.t., to make again the standard money of account.

remon'strance, n., the act of remonstrating; a strong statement of reasons against.

remon'strant, adj., expostulatory.

rem'onstrate, v.t., to expostulate.

rem'onstrated, p.p., remonstrate.

rem'onstrating, pr.p., remonstrate.

remonstra'tion, n., the act of protesting.

remon'strative, adj., in a protesting fashion.

rem'onstrator, n., one who remonstrates.

rem'ora, n., the sucking-fish; an obstacle.

remorse', n., anguish, caused by a sense of guilt.

remorse'ful, adj., full of remorse.

remorse'fully, adv., in a remorseful way.

remorse'less, adj., pitiless.

remorse'lessly, adv., pitilessly.

remote', adj., distant; inconsiderable.

remote'ly, adv., at a distance; slightly.

remote'ness, n., distance; the state of being remote.

remo'ter, adj., comp. of remote.

remo'test, adj., super. of remote.

re'mould, n., anything remade to its former shape; v.t., to mould or shape anew.

re'mould'ed, p.p., remould.

re'mould'ing, pr.p., remould.

remount', v.t. and i., to mount again.

re'mount, n., a fresh horse to mount.

remount'ed, p.p., remount.

remount'ing, pr.p., remount.

removabil'ity, n., the quality of being removable.

remov'able, adj., capable of being removed.

remov'ably, adv., in a removable way.

remov'al, n., a moving from one place to another; the displacing from an office.

remove', n., a removal; a step in any scale of gradation; a dish moved to make room for something else; v.i., to change place; v.t., to move from its place in any manner.

removed', adj., distant; p.p., remove.

remov'er, n., one who, or that which, removes.

remov'ing, pr.p., remove.

remunerabil'ity, n., the capability of being remunerated.

remu'nerable, adj., capable of being remunerated.

remu'nerate, v.t., to reward; to recompense.

remu'nerated, p.p., remunerate.

remu'nerating, pr.p., remunerate.

remunera'tion, n., payment; something given to remunerate; the act of remunerating.

remu'nerative, adj., affording remuneration; profitable.

remu'nerator, n., one who rewards or remunerates.

remu'neratory, adj., rewarding.

Renais'sance, n., the revival of learning in the fifteenth century (Fr.).

renais'sance, n., a revival; a fresh start (Fr.).

re'nal, adj., pert. or rel. to the kidneys.

rename', v.t., to give a new name to.

renamed', p.p., rename.

renam'ing, pr.p., rename.

ren'ard, n., i.q. reynard.

renas'cence, n., i.q. renaissance; the state of being renascent.

renas'cent, adj., springing again into existence.

rencon'tre, n., a chance meeting; a slight hostile engagement (Fr.).

rencoun'ter, n., i.q. rencontre; v.i., to meet (an enemy) unexpectedly; to fight hand to hand.

rend, v.t., to tear; to tear asunder.

ren'der, n., one who rends; v.t., to give back; to invest with qualities; to translate; to represent.

ren'dered, p.p., render.

ren'dering, n., a translation; a representation; pr.p., render.

ren'dezvous, n., a meeting-place; v.i., to assemble at a particular place (Fr.).

rend'ible, adj., capable of being torn asunder.

rend'ing, *pr.p.*, rend.

rendi'tion, *n.*, a translation; an artistic performance; surrender.

ren'egade, *n.*, an apostate; a deserter.

reneg(u)e', *v.i.* and *t.*, to fail to follow suit in a card game.

renew', *v.i.*, to become new; to grow afresh; *v.t.*, to restore; to make again; to begin again.

renew'able, *adj.*, capable of being renewed.

renew'al, *n.*, the act of renewing.

renewed', *p.p.*, renew.

renew'er, *n.*, one who renews.

renew'ing, *pr.p.*, renew.

ren'iform, *adj.*, kidney-shaped.

reni'tency, *n.*, the state of being renitent.

reni'tent, *adj.*, resisting pressure; persistently opposed.

ren'net, *n.*, a kind of apple; a preparation for curdling milk.

renounce', *v.i.*, to revoke; *v.t.*, to disown; to abjure; to cast off.

renounced', *p.p.*, renounce.

renounce'ment, *n.*, renunciation.

renoun'cer, *n.*, one who renounces.

renoun'cing, *pr.p.*, renounce.

ren'ovate, *v.t.*, to repair; to renew.

ren'ovated, *p.p.*, renovate.

ren'ovating, *pr.p.*, renovate.

renova'tion, *n.*, the act of renovating; repair; restoration.

ren'ovator, *n.*, one who, or that which, renovates.

renown', *n.*, fame.

renowned', *adj.*, famous.

rent, *n.*, a torn hole; money paid to an owner by a tenant for occupation; *v.i.*, to be let for rent; *v.t.*, to let for rent; *p.p.*, rend.

rent'able, *adj.*, capable of being rented.

rent'al, *n.*, a schedule of rents; an amount of rent.

rente, *n.*, French Government Stock (*Fr.*).

rent'ed, *p.p.*, rent.

rent'er, *n.*, one who pays rent; a lessee; a wholesaler in the film trade.

ren'tier, *n.*, one who derives his income from investments (*Fr.*).

rent'ing, *pr.p.*, rent.

rent'-roll, *n.*, a list of rents.

renum'ber, *v.t.*, to number again or anew.

renum'bered, *p.p.*, renumber.

renum'bering, *pr.p.*, renumber.

renuncia'tion, *n.*, the act of renouncing; disclaiming; disowning.

renun'ciative, *adj.*, renouncing.

renun'ciator, *n.*, one who renounces.

reoc'cupied, *p.p.*, reoccupy.

reoc'cupy, *v.t.*, to occupy anew.

reoc'cupying, *pr.p.*, reoccupy.

reo'pen, *v.t.* and *i.*, to open again.

reo'pened, *p.p.*, reopen.

reo'pening, *pr.p.*, reopen.

reordain', *v.t.*, to ordain again, the first ordination being defective.

reorganiza'tion, *n.*, the act of organizing again; a change of organization.

reor'ganize, *v.t.*, to organize anew.

reor'ganized, *p.p.*, reorganize.

reor'ganizing, *pr.p.*, reorganize.

reorientate', *v.t.*, to reassume an Eastern direction (*liter.*); to rediscover one's true position (*fig.*).

reorienta'ted, *p.p.*, reorientate.

reorientat'ing, *pr.p.*, reorientate.

reorienta'tion, *n.*, a reassessment of position, physical or intellectual.

rep, *n.*, a dress fabric of ribbed appearance; verse learned by heart; repertory theatre or company; a representative (*colloq. abbrev.*).

repack', *v.t.*, to pack again.

repacked', *p.p.*, repack.

repack'ing, *pr.p.*, repack.

repaid', *p.p.*, repay.

repaint', *v.t.*, to restore the paint or colouring of.

repaint'ed, *p.p.*, repaint.

repaint'ing, *pr.p.*, repaint.

repair', *v.i.*, to go to; *v.t.*, to restore or mend; to make amends for.

repair'ability, *n.*, the ability to be repaired.

repair'able, *adj.*, able to be repaired.

repaired', *p.p.*, repair.

repair'er, *n.*, one who repairs.

repair'ing, *pr.p.*, repair.

repand', *adj.*, descriptive of a leaf with an unequal edge (*bot.*).

repap'er, *v.t.*, to put on fresh wallpaper.

repap'ered, *p.p.*, repaper.

repap'ering, *pr.p.*, repaper.

rep'arable, *adj.*, i.q. repairable.

rep'arably, *adv.*, in a reparable way.

repara'tion, *n.*, amends, compensation, atonement.

repar'ative, *adj.*, repairing.

repartee', *n.*, a smart retort; witty answers in general.

reparti'tion, *v.t.*, to redistribute or divide.

repass', *v.t.*, to pass again.

repassed', *p.p.*, repass.

repass'ing, *pr.p.*, repass.

repast', *n.*, a meal; food.

repat'riate, *n.*, a repatriated person; *v.t.*, to restore to one's native country.

repat'riated, *p.p.*, repatriate.

repat'riating, *pr.p.*, repatriate.

repatria'tion, *n.*, the act of sending someone back to his own country.

repay', *v.t.*, to pay back; to make a return for.

repay'able, *adj.*, able to be repaid; that must be repaid.

repay'ing, *pr.p.*, repay.

repay'ment, *n.*, payment of a debt.

repeal', v.t., to cancel; to revoke; to abrogate.

repealabil'ity, n., the quality of being repealable.

repeal'able, adj., able to be repealed.

repealed', p.p., repeal.

repeal'er, n., one who repeals, esp. one who favoured the repeal of the Union of Great Britain and Ireland.

repeal'ing, pr.p., repeal.

repeat', n., repetition; a musical sign directing the repetition of a passage; v.t., to do or to say again; to recite.

repeat'able, adj., fit for repetition.

repeat'ed, adj., frequent; p.p., repeat.

repeat'edly, adv., over and over again.

repeat'er, n., one who repeats; a revolver; a watch that repeats by striking the time; a recurring decimal.

repeat'ing, pr.p., repeat.

repel', v.t., to drive away; to check; to disgust; to protect from.

repel'lant, adj., disgusting; repulsive; driving back; n., anything which repels.

repelled', p.p., repel.

repel'lence, n., the repellent character.

repel'lency, n., i.q. repellence.

repel'lent, adj., i.q. repellant.

repel'lently, adv., in a repellent way.

repel'ler, n., one who, or that which, repels.

repel'ling, pr.p., repel.

rep'ent, adj., creeping (esp. of roots).

repent', v.i., to express sorrow for an offence.

repent'ance, n., sorrow for an offence; a change of heart.

repent'ant, adj., in a state of repentance.

repent'antly, adv., in a repentant way.

repent'ed, p.p., repent.

repent'ing, pr.p., repent.

repeo'ple, v.t., to populate afresh.

repercuss', v.i., to reverberate; v.t., to re-echo.

repercussed', p.p., repercuss.

repercuss'ing, pr.p., repercuss.

repercus'sion, n., reverberation.

repercus'sive, adj., reverberating.

repertoire', n., a store of music, stories, etc., ready for performance; a storehouse.

rep'ertory, n., i.q. repertoire.

rep'etend, n., the part repeated in a recurring decimal; a refrain.

repeti'tion, n., the act of repeating; reiteration; passages memorized.

repeti'tious, adj., repeating.

repeti'tiously, adv., repeatedly.

repet'itive, adj., i.q. repetitious.

repet'itively, adv., in a repetitive way.

repine', v.i., to grieve; to be discontented; to murmur.

repined', p.p., repine.

repi'ner, n., one who repines.

repi'ning, n., expressing discontent; murmuring; pr.p., repine.

replace', v.t., to put back into its place; to substitute one thing for another.

replaceabil'ity, n., the state of being replaceable.

replace'able, adj., capable of being replaced.

replaced', p.p., replace.

replace'ment, n., the act of replacing; a substitute.

repla'cing, pr.p., replace.

replant', v.t., to plant afresh.

replanta'tion, n., the act of replanting.

replant'ed, p.p., replant.

replant'ing, pr.p., replant.

replen'ish, v.t., to fill afresh; to stock.

replen'ished, p.p., replenish.

replen'isher, n., one who, or that which, replenishes.

replen'ishing, pr.p., replenish.

replen'ishment, n., the act of replenishing; the replenished state.

replete', adj., full.

replete'ness, n., the state of being replete.

reple'tion, n., the state of being over-full.

replev'iable, adj., able to be replevied.

replev'ied, p.p., replevy.

replev'in, n., an action for the recovery of wrongfully seized goods (leg.).

replev'y, v.t., to recover goods by replevin.

replev'ying, pr.p., replevy.

rep'lica, n., a duplicate of a work of art by the artist himself; any exact copy.

rep'licant, adj., folding back.

rep'licate, adj., folded back; n., anything folded back.

rep'licate, v.t., to fold back; to echo.

rep'licated, p.p., replicate.

rep'licating, pr.p., replicate.

replica'tion, n., the act or effect of replicating; an echo; a plaintiff's reply to the defendant.

replied', p.p., reply.

repli'er, n., one who replies.

reply', n., an answer; v.i., to answer.

reply'ing, pr.p., reply.

repoint', v.t., to renew mortar joints.

repoint'ed, p.p., repoint.

repoint'ing, pr.p., repoint.

repol'ish, v.t., to polish afresh.

repol'ished, p.p., repolish.

repoli'shing, pr.p., repolish.

repop'ulate, v.t., to populate afresh.

repop'ulated, p.p., repopulate.

repop'ulating, pr.p., repopulate.

repopula'tion, n., the act of repopulating.

report', n., a rumour; a formal statement; a description; a loud noise (as of a gun); v.t., to bring back a message; to relate; to take down in writing; to announce.

report'able, adj., able to be reported.

report'ed, p.p., report.

report′er, *n.*, one who reports, esp. one who takes down a speech, or gives an account of any proceedings.

report′ing, *n.*, the business of a reporter; the art of reporting; *p.p.*, report.

reporto′rial, *adj.*, pert. or rel. to reporters.

repos′al, *n.*, the state of being in repose.

repose′, *n.*, sleep; a restful attitude; *v.i.*, to lie down to rest; to sleep; *v.t.*, to lay to rest; to place (trust or confidence).

reposed′, *adj.*, calm; *p.p.*, repose.

repose′ful, *adj.*, restful.

repose′fully, *adv.*, restfully.

repo′sing, *pr.p.*, repose.

repos′it, *v.t.*, to place in security.

repos′ited, *p.p.*, reposit.

repos′iting, *pr.p.*, reposit.

re-posi′tion, *n.*, a new position; *v.t.*, to place in a different position.

re-posi′tioned, *p.p.*, reposition.

re-posi′tioning, *n.*, a new position; *pr.p.*, reposition.

repos′itory, *n.*, a place of storage.

repossess′, *v.t.*, to regain possession.

repossessed′, *p.p.*, repossess.

repossess′ing, *pr.p.*, repossess.

reposses′sion, *n.*, possession regained.

re-pot′, *v.t.*, to transfer to a larger pot.

re-pot′ted, *p.p.*, re-pot.

re-pot′ting, *pr.p.*, re-pot.

repoussé, *adj.*, said of metal worked in relief; *n.*, metal so worked and chased (*Fr.*).

reprehend′, *v.t.*, to censure.

reprehend′ed, *p.p.*, reprehend.

reprehend′ing, *pr.p.*, reprehend.

reprehen′sible, *adj.*, worthy of censure; blameworthy.

reprehen′sibly, *adv.*, in a reprehensible way.

reprehen′sion, *n.*, the act of reprehending; reproof; censure.

reprehen′sive, *adj.*, reproving.

reprehen′sively, *adv.*, in a reprehensive way.

reprehen′sory, *adj.*, *i.q.* reprehensive.

represent′, *v.t.*, to show in a picture; to personate; to act on behalf of; to make a report of.

re-present′, *v.t.*, to present anew.

represent′able, *adj.*, able to be represented.

representa′tion, *n.*, the act of representing; a likeness; an account.

re′-presenta′tion, *n.*, a new presentation.

represent′ative, *adj.*, personating; acting or standing for; typical; *n.*, one who acts on behalf of others, esp. a Member of Parliament; an heir; a business agent.

represent′ed, *p.p.*, represent.

re′-present′ed, *p.p.*, re-present.

represent′ing, *pr.p.*, represent.

re′-present′ing, *pr.p.*, re-present.

repress′, *v.t.*, to check; to restrain; to put down.

repressed′, *p.p.*, repress.

repress′ible, *adj.*, controllable.

repress′ing, *pr.p.*, repress.

repres′sion, *n.*, the act of repressing; the state of being repressed; restraint; suppression.

repress′ive, *adj.*, tending to repress.

repress′ively, *adv.*, in a repressive way.

repress′or, *n.*, one who, or that which, represses.

reprieve′, *n.*, respite; *v.t.*, to order suspension of punishment.

reprieved′, *p.p.*, reprieve.

repriev′ing, *pr.p.*, reprieve.

reprimand′, *v.t.*, to reprove severely.

rep′rimand, *n.*, a severe reproof.

reprimand′ed, *p.p.*, reprimand.

reprimand′ing, *pr.p.*, reprimand.

reprint′, *v.t.*, to print again.

re′print, *n.*, a printing repeated.

reprint′ed, *p.p.*, reprint.

reprint′ing, *pr.p.*, reprint.

repri′sal, *n.*, retaliation.

reprise′, *n.*, payment out of an estate; a repetition (*mus.*).

reproach′, *n.*, blame, rebuke; *v.t.*, to blame or rebuke.

reproach′able, *adj.*, blameworthy.

reproached′, *p.p.*, reproach.

reproach′ful, *adj.*, expressing rebuke.

reproach′fully, *adv.*, in a reproachful way.

reproach′ing, *pr.p.*, reproach.

rep′robate, *adj.*, depraved; abandoned; *n.*, a depraved sinner; *v.t.*, to condemn; to denounce.

rep′robated, *p.p.*, reprobate.

rep′robating, *pr.p.*, reprobate.

reproba′tion, *n.*, condemnation.

rep′robative, *adj.*, condemnatory.

reproduce′, *v.t.*, to produce in facsimile; to make a likeness of; to bring forth.

reproduced′, *p.p.*, reproduce.

reproduc′ing, *pr.p.*, reproduce.

reproduc′tion, *n.*, the act or result of reproducing.

reproduc′tive, *adj.*, reproducing.

reproduc′tively, *adv.*, in a reproductive way.

reprog′raphy, *n.*, the art of duplication and reproduction.

reproof′, *n.*, blame, rebuke.

re′-proof′, *v.t.*, to render waterproof again; to produce a further (printer's) proof.

reprov′able, *adj.*, worthy of reproof.

reprov′al, *n.*, the act of reproving.

reprove′, *v.t.*, to rebuke; to take to task.

reproved′, *p.p.*, reprove.

reprov′er, *n.*, one who reproves.

reprov′ing, *pr.p.*, reprove.

reprov′ingly, *adv.*, by way of reproof.

rep'tant, *adj.,* creeping, crawling.

repta'tion, *n.,* creeping.

rep'tatory, *adj.,* creeping.

rep'tile, *adj.,* crawling; creeping; grovelling; *n.,* one of the Reptilia.

Repti'lia, *n. pl.,* creatures that creep or crawl.

reptil'ian, *adj.,* pert. or rel. to reptiles.

reptil'iary, *n.,* a reptile-house.

repub'lic, *n.,* the commonwealth; a government by the people.

repub'lican, *adj.,* pert. or rel. to a republic; *n.,* one who is opposed to a monarchical system.

repub'licanism, *n.,* the principles of republicans.

repub'licanize, *v.t.,* to change to a republic; to indoctrinate with republican principles.

repub'licanized, *p.p.,* republicanize.

repub'licanizing, *pr.p.,* republicanize.

republica'tion, *n.,* the act of republishing; a fresh issue of a book.

repub'lish, *v.t.,* to publish afresh; to issue again.

repub'lished, *p.p.,* republish.

repub'lishing, *pr.p.,* republish.

repu'diable, *adj.,* able to be repudiated.

repu'diate, *v.t.,* to reject; to disavow; to refuse to acknowledge.

repu'diated, *p.p.,* repudiate.

repu'diating, *pr.p.,* repudiate.

repudia'tion, *n.,* the act of repudiating; a disavowal.

repu'diator, *n.,* one who repudiates.

repugn', *v.i.,* to offer resistance; *v.t.,* to resist.

repug'nance, *n.,* distaste; aversion.

repug'nancy, *n., i.q.* repugnance.

repug'nant, *adj.,* distasteful; offensive.

repug'nantly, *adv.,* distastefully, offensively.

repulp', *v.t.,* to pulp again.

repulse', *n.,* a driving back; a refusal; a denial; *v.i.,* to beat back; to repel.

repulsed', *p.p.,* repulse.

repuls'ing, *pr.p.,* repulse.

repul'sion, *n.,* the act or effect of repulsing; a feeling of loathing.

repul'sive, *adj.,* tending to repulse; loathsome.

repul'sively, *adv.,* in a repulsive manner.

repul'siveness, *n.,* the quality or state of being repulsive.

repur'chase, *v.t.,* to buy back.

repur'chased, *p.p.,* repurchase.

repur'chasing, *pr.p.,* repurchase.

rep'utable, *adj.,* of good repute.

rep'utably, *adv.,* in a reputable way.

reputa'tion, *n.,* a good name; credit.

repute', *n.,* character; estimation; *v.t.,* to estimate; to think.

repu'ted, *adj.,* of repute; *p.p.,* repute.

repu'tedly, *adv.,* in a reputable way.

repu'ting, *pr.p.,* repute.

request', *n.,* a prayer, petition or demand; *v.t.,* to ask for.

request'ed, *p.p.,* request.

request'ing, *pr.p.,* request.

requick'en, *v.i.,* to revive; *v.t.,* to reanimate.

req'uiem, *n.,* a funeral mass or its music.

requir'able, *adj.,* able to be required.

require', *v.t.,* to need; to demand.

required', *p.p.,* require.

require'ment, *n.,* something required.

requir'ing, *pr.p.,* require.

req'uisite, *adj.,* indispensable; necessary; *n.,* anything indispensable.

requisi'tion, *n.,* the act of requiring; a demand; *v.t.,* to demand.

requisi'tioned, *p.p.,* requisition.

requisi'tioning, *pr.p.,* requisition.

requi'tal, *n.,* the act of requiting.

requite', *v.t.,* to recompense; to pay back; to make a return to.

requi'ted, *p.p.,* requite.

requi'ting, *pr.p.,* requite.

rerail', *v.t.,* to lay down new rails; to put back upon the rails.

re-read', *v.t.,* to read again.

re-read', *p.p.,* re-read.

re-read'ing, *pr.p.,* re-read.

rere'dos, *n.,* a suspended structure behind an altar.

re-resolve', *v.i.,* to resolve afresh.

re-rubb'er, *v.t.,* to replace rubber covering.

resad'dle, *v.t.,* to saddle afresh.

resale', *n.,* a sale over again.

re'sat, *p.p.,* resit.

rescind', *v.t.,* to cancel; to revoke.

rescind'able, *adj.,* able to be rescinded.

rescind'ed, *p.p.,* rescind.

rescind'ing, *pr.p.,* rescind.

rescin'namine, *n.,* a sedative drug.

rescis'sion, *n.,* the act of rescinding.

rescis'sory, *adj.,* annulling.

rescribe', *v.t.,* to write an answer.

re'script, *n.,* a rewriting; a papal decree on a legal question.

rescrip'tive, *adj.,* of the nature of a rescript.

rescrip'tively, *adv.,* in a rescriptive way.

res'cuable, *adj.,* able to be rescued.

res'cue, *n.,* deliverance; recovery by force (*leg.*); *v.t.,* to save from danger; to recover by force (*leg.*).

res'cued, *p.p.,* rescue.

res'cuer, *n.,* a deliverer.

res'cuing, *pr.p.,* rescue.

re'search, *n.,* investigation; seeking the full facts; a scholarly inquiry.

research', *v.t.,* to make a detailed inquiry into.

researched', *p.p.,* research.

researcher', *n.,* one who researches.

research'ing, *pr.p.,* research.

reseat', *v.t.,* to replace in a seat; to put a new seat in.

reseat'ed, *p.p.,* reseat.

reseat'ing, *pr.p.,* reseat.

resect', *v.t.,* to pare.

Res′eda, *n.*, a genus of herbs.

re-seek′, *v.t.*, to research or inquire for.

reseize′, *v.t.*, to take possession of again.

resell′, *v.t.*, to sell again.

resell′ing, *pr.p.*, resell.

resem′blance, *n.*, a likeness or similarity.

resem′ble, *v.t.*, to be similar to.

resem′bled, *p.p.*, resemble.

resem′bling, *pr.p.*, resemble.

resent′, *v.t.*, to feel indignation at.

resent′ed, *p.p.*, resent.

resent′ful, *adj.*, retaining a sense of injury.

resent′fully, *adv.*, in a resentful way.

resent′ing, *pr.p.*, resent.

resent′ment, *n.*, a sense of injury.

reser′pine, *n.*, a drug used in the treatment of high blood-pressure, etc.

reserva′tion, *n.*, the act of reserving; a right reserved; something held back; a setting apart; a booking; a region reserved for a special purpose.

reserve′, *v.t.*, to hold back; to keep possession of; to book (seats); *n.*, something kept back for later use; reticence; a player in a game, available to take the place of another.

reserved′, *adj.*, reticent; understating; *p.p.*, reserve.

reserv′edly, *adv.*, in a reserved manner; with reserve.

reserv′ing, *pr.p.*, reserve.

reserv′ist, *n.*, one held in reserve, as troops, players in games, etc.

res′ervoir, *n.*, an artificial lake for watersupply; any receptacle in which a liquid supply is kept.

reset′, *v.t.*, to set again; *v.t.* and *i.*, to shelter a criminal; to receive stolen goods.

reset′ter, *n.*, one who resets.

reset′ting, *pr.p.*, reset.

reset′tle, *v.t.* and *i.*, to settle again.

reset′tlement, *n.*, the act of resettling; the state of being resettled.

reshape′, *v.i.*, to assume a new shape; *v.t.*, to shape again.

reshaped′, *p.p.*, reshape.

reshap′ing, *pr.p.*, reshape.

reship′, *v.t.* and *i.*, to ship again.

reship′ment, *n.*, the act of reshipping.

reshuf′fle, *n.*, the act of reshuffling; *v.t.*, to rearrange; to shuffle afresh.

reshuf′fled, *p.p.*, reshuffle.

reshuf′fling, *pr.p.*, reshuffle.

reside′, *v.i.*, to dwell; to inhere.

resi′ded, *p.p.*, reside.

res′idence, *n.*, the act of residing; a place of dwelling.

res′idency, *n.*, an official government dwelling.

res′ident, *adj.*, residing; *n.*, one who resides; an agent of a government.

residen′tial, *adj.*, used for residences.

residen′tially, *adv.*, in a residential way.

residen′tiary, *adj.*, residing; required to reside; *n.*, one required to reside officially.

resi′der, *n.*, one who resides.

resi′ding, *pr.p.*, reside.

resid′ual, *adj.*, leaving a remainder; pert. or rel. to a residuum.

resid′uary, *adj.*, *i.q.* residual.

res′idue, *n.*, a remainder after subtraction.

resid′uum, *n.*, that which remains; dregs.

resign′, *v.t.* and *i.*, to give up; to renounce a claim on; to retire.

re′-sign, *v.t.* and *i.*, to sign again.

resigna′tion, *n.*, the act of resigning; an acceptance of the inevitable.

resigned′, *p.p.*, resign.

re′-signed, *p.p.*, re-sign.

resign′edly, *adv.*, with resignation.

resignee′, *n.*, one to whom something is resigned.

resign′er, *n.*, one who resigns.

resign′ing, *pr.p.*, resign.

re′-signing, *pr.p.*, re-sign.

resile′, *v.t.*, to recoil.

resil′ience, *n.*, elasticity; recuperative power; the power of springing back to a previous state.

resil′iency, *n.*, *i.q.* resilience.

resil′ient, *adj.*, elastic; able to recover quickly.

res′in, *n.*, a gummy substance that exudes from plants or is made chemically.

resinif′erous, *adj.*, producing resin.

res′inous, *adj.*, containing resin; like resin.

resipis′cence, *n.*, the recognition of error; a return to sense.

resist′, *n.*, a protective coating; *v.t.* and *i.*, to oppose or withstand.

resist′ance, *n.*, the act of resisting; opposition; the power to resist; non-conductivity.

resist′ant, *adj.*, having power to resist.

resist′ed, *p.p.*, resist.

resist′er, *n.*, one who resists.

resistibil′ity, *n.*, the quality of being resistible.

resist′ible, *adj.*, able to be resisted.

resist′ibly, *adv.*, in a resistible way.

resist′ing, *pr.p.*, resist.

resist′ive, *adj.*, *i.q.* resistant.

resist′less, *adj.*, irresistible.

resis′tor, *n.*, an electrical resistance.

resit′, *n.*, a further attempt at an examination; *v.t.*, to sit again (as for examination).

resit′ting, *pr.p.*, resit.

resold, *p.p.*, resell.

resole′, *v.t.*, to provide a boot or shoe with a fresh sole.

resoled′, *p.p.*, resole.

resol′ing, *pr.p.*, resole.

resol′uble, *adj.*, able to be resolved.

res′olute, *adj.*, firm, determined, bold.

resol′utely, *adv.*, boldly, determinedly.

resolu′tion, *n.*, analysis; a gradual improvement of morbid conditions; the change of a chord from discord to concord (*mus.*); a firm resolve; a motion adopted by a meeting; a fixed purpose.

res′olutive, *adj.*, dissolving; dispersing; *n.*, an application or drug.

resolvabil′ity, *n.*, the quality or state of being resolvable.

resolv′able, *adj.*, capable of analysis or solution.

resolve′, *n.*, a fixed purpose; a resolution; *v.i.*, to decide; to come to a determination; *v.t.*, to change the form of; to break up into parts; to make intelligible; to cause dispersion of pus.

resolved′, *adj.*, determined; *p.p.*, resolve.

resolv′ent, *adj.*, reducing tumours, etc.; solvent; *n.*, an agent that is resolvent.

resolv′er, *n.*, one who, or that which, resolves.

resolv′ing, *pr.p.*, resolve.

res′onance, *n.*, the quality of being resonant; an echoing sound.

res′onant, *adj.*, returning or prolonging sound; full of sound.

res′onantly, *adv.*, in a resonant way.

res′onator, *n.*, a contrivance which, responding to a particular note, detects its presence in a mixed sound; an apparatus giving greater resonance.

resorb′, *v.t.*, to absorb again.

resorbed′, *p.p.*, resorb.

resorb′ent, *adj.*, having the power to resorb.

resorb′ing, *pr.p.*, resorb.

resor′cin, *n.*, a compound used in dyes.

resorp′tion, *n.*, the act or effect of resorbing.

resort′, *n.*, recourse; an expedient; a frequented place; *v.i.*, to have recourse; to go often.

re-sort′, *v.t.*, to sort again.

resort′ed, *p.p.*, resort.

re-sorted, *p.p.*, re-sort.

resort′ing, *pr.p.*, resort.

re-sort′ing, *pr.p.*, re-sort.

resound′, *v.i.*, to make a loud sound; to be resonant; to be celebrated; *v.t.*, to repeat the sound of; to celebrate.

resound′ed, *p.p.*, resound.

resound′ing, *pr.p.*, resound; producing impact.

resource′, *n.*, something to fall back upon for aid; resort; ingenuity. In pl. it = means, pecuniary or other.

resource′ful, *adj.*, versatile, able to devise ways and means of doing things.

resource′fully, *adv.*, in a resourceful way.

resource′fulness, *n.*, the quality of being resourceful; ingenuity.

resource′less, *adj.*, without resources.

resp, *n.*, a disease of sheep.

respect′, *n.*, deference; relation; *v.t.*, to treat with deference; to heed; to refer to.

respect′ability, *n.*, the quality of being respectable.

respect′able, *adj.*, worthy of respect; of good name; moderately good, passable.

respect′ably, *adv.*, in a respectable way.

respect′ant, *adj.*, confronting (*her.*).

respect′ed, *p.p.*, respect.

respect′er, *n.*, one who respects.

respect′ful, *adj.*, deferential, humble.

respect′fully, *adv.*, with deference.

respect′fulness, *n.*, the quality of being respectful.

respect′ing, *prep.*, concerning; *pr.p.*, respect.

respect′ive, *adj.*, individual, separate.

respect′ively, *adv.*, individually; in turn.

respect′less, *adj.*, impolite, careless, without respect.

respell′, *v.t.*, to spell again.

respell′ing, *pr.p.*, respell.

respelt′, *p.p.*, respell.

respirabil′ity, *n.*, the quality of being respirable.

respir′able, *adj.*, fit to breathe.

respira′tion, *n.*, the act of breathing.

respira′tional, *adj.*, pert. or rel. to respiration.

res′pirator, *n.*, a covering for the mouth to keep out cold air, fog, etc.

respir′atory, *adj.*, pert. or rel. to respiration.

respire′, *v.t.* and *i.*, to breathe; to inhale and exhale.

respired′, *p.p.*, respire.

respir′ing, *pr.p.*, respire.

respirom′eter, *n.*, an instrument for measuring respiration; a breathing apparatus used by divers.

res′pite, *n.*, a postponement; a reprieve; temporary relief; *v.t.*, to grant respite.

res′pited, *p.p.*, respite.

res′piting, *pr.p.*, respite.

resplen′dence, *n.*, splendour, magnificence.

resplen′dency, *n.*, *i.q.* resplendence.

resplen′dent, *adj.*, splendid, magnificent.

resplen′dently, *adv.*, magnificently, splendidly.

respond′, *n.*, a chanted response in a religious service; a pilaster or column attached to a wall and supporting an arch; *v.i.*, to answer; to reply.

respond′ed, *p.p.*, respond.

respond′ence, *n.*, an analogy.

respond′ent, *adj.*, responding; *n.*, one who supports an opposing argument; a defendant in a law suit.

responden′tia, *n.*, a loan upon security of a ship's cargo.

respon′der, *n.*, one who, or that which, responds.

respond′ing, *pr.p.*, respond.

respon′sal, *n.*, a response; the reaction caused by an external stimulus.

response′, *n.*, an answer; liturgically, the answer to the priest's versicle.

responsibil'ities, *n. pl.*, obligations.

responsibil'ity, *n.*, an obligation; a charge.

respon'sible, *adj.*, involving responsibilities; answerable; morally and mentally capable; trustworthy.

respon'sibly, *adv.*, in a responsible way.

Respon'sions, *n. pl.*, formerly the name of the first academic examination at Oxford, colloquially called Smalls.

respon'sive, *adj.*, giving answer; sympathetic.

respon'sively, *adv.*, in a responsive way.

respon'siveness, *n.*, the quality of being responsive.

respon'sory, *n.*, an anthem.

rest, *n.*, repose; the cessation from work or worry or movement; remainder; that on which a thing can be rested; an interval of silence shown by an appropriate sign (*mus.*); *v.i.*, to cease from work or movement or care; *v.t.*, to lay to rest; to place.

restamp', *v.t.*, to stamp again.

restamped', *p.p.*, restamp.

restamp'ing, *pr.p.*, restamp.

restart', *v.t.*, to start afresh.

restart'ed, *p.p.*, restart.

restart'er, *n.*, one who, or that which, restarts.

restart'ing, *pr.p.*, restart.

restate', *v.t.*, to state a second or subsequent time.

restated', *p.p.*, restate.

restat'ing, *pr.p.*, restate.

res'taurant, *n.*, a place offering meals for sale and the amenities for eating them (*Fr.*).

restau'rateur, *n.*, a restaurant-keeper (*Fr.*).

rest'-cure, *n.*, quiet repose as a medical treatment.

rest'-day, *n.*, an official day of rest.

rest'ed, *p.p.*, rest.

rest'ful, *adj.*, producing a sense of ease and rest.

rest'fully, *adv.*, in a restful way.

rest'fulness, *n.*, the quality or state of being restful.

rest'-harrow, *n.*, the cammock, a shrub.

rest'-house, *n.*, a house for those needing rest.

rest'ing, *pr.p.*, rest.

restitu'tion, *n.*, an act of reparation; restoring to the lawful owner; compensation.

rest'ive, *adj.*, stubborn; unmanageable; refractory.

rest'ively, *adv.*, in a restive way.

rest'iveness, *n.*, stubbornness; refractoriness.

rest'less, *adj.*, without rest; fidgety; uneasy.

rest'lessly, *adv.*, in a restless way.

rest'lessness, *n.*, fidgetiness; uneasiness.

resto'rable, *adj.*, able to be restored.

Restora'tion, *n.*, the period of re-establishment of the monarchy in England in 1660.

restora'tion, *n.*, the act, or effect, of restoring; a renewal; re-establishment.

restora'tionism, *n.*, the belief in the final happiness of mankind.

restora'tionist, *n.*, a believer in restorationism.

restor'ative, *adj.*, restoring in its effect; *n.*, something that revives or restores.

restore', *v.t.*, to make restitution; to re-establish; to present anew in what is believed to have been the original state.

restored', *p.p.*, restore.

restor'er, *n.*, one who restores.

restor'ing, *pr.p.*, restore.

restrain', *v.t.*, to hold back, check or confine.

re'-strain', *v.t.*, to strain again.

restrain'able, *adj.*, able to be restrained.

restrained', *adj.*, reserved; *p.p.*, restrain.

restrain'edly, *adv.*, in a restrained manner.

restrain'er, *n.*, one who restrains.

restrain'ing, *pr.p.*, restrain (holding back).

restraint', *n.*, the act of restraining; the state of being restrained; self-control; confinement.

restrict', *v.t.*, to limit; to confine.

restrict'ed, *p.p.*, restrict.

restrict'ing, *pr.p.*, restrict.

restric'tion, *n.*, limitation; confinement.

restrict'ive, *adj.*, tending to restrict.

restrict'ively, *adv.*, with restriction.

restring', *v.t.*, to fit a racket with fresh gut.

restring'ing, *v.i.*, the refitting with gut; *pr.p.*, restring.

restrung', *p.p.*, restring.

restuff', *v.t.*, to stuff afresh.

restuffed', *p.p.*, restuff.

restuff'ing, *pr.p.*, restuff.

result', *n.*, a consequence, an effect; *v.i.*, to arise; to issue; to follow as a consequence.

result'ant, *adj.*, resulting; *n.*, a force which is the result of two or more forces combined.

result'ed, *p.p.*, result.

result'ing, *adj.*, consequent; *pr.p.*, result.

resu'mable, *adj.*, able to be resumed.

resume', *v.i.*, to begin speaking again; *v.t.*, to take up again; to recover.

résumé', *n.*, a summary, an abstract, a precis (*Fr.*).

resumed', *p.p.*, resume.

resu'ming, *pr.p.*, resume.

resumm'ons, *n.*, a renewed legal summons.

resump'tion, *n.*, the act of resuming.

resump'tive, *adj.*, taking back or up again.

resu'pinate, *adj.*, inverted.

resurge', *v.i.*, to rise or arise again.

resur'gence, *n.*, the act of surging back.

resur'gent, *adj.*, surging back.

resurrect', *v.i.*, to revive; *v.t.*, to bring back to life and notice.

resurrec'tion, *n.*, the act of rising again; a revival; body-snatching.

resurrec'tionist, *n.,* a body-snatcher.

resurvey', *v.t.,* to survey afresh.

resurveyed', *p.p.,* resurvey.

resurvey'ing, *pr.p.,* resurvey.

resus'citant, *adj.,* tending to revive.

resus'citate, *v.t.,* to revive; to bring back to consciousness; to reanimate.

resus'citated, *p.p.,* resuscitate.

resus'citating, *pr.p.,* resuscitate.

resuscita'tion, *n.,* the act or effect of resuscitating.

resus'citative, *adj.,* aiding recovery.

resus'citator, *n.,* one who, or that which, resuscitates.

ret, *v.t.,* to macerate fibrous plants.

reta'ble, *n.,* an altarpiece; a reredos.

re'tail, *adj.,* (the opposite to wholesale), sold in small quantities; *n.,* sale in small quantities.

retail', *v.t.,* to sell direct to the consumer; to repeat; to recount.

retailed', *p.p.,* retail.

retail'er, *n.,* one who retails; one who sells to consumers; a shopkeeper.

retail'ing, *pr.p.,* retail.

retain', *v.t.,* to hold in possession; to keep; to engage for a fee.

retain'able, *adj.,* able to be retained.

retained', *p.p.,* retain.

retain'er, *n.,* one who retains; a servant in a large household; a camp-follower; a fee for services engaged; legal retention or authority to retain.

retain'ing, *pr.p.,* retain.

retake', *v.t.,* to take back or again.

reta'ken, *p.p.,* retake.

reta'king, *pr.p.,* retake.

retal'iate, *v.i.,* to return evil for evil; to impose fiscal duties; to make rejoinder; *v.t.,* to repay in kind.

retal'iated, *p.p.,* retaliate.

retal'iating, *pr.p.,* retaliate.

retalia'tion, *n.,* the act of retaliating; revenge.

retal'iative, *adj.,* of the nature of retaliation.

retal'iatory, *adj., i.q.* retaliative.

retard', *n.,* delay, esp. in regard to the motion of tides, waves, celestial bodies, etc.; *v.i.,* to delay; *v.t.,* to arrest the progress of; to diminish the velocity of.

retarda'tion, *n.,* the act or process of retarding; hindrance or delay.

retard'ative, *adj.,* tending to retard.

retard'ed, *p.p.,* retard.

retard'ing, *pr.p.,* retard.

retaste, *v.t.,* to taste again.

retast'ed, *p.p.,* retaste.

retast'ing, *pr.p.,* retaste.

retch, *v.i.,* to strain as with vomiting.

retched, *p.p.,* retch.

retch'ing, *n.,* straining as with vomiting; *pr.p.,* retch.

retell', *v.t.,* to repeat, to tell again.

retell'ing, *pr.p.,* retell.

reten'tion, *n.,* the act of retaining; holding back; the power of retaining.

reten'tive, *adj.,* with power to retain, esp. in the memory.

reten'tively, *adv.,* in a retentive way.

reten'tiveness, *n.,* the power of retaining; a good memory.

retenue', *n.,* self-control (*Fr.*).

retex'ture, *n.,* reweaving, a second weaving.

re'tiary, *adj.,* using nets or webs as traps.

ret'icence, *n.,* silence, reserve, taciturnity.

ret'icent, *adj.,* silent, reserved, taciturn.

ret'icently, *adv.,* silently, reservedly.

ret'icle, *n.,* fine lines, like network, drawn across an object glass.

retic'ular, *adj.,* having interstices.

retic'ulate, *adj.,* consisting of, or like, network.

retic'ulate, *v.t. and i.,* to divide in networkfashion.

retic'ulated, *adj., i.q.* reticulate; *p.p.,* reticulate.

retic'ulating, *pr.p.,* reticulate.

reticula'tion, *n.,* network.

ret'icule, *n., i.q.* reticle; also a network bag.

retic'ulum, *n.,* a ruminant animal's second stomach (*Lat.*).

re'tiform, *adj.,* like network.

ret'ina, *n.,* a coat at the back of the eyeball sensitive to light.

ret'inal, *adj.,* pert. or rel. to the retina.

retini'tis, *n.,* inflammation of the retina.

re'tinol(e), *n.,* a resin hydrocarbon.

ret'inue, *n.,* a body of attendants or retainers.

retire', *v.i.,* to withdraw oneself (in several senses); *v.t.,* to withdraw; to remove from active service.

retired', *adj.,* returned to private life; *p.p.,* retire.

retire'ment, *n.,* the act of retiring; the retired state; a secluded place.

retir'ing, *adj.,* shy, unobtrusive; *pr.p.,* retire.

retir'ingly, *adj.,* shyly, unobtrusively.

retold', *p.p.,* retell.

retort', *n.,* a sharp reply; a vessel used for distillation and other purposes; *v.i.,* to make a sharp reply; *v.t.,* to turn back upon another.

retort'ed, *p.p.,* retort.

retort'ing, *pr.p.,* retort.

retor'tion, *n.,* a bending back.

retouch', *v.t.,* to touch over again; to improve by slight addition and alterations.

retouched', *p.p.,* retouch.

retouch'ing, *pr.p.,* retouch.

retour', *n.,* a copy of a return to the Chancery Court (*Scot.*).

retrace', *v.t.,* to trace back; to repeat.

retrace'able, *adj.,* able to be retraced.

retraced', *p.p.,* retrace.

retra'cing, *pr.p.,* retrace.

retract', n., the pricking of a horse's hoof by driving a nail into it; v.t. and i., to draw back; to take back; to recant.

retractabil'ity, n., the state or quality of being retractable.

retract'able, adj., able to be retracted.

retract'ed, p.p., retract.

retract'ile, adj., able to be drawn back.

retract'ing, pr.p., retract.

retrac'tion, n., the act of withdrawing; withdrawal or retreat.

retract'ive, adj., retracting; able to draw back.

retract'ively, adv., in a retractive way.

retract'or, n., that which retracts; a retracting muscle or instrument.

ret'ral, adj., posterior, at the back.

retransfer', n., the act of retransferring; v.t., to transfer back or back again.

retransferred', p.p., retransfer.

retransfer'ring, pr.p., retransfer.

retransform', v.t., to transform again.

retranslate', v.t., to translate back into the original language; to translate again.

retranslated', p.p., retranslate.

retranslat'ing, pr.p., retranslate.

retransla'tion, n., a return to the original language; a second translation.

retrax'it, n., the withdrawal of a suit by the plaintiff, causing loss of action (leg.).

retread', v.t., to tread again; to fit a new tread (to a tyre).

re'tread, n., a tyre fitted with a new tread.

retreat', v.i., to withdraw, to retire, to go back; n., a withdrawal or retirement; a place of retirement.

retreat'ed, p.p., retreat.

retreat'ing, pr.p., retreat.

retrench', v.i., to economize; v.t., to cut down or curtail.

retrenched', p.p., retrench.

retrench'ing, pr.p., retrench.

retrench'ment, n., economy; the cutting down of expenses.

re'tri'al, n., a second trial; a renewed attempt.

retrib'ute, v.t., to repay, to give back.

retribu'tion, n., requital; punishment.

retrib'utive, adj., punitive; in the way of requital.

retrib'utively, adv., in a retributive way.

retrib'utory, adj., making retribution.

retriev'able, adj., able to be retrieved.

retriev'al, n., recovery.

retrieve', v.i., to be a retriever (said of a dog); v.t., to bring back; to restore; to remedy.

retrieved', p.p., retrieve.

retriev'er, n., one who retrieves; a breed of dogs used in shooting game.

retriev'ing, pr.p., retrieve.

retrim, v.t., to trim again.

retrimmed', p.p., retrim.

retrim'ming, pr.p., retrim.

ret'ro-, a prefix = backward.

retroact', v.i., to react; to have a retrospective effect; to act in a contrary direction.

retroac'tion, n., reverse action.

retroact'ive, adj., retrospective; pert. or rel. to past transactions.

retrocede', v.i., to go back; v.t., to give back or restore.

retroce'ded, p.p., retrocede.

retroce'dent, adj., giving back.

retroce'ding, pr.p., retrocede.

retroces'sion, n., the act of giving back, or restoring; a moving inwards or backwards (med.).

retroces'sive, adj., i.q. retrocedent.

re'trochoir, n., the part of a church behind the high altar in the choir.

retroduc'tion, n., a drawing back.

retroflec'ted, adj., turned backwards.

ret'roflex, adj., bent back.

ret'roflexed, adj., i.q. retroflex.

retrograda'tion, n., the act of retrograding.

ret'rograde, adj., going back; deteriorating; n., a degenerate; v.i., to go back; to deteriorate.

ret'rograded, p.p., retrograde.

ret'rograding, pr.p., retrograde.

retrogress', v.i., to go back; to move backwards; to deteriorate.

retrogres'sion, n., a retrograde process.

retrogres'sive, adj., retrograding.

retrogres'sively, adv., in a retrogressive way.

ret'roject, v.t., to cast or throw back.

retropul'sion, n., the shifting of external disease to an internal part (path.); the tendency to walk backwards in paralysis.

retropul'sive, adj., pushing backward.

ret'ro-rock'et, n., an auxilliary rocket for a space vehicle.

retrorse', adj., turned backward.

retrorse'ly, adv., in a retrorse way.

ret'rospect, n., a survey of the past; v.t. and i., to survey the past.

retrospec'tion, n., the act of looking back into the past.

retrospec'tive, adj., looking back on the past; embracing the past.

retrospec'tively, adv., in a retrospective way.

retrous'sé, adj., turned up at the end (of the nose); tip-tilted (Fr.).

retrover'sion, n., the state of being tipped back; a tipping backward.

ret'rovert, v.t., to turn back.

ret'roverted, p.p., retrovert.

ret'roverting, pr.p., retrovert.

retru'sible, adj., obstruse; capable of being thrust back.

rett'ed, p.p., ret.

rett'ery, n., a flax-retting place.

rett'ing, pr.p., ret.

return', n., a coming or going back; a restoration or requital; a formal statement or list; an election; a side of a building receding from the

front. In pl., profits; *v.i.*, to come or go back; to reply; to turn again; *v.t.*, to send back; to repay; to requite; to pay; to elect; to transmit (a statement, etc.); to send back (a tennisball) into the opponent's court.

return'able, *adj.*, able to be returned; due.

returned', *adj.*, used in an architectural sense, as "returned stalls," *i.e.*, arranged L shape; *p.p.*, return.

return'ing, *pr.p.*, return.

retuse', *adj.*, broadened at the end and depressed in the middle (*bot.*).

reu'nion, *n.*, a reuniting; the state of being reunited; a social meeting.

reun'ionist, *n.*, one who supports the policy of reunion.

reunite', *v.t.* and *i.*, to unite again.

reuni'ted, *p.p.*, reunite.

reunit'ing, *pr.p.*, reunite.

rev, *n.*, the revolution of an engine, *v.t.* and *i.*, to revolve; to accelerate (a motor).

revac'cinate, *v.t.*, to vaccinate again.

revac'cinated, *p.p.*, revaccinate.

revac'cinating, *pr.p.*, revaccinate.

revaccina'tion, *n.*, a vaccination repeated.

revalen'ta, *n.*, food prepared from lentil and barley flour.

revaloriza'tion, *n.*, the restoration of ·the value of currency.

reval'orize, *v.t.*, to revalue; to restore the value of a country's currency.

revalua'tion, *n.*, the act of valuing afresh.

reval'ue, *v.t.*, to assess value afresh.

reval'ued, *p.p.*, revalue.

reval'uing, *pr.p.*, revalue.

reveal', *n.*, the internal side surface of an opening or recess (esp. a window or doorway); *v.t.*, to bring into the light; to disclose; to divulge.

reveal'able, *adj.*, able to be revealed.

revealed', *p.p.*, reveal.

reveal'er, *n.*, one who reveals.

reveal'ing, *adj.*, enlightening; *pr.p.*, reveal.

reveil'lé, *n.*, the morning bugle call (*Fr.*).

rev'el, *n.*, wild festivities; a carousal; *v.i.*, to indulge in wild festivities; to delight greatly.

revela'tion, *n.*, the act of revealing; something revealed; an apocalypse.

revela'tionist, *n.*, a believer in divine revelation.

rev'elled, *p.p.*, revel.

rev'eller, *n.*, one who holds revel.

rev'elling, *pr.p.*, revel.

revel'lent, *adj.*, causing revulsion.

rev'elry, *n.*, revelling; riotous festivity.

re'venant, *n.*, one returned from the dead or exile; a ghost (*Fr.*).

revendica'tion, *n.*, a suit demanding back lost property, etc.

revenge', *n.*, the act of revenging; retaliation; vindictiveness; *v.t.*, to exact vengeance for; to inflict punishment for.

revenged', *p.p.*, revenge.

revenge'ful, *adj.*, vindictive.

revenge'fully, *adv.*, vindictively.

reven'ger, *n.*, one who takes revenge.

reven'ging, *pr.p.*, revenge.

rev'enue, *n.*, income, public or private.

rever'berant, *adj.*, resounding.

rever'berate, *v.t.* and *i.*, to echo; to reflect or be reflected.

rever'berated, *p.p.*, reverberate.

rever'berating, *pr.p.*, reverberate.

reverbera'tion, *n.*, the act or effect of reverberating.

reverb'erator, *n.*, a reflector; a reflecting lamp.

reverb'eratory, *adj.*, *i.q.* reverberant.

revere', *v.t.*, to reverence; to respect greatly.

revered', *p.p.*, revere.

rev'erence, *n.*, veneration, honour; an act of respect; a reverend person, as in the expression *Your Rever-*ence, *his Reverence*, etc. (*colloq.*); *v.t.*, to treat or regard with veneration.

rev'erenced, *p.p.*, reverence.

rev'erencing, *pr.p.*, reverence.

rev'erend, *adj.*, worthy of reverence; an ecclesiastical title of a person in Holy Orders.

rev'erent, *adj.*, showing reverence.

reveren'tial, *adj.*, expressive of reverence.

reveren'tially, *adv.*, in a reverential way.

rev'erently, *adv.*, in a reverent way.

reve'rer, *n.*, one who reveres.

rev'erie, *n.*, day-dreaming; musing without method (*Fr.*).

rev'erize, *v.t.*, to revere greatly.

revers', *n.*, (also *n. pl.*), a lapel (*Fr.*).

revers'al, *n.*, the act or effect of reversing; defeat.

reverse', *adj.*, opposite, reversed, annulled; *n.*, the opposite; the back of a coin (as distinguished from the obverse); a change to the contrary; defeat, a setback; *v.t.*, to turn back; to change diametrically the order or position of; to annul; to change to an opposite direction.

reversed', *adj.*, upside down; *p.p.*, reverse.

reverse'ly, *adv.*, in a reverse way.

rever'si, *n.*, an old-fashioned game of draughts (*Fr.*).

revers'ible, *adj.*, able to be reversed.

revers'ing, *pr.p.*, reverse.

rever'sion, *n.*, a return to a former state; the right of inheritance; a deferred annuity.

rever'sionary, *adj.*, pert. or rel. to reversion.

rever'sioner, *n.*, one who is entitled to a reversion.

revert', *v.i.*, to return; to come back to the original owner.

revert'ed, *p.p.*, revert.

revert'ible, *adj.*, able to revert.

revert'ing, *pr.p.*, revert.

revert'ive, *adj.*, retiring.

revest', *v.i.*, to take effect again; *v.t.*, to clothe again; to reinvest in a title or office.

revest'ry, *n.*, *i.q.* vestry.

revet'ment, *n.*, a retaining wall or facing.

revic'tual, *v.t. and i.*, to provide with a fresh supply of victuals.

revict'ualment, *n.*, reprovisioning; restocking with victuals.

review', *n.*, a looking back, retrospect; a critical examination; an inspection; a written criticism; a literary periodical; *v.t.*, to view again; to go over in memory; to scrutinize; to criticize; to inspect; to write an opinion.

review'able, *adj.*, able to be reviewed.

review'al, *n.*, *i.q.* review.

reviewed', *p.p.*, review.

review'er, *n.*, a writer of reviews.

review'ing, *n.*, the business of a reviewer; *pr.p.*, review.

revile', *v.t.*, to slander, to abuse.

reviled', *p.p.*, revile.

revi'ler, *n.*, one who reviles.

revi'ling, *n.*, abuse; *pr.p.*, revile.

revis'able, *adj.*, able to be revised.

revi'sal, *n.*, revision.

revise', *n.*, a revision; *v.t.*, to reconsider for the purpose of correction; to alter.

revised', *p.p.*, revise.

revi'ser, *n.*, one who revises.

revi'sing, *pr.p.*, revise.

revi'sion, *n.*, the act of revising; that which has been revised.

revi'sional, *adj.*, of the nature of revision.

revi'sionary, *adj.*, *i.q.* revisional.

revi'sionism, *n.*, a scheme of revision.

revi'sionist, *n.*, one who supports a policy of revision.

revis'it, *v.t.*, to visit again.

revis'ited, *p.p.*, revisit.

revis'iting, *pr.p.*, revisit.

revitaliza'tion, *n.*, the restoring of vitality.

revit'alize, *v.t.*, to put fresh life into.

revit'alized, *p.p.*, revitalize.

revit'alizing, *pr.p.*, revitalize.

revi'val, *n.*, the act of reviving; restoration; recovery.

revi'valism, *n.*, a movement advocating spiritual revival.

revi'valist, *n.*, an advocate of revivalism.

revive', *v.i.*, to recover; to regain animation; *v.t.*, to restore to animation; to bring back to life; to bring back from oblivion.

revived', *p.p.*, revive.

revi'ver, *n.*, that which revives; a stimulating drink.

revivifica'tion, *n.*, the act of revivifying.

reviv'ified, *p.p.*, revivify.

reviv'ify, *v.t.*, to give fresh life to; to quicken again.

reviv'ifying, *pr.p.*, revivify.

revi'ving, *adj.*, restorative; *pr.p.*, revive.

revivis'cence, *n.*, a renewal of life.

revivis'cent, *adj.*, returning to life.

revi'vor, *n.*, the process of reviving a dormant judgment or suspended action (*leg.*).

revocabil'ity, *n.*, the state of being revocable.

rev'ocable, *adj.*, able to be revoked or recalled.

revoca'tion, *n.*, the act or effect of revoking; annulment.

rev'ocatory, *adj.*, revoking.

revoke', *n.*, an instance of neglect to follow suit; *v.i.*, to fail to follow suit (at cards); *v.t.*, to recall; to cancel; to withdraw.

revoked', *p.p.*, revoke.

revo'king, *pr.p.*, revoke.

revolt', *n.*, a rebellion, a mutiny; *v.i.*, to rebel; to mutiny; to be nauseated; *v.t.*, to shock.

revolt'ed, *p.p.*, revolt.

revolt'er, *n.*, one who revolts.

revolt'ing, *adj.*, shocking, nauseating; *pr.p.*, revolt.

rev'olute, *adj.*, rolled backwards.

revolute', *v.i.*, to take part in a political revolution (*slang*).

revolu'tion, *n.*, a rolling backward; a complete turn round; a complete reversal; a wholesale change of principles of government.

revolu'tionary, *adj.*, pert. or rel. to a revolution.

revolu'tionist, *n.*, one who advocates, or takes part in, a revolution.

revolu'tionize, *v.i.*, to pass through a revolution; *v.t.*, to change completely.

revolu'tionized, *p.p.*, revolutionize.

revolu'tionizing, *pr.p.*, revolutionize.

revolve', *v.i.*, to rotate; to recur in a cycle; *v.t.*, to make go round; to ponder.

revolved', *p.p.*, revolve.

revolv'er, *n.*, a pistol having a revolving cylinder in the breech; anything that revolves.

revolv'ing, *pr.p.*, revolve.

revue', *n.*, a musical stage show (*Fr.*).

revu'ette, *n.*, a short musical revue (*Fr.*).

revul'sion, *n.*, a violent change of feeling; the removal of a disease from one part of the body to another.

revul'sive, *adj.*, producing a revulsion.

reward', *n.*, a recognition of merit; a requital; *v.t.*, to recompense; to requite.

reward'able, *adj.*, worthy of reward.

reward'ed, *p.p.*, reward.

reward'er, *n.*, one who rewards.

reward'ing, *pr.p.*, reward.

rewin', *v.t.*, to win back; to win again.

rewin'ning, *pr.p.*, rewin.

rewon', *p.p.*, rewin.

reword', *v.t.*, to express in different words.

reword'ed, *p.p.*, reword.

reword'ing, *pr.p.*, reword.

rewrite', *n.*, a passage professionally rewritten; *v.t.*, to write over again.

rewrit'ing, *pr.p.*, rewrite.

rewrit'ten, *p.p.*, rewrite.

rex, *n.*, a king (*Lat.*).

Rex'ine, *n.*, a kind of artificial leather.

rey'nard, *n.*, a name for the fox as the most cunning of beasts.

rhabar'barate, *adj.*, tinctured with rhubarb.

rhabdol'ogy, *n.*, *i.q.* rabdology.

rhab'domancy, *n.*, divination by means of rods.

Rhadaman'thine, *adj.*, pert. or rel. to Rhadamanthus, the judge in Hades; rigorous, exact.

Rhae'tian, *adj.*, naming the Alps near the Engadine.

rhapsod'ic, *adj.*, pert. or rel. to rhapsody.

rhapsod'ical, *adj.*, *i.q.* rhapsodic.

rhapsod'ically, *adv.*, in a rhapsodic way.

rhap'sodist, *n.*, one who recites or makes rhapsodies.

rhap'sodize, *v.t.* and *i.*, to recite; to make rhapsodies; to be ecstatic about.

rhap'sodized, *p.p.*, rhapsodize.

rhap'sodizing, *pr.p.*, rhapsodize.

rhap'sody, *n.*, a long epic poem for recitation in whole or part; any artistic composition full of romantic feeling.

rhat'any, *n.*, the root of a Peruvian shrub used medicinally and to flavour port wine.

rhe'a, *n.*, the three-toed S. American ostrich.

Rhen'ish, *adj.*, pert. or rel. to the Rhine; *n.*, Rhine wine.

rhen'ium, *n.*, a rare metallic element of the manganese group, discovered in 1925.

rhe'ograph, *n.*, an instrument for measuring variations in electric current.

rheol'ogy, *n.*, the study of the flow of, and changes in, matter.

rheom'eter, *n.*, an instrument for measuring the force of an electric current.

rheom'etry, *n.*, the science of measuring the force and velocity of electric currents.

rhe'ostat, *n.*, an instrument to regulate the force of currents.

Rhes'us, *n.*, a genus of small monkey common in N. India.

Rhe'tian, *adj.*, *i.q.* Rhaetian.

rhet'or, *n.*, a professor of rhetoric.

rhet'oric, *n.*, the art of discourse; oratory; the science of persuasive speech; insincere or exaggerated speech or writing.

rhetor'ical, *adj.*, pert. or rel. to rhetoric; artificial, extravagant or unnecessary in speech or writing.

rhetor'ically, *adv.*, in a rhetorical way.

rhetori'cian, *n.*, one who speaks or writes rhetoric.

rheum, *n.*, catarrhal discharge.

rheumat'ic, *adj.*, pert. or rel. to, or suffering from, rheumatism; *n.*, one who suffers from rheumatism.

rheumat'ics, *n. pl.*, rheumatic pains (*colloq.*).

rheum'atism, *n.*, a painful disease affecting the joints or muscles.

rheu'matoid, *adj.*, pert. or rel. to rheumatism.

rheumatol'ogy, *n.*, the study of rheumatism.

rheum'y, *adj.*, pert. or rel. to rheum; damp.

rhin'al, *adj.*, pert. or rel. to the nostril or nose.

rhine'stone, *n.*, a kind of rock crystal; an imitation paste gem.

rhi'no, *n.*, money (*slang*); also a *prefix* meaning nose; the abbrev. for rhinoceros.

rhinoce'rial, *adj.*, rhinoceros-like; pug.

rhinoc'eros, *n.*, a large mammal, with a thick, plated skin and a horned nose.

rhinol'ogist, *n.*, one who studies noses and nasal diseases.

rhinol'ogy, *n.*, the study of the nose and nasal diseases.

rhi'noscope, *n.*, an instrument for the examination of the nose.

rhinos'copy, *n.*, the art of examining the nose.

rhizo'ma, *n.*, *i.q.* rhizome.

rhi'zome, *n.*, a prostrate stem producing roots, etc.

rhizoph'agous, *adj.*, root-eating.

Rhode'sian, *adj.*, pert. or rel. to Rhodesia; *n.*, a native of R.

Rho'dian, *adj.*, pert. or rel. to Rhodes, an island in the Aegean Sea; *n.*, a native of R.

rhod'ium, *n.*, a greyish element used in alloys; the Jamaica rosewood.

Rhododen'dron, *n.*, an evergreen shrub with large, fine flowers.

rhodomontade', *n.*, *i.q.* rodomontade.

rhomb, *n.*, a lozenge shape; a parallelogram, equilateral and with opposite angles equal.

rhom'bic, *adj.*, like a rhomb.

rhombohed'ron, *n.*, a solid bounded by six equal rhombs.

rhom'boid, *adj.*, like a rhomb; *n.*, a parallelogram that is neither rectangular nor rhombic.

rhom'boidal, *adj.*, *i.q.* rhomboid.

rhom'bus, *n.*, *i.q.* rhomb; the turbot or brill.

rhopal'ic, *adj.*, *i.q.* ropalic.

rhot'acism, *n.*, the mispronunciation of the sound *r*; the conversion of other sounds into *r*.

rhu'barb, *n.*, a purgative root imported from Turkey, China and Tibet; an edible garden-stalk used in cookery.

rhumb, *n.*, one of the thirty-two points in a mariner's compass.

rhyme, *n.*, the repetition of similar sounds in verse, usually at line ends; *v.i.*, to versify; to make rhymes. (Also *rime.*)

rhymed, *p.p.*, rhyme.

rhyme'less, *adj.*, not rhyming.

rhyme'let, *n.*, a short rhyme.

rhym'er, *n.*, one who rhymes; a versifier.

rhyme'ster, *n.*, a composer of rhymes.

rhym'ic, *adj.*, pert. or rel. to rhyme.

rhym'ing, *n.*, versification in rhyme; *pr.p.*, rhyme.

rhythm, *n.,* the pattern of stress and non-stress in words, music or movements; the measured flow of words or musical notes; the proper correlation of structural parts (*arch.*); the regular succession of strong and weak elements in movement; periodicity.

rhyth′mic, *adj.,* marked by rhythm.

rhyth′mical, *adj., i.q.* rhythmic.

rhyth′mically, *adv.,* in a rhythmic way.

rhythm′less, *adj.,* lacking rhythm.

rhyth′mus, *n., i.q.* rhythm (*Gr.*).

ri′a, *n.,* a long, narrow inlet on the coast (*Span., geol.*).

Rial′to, *n.,* the old business quarter of Venice; the bridge over the Grand Canal.

ri′ancy, *n.,* laughter; gaiety (*Fr.*).

ri′ant, *adj.,* bright, smiling.

rib, *n.,* one of the curved bones extending from the spine and encircling the body; anything like a rib, as the vein of a leaf, a wave-mark on sand, etc.; *v.t.,* to furnish with ribs.

rib′ald, *adj.,* profane, irreverent; obscene in speech.

rib′aldry, *n.,* profanity, obscenity in speech.

rib′(b)and, *n., i.q.* ribbon.

ribbed, *adj.,* having ribs; *p.p.,* rib.

rib′bing, *n.,* an arrangement of ribs; a method of ploughing; *pr.p.,* rib.

rib′bon, *n.,* a strip of silk or other material for a variety of decorative uses; any long continuous strip of material; *v.i.,* to run to ribbons (as melting wax); *v.t.,* to deck with ribbons.

rib′boned, *adj.,* decorated with a ribbon; *p.p.,* ribbon.

rib′boning, *pr.p.,* ribbon.

Rib′bonism, *n.,* the principles of the Irish society of Ribbonmen.

Ri′bes, *n.,* a plant genus which includes the gooseberry and the currant (*bot.*).

Rib′ston pip′pin, *n.,* a variety of eating apple.

rice, *n.,* a cereal producing a seed much used for food.

rice′-bird, *n.,* the bobolink.

rice′-paper, *n.,* a delicate paper made from a Formosan plant and much used by Chinese artists.

rice′-water, *n.,* water in which rice has been boiled.

rich, *adj.,* wealthy, affluent; costly; luxuriant; abounding in; deep and full; very amusing (*colloq.*).

rich′er, *adj., comp.* of rich.

rich′es, *n.,* wealth, possessions.

rich′est, *adj., super.* of rich.

rich′ly, *adv.,* in a rich way; sumptuously; fully.

rich′ness, *n.,* the quality of being rich.

ricinela′idin, *n.,* a compound of castor-oil and nitric peroxide.

Ric′inus, *n.,* a botanical genus incl. the castor-oil plant.

rick, *n.,* a stack of hay, etc.; *v.t.,* to make into ricks.

ricked, *p.p.,* rick.

rick′ets, *n.,* an infantile disease, accompanied by softening of the bones, esp. of the spine. (Also *rachitis.*)

rick′ety, *adj.,* afflicted with rickets; tottering, unsafe.

rick′ing, *pr.p.,* rick.

rick′shaw, *n.,* a handcarriage used in the Orient.

ricochet′, *n.,* the glancing off of a bullet, etc., after striking some object; *v.t.,* to glance off, to rebound (*Fr.*).

ricocheted′, *p.p.,* ricochet.

ricochet′ing, *pr.p.,* ricochet.

ric′tus, *n.,* the vertical width of a person's or animal's mouth; a bird's beak; the mouth of a labate corolla; the fixed expression on the mouth of a corpse (*Lat.*).

rid, *adj.,* free; disencumbered; *v.t.,* to free, relieve or abolish.

ri′d(e)able, *adj.,* able to be ridden.

rid′dance, *n.,* the act of ridding; relief, freedom.

rid′ded, *p.p.,* rid.

rid′den, *p.p.,* ride.

rid′der, *n.,* one who, or that which, rids.

rid′ding, *pr.p.,* rid.

rid′dle, *n.,* a large sort of sieve; an enigma; a puzzle; *v.t.,* to pierce with holes; to sift; to solve.

rid′dled, *p.p.,* riddle.

rid′dler, *n.,* one who, or that which, riddles.

rid′dling, *pr.p.,* riddle.

ride, *v.i.,* to travel on horse back, etc., or in a conveyance; to float; to work its way up; *v.t.,* to be carried on the back of; to sit on or in (as a carriage).

rideau′, *n.,* a curtain; a mound of earth commanding a camp or fortification (*Fr.*).

rid(d)′el, *n.,* an altar-curtain.

ri′der, *n.,* one who rides a horse, bicycle, etc.; a supplementary writing, or clause of a Parliamentary Bill; a corollary; a mathematical problem.

ri′derless, *adj.,* without a rider.

ridge, *n.,* the top of two slopes which meet, as on a mountain, a furrow, etc.; *v.i.* and *t.,* to form into ridges.

ridged, *adj.,* having ridges; *p.p.,* ridge.

ridge′-pole, *n.,* a pole supporting the ridge of a roof or tent.

ridge′-tile, *n.,* a tile used for the ridge of a roof.

ridge′way, *n.,* a road along a ridge.

ridg′ing, *pr.p.,* ridge.

rid′ibund, *adj.,* inclined to laugh; laughing.

rid′icule, *n.,* derisive laughter; an object of derision; *v.t.,* to make fun of; to laugh at; to satirize.

rid′iculed, *p.p.,* ridicule.

rid′iculer, *n.,* one who ridicules.

rid′iculing, *pr.p.*, ridicule.

ridic′ulous, *adj.*, absurd, laughable.

ridic′ulously, *adv.*, in an absurd fashion.

ridic′ulousness, *n.*, absurdity.

ri′ding, *n.*, the act or state of riding; a procession; an administrative division of Yorkshire and Lincolnshire; *pr.p.*, ride.

ri′ding-hood, *n.*, a rider's head-covering.

ri′ding-master, *n.*, a teacher of riding.

ri′ding-school, *n.*, a place where horse-riding is taught.

ridot′to, *adj.*, abbreviated from a full score; *n.*, a masked ball; a shortened score (*It.*).

Ries′ling, *n.*, a dry, white table-wine (*Ger.*).

rifacimen′to, *n.*, a remodelled form of a literary work (*It.*).

rife, *adj.*, commonly occurring; current; abundant.

rife′ly, *adv.*, abundantly.

rife′ness, *n.*, the state or quality of being rife.

rif′fle, *n.*, a device for catching particles in gold-washing; *v.t.* and *i.*, to search the pages of a book quickly.

riff′raff, *n.*, the mob, rabble; rubbish.

ri′fle, *n.*, a firearm having its bore grooved (or rifled); *v.t.*, to rob, to plunder; to groove (a firearm).

ri′fle-bird, *n.*, the Australian bird of Paradise.

ri′fled, *p.p.*, rifle.

ri′fleman, *n.*, a soldier armed with a rifle.

ri′fler, *n.*, one who rifles; a robber.

ri′fle-range, *n.*, the distance a rifle shot will carry; a place for rifle practice.

ri′fle-shot, *n.*, the length to which a rifle shot carries.

ri′fling, *pr.p.*, rifle.

rift, *n.*, a fissure or split; *v.t.*, to cleave, to split.

rift′ed, *p.p.*, rift.

rift′ing, *pr.p.*, rift.

rift′less, *adj.*, without a rift.

rif′ty, *adj.*, full of fissures.

rig, *n.*, a ship's equipment; costume; tackle; a dodge; a partially castrated animal; *v.t.*, to furnish with sails, ropes, etc.; to equip; to manipulate the market fraudulently.

rigadoon′, *n.*, an old Provençal dance and its music.

Ri′gel, *n.*, the star *Beta*, in *Orion*.

riges′cent, *adj.*, stiffening.

rigged, *p.p.*, rig.

rig′ger, *n.*, one who rigs; a handwheel.

rig′ging, *n.*, a ship's equipment of spars, sails, etc.; *pr.p.*, rig.

right, *adj.*, straight; just; morally good; fitting, correct; conservative politically; *adv.*, correctly; justly; greatly; *n.*, just or proper conduct; that which is essentially right; a just claim; the side opposite to the left; *v.t.*, to put right; to remedy a wrong.

right′able, *adj.*, able to be righted.

right′-about, *n.*, the opposite direction.

right′-angle, *n.*, an angle of 90°.

right′-angled, *adj.*, containing right angles.

right′ed, *p.p.*, right.

right′eous, *adj.*, just, virtuous, upright.

right′eously, *adv.*, justly, uprightly.

right′eousness, *n.*, the quality of being righteous.

right′er, *n.*, *comp.* of right; *n.*, one who rights.

right′ful, *adj.*, with a just claim; just.

right′fully, *adv.*, by right.

right′fulness, *n.*, the quality of being rightful.

right′-hand, *adj.*, lying to the right side.

right′-handed, *adj.*, using chiefly the right hand.

right′ing, *pr.p.*, right.

right′ist, *n.*, one who supports the political right.

right′ly, *adv.*, properly, strictly.

right′minded′, *adj.*, upright in disposition.

right′minded′ness, *n.*, the quality of being rightminded.

right′ness, *n.*, the quality of being right.

rig′id, *adj.*, stiff; not flexible.

rigid′ity, *n.*, stiffness; inflexibility.

rig′idly, *adv.*, stiffly.

rig′idness, *n.*, *i.q.* rigidity.

rig′marole, *n.*, incoherent, rambling talk or writing.

ri′gor, *n.*, stiffness, rigidity; a violent chill with shivering (*Lat.*).

rig′orist, *n.*, an austere person of strict principles.

rig′orous, *adj.*, austere, strict; inclement.

rig′orously, *adv.*, in a rigorous way.

rig′our, *n.*, severity, austerity; strictness; the quality or state of being inclement.

Rig-ve′da, *n.*, the chief of the Vedas, or hymns, in praise of the powers of nature.

rig′widdy, *n.*, the band across the horse's back that supports the shafts.

rile, *v.t.*, to annoy or exasperate (*colloq.*).

riled, *p.p.*, rile.

rilie′vo, *n.*, a relief, in sculpture (*It.*).

ri′ling, *adj.*, exasperating; *pr.p.*, rile.

rill, *n.*, a brooklet; *v.i.*, to run in a small stream.

rille, *n.*, a trench or valley on the moon's surface (*astron.*).

rilled, *p.p.*, rill.

rill′et, *n.*, a diminutive of rill.

rillets′ (-ettes′), *n.*, minced meats (*Fr.*).

rill′ing, *pr.p.*, rill.

rim, *n.*, an edging; the circumference of a wheel; a frame; *v.t.*, to put a rim to.

rime, *n.*, a hoar-frost; *v.t.*, to cover with rime; also *i.q.* rhyme.

rimed, *p.p.*, rime.

ri′ming, *pr.p.*, rime.

rimmed, *adj.*, having a rim; *p.p.*, rim.

rim′ming, *pr.p.*, rim.

rimose′, *adj.*, chinky.

rimos′ity, *n.*, the quality or state of being rimose.

ri′mous, *adj.*, i.q. rimose.

rim′ple, *v.i.* and *t.*, to wrinkle into curves.

rim′pled, *p.p.*, rimple.

rim′pling, *pr.p.*, rimple.

ri′my, *adj.*, frosty, cold.

rind, *n.*, the peel or outer coating of fruit, flesh, etc.; *v.t.*, to strip bark from.

rin′derpest, *n.*, a cattle-disease.

rin′dle, *n.*, a runnel.

ring, *n.*, a circle; a circular band for the finger; the sound of a bell; a combination for controlling the market; an enclosure for boxing or wrestling; *v.i.*, to give forth a clear musical sound; to move in spirals; to resound; *v.t.*, to cause to sound clearly; to sound; to encircle; to put a ring in or upon.

ring′-bolt, *n.*, an eye-bolt with a ring.

ring′-bone, *n.*, a disease in horses marked by a bony growth on the pastern-bones.

ring′-dove, *n.*, a wood-pigeon.

ringed, *adj.*, marked with a ring; *p.p.*, ring.

rin′gent, *adj.*, grinning; gaping (*bot.*).

ring′er, *n.*, one who rings bells; an apparatus for ringing; a quoit that encircles the pin.

ring′-fence, *n.*, a fence entirely surrounding a park, etc.

ring′-finger, *n.*, the wedding-ring finger.

ring′hals, *n.*, a S. African cobra.

ring′ing, *adj.*, giving forth a clear metallic sound; *n.*, the act of ringing; the sound of bells; *pr.p.*, ring.

ring′leader, *n.*, one who heads a rebellion, riot, etc.

ring′let, *n.*, a little ring; a spiral lock of hair.

ring′master, *n.*, the manager of a circus performance.

ring′-road, *n.*, a road encircling a town or centre.

ring′-shaped, *adj.*, shaped like a ring.

ring′side, *n.*, the side of a boxing or wrestling ring.

ring′ster, *n.*, a member of a group or consortium.

ring′tail, *n.*, the female of the hen-harrier; the golden eagle.

ring′-tailed, *adj.*, having a tail marked with rings.

ring′worm, *n.*, a skin disease in circular patches.

rink, *n.*, a curling-ground; an artificial skating surface; *v.i.*, to skate on a rink.

rinked, *p.p.*, rink.

rink′er, *n.*, one who rinks.

rink′ing, *n.*, the act or art of rinking; *pr.p.*, rink.

rinse, *n.*, a kind of hair tint; *v.t.*, to swill; to cleanse with liquid, usually water.

rinsed, *p.p.*, rinse.

rins′er, *n.*, a person who, or that which, rinses.

rins′ing, *n.*, the act of rinsing; a liquid for rinsing; *pr.p.*, rinse.

ri′ot, *n.*, tumult, disorder; luxuriant growth; *v.i.*, to make a tumult; to behave violently; to luxuriate.

ri′oted, *p.p.*, riot.

ri′oter, *n.*, one who riots; a tumultuous person.

ri′oting, *n.*, tumult; *pr.p.*, riot.

ri′otous, *adj.*, tumultuous; dissipated; profligate.

ri′otously, *adv.*, in a riotous way.

ri′otousness, *n.*, the state of being riotous.

rip, *n.*, a dissipated person (*colloq.*); *v.i.*, to be torn; to rush along; *v.t.*, to tear, to divide; to pull off; to lay bare.

ripa′rian, *adj.*, pert. or rel. to a river bank.

ripe, *adj.*, mature; ready to be reaped or gathered; *v.i.* and *t.*, to ripen.

ripe′ly, *adv.*, maturely.

ri′pen, *v.i.* and *t.*, to bring or come to maturity.

ri′pened, *p.p.*, ripen.

ripe′ness, *n.*, maturity; the state of being ripe.

ri′pening, *pr.p.*, ripen.

ri′per, *adj.*, comp. of ripe.

ri′pest, *adj.*, super. of ripe.

ripie′no, *adj.*, reinforced; having the parts supplemented (*It., mus.*).

riposte′, *n.*, a quick return with a rapier or the tongue; a repartee (*Fr.*); *v.i.*, to make a quick return.

ripped, *p.p.*, rip.

rip′per, *n.*, one who, or that which, rips.

rip′ping, *pr.p.*, rip.

rip′ple, *n.*, a ruffling of the surface of water; anything resembling ruffled water; a toothed implement; *v.i.*, to make a ripple; *v.t.*, to ruffle (the surface); to treat with a ripple.

rip′pled, *p.p.*, ripple.

rip′pling, *pr.p.*, ripple.

rip′ply, *adj.*, wavy.

rip′-rap, *n.*, broken stones for strengthening or making foundations; *v.t.*, to reinforce with rip-rap.

rip′roaring, *adj.*, boisterous, riotous; first-rate.

rise, *n.*, an ascent; a salary increase; a fish's ascent for bait; the height of a step; any kind of upward advance; humiliation by ridicule (*slang*); *v.i.*, to ascend; to get up from a lying posture; to advance in height in any sense, as to be promoted; to slope upward; to come to the surface (as a fish); *v.t.*, to bring above the horizon; to lift a fish to the top of the water.

ris′en, *p.p.*, rise.

ri′ser, *n.*, one who, or that which, rises; the upright piece between two stair-treads.

risibil′ity, *n.*, the quality of being risible.

ris′ible, *adj.*, disposed to laugh; causing laughter.

ris′ibly, *adv.*, in a risible way.

ri′sing, *n.*, a getting up; an insurrection; *pr.p.*, rise.

risk, *n.*, a hazard; a chance taken; *v.i.* and *t.*, to hazard.

risked, *p.p.*, risk.

risk'ily, *adv.*, dangerously.

risk'ing, *pr.p.*, risk.

risk'y, *adj.*, hazardous, dangerous; somewhat improper.

risott'o, *n.*, a rice-based dish (*It.*).

ris'qué, *adj.*, bordering on indecency (*Fr.*).

ris'sole, *n.*, meat or fish cooked in a sausage-like roll or cake (*Fr.*).

ritardan'do, *adv.*, slower (*mus.*, *It.*).

rite, *n.*, a prescribed form of words and procedure used in liturgical worship or ceremonial observances.

ritornel'lo, *n.*, an instrumental interlude, prelude or refrain (*mus.*, *It.*).

rit'ual, *adj.*, pert. or rel. to rites; *n.*, a prescribed order of religious service; a formal ceremonious procedure.

rit'ualism, *n.*, a system based on rites as opposed to informal or non-liturgical worship.

rit'ualist, *n.*, a student of ceremonial.

ritualis'tic, *adj.*, pert. or rel. to ritual and ritualism.

rit'ually, *adv.*, according to ritual; with rites.

ri'val, *adj.*, in competition; *n.*, one who competes for a prize coveted by another; *v.t.*, to emulate, to oppose; to equal.

ri'val(l)ed, *p.p.*, rival.

ri'val(l)ing, *pr.p.*, rival.

ri'valry, *n.*, an act or state of competing.

ri'valship, *n.*, *i.q.* rivalry.

rive, *v.i.* and *t.*, to split.

rived, *p.p.*, rive.

riv'el, *v.i.* and *t.*, to wrinkle, crumple or shrivel.

riv'en, *p.p.*, rive.

riv'er, *n.*, a large stream of flowing water.

riv'erain, *adj.*, situated near a river; *n.*, a person dwelling by a river.

riv'er-bed, *n.*, the bottom of a river.

riv'er-horse, *n.*, the hippopotamus.

riv'erine, *adj.*, of or on a river or its banks.

riv'er-mouth, *n.*, the outfall point of a river.

riv'erside, *adj.*, by the river; *n.*, the river bank.

riv'et, *n.*, a bolt or nail fixing metal plates together; bearded wheat; *v.t.*, to fix, fasten or clinch.

riv'et(t)ed, *p.p.*, rivet.

riv'eter, *n.*, one engaged in riveting; a riveting-machine.

riv'et(t)ing, *n.*, the act of joining with rivets; a whole system of rivets; *pr.p.*, rivet.

rivière', *n.*, a necklace of diamonds or other gems (*Fr.*).

ri'ving, *pr.p.*, rive.

riv'ulet, *n.*, a very small stream.

roach, *n.*, a freshwater fish; an upward curve in the foot of a square sail (*naut.*).

road, *n.*, a track, path or highway.

road'hog, *n.*, one who drives a motor or rides a motor-cycle without regard for others.

road'less, *adj.*, without a road.

road'man, *n.*, a man who repairs the roads.

road'-met'al, *n.*, broken stone for road-making.

roads, *n.*, *i.q.* roadstead.

road'-sense, *n.*, the instinct to act correctly on the road.

road'side, *n.*, the side of a road.

road'stead, *n.*, an open place of anchorage.

road'way, *n.*, the middle of a road.

road'worthiness, *n.*, reliability on the road.

road'worthy, *adj.*, fit for the road; reliable on the road.

roam, *v.t.*, to wander over; *v.i.*, to go from place to place, to wander.

roamed, *p.p.*, roam.

roam'er, *n.*, one who roams.

roam'ing, *pr.p.*, roam.

roan, *adj.*, of a colour combining chestnut, bay, or sorrel with grey or white; *n.*, the roan colour; a roan-coloured horse; a soft sheep-skin leather.

roar, *n.*, a loud, prolonged sound; *v.i.*, to utter a loud, prolonged sound; *v.t.*, to shout out something.

roared, *p.p.*, roar.

roar'er, *n.*, one who roars, esp. a horse afflicted with roaring.

roar'ing, *adj.*, boisterous; riotously merry; highly successful (*slang*); *n.*, a disease of the larynx affecting horses; *pr.p.*, roar.

roaringly', *adv.*, in a roaring way.

roast, *adj.*, roasted; *n.*, roasted meat, or meat for roasting; *v.t.*, to cook by subjecting to dry heat; to parch; to banter (*slang*).

roast'ed, *p.p.*, roast.

roast'er, *n.*, one who roasts; an oven or other apparatus for roasting.

roast'ing, *pr.p.*, roast.

rob, *v.i.*, to be a thief; *v.t.*, to plunder; to steal from; to deprive.

robbed, *p.p.*, rob.

rob'ber, *n.*, a thief, a plunderer.

rob'bery, *n.*, the act of robbing.

rob'bin, *n.*, a package of rice, spice, etc.

rob'bing, *pr.p.*, rob.

robe, *n.*, a dress, esp. an official garment; a costume; a woman's dress-fabric in a single piece; *v.i.*, to put on dress; *v.t.*, to dress; to invest ceremoniously with dress.

robed, *p.p.*, robe.

rob'in, *n.*, a small bird with a red breast.

ro'bing, *pr.p.*, robe.

Robin'ia, *n.*, a N. American genus of trees.

rob'in-red'breast, *n.*, the robin.

ro'borant, *adj.*, strengthening; *n.*, a tonic.

rob'ot, *n.*, a mechanical man; an automatic rifle; any wholly automated device.

robotesque', *adj.*, robot-like.

ro'botism, *n.*, mechanical behaviour.

ro′botize, v.t., to make robot-like.

ro′burite, n., an explosive.

robust′, adj., vigorous; stout, strenuous.

robust′ious, adj., sturdy, boisterous.

robust′ly, adv., vigorously.

robust′ness, n., the quality of being robust.

roc, n., a fabulous Eastern bird of vast size and strength.

roc′ambole, n., Spanish garlic (Fr.).

Roccel′la, n. pl., a genus of certain lichens; a dye made from the plant (It.).

roccel′lic, adj., pert. or rel. to Roccella.

roch′et, n., a closefitting ecclesiastical linen vestment.

rock, n., the hard crust of the earth; a foundation; v.i., to sway one way and another; v.t., to move from side to side; to move (a cradle).

rock′bot′tom, adj., lowest; n., the rocky bed of the ocean; the very bottom.

rock′bound, adj., fenced round with rocks.

rock′-crystal, n., transparent quartz.

rock′-doe, n., an Alpine deer.

rocked, p.p., rock.

rock′er, n., anything that rocks; one of the curved pieces beneath a rocking-chair; an automobile lever.

rock′ery, n., rock-work in horticulture.

rock′et, n., an explosive device or missile attaining high velocity rapidly; a kind of plant; a reprimand (slang); v.i., to shoot up like a rocket.

rock′etry, n., the science of rockets.

rock′iness, n., the quality or state of being rocky.

rock′ing, pr.p., rock.

rock′ing-chair, n., a chair that swings on rockers.

rock′ing-horse, n., a child's toy-horse on rockers.

rock′ing-stone, n., a stone that rocks without falling over.

rock′less, adj., having no rocks.

rock′n′roll′, n., a form of dancing to swing music; jazz.

rock′-oil, n., petroleum.

rock′-salt, n., natural salt in lump form.

rock′work, n., a structure imitating rock; a rockery.

rock′y, adj., hard, like rock; abounding in rocks.

roco′co, adj., in the rococo style; n., a florid, highly decorated architectural style.

rod, n., a straight slip of wood; a switch; a birch-rod; a lightning-rod; a measure of length; anything rod-like; v.t., to supply with rods.

rode, p.p., ride.

ro′dent, adj., gnawing; n., a mammal with incisor and no canine teeth.

Roden′tia, n. pl., rodent mammals, as the beaver, rat, etc.

rodent′ial, adj., pert. or rel. to a rodent.

rode′o, n., a round-up of cattle; a form of cowboy entertainment associated with a round-up.

rodomontade′, n., rant, bluster; v.i., to rant. (Also rhodomontade.)

roe, n., spawn; the eggs of fishes; the roebuck; the female of the hart.

roe′buck, n., a small kind of deer.

roga′tion, n., the act of supplicating.

roga′tional, adj., pert. or rel. to rogation.

Roga′tion days, n. pl., the Monday, Tuesday and Wednesday preceding Ascension Day.

Roga′tiontide, n., the period of the rogation days.

Roga′tion week, n., the week in which the rogation days occur.

rogue, n., a knave, swindler, or vagabond; v.t., to trick.

rogu′ery, n., the conduct of a rogue; mischievous playfulness.

rogu′ish, adj., inclined to roguery.

rogu′ishly, adv., in a roguish way.

rogu′ishness, n., the quality of being roguish.

roil, v.t., to muddy; to annoy.

roiled, p.p., roil.

roil′ing, pr.p., roil.

roil′y, adj., muddy.

roist′er, v.i., to rollick. (Also royster.)

roist′erer, n., a rollicking person. (Also roysterer.)

rôle, n., a character or part in a play; a function (Fr.).

roll, n., anything rolled into cylindrical form; an official list; a strip of material that can be rolled; a cake formed by rolling; a printer's tool; a rolling sound, as of thunder or drums; v.t., to move by turning round and round; to wrap; to fold cylindrically; to flatten by rolling; v.i., to move onward by revolving; to rotate; to thunder.

roll′-call, n., a calling over of names on a roll.

rolled, p.p., roll.

roll′er, n., anything with which rolling is done.

roll′er-skate, n., a skate on wheels.

roll′ey, n., i.q. rulley.

rol′lick, v.i., to indulge in boisterous amusement.

rol′licked, p.p., rollick.

rol′licking, adj., boisterous, frolicsome; pr.p., rollick.

roll′ing, adj., moving circularly; undulating; pr.p., roll.

roll′ing-mill, n., a mill where metal is rolled out into sheets and bars.

roll′ing-pin, n., a kitchen utensil for rolling out paste, etc.

roll′ing-stock, n., a railway's carriages, trucks, etc.

roll′-on, n., a stretch-corset; v.t., to put on with a roller.

ro′ly-po′ly, n., pastry rolled round jam or fruit.

Roma′ic, adj., pert. or rel. to modern Greek; n., the modern Greek language.

romal′, n., a Spanish-American thong used instead of a whip; a silk handkerchief.

Ro'man, adj., pert. or rel. to Rome and the Romans; like an ancient Roman, stern; n., a citizen of Rome; a kind of type.

Ro'man Cath'olic, adj., bel. to the Roman Church; n., one who belongs to the Roman obedience.

Romance', adj., pert. or rel. to languages deriving from Latin.

romance', n., an imaginative story about chivalry, whether in verse or prose; the sentiment of chivalry, love or mystery; v.i., to fabricate stories.

romanced', p.p., romance.

roman'cer, n., one who romances; a fantastic liar.

roman'cing, pr.p., romance.

roman'cist, n., i.q. romancer.

Rom'anes, n., the Gipsy language.

Romanesque', adj., pert. or rel. to romanesque architecture, a style prevailing between Roman [500 A.D.] and Gothic [1100 A.D.].

Roman'ic, adj., i.q. Romance or Roman.

Ro'manism, n., the Roman Catholic system.

Ro'manist, adj., pert. or rel. to Romanism; n., an adherent of the Roman Catholic Church.

Ro'manize, v.i., to become Roman Catholic; v.t., to make Roman in any sense.

Ro'manized, p.p., Romanize.

Ro'manizing, pr.p., Romanize.

roman'tic, adj., pert. or rel. to romance; full of mysterious suggestion; appealing to the historic sentiment; sentimental.

roman'tically, adv., in a romantic way.

roman'ticism, n., a romantic style of writing; the appeal to mediaevalism.

roman'ticist, n., one who leans to romanticism.

roman'ticize, v.i. and t., to make romantic.

roman'ticized, p.p., romanticize.

roman'ticizing, pr.p., romanticize.

Rom'any, adj., pert. or rel. to the gipsies; n., a gipsy; gipsy speech.

Ro'mic, n., a phonetic system of writing based on the Roman alphabet.

Ro'mish, adj., Roman Catholic (in popular language).

romp, n., one who romps, esp. a tomboy; v.i., to play roughly; to gain an easy win.

romped, p.p., romp.

romp'er, n., one who romps; n. pl., a child's playsuit.

romp'ing, pr.p., romp.

romp'ish, adj., given to romping.

romp'ishly, adv., in a rompish way.

romp'ishness, n., active frolic.

ron'deau, n., a poetical form, consisting of ten or thirteen lines with two rhymes only and two refrains (Fr.).

ron'del, n., a poetical form, more or less resembling the rondeau, but differing esp. in the treatment of the refrain.

ron'do, n., a composition with repeating leading theme (mus.); a game of hazard.

ron'dure, n., a round outline or object.

rone, n. roof-guttering (Scot.).

Ro'neo, n., a duplicating machine; v.t., to reproduce letters, circulars, etc.

Rönt'genogram, n., a photograph taken by Röntgen rays.

Rönt'gen rays, n. pl., rays which penetrate many substances otherwise impervious to light.

rood, n., the Cross, with or without the figure of Christ upon it; a square land-measure; an old measure of length = a rod.

rood'screen, n., a stone or wooden carved screen.

roof, n., the upper covering of a house, building or conveyance; v.t., to cover with a roof in any sense.

roofed', adj., covered with a roof; p.p., roof.

roof'er, n., a man who builds or repairs roofs.

roof'ing, n., the structural materials of a roof; pr.p., roof.

roof'less, adj., uncovered; without a roof.

roof'-tree, n., a ridgepole; a roof.

rook, n., a kind of crow; a swindler (slang); the castle in chess; v.t., to swindle; to overcharge (slang).

rooked, p.p., rook.

rook'ery, n., a colony of rooks, penguins, seals, etc.

rook'ie, n., a recruit (army slang).

rook'ing, pr.p., rook.

room, n., space enough for a given purpose; opportunity; a chamber or apartment.

room'ful, n., as many, or as much, as a room holds.

room'ily, adv., spaciously.

room'iness, n., the quality of being roomy or spacious.

room'y, adj., spacious.

roon, n., a strip of cloth (Scot.).

roop, n., hoarseness.

roost, n., a perch; a garret (Scot.); a dangerous tidal current; v.i., to sit on a perch.

roost'ed, p.p., roost.

roost'er, n., a domestic cock.

roost'ing, pr.p., roost.

root, n., a plant's growth beneath the soil, giving it fixity and nourishing it from the soil; foundation; source; the primitive of a word; a number that, being multiplied by itself a given number of times, gives its power; a chord's fundamental note (mus.); v.i., to get fixed in the soil; to turn up with the snout; to cheer (Amer.); v.t., to plant; to dig up.

root'-crop, n., a crop of turnips, potatoes, etc.

root'ed, adj., established, fixed; p.p., root.

root'er, n., an animal that roots; one who shouts and cheers.

root'ery, *n.*, a pile of roots and stumps used as a rockery.

root'ing, *pr.p.*, root.

roo'tle, *v.t.* and *i.*, to root.

root'less, *adj.*, without a root.

root'let, *n.*, a little root.

root'-stock, *n.*, a rhizome; an original root.

root'y, *adj.*, full of roots; *n.*, bread (*mil. slang*).

ropal'ic, *adj.*, containing words each a syllable longer than the preceding word.

rope, *n.*, fibres twisted into a thick cord; anything rope-like, as a rope of hair; *v.i.*, to become ropy; *v.t.*, to fasten with a rope, to enclose with a rope.

roped, *p.p.*, rope.

rope-ladder, *n.*, two long ropes with short cross-ropes to make a ladder.

rope'maker, *n.*, one who makes ropes.

rope'making, *n.*, the trade of making ropes.

ro'per, *n.*, a ropemaker; one who binds with rope.

ro'pery, *n.*, a ropewalk.

rope's' end, *n.*, a piece of rope used for flogging sailors.

rope'walk, *n.*, a place where rope is made.

rope'-yarn, *n.*, fibres forming a smaller strand.

ro'piness, *n.*, the state or quality of being ropy.

ro'ping, *n.*, cordage; *pr.p.*, rope.

ro'py, *adj.*, stringy, viscous.

Roque'fort, *n.*, kind of French cheese.

roqu'elaure, *n.*, an eighteenth century French cloak for men.

roq'uet, *v.t.*, to strike an opponent's ball when playing croquet.

ro'ral, *adj.*, pert. or rel. to dew.

rorif'erous, *adj.*, dew-producing.

ror'qual, *n.*, a variety of whale, having a dorsal fin.

ror'ty, *adj.*, enjoyable (*slang*). (Also *raughty.*)

Rosa'ceae, *n. pl.*, the generic name for flowers of the rose type.

rosa'ceous, *adj.*, pert. or rel. to the Rosaceae.

rosan'iline, *n.*, an analine red dye.

rosar'ian, *n.*, a rose-fancier.

rosar'ium, *n.*, a rose-garden (*Lat.*).

ro'sary, *n.*, a rose-garden; a chaplet of roses; a string of beads used in a sequence of prayers.

rose, *n.*, a plant bel. to the Rosaceae; the flower of this shrub; rose-colour; the nozzle of a watering-pot; *p.p.*, rise.

ro'sé, *n.*, a light pink table wine (*Fr.*).

ro'seal, *adj.*, i.q. roseate.

ro'seate, *adj.*, rose-coloured; blooming; promising.

rose'bud, *n.*, the bud of a rose.

rose'-colour, *n.*, the colour of the rose.

rose'-coloured, *adj.*, of the colour of the rose.

rose'mary, *n.*, a sweet-scented evergreen shrub.

ro'seola, *n.*, a red rash.

roset(te'), *n.*, a rose-shaped badge or architectural ornament.

rose'-water, *n.*, a perfume prepared from roses.

rose'wood, *n.*, the name of a Brazilian timber much used in cabinet work.

Rosicru'cian, *adj.*, pert. or rel. to the Rosicrucians and their magic; *n.*, one of the Rosicrucians, an esoteric semi-religious society of occult philosophers.

ros'ied, *adj.*, made rosy.

ro'sier, *adj.*, *comp.* of rosy.

ro'siest, *adj.*, *super.* of rosy.

ros'in, *n.*, i.q. resin, particularly that which results from the distillation of oil of turpentine from crude turpentine; *v.t.*, to rub with rosin.

ros'iny, *adj.*, like, or covered with, rosin.

rosol'io, *n.*, a sweet raisin cordial (*It.*).

ross, *n.*, a rough surface of bark; *v.t.*, to remove bark.

ros'tel, *n.*, a small beak or beak-like protuberance.

ros'tellate, *adj.*, having a rostel.

ros'ter, *n.*, a list or order of names or duties. (Also *rota*.)

ros'tral, *adj.*, ornamented with beaks; pert. or rel. to rostrum.

ros'trate, *adj.*, having a rostrum.

ros'trated, *adj.*, i.q. rostrate.

ros'trum, *n.*, a beak; a platform (*Lat.*).

ros'ulate, *adj.*, arranged like the petals of roses.

ro'sy, *adj.*, of the colour of red roses; cheerful, bright.

rot, *n.*, decay, rottenness; absurdity (*slang*); a virulent liver disease of sheep; *v.i.*, to become rotten, to decay, to pine; to pretend to be serious (*slang*); *v.t.*, to make to rot; to spoil (*slang*); to banter.

ro'ta, *n.*, i.q. roster.

rotam'eter, *n.*, a wheeled instrument for measuring curves.

Rotar'ian, *n.*, a member of a Rotary Club.

Rotar'ianism, *n.*, the Rotarian principles and system.

Ro'tary, *n.*, a world-wide society for service to humanity (Rotary Club).

ro'tary, *adj.*, revolving on its axis; rotating; *n.*, a rotary machine.

rot'ascope, *n.*, a stroboscopic instrument for observing quickly-turning machines.

rotat'able, *adj.*, pert. or rel. to rotation.

rotate', *v.i.*, to revolve; to recur; *v.t.*, to cause to revolve on its axis; to vary the order of (crops).

ro'tate, *adj.*, wheel-shaped.

rota'ted, *adj.*, i.q. rotate; *p.p.*, rotate.

rota'ting, *pr.p.*, rotate.

rota'tion, *n.*, the act of rotating; recurrence or succession in a regular order.

ro'tative, *adj.*, turning like a wheel.

ro'tatively, *adv.*, in a rotative way.

ro'tativism, *n.*, government by political parties in turn.

ro'tativist, *n.*, a supporter of rotativism.

rota'tor, *n.*, a revolving apparatus or a piece of one; a muscle that enables a limb to rotate.

ro'tatory, *adj.*, revolving.

rotava'tor, *n.*, a rotary mechanical cultivator.

rotch(e), *n.*, the little auk.

rote, *n.*, repetition for the purpose of fixing in the memory; mechanical memory.

ro'tifer, *n.*, one of the Rotifera.

Rotif'era, *n. pl.*, animalcules having rotatory organs.

ro'tiform, *adj.*, wheel-shaped.

ro'todyne, *n.*, a vertical take-off aeroplane.

ro'tograph, *n.*, a photostat copy of a print, etc.

rotogravure', *n.*, a photogravure printed by rotary.

rot'or, *n.*, the rotating part of a machine; a helicopter vane.

ro'torcraft, *n.*, an aeroplane with a rotor lift.

rot'ted, *p.p.*, rot.

rot'ten, *adj.*, decaying, putrid, corrupt (in any sense).

rot'tenness, *n.*, the state or quality of being rotten.

rot'ten-stone, *n.*, decomposed limestone.

rot'ter, *n.*, an objectionable person (*slang*).

rot'ting, *pr.p.*, rot.

rotund', *adj.*, round, sonorous.

rotun'da, *n.*, a round building, usu. domed.

rotund'ity, *n.*, roundness.

rotund'ly, *adv.*, sonorously.

rotund'ness, *n.*, i.q. rotundity.

rou'ble, *n.*, the Russian monetary unit.

rou'cou, *n.*, a dye from the roucou tree.

rou'é, *n.*, a dissipated person; a rake (*Fr.*).

rouge, *adj.*, red (*her.*); *n.*, a scrummage or touchdown (Eton football); a red powder; *v.t.* and *i.*, to stain with rouge.

Rouge Croix', *n.*, one of the two pursuivants in the College of Arms (*Fr.*).

Rouge Drag'on, *n.*, i.q. Rouge Croix.

rouge-et-noir', *n.*, a gambling card-game, so named from the stakes being placed on red and black marks (*Fr.*).

rouged, *p.p.*, rouge.

rough, *adj.*, uneven, not level; coarse; shaggy; rude; violent; harsh, imperfect; preliminary; *n.*, a hooligan; a first draft; *v.t.*, to turn up; to rub the wrong way; to treat a horse's hoofs so as to prevent it from slipping; to make a rough sketch of.

rough'age, *n.*, food which stimulates bowel action.

rough'cast, *adj.*, covered with lime and gravel mixed; not completely worked out.

rough'-draft, *n.*, a draft not completely worked out.

rough'-draw, *v.t.*, to draw in outline.

rough'-drawing, *n.*, an outline; *pr.p.*, rough-draw.

rough'-drawn, *adj.*, outlined; *p.p.*, rough-draw.

roughed, *p.p.*, rough.

rough'en, *v.t.*, to make rough.

rough'ened, *p.p.*, roughen.

rough'ening, *pr.p.*, roughen.

rough'er, *adj.*, comp. of rough.

rough'est, *adj.*, super. of rough.

rough'-hew, *v.t.*, to shape incompletely.

rough'-hewed, *p.p.*, rough-hew.

rough'-hewing, *pr.p.*, rough-hew.

rough'-hewn, *adj.*, rough shaped; *p.p.*, rough-hew.

rough'ing, *pr.p.*, rough.

rough'ish, *adj.*, somewhat rough.

rough'ly, *adv.*, in a rough way.

rough'ness, *n.*, the quality of being rough.

rough'rider, *n.*, one who can ride any sort of horse; an irregular horse-soldier.

rough'shod, *adj.*, having the nails of the hoof projecting; *adv.*, in a domineering way.

roug'ing, *pr.p.*, rouge.

roulade', *n.*, a series of rapid runs; a vocal flourish (*Fr.*).

rouleau', *n.*, coins packed cylindrically; a roll (*Fr.*).

roulette', *n.*, a gambling game; a wheel used in engraving and perforating (*Fr.*).

rounce, *n.*, a card-game; a cylindrical contrivance for moving the bed of a hand-press.

roun'cival, *n.*, the name for a variety of pea.

round, *adj.*, spherical; circular; cylindrical; complete; considerable; *adv.*, rotatorily; about; *prep.*, about, surrounding; *n.*, anything round; circumference; a circuit or series; a musical piece for three or more equal voices; a kind of canon (*mus.*); *v.t.*, to make round; to make complete and symmetrical.

round'about, *adj.*, circuitous; circumlocutory; *n.*, a kind of jacket; a merry-go-round; circumlocution.

round'ed, *p.p.*, round.

round'el, *n.*, a circle; a disk; a medallion.

round'elay, *n.*, a song with refrain.

round'er, *adj.*, comp. of round; *n.*, one who rounds; in pl. a game with bat and ball.

round'est, *adj.*, super. of round.

round'-hand, *adj.*, bowling with the arm horizontally swung; *n.*, a round, full style of handwriting.

Round'head, *n.*, one of the seventeenth century Puritans.

round'house, *n.*, a watchhouse; a lockup; a range of cabins in an old sailing-ship (*naut.*).

round'ing, *pr.p.*, round.

round'ish, *adj.*, somewhat round.

round'ly, *adv.*, in a round way; very thoroughly.

round'ness, *n.*, the quality of being round.

round'-rob'in, *n.*, a petition, the signatures to which are arranged in a circle.

round'-shouldered, *adj.*, with shoulders inclined forward from the horizontal.

rounds'man, *n.*, one who goes round from house to house.

round'-ta'ble, *adj.*, meeting on equal terms; *n.*, a circular table.

round'up, *n.*, the herding of cattle for branding; *v.t.*, to gather up cattle or stragglers.

roup, *n.*, an auction sale (*Scot.*); a disease in poultry; *v.t.*, to sell by auction.

rouse, *n.*, a reveillé, a bumper; *v.i.*, to awake; to haul (*naut.*); *v.t.*, to awaken, excite or stir up; to sprinkle with salt in curing (esp. herrings).

roused, *p.p.*, rouse.

rous'er, *n.*, one who, or that which, rouses; an implement used for stirring beer during brewing.

rous'ing, *adj.*, startling, outrageous; *pr.p.*, rouse.

rous'ingly, *adv.*, excitingly, stirringly.

roust'about, *n.*, a wharf labourer, a deckhand.

rout, *n.*, a disorderly flight; an unlawful assembly; an evening party (*obs.*); *v.t.*, to put to disorderly flight; to fetch out.

route, *n.*, a road or direction; marching orders.

rout'ed, *p.p.*, rout.

route'-march, *n.*, a long march over a prepared route; a training march.

routine', *n.*, a regular, ordered succession of tasks or procedure; a series of movements in a dance.

rout'ing, *pr.p.*, rout.

rove, *n.*, a strand of fibre; a small metal plate used in rivetting; *v.i.*, to wander, to stray; to rave (*Scot.*); *v.t.*, to stray through; to ravel out; to reduce in diameter.

roved, *p.p.*, rove.

ro'ver, *n.*, one who roves; a pirate or brigand; the name of a croquet player or ball when all the hoops have been made.

ro'ving, *adj.* and *n.*, rambling; *pr.p.*, rove.

row, *n.*, a line; a rank or file; a series; *v.t.*, to propel with oars; to place in line.

row, *n.*, a brawl; a loud noise; *v.i.*, to make a disturbance; *v.t.*, to abuse; to rebuke severely (*colloq.*).

row'an, *n.*, the mountain ash.

row'boat, *n.*, a boat propelled with oars.

row'dily, *adv.*, in a boisterous, rough manner; roughly.

row'diness, *n.*, boisterousness, noisiness; rough behaviour.

row'dy, *adj.*, boisterous, rough; *n.*, a rough, disorderly person.

row'dyish, *adj.*, inclined to rowdyism.

row'dyism, *n.*, turbulence.

rowed, *p.p.*, row (oars).

rowed, *p.p.*, row (noise).

row'el, *n.*, the little toothed wheel in a spur; *v.t.*, to prick with a spur.

row'el(l)ed, *p.p.*, rowel.

row'el(l)ing, *pr.p.*, rowel.

row'en, *n.*, an aftermath of hay.

row'er, *n.*, one who rows with an oar.

row'ing, *pr.p.*, row (oars).

row'ing, *pr.p.*, row (noise).

row'lock, *n.*, a contrivance on a gunwale for retaining oars and providing a fulcrum for them.

roy'al, *adj.*, kingly; pert. or rel. to kings; regal; *n.*, a size of paper; the sail immediately above the topgallant mast.

roy'alism, *n.*, adherence to the principles of monarchy.

roy'alist, *n.*, a supporter of monarchy, esp. a supporter of the Crown against the Cromwellian rebellion.

roy'ally, *adv.*, in a royal way.

roy'alty, *n.*, the rank or office of a sovereign; the sovereign's privileges; kingly character; princes collectively; payment to an author or patentee on the proceeds of his book, invention, etc.

roys'ter, *v.i.*, *i.q.* roister.

roys'terer, *n.*, *i.q.* roisterer.

rub, *n.*, the act of rubbing; a cause of difficulty; *v.i.*, to graze or scrape; to make difficult progress; *v.t.*, to apply friction by moving something over the surface of; to chafe; to polish; to graze; to erase by rubbing; to take a copy by rubbing.

rub'-a-dub, *n.* and *v.i.*, (to make) the rolling sound of a drum.

ruba'to, *adv.* time varied for expression (*mus.*); *n.*, a certain freedom as to tempo (*It.*).

rubbed, *p.p.*, rub.

rub'ber, *adj.*, made of rubber; *n.*, one who rubs; any appliance for rubbing; a masseur; caoutchouc; the winning game at cards; a series of games; a collision (in the game of bowls); *v.t.*, to apply a rubber coating to.

rub'berize, *v.t.*, to treat with rubber.

rub'berized, *adj.*, treated with rubber; *p.p.*, rubberize.

rub'berizing, *pr.p.*, rubberize.

rub'bery, *adj.*, like rubber.

rub'bing, *n.*, the act of rubbing; a reproduction of a brass, drawing, etc., obtained by rubbing heel-ball or graphite over paper placed above the design, etc.; *pr.p.*, rub.

rub'bish, *interj.*, nonsense; *n.*, waste matter, refuse, trash.

rub'bishy, *adj.*, worthless.

rub'ble, *n.*, broken stone; water-worn stones.

rub'bly, *adj.*, full of rubble.

rube, *n.*, a country bumpkin (*colloq.*).

rubefa'cient, *adj.*, producing redness or blushing; *n.*, a counter-irritant.

rubefac'tion, *n.*, a making red.

ru'befied, *p.p.*, rubefy.

ru'befy, *v.t.*, to redden.

ru'befying, *pr.p.*, rubefy.

rubel'la, *n.*, German measles.

ru'bellite, *n.*, a red silicate.

Rubenesque', *adj.*, pert. or rel. to the painter, Rubens.

rube'ola, *n.*, measles.

rubes'cence, *n.*, the state of being rubescent.

rubes'cent, *adj.*, growing red.

ru'bican, *adj.*, with grey or white flecks.

ru'bicelle, *n.*, a precious stone resembling a ruby.

Ru'bicon, *n.*, a river in Italy. In his quarrel with Pompey, Caesar crossed the river and so committed himself to a war. Hence, the word means any irrevocable decision or proceeding.

ru'bicund, *adj.*, ruddy; flushed.

rubicun'dity, *n.*, the state of being rubicund.

rubid'ium, *n.*, a soft metallic element.

ru'bied, *adj.*, ornamented with rubies.

rubif'ic, *adj.*, *i.q.* rubefacient.

ru'biform, *adj.*, reddish.

ru'bify, *v.t.*, *i.q.* rubefy.

rubig'inous, *adj.*, rusty; rust-coloured.

ru'bious, *adj.*, ruby coloured.

ru'bric, *n.*, a heading or caption; a liturgical direction written in red; a written instruction, esp., on an examination paper.

ru'brical, *adj.*, pert. or rel. to, or of the nature of, a rubric.

ru'brically, *adv.*, in a rubrical way.

ru'bricate, *v.t.*, to illuminate with red; to furnish with rubrics.

ru'bricated, *p.p.*, rubricate.

ru'bricating, *pr.p.*, rubricate.

rubrica'tion, *n.*, the act of rubricating.

rubri'cian, *n.*, a student of the ecclesiastical rubrics; a stickler for rubrics.

ru'bricist, *n.*, a stickler for rubrics.

rub'stone, *n.*, the stone of which whetstones are made; a whetstone.

Ru'bus, *n.*, the blackberry or loganberry.

ru'by, *n.*, a gem of varying degrees of red; a size of printer's type.

ruche, *n.*, a frill; *v.t.*, to ornament with a frill.

ruch'ing, *n.*, *i.q.* ruche.

ruck, *n.*, a crease; a heap; a crowd in the end of a race; *v.t.* and *i.*, to crease.

ruck'le, *n.*, *v.t.* and *i.*, *i.q.* ruck, wrinkle or crease; a death-rattle; *v.i.*, to gurgle.

ruck'led, *p.p.*, ruckle.

ruck'ling, *n.*, *i.q.* ruckle; *pr.p.*, ruckle.

ruck'sack, *n.*, a capacious bag carried on the back by walkers and climbers.

ruc'tion, *n.*, trouble; a row.

rudbeck'ia, *n.*, a plant of the aster family.

rudd, *n.*, a freshwater fish.

rud'der, *n.*, a steering apparatus.

rud'dier, *adj.*, *comp.* of ruddy.

rud'diest, *adj.*, *super.* of ruddy.

rud'diness, *n.*, the quality of being ruddy.

rud'dle, *n.*, red ochre.

rud'dock, *n.*, a robin; a red apple.

rud'dy, *adj.*, inclined to red; florid; *v.t.*, to make ruddy.

rude, *adj.*, rough, barbarous, impolite, uncultivated, robust.

rude'ly, *adv.*, in a rude way.

rude'ness, *n.*, impoliteness.

ruden'ture, *n.*, cabling.

ru'der, *adj.*, *comp.* of rude.

ru'dest, *adj.*, *super.* of rude.

ru'diment, *n.*, an element; the first principle; something undeveloped.

rudimen'tal, *adj.*, *i.q.* rudimentary.

rudimen'tarily, *adv.*, in a rudimentary way.

rudimen'tary, *adj.*, elementary; undeveloped.

ru'dish, *adj.*, inclined to be rude.

rue, *n.*, a bitter herb; *v.t.*, to lament for; to repent of.

rued, *p.p.*, rue.

rue'ful, *adj.*, dolorous, mournful.

rue'fully, *adv.*, mournfully.

rue'fulness, *n.*, sadness.

rue'ing, *pr.p.*, rue.

rue'raddy, *n.*, a dragrope.

rufes'cent, *adj.*, tending to yellow redness.

ruff, *n.*, a frilled neck ornament; a freshwater fish; a snipe; a pigeon; *v.t.*, to ruffle; to play a trump card on a lead of another suit.

ruffed, *p.p.*, ruff.

ruf'fian, *n.*, a coarse villain.

ruf'fianism, *n.*, the character of a ruffian.

ruf'fianly, *adj.*, brutal.

ruff'ing, *pr.p.*, ruff.

ruf'fle, *n.*, a laced or plaited article of dress; *v.i.*, to become rough; to flutter; to fall out of temper; *v.t.*, to disorder, to flutter; to put out of temper; to put a ruffle on; to make a drum roll.

ruf'fled, *p.p.*, ruffle.

ruf'fling, *pr.p.*, ruffle.

ru'fous, *adj.*, yellowish red.

rug, *n.*, a wrap or coverlet; a loose covering for the floor.

ru'gate, *adj.*, *i.q.* rugous.

Rug'by, *n.*, Rugby football originally played at Rugby school in Warwickshire, England.

rug'ged, *adj.*, rough; uneven; uncouth; shaggy.

rug'gedly, *adv.*, in a rugged way.

rug'gedness, *n.*, the quality or state of being rugged.

rug'ger, *n.* Rugby football (*colloq.*).

ru'gose, *adj.*, wrinkled.

ru'in, *n.*, destruction, overthrow; moral or financial destruction; a ruinous building; *v.t.*, to destroy, to overthrow; to bring to poverty.

ru'inate, *adj.*, ruined.

ruina'tion, *n.*, destruction.

ru'ined, *p.p.*, ruin.

ru'ining, *pr.p.*, ruin.

ru'inous, *adj.*, in a ruined state; leading to ruin.

ru'inously, *adv.*, in a ruinous way.

rule, *n.*, a standard, law or regulation; regular mode; an order of court; an instrument for ruling lines; *v.i.*, to be a ruler; to prevail; *v.t.*, to govern; to give a decision on; to mark with lines.

ruled, *p.p.*, rule.

ru'ler, *n.*, one who rules; an instrument for ruling and measuring.

ru'ling, *pr.p.*, rule.

rull'ey, *n.*, a flat, four-wheeled dray or lorry.

ru'ly, *adj.*, orderly; well-behaved.

rum, *adj.*, queer, strange (*slang*); *n.*, an alcoholic liquor distilled from sugar-cane juice.

R(o)uman'ian, *adj.*, pert. or rel. to Rumania; *n.*, a native of R.

rum'ba, *n.*, a Latin-American dance (*Span.*).

rum'ble, *n.*, a long, heavy sound; a servant's seat behind a carriage; *v.i.*, to make a prolonged heavy sound; *v.t.*, to see through, to detect (*slang*).

rum'bled, *p.p.*, rumble.

rum'bling, *n.*, i.q. rumble; *pr.p.*, rumble.

rumbus'tious, *adj.*, boisterous, uproarious (*colloq.*).

ru'men, *n.*, a ruminant's first stomach.

ru'minal, *adj.*, chewing the cud.

ru'minant, *adj.*, i.q. ruminal; *n.*, a cud-chewing animal.

ru'minate, *v.i.*, to chew the cud; to ponder.

ru'minated, *p.p.*, ruminate.

ru'minating, *pr.p.*, ruminate.

rumina'tion, *n.*, the act of ruminating; calm reflection.

ru'minator, *n.*, one who ponders.

rum'mage, *n.*, a close search; *v.i.*, to search with care; *v.t.*, to ransack.

rum'maged, *p.p.*, rummage.

rum'mage-sale, *n.*, a sale of old odds and ends for charity.

rum'maging, *pr.p.*, rummage.

rum'mer, *n.*, a drinking glass for toddy.

rum'my, *adj.*, odd, strange (*slang*); *n.*, a simple card game.

ru'mour, *n.*, a report; a current story; *v.t.*, to report.

ru'moured, *p.p.*, rumour.

ru'mouring, *pr.p.*, rumour.

rump, *n.*, the buttocks; tail-end.

rum'ple, *n.*, a plait; *v.t.*, to make uneven; to plait.

rum'pled, *p.p.*, rumple.

rum'pling, *pr.p.*, rumple.

rum'pus, *n.*, a great fuss; a disturbance (*slang*).

rum'py, *n.*, a manx cat.

rum'-tum', *n.*, a light sculling boat.

run, *n.*, the act of running; a distance covered by running or sailing; a sudden demand; a space for moving in; continuance; a score for running the distance between wickets; a snag in silk or nylon material; *v.i.*, to move swiftly above a walk; to flow or melt; to go on continuously; *v.t.*, to make to run; to push; to carry on.

run'about, *adj.*, roving; *n.*, a light motor car; a person who runs about from place to place.

run'agate, *n.*, a renegade (of which *runagate* is an altered form); a fugitive.

run'away, *adj.*, running away; *n.*, a fugitive.

run'cinate, *adj.*, having leaves convex on one side and straight on the other (*bot.*).

run'dle, *n.*, a rung in a ladder.

rund'let, *n.*, a wine-cask; a measure of wine. (Also *runlet*.)

run-down', *adj.*, stopped for want of winding; in poor health; *v.t.*, to knock down.

rune, *n.*, a runic letter or poem.

rung, *n.*, a step in a ladder; *p.p.*, ring.

ru'nic, *adj.*, pert. or rel. to runes; *n.*, a primitive Teutonic alphabet.

run'let, *n.*, a little stream; a small barrel; i.q. rundlet.

run'nel, *n.*, a small brook.

run'ner, *n.*, one who runs; a scout; the keel on which a sleigh runs; a shooting sprig; a mill-stone that revolves; a supplementary rope in mechanical tackle; a strip of decorative textile material for a table or sideboard; a kind of twining bean.

run'net, *n.*, i.q. rennet.

run'ning, *n.*, the act of running; that which flows; *pr.p.*, run.

run'ning-board, *n.*, the foot-platform on the side of a vehicle.

run'ning-jump, *n.*, a jump taken after a run.

runt, *n.*, a stunted animal; a stump; a large breed of domestic pigeon.

run'way, *n.*, a track; a path for aircraft to take off and land.

rupee', *n.*, the Indian monetary unit.

rup'tion, *n.*, i.q. rupture.

rup'ture, *n.*, a breach, a severance; a hernia; *v.t.*, to break, burst or sever; to produce hernia.

rup'tured, *p.p.*, rupture.

rup'turing, *pr.p.*, rupture.

ru'ral, *adj.*, pert. or rel. to the country; rustic.

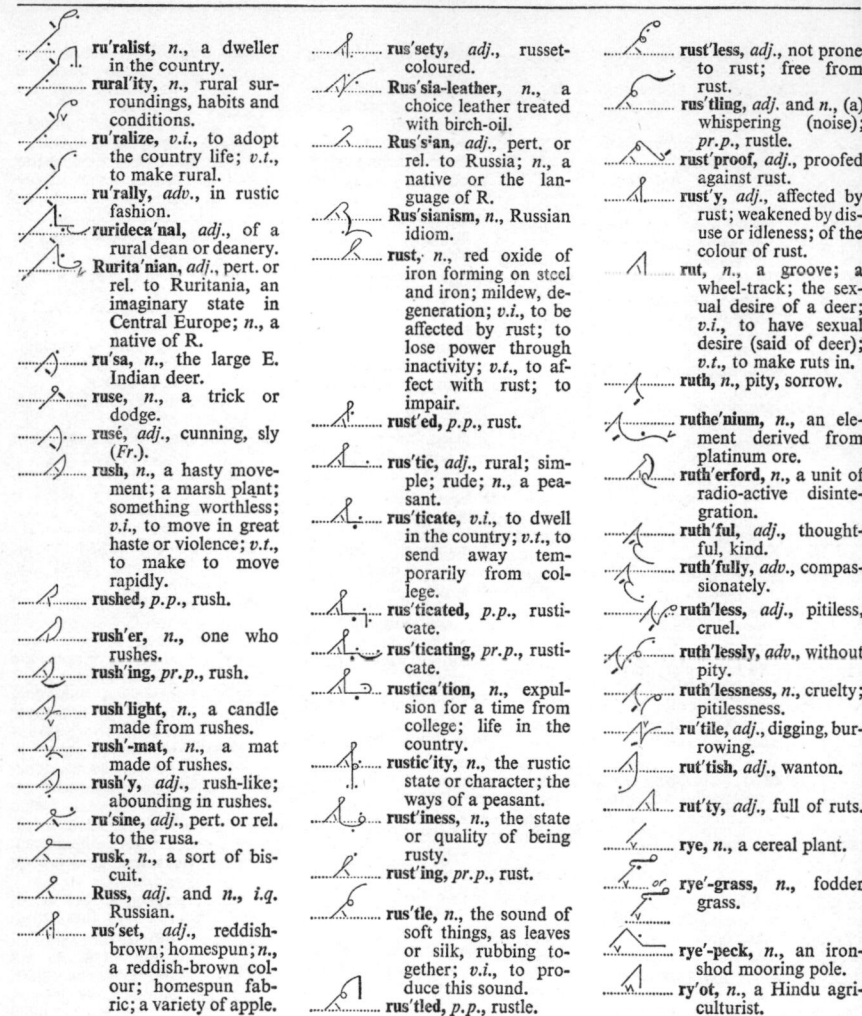

ru′ralist, *n.,* a dweller in the country.

rural′ity, *n.,* rural surroundings, habits and conditions.

ru′ralize, *v.i.,* to adopt the country life; *v.t.,* to make rural.

ru′rally, *adv.,* in rustic fashion.

rurideca′nal, *adj.,* of a rural dean or deanery.

Rurita′nian, *adj.,* pert. or rel. to Ruritania, an imaginary state in Central Europe; *n.,* a native of R.

ru′sa, *n.,* the large E. Indian deer.

ruse, *n.,* a trick or dodge.

rusé, *adj.,* cunning, sly (*Fr.*).

rush, *n.,* a hasty movement; a marsh plant; something worthless; *v.i.,* to move in great haste or violence; *v.t.,* to make to move rapidly.

rushed, *p.p.,* rush.

rush′er, *n.,* one who rushes.

rush′ing, *pr.p.,* rush.

rush′light, *n.,* a candle made from rushes.

rush′-mat, *n.,* a mat made of rushes.

rush′y, *adj.,* rush-like; abounding in rushes.

ru′sine, *adj.,* pert. or rel. to the rusa.

rusk, *n.,* a sort of biscuit.

Russ, *adj.* and *n.,* *i.q.* Russian.

rus′set, *adj.,* reddish-brown; homespun; *n.,* a reddish-brown colour; homespun fabric; a variety of apple.

rus′sety, *adj.,* russet-coloured.

Rus′sia-leather, *n.,* a choice leather treated with birch-oil.

Rus′s¹an, *adj.,* pert. or rel. to Russia; *n.,* a native or the language of R.

Rus′sianism, *n.,* Russian idiom.

rust, *n.,* red oxide of iron forming on steel and iron; mildew, degeneration; *v.i.,* to be affected by rust; to lose power through inactivity; *v.t.,* to affect with rust; to impair.

rust′ed, *p.p.,* rust.

rus′tic, *adj.,* rural; simple; rude; *n.,* a peasant.

rus′ticate, *v.i.,* to dwell in the country; *v.t.,* to send away temporarily from college.

rus′ticated, *p.p.,* rusticate.

rus′ticating, *pr.p.,* rusticate.

rustica′tion, *n.,* expulsion for a time from college; life in the country.

rustic′ity, *n.,* the rustic state or character; the ways of a peasant.

rust′iness, *n.,* the state or quality of being rusty.

rust′ing, *pr.p.,* rust.

rus′tle, *n.,* the sound of soft things, as leaves or silk, rubbing together; *v.i.,* to produce this sound.

rus′tled, *p.p.,* rustle.

rust′less, *adj.,* not prone to rust; free from rust.

rus′tling, *adj.* and *n.,* (a) whispering (noise); *pr.p.,* rustle.

rust′proof, *adj.,* proofed against rust.

rust′y, *adj.,* affected by rust; weakened by disuse or idleness; of the colour of rust.

rut, *n.,* a groove; a wheel-track; the sexual desire of a deer; *v.i.,* to have sexual desire (said of deer); *v.t.,* to make ruts in.

ruth, *n.,* pity, sorrow.

ruthe′nium, *n.,* an element derived from platinum ore.

ruth′erford, *n.,* a unit of radio-active disintegration.

ruth′ful, *adj.,* thoughtful, kind.

ruth′fully, *adv.,* compassionately.

ruth′less, *adj.,* pitiless, cruel.

ruth′lessly, *adv.,* without pity.

ruth′lessness, *n.,* cruelty; pitilessness.

ru′tile, *adj.,* digging, burrowing.

rut′tish, *adj.,* wanton.

rut′ty, *adj.,* full of ruts.

rye, *n.,* a cereal plant.

rye′-grass, *n.,* fodder grass.

rye′-peck, *n.,* an iron-shod mooring pole.

ry′ot, *n.,* a Hindu agriculturist.

S

sabadil′la, *n.*, a drug prepared from the seeds of the sabadilla or cevadilla plant, found in S. America.

Sabae′an, *adj.*, pert. or rel. to Saba or Yemen; Arabian.

Sab′aism, *n.*, star worship.

Sab′aoth, *n. pl.*, hosts; armies.

Sabbata′rian, *adj.*, pert. or rel. to the Sabbath and Sabbatarianism; *n.*, a precisian in regard to sabbatic observance.

Sabbata′rianism, *n.*, the principles of Sabbatarians.

Sab′bath, *n.*, the day of rest and religious observance.

sabbat′ic, *adj.*, pert. or rel. to the Sabbath.

sabbat′ical, *adj.*, *i.q.* sabbatic; related to rest or a change of occupation.

sab′batism, *n.*, the observance of the sabbatic rest.

sab′batize, *v.i.*, to keep the Sabbath; *v.t.*, to make into the Sabbath.

Sabe′an, *adj.*, *i.q.* Sabaean.

Sa′beism, *n.*, *i.q.* Sabianism.

Sabel′lian, *adj.*, pert. or rel. to Sabellius, an African heretic.

Sabel′lianism, *n.*, the heresy of Sabellius.

Sa′bian, *adj.*, pert. or rel. to Sabianism.

Sa′bianism, *n.*, a system of nature-worship, in which the heavenly hosts were taken to symbolize God.

Sab′ine, *adj.*, pert. or rel. to the Sabines, an old Italian people.

sa′ble, *adj.*, black; of dark hue; *n.*, a species of weasel esteemed for its fine fur; in pl., mourning attire.

sabot′, *n.*, a rustic wooden shoe (*Fr.*).

sabotage′, *n.*, deliberate destruction for political or economic motives (*Fr.*).

saboteur′, *n.*, one who commits sabotage (*Fr.*).

sa′bre, *n.*, a cavalryman's sword; *v.t.*, to put to the sword.

sab′retache, *n.*, a cavalryman's leather bag attached to the left side of his sword-belt (*Fr.*).

sab′ulous, *adj.*, sandy, gritty; granular (*med.*).

sabu′rra, *n.*, foul granular matter found in the stomach (*med.*).

sac, *n.*, a bag; a cyst; a manorial lord's privilege of holding a court.

saccade′, *n.*, a jerk on a bridle; pressure with a violin bow.

sac′cate, *adj.*, bag-shaped.

sacchar′ic, *adj.*, pert. or rel. to sugar.

sacchar′ify, *v.t.*, to change into sugar.

sac′charin, *n.*, a compound for sweetening prepared from coal-tar.

sac′charine, *adj.*, sugary; pert. or rel. to sugar.

sac′charoid, *adj.*, resembling loaf sugar.

saccharom′eter, *n.*, an apparatus showing the quantity of saccharine matter in liquids.

sac′ciform, *adj.*, sac-shaped.

sac′cule, *n.*, a small cyst or sac.

sacerdo′cy, *n.*, a priestly function.

sacerdo′tage, *n.*, a priest-ridden state.

sacerdo′tal, *adj.*, pert. or rel. to a priest; priestly.

sacerdo′talism, *n.*, the priestly system.

sacerdo′tally, *adv.*, in a priestly way or sense.

sa′chem, *n.*, a chief (*Amer. Ind.*).

sachet′, *n.*, a scent-bag (*Fr.*).

sack, *n.*, a bag or pouch; a sackful; a loose garment; an old wine; the plunder of a besieged place; dismissal from service (*colloq.*); *v.t.*, to pillage; to fill sacks with; to dismiss (*colloq.*).

sack′age, *n.*, plundering.

sack′but, *n.*, an ancient musical instrument resembling a trombone.

sack′cloth, *n.*, cloth of which sacks are made; a sign of sorrow.

sackdoo′dle, *v.i.*, to play the bagpipes.

sacked, *p.p.*, sack.

sack′er, *n.*, a pillager.

sack′ful, *n.*, what a sack will hold.

sack′ing, *n.*, the material of which sacks are made; *pr.p.*, sack.

sack′less, *n.*, innocent, without blame, quiet.

sacque, *n.*, a woman's robe (*Fr.*).

sa′cral, *adj.*, pert. or rel. to the sacrum (*anat.*).

sac′rament, *n.*, originally a military oath; a mystery; "an outward and visible sign of an inward and spiritual grace given unto us."

sacramen′tal, *adj.*, pert. or rel. to sacraments; of the nature of a sacrament; *n.*, something akin to a sacrament.

sacramen′talist, *n.*, one with exalted views on the sacraments.

sacramenta′rian, *adj.*, pert. or rel. to sacraments; *n.*, a professor of Zwinglian doctrines.

Sacramen′tary, *adj.*, *i.q.* sacramentarian; *n.*, an ancient ritual book rel. to the celebration of Mass.

sacra′rium, *n.*, a piscina; anciently, a shrine (*Lat.*).

sa′cred, *adj.*, consecrated; holy; inviolate.

sa′credly, *adv.*, in a sacred way.

sa'credness, *n.,* the state or quality of being sacred.

sac'rifice, *n.,* an offering in worship; that which is sacrificed; loss with a purpose; a sale below value; *v.i.,* to make an offering; *v.t.,* to offer as an act of worship; to suffer a loss for the sake of gaining something; to sell below value.

sac'rificed, *p.p.,* sacrifice.

sac'rificer, *n.,* one who sacrifices; a priest.

sacrifi'cial, *adj.,* of the nature of sacrifice.

sacrifi'cially, *adv.,* in a sacrificial way.

sac'rificing, *pr.p.,* sacrifice.

sac'rilege, *n.,* an act of impiety in a sacred place; the diversion of sacred property to secular uses.

sacrile'gious, *adj.,* of the nature of sacrilege.

sacrile'giously, *adv.,* in a sacrilegious way.

sacrile'gist, *n.,* a sacrilegious person.

sac'ring, *n.,* the consecration of elements in mass.

sa'crist, *n.,* a minor canon who is the sacristan.

sac'ristan, *n.,* a church official whose duties are connected with the altar; a sexton.

sac'risty, *n.,* the part of a church where the vestments are kept.

sac'rosanct, *adj.,* peculiarly sacred; inviolable.

sa'crum, *n.,* the bone at the lower end of the vertebral column (*Lat.*).

sad, *adj.,* sorrowful, depressed, grave; of dark hue.

sad'den, *v.i.,* to become sad; *v.t.,* to make sad.

sad'dened, *p.p.,* sadden.

sad'dening, *pr.p.,* sadden.

sad'der, *adj.,* comp. of sad.

sad'dest, *adj.,* super. of sad.

sad'dle, *n.,* a rider's seat on a horse or cycle; *v.t.,* to lay a saddle on; to encumber.

sad'dle-bag, *n.,* a bag carried on a saddle.

sad'dle-bar, *n.,* a bar joining the pommel and cantle of a saddle; the stay in a stained glass window.

sad'dle-bow, *n.,* the curved part of a saddle or pommel.

sad'dled, *p.p.,* saddle.

sad'dler, *n.,* one who makes or repairs harness.

sad'dlery, *n.,* the articles made by a saddler; a saddler's shop.

sad'dle-shaped, *adj.,* shaped like a saddle.

sad'dle-tree, *n.,* the frame of a saddle.

sad'dling, *pr.p.,* saddle.

Sadduce'an, *adj.,* pert. or rel. to the Sadducees.

Sad'ducee, *n.,* a member of a Jewish sceptical sect.

Sad'duceeism, *n.,* the principles and system of the Sadducees.

sad(d)hu, *n.,* a holy man (*Ind.*).

sad'-iron, *n.,* a flat-iron, usually containing a heater.

sa'dism, *n.,* a form of sexual perversion and cruelty; pleasure derived from seeing and inflicting cruelty.

sa'dist, *n.,* a person who gains sexual pleasure from cruelty.

sadis'tic, *adj.,* pert. or rel. to sadism.

sad'ly, *adv.,* in a mournful way; unhappily; excessively.

sad'ness, *n.,* the state of being sad.

safa'ri, *n.,* a hunting expedition; a tour in wild game country.

safe, *adj.,* secure; in shelter; harmless; *n.,* a strong chest.

safe-con'duct, *n.,* a permit or guard guaranteeing a safe journey.

safe'-depos'it, *n.,* a building containing strong rooms and safes for renting.

safe'guard, *n.,* a protector; protection; a guarantee of safety; *v.t.,* to protect or secure.

safe'guarded, *p.p.,* safeguard.

safeguard'ing, *pr.p.,* safeguard.

safe'-keeping, *n.,* care, protection.

safe'ly, *adv.,* out of danger; securely.

sa'fer, *adj.,* comp. of safe.

sa'fest, *adj.,* super. of safe.

safe'ty, *n.,* security, shelter, freedom from danger.

safe'ty-belt, *n.,* a strap to secure occupant to the seat of a motorcar, aeroplane, etc.

safe'ty-lamp, *n.,* a miner's lamp, the flame protected by gauze.

safe'ty-pin, *n.,* a pin with a point that returns to a guard to protect the wearer.

safe'ty-razor, *n.,* a razor mounted on a guard to prevent cutting the skin.

safe'ty-valve, *n.,* a valve that allows liquid or gas to escape when the pressure becomes dangerous.

saff'ian, *n.,* brightly coloured leather of goat or sheep skins.

saf'flower, *n.,* a kind of thistle used for the dye which it yields.

saf'fron, *adj.,* of the colour of saffron; *n.,* a plant which yields a yellow dye; yellow.

saf'frony, *adj.,* yellowish; orange-coloured.

sag, *n.,* a tendency to sink or incline; *v.i.,* to sink in; to incline to one side; *v.t.,* to make to sag.

sa'ga, *n.,* a Scandinavian prose epic.

saga'cious, *adj.,* prudent, clear-sighted.

saga'ciously, *adv.,* in a sagacious way.

saga'ciousness, *i.q.* sagacity.

sagac'ity, *n.,* prudence, clear-sightedness, wisdom.

sag'amore, *n.,* a chief (*N. Amer. Ind.*).

sage, *adj.,* wise, discreet; *n.,* an elder noted for wisdom; an aromatic garden herb.

sage'-green, *n.,* a greyish green; the colour of sage.

sage'ly, *adv.,* in a sage way.

sage'ness, *n.,* wisdom.

sag'gar, *n.,* a fireclay casing used in a kiln.

sagged, *p.p.,* sag.

sag'ging, *pr.p.,* sag.

sag'gy, *adj.,* sinking or inclining.

sagit'ta, *n.*, an arrow (*Lat.*).

sag'ittal, *adj.*, arrow-like.

Sagitta'rius, *n.*, the Archer, the ninth sign of the Zodiac.

sag'ittary, *adj., i.q.* sagittal.

sag'ittate, *adj.*, arrow-shaped.

sa'go, *n.*, a starch-like article of food prepared from the pith of a species of palm.

sagoin', *n.*, a variety of monkey.

sa'gy, *adj.*, flavoured with sage.

Sahar'a, *n.*, the great Libyan dessert.

Sahar'ian, *adj.*, pert. or rel. to Sahara.

sah'ib, *n.*, a male title of respect in the East.

sa'ic, *n.*, a Levantine sailing-vessel.

saice, *n.*, a Bengalese word for groom.

said, *adj.*, before-mentioned; declared; *p.p.*, say.

saig'a, *n.*, an antelope of the steppes (*Russ.*).

sail, *n.*, a canvas sheet stretched out to catch the breeze; a ship; a pleasure trip on the water; *v.i.*, to be carried in a boat or ship; to start on a voyage; *v.t.*, to cause to sail; to navigate; to traverse with a ship.

sail'able, *adj.*, fit for sailing.

sail'cloth, *n.*, canvas or other fabric of which sails are made.

sailed, *p.p.*, sail.

sail'er, *n.*, a sailing ship.

sail'ing, *n.*, navigation; starting on a voyage; *pr.p.*, sail.

sail'-less, *adj.*, without sails.

sail'-loft, *n.*, a place for the storage of sails.

sail'maker, *n.*, a maker of sails.

sail'or, *n.*, a mariner; a seaman.

sain, *v.t.*, to bless; to protect by divine power.

sain'foin, *n.*, a plant resembling clover grown for fodder.

saint, *n.*, a person of especial sanctity; one of the blest in Paradise; one who has been canonized; *v.t.*, to canonize.

saint'ed, *adj.*, holy; dead; *p.p.*, saint.

saint'like, *adj.*, resembling a saint.

saint'liness, *n.*, the quality of being a saint.

saint'ly, *adj.*, saintlike.

Saint-Simo'nian, *adj.*, pert. or rel. to St.-Simonism.

Saint-Si'monism, *n.*, the socialistic doctrines of Saint-Simon, a French writer and thinker (1760–1825).

Saint-Si'monist, *n.*, a disciple of Saint-Simon.

Saint-Si'monite, *n., i.q.* Saint-Simonist.

saith, *pr.p.*, say; *v.t.*, the old 3rd pers. sing.

saithe, *n.*, the coal-fish (*Scot.*).

sake, *n.*, purpose; cause; account.

sak'é, *n.*, fermented liquor obtained from rice, a Japanese beverage.

sa'ker, *n.*, a large breed of falcon.

sa'ki, *n.*, a type of S. American monkey.

sa'kia, *n.*, a water-wheel for irrigation.

sal, *n.*, the Lat. name for salt, used frequently as a prefix.

sa(u)l, *n.*, a valuable Indian timber tree.

salaam', *n.*, an exclamation of greeting or obeisance; *v.i.*, to make obeisance or greeting.

salabil'ity, *n.*, the quality of being salable.

sal'able, *adj.*, able to be sold.

sal'ableness, *n., i.q.* salability.

sala'cious, *adj.*, lustful.

sala'ciously, *adv.*, lustfully.

sala'ciousness, *n., i.q.* salacity.

salac'ity, *n.*, lustfulness.

sal'ad, *n.*, uncooked herbs and vegetables shredded and mixed with oil, etc.

salaman'der, *n.*, a kind of newt, reputed in ancient times to live in fire.

salaman'drine, *adj.*, pert. to, or resembling, a salamander.

sala'me, *n.*, highly flavoured Italian sausage.

sal-ammon'iac, *n.*, ammonium chloride.

sal'angane, *n.*, a swallow constructing an edible nest.

sal'aried, *adj.*, in receipt of a salary.

sal'ary, *n.*, a periodical payment for service.

sale, *n.*, selling; the exchange of a commodity for money; demand.

sale'able, *adj.*, that can be sold.

sale'ableness, *n.*, the quality of being saleable.

sal'ep, *n.*, a farinaceous meal obtained from the tubers of certain orchids.

sale'-price, *n.*, the price asked at a sale.

salera'tus, *n.*, cooking-soda.

sale'-room, *n.*, a place where goods are sold by auction.

sales'man, *n.*, one who earns a livelihood by selling; a retail shop assistant.

sales'manship, *n.*, the skill of selling.

sales'-talk, *n.*, talk used to influence a sale.

sales'-tax, *n.*, a tax on sales and services.

sales'woman, *n.*, the fem. of salesman.

Sal'ian, *adj.*, pert. or rel. to the Salii or priests of Mars.

Sal'ic, *adj.*, pert. or rel. to the Salii, an ancient Frankish tribe.

sal'icin, *n.*, an extract from the willow or poplar.

sali'cional, *n.*, an organ stop.

sali'cylate, *n.*, a salt of salicylic acid.

salicyl'ic, *adj.*, pert. or rel. to willows or derived from some of them.

salicyl'ic-ac'id, *n.*, an antiseptic.

sa'lience, *n.*, a projection.

sa'lient, *adj.*, leaping; prominent; at an angle less than two right angles; *n.*, a projection in a military line or fortification.

sa'liently, *adv.*, prominently.

salif'erous, *adj.*, producing salt (*geol.*).

sal'ifiable, *adj.*, able to be salified.

salifica'tion, *n.*, the act or effect of salifying.

sal'ified, *p.p.*, salify.

sal'ify, *v.t.*, to impregnate with a salt.

sal'ifying, *pr.p.*, salify.

sali'na, *n.*, salt-marsh; salt-water lying on land.

salina'tion, *n.*, the act of steeping in a saline liquor.

sa'line, *adj.*, possessing the properties of salt; *n.*, a salt spring.

salin'ity, *n.*, saltiness.

salino'meter, *n.*, an instrument for measuring brine in marine boilers.

sali'va, *n.*, the secretion of the mouth.

sali'val, *adj.*, pert. or rel. to saliva.

sal'ivant, *adj.*, promoting the secretion of saliva; *n.*, that which promotes saliva.

sal'ivary, *adj.*, *i.q.* salival.

sal'ivate, *v.i.*, to secrete saliva.

sal'ivated, *p.p.*, salivate.

sal'ivating, *pr.p.*, salivate.

saliva'tion, *n.*, the act of secreting saliva in an abnormal quantity.

Sa'lix, *n.*, the willow genus of trees.

sal'landers, *n. pl.*, *i.q.* sallenders.

salle, *n.*, a hall or room (*Fr.*).

sal'lenders, *n. pl.*, an eruption on a horse's hind leg. (Also *sallanders*.)

sal'let, *n.*, a light helmet.

sal'lied, *p.p.*, sally.

sal'low, *adj.*, pallid, yellowish; *n.*, a small willow-like tree.

sal'lowish, *adj.*, somewhat sallow.

sal'lowness, *n.*, the state of being sallow.

sal'ly, *n.*, a sudden dash out from a besieged place (*mil.*); an excursion; a lively encounter of wits; raillery; the first pull on a bell rope; *v.i.*, to rush forth suddenly.

sal'ly-hole, *n.*, the hole through which a bell rope passes.

sal'lying, *pr.p.*, sally.

sally'lunn', *n.*, a variety of tea-cake.

sal'ly-port, *n.*, a postern in a castle for the passage of troops (*mil.*).

salmagun'di, *n.*, a dish of mixed ingredients; a medley.

sal'mi(s), *n.*, a ragout of game (*Fr.*).

salm'on, *n.*, a pink-fleshed fish found in the temperate waters of Europe.

Salmonel'la, *n.*, a bacteria genus associated with food poisoning.

salm'onet, *n.*, a young salmon; parr.

salm'onoid, *adj.*, like a salmon.

salm'on-trout, *n.*, a marine trout, resembling the salmon.

salon', *n.*, a saloon; an art gallery; a social or literary circle (*Fr.*).

saloon', *n.*, a state apartment; a large room; a divan.

saloon'-bar, *n.*, a first-class bar in an English public-house.

saloop', *n.*, a medicinal infusion of sassafras; a substitute for coffee.

Salop'ian, *adj.*, pert. or rel. to the English county of Shropshire; *n.*, a native of S.

sal'picon, *n.*, a rechauffé of meat, bread and vegetables.

salpigloss'is, *n.*, a garden flowering plant allied to the petunia.

salpingi'tis, *n.*, inflammation of the salpinx.

sal'pinx, *n.*, the Eustachian and Fallopian tubes (*Gr.*).

salse, *n.*, a mud volcano.

sal'sify, *n.*, the oyster-plant, chiefly valued for its edible root.

salsil'la, *n.*, an edible plant resembling the Jerusalem artichoke.

salt, *adj.*, saline; impregnated or flavoured with salt; *n.*, a mineral found in the earth or obtained from the sea by evaporation; chloride of sodium; an acid combined with a base; wit; flavour; a seaman; *v.t.*, to sprinkle salt upon; to season.

sal'tant, *adj.*, leaping, dancing (*her.*).

saltarell'o, *n.*, an Italian and Spanish dance.

sal'tate, *v.i.*, to dance, to leap.

salta'tion, *n.*, the act of leaping or dancing.

saltato'rial, *adj.*, pert. or rel. to dancing.

saltato'rious, *adj.*, *i.q.* saltatorial.

sal'tatory, *adj.*, *i.q.* saltatorial.

salt'-cellar, *n.*, a receptacle for table-salt; an especially deep hollow above the collarbone in a woman's neck (*colloq.*).

salt'ed, *p.p.*, salt.

salt'er, *n.*, a dealer in salt; a fish-curer.

salt'ern, *n.*, a salt factory.

sal'tier, *adj.*, *comp.* of salty.

sal'tiest, *adj.*, *super.* of salty.

Saltigra'da, *n. pl.*, a genus of leaping spiders.

saltimban'co, *n.*, a quack (*It.*).

salt'iness, *n.*, the state of being salty.

salt'ing, *pr.p.*, salt.

sal'tire, *n.*, a St. Andrew's Cross (×) used in heraldry.

salt'ish, *adj.*, somewhat salty.

salt'less, *adj.*, insipid.

salt'marsh, *n.*, land flooded with salt-water.

salt'ness, *n.*, the saline quality.

saltpe'tre, *n.*, nitre.

sal'tus, *n.*, a sudden change (*Lat.*).

salt'y, *adj.*, tasting of salt.

salu'brious, *adj.*, healthy.

salu'briously, *adv.*, healthily.

salu'briousness, *n.*, *i.q.* salubrity.

salu'brity, *n.*, the quality of being salubrious.

Salu'ki, *n.*, a breed of Arabian dog.

sal'utarily, *adv.*, in a salutary way.

sal'utariness, *n.*, the quality of being salutary.

sal'utary, *adj.*, healthful; wholesome.

saluta'tion, *n.*, the act of saluting; a word of greeting.

salu'tatory, *adj.*, greeting, saluting.

salute', *n.*, an act of greeting; a sign of respect to a superior or to a flag, etc.; *v.t.*, to make a salute; *v.t.*, to greet; to welcome; to pay honour to.

salu'ted, *p.p.*, salute.

salu'ter, *n.*, one who salutes.

salutif'erous, *adj.*, health-giving.

salu'ting, *pr.p.*, salute.

salvabil'ity, *n.*, the state of being salvable.

sal'vable, *adj.*, able to be saved.

sal'vage, *n.*, reward for saving a cargo, vessel or other property; the property saved; *v.t.*, to rescue, to recover property endangered.

sal'vaged, *p.p.*, salvage.

sal'vager, *n.*, one who salvages.

sal'vaging, *pr.p.*, salvage.

sal'varsan, *n.*, a drug especially used for the treatment of syphilis.

salva'tion, *n.*, the act of saving; rescue; spiritual saving.

Salva'tionist, *adj.*, pert. or rel. to the Salvation Army; *n.*, a member of the Salvation Army.

salvator'ian, *n.*, a Roman Catholic Order.

salve, *n.*, a soothing remedy, usually an ointment; *v.t.*, to save from loss or destruction; to remedy, to soothe.

salved, *p.p.*, salve.

sal'ver, *n.*, a tray.

sal'via, *n.*, a flowering plant of the sage family.

salv'ing, *pr.p.*, salve.

sal'vo, *n.*, an artillery salute; a mental reservation.

sal volat'ile, *n.*, spirit of ammonia (*Lat.*).

sal'vor, *n.*, one who salvages a ship.

sam'ara, *n.*, winged fruit, as of the elm, etc.

Samar'itan, *adj.*, pert. or rel. to Samaria; *n.*, a native of S.

sam'ba, *n.*, a Brazilian dance; its music.

Sam Browne, *n.*, an Army officer's belt and shoulder strap.

same, *adj.*, identical; already mentioned.

sam'el, *adj.*, imperfectly baked (of brick).

same'ness, *n.*, identity; similarity.

Sa'mian, *adj.*, pert. or rel. to the island of Samos; *n.*, a native of S.

sa'miel, *n.*, the simoom.

sam'isen, *n.*, a kind of Japanese guitar.

sam'ite, *n.*, a silk or satin fabric.

sam'let, *n.*, a small salmon.

Samothra'cian, *adj.*, pert. or rel. to Samothrace; *n.*, a native of S.

samovar', *n.*, a Russian tea-urn.

Sam'oyed, *n.*, a Siberian Mongol; an Arctic breed of dog.

samp, *n.*, maize boiled in milk (*Amer.*).

sam'pan, *n.*, a Chinese or Indonesian fisherman's boat and house combined. (Also *sanpan.*)

sam'phire, *n.*, an aromatic marine plant found on cliffs.

sam'ple, *n.*, a specimen, an example; *v.t.*, to take as a specimen; to exhibit a thing of the same kind.

sam'pled, *p.p.*, sample.

sam'pler, *n.*, a piece of needlework made as a pattern, or as an example of a beginner's work; one who samples; a young tree left standing when others are felled.

sam'pling, *pr.p.*, sample.

sam'sonite, *n.*, a proprietary adhesive; a kind of dynamite; a mineral containing manganese.

sam'urai, *n.*, the Japanese noble and military caste.

sanabil'ity, *n.*, the state of being sanable.

san'able, *adj.*, curable.

san'ative, *adj.*, curative.

sanato'rium, *n.*, a home where patients are placed for cure. (Also *sanitorium.*)

san'atory, *adj.*, conducive to cure or health.

sanctifica'tion, *n.*, the act of sanctifying; the sanctified state.

sanc'tified, *p.p.*, sanctify.

sanc'tifier, *n.*, one who sanctifies; the Holy Ghost.

sanc'tify, *v.t.*, to make holy; to consecrate; to make into a means of sanctity.

sanc'tifying, *pr.p.*, sanctify.

sanctil'oquent, *adj.*, speaking of holy things.

sanctimo'nious, *adj.*, affectedly pious.

sanctimo'niously, *adv.*, in a sanctimonious way.

sanctimo'niousness, *n.*, affected piety.

sanc'timony, *n.*, *i.q.* sanctimoniousness.

sanc'tion, *n.*, the act of authorizing or sanctioning; authority; a compelling principle; *v.t.*, to authorize or permit.

sanc'tionable, *adj.*, able to be sanctioned.

sanc'tioned, *p.p.*, sanction.

sanc'tioning, *pr.p.*, sanction.

sanc'titude, *n.*, holiness.

sanc'tity, *n.*, holiness; inviolability.

sanctor'um, *n.*, *i.q.* sanctum.

sanc'tuary, *n.*, a sacred place; a place of privileged asylum; the part of a church where the altar stands.

sanc'tum, *n.*, a specially private room; a study (*Lat.*).

sanc'tus, *n.*, a prose anthem sung in religious services (*Lat.*).

sand, *n.*, rock worn into minute particles; *v.t.*, to sprinkle sand over.

san'dal, *n.*, a shoe strapped to the foot; a kind of slipper.

san'dal(l)ed, *adj.*, wearing sandals.

san'dalwood, *n.*, a white wood used by cabinetmakers.

san'darac, *n.*, a resinous gum.

sand'bag, *n.*, a bag filled with sand and used for defensive purposes.

sand'bank, *n.*, a sandy shoal.

sand'blind, *adj.*, semiblind.

sand-dune, *n.*, a hill or ridge of shifting sand.

sand'ed, *p.p.*, sand.

sand'-eel, *n.*, an eel that disappears into the sand at ebb-tide.

san'derling, *n.*, a little wading-bird.

san'ders, *n.*, a red sandal-wood. (Also *saunders*.)

san'dever, *n.*, *i.q.* sandiver.

sand'-fly, *n.*, a stinging fly.

sand'-glass, *n.*, a reversible glass with sand for measuring time.

sand'hill, *n.*, sand mounded into a hill.

sand'iness, *n.*, the quality of being sandy.

sand'ing, *n.*, a spreading with sand; *pr.p.*, sand.

sand'-iron, *n.*, a special golf club for lofting the ball out of sand.

san'diver, *n.*, saline liquid from a glass making process.

sand'paper, *n.*, paper on which sand is fixed and used for polishing; *v.t.*, to rub or polish with sand-paper.

sand'piper, *n.*, a snipe or woodcock.

sand'-shoe, *n.*, a light canvas, rubber-soled shoe for walking on sand.

sand'stone, *n.*, rock composed of quartz and silica.

sand'storm, *n.*, a desert wind carrying clouds of sand.

sand'wich, *n.*, meat, etc., between two slices of bread; *v.t.*, to put one thing between two others.

sand'wich-man, *n.*, a man who carries advertisement boards.

sand'y, *adj.*, full of, or resembling, sand; sand-coloured; plucky (*colloq.*).

sand'-yacht, *n.*, a boat with sails and wheels.

sand'yish, *adj.*, somewhat sandy.

sane, *adj.*, of sound mind; reasonable.

sane'ness, *n.*, soundness of mind; reasonableness.

san'forize, *v.t.*, to proof against shrinkage.

san'forized, *p.p.*, san-forize.

san'forizing, *pr.p.*, san-forize.

sang, *p.p.*, sing.

sang'a(r), *n.*, stone breastwork (*Ind.*).

sangaree', *n.*, spiced brandy and water.

sangfroid', *n.*, coolness, composure (*Fr.*).

san'giac, *n.*, a Turkish administrative area. (Also *Sanjac*.)

Sangrail', -greal', *n.*, the Holy Grail, a sacred chalice reputedly brought to Glastonbury by St. Joseph of Arimathea. (Also *Sangraal*.)

sanguif'erous, *adj.*, conveying blood.

sanguifica'tion, *n.*, the production of blood.

san'guify, *v.i.*, to form blood.

san'guinarily, *adv.*, in a sanguinary way; with much bloodshed.

san'guinary, *adj.*, bloody; with much bloodshed.

san'guine, *adj.*, of blood colour; ardent; hopeful; *v.t.*, to stain with blood.

san'guinely, *adv.*, in a hopeful way.

sanguin'eous, *adj.*, bloody.

sanguiniv'orous, *adj.*, living on blood. (Also *sanguivorous*.)

sanguisu'gous, *adj.*, blood-sucking.

sanguiv'orous, *adj.*, *i.q.* sanguinivorous.

San'hedrim, *n.*, the Jewish Council of judges, presided over by the High Priest.

San'hedrin, *n.*, *i.q.* San-hedrim.

san'icle, *n.*, a perennial herb.

sa'nies, *n.*, blood from a wound.

san'ify, *v.t.*, to make hygienic and healthy.

sa'nious, *adj.*, resembling or producing sanies.

sanita'rian, *adj.*, *i.q.* sanitary.

san'itary, *adj.*, pert. or rel. to health; hygienic.

sanita'tion, *n.*, hygiene; the means for the hygienic disposal of waste products.

sanito'rium, *n.*, *i.q.* sana-torium.

san'ity, *n.*, mental soundness; reasonableness.

san'jak, *n.*, *i.q.* sangiac.

sank, *p.p.*, sink.

san'pan, *n.*, *i.q.* sampan.

sans, *prep.*, without (*Fr.*).

Sanscrit, *n.*, *i.q.* San-skrit.

sansculotte', *n.*, a person without breeches, a term disparagingly applied to a French Revolutionist (*Fr.*).

sanse'rif, *adj.*, (type) without serifs; *n.*, a form of type.

San'skrit, *n.*, the ancient Aryan language of India. (Also *Sanscrit*.)

sans souci', a French phrase = without care.

San'ta Claus', *n.*, Father Christmas, a legendary figure.

san'talin, *n.*, red colouring matter derived from sandalwood.

san'ton, *n.*, a Mohammedan monk or hermit (*Fr.* or *Span.*).

santon'ica, *n.*, a kind of wormwood.

san'tonin, *n.*, a vermifuge obtained from the plant santonica.

san(n)yasi, *n.*, an Indian religious mendicant.

sap, *n.*, the vital juice in the stem of a plant or tree; any vital fluid; a trench dug for besiegers to approach a fort under shelter; one who studies hard (*colloq.*); *v.t.*, to undermine; to impair the vitality of.

sap'ajou, *n.*, a S. Amer. monkey.

sap'an-wood, *n.*, the wood of an E. Indian tree, the sapan.

sap'id, *adj.*, savoury.

sapid'ity, *n.*, flavour, savour.

sa'pience, *n.*, wisdom; knowledge.

sa'pient, *adj.*, wise, learned.

sapien'tial, *adj.*, pert. or rel. to wisdom, esp. the Jewish Sapiential writings, as Proverbs, Book of Wisdom, etc.

sa'piently, *adv.*, wisely.

sapinda'ceous, *adj.*, bel. to the Sapindaceae, the soap-berry family.

sap'less, *adj.*, without sap.

sap'ling, *n.*, a young tree.

sapodil'la, *n.*, a tropical tree.

sapona'ceous, *adj.*, soapy.

saponac'ity, *n.*, soapiness.

sapon'ifiable, *adj.*, able to be saponified.

saponifica′tion, *n.*, the state of being saponified; a change into soap.

sapon′ified, *p.p.*, saponify.

sapon′ify, *v.t.*, to change into soap.

sapon′ifying, *pr.p.*, saponify.

sap′onin, *n.*, an extract from soapwort, horse-chestnut and other plants.

sap′onine, *n.*, *i.q.* saponin.

sap′onite, *n.*, a non-crystalline silicate of magnesium - aluminium.

sap′onule, *n.*, a magnesium - aluminium silicate.

sa′por, *n.*, taste.

saporif′ic, *adj.*, producing ample taste; appetizing; *n.*, a producer of taste.

saporos′ity, *n.*, the power of producing taste.

sap′orous, *adj.*, exciting taste.

sa′pour, *n.*, *i.q.* sapor.

sapped, *p.p.*, sap.

sap′per, *n.*, one who saps; a private of the Royal Engineers.

Sap′phic, *adj.*, pert. or rel. to Sappho, the Greek poetess, and to the metre associated with her name.

sapph′ire, *n.*, a precious blue stone.

sapph′irine, *adj.*, resembling sapphire.

sapph′ism, *n.*, sexual passion between women.

sap′piness, *n.*, the quality of being sappy.

sap′ping, *pr.p.*, sap.

sap′py, *adj.*, full of sap.

saproph′agan, *n.*, a kind of beetle which feeds on decomposed vegetable matter.

saproph′agous, *adj.*, eating rotten food.

sap′-rot, *n.*, dry-rot.

sap′-wood, *n.*, new wood, next to the bark.

sar, *n.*, sea bream.

sar′aband, *n.*, a Spanish dance and its music.

Sar′acen, *n.*, the old name for a Turk.

Saracen′ic, *adj.*, pert. or rel. to the Saracens.

sarato′ga, *n.*, a lady's large travelling trunk.

sar′casm, *n.*, caustic expression.

sarcas′tic, *adj.*, caustic, biting, satirical.

sarcas′tically, *adv.*, in a sarcastic way.

sarcelle′, *n.*, a small duck or teal.

sarce′net, *n.*, a fine silken fabric. (Also *sarsenet*.)

sar′cocarp, *n.*, the flesh of a fruit.

sar′cocele, *n.*, a tumour of the testicles.

sar′cocol, *n.*, an African gum-resin.

sarcocol′la, *n.*, a gum-resin from Arabia and Persia.

sar′code, *n.*, animal protoplasm.

sar′colite, *n.*, mineral of the colour of flesh.

sarcol′ogy, *n.*, the study of flesh or the soft bodily tissue.

sarco′ma, *n.*, a fleshy tumour.

sarco′matous, *adj.*, pert. or rel. to sarcoma.

sarcoph′agi, *n. pl.*, flesh-eaters.

sarcoph′agus, *n.*, a stone coffin.

sarcoph′agy, *n.*, the habit of eating flesh.

sar′coplasm, *n.*, the material between muscle fibres.

sar′cous, *adj.*, pert. or rel. to flesh.

sard, *n.*, a yellowish-red or brown precious stone.

sardelle′, *n.*, a sardine-like fish.

sar′dine, *n.*, *i.q.* sard.

sardine′, *n.*, a Mediterranean fish like the pilchard; the young of the herring, etc., prepared.

Sardin′ian, *adj.*, pert. or rel. to Sardinia; *n.*, a native of S.

sar′dius, *n.*, *i.q.* sard.

sardon′ic, *adj.*, forced and harsh (said of a grin or cruel laugh).

sardon′ically, *adv.*, in a sardonic way.

sar′donyx, *n.*, a kind of agate.

sargass′o, *n.*, *i.q.* sargassum.

sargas′sum, *n.*, a weed growing in the N. Atlantic. (Also *sargasso*.)

sa′ri, *n.*, a Hindu woman's dress.

sariss′a, *n.*, a Macedonian lance (*Gr.*).

sark, *n.*, a shirt (*Scot.*).

sark′ing, *n.*, material for sarks; thin boarding.

sar′lak, *n.*, a Tartary yak.

Sarma′tian, *adj.*, pert. or rel. to Sarmatia (Russia and Poland); *n.*, a native of S.

Sarmat′ic, *adj.*, *i.q.* Sarmatian.

sar′ment, *n.*, a runner.

sarong′, *n.*, an Asian garment worn by either sex.

sar′plar, *n.*, a large wool-sack, containing 2,240 lb.

sar′rasin, *n.*, a portcullis.

sarsaparil′la, *n.*, a Mexican medicinal shrub; drink made from this.

sar′sen, *adj.*, a stone erected by Celts on the chalk downs.

sarse′net, *n.*, *i.q.* sarcenet.

sar′tor, *n.*, a tailor (*Lat.*).

sarto′rial, *adj.*, pert. or rel. to tailors and clothes.

sarto′rially, *adv.*, with regard to clothes.

sarto′rius, *n.*, a muscle in the thigh used to squat cross-legged.

sash, *n.*, a scarf or band worn over the shoulder or round the waist; the frame-work of window-glass; *v.t.*, to fit with sashes.

sash′cord, *n.*, specially stout cord used to carry the balancing weights in a sash-window.

sashed, *adj.*, wearing a sash; *p.p.*, sash.

sash′-frame, *n.*, the framework enclosing a sash window.

sash′ing, *pr.p.*, sash.

sash′-line, *n.*, a cord for raising or lowering a sash.

sash′-window, *n.*, a window with sliding sashes.

sas′in, *n.*, an Indian antelope.

sassab′y, *n.*, a large S. African antelope.

sas′safras, *n.*, a fragrant tree.

Sas′senach, *adj.*, Saxon; *n.*, a Saxon (a Gaelic word); hence, to a Scot, an Englishman.

sas'soline, *n.*, a natural boracic acid.

sas'tra, *n. pl.*, laws, institutes, esp. those of the Brahmins.

sastru'gi, *n. pl.*, wavelike irregularities on snow or sand.

sat, *p.p.*, sit.

Sa'tan, *n.*, the Devil.

satan'ic, *adj.*, pert. to, or resembling, Satan; devilish.

satan'ical, *adj.*, *i.q.* Satanic.

satan'ically, *adv.*, in a satanic way.

satar'a, *n.*, ribbed cloth from India.

satch'el, *n.*, a light bag suspended from the arm or slung over the shoulder.

sate, *v.t.*, to satisfy (a desire or appetite).

sa'ted, *p.p.*, sate.

sateen', *n.*, an imitation satin.

sat'ellite, *n.*, an attendant; a small planet revolving round a larger one; an artificial body launched from and encircling the earth.

satiabil'ity, *n.*, the quality of being satiable.

sa'tiable, *adj.*, able to be sated.

sa'tiate, *adj.*, glutted; *v.t.*, to fill to the full; to glut.

sa'tiated, *p.p.*, satiate.

sa'tiating, *adj.*, glutting; *pr.p.*, satiate.

satia'tion, *n.*, quenching; surfeit.

sati'ety, *n.*, overfulness.

sat'in, *n.*, a smooth, glossy fabric of silk.

satinet(te)', *n.*, an imitation thin satin.

sa'ting, *pr.p.*, sate.

sat'in-wood, *n.*, a wood with a satin-like surface.

sat'iny, *adj.*, like satin.

sat'ire, *n.*, ridicule, sarcasm; literature holding folly or vice up to ridicule.

satir'ic, *adj.*, of the nature of satire.

satir'ical, *adj.*, *i.q.* satiric.

satir'ically, *adv.*, in a satirical way.

sat'irist, *n.*, a writer of satire.

sat'irize, *v.t.*, to ridicule with satire.

sat'irized, *p.p.*, satirize.

sat'irizing, *pr.p.*, satirize.

satisfac'tion, *n.*, the giving of content; complete content; appeasing.

satisfac'torily, *adv.*, in a satisfactory way.

satisfac'tory, *adj.*, giving satisfaction; removing doubt.

sat'isfiable, *adj.*, able to be satisfied.

sat'isfied, *p.p.*, satisfy.

sat'isfier, *n.*, one who gives satisfaction.

sat'isfy, *v.i.*, to make atonement; *v.t.*, to give satisfaction to; to content; to make full discharge; to remove doubt.

sat'isfying, *adj.*, contenting; *pr.p.*, satisfy.

sa'tive, *adj.*, sown artificially as in a garden.

satrang'i, *n.*, cheap Indian cotton carpet.

sa'trap, *n.*, a Persian provincial governor.

sa'trapy, *n.*, the office or province of a satrap.

sat'suma, *n.*, a yellow Japanese ware; a small, sweet orange.

sat'urable, *adj.*, able to be saturated.

sat'urant, *adj.*, saturating; *n.*, an antacid substance.

sat'urate, *adj.*, saturated; impregnated; *v.t.*, to impregnate, to soak.

sat'urated, *p.p.*, saturate.

sat'urating, *pr.p.*, saturate.

satura'tion, *n.*, the act or effect of saturating.

Sat'urday, *n.*, the seventh day of the week; the Sabbath; (named after Saturn).

Sat'urn, *n.*, the most ancient of the Roman deities; a god of creation; a planet.

saturna'lia, *n. pl.*, the festival in honour of Saturn, attended by great revelry and licence, hence = noisy revel.

saturna'lian, *adj.*, pert. or rel. to saturnalia; riotous.

satur'nian, *adj.*, pert. or rel. to Saturn and the Golden Age of primitive goodness and happiness.

saturn'ic, *adj.*, affected with lead poisoning.

sat'urnine, *adj.*, grim, morose; pert. or rel. to the influence of the planet Saturn.

satya'graha, *n.*, passive resistance (*Ind.*).

sat'yr, *n.*, a fabulous creature, half man, half goat, attending on Bacchus.

satyri'asis, *n.*, excessive sexual desire in males.

sauce, *n.*, a liquid preparation for flavouring purposes; a relish; impertinence (*colloq.*); *v.t.*, to add as a relish to; to be impertinent to (*colloq.*).

sauce'boat, *n.*, a boat-shaped piece of tableware to hold a sauce or gravy.

sauce'-box, *n.*, an impertinent person (*colloq.*).

sauced, *p.p.*, sauce.

sauce'less, *adj.*, without sauce.

sauce'pan, *n.*, a pan for cooking purposes.

sau'cer, *n.*, a shallow piece of ware to hold a cup.

sau'cier, *adj.*, *comp.* of saucy.

sau'ciest, *adj.*, *super.* of saucy.

sau'cily, *adv.*, impertinently.

sau'ciness, *n.*, pertness; impertinence.

sauc'ing, *pr.p.*, sauce.

saucisse', *n.*, a fuse; faggots' in a bundle to keep earth in a trench from falling in; a sausage (*Fr.*).

saucisson', *n.*, *i.q.* saucisse.

sau'cy, *adj.*, pert; impertinent.

sauer'kraut, *n.*, cabbage in pickle.

saul, *n.*, the resin of the saul tree of the Himalayas.

Saumur, *n.*, a white French wine.

saun'ders, *n.*, *i.q.* sanders.

saun'ter, *n.*, a stroll; a place for rambling in; *v.i.*, to stroll; to walk idly.

saun'tered, *p.p.*, saunter.

saun'terer, *n.*, one who saunters.

saun'tering, *pr.p.*, saunter.

Sau′ria, *n. pl.*, an order of scaly, four-footed reptiles, as the crocodile, etc.

sau′rian, *n.*, one of the Sauria.

sau′roid, *adj.*, like a saurian.

saur′y, *n.*, a long-billed sea-fish.

sau′sage, *n.*, chopped meat or other ingredients packed with preservative in a translucent wrapping.

sau′sage-meat′, *n.*, minced meat used in sausages or for stuffing.

sau′sage-roll′, *n.*, a roll filled with sausage-meat.

sauté, *adj.*, cooked in a frying pan and tossed (*Fr.*).

Sauterne′, *n.*, a French white wine.

sa′vable, *adj.*, able to be saved.

sav′age, *adj.*, fierce, wild, angry; *n.*, a cruel person; *v.t.*, to bite.

sav′agely, *adv.*, fiercely, angrily.

sav′ageness, *n.*, fierceness.

sav′agery, *n.*, the acts of a savage; the state of a savage.

savan′nah, *n.*, an open plain.

savant′, *n.*, a learned or scientific person (*Fr.*).

savate′, *n.*, French boxing with fists and feet.

save, *prep.*, excepting; *v.i.*, to practise economy; *v.t.*, to rescue, to redeem; to prevent; to put by.

saved, *p.p.*, save.

sav′eloy, *n.*, a kind of cooked sausage.

sa′ver, *n.*, one who saves or economizes.

sav′in(e), *n.*, an evergreen shrub, the leaves of which have medicinal properties.

sa′ving, *adj.*, excepting, redeeming; *n.*, economy; *prep.*, except; *pr.p.*, save.

sa′vingly, *adv.*, in a saving way.

sa′vings, *n. pl.*, money economized.

sa′vings-bank, *n.*, a bank where savings are deposited.

Sa′viour, *n.*, Jesus Christ; the Redeemer in the Christian faith.

sa′viour, *n.*, one who saves.

sav′onette, *n.*, a kind of soap; an Indian tree bark which serves as soap.

sa′vory, *n.*, an aromatic plant, allied to thyme.

sa′vour, *n.*, flavour; relish; scent; *v.i.*, to possess an agreeable taste or smell; *v.t.*, to taste or smell agreeably.

sa′voured, *p.p.*, savour.

sa′vourily, *adv.*, in a savoury way.

sa′vouriness, *n.*, the quality of being savoury.

sa′vouring, *pr.p.*, savour.

sa′vourless, *n.*, insipid, tasteless.

sa′voury, *adj.*, good to taste or smell.

savoy′, *n.*, a winter cabbage.

Savoy′ard, *n.*, a native of Savoy; a member of the Savoy Theatre company who acted in the original Gilbert and Sullivan operas.

savv′y, *n.*, understanding, wit; *v.t.*, to understand, to know (*slang*).

saw, *n.*, a serrated instrument for cutting; a wise saying; *p.p.*, see; *v.i.*, to yield to the saw; *v.t.*, to cut with a saw.

saw′bench, *n.*, a table for sawing.

saw′dust, *n.*, the dust produced by sawing.

sawed, *p.p.*, saw.

saw′fish, *n.*, a fish with a spined snout.

saw′ing, *pr.p.*, saw.

saw′mill, *n.*, a factory where timber is sawn.

sawn, *p.p.*, saw.

saw′ney, *n.*, an idiot, a lout; a rude nickname for a Scot.

saw′pit, *n.*, a pit in which sawyers work.

saw′yer, *n.*, a workman who saws wood.

sax, *n.*, a slater's chopper; the abbrev. for saxophone.

sax′atile, *adj.*, pert. or rel. to rocks.

saxe, *n.*, a kind of photographic paper; a light-blue colour.

sax′horn, *n.*, a brass wind-instrument.

saxic′avous, *adj.*, rock-boring.

saxic′oline, *adj.*, *i.q.* saxatile.

Sax′ifrage, *n.*, a genus of rock-grown plants.

Sax′on, *adj.*, pert. or rel. to Saxony and the Saxons; *n.*, a native of S; an Anglo-Saxon.

Sax′onism, *n.*, Saxon idiom.

sax′ony, *n.*, a kind of wool; cloth made from it.

sax′ophone, *n.*, a metal wind-instrument.

sax′tuba, *n.*, a large sax-horn.

say, *n.*, a remark, speech; *v.i.*, to speak, to answer; *v.t.*, to speak, recite, declare or pronounce.

say′est, 2nd pers. sing. (present tense), say.

say′ing, *n.*, something said; a proverb; *pr.p.*, say.

says, 3rd pers. sing. (present tense), say.

scab, *n.*, a cover formed over a wound; a disease in sheep; one who stands out of a workmen's strike (*slang*).

scab′bard, *n.*, the sheath of a sword; *v.t.*, to sheathe.

scabbed, *adj.*, troubled with scab.

scab′bier, *adj.*, *comp.* of scabby.

scab′biest, *adj.*, *super.* of scabby.

scab′biness, *n.*, the condition of being scabby.

scab′by, *adj.*, covered with scabs; suffering from scab.

sca′bies, *n.*, the itch.

Sca′bious, *n.*, a genus of herbaceous plants.

sca′bious, *adj.*, troubled with scabies.

sca′brous, *adj.*, rough, scaly, dotted; indelicate, indecent.

scad, *n.*, the shad.

scaf′fold, *n.*, a raised platform or stage; the place for the gallows; a temporary erection adjacent to a building.

scaf′folder, *n.*, one who builds scaffolding.

scaf′folding, *n.*, the timber, poles, etc., for a scaffold; the framework of a scaffold.

scagl′ia, *n.*, a special kind of limestone (*It.*).

scaglio′la, *n.*, plaster imitating scaglia (*It.*).

sca'la, *n.,* a ladder or staircase (*Lat.*).

scal'able, *adj.,* able to be scaled.

scala'riform, *adj.,* ladder-shaped.

scald, *n.,* a burn from hot liquid or steam; scurf; a Scandinavian minstrel; *v.t.,* to burn with hot liquid or steam; to heat (cream); to let the fire taint what is being boiled.

scald'ed, *p.p.,* scald.

scald'er, *n.,* one who, or that which, scalds.

scald'-head, *n.,* a scab on the head.

scal'dic, *adj.,* pert. or rel. to the scalds (i.e. minstrels).

scald'ing, *pr.p.,* scald.

scale, *n.,* the pan of a balance; a weighing instrument; one of the small plates on a fish's body; any scale like layer; a graduated measure; a complete series of musical intervals; a standard of measurement; the Zodiac sign Libra; a ladder or flight of steps; *v.i.,* to come off in layers; to weigh (so much); *v.t.,* to mount, to ascend; to remove scales from.

scaled, *p.p.,* scale.

scalene', *adj.,* (of a triangle) having unequal angles and sides.

scale'less, *adj.,* without scales.

sca'ler, *n.,* one who scales.

sca'liness, *n.,* the quality of being scaly.

sca'ling, *pr.p.,* scale.

scall, *n.,* a skin eruption.

scal'lawag, *n.,* i.q. scallywag.

scall'ion, *n.,* the eschalot.

scal'lop, *n.,* a sea bivalve; a recessed border; *v.t.,* to cut a border with curves or recesses. (Also *scollop*.)

scal'loped, *adj.,* said of oysters baked with bread crumbs; *p.p.,* scallop.

scal'loping, *pr.p.,* scallop.

scal'lop-shell, *n.,* the shell of a scallop;

the emblem of a pilgrim to the Shrine of St. Iago of Compostella; the emblem of St. James.

scal'lywag, *n.,* a poor, lean animal; a scamp. (Also *scallawag*.)

scalp, *n.,* the skin on the top of a head; that part torn or cut off by Red Indians; *v.i.,* to profit quickly on market fluctuations (*colloq.*); *v.t.,* to cut off the scalp from.

scalped, *p.p.,* scalp.

scal'pel, *n.,* a small, sharp surgical knife.

scalp'er, *n.,* one who scalps; a gouge used by engravers; a surgical instrument.

scalp'ing, *pr.p.,* scalp.

scalp'ing-knife, *n.,* a knife used for the purpose of scalping.

scal'priform, *adj.,* chisel-shaped.

scalp'rum, *n.,* a surgeon's rasp.

scal'y, *adj.,* covered with scales; scale-like.

scam'ble, *v.i.,* to trespass on hospitality (*Scot.*).

scam'bled, *p.p.,* scamble.

scam'bler, *n.,* an intruder who scambles (*Scot.*).

scam'bling, *pr.p.,* scamble.

scam'mony, *n.,* a purging medicine obtained from the sap of a convolvulus-like plant.

scamp, *n.,* a worthless fellow; a rascal; *v.t.,* to stint labour on a task.

scamped, *p.p.,* scamp.

scam'per, *n.,* a hurried flight; a quick run or ride; *v.i.,* to run very fast; to hurry off.

scam'pered, *p.p.,* scamper.

scam'pering, *pr.p.,* scamper.

scam'pi, *n. pl.,* scampo (*It.*).

scam'po, *n.,* a small prawn-like crustacean, an edible delicacy (*It.*).

scan, *v.i.,* to obey the rules of scansion; to survey with radar beam; *v.t.,* to run the eyes over; to survey; to examine the metre of.

scan'dal, *n.,* offence; cause of offence; defamatory talk; disgrace.

scan'dalize, *v.t.,* to shock; to reduce the area of (a sail) (*naut.*).

scan'dalized, *p.p.,* scandalize.

scan'dalizing, *pr.p.,* scandalize.

scan'dalmonger, *n.,* one who talks scandal.

scan'dalous, *adj.,* causing scandal; infamous.

scan'dalously, *adv.,* in a scandalous way.

scan'dent, *adj.,* climbing, as the ivy.

Scandina'vian, *adj.,* pert. or rel. to Scandinavia; *n.,* a native of S.

scanned, *p.p.,* scan.

scan'ner, *n.,* a rotating radar aerial.

scan'ning, *n.,* i.q. scansion; *pr.p.,* scan.

scan'sion, *n.,* the act of scanning, *i.e.,* of marking the metrical construction of verse.

Scanso'res, *n. pl.,* climbing birds, as the woodpecker, etc.

scanso'rial, *adj.,* pert. or rel. to Scansores, climbing.

scant, *adj.,* i.q. scanty; with the minimum amount; *n.,* lack; stint; *v.i.,* to fall off in quantity or amount; *v.t.,* to stint, to limit.

scant'ed, *p.p.,* scant.

scant'ier, *adj.,* comp. of scanty.

scan'ties, *n. pl.,* the abbrev. of panties (*colloq.*).

scant'iest, *adj.,* super. of scanty.

scant'ily, *adv.,* in a scanty way.

scant'iness, *n.,* stint; insufficiency.

scant'ing, *pr.p.,* scant.

scan'tle, *n.,* a gauge used in slate-making; *v.t.,* to partition.

scant'ling, *n.,* a small piece of sawn timber; the size to which it should be sawn.

scant'ly, *n.,* barely; insufficiently.

scant'ness, *n.,* bareness, insufficiency.

scant'y, *adj.,* not abundant; not sufficing; scant.

scape, *n.*, the shaft of a column (in architecture).

scape'goat, *n.*, orig., a goat which was sent out into the wilderness, the Jewish High Priest having confessed the sins of the people over it; any one on whom blame for others is cast.

scape'grace, *n.*, a ne'er-do-well.

scape'ment, *n.*, *i.q.* escapement.

scaph'oid, *adj.*, boat-shaped; *n.*, a bone in the hand.

scap'ple, *v.t.*, to rough-dress stone.

scap'ula, *n.*, the shoulder-blade (*Lat.*).

scap'ular, *adj.*, pert. or rel. to the shoulder-blade; *n.*, a part of the religious habit worn over the shoulders.

scap'ulary, *n.*, *i.q.* scapular.

scap'ulo, *n.*, a form of scapula.

scar, *n.*, a mark or scratch; a steep rock; the mark on the body left by a wound; *v.i.*, to form a scar; *v.t.*, to make a mark upon.

scar'ab, *n.*, a beetle, scarabaeus; an Egyptian beetle-shaped charm. (Also *scarabee*.)

scarabae'id, *n.*, a species of beetle.

scarabae'oid, *adj.*, like a scarab; *n.*, a counterfeit scarab.

scarabae'us, *n.*, *i.q.* scarab.

scar'abee, *n.*, *i.q.* scarab.

scar'amouch, *n.*, a buffoon dressed in black; a bragging, cowardly character in old Italian comedy.

scarce, *adj.*, rare, stinted; in short supply.

scarce'ly, *adv.*, hardly, stintedly.

scarce'ment, *n.*, a setback or ledge, in a wall.

scarce'ness, *n.*, want, rarity; the state of being scarce.

scar'city, *n.*, *i.q.* scarceness.

scare, *n.*, a fright or panic; *v.t.*, to frighten, to terrify.

scare'crow, *n.*, anything set up to frighten birds away; a ridiculous figure.

scared, *p.p.*, scare.

scare'mon'ger, *n.*, an alarmist; one who indulges in creating fear and panic.

scarf, *n.*, a neckwrap or tie; a sash; *v.t.*, to cover with a scarf; to dovetail.

scarfed, *p.p.*, scarf.

scarf'ing, *n.*, the straight, joining of two pieces of timber; *pr.p.*, scarf.

scarf'pin, *n.*, a pin for fastening a scarf or necktie.

scarf'skin, *n.*, the cuticle.

scarifica'tion, *n.*, the act of scarifying.

scar'ificator, *n.*, a scarifying surgical instrument.

scar'ified, *p.p.*, scarify.

scar'ifier, *n.*, anything that scarifies; *i.q.* scarificator; an implement used in agriculture.

scar'ify, *v.t.*, to cut or scratch a surface, as the skin or the soil.

scar'ifying, *pr.p.*, scarify.

sca'ring, *pr.p.*, scare.

sca'rious, *adj.*, dry, scaly.

scarlati'na, *n.*, a mild type of scarlet fever.

scarlati'nous, *adj.*, of the nature of scarlatina.

scar'less, *adj.*, without a scar; unmarked; unhurt.

scar'let, *adj.*, bright red; *n.*, a bright red colour; a scarlet-coloured robe or material.

sca'roid, *adj.*, resembling scarus; *n.*, a fish (scarus).

scarp, *n.*, a steep slope; the sloping ground beneath a parapet; *v.t.*, to cut like a scarp.

scarped, *p.p.*, scarp.

scarp'ing, *pr.p.*, scarp.

scarred, *adj.*, marked; *p.p.*, scar.

scar'ring, *pr.p.*, scar.

scar'us, *n.*, a kind of fish.

scat, *interj.*, begone; *n.*; a kind of duty or tax.

scathe, *n.*, a hurt or injury; *v.t.*, to injure.

scathed, *p.p.*, scathe.

scathe'less, *adj.*, unhurt.

sca'thing, *adj.*, cutting, severe, injurious; *pr.p.*, scathe.

scatol'ogy, *n.*, the study of obscene literature.

scatoph'agous, *adj.*, feeding on dung.

scat'ter, *v.i.*, to be broken up or dispersed; *v.t.*, to disperse; to throw broadcast.

scat'ter-brain, *n.*, a thoughtless, silly person.

scat'terbrained, *adj.*, frivolous, giddy.

scat'tered, *p.p.*, scatter.

scat'terer, *n.*, one who, or that which, scatters.

scat'tering, *pr.p.*, scatter.

scat'ty, *adj.*, feeble-minded; hare-brained (*slang*).

scaup, *n.*, a certain kind of duck.

scau'per, *n.*, a gouge used by engravers.

scav'enge, *v.i.*, and *t.* to cleanse (streets) from filth; to search for objects of use among trash or filth.

scav'enged, *p.p.*, scavenge.

scav'enger, *n.*, one who scavenges; a refuse-eating animal.

scav'enging, *pr.p.*, scavenge.

sce'na, *n.*, an Italian operatic scene.

scenar'io, *n.*, a sketch of the plot or libretto of a play (*It.*).

scena'rist, *n.*, one who prepares a scenario.

scene, *n.*, a spectacle; a show; a disagreeable exhibition of quarrelling; the general setting of an action or occurrence.

scene'painter, *n.*, one who paints stage-scenery.

sce'nery, *n.*, the general aspect of ground or country; stage-paintings.

scene'shifter, *n.*, one who moves the scenery in a theatre.

sce'nic, *adj.*, pert. or rel. to scenery and the stage.

sce'nical, *adj.*, *i.q.* scenic.

scenograph'ic, *adj.*, drawn perspectively.

scenog'raphy, *n.,* drawing in perspective.

scent, *n.,* smell, odour, perfume; the sense of smell; *v.t.,* to detect by the smell; to perfume.

scent'ed, *adj.,* odorous, fragrant; *p.p.,* scent.

scent'ing, *pr.p.,* scent.

scent'less, *adj.,* inodorous; without smell.

scep'sis, *n.,* sceptical philosophy.

scep'tic, *n.,* one who accepts nothing on trust, but inquires into truth or falsehood; a doubter. (Also *skeptic.*)

scep'tical, *adj.,* doubting, inquiring; disbelieving.

scep'tically, *adv.,* in a sceptical way.

scep'ticism, *n.,* the philosophical position that experience is the only test of truth; doubt, negation.

scep'tre, *n.,* a staff, the emblem of royal power.

scep'tred, *adj.,* wielding a sceptre.

scep'treless, *adj.,* without a sceptre.

schappe, *n.,* fabric made from silk waste (*Ger.*).

sched'ule, *n.,* a document containing an inventory, timetable or list; a document appended to another; *v.t.,* to enter in a schedule. (*U.S.*)

sched'uled, *p.p.,* schedule.

sched'uling, *pr.p.,* schedule.

scheel'ite, *n.,* calcium tungstate.

sche'ma, *n.,* an outline, a plan; a type; a syllogistic figure.

schemat'ic, *adj.,* pert. or rel. to a schema.

sche'matism, *n.,* an outline; a design.

sche'matist, *n.,* one who frames a scheme.

scheme, *n.,* a plan, purpose or plot; *v.i.,* to form a plot or design; *v.t.,* to design.

schemed, *p.p.,* scheme.

sche'mer, *n.,* a designing person.

sche'ming, *pr.p.,* scheme.

scherzan'do, *adv.,* brightly and lightly (*mus., It.*).

scher'zo, *n.,* a quick, bright, musical movement (*mus., It.*).

Schiedam', *n.,* Holland gin.

schill'ing, *n.,* an Austrian coin; the Austrian unit of currency.

schipp'erke, *n.,* a kind of lap-dog from Belgium.

schism, *n.,* a rent, separation or division, especially religious.

schismat'ic, *adj.,* pert. or rel. to schism; *n.,* one guilty of schism.

schismat'ical, *adj., i.q.* schismatic.

schist, *n.,* fissile rock.

schist'ose, *adj.,* fissile; schist-like.

schist'ous, *adj., i.q.* schistose.

schizan'thus, *n.,* a Chilian flowering plant.

schizogen'esis, *n.,* reproduction by fission (*biol.*).

schiz'oid, *adj.,* of, or resembling, a schizophrenic; *n.,* a schizophrenic.

schizomycete', *n.,* singlecell vegetable organisms.

schizophren'ia, *n.,* a mental disease in which the personality appears to be divided.

schizophren'ic, *n.,* one who suffers from schizophrenia.

schmaltz, *n.,* sugary sentimentalism in art.

schnap(p)s, *n.,* Dutch gin (*Ger.*).

schnauz'er, *n.,* a German breed of dog.

schnor'kel, *n.,* the air intake on a submarine or diving mask.

schno'rrer, *n.,* a Jewish beggar.

schol'ar, *n.,* one who goes to school; a learner; a man of learning; a title of an undergraduate foundationer in a college.

schol'arlike, *adj., i.q.* scholarly.

schol'arly, *adj.,* learned.

schol'arship, *n.,* learning, erudition; an exhibition held by a scholar of a college.

scholas'tic, *adj.,* pert. or rel. to schools and scholars; bel. to the mediaeval philosophy of the schoolmen; *n.,* their philosophical system.

scholas'tically, *adv.,* in a scholastic way.

scholas'ticism, *n., i.q.* scholastic.

schol'ia, *n. pl.,* scholium.

scho'liast, *n.,* a learned commentator.

scho'lium, *n.,* the comment or annotation of a scholiast.

school, *n.,* a place of instruction; a group of adherents to a particular set of opinions; a great collection; a shoal of fish; *v.t.,* to train; to discipline.

school'book, *n.,* a book of instruction.

school'boy, *n.,* a boy under instruction at school.

school'-days, *n.,* the time of life when one is at school.

schooled, *adj.,* trained; *p.p.,* school.

school'fellow, *n.,* a contemporary at school.

school'girl, *n.,* a girl who is at school.

school'house, *n.,* a schoolmaster's residence *in situ.*

school'ing, *n.,* education; *pr.p.,* school.

school'man, *n.,* a mediaeval teacher of scholastic.

school'master, *n.,* a teacher.

school'mate, *n., i.q.* schoolfellow.

school'mistress, *n.,* a woman teacher.

school'room, *n.,* a room where school is held.

school'teacher, *n.,* a teacher in a school.

school'teaching, *n.,* the profession of teaching in school.

schoon'er, *n.,* a two-, three- or four-masted sailing vessel with mainsails, and rigged fore and aft; a tall glass.

schorl, *n.,* black tourmaline.

schottische', *n.,* a variety of polka (*Ger.*).

Schuber'tian, *adj.,* pert. or rel. to Franz Schubert, the Austrian composer.

sci'agram, *n.,* an x-ray picture; an outline or shadow of an object.

sci'agraph, *n.,* the interior of a building shown in section (*archit.*).

sciagraph'ic, *adj.*, pert. or rel. to a sciagraph.

sciag'raphy, *n.*, the art of representing shadows.

sciam'achy, *n.*, shadow boxing.

sciat'ic, *adj.*, pert. or rel. to the hip.

sciat'ica, *n.*, neuralgia affecting the sciatic nerve.

sciat'ical, *adj.*, pert. or rel. to the hip and sciatica.

sci'ence, *n.*, knowledge; systematized discoveries in nature or other departments of inquiry.

scien'ter, *adv.*, wittingly (*leg.*).

scien'tial, *adj.*, pert. or rel. to science.

scien'tially, *adv.*, in a sciential way.

scientif'ic, *adj.*, pert. or rel. to science; versed in science.

scientif'ical, *adj.*, *i.q.* scientific.

scientif'ically, *adv.*, in a scientific way.

sci'entist, *n.*, a man of science.

scientol'ogist, *n.*, one who practises scientology.

scientol'ogy, *n.*, a belief in the ability of prescribed study to improve human life on earth.

sci'licet, *conj.*, namely, to wit (*Lat.*).

Scill'a, *n.*, a genus of bulbous plants including the bluebell.

scim'itar, *n.*, a curved Oriental sword.

scintil'la, *n.*, a spark; a tiny trace (*Lat.*).

scin'tillant, *adj.*, sparkling.

scin'tillate, *v.i.*, to sparkle; to emit sparks.

scin'tillated, *p.p.*, scintillate.

scin'tillating, *pr.p.*, scintillate.

scintilla'tion, *n.*, the act of scintillating; a flash; a twinkle.

scin'tillator, *n.*, an instrument used to detect radio-activity.

scintillom'eter, *n.*, an instrument for trapping and measuring radio-activity.

sci'olism, *n.*, shallow learning.

sci'olist, *n.*, a false pretender to learning.

sciol'to, in free manner; staccato (*mus.*, *It.*).

sciom'achy, *n.*, *i.q.* sciamachy.

sci'on, *n.*, a branch, a shoot; a descendant.

sciop'tic, *adj.*, pert. or rel. to a *camera obscura* . or the art of producing luminous images in the dark.

scios'ophy, *n.*, a system based on unfounded beliefs, as astrology.

scirrhos'ity, *n.*, hardness.

scir'rhous, *adj.*, hardened.

scir'rhus, *n.*, a hard cancer.

scis'sel, *n.*, clippings of metal.

scis'sile, *adj.*, with cutting power.

scis'sion, *n.*, a cutting; the act of cutting.

scis'sor, *v.t.*, to cut or clip with scissors.

scis'sors, *n. pl.*, a small kind of shears.

scis'sure, *n.*, a cut.

sci'urine, *adj.*, pert. or rel. to squirrels.

Sci'urus, *n.*, the squirrel genus.

scler'a, *n.*, *i.q.* sclerotic.

scleri'asis, *n.*, a hardening of tissue.

scler'ogen, *n.*, the thickening substance in wood cells.

scler'oid, *adj.*, of hard texture (*bot.*, *zool.*).

scler'oscope, *n.*, an instrument for measuring hardness of metals.

sclero'sis, *n.*, a hardening; thickening.

sclerot'ic, *adj.*, hard; *n.*, the external membrane of the eye.

scler'ous, *adj.*, indurated, bony.

scobs, *n.*, the raspings of hard substances.

scoff, *n.*, anything to eat (*slang*); derision; ridicule; *v.i.*, to be derisive; *v.t.*, to eat greedily; to deride.

scoffed, *p.p.*, scoff.

scoff'er, *n.*, one who scoffs.

scoff'ing, *pr.p.*, scoff.

scoff'ingly, *adv.*, sneeringly.

scold, *n.*, a woman who habitually finds fault; *v.t.* and *i.*, to reprove angrily; to find fault.

scold'ed, *p.p.*, scold.

scold'er, *n.*, one who scolds.

scold'ing, *n.*, a chiding; *pr.p.*, scold.

sco'lecite, *n.*, a fossilized worm.

sco'lex, *n.*, a tape-worm larva (*Gr.*).

scol'lop, *n.*, *i.q.* scallop.

scolopa'ceous, *adj.*, of, or like, the snipes.

scol'opacine, *adj.*, *i.q.* scolopaceous.

Scolopen'dra, *n. pl.*, centipede venomous insects.

scolopen'drine, *adj.*, pert. or rel. to centipede(s).

scolopen'drium, *n.*, a kind of fern.

scom'ber, *n.*, the mackerel.

scon, *n.*, *i.q.* scone.

sconce, *n.*, a bulwark; protection; a candle or lamp-holder; a head; a penalty; *v.t.*, to inflict a penalty on.

scone, *n.*, a kind of tea-cake.

scoop, *n.*, a shovel, ladle or scuttle; a substantial gain; an exclusive news story (*colloq.*); *v.t.*, to shovel up; to hollow.

scooped, *p.p.*, scoop.

scoop'er, *n.*, anything that scoops.

scoop'ing, *pr.p.*, scoop.

scoot, *v.i.*, to hurry off, to run away hurriedly (*slang*).

scoot'er, *n.*, a two-wheeled children's toy.

scop'a, *n.*, a small tuft of hairs (esp. of bees).

scope, *n.*, range; outlook; room for action; aim.

scorbu'tic, *adj.*, pert. or rel. to scurvy.

scorch, *v.i.*, to cycle or motor at high speed (*slang*); *v.t.* and *i.*, to singe; to shrivel up with heat.

scorched, *p.p.*, scorch.

scorch'er, *n.*, one who cycles or motors at high speed; anything extreme (*slang*); that which scorches.

scorch'ing, *pr.p.*, scorch.

scorch'ingly, *adv.*, with a scorching effect.

score, *n.*, a mark; a notch; a reckoning; behalf; the number 20; musical parts written down; *v.t.*, to

mark; to notch; to reckon up; to win (a number of runs, etc.).

scored, *p.p.*, score.

scor'er, *n.*, one who scores; a recorder of scores.

sco'ria, *n.*, a volcanic débris; slag.

scoria'ceous, *adj.*, pert. or rel. to scoria.

scorifica'tion, *n.*, the formation of scoria.

sco'rified, *p.p.*, scorify.

sco'riform, *adj.*, like scoria.

sco'rify, *v.t.* and *i.*, to form scoria.

sco'rifying, *pr.p.*, scorify.

scor'ing, *pr.p.*, score.

sco'rious, *adj.*, *i.q.* scoriaceous.

scorn, *n.*, contempt, disdain; *v.t.*, to despise or disdain.

scorned, *p.p.*, scorn.

scorn'er, *n.*, one who scorns.

scorn'ful, *adj.*, disdainful, contemptuous.

scorn'fully, *adv.*, in a scornful way.

scorn'ing, *pr.p.*, scorn.

Scor'pio, *n.*, the Scorpion, the eighth sign of the Zodiac.

scorp'ioid, *adj.* and *n.*, scorpion-like (*bot.*).

scor'pion, *n.*, a creature with claws like a lobster and a sting in its tail.

scor'tatory, *adj.*, pert. or rel. to prostitution, fornication or lewdness.

scorzoner'a, *n.*, viper's grass.

Scot, *n.*, a native of Scotland.

scot, *n.*, a fine; tax.

Scotch, *adj.*, *i.q.* Scottish; *n. pl.*, the Scots; (generally used only for whisky and potatoes).

scotch, *n.*, a cut; a chock or block; *v.t.*, to score, to hack; to cripple; to block; to frustrate.

scotched, *p.p.*, scotch.

scotch'ing, *pr.p.*, scotch.

Scotch'man, *n.*, *i.q.* Scotsman.

Scotch'woman, *n.*, *i.q.* Scotswoman.

sco'ter, *n.*, a variety of sea-duck.

scot'free', *adj.*, free from the duty of paying scot; unpunished; safe and sound.

Sco'tia, *n.*, the Latin name for Scotland.

sco'tia, *n.*, a hollow moulding in a pillarbase in classical architecture.

Scot'ice, *adv.*, after the Scottish manner; in Scots speech.

Sco'tist, *n.*, a disciple of Duns Scotus, the famous 13th cent. philosopher.

sco'tograph, *n.*, a contrivance enabling the blind to read or anyone to write in the dark.

scoto'ma, *n.*, vertigo; difficulty in discerning objects.

Scots, *adj.*, Scottish; *n.*, the speech of Scotland; the pl. of Scot.

Scots'man, *n.*, a man born in Scotland.

Scots'woman, *n.*, a woman born in Scotland.

Scot'ticism, *n.*, Scottish idiom.

Scot'tish, *adj.*, Scots, Scotch.

scoun'drel, *n.*, a villain, a rascal.

scoun'drelism, *n.*, the conduct of a scoundrel; rascality.

scoun'drelly, *adj.*, like a scoundrel.

scour, *n.*, the effect of rushing water on a channel; something used for scouring; *v.t.*, to cleanse by rubbing or polishing; to range over; to sweep along.

scoured, *p.p.*, scour.

scour'er, *n.*, one who, or that which, scours.

scourge, *n.*, a whip for flogging; any plague or vengeance; *v.t.*, to lash, to punish with scourging, to harass.

scourged, *p.p.*, scourge.

scour'ger, *n.*, one who scourges.

scour'ging, *n.*, a whipping; *pr.p.*, scourge.

scour'ing, *n.*, the act of scouring in all senses; *pr.p.*, scour.

scouse, *n.*, a native or the dialect of Liverpool (*slang*); a mixture of meat and vegetables.

scout, *n.*, someone sent out to reconnoitre and bring information; a lookout; a member of the organization of boy scouts; a college servant at Oxford; a small, fast military aircraft; *v.i.*, to mock; to act as a scout; *v.t.*, to reject or dismiss with contempt.

scout'ed, *p.p.*, scout.

scout'er, *n.*, one who goes scouting; a patrolman; a senior scout.

scouth, *n.*, plenty of scope for achievement.

scout'ing, *pr.p.*, scout.

scout'master, *n.*, an officer in charge of boy scouts.

scov'el, *n.*, a mop to clean ovens.

scow, *n.*, a flat-bottomed boat, square-ended (*Dutch*).

scowl, *n.*, an angry frown; *v.i.*, to put on a sullen look; to frown angrily.

scowled, *p.p.*, scowl.

scowl'ing, *pr.p.*, scowl.

scrab'ble, *n.*, scrambling; a word game; *v.i.*, to scrawl, to scribble; to scramble; *v.t.*, to scratch writings on.

scrab'bled, *p.p.*, scrabble.

scrab'bling, *pr.p.*, scrabble.

scrag, *n.*, a lean person or thing; the thin end of a neck of mutton; *v.t.*, to kill by hanging (*colloq.*); to collar (at football).

scragged, *p.p.*, scrag.

scrag'gily, *adv.*, in a scraggy way.

scrag'giness, *n.*, the condition of being scraggy.

scrag'gy, *adj.*, lean and unsightly.

scram'ble, *n.*, a struggle; a clambering; an informal kind of race; *v.i.*, to clamber on hands and feet; to struggle; to run in all directions, as a creeper; *v.t.*, to cook eggs broken into a pan and mixed with butter, etc.; to gather up in confusion; to mix sounds so as to make them unintelligible.

scram'bled, *p.p.*, scramble.

scram'bler, *n.*, one who scrambles; a device for distorting sound.

scram'bling, *pr.p.*, scramble.

scran, *n.*, food (*slang*).

scranch, *v.t.*, to crunch (*colloq.*).

scrann'el, *adj.*, weak, feeble (of sound); *n.*, a thin person.

scrann'y, *adj.*, lean, scraggy.

scrap, *n.*, something scraped off; a fragment; a small portion; a fight (*slang*); *v.t.*, to throw away as refuse; to engage in a fight (*slang*).

scrap'book, *n.*, a book of extracts, cuttings, pictures, etc.

scrape, *n.*, the act of scraping; a troublesome situation created by one's own fault; a movement with the foot in making a bow; *v.i.*, to rub a surface; to save money; to make a bow by scraping the feet; to play a fiddle indifferently; *v.t.*, to scratch; to take the surface off; to rub hard on; to gather up by scraping.

scraped, *p.p.*, scrape.

scra'per, *n.*, that which scrapes; an appliance for scraping.

scrap'heap, *n.*, orig. a heap of scrap metal, a rubbish heap.

scra'ping, *pr.p.*, scrape.

scra'pingly, *adv.*, in a scraping way.

scra'pings, *n. pl.*, remains, leavings.

scrapped, *p.p.*, scrap.

scrap'ping, *pr.p.*, scrap.

scratch, *adj.*, chosen indiscriminately; having no handicap allowance; *n.*, a mark of scratching; the sound of scratching; a slight wound; the starting line in a race; *v.t.*, to tear or abrade a surface; to write clumsily; to erase from a list.

scratched, *p.p.*, scratch.

scratch'ily, *adv.*, in a scratchy way.

scratch'iness, *n.*, the state of being scratchy.

scratch'ing, *pr.p.*, scratch.

scratch'y, *adj.*, making the sound of scratching; poorly drawn.

scrawl, *n.*, a piece of bad writing; *v.t.*, to scribble, to write more or less illegibly.

scrawled, *p.p.*, scrawl.

scrawl'er, *n.*, one who scrawls.

scrawl'ing, *pr.p.*, scrawl.

scrawl'y, *adj.*, badly written.

scrawn'y, *adj.*, skinny.

scray, *n.*, a tern.

scream, *n.*, a piercing cry or sound, usually of anguish or terror; a comical person (*slang*); *v.i.*, to make a piercing cry; *v.t.*, to utter in a piercing voice.

screamed, *p.p.*, scream.

scream'er, *n.*, one who screams; a kind of S. American bird; anything that excites great laughter or astonishment (*slang*); an exclamation mark (*colloq.*).

scream'ing, *adj.*, provoking great laughter (*slang*); *pr.p.*, scream.

scream'ingly, *adv.*, in a screaming way.

scree, *n.*, a mountain slope of loose stones.

screech, *v.i.*, to make a sharp, screaming sound or cry; *v.t.*, to utter in a high, harsh voice.

screeched, *p.p.*, screech.

screech'ing, *pr.p.*, screech.

screech'-owl, *n.*, an owl that screeches instead of hoots.

screed, *n.*, a long, boring tale; a strip of mortar or wood fixed at intervals on a surface to be plastered, and showing the compartments of the plastering.

screen, *n.*, a barrier of any kind protecting against heat, cold, etc.; the barrier between nave and choir, or between one division of a church and another; a sheet on to which films or pictures are thrown; *v.t.*, to cover, conceal or protect; to riddle.

screened, *p.p.*, screen.

screen'ing, *pr.p.*, screen.

screes, *n. pl.*, loose stones; *i.q.* scree.

screeve, *v.i.*, to do pavement art.

screev'er, *n.*, a pavement artist.

screw, *n.*, a cylindrical piece of wood or metal, spirally grooved on the outside or inside; a miser; a broken-down horse; a prison officer (*slang*); *v.i.*, to turn screw-fashion; to be a miser; *v.t.*, to apply a screw or a screwing motion to; to use pressure with; to distort; to put a twist on a ball.

screw'driver, *n.*, a tool for forcing a screw in.

screwed, *p.p.*, screw.

screw'ing, *pr.p.*, screw.

screw'-jack, *n.*, a lifting jack with a screw; a dentist's apparatus for changing the position of overcrowded teeth.

screw'-pine, *n.*, a plant with spiral leaves.

screw'y, *adj.*, slightly crazy (*slang*).

scriba'cious, *adj.*, given to writing.

scrib'ble, *n.*, hasty writing; poor literature; *v.i.*, to be a writer or scribbler; to card wool; *v.t. and i.*, to write hastily or carelessly.

scrib'bled, *p.p.*, scribble.

scrib'bler, *n.*, one who scribbles; an indifferent author; a machine for scribbling wool.

scrib'bling, *n.*, wool-carding; *pr.p.*, scribble.

scribe, *n.*, a writer, a penman; specifically an expounder and recorder of the Jewish law and tradition; *v.t.*, to scratch with a marking tool, for the purpose of guiding a saw, etc.

scribed, *p.p.*, scribe.

scri'bing, *pr.p.*, scribe.

scrim, *n.*, open canvas for lining in upholstery, for camouflage, etc.

scrim'mage, n., a tussle, row or skirmish; v.i., to join in a scrimmage (colloq.).

scrimp, adj., skimped; n., a niggard; v.i. and t., to stint, to skimp.

scrimped, p.p., scrimp.

scrimp'ing, pr.p., scrimp.

scrim'shank, v.i., to shirk duty (slang).

scrim'shanked, p.p., scrimshank.

scrim'shanker, n., a shirker.

scrimshank'ing, n., the shirking of duty; pr.p., scrimshank.

scrim'shaw, n., a decorated shell, etc.; v.i. and t., to decorate ivory, shells, etc., with coloured drawings.

scrin'ium, n., a manuscript box.

scrip, n., a bag, a wallet; a document showing the holder's title to payment of interest, dividend, etc.

scrip'-holder, n., the owner of a piece of scrip.

script, n., writing; style of writing; imitation writing; a draft; the working copy for a film or play.

scripto'rial, adj., pert. or rel. to writing or authorship.

scripto'rium, n., a part of a monastery where manuscripts are written (Lat.).

scrip'tural, adj., pert. or rel. to the scriptures.

scrip'turalist, n., one who interprets the scriptures in the most literal sense.

scrip'turally, adv., according to scripture.

scrip'ture, n., writing, esp. the Bible; a passage from the Bible.

scrip'ture-reader, n., a layman who instructs the poor and unlearned.

scrip'turist, n., one learned in the scriptures.

scriv'ener, n., a person who draws up deeds, drafts or documents, lends money, or acts as a notary.

scriv'enery, n., a scrivener's calling.

scrobic'ulate, adj., furrowed, marked (bot.).

scrobic'ulated, adj., i.q. scrobiculate.

scrof'ula, n., a morbid predisposition to glandular tumours (formerly known as King's Evil).

scrof'ulous, adj., suffering from scrofula; of the nature of scrofula.

scroll, n., a roll of parchment or paper; an artistic scroll-like ornament; anything resembling a scroll, as a fiddle-head; v.i., to curl up in a roll; v.t., to write in a scroll; to draft; to curl up; to adorn with scrolls.

scrolled, adj., decorated with scrolls; like a scroll; encased in a scroll; p.p., scroll.

scroll'work, n., ornamental scroll-like design.

scroop, n., a grating noise; v.i., to make a grating noise.

scro'tal, adj., pert. or rel. to the scrotum.

scro'titis, n., inflammation of the scrotum.

scro'tum, n., the pouch containing the testicles (Lat.).

scrounge, v.i., to sponge (colloq.); v.t., to appropriate things; to cadge.

scrounged, p.p., scrounge.

scroun'ger, n., one who scrounges.

scroung'ing, pr.p., scrounge.

scrub, n., the act of scrubbing; a stunted shrub; ground covered with stunted trees or shrubs; any person or thing particularly mean; v.i., to be a drudge; v.t. and i., to cleanse by rubbing.

scrubbed, p.p., scrub.

scrub'ber, n., one who, or that which, scrubs; a prostitute (slang).

scrub'bier, adj., comp. of scrubby.

scrub'biest, adj., super. of scrubby.

scrub'bing, n., a thorough cleaning; pr.p., scrub.

scrub'by, adj., mean, undersized, shabby.

scruff, n., the back of the neck.

scrum, n., a scrummage; a formal, physical arrangement of players to allow for a struggle for possession of the ball (Rugby football) (colloq.).

scrum'mage, n., i.q. scrimmage.

scrump'tious, adj., especially delightful or beautiful (colloq.).

scrunch, v.t., i. and n., i.q. crunch.

scru'ple, n., hesitation on moral or conscientious grounds; an apothecary's weight-unit (= 20 grains); v.i., to hesitate on conscientious grounds.

scru'pled, p.p., scruple.

scru'pling, pr.p., scruple.

scrupulos'ity, n., i.q. scrupulousness.

scru'pulous, adj., conscientious, punctilious; sensitive about moral issues.

scru'pulously, adv., conscientiously.

scru'pulousness, n., the state or quality of being scrupulous.

scruta'tor, n., a careful enquirer or examiner (Lat.).

scru'tatory, adj., scrutinizing.

scru'tin, n., a method of voting (Fr.).

scrutineer', n., a scrutinizer; one who conducts a scrutiny, particularly at Parliamentary or municipal elections.

scru'tinize, v.t., to investigate or examine closely.

scru'tinized, p.p., scrutinize.

scru'tinizer, n., one who scrutinizes.

scru'tinizing, pr.p., scrutinize.

scru'tiny, n., a close investigation; a strict inquiry; the examination of voting-papers at an election; a mode of electing a Pope.

scrutoire', n., a writing-table; an escritoire (Fr.).

scry, v.i., to use the crystal in crystal-gazing.

scud, n., a rapid rushing; light cloud or spray driven before the wind; v.i., to drive along swiftly.

scud'ded, p.p., scud.

scud'ding, pr.p., scud.

scu'di, n., the pl. of scudo.

scu′do, *n.*, an old Italian silver-piece.

scuff, *n.*, the nape (of the neck) (usu. scruff); *v.i.*, to walk in a shuffling manner; *v.t.*, to scrape the surface of shoes.

scuf′fle, *n.*, a disordered, physical struggle; *v.i.*, to struggle in a disorderly contest; *v.t.*, to hustle.

scuf′fled, *p.p.*, scuffle.

scuf′fler, *n.*, one who scuffles.

scuf′fling, *pr.p.*, scuffle.

sculk, *v.i.*, *i.q.* skulk.

sculked, *p.p.*, sculk.

sculk′er, *n.*, *i.q.* skulker.

sculk′ing, *pr.p.*, sculk.

scull, *n.*, a small oar used by one hand only; *v.t.* and *i.*, to propel a boat with sculls.

sculled, *p.p.*, scull.

scull′er, *n.*, one who sculls.

scull′ery, *n.*, the part of a house where dishes, etc., are washed up.

scull′ing, *n.*, the practice or art of rowing with sculls; *pr.p.*, scull.

scull′ion, *n.*, a cook's help, the boy who washes dishes, etc.

sculp, *v.t.* and *i.*, to carve, to practise a sculptor's art.

scul′pin, *n.*, an American sea-fish..

sculp′tor, *n.*, an artist who carves or models in solid materials; an artist in sculpture.

sculp′tress, *n.*, a woman who sculptures.

sculp′tural, *adj.*, pert. or rel. to sculpture.

sculp′ture, *n.*, the art of carving in stone, marble, etc.; modelling in clay, casting in metals; a piece of sculptured work; *v.t.*, to carve; to adorn with sculpture.

sculp′tured,′ *adj.*, with superficial marking; *p.p.*, sculpture.

sculpturesque′, *adj.*, with the manner or appearance of a sculptured work; clean-cut, statue-like.

sculp′turing, *n.*, *i.q.* sculpture; *pr.p.*, sculpture.

scum, *n.*, impurities that have risen to the surface of a liquid; refuse; off-scouring; *v.i.*, to form a scum; *v.t.*, to skim.

scum′ble, *n.*, the softening of colours or outlines; *v.t.*, to soften the colours or hard outlines of a picture.

scum′bled, *p.p.*, scumble.

scumb′ling, *pr.p.*, scumble.

scummed, *p.p.*, scum.

scum′ming, *pr.p.*, scum.

scum′mings, *n. pl.*, skimmings.

scun′ner, *n.*, loathing (*Scot.*).

scup, *n.*, a kind of fish found on the eastern coast of America.

scup′per, *n.*, an opening in the side of a ship to let water off the deck; *v.t.*, to sink; to ruin.

scup′pered, *p.p.*, scupper.

scupper′ing, *pr.p.*, scupper.

scup′pet, *n.*, a shovel.

scurf, *n.*, skin flaked off; scaly matter on a surface.

scurf′ier, *adj.*, *comp.* of scurfy.

scurf′iest, *adj.*, *super.* of scurfy.

scurf′iness, *n.*, the state of being scurfy.

scurf′y, *adj.*, covered with scurf; forming scurf.

scur′ried, *p.p.*, scurry.

scur′rile, *adj.*, *i.q.* scurrilous.

scurril′ity, *n.*, gross or obscene abuse.

scur′rilous, *adj.*, grossly or obscenely abusive.

scur′rilously, *adv.*, in a scurrilous way.

scur′ry, *n.*, a hurried run; a whirl; *v.i.*, to run hastily; to scamper.

scur′rying, *pr.p.*, scurry.

scur′vily, *adv.*, shabbily; basely.

scur′viness, *n.*, meanness; shabbiness.

scur′vy, *adj.*, mean, base (*colloq.*); covered with scurf; *n.*, a deficiency disease affecting the blood and producing painful effects internally and externally.

scut, *n.*, a short tail, as of a rabbit, etc.

scu′tage, *n.*, an old English assessment of feudal landlords in lieu of personal service.

scu′tate, *adj.*, buckler-shaped; covered with shield-shaped scales.

scutch, *n.*, a scutching machine; a tow separated by scutching; *v.t.*, to dress fibrous material by beating; to beat (*Scot.*).

scutched, *p.p.*, scutch.

scutch′eon, *n.*, *i.q.* escutcheon.

scutch′er, *n.*, a scutching implement.

scutch′ing, *pr.p.*, scutch.

scute, *n.*, *i.q.* scutum.

scu′tel, *n.*, *i.q.* scutellum.

scu′tellate, *adj.*, like a scutellum; platter-like.

scu′tellated, *adj.*, *i.q.* scutellate.

scutel′lum, *n.*, a little plate, shield or scale formed on insects, birds, plants, etc.

scutif′erous, *adj.*, shield-bearing.

scu′tiform, *adj.*, shield-shaped; peltate.

scut′ter, *v.i.*, *i.q.* scurry.

scut′tle, *n.*, a hatchway; any hole; a vessel to hold coal; a running in haste; *v.i.*, to run in a hurry; to desert dishonourably; *v.t.*, to make holes in a ship in order to sink it.

scut′tled, *p.p.*, scuttle.

scut′tling, *pr.p.*, scuttle.

scu′tum, *n.*, a shield (*Lat.*); a knee-pan; a shield-like plate or scale on turtles, alligators, etc.

scym′itar, *n.*, *i.q.* scimitar.

scy′phus, *n.*, a Greek drinking-cup; in botany, a cup-shaped organ.

scythe, *n.*, an implement for mowing and reaping; *v.t.*, to mow; to arm with a scythe.

scythed, *adj.*, having scythes fixed to the axles; *p.p.*, scythe.

Scyth′ian, *adj.*, pert. or rel. to Scythia, the region north of the Black Sea; *n.*, a native of S.; a savage.

scyth'ing, *pr.p.*, scythe.

sea, *n.*, a large body of salt water, the ocean; a large inland lake.

sea'-anc'hor, *n.*, a floating drag-anchor used in adverse weather.

sea'board, *n.*, the coast or seashore.

sea'-born, *adj.*, born of the sea.

sea'borne, *adj.*, carried by sea.

sea'-breach, *n.*, the bursting of a dyke.

sea'breeze, *n.*, a breeze coming from the sea.

sea'-captain, *n.*, the captain of a ship.

sea'-chart, *n.*, a marine map.

sea'-coast, *n.*, the land where it fringes the sea; the shore.

sea'-cow, *n.*, the walrus.

sea'-dog, *n.*, the harbour-seal; dogfish; a tough old sailor.

sea'drome, *n.*, a floating stage for aircraft.

sea-elephant, *n.*, an elephant-seal.

sea'farer, *n.*, a mariner.

sea'faring, *adj.*, living a sailor's life; *n.*, the life of a sailor.

sea'-fight, *n.*, a battle at sea.

sea'front, *n.*, that edge of a place which adjoins the sea.

sea'-gauge, *n.*, a sounding apparatus; a ship's draught.

sea'-girt, *adj.*, surrounded by the sea.

sea'green, *adj.*, green like the sea; *n.*, the colour of the sea.

sea'gull, *n.*, a gull; a large tern.

sea'-horse, *n.*, a walrus; a hippocampus.

sea'-kale, *n.*, a perennial edible herb.

sea'-king, *n.*, an ancient Scandinavian sea-rover.

seal, *n.*, a stamp for making impressions in wax, lead, etc.; the impression thus made; a pledge; a ratification; an amphibious marine mammal, much prized for its fur; *v.i.*, to affix a seal; to go sealing; *v.t.*, to impress with a stamp bearing a device; to close; to confirm.

sealed, *p.p.*, seal.

sea-legs, *n. pl.*, the art of walking on a ship's deck in rough weather.

sea'-leopard, *n.*, a variety of seal marked with spots.

seal'er, *n.*, one who, or that which, seals in any sense; a ship used in sealing; any material used to seal.

sea'-level, *n.*, the level of a line halfway between high and low tide.

seal'ing, *n.*, the occupation of hunting seals; the act of affixing a seal to a document; *pr.p.*, seal.

seal'ing-wax, *n.*, wax to receive the impression of a seal.

sea'lion, *n.*, a large seal.

sea'lord, *n.*, naval member of the board of Admiralty.

seal'skin, *adj.*, made of sealskin; *n.*, the skin and fur of a seal.

seal'yham, *n.*, a breed of terrier.

seam, *n.*, a line showing the junction of two parts; a line of fissure; a stratum of rock or coal; a joining; *v.t.*, to join with a seam; to mark, to scar; to produce a seam-like appearance in knitting.

sea'man, *n.*, a mariner, a sailor.

sea'manlike, *adj.*, in the manner of a seaman.

sea'manship, *n.*, the mariner's art; the skill in navigating and handling a boat.

sea'mark, *n.*, a lighthouse, beacon, etc.

seamed, *p.p.*, seam.

seam'er, *n.*, one who seams; a machine for seaming.

sea'mew, *n.*, a gull.

seam'ing, *pr.p.*, seam.

seam'less, *adj.*, without seam.

sea'-mouse, *n.*, an iridescent sea-worm.

seam'ster, *n.*, one whose business it is to sew.

seam'stress, *n.*, *i.q.* seamster.

seam'y, *adj.*, having or showing seams; showing the less favourable aspect.

séance, *n.*, a sitting, a session, esp. of spiritualists (*Fr.*).

sea'-nettle, *n.*, a class of jelly-fish.

sea'-pie, *n.*, a sailor's dish of meat and crust in layers.

sea'plane, *n.*, an aircraft designed to touch down on or take off from water.

sea'port, *n.*, a harbour; a town or city with a harbour.

sear, *adj.*, dry, withered (also *sere*); *n.*, the catch that keeps a gun-hammer at half-cock; *v.t.*, to wither, to scorch.

search, *n.*, the act of searching; an investigation; an inquiry; *v.t.*, to explore, to overhaul; to ransack, to investigate.

search'able, *adj.*, able to be searched.

searched, *p.p.*, search.

search'er, *n.*, one who searches.

search'ing, *adj.*, penetrating, critical; *pr.p.*, search.

search'ingly, *adv.*, in a penetrating or critical way.

search'light, *n.*, a strong beam of light.

search'-party, *n.*, a number of people detailed to look for a lost person or thing.

search'-warrant, *n.*, a warrant granted by a magistrate to search suspected premises.

seared, *p.p.*, sear.

sear'ing, *pr.p.*, sear.

sea'-room, *n.*, space enough for a ship to move freely.

sea'-rover, *n.*, a pirate or pirate-ship.

sea'scape, *n.*, a picture of a marine subject.

sea'-serpent, *n.*, a supposed marine monster.

sea'shell, *n.*, the shell of a marine creature.

sea'shore, *n.*, the land by the sea; the coast.

sea'sick, *adj.*, suffering from sea-sickness.

sea'-sickness, *n.*, a sickness induced by the motion of a ship.

sea'side, *adj.*, adjacent to the sea; *n.*, the land near the sea.

sea'-snail, *n.*, a marine snail-like gasteropod.

sea′son, n., a period of time; a division of the year; the fitting time; v.t., to spice, flavour, temper or inure.

sea′sonable, adj., fitting to the season; opportune.

sea′sonably, adv., in a seasonable way.

sea′sonal, adv., according to season.

sea′sonally, adv., in a seasonal way.

sea′soned, p.p., season.

sea′soner, n., that which seasons.

sea′soning, n., a relish; anything added to food to increase the flavour; pr.p., season.

sea′son-ticket, n., a railway or other ticket allowing the holder to use it for a stated period (colloq.).

sea′squirt, n., an ascidium; a marine organism with leathery enveloping tissue.

seat, n., that on which one sits, as a chair, settee, etc.; the buttocks; the part of pants, trousers, etc., that covers the buttocks; a place where a landowner resides or anything is situated; a constituency; the right to sit; v.t., to place in a seat; to establish; to fit firmly.

seat′ed, p.p., seat.

sea′-term, n., a nautical expression.

seat′ing, n., the collective seats, or method of arranging them, in a building; the material for seat-covering; pr.p., seat.

sea′-urchin, n., the echinus.

sea′wall, n., a wall built to keep out the sea.

sea′ward, adj. and adv., toward the sea.

sea′wards, adj. and adv., i.q. seaward.

sea′water, n., the water of the sea.

sea′weed, n., a plant that grows in sea-water.

sea′worthiness, n., the state or quality of being seaworthy.

sea′worthy, adj., fit to go to sea; in sound condition.

seba′ceous, adj., pert. or rel. to fat.

sebac′ic, adj., fatty; made from fat.

se′bate, n., a sebacic acid salt.

sebes′tan, n., a plum-like fruit used for medicine in the East.

sebes′ten, n., i.q. sebestan.

sebife′rous, adj., producing fat.

seborrhoe′a, n., excessive secretion of the sebaceous glands, causing a greasy skin, acne, etc.

se′bum, n., the product of the sebaceous glands; a fatty secretion.

sebun′dy, n., an Anglo-Indian word for the native militia and police.

sec, adj., (of wines) dry (Fr.).

se′cant, adj., cutting, intersecting.

sec′ateur, n., a garden tool for pruning purposes (Fr.).

secc′o, adj. unaccompanied (mus.); n., a painting on any dry plaster; tempera work (It.).

secc′otine, n., a kind of adhesive; v.t., to affix with adhesive.

secede′, v.i., to withdraw, to separate.

sece′ded, p.p., secede.

sece′der, n., one who secedes; a separatist.

sece′ding, pr.p., secede.

secern′, v.t., to distinguish.

secerned′, p.p., secern.

secern′ent, adj., secreting; n., that which secretes; a secreting organ; a drug causing secretion.

secern′ing, pr.p., secern.

seces′sion, n., the act of seceding.

seces′sionist, n., a supporter of secession, esp. a supporter of the doctrine that a State had the right to secede from the United States of America.

seclude′, v.t., to shut up; to put into retirement; to remove from intercourse.

seclu′ded, adj., retired; p.p., seclude.

seclu′ding, pr.p., seclude.

seclu′sion, n., the act of secluding; retirement; solitariness.

seclu′sionist, n., one who seeks seclusion or solitude.

seclu′sive, adj., having a tendency to seclude.

sec′odont, adj., with cutting back teeth.

Sec′onal, n., a hypnotic drug.

sec′ond, adj., the ordinal of two; next after the first; below in pitch (mus.); n., a short interval (one-sixtieth of a minute); a supporter to a protagonist; an inferior to the first; a subordinate part; v.t., to support or promote.

second′, v.t., to retire (an officer) temporarily before appointing him to some duty outside his regiment; to shift (a person) to a different employment temporarily.

sec′ondarily, adv., in a secondary degree.

sec′ondary, adj., of lower rank, influence or grade; less important; delegated; subsequent; in the middle stage between primary and tertiary; n., a delegate; a minor official in a cathedral; one of an insect′s hind wings; a feather on the second joint of a bird′s wings.

sec′ond-best, adj., not quite the first; inferior.

seconde′, n., a fencing-position (Fr.).

sec′onded, p.p., sec′ond.

second′ed, p.p., second′.

sec′onder, n., one who seconds or formally supports a resolution.

sec′ond-hand, adj., not new; previously owned; indirect; not original; n., the pointer that indicates the seconds on a clock or watch dial.

sec′onding, pr.p., se′cond.

second′ing, pr.p., second′.

sec′ondly, adv., in the second place.

second′ment, n., to second to another place, service or position.

secon′do, n., second performer (part) in a duet (It.).

sec'ond-rate, *adj.*, not first rate; of indifferent quality.

sec'ond-rat'er, *n.*, one who is of inferior class.

sec'onds, *n. pl.*, articles not of the first quality, as seconds in flour or tobacco.

sec'onds-hand, *n.*, a watch-finger indicating the seconds.

sec'ond sight, *n.*, a supposed faculty of seeing future or distant events.

se'crecy, *n.*, concealment, seclusion, secretiveness.

se'cret, *adj.*, concealed, hidden, private, reticent; *n.*, something not revealed; a mystery; something not to be told.

secretaire', *n.*, a writing desk; *i.q.* escritoire.

secreta'rial, *adj.*, pert. or rel. to a secretary and a secretary's duties.

secreta'rially, *adv.*, in the manner of a secretary.

secreta'riat, *n.*, offices, functions or a body of people concerned in secretarial work.

sec'retary, *n.*, one who acts as the confidential assistant of another, or attends to the correspondence and records of a society, or superintends a Department of State, or who conducts the communications and private aspects of an executive's work.

sec'retary-bird, *n.*, a S. African bird with a crest that suggests a quill pen.

sec'retaryship, *n.*, a secretary's post.

secrete', *v.t.*, to place in concealment; to separate from blood and sap by secretion; to exude a liquid.

secre'ted, *p.p.*, secrete.

secre'tin, *n.*, a pancreatic hormone.

secre'ting, *pr.p.*, secrete.

secre'tion, *n.*, the act or result of secreting; the process by which materials are separated from blood and sap and made into new substances, as milk, urine, etc.

se'cretive, *adj.*, reserved, reticent.

se'cretively, *adv.*, in a secretive way.

se'cretiveness, *n.*, the quality or state of being secretive.

se'cretly, *adv.*, in a secret way.

se'cretness, *n.*, the quality or state of being secret.

secre'tory, *adj.*, secreting.

sect, *n.*, a body that dissents from a church or other body holding defined philosophical views, or sets up its own particular standard of religion or philosophy.

secta'rial, *adj.*, peculiar to a particular sect; a token worn on the forehead of Indian natives.

secta'rian, *adj.*, pert. or rel. to sects and sectarianism.

secta'rianism, *n.*, the spirit of sects.

secta'rianize, *v.t.*, to make sectarian.

sect'arist, *n.*, *i.q.* sectary.

sect'ary, *n.*, the adherent of a sect, religious, philosophical, etc.; a fanatic.

secta'tor, *n.*, a follower or disciple of an exclusive sect.

sec'tile, *adj.*, able to be cut.

sec'tion, *n.*, the act of cutting; a portion cut or marked off.

sec'tional, *adj.*, pert. or rel. to a section; divided into sections; pert. or rel. to a portion of a community or territory.

sectionaliza'tion, *n.*, the division into sections.

sec'tionalize, *v.t.*, to divide into sections; to separate.

sec'tionalized, *adj.*, divided into sections; *p.p.*, sectionalize.

sec'tionalizing, *pr.p.*, sectionalize.

sec'tionally, *adv.*, in a sectional way.

sec'tionize, *v.t.*, *i.q.* sectionalize.

sec'tor, *n.*, a plane figure contained within two radii of a circle and the subtending arc; a mathematical rule consisting of two flat pieces strongly jointed at one end and marked with lines to represent sines, tangents, etc.; any defined area.

sector'ial, *adj.*, of or like the sector of a circle; *n.*, a tooth adapted for cutting.

sector'ially, *adv.*, in a sectorial way.

sec'ular, *adj.*, pert. or rel. to this age or world, and so the opposite to religious; recurring through the ages; happening once in a century; nonmonastic; *n.*, a nonmonastic priest.

sec'ularism, *n.*, the quality of being secular; the principles of the secularists.

sec'ularist, *n.*, one who repudiates religion and worship; specifically, one who opposes religious teaching in schools.

secular'ity, *n.*, the quality or state of being secular.

seculariza'tion, *n.*, the act or effect of secularizing.

sec'ularize, *v.t.*, to make secular; to exclude religion from.

sec'ularized, *p.p.*, secularize.

sec'ularizing, *pr.p.*, secularize.

sec'ularly, *adv.*, in a secular way.

sec'und, *adj.*, having organs on one side only.

sec'undine, *n.*, the inside coat of an ovule.

secur'able, *adj.*, able to be secured.

secure', *adj.*, free from care or anxiety; safe; sure; firm; *v.t.*, to make secure; to guarantee; to obtain; to get hold of.

secured', *p.p.*, secure.

secure'ly, *adv.*, safely.

secu'rer, *adj.*, *comp.* of secure; *n.*, one who, or that which, secures.

secu'rest, *adj.*, *super.* of secure.

secu'riform, *adj.*, hatchet-shaped.

secu'ring, *pr.p.*, secure.

secu'rity, *n.*, freedom from anxiety; safety; a guarantee; something hypothecated; a documentary proof of loan.

sedan', *n.*, a portable chair borne on poles.

sedate′, *adj.*, dignified, grave, composed.

sedate′ly, *adv.*, in a sedate manner.

sedate′ness, *n.*, the quality or state of being sedate.

sed′ative, *adj.*, soothing; *n.*, a soothing drug.

sed′entarily, *adv.*, in a sedentary way.

sed′entariness, *n.*, the sedentary habit.

sed′entary, *adj.*, not active; requiring or involving much sitting.

sed′er, *n.*, the ritual carried out on the first night of the Passover.

sede′runt, *v.i. p.t.*, 3rd per. pl. = "there sat" or "were present" (said of persons attending at a council, meeting, etc.) (*Lat.*); thence used as a *n.*, a session or sitting.

sedge, *n.*, a general name for many waterside plants.

sedg′y, *adj.*, abounding in, or like, sedge.

sedi′le, *n.*, a seat (*Lat.*); specifically a seat let into a church wall near an altar or in a chapter-house.

sedil′ia, *n.*, the pl. of sedile, seats for priests.

sed′iment, *n.*, a deposit at the bottom of a liquid; lees.

sedimen′tary, *adj.*, of the nature of sediment.

sedimenta′tion, *n.*, the precipitation or formation of sediment.

sedi′tion, *n.*, revolt, strife; opposition to a government with the object of its overthrow.

sedi′tionary, *adj.*, pert. or rel. to sedition.

sedi′tious, *adj.*, of the character of sedition; engaged in sedition.

sedi′tiously, *adv.*, in a seditious way.

sedi′tiousness, *n.*, the state of sedition.

se′dra, *n.*, one of the 54 sections of the Pentateuch.

seduce′, *v.t.*, to draw away; to tempt, esp. to corrupt a person sexually.

seduced′, *p.p.*, seduce.

seduce′ment, *n.*, *i.q.* seduction.

sedu′cer, *n.*, one who seduces.

sedu′cible, *adj.*, able to be seduced.

sedu′cing, *pr.p.*, seduce.

seduc′tion, *n.*, the act of seducing; enticement.

seduc′tive, *adj.*, attractive, enticing.

seduc′tively, *adv.*, in a seductive way.

sedu′lity, *n.*, industry, diligence.

sed′ulous, *adj.*, diligent, industrious, busy.

sed′ulously, *adv.*, in a sedulous way.

sed′ulousness, *n.*, the quality or state of being sedulous.

see, *n.*, the seat of a bishop's jurisdiction; *v.i.*, to perceive; to reflect, to consider; *v.t.*, to perceive with the eyes; to perceive with the mind; to understand; to visit; to attend upon.

seed, *n.*, the germ of a plant; semen; milt; progeny; *v.i.*, to yield seed; *v.t.*, to plant with seed; to extract the seeds from; in sport, to distinguish between strong and weak competitors.

seed′-bed, *n.*, ground specially prepared for the sowing of seeds.

seed′-bud, *n.*, the ovule of a seed.

seed′-cake, *n.*, a sweet cake which is flavoured with caraway seeds.

seed′ed, *adj.*, bearing seed; *p.p.*, seed.

seed′er, *n.*, a seed-drill; a spawning fish.

seed′ier, *adj.*, comp. of seedy.

seed′iest, *adj.*, super. of seedy.

seed′iness, *n.*, the state of being seedy.

seed′ing, *pr.p.*, seed.

seed′less, *adj.*, without seeds.

seed′ling, *n.*, a young plant grown or raised from seed.

seed′-pearl, *n.*, a very small pearl.

seeds′man, *n.*, one who sells seeds.

seed′-time, *n.*, the time for sowing.

seed′-vessel, *n.*, the pericarp.

seed′y, *adj.*, full of seed; running to seed; having the flavour of weeds growing among (grape) vines; shabby, mean; unwell (*colloq.*).

see′ing, *adj.*, intelligent; understanding; *pr.p.*, see.

seek, *v.i.*, to make search or inquiry; *v.t.*, to go in quest of; to look for; to aim at acquiring; to ask for.

seek′er, *n.*, one who seeks; an inquirer.

seek′ing, *pr.p.*, seek.

seel, *v.t.*, to close (eye of hawk) by sewing up lids; to dupe.

seem, *v.i.*, to appear; to present the appearance of being.

seemed, *p.p.*, seem.

seem′ing, *adj.*, apparent; not real or genuine; *pr.p.*, seem.

seem′ingly, *adv.*, apparently.

seem′lier, *adj.*, comp. of seemly.

seem′liest, *adj.*, super. of seemly.

seem′liness, *n.*, the quality of being seemly; grace, comeliness.

seem′ly, *adj.*, fitting, becoming, decorous.

seen, *p.p.*, see.

seep, *v.i.*, to ooze out; to percolate slowly.

see′page, *n.*, slow percolation.

seeped, *p.p.*, seep.

seep′ing, *pr.p.*, seep.

se′er, *n.*, one who sees.

seer, *n.*, a prophet; an Indian measure of weight and liquid.

seer′craft, *n.*, the craft of a prophet.

seer′-fish, *n.*, an Indian fish.

seer′hand, *n.*, a fine muslin.

seer′sucker, *n.*, crimped, textile material.

sees, *v.t. and i.*, 3rd per. sing., *pr.t.* tense.

see′-saw, *adj. and adv.*, with a backward and forward or upward and downward movement; *n.*, a children's game with a plank, balanced so that the players move up and down alternately; *v.i.*, to move up and down or backward and forward.

see′-sawed, *p.p.*, see-saw.

see′-sawing, *pr.p.*, see-saw.

seethe, *v.i.*, to be in a boiling state; to be hot; *v.t.*, to boil.

seethed, *p.p.*, seethe.

seeth′er, *n.,* one who, or that which, seethes; a pot for boiling.

seeth′ing, *adj.,* agitated; *pr.p.,* seethe.

see′-through, *adj.,* transparent.

seg′gar, *n., i.q.* saggar.

seg′ment, *n.,* a portion cut off or marked off.

segment′al, *adj.,* of the nature of a segment.

segment′ally, *adv.,* in a segmental way.

segmenta′tion, *n.,* the act of dividing into segments.

seg′mented, *adj.,* divided into segments.

se′gno, *n.,* the repeat sign (*It., mus.*).

seg′regable, *adj.,* capable of segregation.

seg′regate, *v.i.,* to separate; *v.t.,* to place apart; to isolate.

seg′regated, *p.p.,* segregate.

seg′regating, *pr.p.,* segregate.

segrega′tion, *n.,* the act or result of segregating.

segrega′tionist, *n.,* one who advocates racial or other segregation.

seg′regator, *n.,* an instrument for obtaining urine from each kidney separately.

Seid′litz, *adj.,* pert. or rel. to Seidlitz, in Bohemia, noted for its alkaline waters.

seign′eur, *n.,* a feudal, manorial lord. (Also *seignior.*)

seigneu′rial, *adj.,* pert. or rel. to a seigneur and a seigneurie.

seigneurie, *n.,* the fem. of seigneur.

seign′ior, *n., i.q.* seigneur.

sei′gniorage, *n.,* the prerogatives of a seigneur.

sei′gniory, *n.,* lordship; sovereign authority.

seigno′ral, *adj., i.q.* seigneurial.

seine, *n.,* a large fishing-net; *v.t.,* to fish with a seine.

seined, *p.p.,* seine.

sein′er, *n.,* a fisher with a seine.

sein′ing, *pr.p.,* seine.

seise, *v.t.,* to put in possession (*leg.*).

seis′in, *n.,* the possession of land freehold (*leg.*). (Also *seizin.*)

seis′mic, *adj.,* pert. or rel. to earthquakes.

seis′mogram, *n.,* the record given by a seismograph.

seis′mograph, *n.,* an instrument for recording the phenomena of earthquakes.

seismol′ogy, *n.,* the science of earthquakes.

seismom′eter, *n.,* an apparatus for measuring the length, etc., of a seismic wave.

seis′moscope, *n.,* a simple instrument for recording the details of earthquakes.

seiz′able, *adj.,* able to be seized.

seize, *v.t.,* to take hold or possession of; to grasp, to snatch; to perceive the meaning of.

seized, *p.p.,* seize.

seiz′er, *n.,* one who seizes.

sei′zin, *n., i.q.* seisin.

seiz′ing, *pr.p.,* seize.

sei′zure, *n.,* the act or result of seizing; a sudden attack of apoplexy; the sudden onset of illness.

sej′ant, *adj.,* sitting upright on the haunches (*her.*).

sek′os, *n.,* a sacred enclosure (*Gr.*).

selach′ian, *adj.,* shark-like; *n.,* a shark or dog-fish.

sela′dang, *n.,* the Malayan wild ox.

se′lah, *n.,* a supposed Hebrew musical direction.

selam′lik, *n.,* the part of a Mohammedan house assigned to the men (*Turk.*).

sel′dom, *adv.,* infrequently; rarely; not often.

select′, *adj.,* picked, chosen; exclusive; *v.t.,* to pick out.

select′ed, *p.p.,* select.

select′ing, *pr.p.,* select.

selec′tion, *n.,* the act of selecting; anything selected.

select′ive, *adj.,* particular and careful in choice.

select′ively, *adv.,* tending to select; exercising informed choice.

selectiv′ity, *n.,* the selective quality; the ability to choose or discriminate.

select′man, *n.,* one of three New England urban officials.

select′ness, *n.,* the quality of being select; exclusiveness.

select′or, *n.,* one who, or that which, selects.

sel′enate, *n.,* a selenic acid salt.

selen′ic, *adj.,* pert. or rel. to selenium.

sel′enide, *n.,* a compound of selenium and a radical or element.

selenif′erous, *adj.,* producing or containing selenium.

sel′enite, *n.,* a variety of gypsum; an acid gas of the nature of selenium; an inhabitant of the moon.

selenit′ic, *adj.,* pert. or rel. to selenite.

sele′nium, *n.,* a non-metallic element.

sele′nograph, *n.,* a drawing of the moon's surface.

selenog′rapher, *n.,* one who studies the moon's surface.

selenograph′ic, *adj.,* pert. or rel. to selenography.

selenog′raphy, *n.,* the study or mapping of the moon.

selenol′ogist, *n.,* one who specializes in selenology.

selenol′ogy, *n.,* that branch of astrology which deals with the moon.

self, *adj.,* identical, same; unmixed; *n.,* the personal individuality; a person or thing regarded from its individual point of view.

self′-aban′donment, *n.,* the forsaking of oneself.

self′-abase′ment, *n.,* the degradation or humiliation of oneself.

self′-absorbed′, *adj.,* concerned only with one's own affairs.

self′-absorp′tion, *n.,* the state of being self-absorbed.

self′-abuse′, *n.,* the abuse of one's own abilities.

self′-accusa′tion, *n.,* the accusation of oneself.

self′-act′ing, *adj.,* able to operate automatically.

self′-adhe′sive, *adj.,* (of labels, etc.) already prepared for affixing.

self'-adjust'ing, *adj.*, adjusting by oneself or itself.

self'-advert'isement, *n.*, the drawing of attention to oneself.

self'-aggran'dizement, *n.*, the exaltation of oneself.

self'-appoint'ed, *adj.*, chosen by oneself.

self'assert'ing, *adj.*, forward in making claims for oneself.

self'asser'tion, *n.*, the quality of being self-assertive.

self'asser'tive, *adj.*, *i.q.* self-asserting.

self'-assur'ance, *n.*, self-confidence.

self'-assured, *adj.*, confident of one's own ability.

self'-cen'tred, *adj.*, egotistic.

self'-clos'ing, *adj.*, closing automatically.

self'-col'our, *n.*, uniformity of colour.

self'-col'oured, *adj.*, pert. or rel. to self-colour.

self'-command', *n.*, the power of self-control.

self'-compla'cent, *adj.*, pleased with oneself.

self'-condemna'tion, *n.*, the blaming of oneself.

self'-condemned, *adj.*, blamed by oneself.

self'-con'fidence, *n.*, confidence in oneself.

self-con'fident, *adj.*, relying upon oneself; having confidence in one's ability.

self'-con'fidently, *adv.*, in a self-confident way.

self'-congratula'tion, *n.*, the act of expressing joy with oneself.

self-con'scious, *adj.*, thinking too much about other people's opinion of oneself.

self-con'sciously, *adv.*, in a self-conscious way.

self-con'sciousness, *n.*, the quality or state of being self-conscious.

self'-con'sequence, *n.*, self-importance.

self'-contained', *adj.*, calm; not communicative; complete in itself.

self'-content', *n.*, the state of being satisfied with oneself or one's position.

self'-control', *n.*, command over oneself.

self'-crit'icism, *n.*, the finding of fault in oneself or one's own work.

self'-decep'tion, *n.*, deception arising from one's own mistake.

self'-defence', *n.*, the protection of oneself; the art of protecting oneself against physical attack.

self'-delu'sion, *n.*, the deluding of oneself.

self'-deni'al, *n.*, unselfishness; the denying of oneself.

self'-determina'tion, *n.*, the act of deciding for oneself; free will.

self'-dis'cipline, *n.*, the strict control of oneself.

self'-drive, *adj.*, driven by the hirer, esp. motor vehicles.

self'-ed'ucated, *adj.*, taught by oneself.

self'efface'ment, *n.*, the withdrawal of oneself from notice.

self'-effac'ing, *adj.*, pert. or rel. to self-effacement.

self'-elec'ted, *adj.*, elected by oneself, or itself, from its own members.

self'-employed', *adj.*, working for oneself.

self-esteem', *n.*, a good opinion of oneself.

self'-ev'ident, *adj.*, obvious; needing no outside proof.

self'-evidently, *adv.*, in a self-evident manner.

self'-explan'atory, *adj.*, needing no explanation.

self'-expre'ssion, *n.*, the expression of one's personality and ideas.

self'-govern'ing, *adj.*, autonomic.

self-gov'ernment, *n.*, autonomy.

self-help', *n.*, independence.

self'hood, *n.*, one's personality or identity.

self'-import'ance, *n.*, the holding of an excessive opinion of oneself.

self'-import'ant, *adj.*, pert. or rel. to self-importance.

self'-imposed', *adj.*, voluntarily taken upon oneself.

self'-indul'gence, *n.*, the excessive satisfaction of one's own pleasures.

self'-indul'gent, *adj.*, satisfying one's own pleasures.

self'-inflict'ed, *adj.*, imposed by, or on, oneself.

self'-insurance, *n.*, the creation of a fund to offset one's own losses.

self-in'terest, *n.*, one's own interest.

self-in'terested, *adj.*, with an eye to one's own interest and benefit.

self'-invi'ted, *adj.*, present without invitation.

self'ish, *adj.*, loving self and disregarding others.

self'ishly, *adv.*, in a selfish way.

self'ishness, *n.*, the quality or state of being selfish.

self'less, *adj.*, unselfish.

self'lessness, *n.*, unselfishness.

self'-light'ing, *adj.*, lighting or igniting automatically.

self'-lock'ing, *adj.*, fastening or securing without external intervention.

self-love', *n.*, love of self.

self-made', *adj.*, made by one's own efforts.

self'-neglect', *n.*, the lack of care of oneself.

self'-opin'ionated, *adj.*, stubbornly following one's own opinion.

self'-pity', *n.*, a feeling of sorrow for one's own situation.

self'-por'trait, *n.*, a drawing or picture of oneself, produced or painted by oneself.

self-possessed', *adj.*, with perfect command of oneself.

self-posses'sion, *n.*, command of oneself.

self'-praise', *n.*, the commendation of self.

self'-preserva'tion, *n.*, the instinctive avoidance of death or injury.

self'-propelled, *adj.*, motivated from within.

self'-protec'tion, *n.*, self-defence.

self'-rais'ing, *adj.*, requiring no additional rising agent (esp. of flour).

self'-record'ing, *adj.*, making its own records.

self'-reg'ulating, *adj.*, controlling itself.

self'-reli'ance, *n.,* reliance on one's own strength and abilities.

self-reli'ant, *adj.,* relying on one's own strength.

self-rely'ing, *adj., i.q.* self-reliant.

self'-reproach', *n.,* the voice of conscience.

self'-respect', *n.,* regard for, and pride in, one's person or position.

self'-restraint', *n., i.q.* self-control.

self'-right'eous, *adj.,* righteous in one's own eyes; pharisaical.

self'-right'eousness, *n.,* the quality or state of being self-righteous.

self-sac'rifice, *n.,* the surrendering of one's own private interests and wishes for the benefit of others.

self'-sac'rificing, *adj.,* pert. or rel. to self-sacrifice.

self'-same, *adj.,* the very same.

self'-satisfac'tion, *n.,* conceit.

self-sat'isfied, *adj.,* conceited.

self'-satisfy'ing, *adj., i.q.* self-satisfied.

self'-service', *adj.* and *n.,* helping oneself.

self'-sown', *adj.,* sown naturally without human intervention.

self'-start'er, *n.,* the electrical starter for a car, etc.

self'-start'ing, *adj.,* able to start by itself.

self'-ster'ile, *adj.,* unable to reproduce itself.

self'-styled', *adj.,* so-called; pretended.

self'-suffi'ciency, *n.,* the quality or state of being independent of outside help.

self-suffi'cient, *adj.,* pert. or rel. to self-sufficiency.

self'-support'ing, *adj.,* able to support oneself or itself.

self'-taught', *adj., i.q.* self-educated.

self'-tor'ture, *n.,* self-inflicted pain or suffering.

self-will', *n.,* obstinacy; wilfulness.

self-willed', *adj.,* obstinate; following one's own will exclusively.

self'-wind'ing, *adj.,* automatically wound, by movement or electrically, esp. timepieces.

self'-wor'ship, *n.,* idolizing of oneself.

sell, *n.,* the disappointment caused by falsely-roused anticipation (*slang*); *v.i.,* to be sold; *v.t.,* to barter for a consideration; to betray; to disappoint by not doing what was expected or promised (*slang*).

sell'er, *n.,* one who sells.

sell'ing, *pr.p.,* sell.

Sel'lotape, *n.,* an adhesive tape; *v.t.,* to stick with adhesive tape.

sel'lotaped, *p.p.,* sellotape.

sellotap'ing, *pr.p.,* sellotape.

sell'zogene, *n.,* an apparatus for making aerated waters.

selt'zer, *n.,* medicinal mineral water.

sel'vage, *n.,* the edge of woven fabric; *v.t.,* to finish with a selvage, i.e. a prepared edge.

sel'vaged, *adj.,* having a selvage; *p.p.,* selvage.

sel'vagee, *n.,* a strap or ring of rope yarns.

sel'vedge, *n., i.q.* selvage.

sel'vedged, *adj.* and *p.p., i.q.* selvaged.

selves, *n.,* the pl. of self.

seman'tic, *adj.,* relating to meaning and the associations of words in language.

seman'tics, *n. pl.,* the study of meanings and associations of words.

sem'aphore, *n.,* an apparatus for signalling, having movable arms, discs, etc.

semaphor'ic, *adj.,* pert. or rel. to a semaphore.

semasiol'ogy, *n.,* the scientific study of words.

semat'ic, *adj.,* significant (*biol.*).

sematol'ogy, *n.,* the study of signs or characters.

sem'blance, *adj.,* likeness; *n.,* the outward appearance; something imaginary.

semé(e), *adj.,* covered with small (heraldic) bearings.

semeiog'raphy, *n.,* the science of morbid symptoms.

semeiolog'ical, *adj.,* pert. or rel. to semeiology.

semeiol'ogy, *n.,* that department of

pathology that relates to symptoms.

semeiot'ic, *adj.,* symptomatic.

sem'en, *n.,* male sperms.

semes'ter, *n.,* a six months' academic course; a division of the academic year (*Amer.*).

semes'tral, *adj.,* pert. or rel. to a semester.

semi-an'nual, *adj.,* half-yearly.

sem'i-automatic, *adj.,* partly automatic.

sem'ibreve, *n.,* a musical note, half the length of a breve.

sem'i-centen'nial, *adj.,* occurring every fifty years.

sem'icircle, *n.,* a half-circle.

semicir'cular, *adj.,* in the form of a half-circle.

semico'lon, *n.,* a punctuation mark (;), ranking in importance between a comma and a full-stop.

semico'ma, *n.,* a condition close to coma.

semico'matose, *adj.,* in a semicoma.

semiconduc'tor, *n.,* any substance which partly, or in some conditions, conducts electrically.

semi-con'scious, *adj.,* barely conscious.

semi-detached', *adj.,* joined at one side, free on the other (esp. of buildings).

semi-diam'eter, *n.,* a half-diameter.

sem'i-diur'nal, *adj.,* taking twelve hours to complete.

semi-documen'tary, *n.,* a film with factual background but an invented plot.

sem'i-domes'ticated, *adj.,* only partly domesticated or tamed.

sem'i-dou'ble, *adj.,* having the outer flowers as petals while the inner ones are perfect.

semifi'nal, *n.,* the contest before the final one.

semifi'nalist, *n.,* one who takes part in a semi-final.

sem'i-independ'ent, *adj.,* only partly independent.

sem'i-li'quid, *adj.,* only half liquid.

semilu'nar, *adj.,* crescent-shaped.

sem'inal, adj., pert. or rel. to seed and reproduction; imaginative, creative.

sem'inally, adv., in a seminal way.

sem'inar, n., a discussion group; a short, intensive course.

sem'inarist, n., a member of a seminary.

sem'inary, n., a place of education.

semina'tion, n., seeding.

seminif'erous, adj., producing seed.

seminif'ic, adj., i.q. seminiferous.

semi-nude', adj., partly naked.

sem'i-offi'cial, adj., only partly official.

sem'i-opaque', adj., almost opaque.

sem'iped, n., a half-foot.

sem'i-prec'ious, adj., (of gemstones) not as valuable as real gems.

sem'iquaver, n., a musical note, half the value of a quaver.

sem'i-skilled', adj., partly skilled.

Se'mite, n., one bel. to a race descended from Shem, as the Hebrews.

semit'ic, adj., pert. or rel. to the Semites.

sem'itism, n., the advocacy of semitic interests.

sem'itone, n., a half tone interval (mus.).

semitranspa'rency, n., the state of being partly transparent.

semitranspa'rent, adj., partly transparent.

sem'i-trop'ical, adj., subtropical.

semivow'el, n., a sound half vowel and half consonant (as w and y).

sem'i-week'ly, adj., occurring twice each week.

semoli'na, n., what remains of wheat when the flour has been bolted, used in puddings, etc.

sempervi'rent, adj., evergreen.

sempiter'nal, adj., everlasting.

sem'pre, adv., always, throughout (It.).

sen'ate, n., the supreme council at Rome; the upper legislative chamber in modern states; the governing body of some universities.

sen'ate-house, n., the meeting-place of a senate.

sen'ator, n., a member of a senate.

senato'rial, adj., pert. or rel. to a senate and senators.

senato'rially, adv., in a senatorial way.

sen'atorship, n., the office or rank of a senator.

send, n., a forward impulse; v.i., to dispatch a messenger; v.t., to dispatch, to dismiss; to order to go; to throw; to grant.

sen'dal, n., silken fabric.

send'er, n., one who sends.

send'ing, pr.p., send.

sen'ega, n., an expectorant drug made from snakeroot.

senes'cence, n., the state of growing old.

senes'cent, adj., growing old.

sen'eschal, n., a steward in a great establishment.

sen'green, n., the houseleek.

se'nile, adj., decaying with age.

senil'ity, n., the state of being senile; infirm old age.

se'nior, adj., older; superior in age or standing; n., one who is older, or superior on account of age or standing.

senior'ity, n., the state of being senior.

sen'na, n., an aperient drug, being the dried leaves of the cassia.

senn'et, n., a signal call on a trumpet.

sen'night, n., a week.

sen'nit, n., braided cord.

senoc'ular, adj., with six eyes.

señor', n., the Spanish equivalent of Sir or Mr.

seño'ra, n., the fem. of señor.

señori'ta, n., the Spanish equivalent of Miss.

sen'sate, adj., apprehended by the senses; perceptible to the senses.

sensa'tion, n., perception by the senses; feeling; a condition of excitement or interest.

sensa'tional, adj., pert. or rel. to sensation; exciting, thrilling.

sensa'tionalism, n., a pandering to excitement; the theory that ideas are but sensations transformed.

sensa'tionalist, adj., of a sensational character; n., a believer in sensationalism.

sensa'tionally, adv., in a sensational way.

sensa'tionary, adj., i.q. sensational.

sense, n., the perception of objects; means by which we receive information of the external world; understanding; meaning.

sense'less, adj., unable to feel; unconscious; silly; contrary to reason.

sense'lessly, adv., in a senseless fashion.

sense'lessness, n., the quality or state of being senseless.

sensibil'ity, n., the quality or state of being sensible; the ability to be sensitive; fine feeling.

sen'sible, adj., apprehended by the senses; of good judgment; reasonable.

sen'sibly, adv., judiciously, reasonably; perceptibly.

sensif'erous, adj., conveying sense impressions.

sensif'ic, adj., causing sensation.

sen'sitive, adj., readily perceptive of objects; easily affected by the acts, words and attitude of others; responsive to external impressions.

sen'sitively, adv., in a sensitive way.

sen'sitiveness, n., the quality or state of being sensitive.

sen'sitize, v.t., to make sensitive, esp. to cause to be acted upon by the sun's rays.

sen'sitized, p.p., sensitize.

sen'sitizing, pr.p., sensitize.

sensitom'eter, n., an instrument which tests the sensitiveness of plates and films to light.

senso'rial, adj., pert. or rel. to the sensorium.

senso'rium, n., the brain.

sen'sory, *adj.*, *i.q.* sensorial; pert. or rel. to the senses.

sen'sual, *adj.*, controlled by the senses and bodily appetites; licentious; carnal.

sen'sualism, *n.*, sensual conduct.

sen'sualist, *n.*, a sensual person.

sensual'ity, *n.*, *i.q.* sensualism.

sen'sualize, *v.t.*, to make sensual.

sen'sualized, *p.p.*, sensualize.

sen'sualizing, *pr.p.*, sensualize.

sen'sually, *adv.*, in a sensual way.

sen'suous, *adj.*, pert. or rel. to the senses; pert. or rel. to the objects of sense.

sen'suously, *adv.*, in a sensuous way.

sen'suousness, *n.*, the quality or state of being sensuous.

sent, *p.p.*, send.

sen'tence, *n.*, judgment; meaning; the judgment of a court; a complete verbal expression of a thought; *v.t.*, to condemn from the judicial bench.

sen'tenced, *p.p.*, sentence.

sen'tencing, *pr.p.*, sentence.

senten'tial, *adj.*, pert. or rel. to a sentence.

senten'tious, *adj.*, composed of sentences; full of maxims; axiomatic; moralizing pompously.

senten'tiously, *adv.*, in a sententious style.

senten'tiousness, *n.*, the quality or state of being sententious.

sen'tience, *n.*, *i.q.* sentiency.

sen'tiency, *n.*, the quality or state of being sentient.

sen'tient, *adj.*, capable of, or in fact, feeling and perceiving.

sen'timent, *n.*, a thought influenced by emotion; an opinion; common opinion; a toast.

sentimen'tal, *adj.*, emotional; led by emotion rather than by reason; inclined to the romantic.

sentimen'talism, *n.*, a tendency to the romantic and emotional.

sentimen'talist, *n.*, one who thinks, or pretends to think, sentimentally.

sentimental'ity, *n.*, *i.q.* sentimentalism.

sentimen'talize, *v.i.*, to act or think in a sentimental way.

sentimen'talized, *p.p.*, sentimentalize.

sentimen'talizing, *pr.p.*, sentimentalize.

sentimen'tally, *n.*, in a sentimental way.

sen'tinel, *n.*, one on guard, esp. on military guard; *v.t.*, to guard; to appoint a sentinel for.

sen'try, *n.*, a sentinel's post and duty; a sentinel.

sen'try-box, *n.*, a sentry's shelter.

sen'try-go, *n.*, the sentry's job of pacing to and fro.

sen'za, *prep.*, without strict time (*It.*, *mus.*).

sep'al, *n.*, a division of a calyx (*bot.*).

sep'aloid, *adj.*, like a sepal.

separabil'ity, *n.*, the quality or state of being separable.

sep'arable, *adj.*, able to be parted or separated.

sep'arate, *adj.*, parted, divided, distinct.

sep'arate, *v.i.*, to disperse; to come apart; *v.t.*, to divide; to part; to set apart.

sep'arated, *p.p.*, separate.

sep'arately, *adv.*, apart; individually; in a separate way.

sep'arateness, *n.*, the quality or state of being separate.

sep'arates, *n. pl.*, individual items as blouse, jumper and skirt when worn together.

sep'arating, *pr.p.*, separate.

separa'tion, *n.*, the act of separating; the state of being separate.

sep'aratism, *n.*, the principles of the separatists.

sep'aratist, *n.*, one who advocates separation; specifically, one who has parted from the Church.

sep'arative, *adj.*, disjunctive.

sep'arator, *n.*, one who, or that which, separates.

sep'aratory, *adj.*, tending to separate; *n.*, an instrument used in surgery; an apparatus for the chemical separation of liquors.

se'pia, *adj.*, of the colour of sepia; drawn in sepia; *n.*, a brown pigment obtained from the cuttle-fish.

se'poy, *n.*, an Indian native soldier.

sep'sis, *n.* blood-poisoning (*med.*).

sept, *adj.*, *i.q.* septangular; *n.*, a tribe, a part of a clan.

sep'ta, *n. pl.*, of septum (*Lat.*).

sep'tal, *adj.*, pert. or rel. to septum or septa.

septan'gular, *adj.*, having seven angles. (Also *sept.*)

septa'ria, *n. pl.*, geological nodules.

sep'tate, *adj.*, divided by septa.

septcente'nary, *n.*, the 700th anniversary.

Septem'ber, *n.*, the ninth month.

Septem'brist, *n.*, a French Revolutionist who took part in the massacre of Sept. 3, 1792.

septem'vir, *n.*, one of a commission of seven in ancient Rome. (In pl., *septemviri.*, *Lat.*)

sep'tenary, *adj.*, pert. or rel. to, or lasting for, seven years.

sep'tenate, *adj.*, growing in sevens, having seven divisions (*bot.*).

septenn'ate, *n.*, a period of seven years.

septen'nial, *adj.*, recurring every seven years; lasting seven years.

septen'trional, *adj.*, pert. or rel. to the north.

septet'(te), *n.*, a musical piece for seven instruments.

sept'foil, *n.*, the tormentil (*bot.*); an architectural ornament resembling seven leaves.

sep'tic, *adj.*, causing putrefaction; *n.*, that which causes putrefaction.

septicae'mia, *n.*, putrefaction in the blood; blood-poisoning.

sep'tical, *adj.*, putrefying.

sep'ticidal, *adj.*, splitting through septa.

septic'ity, *n.*, a septic condition.

septifa'rious, *adj.*, in seven different ways.

septif'erous, *adj.*, conveying septic poison.

septilat'eral, *adj.*, seven-sided.

septill'ion, *n.*, the seventh power of a million.

sep'timal, *adj.*, pert. or rel., to number seven.

sep'time, *n.*, a fencing position.

septin'sular, *adj.*, having seven islands.

septuagena'rian, *adj.*, seventy years old; *n.*, a person seventy years of age.

septuage'nary, *adj.*, composed of seventy; *n.*, the number 70.

Septuages'ima, *n.*, the name of the third Sunday (and its week) before Lent.

Sep'tuagint, *n.*, the Greek version of the Old Testament scriptures, named from the 70 translators supposedly employed.

sep'tum, *n.*, a barrier; a partition; the membranous partition between organs or cavities. (In pl., *septa*, *Lat.*)

sep'tuple, *adj.*, sevenfold.

sepul'chral, *adj.*, pert. or rel. to sepulchres or tombs; hollow-sounding.

sep'ulchre, *n.*, a tomb, a grave; *v.t.*, to bury.

sep'ulture, *n.*, burial.

sequa'cious, *adj.*, following.

sequac'ity, *n.*, the quality or state of being sequacious.

se'quel, *n.*, something that follows as a consequence; a continuation to a story or incident.

seque'la, *n.*, a morbid state consequent on another (*Lat.*).

se'quence, *n.*, successive order; a series; cards of successive values in the same suit; a musical phrase repeated at another pitch; a hymn.

se'quent, *adj.*, following in sequence; *n.*, a sequence.

sequen'tial, *adj.*, in succession.

sequen'tially, *adv.*, in succession.

seques'ter, *v.i.*, to forgo a wife's claim on her husband's estate; *v.t.*, to take away temporarily; to seclude.

seques'tered, *adj.*, remote, secluded, shut off; *p.p.*, sequester.

seques'tering, *pr.p.*, sequester.

seques'trate, *v.t.*, to withhold for a time the income of a benefice from the incumbent; to take under state control a debtor's property for the benefit of the creditors.

seques'trated, *p.p.*, sequestrate.

seques'trating, *pr.p.*, sequestrate.

sequestra'tion, *n.*, the act or effect of sequestrating.

se'questrator, *n.*, one who sequesters property.

sequestrot'omy, *n.*, the study of bone structure.

seques'trum, *n.*, a section of dead bone.

se'quin, *n.*, an old Venetian gold coin; a glittering spangle.

sequoi'a, *n.*, the Californian redwood tree.

sérac', *n.*, a pinnacle of glacial ice; a Swiss cheese (*Fr.*).

sera'glio, *n.*, a harem.

sera'i, *n.*, an Eastern inn.

seralbu'men, *n.*, albumen in the blood.

serang', *n.*, an East-Indian boatswain.

sera'pe, *n.*, shawl or blanket work by South Americans.

ser'aph, *n.*, an angelic being of the highest rank.

seraph'ic, *adj.*, pert. or rel. to, or resembling, a seraph; blissful.

seraph'ically, *adv.*, like a seraph.

ser'aphim, *n. pl.*, seraphs.

ser'aphine, *n.*, a small instrument of the harmonium type.

seraskier', *n.*, a high military authority in the Turkish army.

Ser'bian, *adj.*, *i.q.* Servian.

Serbo'nian, *adj.*, pert. or rel. to Serbonis, an Egyptian bog that swallowed everything up.

sere, *adj.* and *v.t.*, *i.q.* sear.

serenade', *n.*, outdoor evening music; a song sung by a lover at the window of his loved one; *v.t.*, to honour with a serenade.

serena'ded, *p.p.*, serenade.

serena'der, *n.*, one who serenades.

serena'ding, *pr.p.*, serenade.

serena'ta, *n.*, a cantata to be performed in the open air; a form of symphony (*It.*).

serendip'ity, *n.*, the ability to make accidentally fortuitous discovery whilst engaged in other unrelated activity.

serene', *adj.*, calm, unruffled.

serene'ly, *adv.*, calmly.

serene'ness, *n.*, the quality or state of being serene. (Also *serenity*.)

seren'ity, *n.*, *i.q.* sereneness.

serf, *n.*, a slave attached to the land; a villein.

serf'dom, *n.*, the state of being a serf.

serge, *n.*, a rough-surfaced, woollen fabric (*Fr.*).

ser'geancy, *n.*, a sergeant's office.

ser'geant, *n.*, a non-commissioned military officer.

ser'geantcy, *n.*, *i.q.* sergeancy.

ser'geant-ma'jor, *n.*, a warrant officer.

ser'geantship, *n.*, *i.q.* sergeancy.

sergette', *n.*, thin serge.

se'rial, *adj.*, bel. to a series; *n.*, a story appearing in parts.

se'rialize, *v.t.*, to issue in parts.

se'rialized, *adj.*, issued in parts; *p.p.*, serialize.

se'rializing, *pr.p.*, serialize.

se'rially, *adv.*, in part publication.

se'riate, *adj.*, arranged in order.

se'riate, *v.t.*, to arrange in order.

seria'tim, *adv.*, in order (*Lat.*).

seri'ceous, *adj.*, silky (*bot.*).

sericiculture, *n.*, *i.q.* sericulture.

se′riculture, n., silkworm breeding; raw silk production. (Also sericiculture.)

se′ricul′turist, n., a silkworm breeder.

seriem′a, n., a Brazilian heron-type bird.

se′ries, n., a connected or related order; succession.

se′rif, n., the little stroke projecting from the main strokes of an alphabetical character. (Also ceriph.)

ser′in, n., a finch.

serinette′, n., a musical box; a small barrelorgan; a gadget used to teach birds to sing.

sering′a, n., the Brazilian rubber tree.

serio-com′ic, adj., combining grave and comic.

se′rious, adj., grave, earnest.

se′riously, adv., in a serious way.

se′riousness, n., the quality or state of being serious.

ser′jeant, n., a member of a now extinct order of serjeants-at-law, from whom the judges were selected.

ser′jeanty, n., a mode of legal tenure.

ser′mon, n., a homily or discourse, usually on a text.

ser′monize, v.i., to preach; v.t., to address.

ser′monized, p.p., sermonize.

ser′monizer, n., one who sermonizes.

ser′monizing, pr.p., sermonize.

serol′ogy, n., the study of serums.

seron′, n., a crate for dried fruits. (Also seroon.)

seros′ity, n., the quality or state of being serous; the thin exudation from serum.

ser′otine, n., a reddishcoloured bat.

serot′inous, adj., seasonably late (bot.).

se′rous, adj., pert. or rel. to serum.

ser′pent, n., a reptile of the snake order; a musical instrument of brass; a firework; anyone of snake-like qualities.

serpen′tiform, adj., shaped like a snake.

ser′pentine, adj., pert. or rel. to, or resembling, a snake in form or movement; n., a variety of rock formation.

ser′pentry, n., a place of serpents.

serpi′ginous, adj., suffering from herpes; creeping.

serpi′go, n., herpes (med.).

serp′ula, n., a marine worm.

ser′ra, n., a serrated organ, structure or edge (anat., bot.).

se′rrate′, v.t., to notch.

ser′rate, adj., like a saw; with toothed edge.

ser′rated, adj., i.q. serrate; p.p., serrate.

serra′tion, n., the state of being serrated; a saw-like edge.

ser′rature, n., sawlike edging; a serrated structure.

ser′refile, n. pl., the supporting line of N.C.O′s in rear (mil.).

ser′ried, adj., in close order; packed.

ser′rulate, adj., finely notched.

serrula′tion, n., an arrangement of fine notches.

se′rum, n., the fluid secretion of serous membranes; a fluid to prevent or treat disease.

serv′al, n., the African tiger-cat.

serv′ant, n., one who serves in any capacity.

serve, v.i., to be a servant; to fit; to hold an office; v.t., to be the servant of; to worship; to wait upon; to deliver (food) to; to conduce to; to work on behalf of others.

served, p.p., serve.

serv′er, n., one who serves, esp. one who assists the priest at the altar.

Ser′vian, adj., pert. or rel. to Servia (or Serbia, now a part of Yugo-Slavia); n., a native of S. (Also Serbian.)

serv′ice, n., the status or occupation of a servant; a kind office; naval, military, and air force employ; an outfit of plate, china or crockery; regular traffic between place and place; waiting at table; waiters collectively; a religious office; a musical setting; v.t., to adjust and maintain.

serv′iceable, adj., handy, convenient.

serv′iceableness, n., the quality of being serviceable.

serv′iceably, adv., in a serviceable manner.

serv′iced, p.p., service.

serv′iceman, n., a member of the armed forces.

serv′icing, pr.p., service.

serviette′, n., a tablenapkin (Fr.).

serv′ile, adj., slavish; mean; obsequious.

serv′ilely, adv., in a servile way.

servil′ity, n., the quality or state of being servile.

serv′ing, pr.p., serve.

serv′ing-man, n., a manservant.

serv′itor, n., a servant, a retainer; formerly the name for certain undergraduates at Oxford who performed some menial offices in return for their keep.

serv′itorship, n., the office of a servitor.

serv′itude, n., the state of slavery.

serv′o-mech′anism, n., a power-assisted device for controlling and reinforcing movement (e.g. brakes).

serv′o-mot′or, n., an auxiliary (marine) motor.

ses′ame, n., an oil-yielding plant of Southern Asia.

ses′amoid, adj., like sesame.

ses′amum, n., i.q. sesame.

ses′eli, n., a perennial plant.

sesquial′tera, n., an organ-stop of several ranks.

sesquial′teral, adj., being one-half more.

sesquidu′plicate, adj., in the ratio of 2½ to 1.

sesquip′edal, adj., i.q. sesquipedalian.

sesquipeda′lian, adj., a foot and a half long; expressed in long words.

ses'quitone, *n.*, the interval of a minor third (*mus.*).

sess, *n.*, *i.q.* cess.

ses'sile, *adj.*, not having a footstalk or peduncle (*bot., zool.*).

ses'sion, *n.*, the act of sitting; a meeting; a period of being assembled (as a Session of Parliament). In the pl. the sittings of magistrates.

ses'sional, *adj.*, pert. or rel. to a session.

ses'sionally, *adv.*, in a sessional way.

ses'terce, *n.*, an old Roman coin of small value.

sester'tium, *n.*, ancient Roman money.

sestet(te'), *n.*, a composition for six voices or instruments; the last six lines of the second section of a sonnet. (Also *sextet.*)

sesti'nn, *n.*, a form of poem (*It.*).

Sesu'to, *n.*, the language of the African country Botswana.

set, *adj.*, fixed, regular; resolute; prescribed; *n.*, the act of setting; a tendency or direction; the sinking of a heavenly body; a clique; a group; a number of games in lawn tennis; *v.i.*, to decline (said of the heavenly bodies); to become fixed or congealed; to take a certain direction; *v.t.*, to fix, place or plant; to spread (sails); to give a start to; to adjust; to appoint; to arrange printer's type.

se'ta, *n.*, a bristle (*Lat.*).

seta'ceous, *adj.*, bristly.

set'back, *n.*, a rebuff; a disappointment; a check.

setif'erous, *adj.*, having bristles.

se'tiform, *adj.*, like a bristle.

set'-off, *n.*, a counterbalance; a *quid pro quo.*

se'ton, *n.*, a surgical contrivance for keeping a sore open.

se'tose, *adj.*, bristly.

se'tous, *adj.*, *i.q.* setose.

setsquare, *n.*, a draughtsman's appliance made of wood, metal or plastic.

sett, *n.*, mines leased in a number; wood or metal laid on the top of a pile too short for the hammer to reach it otherwise; a stone for roadmaking.

settee', *n.*, a lounge-seat; a Mediterranean boat.

set'ter, *n.*, one who, or that which, sets; a breed of sporting dog.

set'terwort, *n.*, a plant of the Helleborus genus.

set'ting, *n.*, the act of setting; environment; the mount of a jewel.; *pr.p.*, set.

set'tle, *n.*, a high-backed bench with arms; *v.i.*, to steady down and remain at rest; to alight; to sink to the bottom; to pay an account; to colonize; to set up a home with a wife; *v.t.*, to make to remain at rest; to establish; to make to sink; to adjudicate; to compose; to discharge (a debt); to colonize.

set'tled, *p.p.*, settle.

set'tlement, *n.*, the act or effect of settling; a composition or agreement; a colony; money legally assigned to a wife.

set'tler, *n.*, a colonist; a decisive act or occurrence.

set'tling, *pr.p.*, settle.

set'tlor, *n.*, one who settles an estate.

set'-to, *n.*, a contest; a bout of fencing, boxing, etc.; a violent, noisy discussion.

set'wall, *n.*, the valerian.

sev'en, *adj.*, containing seven persons or things; *n.*, a cardinal number = 6 + 1; the symbol 7.

sev'enfold, *adj.*, seven times over.

sev'ennight, *n.*, *i.q.* sennight (a week).

sevenpence, *n.*, the value of seven pence.

sevenpenny, *adj.*, worth seven pence.

seventeen, *adj.*, containing seven + ten; *n.*, a cardinal number = 7 + 10; the symbol 17.

seventeenth, *adj.*, the next after the sixteenth; *n.*, the ordinal of seventeen.

sev'enth, *adj.*, the next after the sixth; *n.*, the ordinal of seven.

sev'enthly, *adv.*, in the seventh place.

sev'entieth, *adj.*, the next after the sixty-ninth; *n.*, the ordinal of seventy.

sev'enty, *adj.*, containing seven × ten persons or things; *n.*, the cardinal number next after 69 = 7 × 10; in pl., one of the years in the seventh decade.

Sev'enty, The, *n. pl.*, the traditional 70 translators of the Septuagint, often referred to as LXX.

sev'er, *v.i.*, to come apart; *v.t.*, to cut; to part; to divide.

sev'erable, *adj.*, capable of being severed.

sev'eral, *adj.*, separate, distinct; composed of more than two but only a few.

sev'erally, *adv.*, separately.

sev'eralty, *n.*, the state of being several.

sev'erance, *n.*, the act of severing; the state of being severed.

severe', *adj.*, harsh; stern; inclement; hard to bear; extremely critical.

sev'ered, *p.p.*, sever.

severe'ly, *adv.*, in a severe way.

seve'rer, *adj.*, *comp.* of severe.

seve'rest, *adj.*, *super.* of severe.

sev'ering, *pr.p.*, sever.

sever'ity, *n.*, harshness, strictness; inclemency; rigour.

sev'ery, *n.*, one of the compartments or divisions of a vaulted roof (*archit.*).

sew, *v.i.*, to use a needle and thread; *v.t.*, to stitch together with a needle and thread.

sew'age, *n.*, waste matter discharged into a sewer.

sewed, *p.p.*, sew.

sew'er, *n.*, one who sews.

sew'er, *n.*, a drain; an attendant at a banquet who tasted dishes, placed guests, etc.

sew'erage, n., the system of sewers; drainage.

sew'ing, n., the act of sewing; work done with a thread and needle; pr.p., sew.

sew'ing-machine, n., a machine that sews.

sewn, p.p., sew.

sex, n., the physical and other characteristics differentiating male or female; the physical relationships between male and female.

sexagena'rian, adj., sixty years old; n., a person of that age.

sexag'enary, adj., pert. or rel. to the number sixty.

Sexages'ima, n., the second Sunday before Lent.

sexan'gular, adj., having six angles.

sex'-appeal, n., attractiveness due to sex differences.

sexen'nial, adj., occurring every six years; lasting six years.

sex'-kitten, n., a young woman having sex-appeal.

sex'less, adj., of no sex.

sexol'ogy, n., branch of biology dealing with sex.

Sext, n., the Breviary office for midday (the sixth hour) (Lat.).

sex'tain, n., a stanza containing six lines.

sex'tan, adj., happening every sixth day.

sex'tant, n., the one-sixth of a circle; a mathematical instrument for finding angular distances between objects, especially in navigation.

sextet', n., i.q. sestet.

sex'tile, adj., pert. or rel. to the position of planets at a distance of 60 degrees from each other.

sextil'lion, n., a million raised to the sixth power.

sex'to, n., a book formed by folding sheets in six.

sextode'cimo, n., a sheet of paper folded in 16 leaves.

sex'ton, n., originally a sacristan; later a gravedigger and lower official of a church.

sex'toness, n., the fem. of sexton, whose duties are to look after the church.

sex'tuple, adj., six times multiplied.

sex'ual, adj., pert. or rel. to sex and the relations between the sexes.

sex'ualist, n., one who is interested in sex problems.

sexual'ity, n., the quality or state of being sexual.

sex'ualize, v.t., to attribute to sex.

sex'ually, adv., in relation to the sexes.

sex'y, adj., arousing sex feelings.

sforzan'do, adv., with sudden emphasis; forcefully (It., mus.).

sforza'to, adv., forcibly, emphatically (It., mus.).

sfuma'to, adj., misty in appearance; blurred in outline (It.).

sgraffi'to, adj., painted in lines cut through a white overlaid surface down to a dark stucco beneath (It.).

shab, n., i.q. scab.

shab'bier, adj., comp. of shabby.

shab'biest, adj., super. of shabby.

shab'bily, adv., in a mean, shabby way.

shab'biness, n., the quality or state of being shabby.

shab'by, adj., with a worn-out appearance; mean and unworthy.

shab'rack, n., a cavalry officer's horse-covering.

shack, n., the right of pasturage in the winter; a tramp; a log cabin; any roughly constructed small building.

shack'le, n., a fetter; the bar of a padlock; v.t., to fetter; to impede.

shack'led, p.p., shackle.

shack'les, n., the pl. of shackle.

shack'ling, pr.p., shackle.

shad, n., a small herring fish.

shad'dock, n., an orange-like fruit.

shade, n., the darkened state resulting from the sun's rays being screened off; a gradation of colour; a ghost; v.t., to screen from heat or light; to darken parts of a map, drawing, etc.

sha'ded, p.p., shade.

shades, n. pl., wine vaults.

sha'dier, adj., comp. of shady.

sha'diest, adj., super. of shady.

sha'dily, adv., in a shady way.

sha'diness, n., the quality or state of being shady.

sha'ding, n., the act of shading; the act of depicting the effect of light and shade; pr.p., shade.

shadoof', n., an Egyptian water bucket and pole used in irrigation.

shad'ow, n., shade that more or less resembles the form of the object that casts it; a dark part of a painting, drawing, etc.; safety; a close attendant; a wasted body; v.t., to darken; to pursue closely and secretly.

shad'owed, p.p., shadow.

shad'owing, pr.p., shadow.

shad'owy, adj., giving shade; dim; unreal.

sha'dy, adj., spreading a shade; covering; of questionable, moral or ethical, character.

shaft, n., an arrow; the straight length of a spear or similar weapon; a mine entrance; a straight chimney; a handle; the middle members of a column; a connecting member, often cylindrical, in a machine.

shaft'ed, adj., having a shaft.

shaft'ing, n., power-transmitting shafts.

shag, n., a tobacco; a rough mass of hair; the crested cormorant.

shag'bark, n., the white hickory.

shag'gily, adv., in a shaggy way.

shag'giness, n., the quality or state of being shaggy.

shag'gy, adj., with rough or long hair.

shagreen', *adj.*, made of shagreen; *n.*, leather made of, or resembling, shark's skin.

shah, *n.*, the sovereign of Persia (Iran).

shak'able, *adj.*, able to be shaken.

shake, *v.i.*, to shiver; to tremble; to put a quiver into a musical note with the voice or an instrument; *v.t.*, to make to shiver; to move with short, quick jerks; to weaken; to cause to vibrate.

shake-down, *n.*, a temporary bed (*Amer.*).

sha'ken, *adj.*, weakened; broken.

sha'ker, *n.*, one who, or that which, shakes; a member of a fanatical religious sect.

Sha'kerism, *n.*, the system of the Shaker sect.

shake-up, *n.*, a severe shock.

sha'kier, *adj.*, *comp.* of shaky.

sha'kiest, *adj.*, *super.* of shaky.

sha'kily, *adj.*, in a shaky way.

sha'kiness, *n.*, the quality or state of being shaky.

sha'king, *n.*, the act of shaking; *pr.p.*, shake.

shak'o, *n.*, a soldier's cap.

Shak(e)spe(a)'rian, -ean, *adj.*, pert. of rel. to Shakespere.

sha'ky, *adj.*, in a shaking condition; unsafe; unsound.

shale, *n.*, loose flaked stone; a husk.

shall, *v. aux.*, *future tense*, to be about to do or be = to intend. (Also *shalt.*)

shalloon', *n.*, a worsted fabric.

shal'lop, *n.*, a small fishing boat.

shal(l)ot', *n.*, a type of onion. (Also *eschalot.*)

shal'low, *adj.*, not deep; not intellectually profound; without deep feeling; insincere; *n.*, a part of a river, etc., where the water is not deep; a shoal; *v.i.*, to lessen in depth.

shal'lower, *adj.*, *comp.* of shallow.

shal'lowest, *adj.*, *super.* of shallow.

shal'lowness, *n.*, a want of depth in all senses.

shalt, *v. aux., pres. tense*, 2nd person. sing.; *i.q.* shall.

sha'ly, *adj.*, abounding in, or resembling, shale.

sham, *adj.*, false; imitation; *n.*, a person or thing that is false or counterfeit; *v.i.*, to pretend.

sha'man, *n.*, a priestly practitioner of Shamanism.

Sha'manism, *n.*, a system of doctrines and functions based on a belief in good and evil spiritual agencies and in magic.

sham'ash, *n.*, a synagogue official.

sham'ateur, *n.*, an amateur sportsman who makes monetary gains from playing.

sham'ble, *v.t.*, to shuffle along with a clumsy gait.

sham'bled, *p.p.*, shamble.

sham'bles, *n. pl.*, a place where meat is sold or cattle are slaughtered; disastrous disorder.

sham'bling, *adj.*, with a clumsy gait; *pr.p.*, shamble.

shame, *n.*, the sense of having done something wrong or improper; disgrace; infamy; *v.t.*, to disgrace; to confound; to humiliate.

shamed, *p.p.*, shame.

shame'faced, *adj.*, modest, bashful; repentant.

shame'ful, *adj.*, disgraceful, shocking.

shame'fully, *adv.*, in a shameful way.

shame'less, *adj.*, without shame; immodest.

shame'lessly, *adv.*, in a shameless way.

shame'lessness, *n.*, the quality or state of being shameless.

sha'ming, *pr.p.*, shame.

shammed, *p.p.*, sham.

sham'mer, *n.*, one who shams.

sham'ming, *n.*, pretending; *pr.p.*, sham.

sham'my, *n.*, chamois leather.

shampoo', *n.*, a wash for the hair; friction and pressure of the limbs and joints; *v.t.*, to subject to the process of shampooing.

shampooed', *p.p.*, shampoo.

shampoo'er, *n.*, one who shampoos.

shampoo'ing, *pr.p.*, shampoo.

sham'rock, *n.*, a trefoil plant, the national emblem of the Irish.

shan'drydan, *n.*, an Irish one-horse cart.

shan'dy(gaff), *n.*, a beverage of ale and ginger beer combined.

shanghai', *v.t.*, to force into service (*naut. slang*).

shanghaied', *p.p.*, shanghai.

shank, *n.*, the part of the leg between the knee and the ankle; the shaft of a column; the part of a tool between the head and the handle; the straight part of a fish hook; *v.i.*, to drop off in decay.

shanked, *adj.*, having a shank; *p.p.*, shank.

shank'er, *n.*, one who makes shanks.

shank'ing, *pr.p.*, shank.

shann'y, *n.*, a small sea fish.

shan't, *v. aux.*, an abbreviation for *shall not*.

shantung', *n.*, a kind of Chinese silk.

shan'ty, *n.*, a rough sort of dwelling; a sailor's song.

shape, *n.*, form, outline, figure; *v.i.*, to conform to a type or pattern; *v.t.*, to form, to fashion.

shape'able, *adj.*, able to be shaped.

shaped, *p.p.*, shape.

shape'less, *adj.*, without any particular shape.

shape'lessly, *adv.*, in a shapeless way.

shape'lessness, *n.*, the state of being shapeless.

shape'liness, *n.*, the quality of being shapely.

shape'ly, *adj.*, well formed.

shap'er, *n.*, a kind of planing, turning, etc., machine.

shap'ing, *pr.p.*, shape.

shar'able, *adj.*, capable of being shared.

shard, *n.*, a piece of broken earthenware; a potsherd; the wing-case of a beetle. (Also *sherd.*)

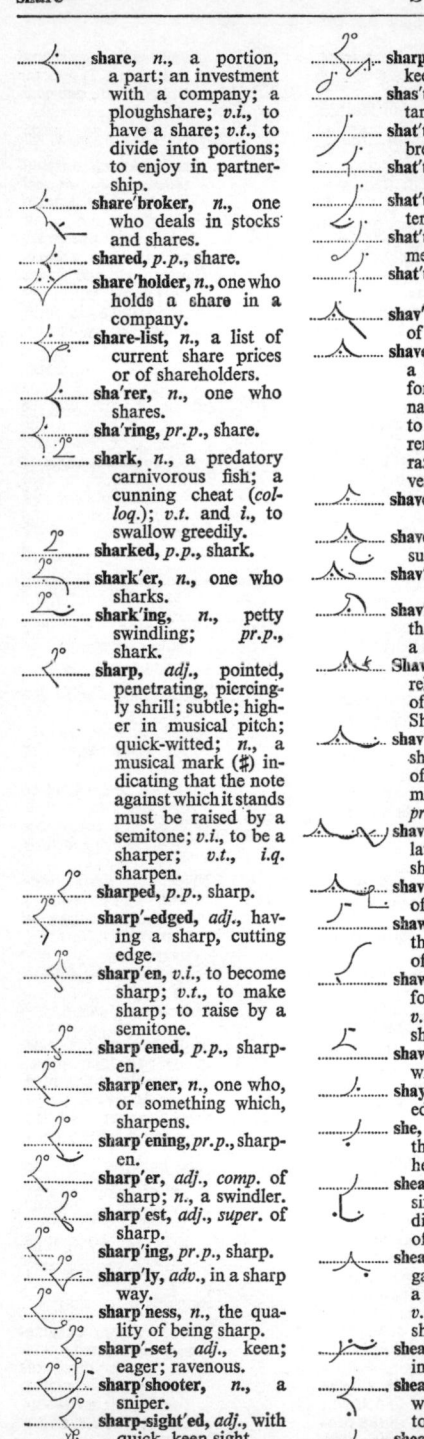

share, *n.*, a portion, a part; an investment with a company; a ploughshare; *v.i.*, to have a share; *v.t.*, to divide into portions; to enjoy in partnership.

share'broker, *n.*, one who deals in stocks and shares.

shared, *p.p.*, share.

share'holder, *n.*, one who holds a share in a company.

share-list, *n.*, a list of current share prices or of shareholders.

sha'rer, *n.*, one who shares.

sha'ring, *pr.p.*, share.

shark, *n.*, a predatory carnivorous fish; a cunning cheat (*colloq.*); *v.t.* and *i.*, to swallow greedily.

sharked, *p.p.*, shark.

shark'er, *n.*, one who sharks.

shark'ing, *n.*, petty swindling; *pr.p.*, shark.

sharp, *adj.*, pointed, penetrating, piercingly shrill; subtle; higher in musical pitch; quick-witted; *n.*, a musical mark (♯) indicating that the note against which it stands must be raised by a semitone; *v.i.*, to be a sharper; *v.t.*, *i.q.* sharpen.

sharped, *p.p.*, sharp.

sharp'-edged, *adj.*, having a sharp, cutting edge.

sharp'en, *v.i.*, to become sharp; *v.t.*, to make sharp; to raise by a semitone.

sharp'ened, *p.p.*, sharpen.

sharp'ener, *n.*, one who, or something which, sharpens.

sharp'ening, *pr.p.*, sharpen.

sharp'er, *adj.*, *comp.* of sharp; *n.*, a swindler.

sharp'est, *adj.*, *super.* of sharp.

sharp'ing, *pr.p.*, sharp.

sharp'ly, *adv.*, in a sharp way.

sharp'ness, *n.*, the quality of being sharp.

sharp'-set, *adj.*, keen; eager; ravenous.

sharp'shooter, *n.*, a sniper.

sharp-sight'ed, *adj.*, with quick, keen sight.

sharp-wit'ted, *adj.*, of keen wit.

shas'ter, *n.*, a commentary on the Vedas.

shat'ter, *v.t.*, to shake or break to pieces.

shat'tered, *p.p.*, shatter.

shat'tering, *pr.p.*, shatter.

shat'ters, *n. pl.*, fragments.

shat'tery, *adj.*, brittle.

shav'able, *adj.*, capable of being shaved.

shave, *n.*, the removal of a beard, etc.; a tool for shaving wood; a narrow escape; *v.i.*, to use a razor; *v.t.*, to remove hairs with a razor; to pare; to go very close to.

shaved, *p.p.*, shave.

shave'ling, *n.*, a tonsured cleric; a monk.

shav'en, *adj.*, shaved.

shav'er, *n.*, one who, or that which, shaves; a small boy (*colloq.*).

Shav'ian, *adj.*, pert. or rel. to the philosophy of George Bernard Shaw.

shav'ing, *n.*, the act of shaving; a thin slice of wood or other material shaved off; *pr.p.*, shave.

shav'ing-brush, *n.*, a lather-brush used in shaving.

shav'ing-stick, *n.*, a stick of shaving soap.

shaw, *n.*, thicket wood; the stalks and leaves of some plants.

shawl, *n.*, a loose wrap for the shoulders, etc.; *v.t.*, to wrap in a shawl.

shawm, *n.*, a Biblical wind-instrument.

shay, *n.*, an old-fashioned carriage.

she, *n.*, the fem. of the personal pronoun, he.

shead'ing, *n.*, one of the six administrative divisions of the Isle of Man.

sheaf, *n.*, a bundle of gathered wheat, etc.; a quiverful of arrows; *v.i.*, to make up into sheaves.

sheal'ing, *n.*, *i.q.* shieling.

shear, *v.t.*, to clip the wool from; to reap; to cut through.

sheared, *p.p.*, shear.

shear'er, *n.*, one who, or that which, shears.

shear'-hulk, *n.*, *i.q.* sheerhulk.

shear'ing, *n.*, the act or the time of shearing; *pr.p.*, shear.

shearling, *n.*, a sheep once shorn.

shear'man, *n.*, a man who shears.

shears, *n. pl.*, an instrument with two-edged blades used for cutting or shearing; a mechanical weight-raising apparatus.

shear'-steel, *n.*, drawn steel.

shear'water, *n.*, a kind of puffin. (Also *sheerwater*.)

sheat'-fish, *n.*, a catfish.

sheath, *n.*, a scabbard; an outside casing; an enveloping membrane, skin, etc.

sheathe, *v.t.*, to enclose in a scabbard or a casing.

sheathed, *p.p.*, sheathe.

sheath'er, *n.*, one who sheathes.

sheath'ing, *pr.p.*, sheathe.

sheath'-knife, *n.*, a dagger-type knife, kept in a sheath.

sheath'y, *adj.*, like a sheathe.

sheave, *n.*, a pulley wheel, grooved; *v.t.*, to make up into sheaves.

shebang', *n.*, a gambling house, a saloon; the whole concern (*slang*).

shebeen', *n.*, a drinking den.

shed, *n.*, a sloping surface (as a watershed); a one-storeyed building to shelter cattle, goods, etc.; *v.t.*, to drop off; to let fall; to spread abroad.

shed'der, *n.*, one who sheds.

shed'ding, *pr.p.*, shed.

shee'lah, *n.*, a young woman (*Austral.*).

sheen, *n.*, brightness, radiance.

sheen'y, *adj.*, radiant, bright; *n.*, a Jewish errand-boy (*colloq.*).

sheep, *n.*, a ruminant, woolbearing animal.

sheep'-cot, *n.*, a pen for sheep.

sheep'dog, *n.*, a shepherd's dog.

sheep'-farmer, *n.*, a breeder of sheep.

sheep'fold, *n.*, an enclosure for sheep.

sheep'-hook, *n.*, a shepherd's crook.

sheep'ish, *adj.*, like a sheep; bashful and silly-looking.

sheep'ishly, *adv.*, in a sheepish way.

sheep'ishness, *n.*, the quality of being sheepish.

sheep'-pen, *n.*, a pen to hold sheep.

sheep'-run, *n.*, a pasturage ground.

sheep's'-eye, *n.*, an amorous look.

sheep'shank, *n.*, a bight and hitch used to shorten the length of a rope for the time being.

sheep'skin, *n.*, the skin of a sheep; parchment.

sheep'-stealer, *n.*, one who steals sheep.

sheep'-stealing, *n.*, the practice of stealing sheep.

sheep'wash, *n.*, a pond where sheep are washed; an insecticide lotion.

sheer, *adj.*, downright; mere; precipitous; *adv.*, precipitously; *n.*, the slope upwards of a ship's lines towards the bow or stern; a swerving course; *v.i.*, to turn sharply from a course (*naut.*).

sheered, *p.p.*, sheer.

sheer'-hulk, *n.*, a dismasted ship used for hoisting purposes. (Also *shear-hulk*.)

sheer'ing, *pr.p.*, sheer.

sheers, *n. pl.*, a hoisting apparatus (*naut.*).

sheer'water, *n.*, *i.q.* shearwater.

sheet, *n.*, a thin expanse of anything, as linen, paper, etc., esp. a rectangular piece of linen cloth used as one of the bed-clothes; a stretch of water; a rope attached to the lower corner of a sail; *v.t.*, to cover with a sheet.

sheet'-anchor, *n.*, an emergency anchor.

sheet'ing, *n.*, material of which bed-sheets are made; *pr.p.*, sheet.

sheik(h), *n.*, an Arab or Mohammedan chief.

shei'la, *n.*, a white girl of inferior type (*S. African*).

sheka'rry, *n.*, *i.q.*shikaree.

shek'el, *n.*, an ancient Hebrew coin or weight.

shek'els, *n. pl.*, money (*colloq.*).

Shel'donian, *adj.*, pert. or rel. to Archbishop Sheldon (1598–1677) founder of the theatre at Oxford which bears this name.

shel'drake, *n.*, a variety of wild duck.

shel'duck, *n.*, the female sheldrake.

shelf, *n.*, a slab or board let into a wall; a book-case, cupboard or plane surface parallel to the ground to stand things upon.

shelf'y, *adj.*, abounding in, or resembling, shelves.

shell, *n.*, the outer case or covering of nuts, fruits, seeds, eggs, molluscs, etc.; the walls of a ruined or partly finished building; an inner coffin; the case of an explosive; a projectile; *v.i.*, to throw off scales; *v.t.*, to take out of its shell; to fire at with shells.

shellac', *n.*, thin flakes of lac used for varnish; *v.t.*, to varnish with this.

shellacked', *p.p.*, shellac.

shellack'ing, *n.*, a telling off (*slang*); *pr.p.*, shellac.

shell'-crater, *n.*, a crater made by an exploding shell.

shelled, *p.p.*, shell.

shell'fish, *n.*, a crustacean or mollusc.

shell'-hole, *n.*, a hole made by an exploding shell.

shell'ing, *pr.p.*, shell.

shell'-less, *adj.*, having no shell.

shell'-proof, *adj.*, proof against an exploding shell.

shell'shock, *n.*, mental disturbance arising from exposure over time to detonations.

shell'work, *n.*, ornamentation with shells.

shell'y, *adj.*, resembling, or abounding in, shells.

shel'ta, *n.*, Irish gypsy language.

shel'ter, *n.*, protection against danger, wind, rain, etc., a place of refuge; *v.i.*, to seek refuge; *v.t.*, to protect.

shel'tered, *p.p.*, shelter.

shel'tering, *pr.p.*, shelter.

shel'terless, *adj.*, without shelter.

shel'tie, *n.*, a Shetland pony.

shel'ty, *n.*, a rough cabin; *n.*, *i.q.* sheltie.

shelve, *v.i.*, to slope gradually; *v.t.*, to put aside or on a shelf.

shelved, *p.p.*, shelve.

shelves, *n.*, the pl. of shelf.

shelv'ing, *adj.*, gently sloping; *n.*, material for shelves; *pr.p.*, shelve.

shelv'y, *adj.*, sloping.

Shem'ite, *adj.*, *i.q.* Semite.

shemit'ic, *adj.*, *i.q.* semitic.

shemoz'zle, *n.*, muddle; a rumpus; a brawl; (*slang*).

shenan'igan, *n.*, nonsense, trickery, (*colloq.*).

She'ol, *n.*, the place of the dead; the Hebrew Hades.

shep'herd, *n.*, one who tends sheep; *v.t.*, to care for as a shepherd; to watch over.

shep'herded, *p.p.*, shepherd.

shep'herdess, *n.*, the fem. of shepherd.

shep'herding, *pr.p.*, shepherd.

shep'pey, *n.*, a pen for sheep.

She'raton, *n.*, an 18th. century style of furniture.

sher'bet, *n.*, an Oriental drink, composed of fruit juice with flavouring, and cooled with snow. The Western imitation is effervescing.

sherd, *n.*, *i.q.* shard.

sherif', -eef', *n.*, one descended from Mohammed through Fatima, and distinguished by a green turban or veil; the chief magistrate of Mecca.

sher'iff, *n.*, a shire-reeve; the chief administrative officer of a shire or county. His duties are partly judicial, partly concerned with the writs, presiding at elections, etc.

Sher'pa, *n.*, an Eastern Tibetan from the Himalayas noted as a mountaineer.

sher'ry, *n.*, a popular wine originally from Xeres, in Southern Spain.

Shet'land, *adj.*, a kind of pony bred in the Shetland islands off Scotland.

Shet'lander, *n.*, a native of the S. islands.

Shevat', *n.*, the fifth month of the Jewish civil year.

shew, *v.t.*, *i.q.* show.

shew'bread, *n.*, *i.q.* showbread.

Shi'ah, *n.*, one of the two great Mohammedan sects, Sunni and Shiah. A Shiite professes to be a follower of Ali as the first legitimate Imam.

shib'boleth, *n.*, a testword; a party phrase; an irrational belief.

shield, *n.*, a body protection worn on the left arm; any protective person or thing, such as a screen in machinery or gunnery; an escutcheon; *v.t.*, to protect, defend or screen.

shield'ed, *p.p.*, shield.

shield'ing, *pr.p.*, shield.

shield'less, *adj.*, without a shield.

shiel'ing, *n.*, a shelter, a hut (*Scot.*).

shift, *n.*, a change; a substitution; a relay; a dodge; a device; a chemise or shirt; an expedient; a working period; *v.i.*, to change one's position; to equivocate; to do as well as one can for oneself; *v.t.*, to move from one place to another; to substitute one for another.

shift'ed, *p.p.*, shift.

shift'er, *n.*, one who shifts, esp. one who shifts scenes in a theatre.

shift'ier, *adj.*, *comp.* of shifty.

shift'iest, *adj.*, *super.* of shifty.

shift'ily, *adv.*, craftily.

shift'ing, *adj.*, moving; *pr.p.*, shift.

shift'ingly, *adv.*, in a shifting way.

shift'less, *adj.*, helpless; without resource; incapable.

shift'y, *adj.*, prevaricating; crafty; evasive.

Shih' Tzus, *n.*, a breed of small long-coated dog from China.

Shi'ite, *n.*, a member of the Shiah sect.

shikar', *n.*, hunting.

shikar'ee, *n.*, a hunter. (Also *shekarry*.)

shille'la(g)h, shilla'lah, *n.*, an Irish oak or blackthorn cudgel.

shil'ling, *n.*, an English silver coin originally worth twelve pence = five new pence; (in Kenya) a coin worth 100 cents.

shil'ly-shally, *n.*, indecision, vacillation; *v.i.*, to waste time in making up one's mind; to vacillate.

shi'ly, *adv.*, *i.q.* shyly.

shim, *n.*, a thin slip or wedge; *v.t.*, to wedge up.

shim'mer, *n.*, a tremulous gleam; a faint quivering light; *v.i.*, to give a faint quivering light; to gleam tremulously.

shim'mered, *p.p.*, shimmer.

shim'mering, *pr.p.*, shimmer.

shimm'y, *n.*, a ballroom dance, a shaking body motion.

shin, *n.*, the front part of the leg from the knee downward; the shank; *v.i.*, to climb; *v.t.*, to kick or hit on the shin.

shin'dy, *n.*, a row or brawl (*slang*).

shine, *n.*, light, brightness, polish; *i.q.* shindy; *v.i.*, to give light; to be bright; to be brilliant (in any sense); *v.t.*, to make to shine; to polish (*colloq.*).

shined, *p.p.*, shine, in the sense of polishing.

shi'ner, *n.*, one who, or that which, shines.

shin'gle, *n.*, rounded beach pebbles; a wooden roof-tile; *v.t.*, to roof with shingles; to trim hair closely at the neck.

shin'gled, *adj.*, covered with shingle(s); *p.p.*, shingle.

shin'gles, *n.*, herpes; a nervous cutaneous affection, marked by an eruption on any part of the body but esp. the torso. (Also *gingles*.)

shin'gling, *n.*, a process in puddling, which consists in pressing or hammering out iron impurities; *pr.p.*, shingle.

shin'gly, *adj.*, composed of shingle(s); covered with shingle(s); like shingle(s).

shi'nier, *adj.*, *comp.* of shiny.

shi'niest, *adj.*, *super.* of shiny.

shi'ning, *adj.*, radiant, eminent; *pr.p.*, shine.

shinn'y, *v.i.*, to shin (up) a tree, etc., (*colloq.*).

Shinto, *n.*, the earliest religion of Japan. (Also *Sintoo*.)

Shin'toism, *n.*, the cult of Shinto, a Japanese religion.

shi'ny, *adj.*, bright, polished.

ship, *n.*, a vessel for transporting people or goods on water; anything resembling a ship; *v.i.*, to go aboard; to join a ship as a common sailor; *v.t.*, to place on board for transport; to take (a crew) on board; to draw (oars) in from the water.

ship'board, *n.*, a ship's deck or side; the area within the ship itself.

ship'broker, *n.*, a dealer in ships; an agent for marine insurance.

ship'builder, *n.*, a builder of ships.

ship'building, *n.*, the shipbuilder's craft; naval construction.

ship'-carpenter, *n.*, a carpenter on board ship or employed in building ships.

ship'chandler, *n.*, a dealer in ship requirements, as canvas, cordage, lockers, etc.

ship'master, *n.*, the commander of a merchant-vessel.

ship'mate, *n.*, a member of one's own crew.

ship'ment, *n.*, the act of shipping; anything shipped.

ship'-money, *n.*, a tax imposed on coast towns and villages, compelling them to provide the King with ships.

ship'owner, n., one who owns ships.

shipped, p.p., ship.

shipp'en, n., a cattle shelter.

ship'per, n., one who ships.

ship'ping, n., ships collectively; pr.p., ship.

ship'shape, adj., neat and tidy as is customary in ships; adv., in perfect order.

ship'way, n., the structure on which a ship is built and launched.

ship'wreck, n., the wrecking of a ship; complete ruin; v.t., to destroy by wrecking; to ruin.

ship'wrecked, p.p., shipwreck.

ship'wrecking, pr.p., shipwreck.

ship'wright, n., a builder or repairer of ships.

ship'yard, n., a place where ships are built or repaired.

shir(r), n., elastic webbing or thread; v.t., to gather with thread, to pucker.

shire, n., a political division of Great Britain, corresponding to a county.

shire'-horse, n., a large breed of draught horse.

shire'-town, n., the chief town of a shire or county.

shirk, n., i.q. shirker; v.i., to be a shirker; v.t., to evade; to try to wriggle out of.

shirked, p.p., shirk.

shirk'er, n., one who evades his duty.

shirk'ing, pr.p., shirk.

shir'ring, n., a gathered fabric.

shirt, n., a light body garment, usually for men.

shirt'ed, adj., wearing, or covered with, a shirt.

shirt'front, n., the starched front of a shirt.

shirt'ing, n., material for shirts.

shirt'less, adj., without a shirt.

shirt'sleeves, n. pl., the sleeves of a shirt; partial undress, without a jacket.

shirt'y, adj., annoyed, ill-tempered.

shit'tah, n., a kind of acacia.

---

shit'tim-wood, n., the timber of the shittah.

shive, n., a shiver or thin fragment.

shiv'er, n., a trembling with cold or emotion; v.i., to shudder or tremble with cold; v.t., to break or smash to shivers.

shiv'ered, p.p., shiver.

shiv'ering, n., an attack of the shivers; pr.p., shiver.

shiv'eringly, adv., in a shivering way.

shiv'ery, adj., like a shiver; feeling cold and inclined to shiver.

shoad, n., a fragment of ore. (Also shode.)

shoal, adj., shallow; n., a school or multitude of fishes; any throng; shallow water; a sandbar; v.i., to run shallow; to swarm; v.t., to make shallow.

shoal'iness, n., the state of being shoaly.

shoal'y, adj., abounding in shoals.

shoat, n., i.q. shote.

shock, n., a concussion; a sudden shaking or collision; the effect of a sudden blow or concussion; the passage of an electric current; sheaves set up to ripen; a disordered mass (as of hair); v.i., to collide; v.t., to jar; to shake; to horrify.

shock'-absorber, n., any device for preventing damage, from vibration or collision, to machinery or vehicles.

shocked, p.p., shock.

shock'er, n., a sensational novel; a very bad specimen of anything (colloq.).

shock'-headed, adj., with rough, tumbled hair.

shock'ing, adj., disgusting, horrifying; pr.p., shock.

shock'-troops, n., troops specially trained for swift offensive action.

shod, p.p., shoe.

shod'dy, adj., made of shoddy; sham; of inferior quality; n., old fabrics and rags shredded and made up into a cloth; sham; v.t., to convert into shoddy cloth.

shode, n., i.q. shoad.

---

shoe, n., a low outer covering for the foot; anything resembling a shoe in shape or use; v.t., to supply with shoes; to put a ferrule on.

shoe'black, n., one who polishes shoes with blacking.

shoe'horn, n., an instrument made of horn or other substance, to enable the foot to slide easily into a shoe.

shoe'ing, n., the act of shoeing a horse, etc.; pr.p., shoe.

shoe'-leather, n., the material for making shoes.

shoe'less, adj., without shoes.

shoe'maker, n., one who makes shoes.

shoe'making, n., a shoemaker's or cobbler's craft.

sho'er, n., one who shoes, esp. horses.

shoe'-string, n., the lace of a shoe; slender resources (colloq.).

shog'un, n., a Japanese military chief.

shone, p.p., shine.

shoo, interj., the sound shoo; v.i., to make the sound shoo; v.t., to scare birds or animals with the voice.

shook, p.p., shake.

shoon, n., the pl. of shoe (obs.).

shoot, n., a young growth, a sprout; a swift flow of water; a sloping passage down which things can be shot; a district owned or hired for shooting game; a shooting party; v.i., to fire a gun or pistol; to let fly an arrow; to dart; to grow up quickly; to project; v.t., to discharge a missile; to hit or kill by shooting; to put forth; to protrude; to discharge; to shoot [game] over (colloq.).

shoot'able, adj., able to be shot.

shoot'er, n., one who, or that which, shoots.

shoot'ing, n., the act of shooting; the ownership of land where game can be shot; the land so owned or hired; pr.p., shoot.

shoot'ing-box, n., a lodge where a shooting-party lives temporarily.

shoot'ing-brake, n., an estate car.

shoot'ing-star, n., a star-like meteorite incandescent by friction as it falls through the atmosphere.

shoot'ing-stick, n., a walking-stick convertible into a seat; a printer's tool.

shop, n., a place where goods of any sort are sold; a building or room where an artisan's or craftsman's work is done; unseasonable talk about one's profession or business (colloq.); v.i., to visit shops; v.t., to expose another person's errors or failings to authority (colloq.).

shop'keeper, n., a tradesman.

shop'lifter, n., one who steals from a shop.

shop'man, n., one who serves in a shop.

shopped, p.p., shop.

shop'per, n., one who shops.

shop'ping, n., the act or practice of visiting shops; pr.p., shop.

shop'-stew'ard, n., the workers' elected negotiator in industry.

shop'walker, n., a person whose function is to help customers in large shops and supervise retail staff.

shore, n., the land skirting the sea; a prop to hold up a structure; v.t., to prop up; to surround with a shore.

shored, p.p., shore.

shore'less, adj., without a shore; boundless.

shore'ward, adv., toward the shore.

shore'wards, adv., i.q. shoreward.

shor'ing, n., the act of shoring; an arrangement of props; pr.p., shore.

shorn, p.p., shear.

short, adj., the opposite to long; of little length; insufficient; in want of, or inadequately supplied with; quick-tempered; crisp or brittle; unmixed; adv., not enough;

abruptly; n., something short, essence or pith; a syllable pronounced short; a drink of spirit (as opposed to beer) (colloq.); v.t. and i., to shorten.

short'age, n., deficiency.

short'bread, n., a crisp sweet biscuit.

short'cake, n., i.q. shortbread.

short'-circ'uit, n., an electrical circuit made through a small resistance and thus failing to make the complete intended circuit; such a circuit caused by a fault; v.t., to create a short circuit.

short'coming, n., a failure; a defect; deficiency.

short'en, v.i., to become shorter; v.t., to make shorter; to curtail; to check.

short'ened, p.p., shorten.

short'ener, n., one who shortens.

short'ening, n., fat used in pastry cooking; pr.p., shorten.

short'er, adj., comp. of short.

short'est, adj., super. of short.

short'fall, n., the fact or amount of falling short.

short'hand, n., a method or system of writing compendiously and in a labour-saving way; stenography.

short-han'ded, adj., without enough helpers.

short'horn, n., a special breed of cattle.

short'horned, adj., having short horns.

short'ish, adj., on the short side.

short'lived, adj., living or lasting only for a short time.

short'ly, adv., immediately; curtly.

short'ness, n., the quality or state of being short.

shorts, n. pl., a poorer quality of hemp; trousers not reaching to the knee.

short'sighted, adj., myopic; near-sighted; not discerning.

shortsightedly, adv., lacking foresight.

shortsight'edness, n., the quality or state of being shortsighted.

short-temp'ered, adj., irritable.

short'-term, adj., over a short period; n., a short period.

shortwin'ded, adj., suffering from a shortness of breath.

shot, n., a missile (non-explosive) discharged from a cannon, gun or pistol; an act of shooting; one who shoots; a reckoning; an attempt; an injection; a short measure of a liquid; p.p., shoot.

shote, n., a young hog. (Also shoat.)

shot-free, adj., i.q. scot-free.

shot'gun, n., a smooth-bore gun used to fire small pellets or shot.

shot'ted, adj., loaded with shot.

should, past and conditional of shall; sometimes implying further action as contemplated in the past; sometimes forming the apodosis of a conditional sentence; sometimes implying obligation.

shoul'der, n., that part of a body to which an arm, wing or fore-leg is joined; anything like a shoulder, as, e.g., an abutment; v.t., to raise on to one's shoulder; to hustle or push aside; to assume responsibility for.

shoul'der-belt, n., a belt worn over one shoulder and across back and chest.

shoul'der-blade, n., the scapula; one of the large, flat bones in the upper back.

shoul'dered, adj., having a shoulder or shoulders; p.p., shoulder.

shoul'dering, pr.p., shoulder.

shoul'der-knot, n., a distinctive badge or ornament worn on the shoulders.

shout, n., a loud cry or call; v.i., to speak with a loud voice; to cry out lustily; v.t., to pronounce loudly.

shout'ed, p.p., shout.

shout'er, n., one who shouts.

shout'ing, n., loud applause or excitement; pr.p., shout.

shove, *n.*, a push; *v.t. and i.*, to thrust or push.

shoved, *p.p.*, shove.

shov'el, *n.*, a spadelike implement for scooping up earth, coal, etc.; *v.t.*, to scoop up.

shov'elboard, *n.*, a game with coins or discs, now a ship's deck game. (Also *shuffleboard*.)

shov'elful, *n.*, as much as a shovel holds.

shov'elled, *p.p.*, shovel.

shov'eller, *n.*, one who, or that which, shovels.

shov'elling, *pr.p.*, shovel.

shov'er, *n.*, one who, or that which, shoves anything.

shov'ing, *pr.p.*, shove.

show, *n.*, an exhibition; a spectacle; a display; an appearance; *v.i.*, to be seen; *v.t.*, to make to be seen; to reveal; to prove; to exhibit. (Also *shew*.)

show'bill, *n.*, a placard advertising an exhibition, etc.

show'bread, *n.*, the twelve loaves laid every Sabbath on a table near the altar of incense in the tabernacle and the Temple. (Also *shewbread*.)

show'case, *n.*, a case containing samples.

show'down, *n.*, placing cards face-up in a card game; a revaluation of true facts; a confrontation to reach a decision.

showed, *p.p.*, show.

show'er, *n.*, one who shows.

show'er, *n.*, a brief fall (of rain, hail, etc.); *i.q.* showerbath; *v.i.*, to fall in a shower; *v.t.*, to discharge as in a shower; to sprinkle.

show'erbath, *n.*, a bath with an apparatus for letting water fall from above.

show'ered, *p.p.*, shower.

show'ering, *pr.p.*, shower.

show'erless, *adj.*, without a shower.

show'ery, *adj.*, coming in showers, not in steady rain.

show'girl, *n.*, a girl engaged for her beauty in the entertainment world.

show'ground, *n.*, place where shows are staged; a fair-ground.

show'ily, *adv.*, in a showy way.

show'iness, *n.*, the quality or state of being showy.

show'ing, *pr.p.*, show.

show'man, *n.*, one who gives an exhibition; a pretentious person.

show'manship, *n.*, the act of the showman; a capacity for display.

shown, *p.p.*, show.

show'room, *n.*, a room where articles for sale, etc., are exhibited.

show'y, *adj.*, gaudy; ostentatious.

shram, *adj.*, numb with cold.

shrank, *p.p.*, shrink.

shrap'nel, *n.*, bullets contained in an explosive shell or pieces of an exploded missile.

shred, *n.*, a torn piece; any small bit; *v.t.*, to tear into fragments.

shred'ded, *p.p.*, shred.

shred'ding, *n.*, a tearing into small pieces; *pr.p.*, shred.

shreds, *n. pl.*, tatters.

shrew, *n.*, a scold, usually a woman.

shrewd, *adj.*, sagacious, farseeing, judicious.

shrewd'ly, *adv.*, in a shrewd way.

shrewd'ness, *n.*, the quality or state of being shrewd.

shrew'ish, *adj.*, inclined to be a scold.

shrew'-mole, *n.*, an American mole.

shrew'-mouse, *n.*, a very small, mouse-like, insect-eating creature.

shriek, *n.*, a wild, shrill cry; *v.t. and i.*, to call out in piercing or agonized tones; to laugh uncontrollably.

shrieked, *p.p.*, shriek.

shriek'er, *n.*, one who shrieks.

shriek'ing, *n.*, shrill cries; *pr.p.*, shriek.

shrie'valty, *n.*, the office, and term of office, of a sheriff.

shrift, *n.*, absolution after confession.

shrike, *n.*, the butcherbird, which impales its victims on thorns.

shrill, *adj.*, high-sounding; *n.*, a high, penetrating sound; *v.i.*, to make a shrill sound; *v.t.*, to utter shrilly.

shrill'ness, *n.*, the quality or state of being shrill.

shril'ly, *adv.*, in a shrill way.

shrimp, *n.*, a small seawater crustacean; anyone very small; *v.i.*, to catch shrimps.

shrimped, *p.p.*, shrimp.

shrimp'er, *n.*, one who catches shrimps.

shrimp'ing, *n.*, catching shrimps; *pr.p.*, shrimp.

shrimp'-net, *n.*, a fine-mesh net for catching shrimps.

shrine, *n.*, a chest, casket or tomb containing relics; a place hallowed by a saint's relics; a place of pilgrimage; *v.t.*, *i.q.* enshrine.

shrink, *v.i.*, to become smaller, to recoil; *v.t.*, to cause to contract or shrivel.

shrink'age, *n.*, contraction, diminution.

shrink'er, *n.*, one who, or an agent that, shrinks.

shrink'ing, *n.*, contraction; *pr.p.*, shrink.

shrive, *v.t.*, to minister to in the tribunal of penance; to absolve.

shrived, *p.p.*, shrive.

shriv'el, *v.i.*, to contract; to wither; *v.t.*, to cause to contract or wither.

shriv'elled, *p.p.*, shrivel.

shriv'elling, *pr.p.*, shrivel.

shriv'en, *p.p.*, shrive.

shri'ving, *pr.p.*, shrive.

shri'ving-pew, *n.*, the mediaeval predecessor of the confessional-box.

shroff, *n.*, an E. Indian money-changer or banker; *v.t.*, to inspect coins and coining.

shroff'age, *n.*, the inspection of coins and coining, and the cost of making such an inspection.

shroud, n., a wrapper for a corpse; in pl., a ship's ropes steadying the mast; v.t., to cover or conceal.

shroud'ed, p.p., shroud.

shroud'ing, pr.p., shroud.

shroud'-line, n., a parachute cord.

Shrove'tide, n., the period for being shriven.

Shrove Tues'day, n., the day before Ash Wednesday. Its name comes from the fact that at this season penitents especially made their confession.

shrub, n., a plant growth of smaller size than a tree, and commonly springing from several stems; a kind of liquor made generally of rum with fruit juices.

shrub'bery, n., a place abounding in shrubs.

shrub'biness, n., the quality or state of being shrubby.

shrub'by, adj., abounding in shrubs; like shrubs.

shrug, n., a quick raising of the shoulders; v.t., to lift the shoulders slightly by way of expressing contempt, annoyance, etc.

shrugged, p.p., shrug.

shrug'ging, pr.p., shrug.

shrunk, p.p., shrink.

shrunk'en, adj., contracted, diminished.

shuck, n., a husk pod; v.t., to remove a husk or shell (U.S.A.).

shud'der, n., a quivering with fear or horror; v.i., to shiver with fear, horror, etc.

shud'dered, p.p., shudder.

shud'dering, pr.p., shudder.

shuf'fle, v.i., to move along, the feet scraping the ground; to prevaricate; to be evasive; v.t., to move in a random way (esp. playing cards); to change the positions of.

shuf'fleboard, n., i.q. shovelboard.

shuf'fled, p.p., shuffle.

shuf'fler, n., one who shuffles; a prevaricator.

shuf'fling, pr.p., shuffle.

shu'mac, n., dried leaves, ground, and used in dyeing and tanning processes. (Also sumac.)

shun, v.t., to avoid.

shunned, p.p., shun.

shun'ning, pr.p., shun.

shunt, n., the act of shunting or the state of being shunted; an electric conductor, by means of which the current may in different degrees be diverted; v.i., to diverge; v.t., to remove from a main to a side line; to divert.

shunt'ed, p.p., shunt.

shunt'er, n., one who, or that which, shunts.

shunt'ing, pr.p., shunt.

shut, v.i., to be closed; v.t., to close, lock, or bar.

shut'-eye, n., a nap or short sleep (colloq.).

shut'ter, n., one who, or that which, shuts; a cover to a window.

shut'ting, pr.p., shut.

shut'tle, n., a weaving implement.

shut'tlecock, n., a feathered cork, used in the game of battledore and shuttlecock.

shwan'pan, n., a Chinese calculating apparatus.

shy, adj., nervously retiring; bashful; reserved; n., a throw (colloq.); a starting aside; v.i., to start aside in fear; v.t., to throw (colloq.).

shy'er, adj., comp. of shy; n., one who, or that which, shies.

shy'est, adj., super. of shy.

shy'ing, adj., apt to shy; n., the act of shying; pr.p., shy.

shy'ly, adv., in a shy way. (Also shily.)

shy'ness, n., the character of being shy.

shys'ter, n., a person without professional honour.

si, n., the seventh note in the musical scale.

si'al, n., the outer shell of the earth's crust, rich in silica and aluminium.

sial'agogue, n., a saliva-inducing agent.

si'amang, n., a Malayan gibbon.

Siamese', adj., the older name for Thai; pert. or rel. to Siam (Thailand); n., a native of S; the language of S.

Sibe'rian, adj., pert. or rel. to Siberia; n., a native of S.

sib'ilance, n., the quality or state of being sibilant.

sib'ilancy, n., i.q. sibilance.

sib'ilant, adj., hissing; n., a sibilant consonant (e.g. S or Z).

sib'ilate, v.t. and i., to pronounce with a hissing sound.

sibila'tion, n., pronouncing with a sibilant sound.

sib'lings, n. pl., brothers and sisters born at different times; half brothers and sisters.

sib'yl, n., a woman who prophesies.

sib'ylline, adj., pert. or rel. to a sibyl.

sic, adj., such (Scot.); adv., thus; so (Lat.). A word used to express the fact that an apparent error is intended.

sic'ca, n., an Indian jeweller's weight.

sic'cative, adj., drying.

sic'city, n., aridity.

sice, n., the number six in dicing; an Indian groom.

Sicil'ian, adj., pert. or rel. to Sicily; n., a native of S., a large Italian island.

sick, adj., ill, unwell, vomiting, disgusted.

sick'-bay, n., a special bay reserved for the sick (esp. on a ship); a sick-berth.

sick'-bed, n., a bed of illness.

sick'-berth, n., a ship's sick-room.

sick'en, v.i., to be on the point of becoming ill; to feel disgust; v.t., to disgust; to make sick.

sick'ened, p.p., sicken.

sick'ening, adj., disgusting; pr.p., sicken.

sick'ish, adj., inclined to sickness.

sick'le, n., a reaper's hook.

sick'-leave, n., absence from duty owing to sickness.

sick'led, adj., supplied with a sickle.

sickle'wort, n., a plant otherwise known as heal-all (bot.).

sick'lied, adj., made to look sickly.

sick'liness, n., a tendency to ill-health; the quality or state of being sickly.

sick'-list, n., a list of persons regarded as ill.

sick'ly, adj., ailing; causing nausea; adv., in a sick way.

sick'ness, n., illness; nausea.

sick'-room, n., a room for a sick person.

side, n., a surface of a solid body; the part from the shoulder to the hip; a hill-slope; a party; the bias given to a billiard ball struck not quite in the centre; arrogance (slang); v.i., to take a side (i.e., to support a party).

side'band, n., the frequency band on each side of the carrier frequency (radio).

side'board, n., a side serving table in a dining room.

side'-car, n., a passenger car attached to a motor-cycle.

si'ded, p.p., side.

side'-effect, n., an effect additional to the main one.

side'-glance, n., a quick glance to one side.

side'-iss'ue, n., a topic subordinate to the main one.

side'light, n., a small light on the side of vehicles.

side'-line, n., work or business carried on as an additional activity to one's main work.

side'ling, adj., sloping.

side'long, adj., on the side; adv., laterally.

si'deral, adj., i.q. sidereal.

side'real, adj., pert. or rel. to stars.

sid'erite, n., a meteoric stone.

siderog'raphy, n., engraving on steel.

sid'eroscope, n., a scientific apparatus for discovering iron particles.

side'-saddle, adv., riding with both legs on the one side; n., a lady's saddle.

side'show, n., a subsidiary show or exhibition.

side'slip, n., a skid; a slip to one side.

sides'man, n., a church official assistant to the churchwardens; one who takes sides.

side'-splitting, adj., extremely funny.

side'-step, n., a step to the side; v.t. and i., to avoid by stepping to one side; to evade.

side'stroke, n., a kind of stroke in swimming.

side'-table, n., a supplementary table.

side'track, n., a track alongside the main one; v.t., to postpone considering; to evade; to prevent discussion deliberately.

side'walk, n., a footpath (Amer.).

side'ward, adj. and adv., laterally, to or from the side.

side'wards, adj., i.q. sideward.

side'ways, adj. and adv., laterally.

side'wise, adv., laterally.

si'di, n., an E. Indian word used in addressing a Mohammedan gentleman.

si'ding, n., a railway line off the main track; pr.p., side.

si'dle, v.i., to walk sideways.

si'dled, p.p., sidle.

si'dling, pr.p., sidle.

siege, n., an attempt to reduce a fortified place to surrender; the floor in a glass furnace; v.t., i.q. besiege.

sieg'ing, pr.p., siege.

si'enite, n., i.q. syenite.

sien'na, n., a reddish-brown pigment brought from the Italian town of Sienna.

sier'ra, n., a serrated range of mountains (Span.).

sies'ta, n., a midday rest or sleep in hot countries (Span.).

sieve, n., an implement used for straining out finer particles.

siffleur, n., a whistling artist (Fr.).

sift, v.t., to separate by means of a sieve; to investigate closely.

sift'ed, p.p., sift.

sift'er, n., one who, or that which, sifts.

sift'ing, pr.p., sift.

sigh, n., a long, deep breath; a sound of grief or sorrow; v.i., to breathe deep and long; to mourn.

sighed, p.p., sigh.

sigh'er, n., one who sighs.

sigh'ing, n., the act of sighing; pr.p., sigh.

sight, n., the power of seeing; vision; appearance; a contrivance for improving one's aim with a gun; a spectacle; v.t., to catch sight of; to adjust the sight of (a gun).

sight'ed, p.p., sight.

sight'ing, pr.p., sight.

sight'less, adj., blind.

sight'lessness, n., blindness.

sight'liness, n., the quality or state of being sightly.

sight'ly, adj., good to look on.

sight'-play'er, n., one who can play music at first sight.

sight'-read'er, n., one who can read music at first sight.

sight'seeing, n., going to see places and things worth seeing.

sight'seer, n., one who indulges in sight-seeing.

sight'-sing'er, n., a singer who can read vocal music at sight.

sig'il, n., a seal or signature.

sigilla'ria, n. pl., coal-fossils.

si'gillate, adj., impressed with pattern (pottery); marked with a seal.

sigil'lum, n., a seal (Lat.).

sig'ma, n., the Greek equivalent of the letter S.

sig'mate, *adj.*, sigma or S-shaped; *v.t.*, to add a sigma or S to.

sigmat'ic, *adj.*, formed with sigma.

sig'moid, *adj.*, like an S.

sigmoid'al, *adj.*, *i.q.* sigmoid.

sign, *n.*, a mark; a token; an indication; wonder; a board bearing a device and hung outside a shop or inn; any public notice; *v.i.*, to signal; *v.t.*, to mark with a signature.

sig'nal, *adj.*, worthy of note; remarkable; *n.*, a means of giving notice or warning; *v.t.* and *i.*, to convey (a message) by signals.

sig'nalize, *v.t.*, to make noteworthy.

sig'nalized, *p.p.*, signalize.

sig'nalizing, *pr.p.*, signalize.

sig'nalled, *p.p.*, signal.

sig'naller, *n.*, one who gives signals.

sig'nalling, *n.*, the act of signalling; *pr.p.*, signal.

sig'nally, *adv.*, in a conspicuous manner.

sig'nalman, *n.*, a man who attends to railway signals.

sig'nary, *n.*, the symbols forming an alphabet.

sig'natory, *adj.*, signing; *n.*, one who appends his name to a document.

sig'nature, *n.*, a handwritten name subscribed to a letter or document; a stamp; the indication of a musical key by means of signs—flats and sharps; a section of a book produced from one printed sheet.

sig'nature-tune', *n.*, a tune used to introduce and identify an artist or show.

sign'board, *n.*, a board bearing a device and hung outside a shop or inn.

signed, *p.p.*, sign.

sign'er, *n.*, one who signs.

sig'net, *n.*, a device used for sealing; a signet-ring.

sig'net-ring, *n.*, a finger ring with an inset seal.

signif'icance, *n.*, the quality or state of being significant; meaning; importance.

signif'icancy, *n.*, *i.q.* significance.

signif'icant, *adj.*, full of meaning; important; *n.*, a symbol.

signif'icantly, *adv.*, meaningly; with importance.

significa'tion, *n.*, the act or effect of signifying; import.

signif'icative, *adj.*, *i.q.* significant.

sig'nificator, *n.*, one who, or that which, signifies; a ruling planet.

signif'icatory, *adj.*, signifying.

sig'nified, *p.p.*, signify.

sig'nify, *v.i.*, to have importance; *v.t.*, to indicate; to exhibit; to imply; to mean.

sig'nifying, *pr.p.*, signify.

sign'ing, *pr.p.*, sign.

si'gnior, *n.*, a lord; the Italian for Mr. or Sir.

sign'-manual, *n.*, an autograph signature.

si'gnor, *n.*, *i.q.* signior.

signo'ra, *n.*, the fem. of signor (*It.*).

signori'na, *n.*, a young lady; Miss (*It.*).

si'gnory, *n.*, a lordship.

sign'painter, *n.*, an artist in sign-boards.

sign'post, *n.*, a post with pointers showing direction to places.

sign'writer, *n.*, a person who writes signs for shop fronts, etc.

Sikh, *n.*, a Pakistani of a particular religious sect from the Punjab.

sik'ra, *n.*, a pyramidal tower on a Hindu temple.

sil'age, *n.*, preserved cattle fodder; *v.t.*, to put into silo.

sil'cot, *n.*, a silky-finished cotton material.

si'lence, *n.*, the absence of sound; stillness; hush; *v.t.*, to reduce to silence.

si'lenced, *adj.*, hushed; *p.p.*, silence.

si'lencer, *n.*, one who, or that which, silences; the exhaust muffling device on a motorcar.

si'lencing, *pr.p.*, silence.

si'lent, *adj.*, without sound; still; mute; reserved.

si'lently, *adv.*, noiselessly.

sile'sia, *n.*, a cloth, so named, from Silesia whence it originally came.

Sile'sian, *adj.*, pert. or rel. to Silesia; *n.*, a native of S., a region of Central Europe.

si'lex, *n.*, *i.q.* silica.

silhouette', *n.*, a profile portrait; a likeness cast on a wall or other surface; an outline; *v.t.*, to show in profile or outline.

silhouet'ted, *p.p.*, silhouette.

silhouet'ting, *pr.p.*, silhouette.

sil'ica, *n.*, silicon dioxide. (Also *silex*.)

sil'icate, *n.*, a siliceous acid salt.

sil'icated, *adj.*, impregnated with silica.

sili'ceous, *adj.*, containing, or pert. to, silica.

silicif'erous, *adj.*, producing silica.

silic'ified, *p.p.*, silicify.

silic'ify, *v.t.*, to change into silica.

silic'ifying, *pr.p.*, silicify.

silic'ium, *n.*, *i.q.* silicon.

sil'icle, *n.*, a small pod.

sil'icon, *n.*, a nonmetallic element.

silicos'is, *n.*, a disease of the lungs caused by breathing silica dust.

silic'ulose, *adj.*, pod-like.

sil'iqua, *n.*, a pod (*Lat.*).

sil'iquiform, *adj.*, like a siliqua.

sil'iquose, *adj.*, pod-like.

silk, *adj.*, made of silk; *n.*, a fibrous substance produced by silkworms in forming their cocoons; fine, very smooth cloth or thread made of silk; the silk gown of a Queen's or King's Counsel; the lustre of certain precious stones.

silk'en, *adj.*, made of silk; like silk; soft and smooth.

silk'iness, *n.*, the quality or state of being silky.

silk'screen, *n.*, fine silk mesh used in stencilling and printing.

silk'worm, *n.*, the worm (*bombyx mori*) that produces silk.

silk'y, *adj.*, like silk; smooth, soft, and lustrous.

sill, *n.*, a horizontal base of a window or door.

sil'labub, *n.*, milk or cream curded by the addition of wine, and often whipped. (Also *syllabub.*)

sill'er, *n.*, silver; money.

Sil'lery, *n.*, a champagne.

sil'lier, *adj.*, comp. of silly.

sil'liest, *adj.*, super. of silly.

sil'lily, *adv.*, in a silly way.

sil'liness, *n.*, the quality or state of being silly.

sillom'eter, *n.*, a nautical instrument for ascertaining a ship's rate of sailing.

sil'ly, *adj.*, simple, foolish, senseless, imbecile.

si'lo, *n.*, an airtight enclosure, whether a pit or a building, in which green fodder or grain can be stored and kept fit for eating; *v.t.*, to treat in this way; to turn to ensilage.

silt, *n.*, sediment carried down by flowing water; *v.i.*, to become choked up with an earthy deposit; *v.t.*, to choke up with an earthy deposit.

silt'ed, *p.p.*, silt.

silt'ing, *pr.p.*, silt.

Silu'rian, *adj.*, pert. or rel. to the Silures, early Celtic inhabitants of Wales; bel. to the Silurian geological division of the Palaeozoic period.

sil'va, *n.*, a wood, forest or glade (*Lat.*).

sil'van, *adj.*, wooded; rustic; shady; pert. or rel. to forests and woods; rural. (Also *sylvan.*)

sil'ver, *n.*, one of the precious metals, white and lustrous; a silver coin; a sheen as of silver; *v.i.*, to become silvery; *v.t.*, to coat or cover with silver.

sil'vered, *p.p.*, silver.

sil'verer, *n.*, one who silvers.

sil'vergilt', *adj.* and *n.*, silver, coated with gold.

sil'ver-grey, *adj.*, grey with a look of silver.

sil'veriness, *n.*, the appearance or quality of silver.

sil'vering, *n.*, silver-plating; the art of silvering; *pr.p.*, silver.

sil'ver-leaf, *n.*, silver beaten out into very thin leaves; a disease of plants and trees.

sil'verling, *n.*, an ancient silver coin.

sil'verside, *n.*, the best side of a round of beef.

sil'versmith, *n.*, a craftsman in silver.

sil'ver-stick, *n.*, a field officer of the Life Guards in attendance at Court, whose emblem of office is a silver wand.

sil'verware, *n.*, ware made from silver.

sil'very, *adj.*, like silver; containing silver.

sil'viculture, *n.*, the growing of trees.

simar', *n.*, a kind of scarf.

Sim'ia, *n.*, an anthropoid genus of apes.

sim'ian, *adj.*, ape-like; pert. or rel. to apes. (Also *simious.*)

sim'ilar, *adj.*, like, resembling.

similar'ity, *n.*, likeness; the state of being similar.

sim'ilarly, *adv.*, in like manner.

sim'ile, *adv.*, in similar style (*mus.*); *n.*, a comparison; the likening of one thing to another in express words, alike in only one or two respects; (a metaphor is a simile condensed into a single word or phrase).

simil'itude, *n.*, likeness; appearance.

sim'ilize, *v.i.*, to use similes; *v.t.*, to compare by means of a simile.

sim'ilor, *n.*, an alloy of copper and zinc.

sim'ious, *adj.*, *i.q.* simian.

sim'itar, *n.*, *i.q.* scimitar.

sim'mer, *n.*, the simmering state; *v.i.*, to keep gently boiling; *v.t.*, to keep near the boiling point.

sim'mered, *p.p.*, simmer.

sim'mering, *pr.p.*, simmer.

sim'nel-cake, *n.*, a rich cake, often decorated, and eaten principally on Mothering Sunday, but also at Christmas and Easter.

simo'niac, *n.*, one who has committed an act of simony.

simoni'acal, *adj.*, of the nature of simony.

Simo'nian, *adj.*, rel. to Simon Magus; *n.*, a member of an Early Christian heretical sect.

sim'ony, *n.*, the sin of Simon Magus; purchasing preferment in the Church.

simoom', *n.*, a hot, dry wind met with mostly in the Arabian desert.

simoon', *n.*, *i.q.* simoom.

si'mous, *adj.*, snub-nosed.

simp, *n.*, a simpleton (*colloq.*).

sim'per, *n.*, a silly, affected smile; *v.i.*, to laugh or smile in a silly fashion; to smirk.

sim'pered, *p.p.*, simper.

sim'perer, *n.*, one who simpers.

sim'pering, *pr.p.*, simper.

sim'peringly, *adv.*, in a simpering, foolish way.

sim'ple, *adj.*, not combined with another thing; single; unaffected; plain; easy; unlettered; uncultivated; ordinary; uncomplicated; *n.*, an element; a medicinal herb; ecclesiastically, a feast of the lowest rank.

sim'ple-minded, *adj.*, ingenuous.

simple-mind'edness, *n.*, ingenuousness.

sim'pleness, *n.*, the quality or state of being simple.

sim'pler, *adj.*, comp. of simple.

sim'plest, *adj.*, super. of simple.

sim'pleton, *n.*, a silly person; a dolt.

simplic'ity, *n.*, *i.q.* simpleness; ease.

simplifica'tion, *n.*, the act or effect of simplifying.

sim'plified, *adj.*, made easy; *p.p.*, simplify.

simplifi'er, *n.*, one who, or that which, makes things simple or easy to understand.

sim'plify, *v.t.,* to make simple; to explain.

sim'plifying, *pr.p.,* simplify.

sim'plism, *n.,* affected simplicity.

sim'ply, *adv.,* in a simple way; merely.

simula'crum, *n.,* an image, likeness, ghost or pretender (*Lat.*).

sim'ulant, *adj.,* simulating.

sim'ulate, *v.t.,* to pretend; to present oneself in the character of; to assume the form of.

sim'ulated, *p.p.,* simulate.

sim'ulating, *pr.p.,* simulate.

simula'tion, *n.,* the act of simulating.

simultane'ity, *n.,* the state of occurring or operating at the same moment.

simulta'neous, *adj.,* occurring at the same moment.

simulta'neously, *adv.,* at the same moment.

simultan'eousness, *n., i.q.* simultaneity.

simurg', *n.,* a Persian mythical bird.

sin, *n.,* offence against God and right; transgression; a moral offence; *v.i.,* to offend against divine or moral law.

Sinait'ic, *adj.,* pert. or rel. to Sinai or the Peninsula of S., in the Near East.

sin'apism, *n.,* a mustard plaster.

since, *adv.,* ago; from a past time till now; *conj.,* from a past time till now and during the interval; because; *prep.,* throughout the interval between then and now.

sincere', *adj.,* ingenuous; honest without deceit; genuine.

sincere'ly, *adv.,* with sincerity.

sincer'ity, *n.,* the quality or state of being sincere.

sincip'ital, *adj.,* pert. or rel. to the sinciput.

sin'ciput, *n.,* the front part of the top of the head.

sin'don, *n.,* a fine Oriental fabric; a robe made of sindon.

sine, *adv.,* ago (*Scot.*); *n.,* a line drawn from one end of an arc

perpendicular to the radius at the other end (*math.*).

si'ne, *prep.,* without (*Lat.*).

si'necure, *n.,* a post or office with no duties, esp. an ecclesiastical benefice without cure of souls.

si'necurism, *n.,* the state of being the holder of a sinecure.

si'necurist, *n.,* one who holds a sinecure.

sin'ew, *n.,* a tendon or cord-like tissue.

sin'ewed, *adj.,* having sinews.

sin'ewless, *adj.,* without sinews.

sin'ewy, *adj.,* strong, well-knit.

sinfo'nia, *n.,* a symphony (*mus.*).

sin'ful, *adj.,* wicked.

sin'fully, *adv.,* wickedly.

sin'fulness, *n.,* wickedness; a state of sin.

sing, *v.t.,* to celebrate in song or verse; *v.i.,* to utter musical sounds; to make a sound as of singing; to speak words to a melody.

sing'able, *adj.,* that can be sung.

singe, *n.,* the act or effect of singeing; *v.t.* and *i.,* to scorch; to burn superficially.

singed, *p.p.,* singe.

singe'ing, *pr.p.,* singe.

sin'ger, *n.,* one who singes.

sing'er, *n.,* one who sings; a cantor or chorister.

singh, *n.,* a Sikh warrior.

sing'ing, *pr.p.,* sing.

sing'ing-book, *n.,* a song-book.

sing'ing-master, *n.,* an instructor in singing.

sin'gle, *adj.,* individual; one only; unmarried; unaided; ingenuous; *n.,* a hit for one in cricket; *v.t.,* to pick out as typical or exemplary.

sin'gle-breasted, *adj.,* having only one row of buttons.

sin'gled, *p.p.,* single.

sin'gle-en'try, *n.,* a system of book-keeping.

sin'gle-handed, *adj.,* unaided.

sin'gle-hearted, *adj.,* sincere.

sin'gle-minded, *adj.,* purposeful; concentrated on one purpose.

single'mind'edness, *n.,* the quality or state of being single-minded.

sin'gleness, *n.,* the quality or state of being single or distinct; simplicity; ingenuousness.

sin'gle-seater, *n.,* anything having only one seat.

sin'gle-stick, *n.,* a thick cudgel; esp. a stick used in a kind of fencing game.

sin'glet, *n.,* a light undergarment.

sin'gleton, *n.,* the only card of a suit; a single thing.

sin'gling, *pr.p.,* single.

sin'gly, *adv.,* one at a time; by oneself.

sing'song, *adj.,* monotonous, droning; *n.,* a monotonous, droning kind of speech; an amateur, free-and-easy vocal concert.

sin'gular, *adj.,* not plural; single; remarkable; strange.

singular'ity, *n.,* the quality or state of being singular.

sin'gularize, *v.t.,* to make singular; to single out.

sin'gularized, *p.p.,* singularize.

sin'gularizing, *pr.p.,* singularize.

sin'gularly, *adv.,* in a surprising or strange way.

sin'gult, *n.,* a hiccough or sob.

Sinha'la, *n.,* the language of Ceylon. (Also *Sinhalese.*)

Singhalese', *adj.,* pert. or rel. to Ceylon; *n.,* a native of C.

Sin'halese, *adj.* and *n., i.q.* Singhalese.

sin'ical, *adj.,* pert. or rel. to a sine.

sin'ister, *adj.,* of ill omen; malignant; villainous; on the left side (*her.*).

sin'istral, *adj.,* pert. or rel. to the left hand.

sin'istrous, *adj.,* towards the left.

sink, *n.,* a drain for dirty water, etc.; *v.i.,* to descend or decline; to fall towards the bottom; *v.t.,* to submerge; to excavate downward; to lower or degrade; to suppress; to engrave.

sink'er, *n.*, one who, or that which, sinks; a weight attached to a fishing or sounding line.

sink'hole, *n.*, the hole in a sink for the outflow.

sink'ing, *n.*, an internal feeling of hunger or exhaustion; *pr.p.*, sink.

sink'ing-fund, *n.*, a reserve of money, the accumulation of which will, at maturity, pay off a debt.

sin'less, *adj.*, without sin; pure.

sin'lessness, *n.*, the quality or state of being sinless.

sinned, *p.p.*, sin.

sin'ner, *n.*, one who sins.

sin'net, *n.*, *i.q.* sennet.

Sinn Fein', *n.*, an Irish patriotic movement ("ourselves alone").

sin'ning, *pr.p.*, sin.

sin'-offering, *n.*, a sacrifice in atonement for sin.

sin'ogram, *n.*, a Chinese written character.

sinol'ogist, *n.*, *i.q.* a sinologue.

sin'ologue, *n.*, a person versed in sinology.

sinol'ogy, *n.*, the study of Chinese culture, art, religion, etc.

sinophob'ia, *n.*, a dislike of the Chinese.

sin'ter, *n.*, a siliceous deposit in springs (*Ger.*).

Sin'too, *n.*, *i.q.* Shinto.

sin'uate, *adj.*, with a margin curving inward and outward.

sin'uated, *adj.*, *i.q.* sinuate.

sinua'tion, *n.*, a curving inward and outward.

sin'uose, *adj.*, wavy.

sinuos'ity, *n.*, waviness.

sin'uous, *adj.*, curving, winding.

sin'uously, *adv.*, in a winding or curving way.

si'nus, *n.*, a hollow; a depression (*anat.*); a fistula (*path.*, *Lat.*).

sinusi'tis, *n.*, inflamation of the sinus of the nose.

Sioux, *n.*, a N. American Indian tribe; the language of the tribe; a member of the tribe.

sip, *n.*, a small draught; a taste; *v.t.*, to drink lightly and in small draughts; to taste.

si'phon, *n.*, a bent tube with one part shorter than the other, used for drawing water, etc., down to a lower level; an aerated water bottle containing a siphon; a tube-like organ. (Also **syphon**.)

si'phonet, *n.*, a tube through which aphides exude honey-dew.

siphon'ic, *adj.*, pert. or rel. to a siphon.

si'phuncle, *n.*, a canal-like tube in certain molluscs and shells; a tube with which some insects suck.

siphun'cular, *adj.*, pert. or rel. to a siphuncle.

sipped, *p.p.*, sip.

sip'per, *n.*, one who drinks constantly.

sip'pet, *n.*, a small piece of fried or toasted bread.

sip'ping, *pr.p.*, sip.

sir, *n.*, a courtesy title in speaking to a man; the courtesy title of a knight or baronet.

sir'car, *n.*, an E. Indian name for the Government or the head of a business house. (Also **sirkar**.)

sir'dar, *n.*, a military commander; a chief (*Hind.*).

sire, *n.*, the title of address in speaking to the sovereign; a father; a male animal; *v.t.*, to be the father of.

si'ren, *adj.*, enchanting, bewitching; *n.*, one of the three melodious divinities who lured mariners to destruction; a ship's foghorn; a dangerously seductive woman.

sirene', *n.*, an apparatus that marks the vibrations of a musical note.

siren'ian, *n.*, an aquatic fish-like mammal.

sirg'ang, *n.*, the green jackdaw.

siri'asis, *n.*, sunstroke; a sun-bath.

Sir'ius, *n.*, the dog-star (*astron.*).

sir'kar, *n.*, *i.q.* sircar.

sir'loin, *n.*, the upper part of a loin of beef.

siroc'co, *n.*, a hot, dry wind rising in the Libyan desert (*It.*).

sir'rah, *n.*, an angry or scornful expression (*arch.*).

sir'up, *n.*, *i.q.* syrup.

sir'upy, *adj.*, *i.q.* syrupy.

sis'al, *n.*, the fibre plant *Agave rigida* used for making rope and mats.

sis'kin, *n.*, a variety of finch.

siss'y, *adj.*, effeminate (*colloq.*); *n.*, an effeminate male; a young girl.

sist, *v.t.*, to stay or stop; to summon (*leg.*).

sis'ter, *n.*, a daughter of the same parents as those of another person; the title of a woman belonging to a religious or a nursing order; one of the same kind, as "the sister university."

sis'terhood, *n.*, the relation of a sister; a religious community of sisters; sisters collectively.

sis'ter-in-law, *n.*, a wife's or a husband's sister; a brother's wife.

sis'terly, *adj.*, like a sister.

Sis'tine, *adj.*, rel. specifically to Pope Sixtus IV and the Sistine Chapel named after him and built by him in Rome.

sis'trum, *n.*, a sort of musical rattle (*Lat.*).

sisyphe'an, *adj.*, pert. or rel. to Sisyphus and his perpetual punishment of having to push uphill a stone that continually rolled back; hopelessly laborious.

sit, *v.i.*, to support the body on the buttocks; to rest; to weigh upon; to enter for an examination; to represent a constituency; to hold a court; to incubate; *v.t.*, to have a firm seat on.

site, *n.*, a place where a building stands or is about to be erected; *v.t.*, to place or locate.

si'ted, *p.p.*, site.

sith, *conj.*, since.

sithe, *n.*, the old form of the word *scythe*.

sit'ing, *n.*, *i.q.* site; *pr.p.*, site.

sitol'ogy, *n.*, the science of food and diet.

sit'ter, *n.*, one who sits, esp. to an artist, etc.; a brooding hen.

sitt'er-in, *n.*, a babysitter (*colloq.*).

sit'ting, *n.*, the act of sitting; a session; the collective eggs under a sitting hen; *pr.p.*, sit.

sit'ting-room, *n.*, a room to sit in.

sit'uate, *adj.*, placed; *v.t.*, to place.

sit'uated, *adj.*, *i.q.* situate; *p.p.*, situate.

situa'tion, *n.*, position, place; a post of service; a job.

situa'tional, *adj.*, pert. or rel. to a situation or position.

situa'tionally, *adv.*, in a situational way.

sitz'-bath, *n.*, a bath in which one sits.

Si'vaism, *n.*, the worship of Siva.

Si'vaite, *n.*, a worshipper of the Hindu deity, Siva.

Sivan', *n.*, the ninth month of the Jewish civil year.

six, *adj.*, exceeding five by one; *n.*, the number next above five; the sign 6.

six'ain, *n.*, a six-line stanza.

six'er, *n.*, a hit for six in cricket.

six'fold, *adj.*, six times as many; multiplied by six.

six'foo'ter, *n.*, a person who is six feet tall.

six'pence, *n.*, the value of six pence.

six'penny, *adj.*, worth six pence.

six'score, *adj.*, 120; six time twenty.

six'-seater, *n.*, anything having six seats.

sixte, *n.*, a position in fencing.

sixteen', *adj.*, six added to ten.

sixteenth, *adj.*, the ordinal of sixteen.

sixth, *adj.*, the ordinal of six.

sixth'ly, *adv.*, in the sixth place.

six'tieth, *adj.*, the ordinal of sixty.

six'ty, *adj.*, six times ten.

si'zable, *adj.*, proper as regards size; not small. (Also *sizeable*.)

si'zar, *n.*, an undergraduate at Cambridge or Dublin holding a small benefaction from his college.

size, *n.*, bulk, dimensions; a sort of glue; *v.i.*, to draw food supplies from a college buttery at Cambridge; *v.t.*, to group according to size; to cover with size.

size'able, *adj.*, *i.q.* sizable.

sized, *p.p.*, size.

siz'el, *n.*, *i.q.* scissel.

si'zer, *n.*, one who sizes.

si'zing, *n.*, the act of sizing in all senses; the materials used in the process of sizing; *pr.p.*, size.

si'zy, *adj.*, like, or containing, size.

siz'zle, *n.*, a spluttering or sizzling sound; *v.i.*, to make a spluttering sound.

siz'zled, *p.p.*, sizzle.

siz'zling, *n.*, *i.q.* sizzle; *pr.p.*, sizzle.

sjam'bok, *n.*, a S. African Boer's whip; *v.t.*, to flog with a sjambok.

skain, *n.*, *i.q.* skean.

skald, *n.*, *i.q.* scald.

skat, *n.*, a German card-game.

skate, *n.*, a flat fish; an attachment to the foot enabling the wearer to travel over ice or on rollers; *v.i.*, to travel on skates.

ska'ted, *p.p.*, skate.

ska'ter, *n.*, one who skates.

ska'ting, *pr.p.*, skate.

skean, *n.*, a Gaelic dagger. (Also *skain* and *skene*.)

skedad'dle, *v.i.*, to make one's escape; to clear off (*Amer.*).

skee, *n.* and *v.i.*, *i.q.* ski.

skee'ball, *n.*, a bowls game played in an alley humped in the middle.

skeel, *n.*, a Scottish wooden milk vessel.

skeet, *n.*, a scoop for throwing water on sails and decks (*naut.*).

skein, *n.*, silk, thread, etc., in a coil; a group of geese when flying.

skel'etal, *adj.*, pert. or rel. to the skeleton (*biol.*).

skel'eton, *n.*, the bony structure of animals when stripped of the flesh; an outline; a fleshless person.

skel'etonize, *v.i.*, to become a skeleton; *v.t.*, to make a skeleton of.

skelp, *n.*, a smart smack; *v.t.*, to hit or smack (*Scot.*).

skene, *n.*, *i.q.* skean.

skep, *n.*, a wicker basket; a straw or wicker beehive. (Also *skip*.)

skep'tic, *n.*, *i.q.* sceptic.

skep'ticism, *n.*, *i.q.* scepticism.

sker'ry, *n.*, a reef (*Scot.*).

sketch, *n.*, an incomplete or rapid drawing; a rough draft; *v.i.*, to act as a sketcher; *v.t.*, to draw in rough outline; to make a sketch of.

sketch'-book, *n.*, a book in which sketches can be drawn.

sketched, *p.p.*, sketch.

sketch'er, *n.*, one who sketches.

sketch'ily, *adv.*, in a sketchy way.

sketch'iness, *n.*, the state of being sketchy.

sketch'ing, *n.*, the occupation of a sketcher; *pr.p.*, sketch.

sketch'y, *adj.*, in outline; imperfect.

skew, *adj.*, slanting; *adv.*, slantwise.

skew'-back, *n.*, the bevelled support at the spring of a segmented arch.

skew'bald, *adj.*, (of a horse) with brown and white patches (not black).

skew'-bridge, *n.*, a bridge crossing a road or river slant-wise.

skewed, *p.p.*, skew.

skew'er, *n.*, a metal or wooden pin for holding meat together.

skew'ing, *pr.p.*, skew.

ski, *n.,* a long snow-shoe; *v.i.,* to slide on skis. (Also *skee.*)

ski'agram, *n.,* *i.q.* sciagram.

ski'agraph, *n.,* *i.q.* sciagraph.

ski'agraphy, *n.,* *i.q.* sciagraphy.

skid, *n.,* a drag on a wheel; a ship's fender; the lateral movement of an automobile; *v.i.,* to side-slip; *v.t.,* to check with a skid.

skid'ded, *p.p.,* skid.

skid'ding, *pr.p.,* skid.

skied, *p.p.,* ski.

ski'er, *n.,* one who skis.

skiff, *n.,* a small boat.

skif'fle, *n.,* a kind of jazz type folk music.

ski'-ing, *pr.p.,* ski.

skil'ful, *adj.,* clever; handy; expert.

skil'fully, *adv.,* with skill.

skil'fulness, *n.,* cleverness, dexterity.

skill, *n.,* cleverness; expertness.

skilled, *adj.,* expert; skilful.

skil'let, *n.,* a small shallow cooking utensil.

skill-less, *adj.,* without skill.

skil'ly, *n.,* a thin gruel in which meat has been boiled.

skim, *v.i.,* to pass quickly and lightly over anything; *v.t.,* to take the scum off; to remove cream from.

skimmed, *p.p.,* skim.

skim'mer, *n.,* one who, or that which, skims.

skim'-milk, *n.,* milk from which the cream has been skimmed.

skim'ming, *pr.p.,* skim.

skim'mington, *n.,* orig. a rowdy demonstration against a henpecked man; a row; now, any disturbance.

skimp, *adj.,* scanty; *v.i.,* to be mean or parsimonious; *v.t.,* to stint; to supply meagrely.

skimped, *p.p.,* skimp.

skimp'ing, *pr.p.,* skimp.

skin, *n.,* an animal's outer covering; anything like a skin; *v.i.,* to form a coating; *v.t.,* to remove the skin; to flay.

skin'-deep, *adj.* and *adv.,* only just below the surface; insincere.

skin'flint, *n.,* a screw; a niggardly person.

skin'ful, *n.,* as much as one can hold of food or drink (*slang*).

skin'-grafting, *n.,* the surgical operation of replacing injured or diseased skin by healthy skin from the same person's body.

skink, *n.,* a variety of lizard.

skin'less, *adj.,* having little or no skin; having a thin skin.

skinned, *p.p.,* skin.

skin'ner, *n.,* a dealer in skins.

skin'nier, *adj.,* comp. of skinny.

skin'niest, *adj.,* super. of skinny.

skin'niness, *n.,* the quality or state of being skinny.

skin'ning, *pr.p.,* skin.

skin'ny, *adj.,* lean; mean (*slang*); niggardly.

skin'-tight, *adj.,* very close-fitting.

skip, *n.,* a light leap; an omission; a basket; (Also *skep.*); a college servant; a scout; a large container for débris; the captain of a bowling or curling side; a cage or bucket for raising or lowering men in quarries, mines, etc. or over the side of a ship; *v.i.,* to take light leaps; *v.t.,* to omit (passages from a book or letter).

skipped, *p.p.,* skip.

skip'per, *n.,* one who skips; a sea-captain; a small brown butterfly.

skip'pet, *n.,* a deed seal protector.

skip'ping, *pr.p.,* skip.

skip'ping-rope, *n.,* a rope used in a children's skipping game.

skirl, *n.,* the sound of bagpipes; *v.i.,* to make a sound like bagpipes.

skir'ling, *pr.p.,* skirl.

skir'mish, *n.,* a small fight; a brush; *v.i.,* to engage in a small fight, not a regular battle.

skir'mished, *p.p.,* skirmish.

skir'misher, *n.,* one who skirmishes.

skir'mishing, *n.,* *i.q.* skirmish; *pr.p.,* skirmish.

skir'ret, *n.,* a water-parsnip.

skirt, *n.,* the lower part of any garment; the part of a dress from the waist downward; a separate garment from the waist downwards; a border; *v.i.,* to extend along; *v.t.,* to go close by anything.

skirt'ed, *adj.,* having a skirt attached; *p.p.,* skirt.

skirt'ing, *n.,* dress material; *i.q.* skirting-board; *pr.p.,* skirt.

skirt'ing-board, *n.,* upright boarding laid along the bottom of an inner wall.

skit, *n.,* a take-off; a satire.

skit'ter, *v.i.,* to fish by surface baiting; to go splashing lightly along a water surface.

skit'tish, *adj.,* playful; wanton; easily startled.

skit'tishly, *adv.,* in a skittish way.

skit'tle, *n.,* a wooden pin used in the game of skittles; *v.t.,* to dismiss batsmen in rapid succession; to knock down.

skit'tle-alley, *n.,* an alley in which skittles or ninepins are played.

skit'tles, *n. pl.,* the game of ninepins.

skive, *v.i.,* to dodge work or responsibilities (*colloq.*).

skived, *p.p.,* skive.

ski'ver, *n.,* an instrument used in leather dressing; split sheep skin; a person who skives (*colloq.*).

skiv'ing, *pr.p.,* skive.

skiv'vy, *n.,* a female domestic servant (*colloq.*).

skow, *n.,* *i.q.* scow.

sku'a, *n.,* a gull-like sea-bird.

skuldugg'ery, *n.,* trickery; corrupt behaviour.

skulk, *n.,* an idler; *v.i.,* to keep out of sight; to hang back; to idle. (Also *sculk.*)

skulked, *p.p.*, skulk.

skulk'er, *n.*, one who skulks. (Also *sculker*.)

skulk'ing, *pr.p.*, skulk.

skull, *n.*, the bony structure containing the brain.

skull'cap, *n.*, a cap fitting close to the skull.

skunk, *n.*, a carnivorous American beast, highly malodorous when chased; a mean, worthless person.

skur'ry, *v.i.*, *i.q.* scurry.

sky, *n.*, the upper air; the ethereal vault; *v.t.*, to hang (pictures) too high to be properly seen; to strike a ball very high.

sky'-blue, *adj.*, blue like the colour of the sky.

sky'er, *n.*, a high hit at cricket.

Skye-ter'rier, *n.*, a kind of Scotch terrier.

sky'ey, *adj.*, like the sky; up in the sky.

sky'high, *adj.* and *adv.*, high up towards the sky; excessive.

sky'ish, *adj.*, sky-like.

sky'-jack, *v.t.*, to steal or take away an aircraft.

sky'lark, *n.*, a soaring lark; a frolic; *v.i.*, to indulge in a frolic (*colloq.*).

sky'larked, *p.p.*, skylark.

sky'larking, *n.*, frolicking; *pr.p.*, skylark.

sky'light, *n.*, a window in a roof.

sky'line, *n.*, the outline of buildings, etc., defined against the sky.

sky'man, *n.*, a paratrooper.

sky'rocket, *n.*, a rocket with a high flight.

sky'-sail, *n.*, a light sail above the royal.

sky'scraper, *n.*, a very tall building; a sail above the royal.

sky'troops, *n.*, airborne troops; paratroopers.

sky'way, *n.*, a route for aircraft; airways.

sky'-writing, *n.*, the use of an aircraft to make sky-signs in smoke.

slab, *adj.*, thick, sticky; *n.*, a flat piece of stone; mire.

slab'ber, *n.*, saliva; *v.i.*, to dribble saliva. (Also *slobber*.)

slab'bered, *p.p.*, slabber.

slab'berer, *n.*, one who slabbers. (Also *slobberer*.)

slab'bering, *pr.p.*, slabber.

slab'biness, *n.*, the quality or state of being slabby.

slab'by, *adj.*, viscous; sloppy.

slack, *adj.*, loose; unenergetic; idle; at ease; *n.*, the loose part of a rope; *v.i.*, to be lazy (*colloq.*).

slacked, *p.p.*, slack.

slack'en, *v.i.*, to become looser; to relax in effort; *v.t.*, to make looser.

slack'ened, *p.p.*, slacken.

slack'ening, *pr.p.*, slacken.

slack'er, *adj.*, *comp.* of slack; *n.*, a lazy, indolent person; an idler.

slack'est, *adj.*, *super.* of slack.

slack'ing, *pr.p.*, slack.

slack'ly, *adv.*, loosely, lazily.

slack'ness, *n.*, the quality or state of being slack.

slacks, *n. pl.*, long trousers (*colloq.*).

slag, *n.*, metal refuse; cinders vitrified.

slag'gy, *adj.*, containing or resembling slag.

slain, *p.p.*, slay.

slake, *v.i.*, to be watered; *v.t.*, to quench (thirst); to weaken by watering.

slaked, *p.p.*, slake.

slake'less, *adj.*, unquenchable.

sla'king, *pr.p.*, slake.

sla'lom, *n.*, a downhill ski race through obstacles; an obstacle race in canoes.

slam, *n.*, a loud bang; *v.i.*, to close with a noise; *v.t.*, to bang to with a noise.

slammed, *p.p.*, slam.

slam'ming, *pr.p.*, slam.

slan'der, *n.*, calumny; spiteful rumour; *v.t.*, to defame; to speak untruth about spitefully.

slan'dered, *p.p.*, slander.

slan'derer, *n.*, one who slanders.

slan'dering, *n.*, calumniation; *pr.p.*, slander.

slan'derous, *adj.*, calumnious; speaking slander.

slan'derously, *adv.*, in a slanderous manner.

slang, *n.*, words or expressions only acceptable in informal speech or writing; colloquial jargon; argot; *v.t.*, to address abusively (*colloq.*).

slanged, *p.p.*, slang.

slang'ing, *pr.p.*, slang.

slan'guage, *n.*, slang language (*colloq.*).

slang'y, *adj.*, given to the use of slang.

slant, *adj.*, oblique, sloping; *n.*, a sloping direction; an inclined plane; *v.i.* to slope; *v.t.*, to make to slope.

slant'ed, *p.p.*, slant.

slant'ing, *adj.*, sloping; *pr.p.*, slant.

slant'ingly, *adv.*, in a slanting way; slantwise; aslant.

slant'wise, *adv.*, *i.q.* slantingly.

slap, *adv.*, directly; *n.*, an attempt (*colloq.*); a blow with the open hand; *v.t.*, to deliver such a blow.

slap-bang', *adv.*, thoughtlessly, carelessly.

slap'dash, *adj.*, done at random; *adv.*, in a free, careless manner.

slap'happy, *adj.*, made complacent or indifferent (*slang*).

slap'jack, *n.*, a pancake cooked on a griddle.

slapped, *p.p.*, slap.

slap'ping, *pr.p.*, slap.

slap'stick, *n.*, a kind of boisterous low comedy.

slash, *n.*, a slit; *v.i.*, to use a whip at random; *v.t.*, to cut with repeated strokes; to slit; to whip savagely.

slashed, *p.p.*, slash.

slash'er, *n.*, one who slashes.

slash'ing, *adj.*, caustic, severely critical; *pr.p.*, slash.

slat, *n.*, a narrow metal or wooden strip.

slatch, *n.*, the slack of a rope; the duration of a transitory breeze.

slate, *n.*, laminated rock that can be used in place of roof-tiles; *v.t.*, to roof with slates; to rebuke or condemn.

sla'ted, *p.p.*, slate.

sla'ter, *n.*, a man who slates roofs; a leather-dresser's implement for removing the hair from hides.

sla'ting, *n.*, a condemnation; *pr.p.*, slate.

slat'ted, *adj.*, made with slats.

slat'tern, *n.*, a slovenly woman.

slat'ternliness, *n.*, slovenliness.

slat'ternly, *adj.*, slovenly; *adv.*, untidily.

sla'ty, *adj.*, like, or abounding in, slate.

slaugh'ter, *n.*, killing on a large scale; massacre; the killing of cattle; *v.t.*, to slay; to kill (cattle) for eating.

slaugh'tered, *p.p.*, slaughter.

slaugh'terer, *n.*, one who kills cattle for the butcher.

slaugh'ter-house, *n.*, an abattoir.

slaugh'tering, *pr.p.*, slaughter.

slaugh'terous, *adj.*, murderous.

Slav, *n.*, a member of the Slavonic race in Central and Eastern Europe.

slave, *n.*, a person held in bondage; a serf; a downtrodden person; *v.i.*, to drudge; to work laboriously.

slaved, *p.p.*, slave.

slave'driver, *n.*, one who compels slaves to work; anyone like him.

slave'holder, *n.*, an owner of slaves.

slave'holding, *n.*, the practice of keeping slaves.

slave'-owner, *n.*, *i.q.* slaveholder.

sla'ver, *n.*, a dealer in slaves; a ship for exporting slaves.

slav'er, *n.*, dribbled saliva; *v.i.*, to dribble; *v.t.*, to foul with dribble.

slav'ered, *p.p.*, slaver.

slav'erer, *n.*, one who slavers.

slav'ering, *pr.p.*, slaver.

sla'very, *n.*, the condition of being a slave.

slave'-ship, *n.*, a ship used in the slave-trade; *i.q.* slaver.

slave'-trade, *n.*, traffic in slaves.

sla'vey, *n.*, a young, overworked maid-servant (*colloq.*).

sla'ving, *pr.p.*, slave.

sla'vish, *adj.*, like a slave; abject.

sla'vishly, *adv.*, abjectly.

sla'vishness, *n.*, abjectness.

Slavon'ic, *adj.*, pert. or rel. to the Slavs; the language of the Slavs.

slaw', *n.*, a sliced cabbage salad, usually in *coleslaw.*

slay, *n.*, *i.q.* sley; *v.t.*, to kill, to destroy.

slay'er, *n.*, one who kills.

slay'ing, *pr.p.*, slay.

sleave, *n.*, floss; entangled thread.

slea'zy, *adj.*, flimsy; slatternly (*colloq.*). (Also *sleezy.*)

sled, *n.*, a sledge; *v.t.*, to carry in a sled.

sled'ded, *p.p.*, sled.

sled'ding, *pr.p.*, sled.

sledge, *n.*, *i.q.* sled; *i.q.* sledge-hammer.

sledge'-hammer, *n.*, a great heavy hammer.

sleek, *adj.*, smooth, shiny; *v.t.*, to smooth; to put a gloss on.

sleeked, *p.p.*, sleek.

sleek'ing, *pr.p.*, sleek.

sleek'ly, *adv.*, in a sleek way.

sleek'ness, *n.*, smoothness, glossiness.

sleep, *n.*, slumber; *v.i.*, to slumber; to rest in the almost unconscious state of complete nervous relaxation; to become motionless.

sleep'er, *n.*, one who sleeps; one of the timbers on which railway metals are laid; an animal that hibernates; a sleeping compartment.

sleep'ier, *adj.*, comp. of sleepy.

sleep'iest, *adj.*, super. of sleepy.

sleep'ily, *adv.*, in a sleepy way.

sleep'iness, *n.*, the state of being sleepy.

sleep'ing, *pr.p.*, sleep.

slee'ping-draught, *n.*, a drug taken to induce sleep.

slee'ping-part'ner, *n.*, a partner in a business who takes no active part.

sleep'ing-sick'ness, *n.*, a disease causing a half-sleepy condition and fever, borne by the tsetse fly.

sleep'less, *adj.*, unable to sleep.

sleep'lessness, *n.*, the state of being sleepless; insomnia.

sleep'walker, *n.*, one who walks in his sleep; a somnambulist.

sleep'walking, *n.*, the habit of walking in sleep; somnambulism.

sleep'y, *adj.*, wanting to go to sleep; tired; slow; over-ripe.

sleet, *n.*, driving snow or hail mixed with rain; *v.i.*, to come in a shower of sleet.

sleet'iness, *n.*, the state of being sleety.

sleet'y, *adj.*, falling in sleet.

sleeve, *n.*, an arm-covering; *v.t.*, to put sleeves into a garment; any exterior fitting into which another part slides.

sleeve'-links, *n. pl.*, a contrivance for fastening shirt cuffs.

slee-worm, *n.*, *i.q.* slow-worm.

slee'zy, *adj.*, *i.q.* sleazy.

sleigh, *n.*, a sledge; *v.i.*, to ride in a sleigh or sledge.

sleigh'-bell, *n.*, a bell on a horse drawing a sleigh.

sleighed, *p.p.*, sleigh.

sleigh'ing, *n.*, driving in a sleigh; *pr.p.*, sleigh.

sleight, *n.*, dexterity; prestidigitation.

slen'der, *adj.*, thin, tapering, slight.

slen'derly, *adv.*, slightly.

slen'derness, *n.*, the quality or state of being slender.

slept, *p.p.*, sleep.

sleuth, *n.*, trail; a person who tracks another; detective; *v.i.*, to trail.

sleuth'-hound, *n.*, a bloodhound; a detective (*colloq.*).

slew, *v.i.* and *t.*, to turn round; (Also *slue*.); *p.p.*, slay.

sley, *n.*, a weaver's reed. (Also *slay*.)

slice, *n.*, a piece cut out of or off something; a table-implement for serving fish; the flight of a sliced golf-ball; *v.t.*, to cut into slices; to hit a golf-ball so that it flies off to one side.

sliced, *p.p.*, slice.

sli'cer, *n.*, one who, or that which, slices.

sli'cing, *pr.p.*, slice.

slick, *n.*, metal ore in a state to be worked; *adj.*, smart, quick-thinking; *adv.*, right away; entirely.

slid, *p.p.*, slide.

slid'able, *adj.*, capable of being slid.

slid'der, *v.i.*, to slide; *v.t.*, to slip (*Scot.*).

slide, *v.i.*, to skim over ice or any other smooth surface; *v.t.*, to slip a thing along; *n.*, smooth ice on which one can slide; a slip; a slope; a picture for photographic projection.

sli'der, *n.*, one who slides.

slide'-rule, *n.*, a rule with a sliding part, used in mathematical calculations.

sli'ding, *pr.p.*, slide.

sli'ding-scale, *n.*, a graduated scale.

slight, *adj.*, slim, frail, small; insignificant; unimportant; *n.*, contemptuous treatment; an affront; *v.t.*, to treat contemptuously; to affront.

slight'ed, *p.p.*, slight.

slight'er, *adj.*, *comp.* of slight.

slight'est, *adj.*, *super.* of slight.

slight'ing, *pr.p.*, slight.

slight'ingly, *adv.*, in a slighting way.

slight'ly, *adv.*, in small degree; insignificantly.

slight'ness, *n.*, the quality or state of being slight.

sli'ly, *adv.*, in a sly way.

slim, *adj.*, slender, thin; crafty (*colloq.*); *v.i.*, to reduce one's weight.

slime, *n.*, sticky mud; any sticky substance; *v.i.*, to become slimy; *v.t.*, to daub.

slimed, *p.p.*, slime.

sli'miness, *n.*, the quality or state of being slimy.

sli'ming, *pr.p.*, slime.

slimmed, *p.p.*, slim.

slim'ming, *adj.*, producing slimness; *n.*, reducing weight; *pr.p.*, slim.

slim'ness, *n.*, the quality or state of being slim.

sli'my, *adj.*, viscous, sticky; covered with slime.

sling, *n.*, an implement for hurling stones; a contrivance for supporting an injured arm or hand; a kind of toddy or alcoholic drink; a hoist for loading goods.

sling'er, *n.*, one who slings.

sling'ing, *pr.p.*, sling.

slink, *v.i.*, to steal away; to sneak off; *v.t.*, to give birth prematurely to (said of the lower animals).

slink'er, *n.*, one who slinks; a slacker.

slink'ing, *pr.p.*, slink.

slink'y, *adj.*, slender; graceful and flowing; close-fitting.

slip, *n.*, a fall; a fault; an omission; a twig; a young growth or shoot; a petticoat; the cover of a pillow, etc.; a little sole; one of the fielders in cricket; a position in the cricket field; *v.i.*, to miss one's footing; to fall; to move unperceived; to commit a fault; *v.t.*, to let loose; to omit.

slip'-knot, *n.*, a running-knot.

slipped, *p.p.*, slip.

slip'per, *n.*, a loose, easy shoe; one who slips.

slip'periness, *n.*, the quality or state of being slippery.

slip'perwort, *n.*, the calceolaria or campanula.

slip'pery, *adj.*, excessively smooth, causing one to slip; infirm; crafty.

slip'piness, *n.*, *i.q.* slipperiness.

slip'ping, *pr.p.*, slip.

slipp'y, *adj.*, *i.q.* slippery; quick, nimble (*colloq.*).

slip'road, *n.*, a local by-pass.

slips, *n. pl.*, fielders in cricket; bathing drawers.

slip'shod, *adj.*, careless, slovenly.

slip'-slop, *adj.*, *i.q.* slipshod; *n.*, a poor, weak drink; careless work.

slip'way, *n.*, a launching plane for a seaplane, ship, etc.

slit, *n.*, a narrow cut or opening; *v.t.*, to make a slit in.

slith'er, *v.i.*, to slip, to slide.

slit'ter, *n.*, one who, or that which, slits.

slit'ting, *pr.p.*, slit.

slit'ting-mill, *n.*, a mill where metal plates are slit.

slit'-trench, *n.*, a narrow trench.

sliv'er, *n.*, a small piece cut from something; *v.t.*, to cut up small.

sloam, *n.*, earth between coal layers.

sloat, *n.*, *i.q.* slot.

slob'ber, *v.i.*, *i.q.* slabber.

slob'bered, *p.p.*, slobber.

slob'berer, *n.*, *i.q.*, slabberer.

slob'bering, *pr.p.*, slobber.

slob'ice, *n.*, floating ice mixed with snow.

sloe, *n.*, a bitter sort of plum.

slog, *n.*, a wild hit; *v.t.* and *i.*, to strike hard and wildly; to work very hard. (Also *slug*.)

slo'gan, *n.*, a war-cry of a clan; any catch-phrase (*Scot.*).

slogged, *p.p.*, slog.

slog'ger, *n.*, one who slogs.

slog'ging, *pr.p.*, slog.

sloid, *n.*, a Swedish system of manual instruction. (Also *sloyd*.)

sloop, *n.*, a single-masted vessel rigged fore and aft.

sloot, *n.*, *i.q.* sluit.

slop, *n.*, spilt liquid; drink or liquid food of poor quality; a policeman (from "backslang"); *v.t.*, to spill carelessly or by accident; to wet.

slop'-basin, *n.*, a basin into which dregs of tea may be poured. (Also *slop-bowl*.)

slope, *n.*, a declivity; *v.i.*, to slant; to run away (*colloq.*); *v.t.*, to make to incline; to cause to slant.

sloped, *p.p.*, slope.

slo'ping, *adj.*, slanting; *pr.p.*, slope.

slo'pingly, *adv.*, in a sloping way.

slop'-pail, *n.*, a pail to hold dirty water.

slopped, *p.p.*, slop.

slop'pily, *adv.*, in a sloppy way.

slop'piness, *n.*, the quality or state of being sloppy.

slop'ping, *pr.p.*, slop.

slop'py, *adj.*, wet, slopped, splashed; careless; untidy.

slops, *n. pl.*, readymade, reach-me-down clothes; an invalid's food; used water.

slop'-seller, *n.*, one who sells cheap, readymade clothing.

slop'-shop, *n.*, a shop where cheap, readymade clothes are sold.

slosh, *n.*, mud, slush; *v.t.*, to thrash or beat (*colloq.*).

slosh'y, *adj.*, muddy (*colloq.*).

slot, *n.*, a slit or aperture; a mortise; a deer's trail; a stage trap-door; *v.t.*, to furnish with a slot; to track; to fit in. (Also *sloat*.)

sloth, *n.*, inertness, laziness; a slow-moving quadruped that lives in trees.

sloth'ful, *adj.*, inert, lazy.

sloth'fully, *adv.*, lazily.

sloth'fulness, *n.*, idleness, inertness.

slot'ted, *p.p.*, slot.

slot'ting, *pr.p.*, slot.

slouch, *n.*, a stoop with the head or shoulders; an awkward gait; a clumsy fellow; *v.i.*, to walk in an ungainly way; *v.t.*, to tilt to one side.

slouched, *p.p.*, slouch.

slouch'-hat, *n.*, a hat that tilts down.

slouch'ing, *adj.*, ungainly; stooping; *pr.p.*, slouch.

slouch'ingly, *adv.*, in a slouching way.

slough, *n.*, a bog.

slough, *n.*, a skin that is cast by a snake; that which comes away from a malignant sore; *v.i.*, to come away from the skin; to cast off a skin.

sloughed, *p.p.*, slough.

slough'ing, *pr.p.*, slough.

slough'y, *adj.*, miry.

slough'y, *adj.*, sloughing; tending to slough.

Slov'ak, *adj.*, pert. or rel. to the Slavonic race which inhabits part of Hungary; *n.*, a native of that part of H.

slov'en, *n.*, a careless, untidy person.

Slovene', *adj.*, pert. or rel. to a southern Slavic people in Yugoslavia; *n.*, a member of this race.

Sloven'ian, *adj.* and *n.*, *i.q.* Slovene; the language of the Slovenes.

slov'enliness, *n.*, the state of being slovenly.

slov'enly, *adj.*, carelessly untidy.

slow, *adj.*, not quick; behind in point of time; dull.

slow'coach, *n.*, a dull, slow person; a laggard.

slow'er, *adj.*, *comp.* of slow.

slow'est, *adj.*, *super.* of slow.

slow'ly, *adv.*, not quickly.

slow'-march, *n.*, a military funeral pace, as opposed to the quick march.

slow'-match, *n.*, a slow-burning rope for igniting explosives.

slow'-motion, *n.*, a film shown at slow speed to show the detail of movement.

slow'ness, *n.*, the quality or state of being slow.

slow'-worm, *n.*, the blind-worm. (Also *slee-worm*.)

sloyd, *n.*, *i.q.* sloid.

slub, *n.*, twisted wool; *v.t.*, to give (wool) a slight twist.

slub'ber, *n.*, and *v.t.* *i.q.* slub.

slub'bered, *p.p.*, slubber.

slub'bering, *pr.p.*, slubber.

sludge, *n.*, *i.q.* slush; a semi-liquid mixture (esp. of waste).

sludg'y, *adj.*, muddy, slushy.

slue, *v.t.* and *i.*, *i.q.* slew.

slued, *p.p.*, slue.

slug, *n.*, a kind of snail without a shell; a form of bullet; *i.q.* sluggard; *n.*, *v.t.* and *i.*, *i.q.* slog.

slug'abed, *n.*, a lazy, sluggish person.

slug'gard, *n.*, one who loves lying abed.

slugged, *p.p.*, slug.

slug'ging, *pr.p.*, slug.

slug'gish, *adj.*, torpid; inert, slow.

slug'gishly, *adv.*, in a sluggish way.

slug'gishness, *n.*, laziness, idleness, inactivity.

sluice, *n.*, a barrier in a river, etc., controlling the water's flow; the rush of water through a floodgate; *v.t.*, to throw water over oneself.

sluice'-gate, *n.*, a floodgate.

slui'cy, *adj.*, rushing out like water from a sluice.

slu'ing, *pr.p.*, slue.

sluit, *n.*, a narrow water channel. (Also *sloot*.)

slum, *n.*, a wretchedly poor quarter in a town; residue formed in lubricating oil during use; *v.i.*, to visit the slums.

slum'ber, *n.*, sleep; *v.i.*, to sleep soundly.

slum'bered, *p.p.*, slumber.

slum'berer, *n.*, one who slumbers.

slum'bering, *pr.p.*, slumber.

slum'berless, *adj.*, without sleep.

slum'berous, *adj.*, inducing sleep; sleeping; quiet.

slum'berously, *adv.*, sleepily.

slum'berwear, *n.*, night clothes.

slummed, *p.p.*, slum.

slum'ming, *n.*, the practice of visiting slums; *pr.p.*, slum.

slum'mock, *v.i.* and *t.*, to eat greedily; to stumble; to lounge ungracefully (*colloq.*).

slum'my, *adj.*, like a slum.

slump, *n.*, a rapid fall in prices, etc.; a fall through a coating of ice; *v.i.*, to fall helplessly; to sink through ice or into mud; to fall in value; to fail.

slung, *p.p.*, sling

slunk, *p.p.*, slink.

slur, *n.*, a disparaging remark; a stigma; a curve over two or more musical notes which are to be sung to the same syllable or played without a break; *v.t.*, to disparage; to speak or write indistinctly; to do anything carelessly; to sing with a slur.

slurred, *p.p.*, slur.

slur'ring, *pr.p.*, slur.

slush, *n.*, wet snow; soft mud.

slush'y, *adj.*, full of slush.

slut, *n.*, an untidy, dirty girl or woman.

slut'tish, *adj.*, inclined to be a slut.

slut'tishly, *adv.*, in a slatternly way.

slut'tishness, *n.*, the state of being sluttish.

sly, *adj.*, cunning, hypocritical, playful.

sly'-boots, *n.*, a sly person or animal.

sly'-goose, *n.*, a sheldrake.

sly'ly, *adv.*, in a sly way.

sly'ness, *n.*, the quality of being sly.

slype, *n.*, a covered passage from a cathedral transept to the chapter house.

smack, *adv.*, clean, outright; with a smacking noise; *n.*, a blow with the hands; a noise made with the lips; a flavour or taste; a small fishingboat; *v.i.*, to have a flavour; *v.t.*, to hit with the hand; to make a cracking noise with; to part the lips explosively.

smacked, *p.p.*, smack.

smack'er, *n.*, one who, or that which, smacks; a loud kiss (*slang*); a £1 note (*slang*).

smack'ing, *n.*, a smack or succession of smacks; *pr.p.*, smack.

small, *adj.*, not large; of little size, amount, quantity, etc.; weak; mild, humble; *adv.*, in a low tone; *n.*, a small part, esp. of the back.

small'age, *n.*, wild celery.

small'-arms, *n. pl.*, military weapons of the smaller kind, as rifles, etc.

small'er, *adj.*, *comp.* of small.

small'est, *adj.*, *super.* of small.

small'hold'ing, *n.*, a leased small farm or cultivated plot.

small'holder, *n.*, one who works a smallholding.

small'ish, *adj.*, rather small.

small'ness, *n.*, the quality or state of being small.

small'pox, *n.*, a virulent and highly infectious disease.

small-talk, *n.*, gossip.

smalt, *n.*, a glass of a deep cobalt-blue colour; when pulverized, it is used for a pigment.

smarag'dine, *adj.*, of emerald green.

smarm, *v.i.* and *t.* to smear; *v.i.*, to toady (*colloq.*).

smarm'y, *adj.*, ingratiating, fulsome; obsequious.

smart, *adj.*, alert; trim; fashionably attired; sharp; *n.*, an acute feeling of pain, physical or mental; *v.i.*, to feel an acute pain; to induce a feeling of pain.

smart'ed, *p.p.*, smart.

smart'en, *v.t.*, to brisk up; to improve the appearance of.

smart'ened, *p.p.*, smarten.

smart'ening, *pr.p.*, smarten.

smart'er, *adj.*, *comp.* of smart.

smart'est, *adj.*, *super.* of smart.

smart'ing, *pr.p.*, smart.

smart'ly, *adv.*, in a smart way.

smart'-money, *n.*, exemplary legal damages.

smart'ness, *n.*, the quality or state of being smart.

smash, *n.*, a breaking to pieces; a great fall; bankruptcy; *v.i.*, to become bankrupt; to fall in pieces; *v.t.*, to break in pieces; to hit downward with violence.

smash-and-grab, *n.*, robbery by a sudden breaking of a shop window and seizing hold of the nearest contents.

smashed, *p.p.*, smash.

smash'er, *n.*, one who, or that which, smashes; a smashing or complete blow; a very attractive person (*colloq.*).

smash'ing, *adj.*, very attractive; *pr.p.*, smash.

smash'-up, *n.*, a violent accident or collision.

smatch, *n.*, *i.q.* smack.

smat'ter, *n.*, scanty and superficial knowledge; *v.i.*, to have a smattering; *v.t.*, to show only a superficial knowledge of.

smat'tered, *p.p.*, smatter.

smat'terer, *n.*, one who has a superficial knowledge.

smat'tering, *n.*, a slight superficial knowledge; *pr.p.*, smatter.

smaze, *n.*, a mixture of smoke and haze.

smear, *n.*, a daub, stain or spot; a libel (*colloq.*); *v.t.*, to daub with some sticky or greasy substance; to mark with a stain, smudge or blot.

smeared, *p.p.*, smear.

smear'ing, *n.*, a daubing; *pr.p.*, smear.

smear'y, *adj.*, smeared.

smec'tite, *n.*, a clay used for cleaning purposes.

smeech, *n.*, a smell of burning. (Also *smitch*).

smeg'ma, *n.*, a soapy secretion in folds of the skin.

smell, *n.*, the nasal sense; an odour; *v.i.*, to emit an odour; *v.t.*, to perceive an odour.

smelled, *p.p.*, smell.

smell'er, *n.*, one who, or that which, smells; the nose (*slang*).

smell'ing, *adj.*, odoriferous; *pr.p.*, smell.

smell'ing-bottle, *n.*, a bottle containing smelling-salts.

smell'ing-salts, *n.*, an olfactory stimulant made of ammonium carbonate, and scented.

smell'-less, *adj.*, inodorous.

smell'y, *adj.*, giving off an unpleasant odour.

smelt, *n.*, an extract from ore; a small edible fish; *p.p.*, smell; *v.t.*, to extract metal from ore.

smelt'ed, *p.p.*, smelt.

smelt'er, *n.*, one who works at smelting.

smelt'ery, *n.*, a factory where metal is extracted from ore by roasting.

smelt'ing, *n.*, the process of smelting; *pr.p.*, smelt.

smew, *n.*, a variety of merganser.

smi'lax, *n.*, a climbing shrub of the Liliaceae.

smile, *n.*, a kind, pleased or contemptuous expression on the face; *v.i.*, to show pleasure, kindness or contempt with a facial expression; to be favourable; to be auspicious.

smiled, *p.p.*, smile.

smi'ler, *n.*, one who smiles.

smi'ling, *adj.*, favourable, auspicious; *pr.p.*, smile.

smi'lingly, *adv.*, with a pleased expression.

smirch, *v.t.*, to stain, pollute or defame.

smirched, *p.p.*, smirch.

smirch'ing, *pr.p.*, smirch.

smirk, *v.i.*, to smile in a silly way; to simper.

smirked, *p.p.*, smirk.

smir'ker, *n.*, one who smirks.

smirk'ing, *pr.p.*, smirk.

smirk'ingly, *adv.*, in a smirking way.

smitch, *n.*, *i.q.* smeech.

smite, *n.*, a blow; a hit; *v.t.*, to strike, to hit.

smi'ter, *n.*, one who smites.

smith, *n.*, one who works in metals, esp. iron.

smithereens', *n. pl.*, fragments.

smith'ery, *n.*, the smith's art.

smith'ing, *n.*, *i.q.* smithery.

smith'y, *n.*, a blacksmith's shop; a forge.

smi'ting, *pr.p.*, smite.

smit'ten, *p.p.*, smite.

smock, *n.*, a shift; a smock-frock; an insertion like the collar of a smock-frock; *v.t.*, to dress in a smock; to gather with pleats.

smocked, *p.p.*, smock.

smock'-frock, *n.*, an old-fashioned rustic outer garment.

smock'ing, *n.*, pleating closely in the form of a honeycomb; *pr.p.*, smock.

smog', *n.*, a mixture of smoke and fog.

smok'able, *adj.*, able to be smoked.

smoke, *n.*, a volatilized product of combustion; vapour; fume; the act of smoking a cigarette, pipe or cigar; *v.i.*, to emit smoke; to perform the act of smoking; to rage; *v.t.*, to cure by smoking; to blacken with smoke; to inhale smoke from a pipe, a cigar or a cigarette.

smoke'able, *adj.*, *i.q.* smokable.

smoke'-bomb, *n.*, a bomb discharging smoke to form a protective screen.

smoked, *adj.*, smoke-cured; *p.p.*, smoke.

smoke'less, *adj.*, free from smoke.

smo'ker, *n.*, one who, or that which, smokes.

smoke'-screen, *n.*, dense smoke cloud used to conceal movement.

smoke'-test, *n.*, the introduction of smoke to test the condition of a drain.

smo'kier, *adj.*, *comp.* of smoky.

smo'kiest, *adj.*, *super.* of smoky.

smo'kily, *adv.*, in a smoky way.

smo'kiness, *n.*, the quality or state of being smoky.

smo'king, *n.*, the act of a smoker; *pr.p.*, smoke.

smok'ing-room, *n.*, a room specially reserved for smokers, in hotels, ships, etc.

smo'ky, *adj.*, full of, or resembling, smoke; smoke-stained.

smolt, *n.*, young salmon or sea trout.

smooth, *adj.*, with an even, not rough, surface; easy, without obstructions; easily flowing; hairless; not aspirated; *v.t.*, to remove roughness, obstructions, difficulties, etc.

smoothed, *p.p.*, smooth.

smooth'er, *adj.*, *comp.* of smooth.

smooth'est, *adj.*, *super.* of smooth.

smooth'-faced, *adj.*, beardless; hypocritical.

smooth'ing, *pr.p.*, smooth.

smooth'ly, *adv.*, in a smooth way.

smooth'ness, *n.*, the quality or state of being smooth.

smooth'-spoken, *adj.*, plausible.

smooth'-tongued, *adj.*, plausible, flattering.

smorzan'do, *adv.*, decreasing in tone (*It.*, *mus.*).

smorza'to, *adv.*, *i.q.* smorzando.

smote, *p.p.*, smite.

smoth'er, *n.*, stifling dust; the state of being smothered; *v.t.*, to suffocate; to overwhelm; to cover up; to conceal.

smoth'ered, *p.p.*, smother.

smoth'ering, *adj.*, suffocating; *pr.p.*, smother.

smoth'ery, *adj.*, stifling.

smoul'der, *v.i.*, to burn slowly without flame; to burn inwardly; to exist but not to be outwardly perceived.

smoul'dered, *p.p.*, smoulder.

smoul'dering, *pr.p.*, smoulder.

smoul'dry, *adj.*, smouldering.

smudge, *n.*, an ugly stain; a smear; a dampened fire; *v.i.*, to show smears; *v.t.*, to draw a smudge over.

smudged, *p.p.*, smudge.

smudg'ily, *adv.*, in a smudgy way.

smudg'iness, *n.*, the state of being smudgy or smeared.

smudg'ing, *pr.p.*, smudge.

smug, *adj.*, affectedly correct; self-satisfied; *n.*, an outsider (*colloq.*); a person not interested in games and society doings.

smug'gle, *v.t.*, to convey secretly; to import or export goods without paying duty.

smug'gled, *p.p.*, smuggle.

smug'gler, *n.*, one who smuggles.

smug'gling, *n.*, the practices of a smuggler; *pr.p.*, smuggle.

smug'ly, *adv.*, in a smug manner.

smut, *n.*, a sooty stain; a floating particle of soot; a disease in corn and other plants; filthy talk; *v.i.*, to be infected with smut; *v.t.*, to stain with soot; to induce the disease of smut.

smutch, *n.*, a stain; defilement; *v.t.*, to soil.

smutched, *p.p.*, smutch.

smutch'ing, *pr.p.*, smutch.

smut'ted, *p.p.*, smut.

smut'tily, *adv.*, in a smutty way.

smut'tiness, *n.*, the quality or state of being smutty.

smut'ting, *pr.p.*, smut.

smut'ty, *adj.*, stained or infected with smut; lewd.

snack, *n.*, a small portion of food; a small, quick meal; a share.

snack'-bar, *n.*, a bar from which light refreshments are served.

snaf'fle, *n.*, a light bridle without a curb for a horse.

snaf'fled, *adj.*, having a snaffle bit.

snafu', *adj.*, chaotic; *n.*, utter confusion (*colloq.*, from "Situation Normal—All Fouled Up").

snag, *n.*, a jagged projection from a tree-stump or a broken tooth; a sunken piece of timber just below the surface of water and dangerous to boats.

snagged, *adj.*, *i.q.* snaggy.

snag'gy, *adj.*, full of, or resembling, snags.

snail, *n.*, a slimy gasteropod mollusc.

snail'-like, *adj.*, like a snail.

snail'-shell, *n.*, the shell of a snail.

snake, *n.*, a serpent; any person or thing resembling a snake; *v.i.*, to steal along in snake-like fashion.

snake'-root, *n.*, the name for some medicinal plants useful in cases of snake-bite.

snake'-stone, *n.*, ammonite.

snake'-wood, *n.*, a climbing plant, from the root of which is derived a medicine for snake-bite.

sna'kish, *adj.*, like a snake.

sna'ky, *adj.*, *i.q.* snakish; looped; infested with snakes.

snap, *adj.*, done immediately without deliberation; *n.*, an act of biting or attempting to bite; a touch of frost; a breaking; a vigorous style of writing; *v.i.*, to make a short crackling sound; to come apart with a short, sharp sound; to rap out a cross word; *v.t.*, to bite suddenly and with a sound; to break with a jerk; to cut off short.

snap'dragon, *n.*, an antirrhinum; a Christmas game.

snapped, *p.p.*, snap.

snap'per, *n.*, one who, or that which, snaps; a tropical fish.

snap'ping, *pr.p.*, snap.

snap'pish, *adj.*, inclined to be cross or peevish.

snap'pishly, *adv.*, in a snappish way.

snap'py, *adj.*, *i.q.* snappish.

snap'shot, *n.*, a random shot; an instantaneous photograph; *v.t.*, to photograph instantaneously.

snapt, *p.p.*, snap.

snare, *n.*, a trap, a gin; *v.t.*, to trap; to entangle.

snared, *p.p.*, snare.

sna'rer, *n.*, one who, or that which, snares.

sna'ring, *pr.p.*, snare.

snark, *n.*, a chimerical animal.

snark'y, *adj.*, irritable, unpleasant; bad-tempered (*colloq.*).

snarl, *n.*, tangled thread, hair, etc.; a knot in timber; the angry growl of a dog; *v.i.*, to growl angrily as a dog does; to speak harshly or angrily; to become entangled; *v.t.*, to say in harsh tones; to entangle; to emboss.

snarled, *p.p.*, snarl.

snarl'er, *n.*, one who, or that which, snarls.

snarl'ing, *n.*, a way of raising hollow work in metal by percussion; *pr.p.*, snarl.

snar'ly, *adj.*, bad-tempered.

sna'ry, *adj.*, entangling.

snatch, *n.*, the act of snatching; a fragment; a short spell; a short fragment of song or speech; *v.t.*, to seize quickly or rudely.

snatched, *p.p.*, snatch.

snatch'er, *n.*, one who snatches.

snatch'ing, *pr.p.*, snatch.

snatch'ingly, *adv.*, in a snatching way.

snath, *n.*, a scythe-handle.

sneak, *n.*, a furtive person; a telltale; *v.i.*, to go about stealthily; to act in an underhand way; to tell tales (*colloq.*); *v.t.*, to steal (*colloq.*).

sneaked, *p.p.*, sneak.

sneak'er, *n.*, one who sneaks.

sneak'ers, *n. pl.*, soft shoes (*colloq.*).

sneak'ier, *adj.*, *comp.* of sneaky.

sneak'iest, *adj.*, *super.* of sneaky.

sneak'ily, *adv.*, *i.q.* sneakingly.

sneak'ing, *pr.p.*, sneak.

sneak'ingly, *adv.*, in a sneaking way.

sneak'ish, *adj.*, befitting a sneak.

sneak'ishly, *adv.*, in a sneaky way; stealthily.

sneak'-thief, *n.*, one who steals sneakily from open doors or windows.

sneak'y, *adj.*, like a sneak.

sneck, *n.* and *v.t.*, latch.

sneer, *n.*, a contemptuous look or word; *v.i.*, to express contempt in the face or in speech; to deride.

sneered, *p.p.*, sneer.

sneer'er, *n.*, one who sneers.

sneer'ing, *pr.p.*, sneer.

sneer'ingly, *adv.*, in a sneering way.

sneeze, *n.*, the sound of sneezing; *v.i.*, to emit a spasmodic noise and drops of moisture from the mouth or nostrils.

sneezed, *p.p.*, sneeze.

sneeze'wood, *n.*, a S. African tree.

sneez'ing, *pr.p.*, sneeze.

snell, *adj.*, cold; harsh (*Scot.*).

snib', *n.*, a bolt or catch; *v.t.*, to bolt or fasten.

snick, *n.*, a notch; a slightly deflected hit; *v.t.*, to notch; to cut a small notch in; to hit (a cricket ball) with a slight deflection.

snick'er, *v.i.*, *i.q.* snigger.

snick'ered, *p.p.*, snicker.

snick'ering, *pr.p.*, snicker.

snick'ersnee, *n.*, a comic word for a knife (*Dutch*).

snide, *adj.*, bogus; counterfeit; insinuating; *n.*, false jewellery or coins; a bogus person.

sniff, *n.*, an expression of contempt; a slight smell; the act of sniffing; *v.i.* and *t.*, to draw into the nostrils; to make a contemptuous sound through the nostrils.

sniffed, *p.p.*, sniff.

sniff'ing, *pr.p.*, sniff.

snif'fle, *v.i.*, *i.q.* snuffle.

sniff'y, *adj.*, contemptuous; disdainful (*colloq.*).

snift'ing-valve, *n.*, the air escape in a steam-engine cylinder.

snig'ger, *n.*, a silly or sly laugh; *v.i.*, to laugh in a silly or sly way. (Also *snicker*.)

snig'gered, *p.p.*, snigger.

snig'gering, *pr.p.*, snigger.

snig'geringly, *adv.*, in a sniggering way.

snig'gle, *v.i.*, to fish for eels by baiting their hiding-holes.

snig'gled, *p.p.*, sniggle.

snig'gling, *pr.p.*, sniggle.

snip, *n.*, a cut with scissors; a small portion; *v.t.*, to cut off quickly.

snipe, *n.*, a bird of the fens; *v.t.*, to kill one by one (said of a sharpshooter).

sniped, *p.p.*, snipe.

sni'per, *n.*, one who shoots from a concealed position.

snip'ing, *pr.p.*, snipe.

snipped, *p.p.*, snip.

snip'pet, *n.*, a small piece or share.

snip'ping, *pr.p.*, snip.

snip-snap-snor'um, *n.*, a child's card game.

sniv'el, *n.*, discharge from the nose; cant, hambug; *v.i.*, to run at the nose; to cry from fear or misery.

sniv'elled, *p.p.*, snivel.

sniv'eller, *n.*, one who snivels.

sniv'elling, *pr.p.*, snivel.

snob, *n.*, one who gives himself airs for his supposed social distinction; one who affects to be of higher standing than he is; a repairer of shoes (*colloq.*).

snob'bery, *n.*, the conduct of a snob.

snob'bing, *n.*, a cobbler's trade (*colloq.*).

snob'bish, *adj.*, like a snob.

snob'bishly, *adv.*, in a snobbish way.

snob'bishness, *n.*, the state of being snobbish.

snoek, *n.*, a large sea fish.

snood, *n.*, a net to hold long hair.

snook, *n.*, *i.q.* snoek; a rude gesture with a thumb to the nose.

snook'er, *n.*, a game played on a billiard-table.

snook'ered, *adj.*, beaten, defeated.

snoop, *v.i.*, to pry into another's business; to sneak around nosily.

snoop'er, *n.*, one who snoops.

snooty, *adj.*, disdainful, condescending; *n.*, *i.q.* snout.

snooze, *n.*, a nap; *v.i.*, to sleep lightly and for a short spell; to nap.

snoozed, *p.p.*, snooze.

snooz'ing, *pr.p.*, snooze.

snore, *n.*, a stertorous noise; *v.i.*, to breathe heavily and stertorously in sleep.

snored, *p.p.*, snore.

snor'er, *n.*, one who, or that which, snores.

snor'ing, *n.*, the act of snoring; *pr.p.*, snore.

snor'kel, *n.*, *i.q.* schnorkel.

snort, *n.*, a contemptuous sound made through the nostrils; air intake on submarines; *v.i.*, to make a sound through the nostrils, expressing anger, contempt, surprise, etc.

snort'ed, *p.p.*, snort.

snort'er, *n.*, one who, or that which, snorts.

snort'ing, *pr.p.*, snort.

snot, *n.*, mucus of the nose; a word of abuse (*slang*).

snot'ters, *n.p.l.*, a turkey-cock's wattles.

snott'y, *adj.*, stand-offish; *n.*, a midshipman (*slang*).

snout, *n.*, a beast's nose. (Also *snooty*.)

snow, *n.*, frozen vapour in flakes in the air; a small brig-like sailing vessel; *v.i.*, to come down as snow.

snow'ball, *n.*, snow packed into a ball; a kind of alcoholic drink; *v.t.*, to pelt with snowballs.

snow'bird, *n.*, the snow-bunting.

snow'blind, *adj.*, made blind by the snow.

snow'blindness, *n.*, the state of being snow-blind.

snow'drift, *n.*, a drift of snow.

snow'drop, *n.*, an early spring white flower.

snowed, *p.p.*, snow.

snow'fall, *n.,* a fall of snow; the amount of snow that falls in a given time or place.

snow'flake, *n.,* a flake of snow.

snow'ing, *pr.p.,* snow.

snow'line, *n.,* the contour height at which snow becomes perpetual.

snow'man, *n.,* a human figure modelled in snow.

snow'plough, *n.,* a special vehicle used for clearing snow from a railway or road.

snow'shoe, *n.,* a long shoe for travelling over snow.

snow'-slip, *n.,* an avalanche.

snow'storm, *n.,* a storm of snow.

snow'-white, *adj.,* white as snow.

snow'y, *adj.,* like snow; full of, covered with, snow.

snub, *n.,* an intentional slight; a reproof; a short turned-up nose; *adj.,* short; stumpy; *v.t.,* to put a person down with a slight.

snubbed, *p.p.,* snub.

snub'ber, *n.,* a shock absorber.

snub'bing, *n.,* a reprimand; *pr.p.,* snub.

snub'-nose, *n.,* a short, flat, turned-up nose.

snub'-nosed, *adj.,* having a short, flat nose.

snuff, *n.,* tobacco in the form of powder; burnt wick; *v.t.,* to draw up into the nose; to smell; to cut the wick of a candle.

snuff'box, *n.,* a box to hold snuff.

snuffed, *p.p.,* snuff.

snuff'er, *n.,* a person addicted to snuff-taking.

snuff'ers, *n. pl.,* a scissors-like instrument for snuffing a candle.

snuff'ing, *n.,* snuff-taking; *pr.p.,* snuff.

snuf'fle, *n.,* the noise of breathing through the nose; a nasal way of speaking; cant; *v.i.,* to breathe or speak through the nose.

snuf'fled, *p.p.,* snuffle.

snuf'fler, *n.,* one who snuffles.

snuf'fles, *n. pl.,* an attack of snuffling.

snuf'fling, *pr.p.,* snuffle.

snuff'-taker, *n., i.q.* snuffer.

snuff'y, *adj.,* covered or stained with snuff.

snug, *adj.,* concealed; cosy; comfortable; *v.i.,* to snuggle.

snugged, *p.p.,* snug.

snug'gery, *n.,* a cosy room.

snug'ging, *pr.p.,* snug.

snug'gle, *v.i.,* to lie close; *v.t.,* to clasp close for warmth and/or affection.

snug'gled, *p.p.,* snuggle.

snug'gling, *pr.p.,* snuggle.

snug'ly, *adv.,* cosily.

so, *adv.,* thus; in such a way or degree; thereabouts; on that condition; *conj.,* provided that; *interj.,* stay there; stop.

soak, *v.i.,* to become wet through; to drink to excess; *v.t.,* to make to absorb moisture; to steep.

soak'age, *n.,* the extent of soaking.

soak'away, *n.,* a form of drainage into which water percolates.

soaked, *p.p.,* soak.

soak'er, *n.,* a hard drinker (*colloq.*).

soak'ing, *n.,* a wetting through; *pr.p.,* soak.

soap, *n.,* a manufactured article for cleansing, made from fats and alkali; *v.t.,* to cleanse with soap; to cajole.

soap-box, *n.,* a box for holding soap; a makeshift platform for a street orator.

soap'-bubble, *n.,* a bubble produced by blowing through soapy water.

soaped, *p.p.,* soap.

soap'ier, *adj., comp.* of soapy.

soap'iest, *adj., super.* of soapy.

soap'ily, *adv.,* in a soapy way.

soap'iness, *n.,* the state of being soapy.

soap'ing, *pr.p.,* soap.

soap'less, *adj.,* without soap.

soap'stone, *n.,* steatite.

soap'suds', *n. pl.,* frothy, soapy water.

soap'wort, *n.,* a perennial plant, juice from the roots of which produces a lather.

soap'y, *adj.,* like soap; covered with soap; softly flattering.

soar, *n.,* a flight; *v.i.,* to rise or fly upwards.

soared, *p.p.,* soar.

soar'ing, *pr.p.,* soar.

soar'ingly, *adv.,* in a soaring way.

soa've, *adv.,* with tenderness (*It., mus.*).

sob, *n.,* a convulsive sigh in weeping; *v.i.,* to utter a sound of grief convulsively with weeping.

sobbed, *p.p.,* sob.

sob'bing, *pr.p.,* sob.

so'ber, *adj.,* not given to drunkenness; abstemious; grave; earnest; quiet; *v.i.,* to become sober; *v.t.,* to make sober.

so'bered, *p.p.,* sober.

so'bering, *adj.,* serious; *pr.p.,* sober.

so'berly, *adv.,* sedately; in a sober way.

so'berness, *n.,* the quality or state of being sober.

so'bersides, *n.,* the nickname for a solemn person.

Sobran'je, *n.,* the Bulgarian national assembly.

sobri'ety, *n.,* abstinence from alcoholic drink; seriousness.

so'briquet, *n.,* a nickname (*Fr.*).

sob'sis'ter, *n.,* a woman journalist who writes sentimental stories.

sob'stuff, *n.,* artificial pathos; sentimental writing or speech.

soc, *n.,* a feudal tenant-right; the lord of the manor's power of holding a court.

soc'age, *n.,* a feudal form of tenure.

so'-called, *adj.,* pretended; not as in fact.

socc'er, *n.,* association football.

sociabil'ity, *n.,* the quality or state of being sociable.

so'ciable, *adj.,* fond of company; agreeable; friendly.

so'ciably, *adv.*, in a sociable way.

so'cial, *adj.*, pert. or rel. to society; sociable; convivial; *n.*, a friendly party; a get-together.

so'cialism, *n.*, the principles of socialists, who advocate community of property and co-operation of labour.

so'cialist, *n.*, an advocate of community of property and co-operation of labour.

socialist'ic, *adj.*, pert. or rel. to socialists and socialism.

social'ity, *n.*, conviviality; the quality or state of being social.

socializa'tion, *n.*, the act of arranging socialistically.

so'cialize, *v.t.*, to bring under socialistic conditions.

so'cialized, *p.p.*, socialize.

so'cializing, *pr.p.*, socialize.

so'cially, *adv.*, in a social way; in rel. to society.

soci'ety, *n.*, company; fraternity; people collectively; an association for a common purpose and with common interests; people collectively of the wealthier and more educated class.

Socin'ian, *adj.*, pert. or rel. to Socinus, a 16th Cent. writer, who advocated Unitarianism.

Socin'ianism, *n.*, the doctrines of Socinus; Unitarianism.

so'ciogram, *n.*, a chart showing social relationships.

sociolog'ical, *adj.*, pert. or rel. to sociology.

sociol'ogist, *n.*, a student of sociology.

sociol'ogy, *n.*, the study of social phenomena; social science.

sociomet'ric, *adj.*, pert. or rel. to sociometry.

sociom'etry, *n.*, the measurement of social phenomena.

sock, *adj.*, hit with a fist blow; *n.*, originally a low shoe, worn by the players in a classical comedy; a shortened stocking; a removable lining to footwear; a blow with the fist; *v.t.*, to treat, to give; to fling at, to hit, to punch.

sockdol'oger, *n.*, a decisive blow or argument (*slang*).

sock'et, *n.*, a tubelike arrangement or recess into which a bolt, bar, etc., fits.

sock'eye, *n.*, the blueback salmon.

so'cle, *n.*, a low plinth.

soc'man, *n.*, one whose tenure is by socage.

Soc'otrine, *adj.*, pert. or rel. to Socotra, an island E. of Africa.

Socrate'an, *n.*, an adherent to the philosophy of Socrates.

Socrat'ic, *adj.*, pert. or rel. to Socrates and his philosophy.

Socrat'ical, *adj.*, i.q. Socratic.

socrat'ically, *adv.*, after the manner of Socrates.

Soc'ratism, *n.*, the method of Socrates.

sod, *n.*, turf; abbrev. of sodomite (term of abuse); *v.t.*, to put turf on.

so'da, *n.*, sodium oxide.

sodal'ity, *n.*, a brotherhood or company.

so'da-water, *n.*, water impregnated with bicarbonate of soda and aerated.

sod'ded, *p.p.*, sod.

sod'den, *adj.*, soaked with wet; flabby.

sod'ding, *pr.p.*, sod.

sod'dy, *adj.*, turfy.

so'dium, *n.*, a metallic element.

sod'omite, *n.*, a person practising sodomy.

sod'omy, *n.*, homosexuality (male) or copulation with animals.

soev'er, a separable suffix giving an indefinite and general meaning to adjectives, adverbs and relative pronouns.

so'fa, *n.*, a kind of couch.

sof'fit, *n.*, the undersurface of an arch, cornice, etc.

soft, *adj.*, not hard; yielding to pressure; smooth; subdued; weak-headed.

sof'ta, *n.*, a Moslem theological student.

sof'ten, *v.i.*, to become soft; *v.t.*, to make soft.

sof'tened, *p.p.*, soft.

sof'tener, *n.*, one who, or that which, softens.

sof'tening, *pr.p.*, soften.

soft'er, *adj.*, comp. of soft.

soft'est, *adj.*, super. of soft.

soft'-hearted, *adj.*, tender, kind.

soft'-heartedness, *n.*, the quality or state of being soft-hearted.

soft'ly, *adv.*, in a soft way.

soft'ness, *n.*, the quality or state of being soft.

soft'soap, *n.*, flattery; potash soap.

soft'-spoken, *adj.*, affable, plausible.

soft'ware, *n.*, programmes for computers, etc.

soft'wood, *n.*, wood of coniferous trees.

sof'ty, *n.*, a foolish person.

sog'gy, *adj.*, impregnated with wet.

soho', *interj.*, used by huntsmen.

soi-disant', *adj.*, pretended; self-styled (*Fr.*).

soigné, *adj.*, well-groomed and dressed (fem. soignée) (*Fr.*).

soil, *n.*, surface earth; land; stain; impurity; *v.i.*, to become soiled; *v.t.*, to stain, defile or damage; to feed on fresh fodder.

soiled, *p.p.*, soil.

soil'ing, *pr.p.*, soil.

soirée', *n.*, an evening entertainment (*Fr.*).

soj'ourn, *n.*, a visit or stay; *v.i.*, to stay in a place for a while.

soj'ourned, *p.p.*, sojourn.

soj'ourner, *n.*, a visitor to a place.

soj'ourning, *pr.p.*, sojourn.

soke, *n.*, i.q. soc.

so'ken, *n.*, territory held in socage.

Sol, *n.*, the Sun (*Lat.*); the fifth note in the diatonic scale (*mus.*).

so'la, *adj.*, the fem. of solus, "alone" (*Lat.*); *n.*, the hat-plant of India and its pith; a sun-helmet made of the pith.

sol'ace, *n.*, comfort, consolation; *v.t.*, to comfort, to console.

sol'aced, *p.p.*, solace.

sol'acement, *n.*, *i.q.* solace.

sol'acing, *pr.p.*, solace.

Solana'ceae, *n. pl.*, plants of the nightshade family.

solana'ceous, *adj.*, pert. or rel. to the Solanaceae.

solan'der, *n.*, a case for botanical papers, specimens, drawings, etc.

so'lan-goose, *n.*, the gannet.

sol'anine, *n.*, a poisonous compound derived from the solanum.

sola'no, *n.*, a hot wind felt in the Mediterranean (*Span.*).

Sola'num, *n.*, a plant genus including the nightshade and the potato.

so'lar, *adj.*, pert. or rel. to the sun; *n.*, the dwelling-room in a mediaeval house.

sol'arism, *n.*, belief in solar myths.

sola'rium, *n.*, *i.q.* solar; a sun-bath.

solariza'tion, *n.*, the act or effect of solarizing.

so'larize, *v.t.*, to expose too long to the sun's light.

so'larized, *p.p.*, solarize.

so'larizing, *pr.p.*, solarize.

solar-plex'us, *n.*, the network of nerves at the pit of the stomach.

sola'tium, *n.*, compensation (*Lat.*).

sold, *adj.*, tricked or cheated (*colloq.*); *p.p.*, sell.

sol'dan, *n.*, a sultan.

soldanell'a, *n.*, a kind of alpine plant.

sol'der, *n.*, a fusible cement for joining metal; *v.t.*, to join metal.

sol'dered, *p.p.*, solder.

sol'derer, *n.*, one who solders.

sol'dering, *pr.p.*, solder.

sol'dier, *n.*, a fighting man; a private; *v.i.*, to act as a soldier.

sol'diered, *p.p.*, soldier.

sol'diering, *n.*, the profession of arms; *pr.p.*, soldier.

sol'dierly, *adj.*, like a true soldier.

sol'diery, *n.*, soldiers collectively.

sol'do, *n.*, formerly an Italian coin.

sole, *adj.*, alone; single; *n.*, a flat fish; the bottom of the foot or shoe; *v.t.*, to put a sole on (a shoe).

sol'ecism, *n.*, an error in language betraying gross ignorance; an impropriety.

sol'ecist, *n.*, one who commits a solecism.

solecis'tic, *adj.*, of the nature of a solecism.

sol'ecize, *v.i.*, to commit a solecism.

soled, *p.p.*, sole.

sole'ly, *adv.*, singly; by oneself, alone.

sol'emn, *adj.*, ceremonial; grave; awful; reverential.

solem'nity, *n.*, *i.q.* solemnness; a solemn rite.

solemniza'tion, *n.*, the act of solemnizing.

sol'emnize, *v.t.*, to give solemnity to; to perform (a rite, as marriage).

sol'emnized, *p.p.*, solemnize.

sol'emnizer, *n.*, one who solemnizes.

sol'emnizing, *pr.p.*, solemnize.

sol'emnly, *adv.*, with solemnity.

sol'emnness, *n.*, the quality or state of being solemn.

so'len, *n.*, the razorshell mollusc.

so'lenite, *n.*, a fossil solen.

so'lenoid, *adj.*, like a solen; *n.*, a controllable, electromagnetic device.

sol'-fa, *n.*, the name for the gamut or diatonic scale; *v.i.*, to sing the scale.

sol'-faing, *pr.p.*, sol-fa.

solfana'ria, *n.*, a sulphur mine (*It.*).

solfata'ra, *n.*, a vent in a volcano (*It.*).

solfe'ggio, *n.*, vocal solfa exercises (*It.*).

solferi'no, *n.*, a purplish-red coloured dye (*It.*).

solic'it, *v.t.*, to importune, to beg.

solic'itant, *adj.*, importuning.

solic'itate, *v.t.*, *i.q.* solicit.

solicita'tion, *n.*, the act of soliciting.

solic'ited, *p.p.*, solicit.

solic'iting, *pr.p.*, solicit.

solic'itor, *n.*, a member of the legal profession who acts on one's behalf in the courts and gives professional, legal advice.

solic'itor-gen'eral, *n.*, the second in rank of the law officers of the Crown.

solic'itous, *adj.*, concerned for; anxious.

solic'itously, *adv.*, concernedly; anxiously.

solic'itude, *n.*, concern; anxiety.

solicitud'inous, *adj.*, anxious about.

sol'id, *adj.*, substantial; firm; compact; the opposite to hollow; unanimous; *n.*, a body having its particles closely compacted.

solidar'ity, *n.*, community of interests; *esprit de corps*.

solid'ifiable, *adj.*, capable of being made solid.

solidifica'tion, *n.*, the act or effect of solidifying.

solid'ified, *p.p.*, solidify.

solid'ify, *v.i.*, to become solid; *v.t.*, to make solid.

solid'ifying, *pr.p.*, solidify.

sol'idism, *n.*, the theory of the solidists.

sol'idist, *n.*, one who believes in the theory that diseases are due to morbid alterations in the solid parts of the system.

solid'ity, *n.*, the quality or state of being solid.

sol'idly, *adv.*, in a solid way.

solidung'ular, *adj.*, solid-hoofed; equine.

solidung'ulate, *adj.*, having hooved feet. (Also *soliped*.)

solidung'ulous, *adj.*, having the hoof solid.

sol'idus, *n.*, an old Roman gold coin; the oblique used in printing, writing and typewriting (*Lat.*).

solifid'ian, *adj.*, pert. or rel. to the belief that faith only (*i.e.*, without works) suffices for salvation.

solifid'ianism, *n.*, the belief in faith alone, without works.

solil'oquize, *v.i.*, to speak in soliloquy.

solil'oquized, *p.p.*, soliloquize.

solil'oquizing, *pr.p.*, soliloquize.

solil'oquy, *n.*, speaking to oneself.

sol'iped, *adj.*, *i.q.* solidungulate.

solip'edous, *adj.*, *i.q.* soliped.

sol'ipsism, *n.*, the theory that the universe exists only in a person's mind.

solitaire', *n.*, a button; a single stone in its setting; a solo game.

solita'rian, *n.*, a recluse.

sol'itarily, *adv.*, in a solitary way.

sol'itariness, *n.*, the state of being solitary.

sol'itary, *adj.*, lonely, single; *n.*, a recluse.

sol'itude, *n.*, loneliness; remoteness.

soliv'agant, *adj.*, wandering solitary.

sol'mizate, *v.i.*, to sing the scale with the use of syllables as the names of the notes; to sol-fa.

solmiza'tion, *n.*, the use of syllables as the names of the notes in the musical scale.

so'lo, *n.*, any form of self-expression performed by a single person or on a single instrument.

so'loist, *n.*, one who performs a solo.

Solomon's-seal', *n.*, a plant of the lily family.

Sol'on, *n.*, a sage.

sol'stice, *n.*, one of the two half-yearly periods when the sun seems to pause after reaching its farthest distance N. and S. of the equator (these occur about June 21 and Dec. 22); one of the two points in the ecliptic which the sun reaches at the time of solstice.

solsti'tial, *adj.*, pert. or rel. to the solstices.

solubil'ity, *n.*, the quality or state of being soluble.

sol'uble, *adj.*, able to be solved or dissolved.

so'lus, *adj.*, alone (*Lat.*).

solute', *adj.*, separated.

solu'tion, *n.*, the act or effect of solving or dissolving.

solu'tionist, *n.*, a professional solver of newspaper puzzles.

solvabil'ity, *n.*, the quality or state of being solvable.

solv'able, *adj.*, capable of solution.

solve, *v.t.*, to work out (a problem or puzzle); to explain.

solved, *p.p.*, solve.

solv'ency, *n.*, the state of being solvent.

solv'end, *n.*, something to be solved.

solv'ent, *adj.*, able to pay all debts; able to dissolve; *n.*, an agent that dissolves another substance.

solv'er, *n.*, one who solves.

solv'ing, *pr.p.*, solve.

Soma'li, *n.*, a native of Somaliland; the language of S.

so'mascope, *n.*, an instrument used for examining internal tissues of the body.

somat'ic, *adj.*, pert. or rel. to the body, physical; corporeal.

somat'ical, *adj.*, *i.q.* somatic.

somat'ically, *adv.*, in a physical way.

somatol'ogy, *n.*, the study of the properties of material bodies.

somatot'omy, *n.*, the dissection of bodies.

som'bre, *adj.*, dark, lowering, gloomy.

som'brely, *adv.*, in a dark, gloomy way.

som'breness, *n.*, the quality or state of being sombre.

sombrer'o, *n.*, a broadbrimmed hat, worn in Spanish-speaking countries (*Span.*).

som'brous, *adj.*, gloomy.

some, a suffix indicating degree; *adj.*, to a certain extent; describing without defining a number, amount, extent, etc.; approximately.

some'body, *n.*, some person; an important person.

some'how, *adv.*, in some way or other.

some'one, *n.*, *i.q.* somebody.

som'ersault, *n.*, a turning head over heels; *v.i.*, to do a somersault.

som'ersaulted, *p.p.*, somersault.

som'ersaulting, *pr.p.*, somersault.

som'erset, *n.*, a padded saddle; *n.* and *v.i.*, *i.q.* somersault.

some'thing, *adv.*, somewhat; to a certain extent; *n.*, a thing alluded to but not specified; a part.

some'time, *adv.*, at one time or another; once upon a time.

some'times, *adv.*, at times; occasionally.

some'what, *adv.*, to some extent.

some'where, *adv.*, in some place or other.

some'while, *adv.*, at some time or other; formerly.

so'mite, *n.*, a segment of a vertebrate.

somnam'bulance, *n.*, sleepwalking.

somnam'bulant, *adj.*, walking in sleep.

somnam'bulate, *v.i.*, to walk in sleep.

somnambula'tion, *n.*, sleepwalking.

somnam'bulator, *n.*, *i.q.* somnambulist.

somnam'bulism, *n.*, *i.q.* somnambulation.

somnam'bulist, *n.*, a sleepwalker.

somnif'erous, *adj.*, producing sleep.

somnif'ic, *adj.*, *i.q.* somniferous.

somnil'oquence, *n.*, talking in sleep.

somnil'oquism, *n.*, *i.q.* somniloquence.

somnil'oquist, *n.*, a talker in sleep.

somnip'athy, *n.*, sleep produced by hypnotism.

som'nolence, *n.*, sleepiness.

som'nolency, *n.*, *i.q.* somnolence.

som'nolent, *adj.*, sleepy, drowsy.

som'nolently, *adv.*, in a sleepy way.

som'nolism, *n.*, hypnotic sleep.

son, *n.*, a male offspring or descendant.

so'nance, *n.*, sounding, resonance.

so'nant, *adj.*, sounding.

sonan'tal, *adj.*, of a sonant quality or character.

so'nar, *n.*, sound navigation ranging; location by means of reflected sound waves.

sona'ta, *n.*, a musical composition, of a particular structure, performed on a solo instrument (*It.*).

sonati'na, *n.*, a simpler form of the sonata (*It.*).

song, *n.*, that which is sung or intended for singing; verse; a lyric; a bird's vocal utterance; a bagatelle.

song'-bird, *n.*, any bird which sings.

song'ful, *adj.*, abounding in song; melodious.

song'fully, *adv.*, in a songful way.

song'less, *adj.*, without a song; unable to sing.

song'ster, *n.*, a singer, esp. a bird.

song'stress, *n.*, the fem. of songster.

son'ic, *adj.*, pert. or rel. to sound or sound waves.

sonif'erous, *adj.*, producing a sound; conducting sound.

son'-in-law, *n.*, the husband of one's daughter.

son'net, *n.*, a lyrical composition of fourteen lines, conforming to several different types.

sonneteer', *n.*, a writer of sonnets.

Son'nite, *adj.*, pert. or rel. to the Sunnites; *n.*, an orthodox Mohammedan who accepts tradition (Sunna) as well as the Koran.

son'ny, *n.*, a form of address to a young boy.

son'obuoy, *n.*, a floating buoy for detecting underwater sounds.

sonom'eter, *n.*, an instrument for ascertaining sound-values, or for testing the hearing capacity.

sonores'cence, *n.*, the quality or state of being sonorescent.

sonores'cent, *adj.*, capable of emitting sound when affected by heat and light.

sonorif'ic, *adj.*, producing sound.

sonor'ity, *n.*, the quality or state of being sonorous.

sono'rous, *adj.*, resounding; clearly audible; deep sounding.

sono'rously, *adv.*, clearly, loudly.

son'sy, *adj.*, buxom, plump; cheerful (*Scot.*); lucky.

son'tag, *n.*, a kind of knitted cape.

Soo'der, *n.*, *i.q.* Sudra.

Soo'dra, *n.*, *i.q.* Sudra.

soon, *adv.*, in a short time, hence; shortly; immediately.

soon'er, *adv.*, more quickly; in preference.

soon'est, *adj. super.*, of soon.

soot, *n.*, a black, powdery product of coal combustion; *v.t.*, to cover with soot.

soot'ed, *p.p.*, soot.

soot'erkin, *n.*, a kind of false birth; an abortive proposal or scheme.

sooth, *n.*, truth.

soothe, *v.t.*, to stroke, calm or allay; to blandish.

soothed, *p.p.*, soothe.

sooth'er, *n.*, one who, or that which, soothes.

sooth'fast, *adj.*, truthful, loyal.

sooth'ing, *adj.*, comforting; *pr.p.*, soothe.

sooth'ingly, *adv.*, in a soothing way; with a soothing effect.

sooth'say, *v.i.*, to prognosticate.

sooth'sayer, *n.*, a prophet, a foreteller.

sooth'saying, *n.*, the profession of a soothsayer; *pr.p.*, soothsay.

soot'ier, *adj.*, comp. of sooty.

soot'iest, *adj.*, super. of sooty.

soot'iness, *n.*, the quality or state of being sooty.

soot'y, *adj.*, full of, or covered with, soot.

sop, *n.*, something dipped and soaked in broth, etc.; something intended to appease; *v.t.*, to dip into broth; to absorb.

soph, *n.*, an abbreviation of sophister and sophomore.

soph'ism, *n.*, a false argument; a fallacy.

soph'ist, *n.*, an ancient Greek teacher of philosophy and rhetoric. The sophists were noted for their specious and fallacious arguments; hence a sophist now means a false reasoner.

soph'ister, *n.*, a second or third year man at Cambridge.

sophis'tic, *adj.*, pert. or rel. to sophists; fallacious.

sophis'tical, *adj.*, *i.q.* sophistic.

sophis'tically, *adv.*, fallaciously.

sophis'ticate, *v.t.*, to obscure with sophistry; to mislead; to adulterate.

sophis'ticated, *adj.*, knowledgeable in worldy things; *p.p.*, sophisticate.

sophis'ticating, *pr.p.*, sophisticate.

sophistica'tion, *n.*, the quality or state of being sophisticated.

sophis'ticator, *n.*, one who indulges in sophistry.

soph'istry, *n.*, the practices of sophists; deception, quibbling, perverted casuistry.

soph'omore, *n.*, a second-year student in an American University.

sophomor'ic, *adj.*, pert. or rel. to a sophomore; callow.

So'phy, *n.*, *i.q.* Sufi.

soporif'erous, *adj.*, producing sleep.

soporif'erously, *adv.*, in a soporiferous way.

soporif'ic, *adj.*, *i.q.* soporiferous; *n.*, an anodyne producing sleep.

so'porous, *adj.*, *i.q.* soporiferous.

sopped, *p.p.*, sop.

sop'ping, *adj.*, wet through; *pr.p.*, sop.

sop'py, *adj.*, soaked through; sentimental (*slang*).

sopra'nist, *n.*, a soprano vocalist.

sopra'no, *n.*, the highest treble voice; one who sings soprano.

sor'a, *n.*, a Carolina marsh bird.

sorb, *n.*, the service-tree or its fruit.

sorbefa'cient, *adj.* and *n.*, causing absorption (*med.*).

sor'bet, n., flavoured water-ice (Fr.).

Sorbonne', n., originally, the theological faculty in the University of Paris, and named after its founder, Robert de Sorbon, a 13th Cent. theologian; now the centre for the Académie and for science and literature.

sor'cerer, n., one who uses magic, enchantments, etc.

sor'ceress, n., the fem. of sorcerer.

sor'cerous, adj., pert. or rel. to sorcery.

sor'cery, n., magic arts, wizardry, witchcraft.

sor'des, n., foul discharge from ulcers, etc. (Lat.).

sor'det, n., i.q. sordine.

sor'did, adj., filthy, squalid, mercenary.

sor'didly, adv., in a sordid way.

sor'didness, n., the state of being sordid.

sor'dine, n., a mute, a damper (mus.). (Also sordet and sordino.)

sordi'ni, n., the pl. of sordino.

sordi'no, n., i.q. sordine (It.).

sordor, n., uncleanliness of mind or body.

sore, adj., morbidly sensitive to pain; causing pain; offended; adv., i.q. sorely; n., a sore place on the body; something rankling in the mind.

sorel, n., i.q. sorrel.

sore'ly, adv., in a sore manner; in a way to cause distress; very greatly.

sore'ness, n., the quality or state of being sore.

sor'er, adj., comp., of sore.

sor'est, adj., super. of sore.

Sor'ghum, n., a genus of tropical cereal grasses.

sor'go, n., a kind of sugar-cane; the Sorghum.

sor'icine, adj., of, or related to, the shrewmouse.

sori'tes, n., an extended syllogism or chain of syllogisms; a sophistical method of leading a person to the acceptance of an absurd conclusion.

sorn, v.i., to sponge on friends for hospitality (Scot.).

sorned, p.p., sorn.

sorn'er, n., one who sorns.

sorn'ing, pr.p., sorn.

sorop'timist, n., member of a woman's international club.

soror'icide, n., the murder of a sister.

soro'rity, n., devotional sisterhood.

soro'sis, n., a fleshy kind of fruit, such as the pineapple, mulberry, etc.

sor'rel, adj. and n., reddish-brown colour; n., a perennial herb with a slightly sour taste. (Also sorel.)

sor'rier, adj., comp. of sorry.

sor'riest, adj., super. of sorry.

sor'rily, adv., in a sorry way.

sor'row, n., grief; repentance; misfortune; v.i., to feel sorrow.

sor'rowed, p.p., sorrow.

sor'rowful, adj., full of sorrow; sad.

sor'rowfully, adv., sadly, mournfully.

sor'rowfulness, n., the state of being sorrowful.

sor'rowing, pr.p., sorrow.

sor'ry, adj., filled with regret; poor, mean, shabby.

sort, n., kind, class, way; in printer's type, a letter or portion of a fount; a group; v.i., to correspond; v.t., to separate into groups; to pick out from a mixed number.

sort'able, adj., able to be sorted.

sort'ed, p.p., sort.

sort'er, n., one who sorts (esp. letters).

sor'tie, n., a sally; a dash out from a besieged place (Fr.).

sor'tilege, n., divination by casting lots.

sortile'gious, adj., pert. or rel. to sortilege.

sort'ing, pr.p., sort.

sorti'tion, n., the casting of lots.

sor'us, n., a heap or cluster (esp. of spores).

so'-so, adj. and adv., not up to much; indifferent(ly).

sostenu'to, adv., in a sustained way (It., mus.).

sot, n., a drunkard, a toper; v.i., to be a toper.

sote'rial, adj., pert. or rel. to salvation.

soteriol'ogy, n., the branch of theological science rel. to the scheme of salvation (theol.).

so'thic, adj., pert. or rel. to the dog-star (of which Sothis was the Egyptian name).

sot'tise, n., a foolish action or remark (Fr.).

sot'tish, adj., like a sot; characteristic of a sot.

sot'tishly, adv., in a sottish way.

sot'tishness, n., habitual drunkenness.

sot'to vo'ce, adverbial phrase = under the breath; softly; aside (It., mus.).

sou, n., formerly a French coin.

soubrette', n., a French actress in the character of a pert maidservant or lady's maid (Fr.).

sou'briquet, n., i.q. sobriquet.

sou'car, n., a Hindu banker or moneylender. (Also sowkar.)

sou'chet, n., fish served in the water in which it is boiled (Fr.).

souchong', n., a black China tea.

souf'fle, n., a low murmur heard in the auscultation of an organ or part.

souf'flé, adj., mottled; prepared with beaten white of egg; n., a dish so prepared (Fr.).

sough, n., a gentle, whistling or sighing sound as of wind; a drain or sewer; v.i., to make a whistling sound.

sought, p.p., seek.

soul, n., the spiritual part, as distinct from the material part, of a person; a human being; the vital principle and mental powers common to all the animal world; the essence; the animating influence; emotional feeling.

soul'ful, adj., full of soul; emotional.

soul'fully, adv., in a soulful way.

soul'fulness, n., the quality or state of being soulful.

soul'less, adj., without emotional feeling; heartless.

soul'lessly, adv., in a soulless way.

soul'lessness, n., the quality or state of being soulless.

soul'-stirring, adj., rousing, exciting.

sound, adj., healthy; to be relied upon; judicious; solvent; n., the sensation produced through the hearing; tone; noise; ear-shot; one of a series of articulate utterances, as vowel sounds; a strait; a fish's air-bladder; v.i., to give forth a sound; to appear like; to plunge to deep water; v.t., to make a sound with; to express by means of sound; to celebrate; to auscultate; to try the depth of; to inquire into.

sound'board, n., a canopy over a pulpit or platform to enable the voice to carry; a thin piece of wood in some musical instruments to improve the resonance; in a pianoforte, the wood on which the strings are stretched; in an organ, the top of the wind-chest having the pipes inserted into it.

sound'ed, p.p., sound.

sound'er, adj., comp. of sound; n., a herd of wild swine; young boar; a sounding device used at sea.

sound'est, adj., super. of sound.

sound'ing, adj., resonant; n., the act of sounding in any sense; the taking of the depth of water; pr.p., sound.

sound'ing-board, n., i.q. soundboard.

sound'ings, n. pl., the result of making a sounding; specimens brought up as the result of sounding.

sound'less, adj., without a sound; still; silent.

sound'lessly, adv., silently.

sound'ly, adv., in a sound way.

sound'ness, n., the quality or state of being sound.

sound'proof, adj., insulated against interference from sound; v.t., to insulate thus.

sound'proofed, p.p., soundproof.

sound'proof'ing, n., the material used to make a room soundproof.

sound'track, n., the strip on a film to carry the recording of sound.

soup, n., a liquid food produced by boiling meat, vegetables, etc., in water or stock.

soupçon, n., a very small quantity; just a taste. (The French word properly means "a suspicion.")

soup'-spoon, n., a specially shaped spoon for soup.

sour, adj., acid, tart; without sweetness of temper; peevish, morose; bad for crops; v.i., to become acid; v.t., to make acid.

source, n., a spring, fount or origin.

sour'crout, n., i.q. sauerkraut.

sourdine', n., a harmonium or organ stop.

sour'dough, n., one who has spent more than one winter in Alaska; an old timer.

soured, p.p., sour.

sour'er, adj., comp. of sour.

sour'est, adj., super. of sour.

sour'ing, pr.p., sour.

sour'krout, n., i.q. sauerkraut.

sour'ly, adv., in a sour way.

sour'ness, n., the quality or state of being sour.

sour'sop, n., a W. Indian fruit and tree.

sous, prep., under (Fr.).

sou'saphone, n., an instrument resembling a French horn.

souse, adv., headlong; v.t., to plunge or dip in water; to give a wetting to; to steep in vinegar; to put into pickle made with salt.

soused, p.p., souse.

sous'ing, n., a drenching with water; pr.p., souse.

soutache', n., ornamental braid.

soutane', n., a cassock (Fr.).

souteneur', n., a man who lives on prostitutes' earnings.

sout'er, n., a cobbler.

sou'terrain, n., a cellar or grotto (Fr.).

south, adj., rel. to the south; situated in, or looking towards, the south; adv., southward; from the south; n., the point of the compass opposite to the north; v.i., to cross the meridian of a place.

Southcott'ian, n., a follower of Joanna Southcott, an 18th and early 19th Cent. religious impostor.

South'down, adj., pert. or rel. to a district of Sussex and Hants. known as the South Downs; n., the mutton of Southdown sheep.

south-east', adj., adv., and n., midway between S. and E.

south-east'er, n., a wind blowing from the S.E.

south-east'erly, adj., blowing from, or in the direction of, the S.E.

south-east'ern, adj., pert. or rel. to the S.E.

south'erly, adj., in or towards the south; blowing from the south.

south'ern, adj., pert. or rel. to, situated in, looking or tending towards, the south.

south'erner, n., one who lives in the south country, esp. in the southern part of the U.S.A.

south'ernish, adj., southern in character.

south'ernmost, adj., farthest south.

south'ing, n., the difference of latitude in sailing south; pr.p., south.

south'most, adj. and adv., farthest south.

south'ron, n., a dweller in the south; esp. south of the Scottish border. (It was supposed, in Scotland, to be felt in England as a term of contempt.)

south'ward, adj. and adv., toward the S.

south'wards, *adv.*, in a southerly direction.

south'west', *adj.*, *adv.* and *n.*, midway between S. and W.

south-west'er, *n.*, a S.W. wind.

south-west'erly, *adj.*, toward, or blowing from, the S.W.

south-west'ern, *adj.*, situated in, pert. or rel. to, the S.W.

souvenir', *n.*, a memento; recollection (*Fr.*).

souwest'er, *n.*, a strong gale blowing from the S.W.; a sailor's waterproof storm hat.

sov'ereign, *adj.*, supreme; pre-eminent; very potent; *n.*, a supreme ruler; formerly an English gold coin.

sov'ereignty, *n.*, the quality or state of being sovereign.

Sov'iet, *n.*, a local or national unit of the U.S.S.R. Government.

Sov'ietism, *n.*, the Soviet system.

Sov'ietize, *v.t.*, to impose or convert to a Soviet form of government.

sow, *n.*, the female pig.

sow, *v.t.*, to scatter seeds on; to plant.

sowar', *n.*, an Indian cavalryman.

sow'bread, *n.*, a variety of cyclamen.

sowed, *p.p.*, sow.

sow'ens, *n.*, a Scottish flummery; a paste used by weavers.

sow'er, *n.*, one who, or that which, sows; one who causes.

sow'ing, *n.*, the act of sowing; the thing sown; *pr.p.*, sow.

sow'kar, *n.*, *i.q.* soucar.

sown, *p.p.*, sow.

soy, *n.*, a sauce or flavouring used by the Chinese and the Japanese. It is made from the soya-bean or pea.

soy'a-bean, *n.*, an edible bean from S.E. Asia.

soz'zled, *adj.*, very drunk (*slang*).

spa, *n.*, any place where there is a mineral spring.

space, *n.*, continuous extension in three dimensions; the interval between one point and another, whether of time or material objects; a printer's device to separate words; room; *v.t.*, to arrange that a space separates each object or group of objects.

space'-bar, *n.*, the bar on a typewriter for making space between words.

space'-craft, *n.*, *i.q.* space-ship.

spaced, *p.p.*, space.

space'less, *adj.*, without space; unlimited.

space'-man, *n.*, one who travels in outer space.

space'-ship, *n.*, a vehicle for travel in space.

space'-sta'tion, *n.*, a halting place for travellers in outer space.

space'-suit, *n.*, the suit worn by astronauts.

space'-travel, *n.*, travel in space.

spa'cing, *n.*, the act of spacing; the distance spaced; *pr.p.*, space.

spa'cious, *adj.*, vast in extent; roomy; with scope for activity.

spa'ciously, *adv.*, in a spacious way.

spa'ciousness, *n.*, roominess, extent.

spad'dle, *n.*, a little spade.

spade, *n.*, an implement for digging; the name of one of the suits in a pack of cards; *v.t.*, to dig over.

spade'ful, *n.*, as much as a spade will hold.

spade'work, *n.*, preparatory drudgery; the hard work.

spadi'ceous, *adj.*, pert. or rel. to a spadix.

spadille', *n.*, the ace of spades in the games of quadrille and ombre.

spa'dix, *n.*, a spike of flowers having a fleshy axis, which is usually enclosed in a spathe.

spad'o, *n.*, a person unable to procreate; a eunuch.

spado'ne, *n.*, a light broadsword.

spae, *v.i.* and *t.*, to prophesy.

spaghet'ti, *n. pl.*, a smaller kind of macaroni (*It.*).

spa'hi, *n.*, an old name for a corps of Turkish cavalry; an Algerian cavalryman.

spake, *p.p.*, speak.

spall, *n.*, a flake, a chip; *v.i.*, to chip; *v.t.*, to break up; to chip.

spalpeen', *n.*, a rascal (*Ir.*).

spalt, *n.*, a white, scaly mineral of use in fusing metals.

Spam, *n.*, a brand of chopped ham.

span, *n.*, any interval of space or time; the extreme distance from one fixed point to another, as, for instance, the width of an arch or of the space between the abutments of a bridge; *v.i.*, to extend; *v.t.*, to measure; to cover the width of; to hobble.

spanaem'ia, *n.*, a shortage of red corpuscles in the blood (*med.*).

spanaem'ic, *adj.*, suffering from a shortage of red corpuscles (*med.*).

span'drel, *n.*, the space between the shoulder of an arch and the rectangular moulding surrounding it, or the space between adjoining arches.

span'gle, *n.*, a little glittering piece of metal, often used as a dress ornament; *v.t.*, to ornament with spangles.

span'gled, *p.p.*, spangle.

span'gling, *pr.p.*, spangle.

Span'iard, *n.*, a native of Spain.

span'iel, *n.*, a sporting dog.

Span'ish, *adj.*, pert. or rel. to Spain and the Spaniards; *n.*, the language of S.

spank, *n.*, a smack; *v.i.*, to career along; *v.t.*, to smack.

spanked, *p.p.*, spank.

spank'er, *n.*, one who spanks; an aftersail.

spank'ing, *adj.*, brisk, striking; *n.*, a smacking; *pr.p.*, spank.

span'less, *adj.*, beyond measure.

spanned, *p.p.*, span.

span'ner, *n.*, one who, or that which, spans; a tool for tightening bolts.

span'ning, *pr.p.*, span.

span'-roof, n., a roof which has two sloping sides.

spar, n., a shining mineral; a ship's mast, boom, etc.; a boxing contest; a verbal dispute; v.i., to engage in a contest of blows or words.

spa'rable, n., a headless nail.

spar'-deck, n., a light, upper deck.

spare, adj., meagre, thin, economical; n., a duplicate thing or part kept for an emergency; v.i., to live in a poor way; to forbear; v.t., to show mercy to; to do without; to part with.

spared, p.p., spare.

spare'ness, n., the quality or state of being spare.

spa'rer, n., one who spares.

spare'rib, n., a joint of pork consisting of ribs specially treated.

sparge, v.t., to sprinkle.

spar'ger, n., a sprinkler, used esp. by brewers.

spar'ing, adj., thrifty; pr.p., spare.

spar'ingly, adv., in a sparing way.

spark, n., a flash of light as from a fire; a smart youth; a beau; v.i., to give off sparks when electric continuity is broken.

spark'ing-plug, n., an automobile device causing an electric spark to leap between two electrodes, thus exploding the charge in the cylinder.

spark'le, n., a coruscation; a flash; v.i., to flash; to coruscate.

spark'led, p.p., sparkle.

spark'ler, n., one who, or that which, sparkles; a kind of firework.

spark'ling, pr.p., sparkle.

spark'lingly, adv., in a sparkling way.

sparks, n., a wireless operator (colloq.).

spar'ling, n., a smelt.

sparred, adj., fitted with spars; p.p., spar

spar'ring, pr.p., spar.

spar'row, n., a small, common British bird.

spar'row-hawk, n., a small bird that preys on sparrows and other small birds.

spar'ry, adj., like, full of, spar.

sparse, adj., thin, scanty.

sparse'ly, adv., scantily.

sparse'ness, n., the quality or state of being sparse.

spar'sity, n. i.q., sparseness.

Spar'tan, adj., pert. or rel. to Sparta and the Spartans; austere; hardy; following a severe regimen; n., a native of S.

spar'terie, n., articles made from esparto grass.

spasm, n., a sudden, violent muscular contraction.

spasmod'ic, adj., sudden and violent; convulsive.

spasmod'ical, adj., i.q. spasmodic.

spasmod'ically, adv., in a spasmodic way.

spasmol'ogy, n., the study of spasms.

spas'tic, adj., i.q. spasmodic; n., a person having severe physical handicaps.

spastic'ity, n., the quality or state of being spastic.

spat, n., the spawn of shellfish; a short gaiter; a splash; a cover over a wheel; p.p., spit.

spatch'cock, n., a fowl cooked immediately after killing; v.t., to insert (words) hastily in a telegram, etc. (colloq.).

spate, n., a sudden flood, (esp. river).

spatha'ceous, adj., producing or resembling spathes.

spathe, n., the calix of a spadix.

spath'ic, adj., like spar, easy to split.

spath'iform, adj., like a spathe.

spa'tial, adj., pert or rel. to space.

spattee', n., women's or children's woollen leggings.

spat'ter, v.t., to moisten by sprinkling; to destroy the character of.

spat'terdashes, n. pl., long gaiters.

spat'tered, p.p., spatter.

spat'tering, pr.p., spatter.

spat'ula, n., a flat, broad knife used in spreading plasters, mixing paints, etc.

spat'ulate, adj., like a spatula.

spat'ule, n., a spatulate formation.

spav'in, n., a disease in a horse's hock; v.t., to affect with spavin.

spav'ined, p.p., spavin.

spawn, n., offspring; ova; the mycelium of mushrooms and other fungi.

spawned, p.p., spawn.

spawn'er, n., one who, or that which, spawns.

spawn'ing, pr.p., spawn.

spay, v.t., to remove ovaries from a female animal; to castrate.

spay'ad, n., a red deer stag of the third year.

spayed, p.p., spay.

spay'ing, pr.p., spay.

speak, v.i., to communicate in words; to talk; to deliver an oration; v.t., to utter, to say, to reveal.

speak'able, adj., able to be spoken.

Speak'er, n., the elected M.P. who acts as Chairman for the House of Commons.

speak'er, n., one who speaks.

speak'ing, adj., life-like; pr.p., speak.

speak'ing-trumpet, n., a device enabling deaf persons to hear.

speak'ing-tube, n., a tube conveying the voice.

speak'ing-voice, n., the voice used when speaking.

spear, n., a pointed weapon; anything resembling it; v.t., to pierce with a spear.

speared, p.p., spear.

spear'head, n., a group or an individual chosen to lead an attack.

spear'ing, pr.p., spear.

spear'mint, n., common garden mint; a chewing sweetmeat impregnated with mint.

spear'wort, n., a variety of ranunculus.

spec'ial, adj., pert. or rel. to a species; appropriate to a particular end; distinctive; particular.

spec′ialism, *n.*, that in which one specializes.

spec′ialist, *n.*, a professional man who devotes himself to a particular department of his work; an expert in a particular subject.

specialis′tic, *adj.*, pert. or rel. to specialist.

special′ity, *n.*, a distinct department; a special aptitude.

specializa′tion, *n.*, the act or process of specializing.

spec′ialize, *v.i.*, to act as a specialist; to intensify study in a narrower field of knowledge or skill.

spec′ialized, *p.p.*, specialize.

spec′ializing, *pr.p.*, specialize.

spec′ially, *n.*, in a special manner or degree.

spec′ialty, *n.*, a special characteristic or obligation.

specia′tion, *n.*, the process of evolution (*zool.*).

spe′cie, *n.*, coin (money).

spe′cies, *n.*, a group within a genus; a kind.

speci′fiable, *adj.*, able to be specified.

specif′ic, *adj.*, pert. or rel. to a species; detailed; *n.*, a cure for a disease.

specif′ically, *adv.*, in detail; precisely.

specifica′tion, *n.*, the act or result of specifying; the setting out of the precise details of a plan.

spec′ified, *p.p.*, specify.

spec′ify, *v.t.*, to particularize; to give details of.

spec′ifying, *pr.p.*, specify.

spec′imen, *n.*, a proof, an example, an exhibit.

spe′cious, *adj.*, outwardly attractive; plausible.

spe′ciously, *adv.*, in a specious way.

speck, *n.*, a small spot; a flaw; bacon, whaleblubber (*Dutch*); *v.t.*, to spot.

specked, *p.p.*, speck.

speck′ing, *pr.p.*, speck.

speck′le, *n.*, a small spot; *v.t.*, to cover with speckles; to variegate.

speck′led, *p.p.*, speckle.

speck′less, *adj.*, clean, free from blemishes.

speck′ling, *pr.p.*, speckle.

speck′ly, *adj.*, covered with specks.

specs, *n.*, a pair of spectacles (*colloq.*).

spec′tacle, *n.*, a sight; a show.

spec′tacled, *adj.*, wearing spectacles.

spec′tacles, *n. pl.*, a pair of framed eyeglasses.

spectac′ular, *adj.*, pert. or rel. to a spectacle; shown in picture; scenic; of dramatic visual interest.

specta′tor, *n.*, one who looks on.

spectato′rial, *adj.*, pert. or rel. to spectators.

specktioneer′, *n.*, a chief harpooner (whaling).

spec′tral, *adj.*, pert. or rel. to a spectre; ghostly.

spec′tre, *n.*, a ghost.

spectrol′ogy, *n.*, the study of spectrum analysis.

spectrom′eter, *n.*, an instrument for measuring refraction indices.

spec′trophotom′eter, *n.*, a photometer and spectroscope combined.

spec′troscope, *n.*, a scientific instrument for the examination of the spectrum.

spec′trum, *n.*, light rays broken into their constituent wavelengths (hence colours).

spec′ular, *adj.*, like a mirror or speculum.

spec′ulate, *v.i.*, to meditate inquiringly; to invest money for profit.

spec′ulated, *p.p.*, speculate.

spec′ulating, *pr.p.*, speculate.

specula′tion, *n.*, meditation; theorizing; the investment of money for profit.

spec′ulative, *adj.*, meditative; theorizing; involving risk.

spec′ulatively, *adv.*, in a speculative way.

spec′ulator, *n.*, one who speculates.

spec′ulatory, *adj.*, theoretical.

spec′ulum, *n.*, a mirror; a surgical instrument used in internal examinations.

sped, *p.p.*, speed.

speech, *n.*, articulate utterance; an oration; language.

speech′-day, *n.*, an annual school function for prize-giving.

speech′ified, *p.p.*, speechify.

speech′ifier, *n.*, one who likes to make speeches.

speech′ify, *v.i.*, to make speeches.

speech′ifying, *pr.p.*, speechify.

speech′less, *adj.*, unable to speak; silent; dumb.

speech′lessness, *n.*, the state of being speechless.

speed, *n.*, haste; swiftness; success; *v.i.*, to move swiftly; to prosper; *v.t.*, to give a good send-off to; to accelerate.

speed′-boat, *n.*, a motorboat of high speed.

speed′er, *n.*, a device for regulating the speed of machinery.

speed′ily, *adv.*, quickly.

speed′ing, *pr.p.*, speed.

speedom′eter, *n.*, an instrument to indicate speed.

speed′ster, *n.*, one who drives at excessive speed.

speed-up′, *v.i.* and *t.*, to quicken.

speed′way, *n.*, a motorcycle racing track.

speed′well, *n.*, veronica.

speed′y, *adj.*, quick, hasty.

speiss, *n.*, a compound obtained in smelting certain ores.

spelae′an, *adj.*, pert. or rel. to the inhabitants of caves.

spelicans, *n.*, *i.q.* spillikin.

spelk, *n.*, a thatching spike.

spell, *n.*, a charm or incantation; a turn of labour; a period of working; *v.i.*, to make words from letters; to signify; *v.t.*, to write or recite the separate letters of a word; to mean.

spell′bound, *adj.*, charmed, fascinated.

spelled, *p.p.*, spell.

spell′er, *n.*, one who spells; a spelling-book.

spell'ing, n., the act of spelling; pr.p., spell.

spell'ing-bee, n., a spelling competition.

spell'ing-book, n., a book from which spelling is learnt.

spelt, n., a variety of wheat; p.p., spell.

spel'ter, n., zinc.

spence, n., a buttery or larder. (Also spense.)

spen'cer, n., a short overcoat; a bodice; a trysail.

Spence'rian, adj., pert. or rel. to Herbert Spencer and his philosophy.

spend, v.i., to incur expense; v.t., to lay out; to pay out; to pass; to use.

spend'er, n., one who spends; an extravagant person.

spend'ing, n., the habit of spending; pr.p., spend.

spend'thrift, n., a wasteful spender.

spense, n., i.q. spence.

Spense'rian, adj., pert. or rel. to Edmund Spenser and his poetry.

spent, adj., exhausted; p.p., spend.

sperm, n., a sperm whale; semen.

spermace'ti, n., a fatty secretion in the head of a sperm whale.

sperm'ary, n., the male germ-gland.

spermat'ic, adj., pert. or rel. to sperm or semen.

spermatorrhœ'a, n., the persistent involuntary issue of semen.

spermatozo'a, n. pl., the living fertilizing elements in semen.

spermatozo'on, n. sing., the germ cell in male semen.

spermo'logy, n., the study of sperm.

spew, v.i. and t., to vomit; to spit forth; to droop at the muzzle (said of a gun). (Also spue.)

spewed, p.p., spew.

spew'ing, pr.p., spew.

sphac'elate, v.i., to become gangrenous; v.t., to make gangrenous.

sphacela'tion, n., a gangrenous condition.

sphac'elus, n., gangrene (Gr.).

sphag'nous, adj., covered with bog-moss.

sphag'num, n., a kind of moss.

sphe'nogram, n., a cuneiform sign.

sphe'noid, adj., wedge-shaped.

sphenoid'al, adj., i.q. sphenoid.

sphere, n., a solid body, every point on the surface of which is equally distant from the centre; a globe; a ball; the sky; a celestial body; the range of duty; social position; v.t., to include in a sphere or among the heavenly bodies; to make spherical.

spher'ic, adj., i.q. spherical.

spher'ical, adj., of the shape of a sphere.

spher'ically, adv., in a spherical way.

spheric'ity, n., the quality or state of being spherical.

spher'icle, n., a small sphere. (Also spherule.)

spher'ics, n. pl., spherical geometry and trigonometry.

spher'ograph, n., a device for measuring spherical triangles.

sphe'roid, adj., spherelike.

spheroi'dal, adj., i.q. spheroid.

spherom'eter, n., an apparatus for measuring the length of the radii of spherical surfaces.

spher'ule, n., i.q. sphericle.

spher'ulite, n., glassy globules in some rock formations.

sphe'ry, adj., starry.

sphinc'ter, n., a muscle that closes an opening or a tube (esp. the anus).

sphinx, n., the winged monster of Thebes; the name also of Egyptian figures with a lion's body and a human face; any mysterious person.

sphragis'tics, n. pl., the study of engraved seals.

sphyg'mic, adj., pert. or rel. to the pulse.

sphyg'mograph, n., an instrument that records pulse-beats.

sphygmom'eter, n., a contrivance for ascertaining the blood pressure in the arteries.

sphyg'mus, n., the pulse, pulsation (physiol.).

spic'a, n., a spike (bot.).

spi'cate, adj., like a spike; consisting of spikes.

spi'cated, adj., i.q. spicate.

spicca'to, adv., the opposite to legato (It., mus.).

spice, n., an aromatic vegetable substance; anything that adds a flavour or zest; v.t., to season with spice.

spiced, p.p., spice.

spi'cer, n., one who deals in spices.

spi'cery, n., spices collectively; a store of spices; the quality of spice.

spi'cier, adj., comp. of spicy.

spi'ciest, adj., super. of spicy.

spic'ily, adv., in a spicy way.

spi'ciness, n., the quality or state of being spicy.

spi'cing, pr.p., spice.

spick, adj., fresh, smart (generally found only in spick and span = fresh and new).

spic'ular, adj., pert. or rel. to a spicule; pointed; pungent.

spic'ulate, adj., having spicules.

spic'ule, n., a thin, pointed body.

spic'uliform, adj., shaped like a spicule.

spiculig'enous, adj., bearing spicules.

spic'y, adj., aromatic, pungent, piquant; showy; indelicate (colloq.).

spi'der, n., one of the arachnida; a creature with eight legs; the name for various objects with spider-like legs.

spi'derman, n., a man who erects steel structures.

spi'der's-web, n., the web a spider spins.

spi'dery, adj., spider-like; very thin.

spied, p.p., spy.

spieg'eleisen, n., cast iron (Ger.).

spiel, *n.*, a speech or story; *v.i.* and *t.*, to orate (*Ger.*).

spif(f)'licate, *v.t.*, to crush; to trounce; to treat roughly.

spig'ot, *n.*, the plug of a vent in a cask.

spike, *n.*, a sharp point or end; a flower-cluster; *v.t.*, to fasten, to supply or pierce with spikes; to render useless.

spiked, *p.p.*, spike.

spike'let, *n.*, a sub-ordinate spike.

spike'nard, *n.*, costly aromatic ointment.

spi'king, *pr.p.*, spike.

spi'ky, *adj.*, like a spike; set with spikes.

spile, *n.*, a spigot; a wooden pile; *v.t.*, to make a hole for a spigot.

spil'ikin, *n.*, a little pin.

spil'ing, *n.*, a set of piles; the edge-curve in the plank of a vessel's hull (*naut.*).

spill, *n.*, a fall; a thin roll or strip of paper or wood for lighting a candle, etc.; *v.t.*, to let liquid drop; to upset.

spilled, *p.p.*, spill.

spill'er, *n.*, one who spills; a small mack-erel-net inside a large one.

spill'ikin, *n.*, the splin-ters of wood, bone, etc. (Also *spelicans*.)

spill'ing, *pr.p.*, spill.

spilt, *p.p.*, spill.

spilth, *n.*, that which is spilt; an excess.

spin, *n.*, a whirl; a short, brisk run or walk; *v.i.*, to practise the art of spinning; to make webs; to troll; *v.t.*, to twist into threads; to form a web; to make to re-volve; to compose; to reject a candidate in an examination (*col-loq.*).

spina'ceous, *adj.*, like spinach.

spin'ach, *n.*, a garden vegetable.

spi'nal, *adj.*, pert. or rel. to the spine.

spin'dle, *n.*, a pin that twists and winds thread on a spinning wheel; a bar used in the same manner in hand spinning; any axis on which a larger object rotates; *v.i.*, to grow like a spindle.

spin'dleage, *n.*, the num-ber of spindles in use.

spin'dled, *p.p.*, spindle.

spin'dle-legged, *adj.*, with very long, thin legs.

spin'dle-tree, *n.*, a tree or shrub with hard wood used for spin-dles.

spin'dling, *n.*, a shoot on a plant; *pr.p.*, spindle.

spin'dly, *adj.*, slender, attenuated.

spin'drier, *n.*, a high-speed rotary machine for drying washed clothes.

spin'drift, *n.*, windblown sea-spray.

spine, *n.*, the column of the vertebrae; the backbone; a ridge; a thorn (*bot.*).

spined, *adj.*, having a spine or spines.

spin'el, *n.*, the name of certain minerals found in regular crystals.

spine'less, *adj.*, without a spine; invertebrate.

spines'cent, *adj.*, ending in a spine.

spin'et, *n.*, an old musi-cal instrument with one string to each note, a predecessor of the pianoforte.

spinif'erous, *adj.*, pro-ducing spines.

spin'naker, *n.*, a large supplementary sail carried on the main-mast and used by racing yachts.

spin'ner, *n.*, one who, or that which, spins, or turns in a lathe.

spin'neret, *n.*, a spinning organ in silkworms, etc.

spin'nery, *n.*, a spinning-mill.

spin'ney, *n.*, a thicket.

spin'ning, *pr.p.*, spin.

spin'ning-jenny, *n.*, a machine for spinning two or more strands at once.

spin'ning-wheel, *n.*, an old family implement with which yarn or thread was spun.

spi'nose, *adj.*, *i.q.* spin-ous.

spinos'ity, *n.*, the qua-lity or state of being spinous.

spi'nous, *adj.*, having spines. (Also *spinose*.)

Spino'zism, *n.*, the philosophical doc-trines of Spinoza (died 1677).

Spino'zist, *n.*, a follower of Spinoza.

spin'ster, *n.*, orig. a woman who spins; now an unmarried one.

spinster'hood, *n.*, the state of being a spins-ter.

spintha'riscope, *n.*, a de-vice for showing the effects of the dis-integration of radium.

spin'ule, *n.*, a small spine.

spin'ulose, *adj.*, *i.q.* spinulous.

spin'ulous, *adj.*, having spinules.

spi'ny, *adj.*, full of spines, thorny.

spi'racle, *n.*, a breath-ing-hole; a blow-hole.

spirae'a, *n.*, a rosaceous garden flowering plant.

spi'ral, *adj.*, pointed like a spire; twisted, coil-ed, winding round in one direction and along a straight line simultaneously; *n.*, a curve; a spring, a spiral formation in shells, etc.; *v.t.*, to make spiral.

spi'rally, *adv.*, in a spiral way.

spi'rant, *adj.*, produced by the breath; *n.*, a consonant pronounc-ed through a not quite closed aper-ture of the mouth and continued.

spira'tion, *n.*, breathing.

spire, *n.*, a tapering pyramidal body; a pyramidal termina-tion to a church-tower; a shoot; *v.i.*, to shoot upward; *v.t.*, to furnish with spires.

spir'it, *n.*, breath, soul; a ghost; an incor-poreal, rational be-ing; energy, courage; the inner meaning; a state of mind; an un-seen influence; strong distilled liquor; *v.t.*, to convey away secret-ly; to inspirit.

spir'ited, *adj.*, dashing, courageous; *p.p.*, spirit.

spir'itedly, *adv.*, courageously, with spirit.

*spir'it*ing, *pr.p.*, spirit.

*spir'it*ism, *n.*, *i.q.* spiritualism.

*spir'it*ist, *n.*, a spiritualist; a medium.

spi'rit-lamp, *n.*, a small cooking appliance heated with methylated spirits.

*spir'it*less, *adj.*, tame; without fire or energy.

spi'rit-level, *n.*, an instrument which shows a true horizontal line by means of an air bubble in alcohol.

spirito'so, *adv.*, with spirit (*It.*, *mus.*).

spir'itous, *adj.*, of the nature of spirits.

*spir'it*ual, *adj.*, pert. or rel. to the spirit; the opposite to the material; inspired or divinely bestowed; marked by the highest qualities of the soul; ecclesiastical; *n.*, something pert. to the spirit; a religious song.

*spir'it*ualism, *n.*, the belief in the power to hold intercourse with the dead; the philosophic doctrine that spirit alone exists. (Also *spiritism*.)

*spir'it*ualist, *n.*, a believer in spiritualism.

*spir'it*ualis'tic, *adj.*, pert. or rel. to spiritualism and spiritualists.

*spir'it*ual'ities, *n. pl.*, the sources of revenue arising out of the performance of ecclesiastical functions (as the spiritualities of a see).

*spir'it*ual'ity, *n.*, the quality or state of being spiritual.

*spir'it*ualiza'tion, *n.*, the act or result of spiritualizing.

*spir'it*ualize, *v.t.*, to make spiritual; to raise morally, intellectually or religiously; to interpret in a spiritual rather than a literal-sense.

*spir'it*ualized, *p.p.*, spiritualize.

*spir'it*ualizer, *n.*, one who spiritualizes.

*spir'it*ualizing, *pr.p.*, spiritualize.

*spir'it*ually, *adv.*, in a spiritual way.

*spir'it*ualty, *n.*, the clergy.

spirituelle', *adj.*, pure; graceful; delicate (gen. of women) (*Fr.*).

spir'ituous, *adj.*, of the nature of spirit; markedly alcoholic.

spirivalve, *adj.*, having a spiral shell.

spirk'eting, *n.*, the inside planking of a ship (*naut.*).

spi'rograph, *n.*, an instrument to record the movements in breathing.

spirom'eter, *n.*, an instrument to measure lung capacity.

Spirrill'um, *n.*, one of the genus of blood parasites.

spirt, *n.*, *v.i.* and *t.*, *i.q.* spurt.

spirt'ed, *p.p.*, spirt.

spirt'ing, *pr.p.*, spirt.

spi'ry, *adj.*, like a spire; tapering.

spis'sated, *adj.*, thickened.

spis'situde, *n.*, thickness.

spit, *n.*, a pointed piece of metal on which meat can be roasted; a pointed shoal of sand; saliva from the mouth; a spade's depth in digging; *v.i.*, to discharge saliva; to drizzle; *v.t.*, to put on a spit for roasting; to impale; to send out from the mouth.

spitch'cock, *n.*, a broiled eel; *v.t.*, prepare an eel for broiling.

spite, *n.*, a feeling of envy or hatred; a grudge; *v.t.*, to injure maliciously and in revenge.

spi'ted, *p.p.*, spite.

spite'ful, *adj.*, malicious; full of spite.

spite'fully, *adv.*, in a spiteful way.

spite'fulness, *n.*, the quality or state of being spiteful.

spit'fire, *n.*, one who habitually expresses his feelings overtly; one quick to react angrily.

spi'ting, *pr.p.*, spite.

spit'ted, *p.p.*, spit (in the sense of impaling or putting on a spit).

spit'ter, *n.*, one who spits.

spit'ting, *pr.p.*, spit.

spit'tle, *n.*, saliva.

spittoon', *n.*, an antiquated smoking-room receptacle for spitting.

spitz, *n.*, a breed of dog.

spiv, *n.*, a shady character who lives by his wits.

splanch'nic, *adj.*, pert. or rel. to the viscera.

splanchnol'ogy, *n.*, the study of the internal organs.

splash, *n.*, water or other liquid dashed up or down; the displacement of liquid when an object falls into it; *v.i.*, to dash water about; to brag (*colloq.*); *v.t.*, to wet with water thrown upon a person or thing.

splash'board, *n.*, a protection at the front of a driver's seat of a vehicle to catch splashed mud.

splashed, *p.p.*, splash.

splash'er, *n.*, one who, or that which, splashes.

splash'ing, *pr.p.*, splash.

splash'y, *adj.*, splashing.

splatt'er, *v.i.* and *t.*, to spatter, to splash lightly; to speak unintelligibly.

splay, *adj.*, sloping or extending inwards or outwards; *n.*, a sloping surface; *v.t.*, to slant; to put out of joint.

splayed, *adj.*, widening outwards or inwards; *p.p.*, splay.

splay'-foot, *n.*, a foot which turns outwards.

splay'-footed, *adj.*, having splay feet.

spleen, *n.*, an internal organ, believed by the ancients to be the seat of some of the feelings; melancholy; suppressed spite; bad temper.

spleen'ish, *adj.*, ill-humoured; melancholy.

spleenwort, *n.*, kinds of fern, such as maidenhair.

spleen'y, *adj.*, *i.q.* spleenish.

splen'dent, *adj.*, shining; gleaming.

splen'did, *adj.*, shining; bright; glorious.

splen'didly, *adv.*, in a splendid way.

splendif'erous, *adj.*, splendid (*colloq.*).

splen'dour, *n.*, brightness, glory, **magnificence**.

splenet'ic, *adj.*, given to spleen; melancholy; peevish.

splenet'ical, *adj.*, *i.q.* splenetic.

splen'ial, *adj.*, splint-like; of the splenius muscle (*anat.*).

splen'ic, *adj.*, **pert. or** rel. to the spleen.

spleni'tis, *n.*, inflammation of the spleen.

splen'ius, *n.*, a cervical muscle moving the head.

spleniza'tion, *n.*, the conversion of organic tissue into substance resembling the spleen.

sple'nocele, *n.*, the rupture of the spleen.

splenol'ogy, *n.*, the study of the spleen.

spleu'chan, *n.*, a bag; a pouch (*Scot.*).

splice, *n.*, the joining of a fracture; the binding together of two rope-ends; *v.t.*, to join together by uniting the strands (of two ropes); to bind round a lecture; to unite in marriage (*slang*).

spliced, *p.p.*, splice.

spli'cing, *pr.p.*, splice.

spline, *n.*, a draughtsman's implement, part of a hub or shaft assembly to allow lateral movement.

splint, *n.*, *i.q.* splinter; wood or plaster used for keeping fractured limbs, etc., in position; a growth on a horse's shank bone.

splin'ter, *n.*, a small piece broken off longitudinally; any fragment; *v.i.* and *t.*, to break into splinters.

splin'tered, *p.p.*, splinter.

splin'tering, *pr.p.*, splinter.

splin'tery, *adj.*, like splinters.

split, *n.*, a fissure; a cleavage; *v.i.* and *t.*, to make a fissure; to rupture or be ruptured; to give away a secret (*colloq.*).

split'ter, *n.*, one who, or that which, splits.

split'ting, *pr.p.*, split.

splodge, *n.*, a daub; a smear; a splash.

splosh, *n.*, a splash of water (*colloq.*).

splotch, *n.*, *i.q.* splodge.

splotch'y, *adj.*, dauby; discoloured.

splurge, *n.* and *v.i.*, noisy display.

splutter', *n.*, an inarticulate, confused noise; a muddle; *v.i.*, to speak in an indistinct and rapid way; to shed ink (of a pen).

splut'tered, *p.p.*, splutter.

splut'terer, *n.*, one who splutters.

splut'tering, *pr.p.*, splutter.

splut'teringly, *adv.*, in a spluttering way.

spod'omancy, *n.*, divination with dust.

spoff'ish, *adj.*, bustling, fussy.

spoil, *n.*, plunder; pillage; earth removed from a hole; *v.i.*, to deteriorate; *v.t.*, to plunder; to pillage; to mar; to vitiate.

spoil'age, *n.*, waste during manufacture.

spoiled, *p.p.*, spoil.

spoil'er, *n.*, one who spoils.

spoil'ing, *adj.*, eager; *pr.p.*, spoil.

spoilt, *p.p.*, spoil.

spoke, *n.*, one of the parts of a wheel connecting the hub with the rim; a rung in a ladder; *p.p.*, speak; *v.t.*, to fit with spokes.

spo'ken, *p.p.*, speak.

spoke'shave, *n.*, a small two-handled plane for working on curved wood.

spokes'man, *n.*, one who acts as a mouthpiece.

spo'liate, *v.t.*, to despoil.

spo'liated, *p.p.*, spoliate.

spo'liating, *pr.p.*, spoliate.

spolia'tion, *n.*, plundering; pillaging.

spo'liative, *adj.*, having the effect of pillage.

spo'liator, *n.*, a plunderer.

sponda'ic, *adj.*, pert. or rel. to a spondee.

sponda'ical, *adj.*, *i.q.* spondaic.

spon'dee, *n.*, a metrical foot consisting of two long syllables.

spondul'icks, *n. pl.*, money (*slang*).

spon'dyl(e), *n.*, a vertebra.

sponge, *n.*, a porous, elastic, marine and fibrous growth used for cleaning; a gun-mop; a horseshoe point; a cadger (*colloq.*); *v.i.*, to cadge (*colloq.*); *v.t.*, to cleanse with a sponge. (Also *spunge.*)

sponged, *p.p.*, sponge.

spon'ger, *n.*, a person who relies on others to pay his share (*colloq.*).

spon'giform, *adj.*, like a sponge.

spon'giness, *n.*, the quality or state of being spongy.

spon'ging, *pr.p.*, sponge.

spon'ging-house, *n.*, a house where debtors were kept by the bailiff before being committed to prison.

spon'giole, *n.*, a sponge-like material in plant roots.

spon'giolite, *n.*, a fossilized sponge.

spongiopil'ine, *n.*, a kind of poultice.

spon'gious, *adj.*, sponge-like.

spon'gy, *adj.*, like sponge; oozing under pressure.

spon'sal, *adj.*, pert. or rel. to godparents or sureties.

spon'sion, *n.*, the act of a sponsor; a solemn undertaking.

spon'son, *n.*, a platform projecting from the side of a ship.

spon'sor, *n.*, a surety; a person who gives financial backing; a godparent.

spon'sored, *p.p.*, sponsor.

sponso'rial, *adj.*, pert. or rel. to a sponsor.

sponsor'ing, *n.*, the act of being a sponsor; *pr.p.*, sponsor.

spon'sorship, *n.*, the office of a sponsor.

spontane'ity, *n.*, the quality or state of being spontaneous.

sponta'neous, *adj.*, of one's own accord; done as the result of a natural impulse; occurring without apparent cause.

sponta′neously, *adv.*, in a spontaneous way.

spontoon′, *n.*, a short halberd.

spoof, *n.*, a hoax; *v.t.*, to swindle, to hoax.

spook, *n.*, a ghost (*colloq.*).

spool, *n.*, a cylinder or circular container round which thread or tape is wound.

spoon, *n.*, a small ladle for domestic or table use; a variety of golf club; *v.i.*, to play the lover (*colloq.*); *v.t.*, to lift with a spoon.

spoon′bill, *n.*, a wading-bird.

spoon′erism, *n.*, the involuntary transposition of initial sounds in two or more words, e.g. "boiling your icicles" for "oiling your bicycles".

spoon′-fed, *adj.*, artificially fostered; taught by cut and dried information; fed with a spoon; given excessive help; *p.p.*, spoon-feed.

spoon′-feed, *v.t.*, to feed by means of a spoon; to teach by cut and dried information; to give excessive help.

spoon′-feeding, *pr.p.*, spoon-feed.

spoon′ful, *n.*, the quantity contained in a spoon.

spoon′meat, *n.*, food conveyed in a spoon.

spoon′y, *adj.*, foolishly amatory; idiot-like.

spoor, *n.*, scent; trail.

sporad′ic, *adj.*, scattered; occurring here and there.

sporad′ically, *adv.*, in a sporadic way.

sporan′gium, *n.*, a spore case.

spore, *n.*, a minute seed of plants and other organisms.

spor′ran, *n.*, a Highlander's pouch.

sport, *n.*, a game; jest; mockery; recreative games; athletics; a freak; *v.i.*, to indulge in games or frolics; *v.t.*, to wear or exhibit.

sport′ed, *p.p.*, sport.

sport′ful, *adj.*, fond of jest; merry.

sport′fully, *adv.*, in a sportful way.

sport′fulness, *n.*, the quality or state of being sportful.

sport′ily, *adv.*, in a sporty way.

sport′ing, *adj.*, fond of sport; conforming to the courteous ideals of sport; *pr.p.*, sport.

sport′ive, *adj.*, merry, lively.

sport′ively, *adv.*, in a sportive way.

sport′iveness, *n.*, frolicsomeness.

sports′man, *n.*, one addicted to sport; a man who "plays the game".

sports′manlike, *adj.*, acting as befitting a sportsman.

sports′manship, *n.*, the behaviour of a sportsman.

sports′wear, *n.*, clothes worn especially for sports.

sports′wo′man, *n.*, the fem. of sportsman.

sport′y, *adj.*, sportsman-like (*colloq.*).

spor′ule, *n.*, a granule with spore.

sporulif′erous, *adj.*, producing sporules.

spot, *n.*, a speck; a blemish; a round mark; a place or locality; the spot-stroke at billiards; *v.i.*, to become spotty; *v.t.*, to blemish; to mark with spots; to detect (*colloq.*).

spot′-check, *n.*, an impromptu check; *v.i.* and *t.*, to carry out such a check.

spot′less, *adj.*, without spot or blemish; pure; innocent.

spot′lessly, *adv.*, in a spotless way.

spot′lessness, *n.*, the quality or state of being spotless.

spot′light, *n.*, a light which can be directed on to one spot, especially on a stage; *v.t.*, to pick out; to direct special attention to.

spot-on′, *adj.*, accurate (*colloq.*).

spot′ted, *p.p.*, spot.

spot′ter, *n.*, one who, or that which, spots.

spot′tiness, *n.*, the quality or state of being spotty.

spot′ting, *pr.p.*, spot.

spot′ty, *adj.*, marked with spots.

spou′sal, *adj.*, nuptial; matrimonial.

spouse, *n.*, a married person; a husband or wife.

spout, *n.*, the lip of a can, jug, etc.; a projecting pipe for discharging a liquid; *v.i.*, to gush forth; to make a wordy speech (*colloq.*); *v.t.*, to discharge liquid as from a pipe; to deposit with a pawnbroker.

spout′ed, *p.p.*, spout.

spout′er, *n.*, one who makes wordy speeches (*colloq.*).

spout′ing, *pr.p.*, spout.

sprack, *adj.*, vivacious (*Scot.*).

sprag, *n.*, a young salmon or codling; a block placed against a vehicle wheel to prevent its turning.

sprain, *n.*, a violent straining of muscles or ligaments; *v.t.*, to strain the muscles or ligaments violently.

sprained, *p.p.*, sprain.

sprain′ing, *pr.p.*, sprain.

spraints, *n. pl.*, the otter's dung.

sprang, *p.p.*, spring.

spran′gle, *v.i.*, to wander or spread irregularly.

sprat, *n.*, a diminutive fish.

sprawl, *v.i.*, to stretch oneself loosely or awkwardly; to spread out.

sprawled, *p.p.*, sprawl.

sprawl′er, *n.*, one who, or that which, sprawls.

sprawl′ing, *pr.p.*, sprawl.

spray, *n.*, water or liquid blown into small particles; a small branch; a number of small shoots; a corsage; a small bouquet of flowers; *v.t.*, to sprinkle.

sprayed, *p.p.*, spray.

spray′er, *n.*, one who, or that which, sprays.

spray′-gun, *n.*, an apparatus for spraying paint, etc.

spray′ing, *pr.p.*, spray.

spread, *n.*, a measure of extension; a feast (*colloq.*); *v.i.*, to be stretched or extended; *v.t.*, to extend; to scatter; to unfurl; to circulate; to furnish a table.

spread'-eagle, *adj.*, tall-talking; *n.*, the emblem of the U.S.A.; *v.t.*, to secure with limbs outstretched.

spread'er, *n.*, one who, or that which, spreads.

spread'ing, *pr.p.*, spread.

spree, *n.*, a frolic.

sprent, *adj.*, sprinkled; scattered.

sprig, *n.*, a young shoot; a small nail or brad; *v.t.*, to drive sprigs into.

sprigged, *p.p.*, sprig.

sprig'ging, *pr.p.*, sprig.

sprig'gy, *adj.*, full of, or resembling, sprigs.

spright, *n.*, *i.q.* sprite.

spright'liness, *n.*, the quality or state of being sprightly.

spright'ly, *adj.*, lively, vivacious, alert, gay.

spring, *n.*, the season of the year after winter; a leap or bound; an elastic piece of mechanism; a dart forward or a recoil; a fountain or source; a crack in the handle of a cricket bat, etc.; a rope securing a ship to a quayside; *v.i.*, to arise; to take origin; to leap; to bound; to fly backward or forward; *v.t.*, to arouse; to start; to strain.

spring'board, *n.*, a diving platform.

spring'bok, *n.*, a S. African variety of deer.

spring'-clean, *n.*, *i.q.* spring-cleaning; *v.t.*, to carry out spring-cleaning.

spring'-cleaned, *p.p.*, spring-clean.

spring'-clean'ing, *n.*, the seasonal cleaning of houses in spring; *pr.p.*, spring-clean.

springe, *n.*, a gin.

spring'er, *n.*, one who, or that which, springs; architecturally, the part where an arch begins to curve; the impost; the bottom stone laid on the impost; the lowest of the stones in a gable; a rib in a vault; a breed of spaniel.

spring'-halt, *n.*, a sort of chorea in horses.

spring'iness, *n.*, the quality or state of being springy.

spring'ing, *pr.p.*, spring.

spring'-like, *adj.*, resembling the conditions of the spring season; *adv.*, in a springy manner.

spring'-mattress, *n.*, a mattress which contains springs.

spring'tide, *n.*, the tide at the new and the full moon, having the largest rise and fall.

spring'time, *n.*, the season of spring.

spring'y, *adj.*, soft, elastic.

sprin'kle, *n.*, a light fall in drops; *v.i.*, to fall in thin drops, as a light rain; *v.t.*, to scatter into drops; to pour over.

sprin'kled, *p.p.*, sprinkle.

sprin'kler, *n.*, one who, or that which, sprinkles.

sprin'kling, *adj.*, in small drops; *n.*, a small quantity dropping; any small number; *pr.p.*, sprinkle.

sprint, *n.*, a short run at top speed; *v.i.*, to run at top speed for a short distance.

sprint'er, *n.*, a short distance runner; one who sprints.

sprit, *n.*, a shoot; a small spar.

sprite, *n.*, a spirit, fairy or elf. (Also *spright.*)

sprit'sail, *n.*, a sail stretched on a sprit.

sprock'et, *n.*, a little tooth on a wheel.

sprod, *n.*, a second year salmon.

sprout, *n.*, a young growth; a shoot; *v.i.*, to shoot.

sprout'ed, *p.p.*, sprout.

sprout'ing, *pr.p.*, sprout.

sprouts, *n. pl.*, Brussels sprouts, a green vegetable.

spruce, *adj.*, trim, tidy, smart; *n.*, the spruce fir; a fermented drink produced from spruce-leaves; *v.t.*, to make spruce.

spruced, *p.p.*, spruce.

spruce'ly, *adv.*, in a spruce manner.

spruce'ness, *n.*, the quality or state of being spruce.

spru'cing, *pr.p.*, spruce.

sprue', *n.*, a passage for metal being moulded to flow through; a tropical disease; inferior asparagus.

spruit, *n.*, a watercourse that is dry except after rain (*S. Africa*).

sprung, *p.p.*, spring.

spry, *adj.*, alert.

spry'ly, *adv.*, in a spry fashion.

spud, *n.*, a small weeding spade; a potato (*slang*).

spud'dle, *v.i.*, to dig lightly.

spue, *v.i.* and *t.*, *i.q.* spew.

spume, *n.*, foam, froth; *v.i.*, to throw off froth.

spumed, *p.p.*, spume.

spumes'cence, *n.*, the state of being spumescent.

spumes'cent, *adj.*, foaming.

spumif'erous *adj.*, producing froth.

spu'miness, *n.*, the state of foaming.

spu'ming, *pr.p.*, spume.

spu'mous, *adj.*, frothy, foamy.

spun, *p.p.*, spin.

spunge, *n.* and *v.t.*, *i.q.* sponge.

spunk, *n.*, courage; spirit.

spur, *n.*, a rowelled instrument attached to the heel for pricking a horse; anything spurlike, as a projection from a mountain or a flower, etc.; *v.t.*, to prick (a horse); to stimulate; to put spurs on to.

spur'gall, *n.*, a gall produced by spurring.

spurge, *n.*, a type of plant, acrid, milky, and juicy.

spu'rious, *adj.*, false; sham.

spu'riously, *adv.*, in a spurious way.

spu'riousness, *n.*, the quality or state of being spurious.

spurl'ing-line, *n.*, a cord connecting the steering-wheel with a cabin indicator to show the helm position.

spurn, *n.*, a contemptuous action; *v.i.* and *t.*, to scorn; to contemn; to reject.

spurned, *p.p.*, spurn.

spurn'er, *n.*, one who spurns.

spurn'ing, *pr.p.*, spurn.

spurred, *p.p.*, spur.

spur'rer, *n.*, one who spurs.

spur'rier, *n.*, a spurmaker.

spur'ring, *pr.p.*, spur.

spur'royal, *n.*, an old coin of James the First's reign, stamped with a device resembling the rowel of a spur.

spur'ry, *n.*, the name for certain kinds of plants, esp. the common weed, the cornspurry.

spurt, *n.*, a sudden, fresh effort; a sudden increase in speed; *v.i.*, to flow suddenly in a jet; to make a sudden and fresh start or effort; *v.t.*, to make a sudden flow. (Also *spirt*.)

spurt'ed, *p.p.*, spurt.

spurt'ing, *pr.p.*, spurt.

spur'-wheel, *n.*, a cogwheel with radial teeth.

spu'ta, *n.*, the pl. of sputum.

sput'nik, *n.*, a man-made space satellite.

sput'ter, *n.*, rapid, incoherent talk; *v.i.*, to speak with a spitting noise; *v.t.*, to utter incoherently or excitedly.

sput'tered, *p.p.*, sputter.

sput'terer, *n.*, one who sputters.

sput'tering, *pr.p.*, sputter.

sput'teringly, *adv.*, in a sputtering manner.

spu'tum, *n.*, saliva; matter expectorated.

spy, *n.*, a person who secretly keeps watch on an enemy's plans, and communicates the results of his observations to his own country; one who informs against anyone; *v.i.*, to play the spy; *v.t.*, to catch sight of; to perceive.

spy'-glass, *n.*, a hand telescope.

spy'hole, *n.*, an inconspicuous observation hole, a peep-hole.

spy'ing, *pr.p.*, spy.

squab, *adj.*, squat; *n.*, a squat person; a young pigeon.

squab'bish, *adj.*, somewhat squat.

squab'ble, *n.*, a quarrel; *v.i.*, to bicker; to wrangle.

squab'bled, *p.p.*, squabble.

squab'bler, *n.*, one who squabbles.

squab'bling, *n.*, the act of squabbling; *pr.p.*, squabble.

squab'by, *adj.*, dumpy.

squab'pie, *n.*, pigeon pie; a pie of mutton, onions and apples.

squacc'o, *n.*, a small crested heron.

squad, *n.*, a small force of soldiers, etc.

squad'ron, *n.*, a division of a cavalry regiment containing two troops; a group of fighting aircraft; a group of war-vessels detached for particular service.

squa'dron-lead'er, *n.*, an officer commanding an airforce squadron.

squails, *n.*, a game similar to shove-halfpenny, but played with wooden discs.

squal'id, *adj.*, dirty, mean, wretched-looking.

squalid'ity, *n.*, *i.q.* squalidness.

squal'idness, *n.*, the quality or state of being squalid.

squall, *n.*, a scream; a sudden storm of wind, often accompanied by rain or snow; *v.i.*, to blow a squall; *v.i.* and *t.*, to cry out; to scream.

squalled, *p.p.*, squall.

squall'er, *n.*, one who squalls.

squall'ing, *pr.p.*, squall.

squall'y, *adj.*, stormy; blustering.

squa'loid, *adj.*, sharklike.

squal'or, *n.*, wretched appearance; poverty; destitution.

squa'ma, *n.*, a scale, or a scale-like structure (*Lat.*).

squama'ceous, *adj.*, scaly.

squamif'erous, *adj.*, *i.q.* squamaceous.

squa'miform, *adj.*, like scales.

squamig'erous, *adj.*, having scales.

squa'mipen, *n.*, a penguin.

squa'moid, *adj.*, scaly.

squa'mous, *adj.*, covered with, or resembling, scales.

squam'ula, *n.*, a small scale.

squam'ule, *n.*, *i.q.* squamula.

squan'der, *v.t.*, to waste; to spend extravagantly.

squan'dered, *p.p.*, squander.

squan'derer, *n.*, one who squanders.

squan'dering, *pr.p.*, squander.

squan'derma'nia, *n.*, a craze for extravagant expenditure (*colloq.*).

square, *adj.*, having four equal sides and four right-angles; honest, outright; ample (*colloq.*); multiplied by itself; old-fashioned (*colloq.*); *n.*, a four-sided equilateral figure; an open area surrounded by buildings; the product of a number or quantity multiplied by itself; a T-shaped right-angular rule; *v.i.*, to be at right angles; to agree; to take a boxer's attitude; *v.t.*, to multiply a number by itself; to make square or rectangular; to make to balance; to adjust; to bribe, to win over; to lay (yards) at right angles to the keel.

square'-built, *adj.*, of a comparatively broad shape.

squared, *p.p.*, square.

square'leg, *adv.*, in a fielding position in cricket; *n.*, a fielding position in a game of cricket.

square'ly, *adv.*, in a square way; fairly.

square'ness, *n.*, the quality or state of being square.

squar'er, *adj.*, *comp.* of square; *n.*, one who squares.

square'-rigged, *adj.*, having the principal sails rigged on horizontal yards suspended by the middle from the mast.

square'root', *n.*, the base or root of a number, which when multiplied by itself gives that number (the root of 4 is 2, 2 × 2 = 4).

squar'est, *adj.*, *super.* of square.

square'-toed, *adj.*, having square toes or toe-caps.

squar'ing, *pr.p.*, square.

squar'ish, *adj.*, generally, but not precisely, square.

squarrose', *adj.*, *i.q.* squarrous.

squar'rous, *adj.*, rough and having scale-like processes.

squash, *n.*, a close crowd; the name of certain gourds; *v.i.*, to become pulpy; to crowd; *v.t.*, to squeeze and make pulpy; to snub a person.

squashed, *p.p.*, squash.

squash'er, *n.*, one who, or that which, squashes.

squash'iness, *n.*, the state of being squashy.

squash'ing, *pr.p.*, squash.

squash'y, *adj.*, soft, pulpy.

squat, *adj.*, dwarfish, dumpy; squatting; *n.*, the posture of squatting; *v.i.*, to crouch in a sitting posture; to settle in a new country; to take over accommodation illegally.

squat'ted, *p.p.*, squat.

squat'ter, *n.*, a settler; one who squats.

squat'ting, *pr.p.*, squat.

squaw, *n.*, an American Indian woman or girl.

squawk, *v.i.*, to make a shrill, harsh cry of fear, pain or complaint; to betray information (*slang*); *n.*, a shrill, harsh cry.

squawked, *p.p.*, squawk.

squawk'er, *n.*, one who squawks.

squawk'ing, *pr.p.*, squawk.

squaw'-man, *n.*, a white man with an American Indian wife.

squeak, *n.*, a thin, small noise; *v.i.*, to make a thin, small noise.

squeaked, *p.p.*, squeak.

squeak'er, *n.*, one who, or that which, squeaks.

squeak'ing, *n.*, *i.q.* squeak; *pr.p.*, squeak.

squeak'y, *adj.*, making a squeak.

squeal, *n.*, a shrill, prolonged cry; *v.i.* and *t.*, to utter with a sharp, loud noise, as in pain.

squealed, *p.p.*, squeal.

squeal'er, *n.*, one who, or that which squeals.

squeal'ing, *n.*, *i.q.* squeal; *pr.p.*, squeal.

squeam'ish, *adj.*, readily nauseated; over-scrupulous; easily disgusted by unpleasant appearances.

squeam'ishly, *adv.*, in a squeamish way.

squeam'ishness, *n.*, the quality or state of being squeamish.

squee'gee, *n.*, an implement for absorbing and removing wet.

squeezabil'ity, *n.*, the quality of being squeezable.

squeez'able, *adj.*, able to be squeezed.

squeeze, *n.*, the act of pressing; a tight fit; mental pressure or intimidation; *v.i.*, to press one's way; to penetrate by pressing; to clasp affectionately; *v.t.*, to crush or press; to extract by pressing; to extort; to take an impression of.

squeezed, *p.p.*, squeeze.

squeez'er, *n.*, one who, or that which, squeezes.

squeez'ing, *pr.p.*, squeeze.

squelch, *v.i.*, to move through muddy or marshy terrain; *v.t.*, to suppress.

squelched, *p.p.*, squelch.

squelch'ing, *pr.p.*, squelch.

squib, *n.*, a small explosive firework; a lampoon; *v.i.*, to throw squibs at; to lampoon.

squibbed, *p.p.*, squib.

squib'bing, *pr.p.*, squib.

squid, *n.*, a cuttlefish.

squidg'y, *adj.*, soft and moist.

squiff'er, *n.*, a concertina (*slang*).

squi'ffy, *adj.*, slightly drunk; tipsy (*slang*); feeling fuddled.

squig'gle, *n.*, a wriggly line (*colloq.*); a twist; *v.i.*, to squirm.

squig'gled, *p.p.*, squiggle.

squig'gling, *pr.p.*, squiggle.

squil'gee, *n.*, *i.q.* squeegee.

squill, *n.*, a medicinal bulbous plant; its sliced bulb.

squinch, *n.*, a kind of support (*archit.*).

squint, *adj.*, having a squint; not correctly aligned; *n.*, strabismus; a difference between the axes of the two eyes; a hurried look; a little opening in a church wall to give a view of the altar; *v.i.*, to look obliquely; to suffer from strabismus.

squint'ed, *p.p.*, squint.

squint'er, *n.*, one who squints.

squint'-eyed, *adj.*, having cross-eyes.

squint'ing, *pr.p.*, squint.

squir(e)'archy, *n.*, squires collectively as country magnates; government by these.

squire, *n.*, the attendant on a knight; an esquire; a country gentleman with a landed estate; a flourish in handwriting (*colloq.*); *v.t.*, to attend upon.

squire'dom, *n.*, *i.q.* squirearchy.

squireen', *n.*, a smaller landowner, particularly in Ireland.

squire'ship, *n.*, the position of a squire.

squirl, *n.*, a squiggle or flourish in handwriting.

squirm, *n.*, an evasive wriggle; *v.i.*, to wriggle uncomfortably; to cower and shudder.

squirmed, *p.p.*, squirm.

squirm'ing, *n.*, the act of wriggling uncomfortably; *pr.p.*, squirm.

squir'rel, *n.*, a tree-dwelling rodent with a bushy tail.

squirt, *n.*, a syringe; a jet; *v.i.*, to be propelled as from a syringe; *v.t.*, to jet water or other liquid with a syringe.

squirt'ed, *p.p.*, squirt.

squirt'er, *n.,* one who, or that which, squirts.

squirt'ing, *pr.p.,* squirt.

squit, *n.,* a small insignificant person (*slang*).

stab, *n.,* a blow with a knife; a stabbing pain; *v.i.* and *t.* to pierce with a knife, dagger, etc.; to cause a stabbing pain.

stabbed, *p.p.,* stab.

stab'ber, *n.,* one who, or that which, stabs.

stab'bing, *pr.p.,* stab.

stabil'ity, *n.,* firmness; strength; steadfastness; equilibrium.

stabiliza'tion, *n.,* the process of making or becoming stable.

sta'bilizator, *n., i.q.* stabilizer.

sta'bilize, *v.t.,* to make stable.

sta'bilized, *p.p.,* stabilize.

sta'bilizer, *n.,* one who, or that which, stabilizes; a device on a ship to prevent rolling.

sta'bilizing, *pr.p.,* stabilize.

sta'ble, *adj.,* firm, steady, lasting; *n.,* a shed or other building to shelter horses or cattle; *v.i.* and *t.,* to shelter in a stable.

sta'ble-boy, *n.,* a boy/man employed in a stable.

sta'bled, *p.p.,* stable.

sta'ble-keeper, *n.,* one who keeps stables and hires out horses.

sta'bleness, *n., i.q.* stability.

sta'bler, *n.,* a stable keeper.

sta'bling, *n.,* accommodation for horses; *pr.p.,* stable.

stab'lish, *v.t., i.q.* establish.

sta'bly, *adv.,* in a stable way.

stacca'to, *adj.* and *adv.,* in a sharp, quick way; with a swift, separate action (*It., mus.*).

stack, *n.,* a pile of wheat sheaves or of hay or straw; anything piled; a smoke-funnel or chimney; *v.t.,* to arrange in stacks; to file.

stacked, *adj.,* (of aircraft) circling in a queue awaiting landing instructions; *p.p.,* stack.

stack'er, *n.,* one who stacks.

stack'ing, *pr.p.,* stack.

stack'-yard, *n.,* a yard for corn or hay stacks.

stac'te, *n.,* a spice used as an ingredient of incense.

stactom'eter, *n.,* a tube for measuring liquid in drops.

stad(t)'holder, *n.,* a provincial governor of the Netherlands.

stad(t)'holderate, *n.,* the position or office of a stadtholder.

sta'dia, *n.,* an instrument for measuring distances. Also the pl. of stadium.

sta'dium, *n.,* an ancient Greek measure of length; a racecourse; an enclosed campus for sports; the interval between insect moults; in medicine, the period of a disease.

staff, *n.,* a stick, a support; a pole; a body of officers closely attached to headquarters, or of persons employed in a firm, school, etc.; the lines, with spaces between, on which music is printed; *v.t.,* to provide personnel for.

staff'-college, *n.,* a college for training staff officers in the armed forces.

staffed, *p.p.,* staff.

staffing, *pr.p.,* staff.

staff'room, *n.,* a room used by the staff of a school or college.

stag, *n.,* a male deer; a bull castrated when fully grown.

stage, *n.,* a platform for actors; the theatrical profession; any sort of platform; a storey; a halting-place; the distance between two places in a journey; a defined period or point arrived at in a logical progression; *i.q.* stage-coach; *v.t.,* to mount a play; to contrive a situation.

stage'-coach, *n.,* a public conveyance travelling from one place to another by stages.

stage'craft, *n.,* the skill in staging or writing plays.

staged, *p.p.,* stage.

stage'-door, *n.,* the actors' entrance at the back of a theatre.

stage'-fright, *n.,* the nervousness of an actor on facing an audience.

stage'-manager, *n.,* the person who superintends a stage performance.

stage'-name, *n.,* the professional name of an actor or actress.

stage'-player, *n.,* an actor.

stage'-property, *n.,* the scenery, furniture, etc. required in a play.

sta'ger, *n.,* a stage-horse.

stage'struck, *adj.,* excessively desirous of becoming an actor.

stage'-whisper, *n.,* a whisper intended for the audience and not heard by the other players; any loud whisper.

sta'gey, *adj.,* theatrical; unnatural. (Also stagy.)

stag'gard, *n.,* a four year old stag.

stag'ger, *n.,* a reeling movement; in the *pl.,* a brain disease in cattle and horses; a state of giddiness; *v.i.,* to reel; to waver; *v.t.,* to shake; to dismay; to cause to doubt; to arrange the spokes of wheels; to separate over time.

stag'gered, *p.p.,* stagger.

stag'gerer, *n.,* one who staggers.

stag'gering, *adj.,* amazing; *pr.p.,* stagger.

stag'geringly, *adv.,* in a staggering way.

stag'horn, *n.,* a stag's antler.

stag'hound, *n.,* a hound used in stag hunting.

sta'ging, *n.,* scaffolding; *pr.p.,* stage.

sta'ging-post, *n.,* an air-route station.

Stag'irite, *n.,* a native of Stagira in Macedonia, esp. Aristotle.

stag'nancy, *n.,* the quality or state of being stagnant.

stag'nant, *adj.,* motionless; not flowing; lifeless, dull, foul.

stag'nantly, *adv.*, in a stagnant way.

stag'nate, *v.i.*, to have no movement; to become inert.

stag'nated, *p.p.*; stagnate.

stag'nating, *pr.p.*, stagnate.

stagna'tion, *n.*, the state of being stagnant.

stagnic'olous, *adj.*, living in swamps or stagnant water.

stag'-party, *n.*, a party for men only.

sta'gy, *adj.*, i.q. stagey.

staid, *adj.*, steady, sober.

stain, *n.*, a spot, blemish or discoloration; colouring for wood, walls, etc.; *v.t.*, to discolour; to blemish; to colour.

stained, *p.p.*, stain.

stain'er, *n.*, one who stains or paints.

stain'ing, *n.*, the act of staining; stained work; *pr.p.*, stain.

stain'less, *adj.*, unblemished.

stain'lessness, *n.*, the quality or state of being stainless.

stair, *n.*, a step, or series of ascending or descending steps.

stair'case, *n.*, a set of stairs. (Also *stairway*.)

stair'-rod, *n.*, a rod to keep a stair-carpet in its place.

stair'way, *n.*, i.q. staircase.

stair'wise, *adv.*, by steps.

staith(e), *n.*, a wharf.

stake, *n.*, a pole, stick or pale with a sharpened end; an upright post; a hazard; an amount wagered; *v.t.*, to impale; to defend with stakes; to wager; to curry (a skin).

staked, *p.p.*, stake.

stake'holder, *n.*, one who holds the wagers of two or more parties.

stakhan'ovite, *n.*, a worker who increases output considerably (*Russ.*).

sta'king, *pr.p.*, stake.

stalac'tic, *adj.*, formed by a dripping deposit.

stalac'tiform, *adj.*, like a stalactite.

stal'actite, *n.*, a mineral pendulous formation, the result of a dripping deposit.

stalactit'ic, *adj.*, i.q. stalactic.

stal'ag, *n.*, a German prison camp (*Ger.*).

stal'agmite, *n.*, a deposit on the ground, formed by a drip from above, and sometimes growing till it meets the gradually descending stalactite and joins with it.

stalagmit'ic, *adj.*, pert. or rel. to stalagmites.

stalagmom'eter, *n.*, an instrument for measuring surface tensions.

stal'der, *n.*, a cask stand.

stale, *adj.*, vapid through age; worn out; trite; *n.*, the urine of cattle; a broomhandle; a decoy bird, a dupe; *v.i.*, to become stale; to urinate; *v.t.*, to make stale; to take the life out of.

stale'mate, *n.*, a position (in chess) where neither side can claim a win; hence a position where further action or progress is impossible; *v.t.*, to reduce to a stalemate.

stale'ness, *n.*, the quality or state of being stale.

Stalinism, *n.*, the policy and theories of Joseph Stalin, the former Russian dictator.

stalk, *n.*, a stem; a gait; *v.i.*, to walk in a stately way; to pursue game stealthily; *v.t.*, to track stealthily; to pass with a stately step.

stalked, *p.p.*, stalk.

stalk'er, *n.*, one who stalks.

stalk'ing, *n.*, the act of stalking; *pr.p.*, stalk.

stalk'less, *adj.*, without a stalk.

stalk'y, *adj.*, like a stalk; with a large stalk.

stall, *n.*, a compartment in a row of seats in a choir or a theatre; a compartment in a stable; a booth or barrow for display; a pickpocket's confederate; *v.i.*, to be stuck in mud, etc.; to come to an unintended halt; to lose flying speed; to stop working (as engine); *v.t.*, to put into a stall; to put stalls into; to fix in a drift or mud; to obstruct.

stall'age, *n.*, stall-accommodation; payment for the right to erect stalls at a fair.

stalled, *p.p.*, stall.

stall'-fed, *adj.*, fed in a stable; *p.p.*, stall-feed.

stall'-feed, *v.t.*, to feed cattle in a stable or stall.

stall'-feeding, *pr.p.*, stallfeed.

stall'ing, *pr.p.*, stall.

stal'lion, *n.*, a horse not castrated and kept for breeding purposes.

stal'wart, *adj.*, sturdy, strong, bold; *n.*, a strong partisan.

sta'men, *n.*, the organ that contains the pollen of a flowering plant (*Lat.*).

sta'mened, *adj.*, having stamens.

stam'ina, *n.*, strength of constitution; lasting power.

stam'inal, *adj.*, pert. or rel. to stamina and stamens.

stam'inate, *adj.*, having stamens.

stamin'eous, *adj.*, pert. or rel. to stamens.

staminif'erous, *adj.*, having stamens.

stam'inode, *n.*, i.q. staminodium.

staminod'ium, *n.*, a sterile stamen (*bot.*).

stam'inoid, *adj.*, stamenlike.

stam'mel, *n.*, dull red woollen cloth.

stam'mer, *n.*, defective, stuttering speech; utterance with an impediment; *v.t.* and *i.*, to speak with pauses and repeated partial utterances.

stam'mered, *p.p.*, stammer.

stam'merer, *n.*, one who stammers.

stam'mering, *adj.* and *n.*, stuttering; *pr.p.*, stammer.

stam'meringly, *adv.*, in a stammering way.

stamp, *n.*, a pattern or impress; a stamping machine; an official mark on deeds, bills, etc.; an official paper marked as a receipt for payment of a fee for postage, etc.; character; heavy pressure with the foot; *v.i.*, to press down sharply and heavily with the foot; *v.t.*, to make an impress; to affix a stamp.

stamp′-album, *n.,* a book for storing collected postage-stamps.

stamp′-collecting, *n.,* philately.

stamp′-collector, *n.,* a philatelist.

stamp-duty, *n.,* duty collected by means of stamps affixed to certain legal and business documents.

stamped, *p.p.,* stamp.

stampede′, *n.,* a wild flight in alarm; *v.i.,* to run wildly away in a frightened crowd; *v.t.,* to cause to stampede.

stamped′ed, *p.p.,* stampede.

stamped′ing, *pr.p.,* stampede.

stamp′er, *n.,* one who, or that which, stamps.

stamp′ing, *pr.p.,* stamp.

stamp′ing-ground, *n.,* a wild animal resort (U.S.A.); a place of habitual visitation.

stamp′-machine, *n.,* an automatic slot-machine which sells postage stamps.

stance, *n.,* a standing position adopted for a particular purpose.

stanch, *v.t.,* to stop the flow; to check the flow of blood from. (Also *staunch.*)

stanched, *p.p.,* stanch.

stanch′ing, *pr.p.,* stanch.

stan′chion, *n.,* a vertical support; an upright bar from which chains or ropes are hung; *v.t.,* to enclose (cattle); to secure.

stand, *n.,* a firm position; a halt; resistance; a support; a platform; a rack; a set of shelves; *v.i.,* to assume an upright position; to keep one's footing; to endure; to be still; to be based; *v.t.,* to set upright; to bear; to give as a treat.

stand′ard, *adj.,* according to pattern or recognized degree of quality or excellence; *n.,* a measure, rule or type; a flag; an educational grade; an upright shrub or tree.

stand′ard-bearer, *n.,* one who carries a standard.

stand′ardizable, *adj.,* capable of standardization.

standardiza′tion, *n.,* the reduction of a group of items to a single pattern or rule.

stand′ardize, *v.t.,* to make according to one pattern; to obtain analytically the specific value of, for the purpose of comparing with other solutions, etc.

stand′ardized, *p.p.,* standardize.

stand′ardizing, *pr.p.,* standardize.

stand′-by, *n.,* a basis of reliance; *v.i.* and *t.,* to support; to abide by; to side with; to be ready for action.

stan′del, *n.,* a young tree specially grown for timber.

stand′er, *n.,* one who, or that which, stands.

stand′-in, *n.,* a deputy or substitute.

stand′ing, *adj.,* permanent; stock; *n.,* a rank, position or repute; *pr.p.,* stand.

stand′ish, *n.,* an ink-stand.

stand′-off′ish, *adj.,* distant; reserved, not affable.

stand′-off′ishness, *n.,* the quality or state of being stand-offish.

stand′patter, *n.,* a loyal party politician.

stand′-pipe, *n.,* a vertical water-pipe.

stand′point, *n.,* a point from which one views a question.

stand′still, *n.,* a halt.

stand′-to, *n.,* the occupation of a post in readiness; *v.i.,* to abide by; to stick to (a promise).

stang, *n.,* a long wooden pole or shaft.

stan′hope, *n.,* a light, open carriage.

stan′iel, *n.,* the kestrel. (Also *stannel, stannyel.*)

stank, *p.p.,* stink.

stan′nary, *adj.,* pert. or rel. to tin mining; *n.,* a tin mine; a tin mining district.

stan′nate, *n.,* a stannic acid salt.

stan′nel, *n., i.q.* staniel.

stan′nic, *adj.,* pert. or rel. to tin.

stannif′erous, *adj.,* producing tin.

stan′notype, *n.,* a photo-mechanical process with tinfoil.

stan′nous, *adj.,* containing tin.

stann′yel, *n., i.q.* staniel.

stan′za, *n.,* a group of rhymed lines in a poem.

stanza′ic, *adj.,* arranged in, pert. or rel. to, stanzas.

staph′yle, *n.,* the uvula.

staph′yline, *adj.,* pert. or rel. to the uvula.

staphyli′tis, *n.,* inflammation of the uvula.

staphylococc′us, *n.,* a bacterial infection (usu. of the throat).

staphylo′ma, *n.,* a protrusion of the cornea or other surface of the eye.

staphylom′atous, *adj.,* pert. or rel. to staphyloma.

sta′ple, *adj.,* regularly on the market; principal; *n.,* a leading article of commerce; the chief element; cotton-fibre; a great mart; a monopoly; a piece of metal, pointed at both ends and driven into a door, etc., to receive a hook or hasp; *v.t.,* to fasten with a staple.

sta′pled, *p.p.,* staple.

sta′pler, *n.,* one who sorts wool; a wool merchant with a monopoly.

sta′pling, *pr.p.,* staple.

star, *n.,* a self-luminous heavenly body like the Sun, but outside the solar system; an asterisk; the principal actor in a company; any outstanding member of a profession; *v.i.,* to play a leading part as an actor; to get a new innings in the game of pool; *v.t.,* to adorn with stars; to mark with an asterisk; to break so as to produce a starlike appearance.

star′board, *n.,* the right-hand side of a ship looking forward; *v.t.,* to turn a ship to the right.

starch, *adj.*, prim, stiff; *n.*, a carbohydrate found in all plants except fungi; in its prepared form, when mixed with boiling water, it is used for stiffening linen, etc.; *v.t.*, to stiffen.

Star' Chamber, *n.*, an historical, legal tribunal, so named from a chamber with a star-spangled roof in which it met. (Abolished 1640.)

starched, *p.p.*, starch.

starch'er, *n.*, one who, or that which, starches.

starch'ily, *adv.*, stiffly.

starch'iness, *n.*, stiffness from being starched; formality; stiffness of manner.

starch'ing, *pr.p.*, starch.

starch'y, *adj.*, stiff in any sense.

star'dom, *n.*, the status of a stage or screen star.

star'-dust, *n.*, groups of distant stars, seen like dust particles; meteoric dust.

stare, *n.*, a fixed look expressing horror, fright, astonishment, etc.; *v.i.*, to look with a stare; *v.t.*, to put out of countenance.

stared, *p.p.*, stare.

sta'rer, *n.*, one who stares.

star'fish, *n.*, a sea creature with five or more radiating arms.

star'-flower, *n.*, any star-shaped flower.

star'gaze, *v.i.*, to gaze at the stars.

star'gazer, *n.*, an astronomer; an astrologer; a dreamy idealist.

star'gazing, *adj.*, studying the stars; *n.*, astronomy; the study of the stars; absent-mindedness; *pr.p.*, stargaze.

sta'ring, *adj.*, with a stare; prominent; gaudy; *pr.p.*, stare.

star'ingly, *adv.*, in a staring manner.

stark, *adj.*, stiff; downright; *adv.*, quite.

star'less, *adj.*, without stars; dark.

star'let, *n.*, a small star; a promising young actress; a kind of starfish.

star'light, *n.*, the light of the stars.

star'like, *adj.*, like a star.

star'ling, *n.*, a common bird noted for its powers of imitation; an arrangement of piles round a bridge-pier.

star'lit, *adj.*, illuminated by the stars.

star'ost, *n.*, a Polish noble (*hist.*).

star'osta, *n.*, *i.q.* starost.

star'osty, *n.*, a Polish noble's seigniory.

starred, *p.p.*, star.

star'riness, *n.*, the quality or state of being starry.

star'ring, *pr.p.*, star.

star'ry, *adj.*, bright with stars.

star'ry-eyed, *adj.*, unrealistic; having a tendency to romanticize.

star'shaped, *adj.*, shaped like a star.

star'shell, *n.*, a shell, which on bursting, emits intense light.

star'spangled, *adj.*, spangled or dotted over with stars.

star'-stone, *n.*, a kind of sapphire.

start, *n.*, a beginning; a setting out; the distance allowed on a handicap; a sudden movement of surprise or fright; *v.i.*, to make a beginning; to set out on a journey; to spring up in alarm, to surprise, etc.; *v.t.*, to cause to begin; to make a beginning of.

start'ed, *p.p.*, start.

start'er, *n.*, one who, or that which, starts; one who gives the signal to start to competitors in a race; anything that sets machinery in motion; the first course of a meal.

start'ful, *adj.*, jumpy, nervous.

start'ing, *pr.p.*, start.

start'ing-point, *n.*, a point or place from which one starts.

start'ing-post, *n.*, a post from which racers start.

start'le, *v.t.*, to fill with sudden alarm; to surprise.

start'led, *p.p.*, startle.

start'ler, *n.*, one who, or that which, startles.

start'ling, *adj.*, alarming; surprising; *pr.p.*, startle.

start'lingly, *adv.*, alarmingly.

star'-turn, *n.*, an outstanding performer.

starva'tion, *n.*, the act or effect of starving; the starved state.

starve, *v.i.*, to perish, or to be perishing, from hunger or cold; *v.t.*, to destroy with hunger or cold; to deprive of necessaries.

starved, *p.p.*, starve.

starve'ling, *adj.*, starving; improperly fed; *n.*, a starving or ill-fed person.

starv'ing, *pr.p.*, starve.

star'wort, *n.*, an aster.

sta'sis, *n.*, the stoppage of blood circulation.

stat'able, *n.*, capable of being stated.

sta'tant, *adj.*, standing still (*her.*).

state, *adj.*, pert. or rel. to the State; ceremoniously formal; *n.*, condition; a mode of existence; a community with an organized government; *v.i.* and *t.*, to say expressly in word or writing; to fix definitely.

state'-aided, *adj.*, subsidized by public funds.

state'craft, *n.*, skill in government.

sta'ted, *adj.*, fixed; regular; *p.p.*, state.

sta'tedly, *adv.*, expressly.

state'hood, *n.*, the quality or status of a state.

state'less, *adj.*, without nationality.

state'lier, *adj.*, *comp.* of stately.

state'liest, *adj.*, *super.* of stately.

state'liness, *n.*, the quality or state of being stately.

state'ly, *adj.*, majestic, dignified, ceremonious.

state'ment, *n.*, the act of stating; that which is stated.

sta'ter, *n.*, one who states; an old Greek coin varying in value.

state′room, *n.*, an officer's sleeping-room in a ship; a private sleeping-room in a passenger ship.

States-Gen′eral, *n. pl.*, a general legislative body representing various estates of the citizens of a country.

states′man, *n.*, one engaged or skilled in government.

states′manlike, *adj.*, showing skill in government.

states′manship, *n.*, the quality of being statesmanlike.

stat′ic, *adj.*, pert. or rel. to bodies in equilibrium and at rest, or to electricity at rest; acting as weight without motion.

stat′ical, *adj.*, *i.q.* static.

stat′ically, *adv.*, without movement.

stat′ics, *n. pl.*, the study or science of bodies at rest.

sta′ting, *pr.p.*, state.

sta′tion, *n.*, a position or place where people stay or it is appointed for them to stay or halt; rank; the collected officers and society residing at a military post; a point from which surveying measurements are taken; a stated fast on Wednesday or Friday; a halting-point in a procession; a place where trains or buses pick up or set down passengers; one of the set of fourteen pictures or sculptures illustrating the events of the death of Christ; *v.t.*, to place; to assign a position to.

sta′tional, *adj.*, pert. or rel. to a station.

sta′tionary, *adj.*, standing still; not moving or advancing.

sta′tioned, *p.p.*, station.

sta′tioner, *n.*, one who sells paper, pens, pencils, etc.

sta′tionery, *n.*, writing materials.

sta′tion-house, *n.*, a police-station; a house for a station-master.

sta′tioning, *pr.p.*, station.

sta′tion-man′ager, *n.*, *i.q.* station-master.

sta′tion-mas′ter, *n.*, the person responsible for a railway station.

sta′tion-wagon, *n.*, an estate car; a dual-purpose car for goods and passengers.

stat′ism, *n.*, the state control of the individual.

sta′tist, *n.*, one who handles statistics; *i.q.* statistician; one concerned with the craft of politics.

statis′tic, *n.*, the sing. of statistics.

statis′tical, *adj.*, pert. or rel. to statistics.

statis′tically, *adv.*, in a statistical way.

statisti′cian, *n.*, one who compiles and tabulates statistics.

statis′tics, *n. pl.*, facts, often numerical, compiled and systematically tabulated to reveal their significance.

sta′tive, *adj.*, pert. or rel. to a permanent camp.

stat′or, *n.*, the stationary part of a generator.

stat′oscope, *n.*, an aneroid barometer capable of recording minor variations of pressure.

stat′uary, *adj.*, pert. or rel. to statues; *n.*, statues collectively; the sculptor's art; a sculptor.

stat′ue, *n.*, a sculptured, cast or moulded representation of a human or animal figure.

stat′ued, *adj.*, ornamented with statues.

statuesque′, *n.*, like a statue for grace, dignity or repose.

statuette′, *n.*, a little statue.

stat′ure, *n.*, height, chiefly of a human being.

sta′tus, *n.*, position, standing (*Lat.*).

sta′tus quo, *n.*, the former and present existing position (*Lat.*)

stat′utable, *adj.*, *i.q.* statutory.

stat′ute, *n.*, a legislative enactment; a law; *adj.*, pert. or rel. to statutes; authorized by statute.

stat′ute-book, *n.*, a book recording legal enactments.

stat′utory, *adj.*, regulated by statute; having the authority of law. (Also *statutable*.)

staunch, *adj.*, trustworthy; steadfast; airtight; watertight; *v.t.*, *i.q.* stanch.

staur′o-, a Greek prefix denoting a cross.

staur′oscope, *n.*, an optical instrument for determining the effect of polarized light on crystals.

stau′rotypous, *adj.*, with markings like crosses.

stave, *n.*, one of the bent timbers in the side of a cask; a staff (*mus.*); a verse or stanza; *v.i.*, to be broken in; *v.t.*, to break the staves or sides of; to fix with staves; (with the word *off*) to avert.

staved, *p.p.*, stave.

staves, *n.*, the pl. of staff.

staves′acre, *n.*, a kind of larkspur.

sta′ving, *pr.p.*, stave.

stay, *n.*, a support; continuance (in a place); the suspension of proceedings (*leg.*); a rope supporting a mast or sail; *v.i.*, to remain (in a place); to stand still; *v.t.*, to stop; to arrest; to support.

stay′-at-home, *n.*, an untravelled person.

stay′bar, *n.*, a horizontal iron bar across the top of a window mullion (*archit.*).

stay′bolt, *n.*, a bolt used for binding plates together.

stayed, *p.p.*, stay.

stay′er, *n.*, one who stays; one who can last.

stay′ing, *pr.p.*, stay.

stay′ing-pow′er, *n.*, extreme endurance.

stays, *n. pl.*, the act of going about (*naut.*).

stay′sail, *n.*, a sail on a stay.

stay′-tape, *n.*, a binding tape.

stead, *n.*, place or room; avail.

stead′fast, *adj.*, firm, loyal.

stead′fastly, *adv.*, loyally, firmly.

or stead'fastness, n., firmness, loyalty.

stead'ied, p.p., steady.

stead'ier, adj., comp. of steady.

stead'iest, adj., super. of steady.

stead'ily, adv., in a steady way.

stead'iness, n., the quality or state of being steady.

stead'y, adj., not easily shaken; firm; temperate; regular; n., a support; v.t., to make steady; to keep (a ship) on its course.

stead'y-go'ing, adj., persistent; not frivolous.

stead'ying, pr.p., steady.

steak, n., a cut from meat or fish.

steal, v.i., to be a thief; to move secretly or silently; v.t., to take by theft or by surprise; to take secret or complete possession of.

steal'er, n., one who steals.

steal'ing, n., theft; pr.p., steal.

stealth, n., secrecy or silence.

stealth'ily, adv., in a stealthy way.

stealth'iness, n., the quality or state of being stealthy.

stealth'y, adj., surreptitious; furtive.

steam, n., the vapour of water; the gas emanating from boiling water; any exhalation like steam; energy; v.i., to give forth steam; to travel by means of steam; v.t., to treat or cook with steam.

steam'boat, n., a boat driven by steampower.

steam'-chest, n., a chamber through which steam passes from a boiler to a cylinder.

steamed, p.p., steam.

steam'-engine, n., an engine worked by steam.

steam'er, n., one who, or that which, steams; a steamship.

steam'-gauge, n., a gauge showing the steam pressure in a boiler.

steam'-hammer, n., a hammer worked by steam.

steam'ing, pr.p., steam.

steam'-jacket, n., a hollow cylinder casing holding steam for heating the cylinder, etc.

steam'-jet, a blast of steam emitted from a nozzle.

steam'nav'y, n., a steam-driven excavator.

steam'-packet, n., a steam-vessel used for port-to-port services.

steam'-pipe, n., a pipe providing for the conveyance of steam.

steam'-proof, adj., protected against steam.

steam'roller, n., a steam-engine used for road making; a crushing power; v.t., to crush.

steam'ship, n., a ship propelled by steam.

steam'-tug, n., a tug propelled by steam.

steam'y, adj., like steam; full of steam.

ste'arate, n., a stearic acid salt.

stear'ic, adj., pert. or rel. to stearin.

ste'arin, n., the principal ingredient in animal and vegetable fats; stearic acid for candles.

ste'atite, n., soap-stone.

steatit'ic, adj., pert. or rel. to steatite.

steato'ma, n., a fatty tumour.

steatom'atous, adj., pert. or rel. to a steatoma.

steatopyg'ia, n., fatness of the buttocks.

steatop'ygous, adj., fat buttocked.

steato'sis, n., fatty degeneration.

sted'fast, adj., i.q. steadfast.

steed, n., a horse.

steel, adj., made of, or resembling steel; n., a malleable alloy of iron; an instrument for sharpening knives; v.t., to harden.

steeled, p.p., steel.

steel'iness, n., the quality or state of being steely.

steel'ing, pr.p., steel.

steel'-plated, adj., protected with steel plates.

steel'-wool, n., steel shavings; an abrasive steel pad.

steel'work, n., work done in steel.

steel'y, adj., like steel; inflexible.

steel'yard, n., a weighing apparatus with a short arm from which the thing to be weighed is suspended, and a long arm that is graduated and along which a weight slides until it registers the exact weight of the suspended object.

steen'bok, n., a small African antelope.

steen'ing, n., the stone casing of a well.

steen'kirk, n., a cravat.

steep, adj., greatly inclining; sheer; precipitous; outrageous, exorbitant (colloq.); n., a precipice, a mountain or ascent; liquid for steeping; the process of steeping; v.t., to soak in a liquid; to impregnate.

steeped, p.p., steep.

steep'en, v.i. and t., to make or become steep.

steep'er, adj., comp. of steep.

steep'est, adj., super. of steep.

steep'ing, pr.p., steep.

steep'ish, adj., rather steep.

stee'ple, n., a tower and spire.

stee'plechase, n., a horse race over obstacles.

stee'plechaser, n., one who takes part in a steeplechase; a horse specially trained for these races.

stee'plejack, n., one who works on steeples or tall chimneys.

steep'ly, adv., precipitously.

steep'ness, n., the quality or state of being steep.

steep'y, adj., i.q. steep.

steer, n., a young male ox; v.i., to guide the rudder of a boat; to direct one's course; v.t., to direct the course of (a ship or boat).

steer'able, adj., able to be steered.

steer'age, *n.*, the act of steering; the action of a ship's helm; the part of a passenger ship where the cheaper berths are placed.

steer'age-way, *n.*, sufficient motion of a vessel to permit effective use of the helm.

steered, *p.p.*, steer.

steer'er, *n.*, one who, or that which, steers.

steer'ing, *pr.p.*, steer.

steers'man, *n.*, *i.q.* steerer.

steeve, *n.*, the angle a bowsprit makes with the horizon; a spar used in shifting cargo; *v.i.*, to work with a steeve; *v.i. and t.*, to make an angle with the horizon.

steeved, *p.p.*, steeve.

steev'ing, *pr.p.*, steeve.

steg'anogram, *n.*, a cryptogram.

steganog'raphy, *n.*, cryptic writing; cipher.

steg'anopod, *n.*, any bird with four webbed toes.

stegno'sis, *n.*, constipation.

stegnot'ic, *adj.*, constipating.

stegoph'ilist, *n.*, one who enjoys climbing buildings.

stein, *n.*, a beer mug (*Ger.*).

Stein'berger, *n.*, a Rhenish white wine (*Ger.*).

stein'bock, *n.*, the Alpine ibex; the wild goat.

ste'la, *n.*, *i.q.* stele.

ste'le, *n.*, a plain pillar with neither base nor capital (*Gr.*).

stel'lar, *adj.*, pert. or rel. to the stars.

stel'larator, *n.*, a device used in controlling thermo-nuclear energy.

stel'lary, *adj.*, *i.q.* stellar.

stel'late, *adj.*, starlike, radiating.

stel'lated, *adj.*, *i.q.* stellate.

stell'enbosch, *v.t.*, to appoint to lower rank.

stellif'erous, *adj.*, starry.

stel'liform, *adj.*, shaped like a star.

stel'lify, *v.t.*, to transform into or set among stars.

stel'lular, *adj.*, radiated.

stelog'raphy, *n.*, the art of writing on pillars.

stem, *n.*, the trunk of a tree; the main axis of any plant; any stem-like thing (as the stem of a pipe); the forepart of a ship; the uninflected base of a word; *v.i.*, to arise from; *v.t.*, to arrest; to oppose; to dam.

stem'less, *adj.*, without a stem.

stem'ma, *n.*, a genealogical tree, a pedigree.

stemmed, *p.p.*, stem.

stem'ming, *pr.p.*, stem.

stem'ple, *n.*, a cross-bar enabling miners to ascend and descend in a pit.

sten-gun, *n.*, a small machine gun.

stench, *n.*, an obnoxious smell or stink.

sten'cil, *n.*, a flat piece of material perforated with a pattern or lettering; *v.t.*, to mark by means of such a device.

sten'cilled, *p.p.*, stencil.

sten'cilling, *pr.p.*, stencil.

sten'ciller, *n.*, one who produces stencils.

stenoch'romy, *n.*, multicolour printing at one impression.

sten'ograph, *n.*, a shorthand writing machine; a character or passage written in shorthand; *v.t.*, to write in shorthand.

stenog'rapher, *n.*, a writer of stenography or shorthand.

stenograph'ic, *adj.*, pert. or rel. to stenography.

stenograph'ical, *adj.*, *i.q.* stenographic.

stenog'raphist, *n.*, *i.q.* stenographer.

stenog'raphy, *n.*, the art and practice of shorthand writing.

sten'otype, *n.*, a shorthand-writing machine.

sten'otypist, *n.*, one who uses a stenotype machine.

sten'otypy, *n.*, shorthand printing.

sten'tor, *n.*, a loud-voiced person.

stento'rian, *adj.*, loud-voiced: like the ancient Greek herald, Stentor.

sten'torphone, *n.*, a device for intensifying sound.

step, *n.*, a movement of the foot in walking; a footstep; the distance measured by the foot in stepping; a rung in a ladder; a stair; *v.i.*, to move on foot; to walk; *v.t.*, to measure a distance by pacing it; to make a step of; to fix up (a mast).

step'brother, *n.*, a brother by marriage only; the son of one's father or mother by a later or previous marriage.

step'child, *n.*, the child of one's wife or husband by a previous marriage.

step'dame, *n.*, a grandmother by marriage only.

step'-dance, *n.*, a display dance.

step'daughter, *n.*, the daughter of one's wife or husband by a previous marriage.

step'father, *n.*, the husband of one's mother by a later marriage.

steph'anite, *n.*, a brittle silver ore.

stephano'tis, *n.*, a climbing, white-flowered plant.

step'-ladder, *n.*, a small, folding ladder with flat treads.

step'mother, *n.*, the wife of one's father by a later marriage.

step'-par'ent, *n.*, a stepmother or stepfather.

steppe, *n.*, a Russian plain.

stepped, *p.p.*, step.

step'per, *n.*, one who steps.

step'ping, *pr.p.*, step.

step'ping-stone, *n.*, a stone used for mounting or for crossing a stream.

step'-rocket, *n.*, a rocket with successive firing stages.

step'sister, *n.*, the daughter of one's father or mother by a previous or later marriage.

step'son, *n.*, the son of a wife or husband by a previous marriage.

stercora'ceous, *adj.*, pert. or rel. to dung.

ster'corary, *adj.*, *i.q.* stercoraceous.

ster'corate, *v.t.*, to manure.

stere, *n.*, a cubic metre.

ster'eo, a prefix = hard, solid, firm; three-dimensional; *n.*, abbrev. of stereotype; *adj.*, stereophonic.

ster'eobate, *n.*, a solid structure for building.

ster'eogram, *n.*, *i.q.* stereograph; a stereo-gramophone.

ster'eograph, *n.*, one of twin photographs for use in a stereoscope.

stereograph'ic, *adj.*, pert. or rel. to stereography.

stereog'raphy, *n.*, showing solid figures on a plane so that they appear three-dimensional.

stereom'eter, *n.*, a scientific apparatus for finding specific gravity.

steromet'ric, *adj.*, pert. or rel. to stereometry.

stereom'etry, *n.*, the art of finding the specific gravity of bodies, or their cubic contents.

ster'eophonic, *adj.*, sounding from three different directions, hence very realistic.

ster'eoph'ony, *n.*, stereophonic sound; sound represented with high fidelity.

ster'eop'tics, *n. pl.*, the optics of stereoscopic imagery.

ster'eoscope, *n.*, an optical binocular apparatus showing a picture as though in relief.

stereoscop'ic, *adj.*, pert. or rel. to stereoscopes.

stereos'copist, *n.*, one who makes stereoscopes.

stereos'copy, *n.*, the presentation of pictures in relief.

stereoson'ic, *adj.*, *i.q.* stereophonic.

ster'eotype, *adj.*, pert. or rel. to stereotype; *n.*, a metal or plastic casting of matter printed in movable types; *v.t.*, to make such a casting; to make permanent.

ster'eotyped, *adj.*, fixed, unchangeable; *p.p.*, stereotype.

stereotyp'er, *n.*, one who stereotypes.

stereotyp'ic, *adj.*, in stereotype.

stereotyp'ing, *n.*, the act of making stereotype; *pr.p.*, stereotype.

stereotyp'ist, *n.*, one who uses the stereotype process.

stereotypog'raphy, *n.*, *i.q.* stereotyping.

ster'eotypy, *n.*, *i.q.* stereotyping.

ster'ile, *adj.*, barren, unfruitful.

steril'ity, *n.*, the state of being sterile.

steriliza'tion, *n.*, the act of sterilizing.

ster'ilize, *v.t.*, to make sterile; to make incapable of reproduction; to purify.

ster'ilized, *p.p.*, sterilize.

ster'ilizer, *n.*, one who, or that which, sterilizes; an apparatus used for sterilization.

ster'ilizing, *pr.p.*, sterilize.

ster'let, *n.*, a small sturgeon giving the best roe for caviare.

ster'ling, *adj.*, pure; of the best quality; according to the English money standard.

stern, *adj.*, severe; harsh; in the stern; *n.*, the after part of a ship or boat; hindquarters (*colloq.*).

ster'nal, *adj.*, pert. or rel. to the sternum.

sternalg'ia, *n.*, angina pectoris.

stern'-board, *n.*, a board on a vessel's stern.

stern'-chase, *n.*, pursuit from the rear.

stern'er, *adj.*, comp. of stern.

stern'est, *adj.*, super. of stern.

stern'ly, *adv.*, in a stern way.

stern'most, *adj.*, furthest in the rear.

stern'ness, *n.*, the quality or state of being stern; severity.

sternocos'tal, *adj.*, pert. or rel. to the chest and ribs.

stern'-post, *n.*, the timber support of the stern.

stern'-sheets, *n. pl.*, the part of a small sailing boat devoted to the passengers' seats.

ster'num, *n.*, the breastbone (*Lat.*).

sternuta'tion, *n.*, sneezing.

sternu'tative, *adj.*, exciting a sneeze.

ster'nutator, *n.*, the material or device producing sneezing.

sternu'tatory, *adj.*, pert. or rel. to sneezing.

ster'torous, *adj.*, snoring.

stet, *v.i.*, *pr. subjunct.* 3rd pers. sing. of the Latin word for *stand* = "let it stand." It has become an English transitive verb, meaning to leave uncorrected anything that has been corrected.

stethom'eter, *n.*, an instrument measuring the chest in the act of respiration.

steth'oscope, *n.*, a medical instrument enabling the user to hear sounds in a patient's thorax.

stethoscop'ic, *adj.*, pert. or rel. to a stethoscope.

stethoscop'ical, *adj.*, *i.q.* stethoscopic.

stet'son, *n.*, a broad-brimmed slouch hat.

ste'vedore, *n.*, a man engaged in loading or unloading cargo.

stew, *n.*, meat cooked slowly with vegetables, etc.; a fishpond or tank; an artificial oyster-bed; *v.i.*, to be cooking slowly; *v.t.*, to cook meat slowly in a pan; to let it simmer.

stew'ard, *n.*, one who looks after the domestic accounts of a family or master; one who manages a landed estate; one who superintends the culinary affairs of a ship, a club, etc.; one who performs duties akin to those of a steward.

stew'ardess, *n.*, a female attendant.

stew'ardship, *n.*, the office of a steward.

stewed, *p.p.*, stew.

stew'ing, *adj.*, excessively hot (*colloq.*); *pr.p.*, stew.

sthen'ic, *adj.*, showing a morbid condition of the heart and blood vessels.

stib'ial, *adj.*, like antimony.

stib'ialism, *n.*, antimony poisoning.

stib'iated, *adj.*, *i.q.* stibious.

stib'ious, *adj.*, containing antimony.

stib'ium, *n.*, antimony (*Lat.*).

stic'cado, *n.*, a kind of xylophone.

stich, *n.*, a metrical line or verse.

stichar'ion, *n.*, a stanza or short hymn.

sticher'on, *n.*, *i.q.* sticharion.

stich'ic, *adj.*, pert. or rel. to a stich.

stichom'etry, *n.*, verse-measurement.

stichomyth'ia, *n.*, a dialogue in alternate lines.

stick, *n.*, a cutting from a tree; a walking-staff; a line or verse; a printer's composing stick; any long, roundish piece of wood; a dull fellow (*colloq.*); *v.i.*, to adhere; to remain; to be unable to move; *v.t.*, to cause to adhere; to fasten; to stab; to set with points; to compose (type).

stickabil'ity, *n.*, endurance (*colloq.*).

stick'er, *n.*, one who, or that which, sticks; an adhesive label.

stick'iness, *n.*, the quality or state of being sticky.

stick'ing, *pr.p.*, stick.

stick'ing-plas'ter, *n.*, adhesive plaster.

stick'le, *v.i.*, to insist on an unimportant point; to cling tenaciously to some observance or rule.

stick'leback, *n.*, a small fish with a spiny back.

stick'led, *p.p.*, stickle.

stick'ler, *n.*, one who stickles.

stick'ling, *pr.p.*, stickle.

stick'-up, *n.*, an armed robbery.

stick'y, *adj.*, adhesive; viscous; awkward.

stiff, *adj.*, unyielding to the touch; firm; precise; severe.

stiff'en, *v.i.*, to become stiff; *v.t.*, to make stiff.

stiff'ened, *p.p.*, stiffen.

stiff'ener, *n.*, one who, or that which, stiffens.

stiff'ening, *n.*, material that makes something stiff; *pr.p.*, stiffen.

stiff'er, *adj.*, *comp.* of stiff.

stiff'est, *adj.* *super.* of stiff.

stiff'ish, *adj.*, somewhat stiff.

stiff'ly, *adv.*, in a stiff way.

stiff'neck, *n.*, an obstinate person.

stiff'necked, *adj.*, stubborn; obstinate.

stiff'ness, *n.*, the quality or state of being stiff.

sti'fle, *n.*, the joint next below a horse's buttock; *v.i.*, to be suffocated; to suffer from lack of air; *v.t.*, to smother; to suffocate; to deaden.

sti'fled, *p.p.*, stifle.

sti'fling, *adj.*, suffocating; *pr.p.*, stifle.

stig'ma, *n.*, a mark; a stamp; a brand of censure or of shame; the top of a pistil.

stig'mata, *n.*, the pl. of stigma; the marks of Christ's wounds received at his crucifixion.

stigmat'ic, *adj.*, pert. or rel. to a stigma.

stigmat'ical, *adj.*, *i.q.* stigmatic.

stigmatiza'tion, *n.*, the action of stigmatizing.

stig'matize, *v.t.*, to brand with a stigma; to hold up to infamy.

stig'matized, *p.p.*, stigmatize.

stig'matizing, *pr.p.*, stigmatize.

stile, *n.*, an arrangement of steps over a fence or wall; an upright in panelled work; a gnomon.

stilet'to, *n.*, a small dagger; a pointed instrument for making eyelet holes; a kind of lady's shoe heel.

still, *adj.*, quiet; calm; not effervescent (also *stilly*); *adv.*, continuing now; nevertheless; *n.*, a distilling appliance; *v.t.*, to make still; to calm.

still'age, *n.*, a low stand for articles whilst draining or waiting to be packed.

still'born, *adj.*, born dead.

stilled, *p.p.*, still.

still'er, *adj.*, *comp.* of still; *n.*, one who, or that which, stills.

still'est, *adj.*, *super.* of still.

still'ing, *pr.p.*, still.

still-life, *n.*, inanimate objects in art.

still'ness, *n.*, the quality or state of being still.

still'room, *n.*, a room in a house for making or storing drinks.

stil'ly, *adj.*, *i.q.* still.

stilt, *n.*, one of two poles with a notch some way up each of them, on which the foot can be rested; a pole on which (with others) a habitation is erected; *v.t.*, to place on stilts.

stilt'ed, *adj.*, artificial; pompous; in architecture, elongated; *p.p.*, stilt.

stilt'ing, *pr.p.*, stilt.

Stil'ton, *n.*, a make of cheese.

stilt'-walk'er, *n.*, one who walks with stilts.

stilus, *n.*, *i.q.* stylus.

stim'ulant, *adj.*, stimulating; *n.*, that which stimulates, esp. an alcoholic liquor.

stim'ulate, *v.t.*, to give a stimulus to; to spur on; to inspirit.

stim'ulated, *p.p.*, stimulate.

stim'ulating, *pr.p.*, stimulate.

stimula'tion, *n.*, the act or effect of stimulating.

stim'ulative, *adj.*, having the effect of a stimulant.

stim'ulator, *n.*, one who, or that which, stimulates.

stim'ulus, *n.*, an impetus; a spur; an incentive (*Lat.*).

stim'y, *n.*, *v.i.* and *t.*, *i.q.* stymie.

sting, *n.*, the poisonous pointed weapon of certain creatures; a sharp, temporary pain; *v.t.*, to cause pain with a sting; to provoke.

sting'er, *n.*, one who, or that which, stings.

stin'gier, *adj.*, *comp.* of stingy.

stin'giest, *adj.*, *super.* of stingy.

stin'gily, *adv.*, in a stingy way.

stin'giness, *n.*, the quality or state of being stingy.

sting'ing, *pr.p.*, sting.

sting'less, *adj.*, harmless; without a sting.

sting'o, *n.*, strong ale.

stin'gy, *adj.*, niggardly, mean, parsimonious.

sting'y, *adj.*, apt to sting.

stink, *n.*, a foul smell; stench; *v.i.*, to give forth a foul smell; *v.t.*, to make to stink.

stink'ard, *n.*, an offensive person.

stink'-bomb, *n.*, a hand-thrown bomb which, on explosion, gives out an evil-smelling vapour.

stink'er, *n.*, one who, or that which, stinks.

stink'ing, *adj.*, foully smelling; offensive; *pr.p.*, stink.

stint, *n.*, a niggardly or scanty supply; an allotted task; *v.t.*, to supply in scanty or niggardly amount or quantity.

stint'ed, *p.p.*, stint.

stint'er, *n.*, one who stints.

stint'ing, *pr.p.*, stint.

stip'ate, *adj.*, close set, crowded.

stipe, *n.*, a stalk.

stip'el, *n.*, a secondary stipule.

sti'pend, *n.*, pay; a fixed salary.

stipend'iary, *adj.*, in receipt of a fixed stipend; *n.*, one so paid, esp. a magistrate.

stip'ple, *n.*, dotted work; *v.i.* and *t.*, to employ dots for lines in engraving, drawing or painting.

stip'pled, *adj.*, dotted; *p.p.*, stipple.

stip'pler, *n.*, one who, or that which, stipples.

stip'pling, *n.*, the act of engraving, etching, etc., in dots; *pr.p.*, stipple.

stipula'ceous, *adj.*, *i.q.* stipular.

stip'ular, *adj.*, growing on stipules; near or resembling stipules.

stip'ulary, *adj.*, *i.q.* stipular.

stip'ulate, *adj.*, having stipules; *v.i.* and *t.*, to require as the terms of an agreement; to demand.

stip'ulated, *p.p.*, stipulate.

stip'ulating, *pr.p.*, stipulate.

stipula'tion, *n.*, the act of stipulating; the terms demanded.

stip'ulator, *n.*, one who stipulates.

stip'ule, *n.*, an appendage at the base of some leaves.

stip'uled, *adj.*, having stipules.

stir, *n.*, a bustle or disturbance; public interest; prison (*slang*); *v.i.*, to arouse oneself; to move; *v.t.*, to move liquid round and round; to arouse, to stimulate; to agitate.

stirk, *n.*, a bovine yearling.

stirp'iculture, *n.*, selective breeding.

stirps, *n.*, a progenitor; a man who founds a family.

stirred, *p.p.*, stir.

stir'rer, *n.*, one who, or that which, stirs.

stir'ring, *adj.*, exciting, busy; *n.*, the act of stirring; *pr.p.*, stir.

stir'ringly, *adv.*, in a stirring manner.

stir'rup, *n.*, a rider's foot-rest suspended from the saddle.

stitch, *n.*, one passing of the needle and thread in sewing; a sharp pain in the side; *v.i.* and *t.*, to sew; to pass thread through and back.

stitched, *p.p.*, stitch.

stitch'er, *n.*, one who, or that which, stitches.

stitch'ing, *pr.p.*, stitch.

Stitchwort, *n.*, a genus of slender plants, including chickweed.

stith'y, *n.*, a forge.

stive, *n.*, a stew; flourdust; *v.t.*, to stew.

stived, *p.p.*, stive.

sti'ver, *n.*, a Dutch coin of the very smallest value.

sti'ving, *pr.p.*, stive.

sto'a, *n.*, a Greek portico, esp. one in Athens, where Zeno and his school expounded their philosophy. Hence the name *Stoics*.

stoat, *n.*, the ermine, a small furry animal; *v.t.*, to invisibly mend.

stocca'do, *n.*, a sword or dagger thrust.

stock, *adj.*, always in store; commonplace; *n.*, a tree-trunk or stem; lineage; animals on a farm; company capital; accumulated goods; a handle; the part of a gun supporting the barrel, etc.; a stiff neck-band; a variety of gilly-flower; *v.t.*, to furnish with cattle, goods or seed; to fit with a handle or support.

stockade', *n.*, a fortification of stakes; a palisade; *v.t.*, to fence with stakes.

stock'-breed'er, *n.*, one who breeds livestock.

stock'broker, *n.*, one who negotiates the purchase and sale of stocks.

stock'-dove, *n.*, a wood pigeon.

stocked, *p.p.*, stock.

stock' *exchange*, *n.*, a place where deals in securities are made.

stock'fish, *n.*, dried salted fish.

stock'holder, *n.*, one who holds stocks.

stock'hold'ing, *n.*, the holding of stock in the public funds or companies.

stockinet' -te, *n.*, an elastic material.

stock'ing, *n.*, a leg-covering up to, or beyond the knee; *pr.p.*, stock.

stock'ingless, *adj.*, without stockings.

stock'-in-*trade*, *n.*, a dealer's collective goods.

stock'ish, *adj.*, stunted.

stock'ist, *n.*, one who keeps goods in stock.

stock'jobber, *n.*, a dealer in stocks and shares.

stock'jobbing, *n.*, a stockjobber's business.

stock'list, *n.*, a list of stocks and shares.

stock'pile, *n.*, a reserve supply; *v.i.* and *t.*, to build up a reserve.

stock'piling, *n.*, the accumulation of supplies for emergencies.

stock'-room, *n.*, a storeroom.

stocks, *n. pl.*, public funds; an old instrument of punishment, the offender's legs being confined in a wooden frame.

stock'-size, *adj.*, able to fit the average figure.

stock'still, *adj.* and *adv.*, absolutely at rest; motionless.

stock'taking, *n.*, a periodical overhauling of one's possessions or merchandise.

stock'y, *adj.*, stumpy.

stock'yard, *n.*, an enclosure for cattle on a ranch, etc.

stodge', *n.*, heavy food (*slang*); *v.i.*, to trudge; *v.t.*, to gorge (*slang*).

stodg'y, *adj.*, dull, heavy.

stoep, *n.*, a veranda (*S. Africa*).

stog'y, *n.*, a kind of heavy boot or shoe; a roughly made cigar.

Sto'ic, *adj.*, pert. or rel. to the Stoa and the Stoics; contemptuous of pain or privation; *n.*, a disciple of Zeno and the Stoic philosophers.

sto'ical, *adj.*, *i.q.* stoic.

sto'ically, *adv.*, in a stoic way.

stoicheiol'ogy, *n.*, the study of first principles.

stoicheiom'etry, *n.*, the art of calculating the weight of atoms in chemical elements.

sto'icism, *n.*, the doctrines of the Stoics; indifference to pain and misfortune.

stoke, *v.i.* and *t.*, to make up a fire.

stoked, *p.p.*, stoke.

stoke'hold, *n.*, *i.q.* stokehole.

stoke' hole, *n.*, the part of a ship's interior containing the boilers and furnaces.

stok'er, *n.*, a furnaceman on an engine.

stok'ing, *n.*, the act or business of a stoker; *pr.p.*, stoke.

stole, *n.*, a long, narrow strip of silk or other material worn scarf-fashion by officiating clergy; a long, broad piece of decorative material worn by women over their shoulders; *p.p.*, steal.

stoled, *adj.*, vested in a stole.

sto'len, *p.p.*, steal.

stol'id, *adj.*, unmoving, slow, stupid.

stolid'ity, *n.*, the quality or state of being stolid.

stol'idly, *adv.*, in a stolid way.

stolid'ness, *n.*, *i.q.* stolidity.

sto'lon, *n.*, a branch which trails or a sucker which takes root.

stolonif'erous, *adj.*, producing stolons or (*colloq.*) suckers.

sto'ma, *n.*, a breathing-pore or orifice (esp., in a leaf).

stom'ach, *n.*, the chief digestive organ; appetite; liking; pride; *v.t.*, to tolerate.

stom'ach-ache, *n.*, a pain in the stomach or intestines.

stom'achal, *adj.*, pert. or rel. to the stomach.

stom'ached, *p.p.*, stomach.

stom'acher, *n.*, the front piece, covering breasts and stomach in mediaeval female dress.

stomach'ic, *adj.*, pert. or rel. to the stomach; appetising; good for the stomach; *n.*, a stomach medicine.

stomach'ical, *adj.*, *i.q.* stomachic.

stomach'ing, *pr.p.*, stomach.

stom'achless, *adj.*, without a stomach.

stom'ach-pump, *n.*, an instrument for evacuating the stomach.

stom'achy, *adj.*, paunchy.

sto'mapod, *n.*, one of the Stomapoda, an order of crustaceans.

stoma'ta, *n.pl.*, of stoma.

stomatit'is, *n.*, inflammation of the mouth.

stomat'opod, *n.*, the crustacean with legs mostly near the mouth.

stomat'oscope, *n.*, an instrument for examining the inside of the mouth.

stomp, *n.*, a dance involving stamping; a stamp.

stone, *n.*, hard earth formation; a gem; stony matter in the bladder; the hard seed-shell of stone-fruit; a weight (14 lb.); *v.t.*, to throw stones at; to extract the stones from; to pave, etc., with stones.

stone'-blind, *adj.*, absolutely sightless.

stone'chat, *n.*, a little bird.

stone'-cold, *adj.*, as cold as stone.

stone'crop, *n.*, a small, rock plant bearing yellow flowers.

stone'-cutter, *n.*, a cutter of stone.

stoned, *p.p.*, stone.

stone'-dead, *adj.*, quite dead.

stone'-deaf, *adj.*, completely deaf.

stone'-dress'er, *n.*, one who shapes or dresses stones.

stone'-fruit, *n.*, fruit containing a hard seed-shell.

stone'less, *n.*, without stones.

stone'mason, *n.*, a worker in stone.

stone'pit, *n.*, a quarry.

sto'ner, *n.*, one who stones.

stone's'-throw, *n.*, a short distance.

stone'-still, *adj.*, absolutely still.

stone'wall, *v.i.* and *t.*, to obstruct or block; (cricket) to bat defensively.

stone'waller, *n.*, a cricketer who stays in for a long time, but makes few runs; an obstructionist.

stone'wall'ing, *n.*, a defence by obstructing (esp., cricket); batting defensively.

stone'ware, *n.*, a common kind of pottery.

stone'work, *n.*, masonry.

ston'ily, *adv.*, in a stony fashion; unfeelingly.

ston'iness, *n.*, the quality or state of being stony.

ston'ing, *pr.p.*, stone.

ston'y, *adj.*, hard like stone; abounding in stone.

ston'ybroke, *adj.*, penniless, without money (*slang*).

ston'y-heart'ed, *adj.*, hard-hearted.

stood, *p.p.*, stand.

stooge', *n.*, a dupe; a scapegoat; *v.i.*, to act as a stooge.

stook, *n.*, corn-sheaves gathered into a shock; *v.t.*, to gather into shocks.

stool, *n.*, a moveable unbacked seat; the seat of a commode, etc.; an excretion; *v.i.*, to evacuate the bowels.

stool'ball, *n.*, a bat and ball game.

stool'pi'geon, *n.*, a decoy.

stoop, *n.*, a bending down and forward; a bird's swoop; a verandah or porch (*Amer.*); *v.i.*, to incline the body; to abase oneself; to condescend; to make submission; to swoop.

stooped, *p.p.*, stoop.

stoop'er, *n.*, one who stoops.

stoop'ing, *pr.p.*, stoop.

stoop'ingly, *adv.*, in a stooping way.

stop, *n.*, the cessation of movement; an arrest, a standstill; a punctuation mark; a slide opening or closing; a range of pipes in an organ or musical instrument; *v.i.*, to come to a standstill; *v.t.*, to bring to rest; to hinder; to punctuate; to withhold payment.

stop'cock, *n.*, a tap, by means of which the flow of water can be controlled.

stop'gap, *n.*, that which fills any gap or vacancy.

stop'page, *n.*, the effect or act of stopping; a hindrance; a suspension of pay.

stopped, *p.p.*, stop.

stop'per, *n.*, one who, or that which, stops; esp. that which closes the mouth of a bottle.

stop'ping, *n.*, stoppage; that which stops; *pr.p.*, stop.

stop'ple, *n.*, a plug; *v.t.*, to plug.

stop'-press, *adj.* and *n.*, (news) inserted after printing has begun.

stop'watch, *n.*, a watch that can be stopped at will.

stor'able, *adj.*, able to be stored.

stor'age, *n.*, accommodation for goods of all kinds; the storing of electricity; the charge for storing.

sto'rax, *n.*, a resin.

store, *n.*, a collection of things that are to be kept; an abundance; a miscellaneous shop; *v.t.*, to place in a warehouse; to accumulate; to furnish with stores.

stored, *p.p.*, store.

store'house, *n.*, a place for storing.

store'keeper, *n.*, one who keeps a store.

stor'er, *n.*, one who stores.

store'room, *n.*, a room where stores are kept.

store'ship, *n.*, a ship carrying stored goods.

stor'eyed, *adj.*, divided into storeys or tiers.

sto'riated, *adj.*, with elaborate decorative designs.

stor'ied, *adj.*, supplied with stories; told in story.

stor'ing, *pr.p.*, store.

stork, *n.*, a large wading bird.

storm, *n.*, a violent outburst of wind, rain, thunder, passion, etc.; an attack on a fortified position; *v.i.*, to make much noise in angry abuse; *v.t.*, to besiege.

storm'bound, *adj.*, confined to port or cut off by storms.

storm'-cen'tre, *n.*, a centre of cyclonic disturbance.

stormed, *p.p.*, storm.

storm'ier, *adj.*, *comp.* of stormy.

storm'iest, *adj.*, *super.* of stormy.

storm'ily, *adv.*, in a stormy way.

storm'iness, *n.*, the quality or state of being stormy.

storm'ing, *pr.p.*, storm.

storm'-lantern, *n.*, a lantern with the light protected from the elements.

storm'proof, *adj.*, proof against storms.

storm'-troops, *n.*, shock troops.

storm'y, *adj.*, tempestuous; threatening storm.

Stor'thing, *n.*, the Parliament of Norway.

stor'(e)y, *n.*, a stage in a building at one level.

stor'y, *n.*, history; narrative; a tale; a novel; a report; the plot of a book, play, etc.;

a lie; *v.t.*, to chronicle; to record in history.

stor'y-book, *n.*, a book of stories for children.

stor'yteller, *n.*, one who tells stories professionally; a liar.

stor'ytelling, *n.*, the art or practice of telling stories.

stot, *n.*, a young ox.

stoup, *n.*, a drinking-vessel; a holy-water receptacle.

stout, *adj.*, corpulent; strongly built; firm, resolute; *n.*, a dark ale or porter.

stout'er, *adj.*, *comp.* of stout.

stout'est, *adj.*, *super.* of stout.

stout'heart'ed, *adj.*, brave; courageous.

stout'ish, *adj.*, somewhat stout.

stout'ly, *adv.*, firmly, solidly.

stout'ness, *n.*, the quality or state of being stout.

sto'vaine, *n.*, a local anaesthetic.

stove, *n.*, a closed or partially closed firebox, used for heating, cooking, etc.; *p.p.*, stave; *v.t.*, to force (plants) in a hothouse.

stove'-pipe, *n.*, a pipe from a stove into a chimney; a tall silk hat (*colloq.*).

stow, *v.t.*, to pack; to fill compactly and neatly; to leave off doing (*slang*).

stow'age, *n.*, the act of stowing; capacity; the charge for stowing.

stow'away, *n.*, one who secretes himself on transport vessels to obtain a free passage.

stowed, *p.p.*, stow.

stow'er, *n.*, one who stows.

stow'ing, *pr.p.*, stow.

stra'bism, *n.*, *i.q.* strabismus.

strabis'mus, *n.*, a squint.

strabot'omy, *n.*, the operation to cure a squint.

strad, *n.*, the abbrev. for *Stradivarius* (*colloq.*).

strad'dle, *n.*, a straddling posture; the extent to which the legs are stretched apart; an arrangement in a

stock exchange by which a purchaser secures the right to call or deliver stock; *v.i.*, to stand, ride or sit with the legs far apart; *v.t.*, to sit across.

strad'dled, *p.p.*, straddle.

strad'dler, *n.*, one who straddles.

strad'dling, *pr.p.*, straddle.

Stradiva'rius, *n.*, a violin or some other stringed instrument by the 18th Cent. maker, Stradivarius of Cremona. (Also *strad*.)

strafe', *n.*, gunfire, bombardment; a punishment (*colloq.*); *v.t.*, to punish severely; to bombard or shoot (*Ger.*).

strafed, *p.p.*, strafe.

straf'ing, *pr.p.*, strafe.

strag'gle, *v.i.*, to go astray from a company or main body; to fall behind; to ramble; to grow irregularly and be spread; to occur irregularly.

strag'gled, *p.p.*, straggle.

strag'gler, *n.*, one who, or that which, straggles.

strag'gling, *pr.p.*, straggle.

straight, *adj.*, lying evenly between any two points; keeping to one direction; not bent or curving; erect; upright, frank; *n.*, a straight part; a reach in a river; the condition of being straight; a sequence at poker.

straight'away, *adv.*, *i.q.* straightway.

straight'-edge, *n.*, a bar with one edge perfectly straight, for measuring, drawing, etc.

straight'en, *v.i.*, to become straight; *v.t.*, to make straight.

straight'ened, *p.p.*, straighten.

straight'ener, *n.*, one who, or that which, straightens.

straight'ening, *pr.p.*, straighten.

straight'er, *adj.*, comp. of straight.

straight'est, *adj.*, super. of straight.

straightfor'ward, *adj.*, honest, frank, ingenuous.

straightfor'wardness, *n.*, the quality or state of being straightforward.

straight'ly, *adv.*, without deviating.

straight'ness, *n.*, the quality or state of being straight.

straight'way, *adv.*, immediately, forthwith.

strain, *n.*, the act or effect of straining; stress; tension; a snatch of poetry or musical sound; a style of speaking, thinking or writing; family descent; a natural disposition; *v.i.*, to exert oneself greatly; to percolate; *v.t.*, to apply tension to; to exert to the utmost; to over-exert; to pass through a sieve or colander.

strained, *p.p.*, strain.

strain'er, *n.*, one who, or that which, strains; a sieve-like utensil; a strengthening support behind the panel of a carriage.

strain'ing, *n.*, the act of straining; *pr.p.*, strain.

strain'less, *adj.*, free from strain.

strait, *adj.*, narrow; strict; *n.*, a narrow waterway connecting two seas.

strait'en, *v.t.*, to narrow, to confine; to tighten.

strait'ened, *p.p.*, straiten.

strait'jacket, *n.*, a strong jacket confining the wearer's arms.

straight'-jet, *adj.*, (of aircraft) driven only by jet.

strait'laced, *adj.*, tightly laced; prim; prudish.

strait'ly, *adv.*, narrowly, strictly.

strait'ness, *n.*, narrowness; poverty.

straits, *n. pl.*, difficulties; narrow means.

strait'-waistcoat, *n.*, *i.q.* strait-jacket.

strake, *n.*, a single breadth of the planking in a ship continuously from end to end.

stramin'eous, *adj.*, like straw.

stramo'nium, *n.*, the thorn-apple, a dangerous narcotic weed akin to the nightshade.

stram'ony, *n.*, *i.q.* stramonium.

strand, *n.*, a shore; a fibre; a loose hair; one of the strings or wires in a rope; *v.t.*, to run (a vessel) ashore; to leave in difficulties.

strand'ed, *adj.*, hopelessly in difficulties; *p.p.*, strand.

strand'ing, *pr.p.*, strand.

strange, *adj.*, alien; unfamiliar; extraordinary; eccentric.

strange'ly, *adv.*, in a strange manner.

strange'ness, *n.*, the quality or state of being strange.

stran'ger, *adj.*, comp. of strange; *n.*, an alien; a foreigner.

stran'gest, *adj.*, super. of strange.

stran'gle, *v.i.*, to be throttled; *v.t.*, to choke; to throttle; to suppress.

stran'gled, *p.p.*, strangle.

stran'glehold, *n.*, a deadly grip.

stran'gler, *n.*, a person or thing that strangles.

stran'gles, *n. pl.*, a catarrhal affection in horses.

stran'gling, *pr.p.*, strangle.

stran'gulate, *v.t.*, to strangle; to constrict.

stran'gulated, *adj.*, constricted, strangled; *p.p.*, strangulate.

stran'gulating, *pr.p.*, strangulate.

strangula'tion, *n.*, the act or effect of strangulating.

stran'gury, *n.*, difficulty in passing urine; a swelling in plants as the result of bandaging.

strap, *n.*, a leather thong, usually with a buckle or some means of fastening; a strip or band, etc., for joining or holding things together; *v.t.*, to bind with a strap; to flog; to whet; to close a wound by strapping.

straphang'er, *n.*, a passenger in public transport who, unable to get a seat, hangs on to straps suspended for the purpose.

strappa'do, *n.*, torture by hanging the victim up to a pulley, letting him down with violence, and pulling him up again; *v.t.*, to torture in this way.

strapped, *p.p.*, strap.

strap'per, *n.*, one who straps; a big, lusty person.

strap'ping, *adj.*, big, bulky, lusty; *pr.p.*, strap.

strass, *n.*, silk refuse; a compound used in imitation gems.

stra'ta, *n.*, the pl. of stratum (*Lat.*).

strat'agem, *n.*, a cunning plan to trick an enemy.

stratarith'metry, *n.*, the art of estimating the number of items enclosed in a geometrical space.

strateg'ic, *adj.*, pert. or rel. to strategy.

strateg'ical, *adj.*, i.q. strategic.

strateg'ically, *adv.*, in a strategic way.

strat'egist, *n.*, one skilled in strategy.

strateg'us, *n.*, a military commander (*Gr.*).

strat'egy, *n.*, generalship; military science; the art of planning movements of armies so as to prevent the enemy from choosing his own time and place for fighting; an overall plan for coping with a series of related problems.

Strat'fordian, *adj.*, pert. or rel. to Stratford-on-Avon; one who believes that William Shakespeare wrote the Shakespeare plays.

strath, *n.*, a mountain valley or river-course.

strathspey', *n.*, a Scottish dance of a lively character and resembling a reel.

stratic'ulate, *adj.*, arranged in thin layers.

stratifica'tion, *n.*, the arrangement of strata; the act or effect of laying sedimentary deposits.

strat'ified, *p.p.*, stratify.

strat'iform, *adj.*, formed like a stratum.

strat'ify, *v.i.*, to form in layers; *v.t.*, to deposit sedimentary layers.

strat'ifying, *pr.p.*, stratify.

stratig'raphy, *n.*, the geological study of strata.

stratoc'racy, *n.*, government by the military.

stra'tocruis'er, *n.*, an aircraft designed to fly through the stratosphere.

stratog'raphy, *n.*, a description of a military establishment.

strat'osphere, *n.*, the upper part of the atmosphere where height does not affect temperature.

stratospher'ic, *n.*, *adj.*, pert. or rel. to stratosphere.

stra'tum, *n.*, a layer naturally deposited (*Lat.*).

stra'tus, *n.*, a layer of cloud near to the horizon.

straw, *adj.*, made of straw; *n.*, the dry stalk of cut wheat, barley, oats, etc.; something valueless; *v.t.*, to strew.

straw'berry, *n.*, a perennial plant and its fruit.

straw'berry-mark, *n.*, a birthmark, coloured and shaped like a strawberry.

straw'board, *n.*, coarse cardboard made of straw pulp.

straw'-colour, *n.*, yellow in colour, like straw.

straw'sonizer, *n.*, an instrument which distributes liquid in the form of a fine spray.

straw'y, *adj.*, made of, or resembling, straw.

stray, *adj.*, wandering; sporadic; *n.*, a domestic animal gone astray; the escheated property of a deceased person; *v.i.*, to wander, to straggle.

strayed, *p.p.*, stray.

stray'er, *n.*, one who, or that which, strays.

stray'ing, *pr.p.*, stray.

stray'ling, *n.*, a little waif.

streak, *n.*, a line or stripe; a trace; *v.i.*, to stretch; to move very swiftly (*colloq.*); *v.t.*, to mark with streaks.

streaked, *p.p.*, streak.

streak'ily, *adv.*, in a streaky way.

streak'iness, *n.*, the quality or state of being streaky.

streak'ing, *pr.p.*, streak.

streak'y, *adj.*, in layers or stripes.

stream, *n.*, running water; the flow of any liquid or gas; a current; the continuous flow (of speech, people moving, etc.); *v.i.*, to flow in a stream or like a stream.

streamed, *p.p.*, stream.

stream'er, *n.*, anything that streams; a flag, pennon, ribbon, etc.

stream'ing, *adj.*, flowing in large quantities; *pr.p.*, stream.

stream'less, *adj.*, without a stream or streams.

stream'let, *n.*, a small stream.

stream'line, *n.*, a natural course for water or air; *v.t.*, to shape so as to minimize the resistance to air or water.

stream'lined, *adj.*, designed so as to offer the minimum resistance; *p.p.*, streamline.

stream'lin'ing, *pr.p.*, streamline.

stream'y, *adj.*, abounding in streams; stream-like.

street, *n.*, orig. a paved road; now, a road through a town or village.

street'-car, *n.*, a tram car (*Amer.*).

street'-cor'ner, *n.*, the point where two or more streets intersect.

street'wal'ker, *n.*, one who walks the streets; a prostitute.

strength, *n.*, physical power; the quality or state of being strong.

strength'en, *v.i.*, to become stronger; *v.t.*, to make strong.

strength'ened, *p.p.*, strengthen.

strength'ener, *n.*, one who, or that which, strengthens.

strength'ening, *adj.*, nourishing; invigorating; *pr.p.*, strengthen.

strength'less, *adj.*, weak; without strength.

stren'uous, *adj.*, vigorous; exacting; calling for exertion.

stren'uously, *adv.*, in a strenuous way.

stren'uousness, *n.*, the quality or state of being strenuous.

strepi'tant, *adj.*, very noisy.

strepitos'o, *adv.*, noisily (*It., mus.*).

Streptococ'ci, *n.*, the pl. of Streptococcus.

Streptococ'cus, *n.*, a genus of bacteria which come in twos or chains.

streptomy'cin, *n.*, an antibiotic medical treatment.

stress, *n.*, force; pressure; a need of effort; emphasis; in mechanics, the force acting between adjoining bodies or parts of bodies; *v.t.*, to emphasize; to accentuate.

stressed, *adj.*, emphasized; *p.p.*, stress.

stress'ing, *pr.p.*, stress.

stretch, *n.*, the act of stretching; the state of being stretched; an extent of country or expanse of water; a measured period; *v.i.*, to extend oneself; to exaggerate; *v.t.*, to strain, to tighten; to make longer or wider; to extend; to use extra effort.

stretched, *p.p.*, stretch.

stretch'er, *n.*, one who, or that which, stretches; a contrivance for carrying disabled persons; a footrest in a boat; an instrument for enlarging shoes, gloves, etc.; a brick or stone set in a wall so as to show its side; a lie (*colloq.*).

stretch'ing, *pr.p.*, stretch.

stret'to, *adj.*, in quicker time (*It., mus.*).

strew, *v.t.*, to spread or scatter on the ground; to shower; to partly cover. (Also *strow*.)

strewed, *p.p.*, strew.

strew'ing, *n.*, scattering; *pr.p.*, strew.

strewn, *p.p.*, strew.

stri'a, *n.*, superficial marking; a line; a low ridge.

stri'ae, *n.*, the pl. of stria.

stri'ate, *adj.*, *i.q.* striated; *v.t.*, to mark with striae.

stri'ated, *adj.*, marked with striae.

stria'tion, *n.*, marking with striae.

strick'en, *adj.*, afflicted; *p.p.*, strike.

strick'le, *n.*, a straightedged piece of metal or wood for levelling the top of a measure of grain.

strict, *adj.*, severe, formal, precise, ascetic.

strict'er, *adj.*, *comp.* of strict.

strict'est, *adj.*, *super.* of strict.

strict'ish, *adj.*, rather strict.

strict'ly, *adv.*, in a strict way; accurately, precisely.

strict'ness, *n.*, the quality or state of being strict.

stric'ture, *n.*, the contraction of some bodily organ; animadversion; censure.

stric'tured, *adj.*, suffering from stricture.

strid'den, *p.p.*, stride.

stride, *n.*, a long step; the space covered in a stride; *v.i.*, to walk in strides or long steps; *v.t.*, to span in striding.

stri'dent, *adj.*, harsh; raucous.

stri'dently, *adv.*, harshly; raucously.

stri'ding, *pr.p.*, stride.

stri'dor, *n.*, a harsh noise.

strid'ulant, *adj.*, strident; chirping in a shrill manner.

stri'dulate, *v.i.*, to make a creaking noise, like that of a grasshopper, cricket, etc.

stri'dulous, *adj.*, creaking.

strife, *n.*, dissension, a feud, a quarrel.

strife'less, *adj.*, without strife.

stri'ga, *n.*, in botany, a hair-like scale; in architecture, fluting.

strig'il, *n.*, a flesh-scraper; a brush (*Lat.*).

stri'gose, *adj.*, having strigae.

stri'gous, *adj.*, *i.q.* strigose.

strik'able, *adj.*, that which may be struck.

strike, *n.*, a blow; a refusal to work; *i.q.*

strickle; flax ready for heckling; a full measure of ale; *v.i.*, to come in sudden contact; to give out a sound that results from striking; to refuse to work; to impinge, etc.; *v.t.*, to hit or beat; to create an impression on; to occur to; to haul down (and many metaphorical senses).

strike'bound, *adj.*, immobilized by a strike.

strike'-break'er, *n.*, a blackleg; a workman brought in to replace a striker.

strike'-pay, *n.*, weekly compensation to a Trade Union member for loss of earnings during an official strike.

stri'ker, *n.*, one who, or that which, strikes.

stri'king, *adj.*, remarkable; noteworthy; *pr.p.*, strike.

stri'kingly, *adv.*, in a striking manner.

strine, *n.*, the Australian dialect.

string, *n.*, a thin rope, line, twine or cord; a series of things strung together, as beads or a string of horses; a billiard scoring-board, on which the scored numbers slide; *v.i.*, to form a string or continuous line; *v.t.*, to thread; to supply with strings; to tighten up.

string'-band, *n.*, an orchestra composed of stringed instruments only.

string'bean, *n.*, a French bean.

string'-board, *n.*, *i.q.* string-course.

string'-course, *n.*, a projecting moulding on a building.

stringed, *adj.*, furnished with strings (*mus.*); *p.p.*, string.

strin'gency, *n.*, the quality or state of being stringent.

stringen'do, *adv.*, quickening up (*It. mus.*).

strin'gent, *adj.*, exacting; severe; difficult.

strin'gently, *adv.*, severely.

string'er, *n.*, one who, or that which, strings; a supporting timber running along the length of a structure.

string'iness, *n.*, the quality or state of being stringy.

string'ing, *pr.p.*, string.

string'less, *adj.*, without strings.

strings, *n. pl.*, imposed conditions; the string section of an orchestra.

string'tie, *n.*, a very narrow tie.

string'y, *adj.*, like string; fibrous.

strip, *n.*, a narrow piece; *v.i.*, to take off one's clothes; to peel off; *v.t.*, to remove the outer covering from; to despoil; to denude; to cut into strips.

stripe, *n.*, a distinguishing line or band; a blow; *v.t.*, to mark with stripes.

striped, *adj.*, marked with stripes; *p.p.*, stripe.

stri'ping, *pr.p.*, stripe.

strip'ling, *n.*, a youth; one not fully matured.

strip'mine, *n.*, an opencast mine.

stripped, *p.p.*, strip.

strip'per, *n.*, one who, or that which, strips.

strip'ping, *pr.p.*, strip.

stript, *p.p.*, strip.

strip'tease, *n.*, an act of undressing as entertainment.

strip'y, *adj.*, marked with stripes.

strive, *v.i.*, to endeavour; to struggle; to dispute; to quarrel.

striv'en, *p.p.*, strive.

stri'ver, *n.*, one who strives.

stri'ving, *pr.p.*, strive.

Strix, *n.*, a genus of birds, including the owl.

strob'ile, *n.*, a pine-cone.

strobo'scope, *n.*, an instrument for measuring the rotation of turn-tables (e.g., record-player); an instrument for projecting whirling coloured lights.

strobo'scopic, *adj.*, pert. or rel. to a stroboscope.

strode, *p.p.*, stride.

stroke, *n.*, the act of striking; repeated action; a line, etc., made by a single movement of the hand; an accident; a paralytic seizure; the first oarsman in a boat who controls the rate of rowing; *v.t.*, to move the hand gently along; to smooth; to flatter; to be the stroke oarsman of.

stroked, *p.p.*, stroke.

strok'er, *n.*, one who, or that which, strokes.

strokes'man, *n.*, a man who rows stroke, *i.e.*, who sits nearest the stern and sets the pace and strength.

strok'ing, *pr.p.*, stroke.

stroll, *v.i.*, to take a ramble; to walk casually.

strolled, *p.p.*, stroll.

stroll'er, *n.*, one who strolls.

stroll'ing, *pr.p.*, stroll.

stro'ma, *n.*, the connecting tissue in the framework of a cell, etc. (*biol.*).

strom'ata, *n.*, the pl. of stroma.

stromat'ic, *adj.*, pert. or rel. to a stroma.

stromb, *n.*, a gastropod.

strom'bite, *n.*, a fossil stromb.

strom'bus, *n.*, *i.q.* stromb.

strong, *adj.*, vigorous; full of strength; healthy; loud; clear; staunch; inflecting or modifying the stem rather than the endings of words.

strong'-box, *n.*, a safe for storing money, jewellery, etc.

stron'ger, *adj.*, comp. of strong.

stron'gest, *adj.*, super. of strong.

strong'hold, *n.*, a fortified place.

strong'ish, *adj.*, rather strong.

strong'ly, *adv.*, with strength; firmly.

strong'minded, *adj.*, not squeamish; courageous.

strong-mind'edness, *n.*, the quality or state of being strongminded.

strong'room, *n.*, a room specially built to keep things safe from fire and burglary.

stron'tia, *n.*, a strontium oxide.

stron'tian, *adj.*, pert. or rel. to strontium.

stron'tium, *n.*, a metallic element.

strop, *n.*, a leather strap to sharpen razors on; *v.t.*, to sharpen (a razor) by stropping.

strophan'thin, *n.*, a poisonous drug.

stro'phe, *n.*, in a Greek drama, one section of a song chanted by the chorus; the first of two stanzas.

stroph'ic, *adj.*, pert. or rel. to a strophe.

stroph'iolate, *adj.*, having a strophiole.

stroph'iolated, *adj.*, *i.q.* strophiolate.

stroph'iole, *n.*, an appendage to the base of some seeds.

stro'phulus, *n.*, a skin infection in children, esp. of the gums.

strove, *p.p.*, strive.

strow, *v.t.*, *i.q.* strew.

strowed, *p.p.*, strow.

strow'ing, *pr.p.*, strow.

strown, *p.p.*, strow.

struck, *p.p.*, strike.

struc'tural, *adj.*, pert. or rel. to structure.

struc'turally, *adv.*, in a structural way.

struc'ture, *n.*, a construction; a building; a make; a disposition of parts in any living or inanimate thing.

struc'tureless, *adj.*, without structure.

strug'gle, *n.*, a striving; great effort; pain; labour; *v.i.*, to make a great effort; to strive with difficulty.

strug'gled, *p.p.*, struggle.

strug'gling, *pr.p.*, struggle.

strum, *v.i.* and *t.*, to play a musical instrument casually and informally.

stru'ma, *n.*, scrofula.

strumi'tis, *n.*, inflammation of the thyroid gland.

strummed, *p.p.*, strum.

strum'ming, *pr.p.*, strum.

stru'mous, *adj.*, affected with struma.

strum'pet, *adj.*, false; *n.*, a brazen prostitute.

strung, *p.p.*, string.

strut, *n.*, a proud, conceited way of walking; a wooden support; *v.i.*, to march about in a proud way.

stru'thioid, *adj.*, like an ostrich.

stru'thious, *adj.*, pert. or rel. to the Struthio (ostrich) genus of birds.

strut'ted, *p.p.*, strut.

strut'ter, *n.*, one who, or that which, struts.

strut'ting, *pr.p.*, strut,

strut'tingly, *adv.*, in a strutting manner.

strych'nia, *n.*, *i.q.* strychnine.

strych'nine, *n.*, a poisonous extract of nux vomica.

stub, *n.*, a tree-stump; a stub-nail; the retained record of a written cheque; any portion left after the main part has been detached; *v.t.*, to root up; to extinguish (a cigarette).

stubbed, *adj.*, full of stubs; broken off short; *p.p.*, stub.

stub'bing, *pr.p.*, stub.

stub'ble, *n.*, what is left in a cornfield after reaping.

stub'bly, *adj.*, like stubble; covered with stubble; bristly (a man's beard).

stub'born, *adj.*, obstinate; mulish; difficult to work.

stub'bornly, *adv.*, in a stubborn way.

stub'bornness, *n.*, the quality or state of being stubborn.

stub'by, *adj.*, short and thick.

stuc'co, *n.*, plaster for overlaying wall surfaces; stucco-work; *v.t.*, to overlay with plaster.

stuc'coed, *p.p.*, stucco.

stuc'coer, *n.*, a worker or dealer in stucco.

stuc'coing, *pr.p.*, stucco.

stuck, *p.p.*, stick.

stuck'-up, *adj.*, conceited.

stud, *n.*, a knob; a button; a fastener; a collection of horses for racing or breeding purposes; *v.t.*, to furnish with studs; to ornament.

stud'-bolt, *n.*, a bolt with a thread at each end.

stud'ded, *p.p.*, stud.

stud'ding, *pr.p.*, stud.

stu'dent, *n.*, one who studies; a scholar.

stu'dentship, *n.*, the state of being a student; scholarship.

stud'-horse, *n.*, a horse kept for breeding purposes.

stud'ied, *adj.*, premeditated; precise; *p.p.*, study.

stu'dio, *n.*, a workroom for artistic or craft work.

stu'dious, *adj.*, given to study; zealous.

stu'diously, *adv.*, in a studious way.

stu'diousness, *n.*, the state of being studious.

stud'-mare, *n.*, a mare kept for breeding purposes.

stud'y, *n.*, mental application to learning; a learned pursuit; a preliminary sketch; a room to study in; *v.t.*, to apply the mind to; to look minutely into; to be mindful of.

stud'ying, *pr.p.*, study.

stu'fa, *n.*, steam exhaling from the ground.

stuff, *n.*, fabric or material; furniture; worthless material; nonsense; *v.i.*, to overeat oneself; *v.t.*, to pack; to cram into; to put stuffing into; to fill a dead animal's skin to retain its natural appearance.

stuffed, *adj.*, filled; *p.p.*, stuff.

stuff'er, *n.*, one who stuffs; a taxidermist.

stuff'ier, *adj.*, *comp.* of stuffy.

stuff'iest, *adj.*, *super.* of stuffy.

stuff'ily, *adv.*, in a stuffy way.

stuff'iness, *n.*, the quality or state of being stuffy.

stuff'ing, *n.*, forcemeat; anything used for the purpose of stuffing; *pr.p.*, stuff.

stuff'y, *adj.*, stifling; without proper ventilation; narrow and inconsiderate in attitude.

stul'm, *n.*, a mining shaft (*Ger.*).

stultifica'tion, *n.*, the act or effect of stultifying.

stul'tified, *p.p.*, stultify.

stul'tifier, *n.*, one who stultifies.

stul'tify, *v.t.*, to make foolish; to make of no effect.

stul'tifying, *pr.p.*, stultify.

stultil'oquence, *n.*, foolish, vain talk.

stum, *n.*, must; grape juice before fermentation.

stum'ble, *n.*, a false step; a trip; *v.i.*, to trip up; to walk haltingly; to fall.

stum'bled, *p.p.*, stumble.

stum'bler, *n.*, one who stumbles.

stum'bling, *pr.p.*, stumble.

stum'bling-block, *n.*, a cause of offence; a difficulty in the way.

stu'mer, *n.*, a sham; a forgery (*colloq.*).

stump, *n.*, what is left above ground of a tree cut down; a mutilated limb; an artist's pencil; one part of the wicket on a cricket ground; *v.i.*, to make a round of speeches or lectures; to walk stiffly and heavily; *v.t.*, to reduce to a stump; to hit a wicket down while the batsman is out of his ground; to baffle (*colloq.*)..

stumped, *p.p.*, stump.

stump'er, *n.*, a wicketkeeper; a difficulty (*colloq.*).

stump'iness, *n.*, the quality or state of being stumpy.

stump'ing, *pr.p.*, stump.

stump-or'ator, *n.*, one who stumps the country making speeches extempore.

stump-or'atory, *n.*, a stump-orator's performances.

stump'-up, *v.i.*, to pay (*colloq.*).

stump'y, *adj.*, stunted; abounding in stumps.

stun, *v.t.*, to make senseless with a violent blow; to deafen; to overwhelm with surprise, grief, etc.

Stund'ist, *n.*, one of a Russian religious sect resembling Puritans.

stung, *p.p.*, sting.

stunk, *p.p.*, stink.

stunned, *p.p.*, stun.

stun'ner, *n.*, one who, or that which, stuns.

stun'ning, *adj.*, overwhelming; delightful (*colloq.*); *pr.p.*, stun.

stunt, *n.*, the arrest of growth; a special feat or display; *v.i.*, to have the growth arrested; *v.t.*, to shorten the growth of; to perform in a special way.

stunt'ed, *p.p.*, stunt.

stunt'ing, *pr.p.*, stunt.

stupe, *n.*, a compress.

stupefa'cient, *adj.*, stupefying.

stupefac'tion, *n.*, the act or effect of stupefying.

stupefac'tive, *adj.*, causing stupefaction.

stu'pefied, *p.p.*, stupefy.

stu'pefier, *n.*, one who, or that which, stupefies.

stu'pefy, *v.t.*, to reduce to a state of stupor; to make insensible to pain, etc.; to make stupid.

stu'pefying, *pr.p.*, stupefy.

stupen'dous, *adj.*, amazing in greatness.

stupen'dously, *adv.*, in a stupendous way.

stu'pid, *adj.*, dull; insensible; unreasonable; obstinate.

stupid'ity, *n.*, the quality or state of being stupid.

stu'pidly, *adv.*, in a stupid way.

stupid'ness, *n.*, *i.q.* stupidity.

stu'por, *n.*, insensibility; lethargy.

stu'pose, *adj.*, with towlike hairs (*bot.*).

stu'prate, *v.t.*, to ravish.

stupra'tion, *n.*, the act of ravishing.

stur'dier, *adj.*, *comp.* of sturdy.

stur'diest, *adj.*, *super.* of sturdy.

stur'dily, *adv.*, in a sturdy way.

stur'diness, *n.*, the quality or state of being sturdy.

stur'dy, *adj.*, strong; well-set; vigorous; *n.*, a brain disease of sheep.

stur'geon, *n.*, a large fish, much valued for its roe, from which caviare is made.

stut'ter, *v.i.*, to stammer; *v.t.*, to say with a stammer.

stut'tered, *p.p.*, stutter.

stut'terer, *n.*, one who stutters.

stut'tering, *n.*, hesitation in speaking; *pr.p.*, stutter.

stut'teringly, *adv.*, in a stuttering fashion.

sty, *n.*, a pig's shelter; a swelling on the eye (also *stye*); *v.t.*, to enclose in a sty.

Styg'ian, *adj.*, pert. or rel. to the Styx, the river of Hades; hellish; very black.

stylagalma'ic, *adj.*, like a caryatid.

sty'lar, *adj.*, pert. or rel. to a style.

sty'late, *adj.*, pointed (*bot.*).

style, *n.*, a pointed instrument for writing on waxen tablets; fashion; mode; a distinctive title; distinguishing characteristics of expression in speech or the arts; the stalk between a flower's ovary and its stigma; *v.t.*, to address; to call by a distinctive name.

styled, *p.p.*, style.

style'less, *adj.*, without style.

styl'et, *n.*, a small style.

styl'i, *n. pl.*, of stylus.

stylif'erous, *adj.*, bearing styles.

sty'liform, *adj.*, like a style.

sty'ling, *n.*, shaping; *pr.p.*, style.

sty'lish, *adj.*, smart; in the fashion.

sty'lishly, *adv.*, in a stylish way.

sty'lishness, *n.*, the condition of being stylish.

sty'list, *n.*, one who is particular in regard to style in writing.

stylis'tic, *adj.*, of literary style; showing the characteristics of style.

sty'lite, *n.*, an eremite who lived on the top of a pillar, as St. Simeon Stylites.

styl'ize, *v.t.*, to bring into line with a style; to conventionalize.

styl'o, *n.*, the abbrev. for stylograph.

sty'lobate, *n.*, the base of a row of pillars.

sty'lograph, *n.*, a stylographic pen.

stylograph'ic, *adj.*, pert. or rel. to a stylograph and stylography.

stylog'raphy, *n.*, writing with a style.

sty'loid, *adj.*, like a style or a pillar.

sty'lus, *n.*, a style for writing on wax.

stym'ie, *n.*, a position in which the path of a putt is obstructed by an opponent's ball in golf; any position in which it is difficult to proceed.

stym'ied, *adj.*, prevented from going on.

styp'tic, *adj.*, having the effect of staunching blood; *n.*, a substance that stops bleeding.

styptic'ity, *n.*, the quality of being styptic.

Styr'ax, *n.*, a genus of tree and shrub from which benzoin and storax are obtained.

Sty'rian, *adj.*, pert. or rel. to Styria, formerly a province of Austria.

sua'be, *n.*, an organ flute-stop (*mus.*).

suabil'ity, *n.*, the state of being suable.

su'able, *adj.*, in a position to be sued.

sua'sible, *adj.*, easily persuaded.

sua'sion, *n.*, advice; entreaty.

sua'sive, *adj.*, conveying advice or entreaty.

sua'sively, *adv.*, in a persuasive way.

suave, *adj.*, gentle, bland; smooth and courteous in manner.

suave'ly, *adv.*, in a suave way.

suav'ity, *n.*, gentleness; blandness.

sub, a Lat. preposition = "under", used in many words as a prefix, meaning *under*, *beneath*, *somewhat*.

subac'etate, *adj.*, somewhat acetate.

subacute', *adj.*, moderately acute.

sub-a'gency, *n.*, an agency under another agent.

sub-a'gent, *n.*, an agent's deputy.

subal'pine, *adj.*, situated below the Alps.

subal'tern, *adj.*, inferior; *n.*, a commissioned officer below a captain's rank.

subalter'nate, *adj.*, alternate, but with a tendency to become opposite; a broad proposition (*logic*).

subaquat'ic, *adj.*, partly aquatic; *i.q.*, subaqueous.

suba'queous, *adj.*, beneath the water.

subarc'tic, *adj.*, pert. or rel. to the region next to the arctic.

subar'id, *adj.*, moderately dry.

subas'tral, *adj.*, beneath the stars.

subat'om, *n.*, part of an atom.

subaudi'tion, *n.*, the understanding of something not expressed, as "St. Paul's" the word "Cathedral" being understood.

subax'illary, *adj.*, below the armpit; beneath the axil (*bot.*).

sub'base, *n.*, a lower base.

subbra'chial, *adj.*, having ventrals under pectorals.

subbra'chian, *adj.*, *i.q.* subbrachial.

sub'bing, *adj.*, acting as a substitute; seeking or receiving payment in advance (*colloq.*).

subcla'vian, *adj.*, below the shoulder.

sub-commis'sioner, *n.*, a deputy commissioner.

subcommit'tee, *n.*, an inner committee.

subcon'scious, *adj.*, partially conscious; pert. or rel. to acts done without full consciousness.

subcon'sciously, *adv.*, in a sub-conscious way.

subcon'tract, *n.*, a contract within another.

sub'contractor, *n.*, one who undertakes part of a large job or contract.

subcon'trary, *adj.*, contrary in a lesser degree.

subcor'date, *adj.*, below the heart.

subcos'tal, *adj.*, below the ribs.

subcuta'neous, *adj.*, beneath the skin.

sub'deacon, *n.*, a minister next below the deacon.

sub'dean, *n.*, the dean's deputy.

subdivide', *v.t.*, to divide what has been already divided.

subdivi'ded, *p.p.*, subdivide.

subdivi'ding, *pr.p.*, subdivide.

subdivis'ible, *adj.*, capable of subdivision.

subdivi'sion, *n.*, division into still smaller parts after a first division.

subdom'inant, *adj.*, below the dominant; *n.*, the fourth note in the scale.

subdu'able, *adj.*, able to be subdued.

subdu'al, *n.*, the act or result of subduing.

subduce', *v.t.*, to withdraw.

subduced', *p.p.*, subduce.

subdu'cing, *pr.p.*, subduce.

subduct', *v.t.*, to withdraw.

subduct'ed, *p.p.*, subduct.

subduct'ing, *pr.p.*, subduct.

subduc'tion, *n.*, the act of subducting; that which is subducted.

subdue', *v.t.*, to overcome; to conquer; to lower.

subdued', *adj.*, depressed; lowered; *p.p.*, subdue.

subdu'er, *n.*, one who subdues.

subdu'ing, *pr.p.*, subdue.

subed'it, *v.t.*, to assist in editing.

subed'ited, *p.p.*, subedit.

subed'iting, *pr.p.*, subedit.

subed'itor, *n.*, one who subedits.

sube'qual, *adj.*, nearly equal.

su'berate, *n.*, a salt of suberic acid.

suber'ic, *adj.*, pert. or rel. to cork.

su'berin, *n.*, the cellular tissue of cork.

su'berine, *n.*, *i.q.* suberin.

su'berose, *adj.*, *i.q.* suberous.

su'berous, *adj.*, pert. or rel. to cork; elastic.

sub'genus, *n.*, a genus within a genus.

sub'-head, *n.*, *i.q.* subheading.

sub'-head'ing, *n.*, a subordinate heading.

sub'hu'man, *adj.*, less than human.

subirriga'tion, *n.*, underground irrigation.

su'bito, *adv.*, suddenly; quickly (*It.*, *mus.*).

subja'cent, *adj.*, lying close to, or below.

sub'ject, *adj.*, under another's authority; liable to; *n.*, one who is under another's authority; a matter for discussion, writing, etc.; a musical theme; a design; the *Ego* as distinguished from the object.

subject', *v.t.*, to reduce to submission; to expose.

subject'ed, *p.p.*, subject.

subject'ing, *pr.p.*, subject.

subjec'tion, *n.*, subjugation; the state of being subjected.

subjec'tive, *adj.*, pert. or rel. to the subject, or to one's own consciousness.

subjec'tively, *adv.*, in a subjective sense.

subjec'tiveness, *n.*, *i.q.* subjectivity.

subjec'tivism, *n.*, the teaching of thinkers who believe that knowledge is relative.

subjectiv'ity, *n.*, the quality or state of being subjective.

sub'ject-matter, *n.*, a theme or question under discussion or written about.

subjoin', *v.t.*, to add; to affix.

subjoined', *p.p.*, subjoin.

subjoin'ing, *pr.p.*, subjoin.

sub ju'dice, *Lat. phrase* = still before a judge; not yet determined.

sub'jugate, *v.t.*, to conquer or subdue.

sub'jugated, *p.p.*, subjugate.

sub'jugating, *pr.p.*, subjugate.

subjuga'tion, *n.*, the act or effect of subjugating.

sub'jugator, *n.*, one who subjugates.

subjunc'tion, *n.*, the act or effect of subjoining.

subjunc'tive, *adj.*, denoting contingency; *n.*, the verbal mood which expresses contingency, hypothesis or wish.

sublapsa'rian, *adj.*, pert. or rel. to sublapsarianism.

sublapsa'rianism, n., the opinions of sublapsarians, or moderate Calvinists, who hold that election was subsequent to the Fall.

sublate', v.t., to deny in argument.

subla'tion, n., the act of sublating.

sublease', n., a lease within a lease; v.t., said of a leasehold tenant who leases his house to another holder.

sublet', n., a let within a let; v.t., said of the occupant of a rented house who lets the house or part of it to another tenant.

subleva'tion, n., removal.

sublibra'rian, n., a librarian's assistant.

sub'lieuten'ant, n., the naval rank below lieutenant.

sub'limate, adj., said of a substance that has been sublimated; n., a sublimated substance; v.t., to reduce a solid to vapour and then condense it.

sub'limated, p.p., sublimate.

sub'limating, pr.p., sublimate.

sublima'tion, n., the process of sublimating.

sublime', adj., high, exalted, awe-inspiring; n., the awe-inspiring as distinct from the beautiful; v.i., to be able to be sublimated; v.t., to elevate; to ennoble.

sublimed', p.p., sublime.

sublime'ly, adv., in a sublime way.

sublim'inal, adj., behind or beneath the conscious state.

sublim'ing, pr.p., sublime.

sublim'ity, n., the quality or state of being sublime.

sub'lin'ear, adj., below the line.

sublu'nar, adj., i.q. sublunary.

sub'lunary, adj., beneath the moon.

sub'man, n., a man of poor physique or low intellect.

sub'marine, adj., beneath the sea; n., a boat for sailing below as well as on the surface.

submax'illary, adj., lying under the maxilla.

subme'diant, n., the sixth note in the scale.

submerge', v.i., to sink below the water; v.t., to sink or depress below water; to overwhelm.

submerged', p.p., submerge.

submer'gence, n., the act of submerging; the state of being submerged.

submer'ging, pr.p., submerge.

submerse', v.t., i.q. submerge.

submersed', p.p., submerse.

submers'ibility, n., the capacity to submerge.

submers'ible, adj., capable of being submerged.

submers'ing, pr.p., submerse.

submer'sion, n., i.q. submergence.

submis'sion, n., subjection; yielding; deference.

submiss'ive, adj., yielding; obedient.

submiss'ively, adv., in a submissive way.

submiss'iveness, n., the state of being submissive.

submit', v.i., to yield; to place oneself under another; v.t., to place under another's authority; to yield; to offer for judgment.

submit'ted, p.p., submit.

submit'ting, pr.p., submit.

submon'tane, adj., at the foot of a mountain.

submul'tiple, n., a quantity or number contained within another an exact number of times.

subnas'cent, adj., growing underneath.

subnor'mal, adj., less than normal.

subor'dinacy, n., the state or being subordinate.

subor'dinate, adj., of lower rank; under authority; n., a person under authority.

subor'dinate, v.t., to place in subjection; to rank as of lower importance.

subor'dinated, p.p., subordinate.

subor'dinately, adv., in a subordinate way.

subor'dinating, pr.p., subordinate.

subordina'tion, n., the act of subordinating; submissiveness.

subordina'tionism, n., the doctrine that the second and third persons of the Trinity are inferior to the Father.

subord'inative, adj., involving subordination.

suborn', v.t., to make to give false witness; to obtain by collusion.

suborna'tion, n., the act of suborning.

suborned', p.p., suborn.

suborn'er, n., one who suborns.

suborn'ing, pr.p., suborn.

subo'vate, adj., slightly ovate.

subpoe'na, n., a command from a lawcourt for the appearance of a witness; v.t., to summon a witness under a penalty.

subpoe'naed, p.p., subpoena.

subpoe'naing, pr.p., subpoena.

subprin'cipal, adj., principal in a secondary degree.

subrep'tion, n., the act of snatching away.

sub'rogate, v.t., to substitute; to replace one party for another as creditor.

subroga'tion, n., succession; substitution.

sub ro'sa, an adverbial Lat. phrase = under the rose (i.e., in secret).

sub'salt, adj., slightly salt.

subscribe', v.i., to consent; v.t., to sign; to contribute; to get a book published by subscription.

subscribed', p.p., subscribe.

subscri'ber, n., one who subscribes.

subscri'bing, pr.p., subscribe.

sub'script, adj., written underneath.

subscrip'tion, n., the act of subscribing; something subscribed; formal assent; payment for a fixed term or precise purpose.

sub'section, *n.*, a section within a section.

sub'sequence, *n.*, the act or state of being subsequent.

sub'sequent, *adj.*, following on; later.

sub'sequently, *adv.*, later.

subserve', *v.t.*, to be to the interest of; to promote.

subserved', *p.p.*, subserve.

subserv'ience, *n.*, the state of being subservient.

subserv'iency, *n.*, *i.q.*, subservience.

subserv'ient, *adj.*, helping; subordinate to.

subserv'iently, *adv.*, in a subservient way.

subserv'ing, *pr.p.*, subserve.

subside', *v.i.*, to sink down; to collapse; to grow calm.

subsi'ded, *p.p.*, subside.

subsi'dence, *n.*, the act or result of subsiding.

subsid'iarily, *adv.*, in a subsidiary way.

subsid'iary, *adj.*, aiding; additional; auxiliary.

subsi'ding, *pr.p.*, subside.

sub'sidist, *n.*, one who proposes a subsidy.

sub'sidize, *v.t.*, to help with a money grant.

sub'sidized, *p.p.*, subsidize.

sub'sidizing, *pr.p.*, subsidize.

sub'sidy, *n.*, money granted in aid.

subsist', *v.i.*, to live; to inhere.

subsist'ed, *p.p.*, subsist.

subsist'ence, *n.*, the act or state of subsisting; the necessities of life.

subsist'ent, *adj.*, subsisting.

subsist'ing, *pr.p.*, subsist.

sub'soil, *n.*, soil beneath the surface soil.

subson'ic, *adj.*, below the speed of sound.

subspe'cies, *n.*, a species within a species.

sub'stance, *n.*, matter; meaning; wealth.

substan'dard, *adj.*, below standard.

substan'tial, *adj.*, pert. or rel. to substance; solid; bodily; having plenty of means.

substan'tialism, *n.*, the doctrine that behind all phenomena there are realities.

substantial'ity, *n.*, the quality or state of being substantial.

substan'tialize, *v.i.* and *t.*, to make substantial.

substan'tially, *adv.*, in a substantial way or sense.

substan'tials, *n. pl.*, parts that are of the essence of a thing.

substan'tiate, *v.t.*, to prove the truth of.

substan'tiated, *p.p.*, substantiate.

substan'tiating, *pr.p.*, substantiate.

substantia'tion, *n.*, the act or effect of substantiating.

substantiv'al, *adj.*, pert. to, or serving as, a substantive.

sub'stantive, *adj.*, denoting existence or reality; material; *n.*, a noun, denoting individual things, actions or qualities.

sub'stantively, *adv.*, in a substantive way.

sub'stitute, *n.*, a person or thing taking the place of another; *v.t.*, to put (one thing) in the place of another.

sub'stituted, *p.p.*, substitute.

sub'stituting, *pr.p.*, substitute.

substitu'tion, *n.*, the act or result of substituting.

substitu'tional, *adj.*, pert. or rel. to substitution.

substitu'tionary, *adj.*, *i.q.* substitutional.

sub'stitutive, *adj.*, effecting substitution.

sub'strate, *adj.*, lying beneath.

substra'tum, *n.*, a lower stratum (*Lat.*).

substruc'ture, *n.*, a structure supporting another.

subsul'phate, *n.*, a salt allied to a sulphate.

subsume', *v.t.*, to put into a stated category; to subordinate.

subsump'tion, *n.*, an inclusion or comprehension as subordinate.

subtan'gent, *n.*, that part of a curve's axis which is intercepted between the tangent and the ordinate.

sub'ten'ant, *n.*, the holder of a sublease.

subtend', *v.t.*, to lie opposite to.

subtend'ed, *p.p.*, subtend.

subtend'ing, *pr.p.*, subtend.

subtense', *adj.*, subtending.

subter'fluent, *adj.*, flowing beneath.

sub'terfuge, *n.*, an evasion; a dodge.

subterra'nean, *adj.*, underground.

subterra'neous, *adj.*, *i.q.* subterranean.

sub'tile, *adj.*, *i.q.* subtle.

subtil'ity, *n.*, the quality or state of being subtile.

subtiliza'tion, *n.*, the act or effect of subtilizing.

sub'tilize, *v.t.*, to make subtile.

sub'tilized, *p.p.*, subtilize.

sub'tilizing, *pr.p.*, subtilize.

sub'title, *n.*, the secondary title of a book; a film caption.

sub'tle, *adj.*, clever; cunning; refined; penetrating; acute; tenuous.

sub'tlety, *n.*, cunning; acuteness.

sub'tly, *adv.*, in a subtle way.

subton'ic, *n.*, the leading note of the diatonic scale (*mus.*).

subto'pia, *n.*, badly planned, sprawling suburbs.

subtract', *v.t.*, to take from; to take a smaller from a larger number or quantity.

subtract'ed, *p.p.*, subtract.

subtract'er, *n.*, one who subtracts.

subtract'ing, *pr.p.*, subtract.

subtrac'tion, *n.*, the act of subtracting; one of the rules of arithmetic.

subtract'ive, *adj.*, having the effect of subtracting.

sub'trahend, *n.*, the smaller number or amount to be subtracted from a larger.

subtrop'ical, *adj.*, nearly tropical.

su'bulate, *adj.*, like an awl.

sub'urb, *n.*, a residential district at a distance from a city centre.

subur'ban, *adj.*, pert. or rel. to a suburb.

suburb'ia, *n.*, the suburbs and their characteristics.

suburb'ian, *adj.*, pert. or rel. to suburbia.

sub'urbs, *n. pl.*, the environs of a town.

subven'tion, *n.*, a grant; a subsidy.

subver'sion, *n.*, the act or result of subverting.

subver'sive, *adj.*, tending to subvert.

subvert', *v.t.*, to overthrow; to turn upside down; to demoralize.

subvert'ed, *p.p.*, subvert.

subvert'er, *n.*, one who subverts.

subvert'ible, *adj.*, able to be subverted.

subvert'ing, *pr.p.*, subvert.

sub'way, *n.*, an underground passage.

succade, *n.*, candied fruit in syrup.

succeda'neous, *adj.*, substitutional.

succeda'neum, *n.*, a deputy; a substitute.

succeed', *v.i.*, to come after; to prosper; to do what one attempts to do; *v.t.*, to follow next after.

succeed'ed, *p.p.*, succeed.

succeed'ing, *pr.p.*, succeed.

succen'tor, *n.*, one who acts for a precentor.

success', *n.*, the accomplishment of an endeavour; prosperity.

success'ful, *adj.*, having success.

success'fully, *adv.*, with success.

succes'sion, *n.*, the act of following; the right to take another's place or possessions; rotation.

succes'sional, *adj.*, pert. or rel. to succession.

succes'sionist, *n.*, one who believes in some principle of succession.

succes'sive, *adj.*, consecutive; repeated.

succes'sively, *adv.*, consecutively.

succes'siveness, *n.*, the state of being successive.

success'or, *n.*, one who takes another's place or property.

succif'erous, *adj.*, producing sap or juice.

suc'cinate, *n.*, a salt of succinic acid.

suc'cinated, *adj.*, pert. or rel. to succinate.

succinct', *adj.*, brief; terse.

succinct'ly, *adv.*, tersely.

succinct'ness, *n.*, the quality or state of being succinct.

succin'ic, *adj.*, derived from amber; contained in amber.

suc'cinite, *n.*, amber.

suc'cinous, *adj.*, sappy; juicy.

succ'ory, *n.*, *i.q.* chicory.

succ'otash, *n.*, a boiled dish of green maize and beans.

suc'cour, *n.*, help, aid; *v.t.*, to help.

suc'coured, *p.p.*, succour.

suc'courer, *n.*, a helper.

suc'couring, *pr.p.*, succour.

suc'culence, *n.*, juiciness.

suc'culency, *n.*, *i.q.* succulence.

suc'culent, *adj.*, juicy.

suc'culently, *adv.*, juicily.

succumb', *v.i.*, to give in; to yield.

succumbed', *p.p.*, succumb.

succumb'ing, *pr.p.*, succumb.

succus'sion, *n.*, a shaking.

succus'sive, *adj.*, shaking.

such, *adj.*, of that kind or degree; certain; so great.

such'like, *adj.*, of such a kind.

suck, *n.*, an act of sucking; *v.i.*, to draw a mother's milk; *v.t.*, to extract with the lips.

sucked, *p.p.*, suck.

suck'er, *n.*, one who sucks; that which sucks or by which anything is sucked; a shoot thrown out by a plant at its stem; one easily duped (*slang*).

suck'ing, *pr.p.*, suck.

suck'le, *v.t.*, to feed from the breast.

suck'led, *p.p.*, suckle.

suck'ling, *n.*, a child or animal at the breast; *pr.p.*, suckle.

suc'rose, *n.*, sugar cane.

suc'tion, *n.*, the act of sucking or of drawing liquids or air.

suc'tion-stroke, *n.*, in a motor engine, the outward movement of the piston.

sucto'rial, *adj.*, living by sucking.

sucto'rian, *adj.*, *i.q.* suctorial.

Sudanese', *adj.*, pert. or rel. to the Sudan; *n.*, a native of the S.

suda'tion, *n.*, sweating.

sudator'ium, *n.*, a room where a hot-air bath is taken (*Lat.*).

su'datory, *adj.*, promoting sweat; *n.*, a hot-air bath.

sudd, *n.*, floating plants and trees *en masse*.

sud'den, *adj.*, happening unexpectedly or in an instant.

sud'denly, *adv.*, instantaneously; unexpectedly.

sud'denness, *n.*, the quality or state of being sudden.

Sude'tan, *n.*, a range of mountains bordering Czechoslovakia and Silesia; *adj.*, pert. or rel. to the German nationals formerly resident in this region.

su'dor, *n.*, sweat (*med.*).

sudore'sis, *n.*, a state of perspiration.

sudorif'erous, *adj.*, causing sweat.

sudorif'ic, *adj.*, *i.q.* sudoriferous.

sudorip'arous, *adj.*, *i.q.* sudoriferous.

Su'dra, *n.*, the lowest Hindu caste.

suds, *n. pl.*, dirty soapy water.

sue, *v.i.*, to petition; to court; to take out a summons; *v.t.*, to take out a summons against.

sued, *p.p.*, sue.

suède, *n.*, leather or smooth hide, undressed, and used for gloves, footwear and top garments.

suèdette, *n.*, imitation suède fabric.

su'er, *n.*, one who sues.

su'et, *n.*, a fatty substance in oxen and sheep.

su'ety, *adj.*, like, or abounding in, suet.

suf'fer, *v.i.*, to have pain; to be injured; *v.t.*, to endure (pain, hardship, etc.); to permit.

suf'ferable, *adj.*, able to be suffered.

suf'ferance, *n.*, tolerance; contemptuous permission.

suf'fered, *p.p.*, suffer.

suf'ferer, *n.*, one who suffers.

suf'fering, *n.*, pain, misery; *pr.p.*, suffer.

suffice', *v.i.*, to be enough; *v.t.*, to content; to satisfy.

sufficed', *p.p.*, suffice.

suffi'ciency, *n.*, the quality or state of being sufficient; adequate means; self-satisfaction; adequacy.

suffi'cient, *adj.*, enough, satisfying.

suffi'ciently, *adv.*, enough.

suffi'cing, *pr.p.*, suffice.

suf'fix, *n.*, a syllable or word added to the end of a word.

suffix', *v.t.*, to add to the end of a word.

suffixed', *p.p.*, suffix.

suffix'ing, *pr.p.*, suffix.

suffla'tion, *n.*, a filling with air.

suf'focate, *v.i.* and *t.*, to stifle; to stop the breathing of; to perish through lack of air.

suf'focated, *p.p.*, suffocate.

suf'focating, *pr.p.*, suffocate.

suf'focatingly, *adv.*, in a suffocating way.

suffoca'tion, *n.*, the act or effect of suffocating.

suf'focative, *adj.*, causing suffocation.

suf'fragan, *adj.*, assistant (*lit.*, voting with), said of the bishops of a Province who are the supporters of their Metropolitan; *n.*, an assistant bishop.

suf'frage, *n.*, the vote; franchise; a vote given at any discussion.

suf'fragette, *n.*, a woman who worked for the Parliamentary vote.

suf'fragism, *n.*, the theory that women ought to have equal political rights.

suf'fragist, *n.*, an advocate of wider franchise.

suffuse', *v.t.*, to tinge.

suffused', *p.p.*, suffuse.

suffu'sing, *pr.p.*, suffuse.

suffu'sion, *n.*, the act or effect of suffusing.

Su'fi, *n.*, a dervish; one of the Persian Shah's titles. (Also *Sophy*.)

su'fism, *n.*, the doctrines of the dervishes.

sug, *n.*, a parasite of the trout.

sug'ar, *adj.*, made of sugar; *n.*, a sweet extract from cane, beet, etc.; adulation; *v.t.*, to sweeten.

sug'ar-beet, *n.*, a variety of beet grown for sugar.

sug'ar-cane, *n.*, the cane from which sugar is extracted.

sug'ared, *adj.*, sweetened; flattering; *p.p.*, sugar.

sug'ariness, *n.*, the quality or state of being sugary; sweetness.

sug'aring, *pr.p.*, sugar.

sug'arless, *adj.*, without sugar.

sug'ar-loaf, *n.*, sugar made into a conical pyramid.

sug'ar-plum, *n.*, a plum preserved and covered with sugar.

sug'ary, *adj.*, full of, or resembling, sugar.

suggest', *v.t.*, to convey a thought or hint; to intimate.

suggest'ed, *p.p.*, suggest.

suggest'er, *n.*, one who suggests.

suggestibil'ity, *n.*, the quality or state of being suggestible.

suggest'ible, *adj.*, capable of being influenced by suggestion.

suggest'ing, *pr.p.*, suggest.

sugges'tion, *n.*, the act of suggesting; a hint.

sugges'tive, *adj.*, conveying a suggestion; implying.

sugges'tively, *adv.*, in a suggestive way.

sugges'tiveness, *n.*, the quality or state of being suggestive.

suici'dal, *adj.*, self-destructive.

suici'dally, *adv.*, in a suicidal way.

su'icide, *n.*, one who takes his own life; the act of taking one's own life.

su'illine, *adj.*, of the hog family.

su'ing, *pr.p.*, sue.

suit, *n.*, a set of matching top garments

worn together; an action-at-law to recover something; a series of cards of the same name; *v.i.*, to agree; *v.t.*, to fit; to accord with; to please.

suitabil'ity, *n.*, the quality or state of being suitable.

suit'able, *adj.*, fitting; convenient; appropriate.

suit'ableness, *n.*, *i.q.* suitability.

suit'ably, *adv.*, fittingly.

suit'case, *n.*, a carrying case for personal belongings.

suite, *n.*, a company of followers or attendants; a series; a set (of rooms, furniture, etc.).

suit'ed, *p.p.*, suit.

suit'ing, *n.*, material for suits of clothes; *pr.p.*, suit.

suit'or, *n.*, one who makes an application; a wooer; a plaintiff.

sul'cate, *adj.*, furrowed; grooved (*anat.*, *bot.*).

sul'cated, *adj.*, *i.q.* sulcate.

sul'fate, *n.*, *i.q.* sulphate (*Amer.*).

sul'fur, *n.*, *i.q.* sulphur (*Amer.*).

sulk, *v.i.*, to be angrily silent.

sulk'ily, *adv.*, in a sulky way.

sulk'iness, *n.*, the quality of state of being sulky.

sulks, *n. pl.*, a sulky fit.

sulk'y, *adj.*, sullen and silent; *n.*, a light carriage for one person.

sull'age, *n.*, sewage, refuse, filth.

sul'len, *adj.*, morose; refusing to speak.

sul'lenly, *adv.*, in a sullen way.

sul'lenness, *n.*, the state of being sullen.

sul'lied, *p.p.*, sully.

sul'ly, *v.t.*, to stain; to defile; to tarnish.

sul'lying, *pr.p.*, sully.

sul'phate, *n.*, a sulphurous acid salt.

sulphat'ic, *adj.*, pert. or rel. to sulphate.

sul'phide, *n.*, sulphur and some element or metal combined.

sul'phite, *n.*, *i.q.* sulphate.

sul′phonal, *n.,* a narcotic drug.

sulphon′amide, *n.,* a drug having antibacterial properties.

sul′phoral, *n.,* a narcotic compound.

sul′phur, *n.,* an element, non-metallic, yellow, not soluble in water.

sul′phurate, *v.t.,* to impregnate or to act upon with sulphur.

sul′phurated, *p.p.,* sulphurate.

sul′phurating, *pr.p.,* sulphurate.

sulphura′tion, *n.,* the act or effect of sulphurating.

sulphu′reous, *adj.,* full of, or resembling, sulphur.

sul′phuret, *n., i.q.* sulphide.

sul′phuretted, *adj.,* treated with sulphur.

sulphu′ric, *adj.,* pert. or rel. to, or containing, sulphur.

sul′phurize, *v.t., i.q.* sulphurate.

sul′phurous, *adj.,* produced by sulphur; like sulphur.

sul′phury, *adj.,* like sulphur.

sul′tan, *n.,* the head of the Ottoman Empire; any Mohammedan ruler.

sulta′na, *n.,* the fem. of sultan; a variety of raisin.

sul′tanate, *n.,* the office of a sultan.

sul′tanship, *n.,* the office or rank of a sultan.

sul′trily, *adv.,* in a sultry way.

sul′triness, *n.,* the quality or state of being sultry.

sul′try, *adj.,* hot and oppressive.

sum, *n.,* a total amount; the whole; an arithmetical problem; an aggregate of money; *v.t.,* to reckon up the total; to summarize.

su′mac(h), *n.,* a tree or shrub of the Rhus genus; also *i.q.* shumac.

Suma′tran, *adj.,* pert. or rel. to Sumatra, an Indonesian island; *n.,* a native of S.

sum′marily, *adv.,* in a summary fashion.

sum′marize, *v.t.,* to reduce to a concise statement.

sum′marized, *p.p.,* summarize.

sum′marizing, *pr.p.,* summarize.

sum′mary, *adj.,* done on the spot or at once; abrupt; concise; *n.,* a concise abstract.

summa′tion, *n.,* the act of summing; the aggregate.

summed, *p.p.,* sum.

sum′mer, *n.,* the second season of the year; the period of maximum growth and maturity; a timber on which the end of a joint rests; *v.i.,* to pass the summer.

sum′mered, *p.p.,* summer.

sum′mer-house, *n.,* a shelter in a garden.

sum′mering, *pr.p.,* summer.

sum′merish, *adj., i.q.* summery.

sum′mersault, *n., i.q.* somersault.

sum′merset, *n., i.q.* somersault.

sum′mer-time, *n.,* the period of summer; the time adjusted to prolong the use of daylight.

sum′mery, *adj.,* like, or suitable for, summer.

sum′ming, *pr.p.,* sum.

sum′ming-up, *n.,* a recapitulation (esp. of evidence by a judge to a jury).

sum′mit, *n.,* the top; the highest point.

sum′mitless, *adj.,* without a top; too high to be scaled.

sum′mon, *v.t.,* to call upon; to command the appearance of; to rally.

sum′moned, *p.p.,* summon.

sum′moner, *n.,* one who summons.

sum′moning, *pr.p.,* summon.

sum′mons, *n. pl.,* a writ commanding appearance in court; a call; *v.t.,* to serve with a summons.

sump, *n.,* a pit or well for drainage; a cesspool; in a car, the container for engine oil.

sumph, *n.,* a stupid fellow (*Scot.*).

sump′ter, *adj.,* used for carrying baggage; *n.,* a baggage-horse.

sump′tion, *n.,* the major premiss of syllogism.

sump′tuary, *adj.,* pert. or rel. to expenditure and in restraint of extravagance, especially in matters of dress and diet.

sump′tuous, *adj.,* costly, luxurious.

sump′tuously, *adv.,* in a sumptuous way.

sump′tuousness, *n.,* costliness; magnificence.

sun, *n.,* the star which is the centre of our solar system; any central orb; the sunshine; *v.t.,* to expose to the sun's influence.

sun′-bath, *n.,* exposure of the body to the sun.

sun′bathe, *v.i.,* to take a sun-bath.

sun′bathed, *p.p.,* sunbathe.

sun′bather, *n.,* one who sunbathes.

sun′bathing, *pr.p.,* sunbathe.

sun′beam, *n.,* a ray from the sun.

sun′blind, *n.,* a window shade.

sun′burn, *n.,* the burning of the skin by the sun; sun-tan; a colour used in textiles.

sun′burned, *adj., i.q.* sunburnt.

sun′burnt, *adj.,* tanned by the sun.

sun′dae, *n.,* an ice-cream confection with crushed fruit, etc.

Sun′day, *n.,* the first day of the week; the Lord's Day in the Christian faith; *adj.,* pert. or rel. to Sunday.

Sun′dayfied, *adj.,* Sunday-like.

sun′der, *v.t.,* to sever; to divide.

sun′dew, *n.,* a small bog plant.

sun′dial, *n.,* a dial showing the time by means of a shadow cast by the sun.

sun′down, *n.,* sunset.

sun′dried, *adj.,* dried in the sun.

sun′dries, *n. pl.,* odds and ends; a variety of things.

sun′dry, *adj.,* several; various.

sun′fish, *n.,* a circular fish.

sun′flower, *n.,* a tall, yellow flower with ray-like petals.

sung, *p.p.,* sing.

sun'glasses, n., glasses to protect the eyes from the sun's rays.

sun'-hat, n., a hat worn to give protection against the sun.

sunk, p.p., sink.

sunk'en, adj., sunk; pressed down.

sun'-lamp, n., a sun-ray lamp.

sun'less, adj., without sun.

sun'lessness, n., the state of being without sun.

sun'light, n., the light of the sun.

sun'lighted, adj., lighted by the sun.

sun'like, adj., like a sun.

sun'lit, adj., i.q. sunlighted.

sunn, n., i.q. sunnin.

Sun'na, n., traditional Mohammedan laws orally handed down.

sunned, p.p., sun.

sun'ni, n., a Mohammedan who accepts the Sunna as well as the Koran (see Shiah).

sun'nier, adj., comp. of sunny.

sun'niest, adj., super. of sunny.

sun'nily, adv., in a sunny fashion.

sunnin, n., hemp-like fibre.

sun'niness, n., the quality or state of being sunny.

sun'ning, pr.p., sun.

Sun'nite, n., a Mohammedan adherent of the precepts of the Sunna.

sun'ny, adj., bright; warmed and brightened by the sun; cheerful.

sun'proof, adj., impervious to the sun's rays.

sun'-ray, adj., by ultraviolet rays; n., a sunbeam.

sun'rise, n., the dawn.

sun'rising, n., the coming of the dawn.

sun'roof, n., a roof (usu. motor car) which will open to admit sunlight.

sun'set, n., the setting of the sun below the horizon.

sun'shade, n., a parasol.

sun'shine, n., the shining of the sun; warmth and brightness.

sun'shiny, adj., full of sunshine.

sun'spot, n., a dark patch on the sun's surface.

sun'stone, n., a kind of quartz (felspar).

sun'stroke, n., a brain affection caused by excessive exposure to sun-heat.

sun'struck, adj., affected with sunstroke.

sun'wards, adv., towards the sun.

sun'-wor'ship, n., the cult of worshipping the sun.

sup, n., a small quantity of liquid food; v.i., to take supper; v.t., to sip.

su'per, a Lat. prep. used as a prefix in the sense of over, to excess, beyond; adj., excellent (colloq.); n., a supernumerary actor (colloq.).

su'perable, adj., able to be overcome.

superabound', v.i., to abound to excess.

superabun'dance, n., abundance beyond what is needed.

superabun'dant, adj., abounding to excess.

superabun'dantly, adv., in a superabundant way.

superadd', v.t., to add over and above.

superaddi'tion, n., addition over and above.

superangel'ic, adj., above ordinary angelic rank.

superan'nuate, v.t., to discharge on account of age; to pension off.

superan'nuated, p.p., superannuate.

superan'nuating, pr.p., superannuate.

superannua'tion, n., retirement on account of age; retirement pension.

superb', adj., proud, magnificent.

superb'ly, adv., in a superb way.

supercar'go, n., one who has the charge of the cargo on a merchant vessel; a person with no defined position in a ship's complement.

sup'erceles'tial, adj., more than heavenly.

super'charger, n., a device for increasing the pressure of a power unit.

supercil'iary, adj., over the eye.

supercil'ious, adj., disdainful; haughty.

supercil'iously, adv., in a supercilious way.

supercil'iousness, n., the quality or state of being supercilious.

su'per-du'per, adj., superlatively good (slang).

superem'inence, n., very high eminence.

superem'inent, adj., very eminent.

supereroga'tion, n., doing more than one is called upon to do.

supererog'atory, adj., of the nature of supererogation.

superex'cellence, n., excellence in a high degree.

superex'cellent, adj., excellent in a high degree.

superfi'cial, adj., pert. or rel. to the surface; shallow; unsound; not thorough.

superficial'ity, n., the quality or state of being superficial.

superfi'cially, adv., in a superficial way; on the surface.

superfi'cies, n., surface; the superficial area.

su'perfine, adj., exceedingly fine; very choice.

superflu'ity, n., an overabundance.

super'fluous, adj., overabundant; unnecessary.

super'fluously, adv., over-abundantly.

superheat', v.t., to heat to a very high temperature (esp. water to steam).

superhet', n., the abbrev. for superheterodyne.

superhet'erodyne, n., a selective radio receiving circuit.

superhigh'way, n., a motorway.

superhu'man, adj., more than human.

superimpose', v.t., to lay on the top.

superimposed', p.p., superimpose.

superimpo'sing, pr.p., superimpose.

superimposi'tion, n., a laying on top of something else.

superincum'bent, adj., lying on the top.

superinduce', v.t., to bring on in addition.

superinduced', p.p., superinduce.

superindu'cing, *pr.p.,* superinduce.

superintend', *v.t.,* to look after; to have the oversight of.

superintend'ed, *p.p.,* superintend.

superintend'ence, *n.,* the act of superintending; the duty of a superintendent.

superintend'ency, *n., i.q.* superintendence.

superintend'ent, *n.,* one who superintends.

superintend'ing, *pr.p.,* superintend.

supe'rior, *adj.,* higher; of better quality; surpassing; affectedly better than others; *n.,* the head of a religious community.

superior'ity, *n.,* the quality or state of being superior; advantage.

super'lative, *adj.,* excellent in the highest degree; *n.,* a degree of comparison denoting the highest.

super'latively, *adv.,* in a superlative degree.

superlu'nar, *adj.,* above the moon. (Also *supralunar.*)

superlu'nary, *adj., i.q.* superlunar.

su'perman, *n.,* an ideal, superior man.

su'permarine, *n.,* a type of seaplane.

su'permarket, *n.,* a large, usu. self-service store.

supermun'dane, *adj.,* above the world; not concerned with everyday things.

super'nal, *adj.,* pert. or rel. to the upper regions; heavenly.

superna'tant, *adj.,* floating above the surface.

supernat'ural, *adj.,* outside and above the ordinary laws of nature.

supernat'uralism, *n.,* the quality or state of being supernatural; the teaching that God is known only through revelation.

supernat'uralist, *n.,* a believer in supernaturalism.

supernat'urally, *adv.,* in a supernatural way or sense.

super'nova, *n.,* a newly formed starry mass of great size and energy.

supernu'merary, *adj.,* additional beyond a required number; *n.,*

a person taken on above the full complement.

superphos'phate, *n.,* a phosphate of extra strength as regards the proportion of phosphoric acid.

superpose', *v.t.,* to put on the top.

superposed', *p.p.,* superpose.

superposi'tion, *n.,* the act of putting on top; the state of being put on top.

super'-roy'al, *adj.,* more than royal; *adj.* and *n.,* the paper size next above royal.

superscribe', *v.t.,* to write over, or at the head.

superscribed', *p.p.,* superscribe.

superscri'bing, *pr.p.,* superscribe.

superscrip'tion, *n.,* the act of superscribing; that which is superscribed.

supersede', *v.t.,* to take the place of; to depose.

superse'deas, *n.,* the legal permission to supersede (*Lat.*).

superse'ded, *p.p.,* supersede.

superse'ding, *pr.p.,* supersede.

supersen'sitive, *adj.,* touchy; excessively sensitive.

supersen'sory, *adj.,* beyond the ordinary senses.

supersen'sual, *adj.,* above the senses; spiritual.

superses'sion, *n.,* the act or result of superseding.

superson'ic, *adj.,* relating to sound-waves of too high a frequency to be audible; of a speed faster than sound.

su'persound, *n.,* vibrations of the same type as sound, but too rapid to be audible.

supersti'tion, *n.,* excessive devotion to illogical beliefs or unworthy religious observances.

supersti'tious, *adj.,* believing in irrational occurrences or possibilities; having primitive religious beliefs.

supersti'tiously, *adv.,* in a superstitious way.

superstra'tum, *n.,* a layer over another.

superstruc'ture, *n.,* a structure over a substructure.

su'pertax, *n., i.q.* surtax.

superton'ic, *n.,* the second note in the diatonic scale (*mus.*).

supervene', *v.i.,* to come on, not as a consequence but merely as an after event.

supervened', *p.p.,* supervene.

superve'nient, *adj.,* supervening.

superve'ning, *pr.p.,* supervene.

superven'tion, *n.,* the act or state of supervening.

supervi'sal, *n., i.q.* supervision.

supervise', *v.t.,* to superintend; to look after as an overseer.

supervised', *p.p.,* supervise.

supervi'sing, *pr.p.,* supervise.

supervi'sion, *n.,* the act of supervising; an overseer's duty.

supervi'sor, *n.,* one who supervises.

supervi'sory, *adj.,* of the nature of supervision.

su'pinate, *v.t.,* to turn on its back.

supina'tion, *n.,* the act of laying on its back; the state of being so placed.

sup'inator, *n.,* a muscle enabling a part of the body to be turned through 180°.

supine', *adj.,* lying on the back; indolent; feeble.

su'pine, *n.,* one of the two Lat. verbal nouns in *-um* and *-u.*

supine'ly, *adv.,* in a supine way.

supine'ness, *n.,* the quality or state of being supine.

supped, *p.p.,* sup.

sup'per, *n.,* an evening meal.

sup'perless, *adj.,* without a supper.

sup'ping, *pr.p.,* sup.

supplant', *v.t.,* to supersede; to take another's place.

supplanta'tion, *n.,* the act of supplanting.

supplant'ed, *p.p.,* supplant.

supplant'er, n., one who supplants.

supplant'ing, pr.p., supplant.

sup'ple, adj., lissom; very free and flexible in movement; obsequious; v.i., to become flexible; v.t., to make flexible.

sup'pled, p.p., supple.

sup'plement, n., something added to fill up; an addition at the end of, or inserted into, a book or treatise; an extra sheet or sheets in a newspaper; v.t., to make additions to.

supplemen'tal, adj., pert. or rel. to a supplement; additional.

supplemen'tary, adj., i.q. supplemental.

supplementa'tion, n., the act of providing a supplement; the actual supplement itself.

sup'pleness, n., the quality or state of being supple; flexibility.

sup'pliant, n., a petitioner; one who supplicates.

sup'plicant, adj., supplicating; n., i.q. suppliant.

sup'plicate, v.t., to implore; to entreat humbly.

sup'plicated, p.p., supplicate.

sup'plicating, pr.p., supplicate.

supplica'tion, n., the act of supplication.

sup'plicator, n., one who supplicates.

sup'plicatory, adj., making supplication; in the character of a suppliant.

supplied', p.p., supply.

suppli'er, n., one who supplies.

supplies', n. pl., stores; provisions; money for necessary purposes.

supply', n., an adequate amount or quantity; v.t., to furnish; to give what is necessary; to provide; to stand for; to fill a vacant post.

supply'ing, pr.p., supply.

support', n., help; countenance; maintenance; confirmation; v.t., to hold up; to defend; to take the side of; to supply with maintenance.

support'able, adj., able to be supported.

support'ed, p.p., support.

support'er, n., one who, or that which, supports. In the pl., the savage men, or strange beasts, or other heraldic emblems (as the lion and the unicorn) supporting certain privileged coats of arms (her.).

support'ing, pr.p., support.

suppo'sable, adj., able to be supposed.

suppose', v.i. and t., to imagine; to assume; to think.

supposed', p.p., suppose.

suppos'edly, adv., according to what is believed or said.

suppos'ing, pr.p., suppose.

supposi'tion, n., the act of supposing; that which is supposed.

supposi'tional, adj., of the nature of supposition.

suppositi'tious, adj., imaginary; false.

suppos'itive, adj., making supposition.

suppos'itory, adj., a solid medicine introduced into the body through an orifice, usu. the anus.

suppress', v.t., to crush down; to quell; to conceal.

suppressed', p.p., suppress.

suppress'ible, adj., capable of being suppressed.

suppress'ing, pr.p., suppress.

suppres'sion, n., the act or effect of suppressing.

suppress'ive, adj., with the effect of suppressing.

suppress'or, n., one who suppresses; an electrical device to prevent interference with other electrical devices.

sup'purate, v.i., to discharge pus.

sup'purated, p.p., suppurate.

sup'purating, pr.p., suppurate.

suppura'tion, n., the discharge of pus.

sup'purative, adj., suppurating.

sup'ra, adv., above; previously (Lat.).

supra-ax'illary, adj., above the armpit.

supracil'iary, adj., above the eyelids.

supralapsa'rian, adj., pert. or rel. to the high Calvinistic doctrine that election was decreed before the Fall.

supralapsa'rianism, n., the supralapsarian doctrine.

supralun'ar, adj., i.q. superlunar.

supramun'dane, adj., above the world or the worldly.

suprana'tional, adj., overriding national authority.

supra-or'bital, adj., above the orbit.

suprem'acy, n., the quality or state of being supreme; a position of complete command.

supreme', adj., highest above all; utmost.

supreme'ly, adv., in the highest degree.

su'ra(h), n., a division of the Koran.

su'ra, n., cocoa-palm juice.

su'rah, n., a silky material.

su'ral, adj., pert. or rel. to the calf of the leg.

surat', n., a coarse make of cotton.

surbase', v.t., to flatten.

sur'base, n., mouldings, etc., on the base of a column, etc.

surbase'ment, n., a flattened state.

surbed', adj., laid edgeways (as of stone setts).

surcease', n., cessation; v.i., to cease.

surcharge', v.t., to charge in excess.

sur'charge, n., an overcharge.

surcharged', p.p., surcharge.

surcharg'ing, pr.p., surcharge.

sur'cingle, n., a girdle, belt or band going round a body.

sur'coat, n., a topcoat.

surc'ulose, adj., producing suckers.

surd, adj., not to be expressed in rational numbers; n., in mathematics, a quantity not to be expressed in rational numbers.

sure, *adj.*, certain; reliable; safe; *adv.*, *i.q.* surely.

sure′footed, *adj.*, steady on the foot; not tripping.

sure′ly, *adv.*, certainly; truly; without danger.

sure′ness, *n.*, the quality or state of being sure.

sur′er, *adj.*, *comp.* of sure.

sur′est, *adj.*, *super.* of sure.

sûreté, *n.*, the criminal investigation department in France.

sure′ty, *n.*, a sponsor; one who gives guarantees; bail; an amount pledged as a guarantee.

sure′tyship, *n.*, the office or obligation of a surety.

surf, *n.*, broken foaming water, moving in on a shore.

sur′face, *n.*, the upper or outside face of a thing; superficies.

sur′face-car, *n.*, a tramcar (*Amer.*).

surf′board, *n.*, a board for riding on waves breaking into surf.

surf′boat, *n.*, a buoyant boat for use in surf.

sur′feit, *n.*, fulness to satiety; eating and drinking to excess; an excess; *v.i.*, to eat and drink to excess; *v.t.*, to fill to satiety.

sur′feited, *p.p.*, surfeit.

sur′feiting, *pr.p.*, surfeit.

surfi′cial, *adj.*, superficial.

surf′riding, *n.*, riding on a surfboard.

surge, *n.*, a great wave; a swell; *v.i.*, to flow in a great wave.

surged, *p.p.*, surge.

sur′geon, *n.*, a person qualified to perform operations for the relief of bodily diseases or injuries.

sur′geoncy, *n.*, an army or naval surgeon's position.

sur′gery, *n.*, a doctor's consulting room; the art and science of performing operations on bodily tissue; a place for such operations.

sur′gical, *adj.*, pert. or rel. to surgeons and surgery.

sur′gically, *adv.*, in a surgical way.

sur′ging, *pr.p.*, surge.

sur′gy, *adj.*, surging.

sur′icate, *n.*, a S. African ferret-like animal.

sur′liness, *n.*, the quality or state of being surly.

surloin, *n.*, *i.q.* sirloin.

sur′ly, *adj.*, morose; gruff; ill-conditioned.

sur′master, *n.*, a second master.

surmis′able, *adj.*, able to be surmised.

surmise′, *n.*, conjecture; suspicion; *v.t.*, to conjecture; to suppose; to suspect.

surmised′, *p.p.*, surmise.

surmi′sing, *pr.p.*, surmise.

surmount′, *v.t.*, to overcome; to ascend above.

surmount′able, *adj.*, able to be surmounted.

surmount′ed, *p.p.*, surmount.

surmount′er, *n.*, one who surmounts.

surmount′ing, *pr.p.*, surmount.

surmull′et, *n.*, the red mullet.

sur′name, *n.*, a family or additional name; *v.t.*, to give this additional name.

sur′named, *p.p.*, surname.

sur′naming, *pr.p.*, surname.

surpass′, *v.t.*, to go beyond; to exceed; to excel.

surpass′able, *adj.*, able to be surpassed.

surpassed′, *p.p.*, surpass.

surpass′ing, *adj.*, exceeding; *pr.p.*, surpass.

surpass′ingly, *adv.*, exceedingly.

sur′plice, *n.*, a white linen vestment.

sur′pliced, *adj.*, wearing a surplice.

sur′plus, *n.*, an overplus; something over and above what is necessary.

sur′plusage, *n.*, the amount of a surplus.

surpri′sal, *n.*, the act of surprising; the state of being surprised.

surprise′, *n.*, the state of being caught unawares; astonishment; an unexpected event; *v.t.*, to take unexpectedly; to attack suddenly; to amaze.

surprised′, *p.p.*, surprise.

surpri′sing, *adj.*, astonishing; *pr.p.*, surprise.

surpri′singly, *adv.*, in a surprising way.

sur′ra, *n.*, a form of anaemia affecting horses and cattle in the tropics.

surre′alism, *n.*, a 20th century movement in art and literature purporting to express the subconscious mind.

surre′alist, *n.*, a sculptor, writer or artist who practises surrealism.

surre′alistic, *adj.*, pert. or rel. to surrealism.

surrebut′, *v.i.*, to answer a rebut.

surrebut′ted, *p.p.*, surrebut.

surrebut′ter, *n.*, one who surrebuts.

surrebut′ting, *pr.p.*, surrebut.

surrejoin′, *v.i.*, to reply to a rejoinder.

surrejoin′der, *n.*, a reply to a rejoinder.

surren′der, *n.*, the act of surrendering; *v.i.*, to yield; to give up; *v.t.*, to resign the possession of or claim to; to yield.

surren′dered, *p.p.*, surrender.

surrenderee′, *n.*, one to whom anything is surrendered.

surren′derer, *n.*, one who surrenders.

surren′dering, *pr.p.*, surrender.

surrepti′tious, *adj.*, stealthy; underhand; secret.

surrepti′tiously, *adv.*, in a surreptitious way.

sur′rey, *n.*, a light, two-seater, four-wheeled carriage.

sur′rogate, *n.*, a bishop's official, having licensing powers.

surround′, *n.*, a panel, planking or decoration going round a wall or fireplace; *v.t.*, to encircle; to encompass; to invest.

surround′ed, *p.p.*, surround.

surround'ing, *pr.p.,* surround.

surtax', *v.t.,* to overtax.

sur'tax, *n.,* a graduated additional tax on incomes above an imposed limit.

surtout', *n.,* a long coat (*Fr.*).

surveil'lance, *n.,* supervision; watch; overseeing (*Fr.*).

survey', *v.t.,* to examine visually; to scan; to estimate a land surface by measurement.

sur'vey, *n.,* the act of surveying; an examination.

survey'al, *n.,* the act of surveying.

surveyed, *p.p.,* survey.

survey'ing, *n.,* the profession of a surveyor; *pr.p.,* survey.

survey'or, *n.,* one who surveys; one qualified in land or property surveying.

survey'orship, *n.,* the office of a surveyor.

survi'val, *n.,* the act of surviving; that which has survived.

survive', *v.i.* and *t.,* to outlive; to live on.

survived', *p.p.,* survive.

survi'ving, *pr.p.,* survive.

survi'vor, *n.,* one who has survived.

survi'vorship, *n.,* the state of being a survivor; a reversion that depends upon some life.

susceptibil'ity, *n.,* the state of being susceptible.

suscep'tible, *adj.,* able to be influenced by changes, appeals to the affection, sensations, etc.; capable of being impressed; having sensibility; easily influenced.

suscep'tibly, *adv.,* in a susceptible way.

suscep'tive, *adj., i.q.* susceptible.

sus'citate, *v.t.,* to bring to life; to rouse.

sus'citated, *p.p.,* suscitate.

sus'citating, *pr.p.,* suscitate.

sus'citation, *n.,* a bringing to life.

sus'i, *n.,* silk striped cotton fabric (*Hind.*).

sus'pect, *n.,* a suspected person.

suspect', *v.t.,* to have under suspicion; to believe, but without proof; to mistrust.

suspect'able, *adj.,* able to be suspected.

suspect'ed, *p.p.,* suspect.

suspect'er, *n.,* one who suspects.

suspect'ing, *pr.p.,* suspect.

suspend', *v.t.,* to hang up; to defer; to debar from office; to temporarily withdraw privileges.

suspend'ed, *p.p.,* suspend.

suspend'er, *n.,* one who, or that which, suspends.

suspen'ders, *n. pl.,* braces to hold up trousers, stockings, etc.

suspend'ing, *pr.p.,* suspend.

suspense', *n.,* an anxious state of mind while something is awaited; the reservation of judgment; a temporary abeyance of one's rights.

suspensibil'ity, *n.,* the quality or state of being suspensible.

suspen'sible, *adj.,* able to be suspended or held up.

suspen'sion, *n.,* the act of suspending; the state of being suspended or in suspense; abeyance; in music, the holding of a note while passing from one chord to another.

suspen'sor, *n.,* that which suspends, esp. a supporting bandage.

suspen'sory, *adj.,* having the effect of holding up or delaying.

suspi'cion, *n.,* a feeling of mistrust; a conjecture; a hint; just a little; a very small quantity.

suspi'cious, *adj.,* feeling suspicion; arousing suspicion.

suspi'ciously, *adv.,* in a suspicious way.

suspira'tion, *n.,* sighing.

suspire', *v.i.,* to sigh.

suspired', *p.p.,* suspire.

suspi'ring, *pr.p.,* suspire.

sustain', *v.t.,* to support; to bear; to nourish; to continue.

sustain'able, *adj.,* able to be sustained.

sustained', *p.p.,* sustain.

sustain'er, *n.,* one who, or that which, sustains.

sustain'ing, *adj.,* nourishing; *pr.p.,* sustain.

sustain'ment, *n.,* the act or result of sustaining.

sus'tenance, *n.,* support; a means of living; nourishment.

sustenta'tion, *n.,* support; relief.

susurra'tion, *n.,* whispering, rustling.

susur'rous, *adj.,* pert. or rel. to susurration.

sut'ler, *n.,* a camp follower who sells provisions, etc.

suttee', *n.,* the old Hindu custom for a widow to offer her life on her husband's funeral pyre.

suttee'ism, *n.,* the system of suttee.

sut'tle, *n.,* weight after the deduction of tare before tret has been reckoned.

Sut'ra, *n.,* a set of aphorisms in Sanscrit literature.

su'tural, *adj.,* pert. or rel. to a suture.

su'ture, *n.,* a joint by sewing; the markings of the skull's joints; a seam.

su'tured, *adj.,* pert. or rel. to suture.

su'zerain, *n.,* a supreme ruler; an overlord.

su'zerainty, *n.,* the rank or office of a suzerain.

svelte, *adj.,* lightly built; supple; lissom (*Fr.*).

swab, *n.,* a ship's mop; a lout; *v.t.,* to mop up.

swabbed, *p.p.,* swab.

swab'ber, *n.,* one who swabs.

swab'bing, *pr.p.,* swab.

swad'dle, *v.t.,* to wrap in long loose robes; to swathe.

swad'dled, *p.p.,* swaddle.

swad'dling, *pr.p.,* swaddle.

swad'dling-band, *n., i.q.* swaddling-clothes.

swad'dling-clothes, *n.,* a newborn infant's wrapping.

swag, *n.,* a sagging movement; a thief's booty (*slang*); *v.i.,* to sink down heavily.

swage, *n.,* a die used in wrought iron work; *v.t.,* to shape with a swage.

swagged, *p.p.*, swag.

swag'ger, *n.*, bragging; walking in a conceited way; *v.i.*, to give oneself airs; to walk with a strut.

swag'ger-coat, *n.*, a short, loose jacket.

swag'gered, *p.p.*, swagger.

swag'gerer, *n.*, one who swaggers.

swag'gering, *pr.p.*, swagger.

swag'ging, *pr.p.*, swag.

Swahi'li, *n.*, the natives of Zanzibar and the adjacent coasts; an E. African language.

swain, *n.*, a rustic; a lover.

swale, *v.t.*, *i.q.* sweal.

swaled, *p.p.*, swale.

swa'ling, *pr.p.*, swale.

swal'let, *n.*, an underground stream.

swal'low, *n.*, a migratory bird; the act of swallowing; the amount swallowed; *v.i.*, to take down through the mouth; to engulf; to submit to; to accept with credulity (*colloq.*).

swal'lowed, *p.p.*, swallow.

swal'lower, *n.*, one who swallows.

swal'lowing, *pr.p.*, swallow.

swal'lowtail, *n.*, something resembling a swallow's tail; a dress-coat.

swal'low-tailed, *adj.*, shaped like a swallow's tail.

swal'lowwort, *n.*, a herb; celandine.

swam, *p.p.*, swim.

swa'mi, *n.*, an Hindu idol; a Hindu religious teacher.

swamp, *n.*, a marsh; a morass; *v.t.*, to plunge into a swamp; to overturn a boat; to overwhelm; to over-fill with water.

swamped, *p.p.*, swamp.

swamp'ing, *pr.p.*, swamp.

swamp'y, *adj.*, marshy.

swan, *n.*, a large, long-necked, web-footed aquatic bird.

swan'herd, *n.*, an officer in charge of swans.

swank, *n.*, swagger; *v.i.*, to show off, to bluff; to show conceit (*slang*).

swanked, *p.p.*, swank.

swank'er, *n.*, one who swanks.

swank'iness, *n.*, *i.q.* swank.

swank'ing, *pr.p.*, swank.

swank'y, *adj.*, showy, ostentatious.

swan'like, *adj.*, resembling a swan.

swan'neck, *n.*, a curved end of a discharge-pipe; an S bend.

swan'nery, *n.*, a place where swans are kept.

swan'pan, *n.*, a Chinese abacus.

swans'down, *n.*, the soft down of a swan.

swan'song, *n.*, a person's last production, etc.; the fabled song of a dying swan.

swan'-up'per, *n.*, a man charged with the duty of marking swans.

swan'-up'ping, *n.*, the annual stock-taking and marking of swans.

swap, *n.* and *v.t.*, *i.q.* swop.

swapped, *p.p.*, swap.

swap'ping, *pr.p.*, swap.

swaraj', *n.*, an Indian self-government move-ment.

sward, *n.*, a stretch of grass.

swarf, *n.*, wood or metal filings.

swarm, *n.*, a moving crowd; a cluster, esp. of bees; *v.i.*, to move in crowds; to grow multitudinously; to migrate from a hive; *v.t.*, (with the added word *up*) to climb.

swarmed, *p.p.*, swarm.

swarm'ing, *pr.p.*, swarm.

swart, *adj.*, *i.q.* swarthy.

swart'back, *n.*, the black-headed gull.

swarth, *adj.*, *i.q.* swarthy; *n.*, a phantom (*Scot.*).

swarth'ily, *adv.*, in a swarthy way.

swarth'iness, *n.*, the state of being swarthy.

swarth'y, *adj.*, dark-complexioned.

swash, *n.*, water dashed about; slush; *v.t.*, to make a splash with water; to bluster.

swash'buckler, *n.*, a swaggering soldier of fortune.

swashed, *p.p.*, swash.

swash'ing, *adj.*, slashing; blustering; *pr.p.*, swash.

swas'tika, *n.*, the fylfot; the ancient emblem, a cross with equal arms, the ends of which are returned at right angles.

swat, *n.*, a sharp blow; *v.t.*, to slap or crush.

swatch, *n.*, a sample or pattern; a bunch or collection of samples or patterns.

swath, *n.*, the sweep of a scythe; the line where a scythe has mown.

swathe, *n.*, a rolled bandage; *v.t.*, to wrap a bandage round.

swathed, *p.p.*, swathe.

swa'thing, *pr.p.*, swathe.

swat'ted, *p.p.*, swat.

swat'ter, *n.*, a fly-whisk.

swat'ting, *pr.p.*, swat.

sway, *n.*, rule, dominion; the inclination of a balance; *v.i.*, to waver; to fall on one side, or backward and forward unsteadily; *v.t.*, to rule; to influence.

swayed, *p.p.*, sway.

sway'er, *n.*, one who sways.

sway'ing, *pr.p.*, sway.

sweal, *v.i.*, to melt away; to extinguish; *v.t.*, to scorch; to singe. (Also swale.)

swealed, *p.p.*, sweal.

sweal'ing, *pr.p.*, sweal.

swear, *v.i.*, to take oath; to use bad language; *v.t.*, to cause to take oath.

swear'er, *n.*, one who swears.

swear'ing, *pr.p.*, swear.

swear'-word, *n.*, a profane oath or word.

sweat, *n.*, perspiration; toil; *v.i.*, to perspire; to labour; *v.t.*, to overwork and under-pay.

sweat'ed, *p.p.*, sweat.

sweat'er, *n.*, one who sweats; a thick jersey.

sweat'ily, *adv.*, in a sweaty way.

sweat'iness, *n.*, the state of being sweaty.

sweat'ing, *n.*, employing people for an inadequate wage; *pr.p.*, sweat.

sweat'-shirt, *n.*, a short-sleeved, absorbent shirt.

sweat'y, *adj.*, perspiring; covered with sweat.

Swede, *n.*, a Swedish native; (without cap.) a kind of turnip.

Swedenbor'gian, *adj.*, pert. or rel. to Emanuel Swedenborg and his doctrines.

Swedenbor'gianism, *n.*, the religious system of Swedenborg's followers; the New Jerusalem.

Swe'dish, *adj.*, pert. or rel. to Sweden and the Swedes; *n.*, the language of Sweden.

sween'y, *n.*, muscular atrophy in horses.

sweep, *n.*, the act of sweeping; a range; the force of a blow; a large-sized oar; a broad movement across country; a chimney sweep; a low fellow (*colloq.*); *v.i.*, to rush along with violence or majestically; to make a long or wide movement; *v.t.*, to clear up with a broom; to drive or carry off with a violent rush; to gaze.

sweep'er, *n.*, one who, or that which, sweeps.

sweep'ing, *adj.*, wide in its application; *pr.p.*, sweep.

sweep'ingly, *adv.*, in a sweeping manner.

sweep'ings, *n. pl.*, what is swept up.

sweep'stakes, *n. pl.*, money staked on horse races or other competitions.

sweet, *adj.*, sugary; agreeable to taste; luscious; kind; gentle; fresh (*i.e.*, not stale); dear; in pl., as a *n.*, confectionery.

sweet'bread, *n.*, the pancreas in a calf.

sweet'-briar, *n.*, *i.q.* sweet-brier.

sweet'-brier, *n.*, the eglantine.

sweet'en, *v.t.*, to make sweet in any sense.

sweet'ened, *p.p.*, sweeten.

sweet'ener, *n.*, one who, or that which, sweetens.

sweet'ening, *n.*, something used in order to sweeten; *pr.p.*, sweeten.

sweet'er, *adj.*, *comp.* of sweet.

sweet'est, *adj.*, *super.* of sweet.

sweet'heart, *n.*, a lover; *v.t.*, to court.

sweet'ie, *n.*, a sweetheart (*colloq.*).

sweet'ing, *n.*, *i.q.* sweetheart (*obs.*).

sweet'ish, *adj.*, somewhat sweet.

sweet'ly, *adv.*, in a sweet way.

sweet'meat, *n.*, a sugary confection.

sweet'ness, *n.*, the quality or state of being sweet.

sweet'pea, *n.*, a flowering garden plant.

sweet'-scented, *adj.*, fragrant.

sweet'-smelling, *adj.*, fragrant.

sweet-will'iam, *n.*, a colourful flowering plant.

swell, *n.*, the state of swelling; increase; the rising of waves; a part of an organ in which the pipes are screened off by shutters, the gradual opening of which produces a swelling sound; a personage; a dandy (*colloq.*); *adj.*, distinguished; dandified; good; (*colloq.*); *v.i.*, to be inflated; to expand; to grow stronger or more violent; *v.t.*, to make to expand; to fill out; to increase.

swelled, *p.p.*, swell.

swell'ing, *n.*, a tumorous growth; *pr.p.*, swell.

swel'ter, *v.i.*, to sweat excessively; to be oppressed by heat.

swel'tered, *p.p.*, swelter.

swel'tering, *adj.*, overpoweringly hot; *pr.p.*, swelter.

swel'try, *adj.*, sultry.

swept, *p.p.*, sweep.

swerve, *n.*, a turning aside; a deviation; *v.i.*, to turn aside.

swerved, *p.p.*, swerve.

swerve'less, *adj.*, unswerving.

swerv'er, *n.*, one who, or that which, swerves.

swerv'ing, *pr.p.*, swerve.

swift, *adj.*, fast; rapid; sudden; *n.*, a kind of swallow; a rapid current.

swift'er, *adj.*, *comp.* of swift; *n.*, a temporary rope to tighten or steady things (*naut.*).

swift'est, *adj.*, *super.* of swift.

swift'let, *n.*, a young swift.

swift'ly, *adv.*, rapidly, suddenly, fast.

swift'ness, *n.*, the quality or state of being swift.

swig, *v.i.*, to be a drinker; *v.t.*, to drink.

swigged, *p.p.*, swig.

swig'ging, *pr.p.*, swig.

swill, *v.i.* and *t.*, to drink to excess; *v.t.*, to wash by pouring water over.

swilled, *p.p.*, swill.

swill'er, *n.*, one who, or that which, swills.

swill'ing, *pr.p.*, swill.

swim, *n.*, the act of swimming; a fish's air-bladder; the part of a lighter or boat that slopes towards the water; *v.i.*, to float and move through water; to be full to overflowing; to become dizzy; *v.t.*, to make to swim or float.

swim'mable, *adj.*, capable of being swum.

swim'mer, *n.*, one who, or that which, swims.

swim'meret, *n.*, a swimming-foot in crustaceans.

swim'ming, *n.*, supporting and moving oneself in the water; *pr.p.*, swim.

swim'mingly, *adv.*, easily; with success.

swin'dle, *n.*, the act of a swindler; *v.i.*, to be a swindler; *v.t.*, to cheat, esp. in money matters.

swin'dled, *p.p.*, swindle.

swin'dler, *n.*, one who swindles; a fraudulent person who cheats over money dealings.

swin'dling, *n.*, the practices of a swindler; *pr.p.*, swindle.

swine, *n.* and *n. pl.*, a pig or pigs.

swine'herd, n., one who tends swine.

swing, n., the act of swinging; the state of being swung; a hanging seat that can be swung to and fro; v.t. and i., to move to and fro; to oscillate; to be hanged; to move with freedom and enjoyment.

swing'-bridge, n., a bridge that is swung to make room for traffic.

swing'door, n., a self-closing door that opens inwards or outwards.

swinge, n., movement to and fro; sway; v.t., to thrash.

swinged, p.p., swinge.

swinge'ing, adj., violent, severe, vigorous; pr.p., swinge.

swin'gel, n., the striking part of a flail.

swing'er, n., one who swings.

swing'ing, adj., fashionable (colloq.); pr.p., swing.

swing'ingly, adv., in a swinging way.

swin'gle, v.i., to be pendent; v.t., to beat flax.

swin'gled, p.p., swingle.

swin'gletree, n., a crossbar pivoted in the centre to the ends of which a horse's traces are attached.

swin'gling, pr.p., swingle.

swin'ish, adj., like a swine; beastly.

swink, n. and v.i., toil.

swipe, n., a sweeping blow with a cricket bat; v.i. and t., to hit with a wild stroke.

swiped, p.p., swipe.

swip'er, n., one who swipes.

swipes, n. pl., thin beer; the collected remains of beer.

swip'ing, pr.p., swipe.

swirl, n., the motion of eddying water; v.i., to eddy.

swirled, p.p., swirl.

swirl'ing, pr.p., swirl.

swish, adj., very smart (colloq.); n., the sound of a stroke with a birch, etc.; v.t., to flog.

Swiss, adj., pert. or rel. to Switzerland and the Swiss; n., a native of S.

switch, n., a thin rod; a device for shunting on a railway; a device for controlling electric currents; v.t., to shunt; to turn on or off; to thrash.

switch'back, adj., with a succession of ascents and descents; n., an up-and-down track.

switch'band, n., a contrivance for cutting or making an electric current.

switch'board, n., a board on which electric switches are placed, showing their controls; a central control for telephones.

switched, p.p., switch.

switch'ing, pr.p., switch.

switch'man, n., a man in charge of switches.

swith'er, n., uncertainty; v.i., to hesitate.

Swit'zer, n., a Swiss.

swiv'el, n., something that revolves within another thing; a revolving cannon; v.i., to turn; v.t., to make to move on a pivot.

swiz(z), n., a swindle. (colloq.).

swiz'zle, n., compounded intoxicating drink; v.i., to drink excessively; to mix a drink.

swiz'zle-stick, n., an ornamental stick for mixing a drink.

swoll'en, p.p., swell.

swoon, n., a fainting-fit; v.i., to faint.

swooned, p.p., swoon.

swoon'ing, n., a syncope; pr.p., swoon.

swoon'ingly, adv., in a swooning way.

swoop, n., the act of swooping and seizing; v.i. and t., to fly or spring down upon a thing.

swooped, p.p., swoop.

swoop'ing, pr.p., swoop.

swop, n., exchange, barter; v.t., to barter, to exchange. (Also swap.)

swopped, p.p., swop.

swop'ping, pr.p., swop.

sword, n., a cutting and stabbing weapon; the emblem of war, power of life and death, justice, etc.

sword'-bayonet, n., a bayonet shaped like a short sword.

sword'-belt, n., a belt from which a sword is suspended.

sword'-blade, n., the blade of a sword.

sword'-cane, n., a cane containing a sword.

sword'-dance, n., a dance with or amongst swords.

sword'fish, n., a fish with a sword-like projection.

sword'-shaped, adj., shaped like a sword.

swords'man, n., one skilled in the use of the sword.

swords'manship, n., the art of the swordsman.

swore, p.p., swear.

sworn, adj., bound by promise or oath; p.p., swear.

swot, n., one who studies; v.i. and t., to study hard (slang).

swot'ted, p.p., swot.

swot'ting, pr.p., swot.

swum, p.p., swim.

swung, p.p., swing.

Syb'arite, n., a luxurious person; a native of the ancient Italian city, Sybaris, notorious for extravagance.

Sybarit'ic, adj., like a Sybarite.

syc'amine, n., a black mulberry tree.

syc'amore, n., a large timber tree of the maple variety.

syce, n., a groom (India).

sycee', n., Chinese silver currency.

sychnocarp'ous, adj., semi-perennial fruit bearing (bot.).

sycon'ium, n., a multiple fruit (bot.).

syc'ophancy, n., the act or character of a sycophant.

syc'ophant, n., a hypocritical flatterer, a parasite.

sycophan'tic, adj., like a sycophant.

sycophan'tish, adj., i.q. sycophantic.

sycophan'tize, v.i., to play the sycophant.

sycos'is, *n.*, barber's itch, a skin disease of the face and scalp.

sy'enite, *n.*, an Egyptian granite rock. (Also *sienite*.)

syenit'ic, *adj.*, pert. or rel. to syenite.

syllaba'rium, *n.*, a list of the root syllables of a language.

syl'labary, *n.*, *i.q.* syllabarium.

syllab'ic, *adj.*, pert. or rel. to syllables.

syllab'ically, *adv.*, syllable by syllable.

syllab'icate, *v.t.*, to form into or pronounce as separate syllables.

syllabica'tion, *n.*, formation into syllables.

syllab'ify, *v.t.*, *i.q.* syllabicate.

syll'abize, *v.t.*, to divide into or articulate by syllables.

syl'lable, *n.*, a letter or group of letters that can be pronounced by a single vocal effort.

syl'labub, *n.*, *i.q.* sillabub.

syl'labus, *n.*, a conspectus; an abstract (esp. of a course of study).

syllep'sis, *n.*, the application of a word to others in different senses in the same expression.

syl'logism, *n.*, a logical term describing the drawing of a conclusion from two premises.

syllogis'tic, *adj.*, pert. or rel. to syllogism; in the form of a syllogism.

syllogiza'tion, *n.*, the act of making syllogisms.

syl'logize, *v.i.*, to make syllogisms; *v.t.*, to throw into the form of a syllogism.

syl'logized, *p.p.*, syllogize.

syl'logizer, *n.*, one who syllogizes.

syl'logizing, *pr.p.*, syllogize.

sylph, *n.*, a fairy; a sprite.

sylph'id, *adj.*, sylphlike.

sylph'like, *adj.*, slender; graceful.

syl'va, *n.*, *i.q.* silva.

syl'van, *adj.*, *i.q.* silvan.

syl'vanite, *n.*, a tellurid.

syl'viculture, *n.*, *i.q.* silviculture.

sym'bol, *n.*, a token, pledge, sign or creed.

symbol'ic, *adj.*, pert. or rel. to a symbol; expressed in symbols.

symbol'ical, *adj.*, *i.q.* symbolic.

symbol'ically, *adv.*, in a symbolic way.

symbol'ics, *n. pl.*, the study of creeds.

sym'bolism, *n.*, expression by means of symbols; the meaning of a thing interpreted by metaphors and tokens.

sym'bolist, *n.*, one who studies creeds.

symboliza'tion, *n.*, the use of symbols.

sym'bolize, *v.t.*, to mean symbolically.

sym'bolized, *p.p.*, symbolize.

sym'bolizing, *pr.p.*, symbolize.

symbol'ogy, *n.*, the study of symbols.

sym'centre, *n.*, a centre of symmetry.

symmet'allism, *n.*, a monetary system using a silver-gold alloy as the standard metal.

symmet'ric, *adj.*, commensurate; in exact proportion; harmonious.

symmet'rical, *adj.*, *i.q.* symmetric.

symmet'rically, *adv.*, in a symmetrical way.

sym'metrize, *v.t.*, to make symmetrical.

sym'metrized, *p.p.*, symmetrize.

sym'metrizing, *pr.p.*, symmetrize.

sym'metry, *n.*, perfect proportion of parts; regularity of form; harmony.

sympathec'tomy, *n.*, an operation for the division of fibres which control specific involuntary muscles.

sympathet'ic, *adj.*, being in sympathy; compassionate; congenial.

sympathet'ical, *adj.*, *i.q.* sympathetic.

sympathet'ically, *adv.*, in a sympathetic way.

sym'pathize, *v.i.*, to show or feel sympathy or compassion.

sym'pathized, *p.p.*, sympathize.

sym'pathizer, *n.*, one who sympathizes.

sym'pathizing, *adj.*, *i.q.* sympathetic; *pr.p.*, sympathize.

sym'pathizingly, *adv.*, in a sympathizing way.

sym'pathy, *n.*, compassion; a feeling for another's sorrow or sharing in his pleasure; reciprocal action of bodily organs.

symphon'ic, *adj.*, pert. or rel. to symphony; concordant.

sympho'nious, *adj.*, *i.q.* symphonic.

sympho'niously, *adv.*, in a symphonic way.

sym'phonist, *n.*, a composer of symphonies (*mus.*).

sym'phony, *n.*, harmony; a concord of sounds; a musical orchestral work of a particular form; an instrumental beginning or ending to a vocal work.

sym'physis, *n.*, a union of parts; coalescence.

sympiesom'eter, *n.*, a barometer working by compression.

sympo'siac, *adj.*, pert. or rel. to a symposium.

sympo'siarch, *n.*, the master of a banquet.

sympo'siast, *n.*, one who shares in a literary symposium.

sympo'sium, *n.*, a drinking in company; a banquet; a joint literary work.

symp'tom, *n.*, a perceptible sign of a hidden cause; a token.

symptomat'ic, *adj.*, betokening.

symptomat'ically, *adv.*, in a symptomatic way.

symptomatol'ogy, *n.*, the study of symptoms.

syn, a Greek prefix = with, together.

synae'resis, *n.*, the combination of two vowels into a single sound.

synagog'ic, *adj.*, pert. or rel. to a synagogue.

synagog'ical, *adj.*, *i.q.* synagogic.

syn'agogue, *n.*, a congregation; an assembly; a Jewish place of worship.

syn'archy, *n.*, joint rule.

synarthro'sis, *n.*, congestion.

syncar'pous, *adj.*, having coherent carpels.

synch'romesh, *n.*, a system of gear changing with automatic correct timing of gear parts.

syn'chronal, *adj.*, *i.q.* synchronous.

synchron'ic, *adj.*, *i.q.* diachronic.

syn'chronism, *n.*, the coincidence of times.

synchroniza'tion, *n.*, the act or result of syncronizing.

syn'chronize, *v.i.*, to occur simultaneously; *v.t.*, to date simultaneously; to align in time.

syn'chronized, *p.p.*, synchronize.

syn'chronizing, *pr.p.*, synchronize.

syn'chronous, *adj.*, simultaneous. (Also *synchronal*.)

syn'chronously, *adv.*, simultaneously.

syncli'nal, *adj.*, pert. or rel. to a line that inclines till it meets a common line or point.

syn'copal, *adj.*, pert. or rel. to syncope.

syn'copate, *v.t.*, to shorten by cutting something out; in music, to borrow from a following note part of its accent and throw it on to part of the preceding note; to carry the sound of the last note of a bar into the first beat of the next bar.

syn'copated, *p.p.*, syncopate.

syn'copating, *pr.p.*, syncopate.

syncopa'tion, *n.*, the act of syncopating; the result of syncopating.

syn'copator, *n.*, a performer of syncopated music.

syn'cope, *n.*, a cutting out from the middle of a word; a fainting fit.

syncop'ic, *adj.*, *i.q.* syncoptic.

syn'copist, *n.*, one who practises syncopation.

syncop'tic, *adj.*, pert. or rel. to syncopation.

syncret'ic, *adj.*, pert. or rel. to syncretism.

syn'cretism, *n.*, the act of harmonizing contradictory beliefs; the result so obtained.

syn'cretist, *n.*, one who makes a syncretism.

syndac'tylous, *adj.*, having the same kind of toes or fingers.

syndesmo'sis, *n.*, a binding together.

syn'dic, *n.*, a Government official; a chief magistrate; one charged with special business duties.

syn'dicalism, *n.*, a socialistic labour doctrine, insisting on the control of all industries by the workers.

syndicalis'tic, *adj.*, pert. or rel. to syndicalism.

syn'dicate, *n.*, syndics in council; business men combined in a speculation or a particular mission.

syndica'tion, *n.*, *i.q.* syndicate; the act of syndicating.

syn'drome, *n.*, the combination of disease symptoms; a particular mental state and its manifestations.

synec'doche, *n.*, mentally taking a part for the whole, or a whole for the part.

syner'esis, *n.*, *i.q.* synaeresis.

synerget'ic, *adj.*, working or energizing in union.

syn'ergism, *n.*, the belief in combined endeavour as opposed to two or more separate similar activities.

syn'ergy, *n.*, the correlation of different organs; co-operation.

syngen'esis, *n.*, the view that the male and the female jointly produce the embryo.

synize'sis, *n.*, pronouncing as one syllable two vowels, which do not form a diphthong.

syn'od, *n.*, a formal gathering of the clergy under their bishop; a Presbyterian council.

syn'odal, *adj.*, *i.q.* synodic.

syn'odals, *n. pl.*, a money payment of the clergy to the bishop at Easter.

synod'ic, *adj.*, pert. or rel. to a synod; done in synod. (Also *synodal*.)

synod'ical, *adj.*, *i.q.* synodic.

synod'ically, *adv.*, in a synodical way.

syn'odist, *n.*, a member of a synod.

syn'onym, *n.*, a word that has the same meaning as another.

synonym'ic, *adj.*, being synonymous.

synonym'ity, *n.*, the state of being synonamous. (Also *synonymy*.)

synon'ymize, *v.i.*, to use a synonym; *v.t.*, to make synonymous.

synon'ymous, *adj.*, having identical meaning.

synon'ymously, *adv.*, in a synonymous way.

synon'ymy, *n.*, *i.q.* synonymity.

synop'sis, *n.*, a general view; a brief summary.

synop'tic, *adj.*, in the nature of a synopsis; agreeing in point of view and in statement, with special reference to the first three Gospels.

synop'tical, *adj.*, *i.q.* synoptic.

synop'tically, *adv.*, in a synoptic way.

synop'tist, *n.*, a name given severally to St. Matthew, St. Mark and St. Luke.

syno'via, *n.*, the fluid secretion in joints.

syno'vial, *adj.*, pert. or rel. to synovia.

synovi'tis, *n.*, inflammation of a synovial membrane.

syntac'tic, *adj.*, pert. or rel. to syntax.

syntac'tical, *adj.*, *i.q.* syntactic.

syn'tax, *n.*, the rules of grammatical construction; the relation of phrases and clauses to one another.

syntax'is, *n.*, *i.q.* syntax.

synther'mal, *adj.*, of the same temperature.

syn'thesis, *n.*, a combination; a composition; the opposite to analysis; the result of combining into a whole.

syn'thesize, *v.t.*, to unite.

syn'thesized, *p.p.*, synthesize.

syn'thesizing, *pr.p.*, synthesize.

synthet'ic, *adj.*, not analytic; man-made as opposed to natural; pert. or rel. to synthesis.

synthet'ical, *adj.*, *i.q.* synthetic.

synthet'ically, *adv.*, by way of synthesis; in a synthetic way.

synthetiza'tion, *n.*, the act of synthetizing.

syn'thetize, *v.t.*, to make a synthesis of; i.e., to unite elements into a complex whole.

syn'thetized, *p.p.*, synthetize.

syn'thetizing, *pr.p.*, synthetize.

syn'tomy, *n.*, brevity.

synton'ic, *adj.*, alike in tone.

syn'tony, *n.*, agreement in frequencies (*radio*).

syph'er, *v.t.*, to join up flush with overlapping edges (*planks*).

syph'ilis, *n.*, a venereal disease.

syphilit'ic, *adj.*, pert. or rel. to syphilis.

syphilol'ogy, *n.*, the study of syphilis.

sy'phon, *n.*, *i.q.* siphon.

sy'ren, *n.*, *i.q.* siren.

Syr'iac, *adj.*, pert. or rel. to Syria, a country of the Middle East; *n.*, the old language of S.

Syr'iacism, *n.*, the Syriac idiom.

Syr'ian, *adj.*, rel. to Syria; *n.*, a native of S.

Syr'ianism, *n.*, *i.q.* Syriacism.

Syrin'ga, *n.*, a plant genus including the lilac.

syr'inge, *n.*, a small pump or squirt; *v.t.*, to inject.

syr'inged, *p.p.*, syringe.

syr'inging, *pr.p.*, syringe.

syringot'omy, *n.*, cutting for fistula.

syr'inx, *n.*, fistula; the lower larynx; Pan pipes (*med.*).

syr'tic, *adj.*, pert. or. rel. to a syrtis.

syrt'is, *n.*, a quicksand (*Lat.*).

syr'up, *n.*, sugar saturated in water; a liquid product of sugar; any sweet, viscous liquid.

syr'upy, *adj.*, like, or full of, syrup.

syssarcos'is, *n.*, connexion between bones by intervening muscle.

systal'tic, *adj.*, pulsing.

sys'tem, *n.*, a whole in relation to parts; a regular arrangement or routine; method; a code of doctrines, etc.

systemat'ic, *adj.*, methodical; regular.

systemat'ical, *adj.*, *i.q.* systematic.

systemat'ically, *adv.*, in a systematic way.

sys'tematism, *n.*, the attempt to systematize.

sys'tematist, *n.*, one who systematizes.

systematiza'tion, *n.*, the act or result of systematizing.

sys'tematize, *v.t.*, to reduce to system.

sys'tematized, *p.p.*, systematize.

sys'tematizer, *n.*, *i.q.* systematist and systemizer.

sys'tematizing, *pr.p.*, systematize.

sys'tematy, *n.*, systematic classification.

system'ic, *adj.*, pert. or rel. to the whole bodily system (*physiol.*); *n.*, a type of insecticide.

system'ically, *adv.*, in a systemic way.

systemiza'tion, *n.*, the act or result of systematizing.

sys'temize, *v.t.*, *i.q.* systematize.

sys'temized, *p.p.*, systemize.

sys'temizer, *n.*, *i.q.* systematist.

sys'temless, *adj.*, without a system or organic structure.

sys'tem-maker, *n.*, one who makes systems.

sys'tole, *n.*, the shortening of a long syllable; one of the heart movements, consisting of the contraction of the auricles and ventricles (*physiol.*).

systol'ic, *adj.*, pert. or rel. to systole.

sys'tyle, *adj.*, with pillars closely set in a row; with pillars placed at a distance of two diameters from each other.

sys'tylous, *adj.*, possessing united styles (*bot.*).

syz'ygy, *n.*, a conjunction. In the pl., the point of conjunction of the moon or a planet with the sun (*astron.*).

T

Taal, *n.*, a S. African Dutch dialect.

tab, *n.*, a border, shoe latchet, tag, check (*colloq.*).

Taba′nus, *n.*, the genus of gadflies.

tab′ard, *n.*, a short coat worn over a suit of armour, and still worn by heralds.

tab′aret, *n.*, a striped upholstering fabric.

tabas′co, *n.*, a kind of hot-pepper sauce.

tabasheer′, *n.*, an Oriental drug extracted from bamboo.

tab′bied, *p.p.*, tabby.

tab′binet, *n.*, a mixed fabric used in upholstery and furnishing.

tab′by, *v.t.*, to give a wavy appearance to; *adj.*, brindled, wavy; *n.*, a wavy silken fabric; stone, etc., mixed with mortar; a brindled cat.

tab′bying, *pr.p.*, tabby; *n.*, a calendering process producing a wavy appearance.

tabefac′tion, *n.*, consumption, wasting.

tab′erdar, *n.*, the title of certain scholars of Queen's College, Oxford.

tab′ernacle, *v.i.*, to dwell for a while; sojourn; *n.*, a tent; specifically the Tabernacle in the wilderness.

tab′ernacled, *p.p.*, tabernacle.

tab′ernacle-work, *n.*, carved or sculptured canopy-work.

tab′ernacling, *pr.p.*, tabernacle.

ta′bes, *n.*, a wasting away (*Lat.*).

tabet′ic, *adj.*, atrophied.

tab′idly, *adv.*, in a wasting manner.

tab′idness, *n.*, a state of wasting.

tabif′ic, *adj.*, causing wasting away.

tab′lature, *n.*, decorative painting; the division of the skull.

ta′ble, *v.t.*, to place (a document, etc.) on a table; to register or index; *v.i.*, to share a table; *n.*, a flat board on legs; any flat surface; food; an index or catalogue.

tableau′, *n.*, a picture; lively scene.

tableau′-vivant′, *n.*, a living picture.

tab′le-cloth, *n.*, a cloth to cover a table.

ta′bled, *p.p.*, table.

ta′ble d′hôte, *n.*, a set meal for a fixed price.

ta′bleful, *n.*, as much as a table will hold.

ta′ble-knife, *n.*, an ordinary knife used at table.

ta′ble-land, *n.*, high, flat land; a plateau.

ta′ble-linen, *n.*, the cloths, napkins, etc., used on meal tables.

ta′ble-money, *n.*, money paid to reserve a table, or for the use of a table, in a restaurant.

ta′blespoon, *n.*, a large spoon used at table.

ta′ble-spoon′ful, *n.*, quantity held by a tablespoon.

tab′let, *n.*, a little table; a flat surface for inscriptions or for memoranda; a cake of soap, etc.

ta′ble-talk, *n.*, conversation of a desultory kind.

ta′ble-ten′nis, *n.*, a game like tennis, but played on a large table.

ta′bleware, *n.*, items to go on a table.

ta′ble-wa′ter, *n.*, a mineral water served with meals.

ta′bling, *pr.p.*, table.

tab′loid, *n.*, small format of newspaper.

taboo′, tabú, *n.*, a barbarous rite of consecration; *v.t.*, to pronounce inviolable; to prohibit the use of.

tabooed′, *p.p.*, taboo.

taboo′ing, *pr.p.*, taboo.

ta′bor, *n.*, a little drum.

tab′oret, *n.*, a diminutive tabor.

tab′ouret, *n.*, a footstool of ornamental work.

tab′ret, *n.*, *i.q.* taboret.

tab′ular, *adj.*, pert. to a table; like a table; laminated; in catalogue or index form.

tab′ula ra′sa, *n.*, a blank page (*Lat.*).

tab′ularize, *v.t.*, to arrange in tabular form.

tab′ulate, *v.t.*, to put a flat surface on; to reduce to tabular form.

tab′ulated, *p.p.*, tabulate.

tab′ulating, *pr.p.*, tabulate.

tabula′tion, *n.*, the act of tabulating; a tabular arrangement.

tab′ulator, *n.*, one who, or that which, tabulates.

tac′amahac, *n.*, a resin.

tac′-au-tac′, *n.*, the to-and-fro of fencing.

tac′ca, *n.*, a species of arrowroot.

ta′cet, *n.*, a musical term indicating a silence.

tache, *v.t.*, to mark; to blemish; *n.*, a blemish.

tache, *n.*, a pan used in sugar making.

tacheom′eter, *n.*, a surveyor's instrument for measuring distance.

tachom′eter, *n.*, a speed-measuring instrument.

tachycard′ia, *n.*, a medical condition of quick heartbeats.

tachygraph′ic, *adj.*, pert. to tachygraphy.

tachyg′raphy, *n.*, stenography.

tach′ylyte, *n.*, glassy basalt.

tac′it, *adj.*, silent, secret, unspoken.

tac′itly, *adv.*, in a tacit way.

tac′iturn, *adj.*, gloomily silent.

taciturn′ity, *n.*, the quality or state of being taciturn.

taciturn′ly, *adv.*, in a taciturn way.

tack, *n.*, a small kind of nail; something appended; a boat's or ship's sailing direction; *v.t.*, to drive a tack into; to append; *v.i.*, to change a ship's sailing direction.

tacked, *p.p.*, tack.

tack'er, *n.*, one who tacks.

tack'iness, *n.*, stickiness.

tack'ing, *pr.p.*, tack; *n.*, a ship's change of direction.

tack'le, *n.*, a ship's outfit of rigging, etc.; an arrangement of pulleys; fishing implements; *v.t.*, to grapple with; to harness.

tack'led, *p.p.*, tackle.

tack'ling, *pr.p.*, tackle; *n.*, gear; sails, ropes, etc., on a ship.

tacks'man, *n.*, a Scottish leaseholder.

ta'cky, *adj.*, sticky.

tact, *n.*, skilfulness in handling a difficult position without giving offence.

tact'ful, *adj.*, possessing tact.

tact'fully, *adv.*, in a tactful way.

tac'tic, *adj.*, *i.q.* tactical; *n.*, a method.

tac'tical, *adj.*, rel. to tactics.

tact'ically, *adv.*, in a tactical way.

tacti'cian, *n.*, one skilled in tactics.

tac'tics, *n. pl.*, that part of military science which relates to movements of Forces in battle; plans of action.

tac'tile, *adj.*, sensible to the touch; that can be touched.

tactil'ity, *n.*, the quality of being tactile.

tac'tion, *n.*, the act of touching.

tact'less, *adj.*, without tact.

tact'lessly, *adv.*, in a tactless way.

tact'lessness, *n.*, state of being without tact.

tac'tual, *adj.*, rel. to touch.

tac'tually, *adv.*, in a tactual way.

tad'pole, *n.*, a young frog.

tael, *n.*, a Chinese coin.

tae'nia, *n.*, the tapeworm; a fillet or band

ornament on a Doric architrave (*Lat.*).

tae'noid, *adj.*, ribbonlike.

taff'erel, *n.*, *i.q.* taffrail.

taff'eta, *n.*, a thin silken fabric with a glossy surface.

taff'rail, *n.*, the rail of a boat's stern.

Taf'fy, *n.*, a Welshman (*colloq.*).

tafi'a, *n.*, a kind of rum.

tag, *n.*, the metal tubing at the end of a lace; an appendage; a trite quotation of a familiar passage; *v.t.*, to append.

Taga'log, *n.*, a race of people in the Phillipine Islands; their language.

Tag'etes, *n.*, a genus of yellow flowering plants.

tagged, *p.p.*, tag; *adj.*, having tags.

tag'ger, *n.*, pursuer; low gauge iron sheet.

tag'ging, *pr.p.*, tag.

tag'na, *n.*, a pulley arrangement.

Tagliaco'tian, *adj.*, pert. to the 16th cent. Bolognese surgeon, Taliacotius, and the operation for making a new nose.

tag'rag, *n.*, the multitude; rabble.

Tahi'tian, *adj.*, pert. or rel. to the Polynesian island of Tahiti; *n.*, the language of T.; a native of T.

tahsil', *n.*, a tax division of India.

tai'ga, *n.*, tundra forest.

tail, *n.*, an appendage to an animal's backbone; anything hanging down or appended; limitation; *v.i.*, to dwindle.

tail'age, *n.*, *i.q.* tallage.

tail'-board, *n.*, a hinged board at the rear of a vehicle.

tail'dive, *n.*, an aircraft dive, tail first.

tailed, *p.p.*, tail; *adj.*, having a tail.

tail'-end', *n.*, the last part or item.

tail'ing, *pr.p.*, tail; *n.*, that part of a projecting brick or stone which does not project from the wall; stamped ore refuse.

tail'less, *adj.*, lacking a tail.

tail'-light, *n.*, a light at the rear of a train or road vehicle.

tail'or, *n.*, a man who makes clothes; *v.t.*, to make clothes for; *v.i.*, to practise tailoring.

tail'ored, *p.p.*, tailor; *adj.*, turned out by one's tailor.

tail'oress, *n.*, fem. of tailor.

tail'oring, *pr.p.*, tailor; *n.*, a tailor's trade; tailor's materials.

tail'or-made', *adj.*, made by a tailor.

tail'-piece, *n.*, an appendage to a page or chapter.

tail'-spin, *n.*, a special form of spinning dive of aircraft.

tail'zie, *n.*, the legal cutting of entail (*Scots Law*).

tain, *n.*, foil or tinplate.

taint, *v.t.*, to infect with an odour or bad taste; to tinge; *n.*, an infecting smell or taste.

taint'ed, *p.p.*, taint.

taint'ing, *pr.p.*, taint.

taint'less, *adj.*, without a taint.

taint'ure, *n.*, stain.

taj, *n.*, an eastern coneshaped head-dress.

take, *v.t.*, to assume possession of; to lay hands on; to seize; to adopt; to regard; to obtain; to contract; to apprehend; to conduct; to go across or through; *v.i.*, to derogate from; to have effect; to form a liking for; to make a good picture; *n.*, a catch (as of fish); amount of copy furnished to a compositor; takings.

take'down, *n.*, a lowering of one's dignity by another.

take'-in, *n.*, a trick, deception.

ta'ken, *p.p.*, take.

take'-off, *n.*, a satirical representation; a piece of mimicry; a drawback; a starting-point.

take'-over, *n.*, control of one business surrendered to another.

ta'ker, *n.*, one who takes.

ta′kin, *n.*, the cow of Tibet.

ta′king, *pr.p.*, take; *adj.*, attractive, pleasing.

ta′kingly, *adv.*, attractively.

ta′kingness, *n.*, agreeableness, charm.

ta′kings, *n. pl.*, money received for seats in a theatre or by sales in a business.

tal′apoin, *n.*, a species of monkey; a Siamese bonza.

tala′ria, *n. pl.*, Mercury's winged sandals.

tal′bot, *n.*, a variety of hunting-dog, noted for its quick scent.

talc, *n.*, a flaky substance, hydrous silicate of magnesia.

talc′ite, *n.*, talc in the mass.

talck′y, *adj.*, *i.q.* talcous.

talc′ose, *adj.*, *i.q.* talcous.

talc′ous, *adj.*, of the nature of talc.

tal′cum, *n.*, powdered talc for the toilet.

tale, *n.*, a story, anecdote; a reckoning; a number.

tale′bearer, *n.*, one who carries gossip from one person to another.

tale′bearing, *adj.*, idly gossiping; *n.*, idle gossip.

tal′ent, *n.*, in the classical age, a weight, coin, sum of money; mental endowment; intellectual gifts.

tal′ented, *adj.*, intellectually endowed; clever.

ta′les, *n. pl.*, a writ for summoning extra jurors; a list of them.

ta′lesman, *n.*, an extra juryman.

tal′ion, *n.*, retaliatory law.

tal′iped, *adj.*, clubfooted.

tal′ipes, *n.*, club-foot.

tal′ipot, *n.*, a Ceylon giant palm.

tal′isman, *n.*, a stone or metal charm, defensive against evil or productive of great good.

talisman′ic, *adj.*, of the nature of a talisman.

talk, *v.t.*, to utter; converse about; *v.i.*, to speak; to converse.

talk′ative, *adj.*, too much given to talking.

talk′atively, *adv.*, in a talkative way.

talked, *p.p.*, talk.

talk′ee-talk′ee, *n.*, rubbish, nonsense.

talk′er, *n.*, one who talks, esp. one who talks overmuch.

talk′ing, *pr.p.*, talk; *n.*, the act of talking; conversation.

talk′ing-point, *n.*, a matter for discussion.

talk′ing-to, *n.*, a rebuke.

tall, *adj.*, lofty; high of stature; exaggerated (*slang*).

tall′age, *n.*, toll, tax. Also *tailage*.

tall′boy, *n.*, a tall chest of drawers.

tall′er, *adj.*, *comp.* of tall.

tallest, *adj.*, *super.* of tall.

tal′lied, *p.p.*, tally.

tallith, *n.*, a Jewish prayer scarf.

tall′ness, *n.*, loftiness; height of stature.

tal′low, *v.t.*, to smear with tallow; *n.*, melted fat; material for candles.

tal′low-can′dle, *n.*, a candle made mainly from tallow.

tal′low-chandler, *n.*, one who sells tallow.

tal′lowish, *adj.*, like tallow.

tall′ow-tree, *n.*, vegetable-yielding tree.

tal′lowy, *adj.*, pert. to tallow.

tal′ly, *n.*, a notched stick once used for keeping accounts; something that matches; *v.t.* and *i.*, to match.

tally-ho′, *n.*, a huntsman's cry.

tal′lying, *pr.p.*, tally; *n.*, the act of tallying.

tal′lyman, *n.*, a seller of goods for payment in instalments.

tal′mi-gold, *n.*, brass lightly gold coated.

Tal′mud, *n.*, a Rabbinical book, consisting of the Mishna and the Gemara, and treating of Jewish traditions, law, etc.

Talmud′ic, *adj.*, pert. to the Talmud.

Tal′mudist, *n.*, one learned in the Talmud.

tal′on, *n.*, a bird's claw.

tal′oned, *adj.*, furnished with talons.

talook′, taluk′, *n.*, an Indian territorial area.

taluk′dar, *n.*, one who holds a taluk.

ta′lus, *n.*, the anklebone; a slope; sloping débris below a rock.

tamabil′ity, *n.*, the quality of being tamable.

ta′mable, tame′able, *adj.*, able to be tamed; gentle.

ta′mableness, tame′ableness, *n.*, the quality of being tamable.

tam′arack, *n.*, the black larch of America.

tam′arin, *n.*, a species of monkey.

tam′arind, *n.*, a leguminous tree.

tam′arisk, *n.*, an evergreen shrub with pink or white flowers.

tama′sha, *n.*, an entertainment.

tam′bour, *n.*, a drum; a drum-shaped structure; an embroidery frame; *v.t.*, to embroider on a tambour.

tambourine′, *n.*, a musical instrument, tapped with the hand, and having jingling cymbals in the encircling frame.

tame, *v.t.*, to bring under control; to change from wild to gentle; to subdue; *adj.*, subdued; rendered gentle; dull; without spirit.

tameabil′ity, tamabil′ity, *n.*, *i.q.* tamableness.

tamed, *p.p.*, tame.

tame′less, *adj.*, untamable.

tame′ly, *adv.*, in a tame manner.

tame′ness, *n.*, gentleness; insipidity.

ta′mer, *n.*, one who tames, esp. wild animals.

Tam′il, *n.*, a language spoken in Ceylon and S.E. India.

ta′ming, *pr.p.*, tame.

Tam′many, *n.*, an American political organization.

Tammuz′, *n.*, the tenth month of the Jewish civil year; also *i.q.* Thammuz.

tam′my, *n.*, *i.q.* tam-o′-shanter.

tam-o′-shan′ter, *n.*, a soft flat cap (*Scot.*).

tamp, *v.t.*, to stop a blasting-hole; to hammer gently.

tamped, *p.p.*, tamp.

tam'per, *v.t.*, to meddle; interfere; bribe.

tam'pered, *p.p.*, tamper.

tam'perer, *n.*, one who tampers.

tam'pering, *pr.p.*, tamper.

tamp'ing, *pr.p.*, tamp.

tam'pion, *n.*, a stopper, esp. of a cannon's mouth.

tam'poe, *n.*, an edible Malayan fruit.

tam'pon, *n.*, a plug to stop blood flowing.

tam'tam, *n.*, a native drum; *i.q.* tom-tom.

tan, *n.*, bark of a tree, esp. the oak, used for the preparation of hides; the abbrev. of tangent; *adj.*, brown-like tan; *v.t.*, to make leather from hides treated with an infusion of bark; to sunburn; to beat (*colloq.*); *v.i.*, to be browned by the sun.

tan'ager, *n.*, an American finch-like bird.

tan'agra, *n.*, *adj.*, a terracotta statue.

ta'nais'te, *n.*, a deputy; an heir; the deputy prime minister in the Republic of Ireland.

tan'dem, *adv.*, with one horse in front of another; *n.*, a carriage drawn by two horses, one in front of the other; a bicycle for two or more riders seated tandem-fashion.

tang, *n.*, a strong flavour; the part of a knife, tool, etc., that goes into the handle; the sound of a bell; *v.i.*, to give forth a bell-like sound.

tan'gency, *n.*, contact.

tan'gent, *adj.*, touching; *n.*, a straight line which touches a curve but, being produced beyond the point of contact, does not cut the curve.

tangen'tial, *adj.*, pert. to a tangent.

tangen'tially, *adv.*, in a tangential way.

tangerine', *n.*, a small orange-like fruit.

tangibi'lity, *n.*, the quality of being tangible.

tan'gible, *adj.*, able to be touched, attained, or perceived; real.

tan'gibly, *adv.*, in a tangible way.

tan'gle, *v.t.*, to twist into a confused knot; to complicate; *v.i.*, to become entangled; *n.*, a confused knot; a complication; a seaweed.

tan'gled, *adj.*, twisted; complicated; *p.p.*, tangle.

tan'gling, *pr.p.*, tangle.

tan'gly, *adj.*, in a tangle.

tan'go, *n.*, a ballroom dance.

tan'gram, *n.*, a seven-piece square; a Chinese puzzle.

tan'ist, *n.*, an Irish popularly elected head of a clan or a landowner.

tan'istry, *n.*, the custom of electing tanists.

tank, *n.*, a reservoir or large cistern; an armoured military vehicle with gun(s).

tank'ard, *n.*, a drinking vessel.

tank'er, *n.*, a truck or ship to transport liquid.

tank'ful, *n.*, the quantity a tank will hold.

tan'nage, *n.*, the process of tanning.

tan'nate, *n.*, a tannic acid salt.

tanned, *p.p.*, tan.

tan'ner, *n.*, one who makes hides into leather.

tan'nery, *n.*, a place where hides are tanned.

tan'nic, *adj.*, rel. to, or obtained from, bark.

tan'nier, *n.*, the spoonflower.

tan'nin, *n.*, tannic acid.

tan'ning, *pr.p.*, tan; *n.*, the tanning industry.

tan'sy, *n.*, an aromatic herb.

tantaliza'tion, *n.*, the act of tantalizing; being tantalized.

tan'talize, *v.t.*, to tempt with vain hopes.

tan'talized, *p.p.*, tantalize.

tan'talizer, *n.*, one who tantalizes.

tan'talizing, *pr.p.*, tantalize; *adj.*, provoking.

tan'talizingly, *adv.*, in a tantalizing way.

tan'talum, *n.*, a metallic element (*chem.*).

tan'talus, *n.*, an open stand for spirit decanters secured with a lock.

tan'tamount, *adj.*, equal; equivalent.

tantar'a, *n.*, a trumpet call.

tan'tivy, *n.*, a gallop; *adv.*, at a gallop.

tan'trum, *n.*, a petulant attitude.

tan'yard, *n.*, *i.q.* tannery.

taoi'seach, *n.*, a prime minister (*Gaelic*).

tap, *v.t.*, to beat or hammer lightly; to make an opening in a vessel for the liquid to flow out; to sole or heel a shoe; to bore; *n.*, a light blow with a hammer or the hand; an outlet for fluid; the part of a tavern where liquor is drawn.

tap'-bolt, *n.*, a threaded bolt which screws in and requires no nut.

tap'-dance, *n.*, a feet-tapping dance.

tap'-dancer, *n.*, one who performs tap-dancing.

tap'-dancing, *n.*, *i.q.* tap-dance.

tape, *n.*, a narrow strip of linen or cotton cloth.

tape'-machine, *n.*, a telegraphic device which automatically prints each message received.

tape'measure, *n.*, a tape marked in linear measurement.

ta'per, *v.t.*, to narrow; *v.i.*, to become slender towards one end; *n.*, a slender candle.

tape'-record, *v.t.*, to make a sound record with a tape-recorder.

tape'-recorded, *p.p.*, tape-record.

tape'-recorder, *n.*, an audio machine to record speech and sound.

tape'-record'ing, *n.*, a sound record on a magnetic tape; *pr.p.*, tape-record.

ta'pered, *p.p.*, taper.

ta'pering, *pr.p.*, taper; *adj.*, narrowing towards one end.

tap'estried, *adj.*, hung, furnished, or upholstered with tapestries.

tap'estry, *n.*, a woven fabric with figures, pictures, etc., worked in.

tap'eti, *n.*, a S. Amer. hare.

tape′worm, *n.,* an intestinal worm like a tape.

tap′house, *n.,* a beerhouse.

tapio′ca, *n.,* a product from cassava root.

ta′pir, *n.,* a quadruped of the hog genus.

tap′is, *n.,* a carpet (*Fr.*); ("on the tapis") for discussion.

tapote′ment, *n.,* tapping for massage.

tapped, *p.p.,* tap.

tap′per, *n.,* one who, that which, taps.

tap′pet, *n.,* a little lever arrangement, altering or regulating motion.

tap′ping, *pr.p.,* tap.

tap′-room, *n.,* a public-house bar.

tap′-root, *n.,* a plant's chief root.

tap′ster, *n.,* one who draws liquor. (This word originally was the feminine form of tapper, women being often employed as drawers.)

tar, *n.,* a thick, black, oily substance distilled from coal, pine, etc.; a sailor; *v.t.,* to cover with tar.

ta′raddidle, *n.,* a roll of drums; a lie.

tarantel′la, *n.,* a fast Neapolitan dance and its music.

tar′antism, *n.,* an affection produced by the bite of a tarantula.

taran′tula, *n.,* a great poisonous spider, alleged to affect with a dancing madness those whom it bites.

tarax′acum, *n.,* a plant genus, containing the dandelion.

tarboosh′, *n.,* a blue-tasselled fez.

tar′digrade, *n.,* one of the Tardigrada, such as the sloth.

tar′dily, *adv.,* slowly; hesitatingly.

tar′diness, *n.,* slowness, dilatoriness.

tar′do, *adj.,* played slowly (*It., mus.*).

tar′dy, *adj.,* slow; belated; dilatory.

tare, *n.,* a darnel; allowance for the weight of a cask, wrapper, case, etc., after it has been weighed with its contents.

tar′entism, *n., i.q.* tarantism.

tar′get, *n.,* a marked disk or butt used in archery and rifle or artillery practice; a light shield; neck and breast of lamb (as a joint for the table).

targeteer′, *n.,* one armed with a shield.

Tar′gum, *n.,* the Chaldaic version of the Old Testament Scriptures.

Tar′gumist, *n.,* one learned in the Targum.

tar′iff, *n.,* list of dutiable commodities, whether imports or exports.

tar′iff-reform′, *n.,* a change in existing tariffs; a movement to tax imports.

ta′riff-wall′, *n.,* a system of tariffs on imported goods.

tar′in, *n.,* a French bird like a gold-finch.

tar′latan, *n.,* a fine dress fabric.

tar′mac, *n.,* the proprietary name for a kind of tarmacadam.

tarmacad′am, *n.,* a road surfacing.

tarn, *n.,* a small mountain lake.

tar′nish, *v.t.,* to sully; to stain; *v.i.,* to be sullied.

tar′nishable, *adj.,* capable of being tarnished.

tar′nished, *p.p.,* tarnish.

tar′nisher, *n.,* one who, or that which, tarnishes.

tar′nishing, *pr.p.,* tarnish.

tar′o, *n.,* a tropical root plant.

tar′ot, *n.,* a special pack of 78 playing cards; a card game.

tarp′an, *n.,* a Turkish wild horse.

tarpau′lin, *n.,* heavy canvas waterproof.

Tarpe′ian, *adj.,* rel. to Tarpeia and the rock named after her at Rome.

tar′pon, *n.,* a Pacific game-fish.

tar′ragon, *n.,* a vinegar.

Tarragon′a, *n.,* a Spanish wine, like port.

tarred, *p.p.,* tar.

tar′ried, *p.p.,* tarry.

tar′rier, *n.,* one who tarries.

tarri′ness, *n.,* the state of being tarry.

tar′ring, *pr.p.,* tar.

tar′rock, *n.,* a young kittiwake.

tar′ry, *adj.,* like tar; covered with tar.

tar′ry, *v.i.,* to wait; linger; in older English, *v.t.,* to wait for; await.

tar′rying, *pr.p.,* tarry.

tar′sal, *adj.,* rel. to the tarsus.

tarsal′gia, *n.,* pain in the tarsal region.

tarse, *n., i.q.* tarsus.

tar′sia, *n.,* marquetry mosaic.

tar′sus, *n.,* the instep.

tart, *adj.,* sharp; acid; cutting; *n.,* an uncovered pie; a woman of low moral character (*slang*).

tar′tan, *n.,* a many-coloured plaid.

Tar′tar, tar′tar, *n.,* a native of Tartary; a dangerous-tempered person; a dental deposit; *adj.,* rel. to Tartary.

tar′tare, *n.,* the name of a savoury fish sauce.

Tarta′rean, *adj.,* pert. to Tartarus.

tar′tar-emet′ic, *n.,* a compound of antimony, potassium, and tartaric acid.

tartar′ic, *adj.,* pert. to acid of calcium phosphate.

Tar′tarus, *n.,* a sunless place below Hades; the darkest of the infernal regions.

tart′ish, *adj.,* somewhat sharp or acid.

tart′let, *n.,* small tart.

tartly, *adv.,* in a tart manner.

tart′ness, *n.,* the state or quality of being tart.

tar′trate, *n.,* a tartaric acid salt.

Tartuffe′, *n.,* one of Molière's comic characters; a precise hypocrite.

Tartuf′fish, *adj.,* like Tartuffe.

tar′-water, *n.,* a decoction from tar.

taseo′meter, *n.,* electrical apparatus for fine measurement of temperature, moisture, strain, etc.

tasi′meter, *n., i.q.* taseometer.

task, n., an imposed piece of work; something to be learnt; v.t., to impose a task upon; to try severely.

tasked, p.p., task.

task'er, n., one who imposes a task.

task'-force, n., a specially selected military group for a specific task.

task'ing, pr.p., task.

task'master, n., i.q. tasker.

task'-work, n., a definite amount of work required to be done.

Tasma'nian, adj., pert. to Tasmania; n., a native of Tasmania.

tas'sel, n., a hanging ornament made of cord, gold lace, etc.; a male goshawk; anything like a tassel.

tas'sel(l)ed, adj., ornamented with tassels.

tas'sel(l)ing, n., ornamentation with tassels.

ta'stable, adj., able to be tasted.

taste, n., a sensation by means of the tongue and palate; relish; flavour; savour; experimental trial; fine discrimination and a sense of the good and beautiful; v.t., to experience the sensation of tasting; to make trial of; to eat or sip just a little of.

ta'sted, p.p., taste.

taste'ful, adj., marked by good taste.

taste'fully, adv., in a tasteful way.

tastefulness, n., the quality of good taste.

taste'less, adj., without taste (in any sense).

taste'lessness, n., the state or quality of being tasteless.

ta'ster, n., one who tastes, esp. an expert in wines, teas, etc.

ta'stily, adv., in a tasty way.

ta'sting, pr.p., taste.

ta'sty, adj., pleasant to the taste; exhibiting good taste.

tat, n., a cloth of jute; v.t. and i., to do tatting.

ta'-ta', interj. = goodbye (colloq.).

tat'ou, n., an armadillo.

tatt, n., a rag; n. pl., old oddments.

tat'ter, n., one who tats; a torn fragment.

tatterdema'lion, n., a fellow in rags.

tat'tered, adj., torn and ragged.

tat'tily, adv., in a tatty way.

tat'tiness, n., the state of being tatty.

tat'ting, pr.p., tat; n., a sort of hand lacework; the act of tatting.

tat'tle, v.i., to prattle; to talk small scandal; n., prating talk.

tat'tled, p.p., tattle.

tat'tler, n., one who tattles.

tat'tling, pr.p., tattle.

tattoo', n., pictorial and emblematic drawings in colour worked into the skin after puncturing; a drum-beat; v.t., to mark the skin with tattoo.

tattooed', p.p., tattoo.

tattooing, pr.p., tattoo; n., the act of tattooing; tattoo marks.

tat'ty, adj., over-fussy; of low quality.

taught, p.p., teach.

taunt, n., a bitter, spiteful reproach; v.t., to level reproach at.

taunt'ed, p.p., taunt.

taunt'er, n., one who taunts.

taunt'ing, pr.p., taunt.

taunt'ingly, adv., in a taunting way.

tau'riform, adj., like a bull.

tau'rine, adj., pert. to bulls.

tau'rocol, n., glue made from a bull's hide.

taurom'achy, n., the science of bull-fighting.

Tau'rus, n., the Bull, one of the signs of the Zodiac (Lat.).

taut, adj., stretched; tight; secure.

tautolog'ical, adj., saying the same thing repeatedly; unnecessarily repetitious.

tautolog'ically, adv., in a tautological way.

tautol'ogist, n., one who tautologizes.

tautol'ogize, v.i., to say the same thing in different words.

tautol'ogized, p.p., tautologize.

tautol'ogizing, pr.p., tautologize.

tautol'ogy, n., saying the same thing though in different words.

tautophon'ical, adj., identical in sound or speech.

tautoph'ony, n., identity of sound or speech.

tav'ern, n., an inn.

tav'erner, n., i.q. tavern-keeper; a publican.

tav'ern-keeper, n., an innkeeper.

taw, v.t., to make white leather from skins; n., a marble for playing.

taw'drily, adv., in a tawdry way.

taw'driness, n., the state or quality of being tawdry.

taw'dry, adj., cheap, showy, gaudy. The word is derived from St. Audrey (Etheldreda), on whose festival St. Audrey (called tawdry) beads were sold.

tawed, p.p., taw.

taw'er, n., a leather-dresser.

taw'ery, n., a place where tawing is done.

taw'ing, pr.p., taw.

taw'niness, n., the state or quality of being tawny.

taw'ny, adj., brown, with a tinge of yellow.

taws, n., n.pl., a Scottish instrument for punishing youth. It consists of a leather strap with a fringed end.

tax, n., an impost; v.t., to impose a tax on income, etc.; to oppress; to put a strain on; to accuse.

taxabil'ity, n., the state of being taxable.

tax'able, adj., subject to tax.

taxa'tion, n., the act of taxing; imposed rate.

tax'-collector, n., one who collects taxes.

taxed, p.p., tax.

tax'er, n., one who taxes.

tax'-free, adj., without payment of tax.

tax'-gatherer, n., a collector of taxes.

tax'i, n., an abbreviation for taxicab; v.i., move along the ground (aircraft).

tax'icab, n., a motor-cab.

tax'i-dancer, *n.*, a female dancing partner, available for hire in a dance-hall.

taxider'mic, *adj.*, rel. to taxidermy.

tax'idermist, *n.*, one who stuffs dead beasts, birds, etc.

tax'idermy, *n.*, the art of preserving the natural appearance of dead beasts, etc., by stuffing them.

tax'ied, *p.p.*, taxi.

taxi'meter, *n.*, a register of the fare on a taxi-cab or other public vehicle.

tax'in, *n.*, a resin obtained from yew trees.

tax'ing, *pr.p.*, tax.

tax'ing-master, *n.*, a court official who examines bills of costs.

Taxo'dium, *n.*, the genus of the swamp-cypress.

tax'on, *n.*, a kind of division or category (*biol.*).

taxon'omist, *n.*, a specialist in taxonomy.

taxon'omy, *n.*, classification—a department of natural history.

tax'payer, *n.*, one who pays tax.

Tax'us, *n.*, the yew genus.

tax'ying, *pr.p.*, taxi.

taz'za, *n.*, a wide open bowl, with or without handles (*It.*).

tea, *n.*, a plant so named; the dried leaves of the same; a drink made by an infusion of the leaves; any infusion of the kind.

tea'-bag, *n.*, a porous bag containing tea ready for infusion.

tea'-break, *n.*, an interval for tea.

tea'-caddy, *n.*, a small chest to contain the dried leaves of the tea plant.

tea'-cake, *n.*, a cake, usually toasted, and containing dried fruits.

teach, *v.t.*, to instruct; inform; *v.i.*, to practise as a teacher.

teach'able, *adj.*, able to be taught; apt to learn.

teach'ableness, *n.*, the state of being teachable.

teach'er, *n.*, one who teaches.

tea'-chest, *n.*, a box in which tea is packed.

teach'-in, *n.*, a kind of seminar.

teach'ing, *pr.p.*, teach; *n.*, the act or profession of teaching.

tea'-cloth, *n.*, a cloth used for drying washed dishes, etc.

tea'cup, *n.*, a cup to hold tea.

tea'cupful, *n.*, the quantity that will fill a cup.

tea'-dealer, *n.*, one who deals in tea.

tea'-garden, *n.*, a pleasure garden where tea can be drunk.

teak, *n.*, an Indian tree; its timber.

tea'kettle, *n.*, a kettle to hold boiling water for the making of tea.

teal, *n.*, a fresh-water wild duck.

team, *n.*, horses harnessed for driving a plough, etc.; players in a game; *v.t.*, to join to achieve a combined effort.

teamed, *p.p.*, team.

team'ing, *pr.p.*, team.

team'ster, *n.*, the driver of a team.

team'-work, *n.*, co-operation; the work of an organized team.

tea'pot, *n.*, a pot from which tea is poured.

tear, *n.*, a drop of fluid secreted from the lachrymal gland.

tear, *n.*, a rent; *v.t.*, to rend; make a tear in; to snatch away; *v.i.*, to be rent; come apart.

tear'away, *adj.*, reckless, impetuous; *n.*, a reckless and sometimes violent person.

tear'-drop, *n.*, *i.q.* tear.

tear'er, *n.*, one who tears.

tear'ful, *adj.*, weeping.

tear'fully, *adv.*, in a tearful way.

tear'fulness, *n.*, the state of being tearful.

tear'-gas, *n.*, a gas to provoke tears and thus disable.

tear'ing, *pr.p.*, tear.

tear'jerker, *n.*, a film or play which provokes sentimental reactions.

tea'-rose, *n.*, a class of rose.

tear'-shell, *n.*, a projectile for dispersing tear-gas.

tear'-stained, *adj.*, marked by tears.

tease, *v.t.*, to annoy by frequent provocation or raillery; irritate; to unravel (flax, etc.); *n.*, one given to teasing.

teased, *p.p.*, tease.

teas'el, **tea'zle**, *n.*, a plant so named, and used in wool manufacture; *v.t.*, to treat cloth with a prickly plant, or mechanical substitute.

teas'elled, *p.p.*, teasel.

teas'eller, *n.*, one whose work it is to teasel.

teas'elling, *pr.p.*, teasel.

teas'er, *n.*, one who teases; a difficult problem.

tea'-service, *n.*, a set of crockery for serving tea.

tea'-shop, *n.*, a small restaurant where afternoon tea (and other light refreshment) is served.

teas'ing, *pr.p.*, tease.

tea'spoon, *n.*, a small spoon used to stir tea.

tea'spoonful, *n.*, the quantity that a teaspoon will contain. (In pl., *teaspoonfuls*.)

teat, *n.*, the nipple of a female mammal's breast.

tea'-table, *n.*, a table on which tea is served.

tea'-taster, *n.*, one whose work is tasting tea.

tea'-towel, *n.*, *i.q.* tea-cloth.

tea'-urn, *n.*, an urn containing tea, or used in making tea.

tea'zle, *n.*, *i.q.* teasle; *v.t.*, to raise the nap of woollen cloth.

tea'zled, *p.p.*, teazle.

tea'zler, *n.*, one who, that which, teazles.

tea'zling, *pr.p.*, teazle.

tech'ily, *adv.*, *i.q.* tetchily.

tech'iness, *n.*, *i.q.* tetchiness.

tech'nical, *adj.*, embodying elements of specialized skill and knowledge.

technical'ity, *n.*, the quality of being technical; something exclusively relating to a

particular industry, art, etc.; a minor point.

tech'nically, *adv.*, in a technical sense or manner.

technician, *n.*, a trained expert in a technique.

tech'nicist, *n.*, a skilled practical person.

tech'nicolour, *adj.*, in full, bright colour.

tech'nics, *n. pl.*, studies rel. to the arts.

technique', *n.*, skill in an art (*Fr.*).

technoc'racy, *n.*, government by technologists.

tech'nocrat, *n.*, an advocate of technocracy.

technolog'ic, *adj.*, pert. to technology.

technolog'ical, *adj.*, *i.q.* technologic.

technolo'gically, *adv.*, in a technological way.

technol'ogist, *n.*, a student of technology.

technol'ogy, *n.*, the science or study of the arts in industry.

tech'y, *adj.*, *i.q.* tetchy.

tect'iform, *adj.*, roof-shaped.

tectol'ogy, *n.*, morphology of structures.

tecton'ic, *n.*, *adj.*, pert. to construction.

tecton'ically, *adv.*, in a tectonic way.

tecton'ics, *n. pl.*, the science of construction.

tector'ial, *adj.*, covering (as of body membranes).

ted, *v.t.*, to spread out; to dry.

ted'ded, *p.p.*, ted.

ted'der, *n.*, one who, that which, teds.

ted'ding, *pr.p.*, ted.

Ted'dy-bear, *n.*, an animal toy. (Its name comes from Theodore Roosevelt, a former President of the U.S.)

Te De'um, *n.*, a prose-hymn of the Church, recited in the daily offices, and sung solemnly on occasions of national rejoicing.

te'dious, *adj.*, wearisome; boring; lengthy.

te'diously, *adv.*, in a tedious way.

te'dium, *n.*, wearisomeness.

tee, *n.*, the starting-place for each hole in a golf-course; the mark aimed at in curling and quoits; a short length of piping; *v.t.*, to set up a golf ball on a raised cone of sand.

teem, *v.i.*, to be very full; to be fertile; *v.t.*, to pour.

teemed, *p.p.*, teem.

teem'ing, *pr.p.*, teem.

teen'age, *n.*, period from thirteen to nineteen years of age.

teen'ager, *n.*, one who is of teenage.

teens, *n. pl.*, the years numbered from thirteen to nineteen.

tee'ny, *adj.*, colloquial variant of *tiny* (*q.v.*).

tee'ter, *v.i.*, to totter, sway unsteadily.

teeth, *n.*, pl. of tooth.

teethe, *v.t.*, to cut the teeth; to go through the process of dentition.

teethed, *p.p.*, teeth.

teeth'ing, *pr.p.*, teethe; *n.*, dentition.

teeto'tal, *adj.*, completely abstaining from alcohol.

teeto'tal(l)er, *n.*, a total abstainer from alcohol.

teeto'talism, *n.*, total abstinence from alcohol.

teeto'tum, *n.*, a child's spinning toy.

teg, *n.*, a young sheep; a second-year doe.

teg'men, *n.*, a covering; in botany, the under layer of a seed's coating (*Lat.*).

tegment'al, *adj.*, pert. or rel. to a tegmen.

tegmen'tum, *n.*, a covering; protection (*Lat.*).

teg'ular, *adj.*, like a tile; covering.

teg'ularly, *adv.*, in a tegular way.

teg'ulated, *adj.*, (of armour) composed of small plates, overlapping like tiles.

teg'ument, *n.*, a covering; envelope; skin.

tegumen'tal, *adj.*, in the nature of a tegument.

tegumen'tary, *adj.*, *i.q.* tegumental.

tehee', *n.*, a comic titter; *v.i.*, to titter in an absurd way.

teichop'sia, *n.*, a temporary sight disorder, involving partial blindness.

teil, *n.*, the linden.

tei'noscope, *n.*, a telescope furnished with prisms to correct the chromatic aberration of light.

telaesthe'sia, *n.*, seeing things far off without sensory aid.

telaesthet'ic, *adj.*, pert. or rel. to telaesthesia.

Telamo'nes, *n. pl.*, in architecture, figures of men used as pillars or pilasters.

tela'rian, *adj.*, spinning a web.

telaut'ograph, *n.*, hand-writing transmitted by telegraph.

telaut'ographic, *adj.*, pert. or rel. to telautography.

telauto'graphy, *n.*, the transmission of hand-writing or drawing by telegraph.

telecam'era, *n.*, a long-distance camera.

tel'ecast, *n.*, a broadcast by television.

telecine', *n.*, the telecast of a film.

telecommunica'tion, *n.*, communication by telephone or radio.

tele'control', *n.*, the remote control of mechanical things by radio or sound waves.

tel'edu, *n.*, an Indonesian badger.

tel'efilm, *n.*, a film made for televising.

telegen'ic, *adj.*, pictorially suitable for television.

tel'egram, *n.*, a message transmitted by telegraph.

tel'egraph, *n.*, an instrument for transmitting messages; *v.t.*, to transmit a message; *v.i.*, to make use of the telegraph.

tele'graph-cable, *n.*, *i.q.* telegraph-wire.

tel'egraphed, *p.p.*, telegraph.

tele'graphese', *n.*, a specially abbreviated language used in telegrams.

telegraph'ic, *adj.*, rel. to telegraphy.

telegraph'ically, *adv.*, by telegraphy.

tel'egraphing, *pr.p.*, telegraph.

teleg'raphist, *n.*, a telegraphic operator.

tele'graph-pole, *n.*, a pole erected to support overhead telegraph-wires, etc.

tele'graph-wire, *n.*, the special wire used for telegraphic transmission.

teleg'raphy, *n.*, the system or science of the telegraph.

telekines'is, *n.*, distant movement without normal material connection.

tele'lens, *n.*, a tele-photographic lens.

tel'emark, *n.*, an expert ski-ing movement to stop or turn.

tel'emeter, *n.*, an instrument to record at a distance, usually radio controlled.

teleolog'ical, *adj.*, pert. to teleology.

teleol'ogist, *n.*, one who investigates final causes or purposes of phenomena.

teleol'ogy, *n.*, the philosophy of final causes.

Teleosau'rus, *n.*, a genus of Oolitic fossil reptiles.

telepath'ic, *adj.*, rel. to telepathy.

telepath'ically, *adv.*, in a telepathic way.

telep'athist, *n.*, one who has the gift of telepathy.

telep'athy, *n.*, thought transference by an effort of the mind.

tel'epheme, *n.*, a telephone message.

tel'ephone, *n.*, an instrument conveying sound by means of electricity; *v.t.*, to use a telephone for communication.

tel'ephoned, *p.p.*, telephone.

tel'ephoner, *n.*, one who telephones.

telephon'ic, *adj.*, rel. to, or transmitted by, the telephone.

telephon'ically, *adv.*, in a telephonic way.

tel'ephoning, *pr.p.*, telephone.

teleph'onist, *n.*, one who operates a telephone or a telephone switchboard.

teleph'ony, *n.*, the technical craft of communication by telephone.

tele'photo., *n.*, the abbrev. of telephotograph.

telepho'tograph, *n.*, a photograph taken at long distance.

telephotograph'ic, *adj.*,

pert. or rel. to telephotography.

telephotog'raphy, *n.*, the craft of long-distance photography.

tel'eprinter, *n.*, a device for instantaneous sending of typed messages by telegraphy.

telepromp'ter, *n.*, a device which reveals to a television speaker, a script which is invisible to viewers.

telerecor'ding, *n.*, a recording made for later transmission by television.

tel'escope, *n.*, an instrument making distant objects more visible; *v.t.*, to crush in; *v.i.*, to slide together.

telescop'ic, *adj.*, pert. to the telescope.

telescop'ically, *adv.*, by means of a telescope; like a telescope.

teles'copist, *n.*, one who makes skilled use of the telescope.

teles'copy, *n.*, the use of the telescope.

tele'screen, *n.*, the screen of a television receiver.

tele'seme, *n.*, an electric signalling device which automatically indicates what is required.

telesmat'ic, *adj.*, magical.

tele'stich, *n.*, a poem, the final letters of each line of which make a word.

tele'type, *n.*, a kind of telegraphic printing device.

tele'view, *v.i.*, to watch television.

tele'viewer, *n.*, one who watches television.

televise, *v.t.*, to transmit sound and moving pictures for reception.

televised, *p.p.*, televise.

televising, *pr.p.*, televise.

tel'evision, *n.*, the radio transmission of pictures, over a distance simultaneously with the occasion.

tele'visional, *adj.*, pert. or rel. to television.

tele'visionary, *adj.*, i.q. televisional.

televi'sor, *n.*, a television receiver.

tel'ewriter, *n.*, an instrument transmitting facsimile telegrams.

tel'ex, *n.*, the Post Office system of immediate

telegraphic communication.

tell, *v.t.*, to convey in words; relate; count; *v.i.*, to lay information; to be effective; to produce an effect.

tell'er, *n.*, one who tells; a bank official at the counter; one who counts votes in the Parliamentary lobbies.

tell'ing, *pr.p.*, tell; *adj.*, effective.

tell'ingly, *adv.*, in an effective way.

tell'-tale, *n.*, one who reveals secrets; an automatic monitor; *adj.*, telling tales.

tellu'ral, *adj.*, i.q. telluric.

tel'lurate, *n.*, a telluric acid salt.

tellu'rian, *adj.*, rel. to tellurium.

tellu'ric, *adj.*, pert. to the earth.

tell'uride, *n.*, tellurium compounded with an organic radical.

tellu'rium, *n.*, a rare silver-coloured metal (*chem.*).

tel'lurous, *adj.*, pert. to tellurium.

tel'pher, *adj.*, pert. or rel. to telpherage.

tel'pherage, *n.*, automatic electric transportation.

tel'star, *n.*, a radio and television communication satellite.

tel'ugu, *n.*, a language of S.E. India.

temera'rious, *adj.*, i.q. temerous.

temera'riously, *adv.*, i.q. temerously.

temer'ity, *n.*, rashness.

tem'erous, *adj.*, rash; foolhardy.

tem'erously, *adv.*, rashly or recklessly.

tem'per, *n.*, the quality of metal; a state of mind; natural tendency; passion; *v.t.*, to reduce to sufficient strength, coolness, etc.; to calm.

tem'pera, *n.*, a method of painting on a prepared medium. Also *distemper*.

tem'perament, *n.*, mental qualities.

temperamen'tal, *adj.*, pert. to temperament.

temperamen'tally, *adv.*, according to temperament.

tem'perance, *n.*, self-restraint in all matters.

tem'perate, *adj.*, self-restrained; moderate; not excessive.

tem'perately, *adv.*, in a temperate way.

tem'perative, *adj.*, restraining; gratifying.

tem'perature, *n.*, the degree of warmth or cold.

tem'pered, *p.p.*, temper.

tem'pering, *pr.p.*, temper.

tem'perish, *adj.*, pert. or rel. to temper.

tem'persome, *adj.*, of good quality.

tem'pest, *n.*, a violent storm.

tempes'tuous, *adj.*, stormy; violent.

tempes'tuously, *adv.*, in a tempestuous way.

tempes'tuousness, *n.*, the state or quality of being tempestuous.

tempi, *n.*, pl. of tempo.

tem'plar, *n.*, a knight of the Order of Templars; a student in law attached to the Inner or the Middle Temple, London.

tem'plate, *n.*, *i.q.* templet.

tem'ple, *n.*, a place of divine worship, esp. the Temple in Jerusalem; one of the flat sides of the head by the forehead.

tem'plet, *n.*, a shaping pattern; a gauge.

tem'po, *n.*, the rate of musical speed (*Ital.*).

tem'poral, *adj.*, rel. to time; secular.

temporal'ities, *n. pl.*, the revenues from ecclesiastical property.

temporal'ity, *n.*, the state or quality of being temporal.

tem'porally, *adv.*, in a temporal way or sense.

tempora'neous, *adj.*, *i.q.* temporary.

tem'porarily, *adv.*, for a time only.

tem'porariness, *n.*, the quality of lasting only a short time.

tem'porary, *adj.*, lasting only for a time.

tem'pore, in the time of (*Lat.*).

temporiza'tion, *n.*, the act of temporizing.

tem'porize, *v.i.*, to play for time; to be a trimmer.

tem'porized, *p.p.*, temporize.

tem'porizer, *n.*, one who temporizes.

tem'porizing, *pr.p.*, temporize.

tempt, *v.t.*, to try; persuade to wrong; allure.

temptabil'ity, *n.*, the state of being temptable.

tempt'able, *adj.*, able to be tempted.

tempta'tion, *n.*, the act of tempting; state of being tempted; something alluring or enticing to wrong.

tempta'tious, *adj.*, alluring; enticing.

tempt'ed, *p.p.*, tempt.

tempt'er, *n.*, one who tempts, esp. Satan.

tempt'ing, *pr.p.*, tempt; *adj.*, alluring; attractive.

tempt'ingly, *adv.*, alluringly.

tempt'ress, *n.*, fem. of tempter.

ten, *n.*, the cardinal number next above nine; *adj.*, one more than nine.

tenabil'ity, *n.*, the state or quality of being tenable.

ten'able, *adj.*, able to be held.

ten'ace, *n.*, a particular holding of playing cards.

tena'cious, *adj.*, grasping; clinging; obstinate.

tena'ciously, *adv.*, in a tenacious way.

tenac'ity, *n.*, the quality of being tenacious.

tenac'ulum, *n.*, a surgical hooked instrument.

ten'ancy, *n.*, the status of a tenant; temporary occupancy.

ten'ant, *n.*, a temporary occupant of land or premises; *v.t.*, to hold in tenancy.

ten'antable, *adj.*, fit for occupation.

ten'anted, *p.p.*, tenant.

ten'ant-in-chief', *n.*, a leading tenant.

ten'anting, *pr.p.*, tenant.

ten'antless, *adj.*, unoccupied.

ten'antry, *n.*, collective tenants.

tench, *n.*, a fresh-water fish.

tend, *v.t.*, to look after; care for.

tend'ed, *p.p.*, tend.

ten'dency, *n.*, disposition; proneness; direction.

tenden'tious, *adj.*, pursuing a purpose in argument.

tenden'tiously, *adv.*, objectively.

tenden'tiousness, *n.*, the quality of being tendentious.

ten'der, *adj.*, soft; kind-hearted; sore; *n.*, a detachable part of a locomotive engine, containing the fuel, etc.; an attendant ship; a proposal or offer; *v.t.*, to offer; propose; *v.i.*, to send in an estimate for the performance of work or supply of goods.

ten'dered, *p.p.*, tender.

ten'derer, *adj.*, *comp.* of tender.

ten'derest, *adj. super.*, most tender.

ten'derfoot, *n.*, an inexperienced person.

ten'der-hearted, *adj.*, compassionate; easily moved to pity.

ten'der-heart'edly, *adv.*, feelingly.

ten'der-heart'edness, *n.*, compassion; feeling.

ten'dering, *pr.p.*, tender.

ten'derly, *adv.*, in a tender way.

ten'derness, *n.*, the state or quality of being tender.

tend'ing, *pr.p.*, tend.

ten'dinous, *adj.*, rel. to a tendon.

ten'don, *n.*, a sinew; the connecting link between bone and muscle.

ten'dril, *n.*, a feeler thrown out by a plant.

ten'drilled, *adj.*, having tendrils.

ten'dron, *n.*, *i.q.* tendril.

ten'ebrae, *n.*, the offices of matins and lauds for Thursday, Friday and Saturday in Holy Week (R.C.).

tenebrif'ic, *adj.*, creating darkness.

tene'brio, *n.*, one who moves by night; a meal worm.

teneb'rious, *adj.*, *i.q.* tenebrous.

ten'ebrist, *n.*, a painter who uses predominantly dark colours.

ten'ebrous, *adj.*, dark, gloomy.

ten'ement, n., a building held by a tenant; esp. a room or set of rooms in a house; permanent property.

tenemen'tal, adj., pert. to a tenement.

tenemen'tary, adj., i.q. tenemental.

tenes'mus, n., a painful tendency to void excrement or urine.

ten'et, n., a belief; an accepted principle.

ten'fold, adj., ten times as much or great.

te'nioid, adj., like a band.

ten'nis, n., an old game known as court tennis; also a modern game known as lawn tennis.

ten'nis-ball, n., a cloth-covered ball used in tennis.

ten'nis-court, n., a court where tennis is played.

ten'nis-lawn, n., a lawn where lawn tennis is played.

ten'nis-racket, n., an elliptical bat, strung with nylon or gut.

ten'on, n., the wedge-shaped end of a timber so shaped for mortising.

ten'or, n., course; drift; purport; male voice between bass and alto; adj., rel. to the tenor voice or pitch.

tenot'omy, n., cutting a tendon.

ten'pence, n., the amount or value of ten pennies.

ten'penny, adj., worth or costing tenpence.

ten'pins, n., a bowling game.

tense, adj., on the stretch; n., one of the verb inflections varying in relation to the time expressed, whether past, present, or future.

tense'ly, adv., in a tense way.

tense'ness, n., the state or quality of being tense.

tensibil'ity, n., the state or quality of being tensible.

ten'sible, adj., able to be stretched.

ten'sile, adj., ductile.

ten'sility, n., i.q. tensibility.

ten'sion, n., the act of stretching; the state of being stretched or tense; suspense; mental excitement.

ten'sity, n., i.q. tenseness.

ten'sive, adj., producing tension.

ten'son, n., a French mediaeval verse contest.

ten'sor, n., a muscle that stretches.

tent, n., a movable habitation or shelter; a surgical roll; a variety of wine.

ten'tacle, n., an organ by means of which certain invertebrates feel, move, etc.

ten'tacled, adj., having tentacles.

tentac'ular, adj., of the nature of tentacles.

tentac'ulum, n., a tentacle (Lat.).

ten'tative, adj., attempting; making experiment.

ten'tatively, adv., in a tentative way.

tent'ed, adj., having tents.

ten'ter, n., a frame holding tenterhooks; v.t., to hang on tenterhooks.

ten'terhook, n., a hook on which to hang clothes, etc. In pl., a state of strain.

tenth, adj., the ordinal of ten; next after ninth.

tenth'ly, adv., in the tenth place.

tent'ing, n., material for making tents.

tento'rium, n., a tent (Lat.); a tent-like formation between the cerebrum and the cerebellum.

tenuifo'lious, adj., having thin leaves.

tenu'ity, n., thinness; rarity.

ten'uous, adj., thin; slender.

ten'uously, adv., in a tenuous way.

ten'uousness, n., the state or quality of being tenuous.

ten'ure, n., a holding; an occupancy; rights or conditions of occupancy.

ten'uto, adj., sustained.

tep'ee, n., a Red Indian tent.

tepefac'tion, n., the act of tepefying; the state of being tepefied.

tep'efied, p.p., tepefy.

tep'efy, v.t., to warm; make tepid.

tep'efying, pr.p., tepefy.

tep'id, adj., neither hot nor cold; fairly warm.

tepid'ity, n., the state of being tepid.

ter'aph, n., a household god, or image of one.

ter'aphim, n., pl. of teraph.

ter'atoid, adj., hideous; abnormal.

teratol'ogy, n., the study of abnormal animal or plant structures.

terato'ma, n., a growth or swelling; a tumour.

terce, n., a large cask (42 gallons); a card sequence of the same colour; a musical interval of a third; one of the day offices said at the third hour (i.e., 9 a.m.).

ter'cel, n., the male falcon. Also tiercel.

tercen'tenary, adj., rel. to a period of 300 years; n., the three hundredth anniversary.

ter'ebene, n., a turpentine-based disinfectant.

ter'ebinth, n., the turpentine tree.

terebin'thine, adj., rel. to the terebinth; like turpentine.

tere'do, n., a boring worm; the ship-worm.

terete', adj., cylindrical.

tergem'inal, adj., three times double.

tergem'inate, adj., i.q. tergeminal.

tergif'erous, adj., bearing on the back.

ter'giversate, v.i., to shuffle; evade.

tergiversa'tion, n., evasion; shuffling.

ter'giversator, n., one who changes party or opinions.

ter'gum, n., the upper-surface of an insect's abdomen (Lat.).

term, n., an end; limit; subject or predicate of a logical proposition; the number of a compound mathematical quantity; an expression; a period; the time when the law courts or universities are open; v.t., to name; to phrase.

ter'magancy, n., the conduct of a termagant.

ter'magant, n., a violent, loud-tongued woman; adj., noisily violent.

termed, p.p., term.

Ter'mes, n., a variety of insects, as white ants, etc.

terminabil'ity, n., the state of being terminable.

ter'minable, adj., able to be terminated.

ter'minably, adv., in a terminable way.

ter'minal, adj., rel. to a term or to an end; disposed according to termination; n., a boundary; an end of a circuit on a dynamo.

term'inally, adv., finally.

ter'minate, adj., limited; bounded.

ter'minate, v.t., to put a finish to; to end; v.i., to be limited; to end.

ter'minated, p.p., terminate.

ter'minating, pr.p., terminate.

termina'tion, n., the act of terminating; an end.

termina'tional, adj., pert. to a termination.

ter'minative, adj., placing a limit; fixing an end.

ter'minatively, adv., in a terminative way.

ter'minator, n., one who, that which, terminates; the line marking the division between the bright and the dark parts of the moon.

ter'minatory, adj., i.q. terminative.

ter'miner, n., the fact of determining.

term'ing, pr.p., term.

ter'mini, n., pl. of terminus.

ter'minism, n., the teaching that the period of Divine grace is limited.

ter'minist, n., a believer in terminism.

terminolog'ical, adj., ref. to terms.

terminolog'ically, adv., according to terminology.

terminol'ogy, n., the definition or use of special terms.

ter'minus, n., an end; a boundary; a railway station where a line begins or ends.

ter'mite, n., a white ant.

term'less, adj., without a term.

term'ly, adj. and adv., happening once a term.

tern, n., a kind of gull; adj., containing three; three-fold.

ter'nary, adj., going in threes; n., the number three.

ter'nate, adj., grouped in threes.

tero'technol'ogy, n., the study of industrial plant installation, maintenance and removal.

terpsichore'an, n., pert. to Terpsichore the Muse of dancing.

ter'ra, n., the earth (Lat.).

ter'race, n., ground levelled on a hill or sloping ground; a row of houses; the flat top of an Eastern house; v.t., to make a terrace of.

ter'raced, p.p., terrace.

ter'racing, pr.p., terrace.

ter'ra-cot'ta, n., burnt clay and sand, used for making statues, medallions, architectural ornaments, etc.

ter'ra fir'ma, n., the land as distinct from water.

terrain', n., the nature of land from a military or sociologist's viewpoint.

ter'ra incog'nita, n., an unknown, strange land.

terramare', n., phosphate earth deposits used as fertilizers.

ter'rapin, n., an edible fresh-water tortoise.

terra'queous, adj., consisting of land and water.

ter'ras, n., flaws in marble, filled in with a substitute (trass).

terraz'zo, n., a kind of mosaic floor-covering, sometimes prefabricated, made of marble chippings (It.).

terrene', adj., pert. to the earth.

ter'reous, adj., earthy.

terre'plein, n., the terrace behind a rampart.

terres'trial, adj., rel. to the earth or the world, as distinct from celestial.

terres'trially, adv., in a terrestrial way.

ter'ret, n., a ring on harness for reins.

ter'rible, adj., fearful; frightful; dreadful.

ter'ribly, adv., in a terrible degree.

terricole, n., a burrowing animal or plant.

terri'colous, adj., living in the earth.

ter'rier, n., a canine breed; a scheduled statement of landed property.

terrif'ic, adj., terrifying.

terrif'ically, adv., terrifyingly.

ter'rified, p.p., terrify.

ter'rify, v.t., to fill with terror; to frighten.

ter'rifying, pr.p., terrify.

terrify'ingly, adv., in a terrifying way.

terrig'enous, adj., earthborn.

territo'rial, adj., rel. to territory or a specified district.

territo'rialism, n., the principle of territorial division.

territo'rialize, v.t., to take over as a territory.

territo'rialized, p.p., territorialize.

territo'rializing, pr.p., territorialize.

territo'rially, adv., in a territorial way.

Territo'rials, n. pl., a British military force created in 1908, now part of the Reserve.

ter'ritory, n., the area contained within the jurisdiction of a king, bishop, etc.; a large extent of land; a region.

ter'ror, n., fear, alarm; a frightful person.

ter'rorism, n., ruling by fear; intimidation.

ter'rorist, n., one who advocates terrorism.

ter'rorize, v.t. and i., to rule by fear; to intimidate.

ter'rorized, p.p., terrorize.

ter'rorizer, n., one who frightens or intimidates.

ter'rorizing, pr.p., terrorize.

ter'ry, n., an uncut-pile fabric.

Ter Sanc'tus, n., a liturgical hymn.

terse, adj., neat; concise.

terse'ly, adv., neatly, concisely.

terse'ness, n., neatness; elegance; conciseness.

ter'tial, *adj.*, rel to the third row.

ter'tian, *adj.*, recurring on each third day; *n.*, a fever or ague recurring each third day.

ter'tiary, *adj.*, of the third order, etc.; rel. to geological strata that overlie the chalk; *n.*, a member of the third order of St. Francis or St. Dominic.

Terylene', *n.*, a man-made fibre and textile.

ter'za-ri'ma, *n.*, an Italian poetic form in which the middle line of the first triplet rhymes with a first and third of the next triplet.

terzet'to, *n.*, a short three-voice composition (*mus.*).

tessel'la, *n.*, a small tessera.

tes'sellate, *v.t.*, to cover with tile-work.

tes'sellated, *p.p.*, tessellate.

tes'sellating, *pr.p.*, tessellate.

tessella'tion, *n.*, the act of tessellating; the state of being tessellated.

tes'sera, *n.*, one of the cubes in a piece of mosaic.

tes'serae, *n.*, pl. of tessera.

tes'seral, *adj.*, rel. to tesserae.

tessitur'a, *n.*, the singing voice range.

tes'sular, *adj.*, of equal measure.

test, *n.*, a trial; proof; experiment; *v.t.*, to put to the proof; make trial of; experiment with; refine.

tes'ta, *n.*, a tile; the integument of a seed; the shell of testaceae (*Lat.*).

test'able, *adj.*, able to be tested.

testa'cea, *n.*, a mollusc. (In pl., testaceae.)

testa'cean, *adj.*, pert. to testaceae.

testacel'la, *n.*, a slug-like gastropod.

testaceol'ogy, *n.*, the study of testacean creatures.

testa'ceous, *adj.*, covered with a shell.

tes'tacy, *n.*, the position of leaving a proper will.

tes'tament, *n.*, a will; one of the two sections of the Bible, the Old and the New Testament.

testamen'tal, *adj.*, i.q. testamentary.

testamen'tary, *adj.*, pert. to a will; bequeathed.

testam'ur, *n.*, a certificate of passing an examination.

tes'tate, *adj.*, leaving a valid will; *n.*, one whose will is valid.

testa'tion, *n.*, the disposing of property by a will.

testa'tor, *n.*, one who bequeathes property by a will.

testa'trix, *n.*, fem. of testator.

test'ed, *p.p.*, test.

test'er, *n.*, one who tests; the old name for sixpence; a canopy.

test'-flight, *n.*, a proving flight for a new aircraft.

tes'ticle, *n.*, a gland that secretes spermatozoa.

testifica'tion, *n.*, the act of testifying; witness.

tes'tified, *p.p.*, testify.

tes'tifier, *n.*, one who testifies.

tes'tify, *v.i.*, to bear witness; give evidence; *v.t.*, to state in evidence.

tes'tifying, *pr.p.*, testify.

tes'tily, *adv.*, in a testy way.

testimo'nial, *n.*, an expression of approval; witness to character; a gift to mark high esteem; *adj.*, rel. to testimony.

tes'timony, *n.*, witness's evidence.

tes'tiness, *n.*, the state or quality of being testy.

test'ing, *pr.p.*, test; *n.*, an assay; a trial.

test'-match, *n.*, a game between national sides.

test'-paper, *n.*, a sensitive paper used in chemical experiments.

test'-tube, *n.*, a cylindrical glass container used in scientific work.

testu'dinal, *adj.*, like a tortoise.

testudinar'ious, *adj.*, coloured marking like tortoise-shell.

testu'dinate, *adj.*, arched tortoise-like.

testudin'eous, *adj.*, like the shell of a tortoise.

testu'do, *n.*, an ancient Roman device of locking shields together, under cover of which soldiers advanced to a siege; a tortoise (*Lat.*).

tes'ty, *adj.*, quick-tempered and peevish; irritable.

tetan'ic, *adj.*, rel. to tetanus.

tet'anus, *n.*, lockjaw.

tetch'ily, *adv.*, in a tetchy way.

tetch'iness, *n.*, the state of being tetchy.

tetch'y, *adj.*, easily vexed; irritable.

tête, *n.*, a head; a headdress (*Fr.*).

tête'-à-tête', *n.*, a private conversation; *adv.*, in private conversation (*Fr.*).

teth'er, *n.*, a rope for fastening animals; liberty of action up to a point; *v.t.*, to confine.

teth'ered, *p.p.*, tether.

teth'ering, *pr.p.*, tether.

tet'ra, a *Gr.* prefix = four.

tetrabran'chiate, *adj.*, with four gills or branchiae.

tet'rachord, *n.*, the four notes of the half-scale.

tet'ract, *adj.*, having four rays.

tet'rad, *n.*, the number four; a group of four.

tet'radrachm, *n.*, a coin of four drachmae value.

tet'ragon, *n.*, a four-sided figure having four angles.

tetrag'onal, *adj.*, rel. to a tetragon.

tet'ragram, *n.*, a four-letter inscription.

tetrahe'dral, *adj.*, with four sides.

tetrahe'dron, *n.*, a solid figure with four triangular surfaces.

tetram'eter, *n.*, a metrical verse of four feet.

tetran'drous, *adj.*, with four stamens.

tet'rapla, *n.*, the Holy Scriptures set out in four parallel columns each containing a different version.

tet'rapod, *n.*, a quadrupedal insect.

tet'rarch, *n.*, a Roman governor of the fourth part of a province.

tet′rarchate, *n.*, the rule or term of office, of a tetrarch.

tet′rarchy, *n.*, the province of a tetrarch.

tet′rastich, *n.*, a stanza of four lines.

tet′rastyle, *n.*, a structure fronted by four pillars.

tetrasyl′lable, *n.*, a four-syllabled word.

tetrath′lon, *n.*, a four-part athletic contest.

tet′ronal, *n.*, a drug.

tet′ter, *n.*, a skin disease; herpes.

Teu′ton, *adj.*, *i.q.* Teutonic; *n.*, a German.

Teuton′ic, *adj.*, German.

Teu′tonism, *n.*, German idiom.

Teu′tonize, *v.t.*, to make Germanic.

Teu′tonized, *p.p.*, Teutonize.

Teu′tonizing, *pr.p.*, Teutonize.

Tevet′, *n.*, the fourth month of the Jewish civil year.

tew′el, tu′el, *n.*, the anus of an animal, esp. horse.

te′whit, *n.*, the lapwing.

Tex′an, *adj.*, rel. to Texas; *n.*, a native of T.

text, *n.*, a subject of discourse; a writing.

text′book, *n.*, an authoritative book of instruction.

text′-hand, *n.*, a large style of hand-writing.

tex′tile, *adj.*, woven; *n.*, a woven fabric.

texto′rial, *adj.*, rel. to weaving.

tex′tual, *adj.*, rel. to text.

tex′tualist, *n.*, a student of text.

textual′ity, *n.*, the quality of being textual.

tex′tually, *adv.*, according to text.

tex′tuary, *adj.*, *i.q.* textual.

tex′tural, *adj.*, pert. or rel. to texture.

tex′turally, *adv.*, in a textural way.

tex′ture, *n.*, weaving; a thing woven; a manner of weaving; *v.t.*, to weave.

tex′tured, *p.p.*, texture.

tex′turing, *pr.p.*, texture.

Thai, *adj.*, pert. or rel. to Thailand; *n.*, the language of T.; a native of T.

thal′amus, *n.*, the reputed starting-point of a nerve; the receptacle of a flower (*Lat.*).

thalas′sic, *adj.*, related to inland seas.

tha′ler, *n.*, an old German coin.

Thali′a, *n.*, the Muse of Comedy.

Thali′an, *adj.*, rel. to Thalia; comic.

thali′domide, *n.* and *adj.*, (a drug) producing aberrant human forms.

thal′lium, *n.*, a metallic element so named.

thall′us, *n.*, a plant with root, leaves and stem all in one.

Tham′muz, *n.*, an ancient deity. (Also *Tammuz*.)

than, *conj.*, used in comparisons, as *more than, greater than.*

than′atism, *n.*, the belief in death of the soul with bodily decease.

than′atoid, *adj.*, looking as though dead.

thanatol′ogy, *n.*, the study of death.

thanatopho′bia, *n.*, excessive fear of death.

thanatop′sis, *n.*, a morbid contemplation of death.

thanato′sis, *n.*, a gangrenous condition.

thane, *n.*, an Anglo-Saxon landowner.

thank, *v.t.*, to profess gratitude to.

thanked, *p.p.*, thank.

thank′ful, *adj.*, grateful.

thank′fully, *adv.*, gratefully.

thank′fulness, *n.*, gratitude.

thank′ing, *pr.p.*, thank.

thank′less, *adj.*, ungrateful; earning no return of thanks.

thank′lessness, *n.*, the state or quality of being thankless.

thank′offering, *n.*, a sacrifice in gratitude.

thanks, *n. pl.*, the expression of gratitude.

thanks′giving, *n.*, the act of giving thanks; a public festival of thanks.

thank′worthy, *adj.*, deserving of gratitude.

thar, *n.*, the Nepalese antelope.

that, *demonstrative pron.* and *adj.*, yonder one; not this; *conj.*, because; since. The word is also used as a *relative pron.* = who or which.

thatch, *n.*, a straw covering for houses, sheds, etc.; *v.t.*, to protect with thatch.

thatched, *p.p.*, thatch.

thatch′er, *n.*, a man who thatches houses, stacks, etc.

thatch′ing, *pr.p.*, thatch.

thaumato′graphy, *n.*, the written description of natural wonders or phenomena.

thaumatol′atry, *n.*, miracle- or wonder-worship.

thau′matrope, *n.*, an optical device causing an impression of a visible object to remain after its actual withdrawal.

thaumatur′gic, *adj.*, wonder-working; rel. to miracles.

thaumatur′gist, *n.*, a wonder-worker.

thau′maturgy, *n.*, wonder-working; performing of miracles; sleight of hand.

thaw, *v.i.*, to melt; to become milder; *v.t.*, to melt; *n.*, a state in which ice melts when the temperature rises above freezing-point.

thawed, *p.p.*, thaw.

thaw′er, *n.*, a substance or apparatus for melting ice.

thaw′ing, *pr.p.*, thaw.

thaw′y, *adj.*, inclined to thaw.

the, *adj.*, the definite article.

The′a, *n.*, the tea plant genus.

thean′dric, *adj.*, simultaneously human and divine.

thean′thropic, *adj.*, *i.q.* theandric.

thean′thropism, *n.*, a belief that deity and humanity can be combined in one person.

thean′thropy, *n.*, *i.q.* theanthropism.

the′archy, *n.*, government by God or by divine rulers.

The′atine, *n.*, a member of the Theatine Order, which was founded in order to promote the Counter Reformation.

the′atre, *n.*, a place for spectacular or dramatic exhibitions; a scene of action; a room arranged for lectures, etc.

theatre′-goer, *n.*, a regular visitor to the theatre.

theat′ric, *adj.*, pert. to a theatre.

theat′rical, *adj.*, *i.q.* theatric; histrionic; affected like an actor.

theat′rically, *adv.*, in a theatrical way.

theat′ricals, *n. pl.*, dramatic performances (usually amateur).

The′ban, *adj.*, rel. to Thebes; *n.*, a native of Thebes.

the′ca, *n.*, a sheath; a fern's seed-case (*Gr.*).

the′codont, *adj.*, with sheathed teeth.

thee, *pers. pron.*, accusative or objective case of thou.

theft, *n.*, the act of stealing.

thegn, *n.*, *i.q.* thane.

the′ic, *n.*, a tea-drinker to excess.

the′ine, *n.*, the essential principle of tea.

their, *poss. adj.*, bel. to them.

theirs, *pers. pron.*, possessive case of they.

the′ism, *n.*, belief in a personal God.

the′ist, *n.*, a believer in a personal God.

theistic, *adj.*, rel. to theism.

theist′ical, *adj.*, *i.q.* theistic.

theli′tis, *n.*, inflammation of the nipple.

them, *pers. pron.*, objective or accusative case of they.

thema′tic, *adj.*, related to a main subject.

theme, *n.*, a subject for discourse or argument; a short essay; a musical subject.

Them′is, *n.*, the Greek goddess of justice.

themselves′, *reflexive pron.*, pl. of himself, etc.

then, *adv.*, at that time; immediately; in addition or next after; *conj.*, therefore; so; in consequence.

then′abouts, *adv.*, at about that time.

then′ar, *n.*, the palm of the hand, the sole of the foot.

thence, *adv.*, from that place or time.

thenceforth′, *adv.*, from that time forward.

thencefor′ward, *adv.*, from that time or place forward.

Theobro′ma, *n.*, a genus of trees from which cacao is derived.

theobro′mine, *n.*, an alkaloid obtained from the chocolate nut.

theoc′racy, *n.*, government by God; a kingdom ruled directly by God.

theoc′rasy, *n.*, the worship of more than one god; the neoplatonic philosophy of union of the soul with God through contemplation.

the′ocrat, *n.*, a divine ruler; one who is ruled directly by God in all matters.

theocrat′ic, *adj.*, rel. to theocracy.

theocrat′ical, *adj.*, *i.q.* theocratic.

theocrat′ically, *adv.*, in a theocratic way.

theod′icy, *n.*, the justification of God's Providence.

theod′olite, *n.*, a surveying instrument.

theodolit′ic, *adj.*, rel. to the use of the theodolite.

theog′onist, *n.*, a student of theogony.

theog′ony, *n.*, the study of the origin of heathen deities; a poem on the subject.

theolo′gian, *n.*, a student or professor of theology.

theolog′ic, *adj.*, *i.q.* theological.

theolog′ical, *adj.*, pert. to theology.

theolog′ically, *adv.*, according to theology.

theol′ogist, *n.*, *i.q.* theologian.

theo′logize, *v.t. and i.*, to speculate about nature of God.

the′ologue, *n.*, *i.q.* theologian.

theol′ogy, *n.*, the study of divinity.

theom′achy, *n.*, a strife among deities.

theoma′nia, *n.*, madness associated with religious melancholy.

theomor′phic, *adj.*, like a god.

theop′athy, *n.*, a sense of piety.

theoph′any, *n.*, a visible appearance of a deity.

theophilosoph′ic, *adj.*, philosophic about religion.

theo′phobia, *n.*, an unwholesome fear of God; a hatred of God.

theopneus′tic, *adj.*, divinely inspired.

theopneu′sty, *n.*, a divine inspiration.

theor′bo, *n.*, a double lute.

the′orem, *n.*, a proposition for proof.

theoret′ic, *adj.*, pert. to theory; speculative.

theoret′ical, *adj.*, *i.q.* theoretic.

theoret′ically, *adv.*, in a theoretical way.

theoreti′cian, *n.*, one who is concerned only with theory.

the′orist, *n.*, one who theorizes.

the′orize, *v.i.*, to indulge in theories; to speculate.

the′orized, *p.p.*, theorize.

the′orizer, *n.*, *i.q.* theorist.

the′orizing, *pr.p.*, theorize.

the′ory, *n.*, a speculation, a hypothesis; abstract principles.

theosoph′ic, *adj.*, pert. to theosophy.

theosoph′ical, *adj.*, *i.q.* theosophic.

theos′ophist, *n.*, one who practises theosophy.

theos′ophy, *n.*, an esoteric system of philosophy which affects a privileged knowledge of the occult powers of nature.

therapeu′tic, *adj.*, curative.

therapeu′tical, *adj.*, *i.q.* therapeutic.

therapeu′tically, *adv.*, in a therapeutic way.

therapeu′tics, *n. pl.*, that part of medical science which relates to the curative treatment of disease.

ther′apy, *n.*, treatment for cure.

there, *adv.*, yonder; not here; at that point.

there′abouts, *adv.*, somewhere in that direction.

thereaf′ter, *adv.*, after that time; subsequently.

there′at, *adv.*, at that.

thereby′, *adv.*, by that; consequently.

there'for, *adv.*, for that.

there'fore, *adv.* and *conj.*, because of that; for that reason.

therefrom', *adv.*, from that time, place, or cause.

therein', *adv.*, in that.

therein'after, *adv.*, later in the same deed or document.

therein'before, *adv.*, earlier, or previously, in the same deed or document.

therein'to, *adv.*, into that.

thereof', *adv.*, of that.

thereon', *adv.*, upon that; subsequently.

thereout', *adv.*, from out of that.

thereto', *adv.*, to that; in addition.

there'tofore, *adv.*, before that (time).

thereun'der, *adv.*, under that.

thereun'to, *adv.*, to that.

thereupon', *adv.*, consequently; from that moment.

therewith', *adv.*, with that.

therewithal', *adv.*, *i.q.* therewith.

the'riac, *adj.*, pert. to the lower animals and their bites.

theri'acal, *adj.*, *i.q.* theriac.

theriantro'pic, *adj.*, combining man and beast.

theriol'atry, *n.*, the worship of animals.

the'riomorph, *n.*, art form with animals.

theriomorph'ic, *adj.*, like an animal.

theriomorpho'sis, *n.*, a change into animal form.

theriot'omy, *n.*, the anatomy of lower animals.

therm, *n.*, a unit of gas supply.

ther'mae, *n. pl.*, hot springs; baths (*Gr.*).

ther'mal, *adj.*, rel. to temperatures; warm.

ther'mally, *adv.*, with reference to heat.

ther'mic, *adj.*, rel. to heat.

therm'ically, *adv.*, in a thermic way.

Thermidor', *n.*, the eleventh month in the Kalendar of the French Revolution.

therm'ion, *n.*, emitted ion from hot substance.

thermion'ic, *adj.*, relating to thermions.

thermion'ics, *n.*, the study of electronic flow in radio.

ther'mite, *n.*, a substance which burns with intense heat.

thermochem'istry, *n.*, the study of heat in relation to chemical change or reaction.

thermodu'ric, *adj.*, resisting heat.

thermo-dynam'ics, *n. pl.*, the science of the dynamics of heat.

thermo-electric'ity, *n.*, electricity in relation to heat.

therm'ogram, *n.*, a record made by a thermograph.

therm'ograph, *n.*, a self-recording thermometer.

thermograph'ic, *adj.*, pert. or rel. to a thermograph or to thermography.

theromo'graphy, *n.*, the method of recording by the use of heat.

thermol'ogy, *n.*, the study of heat phenomena.

thermom'eter, *n.*, an apparatus showing degrees of temperature.

thermomet'ric, *adj.*, pert. to a thermometer.

thermomet'rical, *adj.*, *i.q.* thermometric.

ther'mo-nu'clear, *adj.*, concerned with fission of atoms in intense heat.

ther'mopla'stic, *adj.* and *n.*, resin or plastic softening with heat.

ther'mos, *n.*, a heat-conserving flask.

ther'moscope, *n.*, an apparatus recording relative differences of temperature.

ther'mostat, *n.*, an instrument which automatically regulates temperature.

ther'most'atic, *adj.*, regulated by heat.

thermot'ic, *adj.*, pert. to heat.

thermot'ics, *n. pl.*, the study of heat phenomena.

ther'motypy, *n.*, the developing of pictures by the application of heat.

ther'oid, *adj.*, beast-like.

therol'ogy, *n.*, the study of animals.

thesau'rus, *n.*, a treasury; a dictionary; a lexicon (*Gr.* and *Lat.*).

these, *demonstrative pron.*, pl. of this.

the'sis, *n.*, a subject for an essay, or for treatment as an academic exercise; the exercise or essay itself.

Thes'pian, *adj.*, pert. to Thespis, the reputed originator of the drama; dramatic.

Thessalian, *adj.*, relating to Thessaly; *n.*, a native of T.

Thessalo'nian, *adj.*, pert. to Thessalonica; *n.*, a native of T.

thet'ic, *adj.*, rel. to a thesis.

thet'ical, *adj.*, *i.q.* thetic.

theur'gic, *adj.*, rel. to theurgy.

theur'gist, *n.*, one who professes theurgy.

the'urgy, *n.*, magic.

thews, *n. pl.*, muscles; physical strength.

they, *pers. pron.*, pl. of he, she, it.

Thibe'tan, *adj.*, *i.q.* Tibetan.

thick, *adj.*, not thin; dense; closely compacted; cloudy; not transparent; quickly following; *adv.*, indistinctly; in rapid succession; *n.*, the thick part.

thick'en, *v.t.*, to make thick; *v.i.*, to become thicker.

thick'ened, *p.p.*, thicken.

thick'ener, *n.*, anything that thickens or adds substance.

thick'ening, *pr.p.*, thicken.

thick'er, *adj.*, *comp.* of thick.

thick'est, *adj.*, *super.* of thick.

thick'et, *n.*, a copse; a close group of trees.

thick'head, *n.*, a dolt; a stupid fellow.

thick'headed, *adj.*, stupid; mentally dense.

thick'ish, *adj.*, somewhat thick.

thick'ly, *adv.*, in a thick way.

thick'ness, *n.*, the state or quality of being thick.

thick'-set, *adj.*, stoutly built; closely planted; *n.*, a closely planted hedge.

thick'-skinned, *adj.,* insensitive, impervious to criticism.

thief, *n.,* one who steals.

thieve, *v.t.* and *i.,* to steal.

thieved, *p.p.,* thieve.

thiev'ery, *n.,* stealing.

thieves, *n.,* pl. of thief.

thiev'ing, *pr.p.,* thieve; *n.,* the art or practice of a thief.

thiev'ish, *adj.,* inclined to stealing; stolen.

thiev'ishly, *adv.,* in a thievish way.

thigh, *n.,* the upper leg between the knee and the body.

thigh'bone, *n.,* the bone of the thigh; the femur.

thill, *n.,* a cart or carriage shaft; a mine floor.

thill'er, *n.,* a shaft horse.

thim'ble, *n.,* a finger-guard used in sewing; a ring on a sail.

thim'bleful, *n.,* a mere drop; a very minute draught.

thim'blerig, *n.,* a juggling trick with a pea and three thimbles; *v.t.,* to play the trick on.

thim'blerigged, *p.p.,* thimblerig.

thim'blerigger, *n.,* one who thimblerigs.

thim'blerigging, *pr.p.,* thimblerig.

thin, *adj.,* not thick; spare; narrow; fine; clear but not strong; meagre; *v.t.,* to make thin; *v.i.,* to become thin.

thine, *posses. adj.,* bel. to thee.

thing, *n.,* that which exists as imaginable or manifest to the senses; an inanimate object; a contemptible object; a Scandinavian legislative assembly.

think, *v.t.,* to conceive in the mind; to hold in opinion; to decide; to purpose; *v.i.,* to imagine; to ponder; to be of opinion.

think'able, *adj.,* able to be thought.

think'er, *n.,* one who thinks; a philosopher.

think'ing, *pr.p.,* think; *adj.,* contemplative; philosophic; *n.,* contemplation; foresight.

think'ingly, *adv.,* in a thoughtful way.

thin'ly, *adv.,* in a thin way.

thinned, *p.p.,* thin.

thin'ner, *adj.,* *comp.* of thin.

thin'ness, *n.,* the state or quality of being thin.

thin'nest, *adj.,* *super.* of thin.

thin'ning, *pr.p.,* thin.

thin'nish, *adj.,* somewhat thin.

thin'-skinned, *adj.,* having a thin skin; morbidly sensitive and touchy.

third, *adj.,* the ordinal of three; the next after the second; rel. to one of three equal parts; *n.,* a third part; a musical interval of three diatonic sounds.

third'-class', *adj.,* next after second-class.

third'ing, *n.,* a third part or division. (Politically, a Riding.)

third'ly, *adv.,* in the third place.

third-par'ty, *n.,* one who is not a principal in a transaction or incident.

third'-rate', *adj.,* inferior.

thirds, *n.,* pl. of third.

thirl'age, *n.,* a mill-owner's power to make his tenants bring their corn to his mill.

thirst, *n.,* a desire for drink; any strong desire; *v.i.,* to have a desire for drink; to be thirsty.

thirst'ed, *p.p.,* thirst.

thirst'er, *n.,* one who thirsts.

thirst'ier, *adj.,* *comp.* of thirsty.

thirst'iest, *adj.,* *super.* of thirsty.

thirst'ily, *adv.,* in a thirsty way.

thirst'iness, *n.,* the state of being thirsty.

thirst'ing, *pr.p.,* thirst.

thirst'y, *adj.,* feeling thirst; eagerly desiring.

thirteen', *adj.,* ten plus three; *n.,* the cardinal number next after twelve.

thirteenth', *adj.,* the ordinal of thirteen; next after twelfth.

thir'tieth, *adj.,* the ordinal of thirty; next after twenty-ninth.

thir'ty, *adj.,* three times ten; *n.,* the cardinal number = 10 × 3.

thir'tyfold, *adj.,* thirty times as much or great.

thirtyish, *adj.,* approximately thirty.

thir'ty-two'mo, *adj.,* of a printer's sheet folded to produce 32 leaves = 64 pages.

this, *pron.* and *adj.,* that which is here or now, or last referred to.

this'tle, *n.,* a plant of the Carduus genus.

this'tly, *adj.,* full of, resembling, thistles.

thith'er, *adv.,* in that direction.

thith'erward, *adv.,* towards that end or direction.

thixotro'pic, *adj.,* pert. or rel. to thixotropy; usu. of paint, meaning non-drip (from the brush).

thixo'tropy, *n.,* the quality or state of reducing in viscosity when stirred.

thole, *n.,* a pin on which a boat's oar turns; *v.t.,* to put up with (*Scot.*).

thole'-pin, *n.,* i.q. thole.

tho'lus, *n.,* a tomb.

Thomae'an, *adj.,* pert. to Thomism.

Tho'mism, *n.,* the teachings of the scholastic doctor, St. Thomas Aquinas (13th cent.).

Tho'mist, *n.,* a disciple of St. Thomas Aquinas.

Tho'mite, *n.,* i.q. Thomist.

thong, *n.,* a thin leather strip for various purposes; a lash.

Thor, *n.,* the Scandinavian god of thunder, etc., whose name is perpetuated in Thursday.

thorac'ic, *adj.,* pert. to the thorax.

tho'rax, *n.,* the chest; a breastplate (*Gr.*).

tho'rium, *n.,* a radioactive metallic element.

thorn, *n.,* a prickly growth on certain trees and shrubs; a prickly shrub or tree; anything that annoys.

thorn'-apple, *n.,* stramonium.

thorn'-bush, *n.,* a thorn-bearing bush.

thorn'-hedge, *n.*, a hedge composed of thorns.

thorn'less, *adj.*, having no thorns.

thorn'y, *adj.*, covered with, resembling, thorns; full of difficulty and trouble.

tho'ron, *n.*, a gas produced from thorium.

thor'ough, *adj.*, complete; entire; insisting on perfection.

thor'oughbass, *n.*, the science of harmony; a kind of musical shorthand, in which chords are represented by figures.

thor'oughbred, *adj.*, bred from the best stock; high-spirited; *n.*, an animal of the best breeding.

thor'oughfare, *n.*, a road open to traffic.

thor'oughgoing, *adj.*, uncompromising; complete.

thor'oughly, *adv.*, completely; entirely.

thor'oughness, *n.*, the state or quality of being thorough.

thor'ough-paced, *adj.*, complete.

thor'oughwort, *n.*, a plant (Eupatorium perfoliatum).

thorp, *n.*, a hamlet. Also *thorpe*.

those, *pron.* and *adj.*, pl. of this.

Thoth, *n.*, the Egyptian god of wisdom.

thou, *pers. pron.*, 2nd person, you.

though, *conj.* (implying concession), granted that; notwithstanding the fact that; *i.q.* although; *adv.*, however.

thought, *p.p.*, think; *n.*, the act of thinking; that which one thinks; reflection; circumspection; regard for others.

thought'ful, *adj.*, reflecting; considerate; anxious.

thought'fully, *adv.*, in a thoughtful way.

thought'fulness, *n.*, the state of being thoughtful.

thought'less, *adj.*, inconsiderate; reckless; unthinking.

thought'lessly, *adv.*, in a thoughtless way.

thought'lessness, *n.*, the state of being thoughtless.

thought'-pro'cess, *n.*, a method of thinking.

thought'-read'er, *n.*, one who can detect another's unspoken thoughts.

thought'-read'ing, *n.*, the act of detecting another's unspoken thoughts.

thou'sand, *adj.*, ten hundred; *n.*, the cardinal number = 100 × 10.

thou'sandfold, *adj.*, a thousand times as many.

thou'sand-pound', *adj.*, weighing one thousand pounds; worth or costing one thousand pounds.

thous'andth, *adj.*, the ordinal of 1,000; next after 999th.

Thra'cian, *adj.*, rel. to Thrace; *n.*, a native of Thrace.

thral'dom, *n.*, servitude.

thrall, *n.*, a serf.

thrap'ple, *n.*, the windpipe (*Scot.*); *i.q.* thropple.

thrash, *v.t.*, to beat corn in order to extract the grain; to flog; *v.i.*, to do thrashing.

thrashed, *p.p.*, thrash.

thrash'er, *n.*, one who, that which, thrashes.

thrash'ing, *pr.p.*, thrash; *n.*, a flogging; the process of beating corn.

thrason'ic, *adj.*, resembling Thraso, a braggart soldier in Terence's *Eunuchus*; bragging.

thrason'ical, *adj.*, pert. or rel. to thrasonic.

thrason'ically, *adv.*, braggingly.

thrave, *n.*, a drove.

thread, *n.*, a very fine line of silk, cotton, etc., a filament; unbroken continuity in a story, an argument, etc.; the spiral of a screw; *v.t.*, to pass thread through; to penetrate; to string together.

thread'bare, *adj.*, worn out; shabby; hackneyed.

thread'ed, *p.p.*, thread.

thread'en, *adj.*, made of thread.

thread'er, *n.*, one who threads.

thread'iness, *n.*, the quality or state of being thready.

thread'ing, *pr.p.*, thread.

thread'like, *adj.*, fine; like a thread.

thread'shaped, *adj.*, like a thread.

thread'-worm, *n.*, a small intestinal worm.

thread'y, *adj.*, like thread.

threap, *v.t.* and *i.*, to cry out; to complain; to persist; to assert or contend.

threat, *n.*, a menace; an indication of harm, trouble or evil.

threat'en, *v.t.*, to try to frighten by menacing; to give sinister indications (as of storm, rain, etc.).

threat'ened, *p.p.*, threaten.

threat'ener, *n.*, one who threatens.

threat'ening, *pr.p.*, threaten; *adj.*, indicating the approach of danger, storm, etc.

threat'eningly, *adv.*, menacingly.

three, *adj.*, containing one more than two; *n.*, the cardinal number 3.

three'-card, *adj.*, played with three cards.

three'-col'our, *adj.*, having or using three colours.

three'-cornered, *adj.*, having three corners; in which three parties are engaged.

three'-decker, *n.*, an old man-of-war with three decks; a church pulpit having desks in three tiers; a sandwich with two layers of filling.

three'-dimen'sional, *adj.*, having height, length, breadth.

three'fold, *adj.*, three times multiplied.

three'-foot, *adj.*, measuring three feet.

three'-footed, *adj.*, having three feet.

three'-lane, *adj.*, applied to three section highway.

three'-leg'ged, *adj.*, having three legs.

three'-mast'ed, *adj.*, (a ship) having three masts.

three'-monthly, *adj.*, every three months; quarterly.

three'pence, *n.*, the amount of three pennies.

three′penny, *adj.*, costing threepence.

three′-ply, *adj.*, having three layers.

three′-point, *adj.*, (of the landing of aircraft) all wheels touching the ground simultaneously.

three′-quar′ter, *adj.* and *adv.*, midway between half and full; the amount of three-fourths.

three′-sea′ter, *adj.*, having three seats or space for three to sit.

three′score, *adj.*, sixty; 20 × 3.

three′some, *n.*, any activity in which three persons are engaged.

thremmatol′ogy, *n.*, the study of breeding domestic animals.

threne, *n.*, a lament.

thren′ody, *n.*, a song of lamentation; a dirge.

thresh, *v.t.*, *i.q.* to thrash, in the sense of beating out grain.

thresh′er, *n.*, one who threshes; a machine for threshing.

thresh′ing, *n.*, the action of separating grain.

thresh′old, *n.*, a door sill; the entrance to a building; the extreme limit or beginning.

threw, *p.p.*, throw.

thrice, *adv.*, three times.

thrid′ace, *n.*, a sedative from lettuce juice.

thrift, *n.*, economy; frugality; improvement of property; a kind of plant.

thrift′ier, *adj.*, *comp.* of thrifty.

thrift′iest, *adj.*, *super.* of thrifty.

thrift′ily, *adv.*, in a thrifty way.

thrift′iness, *n.*, the quality of being thrifty.

thrift′less, *adj.*, not thrifty; wasteful.

thrift′lessness, *n.*, the quality of being thriftless.

thrift′y, *adj.*, economical; saving; industrious.

thrill, *n.*, the feeling of being pierced; something exciting; *v.t.*, to pierce; to fill with excitement; *v.i.*, to feel excited; to quiver.

thrilled, *p.p.*, thrill.

thrill′er, *n.*, a film or book designed to thrill.

thrill′ing, *pr.p.*, thrill, *adj.*, exciting.

thrip, *n.*, a coin between a dime and a nickel (U.S.A.).

thrips, *n. pl.*, insects attacking vines.

thrive, *v.i.*, to prosper; to grow; to grow strong; to grow rich.

thrived, *p.p.* thrive.

thriv′en, *i.q.* thrived.

thri′ving, *pr.p.*, thrive; *adj.*, prosperous.

thriv′ingly, *adv.*, prosperously.

throat, *n.*, the front part of the neck through which food is taken and breath drawn.

throat′ed, *adj.*, having a throat.

throat′ily, *adv.*, gutturally.

throat′iness, *n.*, the quality of being throaty.

throat′wort, *n.*, the nettle-leaved bellflower.

throat′y, *adj.*, produced by the throat; guttural.

throb, *v.i.*, to beat; to pulsate; *n.*, a pulsation.

throbbed, *p.p.*, throb.

throb′bing, *pr.p.*, throb.

throe, *n.*, great pain; agony; *v.i.*, to be in extreme pain.

thrombo′sis, *n.*, a clotted condition of the blood-vessels (*Gr.*).

throm′bus, *n.*, a clot of blood.

throne, *n.*, a seat of authority, as a king's, a bishop's, etc.; *v.t.*, to enthrone.

throned, *p.p.*, throne.

throne′less, *adj.*, without a throne.

throng, *n.*, a crowd; a press; *v.t.*, to fill with a multitude; to press; *v.i.*, to come in crowds.

thronged, *p.p.*, throng.

throng′ing, *pr.p.*, throng.

thro′ning, *pr.p.*, throne.

throp′ple, *n.*, the windpipe of an animal.

thros′tle, *n.*, a song-thrush; a machine used in a cotton mill.

thros′tling, *n.*, a throat disease in cattle.

throt′tle, *v.t.*, to seize by the throat and

strangle; *n.*, the windpipe; a valve regulating the flow of gas to the engine of a motor.

throt′tled, *p.p.*, throttle.

throt′tle-valve, *n.*, *i.q.* throttle (last meaning).

throt′tling, *pr.p.*, throttle.

through, *prep.*, from one end of a thing to the other; by means of; *adv.*, from end to end.

throughout′, *adv.*, all the time; from beginning to end; *prep.*, during the whole of.

through′-put, *n.*, the quantity going through a process.

through′-traf′fic, *n.*, traffic passing through an area on journeys between other places.

through′way, *n.*, a non-stop highway.

throve, *p.p.*, thrive.

throw, *v.t.*, to fling; to cast; to hurl; to bring down; to cast off; to overturn; to spin; *n.*, the act of throwing; a cast of the dice; the length that a thing is thrown.

throw′back, *n.*, a reversion to a former state.

throw′er, *n.*, one who throws; that which throws.

throw-in, *n.*, the act of throwing (anything) in; returning the ball to play (football).

throw′ing, *pr.p.*, throw.

thrown, *adj.*, cast or flung; *p.p.*, throw.

throw′-out, *n.*, a reject.

throw′ster, *n.*, a gamester; a silk-thrower.

thrum, *n.*, coarse yarn; fringe; the sound of strumming; *v.t.*, to tuft; to beat out a tune.

thrummed, *p.p.*, thrum.

thrum′ming, *pr.p.*, thrum.

thrush, *n.*, a song-bird so named; an infantile complaint affecting the mouth and throat.

thrust, *v.t.*, to push; to project; to drive; *v.i.*, to make a push; to aim a blow with a rapier, bayonet, etc.; *n.*, a push; a stab.

thrust′er, *n.*, one who thrusts.

thrust'ing, *pr.p.*, thrust.

thrust'ings, *n. pl.*, white whey pressed out of curd.

Thu'cydide'an, *adj.*, pert. or rel. to Thucydides, a Greek historian in 5 B.C.

thud, *n.*, the heavy sound of a falling body.

thud'ded, *p.p.*, thud.

thud'ding, *pr.p.*, thud.

Thug, *n.*, one of a secret band of Indian assassins; also *thug*, a villain.

Thug'gee, *n.*, the Thug's method of murder.

Thug'gery, *n.*, *i.q.* Thuggee.

Thug'gism, *n.*, *i.q.* Thuggee.

thu'ja, *n.*, an African tree of the cupressus type, used for furniture-making.

Thu'le, *n.*, the ancient classical name for the remotest north (*Ultima Thule*).

thumb, *n.*, the short, thick digit of the human hand; *v.t.*, to soil by rubbing with the thumb; *v.i.*, to handle things awkwardly.

thumbed, *p.p.*, thumb.

thum'ber, *n.*, one who sews thumbs into gloves.

thumb'hole, *n.*, a hole for the insertion of the thumb.

thumb'index, *n.*, one in which portions of the outer edges of a book are cut away to facilitate speedy reference.

thumb'ing, *pr.p.*, thumb.

thumb'less, *adj.*, without a thumb.

thumb'-mark, *n.*, a mark *or* made by a thumb (on paper, paintwork, etc.).

thumb'-marked, *adj.*, having thumb-marks.

thumb'nail, *n.*, the nail of the thumb.

thumb'pot, *n.*, a small plant-pot.

thumb'-print, *n.*, a thumb impression for identification.

thumb'screw, *n.*, an instrument of torture by violent pressure on the thumb.

thumb'-stall, *n.*, a cover for a bandaged thumb.

thum'mim, *n. pl.*, the mysterious ornament of the Jewish high-priest's breastplate.

thump, *v.t.*, to deal hard blows upon; *v.i.*, to beat heavily; *n.*, a heavy blow.

thumped, *p.p.*, thump.

thump'er, *n.*, one who, that which, thumps; a lie; a very big thing (*colloq.*).

thump'ing, *pr.p.*, thump; *adj.*, very big (*colloq.*).

thun'der, *n.*, the noisy discharge of electricity from clouds; any very loud noise; *v.i.*, to make a thundering noise; *v.t.*, to utter in loud denunciation.

thun'derbolt, *n.*, a lightning discharge; something startling for its suddenness or violence.

thun'derclap, *n.*, a clap of thunder.

thun'dercloud, *n.*, an electrically charged storm cloud.

thun'dered, *p.p.*, thunder.

thun'derer, *n.*, one who thunders.

thun'dering, *pr.p.*, thunder; *adj.*, emitting the sound of thunder; very big (*colloq.*).

thun'deringly, *adv.*, in a thundering manner.

thun'derous, *adj.*, loud like thunder.

thun'derously, *adv.*, with the noise of thunder.

thun'der-shower, *n.*, a shower accompanied by thunder.

thun'derstorm, *n.*, a storm accompanied by thunder.

thun'derstruck, *adj.* overcome with sudden astonishment.

thun'dery, *adj.*, inclined to thunder; accompanied by thunder.

thu'rible, *n.*, a censer.

thu'rifer, *n.*, one who carries and swings the censer in church ceremonies.

thurif'erous, *adj.*, producing incense.

thurifica'tion, *n.*, the production of incense.

Thurin'gian, *adj.*, from Thuringia, a part of central Germany.

thurl, *v.t.*, to bore; *n.*, a perforation; a bore-hole (*mining*).

Thurs'day, *n.*, the fifth day of the week.

thus, *adv.*, in this way; so.

thu'ya, *n.*, *i.q.* thuja.

thwack, *v.t.*, to beat with a flat, heavy thing; *n.*, a blow so delivered.

thwacked, *p.p.*, thwack.

thwack'ing, *pr.p.*, thwack.

thwaite, *n.*, land reclaimed for tilling.

thwart, *v.t.*, to cross; to frustrate; *adj.* and *adv.*, crosswise; *n.*, a rower's seat across a boat.

thwart'ed, *p.p.*, thwart.

thwart'ing, *pr.p.*, thwart.

thwart'ingly, *adv.*, in a frustrating way.

thy, *poss. adj.*, bel. to thee.

thy'ine, *adj.*, producing Sandarac.

thy'lacine, *n.*, the striped wolf of Tasmania.

thyme, *n.*, an aromatic herb.

thym'ol, *n.*, an antiseptic, distilled from thyme oil.

thy'mus, *n.*, a generic name of certain shrubs; a gland of the neck and thorax.

thym'y, *adj.*, abounding in, smelling of, thyme.

thy'roid, *adj.*, like a shield; *n.*, a laryngeal cartilage.

thyroidi'tis, *n.*, inflammation of the thyroid.

thyrse, *n.*, *i.q.* thyrsus.

thyr'soid, *adj.*, thyrsus-shaped.

thyr'sus, *n.*, the emblem of Bacchus—a wand adorned with ivy, vine leaves, and grape-clusters.

thyself', *pron.*, an emphatic form of thou or thee.

ti'ang, *n.*, an African antelope.

tia'ra, *n.*, a head-ornament; a diadem.

tia'ra'd, **tia'raed**, *adj.*, wearing a tiara.

Tibe'tan, *adj.*, pert. or rel. to Tibet; *n.*, a native of T.; the language of T.

tib'ia, *n.*, the shin bone (*Lat.*).

tib'ial, *adj.*, pert. to the tibia.

tic, *n.*, neuralgia.

tic'ca, *adj.*, hired on contract (*Indian*).

tic'-douloureux', *n.*, *i.q.* tic.

tick, *n.*, a parasitic insect; a cover for bedding; a little mark; the beat of a clock or watch; credit (*colloq.*); *v.i.*, to make a short, quick beat (as a clock, etc.); *v.t.*, to put a tick against.

ticked, *p.p.*, tick.

tick′en, *n.*, *i.q.* ticking.

tick′et, *n.*, a card, etc., marked in a way to show the owner's right to something; a label; a political party programme; *v.t.*, to label; to mark.

tick′eted, *p.p.*, ticket.

tick′eting, *pr.p.*, ticket.

ti′cket-wri′ter, *n.*, a writer expert in lettering.

tick′ing, *pr.p.*, tick; *n.*, the cover of bedding.

tick′le, *v.t.*, to cause to laugh by touching lightly in a sensitive part; to amuse; *v.i.*, to have the feeling of tickling.

tick′led, *p.p.*, tickle.

tick′ler, *n.*, one who, that which, tickles; a difficult problem.

tick′ling, *pr.p.*, tickle.

tick′lish, *adj.*, having the feeling of being tickled; easily tickled; awkward; critical.

tick′lishly, *adv.*, in a ticklish manner.

tick′lishness, *n.*, the state of being ticklish; precariousness.

tick′ly, *adj.*, *i.q.* ticklish.

tick′seed, *n.*, a plant with prickly joints to its pods.

tick′-tack, *n.*, a mode of signalling on a racecourse; a tapping sound; *adv.*, with a sound of tapping.

tid, *adj.*, nice; soft.

ti′dal, *adj.*, rel. to tide.

tid′bit, *n.*, *i.q.* titbit.

tidd′ler, *n.*, a small fish; anything small.

tidd′lywinks, *n.*, an indoor game.

tide, *n.*, the rise and fall of the sea or a river; season (as Eastertide, etc.); drift; *v.t.*, to drive with the tide; *v.i.*, to drift.

ti′ded, *p.p.*, tide.

tide′-gauge, *n.*, an apparatus showing the degrees in the rise and fall of tides.

tide′less, *adj.*, having no tides.

tide′mark, *n.*, the mark or line left on the shore by the tide; the edge of a washed area.

tide′mill, *n.*, a mill worked by the tide.

tides′man, *n.*, an official of the custom house whose duty is to see to the discharge of ships.

tide′-table, *n.*, a schedule or table showing the times of high- and low-tide.

tide′waiter, *n.*, *i.q.* tidesman.

tide′way, *n.*, the passage in a river where vessels can use the tides.

ti′died, *p.p.*, tidy.

ti′dier, *adj.*, *comp.* of tidy.

ti′diest, *adj.*, *super.* of tidy.

ti′dily, *adv.*, in a tidy way.

ti′diness, *n.*, the state or quality of being tidy.

ti′ding, *pr.p.*, tide.

ti′dings, *n. pl.*, news.

ti′dy, *adj.*, neat; trim; orderly; *n.*, a small receptacle for odds and ends; a movable chair cover.

ti′dying, *pr.p.*, tidy.

tie, *n.*, a fastening; a band; a knot; a close connection; an obligation; a mark showing that a musical note is held for the duration of the following note; a decorative article of neckwear; *v.t.*, to fasten, to join; *v.i.*, to be equal in a contest.

tied, *p.p.*, tie.

ti′er, *n.*, one who, that which, ties.

tier, *n.*, a row, esp. one of a series of ascending stages.

tierce, *n.*, a 42 gal. cask; a fencing thrust; a musical third; an organ stop sounding the seventeenth above the diapason; in card games, a sequence of three cards of the same colour.

tier′cel, *n.*, the male hawk. Also *tercel.*

tierce′let, *n.*, a male bird of prey. Also *tercelet.*

tiff, *n.*, a quarrel; a wordy dispute; a sip; *v.t.*, to sip.

tif′fany, *n.*, a thin gauze fabric.

tif′fin, *n.*, the Anglo-Indian name for luncheon.

tig, *n.*, a childish game of chasing and touching.

tige, *n.*, the shaft of a pillar.

ti′ger, *n.*, a fierce carnivore; a boy groom.

ti′ger-cat, *n.*, a wild-cat.

ti′gerish, *adj.*, like a tiger.

ti′ger-lily, *n.*, a variety of lily with scarlet and orange black-spotted blooms.

ti′ger-moth, *n.*, a large brown-winged moth.

ti′ger-shark, *n.*, a large yellowish-brown shark, with dark spots and transverse bands.

tight, *adj.*, drawn close together; constricted; close fitting; not leaking; difficult; drunk (*colloq.*).

tight′en, *v.t.*, to make tight; *v.i.*, to become tight.

tight′ened, *p.p.*, tighten.

tight′ener, *n.*, one who tightens; a tightening device.

tight′ening, *pr.p.*, tighten.

tight′er, *adj.*, *comp.* of tight.

tight′est, *adj.*, *super.* of tight.

tight′-fisted, *adj.*, mean, stingy.

tight′ish, *adj.*, fairly tight.

tight′ishly, *adv.*, firmly; fairly tightly.

tight′-lipped, *adj.*, uncommunicative.

tight′ly, *adv.*, in a tight way.

tight′ness, *n.*, the state or quality of being tight.

tight′-rope, *n.*, a taut rope used in acrobatics or rope-dancing.

tights, *n. pl.*, an actor's close-fitting underclothes; a garment combining pants and stockings.

ti′gon, *n.*, a lion-tiger offspring.

ti′gress, *n.*, fem. of tiger.

ti′grine, *adj.*, rel. to tigers.

ti′groid, *adj.*, like a tiger.

tike, *n.*, *i.q.* tyke.

til'bury, *n.*, a variety of carriage.

til'de, *n.*, the Spanish writing mark over letter n, as in Señor.

tile, *n.*, a thin flat slab, used for roofing, flooring, etc.; a hat (*colloq.*); *v.t.*, to guard (the door of a Masonic lodge); to roof or cover with tiles.

tiled, *p.p.*, tile.

tile'-earth, *n.*, a clay.

til'er, *n.*, one who lays tiles; a Masonic door-keeper.

til'ery, *n.*, tile works.

til'ing, *pr.p.*, tile; *n.*, the act of tiling; roofing.

till, *v.t.*, to plough; to cultivate; *n.*, a money-receptacle in a shop; a stiff clay.

till, *prep.*, until; as far as.

till'able, *adj.*, fit for tilling.

till'age, *n.*, agriculture; tilled land.

tilled, *p.p.*, till.

till'er, *n.*, one who tills; a rudder-handle; *v.i.*, to send out a number of stems from the root.

till'ering, *pr.p.*, tiller.

till'ing, *pr.p.*, till.

tilt, *n.*, a tent cover; the cover of a wagon or a boat's stern; a jousting; an incline upwards; *v.t.*, to cover with a tilt; to level a tilting-lance; to make to incline; *v.i.*, to incline; to joust.

tilt'ed, *p.p.*, tilt.

tilt'er, *n.*, one who tilts.

tilth, *n.*, tilled soil.

tilt'-hammer, *n.*, a large steam or hydraulic hammer.

tilt'ing, *pr.p.*, tilt; *n.*, the act of tilting; forging with a tilt-hammer.

tim'bal, *n.*, a kettle-drum.

tim'ber, *n.*, wood; trees collectively; *v.t.*, to lay timber on.

tim'bered, *p.p.*, timber; *adj.*, covered with trees.

tim'bering, *pr.p.*, timber.

tim'bre, *n.*, the quality of sound in a voice or musical instrument (*Fr.*).

tim'brel, *n.*, a Hebrew tambourine.

time, *n.*, measured continuance; a date; a period; the opposite to eternity; a season; the duration of opportunity; measured musical beats; *v.t.*, to measure time; to do at the fitting moment.

time-bomb, *n.*, a bomb controlled by a time-fuze.

time-consum'ing, *adj.*, taking or requiring much time.

timed, *p.p.*, time.

time'-expired, *adj.*, having completed a tour of duty or passed a period of validity.

time'-exposure, *n.*, an exposure (usu. in photography) for a period of time longer than the ordinary momentary one.

time'-fuze, *n.*, a fuze designed to operate at a certain time.

time'-honoured, *adj.*, honoured for a long past time; venerable.

time'ist, *n.*, one who observes strict time (*mus.*).

time'keeper, *n.*, a person who records the time when employees begin and leave off work; a watch or clock.

time'-lag, *n.*, the gap between stimulus and response.

time'less, *adj.*, eternal; unconnected with time.

time'lessly, *adv.*, in a timeless way.

time'lessness, *n.*, the state or quality of being timeless.

time'-limit, *n.*, a fixed period of time for the completion of anything.

time'liness, *n.*, the state or quality of being timely.

time'ly, *adj.*, in good or convenient time; seasonable.

time'ous, *adj.*, in good time (*Scot.*).

time'ously, *adv.*, in a timeous way.

time'piece, *n.*, a clock.

tim'er, *n.*, one who, or that which, times or regulates.

time'-saving, *adj.*, pert. or rel. to the saving of time.

time'-server, *n.*, one who takes selfish advantage of every opportunity with no regard to principles.

time'-serving, *adj.*, looking after one's own interests without reference to principles; *n.*, self-interest.

time'-sig'nal, *n.*, a radio or electrical indication of the exact time.

time'-signature, *n.*, the figures showing measure or beat in music.

time'-switch', *n.*, an electrical switch which can be set to operate at a predetermined time.

time'table, *n.*, a register of the times at which trains, etc., depart and arrive, work is to be done, etc.

time'work, *n.*, work paid for by time (as opposed to amount completed).

time'-worn, *adj.*, ancient and decaying.

tim'id, *adj.*, fearful; nervous; cowardly.

timid'ity, *n.*, faint-heartedness; lack of courage.

tim'idly, *adv.*, in a timid way.

ti'ming, *pr.p.*, time.

ti'mist, *n.*, *i.q.* timeist.

timoc'racy, *n.*, a form of polity under which property is a qualification for office.

timocrat'ic, *adj.*, pert. or rel. to timocracy.

timoneer', *n.*, a lookout man; a helmsman.

tim'orous, *adj.*, dreading danger.

tim'orously, *adv.*, in a timorous way.

Timoth'ean, *adj.*, rel. to Timotheus.

tim'othy, *n.*, a species of fodder-grass.

tim'panist, *n.*, an orchestral percussion player.

tim'pano, -i, *n.*, kettle-drum(s).

tin, *n.*, a white, malleable metal; a vessel made of tin; money (*slang*); *v.t.*, to overlay with tin; to preserve in tins.

tin'amou, *n.*, a S. American game bird.

tin'cal, *n.*, native borax.

tin'can', *n.*, a vessel made of tin.

tincto'rial, *adj.*, pert. to colouring and dyeing.

tinc′ture, *n.*, colouring; a medical solution; the colouring in a shield (*her.*); *v.t.*, to tinge; to colour.

tinc′tured, *p.p.*, tincture.

tinc′turing, *pr.p.*, tincture.

tin′der, *n.*, rotten wood, etc., for kindling into a flame.

tin′der-box, *n.*, a box to contain tinder.

tin′dery, *adj.*, like tinder; quick-tempered.

tine, *n.*, a spike; a prong.

tin′ea, *n.*, a moth (*Lat.*); a ringworm.

tin′foil, *n.*, tin beaten exceedingly thin.

tin′ful, *n.*, the measure of the contents of a tin.

ting, *n.*, a sound as of a bell; *v.i.*, to give forth such a sound.

tinge, *v.t.*, to stain; to infect with a faint colour, etc.; *n.*, a colouring; a slight addition of taste, colour, etc.

tinged, *p.p.*, tinge.

tinge′ing, *pr.p.*, tinge.

ting′ing, *pr.p.*, ting.

tin′gle, *v.i.*, to have a pricking sensation; *n.*, such a sensation.

tin′gled, *p.p.*, tingle.

tin′gling, *adj.*, prickling; *pr.p.*, tingle.

tin′gly, *adj.*, *i.q.* tingling.

tin′ier, *comp. adj.*, tiny.

tin′iest, *super. adj.*, tiny.

tink, *v.i.*, to chink; *n.*, a chinking or tinkling sound.

tinked, *p.p.*, tink.

tink′er, *n.*, one who repairs pots and pans; *v.t.*, to mend pots, etc.; to botch; *v.i.*, to be meddlesome.

tink′ered, *p.p.*, tinker.

tink′ering, *pr.p.*, tinker.

tink′ing, *pr.p.*, tink.

tin′kle, *n.*, a sound as of ringing; *v.t.*, to set tinkling.

tin′kled, *p.p.*, tinkle.

tin′kling, *pr.p.*, tinkle.

tin′klingly, *adv.*, in a tinkling way.

tin′kly, *adj.*, pert. or rel. to tinkle.

tin′man, *n.*, a worker in tin.

tinned, *p.p.*, tin; *adj.*, packed or preserved in tins or cans.

tin′ner, *n.*, a worker in a tin mine.

tin′ning, *pr.p.*, tin.

tinnit′us, *n.*, a ringing in the ears.

tin′ny, *adj.*, like tin; making the sound of tin when beaten.

tin′op′ener, *n.*, a device for opening a tin by cutting or tearing the metal.

tin′-pan′, *adj.*, (with **alley**) popular music world.

tin′plate, *n.*, iron-plate overlaid with tin; *adj.*, made of tinplate.

tin′pot′, *adj.*, worthless, rubbishy.

tin′sel, *n.*, cloth with gold or silver woven in; thin metal work; a gaudy, cheap ornament; *adj.*, cheap and gaudy; very showy; *v.t.*, to adorn with tinsel.

tin′selled, *p.p.*, tinsel.

tin′selling, *pr.p.*, tinsel.

tin′smith, *n.*, a worker in tin.

tint, *n.*, a colour; a hue; a shade of colour; *v.t.*, to impart a colour to.

tint′ed, *p.p.*, tint.

tin′ter, *n.*, one who, that which, tints.

tint′ing, *pr.p.*, tint.

tintinnab′ulary, *adj.*, rel. to bells.

tintinnabula′tion, *n.*, the sound of bells.

tintinnab′ulum, *n.*, a bell (*Lat.*).

tintom′eter, *n.*, a device for measuring colour.

tin′ware, *n.*, goods made of tin.

ti′ny, *adj.*, minute; very small.

tip, *n.*, the point of a thing; a tilt; a gift (*colloq.*); a private hint; *v.t.*, to point; to put a tip to; to give a present to (*colloq.*); to help with a private hint.

tip′-cat, *n.*, a boy's game with a stick and a small piece of wood pointed at the ends.

tip′off, *n.*, a secret warning.

tipped, *p.p.*, tip.

tip′per, *n.*, one who, that which, tips (in all senses); a Sussex brew of ale.

tip′pet, *n.*, a shoulder-wrap of fur or other material, esp. the scarf-like tippet of silk or stuff worn by the English clergy.

tip′ping, *pr.p.*, tip; *n.*, the practice of giving tips or gratuities (*colloq.*).

tip′ple, *v.t.* and *i.*, to drink as a habit; *n.*, an alcoholic drink; any sort of drink.

tip′pled, *p.p.*, tipple.

tip′pler, *n.*, a habitual drinker.

tip′pling, *pr.p.*, tipple; *n.*, the alcoholic habit.

tip′sily, *adv.*, in a tipsy way.

tip′staff, *n.*, a sheriff's officer; a constable.

tip′ster, *n.*, a seller of horse-racing information.

tip′sy, *adj.*, partially intoxicated; fuddled; inclined to turn topsy-turvy.

tip′toe, *n.*, the toe-tips; *adj.*, standing on tiptoe; stealthy.

tip′toed, *p.p.*, tiptoe.

tip′toeing, *pr.p.*, tiptoe.

tip′top, *adj.*, supremely good; *n.*, the very summit; *adv.*, in first-rate style (*colloq.*).

Tip′ula, *n.*, the crane-fly or "daddy-long-legs" genus.

tirade′, *n.*, a long-drawn-out declamation; a prolonged scolding; a diatonic run completing the interval between two notes.

tirailleur′, *n.*, a skirmisher; a sharpshooter; a marksman (*Fr.*).

tire, *v.t.*, to weary; to attire; *v.i.*, to grow weary; *n.*, a band round the fellies of wheels.

tired, *p.p.*, tire; *adj.*, weary.

tired′ness, *n.*, the state of being tired, fatigued, weary.

tire′less, *adj.*, without a tire; untiring.

tire′lessly, *adv.*, in a tireless way; untiringly.

tire′lessness, *n.*, the state of being tireless.

tire′some, *adj.*, worrying, annoying, tedious.

tire′somely, *adv.*, in a tiresome, tedious way.

tire′someness, n., the state or quality of being tiresome.

ti′ring, pr.p., tire; adj., wearisome.

tir′ingly, adv., in a tiring way.

ti′ro, n., a beginner.

tirocin′ium, n., the first stage of training or experience (Lat.).

Tiro′nian, adj., pert. to Tiro, Cicero's freedman, the inventor of the shorthand system long known by his name and long in use. It is said to have contained 5,000 shorthand signs.

'tis, an abbreviation for "it is".

tisane′, n., any nourishing drink esp. of barley water; i.q. ptisan.

Tishri′, n., the first month of the Jewish civil year.

tis′sue, n., fabric woven, and sometimes crossed with gold or silver threads; a fine texture; closely connected cellular substance; a connected series, as "a tissue of lies"; v.t., to form into a tissue.

tis′sued, p.p., tissue.

tis′suing, pr.p., tissue.

tit, n., a morsel; a little horse; a titmouse; the name of several small songsters; a colloq. variant of teat.

Ti′tan, n., one of the fabled classical giants; a giant.

ti′tanate, n., a titanic-acid salt.

Tita′nian, adj., i.q. Titanic; rel. to titanium.

Titan′ic, adj., rel. to the Titans; gigantic; immensely strong; pert. or rel. to titanium.

titanif′erous, adj., producing titanium.

ti′tanite, n., a mineral compound of calcium silicate and titanate.

tita′nium, n., a hard, light metal.

tit′-bit, n., a dainty morsel.

ti′thable, adj., subject to payment of tithe.

tithe, n., a tenth part; tax to the amount of one-tenth of profits; a rent; v.t., to levy such a tax.

tithe′-barn, n., a barn where tithe payments in kind instead of money were deposited.

tithed, p.p., tithe.

ti′ther, n., one who tithes.

ti′thing, pr.p., tithe; n., the levying of tithe; a group of ten householders, whose duty it was to keep order in their district; a civil territorial division corresponding to the Hundred.

ti′thing-man, n., the head of a tithing.

ti′tian, n., a reddish-yellow colour, noted for its use by the Venetian painter called by that name.

tit′illate, v.t., to tickle.

tit′illated, p.p., titillate.

tit′illating, pr.p., titillate.

titilla′tion, n., the act or effect of titillating.

tit′ivate, v.t. and i., to make smart.

titi′vated, p.p., titivate.

tit′ivating, pr.p., titivate.

titiva′tion, n., the act of titivating.

tit′lark, n., a small songster.

ti′tle, n., an inscription or heading; a name; a distinctive or honorific appellation; a right to anything; a spiritual charge as a condition of admission to Holy Orders; v.t., i.q. entitle.

tit′led, p.p., title; adj., possessing an honorific title, as Sir, Lord, etc.

ti′tle-deed, n., a document establishing a person's claim to possession.

ti′tle-page, n., the front page of a book setting out its name, description, authorship, imprint, etc.

tit′ler, n., one who writes titles.

ti′tle-role, n., the name part in a film, story or play.

ti′tling, pr.p., title.

tit′ling, n., a small fish; the little hedge-sparrow.

tit′mouse, n., a little bird, noted for its quick, irregular movements.

Ti′toism, n., communism with national independence (after the Yugoslavian, Marshal Tito).

tit′rate, v.t., to measure by titration.

tit′rated, p.p., titrate.

tit′rating, pr.p., titrate.

ti′tration, n., the measurement of the strength of a solution by comparison with others of known strength.

tit′ter, v.i., to laugh in a silly way; n., a giggle.

tit′tered, p.p., titter.

tit′terer, n., one who titters.

tit′tering, pr.p., titter.

tit′tle, n., a tiny particle.

tit′tle-tattle, n., small-talk; silly gossip; v.i., to gossip.

ti′tubate, v.i., to stumble, to roll, to stagger, as the result of nervous disorder.

tituba′tion, n., nervous fidgetting or stumbling.

tit′ular, adj., rel. to title; nominal; n., a person who has an empty title and no authority.

tit′ularly, adv., in a titular way.

tit′ulary, adj., i.q. titular.

ti′tule, n. and v.t., i.q. title.

tiv′y, adv., a hunting term = at full gallop.

tiz′zy, n., a state of nervous agitation (slang).

tme′sis, n., a cutting into two of a compound word (Gr.).

to, prep., towards; in the direction of; as far as.

toad, n., a frog-like reptile; the bufo.

toad′-eater, n., a sycophant.

toad′ied, p.p., toady.

toad′stone, n., a variety of rock.

toad′stool, n., a fungus; one of the agarics.

toad′y, n., a sycophant; a parasite; v.t. to flatter; to curry favour of; to fawn upon.

toad′ying, pr.p., toady.

toad′yism, n., sycophancy; fawning.

toast, *n.*, bread roasted; a health; *v.t.*, to make into toast; to warm before the fire; to drink a health to a person, country, cause, etc., honoured at a banquet by toasting.

toast'ed, *p.p.*, toast.

toast'er, *n.*, one who, that which, toasts.

toast'ing, *pr.p.*, toast.

toast'ing-fork, *n.*, a fork on which bread is held before a fire.

toast'master, *n.*, a person who proclaims the toasts at a banquet.

toast'-rack, *n.*, a rack in which pieces of toast are served.

tobac'co, *n.*, a plant of the genus *Nicotiana*, the leaves of which are smoked in various forms, or ground into snuff.

tobac'conist, *n.*, one who sells tobacco, cigars, pipes, etc.

tobog'gan, *n.*, a sort of sledge for coasting down inclines; *v.i.*, to slide in a toboggan.

tobog'ganing, *pr.p.*, toboggan.

tobog'ganist, *n.*, one who uses a toboggan.

to'by, *n.*, a pottery jug fashioned with male likeness.

tocca'ta, *n.*, a musical piece to exhibit accomplishment; an overture.

toch'er, *n.*, a marriage portion; a dowry (*Scot.*).

toc'sin, *n.*, a bell to sound an alarm.

tod, *n.*, a measure of wool (28 lb.).

today', *adv.*, on this present day; in our time.

tod'dle, *v.i.*, to walk with short, weak steps; *n.*, such a manner of walking.

tod'dled, *p.p.*, toddle.

tod'dler, *n.*, one who toddles; an infant.

tod'dling, *pr.p.*, toddle.

tod'dy, *n.*, a palm-juice; hot spirits and water with sugar, etc.

to-do', *n.*, a fuss.

to'dy, *n.*, a little West Indian bird.

toe, *n.*, one of the separate ends of the forepart of a foot; anything like a toe; *v.t.*, to touch with the toe (as "to toe the line").

toe'cap, *n.*, the part of a boot or shoe which covers the toes.

toed', *adj.*, having toes; *p.p.*, toe.

toe'ing, *pr.p.*, toe.

toe'-nail, *n.*, the nail of a toe.

tof'fee, *n.*, a sweet-meat made with butter, sugar, etc.

toft, *n.*, a grove.

to'ga, *n.*, the robe of a Roman citizen (*Lat.*).

togeth'er, *adv.*, in company; all united or combined.

togeth'erness, *n.*, euphoric companionship.

tog'gery, *n.*, clothes (*colloq.*).

tog'gle, *n.*, a tapering pin of wood grooved in the middle.

togs, *n. pl.*, clothes (*colloq.*).

toil, *n.*, labour; a snare; *v.i.*, to labour.

toile, *n.*, a dress fabric.

toiled, *p.p.*, toil.

toil'er, *n.*, one who labours.

toi'let, *n.*, the business of good grooming; a lavatory (*colloq.*).

toi'letry, *n.*, an article used for one's personal toilet.

toi'let-soap, *n.*, soap for personal toilet.

toilinet(te'), *n.*, a cloth of woollen yarn with cotton and silk interwoven.

toil'ing, *pr.p.*, toil.

toil'less, *adj.*, without toil.

toil'some, *adj.*, laborious.

toil'-worn, *adj.*, worn out with labour.

Toison-d'Or', *n.*, the Order of the Golden Fleece.

tokay', *n.*, a choice wine of Hungary.

tok'en, *n.*, a symbol, a pledge, a voucher, an indicator.

to'la, *n.*, an Indian gold and silver weight (180 grains troy).

to'lbooth, *n.*, a prison (*Scot.*).

told, *p.p.*, tell.

tole, *v.t.*, to attract.

Tole'do, *n.*, a sword of Toledo, a Spanish city noted for its manufacture of finely-tempered sword blades.

tolerabil'ity, *n.*, the quality or state of being tolerable.

tol'erable, *adj.*, endurable; moderately good.

tol'erably, *adv.*, to a tolerable degree.

tol'erance, *n.*, *i.q.* toleration, patience.

tol'erant, *adj.*, patient; indulgent.

tol'erantly, *adv.*, patiently.

tol'erate, *v.t.*, to endure; to allow; not to interfere with.

tol'erated, *p.p.*, tolerate.

tol'erating, *pr.p.*, tolerate.

tolera'tion, *n.*, the act of tolerating; putting up with things not approved; patience with opinions one dislikes.

toll, *n.*, the slow sound of a bell at intervals; a charge at turnpikes, bridges, etc.; duty demanded; *v.i.*, to sound a bell solemnly and at intervals.

toll'-bar, *n.*, the barrier at a toll station.

toll'booth, *n.*, *i.q.* tolbooth.

toll'bridge, *n.*, a bridge on which passengers are charged a fee.

tolled, *p.p.*, toll.

toll'er, *n.*, one who, that which, tolls.

toll'-gate, *n.*, a gate across a road where a fee is demanded of passengers.

toll'-gath'erer, *n.*, a collector of tolls.

toll'-house, *n.*, a toll-gatherer's house.

toll'ing, *pr.p.*, toll.

toll'man, *n.*, *i.q.* toll-gatherer.

tolt, *v.t.*, to remove; *n.*, in old English law, a writ withdrawing a case from the Court baron to the County Court.

tolu', *n.*, a balsam.

tol'uene, *n.*, a methyl chemical used in dyes and explosives.

tol'uol, *n.*, *i.q.* toluene.

tol'zey, *n.*, *i.q.* toll-booth.

tom'ahawk, *n.*, a N. Amer. Indian hatchet; *v.t.*, to hit with a tomahawk.

to'man, *n.*, ten thousand.

toma'to, *n.*, a S. Amer. plant; its edible fruit.

tomb, *n.*, a grave; a sepulchral monument; *v.t.*, to place in a tomb.

tom'bac, *n.*, copper and zinc alloy.

tombed, *p.p.*, tomb.

tombo'la, *n.*, a lottery game.

tom'boy, *n.*, a high-spirited girl.

tomb'stone, *n.*, a stone over a grave.

tom'cat, *n.*, a male cat.

tom'-cod, *n.*, a small variety of cod.

tome, *n.*, a large volume.

tomen'tous, *adj.*, covered with nap. Also *tomentose*.

tom'fool, *n.*, an idiot; a silly fellow.

tomfool'ery, *n.*, nonsense; silly conduct.

tomin', *n.*, a weight of 12 grains, used in the jewellery trade.

tom'my, *n.*, food (*slang*); a private in the army (*colloq.*).

tom'my-gun, *n.*, a light automatic gun.

tom'my-rot, *n.*, nonsense (*slang*).

tom-nod'dy, *n.*, a fool.

tomor'row, *adv.*, on the day after today.

tom'pion, *n.*, a cannon's stopper.

tom'tit, *n.*, the titmouse.

tom'-tom, *n.*, a kind of drum used by African and Indian natives.

ton, *n.*, twenty hundredweights; 40 cubic feet (*naut.*).

ton, *n.*, fashion; the mode (*Fr.*).

to'nal, *adj.*, rel. to tone.

tonal'ity, *n.*, the key-relationship.

tone, *n.*, sound and its quality; a note; a style; a healthy condition; a blend of colours; a musical interval of two semitones; *v.t.*, to invigorate; to temper; to blend the colours of; *v.i.*, to agree in colour or shade.

tone'-control, *n.*, a manually-adjusted amplitude control on a radio-receiver.

toned, *p.p.*, tone.

tone'-deaf, *adj.*, unable to distinguish between musical notes.

tone'less, *adj.*, lacking tone.

toneless'ly, *adv.*, in a toneless way.

tone'-poem, *n.*, a musical version of the non-musical.

ton'ga, *n.*, a British-Indian two-wheeled carriage.

tongs, *n. pl.*, an appliance for grasping objects.

tongue, *n.*, the organ of taste; that with which one speaks; a language; anything tongue-like; *v.i.*, to use the tongue in any sense; to produce a staccato effect on a flute, etc., by using the tongue.

tongued, *p.p.*, tongue; *adj.*, having a tongue.

tongue'-less, *adj.*, without a tongue.

tongue'-shaped, *adj.*, like a tongue in shape.

tongue'-tied, *adj.*, unable to speak; silent.

tongu'ing, *pr.p.*, tongue.

ton'ic, *adj.*, invigorating; rel. to the keynote; *n.*, a medicine that gives tone; the keynote.

ton'ically, *adv.*, in a tonic sense or relation.

tonic'ity, *n.*, the quality of being tonic.

tonight', *adv.*, on this present night; *n.*, the night of this day.

to'ning, *pr.p.*, tone.

ton'ka, *n.*, a scent derived from the tonka bean.

ton'nage, *n.*, the capacity or weight reckoned in tons; ship-duty; shipping collectively.

tonn'eau, *n.*, the boot section of a motor-car.

ton'nelle, *n.*, a kind of arbour for vines, etc. (*Fr.*).

tono'meter, *n.*, a device for measuring musical pitch.

ton'sil, *n.*, one of the glands attached to the sides of the throat.

ton'sillar, *adj.*, pert. to the tonsils.

tonsillec'tomy, *n.*, the surgical excision of tonsils.

tonsillit'ic, *adj.*, pert. to tonsillitis.

tonsilli'tis, *n.*, inflammation of the tonsils.

tonsillot'omy, *n.*, *i.q.* tonsillectomy.

ton'sor, *n.*, a barber.

tonso'rial, *adj.*, rel. to shaving and barbers.

ton'sure, *n.*, the act of shaving the head; the crown left round the head after the top has been shaved; a mark of admission to a religious order; *v.t.*, to confer the tonsure upon.

ton'sured, *p.p.*, tonsure.

tontine', *n.*, an arrangement by which the last survivor of a number of annuitants succeeds to the whole amount secured.

too, *adv.*, also; in addition; excessively.

took, *p.p.*, take.

tool, *n.*, an implement; anyone of whom another makes use for his own purposes; *v.t.*, to use a tool upon.

tooled, *p.p.*, tool.

toolholder, *n.*, a chuck or grip to hold a tool in place.

tool'ing, *pr.p.*, tool; *n.*, work done with a tool (esp. by a bookbinder).

toolmaker, *n.*, a person who makes tools, particularly industrial machine tools.

toolroom, *n.*, a place for the storage and maintenance of machine tools.

tool'shed, *n.*, a shed for storing tools, etc.

toon, **tun**, *n.*, a town (*Scot.*).

toon'wood, *n.*, a dark kind of cedar.

toot, *v.t.*, to blow a horn, flute, etc.; *n.*, a single sound on a horn, flute, etc.

toot'ed, *p.p.*, toot.

toot'er, *n.*, one who, that which, toots.

tooth, *n.*, a bony outgrowth from the jaws with which an animal chews and bites; anything tooth-like; *v.t.*, to supply with tooth-like indentations.

tooth'ache, *n.*, pain in the teeth.

tooth'brush, *n.*, a brush for cleaning teeth.

toothed, *p.p.*, tooth; *adj.*, indented.

tooth'ing, *pr.p.*, tooth.

tooth'less, *adj.*, having no teeth.

tooth'let, *n.*, a small tooth.

tooth'leted, *adj.*, having small teeth.

tooth'paste, *n.*, a dental cleaning preparation.

tooth'pick, *n.*, a quill or metal pointed instrument for picking the teeth.

tooth'some, *adj.*, tasty.

tooth'wort, *n.*, a plant with toothed or indented leaves.

toot'ing, *pr.p.*, toot.

too'tle, *v.i.*, to toot gently or repeatedly.

too'tled, *p.p.*, tootle.

too'tling, *pr.p.*, tootle.

top, *n.*, the summit; the highest part; a revolving toy; *v.t.*, to put a top on; to surpass; to remove the top from.

to'paz, *n.*, a precious stone, yellow, green or blue in colour (sometimes colourless).

top'-boots, *n. pl.*, boots with tops coming well up the leg.

top'coat, *n.*, an overcoat.

top'dress, *v.t.*, to apply a surface dressing of manure or fertilizer to the soil.

top'dressed, *p.p.*, topdress.

topdres'sing, *pr.p.*, topdress.

tope, *n.*, a grove; a shark; a Buddhist monument; *v.i.*, to drink to excess habitually.

topec'tomy, *n.*, the surgical excision of a lobe.

toped, *p.p.*, tope.

to'pee, *n.*, *i.q.* topi.

to'per, *n.*, a hard drinker.

topgal'lant, *adj.*, above the gallant mast; *n.*, a topgallant mast or sail.

toph, *n.*, chalky formation round the teeth and on the surface of joints. Also *tophus*.

topha'ceous, *adj.*, pert. to toph.

top'-hat, *n.*, a high hat worn on special social occasions.

top'-heavy, *adj.*, with too much weight on the top.

To'phet, *n.*, the place in the valley of Hinnom where Moloch was worshipped with a perpetual fire; hell.

top'-hole, *adj.*, first-class, very good (*slang*).

to'phus, *n.*, *i.q.* toph.

topi, *n.*, a tropical sun hat or helmet (*Ind.*).

to'piarist, *n.*, one who is expert in topiary.

to'piary, *n.*, the art of foliage trimming.

top'ic, *n.*, a subject of talk or discourse.

top'ical, *adj.*, rel. to a place; rel. to current events.

top'icality, *n.*, the quality of being topical.

top'ically, *adv.*, in a topical way.

to'ping, *pr.p.*, tope.

top'knot, *n.*, a knot of hair on the top of the head.

top'less, *adj.*, having no top.

top'-level, *adj.*, senior; rel. to those at the top of an administration.

top'man, *n.*, one who is posted in the tops (*naut.*).

top'mast, *n.*, the upper mast.

top'most, *adj.*, the highest.

topog'rapher, *n.*, an expert in topography.

topograph'ic, *adj.*, rel. to topography.

topograph'ically, *adv.*, in a topographical way.

topog'raphy, *n.*, the study of places.

topon'ymic, *adj.*, pert. or rel. to toponymy.

topon'ymy, *n.*, the study of place names.

topped, *p.p.*, top.

top'per, *n.*, one who, that which, tops; a tall hat.

top'ping, *pr.p.*, top.

top'ple, *v.t.*, to overthrow; knock down; *v.i.*, to fall over.

top'pled, *p.p.*, topple.

top'pling, *pr.p.*, topple.

top'-priority, *adj.*, extremely urgent; taking precedence.

tops, *n.*, excellent; the best (*slang*).

top'sail, *n.*, an upper sail.

top'sy-tur'vy, *adj.*, upside down; in a muddle.

toque, *n.*, a lady's close-fitting hat.

tor, *n.*, a high rock or hill.

tor'ah, *n.*, Mosaic law.

torch, *n.*, a portable light.

torch'bearer, *n.*, one who carries a torch.

torch'light, *n.*, the light of a torch.

tore, *p.p.*, tear.

tor'eador, *n.*, a bullfighter.

toreu'tic, *adj.*, sculptured; worked in bas-relief on metal.

tor'ment, *n.*, torture; pain.

torment', *v.t.*, to torture, to cause anguish to.

torment'ed, *p.p.*, torment.

torment'er, *n.*, one who torments.

tor'mentil, *n.*, an astringent drug.

torment'ing, *pr.p.*, torment.

torment'or, *n.*, *i.q.* tormenter.

torment'ress, *n.*, fem. of tormenter.

tor'mina, *n.*, severe bowel pains.

torn, *p.p.*, tear.

torna'do, *n.*, a tempest.

to'rous, *adj.*, having knobs at intervals (*bot.*).

torpe'do, *n.*, a crampfish; a projectile discharged from a submarine; *v.t.*, to discharge a torpedo at; to destroy a project.

torpe'do-boat, *n.*, a small, fast, naval vessel, specially for the firing of torpedoes.

torpe'doed, *p.p.*, torpedo.

torpe'doing, *pr.p.*, torpedo.

torpe'do-tube, *n.*, a tubular device from which torpedoes are fired.

tor'pid, *adj.*, sleepy; sluggish; inactive.

torpid'ity, *n.*, the state or quality of being torpid.

tor'pified, *p.p.*, torpify.

tor'pify, *v.t.*, to make torpid or numb.

tor'pifying, *pr.p.*, torpify.

tor'pitude, n., a state of torpor.

tor'por, n., the state of being torpid; numbness.

tor'quated, adj., furnished with a collar.

torque, n., a neck-ornament; a twisting force.

torqued, adj., having a torque.

torrefac'tion, n., the act of torrefying; the state of being torrefied.

tor'refied, p.p., torrefy.

tor'refy, v.t., to heat, to parch by fire.

tor'refying, pr.p., torrefy.

tor'rent, n., a strongly rushing stream; a copious flood.

torren'tial, adj., pert. to, resembling, a torrent.

torren'tially, adv., in a torrential way.

torren'tuous, adj., i.q. torrential.

Torricel'lian, adj., rel. to Torricelli, the 17th cent. inventor of the barometer.

tor'rid, adj., scorching; dried by the sun.

torrid'ity, n., the state of being torrid.

torse, n., a wreath (her.).

tor'sel, n., scroll-work; a wooden insertion in a wall to support a joist, etc.

tor'siograph, n., an instrument for measuring torsion in machinery.

tor'sion, n., the act of twisting or wrenching.

tor'sional, adj., pert. or rel. to torsion.

tor'sive, adj., twisted spirally (bot.).

tor'so, n., in sculpture, a mutilated statue; the trunk without head or limbs.

tort, n., an injury, damage (leg.).

torteau', n., a circular heraldic emblem.

tor'tile, adj., twisted; twined.

tor'tility, n., the state of being tortile.

tort'illa, n., a Mexican maize cake.

tor'tious, adj., rel. to a tort.

tor'tive, adj., twisted.

tor'toise, n., a shell-covered reptile so named; a testudo.

tor'toiseshell, n., the shell of a tortoise; adj., made of polished tortoiseshell.

tortuos'ity, n., the state or quality of being tortuous.

tor'tuous, adj., twisting; winding; crooked; deceitful.

tor'tuously, adv., in a tortuous way.

tor'ture, n., extreme pain; pain cruelly inflicted; v.t., to inflict cruel pain for the purpose of extorting a confession or evidence; to distort.

tor'tured, p.p., torture.

tor'turer, n., one who inflicts torture.

tor'turing, pr.p., torture.

tor'turingly, adv., in a way to torture.

tor'turous, adj., pert. or rel. to torture.

tor'ulous, adj., ridged; swelling.

to'rus, n., a semi-circular moulding at the bottom of a pillar; the support of carpels in a flower.

To'ry, n., once, a Church and King man; now, a Conservative.

To'ryism, n., the principles professed by Tories.

tosh, n., comfortable, friendly (Scot.); nonsense (slang).

toss, v.t., to heave up into the air; to jerk upward; v.i., to pitch; to roll; n., an upward throw.

tossed, p.p., toss.

toss'ily, adv., partly.

toss'ing, pr.p., toss.

toss'up', n., an even chance; the spinning of a coin to reach a decision.

toss'y, adj., pert.

tos'to, adj., fast (mus.).

tot, n., a tiny thing; v.t., to add up.

to'tal, adj., aggregate; complete; n., the sum; the full amount; v.t., to add up.

totalitar'ian, adj., allowing no political opposition.

totalitar'ianism, n., the advocacy of totalitarian government.

total'ity, n., the state or quality of being total; completeness.

totaliza'tion, n., the state of being totalled.

totaliza'tor, n., a calculating machine for betting.

to'talize, v.t., to work out the total.

to'talizer, n., i.q. totalizator.

to'talled, p.p., total.

to'talling, pr.p., total.

to'tally, adv., completely; entirely.

tote, n., a shortened form of totalizator; v.t., to carry.

to'tem, n., a symbol regarded as the emblem or distinguishing mark of a tribe.

to'temism, n., the practice of distinguishing families or tribes by their totem.

toth'er, pron. = the other (colloq.).

tot'ing, pr.p., tote.

tot'ted, p.p., tot.

tot'ter, v.i., to shake as though on the point of falling.

tot'tered, p.p., totter.

tot'tering, pr.p., totter.

tot'teringly, adv., in a tottering way.

tot'tery, adj., shaky; unstable.

tot'ting, pr.p., tot.

toucan', n., a S. Amer. bird with a very large beak.

touch, n., the sense of feeling; the act of touching; close relation; the power of impression through the hand or fingers; a stroke with a painter's brush, a sculptor's chisel, etc.; v.t., to apply the hand to; to feel; to reach; to affect emotionally or injuriously; v.i., to be in close relation; to put in with a ship.

tou'chable, adj., able to be touched.

tou'ché, interj., a hit in fencing; an acknowledgement of a point won in an argument (Fr.).

touched, p.p., touch.

touch'er, n., one who, that which, touches.

touch'-hole, n., the hole in a firearm where the charge was ignited.

touch'ily, adv., in a touchy way.

touch'iness, *n.*, the state or quality of being touchy.

touch'ing, *pr.p.*, touch; *adj.*, affecting; moving; *prep.*, in regard to.

touch'-line, *n.*, the side line of a football pitch.

touch'-me-not, *n.*, a balsam plant.

touch'-paper, *n.*, chemically treated paper which ignites immediately and burns without flaming.

touch'stone, *n.*, a testing stone; a test.

touch'-type, *v.t.* and *i.*, to operate a typewriter without looking at the keys.

touch'-typing, *pr.p.*, touch-type.

touch'-typist, *n.*, one who is able to touch-type.

touch'wood, *n.*, any dried wood for kindling.

touch'y, *adj.*, quick to take offence; irritable.

tough, *adj.*, hard to break; not easily chewed; sturdy; capable of endurance; *n.*, a hooligan.

tough'en, *v.t.*, to harden; to make tough; *v.i.*, to become tough.

tough'ened, *p.p.*, toughen.

tough'ening, *pr.p.*, toughen.

tough'er, *adj.*, *comp.* of tough.

tough'est, *adj.*, *super.* of tough.

tough'ish, *adj.*, somewhat tough.

tough'ly, *adv.*, in a tough way.

tough'ness, *n.*, the state or quality of being tough.

toupee', *n.*, a wig.

toupet', *n.*, *i.q.* toupee (*Fr.*).

tour, *n.*, a continued journey; travel; *v.i.*, to go on a tour.

tourbil'lion, *n.*, a revolving firework; a whirlwind.

toured, *p.p.*, tour.

tou'rer, *n.*, a kind of motor-car used for touring.

tour'ing, *pr.p.*, tour; *n.*, travel.

tou'rism, *n.*, the business of travelling, especially abroad.

tour'ist, *n.*, one who goes on a tour.

tour'maline, *n.*, a lustrous mineral usu. black.

tour'nament, *n.*, a contest of mounted knights; any formal contest.

tournedos, *n.*, a dish of fillet beef (*Fr.*).

tour'ney, *n.*, *i.q.* tournament.

tour'niquet, *n.*, a surgical appliance for stopping the flow of blood from a severed artery.

tournure', *n.*, a shape; a figure (*Fr.*).

touse, *v.t.*, to pull about; to disarrange.

toused, *p.p.*, touse.

tous'er, *n.*, one who worries or creates a disturbance.

tou'sing, *n.*, a pulling about; a rough handling; *pr.p.*, touse.

tou'sle, *v.t.*, to disarray; to disorder.

tou'sled, *p.p.*, tousle.

tou'sling, *pr.p.*, tousle.

tous'y, *adj.*, shaggy.

tout, *n.*, a person who hangs about to give information, get tips, etc.; *v.t.*, to act as a tout.

tout'ed, *p.p.*, tout.

tout'er, *n.*, one who touts; a tout.

tout'ing, *pr.p.*, tout.

tou'zle, *v.t.*, *i.q.* tousle.

tow, *n.*, coarse hemp or flax; *v.t.*, to haul; *n.*, the action of towing.

tow'able, *adj.*, able to be towed.

tow'age, *n.*, a charge for towing.

to'ward, *adv.*, close at hand; *prep.*, in the direction of; in regard to.

to'wardly, *adj.*, agreeable.

to'wardness, *n.*, the quality of being towardly.

to'wards, *prep.*, *i.q.* toward.

towed, *p.p.*, tow.

tow'el, *n.*, a cloth to dry oneself after washing; *v.t.*, to rub or wipe with a towel.

tow'elled, *p.p.*, towel.

tow'elling, *n.*, absorbent material for towels; *pr.p.*, towel.

tow'el-rail, *n.*, a rod or rail over which to hang towels.

tow'er, *n.*, a fortress-like tall building, or part of a building; *v.i.*, to stand up very high.

tow'ered, *p.p.*, tower.

tow'ering, *pr.p.*, tower; *adj.*, tall.

tow'ery, *adj.*, like a tower.

tow'ing, *pr.p.*, tow.

to-wit', phrase = that is to say.

tow'-line, *n.*, a rope for towing.

town, *n.*, an inhabited place larger than a village.

town'-clerk', *n.*, an official in charge of municipal business.

town'-council, *n.*, a locally elected controlling body.

town'-councillor, *n.*, a member of a town council.

town'-cri'er, *n.*, an official who makes public announcements.

town'-dweller, *n.*, one who lives in a town.

town'-hall', *n.*, a municipal assembly hall.

town'house, *n.*, a residence in town.

town'-planning, *n.*, the controlled development of a town.

towns'folk, *n.*, inhabitants of a town.

town'ship, *n.*, a town; in the U.S., a territorial division of the county.

towns'man, *n.*, a dweller in a town.

towns'people, *n.*, inhabitants of a town.

towns'woman, *n.*, a woman town-dweller.

town'-talk', *n.*, the talk of a town.

tow'path, *n.*, a track by canal or river for towing.

towse, *v.t.*, *i.q.* touse.

tow'y, *adj.*, like tow; full of tow.

toxae'mia, *n.*, blood-poisoning.

toxaem'ic, *adj.*, poisoning.

tox'ic, *adj.*, poisonous.

tox'ical, *adj.*, *i.q.* toxic.

tox'icity, *n.*, the state or quality of being poisonous.

toxicol'ogist, *n.*, an expert in toxicology.

toxicol'ogy, *n.,* the study of poisons.

tox'in, *n.,* an organic poison.

toxipho'bia, *n.,* a fear of being poisoned.

toxoph'ilite, *n.,* an amateur archer; *adj.,* rel. to archery.

toxoph'ily, *n.,* the craft of archery.

toy, *n.,* a plaything; something worthless; *v.i.,* to play; to trifle (with).

toyed, *p.p.,* toy.

toy'ing, *pr.p.,* toy.

toy'shop, *n.,* a shop where toys are sold.

trabe'ated, *adj.,* having beams instead of arches or vaults.

trabea'tion, *n.,* the use of beams instead of vaulting (*archit.*).

trace, *n.,* a mark; a trail; a footprint; a vestige; *v.t.,* to track; to copy by following marks.

trace'able, *adj.,* able to be traced.

traced, *p.p.,* trace.

tra'cer, *n.,* one who traces.

tra'cery, *n.,* the ornamental work in Gothic windows and arches.

tra'ces, *n. pl.,* the bands or ropes by which animals draw a vehicle.

trache'a, *n.,* the windpipe.

trache'ae, *n. pl.,* the tubes through which insects breathe.

trache'al, *adj.,* pert. to the trachea.

trache'itis, *n.,* inflammation of the wind-pipe.

trache'ocele, *n.,* a tracheal hernia.

tracheot'omy, *n.,* the operation of opening the windpipe.

tracho'ma, *n.,* a disease of the inner eyelids.

trac'hyte, *n.,* a kind of igneous rock.

tra'cing, *pr.p.,* trace; *n.,* a copy through thin paper of a picture, etc., beneath.

tra'cing-paper, *n.,* thin paper used for tracing purposes.

track, *n.,* a trail; a footmark; an unmade road; a running path; a railroad; *v.t.,* to follow in the trail of.

tracked, *p.p.,* track.

track'er, *n.,* one who tows or one who follows a track or trail.

track'ing, *pr.p.,* track.

track'less, *adj.,* showing no track.

track'suit, *n.,* special sports clothing.

tract, *n.,* a pamphlet; a short treatise; a large extent of country.

tractabil'ity, *n.,* the state or quality of being tractable.

tract'able, *adj.,* docile, manageable.

tract'ably, *adv.,* in a tractable way.

Tracta'rian, *adj.,* rel. to the "Tracts for the Times", which were published during the period 1833–41, the most famous of the writers being Pusey and Newman; *n.,* a High Churchman.

Tracta'rianism, *n.,* the principles laid down and defended in the "Tracts", which developed into what is known as the Oxford or the Catholic Movement.

trac'tate, *n.,* a treatise.

trac'tile, *adj., i.q.* ductile.

tractil'ity, *n.,* the state or quality of being tractile.

trac'tion, *n.,* the act of drawing; the state of being drawn.

trac'tion-engine, *n.,* a locomotive specially designed for hauling or pulling.

trac'tive, *adj.,* drawing.

trac'tor, *n.,* that which draws; a vehicle for pulling.

trac'tory, *adj., i.q.* tractive.

tract'rix, *n.,* a special kind of curve.

trad, *adj.,* abbrev. of traditional or traditional jazz (*colloq.*).

trade, *n.,* traffic; commerce; a business or craft; *v.t.,* to traffic in; *v.i.,* to engage in commerce.

tra'ded, *p.p.,* trade.

trade'mark, *n.,* a mark protecting a trader's manufacture against the makers of similar, but not genuine, articles.

trade'-name, *n., i.q.* trademark.

trade'-price, *n.,* the price charged to a retailer.

tra'der, *n.,* one who trades; a trading-vessel.

trade'-sale, *n.,* an auction confined to the members of a particular trade.

Trad'escantia, *n.,* the genus of the spiderwort.

trades'folk, *n. pl.,* tradespeople.

trades'man, *n.,* one following a trade.

tradespeople, *n. pl.,* those who follow a trade.

trades-u'nion, an association of trade unions.

trades-u'nionism, *n.,* the principle of association among trade-unions.

tradeswoman, *n.,* a woman who follows a trade.

trade-u'nion, *n.,* an organized mutual association of the workmen of a particular industry.

trade-un'ionism, *n.,* the principle of association of workers.

trade-un'ionist, *n.,* one who supports trade-unionism.

trade'wind, *n.,* a wind that blows steadily for periods in the same direction along ocean trade routes.

tra'ding, *pr.p.,* trade; *adj.,* rel. to trade.

tradi'tion, *n.,* an unwritten delivery of a doctrine or story from generation to generation; an orally transmitted legend or doctrine.

tradi'tional, *adj.,* according to or by tradition.

tradi'tionalism, *n.,* the belief in tradition as a principle.

tradi'tionalist, *n.,* a supporter of traditionalism.

traditional'ity, *n.,* the state of being traditional.

tradi'tionally, *adv.,* by tradition.

tradi'tionary, *adj., i.q.* traditional.

tradi'tionist, *n.,* one who favours tradition.

trad'itor, *n.,* one who, to save his life, makes surrender of sacred property.

traduce', *v.t.,* to slander; grossly to misrepresent.

traduced', *p.p.,* traduce.

tradu'cement, *n.*, calumny, misrepresentation.

tradu'cer, *n.*, a slanderer.

tradu'cian, *n.*, a believer in the propagation of both body and soul.

tradu'cing, *pr.p.*, traduce.

tradu'cingly, *adv.*, in a traducing manner.

traduc'tion, *n.*, the act of traducing.

traduc'tive, *adj.*, slanderous.

traf'fic, *n.*, trade; goods being conveyed; concourse; thronging; the users of a thoroughfare (collectively); *v.t.*, to exchange; *v.i.*, to do business.

traf'ficator, *n.*, a direction indicator on an automobile.

traf'ficked, *p.p.*, traffic.

traf'ficker, *n.*, one who traffics.

traf'ficking, *pr.p.*, traffic.

traffic-lights, *n. pl.*, coloured lights to regulate traffic at road junctions and intersections.

traffic-signals, *n. pl.*, *i.q.* traffic-lights.

trag'acanth, *n.*, a species of gum plant.

trage'dian, *n.*, a writer or actor of tragedies.

tragedienne, *n.*, a woman actor of tragedy.

trag'edy, *n.*, a drama of an exalted character, illustrating the working out of fate; an overwhelmingly sad event.

trag'ic, *adj.*, pert. to tragedy; terrible.

trag'ical, *adj.*, *i.q.* tragic.

trag'ically, *adv.*, in a tragical way.

tragi-com'edy, *n.*, a play containing both tragedy and comedy.

tragi-com'ic, *adj.*, partly tragic and partly comic.

tragi-com'ical, *adj.*, *i.q.* tragi-comic.

tra'gicose, *adj.*, having a tragic style.

trag'opan, *n.*, a horned pheasant.

trag'ule, *n.*, a small hornless deer.

tra'gus, *n.*, the prominence protecting the entrance to the ear.

trail, *n.*, a track; a scent; a string of things; *v.t.*, to drag on the ground; *v.i.*, to be dragged along; to climb or depend (as a creeping plant).

trailed, *p.p.*, trail.

trail'er, *n.*, a trail-car.

trail'ing, *pr.p.*, trail.

train, *n.*, a body of followers; a retinue; railway carriages linked up together; a trailing robe; a state of preparedness; gunpowder laid up to a firing point; *v.t.*, to discipline; to educate; to aim a gun; *v.i.*, to prepare oneself for any skilled performance.

train'able, *adj.*, able to be trained.

train'-band, *n.*, an old English volunteer force.

train'bearer, *n.*, one who supports a train (in the sense of a robe).

trained, *p.p.*, train.

trainee', *n.*, a person under training.

train'er, *n.*, one who trains people, horses, etc.

train'ing, *pr.p.*, train; *n.*, preparation.

train'-oil, *n.*, whale-oil.

traipse, *v.i.*, to walk idly or slovenly; *n.*, a saunter; a sloven. Also *trapes*.

trait, *n.*, a characteristic.

trai'tor, *n.*, one who betrays a cause; one who is guilty of treason or treachery.

trai'torous, *adj.*, pert. to a traitor.

trai'torously, *adv.*, in a traitorous way.

trai'tress, *n.*, fem. of traitor.

traject', *v.t.*, to throw across.

traj'ect, *n.*, *i.q.* trajectory; a ford.

trajec'tion, *n.*, the act of trajecting or transporting; a passage.

traject'ory, *n.*, the curve of a flying missile, comet, etc.

tralati'cious, *adj.*, traditional.

tram, *n.*, *i.q.* tram-car; a tram-line; *v.i.*, to go in a tram-car.

tram'-car, *n.*, a car running on tram lines.

tram'mel, *v.t.*, to encumber; to impede; *n.*, a fishing or fowling net; an impediment.

tram'melled, *p.p.*, trammel.

tram'melling, *pr.p.*, trammel.

tramonta'na, *n.*, the bitter north wind from the Alps (*It.*).

tramon'tane, *adj.*, beyond the mountains.

tramp, *v.t.*, to travel over; *v.i.*, to walk with a regular and heavy tread; to go for a long walk; *n.*, a vagrant; the beat of feet on the ground; a long walk.

tramped, *p.p.*, tramp.

tramp'ing, *pr.p.*, tramp.

tram'ple, *v.t.*, to tread under foot; to treat with rude contempt.

tram'pled, *p.p.*, trample.

tram'pler, *n.*, one who tramples.

tram'pling, *pr.p.*, trample.

tram'poline, *n.*, an athlete's elastic spring apparatus.

tram'-road, *n.*, *i.q.* tramway.

tram'way, *n.*, a track for trams to run on.

trance, *n.*, a condition in which, though unconscious, one sees visions; a cataleptic state; *v.t.*, to throw into a trance.

tran'quil, *adj.*, calm; peaceful.

tranquil'lity, *n.*, the state of being tranquil.

tranquilliza'tion, *n.*, the act of tranquillizing; the state of being tranquillized.

tran'quillize, *v.t.*, to make tranquil; to appease; to calm.

tran'quillized, *p.p.*, tranquillize.

tran'quillizer, *n.*, one who, that which, tranquillizes.

tran'quillizing, *pr.p.*, tranquillize.

tranquilli'zingly, *adv.*, in a tranquillizing way.

tran'quilly, *adv.*, in a tranquil way.

trans, a *Lat. prep.*, across; used as a prefix to many words.

transact', *adj.*, to perform; to carry through; to negotiate.

transact'ed, *p.p.*, transact.

transact'ing, *pr.p.*, transact.

transac'tion, *n.*, the process of transacting; a negotiation; an affair carried through.

transac'tor, *n.*, one who transacts.

transal'pine, *adj.*, on the other side of the Alps.

or **transatlan'tic,** *adj.*, across the Atlantic.

transcei'ver, *n.*, a radio combining transmission and reception facilities.

transcend', *v.t.*, to surpass; to exceed.

transcend'ed, *p.p.*, transcend.

transcend'ence, *n.*, the state or quality of being transcendent.

transcend'ency, *n.*, *i.q.* transcendence.

transcend'ent, *adj.*, surpassing; supereminent.

transcenden'tal, *adj.*, outside or beyond experience; metaphysical.

transcenden'talism, *n.*, the Kantian *a priori* philosophy.

transcenden'talist, *n.*, an adherent of transcendentalism.

transcenden'tally, *adv.*, in a transcendental way.

transcend'ently, *adv.*, in a transcendent way.

transcend'ing, *pr.p.*, transcend.

transcontinent'al, *adj.*, across a continent.

transcribe', *v.t.*, to make an exact copy of.

transcribed', *p.p.*, transcribe.

transcri'ber, *n.*, a copyist; one who transcribes.

transcri'bing, *pr.p.*, transcribe.

tran'script, *n.*, an exact copy in writing.

transcrip'tion, *n.*, the act of transcribing; *i.q.* transcript.

transcrip'tional, *adj.*, pert. or rel. to transcription.

transcrip'tive, *adj.*, transcribing.

transcrip'tively, *adv.*, in a transcriptive way.

transdu'cer, *n.*, a device for transference of power.

transduc'tion, *n.*, a transfer, esp. between bacterial cells.

tran'sept, *n.*, a part of a building that crosses another part at right angles.

transept'al, *adj.*, pert. or rel. to a transept.

transfer', *v.t.*, to remove from one place to another; to hand over; to reproduce, as in lithography.

trans'fer, *n.*, a handing over from one person to another; a reproduction of a picture by printing; a soldier drafted into another regiment, etc.

transferabi'lity, *n.*, the quality of being transferable.

trans'ferable, *adj.*, able to be transferred.

transferee', *n.*, one to whom property is transferred by a deed of conveyance.

trans'ference, *n.*, the act of transferring; the state of being transferred.

trans'feror, *n.*, one who transfers property.

transferred', *p.p.*, transfer.

transfer'rer, *n.*, one who transfers (in a general sense).

transfer'ring, *pr.p.*, transfer.

transfigura'tion, *n.*, the act of transfiguring; the change wrought by transfiguring.

transfig'ure, *v.t.*, to change in form and appearance.

transfig'ured, *p.p.*, transfigure.

transfig'uring, *pr.p.*, transfigure.

transfix', *v.t.*, to pierce through.

transfixed', *p.p.*, transfix.

transfix'ing, *pr.p.*, transfix.

transfix'ion, *n.*, the act of transfixing; the state of being transfixed.

trans'fluent, *adj.*, flowing through or across.

or **transform',** *v.t.*, to change completely.

transform'able, *adj.*, capable of transformation.

or **transforma'tion,** *n.*, the act of transforming; the state of being transformed.

transforma'tional, *adj.*, pert. or rel. to transformation.

transform'ative, *adj.*, producing transformation.

or **transformed',** *p.p.*, transform.

or **transform'er,** *n.*, one who transforms; the apparatus for changing electric voltage.

or **transform'ing,** *pr.p.*, transform.

transfuse', *v.t.*, to remove (liquid) from one vessel to another; to convert into a new form; medically, to take blood from a person's veins and inject it into a patient.

transfused', *p.p.*, transfuse.

transfu'ser, *n.*, one who, or that which, transfuses.

transfu'sible, *adj.*, able to be transfused.

transfu'sing, *pr.p.*, transfuse.

transfu'sion, *n.*, the act of transfusing.

transfu'sive, *adj.*, effecting transfusion.

transfu'sively, *adv.*, in a transfusive way.

transgress', *v.t.*, to overstep; to offend against; *v.i.*, to sin; to offend.

transgressed', *p.p.*, transgress.

transgress'ing, *pr.p.*, transgress.

transgres'sion, *n.*, the act of transgressing; an offence; a sin.

transgres'sional, *adj.*, rel. to transgression.

transgress'ive, *adj.*, transgressing; guilty.

transgress'ively, *adv.*, guiltily.

transgress'or, *n.*, one who transgresses; a sinner.

tranship', *v.t.* and *i.*, to remove from one ship to another. Also *transship*.

tranship'ment, *n.*, the act or process of transhipping.

transhipped', *p.p.*, tranship.

tranship'per, *n.*, one who tranships.

tranship'ping, *pr.p.*, tranship.

transhu'mance, *n.*, the change from summer to winter or vice versa; the seasonal movement of grazing animals.

transhume', *v.t.*, to change from summer to winter (grazing) or vice versa.

tran'sience, *n.*, *i.q.* transientness.

tran'sient, *adj.*, passing; ephemeral.

tran'siently, *adv.*, in a transient way.

tran'sientness, *n.*, the state or quality of being transient.

transil'ience, *n.*, the state of being transilient.

transil'iency, *n.*, *i.q.* transilience.

transil'ient, *adj.*, leaping or stretching from one supporting point to another.

transillu'minate, *v.t.*, to project a strong light through, esp. for the purpose of medical diagnosis.

transillumina'tion, *n.*, the projection of a strong light.

transire', *n.*, a customs permit to shift goods.

transis'tor, *n.*, an electronic semi-conducting device; a radio receiving apparatus (*colloq.*).

transis'torize, *v.t.*, to equip with a transistor.

transis'torized, *adj.*, converted into transistor form; *p.p.*, transistorize.

transis'torizing, *pr.p.*, transistorize.

trans'it, *n.*, a passage; a conveyance; the apparent passage of a celestial body over the meridian of a place.

transi'tion, *n.*, the act of passing; the state of passing; change; a period of change or of changing style; in music, a change from key to key; or from major to relative minor and *vice versa*.

transi'tional, *adj.*, pert. to, or in a stage of, transition. Often esp. applied to the architectural period when Norman was giving way to First Pointed.

transi'tionally, *adv.*, in a transitional way.

transi'tionary, *adj.*, passing, changing, going through a period of change.

trans'itive, *adj.*, acting directly upon an object (said of a verb which expresses an effect upon some person or thing and requires to be followed by the objective or accusative case).

trans'itively, *adv.*, in a transitive way.

trans'itorily, *adv.*, in a transitory way.

trans'itoriness, *n.*, the state or quality of being transitory.

trans'itory, *adj.*, *i.q.* transient; impermanent.

transjorda'nian, *adj.*, lying beyond the River Jordan.

transla'table, *adj.*, able to be translated.

translate', *v.t.*, to convey from one language to another; to remove or promote from one position (as a bishopric) to another; to change the form of; to carry away; to transform; to retransmit (a telegraphic message).

transla'ted, *p.p.*, translate.

transla'ting, *pr.p.*, translate.

transla'tion, *n.*, the act of translating; something translated; removal; a non-rotating motion.

transla'tional, *adj.*, translatory.

transla'tive, *adj.*, metaphorical.

transla'tor, *n.*, one who translates; an instrument converting one form of energy to another; a telegraph repeater; a cobbler who converts old shoes into new ones (*colloq.*). In pl., old shoes so converted (*colloq.*).

translatorese', *n.*, the style of language used by translators.

transla'tory, *adj.*, pert. to, of the nature of, translation.

translit'erate, *v.t.*, to reproduce a foreign word in the alphabetic characters of one's own language according to the sound.

translit'erated, *p.p.*, transliterate.

translit'erating, *pr.p.*, transliterate.

translitera'tion, *n.*, the state of being transliterated.

translocate', *v.t.*, to change position.

transloca'tion, *n.*, the act of changing position.

translu'cence, *n.*, the state or quality of being translucent.

translu'cency, *n.*, *i.q.* translucence.

translu'cent, *adj.*, letting light through but not being quite transparent.

translu'cently, *adv.*, in a translucent way.

translu'cid, *adj.*, *i.q.* translucent.

translucid'ity, *n.*, *i.q.* translucence.

transmarine', *adj.*, situated across the sea.

transmi'grant, *n.*, an alien passing through from one country to another.

trans'migrate, *v.i.*, to pass from one place or state to another.

trans'migrated, *p.p.*, transmigrate.

trans'migrating, *pr.p.*, transmigrate.

transmigra'tion, *n.*, the act of transmigrating, esp. the passing of a soul from one state or body into another; metempsychosis.

transmigra'tionism, *n.*, belief in metempsychosis.

trans'migrator, *n.*, one who transmigrates.

transmi'gratory, *adj.*, passing from one state into another.

transmissibil'ity, *n.*, the state or quality of being transmissible.

transmis'sible, *adj.*, able to be transmitted.

transmis'sion, *n.*, the act of transmitting, esp. of allowing the passage of ether-waves through a medium.

transmis'sional, *adj.*, *i.q.* transmissive.

transmis'sive, *adj.*, permitting transmission; derivable.

transmit', *v.t.*, to convey through or across; to hand down or on; to convey ether-waves through a medium.

transmit'table, *n.*, *adj.*, able to be transmitted.

transmit'tal, *n.*, the act of transmitting.

transmit'ted, *p.p.*, transmit.

transmit'ter, *n.*, one who, that which, transmits; a telegraphic instrument for transmitting messages; also a radio instrument.

transmit'ting, *pr.p.*, transmit.

transmogrifica'tion, *n.*, the state of being transmogrified.

transmo'grified, *p.p.*, transmogrify.

transmog′rify, *v.t.*, to transform in a surprising or humorous fashion.

transmo′grifying, *pr.p.*, transmogrify.

transmutabil′ity, *n.*, the state or quality of being transmutable.

transmu′table, *adj.*, able to be transmuted.

transmu′tably, *adv.*, in a transmutable way.

transmuta′tion, *n.*, the act or result of transmuting, esp. the alchemistic pretended conversion of base metals into gold; the change of one species into another.

transmuta′tionist, *n.*, one who holds the biological theory that one species can be changed into another; an alchemist.

transmuta′tive, *adj.*, serving to transmute.

transmute′, *v.t.*, to change in form, nature, or substance.

transmu′ted, *p.p.*, transmute.

transmu′ter, *n.*, one who, that which, transmutes.

transmu′ting, *pr.p.*, transmute.

transna′tional, *adj.*, extending beyond national boundaries.

transocean′ic, *adj.*, beyond, or crossing, the ocean.

tran′som, *n.*, a horizontal wood or stone bar across a window or a door-head; a beam across a ship; a stern-post; a beam across a sawpit.

tran′somed, *adj.*, having a transom.

transpacif′ic, *adj.*, beyond, or crossing, the Pacific Ocean.

transpa′dane, *adj.*, situated on the other side of the River Po (Padus).

transpa′rence, *n.*, the state or quality of being transparent.

transpa′rency, *n.*, *i.q.* transparence; lucidity; a picture, etc., on a thin canvas or muslin allowing the light to come through it; a photograph, etc., on film to be seen with the light behind it.

transpa′rent, *adj.*, admitting the light through without diffusion; clear; easy to see through; frank.

transpa′rently, *adv.*, in a transparent way.

transpierce′, *v.t.*, to pierce through.

transpierced′, *p.p.*, transpierce.

transpierc′ing, *pr.p.*, transpierce.

transpi′rable, *adj.*, able to be transpired.

transpira′tion, *n.*, the process of transpiring; exhalation.

transpi′ratory, *adj.*, exhaling.

transpire′, *v.t.*, to emit through the excretory organs of the lungs or the skin; to exhale; *v.i.*, to be exhaled.

transpired′, *p.p.*, transpire.

transpi′ring, *pr.p.*, transpire.

transplant′, *n.*, anything removed from one place and implanted in another; *v.t.*, to remove from one place and to plant in another; in surgery, to take tissue from one part of a person's body, or that of another body, and plant it where it is needed.

transplanta′tion, *n.*, the process of transplanting.

transplant′ed, *p.p.*, transplant.

transplant′er, *n.*, one who, that which, transplants.

transplant′ing, *n.*, *i.q.* transplant; *pr.p.*, transplant.

transplend′ent, *adj.*, very resplendent.

transpont′ine, *adj.*, across a bridge; south of London.

transport′, *v.t.*, to convey from one place to another; to take or send away emotionally.

trans′port, *n.*, transportation; conveyance; a ship to carry troops, stores, etc.; rapture.

transportabil′ity, *n.*, the state of being transportable.

transport′able, *adj.*, able to be transported.

transporta′tion, *n.*, the act of transporting; the state of being transported.

transport′ed, *p.p.*, transport.

transport′er, *n.*, one who, that which, transports.

transport′ing, *pr.p.*, transport.

transport′ingly, *adv.*, in a transporting way.

transpor′tive, *adj.*, able to transport.

transpos′able, *adj.*, able to be transposed.

transpo′sal, *n.*, the act of transposing; a piece of music written or played in a different key from the original.

transpose′, *v.t.*, to change the position or order of; to write or play a piece of music in another key than the original.

transposed′, *p.p.*, transpose.

transpo′sing, *pr.p.*, transpose.

transposi′tion, *n.*, the act of transposing; the state of being transposed.

transposi′tional, *adj.*, rel. to transposition.

transpos′itive, *adj.*, causing or caused by transposition.

transship′, *v.t.* and *i.*, *i.q.* tranship.

transship′ment, *n.*, *i.q.* transhipment.

transshipped′, *p.p.*, transship.

transship′ping, *pr.p.*, transship.

transubstan′tiate, *v.t.*, to change the substance of; esp., in the Christian Faith, to change the substance (*i.e.*, the essential, non-material nature) of Bread and Wine in the Eucharist into the Body and Blood of Christ.

transubstan′tiated, *p.p.*, transubstantiate.

transubstan′tiating, *pr.p.*, transubstantiate.

transubstantia′tion, *n.*, the act of transubstantiating, esp. the change in the Eucharistic elements.

transuda′tion, *n.*, the passage of fluid through the pores or membranes.

transu′datory, *adj.*, rel. to transudation.

transude′, *v.i.*, to pass through the pores or membranes.

transu'ded, *p.p.*, transude.

transu'ding, *pr.p.*, transude.

transump'tion, *n.*, a transcription.

transuran'ic, *adj.*, having higher atomic number than uranium.

transvec'tion, *n.*, the act of transporting.

transver'sal, *adj.*, transverse; *n.*, a straight line that cuts a system of lines.

transversal'ity, *n.*, the state of being transverse.

transvers'ally, *adv.*, *i.q.* transversely.

transverse', *v.t.*, to transpose; *adj.*, lying across or in a crosswise relation; *n.*, anything transverse; a muscle so named.

transverse'ly, *adv.*, in a transverse direction; crosswise.

transvest', *v.t. and i.*, to dress in clothes of the opposite sex.

transvest'ism, *n.*, the sexual characteristic of dressing in clothes of the opposite sex.

transvest'ite, *n.*, a person who transvests.

transvola'tion, *n.*, the act of flying across.

Transylvan'ian, *adj.*, pertaining to Transylvania (eastern Austria-Hungary, now Romania).

trap, *v.t.*, to snare; to take in a trap; to prevent the escape of (liquid, gas, etc.); *v.i.*, to snare game; *n.*, a snare; a gin; a pitfall; an arrangement within a pipe to prevent the escape of foul smell, noxious gas, etc.; a carriage (*col-loq.*).

trapan', *v.t.*, *i.q.* trepan.

trapanned', *p.p.*, trapan.

trapan'ning, *pr.p.*, trapan.

trap'-door', *n.*, a hinged door in a roof, floor, deck, etc.

trapes, *v.i.*, to make a needless or wearisome journey. Also *traipes*.

trapeze', *n.*, a bar hung from two ropes and used by athletes, acrobats, etc.

trape'zian, *adj.*, with opposed trapeziform faces.

trape'ziform, *adj.*, like a trapezium.

trape'zium, *n.*, a quadrilateral figure having no two sides parallel.

trapezohe'dron, *n.*, a solid with all its faces bounded by trapezoids.

trap'ezoid, *n.*, a quadrilateral plane figure with two sides parallel but not the others.

trapezoid'al, *adj.*, like a trapezoid.

trap'pean, *adj.*, pert. to trap rock.

trapped', *p.p.*, trap.

trap'per, *n.*, one who traps; a hunter of fur-bearing game; a miner whose duty it is to look after the air-doors.

trap'ping, *pr.p.*, trap; *n.*, the trade of supplying traps; the pursuit of furred game; a harness; an outward adornment.

trap'pings, *n.*, pl. of trapping; in the sense of harness, adornment.

trap'pist, *n.*, a member of the extremely severe Order of Trappists, a reformed Cistercian Order. Among its most ascetic requirements is the obligation of silence.

trap'pous, *adj.*, *i.q.* trappean.

trap'py, *adj.*, full of snares or pit-falls.

trap'-rock, *n.*, an igneous rock useful for road-making and railway ballast.

traps, *n. pl.*, belongings; luggage.

trash, *n.*, nonsense; worthless stuff.

trash'iness, *n.*, the quality or state of being trashy.

trash'y, *adj.*, worthless; rubbishy.

trass, *n.*, an earth used in the making of hydraulic cement.

trattori'a, *n.*, an eating-house (*It.*).

trau'ma, *n.*, a wound; a psychical or emotional shock.

traumat'ic, *adj.*, pert. to a trauma.

traumat'ically, *adv.*, in a traumatic way.

trav'ail, *n.*, labour; toil; labour in childbirth; anguish; *v.i.*, to labour.

trav'ailed, *p.p.*, travail.

trav'ailing, *pr.p.*, travail.

trav'el, *v.t.*, to pass over in travelling; to convey (books, articles, etc.) for orders; *v.i.*, to journey; to move; to go about for a business house; *n.*, journeying. In pl., a story of wanderings.

trav'elled, *p.p.*, travel; *adj.*, having visited many countries.

trav'eller, *n.*, one who, that which, travels; one who has visited many countries; one who travels for a business house.

trav'elling, *pr.p.*, travel.

trav'elogue, *n.*, an account of a journey, usually illustrated.

trav'ersable, *adj.*, able to be traversed.

trav'erse, *v.t.*, to go across or over; to wander over; to question; to oppose; *v.i.*, to swivel; *n.*, a crosspiece; a transom, etc.; a gallery across a building; a screened bench; a ship's zigzag course; a crossing from one face to another in mountain climbing.

trav'ersed, *p.p.*, traverse.

trav'erser, *n.*, one who traverses.

trav'erse-table, *n.*, a nautical table for dealing with traverses; a railway turntable.

trav'ersing, *pr.p.*, traverse.

trav'ertine, **trav'ertin**, *n.*, a porous yellow Italian rock, quarried for building purposes.

trav'estied, *p.p.*, travesty.

trav'esty, *n.*, a caricature; a ridiculous imitation; *v.t.*, to imitate in an absurd way and make ridiculous.

trav'estying, *pr.p.*, travesty.

trav'olator, *n.*, a moving floor to convey pedestrians.

trawl, *n.*, a drag net; *v.t.*, to fish with a trawl.

trawled, *p.p.*, trawl.

trawl'er, *n.*, one who trawls; a boat for trawling.

trawl'ing, *pr.p.*, trawl; *n.*, the business of fishing with a trawl

trawl'-net, *n.*, a large bag net for trawling or dragging.

tray, *n.*, a flat portable, shallow vessel for carrying things; a movable shelf in a trunk.

tray'-cloth, *n.*, a cloth for use of a tray.

tray'ful, *n.*, as much as a tray will hold.

treach'erous, *adj.*, traitorous; betraying; false.

treach'erously, *adv.*, in a treacherous way.

treach'ery, *n.*, betrayal; perfidy.

treac'le, *n.*, a thick syrup derived from sugar.

treac'liness, *n.*, the state or quality of being treacly; stickiness.

trea'cly, *adj.*, having nature of treacle.

tread, *n.*, the planting of one's foot on the ground; a manner of walking; the sound of feet; the upper surface of a stair; the part of a wheel that touches the ground or a rail; a male bird's act of copulation; *v.t.*, to walk on; to press with the feet; to crush; to copulate with (said of the male bird); *v.i.*, to step.

tread'er, *n.*, one who treads.

tread'ing, *pr.p.*, tread.

tread'le, *n.*, a lever worked by the foot; *v.i.*, to operate a treadle.

tread'led, *p.p.*, treadle.

tread'ler, *n.*, one who treadles.

tread'ling, *pr.p.*, treadle.

tread'mill, *n.*, a mechanical device for obtaining rotation by means of walking up steps.

trea'son, *n.*, active disloyalty to the State; treachery.

trea'sonable, *adj.*, guilty of treason; involving treason.

trea'sonably, *adv.*, in a treasonable way.

treas'ure, *n.*, accumulated and hoarded wealth; a highly valued possession; *v.t.*, to hoard; to value very highly; to preserve.

treas'ured, *p.p.*, treasure.

treas'urer, *n.*, an official who is responsible for monetary funds.

treas'urership, *n.*, the office of treasurer.

treas'ure-trove, *n.*, treasure of unknown ownership found anywhere.

treas'uring, *pr.p.*, treasure.

treas'ury, *n.*, a repository of treasure; the department of public finance and revenue.

treat, *n.*, something to give enjoyment; *v.t.*, to act or behave towards; to deal with; to entertain; *v.i.*, to arrange terms.

treat'able, *adj.*, able to be treated.

treat'ed, *p.p.*, treat.

treat'er, *n.*, one who treats.

treat'ing, *pr.p.*, treat.

trea'tise, *n.*, a tract; an essay on a special subject.

treat'ment, *n.*, the act or manner of dealing with a person or thing.

treat'y, *n.*, an arrangement of terms between nations or persons.

treb'le, *adj.*, threefold; soprano; *n.*, the treble voice or part (*mus.*); *v.t.*, to multiply by three; *v.i.*, to increase threefold.

treb'le clef, *n.*, the uppermost clef (*mus.*).

treb'led, *p.p.*, treble.

treb'ling, *pr.p.*, treble.

treb'ly, *adv.*, threefold.

treb'uchet, *n.*, an old military engine for hurling heavy missiles; a scale-balance that tilts; a small tilting-trap for birds.

trecen'to, *n.*, 14th century Italian art and literature.

tree, *n.*, a branching plant growing from one stem; the Cross; *v.t.*, to compel to take refuge in a tree; to place in an embarrassing position.

tree'-frog, *n.*, an arboreal amphibian.

tree'less, *adj.*, devoid of trees.

tree'-nail, *n.*, a wooden timber-fastener.

tref'le, *n.*, *i.q.* trefoil.

tre'foil, *n.*, a three-leaved plant, such as the clover; an architectural ornament so named.

treil'lage, *n.*, an espalier.

trek, *v.i.*, to migrate in wagons; *n.*, a migration. (An Africaans word.)

trekked, *p.p.*, trek.

trek'ker, *n.*, one who treks.

trek'king, *pr.p.*, trek.

trel'lis, *n.*, lattice-work for fencing, etc.; *v.t.*, to cover with trellis work.

trel'lised, *adj.*, having trellis-work; *p.p.*, trellis.

trel'lising, *pr.p.*, trellis.

trel'lis-work, *n.*, wooden laths arranged crosswise.

trem'ble, *v.i.*, to quake with fear, cold, etc.; to quaver; *n.*, a fit of shaking.

trem'bled, *p.p.*, tremble.

trem'bler, *n.*, one who trembles.

trem'bling, *pr.p.*, tremble.

trem'blingly, *adv.*, in a trembling or fearful way.

trem'bly, *adj.*, tremulous.

Tremel'la, *n.*, a genus of fungi of jelly-like substance.

trem'ellose, *adj.*, shaking like a jelly.

tremen'dous, *adj.*, alarming; terrible; amazing.

tremen'dously, *adv.*, to a tremendous degree.

tremoland'o, *adv.*, in tremulous fashion (*mus.*).

trem'olant, *adj.*, tremolo; *n.*, an organ stop which produces a quavering note.

trem'olite, *n.*, a species of hornblende.

trem'olo, *adj.*, quavering; *n.*, a quavering effect produced by the voice, or mechanically (*mus.*).

trem'or, *n.*, a shaking fit; a thrill; a seismic wave.

trem'ulous, *adj.*, trembling; quavering; timid.

trem'ulously, *adv.*, tremblingly.

trem'ulousness, *n.*, the state of being tremulous.

trench, *n.*, an extended excavation; a drain; a dug-out; *v.t.*, to cultivate with trenches; to excavate; *v.i.*, to encroach.

trench'ant, *adj.*, cutting; severe.

trench'antly, *adv.*, sharply; severely.

trenched, *p.p.*, trench.

trench'er, *n.*, one who trenches; a wooden plate; a college cap.

trench'erman, *n.*, one blessed with a good appetite.

trench'ing, *pr.p.*, trench.

trend, *n.*, tendency in a certain direction; bearing; *v.i.*, to tend in a certain direction.

trend'ed, *p.p.*, trend.

trend'ing, *pr.p.*, trend.

trend'-set'ter, *n.*, a leader in fashion.

trend'-set'ting, *adj.*, leading a new fashion.

trendy, *adj.*, in the latest fashion (*colloq.*).

tren'tal, *n.*, thirty things in a series; a daily succession of thirty masses.

trepan', *v.t.*, to perforate (the skull); *n.*, the surgical instrument used in trepanning. Also *trephine* and *trapan*.

trepang', *n.*, bêche-de-mer; a sea-slug.

trepanned', *p.p.*, trepan.

trepan'ner, *n.*, one who trepans.

trepan'ning, *pr.p.*, trepan; *n.*, the surgical operation of trepanning.

trephine', *n.* and *v.t.*, *i.q.* trepan.

trepida'tion, *n.*, alarm; a state of anxious fear.

tres'pass, *n.*, a transgression; a sin; an intrusion in another's domain; an offence; *v.i.*, to transgress; to intrude into another's domain; to offend against custom, etc.

tres'passed, *p.p.*, trespass.

tres'passer, *n.*, one who trespasses.

tres'passing, *pr.p.*, trespass.

tress, *n.*, a lock of hair.

tressed, *adj.*, having tresses.

tress'ure, *n.*, a heraldic border.

tress'ured, *adj.*, bordered with a tressure.

tress'y, *adj.*, covered with tresses.

tres'tle, *n.*, a support; the movable under-part of a temporary table.

tres'tle-board, *n.*, a designing-board for a draughtsman.

tres'tle-ta'ble, *n.*, a table made of boards supported by trestles.

tres'tle-tree, *n.*, a wooden support of the cross-trees (*naut.*).

tret, *n.*, a rebate on the price of certain commodities as compensation for damage or loss in transport.

trev'et, *n.*, *i.q.* trivet.

trews, *n. pl.*, plaid trousers.

trey, *n.*, a three in dice or cards.

tri'able, *adj.*, able to be tried.

tri'ad, *n.*, a group of three; the common chord of a tone, its third and fifth (*mus.*); in chemistry, an atom, etc., with a combining power of three.

tri'al, *n.*, putting to the proof; a test; a trying affliction; an examination in a court of law.

tri'alogue, *n.*, a conversation among three speakers.

trian'drian, *adj.*, with three equal stamens.

trian'drous, *adj.*, *i.q.* triandrian.

tri'angle, *n.*, a plain three-sided figure with three angles; a triangular musical instrument of percussion; a military instrument of punishment.

tri'angled, *adj.*, *i.q.* triangular.

trian'gular, *adj.*, in the form of a triangle.

triangular'ity, *n.*, the state or quality of being triangular.

trian'gularly, *adv.*, in a triangular way.

trian'gulate, *v.t.*, to survey by dividing into triangles.

trian'gulated, *p.p.*, triangulate.

triangulate'ly, *adv.*, in a triangulating way.

trian'gulating, *pr.p.*, triangulate.

triangula'tion, *n.*, the process of triangulating; a survey.

tri'archy, *n.*, a province governed by three persons; the rule of three persons.

Tri'as, tri'as, *n.*, the lowest division of the Mesozoic period.

Trias'sic, *adj.*, pert. to the Trias; *n.*, *i.q.* trias.

tri'atom'ic, *adj.*, containing three atoms.

triax'ial, *adj.*, having three axes.

trib'ade, *n.*, a woman homosexual.

trib'adism, *n.*, sex practices between women.

tri'bal, *adj.*, pert. to a tribe or tribes.

trib'ally, *adv.*, in a tribal way; by tribe.

trib'ble, *n.*, a wire frame used for drying in paper-making.

tribe, *n.*, a group of related families under one chief; a political group; an ethnical division.

tribes'man, *n.*, a member of a tribe.

tribes'woman, *n.*, a female member of a tribe.

trib'let, *n.*, a mandrel for forging rings, nuts, etc.

tribol'ogy, *n.*, the study of the interaction of surfaces in relative motion.

tribom'eter, *n.*, an apparatus for measuring sliding motion.

trib'rach, *n.*, a metrical foot consisting of three short syllables.

tribrach'ic, *adj.*, having three short syllables.

tribula'tion, *n.*, great trouble; affliction.

tribu'nal, *n.*, a seat of authority; a court of justice.

trib'unary, *adj.*, pert. to a tribune.

trib'unate, *n.*, the office of a tribune; the term of a tribune's office.

trib'une, *n.*, an old Roman officer chosen by the people as the guardian of their rights and liberties; a platform.

tribuni'cial, *adj.*, *i.q.* tribunary.

trib'utarily, *adv.*, in a tributary way.

trib'utariness, *n.*, the state of being a tributary.

trib'utary, *adj.*, paying tribute; contributing; *n.*, a nation or prince in subjection to another; a smaller river running into a larger one.

trib'ute, *n.*, a tax; an impost; an acknowledgment.

tricap'sular, *adj.*, having three capsules.

tri'car, *n.*, a three-wheeled automobile.

tricar'pellary, *adj.*, consisting of three carpels (*bot.*).

trice, *n.*, an instant of time; *v.t.*, to fasten up.

Tri'cel, *n.*, a proprietary man-made fibre for textiles.

tricenten'ary, *adj.*, pert. to a period of three hundred years; *n.*, the commemoration of an event of three hundred years ago.

tri'ceps, *n.*, a three-part muscle in the brachial region of the upper arm.

tricer'ion, *n.*, a three-branched candelabra.

trichias'is, *n.*, a urinary disease; inversion of the eyelashes.

trichi'na, *n.*, a parasite in swine and human beings.

trichino'sis, *n.*, a disease produced by the trichina.

trichinot'ic, *adj.*, pert. to trichinosis.

tri'choid, *adj.*, like hair.

tricholog'ical, *adj.*, pert. or rel. to trichology.

trichol'ogist, *n.*, a student of trichology.

trichol'ogy, *n.*, the study of human hair.

Trichoph'yton, *n. pl.*, a kind of fungus genus which causes ringworm.

trichophy'tosis, *n.*, ringworm.

Trichop'tera, *n.*, an order of caddis-flies.

tri'chord, *adj.*, having three strings; *n.*, an instrument of three strings; a pianoforte having three strings to each note.

tricho'sis, *n.*, a hair disease.

trichot'omize, *v.t. and i.*, to divide into threes.

trichot'omous, *adj.*, pert. to trichotomy.

trichot'omously, *adv.*, in a trichotomous way.

trichot'omy, *n.*, division into three.

trick, *n.*, a deception; a dodge; an imposition; a piece of legerdemain; a completed single round in a game of cards; *v.t.*, to deceive; to impose upon; to adorn.

tricked, *p.p.*, trick.

trick'ery, *n.*, deceit; an imposition; stratagem.

trick'ing, *pr.p.*, trick.

trick'ish, *adj.*, i.q. tricky.

trick'ishly, *adv.*, in a trickish or tricky manner.

trick'ishness, *n.*, the quality of being trickish.

trick'le, *v.t.*, to cause to flow in a thin stream or in drops; *v.i.*, to flow in a thin stream or in drops; *n.*, a thin flow.

trick'led, *p.p.*, trickle.

trick'ling, *pr.p.*, trickle.

trick'ster, *n.*, one who plays tricks; a cheat.

trick'sy, *adj.*, up to tricks; pretty.

trick'y, *adj.*, full of tricks; puzzling; difficult.

tric'linate, *adj.*, asymmetric; i.q. triclinic.

triclin'ic, *adj.*, with three unequal axes intersecting obliquely.

triclin'ium, *n.*, the Roman arrangement of a dining-room, having three couches arranged as three sides of a square or oblong.

tricoc'cous, *adj.*, with three carpels.

Tri'coline, *n.*, a silky cotton poplin.

tri'colour, *n.*, a flag in three colours arranged in equal stripes.

tri'coloured, *adj.*, having three colours.

triconsonant'al, *adj.*, having three consonants.

tri'corn, *n.*, a three-cornered hat.

tricor'poral, *adj.*, having three bodies.

tricor'porate, *adj.*, i.q. tricorporal.

tricos'tate, *adj.*, having three ribs.

tri'cot, *n.*, knitted material.

tricus'pid, *adj.*, having three cusps.

tricus'pidate, *adj.*, three-pointed.

tri'cycle, *n.*, a three-wheeled cycle; *v.i.*, to ride a tricycle.

tridac'tyl, *adj.*, i.q. tridactylous.

tridac'tylous, *adj.*, having three toes or fingers.

tri'dent, *n.*, a three-pronged sceptre; the emblem of Neptune and of sovereignty over the sea.

triden'tate, *adj.*, three-pronged.

Triden'tine, *adj.*, rel. to the Council of Trent, in the South Tyrol.

tridiapa'son, *n.*, a triple octave.

tridimen'sional, *adj.*, having three dimensions.

tridomin'ium, *n.*, the rule by three powers.

tridu'an, *adj.*, lasting three days.

tridu'um, *n.*, a special period of three days.

tried, *p.p.*, try; *adj.*, tested; proved; afflicted.

trien'nial, *adj.*, occurring every three years; lasting for three years.

trien'nially, *adv.*, once every three years.

tri'er, *n.*, one who tries; a trial.

tri'erarch, *n.*, the commander of an ancient Greek trireme; one who performed the *leitourgia* or liturgy of supplying a trireme to the State.

tri'eteric, *adj.*, triennial.

trifa'rious, *adj.*, arranged in three upright rows.

tri'fid, *adj.*, split into three.

trifist'ulary, *adj.*, with three pipes.

tri'fle, *n.*, something of little or no value; a sweet dish; *v.i.*, to dally; to be frivolous; *v.t.*, to waste in idleness.

tri'fled, *p.p.*, trifle.

tri'fler, *n.*, one who trifles.

tri'fling, *pr.p.*, trifle; *adj.*, of no importance.

tri'flingly, *adv.*, in a trifling way.

triflo'ral, *adj.*, bearing three flowers.

triflo'rous, *adj.*, i.q. trifloral.

trifoc'al, *adj.*, providing for three distances in vision.

trifo'liate, *adj.*, having three leaves.

trifo'liated, *adj.*, *i.q.* trifoliate.

trifo'liolate, *adj.*, *i.q.* trifoliate.

Trifo'lium, *n.*, a botanical genus containing the clovers.

tri'foly, *n.*, *i.q.* trefoil (*obs.*).

trifo'rium, *n.*, a gallery in the space between the inner vault of an aisle and the outer roof.

tri'form, *adj.*, in three divisions.

triform'ity, *n.*, the state of being triform.

tri'furcated, *adj.*, with three forks or branches.

trifurca'tion, *n.*, the state of being divided into three forks or branches.

trig, *adj.*, neat; trim; *v.t.*, to stop; to skid.

trigam'ist, *n.*, one guilty of trigamy.

trig'amous, *adj.*, pert. to trigamy; bearing three kinds of flowers.

trig'amy, *n.*, the state of being married to three wives or husbands at once.

trigged, *p.p.*, trig.

trig'ger, *n.*, the contrivance in a pistol lock or gun lock by which the hammer is caused to act.

trig'ging, *pr.p.*, trig.

tri'glot, *adj.*, in three languages; *n.*, a work produced in three languages.

tri'glyph, *n.*, a Doric frieze ornament vertically grooved, alternating with the metopes.

tri'gon, *n.*, a triangle.

trig'onal, *adj.*, triangular.

trigon'ic, *adj.*, pert. or rel. to a trigon.

trigonom'eter, *n.*, an instrument for solving right-angled triangles.

trigonomet'ric, *adj.*, pert. to trigonometry.

trigonomet'rically, *adv.*, by the rules of trigonometry.

trigonom'etry, *n.*, a department of mathematics rel. to the angles and sides of triangles.

tri'gram, *n.*, *i.q.* trigraph.

trigrammat'ic, *adj.*, containing three letters or groups of letters.

tri'graph, *n.*, a group of three letters for one sound.

Trigyn'ia, *n. pl.*, Linnaeus's third order in his plant system.

trigyn'ian, *adj.*, having three pistils or styles, or three carpels.

trihe'dral, *adj.*, with three intersecting surfaces as sides.

trihe'dron, *n.*, a three-sided figure.

trilat'eral, *adj.*, three-sided.

tril'by, *n.*, a soft, brimmed hat.

trilem'ma, *n.*, a situation involving a choice of three.

Tri'lene, *n.*, a proprietary brand of trichlorethylene.

tri'linear, *adj.*, composed of three lines.

trilin'gual, *adj.*, speaking three languages.

trilit'eral, *adj.*, containing three letters.

tri'lith, *n.*, *i.q.* trilithon.

tri'lithon, *n.*, a monumental structure of two upright stones supporting a horizontal stone.

trill, *n.*, a tremulous, quavering sound; a musical shake; *v.t.*, to sound with a quaver; to pipe; to roll (certain sounds, as the *r*); *v.i.*, to sound tremulously.

trilled, *p.p.*, trill.

trill'ing, *pr.p.*, trill.

tril'lion, *n.*, a cardinal number, a million million millions; in U.S.A., a million millions.

trilo'bate, *adj.*, having three lobes.

tri'lobed, *adj.*, *i.q.* trilobate.

tri'lobite, *n.*, one of the trilobites, a very early and common order of fossils.

triloc'ular, *adj.*, with three cells.

tril'ogy, *n.*, a series of three tragedies; any group of three related items, esp. in the arts.

trim, *adj.*, tidy; spruce; *n.*, a state or condition as regards being in good order; *v.t.*, to put in good order; to adjust; to make shapely by cutting off

ragged edges; to clip; to prune; to adorn.

tri'maran, *n.*, a craft with three hulls.

trimes'ter, *n.*, a quarterly period.

trimes'tral, *adj.*, quarterly; every three months.

trimes'trial, *adj.*, *i.q.* trimestral.

trim'eter, *n.*, a verse of three metrical feet; or of trimetrical lines.

trimet'ric, *adj.*, pert. to trimeter.

trim'ly, *adv.*, in a trim way.

trimmed, *p.p.*, trim.

trim'mer, *n.*, one who trims; a time-serving person who changes sides when it suits his purpose.

trim'ming, *pr.p.*, trim; *n.*, a decoration.

trim'ness, *n.*, the state or quality of being trim.

trimonth'ly, *adj.*, once every three months.

Trimur'ti, *n.*, the triad of the Hindu religion, Brahma, Vishnu and Siva.

tri'nal, *adj.*, rel. to three.

trine, *adj.*, consisting of three; *n.*, a triad.

trinerv'ate, *adj.*, three-nerved.

trinerved', *adj.*, *i.q.* trinervate.

tring'a, *n.*, birds of the sandpiper genus.

trin'gle, *n.*, a rod for curtain-rings.

tri'niscope, *n.*, a colour-television cathode ray tube.

Trinita'rian, *adj.*, rel. to the Holy Trinity and Trinitarian doctrine.

Trinita'rianism, *n.*, belief in the Holy and Undivided Trinity.

trinitrotol'uene, *n.*, (TNT), a powerful explosive.

Trin'ity, *n.*, the union of Three Persons in One Godhead.

trin'ity, *n.*, a group of three.

trin'ket, *n.*, a little jewel or ornament of no great value.

trin'ketry, *n.*, trinkets collectively.

trinoc'tial, *adj.*, lasting three nights.

trino'mial, *adj.*, involving three terms.

tri'o, *n.*, a group of three; a musical

composition for three voices or instruments; a special musical form.

tri'ode, *n.*, a three-electrode radio valve.

tri'olet, *n.*, an eight-lined stanza of peculiar construction.

tri'onal, *n.*, a narcotic drug.

tri'or, *i.q.* trier (*leg.*).

triox'ide, *n.*, a compound in which one atom of a metal is combined with three atoms of oxygen (*chem.*).

trip, *n.*, a short, quick step; a slip; an error; a short excursion; a small flock of sheep, etc.; *v.i.*, to step quickly; to slip; to err; to go for a short excursion.

tripar'tite, *adj.*, in three parts.

triparti'tion, *n.*, division into three parts.

tripe, *n.*, a cow's stomach; worthless nonsense (*colloq.*).

trip'edal, *adj.*, on three feet.

triper'sonal, *adj.*, consisting of three persons.

tripet'alous, *adj.*, having three petals.

trip'-hammer, *n.*, a machine hammer.

triphib'ious, *adj.*, moving on land, water, and air.

tri'phone, *n.*, a Pitman shorthand sign for three vowels.

triph'thong, *n.*, a union of three vowels.

triphthon'gal, *adj.*, of the nature of a triphthong.

triph'ylline, *adj.*, *i.q.* triphyllous.

triphyl'lous, *adj.*, with three leaves.

tripin'nate, *adj.*, having leaves, branches or feathers on three sides of an axis; three times pinnate.

tri'plane, *n.*, an aircraft with three pairs of wings.

trip'le, *adj.*, threefold; three times over; *v.i.*, to increase threefold.

trip'led, *p.p.*, triple.

tri'ple-headed, *adj.*, having three heads.

trip'let, *n.*, three taken together; in pl., three children at a birth.

tri'plex, *adj.*, threefold in thickness.

trip'licate, *adj.*, threefold; *n.*, a third example of the same original.

trip'licate, *v.t.*, to increase threefold.

triplica'tion, *n.*, the act or result of triplicating.

triplic'ity, *n.*, the state or quality of being threefold.

trip'ling, *pr.p.*, triple.

tri'pod, *n.*, a three-legged stool or table; the altar of the oracular Pythoness at Delphi.

tripod'al, *adj.*, three-legged.

tripo'dian, *n.*, an ancient musical instrument.

trip'ody, *n.*, a verse containing three feet.

trip'oli, *n.*, rotten stone.

Tripol'itan, *adj.*, from Tripoli; *n.*, a native of Tripoli.

tri'pos, *n.*, a list of persons gaining honours in the University examinations at Cambridge.

tri'potage, *n.*, a medley; an intrigue (*Fr.*).

tripped, *p.p.*, trip.

trip'per, *n.*, one who trips; a tourist.

trip'pery, *adj.*, pert. or rel. to tripping or (noisy) trippers, usu. derog.

trip'ping, *pr.p.*, trip.

trip'pingly, *adv.*, in a tripping way; with a light, quick step.

trip'sis, *n.*, massage.

trip'tane, *n.*, an aviation fuel.

trip'terous, *adj.*, having three wings.

trip'tote, *n.*, a noun having only three cases.

trip'tych, *n.*, a picture or writing-tablet in three parts (the two outer ones usually fold over the middle one).

trip'tyque, *n.*, a customs permit for temporary import of an automobile.

tripud'iate, *v.i.*, to dance for joy.

tripu'dium, *n.*, an ancient Roman dance.

triquet'ra, *n.*, an ornamental interlacing of three arcs.

trira'diate, *n.*, having three rays.

tri'reme, *n.*, an ancient Greek war galley with three banks of oars.

trirhomboid'al, *adj.*, with three rhombic faces.

Trisag'ion, *n.*, an ancient hymn of the Eastern liturgies.

trisect', *v.t.*, to cut equally into three parts.

trisect'ed, *p.p.*, trisect.

trisect'ing, *pr.p.*, trisect.

trisec'tion, *n.*, the act or result of trisecting.

tri'seme, *adj.*, equiv. to three short syllables; a trochee.

trisep'alous, *adj.*, having three sepals.

tri'shaw, *n.*, a three-wheeled rickshaw.

tris'mus, *n.*, lockjaw.

trisper'mous, *adj.*, three-seeded.

triste, *adj.*, sad (*Fr.*).

tri'stich, *n.*, a three-line verse.

trisul'cate, *adj.*, with three grooves.

trisul'phide, *n.*, a sulphide containing three atoms of sulphur.

trisyllab'ic, *adj.*, containing three syllables.

trisyl'lable, *n.*, a word of three syllables.

trite, *adj.*, worn; threadbare; commonplace.

trite'ly, *adv.*, in a trite way.

trite'ness, *n.*, the quality of being trite.

tri'theism, *n.*, the doctrine that there are three distinct Gods in the Trinity.

tri'theist, *adj.*, a believer in tritheism.

tritheist'ic, *adj.*, pert. to tritheism.

Tri'ton, *n.*, a marine demigod; a genus of molluscs; a newt.

tri'tone, *n.*, an interval of three full tones; an augmented fourth (*mus.*).

trit'urable, *adj.*, able to be triturated.

trit'urate, *v.t.*, to crush; to reduce to powder.

trit'urated, *p.p.*, triturate.

trit'urating, *pr.p.*, triturate.

tritura'tion, *n.*, the act or result of triturating.

tri'umph, *n.*, a State ceremonial of rejoicing over a victory;

victory; elation over a success; *v.i.*, to rejoice; to celebrate a victory.

trium′phal, *adj.*, of the nature of a triumph.

trium′phant, *adj.*, rejoicing over a conquest.

trium′phantly, *adv.*, in a triumphant way.

tri′umphed, *p.p.*, triumph.

tri′umpher, *n.*, one who triumphs.

tri′umphing, *pr.p.*, triumph.

trium′vir, *n.*, one of three colleagues in office (*triumviri*) in ancient Rome.

trium′viral, *adj.*, pert. to triumviri.

trium′virate, *n.*, the office of the triumviri; a term of office.

tri′une, *adj.*, three in one.

triu′nity, *n.*, the unity of the Three Persons of the Blessed Trinity.

tri′valent, *adj.*, with a valency of three.

tri′valve, *adj.*, with three valves; *n.*, a three-valved shell.

trivalv′ular, *adj.*, having three valves.

triv′et, *n.*, an attachment to a grate for holding a kettle, etc.

triv′ia, *n. pl.*, small, unimportant things.

triv′ial, *adj.*, trifling; ordinary; common-place.

trivial′ity, *n.*, the state or quality of being trivial.

triv′ially, *adv.*, in a trifling way.

triv′ium, *n.*, the mediaeval curriculum comprising grammar, logic, and rhetoric. (This, with the *quadrivium*, i.e., geometry, astronomy, arithmetic and music, made up the complete system of the seven liberal arts.)

triweek′ly, *adj.*, occurring three times in the week.

tri′zone, *n.*, the part of W. Germany occupied by British, French and U.S. forces after World War II.

tro′car, *n.*, a surgical draining instrument.

trocha′ic, *adj.*, pert. to a trochee.

tro′chal, *adj.*, like a wheel.

trochan′ter, *n.*, a bony process on the upper thigh.

tro′chee, *n.*, a metrical foot consisting of a long syllable followed by a short one.

tro′chil, *n.*, *i.q.* trochilus.

troch′ilus, *n.*, the crocodile bird.

tro′chings, *n. pl.*, small antler-points.

troch′lea, *n.*, a pulley-like muscle.

tro′choid, *adj.*, pivotal.

trod, *p.p.*, tread.

trodd′en, *p.p.*, tread.

trog′lodyte, *n.*, a cave-dweller.

troglody′tic, *adj.*, dwelling in caves.

troik′a, *n.*, a three-horse vehicle (*Russ.*).

Tro′jan, *adj.*, pert. to Troy; *n.*, a native of Troy.

troll, *n.*, a fabulous giant; a powerful dwarf; a form of vocal music such as a catch; a fishing-reel; *v.t.*, to sing in the form of a troll; *v.i.*, to fish with a running line.

trolled, *p.p.*, troll.

trol′ley, *n.*, a special form of truck.

troll′ing, *pr.p.*, troll.

trol′lop, *n.*, a slut.

trom′bone, *n.*, a musical wind instrument of brass.

trom′bonist, *n.*, a trombone player.

trom′mel, *n.*, a cylindrical sieve used in mining.

tromom′eter, *n.*, an instrument for measuring earth tremors.

trompe, *n.*, a device for making an air blast in a furnace.

tronc, *n.*, the system of pooling tips and sharing out at intervals (*Fr.*).

troop, *n.*, a host; a cavalry unit; a troupe; *v.i.*, to march in a multitude; to assemble in a large number; *v.t.*, to carry the colours (military) in ceremonious procession.

troop′-carrier, *n.*, a ship or aircraft for conveying troops.

trooped, *p.p.*, troop.

troop′er, *n.*, a private

soldier of cavalry; a troopship.

troop′ing, *pr.p.*, troop.

troop′ship, *n.*, a ship that conveys troops.

trope, *n.*, a figurative expression.

tro′phesy, *n.*, a nutritional upset.

troph′ic, *adj.*, rel. to nutrition.

tro′phied, *adj.*, containing trophies.

tro′phy, *n.*, a memento of some achievement.

trop′ic, *adj.*, one of two circular areas N. and S. of the equator, where the sun's course appears to turn.

trop′ical, *adj.*, rel. to, bel. to, the tropics; figurative.

trop′ically, *adv.*, in a tropical way.

tro′pist, *n.*, one who makes use of tropes.

tropolog′ical, *adj.*, pert. to tropology.

tropol′ogy, *n.*, figurative expression.

trop′opause, *n.*, the gap between troposphere and stratosphere.

trop′osphere, *n.*, the lowest atmospheric layer.

trot, *n.*, a pace between walking and galloping or running; a short walk (*colloq.*); *v.i.*, to go at a trotting pace.

troth, *n.*, a pledge; a word of honour.

Trots′kyism, *n.*, the type of communism, involving world revolution, advocated by Leon Trotsky.

trot′ted, *p.p.*, trot.

trot′ter, *n.*, one who trots, esp. a horse; a pig's or sheep's foot.

trot′ting, *pr.p.*, trot.

trottoir′, *n.*, the foot-path (*Fr.*).

trou′badour, *n.*, an old French lyric poet.

troub′le, *n.*, distress; worry; painstaking; *v.t.*, to cause distress or wrong to; to entail labour upon; *v.i.*, to be painstaking.

troub′led, *p.p.*, trouble.

troub′ler, *n.*, one who troubles.

troub′lesome, *adj.*, annoying; worrying.

troub′lesomely, *adv.*, in a troublesome way.

troub′lesomeness, *n.*, the state of being troublesome.

troub'ling, *pr.p.*, trouble.

troub'lous, *adj.*, disquieting; anxious.

trough, *n.*, a long, narrow tank for holding liquid; anything like a trough.

trounce, *v.t.*, to flog; to dress down with scolding or argument.

trounced, *p.p.*, trounce.

troun'cing, *pr.p.*, trounce.

troupe, *n.*, a theatrical or performing company.

troup'er, *n.*, a member of a performing company.

trou'pial, *n.*, a song bird.

trou'sered, *adj.*, wearing trousers.

trou'sers, *n. pl.*, a divided garment from the waist to the feet.

trousseau', *n.*, a bride's outfit of clothes.

trout, *n.*, a fresh-water fish.

trout'ing, *n.*, trout fishing.

trout'let, *n.*, a young trout.

trout'ling, *n.*, a young trout.

trout'-stream, *n.*, a natural stream abounding in trout.

trou'vaille, *n.*, a lucky find (*Fr.*).

trouvère, *n.*, one of the epic poets of mediaeval France.

trove, *n.*, what is discovered of value, *e.g.* *treasure-trove*.

tro'ver, *n.*, the act of finding lost property; a legal suit for the recovery of found property.

trow, *n.*, to think; to believe.

trow'el, *n.*, an implement with which mortar is spread; a gardening tool.

trow'elled, *adj.*, laid on with a trowel.

troy'weight, *n.*, a weight used in the jewellery and goldsmith's business; *adj.*, weighing 12 oz. to the lb.

tru'ancy, *n.*, playing the truant.

tru'ant, *n.*, one who shirks school or business; *adj.*, pert. to a truant; idle.

Tru'benize, *v.t.*, to stiffen textile materials by this proprietary method.

truce, *n.*, a suspension of hostilities.

tru'cial, *adj.*, bound by truce.

truck, *n.*, a vehicle for goods; a railway goods-wagon; barter; *v.i.*, to barter goods; payment in kind.

truck'age, *n.*, the cost of carriage by truck; trucks collectively; barter.

trucked, *p.p.*, truck.

truck'er, *n.*, one who trucks.

truck'ing, *pr.p.*, truck.

truck'le, *n.*, a small roller; *v.i.*, to give in in a servile way.

truck'le-bed, *n.*, a low bed on wheels.

truck'led, *p.p.*, truckle.

truck'ler, *n.*, one who truckles.

truck'ling, *pr.p.*, truckle.

truck'man, *n.*, a man in charge of a truck.

tru'culence, *n.*, aggressive temper; ferocity.

tru'culent, *adj.*, aggressively ill-tempered.

tru'culently, *adv.*, in a truculent way.

trudge, *v.i.*, to tramp on foot.

trudged, *p.p.*, trudge.

trudg'en, *n.*, a swimming stroke.

trudg'ing, *pr.p.*, trudge.

true, *adj.*, veracious; correct; right.

true'-heart'ed, *adj.*, sincere.

tru'er, *adj.*, *comp.* of true.

tru'est, *adj.*, *super.* of true.

truf'fle, *n.*, an underground fungus eaten as a delicacy; a rich confection.

trug, *n.*, a wooden basket.

tru'ism, *n.*, a truth that no one can dispute.

trull, *n.*, a prostitute.

tru'ly, *adv.*, in truth; sincerely.

tru'meau, *n.*, a pillar or wall dividing an opening.

trump, *n.*, a trumpet; a winning card; a suit superior to any other suit; *v.i.*, to take with a trump card; *v.i.*, to play out a trump.

trump'-card, *n.*, one of the trump suit in a card game; a successful expedient.

trumped, *p.p.*, trump.

trump'ery, *n.*, cheap stuff; *adj.*, cheap; rubbishy.

trump'et, *n.*, a brass or silver musical instrument with a flared or bell-shaped end; *v.t.*, to proclaim aloud; to blazon abroad; *v.i.*, to make a trumpet-like sound (as elephant).

trum'pet-call, *n.*, a signal sounded on a trumpet.

trump'eted, *adj.*, blazoned abroad; *p.p.*, trumpet.

trump'eter, *n.*, a performer on the trumpet; a species of pigeon.

trum'peting, *pr.p.*, trumpet.

trum'pet-shaped, *adj.*, flared, like a trumpet.

trump'ing, *pr.p.*, trump.

trun'cal, *adj.*, pert. or rel. to the trunk.

truncate', *adj.*, shortened; *v.t.*, to cut short, to lop.

truncat'ed, *adj.*, lopped; *p.p.*, truncate.

truncat'ing, *pr.p.*, truncate.

trunca'tion, *n.*, the act of truncating; the state of being truncated.

trun'cheon, *n.*, a short staff; a bâton; *v.t.*, to beat with a truncheon.

trun'dle, *v.t.*, to roll or push along on low wheels; *n.*, a truck.

trun'dled, *p.p.*, trundle.

trun'dling, *pr.p.*, trundle.

trunk, *n.*, a tree-stem; an animal's body apart from the limbs and head; a proboscis; a box for travelling purposes; *adj.*, main.

trunk'-call, *n.*, a telephone message on a trunk line.

trunk'ful, *n.*, as much as fills a trunk.

trunk'ing, *n.*, a covering or casing.

trunk'line, *n.*, a main railway, etc., line.

trunk'-road, *n.*, a main road.

trun'nion, *n.*, a projection.

truss, *n.*, a support; a surgical support in hernia cases; a bundle (as of hay); *v.t.*, to bind; to tuck up.

trussed, *p.p.*, truss.

truss'ing, *pr.p.*, truss.

trust, *n.*, belief; confidence; faith; a combination for establishing a monopoly; the holding of a person's property in his behalf by another person.

trust'-deed, *n.*, a document creating a trust.

trust'ed, *p.p.*, trust; *adj.*, confidential; to be relied on.

trustee', *n.*, one who takes the charge of another's property.

trustee'ship, *n.*, the office of a trustee.

trust'er, *n.*, one who trusts.

trust'ful, *adj.*, confiding; full of trust.

trust'fully, *adv.*, in a trustful way.

trust'fulness, *n.*, the state or quality of being trustful.

trust'-house, *n.*, a hotel or inn owned by a trust company.

trust'ier, *adj.*, *comp.* of trusty.

trust'iest, *adj.*, *super.* of trusty.

trust'ily, *adv.*, in a trusty manner; honestly.

trust'iness, *n.*, the quality of being trusty.

trust'ing, *pr.p.*, trust; *adj.*, confiding.

trust'ingly, *adv.*, in a trusting way.

trust'less, *adj.*, unreliable.

trust'lessness, *n.*, the quality or state of being trustless.

trust'worthily, *adv.*, in a trustworthy manner.

trust'worthiness, *n.*, the state or quality of being trustworthy.

trust'worthy, *adj.*, worthy of confidence.

trust'y, *adj.*, to be relied on; loyal.

truth, *n.*, the quality of being true; that which is true; loyalty.

truth'ful, *adj.*, loyal to truth; speaking the truth.

truth'fully, *adv.*, in a truthful way.

truth'fulness, *n.*, the quality of being truthful.

truth'less, *adj.*, false.

truth'lessness, *n.*, the quality or state of being truthless.

truth'like, *adj.*, pert. or rel. to truth.

truths, *n. pl.*, accepted or revealed beliefs.

trutta'ceous, *adj.*, rel. to trout.

try, *v.t.*, to attempt; to make trial of; to judge; to vex; to refine; *n.*, an attempt.

try'er, *n.*, one who tries.

Try'gon, *n.*, the genus of sting-rays.

try'ing, *pr.p.*, try; *adj.*, vexatious.

try'ingly, *adv.*, in a trying way.

try'-on, *n.*, an attempt to impose on another.

try'-out, *n.*, a test, a trial.

tryp'anosome, *n.*, a blood parasite.

try'sail, *n.*, a sail on the fore and main masts.

tryst, *n.*, an appointed meeting; *v.t.* and *i.*, to arrange a meeting.

tryst'ing, *adj.*, pert. to a rendezvous; *p.p.*, tryst.

Tsar, *n.*, the slav title of a king or emperor. Also *Czar*.

Tsar'evitch, *n.*, the son of a Tsar.

Tsar'evna, *n.*, the daughter or daughter-in-law of a Tsar.

Tsari'na, *n.*, *i.q.* Tsaritsa.

Tsar'ism, *n.*, the old Russian government of the Tsars.

Tsar'ist, *n.*, a supporter of Tsarism.

Tsarit'sa, *n.*, a queen or empress.

tset'se, *n.*, a disease-carrying African fly.

tsuna'mi, *n.*, a sea wave caused by sea bed disturbance.

Tswa'na, *n.*, a race of Bantu people in S. Africa; their language.

tuan', *n.*, (*Malay*) sir; a title of respect.

tub, *n.*, an open vessel; a bath (*colloq.*); *v.t.*, to give a bath to (*colloq.*).

tu'ba, *n.*, a trumpet (*Lat.*).

tu'bal, *adj.*, rel. to tubes and ducts.

tubbed, *p.p.*, tub.

tub'bing, *pr.p.*, tub.

tub'by, *adj.*, tub-shaped; short and stout.

tube, *n.*, a cylindrical pipe or passage.

tubed, *adj.*, having a tube.

tu'ber, *n.*, a thick plant-stem underground.

tu'bercle, *n.*, a small tuber; a morbid growth on tissue.

tu'bercled, *adj.*, having a tubercle.

tuber'cular, *adj.*, *i.q.* tubercled.

tuber'culate, *adj.*, *i.q.* tubercled.

tuber'culin, *n.*, a liquid preparation from tubercle bacilli.

tuber'culize, *v.t.*, to inject with tuberculosis.

tuberculo'sis, *n.*, the disease of tubercle.

tuber'culous, *adj.*, pert. to tubercle.

tuber'culum, *n.*, a tubercle.

tuberif'erous, *adj.*, producing tubers.

tu'beriform, *adj.*, formed like a tuber.

tu'berose, *n.*, a strong scented tuberous plant.

tuberos'ity, *n.*, the state or quality of being tuberous.

tu'berous, *adj.*, consisting of tubers.

tub'ful, *n.*, as much as a tub will hold.

tu'biform, *adj.*, like a tube.

tu'bing, *n.*, the material of which tubes are made.

tu'bipore, *n.*, a kind of coral.

tub'-thum'per, *n.*, a ranter.

tu'bular, *adj.*, like a tube; composed of tubes.

tu'bule, *n.*, a small tube.

tu'buliform, *adj.*, like a tubule.

tu'bulous, *adj.*, containing tubules.

tuck, *n.*, a pleat; a fold; a roll of drum; food (*slang*); *v.t.*, to put a tuck in; to wrap closely.

tucked, *p.p.*, tuck.

tuck'et, *n.*, a roll of a drum or trumpet.

tuck'ing, *pr.p.*, tuck.

tuck'shop, *n.*, a sweet-shop (esp. in schools).

Tu'dor, *adj.*, rel. to the Tudor dynasty; *n.*, one of the Tudor family; the architectural style of the Tudor era.

tudoresque', *adj.*, in Tudor style.

Tues'day, *n.*, the third day of the week.

tu'fa, *n.*, a soft kind of stone; scoria.

tufa'ceous, *adj.*, like, consisting of, tufa.

tuft, *n.*, hair or other substances gathered into a bunch; *v.t.*, to make tufts of; to cover with tufts.

tuft'ed, *adj.*, covered with tufts.

tuft'ing, *pr.p.*, tuft.

tuft'y, *adj.*, abounding in tufts.

tug, *n.*, a pull; a vessel that tows other vessels; *v.t.*, to pull; to draw; to tow.

tug'boat, *n.*, a towboat.

tugged, *p.p.*, tug.

tug'ger, *n.*, one who, that which, tugs.

tug'ging, *pr.p.*, tug.

tug'gingly, *adv.*, in a tugging way.

tu'ism, *n.*, the doctrine that all thought is addressed to one's future self, "you"; an apostrophe.

tui'tion, *n.*, teaching, instruction; a tutor's profession.

tui'tional, *adj.*, pert. or rel. to tuition.

tui'tionary, *adj.*, pert. to tuition.

tul'chan, *n.*, straw-stuffed calf skin to induce cows to give milk.

tu'lip, *n.*, a flowering bulb.

tulipoma'nia, *n.*, a passion for tulip-growing.

tu'lip-tree, *n.*, a N. Amer. tree of the Magnolia genus.

tulle, *n.*, a fine fabric of silk.

tum'ble, *n.*, a fall; *v.t.*, to throw down; *v.i.*, to disorder; *v.i.*, to fall.

tum'bled, *p.p.*, tumble.

tum'bledown, *adj.*, rickety; ruinous.

tum'bler, *n.*, one who tumbles; an acrobat who does tumbling-tricks; a drinking-glass; a variety of pigeon.

tum'blerful, *n.*, what a tumbler will contain.

tum'bler-switch, *n.*, kind of electric switch.

tum'bling, *pr.p.*, tumble.

tum'brel, *n.*, a cart that tilts up; a military wagon.

tum'bril, *n.*, *i.q.* tumbrel.

tumefac'tion, *n.*, a swelling.

tu'mefied, *p.p.*, tumefy.

tu'mefy, *v.i.*, to swell.

tu'mefying, *pr.p.*, tumefy.

tumes'cence, *n.*, a swelling, growing larger.

tumes'cent, *adj.*, *i.q.* tumid.

tu'mid, *adj.*, in a swollen state; bombastic.

tumid'ity, *n.*, the state or quality of being tumid.

tu'morous, *adj.*, pert. or rel. to a tumour.

tu'mour, *n.*, an internal cellular growth or swelling.

tu'mular, *adj.*, like a tumulus.

tu'muli, *n.*, pl. of tumulus.

tu'mult, *n.*, a wild disturbance; a riot.

tumul'tuary, *adj.*, pert. to a tumult.

tumul'tuous, *adj.*, of the nature of a tumult; very disorderly.

tumul'tuously, *adv.*, in a tumultuous way.

tumul'tuousness, *n.*, the state or quality of being tumultuous.

tu'mulus, *n.*, a large artificial mound.

tun, *n.*, a large cask; a wine measure of 252 gallons.

tu'na, *n.*, *i.q.* tunny.

tu'nable, *adj.*, able to be tuned; agreeable to hear.

tun'ably, *adv.*, in a tunable way.

tun'dish, *n.*, a funnel.

tun'dra, *n.*, the frozen Arctic plain.

tune, *n.*, a melodic series; a true sound; a proper state; *v.t.*, to bring (instruments) to exact pitch.

tuned, *p.p.*, tune.

tune'ful, *adj.*, melodious.

tune'fully, *adv.*, in a tuneful way.

tune'less, *adj.*, not melodious.

tu'ner, *n.*, one who tunes organs, pianofortes, etc.

tung'-oil, *n.*, Chinese varnishing oil.

tung'state, *n.*, a tungstic acid salt.

tung'sten, *n.*, a rare white metal.

tung'stic, *adj.*, pert. or rel. to tungsten.

Tun'gus, *n.*, an Asiatic Turanian race.

tu'nic, *n.*, an ancient Roman inner garment; a loose garment; a soldier's coat;

an outer covering or membrane.

tu'nicate, *adj.*, covered with a membrane.

tu'nicated, *adj.*, *i.q.* tunicate.

tu'nicle, *n.*, the vestment of a subdeacon or epistoler.

tu'ning, *pr.p.*, tune.

tu'ning-fork, *n.*, a metal two-pronged instrument, carefully tuned, and giving the pitch.

Tunis'ian, *adj.*, rel. to Tunis; *n.*, a native of Tunis.

tun'nage, *n.*, the tax (by the tun) on wine imports.

tun'nel, *n.*, a bored passage underground; *v.t.*, to bore (a passage) through.

tun'nelled, *p.p.*, tunnel.

tun'neller, *n.*, one who tunnels.

tun'nelling, *pr.p.*, tunnel.

tun'ny, *n.*, a sea-water fish.

tup, *n.*, a ram; *v.t.*, to copulate (orig. with ewe).

tu'pelo, *n.*, a tree noted for the hardness of its wood.

Tu'pi, *n.*, a race of S. Amer. Indians; their language.

tuque, *n.*, a kind of Canadian cap.

tu'racin, *n.*, a red colouring agent, obtained from the feathers of the touracos bird.

Tura'nian, *adj.*, pert. to the races other than the Aryans and Semites.

tur'ban, *n.*, an Oriental head covering.

tur'baned, *adj.*, wearing a turban.

tur'bary, *n.*, the right to cut turf; the ground where it may be cut.

Turbella'ria, *n. pl.*, a group of flat worms.

tur'bid, *adj.*, muddy.

turbid'ity, *n.*, the state or quality of being turbid.

tur'bidly, *adv.*, in a turbid way.

tur'bidness, *n.*, *i.q.* turbidity.

tur'binate, *adj.*, driven by a turbine.

tur'bine, *n.*, a rotary driving mechanism actuated by jets of water or air.

tur′bit, *n.,* a breed of pigeons.

turbo′-jet, *n.,* a jet-propelled gas-turbine.

turbo′-prop, *n.,* an aircraft propeller driven by a gas-turbine.

tur′bot, *n.,* a flat, edible fish.

tur′bulence, *n.,* disorderliness; storminess.

tur′bulent, *adj.,* riotous; disorderly; stormy.

tur′bulently, *adv.,* in a turbulent way.

Turc′ism, Turk′ism, *n.,* a characteristic of the Turks; Turkish idiom.

Tur′co, *n., i.q.* Turcoman.

Turc′oman, *adj.,* a French Algerian infantry soldier.

tur′cophil, *n.,* an admirer of Turks.

tur′cophobe, *n., adj.,* hater of Turks.

tur′dine, *adj.,* pert. or rel. to the thrush (*Lat.*).

Tur′dus, *n.,* the thrush genus (*Lat.*).

tureen′, *n.,* a kind of bowl for soup or sauce.

turf, *n.,* grass; a piece of earth with grass upon it; the business of horse-racing; *v.t.,* to lay down with turf.

turfed, *p.p.,* turf.

turf′iness, *n.,* the state or quality of being turfy.

turf′ing, *pr.p.,* turf.

turf′ing-iron, *n.,* a tool for cutting turf.

turf′y, *adj.,* like turf; covered with turf.

tur′gent, *adj.,* swelling; inflated.

tur′gently, *adv.,* in turgent way.

turges′cence, *n.,* the state of becoming turgent.

turges′cent, *adj.,* becoming turgent or inflated.

tur′gid, *adj.,* inflated; distended; bombastic.

turgid′ity, *n.,* the state or quality of being turgid.

tur′gidly, *adv.,* in turgid way.

tur′ion, *n.,* a growing shoot of a plant.

Turk, *n.,* a native of Turkey; a Mohammedan; an unruly child.

tur′key, *n.,* a large edible bird.

tur′key-buzzard, *n.,* an Amer. vulture.

tur′key-cock, *n.,* a male turkey.

tur′key-trot, *n.,* a kind of dance.

Turk′ish, *adj.,* pert. to Turkey and the Turks.

Turk′ism, *n.,* Turkish idiom or characteristic.

tur′meric, *n.,* a pungent aromatic root used in making curries.

tur′moil, *n.,* a disturbance; confusion.

turn, *v.t.,* to make to go or point in a different direction, or completely round; to transform; to make a version of; to shape with a lathe; *v.i.,* to move round or in a different direction; *n.,* the act of turning a curve; a short period of action; a good or evil deed; a fright.

turn′coat, *n.,* one who changes his opinions and abandons his principles.

turn′cock, *n.,* an official regulating the water supply; a valve.

turned, *p.p.,* turn.

turn′er, *n.,* one who turns; a workman using a lathe.

Turneresque′, *adj.,* like the work of the painter, Turner.

turn′ery, *n.,* things made with a lathe; a turner's trade.

turn′ing, *pr.p.,* turn; *n.,* a bend in a road.

turn′ing-point, *n.,* a point where a turn is made; a crisis.

tur′nip, *n.,* an edible spherical root.

turn′key, *n.,* a keeper of prison-cells; a warder.

turn′out, *n.,* equipment; a show.

turn′over, *n.,* money receipts in a business; an apple roll, etc.

turn′pike, *n.,* a toll-bar across a road.

turn′plate, *n.,* a turntable.

turn′sole, *n.,* the name of some flowers that turn toward the sun (*e.g.,* the heliotrope).

turn′spit, *n.,* one who turns the roasting spit; a variety of dog trained for this purpose.

turn′stile, *n.,* a revolving barrier.

turn′stone, *n.,* a bird so named for its turning over of stones in quest of food.

turn′table, *n.,* a revolving table, used for reversing engines, or turning them on to another line, or holding a gramophone record, etc.

tur′pentine, *n.,* an exudation from pine and fir trees.

tur′peth, *n.,* an E. Indian drug.

tur′pitude, *n.,* baseness; infamy.

turquoise′, *n.,* a blue precious stone.

tur′ret, *n.,* a little tower.

tur′reted, *adj.,* furnished with turrets.

tur′tle, *n., i.q.* a turtle dove; a large kind of edible amphibian.

tur′tle-dove, *n.,* a very gentle breed of doves.

tur′tle-soup, *n.,* a soup made from the flesh, etc., of the turtle.

turves, *n. pl.,* sods; pl. of turf.

Tus′can, *adj.,* pert. to Tuscany or Etruria; *n.,* a native of Tuscany.

tusk, *n.,* a large tooth.

tusked, *adj.,* having tusks.

tusk′er, *n.,* a wild boar.

tusk′y, *adj.,* tusk-like.

tuss′er, *n.,* a kind of silkworm.

tus′sle, *n.,* a fight; a struggle; *v.i.,* to struggle.

tus′sled, *p.p.,* tussle.

tus′sock, *n.,* a tuft or clump of grass.

tus′socky, *adj.,* full of tussocks.

tuss′ore, *n.,* silk from the tusser.

tu′telage, *n.,* the act of protecting; the state of being under protection.

tu′telar, *adj.,* guarding; protecting.

tu′telary, *adj., i.q.* tutelar.

tu′tenag, *n.,* a white alloy; spelter.

tu′tor, *n.,* an instructor; a guardian; *v.t.,* to teach; to bring under discipline.

tu′torage, *n.,* a tutor's fee.

tu′tored, *p.p.,* tutor.

tuto′rial, *adj.,* pert. to tutors or tuition.

tu′toring, *pr.p.,* tutor; *n.,* the act or profession of a tutor.

tu'torship, *n.*, a tutor's appointment.

tut'san, *n.*, St. John's wort.

tut'ti, *n. pl.*, all (*mus.*).

tutt'i-frutt'i, *n.*, a mixed fruit confection.

tut'ty, *n.*, the oxide of zinc ointment.

tu'tu, *n.*, a ballet skirt.

tuxe'do, *n.*, a dinner jacket (*Amer.*).

twad'dle, *n.*, silly talk; nonsense; *v.i.*, to talk twaddle.

twad'dled, *p.p.*, twaddle.

twad'dling, *pr.p.*, twaddle.

twain, *n.* and *adj.*, two.

twaite, *n.*, a shad.

twang, *n.*, a peculiar quality of sound; a disagreeable intonation or pronunciation; *v.t.*, to sound with a peculiar tone.

twanged, *p.p.*, twang.

twang'ing, *pr.p.*, twang.

twan'gle, *v.t.*, *i.q.* twang.

twan'gling, *adj.*, twanging, noisy.

twan'glingly, *adv.*, noisily; disagreeably.

twan'gy, *adj.*, pert. or rel. to twang.

twan'kay, *n.*, a green tea.

'twas, *phrase* = it was.

twat'tle, *v.i.*, to tattle.

twat'tled, *p.p.*, twattle.

twat'tling, *pr.p.*, twattle.

tway'blade, *n.*, a two-bladed knife or sword; a kind of orchid.

tweak, *v.t.*, to pinch; *n.*, a pinch.

tweaked, *p.p.*, tweak.

tweak'ing, *pr.p.*, tweak.

tweed, *n.*, a woollen fabric.

twee'dy, *adj.*, pertaining to tweed, hence "county", countrified.

twee'zers, *n. pl.*, pincers.

twelfth, *adj.*, the ordinal of twelve; next after the eleventh; *n.*, a twelfth part.

twelfth'ly, *adv.*, in twelfth place.

twelfth'-night, *n.*, the Feast of the Epiphany, Jan. 6, being the twelfth day from Christmas.

twelve, *n.*, a cardinal number, next after eleven; *adj.*, containing one more than eleven.

twelve'fold, *adj.*, twelve times as much or great.

twelve'-mo, *n.*, a duodecimo (*colloq.*).

twelve'month, *n.*, the space of a year.

twen'tieth, *adj.*, the ordinal of twenty; *n.*, a twentieth part.

twen'ty, *adj.*, consisting of twice ten; *n.*, the cardinal number of twice ten.

twen'tyfold, *adj.*, twenty times as much.

Twi, *n.*, a Ghanaian language.

twi'bill, *n.*, a double-bladed battle axe.

twice, *adv.*, two times; doubly.

twice'-told, *adj.*, repeated; stale.

twid'dle, *n.*, a twist with the fingers; *v.t.*, to twist about in the fingers; *v.i.*, to twirl.

twid'dled, *p.p.*, twiddle.

twid'dling, *pr.p.*, twiddle.

twig, *n.*, a small branch; *v.t.* and *i.*, to understand; to perceive (*colloq.*).

twig'gy, *adj.*, like, full of, twigs.

twi'light, *n.*, the time just before dawn and sunset; dim light; *adj.*, semi-obscure.

twill, *n.*, a marking as with diagonal lines in a cloth fabric; the fabric itself; *v.t.*, to weave with a twill.

twilled, *p.p.*, twill.

twill'ing, *pr.p.*, twill.

twin, *adj.*, in a pair; double; strongly alike; *n.*, one of two at a birth; a counterpart; *v.t.*, to couple; to join.

twin-broth'er, *n.*, a brother born at the same birth.

twine, *n.*, fine string; strong thread; *v.t.* and *i.*, to wind round.

twined, *p.p.*, twine.

twi'ner, *n.*, one who, or that which, twines.

twinge, *n.*, a short, sharp pain; *v.t.*, to cause such a pain; *v.i.*, to feel such a pain.

twinged, *p.p.*, twinge.

twinge'ing, *pr.p.*, twinge.

twi'ning, *pr.p.*, twine; *n.*, a turn in a road.

twi'ningly, *adv.*, in a twining way.

twink, *n.* and *v.i.*, *i.q.* twinkle.

twin'kle, *n.*, an intermittent rapid movement; a tremulous gleam; a moment; *v.i.*, to open and close (the eyes) rapidly; to give forth a rapid intermittent light.

twin'kled, *p.p.*, twinkle.

twin'kling, *pr.p.*, twinkle.

twinned, *p.p.*, twin.

twin'ning, *pr.p.*, twin.

twin'screw', *adj.*, having two propellers.

twin'-set, *n.*, a matching jumper and cardigan.

twin-sis'ter, *n.*, a sister born at the same birth.

twirl, *v.t.*, to cause to revolve rapidly; *v.i.*, to revolve rapidly; *n.*, a quick revolution.

twirled, *p.p.*, twirl.

twirl'ing, *pr.p.*, twirl.

twist, *n.*, the act of twisting; a turn; a convolution; twisted cord; coiled tobacco; a popular dance; *v.t.*, to wind together; to turn round; *v.i.*, to be twisted or turned round.

twist'ed, *p.p.*, twist.

twist'er, *n.*, one who, that which, twists; a dishonest person.

twist'ing, *pr.p.*, twist.

twit, *n.*, a silly person; *v.t.*, to tease by recalling some act.

twitch, *n.*, a jerk; a short spasm; *v.t.*, to pull with a jerk; *v.i.*, to be affected by a short spasm.

twitched, *p.p.*, twitch.

twitch'er, *n.*, one who, that which, twitches.

twitch'ing, *pr.p.*, twitch.

twit'ted, *p.p.*, twit.

twit'ter, *n.*, a repeated small cry as of birds; *v.t.*, to express in twittering; *v.i.*, to keep up a succession of small sounds.

twit'tered, *p.p.*, twitter.

twit'tering, *pr.p.*, twitter.

twit′teringly, *adv.*, in a twittering way.

twit′ting, *pr.p.*, twit.

twit′tingly, *adv.*, teasingly.

′twixt, *prep.*, betwixt; between.

two, *n.*, the cardinal number next after one; *adj.*, consisting of one more than one.

two′-decker, *n.*, a ship with two decks.

two′-edged, *adj.*, double-edged.

two′-faced′, *adj.*, hypocritical.

two-fisted, *adj.*, awkward; clumsy.

two′fold, *adj.*, double.

two′-handed, *adj.*, wielded by both hands.

two′-headed, *adj.*, having two heads.

two′-legged, *adj.*, having two legs.

two′-lobed, *adj.*, having two lobes.

two′-part, *adj.*, having two parts.

two′pence, *n.*, the sum of two pence.

two′penny, *adj.*, costing twopence; of little value.

two-roomed, *adj.*, having two rooms.

two′-seat′er, *n.*, an object having two seats.

two′-some, *n.*, a game or dance for two.

two′-step, *n.*, a dance.

two-tone, *adj.*, having two colours or matching shades of colour.

two′-year-old, *adj.* and *n.*, (anything) aged two years.

tycoon′, *n.*, the old title of the Japanese Commander-in-chief; a business magnate.

tye, *n.*, a shallow vat used in washing ore.

ty′ing, *pr.p.*, tie.

tyke, *n.*, a dog; a low fellow; a Yorkshireman (*colloq.*).

ty′ler, *n.*, *i.q.* tiler.

tylo′sis, *n.*, inflammation of eyelids.

tym′bal, *n.*, *i.q.* timbal.

tym′pan, *n.*, the parchment frame used by printers for laying sheets upon.

tym′pani, *n. pl.*, drums.

tympan′ic, *adj.*, rel. to the typanum.

tympanit′ic, *adj.*, pert. to tympanitis.

tympani′tis, *n.*, inflammation of the tympanum.

tym′panum, *n.*, the drum of the ear; the surface of the space within a pediment; a drum-like wheel.

tym′pany, *n.*, conceit; self-glorification.

Tyn′wald, *n.*, the parliament of the Isle of Man.

type, *n.*, a pattern; a model; an emblem; a prefigurement; a structural form; letters for printing; *v.t.*, to prefigure; to typify; to manipulate a typewriter.

type′cast, *adj.*, cast to act in same sort of roles.

typed, *p.p.*, type; *adj.*, written by typewriter.

type′-face, *n.*, the printing surface of a piece of type; its style.

type′-high, *adj.*, of the standard height of type.

type′script, *n.*, a script in typed form.

type′setter, *n.*, one who composes type for printing.

type′writer, *n.*, a typewriting machine.

type′writing, *n.*, the use of a mechanical contrivance which makes letters by means of types.

type′written, *adj.*, written with a typewriter.

Typho′ean, *adj.*, pert. to Typhoeus, a mythological monster (*Gr.*).

ty′phoid, *adj.*, resembling typhus; *n.*, an enteric disease.

typhoon′, *n.*, a tornado.

ty′phus, *n.*, a dangerous epidemic disease.

typ′ical, *adj.*, emblematic; prefigurative; ordinary; characteristic.

typical′ity, *n.*, the quality or state of being typical.

typ′ically, *adv.*, in a typical way.

typifica′tion, *n.*, prefiguration.

typ′ified, *p.p.*, typify.

typ′ify, *v.t.*, to prefigure; to foreshadow.

typ′ifying, *pr.p.*, typify.

typ′ing, *pr.p.* and *n.*, the act of typewriting; the quality of this.

ty′pist, *n.*, one who uses a typewriter.

ty′po-, *prefix*, rel. to type.

typog′rapher, *n.*, a printer.

typograph′ic, *adj.*, pert. to typography.

typograph′ical, *adj.*, *i.q.* typographic.

typograph′ically, *adv.*, in a typographical way.

typog′raphy, *n.*, the art of printing.

typ′olite, *n.*, a fossil or stone marked with an animal or plant figure.

typol′ogist, *n.*, one who studies typology.

typol′ogy, *n.*, the study of types in scripture, biology, etc.

tyran′nic, *adj.*, *i.q.* tyrannical.

tyran′nical, *adj.*, despotic; overbearing; cruel.

tyran′nically, *adv.*, in a tyrannical way.

tyran′nicide, *n.*, the murder or murderer of a tyrant.

tyr′annize, *v.i.*, to act despotically or with cruelty.

tyr′annized, *p.p.*, tyrannize.

tyr′annizing, *pr.p.*, tyrannize.

tyr′annous, *adj.*, *i.q.* tyrannical.

tyr′anny, *n.*, the rule of a tyrant; despotism.

ty′rant, *n.*, a despot; an oppressor.

tyre, *n.*, the outer covering of the edge of a wheel.

Tyr′ian, *adj.*, rel. to Tyre and the Tyrians; purple; *n.*, a native of Tyre.

ty′ro, *n.*, a novice.

Tyrole′an, *adj.* and *n.*, *i.q.* Tyrolese.

Tyrolese′, *adj.*, pert. to the Tyrol and the Tyrolese; *n.*, a native of the Tyrol.

ty′rotox′icon, *n.*, poisoning from lactic preparations.

Tzi′gane, *adj.*, rel. to Hungarian gypsies or their music; *n.*, a Hungarian gypsy.

U

u′berous, *adj.*, fruitful.

ubi′ety, *n.*, whereness; the state of being locally.

u′biquist, *n.*, one who believes in the omnipresence of Christ.

ubiquita′rian, *adj.*, pert. or rel. to the ubiquists; *n.*, *i.q.* ubiquist.

ubiquita′rianism, *n.*, the teaching of the ubiquists.

ubiq′uitary, *adj.*, *i.q.* ubiquitous.

ubiq′uitous, *adj.*, being or occurring everywhere.

ubi′quitously, *adv.*, in a ubiquitous manner.

ubiq′uity, *n.*, the quality or state of being ubiquitous.

u′-boat, *n.*, a German submarine.

u′dal, *adj.*, allodial; *n.*, a special kind of freehold right in Orkney and Shetland.

ud′der, *n.*, the milksecreting organ in mammals.

udom′eter, *n.*, a raingauge.

u′fo, an *unidentified flying object.

ugh, *interj.*, an exclamation of revulsion.

ug′lier, *adj.*, *comp.* of ugly.

ug′liest, *adj.*, *super.* of ugly.

ug′lily, *adv.*, in an ugly way.

ug′liness, *n.*, the quality or state of being ugly.

ug′ly, *adj.*, ill-favoured; unsightly; aesthetically displeasing; shocking to the moral sense.

uh′lan, *n.*, a German lancer.

uhu′ru, *n.*, independence (*Swahili*).

uit′lander, *n.*, an alien resident (*S. Africa*).

ukase′, *n.*, an imperial decree in Russia.

Ukrain′ian, *adj.*, pert. or rel. to the Ukraine in Russia; *n.*, a native of the U.

ukule′le, *n.*, a stringed, musical instrument.

ul′cer, *n.*, a malignant sore.

ul′cerate, *v.i.*, to become ulcerated; *v.t.*, to produce an ulcer in.

ul′cerated, *p.p.*, ulcerate.

ul′cerating, *pr.p.*, ulcerate.

ulcera′tion, *n.*, the process or result of forming an ulcer.

ul′cerative, *adj.*, caused by ulcers.

ul′cerous, *adj.*, of the nature of an ulcer.

Ulema′, *n.*, the collective Turkish hierarchy.

ulig′inose, *adj.*, growing in swamps (*bot.*).

ulig′inous, *adj.*, moist.

ul′lage, *n.*, the difference between a full and an empty cask; collected waste and spillage of liquors.

ulma′ceous, *adj.*, pert. or rel. to elms.

ul′mic, *adj.*, obtained from ulmin.

ul′min, *n.*, a gum derived from the elm and other trees (*chem.*).

ul′na, *n.*, the large bone of the forearm (*Lat.*).

ul′nar, *adj.*, of the forearm.

ulot′richan, *adj.*, woollyhaired.

ul′ster, *n.*, a long heavy overcoat.

ulte′rior, *adj.*, further; remoter; secondary; concealed.

ulte′riorly, *adv.*, in an ulterior way.

ul′tima, *n.*, a word's final syllable.

ul′timate, *adj.*, last; furthest.

ul′timately, *adv.*, finally.

ultima′tum, *n.*, a final demand.

ul′timo, *n.*, the month before this one (*Lat.*, *jargon*).

ul′timogen′iture, *n.*, inheritance by the youngest of the family.

Ulto′nian, *adj.*, pert. or rel. to Ulster; *n.*, a native of U.

ul′tra, *adj.*, excessive; *adv.*, *prep.* and *prefix*, beyond (*Lat.*).

ul′tra-high, *adj.*, extremely high.

ul′traism, *n.*, going to extremes.

ul′traist, *n.*, an extremist.

ultramarine′, *adj.*, beyond the seas; *n.*, a blue colour.

ul′tramicrosco′pic, *adj.*, beyond microscope range.

ultramon′tane, *adj.*, beyond the mountains (*i.e.*, the Alps); pert. or rel. to ultramontanism; *n.*, a supporter of ultramontanism.

ultramon′tanism, *n.*, the view concerning the Pope's authority held, or supposed to be held, south of the Alps.

ultramon′tanist, *adj.* and *n.*, *i.q.* ultramontane.

ultramun′dane, *adj.*, beyond the world or solar system.

ul′tra-red, *adj.*, beyond the red band of the spectrum.

ul′trasonic, *adj.*, beyond the range or speed of sound.

ul′trasonics, *n.*, the study of waves beyond the speed of sound.

ul′tra-vi′olet, *adj.*, beyond the violet band of a spectrum.

ul′tra vi′res, *adj.* and *adv.*, beyond one's authority (*Lat.*).

ul′ulate, *v.i.*, to howl.

ulula′tion, *n.*, howling.

um′bel, *n.*, inflorescence in the shape of a fan.

um′bellar, *adj.*, like an umbel.

um′bellate, *adj.*, having umbels.

um′bellated, *adj.*, *i.q.* umbellate.

umbellif′erous, *adj.*, *i.q.* umbellate.

um′ber, *adj.*, umbercoloured; *n.*, a brown colour.

um′bered, *adj.*, stained umber.

umbil'ical, *adj.*, pert. or rel. to the umbilicus.

umbil'icate, *adj.*, like a navel.

umbil'icus, *n.*, the navel (*Lat.*).

um'ble-pie, *n.*, *i.q.* humble-pie.

um'bles, *n. pl.*, the edible viscera of a deer.

um'bo, *n.*, the boss of a shield; a projection on the shell of a bivalve (*Lat.*).

um'bonate, *adj.*, having a boss.

um'bonated, *adj.*, *i.q.* umbonate.

um'bra, *n.*, a shadow (*Lat.*, *astron.*).

umbra'culum, *n.*, an umbrella-like appendage.

um'brage, *n.*, offence; shelter afforded by foliage.

umbra'geous, *adj.*, shady.

umbra'geously, *adv.*, shadily.

umbra'ted, *adj.*, traced faintly.

umbrel'la, *n.*, a portable protection against rain and sun.

Um'brian, *adj.*, of Umbria (in Italy); of that school of painting.

umbrif'erous, *adj.*, shade-giving.

um'laut, *n.*, the modification of a vowel sound by its surrounding sounds.

um'pirage, *n.*, the exercise of an umpire's authority.

um'pire, *n.*, an arbitrator; one who supervises a game.

ump'teen, *n.*, an indeterminate large number (*slang*).

un-, a prefix used unrestrictedly with English words to indicate *not* or negation, reversal, removal, etc. Only a limited selection can be included here.

unabashed', *adj.*, unashamed; not disconcerted.

unaba'ted, *adj.*, without ceasing; undiminished.

una'ble, *adj.*, not able.

unabridged', *adj.*, not abridged or shortened.

unaccent'ed, *adj.*, not accented.

unaccept'able, *adj.*, not acceptable; unpleasant.

unaccom'modating, *adj.*,

inconsiderate; obstinate.

unaccom'panied, *adj.*, alone; not accompanied.

unaccount'able, *adj.*, not to be explained or accounted for.

unaccount'ably, *adv.*, in an unaccountable way.

unaccus'tomed, *adj.*, strange; unused.

unacknowl'edged, *adj.*, not acknowledged.

unacquaint'ed, *adj.*, ignorant; not knowing.

unadap'table, *adj.*, cannot be adapted.

unadap'ted, *adj.*, not fitted or suited.

unad'ept, *adj.*, not skilled.

unadorned', *adj.*, simple; without ornament.

unadul'terated, *adj.*; pure; not adulterated.

unadvi'sable, *adj.*, not to be recommended; unwise; unsafe.

unadvised', *adj.*, rash, hasty.

unadvi'sedly, *adv.*, without considering.

unaffect'ed, *adj.*, not affected; simple; natural.

unaffect'edly, *adv.*, in an unaffected way.

unafraid', *adj.*, not afraid.

unaid'ed, *adj.*, without help.

unallied', *adj.*, not allied.

unalloyed', *adj.*, pure; unmixed; without alloy.

unal'terable, *adj.*, not able to be altered.

unal'terably, *adv.*, in an unalterable way.

unal'tered, *adj.*, unchanged.

unambi'guous, *adj.*, clear, not doubtful.

unambi'guously, *adv.*, clearly.

unambi'tious, *adj.*, without ambition.

unambi'tiously, *adv.*, in an unambitious way.

una'miable, *adj.*, disagreeable; lacking in kindness.

unanim'ity, *n.*, absolute agreement; being of one mind.

unan'imous, *adj.*, entirely agreed; without a dissentient.

unan'imously, *adv.*, entirely in agreement; by a solid vote.

unan'swerable, *adj.*, incapable of being answered.

unan'swerably, *adv.*, in an unanswerable way.

unan'swered, *adj.*, not answered.

unap'petizing, *adj.*, tasteless; badly cooked and served (of food).

unappre'ciated, *adj.*, not appreciated.

unapprised', *adj.*, not informed.

unapproach'able, *adj.*, not to be approached; haughty and reserved.

unappro'priated, *adj.*, not appropriated.

unapt', *adj.*, not handy or ready; slow to learn.

unarmed', *adj.*, without armour; defenceless.

unartistic, *adj.*, not showing an interest in art.

unascertained', *adj.*, not ascertained.

unashamed', *adj.*, not ashamed.

unasham'edly, *adv.*, in an unashamed way.

unasked', *adj.*, without being asked; voluntarily.

unas'pirated, *adj.*, not spoken or written with an aspirate.

unaspi'ring, *adj.*, not ambitious.

unassail'able, *adj.*, safe against assault; impregnable.

unassailed', *adj.*, not assailed.

unassayed', *adj.*, not tried; unattempted.

unassist'ed, *adj.*, without help.

unassort'ed, *adj.*, not assorted; mixed up.

unassu'ming, *adj.*, modest; not giving oneself airs.

unassured', *adj.*, not assured or insured.

unaton'able, *adj.*, unforgiveable.

unattached', *adj.*, not attached; independent.

unattain'able, *adj.*, unreachable; not to be attained.

unattempt'ed, *adj.*, not attempted.

unattend'ed, *adj.*, alone; without attendants.

unattract'ive, *adj.*, not attractive; displeasing.

unattrac′tively, *adv.*, displeasingly.

u′nau, *n.*, a variety of sloth.

unauthen′tic, *adj.*, not authentic; not genuine.

unauthen′ticated, *adj.*, not proved genuine.

unau′thorized, *adj.*, not authorized; without permission.

unavail′able, *adj.*, not available.

unavail′ing, *adj.*, useless; done in vain.

unavail′ingly, *adv.*, ineffectually.

unavoid′able, *adj.*, not able to be avoided.

unavoid′ably, *adv.*, in an unavoidable way.

unaware′, *adj.*, not aware; not cognisant.

unawares′, *adv.*, off one's guard; without warning.

unbal′anced, *adj.*, not balanced; intemperate.

unband′age, *v.t.*, to remove a bandage.

unbandaged′, *adj.*, not bandaged; *p.p.*, unbandage.

unbar′, *v.t.*, to remove the bars from; to open.

unbear′able, *adj.*, intolerable.

unbear′ably, *adv.*, in an unbearable way.

unbeaten, *adj.*, not beaten.

unbecom′ing, *adj.*, not becoming; unseemly; not suiting.

unbefit′ting, *adj.*, unseemly; not proper.

unbegot′ten, *adj.*, not begotten.

unbeknown′, *adj.*, without another's knowledge.

unbelief′, *n.*, the refusal to believe; doubt.

unbeliev′able, *adj.*, incredible.

unbeliev′er, *n.*, a sceptic; a doubter; a heathen.

unbeliev′ing, *adj.*, not believing.

unbeloved′, *adj.*, loved by no one.

unbend′, *v.i.*, to be condescending; to become unbent; *v.t.*, to relax.

unbend′ing, *adj.*, not bending; stiff; not condescending.

unbent′, *adj.*, in a relaxed state.

unbesought′, *adj.*, not solicited.

unbi′as, *v.t.*, to set free from prejudice.

unbi′assed, *adj.*, without bias; not prejudiced.

unbid′den, *adj.*, without invitation.

unbind′, *v.t.*, to loosen what is bound.

unblam′able, *adj.*, cannot be blamed.

unbleached′, *adj.*, in the natural state; not bleached.

unblem′ished, *adj.*, spotless; without blemish.

unblest′, *adj.*, not blest; unhallowed; miserable.

unblushing′, *adj.*, unabashed; shameless.

unblush′ingly, *adv.*, in an unblushing way.

unbolt′, *v.t.*, to remove the bolts from; to open.

unbolt′ed, *adj.*, unlocked; *p.p.*, unbolt.

unbolt′ing, *pr.p.*, unbolt.

unborn′, *adj.*, not yet born.

unbor′rowed, *adj.*, not borrowed; one's own.

unbos′om, *v.t.*, *reflex.*, to show one's feelings or secrets.

unbought′, *adj.*, not bought.

unbound′, *adj.*, not bound; free; *p.p.*, unbind.

unbound′ed, *adj.*, without limit; immense.

unbreak′able, *adj.*, cannot be broken or tamed.

unbri′dle, *v.t.*, to remove the bridle from; to lift restraint.

unbri′dled, *adj.*, without restraint; excessive; *p.p.*, unbridle.

unbrok′en, *adj.*, not broken; continuous.

unbroth′erly, *adj.*, not like a brother; without brotherly feeling.

unbrushed′, *adj.*, not brushed.

unbuck′le, *v.t.*, to loosen the buckles of.

unbur′den, *v.t.*, *reflex.*, to make confession.

unbur′ied, *adj.*, not buried.

unbus′inesslike, *adj.*, not businesslike; slipshod.

unbut′ton, *v.t.*, to undo the buttons of.

uncalled′, *adj.*, without being called.

uncalled′-for, *adj.*, unnecessary.

uncan′did, *adj.*, not candid; disingenuous.

uncan′ny, *adj.*, weird, supernatural.

uncapsiz′able, *adj.*, cannot be capsized.

uncared′-for, *adj.*, neglected.

uncar′ing, *adj.*, indifferent, not caring.

uncar′peted, *adj.*, not covered with carpet.

uncat′alogued, *adj.*, not catalogued.

uncaught′, *adj.*, not caught.

unceas′ing, *adj.*, without pause; neverending.

unceas′ingly, *adv.*, endlessly.

uncel′ebrated, *adj.*, not celebrated, ignored.

uncen′sored, *adj.*, not censored.

unceremo′nious, *adj.*, informal; rude; ill-mannered; without consideration.

unceremo′niously, *adv.*, informally.

uncer′tain, *adj.*, not certain; in doubt; doubtful.

uncer′tainly, *adv.*, in an uncertain way.

uncer′tainty, *n.*, the quality or state of being uncertain.

uncertif′icated, *adj.*, without a certificate.

unchain′, *v.t.*, to remove the chain from; to let loose.

unchal′lengeable, *adj.*, unable to be challenged.

unchal′lenged, *adj.*, not challenged.

unchange′able, *adj.*, unable to be changed; not changing.

unchanged′, *adj.*, not changed.

unchang′ing, *adj.*, not changing; remaining the same.

unchar′itable, *adj.*, not charitable; censorious.

unchar′itableness, *n.*, the state of being uncharitable.

unchar′itably, *adv.*, in an uncharitable way.

unchar′ted, *adj.*, not planned; unknown.

unchaste′, *adj.*, not chaste; impure.

unchaste′ly, *adv.*, impurely.

unchecked′, *adj.*, not examined; not restrained.

unchiv′alrous, *adj.*, discourteous; not gallant.

unchris′tian, *adj.*, not Christian.

unchri'stianlike, *adj.*, not in the manner of a Christian.

unchurch', *v.t.*, to exclude from the Church.

un'cial, *adj.*, written in large Greek capitals; *n.*, an uncial letter.

un'cicatrized, *adj.*, devoid of skin, esp. a wound scar.

un'ciform, *adj.*, like a hook.

un'cinate, *adj.*, having a hook at the end.

uncir'cumcised, *adj.*, not circumcised; Gentile.

unciv'il, *adj.*, rude; impolite.

unciv'ilized, *adj.*, rude; barbarous.

unciv'illy, *adv.*, in an uncivil way.

unclad, *adj.*, not clothed.

unclaimed', *adj.*, not claimed.

unclasp', *v.t.*, to unfasten the clasp of; to untie the hands.

un'cle, *n.*, the brother of one's father or mother; the husband of one's aunt; a pawnbroker (*slang*).

unclean', *adj.*, not clean; ceremonially impure.

unclean'ly, *adv.*, not cleanly; filthy.

unclean'ness, *n.*, the quality or state of being unclean.

uncleansed, *adj.*, *i.q.* unclean.

uncleri'cal, *adj.*, not befitting a clergyman.

uncloak', *v.t.*, to uncover; to take away a cloak.

unclose', *v.i.* and *t.*, to open.

unclosed', *adj.*, open; *p.p.*, unclose.

unclos'ing, *pr.p.*, unclose.

unclothed', *adj.*, naked.

unclouded', *adj.*, without a cloud; bright; clear.

un'co, *adj.*, uncommon; *adv.*, extremely (*Scot.*).

uncock', *v.t.*, to release a gun's hammer without actually firing.

uncoil', *v.i.* and *t.*, to release; to straighten.

uncome'ly, *adj.*, wanting in grace or beauty.

uncom'fortable, *adj.*, not comfortable; uneasy.

uncom'fortably, *adv.*, in an uncomfortable way.

uncommit'ted, *adj.*, not pledged.

uncom'mon, *adj.*, not common; rare.

uncom'monly, *adv.*, in an uncommon manner or degree.

uncommu'nicative, *adj.*, reticent.

uncompan'ionable, *adj.*, unsociable.

uncomplain'ing, *adj.*, making no complaint; acquiescing; patient.

uncomplain'ingly, *adv.*, in an uncomplaining way.

uncomplai'sant, *adj.*, uncivil.

uncomplimen'tary, *adj.*, not flattering, critical.

uncom'promis'ing, *adj.*, unyielding; inflexible.

unconcern', *n.*, calm indifference.

unconcerned', *adj.*, calmly indifferent.

unconcern'edly, *adv.*, without any concern.

uncondi'tional, *adj.*, without conditions; absolute.

uncondi'tionally, *adv.*, absolutely; without conditions.

uncondi'tioned, *adj.*, without limitations; absolute.

unconfirmed', *adj.*, not confirmed; not having received the Confirmation rite in the Christian Church.

unconge'nial, *adj.*, not congenial; not agreeable; not suited; unpleasant.

unconject'urable, *adj.*, cannot be inferred or guessed.

unconnect'ed, *adj.*, not connected; disjoined; separate.

uncon'querable, *adj.*, invincible.

uncon'scionable, *adj.*, unreasonable; not controlled by conscience.

uncon'scionably, *adv.*, unreasonably.

uncon'scious, *adj.*, not conscious; insensible; unaware; *n.*, the unconscious mind.

uncon'sciously, *adv.*, insensibly; not consciously.

uncon'sciousness, *n.*, the state of being unconscious.

uncon'secrated, *adj.*, not consecrated or set apart.

unconsid'ered, *adj.*, not considered.

unconsolidated, *adj.*, not firmly settled.

unconstitu'tional, *adj.*, not according to the constitution.

unconstitu'tionally, *adv.*, in an unconstitutional way.

unconstrained', *adj.*, without constraint.

unconstrain'edly, *adv.*, in an unconstrained way.

unconsumed', *adj.*, not consumed.

uncon'templated, *adj.*, not planned or intended.

uncontest'ed, *adj.*, not disputed.

uncontrol'lable, *adj.*, unable to be controlled; violent.

uncontrol'lably, *adv.*, in an uncontrollable way.

uncontrolled', *adj.*, not under control; excessive.

unconven'tional, *adj.*, not conforming to the accepted pattern; informal.

unconvert'ed, *adj.*, not converted.

unconvert'ible, *adj.*, unable to be converted.

unconvinced', *adj.*, not persuaded.

uncord', *v.t.*, to untie.

uncord'ed, *adj.*, not tied; *p.p.*, uncord.

uncork', *v.t.*, to draw the cork from.

uncorrec'ted, *adj.*, not corrected.

uncount'able, *adj.*, not able to be counted; innumerable.

uncount'ed, *adj.*, not counted; innumerable.

uncoup'led, *adj.*, disjoined; set free.

uncourt'eous, *adj.*, uncivil; rude.

uncourt'ly, *adj.*, wanting in courtesy.

uncouth', *adj.*, ungainly; awkward; coarse.

uncouth'ness, *n.*, the quality or state of being uncouth.

uncov'enanted, *adv.*, not pledged; not under agreement or promise.

uncov'er, *v.t.*, to remove the cover from.

uncov'ered, *adj.*, without a cover; *p.p.*, uncover.

uncov'ering, *pr.p.*, uncover.

uncrea'ted, *adj.*, not created.

uncriti'cal, *adj.*, not critical.

unc'tion, *n.*, an anointing; ointment; fervour in speech; pretended fervour; cant.

unc'tuous, *adj.*, full of unction; fatty; canting.

unc'tuously, *adv.*, in an unctuous way.

uncul'tivated, *adj.*, rude; waste.

uncul'tured, *adj.*, unrefined; uneducated.

uncurbed', *adj.*, unrestrained.

uncurl', *v.i.*, to unwind from a curled condition.

uncut', *adj.*, not cut; with the margins untrimmed; not shortened (of films, plays, etc.).

undam'aged, *adj.*, uninjured.

unda'ted, *adj.*, not dated.

undaunt'able, *adj.*, unable to be daunted.

undaunt'ed, *adj.*, dauntless; without fear.

undaunt'edly, *adv.*, in an undaunted way.

undec'agon, *n.*, a figure having eleven angles and eleven sides.

undeceive', *v.t.*, to remove a misconception from.

undeci'ded, *adj.*, not decided; hesitating.

undecked', *adj.*, not ornamented.

undefeat'able, *adj.*, unconquerable.

undefend'ed, *adj.*, not defended; where a person accused makes no defence.

undefiled', *adj.*, pure; unstained.

undefined', *adj.*, not defined; indefinite.

undeliv'ered, *adj.*, not delivered.

un'democratic, *adj.*, not democratic.

undemon'strative, *adj.*, reserved.

undeni'able, *adj.*, not to be denied; indisputable.

undeni'ably, *adv.*, indisputably.

undenomina'tional, *adj.*, not distinctive of any denomination.

un'der, *adj.*, inferior; lower; *adv.*, in a lower state or position; *prep.*, beneath; lower than; subject to; in the time or reign of.

underact', *v.i.*, to act without emphasis.

under-age', *adj.*, not of the full (legal) age.

un'der-agent, *n.*, a subagent.

underbid', *v.t.*, to make a lower offer than.

un'derbidder, *n.*, one who underbids.

un'derbred, *adj.*, not thoroughbred; not well bred; vulgar.

un'derbrush, *n.*, *i.q.* undergrowth.

un'dercarriage, *n.*, the wheels and related structures of an aircraft.

un'dercharge', *n.*, a charge less than the price; *v.i.*, to charge less than the price.

un'der-clerk, *n.*, an inferior clerk.

underclothed', *adj.*, without sufficient clothing.

un'derclothes, *n. pl.*, *i.q.* underclothing.

un'derclothing, *n.*, garments worn beneath others, esp. next to the skin.

un'dercoat, *n.*, a coat of paint before the final coat.

un'derco'ver, *adj.*, secret [as in espionage].

un'dercroft, *n.*, a crypt, or vault.

un'dercurrent, *n.*, a current beneath an upper current; a secret influence.

un'dercut, *adj.*, carved so as to stand out in relief; *n.*, the under part of a sirloin.

undercut', *v.t.*, to carve stone, etc., so that it stands out in relief; to underbid.

un'derdog, *n.*, one in a subordinate or disadvantageous position.

un'derdone', *adj.*, not done enough; not properly cooked.

underdose', *v.t.*, to administer an insufficient dose.

un'derdose, *n.*, an insufficient dose.

un'derdrain, *n.*, a drain under the surface.

underdrain', *v.t.*, to drain below the surface.

un'derdress', *v.i.*, to dress inadequately for the occasion.

under-es'timate, *n.*, an estimate lower than it should be.

under-es'timate, *v.i.*, to form too low an opinion of.

under-es'timated, *p.p.*, under-estimate.

under-es'timating, *pr.p.*, under-estimate.

un'derfelt, *n.*, material floor-covering under a carpet.

underfoot', *adv.*, beneath the feet; below.

undergo', *v.t.*, to go through; to endure; to submit to.

undergo'ing, *pr.p.*, undergo.

undergone', *p.p.*, undergo.

undergrad'uate, *n.*, an academic student not yet admitted to a degree, being still *in statu pupillari* (in the position of a pupil).

un'derground, *adj.*, subterraneous; *adv.*, below the ground; *n.*, a subterranean train system.

un'dergrowth, *n.*, shrubs, etc., growing beneath higher plants. (Also *underbrush* and *underwood*.)

un'derhand, *adj.*, done behind one's back; mean; deceitful; delivered with the hand kept below the (cricket) ball and the elbow; *adv.*, secretly; clandestinely; in an underhand way; deceitfully.

un'derhanded, *adj.*, done clandestinely.

underhan'dedly, *adv.*, in an underhand way.

underhung', *adj.*, projecting further than the upper jaw.

underlaid', *p.p.*, underlay.

underlay', *v.t.*, to lay under another thing; to put underlays under types.

un'derlay, *n.*, paper, etc., laid underneath types.

underlease', *v.t.*, to grant a sub-lease of.

un'derlease, *n.*, a sublease.

underlet', *v.t.*, to sublet.

un'derlet, *n.*, a sublet.

underlie', *v.t.*, to lie under; to support.

underline', *v.t.*, to score a line under; to emphasize.

underlined', *p.p.*, underline.

un'derlinen, *n.*, underclothing.

un'derling, *n.*, a subordinate.

underli'ning, *pr.p.*, underline.

underly'ing, *pr.p.*, underlie.

un'dermanned, *adj.*, short staffed.

un'dermentioned, *adj.*, noted below.

undermine', *v.t.*, to lay a mine under; to excavate beneath; to weaken in an underhand way.

undermined', *p.p.*, undermine.

undermin'ing, *pr.p.*, undermine.

un'dermost, *adj.*, lowest.

underneath', *adv.* and *prep.*, beneath; below.

un'dernourished, *adj.*, not adequately fed.

underpaid', *adj.*, insufficiently rewarded; *p.p.*, underpay.

un'derpass, *n.* and *v.t.*, a road passing under another; to go beneath.

un'derpay, *v.t.*, to pay inadequately.

underpay'ing, *pr.p.*, underpay.

underpin', *v.t.*, to secure with props or piers.

un'derpinned', *p.p.*, underpin.

underpin'ning, *n.*, a support from below; *pr.p.*, underpin.

un'derpri'vileged, *adj.*, without the average social and economic advantages.

un'derproduction, *n.*, production short of demand.

un'der-quote, *v.t.*, to offer at a lower price.

underrate', *v.t.*, to value too little.

underrun', *v.t.*, to run beneath.

underscore', *v.t.*, to underline; to emphasize.

under-sec'retary, *n.*, an assistant secretary.

undersell', *v.t.*, to sell at less than another's price.

undersel'ling, *pr.p.*, undersell.

un'dershot, *adj.*, driven by water that flows beneath.

un'derside, *n.*, the lower surface of an object.

un'dersign, *v.t.*, to sign below.

un'dersigned, *adj.* and *n.*, whose signature is below.

un'dersized, *adj.*, below standard size; small; dwarfish.

un'derskirt, *n.*, a skirt worn below another.

un'dersoil, *n.*, subsoil.

undersold', *p.p.*, undersell.

un'derstaffed, *adj.*, insufficiently provided with staff.

understand', *v.i.*, to have understanding; *v.t.*, to perceive the meaning of; to suppose; to be informed; to take as meant though not expressed.

understand'able, *adj.*, capable of being understood; excusable.

understand'ably, *adv.*, in an understandable way.

understand'ing, *adj.*, intelligent; *n.*, intelligence; an agreement; *pr.p.*, understand.

understand'ingly, *adv.*, in an understanding way.

understate', *v.t.*, to state less than is justified or correct.

understa'ted, *p.p.*, understate.

understate'ment, *n.*, a statement that says less than the facts would justify.

understat'ing, *pr.p.*, understate.

understock', *v.t.*, to provide insufficient stock.

understood', *p.p.*, understand.

un'derstudy, *n.*, one preparing or prepared to take another's rôle.

undertake', *v.i.*, to promise; to engage oneself; *v.t.*, to take upon oneself; to assume; to contract for doing.

underta'ken, *p.p.*, undertake.

un'dertaker, *n.*, one who carries out funeral arrangements; a contractor.

underta'king, *n.*, an enterprise; a contract; *pr.p.*, undertake.

un'dertone, *n.*, subdued speech.

undertook', *p.p.*, undertake.

underval'ue, *v.t.*, to put too low a value on.

underval'ued, *p.p.*, undervalue.

undervalu'ing, *pr.p.*, undervalue.

un'derwater, *adj.*, below the surface of water; submarine.

un'derwear, *n.*, underclothing.

underwent', *p.p.*, undergo.

un'derwood, *n.*, *i.q.* undergrowth.

underwork', *v.i.*, to do too little work; *v.t.*, to work for lower wages than; to scamp.

un'derworld, *n.*, Hades; the sub-society of criminals.

underwrite', *v.i.*, to be an underwriter; *v.t.*, to subscribe; to execute an insurance policy on; to subscribe for company stock not taken by the public.

un'derwriter, *n.*, one who executes or guarantees insurance.

un'derwriting, *n.*, an underwriter's business; *pr.p.*, underwrite.

under'written, *p.p.*, underwrite.

undeserved', *adj.*, not merited.

undeserv'edly, *adv.*, without being deserved.

undeserv'ing, *adj.*, not meriting; unworthy.

undeserv'ingly, *adv.*, in an unworthy way.

undesigned', *adj.*, not designed; not intended.

undesign'ing, *adj.*, not intending; ingenuous.

undesir'able, *adj.*, not to be desired; unpleasant.

undesir'ably, *adv.*, in an undesirable way.

undetect'ed, *adj.*, not discovered.

undeter'mined, *adj.*, not settled or known.

undeterred', *adj.*, not put off by obstacles.

undevel'oped, *adj.*, immature.

unde'viating, *adj.*, keeping straight onwards; not turning aside.

undid', *p.p.*, undo.

un'dies, *n. pl.*, women's underwear (*colloq.*).

undigest'ed, *adj.*, not digested.

undig'nified, *adj.*, wanting in dignity.

undilu'ted, *adj.*, neat; not mixed with water.

undimin'ished, *adj.*, not diminished.

undimmed', *adj.*, not dimmed.

un'dine, *n.*, a female water sprite.

undiscern'ible, *adj.*, cannot be seen.

undiscern'ing, *adj.*, lacking discernment.

un*discharged*', *adj.*, not fulfilled, not discharged (esp. of bankrupts).

undis'ciplined, *adj.*, uncontrolled; not under discipline.

undisclosed', *adj.*, not revealed.

undiscov'erable, *adj.*, cannot be found.

undiscov'ered, *adj.*, not found.

undiscrim'inating, *adj.*, not discerning.

undisguised', *adj.*, open; not concealed.

undismayed', *adj.*, unafraid.

undisplayed', *adj.*, not displayed.

undispu'table, *adj.*, cannot be disputed.

undispu'ted, *adj.*, not challenged, unrivalled.

undispu'tedly, *adv.*, unquestionably.

undissolved', *adj.*, not dissolved.

un*disting'uishable*, *adj.*, unable to be distinguished.

un*distin'guished*, *adj.*, not famous, mediocre.

undisturbed', *adj.*, not disturbed; left in the original state.

undivi'ded, *adj.*, whole; not divided.

undo', *v.t.*, to cancel; to make undone; to inflict irreparable injury on.

undo'er, *n.*, one who undoes.

undo'ing, *n.*, ruin; *pr.p.*, undo.

undone', *adj.*, not done; *p.p.*, undo.

undoubt'ed, *adj.*, certain; beyond doubt.

undoubt'edly, *adv.*, certainly.

undraped', *adj.*, without drapery; nude.

undreamed', *adj.*, not thought of.

undress', *adj.*, in mufti; *n.*, mufti; *v.i.* and *t.*, to remove the clothing.

undressed', *adj.*, not dressed; *p.p.*, undress.

undress'ing, *pr.p.*, undress.

undrink'able, *adj.*, not fit to drink.

undue', *adj.*, not legally due; excessive.

un'dulant, *adj.*, undulating; or recurring nature (as of fever).

un'dulate, *v.i.*, to move in waves; *v.t.*, to cause to wave or vibrate.

un'dulated, *adj.*, wavy; *p.p.*, undulate.

un'dulating, *adj.*, wavy; *pr.p.*, undulate.

undula'tion, *n.*, a waving motion.

un'dulator, *n.*, a Morse signal recorder.

un'dulatory, *adj.*, vibrating.

undu'ly, *adv.*, improperly; excessively.

undu'tiful, *adj.*, without respect for moral responsibilities.

undu'tifully, *adv.*, unrespectfully.

undy'ing, *adj.*, not dying; neverending.

unearned', *adj.*, not earned; obtained without labour.

unearth', *v.t.*, to disclose; to bring to light.

unearthed', *p.p.*, unearth.

unearth'ing, *pr.p.*, unearth.

unearth'ly, *adj.*, unlike anything on earth.

uneas'ily, *adv.*, uncomfortably.

uneas'iness, *n.*, the state of being uneasy.

uneas'y, *adj.*, uncomfortable; not at ease.

unea'table, *adj.*, not fit to eat.

uneconom'ic, *adj.*, not producing a profitable result.

uneconom'ical, *adj.*, wasteful.

unedi'fying, *adj.*, not morally or ethically stimulating.

uned'ucated, *adj.*, ignorant; not educated.

unembar'rassed, *adj.*, without embarrassment.

unembod'ied, *adj.*, without a body.

unemploy'able, *adj.*, not capable of paid work.

unemployed', *adj.*, without employment.

unemploy'ment, *n.*, the state of being unemployed.

unenclosed', *adj.*, not closed in.

unencum'bered, *adj.*, without encumbrance.

unend'ing, *adj.*, unceasing.

unendur'able, *adj.*, intolerable.

unendur'ably, *adv.*, intolerably.

unengaged', *adj.*, disengaged; not engaged.

un-*English*, *adj.*, not English in character.

unenlight'ened, *adj.*, ignorant; barbarous; without enlightenment.

unen'terprising, *adj.*, not adventurous.

unenthralled', *adj.*, not fascinated.

unen'viable, *adj.*, not to be envied.

unen'viably, *adv.*, in an unenviable way.

une'quable, *adj.*, not equable; of uncertain temper.

une'qual, *adj.*, not equal; not uniform; incapable.

une'qualled, *adj.*, not equalled; not matched.

une'qually, *adv.*, in an unequal way.

unequiv'ocal, *adj.*, not ambiguous; certain.

unequiv'ocally, *adv.*, in an unequivocal way.

uner'ring, *adj.*, certain; making no mistake.

uner'ringly, *adv.*, in an unerring way.

Unesco, *n.*, the United Nations Educational, Scientific and Cultural Organization.

unessen'tial, *adj.*, not essential; immaterial.

une'ven, *adj.*, not even; rough; up and down.

une'venly, *adv.*, in an uneven way.

une'venness, *n.*, the quality or state of being uneven.

unevent'ful, *adj.*, quiet; with nothing of importance happening.

unevent'fully, *adv.*, quietly; in an uneventful way.

unexam'pled, *adj.*, unequalled; unique.

unexcelled', *adj.*, unsurpassed.

unexcep'tionable, *adj.*, to which or whom no'one can take exception; blameless.

unexcep'tionably, *adv.*, in an unexceptionable way.

unexcep'tional, *adj.*, not unusual.

unexcep'tionally, *adv.*, not unusually.

unexhaust'ed, *adj.*, not exhausted; not used up.

unexpect'ed, *adj.*, sudden; coming on one unawares.

unexpect'edly, *adv.*, in an unexpected way.

unexpen'ded, *adj.,* not used or spent.

unexpired', *adj.,* not terminated.

unexplain'able, *adj.,* inexplicable.

unexplained', *adj.,* not explained; mysterious.

unexploi'ted, *adj.,* not used.

unexplored', *adj.,* never travelled over; unknown.

unexposed', *adj.,* not exposed.

unexpressed', *adj.,* not spoken.

unexpress'ive, *adj.,* meaningless.

unexpress'ively, *adv.,* in a meaningless way.

unextin'guishable, *adj.,* that cannot be extinguished.

un'extin'guished, *adj.,* burning; shining; not put out.

unfad'able, *adj.,* cannot fade.

unfa'ded, *adj.,* still fresh and blooming.

unfa'ding, *adj.,* never fading.

unfail'ing, *adj.,* always to be relied on; never found wanting.

unfail'ingly, *adv.,* in an unfailing way.

unfair', *adj.,* unjust; partial.

unfair'ly, *adv.,* in an unfair way; unjustly.

unfair'ness, *n.,* injustice; partiality.

unfaith'ful, *adj.,* disloyal; not keeping a promise or vow.

unfaith'fully, *adv.,* in a disloyal way.

unfaith'fulness, *n.,* the state of being unfaithful.

unfal'tering, *adj.,* not hesitating.

unfal'teringly, *adv.,* unhesitantly.

unfamil'iar, *adj.,* strange; unknown.

unfamil'iarity, *n.,* the state of strangeness.

unfamil'iarly, *adv.,* in an unfamiliar way.

unfash'ionable, *adj.,* not conforming to the fashion.

unfash'ionably, *adv.,* in an unfashionable way.

unfash'ioned, *adj.,* shapeless, not wrought by art.

unfast'en, *v.t.,* to loose; to untie.

unfast'ened, *p.p.,* unfasten.

unfast'ening, *pr.p.,* unfasten.

unfath'omable, *adj.,* that cannot be fathomed; inexplicable.

unfath'omed, *adj.,* unsolved.

unfa'vourable, *adj.,* unpromising; adverse.

unfa'vourably, *adv.,* in an unfavourable way.

unfeared', *adj.,* not feared.

unfear'ing, *adj.,* not afraid.

unfear'ingly, *adv.,* in an unfearing way.

unfeas'ible, *adj.,* impracticable, impossible.

unfed', *adj.,* without food.

unfeel'ing, *adj.,* wanting in feeling; unsympathetic.

unfeel'ingly, *adv.,* in an unfeeling way.

unfeigned', *adj.,* sincere; genuine.

unfeign'edly, *adv.,* sincerely; genuinely.

unfelt', *adj.,* not felt; unperceived.

unfem'inine, *adj.,* unlike what a woman should be, as conventionally understood.

unfenced', *adj.,* not enclosed or protected by a fence.

unfermen'ted, *adj.,* not fermented.

unfer'tile, *adj.,* not prolific.

unfer'tilized, *adj.,* not made fruitful.

unfet'ter, *v.t.,* to set free; to unchain.

unfet'tered, *adj.,* free; loose; *p.p.,* unfetter.

unfil'ial, *adj.,* not filial; not dutiful to parents.

unfilled', *adj.,* empty; not full.

unfin'ished, *adj.,* incomplete.

unfit', *adj.,* not fit; incompetent; *v.t.,* to make unfit.

unfit'ly, *adv.,* in an unfit way.

unfit'ness, *n.,* the quality or state of being unfit.

unfit'ted, *adj.,* not suited; *p.p.,* unfit.

unfit'ting, *adj.,* unsuitable; *pr.p.,* unfit.

unfix', *v.t.,* to release what is fixed.

unfixed', *p.p.,* unfix.

unfix'ing, *pr.p.,* unfix.

unflag'ging, *adj.,* not flagging; keeping on

without relaxing effort.

unflat'tering, *adj.,* uncomplimentary.

unflat'teringly, *adv.,* in an uncomplimentary way.

unfla'voured, *adj.,* without added flavour.

unfledged', *adj.,* raw; callow; inexperienced.

unflinch'ing, *adj.,* absolutely resolute.

unflinch'ingly, *adv.,* steadfastly.

unfold', *v.i.,* to come unfolded; *v.t.,* to open what is folded; to disclose.

unfold'ed, *adj.,* not folded; flat; *p.p.,* unfold.

unfold'ing, *pr.p.,* unfold.

unforced', *adj.,* natural.

unforesee'able, *adj.,* not able to be known beforehand.

unforeseen', *adj.,* sudden; coming on one unawares.

unforetold', *adj.,* not predicted.

unforewarned', *adj.,* not previously warned.

unfor'feited, *adj.,* not given up.

unforget'ful, *adj.,* not forgetful.

unforget'table, *adj.,* not to be forgotten; memorable.

unforgiv'able, *adj.,* inexcusable, unpardonable.

unforgiv'en, *adj.,* not forgiven.

unforgiv'ing, *adj.,* implacable; relentless.

unforgot'ten, *adj.,* remembered.

unformed', *adj.,* not completely formed; undeveloped in character.

unforsa'ken, *adj.,* not forsaken.

unfort'ified, *adj.,* not strengthened; weak.

unfor'tunate, *adj.,* illfated; unlucky.

unfor'tunately, *adv.,* by ill-luck.

unfound'ed, *adj.,* not based on fact.

unframed', *adj.,* without a frame.

unfranked', *adj.,* not cleared for postal charges.

unfrequent'ed, *adj.,* solitary; rarely visited.

unfre'quently, *adv.,* seldom.

unfriend'liness, *n.,* the state of being unfriendly.

unfriend'ly, *adj.*, unsociable; bearing ill-will.

unfrock', *v.t.*, *i.q.* disfrock.

unfruit'ful, *adj.*, not productive.

unfruit'fully, *adv.*, in an unproductive way.

unfruit'fulness, *n.*, the state of being unfruitful.

unfulfilled', *adj.*, never fulfilled.

unfurl', *v.t.*, to unroll (as a flag).

unfurled', *p.p.*, unfurl.

unfurl'ing, *pr.p.*, unfurl.

unfur'nished, *adj.*, without furniture.

ungain'liness, *n.*, clumsiness.

ungain'ly, *adj.*, clumsy; awkward.

ungallant', *adj.*, not courteous.

ungallant'ly, *adv.*, discourteously.

ungar'nered, *adj.*, not harvested.

ungar'risoned, *adj.*, without a garrison.

ungath'ered, *adj.*, not centrally assémbled or brought together.

ungen'erous, *adj.*, lacking in generosity.

ungen'erously, *adv.*, in an ungenerous way.

unge'nial, *adj.*, cold; not kindly.

ungen'tle, *adj.*, rough.

ungen'tlemanly, *adj.*, unlike a gentleman.

unget-at-able, *adj.*, inaccessible.

ungif'ted, *adj.*, not talented.

ungil'ded, *adj.*, not decorated with gold.

ungird'ed, *adj.*, unbound.

unglazed', *adj.*, without glass.

unglue', *v.t.*, to separate.

ungod'liness, *n.*, the state of being ungodly.

ungod'ly, *adj.*, wicked; at enmity with God.

ungov'ernable, *adj.*, uncontrollable.

ungov'ernably, *adv.*, in an ungovernable way.

ungrace'ful, *adj.*, awkward; lacking in grace.

ungrace'fully, *adv.*, in an ungraceful way.

ungrace'fulness, *n.*, the want of charm or elegance.

ungra'cious, *adj.*, lacking in courtesy or condescension.

ungra'ciously, *adv.*, in an ungracious manner.

ungrammat'ical, *adj.*, not according to the rules of grammar.

ungrammat'ically, *adv.*, in an ungrammatical way.

ungrate'ful, *adj.*, without gratitude; unpleasing.

ungrate'fully, *adv.*, in an ungrateful way.

ungrate'fulness, *n.*, the state of being ungrateful.

unground'ed, *adj.*, wanting in support or proof.

ungrudg'ing, *adj.*, generous.

ungrudg'ingly, *adv.*, generously.

un'gual, *adj.*, pert. or rel. to a claw or nail.

unguard'ed, *adj.*, not protected; careless.

unguard'edly, *adv.*, in an unguarded way.

un'guent, *n.*, ointment.

un'guentary, *adj.*, pert. or rel. to unguent.

unguessed', *adj.*, unsuspected.

unguic'ulate, *adj.*, having claws; having a claw-like base (*bot.*).

unguic'ulated, *adj.*, *i.q.* unguiculate.

ungui'ded, *adj.*, not directed.

un'guiform, *adj.*, claw-shaped.

un'guinous, *adj.*, like fat or oil.

ungulat'a, *n. pl.*, animals with hoofs.

un'gulate, *adj.*, hoofed; hoof-like.

un'gulated, *adj.*, *i.q.* ungulate.

unhack'neyed, *adj.*, not over-used or over-familiar.

unhal'lowed, *adj.*, unblest; not consecrated.

unham'pered, *adj.*, unimpeded.

unhand', *v.t.*, to let go of.

unhan'dled, *adj.*, not dealt with.

unhand'some, *adj.*, stingy; ungenerous; wanting good looks.

unhand'somely, *adv.*, in an unhandsome way.

unhan'dy, *adj.*, clumsy.

unhang', *v.t.*, to remove from hinges or hooks.

unhap'pily, *adv.*, sadly; unfortunately.

unhap'piness, *n.*, the state of being unhappy.

unhap'py, *adj.*, joyless; unfortunate.

unharmed', *adj.*, not hurt; not injured; safe and sound.

unharm'ful, *adj.*, not harmful.

unhar'ness, *v.t.*, to remove the harness from.

unhar'nessed, *p.p.*, unharness.

unhar'nessing, *pr.p.*, unharness.

unhealth'ily, *adv.*, in an unhealthy way.

unhealth'iness, *n.*, the state of being unhealthy.

unhealth'y, *adj.*, not in good health; unwholesome.

unheard', *adj.*, not heard; without a hearing.

unheard'-of, *adj.*, unprecedented.

unheed'ed, *adj.*, not noticed; not regarded.

unheed'ful, *adj.*, careless.

unheed'fully, *adv.*, carelessly.

unheed'ing, *adj.*, regardless; rash.

unheed'ingly, *adv.*, rashly.

unhelp'ful, *adj.*, affording no help.

unheral'ded, *adj.*, unannounced.

unhero'ic, *adj.*, not brave.

unhes'itating, *adj.*, prompt in decision.

unhes'itatingly, *adv.*, without hesitation.

unhewn', *adj.*, rough, not sawn.

unhin'dered, *adj.*, not hindered or stopped.

unhinge', *v.t.*, to take off its hinges; to upset the balance of; to make mad.

unhinged', *p.p.*, unhinge.

unhing'ing, *pr.p.*, unhinge.

unhistor'ical, *adj.*, not founded by history.

unhitch', *v.t.*, to loose; to unfasten.

unho'liness, *n.*, the quality of state of being unholy.

unho'ly, *adj.*, profane; not consecrated; irreligious.

unhon'oured, *adj.*, inglorious; without honour.

unhook', v.t., to remove from a hook; to undo the hooks of.

unhooked', p.p., unhook.

unhook'ing, pr.p., unhook.

unhope'ful, adj., not optimistic.

unhope'fully, adv., hopelessly.

unhorse', v.t., to unseat; to throw from a horse.

unhorsed', p.p., unhorse.

unhors'ing, pr.p., unhorse.

unhuman, adj., supernatural.

unhur'ried, adj., easy-paced, without stress or urgency.

unhurt', adj., unharmed; without injury.

unhygien'ic, adj., contrary to the rules of cleanliness and health.

u'niate, adj., pert. or rel. to Eastern churches accepting the supremacy of Roman Catholicism.

uniax'ial, adj., having but one axis.

unicam'eral, adj., having one chamber (a single, legislative assembly).

U'nicef, n., United Nations Children's Fund.

unicel'lular, adj., having only one cell.

u'nicorn, n., a legendary beast with a single horn; a narwhal; a variety of beetles and gasteropods; three horses in harness, a pair and a leader (colloq.).

unicorn'ous, adj., having a single horn.

u'nicycle, n., a one-wheeled cycle.

un'ideal', adj., the opposite to ideal; unimaginative; materialistic.

uni'dimen'sional, adj., with only one dimension.

unifa'cial, adj., having a single face.

unif'ic, adj., unifying.

unifica'tion, n., the act or result of unifying; union.

u'nified, p.p., unify.

uniflo'rous, adj., producing a single flower.

unifo'liate, adj., having only one leaflet.

u'niform, adj., always preserving a single form; never varying; in conformity with a standard; n., dress of one and the same pattern; v.t., to make uniform; to put into uniform.

uniform'ity, n., the being of one pattern, standard, etc.; regularity.

u'niformly, adv., regularly; in one and the same way or degree.

u'nify, v.t., to make one; to bring into uniformity.

u'nifying, pr.p., unify.

Unigen'itus, n., the famous Bull of Pope Clement XI, issued against the Jansenists in 1713.

unig'enous, adj., of the same genus.

unila'biate, adj., with one lip.

unilat'eral, adj., one-sided.

unilin'gual, adj., having or using only one language.

unilit'eral, adj., containing a single letter; of one style of lettering.

un'illu'minated, adj., not lit, dark.

unimag'inable, adj., cannot be imagined.

unimag'inably, adv., in an unimaginable way.

unimag'inative, adj., lacking imagination.

unimag'inatively, adv., in an unimaginative way.

unimag'ined, adj., not thought of.

unimbued', adj., not imbued.

unimpaired', adj., uninjured; whole.

unimpas'sioned, adj., without emotion.

unimpeach'able, adj., not to be impeached; without a flaw; blameless.

unimpe'ded, adj., unhindered.

unimpor'tant, adj., of no importance or significance.

unimpos'ing, adj., not imposing.

unimpres'sible, adj., not easily impressed.

unimpres'sive, adj., unemotional.

unimpres'sively, adv., in an unemotional way.

unimproved', adj., not improved; unamended.

unimpugn'able, adj., cannot be gainsaid.

uninflam'mable, adj., that cannot be set on fire.

unin'fluenced, adj., not influenced.

uninfluen'tial, adj., not influential.

uninformed', adj., not informed; unenlightened.

uninhab'itable, adj., not fit to be lived in; desert.

uninhab'ited, adj., without inhabitants; deserted.

uninhib'ited, adj., without mental or social restraint.

uninjured', adj., unhurt.

un'inspired', adj., mediocre, commonplace, dull.

uninspir'ing, adj., i.q. uninspired.

uninstruct'ed, adj., ignorant.

uninstruct'ive, adj., not informing.

uninstruct'ively, adv., in an uninstructive way.

unintel'ligent, adj., without intelligence.

unintel'ligently, adv., in an unintelligent way.

unintel'ligible, adj., past understanding.

unintel'ligibly, adv., in an unintelligible way.

unintend'ed, adj., not designed; not premeditated.

uninten'tional, adj., i.q. unintended.

uninten'tionally, adv., without intention.

unin'terested, adj., taking no interest.

unin'teresting, adj., not interesting; dull.

unin'terestingly, adv., dully.

uninter'preted, adj., not interpreted.

uninterred', adj., not yet buried.

uninterrupt'ed, adj., without interruption.

uninterrupt'edly, adv., without a break or interruption.

uninured', adj., not hardened; not accustomed.

uninvi'ted, adj., unbidden; without invitation.

uninvi'ting, adj., not attractive.

uninvolved', adj., not involved.

u'nion, n., the act of uniting; a state of being united; a combination; a junction.

U'nionism, *n.,* the principle of combination, esp. Trade Union.

U'nionist, *n.,* an adherent of the continued union of Great Britain and Northern Ireland; a supporter of the Conservative Party.

U'nion Jack, *n.,* the Jack or national flag, showing the national crosses of the countries of the United Kingdom.

unip'arous, *adj.,* having one stem; producing only one.

u'niped, *adj.,* having a single foot.

uniper'sonal, *adj.,* consisting of a single person.

unipla'nar, *adj.,* moving in one plane only.

unipol'ar, *adj.,* having one magnetic pole (*elec.*).

unique', *adj.,* being the only one; sole; unequalled.

unique'ly, *adv.,* in a unique way.

unise'rial, *adj.,* single-ranked.

unise'riate, *adj., l.q.* uniserial.

uni'sex, *n.,* the state of being unisexual.

unisex'ual, *adj.,* of a single sex.

u'nison, *adj.,* vibrating in the same number; of identical pitch; sounding alone; *n.,* exact agreement; a state of sounding alone, or of several voices or instruments sounding the same notes, if not at the same pitch; harmony; the interval of an octave.

unis'onance, *n.,* the identity of musical pitch.

unis'onant, *adj.,* sounding in unison.

unis'onous, *adj., i.q.* unisonant.

u'nit, *n.,* an individual person or thing; a particular group or body; a quantity or value taken as the standard to which other quantities or values must be referred; a part treated as a whole within a greater whole; one of the first nine numbers.

Unita'rian, *adj.,* pert. or rel. to Unitarianism; *n.,* a member of the Unitarian body.

Unita'rianism, *n.,* the principles of the Unitarians, who deny the deity of Christ and the concept of the Trinity.

u'nitary, *adj.,* pert. or rel. to units and unity; integral.

unite', *v.i.,* to combine; to join together; *v.t.,* to join in one; to combine; to attach.

uni'ted, *adj.,* harmonious; loving; combined; *p.p.,* unite.

uni'tedly, *adv.,* in an united way.

uni'ter, *n.,* one who, or that which, unites.

uni'ting, *pr.p.,* unite.

u'nity, *n.,* the state of being one; oneness; harmony; agreement; the number one.

univ'alent, *adj.,* having a valency of one (*chem.*).

u'nivalve, *adj.,* having a single valve; *n.,* a gasteropod; a mollusc with a single-valved shell.

u'nivalved, *adj., i.q.* univalve.

univalv'ular, *adj., i.q.* univalve.

univer'sal, *adj.,* bel. to, pert. or rel. to, all mankind; applicable to all; existing everywhere; *n.,* a logical proposition which predicates something of every individual denoted by the subject; philosophically, a general concept, predicable of many individual things.

Univer'salism, *n.,* the doctrine that all men will finally be saved.

Univer'salist, *n.,* one who accepts Universalism.

universal'ity, *n.,* the quality or state of being universal.

univer'salize, *v.t.,* to generalize.

univer'salized, *p.p.,* universalize.

univer'salizing, *pr.p.,* universalize.

univer'sally, *adv.,* in regard to all; with no exceptions.

u'niverse, *n.,* all created things; the visible world; the total material environment.

univer'sity, *n.,* a corporation or gild; now understood to be a corporation of tea-

chers and scholars dedicated to advanced knowledge and research.

univo'cal, *adj.,* having only one meaning.

unjaun'diced, *adj.,* unaffected by jealousy or prejudice.

unjoin', *v.t.,* to disjoin.

unjoin'ted, *adj.,* without a join.

unjust', *adj.,* not just; unfair; cruel.

unjust'ifiable, *adj.,* without justification; inexcusable.

unjust'ifiably, *adv.,* in an unjustifiable way.

unjust'ified, *adj.,* not warranted by justice or reason; not arranged with regular margins.

unjust'ly, *adv.,* in an unjust way.

unkempt', *adj.,* untidy; dishevelled.

unken'nel, *v.t.,* to bring or drive out of retreat.

unken'nelled, *p.p.,* unkennel.

unken'nelling, *pr.p.,* unkennel.

unkind', *adj.,* harsh; cruel.

unkind'ly, *adj.,* wanting in kindliness; *adv.,* in an unkind way.

unkind'ness, *n.,* the state of being unkind.

unking'ly, *adj.,* not like a king.

unknight'ly, *adj.,* unchivalrous.

unknit', *v.t.,* to unravel; to relax.

unknow'able, *adj.,* not able to be known or recognized.

unknow'ingly, *adv.,* without knowing.

unknown', *adj.,* not known; obscure.

unla'belled, *adj.,* without a label.

unla'boured, *adj.,* easy, spontaneous.

unlace', *v.t.,* to undo the laces of.

unlaced', *p.p.,* unlace.

unla'cing, *pr.p.,* unlace.

unlad'derable, *adj.,* not able to be laddered (of finely woven material in which one thread snaps and opens up the weave).

unlade', *v.t.,* to unload.

unla'den, *adj.,* without burden or cargo.

unla'dylike, *adj.,* not becoming or befitting a lady.

unlaid', *adj.*, not fixed or laid.

unlamen'ted, *adj.*, not regretted, not deplored.

unlar'ded, *adj.*, not dressed with lard; not adulterated.

unlash', *v.t.*, to untie (*naut.*).

unlashed', *p.p.*, untie.

unlash'ing, *pr.p.*, unlash.

unlatch', *v.t.*, to undo the latch of.

unlatched', *p.p.*, unlatch.

unlatch'ing, *pr.p.*, unlatch.

unlaw'ful, *adj.*, not lawful; illegal.

unlaw'fully, *adj.*, illegally.

unlaw'fulness, *n.*, the state of being unlawful; illegality.

unlay', *v.t.*, to untwist (rope stands).

unlearn', *v.t.*, to forget; to banish from the mind.

unlearned', *p.p.*, unlearn.

unlearn'ed, *adj.*, not educated; illiterate.

unlearned'ly, *adv.*, ignorantly.

unlearn'ing, *pr.p.*, unlearn.

unleash', *v.t.*, to let loose.

unleashed', *p.p.*, unleash.

unleash'ing, *pr.p.*, unleash.

unleav'ened, *adj.*, not leavened; not containing leaven.

unled', *adj.*, without a guide.

unless', *conj.*, if not; except.

unlet'tered, *adj.*, illiterate.

unli'censed, *adj.*, not licensed; unrestrained.

unlicked', *adj.*, not licked (into shape) (*colloq.*).

unligh'ted, *adj.*, not lit; dim.

unlike', *adj.*, not like; different from.

unlike'lihood, *n.*, the state of being unlikely.

unlike'liness, *n.*, *i.q.* unlikelihood.

unlike'ly, *adj.*, not probable.

unlike'ness, *n.*, the state of being not like.

unlim'ited, *adj.*, without limit.

unlim'itedly, *adv.*, unrestrictedly.

unlink', *v.t.*, to loosen.

unlinked', *adj.*, loosened; *p.p.*, unlink.

unlink'ing, *pr.p.*, unlink.

unliq'uidated, *adj.*, not liquidated; not ascertained as regards amount.

unload', *v.i.*, to discharge cargo; *v.t.*, to remove a load from; to disburden; to take the charge from a firearm.

unload'ed, *adj.*, (of a firearm) not charged; *p.p.*, unload.

unload'ing, *pr.p.*, unload.

unloca'ted, *adj.*, not fixed in place.

unlock', *v.t.*, to unfasten the lock of; to disclose.

unlocked', *adj.*, not locked; *p.p.*, unlock.

unlock'ing, *pr.p.*, unlock.

unloose', *v.t.*, to unfasten or untie.

unloos'en, *v.t.*, *i.q.* unloose.

unlov'able, *adj.*, not evoking love.

unloved', *adj.*, not loved.

unlove'liness, *n.*, the quality or state of being unlovely.

unlove'ly, *adj.*, not worthy to be loved.

unlov'ing, *adj.*, not loving.

unloving'ly, *adv.*, in an unloving way.

unluck'ily, *adv.*, by illluck.

unluck'y, *adj.*, unfortunate; ill-starred.

unmade', *adj.*, not yet made; taken to pieces; *p.p.*, unmake.

unmaid'enly, *adj.*, unlike, or not befitting, a maiden.

unmake', *v.t.*, to take to pieces.

unma'king, *pr.p.*, unmake.

unmalleabil'ity, *n.*, the quality or state of being unmalleable.

unmal'leable, *adj.*, cannot be hammered out.

unman', *v.t.*, to take the courage out of; to conquer.

unman'ageable, *adj.*, uncontrollable.

unman'liness, *n.*, the state of being unmanly.

unman'ly, *adj.*, not like a man; effeminate; cowardly.

unmanned', *adj.*, without men; *p.p.*, unman.

unman'nered, *adj.*, illbred.

unman'nerliness, *n.*, the state of being unmannerly.

unman'nerly, *adj.*, *i.q.* discourteous.

unmanufac'tured, *adj.*, natural; not manufactured.

unmarked', *adj.*, not marked; unobserved.

unmar'ketable, *adj.*, unsaleable.

unmarred', *adj.*, unspoiled.

unmar'riageable, *adj.*, unfitted for marriage.

unmar'ried, *adj.*, not married.

unmask', *v.t.*, to remove the mask from; to reveal.

unmasked', *adj.*, not wearing a mask; *p.p.*, unmask.

unmask'ing, *pr.p.*, unmask.

unmas'tered, *adj.*, not mastered.

unmatch'able, *adj.*, cannot be matched.

unmatched', *adj.*, unequalled; matchless.

unmean'ing, *adj.*, unintelligible; without any sense.

unmean'ingly, *adv.*, senselessly.

unmeant', *adj.*, not intended.

unmeasur'ably, *adv.*, boundlessly.

unmeas'ured, *adj.*, boundless; not measured.

unmel'lowed, *adj.*, not mellowed.

unmelo'dious, *adj.*, not melodious.

unmelo'diously, *adv.*, in an unmelodious way.

unmen'tionable, *adj.*, unfit to be mentioned.

unmen'tioned, *adj.*, not mentioned.

unmer'chantable, *adj.*, unfit for sale.

unmer'ciful, *adj.*, cruel.

unmer'cifully, *adv.*, in an unmerciful way.

unmer'ited, *adj.*, undeserved.

unmind'ful, *adj.*, forgetful; disregarding.

unmind'fully, *adv.*, forgetfully.

unmin'gled, *adj.*, not mixed; unadulterated.

unmista'kable, *adj.*, that cannot be mistaken.

unmista'kably, adv., in an unmistakable way.

unmit'igated, adj., in full force; without abatement.

unmixed', adj., i.q. unmingled.

unmod'ified, adj., not altered.

unmoist'ened, adj., not moistened.

unmoles'ted, adj., not molested.

unmoor', v.t., to loose from its mooring.

unmor'al, adj., not subject to anything moral.

unmoth'erly, adj., unlike a mother.

unmoun'ted, adj., not mounted (on a horse or in a frame).

unmourned', adj., not lamented.

unmov'able, adj., not movable.

unmov'ably, adv., calmly.

unmoved', adj., not moved; firm, steady; calm.

unmur'muring, adj., without complaining.

unmur'muringly, adv., uncomplainingly.

unmu'sical, adj., lacking the musical sense or quality.

unmu'tilated, adj., without deformation; whole.

unmuz'zle, v.t., to loose the muzzle of; to allow freedom of speech to.

unmuz'zled, p.p., unmuzzle.

unmuz'zling, pr.p., unmuzzle.

unname'able, adj., cannot be named; horrible.

unnamed', adj., not named; unmentioned.

unnat'ural, adj., contrary to nature; monstrous.

unnat'urally, adv., in an unnatural way.

unnav'igable, adj., not capable of being navigated.

unnec'essarily, adv., needlessly.

unnec'essary, adj., needless; not essential.

unneed'ed, adj., not wanted.

unnego'tiable, adj., cannot be negotiated.

unneigh'bourly, adj., not like a neighbour; churlish.

unnerve', v.t., to upset the nerves of; to debilitate; to weaken the resolution of.

unnerved', p.p., unnerve.

unnerv'ing, pr.p., unnerve.

unno'ted, adj., not noted; undistinguished; forgotten.

unno'ticed, adj., not noticed; unperceived.

unnum'bered, adj., not numbered; innumerable.

unobjec'tionable, adj., to which no objection can be raised.

unobjec'tionably, adv., in an unobjectionable way.

unoblig'ing, adj., churlish; selfish.

unobserv'able, adj., unable to be observed.

unobserv'ant, adj., not quick at taking notice of things; paying no regard.

unobserv'ing, adj., i.q. unobservant.

unobtain'able, adj., not to be got.

unobtru'sive, adj., not obtrusive; retiring.

unobtru'sively, adv., without attracting attention.

unobtru'siveness, n., the quality or state of modesty, self-effacement.

unoc'cupied, adj., without occupation; empty; at leisure.

unoffend'ing, adj., harmless.

unoffen'sive, adj., i.q. unoffending.

unoffi'cial, adj., informal; not official.

unoffi'cially, adv., informally.

unoffi'cious, adj., not officious.

uno'pened, adj., not opened; shut.

unopposed', adj., unresisted.

unordained', adj., not decreed; not ordained in the ecclesiastic sense.

unor'ganized, adj., not well arranged or administered.

unor'thodox, adj., not according to accepted practice or custom.

unostenta'tious, adj., without ostentation; without pretentious display.

unostenta'tiously, adv., in an unostentatious way.

unowned', adj., not owned.

unpac'ified, adj., not comforted; not rendered peaceful.

unpack', v.t., to remove the contents from a packed trunk, etc.

unpacked', p.p., unpack.

unpack'ing, pr.p., unpack.

unpaged', adj., with pages not numbered; not yet in page form.

unpaid', adj., not paid; still owing; unsalaried.

unpal'atable, adj., not pleasing to the palate; nauseous; unpleasant.

unpar'alleled, adj., unequalled; without a parallel.

unpar'donable, adj., unforgivable.

unpar'donably, adv., in an unpardonable way.

unparliament'ary, adj., not in accordance with the rules of Parliament; rude.

unpa'tented, adj., not patented.

unpatriot'ic, adj., lacking in patriotism.

unpaved', adj., rough; not paved.

unpeeled', adj., having the peel on.

unperceiv'able, adj., imperceptible; not able to be perceived.

unperceived', adj., unobserved; unnoticed.

unper'forated, adj., not pierced.

unperformed', adj., not done.

unperturbed', adj., not anxious; unworried.

unphilosoph'ical, adj., not philosophical.

unphilosoph'ically, adv., in an unphilosophical way.

unpick', v.t., to take out stitches.

unpicked', adj., unstitched; not gathered (fruit); not opened (lock); p.p., unpick.

unpick'ing, pr.p., unpick.

unpin', v.t., to take the pins out of.

unpinned', p.p., unpin.

unpin'ning, pr.p., unpin.

unpit'ied, adj., pitied by no one.

unpit'ying, adj., showing no pity.

unplaced', adj., not placed; having no office; not in the first three in a (horse) race.

unplant'ed, *adj.,* not planted; uncolonized.

unpleas'ant, *adj.,* disagreeable.

unpleas'antly, *adv.,* disagreeably.

unpleas'antness, *n.,* the quality or state of being unpleasant.

unpleas'ing, *adj.,* disagreeable; not pleasing.

unploughed', *adj.,* not cultivated.

unpoet'ical, *adj.,* prosaic; not poetical; unimaginative.

unpol'ished, *adj.,* in the rough state; dull; rude.

unpollu'ted, *adj.,* clear; pure; not affected by pollution.

unpop'ular, *adj.,* not approved by the people; disliked.

unpopular'ity, *n.,* the state of being unpopular.

unpop'ularly, *adv.,* in an unpopular way.

unpossessed', *adj.,* not possessed or in possession of.

unpost'ed, *adj.,* not kept up to date.

unprac'tical, *adj.,* not practical; given to speculation rather than to action.

unprac'tised, *adj.,* unskilful.

unpraised', *adj.,* not praised.

unprec'edented, *adj.,* unexampled; without precedent.

unpredictabil'ity, *n.,* the quality or state of being unpredictable.

unpredict'able, *adj.,* not to be foreseen.

unprej'udiced, *adj.,* free from bias or predilections.

unpremed'itated, *adj.,* not thought out beforehand; done or said on the impulse of the moment.

unpremed'itatedly, *adv.,* impulsively.

unprepared', *adj.,* unready; not prepared.

unprepossess'ing, *adj.,* wanting in attractiveness.

unpresent'able, *adj.,* not fit to be seen.

unpresum'ing, *adj.,* modest.

unpretend'ing, *adj.,* simple; modest.

unpretend'ingly, *adv.,* modestly.

unpreten'tious, *adj.,* making no special claims; unassuming.

unprevent'able, *adj.,* cannot be prevented.

unprin'cipled, *adj.,* unscrupulous; wanting in principle.

unprint'able, *adj.,* not fit to be printed; obscene.

unprint'ed, *adj.,* not printed.

unproduc'tive, *adj.,* barren; not fertile.

unproduc'tiveness, *n.,* the state of being unproductive.

unprofes'sional, *adj.,* not professional; not showing high standards or values; amateurish.

unprofes'sionally, *adv.,* in an unprofessional way.

unprof'itable, *adj.,* not profitable; not advantageous; useless.

unprof'itably, *adv.,* in an unprofitable way.

unprogres'sive, *adj.,* not progressive.

unprojec'ted, *adj.,* not planned.

unprom'ising, *adj.,* unfavourable in appearance.

unprompt'ed, *adj.,* not prompted; unaided.

unpronounce'able, *adj.,* not able to be pronounced.

unpropi'tious, *adj.,* ill-omened; unfavourable.

unprotect'ed, *adj.,* without protection.

unproved', *adj.,* not shown to be real.

unprovi'ded, *adj.,* not provided.

unprovoked', *adj.,* not incited; spontaneous.

unpub'lished, *adj.,* not hitherto published.

unpunc'tual, *adj.,* habitually not in time.

unpunctual'ity, *n.,* failure to be exact in matters of time.

unpunc'tuated, *adj.,* without punctuation marks.

unpun'ished, *adj.,* without punishment.

unpur'chased, *adj.,* not bought.

unpur'ified, *adj.,* not purified.

unpur'posed, *adj.,* not intended.

unqual'ified, *adj.,* absolute; without conditions; not having the attainments prescribed.

unquench'able, *adj.,* not capable of being extinguished or allayed.

unques'tionable, *adj.,* beyond question; indisputable.

unques'tionably, *adv.,* indisputably.

unques'tioned, *adj.,* not called in question.

unques'tioning, *adj.,* not calling in question.

unqui'et, *adj.,* disturbed; anxious; *n.,* a state of being unquiet.

unqui'etly, *adv.,* in an unquiet way.

unracked', not drawn off the lees (liquor).

unra'tioned, *adj.,* not regulated in supply.

unrav'el, *v.t.,* to disentangle; to clarify.

unrav'elled, *p.p.,* unravel.

unrav'elling, *pr.p.,* unravel.

unrav'elment, *n.,* the state of being unravelled.

unreached', *adj.,* not reached.

unread', *adj.,* not read; illiterate.

unread'able, *adj.,* not capable of being read because of inferiority of expression or content.

unread'y, *adj.,* unprepared; not ready; slow to act.

unre'al, *adj.,* without reality; non-existent; imaginary.

unrealis'tic, *adj.,* not practical; failing to take facts into account.

unrealis'tically, *adv.,* in an unrealistic way.

unreal'ity, *n.,* the quality or state of being unreal.

unre'alizable, *adj.,* that cannot be realized.

unre'alized, *adj.,* not realized.

unrea'sonable, *adj.,* perverse; irrational.

unrea'sonableness, *n.,* the quality or state of being unreasonable.

unrea'sonably, *adv.,* in an unreasonable way.

unrea'soning, *adj.,* not actuated by reason.

unreceived', *adj.,* not received.

unrecep'tive, *adj.,* slow, dull.

unreck'oned, *adj.,* not counted.

unreclaim'able, *adj.,* unable to be reclaimed.

unrecogniz'able, *adj.,* not capable of being recognized.

unrecommend'ed, *adj.,* not recommended.

unre'compensed, *adj.,* not recompensed.

unreconcil'able, *adj.,* unforgiving; cannot be made to agree.

unrecord'ed, *adj.,* not recorded.

unrecov'erable, *adj.,* cannot be recovered.

unredeem'able, *adj.,* cannot be redeemed.

unredeemed', *adj.,* not redeemed; hopelessly bad.

unrefined', *adj.,* unpolished; ill-mannered.

unreflect'ing, *adj.,* thoughtless.

unreformed', *adj.,* not cured of bad ways.

unrefreshed', *adj.,* not refreshed.

unrefresh'ing, *adj.,* not refreshing.

unrefut'ed, *adj.,* not proved false.

unregard'ed, *adj.,* ignored.

unregen'eracy, *n.,* the state of being unregenerate.

unregen'erate, *adj.,* not regenerate; sinful; confirmed in evil ways.

unreg'istered, *adj.,* not registered.

unregret'ted, *adj.,* not regretted.

unreg'ulated, *adj.,* not regulated.

unrehearsed', *adj.,* not planned beforehand; spontaneous.

unrela'ted, *adj.,* not connected.

unrelax'ing, *adj.,* strenuous.

unrelent'ing, *adj.,* ruthless; pitiless; unforgiving.

unrelent'ingly, *adv.,* ruthlessly.

unreli'able, *adj.,* not to be relied upon.

unrelieved', *adj.,* continuous, monotonous, boring.

unremark'able, *adj.,* not meriting special notice.

unremem'bered, *adj.,* forgotten.

unremit'ting, *adj.,* never relaxing; continuous.

unremit'tingly, *adv.,* continuously.

unremorse'ful, *adj.,* without remorse or pity.

unremorse'fully, *adv.,* pitilessly.

unremov'able, *adj.,* cannot be removed.

unremu'nerative, *adj.,* bringing no reward.

unrepeat'able, *adj.,* unfit to be spoken; cannot be repeated.

unrepen'tant, *adj.,* not showing regret or remorse.

unrepent'ing, *adj.,* not repenting.

unreport'ed, *adj.,* not reported.

unrepresent'ed, *adj.,* not represented.

unrepressed', *adj.,* not checked.

unreprieved', *adj.,* not reprieved.

unrequest'ed, *adj.,* not asked.

unrequired', *adj.,* not wanted.

unrequi'ted, *adj.,* unrewarded; not reciprocated.

unreserve', *n.,* a want of reserve.

unreserved', *adj.,* not reserved; frank.

unreserv'edly, *adv.,* without reserve or qualification.

unresist'ing, *adj.,* not offering resistance; passive.

unresolved', *adj.,* left unanswered, unsolved.

unrest', *n.,* disquietude.

unrest'ing, *adj.,* restless; without pause.

unrestored', *adj.,* not renewed.

unrestrained', *adj.,* violent; without restraint.

unrestraint', *n.,* a want of control.

unrestrict'ed, *adj.,* without restriction.

unrestrict'edly, *adv.,* in an unrestricted way.

unrevealed', *adj.,* hidden.

unrevised', *adj.,* not corrected.

unreward'ed, *adj.,* not recompensed.

unreward'ing, *adj.,* thankless.

unrifled', *adj.,* not plundered.

unrig', *v.t.,* to remove the rigging from.

unright'eous, *adj.,* unjust; unholy.

unright'eously, *adv.,* in an unrighteous way.

unright'eousness, *n.,* wickedness; the quality or state of being unrighteous.

unripe', *adj.,* not yet ripe; immature; sour.

unri'valled, *adj.,* without a rival.

unrobe', *v.i. and t.,* to divest oneself of clothing.

unroll', *v.i.,* to unfold; *v.t.,* to spread open that which is rolled up.

unrolled', *p.p.,* unroll.

unroll'ing, *pr.p.,* unroll.

unroman'tic, *adj.,* prosaic; without sentiment.

unroof', *v.t.,* to remove the roof from.

unroofed', *p.p.,* unroof.

unroof'ing, *pr.p.,* unroof.

unruf'fled, *adj.,* calm; without a ripple; undisturbed in adverse circumstances.

unru'liness, *n.,* the state of being unruly.

unru'ly, *adj.,* disorderly; turbulent.

unsad'dle, *v.t.,* to remove the saddle from; to eject from the saddle.

unsad'dled, *p.p.,* unsaddle.

unsad'dling, *pr.p.,* unsaddle.

unsafe', *adj.,* insecure; dangerous.

unsafe'ly, *adv.,* in an unsafe way.

unsaid', *adj.,* not spoken; *p.p.,* unsay.

unsale'able, *adj.,* without the qualities which would make sale possible.

unsalt'ed, *adj.,* not salted.

unsanc'tified, *adj.,* not sanctified; unholy.

unsanc'tioned, *adj.,* not permitted.

unsan'itary, *adj.,* not conducing to health.

unsa'ted, *adj.,* not satisfied.

unsatisfac'torily, *adv.,* in an unsatisfactory way.

unsatisfac'tory, *adj.,* not giving satisfaction.

unsat'isfied, *adj.,* not having enough; doubtful.

unsat'isfying, *adj.,* not satisfying.

unsa'voury, *adj.,* not savoury; not pleasant to taste or smell; having implications of immorality.

unsay', *v.t.,* to recall what has been said.

unsay'ing, *pr.p.,* unsay.

unscal'able, *adj.,* cannot be climbed.

unscale', *v.t.*, to remove the scales from.

unscarred', *adj.*, not scarred or marked.

unscathed', *adj.*, scatheless; unharmed.

unscent'ed, *adj.*, without aroma.

unschol'arly, *adj.*, unlearned; not like a scholar.

unschooled', *adj.*, not trained; not disciplined.

unscientif'ic, *adj.*, not scientific; inexpert.

unscientif'ically, *adv.*, in an unscientific way.

unscram'ble, *v.t.*, to sort out; to decode.

unscratched', *adj.*, not scratched.

unscrew', *v.t.*, to withdraw a screw from.

unscrewed', *p.p.*, unscrew.

unscrew'ing, *pr.p.*, unscrew.

unscrip'tural, *adj.*, contrary to Holy Scripture.

unscru'pulous, *adj.*, devoid of scruples.

unscru'pulously, *adv.*, in an unscrupulous way.

unscru'pulousness, *n.*, the quality or state of being unscrupulous.

unscru'tinized, *adj.*, not closely examined.

unseal', *v.t.*, to break the seal of; to open.

unsealed', *adj.*, not sealed up; *p.p.*, unseal.

unseal'ing, *pr.p.*, unseal.

unseam', *v.t.*, to undo needlework.

unsearch'able, *adj.*, past finding out.

unsea'sonable, *adj.*, untimely; inopportune; not in season.

unsea'sonably, *adv.*, in an unseasonable way.

unsea'soned, *adj.*, not seasoned; not trained or experienced.

unseat', *v.t.*, to displace from a seat; to throw from a saddle.

unseat'ed, *p.p.*, unseat.

unseat'ing, *pr.p.*, unseat.

unseaworth'iness, *n.*, the state of being unseaworthy.

unsea'worthy, *adj.*, unfit for going to sea; leaky.

unsec'onded, *adj.*, not supported.

unsecon'ded, *adj.*, not allocated for special duty.

unsecta'rian, *adj.*, not confined to the principles of a single sect.

unsee'ing, *adj.*, unobservant.

unseem'liness, *n.*, the state of being unseemly.

unseem'ly, *adj.*, indecorous.

unseen', *adj.*, not seen; invisible; *n.*, a passage given for translation on sight.

unselfcon'scious, *adj.*, without embarrassment or awareness of self.

unself'ish, *adj.*, not selfish; considerate of others.

unself'ishly, *adv.*, in an unselfish way.

unself'ishness, *n.*, the quality or state of being unselfish.

unsentimen'tal, *adj.*, not sentimental.

unser'viceable, *adj.*, not fit for use.

unset'tle, *v.t.*, to disturb; to upset.

unset'tled, *p.p.*, unsettle.

unset'tling, *pr.p.*, unsettle.

unsex', *v.t.*, to take away the sex characteristics of.

unshack'le, *v.t.*, to remove the shackles from.

unshad'ed, *adj.*, not shaded.

unshad'owed, *adj.*, unobscured; not clouded.

unsha'kable, *adj.*, resolute, not to be shaken.

unsha'ken, *adj.*, not shaken; immovable; firm.

unshape'ly, *adj.*, not of normal shape; misshapen.

unshared', *adj.*, not shared.

unshar'pened, *adj.*, not sharpened.

unsha'ven, *adj.*, whiskery, not shaved.

unsheathe', *v.t.*, to withdraw from the sheath.

unsheathed', *p.p.*, unsheathe.

unsheath'ing, *pr.p.*, unsheathe.

unshel'tered, *adj.*, without shelter.

unshield'ed, *adj.*, unprotected.

unshift'ing, *adj.*, steadfast.

unship', *v.t.*, to disembark; to unload; to take inboard.

unshipped', *p.p.*, unship.

unship'ping, *pr.p.*, unship.

unshod', *adj.*, without shoes.

unshrink'able, *adj.*, that cannot be shrunk.

unshrink'ing, *adj.*, not shrinking; fearless.

unshrink'ingly, *adv.*, in an unshrinking way.

unsight'ed, *adj.*, not observed; without a view of an object.

unsight'liness, *n.*, the quality or state of being unsightly.

unsight'ly, *adj.*, unpleasant to the eye.

unsigned', *adj.*, not signed.

unsinged', not scorched or singed.

unsis'terly, *adj.*, not becoming a sister.

unskil'ful, *adj.*, clumsy; inexpert.

unskil'fully, *adv.*, clumsily.

unskil'fulness, *n.*, the quality or state of being unskilled.

unskilled', *adj.*, not expert; requiring no skilled effort.

unsleep'ing, *adj.*, not sleeping; watchful.

unsmil'ing, *adj.*, serious, without a smile.

unsmoked', *adj.*, not smoked.

unso'ciable, *adj.*, not companionable, shunning society.

unso'ciably, *adv.*, in an unsociable way.

unso'cial, *adj.*, not social; not convivial.

unsoiled', *adj.*, unstained; fresh; clean.

unsold', *adj.*, not sold.

unsolic'ited, *adj.*, unasked for.

unsolic'itous, *adj.*, not anxious.

unsolv'able, *adj.*, not capable of a solution.

unsolved', *adj.*, not solved.

unsophis'ticated, *adj.*, unadulterated; simple; ingenuous.

unsort'ed, *adj.*, not sorted; mixed up.

unsought', *adj.*, not sought for.

unsound', *adj.*, unhealthy; rotten.

unsound'ly, *adv.*, in an unsound way.

unsound'ness, *n.*, the quality or state of being unsound.

unsown', *adj.*, not planted with seeds.

unspa'ring, *adj.,* not sparing; generous; lavish; severe.

unspa'ringly, *adv.,* in an unsparing way.

unspeak'able, *adj.,* unutterable; shocking.

unspeak'ably, *adv.,* in an unspeakable way.

unspe'cified, *adj.,* not explicitly mentioned.

unspent', *adj.,* not spent; not wearied.

unspi'ritual, *adj.,* worldly, material.

unspoiled', *adj.,* not spoiled.

unspoilt', *adj., i.q.* unspoiled.

unspo'ken, *adj.,* not said.

unsports'manlike, *adj.,* unlike a sportsman.

unspot'ted, *adj.,* without blemish; innocent.

unsta'ble, *adj.,* unsteady; fickle.

unstained', *adj.,* without a stain.

unstamped', *adj.,* not stamped.

unstand'ardized, *adj.,* not standardized.

unstarched', *adj.,* not starched.

unstat'ed, *adj.,* not mentioned.

unstates'manlike, *adj.,* not in the manner of a statesman.

unstead'fast, *adj.,* not firm; lacking in loyalty.

unstead'fastly, *adv.,* not firmly.

unstead'ily, *adv.,* in an unsteady way.

unstead'iness, *n.,* the quality or state of being unsteady.

unstead'y, *adj.,* not steady; inclined to fall.

unstep', *v.t.,* to remove a mast.

unster'ilized, *adj.,* not sterilized; tainted.

unstick', *v.t.,* to separate what was stuck; to become airborne.

unstim'ulated, *adj.,* not moved; not excited.

unstint'ed, *adj.,* without stint; lavish.

unstint'ing, *adj.,* liberal; generous.

unstint'ingly, *adv.,* generously.

unstitch', *v.t.,* to remove the stitches from.

unstitched', *p.p.,* unstitch.

unstitch'ing, *pr.p.,* unstitch.

unstop', *v.t.,* to remove the stopper from; to open.

unstopped', *p.p.,* unstop.

unstop'ping, *pr.p.,* unstop.

unstrained', *adj.,* natural.

unstrap', *v.t.,* to undo the straps of.

unstressed', *adj.,* not emphasized.

unstretch', *v.i.,* to become relaxed.

unstring', *v.t.,* to loosen the strings of.

unstrung', *adj.,* in a state of nervous disorder; *p.p.,* unstring.

unstuck', *adj.,* separated from being stuck.

unstud'ied, *adj.,* natural; unpremeditated.

unstyl'ish, *adj.,* without style.

unsub'sidized, *adj.,* not supported by a State grant or loan.

unsubstan'tial, *adj.,* not substantial; etherial.

unsubstan'tiated, *adj.,* unproved; not borne out by facts.

unsuccess'ful, *adj.,* not succeeding.

unsuccess'fully, *adv.,* without success.

unsuit'able, *adj.,* unfitting; improper.

unsuit'ably, *adv.,* in an unsuitable way.

unsuit'ed, *adj.,* unfitted.

unsul'lied, *adj.,* unstained; pure.

unsum'moned, *adj.,* not having been summoned.

unsung', *adj.,* not sung; not celebrated in song; disregarded.

unsupport'ed, *adj.,* without support.

unsuppressed', *adj.,* not restrained or quelled; not rendered electrically non-interfering.

unsurpass'able, *adj.,* cannot be excelled.

unsurpassed', *adj.,* not exceeded.

unsuscep'tible, *adj.,* not sensitive to external influence.

unsuspect'ed, *adj.,* not suspected.

unsuspect'ing, *adj.,* not mistrustful.

unsuspect'ingly, *adv.,* without suspicion.

unsuspi'cious, *adj., i.q.* unsuspecting.

unsuspi'ciously, *adv.,* in an unsuspicious way.

unsustained', *adj.,* not sustained; not kept up.

unswal'lowed, *adj.,* not swallowed; not believed.

unswathe', *v.t.,* to remove the bandages from.

unswathed', *p.p.,* unswathe.

unswa'thing, *pr.p.,* unswathe.

unswayed', *adj.,* unmoved.

unsweet'ened, *adj.,* without sweetening.

unswept', *adj.,* not swept.

unswerv'ing, *adj.,* not deviating to either side; keeping straight on; resolute.

unswerv'ingly, *adv.,* resolutely.

unsworn', *adj.,* not solemnly declared.

unsymmet'rical, *adj.,* lacking symmetry; out of balance.

unsympathet'ic, *adj.,* wanting in sympathy.

unsympathet'ically, *adv.,* in a manner wanting in sympathy.

unsystemat'ic, *adj.,* not systematic; not methodical.

unsystemat'ically, *adv.,* unmethodically.

untack'led, *adj.,* not attempted; untried.

untact'ful, *adj.,* tactless.

untact'fully, *adv.,* tactlessly.

untaint'ed, *adj.,* without taint; not polluted.

unta'ken, *adj.,* not swallowed; not captured.

untal'ented, *adj.,* lacking in any particular skill.

untam(e)'able, *adj.,* not docile; impossible to tame.

untamed', *adj.,* wild.

untan'gle, *v.t.,* to disentangle.

untar'nished, *adj.,* unsoiled.

untast'ed, *adj.,* not tasted.

untaught', *adj.,* not taught; unlearned.

untaxed', *adj.,* not taxed.

unteach'able, *adj.,* not capable of being taught.

unten'able, *adj.,* not tenable; unable to be held.

unten'antable, *adj.,* unfit for habitation.

unten'anted, *adj.,* not habited.

untend'ed, *adj.*, uncared for.

untest'ed, *adj.*, not tested.

unteth'ered, *adj.*, untied, free.

unthanked', *adj.*, not thanked.

unthank'ful, *adj.*, ungrateful.

unthank'fully, *adv.*, ungratefully.

unthank'fulness, *n.*, ingratitude.

unthink'able, *adj.*, inconceivable.

unthink'ing, *adj.*, inconsiderate; careless.

unthink'ingly, *adv.*, in an unthinking way.

unthought'ful, *adj.*, inconsiderate.

unthought'fully, *adv.*, inconsiderately.

unthrift'ily, *adv.*, extravagantly.

unthrift'y, *adj.*, extravagant; not economizing.

unti'dily, *adv.*, in a disorderly way.

unti'diness, *n.*, disorderliness.

unti'dy, *adj.*, disorderly; slovenly.

untie', *v.t.*, to unfasten; to loose.

untied', *p.p.*, untie.

until', *conj.*, *i.q.* till; up to a specified time.

untilled', *adj.*, uncultivated.

untime'ly, *adj.*, premature; inopportune.

untir'ing, *adj.*, indefatigable.

untir'ingly, *adv.*, in an untiring way.

unti'tled, *adj.*, with no title.

un'to, *prep.*, to (*arch.*).

untold', *adj.*, not told; past all telling.

untouch'able, *adj.*, unable to be touched.

untouch'ables, *n. pl.*, the lowest Hindu caste in India.

untouched', *adj.*, unaffected.

unto'ward, *adj.*, adverse; unpleasant; unexpected.

untrace'able, *adj.*, cannot be found.

untrained', *adj.*, not trained; amateur.

untram'melled, *adj.*, free; unfettered.

untrav'elled, *adj.*, stay-at-home; lacking in experience of other places.

untrav'ersed, *adj.*, not crossed over.

untried', *adj.*, strange; new.

untrod', *adj.*, *i.q.* untrodden.

untrod'den, *adj.*, never before trodden; unexplored.

untroub'led, *adj.*, unworried; calm (waters).

untrue', *adj.*, false.

untru'ly, *adv.*, falsely.

untrust'worthy, *adj.*, cannot be relied upon.

untruth', *n.*, what is not true; a lie.

untruth'ful, *adj.*, lying.

untruth'fully, *adv.*, in an untruthful way.

untu'tored, *adj.*, undisciplined; not taught.

untwine', *v.t.*, to disentangle.

untwined', *p.p.*, untwine.

untwin'ing, *pr.p.*, untwine.

untwist', *v.t.*, to restore to its original state what has become twisted.

untwist'ed, *p.p.*, untwist.

untwist'ing, *pr.p.*, untwist.

unty'ing, *pr.p.*, untie.

unused', *adj.*, not previously used; new; unaccustomed.

unu'sual, *adj.*, out of the ordinary.

unu'sually, *adv.*, in an unusual way or degree.

unut'terable, *adj.*, unspeakable.

unut'terably, *adv.*, unspeakably.

unval'ued, *adj.*, not valued.

unva'ried, *adj.*, without varying.

unvar'nished, *adj.*, not varnished; plain, not embellished.

unva'rying, *adj.*, unchanging.

unveil', *v.t.*, to remove the veil from; to reveal; to disclose.

unveiled', *adj.*, not wearing a veil; *p.p.*, unveil.

unveil'ing, *pr.p.*, unveil.

unven'tilated, *adj.*, not ventilated.

unver'ified, *adj.*, not proved to be true.

unversed', *adj.*, unskilled.

unvoiced', *adj.*, not involving the use of the vocal chords; unspoken.

unwa'rily, *adv.*, incautiously.

unwa'riness, *n.*, the state of being unwary.

unwar'like, *adj.*, not warlike.

unwarned', *adj.*, not cautioned.

unwarped', *adj.*, not prejudiced; not warped.

unwar'rantable, *adj.*, without any justification.

unwar'rantably, *adv.*, in an unwarrantable way.

unwar'ranted, *adj.*, without warrant or justification.

unwa'ry, *adj.*, lacking caution.

unwash'able, *adj.*, unable to be washed.

unwashed', *adj.*, not washed.

unwast'ed, *adj.*, not wasted.

unwatched', *adj.*, unguarded.

unwa'tered, *adj.*, not watered; arid.

unwa'vering, *adj.*, unhesitating.

unwa'veringly, *adv.*, steadily, firmly.

unweak'ened, *adj.*, unimpaired.

unweaned', *adj.*, not weaned.

unwea'ried, *adj.*, indefatigable; not tired.

unwear'iedly, *adv.*, indefatigably.

unwear'y, *adj.*, *i.q.* unwearied.

unweary'ing, *adj.*, tireless.

unweave', *v.t.*, to take to pieces what is woven.

unweav'ing, *pr.p.*, unweave.

unwed', *adj.*, not married.

unweighed', *adj.*, not weighed.

unwel'come, *adj.*, not acceptable; not welcomed.

unwell', *adj.*, indisposed; sick.

unwept', *adj.*, not wept for.

unwhole'some, *adj.*, not wholesome; indigestible; lacking goodness.

unwhole'someness, *n.*, the quality or state of being unwholesome.

unwield'iness, *n.*, the state of being unwieldy.

unwield'y, *adj.*, big and clumsy; awkward to handle.

unwil'ling, *adj.*, reluctant; not willing.

unwil'lingly, *adv.*, in an unwilling way; against one's will.

unwil'lingness, *n.*, the state of being unwilling.

unwind', *v.i.*, to relax; *v.t.*, to loosen what is wound up.

unwind'ing, *pr.p.*, unwind.

unwise', *adj.*, not wise; indiscreet; foolish; imprudent.

unwise'ly, *adv.*, in an unwise way.

unwit'nessed, *adj.*, not seen; not attested.

unwit'tingly, *adv.*, without one's knowledge.

unwom'anly, *adj.*, not as a woman should be or do.

unwont'ed, *adj.*, unaccustomed; unusual.

unwont'edness, *n.*, the quality or state of being unwonted.

unword'ed, *adj.*, not expressed in words.

unwork'able, *adj.*, not practicable.

unwork'manlike, *adj.*, not well-made; unskilful.

unworld'liness, *n.*, the state of being unworldly.

unworld'ly, *adj.*, not given up to worldly pleasures; spiritual.

unworn', *adj.*, never yet worn; new; not worn out.

unwor'ried, *adj.*, not perturbed; relaxed.

unwor'thily, *adv.*, in an unworthy way.

unwor'thiness, *n.*, the quality or state of being unworthy.

unwor'thy, *adj.*, undeserving.

unwound', *p.p.*, unwind.

unwove', *p.p.*, unweave.

unwo'ven, *adj.*, not woven; *p.p.*, unweave.

unwrap', *v.t.*, to take off wrappings; to open; to unfold.

unwrit'ten, *adj.*, not put down in writing; implicit.

unwrought', *adj.*, not wrought; unworked.

unyield'ing, *adj.*, inflexible.

unyield'ingly, *adv.*, obstinately.

unyoke', *v.t.*, to remove the yoke from.

up, *adv.*, against gravity; upwards; from below to above.

u'pas, *n.*, a poisonous Javanese tree.

up'beat, *n.*, the upward movement of a conductor's hand when conducting; the unaccented part of a musical bar.

upbraid', *v.t.*, to reproach.

upbraid'ed, *p.p.*, upbraid.

upbraid'er, *n.*, one who upbraids.

upbraid'ing, *n.*, reproach; *pr.p.*, upbraid.

upbraid'ingly, *adv.*, reproachfully.

up'bringing, *n.*, education, early training.

upcast', *adj.*, pointed upwards; *n.*, a ventilating shaft in a mine.

up-coun'try, *n.*, the heart of a country.

up-end', *v.t.*, to put a thing on its end; to tip a thing over.

up'grade, *v.t.*, to raise in status, health, etc.

up'graded, *p.p.*, upgrade.

up'grading, *pr.p.*, upgrade.

upheav'al, *n.*, a general commotion; widespread change of state or position.

upheave', *v.t.*, to heave up; to lift up with a thrust from below.

upheaved', *p.p.*, upheave.

upheav'ing, *pr.p.*, upheave.

upheld', *p.p.*, uphold.

uphill', *adj.*, going uphill; laborious; *adv.*, climbing upwards.

uphold', *v.t.*, to support; to maintain.

uphold'er, *n.*, one who upholds.

uphold'ing, *pr.p.*, uphold.

uphol'ster, *v.t.*, to put coverings on furniture; to supply a house with furnishings.

uphol'sterer, *n.*, one who is expert in covering furniture.

uphol'stery, *n.*, an upholsterer's business; house-furnishing.

up'keep, *n.*, maintenance.

up'land, *adj.*, pert. or rel. to the hills; *n.*, high ground.

uplift', *v.t.*, to lift up; to exalt; to elevate; *n.*, support; mental or emotional stimulation.

uplift'ed, *adj.*, being above oneself; *p.p.*, uplift.

uplift'ing, *adj.*, inspiring; elevating; *pr.p.*, uplift.

up'most, *adj.*, *i.q.* uppermost.

upon', *prep.*, on; on the surface of; in regard to.

up'per, *adj.*, higher.

up'permost, *adj.*, super. of upper.

uppers, *n. pl.*, the parts of footwear above the soles.

up'pish, *adj.*, vain, arrogant, overweening.

up'pishly, *adv.*, with affected and pretentious superiority.

up'pishness, *n.*, the state of being uppish.

upraise', *v.t.*, to raise up; to lift up.

upraised', *p.p.*, upraise.

uprais'ing, *pr.p.*, upraise.

uprear', *v.i.* and *t.*, to rear up.

upreared', *p.p.*, uprear.

uprear'ing, *pr.p.*, uprear.

up'right, *adj.*, erect; vertical; honest; *n.*, a support; a piano with vertically placed strings.

upright'ly, *adv.*, in an upright way.

upright'ness, *n.*, the quality or state of being upright.

uprise', *v.i.*, to rise up; to spring up.

upris'en, *p.p.*, uprise.

upris'ing, *n.*, a rising-up; *pr.p.*, uprise.

up-riv'er, *adj.*, towards a river's source.

up'roar, *n.*, a din; a tumult.

uproar'ious, *adj.*, boisterous; noisy.

uproar'iously, *adv.*, noisily.

uproot', *v.t.*, to pull up by the roots; to dislodge; to eradicate.

uproot'ed, *p.p.*, uproot.

uproot'ing, *n.*, a disturbance, a move (*colloq.*); *pr.p.*, uproot.

uprose', *p.p.*, uprise.

up'rush, *n.*, a sudden rise into consciousness.

up'saddle, *v.i.*, to saddle a horse (in S. Africa).

upset', *v.t.*, to overthrow; to disturb; to affect seriously.

up'set, *adj.*, fixed; *n.*, the act of upsetting; a disturbance; a state of being upset; temporary indisposition.

upset'ting, *adj.*, disquieting; *pr.p.*, upset.

upset'tingly, *adv.*, in a way so as to cause distress or anxiety.

up'shot, *n.*, the final issue; the result or purport.

upside'-down', *adj.* and *adv.*, bottom upwards; the wrong way up; in confusion.

upspring', *v.i.*, to spring up.

up'stage', *adj.* and *adv.*, near the back of the stage; aloof, reserved.

upstairs', *adv.*, in a position in a building above the level referred to; above stairs.

up'standing, *adj.*, erect; honest.

upstart', *v.i.*, to start up.

up'start, *n.*, one who has too suddenly emerged from obscurity.

up'-stream, *adj.*, near the upper part of a river; *adv.*, against a river's current.

up'stroke, *n.*, an upward stroke with a pen or pencil.

up'surge, *n.*, a rapid rise.

up'swing, *n.*, a change of direction upwards.

up'take, *n.*, comprehension; a ventilating flue.

up'throw, *n.*, an upward fault in the surface of the earth (*geol.*).

up'tight, *adj.*, tense, mentally hostile.

up'town, *adj.*, rel. to the part of a city away from the centre (*Amer.*).

up'-train, *n.*, a train going in the direction of the capital.

upturn', *v.t.*, to overthrow.

upturned', *adj.*, turned upwards; *p.p.*, upturn.

upturn'ing, *pr.p.*, upturn.

up'ward, *adj.*, tending towards a higher level.

up'wards, *adv.*, towards a higher level.

up'-wind, *adv.*, against the wind.

urae'mia, *n.*, the morbid condition of waste matter retained in the blood.

urae'mic, *adj.*, pert. or rel. to uraemia.

urae'us, *n.*, a snake headdress of Egyptians.

Ura'lian, *adj.*, pert. or rel. to the Ural Mountains in Russia.

ura'nium, *n.*, a very hard metallic element.

uranog'raphy, *n.*, the description of the heavens; the art of making celestial maps, etc.

uranol'ogy, *n.*, the science of the heavens.

uranom'etry, *n.*, the measurement of star distances.

uranos'copy, *n.*, the surveying of the heavens.

Uran'us, *n.*, a planet situated between Neptune and Saturn.

u'rate, *n.*, a uric acid salt.

ur'ban, *adj.*, pert. or rel. to the town as distinct from the country.

urbane', *adj.*, polite; courteous; cultivated.

urbane'ly, *adv.*, politely.

ur'banism, *n.*, town planning; the science of town life.

ur'banist, *n.*, a specialist in urbanism.

ur'banite, *n.*, a towndweller.

urban'ity, *n.*, politeness; polished and sophisticated behaviour.

ur'ceolate, *adj.*, pitchershaped (*bot.*).

ur'chin, *n.*, a small boy; a hedgehog.

Ur'du, *n.*, Hindustani, a language spoken in India and Pakistan.

ure'a, *n.*, the chief constituent of urine.

ure'ter, *n.*, one of the urinary ducts.

ure'thra, *n.*, the duct by which urine is voided.

urge, *v.t.*, to push; to impel; to encourage; to advise.

urged, *p.p.*, urge.

ur'gency, *n.*, the state of being urgent.

ur'gent, *adj.*, insistent; imperative; immediately important.

ur'gently, *adv.*, in an urgent way.

ur'ger, *n.*, one who urges.

ur'ging, *pr.p.*, urge.

u'ric, *adj.*, pert. or rel. to urea.

U'rim, *n. pl.*, one of the oracular ornaments (Urim and Thummim) worn by the Jewish High Priests.

u'rinal, *n.*, a place for urinating.

u'rinary, *adj.*, pert. or rel. to urine.

u'rinate, *v.i.*, to void urine.

u'rinated, *p.p.*, urinate.

u'rinating, *pr.p.*, urinate.

urina'tion, *n.*, the process of urinating.

u'rinative, *adj.*, promoting the flow of urine.

u'rine, *n.*, a kidney excretion, the waste from the liquid intake of the body.

u'rinous, *adj.*, *i.q.* urinary.

urn, *n.*, a vessel enlarged centrally and having a foot or base pedestal; a vase for holding water; a receptacle for the ashes of the dead.

urn'-shaped, *adj.*, shaped like an urn.

urol'ogy, *n.*, the study of urine and urination.

uros'copy, *n.*, the examination of urine for the purposes of diagnosis.

Ur'sa Ma'jor, *n.*, the Great Bear, a constellation.

Ur'sa Mi'nor, *n.*, the Little Bear, a constellation.

ur'siform, *adj.*, like a bear.

ur'sine, *adj.*, pert. or rel. to bears.

urs'on, *n.*, a N. American porcupine.

Ur'suline, *adj.*, bel. to the Roman Catholic Order of St. Ursula.

Ur'tica, *n.*, a plant genus which includes the nettle.

urtica'ria, *n.*, nettlerash.

ur'ticate, *v.t.*, to sting with nettles.

urtica'tion, *n.*, a stinging sensation.

ur'ubu, *n.*, a black vulture found in Central and S. America.

Uruguay'an, *adj. n.*, pert. or rel. to Uruguay; a native of U.

u'rus, *n., i.q.* aurochs, a primitive ox.

us, *pron. pers.,* the objective case of we.

u'sable, *adj.,* able to be used.

u'sage, *n.,* custom; treatment.

u'sance, *n.,* the stated period for paying bills of exchange.

use, *n.,* the act of using; custom; treatment; advantage.

use, *v.i.,* to be wont; *v.t.,* to employ; to put to use; to treat; to accustom.

used, *adj.,* accustomed; *p.p.,* use.

use'ful, *adj.,* serviceable; advantageous.

use'fully, *adv.,* in a useful way.

use'fulness, *n.,* the quality or state of being useful.

use'less, *adj.,* of no use.

use'lessly, *adv.,* to no purpose.

use'lessness, *n.,* the quality or state of being useless.

u'ser, *n.,* one who uses; the enjoyment of a right without ownership (*leg.*).

ush'er, *n.,* a doorkeeper; formerly an undermaster in a school; an officer in a law court, etc.; *v.t.,* to introduce; to show into.

ush'ered, *p.p.,* usher.

usherette', *n.,* a girl attendant in a cinema or theatre.

ush'ering, *pr.p.,* usher.

u'sing, *pr.p.,* use.

us'quebaugh, *n.,* whisky (*Ir.*).

ust'ion, *n.,* burning.

ustula'tion, *n.,* searing.

u'sual, *adj.,* customary; ordinary.

u'sually, *adv.,* customarily; commonly.

usucap'tion, *n.,* the right to title or property for a fixed term (*leg.*).

u'sufruct, *n.,* benefit arising from possession (*leg.*).

usufruct'uary, *adj.,* in temporary possession.

u'surer, *n.,* one who practises usury; an extortioner.

usu'rious, *adj.,* pert. or rel. to usury; practising usury; money-grasping.

usu'riously, *adv.,* in an usurious way.

usurp', *v.t.,* to take unlawful possession of.

usurpa'tion, *n.,* the act of usurping.

usurped', *p.p.,* usurp.

usurp'er, *n.,* one who usurps.

usurp'ing, *pr.p.,* usurp.

usurp'ingly, *adv.,* in a usurping way.

u'sury, *n.,* lending money at interest; extortion.

uten'sil, *n.,* a domestic or culinary appliance.

u'terine, *adj.,* pert. or rel. to the womb; having a common mother but another father.

uteri'tis, *n.,* inflammation of the womb.

u'terus, *n.,* the womb (*Lat.*).

utilita'rian, *adj.,* pert. or rel. to utility; *n.,* one who professes utilitarianism.

utilita'rianism, *n.,* the doctrine of shaping policy to attain the greatest good for the greatest number.

util'ity, *n.,* advantage; usefulness.

u'tilizable, *adj.,* able to be used.

utiliza'tion, *n.,* the act or result of utilizing.

u'tilize, *v.t.,* to put to use.

u'tilized, *p.p.,* utilize.

u'tilizer, *n.,* one who uses.

u'tilizing, *pr.p.,* utilize.

ut'most, *adj.,* furthest; to the largest extent.

uto'pia, *n.,* an imagined country of ideal social and economic conditions.

uto'pian, *adj.,* pert. or rel. to utopia; visionary; ideal.

uto'pianism, *n.,* idealism in politics and social affairs.

u'tricle, *n.,* a cell with a thin wall; fruit thin-skinned and with a single cell.

utric'ular, *adj.,* pert. or rel. to the utricle.

ut'ter, *adj.,* complete; absolute; without qualification; *v.t.,* to publish; to speak; to pronounce; to put into circulation.

ut'terable, *adj.,* able to be uttered.

ut'terance, *n.,* speech; a manner of speaking.

ut'tered, *p.p.,* utter.

ut'terer, *n.,* one who utters.

ut'tering, *pr.p.,* utter.

ut'terly, *adv.,* entirely; absolutely.

ut'termost, *adj.,* extreme.

u'vea, *n.,* a layer of the iris.

u'veous, *adj.,* like a grape.

u'vula, *n.,* the fleshy appendage of the soft palate, used in speech.

u'vular, *adj.,* pert. or rel. to the uvula.

uvuli'tis, *n.,* inflammation of the uvula.

uxo'rial, *adj.,* pert. or rel. to a wife.

uxo'rious, *adj., i.q.* uxorial; doting on a wife.

uxo'riously, *adv.,* in an uxorious way.

uxo'riousness, *n.,* the state of being uxorious.

Uz'beg, *n., i.q.* Uzbek.

Uz'bek, *n.,* a Turk of Central Asia; his language.

V

vac, n., the abbrev. for vacation for schools, universities, etc.

va'cancy, n., emptiness; the state of being vacant; an office without its incumbent; an empty space.

va'cant, adj., empty; unoccupied; unintellectual.

va'cantly, adv., in a vacant way.

vacate', v.t., to leave unoccupied; to resign (an office).

vaca'ted, p.p., vacate.

vaca'ting, pr.p., vacate.

vaca'tion, n., the act of vacating; a time of holiday.

vaca'tionist, n., one who is on vacation.

vac'cinal, adj., pert. or rel. to vaccine or vaccination.

vac'cinate, v.t., to inoculate with vaccine lymph; to protect against disease.

vac'cinated, p.p., vaccinate.

vac'cinating, pr.p., vaccinate.

vaccina'tion, n., the act of vaccinating.

vac'cinator, n., one who performs vaccination.

vac'cine, adj., pert. or rel. to cows; n., vaccine lymph.

vaccin'ia, n., cowpox.

vac'cinist, n., one who supports the practice of vaccination.

Vaccin'ium, n., a genus of plants including the bilberry.

vac'illancy, n., i.q. vacillation.

vac'illant, adj., vacillating.

vac'illate, v.i., to waver; to fluctuate in mind.

vac'illated, p.p., vacillate.

vac'illating, pr.p., vacillate.

vac'illatingly, adv., in an uncertain way.

vacilla'tion, n., the state of being unsteady in mind. (Also vacillancy.)

vacua, n. pl., vacuum.

vacu'ity, n., emptiness; the state of being vacuous.

vac'uole, n., a small cavity containing air or fluid.

vac'uous, adj., empty; brainless; with an unintellectual look.

vac'uously, adv., in a vacuous way.

vac'uousness, n., the state of being vacuous.

vac'uum, n., a void space.

vac'uum-clea'ner, n., a cleaner which removes dust and dirt by a suction action.

vac'uum-flask', n., a container with a double wall round a vacuum so that the contents of the inner receptacle retains its original temperature.

va'de-me'cum, n., a pocket guide. (Lat. = go with me.)

vag'abond, adj., vagrant; good for nothing; n., a vagrant; a ne'er-do-well.

vag'abondage, n., the state of being a vagabond.

vag'abondish, adj., like a vagabond.

vag'abondism, n., i.q. vagabondage.

vag'abondize, v.i., to act as a vagrant.

vag'abondry, n., the class of vagabonds.

vaga'ry, n., an eccentric proceeding; a whim.

vagi'na, n., a sheath (Lat., bot.); the female sex passage (anat.).

vagi'nal, adj., pert. or rel. to the vagina.

vag'inate, adj., having a sheath.

vag'inated, adj., i.q. vaginate.

vag'initis, n., inflammation of the vagina (med.).

vag'otomy, n., section of the vagus nerve (med.).

va'grancy, n., the state of being a vagrant.

va'grant, adj., wandering; homeless; n., one who lives a wandering, unsettled life.

va'grantly, adv., in a wandering way.

vague, adj., obscure; uncertain; indefinite; hazy.

vague'ly, adv., in a vague way.

vague'ness, n., the quality or state of being vague.

va'gus, n., the nerve rel. to the lungs and stomach (anat.).

vail, n., submission; a parting gift to a servant; v.i., to give way; v.t., to lower in respect.

vain, adj., useless; without result; ineffectual; conceited.

vain'er, adj., comp. of vain.

vain'est, adj., super. of vain.

vainglo'rious, adj., boastful; ostentatious.

vainglo'riously, adv., boastingly.

vain'glo'ry, n., boastfulness; self-glorification.

vain'ly, adv., to no purpose; conceitedly.

vain'ness, n., the state of being vain.

vair, n., fur (her.).

vair'y, adj., furry; furred (her.).

Vai'sya, n., a Hindu caste.

vai'vode, n., the title of a prince in Roumania and other countries. (Also voivode.)

vakeel', n., an Indian attorney; a delegate.

val'ance, n., drapery hanging from a bed.

vale, n., i.q. valley, but broader and less steep.

va'le, v.i., imperative mood = farewell (Lat.).

valedic'tion, n., a farewell.

valedic'tory, adj., bidding farewell.

va'lence, n., the combining powers of an atom (chem.).

Valenciennes', *n.*, a special kind of lace (*Fr.*).

va'lency, *n.*, a unit of capacity to combine chemically (*chem.*).

val'entine, *n.*, a sweetheart; a gift, especially an anonymous affectionate card, sent on St. Valentine's Day, 14 Feb.

Valentin'ian, *n.*, a follower ·of Valentinus, an Egyptian gnostic.

vale'rian, *n.*, a medicinal plant.

val'et, *n.*, a male personal attendant or body-servant; *v.t.*, to attend upon (*Fr.*).

vale'ta, *n.*, *i.q.* veleta.

valetudina'rian, *adj.*, pert. or rel. to sickness and health; *n.*, a confirmed invalid.

valetudina'rianism, *n.*, excessive and habitual worrying about one's health.

valetu'dinary, *adj.*, *i.q.* valetudinarian.

val'gus, *n.*, a kind of club-foot (*Lat.*).

Valhal'la, *n.*, the place of dead heroes, according to Scandinavian mythology.

val'iance, *n.*, valour, courage.

val'iant, *adj.*, brave; stout-hearted.

val'iantly, *adv.*, heroically; stoutly.

val'id, *adj.*, strong; established; ratified; legally confirmed; having the force of reason and logic.

val'idate, *v.t.*, to ratify, to test the accuracy of; to make valid.

val'idated, *p.p.*, validate.

val'idating, *pr.p.*, validate.

valida'tion, *n.*, *i.q.* validity.

valid'ity, *n.*, the quality or state of being valid.

val'idly, *adv.*, in a valid way.

val'inch, *n.*, a sampling-tube.

valise', *n.*, a travelling case (*U.S.A.*).

Val'kyrie, *n.*, one of Odin's twelve maidens, whose mission it was to lead slain heroes to Valhalla.

vallec'ula, *n.*, a deep groove or valley.

val'ley, *n.*, lower ground between hills.

val'lum, *n.*, a rampart (*Lat.*).

val(l)o'nia, *n.*, the acorn-cup; the Holm or Scarlet Oak.

valoriza'tion, *n.*, an assessment of value.

val'orize, *v.t.*, to establish the value of.

val'orous, *adj.*, brave; heroic.

val'orously, *adv.*, in a valorous way.

val'our, *n.*, bravery; heroism.

valse, *n.* and *v.i.*, *i.q.*, waltz (*Fr.*).

val'uable, *adj.*, of worth; costly; precious.

valua'tion, *n.*, the act of appraising or estimating value; an estimate made.

val'uator, *n.*, *i.q.* valuer.

val'ue, *n.*, worth; price; *v.t.*, to appraise; to esteem.

val'ued, *p.p.*, value.

val'ueless, *adj.*, worthless.

val'uer, *n.*, one whose profession it is to appraise.

val'uing, *pr.p.*, value.

valu'ta, *n.*, standard money (*It.*).

val'vate, *adj.*, having a valve or valves (*anat.*).

valve, *n.*, a covering over an opening; a mechanical or electrical device for opening or closing a passage or allowing movement in one direction only; a division in a shell.

valved, *adj.*, closed with a valve.

valve'let, *n.*, a little valve.

valv'ular, *adj.*, like a valve.

valv'ule, *n.*, *i.q.* valvelet.

vam'brace, *n.*, armour for the forearm.

vamoos(e)', *v.i.* and *t.*, to abscond; to leave (*Span., slang*).

vamose', *v.i.*, *i.q.* vamoose.

vamp, *n.*, a boot's upper leather; a patch on an old garment, etc., intended to make it appear new; a made-up accompaniment; an adventuress; *v.t.*, to put a vamp on; to make up an accompaniment to a song; to improvise; abbrev. of *vampire* = to flirt unscrupulously.

vamped, *p.p.*, vamp.

vamp'er, *n.*, one who vamps.

vamp'ing, *pr.p.*, vamp.

vam'pire, *n.*, a nocturnal, bloodsucking ghoul.

vam'plate, *n.*, a plate to guard the hand in couching a lance.

vam'plet, *n.*, *i.q.* vamplate.

van, *n.*, the front of an army or fleet; a large vehicle for conveying goods such as furniture, etc.; a goods carriage on a train.

vana'dium, *n.*, a metallic element.

Van'dal, *n.*, one of the 5th Cent. invading barbarians who ravaged Europe and destroyed libraries, works of art, etc.

van'dal, *n.*, a senselessly destructive person.

vandal'ic, *adj.*, pert. or rel. to the Vandals.

van'dalism, *n.*, a spirit opposed to art and literature; barbarism; wanton destructiveness.

vandyke', *adj.*, pert. or rel. to the painter Vandyke and his style; *n.*, a picture by him; a particular kind of lace collar; *v.t.*, to cut an ornamental collar in points.

vane, *n.*, a weathercock.

Vanes'sa, *n.*, a genus of butterflies.

vang, *n.*, a steadying-rope (*naut.*).

van'guard, *n.*, the advance guard of an army.

vanil'la, *n.*, a flavouring made from a dried orchid-fruit.

van'ish, *v.i.*, to disappear.

van'ished, *p.p.*, vanish.

van'ishing, *pr.p.*, vanish.

van'ity, *n.*, emptiness; foolish conceit; a vain show.

van'quish, *v.t.*, to overcome; to conquer.

van'quishable, *adj.*, able to be vanquished.

van'quished, *p.p.*, vanquish.

van'quisher, *n.*, one who conquers.

van'quishing, *pr.p.*, vanquish.

van'quishment, *n.*, the state of being vanquished.

van'tage, n., advantage.

van'tage-ground, n., a position of advantage.

van'tage-point, n., i.q. vantage-ground.

vap'id, adj., tasteless; dull.

vapid'ity, n., the quality or state of being vapid.

vap'idly, adv., in a vapid way.

vaporif'ic, adj., producing vapour.

va'porizable, adj., able to be vaporized.

vaporiza'tion, n., conversion into vapour.

va'porize, v.i. and t., to turn to vapour.

va'porized, p.p., vaporize.

va'porizer, n., an apparatus for producing a fine spray.

va'porizing, pr.p., vaporize.

va'porous, adj., filled with, or resembling, vapour.

va'pour, n., the result of converting solids or liquids by means of heat; mist; v.i. to become vapour.

va'pour-bath, n., a bath of steam.

va'poured, p.p., vapour.

va'pourer, n., one who vapours; a bragger.

va'pouring, n., bragging, foolish talk; pr.p., vapour.

va'pourish, adj., like vapour, misty.

va'pours, n. pl., hysterical fancies; melancholia.

va'poury, adj., filled with vapour.

vaquero, n., a Spanish-American cattle drover.

variabil'ity, n., the quality or state of being variable.

va'riable, adj., changeable; fickle.

va'riableness, n., i.q. variability.

va'riably, adv., changeably.

va'riance, n., difference; strife.

va'riant, adj., different; n., an alternative form; a species.

varia'tion, n., the act of varying; change; deviation.

varicell'a, n., chickenpox.

var'ices, n., the pl. of varix (Lat.).

var'icocele, n., a swelling in the scrotum or spermatic cord.

var'icoloured, adj., varied in colour.

var'icose, adj., excessively swollen.

varicos'ity, n., abnormal dilation, as in varicose veins.

va'ried, p.p., vary.

va'riegate, v.t., to introduce a variety of colours in.

va'riegated, adj., multicoloured; p.p., variegate.

va'riegating, pr.p., variegate.

variega'tion, n., the act or effect of variegating.

vari'ety, n., diversity; a blend of diverse things; a peculiar kind; separate stage performances constituting a show.

va'riform, adj., of diverse form.

va'riformed, adj., i.q. variform.

vari'ola, n., smallpox.

vari'olar, adj., pert. or rel. to variola.

var'iolate, adj., pockmarked.

variola'tion, n., inoculation with smallpox virus.

var'iole, n., a pockmark.

variol'ic, adj., marked with smallpox.

va'riolite, n., a greenstone having a pustular appearance.

va'rioloid, adj., like smallpox.

vari'olous, adj., i.q. variolar.

variom'eter, n., an instrument for measuring inductances.

vario'rum, n., an edition containing the notes and opinions of different authorities (Lat.).

va'rious, adj., different; several.

va'riously, adv., differently; here and there.

va'rix, n., the distention of a vein (Lat.).

var'let, n., a footman; a scamp (hist.).

var'mint, n., a troublesome person or animal (slang).

var'nish, n., a liquid used to give a polished surface; v.t., to apply varnish to; to gloss.

var'nished, p.p., varnish.

var'nisher, n., one who varnishes.

var'nishing, pr.p., varnish.

var'sity, n., the abbrev. of university (colloq.).

var'us, n., a bandy-legged person (Lat.).

va'ry, v.i., to change; to deviate; to disagree; v.t., to alter; to diversify.

va'rying, pr.p., vary.

vas'cular, adj., containing vessels; pert. or rel. to veins and arteries.

vascular'ity, n., the quality or state of being vascular.

vasculif'erous, adj., producing vessels.

vase, n., a vessel, usually ornamental.

vasec'tomy, n., castration.

Vas'eline, n., the trade mark of a brand of petroleum jelly and other products.

vas'iform, adj., like a duct.

vas'sal, adj., in subjection; n., the tenant of a feudal lord.

vas'salage, n., the state of a vassal; servitude.

vast, adj., wide; huge; n., space; the sea.

vast'er, adj., comp. of vast.

vast'est, adj., super. of vast.

vast'ly, adv., to a vast extent.

vast'ness, n., spaciousness; extent.

vast'y, adj., vast.

vat, n., a large vessel used by brewers, etc.; (caps.) value added tax.

Vat'ican, n., the great palace of the Popes in Rome.

Vat'icanism, n., the policy of the papal curia.

va'ticide, n., the murder of a prophet; the murderer of a prophet.

vatic'inal, adj., foreboding; soothsaying.

vatic'inate, v.t., to predict.

vatic'inated, p.p., vaticinate.

vatic'inating, pr.p., vaticinate.

vaticina'tion, n., soothsaying; prediction.

vaude'ville, n., a short musical comedy; a topical song; variety entertainment.

Vaudois', adj., pert. or rel. to the Waldenses, or people of Vaud in Switzerland; n., the language of V.; n. pl., the people of V.

vault, n., an arched roof; a vaulted cellar; a tomb; a leap; v.i., to leap over, using some support; v.t., to construct an arched roof over.

vault'ed, adj., having an arched roof of masonry; p.p., vault.

vault'er, n., one who vaults.

vault'ing, pr.p., vault.

vault'ing-horse, n., gymnasium apparatus for vaulting exercises.

vaunt, n., a boast; v.i., to boast.

vaunt'ed, p.p., vaunt.

vaunt'er, n., one who vaunts.

vaunt'ing, n., boasting; pr.p., vaunt.

vaunt'ingly, adv., in a boastful way.

veal, n., calf's flesh prepared as meat.

vec'tis, n., a surgical instrument.

vec'tor, n., a line conceived to have direction and length fixed but not its position; the quantity determining position in space of one point in relation to another.

vec'tograph, n., a three-dimensional picture.

Ve'da, n., one of the Vedas, the four sacred books of the Hindus.

Vedd'a, n., a native of the Ceylon forests.

vedette', n., a sentinel on horseback (Fr.).

veer, v.i., to turn about; v.t., to cause to turn about; (of wind) to change clockwise; to slacken rope, etc. (naut.).

veered, p.p., veer.

veer'ing, adj., turning; pr.p., veer.

veer'ingly, adv., in a veering way.

Ve'ga, n., the brightest star in the Lyra constellation.

ve'ga, n., extensive, moist, grassy tracts in Spain or Cuba (Span.).

Veg'an, n., a vegetarian.

veg'etable, adj., pert. or rel. to plants; n., a plant growing in the ground; an edible plant for the table.

veg'etable-ma'rrow, n., the edible fruit of a kind of gourd.

veg'etal, adj., of the nature of a plant.

vegeta'rian, adj., pert. or rel. to a vegetable diet; n., one who adopts vegetarianism.

vegeta'rianism, n., the principle of excluding flesh, fish and fowl from the diet.

veg'etate, v.i., to grow; to sprout; to live an unintellectual, uninteresting life.

veg'etated, p.p., vegetate.

veg'etating, pr.p., vegetate.

vegeta'tion, n., the act of vegetating; plant-growth; plants collectively.

vegeta'tional, adj., pert. or rel. to vegetation.

veg'etative, adj., growing like plants.

vegete', adj., active; growing strong and healthy.

ve'hemence, n., impetuosity; vigour; passion.

ve'hemency, n., i.q. vehemence.

ve'hement, adj., impetuous; ardent; passionate.

ve'hemently, adv., in a vehement way.

ve'hicle, n., a means of conveyance; a medium.

vehic'ular, adj., pert. or rel. to vehicles.

vehm'gericht, n., an old German secret council.

veh'mic, adj., pert. or rel. to the vehmgericht.

veil, n., a covering for the head or face; anything like a veil; v.t., to cover with a veil; to conceal.

veiled, p.p., veil.

veil'ing, n., material of which veils are made; pr.p., veil.

veil'less, adj., without a veil or cover.

vein, n., a blood-vessel; a leaf-rib; a seam in a mine; mood; style; v.t., to mark with veins.

veined, p.p., vein.

vein'ing, pr.p., vein.

vein'less, adj., wanting veins.

vein'ous, adj., filled with veins.

vein'y, adj., veined.

vel'ar, adj., soft palatal.

veld(t), n., wide, open country in S. Africa.

vele'ta, n., a sequence dance. (Also valeta.)

velle'ity, n., lack of will power.

vel'licate, v.i., to twitch; v.t., to make to twitch convulsively.

vel'licated, p.p., vellicate.

vel'licating, pr.p., vellicate.

vellica'tion, n., twitching.

vel'lum, n., fine parchment.

velo'ce, adv., very quickly (It., mus.).

veloc'ipede, n., a vehicle driven by the feet.

veloc'itous, adj., very rapid.

veloc'ity, n., speed; the rate of speed.

velom'eter, n., an instrument measuring aircraft speed.

velours', n., a velvety plush material (Fr.).

velou'té, n., a rich sauce (Fr.).

veloutine', n., a velvety corded fabric.

ve'lum, n., a membranous covering (Lat.).

velure', n., plush fabric.

velut'inous, adj., velvety (bot.).

vel'vet, n., silk material with a close, soft nap.

vel'veted, adj., covered with velvet.

velveteen', n., a fabric like velvet.

vel'veting, n., collective velvet goods; velvet fabric.

vel'vety, adj., soft and smooth like velvet.

ve'nal, adj., open for sale; mercenary.

venal'ity, n., mercenariness.

venat'ic, adj., pert. or rel. to hunting.

vena'tion, n., the arrangement of veins; hunting.

vend, v.t., to sell.

ven'dace, n., a small fish found in lakes.

vend'ed, p.p., vend.

vendee', n., one to whom something is sold.

vend'er, *n.*, one who sells. (Also *vendor*.)

vendet'ta, *n.*, a system of vengeance; a blood-feud (*It.*).

vendibil'ity, *n.*, the quality or state of being vendible.

vend'ible, *adj.*, saleable; marketable.

vend'ing, *pr.p.*, vend.

vend'ing-machine', *n.*, a machine from which goods may be purchased by the insertion of coins.

vendi'tion, *n.*, the act of vending.

vend'or, *n.*, in law, chiefly a seller of lands and tenements; *i.q.* vender.

vendue', *n.*, an auction-sale (*U.S.A.*).

veneer', *n.*, a thin layer of wood, ivory, etc., laid over an inferior surface; an outer coating; external polish concealing bad qualities; *v.t.*, to cover with veneer; to gloss over.

veneered', *p.p.*, veneer.

veneer'er, *n.*, one who veneers.

veneer'ing, *n.*, the process of adding veneer; material used for veneer; *pr.p.*, veneer.

ven'erable, *adj.*, worthy of veneration; honoured for old age; the honorific title of an Archdeacon; the earliest of the three degrees in canonization.

ven'erate, *v.t.*, to regard with great reverence.

ven'erated, *p.p.*, venerate.

ven'erating, *pr.p.*, venerate.

venera'tion, *n.*, reverence.

ven'erator, *n.*, one who venerates.

vene'real, *adj.*, pert. or rel. to sexual passion or intercourse.

venereo'logy, *n.*, the study of venereal diseases.

ven'ery, *n.*, hunting; the chase; sexual indulgence.

venesec'tion, *n.*, phlebotomy; blood-letting.

Vene'tian, *adj.*, pert. or rel. to Venice and the Venetians; *n.*, a native of V., in Italy.

vene'tian-blind, *n.*, a window blind of slats of wood or plastic which are turned to admit or exclude light.

vene'tian-glass, *n.*, fine glassware made at or near Venice by Venetian glass-makers.

ven'geance, *n.*, revenge; retribution; requital.

venge'ful, *adj.*, vindictive.

venge'fully, *adv.*, in a vengeful way.

venge'fulness, *n.*, the state of being vengeful.

ve'nial, *adj.*, pardonable; excusable.

venial'ity, *n.*, the quality or state of being venial.

ve'nially, *adv.*, pardonably.

veni're, *n.*, a writ bidding the sheriff or coroner call a jury (from *venire facias*, cause to come). (*Lat.*).

ven'ison, *n.*, deer's flesh.

Ven'ite, *n.*, the 95th Psalm.

ven'om, *n.*, poison; malice; spite.

ven'omed, *adj.*, *i.q.* venomous.

ven'omous, *adj.*, containing venom; poisonous; malicious.

ven'omously, *adv.*, in a venomous way.

ve'nose, *adj.*, having marked veins (*bot.*).

ve'nous, *adj.*, full of veins; carried in the veins.

vent, *n.*, an opening for letting in or out; utterance; scent (of an animal); a sale-mark; *v.i.*, to take breath (said of a hunted animal); to sniff the air; *v.t.*, to utter; to emit.

vent'age, *n.*, a small opening.

vent'ed, *p.p.*, vent.

ven'ter, *n.*, the belly; a belly-like protuberance (*Lat.*).

vent'-hole, *n.*, *i.q.* vent.

ven'tiduct, *n.*, an air-passage.

ven'til, *n.*, a shutter arrangement within the wind-chest of an organ, regulating the admission of air.

ven'tilate, *v.t.*, to cause the air to circulate in; to make publicly known.

ven'tilated, *p.p.*, ventilate.

ven'tilating, *pr.p.*, ventilate.

ventila'tion, *n.*, the act of ventilating; public discussion.

ven'tilative, *adj.*, providing ventilation.

ven'tilator, *n.*, any appliance for freshening the air in a room or building; one who, or that which, ventilates.

vent'ing, *pr.p.*, vent.

ven'tose, *adj.*, flatulent; windy.

vent'-peg, *n.*, a peg to stop up a vent.

ven'tral, *adj.*, pert. or rel. to the abdomen; situated on the anterior surface.

ven'tricle, *n.*, a small cavity in the body.

ven'tricose, *adj.*, with a large belly; inflated.

ventrilocu'tion, *n.*, *i.q.* ventriloquism.

ventrilo'quial, *adj.*, pert. or rel. to ventriloquism.

ventril'oquism, *n.*, the art of speaking so that the voice seems to come from some other source than oneself. (Also *ventrilocution* and *ventriloquy*.)

ventril'oquist, *n.*, one who practises ventriloquism.

ventril'oquize, *v.i.*, to practise ventriloquism.

ventril'oquized, *p.p.*, ventriloquize.

ventril'oquizing, *pr.p.*, ventriloquize.

ventril'oquy, *n.*, *i.q.* ventriloquism.

ven'ture, *n.*, a hazard, attempt or trial; *v.i.* and *t.*, to attempt; to dare; to risk.

ven'tured, *p.p.*, venture.

ven'turer, *n.*, an adventurer.

ven'turesome, *adj.*, daring; taking risks; risky. (Also *venturous*.)

ven'turesomely, *adv.*, in a venturesome way.

ven'turin, *n.*, a yellow powder imitating gold.

ven'turing, *pr.p.*, venture.

ven'turous, *adj.*, *i.q.* venturesome.

ven'turously, *adv.*, in a venturous way.

ven'ue, *n.*, the place or district where a trial is appointed to be held; any location for a meeting.

ven'ulose, *adj.*, full of little veins.

Ve'nus, *n.*, the Roman goddess of love; one of the planets.

vera'cious, *adj.*, truthful.

vera'ciously, *adv.*, truthfully.

verac'ity, *n.*, truthfulness.

veran'da(h), *n.*, an open, roofed portico or gallery of a house.

vera'tria, *n.*, *i.q.* veratrine.

ver'atrine, *n.*, a compound medicine derived from hellebore and other plants, and used in cases of rheumatism and neuralgia.

verb, *n.*, a part of speech which predicates something of the subject.

ver'bal, *adj.*, pert. or rel. to a verb or to a word; spoken; oral; literal.

ver'balism, *n.*, something spoken; mere words.

ver'balist, *n.*, a merely verbal critic; one interested merely in words.

verbal'ity, *n.*, the state of being verbal.

ver'balize, *v.i.*, to be wordy; *v.t.*, to convert into a verb; to put into words.

ver'balized, *p.p.*, verbalize.

ver'balizing, *pr.p.*, verbalize.

ver'bally, *n.*, by word of mouth; word for word.

verba'tim, *adj.* and *adv.*, word for word (*Lat.*).

Verbe'na, *n.*, the vervain genus.

ver'berate, *v.t.*, to strike severely.

verbera'tion, *n.*, a severe blow.

ver'biage, *n.*, wordiness; using more words than the sense requires.

verbose', *adj.*, wordy; too fond of words.

verbose'ly, *adv.*, in a verbose style.

verbos'ity, *n.*, wordiness.

ver'dancy, *n.*, the quality or state of being verdant; greenness.

ver'dant, *adj.*, green; fresh.

verd'-antique', *n.*, a green decorative building-stone.

ver'dantly, *adv.*, in a verdant way.

ver'derer, *n.*, an official in the royal forests.

ver'dict, *n.*, the finding of a jury; judgment; a decision.

ver'digris, *n.*, a deposit on copper, brass or bronze, produced by the action of acid; green rust.

ver'diter, *n.*, one of certain pigments obtained from copper nitrate.

ver'dure, *n.*, greenness; vegetation.

ver'dured, *adj.*, covered with verdure.

ver'durous, *adj.*, *i.q.* verdured.

ver'ecund, *adj.*, shy.

verge, *n.*, the edge or brink; an emblematic wand or staff; area; *v.i.*, to border on.

verged, *p.p.*, verge.

ver'ger, *n.*, a wand-bearer; an official who bears a wand or staff before ecclesiastical and academic dignitaries; a minor church official. (Also *virger*.)

Vergil'ian, *adj.*, *i.q.* Virgilian.

ver'ging, *pr.p.*, verge.

verid'ical, *adj.*, speaking the truth.

ver'iest, *adj.*, *super.* of very.

verifiabi'lity, *n.*, the capacity to be verified.

ver'ifiable, *adj.*, capable of verification.

verifica'tion, *n.*, proving to be true; an affidavit in proof.

ver'ified, *p.p.*, verify.

ver'ify, *v.t.*, to establish the truth of; to bring to the test of truth or fact; to bear out; to add an affidavit to pleadings.

ver'ifying, *pr.p.*, verify.

ver'ily, *adv.*, truly; really.

verisim'ilar, *adj.*, probable; likely.

verisimil'itude, *n.*, likeliness; the nearness to truth; a thing resembling the reality.

ver'itable, *adj.*, genuine; actual.

ver'itably, *adv.*, actually; genuinely.

ver'itas, *n.*, the shipping register in France (like Lloyd's in England).

ver'ity, *n.*, truth; a fact; an eternally true doctrine.

ver'juice, *n.*, the juice of sour fruit.

ver'meil, *n.*, silver gilt; a varnish that produces lustre.

vermeol'ogist, *n.*, one who studies worms.

vermeol'ogy, *n.*, the study of worms.

ver'mian, *adj.*, worm-like.

vermicel'li, *n.*, a finer kind of macaroni (*It.*).

vermic'eous, *adj.*, pert. or rel. to, or resembling, worms.

ver'micide, *adj.*, destructive of worms; *n.*, a worm-killer.

vermic'ular, *adj.*, pert. or rel. to worms; like worms.

vermic'ulate, *adj.*, *i.q.* vermicular; worm-eaten; ornamented with wavy lines; *v.t.*, to ornament with wavy lines.

vermic'ulated, *p.p.*, vermiculate.

vermic'ulating, *pr.p.*, vermiculate.

vermicula'tion, *n.*, worm-like motion.

ver'micule, *n.*, a little worm.

vermic'ulous, *adj.*, worm-eaten.

ver'miform, *adj.*, like a worm.

ver'mifuge, *n.*, a remedy against worms.

vermil'ion, *n.*, cinnabar; a bright-red pigment.

ver'min, *n.*, any noxious creature, whether beast or insect; such creatures collectively.

ver'minate, *v.i.*, to produce worms or parasites.

vermina'tion, *n.*, the act or state of verminating.

vermin'icide, *n.*, poison used for vermin.

ver'minous, *adj.*, full of vermin.

vermiv'orous, *adj.*, eating worms.

ver'mouth, *n.*, a wine drink flavoured with wormwood or herbs.

vernac′ular, *adj.*, native; pert. or rel. to one's own country; local; *n.*, the language of a particular country.

vernac′ularist, *n.*, a specialist in the vernacular.

ver′nal, *adj.*, pert. or rel. to spring.

ver′nally, *adv.*, in a springlike way.

verna′tion, *n.*, the disposition of leaves with the leaf-bud (*bot.*).

Ver′nicle, *n.*, the handkerchief of St. Veronica with which she is said to have wiped Christ's face on the way to his crucifixion. (Also *Veronica*.)

ver′nicose, *adj.*, with the appearance of being varnished.

ver′nier, *n.*, a small, adjustable scale which ascertains fractional parts of the sub-divisions on a fixed scale.

ver′onal, *n.*, a poisonous, sedative drug.

Veronese′, *adj.*, pert. or rel. to Verona in Italy; *n.*, a native of V.

Veron′ica, *n.*, *i.q.* Vernicle; *n.*, a plant genus which includes the speedwell.

verru′ca, *n.*, a wart (*Lat.*).

verru′cae, *n.*, the pl. of verruca.

verr′ucose, *adj.*, warty.

verr′ucous, *adj.*, wartlike.

ver′sal, *n.*, a style of decorated letter beginning a paragraph or passage.

ver′sant, *adj.*, conversant with; *n.*, a slope of land.

ver′satile, *adj.*, able to turn one's hand to anything; apt at many pursuits; turning on a pivot.

versatil′ity, *n.*, all-round aptitude.

verse, *n.*, a metrical line; poetry; a single stanza; one of the short sections into which a chapter of the Bible is divided; a short liturgical sentence; a part of an anthem that is reserved for single voices.

versed, *adj.*, familiar with; conversant with; steeped in; proficient.

ver′sicle, *n.*, a short verse; esp. the liturgical short responses during prayers.

ver′sicolour, *adj.*, variegated; of many colours.

ver′sicoloured, *adj.*, *i.q.* versicolour.

versifica′tion, *n.*, poetry-writing; the act of versifying.

ver′sifica′tor, *n.*, a poet.

ver′sified, *p.p.*, versify.

ver′sifier, *n.*, one who makes verses, esp. poor ones.

ver′sify, *v.i.*, to compose poetry; *v.t.*, to turn into metrical writing.

ver′sifying, *pr.p.*, versify.

ver′sion, *n.*, a turning; translation; a special narration from one viewpoint.

ver′so, *n.*, the left hand page of a book; the reverse.

verst, *n.*, a Russian measure of distance (1,166 yards).

ver′sus, *prep.*, against (*Lat.*).

versute′, *adj.*, cunning; tricky.

vert, *n.*, the tincture green (*her.*); a convert to another faith (*colloq.*); all that grows green leaves in a forest, and the right to cut it (*leg.*); *v.i.*, to change one's faith (*colloq.*).

ver′tebra, *n.*, one of the segments of the backbone.

ver′tebrae, *n.*, the pl. of vertebra.

ver′tebral, *adj.*, pert. or rel. to the vertebrae.

Vertebra′ta, *n.*, the division of the animal kingdom distinguished by the possession of a spinal column (*Lat.*).

ver′tebrate, *adj.*, possessing a spinal column; *n.*, one of the Vertebrata; *v.t.*, to cause to be back-boned; to invigorate.

ver′tebrated, *adj.*, *i.q.* vertebrate; *p.p.*, vertebrate.

ver′tebrating, *pr.p.*, vertebrate.

vertebra′tion, *n.*, a formation resembling, or a division into, the spinal column.

ver′tex, *n.*, the turning point at the summit; the apex; the crown of the head.

ver′tible, *adj.*, able to be turned.

ver′tical, *adj.*, pert. or rel. to the vertex; pert. or rel. to the crown of the head; upright; at right angles to the surface of the earth.

verticality, *n.*, the state of being vertical.

ver′tically, *adv.*, uprightly; perpendicularly.

ver′tices, *n.*, the pl. of vertex.

ver′ticil, *n.*, a whorl (*bot.*, *zool.*).

vertic′illate, *adj.*, whorled.

vertig′inous, *adj.*, giddy; producing giddiness.

ver′tigo, *n.*, giddiness.

Vert′oscope, *n.*, a proprietary device for showing photographic negatives as positive.

ver′tu, *n.*, *i.q.* virtu.

ver′vain, *n.*, a weedy plant of the Verbena genus.

verve′, *n.*, spirit; enthusiasm, as shown in artistic or literary production (*Fr.*).

verv′et, *n.*, a small S. African monkey which often accompanied organ-grinders (*Fr.*).

ver′y, *adj.*, true; real; actual; *adv.*, really; in a high degree.

Ve′ry light, *n.*, a brilliant light used for signalling (after the inventor *Véry*, 1877).

vesi′ca, *n.*, a bladder; a cyst (*Lat.*).

ves′ical, *adj.*, pert. or rel. to the bladder.

ves′icant, *adj.*, blistering; *n.*, a blister.

vesi′ca pis′cis, *n.*, a fish-bladder, a name given in art to the pointed oval glory within which a pictorial representation or emblem was painted or carved.

ves′icate, *v.t.*, to blister.

ves′icated, *p.p.*, vesicate.

ves′icating, *pr.p.*, vesicate.

vesica′tion, *n.*, blistering.

ves'icatory, *adj.*, producing a blister.

ves'icle, *n.*, a small cyst.

vesic'ular, *adj.*, pert. or rel. to, or resembling, vesicles.

vesic'ulate, *adj.*, having vesicles.

vesicula'tion, *n.*, the state of having vesicles.

vesic'ulous, *adj.*, *i.q.* vesiculate.

ves'pa, *n.*, a wasp; a hornet (*Lat.*).

ves'per, *adj.*, pert. or rel. to evening; *n.*, the evening star (Venus).

ves'peral, *n.*, a book containing the chants used at vespers.

ves'pers, *n. pl.*, the last but one of the Day Hours or divine offices.

vespertil'io, *n.*, a kind of bat (*zool.*).

ves'pertine, *adj.*, pert. or rel. to the evening; opening or flying in the evening, as flowers, birds, etc.

ves'piary, *n.*, a wasps' nest.

ves'pine, *adj.*, pert. or rel. to wasps.

ves'sel, *n.*, a hollow receptacle to hold liquid; a ship; a duct or canal which conveys blood, etc. (*anat.*); a person viewed as in receipt of blessings poured into him (*religious*).

vest, *n.*, a robe; a dress; a waistcoat; a close-fitting body undergarment; *v.i.*, to assume a robe; (with the addition of *in*) to come to; *v.t.*, to robe; to bestow power or office on; to confer ownership.

Ves'ta, *n.*, the Roman goddess of the hearth.

ves'ta, *n.*, a striking match.

ves'tal, *adj.*, pert. or rel. to Vesta; chaste; *n.*, one of the Virgins who kept the sacred light in the temple of Vesta burning.

vest'ed, *adj.*, fixed without contingency; established; *p.p.*, vest.

vestia'rian, *adj.*, pert. or rel. to vestments and dress.

ves'tiary, *n.*, a place for storing vestments.

vestib'ular, *adj.*, pert. or rel. to a vestibule.

ves'tibule, *n.*, a porch; an entrance-chamber; anatomically, a connecting chamber.

vestib'ulum, *n.*, *i.q.* vestibule (*Lat.*).

ves'tige, *n.*, a trace; a footmark; an atrophied organ.

vestig'ial, *adj.*, pert. or rel. to a trace.

vest'ing, *pr.p.*, vest.

vest'ment, *n.*, a robe; dress or garment.

vest'ments, *n. pl.*, Eucharistic robes.

ves'try, *n.*, a room in a church where the clergy and others robe; the collective ratepayers of a parish; their assembly. (Also *revestry*.)

ves'tryman, *n.*, a member of the vestry.

ves'ture, *n.*, clothing; raiment.

ves'tured, *adj.*, robed.

ves'turer, *n.*, a church official.

vesu'vian, *adj.*, pert. or rel. to Mt. Vesuvius, an Italian volcano; volcanic; *n.*, a fusee.

vet, *n.*, a veterinary surgeon (*colloq.*); *v.t.*, to check for accuracy and acceptability (*colloq.*).

vetch, *n.*, a bean-like plant, much used for forage.

vet'eran, *adj.*, of old standing; experienced; *n.*, an old soldier or sailor; one who has grown old in any service or employment.

veterina'rian, *adj.*, pert. or rel. to veterinary practice.

vet'erinary, *adj.*, pert. or rel. to the treatment of diseases in animals; *n.*, a veterinary surgeon.

vet'iver, *n.*, a sweet-smelling grass.

ve'to, *n.*, the right of vetoing; the act of vetoing; a prohibition; *v.t.*, to forbid; to prohibit officially; to throw out a measure.

ve'toed, *p.p.*, veto.

ve'toer, *n.*, one who vetoes.

ve'toing, *pr.p.*, veto.

ve'toist, *n.*, *i.q.* vetoer.

vet'ted, *p.p.*, vet.

vet'ting, *pr.p.*, vet.

vettu'ra, *n.*, a four-wheeled carriage (*It.*).

vetturi'no, *n.*, the driver of a vettura (*It.*).

vex, *v.t.*, to annoy; to harass or tease.

vexa'tion, *n.*, the act of vexing; disappointment.

vexa'tious, *adj.*, annoying; disappointing. (Also *vexing*.)

vexa'tiously, *adv.*, in a vexatious way.

vexed, *p.p.*, vex.

vex'er, *n.*, one who vexes.

vex'il, *n.*, *i.q.* vexillum.

vex'illar, *adj.*, pert. or rel. to a vexillum.

vex'illary, *n.*, a standard-bearer.

vexilla'tion, *n.*, a Roman army division grouped under one standard.

vexil'lum, *n.*, a Roman military standard; a feather's vane; the large upper petal of a papilionaceous flower; the pennon sometimes hung round a bishop's crozier; a processional cross, etc. (*Lat.*; also *vexil*.)

vex'ing, *adj.*, *i.q.* vexatious; *pr.p.*, vex.

vex'ingly, *adv.*, in a vexing way.

vi'a, *n.*, a road; a way.

vi'a, *prep.*, "by the way of," "through" (*Lat.*).

viabil'ity, *n.*, the quality or state of being viable.

vi'able, *adj.*, able to maintain life; workable; capable of effecting a purpose.

vi'aduct, *n.*, a road supported on arches and carried across a valley or a depression in the country.

vi'al, *n.*, *i.q.* phial.

viam'eter, *n.*, an appliance for measuring distance travelled.

vi'and, *n.*, food; meat.

viat'ic, *adj.*, pert. or rel. to a journey.

viat'ical, *adj.*, *i.q.* viatic.

viat'icum, *n.*, the last sacrament (a rite for one setting out on a journey); a portable altar; provisions for a journey.

via′tor, n., a traveller (Lat.).

vi′bex, n., a weal (Lat.).

vi′bices, n. pl., vibex.

vi′brant, adj., vibrating; resounding.

vi′brate, v.i., to oscillate; to quiver.

vi′brated, p.p., vibrate.

vi′bratile, adj., tending to vibrate.

vi′brating, pr.p., vibrate.

vibra′tion, n., the act of vibrating; resonance.

vi′brative, adj., i.q. vibratory.

vibra′to, adj. and n., a tremulous effect in music (It.).

vibra′tor, n., a device for producing vibration.

vi′bratory, adj., making vibrations.

vibriss′ae, n. pl., stiff hairs round the mouth and nostrils.

vib′roscope, n., an instrument for measuring vibrations.

Vibur′num, n., a genus of shrubs including the guelder-rose and kindred plants.

vic′ar, n., a parish priest.

vic′arage, n., the benefice or the residence of a vicar.

vic′aress, n., formerly the wife of a vicar; now the one below the mother superior or abbess in a convent.

vica′rial, adj., pert. or rel. to a vicar and a vicar's tithes.

vica′riate, n., the office, and tenure of office, of a vicar.

vica′rious, adj., in substitution; done by deputy.

vica′riously, adv., by deputy.

vice, n., a fault; an evil habit; a clamp for firmly holding in its place anything that has to be worked upon. The word is also used as a prefix = in place of; deputy.

vi′ce = a Lat. ablative = in place of.

vice-ad′miral, n., an admiral of the second rank; the next to a full admiral.

vice-chair′man, n., a deputy chairman.

vice-cham′berlain, n., a deputy chamberlain.

vice′-chan′cellor, n., a chancellor's deputy.

vice-con′sul, n., a consul's deputy.

vicege′rency, n., the office, and tenure of office, of a vicegerent.

vicege′rent, n., one who is deputed to exercise another's authority.

vice-gov′ernor, n., a governor's deputy.

vic′enary, adj., containing twenty.

vicen′nial, adj., pert. or rel. to a period of twenty years.

vice-pre′sidency, n., the office, and tenure of office, of a vice-president.

vice-pres′ident, n., one who ranks after a president.

vice-prin′cipal, n., the second in command of an institution presided over by a principal.

vice-re′gal, adj., pert. or rel. to a viceroy.

vicere′gent, n., one who acts in place of a regent.

vice′reine, n., the wife of a viceroy.

vice′roy, n., the king's deputy in a subject or united country.

viceroy′alty, n., the office or jurisdiction of a viceroy.

vi′ce ver′sa, adverbial phrase = exactly in the reverse way (Lat.).

vic′inage, n., neighbourhood.

vic′inal, adj., neighbouring.

vicin′ity, n., neighbourhood; proximity.

vic′ious, adj., depraved; faulty.

vic′iously, adv., in a vicious way.

vic′iousness, n., the state of being vicious.

vicis′situde, n., change.

vicissitud′inous, adj., pert. or rel. to vicissitude.

vic′tim, n., a sacrifice; a person suffering from cruelty, oppression, misfortune, etc.

victimiza′tion, n., the state of being victimized.

vic′timize, v.t., to make a victim of; to make to suffer; to cheat.

vic′timized, p.p., victimize.

vic′timizing, pr.p., victimize.

vic′tor, n., a conqueror (Lat.).

victo′ria, n., victory (Lat.); an open, light carriage; a variety of large water-lily; a kind of pigeon; a red plum.

Victo′ria Cross, n., a decoration awarded for conspicuous bravery in battle, first instituted by Queen Victoria in 1856.

Victo′rian, adj., pert. or rel. to Victoria (the Australian province) or the era of Queen Victoria.

Victo′riana, n. pl., relics of the era of Queen Victoria.

victo′rianism, n., the social, ethical and artistic outlook of the Victorian age.

victorine′, n., a lady's small boa.

victo′rious, adj., conquering.

victo′riously, adv., in a victorious way.

vic′tory, n., triumph; success in battle.

vict′ual, n., food; v.t., to supply with food.

vict′ualled, p.p., victual.

vict′ualler, n., a licensed inn-keeper, who provides food as well as drink.

vict′ualling, n., a victualler's trade; pr.p., victual.

vict′uals, n. pl., food; eatables.

vicu′ña, n., a kind of S. American llama, noted for the fine quality of its fleece.

vi′de, v.t., imperative mood = see (Lat.). Abbreviated to v. and used in footnotes as an instruction.

videl′icet, adv., namely (Lat.). Normally abbreviated to viz.

vi′deo, adj. and n., of television; recorded visual transmission.

vidette′, n., i.q. vedette.

vie, v.i., to engage in rivalry.

vied, p.p., vie.

Viennese′, adj., pert. or rel. to Vienna in Austria and its inhabitants; n., a native of V.

view, *n.*, sight; scenery; the act of seeing; an opinion; a picture; *v.t.*, to inspect with the eye; to consider a situation mentally or intellectually.

viewed, *p.p.*, view.

view'er, *n.*, one who views.

view'-finder, *n.*, that part of a camera through which the photographer can see the limits of his picture.

view'ing, *pr.p.*, view.

view'less, *adj.*, without a view.

view'point, *n.*, an attitude; a position of viewing.

viges'imal, *adj.*, twentieth.

vig'il, *n.*, a watching; the eve of a feast.

vig'ilance, *n.*, watchfulness; wariness.

vig'ilant, *adj.*, watchful; wary.

vigilan'te, *n.*, a member of a vigilance committee (*Span.*).

vig'ilantly, *adv.*, warily; with vigilance.

viginten'nial, *adj.*, once in twenty years.

vignette', *n.*, a photograph or engraving not enclosed in a border; a picture of the head and bust (*archit.*); a short, summing-up of a person's character or appearance; *v.t.*, to make a vignette.

vigoros'o, *adv.*, with vigour (*It.*, *mus.*).

vig'orous, *adj.*, energetic; healthily strong.

vig'orously, *adv.*, in a vigorous way.

vig'our, *n.*, strength; energy; robust health.

vik'ing, *n.*, an armed raider from the fjords or viks of Scandinavia. (Another explanation of the name connects it with *vig* = war.)

vila'yet, *n.*, a province (*Turk.*).

vile, *adj.*, worthless; depraved.

vile'ly, *adv.*, in a vile way.

vile'ness, *n.*, the quality or state of being vile.

vi'ler, *adj.*, *comp.* of vile.

vi'lest, *adj.*, *super.* of vile.

vilifica'tion, *n.*, the act or effect of vilifying.

vil'ified, *p.p.*, vilify.

vil'ifier, *n.*, one who vilifies.

vil'ify, *v.t.*, to slander; to defame; to take away the character of.

vil'ifying, *pr.p.*, vilify.

vil'ipend, *v.t.*, to disparage (*lit.*).

vil'la, *n.*, a country residence (*Lat.*); a suburban house, detached or semidetached, with a certain amount of garden.

vil'lage, *n.*, a small settlement or community in the country.

vil'lager, *n.*, a dweller in a village.

vil'lain, *n.*, a worthless person; a scoundrel; formerly, a serf under feudal conditions.

vil'lainous, *adj.*, rascally; scoundrelly; vile.

vil'lainously, *adv.*, in a villainous way.

vil'lainy, *n.*, depravity; wickedness.

villat'ic, *adj.*, pert. or rel. to a villa; rustic.

vil'lein, *n.*, a feudal serf.

vil'leinage, *n.*, the system of serfdom; the condition of a serf.

vil'li, *n. pl.*, hairs; the hairy growth on plants.

vil'lose, *adj.*, *i.q.* villous.

villos'ity, *n.*, a covering of fine hair (*bot.*).

vil'lous, *adj.*, covered with villi.

vim, *n.*, force (*colloq.*).

vim'inal, *adj.*, pert. or rel. to shoots (*bot.*).

vimin'eous, *adj.*, *i.q.* viminal.

vi'na, *n.*, a seven-stringed, Indian musical instrument.

vina'ceous, *adj.*, pert. or rel. to vines and grapes; like grapes in colour.

vinaigrette', *n.*, a perforated box containing aromatic salts; a piquant, creamy sauce (*Fr.*).

vincibil'ity, *n.*, the quality or state of being vincible.

vin'cible, *adj.*, able to be conquered.

vin'culum, *n.*, a tie; a bond (*Lat.*).

vin'dicable, *adj.*, able to be vindicated.

vin'dicate, *v.t.*, to defend; to prove the justice or truth of; to justify.

vin'dicated, *p.p.*, vindicate.

vin'dicating, *pr.p.*, vindicate.

vindica'tion, *n.*, the act or result of vindicating.

vindic'ative, *adj.*, vindicating.

vin'dicator, *n.*, one who vindicates.

vin'dicatory, *adj.*, justifying.

vindic'tive, *adj.*, revengeful.

vindic'tively, *adv.*, in a vindictive way.

vindic'tiveness, *n.*, the quality or state of being vindictive.

vine, *n.*, the plant which produces grapes. (The name is sometimes given to other climbing plants.)

vine'-clad, *adj.*, covered with vines.

vine'dresser, *n.*, one who cultivates vines.

vin'egar, *n.*, an acid, sharp-tasting liquid produced by fermentation, and used as a condiment or pickling agent.

vi'negarish, *adj.*, like vinegar in sharpness of taste; acidulous.

vin'egary, *adj.*, tasting like vinegar.

vi'nery, *n.*, a greenhouse in which grapes are cultivated.

vine'yard, *n.*, land on which vines are cultivated.

vingt-et-un, *n.*, a gambling game with playing cards (*Fr.*).

vin'ic, *adj.*, obtained from wine.

vin'iculture, *n.*, the craft of growing vines.

vinifica'tion, *n.*, the making of grapes into wine.

vi'no-, a Latin prefix meaning "wine".

vin'ology, *n.*, the study of wines.

vino'meter, *n.*, an instrument for measuring the alcoholic content of wines.

vin or'dinaire, *n.*, a cheap wine for common use (*Fr.*).

vinos'ity, *n.*, a wine's character or flavour.

vi'nous, *adj.*, pert. or rel. to wine; addicted to wine.

vin rosé', n., a light red wine (Fr.).

vint, n., a Russian card game; v.t., to make wine.

vin'tage, n., the time of gathering the grapes for wine; the crop; the wine of a particular year.

vin'tager, n., one who gathers in the vintage.

vint'ner, n., a wine-seller.

vin'try, n., a storehouse or shop for wines.

vi'ny, adj., like a vine; full of vines.

vi'nyl, n., a chemical product used in plastics.

vi'ol, n., the family name of the violin, violoncello, etc.; specifically, the bass-viol.

Vi'ola, n., a plant genus including violets and pansies.

viol'a, n., the tenor violin.

vio'lability, n., the capacity for being violated.

vi'olable, adj., able to be violated.

viola'ceous, adj., pert. or rel. to violets.

vi'olate, v.t., to break; to transgress; to ravish.

vi'olated, p.p., violate.

vi'olating, pr.p., violate.

viola'tion, n., the act of violating.

vi'olator, n., one who violates.

vi'olence, n., the quality or state of being violent; fury; brutality.

vi'olent, adj., furious; vehement; impetuous; using uncontrolled physical force.

vi'olently, adv., in a violent way.

violes'cent, adj., with a violent tinge.

vi'olet, n., a plant of the Viola genus; the purple colour of the same.

violin', n., a wooden musical instrument, having four strings and played with a bow.

violin'ist, n., a player on a violin.

vi'olist, n., a player on the viol.

violoncel'list, n., a player on the violoncello.

violoncel'lo, n., a four-stringed bass instrument, played with a bow and held between the knees (It.).

violo'ne, n., the double-bass (mus.).

vi'per, n., a poisonous snake; a venomous person.

vi'perine, adj., pert. or rel. to, or resembling, a viper.

vi'perish, adj., spiteful, venomous.

vi'perous, adj., venomous.

vira'go, n., a violent, noisy woman.

vi'ral, adj., pert. or rel. to virus.

vire'ment, n., the transfer between accounts of money (Fr.).

vi'reo, n., a small greenish-coloured American singing bird. (Also greenlet.)

vires'cence, n., the quality or state of growing green (Lat.).

vires'cent, adj., becoming green (Lat.).

vir'gate, adj., wand-like; straight; n., an old land-measure.

vir'ger, n., i.q. verger.

Virgil'ian, adj., pert. or rel. to Virgil, the Roman poet.

vir'gin, adj., chaste; maidenly; pure; n., one who is chaste, not having had sexual intercourse; a maiden.

vir'ginal, adj., pert. or rel. to, or resembling, a virgin; n., a musical instrument like a spinet.

vir'ginhood, n., virginity.

Virgin'ia, n., one of the states of U.S.A.; a kind of tobacco.

Virgin'ia cree'per, n., a climbing plant.

Virgin'ian, adj., pert. or rel. to Virginia; a native of V.

virgin'ity, n., the quality or state of being a virgin; maidenhood.

vir'gin-soil, n., soil that has never been cultivated.

Vir'go, n., a virgin (Lat.); the name of the sixth sign of the Zodiac; a constellation.

vir'gulate, adj., like a small wand.

vir'gule, n., an oblique stroke; the old form of the comma.

vi'ricide, n., a virus-killer.

virides'cence, n., the state of becoming green.

virides'cent, adj., becoming green.

virid'ity, n., greenness.

vir'ile, adj., manly; masculine; vigorous.

viril'ity, n., manliness; the masculine character; sexual vigour.

virol'ogy, n., the study of viruses.

virtu', n., the skill of an artist; a work of art; a curio. (Also vertu.)

vir'tual, adj., equal in effect, though not actual.

vir'tualism, n., the doctrine of Christ's physical presence in the Eucharist.

vir'tuality, n., the quality or state of being virtual; potential existence.

vir'tually, adv., essentially, though not actually; to all intents and purposes.

vir'tue, n., goodness; merit; purity; essential spirit.

virtuo'sity, n., exceptional skill, esp. in music.

virtuo'so, n., an expert in an art; specifically, a fine player on a musical instrument (It.).

vir'tuous, adj., good; pure.

vir'tuously, adv., in a virtuous way.

vir'tuousness, n., the quality or state of being virtuous.

vir'ulence, n., the quality or state of being virulent.

vir'ulent, adj., venomous; bitter; spiteful.

vir'ulently, adv., in a virulent way.

vi'rus, n., poison (Lat.); a sub-microscopic organism producing illness or disease.

vis, n., power (Lat.).

visa', n., the confirmation of a passport; v.t., to endorse a passport after examination (Fr.).

vi'saed, p.p., visa.

vis'age, n., countenance.

vis-à-vis′, *adv.*, face to face; in relation to an opposite viewpoint; *n.*, an opposite neighbour (*Fr.*).

viscach′a, *n.*, a S. American burrowing rodent with a valuable fur.

vis′cera, *n. pl.*, entrails; bowels (*Lat.*).

vis′ceral, *adj.*, pert. or rel. to viscera.

vis′cerate, *v.t.*, to disembowel.

visceropto′sis, *n.*, a dropping of the abdominal organs.

vis′cid, *adj.*, sticky; glutinous.

viscid′ity, *n.*, the quality or state of being viscid.

vis′cin, *n.*, a sticky substance found in mistletoe.

viscom′etry, *n.*, the measurement of viscosity.

vi′scose, *n.*, a cellulose for yarn making.

viscosim′eter, *n.*, a device for measuring viscidity.

viscos′ity, *n.*, the quality or state of being viscous.

vis′count, *n.*, a titled person ranking between an earl and a baron.

vis′countess, *n.*, the fem. of viscount.

vis′county, *n.*, the title and honours of a viscount.

vis′cous, *adj.*, *i.q.* viscid.

vi′sé, *v.t.*, *i.q.* visa.

viséed, *p.p.*, visé.

Vish′nu, *n.*, the second in rank of the three Hindu deities.

visibil′ity, *n.*, the quality or state of being visible.

vis′ible, *adj.*, able to be seen; within sight; apparent.

vis′ibly, *adv.*, in a visible way.

Vis′igoth, *n.*, one of the Visigoths, a division of the Goths who settled in France and Spain.

Visigoth′ic, *adj.*, pert. or rel. to the Visigoths.

vi′sile, *adj.*, concerning sight.

vi′sioge′nic, *adj.*, artistically viewable.

vi′sion, *n.*, the act or power of seeing; a dream; an apparition; a prophetic sight.

vi′sionariness, *n.*, the quality or state of being visionary.

vi′sionary, *adj.*, given to dreaming; imaginative; unreal; *n.*, one who indulges in fanciful schemes.

vis′it, *n.*, the act of calling on a person; a stay in a place; an inspection; *v.t.*, to go to see a person or to stay in a place; to punish; to inspect.

vis′itable, *adj.*, able to be visited.

vis′itant, *n.*, *i.q.* visitor.

visita′tion, *n.*, the act of visiting; a visit of official inspection; punishment; chastisement.

visitato′rial, *adj.*, concerned with official visitation.

visite′, *n.*, a light, outdoor feminine costume, which was the mode in the early part of the 19th Cent. (*Fr.*).

vis′ited, *p.p.*, visit.

vis′iting, *pr.p.*, visit.

vis′iting-card, *n.*, a small card bearing the owner's name, address, etc., and left on visiting.

vis′itor, *n.*, one who visits in any sense; specifically, a person authorized to visit a college or church, etc., for the purpose of official inspection. (Also *visitant*.)

visito′rial, *adj.*, pert. or rel. to an official visitor.

vis′ive, *adj.*, pert. or rel. to sight; able to be seen.

vi′son, *n.*, the American mink.

vis′or, *n.*, the openwork, usually hinged to lift from the face, in the front of a helmet. (Also *vizor*.)

vis′ored, *adj.*, furnished with a visor. (Also *vizored*.)

vis′ta, *n.*, a view (*It.*).

vis′ual, *adj.*, pert. or rel. to vision or sight; *n.*, the component of a learning system requiring to be seen.

visual′ity, *n.*, the quality or state of being visual.

visualiza′tion, *n.*, representation in a visual form.

vis′ualize, *v.t.*, to form a mental picture of.

vis′ualized, *p.p.*, visualize.

vis′ualizing, *pr.p.*, visualize.

vis′ually, *adv.*, in a visual way.

vi′taglass, *n.*, glass transparent to ultra-violet rays.

vi′tal, *adj.*, pert. or rel. to life; essential; indispensable.

vi′talism, *n.*, the theory that life owes its origin to a vital, as distinct from a chemical or material, principle.

vi′talist, *n.*, a believer in vitalism.

vital′ity, *n.*, the quality or state of being vital; living power.

vitaliza′tion, *n.*, the act of vitalizing; the state of being vitalized.

vi′talize, *v.t.*, to put life into.

vi′talized, *p.p.*, vitalize.

vi′talizer, *n.*, one who, or that which, vitalizes.

vi′talizing, *pr.p.*, vitalize.

vi′tally, *adv.*, in a vital way or sense.

vi′tals, *n. pl.*, the vital parts of an animal organism.

vi′tamin, *n.*, a lifeenhancing element in food.

vi′tamine, *n.*, *i.q.* vitamin.

vi′taminize, *v.t.*, to add vitamins to food.

vitam′inous, *adj.*, pert. or rel. to vitamins.

vi′tascope, *n.*, a moving picture projector.

vitel′li, *n. pl.*, vitellus.

vitel′lin, *n.*, the protein of the yolk of egg (*chem.*).

vitel′lus, *n.*, the yolk of an egg (*Lat.*).

vi′tiable, *adj.*, likely to be vitiated.

vi′tiate, *v.t.*, to corrupt; to debase.

vi′tiated, *p.p.*, vitiate.

vi′tiating, *pr.p.*, vitiate.

vitia′tion, *n.*, the act or effect of vitiating.

vi′tiator, *n.*, one who vitiates.

vit'iculture, *n.*, the cultivation of the vine.

viticul'turist, *n.*, one who cultivates the vine.

vit'reous, *adj.*, pert. or rel. to glass; glassy.

vitres'cence, *n.*, the quality or state of becoming vitreous.

vitres'cent, *adj.*, becoming vitreous.

vitres'cible, *adj.*, vitrifiable.

vitrifac'tion, *n.*, the act or effect of vitrifying.

vit'rifiable, *adj.*, able to be vitrified.

vitrifica'tion, *n.*, *i.q.* vitrifaction.

vit'rified, *adj.*, glazed; *p.p.*, vitrify.

vit'riform, *adj.*, of a glassy appearance.

vit'rify, *v.i.*, to become glassy; *v.t.*, to turn into glass; to glaze.

vit'rifying, *pr.p.*, vitrify.

vit'rine, *n.*, a glass showcase (*Fr.*).

vit'riol, *n.*, sulphuric acid.

vit'riolate, *v.t.*, to convert into a sulphate.

vit'riolated, *p.p.*, vitriolate.

vit'riolating, *pr.p.*, vitriolate.

vitriola'tion, *n.*, the act or effect of vitriolating.

vitriol'ic, *adj.*, pert. or rel. to vitriol; destructive; caustic.

vitriol'ically, *adv.*, in a vitriolic way.

vit'riolizable, *adj.*, able to be vitriolized.

vitrioliza'tion, *n.*, *i.q.* vitriolation.

vit'riolize, *v.i.* and *t.*, *i.q.* vitriolate.

vit'riolized, *p.p.*, vitriolize.

vit'riolizing, *pr.p.*, vitriolize.

Vitru'vian, *adj.*, pert. or rel. to Vitruvius, the Roman architect.

vitt'a, *n.*, a coloured stripe in fish or animals (*Lat.*).

vitt'ate, *adj.*, marked with bands of colour (*Lat.*).

vit'uline, *adj.*, pert. or rel. to a calf and veal; like veal or a calf.

vitu'perable, *adj.*, shameful.

vitu'perate, *v.t.*, to abuse; to revile.

vitu'perated, *p.p.*, vituperate.

vitu'perating, *pr.p.*, vituperate.

vitupera'tion, *n.*, the act of vituperating; abuse; reviling.

vitu'perative, *adj.*, abusive; reviling.

vitu'peratively, *adv.*, abusively.

vitu'perator, *n.*, one who vituperates.

vi'va, *int.* and *n.*, a shout of greeting; long live — (*It.*).

viva'ce, *adv.*, in a lively manner; quickly (*It.*, *mus.*).

viva'cious, *adj.*, lively; sprightly.

viva'ciously, *adv.*, in a vivacious way.

viva'ciousness, *n.*, *i.q.* vivacity.

vivac'ity, *n.*, liveliness; sprightliness.

vivandière, *n.*, a woman camp-follower (*Fr.*).

vivar'ia, *n. pl.*, vivarium (*Lat.*).

viva'rium, *n.*, a place where live animals are kept (*Lat.*).

viv'ary, *n.*, *i.q.* vivarium.

vi'va vo'ce, *adj.*, oral; *adv.*, orally (*Lat.*).

vive, *adj.*, bright; full of life; *int.*, long live — (*Fr.*).

vi'vency, *n.*, liveliness; vitality.

viv'erine, *adj.*, pert. or rel. to the civet; *n.*, a member of this group of animals.

vive'rra, *n.*, the civet.

viv'ers, *n. pl.*, food, victuals (*Scot.*).

vives, *n. pl.*, an ear disease, esp. in horses.

viv'id, *adj.*, with a look of life; exceedingly bright; realistic.

viv'idly, *adv.*, in a vivid way.

viv'idness, *n.*, the quality or state of being vivid.

vivifica'tion, *n.*, the act or result of vivifying.

viv'ified, *p.p.*, vivify.

viv'ify, *v.t.*, to put life into; to animate.

viv'ifying, *pr.p.*, vivify.

vivipa'rity, *n.*, state of being viviparous.

vivip'arous, *adj.*, bringing forth living offspring.

vivip'arously, *adv.*, in a viviparous way.

viv'isect, *v.i.* and *t.*, to dissect a living body for experimental reasons.

vivisec'tion, *n.*, dissection of the living body.

vivisec'tional, *adj.*, pert. or rel. to vivisection.

vivisec'tionist, *n.*, one who approves of, and practises, vivisection.

viv'isector, *n.*, one who practises vivisection.

vix'en, *n.*, a female fox; a termagant woman.

vix'enish, *adj.*, like a vixen.

viz., the abbrev. of videlicet (*Lat.*).

viz'ard, *n.*, a mask.

vizi(e)r', *n.*, a high Mohammedan state official.

vizi(e)r'ate, *n.*, the office of a vizier.

viz'or, *n.*, *i.q.* visor.

viz'ored, *adj.*, *i.q.* visored.

vo'cable, *n.*, a word.

vocab'ulary, *n.*, a list of words in alphabetical order; the total range of word power.

vocab'ulist, *n.*, the maker of a vocabulary.

vo'cal, *adj.*, pert. or rel. to the voice and utterance.

vocal'ic, *adj.*, pert. or rel. to, or containing, vowels.

vo'calism, *n.*, *i.q.* vocalization.

vo'calist, *n.*, a singer.

vocal'ity, *n.*, the quality or state of being vocal; the quality of vowels.

vocaliza'tion, *n.*, the act of vocalizing. (Also *vocalism*.)

vo'calize, *v.i.*, to give utterance; *v.t.*, to make vocal; to form or utter with the mouth; to add vowel points to (in shorthand or in a language, such as Hebrew, which has only consonantal letters).

vo'calized, *p.p.*, vocalize.

vo'calizing, *pr.p.*, vocalize.

vo'cally, *adv.*, in a vocal way; orally; with the voice.

voca'tion, *n.*, a calling, esp. in the sense of a call to a career in religion; a profession; a career.

voca'tional, *adj.*, concerned with livelihood earning.

voca'tionally, *adv.*, in a vocational way.

voc′ative, adj., pert. or rel. to calling; n., the vocative case, so named from its being used in direct address.

vocif′erant, adj., noisy, clamorous.

vocif′erate, v.i. and t., to shout out; to bawl.

vocif′erated, p.p., vociferate.

vocif′erating, pr.p., vociferate.

vocifera′tion, n., the act of vociferating.

vocif′erator, n., one who shouts and bawls.

vocif′erous, adj., loud; bawling.

vocif′erously, adv., in a vociferous way.

voc′ular, adj., pert. or rel. to the voice.

voc′ule, n., a light vowel sound.

vod′ka, n., a strong, colourless, alcoholic drink, originally from Slav countries.

vogue, n., fashion; popular use or trend.

voice, n., the power of sound produced by the mouth; the spoken word; a sound like a human voice; suffrage, or share in voting, etc.; a resonant vocal note; tone; a verb-form distinguishing between active and passive; v.t., to give expression to; to adjust the tone of an organ pipe.

voiced, p.p., voice.

voice′less, adj., without a voice; silent; without resonance of the vocal chords.

voic′ing, n., the act of regulating the tone of an organ pipe; pr.p., voice.

void, adj., empty; useless; invalid; without effect; n., an empty space; v.t., to make invalid; to excrete.

void′able, adj., able to be voided.

void′ance, n., voiding; the state of being void or vacant, esp. the vacancy of a benefice.

void′ed, p.p., void.

void′er, n., one who, or that which, voids.

void′ing, pr.p., void.

void′ness, n., the quality or state of being void.

voile, n., translucent dress material (Fr.).

voi′vode, n., i.q. vaivode.

vo′lant, adj., flying. (Also volitant.)

volan′te, adv., quickly and lightly (It., mus.).

Volapuk′, n., a universal language, invented by Johann M. Schleyer (1879).

vol′ar, adj., pert. or rel. to the palm of the hand or sole of the foot (anat.).

vol′atile, adj., quickly evaporating; gay; fickle.

volatil′ity, n., the quality or state of being volatile.

volatiliz′able, adj., able to be volatilized.

volatiliza′tion, n., the act or effect of volatilizing.

vol′atilize, v.i., to evaporate; v.t., to make to evaporate.

vol′atilized, p.p., volatilize.

vol′atilizing, pr.p., volatilize.

vol′-au-vent′, n., a pastry filled with a savoury (Fr.).

volcan′ic, adj., pert. or rel. to volcanoes.

volcanic′ity, n., the quality or state of being volcanic.

vol′canist, n., one who investigates volcanic phenomena.

volcan′ity, n., i.q. volcanicity.

vol′canize, v.t., to expose to volcanic heat.

volca′no, n., an opening in the earth's crust through which molten lava is ejected or has at some time been ejected.

volcanol′ogy, n., i.q. vulcanology.

vole, n., a field-mouse; the winning of all the tricks in one deal at cards.

volée′, n., a rush of musical notes (Fr.).

vol′et, n., the panel of a triptych; a short veil.

voli′tant, adj., i.q. volant.

vol′itate, v.i., to fly.

volita′tion, n., flight.

voli′tion, n., an act of will; will-power.

vol′itive, adj., pert. or rel. to the will.

volks′lied, n., a folk-song (Ger.).

volks′raad, n., the Orange State's legislative assembly (hist.).

vol′ley, n., a simultaneous discharge of missiles; the immediate return of a tennis-ball while it is in flight and before it has struck the ground; v.i., to be discharged or to sound together; to volley at tennis; v.t., to discharge in a volley; to return a tennis-ball while in flight.

vol′leyed, p.p., volley.

vol′leying, pr.p., volley.

vol′plane, n., a gliding descent; v.i., to glide.

volt, n., a quick movement to avoid a thrust in fencing; a unit of electromotive force required to drive one ampere of current through one ohm of resistance.

vol′ta, n., a turn (It., mus.).

vol′tage, n., the measurement of volts in an electric instrument or circuit.

volta′ic, adj., galvanic.

Voltair′ism, n., the scepticism of Voltaire, the French philosopher.

vol′taism, n., galvanism.

voltam′eter, n., an instrument measuring voltage in electrolytic processes.

vol′taplast, n., a battery used in the electrotype process.

vol′tatype, n., electrotype.

volte, n., a turn; in fencing, an avoiding movement.

volte-face′, n., a reversal of a state of affairs (Fr.).

voltigeur′, n., a vaulter; a tumbler; an irregular sort of French rifleman (Fr.).

volt′meter, n., an apparatus for measuring the force of an electric current.

volubil′ity, n., the quality or state of being voluble.

vol′uble, adj., glib; talkative; quick and fluent in speech.

vol′ubly, adv., in a voluble way.

vol′ume, n., sheets or pages bound up

together to make one book; a book; a coil; bulk; content; the strength of sound.

vol'umed, *adj.*, convolute; bulky.

volu'meter, *n.*, an instrument for measuring the volume of gas.

volumet'ric, *adj.*, pert. or rel. to the measurement of the volume of gases.

volu'minous, *adj.*, bulky; containing many volumes; (of writing) of great length.

volu'minously, *adv.*, in a bulky way.

vol'untarily, *adv.*, of one's own free will.

vol'untary, *adj.*, done of one's own free will; *n.*, an organ solo.

vol'untaryism, *n.*, the principle of refusing State aid to religious or educational institutions.

vol'untative, *adj.*, showing a desire.

volunteer', *n.*, one who offers his services gratuitously; *v.i.*, to offer oneself for doing anything; to undertake; *v.t.*, to offer; to propose.

volunteered', *p.p.*, volunteer.

volunteer'ing, *n.*, service as a volunteer; *pr.p.*, volunteer.

volupt'uary, *adj.*, pert. or rel. to luxury; *n.*, one addicted to luxury and self-indulgence.

volupt'uous, *adj.*, pert. or rel. to sensual or material pleasures.

volupt'uously, *adv.*, in a voluptuous way.

volupt'uousness, *n.*, the state of being voluptuous.

volute', *adj.*, spiral; *n.*, a classical architectural ornament curved like a scroll; a kind of gasteropod.

volu'ted, *adj.*, having a volute.

volu'tion, *n.*, *i.q.* convolution.

Vol'vox, *n.*, a genus of globular water plants.

vo'mer, *n.*, the thin bone partitioning the nose.

vo'mica, *n.*, an abscess in the lungs.

vom'it, *n.*, matter thrown up from the stomach; an emetic; *v.i.*, to be sick; *v.t.*, to throw up from the stomach.

vom'ited, *p.p.*, vomit.

vom'iting, *n.*, sickness; *pr.p.*, vomit.

vom'itive, *adj.*, causing vomiting; emetic.

vom'ito, *n.*, a type of yellow fever (*Span.*).

vom'itory, *adj.*, *i.q.* vomitive; *n.*, an emetic.

vomituri'tion, *n.*, retching.

voo'doo, *n.*, West Indian witchcraft.

vora'cious, *adj.*, greedy; with a huge appetite.

vora'ciously, *adv.*, in a voracious way.

vorac'ity, *n.*, greediness.

vor'tex, *n.*, a whirlpool; a whirling motion (*Lat.*).

vor'tical, *adj.*, pert. or rel. to a vortex.

vor'tically, *adv.*, in a vortical way.

vor'ticel, *n.*, a bell-animalcule.

vor'ticella, *n.*, *i.q.* vorticel.

vor'tices, *n.*, the pl. of vortex (*Lat.*).

vor'ticism, *n.*, a theory of modern art, in which vortices are a feature.

vor'ticist, *n.*, one who supports vorticism; a person supporting Descartes' view of the universe.

vo'tal, *adj.*, pert. or rel. to vows.

vo'taress, *n.*, the fem. of votary.

vo'tarist, *n.*, one who is tied by vows.

vo'tary, *n.*, one vowed to another person, a deity, a study, etc.

vote, *n.*, a written or spoken assent; *v.i.*, to give a vote; *v.t.*, to grant.

vo'ted, *p.p.*, vote.

vo'ter, *n.*, one who possesses or exercises the vote.

vo'ting, *n.*, votes collectively; *pr.p.*, vote.

vo'tive, *adj.*, given in performance of a vow.

vo'tively, *adv.*, in a votive way.

vouch, *v.i.* and *t.*, to confirm; to support.

vouched, *p.p.*, vouch.

vouchee', *n.*, one who is called upon to defend a legal title.

vouch'er, *n.*, one who vouches; an attesting document; a document having monetary value or value in

kind; the calling in of a vouchee.

vouch'ing, *pr.p.*, vouch.

vouch'or, *n.*, *i.q.* voucher (in the legal sense).

vouchsafe', *v.t.*, to grant; to condescend (to do or give).

vouchsafed', *p.p.*, vouchsafe.

vouchsafe'ment, *n.*, an act of condescension; the favour granted.

vouchsaf'ing, *pr.p.*, vouchsafe.

voussoir', *n.*, a wedge-shaped stone in an arch (*Fr.*, *archit.*).

vow, *n.*, a solemn pledge; *v.i.*, to declare; *v.t.*, to pledge; to promise.

vowed, *p.p.*, vow.

vow'el, *n.*, an open sound as distinguished from a consonant; a sound in which the vocal chords vibrate continuously; the letter which names each vowel.

vow'elize, *v.t.*, to vocalize in the sense of adding vowel points.

vow'elled, *adj.*, having vowels.

vow'er, *n.*, one who vows.

vow'ing, *pr.p.*, vow.

vox, *n.*, the voice (*Lat.*).

vox huma'na, *n.*, a reed-stop on the organ, the sound from which bears some likeness to the human voice (*Lat.*).

vox pop'uli, a Lat. phrase = the voice of the people.

voy'age, *n.*, a journey by water; *v.i.*, to go by water; *v.t.*, to traverse.

voy'aged, *p.p.*, voyage.

voy'ager, *n.*, one who voyages.

voyageur', *n.*, a fur-trader; a Canadian boatman (*Fr.*).

voy'aging, *pr.p.*, voyage.

vraic, *n.*, a kind of sea-weed found in the Channel Islands.

vraisemblance', *n.*, the appearance of truth; plausibility (*Fr.*).

Vul'can, *n.*, the god of fire and metal (*myth.*).

Vulca'nian, *adj.*, pert. or rel. to Vulcan and metallurgy; also to Vulcanism.

Vulcan'ic, *adj.*, *i.q.* Vulcanian.

vulcan'ism, *n.*, the phenomena caused by internal fire or heat.

Vul'canist, *n.*, one who holds the Plutonic theory of rock formation.

vul'canite, *n.*, vulcanized rubber.

vulcaniza'tion, *n.*, the act or effect of vulcanizing.

vul'canize, *v.t.*, to treat rubber with sulphur at a high temperature to harden it.

vul'canized, *p.p.*, vulcanize.

vul'canizing, *pr.p.*, vulcanize.

vulcanol'ogy, *n.*, the study of volcanoes.

vul'gar, *adj.*, rel. to the people; vernacular; common; low; unrefined.

vulga'rian, *n.*, a rich person with unrefined manners.

vul'garism, *n.*, coarseness; vulgarity; a mode of expression not in good literary taste.

vulgar'ity, *n.*, the quality or state of being vulgar; coarseness.

vul'garize, *v.t.*, to make vulgar; to debase.

vul'garized, *p.p.*, vulgarize.

vul'garizing, *pr.p.*, vulgarize.

vul'garly, *adv.*, in a vulgar way; commonly.

Vul'gate, *n.*, the Lat. version of the bible made by St. Jerome in the 4th Cent.

vulnerabil'ity, *n.*, the quality or state of being vulnerable.

vul'nerable, *adj.*, able to be wounded; not proof against attack; being one game ahead in a rubber of contract bridge.

vul'nerary, *adj.*, healing; *n.*, a remedy for wounds.

vul'picide, *n.*, a fox killer (other than by fox-hunting).

vul'pine, *adj.*, pert. or rel. to foxes; fox-like; crafty.

vul'ture, *n.*, a large bird of prey.

vul'turine, *adj.*, pert. or rel. to vultures.

vul'turish, *adj.*, resembling a vulture.

vul'va, *n.*, an opening, esp. of the female genital organs (*Lat.*, *anat.*).

vul'viform, *adj.*, oval-shaped.

vulvi'tis, *n.*, inflammation of the vulva.

vy'ing, *pr.p.*, vie.

vyn'ide, *n.*, a plastic substitute for leather.

W

Waac, *n.*, a member of the Women's Auxiliary Army Corps.

Waaf, *n.*, a member of the Women's Auxiliary Air Force.

wab'ble, *n.* and *v.i.*, *i.q.* wobble.

wab'bled, *p.p.*, wabble.

wab'bler, *n.*, *i.q.* wobbler.

wab'bling, *pr.p.*, wabble.

wab'bly, *n.*, *i.q.* wobbly.

wack'e, *n.*, the German equivalent for trap-rock (decomposed limestone).

wad, *n.*, a pad of soft material used for stuffing; a tow rammed into a gun to keep the powder in; a cake (*services slang*); *v.t.*, to use as a wad; to stuff with a wad.

wad'ded, *p.p.*, wad.

wad'ding, *n.*, material for stuffing of partly compressed and unwoven fibres; *pr.p.*, wad.

wad'dle, *n.*, a walking from side to side; *v.i.*, to walk with a gooselike movement.

wad'dled, *p.p.*, waddle.

wad'dler, *n.*, one who waddles.

wad'dling, *pr.p.*, waddle.

wad'dlingly, *adv.*, in a waddling way.

wadd'y, *n.*, a native club or stick (*Austral.*).

wade, *v.i.*, to walk through water; *v.t.*, to cross by wading.

wa'ded, *p.p.*, wade.

wa'der, *n.*, one who wades; any bird that wades in water, e.g. the heron.

wa'ders, *n. pl.*, waterproof thigh-boots used in fishing, etc.

wa'di, *n.*, a watercourse (*Arabic*).

wa'ding, *pr.p.*, wade.

wa'dy, *n.*, *i.q.* wadi.

Wafd, *n.*, an Egyptian political party.

Wafd'ist, *adj.*, pert. or rel. to the Wafd; a member of the W.

wa'fer, *n.*, a very thin piece of material, used for various purposes and sometimes edible; *v.t.*, to seal up with a wafer.

wa'fered, *p.p.*, wafer.

wa'fering, *pr.p.*, wafer.

waf'fle, *n.*, a cake made with batter; *v.i.*, to talk senselessly (*colloq.*).

waft, *v.t.*, to carry or send with a wind.

waft'age, *n.*, wafting; the distance wafted.

waft'ed, *p.p.*, waft.

waft'er, *n.*, one who, or that which, wafts.

waft'ing, *n.*, a carrying along; *pr.p.*, waft.

wag, *n.*, the act of wagging; a funny fellow; *v.i.* and *t.*, to shake or nod backwards and forwards.

wage, *n.*, pay for work (usu. manual); *v.t.*, to carry on (a war or battle); to hazard.

waged, *p.p.*, wage.

wage'-freeze, *n.*, the pegging of wage levels.

wa'ger, *n.*, a bet; *v.i.* and *t.*, to bet.

wa'gered, *p.p.*, wager.

wa'gerer, *n.*, one who wagers.

wa'gering, *pr.p.*, wager.

wa'ges, *n. pl.*, of wage. (This form is more commonly used than *wage*.)

wagged, *p.p.*, wag.

wag'ger, *n.*, one who wags.

wag'gery, *n.*, drollery; playful joking.

wag'ging, *pr.p.*, wag.

wag'gish, *adj.*, droll; playful.

wag'gishly, *adv.*, in a waggish way.

wag'gishness, *n.*, the quality or state of being waggish.

wag'gle, *v.i.* and *t.*, to shake from side to side.

wag'gled, *p.p.*, waggle.

wag'gling, *pr.p.*, waggle.

wa'ging, *pr.p.*, wage.

wag'(g)on, *n.*, a large cart; a truck on a railway.

wag'(g)onage, *n.*, wagons collectively; the charge for freight on wagons.

wag'(g)oner, *n.*, a wagon-driver.

wagonette', *n.*, a light carriage.

wagon-lit, *n.*, a Continental railway sleeping car (*Fr.*).

wag'tail, *n.*, a bird that constantly wags its tail.

Waha'bi, *n.*, a member of the Arabian sect founded by Abd-el-Wahab.

waif, *n.*, a lost thing; a stray.

wail, *n.*, a cry in lament; *v.i.* and *t.*, to lament.

wailed, *p.p.*, wail.

wail'er, *n.*, one who wails.

wail'ing, *n.*, loud lamentation; *pr.p.*, wail.

wain, *n.*, a wagon; a constellation.

wain'scot, *n.*, the panelling of a wall; *v.t.*, to cover with panelling.

wain'scot(t)ed, *p.p.*, wainscot.

wain'scot(t)ing, *n.*, panelling; *pr.p.*, wainscot.

wain'wright, *n.*, a maker of wagons.

waist, *n.*, the part of the body immediately above the hips; the middle.

waist'band, *n.*, a belt.

waist'coat, *n.*, a short, sleeveless coat worn beneath a jacket.

waist'-deep, *adj.*, *i.q.* waist-high.

waist'ed *adj.*, having a waist, shaped at the waist.

waist'-high, *adj.*, reaching up to the waist.

waist'line, *n.*, the position of the waist in fashion.

wait, *v.i.*, to be in a state of expectancy; to stand still; to serve at a table; to attend on someone; *v.t.*, to await.

wait'ed, *p.p.*, wait.

wait'er, *n.*, one who waits in any sense, esp. who serves at table.

wait'ing, *adj.*, serving at table; *n.*, a waiter's calling; *pr.p.*, wait.

wait'ing-list, *n.*, a list of persons waiting.

wait'ing-maid, *n.*, a female attendant.

wait'ing-room, *n.*, a room for people to wait in.

wait'ress, *n.*, the fem. of waiter.

waits, *n. pl.*, Christmas open-air singers and musicians.

waive, *v.t.*, to concede; to resign one's claim to.

waived, *p.p.*, waive.

waiv'er, *n.*, the voluntary renouncement of a right or claim (*leg.*).

waiv'ing, *pr.p.*, waive.

wake, *n.*, the track of a vessel, etc.; to vigil for the dead; *v.i.*, to be awake; to arise from sleep; *v.t.*, to rouse out of sleep.

waked, *p.p.*, wake.

wake'ful, *adj.*, sleepless; vigilant.

wake'fully, *adv.*, in a wakeful way.

wake'fulness, *n.*, the state of being wakeful.

wa'ken, *v.i.* and *t.*, *i.q.* wake.

wa'kened, *p.p.*, waken.

wa'kener, *n.*, one who wakens.

wa'kening, *pr.p.*, waken.

wa'ker, *adj.*, on the watch; vigilant; *n.*, one who watches or is wakeful.

wakes, *n. pl.*, an annual, communal holiday, esp. in Lancashire.

wa'king, *pr.p.*, wake.

Wal(l)a'chian, *adj.*, pert. or rel. to Wallachia in Roumania; *n.*, a native of W.

Walden'ses, *n. pl.*, the followers of Peter Waldo, a Piedmontese Protestant preacher who founded a sect, *circa* 1170.

wale, *n.*, the scar or mark produced by a blow with a whip, etc.; *v.t.*, to scar. (Also *weal*.)

waled, *p.p.*, wale.

Walhal'la, *n.*, *i.q.* Valhalla.

wal'ing, *pr.p.*, wale.

walk, *n.*, a movement slower than trotting or running; an act of walking; a place to walk in; a manner of life; *v.i.*, to move at a pace slower than trotting or running; to take walking exercise; to conduct oneself; *v.t.*, to make to walk; to travel over.

walk'about, *adv.*, on the move; *n.*, a tour on foot (*Austral.*, *slang*).

walked, *p.p.*, walk.

walk'er, *n.*, one who walks.

wal'kie-tal'kie, *n.*, a portable radio transceiver.

walk'ing, *pr.p.*, walk.

walk'ing-stick, *n.*, a stick used as a help in walking.

walk'-out, *n.*, a sudden labour strike.

walk'-over, *n.*, an easy or undisputed victory.

wall, *n.*, a defence round an enclosure; the side of a house or a room; *v.t.*, to furnish with a wall; to protect.

wal'laby, *n.*, a species of kangaroo.

wal'lah, *n.*, a fellow; a man employed.

wallaroo', *n.*, a large kangaroo.

wall'-chart, *n.*, a graphical or tabulated presentation of information for affixing to a wall or notice-board.

walled, *adj.*, fortified; *p.p.*, wall.

wall'er, *n.*, a wall-builder.

wal'let, *n.*, a satchel; a bag; a flat case for carrying money or documents.

wall'-eye, *n.*, an eye with a white iris.

wall'-eyed, *adj.*, having a wall-eye.

wall'flower, *n.*, a fragrant flower; at a dance, a woman seldom invited to be a partner.

wall'-fruit, *n.*, cultivated fruit grown against a wall.

wall'-game, *n.*, a ball game peculiar to Eton.

wall'ing, *pr.p.*, wall.

wall'-less, *adj.*, having no walls.

Walloon', *adj.*, pert. or rel. to the Walloons (of Flanders) and to the Walloon language; *n.*, the language spoken by some Belgians.

wal'lop, *n.*, a thrashing (*colloq.*); beer (*slang*); *v.i.*, to make a bubbling noise (said of anything boiling); *v.t.*, to thrash.

wal'loped, *p.p.*, wallop.

wal'loper, *n.*, one who wallops.

wal'loping, *n.*, a beating (*colloq.*); *pr.p.*, wallop.

wal'low, *v.i.*, to roll in mud; to revel in vice.

wal'lowed, *p.p.*, wallow.

wal'lower, *n.*, one who wallows.

wal'lowing, *pr.p.*, wallow.

wall'paper, *n.*, decorative paper hung on walls.

wal'nut, *n.*, a tree, its wood (used for furniture) and its fruit.

wal'rus, *n.*, a tusked marine mammal.

waltz, *n.*, a variety of dance; waltz music; *v.i.*, to dance a waltz.

waltzed, *p.p.*, waltz.

waltz'er, *n.*, one who dances the waltz.

waltz'ing, *n.*, the act of dancing the waltz; *pr.p.*, waltz.

wam'ble, *v.i.*, to feel symptoms of nausea; to rumble internally.

wampee', *n.*, a Chinese fruit.

wam'pum, *n.*, the N. Amer. name for a string of beads.

wan, *adj.*, pale; sickly; *v.i.*, to become wan.

wand, *n.*, a rod.

wan'der, *v.i.*, to stray; to ramble; to become light-headed.

wan'dered, *p.p.*, wander.

wan'derer, *n.*, one who wanders.

wan'dering, *pr.p.*, wander.

wan′deringly, *adv.*, in an inattentive fashion.

wan′derlust, *n.*, the urge to travel (*Ger.*).

wanderoo′, *n.*, a large, bearded Ceylon monkey.

wan′doo, *n. pl.*, white gum trees found in W. Australia.

wane, *n.*, a growing less, esp. to the diminution of the moon's brightness; *v.i.*, to grow less; to decline.

waned, *p.p.*, wane.

wanghee′, *n.*, *i.q.* whangee.

wan′gle, *v.t.*, to accomplish by cunning or suspect methods (*colloq.*).

wan′gled, *p.p.*, wangle.

wan′gler, *n.*, one who wangles.

wan′gling, *pr.p.*, wangle.

wa′ning, *adj.*, on the wane; *pr.p.*, wane.

wan′ly, *adv.*, in a sickly way.

wanned, *p.p.*, wan.

wan′ness, *n.*, the quality or state of being wan.

wan′ning, *pr.p.*, wan.

want, *n.*, lack; need; poverty; desire; *v.i.*, to be lacking; to fail; *v.t.*, to be without; to desire.

want′ed, *p.p.*, want.

want′ing, *pr.p.*, want.

wan′ton, *adj.*, lascivious; sportive; without restraint; irresponsible; *n.*, a lustful person; *v.i.*, to play the wanton.

wan′toned, *p.p.*, wanton.

wan′toning, *pr.p.*, wanton.

wan′tonly, *adv.*, in a wanton way.

wan′tonness, *n.*, the state of being wanton.

want′wit, *n.*, silliness; lack of sense.

wap, *n.* and *v.t.*, *i.q.* whop.

wap′entake, *n.*, a Saxon country subdivision for defence purposes.

wap′iti, *n.*, the elk of America.

wapp′ens(c)haw, *n.*, an old Scottish form of sports; a rifle meeting.

war, *n.*, conflict between nations; any state of enmity; *v.i.*, to be engaged in conflict.

war′ble, *n.*, singing with a trill; a boil; *v.i.* and *t.*, to sing in a bird-like way.

war′bled, *p.p.*, warble.

war′bler, *n.*, one who warbles; a bird.

war′bling, *n.*, song; *pr.p.*, warble.

war′cry, *n.*, words shouted in a fight to rally one's own side and strike terror into the enemy, as, "St. George for England".

ward, *n.*, guard; a municipal division; prison; one under the care of a guardian; one of the divisions in a lock or key; a room for patients in a hospital; *v.i.*, to keep watch; *v.t.*, to guard.

war′-dance, *n.*, the dance of warriors.

ward′ed, *p.p.*, ward.

ward′en, *n.*, a guardian; a custodian; a head of certain colleges, guilds, etc.; a churchwarden; a variety of pear.

ward′enry, *n.*, the office of a warden.

ward′enship, *n.*, the office of a warden.

ward′er, *n.*, a keeper; a guard (esp. in prison).

ward′ing, *pr.p.*, ward.

ward′mote, *n.*, the meeting of the inhabitants in a ward.

ward′ress, *n.*, the fem. of warder.

ward′robe, *n.*, a place to keep clothes in; personal clothing.

ward′room, *n.*, the messroom of the officers on a naval vessel.

ward′ship, *n.*, the position of a ward; guardianship.

ware, *adj.*, *i.q.* aware; *n.*, manufactured goods; *v.*, *i.q.* beware.

ware′house, *n.*, a store for wares; *v.t.*, to put into store.

ware′housed, *p.p.*, warehouse.

ware′houseman, *n.*, a storer of goods.

ware′housing, *n.*, the storing of goods; *pr.p.*, warehouse.

wares, *n. pl.*, goods; merchandise.

war′fare, *n.*, a state of war; conflict.

war′head, *n.*, the detachable explosive portion of a missile.

war′horse, *n.*, a charger.

wari′ly, *adv.*, in a wary way.

wari′ness, *n.*, the quality or state of being wary.

war′like, *adj.*, brave; fierce.

war′lock, *n.*, a wizard.

warm, *n.*, moderately hot; excited; passionate; *v.i.*, to grow warm; *v.t.*, to make warm.

warmed, *p.p.*, warm.

warm′er, *adj.*, *comp.* of warm.

warm′est, *adj.*, *super.* of warm.

warm-heart′ed, *adj.*, affectionate; kind.

warm-heart′edly, *adv.*, affectionately, kindly.

warm-heart′edness, *n.*, the quality or state of being warm-hearted.

warm′ing, *pr.p.*, warm.

warm′ing-pan, *n.*, a pan to contain coals formerly used for warming a bed, etc.

warm′ly, *adv.*, with warmth.

war′monger, *n.*, one who advocates war.

warmth, *n.*, the quality or state of being warm; moderate heat; excitement; passion; rich colouring.

warn, *v.t.*, to admonish; to caution; to put on guard; to summon officially.

warned, *p.p.*, warn.

warn′er, *n.*, one who warns.

warn′ing, *n.*, a caution; an admonition; a notice of dismissal; *pr.p.*, warn.

warn′ingly, *adv.*, in a warning way.

War′-Office, *n.*, formerly the office of a War Minister.

warp, *n.*, lengthwise threads crossed by the woof; a twist; a rope for warping; *v.t.*, to twist awry; to haul a ship by means of a hawser round something fixed (*naut.*); to fertilize by means of flooding.

war'paint, *n.*, a N. Amer. face decoration of warriors.

war'path, *n.*, the state of being aggressive.

warped, *p.p.*, warp.

warp'ing, *pr.p.*, warp.

warp'ing-bank, *n.*, a raised bank round a field to retain alluvial mud.

war'rant, *n.*, a guarantee; security; authorization; commission; *v.t.*, to give authority for; to guarantee; to assure.

war'rantable, *adj.*, able to be warranted.

war'rantably, *adv.*, permissibly.

war'ranted, *p.p.*, warrant.

warrantee', *n.*, one to whom a warranty is issued.

war'ranter, *n.*, one who warrants.

war'ranting, *pr.p.*, warrant.

war'rant-of'ficer, *n.*, the highest category of non-commissioned service in the British Army and Air Force.

war'rantor, *n.*, *i.q.* warranter (*leg.*).

war'ranty, *n.*, security; a warrant.

warred, *p.p.*, war.

war'ren, *n.*, a preserve, esp. for rabbits; the right to preserve wild animals (*leg.*).

war'rener, *n.*, the keeper of a warren.

war'ring, *pr.p.*, war.

war'rior, *n.*, a fighting man; a soldier.

war'ship, *n.*, an armed vessel.

war'-song, *n.*, a song for warriors.

wart, *n.*, a morbid growth on the skin.

wart'-hog, *n.*, a kind of African wild pig with warty lumps on its face.

war'time, *n.*, a period of war.

wart'wort, *n.*, one of several plants useful for the cure of warts.

wart'y, *adj.*, covered with, or like, warts.

war'-whoop, *n.*, the yell of warriors fighting.

war'-worn, *adj.*, veteran.

wa'ry, *adj.*, discreet; cautious.

was, *p.t.*, be.

wase, *n.*, a porter's head-pad on which to rest a burden.

wase'goose, *n.*, *i.q.* wayz-goose.

wash, *n.*, the act of washing; a shallow part of the sea, etc.; the effect of displacement of water by a ship; a lotion; a thin layer or coating; indifferent drink (*colloq.*). *v.i.*, to perform the act of washing; *v.t.*, to cleanse with water; to bathe; to lay a thin surface over; to purify.

wash'able, *adj.*, capable of being washed.

wash'ball, *n.*, a form of toilet soap.

wash'-basin, *n.*, *i.q.* washbowl.

wash'board, *n.*, a board formerly used in washing clothes.

wash'bowl, *n.*, a bowl to wash in.

washed, *p.p.*, wash.

wash'er, *n.*, one who washes; a device for making a screw, a joint, etc., secure.

wash'erwoman, *n.*, a woman who washes clothes.

wash'house, *n.*, a building where washing is done.

wash'ing, *n.*, the act of washing; the employment of washing; clothes to be washed; *pr.p.*, wash.

wash'ing-ma'chine, *n.*, a machine for washing clothes, etc.

wash'ing-up, *n.*, the cleaning of table utensils after a meal.

wash'-leather, *n.*, chamois-leather.

wash'out, *n.*, a complete failure (*colloq.*).

wash'stand, *n.*, a table on which washing utensils were placed.

wash'-tub, *n.*, a laundry tub.

wash'y, *adj.*, poor; thin (*colloq.*).

wasn't, abbrev. of was not (*colloq.*).

wasp, *n.*, a stinging winged insect.

wasp'ish, *adj.*, like a wasp; irritable and vexatious; thin about the waist.

wasp'ishly, *adv.*, in a waspish way; spitefully.

was'pishness, *n.*, the state of being irritable.

wasp-waist'ed, *adj.*, very slender about the waist.

was'sail, *n.*, Christmas merriment; a drink of various ingredients; *v.i.*, to revel; to feast; *v.t.*, to pledge in wine or ale.

was'sailer, *n.*, one who wassails.

wast'age, *n.*, loss.

waste, *adj.*, uncultivated; not in use; *n.*, loss; consumption; extravagance; uncultivated land; refuse; *v.t.*, to devastate; to destroy; to expend extravagantly; to dissipate.

waste'book, *n.*, a daybook.

wast'ed, *p.p.*, waste.

waste'ful, *adj.*, extravagant; not thrifty.

waste'fully, *adv.*, in a wasteful way.

waste'fulness, *n.*, the state of being wasteful.

waste'-gate, *n.*, an escape for the surplus water of a dam, etc.

was'tel, *n.*, pastry or thin white bread (*Fr.*).

waste'ness, *n.*, the state of being waste.

waste'paper, *n.*, paper having no further use.

waste'pipe, *n.*, a pipe to allow an overflow to escape.

wa'ster, *n.*, one who wastes; a person of reprehensible conduct (*slang*).

wa'sting, *pr.p.*, waste.

wa'strel, *n.*, a spendthrift; a waif.

watch, *n.*, keeping a look-out; vigilance; one who keeps watch; a division of the night-time; a small, mechanical or electronic time-keeper; a group of men acting as police at night; *v.i.*, to be awake; to keep guard; *v.t.*, to observe closely; to keep an eye on; to protect.

watch'-case, *n.*, the outer cover of a watch.

watch'-chain, *n.*, a metal chain to secure a pocket watch.

watch'-commit'tee, *n.*, the committee of a town council which deals with the lighting, policing and moral welfare of the borough.

watch'dog, *n.*, a dog that keeps guard.

watched, *p.p.*, watch.

watch'er, *n.*, one who watches.

watch'ful, *adj.*, wakeful; vigilant.

watch'fully, *adv.*, in a watchful way.

watch'fulness, *n.*, the quality or state of being watchful.

watch'-glass, *n.*, the glass over a watch face.

watch'-guard, *n.*, a chain, etc., to secure a watch to one's person.

watch'-house, *n.*, a building for watchmen.

watch'ing, *pr.p.*, watch.

watch'ing-brief, *n.*, instructions to counsel to observe a case (*leg.*).

watch'maker, *n.*, a maker of watches.

watch'man, *n.*, one who keeps watch.

watch'night, *n.*, the last night of the year.

watch'spring, *n.*, the spring of a watch.

watch'tower, *n.*, a lookout place.

watch'word, *n.*, a password.

wa'ter, *n.*, a liquid essential for life containing two parts of hydrogen to one of oxygen; the sea; water-like fluid; a diamond's brilliancy; *v.i.*, to take in water; to discharge water; *v.t.*, to give to drink; to irrigate; to supply with water; to dilute.

wa'terage, *n.*, the charge for carrying by water.

wa'ter-borne, *adj.*, carried by water.

wa'ter-bot'tle, *n.*, a container for water, usu. of metal, glass or rubber.

wa'ter-butt, *n.*, a butt to hold rain-water.

wa'ter-cart, *n.*, a cart used to carry water.

wa'terchute, *n.*, a downward channel of water for transporting boats, treetrunks, etc.

wa'ter-col'our, *n.*, a water-colour drawing.

wa'tercourse, *n.*, the course of a stream.

wa'tercress, *n.*, an aquatic, edible plant.

wa'ter-divin'er, *n.*, one who finds water with a divining-rod.

wat'er-divining, *n.*, locating underground water with a divining-rod.

wa'tered, *adj.*, wavy in appearance; diluted with water; *p.p.*, water.

wa'terfall, *n.*, a fall of water from a height.

wa'ter-finder, *n.*, an instrument for detecting water.

wa'ter-flag, *n.*, the yellow iris.

wa'terfowl, *n.*, a bird that lives partly on the water.

wa'terfront, *n.*, the area adjacent to water in an urban area.

wa'terglass, *n.*, egg-preserving liquid.

wa'ter-hen, *n.*, the moorhen.

wa'teriness, *n.*, the quality or state of being watery.

wa'tering, *pr.p.*, water.

wa'tering-place, *n.*, a seaside resort or a place where mineral baths can be obtained.

wa'tering-pot, *n.*, a pot used to water the garden.

wa'terish, *adj.*, thin; watery.

wa'ter-jump, *n.*, an obstacle in the form of a sheet of water in a steeplechase.

wa'ter-lily, *n.*, a lily-like aquatic plant.

wa'terlogged, *adj.*, filled or soaked with water.

wa'terloo', *n.*, final failure or defeat.

wa'ter-main, *n.*, a large underground water pipe.

wa'terman, *n.*, a professional boatman.

wa'termark, *n.*, an identifying mark in the texture of paper or silk.

wa'termelon, *n.*, a melon containing a watery juice.

wa'termill, *n.*, a mill driven by water.

wa'ter-plane, *n.*, the plane of a ship's water-line.

wa'ter-polo', *n.*, a game played by swimmers.

wa'ter-pot, *n.*, a pot to hold water.

wa'ter-pow'er, *n.*, the use of the force of water.

wa'terproof, *adj.*, impervious to wet; *n.*, a coat, etc., of waterproof material.

wa'ter-ram, *n.*, a hydraulic ram.

wa'ter-rat, *n.*, a rat that lives in the banks of rivers, etc.

wa'ter-rate, *n.*, the rate paid for the public supply of water.

wa'ter-rot, *v.t.*, to produce rottenness in by means of soaking.

wa'tershed, *n.*, high ground from which water descends into a river; the line of division between two river basins.

wa'tersider, *n.*, a dock labourer.

wa'ter-ski'ing, *n.*, skiing on water, behind a towing power-boat.

wa'ter-soak, *v.t.*, to fill interstices of with water.

wa'terspout, *n.*, a cyclonic column of water; a spout to carry off water.

wa'ter-sup'ply, *n.*, the public distribution of water.

wa'ter-tank, *n.*, a cistern for holding water.

wa'tertight, *adj.*, able to keep out water.

wa'tertower, *n.*, a tank mounted on a tower to provide supply pressure.

wa'ter-wagon, *n.*, a wagon to convey water; metaphorically representative of abstinence from alcohol.

wa'terway, *n.*, the fairway in a river channel.

wa'terworks, *n. pl.*, pumping stations; in sing., an ornamental cascade, fountain, etc.

wa'terwort, *n.*, a marsh annual plant.

wa'tery, *adj.*, like water; pert. or rel. to water; thin; poor in taste.

watt, *n.*, a unit of electric power.

watt'age, *n.*, electric power expressed in watts.

Wat'teau, *adj.*, pert. or rel. to Watteau and the style of dress exhibited in his pictures (early 18th cent.).

wat'tle, *adj.*, made with wattle; *n.*, a flexible twig; a hurdle; the growth beneath a turkey's or fowl's throat; acacia; *v.t.*, to fasten with wattles.

wat'tled, *p.p.*, wattle.

wat'tling, *n.*, wattlework; the art of wattling; *pr.p.*, wattle.

watt′meter, *n.*, an instrument for measuring electric power.

waul, *n.*, a cat's cry. (Also *wawl*.)

wave, *n.*, an undulating movement of water; a like movement of light, sound, etc.; *v.i.*, to undulate; *v.t.*, to move this way and that; to brandish; to give a wavy appearance to.

wave′band, *n.*, a range of wavelengths.

waved, *p.p.*, wave.

wave′length, *n.*, the distance between two successive waves (*naut.* and *radio*).

wave′less, *adj.*, without waves; calm.

wave′let, *n.*, a little wave.

wave′-like, *adj.*, like a wave.

wave′-offering, *n.*, a Jewish offering by waving towards the points of the compass.

wa′ver, *n.*, one who waves; *v.i.*, to falter; to hesitate between alternative choices; to flicker.

wa′vered, *p.p.*, waver.

wa′verer, *n.*, one who wavers.

wa′vering, *pr.p.*, waver.

wa′veringly, *adv.*, hesitantly.

wa′very, *adj.*, fluttering; unsteady.

wave′son, *n.*, floating wreckage.

wa′viness, *n.*, the quality or state of being wavy.

wa′ving, *pr.p.*, wave.

wa′vy, *adj.*, like a wave; undulating.

wawl, *n.*, *i.q.* waul.

wax, *n.*, a thick clinging substance, such as bees-wax; a like substance formed in the ear; cerumen; a rage (*slang*); *v.i.*, to increase in growth, strength, etc.; to become.

wax′bill, *n.*, a species of small bird with a bill like red sealing wax.

wax′-chandler, *n.*, one who makes or sells wax candles.

wax′cloth, *n.*, a wax-coated cloth usu. for tables.

waxed, *p.p.*, wax.

wax′en, *adj.*, made of, or resembling wax.

wax′-end, *n.*, the end of a piece of thread stiffened with wax.

wax′iness, *n.*, the quality or state of being waxy.

wax′ing, *pr.p.*, wax.

wax-paper, *n.*, paper coated with wax to make it waterproof.

wax′wing, *n.*, a bird so named from the resemblance of some of its feathers to sealing-wax.

wax′work, *n.*, anything made of wax, esp. a representation of a human figure.

wax′worker, *n.*, one who models in wax.

wax′y, *adj.*, wax-like; made of wax; angry (*slang*).

way, *n.*, a road; direction; means; manner.

way′bill, *n.*, a list of passengers or goods to be conveyed, or of places of call.

way′bread, *n.*, the plantain.

way′farer, *n.*, a traveller.

way′faring, *adj.*, travelling.

waylaid′, *p.p.*, waylay.

waylay′, *v.t.*, to attack on the road; to watch for.

way′layer, *n.*, one who waylays.

way′laying, *pr.p.*, waylay.

way′leave, *n.*, a rented right of way.

way′less, *adj.*, without paths or roads.

way′-mark, *n.*, a milestone; a guidepost.

way′side, *adj.*, beside the road; *n.*, the side of the road.

way′ward, *adj.*, perverse; going one's own way.

way′wardly, *adv.*, in a wayward way.

way′wardness, *n.*, the state of being wayward.

way′worn, *adj.*, tired; weary.

wayz′goose, *n.*, a yearly outing or festivity, esp. of printers.

we, *pers. pron.*, 1st person, pl.

weak, *adj.*, not strong; feeble; without influence; yielding; easily led astray.

weak′en, *v.i.*, to become weak; to yield; *v.t.*, to make weak; to undermine.

weak′ened, *p.p.*, weaken.

weak′ener, *n.*, one who, or that which, weakens.

weak′ening, *pr.p.*, weaken.

weak′er, *adj.*, *comp.* of weak.

weak′est, *adj.*, *super.* of weak.

weak′-eyed, *adj.*, having weak eyes.

weak′-kneed, *adj.*, with weak knees; weak-willed.

weak′ling, *n.*, a poor, weak creature.

weak′ly, *adj.*, in frail health; *adv.*, in a weak way.

weak-mind′ed, *adj.*, weak in character; mentally deranged.

weak′ness, *n.*, the quality or state of being weak.

weak-sight′ed, *adj.*, having poor eyesight.

weal, *n.*, happiness; prosperity; *i.q.* wale and wheal; *v.t.*, *i.q.* wale.

weald, *n.*, a forest; *i.q.* wold.

weald′en, *adj.*, pert. or rel. to a weald; *n.*, the lower cretaceous strata, esp. of the weald.

wealth, *n.*, well-being; prosperity; riches.

wealth′ier, *adj.*, *comp.* of wealthy.

wealth′iest, *adj.*, *super.* of wealthy.

wealth′ily, *adv.*, richly.

wealth′y, *adj.*, rich; affluent.

wean, *v.t.*, to cease suckling; to alienate.

weaned, *p.p.*, wean.

wean′ing, *pr.p.*, wean.

wean′ling, *n.*, an infant just weaned.

weap′on, *n.*, an instrument of destruction or violence.

weap′oned, *adj.*, armed with a weapon.

weap′onless, *adj.*, unarmed.

wear, *n.*, the act of wearing; the state of being worn; what is worn as dress; *v.i.*, to become worn; to stand wear; *v.t.*, to destroy by gradual friction, long use, etc.; to assume; to be clothed with.

wearabi′lity, *n.*, the capacity for being worn.

wear'able, *adj.*, able to be worn.

wear'er, *n.*, one who wears.

wear'ied, *p.p.*, weary.

wear'ier, *adj.*, *comp.* of weary.

wear'iest, *adj.*, *super.* of weary.

wear'iless, *adj.*, untiring.

wear'ily, *adv.*, in a weary way.

wear'iness, *n.*, the state of being weary, fatigue.

wear'ing, *adj.*, distressing; *pr.p.*, wear.

wear'isome, *adj.*, tiring; tedious; boring.

wear'isomeness, *n.*, the quality or state of being wearisome.

wear'y, *adj.*, tired; fatigued; tiring; *v.i.*, to grow tired; *v.t.*, to make weary; to tire.

wear'ying, *pr.p.*, weary.

wea'sand, *n.*, the windpipe.

wea'sel, *n.*, a small carnivore; a mean person (*slang*); a snow tractor.

weath'er, *adj.*, on the windward side; *n.*, the atmospheric state; *v.i.*, to be changed by exposure to the atmosphere; *v.t.*, to waste by the action of the air; to overcome by enduring.

weath'er-beaten, *adj.*, hardened by exposure to wind and rain; worn and ancient.

weath'er-board, *n.*, a horizontal board placed as the cover or protection of a wall, etc., to throw off the rain; *v.t.*, to protect with weatherboards.

weath'er-boarding, *n.*, overlapping weatherboards used in the structure of buildings.

weath'er-bound, *adj.*, unable to move by reason of the weather.

weath'er-chart, *n.*, a diagram of weather conditions.

weath'ercock, *n.*, *i.q.* weather-vane.

weath'ered, *p.p.*, weather.

weath'er-eye, *n.*, watchfulness.

weath'er-forecast, *n.*, a prophecy of the weather by experts.

weath'er-gauge, *n.*, a ship's position to windward of another ship.

weath'er-glass, *n.*, a barometer.

weath'ering, *n.*, architecturally, a slight slant in a horizontal surface in order to throw off the water; decay, waste, etc., due to atmospheric action; *pr.p.*, weather.

weath'erly, *adj.*, able to keep on its course without drifting to leeward.

weath'erproof, *adj.*, resistant to the effects of weather.

weath'er-ship, *n.*, one used to collect meteorological data.

weath'er-side, *n.*, the windward side.

weath'er-vane, *n.*, a figure placed at the top of a building or spire which, by rotating with the wind, shows its direction. (Also *weathercock*.)

weath'erwise, *adj.*, possessing, or affecting a knowledge of weather-signs.

weave, *v.i.*, to do weaving; *v.t.*, to intertwine; to work with a loom; to produce textiles by interlacing fibres.

weav'er, *n.*, one who weaves.

weav'ing, *n.*, the weaver's art; *pr.p.*, weave.

wea'zen, *adj.*, withered-looking.

web, *n.*, threads woven together; texture; anything weblike, as the membrane in web-footed creatures, etc.; *v.t.*, to form as a web.

webbed, *p.p.*, web.

web'bing, *n.*, strong, woven braid used in upholstering; *pr.p.*, web.

web'by, *adj.*, weblike; full of webs.

web'-foot, *n.*, a web-footed creature.

web'footed, *adj.*, having a membrane between the divisions of the foot.

Web'ley, *n.*, a type of pistol.

web'ster, *n.*, a weaver.

wed, *v.i.* and *t.*, to marry.

wed'ded, *p.p.*, wed.

wed'ding, *n.*, the marriage ceremony and its celebration; *pr.p.*, wed.

wed'ding-bells, *n.*, bells which are rung by the church where the wedding ceremony takes place.

wed'ding-break'fast, *n.*, the entertainment of guests after the wedding ceremony before the departure for the honeymoon.

wed'ding-cake, *n.*, an ornamental, iced cake eaten at the wedding and distributed to absent friends and relatives.

wed'ding-day, *n.*, the day or anniversary of marriage.

wed'ding-march, *n.*, the music played at a wedding when the bride leaves the church.

wed'ding-ring, *n.*, usu. a gold ring given by the bridegroom to his bride (and sometimes to each other) during the wedding ceremony.

wedge, *n.*, a V-shaped piece of wood or metal, used for forcing into anything or securing it in position; anything wedge-shaped; *v.t.*, to drive a wedge into; to fix tight.

wedged, *adj.*, *i.q.* wedge-shaped; *p.p.*, wedge.

wedge'-shaped, *adj.*, like a wedge.

wedg'ing, *pr.p.*, wedge.

Wedg'wood, *n.*, pottery made at Wedgwood's works, Etruria, Staffordshire.

wed'lock, *n.*, the state of being contractually married.

Wednes'day, *n.*, the fourth day of the week, named after Woden or Odin.

wee, *adj.*, tiny (*Scot.*).

weed, *n.*, a wild, useless plant, often interfering with the growth of cultivated plants; tobacco, a cigar (*colloq.*); a poor sort of animal; *v.i.*, to do weeding; *v.t.*, to pull weeds up.

weed'ed, *p.p.*, weed.

weed'er, *n.*, one who, or that which, weeds.

weed'ery, *n.,* weeds growing in great numbers.

weed'icide, *n.,* a weed-killer.

weed'iness, *n.,* sickly growth; of feeble muscular physique.

weed'ing, *n.,* the act or employment of weeding; *pr.p.,* weed.

weed'ing-hook, *n.,* a hooked implement used in weeding; a bill-hook.

weed'killer, *n.,* a preparation, in solid, liquid or spray form, for the destruction of weeds.

weed'less, *adj.,* free from weeds.

weed'y, *adj.,* full of weeds; weed-like, rank, overgrown and weakly (*colloq.*).

week, *n.,* a period of seven days; sennight.

week'day, *n.,* one of the six days exclusive of Sunday.

week'-end, (week-end'), *n.,* the period at the end of a week (from Friday or Saturday to Monday).

week-en'der, *n.,* one who comes to a place only for week-ends.

week'ly, *adj.,* happening, being published etc., every week; once a week; lasting for a week.

weel, *n.,* a willow or rush fish-trap.

weem, *n.,* a cave.

ween, *v.i.,* to think; to have the opinion.

weened, *p.p.,* ween.

ween'ing, *pr.p.,* ween.

ween'y, *adj.,* very small.

weep, *v.i.,* to shed tears; to cry; *v.t.,* to lament for.

weep'er, *n.,* one who weeps; a mourning-band; *pl.,* the cuffs of a mourning dress.

weep'ing, *pr.p.,* weep.

weep'ing-wil'low, *n.,* a variety of willow distinguished by its pendulous branches.

weev'er, *n.,* a fish genus with sharp spines on the back.

weev'il, *n.,* a beetle, destructive to grain, roots, etc.; any insect that gets into a grain store and destroys the grain.

wee'vil(l)ed, *adj.,* attacked by weevils.

weft, *n.,* the cross-threads of a web.

weige'lia, *n.,* a flowering shrub, originally from the Far East.

weigh, *n.,* the act of weighing; *v.i.,* to be of a certain weight; to set sail; *v.t.,* to balance for the purpose of ascertaining the weight; to balance in the mind; to ponder; to press down; to lift up (an anchor).

weigh'able, *adj.,* able to be weighed.

weigh'age, *n.,* the market charge for weighing.

weigh'bridge, *n.,* platform scales usually flush with the ground.

weighed, *p.p.,* weigh.

weigh'er, *n.,* one who, or that which, weighs.

weigh'-house, *n.,* a building where freight, etc., can be weighed.

weigh'ing, *pr.p.,* weigh.

weigh'ing-machine', *n.,* a machine used to weigh people, animals or heavy objects.

weight, *n.,* the measure of the force which attracts bodies to the earth's centre; the amount that a thing weighs; the relative quantity or mass; a heavy object; a standard by which things are weighed, as a pound weight, etc.; influence; import; *v.t.,* to load; to burden; to adulterate; to give emphasis to, statistically.

weight'ed, *p.p.,* weight.

weight'ier, *adj.,* *comp.* of weighty.

weight'iest, *adj.,* *super.* of weighty.

weight'ily, *adv.,* in a weighty way.

weight'iness, *n.,* the quality or state of being weighty.

weight'ing, *pr.p.,* weight.

weight'less, *adj.,* without weight.

weight'y, *adj.,* heavy; ponderous; influential; important.

weir, *n.,* a dam across a river.

weird, *adj.,* strange; mysterious; uncanny.

weird'ly, *adv.,* in a weird way.

weird'ness, *n.,* the state of being weird.

Weis'mannism, *n.,* the doctrine that acquired characteristics are not transmitted (*biol.*).

Welch, *adj.,* Welsh (applying only to the Welch Regiment and the Royal Welch Fusiliers).

wel'come, *adj.,* gladly received or admitted; timely and agreeable; *interj.,* delighted to see you!; *n.,* a hospitable greeting; hospitality; *v.t.,* to greet on arriving; to receive with hospitality.

wel'comed, *p.p.,* welcome.

wel'comer, *n.,* one who welcomes.

wel'coming, *pr.p.,* welcome.

weld, *n.,* the result of welding; dyer's-weed, formerly used for a yellow dye; *v.t.,* to join by hammering or by pressure; to combine pieces into a homogeneous whole.

weldabil'ity, *n.,* the ability to be welded.

weld'able, *adj.,* able to be welded.

weld'ed, *p.p.,* weld.

weld'er, *n.,* a craftsman in welding.

weld'ing, *n.,* the act of joining together; *pr.p.,* weld.

weld'ing-rod, *n.,* a rod which, when melted, supplies the metal for welding.

wel'fare, *n.,* well-being; happiness; prosperity.

wel'farism, *n.,* the policy of state social welfare.

wel'kin, *n.,* the sky (*poet.*).

we'll, abbrev. of we will (*colloq.*).

well, *adj.,* in good health; *adv.,* in a good state; in a good manner; satisfactorily; sufficiently; *interj.* expressing surprise; *v.i.,* to gush forth; to spring up; *n.,* a spring of water or oil; a shaft sunk into the ground down to the water or oil; anything like a well.

well'aday, *interj.,* expressing grief. (Also *wellaway.*)

well-advised, *adj.,* wise; prudent.

well-*bal'anced*, *adj.,* equally matched; sane; of good proportions; sensible.

well'-behaved, *adj.,* acting with propriety.

well'-being, *n., i.q.* welfare.

well-born', *adj.,* of a good family; aristocratic.

well'-bred, *adj.,* of good breeding; of good manners.

well-connec'ted, *adj.,* knowing the right people; of a good family.

well-disposed, *adj.,* friendly.

well'-doer, *n.,* a virtuous person; a doer of good deeds.

well'-doing, *n.,* good conduct; good deeds.

well-done', *adj.,* done well; rightly formed; cooked rather more than normally; *interj.,* splendid!

well-dressed', *adj.,* smartly attired.

welled, *p.p.,* well.

well'-educated, *adj.,* having a good education.

well-fav'oured, *adj.,* handsome.

well-found'ed, *adj.,* believable.

well-groomed', *adj.,* clean and neat and tidily dressed.

well-grown', *adj.,* big, strong and healthy.

well-*informed'*, *adj.,* having correct information.

wel'ling, *pr.p.,* well.

Wellingto'nia, *n.,* a large Californian tree.

Wellingto'nian, *adj.,* pert. or rel. to Wellington, either to the school or to the 19th Cent. Duke.

well'ingtons, *n. pl.,* tall waterproof boots.

well-knit', *adj.,* compact, tight and strong.

well-known', *adj.,* celebrated; famous; familiar.

well-man'nered, *adj.,* courteous.

well-mean'ing, *adj.,* having good intentions.

well-meant', *adj.,* with good intentions.

well-met', *adj.,* welcome.

wellnigh', *adv.,* nearly; almost.

well-off, *adj.,* rich; in good circumstances.

well-oiled', *adj.,* lubricated; intoxicated *(slang).*

well'-ordered, *adj.,* correctly arranged.

well-preserved', *adj.,* not showing age.

well-read', *adj.,* cultured.

Well'sian, *adj.,* pert. or rel. to H. G. Wells or his writings.

well-spok'en, *adj.,* polite and articulate.

well'spring, *n.,* a fount; the source.

well-timed', *adj.,* opportune.

well-*to-do'*, *adj.,* in sound financial circumstances.

well'-water, *n.,* water from a well.

well'wisher, *n.,* a person with friendly intent.

well-worn', *adj.,* long-used; trite.

Welsh, *adj.,* pert. or rel. to Wales and the people of W. or their language; *n.,* the Welsh language or the people.

welsh, *v.t.,* to cheat on a racecourse.

welsh'er, *n.,* one who welshes.

Welsh'ism, *n.,* the idiom peculiar to Wales.

Welsh'man, *n.,* a native of Wales.

welsh-rab'bit, *n.,* cheese melted on toast.

welt, *n.,* a piece of leather between the sole and the upper of a boot; a weal; *v.t.,* to put welts in.

welt'ed, *p.p.,* welt.

wel'ter, *adj.,* of a particular weight for a race or contest; *n.,* a state of weltering; turmoil; *v.i.,* to wallow.

wel'tered, *p.p.,* welter.

wel'tering, *adj.,* wallowing; *pr.p.,* welter.

wel'terweight, *n.,* a boxer who is between middle and lightweight.

welt'ing, *pr.p.,* welt.

wen, *n.,* a fleshy neck or scalp tumour.

wench, *n.,* a girl; *v.i.,* to associate with loose women.

Wend, *n.,* a Slavic person of E. Germany.

wend, *v.i.,* to go.

wend'ed, *p.p.,* wend.

wend'ing, *pr.p.,* wend.

Wend'ish, *adj.,* pert. or rel. to the Wends.

wen'ny, *adj.,* like a wen; troubled with wens.

Wen'sleydale, *n.,* a type of cheese.

went, *p.p.,* go and wend.

wen'tletrap, *n.,* a spirally shaped shellfish.

wept, *p.p.,* weep.

we're, abbrev. of we are *(colloq.).*

were, *p.t.,* be; also the past subjunctive.

weren't, abbrev. of were not *(colloq.).*

were'wolf, *n.,* a human being changed into a wolf.

Werne'rian, *adj.,* pert. or rel. to Werner and his geological doctrines.

wert, 2nd person sing. of were *(arch.).*

Wes'leyan, *adj.,* pert. or rel. to John Wesley and Wesleyanism; *n.,* a follower of Wesley.

Wes'leyanism, *n.,* the religious principles of Wesley's followers; Methodism.

west, *adj.,* situated in the west, or to the west of some other place; *n.,* one of the four points of the compass, opposite to the East; the quarter of the sky where the sun sets; the West country; a Western land.

west'ering, *adj.,* moving westwards.

west'erly, *adj.,* from or towards the west.

west'ern, *adj.,* pert. or rel. to, or toward, the west.

wes'ternism, *n.,* a characteristic of western culture.

west'ernize, *v.t.,* to change a culture or society into the western pattern.

west'ing, *n.,* the distance between east and west; the distance covered going westward.

Westpha'lian, *adj.,* pert. or rel. to Westphalia, the old Prussian Kingdom; *n.,* a native of W.

west'ward, *adj.,* towards the west.

west'wardly, *adj., i.q.* westwards.

west'wards, *adv.,* in a westerly direction.

wet, *adj.,* humid; damp; rainy; *n.,* moisture; rain; *v.t.,* to make wet; to moisten.

wet'-blank'et, *n.,* a spoilsport (*colloq.*).

weth'er, *n.,* a castrated ram.

wet'ness, *n.,* the quality or state of being wet; moisture; dampness.

wet'-nurse, *n.,* a nurse who suckles another person's child; *v.i.,* to act the wet-nurse; to treat as a child (*colloq.*); *v.t.,* to suckle another person's child.

wet'shod, *adj.,* with wet shoes and feet.

wet'ted, *p.p.,* wet.

wet'ter, *adj., comp.* of wet.

wet'test, *adj., super.* of wet.

wet'ting, *n.,* the result of exposure to wet; *pr.p.,* wet.

wet'tish, *adj.,* inclined to be wet.

wey, *n.,* a varying measure of weight.

whack, *n.,* a flat blow; a big slice (*colloq.*); *v.t.,* to strike.

whacked, *p.p.,* whack.

whack'er, *n.,* one who whacks; a big lie (*colloq.*).

whack'ing, *n.,* a beating; *pr.p.,* whack.

whale, *n.,* a huge cetaceous mammal.

whale'boat, *n.,* a boat used in whale-fishing.

whale'bone, *n.,* a flexible material obtained from the upper jaw of a whale.

whale'man, *n.,* a whalefisher; a whaler.

whale'-oil, *n.,* oil from a whale's blubber.

wha'ler, *n.,* a boat used for whale-fishing; a whaleman.

wha'lery, *n.,* whale fishing.

wha'ling, *n.,* the occupation of catching whales.

whang, *n.,* a thong or string of leather; *v.t.,* to flog; to beat.

whangee', *n.,* a kind of bamboo cane.

whap, *v.t., i.q.* whop.

whare, *n.,* a Maori hut.

wharf, *n.,* a landingstage or quay; *v.t.,* to moor at a wharf; to store on a wharf.

wharf'age, *n.,* the toll on a wharf.

wharf'ing, *n.,* wharves collectively; a wharflike erection; *pr.p.,* wharf.

wharf'inger, *n.,* a wharfowner.

wharf'master, *n.,* an official in charge of a wharf.

what, *exclamation,* expressing surprise, doubt, etc.; *interrog.,* *adj.* and *pron.,* asking for specific information, as "What noise was that?"; *rel. pron.,* what being used for "that which".

what'ever, *adj.* and *indef. rel. pron.,* anything which; no matter what. (Also *whatsoever.*)

what'-not, *n.,* a bracket or set of shelves for bric-a-brac.

whatsoev'er, *adj., i.q.* whatever.

wheal, *n.,* a principle; a mine, esp. a tinmine. (Also *weal.*)

wheat, *n.,* the most important of the cereals and the grain it produces.

wheat'ear, *n.,* the stonechat.

wheat'en, *adj.,* made of wheat.

wheat'grower, *n.,* one who grows wheat.

wheat'meal, *adj. n.,* of wheat flour constituents; meal from wheat.

wheat'sheaf, *n.,* a sheaf of wheat.

Wheat'stone bridge, *n.,* a device for measuring electrical resistance.

whee'dle, *v.t.,* to coax; to cajole.

whee'dled, *p.p.,* wheedle.

wheed'ler, *n.,* one who wheedles.

whee'dling, *n.,* coaxing; *pr.p.,* wheedle.

wheel, *n.,* a mechanical or transportation device, consisting either of a disc revolving about its centre or radially spoked; *v.i.,* to swing round; to gyrate; to ride a bicycle, etc.; *v.t.,* to turn round; to roll on wheels; to push a wheeled cart.

wheel'barrow, *n.,* a kind of hand-cart mounted on a wheel or wheels.

wheel'-base, *n.,* the distance between the front and rear axles of a vehicle.

wheel'-carriage, *n.,* a wheeled vehicle.

wheel'-chair, *n.,* a chair on wheels, esp. for invalids.

wheeled, *adj.,* provided with wheels; *p.p.,* wheel.

wheel'er, *n.,* one who wheels; *i.q.* wheelhorse.

wheel'-horse, *n.,* a horse in the shafts; a polehorse in a four-inhand, etc.

wheel'house, *n.,* a structure aboard ship giving shelter to the navigator and controller of the vessel.

wheel'ing, *pr.p.,* wheel.

wheel'wright, *n.,* a maker of wheels and wheeled vehicles.

wheeze, *n.,* the sound of wheezing; *v.i.,* to breathe with a distressing sound.

wheezed, *p.p.,* wheeze.

wheezing', *n.,* the act of wheezing; *pr.p.,* wheeze.

wheez'y, *adj.,* suffering from wheezing.

whelk, *n.,* a pimple; an edible shellfish.

whelm, *v.t.,* to submerge; to overwhelm.

whelmed, *p.p.,* whelm.

whelm'ing, *pr.p.,* whelm.

whelp, *n.,* the young of a dog, lion, wolf, etc.; a cubbish boy; *v.i.,* to have cubs; *v.t.,* to give birth to.

whelped, *p.p.,* whelp.

whelp'ing, *pr.p.,* whelp.

when, *interrog. pron.,* at what time? *rel. pron.,* (at the time) in which.

whence, *interrog. pronominal adv.,* from which place? *rel. pronominal adv.,* from which (place); (the place) from which.

whencesoe'ver, *adv.,* from any place or source.

whenev'er, *adv.,* at whatever time.

whensoev'er, *adv.,* rather more emphatic than whenever = at any time whatever.

where, *interrog. adv.*, in which place, part, direction? *rel. pron. adv.*, (at the place, to the place, etc.) in which; *n.*, with *the* = locality.

where′about, *adv.*, in regard to which; *i.q.* whereabouts.

where′abouts, *adv.*, a vague equivalent of where; *n.*, locality.

whereas′, *conj.*, the fact being considered that . . .; compared with the fact that . . .; seeing that.

whereat′, *interrog. adv.*, at what? *rel. adv.*, at which.

whereby′, *interrog. adv.*, by what? *rel. adv.*, by which.

where′fore, *interrog. adv.*, for what? why? *rel. adv.*, because of which.

where′in, *interrog. adv.*, in what? *rel. adv.*, in which.

whereinsoev′er, *rel. adv.*, in whatsoever particular or point.

wherein′to, *adv.*, into what or which.

whereof′, *rel. pron.*, of which.

whereon′, *rel. adv.*, on which.

wheresoev′er, *rel. adv.*, in whatever place.

whereto′, *rel. adv.*, to which.

whereun′to, *rel. adv.*, *i.q.* whereto.

whereupon′, *rel. adv.*, immediately after, or in consequence of, which.

wherev′er, *rel. adv.*, in whatever place.

wherewith′, *rel. adv.*, with which.

wherewithal′, *rel. adv.*, with which; *n.*, means.

wher′ry, *n.*, a type of boat, with sails, for navigating shallow waters; a light, oared boat; a fishing-boat decked; a drink made from crab-apples.

whet, *v.t.*, to sharpen; to make keen.

wheth′er, *conj.*, which of one or the other of two courses or alternatives; *pron. interrog.*, which of two.

whet′slate, *n.*, a hard stone used for sharpening blades, etc.

whet′stone, *n.*, a stone on which knives, etc., are sharpened.

whet′ted, *p.p.*, whet.

whet′ter, *n.*, one who whets.

whet′ting, *pr.p.*, whet.

whew, *interj.*, expressing a feeling of heat, discomfort, etc.

whew′ellite, *n.*, a hydrous calcium oxalate.

whey, *n.*, the thin part of milk after the curd has been separated.

whey′-butter, *n.*, butter made from whey.

whey′ey, *adj.*, like, containing, whey.

whey′ish, *adj.*, like whey.

which, *pron. interrog.*, asking what person or thing; the *rel. pron.* stands as the non-personal of who.

whichev′er, *rel. pron. indef.* any one.

whichsoev′er, *i.q.* whichever, but slightly more emphatic.

whiff, *n.*, a slight puff; a small outrigger; a thin, small cigar; *v.t.*, to draw or emit a whiff.

whiffed, *p.p.*, whiff.

whiff′ing, *pr.p.*, whiff.

whif′fle, *v.i.* and *t.*, to change capriciously.

whif′fled, *p.p.*, whiffle.

whif′fler, *n.*, one who whiffles.

whif′fletree, *n.*, a cross-bar swinging on a pivot, having the traces of a cart or plough attached to its ends. (Also *swingletree*.)

whif′fling, *pr.p.*, whiffle.

Whig, *n.*, a member of a political party opposed to the Tories. Its interests were largely bound up with certain powerful landed families.

Whig′garchy, *n.*, the rule of the Whigs.

Whig′gery, *n.*, the principles of Whigs.

Whig′gish, *adj.*, favourable, pert. or rel. to, Whiggery.

Whig′gism, *n.*, *i.q.* Whiggery.

while, *conj.*, during the time when; whereas; *n.*, a period of time; *v.t.*, to make time pass agreeably.

whiled, *p.p.*, while.

whiles, *adv.*, at times (*Scot.*).

whil′ing, *pr.p.*, while.

whi′lom, *adv.*, in former time (*arch.*).

whilst, *conj.*, *i.q.* while.

whim, *n.*, a caprice; a freak; a crotchet.

whim′brel, *n.*, a variety of curlew.

whim′per, *n.*, a low whine indicating distress; *v.i.*, to make a low whine; *v.t.*, to utter with a whimper.

whim′pered, *p.p.*, whimper.

whim′perer, *n.*, one who, or that which, whimpers.

whim′pering, *n.*, *i.q.* whimper; *pr.p.*, whimper.

whim′peringly, *adv.*, in a whimpering way.

whim′sey, *n.*, *i.q.* whim and whimsy.

whim′sical, *adj.*, full of whims; crotchety; fanciful.

whimsical′ity, *n.*, the state of being whimsical.

whim′sically, *adv.*, in a whimsical way.

whim′sy, *n.*, an idle or unusual fancy.

whim′wham, *n.*, an absurd idea; a toy.

whin, *n.*, furze; heath bushes.

whin′chat, *n.*, a small bird similar to the stonechat.

whine, *n.*, a plaintive cry; *v.i.*, to cry in a self-pitying way.

whined, *p.p.*, whine.

whi′ner, *n.*, one who whines or complains.

whi′ning, *pr.p.*, whine.

whi′ningly, *adv.*, in a whining way.

whin′nied, *p.p.*, whinny.

whin′ny, *n.*, the neigh of a horse; *v.i.*, to make the sound.

whin′nying, *pr.p.*, whinny.

whin′stone, *n.*, a hard kind of rock.

whin′yard, *n.*, a short sword.

whip, *n.*, an instrument for punishing or driving; a lash; a driver; a Parliamentary party summoner; the summons he sends out; *v.t.*, to punish; to correct; to drive; to beat; to oversew.

whip'cord, *n.*, cord with which whip-lashes are made.

whip'hand, *n.*, the superior position.

whip'maker, *n.*, a maker of whips.

whipped, *p.p.*, whip.

whip'per, *n.*, one who whips.

whip'per-in, *n.*, a huntsman in charge of the hounds.

whip'per-snap'per, *n.*, a youngster; an insignificant little person.

whip'pet, *n.*, a breed of small, fast-running dogs.

whip'piness, *n.*, the quality or state of being whippy.

whip'ping, *n.*, punishment with a whip; *pr.p.*, whip.

whip'ping-post, *n.*, a post to which a person was tied when about to be whipped.

whip'pletree, *n.*, the cornel or dogwood.

whip'poorwill, *n.*, a goatsucker bird.

whippy, *adj.*, flexible; easily bent.

whip-round', *n.*, a small-scale appeal for contributions.

whip'-saw, *n.*, a fret-saw.

whip'-staff, *n.*, a whip handle.

whip'stick, *n.*, the handle of a whip.

whip'stitch, *n.*, an overhand stitch; *v.t.*, to gather with overhand stitching.

whip'-stock, *n.*, a receptacle for a whip.

whip'top, *n.*, a top which is kept spinning by whipping.

whir, *n.*, a trilling noise of rapid unmusical vibration; *v.i.*, to make the sound. (Also *whirr*.)

whirl, *n.*, a rapid twisting round; *v.i.* and *t.*, to turn; to twist; to hurry along.

whirl'about, *n.*, a whirligig.

whirl'bone, *n.*, the socket bone of a ball-and-socket joint; the patella (knee-cap).

whirled, *p.p.*, whirl.

whirl'er, *n.*, one who, or that which, whirls.

whirl'igig, *n.*, a child's spinning toy.

whirl'ing, *pr.p.*, whirl.

whirl'pool, *n.*, a vortex in water.

whirl'wind, *n.*, a rotatory wind-storm.

whirly'-bird, *n.*, a helicopter (*colloq.*).

whirr, *n.* and *v.i.*, *i.q.* whir.

whirred, *p.p.*, whir.

whir'ring, *pr.p.*, whir.

whisht, *interj.*, *i.q.* whist.

whisk, *n.*, a swift movement; a housemaid's brush; a kitchen implement for beating up the constituents of a dish; *v.i.*, to move along rapidly; *v.t.*, to carry off, to brush away rapidly.

whisked, *p.p.*, whisk.

whisk'ered, *adj.*, having whiskers.

whisk'ers, *n. pl.*, hair on the side of the face.

whis'kery, *adj.*, resembling whiskers.

whis'key, *n.*, *i.q.* whisky; (*Ir.* and *U.S.A.*).

whisk'ing, *pr.p.*, whisk.

whis'ky, *n.*, a spirituous liquor distilled from malt and barley; a light gig.

whis'per, *n.*, utterance in a subdued voice; *v.i.*, to speak in a whisper; *v.t.*, to say in a whisper or secretly.

whis'pered, *p.p.*, whisper.

whis'perer, *n.*, one who whispers.

whis'peringly, *adv.*, in a whispering manner.

whis'pering, *adj.*, pert. or rel. to whisper; *pr.p.*, whisper.

whist, *interj.*, hush!; *n.*, a card game for four.

whist-drive, *n.*, an organized progressive game of whist.

whis'tle, *n.*, a musical sound forced through the lips; a wind instrument for signalling, etc.; *v.i.* and *t.*, to force a sound through an aperture of the lips; to indicate surprise or appreciation by whistling.

whis'tled, *p.p.*, whistle.

whis'tler, *n.*, one who whistles.

whis'tle-stop, *n.*, a short halt on a tour of such halts.

whis'tling, *n.*, the act of whistling; *pr.p.*, whistle.

whit, *n.*, a small portion.

white, *adj.*, of the hue of all the colours combined; like snow or salt in colour; pure; *n.*, a white man; the white part of an egg; *v.t.*, to make white.

white'bait, *n.*, a diminutive edible fish.

white'-coll'ar, *adj.*, non-manual.

whi'ted, *adj.*, white-washed; *p.p.*, white.

white'-feather, *n.*, a coward; fear.

White' Friars, *n. pl.*, members of the Carmelite Order.

white'-heat, *n.*, intense heat which makes a body look white.

white'-hot, *adj.*, at white-heat; intensely emotional.

white'-lie, *n.*, a well-intended lie.

white'-liv'ered, *adj.*, cowardly.

whi'ten, *v.t.*, to make white.

whi'tened, *p.p.*, whiten.

whi'tener, *n.*, one who whitens; a substance for whitening.

white'ness, *n.*, state of being white.

whi'tening, *n.*, a white-wash; *pr.p.*, whiten.

whi'ter, *adj. comp.* of white.

white'smith, *n.*, a tinsmith.

whi'test, *adj.*, *super.* of white.

white'thorn, *n.*, the hawthorn.

white'throat, *n.*, a small song bird.

white'wash, *n.*, a mixture used to whiten walls, ceilings, etc.; *v.t.*, to wash with the mixture; to act so as to give the semblance of innocence or legality; to beat a person at a game without his having scored.

white'washed, *p.p.*, whitewash.

white'washer, *n.*, one who whitewashes.

white'washing, *n.*, the act of whitewashing; *pr.p.*, whitewash.

white'weed, *n.*, the oxeye daisy.

white'wing, *n.*, the chaffinch.

white'wood, *n.*, the wood of the tulip-tree.

whith'er, *adv.*, *interrog.*, towards what place? *adv. rel.*, (place) toward which.

whithersoev'er, *adv. rel.*, towards whatsoever place.

whi'ting, *n.*, powdered chalk; a fish; *pr.p.*, white.

whi'tish, *adj.*, somewhat white or pale in colour.

whit'low, *n.*, a painful growth at the quick of the nail; a similar growth in a sheep's foot.

Whit'sun, *adj.*, pert. or rel. to Whitsuntide.

Whit'sunday, *n.*, the Christian Church's Pentecostal Feast; the seventh Sunday after Easter.

Whit'suntide, *n.*, the week between Whit-Sunday and Trinity Sunday.

Whit'sun-week, *n.*, the week beginning with Whitsunday.

whit'tle, *v.t.*, to cut away bit by bit; to shorten.

whit'tled, *p.p.*, whittle.

whit'tling, *pr.p.*, whittle.

Whit'week, *n.*, *i.q.* Whitsuntide, Whitsunweek.

whiz, *n.*, a sound part hum, part hiss; *v.i.*, to make the sound; to fly with a whizzing sound; to move rapidly.

whizzed, *p.p.*, whiz.

whiz'zing, *pr.p.*, whiz.

who, *interrog. pron.*, what or which person? *rel. pron.*, the person referred to.

whoa, *exclam.*, used by carters to their horses when they wish them to stop.

whoev'er, *rel. pron.*, any or every one who.

whole, *adj.*, entire; sound; in good health; *n.*, entirety; the entire collection.

whole'heart'ed, *adj.*, with sincerity and concentration.

wholeheart'edly, *adv.*, in an enthusiastic and concentrated way.

wholeheart'edness, *n.*, quality of sincerity and effort.

whole'meal, *adj. and n.*, (flour) of complete wheat grains; of that constituency.

whole'ness, *n.*, the quality or state of being whole.

whole'sale, *adj.*, sold in bulk; not retail; *n.*, sale in bulk not retail.

whole'saler, *n.*, one who sells in bulk.

whole'some, *adj.*, healthy; sound; salutary.

whole'somely, *adv.*, in a wholesome way.

whole'someness, *n.*, the quality or state of being wholesome.

whol'ly, *adv.*, entirely; completely.

whom, *interrog. and rel. pron. obj. case of* who.

whomsoev'er, *rel. pron. obj. case of* whosoever.

whoop, *n.*, a yell; *v.i.*, to yell; to shriek.

whooped, *p.p.*, whoop.

whoopee, *n.*, riotous enjoyment.

whoop'ing, *pr.p.*, whoop.

whoop'ing-cough, *n.*, an infectious disease, distinguished by a cough having a whooping sound.

whop, *n.*, a fall; a blow; *v.t.*, to beat. (Also *wap*.)

whopped, *p.p.*, whop.

whop'per, *n.*, a big lie (*slang*); anything very big.

whop'ping, *pr.p.*, whop.

whore, *n.*, a prostitute; *v.i.*, to keep company with prostitutes.

whore'dom, *n.*, prostitution.

whore'monger, *n.*, one who has dealings with prostitutes.

whor'ish, *adj.*, like a prostitute.

whor'ishly, *adv.*, in a whorish way.

whorl, *n.*, a ring of leaves or other growth round the stem of a plant; a turn of a spiral; the fly of a spinning wheel; one distinguishing mark of fingerprints.

whorled, *adj.*, having whorls.

whort, *n.*, *i.q.* whortleberry.

whor'tleberry, *n.*, an edible fruit.

whose, *interrog. poss. pron.*, of whom? bel. to whom? *rel. poss. pron.* of whom; bel. to whom.

whosesoev'er, *rel. poss. pron.*, of whomsoever.

who'so, *indef. rel. pron.*, anyone who.

whosoev'er, *indef. rel. pron.*, somewhat more indefinite than whoso.

why, *interj.*, expressing curiosity or surprise; *interrog. adv.*, for what reason? with what purpose?; *n.*, the reason; the wherefore.

wick, *n.*, the part of a candle or lamp that is lighted; an inhabited place (used in place names like *Berwick*, *Giggleswick*).

wick'ed, *adj.*, sinful; depraved; evil.

wick'edly, *adv.*, in a wicked way.

wick'edness, *n.*, the quality or state of being wicked.

wick'er, *adj.*, plaited with osier; *n.*, osier.

wick'ered, *adj.*, made of wickerwork.

wick'erwork, *n.*, plaited osier.

wick'et, *n.*, a little gate, sometimes forming part of a larger one; a set of three stumps and two bails.

wick'et-keeper, *n.*, in cricket, the player who is positioned behind the wicket.

widd'ershins, *adv.*, *i.q.* withershins.

wide, *adj.*, broad; spacious; vast; away from a mark; *adv.*, to a distance; *n.*, in cricket, a ball bowled outside the limits of the ends of the crease.

wide'awake, *adj.*, on the alert; free from sleepiness; *n.*, a soft felt hat.

wide-eyed', *adj.*, with eyes open to full extent.

wide'ly, *adv.*, far; to a distance.

wide-mouthed', *adj.*, agape.

wi'den, *v.i.*, to become wider; *v.t.*, to make wider.

wi'dened, *p.p.*, widen.

wide'ness, *n.*, *i.q.* width.

wi'dening, *n.*, the act of making or becoming wider or open; *pr.p.*, widen.

wide'-open, *adj.*, opened to the maximum extent.

wi'der, *adj.*, *comp.* of wide.

wide'spread, *adj.*, extending over a great distance or range.

wi'dest, *adj.*, *super.* of wide.

widge'on, *n.*, a variety of wild duck.

wid'ish, *adj.*, fairly wide.

wid'ow, *n.*, a woman whose husband is dead, and who remains single; *v.t.*, to bereave of a husband or of a wife.

wid'owed, *adj.*, in the state of a widow or widower; *p.p.*, widow.

wid'ower, *n.*, a man whose wife is dead and who remains single.

wid'owhood, *n.*, the state or period of being a widow.

width, *n.*, breadth; a stretch from side to side.

wield, *v.t.*, to brandish; to move with the hands.

wield'ed, *p.p.*, wield.

wield'er, *n.*, one who wields.

wield'ing, *pr.p.*, wield.

wield'y, *adj.*, easy to handle.

wife, *n.*, a married woman.

wife'hood, *n.*, the state of being a wife.

wife'less, *adj.*, without a wife.

wife'like, *adj.*, as a wife should be.

wife'ly, *adj.*, *i.q.* wifelike.

wig, *n.*, a false head of hair; *v.t.*, to scold (*colloq.*).

wig'an, *n.*, a canvas used as stiffening.

wigged, *adj.*, wearing a wig; *p.p.*, wig.

wig'ging, *n.*, a scolding (*colloq.*); *pr.p.*, wig.

wig'gle, *v.i.*, to wriggle.

wig'gled, *p.p.*, wiggle.

wig'gling, *n.*, a wriggling; *pr.p.*, wiggle.

wig'gly, *adj.*, wriggly.

wight, *n.*, a being; a person.

wig'-maker, *n.*, one who makes wigs.

wig'wag, *adv.*, to and fro.

wig'wam, *n.*, a N. Amer. Indian's hut or tent.

wild, *adj.*, untamed; fierce; violent; blustering; dissipated; *n.*, the wilderness.

wild'cat, *adj.*, risky; very speculative.

wild'-duck, *n.*, the mallard.

wil'debeest, *n.*, a common type of African game; the gnu.

wild'er, *adj.*, *comp.* of wild.

wil'der, *v.t.*, *i.q.* bewilder (*poet.*).

wil'dered, *p.p.*, wilder.

wil'dering, *adj.*, perplexing; bewildering; *pr.p.*, wilder.

wil'derment, *n.*, *i.q.* bewilderment.

wil'derness, *n.*, a desert; a barren, uninhabited area.

wild'est, *adj.*, *super.* of wild.

wild'fire, *n.*, an old destructive device, consisting of combustible material for setting fire to an enemy's ships; heat-lighting; a symbol used for rapid spread or growth.

wild'-fowl, *n. pl.*, wild birds, esp. game.

wild-goose-chase, *n.*, a hopeless pursuit.

wild'ing, *n.*, a plant sown by nature, esp. the wild crab-apple.

wild'ish, *adj.*, rather wild.

wild'ly, *adv.*, in a wild way.

wild'ness, *n.*, the quality or state of being wild.

wile, *n.*, a trick; cunning; *v.t.*, to deceive; to entrap.

wile'less, *adj.*, free from wiles.

wil'ful, *adj.*, self-willed; obstinate.

wil'fully, *adv.*, in a wilful way.

wil'fulness, *n.*, the state of being wilful.

wi'lier, *adj.*, *comp.* of wily.

wi'liest, *adj.*, *super.* of wily.

wi'lily, *adv.*, in a wily way.

wi'liness, *n.*, cunning; craftiness.

will, *n.*, determination; the mental power of choice; command; desire; testamentary disposition; *v.t.*, to resolve; to determine to ordain; to bequeath. (The word is also used as an auxiliary to form the future tense.)

willed, *p.p.*, will.

wil'let, *n.*, a snipe.

wil'lies, *n. pl.*, a fit of distaste or revulsion (*colloq.*).

wil'ling, *adj.*, ready; complying; *pr.p.*, will.

wil'lingly, *adv.*, in a willing way; voluntarily; readily.

wil'lingness, *n.*, the state of being willing.

will-o'-the-wisp, *n.*, a curious, moving light that plays over marshes; *ignis fatuus*; a person always difficult to locate.

wil'low, *n.*, a tree; a cricketbat (*poet.*).

wil'lowed, *adj.*, planted with willows.

wil'low-herb, *n.*, a perennial herb.

wil'low-pattern, *n.*, a Chinese-style pattern usu. in blue on white china.

wil'low-ware, *n.*, articles made from osiers.

wil'lowy, *adj.*, like a willow; lithe, lissom.

wil'ly, *adj.*, *i.q.* wilful (*Scot.*).

wil'ly-nil'ly, *adv.*, whether one likes or not; *n.*, a tropical storm.

wil'some, *adj.*, obstinate; wilful.

wilt, 2nd *per.* sing., will (*arch.*); *v.t.*, to cause to droop; *v.i.*, to droop; to fade.

wilt'ed, *p.p.*, wilt.

wilt'ing, *pr.p.*, wilt.

Wil'ton, *n.*, cut pile carpet of a special kind, named after W. in Wiltshire.

Wilt'shire, *n.*, a whole side of bacon; a county in S.W. England.

wi'ly, *adj.*, crafty; cunning.

wim'ble, *n.*, a boring-tool; *v.t.*, to bore.

Wim'bledon, *n.*, the headquarters of lawn-tennis in Great Britain.

wim'ple, *n.*, a head-covering once commonly worn by women, and now retained by nuns; *v.i.*, to undulate; *v.t.*, to cover with a wimple.

wim'pled, *adj.*, wearing a wimple.

wim'pling, *adj.*, rippling.

win, *n.*, an achieved success; *v.i.*, to gain a victory or success; *v.t.*, to gain; to obtain.

wince, *n.*, the act of wincing; *v.i.*, to cower; to shrink; to feel repugnance.

winced, *p.p.*, wince.

winc'er, *n.*, one who winces.

win'cey, *n.*, dress fabric.

winceyette', *n.*, strong part-woollen material.

winch, *n.*, a windlass; a crank; *v.t.*, to move by means of a winch.

winched, *p.p.*, winch.

win'chester, *n.*, a repeating rifle; a half-gallon glass jar.

winch'ing, *pr.p.*, winch.

winc'ing, *pr.p.*, wince.

wind, movement of air; breath; air or gas in the stomach; *v.t.*, to take the breath from; to scent.

wind, *v.i.*, to revolve; to take a devious course; *v.t.*, to twist; to coil.

wind'age, *n.*, the difference between the diameter of a projectile and the bore of the gun; the action of the wind on the flight of a projectile.

wind'bag, *n.*, bagpipe bellows; a garrulous person (*colloq.*).

wind'bound, *adj.*, held up by wind.

wind'-break, *n.*, a protection against the wind.

wind'cheater, *n.*, a top garment designed to exclude the wind.

wind'-cone, *n.*, *i.q.* windsock.

wind'ed, *adj.*, with the breath knocked out; breathless; *p.p.*, wind.

wind'er, *n.*, one who, or that which, winds.

wind'fall, *n.*, fruit blown off a tree; an unexpected piece of good luck.

wind'flower, *n.*, the wood anemone.

wind'gall, *n.*, a swelling on a horse's fetlock-joint.

wind'gauge, *n.*, an instrument for measuring the force and direction of wind.

wind'hover, *n.*, the kestrel.

wind'ier, *adj.*, *comp.* of windy.

wind'iest, *adj.*, *super.* of windy.

wind'iness, *n.*, the state of being windy.

wind'ing, *pr.p.*, wind (to take breath from).

wind'ing, *adj.*, twisting; *n.*, a turning; a twisting; *pr.p.*, wind.

wind'ing-sheet, *n.*, the wrapping of a corpse; a cerecloth.

wind'jammer, *n.*, a merchant full-rigged sailing ship.

wind'lass, *n.*, a roller round which a rope or chain is wound.

win'dle, *n.*, a reel; a spindle.

wind'less, *adj.*, out of breath.

wind'lestraw, *n.*, long-stemmed grass.

wind'mill, *n.*, a mill, usually to grind grain, worked by the wind.

win'dow, *n.*, an opening in the wall of a building to let in light and air.

win'dow-box, *n.*, a box (usu. wooden), fitted to a sill or wall, in which small flowering plants are grown.

win'dow-dresser, *n.*, one who arranges goods in a shop window.

win'dow-dressing, *n.*, presenting a situation in a more favourable light than is warranted; the art of displaying goods.

win'dow-en'velope, *n.*, an envelope with an opening to permit the name and address to show through.

win'dow-frame, *n.*, the frame of a window which holds the sashes.

win'dow-glass, *n.*, glazing for a window.

win'dow-pane, *n.*, a sheet of glass in a window-frame.

win'dow-sash, *n.*, the frame of a window-pane.

win'dow-seat, *n.*, a seat in a window.

wind'pipe, *n.*, *i.q.* trachea.

wind'-proof, *adj.*, impervious to the wind.

wind'row, *n.*, a row or pile shaped by the wind's action.

wind'screen, *n.*, a protective glass window for a car, boat, etc.

wind'sock, *n.*, a drogue; a tapered, cylindrical streamer fixed to a mast to show wind direction.

wind'-tunnel, *n.*, a tunnel for flight-testing of model prototypes of aircraft.

wind'ward, *adv.*, toward the wind; *n.*, the quarter from which the wind blows.

wind'y, *adj.*, pert. or rel. to, or full of, wind; blowing; boisterous; empty; frightened (*colloq.*).

wine, *n.*, the juice of the grape.

wine'-bibber, *n.*, one who is too much addicted to wine.

wine'-cellar, *n.*, an underground wine-store.

wine'-glass, *n.*, a glass from which wine is drunk.

wine'-merchant, *n.*, one who deals in wines.

wine'-press, *n.*, a press for crushing grapes for wine.

wine'sap, *n.*, a type of red apple.

wing, *n.*, a bird's pinion with which it flies; any wing-like thing, as one partly detached section of a building; an aisle; *v.i.*, to fly; *v.t.*, to furnish with wings; to wound with a gunshot; to stop the flight of.

wing'-comman'der, *n.*, an air force officer rank.

winged, *p.p.*, wing.

wing'ed, *adj.*, having wings.

wing'ing, *pr.p.*, wing.

wing'less, *adj.*, lacking wings.

wing'let, *n.*, a small wing.

wing'y, *adj.*, having wings; swift.

wink, *n.*, a twitching movement with the eyelids; a suggestive look; *v.i.*, to twitch the eyelids; to give a hint; to pretend not to see; to emit and occlude light in turn; to connive; *v.t.*, to twitch (the eye).

winked, *p.p.*, wink.

wink'er, *n.*, one who winks.

wink'ing, *pr.p.*, wink.

win'kle, *n.*, an edible sea-snail.

win'ner, *n.*, one who, or that which wins.

win'ning, *adj.*, engaging; attractive; *pr.p.*, win.

win'ningly, *adv.*, charmingly.

win'ning-post, *n.*, the end of a race.

win'nings, *n. pl.*, any sum of money that is won.

win'now, v.i., to do winnowing; v.t., to separate (grain) from the husks; to fan.

win'nowed, p.p., winnow.

win'nower, n., one who, or that which, winnows.

win'nowing, n., the process of separating grain and husks; pr.p., winnow.

win'some, adj., engaging; charming.

win'somely, adv., attractively.

win'ter, adj., pert. or rel. to winter; n., the coldest season of the year; the period of least sunlight during the year; v.i., to spend the winter; v.t., to protect or lay up for the winter.

win'tered, p.p., winter.

win'tergreen, n., the name of certain plants which are green through the winter; a medicinal oil.

win'tering, pr.p., winter.

win'terish, adj., rather wintry.

win'terly, adj., i.q. wintery.

win'tery, adj., like winter; cold.

win'try, adj., i.q. winterly.

wi'ny, adj., like wine.

winze, n., a ventilating shaft in a mine.

wipe, n., the act of wiping; a hit; defeat in argument; v.t., to rub; to cleanse or dry by rubbing.

wiped, p.p., wipe.

wi'per, n., one who, or that which, wipes.

wi'ping, pr.p., wipe.

wir'able, adj., able to be wired.

wire, n., metal drawn out into a thread; a telegram (colloq.); v.t., to fence with wire; to snare with wire; a telegraph (colloq.).

wired, p.p., wire.

wire'draw, v.i., to draw wire.

wire'drawer, n., one who draws wire.

wire'drawing, n., a wiredrawer's occupation; pr.p., wiredraw.

wire'drawn, adj., subtle; excessively fine; p.p., wiredraw.

wire'-gauze, n., gauze made of wire.

wire'haired, adj., having stiff hair (dogs).

wire'less, n., the transmission of telegraphic messages without the use of wires (obs.).

wire'puller, n., an intriguer; one who uses secret influence.

wire'pulling, n., intrigue; using secret influence.

wir'er, n., one who wires.

wire'worm, n., a wire-like worm.

wir'iness, n., the quality or state of being wiry.

wir'ing, n., the arrangement of wires in an electrical installation; pr.p., wire.

wir'y, adj., like wire; strong and flexible; able to stand strain; thin but strong.

wis'dom, n., the quality or state of being wise; sagacity; experience; learning, intelligently applied.

wise, adj., sagacious; prudent; learned; experienced.

wise'acre, n., one who lays an unfounded claim to wisdom.

wise'crack, n., a witty, usually caustic, remark or joke.

wise'ly, adv., in a wise way.

wi'ser, adj., comp. of wise.

wi'sest, adj., super. of wise.

wish, n., a desire; something desired; v.i., to have a longing; v.t., to desire.

wish'bone, n., the front bone of a chicken's breast; the merry-thought.

wished, p.p., wish.

wish'er, n., one who wishes.

wish'ful, adj., longing; desiring.

wish'fully, adv., longingly.

wish'fulness, n., the state of being wishful.

wish'ing, pr.p., wish.

wish'tonwish, n., an American prairie dog. (Also wistonwish.)

wish'y-washy, adj., poor, thin.

wisp, n., a thin bunch.

wist, an obsolete word = knew.

Wista'ria, n., a genus of climbing plants.

wist'ful, adj., sad; longing.

wist'fully, adv., in a wistful way.

wist'fulness, n., the state of being wistful.

wis'titi, n., a S. American monkey.

wis'tonwish, n., i.q. wish-tonwish.

wit, n., knowledge; good sense; talent; the power of saying a pointed or clever thing with a touch of the humorous; quickness and sharpness of mind; a person noted for his wit.

Wit'an, n. pl., i.q. witenagemot.

witch, n., a woman supposed to possess supernatural powers through familiarity with evil spirits; a sorceress; a bewitchingly charming woman; v.t., to fascinate.

witch'craft, n., sorcery.

witch'-doctor, n., a priest with magical powers.

witch'-elm, n., a feathery kind of elm tree.

witch'ery, n., enchantment; the power of fascinating.

witch'-hazel, n., a tree (Hamamelis virginica) from which a medicinal extract is made.

witch'ing, adj., enchanting; pr.p., witch.

witch'ingly, adv., enchantingly.

witchol'ogy, n., the study of witchcraft.

Wit'enagemot, n., the ancient Anglo-Saxon national council.

with, prep., in the company of; by means of; as a prefix it indicates antagonism, removal, deprivation.

withal', adv., likewise; also.

withdraw', v.i., to go away; to recede; v.t., to take away; to hold back; to take out.

withdraw'al, n., the act of withdrawing.

withdraw'er, n., one who withdraws.

withdraw'ing, pr.p., withdraw.

withdraw'ing-room, n., what is now called the drawing-room (i.e., a room to which one withdraws from the banqueting-hall).

withdrawn', *p.p.*, withdraw.

withdrew', *p.p.*, withdraw.

withe, *n.*, a twig, usually of willow; twisted twigs. (Also *withy*.)

withed, *adj.*, made of withes.

with'er, *v.i.*, to fade away; to decay; *v.t.*, to cause to fade; to dry up.

with'ered, *p.p.*, wither.

with'ering, *adj.*, crushingly sarcastic; *pr.p.*, wither.

with'eringly, *adv.*, in a withering manner.

with'ers, *n. pl.*, the part between a horse's shoulder-bones.

with'ershins, *adv.*, counter clockwise; contrary in direction to that expected.

withheld', *p.p.*, withhold.

withhold', *v.i.* and *t.*, to keep back; to refuse to give.

withhold'en, *p.p.*, withhold.

withhold'er, *n.*, one who withholds.

withhold'ing, *pr.p.*, withhold.

with'ies, *n. pl.*, of withy.

within', *adv.*, inside.

without', *adv.*, outside; *prep.*, not having; with the omission of.

withstand', *v.t.*, to oppose; to resist.

withstand'ing, *pr.p.*, withstand.

withstood', *p.p.*; withstand.

with'y, *n.*, *i.q.* withe.

wit'less, *adj.*, lacking wits.

wit'lessly, *adv.*, without understanding.

wit'lessness, *n.*, a lack of understanding.

wit'ling, *n.*, an unintellectual person; an idiot.

wit'ness, *n.*, one who testifies; testimony; evidence; *v.i.*, to act as a witness; *v.t.*, to see with one's own eyes; to attest.

wit'nessed, *p.p.*, witness.

wit'nessing, *pr.p.*, witness.

wit'ted, *adj.*, possessed of understanding.

wit'ticism, *n.*, a witty saying.

wit'tier, *adj.*, *comp.* of witty.

wit'tiest, *adj.*, *super.* of witty.

wit'tily, *adv.*, in a witty way.

wit'tiness, *n.*, the quality of being witty.

wit'ting, *adj.*, with full knowledge.

wit'tingly, *adv.*, consciously.

wit'ty, *adj.*, full of wit; characterized by wit; smartly funny.

wit'wall, *n.*, a variety of woodpecker.

wive, *v.i.*, to marry; *v.t.*, to find a wife for.

wived, *p.p.*, wive.

wi'vern, *n.*, *i.q.* wyvern.

wi'ving, *pr.p.*, wive.

wiz'ard, *n.*, the masc. of witch; a sorcerer; a conjurer.

wiz'ardly, *adv.*, like a wizard.

wiz'ardry, *n.*, the arts of a wizard; dazzling expertise.

wiz'en, *adj.*, shrivelled up and faded-looking; *v.t.*, to wither and shrivel up.

wiz'ened, *adj.*, *i.q.* wizen; *p.p.*, wizen.

woad, *n.*, a plant of the Isatis genus formerly used as blue dye.

wob'ble, *n.*, an unsteady motion; *v.i.*, to totter, to show feebleness or unsteadiness.

wob'bled, *p.p.*, wobble.

wob'bling, *pr.p.*, wobble.

Wo'den, *n.*, *i.q.* Odin.

wodge, *n.*, a chunk (*colloq.*).

woe, *n.*, sorrow; grief; calamity.

woe'begone, *adj.*, full of misery.

wo(e)'ful, *adj.*, full of woe; sad; pitiful.

wo(e)'fully, *adv.*, in a woeful manner.

woke, *p.p.*, wake.

wold, *n.*, forest land; open country of an upland character.

wolds, *n. pl.*, a range of hills.

wolf, *n.*, a dog-like wild carnivore; *v.t.*, to eat ravenously.

wolf'-cub, *n.*, a junior (Cub) Scout.

wolf'fish, *n.*, a kind of fish.

wolf'-hound, *n.*, a large hunting dog.

wolf'ish, *adj.*, like a wolf; rapacious.

wolf'ishly, *adv.*, ferociously.

wolf'ram, *n.*, a variety of tungstate (*Ger.*).

wolf's'-bane, *n.*, the aconite.

wolf'-whistle, *n.*, a male whistle of appreciation of a woman's appearance.

wolverine', *n.*, a carnivore.

wom'an, *n.*, the fem. of man; the mature human female.

wom'an-ha'ter, *n.*, a misogynist; one who hates (or pretends to hate) womankind.

wom'anhood, *n.*, the state of being a woman; female maturity.

wom'anish, *adj.*, like a woman; unmanly.

wom'anishly, *adv.*, in a womanish way.

wom'anize, *v.i.*, (of men) to act licentiously; to pursue woman lustfully.

wom'ankind, *n.*, women collectively.

wom'anlike, *adj.*, in the way of a woman.

wom'anliness, *n.*, the qualities appropriate to a woman.

wom'anly, *adj.*, as a woman ought to be.

womb, *n.*, the uterus.

wom'bat, *n.*, a marsupial of Australia.

wom'en, *n.*, the pl. of woman.

wom'enfolk, *n. pl.*, the women of a family; women collectively.

won, *p.p.*, win.

won'der, *n.*, astonishment; surprise; a marvel; a prodigy; *v.i.*, to feel astonishment or surprise; to ponder the truth of.

won'dered, *p.p.*, wonder.

won'derful, *adj.*, surprising; amazing.

won'derfully, *adv.*, in a wonderful way.

won'derfulness, *n.*, the quality or state of being wonderful.

won'dering, *pr.p.*, wonder.

won'deringly, *adv.*, in a wondering way.

won'derland, *n.*, a region of marvels.

won'derment, *n.*, astonishment; perplexity.

won'drous, *adj.*, marvellous.

won'drously, *adv.*, marvellously.

won'ky, *adj.*, insecure, unsound (*slang*).

won't, a colloquialism for "will not."

wont, *adj.*, accustomed; *n.*, usage; custom.

wont'ed, *adj.*, accustomed.

wont'edness, *n.*, the state of being wont.

woo, *v.i.*, to make love; *v.t.*, to count; to importune; to try to win to one's side.

wood, *n.*, timber; a collection of trees; the hard part of a tree.

wood'-ashes, *n.*, ashes from burnt wood.

wood'bine, *n.*, a creeping plant; the honeysuckle.

wood'-carving, *n.*, the art of engraving or making articles in wood.

wood'chat, *n.*, a small bird, a shrike.

wood'chuck, *n.*, a small quadruped, a marmot.

wood'cock, *n.*, a wild fowl.

wood'craft, *n.*, skill in forest life.

wood'cut, *n.*, an engraving on wood.

wood'cutter, *n.*, one who fells trees.

wood'ed, *adj.*, covered with timber.

wood'en, *adj.*, made of wood; stiff; solid; unemotional.

wood'house, *n.*, a building in which wood is stored.

wood'iness, *n.*, the quality or state of being woody.

wood'land, *n.*, country covered with woods.

wood'less, *adj.*, without wood.

wood'-louse, *n.*, an insect found in damp places and in old timber.

wood'man, *n.*, a forester; a woodcutter. (Also *woodsman*.)

wood'-note, *n.*, the song of forest birds.

wood'-nymph, *n.*, a nymph that haunts a wood; a dryad.

wood'pecker, *n.*, a bird which pecks trees with a tapping sound.

wood'pigeon, *n.*, a wild pigeon.

wood'-pile, *n.*, a heap or collection of firewood.

wood'-pulp, *n.*, pulped wood, the base for paper-making.

wood'roof, *n.*, a herb.

wood'ruff, *n.*, a woodland plant.

wood'shed, *n.*, a shed for storing wood (usu. firewood).

woods'man, *n.*, *i.q.* woodman.

wood'ward, *n.*, a forester.

wood'wind, *n.*, the section of an orchestra using musical instruments of wood.

wood'-wool, *n.*, fine wood shavings.

wood'work, *n.*, things constructed of wood; the craft of working in wood.

wood'worker, *n.*, a worker in wood.

wood'worm, *n.*, a destructive wood-boring insect.

wood'y, *adj.*, covered with timber; like wood.

wooed, *p.p.*, woo.

woo'er, *n.*, a suitor.

woof, *n.*, cross-threads in weaving; wovenwork.

woo'ing, *adj.*, courting; *n.*, love-making; *pr.p.*, woo.

woo'ingly, *adv.*, in a wooing manner.

wool, *n.*, fleece; a basic textile from the hairy growth on sheep and other animals.

wool'carder, *n.*, one who does woolcarding.

wool'carding, *n.*, the separation of wool fibres ready for spinning.

wool'comber, *n.*, one who combs wool.

woold, *v.t.*, to wind round.

woold'ed, *p.p.*, woold.

woold'er, *n.*, a pin or stick used in woolding.

woold'ing, *pr.p.*, woold.

wool'fell, *n.*, a fleece.

wool'gathering, *adj.*, abstracted; not collected in thought.

wool'-grower, *n.*, one who rears sheep for their wool.

wool'len, *adj.*, made of wool; *n.*, a woollen cloth; woollen materials.

woollies, *n. pl.*, garments made of wool (*colloq.*).

wool'liness, *n.*, the quality or state of being woolly.

wool'ly, *adj.*, fleecy; soft; like wool.

wool'ly-bear, *n.*, a large hairy caterpillar.

wool'pack, *n.*, a bale of wool.

wool'sack, *n.*, a sack of wool; the Lord Chancellor's cushion; the emblem of the Lord Chancellor's office.

wootz, *n.*, a fine Indian steel.

woozy, *adj.*, confused.

wop, *n.*, an Italian immigrant in America (*pejorative word*).

word, *n.*, a spoken utterance; a unit of meaning; a message; command; tidings; discussion; *v.t.*, to express in words.

word'able, *adj.*, expressible in words.

word'-blindness, *n.*, inability to recognize words.

word'-book, *n.*, a vocabulary; a dictionary.

word'-building, *n.*, the formation of words.

word'ed, *adj.*, expressed in precise words; *p.p.*, word.

word'ily, *adv.*, in a wordy way.

word'iness, *n.*, the quality or state of being wordy.

word'ing, *n.*, the exact words; *pr.p.*, word.

word'-perfect, *adj.*, knowing every word (student or actor).

word'y, *adj.*, full of words; verbose.

wore, *p.p.*, wear.

work, *n.*, labour; toil; employment; duty; something worked; a book or other composition; in pl., mechanism; a manufactory; deeds as distinct from faith; *v.i.*, to labour; to do work; to ferment; *v.t.*, to effect; to cause to work; to sew, etc.

workabili'ty, *n.*, the quality or state of being workable.

work'able, *adj.*, practicable; able to be worked.

work'aday, *adj.*, ordinary; everyday.

work'bag, *n.,* a bag in which needle work is carried.

work'-basket, *n.,* a wicker basket for needlework accessories.

work'-bench, *n.,* a bench on which work (esp. manual) is done.

work'book, *n.,* a student's exercise book.

work'box, *n.,* a box containing sewing materials, etc.

work'-day, *n.,* one of the days in the week exclusive of Sunday.

worked, *p.p.,* work.

work'er, *n.,* one who works, esp. manually.

work'fellow, *n.,* a colleague.

work'house, *n.,* the old name for a house for paupers.

work'ing, *pr.p.,* work.

work'ing-class, *n.,* that part of the community engaged in manual work or industry.

work'ing-day, *n.,* *i.q.* work-day.

work'ing-man, *n.,* *i.q.* workman.

work'less, *adj.,* without work.

work'man, *n.,* one engaged in manual labour.

work'manlike, *adj.,* skilful; done in finished style.

work'manly, *adj.,* *i.q.* workmanlike.

work'manship, *n.,* the quality of work done.

work'mate, *n.,* an associate or companion at work.

work'people, *n.,* *i.q.* working-class.

work'room, *n.,* a room equipped for work.

works, *n. pl.,* a factory or place where (manual) work is done.

work'shop, *n.,* a place where manual work is carried on.

work'shy, *adj.,* not fond of work; *n.,* a shirker.

work'-study, *n.,* the time and motion study of manual operations.

work'-table, *n.,* a table used for work.

work'woman, *n.,* the fem. of workman.

world, *n.,* the universe; this earth; life on earth; society.

world'-fam'ous, *adj.,* renowned throughout the world.

world'liness, *n.,* the quality or state of being worldly.

world'ling, *n.,* one who lives only for this world.

world'ly, *adj.,* pert. or rel. to the world; living only for this world.

world'ly-minded, *adj.,* having no thought for anything but this world.

world'ly-wise, *adj.,* knowing all about worldly things.

world'wide, *adj.,* extending over the whole world.

worm, *n.,* a creeping animal; the thread of a screw; a poor, mean creature; *v.i.,* to creep in; to wriggle in; *v.t.,* to destroy gradually.

worm'cast, *n.,* a small mound of earth voided by the earthworm.

worm'eaten, *adj.,* destroyed by worms; old; decayed.

wormed, *p.p.,* worm.

worm'il, *n.,* a parasitic worm; a bot. (Also *wornil.*)

worm'ing, *pr.p.,* worm.

worm'like, *adj.,* like a worm.

worm'wood, *n.,* a very bitter plant; absinthe.

worm'y, *adj.,* like a worm; full of worms.

worn, *adj.,* weary looking; *p.p.,* wear.

worn'il, *n.,* *i.q.* wormil.

worn'-out, *adj.,* tired out; made useless by long wear.

wor'ried, *p.p.,* worry.

wor'rier, *n.,* one who worries.

wor'risome, *adj.,* causing anxiety or worry.

wor'ry, *n.,* care; trouble; anxiety; *v.i.,* to be over-anxious; to fret; *v.t.,* to harass; to tear with the teeth; to perplex.

wor'rying, *adj.,* harassing; vexing; *pr.p.,* worry.

wor'ryingly, *adv.,* harassingly.

worse, *adj.,* comp. of bad or ill; *adv.,* comp. of badly or ill.

wor'sen, *v.i.,* to deteriorate; *v.t.,* to impair.

wor'sened, *p.p.,* worsen.

wor'sening, *n.,* becoming worse; *pr.p.,* worsen.

wor'ship, *n.,* adoration; divine service; honour; reverence; the title of mayors and other magistrates; *v.i.,* to engage in worship; *v.t.,* to adore; to pay divine honour to; to reverence.

wor'shipable, *adj.,* deserving to be worshipped.

wor'shipful, *adj.,* worthy of reverence.

wor'shipfully, *adv.,* in a worshipful way.

wor'shipped, *p.p.,* worship.

wor'shipper, *n.,* one who worships.

wor'shipping, *pr.p.,* worship.

worst, *adj.,* super. of bad; *adv.,* super. of badly; *v.t.,* to defeat; to get the better of.

worst'ed, *p.p.,* worst.

wors'ted, *adj.,* made of worsted; *n.,* twisted woollen thread.

worst'ing, *pr.p.,* worst.

wort, *n.,* a herb; the infusion of malt.

worth, *adj.,* of such and such value; possessing so much wealth; deserving of; *n.,* *i.q.* worthiness; value.

wor'thier, *adj.,* comp. of worthy.

wor'thiest, *adj.,* super. of worthy.

wor'thily, *adv.,* in a worthy way.

wor'thiness, *n.,* the quality or state of being worthy; moral excellence.

worth'less, *adj.,* of no value; depraved.

worth'lessly, *adv.,* in a worthless way.

worth'lessness, *n.,* the quality or state of being worthless.

worthwhile', *adj.,* worth an effort, worth doing.

wor'thy, *adj.,* deserving; morally excellent; *n.,* a person to be esteemed.

wot, *v.t.,* to know.

would, *p.t.,* will.

would'-be, *adj.,* desiring to be; making pretence; *n.,* one who pretends.

wouldn't, abbrev. of would not (*colloq.*).

wound, *n.*, a hurt that pierces the skin; mental injury; *v.t.*, to inflict a wound upon; to injure the sensibilities of.

wound, *p.p.*, wind.

wound'ed, *p.p.*, wound.

woun'der, *n.*, one who, or that which, wounds.

wound'ing, *pr.p.*, wound.

wound'wort, *n.*, kidneyvetch.

woura'li, *n.*, curare.

wove, *p.p.*, weave.

wo'ven, *adj.*, made on a loom; *p.p.*, weave.

wow, *interj.*, expressive of appreciation or wonder (*colloq.*); *n.*, a particular distortion in recorded sound.

wow'-wow, *n.*, a Java ape.

wrack, *n.*, drifted seaweed; destruction; scudding clouds.

Wraf, *n.*, a member of the Women's Royal Air Force.

wraith, *n.*, a ghost; a spirit.

wran'gle, *n.*, an angry dispute; *v.i.*, to squabble.

wran'gled, *p.p.*, wrangle.

wran'gler, *n.*, one who wrangles; formerly, one who was placed in the first class of the Mathematical Tripos at Cambridge University.

wran'glership, *n.*, a place in the first class of the Mathematical Tripos.

wran'gling, *n.*, the act of quarreling; *pr.p.*, wrangle.

wran'nock, *n.*, the wren.

wrap, *n.*, a covering; a rug; a stole; *v.t.*, to fold something round an object to cover it.

wrap'page, *n.*, a wrapper; wraps collectively.

wrapped, *p.p.*, wrap.

wrap'per, *n.*, a covering; a loose outer garment.

wrap'ping, *pr.p.*, wrap.

wrasse, *n.*, a brightly coloured rock fish.

wrath, *n.*, anger.

wrath'ful, *adj.*, angry.

wrath'fully, *adv.*, in a wrathful way.

wrath'fulness, *n.*, a state of extreme anger.

wrath'y, *adj.*, extremely angry.

wreak, *v.t.*, to carry out in revenge.

wreaked, *p.p.*, wreak.

wreak'ing, *pr.p.*, wreak.

wreath, *n.*, a garland; a chaplet.

wreathe, *v.t.*, to encircle with a wreath; to entwine.

wreathed, *p.p.*, wreathe.

wreath'ing, *pr.p.*, wreathe.

wreath'y, *adj.*, like a wreath.

wreck, *n.*, destruction, esp. of a ship; a wrecked ship; a ruin; anything ruined; *v.t.*, to destroy utterly; to drive to ruin.

wreck'age, *adj.*, the remains from a shipwreck.

wrecked, *p.p.*, wreck.

wreck'er, *n.*, one who causes wrecks; one who steals shipwrecked goods that come ashore.

wreck'ing, *pr.p.*, wreck.

Wren, *n.*, a member of the Women's Royal Naval Service.

wren, *n.*, a small bird.

wrench, *n.*, a sudden and forcible twisting pull; a tool for wrenching; *v.t.*, to pull by twisting.

wrenched, *p.p.*, wrench.

wrench'ing, *pr.p.*, wrench.

wren'let, *n.*, young wren.

wrest, *n.*, a violent pull; *v.t.*, to seize away; to twist; to misinterpret intentionally.

wrest'ed, *p.p.*, wrest.

wrest'er, *n.*, one who, or that which, wrests.

wrest'ing, *pr.p.*, wrest.

wres'tle, *v.i.*, to struggle by grappling; *v.t.*, to contend earnestly; to join in a wrestling contest.

wres'tled, *p.p.*, wrestle.

wres'tler, *n.*, one who wrestles.

wrest'ling, *n.*, the act of wrestling; *pr.p.*, wrestle.

wretch, *n.*, one in misery; a worthless person.

wretch'ed, *adj.*, in great distress; poor; mean.

wretch'edly, *adv.*, in a wretched way.

wretch'edness, *n.*, the state of being wretched.

wrick, *n.*, a sprain; *v.t.*, to sprain or injure a joint.

wrig'gle, *n.*, a twisting motion; *v.i.*, to twist about; *v.t.*, to give a wriggling motion to.

wrig'gled, *p.p.*, wriggle.

wrig'gler, *n.*, one who wriggles.

wrig'gling, *pr.p.*, wriggle.

wright, *n.*, a workman; a carpenter.

wring, *n.*, a twisting squeeze; *v.t.*, to squeeze with a twist; to excruciate.

wring'er, *n.*, one who, or that which, wrings.

wring'ing, *pr.p.*, wring.

wring'ing-wet, *adj.*, wet enough to have water wrung out of it.

wrin'kle, *n.*, a corrugation; a crease; a new, good idea (*colloq.*); *v.i.*, to become wrinkled; *v.t.*, to corrugate; to make into folds.

wrin'kled, *adj.*, furrowed; *p.p.*, wrinkle.

wrin'kling, *pr.p.*, wrinkle.

wrin'kly, *adj.*, full of wrinkles; puckered.

wrist, *n.*, the part of the arm next to the hand.

wrist'band, *n.*, a cuff.

wrist'-drop, *n.*, paralysis of the forearm.

wrist'let, *n.*, anything worn round the wrist.

wrist'-shot, *n.*, a quartershot in golf.

wrist'watch, *n.*, a watch designed for wear on the wrist.

writ, *n.*, a legal document commanding or summoning; *p.p.*, write (*obs.*).

wri'table, *adj.*, able to be written.

write, *v.i.*, to use the pen; to be an author or composer; *v.t.*, to set down words on

paper with a pen or pencil; to indite; to compose.

write'-off, *n.*, a complete loss; anything damaged or worn beyond the point of economical repairability.

wri'ter, *n.*, one who, or that which, writes; a clerk; an author.

wri'tership, *n.*, the status of a writer to the signet or legal practitioner (*Scots law*).

write'-up, *n.*, a written account of a book, play, etc. (*colloq.*).

writhe, *v.i.*, to turn and twist as in pain; *v.t.*, to twist.

writhed, *p.p.*, writhe.

wri'thing, *pr.p.*, writhe.

wri'ting, *n.*, written work; script; composition; authorship; a written document; *pr.p.*, write.

wri'ting-book, *n.*, a book to write in.

wri'ting-desk, *n.*, a desk to write upon.

wri'ting-master, *n.*, a teacher of writing.

wri'ting-paper, *n.*, paper for letter-writing.

writ'ten, *p.p.*, write.

wrong, *adj.*, the opposite to right; wicked; false; mistaken, incorrect; *adv.*, erroneously; unjustly; *n.*, an injury; an injustice; *v.t.*, to do unjustly to.

wrong'doer, *n.*, one who does wrong.

wrong'doing, *n.*, evil doing.

wronged, *p.p.*, wrong.

wrong'ful, *adj.*, injurious; unjust.

wrong'fully, *adv.*, in a wrongful way.

wrong'fulness, *n.*, misdoing; error.

wrong'headed, *adj.*, perverse; irrational.

wrong'ing, *pr.p.*, wrong.

wrong'ly, *adv.*, in a wrong way.

wrong'ness, *n.*, an error; the state of being wrong.

wrote, *p.p.*, write.

wroth, *adj.*, angry.

wrought, *p.p.*, of work.

wrought'-iron', *n.*, malleable iron.

wrung, *p.p.*, wring.

wry, *adj.*, twisted; expressive of disgust, nausea, cynicism.

wry'ly, *adv.*, in a wry manner.

wry'neck, *n.*, a bird that twists its head; a neck that is twisted.

wry'necked, *adj.*, having a twisted neck.

wyan'dotte, *n.*, a breed of poultry.

wych'-elm, *n.*, the Scotch elm or witch-hazel.

wych'-hazel, *n.*, *i.q.* witch-hazel.

Wyc'liffite, *n.*, a follower of Wycliffe; *adj.*, pert. or rel. to Wycliffe.

Wyke'hamist, *n.*, a pupil, or former pupil, of Winchester College; originally the founder's kin to William of Wykeham, the founder of the two Colleges at Winchester and Oxford. (The latter, being founded after Winchester, is commonly known as New College, though its proper dedication is to St. Mary, like that of the sister foundation.)

wynd, *n.*, an alley in a Scottish town.

wy'vern, *n.*, a winged serpent, two-legged and long-tailed (*her.*).

X

xan'thate, *n.*, xanthic acid salt.

xan'thein(e), *n.*, *i.q.* xanthin.

Xan'thian, *adj.*, pert. or rel. to Xanthus in ancient Asia Minor.

xan'thic, *adj.*, yellowish.

xan'thin(e), *n.*, yellow colouring matter.

Xanthip'pe, *n.*, the name of Socrates' wife, who was the type of all shrewish wives.

xan'thium, *n.*, an aster-like plant.

Xan'tho, *n.*, a genus of crabs.

xanthocar'pous, *adj.*, bearing yellow fruit.

xan'thogen, *n.*, a yellowish substance found in flowers.

xanthogen'ic, *adj.*, *i.q.* xanthic.

xantho'ma, *n.*, a yellow skin disease.

xan'thophyll, *n.*, the yellow colour in dead leaves.

xan'thous, *adj.*, yellow; pert. or rel. to Germanic descent.

xe'bec, *n.*, a small ship, three-masted, having lateen and square sails.

xe'ma, *n.*, Sabine's Gull; the forked-tailed gull.

xe'nial, *adj.*, pert. or rel. to hospitality or guests.

xe'nium, *n.*, the Greek term for a gift to a stranger or an envoy.

xenog'amy, *n.*, marrying with a foreigner; cross-fertilization.

xenogen'esis, *n.*, foreign origin.

xenoglos'(s)ia, *n.*, knowledge of a language without learning it.

xenoma'nia, *n.*, an abnormal liking for things foreign.

xen'on, *n.*, inert gas.

xenopho'bia, *n.*, a morbid dislike of foreigners.

Xen'urus, *n.*, a genus of S. American Armadillo.

xera'sia, *n.*, a kind of Alopecia (dryness of the hair).

xero'graphy, *n.*, a non-chemical photocopying process.

xeroph'agy, *n.*, eating dried food.

xero'philous, *adj.*, appropriate for a dry climate; naturally adapted to dryness.

xerophthal'mia, *n.*, an inflamed eye condition from dryness.

xerophthal'my, *n.*, dryness of the eyeball.

xero'sis, *n.*, dryness.

xe'rotes, *n.*, general dryness of the body.

xiph'ias, *n.*, the swordfish and others of the same genus; a Southern Hemisphere constellation.

xiph'oid, *adj.*, swordlike.

Xmas, *n.*, the abbrev. of Christmas.

X-rays, *n. pl.*, Röntgen rays used for physical examination in medicine, surgery and industry.

xy'lem, *n.*, wood tissue (*bot.*).

xy'locarp, *n.*, a hard, wood fruit (*bot.*).

xy'lograph, *n.*, a wood engraving.

xylog'rapher, *n.*, a wood engraver.

xylograph'ic, *adj.*, pert. or rel. to xylography.

xylog'raphy, *n.*, wood engraving.

xy'loid, *adj.*, pert. or rel. to wood.

xyloi'din(e), *n.*, an explosive.

xylom'eter, *n.*, an instrument for calculating the specific gravity of wood.

xy'lonite, *n.*, a sort of gun-cotton, imitating ivory; celluloid.

xyloph'agous, *adj.*, eating wood.

xy'lophone, *n.*, a musical instrument played with wooden hammers on wooden bars.

xyloph'onist, *n.*, a performer on a xylophone.

Xyr'is, *n.*, a genus of yellow-flowered sedge plants.

xyst, *n.*, *i.q.* xystus.

xys'ter, *n.*, a surgical scraping instrument.

xys'tus, *n.*, a covered portico; scraped lint.

Y

yac′ca, n., a West Indian tree and its wood (*Span.*).

yacht, n., a light, pleasure vessel; v.i., to sail or keep a yacht.

yacht′-club, n., an association of yachtsmen.

yacht′ed, p.p., yacht.

yacht′er, n., one who yachts.

yacht′ing, n., the pastime of sailing a yacht; pr.p., yacht.

yachts′man, n., one who sails a yacht.

yachts′woman, n., fem. of yachtsman.

yaf′fle, n., the green woodpecker.

ya′ger, n., a German sharpshooter. (Also *jäger*.)

Yahoo′, n., one of a savage race described in *Gulliver's Travels*.

yahoo′, n., a bestial person.

yak, n., a variety of ox.

yak′alo, n., the offspring of a yak and a buffalo.

yam, n., a West African, edible tuber.

Ya′ma, n., a Hindu god.

ya′men, n., a residence of a Chinese mandarin or a government office in China.

yank, v.t., to pull sharply.

yanked, p.p., yank.

Yan′kee, adj., pert. or rel. to Yankees; n., a colloquial name for an American (orig. one who took the Union side in the Civil War).

Yan′keeism, n., Americanism.

yank′ing, pr.p., yank.

ya′ourt, n., i.q. yoghurt.

yap, n., a yelp; v.i., to make the yelping noise of a dog.

yap′on, n., a bush, from the leaves of which a kind of tea is made.

yapp, n., overlapping in bookbinding.

yapped, p.p., yap.

yap′ping, pr.p., yap.

yar′borough, n., a card hand with no card above a nine.

yard, n., an enclosed space on a farm or near a house, etc.; a standard measure of length = 36 in.; the timber on which a sail is spread.

yard′age, n., the total amount of yards.

yard′-arm, n., the end of a yard (*naut.*).

yard′stick, n., a yard measure.

yare, adj., alert, quick.

yar′ily, adv., quickly.

yarn, n., spun thread; a strand; a story, usually an extravagant one as told by a sailor (*colloq.*); v.i., to indulge in storytelling.

yar′ner, n., one who yarns.

yar′row, n., milfoil.

yash′mak, n., a Moslem woman's veil.

yat′aghan, n., a peculiar sword-dagger with a double curve.

yaup, n., a loud cry; a blue titmouse; v.i., to cry out loudly.

yaw, v.i., to get out of the course; to swing out of control (*naut.*).

yawed, p.p., yaw.

yaw′ing, pr.p., yaw.

yawl, n., a small two-masted sailing vessel.

yaw′ler, n., a member of a yawl's crew.

yawn, n., a gape; v.i., to gape.

yawned, p.p., yawn.

yawn′ing, adj., open; pr.p., yawn.

yawn′ingly, adv., in a gaping way.

yaws, n. pl., a contagious African disease.

ycleped′, yclept′, n., an old *past participle* = called; named.

ye, 2nd *pers. pron.*, *pl.* of *thou* or *you*.

yea, *particle*, i.q. yes.

yean, v.t., to give birth to a lamb.

yeaned, p.p., yean.

yean′ing, pr.p., yean.

yean′ling, n., a newly born lamb.

year, n., the period of time (= 365¼ days) in which the earth orbits the sun.

year′-book, n., a book brought up to date each year and relating to contemporary matters.

year′ling, n., a one-year old animal.

year′long, adj., lasting for a year.

year′ly, adj., occurring every year; lasting for a year; adv., occurring every year.

yearn, v.i., to have a strong desire.

yearned, p.p., yearn.

yearn′ing, n., a longing; pr.p., yearn.

yearn′ingly, adv., longingly.

yeast, n., barm; froth; any substitute for yeast.

yeast′y, adj., like yeast; foaming; frothing.

yed′da, n., straw for hats.

yegg, n., a travelling burglar (*slang*).

yelk, n., i.q. yolk.

yell, n., a loud cry of pain, anger, etc.; v.i., to raise a loud cry; v.t., to utter in a yell.

yelled, p.p., yell.

yell′ing, pr.p., yell.

yel′low, adj., yellow-coloured; jaundiced; n., a colour as of saffron or gold.

yel′lower, adj., comp. of yellow.

yel′lowest, adj., super. of yellow.

yel′low-fe′ver, n., a mosquito-borne, tropical disease.

yel′low-ham′mer, n., the yellow finch.

yel'lowish, *adj.*, inclined to yellow.

yel'lowness, *n.*, the state of being yellow.

Yel'low Per'il, *n.*, the threat from the development of the power of the yellow races, as seen by the white races.

yel'lowy, *adj.*, of a generally yellow appearance.

yelp, *n.*, a sharp bark, often of pain; *v.i.*, to utter a sharp bark.

yelped, *p.p.*, yelp.

yelp'ing, *pr.p.*, yelp.

yen, *n.*, the Japanese monetary unit; a longing (*slang*).

yeo'man, *n.*, a farmer.

yeo'manry, *n.*, a military force raised among the farmer class.

yep, *i.q.*, yes (*Amer. slang*).

yerk, *n.*, a quick push; *v.i.*, to kick; *v.t.*, *i.q.* jerk.

yerked, *p.p.*, yerk.

yerk'ing, *pr.p.*, yerk.

yes, *adv.*, the word of affirmation.

yes'man, *n.*, an obsequious person too acquiescent to authority.

yes'ter, *adj.*, pert. or rel. to the day before the present one.

yes'terday, *adv.*, on the day before this one; *n.*, the day before the present one.

yes'ternight, *adv.* and *n.*, last night.

yes'teryear', *n.*, bygone days.

yet, *adv.*, still; besides; moreover; up to this time; *conj.*, moreover; however.

yet'i, *n.*, the legendary "abominable" snowman of Tibet.

yew, *n.*, the taxus; a dark-leaved evergreen tree.

yew'en, *adj.*, made of yew.

yew'tree, *n.*, *i.q.* yew.

Yid, *n.*, a jew who speaks Yiddish (*slang*).

Yid'dish, *n.*, a mixed language spoken by Jews in England.

Yid'disher, *adj.*, Jewish; *n.*, a Jew (*slang*).

yield, *n.*, an amount produced or returned; *v.i.*, to give in; to submit; *v.t.*, to give up; to surrender; to produce.

yield'able, *adj.*, that may be yielded.

yield'ed, *p.p.*, yield.

yield'er, *n.*, one who yields.

yield'ing, *adj.*, compliant; submissive; *pr.p.*, yield.

yield'ingly, *adv.*, compliantly.

yield'ingness, *n.*, a readiness to comply.

ylang'-ylang, *n.*, a Malayan perfume.

y'lem, *n.*, the conceived origin of matter.

yo'del, *n.*, a song or cry of Swiss-Tyrolese dwellers in the mountains, natural and falsetto notes alternating; *v.i.* and *t.*, to sing yodelfashion. (Also *jodel*.)

yo'del(l)ed, *p.p.*, yodel.

yo'del(l)ing, *n.*, the practice of yodelling; *pr.p.*, yodel.

yo'ga, *n.*, the Hindu philosophic system entailing a physical discipline.

yo'gi, *n.*, a devotee of yoga.

yog(h)(o)urt, *n.*, a fermentation (semi-liquid) of milk. (Also *yaourt*.)

yo-ho', *interj.*, a sailor's cry (*naut.*).

yoicks, *interj.*, a hunting cry.

yoke, *n.*, a contrivance for fastening draught oxen together by the necks; a wooden frame supported in the middle on a person's neck and having suspended from the ends pails, buckets, etc.; any kind of bond or burden; *v.t.*, to join with a yoke.

yoked, *p.p.*, yoke.

yoke'-fellow, *n.*, a close companion; a fellow-slave.

yo'kel, *n.*, a rustic.

yo'king, *pr.p.*, yoke.

yolk, *n.*, the inner yellow part of an egg. (Also *yelk*); the oil in a sheep's skin.

yon, *adj.*, that over there.

yon'der, *adj.*, that over there; *adv.*, over there.

yore, *adv.*, in long past time; *n.*, old times.

yorker, *n.*, a ball in cricket pitched at the point where the bat meets the ground.

York'ist, *n.*, a supporter of the house of York in the Wars of the Roses.

York'shire, *adj.*, pert. or rel. to the county of Yorkshire and its inhabitants; *n.*, the largest county in England; its dialect.

Yo'ruba, *n.*, a large W. African tribal group; its language.

you, *pron.*, 2nd pers., thou, thee, ye.

young, *adj.*, youthful; early; immature; fresh; *n.*, young offspring.

young'er, *adj.*, comp. of young.

young'est, *adj.*, super. of young.

young'ish, *adj.*, rather young.

young'ling, *n.*, a young creature.

young'ster, *n.*, a child; any comparatively young person.

youn'ker, *n.*, a stripling.

your, *possess. adj.*, belonging to you.

yourself', *pers. pron.*, you individually or personally.

yourselves', the pl. of yourself.

youth, *n.*, the early period of life; a young person; young persons collectively.

youth'ful, *adv.*, young; immature; younglooking.

youth'fully, *adv.*, in a youthful way.

youth'fulness, *n.*, the state of being youthful.

youths, *n.*, the pl. of youth.

you've, abbrev. of you have (*colloq.*).

yowl, *n.*, a prolonged howl of a cat or dog; *v.i.*, to make a prolonged howling noise.

yowled, *p.p.*, yowl.

yowl'er, *n.*, an animal that yowls.

yowl'ing, *pr.p.*, yowl.

yo'-yo, *n.*, a string operated toy.

ytter'bium, *n.*, a rare metal (*chem.*).

yt'tria, *n.*, the oxide of yttrium (*chem.*).

yt'trious, *adj.*, containing, pert. or rel. to, yttrium.

yt'trium, *n.*, a metallic base (*chem.*).

Yuc'ca, *n.*, a S. Amer. plant genus.

yuft, *n.*, a variety of Russian leather.

Yug'oslav, *adj.*, *i.q.* Yugoslavian; *n.*, a native of Yugoslavia.

Yugoslav'ian, *adj.*, pert. or rel. to Yugoslavia, a country of Eastern Europe.

yu'lan, *n.*, a kind of magnolia.

Yule, *n.*, Christmas.

Yule'log, *n.*, a log of wood burnt at Christmas.

Yule'tide, *n.*, Christmas time.

yunx, *n.*, a wryneck.

Yur'ga, *n.*, an Afghan pony.

Z

za'bra, n., a small Spanish ship (hist.).

zac'cho, n., a stone block; a socle.

zaf'fer, n., i.q. zaffre.

zaf'fre, n., a cobalt oxide.

zamindar', n., i.q. zemindar.

za'ny, adj., crazy; n., an idiot; a buffoon.

za'nyish, adj., in a crazy fantastic way.

za'nyism, n., buffoonery of a fantastic kind.

Zanzibar'i, adj., pert. or rel. to Zanzibar; n., a native of Z.

zap'tieh, n., a Turkish policeman.

zare'ba, n., a fortification or palisade (African). (Also zeriba.)

zar'nich, n., an arsenic sulphide.

zax, n., a hatchet used in slating.

za'yat, n., a Burmese caravanserai.

ze'a, n., Indian maize and other grasses.

zeal, n., enthusiasm; ardour.

Zea'lander, n., an inhabitant of Zealand, part of the Netherlands.

zeal'ful, adj., i.q. zealous.

zeal'ot, n., an enthusiast; a fanatic.

zeal'otism, n., the conduct of zealots; fanaticism.

zeal'otry, n., i.q. zealotism.

zeal'ous, adj., full of zeal; ardent.

zeal'ously, adv., in a zealous way.

ze'bra, n., a black and white striped African quadruped; a S. American wood.

ze'bra-crossing, n., a marked pedestrian crossing on a road.

ze'brine, adj., like a zebra.

ze'bu, n., an Indian ox with a hump.

zecchin(e), n., i.q. sequin.

zech'stein, n., magnesium limestone.

zed, n., the name of the letter Z.

zed'oary, n., a digestive, aromatic root, also used in perfume.

zeit'geist, n., the spirit of the age (Ger.).

zelo'so, adv., with fervour (It., mus.).

zemindar', n., an Indian tenant of Government land. (Also zamindar.)

zem'indary, n., land held by a zemindar; the area of a zemindar's jurisdiction.

zen, n., a sect of the Buddhist religion.

zena'na, n., the women's quarters in an Indian house.

Zend, n., the ancient language of Persia.

Zend-Aves'ta, n., the writings deemed sacred by the followers of Zoroaster.

zen'dik, n., an Eastern name for an unbeliever.

zen'ith, n., the highest point in the heavens.

ze'olite, n., a silicate so named from the fact that it froths when acted on by the blow-pipe.

zeolit'ic, adj., pert. or rel. to zeolite.

zeph'yr, n., a soft west wind.

Zeph'yrus, n., the poet's personification of the west wind (Lat.).

Zep'pelin, n., an airship designed by the German, Count Zeppelin, in 1900.

zeri'ba, n., i.q. zareba.

ze'ro, n., a cipher; nought; nothing.

zer'umbet, n., an E. Indian drug.

zest, n., keen relish; enjoyment.

zest'ful, adj., relishing.

zest'fully, adv., in a zestful way.

ze'ta, n., the sixth letter of the Greek alphabet, corresponding to the English Z.

zetet'ic, adj., pert. or rel. to inquiry.

zeug'ma, n., a figure of speech, in which two or more nouns are brought under the government of one verb or into relation with one adjective, the meaning of which fits only one of the nouns.

Zeus, n., the chief of gods in Greek mythology.

zeux'ite, n., a ferriferous species of tourmalin.

zib'et, n., the civet.

zie'ga, n., curd produced in milk by acetic acid.

zigan'ka, n., a Russian country dance; the music of the same.

zig'zag, adj., twisting and turning back upon itself; not keeping straight; n., a path that twists and turns; v.i., to move in twists and turns.

zig'zagged, p.p., zigzag.

zig'zagging, pr.p., zigzag.

zim'ent-water, n., copper-impregnated water.

zinc, n., a metal; spelter; v.t., to cover or coat with zinc.

zinced, p.p., zinc.

zincif'erous, adj., producing zinc.

zinc'ing, pr.p., zinc.

zin'co, n., an impression from a zinc plate.

zin'code, n., the positive pole in a galvanic battery.

zinc'ograph, n., i.q. zinco.

zincog'rapher, n., one who reproduces in zinco.

zincograph'ic, adj., pert. or rel. to zincography.

zincog'raphy, n., the art of reproducing from a zinc plate.

zinc'ous, adj., of the nature of zinc.

zinc(k)'y, adj., like, or containing, zinc.

Zing'ari, n. pl., of Zingaro.

Zing'aro, n., gipsy (It.).

Zin'giber, n., the genus of ginger and other related herbs.

zin'nia, *n.*, a spring flower like an aster.

Zi'on, *n.*, the hill on which Jerusalem stands.

Zi'onism, *n.*, a Jewish movement, originally for the restoration of Palestine to the Jews.

Zi'onist, *n.*, one who supports Zionism.

zip, *n.*, energy; a zip-fastener; a tearing sound.

zip'-fas'tener, *n.*, a fastening device consisting of smoothly interlocking teeth with a sliding securing clip.

zip'per, *n.*, a zip-fastener.

zip'py, *adj.*, full of pep, lively.

zir'con, *n.*, a zirconium silicate; a semi-precious stone; the Indian diamond.

zirco'nia, *n.*, the oxide of zirconium.

zirco'nium, *n.*, a metallic element.

zith'er, *n.*, a musical stringed instrument.

zith'ern, *n.*, *i.q.* zither.

zlo'ty, *n.*, the currency unit of Poland.

zo'diac, *n.*, an area of the heavens embracing the twelve constellations through which the sun appears to travel in the year.

zodi'acal, *adj.*, pert. or rel. to the zodiac.

zo'etrope, *n.*, a toy which, by revolving, makes figures in pictures seem to move.

zo'fra, *n.*, a Moorish name for a carpet.

zo'har, *n.*, cabalistic notes on the Old Testament.

zo'ic, *adj.*, of the strata bearing animal fossils.

Zo'laism, *n.*, realistic writing in the manner of Emile Zola.

Zolaist'ic, *adj.*, pert. or rel. to Zolaism and Zola.

zoll'verein, *n.*, a customs union (*Ger.*).

zom'bie, *n.*, an animated corpse.

zo'nal, *adj.*, pert. or rel. to zones.

zone, *n.*, a belt; a girdle; one of the great circular divisions of the earth's surface; a defined area.

zoned, *adj.*, girdled.

zone'less, *adj.*, without zones.

zo'ning, *adj.*, arranging into groups or areas with similar characteristics.

zo'nular, *adj.*, pert. or rel. to a zonule.

zo'nule, *n.*, a small belt.

zo'ö, *prefix* = animal.

zoo, *n.*, the short form of zoological garden, a place designed to display animal life (*colloq.*).

zoog'amy, *n.*, animal production.

zoog'eny, *n.*, the formation of animal organs. (Also **zoogony**.)

zoogeog'raphy, *n.*, the study and science of animal distribution.

zoog'ony, *n.*, *i.q.* zoogeny.

zoog'rapher, *n.*, one who studies zoography.

zoog'raphy, *n.*, the study of the distribution of fauna over the world.

zool'atry, *n.*, animal worship.

zo'olite, *n.*, a fossil animal.

zoo'litic, *adj.*, pert. or rel. to zoolites.

zool'oger, *n.*, a student of zoology. (Also **zoologist**.)

zoolog'ic, *adj.*, pert. or rel. to zoology.

zoolog'ical, *adj.*, *i.q.* zoologic.

zoolog'ically, *adv.*, in a zoological way.

zool'ogist, *n.*, *i.q.* zoologer.

zool'ogy, *n.*, the study of animals.

zoom, *v.i.*, to climb steeply (aviation); to increase rapidly the magnification of a photo image.

zoomor'phism, *n.*, the representation of deity in animal form.

zoon'omy, *n.*, the study of natural laws in relation to animals.

zoopathol'ogy, *n.*, the study of animal diseases.

zooph'agan, *adj.*, *i.q.* zoophagous.

zooph'agous, *adj.*, carnivorous.

zoopho'bia, *n.*, an abnormal fear of animals.

zoophor'ic, *adj.*, pert. or rel. to zoophorus.

zooph'orus, *n.*, a frieze along which are shown figures of men or animals (*arch.*).

zo'ophyte, *n.*, a low-grade animal, hardly distinguishable from a plant.

zoophyt'ic, *adj.*, pert. or rel. to zoophytes.

zoophytol'ogy, *n.*, the study of zoophytes.

zo'oplasty, *n.*, the grafting of live animal tissue on to man.

zo'osperm, *n.*, the moving constituent of the seminal fluid.

zo'ospore, *n.*, a spore which moves about.

zoot'omist, *n.*, a student of comparative anatomy.

zoot'omy, *n.*, comparative anatomy.

zo'ril, *n.*, a carnivorous quadruped.

zoril'la, *n.*, a small skunk-like animal.

Zoroas'trian, *adj.*, pert. or rel. to Zoroaster and his teaching.

Zoroas'trianism, *n.*, the doctrines of Zoroaster (Sarathustra), the ancient Persian lawgiver and teacher.

zos'ter, *n.*, a girdle; a skin disease on the waist, e.g. shingles.

Zouave', *n.*, a French soldier of a regiment wearing an Arab uniform; a woman's short jacket.

zounds, *n.*, an old exclamation of surprise, anger, etc. (= God's wounds).

zucchett'a, *n.*, the skull cap of a priest (*It.*).

zucchett'o, *n.*, *i.q.* zucchetta.

zu'ffolo, *n.*, a small kind of flute (*It.*).

Zu'lu, *n.*, a member of a once warlike South African tribe.

zumolog'ical, *adj.*, *i.q.* zymological.

zumol'ogist, *n.*, *i.q.* zymologist.

zumol'ogy, *n.*, *i.q.* zymology.

zumom'eter, *n.*, *i.q.* zymometer.

Zwing'lian, *adj.*, pert. or rel. to Zwingli, the 16th Cent. Swiss reformer, or his sacramentarian doctrine.

zy'gal, *adj.*, H-shaped.

zygodac'tyl, *adj.*, having toes in pairs.

zygodac′tylous, *adj., i.q.* zygodactyl.

zygo′ma, *n.,* the bony arch of the cheek.

zygomat′ic, *adj.,* pert. or rel. to the zygoma.

zyg′ote, *adj.,* the fusion of two gametes.

zyme, *n.,* the germ of zymotic diseases.

zymolog′ic, *adj.,* pert. or rel. to zymology.

zymolog′ical, *adj., i.q.* zymologic. (Also *zumological.*)

zymol′ogist, *n.,* a student of zymology. (Also *zumologist.*)

zymol′ogy, *n.,* the study of the phenomena of fermentation. (Also *zumology.*)

zymom′eter, *n.,* an apparatus showing degrees of fermentation. (Also *zumometer.*)

zy′moscope, *n.,* an instrument to test fermenting power.

zymo′sis, *n.,* fermenting.

zymot′ic, *adj.,* pert. or rel. to zymosis; pert. or rel. to diseases in which a virus acts upon the system as though it set up fermentation.

zy′murgy, *n.,* brewing.

zy′thum, *n.,* an Egyptian drink of malt and wheat.

zyxom′ma, *n.,* an Indian name for the dragonfly.

Appendix of Proper Names

NOTE. Names which are already included in the main section of the dictionary, either as names or as other words of like spelling and sound, are not included in this appendix.

A

Aar
Aar'on
Aba'ddin
Abbe'ville
Ab'botsford
Ab'diel
Ab'dul-Hamid'
Abed'nego
A'bel
Ab'elard
Abera'von
Ab'ercorn
Abercrom'bie
Aberdarc'
Aberdeen'
Aberdeen'shire
Aberdoùr'
Abergaven'ny
Ab'ernethy
Aberyst'with
Abie'zer
Abim'elech
Ab'ingdon
Ab'inger
Ab'ney
Aboukir', Abukir'
A'braham
A'bram
Abruz'zo
Ab'salom
Abyssin'ia
Aca'dia
Acapul'co
Accra', Acra'
Ac'crington
Acel'dama
Achai'a
Ach'ill, Ach'il
Achil'les
Achit'ophel
Ach'met
A'cis

Ack'ermann
Ack'worth
Ac'land
A'crilan
Actae'on
A'da
Adair'
Ad'derbury
Ad'dingham
Ad'dington
Ad'dison
Ad'ela
Ad'elaide
Adeli'na
Adel'phi
A'delung
A'den
Adiron'dacks
Ad'ler
Adol'phus
A'drian
Adria'na
Adriano'ple
Adria'tic
Aene'as
Aer'oflot
Aes'chylus
Ae'sop, E'sop
Afghanistan'
Af'rica
Africa'nus
Agamem'non
Ag'atha
Agincourt
Ag'lionby
Ag'nes
Ag'new
A'gra
A'gram
Agric'ola
Agrip'pa
Agrippi'na
A'hab

Ahasue'rus
A'haz
Ahazi'ah
Ahith'ophel
Ah'med
Ai'kin
Aileen
Ains'worth
Ain'tree
Air'drie
Ait'kin
Aix
Aix-la-Chapelle'
Aix-les-Bains'
Ajmir'
Ak'enside
Ak'ron
Alaba'ma
Alad'din
Al'aric
Alas'ka
Al'ban
Alba'ni
Alba'nia
Al'bans, St.
Al'bany
Al'bemarle
Alber'ta
Al'bigenses
Al'bion
Al'can
Al'cester
Alces'tis
Alcibi'ades
Al'cides
Al'cock
Ald'borough
Ald'bourne
Alde'burgh
Al'den
Al'derbury
Al'dermanbury
Ald'ermaston

Al'dersgate
Al'dershot
Al'derson
Al'derston
Ald'gate
Al'dington
Al'dridge
Ald'wych
Alençon
Alep'po
Alessan'dria
Alexan'der
Alexan'dria
Alexandri'na
Alex'is
Alfa-Rome'o
Alfie'ri
Alfon'so
Al'ford
Al'fred
Al'freton
Algeci'ras
Alge'ria
Al'gernon
Algiers'
Algo'a
Al'ice
Alic'ia
Al'ison
Alita'lia
Allahabad'
Al'lan
All'church
All'cott
Al'leghany
Al'legheny (city)
Al'len
Al'lendale
Al'lerton
Al'lingham
Al'lington
Al'loa
Al'lonby
Al'mack
Alm'ondbury
Aln'wick
Alon'zo
Alphe'us
Alphon'so
Alping'ton

Alps
Alsace'
Al'sop
Al'ston
A'ltami'ra
Al'tenburg
Al'thorp
Al'ton
Alto'na
Altoo'na
Al'trincham, Al'tringham
Al'va
Alve'ley
Al'verstoke
Al'verstone
Al'verthorpe
Al'vis
Amade'us
Am'adis
Amazo'nia
Am'berg
Am'berley
Am'bleside
Am'brose
Ame'lia
Amer'ica
Am'ersham
Ames'bury
Am'herst
Amiens'
Am'mon
A'mos
Ampt'hill
Am'sterdam
A'my
Anac'reon
A'nak
An'andale
Anani'as
Andalu'sia
An'daman
An'derson
An'derston
An'des
Andor'ra
An'dover
An'drew
An'drews, St.
An'drocles

Androm'ache
Androm'eda
Androni'cus
An'dros
Aner'ley
Angel'ico
Angeli'na
An'gelo
Ang'kor
An'glesey
Angostu'ra
An'gus
An'jou
An'kara
Ann or Anne
Annam'
An'nan
An'nandale
Annap'olis
Annes'ley
Annette'
An'selm
An'son
An'sted
An'stey
An'struther
An'thony
Antig'onus
Anti'gua
Antilles
An'tioch
Antip'ater
Antip'atris
Antoinette'
Anto'nio
Anto'nius
An'tony
An'trim
Aos'ta
Apel'les
Ap'ennines
Aphrodi'te
Apollo'nius
Ap'pleby
Ap'pledore
Ap'plegate
Ap'pleton
Aps'ley
Aqui'nas
Arabel'la

Ara'bia
Ar'agon
A'ram
Ar'arat
Ara'tus
Arbroath'
{Ar'buthnot
{Arbuth'not
Arca'dia
Archela'us
Arch'ibald
Archime'des
Arco'le
Arcot'
Ar'dagh
Ardee'
Ar'den
Ardennes'
Ard'glass
Ard'ing
Ard'leigh
Ardnamur'chan
Ardros'san
Ard'wick
Arequi'pa
Arethu'sa
Argyll'
Ariad'ne
Arimathae'a
Arios'to
Aristar'chus
Aristi'des
Aristoph'anes
Ar'istotle
Arizo'na
Arka'nsas
Ark'low
Ark'wright
Armagh'
Arme'nia
Armin'ius
Arm'ley
Arm'strong
Arnaud'
Arne
Arn'heim
Ar'nold
Ar'not
Ar'ran

Ar'reton
Ar'rowsmith
Artaxerx'es
Ar'temis
Artemis'ia
Ar'thur
Ar'undel
As'aph
Ascen'sion
As'cham
Ashan'ti, Ashantee
Ash'bourne
Ash'burnham
Ash'burton
Ash'by-de-la-
   Zouch
Ash'cott
Ash'er
Ash'ford
Ash'ley
Ashmole'an
Ash'over
Ash'ton
Ash'ton-*under*-
   Lyne
Ash'well
A'sia
As'kew
As'lib
Asmode'us
Aspa'sia
As'quith
Assam'
Assi'si
Assyr'ia
Ast'bury
Ast'ley
As'ton
As'ton-Mar'tin
Astu'rias
Asun'cion
A'talanta
Athana'sius
Ath'elstan
Ath'ens
Ather'ley
Ath'erstone
Ath'erton
Athlone'

Ath'ol
Athy'
At'kins
At'kinson
Atlan'ta
At'terbury
At'tercliffe
At'tica
At'tila
At'tleborough
Att'wood
Au'brey
Auck'land
Au'denshaw
Au'di
Aud'ley
Au'drey
Augs'burg
Augus'ta
Augus'tine, St.
Augus'tus
Aumale'
Aure'lius
Aus'tell, St.
Aus'terlitz
Aus'tin
Australa'sia
Austra'lia
Aus'tria
Autol'ycus
A'va
A'valon
Ave'bury
Ave'ning
Aver'nus
Av'ignon
Av'ington
A'von
Av'ro
Ax'bridge
Ay'cliffe
Ayles'ford
Ayl'sham
Ayr
Ayr'shire
Azerbaijan'
A'zof *or* A'zov
Azores'

B

Ba'alim
Bab'bage
Bab-el-Man'deb
Bab'ington
Bab'ylon
Bacchana'lia
Bach
Ba'cup
Badajos'
Bad'cock
Ba'den
Ba'den-Pow'ell
Bad'ham
Baed'eker
Baf'fin Bay
Bagdad', Bagh'dad
Bage'hot, Bag'ot
Bag'shaw
Bag'shot
Bag'ster
Baha'ma
Bahrain'
Bail'don
Bain'bridge
Baines
Bain'ton
Bai'reuth, Bay'reuth
Bakerloo'
Bake'well
Baku'
Ba'la
Ba'laam
Bal'beck
Bal'combe
Bal'dock
Bald'win
Bâle
Balfe
Bal'four
Bal'guy
Bal'ham
Bal'lantyne
Ballarat'
Ballina'
Ballinasloe'
Ball'iol
Ballymo'ney
Ballyshan'non

Balzac'
Bam'berg
Bam'ford
Bamp'ton
Ban'bury
Ban'croft
Ban'don
Banff
Bangalore'
Bangkok'
Ban'gla Desh
Ban'gor
Ban'ham
Banks
Ban'nerman
Ban'nister
Ban'nockburn
Ban'quo
Ban'try
Ban'well
Barab'bas
Barba'dos
Bar'bara
Barbaros'sa
Bar'bary
Bar'bauld
Bar'clay
Bar'dolph
Bar'ford
Bar'ham
Bar'men
Bar'mouth
Bar'nabas
Bar'naby
Bar'nard Castle
Barn'by
Barnes
Bar'net
Bar'ningham
Barns'bury
Barns'ley
Barn'staple
Barn'well
Baro'da
Bar'rington
Bar'row-in-Fur'ness
Bar'ry
Barthol'omew

Bartimae'us
Bart'lett
Bar'ton
Ba'ruch
Bas'church
Ba'sel
Bas'ford
Ba'sildon
Ba'singhall
Ba'singstoke
Bas'kerville
Basle
Bassa'nio
Basse'-Terre'
Bas'sett
Bas'singbourne
Bas'sora
Bast'wick
Basu'toland
Bata'via
Bat'combe
Bate'man
Bates
Batheast'on
Bathford'
Bath'gate
Bath'sheba
Bath'urst
Bathwick'
Bat'ley
Bat'tenberg
Bat'tersea
Bava'ria
Baw'try
Bax'ter
Bayeux'
Bay'ley
Bayonne'
Bea'consfield
Beale
Bea'minster
Bea'mish
Be'atrice
Beat'tie
Beau'champ
Beau'fort
Beau'lieu
Beauma'ris
Beau'mont

Beb'ington	Benin'	Bey'rout
Bec'cles	Ben Lo'mond	Be'za
Bechua'naland	Ben'nett	Bhutan'
Beck'ford	Ben Nev'is	Biarritz'
Beck'ingham	Ben'nington	Bices'ter
Beck'ington	Ben'son	Bick'ersteth
Beck'ley	Ben'tham	Bick'ley
Beck'with	Ben'tinck	Bid'denden
Be'dale	Bent'ley	Bid'dulph
Bed'dington	Ben'ton	Bid'eford
Bed'does	Béranger'	Bid'stone
Bede	Berar'	Bier'ley
Bed'ford	Ber'bera	Big'gleswade
Bed'minster	Berbice'	Big'low
Bed'win	Bere Al'ston	Bihar'
Bed'worth	Bereni'ce	Bilba'o
Bee'cher	Bere Re'gis	Billeric'ay
Bee'chey	Ber'esford	Bil'linge
Beer'sheba	Beresi'na	Bil'lingham
Bees, St.	Ber'gen	Bil'lingshurst
Bees'ton	Berke'ley	Bil'ston
Bee'thoven	Berkham'sted	Bin'field
Beh'men	Berks	Bing'ham
Beh'ring	Berk'shire	Bing'hamton
Beirut'	Ber'mondsey	Bing'ley
Belfast'	Bermu'da	Bin'ney
Bel'ford	Ber'nard	Bi'on
Bel'gium	Berne	Birk'beck
Belgrade'	Bern'hardt	Birk'enhead
Bel'grave	Ber'ridge	Bir'kett
Belin'da	Ber'tillon	Bir'mah
Belisa'rius	Ber'tram	or Bir'mingham
Belize'	Ber'trand	Bir'rell
Bel'la	Ber'vie	Bir'stall
Bel'lamy	Ber'wick	Bis'cay
Bel'larmine	Besant'	Bish'op's Cas'tle
Bel'lerby	Bes'ley	Bish'opsgate
Beller'ophon	Bess	Bish'op's Stort'- ford
Bel'lingham	Bes'sie	Bish'opthorpe
Bel'mont	Be'telgeuse	Bish'opton
Bel'more	Beth'any	Bis'marck
Bel'per	Beth'lehem	Bit'ton
Belshaz'zar	Beth'nal Green	Bi'zet
Bel'ton	Beth'une	Black'burn
Bel'voir	Bet'sey	Black'friars
Belzo'ni	Bev'an	Black'heath
Bem'bridge	Bev'eridge	Black'ley
Bena'res	Bev'erley	Black'lock
Ben'digo	Bewd'ley	Black'more
Ben'enden	Bex'hill	Black'pool
Bengue'lla	Bex'ley	

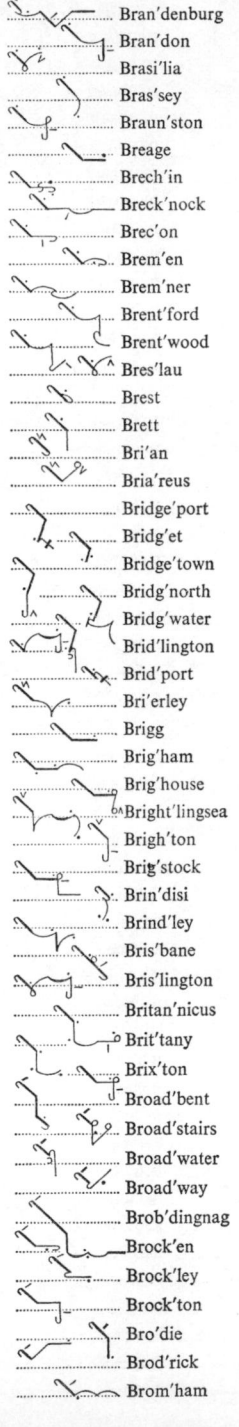

Black'stone	Bor'gia	Bran'denburg
Blackwall'	Bor'neo	Bran'don
Black'wood	Bornu'	Brasi'lia
Blag'don	Bor'oughbridge	Bras'sey
Blai'na	Bor'oughgreen	Braun'ston
Blaine	Bor'stal	Breage
Blair	Bo'sanquet	Brech'in
Blairgow'rie	Bos'castle	Breck'nock
Blake	Bos'cawen	Brec'on
Blake'ney	Bos'nia	Brem'en
Blan'chard	Bos'phorus	Brem'ner
Blanche	Bossuet'	Brent'ford
Bland'ford	Bos'worth	Brent'wood
Blan'tyre	Botes'dale	Bres'lau
Blay'don	Bo'tha	Brest
Blen'kinsopp	Both'well	Brett
Bletch'ingley	Bot'ley	Bri'an
Bloem'fontein	Botswa'na	Bria'reus
Blom'field	Bou'cher	Bridge'port
Bloom'field	Bough'ton	Bridg'et
Blount	Boulanger'	Bridge'town
Blyth	Boulogne'	Bridg'north
Boadice'a	Bour'chier	Bridg'water
Bo'az	Bourne'mouth	Brid'lington
Boccac'cio	Bou'verie	Brid'port
Bod'enham	Bo'vey Tra'cey	Bri'erley
Bod'min	Bow'den	Brigg
Boe'ing	Bowes	Brig'ham
Boe'thius	Bow'ling	Brig'house
Bog'nor	Bowness'	Bright'lingsea
Bogota'	Box'ford	Brigh'ton
Bogue	Boyd	Brig'stock
Bohe'mia	Boyle	Brin'disi
Boileau	Brack'ley	Brind'ley
Bokha'ra	Brack'nell	Bris'bane
Bol'ingbroke	Brad'bourne	Bris'lington
Boliv'ia	Brad'field	Britan'nicus
Bolo'gna	Brad'ford	Brit'tany
Bol'shoi	Brad'laugh	Brix'ton
Bol'ton	Brad'ley	Broad'bent
Bombay'	Brad'ninch	Broad'stairs
Bo'naparte	Brad'well	Broad'water
Bonn	Bra'dy	Broad'way
Bon'nycastle	Braemar'	Brob'dingnag
Bon'sall	Braid'wood	Brock'en
Bon'vilstone	Brails'ford	Brock'ley
Bootan'	Brain'tree	Brock'ton
Boo'tle	Braith'waite	Bro'die
Bordes'ley	Bram'field	Brod'rick
Bore'ham	Bram'ley	Brom'ham
	Bramp'ton	

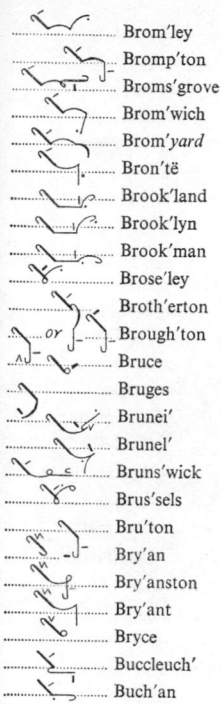

Brom'ley
Bromp'ton
Broms'grove
Brom'wich
Brom'*yard*
Bron'të
Brook'land
Brook'lyn
Brook'man
Brose'ley
Broth'erton
Brough'ton
Bruce
Bruges
Brunei'
Brunel'
Bruns'wick
Brus'sels
Bru'ton
Bry'an
Bry'anston
Bry'ant
Bryce
Buccleuch'
Buch'an

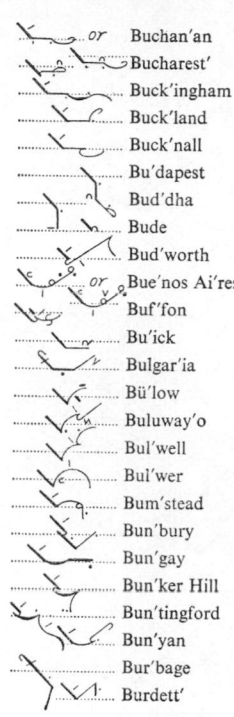

or Buchan'an
Bucharest'
Buck'ingham
Buck'land
Buck'nall
Bu'dapest
Bud'dha
Bude
Bud'worth
or Bue'nos Ai'res
Buf'fon
Bu'ick
Bulgar'ia
Bü'low
Buluway'o
Bul'well
Bul'wer
Bum'stead
Bun'bury
Bun'gay
Bun'ker Hill
Bun'tingford
Bun'yan
Bur'bage
Burdett'

Bu'ren
Bur'ford
Burgh'ley
Bur'lington
Bur'ma
Bur'ney
Burn'ham
Burn'ley
Burns
Burnt'island
Bur'rell
Burslem
Bur'ton-on-Trent
Burun'di
Bur'well
Bur'y St. Ed'munds
Bush'ey
Bushi'do
Bute
But'terley
Bux'ton
Byng
By'rom
By'ron
Byzan'tium

C

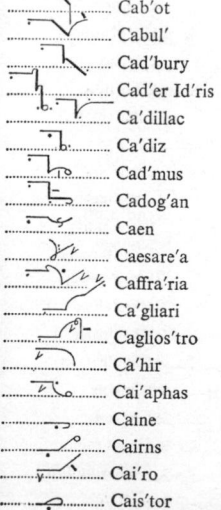

Cab'ot
Cabul'
Cad'bury
Cad'er Id'ris
Ca'dillac
Ca'diz
Cad'mus
Cadog'an
Caen
Caesare'a
Caffra'ria
Ca'gliari
Caglios'tro
Ca'hir
Cai'aphas
Caine
Cairns
Cai'ro
Cais'tor

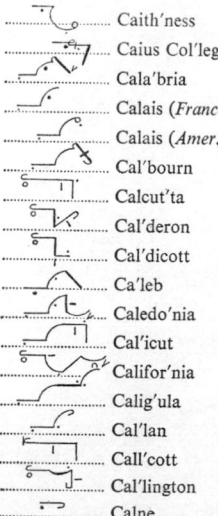

Caith'ness
Caius Col'lege
Cala'bria
Calais (*France*)
Calais (*Amer.*)
Cal'bourn
Calcut'ta
Cal'deron
Cal'dicott
Ca'leb
Caledo'nia
Cal'icut
Califor'nia
Calig'ula
Cal'lan
Call'cott
Cal'lington
Calne

Cal'thorpe
Cal'ton
Cal'vert
Cal'vin
Cam'berwell
Cambo'dia
Cam'bourne
Cambrai'
Cam'bria
Cam'den
Cam'elford
Cam'elot
Cam'eron
Cameroon'
Camil'la
Camil'lus
Cam'oens
Camp'bell
Camp'belltown

Camp'den
Campea'chy
Campe'che
Cam'perdown
Can'ada
Canalet'to
Can'berra
Candahar
Can'dia
Cane'a
Can'ford
Cannes
Can'nington
Can'nock
Can'onbury
Cano'pus
Canos'sa
Cano'va
Canton'
Cantyre'
Canute'
Caper'naum
Cape Town
Capri'
Caracal'la
Cara'cas
Carac'tacus
Caravelle'
Car'diff
Ca'rey
Carew'
Carin'thia
Car'isbrooke
Car'leon
Carlisle'
Car'low
Carls'bad
Carl'ton
Carlyle'
Carmar'then
Car'mel
Carnar'von
Carnat'ic
Carneg'ie
Carn'forth
Caroli'na
Carra'ra
Car'rick
Carrickfer'gus
Car'rington
Car'roll

Car'ron
Carruth'ers
Carshal'ton
Car'son
Car'thage
Carthage'na
Carvair'
Casablan'ca
Cas'bah
Cash'el
Cas'pian Sea
Cas'quets
Cas'sel
Castile'
Castlebar
Cas'tleford
Castlerea'gh
Cas'tleton
Castries'
Cat'aline
Catalo'nia
Cat'ford
Cath'arine
Cath'erine
Ca'ton
Cat'tegat
Cat'terick
Catul'lus
Cau'casus
Caus'ton
Cav'an
Cavour'
Caw'dor
Cawnpore'
Caw'thorne
Cay'ley
Cay'thorpe
Cec'il
Cecil'ia
Ce'dric
Cel'ebes
Ce'lia
Cel'sus
Cen'ci
Cenis'
Ce'res
Cervan'tes
Cetewa'yo
Cetin'je, Cetti'nge
Ceylon'
Chad'wick

Chalde'a
Chal'font
Chal'mers
Chalons'
Cham'bers
Chan'dos
Chan'ning
Chan'trey
Chap'lin
Char'field
Char'ing Cross
Charl'bury
Charlemagne'
Charles
Charles'town
Charleville'
Char'lottetown
Charl'ton
Char'minster
Char'mouth
Cha'ron
Charyb'dis
Chateaubriand'
Chat'ham
Chat'teris
Chat'terton
Chau'cer
Chea'dle
Cheapside'
Cheet'ham
Chelms'ford
Chel'tenham
Che'ops
Chep'stow
Cherbourg'
Cher'iton
Cher'rington
Cher'son
Chert'sey
Ches'ham
Ches'hunt
Ches'ter
Ches'terton
Chet'wynd
Chev'rolet
Chey'ne'
Chey'ne
Chica'go
Chich'ester
Chilcomp'ton
Chil'ders

Chil'e, Chil'i
Chil'ham
Chill'cott
Chil'lingworth
Chil'terns
Chimbora'zo
Ching'ford
Chip'penham
Chip'perfield
Chip'ping Norton
Chip'stead
Chis'holm
Chis'lehurst
Chis'wick
Chitral'
Chlo'e
Cholm'ondeley
Chopin'
Chorassan'
Chor'ley
Chor'leywood
Chorl'ton
Christ'church
Christia'na
Chris'tie
Christi'na
Chris'topher
Chry'sler
Chrys'ostom
Chubb
Chung'king'
Church'ill
Chuz'zlewit
Cic'ero
Cimabu'e
Cincinna'ti
Cincinna'tus
Cin'derford
Cinque
Circas'sia
Cir'ce
Ci'rencester
Ci'troen
Clackman'nan
Clac'ton-on-Sea
Clan'ricarde
Clap'ham
Clap'perton
Clap'ton
Cla'ra

Clare
Clare'mont
Clar'ence
Claris'sa
Clarisse'
Clark
Clark'son
Clat'worthy
Claude'
Clau'dio
Clau'dius
Clav'erhouse
Clavering
Clav'erton
Clay'ton
Clea'ton
Cleck'heaton
Clemenceau'
Clementi'na
Clem'entson
Clerk'enwell
Cler'mont
Cleve'don
Cleve'land
Cleves
Clif'ford
Clif'ton
Clin'ton
Cli'o
Clith'ero(e)
Clive
Clogher
Clonmel'
Clovell'y
Clo'vis
Cloyne
Clut'terbuck
Clyde
Coal'brookdale
Coat'bridge
Cobb
Cob'bett
Cob'den
Cob'lenz
Co'burg
Coch'in Chi'na
Coch'rane
Cock'burn
Cock'erham
Cock'ermouth
Cock'erton

Cod'rington
Coeur de Lion'
Cog'geshall
Co'gnac
Coh'en
Col'chester
Cold'stream
Cole'ford
Cole'man
Colen'so
Coleraine'
Cole'ridge
Coles'hill
Col'lard
Col'lett
Col'lingbrook
Col'lingham
Col'lingwood
Col'lins
Col'linson
Col'man
Colne
Cologne'
Colom'bia
Colom'bo
Colon'na
Colora'do
Colquhoun'
Col'ston
Col'ton
Colum'bia
Colum'bus
Col'ville
Col'vin
Co'mo
Comp'ton
Comte
Con'corde
Concor'dia
Conde'
Confu'cius
Con'gleton
Con'go
Congres'bury
Con'naught
Connect'icut
Con'nell
Con'nor
Conquistador'es
Con'rad
Con'stance

Con'stantine	Courte'nay / Court'ney	Cros'by
Constantino'ple	Coutts	Cross'land
Con'way	Cov'entry	Cross'ley
Cooke	Cov'erdale	Cross'thwaite
Cook'ham	Cov'erley	Cros'ton
Cooks'town	Cov'ington	Crow'combe
Coorg, Kurg	Cow'bridge	Crow'land
Co'os	Cow'den	Crow'ther
Cope'land	Cow'en	Croy'don
Copenha'gen	Cowes	Cru'den
Copern'icus	Cow'ley	Cruik'shank
Cop'ley	Cow'per	Cru'soe
Cop'perfield	Cox	Cu'ba
Cop'pleston	Crabbe	Cuck'field
Copt'hall	Cra'cow	Cud'worth
Cor'by	Craig	Cul'len
Corday'	Craik	Cul'liford
Corde'lia	Crail	Cullod'en
Cordil'leras	Cran'bourne	Cull'ompton
Cor'doba	Cran'brook	Cul'ross
Core'a, Kore'a	Cran'field	Cum'berland
Corel'li	Cran'ford	Cum'bernauld
Corfe	Cran'mer	Cum'bria
Corfu'	Cras'sus	Cum'ming
Cor'inth	Craw'ford	Cum'nock
Coriola'nus	Craw'ley	Cunard'
Corna'ro	Creagh	Cun'ningham
Corneille'	Cré'cy	Cu'par
Corne'lia	Cred'iton	Cur'ran
Corne'lius	Creech	Cur'rie
Corn'hill	Creigh'ton	Cur'tis
Corn'wall	Cres'sida	Cur'tius
Cornwal'lis	Cres'sy	Cur'wen
Coroman'del	Crete	Cur'zon
Correg'gio	Crewe	Cuvier'
Cor'sham	Crew'kerne	Cux'ton
Cor'sica	Crich'ton	Cuz'co
Corun'na	Crick'lade	Cwmbran'
Cos'ham	Crime'a	Cyc'lades
Cos'sington	Crip'plegate	Cym'beline
Cos'ta Bra'va	Croa'tia	Cyn'thia
Cos'ta Ri'ca	Crock'ett	Cy'prus
Cot'ham	Crom'art(h)y	Cyrene'
Cots'wold	Crom'bie	Cyr'il
Cot'tenham	Cro'mer	Cyther'a
Cot'tesmore	Crom'well	Czechoslova'kia
Cott'rell	Cron'stadt, Kron'stadt	Czer'ny
Cour'land		

D

Dac'ca
Dag'enham
Daho'mey
Daim'ler
Dako'ta
Dalhou'sie
Dalkeith'
Dal'las
Dalma'tia
Dalrym'ple
Dal'ston
Dal'ton
Da'ly
Dal'ziel
Dam'aris
Damas'cus
Dam'ien
Damiet'ta
Da'mon
Dam'pier
Dan'bury
Dan'by
Dan'ton
Dan'ube
Dan'vers
Dan'zig
D'Arblay'
Dardanelles'
Dar'field
Da'rien
Dari'us
Darjee'ling
Dar'laston
Dar'lington
Darm'stadt
Dar'racq
Dart'ford
Dart'ington
Dar'ton
Dar'wen
Dar'win
Dauphine'
Dau'phiny
Dav'enham
Dav'entry
Da'vey
Da'vid
Da'vid's, St.
Da'vidson

Da'vies, Da'vis
Da'vison
Dav'itt
Da'vos
Daw'ley
Daw'lish
Daw'son
Day'ton
Dea'kin
Deans
Deans'gate
Deb'enham
Deb'orah
Debrett'
Dec'ca
Dec'can
Deck'er
Ded'dington
Ded'ham
Defoe'
Delago'a
De la Rue'
Del'aware
Del'hi (India)
Del'hi (U.S.A.)
Delisle'
Del'phi
Del'phos
Deme'trius
Demóc'ritus
Demos'thenes
Den'bigh
Den'ham
Den'is
Den'man
Den'mark
Den'sham
Den'ton
Den'ver
Dept'ford
De Quin'cey
Dere'ham
Der'went
Des'borough
Descartes'
Desdemo'na
Des Moines
Det'mold

Detroit'
Det'tingen
Dev'ereux
De Vin'ne
Devi'zes
Dev'lin
Dev'on
Dew'ar
Dew'ey
Dews'bury
Dib'din
Dick'inson
Dick'see
Dick'son
Didot'
Dids'bury
Die'fenbaker
Dieppe
Dig'by
Dijon'
Dilke
Dil'lon
Di'nah
Ding'wall
Din'ton
Diocle'tian
Diodo'rus Sic'ulus
Diog'enes
Dionys'os
Dip'lock
Dis'ley
Disrae'li
Diss
Dix'on
Dnie'per
Dnies'ter
Dodd
Dod'dington
Dodd'ridge
Dods'well
Dod'well
Do'herty
Dolgel'lau
Do'lomites
Dom'bey
Dom'inic
Domini'ca
Domit'ian
Donaghadee'

Don'ald	Dreyfus'	Dundas'
Don'aldson	Drif'field	Dundee'
Don'caster	Drogh'eda	Dundon'ald
Donegal'	Droit'wich	Dune'din
Dongo'la	Dro'more	Dunferm'line
Don'nington	Dron'field	Dungan'non
Don'oghue	Dront'heim	Dungar'van
Dor'chester	Drood	Dungeness'
Doré'	Drum'mond	Dunman'way
Dor'king	Dru'ry	Dunmore'
Dor'noch	Drusil'la	Dun'mow
Dor'othy	Dry'den	Dunn
Dor'rington	Dub'lin	Dunra'ven
Dor'rit	Duck'worth	Dun'stable
D'Orsay'	Dud'dington	Dun'stan
Dor'set	Dud'ley	Dun'ster
Dort	Duf'ferin	Dur'ban
Doug'las	Duf'field	Dü'rer
Doun'reay	Duk'infield	Dur'ham
Dove'dale	Duluth'	Dur'rant
Do'ver	Dul'verton	Durs'ley
Dow'ling	Dul'wich	Dur'ward
Down'end	Dumas'	Dut'ton
Down'ham	Dumbar'ton	Dvor'ak
Dow'ning	Dumfries'	Dwight
Downpat'ric	Dunbar'	Dwi'na
Down'shire	Dunblane'	Dym'oke
Down'ton	Dun'can	Dy'mond
Doyle	Duncan'non	Dy'sart
Drambuie'	Dun'church	Dy'son
Dray'ton	Dundalk'	

E

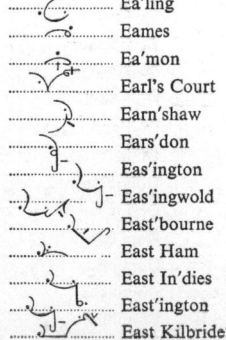

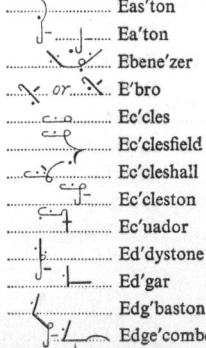

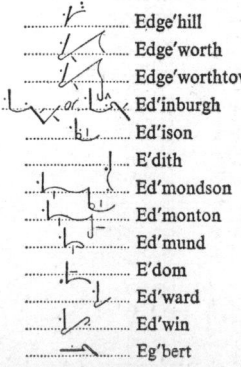

Ea'ling	Eas'ton	Edge'hill
Eames	Ea'ton	Edge'worth
Ea'mon	Ebene'zer	Edge'worthtown
Earl's Court	E'bro	Ed'inburgh
Earn'shaw	Ec'cles	Ed'ison
Ears'don	Ec'clesfield	E'dith
Eas'ington	Ec'cleshall	Ed'mondson
Eas'ingwold	Ec'cleston	Ed'monton
East'bourne	Ec'uador	Ed'mund
East Ham	Ed'dystone	E'dom
East In'dies	Ed'gar	Ed'ward
East'ington	Edg'baston	Ed'win
East Kilbride'	Edge'combe	Eg'bert

Ege'ria	Em'ary	Eth'el
Eg'erton	Em'bleton	Eth'elbald
Eg'ham	Em'den	Eth'elbert
Eg'linton	Em'erson	Eth'elred
Eg'remont	Em'ily	Eth'elwald
E'gypt	Em'ma	Eth'elwulf
Ei'ffel	Emman'uel	Ethio'pia
Ein'stein	Ems'worth	Eto'lia
Eir'e	En'dor	Etru'ria
Ei'senhower	Endym'ion	Eugene'
Elaine'	En'field	Eugénie'
El'ba	Engadine'	Eu'nice
Elbe	Enghien'	Euphra'tes
El'don	Eng'land	Eura'tom
El'eanor	E'nid	Eurip'ides
Elea'zar	En'nis	Eu'rope
Elec'tra	Enniscor'thy	Euryd'ice
Elephan'ta	Enniskil'len	Euse'bius
El'gar	E'noch	Eus'tace
El'gin	En'sor	Eus'ton
E'li	Eph'esus	Eutro'pius
E'lia	E'phraim	Eux'ine
Eli'as	Epicte'tus	E'va
El'ibank	Epp'ing	Ev'an
Elie'zer	Ep'worth	Evan'geline
Eli'hu	Eras'mus	Ev'ans
Eli'jah	E'rewhon	Ev'ansville
El'iot	Er'furt	Ev'elyn, *Eng.*
Eli'sha	Er'ic	Ev'elyn, *Scot.*
Eli'za	E'rie	Ev'erard
Eliz'abeth	*or* E'rith	Ev'erest
El'land	Er'nest	Ev'erett
El'len	Ero'ica	Ev'ersley
El'lenborough	Er'skine	Ev'erton
Elles'mere	Erze'rum	Eve'sham
El'liott	E'sau	Ew'art
El'lis	Escula'pius	Ew'ell
El'lison	Es'dras	Ew'ing
Elm'sley	Esh'er	Ex'bourne
Elo'him	Esk	Ex'bury
El'phinstone	Es'mond	Exca'libur
Elsinore'	Es'senden	Ex'eter
El'tham	Essen'es	Ex'minster
El'ton	Es'sex	Ex'mouth
E'ly	Es'ther	Ex'ton
Ely'sium	Est(h)o'nia	Ey'lau
Eman'uel	Estremadu'ra	Eze'kiel
		Ez'ra

F

Faber'gé
Fabric'ius
Fair'bairn
Fair'fax
Fair'field
Fair'ford
Fa'kenham
Fal'kirk
Falk'land
Fallieres'
Fal'mouth
Fal'staff
Fan'ny
Far'aday
Fare'ham
Far'ingdon
Far'leigh
Farn'borough
Farn'don
Farn'ham
Farn'worth
Far'oe Is'lands
Far'quhar
Far'ragut
Far'rar
Far'ringdon
Fasho'da
Faust
Faus'tus
Fav'ersham
Faw'cett
Fawkes
Faw'ley
Fayette'
Feath'erstone
Fea'therstonehaugh
Felic'ia
Fe'lix
Fel'lenberg
Felt'ham
Fel'ton
Fen'church
Fénelon'
Fen'ning
Fen'ton
Fen'wick
Fer'dinand
Fer'gus

Fer'guson
Ferman'agh
Fermoy'
or Fernan'dez
Ferran'ti
Ferra'ri
Fer'riby
Fer'ro
Festin'iog
Fes'tus
Feth'ard
Fett'es
Fev'ersham
Fez'zan
Fianna Fail
Field'ing
Fie'sole
Figaro'
Fig'gins
Fi'ji
Fildes'
Fill'more
Fil'ton
Finch'ley
or Find'lay
Fin'don
Fi'ne Gael'
Fin'gal
Finisterre'
Fin'land
Fin'lay
Fins'bury
Fish'guard
Fitzclar'ence
Fitzger'ald
Fitzher'bert
Fitzmau'rice
Fitzos'born
Fitzpat'rick
Fitz'roy
Fitzwil'liam
Flam'borough
Flam'steed
Flan'ders
Flat'ford
Flax'man
Flax'ton
Fleet'wood

Fletch'er
Flix'ton
Flod'den
Flo'quet
Flor'ence
Flor'ida
Foles'hill
Fol'jambe
Folke'stone
Folk'ingham
Fol'let
Fontainebleau'
Fon'tenoy
Forbes
Ford'ham
Ford'ingbridge
For'dyce
For'far
Formo'sa
For'res
For'ster
Forsyth'
For'tescue
Fortrose'
Fortuna'tus
Fort Wayne
Foth'ergill
Foth'eringay
Foulis
Fox'hill
Fram'ingham
Fram'lingham
Framp'ton
France
Fran'ces
Fran'cis
Fran'co
Franco'nia
Frank'enstein
Frank'furt
Fra'ser
Fraun'hofer
Fred
Fred'erick
Fred'ericton
Free'ling
Free'man
Free'town

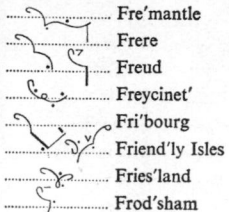

Fre'mantle
Frere
Freud
Freycinet'
Fri'bourg
Friend'ly Isles
Fries'land
Frod'sham

Froe'bel
Frog'more
or Froissart'
Frome
Froude
Fruc'tidor
Fula'ni

Ful'ford
Ful'larton
Ful'ton
Fur'ness
Fur'nival
Fu'seli
Fy'lingdales

G

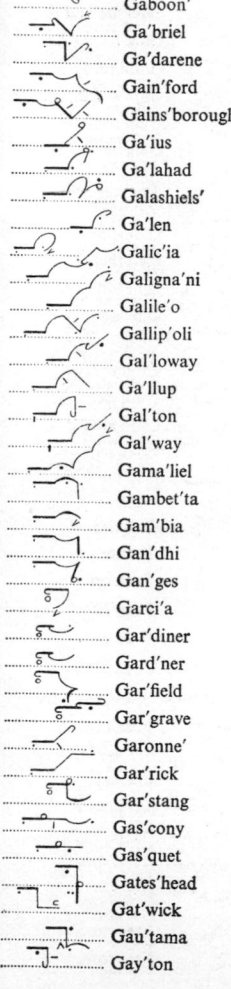

Gaboon'
Ga'briel
Ga'darene
Gain'ford
Gains'borough
Ga'ius
Ga'lahad
Galashiels'
Ga'len
Galic'ia
Galigna'ni
Galile'o
Gallip'oli
Gal'loway
Ga'llup
Gal'ton
Gal'way
Gama'liel
Gambet'ta
Gam'bia
Gan'dhi
Gan'ges
Garci'a
Gar'diner
Gard'ner
Gar'field
Gar'grave
Garonne'
Gar'rick
Gar'stang
Gas'cony
Gas'quet
Gates'head
Gat'wick
Gau'tama
Gay'ton

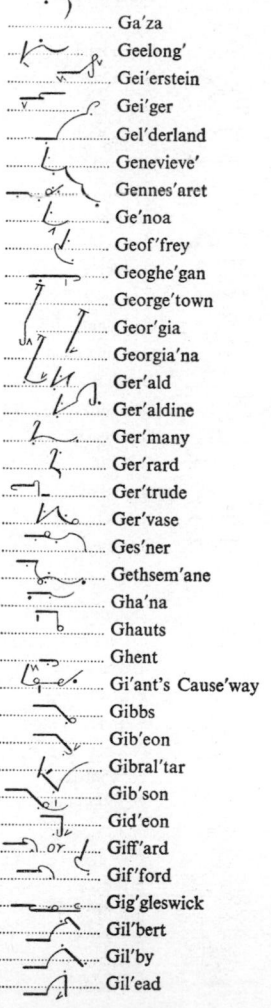

Ga'za
Geelong'
Gei'erstein
Gei'ger
Gel'derland
Genevieve'
Gennes'aret
Ge'noa
Geof'frey
Geoghe'gan
George'town
Geor'gia
Georgia'na
Ger'ald
Ger'aldine
Ger'many
Ger'rard
Ger'trude
Ger'vase
Ges'ner
Gethsem'ane
Gha'na
Ghauts
Ghent
Gi'ant's Cause'way
Gibbs
Gib'eon
Gibral'tar
Gib'son
Gid'eon
or Giff'ard
Gif'ford
Gig'gleswick
Gil'bert
Gil'by
Gil'ead

Giles
Gi'llette
Gil'lies
Gil'ling
or Gil'lingham
Gil'pin
Giot'to
Gis'borough
Glad'stone
Glam'is
Glamor'gan
Glan'ville
Glas'gow
or Glas'tonbury
Glencoe'
Glenelg'
Glenro'thes
Glent'ham
Glos'sop
Glouces'ter
Glouces'tershire
Go'a
God'alming
God'dard
God'frey
Godi'va
or God'manchester
Godol'phin
God'win
Gol'car
Gold Coast
Gol'die
Gol'gotha
Gomor'rah
Gon'dar

Good'enough
Good Hope, Cape of
Good'rich
Good'year
Goon'hilly
Gor'bals
Gor'don
Goree'
Gör'litz
Gorst
Gor'tschakoff'
Gos'berton
Gos'chen
Gos'ford
Gos'port
Gosse
Gos'sett
Gos'well
Go'tha
Goth'ard, St.
Got'henburg
Goth'land
Göt'tingen
Gough
Gould
Gounod'
Gow'er
Go'zo
Grac'chus
Grace'church
Graf'ton
Gra'ham
Gra'hamstown
Grain'ger

Gram'pian
Grana'da
Gran'by
Grand'ison
Grand Rap'ids
Grange'mouth
Grant'ham
Gran'ville
Gras'mere
Grat'tan
Graves'end
Gray''s Inn
Gray'son
Great Brit'ain
Great'ham
Greece
Green'land
Green'law
Green'ock
Green'wich
Greg'ory
Greig
Grena'da
Greno'ble
Gren'ville
Gres'ford
Gresh'am
Gret'na Green
Grev'ille
Grey'stoke
Gries'bach
Grif'fith
Grimal'di
Grims'by
Grin'stead

Grin'ton
Gri'qualand
Grisel'da
Grock
Gro'ningen
Groom'bridge
Gros'venor
Grote
Gro'tius
Grun'dy
Guadalaja'ra
Guadalquiv'ir
Guadeloupe'
Guam
Guatema'la
Guel'derland
Guia'na
Guild'ford
Guin'evere
Guin'ness
Guis'borough
Guizot'
Gul'liver
Gun'ston
Gün'ther
Gun'ton
Gur'ney
Gusta'vus
Gu'tenberg
Guth'rie
Gut'tenberg
Guya'na
Guy'on
Guzerat'
Gwa'lior

H

Haar'lem
Habak'kuk
Häck'el
Hack'et(t)
Had'den
Had'denham
Had'dington
Had'leigh
Ha'drian

Haeck'el
Ha'fiz
Ha'gar
Hagg'ai
Hague
Hah'nemann
Hail'sham
Hai'nau, -ý'nau
Hai'nault

Hai'ti, Hay'ti
Hak'luyt
Hal'dane
Hales
Hales'owen
Hal'ifax
Hal'lam
Ha'llé
Hal'lett

Hal'ley	Har'ris	Hea'viside
Hal'liford	Har'risburg	Heav'itree
Hal'liwell	Har'rison	Heb'denbridge
Hal'sall	Har'rogate	He'ber
Hals'bury	Har'rowby	Heb'rides
Hal'stead	Hart'field	He'bron
Hal'ton	Hart'ford	Hec'ate
Halt'whistle	Hart'ington	Heck'ington
Ham'bleton	Hart'land	Hec'la
Ham'brook	Hart'lebury	Hec'uba
Ham'burg	Hart'lepool	Hed'ingham
Ham'erton	Hart'ley	He'don
Ham'ilton	Hartz	He'gel
Ham'mersmith	Har'vard	Hei'delberg
Ham'mond	Har'vey	Heigh'am
Hamp'den	Har'well	Hei'ne
Hamp'shire	Har'wich	Hel'en(e)
Hamp'stead	Har'wood	Hel'ena
Hamp'ton	Has'lingden	Hele'na, St.
Ham'stead	Has'tings	Hel'ens, St.
Han'cock	Hat'field	Hel'ier, St.
Han'del	Hat'ton	Hel'igoland
Hand'ley	Haugh'ton	Héloise'
Hands'worth	Hav'ant	Helps
Han'ley	Hav'erfordwest	Hel'ston
Han'nah	Hav'erhill	Hel'ton
Han'nan	Ha'vre	Helve'tia
Han'nibal	Hawai'i	Hem'ans
Hants	Hawar'den	Hem'el Hemp'-stead
Han'way	Hawes	Hem'merde
Han'well	Haw'ick	Hem'mings
Han'worth	Hawkes'bury	Hems'well
Haps'burg	Hawkes'worth	Hems'worth
Har'bin	Haw'kins	Hen'bury
Har'borne	Haw'ley	Hen'derson
Har'court	Haw'thorne	Hen'don
Hard'castle	Hay'dn	Hene'age
Hardicanute'	Hay'don	Hen'field
Har'ding	Hayes	Hen'gist
Hard'ing	Hay'ley	Henriet'ta
Hard'wick	Hay'man	Henri'ques
Hares'field	Hay'ti	Hen'ry
Har'lech	Hay'wood	Hen'singham
Har'lem	Haz'litt	Hep'tonstall
Har'ley	Head'ingly	Heracli'tus
Har'lington	Head'ington	Herat'
Har'low(e)	Hea'ly	Her'bert
Har'man	Heath'cote	Hercula'neum
Har'old	Heath'field	Her'komer
Har'penden	Heath'row	Hermi'one
Har'riet	Hea'ton	Herne
Har'rington		

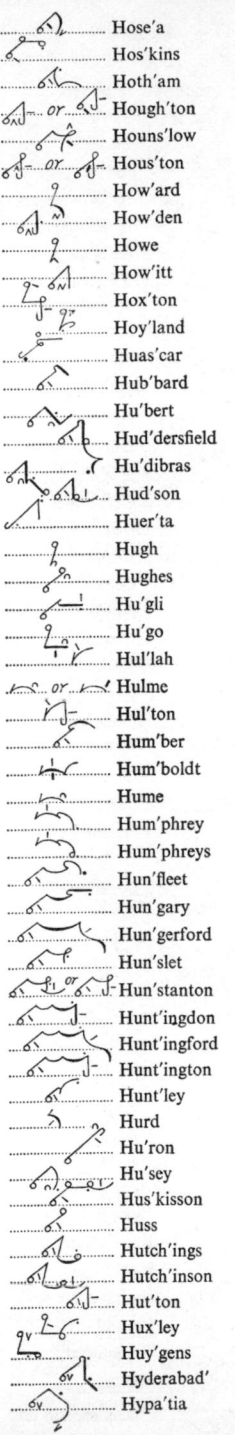

Her'od	Hoad'ly	Hose'a
Herod'otus	Ho'bart	Hos'kins
Her'rick	Hobbes	Hoth'am
Herrn'hutt	Hob'house	Hough'ton
Her'schel(l)	Hobo'ken	Houns'low
Hert'ford	Hodg'es	Hous'ton
Hert'fordshire	Hod'son	How'ard
Her'vey	Hoey	How'den
Herzegovi'na	Ho'fer	Howe
He'siod	Hoff'mann	How'itt
Hes'se Cas'sel	Ho'garth	Hox'ton
Hes'se Darm'stadt	Hogg	Hoy'land
Hes'ter	Hohenlin'den	Huas'car
Hev'ersham	Hohenzol'lern	Hub'bard
Hew'orth	Hol'beach	Hu'bert
Hex'ham	Hol'beck	Hud'dersfield
Hey'sham	Hol'bein	Hu'dibras
Heytes'bury	Hol'born	Hud'son
Hey'wood	Hol'brook	Huer'ta
Hezeki'ah	Hol'croft	Hugh
Hiawa'tha	Holds'worth	Hughes
Hiber'nia	Hol'inshed	Hu'gli
Hicks	Hol'linwood	Hu'go
Hicks'-Beach	Hol'man	Hul'lah
Hig'gins	Holmes	Hulme
High'am	Hol'stein	Hul'ton
High'bury	Hol'yhead	Hum'ber
High'gate	Hol'y Land	Hum'boldt
High'worth	Ho'ly Loch'	Hume
Hil'da	Hol'yoake	Hum'phrey
Hil'desheim	Hol'yoke	Hum'phreys
Hil'lier	Hol'ywell	Hun'fleet
Hill'ingdon	Hom'erton	Hun'gary
Hil'lington	Hondu'ras	Hun'gerford
Hill'man	Hong Kong'	Hun'slet
Hills'borough	Honolu'lu	Hun'stanton
Hil'perton	Hook'ham	Hunt'ingdon
Hil'ton	Hop'kins	Hunt'ingford
Hima'laya	Hop'kinson	Hunt'ington
Him'maleh	Hor'ace	Hunt'ley
Hinch'cliffe	Hora'tio	Hurd
Hinck'ley	Hora'tius	Hu'ron
Hind'ley	Hor'field	Hu'sey
Hindustan'	Horn'castle	Hus'kisson
Hin'ton	Horn'sey	Huss
Hippar'chus	Hor'sa	Hutch'ings
Hiro'shima	Horse'fall	Hutch'inson
His'cock	Hor'sham	Hut'ton
Hispanio'la	Hors'ley	Hux'ley
Hitch'cock	Horten'sius	Huy'gens
Hitch'in	Hor'ton	Hyderabad'
	Hor'wich	Hypa'tia

I

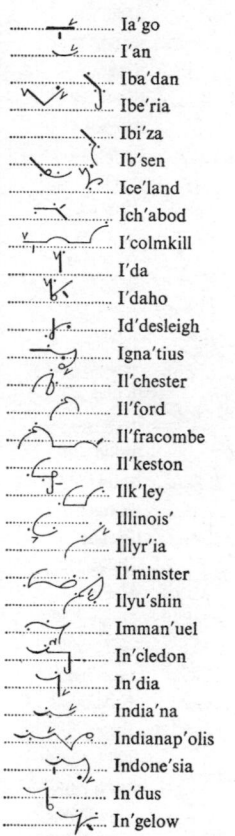

Ia'go
I'an
Iba'dan
Ibe'ria
Ibi'za
Ib'sen
Ice'land
Ich'abod
I'colmkill
I'da
I'daho
Id'desleigh
Igna'tius
Il'chester
Il'ford
Il'fracombe
Il'keston
Ilk'ley
Illinois'
Illyr'ia
Il'minster
Ilyu'shin
Imman'uel
In'cledon
In'dia
India'na
Indianap'olis
Indone'sia
In'dus
In'gelow

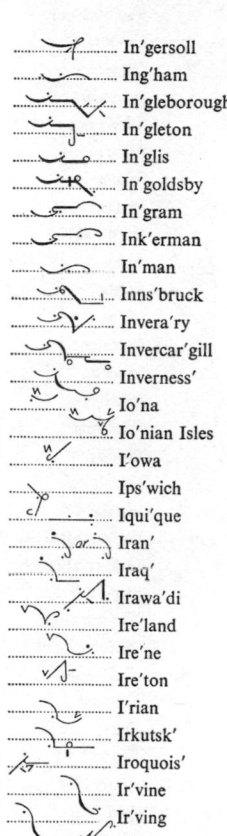

In'gersoll
Ing'ham
In'gleborough
In'gleton
In'glis
In'goldsby
In'gram
Ink'erman
In'man
Inns'bruck
Invera'ry
Invercar'gill
Inverness'
Io'na
Io'nian Isles
I'owa
Ips'wich
Iqui'que
Iran'
Iraq'
Irawa'di
Ire'land
Ire'ne
Ire'ton
I'rian
Irkutsk'
Iroquois'
Ir'vine
Ir'ving
Ir'win

I'saac
I'saacson
Is'abel
Isabel'la
Isai'ah
Iscar'iot
Ish'mael
Ish'maelites
I'sis
I'sla
Isle of Man'
Isle of Wight'
Isle'worth
Is'lington
Isoc'rates
Ispahan'
Is'rael
Is'sachar
Istanbul'
Is'tria
It'aly
Itch'en
Ith'aca
Ithu'riel
Ivan'
I'vanhoe
Ives, St.
Ivi'za
I'vory Coast
Ixi'on
Izves'tia

J

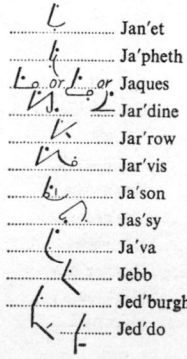

Ja'besh
Ja'bez
Jack'son
Ja'cob
Ja'el
Ja'go, St.
Jakar'ta
Jamai'ca
James
Jame'son
James'town
Janei'ro, Rio de

Jan'et
Ja'pheth
Jaques
Jar'dine
Jar'row
Jar'vis
Ja'son
Jas'sy
Ja'va
Jebb
Jed'burgh
Jed'do

Jeff
Jef'ferson
Jef'feries
Jef'fries
Jef'frey
Jehoi'achin
Jehoi'akim
Jek'yll
Jel'licoe
Jemi'ma
Je'na
Jen'kins
Jen'kinson

Jen'ner
Jen'nings
Jen'sen
Jer'emy
Jer'icho
Je'rome
Jer'rold
Jeru'salem
Jer'vaulx
Jer'vis
Jes'sica
Jes'sie
Jes'sop
Je'sus
Jeune
Jez'ebel
Jil'lian
Jim
Jo'achim
Joan
Joan'na
Job
Jo'drell Bank
Joe

Jo'el
or Johan'nesburg
or a
John
John'son
John'stone
Johore'
Jo'nah
Jo'nas
Jon'athan
Jones
Jor'dan
Jor'tin
Jos'celyn
Jo'seph
Jo'sephine
Jose'phus
Josh'ua
Josi'ah
Josi'as
or Jou'bert (Dutch)
Joubert' (French)
Jove

Joyce
or Juan
Ju'ba
Ju'dah
Judd
Jude
Jude'a
Ju'dith
Ju'dy
Jugur'tha
Ju'lia
Julia'na
Ju'liet
Ju'lius
Jung'frau
Ju'nius
Ju'ra
Jus'tin
Justin'ian
Jus'tus
Jut'land
Ju'venal

K

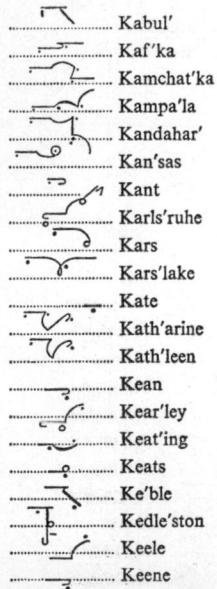

Kabul'
Kaf'ka
Kamchat'ka
Kampa'la
Kandahar'
Kan'sas
Kant
Karls'ruhe
Kars
Kars'lake
Kate
Kath'arine
Kath'leen
Kean
Kear'ley
Keat'ing
Keats
Ke'ble
Kedle'ston
Keele
Keene

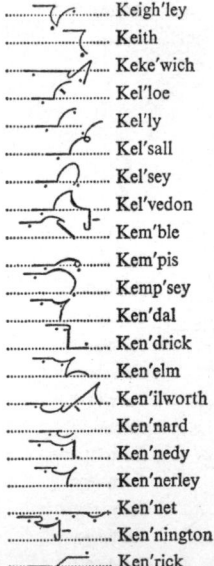

Keigh'ley
Keith
Keke'wich
Kel'loe
Kel'ly
Kel'sall
Kel'sey
Kel'vedon
Kem'ble
Kem'pis
Kemp'sey
Ken'dal
Ken'drick
Ken'elm
Ken'ilworth
Ken'nard
Ken'nedy
Ken'nerley
Ken'net
Ken'nington
Ken'rick

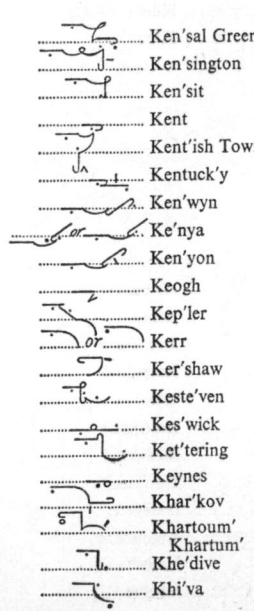

Ken'sal Green
Ken'sington
Ken'sit
Kent
Kent'ish Town
Kentuck'y
Ken'wyn
or Ke'nya
Ken'yon
Keogh
Kep'ler
or Kerr
Ker'shaw
Keste'ven
Kes'wick
Ket'tering
Keynes
Khar'kov
Khartoum'
   Khartum'
Khe'dive
Khi'va

Khorassan'	*or* King'ston-on-Thames	Knollys
Kid'welly	Kings'town	Knot'tingley
Ki'ef(f)	Kingswin'ford	Knowles
Kilbir'nie	Kings'wood	Knox
Kilbride'	King'ton	Knut
Kil'burn	King' Will'iam's Town	Knuts'ford
Kil'da	Kinross'	Ko'be
Kildare'	Kinsale'	Koch
Kild'wick	Kinsha'sha	Kohat'
Kilken'ny	Kin'son	Kon'go
Killal'a	Kintyre'	Kön'igsberg
Killaloe'	Kip'ling	Konti'ki
Killar'ney	Kirk'by	Kore'a
Kil'lyleagh	*or* Kirkcal'dy	Ko'riacs
Kilmain'ham	Kirkcud'bright	Koss'uth
Kilmore'	Kirk'dale	Kra'cow
Kil'ner	Kirk'ham	Krapot'kin
Kil'rush	Kirkhea'ton	Kron'stadt
Kil'wyn	Kirk'lington	Krug'er
Kim'berley	Kirkpat'rick	Ku'belik
Kimbol'ton	Kirkwall'	Kuch'ing
Kincar'dine	Kir'riemuir	Ku Klux Klan
King'lake	Kir'wan	Kumas'(s)i
Kings'bridge	Kiwa'nis	Kuo'mintang'
Kings' Coun'ty	Klon'dike	Kurdistan'
Kings'down	Klop'stock	Kurg
Kings'land	Knares'borough	Ku'rile
Kings'ley	Knel'ler	Kuwait'
King's Lynn	Knight'on	Kyo'to
King's Norton'	Knights'bridge	Kyrle
Kings'ton		

L

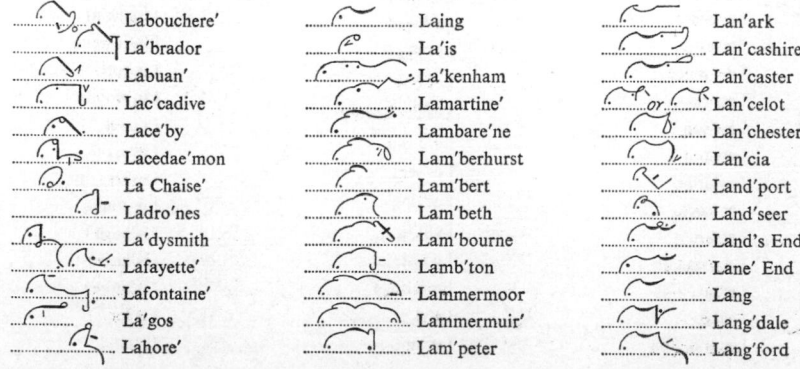

Labouchere'	Laing	Lan'ark
La'brador	La'is	Lan'cashire
Labuan'	La'kenham	Lan'caster
Lac'cadive	Lamartine'	*or* Lan'celot
Lace'by	Lambare'ne	Lan'chester
Lacedae'mon	Lam'berhurst	Lan'cia
La Chaise'	Lam'bert	Land'port
Ladro'nes	Lam'beth	Land'seer
La'dysmith	Lam'bourne	Land's End
Lafayette'	Lamb'ton	Lane' End
Lafontaine'	Lammermoor	Lang
La'gos	Lammermuir'	Lang'dale
Lahore'	Lam'peter	Lang'ford

Lang'ham	Lea'nder	Lew'enhoeck
Lang'horne	Lear	Lew'es, Lew'is
Lang'ley	Leath'erhead	Lew'isham
Lang'port	Leb'anon	Lex'ington
Lan'gridge	Lebrun'	Ley'burn
Lang'ton	Leckhamp'ton	Ley'land
Lans'downe	Leck'y	Ley'ton
Lao'coön	Leclerc'	Ley'tonstone
Laodice'a	Led'bury	Lha'sa
Laos'	Leeds	Lib'anus
Laplace'	Lee'ward Is'lands	Libe'ria
Lap'land	Lefe'vre	Li'berty
La Pla'ta	Legge	Li'bra
Lapu'ta	Legrand'	Lib'ya
Lar'bert	Leib'nitz	Lich'field
Laris'sa	Leices'ter	Lid'dell
Lark'field	Leices'tershire	Lid'don
Lark'ins	Leigh	Lidg'ett
Las'caux	Leigh'ton Buz'zard	Lie'big
Las'celles	Lein'ster	Liech'tenstein
Las'sa	Leip'sic, Leip'zig	Liége'
La'tham	Leith	Lif'ford
La'thom	Lei'trim	Light'foot
Lat'imer	Lel'and	Lille
Lattakoo'	Lem'nos	Lil'leshall
Lat'via	Le'nin	Lil'lian
Lau'ban	Le'ningrad	Lil'liput
Lau'der	Len'nox, Len'ox	Lil'ly
Laugh'ton	Len'ton	Li'ma
Launces'ton	Leomin'ster (*Eng.*)	Lim'burg
Lau'ra	Leon	Lime'house
Lau'rier	Leon'ard	Limps'field
Lausanne'	Leon'idas	Lin'coln
Lavalette'	Leono'ra	Lin'colnshire
Lava'ter	Le'opold	Lind'field
La'venham	Lepan'to	Lind'sey
Lav'ington	Le Queux'	Lin'ley
Lavin'ia	Ler'wick	Linlith'gow
Lavoisier'	Le Sage'	Linnae'us
Lawes	Les'bia	Lin'thwaite
Law'rence	Les'bos	Lin'ton
Law'rie	Les'lie, Les'ley	Lin'wood
Law'son	Leso'tho	Li'onel
Law'ton	Les'seps	Lip'ari
Lay'ard	Les'sing	Lip'pe
Lay'cock	Letit'ia	Lip'ton
Laz'arus	Le'ven	Lis'burn
Lead'enhall	Lev'eridge	Lis'keard
Le'ah	Le'vi	Lis'more
Leake	Lev'in	Lis'ter
Leam'ington		Liszt

Lithua'nia
Lit'tlebury
Lit'tleham
Lit'tlejohn
Lit'tleport
Lit'tleton
Liv'erpool *or*
Liv'ersedge
Li'vingston
Liv'ingstone
Livo'nia
Liv'y
Llan'daff *or*
(And so with the
eight following
words)
Llando'very
Llanel'ly
Llanfyl'lin
Llangol'len
Llan'idloes
Llano'ver
Llanrwst'
Llewel'yn
Lloyd
Loan'go
Locha'ber
Lock'hart
Lock'heed
Lock'wood
Lock'yer
Lo'di
Lofo'ten
Lof'tus
Lo'gan
Loh'engrin
Loire
Lo'mas
Lo'max
Lom'bardy
Lom'broso'
Lo'mond
Lon'don
Londonder'ry
Long'don
Long'fellow
Long'ford
Longi'nus

Long'leat
Long'ley
Long'man
Long'port
Long'ton
Lons'dale
Loo'choo
Lo'pez *or*
Lor'an
Lore'burn
Lo'relei
Loren'zo
Loret'to
Lorne
Lorraine'
Los An'geles
Lostwith'iel
Loth'bury
Lo'thian
Lot'ty
Lou'don
Lough'borough
Loughrea'
Lough'ton
Loui'sa
Lou'isburg
Louise'
Louisia'na
Lou'isville
Lourdes
Louth *or*
Louvre
Love'lace
Lov'ell
Low'ell
Lowes'toft
Lowndes
Lowth
Low'ther
Loyo'la *or*
Lub'bock
Lü'beck
Lu'can
Lu'cas
Luc'ca
Lu'cia
Lu'cian

Lu'cius
Luck'now
Lucre'tius
Lucul'lus
Lu'cy
Lud'denden
Lud'ford
Lud'gate
Lud'low
Lud'wick
Lud'wig
Luft'hansa
Luga'no
Luke
Lul'lington
Lum'ley
Lun'dy
Lu nenbourg
Lu'nik
Lush'ington
Lusita'nia
Lu'ther
Lutine'
Lu'ton
Lut'terworth
Lux'emb(o)urg
Lux'or
Lyc'idas
Lycur'gus
Lydd
Lyd'gate
Lyd'ia
Lyd'ney
Ly'ell
Lyg'on
Lyl'y
Lyme
Lyme Re'gis
Lym'ington
Lyn'combe
Lynd'hurst
Lyne'ham
Lynn
Lyonnesse'
Ly'ons *or*
Lyt'tleton
Lyt'ton

M

Ma'bel
Macao'
Macar'thy
Macart'ney
Macau'lay
Macbeth'
Mac'cabees
Mac'clesfield
Macdon'ald
Macduff'
Macedo'nia
Macgreg'or
Machiavel'li
Ma'chin
Mackay'
Macken'zie
Macknight'
Maclar'en
Maclean'
Macleod'
or MacMah'on

Macmil'lan
Macnama'ra
Macon'ochie
Macpher'son
Macquar'ie
Macrea'dy
Macroom'
Madagas'car
Mad'an
Mad'dox
Madeleine'
Made'ley
Mad'ison
Madras'
Madrid'
Maece'nas
Maes'tricht
Mafeking'
Mag'dala
Mag'dalen
Mag'deburg
Magel'lan
Ma'gog
Mahan'
Mahom'et
or Mahon(e)y
Mai'da Hill
Maid'enhead

Maid'stone
Maine
Main'waring
Mait'land
Major'ca
Maju'ba
Makere're
Mal'abar
Malac'ca
Mal'achi
Malaga'si
Mala'wi
Mala'ya
Malay'sia
Mal'colm
Mal'den
Mal'dive
Mal'don
Ma'li
Mallin'son
Malmes'bury
Malone'
Malo'ny
Mal'pas
Mal'ta
Mal'thus
Mal'ton
Mal'vern
Malvi'na
Mana'gua
Manas'seh
Manas'ses
Man'chester
Mancu'nian
Man'dalay
Mangotsfield'
Manhat'tan
Manito'ba
Man'ley
Man'nering
Mann'heim
Man'ningtree
Mans'field
Man'son
Man'ton
Ma'quis
Marajo'
Marañon'
Mar'burg

Marcel'lus
Marco'ni
Mar'den
Maren'go
Mares'field
Mar'garet
Mar'gate
Mar'gery
Mari'a
Mari'enburg
Mar'ion,
   Mar'ian
Ma'rius
Marjori'banks
Mark'ham
Mark'land
or Marl'borough
Mar'low
Mar'maduke
Mar'mion
Marmontel'
Mar'mora
Mar'ple
Marque'sas
Mars'den
Marseilles'
Mar'shall
Mar'sham
Marsh'field
Mar'ston
Martaban'
Mar'tha
Mar'tineau
Martinique'
Mar'tock
Mar'ton
Marx
Ma'ry
Ma'ryborough
Ma'ryland
Mar'ylebone
Ma'ryport
Ma'sera'ti
Mas'eru
Mash'am
Masho'naland
Massachu'setts
Mass'enet
Mas'sey
Mas'singer

Mas'terman	Mel'ton Mow'bray	Mil'bourne
Matabe'le	Mel'ville	*or* Mil'denhall
Math'er	Me'mel	Mil'dred
Math'eson	Mem'phis	Mile End
Matil'da	Men'ai	Miles
Mat'lock	Men'delssohn	Mil'ford
Matth'ew	Menpes	Millais'
Matthi'as	Men'sa	Mil'lard
Mau'rice	Menton'	Mills
Maurita'nia	Mento'ne	Mil'ner
Maurit'ius	Mentz	Miln'thorpe
Maw'gan	*or* Men'zies	Mil'ton Keynes
Maximil'(l)ian	Mephistoph'eles	Mil'verton
Max'well	Merca'tor	Milwau'kee
Mayence'	Merce'des	Minchinhamp'ton
May'field	Mer'edith	Min'den
May'hew	Merion'eth	Mine'head
May'nard	Mer'riman	Minneap'olis
May'nooth	Mer'ryweather	Minneso'ta
May'o	Mer'sey	Minor'ca
Mazep'pa	Merthyr Tyd'fil	Min'ories
Mazzi'ni	Mer'ton	Mi'nos
M'Car'thy	Me'shech	Min'to
McCor'quodale	Mes'mer	Mirabeau'
McCul'loch	Mesopota'mia	Miran'da
McKay'	Messi'na	Mir'field
McKen'na	Met'calfe	Mir'iam
Mc'Kin'ley	Methu'selah	Mississipp'i
McKin'non	Metz	Missolong'hi
Meagher	*or* Meux	Missou'ri
Meath	Mex'borough	Mitch'am
or Meck'lenburg	Mex'ico	Mitch'ell
	Mey'er	Mitch'elstown
Mede'a	Meyn'ell	Mit'ford
Med'ici	Mi'cah	Mith'ra
Medi'na	Micaw'ber	Mithrida'tes
Med'way	Mi'chael	Mitsubi'shi
Mei'ningen	Mich'ie	Mitsu'i
Mei'ssen	Mich'igan	Miz'pah
Mel'amine	Mick'lethwaite	Mo'ab
Mel'anie	Mi'das	Mod'bury
Mel'ba	Mid'delburg	Mod'der
Mel'bourne	Mid'dleham	Mof'fat
Mel'combe	Mid'dlesbrough	Mogador'
or Mel'huish	*or* Mid'dlesex	Moi'ra
Me'licent	Mid'dleton	Molda'via
Melin'da	Mid'dlewich	Moles'worth
Melis'sa	Mid'hurst	Molière'
Mel'moth	Mid'somer	Mol'ly
Melpom'ene	Nor'ton	Molt'ke
Mel'rose	Milan'	Mol'ton
Mel'tham		

Moluc'ca	Montserrat'	Mountcas'tle
Momba'sa	Moore	Mount'ford
Mon'aco	Mora'via	Mou'sehole
Mon'aghan	Mor'ay	Mow'bray
Monck	Mor'dan	Mo'zambique'
Moncrief'	Mor'decai	Mo'zart
Mond	More	Moz'ley
Monde'go	More'a	Mül'hausen
Mongo'lia	Moreau'	Mü'ller
or Mon'goloid	More'cambe	Mullingar'
Monk'house	Mores'by	Mul'lins
Monk'land	More'ton	Mum'ford
Monk'ton	Mor'gan	Munchau'sen
Mon'mouth	Mor'ison	Mundel'la
Monroe'	Mor'land	Mu'nich
Monro'via	Mor'ley	Munro'
Mon'tagu	Mor'mons	Mun'ster
Montaigne'	Morn'ington	Murat'
Monta'na	Mor'peth	Mur'cia
Mont Blanc'	Mor'rison	Mur'ray
Montcalm'	Mor'timer	Mur'rayfield
Monte'go	Mort'lake	Mus'covy
Montene'gro	Mor'ton	Mus'grave
Montcrcy'	Mos'cow	Mus'lim
Montesquieu	Mose'ley	Mus'selburgh
Montesso'ri	Mo'ses	Mus'well Hill
Montevide'o	Mos'heim	My'att
Montgom'ery	Moss'ley	My'ers
Montpel'lier	Mo'sul	My'ott
Montreal'	Mot'tram	My'ra
Montrose'	Moul'ton	Mysore'

N

Na'aman	Nant'wich	Nathan'iel
Na'both	Na'omi	Na'to
Nagasa'ki	Naph'tali	Nato'lia
Nagoy'a	Na'pier	Naum'burg
Nagpur'	Na'ples	Nau'ru
Na'hum	Na'poli	Nav'an
Nails'worth	Nar'beth	Navari'no
Nairn	Nase'by	Navarre'
Nairo'bi	Nash	Nay'land
Na'mur	Nash'ville	Nay'lor
Nanking'	Na'smyth	Naz'areth
Nan'sen	Nassau'	Neale
Nantuck'et	Na'than	Nebras'ka

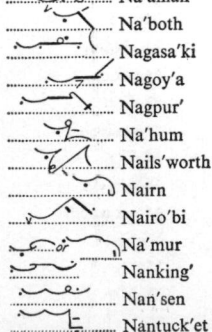
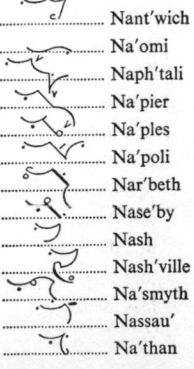
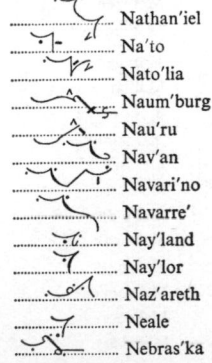

Nebuchadnez′zar	New′market	No′bel
Neck′ar	New Mex′ico	Noot′ka Sound
Neck′er	Newnes	No′ra
Need′ham	Newn′ham	Nord′berg
Neferti′ti	New Or′leans	Nor′dica
Ne′gri Sem′bilan	New′port	Nord′land
Nehemi′ah	New′quay	Nore
Nel′son	New′ry	Nor′folk
Nem′butal	New′som	Nor′ham
Nemours′	New South Wales	Nor′manby
Ne′nagh	New′ton	Nor′mandy
Ne′ots, St.	New′town	Nor′manton
Nepaul′ (Nepal′)	Newtownards′	Nor′ris
Ne′ro	New York	Northal′lerton
Nes′ton	New York City	North′am
Neth′erlands	New Zea′land	Northamp′ton
Neu′burg	Ney	North Caroli′na
Neuchâtel′	Nga′mi	North′cote
Neu′stadt	Niag′ara	North Dako′ta
Neva′da	Nicara′gua	North′field
Nev′ille	Nice	North′fleet
Nev′in	Nich′olas	North′leach
Nev′is	Nich′ols	Nor′throp
New′ark	Nich′olson	Northum′berland
New′berry / New′bery	Nick′leby	Northum′bria
New′borough	Nicobar′	North′wood
New′bridge	Nicode′mus	Nor′ton
New′burg / New′burgh	Nicosi′a	Nor′way
New′burn	Nie′buhr	Nor′wich
New′bury	Nie′per	Nor′wood
New′castle or Newcas′tle	Nie′ster	Nos′tradamus
Newcastle-on-Tyne	Ni′gel	Not′tingham
New′castle under-Lyme	Ni′ger	Not′ting Hill
New′comb / New′come	Nige′ria	No′va Sco′tia
New′digate	Nile	No′va Zem′bla
New′enden	Nil′sson	Novgorod′
New′ent	Nim′rod	No′well
New′foundland or Newfound′land	Nine′ Elms	Nu′bia
New′gate	Nin′eveh	Nu′gent
New Hamp′shire	Nin′field	Nu′ma
Newha′ven	Nin′ian, St.	Nun′eaton
New′ington	Nio′be	Nune′ham
New Jer′sey	Nippon′	Nu′nemberg
New′land	Ni′ssen	Nu′remberg
New′man	Nix′on	Nut′tall
	No′ah	Nyas′(s)aland
	Noakes	Ny′koping

O

Oak'ford
Oak'ham
Oak'hill
Oak'ingham
Oak'land
Oak'ley
Obadi'ah
O'ban
Oberam'mergau
O'berlin
O'beron
O'Bri'en
Ock'brook
O'Con'nell
O'Con'nor
Octa'via
Octa'vius
Odell'
O'der
Odes'sa
Ody'sseus
Oed'ipus
Off'aly
O'gilby
O'gilvie
Og'pu
Ohi'o
Okehamp'ton
Okhotsk'
Oklaho'ma
Old'bury
Old'castle
Ol'denburg
Old'field
Old'ham
Old'land
Olds'worth
Ol'iphant
Olivet'
Oliv'ia
Olleren'shaw
Ol'lerton

Ol'mütz
Ol'ney
Ol'veston
Olym'pia
Olym'pus
Omagh
O'maha
O'mar
Omdurman'
Om'maney
On'ega
O'Neil'
On'gar
Ons'low
Onta'rio
O'pel
O'penshaw
Ophe'lia
O'pie
Opor'to
O'ram
Oran'
Or'egon
O'Reil'ly
O'renburg
Or'ford
Or'igen
Orino'co
Oris'sa
Ork'ney
Orlan'do
Or'leans
Or'monde
Orms'by
Orms'kirk
Or'mus
Or'pen
Or'pheus
Or'ton
Osa'ka
Os'borne
Os'mington

Os'mond
Osnabrück
Os'naburg
Os'sett
Os'sian
Os'tend
Os'tiaks
Os'wald
Os'waldtwistle
Oswe'go
Os'westry
Otahei'te
Ot'ham
Othel'lo
Oth'man
O'tho
Ot'ley
Ot'tawa
Ot'tery St. Ma'ry
Ot'way
Oude, Oudh
Oui'da
Oul'ton
Oun'dle
Ou'ral
Ouse
Ou'tram
O'verbury
O'verend
O'verton
Overys'sel
Ov'id
Ovie'do
O'vingham
O'wen
Ows'ley
Ow'ston
Ox'bridge
Ox'enden
Ox'fam
Ox'ford
Ox'ley

P

Pad'dington
Pa'derborn
Paderew'ski
Pad'iham
Pad'stow
Pad'ua
Pagani'ni
Pag'et
Paign'ton
Paine
Pains'wick
Pais'ley
Pak'enham
Pakistan'
Paler'mo
Pal'estine
Pa'ley
Pal'grave
Pal'issy
Pal'liser
Palm'erston
Palmy'ra
Pa'ludrin
Pamir'
Pampelu'na
Pamphyl'ia
Pan'Am'
Pan'cras, St.
Pang'bourne
Pank'hurst
Pap'ua
Para'
Paracel'sus
Paraguay'
Paramar'ibo
Parana'
Par'fitt
Par'is
Par'ker
Park'gate
Park'hurst
Par'kinson
Par'ma
Parnas'sus
Par'nell
Pa'ros
Par'seval
Par'sons
Par'sonstown

Pas'call
Pass'more
Pasteur'
Patago'nia
Pat'ernoster Row
Pat'erson
Pat'more
Pat'mos
Pat'na
Pa'ton
Patri'cia
Pat'rick
Pat'terson
Pat'tingham
Pat'tison
Paul
Pauli'na
Pauline'
Paul'ton
Paunce'fote
Pausa'nias
Pavi'a
Pav'lov
Pawtuck'et
Pax'ton
Payne
Pea'body
Pearce
Pear'son
Pear'y
Peck'ham
Peck'sniff
Pe'dro
Pee'bles
Peg'gy
Pegu'
Pe'ipus
Pekin'
Peking'
Pela'gius
Pelew' Islands
Pel'ham
Peli'on
Pem'berton
Pem'bridge
or Pem'broke
Pem'bury
Penang'
Penden'nis

Pen'dleton
Pene'lope
Penn
Pen'nefather
Pen'nington
Pen'niston
Pennsylva'nia
Pen'rith
Pen'ryn
Pens'ford
Pent'land
Pen'tonville
Pen'tothal
Pen'wortham
Penzance'
Peo'ria
Pep'in
Pepys
Perak'
Per'cival
Per'cy
Per'gamos
Per'icles
Per'kins
Perks
Pernambu'co
Perranzab'uloe
Per'rin
Perse'phone
Persep'olis
Per'seus
Per'sia
Perth
Peru'
Peru'gia
Peshaw'ar
Pestaloz'zi
Pesth
Pe'terborough
Pe'terchurch
Pe'terhead
Peterlee'
Pe'tersfield
Peth'erton
Pe'tra
Pe'trarch
Pet'rograd
Petulen'gro
Pet'worth

Pev'ensey	Plau'tus	Port'land
Pev'eril	Play'fair	Portmad'oc
Pew'sey	Plev'na	Port'man
Pha'raoh	Plim'soll	Por'tobel'lo
Phe'be	Plin'y	Por'to Ri'co
Phelps	Plumb'land	Port Said'
Pheni'cia, Phoeni'cia	or Plump'tre	Port'sea
Phid'ias	Plum'stead	Ports'mouth
Philadel'phia	Plun'ket	Por'tugal
Phile'mon	Plu'tarch	Po'sen
Phil'ip	Plym'outh	Pos'tlethwaite
Phi'lippi	Plymp'ton	Pot'iphar
Phil'ipstown	Plym'stock	Poto'mac
Philis'tia	Plynlim'mon	Poto'si
Phil'lack	Po	Pots'dam
Phil'lips	Pock'lington	Pot'terne
Phil'lis	Po'cock	Pot'tersham
Phill'pott	Poe	Pou'lett
{Phin'eas {Phin'ehas	Poincaré'	Poul'ton
Phipps	Poitiers'	or Pow'ell
Phoe'be	Po'land	Pow'erscourt
Phryg'ia	Po'laroid	Pow'ick
Phyl'lis	Pole'-Ca'rew	Pow'is, Powys
Pick'ering	Pollokshaws'	Pow'nall
Pick'ett	Pol'ly	Poyn'ter
Pick'ford	Polo'nius	Poyn'ton
Pick'wick	Polyb'ius	Praed
Pied'mont	Polyne'sia	Praesi'dium
Pier'point	Pomera'nia	Prague
Pietermar'itzburg	or Pompe'ii	Pratt
Pig'ott	Pom'pey	Prav'da
Pi'late	Pondicher'ry	Preiss'nitz
Pil'kington	Pon'doland	Pren'dergast
Pil'lau	Pon'sanooth	Pres'burg
Pil'ton	Pon'sonby	Pres'cott
Pin'dar	Pon'tefract	Prest'bury
Piner'o	Pon'tesbury	Presteign'
Pin'kerton	Pon'typool	Pres'ton
Pir'ie	Poole	Pres'tonpans
Pi'sa	Poo'na	Prest'wich
Pit'man	Por'lock	Preto'ria
Pit'manScript	Porsche	Pri'am
Pit'tington	Por'son	Pria'pus
Pitts'burg	Portadown'	Prid'eaux
Pi'us	Port'au-Prince''	Priest'ley
Pizar'ro	Port'bury	Prin'gle
Plais'tow	Port'chester	Pris'cian
Plantag'enet	Por'teus	Priscil'la
Plas'sey	Port Glas'gow	Pritch'ard
Pla'to	Por'tia	Procrus'tes
Platt	Port'ishead	Prome'theus

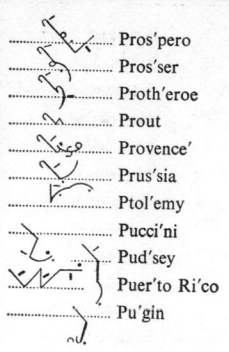

- Pros'pero
- Pros'ser
- Proth'eroe
- Prout
- Provence'
- Prus'sia
- Ptol'emy
- Pucci'ni
- Pud'sey
- Puer'to Ri'co
- Pu'gin

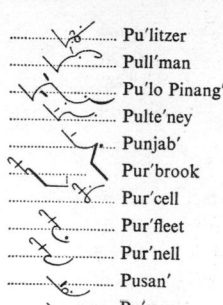

- Pu'litzer
- Pull'man
- Pu'lo Pinang'
- Pulte'ney
- Punjab'
- Pur'brook
- Pur'cell
- Pur'fleet
- Pur'nell
- Pusan'
- Pu'sey

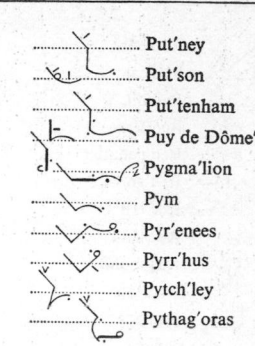

- Put'ney
- Put'son
- Put'tenham
- Puy de Dôme'
- Pygma'lion
- Pym
- Pyr'enees
- Pyrr'hus
- Pytch'ley
- Pythag'oras

Q

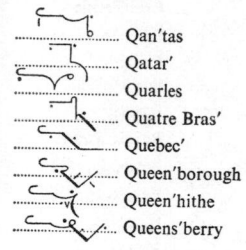

- Qan'tas
- Qatar'
- Quarles
- Quatre Bras'
- Quebec'
- Queen'borough
- Queen'hithe
- Queens'berry

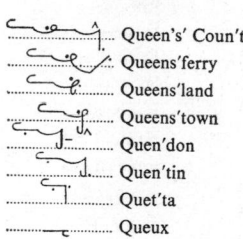

- Queen's' Coun'ty
- Queens'ferry
- Queens'land
- Queens'town
- Quen'don
- Quen'tin
- Quet'ta
- Queux

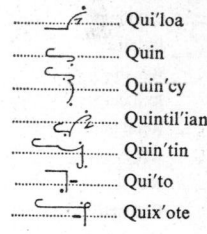

- Qui'loa
- Quin
- Quin'cy
- Quintil'ian
- Quin'tin
- Qui'to
- Quix'ote

R

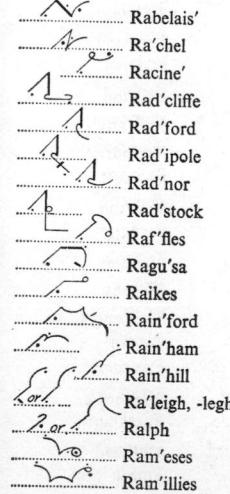

- Rabelais'
- Ra'chel
- Racine'
- Rad'cliffe
- Rad'ford
- Rad'ipole
- Rad'nor
- Rad'stock
- Raf'fles
- Ragu'sa
- Raikes
- Rain'ford
- Rain'ham
- Rain'hill
- Ra'leigh, -legh
- Ralph
- Ram'eses
- Ram'illies

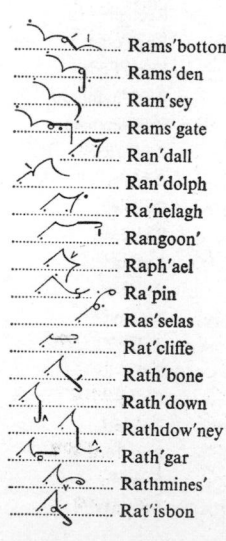

- Rams'bottom
- Rams'den
- Ram'sey
- Rams'gate
- Ran'dall
- Ran'dolph
- Ra'nelagh
- Rangoon'
- Raph'ael
- Ra'pin
- Ras'selas
- Rat'cliffe
- Rath'bone
- Rath'down
- Rathdow'ney
- Rath'gar
- Rathmines'
- Rat'isbon

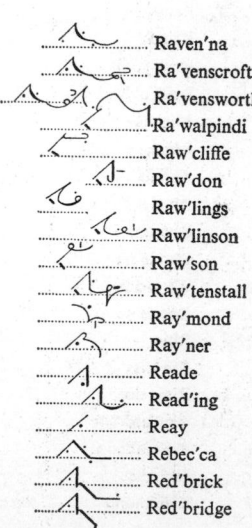

- Raven'na
- Ra'venscroft
- Ra'vensworth
- Ra'walpindi
- Raw'cliffe
- Raw'don
- Raw'lings
- Raw'linson
- Raw'son
- Raw'tenstall
- Ray'mond
- Ray'ner
- Reade
- Read'ing
- Reay
- Rebec'ca
- Red'brick
- Red'bridge

Red'burn	Rich'ter	Rom'sey
Red'car	Rick'etts	Rom'ulus
Red'ditch	Rick'mansworth	Ron'aldshay
Red'fern	Ridd'ell	Ro'nan, St.
Red'gauntlet	Ridge'mount	Rönt'gen
Red'grave	Ridge'well	Roose'velt
Red'hill	Rid'ley	Ror'schach
Red'land	Rien'zi	Ro'sa
Red'mond	Riev'aulx	Ros'alind
Redruth'	Ri'ga	Ros'amond
Red Sea	Ril'lington	Ros'cius
Reeves	Ring'way	Roscoe'
Reg'gio	Ring'wood	Roscom'mon
Reg'inald	Ri'o Janei'ro	Roseau'
Reich'stag	Rip'ley	Rose'bery
Reid	Rip'on	Rosel'la
Rei'gate	Rit'chie	Roset'ta
Rem'brandt	Rit'son	Rosh'erville
Rem'ington	Rivie'ra	Rosinan'te
Re'mus	Riv'ington	Rosset'ti
Renan'	Riz'zio	Rossi'ni
Ren'del	Rob'bins	Rosyth'
Rend'ham	Rob'ert	Roth'erfield
René'	Rob'ertson	Roth'erham
Ren'frew	Rob'espierre	Roth'erhithe
Ren'nell	Rob'in Hood	Rothe'say
Ren'nie	Rob'inson	Roths'child
Ren'shaw	Rob Roy	Roth'well
Ren'wick	Rob'son	Rot'terdam
Rep'ton	Roch'dale	Rouen'
Ret'ford	Rochefort'	Rouma'nia
Reu'ben	Rochefoucauld'	Roume'lia
Reuss	Rochelle', La	Rousseau'
Reu'ter	Roch'ester	Rowe'na
Reyk'javik	Rock Fer'ry	Row'land
Reyn'olds	Rock'hampton	Row'ley
Rheims	Rock'ingham	Row'ton
Rhine	Rod'erick	Rox'burgh
Rho'da	Rodg'er	Rox'bury
Rhode' I'sland	Rod'ney	Rox'well
Rhodes	Roe'dean	Roys'ton
Rhode'sia	Rog'er	Roy'ton
Rhon'dda	Rog'ers	Rua'bon
Rhone	Ro'land	Ru'bens
Rhys	Rollin'	Ru'binstein
Rib'chester	Rolls'-Royce'	Ru'dall
Ricar'do	Rome	Rudge
Rich'ard	Ro'meo	Rudg'wick
Rich'ardson	Rom'ford	Ru'dolph
Richelieu'	Rom'illy	Rud'yard
Rich'mond	Rom'ney	Ru'fus

Ruge'ley
Rum'ford
Rum'sey
Run'ciman
Run'corn
Run'nymede
Ru'pert

Rurita'nia
Rush'ington
Rush'ton
Rus'kin
Rus'sell
Rus'sia
Ruth'erglen

Ru'thin
Ruth'ven
Rut'land
Rwan'da
Ryde
Rys'wick

S

Saab
Saar
Sabe'na
Sabi'na
Sachev'erell
Sack'ville
Sad'dleworth
Saf'fron Wal'den
Sag'inaw
_or_ St. John'
Sal'adin
Salaman'ca
Sal'amis
Sal'combe
Salee'
Sa'lem
Saler'no
Sal'ford
Salis'bury
Salk
Sal'lust
Salo'me
Salon'ica
Sa'lop
Sal'taire
Salt'ash
Salt'ford
Salt' Lake Cit'y
Salu'ki
Salvador'
Salz'burg
Sama'ria
Samarkand'
Samo'a
Sa'mos
Samp'son
Sam'son

Sam'uel
San Anto'nio
San'cho Pan'za
San'croft
Sandakan'
San'dall
San'deman
San'derson
Sand'ford
Sand'gate
Sand'hurst
San'diford
San Domin'go
San'down
Sand'ringham
Sandys
_or_ San Francis'co
San José'
San'key
San Mari'no
San Re'mo
San Sal'vador
_or_ San'ta Cruz
San'ta Fé
Santia'go
Sant'ley
Sa'o Pau'lo
Sapphi'ra
Sapph'o
Saragos'sa
_or_ Sa'rah
Saraje'vo
_or_ Sara'wak
Sardana'palus
Sardin'ia
Sa'rum
Saskatch'ewan

Sau'di Ara'bia
Saun'derson
Savonaro'la
Saw'bridgeworth
Saw'ston
Saw'try
Saxe-Al'tenburg
Saxe-Co'burg, Go'tha
Saxe-Mei'ningen
Saxe-Wei'mar
Saxmund'ham
Sayce
Scal'iger
Scandina'via
Scar'borough
Schaffhau'sen
Scheheraza'de
Schil'ler
Schles'wig
Schnei'der
Schoef'fer
Schrevel'ius
Schu'bert
Schus'ter
Schwartz
Schwarz'burg
Schwerin'
Scillo'nian
Scil'ly Isles
Sci'o
Scip'io
Sclavo'nia
Scot'land
Scott
Scran'ton
Scrym'geour
Scul'coates

Scu'tari	Shar'land	Silves'ter
Scy'lla	Sha'ron	Sil'via
Scyth'ia	She'ba	Sim'ca
Sea'combe	Sheerness'	Sim'eon
Sea'ford	Shef'field	Sim'kin
Sea'forth	Shef'ford	Sim'la
Sea'ham	Shei'la	Sim'mons
Sean'	Shel'burne	Simms
Searle	Shel'don	Si'mon
Sea'ton	Shel'ley	Simp'kin
Seat'tle	Shel'ton	Sim'plon
Sebas'tian	Shen'stone	Simp'son
Sebas'topol	Shep'pard	Si'nai
Sed'berg	Shep'ton Mal'let	Sin'clair
Sedge'field	Sher'borne	Sin'clairtown
Sedge'moor	Sher'idan	Sind, Sindh
Sedg'ley	Sher'lock	Sind'bad
Sedg'wick	Sher'man	Singapore'
See'ley	Sher'win	Sing Sing
Sego'via	Sher'wood	Si'on
Sel'borne	Shil'lingstone	Si'rach
Sel'by	Ship'ton	Sis'era
Sel'den	Shiraz'	Sismon'di
Selec'tric	Shir'ley	Sis'yphus
Seli'na	Shoe'buryness	Sith'ney
Sel'kirk	Shore'ditch	Sit'tingbourne
Selous'	Shore'ham	Ska'raborg
Sel'wyn	Shot'ley	Skeat
Semir'amis	Shrews'bury	Skel'mersdale
Senaar'	Shrop'shire	Skel'ton
Sen'eca	Shuttle'worth	Skibbereen'
Senegal'	Shy'lock	Skid'daw
Senegam'bia	Siam'	Skip'ton
Seoul'	Sibe'ria	Skye
Serampore'	Sib'ford	Slade
Seringapatam	Sic'ily	Slap'ton
Serve'tus	Sid'bury	Slea'ford
Ser'via	Sid'cot	Sles'wick
Seth	Sid'dons	Sli'go
Sev'enoaks	Sid'mouth	Sli'vovitz
Sev'ern	Sid'ney	Sloane
Sev'ille	Si'don	Slo'per
Sévres	Sieg'fried	Small'bridge
Seychelles'	Sie'mens	Smal'ley
Sey'mour	Sienn'a	Smar'den
Sha'drach	Sier'ra Leo'ne	Smea'ton
Shad'well	Sig'ismund	Smeth'wick
Shaftes'bury	Sile'nus	Smith'ers
{Shake'speare	Silk'stone	Smith'field
{Shak'spere	Silva'nus	Smolensk'
Shan'non	Sil'verton	Smol'lett
Shap'wick		

Smyr'na	Soy'uz	Sterne
Smyth	Spain	Ste'venage
Snaith	Spal'ding	Ste'vens
Snel'ling	Spar'ta	Ste'venson
Snen'ton	Speen	Ste'venton
Snod'grass	Speen'hamland	Stew'art
Snow'don	Spen'nithorne	Stew'arton
Snow'hill	Spen'ser	Steyne
Soci'nus	Spils'by	Stil'lington
Soc'rates	Spino'za	Stir'ling
Sod'bury	Spit'alfields	Stock'bridge
Sod'om	Spit'head	Stock'holm
Sofa'la	Spitzberg'en	Stock'land
Sofi'a	Spode	Stock'port
So'ham	Spoon'er	Stocks'field
So'lent	Spring'field	Stock'ton
Soleure'	Spur'geon	Stock'well
Solihull'	Sri Lan'ka	Stock'with
Sol'omon	Sta'cey	Stod'dart
Sol'way Firth	Staf'fa	Sto'gumber
Soma'lia	Staf'ford	Stoke New'ington
Soma'liland	Staines	Stokes'ley
Som'ers	Stain'land	Stone'bridge
Som'ersham	Stal'bridge	Stone'ham
Som'erstown	Sta'lingrad	Stone'haven
Som'erton	Sta'lybridge	Stone'henge
Som'erville	Stamboul'	Stone'house
Sophi'a	Stam'ford	Stony'hurst
Soph'ocles	Stand'lake	Stor'mont
Sophro'nia	Stan'field	Stor'noway
So'phy	Stan'ford	Stort'ford
Soth'eby	Stan'ley	Stoth'ert
South'am	Stan'ningley	Stour
Southamp'ton	Stan'sted	Stour'bridge
South'borough	Stan'ton	Stour'port
South'bourne	Stan'well	Stour'ton
South Caroli'na	Sta'plefield	Stow'ell
South'cott	Sta'pleford	Stow'market
South Dako'ta	Sta'pleton	Strabane'
Southend'-on-sea	Star'key	Stra'bo
Sou'they	Staun'ton	Strachan
South'gate	Stave'ley	Stra'chey
South Mol'ton	Steb'bing	Strad'brooke
South'port	Sted'man	Straf'ford
South'sea	Stel'la	Stral'sund
South Shields	Sten'nett	Strang'ford
South'wark	Ste'phen	Stranraer'
South'well	Ste'phens	Stran'ton
South'wick	Ste'phens, St.	Stras'burg
South'wold	Ste'phenson	Strat'ford
Sow'erby	Step'ney	Strat'ford-on-Avon

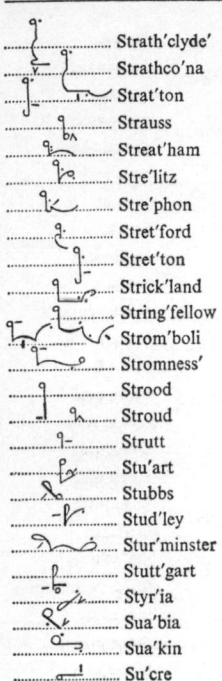

Strath'clyde'
Strathco'na
Strat'ton
Strauss
Streat'ham
Stre'litz
Stre'phon
Stret'ford
Stret'ton
Strick'land
String'fellow
Strom'boli
Stromness'
Strood
Stroud
Strutt
Stu'art
Stubbs
Stud'ley
Stur'minster
Stutt'gart
Styr'ia
Sua'bia
Sua'kin
Su'cre

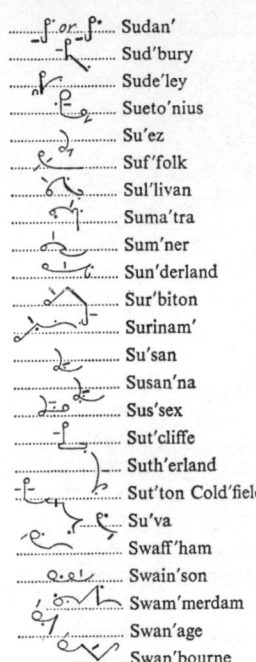

Sudan'
Sud'bury
Sude'ley
Sueto'nius
Su'ez
Suf'folk
Sul'livan
Suma'tra
Sum'ner
Sun'derland
Sur'biton
Surinam'
Su'san
Susan'na
Sus'sex
Sut'cliffe
Suth'erland
Sut'ton Cold'field
Su'va
Swaff'ham
Swain'son
Swam'merdam
Swan'age
Swan'bourne

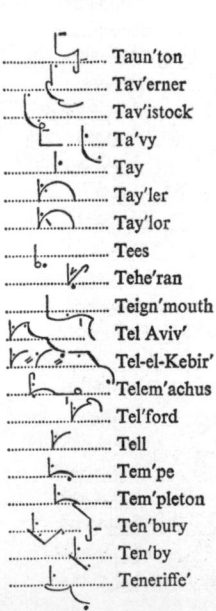

Swan'sea
Swa'ziland
Swe'den
Swe'denborg
Swin'burne
Swin'don
Swine'fleet
Swin'ey
Swin'ford
Swin'stead
Swin'ton
Swith'in, St.
Swith'un, St.
Swit'zerland
Syd'enham
Syd'ney
Sykes
Syl'la
Syl'via
Sy'monds
Sy'mons
Sy'ra
Syr'acuse
Syr'ia

T

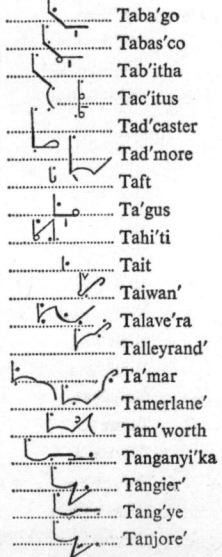

Taba'go
Tabas'co
Tab'itha
Tac'itus
Tad'caster
Tad'more
Taft
Ta'gus
Tahi'ti
Tait
Taiwan'
Talave'ra
Talleyrand'
Ta'mar
Tamerlane'
Tam'worth
Tanganyi'ka
Tangier'
Tang'ye
Tanjore'

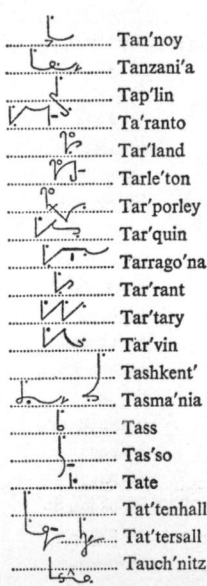

Tan'noy
Tanzani'a
Tap'lin
Ta'ranto
Tar'land
Tarle'ton
Tar'porley
Tar'quin
Tarrago'na
Tar'rant
Tar'tary
Tar'vin
Tashkent'
Tasma'nia
Tass
Tas'so
Tate
Tat'tenhall
Tat'tersall
Tauch'nitz

Taun'ton
Tav'erner
Tav'istock
Ta'vy
Tay
Tay'ler
Tay'lor
Tees
Tehe'ran
Teign'mouth
Tel Aviv'
Tel-el-Kebir'
Telem'achus
Tel'ford
Tell
Tem'pe
Tem'pleton
Ten'bury
Ten'by
Teneriffe'

Ten'nent	Thrap'stone	Tonquin'
Tennessee'	Thucyd'ides	Tooke
Ten'niel	Thur'low	Toot'ing
Ten'nyson	Thur'so	Top'lady
Ten'terden	Thwaites	Tops'ham
Ter'ence	Ti'ber	Top'sy
Terpsich'ore	Tibe'rias / Tibe'rius	Torbay'
Ter'ry	Tibet'	Tor'nea
Tertul'lian	Tibul'lus	Toron'to
Tet'bury	Tice'hurst	Torquay'
Te'viot	Tich'borne	Tor'rington
Tewkes'bury	Tich'field	Torto'la
Tex'as	Tick'ell	Tortu'ga
Tex'el	Tid'denham	Tort'worth
Thack'eray	Tid'dington	Tot'nes
Thai'land	Tides'well	Tot'tenham
Tha'les	Tien' tsin	Tot'tington
Thame	Tierr'a del Fue'go	Toulon'
Thames	Ti'gris	Toulouse'
Than'et	Til'ley	Tournai' / Tournay'
Thatch'am	Tillicoul'try	Tours
Thebes	Til'lingham	Towces'ter
Thel'wall	Til'lotson	Town'er
Themis'tocles	Timbuc'too / Timbuk'tu	Town'ley
The'obald	Timo'leon	Towns'end
Theoc'ritus	Ti'mon	Tox'teth
Theodo'ra	Tims'bury	Toyn'bee
The'odore	Tin'dall	Tra'cey
Theod'oret	Tintag'el	Trafal'gar
Theodo'sia	Tippera'ry	Tra'jan
Theodo'sius	Tippoo Sah'ib	Tralee'
Theoph'ilus	Tip'ton	Tran'mere
There'sa	Tita'nia	Transjordan
Thermop'ylae	Ti'tian	Transvaal'
Thes'saly	Ti'tus	or Transylva'nia
Thet'ford	Tiv'erton	Trapp
Thiers'	Tiv'oli	Travancore'
Thirsk	Toba'go	Treb'izond
Thom'as	Tobi'as	Tred'egar
Thom'asine	To'bit	Trelaw'ny
Thomp'son	Tobolsk'	Tren'chard
Thom'son	Todd	Trent
Thorn'aby	Tod'morden	Trent'ham
Thorn'bury	To'go	Tren'ton
Thorne	To'kyo	Trevel'yan
Thor'ney	Tolle'mache	Treves
Thorn'hill	Tol'stoi	Trev'ithick
Thorn'ley	Tom'kins	Tre'vor
Thorn'ton	Tom'linson	Trichinop'oly
Thorpe	Tomp'kins	Trieste'
Thrace	Ton'bridge	

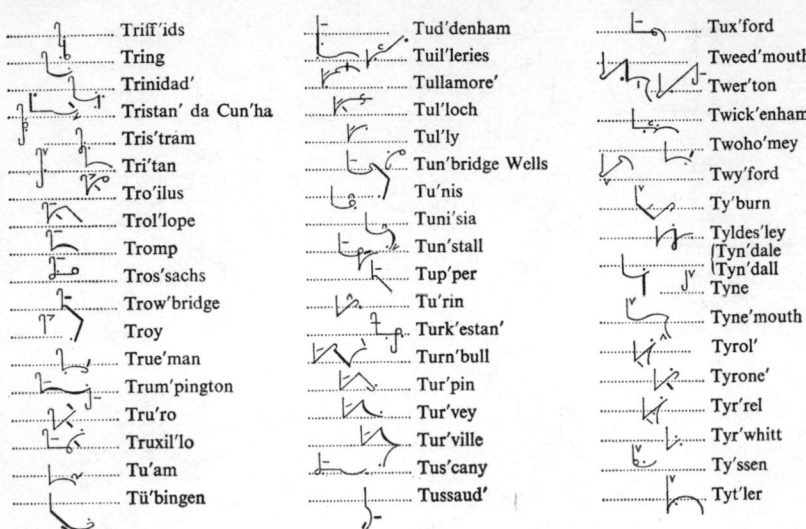

Triff'ids
Tring
Trinidad'
Tristan' da Cun'ha
Tris'tram
Tri'tan
Tro'ilus
Trol'lope
Tromp
Tros'sachs
Trow'bridge
Troy
True'man
Trum'pington
Tru'ro
Truxil'lo
Tu'am
Tü'bingen

Tud'denham
Tuil'leries
Tullamore'
Tul'loch
Tul'ly
Tun'bridge Wells
Tu'nis
Tuni'sia
Tun'stall
Tup'per
Tu'rin
Turk'estan'
Turn'bull
Tur'pin
Tur'vey
Tur'ville
Tus'cany
Tussaud'

Tux'ford
Tweed'mouth
Twer'ton
Twick'enham
Twoho'mey
Twy'ford
Ty'burn
Tyldes'ley
{Tyn'dale
{Tyn'dall
Tyne
Tyne'mouth
Tyrol'
Tyrone'
Tyr'rel
Tyr'whitt
Ty'ssen
Tyt'ler

U

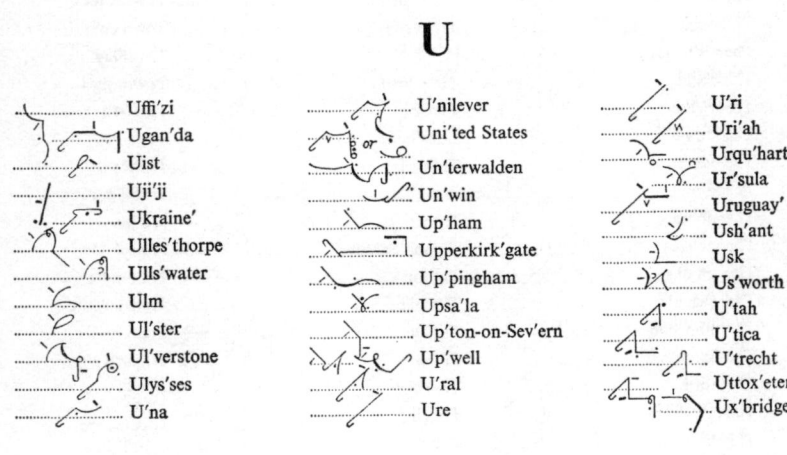

Uffi'zi
Ugan'da
Uist
Uji'ji
Ukraine'
Ulles'thorpe
Ulls'water
Ulm
Ul'ster
Ul'verstone
Ulys'ses
U'na

U'nilever
Uni'ted States
Un'terwalden
Un'win
Up'ham
Upperkirk'gate
Up'pingham
Upsa'la
Up'ton-on-Sev'ern
Up'well
U'ral
Ure

U'ri
Uri'ah
Urqu'hart
Ur'sula
Uruguay'
Ush'ant
Usk
Us'worth
U'tah
U'tica
U'trecht
Uttox'eter
Ux'bridge

V

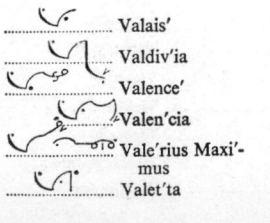

Valais'
Valdiv'ia
Valence'
Valen'cia
Vale'rius Maxi'-
mus
Valet'ta

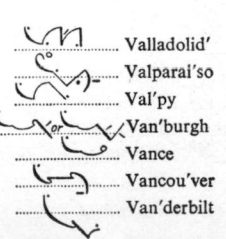

Valladolid'
Valparai'so
Val'py
Van'burgh
Vance
Vancou'ver
Van'derbilt

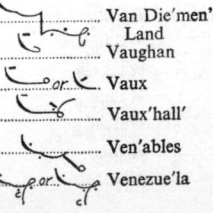

Van Die'men's
Land
Vaughan
Vaux
Vaux'hall'
Ven'ables
Venezue'la

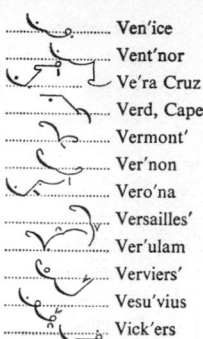

Ven'ice
Vent'nor
Ve'ra Cruz
Verd, Cape
Vermont'
Ver'non
Vero'na
Versailles'
Ver'ulam
Verviers'
Vesu'vius
Vick'ers

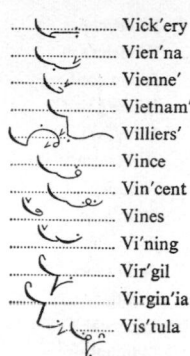

Vick'ery
Vien'na
Vienne'
Vietnam'
Villiers'
Vince
Vin'cent
Vines
Vi'ning
Vir'gil
Virgin'ia
Vis'tula

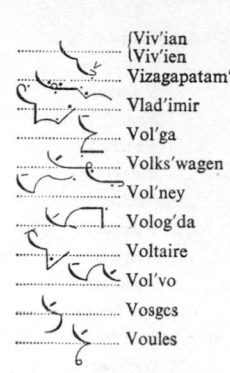

Viv'ian
Viv'ien
Vizagapatam'
Vlad'imir
Vol'ga
Volks'wagen
Vol'ney
Volog'da
Voltaire
Vol'vo
Vosges
Voules

W

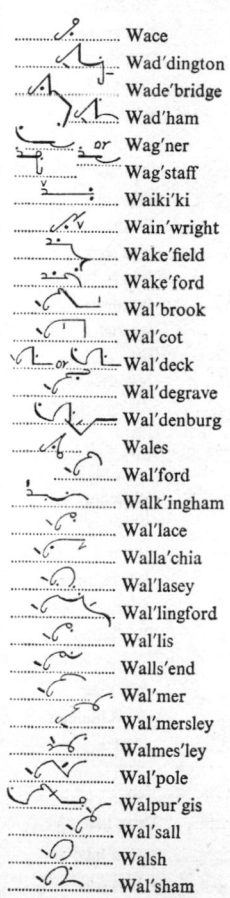

Wace
Wad'dington
Wade'bridge
Wad'ham
Wag'ner
Wag'staff
Waiki'ki
Wain'wright
Wake'field
Wake'ford
Wal'brook
Wal'cot
Wal'deck
Wal'degrave
Wal'denburg
Wales
Wal'ford
Walk'ingham
Wal'lace
Walla'chia
Wal'lasey
Wal'lingford
Wal'lis
Walls'end
Wal'mer
Wal'mersley
Walmes'ley
Wal'pole
Walpur'gis
Wal'sall
Walsh
Wal'sham

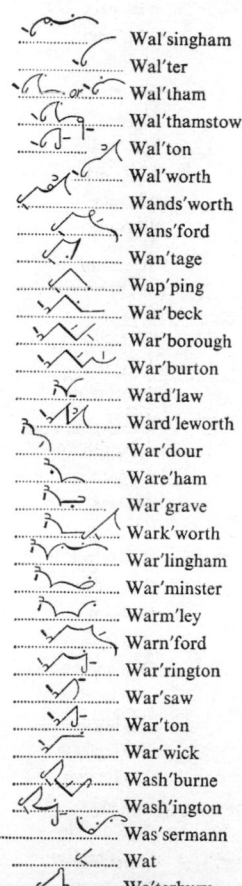

Wal'singham
Wal'ter
Wal'tham
Wal'thamstow
Wal'ton
Wal'worth
Wands'worth
Wans'ford
Wan'tage
Wap'ping
War'beck
War'borough
War'burton
Ward'law
Ward'leworth
War'dour
Ware'ham
War'grave
Wark'worth
War'lingham
War'minster
Warm'ley
Warn'ford
War'rington
War'saw
War'ton
War'wick
Wash'burne
Wash'ington
Was'sermann
Wat
Wa'terbury

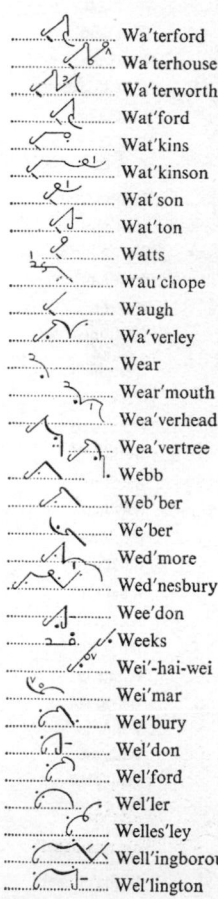

Wa'terford
Wa'terhouse
Wa'terworth
Wat'ford
Wat'kins
Wat'kinson
Wat'son
Wat'ton
Watts
Wau'chope
Waugh
Wa'verley
Wear
Wear'mouth
Wea'verhead
Wea'vertree
Webb
Web'ber
We'ber
Wed'more
Wed'nesbury
Wee'don
Weeks
Wei'-hai-wei
Wei'mar
Wel'bury
Wel'don
Wel'ford
Wel'ler
Welles'ley
Well'ingborough
Wel'lington

Wells
Welsh'pool
Wel'wyn
Wem
Wem'bley
Wemyss
Wen'dover
Wen'ham
Wen'lock
Went'worth
Wer'ner *or*
Wert'heim *or*
Wer'ther *or*
Wes'ley
Wes'sex
West'acott
West'bourne
West'bury
West'cott
West'field
West'gate
West In'dies
West'lake
West'land
West'ley
West'macott
West'meath
West'minster
West'morland
Wes'ton
Wes'ton-su'per-Mare
Westpha'lia
West' Point'
West'port
Weth'erell
Wex'ford
Wey'man *or*
Wey'mouth
Whal'ley
Whal'ton
Wharn'cliffe
Whar'ton
Whate'ly
Wheat'stone
Whips'nade
Whis'ton
Whit'aker
Whit'bread
Whit'by
Whit'church
White'chapel

White'hall
Whiteha'ven
White'head
White'house
Whit'field
Whit'horn
Whit'ley
Whit'man
Whit'minster
Whit'more
Whit'ney
Whit'stable
Whit'taker
Whit'tier
Whit'tingham
Whit'tington
Whit'tlesea
Whit'wick
Wick'ham
Wick'low
Wic'liffe
Wid'ecombe
Wid'nes
Wiesba'den
Wight'man
Wig'ram
Wig'toft
Wig'ton Wig'town
Wil'berforce
Wil'cox
Wil'ford
Wil'frid
Wilhelmi'na
Wilkes
Wilkes'-Barre
Wil'kie
Wil'kins
Wil'kinson
Wil'lenhall
Willes'den
Will'iam
Will'iams
Will'iamsburg
Will'iamson
Wil'lingdon
Wil'lingham
Wil'lington
Wil'lis
Will'oughby
Wills'bridge
Wil'ly

Wil'mington
Wil'mot
Wilms'low
Wil'na
Wil'son
Wim'borne
Wincan'ton
Win'chelsea
Winch'more
Winck'worth
Win'dermere
Wind'ham
Wind'scale
Wind'sor
Win'ford
Win'frith
Win'gate
Wing'field
Wing'ham
Win'grove
Win'ifred
Win'kle
Wink'ton
Win'laton
Winn'ipeg
Wins'low
Win'ster
Win'ston
Win'terbourne
Winter'ton
Win'wick
Wirks'worth
Wis'bech
Wiscon'sin
Wis'den
Wise'man
With'am
With'ers
Wit'ney
Wit'tenberg
Wi'tu
Wo'burn
Wode'house
Wo'king
Wo'kingham
Wol'ga
Wol'laston
Wolse'ley
Wol'sey
Wol'singham
Wol'stanton

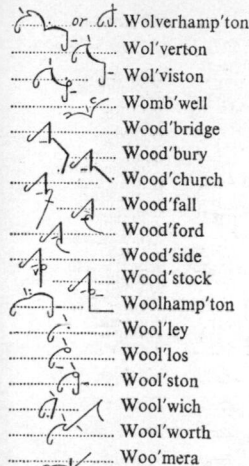

or	Wolverhamp'ton
	Wol'verton
	Wol'viston
	Womb'well
	Wood'bridge
	Wood'bury
	Wood'church
	Wood'fall
	Wood'ford
	Wood'side
	Wood'stock
	Woolhamp'ton
	Wool'ley
	Wool'los
	Wool'ston
	Wool'wich
	Wool'worth
	Woo'mera

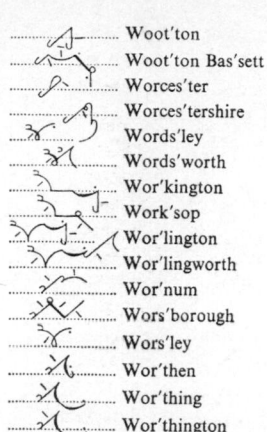

	Woot'ton
	Woot'ton Bas'sett
	Worces'ter
	Worces'tershire
	Words'ley
	Words'worth
	Wor'kington
	Work'sop
	Wor'lington
	Wor'lingworth
	Wor'num
	Wors'borough
	Wors'ley
	Wor'then
	Wor'thing
	Wor'thington
	Wot'ton-*un'der-*Edge

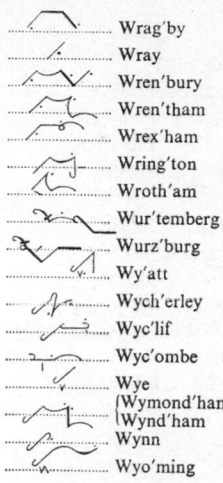

	Wrag'by
	Wray
	Wren'bury
	Wren'tham
	Wrex'ham
	Wring'ton
	Wroth'am
	Wur'temberg
	Wurz'burg
	Wy'att
	Wych'erley
	Wyc'lif
	Wyc'ombe
	Wye
	{Wymond'ham {Wynd'ham
	Wynn
	Wyo'ming

X

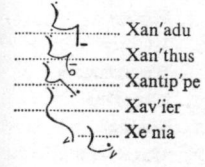

	Xan'adu
	Xan'thus
	Xantip'pe
	Xav'ier
	Xe'nia

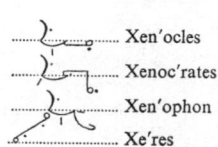

	Xen'ocles
	Xenoc'rates
	Xen'ophon
	Xe'res

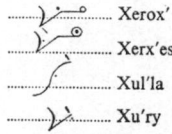

	Xerox'
	Xerx'es
	Xul'la
	Xu'ry

Y

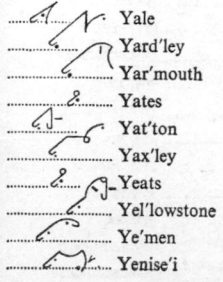

	Yale
	Yard'ley
	Yar'mouth
	Yates
	Yat'ton
	Yax'ley
	Yeats
	Yel'lowstone
	Ye'men
	Yenise'i

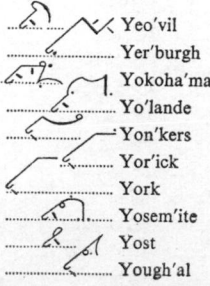

	Yeo'vil
	Yer'burgh
	Yokoha'ma
	Yo'lande
	Yon'kers
	Yor'ick
	York
	Yosem'ite
	Yost
	Yough'al

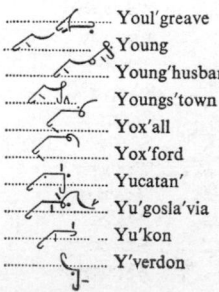

	Youl'greave
	Young
	Young'husband
	Youngs'town
	Yox'all
	Yox'ford
	Yucatan'
	Yu'gosla'via
	Yu'kon
	Y'verdon

Z

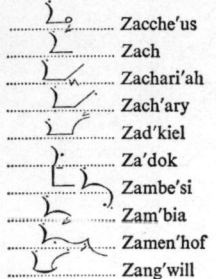

Zacche'us
Zach
Zachari'ah
Zach'ary
Zad'kiel
Za'dok
Zambe'si
Zam'bia
Zamen'hof
Zang'will

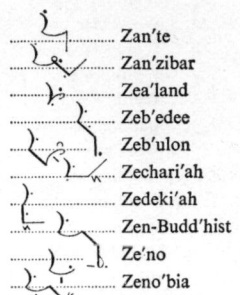

Zan'te
Zan'zibar
Zea'land
Zeb'edee
Zeb'ulon
Zechari'ah
Zedeki'ah
Zen-Budd'hist
Ze'no
Zeno'bia

Zephani'ah
Zer'cho
Zeux'is
Zim'mermann
Zoroas'ter
Zu'luland
Zu'rich
Zut'phen
Zuyder' Zee
Zwing'li